The OXFORD DICTIONARY of Current English

The OXFORD DICTIONARY of Current English

EDITED BY R. E. ALLEN

OXFORD UNIVERSITY PRESS

Oxford University Press, Walton Street, Oxford OX2 6DP
Oxford New York Toronto
Delhi Bombay Calcutta Madras Karachi
Petaling Jaya Singapore Hong Kong Tokyo
Nairobi Dar es Salaam Cape Town
Melbourne Auckland
and associated companies in
Beirut Berlin Ibadan Nicosia

Oxford is a trademark of Oxford University Press

Published in the United States
by Oxford University Press, New York

First published 1984 as seventh edition of The Pocket Oxford Dictionary
First issued as an Oxford University Press paperback 1985

Reprinted 1985, 1986, 1987 (twice)

British Library Cataloguing in Publication Data
Oxford dictionary of current English. – 7th ed.
1. English language–Dictionaries
I. Allen, R. E. (Robert Edward) II. The Pocket
Oxford dictionary of current English
423 PE1625

ISBN 0-19-281919-4

Printed and bound in Great Britain by
Cox & Wyman Ltd, Reading

Contents

Guide to the Use of the Dictionary

1. Headword

1.1 The headword is printed in bold type, or in bold italic type if the word is not naturalized in English and is usually found in italics in printed matter.

1.2 Variant spellings are given before the definition (e.g. **cabby** *n.* (also **cabbie**)); in all such cases the form given as the headword is the preferred form. When the variant form is alphabetically remote from the main form it is given at its proper place in the dictionary (e.g. **caiman** var. of CAYMAN).

1.3 Words that are different but spelt the same way (homographs) are distinguished by superior figures (e.g. **bat**[1] and **bat**[2]).

1.4 Words that are normally spelt with a capital initial are given in this form as the headword; when they are in some senses spelt with a small initial and in others with a capital initial this is indicated by repetition of the full word in appropriate form within the entry (as at **carboniferous**).

1.5 Variant American spellings are indicated by the designation *US* (e.g. **favour** . . . *US* **favor**).

1.6 Verbal forms which can end in either *-ize* or *-ise* (e.g. **centralize**) are given in the *-ize* form but it should be noted that the *-ise* form is also permissible. The same applies to derivative words in *-ization* and *-izer* and so on.

2. Pronunciation

2.1 Guidance on pronunciation follows the system of the International Phonetic Alphabet (IPA). Only the pronunciation standard in southern England is given.

2.1.1 *Consonants*:

b, d, f, h, k, l, m, n, p, r, s, t, v, w, and *z* have their usual English values. Other symbols are used as follows:

g	(*g*ame)	ŋ	(lo*ng*)	ʃ	(*sh*ip)
tʃ	(*ch*air)	θ	(*th*in)	ʒ	(mea*s*ure)
dʒ	(*j*et)	ð	(*th*ere)	j	(*y*es)
x	(Scots etc.: lo*ch*)				

2.1.2 *Vowels*:

short vowels		*long vowels*		*diphthongs*	
æ	(b*a*t)	ɑ:	(d*ar*k)	eɪ	(s*ay*)
e	(b*e*t)	i:	(s*ee*m)	aɪ	(b*uy*)
ə	(*a*noth*er*)	ɔ:	(b*or*n)	ɔɪ	(t*oy*)
ɪ	(s*i*t)	ɜ:	(t*er*m)	əʊ	(s*o*)
ɒ	(t*o*p)	u:	(m*oo*n)	aʊ	(n*ow*)
ʌ	(b*u*t)			ɪə	(p*ee*r)
ʊ	(p*u*t)			eə	(f*air*)
				ʊə	(p*oor*)

(ə) signifies the indeterminate sound as in gard*e*n, carn*a*l, and rhyth*m*.

The following signify sounds not natural in English:

æ̃ (b*ai*n-marie, t*i*mbre)
ɑ̃ (contret*e*mps)
ɔ̃ (b*o*n voyage)

2.1.3 Main stress is indicated by ˈ preceding the relevant syllable; no attempt is made to indicate secondary stress.

2.2 Pronunciation of words of one syllable is not given when it conforms with the following basic pattern:

2.2.1 Single-letter vowels a = /æ/, e = /e/, i = /ɪ/, o = /ɒ/, u = /ʌ/; when lengthened by a succeeding single consonant followed by *e*, a = /eɪ/, e = /i:/, i = /aɪ/, o = /əʊ/, u = /ju:/ (as in m*a*t and m*a*te; m*e*t and m*e*te, s*i*t and s*i*te, tot and tote, t*u*n and t*u*ne).

2.2.2 Other vowels as in g*ai*n, f*air*, f*ar*, d*are*, s*aw*, s*ay*, b*ea*n, f*ear*, s*ee*n, s*eer*, h*er*d, h*ere*, f*ew*, th*ie*f, b*ier*, b*ir*d, t*ire*, bo*a*t, bo*ar*d, ho*e*, j*oi*n, m*oo*n, p*oor*, b*or*n, l*ou*d, s*our*, n*ow*, t*oy*, d*ue*, b*ur*n, p*ure*.

2.2.3 Consonants as in ar*c*, *c*ob, *c*ry (but soft *c* before *e*, *i*, *y* as in i*c*e and *c*ity); *ch*ur*ch*; bla*ck*, lo*dge*; *g*ame, ba*g* (but soft *g* before *e*, *i*, *y* as in a*g*e and *g*in); *j*et; si*ng*; bla*nk*; *ph*oto; *qu*een; *sh*ot; bi*tch*; *th*in; bo*x*; *y*et. Other consonants have their usual English values.

2.2.4 Initial double consonants as in *kn*ot; *rh*yme, *wh*ich; *wr*ing.

2.3 Pronunciation of two-syllable words ending in *-er* preceded by a consonant is also not given when the first syllable is stressed and follows the above pattern (as in **porter**, **matter**, **poker**).

2.4 Pronunciation of compound words of easily recognized elements (e.g. **bathroom**, **jellyfish**) is not given when the stress is on the first element.

2.5 Pronunciation of regularly formed derivatives is not given when it can be easily deduced from the headword or from a preceding main word (e.g. **casually** from **casual** and **catty** from **cat**), unless there is a change of stress or some other notable feature (as with **certification**).

The following suffixes and terminations especially should be noted:

-able /-əb(ə)l/
-age /-ɪdʒ/
-al (preceded by consonant) /-(ə)l/
-dom /-dəm/
-ed (after *d* or *t*) /-ɪd/; (after other voiceless consonant) /-t/; (elsewhere) /-d/
-ess /-ɪs/
-est /-ɪst/
-ful /-fʊl/
-fy /-faɪ/
-ible /-ɪb(ə)l/
-ism /-ɪz(ə)m/
-ive /-ɪv/
-less /-lɪs/
-ment /-mənt/
-ness /-nɪs/
-ous /-əs/
-sion /-ʃ(ə)n or -ʒ(ə)n/
-some /-səm/
-tion /-ʃ(ə)n/
-y (preceded by consonant, but cf. **-fy**) /-ɪ/

3. Part-of-speech label

3.1 This is given for all main entries and derivatives except those consisting of two or more unhyphened words.

3.2 It is not given for compound items listed at the end of entries except where these exist as more than one part of speech.

3.3 Different parts of speech of a single word are listed separately preceded by a bold number (e.g. **turn 1** *n*. . . . **2** *v.t.*).

3.4 Verbs that are both transitive and intransitive are given the simple designation *v.*; those that are only transitive or only intransitive are labelled *v.t.* and *v.i.* respectively. The designation *absol.* denotes use with an implied object (as at **abdicate**).

4. Inflexion

4.1 *Plurals of Nouns*: nouns that form their plural regularly by adding *-s* (or *-es* when they end in *-s*, *-x*, *-z*, *-sh*, or soft *-ch*), or by changing *-y* (preceded by a consonant or *qu*) to *-ies*, receive no comment. Plural forms of those ending in *-o* (preceded by any letter other than another *o*) are always given. Other irregular forms are also given, except when the word is a compound of obvious formation (e.g. **footman**, **schoolchild**).

4.2 *Forms of Verbs*:

4.2.1 The following regular forms receive no comment:

(i) third person singular present forms adding *-s* to the stem (or *-es* to stems ending in *-s*, *-x*, *-z*, *-sh*, or soft *-ch* and stems in *-o* preceded by any letter other than another *o*), or changing *-y* (preceded by a consonant or *qu*) to *-ies* (e.g. *cries*, *defies*).

(ii) past tenses and past participles adding *-ed* to the stem, changing final *-y* (preceded by a consonant or *qu*) to *-ied* (e.g. *cried*, *defied*).

(iii) present participles adding *-ing* to the stem, dropping a final silent *e* (e.g. *changing*, *dancing*).

4.2.2 A doubled consonant in verbal inflexions (e.g. *rubbed*, *rubbing*, *sinned*, *sinning*) is shown in the form (**-bb-**, **-nn-**, etc.). Where practice differs in American usage this is noted (as at **cavil**).

4.3 *Comparative and Superlative of Adjectives and Adverbs*: The following regular forms receive no comment:

4.3.1 Words of one syllable adding *-er* and *-est*, those ending in silent *e* dropping the *e* (e.g. *braver*, *bravest*) and those ending in a final consonant (except *h*, *w*, or *x*) preceded by a single-letter vowel doubling the consonant (e.g. *hotter*, *hottest*).

4.3.2 Words of one or two syllables ending in *-y* (preceded by a consonant or *qu*) changing *-y* to *-ier* and *-iest* (e.g. *drier*, *driest*; *happier*, *happiest*).

4.4 *Adjectives in* -able *formed from Transitive Verbs*:

4.4.1 Verbs generally drop silent final *-e* except after *c* and *g* (e.g. *movable* but *changeable*).

4.4.2 Words of more than one syllable ending in *-y* (preceded by a consonant or *qu*) change *y* to *i* (e.g. *enviable*, *undeniable*).

4.4.3 A final consonant is doubled as in normal inflexion (*conferrable*, *regrettable*): cf. 4.2.2 above.

5. Definition

5.1 Definitions are listed in order of comparative familiarity and importance, with the most current and important senses first.

5.2 They are separated by a semicolon, or by a comma when the two senses are more closely related.

5.3 A word or words in italics forming part of the definition indicates that it is normally used with the headword in the sense concerned (as with *of* and *that* at **certain**). Words such as *one*, *person*, and *do* are simply representative of a type: thus *oneself* implies *myself*, *yourself*, etc., and *do* implies any verb of action.

5.4 Round brackets enclose letters or words that are optional (as at **crash** *v.* where '(cause to) proceed with a crash' can mean either 'proceed with a crash' or 'cause to proceed with a crash'), and indicate typical objects of transitive verbs (such as '*milk*' and '*skin*' in two senses of **cream** *v.*).

6. Subject and Usage labels

6.1 These are used to clarify the particular context in which a word or phrase is normally used.

6.2 Words and phrases more common in informal spoken English than in formal written English are labelled *colloq.* (colloquial) or *sl.* (slang) as appropriate.

6.3 Some subject labels are used to indicate the particular relevance of a term or subject with which it is associated (e.g. *Mus.*, *Law*, *Physics*). They are not used when this is sufficiently clear from the definition itself.

6.4 Two categories of deprecated usage are indicated by special markings: **D** (= disputed) indicates a use that, although widely found, is still the subject of much adverse comment by informed users; **R** (= racially offensive) indicates a use that is regarded as offensive by members of a particular ethnic or religious group.

7. Phrases

Phrases are listed (together with compounds) in alphabetical order after the treatment of the main word, this being the earliest important word in the phrase except when a later word is more clearly the key word. The words *a*, *the*, *one*, and *person* do not count for purposes of alphabetical order.

8. Compounds

8.1 Compound terms forming one word (e.g. **bathroom, jellyfish**) are listed as main entries; those consisting of two or more words (e.g. **chain reaction**) or joined by a hyphen (e.g. **chain-gang**) are given under the first element or occasionally as main entries.

8.2 When a hyphened compound in bold type is divided at the end of a line the hyphen is repeated at the beginning of the next line to show that it is a permanent feature of the spelling and not just an end-of-line hyphen.

9. Derivatives

9.1 Words formed by adding a suffix to another word are in many cases listed in alphabetical order at the end of the entry for the main word (e.g. **chalkiness** and **chalky** at **chalk**). In this position they are not defined since they can be understood from the sense of the main word and that given at the suffix concerned; when further definition is called for they are given main entries in their own right (e.g. **changeable**).

9.2 For reasons of space words formed by certain suffixes are not included at all except when some special feature of spelling or pronunciation or meaning is involved. These suffixes are -ABLE, -ER (in sense '... that does'), -ER and -EST (see also 4.3), -ISH, -LESS, -LIKE, -LY, and -NESS.

10. Etymology

10.1 This is given in square brackets [ ] at the end of the entry. In the space available it can only give the direct line of derivation in outline; the immediate source-language is always given first. Forms in other languages are not given if they are exactly or nearly the same as the English form.

10.2 OE is used for words that are known to have been used in Old English (before AD 1150).

10.3 AF (Anglo-French) denotes the variety of French current in England in the Middle Ages after the Norman Conquest.

10.4 L (Latin) denotes classical and Late Latin up to about AD 600; med.L (medieval Latin) that of the period about 600–1500; AL (Anglo-Latin) denotes Latin as used in medieval England.

10.5 Where the origin of a word cannot be reliably ascertained, the form [orig. uncert.] or [orig. unkn.] is used.

10.6 Names of the rarer languages that have contributed to English (such as Balti at **polo**, and Cree at **wapiti**) are given in full without explanation; they may be found explained in larger dictionaries or in encyclopaedias.

10.7 An etymology is not given when it is identical in essentials with that of the preceding entry, when the word is an abbreviation, or when the derivation is clear from the definition (as at **burgundy**).

11. Prefixes and Suffixes

11.1 A large selection of these is given in the main body of the text; prefixes are given in the form **ex-**, **re-**, etc., and suffixes in the form **-ion**, **-ness**, etc. These entries should be consulted to explain the many derivatives given at the end of entries (see 9.1).

11.2 Prefixes and suffixes are not normally given a pronunciation since this can change considerably when they form part of a word.

12. Cross-Reference

12.1 Cross-reference to main entries is indicated by small capitals (e.g. **calk** *US* var. of CAULK; **change one's tune** see TUNE).

12.2 Cross-reference in italics to a defined phrase or compound refers to the entry for the first word unless another is specified.

12.3 A homograph (see 1.3) is indicated by a superior figure (e.g. **calves** *pl.* of CALF, CALF).

13. Proprietary Status

This dictionary includes some words which are, or are asserted to be, proprietary names or trade marks. Their inclusion does not imply that they have acquired for legal purposes a non-proprietary or general significance, nor is any other judgement implied concerning their legal status. In cases where the editor has some evidence that a word is used as a proprietary name or trade mark this is indicated by the letter **P**, but no judgement concerning the legal status of such words is made or implied thereby.

Abbreviations used in the Dictionary

SOME abbreviations occur only in etymologies. Others may appear in italics. Abbreviations in general use appear in the dictionary

a.	adjective
abbr.	abbreviation
abl.	ablative (case)
Abor.	Aboriginal
absol.	absolute, used absolutely (see 3.4)
acc.	accusative (case)
act.	active
adv.	adverb
Aeron.	Aeronautics
AF	Anglo-French (see 10.3)
Afr.	African
Afrik.	Afrikaans
AL	Anglo-Latin (see 10.4)
alt.	alteration, altered
Amer.	American
Amh.	Amharic
Anat.	Anatomy
anc.	ancient
app.	apparently
approx.	approximately
Arab.	Arabic
Aram.	Aramaic
Archaeol.	Archaeology
Archit.	Architecture
assim.	assimilated
assoc.	associated
Assyr.	Assyrian
Astrol.	Astrology
Astron.	Astronomy
attrib.	attributive, used attributively
Austral.	Australian
aux.	auxiliary

Bibl.	Biblical
Biol.	Biology
Bot.	Botany
Brit.	British

Canad.	Canadian
Carib.	Caribbean
cc.	centuries
Celt.	Celtic
Chem.	Chemistry
Chin.	Chinese
cogn.	cognate
collect.	collective
colloq.	colloquial
comb.	combination, combining
compar.	comparative
conj.	conjunction
contr.	contraction
Corn.	Cornish
corresp.	corresponding
corrupt.	corruption

D	disputed (see 6.4)
Da.	Danish
dat.	dative (case)
dem.	demonstrative
deriv.	derivative
derog.	derogatory
dial.	dialect
diff.	different
dimin.	diminutive
Du.	Dutch

eccl.	ecclesiastical
Econ.	Economics
Egypt.	Egyptian
Electr.	Electricity
ellipt.	elliptically
emphat.	emphatic
Eng.	English
Engl.	England
erron.	erroneous(ly)
esp.	especially
etym.	etymology
euphem.	euphemism
Eur.	Europe, European
exc.	except

excl.	exclamation
F	French
f.	from
fam.	familiar
fem.	feminine
fig.	figurative
Finn.	Finnish
Flem.	Flemish
foll.	following (entry)
form.	formation
frequent.	frequentative
Fris.	Frisian
fut.	future (tense)
G	German
Gael.	Gaelic
gen.	genitive (case)
Geog.	Geography
Geol.	Geology
Geom.	Geometry
Gk	Greek
Gmc	Germanic
Gram.	Grammar
Heb.	Hebrew
Hind.	Hindustani
hist.	with historical reference
i.	intransitive
Icel.	Icelandic
imit.	imitative
imper.	imperative
impers.	impersonal
incl.	including
Ind.	Indian
ind.	indirect
indic.	indicative
infin.	infinitive
infl.	influenced
int.	interjection
interrog.	interrogative
intr.	intransitive
Ir.	Irish
iron.	ironical
It.	Italian
Jap.	Japanese

Jav.	Javanese
joc.	jocular
L	Latin (see 10.4)
lang.	language
LG	Low German
lit.	literal
Math.	Mathematics
Mech.	Mechanics
med.	medieval
Mex.	Mexican
Mil.	Military
mod.	modern
Mus.	Music
Myth.	Mythology
n.	noun
Naut.	Nautical
neg.	negative
Norw.	Norwegian
num.	numeral
O	Old
obj.	objective (case)
obs.	obsolete
occas.	occasionally
OE	Old English (see 10.2)
ON	Old Norse
opp.	as opposed to
orig.	origin, originally
P	Proprietary name (see 13)
parenth.	parenthetically
Parl.	Parliament(ary)
partic.	(esp. present) participle
pass.	passive
perf.	perfect (tense)
perh.	perhaps
Pers.	Persian
pers.	person, personal
Peruv.	Peruvian
Philol.	Philology
Philos.	Philosophy
Photog.	Photography
phr.	phrase
Physiol.	Physiology

pl.	plural
Pol.	Polish
pop.	popular(ly)
Port.	Portuguese
poss.	possessive (case)
p.p.	past participle
pr.	pronounced
prec.	preceding (entry)
predic.	predicative, used predicatively
prep.	preposition
pres.	present (tense)
prob.	probably
pron.	pronoun
pronunc.	pronunciation
Prov.	Provenal
pseud.	pseudonym
Psych.	Psychology
R	racially offensive (see 6.4)
redupl.	reduplication
ref.	reference
refl.	reflexive
rel.	related
repr.	representing
rhet.	rhetorical
Rmc	Romanic
Rom.	Roman
Russ.	Russian
Sc.	Scottish
Scand.	Scandinavian
sing.	singular
Sinh.	Sinhalese
Skr.	Sanskrit
sl.	slang
Slav.	Slavonic
Sp.	Spanish
sp.	spelling
subj.	subject, subjunctive
subord.	subordinate
superl.	superlative
Sw.	Swedish
syll.	syllable
symb.	symbol
t.	transitive
Teut.	Teutonic
Theol.	Theology
thr.	through
trans.	transitive
transf.	by transference
transl.	translation
Turk.	Turkish
ult.	ultimately
uncert.	uncertain
unkn.	unknown
US	American, in American use
usu.	usually
v.	verb
var.	variant(s)
voc.	vocative
W	Welsh
wd(s)	word(s)
Zool.	Zoology
1, 2, 3	1st, 2nd, 3rd person of verb

A

A, a[1] /eɪ/ *n.* (*pl.* **As, A's**). first letter; *Mus.* sixth note in diatonic scale of C major; (as *a*) first known quantity in algebra; (as *A*) first hypothetical person or example; **A1** /eɪ 'wʌn/ first-rate, first-class (orig. of ship in Lloyd's Register).

a[2], **an** /ə, ən; *emphat.* eɪ, æn/ *a.* one, some, any; one like (*a Judas*); one single (*could not see a thing*); the same (*all of a size*); to or for each (*£40 a week, twice a day*: orig. f. A[3]). ¶ *an* is used before vowel sounds (but note *a one, a unit*) and before *heir, honour,* and *hour* (but note *a hotel*). [OE *ān* ONE]

a[3] *prep.* (now chiefly as *prefix*) on, to, in (*afoot, ashore, nowadays*); in the process of (*a-hunting*); with verbs (*aflutter*). [OE *an, on,* ON]

a- *prefix* (**an-** before vowel or *h*) not, without. [Gk]

A *abbr.* ampere(s).

Å *abbr.* ångström(s).

Aaron's beard, rod /'eərənz/ *n.* popular names of plants, esp. St John's wort. [*Aaron* in Ps. 133: 2]

ab- *prefix* (**abs-** before *c, t*; **a-** before *m, p, v*) away, from. [F or L]

aback /ə'bæk/ *adv.* backwards, behind (*archaic* except in **taken aback** surprised). [OE (A[3])]

abacus /'æbəkəs/ *n.* (*pl.* **abacuses**) frame with wires along which beads are slid for calculating; *Archit.* flat upper section of capital. [L f. Gk f. Heb.]

abaft /ə'bɑ:ft/ *Naut.* **1** *adv.* in or towards stern half of ship. **2** *prep.* behind. [A[3], *baft* (see AFT)]

abandon /ə'bænd(ə)n/ **1** *v.t.* give up, forsake, give *oneself* over utterly *to* (passion etc.). **2** *n.* reckless freedom of manner. **3 abandonment** *n.* (esp. = sense 2). [F (AD-, BAN)]

abandoned /ə'bænd(ə)nd/ *a.* forsaken; (of person or behaviour) unrestrained, profligate, depraved.

abase /ə'beɪs/ *v.t.* humiliate, degrade (person; also *refl.*); **abasement** *n.* [F (AD-, BASE)]

abashed /ə'bæʃt/ *a.* embarrassed, disconcerted, ashamed. [F *es-* EX-[1], *baïr* astound]

abate /ə'beɪt/ *v.* become or make less, diminish, weaken; **abatement** *n.* [F *abatre* f. L *batt(u)ereo* beat]

abattoir /'æbətwɑ:/ *n.* slaughterhouse. [F (*abatre* fell, as prec.)]

abbacy /'æbəsɪ/ *n.* office or jurisdiction of abbot or abbess. [L (ABBOT)]

abbé /'æbeɪ/ *n.* abbot or priest in France. [F f. L (ABBOT)]

abbess /'æbes/ *n.* female head of abbey of nuns.

abbey /'æbɪ/ *n.* buildings occupied by community of monks or nuns; the community itself; church or house that was formerly abbey.

abbot /'æbət/ *n.* head of abbey of monks. [OE f. L *abbas* f. Gk f. Aram.]

abbreviate /ə'bri:vɪeɪt/ *v.t.* shorten, esp. represent (word) by a part; **abbreviation** /-'eɪʃ(ə)n/ *n.* [L (BRIEF)]

ABC /-'si:/ *n.* the alphabet; rudiments of subject; alphabetical guide. [*A, B, C*]

abdicate /'æbdɪkeɪt/ *v.t.* renounce or resign from (throne, right, etc., or *absol.*); **abdication** /-'keɪʃ(ə)n/ *n.* [L (*dico* declare)]

abdomen /'æbdəmən/ *n.* belly, including stomach, bowels, and digestive organs; hinder part of insect etc.; **abdominal** /æb'dɒmɪn(ə)l/ *a.* [L]

abduct /æb'dʌkt/ *v.* carry off or kidnap (esp. woman or child) illegally by force or deception; **abduction** *n.*; **abductor** *n.* [L (*duco* lead)]

abeam /ə'bi:m/ *adv.* on line at right angles to ship's or aircraft's length. [A[3]]

Aberdeen Angus /æbə'di:n 'æŋgəs/ *n.* animal of Scottish breed of black hornless cattle. [*Aberdeen* in Scotland]

Aberdeen terrier /'terɪə/ *n.* Scotch terrier.

Aberdonian /æbə'dəʊnɪən/ **1** *a.* of Aberdeen. **2** *n.* native of Aberdeen. [med.L]

aberrant /æ'berənt/ *a.* departing from normal type or accepted standard. [L (ERR)]

aberration /æbə'reɪʃ(ə)n/ *n.* departure from what is normal or accepted or regarded as right, moral or mental lapse; deviation from biological type; distortion of image in optics; apparent displacement of celestial body in astronomy.

abet /ə'bet/ *v.t.* (**-tt-**) encourage or assist (offender or offence; usu. *aid and abet*); **abetter** (in legal use **abettor**) *n.* [F (AD-, BAIT)]

abeyance /ə'beɪəns/ *n.* temporary disuse, suspension (*be in, fall into, abeyance*). [F (AD-, *beer* gape)]

abhor /əb'hɔ:/ *v.t.* (**-rr-**) detest, regard with disgust. [L (HORROR)]

abhorrence /əb'hɒrəns/ *n.* disgust, detestation.

abhorrent *a.* disgusting or hateful (*to* person, one's beliefs).

abide /ə'baɪd/ *v.* (*past* **abode** /ə'bəʊd/ or **abided**) tolerate, endure (usu. in neg. contexts: *can't abide sultanas*); *archaic* remain, continue; **abide by** act on (promise etc.), remain faithful to. [OE (*a*- intensive, BIDE)]

abiding *a.* enduring, permanent.

ability /ə'bɪlɪtɪ/ *n.* capacity or power (*to do* thing); cleverness, talent. [F (ABLE)]

-ability *suffix* forming nouns of quality corresponding to adjectives in *-able*.

ab initio /æb ɪ'nɪʃɪəʊ/ from the beginning. [L]

abject /'æbdʒekt/ *a.* degraded or made humble, miserable, craven; **abjection** /æb'dʒekʃ(ə)n/ *n.* [L (*jacio -ject-* throw)]

abjure /əb'dʒʊə/ *v.t.* renounce or repudiate on oath (opinion, cause, claim, etc.); **abjuration** /-'reɪʃ(ə)n/ *n.* [L (*juro* swear)]

ablative /'æblətɪv/ *Gram.* **1** *n.* case of (esp. Latin) nouns indicating agent, instrument, or location, of action. **2** *a.* of or in the ablative. **3 ablative absolute** see ABSOLUTE. [F or L (*ablatus* taken away)]

ablaut /'æblaʊt/ *n.* change of vowel in related words (*sing, song, sung*). [G]

ablaze /ə'bleɪz/ *predic. a.* on fire; glittering; greatly excited. [A[3]]

able /'eɪb(ə)l/ *a.* having the power or capacity (*to do* thing; used esp. in *is able, will be able, was able*, etc., as tenses of *can*); talented, clever; **able-bodied** healthy, fit; **able-bodied seaman** one fit for all duties; **ably** *adv.* [F f. L *habilis*]

-able *suffix* forming adjectives in sense 'that may *or* may be' (*comfortable, eatable*). [F f. L *-abilis*]

ablution /ə'blu:ʃ(ə)n/ *n.* (usu. in *pl.*) ceremonial washing of hands, vessels, etc.; *colloq.* ordinary washing of the body, place for doing this. [F, or L *ablutio* (*luo lut-* wash)]

ably see ABLE.

-ably *suffix* forming adverbs corresponding to adjectives in *-able*.

abnegate /'æbnɪgeɪt/ *v.t.* give up or renounce (pleasure or right etc.). [L (*nego* deny)]

abnegation /æbnɪ'geɪʃ(ə)n/ *n.* denial, renunciation (of doctrine). [F or L (prec.)]

abnormal /æb'nɔ:m(ə)l/ *a.* exceptional, deviating from a type; **abnormality** /-'mælɪtɪ/ *n.* [F (ANOMALOUS)]

Abo /'æbəʊ/ *n.* & *a.* (also **abo**) *Austral. sl.* (**R**) Aboriginal. [abbr.]

aboard /ə'bɔ:d/ *adv.* & *prep.* on or into a ship, aircraft, train, etc.; alongside. [A[3]]

abode[1] /ə'bəʊd/ *n.* *archaic* dwelling-place. [ABIDE]

abode[2] *past* of ABIDE.

abolish /ə'bɒlɪʃ/ *v.t.* put an end to (esp. custom or institution). [F f. L *aboleo* destroy]

abolition /æbə'lɪʃ(ə)n/ *n.* abolishing or being abolished.

abolitionist *n.* one who favours abolition (esp. of capital punishment).

A-bomb /'eɪbɒm/ *n.* atomic bomb. [*A* for ATOMIC]

abominable /ə'bɒmɪnəb(ə)l/ *a.* detestable, loathsome; *colloq.* unpleasant (*abominable weather*); **Abominable Snowman** unidentified manlike or bearlike animal in Himalayas. [F f. L (*abominor* deprecate)]

abominate /ə'bɒmɪneɪt/ *v.t.* detest, loathe; **abomination** /-'neɪʃ(ə)n/ *n.* [L (prec.)]

aboriginal /æbə'rɪdʒən(ə)l/ **1** *a.* (esp. of a people) indigenous, inhabiting a land from an early period, esp. before arrival of colonists; directly descended from early inhabitants. **2** *n.* aboriginal inhabitant. ¶ Usu. **Aboriginal** with ref. to Australia. [L (ORIGIN)]

aborigines /æbə'rɪdʒəni:z/ *n. pl.* (*sing.* **aborigine** is used informally, but ABORIGINAL is preferable) aboriginal inhabitants, esp. (**Aborigines**) of Australia.

abort /ə'bɔ:t/ *v.* cause or undergo abortion; *Biol.* (cause to) remain undeveloped, shrink away; cause to end fruitlessly or prematurely, esp. terminate space flight, computer program, etc., because of fault. [L (*orior* be born)]

abortion /ə'bɔ:ʃ(ə)n/ *n.* natural or (esp.) induced expulsion of foetus from womb before it is able to survive, esp. in first 28 weeks of pregnancy; stunted or misshapen creature or thing; **abortionist** *n.*

abortive /ə'bɔ:tɪv/ *a.* producing abortion; unsuccessful.

abound /ə'baʊnd/ *v.i.* be plentiful; be rich (*in*), teem (*with*). [F f. L (*unda* wave)]

about /ə'baʊt/ **1** *prep.* pertaining to (*something funny about this*), in connection with, on the subject of (*a book about plants; what are you talking about?*); at a time near to (*come about four*); in, round, surrounding (*wandering about the place*); carried with (*have your wits about you*); here and there in, at points throughout (*strewn about the house*). **2** *adv.* approximately (*costs about a pound; is about right*), *colloq.* in understatement (*just about had enough*); at points nearby, here and there (*a lot of measles about*); on the move, in action (*out and about*); all round, in every direction (*look about*); in the opposite direction (*about face*); in rotation or succession (*turn and turn about*). ¶ Tending to be replaced in many senses by *around* and *round*. **3 about turn** turn made so as to face opposite direction, change of opinion or policy etc.; **be about to** intend to (do something) immediately; **come** (or **bring**) **about** (cause to) happen. [OE]

above /əˈbʌv/ **1** *prep.* over, on the top of, higher (vertically, up a slope or stream etc.) than, over the surface of (*head above water*, *heard above the din*); more than (*above twenty*); higher in rank, position, importance, etc. than (*above all*); beyond the reach of (*above suspicion*); too good etc. for (*above jealousy*, *above one's station*). **2** *adv.* at or to a higher point, overhead (*clear sky above*, *the floor above*); in addition (*over and above*); further back on page or in book; *rhet.* in heaven. **3** *a.* & *n.* (that which is) said, mentioned, or written above (*the above*, *the above argument*, *shows*). **4** **above-board** without concealment, open(ly); **above oneself** arrogant, conceited. [OE (A[3])]

abracadabra /æbrəkəˈdæbrə/ *n.* magic formula, spell; gibberish. [L f. Gk]

abrade /əˈbreɪd/ *v.t.* scrape or wear away by rubbing (skin or fabric or rock etc.). [L (*rado* scrape)]

abrasion /əˈbreɪʒ(ə)n/ *n.* scraping or wearing away; area of damage thus caused.

abrasive /əˈbreɪsɪv/ **1** *a.* capable of (polishing by) rubbing or grinding; harsh and offensive in manner. **2** *n.* abrasive substance.

abreaction /æbrɪˈækʃ(ə)n/ *n.* free expression and consequent release of previously repressed emotion. [AB-]

abreast /əˈbrest/ *adv.* side by side and facing the same way; up to date (*abreast of developments*). [A[3]]

abridge /əˈbrɪdʒ/ *v.t.* condense or shorten (book etc.); **abridgement** *n.* [F f. L (ABBREVIATE)]

abroad /əˈbrɔːd/ *adv.* in or to a foreign country; over a wide area, in different directions (*scatter abroad*); in circulation (*there is a rumour abroad*). [A[3]]

abrogate /ˈæbrəʊgeɪt/ *v.t.* repeal, cancel (law, custom); **abrogation** /-ˈgeɪʃ(ə)n/ *n.* [L (*rogo* propose law)]

abrupt /əˈbrʌpt/ *a.* sudden, hasty (*abrupt departure*); disjointed, not smooth (esp. of thought or speech); steep, precipitous. [L (RUPTURE)]

abscess /ˈæbsɪs/ *n.* swollen area of body tissue in which pus gathers. [L (AB-, CEDE)]

abscissa /æbˈsɪsə/ *n.* (*pl.* **abscissae**/-iː/) *Math.* coordinate measured parallel to horizontal axis. [L (*abscindo* cut off)]

abscond /æbˈskɒnd/ *v.i.* depart hurriedly and furtively, esp. in wrongdoing. [L *abscondo* secrete]

abseil /ˈæbseɪl/ **1** *n.* descent of steep rock-face by using doubled rope fixed at higher point. **2** *v.i.* make abseil. [G (*ab* down, *seil* rope)]

absence /ˈæbsəns/ *n.* being away, time in which one is away; non-existence or lack *of*; **absence of mind** inattentiveness. [F f. L *absentia*]

absent **1** /ˈæbsənt/ *a.* not present; not existing. **2** /æbˈsent/ *v. refl.* keep *oneself* away. **3** **absent-minded** habitually forgetful or inattentive.

absentee /æbsənˈtiː/ *n.* person not present; **absentee landlord** one not residing at property he leases out.

absenteeism *n.* practice of absenting oneself from work etc. esp. frequently or illicitly.

absently *adv.* in absent-minded way.

absinth /ˈæbsɪnθ/ *n.* wormwood; (usu. **absinthe**) liqueur made (orig.) from this. [F f. L]

absolute /ˈæbsəluːt, -ljuːt/ *a.* complete, utter, perfect (*absolute ignorance*, *agony*, *impossibility*, *exhaustion*, *bliss*; *an absolute idiot*); unrestricted, independent, despotic (*absolute submission*, *denial*, *ruler*); not relative (*absolute standard*); *Gram.* (of a construction) not syntactically related to rest of sentence (*ablative absolute* in L, *genitive absolute* in Gk), (of adjective or transitive verb) without expressed noun or object; **the absolute** *Philos.* that which is regarded as self-existent; **absolute majority** majority over all rivals combined; **absolute pitch** see PITCH[1]; **absolute temperature** one measured from absolute zero; **absolute zero** lowest possible temperature. [L (ABSOLVE)]

absolutely *adv.* completely, utterly, unreservedly, in an absolute sense; in actual fact (*he absolutely loves it*); *colloq.* /-ˈluːtlɪ/ quite so, yes (used in reply).

absolution /æbsəˈluːʃ(ə)n, -ljuː-/ *n.* formal forgiveness of sin.

absolutism /ˈæbsəluːtɪz(ə)m, -ljuː-/ *n.* (principle of) government with unlimited powers; **absolutist** *n.*

absolve /əbˈzɒlv/ *v.t.* set or pronounce free (*from* or *of* blame or obligation etc.). [L (SOLVE)]

absorb /əbˈsɔːb/ *v.t.* include or incorporate as part of itself or oneself; take in, suck up (heat etc., liquid, knowledge); deal easily with, reduce effect of (difficulty, shock, etc.); engross the attention of (*absorbed by her work*; *an absorbing film*). [L (*sorbeo* suck in)]

absorbent 1 *a.* having tendency to absorb. **2** *n.* absorbent substance or organ.
absorption /əb'sɔ:pʃ(ə)n/ *n.* incorporation into something else; mental engrossment; **absorptive** *a.*
abstain /əb'steɪn/ *v.i.* restrain oneself (esp. from alcohol; *from* thing or action); decline to use vote. [F f. L (*teneo tent-* hold)]
abstemious /æb'sti:mɪəs/ *a.* sparing or not self-indulgent esp. in eating and drinking. [L (AB-, *temetum* strong drink)]
abstention /əb'stenʃ(ə)n/ *n.* (instance of) abstaining, esp. from voting. [F or L (ABSTAIN)]
abstinence /'æbstɪnəns/ *n.* abstaining from an indulgence, esp. food or alcohol; **abstinent** *a.* [F (ABSTAIN)]
abstract 1 /'æbstrækt/ *a.* to do with or existing in thought or theory rather than matter or practice, not concrete; (of art) achieving effect by form and colour etc., not representational. **2** /æb'strækt/ *v.* remove; summarize (book etc.). **3** /'æbstrækt/ *n.* summary; abstract idea; example of abstract art. **4 abstract noun** noun denoting quality or state. [F or L (TRACT)]
abstracted /æb'stræktɪd/ *a.* inattentive (to matter in hand).
abstraction /æb'strækʃ(ə)n/ *n.* abstracting; abstract idea.
abstruse /æb'stru:s/ *a.* hard to understand, profound. [F or L (*abstrudo -trus-* conceal)]
absurd /əb'sɜ:d/ *a.* wildly inappropriate; ridiculous; **absurdity** *n.* [F or L (SURD)]
abundance /ə'bʌndəns/ *n.* quantity more than enough, plenty; wealth. [F f. L (ABOUND)]
abundant *a.* more than enough, plentiful; rich (*country abundant in fruit*).
abuse 1 /ə'bju:z/ *v.t.* make bad use of; maltreat; attack verbally, revile. **2** /ə'bju:s/ *n.* misuse (*an abuse of his powers*); unjust or corrupt practice; offensive language. [F f. L (USE)]
abusive /ə'bju:sɪv/ *a.* using insulting language, reviling.
abut /ə'bʌt/ *v.* (-**tt**-) (of land) adjoin or border *on* (other land); (of building) touch, lean *on* or *against* (another). [AL (*butta* strip of land), F (BUTT[4])]
abutment *n.* lateral supporting structure of bridge, arch, etc.
abysmal /ə'bɪzm(ə)l/ *a.* extremely bad (*his taste is abysmal*); profound, utter (in bad sense: *abysmal ignorance*). [F f. L (foll.)]
abyss /ə'bɪs/ *n.* bottomless or deep chasm; immeasurable depth. [L f. Gk, = bottomless]
-ac *suffix* forming adjectives (*cardiac*) which are often also used as nouns (*maniac*). [F or L or Gk]
AC *abbr.* alternating current; aircraftman.
a/c *abbr.* account. [*account current*]
Ac *symb.* actinium.
acacia /ə'keɪʃə/ *n.* tree with yellow or white flowers, esp. producing gum arabic. [L f. Gk]
academic /ækə'demɪk/ **1** *a.* scholarly, to do with learning; not of practical relevance. **2** *n.* member of scholarly institution. [ACADEMY]
academy /ə'kædəmɪ/ *n.* place of study; (**Academy**) place of training in a special field (*Military Academy*), society devoted to art etc. (*Royal Academy*); *Sc.* secondary school. [F or L f. Gk *akademeia* place in Athens where Plato taught]
acanthus /ə'kænθəs/ *n.* a kind of herbaceous plant with prickly leaves; *Archit.* representation of its leaf. [L f. Gk]
ACAS /'eɪkæs/ *abbr.* Advisory, Conciliation, and Arbitration Service.
accede /æk'si:d/ *v.i.* take office, become monarch; assent or agree *to* (request, proposal, opinion); **accede to** take up (office), join (party). [L (CEDE)]
accelerate /ək'seləreɪt/ *v.* (cause to) move faster or happen earlier; **acceleration** /-'reɪʃ(ə)n/ *n.* [L (CELERITY)]
accelerator *n.* device for increasing speed, esp. pedal that controls speed of engine etc.; apparatus for producing fast charged particles.
accent 1 /'æksənt/ *n.* prominence given to syllable by stress or pitch; particular (esp. local or national) mode of pronunciation (*BBC, Cockney, Liverpool, accent*); mark on letter or word to indicate pitch, stress, quality of vowel, etc.; distinctive feature or emphasis (*accent on comfort*). **2** /æk'sent/ *v.t.* pronounce with accent; write accents on; accentuate. [F or L (*cantus* song)]
accentuate /æk'sentjʊeɪt/ *v.t.* emphasize, make prominent; **accentuation** /-'eɪʃ(ə)n/ *n.* [med.L (prec.)]
accept /ək'sept/ *v.t.* consent to receive (thing offered, or *absol.*); answer affirmatively (invitation, suitor); regard favourably; believe, receive (opinion, explanation) as valid; receive as adequate or suitable (*hotel accepts traveller's cheques*; *machine only accepts tokens*); undertake (office or responsibility). [F or L (*capio* take)]
acceptable *a.* worth accepting, welcome; tolerable (*an acceptable sacrifice*); **acceptability** /-'bɪlɪtɪ/ *n.* [F (prec.)]
acceptance *n.* consent to receive; affirmative response to invitation;

favourable reception (*of* person or thing), approval (*found wide acceptance*).

access /'ækses/ **1** *n.* approach, way in; right or means of approaching or reaching (*gain access to the building, information*); outburst, esp. *of* emotion. **2** *v.t.* obtain (data) from computer; accession. **3 access time** time taken to retrieve information stored in computer. [F or L (ACCEDE)]

accessary see ACCESSORY.

accessible /ək'sesɪb(ə)l/ *a.* able to be reached or obtained; **accessibility** /-'bɪlɪtɪ/ *n.*

accession /ək'seʃ(ə)n/ **1** *n.* acceding or attaining (*to* position or office, esp. throne); thing added. **2** *v.* record addition of (new item) to library or museum.

accessory /ək'sesərɪ/ (now preferred in all senses to **accessary**) **1** *n.* additional or extra thing, (usu. in *pl.*) small attachment or fitting; one who helps in or is privy *to* an (esp. illegal) act. **2** *a.* additional, contributing in minor way, dispensable. [med.L (ACCEDE)]

accidence /'æksɪdəns/ *n.* part of grammar dealing with the variable parts of words. [L (foll.)]

accident *n.* event that is unexpected or without apparent cause; unintentional act, chance (*did it by accident*); unfortunate esp. harmful event (*killed in a car accident*). [F f. L (*cado* fall)]

accidental /æksɪ'dent(ə)l/ **1** *a.* happening or done by accident. **2** *n. Mus.* sign indicating momentary departure from key signature by raising or lowering of note. [L (prec.)]

acclaim /ə'kleɪm/ **1** *v.t.* welcome or applaud enthusiastically; hail as (*acclaimed him king*). **2** *n.* shout of applause, welcome. [L *acclamo* (CLAIM)]

acclamation /æklə'meɪʃ(ə)n/ *n.* loud and eager assent to proposal; shouting in person's honour.

acclimatize /ə'klaɪmətaɪz/ *v.* accustom or become accustomed to new climate or conditions; **acclimatization** /-'zeɪʃ(ə)n/ *n.* [F *acclimater* (CLIMATE)]

acclivity /ə'klɪvɪtɪ/ *n.* upward slope. [L (*clivus* slope)]

accolade /'ækəleɪd/ *n.* bestowal of praise; touch made with sword at conferring of knighthood. [F f. Prov., f. L *collum* neck]

accommodate /ə'kɒmədeɪt/ *v.t.* provide lodging for (*flat accommodates three people*); do favour to, oblige (person), supply (person *with*); adapt, harmonize, reconcile (*must accommodate himself to new surroundings, cannot accommodate your needs to mine*). [L(COMMODE)]

accommodating *a.* obliging, compliant.

accommodation /əkɒmə'deɪʃ(ə)n/ *n.* lodging; adaptation, adjustment, convenient arrangement; **accommodation address** one used on letters to person unable or unwilling to give permanent address.

accompaniment /ə'kʌmpənɪmənt/ *n.* instrumental or orchestral part supporting or partnering solo instrument, voice, or group; accompanying thing; **accompanist** *n.* (in *Mus.* sense). [foll.]

accompany /ə'kʌmpənɪ/ *v.t.* go with, escort, attend; be done or found with (*speech accompanied with gestures*); supplement (e.g. word *with* blow); *Mus.* support or partner with accompaniment. [F (COMPANION)]

accomplice /ə'kʌmplɪs/ *n.* partner in crime or wrongdoing. [F f. L (COMPLEX)]

accomplish /ə'kʌmplɪʃ/ *v.t.* perform, complete, succeed in doing. [F f. L (COMPLETE)]

accomplished *a.* clever, skilled.

accomplishment *n.* acquired skill, esp. social; completion; thing achieved.

accord /ə'kɔ:d/ **1** *v.* be consistent *with*; grant (permission, request), give (welcome etc.). **2** *n.* harmony, consent (*with one accord*). **3 of one's own accord** spontaneously. [F f. L *cor cord-* heart]

accordance *n.* harmony, agreement (*in accordance with*); **accordant** *a.*

according *adv.* **according as** in a manner or to a degree that varies as (*pays according as he is able*); **according to** in a manner corresponding to, in proportion to (*lives according to her means*); as stated by (*according to Fowler*).

accordingly *adv.* as the (stated) circumstances suggest (*please act accordingly; they had little money and accordingly went home*).

accordion /ə'kɔ:dɪən/ *n.* portable musical instrument with bellows, metal reeds, and keys and/or buttons. [G, f. It. *accordare* to tune]

accost /ə'kɒst/ *v.t.* approach and address, esp. boldly; (of prostitute) solicit. [F, f. L *costa* rib]

account /ə'kaʊnt/ **1** *n.* statement of money, goods, or services received or expended, with balance; relationship or facility for commercial or financial transactions at bank, or firm giving credit (*open an account*); narration, description (*an account of the voyage*); profit, advantage (*to good account*); explanation of administration or behaviour (*called him to account*); appraisal or estimation (*take into account*); importance, value (*of some, no, account*); counting, reckoning. **2** *v.* consider, regard as (*account him a fool, wise*). **3 account for** give reckoning of (money etc. entrusted), answer for (one's conduct), serve as or provide explanation for; kill (game), defeat (player, side), take (wickets); **by all accounts** in the common opinion; **on account** (of goods) to be paid for later, (of money) in part payment; **on account of** because of. [F (COUNT[1])]

accountable *a.* responsible (*for* action or thing, *to* person); explicable.

accountant *n.* one who inspects or keeps financial accounts; **accountancy** *n.*

accoutrements /ə'ku:trəmənts/, *US* **accouterments** /ə'ku:təmənts/ *n. pl.* equipment, trappings; soldier's outfit other than weapons and uniform. [F]

accredit /ə'kredɪt/ *v.t.* attribute (saying etc. *to* person), credit (person *with* saying etc.); send (ambassador etc.) with credentials *to* person, *to* or *at* a court or government; gain belief or influence for (adviser, advice, statement). [F (CREDIT)]

accredited *a.* having credentials, officially recognized; generally accepted or believed.

accretion /ə'kri:ʃ(ə)n/ *n.* growth or increase by accumulation or addition of separate items or by organic enlargement; the resulting whole; (adhesion of) extraneous matter added. [L (*cresco cret-* grow)]

accrue /ə'kru:/ *v.i.* come as natural increase or advantage, esp. financial (*to* person, *from* thing). [F f. L (as prec.)]

accumulate /ə'kju:mjʊleɪt/ *v.* heap up, bring together, get more and more of; produce or acquire thus; become numerous, form an increasing mass or quantity. [L (CUMULUS)]

accumulation /əkju:mjʊ'leɪʃ(ə)n/ *n.* accumulating, being accumulated; growth of capital by continued interest; accumulated mass.

accumulative /ə'kju:mjʊlətɪv/ *a.* arising from accumulation, cumulative.

accumulator /ə'kju:mjʊleɪtə/ *n.* rechargeable electric cell; bet placed on sequence of events with winnings on each staked on next; storage register in computer.

accuracy /'ækjʊrəsɪ/ *n.* precision, exactness, esp. arising from careful effort. [L (*cura* care)]

accurate /'ækjʊrət/ *a.* precise, conforming exactly with truth or a standard.

accursed /ə'kɜ:sɪd/ *a.* lying under a curse; *colloq.* detestable, annoying. [OE (*a-* intensive, CURSE)]

accusation /ækju:'zeɪʃ(ə)n/ *n.* accusing, being accused. [F (ACCUSE)]

accusative /ə'kju:zətɪv/ *Gram.* **1** *n.* case expressing object of action. **2** *a.* of or in the accusative.

accusatory /ə'kju:zətərɪ/ *a.* of or conveying accusation.

accuse /ə'kju:z/ *v.t.* indict, charge with fault or crime (*accused him of murder, of killing his wife*); lay the blame on. [F, f. L *accusare* (CAUSE)]

accustom /ə'kʌstəm/ *v.t.* make (*oneself*, person or thing) used *to* (thing) (esp. in pass.: *she was accustomed to his strange ways*). [F (CUSTOM)]

accustomed *a.* customary; used *to*.

ace *n.* playing-card etc. with single spot and generally having the value 'one'; one who excels in some activity (*an ace batsman*); a stroke (esp. service) in tennis too good for opponent to return; pilot who has shot down many enemy aircraft; **within an ace of** on the verge of. [F f. L *as* unity]

-aceous *suffix* forming adjectives in sense 'of the nature of', esp. in natural sciences (*herbaceous*). [L]

acerbic /ə'sɜ:bɪk/ *a.* harsh and sharp, esp. of speech, temper, etc.; **acerbity** *n.* [F or L (*acerbus* sour)]

acetate /'æsɪteɪt/ *n.* salt or ester of acetic acid, esp. cellulose ester; fabric made from cellulose acetate. [foll.]

acetic /ə'si:tɪk/ *a.* of or like vinegar; **acetic acid** essential ingredient of vinegar. [F, f. L *acetum* vinegar]

acetone /'æsɪtəʊn/ *n.* a colourless volatile liquid that dissolves organic compounds.

acetylene /ə'setɪli:n/ *n.* a hydrocarbon gas burning with bright flame used for welding.

ache /eɪk/ **1** *n.* continuous or prolonged dull pain or mental distress. **2** *v.i.* suffer from or be source of this. [OE]

achieve /ə'tʃi:v/ *v.t.* reach or attain by effort (objective or distinction); gain or earn (*achieved notoriety*); accomplish, perform (feat, task). [F *achever* (CHIEF)]

achievement *n.* feat achieved; act of achieving.

Achilles' heel /ə'kɪli:z/ weak or vulnerable point. [*Achilles*, Gk hero in *Iliad*]

Achilles tendon tendon attaching calf muscles to heel.

achromatic /ækrəʊ'mætɪk/ *a.* free from colour; transmitting light without separating it into constituent colours; **achromatically** *adv.* [F (A-, CHROME)]

achy /'eɪkɪ/ *a.* full of or suffering from aches. [ACHE]

acid /'æsɪd/ **1** *n.* any of a class of substances that contain hydrogen and neutralize alkalis, and of which most are sour; any sour substance; *sl.* the drug LSD. **2** *a.* sour; sharp or bitter (*acid drop,* *wit*). 3 **acid rain** acid formed in atmosphere esp. from industrial waste and falling with rain; **acid test** crucial and conclusive test. 4 **acidic** /ə'sɪdɪk/ *a.*; **acidify** /ə'sɪdɪfaɪ/ *v.t.*; **acidity** /ə'sɪdɪtɪ/ *n.* [F or L (*aceo* be sour)]

acidosis /æsɪ'dəʊsɪs/ *n.* over-acid condition of blood or body tissue. [-OSIS]

acidulate /ə'sɪdjʊleɪt/ *v.t.* make (thing) somewhat acid. [L dimin. (ACID)]

acidulous /ə'sɪdjʊləs/ *a.* somewhat acid.

ack-ack /æk'æk/ *colloq.* 1 *a.* anti-aircraft. 2 *n.* anti-aircraft gun etc. [formerly signallers' name for AA]

ack emma /æk 'emə/ *colloq.* = A.M. [formerly signallers' name for A.M.]

acknowledge /ək'nɒlɪdʒ/ *v.t.* agree to the truth of, admit (*acknowledge it as true, to be true, that it is true*); report receipt of (letter etc.); express appreciation of, reward (service etc.); show that one has noticed (*acknowledged my presence with a grunt*); own, recognize validity of (*the acknowledged king*). [AD-, KNOWLEDGE]

acknowledgement *n.* act of acknowledging; (esp.) thing given or done in return for service etc.

acme /'ækmɪ/ *n.* highest point, point of perfection. [Gk]

acne /'æknɪ/ *n.* skin eruption with red pimples. [L]

acolyte /'ækəlaɪt/ *n.* person assisting priest in a service or procession; assistant, beginner. [L (Gk *akolouthos* follower)]

aconite /'ækənaɪt/ *n.* poisonous plant with yellow or blue flowers (esp. monkshood); drug from this. [F or L f. Gk *akoniton*]

acorn /'eɪkɔ:n/ *n.* fruit of oak, with cuplike base. [OE]

acoustic /ə'ku:stɪk/ 1 *a.* of sound or sense of hearing. 2 *n.* = ACOUSTICS (*hall has a good acoustic*). 3 **acoustical** *a.*; **acoustically** *adv.* [Gk *akouō* hear]

acoustics *n. pl.* properties or qualities (esp. of room, hall, etc.) in transmitting sound; (as *sing.*) science of sound.

acquaint /ə'kweɪnt/ *v.t.* make aware or familiar (*acquaint him, himself, with the facts*); **be acquainted with** know (person) slightly. [F f. L (AD-, COGNIZANCE)]

acquaintance *n.* being acquainted (*with* person or thing); person one knows slightly; **acquaintanceship** *n.*

acquiesce /ækwɪ'es/ *v.i.* agree esp. tacitly; not object; **acquiesce in** accept (arrangement etc.); **acquiescence** *n.*; **acquiescent** *a.* [L (AD-, QUIET)]

acquire /ə'kwaɪə/ *v.t.* gain by and for oneself, come into possession of (*acquire property, skills, a reputation*); **acquired taste** one developed by experience. [F f. L (AD-, *quaero -quisit-* seek)]

acquirement *n.* mental attainment.

acquisition /ækwɪ'zɪʃ(ə)n/ *n.* thing acquired, esp. when useful. [L (ACQUIRE)]

acquisitive /ə'kwɪzɪtɪv/ *a.* keen to acquire things.

acquit /ə'kwɪt/ *v.t.* (-**tt**-) declare (person) not guilty (*of* offence); free or clear (person *of* blame or responsibility etc.); **acquit oneself** perform, conduct oneself *well, badly*, etc. [F f. L (AD-, QUIT)]

acquittal *n.* deliverance from a charge by verdict etc.; performance (*of* duty).

acquittance *n.* payment of or release from debt, receipt in full.

acre /'eɪkə/ *n.* measure of land, 4840 sq. yds., 0.405 ha.; piece of land, field (*broad acres*). [OE]

acreage /'eɪkərɪdʒ/ *n.* number of acres, extent of land.

acrid /'ækrɪd/ *a.* bitterly pungent; bitter in temper etc.; **acridity** /ə'krɪdɪtɪ/ *n.* [L *acer* keen, pungent]

acrimonious /ækrɪ'məʊnɪəs/ *a.* bitter in manner or temper; **acrimony** /'ækrɪmənɪ/ *n.*

acrobat /'ækrəbæt/ *n.* performer of spectacular gymnastic feats; **acrobatic** /ækrə'bætɪk/ *a.*; **acrobatically** /-'bætɪkəlɪ/ *adv.* [F f. Gk *akrobatēs* (*akron* summit, *bainō* walk)]

acrobatics /ækrə'bætɪks/ *n.pl.* acrobatic feats; (as *sing.*) performance of these.

acronym /'ækrənɪm/ *n.* word formed from initial letters of other words (e.g. *Ernie, Nato, laser*). [Gk *akron* end, *onoma* name]

acropolis /ə'krɒpəlɪs/ *n.* citadel or upper fortified part of ancient Greek city, esp. of Athens. [Gk (*akron* summit, *polis* city)]

across /ə'krɒs/ 1 *prep.* from side to side of (*spread across the floor; bridge across the road*); to or on the other side of (*walked across the room; house is across the river*); forming a cross with (*cat across her lap*). 2 *adv.* from side to side (*stretched across*); to or on the other side (*ran across; shall soon be across*). 3 **across the board** general(ly), applying to all. [F *à, en, croix* (CROSS)]

acrostic /ə'krɒstɪk/ *n.* poem in which certain letters (usu. first or first and last in each line) form word(s). [F or Gk (*akron* end, *stikhos* row)]

acrylic /ə'krɪlɪk/ 1 *a.* of material made with synthetic polymer derived from acrylic acid. 2 *n.* an acrylic fibre. 3 **acrylic acid** an unsaturated organic acid. [L *acer* pungent, *oleo* smell]

act 1 *n.* thing done, deed; process of doing, operation (*caught in the act*);

piece of entertainment, usu. one of series in programme; a pretence; main division of play or opera; decree of legislative body etc.; document of legal transaction (*act and deed*). **2** *v.* perform actions, behave (*see how they act under stress*; *you acted wisely*); perform functions (*act as referee*; *brakes did not act*; *we must act quickly*); be actor or actress, personate (character in play or life: *act Othello, the fool*), portray (incident, story) by actions. **3** **act for** be representative of (person); **act of God** operation of uncontrollable natural forces; **get into the act** *sl.* become participant; **put on an act** *colloq.* carry out pretence. [F and L (*ago act-* do)]

acting *attrib. a.* serving temporarily or on behalf of others (*acting manager*; *Acting Captain*).

actinism /'æktɪnɪz(ə)m/ *n.* property of short-wave radiation that produces chemical changes, as in photography. [Gk *aktis* ray]

actinium /æk'tɪnɪəm/ *n.* radioactive element found in pitchblende. [as prec.]

action /'ækʃ(ə)n/ *n.* process of doing or performing, exertion of energy or influence (*demand for action*; *man of action*; *action of acid on metal*); thing done (*useful actions*); series of events in drama, *sl.* events going on around one (*a slice of the action*); battle, fighting (*killed in action*); mechanism of instrument; mode or style of movement of animal or human (*runner has a good action*); legal process (*bring an action*); **action stations** positions of troops etc. ready for battle; **out of action** not working. [F f. L (ACT)]

actionable *a.* providing ground for action at law.

activate /'æktɪveɪt/ *v.t.* make active; make radioactive. [foll.]

active /'æktɪv/ *a.* consisting in or marked by action, energetic, diligent (*active helper, support, life*; *is active for her age*); working, operative (*active volcano*); originating action, not merely passive or inert (*active resistance, ingredients*); radioactive; *Gram.* attributing action of verb to person or thing whence it logically proceeds (e.g. of verbs in *guns kill, we saw him*); **active voice** *Gram.* that comprising active forms of verbs. [F or L (ACT)]

activist *n.* one who follows a policy of vigorous action in a cause, esp. in politics.

activity /æk'tɪvɪtɪ/ *n.* being active, exertion of energy; sphere or kind of action (*outdoor activities*).

actor *n.* performer in drama, film, etc.; **actress** *n. fem.* [L (ACT)]

actual /'æktʃʊəl/ *a.* existing in fact, real; present, current (*the actual situation*). [F f. L (ACT)]

actuality /æktʃʊ'ælɪtɪ/ *n.* reality, (in *pl.*) existing conditions.

actually /'æktʃʊəlɪ/ *adv.* really, for the time being, strange as it seems (*he actually refused!*).

actuary /'æktʃʊərɪ/ *n.* expert in statistics, esp. one who calculates insurance risks and premiums; **actuarial** /-'eərɪəl/ *a.* [L *actuarius* bookkeeper]

actuate /'æktʃʊeɪt/ *v.t.* communicate motion to (machine etc.), cause to function; cause (person) to act. [L]

acuity /ə'kju:ɪtɪ/ *n.* sharpness, acuteness. [F or med.L (ACUTE)]

acumen /'ækjʊmen, ə'kju:men/ *n.* keen insight or discernment. [L, = ACUTE thing]

acupuncture /'ækju:pʌŋktʃə/ *n.* method of pricking body tissue with needles as medical treatment. [L *acu* with needle]

acute /ə'kju:t/ *a.* keen, penetrating (*acute pain, hearing*); shrewd, perceptive (*an acute critic*); (of disease) coming sharply to crisis, severe, not chronic; (of difficulty) sharp in effect, serious (*an acute shortage*); (of sound) high, shrill; **acute accent** mark (´) over vowel to show quality or length; **acute angle** one less than 90°. [L *acutus* pointed]

-acy *suffix* forming nouns esp. (1) of quality (*accuracy, obstinacy*), (2) of state, condition, office, etc. (*lunacy, magistracy, piracy*). [F *-acie*, L *-acia*, *-atia*, Gk *-ateia*]

ad *n. colloq.* advertisement. [abbr.]

ad- *prefix* (altered or assimilated before some letters) implying motion or direction to; change into; addition, adherence, increase; simple intensification. [F or L]

AD *abbr.* of the Christian era. [ANNO DOMINI]

adage /'ædɪdʒ/ *n.* traditional maxim, proverb. [F f. L]

adagio /ə'dɑ:ʒɪəʊ/ *Mus.* **1** *adv.* in slow time. **2** *n.* (*pl.* **adagios**) movement to be played this way. [It.]

Adam /'ædəm/ *n.* the first man; **Adam's apple** projection of cartilage at front of (esp. man's) neck; **not know person from Adam** have no knowledge of his appearance. [Heb., = man]

adamant /'ædəmənt/ *a.* stubbornly resolute, resistant to persuasion. [F f. L f. Gk *adamas adamant-* untameable]

adapt /ə'dæpt/ *v.t.* fit, adjust (thing *to* another); make suitable (*to* or *for* a purpose); alter or modify (esp. a text); **adapt (oneself)** become adjusted (*to* new conditions); **adaptable** *a.*; **adaptation** /-'teɪʃ(ə)n/ *n.* [F f. L (AD-, APT)]

adaptor *n.* device for making equipment compatible; device for connecting several electric plugs to one socket.
add *v.* join (thing *to* another) as increase or supplement; unite numbers to get their total; say further (*she added that I was wrong*); **add in** include; **add up** find the sum of, amount *to*, *colloq.* make sense. [L *addo*]
addendum /ə'dendəm/ *n.* (*pl.* **addenda**) thing to be added; (in *pl.*) additional matter at end of book.
adder *n.* small venomous snake, esp. common viper. [OE, orig. *nadder*]
addict /'ædɪkt/ *n.* person addicted esp. to drug (*heroin addict*); devotee (*chess addict*). [L (AD-, *dico* say)]
addicted /ə'dɪktɪd/ *a.* given over habitually *to* (a drug etc., a practice: *addicted to smoking*); devoted *to* (an interest).
addiction /ə'dɪkʃ(ə)n/ *n.* condition of taking drug etc. habitually and with adverse effects on ceasing.
addictive /ə'dɪktɪv/ *a.* causing addiction.
addition /ə'dɪʃ(ə)n/ *n.* adding; thing added (*a useful addition*); **in addition** as something added (*to*). [F or L (ADD)]
additional *a.* added, extra, supplementary.
additive /'ædɪtɪv/ **1** *n.* thing added, esp. substance with special properties. **2** *a.* involving addition. [L (ADD)]
addle /'æd(ə)l/ *v.* muddle, confuse; (of egg) become addled. [OE, = filth]
addled *a.* (of egg) rotten and producing no chick; muddled.
address /ə'dres/ **1** *n.* place where person lives or firm is situated, particulars of this esp. for postal purposes; discourse to audience; part of computer instruction that specifies location of item of stored information. **2** *v.t.* write postal directions on (envelope etc.); direct in speech or writing (*address remarks, petition*, etc., *to* person); speak or write to, esp. formally (*address the audience, how to address a duke*); direct one's attention to; take aim at (ball in golf). **3 address oneself to** speak or write to; attend to. [F (AD-, DIRECT)]
addressee /ædre'si:/ *n.* person to whom letter etc. is addressed. [-EE]
Addressograph /ə'dresəʊgrɑ:f/ *n.* **(P)** machine for printing addresses on envelopes.
adduce /ə'dju:s/ *v.t.* cite as proof or instance; **adducible** *a.* [L (AD-, *duco* lead)]
adenoids /'ædɪnɔɪdz/ *n.pl.* enlarged lymphatic tissue between back of nose and throat, often hindering breathing. [Gk *adēn* gland]
adept /'ædept, ə'dept/ **1** *a.* thoroughly proficient (*in* or *at* something). **2** *n.* adept person. [L *adipiscor adept-* attain]
adequate /'ædɪkwət/ *a.* sufficient or satisfactory in quantity or quality (*to* requirements); barely sufficient; **adequacy** *n.* [L (AD-, EQUATE)]
adhere /əd'hɪə/ *v.i.* give support or allegiance (*to* person, party, agreement, opinion); behave according *to* (rule, undertaking); stick fast (*to* substance). [F or L (*haereo* stick)]
adherent 1 *n.* supporter or devotee (*of* party, activity). **2** *a.* adhering or sticking *to*. **3 adherence** *n.* [F (prec.)]
adhesion /əd'hi:ʒ(ə)n/ *n.* adhering (*lit.* or *fig.*); unnatural growing together of body tissues due to inflammation. [F or L (ADHERE)]
adhesive /əd'hi:sɪv/ **1** *a.* sticky, having the property of adhering. **2** *n.* adhesive substance. [F (ADHERE)]
ad hoc /æd 'hɒk/ for this purpose, special(ly). [L]
adieu /ə'dju:/ *int.* & *n.* (*pl.* **adieus**) goodbye. [F, = to God]
ad infinitum /æd ɪnfɪ'naɪtəm/ without limit, for ever. [L]
adipose /'ædɪpəʊz/ *a.* of fat, fatty (*adipose tissue*); **adiposity** /-'pɒsɪtɪ/ *n.* [L (*adeps* fat)]
adjacent /ə'dʒeɪsənt/ *a.* lying near, next (*to*); **adjacency** *n.* [L (*jaceo* lie)]
adjective /'ædʒɪktɪv/ *n.* word indicating an attribute, used to describe or modify noun (e.g. *old, French, my, this*; *tall* man; man is *tall*); **adjectival** /-'taɪv(ə)l/ *a.* [F f. L (*jaceo* lie)]
adjoin /ə'dʒɔɪn/ *v.t.* be next to and joined with. [F f. L (*jungo* join)]
adjourn /ə'dʒɜ:n/ *v.* put off, postpone, break off for later resumption (meeting, discussion, etc.); (of assembled persons) suspend proceedings and separate, transfer meeting *to* another place; **adjournment** *n.* [F f. L (AD-, *diurnum* day)]
adjudge /ə'dʒʌdʒ/ *v.t.* pronounce judgement on (matter); pronounce or award judicially; **adjudg(e)ment** *n.* [F f. L (*judex* judge)]
adjudicate /ə'dʒu:dɪkeɪt/ *v.* act as judge in court, tribunal, competition, etc.; adjudge; **adjudication** /-'keɪʃ(ə)n/ *n.*; **adjudicative** *a.*; **adjudicator** *n.*
adjunct /'ædʒʌŋkt/ *n.* thing subordinate or incidental (*to* or *of* another); *Gram.* amplification of predicate, subject, etc. [L (ADJOIN)]
adjure /ə'dʒʊə/ *v.t.* charge or request solemnly or earnestly (*to do* thing); **adjuration** /ædʒʊə'reɪʃ(ə)n/ *n.* [L *adjuro* put to oath (JURY)]
adjust /ə'dʒʌst/ *v.* arrange, put in correct order or position, regulate; make

suitable (*to* need or purpose); harmonize (discrepancies); assess (loss or damages); **adjust oneself** make oneself suited (*to* new conditions); **adjustment** *n*. [F f. L (*juxta* near)]

adjutant /'ædʒʊtənt/ *n*. army officer assisting superior in administrative duties; assistant; **adjutant (bird)** large Indian stork. [L (AD-, *juro jut-* help)]

ad lib /æd 'lɪb/ **1** *v*. speak without formal preparation, improvise. **2** *a*. improvised. **3** *adv*. as one pleases, to any desired extent. [abbr. of L *ad libitum* according to pleasure]

admin /'ædmɪn/ *n*. *colloq*. administration. [abbr.]

administer /əd'mɪnɪstə/ *v*. manage (affairs, person's estate, etc.); formally give out (justice, sacrament), present (oath *to*); furnish, give (*administer a dose, a rebuke*); apply (remedy *to*); act as administrator. [F f. L (AD-, MINISTER)]

administrate /əd'mɪnɪstreɪt/ *v*. administer, esp. manage, act as administrator. [L (prec.)]

administration /ədmɪnɪ'streɪʃ(ə)n/ *n*. administering, esp. of public affairs; the Government. [ADMINISTER]

administrative /əd'mɪnɪstrətɪv/ *a*. of management of affairs.

administrator /əd'mɪnɪstreɪtə/ *n*. manager (of affairs or business); one capable of organizing; one authorized to manage an estate. [L (ADMINISTER)]

admirable /'ædmərəb(ə)l/ *a*. worthy of admiration; excellent; **admirably** *adv*. [F f. L (ADMIRE)]

admiral /'ædmər(ə)l/ *n*. commander-in-chief of navy; naval officer of high rank, commander of fleet or squadron (four grades: **Admiral of the Fleet, Admiral, Vice-Admiral, Rear-Admiral**); any of various butterflies. [F f. L. f. Arab. (AMIR)]

Admiralty *n*. (also **Admiralty Board**) department formerly administering Royal Navy.

admiration /ædmɪ'reɪʃ(ə)n/ *n*. pleased or approving contemplation. [foll.]

admire /əd'maɪə/ *v.t.* regard with approval, respect, or satisfaction; express admiration of. [F or L (AD-, *miror* wonder at)]

admirer *n*. woman's suitor; devotee of able or famous person.

admiring *a*. showing or feeling admiration (*admiring follower, glances*).

admissible /əd'mɪsɪb(ə)l/ *a*. (of idea etc.) worthy of being accepted or considered; (of evidence) allowable in law. [F or L (ADMIT)]

admission /əd'mɪʃ(ə)n/ *n*. acknowledgement (of fact, error); admitting or being admitted, fee for this. [foll.]

admit /əd'mɪt/ *v*. (**-tt-**) recognize as true, acknowledge (*admit it to be so, that it is so*); confess *to* (deed, fault, etc.); let in, allow entrance of (person etc. *to* place, category, privilege, etc.); (of enclosed space) have room for; accept (proof, plea, statement); **admit of** allow as possible (doubt, improvement, etc.). [L (*mitto miss-* send)]

admittance *n*. admitting, being admitted, esp. to place.

admittedly *adv*. as acknowledged fact.

admixture /æd'mɪkstʃə/ *n*. thing added, esp. minor ingredient; adding of this. [AD-, MIXTURE]

admonish /əd'mɒnɪʃ/ *v.t.* reprove; urge, advise, remind (person *to do* thing, *that*); warn; **admonishment** *n*. [F f. L (*moneo* warn)]

admonition /ædmɒ'nɪʃ(ə)n/ *n*. reproof; warning; **admonitory** /əd'mɒnɪtərɪ/ *a*.

ad nauseam /æd 'nɔ:zɪæm/ to an excessive or sickening degree. [L, = to sickness]

ado /ə'du:/ *n*. fuss, busy activity; trouble. [AT, DO[3]; orig. in *much ado* = much to do]

adobe /ə'dəʊbɪ, ə'dəʊb/ *n*. unburnt sun-dried brick. [Sp.]

adolescent /ædə'lesənt/ **1** *a*. between childhood and adulthood. **2** *n*. adolescent person. **3 adolescence** *n*. [F f. L (ADULT)]

adopt /ə'dɒpt/ *v.t.* take (person) into a relationship, esp. *as* one's child or heir; choose (course etc.); take over (another's idea etc.); choose as candidate for office; accept responsibility for maintenance of (road etc.); approve or accept (report, accounts, etc.); **adoption** *n*. [F or L (AD-, OPT)]

adoptive *a*. due to adoption (*adoptive father*). [F f. L (prec.)]

adorable /ə'dɔ:rəb(ə)l/ *a*. worthy of adoration; *colloq*. delightful, charming. [foll.]

adore /ə'dɔ:/ *v.t.* regard with honour and deep affection; worship as divine; *colloq*. like very much; **adoration** /ædə'reɪʃ(ə)n/ *n*. [F f. L *adoro* worship]

adorer *n*. ardent admirer; worshipper.

adorn /ə'dɔ:n/ *v.t.* add beauty to, be an ornament to; furnish with ornament(s); **adornment** *n*. [F f. L (AD-, *orno* decorate)]

adrenal /ə'dri:n(ə)l/ *a*. close to the kidneys; **adrenal gland** one of two ductless glands above the kidney. [AD-, RENAL]

adrenalin /ə'drenəlɪn/ *n*. (also **adrenaline**) hormone secreted by adrenal glands, causing excitement and stimulation; this extracted or synthesized for medicinal use.

adrift /ə'drɪft/ *adv*. & *predic*. *a*. drifting; *fig*. at the mercy of circumstances; *colloq*. amiss, unfastened. [A[3]]

adroit /ə'drɔɪt/ *a.* dextrous, skilful. [F (*à droit* according to right)]
adsorb /æd'sɔ:b/ *v.t.* (of solid) hold (particles of another substance) to its surface; **adsorbent** *a.*; **adsorption** *n.* [AD-, ABSORB]
adulation /ædjʊ'leɪʃ(ə)n/ *n.* obsequious flattery. [F or L (*adulor* fawn on)]
adult /'ædʌlt/ **1** *a.* mature, grown-up. **2** *n.* adult person. **3 adulthood** *n.* [L *adolesco adultus* grow up]
adulterate /ə'dʌltəreɪt/ *v.t.* debase (esp. foods) by admixture of other substances; **adulteration** /-'reɪʃ(ə)n/ *n.* [L *adultero* corrupt]
adulterer /ə'dʌltərə/ *n.* person (esp. man) who commits adultery; **adulteress** *n. fem.* [F f. L (prec.)]
adulterous /ə'dʌltərəs/ *a.* of or committing adultery.
adultery /ə'dʌltərɪ/ *n.* voluntary sexual intercourse of married person with person other than spouse.
adumbrate /'ædʌmbreɪt/ *v.t.* indicate faintly; represent in outline; foreshadow; overshadow; **adumbration** /-'breɪʃ(ə)n/ *n.* [L (AD-, *umbra* shade)]
advance /əd'vɑ:ns/ **1** *v.* come or go forward, progress, rise in rank; lend, pay beforehand; move or put forward; help on, promote (person or plan); present (claim or suggestion); bring (event) to earlier date; raise (price). **2** *n.* going forward, progress; loan, payment beforehand; (in *pl.*) amorous approaches (*to* person); rise in price. **3** *attrib.* done, given, etc., beforehand (*advance warning*). **4 advanced level** higher level in GCE examination; **in advance** ahead in time or place. [F f. L (AB-, *ante* before)]
advancement *n.* promotion of person or plan.
advantage /əd'vɑ:ntɪdʒ/ **1** *n.* favourable or beneficial circumstance (*book has the advantage of brevity*); superiority in particular respect (*over* person); next point after deuce in tennis. **2** *v.t.* be or give advantage to (person or plan). **3 take advantage of** use or exploit for personal benefit; seduce (woman). **4 advantageous** /ædvən'teɪdʒəs/ *a.* [F (prec.)]
Advent /'ædvent/ *n.* season before Christmas; coming of Christ; (**advent**) important arrival. [OE f. F f. L *adventus* (*venio* come)]
Adventist *n.* member of sect believing in second coming of Christ.
adventitious /ædven'tɪʃəs/ *a.* accidental, casual; added from outside; *Biol.* occurring in unusual place. [L (prec.)]
adventure /əd'ventʃə/ **1** *n.* unusual and exciting experience; daring enterprise (*spirit of adventure*). **2** *v.i.* dare, venture; engage in adventure. [F f. L (ADVENT)]
adventurer *n.* one who seeks adventures; mercenary soldier; financial speculator; one ready to take risks for personal gain; **adventuress** *n. fem.*
adventurous *a.* venturesome, enterprising.
adverb /'ædvɜ:b/ *n.* word indicating manner, degree, circumstance, etc., used to modify adjective, verb, or another adverb (e.g. *gently, quite, then, there*; *how* in *cannot explain how*); **adverbial** /əd'vɜ:bɪəl/ *a.* [F or L (AD-, *verbum* word, VERB)]
adversary /'ædvəsərɪ/ *n.* opponent, enemy. [foll.]
adverse /'ædvɜ:s/ *a.* unfavourable (*adverse criticism*); harmful (*adverse effects*). [F f. L (AD-, *verto vers-* turn)]
adversity /əd'vɜ:sɪtɪ/ *n.* misfortune, distress.
advert[1] /'ædvɜ:t/ *n. colloq.* advertisement. [abbr.]
advert[2] /əd'vɜ:t/ *v.i.* refer *to* in speech or writing. [ADVERSE]
advertise /'ædvətaɪz/ *v.* describe and praise (goods etc.) in public medium to promote sales; make generally known; ask *for* by notice in newspaper etc. [F *avertir* (ADVERSE)]
advertisement /əd'vɜ:tɪsmənt/ *n.* public announcement of goods etc. for sale; advertising. [F *avertissement* (ADVERSE)]
advice /əd'vaɪs/ *n.* opinion given as to future action; information, news; formal notice of transaction; **take advice** seek it, act according to it. [ADVISE]
advisable /əd'vaɪzəb(ə)l/ *a.* recommendable, expedient; **advisability** /-'bɪlɪtɪ/ *n.* [foll.]
advise /əd'vaɪz/ *v.* give advice (to), recommend (*she advised caution, me to rest*), inform (*of* thing, *that*); **advised** *a.* (*ill-advised*). [F f. L (AD-, *video vis-* see)]
advisedly /əd'vaɪzɪdlɪ/ *adv.* deliberately.
adviser *n.* (also **advisor**) one who advises, esp. officially.
advisory *a.* giving advice (*advisory committee*).
advocacy /'ædvəkəsɪ/ *n.* pleading in support *of*; function of advocate. [foll.]
advocate **1** /'ædvəkət/ *n.* one who supports or speaks in favour *of* (policy etc.); one who pleads for another, esp. in lawcourt. **2** /'ædvəkeɪt/ *v.t.* support, plead for (policy etc.). [F f. L (AD-, *voco* call)]
adze /ædz/, *US* **adz** *n.* tool like axe, with arched blade at right angles to handle. [OE]
aegis /'i:dʒɪs/ *n.* protection, support. [L f. Gk *aigis* shield of Zeus or Athena]

aeolian /iː'əʊlɪən/ *a.* wind-borne; **aeolian harp** stringed instrument or toy giving musical sounds on exposure to wind. [L (*Aeolus* wind-god, f. Gk)]
aeon /'iːɒn/ *n.* long or indefinite period; an age. [L f. Gk]
aerate /'eəreɪt/ *v.t.* charge (liquid) with carbon dioxide; expose to action of air; **aeration** /-'reɪʃ(ə)n/ *n.* [L *aer* AIR]
aerial /'eərɪəl/ **1** *n.* wire or rod for transmitting or receiving radio waves. **2** *a.* from the air (*aerial attack, photography*); existing in the air; like air. [L f. Gk (AIR)]
aerie var. of EYRIE.
aero- *in comb.* air, aircraft. [Gk *aero-* (*aer* air)]
aerobatics /eərə'bætɪks/ *n.pl.* feats of expert and usu. spectacular flying of aircraft; (as *sing.*) performance of these. [AERO-, after ACROBATICS]
aerobics /eə'rəʊbɪks/ *n.pl.* vigorous exercises designed to increase oxygen intake. [AERO-, Gk *bios* life]
aerodrome /'eərədrəʊm/ *n.* airfield, airport. [AERO-, Gk *dromos* course]
aerodynamics /eərəʊdaɪ'næmɪks/ *n.pl.* (usu. treated as *sing.*) dynamics of solid bodies moving through air; **aerodynamic** *a.* [AERO-]
aerofoil /'eərəfɔɪl/ *n.* structure with curved surfaces (e.g. wing, fin, or tail-plane) designed to give lift in flight.
aeronautics /eərəʊ'nɔːtɪks/ *n.pl.* (usu. treated as *sing.*) science, art, or practice of aerial navigation; **aeronautic** *a.*; **aeronautical** *a.* [AERO-, NAUTICAL]
aeroplane /'eərəpleɪn/ *n.* mechanically driven heavier-than-air aircraft with wings. [F (AERO-, PLANE¹)]
aerosol /'eərəsɒl/ *n.* system of minute particles suspended in gas; device for producing fine spray of substance packed under pressure. [AERO-, SOL]
aerospace /'eərəʊspeɪs/ *n.* earth's atmosphere and outer space; aviation in this. [AERO-, SPACE]
aesthete /'iːsθiːt/ *n.* one who appreciates beauty in art etc. [Gk (*aisthanomai* perceive)]
aesthetic /iːs'θetɪk/ **1** *a.* concerned with or sensitive to the beautiful; artistic, tasteful. **2** *n.* (in *pl.*) philosophy of the beautiful in art etc. **3 aestheticism** /-'sɪz(ə)m/ *n.*
aetiology /iːtɪ'ɒlədʒɪ/ *n.* study of causation or of causes of disease; **aetiological** /-'lɒdʒɪk(ə)l/ *a.* [L f. Gk (*aitia* cause)]
AF *abbr.* audio frequency.
afar /ə'fɑː/ *adv.* at or to a distance. [A³]
affable /'æfəb(ə)l/ *a.* approachable and friendly; kind and courteous; **affability** /-'bɪlɪtɪ/ *n.* [F f. L *affabilis*]
affair /ə'feə/ *n.* matter, concern, thing to be done (*not my affair; the Dreyfus affair*); love-affair; *colloq.* thing or event (*wedding was a grand affair*); (in *pl.*) public or private business. [F *à faire* to do]
affect /ə'fekt/ *v.t.* produce effect on, (of disease) attack (*his liver is affected*); move, touch the feelings of; pretend (*affected ignorance, to be ignorant*); pose as (*affect the aesthete*); make a show of liking or using (*she affects fancy hats*). [F or L *affico affect-* influence]
affectation /æfek'teɪʃ(ə)n/ *n.* studied display (*of* modesty etc.), artificial manner, pretence.
affected *a.* pretended, artificial; full of affectation.
affection /ə'fekʃ(ə)n/ *n.* goodwill, fond feeling (*for, towards*); disease, diseased condition.
affectionate /ə'fekʃənət/ *a.* loving, fond.
affiance /ə'faɪəns/ *v.t.* (usu. in *pass.*) promise in marriage (*affianced to; his affianced bride*). [F f. L (*fidus* trusty)]
affidavit /æfɪ'deɪvɪt/ *n.* written statement confirmed by oath. [L, = has stated on oath]
affiliate /ə'fɪlɪeɪt/ **1** *v.t.* adopt, attach, connect, as member or branch (*to* or *with*). **2** *n.* affiliated person etc. [L (FILIAL)]
affiliation /əfɪlɪ'eɪʃ(ə)n/ *n.* affiliating or being affiliated; **affiliation order** one compelling putative father of illegitimate child to help support it.
affinity /ə'fɪnɪtɪ/ *n.* liking, attraction; relationship esp. by marriage; structural resemblance or similarity of character suggesting relationship; *Chem.* tendency of substances to combine with others. [F f. L (*finis* border)]
affirm /ə'fɜːm/ *v.* assert, state as fact; make legal affirmation. [F f. L (FIRM)]
affirmation /æfə'meɪʃ(ə)n/ *n.* affirming, esp. solemn declaration in place of oath.
affirmative /ə'fɜːmətɪv/ **1** *a.* affirming, answering that a thing is so. **2** *n.* that which affirms.
affix 1 /ə'fɪks/ *v.t.* attach, fasten; add in writing (signature etc.). **2** /'æfɪks/ *n.* thing affixed; *Gram.* prefix or suffix. [F or L (FIX)]
afflict /ə'flɪkt/ *v.t.* distress physically or mentally. [L (*fligo flict-* strike down)]
affliction /ə'flɪkʃ(ə)n/ *n.* distress, suffering; cause of this. [F f. L (prec.)]
affluence /'æflʊəns/ *n.* wealth; abundant supply. [foll.]
affluent 1 *a.* rich, wealthy; abundant. **2** *n.* tributary stream. **3 affluent society** one with wide distribution of wealth. [F f. L (FLUENT)]

afford /ə'fɔ:d/ *v.t.* have enough money, means, time, etc., for, be able to spare (usu. with *can* or *be able*: *can afford £50*; *cannot afford to lose £50*); be in a position to (*can afford to be critical*). [OE (*ge-* prefix implying completeness, FORTH)]

afforest /æ'fɒrɪst/ *v.t.* convert into forest; plant with trees; **afforestation** /-'steɪʃ(ə)n/ *n.* [L (FOREST)]

affray /ə'freɪ/ *n.* breach of the peace by fighting or rioting in public. [AF f. Rmc (= 'remove from peace')]

affront /ə'frʌnt/ **1** *n.* open insult. **2** *v.t.* insult openly; offend, embarrass. [F f. L (FRONT)]

Afghan /'æfgæn/ **1** *n.* native or language of Afghanistan; (**afghan**) kind of woollen blanket or shawl. **2** *a.* of Afghanistan. **3 Afghan hound** hunting dog with long silky hair. [Pashto]

aficionado /əfɪsjə'nɑ:dəʊ/ *n.* (*pl.* ***aficionados***) devotee of a sport or pastime. [Sp.]

afield /ə'fi:ld/ *adv.* away from home, to or at a distance (*far afield*). [OE (A³)]

afire /ə'faɪə/ *adv.* or *predic. a.* on fire (*lit.* or *fig.*). [A³]

aflame /ə'fleɪm/ *adv.* & *predic. a.* in flames; very excited. [A³]

afloat /ə'fləʊt/ *adv.* & *predic. a.* floating in water or air; at sea; out of debt or difficulty; in circulation, current. [OE (A³)]

afoot /ə'fʊt/ *adv.* & *predic. a.* progressing, in operation (*there is a plan afoot*). [A³]

afore /ə'fɔ:/ *adv.* & *prep.* in front of (*archaic* exc. in *Naut.* use); before, previously (*archaic* exc. in **aforementioned, aforesaid,** etc. previously mentioned etc., **aforethought** premeditated). [OE (A³)]

a fortiori /eɪ fɔ:tɪ'ɔ:raɪ/ with stronger reason (than a conclusion already accepted). [L]

afraid /ə'freɪd/ *predic. a.* alarmed, frightened (*afraid of the dark, of falling, that I'll fall, to continue*); *colloq.* politely regretful (*I'm afraid we're late*). [orig. p.p. of AFFRAY]

afresh /ə'freʃ/ *adv.* anew, with fresh beginning. [earlier *of fresh*]

African /'æfrɪkən/ **1** *n.* native (esp. dark-skinned) or inhabitant of Africa. **2** *a.* of Africa. **3 African violet** houseplant with dark leaves. [L]

Afrikaans /æfrɪ'kɑ:ns/ *n.* language derived from Dutch, used in South Africa. [Du., = African]

Afrikaner /æfrɪ'kɑ:nə/ *n.* Afrikaans-speaking white person in South Africa, esp. of Dutch descent.

Afro /'æfrəʊ/ *a.* (of hair) long and bushy, like that of some Blacks. [foll.]

Afro- *in comb.* African (*Afro-Asian*). [L, or abbr.]

Afro-American /æfrəʊə'merɪkən/ **1** *a.* of American Blacks or their culture. **2** *n.* American Black.

aft /ɑ:ft/ *adv.* in, near, or to stern or tail of ship or aircraft. [earlier *baft*]

after /'ɑ:ftə/ **1** *prep.* following in time, later than (*after midnight*; *after a month*; also with causal or concessive force: *after your behaviour tonight what do you expect?*; *after all that trouble he is still no better off*); behind (*shut the door after you*); in pursuit or quest of (*run after them*); about, concerning (*he asked after you*); in allusion to (*named him William after the prince*); according to, in imitation of (*made after the same pattern*; *a painting after Rubens*); next in importance to (*best book on the subject after mine*). **2** *conj.* after the time when (*left after they arrived*). **3** *adv.* later in time (*came soon after*); behind in place (*followed on after*). **4** *a.* later, following (*in after years*); nearer stern of ship (*after cabins*). **5 after all** see ALL; **after-care** attention after leaving hospital etc.; **after-effect** delayed effect following interval or primary effect; **after one's own heart** such as one is devoted to. [OE]

afterbirth *n.* placenta and foetal membrane discharged from womb after childbirth.

afterlife *n.* life after death.

aftermath /'ɑ:ftəmæθ, -mɑ:θ/ *n.* consequences, after-effects (*the aftermath of war*); new grass growing after mowing. [prec., *math* mowing]

aftermost *a.* last; furthest aft. [AFTER]

afternoon /ɑ:ftə'nu:n; *attrib.* 'ɑ:ft-/ *n.* time from noon to evening (*this afternoon*; *tomorrow afternoon*; *during the afternoon*; *afternoon tea*).

afters *n.pl. colloq.* course following main course of meal.

aftershave *n.* lotion used after shaving.

afterthought *n.* thing thought of or added later.

afterwards /'ɑ:ftəwədz/, *US* **afterward** *adv.* later, subsequently. [OE (AFT, -WARD)]

Ag *symb.* silver. [L *argentum*]

again /ə'geɪn, ə'gen/ *adv.* another time, once more (*try again*); as in previous position or condition (*home again, well again*); in addition (*half as much again*); further, besides, likewise (*then, again, who sent it?*); on the other hand (*I might, and again I might not*). [OE]

against /ə'geɪnst, ə'genst/ *prep.* in opposition to (*against hanging*; *against the law*); into collision or in contact with (*ran against a rock*; *lean against the wall*); to the disadvantage of (*his age is *against him*); in contrast to (*against a dark background*); in anticipation of or in preparation for (*against a rainy day*; *against the cold*); as compensating factor to (*income against expenditure*); in return for (*issued against payment of the fee*). [prec., inflexional *-s*]

agape[1] /ə'geɪp/ *predic. a.* gaping, open-mouthed. [A[3]]

agape[2] /'ægəpɪ/ *n.* early Christian Eucharistic feast; Christian love. [Gk, = brotherly love]

agaric /'ægərɪk/ *n.* fungus with cap and stalk, e.g. mushroom. [L f. Gk]

agate /'ægət/ *n.* kind of hard semi-precious stone with streaked colouring. [F f. L f. Gk]

agave /ə'geɪvɪ/ *n.* kind of spiny-leaved plant flowering only once. [*Agave*, woman in Gk myth.]

age 1 *n.* length of past life or existence (*what is your age?*); *colloq.* (esp. in *pl.*) a long time (*waited an age, for ages*); historical or other distinct period (*Bronze, Elizabethan, atomic age*); old age. **2** *v.* (*partic.* **ageing**) (cause to) grow old or show signs of age; (cause to) mature. **3** **come of age** reach legal majority (18, formerly 21); **under age** below this age. [F f. L *aetas*]

-age *suffix* forming nouns denoting action or condition (*breakage, peerage*), aggregate or number (*coverage, mileage*), cost (*postage*), result (*wreckage*), place or abode (*anchorage, orphanage*). [F f. L *-aticus* adj. suffix]

aged *a.* /eɪdʒd/ of the age of (*aged 3*); /'eɪdʒɪd/ old (esp. of person).

ageless *a.* never growing or appearing old; eternal.

agelong *a.* existing for a very long time.

agency /'eɪdʒənsɪ/ *n.* business or establishment of agent (*news agency*); active operation, action; intervening action (*fertilized by the agency of bees*). [L (ACT)]

agenda /ə'dʒendə/ *n. sing.* (*pl.* **agendas**) or *pl.* (list of) items of business to be considered at meeting etc.

agent /'eɪdʒənt/ *n.* one who acts for another in business etc.; one who or that which exerts power or produces effect; (**secret**) **agent** spy.

agent provocateur /ɑ:ʒɑ̃ prəvɒkə'tɜ:/ (*pl.* ***-ts -rs pr.*** same) person employed to detect suspected offenders by tempting them to overt action. [F, = provocative agent]

age-old *a.* having existed for a very long time. [AGE]

agglomerate 1 /ə'glɒməreɪt/ *v.* collect into a mass. **2** /-rət/ *n.* a mass, esp. of fused volcanic fragments. **3** *a.* collected into a mass. **4** **agglomeration** /-'reɪʃ(ə)n/ *n.* [L (*glomus -eris* ball)]

agglutinate /ə'glu:tɪneɪt/ *v.* stick together as with glue, coalesce; **agglutination** /-'neɪʃ(ə)n/ *n.*; **agglutinative** *a.* [L (GLUTEN)]

aggrandize /ə'grændaɪz/ *v.t.* increase power, rank, or wealth of (person, State); make seem greater; **aggrandizement** /-dɪzmənt/ *n.* [F (GRAND[1])]

aggravate /'ægrəveɪt/ *v.t.* increase gravity of (illness, offence, etc.); *colloq.* (**D**) annoy; **aggravation** /-'veɪʃ(ə)n/ *n.* [L (*gravis* heavy)]

aggregate /'ægrɪgət/ **1** *n.* sum total, amount assembled; broken stone etc. used in making concrete; mass of particles or minerals. **2** *a.* combined, collective, total. **3** /-geɪt/ *v.* collect, form into an aggregate; *colloq.* amount to (specified total); unite (individual to company). **4** **in the aggregate** as a whole. **5** **aggregation** /-'geɪʃ(ə)n/ *n.*; **aggregative** *a.* [L *grex greg-* flock]

aggression /ə'greʃ(ə)n/ *n.* unprovoked attacking or attack; hostile act or feeling. [F or L (*gradior gress-* walk)]

aggressive /ə'gresɪv/ *a.* (of person) given to aggression, openly hostile, forceful, self-assertive; (of act) offensive, hostile.

aggressor /ə'gresə/ *n.* one who makes unprovoked attack.

aggrieved /ə'gri:vd/ *a.* having a grievance. [F (GRIEF)]

aggro /'ægrəʊ/ *n. sl.* aggressive trouble-making. [abbr. of *aggravation* or *aggression*]

aghast /ə'gɑ:st/ *a.* filled with dismay or consternation (*at*). [p.p. of obs. v. (*a*)*gast* frighten]

agile /'ædʒaɪl/ *a.* nimble, quick-moving; active, lively; **agility** /ə'dʒɪlɪtɪ/ *n.* [F f. L *agilis* (ACT)]

agitate /'ædʒɪteɪt/ *v.* excite or disturb (feelings, person); stir up esp. public interest or concern (*for, against*); shake briskly (liquid etc.). [L *agito* (ACT)]

agitation /ædʒɪ'teɪʃ(ə)n/ *n.* disturbed mental state; constant pressure on public interest or concern.

agitator /'ædʒɪteɪtə/ *n.* one who agitates, esp. politically; that which agitates.

agley /ə'gleɪ/ *adv. Sc.* askew, awry (see GANG[2]). [A[3], Sc. *gley* squint]

AGM *abbr.* annual general meeting.

agnail /'ægneɪl/ *n.* torn skin at root of finger-nail, the resulting soreness. [OE, = tight (metal) nail, hard excrescence in flesh]

agnostic /æg'nɒstɪk/ **1** *n.* one who believes that nothing can be known of the existence of God or of anything but material phenomena. **2** *a.* of this view. **3** **agnosticism** /-sɪz(ə)m/ *n.* [A-, GNOSTIC]

ago /ə'gəʊ/ *adv.* in the past (*long ago*; *two years ago*). [orig. *agone* = gone by]
agog /ə'gɒg/ *adv.* & *predic. a.* eager, expectant. [F (*gogue* fun)]
agonize /'ægənaɪz/ *v.* undergo mental anguish (*over*), suffer agony; cause agony (*agonizing suspense*). [AGONY]
agonized *a.* expressing agony (*agonized look*).
agony /'ægənɪ/ *n.* extreme mental or physical suffering; severe struggle; **agony column** *colloq.* personal column. [F or L f. Gk (*agōn* struggle)]
agoraphobia /ægərə'fəʊbɪə/ *n.* morbid dread of open spaces; **agoraphobic** *a.* & *n.* [Gk *agora* market-place, -PHOBIA]
agrarian /ə'greərɪən/ **1** *a.* relating to the land or its cultivation; relating to landed property. **2** *n.* advocate of redistribution of landed property. [L (*ager* field)]
agree /ə'gri:/ *v.* hold similar opinion (*with* person); consent (*to* proposal etc., *to do* thing); become or be in harmony (*with* person, *on* matter); approve as correct, reach agreement about (*agree a price*); **agree with** suit, be compatible with, *Gram.* be of same number, gender, case, or person as; **be agreed** have reached similar opinion. [F f. L (AD-, *gratus* pleasing)]
agreeable *a.* pleasing; willing to agree (*to* thing, *to do* thing); **agreeably** *adv.*
agreement *n.* agreeing, sharing of opinion, mutual understanding; contract or promise.
agriculture /'ægrɪkʌltʃə/ *n.* cultivation of soil and rearing of animals; **agricultural** /-'kʌltʃər(ə)l/ *a.*; **agriculturist** /-'kʌltʃərɪst/ *n.* [F or L (*ager* field)]
agrimony /'ægrɪmənɪ/ *n.* perennial plant with small yellow flowers. [F f. L f. Gk]
agronomy /ə'grɒnəmɪ/ *n.* science of soil-management and crop production. [F f. Gk (*agros* land)]
aground /ə'graʊnd/ *adv.* on or on to the bottom of shallow water (*ship is*, *ran*, *aground*). [A[3]]
ague /'eɪgju:/ *n.* malarial fever with cold, hot, and sweating stages; fit of shivering. [F f. L (ACUTE)]
ah /ɑ:/ *int.* expressing esp. surprise, admiration, or delight. [F *a*]
AH *abbr.* of the Muslim era. [L *anno Hegirae* in the year of the Hegira]
aha /ɑ:'hɑ:/ *int.* expressing esp. surprise or triumph. [AH, HA]
ahead /ə'hed/ *adv.* further forward in space or time; in the lead, further advanced (*ahead on points*); **get ahead** make progress (esp. socially). [A[3]]
ahem /(ə)h(ə)m; not usu. clearly articulated/ *int.* used to call attention, fill pause, etc. [HEM[2]]
ahoy /ə'hɔɪ/ *int. Naut.* call used in hailing. [AH, HOY[2]]
aid 1 *n.* help, one who or that which helps. **2** *v.t.* help (person), promote or encourage (*sleep will aid recovery*). **3 in aid of** for the benefit of, *colloq.* for the purpose of (*what's it all in aid of?*). [F f. L (AD-, *juvo* help)]
AID *abbr.* artificial insemination by donor.
aide *n.* aide-de-camp; *US* assistant. [F]
aide-de-camp /eɪd də 'kɑ̃/ *n.* (*pl.* **aides-de-camp** *pr.* same) officer assisting senior officer.
AIDS *abbr.* acquired immune deficiency syndrome.
ail *v.* (*archaic* and only in 3rd person active interrog. or indefinite constructions) trouble, afflict, in mind or body (*what ails you?*); be ill. [OE]
aileron /'eɪlərɒn/ *n.* hinged flap on aeroplane wing, controlling lift and lateral balance. [F (*aile* wing)]
ailing *a.* ill, in poor health or condition. [AIL]
ailment *n.* an illness, esp. a minor one.
aim 1 *v.* intend or make attempt (*aim at winning*, *to win*); point, direct (blow, missile, weapon, remark, action, *at* object of attack); take aim. **2** *n.* object aimed at, purpose (*the aim is to win*); aiming, directing of weapon, missile, etc., at object. **3 take aim** direct weapon at target. [F f. L *aestimare* reckon]
aimless *a.* without aim or purpose.
ain't *colloq.* = *am not, have not.*
air 1 *n.* gaseous mixture mainly of oxygen and nitrogen surrounding earth; atmosphere, open space in it, this as place where aircraft operate; appearance or (esp. affected) manner (*air of mystery*, *give oneself airs*); melody, tune; light wind. **2** *v.t.* expose to fresh air or warmth to remove damp from (room or clothes etc.); make known (opinion, theory, grievance). **3 air commodore** officer of air force next above group captain; **air-conditioning** regulation of humidity and temperature in building, apparatus for this; **air-cushion** inflatable cushion, layer of air supporting hovercraft; **air force** branch of armed forces fighting in the air; **air-hostess** stewardess in passenger aircraft; **air letter** single light sheet forming letter for sending by airmail; **Air (Chief, Vice-) Marshal** high ranks in RAF; **air pocket** apparent vacuum in air causing aircraft in flight to drop suddenly; **air raid** attack by aircraft; **air speed** aircraft's speed relative to air through which it moves; **air terminal** building

in town with transport to and from airport; **by air** in or by aircraft; **in the air** prevalent, (of plan etc.) uncertain, not decided; **on the air** (being) broadcast. [F f. L f. Gk *aēr*; sense 'appearance' F f. L *area*; 'melody' f. It. *aria*]

airborne *a.* transported by air; (of aircraft) in the air after taking off.

airbus *n.* short-range aircraft operating like bus.

aircraft *n.* (*pl.* same) any flying-machine, esp. aeroplane or helicopter; **aircraft-carrier** ship carrying and used as base for aircraft.

aircraftman *n.* lowest rank in RAF.

aircraftwoman *n.* lowest rank in WRAF.

Airedale /'eədeɪl/ *n.* terrier of large rough-coated breed. [*Airedale* in W. Yorkshire]

airfield *n.* area with runway(s) for aircraft. [AIR]

airgun *n.* gun using compressed air.

airless *a.* stuffy; still, calm.

airlift 1 *n.* transport of supplies etc. by air, esp. in emergency. **2** *v.t.* transport thus.

airline *n.* public air transport system or company.

airlock *n.* stoppage of flow by air-bubble in pump or pipe; compartment providing access to pressurized chamber.

airmail *n.* mail carried by air.

airman *n.* pilot or member of crew of aircraft.

airport *n.* airfield with facilities for passengers and goods.

airscrew *n.* propeller of aircraft.

airship *n.* flying machine lighter than air.

airsick *a.* affected with nausea due to motion of aircraft.

airspace *n.* air above country and subject to its jurisdiction.

airstrip *n.* strip of ground for take-off and landing of aircraft.

airtight *a.* impermeable to air.

airway *n.* regular route of aircraft.

airwoman *n.* woman pilot or member of crew of aircraft.

airworthy *a.* (of aircraft) fit to fly.

airy *a.* breezy; well-ventilated; light as air; unsubstantial; lively, flippant; **airily** *adv.*

aisle /aɪl/ *n.* side part of church divided by pillars from main nave; passage between rows of pews or seats. [F f. L *ala* wing]

aitch *n.* letter H; **drop one's aitches** fail to pronounce initial *h* in words. [F *ache*]

aitchbone *n.* rump-bone of animal; cut of beef lying over this. [orig. *nache-bone* f. F f. L *natis* buttock]

ajar /ə'dʒɑː/ *adv.* & *predic. a.* (of door) slightly open. [A[3], obs. *char* turn; see CHAR[1]]

akimbo /ə'kɪmbəʊ/ *adv.* (of arms) with hands on hips and elbows turned outwards. [orig. *in kenebowe*, prob. f. ON]

akin /ə'kɪn/ *predic. a.* similar, related (*a feeling akin to envy*); related by blood. [A[3]]

-al *suffix* forming (1) adjectives with sense of, of the nature of, characteristic of (*postal*, *sensational*, *terrestrial*, *tropical*), (2) nouns esp. of verbal action (*acquittal*, *removal*). [(F f.) L *-alis*]

Al *symb.* aluminium.

alabaster /'æləbɑːstə/ **1** *n.* translucent usu. white form of gypsum, often carved into ornaments. **2** *a.* of, white or smooth as, alabaster. [F f. L f. Gk]

à la carte /ɑː lɑː 'kɑːt/ ordered as separate items from menu. [F]

alacrity /ə'lækrɪtɪ/ *n.* briskness, eager readiness. [L (*alacer* brisk)]

Aladdin's cave /ə'lædɪnz/ store of riches. [*Aladdin* in *Arabian Nights*]

à la mode /ɑː lɑː 'məʊd/ in fashion, fashionable. [F]

alarm /ə'lɑːm/ **1** *n.* warning, warning sound or device (*raise*, *ring*, *the alarm*); frightened expectation of danger or difficulty; = *alarm clock*. **2** *v.t.* disturb, frighten; arouse to sense of danger. **3 alarm clock** clock with device that rings at set time. [F f. It. (*all'arme!* to arms)]

alarmist *n.* one given to spreading needless alarm.

alas /ə'læs/ *int.* expressing esp. sorrow or distress. [F (AH, L *lassus* weary)]

alb /ælb/ *n.* white vestment reaching to feet, worn by priest at service. [OE f. L *albus* white]

albacore /'ælbəkɔː/ *n.* tunny of large W. Indian or related species. [Port. f. Arab., = the young camel]

albatross /'ælbətrɒs/ *n.* long-winged bird related to petrel. [Sp. & Port. *alcatraz* f. Arab., = the jug]

albeit /ɔːl'biːɪt/ *conj.* although. [*all be it*]

albino /æl'biːnəʊ/ *n.* (*pl.* **albinos**) person or animal with congenital lack of colouring pigment in skin and hair (which are white) and eyes (usu. pink); plant lacking normal colouring; **albinism** /'ælbɪnɪz(ə)m/ *n.* [Sp., Port. (ALB)]

album /'ælbəm/ *n.* book for photographs, stamps, etc.; long-playing gramophone record with several items, set of records. [L, = blank tablet (ALB)]

albumen /'ælbjʊmɪn/ *n.* egg-white; (esp. eatable) constituent of many seeds. [L (ALB)]

albumin /'ælbjʊmɪn/ *n.* water-soluble protein found in egg-white, milk, blood, and some plants; **albuminous** /æl'bju:mɪnəs/ *a.*

alchemy /'ælkəmɪ/ *n.* medieval chemistry, esp. seeking transmutation of baser metals into gold; **alchemist** *n.* [F f. L f. Arab.]

alcohol /'ælkəhɒl/ *n.* colourless volatile liquid, intoxicant present in wine, beer, and spirits, also used as solvent and fuel; liquor containing this; *Chem.* compound of same type as alcohol. [F or L f. Arab. (KOHL)]

alcoholic /ælkə'hɒlɪk/ **1** *a.* of, like, containing, caused by, alcohol. **2** *n.* person suffering from alcoholism.

alcoholism /'ælkəhɒlɪz(ə)m/ *n.* continual heavy drinking of alcohol; diseased condition resulting from this.

alcove /'ælkəʊv/ *n.* recess in wall of room, garden, etc. [F f. Sp. f. Arab., = the vault]

aldehyde /'ældɪhaɪd/ *n.* volatile fluid with suffocating smell, got by oxidation of alcohol; *Chem.* compound of same structure as this. [ALCOHOL, DE-, HYDROGEN]

alder /'ɔ:ldə/ *n.* tree related to birch; **black, red, white alder** other trees not related. [OE]

alderman /'ɔ:ldəmən/ *n.* chiefly *hist.* co-opted member of English county or borough council, next below Mayor. [OE (*aldor* chief, MAN)]

Alderney /'ɔ:ldənɪ/ **1** *n.* one of breed of small dairy cattle orig. from Alderney in Channel Islands. **2** *a.* of this breed.

ale *n.* beer; **real ale** beer regarded as brewed in traditional way, with secondary fermentation in cask. [OE]

aleatory /'eɪlɪətərɪ/ *a.* depending on chance or random choice. [L (*alea* DIE[1])]

alembic /ə'lembɪk/ *n.* apparatus formerly used in distilling; means of transforming. [F f. L f. Arab. f. Gk *ambix -ikos* cap of still]

alert /ə'lɜ:t/ **1** *a.* watchful, vigilant; nimble. **2** *n.* alarm-call; state or period of special vigilance. **3** *v.t.* make alert (*to*), warn. [F f. It. *all' erta* to the watch-tower]

A level advanced level in GCE examination. [abbr.]

alexandrine /ælɪg'zændraɪn/ **1** *n.* verse of six iambic feet. **2** *a.* in this metre. [F (*Alexandre* title of romance using metre)]

alfalfa /æl'fælfə/ *n.* clover-like plant used for fodder. [Sp. f. Arab., = a green fodder]

alfresco /æl'freskəʊ/ *a.* & *adv.* in the open air. [It.]

alga /'ælgə/ *n.* (usu. in *pl.* **algae** /'ældʒi:/) non-flowering stemless water-plant, esp. seaweed and plankton. [L]

algebra /'ældʒɪbrə/ *n.* mathematical system that uses letters to represent quantities to be investigated; **algebraic** /-'breɪɪk/ *a.* [It. & Sp. & med.L f. Arab., = reunion of broken parts]

ALGOL /'ælgɒl/ *n.* algebraic computer language. [foll., L(ANGUAGE)]

algorithm /'ælgərɪð(ə)m/ *n.* process or rules for (esp. machine) calculation etc. [F f. L f. Pers. (name of 9th-c. mathematician *al-Kuwārizmī*)]

alias /'eɪlɪəs/ **1** *adv.* called at other times (*Smith, alias Jones*). **2** *n.* assumed name (*his alias was Jones*). [L, = at another time]

alibi /'ælɪbaɪ/ *n.* plea that when alleged act took place one was elsewhere; (D) excuse. [L, = elsewhere]

alien /'eɪlɪən/ **1** *n.* foreign-born resident who is not naturalized; a being from another world. **2** *a.* foreign; not one's own; differing in nature (*from* or *to*), inconsistent; repugnant (*to*). [F f. L (*alius* other)]

alienable *a.* able to be transferred to new ownership.

alienate /'əɪlɪəneɪt/ *v.t.* estrange, make unfriendly or hostile; transfer ownership of; **alienation** /-'neɪʃ(ə)n/ *n.*

alight[1] /ə'laɪt/ *predic. a.* on fire; lighted up. [*on a light* (= lighted) *fire*]

alight[2] /ə'laɪt/ *v.i.* get down or off (*from* train, bus, etc.); settle, come to earth, from the air. [OE]

align /ə'laɪn/ *v.t.* place in or bring into line, co-ordinate; bring several points (e.g. sights of gun) into straight line; ally (country, *oneself*, etc.) with party or cause; **alignment** *n.* [F (*à ligne* into line)]

alike /ə'laɪk/ **1** *predic. a.* similar, like. **2** *adv.* in like manner. [A[3]]

alimentary /ælɪ'mentərɪ/ *a.* pertaining to food or nutrition; nourishing; **alimentary canal** channel through which food passes during digestion. [L (*alo* nourish)]

alimony /'ælɪmənɪ/ *n. hist.* allowance due to woman from (ex-)husband after or pending divorce or legal separation; *US* allowance paid to spouse or child. ¶ In UK use replaced by MAINTENANCE.

aliphatic /ælɪ'fætɪk/ *a. Chem.* (of certain organic compounds) related to fats; in which carbon atoms form open chains. [Gk *aleiphar, -phat-* fat]

aliquot /'ælɪkwɒt/ **1** *a.* that produces quotient without fraction when given larger number is divided by it (*4 is an aliquot part of 12*). **2** *n.* aliquot part; representative portion of a substance. [F f. L, = several]

alive /ə'laɪv/ *predic. a.* living; lively, active; alert, responsive, *to* (circumstance or idea); abounding in, swarming *with* (people or things). [OE (A³, LIFE)]

alkali /'ælkəlaɪ/ *n.* (*pl.* **alkalis**) any of a class of substances that neutralize acids and form caustic or corrosive solutions in water, e.g. caustic soda; other substance with similar but weaker properties, e.g. sodium carbonate; **alkaline** *a.* [med.L f. Arab., = the calcined ashes]

alkaloid /'ælkəlɔɪd/ *n.* nitrogen-containing base of plant origin, e.g. quinine.

alkyl /'ælkɪl/ *a.* derived from or related to a paraffin hydrocarbon. [G (as ALCOHOL)]

all /ɔ:l/ **1** *a.* whole amount, quantity, or extent of (*waited all day*; *we all know why*; *take it all*); greatest possible (*with all speed*); any whatever (*beyond all doubt*). **2** *n.* all persons concerned, everything (*all is lost*; *that is all*); everything one owns or has (*give your all*); (in games) on both sides (*four goals all*). **3** *adv.* entirely, quite (*all covered with mud*; *the all-important thing*); *colloq.* very (*went all shy*). **4 after all** in spite of what has been said or done or expected; **all along** see ALONG; **all but** very nearly; **all-clear** signal that danger or difficulty is over; **all for** *colloq.* very much in favour of; **all in** exhausted; **all-in** *attrib.* inclusive of all; **all in all,** everything considered; **all of** the whole of, every one of; **all out** involving all one's strength etc.; **all over** see OVER; **all-purpose** having many uses; **all round** in all respects, for each person; **all-round** (of person) versatile; **all-rounder** versatile person; **all there** *colloq.* mentally alert; **all-time** (of record) hitherto unsurpassed; **at all** (with neg. or interrog.) in any way, to any extent (*not at all*; *did you see her at all?*); **for all (that)** in spite of, although; **in all** in total, altogether. [OE]

Allah /'ælə/ *n.* Muslim name of God. [Arab.]

allay /ə'leɪ/ *v.t.* diminish (fear, suspicion, etc.); relieve or alleviate (pain). [OE (*a-* intensive, LAY¹)]

allegation /ælɪ'geɪʃ(ə)n/ *n.* assertion, esp. unproved; alleging. [F or L (*allego* adduce)]

allege /ə'ledʒ/ *v.t.* declare to be the case, esp. without proof; advance as argument or excuse. [F f. L (*lis lit-* lawsuit)]

allegedly /ə'ledʒɪdlɪ/ *adv.* as is said to be the case.

allegiance /ə'li:dʒəns/ *n.* duty of subject to sovereign or government; loyalty (*to* person or cause). [F (LIEGE)]

allegorical /ælɪ'gɒrɪk(ə)l/ *a.* in the nature of, by means of, allegory. [ALLEGORY]

allegorize /'ælɪgəraɪz/ *v.t.* treat as or by means of allegory. [foll.]

allegory /'ælɪgərɪ/ *n.* narrative or description of figurative or symbolical application. [F f. L f. Gk]

allegro /ə'legrəʊ/ *Mus.* **1** *adv.* in quick or lively tempo. **2** *n.* (*pl.* **allegros**) movement to be played this way. [It., = lively]

alleluia /ælɪ'lu:jə/ **1** *int.* God be praised. **2** *n.* (song of) praise to God. [L f. Gk f. Heb.]

allergic /ə'lɜ:dʒɪk/ *a.* having an allergy or (*colloq.*) antipathy *to*; caused by allergy. [foll.]

allergy /'ælədʒɪ/ *n.* condition of reacting adversely to certain substances, esp. food or pollen; *colloq.* antipathy. [G, f. Gk *allos* other, ENERGY]

alleviate /ə'li:vɪeɪt/ *v.t.* lessen, make less severe (pain, evil); **alleviation** /-'eɪʃ(ə)n/ *n.*; **alleviator** *n.* [L (*levo* raise)]

alley /'ælɪ/ *n.* narrow passage, esp. between or behind buildings; channel for balls in bowling etc.; walk or lane in garden or park. [F (*aller* go)]

alliance /ə'laɪəns/ *n.* union or agreement to co-operate esp. of States by treaty or families by marriage. [F (ALLY)]

allied /'ælaɪd/ *a.* having similar origin or character *to*. [ALLY]

alligator /'ælɪgeɪtə/ *n.* American or Chinese reptile of crocodile family. [Sp. *el lagarto* the lizard]

alliterate /ə'lɪtəreɪt/ *v.i.* use alliteration. [foll.]

alliteration /əlɪtə'reɪʃ(ə)n/ *n.* recurrence for effect of same letter or sound in several words of phrase etc. (as in *sing a song of sixpence*); **alliterative** /ə'lɪtərətɪv/ *a.* [L (LETTER)]

allocate /'æləkeɪt/ *v.t.* assign or allot (*to* person or purpose); assign to a place; **allocable** *a.*; **allocation** /-'keɪʃ(ə)n/ *n.* [L (LOCAL)]

allot /ə'lɒt/ *v.t.* (-tt-) distribute officially; apportion (share or task) *to*. [F (*a-* to, LOT)]

allotment *n.* small portion of usu. public land let out for cultivation; apportioning; share.

allotropy /ə'lɒtrəpɪ/ *n.* existence at same temperature of different physical forms of a chemical element, e.g. oxygen and ozone; **allotropic** /æləʊ'trɒpɪk/ *a.* [Gk (*allos* different, *tropos* manner)]

allow /ə'laʊ/ *v.* permit (thing, person *to do* thing), let (thing) happen; assign fixed sum to (*allowed him £1000 a year*); provide or set aside for a purpose (*allow £50 for expenses, 10% for inflation*); **allow for** take into consideration, provide for (*allow for wastage, his ex-*

travagance). [orig. = commend, f. F (AD-, L *laudo* praise & *loco* place)]
allowance 1 *n.* amount or sum allowed to person, esp. regularly for a stated purpose; amount allowed in reckoning; deduction or discount (*an allowance on your old cooker*); **make allowances for** regard as mitigating circumstances. **2** *v.t.* make allowance to.
alloy /'ælɔɪ/ **1** *n.* mixture of metals; inferior metal mixed esp. with gold or silver. **2** *v.t.* mix (metals); debase by admixture; moderate (pleasure etc. *with*). [F (ALLY)]
all right *predic.* satisfactory, safe and sound, in good condition; satisfactorily, as desired (*worked out all right*); (as *int.*) I consent (also *iron.*: *all right, you've asked for it!*). [ALL]
allspice *n.* aromatic spice obtained from berry of pimento; the berry. [ALL, SPICE]
allude /ə'lu:d/ *v.i.* refer transiently or indirectly *to* (thing presumed known). [L (AD-, *ludo* play)]
allure /ə'ljʊə/ *v.t.* entice, tempt; attract or charm; **allurement** *n.* [F (AD-, LURE)]
allusion /ə'lu:ʒ(ə)n/ *n.* passing or indirect reference (*to*); **allusive** /ə'lu:sɪv/ *a.* [F or L (ALLUDE)]
alluvial /ə'lu:vɪəl/ **1** *a.* of alluvium. **2** *n.* alluvial deposit. [foll.]
alluvium /ə'lu:vɪəm/ *n.* (*pl.* **alluvia**) deposit of earth, sand, etc., left by flood or flow of water, esp. in river valley. [L (*luo* wash)]
ally /'ælaɪ/ **1** *n.* State or person formally co-operating or united with another for special purpose, esp. by treaty. **2** *v.t.* combine or unite in alliance. [F f. L *alligo* bind]
Alma Mater /ælmə 'mɑ:tə/ university or school one attends or attended. [L, = bounteous mother]
almanac /'ɔ:lmənæk/ *n.* (also **almanack**) calendar of months and days, usu. with astronomical data. [med.L f. Gk]
almighty /ɔ:l'maɪtɪ/ **1** *a.* all-powerful; *sl.* very great. **2** *adv. sl.* very. **3 the Almighty** God. [OE (ALL, MIGHTY)]
almond /'ɑ:mənd/ *n.* nutlike kernel of fruit allied to plum and peach; tree bearing it. [F f. L f. Gk *amugdalē*]
almoner /'ɑ:mənə/ *n.* social worker attached to hospital (¶ now usu. called *medical social worker*); official distributor of alms. [F (ALMS)]
almost /'ɔ:lməʊst/ *adv.* all but, very nearly. [OE (ALL, MOST)]
alms /ɑ:mz/ *n.* (usu. as *sing.*) *hist.* donation of money or food given to the poor. [OE f. L f. Gk *eleēmosunē* pity]
almshouse *n.* house founded by charity for the poor.
aloe /'æləʊ/ *n.* plant with erect spikes of flowers and bitter juice; (in *pl.*) purgative drug from aloe juice. [OE f. L f. Gk]
aloft /ə'lɒft/ *adv.* high up, overhead; upward. [ON *á lopti* in air]
alone /ə'ləʊn/ **1** *predic. a.* by oneself, itself, etc., without company, assistance, or addition. **2** *adv.* only, exclusively. [earlier *al one* (ALL, ONE)]
along /ə'lɒŋ/ **1** *adv.* onward, into more advanced state (*come along*; *getting along nicely*); in company with oneself or others (*have brought my sister along*; *will be along soon*); beside or through part or whole of thing's length (*along by the river*). **2** *prep.* beside or through (part of) the length of (*arranged along the wall*). **3 all along** from the beginning; **along with** in addition to. [OE, orig. adj. = facing against]
alongshore /əlɒŋ'ʃɔ:/ *adv.* along or beside the shore.
alongside /əlɒŋ'saɪd/ **1** *adv.* at or to the side. **2** *prep.* close to the side of.
aloof /ə'lu:f/ **1** *a.* unconcerned, lacking in sympathy. **2** *adv.* away, apart (*stand aloof from*). [orig. *Naut.*, f. A^3 + LUFF]
aloud /ə'laʊd/ *adv.* in normal voice so as to be audible. [A^3]
alp *n.* mountain-peak, esp. (in *pl.*, **the Alps**) in Switzerland and adjacent countries; pasture-land on Swiss mountain-side. [orig. pl., f. F f. L f. Gk]
alpaca /æl'pækə/ *n.* a S. American kind of llama with long wool; its wool; fabric made from this. [Sp. f. Quechua]
alpha /'ælfə/ *n.* first letter of Greek alphabet (Α, α); **Alpha and Omega** beginning and end; **alpha particle** (or **ray**) helium nucleus emitted by radioactive substances, orig. regarded as ray. [L f. Gk]
alphabet /'ælfəbet/ *n.* set of letters (in fixed order) used in a language; symbols or signs for these; **alphabetical** /-'betɪk(ə)l/ *a.* [L f. Gk ALPHA, BETA]
alphanumeric /ælfənju:'merɪk/ *a.* containing both alphabetical and numerical symbols.
Alpine /'ælpaɪn/ **1** *a.* of the Alps or other high mountains. **2** *n.* plant suited to mountain regions. [L (ALP)]
already /ɔ:l'redɪ/ *adv.* before the time in question (*have already seen him*; *had already gone*); as early or soon as this (*he is back already*). [ALL, READY]
alright (D) var. of ALL RIGHT.
Alsatian /æl'seɪʃ(ə)n/ *n.* large dog of a breed of wolfhound. [L *Alsatia* Alsace]
also /'ɔ:lsəʊ/ *adv.* in addition, besides; **also-ran** loser in race, undistinguished person. [OE (ALL, SO)]
altar /'ɒltə, 'ɔ:-/ *n.* table or flat-topped

block, often of stone, for sacrifice or offering to deity; Communion-table. [OE f. L (*altus* high)]
alter /'ɒltə, 'ɔ:-/ *v.* change in character, position, size, shape, etc.; **alteration** /-'reɪʃ(ə)n/ *n.* [F f. L (*alter* other)]
altercate /'ɒltəkeɪt, 'ɔ:-/ *v.i.* dispute, wrangle (*with*); **altercation** /-'keɪʃ(ə)n/ *n.* [L]
alter ego /æltə'ri:gəʊ/ (*pl.* ***alter egos***) intimate friend; other aspect of oneself. [L, = other self]
alternate 1 /ɒl'tɜ:nət, ɔ:l-/ *a.* (of things of two kinds) each following and succeeded by one of the other kind (*alternate joy and misery*); (with *pl.*, of one class of things) every other (*on alternate days*). **2** /'ɒltəneɪt/ *v.* arrange or perform, occur, alternately; consist of alternate things. **3 alternate angles** two angles formed alternately on two sides of line; **alternating current** electric current reversing direction at regular intervals. **4 alternation** /-'neɪʃ(ə)n/ *n.* [L *alterno* do by turns (ALTER)]
alternative /ɒl'tɜ:nətɪv, ɔ:l-/ **1** *a.* available in place of something else. **2** *n.* choice available in place of another, one of two or more possibilities.
alternator /'ɒltəneɪtə/ *n.* dynamo producing alternating current.
although /ɔ:l'ðəʊ/ *conj.* though. [ALL, THOUGH]
altimeter /'æltɪmi:tə/ *n.* instrument measuring altitude. [foll.]
altitude /'æltɪtju:d/ *n.* height, esp. of object above sea-level or star above horizon. [L (*altus* high)]
alto /'æltəʊ/ *n.* (*pl.* **altos**) female singer of low range or adult male singer of highest range; range sung by these; instrument second or third highest in pitch in its family. [It. *alto* (*canto*) high (sing-ing)]
altogether /ɔ:ltə'geðə/ *adv.* entirely, totally; on the whole; **in the altogether** *colloq.* nude. [ALL, TOGETHER]
altruism /'æltrʊɪz(ə)m/ *n.* regard for others as a principle of action; **altruist** *n.*; **altruistic** /-'ɪstɪk/ *a.* [F f. It. *altrui* somebody else]
alum /'æləm/ *n.* double sulphate of aluminium and another element, esp. potassium. [F f. L *alumen -min-*]
alumina /ə'lu:mɪnə/ *n.* aluminium oxide, e.g. corundum.
aluminium /æljʊ'mɪnɪəm/ *n.* a silvery light and malleable metallic element not tarnished by air.
aluminize /ə'lu:mɪnaɪz/ *v.t.* coat with aluminium.
aluminum /ə'lu:mɪnəm/ *US* var. of ALUMINIUM.
alumnus /ə'lʌmnəs/ *n.* (*pl.* **alumni** /-aɪ/) *US* former pupil or student. [L, = nursling, pupil]
always /'ɔ:lweɪz/ *adv.* at all times, on all occasions; whatever the circumstances; repeatedly. [ALL, WAY]
alyssum /'ælɪsəm/ *n.* plant with small usu. yellow or white flowers. [L f. Gk (= curing madness)]
am see BE.
AM *abbr.* amplitude modulation.
a.m. *abbr.* before noon. [L *ante meridiem*]
Am *symb.* americium.
amalgam /ə'mælgəm/ *n.* mixture or blend; alloy of mercury and another metal. [F or med.L]
amalgamate /ə'mælgəmeɪt/ *v.* mix, unite; (of metals) alloy with mercury; **amalgamation** /-'meɪʃ(ə)n/ *n.* [med.L (prec.)]
amanuensis /əmænjʊ'ensɪs/ *n.* (*pl.* **amanuenses** /-i:z/) literary assistant, esp. one who copies from dictation. [L (*a manu* 'at hand')]
amaranth /'æmərænθ/ *n.* kind of plant with coloured foliage, esp. prince's feather and love-lies-bleeding; imaginary unfading flower; purple; **amaranthine** /-'rænθaɪn/ *a.* [F or L f. Gk *amarantos* unfading]
amaryllis /æmə'rɪlɪs/ *n.* bulb plant with lily-like flowers. [L f. Gk (girl's name)]
amass /ə'mæs/ *v.t.* heap together, accumulate. [F (AD-, MASS[1])]
amateur /'æmətə/ *n.* one who engages in sport, interest, etc. as a pastime not a profession (often *attrib.*: *amateur gardener*); one who does something with limited skill. [F f. It. f. L *amator* lover (AMATORY)]
amateurish *a.* suggestive of an amateur (esp. as regards skill).
amatory /'æmətərɪ/ *a.* of or showing (esp. sexual) love. [L (*amo* love)]
amaze /ə'meɪz/ *v.t.* cause to be greatly surprised, fill with wonder; **amazement** *n.* [earlier *amase* f. OE *āmasod*]
amazon /'æməz(ə)n/ *n.* large, strong, or athletic woman; (**Amazon**) female warrior esp. of mythical race in Scythia; **amazonian** /-'zəʊnɪən/ *a.* [L f. Gk]
ambassador /æm'bæsədə/ *n.* diplomat sent by sovereign or State as permanent representative or on mission to another; official messenger; **ambassadorial** /-'dɔ:rɪəl/ *a.* [F f. It. f. L *ambactus* servant]
amber 1 *n.* a yellow translucent fossil resin used in jewellery etc.; colour of this; yellow traffic-light denoting caution. **2** *a.* made of or coloured like amber. [F f. Arab.]
ambergris /'æmbəgrɪs/ *n.* grey waxlike

substance found in tropical seas and intestines of sperm whale, used esp. in perfumery. [F, = grey amber]

ambidextrous /æmbɪ'dekstrəs/ *a.* able to use either hand equally well. [L (*ambi-* on both sides, DEXTER)]

ambience /'æmbɪəns/ *n.* surroundings. [F, or L *ambio* go round]

ambient *a.* surrounding.

ambiguous /æm'bɪgjʊəs/ *a.* having more than one possible meaning; doubtful; uncertain; **ambiguity** /-'gju:ɪtɪ/ *n.* [L (*ambi-* both ways, *ago* drive)]

ambit /'æmbɪt/ *n.* scope or extent; bounds. [L (AMBIENCE)]

ambition /æm'bɪʃ(ə)n/ *n.* desire for advancement or distinction, or for specific attainment (*ambition to see the world*); object of such desire. [F f. L, = canvassing (AMBIENCE)]

ambitious *a.* full of ambition; strongly desirous, eager (*to do* thing); of high aspiration (*an ambitious project*).

ambivalence /æm'bɪvələns/ *n.* coexistence in one person of opposite feelings towards same person or thing; **ambivalent** *a.* [G (L *ambo* both, EQUIVALENCE)]

amble /'æmb(ə)l/ **1** *v.i.* walk in a leisurely or casual manner; (esp. of horse) move with gentle gait. **2** *n.* leisurely walking pace; (esp. horse's) ambling gait. [F f. L *ambulo* walk]

ambrosia /æm'brəʊzɪə, -ʒjə/ *n.* food of the gods in classical mythology; thing delicious to taste or smell. [L f. Gk, = elixir of life]

ambulance /'æmbjʊləns/ *n.* specially equipped vehicle for conveying sick or injured to hospital; mobile hospital serving army. [F f. L (AMBLE)]

ambulatory /'æmbjʊlətərɪ/ **1** *a.* of or for walking; movable. **2** *n.* arcade, cloister. [L (AMBLE)]

ambuscade /æmbəs'keɪd/ *n.* & *v.* = AMBUSH. [foll.]

ambush /'æmbʊʃ/ **1** *n.* surprise attack by persons lying concealed; act or place of concealment for surprise attack. **2** *v.t.* attack from ambush, lie in wait for. [F (IN-¹, BUSH¹)]

ameliorate /ə'mi:lɪəreɪt/ *v.* make or become better; **ameliorative** /-ətɪv/ *a.* [AD-, L *melior* better]

amen /'ɑ:men, 'eɪ-/ *int.* so be it (esp. at end of prayer). [eccl.L f. Gk f. Heb., = certainly]

amenable /ə'mi:nəb(ə)l/ *a.* tractable, responsive (to influence, argument, etc.); answerable (*to* law etc.). [F (AD-, L *mino* drive animals)]

amend /ə'mend/ *v.t.* correct error in (document etc.); make minor alterations in. [F f. L (EMEND)]

amendment *n.* minor alteration or addition in document.

amends *n.* now only in **make amends (for)** give compensation (for).

amenity /ə'mi:nɪtɪ/ *n.* a pleasant or useful feature or facility (freq. in *pl.*); pleasant quality of place etc. [F or L (*amoenus* pleasant)]

American /ə'merɪkən/ **1** *a.* of the continent of America, esp. the United States. **2** *n.* citizen of US; native of America; English as spoken in US; **Americanize** *v.t.* [name of navigator *Amerigo* Vespucci]

Americanism *n.* word or sense or phrase peculiar to or originating in US.

americium /æmə'rɪsɪəm/ *n.* artificial radioactive metallic element. [*America*, where first made]

Amerind /'æmərɪnd/ *n.* an American Indian or Eskimo; **Amerindian** /-'ɪndɪən/ *a.* [AMERICAN, INDIAN]

amethyst /'æməθɪst/ *n.* a precious stone, purple or violet quartz. [F f. L f. Gk, = preventing drunkenness]

Amharic /æm'hærɪk/ **1** *n.* the Semitic official language of Ethiopia. **2** *a.* of or in Amharic. [*Amhara*, region of Ethiopia]

amiable /'eɪmɪəb(ə)l/ *a.* friendly and pleasant in temperament; likeable; **amiably** *adv.* [F f. L (foll.)]

amicable /'æmɪkəb(ə)l/ *a.* friendly, showing friendly feeling (*an amicable meeting*); **amicably** *adv.* [L (*amicus* friend)]

amid /ə'mɪd/ *prep.* in the middle of, among. [OE (ON, MID)]

amide /'æmaɪd/ *n.* compound in which acid radical or metal atom replaces hydrogen atom of ammonia. [AMMONIA]

amidships /ə'mɪdʃɪps/ *adv.* in or to middle of ship. [AMID, alternative form *midships*]

amidst var. of AMID.

amine /'eɪmi:n/ *n.* compound in which alkyl or other non-acidic radical replaces hydrogen atom of ammonia.

amino acid /æmi:nəʊ 'æsɪd/ organic acid derived from ammonia and found in proteins. [AMINE, ACID]

amir /ə'mɪə/ *n.* title of various Muslim rulers. [Arab.]

amiss /ə'mɪs/ **1** *predic. a.* out of order, faulty, wrong. **2** *adv.* wrongly, inappropriately. **3 take amiss** be offended by. [ON *á mis* so as to miss]

amity /'æmɪtɪ/ *n.* friendship. [F f. L (*amicus* friend)]

ammeter /'æmɪtə/ *n.* instrument for measuring electric current, usu. in amperes. [AMPERE, METER]

ammo /'æməʊ/ *n. sl.* ammunition. [abbr.]

ammonia /ə'məʊnɪə/ *n.* pungent gas

with strong alkaline reaction; **(liquid) ammonia** solution of ammonia in water. [as SAL AMMONIAC]

ammonite /'æmənaɪt/ *n.* coil-shaped fossil shell. [L, = horn of Jupiter Ammon]

ammunition /æmjʊ'nɪʃ(ə)n/ *n.* supply of projectiles (esp. bullets, shells, and grenades) fired by guns etc. or hurled; points used to advantage in argument etc. [F *la* MUNITION taken as *l'ammu-*]

amnesia /æm'ni:zjə/ *n.* loss of memory; **amnesiac** *a.* & *n.* [L f. Gk]

amnesty /'æmnɪstɪ/ *n.* general pardon, esp. for political offences. [F or L f. Gk *amnēstia* oblivion]

amnion /'æmnɪɒn/ *n.* (*pl.* **amnia**) innermost membrane enclosing foetus; **amniotic** /-'ɒtɪk/ *a.* [Gk, = caul]

amoeba /ə'mi:bə/ *n.* (*pl.* **amoebas**) microscopic aquatic one-celled organism constantly changing shape. [Gk, = change]

amok /ə'mɒk/ *adv.* now only in **run amok** run about wildly in violent rage. [Malay]

among /ə'mʌŋ/ *prep.* surrounded by; in the category of (*honour among thieves*); in the number of (*among his best works*); between, from the joint resources of (*divided among us*; *not £5 among us*); with one another (*talked among themselves*). [OE, = in a crowd]

amongst var. of AMONG.

amoral /eɪ'mɒr(ə)l/ *a.* beyond morality; having no moral principles. [A-]

amorous /'æmərəs/ *a.* showing or feeling, to do with, sexual love. [F f. L (*amor* love)]

amorphous /ə'mɔ:fəs/ *a.* shapeless; vague, ill organized; *Min. & Chem.* uncrystallized. [Gk (*a-* not, *morphē* form)]

amortize /ə'mɔ:taɪz/ *v.t.* gradually extinguish (debt) by money regularly put aside. [F f. L *ad mortem* to death]

amount /ə'maʊnt/ **1** *n.* total of thing(s) in number, size, value, extent, etc. **2** *v.i.* be equivalent in number, size, etc., *to*. [F f. L *ad montem* upward]

amour /ə'mʊə/ *n.* love-affair, esp. secret one. [F, = love]

amour propre /æmʊə 'prɒpr/ self-respect.

amp *n.* ampere; *colloq.* amplifier. [abbr.]

ampelopsis /æmpɪ'lɒpsɪs/ *n.* climbing plant related to vine. [Gk *ampelos* vine, *opsis* appearance]

amperage *n.* strength of electric current in amperes. [foll.]

ampere /'æmpeə/ *n.* basic unit of electric current. [*Ampère*, physicist]

ampersand /'æmpəsænd/ *n.* the sign & (= 'and'). [corrupt. of *and* PER SE *and*]

amphetamine /æm'fetəmi:n, -ɪn/ *n.* synthetic drug used esp. as stimulant. [abbr. of chem. name]

amphibian /æm'fɪbɪən/ **1** *a.* of class of vertebrates (e.g. frogs) able to live on land and in water. **2** *n.* member of amphibian class; vehicle able to operate on land and in water. [Gk *amphi-* both, *bios* life]

amphibious /æm'fɪbɪəs/ *a.* living or operating on land and in water; involving military forces landed from the sea.

amphitheatre /'æmfɪθɪətə/ *n.* oval or circular unroofed building with tiers of seats surrounding central space. [L f. Gk (*amphi-* round)]

amphora /'æmfərə/ *n.* (*pl.* **amphorae** /-i:/) Greek or Roman vessel with narrow neck and two handles. [L, f. Gk *amphoreus*]

ample /'æmp(ə)l/ *a.* plentiful, abundant, extensive; enough or more than enough; (esp. of person) large, stout; **amply** *adv.* [F, f. L *amplus*]

amplifier /'æmplɪfaɪə/ *n.* apparatus for increasing strength of sounds or electrical signals. [foll.]

amplify /'æmplɪfaɪ/ *v.* increase strength of (sound or electrical signal); add detail to (story etc.); expatiate; **amplification** /-fɪ'keɪʃ(ə)n/ *n.* [F f. L (AMPLE)]

amplitude /'æmplɪtju:d/ *n.* spaciousness, abundance; maximum departure from average of oscillation, alternating current, etc.; **amplitude modulation** that by which amplitude of radio wave is varied. [F or L (AMPLE)]

ampoule /'æmpu:l/ *n.* small sealed jar holding solution for injection. [F (foll.)]

ampulla /æm'pʊlə/ *n.* (*pl.* **ampullae** /-i:/) Roman globular bottle with two handles; vessel for sacred uses. [L]

amputate /'æmpjʊteɪt/ *v.t.* cut off (diseased or injured part of body, esp. limb); **amputation** /-'teɪʃ(ə)n/ *n.* [L (*amb-* about, *puto* prune)]

amuck var. of AMOK.

amulet /'æmjʊlɪt/ *n.* thing worn as charm against evil. [L]

amuse /ə'mju:z/ *v.t.* cause (person) to laugh or smile; interest or occupy (*with* diversion etc.). [F (*a* cause to, *muser* stare)]

amusement *n.* being amused; thing that amuses.

an see A².

an- see A-.

-an *suffix* forming adjectives and nouns in sense '(person) concerned with, born or living in' (*Anglican*, *Roman*) or '(member) of class of' (*reptilian*). [F *-ain*, L *-anus*]

Anabaptist /ænə'bæptɪst/ *n.* member of 16th-c. religious group practising adult baptism. [eccl.L f. Gk (*ana* again)]

anabolism /əˈnæbəlɪz(ə)m/ *n.* synthesis of complex substances in animal or plant to form living tissue. [Gk *anabolē* ascent]
anachronism /əˈnækrənɪz(ə)m/ *n.* attribution of thing (esp. custom or event) to period to which it does not belong; thing thus attributed; person or thing out of harmony with period; **anachronistic** /-ˈnɪstɪk/ *a.* [F or Gk (*ana* against, *khronos* time)]
anaconda /ænəˈkɒndə/ *n.* large tropical S. American snake. [Sinhalese]
anaemia /əˈni:mɪə/ *n.* deficiency of red cells or their haemoglobin in the blood. [Gk, = want of blood]
anaemic /əˈni:mɪk/ *a.* suffering from anaemia; pale, lacking vitality.
anaesthesia /ænɪsˈθi:zɪə/ *n.* absence of sensation, esp. artificially induced insensibility to pain. [Gk]
anaesthetic /ænɪsˈθetɪk/ **1** *n.* drug or gas producing anaesthesia. **2** *a.* producing anaesthesia.
anaesthetist /əˈni:sθətɪst/ *n.* one who administers anaesthetics.
anaesthetize /əˈni:sθətaɪz/ *v.t.* administer anaesthetic to.
anagram /ˈænəgræm/ *n.* word or phrase formed by transposing letters of another.[Gk *ana-* again, *gramma* letter]
anal /ˈeɪn(ə)l/ *a.* of the anus. [ANUS]
analgesia /ænælˈdʒi:zɪə/ *n.* absence or relief of pain. [Gk]
analgesic **1** *n.* drug producing analgesia. **2** *a.* producing analgesia.
analog *US* var. of ANALOGUE.
analogize /əˈnælədʒaɪz/ *v.* represent or explain by analogy; use analogy. [ANALOGY]
analogous /əˈnæləgəs/ *a.* partially similar or parallel (*to*). [L f. Gk (ANALOGY)]
analogue /ˈænəlɒg/ *n.* analogous thing; **analogue computer** one using physical variables, e.g. voltages, to represent numbers. [F f. Gk (ANALOGY)]
analogy /əˈnælədʒɪ/ *n.* correspondence or partial similarity of things; reasoning from parallel cases; inflexion or construction of words in imitation of others; **analogical** /ænəˈlɒdʒɪk(ə)l/ *a.* [F or L f. Gk *analogia* proportion]
analyse /ˈænəlaɪz/ *v.t.* examine in detail; ascertain elements or structure of (substance, sentence, etc.); psychoanalyse. [foll.]
analysis /əˈnæləsɪs/ *n.* detailed examination of elements or structure of substance etc.; statement of this; division of chemical compound into constituent parts; psychoanalysis. [med.L f. Gk (*ana* up, *luō* loose)]
analyst /ˈænəlɪst/ *n.* one skilled in (esp. chemical) analysis; psychoanalyst. [F f. Gk (prec.)]
analytic /ænəˈlɪtɪk/ *a.* of analysis. [L f. Gk (ANALYSIS)]
analytical *a.* using analysis; (of language) using separate words instead of inflexions.
analyze *US* var. of ANALYSE.
anapaest /ˈænəpi:st/ *n.* a metrical foot (⏑⏑–); **anapaestic** /-ˈpi:stɪk/ *a.* [L f. Gk *anapaistos* reversed (dactyl)]
anarchism /ˈænəkɪz(ə)m/ *n.* belief that government and law should be abolished. [F (ANARCHY)]
anarchist /ˈænəkɪst/ *n.* advocate of anarchism; **anarchistic** /-ˈkɪstɪk/ *a.*
anarchy /ˈænəkɪ/ *n.* disorder, esp. political; lack of government; **anarchic** /æˈnɑ:kɪk/ *a.* [med.L f. Gk (*an-* without, *arkhē* rule)]
anathema /əˈnæθəmə/ *n.* detested thing; curse of God or Church. [eccl.L f. Gk, = thing devoted (i.e. to evil)]
anathematize *v.t.* curse.
anatomy /əˈnætəmɪ/ *n.* science of bodily structure; bodily structure of animal or plant; analysis; **anatomical** /ænəˈtɒmɪk(ə)l/ *a.* [F or L f. Gk (*ana-* up, *temnō* cut)]
-ance *suffix* forming nouns denoting quality or state or an instance of this (*arrogance, resemblance*), or action (*assistance*). [F f. L]
ancestor /ˈænsestə/ *n.* any (esp. remote) person from whom one is descended. [F f. L (*ante-* before, *cedo* go)]
ancestral /ænˈsestr(ə)l/ *a.* derived or inherited from ancestors.
ancestry /ˈænsestrɪ/ *n.* one's (esp. remote) family descent; one's ancestors.
anchor /ˈæŋkə/ **1** *n.* heavy metal weight used to moor ship to sea-bottom or balloon to ground; thing affording stability. **2** *v.* secure with anchor; fix firmly; cast anchor; be moored by anchor. **3 anchor man** one who co-ordinates activities, esp. compère in broadcast; **cast anchor** let it down; **weigh anchor** take it up. [OE & F f. L f. Gk *agkura*]
anchorage *n.* place for anchoring; lying at anchor.
anchorite /ˈæŋkəraɪt/ *n.* hermit, religious recluse. [med.L f. Gk (*anakhōreō* retire)]
anchovy /ˈæntʃəvɪ/ *n.* small rich-flavoured fish of herring family. [Sp. & Port. *anchova*]
anchusa /ænˈkju:zə/ *n.* kind of hairy-stemmed plant. [L f. Gk]
ancien régime /ɑ̃sjæ̃ reˈʒi:m/ political and social system formerly in being, esp. in France before Revolution of 1789. [F, = old rule]
ancient /ˈeɪnʃənt/ *a.* of times long past,

esp. before fall of Roman Empire in West; having lived or existed long; **the ancients** people of ancient times. [F f. L *ante* before]

ancillary /æn'sılərı/ *a.* subordinate, subservient, (*to*). [L (*ancilla* handmaid)]

-ancy *suffix* forming nouns denoting quality or state (*constancy*, *infancy*). [L]

and /ənd; *emphat.* ænd/ *conj.* connecting words, clauses, and sentences, in simple relation (*men and women*), implying progression (*better and better*), causation (*she hit him and he cried*), duration (*he cried and cried*), number (*miles and miles*), addition (*two and two*), variety (*there are books and books*); *colloq.* = to (*go and*, *try and*, etc.). [OE]

andante /æn'dæntı/ *Mus.* **1** *adv.* in moderately slow tempo. **2** *n.* (*pl.* **andantes**) movement to be played this way. [It., = going]

andiron /'ændaıən/ *n.* metal stand (usu. one of pair) supporting logs in fireplace. [F *andier*]

and/or either or both of two stated possibilities.

androgynous /æn'drɒdʒınəs/ *a.* hermaphrodite; (of plant) with stamens and pistils in same flower. [Gk *anēr andr-* male, *gunē* woman]

anecdote /'ænıkdəʊt/ *n.* short account of entertaining or interesting incident; **anecdotal** /-'dəʊt(ə)l/ *a.* [(F f.) Gk *anekdota* things unpublished]

anemia *US* var. of ANAEMIA.

anemometer /ænı'mɒmıtə/ *n.* instrument for measuring force of wind. [Gk *anemos* wind]

anemone /ə'nemənı/ *n.* plant akin to buttercup, with white, red, or purple flowers. [Gk, = wind-flower]

aneroid /'ænərɔıd/ **1** *a.* (of barometer) that measures air-pressure without fluid column, by action on lid of box containing vacuum. **2** *n.* aneroid barometer. [F f. Gk (*a-* not, *nēros* water)]

anesthesia *US* var. of ANAESTHESIA.

aneurysm /'ænjʊrız(ə)m/ *n.* (also **aneurism**) excessive enlargement of artery. [Gk (*aneurinō* widen)]

anew /ə'nju:/ *adv.* again; in a different way. [earlier *of newe*]

angel /'eındʒ(ə)l/ *n.* attendant or messenger of God, representation of this conventionally in human form with wings; very virtuous person; obliging person (*be an angel and answer the door*); old English gold coin showing archangel Michael; *sl.* financial backer of enterprise; **angel cake** light sponge cake; **angel-fish** fish with winglike fins. [F f. L f. Gk *aggelos* messenger]

angelic /æn'dʒelık/ *a.* of or like an angel; **angelically** *adv.*

angelica /æn'dʒelıkə/ *n.* aromatic plant or its candied stalks, used in cookery. [med.L, = angelic (herb)]

angelus /'ændʒıləs/ *n.* devotion of the RC Church said at morning, noon, and sunset in commemoration of the Incarnation; bell rung to announce it. [L *Angelus Domini* (= angel of the Lord), opening words]

anger /'æŋgə/ **1** *n.* extreme or passionate displeasure. **2** *v.t.* make angry. [ON *angr* grief]

angina /æn'dʒaınə/ *n.* (in full **angina pectoris** /'pektərıs/) pain in chest brought on by exertion, owing to inadequate blood supply to heart. [L f. Gk *agkhonē* strangling]

angle¹ /'æŋg(ə)l/ **1** *n.* space between two meeting lines or surfaces; inclination of two lines etc. to each other; corner; point of view. **2** *v.* move or place obliquely; present (information) from particular point of view. [F, or L *angulus*]

angle² /'æŋg(ə)l/ *v.i.* fish with line and hook; seek objective deviously.

Angles /'æŋg(ə)lz/ *n.pl.* N. German people who settled in E. Britain in 5th c. [L *Anglus* ult. f. name *Angul* in Germany]

Anglican /'æŋglıkən/ **1** *a.* of Church of England. **2** *n.* member of Anglican Church. **3 Anglicanism** *n.* [L *Anglicanus* (prec.)]

Anglicism /'æŋglısız(ə)m/ *n.* peculiarly English word or custom. [L *anglicus* (ANGLES)]

Anglicize /'æŋglısaız/ *v.t.* make English in form or character.

Anglo- *in comb.* English; of English origin; English or British and. [L (ANGLES)]

Anglo-Catholic /æŋgləʊ'kæθəlık/ **1** *a.* of section of Church of England that emphasizes historical continuity and seeks maximum accordance with doctrine of Catholic Church. **2** *n.* adherent of Anglo-Catholic belief. [ANGLO-]

Anglo-French /æŋgləʊ'frentʃ/ **1** *a.* English and French. **2** *n.* French language developed in England after Norman Conquest.

Anglo-Indian /æŋgləʊ'ındıən/ **1** *a.* of England and India; of British descent but having lived long in India. **2** *n.* Anglo-Indian person.

Anglo-Norman /æŋgləʊ'nɔ:mən/ **1** *a.* English and Norman. **2** *n.* dialect of Normans used in England after Norman Conquest.

Anglophile /'æŋgləʊfaıl/ *n.* one who greatly admires England or the English. [ANGLO-, -PHILE]

Anglo-Saxon /æŋgləʊ'sæks(ə)n/ **1** *a.* of English Saxons before the Norman Conquest. **2** *n.* Anglo-Saxon person or language. [ANGLO-, SAXON]

angora /æŋ'gɔ:rə/ *n.* fabric made from hair of angora goat or rabbit; long-haired variety of cat, goat, or rabbit. [*Angora* (= Ankara) in Turkey]

angostura /æŋgə'stjʊərə/ *n.* aromatic bitter bark used esp. as flavouring. [*Angostura* (= (Ciudad Bolívar) in Venezuela]

angry /'æŋgrɪ/ *a.* feeling or showing anger; (of wound etc.) inflamed, painful; **angrily** *adv.* [ANGER]

ångström /'æŋstrəm/ *n.* unit of wavelength measurement, 10^{-10} metre. [*Ångström*, physicist]

anguish /'æŋgwɪʃ/ *n.* severe esp. mental suffering; **anguished** *a.* [F f. L *angustia* tightness]

angular /'æŋgjʊlə/ *a.* having sharp corners or (of person) features; forming an angle; measured by angle (*angular distance*); **angularity** /-'lærɪtɪ/ *n.* [L (ANGLE¹)]

anhydrous /æn'haɪdrəs/ *a. Chem.* without water, esp. water of crystallization. [Gk (*an-* without, *hudōr* water)]

aniline /'ænɪli:n/ *n.* oily liquid got from coal tar, used in dye-making. [G (*anil* indigo, former source)]

animadvert /ænɪmæd'vɜ:t/ *v.i.* pass criticism or censure (*on*); **animadversion** *n.* [L (*animus* mind, ADVERT²)]

animal /'ænɪm(ə)l/ **1** *n.* living being having sensation and usu. ability to move, esp. such other than man; quadruped; brutish or uncivilized person. **2** *a.* of or like an animal; bestial; carnal. [L *animalis* having breath]

animalcule /ænɪ'mælkju:l/ *n.* microscopic animal. [prec., -CULE]

animalism /'ænɪməlɪz(ə)m/ *n.* nature and activity of animals; belief that humans are mere animals. [ANIMAL]

animality /ænɪ'mælɪtɪ/ *n.* the animal world; animal behaviour.

animalize /'ænɪməlaɪz/ *v.t.* make (person) bestial, sensualize.

animate **1** /'ænɪmət/ *a.* having life; lively. **2** /'ænɪmeɪt/ *v.t.* enliven; give life to. [L (*anima* breath)]

animated /'ænɪmeɪtɪd/ *a.* lively, vigorous; having life; (of film etc.) characterized by animation.

animation /ænɪ'meɪʃ(ə)n/ *n.* vivacity, ardour; being alive; technique of photographing successive drawings or positions of puppets to create illusion of movement.

animism /'ænɪmɪz(ə)m/ *n.* attribution of living soul to inanimate objects and natural phenomena; **animist** *n.*; **animistic** /-'mɪstɪk/ *a.*

animosity /ænɪ'mɒsɪtɪ/ *n.* spirit or feeling of hostility. [F or L (foll.)]

animus /'ænɪməs/ *n.* display of animosity; ill feeling. [L, = spirit, mind]

anion /'ænaɪən/ *n.* negatively charged ion; **anionic** /ænaɪ'ɒnɪk/ *a.* [Gk *ana* up, ION]

anise /'ænɪs/ *n.* plant with aromatic seeds. [F f. L f. Gk *anison*]

aniseed /'ænɪsi:d/ *n.* seed of anise, used for flavouring.

ankle /'æŋk(ə)l/ *n.* joint connecting foot with leg; part of leg between this and calf. [ON]

anklet /'æŋklɪt/ *n.* ornament or fetter for ankle.

ankylosis /æŋkaɪ'ləʊsɪs/ *n.* stiffening of joint by fusion of bones. [Gk (*agkulos* crooked)]

annalist /'ænəlɪst/ *n.* writer of annals; **annalistic** /-'lɪstɪk/ *a.* [foll.]

annals /'æn(ə)lz/ *n.pl.* narrative of events year by year; records. [F or L (*annus* year)]

anneal /ə'ni:l/ *v.t.* heat (metal, glass) and allow to cool slowly, esp. to toughen it. [OE (*ǣlan* bake)]

annelid /'ænəlɪd/ *n.* worm made of segments, e.g. earthworm. [F f. L (*anulus* ring)]

annex /æ'neks/ *v.t.* add or append (thing *to* another) as subordinate part; incorporate (territory of another) into one's own; add as condition or consequence; *colloq.* take without right; **annexation** /-'seɪʃ(ə)n/ *n.* [F f. L (*necto* bind)]

annexe /'æneks/ *n.* separate or added building; addition to document.

annihilate /ə'naɪəleɪt/ *v.t.* destroy utterly; **annihilation** /-'leɪʃ(ə)n/ *n.* [F f. L (*nihil* nothing)]

anniversary /ænɪ'vɜ:sərɪ/ *n.* date on which event took place in a previous year; celebration of this. [L (*annus* year, *verto vers-* turn)]

Anno Domini /ænəʊ 'dɒmɪnaɪ/ **1** *adv.* in the year of the Christian era. **2** *n. colloq.* advancing age. [L, = in the year of the Lord]

annotate /'ænəʊteɪt/ *v.t.* add explanatory notes to (book, document, etc.); **annotation** /-'teɪʃ(ə)n/ *n.* [L (*nota* mark)]

announce /ə'naʊns/ *v.t.* make publicly known; make known the arrival or imminence of (guest, dinner, etc.); be sign of; **announcement** *n.* [F f. L (*nuntius* messenger)]

announcer *n.* one who announces, esp. in broadcasting.

annoy /ə'nɔɪ/ *v.t.* anger or distress slightly; molest; **be annoyed** be somewhat angry *with* person, *at* thing, *to* discover etc.; **annoyance** *n.* [F f. L *in odio* hateful]

annual /'ænjʊəl/ **1** *a.* reckoned by the year; recurring yearly; living or lasting (only) a year. **2** *n.* book etc. published yearly; plant living only a year. [F f. L (*annus* year)]

annuity /ə'nju:ɪtɪ/ *n.* yearly grant or allowance; investment yielding fixed annual sum.

annul /ə'nʌl/ *v.t.* (-ll-) declare invalid; cancel, abolish; **annulment** *n.* [F f. L (*nullus* none)]

annular /'ænjʊlə/ *a.* ring-shaped, forming ring; **annular eclipse** eclipse of sun in which ring of light remains visible. [F or L (*anulus* ring)]

annulate /'ænjʊleɪt/ *a.* marked with or formed of rings.

annunciation /ənʌnsɪ'eɪʃ(ə)n/ *n.* announcement, esp. (**Annunciation**) that of the Incarnation made by Gabriel to Mary; festival of Annunciation. [L (ANNOUNCE)]

anode /'ænəʊd/ *n.* positive electrode or terminal. [Gk *anodos* way up]

anodize /'ænəʊdaɪz/ *v.t.* coat (metal) with protective layer by electrolysis.

anodyne /'ænəʊdaɪn/ **1** *a.* pain-killing, soothing. **2** *n.* anodyne drug or circumstance. [L f. Gk (*an-* without, *odunē* pain)]

anoint /ə'nɔɪnt/ *v.t.* apply oil or ointment to, esp. as religious ceremony; smear (*with* grease etc.). [F f. L *inungo* anoint]

anomalous /ə'nɒmələs/ *a.* deviant, irregular, abnormal. [L f. Gk (*an-* not, *homalos* even)]

anomaly /ə'nɒməlɪ/ *n.* anomalous thing, irregularity.

anomy /'ænəmɪ/ *n.* (also **anomie**) lack of usual social or ethical standards; **anomic** /ə'nɒmɪk/ *a.* [Gk (*a-* without, *nomos* law)]

anon /ə'nɒn/ *adv. archaic* soon, shortly. [OE *on ān* into one]

anon. *abbr.* anonymous.

anonymity /ænə'nɪmɪtɪ/ *n.* state or fact of being anonymous. [foll.]

anonymous /ə'nɒnɪməs/ *a.* of unknown name or authorship; without character, featureless. [L f. Gk (*an-* without, *onoma* name)]

anorak /'ænəræk/ *n.* waterproof jacket of cloth or plastic, usu. with hood. [Eskimo]

anorexia /ænə'reksɪə/ *n.* lack of appetite for food, esp. (in full **anorexia nervosa** /nɜ:'vəʊzə/) as chronic illness. [L f. Gk (*an-* without, *orexis* appetite)]

another /ə'nʌðə/ **1** *a.* additional, one more (*have another pint*); one more of the same sort (*another Callas*); a different (*quite another matter*); some other (*another man's work*). **2** *n.* an additional, other, or different person or thing. [earlier *an other*]

answer /'ɑ:nsə/ **1** *n.* something said or done in reaction to a question, statement, or circumstance; solution to a problem. **2** *v.* make an answer (to); respond to summons or signal of (*answer the door*); suit (need or purpose); be responsible *for* or *to* another; correspond *to* description. **3 answer back** answer rebuke impudently. [OE, = swear against (charge)]

answerable *a.* responsible (*to* person, *for* person or thing); that can be answered.

ant *n.* small usu. wingless insect living in complex social group and proverbial for industry. [OE]

-ant *suffix* forming adjectives denoting attribution of action (*repentant*) or state (*expectant*), and agent nouns (*assistant*, *deodorant*). [F or L (*-ant-* partic. stem of vbs.)]

antacid /ænt'æsɪd/ **1** *a.* that prevents or corrects acidity. **2** *n.* antacid agent. [ANTI-]

antagonism /æn'tægənɪz(ə)m/ *n.* active opposition or hostility. [F (AGONY)]

antagonist *n.* opponent, adversary.

antagonistic /æntægə'nɪstɪk/ *a.* showing antagonism, hostile.

antagonize /æn'tægənaɪz/ *v.t.* evoke hostility or opposition in.

Antarctic /ænt'ɑ:ktɪk/ *a.* of south polar region; **Antarctic Circle** imaginary line round this region at parallel of 66° 33′ S. [F or L (ARCTIC)]

ante /'æntɪ/ **1** *n.* stake offered by player in poker before receiving cards; amount to be paid in advance. **2** *v.t.* put up (an ante); *US* stake, pay *up*. [foll.]

ante- /'æntɪ/ *prefix* before, preceding. [L, = before]

ant-eater /'ænti:tə/ *n.* any of various mammals living on ants. [ANT]

antecedent /æntɪ'si:dənt/ **1** *n.* preceding thing or circumstance; *Gram.* word or phrase to which another word (esp. relative pronoun) refers; in *pl.* person's past history. **2** *a.* previous. [F or L (*cedo* go)]

antechamber /'æntɪtʃeɪmbə/ *n.* anteroom. [ANTE-]

antedate /æntɪ'deɪt/ *v.t.* precede in time; give earlier than true date to.

antediluvian /æntɪdɪ'lu:vɪən/ *a.* of time before the Flood; *colloq.* very old. [ANTE-, DELUGE]

antelope /'æntɪləʊp/ *n.* (*pl.* same or **antelopes**) swift-running deer-like animal (e.g. chamois, gazelle) found esp. in Africa. [F or med.L f. Gk *antholops*]

antenatal /æntɪ'neɪt(ə)l/ *a.* before birth; relating to pregnancy. [ANTE-]
antenna /æn'tenə/ *n.* (*pl.* **antennae** /-i:/) one of pair of sensory organs found on heads of insects, crabs, etc., feeler; (*pl.* **antennas**) radio aerial. [L, = sail-yard]
antepenult /æntɪpɪ'nʌlt/ *n.* last syllable but two in a word. [ANTE-]
antepenultimate /æntɪpɪ'nʌltɪmət/ *a.* last but two.
ante-post /æntɪ'pəʊst/ *a.* (of racing bet) made before runners' numbers are displayed. [ANTE-, POST[1]]
anterior /æn'tɪərɪə/ *a.* nearer the front; prior (*to*). [F or L (ANTE)]
ante-room /'æntɪru:m/ *n.* small room leading to main one. [ANTE-]
anthem /'ænθəm/ *n.* elaborate choral composition usu. based on passage of scripture for (esp. Protestant) church use; song of praise, esp. for nation, or its tune. [OE f. L (ANTIPHON)]
anther /'ænθə/ *n.* part of stamen containing pollen. [(F f.) Gk (*anthos* flower)]
anthill /'ænthɪl/ *n.* mound of soil formed by ants over their nest. [ANT]
anthology /æn'θɒlədʒɪ/ *n.* collection of passages from literature, esp. poetry and song; **anthologist** *n.* [F or med.L f. Gk (*anthos* flower, *-logia* collection)]
anthracite /'ænθrəsaɪt/ *n.* hard form of coal burning with little flame and smoke. [Gk (foll.)]
anthrax /'ænθræks/ *n.* disease of sheep and cattle, transmissible to humans. [L f. Gk, = coal, carbuncle]
anthropocentric /ænθrəpəʊ'sentrɪk/ *a.* regarding man as centre of existence. [Gk *anthrōpos* man]
anthropoid /'ænθrəpɔɪd/ **1** *a.* manlike in form. **2** *n.* anthropoid ape.
anthropology /ænθrə'pɒlədʒɪ/ *n.* study of mankind, esp. as manifested in societies and customs; **anthropological** /-'lɒdʒɪk(ə)l/ *a.*; **anthropologist** *n.* [-LOGY]
anthropomorphism /ænθrəpəʊ'mɔ:fɪz(ə)m/ *n.* attribution of human form to god, animal, or thing; **anthropomorphic** *a.* [Gk (*morphē* form)]
anthropomorphous /ænθrəpəʊ'mɔ:fəs/ *a.* human in form.
anti /'æntɪ/ **1** *prep.* opposed to. **2** *n.* one opposed to a policy etc. [foll.]
anti- /'æntɪ/ *prefix* opposed to; preventing. [Gk]
anti-aircraft /æntɪ'eəkrɑ:ft/ *a.* (of gun or missile) used to attack enemy aircraft. [ANTI-]
antibiotic /æntɪbaɪ'ɒtɪk/ **1** *n.* substance capable of destroying or injuring bacteria or similar organisms. **2** *a.* functioning as antibiotic. [F f. Gk (*bios* life)]
antibody /'æntɪbɒdɪ/ *n.* protein in the body produced in response to and then counteracting antigens. [transl. G *antikörper*]
antic /'æntɪk/ *n.* (usu. in *pl.*) foolish behaviour; absurd or silly action. [It. *antico* ANTIQUE]
Antichrist /'æntɪkraɪst/ *n.* enemy of Christ; **antichristian** /-'krɪstɪən/ *a.* [F f. eccl. L f. Gk (ANTI-, *Khristos* Christ)]
anticipate /æn'tɪsɪpeɪt/ *v.t.* deal with or use before proper time (*anticipate one's income*); (**D**) expect, foresee (*I do not anticipate any trouble*); forestall (person or thing); **anticipation** /-'peɪʃ(ə)n/ *n.*; **anticipatory** *a.* [L (*capio* take)]
anticlerical /æntɪ'klerɪk(ə)l/ *a.* opposed to influence of clergy, esp. in politics. [ANTI-]
anticlimax /æntɪ'klaɪmæks/ *n.* a trivial conclusion to something significant or impressive, esp. where a climax was expected.
anticlockwise /æntɪ'klɒkwaɪz/ *a.* & *adv.* moving in a curve opposite in direction to the hands of a clock.
anticyclone /æntɪ'saɪkləʊn/ *n.* system of winds rotating outwards from area of high barometric pressure, producing fine weather.
antidote /'æntɪdəʊt/ *n.* medicine used to counteract poison; anything counteracting something unpleasant. [F or L f. Gk *antidotos* given against]
antifreeze /'æntɪfri:z/ *n.* substance added to water (esp. in radiator of motor vehicle) to lower its freezing point. [ANTI-]
antigen /'æntɪdʒ(ə)n/ *n.* foreign substance (e.g. toxin) which causes body to produce antibodies. [G (Gk *-genēs* of a kind)]
anti-hero /'æntɪhɪərəʊ/ *n.* central character in story or drama who noticeably lacks conventional heroic attributes. [ANTI-]
antihistamine /æntɪ'hɪstəmɪn, -i:n/ *n.* substance that counteracts effects of histamine, used esp. in treatment of allergies. [ANTI-]
antiknock /'æntɪnɒk/ *n.* substance added to motor fuel to prevent premature combustion.
antilog /'æntilɒg/ *n. colloq.* = ANTILOGARITHM. [abbr.]
antilogarithm /æntɪ'lɒgərɪð(ə)m/ *n.* number to which a logarithm belongs. [ANTI-]
antimacassar /æntɪmə'kæsə/ *n.* (chiefly *hist.*) ornamental or protective covering for back of chair etc.
antimony /'æntɪmənɪ/ *n.* brittle silvery metallic element used esp. in alloys. [med.L]

antinomian /æntɪ'nəʊmɪən/ **1** *a.* of view that Christians are released from obligation of observing moral law. **2** *n.* (**Antinomian**) *hist.* one who holds this view. [med.L (Gk *nomos* law)]

antinomy /æn'tɪnəmɪ/ *n.* contradiction between two laws or authorities in themselves reasonable.

antinovel /'æntɪnɒv(ə)l/ *n.* novel in which conventions of the form are studiously avoided.

antipathy /æn'tɪpəθɪ/ *n.* strong or deep-seated aversion; **antipathetic** /-'θetɪk/ *a.* [F or L f. Gk (PATHETIC)]

antiperspirant /æntɪ'pɜ:spɪrənt/ *n.* substance preventing or reducing perspiration. [ANTI-]

antiphon /'æntɪf(ə)n/ *n.* hymn sung alternately by two bodies of singers; versicle or phrase from this. [eccl.L f. Gk (*phonē* sound)]

antiphonal /æn'tɪfən(ə)l/ *a.* sung alternately by two bodies of singers.

antipodes /æn'tɪpədi:z/ *n.pl.* places diametrically opposite each other on the earth, esp. Australasia in relation to Europe; **antipodal** *a.*; **antipodean** /-'di:ən/ *a.* & *n.* [F or L f. Gk (= having the feet opposite)]

antipope /'æntɪpəʊp/ *n.* person set up as pope in opposition to one (held by others to be) canonically chosen. [ANTI-]

antipyretic /æntɪpaɪ'retɪk/ **1** *a.* that reduces fever. **2** *n.* antipyretic drug.

antiquarian /æntɪ'kweərɪən/ **1** *a.* of or dealing in antiques or rare books. **2** *n.* antiquary. [foll.]

antiquary /æn'tɪkwərɪ/ *n.* student or collector of antiques or antiquities. [L (ANTIQUE)]

antiquated /'æntɪkweɪtɪd/ *a.* out of date, old-fashioned. [foll.]

antique /æn'ti:k/ **1** *n.* object of considerable age, esp. item of furniture or decorative arts having high value. **2** *a.* of, existing from, early date; old-fashioned. [F, or L *antiquus*]

antiquity /æn'tɪkwɪtɪ/ *n.* ancient times, esp. before the Middle Ages; great age; (in *pl.*) remains from ancient times. [F f. L (prec.)]

antirrhinum /æntɪ'raɪnəm/ *n.* flower suggestive of animal's snout in shape, esp. snapdragon. [L f. Gk (= snout)]

antiscorbutic /æntɪskɔ:'bju:tɪk/ **1** *a.* that prevents or cures scurvy. **2** *n.* antiscorbutic medicine. [ANTI-]

anti-Semitic /æntɪsɪ'mɪtɪk/ *a.* hostile to or prejudiced against Jews; **anti-Semite** /-'si:maɪt/ *n.*; **anti-Semitism** /-'semɪtɪz(ə)m/ *n.* [ANTI-]

antiseptic /æntɪ'septɪk/ **1** *a.* that counteracts sepsis, esp. by destroying bacteria. **2** *n.* antiseptic substance.

antiserum /'æntɪsɪərəm/ *n.* serum with high antibody content.

antisocial /æntɪ'səʊʃ(ə)l/ *a.* not sociable; opposed or harmful to existing social order.

antistatic /æntɪ'stætɪk/ *a.* that counteracts effects of static electricity.

antithesis /æn'tɪθəsɪs/ *n.* (*pl.* **antitheses** /-si:z/) direct opposite; contrast; contrast of ideas marked by parallelism of contrasted words; **antithetical** /-'θetɪk(ə)l/ *a.* [L f. Gk (*antitithēmi* set against)]

antitoxin /æntɪ'tɒksɪn/ *n.* antibody that counteracts a toxin; **antitoxic** *a.* [ANTI-]

antitrades /æntɪ'treɪdz/ *n.pl.* winds blowing above and in opposite direction to trade winds.

antler *n.* branched horn of stag or other deer; **antlered** *a.* [F]

antonym /'æntənɪm/ *n.* word opposite in meaning to another. [F (Gk *onoma* name)]

antrum /'æntrəm/ *n.* (*pl.* **antra**) cavity in body, esp. one of pair in upper jawbone. [L f. Gk (= cave)]

anus /'eɪnəs/ *n.* excretory opening at end of alimentary canal. [L]

anvil /'ænvɪl/ *n.* iron block on which metals are worked. [OE]

anxiety /æŋ'zaɪətɪ/ *n.* state of being worried or concerned; eagerness. [F or L (foll.)]

anxious /'æŋkʃəs/ *a.* troubled, uneasy in mind; causing or marked by anxiety (*an anxious moment*); eagerly wanting (*anxious to please*). [L *anxius*]

any /'enɪ/ **1** *a.* one, no matter which, of several (*cannot find any answer*); some, no matter how much or many or of what sort (*have you any coffee, any books?*); minimal amount of (*hardly any difference*); whichever is chosen (*any fool knows that*). **2** *pron.* any one, any number or amount. **3** *adv.* (usu. with neg. or interrog.) at all, in some degree (*is it any good?; it is not any better*). [OE *ǣnig* (ONE, -Y[1])]

anybody *n.* & *pron.* any person; person of importance (*is he anybody?*).

anyhow *adv.* anyway; in disorderly manner.

anyone *n.* & *pron.* anybody.

anything *n.* & *pron.* any thing, thing of any sort (*I'll do anything*); **anything but** not at all.

anyway *adv.* in any way or manner; at any rate.

anywhere **1** *adv.* in or to any place. **2** *pron.* any place (*anywhere will do*).

Anzac /'ænzæk/ *n.* soldier in Australian and New Zealand Army Corps (1914–18). [acronym]

aorist /'eərɪst/ *n.* unqualified past tense of (esp. Greek) verb, without reference to duration or completion. [Gk, = indefinite]
aorta /eɪ'ɔ:tə/ *n.* main artery carrying blood from left ventricle of the heart; **aortic** *a.* [Gk (*aeirō* raise)]
apace /ə'peɪs/ *adv.* swiftly. [F *à pas*]
apart /ə'pɑ:t/ *adv.* separately, not together (*cannot tell them apart*); into pieces (*came apart in my hands*); aside; to or at a distance; **apart from** excepting, not considering. [F *à part* to one side]
apartheid /ə'pɑ:theɪt/ *n.* racial segregation, esp. in S. Africa. [Afrik.]
apartment /ə'pɑ:tmənt/ *n.* (in *pl.*) suite of rooms; single room; *US* flat. [F f. It. (*a parte* apart)]
apathy /'æpəθɪ/ *n.* lack of interest, indifference; insensibility; **apathetic** /-'θetɪk/ *a.* [F f. L f. Gk (*a-* without, PATHOS)]
ape 1 *n.* monkey, esp. of tailless kind; mimic. **2** *v.t.* imitate, mimic. **3 ape-man** extinct primate intermediate between ape and man. [OE]
aperient /ə'pɪərɪənt/ **1** *a.* laxative. **2** *n.* laxative medicine. [L *aperio* open]
aperitif /əperɪ'ti:f/ *n.* alcoholic drink taken before meal. [F f. L (prec.)]
aperture /'æpətjʊə/ *n.* opening or gap, esp. variable one in camera, for admitting light. [L (APERIENT)]
apex /'eɪpeks/ *n.* (*pl.* **apexes**) highest point; pointed end, tip. [L]
aphasia /ə'feɪzjə/ *n.* partial or total loss of speech or understanding of speech, caused by brain damage. [Gk (*aphatos* speechless)]
aphelion /æ'fi:lɪən/ *n.* (*pl.* **aphelia**) point furthest from sun in planet's orbit round it. [Gk *aph' hēliou* from the sun]
aphid /'eɪfɪd/ *n.* small insect infesting and damaging plants, e.g. greenfly. [foll.]
aphis /'eɪfɪs/ *n.* (*pl.* **aphides** /-di:z/) aphid. [invented by Linnaeus: perh. misreading of Gk *koris* bug]
aphorism /'æfərɪz(ə)m/ *n.* short pithy maxim; brief statement of a principle; **aphoristic** /-'ɪstɪk/ *a.* [F or L f. Gk *aphorismos* definition]
aphrodisiac /æfrəʊ'dɪzɪæk/ **1** *a.* arousing sexual desire. **2** *n.* aphrodisiac drug. [Gk (*Aphrodite* goddess of love)]
apiary /'eɪpɪərɪ/ *n.* place where bees are kept; **apiarist** *n.* [L (*apis* bee)]
apical /'eɪpɪk(ə)l/ *a.* of or at or forming an apex. [APEX]
apiculture /'eɪpɪkʌltʃə/ *n.* bee-keeping; **apiculturist** /-'kʌltʃərɪst/ *n.* [L *apis* bee, CULTURE]
apiece /ə'pi:s/ *adv.* for each one, severally. [orig. *a piece*]
apish /'eɪpiʃ/ *a.* of or like an ape; silly, affected. [APE]
aplomb /ə'plɒm/ *n.* assurance, self-confidence. [F, = straight as plummet]
apocalypse /ə'pɒkəlɪps/ *n.* revelation, esp. of the future of the world; **the Apocalypse** last book of New Testament, recounting divine revelation to St John; **apocalyptic** /-'lɪptɪk/ *a.* [F f. eccl.L f. Gk (*apokaluptō* reveal)]
apocrypha /ə'pɒkrɪfə/ *n.pl.* writings not considered genuine, esp. (**Apocrypha**) Old Testament books included in Septuagint and Vulgate but not in Hebrew Bible. [eccl.L f. Gk (*apokruptō* hide away)]
apocryphal /ə'pɒkrɪf(ə)l/ *a.* of doubtful authenticity, not considered genuine.
apogee /'æpədʒi:/ *n.* highest point, climax; point furthest from earth in orbit of moon or satellite round it. [(F f.) Gk *apogeion*]
apolitical /eɪpə'lɪtɪk(ə)l/ *a.* not interested in or concerned with politics. [A-]
apologetic /əpɒlə'dʒetɪk/ *a.* making an apology, showing or expressing regret; in the nature of an apology. [F f. L (APOLOGIA)]
apologetics *n.pl.* reasoned defence, esp. of Christianity.
apologia /æpə'ləʊdʒjə/ *n.* formal defence of belief or conduct. [L f. Gk]
apologist /ə'pɒlədʒɪst/ *n.* one who makes a formal defence of belief etc. by argument. [F f. Gk (prec.)]
apologize /ə'pɒlədʒaɪz/ *v.i.* make an apology, express regret (*to* person, *for* wrong etc.). [Gk (APOLOGIA)]
apology /ə'pɒlədʒɪ/ *n.* regretful acknowledgement of offence or failure; explanation or defence of belief etc.; **apology for** poor or scanty specimen of. [F or L f. Gk (APOLOGIA)]
apophthegm /'æpɒθem/ *n.* terse or pithy saying. [F or L f. Gk]
apoplectic /æpə'plektɪk/ *a.* of, causing, suffering, or liable to apoplexy; *colloq.* extremely enraged. [foll.]
apoplexy /'æpəpleksɪ/ *n.* sudden inability to feel and move, caused by blockage or rupture of brain artery. [F f. L f. Gk (*apoplēssō* disable by stroke)]
apostasy /ə'pɒstəsɪ/ *n.* renunciation of a belief one formerly held, esp. a religious belief. [eccl.L f. Gk (= defection)]
apostate /ə'pɒsteɪt/ *n.* one who renounces his former belief; **apostatize** *v.i.*
a posteriori /eɪ pɒsterɪ'ɔ:raɪ/ from effects to causes; involving reasoning thus. [L, = from what comes after]
apostle /ə'pɒs(ə)l/ *n.* any of the twelve sent out by Christ to preach the Gospel

(**Apostle**); leader, esp. of reform movement. [OE f. eccl.L f. Gk *apostolos* messenger]

apostolate /ə'pɒstələt/ *n.* office or duties of an apostle; leadership in reform. [eccl.L (prec.)]

apostolic /æpə'stɒlɪk/ *a.* of the Apostles or their teaching; of the Pope; **apostolic succession** uninterrupted transmission of spiritual authority from Apostles through popes and bishops. [F or eccl.L (APOSTLE)]

apostrophe /ə'pɒstrəfɪ/ *n.* sign (') showing omission of letter or letters (as in *can't*) or numbers (as in '82 = 1982), or denoting possessive case (as in *boy's*, *boys'*); exclamatory passage addressed to (often absent) person or thing. [L. f. Gk (= turning away)]

apostrophize *v.t.* address in apostrophe.

apothecary /ə'pɒθəkərɪ/ *n. archaic* chemist licensed to dispense medicines and drugs; **apothecaries' measure** (or **weight**) units formerly used in pharmacy. [F f. L (Gk *apothēkē* storehouse)]

apotheosis /əpɒθɪ'əʊsɪs/ *n.* (*pl.* **apotheoses** /-i:z/) elevation to divine status, deification; deified ideal, highest development of thing. [eccl.L f. Gk (*theos* god)]

apotheosize /ə'pɒθɪəʊsaɪz/ *v.t.* make divine, deify; idealize, glorify.

appal /ə'pɔ:l/ *v.t.* (**-ll-**) greatly dismay, shock. [F *apalir* grow pale (PALE[1])]

appalling *a.* greatly dismaying or shocking, frightful; *colloq.* very bad.

apparatus /æpə'reɪtəs/ *n.* equipment for performing particular function, esp. scientific or technical; complicated organization. [L (*paro* prepare)]

apparel /ə'pær(ə)l/ *n. archaic* clothing; **apparelled** *a.* clothed. [F f. Rmc (= make fit, f. L *par* equal)]

apparent /ə'pærənt/ *a.* readily visible or perceivable; seeming. [F f. L (APPEAR)]

apparition /æpə'rɪʃ(ə)n/ *n.* dramatic or remarkable appearance; ghost or phantom.

appeal /ə'pi:l/ **1** *v.* make earnest or formal request; be attractive or of interest *to* (person); call attention or resort *to* (evidence, circumstance) as support; *Law* make request (*to* higher court) for alteration of decision of lower court, refer (case) to higher court; (in cricket) ask umpire to declare batsman out. **2** *n.* act of appealing; urgent or formal request for aid (esp. in support of cause); *Law* referral of case to higher court; appealing quality or attraction. [F f. L *appello* address]

appear /ə'pɪə/ *v.i.* become or be visible; give certain indications, seem (*it appears to be true*); present oneself formally or publicly; act as counsel in court; be published (*it appeared in the papers*; *new edition will appear*). [F f. L *appareo*]

appearance /ə'pɪərəns/ *n.* appearing; outward form as perceived; semblance (*has an appearance of meanness*); **keep up appearances** maintain display or pretence of virtue, affluence, etc.; **put in an appearance** be present, esp. for short time.

appease /ə'pi:z/ *v.t.* make calm or quiet, esp. conciliate (potential aggressor) by making concessions; satisfy (appetite, scruple); **appeasement** *n.* [F (*à* to, *pais* PEACE)]

appellant /ə'pelənt/ *Law* **1** *n.* person who appeals to higher court. **2** *a.* relating to appeal or appellant. [APPEAL]

appellate /ə'pelət/ *a. Law* (esp. of court) concerned with appeals. [L (APPEAL)]

appellation /æpə'leɪʃ(ə)n/ *n.* name, title; nomenclature. [F f. L (APPEAL)]

appellative /ə'pelətɪv/ *a.* naming, esp. *Gram.* (of noun), that designates a class, common. [L (APPEAL)]

append /ə'pend/ *v.t.* attach, affix; add (esp. to written document etc.). [L]

appendage /ə'pendɪdʒ/ *n.* thing attached; addition.

appendectomy /əpen'dektəmɪ/ *n.* (also **appendicectomy**) surgical removal of the appendix. [APPENDIX, -ECTOMY]

appendicitis /əpendɪ'saɪtɪs/ *n.* inflammation of the appendix. [-ITIS]

appendix /ə'pendɪks/ *n.* (*pl.* **appendices** /-si:z/) subsidiary matter at end of book; outgrowth of tissue forming small tube-shaped sac attached to intestine. [L (APPEND)]

appertain /æpə'teɪn/ *v.i.* belong or relate *to*; be appropriate *to*. [F f. L (PERTAIN)]

appetence /'æpɪtəns/ *n.* (also **appetency**) longing or desire *for*; **appetent** *a.* [F or L (foll.)]

appetite /'æpɪtaɪt/ *n.* natural craving or relish, esp. for food or pleasure; desire, inclination; **appetitive** /-'petɪtɪv/ *a.* [F f. L (*peto* seek)]

appetizer /'æpɪtaɪzə/ *n.* small savoury or drink taken before meal to stimulate appetite. [foll.]

appetizing *a.* (of food) stimulating appetite, tasty. [F (APPETITE)]

applaud /ə'plɔ:d/ *v.* express strong approval (of), esp. by clapping; commend, approve (*I applaud your decision*). [L *applaudo* clap hands]

applause /ə'plɔ:z/ *n.* loud approbation, esp. by clapping; warm approval.

apple /'æp(ə)l/ *n.* round, firm, fleshy fruit; tree bearing it; **apple of one's eye**

cherished person or thing; **apple-pie bed** bed with sheets so folded that one cannot stretch out legs; **apple-pie order** extreme neatness. [OE]

appliance /əˈplaɪəns/ *n.* device or equipment for specific task, utensil. [APPLY]

applicable /ˈæplɪkəb(ə)l/ *a.* that may be applied (*to*); **applicability** /-ˈbɪlɪtɪ/ *n.*; **applicably** *adv.* [F or med.L (APPLY)]

applicant /ˈæplɪkənt/ *n.* one who applies for something, esp. employment. [foll.]

application /æplɪˈkeɪʃ(ə)n/ *n.* act of applying, esp. ointment etc. to skin, thing thus applied; formal request usu. in writing; sustained effort, diligence; relevance. [F f. L (APPLY)]

applicator /ˈæplɪkeɪtə/ *n.* device for applying substance to skin or other surface.

applied /əˈplaɪd/ *a.* (esp. of theory or knowledge) put to practical use (*applied mathematics, science*). [foll.]

appliqué /æˈpli:keɪ/ **1** *n.* ornamental work in which fabric is cut out and attached to surface of another fabric. **2** *v.t.* (**appliquéd, -quéing**) decorate with appliqué. [F (foll.)]

apply /əˈplaɪ/ *v.* make formal request (*for* thing, esp. employment); put or spread on (*to* surface); administer (remedy etc. *to*); direct, devote (thing *to* purpose, *to doing* thing); put (knowledge, skill) to practical use; be relevant (*your point does not apply here*); **apply oneself to** undertake (task). [F f. L *applico* fasten to]

appoint /əˈpɔɪnt/ *v.t.* assign job or office to (*appoint him manager, to the post, to act*); fix, decide on (date, place, etc., *for* purpose); equip, furnish; **appointee** /-ˈti:/ *n.* [F (*à point* to a point)]

appointment *n.* appointing, esp. of time and place for meeting; job or office assigned to someone, person appointed; (in *pl.*) fittings, furnishings.

apportion /əˈpɔ:ʃ(ə)n/ *v.t.* share out; assign as share (*to*); **apportionment** *n.* [F or med.L (PORTION)]

apposite /ˈæpəzɪt/ *a.* well expressed, apt, appropriate (*to*). [L (*appono* apply)]

apposition /æpəˈzɪʃ(ə)n/ *n.* juxta position, esp. *Gram.* of elements sharing syntactic function (as in *William the Conqueror; my friend Sue*); **appositional** *a.*

appraisal /əˈpreɪz(ə)l/ *n.* estimation, valuation. [foll.]

appraise /əˈpreɪz/ *v.t.* estimate amount or worth of; fix official price of. [earlier *apprize*, assim. to PRAISE]

appreciable /əˈpri:ʃəb(ə)l/ *a.* significant, considerable. [F (foll.)]

appreciate /əˈpri:ʃɪeɪt/ *v.* regard as valuable, esteem, be grateful for (*we appreciate sincerity, your kindness*); recognize, be sympathetically aware of (*I appreciate your difficulty, that it will be difficult*); assess realistically (*we appreciate the danger ahead*); raise or rise in value. [L (*pretium* price)]

appreciation /əpri:ʃɪˈeɪʃ(ə)n/ *n.* grateful or favourable recognition; sensitive understanding of or reaction to; rise in value. [F (prec.)]

appreciative /əˈpri:ʃɪətɪv/ *a.* (of person) feeling or expressing appreciation. [L (APPRECIATE)]

appreciatory /əˈpri:ʃɪətərɪ/ *a.* (of remarks etc.) expressing appreciation.

apprehend /æprɪˈhend/ *v.t.* arrest, seize; perceive, understand. [F or L (*prehendo* grasp)]

apprehension /æprɪˈhenʃ(ə)n/ *n.* dread, fearful anticipation; arrest, capture; understanding.

apprehensive /æprɪˈhensɪv/ *a.* uneasy, anticipating with fear.

apprentice /əˈprentɪs/ **1** *n.* learner of craft, bound to employer for specified term in return for instruction; novice (esp. jockey). **2** *v.t.* bind (person *to* another) as apprentice. **3 apprenticeship** /-ɪsʃɪp/ *n.* [F (*apprendre* learn)]

apprise /əˈpraɪz/ *v.t.* inform, notify (*of*). [F *appris(e)* learnt, taught]

appro /ˈæprəʊ/ *n. colloq.* approval, chiefly in *on appro*. [abbr.]

approach /əˈprəʊtʃ/ **1** *v.* come near or nearer (to) in space or time (*castle is approached by a path; the time approaches*); be similar to, approximate to; make tentative proposal to; set about (task). **2** *n.* act or means of approaching; way of dealing with person or thing (*needs a new approach*); approximation (*his nearest approach to a smile*); final part of aircraft's flight before landing; (in golf) stroke from fairway to green. [F f. L (*prope* near)]

approachable *a.* friendly, easy to talk to.

approbation /æprəˈbeɪʃ(ə)n/ *n.* approval, consent. [F f. L (*probo* test)]

appropriate **1** /əˈprəʊprɪət/ *a.* suitable, proper. **2** /əˈprəʊprɪeɪt/ *v.t.* take possession of, especially unlawfully for oneself; devote (money etc.) to special purpose. **3 appropriation** /-ˈeɪʃ(ə)n/ *n.* [L (*proprius* own)]

approval /əˈpru:v(ə)l/ *n.* approving; favourable opinion; consent; **on approval** returnable to supplier if not suitable. [foll.]

approve /əˈpru:v/ *v.* confirm, give assent to; **approve of** give or have a favourable opinion of. [F f. L (*probo* test)]

approximate **1** /ə'prɒksɪmət/ *a.* fairly correct, near to the actual (*approximate total, price, result*). **2** /ə'prɒksɪmeɪt/ *v.* be or make approximate or near (*to*). **3 approximation** /-'meɪʃ(ə)n/ *n.* [L (*proximus* nearest)]

appurtenance /ə'pɜ:tɪnəns/ *n.* (in *pl.*) belongings, accessories. [F f. L *pertineo* belong to]

Apr. *abbr.* April.

après-ski /æpreɪ'ski:/ *a.* done or worn after skiing. [F]

apricot /'eɪprɪkɒt/ *n.* orange-yellow stone-fruit allied to plum and peach; its colour; tree bearing it. [Port. or Sp. f. Arab. f. Gk (L *praecox* early-ripe)]

April /'eɪpr(ə)l, -ɪl/ *n.* fourth month of year; **April fool** victim of hoax on 1 April. [L]

a priori /eɪpraɪ'ɔ:raɪ/ from causes to effects, from general principle to particular instance; involving reasoning thus; assumed without investigation; (of knowledge) existing in the mind independently of sensory experience. [L, = from what is before]

apron /'eɪprən/ *n.* garment worn in front of body to protect clothes; area on airfield used for manœuvring and loading aircraft; extension of stage in front of curtain; **tied to mother's apron strings** excessively dependent on her. [orig. *napron*, f. F *nape* table-cloth]

apropos /'æprəpəʊ, -'pəʊ/ **1** *a.* to the point or purpose, appropriate. **2** *adv.* appropriately; *abs.* incidentally. **3 apropos of** in connection with. [F *à propos*]

apse /æps/ *n.* arched or domed recess esp. at end of church. [APSIS]

apsidal /'æpsɪd(ə)l/ *a.* of the form of an apse; of apsides. [foll.]

apsis /'æpsɪs/ *n.* (*pl.* **apsides** /-di:z/) one of two points in orbit of planet or satellite furthest from and nearest to parent planet. [L, f. Gk (*h*)*apsis* arch, vault]

apt *a.* suitable, appropriate; having a tendency (*apt to be careless*); quick-witted (*an apt pupil*). [L *aptus* fitted]

apteryx /'æptərɪks/ *n.* kiwi. [Gk *a-* without, *pterux* wing)]

aptitude /'æptɪtju:d/ *n.* natural talent; ability or fitness, esp. for particular skill. [F (APT)]

aqua /'ækwə/ *n.* the colour aquamarine. [abbr.]

aqua fortis /ækwə 'fɔ:tɪs/ nitric acid. [L, = strong water]

aqualung /'ækwəlʌŋ/ *n.* portable underwater breathing apparatus. [L *aqua* water]

aquamarine /ækwəmə'ri:n/ *n.* bluish-green beryl; its colour. [L *aqua marina* sea water]

aquaplane /'ækwəpleɪn/ **1** *n.* board for riding on water, pulled by speedboat. **2** *v.i.* ride on aquaplane; (of vehicle) glide uncontrollably on wet surface of road. [L *aqua* water, PLANE[1]]

aqua regia /ækwə 'ri:dʒjə/ mixture of acids, able to dissolve gold. [L, = royal water]

aquarelle /ækwə'rel/ *n.* painting in thin usu. transparent water-colours. [F f. It.]

aquarium /ə'kweərɪəm/ *n.* (*pl.* **aquariums**) tank for keeping and showing fish and other aquatic life; building where fish etc. are exhibited. [L *aquarius* of water]

Aquarius /ə'kweərɪəs/ *n.* eleventh sign of zodiac. [L (prec.)]

aquatic /ə'kwætɪk/ **1** *a.* growing or living in water; done in or on water. **2** *n.* aquatic plant or animal; (in *pl.*) aquatic sports. [F or L (*aqua* water)]

aquatint /'ækwətɪnt/ *n.* print resembling water-colour produced from copper plate engraved with nitric acid. [F f. It. *acqua tinta* coloured water]

aqua vitae /ækwə 'vi:taɪ/ *n.* strong alcoholic spirit, esp. brandy. [L, = water of life]

aqueduct /'ækwɪdʌkt/ *n.* channel for conveying water, esp. in form of tall bridge across valley. [L *aquae ductus* conduit]

aqueous /'eɪkwɪəs/ *a.* of or like water; produced by water; **aqueous humour** see HUMOUR. [L *aqua* water]

aquilegia /ækwɪ'li:dʒjə/ *n.* columbine, usu. blue-flowered. [L]

aquiline /'ækwɪlaɪn/ *a.* of or like an eagle; (of nose) curved like eagle's beak. [L (*aquila* eagle)]

-ar *suffix* forming adjectives in sense 'of, of the nature of' (*angular*, *lunar*). [L *-aris*]

Ar *symb.* argon.

Arab /'ærəb/ **1** *n.* member of a Semitic people inhabiting originally Saudi Arabia and neighbouring countries, now the Middle East generally; breed of horse native to Arabia. **2** *a.* of Arabia or the Arabs, esp. with ethnic reference (*Arab hopes of a lasting peace*). [F f. L f. Gk f. Arab.]

arabesque /ærə'besk/ *n.* design of intertwined leaves, scrolls etc.; position of ballet-dancer in which one leg is extended horizontally backwards and the arms are outstretched; *Mus.* short usu. florid piece. [F f. It.]

Arabian /ə'reɪbɪən/ **1** *a.* of Arabia or the Arabs, esp. with geographical reference (*the Arabian desert*). **2** *n.* an Arab (now less usual than *Arab*). [ARAB]

Arabic /'ærəbɪk/ **1** *n.* the Semitic language of the Arabs. **2** *a.* of the Arabs, esp. their language or literature (*Arabic grammar, poetry*). **3 arabic numerals** the numerals 0, 1, 2, 3, etc.

arable /ˈærəb(ə)l/ **1** *a.* (of land) suitable for ploughing and producing crops. **2** *n.* arable land. [F or L (*aro* to plough)]

arachnid /əˈræknɪd/ *n.* any of a class comprising spiders, scorpions, etc. [F or L (Gk *arakhnē* spider)]

arak var. of ARRACK.

Aramaic /ærəˈmeɪɪk/ **1** *n.* branch of Semitic family of languages, esp. language of Syria used as lingua franca in Near East from sixth century BC. **2** *a.* of or in Aramaic. [L f. Gk *Aramaios* of Aram (Heb. name of Syria)]

arbiter /ˈɑːbɪtə/ *n.* person with great control or influence over something (*arbiter of fashion*); judge, arbitrator. [L]

arbitral /ˈɑːbɪtr(ə)l/ *a.* of or by arbitration. [F or L (prec.)]

arbitrary /ˈɑːbɪtrərɪ/ *a.* based on random choice or whim; capricious; despotic; **arbitrarily** *adv.*

arbitrate /ˈɑːbɪtreɪt/ *v.* act, settle (dispute), as arbitrator. [L]

arbitration /ɑːbɪˈtreɪʃ(ə)n/ *n.* settlement of dispute by arbitrator. [F f. L (prec.)]

arbitrator *n.* person appointed by parties involved to settle dispute. [L]

arbor[1] /ˈɑːbə/ *n.* axle or spindle on which wheel etc. revolves in mechanism. [F f. L, = tree]

arbor[2] *US* var. of ARBOUR.

arboraceous /ɑːbəˈreɪʃəs/ *a.* treelike; wooded. [L *arbor* tree]

arboreal /ɑːˈbɔːrɪəl/ *a.* of or living in trees. [L (prec.)]

arborescent /ɑːbəˈresənt/ *a.* treelike in growth or form.

arboretum /ɑːbəˈriːtəm/ *n.* (*pl.* **arboreta**) botanical tree-garden.

arboriculture /ˈɑːbərɪkʌltʃə/ *n.* cultivation of trees and shrubs. [L *arbor* tree, after *agriculture*]

arbor vitae /ɑːbə ˈviːtaɪ/ a kind of evergreen conifer. [L, = tree of life]

arbour /ˈɑːbə/ *n.* shady retreat enclosed by trees or climbing plants. [F f. L *herba* herb; assim. to L *arbor* tree]

arbutus /ɑːˈbjuːtəs/ *n.* a kind of evergreen, esp. strawberry-tree. [L]

arc 1 *n.* part of circumference of circle or other curve; large luminous flow of electric current through gas. **2** *v.i.* (*past* and *p.p.* **arced;** *partic.* **arcing** /-k-/) form arc, move in curve. **3 arc lamp** lamp in which arc is used to produce light. [F f. L *arcus* bow]

arcade /ɑːˈkeɪd/ *n.* covered walk esp. lined with shops; series of arches supporting or along wall. [F f. Rmc (as prec.)]

Arcadian /ɑːˈkeɪdɪən/ **1** *a.* ideally rustic. **2** *n.* one who leads simple rustic life. [L f. Gk *Arkadia* in S. Greece]

arcane /ɑːˈkeɪn/ *a.* mysterious, secret, understood by few. [F or L (*arceo* shut up)]

arch[1] **1** *n.* curved structure supporting bridge, floor, etc., or as ornament; arch-like curvature. **2** *v.* span like arch; (of branches etc.) form arch; provide with or form into arch. [F f. L *arcus* arc]

arch[2] *a.* consciously or affectedly playful. [foll., orig. in *arch rogue* etc.]

arch- *prefix* chief, superior (*archbishop*); pre-eminent, esp. extremely bad (*arch-fiend*). [OE or F f. L f. Gk (*arkhos* chief)]

Archaean /ɑːˈkiːən/ **1** *a.* of the earliest geological period. **2** *n.* this period. [Gk *arkhaios* ancient]

archaeology /ɑːkɪˈɒlədʒɪ/ *n.* study of ancient peoples esp. by scientific excavation of physical remains; **archaeological** /-əˈlɒdʒɪk(ə)l/ *a.*; **archaeologist** *n.* [Gk *arkhaiologia* ancient history]

archaic /ɑːˈkeɪɪk/ *a.* ancient, of early period in culture; antiquated; (of word etc.) no longer in ordinary use; **archaically** *adv.* [F f. Gk (*arkhē* beginning)]

archaism /ˈɑːkeɪɪz(ə)m/ *n.* archaic word or expression; use of the archaic esp. in language and art; **archaistic** /-ˈɪstɪk/ *a.*; **archaize** *v.* [Gk (prec.)]

archangel /ˈɑːkeɪndʒ(ə)l/ *n.* angel of highest rank. [AF (ARCH-, ANGEL)]

archbishop /ɑːtʃˈbɪʃəp/ *n.* chief bishop of province. [OE (ARCH-)]

archbishopric *n.* office or diocese of bishop.

archdeacon /ɑːtʃˈdiːkən/ *n.* church dignitary next below bishop. [OE (ARCH-)]

archdeaconry *n.* office or residence of archdeacon.

archdiocese /ɑːtʃˈdaɪəsɪs/ *n.* diocese of archbishop; **archdiocesan** /-daɪˈɒsɪs(ə)n/ *a.* [ARCH-]

archduchy /ɑːtʃˈdʌtʃɪ/ *n.* territory of an archduke.

archduke /ɑːtʃˈdjuːk/ *n.* chief duke, esp. *Hist.* as title of son of Austrian Emperor. [F f. med.L *archidux*]

Archean *US* var. of ARCHAEAN.

archeology etc. *US* var. of ARCHAEOLOGY etc.

archer *n.* one who shoots with bow and arrows; (**Archer**) sign or constellation Sagittarius. [AF (L *arcus* bow)]

archery *n.* use of bow and arrows, esp. as sport.

archetype /ˈɑːkɪtaɪp/ *n.* original model, prototype; typical example; **archetypal** *a.* [L f. Gk (*tupon* stamp)]

arch-fiend /ɑ:tʃ'fi:nd/ *n.* the Devil. [ARCH-]

archidiaconal /ɑ:kɪdaɪ'ækən(ə)l/ *a.* of an archdeacon or archdeaconry. [med.L]

archiepiscopal /ɑ:kɪɪ'pɪskəp(ə)l/ *a.* of an archbishop or archbishopric. [eccl.L f. Gk]

archimandrite /ɑ:kɪ'mændraɪt/ *n.* superior of large monastery in Orthodox Church; honorary title of monastic priest. [F or eccl.L f. Gk (*arkhi-* chief, *mandritēs* monk)]

archipelago /ɑ:kɪ'pelɪgəʊ/ *n.* (*pl.* **archipelagos**) sea with many islands; group of islands. [It. f. Gk *arkhi-* chief, *pelagos* sea]

architect /'ɑ:kɪtekt/ *n.* designer of buildings and large structures, preparing plans and supervising construction; maker, designer (*architect of his own fortunes*). [F f. It. or L, f. Gk (*arkhi-* chief, *tektōn* builder)]

architectonic /ɑ:kɪtek'tɒnɪk/ *a.* of architecture, constructive; of the systematization of knowledge. [L f. Gk (prec.)]

architecture /'ɑ:kɪtektʃə/ *n.* art or science of designing and constructing buildings; style of building; construction; **architectural** /-'tektʃər(ə)l/ *a.* [F or L (ARCHITECT)]

architrave /'ɑ:kɪtreɪv/ *n.* beam resting on tops of, and parallel with line of, columns; moulded frame round doorway or window. [F f. It. (*archi-* ARCH-, L *trabs* beam)]

archive /'ɑ:kaɪv/ *n.* (freq. in *pl.*) collection of documents or records; place where these are kept. [F f. L f. Gk *arkheia* public records]

archivist /'ɑ:kɪvɪst/ *n.* one in charge of archives.

archway *n.* arched entrance or passage. [ARCH¹]

Arctic /'ɑ:ktɪk/ *a.* of north polar region; (**arctic**) very cold; **Arctic Circle** imaginary line round north polar region at parallel of 66° 33′ N. [F f. L f. Gk (*arktos* Great Bear)]

ardent /'ɑ:dənt/ *a.* eager, fervent, passionate; burning; **ardency** *n.* [F f. L (*ardeo* burn)]

ardour /'ɑ:də/, *US* **ardor** *n.* zeal, enthusiasm, passion.

arduous /'ɑ:djʊəs/ *a.* (of task) hard to accomplish; (of activity) energetic, strenuous. [L, = steep]

are¹ see BE.

are² /ɑ:/ *n.* metric unit of measure, 100 square metres. [F f. L (foll.)]

area /'eərɪə/ *n.* region (*a mountainous area, northern areas*), space set aside for purpose (*dining, picnic area*); extent or measure of surface (*over a large area; 3 acres in area*); scope or range of activity or study; space in front of basement of building. [L, = vacant space]

areca /'ærɪkə, ə'ri:kə/ *n.* a kind of palm-tree; **areca nut** its astringent seed. [Port. f. Malayalam]

arena /ə'ri:nə/ *n.* central part of amphitheatre etc.; scene of conflict, sphere of action. [L, = sand]

aren't /ɑ:nt/ *colloq.* = *are not.*

areola /ə'rɪələ/ *n.* (*pl.* **areolae** /-i:/) circular pigmented area esp. that surrounding nipple; **areolar** *a.* [L dimin. of AREA]

arête /æ'reɪt/ *n.* sharp mountain ridge. [F f. L *arista* spine]

argent /ɑ:dʒənt/ *Heraldry* **1** *n.* silver. **2** *a.* of silver colour. [F f. L *argentum*]

argon /'ɑ:gɒn/ *n.* almost inert gaseous element. [Gk *argos* idle]

argosy /'ɑ:gəsɪ/ *n.* *poetic* large merchant-ship. [It. *Ragusea nave* ship of Ragusa (in Dalmatia)]

argot /'ɑ:gəʊ/ *n.* special jargon of group, formerly esp. criminals. [F]

argue /'ɑ:gju:/ *v.* exchange views, esp. heatedly or contentiously (*with* person, *about* matter); reason (*for* or *against* proposition); maintain by reasoning (*that*); treat (matter) by reasoning; prove, indicate (*that*); persuade (person) *into* or *out of*; **arguable** *a.*; **arguably** *adv.* [F f. L (*arguo* make clear, prove)]

argument /'ɑ:gjʊmənt/ *n.* (esp. contentious) exchange of views, dispute; reason advanced (*for* or *against*); reasoning; summary of reasoning in book etc.

argumentation /ɑ:gjʊmen'teɪʃ(ə)n/ *n.* reasoning, arguing.

argumentative /ɑ:gjʊ'mentətɪv/ *a.* fond of or given to arguing.

Argus /'ɑ:gəs/ *n.* watchful guardian. [L f. Gk *Argos* mythical giant with 100 eyes]

argy-bargy /ɑ:dʒɪ'bɑ:dʒɪ/ *n. colloq.* dispute, wrangle. [orig. Sc.]

aria /'ɑ:rɪə/ *n.* extended piece for solo voice and accompaniment esp. in opera or oratorio. [It.]

Arian /'eərɪən/ **1** *a.* of doctrine of Arius denying full divinity of Christ. **2** *n.* believer in this doctrine. **3** **Arianism** *n.* [*Arius* (4th-c.) who formed doctrine]

arid /'ærɪd/ *a.* dry, parched; dull, uninteresting; **aridity** /æ'rɪdɪtɪ/ *n.* [F or L (*areo* be dry)]

Aries /'eəri:z/ constellation and first sign of zodiac. [L, = ram]

aright /ə'raɪt/ *adv.* rightly. [A³]

arise /ə'raɪz/ *v.i.* (*past* **arose** /ə'rəʊz/; *p.p.* **arisen** /ə'rɪz(ə)n/) emerge, come to one's attention (*a problem has arisen*); originate, result (*from, out of*); rise, esp. from the dead. [OE (*a-* intensive)]

aristocracy /ærɪs'tɒkrəsɪ/ *n.* ruling class or élite, nobility; government by élite, state so governed; best representatives (*of* intellect etc.). [F f. Gk *aristokratia* rule by the best]

aristocrat /'ærɪstəkræt/ *n.* member of aristocracy, noble.

aristocratic /ærɪstə'krætɪk/ *a.* of or like aristocracy; grand, stylish; distinguished.

Aristotelian /ærɪstə'ti:lɪən/ **1** *a.* of Aristotle or his philosophy. **2** *n.* student or follower of Aristotle. [L f. Gk *Aristotelēs* (4th-c. BC), Gk philosopher]

arithmetic 1 /ə'rɪθmətɪk/ *n.* science of numbers; computation, use of numbers. **2** /ærɪθ'metɪk/ *a.* of arithmetic. **3 arithmetic mean** average of two or more numbers obtained by dividing their total by how many there are; **arithmetic progression** sequence of numbers with constant increase or decrease between each and next (as in 1, 3, 5, 7). [F f. L f. Gk (*arithmos* number)]

arithmetical /ærɪθ'metɪk(ə)l/ *a.* = ARITHMETIC 2.

ark *n.* ship in which Noah escaped the Flood with his family and animals, model of this; **Ark of the Covenant** wooden chest or cupboard containing tables of Jewish Law. [OE, f. L *arca*]

arm[1] *n.* upper limb of human body from shoulder to hand; part of clothing covering this, sleeve; raised side part of chair supporting sitter's arm; thing resembling arm in shape or function (*arm of the sea*); control, means of reaching (*arm of the law*); **arm in arm** of two persons with arm of one linked in arm of the other; **at arm's length** at a distance; **with open arms** in friendly manner. [OE]

arm[2] **1** *n.* (usu. in *pl.*) weapon; branch of military forces, e.g. infantry, artillery; (in *pl.*) heraldic devices. **2** *v.* equip with weapons or other requisites; equip oneself with weapons, esp. in preparation for war; make (bomb etc.) ready to explode. **3 arms race** competitive accumulation of weapons by nations; **take up arms** go to war; **under arms** equipped for war; **up in arms** actively resisting, highly indignant. [F f. L *arma* arms]

armada /ɑ:'mɑ:də/ *n.* fleet of warships, esp. (**Armada**) the one sent by Spain against England in 1588. [Sp. f. Rmc]

armadillo /ɑ:mə'dɪləʊ/ *n.* (*pl.* **armadillos**) S. American burrowing mammal with body encased in bony plates. [Sp. (*armado* armed man)]

Armageddon /ɑ:mə'ged(ə)n/ *n.* ultimate or large-scale conflict. [Rev. 16:16]

armament /'ɑ:məmənt/ *n.* (usu. in *pl.*) weapons, military equipment; equipping for war, force equipped. [L (ARM[2])]

armature /'ɑ:mətjʊə/ *n.* wire-wound core of dynamo or electric motor; bar placed in contact with poles of magnet; internal framework supporting sculpture during construction. [F f. L (= armour)]

armchair *n.* chair with side supports for the arms. [ARM[1]]

armful *n.* quantity held in one's arm or arms.

armistice /'ɑ:mɪstɪs/ *n.* stopping of hostilities; truce. [L *arma* arms, *sisto* make stand]

armlet /'ɑ:mlɪt/ *n.* ornamental band worn round arm. [ARM[1]]

armor etc. *US* var. of ARMOUR etc.

armorial /ɑ:'mɔ:rɪəl/ *a.* of heraldry or coats of arms. [foll.]

armour /'ɑ:mə/ *n.* defensive (usu. metal) covering formerly worn in fighting; protective metal covering for armed vehicle, ship, etc.; armoured fighting vehicles collectively; protective covering of animal or plant; heraldic devices. [F f. L (ARM[2])]

armoured *a.* furnished with armour (*armoured car*); equipped with armoured vehicles.

armourer *n.* maker of arms or armour; official in charge of arms.

armoury *n.* arsenal.

armpit *n.* hollow under arm at shoulder. [ARM[1]]

army *n.* organized force armed for fighting on land; *the* military profession; very large number (*army of locusts*); organization devoted to cause (*Salvation Army*). [F (ARM[2])]

arnica /'ɑ:nɪkə/ *n.* a kind of composite plant with yellow flowers; medicine made from it. [orig. unkn.]

aroma /ə'rəʊmə/ *n.* fragrance, sweet or pleasant smell; subtle pervasive quality. [L f. Gk, = spice]

aromatic /ærəʊ'mætɪk/ **1** *a.* of or having an aroma, fragrant; of organic compounds containing rings of six carbon atoms, as benzene. **2** *n.* aromatic substance. [F f. L (prec.)]

arose *past* of ARISE.

around /ə'raʊnd/ **1** *adv.* on every side, all round; *colloq.* near at hand (*good to have you around*); here and there (*shop around; fool around*). **2** *prep.* on or along the circuit of; on every side of; *US* at a time near to (*come around four*). **3 have been around** *colloq.* be widely experienced. [A[3]]

arouse /ə'raʊz/ *v.t.* awake from sleep; stir into activity; cause, induce (*arouse suspicion*); **arousal** *n.* [*a*- intensive pref.]

arpeggio /ɑ:'pedʒɪəʊ/ *n.* (*pl.* **arpeggios**) playing of notes of a chord in rapid succession; chord so played. [It. (*arpa* harp)]
arquebus var. of HARQUEBUS.
arrack /'ærək/ *n.* alcoholic spirit, esp. made from coco sap or rice. [Arab.]
arraign /ə'reɪn/ *v.t.* indict, accuse; find fault with (action, statement); **arraignment** *n.* [F f. L (*ratio* reason)]
arrange /ə'reɪndʒ/ *v.* put into required order, classify; plan or provide for (*arrange a meeting*); take measures or give instructions (*arrange to see him*; *arrange for a taxi to come*); agree *with* person about measures or procedure (*arranged with her to meet at 8*); adapt (piece of music) for performance with different instruments or voices. [F (RANGE)]
arrangement *n.* arranging or result of arranging, thing arranged; (in *pl.*) plans, measures; settlement or agreement on procedure.
arrant /'ærənt/ *a.* downright, utter (*arrant liar, nonsense*). [var. ERRANT, orig. in *arrant* (= outlawed roving) *thief* etc.]
arras /'ærəs/ *n.* richly decorated tapestry or wall-hanging. [*Arras* in France]
array /ə'reɪ/ **1** *n.* imposing series or display; ordered arrangement, esp. of troops (*battle array*). **2** *v.t.* set in order, marshal (forces). [F (L *ad-*, READY)]
arrears /ə'rɪəz/ *n. pl.* amount still outstanding or uncompleted, esp. work undone or debt unpaid; **in arrears** behindhand (in work to be done, debt to be paid, etc.) [F f. med.L *adretro* behindhand]
arrest /ə'rest/ **1** *v.t.* seize (person) by legal authority; stop or check (esp. moving thing, process); attract (person's attention). **2** *n.* act of arresting, esp. legal seizure of person; stoppage (*cardiac arrest*). [F f. L *resto* remain]
arrester *n.* device for slowing aircraft after landing.
arrière-pensée /ærjeəpɑ̃seɪ/ *n.* ulterior motive; mental reservation. [F]
arris /'ærɪs/ *n.* sharp edge formed by meeting of two surfaces. [F *areste*, = ARÊTE]
arrival /ə'raɪv(ə)l/ *n.* arriving, appearance on the scene; person or thing that has arrived; *colloq.* new-born baby. [foll.]
arrive /ə'raɪv/ *v.i.* reach destination or end of journey; (of time) come; achieve fame, position, etc.; (of baby) be born; **arrive at** reach (conclusion). [F, f. L *ripa* shore]
arriviste /ærɪ'vɪst/ *n.* person ruthlessly and obsessively aspiring to advancement. [F (prec.)]
arrogant /'ærəgənt/ *a.* aggressively assertive or presumptuous, overbearing; **arrogance** *n.* [foll.]
arrogate /'ærəʊgeɪt/ *v.t.* claim or seize (thing *to oneself*) without right; attribute unjustly (*to* another); **arrogation** /-'geɪʃ(ə)n/ *n.* [L (*rogo* ask)]
arrow /'ærəʊ/ *n.* pointed slender missile shot from bow; representation of this esp. to show direction. [OE]
arrowhead *n.* pointed tip of arrow; water-plant with arrow-shaped leaves.
arrowroot *n.* nutritious starch; plant from which this comes.
arse /ɑ:s/ *n. sl.* the buttocks. [OE]
arsenal /'ɑ:sən(ə)l/ *n.* place for storing or manufacturing weapons and ammunition. [F or It. f. Arab., = workshop]
arsenic 1 /'ɑ:sənɪk/ *n.* a silvery semi-metallic element; *pop.* arsenic trioxide, a violent poison used in manufacture of insecticides etc. **2** /ɑ:'senɪk/ *a.* of or containing arsenic. [F. ult. f. Pers. *zar* gold]
arson /'ɑ:s(ə)n/ *n.* criminal and deliberate act of setting fire to house or other building; **arsonist** *n.* [F f. L (*ardeo ars-* burn)]
art *n.* human creative skill or its application; branch of creative activity concerned with production of imitative and imaginative designs and expression of ideas, esp. in painting; products of this activity; any skill esp. contrasted with scientific technique or principle; craft or activity requiring imaginative skill; (in *pl.*) branches of learning (esp. languages, literature, and history) associated with imaginative and creative skill as distinct from technical skills of science; specific ability, knack; cunning, artfulness; trick, stratagem. [F f. L *ars, art-*]
artefact /'ɑ:tɪfækt/ *n.* man-made object, esp. tool or vessel as archaeological item. [L *arte* by art, *facio* make]
arterial /ɑ:'tɪərɪəl/ *a.* of or like an artery; (of road etc.) main, important. [F (ARTERY)]
arteriosclerosis /ɑ:tɪərɪəʊsklɪə'rəʊsɪs/ *n.* hardening of the walls of arteries. [ARTERY, SCLEROSIS]
artery /'ɑ:tərɪ/ *n.* any of the tubes conveying blood from the heart; main road or railway line. [L f. Gk (prob. *airō* raise)]
artesian well /ɑ:'ti:ʒ(ə)n/ well in which water rises to surface by natural pressure through vertically drilled hole. [*Artois*, old French province]
artful *a.* crafty, sly; skilful. [ART]
arthritis /ɑ:'θraɪtɪs/ *n.* inflammation of a joint or joints; **arthritic** /ɑ:'θrɪtɪk/ *a.* [L f. Gk (*arthron* joint)]
arthropod /'ɑ:θrəpɒd/ *n.* animal with segmented body and jointed limbs, e.g. insect, spider, crustacean. [Gk *arthron* joint, *pous pod-* foot]

artichoke /'ɑ:tɪtʃəʊk/ *n.* plant allied to thistle; its partly edible flower-head; = JERUSALEM ARTICHOKE. [It. f. Arab.]

article /'ɑ:tɪk(ə)l/ **1** *n.* particular item or commodity; short self-contained piece of writing in newspaper, journal, etc., distinct portion of text (*encyclopaedia article*); clause of agreement. **2** *v.t.* bind by articles of apprenticeship. **3 definite article** 'the' or equivalent in other language; **indefinite article** 'a' or 'an', or equivalent in other language. [F f. L *articulus* (*artus* joint)]

articular /ɑ:'tɪkjʊlə/ *a.* of a joint or joints. [L (prec.)]

articulate 1 /ɑ:'tɪkjʊlət/ *a.* able to express oneself clearly and fluently; (of speech) in which the separate sounds and words are clear; having joints. **2** /ɑ:'tɪkjʊleɪt/ *v.* speak or express clearly, pronounce distinctly; (usu. in *pass.*) connect by or divide with joints; form joint *with*. **3 articulated lorry** one with sections connected by a flexible joint.

articulation /ɑ:tɪkjʊ'leɪʃ(ə)n/ *n.* articulate utterance; jointing or being jointed; joint. [F or L (prec.)]

artifact var. of ARTEFACT.

artifice /'ɑ:tɪfɪs/ *n.* trick, piece of cunning; skill, ingenuity. [F f. L (*ars art-* art, *facio* make)]

artificer /ɑ:'tɪfɪsə/ *n.* craftsman; skilled mechanic in army or navy.

artificial /ɑ:tɪ'fɪʃ(ə)l/ *a.* produced by human art or effort, not originating naturally (*artificial light*); made or done in imitation of the natural (*artificial flowers*); affected, insincere; **artificial insemination** injection of semen into uterus other than by sexual intercourse; **artificial respiration** manual or mechanical stimulation of breathing; **artificiality** /-ʃɪ'ælɪtɪ/ *n.*; **artificially** *adv.* [F or L (ARTIFICE)]

artillery /ɑ:'tɪlərɪ/ *n.* heavy guns used in fighting on land; branch of army equipped with these; **artillerist** *n.*; **artilleryman** *n.* [F (*artiller* equip)]

artisan /ɑ:tɪ'zæn/ *n.* skilled workman or craftsman. [F f. It. (L *artio* instruct in arts)]

artist /'ɑ:tɪst/ *n.* one who practises any of the fine arts, esp. painting; one who does something with skill or taste. [F *artiste* f. It.]

artiste /ɑ:'ti:st/ *n.* professional performer, esp. singer or dancer.

artistic /ɑ:'tɪstɪk/ *a.* of art or artists; showing aptitude for fine arts; skilfully or tastefully done; **artistically** *adv.*

artistry /'ɑ:tɪstrɪ/ *n.* artistic skill; work of artist.

artless *a.* without guile, ingenuous; not resulting from art, natural; crude, clumsy. [ART]

art nouveau /ɑ: nu:'vəʊ/ style of art developed in late 19th-c., with ornamental and flowing designs. [F, = new art]

arty *a. colloq.* pretentiously or quaintly artistic; **artiness** *n.* [ART]

arum /'eərəm/ *n.* a kind of tall plant with small flowers enclosed in bracts. [L f. Gk *aron*]

-ary *suffix* forming adjectives in sense 'of, connected with'. [F *-aire* or L *-ari(u)s*]

Aryan /'eərɪən/ **1** *n.* early speaker of language of Indo-European family; *improperly* (esp. in Nazi Germany) non-Jewish Caucasian. **2** *a.* of Indo-European family of languages. [Skr.]

as[1] /əz, *emphat.* æz/ **1** *adv.* & *conj.* (*adv.* as antecedent; *conj.* in relative clause expressed or implied) to the same extent, ... to the extent to which ... is or does etc. (*I am as tall as he is, as he*, colloq. *as him*; *as like as two peas*; *not as, not so, young as I used to be*; *as sure as death*; *this is just as good*; *I thought as much*); *conj.* with antecedent *so*, expressing result or purpose (*so good as to exceed all hopes*; *came early so as to meet us*); with antecedent *adv.* omitted (*good as it is* = although it is good); in the manner in which (*do as you like*; *was regarded as a mistake, as wrong*; *they rose as one man*); in the capacity or form of (*I speak as your friend*; *Olivier as Hamlet*; *as a matter of fact*); for instance (*books, as Oliver Twist*); during or at the time that (*came up as I was speaking*; *just as I reached the door*); for the reason that, seeing that (*as you are here, we can talk*). **2** *rel. pron.* (with verb of relative clause expressed or implied) that, who, which (*I had the same trouble as you*; *such money as you have, such cities as York*; vulgar *it was him as did it*); a fact that, with sentence as antecedent (*he lost, as you know*). **3 as from** on and after (specified date); **as if** (or **though**) as would be the case if (*acts as if he were in charge*; *as if you didn't know!*; *looks as though we've won*); **as it were** in a way, to some extent; **as of** = *as from*, as at (specified time); **as to** with regard to; **as well** advisable, desirable, reasonably (*it would be as well to try*; *we may as well go*; *you might as well!*); **as well (as)** in addition (to); **as yet** until now (usu. with negative and with implied reserve about the future). [OE, = ALSO]

as[2] /æs/ *n.* (*pl.* **asses**) ancient Roman copper coin. [L]

As *symb.* arsenic.

asafoetida /æsə'fetɪdə/ *n.* resinous strong-smelling plant gum formerly used in medicine. [L f. Pers. *azā* mastic; FETID]

asbestos /æz'bestɒs/ *n.* a fibrous silicate mineral; fire-resistant substance made from this. [F f. L f. Gk, = unquenchable]

ascend /ə'send/ *v.* move upwards, rise (*ascend into the sky, to the highest rank*); mount, climb (*ascend the stairs, the hill*); **ascend the throne** become king or queen. [L (*scando* climb)]

ascendancy *n.* dominant power or control (*over*). [foll.]

ascendant **1** *a.* rising; gaining favour or control; *Astron.* rising towards zenith; *Astrol.* (of sign) just above eastern horizon. **2** *n. Astron.* point of ecliptic that is ascendant at a given time. **3 in the ascendant** at or near the peak of one's fortunes. [F f. L (ASCEND)]

ascension /ə'senʃ(ə)n/ *n.* ascent, esp. (**Ascension**) of Christ to Heaven. [F f. L (ASCEND)]

ascent /ə'sent/ *n.* ascending, rising, climbing; upward path or slope; flight of steps. [ASCEND]

ascertain /æsə'teın/ *v.t.* find out for certain; **ascertainment** *n.* [F (CERTAIN)]

ascetic /ə'setık/ **1** *a.* severely abstinent; self-denying. **2** *n.* person leading ascetic life, esp. in religious cause. [med.L or Gk (*askeō* exercise)]

ascorbic acid /ə'skɔ:bık/ vitamin C, which prevents scurvy. [A-, SCORBUTIC]

ascribe /ə'skraıb/ *v.t.* regard (thing or circumstance) as belonging or causally related *to* (person, event, etc.), attribute (*ascribes difficulties to overspending*; *poems ascribed to Homer*); **ascription** /ə'skrıpʃ(ə)n/ *n.* [L (*scribo* write)]

asdic /'æzdık/ *n.* earlier form of sonar. [*A*llied *S*ubmarine *D*etection *I*nvestigation *C*ommittee]

asepsis /eı'sepsıs/ *n.* absence of sepsis or harmful bacteria; aseptic method in surgery. [A-]

aseptic /eı'septık/ *a.* free from sepsis, surgically sterile; securing absence of septic matter.

asexual /eı'seksjʊəl/ *a.* lacking sex or sexuality; of reproduction not involving fusion of gametes.

ash¹ *n.* whitish grey powdery residue left after a substance has been burned; (in *pl.*) particles of this residue, remains of human body after cremation; (**Ashes**) trophy competed for in Anglo-Australian test cricket. [OE]

ash² *n.* tree with silvery-grey bark; its hard close-grained wood. [OE]

ashamed /ə'ʃeımd/ *a.* (usu. *predic.*) feeling or affected by shame (*am ashamed of myself*); reluctant or hesitant out of shame (*am ashamed to say*). [OE (*a-* intensive pref.)]

ashbin *n.* (*US* **ashcan**) dustbin. [ASH¹]

ashen *a.* like ashes, esp. pale in colour.

Ashkenazi /æʃkə'nɑ:zı/ *n.* (*pl.* **Ashkenazim**) E. European Jew. [Heb.]

ashlar *n.* square-hewn stone or masonry made of this; thin slabs of it used for facing walls. [F f. L (*axis* board)]

ashore /ə'ʃɔ:/ *adv.* to or on shore; on to land (from the sea). [A³]

ashram /'æʃræm/ *n.* in India, retreat for religious meditation. [Skr.]

ashtray *n.* container for discarded tobacco ash. [ASH¹]

ashy *a.* like ash, ashen; covered with ashes.

Asian /'eıʃ(ə)n, 'eıʒ-/ **1** *n.* native or inhabitant of Asia, person descended from one. **2** *a.* of Asia. [L f. Gk]

Asiatic /eızı'ætık/ *a.* of Asia (usu. with geographical reference); (**R**) as *a.* or *n.* of persons.

aside /ə'saıd/ **1** *adv.* to or on one side, away, apart. **2** *n.* words spoken aside, esp. by actor supposedly out of hearing of other actors. [A³]

asinine /'æsınaın/ *a.* like an ass, esp. stupid or stubborn; **asininity** /-'nınıtı/ *n.* [L (*asinus* ass)]

ask /ɑ:sk/ *v.* call for an answer to or about (*ask him a question about it*; *ask a question about it*; *ask him his name*; *ask who he is*; *no questions were asked of us*); seek to obtain or achieve from someone (*ask her for the money*; *ask her a favour*, *a favour of her*; *ask £5 for the book*; *ask them to come in*); invite (*to* dinner etc., *in*, *out*); **ask after** inquire about (esp. person); **ask for** seek to obtain or find or speak to (*ask for the tickets, the bar, the attendant*); **ask for it** invite trouble. [OE]

askance /ə'skæns, -ɑ:ns/ *adv.* with a sideways look; **look askance at** regard with suspicion or disapproval. [orig. unkn.]

askew /ə'skju:/ **1** *adv.* crookedly, out of true position (*hanging askew*). **2** *predic. a.* oblique, crooked. [A³]

aslant /ə'slɑ:nt/ **1** *adv.* on a slant, obliquely. **2** *prep.* obliquely across. [A³]

asleep /ə'sli:p/ **1** *predic. a.* sleeping, *colloq.* inactive, inattentive; (of limb) numb; *euphem.* dead. **2** *adv.* into a state of sleep (*fell asleep*). [A³]

asocial /eı'səʊʃ(ə)l/ *a.* not social; not sociable; *colloq.* inconsiderate. [A-]

asp *n.* small poisonous viper of Africa and S. Europe. [F or L f. Gk *aspis*]

asparagus /ə'spærəgəs/ *n.* plant of lily family with feathery leaves; its edible young shoots as vegetable. [L f. Gk]

aspect /'æspekt/ *n.* viewpoint from which or feature by which a matter is considered (*only one aspect of the* *problem*); way a thing looks (*of pleasing aspect*); side of building facing a particular direction (*southern aspect of the house*); *Astrol.* relative position of planets. [L (*adspico* look at)]

aspen /'æspən/ *n.* a kind of poplar with fluttering leaves. [OE; orig. adj.]

asperity /æ'sperɪtɪ/ *n.* harshness of temper or tone (*spoke with asperity*); roughness of surface. [F or L (*asper* rough)]

aspersion /ə'spɜ:ʃ(ə)n/ *n.* damaging or derogatory remark; **cast aspersions on** attack reputation of (person). [L (*aspergo* besprinkle)]

asphalt /'æsfælt/ **1** *n.* tarlike bitumen made from petroleum; mixture of this with sand or gravel for use in paving etc. **2** *v.t.* cover or surface with asphalt. [L f. Gk]

asphodel /'æsfədel/ *n.* a kind of lily; *poetic* immortal flower growing in Elysium. [L f. Gk]

asphyxia /æs'fɪksɪə/ *n.* lack of oxygen in blood, causing unconsciousness or death; suffocation; **asphyxiant** *a.* & *n.* [Gk (*a-* not, *sphuxis* pulse)]

asphyxiate /æs'fɪksɪeɪt/ *v.t.* cause (person) to have asphyxia; suffocate; **asphyxiation** /-'eɪʃ(ə)n/ *n.*

aspic /'æspɪk/ *n.* savoury of meat, fish, egg, etc., in jelly. [F, = ASP, suggested by various colours of jelly]

aspidistra /æspɪ'dɪstrə/ *n.* plant with broad tapering leaves. [L f. Gk *aspis* shield]

aspirant /'æspɪrənt, ə'spaɪə-/ **1** *n.* one who aspires, esp. to honour or position. **2** *a.* aspiring. [F or L (ASPIRE)]

aspirate 1 /'æspɪreɪt/ *v.t.* pronounce with initial *h* or with release of breath; draw (fluid) by suction from cavity etc. **2** /-ət/ *n.* sound of *h*; consonant pronounced with this. **3** /-ət/ *a.* pronounced with aspirate.

aspiration /æspɪ'reɪʃ(ə)n/ *n.* ambition or desire (*for, to, after*); aspirating; drawing of breath.

aspirator /'æspɪreɪtə/ *n.* apparatus for drawing fluid from cavity etc. [L (foll.)]

aspire /ə'spaɪə/ *v.i.* have ambition or strong desire (*aspire to greatness*), seek *after*. [F, or L *aspiro* breathe upon]

aspirin /'æspərɪn, -prɪn/ *n.* a white powder, acetylsalicylic acid, used to relieve pain and reduce fever; tablet of this. [G]

ass[1] *n.* four-legged animal with long ears, related to horse; stupid person. [OE f. L]

ass[2] *US* var. of ARSE.

assagai var. of ASSEGAI.

assail /ə'seɪl/ *v.t.* attack physically or verbally; begin (task) resolutely; **assailant** *n.* [F f. L (*salio* leap)]

assassin /ə'sæsɪn/ *n.* killer, esp. of important person for political or religious motives. [F or med.L f. Arab., = hashish-eater]

assassinate /ə'sæsɪneɪt/ *v.t.* kill (esp. political or religious leader) treacherously; **assassination** /-'neɪʃ(ə)n/ *n.* [med.L (prec.)]

assault /ə'sɔ:lt, -ɒlt/ **1** *n.* violent physical or verbal attack, *euphem.* rape; *Law* threat or display of violence against person. **2** *v.t.* make an assault on (person, fortification). **3 assault and battery** *Law* violence with actual harm against person. [F f. L (ASSAIL)]

assay /ə'seɪ/ **1** *n.* test of metal or ore to determine ingredients and quality. **2** *v.* make assay of (metal); *archaic* attempt. [F, var. of *essai* ESSAY]

assegai /'æsɪgaɪ/ *n.* light iron-tipped spear of S. African peoples. [F or Port. f. Arab.]

assemblage /ə'semblɪdʒ/ *n.* coming together, concourse; group. [foll.]

assemble /ə'semb(ə)l/ *v.* fit or put (components, the completed whole) together; gather or collect in one place, come together. [F f. L *ad* to, *simul* together]

assembly /ə'semblɪ/ *n.* assembling; group of persons gathered together, esp. as deliberative body; fitting together of components; **assembly line** machinery arranged in stages by which a product is progressively assembled.

assent /ə'sent/ **1** *n.* consent or approval, esp. official. **2** *v.i.* express agreement (*he assented, assented to my view*); consent (*to* proposal, request). **3 assenter** *n.* [F f. L (*sentio* think)]

assert /ə'sɜ:t/ *v.t.* declare, state clearly; enforce claim to (rights); **assert oneself** demand recognition, insist on one's rights; **asserter** *n.* [L *assero -sert-*]

assertion /ə'sɜ:ʃ(ə)n/ *n.* declaration, forthright statement. [F or L (prec.)]

assertive /ə'sɜ:tɪv/ *a.* tending to assert oneself, forthright, positive. [F (ASSERT)]

assess /ə'ses/ *v.t.* estimate magnitude or quality of; estimate value of (property) for taxation; tax or fine (*assessed him at £100*); fix amount of (tax, penalty, etc.); impose (tax etc. *on*); **assessment** *n.* [F f. L *assideo -sess-* sit by]

assessor *n.* one who assesses (esp. for tax or insurance); one who advises judge in court on technical matters.

asset /'æset/ *n.* a possession having value, (often in *pl.*) one's property and possessions esp. regarded as having value in meeting debts, commitments, etc.; useful quality or person. [F *asez* f. L *ad satis* to enough]

asseverate /ə'sevəreɪt/ *v.t.* state solemnly; **asseveration** /-'reɪʃ(ə)n/ *n.* [L (*severus* serious)]

assiduity /æsɪ'dju:ɪtɪ/ *n.* diligence, perseverance. [L (ASSESS)]
assiduous /ə'sɪdjʊəs/ *a.* persevering, working with diligence and close attention.
assign /ə'saɪn/ **1** *v.t.* allot as share or responsibility (*to*); put aside or specify for particular purpose; designate (person) *to* job, duty, etc.; ascribe or attribute (*event assigned to the Bronze Age*; *can assign no motive for it*); *Law* transfer formally (esp. property *to* another). **2** *n.* assignee. **3 assigner** *n.* (in legal use **assignor**). [F f. L *assigno* mark out]
assignation /æsɪg'neɪʃ(ə)n/ *n.* appointment of time and place to meet, esp. by lovers in secret; assigning.
assignee /æsaɪ'ni:/ *n. Law* one to whom a right or property is assigned. [-EE]
assignment /ə'saɪnmənt/ *n.* thing assigned, esp. task or duty; legal transference.
assimilate /ə'sɪmɪleɪt/ *v.* absorb or be absorbed (e.g. with ref. to food into the body, ideas into the mind, people into larger group); make alike (*to* or *with*); make (sound) become similar to next sound in word or phrase; **assimilable** *a.*; **assimilation** /-'leɪʃ(ə)n/ *n.*; **assimilator** *n.*; **assimilative** /-ətɪv/ *a.* [L (*similis* like)]
assist /ə'sɪst/ *v.* help, give help; be present (*at* ceremony etc.); **assistance** *n.* [F f. L *assisto* stand by]
assistant **1** *n.* one who helps; one in subordinate position. **2** *a.* helping.
assizes /ə'saɪzɪz/ *n. pl. hist.* periodical county session for administration of civil and criminal justice. [F (ASSESS)]
Assoc. *abbr.* Association.
associate **1** /ə'səʊsɪeɪt, -ʃɪ- /*v.* connect (one thing *with* another) as idea or concept; join or combine; act together for common purpose, have frequent dealings (*with*); declare *oneself* in agreement *with* (idea, proposal). **2** /ə'səʊsɪət, -ʃɪ-/ *n.* subordinate member of society etc.; partner or colleague. **3** /ə'səʊsət, -ʃɪ-/ *a.* joined or allied. **4 associative** *a.* [L (*socius* allied)]
association /əsəʊsɪ'eɪʃ(ə)n, -ʃɪ-/ *n.* body of persons organized for common purpose; mental connection of ideas; companionship; **Association football** kind played with round ball which only goalkeepers may touch with hands during play. [F or med.L (prec.)]
assonance /'æsənəns/ *n.* resemblance of sound between two syllables; rhyme depending on identity in vowel-sounds only (as *sonnet* and *porridge*), or in consonants only (as *killed* and *cold*); **assonant** *a.* [F f. L (*sonus* sound)]
assort /ə'sɔ:t/ *v.* arrange in sorts, classify; suit or harmonize (*with*). [F (SORT)]
assorted *a.* of various sorts, mixed; classified; matched (*ill-assorted pair*).
assortment *n.* assorted group or mixture; classification.
assuage /ə'sweɪdʒ/ *v.t.* calm or soothe (person, pain); appease (appetite); **assuagement** *n.* [F, f. L *suavis* sweet]
assume /ə'sju:m/ *v.t.* take to be true; take or put on oneself (role, attitude, expression, etc.), undertake (office); simulate (e.g. ignorance). [L (*sumo* take)]
assuming *a.* arrogant, presumptuous.
assumption /ə'sʌmpʃ(ə)n/ *n.* assuming, thing assumed; (**Assumption**) taking of Virgin Mary bodily into Heaven.
assurance /ə'ʃʊərəns/ *n.* emphatic declaration, guarantee; self-confidence, assertiveness; insurance esp. of life; certainty. [foll.]
assure /ə'ʃʊə/ *v.t.* make (person) sure (*of* fact), convince; tell (person) confidently (*assured me of his innocence, that he was innocent*); ensure happening etc. of, guarantee; insure (esp. life). [F f. L (*securus* safe)]
assured *a.* made sure; confident.
assuredly /ə'ʃʊərɪdlɪ/ *adv.* certainly.
Assyriology /əsɪrɪ'ɒlədʒɪ/ *n.* study of language, history, etc., of ancient Assyria in Mesopotamia. [*Assyria*, -LOGY]
astatine /'æstəti:n/ *n.* artificial radioactive element. [Gk *astatos* unstable]
aster *n.* plant with bright daisy-like flowers. [L f. Gk, = star]
asterisk /'æstərɪsk/ *n.* star-shaped symbol (*) used in printing esp. as reference mark. [L f. Gk, = little star]
astern /ə'stɜ:n/ *adv.* in or to rear of ship or aircraft; behind. [A[3]]
asteroid /'æstərɔɪd/ *n.* any of many tiny planets orbiting sun, mainly between orbits of Mars and Jupiter; starfish. [Gk (ASTER)]
asthma /'æsmə/ *n.* disease marked by wheezing and difficulty in breathing. [L f. Gk *azō* breathe hard]
asthmatic /æs'mætɪk/ **1** *a.* of, caused by, or suffering from asthma. **2** *n.* person suffering from asthma.
astigmatism /æ'stɪgmətɪz(ə)m/ *n.* defect in eye or lens in which light rays from a point produce a line image; **astigmatic** /-'mætɪk/ *a.* [A-, STIGMA]
astir /ə'stɜ:/ *adv.* & *predic. a.* in motion; out of bed.
astonish /ə'stɒnɪʃ/ *v.t.* fill with surprise, amaze; **astonishment** *n.* [F (L *ex-* forth, *tono* thunder)]
astound /ə'staʊnd/ *v.t.* astonish greatly.
astraddle /ə'stræd(ə)l/ *a.* & *adv.* in a straddling position. [A[3]]

astrakhan /æstrə'kæn/ *n.* dark curly fur of Astrakhan lamb; imitation of this. [*Astrakhan* in Russia]

astral /'æstr(ə)l/ *a.* of or connected with stars. [L (*astrum* star)]

astray /ə'streɪ/ *adv.* out of the right way; **go astray** be missing. [F, f. L *extra* away, *vagor* wander]

astride /ə'straɪd/ **1** *adv.* with one leg on either side (*of*); with legs wide apart. **2** *prep.* astride of; extending across. [A[3]]

astringent /ə'strɪndʒənt/ **1** *a.* that causes contraction of body tissue and checks bleeding; severe, austere. **2** *n.* astringent substance. **3 astringency** *n.* [F f. L *astringo* draw tight]

astrolabe /'æstrəleɪb/ *n.* instrument used for measuring altitudes of stars etc. [F f. med.L f. Gk, = star-taking]

astrologer /ə'strɒlədʒə/ *n.* one who practises astrology. [foll.]

astrology /ə'strɒlədʒɪ/ *n.* study of planetary movements etc. regarded as an influence on human affairs; **astrological** /æstrə'lɒdʒɪk(ə)l/ *a.* [F f. L f. Gk (*astron* star)]

astronaut /'æstrənɔ:t/ *n.* traveller in space. [Gk *astron* star, *nautēs* sailor]

astronautics /æstrə'nɔ:tɪks/ *n.* science of travel in space; **astronautical** *a.*

astronomer /ə'strɒnəmə/ *n.* one who practises astronomy. [ASTRONOMY]

astronomical /æstrə'nɒmɪk(ə)l/ *a.* vast, gigantic; of astronomy. [F or L (foll.)]

astronomy /ə'strɒnəmɪ/ *n.* science of the heavenly bodies. [F f. L f. Gk (*astron* star, *nemō* arrange)]

astrophysics /æstrəʊ'fɪzɪks/ *n.* study of physics and chemistry of heavenly bodies; **astrophysical** *a.*; **astrophysicist** *n.* [Gk *astron* star]

astute /ə'stju:t/ *a.* shrewd; crafty. [F or L (*astus* craft)]

asunder /ə'sʌndə/ *adv. formal* apart, in pieces (*torn asunder*). [A[3]]

asylum /ə'saɪləm/ *n.* place of refuge or safety, esp. formerly for criminals; (in full **political asylum**) protection given by State to political refugee from another country; *hist.* institution for care and shelter of mentally ill or destitute persons. [L f. Gk (*a-* not, *sulon* right of seizure)]

asymmetry /æ'sɪmətrɪ/ *n.* lack of symmetry; **asymmetrical** /-'metrɪk(ə)l/ *a.* [Gk]

at /ət, *emphat.* æt/ *prep.* **1** expressing position (*wait at the corner*; *at the top of the hill*; *at school*; *at a distance*; *at dinner*); expressing state or scope of activity (*at war*; *at work*); expressing a point in time (*see you at three, at dawn*) or a point in a scale (*at boiling-point*; *at his best*); expressing a value or rate (*sell at £5 each*); with or with reference to (*at a disadvantage*; *annoyed at failing*; *good at cricket*; *play at fighting*; *came at a run*). **2** expressing motion or aim towards (*arrived at the station*; *aim at the target*; *grumble, guess, hint, laugh, at*). **3 at all** see ALL; **at home** see HOME; **at it** working hard; **at once** see ONCE; **at that** at that point (*leave it at that*), moreover (*found one, and a good one at that*). [OE]

At *symb.* astatine.

atavism /'ætəvɪz(ə)m/ *n.* resemblance to remote ancestors rather than parents; reversion to earlier type; **atavistic** /-'vɪstɪk/ *a.* [F f. L *atavus* ancestor]

ataxia /ə'tæksɪə/ *n.* imperfect control of one's bodily movements. [L f. Gk (*a-* without, *taxis* order)]

ate *past* of EAT.

-ate[1] *suffix* forming adjectives in sense 'having, filled or furnished with' (*foliate*, *passionate*). [L participial ending]

-ate[2] *suffix* forming nouns denoting status, function, or office (*doctorate*, *consulate*). [F or L]

atelier /ə'telɪeɪ/ *n.* workshop, artist's studio. [F]

atheism /'eɪθɪɪz(ə)m/ *n.* belief that no God exists; **atheist** *n.*; **atheistic** /-'ɪstɪk/ *a.* [F f. Gk (*a-* not, *theos* god)]

atherosclerosis /æθərəʊsklɪə'rəʊsɪs/ *n.* formation of fatty deposits inside arteries, often with hardening. [G f. Gk *athērē* groat]

athirst /ə'θɜ:st/ *predic. a.* eager (*for*); thirsty. [A[3]]

athlete /'æθli:t/ *n.* one who competes or excels in physical games and exercises; **athlete's foot** fungous disease of the feet. [L f. Gk (*athlon* prize)]

athletic /æθ'letɪk/ *a.* of athletes; physically strong or powerful; **athleticism** /-ɪsɪz(ə)m/ *n.* [F or L (prec.)]

athletics *n.pl.* (occas. *sing.*) competitive sports comprising track and field events.

-ation *suffix* forming nouns denoting action of verb or an instance of it (*creation*, *hesitation*, *flirtation*), or a result or product of it (*in good preservation*; *plantation*). [F or L]

Atlantic /ət'læntɪk/ *a.* of or adjoining the ocean between Europe and Africa to the east and America to the west. [L f. Gk (foll.)]

atlas /'ætləs/ *n.* book of maps, occas. with accompanying illustrations and commentary. [L, f. Gk *Atlas*, titan who held up universe]

atmosphere /'ætməsfɪə/ *n.* body of gas surrounding earth or heavenly body; mental or moral environment, tone or mood pervading book, work of art, etc.; air in room etc., esp. with reference to temperature or purity; pressure of about 1kg. per sq. cm., being that exerted by atmosphere on earth's surface; **atmospheric** /-'ferɪk/ *a.* [Gk *atmos* vapour, SPHERE]

atmospherics /ætməs'ferɪks/ *n.pl.* electrical disturbance in atmosphere; interference with telecommunications caused by this.

atoll /'ætɒl/ *n.* ring-shaped coral reef enclosing lagoon. [Maldive]

atom /'ætəm/ *n.* smallest particle of chemical element; this as source of atomic energy; minute portion or thing; **atom bomb** = *atomic bomb*. [F f. L f. Gk *atomos* indivisible]

atomic /ə'tɒmɪk/ *a.* of atoms; using energy from atoms; **atomic bomb** bomb whose destructive power comes from rapid release of nuclear energy; **atomic energy** nuclear energy; **atomic mass** = *atomic weight*; **atomic number** number of unit positive charges carried by nucleus of atom; **atomic theory** theory that all matter consists of atoms; **atomic weight** ratio between mass of one atom of an element or isotope and $\frac{1}{12}$ weight of an atom of the isotope carbon 12.

atomize /'ætəmaɪz/ *v.t.* reduce to atoms or fine particles.

atomizer *n.* device for reducing liquids to a fine spray.

atonal /eɪ'təʊn(ə)l/ *a. Mus.* not written in any key; **atonality** /-'nælɪtɪ/ *n.* [A-]

atone /ə'təʊn/ *v.i.* make amends (*for* wrong). [foll.]

atonement *n.* atoning; making amends for wrong; (**Atonement**) Christ's making amends for man's sins. [*at one* + -MENT]

atrium /'eɪtrɪəm/ *n.* (*pl.* **atria** or **atriums**) central court of Roman house; either of two upper cavities in the heart. [L]

atrocious /ə'trəʊʃəs/ *a.* very bad or poor (*atrocious puns*); wicked (*atrocious crimes*). [L *atrox* cruel]

atrocity /ə'trɒsɪtɪ/ *n.* wicked act, atrocious behaviour. [F or L (prec.)]

atrophy /'ætrəfɪ/ **1** *n.* wasting away through under-nourishment or lack of use; emaciation. **2** *v.* cause atrophy in; suffer atrophy. [F or L f. Gk (*a-* without, *trophē* food)]

atropine /'ætrəpɪn, -i:n/ *n.* poison of deadly nightshade. [L f. Gk (*Atropos* Fate who cut thread of life)]

attach /ə'tætʃ/ *v.* fasten, affix (*attach label to parcel*); join (*oneself to* a company, enterprise, etc.); accompany, form part of (*no conditions are attached*); attribute, be attributable (*attached importance to your coming*; *no blame attaches to us*); seize (person or property) by legal authority; **be attached to** be fond of. [F f. Gmc]

attaché /ə'tæʃeɪ/ *n.* person with special responsibility attached to ambassador's staff; **attaché case** small rectangular case for carrying documents etc.

attachment *n.* attaching; thing attached, esp. a device; affection, devotion; legal seizure.

attack /ə'tæk/ **1** *v.* act against with (esp. armed) force; make an attack; criticize adversely; act harmfully on (*rust attacks metal*); (in sport) try to score against; undertake (task) with vigour. **2** *n.* act of attacking; sudden onset of illness etc. (*attack of flu*). [F f. It.]

attain /ə'teɪn/ *v.* gain, accomplish (aim, distinction, etc.); reach, come *to* (goal etc.). [F f. L *attingo* reach]

attainment *n.* attaining; (usu. in *pl.*) skills, achievements.

attar /'ætə/ *n.* perfume made from rose-petals. [Pers.]

attempt /ə'tempt/ **1** *v.t.* try (*to do* thing); try to conquer (*attempt the north face*) or accomplish (*attempt the impossible*). **2** *n.* attempting, endeavour (*to do* thing, *at* thing, *on* person's life). [F f. L (*tempto* try)]

attend /ə'tend/ *v.* be present (at), go regularly to (*attend* or *attend at a wedding*; *attend school*); turn or apply one's mind (*to* person or thing); accompany. [F f. L (*tendo* stretch)]

attendance *n.* attending; number of persons present (*a high attendance*); reliability in attending (*poor attendance*).

attendant **1** *n.* person attending, esp. to provide service. **2** *a.* waiting (*on*), accompanying.

attention /ə'tenʃ(ə)n/ *n.* act or faculty of applying one's mind (*pay attention to me*; *attract his attention*); consideration, care (*give it your attention*); attitude of concentration or readiness (*call to attention, stand at attention*: also as command); (in *pl.*) formal courtesies. [L (ATTEND)]

attentive /ə'tentɪv/ *a.* paying attention, assiduous. [F (ATTEND)]

attenuate /ə'tenjʊeɪt/ *v.t.* make slender or thin; reduce in force or value. [L (*tenuis* thin)]

attest /ə'test/ *v.* act as evidence of; certify validity of; bear witness *to*; **attestation** /æte'steɪʃ(ə)n/ *n.* [F f. L (*testis* witness)]

attic[1] /'ætɪk/ *n.* space or room in top storey of house, below roof. [foll., with ref. to archit. feature]

Attic[2] /'ætɪk/ **1** *a.* of Athens or Attica, of Greek dialect used there; elegant in style. **2** *n.* dialect of Attica, used widely in Greek prose. [F f. L f. Gk]

attire /ə'taɪə/ *n.* dress, esp. formal. [F (*à tire* in order)]

attired *a.* dressed, esp. finely or formally.

attitude /'ætɪtju:d/ *n.* way of regarding, considered and permanent disposition or reaction (*to* person or thing); posture of body; position of aircraft etc. relative to given points. [F f. It. f. L (*aptus* fitted)]

attitudinize /ætɪ'tju:dɪnaɪz/ *v.i.* adopt (esp. affected) attitudes, show affectation.

attorney /ə'tɜ:nɪ/ *n.* one appointed to act for another in business or legal affairs; *US* qualified lawyer; **Attorney--General** chief legal officer of government. [F (*atorner* assign)]

attract /ə'trækt/ *v.t.* draw to itself or oneself; arouse interest, pleasure, or admiration in. [L (*traho* draw)]

attraction /ə'trækʃ(ə)n/ *n.* act or power of attracting; thing that attracts by arousing interest etc.; *Physics* tendency of bodies to approach each other. [F or L (prec.)]

attractive /ə'træktɪv/ *a.* that attracts or can attract (esp. interest or admiration); good-looking. [F f. L (ATTRACT)]

attribute **1** /ə'trɪbju:t/ *v.t.* regard as belonging or appropriate *to* person or thing. **2** /'ætrɪbju:t/ *n.* quality ascribed to person or thing, characteristic quality; object associated with or symbolizing person. **3** **attribute to** consider to be caused by. **4** **attribution** /ætrɪ'bju:ʃ(ə)n/ *n.* [F or L (*tribuo* allot)]

attributive /ə'trɪbjʊtɪv/ *a.* expressing an attribute; *Gram.* (of an adjective) coming before the noun it qualifies (as *tall* in *the tall man* but not in *the man is tall*: cf. PREDICATIVE). [F (prec.)]

attrition /ə'trɪʃ(ə)n/ *n.* gradual wearing down (*war of attrition*); friction, abrasion. [L (*tero trit-* rub)]

attune /ə'tju:n/ *v.t.* harmonize or adapt (one's mind etc.) *to* a matter or idea; bring into musical accord (*to*). [TUNE]

atypical /'eɪtɪpɪk(ə)l/ *a.* not belonging to any type. [A-]

Au *symb.* gold. [L *aurum*]

aubergine /'əʊbəʒi:n/ *n.* fruit of egg-plant, used as vegetable; dark pink colour of this. [F ult. f. Skr.]

aubrietia /ɔ:'bri:ʃə/ *n.* small perennial rock-plant with pink and purple flowers. [*Aubriet*, artist]

auburn /'ɔ:bən/ *a.* reddish-brown (esp. of hair). [orig. = yellowish-white, F f. L (*albus* white)]

auction /'ɔ:kʃ(ə)n/ **1** *n.* public sale in which each article is sold to highest bidder. **2** *v.t.* sell by auction. **3** **auction bridge** form of bridge in which players bid for right to name trumps. [L (*augeo auct-* increase)]

auctioneer /ɔ:kʃə'nɪə/ *n.* one whose business is to conduct auctions.

audacious /ɔ:'deɪʃəs/ *a.* daring, bold; foolhardy, impudent; **audacity** /ɔ:'dæsɪtɪ/ *n.* [L (*audax* bold)]

audible /'ɔ:dɪb(ə)l/ *a.* that can be heard, esp. distinctly; **audibility** /-'bɪlɪtɪ/ *n.*; **audibly** *adv.* [L (*audio* hear)]

audience /'ɔ:dɪəns/ *n.* group of listeners or spectators, esp. in theatre or reached by radio etc.; formal interview. [F f. L (prec.)]

audio /'ɔ:dɪəʊ/ *n.* & *comb. form* sound or reproduction of sound; **audio frequency** one comparable to that of ordinary sound; **audio typist** one who types direct from a recording; **audio--visual** using both sight and sound. [L *audio* hear]

audit /'ɔ:dɪt/ **1** *n.* official scrutiny of accounts. **2** *v.t.* conduct audit of (accounts).

audition /ɔ:'dɪʃ(ə)n/ **1** *n.* trial hearing of actor to test suitability for part; faculty of hearing. **2** *v.t.* give trial hearing to (actor etc.). [F or L (*audio* hear)]

auditor /'ɔ:dɪtə/ *n.* one authorized to audit accounts; listener. [F f. L]

auditorium /ɔ:dɪ'tɔ:rɪəm/ *n.* (*pl.* **auditoriums**) part of theatre etc. occupied by audience. [L]

auditory /'ɔ:dɪtərɪ/ *a.* of or concerned with hearing.

au fait /əʊ 'feɪ/ well acquainted *with* subject. [F]

Aug. *abbr.* August.

Augean /ɔ:'dʒi:ən/ *a.* filthy. [L f. Gk *Augeas* mythical king whose filthy stables Hercules cleaned in a day by directing river through them]

auger /'ɔ:gə/ *n.* tool with screw point for boring in wood. [OE]

aught /ɔ:t/ *n. archaic* or *poetic* anything. [OE]

augment **1** /ɔ:g'ment/ *v.t.* increase, make greater. **2** /'ɔ:gmənt/ *n.* vowel prefixed to past tenses in Greek and Sanskrit. **3** **augmentation** /-'teɪʃ(ə)n/ *n.* enlargement, increase. [F or L (AUCTION)]

augmentative /ɔ:g'mentətɪv/ *a.* augmenting, esp. *Gram.* (of affix etc.) increasing in force the idea of the word to which it is attached.

au gratin /əʊ 'grætæ̃/ cooked with a crust of breadcrumbs and grated cheese.

augur /'ɔ:gə/ **1** *n.* Roman religious official who observed favourable or unfavourable omens in natural

phenomena; soothsayer. **2** *v.* portend; serve as an omen (*augur ill, well, for*). **3** **augural** /'ɔ:gjʊr(ə)l/ *a.* [L]
augury /'ɔ:gjʊrɪ/ *n.* divination; omen.
august[1] /ɔ:'gʌst/ *a.* venerable, imposing. [F or L]
August[2] /'ɔ:gəst/ *n.* eighth month of year. [OE, f. L *Augustus* first Roman emperor]
Augustan /ɔ:'gʌst(ə)n/ *a.* of the reign of Augustus esp. as period when Latin literature flourished; (of any literature) classical, stylish. [L (see prec.)]
auk /ɔ:k/ *n.* northern sea-bird with short narrow wings. [ON]
auld lang syne /ɔ:ld læŋ 'saɪn/ *Sc.* days of long ago. [Sc., = old long since]
aunt /ɑ:nt/ *n.* sister or sister-in-law of one's father or mother; *colloq.* unrelated friend of a parent; **Aunt Sally** figure used as target in throwing-game, target of general abuse. [F f. L *amita*]
aunty /'ɑ:ntɪ/ *n.* (also **auntie**) *colloq.* aunt.
au pair /əʊ 'peə/ (in full **au pair girl**) young woman usu. from abroad giving household help in exchange for board and lodging. [F]
aura /'ɔ:rə/ *n.* (*pl.* **auras**) distinctive atmosphere attending person or thing; subtle emanation. [L f. Gk, = breeze]
aural /'ɔ:r(ə)l/ *a.* of or concerning the ear or hearing; **aurally** *adv.* [L (*auris* ear)]
aureate /'ɔ:rɪət/ *a.* golden; brilliant, resplendent. [L (*aurum* gold)]
aureola /ɔ:'rɪələ/, *n.* (also **aureole** /'ɔ:rɪəʊl/) celestial crown or halo, esp. round head or body of portrayed divine figure; corona round sun or moon. [L, = golden (crown)]
au revoir /əʊ rə'vwɑ:/ till we meet again; goodbye. [F]
auricle /'ɔ:rɪk(ə)l/ *n.* external part of ear; atrium of heart. [foll.]
auricula /ɔ:'rɪkjʊlə/ *n.* species of primula with ear-shaped leaves. [L, dimin. of *auris* ear]
auricular *a.* of the ear, ear-shaped; spoken privately in the ear.
auriferous /ɔ:'rɪfərəs/ *a.* yielding gold. [L *aurifer* (*aurum* gold)]
aurochs /'ɔ:rɒks/ *n.* extinct wild ox; European bison. [G]
aurora borealis /ɔ:'rɔ:rə bɔ:rɪ'eɪlɪs/ luminous appearance in upper atmosphere near North Pole; **aurora australis** /ɔ:'streɪlɪs/ this near South Pole. [L, = northern, southern, dawn]
auscultation /ɔ:skʊl'teɪʃ(ə)n/ *n.* listening to sounds of the body for diagnosis. [L *ausculto* listen]
auspice /ɔ:spɪs/ *n.* omen, premonition; (in *pl.*) patronage (*under the auspices of*). [orig. 'observing bird-flight'; F or L (*avis* bird)]
auspicious /ɔ:'spɪʃəs/ *a.* promising well, favourable.
Aussie /'ɒzɪ/ *n.* & *a.* *colloq.* Australian; Australia. [abbr.]
austere /ɒ'stɪə/ *a.* stern, grim; severely simple; morally strict. [F f. L f. Gk]
austerity /ɒ'sterɪtɪ/ *n.* hardship; sternness, severity.
austral /'ɔ:str(ə)l, 'ɒ-/ *a.* southern; (**Austral**) Australian, Australasian. [L (*auster* south)]
Australasian /ɒstrə'leɪʒ(ə)n/ *a.* of the islands of the S. Pacific, including Australia, New Zealand, and New Guinea.
Australian /ɒ'streɪlɪən/ **1** *a.* of Australia. **2** *n.* native or inhabitant of Australia.
autarchy /'ɔ:tɑ:kɪ/ *n.* despotism, absolute rule. [Gk *autos* self, *arkhē* rule]
autarky /'ɔ:tɑ:kɪ/ *n.* self-sufficiency, esp. economic. [Gk (*autos* self, *arkeō* suffice)]
authentic /ɔ:'θentɪk/ *a.* genuine, of legitimate or undisputed origin (*authentic document, signature*); trustworthy (*authentic statement*); **authentically** *adv.*; **authenticity** /-'tɪsɪtɪ/ *n.* [F f. L f. Gk *authentikos*]
authenticate /ɔ:'θentɪkeɪt/ *v.t.* establish (document, claim, etc.) as valid or authentic; **authentication** /-'keɪʃ(ə)n/ *n.*; **authenticator** *n.*
author /'ɔ:θə/ *n.* writer of book, article, etc.; originator *of* idea, event, etc. [F f. L *auctor*]
authoritarian /ɔ:θɒrɪ'teərɪən/ **1** *a.* favouring or characterized by unqualified obedience to authority. **2** *n.* authoritarian person. [AUTHORITY]
authoritative /ɔ:'θɒrɪtətɪv/ *a.* reliable, as having authority; official. [foll.]
authority /ɔ:'θɒrɪtɪ/ *n.* power or right to enforce obedience; this power as delegated; (esp. in *pl.*) body having authority; personal influence arising esp. from knowledge or position, testimony based on such (*on the authority of Plato*); person to whom knowledge or influence is attributed (*an authority on bees*). [F f. L *auctoritas*]
authorize /'ɔ:θəraɪz/ *v.t.* give authority to (person *to do* thing), empower; recognize officially; **Authorized Version** English translation of the Bible (1611), authorized by James I; **authorization** /-'zeɪʃ(ə)n/ *n.*
authorship *n.* origin of book etc.; profession of author. [AUTHOR]
auto /'ɔ:təʊ/ *n.* (*pl.* **autos**) *US colloq.* motor car. [abbr. of AUTOMOBILE]
auto- /'ɔ:təʊ/ *in comb.* self, own, of or by oneself or itself. [Gk *autos*]
autobahn /'ɔ:təʊbɑ:n/ *n.* German, Austrian, or Swiss motorway. [G]

autobiography /ɔ:təʊbaɪ'ɒgrəfɪ/ *n.* story of one's life written by oneself; writing of this; **autobiographer** *n.*; **autobiographical** /-'græfɪk(ə)l/ *a.* [AUTO-]

autochthonous /ɔ:'tɒkθənəs/ *a.* indigenous, aboriginal. [Gk (*khthōn* land)]

autoclave /'ɔ:təʊkleɪv/ *n.* strong vessel used esp. as sterilizer with high-pressure steam. [L *clavus* nail or *clavis* key]

autocracy /ɔ:'tɒkrəsɪ/ *n.* absolute government by one person; dictatorship. [Gk (*kratos* power)]

autocrat /'ɔ:təkræt/ *n.* sole ruler with absolute power; authoritarian person; **autocratic** /-'krætɪk/ *a.*; **autocratically** *adv.* [F f. Gk (prec.)]

autocross /'ɔ:təʊkrɒs/ *n.* motor-racing across country or on unmade roads. [AUTO(MOBILE)]

Autocue /'ɔ:təʊkju:/ *n.* (**P**) device beside camera from which television speaker reads script. [AUTO-]

auto-da-fé /ɔ:təʊdɑ:'feɪ/ *n.* (*pl.* ***autos-da-fé***) ceremonial judgement of heretics by Spanish Inquisition; execution of heretics by public burning. [Port., = act of the faith]

autograph /'ɔ:təgrɑ:f/ **1** *n.* person's own signature or handwriting; manuscript in author's handwriting. **2** *v.t.* sign or write on in one's own hand. **3** **autographic** /-'græfɪk/ *a.* [F or L f. Gk (*graphō* write)]

automat /'ɔ:təʊmæt/ *n.* *US* cafeteria providing meals from slot-machines; slot-machine. [G f. F (AUTOMATON)]

automate /'ɔ:təmeɪt/ *v.t.* apply automation to, operate by automation. [AUTOMATION]

automatic /ɔ:tə'mætik/ **1** *a.* working of itself, without direct human involvement in process; done from habit or without conscious thought; following necessarily (*incurs automatic penalty*); (of firearm) having mechanism for continuous loading and firing. **2** *n.* automatic gun etc.; motor vehicle with automatic transmission. **3** **automatic pilot** device in aircraft or ship to keep it on set course; **automatic transmission** system in motor vehicle for automatic change of gears. **4** **automatically** *adv.* [AUTOMATON]

automation /ɔ:tə'meɪʃ(ə)n/ *n.* production of goods etc. by automatic processes; use of automatic equipment in place of human effort.

automatism /ɔ:'tɒmətɪz(ə)m/ *n.* involuntary action; unthinking routine. [F (foll.)]

automaton /ɔ:'tɒmət(ə)n/ *n.* (*pl.* **automatons** or *collect.* **automata**) machine responding to automatic (esp. electronic) control; person acting mechanically. [L f. Gk, = acting of itself]

automobile /'ɔ:təməbi:l/ *n.* *US* motor car. [F]

automotive /ɔ:tə'məʊtɪv/ *a.* concerned with motor vehicles. [AUTO-]

autonomous /ɔ:'tɒnəməs/ *a.* having self-government; acting independently. [Gk (*nomos* law)]

autonomy *n.* right of self-government.

autopilot *n.* automatic pilot. [AUTO-]

autopsy /'ɔ:tɒpsɪ/ *n.* post-mortem. [(F) f. Gk (*autoptēs* eye-witness)]

autostrada /'ɔ:təʊstrɑ:də/ *n.* (*pl.* ***autostrade*** /-deɪ/) Italian motorway. [It.]

auto-suggestion /ɔ:təʊsə'dʒestʃ(ə)n/ *n.* suggestion made subconsciously by person to himself. [AUTO-]

autumn /'ɔ:təm/ *n.* season between summer and winter; time of incipient decline; **autumnal** /ɔ:'tʌmn(ə)l/ *a.* [F f. L *autumnus*]

auxiliary /ɔ:g'zɪljərɪ/ **1** *a.* giving help; additional, subsidiary. **2** *n.* auxiliary person or thing; (in *pl.*) foreign or allied troops in service of nation at war; verb used to form tenses etc. of other verbs (e.g. *have* in *I have gone*). [L (*auxilium* help)]

AV *abbr.* Authorized Version.

avail /ə'veɪl/ **1** *v.* be of use or help (to). **2** *n.* use, profit (*of no avail*). **3** **avail oneself of** make use of, profit by. [F f. L *valeo* be strong]

available *a.* capable of being used, at one's disposal; **availability** /-'bɪlɪtɪ/ *n.*

avalanche /'ævəlɑ:nʃ/ *n.* mass of dislodged snow, rock, etc., sliding rapidly down mountain; sudden or overwhelming onrush. [F]

avant-garde /ævɑ̃'gɑ:d/ **1** *n.* leading group of innovators esp. in art and literature. **2** *a.* (of ideas) new, progressive. [F, = vanguard]

avarice /'ævərɪs/ *n.* greed for wealth or gain; **avaricious** /-'rɪʃəs/ *a.* [F f. L (*avarus* greedy)]

avatar /'ævətɑ:/ *n.* in Hinduism, descent of god to earth in bodily form. [Skr., = descent]

Ave /'ɑ:vɪ, -veɪ/ *n.* (in full **Ave Maria**) prayer to Virgin Mary (Luke 1: 28, 42). [L]

Ave. *abbr.* avenue.

avenge /ə'vendʒ/ *v.t.* inflict retribution on behalf of (person); take vengeance for (injury); **be avenged** avenge oneself. [F f. L *vindico*]

avenue /'ævənju:/ *n.* road or path, usu. bordered by trees; broad main street; way of approach (*avenues to success*). [F (*avenir* come to)]

aver /ə'vɜ:/ *v.t.* (**-rr-**) assert, affirm; **averment** *n.* [F (L *verus* true)]

average /'ævərɪdʒ/ **1** *n.* usual amount, extent, or rate; number obtained by dividing total of given numbers by how many there are; *Law* damage to or loss of ship or cargo. **2** *a.* usual, ordinary; estimated by average. **3** *v.t.* amount on average to; do on average; estimate average of. **4 average out (at)** result in an average (of); **law of averages** principle that if one of two extremes occurs the other will also; **on (an) average** as an average rate or estimate. [F f. It. f. Arab., = damaged goods]

averse /ə'vɜ:s/ *predic. a.* opposed, disinclined, unwilling (*to* or *from* thing esp. action). [L (*verto vers-* turn)]

aversion /ə'vɜ:ʃ(ə)n/ *n.* strong dislike (*to* or *from* thing), unwillingness; object of dislike.

avert /ə'vɜ:t/ *v.t.* turn away (eyes, thoughts, etc.); prevent (esp. danger) from happening.

Avesta /ə'vestə/ *n.* text of Zoroastrian sacred writings. See also ZEND. [Pers.]

aviary /'eɪvɪərɪ/ *n.* large cage or building for keeping or exhibiting birds. [L (*avis* bird)]

aviation /eɪvɪ'eɪʃ(ə)n/ *n.* practice or science of flying aircraft. [F f. L (prec.)]

aviator /'eɪvɪeɪtə/ *n.* one who flies aircraft.

avid /'ævɪd/ *a.* eager (*an avid collector*); greedy (*of* or *for*); **avidity** /ə'vɪdɪtɪ/ *n.* [F or L (*aveo* crave)]

avionics /eɪvɪ'ɒnɪks/ *n.pl.* (usu. treated as *sing.*) science of electronics applied to aeronautics. [AVIATION, ELECTRONICS]

avocado /ævə'kɑ:dəʊ/ *n.* (*pl.* **avocados**) a pear-shaped tropical fruit with rough skin and yellow creamy flesh. [Sp. f. Aztec]

avocation /ævə'keɪʃ(ə)n/ *n.* secondary activity done in addition to one's main work; *colloq.* one's occupation. [L (*avoco* call away)]

avocet /'ævəset/ *n.* wading bird with long legs and upturned bill. [F f. It.]

avoid /ə'vɔɪd/ *v.t.* keep away or refrain from; prevent, escape from (*just avoided an accident, hitting him*); *Law* annul, quash; **avoidance** *n.* [F]

avoirdupois /ævədə'pɔɪz/ *n.* system of weights based on a pound of 16 ounces or 7,000 grains. [F, = goods of weight]

avow /ə'vaʊ/ *v.t.* declare, confess; **avowal** *n.*; **avowedly** /-ɪdlɪ/ *adv.* [F f. L (*voco* call)]

avuncular /ə'vʌŋkjʊlə/ *a.* of or like an uncle, esp. in manner. [L *avunculus* uncle]

await /ə'weɪt/ *v.t.* wait for; be in store for. [F (WAIT)]

awake /ə'weɪk/ **1** *v.* (*past* **awoke** /ə'wəʊk/, *p.p.* **awoken**) rouse from sleep, cease to sleep; become active. **2** *predic. a.* no longer or not yet asleep; alert. [OE (A[3])]

awaken *v.t.* awake; urgently draw attention of (person *to* fact etc.).

award /ə'wɔ:d/ **1** *v.t.* direct to be given esp. as payment or prize. **2** *n.* judicial decision; amount or prize awarded. [F]

aware /ə'weə/ *a.* conscious, having knowledge (*of* thing, *that*). [OE]

awash /ə'wɒʃ/ *predic. a.* at or near surface of water so that it flows over; covered or flooded by water. [A[3]]

away /ə'weɪ/ **1** *adv.* to or at a distance from the place, person, etc., in question (*give, go, look, away*; *5 miles away*); into non-existence (*explain, fade, away*); constantly, persistently (*work away*); without delay (*fire away*). **2** *a.* played on opponent's ground etc. (*away match*). **3** *n.* away match or win. [OE (A[3], WAY)]

awe /ɔ:/ **1** *n.* wonder or admiration charged with reverence or fear. **2** *v.t.* fill or inspire with awe. [ON]

aweigh /ə'weɪ/ *adv.* (of anchor) just lifted from the bottom in weighing. [A[3]]

awesome /'ɔ:səm/ *a.* inspiring awe, dreaded. [AWE]

awful /'ɔ:fʊl/ *a.* awe-inspiring, terrifying; *colloq.* very bad or poor (*awful weather*), notable of its kind (*an awful bore*).

awfully /'ɔ:fʊlɪ, *colloq.* 'ɔ:flɪ/ *adv.* in a way to inspire awe; *colloq.* very (*awfully nice*), badly (*did it awfully*).

awhile /ə'waɪl/ *adv.* for a short time. [*a while*]

awkward /'ɔ:kwəd/ *a.* clumsy, ungainly, difficult to use; embarrassing or inconvenient (*came at an awkward time*); embarrassed (*felt awkward about it*); hard or dangerous to deal with (*an awkward situation, bend*). [obs. *awk* perverse]

awl *n.* small tool for pricking holes esp. in leather. [OE]

awn *n.* bristly head of sheath of barley etc. [ON]

awning *n.* canvas or plastic sheet stretched by supports from wall as shelter against sun and rain. [orig. uncert.]

awoke, awoken *past* and *p.p.* of AWAKE.

AWOL /'eɪwɒl/ *abbr.* absent without leave.

awry /ə'raɪ/ **1** *adv.* crookedly, out of true position; wrong, amiss (*things went awry*). **2** *predic. a.* crooked. [A[3]]

axe /æks/, *US* **ax 1** *n.* tool with long handle and heavy blade for chopping wood etc. **2** *v.t.* eliminate or reduce drastically (*many jobs have been axed*). **3 have an axe to grind** have one's own purpose to serve. [OE]

axial /'æksɪəl/ *a.* of, forming, or placed round an axis. [AXIS]

axil /'æksɪl/ *n.* upper angle between leaf and stem it springs from. [L *axilla* armpit]

axiom /'æksɪəm/ *n.* established or accepted principle; self-evident truth; **axiomatic** /-'mætɪk/ *a.* [F or L f. Gk (*axios* worthy)]

axis /'æksɪs/ *n.* (*pl.* **axes** /-i:z/) imaginary line about which an object rotates; line about which a regular figure is symmetrically arranged; reference line for measurement of coordinates etc.; **the Axis** alliance of Germany and Italy, and later Japan, in war of 1939–45. [L, = axle]

axle /'æks(ə)l/ *n.* spindle on which or with which wheel revolves; rod connecting pair of wheels of vehicle. [ON]

axolotl /æksə'lɒt(ə)l/ *n.* newtlike amphibian found in Mexican lakes. [Nahuatl, = water-servant]

ayatollah /aɪə'tɒlə/ *n.* Shiite religious leader in Iran. [Pers., f. Arab. = token of God]

aye[1] /aɪ/ **1** *adv.* esp. *archaic* or *formal* yes. **2** *n.* affirmative answer or vote. [prob. f. *I* expr. assent]

aye[2] /aɪ/ *adv. archaic* always (only in *for aye*). [ON]

azalea /ə'zeɪlɪə/ *n.* a kind of rhododendron. [Gk *azaleos* dry]

azimuth /'æzɪməθ/ *n.* arc along horizon from north or south meridian to meridian through given point or celestial body; **azimuthal**/-'mu:θ(ə)l/ *a.* [F f. Arab.]

Aztec /'æztek/ **1** *n.* member of native Mexican people dominant until conquest by Cortes in 1519; their language, also called Nahuatl. **2** *a.* of Aztecs or their language. [F or Sp. f. Nahuatl, = men of the north]

azure /'æʒə, 'æʒjʊə/ **1** *a.* sky-blue. **2** *n.* sky-blue colour; clear sky. [F f. L f. Arab.]

B

B, b /bi:/ *n.* (*pl.* **Bs, B's**). second letter; *Mus.* seventh note in diatonic scale of C major; (as *b*) second known quantity in algebra; (as *B*) second hypothetical person or example.

B *abbr.* black (pencil-lead).

b. *abbr.* born.

B *symb.* boron.

BA *abbr.* Bachelor of Arts.

Ba *symb.* barium.

baa /bɑ:/ **1** *n.* bleat of a sheep or lamb. **2** *v.i.* (**baaed** or **baa'd**) bleat. [imit.]

baba /'bɑ:bɑ:/ *n.* sponge-cake soaked in rum syrup. [F]

babble /'bæb(ə)l/ **1** *v.* make incoherent sounds, talk inarticulately or excessively; say incoherently; repeat or divulge foolishly; (of stream etc.) trickle, murmur. **2** *n.* incoherent or idle talk; murmur of voices, water, etc. [imit.]

babe *n.* baby; innocent or helpless person; *US sl.* young woman. [imit. of child's *ba ba*]

babel /'beɪb(ə)l/ *n.* confused noise esp. of voices; scene of confusion. [Heb., = Babylon (Gen. 11)]

baboon /bə'bu:n/ *n.* large African and Arabian monkey with doglike snout. [F or med.L]

baby /'beɪbɪ/ **1** *n.* very young child; childish person; youngest member of family etc.; thing small of its kind (*baby car*); very young animal; *sl.* sweetheart; *sl.* one's own concern or activity. **2** *v.t.* treat like a baby, pamper. **3 Baby Buggy (P)** kind of child's push-chair; **baby grand** small grand piano; **baby-sit** look after child while its parents are out; **baby-sitter** one who baby-sits. **4 babyhood** *n.* [BABE]

baccalaureate /bækə'lɔ:rɪət/ *n.* university degree of bachelor. [F or med.L (*baccalarius* bachelor)]

baccarat /'bækərɑ:/ *n.* a gambling card-game. [F]

bacchanal /'bækən(ə)l/ **1** *n.* priest or worshipper of Bacchus; drunken reveller or revelry. **2** *a.* of Bacchus; riotous. [L (*Bacchus* f. Gk, god of wine)]

Bacchanalia /bækə'neɪlɪə/ *n.pl.* Roman festival of Bacchus; drunken revelry.

bacchant /'bækənt/ *n.* priest or worshipper of Bacchus; drunken reveller; **bacchante** /bə'kænt, -'kæntɪ/ *n. fem.*

Bacchic /'bækɪk/ *a.* = BACCHANAL 2.

baccy /'bækɪ/ *n. colloq.* tobacco. [abbr.]

bachelor /'bætʃələ/ *n.* unmarried man; person who has taken university first degree (*Bachelor of Arts*); **bachelor flat** one suitable for person living alone; **bachelor girl** young unmarried woman leading independent life; **bachelorhood** *n.* [see BACCALAUREATE]

bacillus /bə'sɪləs/ *n.* (*pl.* **bacilli** /-aɪ/) rodlike bacterium, esp. one causing disease; **bacillary** *a.* [L dimin. of *baculus* stick]

back **1** *n.* rear surface of human body from shoulder to hip; upper surface of animal's body, similar ridge-shaped surface, keel of ship; surface corresponding to human back (*back of the head, the chair*); less active or important or visible part (*back of knife*; *write it on the back*); side or part normally away from spectator or direction of motion (*back of car, house, room*); part of garment covering back; defensive player in field games. **2** *a.* situated behind, esp. as remote or subsidiary (*back teeth, street*); overdue (*back pay*); reversed (*back flow*). **3** *adv.* to the rear, away from the front (*go back a bit*; *sit back*); in or into an earlier or normal position or condition (*go back home, came back to life*; *when will you be back?*); in or into the past (*look back on one's life*; *back in June*; *three years back*); in return (*pay back*); at a distance (*stand back from the road*); in check (*hold him back*). **4** *v.* help with money or moral support; cause (vehicle etc.) to move backwards; go backwards; bet on success of (horse etc.); provide with or serve as a back or support to, *Mus.* accompany; lie at the back of (*house backs* or *backs on to the river*); (of wind) move round in anticlockwise direction. **5 at the back of one's mind** remembered but not consciously thought of; **back and forth** to and fro; **back-bencher** member of parliament without senior office; **back-boiler** one behind domestic fire; **back door** *fig.* secret or ingenious means of gaining objective; **back down** withdraw claim, point of view, etc.; **back-formation** formation of seeming root-word from word which might be (but is not) its derivative (as *laze* from *lazy*); **back number** issue of periodical earlier than current one, *sl.* out-of-date person or thing; **back out** withdraw from commitment; **back-pedal** reverse one's previous action or opinion; **back room** place where secret work is done (*back-room boys*); **the Backs** grounds of Cambridge colleges backing on to River Cam; **back seat** inferior position or status; **back-seat driver** person without responsibility yet eager to advise (orig. of passenger in car etc.); **back slang** slang using words spelt backwards (e.g. *yob*); **back stairs** = back door; **back-to-back** of houses with backs adjoining; **back up** to support (esp. morally); **back-up** *n.* support, reserve; **behind person's back** without his knowledge; **get off person's back** stop troubling him; **get person's back up** annoy him; **go back on** renounce (promise etc.); **on one's back** injured or ill in bed; **see the back of** be rid of; **turn one's back on** abandon, ignore. [OE]

backbite *v.t.* speak badly of.

backblocks *n.pl. Austral.* & *NZ.* land in remote interior.

backbone *n.* spine; main support of structure; firmness of character.

backchat *n. colloq.* impudent repartee.

backcloth *n.* painted cloth at back of stage as main part of scenery.

backdate /bæk'deɪt/ *v.t.* put earlier date to than the actual one; make retrospectively effective.

backdrop *n.* = BACKCLOTH.

backfire /bæk'faɪə/ **1** *v.i.* (of engine or vehicle) undergo premature explosion in cylinder or exhaust-pipe; (of plan etc.) rebound adversely on originator. **2** *n.* instance of backfiring.

backgammon /bæk'gæmən/ *n.* game played on double board with pieces moved according to throw of dice. [BACK + obs. form of GAME[1]]

background *n.* back part of scene etc. esp. as setting for chief part; inconspicuous or obscure position (*kept in the background*); person's education, knowledge, or social circumstances; explanatory or contributory information or circumstances. [BACK]

backhand *n.* stroke esp. in tennis made with back of hand towards opponent.

backhanded *a.* made with backhand; obscure, ambiguous.

backhander *n.* backhanded stroke; blow with back of hand; *sl.* bribe.

backing *n.* help or support, esp. financial; material used to form thing's back or support; musical accompaniment for pop singer.

backlash *n.* excessive or marked reaction; sudden recoil in machinery.

backlog *n.* arrears of uncompleted work etc.

backpack *n.* rucksack.

backside *n.* the buttocks.

backslide *v.i.* relapse into error or bad ways.

backspace *v.i.* cause typewriter carriage or printer to go back one or more spaces.

backspin *n.* backward spin imparted to ball causing it to fly off at angle on hitting surface.

backstage *a.* & *adv.* behind the scenes.

backstroke *n.* stroke made by swimmer lying on back.

backtrack *v.i.* find way back by route one came; *fig.* = *back-pedal*.

backward /'bækwəd/ **1** *adv.* (also **backwards**) away from one's front (*lean, look, backwards*); back foremost (*walk backwards*); in reverse of the usual way (*count, spell, backwards*); (of thing's motion) back to starting-point (*roll backwards*); into a worse state; into the past. 2 *a.* directed to rear or starting-point; reversed; mentally retarded or slow; reluctant, shy. 3 **bend** (or **fall** or **lean**) **over backwards** make every effort, go to opposite extreme to avoid partiality. [-WARD]

backwash *n.* receding waves created by ship etc.; repercussions. [BACK]

backwater *n.* place remote from centre of activity or thought; stagnant water fed from stream.

backwoods *n.pl.* remote uncleared forest land; remote region; **backwoods-man** *n.*

bacon /'beɪkən/ *n.* cured meat from back or side of pig; **save one's bacon** escape injury or difficulty. [F f. Gmc]

bacteriology /bæktɪərɪ'ɒlədʒɪ/ *n.* science of bacteria, esp. in medicine. [foll.]

bacterium /bæk'tɪərɪəm/ *n.* (*pl.* **bacteria**) type of single-celled micro-organism lacking proper nucleus, esp. of kind causing disease; **bacterial** *a.* [Gk, = little stick]

bad 1 *a.* (*compar.* WORSE; *superl.* WORST) inferior, defective, inadequate (*bad piece of work*; *bad light*; *bad driver*); unpleasant, unwelcome (*bad breath*, *news*, *weather*); harmful (*bad for you*); serious, severe (of thing unwelcome: *bad headache*, *mistake*); morally wicked or offensive (*bad man*; *bad language*); naughty, mischievous (*bad child*); decayed, putrid (*meat has gone bad*); ill, injured (*is bad today*; *bad leg*); worthless, not valid (*bad cheque*). 2 *adv.* *US* badly. 3 *n.* ill fortune, ruin. 4 **bad blood** ill feeling; **bad debt** one that cannot be recovered; **bad egg** person of bad character; **not bad** *colloq.* fairly good; **too bad** *colloq.* regrettable. [OE]

bade *past* of BID.

badge *n.* small flat emblem fixed to lapel etc. as mark of office, membership, etc., or as decoration; thing that reveals a quality or condition. [orig. unkn.]

badger 1 *n.* grey burrowing mammal of weasel family. 2 *v.t.* pester. [orig. uncert.]

badinage /'bædɪnɑ:ʒ/ *n.* playful ridicule. [F]

badly *adv.* (*compar.* WORSE; *superl.* WORST) in a bad manner; very much, severely (*need it badly*; *badly defeated*). [BAD]

badminton /'bædmɪntən/ *n.* game with rackets in which shuttlecock is played back and forth across net. [*Badminton* in Avon]

baffle /'bæf(ə)l/ 1 *v.t.* confuse, perplex; frustrate, hinder. 2 *n.* board, panel, etc. that checks flow esp. of fluid or sound waves. 3 **bafflement** *n.* [orig. uncert.]

bag 1 *n.* receptacle of flexible material with opening at top; piece of luggage, woman's handbag; (in *pl.*) *colloq.* large amount (*of*); *sl.* woman; animal's sac; amount of game shot by sportsman. 2 *v.t.* (-**gg**-) secure, get hold of; put in bag. 3 **bags I!** *children's sl.* I claim (it)!; **in the bag** *colloq.* achieved, secured. 4 **bagful** *n.* [orig. unkn.]

bagatelle /bægə'tel/ *n.* board game in which small balls are struck into holes; mere trifle; short piece of music esp. for piano. [F f. It.]

baggage /'bægɪdʒ/ *n.* luggage; portable equipment of army. [F]

baggy *a.* puffed out, hanging loosely; **baggily** *adv.*; **bagginess** *n.* [BAG]

bagpipe *n.* (usu. in *pl.*) reed instrument with air-bag, fingered melody pipe, and drone pipes.

bah *int.* expressing contempt or disgust. [F]

bail[1] 1 *n.* security given for released prisoner's return for trial; person(s) giving bail. 2 *v.t.* (often with *out*) give bail for (person in prison) and secure his release. 3 **on bail** released after payment of bail. [F f. L (*bajulus* carrier)]

bail[2] *n.* one of two cross-pieces over stumps in cricket; bar holding paper against typewriter platen; bar separating horses in open stable. [F]

bail[3], **bale**[2] *v.* scoop water out of (boat etc.); scoop (water etc.); **bale out** make emergency parachute jump from aircraft. [F]

bailey /'beɪlɪ/ *n.* outer wall of castle; court enclosed by it. [F, rel. to BAIL[2]]

Bailey bridge /'beɪlɪ/ prefabricated military bridge designed for rapid construction. [Sir D. *Bailey*, designer]

bailie /'beɪlɪ/ *n.* municipal officer and magistrate in Scotland. [F (BAIL[1])]

bailiff /'beɪlɪf/ *n.* sheriff's officer who executes writs and performs distraints; landlord's agent or steward.

bailiwick /'beɪlɪwɪk/ *n.* district of bailie. [BAILIE, obs. *wick* district]

bain-marie /bæ̃mæ'ri:/ *n.* vessel of hot water in which cooking-pans with contents are slowly heated. [F transl. med.L (*Mary* supposed alchemist)]

bairn /beən/ *n.* *Sc.* child. [OE, rel. to BEAR[1]]

bait 1 *v.t.* harass or annoy (person); torment (chained animal); put bait on (hook, trap, etc.). 2 *n.* food or lure to entice prey; allurement. [ON]

baize *n.* coarse usu. green woollen stuff used for coverings. [F pl. *baies* chestnut-coloured]

bake *v.* cook by dry heat (not direct flame) esp. in oven; harden (clay etc.) by heat; become baked; *colloq.* (of weather) be hot, (of person) become hot; **baked**

beans baked haricot beans usu. tinned in tomato sauce; **baking-powder** mixture of sodium bicarbonate, cream of tartar, etc., used as raising-agent in cooking; **baking soda** sodium bicarbonate used in baking. [OE]

bakelite /'beɪkəlaɪt/ *n.* plastic made from formaldehyde and phenol, etc. [G f. *Baekeland*, inventor]

baker *n.* one who bakes and sells bread, esp. professionally; **baker's dozen** thirteen. [BAKE]

bakery *n.* place where bread is made or sold.

baksheesh /'bækʃi:ʃ/ *n.* gratuity, tip. [Pers.]

Balaclava /bælə'klɑ:və/ *n.* (in full **Balaclava helmet**) woollen covering for whole head and neck, except face. [*Balaclava* in Crimea]

balalaika /bælə'laɪkə/ *n.* stringed instrument like guitar, with triangular body. [Russ.]

balance /'bæləns/ **1** *n.* apparatus for weighing, esp. with scale at each end of beam supported by central pivot; counteracting weight or force; regulating-gear of clock etc.; even distribution of weight or amount; stability of body or mind; preponderating weight or amount (*balance of opinion*); agreement between or difference between credits and debits in an account; difference between amount due and amount paid (*will pay the balance next week*); amount left over; (**Balance**) sign or constellation Libra. **2** *v.* offset or compare (one thing *with* or *against* another); counteract, equal or neutralize weight or importance of; bring into or keep in equilibrium (*balancing a book on her head*), come into equilibrium; weigh (arguments etc.); compare and esp. equalize debits and credits of an account, (of account) have debits and credits equal. **3 balance of payments** difference in value between payments into and out of a country; **balance of power** situation in which chief States have roughly equal power, power held by small group when larger groups are of equal strength; **balance of trade** difference in value between imports and exports; **in the balance** uncertain, at critical stage; **on balance** all things considered. [F f. L *bilanx* scales]

balcony /'bælkənɪ/ *n.* balustraded platform on outside of building, with access from upper-floor window; upper tier of seats in theatre or cinema. [It. prob. f. Gmc (rel. to BALK)]

bald /bɔ:ld/ *a.* with scalp wholly or partly lacking hair; not covered by usual hair, feathers, leaves, etc.; with surface worn away (e.g. of tyre); direct, dull, unelaborated (*bald statement, style*); **balding** *a.* becoming bald. [OE]

balderdash /'bɔ:ldədæʃ/ *n.* senseless talk or writing, nonsense. [orig. unkn.]

bale[1] **1** *n.* bundle of merchandise or straw etc. tightly wrapped and bound with cords or hoops. **2** *v.t.* make up into bales. [Du., rel. to BALL[1]]

bale[2] see BAIL[3].

baleen /bə'li:n/ *n.* whalebone. [F f. L *balaena* whale]

baleful /'beɪlfʊl/ *a.* pernicious, destructive; malignant. [archaic *bale* evil]

balk /bɔ:lk/ **1** *v.* thwart or hinder; disappoint; miss, let slip (chance etc.); refuse to go on, hesitate (*at*). **2** *n.* hindrance, stumbling-block; roughly squared timber beam; (**baulk**) area on billiard-table from which player begins game. [OE]

Balkan /'bɔ:lkən/ *a.* of the peninsula in SE Europe bounded by the Adriatic, the Aegean, and the Black Sea, or of its peoples or countries. [Turk.]

ball[1] /bɔ:l/ **1** *n.* solid or hollow sphere, esp. for use in a game; ball-shaped object, material gathered into shape of ball (*ball of snow, wool*); delivery of ball in a game; rounded part of the body (*ball of foot, thumb*); solid missile for cannon etc., (in *pl.*) *sl.* testicles, nonsense, mess (*made a balls of it*). **2** *v.* form into a ball. **3 ball-bearing** bearing in which parts move round series of small balls, one of these balls; **ball-point (pen)** pen with tiny ball as writing-point; **balls-up** *vulgar sl.* mess, confusion; **get** (or **keep**) **the ball rolling** begin (or continue) (activity or discussion); **have the ball at one's feet** have one's opportunity; **on the ball** *colloq.* alert; **play ball** *colloq.* co-operate (*with*). [ON]

ball[2] /bɔ:l/ *n.* formal social gathering for dancing; *sl.* an enjoyable time. [F f. L f. Gk *ballō* throw]

ballad /'bæləd/ *n.* sentimental song with repeated melody; poem or song in short stanzas narrating popular story; short simple song. [F f. Prov. (prec.)]

ballade /bæ'lɑ:d/ *n.* poem of one or more triplets of stanzas with repeated refrain and envoy; short lyrical piece of music, esp. for piano.

balladry *n.* ballad poetry.

ballast /'bæləst/ **1** *n.* heavy material placed in ship's hold or in balloon-car for stability; coarse stone etc. as bed of railway track or road. **2** *v.t.* furnish with ballast. [LG or Scand.]

ballcock *n.* floating ball on arm, controlling cistern-valve. [BALL[1], COCK[1]]

ballerina /bælə'ri:nə/ *n.* woman ballet-dancer, esp. one taking leading roles in classical ballet. [It. (BALL[2])]

ballet /ˈbæleɪ/ *n.* dramatic performance of dancing and mime to music. [F (BALL[2])]

balletomane /ˈbælɪtəʊmeɪn/ *n.* ballet enthusiast.

ballista /bəˈlɪstə/ *n.* (*pl.* **ballistae** /-iː/) machine of ancient warfare for hurling large stones etc. [L, f. Gk *ballō* throw]

ballistic /bəˈlɪstɪk/ *a.* of projectiles; **ballistic missile** one powered and guided but falling under gravity on target.

ballistics /bəˈlɪstɪks/ *n.pl.* (usu. treated as *sing.*) science of projectiles and firearms.

ballocks /ˈbɒləks/ *n.pl. vulgar* testicles (often as *int.*). [OE, rel. to BALL[1]]

balloon /bəˈluːn/ **1** *n.* small inflatable rubber pouch with neck, as child's toy or decoration; large usu. round envelope inflated with hot air or gas to make it rise in the air, often carrying basket etc. for passengers; balloon shape enclosing words or thoughts of characters in comic strip or cartoon. **2** *v.* swell out like balloon; travel in balloon; hit or kick high in the air. **3** **balloonist** *n.* [F or It. (*balla* ball)]

ballot /ˈbælət/ **1** *n.* voting, in writing and usu. secret; total of votes recorded in ballot. **2** *v.* hold ballot of; vote by ballot. **3** **ballot-box** (usu. sealed) container for ballot-papers; **ballot-paper** slip for marking vote. [It. *ballotta* (prec.)]

bally /ˈbælɪ/ *a.* & *adv. sl.* mild form of BLOODY. [= *bl—y*]

ballyhoo /bælɪˈhuː/ *n.* loud noise, fuss; extravagant publicity. [orig. unkn.]

balm /bɑːm/ *n.* fragrant exudation from certain trees, used as medicine; aromatic ointment; thing that soothes or heals; aromatic herb. [F f. L (BALSAM)]

balmy /ˈbɑːmɪ/ *a.* fragrant, mild, soothing; *sl.* idiotic, crazy; **balmily** *adv.*; **balminess** *n.*

baloney var. of BOLONEY.

balsa /ˈbɒlsə, ˈbɔːl-/ *n.* lightweight strong wood used for making models etc.; tropical American tree from which it comes. [orig. = raft, f. Sp.]

balsam /ˈbɒlsəm, ˈbɔːl-/ *n.* resinous exudation from certain trees, balm; ointment, esp. of substance dissolved in oil or turpentine; tree yielding balsam; a flowering plant; **balsamic** /-ˈsæmɪk/ *a.* [OE f. L *balsamum*]

baluster /ˈbæləstə/ *n.* one in series of short posts or pillars supporting rail. [F ult. f. Gk *balaustion* wild pomegranate flower, from resemblance in shape]

balustrade /bæləˈstreɪd/ *n.* railing supported by balusters, esp. on balcony etc.

bamboo /bæmˈbuː/ *n.* tropical giant grass; its stem used to make canes, furniture, etc., or for food. [Du. f. Port. f. Malay]

bamboozle /bæmˈbuːz(ə)l/ *v.t. colloq.* hoax, cheat; mystify, perplex; **bamboozlement** *n.* [orig. unkn.]

ban **1** *v.t.* (**-nn-**) forbid, prohibit, esp. formally. **2** *n.* formal or authoritative prohibition. [OE, = summon]

banal /bəˈnɑːl/ *a.* trite, feeble, commonplace; **banality** /-ˈnælɪtɪ/ *n.*; **banally** *adv.* [F (as BAN); orig. = compulsory, hence = common]

banana /bəˈnɑːnə/ *n.* long curved fruit with soft flesh and yellow skin; tree bearing it; **banana republic** small State dependent on influx of foreign capital; **go bananas** *sl.* become crazy or angry. [Sp. or Port., f. Afr. name]

band **1** *n.* flat, thin strip of material (e.g. paper, leather, metal) that goes round thing esp. to hold it together or decorate it; strip of cloth forming part of clothing (*hatband*); stripe differing esp. in colour from background; body of musicians, section of orchestra (*wind band*); organized group of persons, esp. robbers; specified range of radio wavelengths; division of gramophone record; (in *pl.*) pair of strips hanging below collar as part of clerical or academic dress. **2** *v.t.* unite, form into a league (*band, banded, together*); put band on; mark with stripes. **3** **band-saw** power saw in form of toothed loop running over wheels. [ON (rel. to BIND) & F]

bandage /ˈbændɪdʒ/ **1** *n.* strip of material used to bind wound or injury. **2** *v.t.* bind (wound etc.) with bandage. [F (BAND)]

bandanna /bænˈdænə/ *n.* large handkerchief with spots or other pattern. [Port. f. Hindi]

bandbox *n.* box for hats etc. [BAND]

bandeau /ˈbændəʊ/ *n.* (*pl.* **bandeaux** /-əʊz/) narrow band worn round head. [F]

banderole /bændəˈrəʊl/ *n.* long narrow flag with cleft end; ribbon-like scroll bearing inscription. [F f. It. (BANNER)]

bandicoot /ˈbændɪkuːt/ *n.* a kind of very large rat in India; ratlike marsupial in Australia. [Telugu, = pig-rat]

bandit /ˈbændɪt/ *n.* robber, outlaw, esp. one of gang that attacks travellers etc.; **banditry** *n.* [It.]

bandmaster *n.* conductor of musical band. [BAND]

bandoleer /bændəˈlɪə/ *n.* (also **bandolier**) shoulder-belt with loops for ammunition. [Du. or F]

bandsman *n.* member of musical band. [BAND]

bandstand *n.* platform for musicians, esp. outdoors.

bandwagon *n.* wagon for musical band to ride in, esp. in a parade; **climb** (or

jump etc.) **on the bandwagon** join a popular or successful cause.

bandy[1] /'bændɪ/ *v.t.* exchange (words etc. *with* person); pass on (rumour etc.) thoughtlessly. [perh. F]

bandy[2] /'bændɪ/ *a.* curved or bending outward in the middle; **bandy-legged** having bandy legs. [perh. obs. *bandy* curved stick]

bane *n.* cause of ruin or trouble; *poetic* ruin; poison (now only in *ratsbane* etc.); **baneful** *a.* [OE]

bang **1** *v.* strike or shut noisily (*bang the drum, the door; the door bangs*); collide (*banged into me, against the wall*); make or cause to make explosive sound (*guns banging all round*); *vulgar sl.* have sexual intercourse with. **2** *n.* sound of blow or explosion; sharp blow. **3** *adv.* with a bang (*went bang*); suddenly or abruptly (*bang go my chances*); *colloq.* exactly (*bang on target*). **4 bang on** *sl.* exactly right. [imit.]

banger *n.* firework made to explode with bang; *sl.* sausage; *sl.* noisy old car.

bangle /'bæŋg(ə)l/ *n.* large decorative ring worn round arm or ankle. [Hindi *bangri*]

banian /'bænɪən/ *n.* Indian fig-tree whose branches take root. [Port. f. Skr., = trader (from tree under which banians built pagoda)]

banish /'bænɪʃ/ *v.t.* condemn to exile; dismiss (esp. thought from one's mind); **banishment** *n.* [F f. Gmc (rel. to BAN)]

banister /'bænɪstə/ *n.* (usu. in *pl.*) stair rail and supporting uprights, these uprights. [corrupt. of BALUSTER]

banjo /'bændʒəʊ/ *n.* (*pl.* **banjos**) stringed instrument like guitar, with circular body; **banjoist** /-əʊɪst/ *n.* [Negro corrupt. of *bandore* (Gk *pandoura* lute)]

bank[1] **1** *n.* establishment where money is deposited in accounts, withdrawn, and borrowed; storage place (*blood bank*); pool of money in gambling-game. **2** *v.* deposit (money) in a bank; have an account *at* or *with* a bank. **3 bank card** = *cheque card*; **bank holiday** day on which banks are officially closed, usu. kept as public holiday; **bank on** *colloq.* base one's hopes on, reckon reliable. **4 bankable** *a.* [F *banque* or It. *banco* (foll.)]

bank[2] **1** *n.* sloping ground on each side of river; raised shelf of ground esp. in sea; stretch of rising ground; mass of cloud, fog, snow, etc. **2** *v.* provide with or form with a bank or slope; (freq. with *up*) heap or rise in banks, pack (fire) close for slow burning; incline (aircraft) laterally in making turn, (of aircraft) incline in this way. [ON (rel. to BENCH)]

bank[3] *n.* series of similar objects grouped in row (*bank of lights, switches; bank of oars*). [F f. Gmc (prec.)]

banker *n.* owner or manager of a bank; keeper of bank in gambling-game. [BANK[1]]

banking *n.* business of running a bank.

banknote *n.* promissory note from central bank payable on demand, serving as money.

bankrupt /'bæŋkrʌpt/ **1** *a.* insolvent, declared in law unable to pay debts; deprived (*of* a quality etc.). **2** *n.* bankrupt person, esp. one whose assets are distributed to repay creditors. **3** *v.t.* make bankrupt. **4 bankruptcy** *n.* [It. *banca rotta* broken bench (BANK[1])]

banksia /'bæŋksɪə/ *n.* a flowering shrub, orig. Australian. [Sir J. *Banks*, naturalist]

banner *n.* large cloth carrying design or slogan, esp. held high at rallies etc.; flag; **banner headline** headline in newspaper extending across page. [F f. L *bandum* standard]

bannister var. of BANISTER.

bannock /'bænək/ *n. Sc. & N. Engl.* round flat meal loaf, usu. unleavened. [OE]

banns *n.pl.* announcement in church etc. (usu. made three times) of intended marriage. [BAN]

banquet /'bæŋkwɪt/ **1** *n.* sumptuous meal; elaborate and formal dinner. **2** *v.* give banquet for; attend banquet. [F dimin. of *banc* bench]

banshee /'bænʃi:/ *n. Ir. & Sc.* female spirit whose wail outside house portends death within. [Ir., = woman of the fairies]

bantam /'bæntəm/ *n.* a kind of small fowl; small but assertive person. [app. f. *Bantan* in Java]

bantamweight *n.* boxing-weight with upper limit of 54 kg.

banter **1** *n.* playful good-humoured teasing. **2** *v.* tease, make fun of; exchange banter. [orig. unkn.]

Bantu /bæn'tu:/ **1** *n.* large group of Negroid peoples of central and southern Africa; group of languages spoken by them. **2** *a.* of Bantu or their languages [Bantu, = people]

Bantustan /bæntu:'stɑ:n/ *n. derog.* any of Bantu homelands, esp. in S. Africa.

banyan var. of BANIAN.

baobab /'beɪəʊbæb/ *n.* African tree with massive trunk and large pulpy fruit. [prob. Afr. dial.]

bap *n.* soft flat bread roll. [Sc.; orig. unkn.]

baptism /'bæptɪz(ə)m/ *n.* sacramental rite of admission to the Christian Church by sprinkling with water or by immersion, administered esp. to infants usu. with name-giving; **baptism of fire** soldier's first experience of fighting; **baptismal** /-'tɪzm(ə)l/ *a.* [F f. eccl.L f. Gk]

baptist *n.* one who baptizes, esp. John the Baptist; **(Baptist)** member of nonconformist Church practising baptism of adults by immersion.

baptistery /'bæptɪstərɪ/ *n.* part of church, or (formerly) separate building, used for baptism; immersion receptacle in Baptist chapel.

baptize /bæp'taɪz/ *v.t.* administer baptism to, christen; give name or nickname to.

bar[1] **1** *n.* long thin piece of rigid material, esp. used to confine or obstruct; oblong piece (*of* chocolate, soap, etc.); counter across which (esp. alcoholic) drinks are served, room containing it; counter for special service (*coffee, heel, snack, bar*); *fig.* obstacle or barrier, restriction (*bar to progress*); place in lawcourt where prisoner stands; **(the bar)** the legal profession at court, a lawcourt; vertical line in music dividing piece into sections of equal time value, music of one such section; band of colour etc., esp. heraldic stripe as part of design; strip of silver below clasp of medal, serving as extra distinction. **2** *v.t.* **(-rr-)** fasten with bar, bolt, etc.; shut (person) *in* or *out*; obstruct or prevent (progress or action); exclude from consideration (*barring accidents*); mark with stripes. **3** *prep.* except, excluding (*all were there bar a few*). **4 bar billiards** form of billiards in which balls are struck into holes on table; **bar sinister** = *baton sinister, bend sinister* (see BEND[2]); **be called to the Bar** be admitted as barrister; **behind bars** in prison. [F]

bar[2] *n.* unit of pressure, 10^5 newton per sq. metre, approx. one atmosphere. [Gk *baros* weight]

barathea /bærə'θi:ə/ *n.* a kind of fine wool cloth. [orig. unkn.]

barb 1 *n.* secondary point of fish-hook, arrow, etc., projecting backward along shaft; wounding remark; fleshy appendage from mouth of some fishes. **2** *v.t.* fit (hook, arrow) with barb. **3 barbed wire** wire with twisted wire spikes along length, used esp. in fences and barriers. [F f. L *barba* beard]

barbarian /bɑ:'beərɪən/ **1** *n.* member of primitive or uncultured people; coarse or cruel person. **2** *a.* coarse, uncivilized; cruel. [F f. L f. Gk *barbaros* foreign]

barbaric /bɑ:'bærɪk/ *a.* primitive; extremely coarse or cruel.

barbarism /'bɑ:bərɪz(ə)m/ *n.* coarse or uncultured state or act; (use of) unacceptable word or expression.

barbarity /bɑ:'bærɪtɪ/ *n.* savage cruelty; brutal act.

barbarous /'bɑ:bərəs/ *a.* uncivilized; brutal or cruel; coarse.

barbecue /'bɑ:bɪkju:/ **1** *n.* metal frame or portable grill for cooking meat esp. above open fire; meat cooked in this way; open-air party with meat cooked on barbecue. **2** *v.t.* cook on barbecue. [Sp. f. Haitian]

barbel /'bɑ:b(ə)l/ *n.* beardlike filament at mouth of some fishes; a freshwater fish having these. [F f. L (BARB)]

barbell *n.* bar used in weight-lifting, with interchangeable discs at each end to determine weight. [BAR[1]]

barber *n.* one who by profession cuts men's hair and shaves beards; **barber's pole** pole with red and white spiral stripes, used as barber's sign. [F f. med. L (*barba* beard)]

barberry /'bɑ:bərɪ/ *n.* shrub with prickly stem and yellow flowers; its long red berry. [F *berberis*]

barbican /'bɑ:bɪkən/ *n.* fortification over gate or bridge as outer defence of city or castle. [F]

barbiturate /bɑ:'bɪtjʊrət/ *n.* soporific or sedative drug derived from barbituric acid. [G, f. name *Barbara*]

barbituric acid /bɑ:bɪ'tjʊərɪk/ an acid from which barbiturates are derived.

barcarole /bɑ:kə'rɒl, -'rəʊl/ *n.* gondolier's song; piece of music with steady lilting rhythm, esp. for piano. [F f. It. *barca* boat]

bard *n.* poet; Celtic poet; **bardic** *a.* [Celt.]

bare 1 *a.* lacking usual clothing or covering (*bare arms, floor, tree*); plain, unfurnished, simple (*bare walls, room, facts*); empty (*cupboard was bare*); scanty, only just sufficient (*bare majority; bare necessities*). **2** *v.t.* uncover, reveal. **3 lay bare** reveal or expose (truth, secret, etc.). [OE]

bareback *a.* & *adv.* on unsaddled horse.

barefaced *a.* shameless, impudent.

barefoot *a.* & *adv.* (also **barefooted**) without shoes or stockings.

bareheaded *a.* & *adv.* without hat.

barely *adv.* scarcely, only just (*barely enough*); scantily (*barely furnished*).

bargain /'bɑ:gɪn/ **1** *n.* agreement on terms of a sale or other transaction, this seen from buyer's viewpoint (*good, bad, bargain*); thing acquired on terms advantageous to buyer (*a bargain at £5*). **2** *v.* discuss terms of transaction (*with* person, *for* thing). **3 bargain for** (or **on**) be prepared for, expect; **bargain on** rely on; **into the bargain** moreover. [F f. Gmc]

barge 1 *n.* long flat-bottomed boat for carrying freight on canal or river; large ornamental boat for pleasure or ceremony. 2 *v.i.* move clumsily (*around*); intrude rudely or awkwardly (*barged in while we were kissing*; *barged into the meeting*); collide *into*. 3 **would not touch with a barge-pole** would have nothing to do with (person or thing). [F, perh. f. med.L & rel. to BARQUE]

bargee /bɑ:'dʒi:/ *n.* person in charge of barge.

baritone /'bærɪtəʊn/ *n.* male singer of range between tenor and bass; range sung by him. [It. f. Gk (*barus* heavy, *tonos* tone)]

barium /'beərɪəm/ *n.* a white metallic chemical element; **barium meal** mixture used in radiography of stomach and intestines. [BARYTA]

bark[1] 1 *n.* tough outer skin of tree trunks and branches. 2 *v.t.* graze or scrape (shin etc.); strip bark from (tree). [Scand.]

bark[2] 1 *v.* (of dog, fox, etc.) utter sharp explosive cry; speak or utter sharply or petulantly; *colloq.* cough fiercely. 2 *n.* sound of or like barking. 3 **bark up the wrong tree** make effort in wrong direction. [OE]

barker *n.* tout at auction, side-show, etc.

barley /'bɑ:lɪ/ *n.* cereal used as food and in malt liquors and spirits; its grain (also **barleycorn**); **barley sugar** hard sweet made from sugar and orig. barley water; **barley water** drink made from water and boiled barley mixture. [OE]

barm *n.* frothy yeast on surface of fermenting malt liquor. [OE]

barman *n.* person who serves (esp. alcoholic drinks) at a bar; **barmaid** *n. fem.* [BAR[1]]

bar mitzvah /bɑ: 'mɪtzvə/ Jewish boy who has reached age of thirteen; religious initiation and celebration of this. [Heb., = son of the commandment]

barmy /'bɑ:mɪ/ *a.* frothy; *sl.* crazy. [BARM]

barn *n.* large farm building for storing grain etc.; **barn dance** a kind of country dance, informal social gathering for dancing, orig. in barn; **barn owl** a kind of owl, brownish above with white under-parts. [OE, = barley house]

barnacle /'bɑ:nək(ə)l/ *n.* marine shellfish that clings to rocks, ships' bottoms, etc.; parasitic companion or follower; **barnacle goose** a kind of wild Arctic goose. [F or med.L]

barney /'bɑ:nɪ/ *n. colloq.* noisy quarrel. [perh. dial.]

barnstorm *v.i.* travel through rural areas as actor or political campaigner; **barnstormer** *n.* [BARN]

barnyard *n.* area around barn.

barograph /'bærəʊgrɑ:f/ *n.* barometer equipped to record its readings. [Gk *baros* weight]

barometer /bə'rɒmɪtə/ *n.* instrument measuring atmospheric pressure, used esp. in forecasting weather; **barometric** /bærəʊ'metrik/ *a.* [as prec.]

baron /'bærən/ *n.* member of lowest order of British or foreign nobility; important business man, other powerful or influential person (*sugar, newspaper, trade union, baron*); *hist.* holder of lands from sovereign; **baron of beef** double sirloin; **baronial** /bə'rəʊnɪəl/ *a.* [F f. med.L, = man]

baroness /'bærənɪs/ *n.* baron's wife or widow; woman with own rank of baron.

baronet /'bærənɪt/ *n.* member of lowest hereditary order of British nobility; **baronetcy** *n.*

barony /'bærənɪ/ *n.* rank or domain of a baron.

baroque /bə'rɒk/ 1 *a.* highly ornate and brilliant in style, esp. of European architecture and music of 17th and 18th centuries; of this period. 2 *n.* baroque style; baroque art collectively. [F f. Port., orig. = misshapen pearl]

barque /bɑ:k/ *n.* sailing ship with rear mast fore-and-aft rigged and other masts square-rigged. [F f. Prov. f. L *barca*]

barrack[1] /'bærək/ *n.* (usu. in *pl.*) building or building complex for housing soldiers; large building resembling barracks. [F f. It. or Sp.]

barrack[2] /'bærək/ *v.t.* shout or jeer at (players in game, performer, speaker, etc.). [perh. f. Austral. sl. *borak* banter]

barracouta /bærə'ku:tə/ *n.* long slender food-fish of South Pacific. [Sp.]

barracuda /bærə'ku:də/ *n.* large sea-fish of W. Indies.

barrage /'bærɑ:ʒ/ *n.* artillery bombardment to keep enemy pinned down; rapid succession of criticisms, questions, etc.; artificial barrier in river; **barrage balloon** large balloon anchored to ground, with cables as barrier against aircraft. [F (*barrer* BAR[1])]

barratry /'bærətrɪ/ *n.* fraud or gross negligence of ship's master or crew at expense of owners or users. [F *barat* deceit]

barre /bɑ:/ *n.* horizontal bar at waist level used in dance exercises. [F]

barrel /'bær(ə)l/ 1 *n.* round wooden vessel made of hooped staves, with flat ends and usu. bulging out in the middle; contents of this, measure of capacity (varying from 30 to 40 gallons); cylindrical tube forming part of thing, esp. gun or pen. 2 *v.t.* (-ll-, *US* -l-) put in a barrel. 3 **barrel-organ** mechanical instrument producing sounds controlled by rotating pin-studded cylinder acting on pipe-valves; **over a barrel** *colloq.* helpless, at the mercy of someone. [F]

barren /'bærən/ *a.* unable to bear young; unable to produce fruit or vegetation (*barren tree, region*); unprofitable, dull; **barrenness** *n.* [F]

barricade /bærɪ'keɪd/ **1** *n.* barrier, esp. one erected hastily across street. **2** *v.t.* block or defend with barricade. [F (*barrique* cask)]

barrier /'bærɪə/ *n.* fence or other obstacle that bars advance or access; obstacle or circumstance that keeps apart (*class barriers*); **barrier cream** cream used to protect skin from damage or infection; **barrier reef** coral reef separated from land by channel. [F f. Rmc (rel. to BAR¹)]

barrister /'bærɪstə/ *n.* person entitled to practise as advocate in higher courts. [BAR¹]

barrow¹ /'bærəʊ/ *n.* two-wheeled hand-cart; = WHEELBARROW. [OE, rel. to BEAR¹]

barrow² /'bærəʊ/ *n.* mound over ancient burial-place. [OE]

barter **1** *v.* trade in commodities without using money; exchange (goods). **2** *n.* such trade or exchange. [perh. F]

baryon /'bærɪɒn/ *n.* heavy elementary particle (nucleon or hyperon). [Gk *barus* heavy]

baryta /bə'raɪtə/ *n.* barium oxide or hydroxide. [Gk *barus* heavy]

barytes /bə'raɪti:z/ *n.* barium sulphate, used in some white paints.

basal /'beɪs(ə)l/ *a.* of, at, or forming, a base. [BASE¹]

basalt /'bæsɔ:lt/ *n.* dark volcanic rock; **basaltic** /bə'sɔ:ltɪk/ *a.* [L *basaltes* f. Gk]

bascule bridge /'bæskju:l/ a kind of drawbridge with action assisted by counterweights. [F, = see-saw]

base¹ **1** *n.* thing that supports from beneath or serves as foundation for object or structure; essential part of system (*database*); place from which operation or activity is directed; principle or starting-point, basis; main ingredient; *Geom.* line or surface on which a figure is regarded as standing; *Math.* number in terms of which other numbers or logarithms are given; *Chem.* substance capable of combining with an acid to form a salt; station or one of stations which player occupies or seeks in game (esp. baseball). **2** *v.t.* found or establish (opinion, hope, etc. *on*). [F, or L f. Gk *basis* stepping]

base² *a.* lacking moral worth, cowardly, despicable; menial; debased, not pure (*base coin*); low in value (*base metal*). [F f. L *bassus*]

baseball *n.* game played esp. in US with bat and ball and circuit of four bases which batsman must complete. [BASE¹]

baseless *a.* unfounded, groundless.

baseline *n.* line used as base or starting-point; line at each end of tennis-court.

basement /'beɪsmənt/ *n.* lowest floor of building, usu. below ground level.

basenji /bə'sendʒɪ/ *n.* small African hunting-dog. [Bantu]

bash **1** *v.t.* strike bluntly and with great force, attack violently, beat *up*. **2** *n.* heavy blow; *sl.* attempt. [imit.]

bashful /'bæʃfʊl/ *a.* shy, reticent, self-conscious. [ABASH]

basic /'beɪsɪk/ *a.* serving as base, fundamental; simplest, lowest in level (*basic pay, requirements*); **basic slag** fertilizer containing phosphates that is by-product in steel manufacture; **basically** *adv.* [BASE¹]

BASIC /'beɪsɪk/ *n.* a computer language using familiar English words. [*B*eginner's *A*ll-purpose *S*ymbolic *I*nstruction *C*ode]

basil /'bæz(ə)l/ *n.* an aromatic herb used as flavouring. [F f. med.L f. Gk *basilikos* royal]

basilica /bə'zɪlɪkə/ *n.* ancient Roman hall with apse and colonnades, used as lawcourt etc.; similar building as Christian church. [L, f. Gk *basilikē (stoa)* royal (portico)]

basilisk /'bæzɪlɪsk/ *n.* mythical reptile with lethal breath and look; tropical crested lizard. [L f. Gk, dimin. of *basileus* king]

basin /'beɪs(ə)n/ *n.* wide shallow vessel, esp. fixed one for holding water; hollow depression, round valley, tract drained by river; land-locked harbour or bay; **basinful** *n.* [F f. med.L *bacinus*]

basis /'beɪsɪs/ *n.* (*pl.* **bases** /-i:z/) foundation, main or determining principle or ingredient; starting-point for discussion etc. [L f. Gk (BASE¹)]

bask /bɑ:sk/ *v.i.* sit or lie back indulgently in warmth (*basking by the fire, in the sun*); derive great pleasure (*in* fame etc.); **basking shark** shark that lies near surface of water. [ON (rel. to BATHE)]

basket /'bɑ:skɪt/ *n.* container made of interwoven cane etc., structure like this; amount held by basket; the goal in basketball, a goal scored; **basket weave** weave resembling that of basket. [F]

basketball *n.* team game in which goals are scored by putting ball through basket fixed high at opponents' end; ball used in this.

basketry *n.* art of weaving in cane etc.; work produced in this way.

basketwork *n.* material woven in style of basket; art of this.

Basque /bɑ:sk/ **1** *n.* member of people living in W. Pyrenees; their language. **2** *a.* of Basques or their language. [F f. L *Vasco*]

bas-relief /'bæsrɪli:f/ *n.* sculpture or carving in which figures project slightly from background; = *low relief* (see RELIEF). [F & It.]

bass[1] /beɪs/ **1** *n.* male singer of lowest range; range sung by him; instrument lowest in pitch in its family, *colloq.* = *double-bass*, bass guitar. **2** *a.* lowest in musical pitch; deep sounding. [BASE[2] alt. after It. *basso*]

bass[2] /bæs/ *n.* (*pl.* **basses** or *collect.* **bass**) common perch; other spiny-finned fish of perch family. [OE]

bass[3] /bæs/ *n.* fibre from inner bark of (esp. lime) tree. [OE]

basset /'bæsɪt/ *n.* (in full **basset-hound**) sturdy hunting-dog with long body and short legs. [F dimin. of *bas* low]

basset-horn *n.* alto clarinet in F, with dark tone. [G, ult. f. It. *corno di bassetto* (BASSO)]

bassinet /bæsɪ'net/ *n.* child's wicker cradle with hood. [F dimin. of *bassin* BASIN]

basso /'bæsəʊ/ *n.* (*pl.* **bassos**) bass voice or singer. [It., = BASS[1]]

bassoon /bə'su:n/ *n.* bass instrument of oboe family, with double reed; **bassoonist** *n.* [F f. It. (prec.)]

bast var. of BASS[3].

bastard /'bɑ:stəd, 'bæ-/ **1** *n.* person born of unmarried parents; *colloq.* person regarded with pity or contempt (*poor, rotten, bastard*); spurious thing. **2** *a.* illegitimate by birth; spurious, counterfeit, hybrid. **3 bastardy** *n.* [F f. med.L]

bastardize *v.t.* declare to be bastard.

baste[1] /beɪst/ *v.t.* moisten (meat) with fat etc. in roasting; beat, thrash. [orig. unkn.]

baste[2] /beɪst/ *v.t.* sew together temporarily with large loose stitches. [F f. Gmc]

bastinado /bæstɪ'neɪdəʊ/ **1** *n.* (*pl.* **bastinados**) beating with stick on soles of feet. **2** *v.t.* punish or torture with bastinado. [Sp. (*baston* stick)]

bastion /'bæstɪən/ *n.* projection from a fortification; *fig.* thing regarded as protecting (*bastion of freedom*). [F f. It. (*bastire* build)]

bat[1] **1** *n.* implement with handle, usu. of wood and with flat or curved surface, for striking balls in games; turn at using this; batsman. **2** *v.* (**-tt-**) strike with or as with bat; have turn at batting. **3 bat around** *sl.* potter aimlessly; **off one's own bat** unaided, unprompted. [OE f. F]

bat[2] *n.* furry mouselike mammal active at night and flying by means of membrane on forelimbs; **blind as a bat** completely blind. [Scand.]

bat[3] *v.t.* (**-tt-**) now only in **not** (or **never**) **bat an eyelid** *colloq.* show no feelings; sleep soundly. [var. of obs. *bate* flutter]

batch 1 *n.* number of things or persons forming group or dealt with together, instalment; loaves produced in one baking. **2** *v.t.* arrange in batches. [rel. to BAKE]

bated /'beɪtɪd/ *a.* now only in **with bated breath** extremely anxiously. [ABATE]

bath /bɑ:θ/ **1** *n.* (*pl.* /bɑ:ðz/) long open vessel for washing oneself in; the water filling it; the process of washing in it; (in *pl.*) building for bathing or swimming in; liquid solution, esp. for developing photographic film. **2** *v.* wash, take a bath. **3 bath cube** (or **salts**) additive for scenting or softening bath water. [OE]

bath bun /bɑ:θ/ round spiced bun with currants and icing; **bath chair** a kind of wheelchair for invalids. [*Bath*, spa town in Avon]

bathe /beɪð/ **1** *v.* immerse in or treat with liquid (*bathe one's eyes*); lie immersed in water etc., esp. to swim or wash oneself; (of sunlight etc.) envelop. **2** *n.* instance of bathing. **3 bathing-suit** garment worn when swimming. [OE]

bathos /'beɪθɒs/ *n.* unintentional lapse in mood from the sublime to the absurd or trivial, anticlimax; **bathetic** /-'θetɪk/ *a.*; **bathotic** /-'θɒtɪk/ *a.* [Gk, = depth]

bathrobe *n.* loose gown of towelling etc. for use when having a bath.

bathroom *n.* room with bath, wash-basin, etc.; *euphem.* lavatory.

bathyscaphe /'bæθɪskæf/ *n.* manned vessel for deep-sea diving. [Gk *bathus* deep, *skaphos* ship]

bathysphere /'bæθɪsfɪə/ *n.* vessel for deep-sea observation. [as prec., SPHERE]

batik /'bætɪk/ *n.* process of printing coloured designs on textiles by applying wax to parts not to be dyed; cloth so treated. [Jav., = painted]

batiste /bæ'ti:st/ *n.* a fine linen or cotton cloth. [F f. *Baptiste*, first maker]

batman /'bætmən/ *n.* attendant serving army officer. [*bat* pack-saddle, f. F]

baton /'bætən/ *n.* thin stick used by conductor to direct performers; short stick carried and passed on in relay race; drum major's stick; staff of office; **baton sinister** (in heraldry) badge of bastardy. [F f. L]

batrachian /bə'treɪkɪən/ **1** *a.* of amphibians that discard gills and tails, e.g. frog and toad. **2** *n.* such an animal. [Gk *batrakhos* frog]

batsman *n.* person who bats, esp. in cricket. [BAT[1]]

battalion /bə'tæljən/ *n.* large body of men ready for battle, esp. infantry unit forming part of brigade; large group of persons with common purpose. [F f. It. *battaglia* BATTLE]

batten[1] /'bæt(ə)n/ **1** *n.* long flat strip of timber, used esp. in joining and fixing; strip used to secure tarpaulin over ship's hatchway. **2** *v.t.* strengthen or fasten with battens. [F (as BATTER)]

batten[2] /'bæt(ə)n/ *v.i.* feed greedily (*on*); thrive or prosper at another's expense. [ON]

batter[1] *v.* strike repeatedly with hard blows; beat out of shape; pound heavily and insistently (*batter at the door*); censure or criticize severely; **battered baby** infant with symptoms of repeated violence by adults, esp. parents; **battered wife** wife subjected to repeated violence by husband; **battering-ram** *hist.* beam orig. with ram's-head end used in breaching fortifications. [F *battre* beat (BATTLE)]

batter[2] *n.* mixture of flour, egg, and milk or water, for cooking. [F (prec.)]

battery /'bætərɪ/ *n.* portable container of cell or cells carrying electric charge; series of cages for intensive breeding of poultry or cattle; set of connected similar units of equipment; emplacement for heavy guns; *Law* physical violence inflicted on person. [F f. L (as foll.)]

battle /'bæt(ə)l/ **1** *n.* prolonged fight between armed forces (*do battle*; *fight a battle*; *Battle of Marathon*); contest (*battle of wits*); battle regarded as potential success (*is half the battle*). **2** *v.i.* do battle, struggle. **3 battle-cruiser** warship of higher speed and lighter armour than battleship; **battle-cry** cry or slogan of participants in battle; **battle royal** battle of many combatants, free fight. [F f. L (*battuo* beat)]

battleaxe *n.* large axe used in ancient warfare; *colloq.* domineering insensitive (usu. middle-aged) woman.

battledore /'bæt(ə)ldɔ:/ *n.* small racket; **battledore and shuttlecock** game in which this is used to strike shuttlecock. [perh. Prov. *batedor* beater]

battledress *n.* everyday uniform of soldier etc. [BATTLE]

battlefield *n.* (also **battleground**) scene of battle.

battlement /'bæt(ə)lmənt/ *n.* (usu. in *pl.*) parapet with recesses along top of wall as part of fortification. [F *batailler* fortify]

battleship *n.* warship with heaviest armour and largest guns. [BATTLE]

batty /'bætɪ/ *a. sl.* crazy; eccentric. [BAT[2]]

bauble /'bɔ:b(ə)l/ *n.* showy trinket; mere toy. [F *ba(u)bel* toy]

baulk var. of BALK.

bauxite /'bɔ:ksaɪt/ *n.* earthy mineral, the chief source of aluminium. [F f. *les Baux* in S. France]

bawd /bɔ:d/ *n.* woman keeper of a brothel. [F *baudetrot*]

bawdy /'bɔ:dɪ/ **1** *a.* humorously indecent. **2** *n.* bawdy talk or writing. **3 bawdy-house** brothel.

bawl /bɔ:l/ *v.* speak or call out noisily; weep loudly; **bawl out** reprimand angrily. [imit.]

bay[1] *n.* broad inlet of sea where land curves inward. [F f. Sp. *bahia*]

bay[2] *n.* section of wall between buttresses or columns, recess; projecting window-space; compartment (*bomb bay*); area specially marked off (*parking bay*); **bay window** window projecting from line of building. [F (*baer* gape)]

bay[3] **1** *v.* bark loudly and plangently (at). **2** *n.* sound of baying, esp. of hounds in close pursuit. **3 at bay** unable to escape, cornered (*lit.* & *fig.*); **bring to bay** approach in pursuit, trap; **keep at bay** hold off (pursuer). [F *bayer* to bark]

bay[4] *n.* a kind of laurel with deep-green leaves and purple berries; (in *pl.*) bay wreath of conqueror or poet, fame, reputation; **bay-leaf** leaf of bay-tree used for flavouring; **bay rum** perfume derived orig. from bayberry leaves in rum. [F f. L *baca* berry]

bay[5] **1** *a.* reddish-brown (esp. of horse). **2** *n.* bay horse. [F f. L *badius*]

bayberry *n.* a fragrant W. Indian tree. [BAY[4]]

bayonet /'beɪənɪt/ **1** *n.* stabbing blade attachable to muzzle of rifle; fitting engaged by pushing into a socket and twisting. **2** *v.t.* stab with bayonet. [F, perh. f. *Bayonne* in SW France]

bazaar /bə'zɑ:/ *n.* market in oriental countries; fund-raising sale of goods, esp. for charity. [Pers.]

bazooka /bə'zu:kə/ *n.* anti-tank rocket-launcher. [orig. unkn.]

BB *abbr.* double black (pencil-lead).

BBC *abbr.* British Broadcasting Corporation; **BBC English** that supposedly spoken by BBC announcers.

BC *abbr.* Before Christ; British Columbia.

BD *abbr.* Bachelor of Divinity.

bdellium /'delɪəm/ *n.* a resin used esp. as perfume; tree yielding it. [L f. Gk]

be /bɪ, *emphat.* bi:/ *v.i.* (*pres.* **am, are** /ɑ:/, **is** /ɪz/; *past* **was** /wɒz/, **were** /wɜ:/; *p.p.* **been;** *partic.* **being)** **1** as simple verb: exist, live (*I think, therefore I am*; *there is a pub up the road*); occur, take place (*dinner is at eight*); occupy position in space or time (*he is in the garden*; *she is from abroad*; *have you been to Paris?*); remain or continue (*let it be*); occupy oneself (*he is at it again*). **2** linking subject and predicate, expressing identity (*she is the person*), condition (*he is better today*), state or quality (*they are my friends*; *we must be firm*), opinion (*I am against hanging*), total (*two and two are four*), cost (*how much is it?*), significance (*it is nothing to me*). **3** as auxiliary verb with past participle to form passive (*it was done, will be done*); with present participle to form continuous tenses (*we are coming*; *it is being cleaned*); with infinitive to express duty or commitment (*I am to tell you*; *we are to wait here*), intention (*he is to come at four*), possibility (*it was not to be found*), destiny (*they were never to meet again*), hypothesis (*if I were to die*). **4 be-all (and end-all)** whole being or essence (*of*); **be off** go away; **-to-be** of the future (*his bride-to-be*). [OE]

be- *prefix* forming verbs implying transitive action (*bemoan, benumb*), completeness (*becalm, befog*), thoroughness (*belabour*), attitude or treatment (*befriend*); forming adjectives with suffix *-ed* in sense 'having' (*bespectacled*). [OE, = BY]

Be *symb.* beryllium.

beach 1 *n.* pebbly or sandy shore esp. of sea between high and low water mark. **2** *v.t.* run or haul up (boat etc.) on beach. **3 beach-head** fortified position set up on beach by landing forces. [orig. unkn.]

beachcomber *n.* vagrant living by beach.

beacon /'bi:kən/ *n.* signal-fire set up in high or prominent position; warning or guiding signal or signal station, lighthouse; radio transmitter whose signal helps fix position of ship or aircraft; = BELISHA BEACON. [OE]

bead 1 *n.* small usu. rounded piece of glass, stone, etc., for threading with others on string or wire; (in *pl.*) a string of beads, a rosary; drop of liquid, bubble; small knob in foresight of gun; inner edge of pneumatic tyre gripping rim of wheel. **2** *v.t.* furnish with beads, string together. **3 draw a bead on** take aim at. [OE, = prayer]

beading *n.* moulding or carving like series of beads; bead of tyre.

beadle /'bi:d(ə)l/ *n.* ceremonial officer of church, college, etc.; *Sc.* church officer attending on minister; *hist.* minor parish officer dealing with petty offenders etc. [F f. Gmc]

beady *a.* (esp. of eyes) small, round, and gleaming like beads. [BEAD]

beagle /'bi:g(ə)l/ *n.* small hound with short coat, used for hunting hares. [F]

beak *n.* bird's horny projecting jaws; similar jaw of turtle etc.; hooked nose; *sl.* magistrate; *hist.* pointed prow of warship; spout. [F f. Celt.]

beaker *n.* small relatively tall cup for drinking; lipped glass vessel for scientific experiments. [ON]

beam 1 *n.* long sturdy piece of squared timber used in house-building etc.; ray or shaft of light or radiation; series of radio or radar signals as guide to ship or aircraft; bright look, smile; cross-bar of balance; chief timber of plough; (in *pl.*) horizontal cross-timbers of ship; ship's breadth. **2** *v.* emit or direct (light, radio waves, affection); shine; look radiantly, smile. **3 off beam** *colloq.* mistaken, wrong; **on the beam** *colloq.* on the right track. [OE, = tree]

bean *n.* a kind of leguminous plant with edible kidney-shaped seeds in long pods; one of these seeds; similar seed of coffee or other plant; **full of beans** *colloq.* lively, in high spirits; **not a bean** *sl.* no money; **spill the beans** divulge secret accidentally or indiscreetly. [OE]

beanfeast *n.* celebration; workers' annual dinner.

beano /'bi:nəʊ/ *n.* (*pl.* **beanos**) *sl.* a party or celebration.

bear[1] /beə/ *v.* (*past* **bore**; *p.p.* BORNE or BORN) carry, bring or take, esp. visibly (*bear gifts*; *bore off a prize*); show, be marked by, have as attribute or characteristic (*bear marks of violence*; *bears no relation to the case*; *bore no name*); produce, yield (fruit etc.); give birth to (*has borne a son*; *was borne by Mary*; *was born on Monday*); sustain (weight, responsibility, cost), stand or endure (test, difficulty); (usu. with negative or interrogative) admit of, be fit for, tolerate (*does not bear thinking about*; *how can you bear it?*); carry in thought or memory (*bear a grudge*; *will bear it in mind*); bring something needed (*bear a hand*); wear (*bear arms*); move in given direction (*bear left, north*); apply pressure or weight (*bring to bear*); **bear down** exert downward pressure; **bear down on** approach rapidly or purposefully; **bear on** (or **upon**) be relevant to; **bear out** confirm (account, person giving it); **bear up** revive one's spirits, not despair; **bear with** tolerate patiently. [OE]

bear[2] /beə/ *n.* large heavy mammal with thick fur; rough or uncouth person; one who sells shares hoping to buy them back at lower price; **bear-hug** tight embrace; **Great Bear, Little Bear** constellations near north pole; **like a bear with a sore head** *colloq.* very irritable. [OE]

bearable *a.* that may be borne or endured. [BEAR[1]]

beard 1 *n.* hair growing on chin and lower cheeks of face; part on animal (esp. goat) resembling beard. 2 *v.t.* oppose or defy. [OE]
bearer *n.* one who bears or carries, esp. document, cheque, etc.; carrier of equipment on expedition. [BEAR¹]
beargarden *n.* rowdy or noisy scene. [BEAR²]
bearing *n.* one's conduct or outward behaviour; endurability (*past bearing*); relation or relevance (*has a bearing on the matter*); part of machine supporting rotating part; direction or position relative to fixed point, (in *pl.*) knowledge of one's position (*have lost my bearings*); heraldic charge or device. [BEAR¹]
bearskin *n.* skin of a bear; wrap etc. made of this; guardsman's tall furry hat. [BEAR²]
beast *n.* animal, usu. four-footed and wild; brutal person, *colloq.* objectionable person; *the* animal nature in man. [F f. L *bestia*]
beastly 1 *a.* like a beast, brutal; *colloq.* objectionable or unpleasant. 2 *adv. colloq.* very, extremely.
beat 1 *v.* (*past* **beat;** *p.p.* **beaten**) strike repeatedly or persistently, esp. to harm or punish; dash or strike repeatedly *against*; deliver rhythmic blows on (drum etc.); remove dust from (carpet etc.) by beating; overcome, surpass, win victory over; perplex, be too hard for; fashion or shape, move or shift, by blows; knock loudly *at* door etc.; stir (eggs etc.) vigorously into frothy mixture; (of heart etc.) pulsate rhythmically; (of bird) move (wings) up and down, (of wings) move thus; mark or follow (time in music) with rhythmic movement, tapping, etc.; make (path) by trampling; strike (bushes etc.) to rouse game. 2 *n.* main accent in music or verse, strongly marked rhythm of popular music; stroke (e.g. on drum), measured sequence of strokes; indication of rhythm by conductor's movements; throbbing movement or sound; route or area allocated to policeman etc., one's habitual round. 3 *predic. a. sl.* exhausted, tired out. 4 **beat about the bush** discuss matter without coming to the point; **beat down** bargain with (seller) to lower price, (of sun, heat, etc.) radiate fiercely; **beat it** *sl.* go away; **beat off** drive back (attack etc.); **beat to it** get there before (another; *lit.* & *fig.*); **beat up** give beating to, esp. with punches and kicks; **(it) beats me** *sl.* I do not understand (it); **take some beating** be difficult to surpass. [OE]
beater *n.* implement for beating (esp. carpet or eggs); person who rouses game at a shoot.
beatific /bi:ə'tɪfɪk/ *a.* making blessed; blissful (*beatific smile*). [F or L (*beatus* blessed)]
beatify /bi:'ætɪfaɪ/ *v.t.* make happy; (in RC Church) declare (person) to be in heaven, as first step to canonization; **beatification** /-fɪ'keɪʃ(ə)n/ *n.*
beatitude /bi:'ætɪtju:d/ *n.* state of perfect bliss or happiness; (in *pl.*) the blessings in Matthew 5: 3–11.
beatnik /'bi:tnɪk/ *n.* member of beat generation. [BEAT, -NIK]
beau /bəʊ/ *n.* (*pl.* **beaux** /bəʊz/) dandy; admirer, suitor. [F f. L *bellus* pretty]
Beaufort scale /'bəʊfət/ scale of wind velocity ranging from 0 (calm) to 12 (hurricane). [Sir F. *Beaufort*, admiral]
Beaujolais /'bəʊʒəleɪ/ *n.* a red or white burgundy wine from Beaujolais district of France.
beauteous /'bju:tɪəs/ *a. literary* beautiful. [BEAUTY]
beautician /bju:'tɪʃ(ə)n/ *n.* specialist in beauty treatment.
beautiful /'bju:tɪf(ə)l/ *a.* having beauty, pleasing to eye or ear or mind; gratifying taste (*beautiful steak*); **beautifully** *adv.*
beautify /'bju:tɪfaɪ/ *v.t.* make beautiful, adorn; **beautification** /-fɪ'keɪʃ(ə)n/ *n.*
beauty /'bju:tɪ/ *n.* qualities of form, complexion, etc., that together please one or more of the senses or the mind; person or thing having these; a fine specimen (*here's a beauty*); pleasing or advantageous feature (*the beauty of it*); **beauty parlour** place where women receive beautifying treatment; **beauty queen** woman judged most beautiful in contest; **beauty spot** place famous for its scenery, mole etc. on woman's face. [F or L (*bellus* pretty)]
beaver¹ *n.* amphibious rodent with soft brown fur and broad tail, able to cut down trees and build dams; its fur, a hat made of this; **beaver away** work hard (*at*). [OE]
beaver² *n.* chin-guard of helmet. [F, = bib]
bebop /'bi:bɒp/ *n.* a kind of jazz music with syncopated rhythms. [imit.]
becalm /bɪ'kɑ:m/ *v.t.* (usu. in *pass.*) make calm, deprive (ship) of wind. [BE-]
became *past* of BECOME.
because /bɪ'kɒz/ *conj.* for the reason that, since; **because of** by reason of. [BY, CAUSE]
beck¹ now only in **at the beck and call of** subject to constant orders from (someone). [BECKON]
beck² *n. Northern* brook, mountain-stream. [ON]
beckon /'bekən/ *v.* make mute signal

(*to*) esp. to approach; summon in this way. [OE]
become /bɪˈkʌm/ *v.* (*past* **became**; *p.p.* **become**) come to be, begin to be (*became king*; *became famous*); suit, look well on (*the dress becomes her*; *it ill becomes you to complain*; *with becoming modesty*); **become of** happen to. [OE (BE-)]
becquerel /ˈbekərel/ *n.* SI unit of radioactivity. [*Becquerel*, physicist]
bed 1 *n.* base or support to sleep or rest on, esp. piece of furniture with mattress and coverings; garden plot for rearing plants; bottom of sea, river, etc.; foundation of road or railway; stratum or layer. **2** *v.* (**-dd-**) put or go to bed, have sexual intercourse with (usu. with *down*); plant in a garden bed (usu. with *out*); arrange in layer; fix firmly. **3 bed and board** use of bedroom and provision of meals; **bed and breakfast** sleeping accommodation and provision of breakfast; **bed of roses** pleasant carefree living; **bed-wetting** (usu. involuntary) urination while asleep in bed; **get out of bed on the wrong side** be (temporarily) bad-tempered in the morning; **go to bed** retire to sleep, have sexual intercourse *with*. [OE]
bedaub /bɪˈdɔːb/ *v.t.* smear over, esp. with paint. [BE-]
bedazzle /bɪˈdæz(ə)l/ *v.t.* confuse, completely dazzle. [BE-]
bedclothes *n.pl.* sheets, pillows, blankets, etc., for use on bed. [BED]
bedding *n.* mattress and bedclothes; litter for animals; geological strata.
bedeck /bɪˈdek/ *v.t.* adorn, decorate. [BE-]
bedevil /bɪˈdev(ə)l/ *v.t.* (**-ll-**, *US* **-l-**) trouble or vex; confuse, perplex; torment or abuse; **bedevilment** *n.* [BE-]
bedizen /bɪˈdɪz(ə)n/ *v.t.* deck out gaudily. [BE-, obs. *dizen* deck out]
bedlam /ˈbedləm/ *n.* scene of confusion or uproar. [St Mary of *Bethlehem*, hospital in London]
Bedlington /ˈbedlɪŋtən/ *n.* (in full **Bedlington terrier**) small sporting terrier with narrow head and curly grey hair. [*Bedlington* in Northumberland]
bedouin /ˈbedʊɪn/ *n.* (*pl.* same) nomadic Arab of the desert; wandering person. [F, f. Arab., = dwellers in desert]
bedpan *n.* pan for use as toilet by invalid in bed. [BED]
bedpost *n.* upright support of bed.
bedraggled /bɪˈdræg(ə)ld/ *a.* dishevelled, untidy. [BE-]
bedridden *a.* confined to bed by infirmity. [BED]
bedrock *n.* solid rock under alluvial deposits etc.; basic principles.
bedroom *n.* room with bed and other furniture, for sleeping in.
bedside *n.* side or area to side of (esp. invalid's) bed; **bedside manner** (esp. doctor's) way of dealing with patients.
bed-sitting-room (also *colloq.* **bed-sitter**) room serving as bedroom and sitting-room.
bedsore *n.* sore developed by lying in bed.
bedspread *n.* cloth or cover put over bed esp. when not in use.
bedstead *n.* framework of bed.
bedstraw *n.* small herbaceous plant.
beduin var. of BEDOUIN.
bee *n.* four-winged hairy insect with sting, living in colony and collecting nectar and pollen to produce wax and honey; busy person; *US* meeting in group for work or pleasure; **bee in one's bonnet** an obsession. [OE]
Beeb *n. sl. the* BBC. [abbr.]
beech *n.* a forest tree with smooth bark and glossy leaves; its hard wood; **beechen** *a.* [OE]
beechmast *n.* fruit of beech.
beef 1 *n.* flesh of ox, bull, or cow; (*pl.* **beeves**) ox etc. bred for meat; *colloq.* human strength, muscle; (*pl.* **beefs**) complaint. **2** *v.i.* complain. **3 beef tea** stewed extract of beef for invalid; **beef up** strengthen, reinforce. [F, f. L *bos bovis* ox]
beefeater *n.* guard at the Tower of London; Yeoman of the Guard.
beefy *a.* like beef; solid, muscular; **beefily** *adv.*; **beefiness** *n.*
beehive *n.* artificial shelter for colony of bees; scene of great activity. [BEE]
beeline *n.* straight line between two places; **make a beeline for** go directly to.
Beelzebub /biːˈelzɪbʌb/ *n.* the Devil, Satan. [OE ult. f. Heb., = lord of flies]
been *p.p.* of BE.
beep 1 *n.* sound of (esp. motor-car) horn. **2** *v.i.* emit beep. [imit.]
beer *n.* alcoholic liquor made from fermented malt flavoured esp. with hops; a glass of this; **beer and skittles** amusement, pleasure. [OE]
beery *a.* like beer; showing effects of beer-drinking.
beeswax /ˈbiːzwæks/ *n.* wax secreted by bees for honeycomb. [BEE]
beeswing /ˈbiːzwɪŋ/ *n.* filmy crust on old port wine.
beet *n.* (*pl.* same or **beets**) plant with succulent root used in sugar-making and in salads; *US* = BEETROOT. [OE]
beetle[1] /ˈbiːt(ə)l/ *n.* insect, esp. large black kind, with hard outer wings. [OE, rel. to BITE]
beetle[2] /ˈbiːt(ə)l/ *n.* tool with heavy head for crushing, beating, etc. [OE, rel. to BEAT]

beetle[3] /'bi:t(ə)l/ **1** *a.* projecting, shaggy, scowling (*beetle brows*). **2** *v.i.* project, overhang (*beetling cliff*). [orig. unkn.]
beetroot *n.* red root of garden beet, used as vegetable. [BEET]
befall /bɪ'fɔ:l/ *v.* (*past* **befell**; *p.p.* **befallen**) happen (to). [OE (BE-)]
befit /bɪ'fɪt/ *v.t.* (**-tt-**) be suited to, be proper for. [BE-]
befog /bɪ'fɒg/ *v.t.* (**-gg-**) confuse, obscure; envelop in fog. [BE-]
before /bɪ'fɔ:/ **1** *prep.* ahead of, in front of (esp. directly: *have your letter before me*); earlier than (*arrived before me*; *before noon*); in the presence of, for the attention of (*appear before the judge*; *plan was put before the committee*); in face of, under impetus of (*drew back before the blast*); rather than (*would die before telling them*). **2** *adv.* in front, ahead (*go before*); previously, in the past (*have heard this before*; *happened long before*). **3** *conj.* earlier than (*arrived before I did*); rather than (*would die before he told them*). **4 Before Christ** of date reckoned backwards from birth of Christ. [OE (BY, FORE)]
beforehand *adv.* in advance, in readiness or anticipation.
befriend /bɪ'frend/ *v.t.* act as a friend to, help. [BE-]
befuddle /bɪ'fʌd(ə)l/ *v.t.* stupefy, confuse with or as with alcoholic drink. [BE-]
beg *v.* (**-gg-**) ask for (gift, favour), ask earnestly or humbly (*beg for mercy*; *begged her for forgiveness*, *to forgive him*); live by seeking charity; ask formally (*beg leave*, *pardon*); take or ask leave (*I beg to differ*); **beg off** decline to take part; **beg the question** assume truth of proposition needing proof; **go begging** be unwanted. [rel. to BID]
began *past* of BEGIN.
beget /bɪ'get/ *v.t.* (**-tt-**; *past* **begot**, *archaic* **begat**; *p.p.* **begotten**) be the father of; give rise to (*anger begets violence*). [OE (BE-)]
beggar /'begə/ **1** *n.* one who begs, esp. who lives by begging; very poor person; *colloq.* person, fellow (*cheeky beggar*; *poor little beggar*). **2** *v.t.* reduce to poverty; render inadequate (*beggar description*). **3 beggarly** *a.* [BEG]
begin /bɪ'gɪn/ *v.* (**-nn-**; *past* **began**; *p.p.* **begun**) perform first part of (*begin work*, *crying*, *to cry*); come *to do* thing at certain time (*began to feel sick*; *radio began to crackle*); *colloq.* show any likelihood (usu. with neg.; *does not begin to compare*); take first step, be first to do something (*shall I begin?*); start speaking; come into being, be begun (*when the world began*; *meeting begins at 8*); have nearest boundary *at* (*Asia begins at the Bosphorus*). [OE]
beginner *n.* one who is just beginning, esp. to learn a skill; **beginner's luck** good luck supposed to attend a beginner.
beginning *n.* first part of thing; time or place at which thing begins; source, origin; **beginning of the end** first clear sign of (esp. unfavourable) outcome.
begone /bɪ'gɒn/ *int.* go away at once! [*be gone*]
begonia /bɪ'gəʊnɪə/ *n.* plant with brilliant foliage and bright flowers. [*Bégon*, patron of science]
begot, begotten *past* and *p.p.* of BEGET.
begrudge /bɪ'grʌdʒ/ *v.t.* resent or be dissatisfied at; envy (person) the possession of. [BE-]
beguile /bɪ'gaɪl/ *v.t.* charm or divert, esp. wilfully; delude, cheat, deprive *of*; **beguilement** *n.* [BE-]
beguine /bɪ'gi:n/ *n.* a W. Indian dance; its music or rhythm. [F (*béguin* infatuation)]
begum /'beɪgəm/ *n.* title of married woman in India and Pakistan; lady of high rank. [Urdu f. Turk. *bīgam* princess]
begun *p.p.* of BEGIN.
behalf /bɪ'hɑ:f/ *n.* now only in **on behalf of** or **on one's behalf** in the interests of, as representative of. [earlier *bihalve* on the part of]
behave /bɪ'heɪv/ *v.* act or react (in specified way); show good manners, conduct *oneself* well (esp. to or of child); (of machine) work well (or in other specified way). [BE-, HAVE]
behaviour /bɪ'heɪvjə/, *US* **behavior** *n.* way of behaving, manners.
behavioural *a.* of or connected with behaviour; **behavioural science** any discipline that studies aspects of human behaviour, esp. anthropology and sociology.
behaviourism *n.* study of human actions by analysis into stimulus and response; advocacy of this as only valid method in psychology.
behead /bɪ'hed/ *v.t.* cut off the head of, esp. as execution. [OE (BE-)]
beheld *past* of BEHOLD.
behemoth /bɪ'hi:mɒθ/ *n.* a huge creature or thing. [Heb. (Job 40: 15)]
behest /bɪ'hest/ *n. literary* command, request. [OE]
behind /bɪ'haɪnd/ **1** *adv.* in or to the rear; further back in space or time; in an inferior or weaker position; in support; remaining after others have left (*were kept behind*); in arrears (*with* payments etc.). **2** *prep.* in or to the rear of; on the far side of (*behind that bush*); later than; in support of (*has party behind her*); in past

time already experienced by (*troubles are behind me*); inferior to or weaker than; hidden or implied by (*what is behind his remark?*). **3** *n. colloq.* the buttocks. **4 behind time** late, not punctual. [OE]

behindhand *adv.* & *predic. a.* in arrears; behind time, out of date.

behold /bɪ'həʊld/ *v.t.* (*past* and *p.p.* **beheld**) look at attentively; (in *imper.*) take notice, observe. [OE (BE-)]

beholden *predic. a.* under obligation (*to*).

behove /bɪ'həʊv/ *v.t. impers.* be incumbent on (*it behoves* person *to do* thing); be fitting (with negative: *it ill behoves you to complain*). [OE (BE-, HEAVE)]

beige /beɪʒ/ **1** *a.* of sandy fawn colour. **2** *n.* this colour. [F]

being /'bi:ɪŋ/ *n.* existence; essence or nature, constitution; existing person (*human being*). [BE]

bejewelled /bɪ'dʒu:əld/, *US* **bejeweled** *a.* adorned with jewels. [BE-]

bel *n.* unit of relative power level, corresponding to intensity ratio 10:1. See also DECIBEL. [*Bell*, inventor of telephone]

belabour /bɪ'leɪbə/, *US* **belabor** *v.t.* attack physically or verbally; labour (a subject). [BE-]

belated /bɪ'leɪtɪd/ *a.* coming late or too late. [BE-]

belay /bɪ'leɪ/ **1** *v.t.* secure (rope) by winding it round peg etc. **2** *n.* securing of rope in this way. [Du. *beleggen*]

bel canto /bel 'kæntəʊ/ lyrical style of singing with beauty of tone and smooth phrasing. [It., = fine song]

belch **1** *v.* emit wind from stomach through mouth; (of volcano, gun, etc.) send out or up (smoke etc.). **2** *n.* act of belching. [OE]

beleaguer /bɪ'li:gə/ *v.t.* besiege; vex or harass. [Du. (*leger* camp)]

belfry /'belfrɪ/ *n.* bell tower; space for bells in church tower. [F f. Gmc, prob. = peace-protector]

Belial /'bi:ljəl/ *n.* the Devil, Satan. [Heb., = worthless]

belie /bɪ'laɪ/ *v.t.* (*partic.* **belying;** *p.p.* **belied**) fail to confirm, show to be untrue; fail to fulfil or justify (promise, hope); give false notion of (*report belies him*). [OE (BE-)]

belief /bɪ'li:f/ *n.* act of believing (*belief in afterlife*); what one firmly believes; trust or confidence (*in* person or thing); acceptance of doctrine etc., one's religion. [foll.]

believe /bɪ'li:v/ *v.* accept as true or as conveying truth (*I believe it, him, what you say, that it is so*); think, suppose; have (esp. religious faith); have faith *in* the existence of (*believe in ghosts*), have confidence *in* (*believe in honesty*); **believable** *a.*; **believer** *n.* [OE]

Belisha beacon /bə'li:ʃə/ flashing orange ball on striped post, marking pedestrian crossing. [Hore-*Belisha*, who introduced it]

belittle /bɪ'lɪt(ə)l/ *v.t.* make (person, achievement) seem insignificant, disparage; **belittlement** *n.* [BE-]

bell[1] **1** *n.* hollow usu. metal object in shape of deep cup made to sound note when struck; sound or stroke of bell as signal etc.; thing which makes bell-like sound; thing with shape of bell. **2** *v.t.* provide with a bell. **3 bell-bottomed** (of trousers) heavily flared below knee; **bell the cat** face danger in common interest; **bell-glass** bell-shaped cover for plants; **bell-jar** bell-shaped jar to cover instruments or contain gas; **bell-pull** handle or cord sounding bell when pulled; **bell-push** button operating electric bell; **bell-wether** leading sheep of flock, ringleader; **sound as a bell** completely sound or well. [OE]

bell[2] **1** *n.* bay of stag. **2** *v.i.* make this sound. [OE]

belladonna /belə'dɒnə/ *n.* deadly nightshade; drug obtained from this. [L f. It., = fair lady]

belle /bel/ *n.* beautiful or the most beautiful woman. [F fem. of BEAU]

belles-lettres /bel 'letr/ *n.pl.* writings or studies of a literary nature. [F, = fine letters]

bellicose /'belɪkəʊz/ *a.* eager to fight, warlike. [L (*bellum* war)]

belligerence /bɪ'lɪdʒərəns/ *n.* (also **belligerency**) pugnacious behaviour; status of a belligerent. [foll.]

belligerent **1** *a.* engaged in war or conflict; given to constant fighting, pugnacious. **2** *n.* belligerent person or (esp.) nation. [L *belligero* wage war]

bellow /'beləʊ/ **1** *v.* emit deep loud roar; utter loudly. **2** *n.* loud roar, orig. that of a bull. [orig. uncert.]

bellows *n.pl.* device with air-bag emitting stream of air when squeezed, esp. two-handled kind for blowing fire; expandable part of camera etc. [rel. to foll.]

belly /'belɪ/ **1** *n.* part of the body below chest, containing stomach, bowels, and digestive organs; the stomach; front of the body from waist to groin; underside of four-legged animal; cavity or bulging part of anything. **2** *v.* swell out, bulge. **3 belly-ache** *n.* & *v.i.* stomach pain, *sl.* complain noisily or persistently; **belly-button** *colloq.* navel; **belly-dance** dance by woman with voluptuous movements of belly; **belly-laugh** loud unrestrained laugh. [OE, = bag]

bellyful *n.* enough to eat, *colloq.* enough

or more than enough of anything (esp. unwelcome).

belong /bɪ'lɒŋ/ *v.i.* **1** (with *to*) be the property of, be rightly assigned to as duty, right, part, etc.; be a member of (club, family, group, etc.). **2** fit a specified environment etc.; be rightly placed or classified (*in*, *under*). [BE-, obs. *long* belong]

belongings *n.pl.* one's movable possessions or luggage.

beloved /bɪ'lʌvɪd/ **1** *a.* much loved. **2** *n.* much loved person. [BE-]

below /bɪ'ləʊ/ **1** *adv.* at or to a lower point or level; further down page or on in book; downstream; *rhet.* on earth, in hell. **2** *prep.* lower in position, amount, status, etc., than; unworthy of. [*be* BY, LOW[1]]

belt 1 *n.* strip of leather etc. worn round waist or across chest; encircling strip of colour etc.; distinct region or extent (*belt of land*, *of rain*); looped strip connecting pulleys etc.; *sl.* heavy blow. **2** *v.* put belt round, fasten with belt; beat with belt; hit hard; *sl.* move rapidly. **3 below the belt** unfair(ly); **belt up** *colloq.* fix safety belt, *sl.* be quiet; **tighten one's belt** live more frugally; **under one's belt** securely acquired. [OE]

beluga /bɪ'lu:gə/ *n.* a kind of large sturgeon; caviare from this; a white whale. [Russ.]

belvedere /'belvɪdɪə/ *n.* summer-house or gallery in raised position for viewing scenery. [It., = beautiful view]

BEM *abbr.* British Empire Medal.

bemoan /bɪ'məʊn/ *v.t.* lament, complain of. [BE-]

bemuse /bɪ'mju:z/ *v.t.* stupefy or bewilder (person). [BE-, MUSE[1]]

bench *n.* long seat of wood or stone; working-table for carpenter, mechanic, scientist, etc.; lawcourt, judge's seat in court, *collect.* judges and magistrates; **King's** (or **Queen's**) **Bench** a division of the High Court of Justice; **on the bench** appointed judge or magistrate. [OE]

bencher *n.* senior member of one of the Inns of Court.

bench-mark *n.* surveyor's mark at point in line of levels; standard or point of reference.

bend[1] **1** *v.* (*past* and *p.p.* **bent** except in *bended knee*; see also BENT[1]) force (thing that was straight) into curve or angle; (of object) be altered in this way; interpret or modify (rule etc.) to suit oneself; direct or devote (attention, energies, *oneself*, *to* or *on*); incline from vertical; turn (steps) in new direction; submit, bow (*to* or *before*); force to submit. **2** *n.* curve, departure from straight course; bent part of thing; (in *pl.*) sickness due to too rapid decompression underwater. **3 bend over backwards** see BACKWARDS; **round the bend** *colloq.* crazy, insane. [OE]

bend[2] *n.* any of various knots for tying ropes; **bend sinister** (in heraldry) diagonal stripe as mark of bastardy. [OE, rel. to BIND]

bender *n. sl.* wild drinking-spree. [BEND[1]]

beneath /bɪ'ni:θ/ *adv.* & *prep.* below, under; not worthy of (*beneath him to reply*); **beneath contempt** not even worth despising. [OE (BE-, NETHER)]

Benedictine /benɪ'dɪktɪn/ **1** *n.* monk or nun of order following rule of St Benedict; (**P**) liqueur of kind orig. made by these monks. **2** *a.* of St Benedict or his order. [L *Benedictus* (foll.)]

benediction /benɪ'dɪkʃ(ə)n/ *n.* utterance of blessing, esp. at end of religious service (or as special RC service); **benedictory** *a.* [F f. L (*benedico* bless)]

benefaction /benɪ'fækʃ(ə)n/ *n.* a donation or gift; act of giving or doing good. [L (BENEFIT)]

benefactor /'benɪfæktə/ *n.* one who has given financial or other help; **benefactress** *n.*

benefice /'benɪfɪs/ *n.* a living from a church office. [F f. L (BENEFIT)]

beneficent /bɪ'nefɪsənt/ *a.* doing good; generous, actively kind; **beneficence** *n.* [L (BENEFIT)]

beneficial /benɪ'fɪʃ(ə)l/ *a.* advantageous, having benefits; **beneficially** *adv.* [F or L (BENEFIT)]

beneficiary /benɪ'fɪʃərɪ/ *n.* receiver of benefits, esp. as designated in a will; holder of benefice. [L (foll.)]

benefit /'benɪfɪt/ **1** *n.* favourable or helpful factor or circumstance; (often in *pl.*) payment made under insurance or social security; public performance or game of which proceeds go to charitable cause etc. **2** *v.* do good to; receive benefit (*from* or *by*). **3 benefit of the doubt** concession that person is innocent, correct, etc., although doubt exists; **benefit society** society for mutual insurance against illness or effects of old age. [F f. L *benefactum* (*bene* well, *facio* do)]

benevolent /bɪ'nevələnt/ *a.* wishing to do good, actively friendly and helpful; charitable (*benevolent fund*); **benevolence** *n.* [F f. L *bene volens* well wishing]

Bengali /beŋ'gɔ:lɪ/ **1** *n.* native or language of Bengal. **2** *a.* of Bengal. [*Bengal*, former Indian province]

benighted /bɪ'naɪtɪd/ *a.* in darkness; intellectually or morally ignorant. [BE-]

benign /bɪ'naɪn/ *a.* gentle, mild, kindly; fortunate, salutary; (of disease) mild, not malignant. [F f. L *benignus*]
benignant /bɪ'nɪgnənt/ *a.* kindly, esp. to inferiors; salutary, beneficial; **benignancy** *n.*
benignity /bɪ'nɪgnɪtɪ/ *n.* kindliness.
bent[1] **1** *a.* (*p.p.* of BEND[1]) curved or having angle; *sl.* dishonest, illicit; *sl.* sexually perverted. **2** *n.* inclination, bias; talent *for*. **3 bent on** determined on. [BEND[1]]
bent[2] *n.* reedy grass with stiff stems; stiff flower stalk of grass. [OE]
Benthamism /'benθəmɪz(ə)m/ *n.* belief in greatest happiness of greatest number as guiding principle of ethics; philosophy based on this. [*Bentham*, philosopher]
benthos /'benθɒs/ *n.* flora and fauna found at bottom of sea or lake. [Gk, = depth of sea]
bentwood *n.* wood artificially curved for making furniture. [BENT[1]]
benumb /bɪ'nʌm/ *v.t.* make numb, deaden; paralyse (mind or feelings). [BE-]
benzene /'benzi:n/ *n.* a substance obtained from coal-tar and used as solvent etc. [BENZOIN]
benzine /'benzi:n/ *n.* a spirit obtained from petroleum and used as cleaning agent.
benzoin /'benzəʊɪn/ *n.* aromatic resin of an E. Asian tree; **benzoic** /-'zəʊɪk/ *a.* [F f. Arab. *lubān jāwī* incense of Java]
benzol /'benzɒl/ *n.* benzene, esp. unrefined.
bequeath /bɪ'kwi:ð/ *v.t.* leave (personal estate) *to* person by will; transmit to posterity. [BE-, rel. to QUOTH]
bequest /bɪ'kwest/ *n.* bequeathing; thing bequeathed. [BE-, obs. *quiste* saying]
berate /bɪ'reɪt/ *v.t.* scold, rebuke. [BE-]
Berber 1 *a.* of N. African stock including aboriginal races of Barbary. **2** *n.* Berber person or language. [Arab.]
berceuse /beə'sɜ:z/ *n.* lullaby; instrumental piece in style of lullaby. [F]
bereave /bɪ'ri:v/ *v.t.* (chiefly in *pass.*; *partic.* **bereaved**) leave desolate, deprive *of* near relative; **bereavement** *n.* [OE (BE-, REAVE)]
bereft /bɪ'reft/ *a.* deprived (*of* life, hope, etc.). [p.p. of BEREAVE]
beret /'bereɪ/ *n.* round flat cap of felt or cloth. [F, rel. to BIRETTA]
berg *n.* iceberg. [abbr.]
bergamot[1] /'bɜ:gəmɒt/ *n.* perfume from fruit of citrus tree; an aromatic herb. [*Bergamo* in Italy]
bergamot[2] /'bɜ:gəmɒt/ *n.* a kind of fine pear. [F f. Turk., = prince's pear]
beriberi /berɪ'berɪ/ *n.* a deficiency disease, esp. in the tropics. [Sinh.]
berk *n. sl.* fool, stupid person. [*Berkshire Hunt*, rhyming sl. for *cunt*]
berkelium /bɜ:'ki:lɪəm/ *n.* artificial radioactive metallic element. [*Berkeley* in USA, where first made]
Bermuda shorts /bɜ:'mju:də/ knee-length shorts. [*Bermuda* in W. Atlantic]
berry /'berɪ/ *n.* any small roundish juicy fruit without stone; *Bot.* fruit with seeds enclosed in pulp (e.g. banana and tomato). [OE]
berserk /bə'sɜ:k/ *a.* wild, frenzied; **go berserk** go into a violent rage, lose control. [orig. = Norse warrior: Icel., = bear-coat]
berth 1 *n.* fixed bunk on a ship, train, etc., for sleeping in; ship's place at wharf; room for ship to swing at anchor; sea-room; situation, appointment. **2** *v.* moor (ship) in berth; (of ship) come to mooring; provide sleeping-berth for. **3 give a wide berth to** stay away from. [BEAR[1]]
beryl /'berɪl/ *n.* a kind of transparent precious stone, esp. pale green; mineral species including this and emerald. [F f. L f. Gk]
beryllium /bə'rɪlɪəm/ *n.* a light hard white metallic element.
beseech /bɪ'si:tʃ/ *v.t.* (*past* and *p.p.* **besought** /-'sɔ:t/) entreat (person *to do* thing, *for* thing); ask earnestly for. [BE-, SEEK]
beset /bɪ'set/ *v.t.* (**-tt-**; *past* and *p.p.* **beset**) attack or harass persistently (*beset by worries*); surround, hem in (person). [OE (BE-)]
beside /bɪ'saɪd/ *prep.* at the side of, near; compared with; irrelevant to (*beside the point*); **beside oneself** frantic with worry or anger etc. [OE (BY, SIDE)]
besides 1 *prep.* in addition to, apart from. **2** *adv.* also, as well.
besiege /bɪ'si:dʒ/ *v.t.* lay siege to; crowd round oppressively; harass with requests. [BE-]
besmirch /bɪ'smɜ:tʃ/ *v.t.* soil, discolour; dishonour. [BE-]
besom /'bi:zəm/ *n.* broom made of twigs tied round stick. [OE]
besot /bɪ'sɒt/ *v.t.* (**-tt-**; usu. in *pass.*) stupefy; infatuate. [BE-]
bespangle /bɪ'spæŋg(ə)l/ *v.t.* adorn with spangles. [BE-]
bespatter /bɪ'spætə/ *v.t.* spatter all over; overwhelm with abuse etc. [BE-]
bespeak /bɪ'spi:k/ *v.t.* (*past* **bespoke**; *p.p.* **bespoken,** as adj. BESPOKE) engage in advance; order (goods); suggest, be evidence of. [BE-]
bespectacled /bɪ'spektək(ə)ld/ *a.* wearing spectacles. [BE-]

bespoke /bɪˈspəʊk/ *a.* ordered in advance, made to order. [partic. of BESPEAK]

best 1 *a.* (*superl.* of GOOD) of most excellent or desirable kind (*my best friend; the best dictionary; best thing would be to confess*); greatest (*best part of an hour*). 2 *adv.* (*superl.* of WELL[1]) in best manner; to greatest degree; most usefully (*is best ignored*). 3 *n.* that which is best; chief merit or advantage (*bring out the best in him*); victory in fight or argument (*get the best of it; best of three games wins*); one's best clothes (*Sunday best*). 4 *v.t. colloq.* defeat, outwit. 5 **as best one can** as well as one can under the circumstances; **at best** on the most optimistic view; **at one's best** in peak of form; **best man** bridegroom's chief attendant at wedding; **do one's best** do all one can; **had best** would find it wisest to; **make the best of** derive all possible advantage from (something of qualified worth). [OE]

bestial /ˈbestɪəl/ *a.* of or like beasts; brutish, cruel; **bestiality** /-ˈælɪtɪ/ *n.*; **bestially** *adv.* [F f. L (BEAST)]

bestiary /ˈbestɪərɪ/ *n.* medieval treatise on beasts. [med.L (BEAST)]

bestir /bɪˈstɜː/ *v.t.* (**-rr-**) exert or rouse (*oneself*). [BE-]

bestow /bɪˈstəʊ/ *v.t.* confer (gift, right, etc.) *on* or *upon* person; **bestowal** *n.* [BE-]

bestrew /bɪˈstruː/ *v.t.* (*p.p.* **bestrewed** or **bestrewn**) strew (surface *with*); lie scattered over. [BE-]

bestride /bɪˈstraɪd/ *v.t.* (*past* **bestrode**; *p.p.* **bestridden**) sit astride on; stand astride over. [BE-]

bet 1 *v.* (**-tt-**; *past* and *p.p.* **bet** or **betted**) risk sum of money against another's, risk (amount) on result of doubtful event. 2 *n.* such an arrangement (*make a bet*), money staked (*put a bet on*); *colloq.* opinion (*my bet is that*). 3 **I bet** *colloq.* I feel sure; **you bet** *colloq.* you may be sure. [orig. uncert.]

beta /ˈbiːtə/ *n.* second letter of Greek alphabet (Β, β); **beta particle** (or **ray**) fast-moving electron emitted by radioactive substances, orig. regarded as ray. [L f. Gk]

betake /bɪˈteɪk/ *v.t.* (*past* **betook**; *p.p.* **betaken**) *refl.* go *to* (place, person). [BE-]

betatron /ˈbiːtətrɒn/ *n. Physics* apparatus for accelerating electrons in circular path. [BETA, (ELEC)TRON]

betel /ˈbiːt(ə)l/ *n.* tropical Asian plant whose leaf is chewed with betel-nut; **betel-nut** = *areca nut.* [Port. f. Malayalam]

bête noire /beɪt ˈnwɑː/ (*pl.* ***bêtes noires*** *pr.* same) person or thing one particularly dislikes. [F, lit. = black beast]

bethink /bɪˈθɪŋk/ *v.t.* (*past* and *p.p.* **bethought**) *refl.* reflect, stop to think, be reminded by reflection (*of, that, how*). [OE (BE-)]

betide /bɪˈtaɪd/ *v.* happen; now chiefly in **woe betide** (person), orig. a curse, now a warning. [BE-, *tide* befall]

betimes /bɪˈtaɪmz/ *adv. literary* in good time, early. [BY]

betoken /bɪˈtəʊkən/ *v.t.* be a sign of, indicate. [OE (BE-)]

betony /ˈbetənɪ/ *n.* plant with purple flowers. [F f. L]

betray /bɪˈtreɪ/ *v.t.* be disloyal to, assist the enemy of (*betrayed his trust, his country*); give up (person etc. *to* enemy); reveal treacherously; reveal involuntarily; be evidence of; lead astray; **betrayal** *n.* [BE-, obs. *tray* f. F f. L *trado* hand over]

betroth /bɪˈtrəʊð/ *v.t.* bind with promise to marry; **betrothal** *n.*; **betrothed** *a.* & *n.* [BE-, TRUTH]

better 1 *a.* (*compar.* of GOOD) of more excellent or desirable kind; partly or fully recovered from illness; greater (*better part of two hours*). 2 *adv.* (*compar.* of WELL[1]) in better manner; to greater degree; more usefully (*is better forgotten*). 3 *n.* that which is better; (in *pl.*) one's superiors. 4 *v.t.* improve; surpass (feat); *refl.* improve one's position etc. 5 **better half** *colloq.* wife or husband; **better off** see OFF; **get the better of** win an advantage over, outwit; **had better** would find it wiser to. [OE]

betterment *n.* making better.

betting-shop *n.* bookmaker's shop or office. [BET]

between /bɪˈtwiːn/ 1 *prep.* in, into, along, or across the extent or interval bounded by two or more points, lines, dates, etc. (*between York and Leeds, Monday and Friday; read between the lines*); separating (*difference between right and wrong*); to and from (*runs between London and Oxford*); shared by, confined to (*£5 between us*); taking one and rejecting the other of (*choose between them*). 2 *adv.* in the space or interval bounded by two or more points etc. 3 **between ourselves** (or **you and me**) in confidence; **in between** intermediately in position. [OE BY, rel. to TWO]

betwixt /bɪˈtwɪkst/ *prep.* & *adv.* between; now only in **betwixt and between** *colloq.* neither one thing nor the other.

bevel /ˈbev(ə)l/ 1 *n.* tool for marking angles in carpentry and stonework; slope from horizontal or vertical; sloping edge or surface. 2 *v.* (**-ll-**, *US* **-l-**)

reduce (square edge) to a sloping one; slope at an angle. **3 bevel gear** gear working another at an angle to it. [F]

beverage /'bevərɪdʒ/ *n.* liquid prepared for drinking. [F f. L (*bibo* drink)]

bevy /'bevɪ/ *n.* a company (*of ladies, roes, quails, larks*). [orig. unkn.]

bewail /bɪ'weɪl/ *v.t.* wail over, mourn for. [BE-]

beware /bɪ'weə/ *v.* (only in *imper.* or *infin.*) take heed, be cautious (of) (*beware of the dog; beware the Ides of March; told us to beware*). [BE, *ware* cautious]

bewilder /bɪ'wɪldə/ *v.t.* perplex, confuse; **bewilderment** *n.* [BE-, obs. *wilder* lose one's way]

bewitch /bɪ'wɪtʃ/ *v.t.* enchant, greatly delight; cast spell on. [BE-]

bey /beɪ/ *n.* Turkish title of rank, esp. *hist.* of Ottoman governor. [Turk.]

beyond /bɪ'jɒnd/ **1** *prep.* at or to the further side of; outside the scope of (*beyond repair*) or understanding of (*quite beyond me*); more than. **2** *adv.* at or to the further side, further on, outside. **3** *n. the* unknown after death. **4 the back of beyond** very remote place. [OE (BY, rel. to YON)]

bezel /'bez(ə)l/ *n.* sloped edge of chisel; oblique face of cut gem; groove holding watch-glass or gem. [F]

bezique /bɪ'zi:k/ *n.* card-game for two players. [F]

b.f. *abbr.* bloody fool.

bhang /bæŋ/ *n.* Indian hemp; its dried leaves smoked or chewed as narcotic and intoxicant. [Port. f. Skr.]

b.h.p. *abbr.* brake horsepower.

bi- /baɪ-/ *prefix* (thing) having two (*bilateral, biplane*); occurring twice in every one or once in every two (*bi-weekly*); *Chem.* substance having a double proportion of the acid etc. indicated by the simple word (*bicarbonate*); *Bot. & Zool.* (of division and subdivision) twice over (*bipinnate*). [L]

Bi *symb.* bismuth.

biannual /baɪ'ænjʊəl/ *a.* occurring twice a year. [BI-]

bias /'baɪəs/ **1** *n.* predisposition or prejudice (*have a bias towards*); distortion of statistical result by neglected factor; (in bowls) oblique course of bowl due to its lopsided form, this form; oblique direction in cutting cloth. **2** *v.t.* (*past* and *p.p.* **biased**) give a bias to; prejudice. **3 bias binding** strip of material cut diagonally, used to bind edges; **on the bias** obliquely, diagonally. [F]

bib *n.* cloth etc. tied under child's chin and over chest while eating; part of apron covering chest. [orig. uncert.]

bib-cock *n.* tap with bent nozzle. [perh. f. prec.]

Bible /'baɪb(ə)l/ *n.* Christian scriptures of Old and New Testament; (**bible**) a copy of these (*three bibles*), any authoritative book; **biblical** /'bɪblɪk(ə)l/ *a.* [F f. L f. Gk *biblia* books]

bibliography /bɪblɪ'ɒgrəfɪ/ *n.* list of books on a particular subject or by a particular author; historical and thematic study of books, their authorship and editions, etc.; **bibliographer** *n.*; **bibliographical** /-'græfɪk(ə)l/ *a.* [F f. L f. Gk (prec.)]

bibliophile /'bɪblɪəʊfaɪl/ *n.* admirer or collector of books.

bibulous /'bɪbjʊləs/ *a.* fond of or addicted to alcoholic drink. [L (*bibo* drink)]

bicameral /baɪ'kæmər(ə)l/ *a.* having two legislative chambers. [BI-, L *camera* chamber]

bicarbonate /baɪ'kɑ:bənɪt/ *n.* salt containing double proportion of carbon dioxide; **bicarbonate of soda** = SODIUM BICARBONATE. [BI-]

bicentenary /baɪsen'ti:nərɪ/ *n.* two-hundredth anniversary; celebration of this. [BI-]

bicentennial /baɪsen'tenɪəl/ **1** *a.* occurring every two hundred years. **2** *n.* bicentenary. [BI-]

biceps /'baɪseps/ *n.* muscle with double head or attachment, esp. that which bends elbow. [L (*caput* head)]

bicker *v.i.* quarrel pettily, wrangle. [orig. unkn.]

bicuspid /baɪ'kʌspɪd/ **1** *a.* having two cusps. **2** *n.* any of eight such teeth in adults. [BI-, CUSP]

bicycle /'baɪsɪk(ə)l/ **1** *n.* metal-framed vehicle with two wheels one behind the other, driven by foot pedals. **2** *v.i.* ride on bicycle. **3 bicyclist** *n.* [F (Gk *kuklos* wheel)]

bid 1 *v.* (**-dd-**; *past* and *p.p.* **bid,** in last two senses *past* **bade** /bæd/, *p.p.* **bid** or **bidden**) offer (certain amount) as price one is willing to pay, esp. at auction; offer service at stated price; state number of tricks one proposes to win at cards; command or invite (*to*); utter (greeting or farewell) to (*I bade her good-night*). **2** *n.* act of bidding; amount bid; attempt, effort. **3 bid fair to** seem likely to; **make a bid for** attempt to secure. [OE]

biddable *a.* obedient.

bidding *n.* command, request, invitation; bids at auction or in card-game.

biddy /'bɪdɪ/ *n. sl.* elderly woman. [name *Bridget*]

bide *v.t.* now only in **bide one's time** await one's best opportunity. [OE]

bidet /'bi:deɪ/ *n.* low basin for sitting astride on to wash genitals. [F, = pony]

biennial /baɪ'enɪəl/ **1** *a.* lasting, recurring every, two years. **2** *n.* plant that springs one year and flowers and dies the next. [L (*annus* year)]

bier *n.* movable stand on which coffin or corpse rests. [OE]

biff *sl.* **1** *n.* smart blow. **2** *v.t.* strike (person). [imit.]

bifid /'baɪfɪd/ *a.* divided by deep cleft into two parts. [L (*findo* cleave)]

bifocal /baɪ'fəʊk(ə)l/ **1** *a.* having two foci, esp. of lens with part for distant and part for near vision. **2** *n.* (in *pl.*) spectacles with bifocal lenses. [FOCUS]

bifurcate /'baɪfɜːkeɪt/ *v.* have or divide into two branches; **bifurcation** /-'keɪʃ(ə)n/ *n.* [L (*furca* fork)]

big **1** *a.* of considerable size, amount, intensity, etc.; of large or largest size (*big drum, game, toe*); older or adult (*big sister*); important (*the Big Four*); boastful (*big words*); *colloq.* ambitious, generous (*big ideas*); outstanding (*my big moment*); advanced in pregnancy (esp. of animals). **2** *adv. colloq.* in a big manner, impressively or grandly (*think big*). **3** **Big Brother** dictatorial person seemingly benevolent; **big end** end of connecting-rod in engine, encircling crankpin; **big-head** *colloq.* conceited person; **big-hearted** generous; **big money** high financial reward; **big shot** *colloq.* important person; **big time** *sl.* highest or most successful level in a profession etc.; **big top** main tent at circus; **in a big way** with great energy, enthusiasm, etc.; **too big for one's boots** *colloq.* very conceited. [orig. unkn.]

bigamy /'bɪgəmɪ/ *n.* act of attempting second marriage while first is still valid; **bigamist** *n.*; **bigamous** *a.* [F f. L f. Gk (*gamos* marriage)]

bight /baɪt/ *n.* loop of rope; recess of coast, bay. [OE]

bigot /'bɪgət/*n.* one who holds obstinately to a belief or opinion intolerantly of others; **bigoted** *a.*; **bigotry** *n.* [F]

bigwig *n. colloq.* important person. [BIG]

bijou /'biːʒuː/ **1** *n.* (*pl.* ***bijoux*** *pr.* same) jewel, trinket. **2** *a.* small and elegant. [F]

bike *colloq.* **1** *n.* bicycle, motor cycle. **2** *v.i.* ride on bicycle or motor cycle. [abbr.]

bikini /bɪ'kiːnɪ/ *n.* brief two-piece bathing-suit worn by women. [*Bikini*, Pacific atoll]

bilateral /baɪ'lætər(ə)l/ *a.* of, on, or with two sides; affecting or between two parties, countries, etc.; **bilateralism** *n.*; **bilaterally** *adv.* [BI-]

bilberry /'bɪlbərɪ/ *n.* a N. European shrub growing esp. on heath-land; its small edible dark-blue berry. [Scand.]

bile *n.* bitter fluid secreted by liver to aid digestion; bad temper, peevish anger. [F f. L *bilis*]

bilge /bɪldʒ/ *n.* nearly flat part of ship's bottom; foul water that collects there (also **bilge-water**); *sl.* nonsense, rubbish. [prob. var. of BULGE]

bilharzia /bɪl'hɑːtsɪə/ *n.* chronic tropical disease caused by flatworm in pelvis. [*Bilharz*, physician]

biliary /'bɪljərɪ/ *a.* of the bile; carrying bile. [F (BILE)]

bilingual /baɪ'lɪŋgw(ə)l/ *a.* speaking or able to speak two languages; written in two languages; **bilingually** *adv.* [L (*lingua* tongue)]

bilious /'bɪljəs/ *a.* affected by disorder of the bile; bad-tempered. [F f. L (BILE)]

bilk *v.t.* cheat, elude; avoid paying (creditor, bill). [orig. uncert.]

bill[1] **1** *n.* statement of charges for goods supplied or services rendered; draft of proposed law; poster or placard; *Law* written statement of facts of case; programme of entertainment; *US* banknote. **2** *v.t.* announce, put in programme; advertise *as*; send statement of charges to. **3** **bill of exchange** written order to pay sum to named person on given date; **bill of fare** menu; **bill of lading** see LADE; **clean bill of health** declaration that there is no disease, or *fig.* that there is no defect. [AF f. med.L *bulla* seal]

bill[2] **1** *n.* bird's beak (esp. if small or slender); narrow promontory. **2** *v.i.* (of doves) stroke bills. **3** **bill and coo** exchange caresses. [OE]

bill[3] *n. hist.* weapon with hook-shaped blade. [OE]

billabong /'bɪləbɒŋ/ *n.* in Australia, branch of river forming backwater. [Abor.]

billboard *n.* large outdoor hoarding for advertisements. [BILL[1]]

billet[1] /'bɪlɪt/ **1** *n.* order to provide lodging for soldier etc., esp. in private house; place so provided; job, appointment. **2** *v.t.* allocate lodging to by billet. [AF dimin. of BILL[1]]

billet[2] /'bɪlɪt/ *n.* thick piece of firewood; small metal bar. [F dimin. of *bille* tree-trunk]

billet-doux /bɪlɪ'duː/ *n.* (*pl.* **billets-doux** /-'duːz/) a love-letter. [F, = sweet note]

billhook *n.* tool with hooked blade, used esp. for pruning. [BILL[3]]

billiards /'bɪljədz/ *n.* game played on oblong cloth-covered table with three balls struck with cues. [F (BILLET[2])]

billion /'bɪljən/ *a.* & *n.* (*pl.* **billion** except as below) million million; *US* (and increasingly *Brit.*) thousand million;

billions *pl. colloq.* very many; **billionth** *a.* [F]

billow /'bɪləʊ/ **1** *n.* large wave; any large mass. **2** *v.i.* rise or surge in billows. **3 billowy** *a.* [ON]

billposter *n.* (also **billsticker**) one who pastes up advertisements on hoardings etc. [BILL[1]]

billy /'bɪlɪ/ *n.* (in full **billycan**) tin or enamelled outdoor cooking vessel with lid and handle, esp. in Australia. [perh. f. Abor. *billa* water]

billy-goat /'bɪlɪgəʊt/ *n.* male goat. [*Billy*, name]

bimetallic /baɪmɪ'tælɪk/ *a.* using or made of two metals. [F]

bin *n.* large box-shaped container for storage; = DUSTBIN. [OE]

binary /'baɪnərɪ/ *a.* consisting of two parts, dual; of arithmetical system using 2 as base; **binary compound** *Chem.* of two elements or radicals; **binary star** system of two stars revolving round common centre. [L (*bini* two together)]

binaural /baɪn'ɔ:r(ə)l, bɪ-/ *a.* of or used with both ears; (of sound) recorded by two microphones and usu. transmitted separately to the two ears. [BI-, AURAL]

bind /baɪnd/ **1** *v.* (*past* and *p.p.* **bound,** BOUND) tie or fasten together; hold together, (cause to) cohere; bandage (*up*); restrain (*was bound hand and foot*); encircle (thing) *with*; wrap (material) *round* or *on*; fasten sheets of (book) into cover; be obligatory; compel, impose duty on; constipate; edge with braid etc. **2** *n. sl.* a nuisance. **3 bind over** *Law* order (person) to do thing, esp. keep the peace. [OE]

binder *n.* loose cover for papers; bookbinder; substance that binds things together; reaping-machine that binds grain into sheaves.

bindery *n.* bookbinder's workshop.

binding 1 *n.* thing that binds, esp. gluing etc. and covers of book. **2** *a.* obligatory (*on*).

bindweed *n.* convolvulus.

bine *n.* twisting stem of climbing plant, esp. hop; flexible shoot. [dial. form of BIND]

binge /bɪndʒ/ *n. sl.* drinking-bout, spree. [prob. dial., = to soak]

bingo /'bɪŋgəʊ/ *n.* game with any number of people, each having card marked off as numbers are drawn. [orig. uncert.]

binnacle /'bɪnək(ə)l/ *n.* case for ship's compass. [Sp. or Port. f. L *habitaculum* dwelling]

binocular /bɪ'nɒkjʊlə, baɪ-/ **1** *n.* (usu. in *pl.* and /bɪ-/) instrument with lens for each eye, for viewing distant objects. **2** *a.* (usu. /baɪ-/) for both eyes. [L *bini* two together, *oculus* eye]

binomial /baɪ'nəʊmɪəl/ **1** *n.* algebraic expression of sum or difference of two terms. **2** *a.* consisting of two terms. **3 binomial theorem** formula giving any power of binomial. [F (Gk *nomos* part)]

bint *n. colloq.* (usu. *derog.*) girl, woman. [Arab.]

bio- *in comb.* biological, of living things; of life (*biography*). [Gk *bios* life]

biochemistry /baɪəʊ'kemɪstrɪ/ *n.* branch of chemistry dealing with animals and plants; **biochemical** *a.*; **biochemist** *n.* [BIO-]

biodegradable /baɪəʊdɪ'greɪdəb(ə)l/ *a.* capable of being decomposed by bacteria.

bioengineering /baɪəʊendʒɪ'nɪərɪŋ/ *n.* application of engineering techniques to biological processes.

biogenesis /baɪəʊ'dʒenɪsɪs/ *n.* hypothesis that living matter arises only from other living matter; synthesis of substances by living matter.

biography /baɪ'ɒgrəfɪ/ *n.* written account of person's life, usu. by another; such writing as branch of literature; **biographer** *n.*; **biographical** /baɪəʊ'græfɪk(ə)l/ *a.* [F f. Gk (BIO-)]

biological /baɪə'lɒdʒɪk(ə)l/ *a.* of biology, of plants and animals; **biological warfare** use of organisms to spread disease among enemy; **biologically** *adv.* [foll.]

biology /baɪ'ɒlədʒɪ/ *n.* science dealing with origin, forms, and behaviour of animals and plants; **biologist** *n.* [F f. G (as BIO-)]

bionic /baɪ'ɒnɪk/ *a.* having electronically operated body-parts, or resulting superhuman strengths; **bionically** *adv.* [BIO- after *electronics*]

biophysics /baɪəʊ'fɪzɪks/ *n.pl.* (usu. treated as *sing.*) science in which laws of physics are applied to biological phenomena. [BIO-]

biopsy /'baɪɒpsɪ/ *n.* examination of tissue cut from living body, as means of diagnosis. [F (Gk *bios* life, *opsis* sight)]

biorhythm /'baɪəʊrɪθ(ə)m/ *n.* any of the recurring cycles of biological processes said to affect one's emotional, intellectual, and physical activity. [BIO-]

biosphere /'baɪəʊsfɪə/ *n.* regions of earth's crust and atmosphere occupied by living matter. [G (as BIO-)]

biotic /baɪ'ɒtɪk/ *a.* relating to life or living things. [F or L f. Gk (*bios* life)]

biotin /'baɪətɪn/ *n.* crystalline vitamin controlling growth and found esp. in yeast and egg-yolk. [G (as prec.)]

bipartisan /baɪpɑ:tɪ'zæn/ *a.* of or involving two parties. [BI-]

bipartite /baɪ'pɑ:taɪt/ *a.* consisting of two parts; concerning two parties (*bipartite agreement*). [L *bipartio* divide in two]

biped /ˈbaɪped/ **1** *n.* two-footed animal. **2** *a.* two-footed. **3 bipedal** *a.* [L *bipes, -pedis*]

biplane /ˈbaɪpleɪn/ *n.* aeroplane with two sets of wings, one above the other. [BI-]

bipolar /baɪˈpəʊlə/ *a.* having two poles or extremities. [BI-]

birch 1 *n.* northern forest tree with hard wood and smooth bark; rod from birch, used for flogging. **2** *v.t.* flog with birch. [OE]

bird *n.* feathered vertebrate with two wings and two feet, egg-laying and usu. able to fly; *sl.* young woman, person (esp. strange one); **bird in the hand** something secured or certain; **bird of paradise** bird with brilliant plumage; **bird of passage** migratory bird, person who travels habitually; **bird's eye view** general view from above; **birds of a feather** people with similar characteristics; **for the birds** *sl.* of no interest; **get the bird** *sl.* be dismissed or rejected out of hand; **kill two birds with one stone** achieve two aims by one action etc. [OE]

birdie *n.* (child's name for) little bird; hole played in one under par in golf.

birdlime *n.* sticky substance spread to catch birds.

birdseed *n.* special seeds for caged birds.

biretta /bɪˈretə/ *n.* square usu. black cap worn by (esp. RC) priest. [It. or Sp. dimin. f. L *birrus* cape]

Biro /ˈbaɪərəʊ/ *n.* **(P)** a kind of ball-point pen. [*Biró*, inventor]

birth *n.* emergence of young from mother's body; origin, parentage, descent; beginning (*birth of socialism*); inherited position, noble lineage; **birth certificate** official document giving date and place of person's birth; **birth-control** control of number of children one has, esp. by contraception; **birth-rate** number of births per thousand of population per year; **give birth to** produce (young), be cause of. [ON]

birthday *n.* day on which one was born; anniversary of this.

birthmark *n.* unusual (esp. brown or red) mark on one's body at or from birth.

birthplace *n.* place where one was born.

birthright *n.* rights one has by birth esp. as eldest son.

biscuit /ˈbɪskɪt/ *n.* flat thin unleavened cake, usu. dry and crisp, and often sweetened; porcelain after firing but before glazing; light-brown colour. [F f. L (*bis* twice, *coquo* cook)]

bisect /baɪˈsekt/ *v.t.* divide into two (strictly, equal) parts; **bisection** *n.*; **bisector** *n.* [BI-, L *seco sect-* cut]

bisexual /baɪˈseksjʊəl/ *a.* sexually attracted by members of both sexes; having both sexes in one individual; **bisexuality** /-ˈælɪtɪ/ *n.* [BI-]

bishop /ˈbɪʃəp/ *n.* senior clergyman in charge of diocese; mitre-shaped chess piece. [OE f. eccl.L f. Gk *episkopos* overseer]

bishopric /ˈbɪʃəprɪk/ *n.* office or diocese of bishop.

bismuth /ˈbɪzməθ/ *n.* reddish-white metallic element used in alloys etc.; compound of it used as medicine. [G]

bison /ˈbaɪs(ə)n/ *n.* (*pl.* same) wild hump-backed ox of Europe and America. [L f. Gmc]

bisque[1] /bɪsk/ *n.* advantage of one free point or stroke awarded to player in certain games. [F]

bisque[2] /bɪsk/ *n.* unglazed white porcelain. [BISCUIT]

bistre /ˈbɪstə/, *US* **bister** *n.* brownish pigment made from soot of burnt wood. [F]

bistro /ˈbiːstrəʊ/ *n.* small bar or restaurant. [F]

bit[1] *n.* small piece or quantity, *iron.* a large amount (*takes a bit of remembering*); short time or distance (*move up a bit; wait a bit*); small part in play or film; small coin; mouthpiece of bridle; tool or piece for boring or drilling; cutting or gripping part of plane, pincers, etc.; **a bit** *colloq.* somewhat (*a bit late*); **bit by bit** gradually; **a bit of** *colloq.* rather (*a bit of a fool*); **do one's bit** *colloq.* make one's useful contribution; **take the bit between one's teeth** escape from control. [OE]

bit[2] *n.* (in computers) unit of information expressed as choice between two possibilities. [*binary digit*]

bit[3] *past* of BITE.

bitch 1 *n.* female dog; female fox, wolf, or otter; *derog.* sly or spiteful woman; *sl.* unpleasant or difficult thing. **2** *v.* grumble; be spiteful or unfair to. [OE]

bitchy *a.* spiteful, bad-tempered; **bitchiness** *n.*

bite 1 *v.* (*past* **bit**; *p.p.* **bitten**) cut into or nip with the teeth, take (piece) *off* or *out* with the teeth; (of insect etc.) sting; snap *at*; penetrate, grip, have (desired) adverse effect; cause smarting pain (*biting wind*), be sharp or effective (*biting wit, sarcasm*); accept bait or enticement; (usu. in *passive*) infect *with* enthusiasm etc., swindle. **2** *n.* act of biting; wound or sting made by biting; mouthful of food; snack or light meal; taking of bait by fish; incisiveness, pungency. **3 bite per-**

son's head off respond fiercely or angrily. [OE]

bitter 1 *a.* having a sharp pungent taste, not sweet; feeling or causing anger or resentment; harsh, biting; virulent, relentless; piercingly cold. **2** *n.* bitter beer strongly flavoured with hops; (in *pl.*) liquor with bitter flavour (esp. of wormwood) used as additive in cocktails. **3 bitter-sweet** *a.* & *n.* sweet with bitter after-taste, woody nightshade; **to the bitter end** to the very end in spite of difficulties. [OE]

bittern /ˈbɪtɜːn/ *n.* kind of marsh bird allied to heron. [F *butor* f. L]

bitty *a.* made up of bits, scrappy. [BIT[1]]

bitumen /ˈbɪtjʊmɪn/ *n.* brown or black mixture of tarlike hydrocarbons derived from petroleum. [L]

bituminous /bɪˈtjuːmɪnəs/ *a.* of or like bitumen; **bituminous coal** coal burning with smoky flame and yielding pitch or tar.

bivalve /ˈbaɪvælv/ **1** *a.* having two valves or (of shellfish) a hinged double shell. **2** *n.* bivalve shellfish; oyster. [BI-]

bivouac /ˈbɪvʊæk/ **1** *n.* temporary open encampment without tents, esp. of soldiers. **2** *v.i.* **(-ck-)** make open camp, esp. overnight. [F prob. f. G]

biz *n. colloq.* business. [abbr.]

bizarre /bɪˈzɑː/ *a.* strange in appearance or effect, eccentric, grotesque. [F]

Bk *symb.* berkelium.

blab *v.* **(-bb-)** chatter, gossip; give away (secret) by indiscreet talk, confess. [imit.]

black 1 *a.* reflecting no light, colourless from lack of light (like coal or soot), completely dark; dark-skinned, **(Black)** of Negroes; (of sky etc.) dusky, heavily overcast; wicked, sinister, deadly; gloomy, depressed, sullen (*black look, mood*); portending trouble or difficulty (*things look black*); comic but with sinister import (*black humour*); (of goods etc.) declared untouchable by workers on strike. **2** *n.* black colour or pigment; black clothes or material (*dressed in black*); black ball or man in game, player of this; credit side of account (*in the black*); **(Black)** Negro. **3** *v.t.* make black; polish with blacking; declare (goods etc.) 'black'. **4 black and blue** discoloured from bruises; **black and white** writing or print (*in black and white*), (of film etc.) not in colour, *fig.* consisting of extremes only; **black art** = *black magic*; **black box** flight-recorder in aircraft; **Black Country** district of Midlands with heavy industry; **Black Death** see DEATH; **black eye** bruised skin round eye, resulting from blow; **black flag** flag of piracy; **Black Friar** Dominican; **black hole** *Astron.* region from which matter and radiation cannot escape; **black ice** thin hard transparent ice, esp. on road; **black magic** magic supposed to invoke evil powers; **Black Maria** police vehicle for transporting prisoners; **black mark** mark of discredit; **black market** illicit traffic in officially controlled or scarce commodities, place of this; **black mass** Requiem Mass, travesty of the Mass in worship of Satan; **Black Monk** Benedictine; **black out** effect black-out, on, undergo black-out; **black-out** *n.* extinguishing of lights and covering of windows etc. to conceal existence from enemy, temporary loss of power, radio reception etc., temporary suppression of information (*news black-out*), temporary loss of consciousness or failure of memory, sudden darkening of theatre stage; **black pepper** pepper made by grinding whole of dried berry including husk; **Black Power** movement seeking rights and political power for Blacks; **black pudding** sausage of dried blood, suet, etc.; **Black Rod** usher of Lord Chamberlain's Department, House of Lords, etc.; **black sheep** unsatisfactory member of family, group, etc., scoundrel; **black spot** place of danger or difficulty; **black tea** tea that is fully fermented before drying; **black tie** black bow-tie worn with dinner-jacket, designation of formal dress; **black velvet** mixture of stout and champagne; **Black Watch** Royal Highland Regiment, having dark tartan; **black widow** American spider, of which female devours male. [OE]

blackamoor /ˈblækəmʊə/ *n.* dark-skinned person, esp. Negro. [MOOR]

blackball *v.t.* reject (candidate, orig. with black ball) in ballot.

blackberry /ˈblækbərɪ/ *n.* dark edible fruit of bramble.

blackbird *n.* European bird of thrush family, of which male is largely black. [BLACK]

blackboard *n.* board with smooth usu. dark surface for writing on with chalk.

blackcap *n.* small songbird with black-topped head.

blackcock *n.* male black grouse.

blackcurrant /blækˈkʌrənt/ *n.* small dark edible berry; shrub on which it grows.

blacken *v.* make or become black; defame, slander.

blackguard /ˈblægɑːd/ **1** *n.* villain, scoundrel. **2** *a.* foul-mouthed, abusive. **3** *v.t.* abuse scurrilously. **4 blackguardly** *a.* [orig. = menial]

blackhead *n.* black-topped pimple on skin; bird with black head. [BLACK]
blacking *n.* black polish, esp. for shoes.
blacklead *n.* graphite.
blackleg 1 *n.* person who refuses to join strike or trade union. **2** *v.i.* act as blackleg.
blacklist 1 *n.* list of persons in disfavour. **2** *v.t.* put on blacklist.
blackmail 1 *n.* extortion of payment in return for not disclosing discreditable information, secret, etc.; payment extorted in this way; use of threats or moral pressure. **2** *v.t.* extort money etc. from by blackmail; threaten, coerce. [obs. *mail* rent]
blackshirt *n.* member of a Fascist organization. [BLACK]
blacksmith *n.* smith who works in iron.
blackthorn *n.* thorny shrub bearing white flowers and sloes.
bladder *n.* sac in bodies of humans and other animals for holding liquid, esp. that holding urine; inflated animal's bladder or bag resembling this; air-filled blister in seaweed etc. [OE]
blade *n.* cutting part of knife etc.; flat part of oar, propeller, etc.; flat narrow leaf esp. of grass and cereals; flat part of leaf; flat bone, esp. of shoulder. [OE]
blain *n.* inflamed sore, blister. [OE]
blame 1 *v.t.* assign fault or responsibility to; fix responsibility for (error or wrong) *on* person. **2** *n.* attribution of responsibility for error or wrong. **3 be to blame** deserve censure, be responsible *for*. **4 blameable** *a.*; **blameless** *a.*; **blameworthy** *a.* [F, rel. to BLASPHEME]
blanch /blɑːntʃ/ *v.* make white or pale by extracting colour; peel (almonds etc.) by scalding; deprive (plants) of light; immerse (vegetables) in boiling water; become pale with cold, fear, etc. [F (BLANK)]
blancmange /bləˈmɒnʒ/ *n.* sweet opaque jelly made with flavoured cornflour and milk. [F, = white food]
bland *a.* mild, feeble, insipid; tasteless, unstimulating; gentle in manner, suave. [L *blandus* smooth]
blandish /ˈblændɪʃ/ *v.t.* flatter, cajole; **blandishment** *n.* (usu. in *pl.*) [F f. L (prec.)]
blank 1 *a.* not written or printed on (*blank sheet*); with spaces left for details or signature (*blank form*); not filled (*blank space*); without interest, result, or expression (*she looked blank*); complete, unrelieved (*blank refusal*; *blank wall*). **2** *n.* unfilled space, esp. in document; document with blank spaces; empty area; dash written in place of word; = *blank cartridge*. **3** *v.t.* screen *off* or *out*. **4 blank cartridge** one without bullet, for sound only; **blank cheque** one with amount left for payee to fill in, *fig.* complete authority; **blank verse** unrhymed verse, esp. iambic pentameters; **draw a blank** be unsuccessful, get no response. [F *blanc* white f. Gmc]
blanket /ˈblæŋkɪt/ **1** *n.* large woollen or fibre sheet for warmth, esp. as bedcovering; thick covering mass or layer (*blanket of fog*). **2** *a.* general, covering all cases or classes. **3** *v.t.* cover; suppress, keep quiet (scandal etc.). [F (prec.)]
blare 1 *v.* make loud sound like trumpet; utter or sound loudly. **2** *n.* blaring sound. [LG or Du., imit.]
blarney /ˈblɑːnɪ/ **1** *n.* empty or flattering talk; nonsense. **2** *v.* flatter, use blarney. [*Blarney*, castle near Cork]
blasé /ˈblɑːzeɪ/ *a.* bored or indifferent esp. through familiarity. [F]
blaspheme /blæsˈfiːm/ *v.* revile, speak profanely of (esp. sacred person or thing); talk impiously. [F f. eccl.L f. Gk *blasphēmeō*]
blasphemy /ˈblæsfəmɪ/ *n.* talk or act reviling sacred person or thing; depreciatory remark or act; **blasphemous** *a.*
blast /blɑːst/ **1** *n.* explosion, destructive wave of air from this; strong gust of air etc.; loud sound of instrument, car horn, etc.; sudden forcible criticism or reprimand. **2** *v.* blow up (esp. rock) with explosives; make blasting or explosive sound; blight (person or thing, or *absol.*; often = *may God blast*, or as *int.* of anger or annoyance); *colloq.* criticize forcibly. **3 (at) full blast** *colloq.* at full capacity or speed; **blast furnace** smelting furnace with heat intensified by hot air driven in; **blast off** take off from launching site; **blast-off** *n.* launching of rocket or space vehicle. [OE]
blasted 1 *a.* annoying, hateful (*blasted nuisance*). **2** *adv.* extremely (*blasted cold*).
blatant /ˈbleɪtənt/ *a.* flagrant, unashamed; loudly obtrusive. [coined by Spenser]
blather /ˈblæðə/ **1** *v.i.* chatter foolishly. **2** *n.* foolish talk. [ON]
blaze[1] **1** *n.* bright flame or fire; dramatic outburst of emotion etc.; brilliant display (*blaze of light, of publicity*). **2** *v.i.* burn or shine fiercely; show great feeling, esp. anger. **3 blaze away** fire gun continuously, work vigorously (*at*); **go to blazes**! go to hell! [OE, = torch]
blaze[2] **1** *n.* white mark on animal's face; mark chipped in bark of tree esp. to show route. **2** *v.t.* mark (tree or path) with blazes. **3 blaze a trail** show the way for others (*lit.* or *fig.*). [orig. uncert.]

blaze[3] *v.t.* proclaim. [LG or Du., rel. to BLOW]

blazer *n.* light jacket, esp. with colours as part of uniform. [BLAZE[1]]

blazon /'bleɪz(ə)n/ **1** *n.* heraldic shield, coat of arms. **2** *v.t.* proclaim; adorn ornamentally; describe or paint (coat of arms). **3 blazonment** *n.*; **blazonry** *n.* [F, orig. = shield]

bleach 1 *v.* make or become white or pale in sunlight or by chemical process. **2** *n.* bleaching substance or process. **3 bleaching-powder** chloride of lime. [OE]

bleak *a.* exposed, wind-swept; dreary, grim. [ON]

bleary /'blɪərɪ/ *a.* filmy, seeing dimly (*bleary-eyed*); indistinct. [LG]

bleat 1 *v.* utter cry of sheep, goat, or calf; say or speak feebly or plaintively. **2** *n.* bleating cry. [OE]

bleed 1 *v.* (*past* and *p.p.* **bled**) emit blood; draw blood from; suffer wounds or death *for* a cause; be sorrowful (*my heart bleeds*); *colloq.* extort money from; emit sap, juice, etc.; (of dye) come out in water; empty (system) of excess air or fluid. **2** *n.* act of bleeding. [OE (BLOOD)]

bleeder *n.* haemophiliac; *derog. sl.* person.

bleeding *a.* & *adv. vulgar* expressing annoyance or antipathy.

bleep 1 *v.i.* emit intermittent high-pitched sound. **2** *n.* such sound. [imit.]

blemish /'blemɪʃ/ **1** *v.t.* spoil the beauty or perfection of, mar. **2** *n.* flaw, defect, stain. [F]

blench *v.i.* flinch, quail. [OE]

blend 1 *v.* mix (various sorts) into required sort; merge or mingle *with*; become one; (of colours etc.) pass imperceptibly into each other, harmonize. **2** *n.* mixture from various sorts. [ON]

blende /blend/ *n.* native zinc sulphide. [G]

blender *n.* device for blending soft or liquid foods. [BLEND]

blenny /'blenɪ/ *n.* small sea-fish with spiny fins and slimy scales. [L f. Gk *blennos* mucus]

bless *v.t.* invoke divine favour on, esp. by making sign of cross over; consecrate (food etc.); glorify (God); attribute one's good luck to (stars etc.); make happy or successful (*blessed with children*); **bless me** *int.* of surprise, dismay, etc.; **bless you** *int.* of endearment etc., or said to person who has sneezed. [OE]

blessed /'blesɪd/ *predic. a.* holy; beatified; *iron. sl.* cursed.

blessing *n.* invocation of divine favour; grace before or after meal; benefit or advantage (*blessing in disguise*).

blether var. of BLATHER.

blew *past* of BLOW.

blight /blaɪt/ **1** *n.* disease of plants caused esp. by insects; such insect; obscure harmful or destructive force; unsightly or neglected urban area. **2** *v.t.* affect with blight; harm, destroy; spoil. [orig. unkn.]

blighter *n. colloq.* contemptible or annoying person.

Blighty /'blaɪtɪ/ *n. Mil. sl.* home (esp. Britain) after service abroad; wound ensuring return home. [Hind., = foreign]

blimey /'blaɪmɪ/ *int.* of astonishment, disappointment, etc. [(*God*) *blind me*]

blimp *n.* small non-rigid airship; soundproof cover for cine-camera; (**Blimp,** in full **Colonel Blimp,** after cartoon character) reactionary person, diehard. [orig. uncert.]

blind /blaɪnd/ **1** *a.* lacking power of sight; preventing or lacking direct observation (*blind corner, flying*); without adequate knowledge, information, or foresight; unable or unwilling to appreciate factor or circumstance (*blind to all his faults*); reckless (*blind hitting*); not governed by purpose (*blind forces*); concealed; closed at one end; *sl.* drunk. **2** *v.* deprive of sight; overwhelm with bright light; beguile so as to deprive of judgement, overawe (*blinded them with science*); *sl.* go recklessly. **3** *n.* anything that prevents sight or obstructs light; screen for window, awning; misleading thing or person. **4** *adv.* blindly (*flying blind*). **5 blind alley** alley closed at one end, fruitless plan or undertaking; **blind date** social engagement between man and woman who have not previously met; **blind spot** insensitive point in retina, area where vision or understanding is lacking; **turn a blind eye to** pretend not to notice. [OE]

blindfold 1 *a.* & *adv.* with the eyes covered; without care or attention. **2** *n.* covering for eyes to prevent person from seeing. **3** *v.t.* cover eyes of (person) with blindfold. [orig. *blindfelled* = struck blind]

blind-man's buff /'bʌf/ game in which blindfold player tries to catch others who push him about. [obs. *buff* = buffet]

blindworm *n.* slow-worm. [BLIND]

blink 1 *v.* move eyelids quickly down and up; look with eyes opening and shutting; shut the eyes for a moment; give off unsteady or intermittent light. **2** *n.* blinking movement; momentary gleam of light. **3 blink at** ignore, shirk; **on the blink** *sl.* out of order. [Du., var. of BLENCH]

blinker *n.* one of two small screens on bridle preventing horse from seeing to side; device that blinks.

blinking *a.* & *adv. sl.* expressing mild annoyance or antipathy.

blip 1 *n.* small spot or image on radar screen; quick popping sound. 2 *v.i.* make blip. [imit.]

bliss *n.* utter joy or happiness; being in heaven; **blissful** *a.*; **blissfully** *adv.* [OE]

blister 1 *n.* small bubble on skin filled with watery fluid, caused by heat or friction; similar swelling on other surface. 2 *v.* come up in blisters; raise blister on; *fig.* attack sharply. [orig. uncert.]

blithe /blaɪð/ *a.* joyous, gay, carefree; casual. [OE]

blithering /ˈblɪðərɪŋ/ *a. colloq.* utter, hopeless (*blithering idiot*); talking senselessly. [BLATHER]

blithesome /ˈblaɪðsəm/ *a.* blithe, gay. [BLITHE]

B.Litt. *abbr.* Bachelor of Letters. [L *Baccalaureus Litterarum*]

blitz /blɪts/ 1 *n.* sudden intensive attack; (**Blitz**) German air raids on Britain in 1940. 2 *v.t.* inflict blitz on; attack overwhelmingly. [abbr. of foll.]

blitzkrieg /ˈblɪtskri:g/ *n.* intensive campaign of war intended to bring about swift victory. [G, = lightning war]

blizzard /ˈblɪzəd/ *n.* severe snowstorm. [orig. unkn.]

bloat *v.* swell, inflate; cure by salting and smoking slightly. [ON]

bloated *a.* inflated, overfed, pampered; (of fish) cured by bloating.

bloater *n.* bloated herring.

blob *n.* small drop or spot. [imit.]

bloc *n.* combination of countries, parties, or groups sharing common purpose or policy. [F, = foll.]

block 1 *n.* large solid piece of wood, stone, or other hard material; this as base, esp. for chopping or beheading; stand for mounting horse; *sl.* head; large building, esp. when subdivided (*block of flats*); group of buildings between streets; obstruction; large quantity as unit, *attrib.* made or regarded as large unit (*block booking*); piece of wood or metal engraved for printing; pulley mounted in case. 2 *v.t.* obstruct, impede; restrict use of; stop (cricket ball) with bat defensively; sketch *in* or *out* roughly. 3 **block and tackle** system of pulleys and ropes, esp. for lifting; **block diagram** diagram showing general arrangement of parts; **block letter** separate capital letter; **block system** system by which train may only enter section if it is clear; **block up** confine, enclose; **block vote** vote proportional in size to number of persons voter represents; **mental block** mental inability due to subconscious factors. [F f. LG or Du.]

blockade /blɒˈkeɪd/ 1 *n.* surrounding or blocking of a place by enemy to prevent entry and exit. 2 *v.t.* subject to blockade.

blockage *n.* obstruction, blocked-up state.

block-buster *n. sl.* highly destructive bomb; thing of great power.

blockhead *n.* stupid person.

blockhouse *n.* reinforced concrete shelter; small fort built of squared logs.

bloke *n. colloq.* man, fellow. [Shelta]

blond (of woman usu. **blonde**) 1 *a.* having golden or pale-coloured hair, flaxen; of fair complexion. 2 *n.* blond person, esp. woman. [F f. L *blondus* yellow]

blood /blʌd/ 1 *n.* liquid, usu. red, circulating in arteries and veins of animals; taking of life; passion, temperament; race, descent, parentage (*blue blood*; *new blood*); relationship, relations, kindred; dandy. 2 *v.t.* give (hound) first taste of blood; initiate (person). 3 **blood-and-thunder** melodrama; **blood bank** place where supply of blood for transfusion is stored; **blood-bath** massacre; **blood count** number of corpuscles in quantity of person's blood; **blood-curdling** horrifying; **blood donor** one who gives blood for transfusion; **blood group** any of types of human blood as regards compatibility in transfusion; **blood-heat** ordinary temperature of healthy human blood, about 37°C (98°F); **blood-letting** surgical removal of blood; **blood-money** money paid to next of kin of person killed, money paid to killer; **blood orange** orange with red-streaked pulp; **blood-poisoning** poisoning due to bacteria in blood; **blood pressure** varying pressure of blood in vessels, measured for diagnosis; **blood-relation** one related by birth; **blood sport** sport involving wounding or killing of animals; **blood-stained** stained with blood, guilty of bloodshed; **blood test** examination of blood esp. for diagnosis; **blood-vessel** vein, artery, or capillary, carrying blood; **in cold blood** deliberately, without passion; **in one's blood** inherent in one's character; **make one's blood boil** infuriate one; **make one's blood run cold** horrify one. [OE]

bloodhound *n.* large keen-scented dog used in tracking.

bloodless *a.* without blood or bloodshed; pale, unemotional; feeble.

bloodshed *n.* shedding of blood; slaughter.

bloodshot *a.* (of eyeball) tinged with blood.

bloodstream *n.* blood in circulation.

bloodsucker *n.* leech; extortioner.
bloodthirsty *a.* eager for bloodshed.
bloody 1 *a.* of, like, running or smeared with blood; involving bloodshed; cruel, bloodthirsty; *sl.* expressing annoyance or antipathy (*bloody fool*), or as intensive (*not a bloody one*). **2** *adv. sl.* extremely (*bloody awful*). **3** *v.t.* (*past* and *p.p.* **bloodied**) stain with blood.
bloody-minded *a. colloq.* deliberately unco-operative, wilfully awkward.
bloom 1 *n.* flower, esp. of plant valued chiefly for this; flowering state (*in bloom*); one's prime; freshness; flush, glow; powdery deposit on fruit and leaves. **2** *v.i.* bear blooms, be in bloom; be in one's prime, flourish. [ON]
bloomer[1] *n.* flower regarded as blooming; *sl.* blunder.
bloomer[2] *n.* long rounded loaf with diagonal marks on top. [orig. uncert.]
bloomers *n.pl.* loose knee-length trousers formerly worn by women; *colloq.* knickers. [Mrs A. *Bloomer*, originator]
blooming *a.* & *adv.* in bloom; *sl.* expressing mild annoyance or antipathy. [BLOOM]
blossom /ˈblɒsəm/ **1** *n.* flower or mass of flowers, esp. of fruit-tree; early stage of growth. **2** *v.i.* open into blossom; mature, thrive. [OE]
blot 1 *n.* small stain, esp. of ink; blemish; act or quality bringing censure. **2** *v.t.* (**-tt-**) make blot on, stain; dry with blotting-paper. **3 blot one's copy-book** mar reputation by small mistake; **blot out** obliterate, remove from view, obscure; **blotting-paper** absorbent paper for drying wet ink. [prob. Scand.]
blotch 1 *n.* inflamed or discoloured patch on skin; dab or stain. **2** *v.t.* cover with blotches. **3 blotchy** *a.* [obs. *plotch*, BLOT]
blotter *n.* pad of blotting-paper. [BLOT]
blotto /ˈblɒtəʊ/ *a. sl.* very drunk. [orig. uncert.]
blouse /blaʊz/ *n.* garment like shirt, worn by women; jacket forming part of military uniform. [F]
blow[1] /bləʊ/ **1** *v.* (*past* **blew** /bluː/; *p.p.* **blown** except as in 3) direct current of air (at) esp. from mouth; move rapidly, as the wind; puff, pant; sound (wind instrument), (of instrument) make sound; send out by breathing (*blew a bubble*); (of fuse, tyre, etc.) break or burst suddenly, cause (fuse etc.) to break; drive or be driven by blowing (*door blew open*), *sl.* depart hurriedly; break into with explosives; send flying (*off* etc.) by explosion; shape (molten glass) by blowing; *sl.* reveal (secret etc.); *sl.* curse, confound (esp. as *int.*); *sl.* squander (money, chance, etc.), bungle; (of whale) eject air and water. **2** *n.* blowing, blast of air; exposure to fresh air. **3 be blowed if one will** *colloq.* be unwilling to; **blow-dry** style (hair) while drying it with blower; **blow-hole** hole for blowing or breathing through, escape for gas etc.; **blow hot and cold** vacillate; **blow in** break or drive inwards by explosion; **blow one's own trumpet** boast; **blow one's top** *sl.* lose one's temper; **blow out** extinguish by blowing, send outwards by explosion; **blow-out** *n.* explosion, forceful escape of liquid etc., bursting of tyre, breaking of fuse etc., *sl.* large meal; **blow over** pass away without great effect; **blow up** explode, inflate with air, *colloq.* enlarge (photograph), *colloq.* lose one's temper, reprove (person), *colloq.* arise, happen; **blow-up** *n.* explosion, *colloq.* enlargement of photograph. [OE]
blow[2] /bləʊ/ *n.* hard stroke with hand or weapon; sudden shock or misfortune; **blow-by-blow** relating details of happening in sequence. [orig. unkn.]
blower *n.* device for blowing; *sl.* telephone. [BLOW[1]]
blowfly *n.* fly that deposits eggs in meat, bluebottle.
blowlamp *n.* burner for directing very hot flame on small area.
blowpipe *n.* tube for blowing air through, esp. to increase heat of flame or to blow glass; tube as weapon to blow darts etc. through.
blowy /ˈbləʊɪ/ *a.* windy. [BLOW[1]]
blowzy /ˈblaʊzɪ/ *a.* coarse-looking, red-faced; dishevelled, slovenly. [obs. *blowze* beggar's wench]
blub *v.i.* (**-bb-**) sob. [foll.]
blubber 1 *n.* whale fat. **2** *v.* sob loudly, sob out (words). **3** *a.* swollen, thick. [prob. imit.]
bludgeon /ˈblʌdʒən/ **1** *n.* club with heavy end. **2** *v.t.* beat with bludgeon; coerce. [orig. unkn.]
blue /bluː/ **1** *a.* having the colour of a clear sky; sad, depressed (*feel blue*); depressing, gloomy; indecent (*blue film*); politically conservative. **2** *n.* blue colour or pigment; blue clothes or material (*dressed in blue*); one who has represented a university in sport, esp. at Oxford or Cambridge; supporter of Conservative party; (in *pl.*) bout of depression, slow melancholy music of Amer. Black origin. **3** *v.t.* (*partic.* **blueing**) make blue; *colloq.* squander. **4 blue baby** one with congenital blueness of skin from heart defect; **blue blood** noble birth; **blue book** report issued by Parliament or Privy Council; **blue cheese** cheese produced with veins of blue fungus; **blue-collar** of manual or unskilled work; **blue-eyed boy** *colloq.*

favourite; **blue-pencil** correct or edit (with blue pencil); **Blue Peter** blue flag with white square raised when ship leaves port; **blue ribbon** high honour; **blue tit** tit with blue wings and markings; **blue whale** rorqual with dark blue body, largest known living animal; **once in a blue moon** very rarely; **out of the blue** unexpected(ly). [F f. Gmc]

bluebell *n.* plant with blue bell-shaped flowers.

bluebottle *n.* large buzzing fly with blue body.

blueprint *n.* photographic print of plans with white on blue ground; *fig.* detailed plan.

bluestocking *n.* intellectual or literary woman. [18th-c. Blue Stocking Society]

bluff[1] 1 *v.* deceive or mislead by a pretence, to secure advantage. **2** *n.* act of bluffing. **3 call person's bluff** challenge him as bluffing. [Du. *bluffen* brag]

bluff[2] 1 *a.* having vertical or steep broad front; frank, abrupt in manner. **2** *n.* high steep cliff or headland. [orig. unkn.]

bluish /'blu:ɪʃ/ *a.* fairly blue. [BLUE]

blunder 1 *v.* make serious mistake, mismanage; stumble, move about clumsily. **2** *n.* serious or foolish mistake. [prob. Scand.]

blunderbuss /'blʌndəbʌs/ *n.* disused type of short gun with large bore. [Du. *donderbus* thunder gun]

blunt 1 *a.* lacking sharp edge or point, not sharp; dull, insensitive; outspoken, abrupt. **2** *v.t.* make blunt or less sharp. [prob. Scand.]

blur 1 *v.* (**-rr-**) make or become less distinct; smear. **2** *n.* thing seen or heard indistinctly; smear. [perh. rel. to BLEARY]

blurb *n.* description of book, esp. as promotion by publishers. [coined by G. Burgess 1907]

blurt *v.t.* (usu. with *out*) utter tactlessly or thoughtlessly. [imit.]

blush 1 *v.i.* develop pink tinge in face from embarrassment or shame, (of face) redden thus; be ashamed or embarrassed (*I blush to think of it*); redden. **2** *n.* blushing of face; pink tinge or glow. [OE]

bluster 1 *v.i.* behave noisily or boisterously; (of wind etc.) blow fiercely. **2** *n.* noisy self-assertive talk, threats. **3 blustery** *a.* [imit.]

BM *abbr.* Bachelor of Medicine; British Museum.

B.Mus. *abbr.* Bachelor of Music.

BO *abbr. colloq.* body odour.

boa /'bəʊə/ *n.* large S. American snake that kills its prey by crushing it; woman's long furry wrap; **boa constrictor** Brazilian species of boa, python. [L]

boar *n.* male wild pig; uncastrated male pig. [OE]

board 1 *n.* flat thin piece of sawn timber, usu. long and narrow; material resembling this, made of compressed fibres; flat piece of wood or other firm substance used in games, for posting notices, etc.; thick stiff card used in bookbinding; provision of meals usu. in return for payment (*board and lodging*); directors of company or other official group meeting together (*board of examiners*); council table; (in *pl.*) theatre stage, acting profession; side of ship. **2** *v.* go on board (ship or aircraft etc.); cover or close *up* with boards; provide or receive meals, usu. for payment. **3 boarding-house** house providing board and lodging; **boarding-school** school providing board and lodging for pupils; **board out** send away from home to receive board and lodging; **go by the board** be discarded or neglected; **on board** on or into ship, aircraft, oil rig, etc. [OE]

boarder *n.* pupil who boards at boarding-school; one who boards a ship, esp. as enemy.

boardroom *n.* room in which board of directors etc. regularly meet.

boast 1 *v.* declare one's achievements or abilities with indulgent pride and satisfaction; own with pride (*boasts a Mercedes*). **2** *n.* act of boasting; thing one is proud of. [AF]

boastful *a.* given to boasting.

boat 1 *n.* small vessel propelled on water by oars, engine, or sails, *loosely* a ship (*travelling by boat*); dish in shape of open boat. **2** *v.i.* go in boat, esp. for pleasure. **3 boat-hook** long pole with hook and spike at end, for moving boats; **boat-house** shed at water's edge for housing boat; **boat-train** train timed to meet or go on boat; **in the same boat** sharing same adverse circumstances; **miss the boat** lose one's opportunity; **rock the boat** disturb equilibrium. [OE]

boater *n.* flat-topped straw hat with brim.

boatman *n.* one who conveys by boat or hires out boats.

boatswain /'bəʊs(ə)n/ *n.* ship's officer in charge of crew and ship's rigging etc.

bob[1] 1 *v.* (**-bb-**) move quickly up and down; bounce buoyantly *back* or *up*; cut (hair) short. **2** *n.* jerking or bouncing movement, esp. upward; hair cut short; horse's docked tail; weight on pendulum etc. **3 bob up** appear or reappear suddenly. [imit.]

bob[2] *n.* (*pl.* same) *sl.* former shilling (now = 5 pence). [orig. unkn.]

bob[3] *n.* now only in **bob's your uncle**

int. expressing completion or success. [pet-form of *Robert*]
bobbin /'bɒbɪn/ *n.* cylinder holding spool of thread, esp. in weaving and machine sewing. [F]
bobble /'bɒb(ə)l/ *n.* small woolly ball as ornament. [dimin. of BOB[1]]
bobby /'bɒbɪ/ *n. colloq.* policeman. [Sir *Robert* Peel]
bob-sled *n.* = BOB-SLEIGH. [BOB[1]]
bob-sleigh *n.* sleigh with two sets of runners in line and body of wood, metal, or plastic.
bobtail *n.* docked tail; horse or dog with bobtail.
Boche /bɒʃ/ *n. sl. derog.* German, esp. soldier. [F]
bod *n. colloq.* person. [BODY]
bode *v.* be a sign of, portend; **bode ill** (or **well**) be a bad (or good) sign. [OE]
bodega /bə'di:gə/ *n.* cellar or shop selling wine. [Sp.]
bodice /'bɒdɪs/ *n.* part of woman's dress above waist; woman's undergarment like vest. [orig. *pair of bodies*]
bodiless /'bɒdɪlɪs/ *a.* lacking (a) body. [BODY]
bodily /'bɒdɪlɪ/ **1** *a.* of or concerning the body. **2** *adv.* as a whole; as regards the body, in person.
bodkin /'bɒdkɪn/ *n.* blunt thick needle for drawing tape etc. through hem. [orig. uncert.]
body /'bɒdɪ/ **1** *n.* physical structure, including bones, flesh and organs, of man or animal (whether dead or alive); corpse; trunk apart from head and limbs; main or central part of thing; group of persons regarded as unit (*governing body*); *colloq.* person; substance (*body of water*); piece of matter (*heavenly body*); bulk, quantity; solid quantity, substantial flavour, tone, etc. (*wine, orchestra, has plenty of body*). **2** *v.t.* give body or substance to. **3 body-blow** severe set-back; **body odour** smell of human body, esp. when unpleasant; **body politic** nation or State as corporate body; **body stocking** woman's undergarment covering trunk and legs; **in a body** all together; **keep body and soul together** struggle to remain alive. [OE]
bodyguard *n.* person or group of persons escorting and guarding dignitary etc.
bodywork *n.* structure of vehicle body.
Boer /'bəʊə, 'bʊə/ **1** *n.* South African of Dutch descent. **2** *a.* of Boers. [Du., = farmer]
boffin /'bɒfɪn/ *n. colloq.* person engaged in scientific research. [orig. unkn.]
bog 1 *n.* wet spongy ground, morass; *sl.* lavatory. **2** *v.t.* (**-gg-**; usu. in *pass.* with *down*) submerge in bog (*lit. & fig.*). **3 boggy** *a.* [Ir. or Gael. *bogach*]
bogey /'bəʊgɪ/ *n.* par or one more than par on a hole in golf. [perh. BOGY as imaginary player]
boggle /'bɒg(ə)l/ *v.i.* be startled or baffled; hesitate, demur (*about* or *at*). [dial., = BOGY]
bogie /'bəʊgɪ/ *n.* wheeled undercarriage pivoted below locomotive etc. [orig. unkn.]
bogus /'bəʊgəs/ *a.* spurious, sham. [orig. unkn.]
bogy /'bəʊgɪ/ *n.* evil spirit, devil, goblin; awkward thing or circumstance. [orig. (*Old*) *Bogey* the Devil]
bogyman *n.* person causing fear or difficulty.
Bohemian /bəʊ'hi:mɪən/ **1** *a.* socially unconventional; of Bohemia, Czech. **2** *n.* Bohemian person, esp. artist. **3 bohemianism** *n.* [*Bohemia*, mod. Czechoslovakia]
boil[1] 1 *v.* bubble up, of liquid reaching temperature at which it gives off vapour or of its vessel; cook or be cooked in boiling liquid, bring to boiling-point; subject to heat of boiling liquid; (of sea etc.) be disturbed like boiling liquid; be disturbed or agitated, esp. with anger. **2** *n.* act or point of boiling. **3 boil down to** amount to essentially; **boiling-point** temperature at which a liquid begins to boil, great excitement; **boil over** spill over in boiling, lose one's temper. [F f. L *bullio* bubble *v.*]
boil[2] *n.* inflamed pus-filled swelling under skin. [OE]
boiler *n.* fuel-burning apparatus for heating hot-water supply; tank for heating water or turning it into steam; vessel for boiling things (e.g. clothes) in. [BOIL[1]]
boiling *a. colloq.* very hot.
boisterous /'bɔɪstərəs/ *a.* lively, noisily exuberant, rowdy; rough, stormy (*boisterous wind*). [orig. unkn.]
bold /bəʊld/ *a.* confidently assertive, adventurous, courageous; impudent; distinct or vivid (*bold colour, relief*); **be** (or **make**) **so bold as to** presume, venture, to. [OE]
bole *n.* stem or trunk of tree. [ON]
bolero /bə'leərəʊ/ *n.* (*pl.* **boleros**) Spanish dance or the music for it; /also 'bɒlərəʊ/ woman's short open jacket. [Sp.]
boll /bəʊl/ *n.* round seed-vessel of cotton, flax, etc. [Du.]
bollard /'bɒlɑ:d/ *n.* short post in road, esp. on traffic island; post on ship or quay for securing rope. [perh. rel. to BOLE]

bollocks var. of BALLOCKS.
boloney /bəˈləʊnɪ/ *n. sl.* nonsense. [orig. uncert.]
Bolshevik /ˈbɒlʃɪvɪk/ **1** *n. hist.* member of radical faction of Russian socialist party becoming communist party in 1918; Russian communist; *loosely* any radical socialist. **2** *a.* of Bolsheviks; communist. **3 Bolshevism** *n.*; **Bolshevist** *n.* [Russ. = member of majority]
Bolshie /ˈbɒlʃɪ/ (also **Bolshy**) *sl.* **1** *a.* uncooperative, awkward; bad-tempered; left-wing. **2** *n.* Bolshevik. [abbr.]
bolster /ˈbəʊlstə/ **1** *n.* long pillow across bed; pad or support. **2** *v.* support with bolster; aid, prop *up*. [OE]
bolt[1] /bəʊlt/ **1** *n.* sliding bar and socket to fasten door; large metal pin with head used with nut to hold things together; act of bolting; discharge of lightning; arrow shot from crossbow. **2** *v.* fasten (door) with bolt, keep (person etc.) *in* or *out* by bolting door; fasten together with bolts; gulp down (food) unchewed; dash off suddenly, (of horse) escape from control; run to seed. **3** *adv.* rigidly, now usu. in **bolt upright. 4 bolt from the blue** complete surprise; **bolt-hole** *fig.* means of escape; **shoot one's bolt** do all in one's power. [OE]
bolt[2] /bəʊlt/ *v.t.* sift; investigate. [F]
bomb /bɒm/ **1** *n.* container with explosive, incendiary, or other contents for explosion when dropped or thrown or by time mechanism or remote control; *the* atomic or hydrogen bomb. **2** *v.t.* attack with bombs; throw or drop bombs on. **3 like a bomb** *colloq.* very successfully. [F ult. f. Gk *bombos* hum]
bombard /bɒmˈbɑːd/ *v.t.* attack with heavy guns or bombs; subject to persistent questioning or abuse; *Physics* direct stream of high-speed particles on; **bombardment** *n.* [F f. L (prec.)]
bombardier /bɒmbəˈdɪə/ *n.* non-commissioned officer in artillery; *US* person in aircraft who releases bombs.
bombast /ˈbɒmbæst/ *n.* pompous or extravagant language; **bombastic** /-ˈbæstɪk/ *a.* [earlier *bombace* cotton wool]
Bombay duck dried fish eaten as relish, esp. with curry. [corrupt. of *bombil*, native name of fish]
bombazine /ˈbɒmbəziːn/ *n.* twilled worsted dress-material. [F f. L f. Gk (*bombux* silk)]
bomber /ˈbɒmə/ *n.* aircraft used to drop bombs; person using bombs, esp. illegally. [BOMB]
bombshell *n.* overwhelming surprise or disappointment.
bona fide /bəʊnə ˈfaɪdɪ/ in good faith, genuine. [L]
bonanza /bəˈnænzə/ *n.* source of wealth or prosperity; large output of gold-mine etc. [Sp., = fair weather]
bon-bon *n.* sweet. [F (*bon* good)]
bond 1 *n.* thing or force that unites or (usu. in *pl.*) restrains; binding agreement; deed binding person to pay specified sum of money; certificate issued by government or company promising to repay borrowed sum and any interest; *Chem.* linkage of atoms in molecule. **2** *v.t.* hold or tie together; connect or reinforce with bond; place (goods) in bond. **3 bond paper** high-quality writing-paper; **in bond** stored by Customs until duty is paid. [var. of BAND]
bondage *n.* slavery; confinement, subjection to constraint or influence. [AL, rel. to BONDMAN]
bonded *a.* stored in or for storing in bond (*bonded whisky, warehouse*). [BOND]
bondman *n.* (also **bondsman**) serf or slave. [OE *bonda* husbandman]
bone 1 *n.* any of hard pieces making up skeleton in vertebrates, (in *pl.*) skeleton, esp. as remains; substance of bones or material like it, thing made of it; (in *pl.*) essential part of thing (*the bare bones*). **2** *v.t.* remove bones from; stiffen with bone. **3 bone china** thin china made of clay mixed with bone ash; **bone-dry** completely dry; **bone idle** (or **lazy**) utterly idle, lazy; **bone of contention** subject of dispute; **bone-shaker** rickety old bicycle, car, etc.; **have a bone to pick** have cause for dispute *with*; **make no bones about** admit or allow without fuss; **to the bone** to the bare minimum. [OE]
bonfire *n.* large open-air fire; **Bonfire Night** 5 November. [BONE, FIRE]
bongo /ˈbɒŋgəʊ/ *n.* (*pl.* **bongos, -oes**) one of pair of small drums usu. held between knees and beaten with fingers. [Amer. Sp.]
bonhomie /ˈbɒnɒmiː/ *n.* geniality, good nature. [F]
bonkers /ˈbɒŋkəz/ *a. sl.* crazy. [orig. unkn.]
bonnet /ˈbɒnɪt/ *n.* outdoor head-dress tied with strings below chin, now worn esp. by babies; man's round brimless Scots cap; hinged cover over engine of motor vehicle. [F]
bonny /ˈbɒnɪ/ *a.* (chiefly *Sc.*) handsome, comely, healthy-looking; pleasant. [perh. f. F *bon* good]
bonsai /ˈbɒnsaɪ/ *n.* dwarf tree or shrub; art of growing these. [Jap.]
bonus /ˈbəʊnəs/ *n.* something paid or given in addition to normal amount; extra benefit. [L, = good]

bon voyage /bɔ̃ vɔrˈjɑːʒ/ expression of good wishes to someone beginning journey. [F]
bony *a.* of or like bone; thin with prominent bones; **boniness** *n.* [BONE]
bonze *n.* Buddhist priest, esp. in Japan. [F or Port. f. Jap.]
boo 1 *int.* expressing disapproval or contempt. **2** *n.* the sound *boo.* **3** *v.* utter boos, jeer at. [imit.]
boob *sl.* **1** *n.* silly mistake; foolish person; *sl.* woman's breast. **2** *v.i.* make silly mistake. [foll.]
booby *n.* foolish or childish person; **booby prize** one awarded to person coming last in contest; **booby trap** disguised exploding device triggered by unknowing victim, device to trick unsuspecting person. [Sp. *bobo*]
boodle /ˈbuːd(ə)l/ *n. sl.* money gained illicitly, esp. as bribe. [Du. *boedel* possessions]
book /bʊk/ **1** *n.* set of printed or written sheets bound at one edge with cover; literary composition intended for printing as book (*is working on her book*); bound set of blank sheets for writing or keeping records in; set of matches, tickets, cheques, etc., bound in form of book; main division of literary work or Bible; (in *pl.*) set of records or accounts; telephone directory (*I am in the book*); *colloq.* magazine; record of bets (*start a book*); libretto, script of play. **2** *v.* enter name of in book or list, bring charge against (*was booked for speeding*); engage (person) or reserve (seat etc.) in advance; make reservation (*no need to book*). **3** **book club** society providing members with specified books on special terms; **book-end** one of props at each end of row of standing books; **book in** register one's arrival, esp. at hotel; **book-plate** (ornamental) slip pasted in book with owner's name; **book token** voucher exchangeable for books of given value; **bring to book** demand an explanation from; **by the book** strictly in accordance with regulations; **in person's good** (or **bad**) **books** in (or out of) favour with him; **the good Book** the Bible; **throw the book at** charge or punish to the utmost. [OE]
bookbinder *n.* one who binds books, esp. professionally; **bookbinding** *n.*
bookcase *n.* case or cabinet with shelves for holding books.
bookie /ˈbʊkɪ/ *n. colloq.* bookmaker. [abbr.]
bookish *a.* fond of reading; having knowledge based only on reading. [BOOK]
bookkeeper *n.* one who keeps accounts, esp. professionally; **bookkeeping** *n.*
booklet /ˈbʊklɪt/ *n.* small book, usu. with paper cover.
bookmaker *n.* professional taker of bets; **bookmaking** *n.*
bookmark *n.* strip of card, leather, etc., inserted in book to mark reader's place.
bookseller *n.* dealer in books.
bookshop *n.* shop selling books.
bookstall *n.* stall or stand selling books.
bookworm *n.* person devoted to reading; larva that feeds on paper etc. in books.
Boolean /ˈbuːlɪən/ *a.* (esp. in **Boolean algebra**) of system using algebraic notation to represent propositions in logic. [*Boole*, mathematician]
boom[1] **1** *n.* deep resonant sound. **2** *v.i.* make or speak with boom. [imit.]
boom[2] **1** *n.* period of prosperity or sudden activity in commerce. **2** *v.i.* be prosperous or very successful. **3** **boom town** one arising or flourishing from boom. [perh. prec.]
boom[3] *n.* long pole fixed at one end, to support bottom of sail, microphone, etc.; barrier across harbour. [Du., = BEAM]
boomerang /ˈbuːməræŋ/ **1** *n.* flat curved strip of wood usu. of kind that can be thrown so as to return to thrower, used esp. in Australia; idea that recoils unfavourably on originator. **2** *v.i.* (of idea) recoil on originator. [Abor.]
boon[1] *n.* advantage or benefit, blessing. [ON]
boon[2] *a.* jolly, usu. in **boon companion.** [F *bon* f. L *bonus* good]
boor *n.* ill-mannered person. [LG or Du.]
boost 1 *v.t.* promote or increase reputation of (person or thing); *colloq.* push from below, increase, assist. **2** *n.* act or result of boosting. [orig. unkn.]
booster *n.* device for increasing power or voltage; auxiliary engine or rocket for initial acceleration; dose, injection, etc., increasing effect of earlier one.
boot[1] **1** *n.* outer covering for foot reaching above ankle; luggage compartment of motor car; *colloq.* firm kick, dismissal (*get, give, the boot*). **2** *v.t.* kick; *colloq.* dismiss forcefully (with *out*). **3** **put the boot in** kick brutally, act decisively against person. [ON]
boot[2] *n.* advantage, now only in **to boot** as well, in addition. [OE]
bootee /buːˈtiː/ *n.* soft shoe worn by a baby. [BOOT[1]]
booth /buːð/ *n.* small temporary structure of canvas, wood, etc., used esp. as market stall; enclosure or compartment for telephoning, voting, etc. [ON]
bootleg *a.* smuggled, illicit.
bootlegger *n.* illicit trader in liquor.
bootless *a.* unavailing. [BOOT[2]]

bootlicker *n.* toady.

booty /'bu:tɪ/ *n.* plunder gained esp. in war; prize, gain. [G]

booze *colloq.* **1** *n.* alcoholic drink; drinking of it (*on the booze*). **2** *v.i.* drink alcoholic liquor, esp. excessively. **3** **boozy** *a.* [Du.]

boozer *n. colloq.* (esp. excessive) drinker of alcoholic liquor; public house.

bop *n.* = BEBOP; **bopper** *n.* [abbr.]

boracic /bə'ræsɪk/ *a.* of borax; **boracic acid** boric acid. [BORAX]

borage /'bɒrɪdʒ/ *n.* plant with blue flowers and hairy leaves, used in salads. [F f. L f. Arab.]

borax /'bɔ:ræks/ *n.* a salt used in making glass and china and as antiseptic. [F ult. f. Pers.]

Bordeaux /bɔ:'dəʊ/ *n.* red or white wine from Bordeaux district of France.

border **1** *n.* edge or boundary or part near it; line separating two countries, district on each side of it; ornamental or strengthening strip round edge. **2** *v.* provide with border; be border to; (usu. with *on*) adjoin, be like, come close to being. **3** **the Border** esp. that between England and Scotland. [F f. Gmc, rel. to BOARD]

borderer *n.* one who lives near a border.

borderland *n.* district near border; condition between two extremes; area for debate.

borderline **1** *n.* line marking boundary (esp. *fig.*). **2** *a.* on the borderline; only just acceptable.

bore[1] **1** *v.* make (a hole) esp. with a revolving tool; drill (shaft of well); make hole (in) thus, hollow out (tube). **2** *n.* hollow of gun barrel or of cylinder in internal-combustion engine; diameter of this; deep hole made esp. to find water. [OE]

bore[2] **1** *v.t.* weary by tedious talk or dullness. **2** *n.* dull or tiresome person or thing. [orig. unkn.]

bore[3] *n.* high tidal wave rushing up estuary. [Scand.]

bore[4] *past* of BEAR[1].

boredom /'bɔ:dəm/ *n.* state of being bored. [BORE[2]]

boric acid /'bɔ:rɪk/ an acid derived from borax, used as antiseptic. [BORON]

born *a.* existing as a result of birth; of natural quality or ability (*a born leader*); destined *to do* thing (*born to lead men*); of certain status by birth (*French-born, well-born*); **born of** owing origin to. [p.p. of BEAR[1]]

borne **1** *p.p.* of BEAR[1]. **2** *a.* with prefixed noun in sense 'carried or transported by' (*airborne*). [BEAR[1]]

boron /'bɔ:rɒn/ *n.* a non-metallic solid element. [BORAX, after *carbon*]

borough /'bʌrə/ *n. hist.* town with municipal corporation conferred by royal charter, town represented in House of Commons; town or district granted status of borough. [OE]

borrow /'bɒrəʊ/ *v.* acquire temporarily with promise or intention of returning; obtain money thus; use (invention, idea, etc.) originated by another, plagiarize. [OE]

Borstal /'bɔ:st(ə)l/ *n.* institution for reforming and training young offenders. [*Borstal* in Kent]

bortsch /bɔ:tʃ/ *n.* Russian beetroot and cabbage soup. [Russ.]

borzoi /'bɔ:zɔɪ/ *n.* large hound with narrow head and silky coat. [Russ., = swift]

bosh *n.* & *int. sl.* nonsense. [Turk., = empty]

bos'n /'bəʊs(ə)n/ *contr.* of BOATSWAIN.

bosom /'bʊz(ə)m/ *n.* person's (esp. woman's) breast; enclosing space formed by breast and arms; emotional centre (*bosom of one's family*); part of dress covering breast; **bosom friend** intimate friend. [OE]

boss[1] *colloq.* **1** *n.* employer or manager, supervisor. **2** *v.t.* control, give orders to; order person *about*. [Du. *baas*]

boss[2] *n.* protuberance, round knob or stud esp. on centre of shield; *Archit.* ornamental projection where ribs of vault cross. [F]

boss-eyed *a.* cross-eyed, blind in one eye; crooked. [*boss* = bad shot, orig. unkn.]

bossy *a. colloq.* domineering; **bossiness** *n.* [BOSS[1]]

bosun, bo'sun /'bəʊs(ə)n/ *contr.* of BOATSWAIN.

botany /'bɒtənɪ/ *n.* science dealing with forms and classification of plants; **botanical** /bə'tænɪk(ə)l/ *a.*; **botanist** *n.* [F or L f. Gk (*botanē* plant)]

botch **1** *v.t.* bungle, do badly; patch clumsily. **2** *n.* bungled or spoilt work. [orig. unkn.]

both /bəʊθ/ **1** *a.* & *pron.* the two, not only one (*both boys, both the boys, both of the boys, are here; the boys are both here*). **2** *adv.* with equal truth in two cases (*both the boy and his sister are here; are both here and hungry*). [ON]

bother /'bɒðə/ **1** *v.* give trouble to, worry, disturb; take trouble (*to do* thing, *about*); be concerned *with*. **2** *n.* person or thing that bothers; minor nuisance. **3** *int.* expressing annoyance or impatience. [orig. unkn.]

botheration /bɒðə'reɪʃ(ə)n/ *n.* & *int. colloq.* bother.

bothersome /'bɒðəsəm/ *a.* causing bother.

bo-tree /'bəʊ-/ *n.* sacred Indian fig-tree. [Sinh.]

bottle /'bɒt(ə)l/ **1** *n.* container usu. of glass or plastic for storing liquid; amount that will fill it; baby's feeding-bottle; *sl.* courage. **2** *v.t.* seal or store in bottles or jars; (with *up*) confine, restrain (*lit.* & *fig.*). **3 bottle-green** dark green; **bottle-neck** point at which flow of traffic, production, etc., is constricted, narrow place; **bottle-party** one to which guests bring bottles of drink; **hit the bottle** *sl.* become drunk. [F f. med.L (BUTT¹)]

bottom /'bɒtəm/ **1** *n.* lowest part or point, part on which thing rests; buttocks; furthest point (*bottom of the garden*); less honourable end of table, class, etc.; ground below water of sea, lake, etc.; ship's keel or hull, ship; basis, origin; essential nature; seat of chair. **2** *a.* lowest, last. **3** *v.* provide with bottom; touch bottom (of), find extent of; (usu. with *out*) reach lowest level. **4 at bottom** basically; **be at the bottom of** be basic cause of; **bottom drawer** woman's clothes etc. stored ready for marriage; **bottoms up!** call to drain one's glass; **get to the bottom of** find real cause of. [OE]

bottomless *a.* without bottom; inexhaustible.

botulism /'bɒtjʊlɪz(ə)m/ *n.* poisoning by bacillus in inadequately preserved food. [G f. L *botulus* sausage]

bouclé /'bu:kleɪ/ *n.* yarn with looped or curled strands; tufted fabric made from it. [F, = curled]

boudoir /'bu:dwɑ:/ *n.* woman's private room. [F (*bouder* sulk)]

bougainvillaea /bu:gən'vɪlɪə/ *n.* tropical plant with large coloured bracts. [*Bougainville*, navigator]

bough /baʊ/ *n.* one of main branches of tree. [OE]

bought *past* and *p.p.* of BUY.

bouillon /'bu:jɒn/ *n.* thin clear broth. [F (*bouillir* boil)]

boulder /'bəʊldə/ *n.* large stone worn smooth by weather or water. [Scand.]

boulevard /'bu:ləvɑ:d/ *n.* broad street usu. lined with trees; *US* broad main road. [F f. G]

boult var. of BOLT².

bounce 1 *v.* rebound, cause to rebound; *sl.* (of cheque) be returned by bank when there are no funds to meet it; rush noisily *in* or *out*, *into* or *out of* (room). **2** *n.* rebounding power, rebound; boast, swagger; *colloq.* energy. **3 bouncy** *a.* [imit.]

bouncer *n.* bumper in cricket; *sl.* person employed to eject troublesome people from night-club etc.

bouncing *a.* big and healthy (usu. of baby).

bound¹ 1 *v.i.* spring or leap, move by leaps; (of ball etc.) recoil from wall or ground. **2** *n.* springy upward or forward movement; recoil of ball etc. [F *bondir* f. L (*bombus* hum)]

bound² 1 *n.* limit of territory; (usu. in *pl.*) limitation, restriction. **2** *v.t.* set bounds to, be boundary of. **3 beat the bounds** go in mass round parish boundary striking certain points with rods; **out of bounds** beyond permitted area. [F f. med.L]

bound³ *a.* ready to start or having started (*for* place); moving in specified direction (*northbound*). [ON, = ready]

bound⁴ *a.* constrained or required by law or duty; certain *to* (*bound to lose*); tied or fastened; **bound up with** closely associated with. [*p.p. of* BIND]

boundary /'baʊndərɪ/ *n.* line marking limit of land etc.; limit of field in cricket, hit to this scoring 4 or 6 runs. [BOUND²]

bounden /'baʊnd(ə)n/ *a. archaic* obligatory (*bounden duty*). [p.p. of BIND]

bounder *n. colloq.* cad. [BOUND¹]

boundless *a.* unlimited. [BOUND²]

bounteous /'baʊntɪəs/ *a. rhet.* freely bestowed. [F (BOUNTY)]

bountiful /'baʊntɪfʊl/ *a.* generous in giving. [foll.]

bounty /'baʊntɪ/ *n.* generosity in giving; gift; sum paid as official reward, esp. by State. [F f. L (*bonus* good)]

bouquet /bu:'keɪ/ *n.* bunch of flowers, esp. arranged for carrying at ceremony; perfume of wine; compliment, praise; **bouquet garni** small bag of mixed herbs for seasoning. [F (*bois* wood)]

bourbon /'bɜ:bən/ *n. US* whisky distilled from maize and rye. [*Bourbon* County, Kentucky]

bourgeois /'bʊəʒwɑ:/ **1** *a.* of or associated with the middle classes; conventional, materialistic. **2** *n.* bourgeois person. [F (BURGESS)]

bourgeoisie /bʊəʒwɑ:'zi:/ *n.* the middle classes, esp. regarded disfavourably.

bourn /bʊən/ *n.* small stream. [var. of BURN²]

bourse /bʊəs/ *n.* money-market, esp. (**Bourse**) stock exchange in Paris. [F (PURSE)]

bout *n.* spell or turn of an activity; attack *of* illness; boxing or wrestling match. [obs. *bought* bending]

boutique /bu:'ti:k/ *n.* small shop or department selling clothes and items of fashion. [F]

bouzouki /bu:'zu:kɪ/ *n.* Greek instrument like mandolin, with long thin neck and metal strings. [mod. Gk]

bovine /'bəʊvaɪn/ *a.* of or like ox or cow; dull, stupid. [L (*bos* ox)]

bow¹ /bəʊ/ **1** *n.* shallow curve or bend,

thing of this form; weapon with string stretched across ends of curved piece of wood etc., for shooting arrows; flexible stick with stretched horsehair etc. for playing violin etc.; ornamental knot with two loops, ribbon etc. so tied. **2** *v.t.* use bow on (violin etc., or *absol.*). **3 bow-legged** having bandy legs; **bow-tie** necktie for tying in double loop; **bow-window** curved bay window. [OE]

bow[2] /baʊ/ **1** *v.* incline head or body, esp. in assent or greeting; bend *down* or kneel in reverence or submission; cause (head etc.) to bend thus. **2** *n.* act of bowing. **3 bow and scrape** be obsequiously polite; **bow out** make formal exit; **take a bow** acknowledge applause. [OE]

bow[3] /baʊ/ *n.* (often in *pl.*) fore-end of boat or ship; rower nearest bow. [LG or Du., rel. to BOUGH]

bowdlerize /ˈbaʊdləraɪz/ *v.t.* expurgate (book or author); **bowdlerization** /-ˈzeɪʃ(ə)n/ *n.* [*Bowdler*, expurgator of Shakespeare]

bowel /ˈbaʊəl/ *n.* division of alimentary canal below stomach, intestine; (in *pl.*) innermost parts. [F f. L *botulus* sausage]

bower /ˈbaʊə/ *n.* arbour, leafy nook, summer-house; *poetic* inner room; **bower-bird** Australian bird-of-paradise that builds decorated runs; **bowery** *a.* [OE, = dwelling]

bowie /ˈbəʊɪ/ *n.* (in full **bowie knife**) kind of long hunting-knife. [*Bowie*, Amer. soldier]

bowl[1] /bəʊl/ *n.* hollow dish esp. for food or liquid; hollow part, esp. of tobacco-pipe or spoon; contents of bowl. [OE]

bowl[2] /bəʊl/ **1** *n.* hard heavy ball made with bias to run in curve; (in *pl.*) game with these on grass. **2** *v.* play bowls; roll (ball); (in cricket) deliver (ball), dismiss (batsman) by delivering ball that hits wicket, put (batsman or side) *out*; move *along* rapidly, esp. in car etc. **3 bowling-alley** one of series of enclosed channels for playing skittles, building containing these; **bowling-green** lawn for playing bowls; **bowl over** knock down, *colloq.* disconcert, amaze, exhaust. [F f. L *bulla* bubble]

bowler[1] *n.* player at bowls; (in cricket) fieldsman who bowls.

bowler[2] *n.* hard felt hat with curved brim and rounded crown. [*Bowler*, hatter]

bowline /ˈbəʊlɪn/ *n.* rope from bow keeping sail taut against wind; knot forming non-slipping loop at end of rope. [BOW[3]]

bowsprit /ˈbəʊsprɪt/ *n.* long spar running forward from ship's bow.

box[1] **1** *n.* container, usu. with flat sides and of firm material such as wood or card; quantity contained in this; separate compartment, as for several persons in theatre, for horses in stable or vehicle, or for witnesses in a law-court; enclosure or receptacle for special purpose (*money-box*, *telephone-box*); enclosed area or space; receptacle at newspaper office for replies to advertisement; small country-house for sporting activity; coachman's seat. **2** *v.t.* put in or provide with box. **3 the box** *colloq.* television; **box girder** one square in cross-section; **box in** (or **up**) shut in, restrict movement of; **box junction** road area marked with yellow grid, which vehicle may enter only if exit is clear; **box number** number identifying box in newspaper office; **box office** office for booking seats at theatre etc.; **box-pleat** pleat of two parallel creases forming raised band; **box-room** room for storing boxes etc.; **box-spring** one of set of vertical springs housed in frame. [OE f. L *buxis* (as BOX[3])]

box[2] **1** *v.* fight with fists, esp. in padded gloves as sport; slap (person's ears). **2** *n.* hard slap, esp. on ears. [orig. unkn.]

box[3] *n.* small evergreen shrub with thick dark leaves; its wood. [OE f. L *buxus*, Gk *puxos*]

Box and Cox two persons sharing accommodation etc. and using it at different times. [people in play 1847]

boxer *n.* one who boxes, esp. for sport; dog of medium-size breed with smooth brown coat. [BOX[2]]

boxing *n.* fighting with fists, esp. as sport; **boxing-glove** padded glove worn in this. [BOX[2]]

Boxing Day first weekday after Christmas. [BOX[1], from custom of giving Christmas boxes]

boy *n.* male child; young man; male servant, attendant, etc.; **boy-friend** girl's or woman's regular male companion; **boyhood** *n.*; **boyish** *a.* [orig. uncert.]

boycott /ˈbɔɪkɒt/ **1** *v.t.* combine in refusing social or commercial relations with (person, group, country); refuse to handle (goods). **2** *n.* such refusal. [Capt. *Boycott*, so treated 1880]

BP *abbr.* boiling-point; before present (era).

Br *symb.* bromine.

bra /brɑː/ *n.* brassière. [abbr.]

brace **1** *n.* device that clamps or fastens tightly; (in *pl.*) straps supporting trousers from shoulders; wire device for straightening teeth; (*pl.* same) pair (esp. of game); rope attached to yard of ship for trimming sail; connecting mark { or } in printing. **2** *v.t.* fasten tightly, give firmness to, make steady by supporting; invigorate. **3 brace and bit** revolving tool with D-shaped handle for boring; **brace oneself** (or **brace up**) prepare for difficulty, enterprise, etc. [F f. L *bracchia* arms]

bracelet /'breɪslɪt/ *n.* ornamental band or chain worn on wrist or arm; *sl.* handcuff.

bracken /'brækən/ *n.* large fern; mass of these esp. on heathland. [ON]

bracket /'brækɪt/ **1** *n.* support (esp. angular) projecting from vertical surface; shelf fixed with angled prop to wall; mark used in pairs () [] {} to enclose words or figures; group classified as similar or falling between given limits (*social bracket*; *age bracket*). **2** *v.t.* enclose in brackets; group in same category. [F or Sp. f. L *bracae* breeches]

brackish /'brækɪʃ/ *a.* (of water) slightly salty. [LG or Du.]

bract *n.* leaf below calyx of flower, usu. small and scaly. [L *bractea* thin sheet]

brad *n.* thin flat nail with head in form of slight enlargement at top. [ON]

bradawl /'brædɔ:l/ *n.* tool with small blade-end for making holes by hand.

brae /breɪ/ *n. Sc.* hillside. [ON]

brag **1** *v.* (**-gg-**) talk boastfully, boast about. **2** *n.* boastful statement or talk; card-game like poker. [orig. unkn.]

braggart /'brægət/ **1** *n.* person given to bragging. **2** *a.* boastful.

Brahma /'brɑ:mə/ *n.* supreme Hindu deity; divine reality of which world is manifestation. [Skr., = creator]

brahmin /'brɑ:mɪn/ *n.* (also **brahman**) member of Hindu priestly caste; **brahminic** /-'mɪnɪk/ *a.*; **brahminism** *n.*

braid **1** *n.* woven band of silk or thread as edging or trimming; plaited tress of hair. **2** *v.t.* trim with braid, plait (hair or thread). [OE]

Braille /breɪl/ **1** *n.* printing or writing for the blind formed by raised points interpreted by touch. **2** *v.t.* transcribe in Braille characters. [*Braille*, its inventor]

brain **1** *n.* organ of convoluted nervous tissue in skull of vertebrates; centre of sensation or thought; intelligent person; person who originates complex plan or idea (*brain behind the robbery*); (often in *pl.*) intelligence; electronic device with functions comparable to brain's. **2** *v.t.* dash out brains of, strike hard on head. **3** **brain-child** idea or plan as result of mental effort; **brain-drain** loss of intellectual or professional people by emigration; **brains trust** group of people giving impromptu answers to questions; **on the brain** obsessively in one's thoughts. [OE]

brainless *a.* lacking intelligence.

brainpower *n.* mental ability, intelligence.

brainstorm *n.* extreme mental disturbance; *loosely* mental confusion.

brainwash *v.t.* systematically implant new ideas in person's mind in place of the established ones; **brainwashing** *n.*

brainwave *n.* electrical impulse in brain; *colloq.* sudden bright idea.

brainy *a.* intellectually clever or active; **braininess** *n.*

braise /breɪz/ *v.t.* stew (esp. meat) with little liquid in closed container. [F (*braise* live coals)]

brake[1] **1** *n.* device for checking motion of wheel or vehicle. **2** *v.* apply brake; retard with brake. **3** **brake-drum** cylinder in wheel on which brake-shoe presses; **brake-horsepower** power of engine measured by force needed to brake it; **brake-shoe** long curved block acting on wheel to brake it. [prob. obs. *brake* = curb]

brake[2] **1** *v.t.* crush (hemp or flax) by beating it. **2** *n.* toothed braking-instrument; heavy harrow. [LG or Du., rel. to BREAK]

brake[3] *n.* thicket, brushwood. [OE]

brake[4] *n.* estate car. [var. of BREAK]

bramble /'bræmb(ə)l/ *n.* wild prickly shrub, esp. blackberry; **brambly** *a.* [OE]

brambling /'bræmblɪŋ/ *n.* small brightly coloured finch. [G, rel. to prec.]

bran *n.* husks separated from flour; **bran-tub** lucky dip with prizes hidden in bran. [F]

branch /brɑ:ntʃ/ **1** *n.* limb extending from tree or bough; lateral extension or subdivision, esp. of river, road, or railway; conceptual subdivision, as of family, knowledge, etc.; local office etc. of large business (e.g. bank, library). **2** *v.i.* diverge from main part (often with *off*); divide into branches; send out branches. **3** **branch out** extend one's field of interest. [F f. L *branca* paw]

brand **1** *n.* particular make of goods, their trade mark, identifying label, etc.; special kind of thing (*brand of humour*); identifying mark burned esp. on livestock with hot iron, iron used for this; stigma, sign of disgrace; piece of burning or charred wood, *poetic* torch. **2** *v.t.* assign trade mark or label to; stigmatize, mark with disgrace (*branded as an outlaw*); mark with hot iron; impress unforgettably. **3** **brand-new** completely or obviously new. [OE]

brandish /'brændɪʃ/ *v.t.* wave or flourish as threat or in display. [F f. Gmc]

brandy /'brændɪ/ *n.* strong alcoholic spirit distilled from wine or fermented fruit-juice; **brandy-snap** crisp rolled gingerbread wafer eaten with cream. [Du. *brandewijn*]

brash *a.* bluntly self-assertive; impudent. [dial.]
brass /brɑːs/ **1** *n.* dark yellow alloy of copper and zinc; brass objects collectively; *Mus.* brass instruments; memorial tablet of brass; brass ornament worn by horse; *colloq.* effrontery; *sl.* money. **2** *a.* made of brass. **3 brass band** band of brass instruments; **brass hat** *colloq.* high-ranking officer, important person; **brass-rubbing** rubbing of paper over memorial brass to get reproduction of design; **brass tacks** *colloq.* essential details.[OE]
brasserie /ˈbræsərɪ/ *n.* restaurant serving beer with food. [F (*brasser* brew)]
brassica /ˈbræsɪkə/ *n.* plant of family including cabbage and turnip. [L, = cabbage]
brassière /ˈbræsɪə/ *n.* undergarment worn by women to support breasts. [F]
brassy /ˈbrɑːsɪ/ *a.* impudent; pretentious, showy; loud and blaring; of or like brass. [BRASS]
brat *n. derog.* child, esp. ill-behaved one. [orig. unkn.]
bravado /brəˈvɑːdəʊ/ *n.* show of boldness. [Sp.]
brave 1 *a.* able or ready to face and endure danger or pain; admirable, spirited. **2** *v.t.* face bravely or defiantly. **3** *n.* American Indian warrior. **4 bravery** *n.* [F f. It. or Sp. f. L *barbarus* barbarian]
bravo[1] /ˈbrɑːvəʊ/ *n.* (*pl.* **bravos**) & *int.* cry of approval; well done! [F f. It.]
bravo[2] /ˈbrɑːvəʊ/ *n.* (*pl.* **bravoes**) hired ruffian or killer. [It. (BRAVE)]
bravura /brəˈvʊərə/ *n.* brilliant display or show; passage of (esp. vocal) music calling for brilliant technique. [It.]
brawl 1 *n.* noisy quarrel. **2** *v.i.* quarrel noisily or roughly; (of stream) flow noisily. [Prov.]
brawn *n.* muscle, muscular strength; pressed jellied meat made esp. from pig's head; **brawny** *a.* [F f. Gmc]
bray 1 *n.* loud strident cry of donkey; harsh sound. **2** *v.* emit bray; utter in braying tone. [F *braire*]
braze *v.t.* solder with alloy of brass and zinc. [F *braser*]
brazen /ˈbreɪz(ə)n/ **1** *a.* shameless, insolent; of or like brass, harsh in tone or colour. **2** *v.t.* (with *out*, esp. in **brazen it out**) face or undergo shamelessly. [OE]
brazier[1] /ˈbreɪzɪə/ *n.* metal stand or pan holding burning coals etc. [F (BRAISE)]
brazier[2] /ˈbreɪzɪə/ *n.* worker in brass. [BRASS]
Brazil /brəˈzɪl/ *n.* large three-sided nut from S. American tree. [*Brazil* in S. Amer.]
breach 1 *n.* breaking of or failure to observe law, contract, etc.; quarrel, breaking of relations; opening, gap. **2** *v.t.* break through, make gap in. **3 breach of the peace** disturbance, affray; **breach of promise** breaking of promise to marry; **step into the breach** take responsibility in crisis. [F f. Gmc, rel. to BREAK]
bread /bred/ **1** *n.* food of baked dough made of flour usu. leavened with yeast and moistened; *sl.* money. **2** *v.t.* coat with breadcrumbs for cooking. **3 bread and butter** one's livelihood; **on the breadline** at subsistence level. [OE]
breadboard *n.* board for cutting bread on; board for making experimental model of electric circuit etc.
breadcrumbs *n.pl.* bread crumbled for use in cooking
breadth /bredθ/ *n.* distance or measure from side to side of thing; freedom from prejudice or intolerance (*breadth of mind*). [OE (BROAD)]
breadwinner *n.* person who works to support family.
break /breɪk/ **1** *v.* (*past* **broke**; *p.p.* BROKEN, BROKE) (cause to) separate into pieces under blow or strain, make or become inoperative (*the machine has broken*); shatter (window etc.); break bone in or dislocate (part of the body), break skin of (head, crown); cause interruption in (journey etc.), disconnect (electric circuit); have interval between spells of work (*break for tea*); fail to observe or keep (law, promise, etc.); quarrel or cease association *with* person; penetrate by breaking; make or become weak or ineffective, destroy; exhaust (*break the bank*); surpass (record); tame, subdue, overcome (person, resistance, spirit, etc.); distress overwhelmingly (*broke his heart*); be no longer subject to (habit); cause (person) to be free *of* habit; solve (code etc.); reveal or be revealed (*the story broke*); weaken effect of (blow, fall); (of day) begin, dawn; (of weather) change suddenly, esp. after fine spell; (of storm) begin violently; (of waves) dissolve into foam on shore or rocks; (of clouds) show gap; (of voice) change tone with emotion or at manhood; move away or change course suddenly; (of troops) disperse in confusion; (of boxers) come out of clinch; make (way) by penetrating obstacles; escape, emerge from (prison, cover). **2** *n.* breaking, point where thing is broken, gap; interval, interruption, pause in work; sudden dash (*make a break for it*); *sl.* piece of luck; (in cricket) change of direction of ball on bouncing; points scored continuously in billiards etc. **3 bad break** *colloq.* piece of bad luck; **break**

away make or become free or separate; **break the back of** accomplish greatest or hardest part of; **break down** fail in mechanical action or (esp. mental) health, lose self-control, collapse, demolish, suppress (resistance), analyse into components; **break even** make neither profit nor loss in transaction etc.; **break in** intrude forcibly esp. as thief, interrupt, accustom to habit, wear etc. until comfortable; **break-in** *n.* forcible entry esp. by thief; **breaking-point** point of greatest strain, at which thing breaks, person gives way, etc.; **break into** enter forcibly or violently, interrupt (talk etc.), suddenly begin (*break into song*); **break off** detach by breaking, bring to an end, cease talking etc.; **break open** open forcibly; **break out** escape by force esp. from prison, emerge suddenly from restraint or concealment, exclaim, become covered *in* rash etc.; **break-out** *n.* forcible escape; **break up** break into small pieces, disperse, end school term, cease friendship; **break wind** emit wind from anus. [OE]

breakable 1 *a.* able to be broken easily. **2** *n.* (esp. in *pl.*) breakable thing.

breakage *n.* breaking; damage caused by breaking, broken thing.

breakaway 1 *n.* breaking away; secession. **2** *a.* that has broken away or seceded, separate.

breakdown *n.* failure of mechanical action or (esp. mental) health; collapse, disintegration; analysis of statistics.

breaker *n.* heavy wave breaking on coast or over reef.

breakfast /ˈbrekfəst/ **1** *n.* first meal of the day. **2** *v.i.* have breakfast.

breakneck *a.* (of speed) dangerously fast.

breakthrough *n.* major advance or discovery; act of breaking through obstacle etc.

breakup *n.* disintegration, collapse; dispersal.

breakwater *n.* barrier breaking force of waves.

bream *n.* (*pl.* same) yellowish freshwater fish with arched back; sea-fish of similar shape. [F f. Gmc]

breast /brest/ **1** *n.* either of two milk-secreting organs on upper front of woman's body, corresponding usu. rudimentary part of man's body; upper front of human body or of garment covering it; corresponding part of animals; breast as source of nourishment or emotion. **2** *v.t.* face up to, contend with; reach top of (hill). **3 breast-feed** feed (baby) from breast; **breast-stroke** stroke made while swimming on breast by extending arms forward and sweeping them back; **make a clean breast of** confess fully. [OE]

breastbone *n.* thin flat vertical bone in chest between ribs.

breastplate *n.* armour covering breast.

breastwork *n.* low temporary defence or parapet.

breath /breθ/ *n.* air drawn into and expelled from the lungs; a breathing in; breathing or ability to breathe; breath as perceived by the senses; slight movement of air; whiff or perfume; hint or slight rumour (*breath of scandal*); **breath test** test of breath to determine level of alcohol in blood; **catch one's breath** cease breathing for a moment esp. in surprise; **hold one's breath** cease breathing temporarily; **out of breath** panting to recover breath after exertion; **save one's breath** keep silent because speaking would be useless; **take one's breath away** cause great surprise, delight, etc.; **under one's breath** in a whisper. [OE]

breathalyser /ˈbreθəlaɪzə/ *n.* device measuring amount of alcohol in breath exhaled into it; **breathalyse** *v.t.* [BREATH, ANALYSE]

breathe /bri:ð/ *v.* draw air into and expel it from the lungs; be or seem alive; draw into or expel from lungs on breath (*breathe in smoke, breathe out fire*); utter or mention (*don't breathe a word*); exude or instil (*breathed defiance, confidence*); speak or sound softly; pause for breath or rest; **breathe again** (or **freely**) feel relieved of fear etc.; **breathing-space** time to breathe, chance to recover from effort. [BREATH]

breather /ˈbri:ðə/ *n.* brief pause from exertion; spell of fresh air.

breathing /ˈbri:ðɪŋ/ *n.* sign indicating whether Greek vowel is aspirated.

breathless /ˈbreθlɪs/ *a.* panting, out of breath; overcome with emotion, surprise, etc.; still, not moved by the wind. [BREATH]

breathtaking *a.* spectacular, very exciting.

bred *past* and *p.p.* of BREED.

breech *n.* back part of rifle or gun barrel; (in *pl.*) short trousers fastened below knee for riding or in ceremonial dress; buttocks (now only in *breech birth*); **breech birth** birth in which baby's buttocks or feet emerge first; **breeches buoy** lifebuoy running along rope over sea, with canvas breeches for user's legs. [OE]

breed 1 *v.* (*past* and *p.p.* **bred**) bear or generate (offspring); keep or raise (animals); result in, lead to; train, bring up; arise, spread; create (fissile material) by nuclear reaction. **2** *n.* stock of animals etc. within species, having similar appearance and usu. developed by deliberate selection; race, lineage; sort, kind. **3 breeder reactor** nuclear reactor that can create more fissile material than it consumes. [OE]

breeding *n.* raising of offspring; result or qualities of upbringing (*shows good breeding*).

breeze[1] **1** *n.* gentle wind; *sl.* quarrel; *sl.* easy task. **2** *v.i. colloq.* come *in*, go *out*, move *along*, etc., in casual or light-hearted manner. [prob. Sp. & Port. *briza*]

breeze[2] *n.* small cinders; **breeze block** lightweight building block made from breeze with sand and cement. [F (BRAISE)]

breezy *a.* slightly windy; cheerful, light-hearted, casual. [BREEZE[1]]

Bren *n.* lightweight quick-firing machine-gun. [*Br*no in Czechoslovakia, *En*field in England]

brent *n.* smallest kind of wild goose. [orig. unkn.]

brethren /'breðrən/ *n.pl.* brothers (*archaic* except with reference to sect or religion). [BROTHER]

Breton /'bret(ə)n/ **1** *n.* native or inhabitant of Brittany; its language. **2** *a.* of Brittany. [F, = BRITON]

breve *n.* mark (˘) over short or unstressed vowel; *Mus.* note twice the length of semibreve. [var. of BRIEF]

breviary /'bri:vɪərɪ/ *n.* book containing RC daily office. [L (BRIEF)]

brevity /'brevɪtɪ/ *n.* conciseness of written or spoken expression; shortness, esp. of time. [AF (BRIEF)]

brew /bru:/ **1** *v.* make (beer etc.) by infusion, boiling, and fermentation; make (tea etc.) by infusion or mixture; (of tea, beer, etc.) undergo these processes; gather force, threaten (*trouble is brewing*); concoct. **2** *n.* liquid or amount brewed at once; process of brewing; quality of what is brewed. [OE]

brewery /'bru:ərɪ/ *n.* place where beer etc. is brewed commercially.

briar[1, 2] var. of BRIER[1, 2].

bribe 1 *n.* inducement (esp. money) offered to procure illegal or dishonest action or decision in favour of giver. **2** *v.* give bribe to (person *to do* thing), give bribes. **3 bribery** *n.* [F *briber* beg]

bric-à-brac /'brɪkəbræk/ *n.* miscellaneous ornaments, trinkets, etc., usu. of little value. [F]

brick 1 *n.* small usu. rectangular block of baked or dried clay, used in building; material of this; child's toy block; thing with shape of a brick; *sl.* loyal or kind-hearted person. **2** *a.* made of brick. **3** *v.t.* block *up*, close *in*, with bricks. **4 drop a brick** *colloq.* say something indiscreet. [LG or Du.]

brickbat *n.* piece of brick esp. as missile; uncomplimentary remark.

bricklayer *n.* one who builds with bricks.

brickwork *n.* structure of or building in bricks.

bridal /'braɪd(ə)l/ *a.* of a bride or wedding. [OE]

bride *n.* woman on or just before her wedding-day; newly-married woman. [OE]

bridegroom *n.* man on or just before his wedding-day; newly-married man. [OE]

bridesmaid *n.* unmarried woman or girl (usu. one of several) attending bride at wedding. [BRIDE]

bridge[1] **1** *n.* structure carrying way over river, road, railway, etc.; thing joining or connecting parts; upper bony part of nose; piece of wood etc. over which strings of violin etc. are stretched; raised platform on ship from which captain and officers direct its course; false tooth or teeth connected to real teeth on each side. **2** *v.t.* be or make bridge over; join, connect. **3 bridging loan** loan to cover short interval between buying one thing and selling another (esp. houses). [OE]

bridge[2] *n.* card-game developed from whist. [orig. unkn.]

bridgehead *n.* fortified position held on far side of river where enemy is.

bridle /'braɪd(ə)l/ **1** *n.* harness round head of horse for rider to control horse; restraining thing or influence. **2** *v.* put bridle on; curb, restrain; show resentment or anger, esp. by throwing up head and drawing in chin. **3 bridle-path** path suitable for horse-riding. [OE]

Brie /bri:/ *n.* a kind of soft ripe cheese. [*Brie* in N. France]

brief 1 *a.* of short duration; concise in expression. **2** *n.* summary of facts or relevant points, esp. as drawn up for legal counsel; case taken on by counsel; (in *pl.*) very short pants; papal letter on discipline. **3** *v.t.* provide (participant) with information on planned operation, activity, etc.; give legal brief to (counsel). **4 hold no brief for** not wish to support. [F f. L *brevis* short]

briefcase *n.* flat case for carrying documents etc.

brier[1] /'braɪə/ *n.* wild rose or other prickly bush. [OE]

brier[2] /'braɪə/ *n.* shrub with woody root used for tobacco-pipes; pipe made from this. [F *bruyère*]

brig[1] *n.* square-rigged sailing-ship with two masts. [abbr. BRIGANTINE]

brig[2] *n. Sc. & N. Engl.* bridge. [BRIDGE[1]]
Brig. *abbr.* Brigadier.
brigade /brɪ'geɪd/ **1** *n.* military unit forming part of division; group of people organized for special purpose. **2** *v.t.* organize into brigade. [F f. It. (*briga* strife)]
brigadier /brɪgə'dɪə/ *n.* officer commanding brigade; staff officer with similar status.
brigand /'brɪgənd/ *n.* bandit, one of band living by robbery and ransom; **brigandage** *n.* [F f. It. (BRIGADE)]
brigantine /'brɪgəntiːn/ *n.* sailing-ship with two masts, the foremast square-rigged. [F or It. (BRIGAND)]
bright /braɪt/ **1** *a.* emitting or reflecting much light, shining; vivid or conspicuous to see or hear; intelligent, talented; cheerful, vivacious. **2** *adv.* brightly. [OE]
brighten /'braɪt(ə)n/ *v.* make or become brighter.
Bright's disease /braɪts/ kidney disease. [*Bright*, physician]
brill *n.* a European flat-fish. [orig. unkn.]
brilliant /'brɪlɪənt/ **1** *a.* bright, sparkling; strikingly talented or intelligent; showy. **2** *n.* diamond of finest cut, with many facets. **3 brilliance** *n.*; **brilliancy** *n.* [F (*briller* shine f. It.)]
brilliantine /'brɪljəntiːn/ *n.* dressing for making hair glossy. [F (prec.)]
brim 1 *n.* edge or lip of cup or other vessel; projecting edge of hat. **2** *v.* (**-mm-**) fill or be full to the brim. **3 brim over** overflow. [orig. unkn.]
brimstone *n. archaic* sulphur. [BURN[1], STONE]
brindled /'brɪnd(ə)ld/ *a.* brownish or tawny with streaks of other colour (esp. of dogs and cattle). [Scand.]
brine 1 *n.* water saturated with salt; sea-water. **2** *v.t.* soak in brine. [OE]
bring *v.t.* (*past* and *p.p.* **brought** /brɔːt/) come with or convey, esp. by carrying or leading, cause to be present; cause, result in (*war brings hardship*); be sold for, produce as income; prefer (charge), initiate (legal action), adduce (evidence, argument); cause to become or reach particular state (*bring low*; *bring to the boil*; *cannot bring himself to agree*); **bring about** cause to happen; **bring-and-buy sale** sale at which participants bring items for sale and buy those brought by others; **bring back** call to mind; **bring down** cause to fall, lower (price); **bring down the house** receive rapturous applause; **bring forth** give birth to, cause; **bring forward** draw attention to, move to earlier time; **bring home to** convince of; **bring in** introduce, yield as income or profit; **bring off** achieve successfully; **bring on** cause to appear or make progress; **bring out** express or emphasize, publish; **bring over** convert to one's own side; **bring round** restore to consciousness, persuade; **bring through** aid (person) through difficulty, esp. illness; **bring to** restore to consciousness (*brought him to*); **bring up** raise (child), vomit, draw attention to, stop suddenly. [OE]
brink *n.* extreme edge of land before precipice, river, etc., esp. when sudden drop follows; furthest point before something dangerous or exciting is encountered; **on the brink of** about to experience or suffer (e.g. success, destruction), in imminent danger of *doing*. [ON]
brinkmanship *n.* art or policy of pursuing dangerous course to brink of catastrophe before desisting.
briny *a.* of brine or sea, salty; **the briny** *sl.* the sea. [BRINE]
brio /'briːəʊ/ *n.* vigour, vivacity. [It.]
briquette /brɪ'ket/ *n.* block of compressed coal-dust as fuel. [F dimin. (BRICK)]
brisk 1 *a.* quick, active, energetic (*brisk pace, trade*); enlivening (*brisk air*). **2** *v.* make or grow brisk (often with *up*). [prob. F BRUSQUE]
brisket /'brɪskɪt/ *n.* animal's breast, esp. as joint of meat. [F]
brisling /'brɪzlɪŋ, 'brɪs-/ *n.* small herring or sprat. [Norw. & Da.]
bristle /'brɪs(ə)l/ **1** *n.* short stiff hair, esp. one of those on animal's back, used in brushes. **2** *v.* show anger or temper; (of hair or feathers) stand up; (esp. of animal) make (hair etc.) bristle, bristle the hair. **3 bristle with** have in abundance. [OE]
bristly /'brɪslɪ/ *a.* full of bristles; rough, prickly.
Britannia /brɪ'tænjə/ *n.* personification of Britain, esp. as helmeted woman with shield and trident; **Britannia metal** silvery alloy of tin, antimony, and copper. [L]
Britannic /brɪ'tænɪk/ *a.* of Britain (chiefly in **Her** or **His Britannic Majesty**).
Briticism /'brɪtɪsɪz(ə)m/ *n.* idiom used in Britain but not US etc. [foll., after *gallicism*]
British /'brɪtɪʃ/ *a.* of Great Britain; **the British** the people of Great Britain; **British Legion** see ROYAL. [OE]
Briton /'brɪt(ə)n/ *n.* one of people in S. Britain before Roman conquest; native or inhabitant of Great Britain. [L *Britto -onis*]
brittle /'brɪt(ə)l/ *a.* hard but fragile; apt to break; **brittlely** *adv.* [OE]

broach[1] 1 *v.t.* raise (subject) for discussion; pierce to draw liquor from (cask); open and start using. **2** *n.* bit for making holes; roasting-spit. **3 broach spire** octagonal spire rising from square tower without parapet. [F, f. L *broccus* projecting]

broach[2] *v.* (often with *to*) veer or cause (ship) to veer and present side to wind and waves. [orig. unkn.]

broad /brɔːd/ **1** *a.* large in extent from one side to the other, wide; in breadth (*2m. broad*); extensive (*broad acres*); full, clear (*broad daylight*); strong (*broad hint*); markedly regional (*in broad Scots*); tolerant, liberal (*broad view*); general in scope (*broad rule, inquiry*); somewhat coarse (*broad humour*); main (*broad facts*). **2** *n.* broad part; *US sl.* woman. **3 broad bean** kind of bean with large flat seeds, one of these seeds; **broad-minded** tolerant, liberal; **the Broads** in E. Anglia, large areas of fresh water formed by widening of rivers. [OE]

broadcast **1** *v.* (*past* and *p.p.* **broadcast**) transmit (programmes, information) by radio or television; speak or perform thus; disseminate (information) widely; scatter (seed). **2** *n.* radio or television programme or transmission. **3** *a.* transmitted by radio or television; scattered widely.

broadcloth *n.* a fine cloth of cotton, wool, or silk.

broadloom *a.* woven in broad widths.

broadsheet *n.* large sheet of paper printed on one side only, esp. with information.

broadside *n.* firing of all guns from one side of ship; fierce verbal attack; side of ship between bow and quarter; **broadside on** sideways on.

broadsword *n.* sword with broad blade, for cutting rather than thrusting.

brocade /brəʊˈkeɪd/ **1** *n.* fabric woven with raised pattern. **2** *v.t.* weave thus. [Sp. & Port. f. It. (*brocco* twisted thread)]

broccoli /ˈbrɒkəlɪ/ *n.* hardy variety of cauliflower with greenish flower-head. [It.]

brochure /ˈbrəʊʃʊə, -ʃə/ *n.* leaflet or pamphlet, esp. one giving descriptive information. [F (*brocher* stitch)]

broderie anglaise /brəʊdrɪ ɑŋˈgleɪz/ open embroidery on white linen or cambric. [F, = English embroidery]

brogue[1] /brəʊg/ *n.* strong outdoor shoe with perforated ornamental bands; rough shoe of untanned leather. [Ir. & Gael. f. ON]

brogue[2] /brəʊg/ *n.* marked accent, esp. Irish. [perh. rel. to prec.]

broil *v.* grill (esp. meat) on fire or gridiron; make or become very hot, esp. from sun. [F *bruler* burn]

broiler *n.* young chicken reared for broiling or roasting.

broke **1** *past* of BREAK. **2** *a. colloq.* having no money, bankrupt. [BREAK]

broken **1** *p.p.* of BREAK. **2** *a.* that has been broken; (of person) reduced to despair, beaten; (of language) spoken imperfectly; disturbed or interrupted (*broken sleep, time*). **3 broken chord** *Mus.* chord in which notes are played successively; **broken-down** worn or sick, out-of-order; **broken-hearted** overwhelmed by sorrow or grief; **broken home** family lacking one parent esp. by divorce or separation; **broken reed** person who has become unreliable or ineffective.

broker *n.* agent buying and selling for others, middleman; stockbroker; official appointed to sell distrained goods; **broking** *n.* [AF]

brokerage *n.* broker's fee or commission.

brolly /ˈbrɒlɪ/ *n. colloq.* umbrella. [abbr.]

bromide /ˈbrəʊmaɪd/ *n.* compound of bromine, used in medicinal sedatives; trite remark. [foll.]

bromine /ˈbrəʊmiːn/ *n.* non-metallic liquid element, poisonous and with rank smell. [F f. Gk *brōmos* stink]

bronchial /ˈbrɒŋkɪəl/ *a.* of the bronchi (see BRONCHUS) or the smaller tubes into which they divide. [BRONCHUS]

bronchitis /brɒŋˈkaɪtɪs/ *n.* inflammation of mucous membrane in bronchial tubes. [foll.]

bronchus /ˈbrɒŋkəs/ *n.* (*pl.* **bronchi** /-aɪ/) either of two main divisions of windpipe, leading to the lungs. [L f. Gk]

bronco /ˈbrɒŋkəʊ/ *n.* (*pl.* **broncos**) wild or half-tamed horse of western US. [Sp., = rough]

brontosaurus /brɒntəˈsɔːrəs/ *n.* large plant-eating dinosaur. [Gk *brontē* thunder, *sauros* lizard]

bronze **1** *n.* alloy of copper and tin; its brownish colour; thing made of bronze, esp. as work of art. **2** *a.* made of or coloured like bronze. **3** *v.* give bronze surface or colour to, (esp. of sun) tan. **4 Bronze Age** period when weapons and tools were commonly made of bronze; **bronze medal** medal given usu. as third prize. [F f. It.]

brooch /brəʊtʃ/ *n.* ornamental hinged pin. [F *broche* (BROACH)]

brood **1** *n.* young of animal (esp. bird) produced at one hatching or birth; children in a family. **2** *v.i.* worry or ponder, esp. resentfully (*on* or *over*); sit as hen on eggs to hatch them. [OE]

broody *a.* (of hen) wanting to brood; sullenly thoughtful.
brook[1] /brʊk/ *n.* small stream. [OE]
brook[2] /brʊk/ *v.t.* (usu. with neg.) tolerate, allow. [OE]
broom *n.* long-handled brush (orig. with twigs from shrub) for sweeping; shrub with yellow flowers; **new broom** newly appointed person eager to make changes. [OE]
broomstick *n.* handle of broom.
Bros. *abbr.* Brothers (esp. in name of firm).
broth *n.* thin clear meat or fish soup. [OE]
brothel /'brɒθ(ə)l/ *n.* house of prostitution. [orig. = worthless fellow, f. OE]
brother /'brʌðə/ *n.* man or boy in relation to other sons and daughters of his parents; close friend or associate; member of religious order, esp. monk; fellow member of Church or other association; fellow man; **brother-in-law** (*pl.* **brothers-in-law**) one's husband's or wife's brother, one's sister's husband; **brotherly** *a.* [OE]
brotherhood *n.* relationship of brothers; comradeship; association of men, its members.
brougham /'bru:əm/ *n. hist.* horse-drawn closed carriage with driver perched outside in front; motor-car with open driver's seat. [Lord *Brougham*]
brought *past* and *p.p.* of BRING.
brow /braʊ/ *n.* eyebrow (usu. in *pl.*); forehead; summit of hill or pass; edge of cliff etc. [OE]
browbeat *v.t.* intimidate with stern looks and words.
brown /braʊn/ **1** *a.* having the colour produced by mixing red, yellow, and black, as of dark wood or rich soil; (of bread) brown from wholemeal flour used; dark-skinned; sun-tanned. **2** *n.* brown colour or pigment; brown clothes or material (*dressed in brown*). **3** *v.* make or become brown. **4 brown coal** lignite; **browned off** *colloq.* fed up, disheartened; **brown sugar** sugar that is only partly refined. [OE]
Brownie *n.* junior Guide; (**brownie**) benevolent elf in folklore.
browning *n.* browned flour or other additive to colour gravy.
browse /braʊz/ **1** *v.* read or look over desultorily; eat, feed *on*, leaves and young shoots. **2** *n.* browsing; leaves etc. for feeding. [F *brost* bud]
brucellosis /bru:sə'ləʊsɪs/ *n.* disease caused by bacteria, affecting esp. cattle. [Sir D. *Bruce*, physician]
bruise /bru:z/ **1** *n.* injury caused esp. by blow, discolouring flesh but not breaking the skin. **2** *v.* inflict bruise on; be susceptible to bruises; hurt mentally. [orig. = crush, f. OE]
bruiser *n.* prize-fighter; large tough person.
bruit /bru:t/ *v.t. archaic* spread (report, fame, *that*) *about* or *abroad*. [F, = noise]
brunch *n. colloq.* meal combining breakfast and lunch. [portmanteau word]
brunette /bru:'net/ *n.* woman with dark brown hair. [F dimin.]
brunt *n.* chief or initial impact *of* attack (esp. in *bear the brunt of*). [orig. unkn.]
brush **1** *n.* implement with bristles, hairs, feathers, or wires, set in block of wood etc., for cleaning, painting, dressing the hair, etc.; application of brush; short esp. unpleasant encounter; fox's bushy tail; brushlike carbon or metal piece serving as electrical contact esp. with moving part. **2** *v.* sweep, clean, arrange, etc., with brush; graze or touch in passing; apply or remove with brush. **3 brush aside** dismiss curtly or lightly; **brush off** dismiss abruptly; **brush-off** *n.* rebuff, abrupt dismissal; **brush up** clean up or smarten, revive former knowledge of; **brush-up** *n.* process of cleaning up. [F]
brushwood *n.* cut or broken twigs etc.; undergrowth, thicket.
brushwork *n.* manipulation of brush in painting; painter's style in this.
brusque /brʊsk/ *a.* blunt or offhand in manner. [F, f. It. *brusco* sour]
Brussels sprouts /'brʌs(ə)lz/ edible buds resembling tiny cabbages, growing on plant of cabbage family.
brutal /'bru:t(ə)l/ *a.* savagely cruel, coarse; harsh, unsparing; **brutality** /-'tælɪtɪ/ *n.*; **brutally** *adv.* [F or med.L (BRUTE)]
brutalize /'bru:təlaɪz/ *v.t.* make brutal; treat brutally.
brute /bru:t/ **1** *n.* brutal or violent person or animal; *colloq.* unpleasant person. **2** *a.* unable to reason; stupid, sensual, animal-like, cruel; unthinking, unsparing (*brute force*). **3 brutish** *a.* [F f. L *brutus* stupid]
bryony /'braɪənɪ/ *n.* either of two kinds of climbing hedge-plant. [L f. Gk]
BS *abbr.* British Standard; Bachelor of Surgery.
B.Sc. *abbr.* Bachelor of Science.
BSI *abbr.* British Standards Institution.
BST *abbr.* British Summer Time.
Bt. *abbr.* Baronet.
bubble /'bʌb(ə)l/ **1** *n.* globular film of liquid enclosing air or gas; ball of air or gas formed in liquid or solid; transparent domed canopy; visionary idea unlikely to succeed. **2** *v.i.* send up or rise in bubbles, boil; make sound of bubbles.

3 **bubble and squeak** cold cooked vegetables mixed and fried in cake; **bubble bath** bath with water made bubbly by additive, the additive; **bubble car** small car with transparent dome; **bubble gum** chewing-gum that can be blown into bubbles. [imit.]

bubbly 1 *a.* having many bubbles. 2 *n. colloq.* champagne.

bubo /'bju:bəʊ/ *n.* (*pl.* **buboes**) inflamed swelling in groin or armpit. [L f. Gk *boubōn* groin]

bubonic /bju:'bɒnɪk/ *a.* (of plague) characterized by buboes.

buccaneer /bʌkə'nɪə/ *n.* pirate; adventurer; **buccaneering** *a.* & *n.* [F]

buck[1] 1 *n.* male deer, hare, or rabbit; *archaic* fashionable young man; *attrib. sl.* male. 2 *v.* (of horse) jump upwards with back arched, throw (rider) thus; *sl.* resist, oppose. 3 **buck up** *sl.* cheer up, hurry up. [OE]

buck[2] *n. sl.* object placed before player next to deal in poker; **pass the buck** *colloq.* shift responsibility (*to*). [orig. unkn.]

buck[3] *n. US sl.* a dollar. [orig. unkn.]

bucket /'bʌkɪt/ 1 *n.* round open container with handle, for carrying or holding liquid, sand, etc.; amount contained in this; (in *pl.*) large quantities (esp. of rain); scoop in water-wheel, dredger, etc. 2 *v.* move or drive fast and bumpily; (of rain etc.) pour down heavily. 3 **bucket-shop** unregistered broking agency, agency dealing in cheap airline tickets; **kick the bucket** *sl.* die. [AF]

buckle /'bʌk(ə)l/ 1 *n.* metal clasp with hinged pin for securing a strap, belt, etc. 2 *v.* fasten with a buckle; (cause to) crumple under pressure. 3 **buckle down** make determined start. [F f. L *buccula* cheek-strap]

buckler *n. hist.* small round shield with handle.

buckram /'bʌkrəm/ *n.* coarse linen or cloth stiffened with paste etc. [F *boquerant*]

buckshee /bʌk'ʃi:/ 1 *a.* & *adv.* free of charge, gratuitously. 2 *n.* free bonus, tip. [corrupt. of BAKSHEESH]

buckshot *n.* coarse lead shot. [BUCK[1]]

buckskin *n.* leather made from buck's skin; thin smooth cotton or woollen cloth.

buckthorn *n.* thorny shrub with berries formerly used as cathartic.

buckwheat *n.* dark-grained cereal used esp. for horse and poultry food. [Du., = beech-wheat]

bucolic /bju:'kɒlɪk/ 1 *a.* of shepherds, rustic, pastoral. 2 *n.* pastoral poem or poetry. 3 **bucolically** *adv.* [L f. Gk (*boukolos* herdsman)]

bud 1 *n.* knoblike projection from which flower, leaf-cluster, or branch develops; flower or leaf not fully open; asexual growth separating from organism as new animal. 2 *v.* (**-dd-**) put forth buds; sprout as bud; begin to grow or develop (*budding lawyer, cricketer*); graft bud of (plant) on another plant. 3 **nip in the bud** suppress or destroy at early stage. [orig. unkn.]

Buddha /'bʊdə/ *n.* title of Indian philosopher Gautama (5th c. BC) and his successors; representation of Gautama. [Skr., = enlightened]

Buddhism /'bʊdɪz(ə)m/ *n.* Asian religion founded by Gautama Buddha; **Buddhist** *n.* & *a.*; **Buddhistic** /-'dɪstɪk/ *a.*

buddleia /'bʌdlɪə/ *n.* shrub or tree with lilac or yellow flowers. [*Buddle*, botanist]

buddy /'bʌdɪ/ *n. colloq.* friend, mate. [perh. f. BROTHER]

budge *v.* move slightly (usu. in negative context: *it won't budge*; *cannot budge it*); (cause to) alter an opinion. [F *bouger*]

budgerigar /'bʌdʒərɪgɑ:/ *n.* Australian grass parakeet, often kept as cage-bird. [Abor.]

budget /'bʌdʒɪt/ 1 *n.* estimate or plan of expenditure in relation to income; periodic (esp. annual) estimate of a country's revenue and expenditure; amount of money needed or available; *attrib.* inexpensive. 2 *v.* allot or allow *for* in budget. 3 **budgetary** *a.* [F f. L *bulga* bag]

budgie /'bʌdʒɪ/ *n. colloq.* budgerigar. [abbr.]

buff 1 *n.* velvety dull-yellow leather; colour of this; *colloq.* enthusiast (*film-buff*). 2 *v.t.* polish (metal etc.); make velvety like buff. 3 **in the buff** naked. [orig. = buffalo, f. F *buffle*]

buffalo /'bʌfələʊ/ *n.* (*pl.* **buffaloes** or *collect.* **buffalo**) wild ox of various kinds; American bison. [Port. f. L f. Gk *boubalos* ox]

buffer[1] *n.* thing that deadens impact, esp. device (usu. one of pair) on railway vehicle or at end of track; *Chem.* substance tending to maintain constant acidity of solution; **buffer State** small one between two great ones, regarded as diminishing danger of quarrels. [imit.]

buffer[2] *n. sl.* man, fellow, esp. an old or incompetent one. [perh. f. prec.]

buffet[1] /'bʊfeɪ/ *n.* place where light meals may be bought (usu. at a counter) and eaten; provision of food where guests serve themselves (*buffet lunch*); sideboard or recessed cupboard for dishes etc.; **buffet car** railway coach in which refreshments are served. [F, = stool]

buffet[2] /'bʌfɪt/ **1** *n.* blow (esp. with the hand), shock. **2** *v.t.* deal blows to; contend with (waves etc). [F dimin. (*bufe* blow)]
buffoon /bə'fu:n/ **1** *n.* silly or ludicrous person, jester. **2** *v.i.* play the buffoon. **3** **buffoonery** *n.* [F f. It. f. L *buffo* clown]
bug **1** *n.* any of various flat-bodied insects with wings hardened at base, esp. foul-smelling one infesting dirty houses and beds; any small insect; *colloq.* virus, infection; *sl.* concealed microphone; *sl.* defect in machine, computer program, etc.; *sl.* enthusiasm, obsession. **2** *v.t.* (**-gg-**) *sl.* conceal microphone in (room etc.); *sl.* annoy. [orig. unkn.]
bugbear *n.* cause of annoyance; object of baseless terror, mental bogy. [*bug* = bogy]
bugger **1** *n.* sodomite; *vulgar* unpleasant or contemptible person or thing. **2** *v.* commit sodomy with; *vulgar* make *off*, fool *about*, mess *up*. **3** *int. vulgar* expressing annoyance or antipathy. **4** **buggery** *n.* [Du. f. F f. L *Bulgarus* Bulgarian heretic]
buggy /'bʌgɪ/ *n.* light horse-drawn vehicle for one or two; small sturdy motor vehicle. [orig. unkn.]
bugle[1] /'bju:g(ə)l/ **1** *n.* brass instrument like small trumpet, used for sounding signals. **2** *v.* sound bugle; sound (call) on bugle. [F f. L *buculus* young bull]
bugle[2] /'bju:g(ə)l/ *n.* creeping plant with usu. blue flowers. [L *bugula*]
bugler *n.* person who sounds bugle. [BUGLE[1]]
buhl /bu:l/ *n.* inlaid work of brass and tortoiseshell. [*Boule*, wood-carver]
build /bɪld/ **1** *v.* (*past* and *p.p.* **built** /bɪlt/) construct by putting parts or material together; develop or establish (reputation etc.); (in *p.p.*) having indicated build (*sturdily built*). **2** *n.* style or form of construction; proportions of human body (*sturdy build*). **3** **build on** use as basis, rely on; **build up** gradually establish or be established; **build-up** *n.* favourable description in advance, gradual approach to climax; **built-up** increased in height etc. by additions, composed of separately made parts, (of locality) fully occupied by houses. [OE]
builder *n.* one who builds, esp. contractor who builds houses.
building *n.* constructing of houses etc.; completed structure such as house, factory, etc.; **building society** society of investors that lends money on mortgage to those buying houses.
bulb *n.* globular base of stem of some plants (e.g. onion, lily) sending roots down and leaves up; electric lamp-filament, its glass container; object or part shaped like a bulb. [L *bulbus* f. Gk, = onion]
bulbous *a.* bulb-shaped; having bulb(s); (of plant) growing from bulb.
bulge **1** *n.* irregular swelling-out of a surface or line; *colloq.* temporary increase in volume or numbers. **2** *v.i.* form bulge. **3** **bulgy** *a.* [F f. L *bulga* bag]
bulk **1** *n.* size or magnitude, esp. when great; the greater part or number *of*; large shape, body, or person; large quantity (*ordered in bulk*); roughage. **2** *v.* increase size or thickness of; seem in terms of size or importance (*bulk large*). **3** **bulk buying** buying in large amounts, esp. by one buyer of much of producer's output. [ON]
bulkhead *n.* upright partition between compartments in ship, aircraft, etc.
bulky *a.* taking up much space, awkwardly large; **bulkily** *adv.*
bull[1] /bʊl/ **1** *n.* uncastrated male of ox family; male of whale, elephant, and other large animals; (**Bull**) sign or constellation Taurus; bull's-eye of target; one who buys shares hoping to sell them at higher price later. **2** *a.* like (that of) bull (*bull neck*). **3** **bull-headed** obstinate, blundering; **bull in a china shop** reckless or clumsy person; **bull market** market with shares rising in price; **bull-nosed** with rounded end; **bull-terrier** cross between bulldog and terrier; **take the bull by the horns** face danger or challenge boldly. [ON]
bull[2] /bʊl/ *n.* papal edict. [F f. L *bulla* seal]
bull[3] /bʊl/ *n.* absurdly illogical statement; *sl.* unnecessary routine tasks. [orig. unkn.]
bulldog *n.* dog of sturdy powerful breed with large head and smooth hair; tenacious courageous person; **bulldog clip** strong sprung clip. [BULL[1]]
bulldoze /'bʊldəʊz/ *v.t.* clear with bulldozer; *colloq.* intimidate, make one's *way* forcibly.
bulldozer *n.* powerful tractor with broad curved vertical blade at front for clearing ground.
bullet /'bʊlɪt/ *n.* small round or cylindrical missile with pointed end, fired from gun or rifle. [F dimin. (*boule* ball)]
bulletin /'bʊlɪtɪn/ *n.* short official statement of news; society's regular list of information etc. [F f. It. dimin. (BULL[2])]
bullfight *n.* sport of baiting and killing bulls as public spectacle, esp. in Spain; **bullfighter** *n.*; **bullfighting** *n.* [BULL[1]]
bullfinch *n.* songbird with strong beak and fine plumage.
bullfrog *n.* large American frog with bellowing cry.
bullion /'bʊljən/ *n.* gold or silver in bulk

before coining, or valued by weight. [F (BOIL[1])]

bullock /'bʊlək/ *n.* castrated bull. [OE dimin. of BULL[1]]

bullring *n.* arena for bullfight. [BULL[1]]

bull's-eye *n.* centre of target; large hard minty sweet; hemisphere or thick disc of glass as window in ship, small circular window; hemispherical lens, lantern with this; boss of glass at centre of blown glass sheet.

bully[1] /'bʊlɪ/ **1** *n.* person using strength and power to coerce others by fear. **2** *v.t.* persecute or oppress by force or threats. **3** *int. sl.* expressing admiration (*bully for you*). [Du.]

bully[2] /'bʊlɪ/ **1** *n.* start of play in hockey, in which two opponents strike each other's sticks three times and then go for ball. **2** *v.i.* start play thus (also with *off*). [orig. unkn.]

bully[3] /'bʊlɪ/ *n.* (in full **bully beef**) corned beef. [F (BOIL[1])]

bulrush /'bʊlrʌʃ/ *n.* kind of tall rush; *Bibl.* papyrus. [perh. BULL[1] = coarse + RUSH[2]]

bulwark /'bʊlwək/ *n.* defensive wall, esp. of earth; protecting person or thing; (usu. in *pl.*) ship's side above deck. [MDu.]

bum[1] *n. sl.* the buttocks. [orig. uncert.]

bum[2] *US sl.* **1** *n.* loafer, dissolute person. **2** *v.* (**-mm-**) loaf *around*, cadge. **3** *a.* of poor quality. [G *bummler* loafer]

bumble /'bʌmb(ə)l/ *v.i.* blunder, act ineptly; ramble *on* in speech; make buzz. [f. BOOM[1]]

bumble-bee *n.* large bee with loud hum.

bumf *n. sl.* documents, papers (esp. depreciatory). [*bum-fodder* = toilet-paper]

bump **1** *n.* dull-sounding blow or collision; swelling caused by it; rounded swelling or lump on a surface, uneven patch on road etc.; prominence on skull, thought to indicate mental faculty. **2** *v.* hit or come against with a bump; collide *against* or *into*; hurt thus; move *along* with jolting action. **3 bump into** *colloq.* meet by chance; **bump off** *sl.* murder; **bump up** *colloq.* increase (prices etc.). **4 bumpily** *adv.*; **bumpy** *a.* [imit.]

bumper *n.* unusually large or fine example (*bumper crop*); horizontal bar across front or back of motor vehicle to reduce damage in collision; (in cricket) ball rising high after pitching; brim-full glass.

bumpkin /'bʌmpkɪn/ *n.* simple country person with awkward manners. [Du.]

bumptious /'bʌmpʃəs/ *a.* offensively conceited or self-assertive. [BUMP, after *fractious*]

bun *n.* small soft round sweet cake, often with dried fruit; hair worn in shape of bun; **bun-fight** *sl.* tea-party. [orig. unkn.]

bunch **1** *n.* set of things growing or fastened together (*bunch of flowers, grapes, keys*); collection, lot (*best of the bunch*); *sl.* gang, group. **2** *v.* make into a bunch; gather into close folds; form group or crowd. **3 bunchy** *a.* [orig. unkn.]

bundle /'bʌnd(ə)l/ **1** *n.* collection of things tied or fastened together; set of nerve fibres etc. banded together; *sl.* large amount of money. **2** *v.* make *up* or tie into a bundle; throw hastily *into* receptacle; go or send (person) hurriedly or unceremoniously *out, off, away*, etc. [LG or Du.]

bung **1** *n.* stopper for closing hole in container, esp. cask. **2** *v.t.* stop with bung; *sl.* throw, put. **3 bunged up** stopped by blockage. [Du.]

bungalow /'bʌŋgələʊ/ *n.* house of one storey. [orig. in India; Gujarati f. Hindi, = of Bengal]

bungle /'bʌŋg(ə)l/ **1** *v.* blunder over, mismanage, or fail at (task); work badly or clumsily. **2** *n.* bungled work or attempt. [imit.]

bunion /'bʌnjən/ *n.* swelling on foot, esp. on big toe. [F]

bunk[1] *n.* shelflike bed against wall, esp. one built into ship etc.; **bunk-bed** two or more bunks one above the other, forming unit. [orig. unkn.]

bunk[2] *n.* only in **do a bunk** *sl.* depart hurriedly, run away. [orig. unkn.]

bunk[3] *n. sl.* nonsense, humbug. [BUNKUM]

bunker **1** *n.* container for fuel; reinforced underground shelter; sandy hollow as obstacle in golf-course. **2** *v.t.* fill fuel bunkers of (ship etc.). [orig. unkn.]

bunkum /'bʌŋkəm/ *n.* nonsense, humbug. [*Buncombe* in US]

bunny /'bʌnɪ/ *n.* child's name for rabbit. [dial. *bun* rabbit]

Bunsen burner /'bʌns(ə)n/ laboratory instrument with vertical tube burning mixture of air and gas to produce great heat. [*Bunsen*, chemist]

bunting[1] /'bʌntɪŋ/ *n.* flags and other decorations; loosely-woven fabric used for these. [orig. unkn.]

bunting[2] /'bʌntɪŋ/ *n.* small bird allied to finches. [orig. unkn.]

buoy /bɔɪ/ **1** *n.* anchored float as navigation mark etc.; lifebuoy. **2** *v.t.* mark with a buoy; keep (thing) afloat; sustain courage or spirits of (often with *up*). [Du., perh. f. L f. Gk]

buoyant /'bɔɪənt/ *a.* able or apt to float or keep something afloat; constantly cheerful or light-hearted; **buoyancy** *n.* [F or Sp. (prec.)]

bur *n.* prickly clinging seed-case or flower-head of plant, plant producing burs; person hard to shake off. [Scand.]

burble /'bɜ:b(ə)l/ *v.i.* make murmuring noise; speak ramblingly. [imit.]

burbot /'bɜ:bət/ *n.* eel-like freshwater fish. [F]

burden /'bɜ:d(ə)n/ **1** *n.* thing carried, heavy load; oppressive duty, obligation, expense, emotion, etc.; bearing of loads (*beast of burden*); ship's carrying capacity; refrain of song, theme or gist of speech etc. **2** *v.t.* load with burden, encumber, oppress. **3 burden of proof** obligation to prove case. [OE (rel. to BIRTH)]

burdock /'bɜ:dɒk/ *n.* plant with prickly flowers and docklike leaves. [BUR, DOCK[3]]

bureau /'bjʊərəʊ/ *n.* (*pl.* **bureaux** or **-eaus** /-əʊz/) writing-desk with drawers; *US* chest of drawers; office or department for transacting specific business; government department. [F, orig. = baize]

bureaucracy /bjʊə'rɒkrəsɪ/ *n.* government by central administration, officialism; officials of State administration, esp. regarded as oppressive and inflexible.

bureaucrat /'bjʊərəʊkræt/ *n.* official in a bureaucracy; one who administers inflexibly; **bureaucratic** /-'krætɪk/ *a.*; **bureaucratically** /-'krætɪkəlɪ/ *adv.*

burette /bjʊə'ret/, *US* **buret** *n.* graduated glass tube with tap at end for measurement of liquid in chemical analysis. [F]

burgee /bɜ:'dʒi:/ *n.* triangular or swallow-tailed flag with colours of sailing-club. [F]

burgeon /'bɜ:dʒ(ə)n/ *v.i.* begin to grow rapidly, flourish. [F f. L *burra* wool]

burgess /'bɜ:dʒɪs/ *n.* inhabitant of a town or borough; *hist.* MP for borough or corporate town or university. [F f. L *burgus* borough]

burgh /'bʌrə/ *n.* Scottish borough. [Sc. form of BOROUGH]

burgher /'bɜ:gə/ *n.* citizen of foreign town. [G or Du.]

burglar /'bɜ:glə/ *n.* person who commits burglary; **burglarious** /-'gleərɪəs/ *a.* [AF]

burglary *n.* entry into building illegally to commit theft, do bodily harm, etc. ¶ See HOUSEBREAKING.

burgle /'bɜ:g(ə)l/ *v.* commit burglary on (house, person); act as burglar.

burgomaster /'bɜ:gəmɑ:stə/ *n.* mayor of Dutch or Flemish town. [Du.]

burgundy /'bɜ:gəndɪ/ *n.* red or white wine from Burgundy in E. France; similar wine from elsewhere.

burial /'berɪəl/ *n.* burying of dead body, funeral; *Archaeol.* grave or its remains. [BURY]

burin /'bjʊərɪn/ *n.* tool for engraving on copper; *Archaeol.* chisel-pointed flint tool. [F]

burlesque /bɜ:'lesk/ **1** *n.* dramatic or literary parody, comic imitation; this as branch of art; *US* variety show, esp. with strip-tease. **2** *a.* in the nature of burlesque. **3** *v.t.* make or give burlesque of. [F f. It. (*burla* mockery)]

burly /'bɜ:lɪ/ *a.* of stout sturdy build. [OE]

burn[1] **1** *v.* (*past* and *p.p.* **burnt** or **burned**) set on fire; be consumed or destroyed by fire, blaze or glow with fire; (cause to) be injured or damaged by fire or sun or great heat; use or be used as fuel; (cause to) give out light or heat; char or scorch in cooking; subject to heat, produce (hole, mark, etc.) by fire or heat; harden (bricks) by fire; tan or colour with heat or light; (cause to) die by fire; cauterize, brand; make or be hot, give or feel sensation or pain of or like heat; (cause to) feel great emotion or passion. **2** *n.* mark or injury caused by burning. **3 burn one's boats** (or **bridges**) commit oneself irrevocably; **burn the candle at both ends** exhaust one's strength or resources by undertaking too much; **burn down** (cause to) be destroyed by burning; **burn one's fingers** suffer for meddling or rashness; **burning-glass** lens for concentrating sun's rays to produce flame; **burn the midnight oil** read or work late into the night; **burnt ochre** (or **sienna** etc.) pigment darkened by burning; **burnt offering** sacrifice offered by burning. [OE]

burn[2] *n. Sc.* brook. [OE]

burner *n.* part of lamp or cooker that emits and shapes the flame. [BURN[1]]

burning *a.* that burns; ardent, intense; hotly discussed, vital.

burnish /'bɜ:nɪʃ/ *v.t.* polish by rubbing. [F *brunir* (*brun* brown)]

burnous /bɜ:'nu:s/ *n.* Arab or Moorish hooded cloak. [F f. Arab. f. Gk]

burnt see BURN[1].

burp *colloq.* **1** *v.* belch; cause (baby) to belch. **2** *n.* belch. [imit.]

burr **1** *n.* whirring sound; rough sound of letter *r*; rough edge on metal or paper; small drill. **2** *v.i.* make burr. [imit.]

burrow /'bʌrəʊ/ **1** *n.* hole or tunnel dug by fox or rabbit or other animal as dwelling. **2** *v.* make or live in burrow; make (hole, one's *way*) by digging; hide oneself; investigate or search (*into*). [var. of BOROUGH]

bursar /'bɜ:sə/ *n.* treasurer, esp. of a

college; student holding bursary. [F or med.L (*bursa* purse)]
bursary *n*. scholarship or grant awarded to student; office of bursar. [med.L (prec.)]
burst **1** *v*. (*past* and *p.p.* **burst**) fly violently apart or open forcibly by expansion of contents or internal pressure; cause to do this; send (container etc.) violently apart; make one's way suddenly or dramatically *in* or *out*, get away from or through; express one's feelings forcibly or suddenly; be full to overflowing; appear or come suddenly (*burst into flame*); be as if about to burst because of effort, excitement, etc. **2** *n*. bursting; sudden issuing forth (*burst of gunfire*); outbreak; spurt, gallop. **3** **burst into** suddenly begin to utter (*burst into song, tears*); **burst out** suddenly begin (*burst out laughing*). [OE]
burton /ˈbɜːt(ə)n/ *n. sl.* only in **go for a burton** be lost or destroyed or killed. [orig. uncert.]
bury /ˈberɪ/ *v.t.* place (dead body) in the earth, tomb, or sea; lose by death (*has buried 4 husbands*); put under ground, hide in earth, cover up; consign to obscurity, put out of sight; involve oneself deeply in (*buried himself, was buried, in his work*); **bury the hatchet** cease to quarrel. [OE]
bus **1** *n*. (*pl*. **buses,** *US* **busses**) large passenger vehicle, esp. one serving public on fixed route; *colloq*. motor car or aeroplane. **2** *v*. (**-s-**, *US* **-ss-**) go by bus, *US* transport by bus, esp. to counteract racial segregation. **3** **bus lane** part of road's length marked off mainly for use by buses; **busman's holiday** leisure time spent in activity similar to one's regular work; **bus-stop** regular stopping-place of bus, sign marking this. [abbr. of OMNIBUS]
busby /ˈbʌzbɪ/ *n*. tall fur hat worn by hussars and guardsmen. [orig. unkn.]
bush[1] /bʊʃ/ *n*. shrub or clump of shrubs; thing resembling this, esp. clump of hair or fur; (esp. in Australia and Africa) wild uncultivated district, woodland or forest; **bush-baby** small African tree-climbing lemur; **bush telegraph** rapid spreading of information, rumour, etc. [OE & ON]
bush[2] /bʊʃ/ **1** *n*. metal lining for round hole enclosing revolving shaft etc.; electrically insulating sleeve. **2** *v.t.* fit with bush. [Du. *buse* box]
bushel /ˈbʊʃ(ə)l/ *n*. measure of capacity for corn, fruit, etc. (8 gallons, c. 36.4 litres). [F]
bushman *n*. inhabitant of or traveller in Australian bush; (**Bushman**) member or language of aboriginal peoples in S. Africa. [BUSH[1]]
bushy *a*. growing thickly like a bush; having many bushes.
business /ˈbɪznɪs/ *n*. one's regular occupation or profession; thing that is one's concern; task, duty; serious work or activity; *derog*. affair, matter (*sick of the whole business*); thing needing to be dealt with; buying and selling, trade; commercial house or firm; action on theatre stage; **business man** (or **woman**) man (or woman) engaged in trade or commerce; **mean business** be in earnest; **mind one's own business** not meddle. [OE (BUSY)]
businesslike *a*. efficient, systematic.
busker *n*. street singer, itinerant entertainer. [obs. *busk* peddle]
bust[1] *colloq*. **1** *v*. (*past* and *p.p.* **bust** or **busted**) break, burst. **2** *a*. broken, burst; bankrupt. **3** *n*. sudden (esp. financial) failure; spree. **4** **bust-up** *sl*. quarrel, explosion, collapse. [f. BURST]
bust[2] *n*. sculptured representation of head, shoulders, and chest; upper front of (esp. woman's) body, measurement round upper part of body; **busty** *a*. [F f. It.]
bustard /ˈbʌstəd/ *n*. large tall swift-running bird. [AF f. L *avis tarda* slow bird ('slow' unexplained)]
bustle[1] /ˈbʌs(ə)l/ **1** *v*. make show of activity, hurry *about*; make (person) hurry or work hard. **2** *n*. excited activity. [perh. f. obs. *busk* prepare]
bustle[2] /ˈbʌs(ə)l/ *n. hist*. padding used to puff out woman's skirt at the back. [orig. uncert.]
busy /ˈbɪzɪ/ **1** *a*. fully occupied, concentrating hard; full of activity (*busy day, town*); engaged to capacity; always employed; fussy, meddlesome. **2** *v.t.* occupy or keep busy (esp. *oneself*). [OE]
busybody *n*. meddlesome person.
but /bət, *emphat*. bʌt/ **1** *conj*. (introducing words of contrary tendency) nevertheless, however (*tried hard but did not succeed, but without success*), on the other hand (*I am old but you are young*); otherwise than (*cannot choose but do it*); that not (*not such a fool but he can see the reason*); without the result that (*justice was never done but someone complained*). **2** *prep*. (occas. indistinguishable from *conj*.) except, apart from, other than (*we are all safe but me, but I* [sc. *am not*]; *but for you I would be safe; last but one, two*, etc.). **3** *adv*. only, no more than, only just (*he is but a child; I can but do it; they had but arrived*); as emphatic (*never do it, but never*). **4** *pron*. who not (*there is not a man but feels pity*). **5** *n*. an objection (*ifs and buts*). **6** *v.t.* only in **but me no buts** do not raise objections. **7** **but that** (or **what**) other than

that (*who knows but that, but what, it is true?*); **but that** (after negative) that (*I do not doubt but that he will come*). [OE]

butane /'bju:teɪn/ *n.* a hydrocarbon of the paraffin series, used in liquefied form as fuel. [f. BUTYL]

butch /bʊtʃ/ *a. sl.* masculine, tough-looking. [orig. uncert.]

butcher /'bʊtʃə/ **1** *n.* one who sells meat; one who slaughters animals for food; one who kills people indiscriminately or brutally. **2** *v.t.* slaughter or cut up (animal); kill needlessly or cruelly; make a mess of (*lit.* & *fig.*). [F (*boc* BUCK[1])]

butchery *n.* butcher's trade; needless or cruel killing.

butler *n.* chief manservant of household, in charge of pantry and wine-cellar. [F (*bouteille* bottle)]

butt[1] **1** *v.* push with head like ram or goat; (cause to) meet edge to edge. **2** *n.* act of butting; join of two edges. **3 butt in** interrupt, meddle. [F f. Gmc]

butt[2] *n.* object of ridicule, person habitually ridiculed or teased; mound behind target, (in *pl.*) shooting-range. [F *but* goal]

butt[3] *n.* thicker end of tool or weapon; stub of cigarette. [Du.]

butt[4] *n.* large cask. [F f. L *buttis*]

butter 1 *n.* edible yellow fatty substance into which cream solidifies on churning, used on bread and in cookery; substance of similar form (*peanut butter*). **2** *v.t.* spread, cook, or serve with butter. **3 butter-bean** bean with yellow pods, dried white Lima bean; **butter-fingers** person likely to drop things; **butter muslin** thin loosely woven cloth orig. for wrapping butter; **butter up** *colloq.* flatter. [OE f. L f. Gk *bouturon*]

buttercup *n.* wild plant with yellow cup-shaped flowers.

butterfly *n.* insect with long thin body and four usu. brightly coloured wings, active by day; (in *pl.*) nervous sensation felt in the stomach; **butterfly nut** a kind of wing-nut; **butterfly stroke** stroke in swimming, with both arms raised and lifted forwards together.

buttermilk *n.* somewhat acid liquid left after churning butter.

butterscotch *n.* brittle sweet made from butter, brown sugar, etc.

buttery[1] *a.* like or containing butter.

buttery[2] /'bʌtərɪ/ *n.* place in college etc. where provisions are kept and supplied. [BUTT[4]]

buttock /'bʌtək/ *n.* (usu. in *pl.*) either of two fleshy protuberances on lower rear part of human body; corresponding part of animal. [*butt* ridge]

button /'bʌt(ə)n/ **1** *n.* small disc or knob sewn to garment to fasten it by passing through buttonhole or as ornament or badge; small rounded object similar in form, esp. knob to operate electrical device. **2** *v.* (usu. with *up*) fasten with buttons, *fig.* complete satisfactorily. **3 button mushroom** small unopened mushroom; **not worth a button** of little or no value. [F f. Gmc]

buttonhole 1 *n.* slit through which fastening button passes; flower worn in buttonhole of coat-lapel. **2** *v.t.* accost and detain (reluctant listener); make buttonholes in.

buttress /'bʌtrɪs/ **1** *n.* projecting support built against wall; thing or person that gives help, encouragement, etc. **2** *v.t.* support with buttress; help, encourage. [F (*bouter* BUTT[1])]

butyl /'bju:tɪl/ *n.* radical C_4H_9 derived from butane. [L *butyrum* BUTTER]

buxom /'bʌksəm/ *a.* (esp. of woman) plump, healthy-looking, large and shapely. [earlier = pliant, rel. to BOW[2]]

buy /baɪ/ **1** *v.t.* (*past* and *p.p.* **bought** /bɔ:t/) obtain in exchange for money or by some sacrifice; be means of obtaining (*the best that money can buy*); bribe (person); *sl.* believe, accept truth of. **2** *n.* buying; thing bought (*bad, good, best,* etc., *buy*). **3 buy in** buy stock of; **buy it** *sl.* be killed; **buy off** pay to get rid of; **buy out** pay (person) to give up ownership or interest; **buy up** buy all available stocks of, absorb (firm) by purchase. [OE]

buyer *n.* one who buys; person employed to purchase stock for large shop; **buyer's market** trading conditions favourable to buyer.

buzz 1 *v.* make humming sound of bee; be filled with activity or excitement; threaten (aircraft) by flying very close to it; *sl.* call (person) on telephone etc. **2** *n.* humming sound; confused sound as of people talking; sound of buzzer; *sl.* telephone call. **3 buzz about** (or **around**) move about excitedly; **buzz off** *sl.* hurry away. [imit.]

buzzard /'bʌzəd/ *n.* large kind of predatory hawk. [F f. L *buteo* falcon]

buzzer *n.* electrical device producing buzzing sound as signal. [BUZZ]

bwana /'bwɑ:nə/ *n.* sir, master (form of address in Africa). [Swahili]

by /baɪ/ **1** *prep.* near, beside (*stand by the door*), in possession or company or region of (*house by the church*; *come and sit by me*; *have not got it by me*); along, passing through or beside (*path by the river*; *travel by Paris, by sea*); avoiding (*pass by him*); in circumstances of (*by day, daylight*); towards, approaching (*north by north-west*); through agency, means, instrumentality, or causation of (*by proxy*; *by skill*; *by train*; *by chance*;

lead by the hand; go by the name of; what do you mean by that?; have been made by robots; opera by Mozart); as soon as, not later than (*by now; by next week*); according to, using as standard or unit (*by your leave; judge by appearances; sold by the metre; paid by the hour*); with succession of (*by degrees; by the minute; day by day; bit by bit*); to the extent of (*missed by a foot; better by far*); in respect of (*Jones by name; pull up by the roots; do as you would be done by*); as surely as one believes in (*by God; swear by all that is sacred*). **2** *adv.* near (*stand by*); aside, in reserve (*put it by*); past (*go, march, by*). **3** *a.* subordinate, incidental, secondary, side. **4** *n.* = BYE¹. **5 by and by** *adv.* & *n.* before long, *the* future; **by and large** on the whole, everything considered; **by the by** (or **bye**) incidentally; **by oneself** alone, unaided. [OE]

bye¹ /baɪ/ *n.* run scored in cricket from ball that passes batsman without being hit; status of unpaired competitor in a sport, who proceeds to next round as if having won. [BY]

bye² /baɪ/ *int.* (also **bye-bye**) *colloq.* = GOODBYE. [abbr.]

by-election *n.* election of MP in single constituency. [BY]

bygone 1 *a.* past, antiquated. **2** *n.* (in *pl.*) past offence (*let bygones be bygones*).

by-law *n.* regulation made by local authority or corporation. [obs. *by* town]

byline *n.* line in newspaper etc. naming writer of article; secondary line of work. [BY]

bypass 1 *n.* main road taking through traffic round town or congested area; secondary channel, pipe, etc., when main one is closed or blocked. **2** *v.t.* avoid, go round; provide with bypass.

bypath *n.* secluded path; minor branch of subject.

by-play *n.* minor action in play, usu. without speech.

by-product *n.* substance or product made in manufacture of something else; secondary result.

byre /'baɪə/ *n.* cow-shed. [OE]

by-road *n.* minor road. [BY]

byssinosis /bɪsɪ'nəʊsɪs/ *n.* lung disease caused by prolonged inhalation of textile fibre dust. [Gk *bussinos* made of linen]

bystander *n.* one who stands by but does not take part, mere spectator. [BY]

by-street *n.* side-street.

byte /baɪt/ *n.* group of binary digits in computer, often representing one character. [orig. uncert.]

byway *n.* by-road or bypath; minor activity. [BY]

byword *n.* person or thing cited as notable example (*is a byword for luxury*); familiar saying.

Byzantine /bɪ'zæntaɪn, baɪ-/ **1** *a.* of Byzantium or the E. Roman Empire; of its style of architecture; resembling its complicated politics, inflexible, underhand. **2** *n.* native or inhabitant of Byzantium. [F or L (*Byzantium*, now Istanbul)]

C

C, c /siː/ *n.* (*pl.* **Cs, C's**) third letter; *Mus.* first note of natural major scale; *Rom. num.* 100; (as *c*) third known quantity in algebra; (as *C*) third hypothetical person or example.

C *abbr.* centigrade; Celsius.

c. *abbr.* century; chapter; cent.

c. abbr. *circa*.

C *symb.* carbon; copyright (also ©).

ca. abbr. *circa*.

Ca *symb.* calcium.

cab *n.* taxi, *hist.* hackney carriage; driver's compartment in train, lorry, or crane. [abbr. CABRIOLET]

cabal /kə'bæl/ *n.* secret intrigue; political clique. [F f. L]

cabaret /'kæbəreɪ/ *n.* entertainment in night-club or restaurant while guests eat or drink at tables; such night-club etc. [F, = tavern]

cabbage /'kæbɪdʒ/ *n.* vegetable with thick green or purple leaves usu. forming round head; *colloq.* person who is inactive or lacks interest. [F *caboche* head]

cabby *n.* (also **cabbie**) *colloq.* taxi-driver. [CAB]

caber /'keɪbə/ *n.* roughly-trimmed tree-trunk used in Scottish sport of **tossing the caber.** [Gael.]

cabin /'kæbɪn/ *n.* small shelter or house, esp. of wood; room or compartment in ship, aircraft, etc., for passengers or crew; driver's cab; **cabin-boy** ship's waiter; **cabin cruiser** large motor boat with cabin. [F f. L]

cabinet /'kæbɪnɪt/ *n.* cupboard or case with drawers, shelves, etc., for storing or displaying articles; piece of furniture housing radio or television set etc.;

(**Cabinet**) group of ministers responsible for controlling government policy; **cabinet-maker** skilled joiner. [dimin. of prec.]

cable /'keɪb(ə)l/ **1** *n.* thick rope of wire or hemp; encased group of insulated wires for transmitting electricity or telecommunications; anchor chain of ship; cablegram. **2** *v.* transmit (message), send message to (person), by undersea cable. **3 cable-car** car (often one of series) mounted on endless cable and drawn up and down mountainside etc. by engine at one end; **cable stitch** knitted stitch resembling twisted rope; **cable television** transmission of television programmes by cable to subscribers. [F f. L *caplum* halter f. Arab.]

cablegram *n.* telegraph message sent by undersea cable.

caboodle /kə'bu:d(ə)l/ *n. sl.* in **the whole caboodle** the whole lot. [orig. uncert.]

caboose /kə'bu:s/ *n.* kitchen on ship's deck; *US* guard's van esp. on goods train. [Du.]

cabriolet /kæbrɪəʊ'leɪ/ *n.* light two-wheeled carriage with hood, drawn by one horse. [F (CAPRIOLE)]

cacao /kə'kɑ:əʊ/ *n.* (*pl.* **cacaos**) seed from which cocoa and chocolate are made; tree producing it. [Sp. f. Nahuatl]

cachalot /'kæʃəlɒt/ *n.* sperm whale. [F f. Sp. & Port.]

cache /kæʃ/ **1** *n.* place for hiding or storing treasure or stores; things so hidden. **2** *v.t.* put in cache. [F (*cacher* hide)]

cachet /'kæʃeɪ/ *n.* distinguishing mark or seal; prestige; internal evidence of authenticity; small capsule of medicine. [F (*cacher* press)]

cack-handed /kæk'hændɪd/ *a. colloq.* awkward, clumsy; left-handed. [dial. *cack* excrement]

cackle /'kæk(ə)l/ **1** *n.* clucking of hen; noisy inconsequential talk; loud silly laugh. **2** *v.i.* emit cackle; utter or express with cackle. **3 cut the cackle** *colloq.* come to the point. [imit.]

cacophony /kə'kɒfənɪ/ *n.* harsh discordant sound; **cacophonous** *a.* [F f. Gk (*kakos* bad, *phōnē* sound)]

cactus /'kæktəs/ *n.* (*pl.* **cacti** /-aɪ/ or **cactuses**) plant with thick fleshy stem, usu. with spines but no leaves. [L f. Gk]

cad *n.* person (esp. man) who behaves dishonourably; **caddish** *a.* [abbr. of CADDIE]

cadaver /kə'deɪvə/ *n.* corpse. [L (*cado* fall)]

cadaverous /kə'dævərəs/ *a.* corpse-like, deathly pale.

caddie /'kædɪ/ **1** *n.* person who assists golfer during match, carrying clubs etc. **2** *v.i.* act as caddie. [F CADET]

caddis-fly /'kædɪs/ *n.* four-winged insect living near water; **caddis(-worm)** larva of caddis-fly. [orig. unkn.]

caddy[1] / kædɪ/ *n.* small box for holding tea. [Malay]

caddy[2] var. of CADDIE.

cadence /'keɪdəns/ *n.* fall of the voice, esp. at end of phrase or sentence; tonal inflection; measured movement of sound; close of musical phrase. [F f. It. f. L *cado* fall)]

cadenza /kə'denzə/ *n.* flourish in a musical cadence, esp. elaborate improvisation by soloist near end of concerto movement. [It. (prec.)]

cadet /kə'det/ *n.* young trainee in armed services or police force. [F f. dimin. of L *caput* head]

cadge /kædʒ/ *v.* beg; get or seek by begging. [orig. unkn.]

cadi /'kɑ:dɪ/ *n.* judge in Muslim country. [Arab.]

cadmium /'kædmɪəm/ *n.* bluish-white metallic element, physically resembling tin. [L f. Gk *kadmia* Cadmean (earth)]

cadre /'kɑ:də, 'kɑ:drə/ *n.* basic unit, esp. of servicemen; politically active group in Communist countries. [F f. It. f. L *quadrus* square]

caecum /'si:kəm/, n. (pl. **caeca**) tubular pouch forming first part of large intestine. [L (*caecus* blind)]

Caenozoic var. of CAINOZOIC.

Caerphilly /keə'fɪlɪ/ *n.* a kind of mild pale cheese. [*Caerphilly* in Wales]

Caesar /'si:zə/ *n.* title of Roman emperors, esp. from Augustus to Hadrian; dictator, autocrat. [L (C. Julius *Caesar*)]

Caesarean /si:'zeərɪən/ *a.* (of birth) effected by cutting into womb through wall of abdomen. [prec. (Julius Caesar supposedly being born this way)]

caesium /'si:zɪəm/ *n.* soft silver-white element. [L *caesius* blue-grey]

caesura /sɪ'zjʊərə/ *n.* short pause in line of verse. [L (*caedo* cut)]

café /'kæfeɪ/ *n.* small coffee-house or restaurant. [F]

cafeteria /kæfɪ'tɪərɪə/ *n.* restaurant in which customers serve themselves from a counter or display. [Amer. Sp., = coffee-shop]

caff *n. sl.* café. [abbr.]

caffeine /'kæfi:n/ *n.* alkaloid stimulant found in tea leaves and coffee beans. [F (*café* coffee)]

caftan /'kæftæn/ *n.* long usu. belted tunic worn by men in countries of Near East; woman's long loose dress. [Turk.]

cage 1 *n.* structure of bars or wires, esp. for confining animals or birds; any similar open framework, esp. enclosed platform or lift in mine. **2** *v.t.* confine in cage. [F f. L *cavea*]

cagey /'keɪdʒɪ/ *a. colloq.* cautious and uncommunicative; wary; **cagily** *adv.*; **caginess** *n.* [orig. unkn.]

cagoule /kə'gu:l/ *n.* thin hooded waterproof jacket reaching to knees. [F]

cahoots /kə'hu:ts/ *n.pl. US sl.* in **in cahoots with** in collusion with. [orig. uncert.]

caiman var. of CAYMAN.

Cain *n.* in **raise Cain** *colloq.* make disturbance. [*Cain*, eldest son of Adam (Gen. 4)]

Cainozoic /kaɪnə'zəʊɪk/ **1** *a.* of the third geological era. **2** *n.* this era. [Gk *kainos* new, *zōion* animal]

cairn *n.* mound of rough stones as monument or landmark; **cairn (terrier)** small shaggy terrier with short legs. [Gael.]

cairngorm /'keəngɔ:m/ *n.* yellow or wine-coloured gem-stone. [*Cairngorms* in Scotland]

caisson /'keɪs(ə)n, kə'su:n/ *n.* watertight chamber in which underwater construction work can be done. [F f. It. *cassone*]

cajole /kə'dʒəʊl/ *v.t.* persuade or soothe by flattery, deceit, etc.; **cajolery** *n.* [F]

cake 1 *n.* mixture of flour, butter, eggs, sugar, etc., baked in oven; this baked in flat round or ornamental shape and often iced and decorated; other food in flat round shape (*fish cake*); flattish compact mass (*cake of soap*). **2** *v.* form into compact mass; cover *with* hard or sticky mass. **3 have one's cake and eat it** enjoy both of two conflicting alternatives; **like hot cakes** rapidly or successfully; **piece of cake** *colloq.* something easily achieved. [ON]

calabash /'kæləbæʃ/ *n.* tropical American tree with fruit in form of large gourds; this or similar gourd whose shell serves for holding liquid etc.; bowl or pipe made from gourd. [F f. Sp.]

calamine /'kæləmaɪn/ *n.* pink powder, chiefly zinc carbonate or oxide, used esp. in skin lotions. [F f. L]

calamity /kə'læmɪtɪ/ *n.* grievous disaster or adversity; deep distress; **calamitous** *a.* [F f. L]

calcareous /kæl'keərɪəs/ *a.* of or containing calcium carbonate. [CALX]

calceolaria /kælsɪə'leərɪə/ *n.* plant with slipper-shaped flower. [L *calceus* shoe]

calces *pl.* of CALX.

calcify /'kælsɪfaɪ/ *v.* harden by deposit of calcium salts; convert or be converted into calcium carbonate; **calcification** /-fɪ'keɪʃ(ə)n/ *n.* [CALX]

calcine /'kælsɪn, -saɪn/ *v.* reduce or be reduced to quicklime or powder by burning or roasting; **calcination** /-'neɪʃ(ə)n/ *n.* [F or med.L (CALX)]

calcium /'kælsɪəm/ *n.* greyish-white metallic element whose oxide is quicklime and which is widely present as calcium carbonate in chalk, bone, etc.; **calcium carbide** carbide used in making acetylene gas. [L (CALX)]

calculate /'kælkjʊleɪt/ *v.* ascertain or forecast, esp. by mathematics or by reckoning; plan deliberately; rely *on*; *US colloq.* suppose, believe; **calculable** *a.* [L (CALCULUS)]

calculated *a.* (of action) done with awareness of likely consequences; designed or suitable *to do* thing.

calculating *a.* (of person) shrewd, scheming.

calculation /kælkjʊ'leɪʃ(ə)n/ *n.* act or result of calculating; scheming. [F f. L (CALCULUS)]

calculator *n.* device (esp. small electronic one) used for making mathematical calculations.

calculus /'kælkjʊləs/ *n.* (*pl.* **calculi** /-aɪ/, **calculuses**) particular method of mathematical calculation (*differential, integral, calculus*), esp. = *infinitesimal calculus*; stone or concretion formed in some part of the body. [L, = small stone (used on abacus)]

caldron var. of CAULDRON.

Caledonian /kælɪ'dəʊnɪən/ **1** *a.* of Scotland. **2** *n.* Scotsman. [L *Caledonia* N. Britain]

calendar /'kælɪndə/ **1** *n.* system fixing year's beginning, length, and subdivision; chart showing days, weeks, and months of a particular year; adjustable device showing day's date etc.; register or list of special dates or events. **2** *v.t.* enter in calendar; analyse and index (documents). [F f. L (CALENDS)]

calender /'kælɪndə/ **1** *n.* machine for rolling cloth or paper etc. to glaze or smooth it. **2** *v.t.* press in calender. [F]

calends /'kælɪndz/ *n.pl.* first of month in ancient Roman calendar. [F f. L *calendae*]

calf[1] /kɑ:f/ *n.* (*pl.* **calves**) young of cow or bull; young of other animals, e.g. deer, elephant, and whale; calfskin; **calf-love** immature feeling of love. [OE]

calf[2] /kɑ:f/ *n.* (*pl.* **calves**) fleshy hind part of human leg below knee. [ON]

calfskin *n.* calf-leather, esp. in bookbinding and shoemaking. [CALF[1]]

calibrate /'kælɪbreɪt/ *v.t.* mark (gauge) with scale of readings; correlate readings of (instrument etc.) with a standard; find calibre of; **calibration** /-'breɪʃ(ə)n/ *n.* [foll.]

calibre /'kælɪbə/, *US* **caliber** *n.* internal diameter of gun or tube; diameter of bullet or shell; strength or quality of character, ability, importance. [F f. It. f. Arab., = mould]

calices *pl.* of **calix.**

calico /'kælɪkəʊ/ **1** *n.* (*pl.* **calicoes**, *US* **-os**) cotton cloth, esp. plain white or unbleached; *US* printed cotton fabric. **2** *a.* of calico; *US* multicoloured. [*Calicut* in India]

californium /kælɪ'fɔ:nɪəm/ *n.* artificial radioactive metallic element. [*California* in USA, where first made]

caliph /'kælɪf, 'keɪ-/ *n.* Muslim chief civil and religious leader. [F f. Arab., = successor (of Muhammad)]

caliphate /'kælɪfeɪt, 'keɪ-/ *n.* rank, domain, or term of office of a caliph.

calix /'keɪlɪks/ *n.* (*pl.* **calices** /-si:z/) cuplike cavity or organ. [L, = cup]

calk *US* var. of CAULK.

call /kɔ:l/ **1** *v.* shout, cry, speak *out* loudly to attract attention; summon (*call the police*); order to take place (*call a strike, a meeting*); invite (*call attention to*); rouse from sleep (*call me at 8*); name, describe, regard as (*call him John*; *I call that silly*); communicate, converse with, by telephone or radio; name (suit) in bidding at cards; predict result of tossing coin etc.; make brief visit (*at* place, *on* person); (of bird etc.) utter characteristic sound. **2** *n.* shout, cry to attract attention; invitation, summons, demand (*calls on one's time*; *call of the wild*); act of telephoning, conversation over telephone; signal on bugle etc.; short esp. formal visit; need, occasion (*no call for violence*; *not much call for it these days*); vocation; player's right or turn to bid at cards, bid thus made; bird's cry, instrument imitating it; option of buying stock at given date. **3** **call-box** telephone-box; **call for** demand, require, go and fetch; **call-girl** prostitute accepting appointments by telephone; **call in** withdraw (thing) from circulation, seek advice from, make brief visit; **call off** cancel (arrangement), order (dog etc.) to stop attacking etc.; **call on** (or **upon**) appeal to, request or require (person *to do* thing etc.); **call out** elicit, summon to action, order (workers) to strike; **call up** telephone, summon (esp. to do military service), bring back to mind; **call-up** *n.* summons to do military service; **on call** ready or available when needed; **pay a call** make short formal visit, *colloq.* go to lavatory. [OE f. ON]

caller *n.* person who calls, esp. one who pays visit or makes telephone call.

calligraphy /kə'lɪgrəfɪ/ *n.* handwriting, esp. when fine or pleasing; art of this; **calligrapher** *n.*; **calligraphic** /-'græfɪk/ *a.*; **calligraphist** *n.* [Gk (*kallos* beauty)]

calling *n.* profession or trade; vocation. [CALL]

calliper /'kælɪpə/ *n.* (usu. in *pl.*) pair of hinged arms for measuring diameters; metal support for weak or injured leg. [var. of CALIBRE]

callisthenics /kælɪs'θenɪks/ *n.pl.* exercises to develop bodily strength and grace. [Gk *kallos* beauty, *sthenos* strength]

callosity /kæ'lɒsɪtɪ/ *n.* abnormal hardness of skin, callus. [F or L (foll.)]

callous /'kæləs/ *a.* unfeeling, insensitive; (of skin) hardened. [L (CALLUS)]

callow /'kæləʊ/ *a.* inexperienced, raw. [OE, = bald]

callus /'kæləs/ *n.* hard thickened part of skin or tissue; bony material formed to aid healing of bone-fracture. [L]

calm /kɑ:m/ **1** *a.* still, tranquil, quiet, windless, not agitated (*lit.* or *fig.*); confident. **2** *n.* calm condition or period. **3** *v.* make calm, pacify. **4** **calm down** become or make calm. [L f. Gk *kauma* heat]

calomel /'kæləmel/ *n.* compound of mercury, used as cathartic. [Gk *kalos* beautiful, *melas* black]

Calor gas /'kælə/ (**P**) liquefied butane etc. stored under pressure in containers for domestic use. [L *calor* heat]

caloric /'kælərɪk/ *a.* of heat; of calories. [F (foll.)]

calorie /'kælərɪ/ *n.* unit of quantity of heat, the amount needed to raise one gram (**small calorie**) or one kilogram (**large calorie**) of water 1°C; large calorie as unit of energy value of foods. [F f. L *calor* heat]

calorific /kælə'rɪfɪk/ *a.* producing heat. [L (prec.)]

calorimeter /kælə'rɪmɪtə/ *n.* instrument for measuring quantity of heat. [CALORIE]

calumniate /kə'lʌmnɪeɪt/ *v.t.* slander, defame. [L]

calumny /'kæləmnɪ/ *n.* slander; malicious misrepresentation; **calumnious** /kə'lʌmnɪəs/ *a.* [L]

Calvary /'kælvərɪ/ *n.* place or representation of the Crucifixion. [L *calvaria* skull]

calve /kɑ:v/ *v.i.* give birth to calf. [OE (CALF[1])]

calves *pl.* of CALF[1], CALF[2].

Calvinism /'kælvɪnɪz(ə)m/ *n.* theology of Calvin and his followers, stressing predestination and divine grace; **Calvinist** *n.* & *a.* [*Calvin*, theologian]

calx *n.* (*pl.* **calces** /'kælsi:z/) powdery or friable substance left after burning of metal or mineral. [L *calx calc-* lime]

calypso /kə'lɪpsəʊ/ *n.* (*pl.* **calypsos**) W. Indian song with improvised usu. topical words and variable rhythm. [orig. unkn.]

calyx /'keɪlɪks/ *n.* (*pl.* **calyces** /-lɪsi:z/, **calyxes**) whorl of leaves forming outer case of bud or envelope of flower. [L f. Gk, = husk]

cam *n.* projecting part of wheel etc. in machinery, shaped to convert circular into reciprocal or variable motion. [Du. *kam* comb]

camaraderie /kæmə'rɑ:dərɪ/ *n.* comradeship; mutual trust and friendship. [F]

camber 1 *n.* convex or arched shape of surface of road, deck, etc. 2 *v.t.* construct (road etc.) with camber. [F f. L *camurus* curved]

Cambrian /'kæmbrɪən/ 1 *a.* Welsh; of the earliest period in the Palaeozoic era. 2 *n.* this period. [L f. W (CYMRIC)]

cambric /'kæmbrɪk/ *n.* fine linen or cotton cloth. [*Cambrai* in N. France]

Cambridge blue /'keɪmbrɪdʒ/ light blue. [*Cambridge* in England]

came *past* of COME.

camel /'kæm(ə)l/ *n.* large four-legged animal with long neck and one hump (**Arabian camel**) or two humps (**Bactrian camel**); fawn colour; **camel('s)-hair** fine soft hair used in artists' brushes, fabric made of this. [OE f. L f. Gk]

camellia /kə'mi:lɪə/ *n.* evergreen shrub with shiny leaves and large flowers. [*Camellus*, botanist]

Camembert /'kæməmbeə/ *n.* a kind of soft rich cheese. [*Camembert* in N. France]

cameo /'kæmɪəʊ/ *n.* (*pl.* **cameos**) small piece of onyx or other hard stone carved in relief with design in different colour from background; short descriptive literary sketch or acted scene. [F & med.L]

camera /'kæmərə/ *n.* apparatus for taking photographs, film, or television pictures; **in camera** in private. [L (CHAMBER)]

cameraman *n.* one who operates camera professionally, esp. in film-making or television.

camomile /'kæməmaɪl/ *n.* aromatic herb with flowers used as tonic, esp. to make medicinal tea. [F f. L f. Gk, = earth-apple]

camouflage /'kæməflɑ:ʒ/ 1 *n.* disguising of guns, ships, etc., by painting or covering them to make them blend with surroundings; such disguise; misleading or evasive precaution. 2 *v.t.* hide by camouflage. [F (*camoufler* disguise, f. It.)]

camp[1] 1 *n.* place where troops are lodged or trained; fortified site; temporary accommodation of tents, huts, etc., for holiday-makers, detainees, etc. 2 *v.i.* live in camp; make camp. 3 **camp-bed** folding bed used in camping; **camp-follower** civilian worker in military camp, disciple or adherent. 4 **camper** *n.* [F f. It. f. L *campus* level ground]

camp[2] 1 *a.* affected, effeminate; homosexual; done in exaggerated way for effect. 2 *n.* camp manner or style. 3 *v.* behave or do in camp way. [orig. uncert.]

campaign /kæm'peɪn/ 1 *n.* organized course of action for particular purpose, esp. to arouse public interest; series of military operations in a definite area or for particular objective. 2 *v.i.* take part in campaign. [F f. It. f. L (CAMP[1])]

campanile /kæmpə'ni:lɪ/ *n.* bell-tower, usu. free-standing, esp. in Italy. [It. (*campana* bell f. L)]

campanology /kæmpə'nɒlədʒɪ/ *n.* study of bells; bell-ringing; **campanologist** *n.* [L *campana* bell]

campanula /kæm'pænjʊlə/ *n.* plant with bell-shaped usu. blue or white flowers. [dimin. (prec.)]

camphor /'kæmfə/ *n.* strong-smelling crystalline substance used in insect repellents and medicines. [F or med. L f. Arab. f. Skr.]

camphorated *a.* containing camphor.

campion /'kæmpɪən/ *n.* wild plant usu. with pink or white notched flowers. [orig. uncert.]

campsite *n.* place for camping, esp. one specially equipped for holiday-makers.

campus /'kæmpəs/ *n.* university or college grounds; university esp. as teaching institution. [L, = field]

camshaft *n.* shaft carrying cams. [CAM]

can[1] /kən, *emphat.* kæn/ *v. aux.* (3 *sing. pres.* **can;** *past* **could** /kʊd/) be able to, know how to; have right to, be permitted to. [OE, = know]

can[2] 1 *n.* metal vessel for liquid; tin container in which food or drink is hermetically sealed; *sl.* prison, *US* lavatory. 2 *v.t.* (-**nn**-) put or preserve in can; (in *p.p.*) *sl.* drunk. 3 **canned music** music recorded for reproduction; **carry the can** bear responsibility or blame. [OE]

Canadian /kə'neɪdɪən/ 1 *a.* of Canada. 2 *n.* native or inhabitant of Canada. [*Canada* in N. America]

canal /kə'næl/ *n.* artificial waterway for inland navigation or irrigation; tubular passage in plant or animal. [F or It. f. L *canalis*]

canalize /'kænəlaɪz/ *v.t.* make canal through; provide with canals; *fig.* give desired direction to. [F (prec.)]

canapé /'kænəpeɪ/ *n.* small piece of

bread or pastry with savoury on top. [F]

canard /kə'nɑ:d, 'kænɑ:d/ *n.* unfounded rumour or story. [F, = duck]

canary /kə'neərɪ/ *n.* small songbird with yellow feathers. [*Canary* Islands]

canasta /kə'næstə/ *n.* card-game using two packs and resembling rummy. [Sp., = basket]

cancan /'kænkæn/ *n.* lively stage-dance with high kicking, performed by women in long skirts and petticoats. [F]

cancel /'kæns(ə)l/ *v.* (**-ll-**, US **-l-**) withdraw or revoke (previous arrangement); discontinue (arrangement in progress); obliterate or delete (writing etc.), mark (ticket, stamp, etc.) to invalidate it; annul, make void; neutralize, counterbalance; *Math.* strike out (equal factor) on each side of equation etc.; **cancel out** neutralize (each other); **cancellation** /-'leɪʃ(ə)n/ *n.* [F f. L (CHANCEL)]

cancer *n.* malignant tumour in the body, disease featuring this; *fig.* evil influence or corruption; (**Cancer**) constellation and fourth sign of the zodiac; **cancroid** *a.*; **cancerous** *a.* [L, = crab]

candela /'kændɪlə/ *n.* unit of luminous intensity. [L, = candle]

candelabrum /kændɪ'lɑ:brəm/ *n.* (*pl.* **candelabra**) large branched candlestick or light-holder. [L (prec.)]

candid /'kændɪd/ *a.* frank, not hiding one's thoughts; informal, of photograph taken usu. without subject's knowledge. [F, or L *candidus* white]

candidate /'kændɪdət/ *n.* person who seeks or is nominated for an office, award, etc.; person or thing likely to gain some distinction or position; person taking an examination; **candidacy** *n.*; **candidature** *n.* [F or L, = white-robed]

candle /'kænd(ə)l/ *n.* cylinder or block of wax or tallow enclosing wick for giving light when burning; **cannot hold a candle to** is very inferior to; **not worth the candle** not worth doing. [OE f. L *candela*]

Candlemas /'kænd(ə)lməs/ *n.* feast of the Purification of the Virgin Mary (2 Feb.) when candles are blessed. [OE (MASS²)]

candlepower *n.* unit of luminous intensity. [CANDLE]

candlestick *n.* holder for one or more candles.

candlewick *n.* thick soft cotton yarn; material with raised tufted pattern in this.

candour /'kændə/, *US* **candor** *n.* candid behaviour or quality, frankness. [F, or L *candor*]

candy /'kændɪ/ **1** *n.* sugar crystallized by repeated boiling and slow evaporation; *US* sweets, a sweet. **2** *v.t.* preserve (fruit etc.) by coating or impregnating with candy. **3 candy-floss** fluffy mass of spun sugar round stick; **candy-stripe** alternate white and coloured stripes. [F f. Arab.]

candytuft /'kændɪtʌft/ *n.* garden plant with white, pink, or purple flowers. [*Candia* in Crete, TUFT]

cane 1 *n.* hollow jointed stem of tall reeds and grasses (*bamboo cane*) or of slender palm; sugar-cane; these used as material for wickerwork etc.; a stem used as walking-stick or to support plant or as instrument of punishment. **2** *v.t.* beat with a cane; weave cane into (chair etc.). **3 cane-sugar** sugar obtained from sugar-cane. [F f. L f. Gk *kanna* reed]

canine /'keɪnaɪn/ **1** *a.* of a dog or dogs. **2** *n.* a dog; = *canine tooth.* **3 canine tooth** pointed tooth between incisors and molars. [F or L (*canis* dog)]

canister /'kænɪstə/ *n.* small container for tea etc.; cylinder of shot or tear-gas, bursting on impact. [L f. Gk *kanastron* wicker basket]

canker 1 *n.* destructive disease of trees and plants; ulcerous disease of animals; *fig.* corrupting influence. **2** *v.t.* consume with canker; corrupt; (in *p.p.*) soured, malignant. **3 cankerous** *a.* [OE & F f. L (CANCER)]

canna /'kænə/ *n.* tropical plant with bright flowers and ornamental leaves. [L (CANE)]

cannabis /'kænəbɪs/ *n.* hemp plant; parts of it used as intoxicant or hallucinogen. [L f. Gk]

cannery /'kænərɪ/ *n.* canning-factory. [CAN²]

cannibal /'kænɪb(ə)l/ **1** *n.* person or animal that eats its own species. **2** *a.* of or like a cannibal. **3 cannibalism** *n.*; **cannibalistic** /-bə'lɪstɪk/ *a.* [Sp. f. Carib]

cannibalize /'kænɪbəlaɪz/ *v.t.* use (machine etc.) as source of spare parts for others.

cannon /'kænən/ **1** *n. hist.* large heavy gun (*pl.* usu. same); in billiards, hitting of two balls successively by player's ball. **2** *v.i.* collide heavily *against* or *into*. **3 cannon-ball** large metal ball fired from cannon; **cannon-fodder** men regarded merely as material to be expended in war. [F f. It. (CANE)]

cannonade /kænə'neɪd/ **1** *n.* continuous heavy gunfire. **2** *v.t.* bombard with cannonade. [F f. It. (prec.)]

cannot = *can not.*

canny /'kænɪ/ *a.* shrewd and cautious; worldly-wise; thrifty; **cannily** *adv.*; **canniness** *n.* [CAN¹]

canoe /kə'nu:/ **1** *n.* light narrow boat

propelled by paddles. **2** *v.i.* (*partic.* **canoeing**) travel by canoe. **3 canoeist** *n.* [Sp. & Haitian]

canon /'kænən/ *n.* general law, rule, principle, or criterion; church decree or law; member of cathedral chapter; body of (esp. sacred) writings accepted as genuine; central unchanging part of the RC Mass; *Mus.* piece with different parts taking up same theme successively. [OE f. L f. Gk *kanōn* rule]

canonical /kə'nɒnɪk(ə)l/ *a.* according to or ordered by canon law; included in canon of Scripture; authoritative, accepted; of cathedral canon or chapter; (in *pl.*) canonical dress of clergy. [med.L (prec.)]

canonist /'kænənɪst/ *n.* expert in canon law. [F or med.L (CANON)]

canonize /'kænənaɪz/ *v.t.* declare officially to be a saint, usu. with ceremony; admit to canon of Scripture; sanction by church authority; **canonization** /-'zeɪʃ(ə)n/ *n.* [med.L (CANON)]

canoodle /kə'nu:d(ə)l/ *v.i. sl.* kiss and cuddle amorously. [orig. unkn.]

canopy /'kænəpɪ/ **1** *n.* covering hung or held up over throne, bed, person, etc.; *fig.* sky, overhanging shelter; *Archit.* roof of niche etc.; expanding part of parachute; cover of aircraft's cockpit. **2** *v.t.* supply or be canopy to. [L f. Gk, = mosquito-net]

cant[1] **1** *n.* insincere pious or moral talk; language peculiar to one class of people, jargon. **2** *v.i.* use cant. [prob. f. L (CHANT)]

cant[2] **1** *n.* slanting surface, bevel; oblique push or jerk; tilted position. **2** *v.* push or pitch out of level; tilt. [LG or Du., = edge]

can't /kɑ:nt/ *colloq.* = *can not.*

Cantab. *abbr.* Cantabrigian.

cantabile /kæn'tɑ:bɪlɪ/ *Mus.* **1** *adv.* in smooth flowing style. **2** *n.* piece to be performed this way. [It., = singable]

Cantabrigian /kæntə'brɪdʒɪən/ **1** *a.* of Cambridge or Cambridge University. **2** *n.* citizen of Cambridge; member of Cambridge University. [*Cantabrigia*, Latinized name of Cambridge]

cantaloup /'kæntəlu:p/ *n.* (also **cantaloupe**) small ribbed melon. [F, f. *Cantaluppi* near Rome]

cantankerous /kæn'tæŋkərəs/ *a.* bad-tempered, quarrelsome. [orig. uncert.]

cantata /kæn'tɑ:tə/ *n. Mus.* short narrative or descriptive composition with vocal solos and usu. chorus and orchestral accompaniment. [It. (CHANT)]

canteen /kæn'ti:n/ *n.* restaurant for employees in office, factory, etc.; shop for provisions or liquor in barracks or camp; case or box containing cutlery; soldier's or camper's water-flask. [F f. It., = cellar]

canter 1 *n.* gentle gallop. **2** *v.i.* go at canter. [*Canterbury gallop* of med. pilgrims]

Canterbury bell /'kæntəbərɪ/ cultivated campanula with large flowers. [*Canterbury* in Kent]

canticle /'kæntɪk(ə)l/ *n.* song or chant on biblical text. [F or L (canticum CHANT)]

cantilever /'kæntɪli:və/ *n.* beam, bracket, etc., projecting from wall to support balcony etc.; beam or girder fixed at one end only; **cantilever bridge** bridge made of two cantilevers projecting from piers and joined by girders. [orig. unkn.]

canto /'kæntəʊ/ *n.* (*pl.* **cantos**) division of long poem. [It. f. L *cantus* (CHANT)]

canton 1 /'kæntɒn/ *n.* subdivision of a country, esp. of Switzerland. **2** /kæn'tu:n/ *v.t.* put (troops) in their quarters. [F, = corner (rel. to CANT[2])]

cantonment /kæn'tu:nmənt/ *n.* lodging of troops; permanent military station in India. [F (prec.)]

cantor /'kæntɔ:/ *n.* choir leader; precentor in synagogue; **cantorial** /-'tɔ:rɪəl/ *a.* [L, = singer]

canvas /'kænvəs/ **1** *n.* strong coarse cloth used esp. for sails and tents and as surface for oil-painting; a painting on canvas, esp. in oils. **2** *v.t.* (**-ss-**, *US* **-s-**) cover with canvas. **3 under canvas** in tents, with sails spread. [F f. L (CANNABIS)]

canvass /'kænvəs/ **1** *v.* solicit votes; solicit votes from (electors in constituency); ascertain opinions of; ask custom from; propose (idea or plan etc.). **2** *n.* canvassing, esp. of electors. [orig. = toss in sheet, f. prec.]

canyon /'kænjən/ *n.* deep gorge. [Sp. *cañón* tube]

caoutchouc /'kaʊtʃʊk/ *n.* unvulcanized rubber. [F f. Carib]

cap 1 *n.* soft brimless head-covering, usu. with peak; head-covering worn in particular profession (*nurse's cap*); cap awarded as sign of membership of sports team; academic mortar-board; cover resembling cap or designed for specific purpose; = *Dutch cap*; = *percussion cap*. **2** *v.t.* (**-pp-**) put cap on; cover top or end of; award sports cap to; form top of; surpass, excel. **3 cap in hand** humbly; **if the cap fits** (said of a generalized comment) it seems to be true of (a particular person). [OE f. L *cappa*]

CAP *abbr.* Common Agricultural Policy (of EEC).

capability /keɪpə'bɪlɪtɪ/ *n.* ability, power; undeveloped or unused faculty. [foll.]

capable /'keɪpəb(ə)l/ *a.* gifted, able, competent; **capable of** having the ability, fitness, or necessary quality for, susceptible or admitting of (explanation or improvement etc.); **capably** *adv.* [F f. L (*capio* hold)]

capacious /kə'peɪʃəs/ *a.* roomy, able to hold much. [L *capax* (prec.)]

capacitance /kə'pæsɪtəns/ *n.* ability to store electric charge; ratio of change in electric charge of a body to corresponding change in its potential. [CAPACITY]

capacitor /kə'pæsɪtə/ *n.* device able to store electric charge.

capacity /kə'pæsɪtɪ/ *n.* power of containing, receiving, experiencing, or producing; maximum amount that can be contained or produced etc.; mental power; function or position (*in my capacity as a critic*); legal competency; **to capacity** fully, to the full. [F f. L (CAPACIOUS)]

caparison /kə'pærɪs(ə)n/ **1** *n.* horse's trappings; equipment, finery. **2** *v.t.* adorn. [F f. Sp., = saddle-cloth]

cape[1] *n.* sleeveless cloak; short sleeveless cloak as attached part of long coat. [F f. L *cappa* CAP]

cape[2] *n.* headland, promontory; **the Cape** Cape of Good Hope. [F f. Prov. f. L *caput* head]

caper[1] **1** *v.i.* jump or run about playfully. **2** *n.* playful jump or leap; prank; *sl.* an activity. **3 cut a caper** act friskily. [abbr. of CAPRIOLE]

caper[2] *n.* bramble-like shrub; (in *pl.*) its buds pickled esp. for use in **caper sauce.** [L f. Gk *kapparis*]

capercaillie /kæpə'keɪlɪ/ *n.* (*also* **capercailzie**) largest kind of European grouse. [Gael., = horse of the forest]

capillarity /kæpɪ'lærɪtɪ/ *n.* capillary attraction or repulsion; power to exert this. [F (foll.)]

capillary /kə'pɪlərɪ/ **1** *a.* of or like a hair; (of tube, blood-vessel, etc.) of hair-like diameter. **2** *n.* capillary tube; one of ramified blood-vessels connecting arteries and veins. **3 capillary attraction (or repulsion)** tendency of liquid to be drawn up (or down) in capillary tube. [L (*capillus* hair)]

capital /'kæpɪt(ə)l/ **1** *n.* most important town or city of a country or region, usu. its seat of government and administrative centre; money or other assets with which company starts business, accumulated wealth; capitalists collectively; capital letter; head of column or pillar. **2** *a.* principal, most important; *colloq.* excellent; involving punishment by death (*capital offence*); (of error etc.) vitally harmful, fatal; (of letters of alphabet) large in size and form, such as begin sentence and name. **3 capital gain** profit from sale of investments or property; **capital levy** general tax on wealth or property; **capital sum** lump sum of money, esp. payable to insured person; **capital transfer tax** tax levied on transfer of capital, as by gift or bequest; **make capital out of** use (esp. circumstance) to one's advantage. [F f. L (*caput -itis* head)]

capitalism *n.* system in which production and distribution of goods depend on private capital and wealth and profit-making; dominance of private owners of capital and production for profit.

capitalist 1 *n.* person using or possessing capital, rich person; believer in capitalism. **2** *a.* of or favouring capitalism. **3 capitalistic** /-'lɪstɪk/ *a.*

capitalize *v.* convert into or provide with capital; write (letter of alphabet) as capital, begin (word) with capital letter; **capitalize on** use to one's advantage; **capitalization** /-'zeɪʃ(ə)n/ *n.* [F (CAPITAL)]

capitation /kæpɪ'teɪʃ(ə)n/ *n.* tax or fee levied per person. [F or L (CAPITAL)]

capitular /kə'pɪtjʊlə/ *a.* of a cathedral chapter. [L (*capitulum* CHAPTER)]

capitulate /kə'pɪtjʊleɪt/ *v.i.* surrender, esp. on stated conditions; **capitulation** /-'leɪʃ(ə)n/ *n.* [med.L, = put under headings]

capon /'keɪpɒn/ *n.* domestic cock castrated and fattened for eating. [OE f. F f. L *capo*]

caprice /kə'pri:s/ *n.* whimsical or unaccountable change of mind or conduct; tendency to this; work of lively fancy in art etc. [F f. It. *capriccio* sudden start]

capricious /kə'prɪʃəs/ *a.* given to caprice, unpredictable.

Capricorn /'kæprɪkɔ:n/ *n.* constellation and tenth sign of zodiac. [F f. L (*caper -pri* goat, *cornu* horn)]

capriole /'kæprɪəʊl/ **1** *n.* caper, leap, esp. of trained horse. **2** *v.i.* make capriole. [F f. It. (prec.)]

capsicum /'kæpsɪkəm/ *n.* tropical plant with hot-tasting seeds; its fruit. [L *capsa* case]

capsize /kæp'saɪz/ *v.* overturn (boat etc.); be overturned. [Sp. *capuzar* sink]

capstan /'kæpst(ə)n/ *n.* thick revolving cylinder with vertical axis round which cable or rope is wound e.g. to raise a ship's anchor; revolving spindle carrying spool on tape-recorder; **capstan lathe** lathe with revolving tool-holder. [Prov.]

capsule /'kæpsju:l/ **1** *n.* small soluble case enclosing dose of medicine and swallowed with it; detachable compartment of spacecraft or nose-cone of rocket; enclosing membrane in the body; plant's seed-case that opens when ripe. **2** *a.* concise, highly condensed. [F f. L (*capsa* case)]

capsulize *v.t.* put (information etc.) into concise form.

Capt. *abbr.* Captain.

captain /ˈkæptɪn/ **1** *n.* chief, leader; commander of ship, naval officer next below commodore; master of merchant ship; army officer next below major; pilot of civil aircraft; leader of side in games. **2** *v.t.* be captain of. **3 captaincy** *n.* [F f. L *caput* head)]

caption /ˈkæpʃ(ə)n/ **1** *n.* heading of chapter, article, etc.; wording on cinema or television screen, wording appended to illustration or cartoon etc. **2** *v.t.* provide with caption. [L (*capio* take)]

captious /ˈkæpʃəs/ *a.* fond of finding fault, raising petty objections, etc. [F or L (prec.)]

captivate /ˈkæptɪveɪt/ *v.t.* overwhelm with charm or affection; fascinate; **captivation** /-ˈveɪʃ(ə)n/ *n.* [L (foll.)]

captive /ˈkæptɪv/ **1** *n.* person or animal taken prisoner or confined. **2** *a.* taken prisoner; restrained; in position of having to comply (*captive audience, market*). **3 captivity** /-ˈtɪvɪtɪ/ *n.* [L (*capio capt-* take)]

captor /ˈkæptə, -ɔː/ *n.* one who captures. [L (prec.)]

capture /ˈkæptʃə/ **1** *v.t.* take prisoner, seize; obtain by force or trickery; portray in permanent form (*picture fails to capture her real beauty*); absorb (atomic particle). **2** *n.* act of capturing; thing or person captured. [F f. L (CAPTIVE)]

Capuchin /ˈkæpjʊtʃɪn/ *n.* friar of branch of Franciscans; (**capuchin**) monkey or pigeon with crown resembling hood. [F f. It. (*cappuccio* cowl)]

capybara /kæpɪˈbɑːrə/ *n.* large S. American rodent. [Tupi]

car *n.* wheeled vehicle, esp. = *motor car*; railway carriage of specified type (*dining-car*); *US* any railway carriage or van; passenger compartment of airship, balloon, cable railway, or lift; **car-park** area for parking cars; **car-sick** affected by nausea through motion of car. [F f. L]

caracul var. of KARAKUL.

carafe /kəˈræf, -ˈrɑːf/ *n.* glass container for water or wine. [F ult. f. Arab.]

caramel /ˈkærəmel/ *n.* burnt sugar or syrup as colouring or flavouring; kind of toffee; light-brown colour; **caramelize** *v.t.* [F f. Sp.]

carapace /ˈkærəpeɪs/ *n.* upper shell of tortoise or crustacean. [F f. Sp.]

carat /ˈkærət/ *n.* unit of weight for precious stones (200 mg) or of purity of gold (pure gold = 24 carats). [F ult. f. Gk]

caravan /ˈkærəvæn/ **1** *n.* large vehicle on wheels, equipped for living in and usu. towed by motor vehicle; company travelling together, esp. across desert. **2** *v.i.* (**-nn-**) travel or live in caravan. [F f. Pers.]

caravanserai /kærəˈvænsərɪ/ *n.* Eastern inn with central court. [Pers., = caravan place]

caravel /ˈkærəvel/ *n. hist.* small light fast ship. [F f. Port. f. Gk]

caraway /ˈkærəweɪ/ *n.* aromatic herb with white flowers; **caraway seed** its spicy fruit, used in cakes and bread. [Sp. f. Arab.]

carb *n. colloq.* carburettor. [abbr.]

carbide /ˈkɑːbaɪd/ *n.* binary compound of carbon, esp. = *calcium carbide*. [CARBON]

carbine /ˈkɑːbaɪn/ *n.* short rifle orig. for cavalry use. [F]

carbohydrate /kɑːbəʊˈhaɪdreɪt/ *n.* energy-producing compound of carbon with oxygen and hydrogen (e.g. starch, sugar, glucose). [CARBON, HYDRATE]

carbolic acid /kɑːˈbɒlɪk/ phenol; **carbolic soap** soap containing this. [foll.]

carbon /ˈkɑːbən/ *n.* non-metallic element occurring as diamond, graphite, and charcoal, and in all organic compounds; = *carbon copy, carbon paper*; rod of carbon used in arc lamp; **carbon copy** copy made with carbon paper, *fig.* exact copy; **carbon dating** determination of age of object from decay of radiocarbon; **carbon dioxide** gas formed by burning carbon or by breathing; **carbon 14** radioisotope used in carbon dating, with mass 14; **carbon monoxide** poisonous gas formed by burning carbon incompletely; **carbon paper** thin carbon-coated paper for making (esp. typed) copies; **carbon tetrachloride** colourless liquid used esp. in fire extinguishers. [F f. L *carbo* charcoal]

carbonaceous /kɑːbəˈneɪʃəs/ *a.* consisting of or containing carbon; of or like coal or charcoal.

carbonate /ˈkɑːbənɪt, -eɪt/ **1** *n.* salt of carbonic acid. **2** /-eɪt/ *v.t.* impregnate with carbon dioxide. [F (CARBON)]

carbonic /kɑːˈbɒnɪk/ *a.* of carbon; **carbonic acid** weak acid formed from carbon dioxide and water. [CARBON]

carboniferous /kɑːbəˈnɪfərəs/ **1** *a.* producing coal; (**Carboniferous**) of the period in the Palaeozoic era after Devonian, with copious creation of coal deposits. **2** *n.* (**Carboniferous**) this period.

carbonize /ˈkɑːbənaɪz/ *v.t.* convert into

carbon; reduce to charcoal or coke; coat with carbon; **carbonization** /-'zeɪʃ(ə)n/ *n.*

carborundum /kɑ:bə'rʌndəm/ *n.* compound of carbon and silicon used esp. as abrasive. [CARBON, CORUNDUM]

carboy /'kɑ:bɔɪ/ *n.* large globular glass bottle enclosed in frame. [Pers.]

carbuncle /'kɑ:bʌŋk(ə)l/ *n.* severe abscess in the skin; bright-red gem. [F f. L (CARBON)]

carburation /kɑ:bjʊ'reɪʃ(ə)n/ *n.* process of charging air with spray of liquid hydrocarbon fuel. [CARBON]

carburettor /kɑ:bjʊ'retə/, *US* **carburetor** *n.* apparatus for carburation of petrol and air in an internal-combustion engine.

carcass /'kɑ:kəs/ *n.* (also **carcase**) dead body of animal, esp. trunk for cutting up as meat; bones of cooked bird; *derog.* human body, living or dead; framework, worthless remains. [F]

carcinogen /kɑ:'sɪnədʒ(ə)n/ *n.* substance that produces cancer; **carcinogenic** /-'dʒenɪk/ *a.* [foll.]

carcinoma /kɑ:sɪ'nəʊmə/ *n.* (*pl.* **carcinomata, -mas**) cancerous tumour. [L f. Gk (*karkinos* crab)]

card[1] *n.* thick stiff paper or thin pasteboard; a piece of this for writing or printing on, esp. to send greetings (*birthday card, postcard*), to identify person (*visiting-card*), or to record information; = *playing-card*, (in *pl.*) card-playing; (in *pl.*) *colloq.* employee's documents held by employer; programme of events of race-meeting etc.; *colloq.* odd or amusing person; **card-carrying** being registered member (esp. of political party or trade union); **card-game** game using playing-cards; **card index** index with separate card for each entry; **card-sharp** swindler at card-games; **card-table** (esp. folding) table for card-playing; **card up one's sleeve** plan in reserve; **card vote** = *block vote*; **get one's cards** *colloq.* be dismissed from one's employment; **on the cards** likely, possible; **play one's cards well** (or **right** etc.) act wisely; **put** (or **lay**) **one's cards on the table** reveal one's resources, intentions, etc. [F f. L *charta* f. Gk, = papyrus-leaf]

card[2] **1** *n.* toothed instrument or wire-brush for raising nap on cloth or for disentangling fibres before spinning. **2** *v.t.* brush or comb with card. [F f. Prov. f. L *caro* card *v.*]

cardamom /'kɑ:dəməm/ *n.* E. Indian spice from seeds of aromatic plant. [F or L f. Gk]

cardboard *n.* stiff paper or pasteboard, esp. for making cards or boxes. [CARD[1]]

cardiac /'kɑ:dɪæk/ *a.* of the heart. [F or L f. Gk (*kardia* heart)]

cardigan /'kɑ:dɪgən/ *n.* knitted jacket with buttons down front. [Earl of *Cardigan*]

cardinal /'kɑ:dɪn(ə)l/ **1** *a.* chief, fundamental; of deep scarlet. **2** *n.* leading dignitary of RC Church, one of college electing Pope; small scarlet American songbird. **3 cardinal numbers** those representing quantity (1, 2, 3, etc.), as opposed to ordinal numbers; **cardinal points** four main points of compass (N., S., E., W.); **cardinal virtues** justice, prudence, temperance, fortitude, faith, hope, charity. [F f. L (*cardo -din-* hinge)]

cardiogram /'kɑ:dɪəʊgræm/ *n.* record of heart movements. [Gk *kardia* heart]

cardiograph /'kɑ:dɪəʊgrɑ:f/ *n.* instrument recording heart movements.

cardiology /kɑ:dɪ'ɒlədʒɪ/ *n.* branch of medicine concerned with diseases and abnormalities of the heart; **cardiologist** *n.*

cardio-vascular /kɑ:dɪəʊ'væskjʊlə/ *a.* of the heart and blood-vessels.

care 1 *n.* worry, anxiety; occasion for these; serious attention, caution (*assembled with care*; *handle with care*); protection, charge, = *child care*; thing to be done or seen to. **2** *v.* feel concern or interest (*about, for, whether*); have liking *for* or wish *to* do (*don't care for jazz*; *would you care to try?*); provide *for*. **3 care of** at the address of; **in care** taken into the care of a local authority; **take care** be cautious, not fail or neglect *to* do; **take care of** look after, deal with, dispose of. [OE, = sorrow]

careen /kə'ri:n/ *v.* turn (ship) on side for repair etc.; tilt, lean over; *US* swerve about. [F f. It. f. L *carina* keel]

career /kə'rɪə/ **1** *n.* one's advancement through life, esp. in a profession; profession or occupation, esp. as offering advancement; *attrib.* of person wishing to pursue career (*career girl*); swift course (*in full career*). **2** *v.i.* move or swerve about wildly. [F ult. f. L (CAR)]

careerist *n.* person predominantly concerned with personal advancement.

carefree *a.* free from anxiety or responsibility, light-hearted.

careful *a.* painstaking, thorough; cautious; done with care and attention; **carefully** *adv.*

careless *a.* lacking care or attention; unthinking, insensitive; done without care, inaccurate; light-hearted.

caress /kə'res/ **1** *v.t.* touch or stroke lovingly, kiss. **2** *n.* loving touch, kiss. [F f. L *carus* dear)]

caret /'kærət/ *n.* mark (‸, ⋏) showing

intended insertion in printing or writing. [L, = is lacking]

caretaker *n.* person employed to look after house, building, etc.; *attrib.* exercising temporary power (*caretaker president*). [CARE]

careworn *a.* showing effects of prolonged worry.

cargo *n.* (*pl.* **cargoes,** *US* **-os**) goods carried on a ship or aircraft. [Sp. (rel. to CHARGE)]

Carib /'kærɪb/ *n.* aboriginal inhabitant or southern W. Indies and adjacent coasts; their language. [Sp. f. Haitian]

Caribbean /kærɪ'bi:ən/ *a.* of the Caribs or the W. Indies generally.

caribou /'kærɪbu:/ *n.* (*pl.* same) N. American reindeer. [F f. Amer. Ind.]

caricature /'kærɪkətjʊə/ **1** *n.* grotesque representation esp. of person by exaggeration of characteristics; ridiculously poor imitation or version. **2** *v.t.* make or give caricature of. **3 caricaturist** *n.* [F f. It. (*caricare* exaggerate)]

caries /'keəriː:z, -ri:z/ *n.* (*pl.* same) decay of tooth or bone. [L]

carillon /kə'rɪljən, 'kærɪljən/ *n.* set of bells sounded either from keyboard or mechanically; tune played on bells. [F]

Carmelite /'kɑ:mɪlaɪt/ **1** *n.* friar of order of Our Lady of Carmel, following rule of extreme asceticism; nun of similar order. **2** *a.* of the Carmelites. [F or med.L (Mt. *Carmel* in Palestine)]

carminative /'kɑ:mɪnətɪv/ **1** *a.* curing flatulence. **2** *n.* carminative drug. [F or L (*carmino* heal by CHARM)]

carmine /'kɑ:maɪn/ **1** *a.* of vivid crimson colour. **2** *n.* this colour. [F or med.L (perh. rel. to CRIMSON)]

carnage /'kɑ:nɪdʒ/ *n.* great slaughter, esp. in battle. [F f. It. f. L (foll.)]

carnal /'kɑ:n(ə)l/ *a.* of the body or flesh, worldly; sensual, sexual; **carnality** /-'nælɪtɪ/ *n.* [L (*caro carn-* flesh)]

carnation /kɑ:'neɪʃ(ə)n/ **1** *n.* cultivated clove-scented pink; rosy-pink colour. **2** *a.* of this colour. [F f. It. (prec.)]

carnelian /kɑ:'ni:lɪən/ var. of CORNELIAN.

carnet /'kɑ:neɪ/ *n.* permit to drive across frontier or use camping site. [F, = notebook]

carnival /'kɑ:nɪv(ə)l/ *n.* a festival or festivities, esp. preceding Lent; merrymaking; *US* fun-fair or circus. [It. f. L (*carnem levo* put away meat)]

carnivore /'kɑ:nɪvɔ:/ *n.* carnivorous animal (e.g. cat, dog, bear) or plant. [foll.]

carnivorous /kɑ:'nɪvərəs/ *a.* flesh-eating. [L (CARNAL, *voro* devour)]

carol /'kær(ə)l/ **1** *n.* joyous song, esp. Christmas hymn. **2** *v.* (**-ll-**, *US* **-l-**) sing carols; sing joyfully. [F]

Carolean /kærə'li:ən/ *a.* (also **Caroline**) of the time of Charles I or II of England. [L *Carolus* Charles]

Carolingian /kærə'lɪndʒɪən/ **1** *a.* of Frankish dynasty founded by Charlemagne. **2** *n.* member of this dynasty. [F f. *Karl* Charles, after MEROVINGIAN]

carotid /kə'rɒtɪd/ **1** *a.* of the two main arteries, one on each side of the neck, carrying blood to the head. **2** *n.* carotid artery. [F or L f. Gk]

carouse /kə'raʊz/ **1** *v.i.* have noisy or lively drinking-party. **2** *n.* such a party. **3 carousal** *n.* [G *gar aus* (drink) right out]

carousel /kærʊ'sel/ *n.* merry-go-round; rotating delivery or conveyor system. [F f. It.]

carp[1] *n.* (*pl.* same) freshwater fish often bred in ponds. [F f. Prov. or L]

carp[2] *v.i.* find fault, complain pettily. [ON, = brag]

carpal /'kɑ:p(ə)l/ *a.* of the wrist-bone. [CARPUS]

carpel /'kɑ:pel/ *n.* one of divisions of a compound pistil of a flower, a cell making up a pistil. [(F f.) Gk *karpos* fruit]

carpenter /'kɑ:pɪntə/ **1** *n.* craftsman in woodwork, esp. of structural kind. **2** *v.* do, make by, carpenter's work. **3 carpentry** *n.* [AF f. L (*carpentum* wagon)]

carpet /'kɑ:pɪt/ **1** *n.* thick fabric for covering floors or stairs; carpet-like expanse, thick layer. **2** *v.t.* cover with or as with carpet; *colloq.* reprimand. **3 carpet-bag** travelling-bag of kind orig. made of carpet-like material; **carpet-bagger** political candidate etc. without local connections, adventurer in southern US after Civil War; **on the carpet** *colloq.* being reprimanded, under consideration; **sweep under the carpet** conceal (problem or difficulty). [F or med.L f. L (*carpo* pluck)]

carport *n.* roofed open-sided shelter for car. [CAR]

carpus /'kɑ:pəs/ *n.* (*pl.* **carpi** /-aɪ/) set of small bones connecting hand and forearm, esp. wrist in man. [L f. Gk]

carriage /'kærɪdʒ/ *n.* wheeled passenger vehicle, esp. with four wheels and pulled by horses; railway passenger vehicle; conveying of goods etc., cost of this; part of machine (e.g. typewriter) that carries other parts into desired position; = *gun-carriage*; manner of carrying oneself, deportment. [F (CARRY)]

carriageway *n.* part of road for use by vehicles.

carrier /'kærɪə/ *n.* person or thing that carries; person or company conveying goods or passengers for payment; = *carrier-bag*; part of bicycle etc. for carrying luggage or passenger; person or animal that transmits disease without suffering from it; = *aircraft-carrier*; **carrier bag** paper or plastic bag for shopping etc.; **carrier pigeon** pigeon trained to carry messages tied to its neck or leg; **carrier wave** high-frequency electromagnetic wave modulated in amplitude or frequency to convey signal. [CARRY]

carrion /ˈkærɪən/ *n.* dead putrefying flesh; something vile or filthy; **carrion crow** black crow living on carrion. [F f. L *caro* flesh]

carrot /ˈkærət/ *n.* plant with tapering orange-coloured root; this root as vegetable; means of enticement; **carroty** *a.* [F f. L f. Gk]

carry /ˈkærɪ/ **1** *v.* support or hold up, esp. while moving; convey with one from one place to another; have on one's person, possess (*carry a watch*); conduct or transmit (*pipe carries water*; *wire carries electric current*); take (process etc.) *to* specified point (*carry into effect*; *carry joke too far*); continue or prolong to (*carry modesty to excess*); involve, imply (*carries 6% interest*; *carries 2-year guarantee*); transfer (figure) to column of higher value; hold, conduct *oneself*, in a certain way; (of newspaper, radio station, etc.) include in contents, publish, broadcast; keep regular stock of (goods for sale); (of sound, voice, etc.), be audible at a distance; (of gun etc.) propel to specified distance; win victory or acceptance for (proposal etc.), win acceptance from (*carried the audience with him*); win, capture (prize, fortress, etc.); endure weight of, support; be pregnant with (*she is carrying twins*). **2** *n.* act of carrying; golf ball's flight before pitching. **3 carry away** remove, inspire, deprive of self-control (*got carried away*); **carry-cot** portable cot for baby; **carry the day** be victorious or successful; **carry forward** transfer to new page or account; **carry off** take away, esp. by force, manage successfully, win, (esp. of disease) kill; **carry on** continue, engage in, *colloq.* behave strangely or excitedly, have love-affair (*with*); **carry out** put (idea etc.) into practice; **carry over** carry forward, postpone; **carry through** complete successfully, bring safely out of difficulties; **carry weight** be important or influential. [AF (CAR)]

cart 1 *n.* small strong vehicle with two or four wheels for carrying loads, usu. drawn by a horse; light vehicle for pulling by hand. **2** *v.t.* convey in cart; *sl.* carry (esp. cumbersome thing) with difficulty. **3 cart-horse** horse of heavy build; **cart-wheel** wheel of cart, sideways somersault with arms and legs extended, large circular hat; **cart-wright** maker of carts; **in the cart** *sl.* in trouble or difficulty; **put the cart before the horse** reverse proper order or procedure. [OE & ON]

carte blanche /kɑːt blɑ̃ʃ/ full discretionary power given to person. [F, = blank paper]

cartel /kɑːˈtel/ *n.* union of manufacturers to control prices etc. [G f. F f. It. dimin. (CARD[1])]

Cartesian /kɑːˈtiːzjən/ **1** *a.* of Descartes or his philosophy. **2** *n.* follower of Descartes. [L (*Cartesius* Descartes)]

Carthusian /kɑːˈθjuːzjən/ **1** *n.* monk of contemplative order founded by St Bruno. **2** *a.* of the Carthusians. [L (CHARTREUSE)]

cartilage /ˈkɑːtɪlɪdʒ/ *n.* tough flexible tissue attached to bones of vertebrates; structure of this; **cartilaginous** /-ˈlædʒɪnəs/ *a.* [F f. L]

cartography /kɑːˈtɒgrəfɪ/ *n.* map-drawing; **cartographer** *n.*; **cartographic** /-ˈgræfɪk/ *a.* [F (*carte* map)]

carton /ˈkɑːt(ə)n/ *n.* light box or container made of cardboard etc. [F, as foll.]

cartoon /kɑːˈtuːn/ **1** *n.* humorous drawing in newspaper etc., esp. as topical comment; sequence of these (*strip cartoon*); animated cartoon on film; full-size drawing as sketch for work of art. **2** *v.t.* draw cartoon of. **3 cartoonist** *n.* [It. (CARD[1])]

cartouche /kɑːˈtuːʃ/ *n.* scroll-like ornamentation; oval ring enclosing name and title of Egyptian king. [F, as prec.]

cartridge /ˈkɑːtrɪdʒ/ *n.* case containing charge of propelling explosive for firearms or blasting, with bullet or shot if for small arms; spool of film, magnetic tape, etc., in sealed container ready for insertion; component carrying stylus on pick-up head of record-player; ink-container for insertion in pen; **cartridge paper** thick strong paper for drawing etc. [F, as CARTOON]

carve *v.* produce or shape by cutting; cut patterns, designs, etc. in (hard material); make (material) *into* object thus; cut up (meat etc.) at or for table; **carve out** take from larger whole, make (career or name etc. *for oneself*); **carve up** subdivide; **carve-up** *n. sl.* sharing-out, esp. of spoils; **carver** *n.* [OE]

carvel /ˈkɑːv(ə)l/ *n.* var. of CARAVEL; **carvel-built** (of boat) made with planks flush, not overlapping.

carving *n.* carved object, esp. as work of art. [CARVE]

Casanova /kæsəˈnəʊvə/ *n.* man

notorious for many love-affairs. [It. adventurer]

cascade /kæs'keɪd/ **1** *n.* small waterfall, esp. one in series; thing arranged like cascade. **2** *v.i.* fall in or like cascade. [F f. It. f. L (CASE[1])]

cascara /kæ'skɑ:rə/ *n.* bark of N. American buckthorn, used as laxative. [Sp.]

case[1] *n.* instance of thing's occurring; actual or hypothetical situation; instance or condition of person receiving professional guidance, esp. by doctor, person being treated; matter under official investigation, esp. by police; suit at law, sum of arguments on one side in suit; set of arguments esp. in relation to persuasiveness (*have a good, a weak, case*); *Gram.* relation of word to other words in sentence, form of noun, adjective, or pronoun expressing this; **case history** information about person for use in professional treatment, e.g. by doctor; **case-law** law as established by decided cases; **in any case** whatever the truth is; **in case** in the event that, lest, because of a possibility; **is (not) the case** is (not) so. [F f. L *casus* (*cado* fall)]

case[2] **1** *n.* container or covering serving to enclose or contain something; this with its contents; outer protective covering of watch, book, etc.; item of luggage, esp. suitcase; *Printing* partitioned receptacle for type. **2** *v.t.* enclose in a case; surround *with*; *sl.* reconnoitre (house etc.) with view to robbery. **3 case-harden** harden surface of (esp. iron by carbonizing), *fig.* make callous; **lower case** small letters; **upper case** capitals. [F f. L *capsa* box]

casemate /'keɪsmeɪt/ *n.* embrasured room in thickness of fortress wall; armoured enclosure for guns on warships. [F & It.]

casement /'keɪsmənt/ *n.* window or part of window hinged to open like door; *poetic* window. [AL (CASE[2])]

casework *n.* social work in relation to person's family and background. [CASE[1]]

cash 1 *n.* money in coin or notes; money paid as full payment at time of purchase; *colloq.* wealth. **2** *v.* give or obtain cash for. **3 cash and carry** system in which buyer pays for goods in cash and takes them away himself; **cash crop** crop produced for sale; **cash flow** movement of money into and out of a business, as measure of profitability; **cash in** obtain cash for, *fig.* profit; **cash in on** take advantage of; **cash on delivery** system of paying carrier for goods when they are delivered; **cash register** machine in shop etc. with drawer for money, recording amount of each sale. [F or It. f. L (CASE[2])]

cashew /'kæʃu:/ *n.* edible kidney-shaped nut; tropical tree from which it comes. [Port. f. Tupi]

cashier[1] /kæ'ʃɪə/ *n.* person in charge of cash transactions in shop, bank, etc. [CASH]

cashier[2] /kæ'ʃɪə/ *v.t.* dismiss from service, especially with disgrace. [Flem. f. F (QUASH)]

cashmere /'kæʃmɪə/ *n.* fine soft wool, esp. that of Kashmir goat; fabric made from this. [*Kashmir* in Asia]

casing /'keɪsɪŋ/ *n.* protective or enclosing material. [CASE[2]]

casino /kə'si:nəʊ/ *n.* (*pl.* **casinos**) public room or building for amusements, esp. gambling. [It. dimin. (*casa* house)]

cask /kɑ:sk/ *n.* barrel, esp. one for alcoholic liquor; its contents. [F or Sp. (*casco* helmet)]

casket /'kɑ:skɪt/ *n.* small usu. ornamental box for valuables; *US* coffin. [AF f. It. f. L (CASE[2])]

Cassandra /kə'sændrə/ *n.* prophet of disaster, esp. if disregarded. [Trojan prophetess]

cassata /kə'sɑ:tə/ *n.* ice-cream cake with fruit and nuts. [It.]

cassava /kə'sɑ:və/ *n.* tropical plant with starchy roots; starch or flour from this, used e.g. in tapioca. [Taino]

casserole /'kæsərəʊl/ **1** *n.* covered dish in which food is cooked and served; food cooked in this. **2** *v.t.* cook in casserole. [F ult. f. Gk *kuathion* little cup]

cassette /kæ'set/ *n.* small sealed case containing magnetic tape or film, ready for insertion. [F dimin. (CASE[2])]

cassia /'kæsɪə/ *n.* inferior kind of cinnamon; plant yielding senna-leaves. [L f. Gk f. Heb.]

cassock /'kæsək/ *n.* long close usu. black or red garment worn by clergy, male members of choir, etc. [F f. It.]

cassowary /'kæsəweərɪ/ *n.* large flightless bird related to emu. [Malay]

cast /kɑ:st/ **1** *v.* (*past* and *p.p.* **cast**) throw or emit, esp. deliberately or forcefully; cause to fall, direct (eyes, glance, light, shadow, spell, etc., *on*, *over*, etc.); throw out (fishing-line, net, etc., esp. into water); let down (anchor); shed or lose (horns, skin, horseshoe, etc.); record or register (vote); shape (molten metal or plastic material) in mould, make (product) thus; assign (actor) *as* character; allocate roles in (play, film, etc.); utter (aspersions *on*); arrange (facts etc.) *into* specified form; reckon or add up (accounts, figures); calculate (horoscope). **2** *n.* throwing of missile, dice, line, net, etc.; object of metal, clay etc., made in mould; moulded mass of solidified material, esp. plaster protecting broken limb; set of actors taking parts in play, film, etc.; form, type, or quality (*of* features, mind, etc.); tinge of colour; slight squint; = *worm-cast*. 3 **cast about** (or **around**) **for** try to find or think of; **cast adrift** leave to drift; **cast down** depress, deject; **casting vote** deciding vote when votes on two sides are equal; **cast iron** hard alloy of iron, carbon, and silicon cast in mould; **cast-iron** *a.* of cast iron, *fig.* hard, unchallengeable; **cast loose** detach (oneself); **cast lots** see LOT; **cast off** abandon, (in knitting) take (stitches) off needle and finish edge, set ship free from quay etc.; **cast-off** *a.* & *n.* abandoned or discarded (thing, esp. garment); **cast on** (in knitting) make first row of loops on needle; **cast up** throw on to shore etc., add up (figures etc.). [ON]

castanet /kæstəˈnet/ *n.* (usu. in *pl.*) small concave piece of hardwood, ivory, etc., in pairs struck with fingers as rhythmic accompaniment, esp. to Spanish dance. [Sp. f. L (CHESTNUT)]

castaway /ˈkɑːstəweɪ/ **1** *n.* shipwrecked person. **2** *a.* shipwrecked. [CAST]

caste /kɑːst/ *n.* any of the Hindu hereditary classes whose members have no social contact with other classes; exclusive social class or system of classes; **lose caste** descend in social order. [Sp. & Port. (CHASTE)]

casteism /ˈkɑːstɪz(ə)m/ *n.* caste system.

castellated /ˈkæstəleɪtɪd/ *a.* built with battlements; castle-like. [med.L (CASTLE)]

caster var. of CASTOR[1].

castigate /ˈkæstɪgeɪt/ *v.t.* rebuke or punish severely; **castigation** /-ˈgeɪʃ(ə)n/ *n.*; **castigator** *n.* [L (*castus* pure)]

casting /ˈkɑːstɪŋ/ *n.* object, esp. of molten metal, made by casting. [CAST]

castle /ˈkɑːs(ə)l/ **1** *n.* large fortified building with towers and battlements; (in chess) = ROOK[2]. **2** *v.i.* (in chess) move rook next to king and king to other side of rook. **3 castles in the air** visionary unattainable scheme, day-dream. [AF f. L *castellum*]

castor[1] /ˈkɑːstə/ *n.* small swivelled wheel (often one of set) fixed to leg or underside of piece of furniture; small bottle etc. with holes in top for sprinkling contents; **castor sugar** finely granulated white sugar. [CAST]

castor[2] /ˈkɑːstə/ *n.* oily substance got from beaver and used in medicine and perfumes. [F or L f. Gk]

castor oil /ˈkɑːstə/ oil from seeds of tropical plant, used as purgative and lubricant. [orig. uncert.]

castrate /kæˈstreɪt/ *v.t.* remove testicles of, geld; deprive of vigour; **castration** *n.* [L *castro*]

castrato /kæˈstrɑːtəʊ/ *n.* (*pl.* **castrati** /-tiː/) *hist.* male singer castrated in boyhood to preserve soprano or alto voice. [It. (prec.)]

casual /ˈkæʒjʊəl/ **1** *a.* accidental, due to chance; not regular or permanent (*casual labour*); unconcerned, made or done without great care or thought (*a casual remark*); (of clothes) informal. **2** *n.* casual worker; (usu. in *pl.*) casual clothes or shoes. **3 casually** *adv.* [F & L (CASE[1])]

casualty /ˈkæʒjʊəltɪ/ *n.* person killed or injured in war or accident; thing lost or destroyed; = *casualty department*; accident, mishap; **casualty department** (or **ward**) part of hospital where casualties are attended to. [med.L (prec.)]

casuist /ˈkæʒjʊɪst/ *n.* person who resolves cases of conscience, duty, etc., often with clever but false reasoning; sophist, quibbler; **casuistic** /-ˈɪstɪk/ *a.*; **casuistry** *n.* [F f. Sp. f. L (CASE[1])]

cat *n.* small soft-furred domesticated animal of carnivorous quadruped family; any of several wild animals of this family (e.g. lion and tiger); *colloq.* spiteful or malicious woman; *sl.* person, esp. jazz enthusiast; = *cat-o'-nine-tails*; **cat-and-dog life** one full of quarrels; **cat-and-mouse game** persistent but ineffectual pursuit of weaker party by stronger; **cat burglar** one who enters by climbing wall to upper storey; **cat-o'-nine-tails** whip of nine rope lashes; **cat's-cradle** child's game with string forming designs between fingers; **Cat's-eye (P)** reflector stud in road; **cat's-eye** precious stone; **cat's-paw** person used as tool by another, slight breeze; **cat's whiskers** *sl.* excellent person or thing; **let the cat out of the bag** reveal secret, esp. involuntarily; **like a cat on hot bricks** very agitated; **set the cat among the pigeons** cause trouble. [OE & AF f. L *cattus*]

cata- *pref.* down; wrongly. [Gk]

catabolism /kəˈtæbəlɪz(ə)m/ *n.* breakdown of complex substances in the body, destructive metabolism. [Gk *katabolē* throwing down]

catachresis /kætəˈkriːsɪs/ *n.* incorrect use of words; **catachrestic** /-ˈriːstɪk/ *a.* [L f. Gk (*khraomai* use)]

cataclysm /ˈkætəklɪz(ə)m/ *n.* violent upheaval or disaster; great change; **cataclysmic** /-ˈklɪzmɪk/ *a.* [F f. L f. Gk (*kluzō* wash)]

catacomb /ˈkætəkuːm/ *n.* (often in *pl.*) underground gallery with side recesses for tombs. [F f. L]

catafalque /ˈkætəfælk/ *n.* wooden framework for supporting coffin of distinguished person in funeral or lying-in-state. [F f. It.]

Catalan /ˈkætəlæn/ **1** *n.* native, inhabitant, or language of Catalonia in Spain. **2** *a.* of Catalonia. [F f. Sp.]

catalepsy /ˈkætəlepsɪ/ *n.* trance or seizure with unconsciousness and rigidity of body; **cataleptic** /-ˈleptɪk/ *a.* & *n.* [F or L f. Gk (*lēpsis* seizure)]

catalogue /ˈkætəlɒg/, *US* **catalog 1** *n.* complete list of items usu. in alphabetical or other systematic order and often with description of each. **2** *v.t.* make catalogue of; enter in catalogue. [F f. L f. Gk (*legō* choose)]

catalpa /kəˈtælpə/ *n.* flowering tree with long pods. [N. Amer. Ind.]

catalyse /ˈkætəlaɪz/, *US* **-yze** *v.t.* accelerate or produce by catalysis. [foll.]

catalysis /kəˈtælɪsɪs/ *n.* (*pl.* **-lyses** /-iːz/) effect produced by substance that, without itself undergoing change, aids chemical change in other substances. [Gk (*lūo* set free)]

catalyst /ˈkætəlɪst/ *n.* substance causing catalysis; person or thing that precipitates a change.

catamaran /kætəməˈræn/ *n.* boat with twin hulls in parallel; raft of yoked logs or boats. [Tamil]

catamite /ˈkætəmaɪt/ *n.* passive partner (esp. boy) in homosexual practices. [L, = Ganymede]

catapult /ˈkætəpʌlt/ **1** *n.* forked stick etc. with elastic for shooting stones; *hist.* military machine for hurling large stones etc.; mechanical device for launching glider, aircraft from deck of ship, etc. **2** *v.* launch with or hurl from catapult; fling forcibly; leap or be hurled forcibly. [F or L f. Gk]

cataract /ˈkætərækt/ *n.* waterfall, esp. large and sheer one; rush of water; condition in which lens of eye becomes progressively opaque. [L *cataracta* f. Gk, = down-rushing]

catarrh /kəˈtɑː/ *n.* inflammation of mucous membrane; watery discharge in nose or throat due to this. **catarrhal** *a.* [F f. L f. Gk (*rheō* flow)]

catastrophe /kəˈtæstrəfɪ/ *n.* great and usu. sudden disaster; disastrous outcome; dénouement of drama; **catastrophic** /-ˈstrɒfɪk/ *a.* [L f. Gk (*strephō* turn)]

catatonia /kætəˈtəʊnɪə/ *n.* schizophrenia with intervals of catalepsy and sometimes violence; **catatonic** /-ˈtɒnɪk/ *a.* & *n.* [Gk (TONE)]

catcall 1 *n.* shrill whistle of disapproval. **2** *v.i.* make catcall. [CAT]

catch 1 *v.* (*past* and *p.p.* **caught** /kɔːt/) capture in trap, in hands, etc., lay hold of; detect or surprise (person esp. in wrongful or embarrassing act: *caught them in the act*; *caught him reading comics*); trap into revelation, contradiction, etc.; receive and hold (moving thing) in hands etc.; dismiss (batsman in cricket) by catching ball direct from bat; get or contract by infection, contagion, or example (*caught measles*, *her enthusiasm*); apprehend with senses or mind (esp. thing occurring quickly or briefly); reach in time (train, person about to leave, etc.); reach or overtake (person ahead); (cause to) become fixed or entangled or be checked (*bolt does not catch*; *caught my foot in the door*); check suddenly (*catch one's breath*); try to grasp *at*; draw attention of, captivate (person's eye, fancy); begin to burn. **2** *n.* act of catching, chance or act of catching the ball in cricket etc.; amount of thing caught, esp. of fish in fishing; thing or person caught or worth catching, esp. in marriage; question, trick, etc., intended to deceive, incriminate, etc.; unexpected or hidden difficulty or disadvantage; device for fastening door, window, etc.; *Mus.* round, esp. with words arranged to produce humorous effect. **3 catch-all** thing for including many items; **catch-as-catch-can** wrestling with few holds barred; **catch fire** see FIRE; **catch hold of** grasp, seize; **catch it** *sl.* be punished; **catch on** *colloq.* become popular, understand what is meant; **catch out** detect in mistake etc., take unawares, (in cricket) get (batsman) out by catching; **catch-phrase** phrase in frequent current use; **catch up** reach (person etc. ahead), make up arrears, pick up hurriedly. [AF f. L *capto* try to catch (*capio* take)]

catching *a.* infectious; catchy.

catchment *n.* collection of rainfall; **catchment area** area from which rainfall flows into river etc., area served by school, hospital, etc.

catchpenny *a.* intended merely to sell quickly; superficially attractive.

catch-22 *n. colloq.* dilemma in which victim cannot escape insurmountable obstacle.

catchweight 1 *a.* unrestricted as regards weight. **2** *n.* catchweight sport.

catchword *n.* word or phrase in frequent current use, slogan; word so placed as to draw attention.

catchy *a.* (of tune) easy to remember, attractive.

catechism /ˈkætɪkɪz(ə)m/ *n.* summary of principles of a religion in form of questions and answers; series of questions. [eccl. L (CATECHIZE)]

catechist /ˈkætɪkɪst/ *n.* religious teacher, esp. one using catechism.

catechize /'kætɪkaɪz/ *v.t.* instruct by means of a catechism. [L f. Gk]
catechumen /kætɪ'kju:mən/ *n.* Christian convert being instructed before baptism. [F or eccl.L (as prec.)]
categorical /kætɪ'gɒrɪk(ə)l/ *a.* unconditional, absolute, explicit; **categorically** *adv.* [CATEGORY]
categorize /'kætɪgəraɪz/ *v.t.* place in category; **categorization** /-'zeɪʃ(ə)n/ *n.*
category /'kætɪgərɪ/ *n.* class or division (of things, ideas, etc). [F or L f. Gk, = statement]
cater /'keɪtə/ *v.i.* supply food; provide meals, amusements, etc., *for*; pander *to* (evil inclinations). [AF *acatour* buyer f. L *capto* (CATCH)]
caterer *n.* one who supplies food for social events, esp. professionally.
caterpillar /'kætəpɪlə/ *n.* larva of butterfly or moth; **Caterpillar track (P)** steel band passing round wheels of tractor etc. for travel on rough ground. [AF, = hairy cat]
caterwaul /'kætəwɔ:l/ *v.i.* make shrill howl of cat. [CAT, *-waul* imit.]
catfish *n.* large fish with whisker-like barbels round mouth. [CAT]
catgut *n.* fine strong thread made from dried intestines of sheep etc., used for strings of musical instruments and for surgical suture.
catharsis /kə'θɑ:sɪs/ *n.* (*pl.* **catharses** /-i:z/) emotional release in drama or art; purgation. [Gk (*katharos* clean)]
cathartic /kə'θɑ:tɪk/ **1** *a.* effecting catharsis, purgative. **2** *n.* cathartic drug.
cathedral /kə'θi:dr(ə)l/ *n.* principal church of bishop's see. [F or L f. Gk *kathedra* seat]
Catherine wheel /'kæθərɪn/ firework that spins when lit. [St *Catherine*, martyred on spiked wheel]
catheter /'kæθɪtə/ *n.* tube inserted into body-cavity (esp. bladder) to drain fluid; **catheterize** *v.t.* [Gk (*kathiemi* send down)]
cathode /'kæθəʊd/ *n.* negative electrode or terminal; **cathode ray** beam of electrons from cathode of high-vacuum tube; **cathode ray tube** vacuum tube in which cathode rays produce luminous image on fluorescent screen. [Gk *kathodos* way down]
catholic /'kæθəlɪk/ **1** *a.* universal, of interest or use to all, all-embracing, of wide sympathies or interests (*has catholic tastes*); (**Catholic**) Roman Catholic; including all Christians, or all of Western Church. **2** *n.* (**Catholic**) a Roman Catholic. **3 Catholicism** /-'θɒlɪsɪz(ə)m/ *n.*; **catholicity** /-'lɪsɪtɪ/ *n.* [F or L f. Gk (*holos* whole)]
cation /'kætaɪən/ *n.* positively charged ion; **cationic** /-'ɒnɪk/ *a.* [CATA-, ION]
catkin *n.* spike of small soft flowers hanging from willow, hazel, etc. [Du., = kitten]
catmint *n.* aromatic plant with blue flowers. [CAT]
catnap 1 *n.* short sleep. **2** *v.i.* (**-pp-**) have catnap.
catnip *n.* = CATMINT.
catsuit *n.* close-fitting garment with trouser legs, covering body from neck to feet.
cattle /'kæt(ə)l/ *n.pl.* cows, bulls, oxen; **cattle-grid** grid covering ditch, allowing vehicles to pass over but not cattle, sheep, etc. [AF *catel*, f. as CAPITAL]
catty *a.* catlike; malicious, spiteful in talk. [CAT]
catwalk *n.* narrow footway.
Caucasian /kɔ:'keɪʒ(ə)n/ **1** *a.* of the 'white' or light-skinned division of mankind; of the Caucasus. **2** *n.* Caucasian person. [*Caucasus* in USSR]
Caucasoid /'kɔ:kəsɔɪd/ *a.* of the Caucasian division of mankind.
caucus /'kɔ:kəs/ *n.* (often *derog.*) local committee for party political organization; party meeting. [perh. f. Algonquin]
caudal /'kɔ:d(ə)l/ *a.* of or like a tail; of posterior part of body. [L (*cauda* tail)]
caudate /'kɔ:deɪt/ *a.* tailed.
caught *past* and *p.p.* of CATCH.
caul /kɔ:l/ *n.* membrane enclosing foetus; part of this sometimes found on child's head at birth. [F]
cauldron /'kɔ:ldrən/ *n.* large deep vessel for boiling. [AF f. L *caldarium* hot bath]
cauliflower /'kɒlɪflaʊə/ *n.* cabbage with large white flower-head; **cauliflower ear** ear thickened by repeated blows. [F *chou fleuri* flowered cabbage]
caulk /kɔ:k/ *v.t.* make (esp. boat) watertight by filling seams or joints with oakum etc. and waterproofing material or by driving plate-joins together. [F f. L *calco* tread]
causal /'kɔ:z(ə)l/ *a.* of or forming a cause; relating to cause and effect; **causally** *adv.* [L (CAUSE)]
causality /kɔ:'zælɪtɪ/ *n.* relation of cause and effect; principle that everything has a cause.
causation /kɔ:'zeɪʃ(ə)n/ *n.* act of causing; causality. [F or L (CAUSE)]
causative /'kɔ:zətɪv/ *a.* acting as or expressing cause.
cause /kɔ:z/ **1** *n.* thing that produces an effect; person or thing that occasions or produces something; reason or motive; justification (esp. *show cause*); principle, belief, or purpose that is advocated or

advanced, esp. zealously; matter to be settled at law; case offered at law (*plead a cause*). **2** *v.t.* be the cause of, produce, make happen. **3 good cause** one deserving support; **lost cause** hopeless undertaking; **make common cause with** combine with in common effort. [F f. L *causa*]

cause célèbre /kəʊz se'lebrə/ (*pl. **causes célèbres***) lawsuit that attracts much interest. [F]

causerie /'kəʊzərɪ/ *n.* informal article or talk, esp. on literary subject. [F]

causeway /'kɔ:zweɪ/ *n.* raised road across low or wet ground; raised path by road. [AF *caucée* f. L CALX]

caustic /'kɔ:stɪk/ **1** *a.* that burns or corrodes organic tissue; sarcastic, biting. **2** *n.* caustic substance. **3 caustic soda** sodium hydroxide. **4 caustically** *adv.*; **causticity** /-'tɪsɪtɪ/ *n.* [L f. Gk (*kaiō* burn)]

cauterize /'kɔ:təraɪz/ *v.t.* burn (tissue) with caustic substance or hot iron, esp. to destroy infection. [F (prec.)]

caution /'kɔ:ʃ(ə)n/ **1** *n.* avoidance of rashness, attention to safety, prudence; warning, esp. formal one by police etc.; warning and reprimand; *colloq.* surprising or amusing person or thing. **2** *v.t.* warn (*against, not to do* thing), admonish; issue caution to. [F f. L (*caveo* take heed)]

cautionary *a.* that gives or serves as warning.

cautious *a.* having or showing caution.

cavalcade /kævəl'keɪd/ *n.* procession or company of riders, motor cars, etc. [F f. It. (CHEVALIER)]

cavalier /kævə'lɪə/ **1** *n.* courtly gentleman; *archaic* horseman; (**Cavalier**) supporter of Charles I in Civil War. **2** *a.* offhand, curt, supercilious.

cavalry /'kæv(ə)lrɪ/ *n.* (usu. treated as *pl.*) soldiers on horseback or in armoured vehicles.

cave 1 *n.* large hollow in side of hill, cliff, etc., or underground. **2** *v.* explore caves. **3 cave in** (cause to) subside or fall in, *fig.* yield to pressure, submit, withdraw opposition. [F f. L (*cavus* hollow)]

caveat /'kævɪæt/ *n.* warning, proviso; *Law* process to suspend court proceedings. [L, = let him beware]

caveman *n.* prehistoric man living in caves; *fig.* primitive or crude person. [CAVE]

cavern /'kæv(ə)n/ *n.* cave, esp. large or dark one; **cavernous** *a.* [F, or L *caverna* (CAVE)]

caviare /'kævɪɑ:/, *US* **caviar** *n.* pickled roe of sturgeon or other large fish. [It. f. Turk.]

cavil /'kævɪl/ **1** *v.i.* (**-ll-**, *US* **-l-**) take exception (*at*), carp, find fault. **2** *n.* petty objection. [F f. L *cavillor*]

cavity /'kævɪtɪ/ *n.* hollow within solid body; **cavity wall** double wall with internal space. [F or L (CAVE)]

cavort /kə'vɔ:t/ *v.i.* prance or caper excitedly. [orig. uncert.]

caw 1 *n.* harsh cry of rook, crow, etc. **2** *v.i.* make caw. [imit.]

cayenne /keɪ'en/ *n.* (in full **cayenne pepper**) pungent red pepper from capsicum. [Tupi]

cayman /'keɪmən/ *n.* S. American alligator. [Sp. & Port. f. Carib]

CB *abbr.* Companion (of the Order) of the Bath; citizens' band.

CBE *abbr.* Commander (of the Order) of the British Empire.

CBI *abbr.* Confederation of British Industry.

cc *abbr.* cubic centimetre(s).

CD *abbr. Corps Diplomatique*; compact disc.

Cd *symb.* cadmium.

Ce *symb.* cerium.

cease 1 *v.* end, stop, bring or come to an end. **2** *n.* in **without cease** not ceasing. **3 cease-fire** *n.* signal in war to stop firing; halt in hostilities. [F f. L *cesso*]

ceaseless *a.* without end.

cecum *US* var. of CAECUM.

cedar /'si:də/ *n.* evergreen coniferous tree; its hard fragrant wood. [F f. L f. Gk]

cede *v.t.* give up one's rights to or possession of. [F, or L *cedo cess-* yield]

cedilla /sɪ'dɪlə/ *n.* mark written under *c* esp. in French, to show that it is sibilant (as in *façade*); similar mark under *s* in Turkish etc. [Sp. dimin. of *zeda* Z]

Ceefax /'si:fæks/ *n.* (**P**) teletext service provided by BBC.

ceilidh /'keɪlɪ/ *n.* (orig. *Sc.* & *Ir.*) informal gathering for music, dancing, etc. [Gael.]

ceiling /'si:lɪŋ/ *n.* upper interior surface of room or other compartment; material forming this; upper limit; maximum altitude a given aircraft can normally reach. [orig. uncert.]

celandine /'seləndaɪn/ *n.* one of two kinds of small wild plant with yellow flowers. [F f. L f. Gk (*khelidōn* a swallow)]

celebrant /'selɪbrənt/ *n.* one who performs rite, esp. priest at Eucharist. [F or L (foll.)]

celebrate /'selɪbreɪt/ *v.* mark (event or festival) with festivities; perform (rite or ceremony), officiate thus; honour or praise publicly; **celebration** /-'reɪʃ(ə)n/ *n.*; **celebrator** *n.* [L (*celeber* renowned)]

celebrated *a.* widely known.

celebrity /sɪ'lebrɪtɪ/ *n.* well-known person; fame. [F or L (CELEBRATE)]

celerity /sɪ'lerɪtɪ/ *n. archaic* swiftness. [F f. L (*celer* swift)]

celery /'selərɪ/ *n.* plant with long crisp stems used as vegetable or in salads. [F ult. f. Gk *selinon* parsley]

celesta /sɪ'lestə/ *n.* small keyboard instrument with metal plates struck for bell-like sound. [F (foll.)]

celestial /sɪ'lestɪəl/ *a.* of the sky or heavenly bodies; heavenly, divinely good, sublime; **celestial equator** great circle of sky in plane perpendicular to earth's axis. [F f. L (*caelum* sky)]

celibate /'selɪbət/ **1** *a.* unmarried, esp. for religious reasons; abstaining from sexual relations. **2** *n.* unmarried person. **3 celibacy** *n.* [F or L (*caelebs* unmarried)]

cell *n.* small room, esp. in prison or monastery; cavity or compartment in honeycomb etc.; small group as nucleus of political activity, esp. of subversive kind; unit of structure of organic matter, portion of protoplasm usu. enclosed in membrane; vessel containing electrodes for current-generation or electrolysis. [F, or L *cella*]

cellar /'selə/ **1** *n.* room below ground level of house, used for storage (esp. of wine); stock of wine in cellar. **2** *v.t.* store in cellar. [AF f. L *cellarium* (CELL)]

cello /'tʃeləʊ/ *n.* (*pl.* **cellos**) bass instrument like very large violin, held upright on floor by seated player; **cellist** *n.* [abbr. of VIOLONCELLO]

Cellophane /'seləʊfeɪn/ *n.* **(P)** thin transparent wrapping material made from viscose. [CELLULOSE, cf. DIAPHANOUS]

cellular /'seljʊlə/ *a.* consisting of cells, of open texture, porous; **cellular radio** system of mobile radio transmission with area divided into 'cells' each served by small transmitter; **cellularity** /-'lærɪtɪ/ *n.* [foll.]

cellule /'selju:l/ *n.* small cell or cavity. [F or L (CELL)]

celluloid /'seljʊlɔɪd/ *n.* plastic made from camphor and cellulose nitrate. [foll.]

cellulose /'seljʊləʊz, -əʊs/ *n.* main constituent of plant-cell walls and textile fibres; *pop.* paint or lacquer consisting of esp. cellulose acetate or nitrate in solution. [F or L (CELL)]

Celsius /'selsɪəs/ *a.* of scale of temperature on which water freezes at 0° and boils at 100°. [astronomer]

Celt /kelt/ *n.* member of a group of W. European peoples including pre-Roman inhabitants of Britain and Gaul and their descendants esp. in Ireland, Wales, Scotland, Cornwall, and Brittany. [L f. Gk]

Celtic /'keltɪk/ **1** *a.* of the Celts. **2** *n.* group of languages spoken by Celtic peoples, including Gaelic, Welsh, Cornish, and Breton.

cement /sɪ'ment/ **1** *n.* powdery substance made by calcining lime and clay, mixed with water to form mortar or concrete that sets to stonelike consistency; any similar substance that hardens and fastens on setting; substance for filling cavities in teeth. **2** *v.t.* unite with or like cement; apply cement to; line or cover with cement. **3 cementation** /si:men'teɪʃ(ə)n/ *n.* [F f. L (*caedo* cut)]

cemetery /'semɪtrɪ/ *n.* burial ground, esp. one not in churchyard.

cenobite *US* var. of COENOBITE.

cenotaph /'senətɑ:f/ *n.* tomblike monument to one whose body is elsewhere. [F f. L f. Gk (*kenos* empty, *taphos* tomb)]

Cenozoic /ki:nə'zəʊɪk/ *US* var. of CAINOZOIC.

censer /'sensə/ *n.* vessel in which incense is burnt. [AF (INCENSE[1])]

censor /'sensə/ **1** *n.* official with power to suppress whole or parts of books, plays, films, letters, news, etc., on grounds of obscenity, threat to security, etc. **2** *v.t.* act as censor of; make deletions or changes in. **3 censorship** *n.*; **censorial** /-'sɔ:rɪəl/ *a.* [L (*censeo* assess)]

censorious /sen'sɔ:rɪəs/ *a.* severely critical.

censure /'senʃə/ **1** *n.* expression of disapproval, reprimand. **2** *v.t.* criticize harshly, reprove. [F f. L (CENSOR)]

census /'sensəs/ *n.* official count of population or of a class of things. [L (CENSOR)]

cent *n.* one hundredth of a US dollar or other metric unit of currency; coin of this value; *colloq.* very small amount. [F or It. or L (*centum* 100)]

centaur /'sentɔ:/ *n.* creature in Greek mythology with head, arms, and trunk of man joined to body and legs of horse. [L f. Gk]

centenarian /sentɪ'neərɪən/ **1** *n.* person a hundred or more years old. **2** *a.* of a hundred years. [foll.]

centenary /sen'ti:nərɪ/ **1** *n.* hundredth anniversary, celebration of this. **2** *a.* of a hundred years; of a centenary. [L (*centeni* 100 each)]

centennial /sen'tenɪəl/ **1** *a.* lasting for or occurring every hundred years; centenary. **2** *n.* centenary. [L *centum* 100, cf. BIENNIAL]

center *US* var. of CENTRE.

centesimal /sen'tesɪm(ə)l/ *a.* reckoning or reckoned by hundredths. [L (*centum* 100)]

centi- *in comb.* one hundredth; hundred. [L *centum* 100]

centigrade /'sentɪgreɪd/ *a.* having 100 degrees, esp. = CELSIUS. [L *gradus* step]

centigram /'sentɪgræm/ *n.* (also **centigramme**) metric unit of mass, equal to 0.01 gram. [CENTI-]

centilitre /'sentɪli:tə/ *n.* metric unit of capacity, equal to 0.01 litre.

centimetre /'sentɪmi:tə/ *n.* metric unit of length, equal to 0.01 metre.

centipede /'sentɪpi:d/ *n.* small crawling creature with long body and many legs. [F or L (*pes ped-* foot)]

central /'sentr(ə)l/ *a.* of, at, or forming the centre; from the centre; chief, most important, basic; **central bank** national bank issuing currency etc.; **central heating** method of warming a building by pipes, radiators, etc., fed from central source of heat; **central nervous system** brain and spinal cord; **central processor** see PROCESSOR; **centrally** *adv.* [F or L (CENTRE)]

centralism *n.* system that centralizes (esp. administration); **centralist** *n.*

centralize *v.* concentrate (esp. administration) at single centre; subject (State etc.) to this system; **centralization** /-'zeɪʃ(ə)n/ *n.*

centre /'sentə/ **1** *n.* middle point or part, esp. of line, circle, or sphere; pivot or axis of rotation; place or group of buildings forming central point in district etc. or main area for an activity (*city centre*; *shopping centre*); point of concentration or dispersion, nucleus, source (*centre of attraction*); political party holding moderate opinions; middle player in line in some field games, kick or hit from side to centre of pitch. **2** *a.* of or at the centre. **3** *v.* concentrate or be concentrated *in*, *on*, **(D)** *around*. **4 centre-board** board lowered through boat's keel to prevent leeway; **centre-forward** (or **-half**) middle player in forward (or half-back) line; **centre of gravity** point round which mass of body etc. is evenly distributed; **centre-piece** ornament for middle of table etc., principal item. [F, or L *centrum* f. Gk *kentron* sharp point]

centric *a.* at or near the centre; from a centre; **centrical** *a.*; **centrically** *adv.*

centrifugal /sen'trɪfjʊg(ə)l, **(D)** -'fju:g(ə)l/ *a.* moving or tending to move from centre, esp. of force with which body revolving round centre seems to tend from it; (of machine etc.) in which rotation causes such motion; **centrifugally** *adv.* [CENTRE, L *fugio* flee]

centrifuge /'sentrɪfju:dʒ/ *n.* rotating machine using centrifugal force to separate solids or liquids (e.g. milk and cream). [F (prec.)]

centripetal /sen'trɪpɪt(ə)l/ *a.* moving or tending to move towards centre. [CENTRE, L *peto* seek]

centrist *n.* one who holds moderate political views; **centrism** *n.* [CENTRE]

centurion /sen'tjʊərɪən/ *n.* commander of a century in ancient Roman army. [L (foll.)]

century /'sentjʊrɪ, -tʃərɪ/ *n.* period of 100 years, esp. reckoned from birth of Christ and beginning with a unit of 1 (1901–2000 = 20th century); 100 runs scored by batsman in one innings at cricket; company in ancient Roman army, orig. of 100 men. [L *centuria* (CENT)]

cephalic /sɪ'fælɪk, ke-/ *a.* of or in the head. [F f. L f. Gk (*kephalē* head)]

cephalopod /'sefələʊpɒd/ *n.* mollusc with distinct tentacled head, e.g. octopus. [prec., Gk *pous pod-* foot]

ceramic /sɪ'ræmɪk/ **1** *a.* of pottery, porcelain, or other articles of baked clay; of ceramics. **2** *n.* pottery etc. article. [Gk *keramos* pottery)]

ceramics *n.pl.* pottery collectively; (usu. treated as *sing.*) art of making pottery etc.

cereal /'sɪərɪəl/ **1** *a.* of edible grain. **2** *n.* any kind of grain used for food, plant producing this; breakfast food made from a cereal. [L (*Ceres* goddess of agriculture)]

cerebellum /serɪ'beləm/ *n.* smaller part of brain, located in back of skull. [L dimin.]

cerebral /'serɪbr(ə)l/ *a.* of the brain; intellectual; **cerebral palsy** spastic paralysis from brain damage before or at birth. [CEREBRUM]

cerebration /serɪ'breɪʃ(ə)n/ *n.* working of the brain.

cerebro-spinal /serɪbrəʊ'spaɪn(ə)l/ *a.* of brain and spine.

cerebrum /'serɪbrəm/ *n.* principal part of brain, located in front area of skull. [L]

ceremonial /serɪ'məʊnɪəl/ **1** *a.* of or with ceremony, formal. **2** *n.* system of rites, ceremonies proper to an occasion. **3 ceremonially** *adv.* [L (CEREMONY)]

ceremonious /serɪ'məʊnɪəs/ *a.* fond of or characterized by ceremony, formal. [F or L (foll.)]

ceremony /'serɪmənɪ/ *n.* formal procedure, esp. on religious or public occasions; observance of formalities, punctilious behaviour; **stand on ceremony** insist on formality. [F, or L *caerimonia* worship]

cerise /sə'ri:z/ *a.* & *n.* light clear red. [F (CHERRY)]

cerium /'sɪərɪəm/ *n.* grey metallic element of lanthanide series. [asteroid *Ceres*]

cert *n. sl.* a certainty, esp. in **dead cert.** [abbr.]

certain /ˈsɜːt(ə)n/ *a.* settled, unfailing, that may be relied on to happen; unerring, reliable; confident, convinced (*of*, *that*); that need not be specified or may not be known to reader or hearer (*a certain person*; *a certain Joe Bloggs*); some but not much (*felt a certain reluctance*); **for certain** without doubt. [F f. L *certus*]
certainly *adv.* without doubt; (in answer) yes, I admit that.
certainty *n.* undoubted fact; indubitable prospect; absolute conviction.
Cert. Ed. *abbr.* Certificate in Education.
certificate 1 /səˈtɪfɪkət/ *n.* document formally attesting a fact (esp. birth or marriage or death), a state (e.g. health), or a qualification attained. 2 /-keɪt/ *v.t.* (esp. in *p.p.*) provide with certificate. 3 **Certificate of Secondary Education** examination set for secondary-school pupils in England and Wales; **General Certificate of Education** public examination for secondary schools, at usu. two levels. 3 **certification** /sɜːtɪfɪˈkeɪʃ(ə)n/ *n.* [F or L (foll.)]
certify /ˈsɜːtɪfaɪ/ *v.t.* declare by certificate; make formal statement of; officially declare (person) insane; **certified cheque** one guaranteed by bank; **certifiable** *a.* [F f. med.L (CERTAIN)]
certitude /ˈsɜːtɪtjuːd/ *n.* feeling of certainty. [L (CERTAIN)]
cerulean /səˈruːlɪən/ *a.* sky-blue. [L *caeruleus*]
cervix /ˈsɜːvɪks/ *n.* (*pl.* **cervices** /-iːz/) neck; necklike structure, esp. neck of the womb; **cervical** /sɜːˈvaɪk(ə)l/ *a.* [L]
cessation /seˈseɪʃ(ə)n/ *n.* ceasing. [L (CEASE)]
cession /ˈseʃ(ə)n/ *n.* ceding. [F or L (CEDE)]
cesspit /ˈsespɪt/ *n.* (also **cesspool**) covered pit for temporary storage of liquid waste or sewage. [orig. uncert.]
cetacean /sɪˈteɪʃ(ə)n/ 1 *n.* member of order of mammals including whales. 2 *a.* of cetaceans. [L f. Gk *kētos* whale]
cetane /ˈsiːteɪn/ *n.* hydrocarbon of paraffin series found in petroleum. [f. SPERMACETI]
cf. *abbr.* compare. [L *confer*]
Cf *symb.* californium.
cg. *abbr.* centigram(s).
CH *abbr.* Companion of Honour.
Chablis /ˈʃæbli/ a white burgundy wine. [*Chablis* in E. France]
chaconne /ʃəˈkɒn/ *n.* music on ground bass; dance to this. [F f. Sp.]
chafe 1 *v.* rub (skin etc.) to restore warmth or sensation; make or become sore or damaged by rubbing; irritate; become annoyed, fret. 2 *n.* sore caused by rubbing. 3 **chafing-dish** vessel in which food is cooked or kept warm at table. [F f. L *calefacio* make warm]
chafer *n.* large slow-moving beetle. [OE]
chaff /tʃɑːf/ 1 *n.* separated husks of corn etc.; chopped hay or straw; worthless stuff; good-humoured teasing. 2 *v.* tease, banter. [OE]
chaffer *v.i.* bargain, haggle. [OE]
chaffinch /ˈtʃæfɪntʃ/ *n.* a common European finch. [OE (CHAFF, FINCH)]
chagrin /ˈʃægrɪn/ 1 *n.* feeling of acute annoyance or disappointment. 2 *v.t.* affect with chagrin. [F]
chain 1 *n.* connected flexible series of links or rings, usu. of metal; length or loop of this for specific purpose (as badge of office; for transmitting power from bicycle pedals to wheel); (in *pl.*) fetters, confinement, restraining force; sequence, series, or set of mountains, posts, facts, events, etc.; line of people; group of associated shops, hotels, newspapers, etc.; unit of length (66 ft.). 2 *v.t.* (often with *up*) fasten or restrain with chain. 3 **chain-gang** group of prisoners chained together for manual work; **chain-mail** armour made from interlaced rings; **chain reaction** chemical or nuclear reaction forming products which themselves cause further reaction, series of events each causing the next; **chain-smoke** smoke continuously, esp. by lighting next cigarette etc. from previous one; **chain store** one of series of shops owned by one firm and selling same class of goods. [F f. L *catena*]
chair 1 *n.* movable backed seat for one; seat of authority, office of chairman etc.; chairman (*address the chair*); *hist.* sedan-chair; *US* electric chair. 2 *v.t.* install in chair of authority; conduct (meeting) as chairman; carry (person) aloft in honour. 3 **chair-lift** series of chairs on endless cable for carrying passengers up mountain etc; **take the chair** be chairman. [F f. L f. Gk *kathedra*]
chairman *n.* person who presides over meeting; regular president of a committee, board of directors, etc.; **chairperson** *n.*; **chairwoman** *n. fem.*
chaise /ʃeɪz/ *n.* (chiefly *hist.*) light open carriage for one or two persons. [F]
chaise longue /ʃeɪz ˈlɒŋg/ long low chair able to support sitter's legs. [F, = long chair]
chalcedony /kælˈsedənɪ/ *n.* type of quartz with many varieties, e.g. onyx. [L f. Gk]
chalet /ˈʃæleɪ/ *n.* Swiss mountain hut or cottage; house in similar style; small cabin in holiday camp etc. [Swiss F]

chalice /ˈtʃælɪs/ *n.* goblet; Eucharist cup. [F f. L CALIX]

chalk /tʃɔːk/ **1** *n.* white soft limestone used for burning into lime; piece of this or similar coloured substance for writing and drawing; = *French chalk.* **2** *v.t.* mark, write, draw, or rub with chalk. **3 by a long chalk** by far; **chalk up** register or gain (success etc.). **4 chalkiness** *n.*; **chalky** *a.* [OE f. L CALX]

challenge /ˈtʃælɪndʒ/ **1** *n.* call to take part in contest etc. or to prove or justify something; demanding or difficult task; calling to respond, esp. sentry's call to give password; exception taken (e.g. to member of jury). **2** *v.t.* issue challenge to; take exception to (evidence, member of jury, etc.); dispute, deny (statement etc.). [F f. L *calumnia* CALUMNY]

challenging *a.* testing and stimulating.

chalybeate /kəˈlɪbɪət/ *a.* (of water etc.) impregnated with iron salts. [L (*chalybs* steel f. Gk)]

chamber /ˈtʃeɪmbə/ *n.* assembly hall, the council or other body that meets in it; one of the houses of a parliament; (in *pl.*) set of rooms let separately from rest of building (esp. in Inns of Court), judge's room for hearing cases not needing to be taken in court; cavity or compartment in body, machinery, etc., esp. part of gun-bore that contains charge; *archaic* room, esp. bedroom; **chamber music** music for a small group of instruments; **chamber of commerce** association to promote local commercial interests; **chamber-pot** receptacle for urine etc., used in bedroom. [F f. L *camera* f. Gk *kamara* vault]

chamberlain /ˈtʃeɪmbəlɪn/ *n.* officer managing royal or noble household; treasurer of corporation etc. [F f. Gmc (prec.)]

chambermaid *n.* woman employed to clean and tidy bedrooms in hotel etc.

chameleon /kəˈmiːlɪən/ *n.* small lizard able to change colour to suit surroundings; variable or inconstant person. [L f. Gk, = ground-lion]

chamfer /ˈtʃæmfə/ **1** *n.* bevelled surface at edge or corner. **2** *v.t.* make chamfer on. [F (*chant* edge, *fraint* broken)]

chamois /ˈʃæmwɑː/ *n.* (*pl.* same /-wɑːz/) small European and Asian mountain antelope; /also ˈʃæmɪ/ soft leather from sheep, goats, deer, etc., piece of this. [F]

chamomile var. of CAMOMILE.

champ[1] **1** *v.* chew noisily or vigorously. **2** *n.* sound of champing. **3 champ at the bit** be restless or impatient. [imit.]

champ[2] *n. sl.* champion. [abbr.]

champagne /ʃæmˈpeɪn/ *n.* wine (esp. sparkling white) from Champagne district of E. France; similar wine from elsewhere; pale straw colour.

champers /ˈʃæmpəz/ *n. sl.* = CHAMPAGNE.

champion /ˈtʃæmpɪən/ **1** *n.* person or thing that has defeated or surpassed all rivals in a competition etc. (often *attrib.* *champion boxer, dog, bloom*); person who fights or argues for another in a cause. **2** *a.* & *adv.* (*colloq.* or *dial.*) splendid(ly), first-class. **3** *v.t.* support the cause of, vigorously defend. [F f. med.L *campio* fighter f. L (CAMP[1])]

championship *n.* contest to decide champion in a sport; position of having defeated all rivals thus.

chance /tʃɑːns/ **1** *n.* way things happen, fortune, absence of design or discoverable cause, course of events regarded as a power, fate; undesigned occurrence, opportunity, possibility, or prospect. **2** *a.* fortuitous, accidental (*a chance meeting, occurrence*). **3** *v.* happen (*it chanced that; I chanced to see*); *colloq.* risk, take no thought for. **4 by chance** fortuitously, as it happens or happened; **chance one's arm** (or **chance it**) *colloq.* make attempt though unlikely to succeed; **chance on** happen to find or meet; **game of chance** one decided by luck not skill; **stand a chance** be likely to succeed; **take a chance** risk failure; **take one's chance** trust to luck; **take chances** behave riskily. [F f. L *cado* fall]

chancel /ˈtʃɑːns(ə)l/ *n.* part of church near altar. [F f. L *cancelli* grating]

chancellery /ˈtʃɑːnsələrɪ/ *n.* chancellor's department, staff, or residence; office attached to embassy or consulate. [foll.]

chancellor /ˈtʃɑːnsələ/ *n.* State or law official; non-resident head of university; chief minister of State in W. Germany and Austria; **Chancellor of the Exchequer** UK finance minister. [AF f. L *cancellarius* secretary]

chancery /ˈtʃɑːnsərɪ/ *n.* Lord Chancellor's division of High Court of Justice (usu. **Chancery**); records office; chancellery. [contr. of CHANCELLERY]

chancy /ˈtʃɑːnsɪ/ *a.* risky, uncertain; **chancily** *adv.* [CHANCE]

chandelier /ʃændəˈlɪə/ *n.* hanging fixture for lighting, usu. ornamental and having several branches. [F (CANDLE)]

chandler /ˈtʃɑːndlə/ *n.* dealer in ropes, canvas, and other supplies for ships; dealer in candles etc.; **chandlery** *n.* [F (CANDLE)]

change /tʃeɪndʒ/ **1** *n.* making or becoming different, difference from previous state; substitution of one for another (*change of air, scene*); variety, variation (*for a change*); money exchanged for coins of larger value or for different currency, money returned as difference between price and higher amount paid; = *small change*; one of different orders in which bells can be rung. **2** *v.* undergo, show, or subject to change; make or become different; take or use another instead of (*change one's shirt, doctor*); interchange, exchange (places, seats, often *with* person); get or give money change for; go from one to another of (houses, sides, trains, etc.), make such change; put fresh clothes, coverings, etc., on (child, bed, etc.); put on other clothes; (of moon) arrive at fresh phase. **3 change down** engage lower gear; **change gear** engage different gear; **change hands** pass to different owner; **change of clothes** second outfit in reserve; **change of heart** see HEART; **change of life** menopause; **change one's mind** see MIND; **change over** change from one system or situation to another; **change-over** *n.* such change; **change one's tune** see TUNE; **change up** engage higher gear; **get no change out of** *sl.* get no satisfaction or help from; **ring the changes** vary ways of doing things. **4 changeful** *a.*; **changefully** *adv.*; **changeless** *a.* [F f. L *cambio* barter]

changeable *a.* liable to change, inconstant; able to be changed.

changeling *n.* child believed to have been substituted for another.

channel /'tʃæn(ə)l/ **1** *n.* bed in which water runs; navigable part of waterway; piece of water (wider than strait) connecting two seas; passage for liquid; groove; course or line of motion; (usu. in *pl.*) medium of communication, agency (*through the usual channels*); narrow band of frequencies used in radio and television transmission, esp. by particular station; path for transmitting electrical signal or (in computers) data. **2** *v.t.* (**-ll-**, *US* **-l-**) form channel(s) in; guide, direct. **3 the Channel** the English Channel. [F f. L CANAL)]

chant /tʃɑːnt/ **1** *n.* song; melody with timeless reciting note(s) for unmetrical texts. **2** *v.* sing; intone, sing to a chant. [F f. L *canto* (*cano* sing)]

chanter *n.* one who chants; melody-pipe of bagpipes.

chanticleer /'tʃæntɪklɪə/ *n.* domestic cock (esp. as personal name in stories). [F (CHANT, CLEAR)]

chantry /'tʃɑːntrɪ/ *n.* endowment for singing of Masses; chapel or priests so endowed. [F (CHANT)]

chanty /'tʃɑːntɪ/ var. of SHANTY².

chaos /'keɪɒs/ *n.* utter confusion or disorder; formless primordial matter; **chaotic** /-'ɒtɪk/ *a.*; **chaotically** /-'ɒtɪkəlɪ/ *adv.* [F or L f. Gk]

chap¹ *n. colloq.* man, boy, fellow. [abbr. of CHAPMAN]

chap² **1** *v.* (**-pp-**) (of skin, hands, etc.) develop cracks or soreness; (of wind, cold, etc.) cause to chap. **2** *n.* (usu. in *pl.*) crack in skin etc. [orig. uncert.]

chap³ *n.* lower jaw or half of cheek, esp. of pig as food. [orig. unkn.; cf. CHOP²]

chaparral /tʃæpə'ræl, ʃæ-/ *n. US* dense tangled brushwood. [Sp.]

chapatti /tʃə'pætɪ/ *n.* (also **chapati**) small flat thin cake of unleavened bread. [Hindi]

chapel /'tʃæp(ə)l/ *n.* small building or room used for Christian worship; separate part of cathedral or church, with its own altar; place of worship of Nonconformist bodies; service in or attendance at chapel; association or meeting of workers in a printing-office. [F f. med.L dimin. of *cappa* cloak; St. Martin's cloak was kept by *cappelani* or chaplains in a sanctuary]

chaperon /'ʃæpərəʊn/ **1** *n.* older or married woman accompanying young unmarried woman for sake of propriety on social occasions. **2** *v.t.* act as chaperon to. **3 chaperonage** *n.* [F (*chape* cope, as CAPE¹)]

chaplain /'tʃæplɪn/ *n.* clergyman attached to private chapel, institution, ship, regiment, etc.; **chaplaincy** *n.* [F f. L (CHAPEL)]

chaplet /'tʃæplɪt/ *n.* garland or circlet for head; string of beads, short rosary. [F f. L (CAP)]

chapman /'tʃæpmən/ *n. hist.* pedlar. [OE (CHEAP, MAN)]

chappie *n. colloq.* = CHAP¹.

chapter *n.* main division of book; period of time (*a sorry chapter in my life*); canons of cathedral or other religious community, meeting of these; **chapter and verse** exact reference or details; **chapter of accidents** series of misfortunes. [F f. L dimin. of *caput* head]

char¹ *v.* (**-rr-**) make or become black by burning, scorch; burn to charcoal. [CHARCOAL]

char² *colloq.* **1** *n.* = CHARWOMAN. **2** *v.i.* (**-rr-**) work as charwoman. [orig. = CHORE]

char³ *n. sl.* tea. [Chin. *ch'a*]

char⁴ *n.* (*pl.* same) a kind of small trout. [orig. unkn.]

charabanc /'ʃærəbæŋ/ *n.* early form of motor coach. [F *char à bancs* carriage with seats]

character /'kærɪktə/ *n.* collective qualities or peculiarities that distinguish an individual or group; idiosyncracy, individuality, mental or moral qualities; moral strength; reputation, good reputation; a person, esp. an eccentric or noticeable one; person in novel, play, etc.; part played by actor; person's role or ways; written description of person's qualities, testimonial; distinctive mark, (often in *pl.*) printed or written letter or symbol; characteristic (esp. of biological species); **in** (or **out of**) **character** consistent (or inconsistent) with person's character. [F f. L f. Gk]

characteristic /kærɪktəˈrɪstɪk/ **1** *a.* typical or distinctive. **2** *n.* characteristic feature or quality. **3 characteristically** *adv.*

characterize /ˈkærɪktəraɪz/ *v.t.* describe character of, describe *as*; give character to, be characteristic of; **characterization** /-ˈzeɪʃ(ə)n/ *n.*

charade /ʃəˈrɑːd/ *n.* guessing of a word from clues given in acted scenes (often in *pl.*); absurd pretence. [F f. Prov. (*charra* chatter)]

charcoal /ˈtʃɑːkəʊl/ *n.* form of carbon consisting of black residue from partially burnt wood; dark grey. [orig. unkn.]

charge 1 *n.* price asked for goods or services, expense or cause of expenditure; accusation (*bring charges against*), discredit (*lay to person's charge*); directions, exhortation; task, duty, commission; care, custody, responsible possession (*I am in charge of him*; *he is in my charge*); impetuous attack or rush, esp. in battle, signal for this; appropriate quantity of material to put into receptacle, mechanism, etc., at one time, esp. of explosive for gun; quantity of electricity carried by a body; energy stored chemically for conversion into electricity; heraldic device or bearing. **2** *v.* ask (amount) as price, ask (person) for amount as price; debit cost of *to* person or account; accuse (*charged them with theft*); make accusation *that*; command, instruct, or urge (*to do* thing); entrust *with* task; attack or rush impetuously, throw oneself bodily (against); give electric charge to; load or fill with charge of explosive etc.; fill *with*; saturate with liquid, vapour, or chemical. **3 in charge** having command; **take charge** assume command. **4 chargeable** *a.* [F f. L (*carrus* car)]

chargé d'affaires /ʃɑːʒeɪ dæˈfeə/ (*pl.* **chargés** /ʃɑːʒeɪ/) ambassador's deputy; ambassador to minor country. [F]

charger *n.* cavalry horse; apparatus for charging battery. [CHARGE]

chariot /ˈtʃærɪət/ *n. hist.* two-wheeled vehicle drawn by horses, used in ancient racing and warfare. [F (CHARGE)]

charioteer /tʃærɪəˈtɪə/ *n.* chariot-driver.

charisma /kəˈrɪzmə/ *n.* ability to inspire followers with devotion and enthusiasm; divinely conferred power or talent; **charismatic** /kærɪzˈmætɪk/ *a.* [L f. Gk (*kharis* grace)]

charitable /ˈtʃærɪtəb(ə)l/ *a.* having or marked by charity; connected with charities or a charity; **charitably** *adv.* [foll.]

charity /ˈtʃærɪtɪ/ *n.* kindness, benevolence, a giving voluntarily to those in need; leniency or tolerance in judging others; institution or organization for helping those in need, help so given; love of fellow men. [F f. L *caritas* (*carus* dear)]

charlady /ˈtʃɑːleɪdɪ/ *n.* = CHARWOMAN.

charlatan /ˈʃɑːlətən/ *n.* one falsely claiming a special knowledge or skill; **charlatanism** *n.* [F f. It., = babbler]

Charleston /ˈtʃɑːlst(ə)n/ *n.* lively American dance of 1920s, with side-kicks from knee. [*Charleston* in S. Carolina]

charlock /ˈtʃɑːlɒk/ *n.* wild mustard, a weed with yellow flowers. [OE]

charlotte /ˈʃɑːlɒt/ *n.* pudding made of stewed fruit with covering of breadcrumbs etc.

charm 1 *n.* power or quality of giving delight or arousing admiration; fascination, attractiveness; trinket on bracelet etc.; speech, action, or object supposedly having occult or magic power. **2** *v.t.* delight, captivate; influence or protect as if by magic (*leads a charmed life*). **3 charmer** *n.* [F f. L *carmen* song]

charming *a.* delightful.

charnel-house /ˈtʃɑːn(ə)lhaʊs/ *n.* repository of corpses or bones. [F f. L (CARNAL)]

chart 1 *n.* geographical map or plan, esp. for navigation by sea or air; sheet of information in form of tables or diagrams; (often in *pl.*) listing of currently most popular gramophone records. **2** *v.t.* make chart of, map. [F f. L *charta* (CARD[1])]

charter 1 *n.* written grant of rights, esp. by sovereign or legislature; written constitution or description of organization's functions etc.; contract to use aircraft, ship, etc., for special purpose. **2** *v.t.* grant charter to; hire (aircraft etc.) for one's own use. **3 chartered accountant, engineer, librarian,** etc., member of professional body that has royal charter; **charter flight** flight by chartered aircraft. [F f. L *chartula* dimin. (prec.)]

Chartist *n. hist.* member of movement in Britain in 1837–8 seeking electoral and social reform; **Chartism** *n.* [prec.; name taken from 'People's Charter']

chartreuse /ʃɑːˈtrɜːz/ *n.* pale green or

yellow brandy liqueur. [*Chartreuse*, monastery in S. France]
charwoman *n.* woman employed to clean rooms in houses or offices. [CHAR²]
chary /'tʃeərɪ/ *a.* cautious, wary; sparing (*chary of giving praise*). [OE, rel. to CARE]
Charybdis see SCYLLA.
chase¹ 1 *v.* pursue; drive *from*, *out of*, *to*, etc.; hurry (*after* person, *round*, etc.); *colloq.* try to attain. **2** *n.* pursuit; unenclosed hunting-land. **3 the chase** hunting, esp. as sport; **chase up** *colloq.* pursue with specific purpose. [F f. L *capto* (CATCH)]
chase² *v.t.* emboss or engrave (metal). [F (CASE²)]
chase³ *n. Printing* metal frame holding composed type. [F f. L *capsa* CASE²]
chaser *n.* horse for steeplechasing; *colloq.* drink taken after another of a different kind.
chasm /'kæz(ə)m/ *n.* deep fissure or opening in earth, rock, etc.; *fig.* wide difference of feeling, interests, etc. [L f. Gk]
chassis /'ʃæsɪ, -i:/ *n.* (*pl.* **chassis** /-i:z/) base-frame of motor vehicle, carriage, etc.; frame to carry radio etc. equipment. [F f. L (CASE²)]
chaste /tʃeɪst/ *a.* abstaining from extramarital, or from all, sexual intercourse; pure, virtuous; simple in style, unadorned. [F f. L *castus*]
chasten /'tʃeɪs(ə)n/ *v.t.* punish, discipline by inflicting suffering; restrain, moderate.
chastise /tʃæ'staɪz/ *v.t.* punish, esp. by beating; **chastisement** *n.*
chastity /'tʃæstɪtɪ/ *n.* being chaste; sexual abstinence; simplicity of style.
chasuble /'tʃæzjʊb(ə)l/ *n.* loose sleeveless usu. ornate outer vestment worn by celebrant of Mass or Eucharist. [F f. L *casubla*]
chat 1 *v.* (**-tt-**) talk in light and familiar way. **2** *n.* informal talk; any of various songbirds. **3 chat up** *colloq.* chat to, esp. flirtatiously or with ulterior motive. [CHATTER]
château /'ʃætəʊ/ *n.* (*pl.* **châteaux** /-əʊz/) large French country-house or castle. [F (CASTLE)]
chatelaine /'ʃætəleɪn/ *n.* mistress of large house; *hist.* set of short chains attached to woman's belt, for carrying keys etc. [F, f. med.L *castellanus* (CASTLE)]
chattel /'tʃæt(ə)l/ *n.* (usu. in *pl.*) movable possession. [F (CATTLE)]
chatter 1 *v.i.* talk quickly, incessantly, trivially, or indiscreetly; (of bird) emit short quick notes; (of teeth) click repeatedly together. **2** *n.* chattering talk or sound. [imit.]
chatterbox *n.* talkative person.
chatty *a.* fond of or resembling chat; **chattily** *adv.*; **chattiness** *n.*
chauffeur /'ʃəʊfə, ʃəʊ'fɜ:/ **1** *n.* person employed to drive a private or hired motor car. **2** *v.t.* drive (car or person) as chauffeur. **3 chauffeuse** /-'fɜ:z/ *n. fem.* [F, = stoker]
chauvinism /'ʃəʊvɪnɪz(ə)m/ *n.* exaggerated or aggressive patriotism; excessive or prejudiced support or loyalty for one's cause or group (*male chauvinism*); **chauvinist** *n.*; **chauvinistic** /-'nɪstɪk/ *a.*; **chauvinistically** /-'nɪstɪkəlɪ/ *adv.* [*Chauvin*, character in French play 1831]
cheap 1 *a.* low in price, worth more than its cost; charging low prices, offering good value; easily got or made; inferior, of poor quality, of little account. **2** *adv.* cheaply (*going cheap*; *got it cheap*). **3 on the cheap** cheaply. [OE, = price, bargain]
cheapen *v.* make or become cheap; depreciate, degrade.
cheapjack 1 *n.* seller of inferior goods at low prices. **2** *a.* inferior, shoddy.
cheat 1 *v.* trick, deceive, deprive *of* by deceit; act fraudulently. **2** *n.* one who cheats, swindler; deception, trick. [ESCHEAT]
check 1 *n.* sudden stopping or slowing of motion; pause; rebuff or rebuke; person or thing that restrains; means or act of testing or ensuring accuracy; cross-lined pattern of small squares, fabric so patterned; bill in restaurant; *US* = CHEQUE; *US* counter used in games; token of identification for left luggage etc.; (announcement of) exposure of chess king to direct attack (also as *int.*); loss of the scent in hunting. **2** *v.* stop or slow motion (of); restrain, curb, rebuke; test, examine, verify; *US* agree on comparison; *US* mark with tick etc., deposit; threaten (opponent's king) at chess. **3 check in** arrive or register at hotel, airport, etc., record arrival of; **check off** mark on list etc. as having been examined; **check on** (*US* **out**) test, verify, investigate; **check out** leave hotel, airport, etc. with formalities; **check-out** *n.* act of checking out, pay-desk in supermarket etc; **check up (on)** = *check on*; **check-up** *n.* thorough (esp. medical) examination. [F ult. f. Pers., = king]
checked *a.* having a check pattern.
checker¹ one who checks.
checker² var. of CHEQUER.
checkmate 1 *n.* check at chess from which king cannot escape (also as *int.*); final defeat or deadlock. **2** *v.t.* put into checkmate; frustrate. [F (CHECK, Pers. *māt* is dead)]

Cheddar /ˈtʃedə/ *n.* a kind of firm smooth cheese. [*Cheddar* in Somerset]
cheek 1 *n.* side-wall of mouth, side of face below eye; impertinent speech; cool confidence, effrontery (*have the cheek to*). **2** *v.t.* speak impertinently to. **3** **cheek-bone** bone below eye; **cheek by jowl** close together, intimate. [OE]
cheeky *a.* impertinent, saucy; **cheekily** *adv.*; **cheekiness** *n.*
cheep 1 *n.* weak shrill cry of young bird. **2** *v.i.* make such a cry. [imit.]
cheer 1 *n.* shout of encouragement or applause; mood or disposition (*of good cheer*). **2** *v.* applaud, urge *on* by shouts; shout with joy; comfort, gladden. **3** **cheer up** make or become happier. [F f. L *cara* face f. Gk]
cheerful *a.* in good spirits, noticeably happy; bright, pleasant; **cheerfully** *adv.*
cheerio /tʃɪərɪˈəʊ/ *int. colloq.* expressing good wishes on parting or before drinking.
cheerless *a.* gloomy, dreary.
cheery *a.* lively, genial; **cheerily** *adv.*; **cheeriness** *n.*
cheese[1] /tʃi:z/ *n.* food made from curds of milk; shaped mass of this with rind; conserve with consistency of soft cheese; **cheese-paring** mean, stingy; **cheesy** *a.* [OE f. L *caseus*]
cheese[2] /tʃi:z/ *n. sl.* important person. [perh. f. Hind. *chīz* thing]
cheese[3] /tʃi:z/ *v.t. sl.* as *imper.* in **cheese it** stop it, leave off; **cheesed off** *sl.* bored, fed up. [orig. unkn.]
cheeseburger /ˈtʃi:zbɜ:gə/ *n.* hamburger with cheese in or on it. [CHEESE[1]]
cheesecake *n.* tart filled with sweetened curds; *colloq.* portrayal of shapely female body esp. in advertising.
cheesecloth *n.* thin loosely woven cloth.
cheetah /ˈtʃi:tə/ *n.* swift-running spotted feline like leopard. [Hindi]
chef /ʃef/ *n.* cook, esp. head cook (usu. a man) in restaurant etc. [F]
Chelsea bun /ˈtʃelsɪ/ a kind of currant bun in form of spiral. [*Chelsea* in London]
Chelsea pensioner inmate of Chelsea Royal Hospital for old or disabled soldiers.
chemical /ˈkemɪk(ə)l/ **1** *a.* of, made by, or employing chemistry or chemicals. **2** *n.* substance obtained by or used in chemistry. **3** **chemical engineering** industrial applications of chemistry; **chemical warfare** warfare using poison gas and other chemicals. **4** **chemically** *adv.* [F or med.L (ALCHEMY)]
chemise /ʃəˈmi:z/ *n. hist.* woman's loose-fitting undergarment or dress. [F f. L *camisia* shirt]
chemist /ˈkemɪst/ *n.* dealer in medicinal drugs etc.; expert in chemistry. [F (ALCHEMY)]
chemistry /ˈkemɪstrɪ/ *n.* science of the elements and compounds and their laws of combination and change resulting from interactions between substances in contact.
chenille /ʃəˈni:l/ *n.* tufty velvety cord or yarn; fabric made of this. [F, = caterpillar f. L dimin. of *canis* dog]
cheque /tʃek/ *n.* written order to bank to pay stated sum from drawer's account; printed form for writing this; **cheque-book** book of printed forms for writing cheques; **cheque card** card issued by bank to guarantee honouring of cheques up to stated amount. [CHECK]
chequer /ˈtʃekə/ **1** *n.* (often in *pl.*) pattern of squares often alternately coloured; *US* (in *pl.*) game of draughts. **2** *v.t.* mark with chequers; variegate; break uniformity of; (in *p.p.*) with varied fortunes (*chequered career*).
cherish /ˈtʃerɪʃ/ *v.t.* protect or tend lovingly; hold dear, cling to (hopes, feelings, etc.). [F (*cher* dear f. L *carus*)]
cheroot /ʃəˈru:t/ *n.* cigar with both ends open. [F f. Tamil]
cherry /ˈtʃerɪ/ **1** *n.* small soft round stone-fruit; tree bearing this, its wood; light red colour. **2** *a.* of light red colour. **3** **cherry brandy** liqueur of brandy in which cherries have been steeped. [F f. L f. Gk *kerasos*]
cherub /ˈtʃerəb/ *n.* angelic being of the second order of the celestial hierarchy (*pl.* **cherubim**); representation of (head of) winged child; beautiful or innocent child; **cherubic** /tʃəˈru:bɪk/ *a.* [OE & Heb.]
chervil /ˈtʃɜ:vɪl/ *n.* salad herb. [OE f. L f. Gk]
Cheshire /ˈtʃeʃə/ *n.* a kind of soft firm cheese; **like a Cheshire cat** with broad fixed grin. [*Cheshire* in England]
chess *n.* game for two with 16 men each played on chessboard. [F (CHECK)]
chessboard *n.* chequered board of 64 squares on which chess and draughts are played.
chest *n.* large strong box, esp. for storage or transport; part of body enclosed by ribs, front surface of body from neck to waist; small cabinet for medicines etc.; **chest of drawers** piece of furniture with set of drawers in frame; **get (thing) off one's chest** *colloq.* admit to (thing) to relieve anxiety about it. [OE f. L *cista* f. Gk]
chesterfield /ˈtʃestəfɪəld/ *n.* sofa with

padded back, seat, and ends. [Earl of *Chesterfield*]

chestnut /'tʃesnʌt/ **1** *n.* a glossy hard brown edible fruit; = *horse-chestnut*; tree bearing it; stale joke or anecdote; reddish-brown colour; horse of this colour. **2** *a.* deep reddish-brown. [F f. L f. Gk *kastanea* nut]

chesty *a. colloq.* inclined to or symptomatic of chest disease; **chestily** *adv.*; **chestiness** *n.* [CHEST]

cheval-glass /ʃə'væl glɑ:s/ *n.* tall mirror swung on upright frame. [F f. L *caballus* horse]

chevalier /ʃevə'lɪə/ *n.* member of certain orders of knighthood, or of French Legion of Honour etc. [F f. L *caballarius* horseman (*caballus* horse)]

cheviot /'tʃevɪət,'tʃi:-/ *n.* sheep of breed with short thick wool; this wool or cloth made from it. [*Cheviot Hills* in N. England & Scotland]

chevron /'ʃevrən/ *n.* bent line or stripe forming V shape, esp. as badge worn on sleeve of uniform indicating rank or length of service. [F f. L *caper* goat]

chew **1** *v.* work (food etc.) between the teeth, crush or indent thus; discuss, talk *over*; meditate *on* or *over*. **2** *n.* act of chewing; thing for chewing. **3 chew the fat** (or **rag**) *sl.* chat, grumble; **chewing-gum** flavoured gum used for chewing. [OE]

chewy *a.* needing much chewing; suitable for chewing; **chewiness** *n.*

chez /ʃeɪ/ *prep.* at the house or home of. [F f. L *casa* cottage]

chi /kaɪ/ twenty-second letter of Greek alphabet (Χ,χ). [Gk]

Chianti /kɪ'æntɪ/ dry, usu. red, Italian wine. [*Chianti* in Tuscany]

chiaroscuro /kɪɑ:rə'skʊərəʊ/ *n.* (*pl.* **chiaroscuros**) treatment of light and shade in painting; use of contrast in literature etc. [It., = clear dark]

chic /ʃi:k/ **1** *n.* stylishness, elegance in dress. **2** *a.* stylish, elegant. [F]

chicane /ʃɪ'keɪn/ **1** *v.* use chicanery; cheat (person *into*, *out of*, etc.). **2** *n.* chicanery; artificial barrier or obstacle on motor-racing track. [F]

chicanery /ʃɪ'keɪnərɪ/ *n.* clever but misleading talk; trickery, deception. [F]

chick *n.* young bird; *sl.* young woman. [OE (CHICKEN)]

chicken /'tʃɪkən/ **1** *n.* young bird, esp. of domestic fowl; flesh of domestic fowl as food; youthful person (*is no chicken*); *sl.* a game testing courage. **2** *a. sl.* cowardly. **3** *v.i.* (usu. with *out*) *sl.* withdraw through cowardice. **4 chicken-feed** food for poultry, *colloq.* unimportant amount, esp. of money; **chicken-pox** infectious disease, esp. of children, with rash of small blisters. [OE]

chick-pea *n.* dwarf pea with yellow seeds. [F f. L *cicer*]

chickweed *n.* a small weed. [CHICK]

chicle /'tʃɪk(ə)l/ *n.* milky juice of tropical American tree, chiefly used in chewing-gum. [Sp. f. Nahuatl]

chicory /'tʃɪkərɪ/ *n.* a blue-flowered plant used for salads; its root, roasted and ground, used with or instead of coffee. [F f. L f. Gk]

chide *v. literary* (*past* **chided** or **chid**; *p.p.* **chided** or **chidden**) scold, rebuke. [OE]

chief **1** *n.* leader or ruler; head of tribe, clan, etc.; head of department, highest official. **2** *a.* first in position, importance, influence, etc.; prominent, leading. **3 Chief of Staff** senior staff officer of a service or command. [F f. L *caput* head]

chiefly *adv.* above all; mainly but not exclusively.

chieftain /'tʃi:ft(ə)n/ *n.* leader of clan, tribe, or other group; **chieftaincy** *n.* [F f. L (CHIEF)]

chiff-chaff /'tʃɪftʃæf/ *n.* small European bird of warbler family. [imit.]

chiffon /'ʃɪfɒn/ *n.* light diaphanous fabric of silk or nylon etc.; very light-textured filling for pudding etc. [F (*chiffe* rag)]

chigger /'tʃɪgə/ *n.* = CHIGOE. [var. of CHIGOE]

chignon /'ʃi:njɔ̃/ *n.* coil or mass of hair at back of woman's head. [F]

chigoe /'tʃɪgəʊ/ *n.* tropical flea, burrowing into skin. [Carib]

chihuahua /tʃɪ'wɑ:wə/ *n.* dog of very small smooth-haired breed originating in Mexico. [*Chihuahua* in Mexico]

chilblain /'tʃɪlbleɪn/ *n.* painful swelling on hand or foot caused by exposure to cold. [CHILL, BLAIN]

child /tʃaɪld/ *n.* (*pl.* **children** /'tʃɪldrən/) young human being below age of puberty; unborn or newborn human being; one's son or daughter; descendant (*lit.* or *fig.*), follower, product, *of*; childish person; **child benefit** regular payment by State to parents of child up to certain age; **child-minder** person who looks after children for payment; **child's play** easy task; **with child** pregnant. [OE]

childbirth *n.* process of giving birth to a child.

childhood *n.* state or period of being a child.

childish *a.* of, like, or proper to a child; immature, silly.

childlike *a.* having good qualities of a child; innocent, frank, etc.

chili var. of CHILLI.

chill 1 *n.* unpleasant cold sensation, lowered body-temperature, feverish cold; unpleasant coldness of air, water, etc.; depressing influence; coldness of manner. **2** *a.* chilly. **3** *v.* make or become cold; depress, dispirit; harden (molten metal) by contact with cold material; preserve (meat etc.) at low temperature without freezing. [OE]

chilli /'tʃɪlɪ/ *n.* (*pl.* **chillies**) hot-tasting dried red capsicum pod. [Sp. f. Aztec]

chilly *a.* somewhat cold; sensitive to cold; unemotional, unfriendly. [CHILL]

Chiltern Hundreds /'tʃɪlt(ə)n/ Crown manor, for administration of which MP applies as a way of resigning from House of Commons. [*Chiltern* Hills in S. England]

chime 1 *n.* set of attuned bells; sounds made by this. **2** *v.* (of bells) ring; (of clock) show (hour) by chiming; be in agreement (*together, with*). **3 chime in** join in harmoniously, interject remark, agree (*with*). [OE (CYMBAL)]

chimera /kɪ'mɪərə/ *n.* monster in Greek mythology with lion's head, goat's body, and serpent's tail; bogy; wild or fanciful conception; **chimerical** /-'merɪk(ə)l/ *a.* [L f. Gk]

chimney /'tʃɪmnɪ/ *n.* structure by which smoke or steam is carried off from fire, furnace, engine, etc.; part of this above roof; glass tube protecting lamp-flame; narrow vertical cleft in rock-face; **chimney-breast** projecting wall round chimney; **chimney-pot** earthenware or metal pipe at top of chimney; **chimney-stack** number of chimneys standing together; **chimney-sweep** one who removes soot from inside chimneys. [F f. L (*caminus* oven f. Gk)]

chimp *n. colloq.* chimpanzee. [abbr.]

chimpanzee /tʃɪmpən'zi:/ *n.* small African anthropoid ape most closely resembling man. [F f. Kongo]

chin *n.* front of lower jaw; **chin-wag** *n.* & *v.i. sl.* talk, chat; **keep one's chin up** remain cheerful; **take on the chin** suffer severe blow from, endure courageously. [OE]

china /'tʃaɪnə/ *n.* fine semi-transparent or white earthenware, porcelain; things made of this; **china clay** kaolin. [*China* in Asia]

Chinaman /'tʃaɪnəmən/ *n.* native of China (usu. *derog.*); (in cricket) off-break or googly by left-handed bowler.

chinchilla /tʃɪn'tʃɪlə/ *n.* small S. American rodent; its soft grey fur; breed of domestic cat and rabbit. [Sp. (*chinche* bug)]

chine[1] **1** *n.* backbone; joint of meat including (part of) this; ridge. **2** *v.t.* cut through backbone of (carcass). [F f. Gmc & L]

chine[2] *n.* deep narrow ravine in Isle of Wight and Dorset. [OE]

Chinese /tʃaɪ'ni:z/ **1** *n.* (*pl.* same) native or language of China; person of Chinese descent. **2** *a.* of China. **3 Chinese lantern** collapsible paper lantern; plant with inflated orange calyx. [CHINA]

chink[1] *n.* narrow opening, slit. [rel. to CHINE[2]]

chink[2] **1** *n.* sound like glasses or coins being struck together. **2** *v.* (cause to) make this sound. [imit.]

Chink *n. sl. derog.* (**R**) a Chinese. [abbr.]

chinless *a.* weak or feeble in character. [CHIN]

chinoiserie /ʃɪn'wɑ:zərɪ/ *n.* imitation of Chinese motifs in furniture and decoration; articles featuring this. [F]

chintz *n.* colour-printed, usu. glazed, cotton fabric. [Hindi f. Skr.]

chintzy *a.* like chintz; gaudy, cheap.

chip 1 *v.* (**-pp-**) break or cut (piece etc.) *off* or *away*; break or cut edge or surface of (something hard), shape or carve thus; be apt to break at edge; cut (potato) into chips. **2** *n.* piece chipped off; place on object where piece has been chipped off; long strip of potato fried; *US* (in *pl.*) potato crisps; counter used in game; microchip. **3 chip in** *colloq.* interrupt, contribute money; **chip off the old block** child resembling parent, esp. in character; **chip on one's shoulder** inclination to feel resentful or aggrieved; **when the chips are down** when it comes to the point. [OE]

chipboard *n.* board made of compressed wood chips.

chipmunk /'tʃɪpmʌŋk/ *n.* small striped N. American animal like squirrel. [Algonquian]

chipolata /tʃɪpə'lɑ:tə/ *n.* small spicy sausage. [F f. It.]

Chippendale /'tʃɪpəndeɪl/ *n.* 18th-c. elegant style of furniture. [cabinet-maker]

chiro- *in comb.* hand. [Gk *kheir*]

chirography /kaɪə'rɒgrəfɪ/ *n.* handwriting; study of this. [-GRAPHY]

chiromancy /'kaɪrəʊmænsɪ/ *n.* palmistry. [Gk *mantis* seer]

chiropody /kɪ'rɒpədɪ/ *n.* treatment of the feet and their ailments; **chiropodist** *n.* [Gk *pous pod-* foot]

chiropractic /kaɪərəʊ'præktɪk/ *n.* treatment of disease by manipulation esp. of spinal column. **chiropractor** /'kaɪərəʊ-/ *n.* [Gk *prattō* do]

chirp 1 *n.* short sharp note made by small bird or grasshopper. **2** *v.* emit chirp(s); express or utter thus; talk merrily. [imit.]

chirpy *a. colloq.* lively, cheerful; **chirpily** *adv.*; **chirpiness** *n.*

chirrup /'tʃɪrəp/ **1** *n.* series of chirps. **2** *v.i.* emit chirrup. [imit.]

chisel /'tʃɪz(ə)l/ **1** *n.* tool with sharp bevelled end for shaping wood, stone, or metal. **2** *v.t.* (**-ll-**, *US* **-l-**) cut or shape with chisel; *sl.* defraud, treat unfairly. [F f. L (*caedo* cut)]

chit[1] *n.* young child; young small woman (usu. *derog.*: *chit of a girl*). [orig. = whelp, cub]

chit[2] *n.* short letter or note; note of order made, sum owed, etc. [Hindi f. Skr.]

chit-chat /'tʃɪttʃæt/ *n.* light conversation, gossip. [redupl. of CHAT]

chivalrous /'ʃɪv(ə)lrəs/ *a.* of or showing chivalry, courteous, honourable. [F f. L (CHEVALIER)]

chivalry /'ʃɪv(ə)lrɪ/ *n.* courtesy and honour, esp. showed to those weaker; medieval knightly system with its religious, moral, and social code; **chivalric** *a.*

chive *n.* small herb of onion and leek family, with onion-flavoured leaves. [F f. L *cepa* onion]

chivvy /'tʃɪvɪ/ *v.t.* pursue, harass. [prob. f. ballad of *Chevy Chase*]

chloral /'klɔ:r(ə)l/ *n.* (in full **chloral hydrate**) white crystalline compound used as sedative and anaesthetic. [F (CHLORINE, ALCOHOL)]

chloride /'klɔ:raɪd/ *n.* binary compound of chlorine; bleaching agent containing this. [CHLORINE]

chlorinate /'klɔ:rɪneɪt/ *v.t.* impregnate or treat with chlorine (esp. to purify water); **chlorination** /-'neɪʃ(ə)n/ *n.* [foll.]

chlorine /'klɔ:ri:n/ *n.* non-metallic element, a yellowish-green heavy gas used as water-purifier etc. [Gk *khlōros* green]

chloroform /'klɒrəfɔ:m/ **1** *n.* thin colourless liquid whose inhaled vapour produces unconsciousness. **2** *v.t.* render (person) unconscious with this. [prec., FORMIC]

chlorophyll /'klɒrəfɪl/ *n.* green colouring-matter of plants. [Gk *khlōros* green, *phullon* leaf]

choc *n. colloq.* chocolate; **choc-bar, choc-ice** bar of ice-cream enclosed in chocolate. [abbr.]

chock **1** *n.* block or wedge for stopping motion of wheel, cask, etc. **2** *v.t.* make fast with chocks. **3 chock-a-block** jammed together, crammed *with*; **chock-full** crammed full (*of*). [F]

chocolate /'tʃɒkələt,-klət/ **1** *n.* edible substance made as paste, powder, or solid block from ground cacao seeds; sweet made of or coated with this; drink of chocolate in hot milk or water; dark-brown colour. **2** *a.* made with chocolate; chocolate-coloured. [F or Sp. f. Aztec]

choice **1** *n.* act or power of choosing; variety to choose from; thing or person chosen. **2** *a.* of special quality. **3 from choice** willingly; **have no choice** have no alternative. [F f. Gmc, rel. to CHOOSE]

choir /'kwaɪə/ *n.* group of trained singers esp. in church; chancel of cathedral or large church. [F f. L CHORUS]

choirboy *n.* boy singer in church choir.

choke **1** *v.* cause to stop breathing by blocking windpipe or (of gas etc.) by being unbreathable; suffer such stoppage; make or become speechless from emotion; suppress (feelings); smother, clog, stifle; fill chock-full; block up or narrow (channel, tube, etc.). **2** *n.* valve in carburettor etc. controlling flow of air into petrol engine; device for smoothing variations of electric current. **3 choke back** suppress (emotion etc.); **choke down** swallow with difficulty; **choke up** block (channel etc.). [OE]

choker *n.* high collar; close-fitting necklace.

choler /'kɒlə/ *n. archaic* anger or irascibility; *hist.* one of the four humours, bile. [L f. Gk (*kholē* bile)]

cholera /'kɒlərə/ *n.* infectious often fatal bacterial disease with severe intestinal symptoms.

choleric /'kɒlərɪk/ *a.* irascible, easily angered.

cholesterol /kə'lestərɒl/ *n.* steroid alcohol found in body cells and fluids and thought to promote arteriosclerosis. [CHOLER, Gk *stereos* stiff]

choose /tʃu:z/ *v.* (*past* **chose** /tʃəʊz/; *p.p.* **chosen**) select out of greater number; select as (*was chosen king*); decide or think fit (*to do* thing, esp. one thing rather than another); make choice (*between* or *from*). [OE]

choosy /'tʃu:zɪ/ *a. colloq.* fussy, fastidious; **choosiness** *n.*

chop[1] **1** *v.* (**-pp-**) cut with strokes of knife, axe, etc.; cut (meat etc.) into small pieces; make chopping blow (*at*); strike (ball) with heavy edgewise blow. **2** *n.* chopping stroke; thick slice of meat, esp. pork or lamb, usu. including rib. **3 the chop** *sl.* action of killing or dismissing (*get the chop*; *be for the chop*). [rel. to CHAP[2]]

chop[2] *n.* (usu. in *pl.*) jaw of animal or person. [var. of CHAP[3]]

chop[3] *v.* (**-pp-**) change suddenly *round* or *about* in direction; **chop and change** vacillate, be inconstant; **chop logic** argue pedantically.[perh. rel. to CHEAP]

chopper *n.* short axe with large blade; butcher's cleaver; *colloq.* helicopter. [CHOP[1]]

choppy *a.* (of the sea) somewhat rough, with short broken waves; jerky, abrupt; **choppily** *adv.*; **choppiness** *n.* [CHOP[1]]

chopsticks *n.pl.* pair of sticks of wood etc. held in one hand, used in Asian countries to lift food to mouth. [pidgin Eng. f. Chin. (= nimble ones)]

chop-suey /tʃɒp'su:ɪ/ *n.* Chinese dish of meat fried with rice and vegetables. [Chin., = mixed bits]

choral /'kɔ:rəl/ *a.* of, for, or sung by, choir; of or with chorus; **choral society** group meeting regularly to sing choral music. [med.L (CHORUS)]

chorale /kɒ'rɑ:l/ *n.* metrical hymn-tune usu. sung in unison; harmonized form of this; choir, choral society. [G (prec.)]

chord[1] /kɔ:d/ *n. Mus.* combination of notes sounded together. [orig. *cord* f. ACCORD]

chord[2] /kɔ:d/ *n.* straight line joining ends of arc or curve; (*poetic* or *fig.*) string of harp etc.; **strike a chord** recall something to person's memory; **touch the right chord** appeal skilfully to emotion. [var. of CORD]

chore *n.* recurrent or tedious task; odd job. [CHAR[2]]

choreograph /'kɒrɪəgrɑ:f/ *v.t.* provide choreography for (ballet etc.). [foll.]

choreography /kɒrɪ'ɒgrəfɪ/ *n.* design or arrangement of dancing, esp. in ballet; **choreographer** *n.*; **choreographic** /-'græfɪk/ *a.* [Gk *khoreia* choral dancing to music]

chorister /'kɒrɪstə/ *n.* member of choir, esp. choirboy. [AN (CHOIR)]

chortle /'tʃɔ:t(ə)l/ **1** *n.* loud gleeful chuckle. **2** *v.* utter chortle; express with chortle. [portmanteau word (CHUCKLE, SNORT)]

chorus /'kɔ:rəs/ **1** *n.* group of singers, choir; such group singing and dancing in opera, musical comedy, etc.; refrain or main part of song; thing sung or said by many at once; any simultaneous utterance by many persons, etc. (*in chorus*); group of dancers and singers in ancient Greek plays and religious rites, any of its utterances; character speaking prologue in play. **2** *v.* say or sing in chorus. [L f. Gk]

chose, chosen *past* and *p.p.* of CHOOSE.

chough /tʃʌf/ *n.* red-legged bird of crow family. [imit.]

choux pastry /ʃu:/ very light pastry enriched with eggs. [F]

chow *n.* long-haired dog of orig. Chinese breed; *sl.* food. [Chin. *chow-chow*]

chrism /'krɪz(ə)m/ *n.* consecrated oil; ritual anointing. [OE f. L *chrisma* f. Gk]

Christ /kraɪst/ *n.* the Messiah of Old Testament prophecy; (title, now treated as name, of) Jesus as fulfilling this prophecy; image or picture of Jesus. [OE f. L f. Gk, = anointed]

christen /'krɪs(ə)n/ *v.t.* admit to Christian Church by baptism; give name or nickname to (person, ship, etc.); *colloq.* use etc. for first time; **christening** *n.* [OE f. L (CHRISTIAN)]

Christendom /'krɪsəndəm/ *n.* all Christians; Christian countries.

Christian /'krɪstjən/ **1** *a.* of Christ or his teaching; believing in, professing, or belonging to the religion of Christ; showing qualities associated with this; charitable, kind. **2** *n.* adherent of Christianity. **3 Christian era,** era reckoned from birth of Christ; **Christian name** forename given (as) at baptism; **Christian Science** system of health and healing without medical treatment by mental effect of patient's Christian faith; **Christian Scientist** adherent of this. [L *Christianus* of CHRIST]

Christianity /krɪstɪ'ænɪtɪ/ *n.* the Christian faith, based on teachings of Christ; being a Christian, Christian quality or character. [F (prec.)]

Christmas /'krɪsməs/ *n.* Christian festival or festive period commemorating Christ's birth; **Christmas-box** small present or gratuity given at Christmas, esp. to tradesmen and employees; **Christmas Day** 25 Dec.; **Christmas Eve** 24 Dec.; **Christmas pudding** rich boiled pudding of flour, suet, dried fruit, etc., eaten at Christmas; **Christmas rose** white-flowered winter-blooming hellebore; **Christmas tree** evergreen tree decorated with lights etc. at Christmas; **Christmassy** *a.* [OE (CHRIST, MASS[2])]

chromatic /krə'mætɪk/ *a.* of colour, in colours; *Mus.* of or having notes not belonging to diatonic scale; **chromatic scale** scale that ascends or descends by semitones; **chromatically** *adv.* [F or L f. Gk (*khrōma -mat-* colour)]

chromatin /'krəʊmətɪn/ *n.* constituent of cell-nucleus that can be readily stained. [G f. Gk (CHROME)]

chromatography /krəʊmə'tɒgrəfɪ/ *n.* separation of substances by slow passage through or over adsorbing etc. material.

chrome /krəʊm/ *n.* chromium, esp. as plating; yellow pigment got from compound of chromium. [F f. Gk *khrōma* colour]

chromite /'krəʊmaɪt/ *n.* mineral composed of chromium and iron oxides.

chromium /'krəʊmɪəm/ *n.* metallic element with coloured compounds; **chromium plate** protective coating of chromium.

chromosome /ˈkrəʊməsəʊm/ *n.* rod-like or threadlike structure occurring in pairs in cell-nucleus of animals and plants, carrying genes. [Gk (CHROME, *sōma* body)]

chronic /ˈkrɒnɪk/ *a.* (of disease) lingering, long-lasting; (of invalid) having chronic disease; *colloq.* bad, intense, severe; **chronically** *adv.*; **chronicity** /krɒˈnɪsɪtɪ/ *n.* [F f. L f. Gk (*khronos* time)]

chronicle /ˈkrɒnɪk(ə)l/ **1** *n.* continuous record of events in order of occurrence. **2** *v.t.* enter or relate in a chronicle. [F f. L f. Gk *khronika* (prec.)]

chronological /krɒnəˈlɒdʒɪk(ə)l/ *a.* of chronology; according to order of occurrence. [foll.]

chronology /krəˈnɒlədʒɪ/ *n.* science of computing dates; arrangement of events in order in which they occurred or in terms of absolute dates. [Gk *khronos* time, -LOGY]

chronometer /krəˈnɒmɪtə/ *n.* time-measuring instrument, esp. one keeping accurate time at all temperatures and used in navigation. [prec., -METER]

chrysalis /ˈkrɪsəlɪs/ *n.* pupa, esp. quiescent one of butterfly or moth; case enclosing it. [L f. Gk (*khrusos* gold)]

chrysanthemum /krɪˈsænθəməm/ *n.* composite garden plant flowering in autumn. [L f. Gk, = gold flower]

chrysoberyl /krɪsəʊˈberɪl/ *n.* a yellowish-green gem. [L f. Gk (*khrusos* gold, BERYL)]

chrysolite /ˈkrɪsəʊlaɪt/ *n.* a precious stone, a variety of olivine. [F f. L f. Gk (prec., *lithos* stone)]

chrysoprase /ˈkrɪsəʊpreɪz/ *n.* apple-green variety of chalcedony. [F f. L f. Gk (*khrusos* gold, *prason* leek)]

chub *n.* (*pl.* same) thick-bodied river-fish of carp family. [orig. unkn.]

chubby *a.* plump and round, esp. in the face. [f. prec.]

chuck[1] *colloq.* **1** *v.t.* throw or fling carelessly or casually (*away, in, out, up,* etc.); touch playfully under the chin. **2** *n.* act of chucking; playful touch. **3 the chuck** *sl.* dismissal; **chuck it** *sl.* stop, desist; **chuck out** expel (troublesome person) from meeting etc. [perh. F *chuquer* knock]

chuck[2] **1** *n.* device in lathe or drill for holding workpiece or bit; cut of beef from neck to ribs. **2** *v.t.* fix in chuck. [var. of CHOCK]

chuckle /ˈtʃʌk(ə)l/ **1** *n.* quiet or suppressed laugh. **2** *v.i.* emit chuckle; exult *over*. [*chuck* cluck]

chuff *v.i.* (of engine etc.) work with regular sharp puffing sound. [imit.]

chuffed *a. sl.* pleased; (*less often*) displeased. [dial. *chuff*]

chug **1** *n.* repeated dull explosive sound made by engine running slowly. **2** *v.* (**-gg-**) make, move (*along*) with, chug. [imit.]

chukker *n.* (also **chukka**) period in game of polo; **chukka boot** ankle-high leather boot. [f. Hindi, f. Skr. *chakra* wheel]

chum *colloq.* **1** *n.* close friend. **2** *v.i.* (**-mm-**) share rooms (*with*). **3 chum up** form friendship (*with*). [abbr. of *chamber-fellow*]

chummy *a. colloq.* friendly; **chummily** *adv.*; **chumminess** *n.*

chump *n.* short thick lump of wood; thick end of loin of lamb or mutton (*chump chop*); *colloq.* foolish person; **off one's chump** crazy. [blend of CHUNK, LUMP]

chunk *n.* thick piece cut or broken off; substantial amount. [var. of CHUCK[2]]

chunky *a.* consisting of or resembling chunks; small and sturdy; **chunkiness** *n.*

chunter *v.i. colloq.* mutter, grumble, complain. [prob. imit.]

chupatty var. of CHAPATTI.

church **1** *n.* building for public Christian worship; public worship (*go to church; meet after church*); (**Church**) body of all Christians, organized Christian society, the clergy or clerical profession (*went into the Church*). **2** *v.t.* perform church service of thanksgiving for (esp. woman after childbirth). **3 Church of England** Church in England recognized by State and rejecting papal authority. [OE f. Gmc f. Gk *kuriakon* Lord's (house)]

churchgoer *n.* person who goes to church, esp. regularly.

churchman *n.* member of clergy or church.

churchwarden *n.* elected lay official (usu. one of two) of parish; long clay pipe.

churchyard *n.* enclosed ground round church, esp. as used for burials.

churl *n.* ill-bred, surly person; *archaic* peasant. [OE, = man]

churlish *a.* ill-mannered, surly, niggardly. [f. prec.]

churn **1** *n.* butter-making machine; large milk-can. **2** *v.t.* agitate (milk or cream) in churn; make (butter) in churn. **3 churn out** produce in large quantities; **churn up** agitate violently. [OE]

chute /ʃuːt/ *n.* sloping channel or slide for conveying things to lower level; *colloq.* parachute. [F (L *cado* fall)]

chutney /ˈtʃʌtnɪ/ *n.* pungent relish of fruits, vinegar, spices, etc. [Hindi]

chutzpah /ˈhuːtspə/ *n. sl.* shameless audacity. [Yiddish]

chyle /kaɪl/ *n.* milky fluid formed from action of pancreatic juice and bile on chyme. [L f. Gk *khulos* juice]
chyme /kaɪm/ *n.* acid pulp formed from digested food. [L f. Gk *khumos* juice]
CIA *abbr.* Central Intelligence Agency.
ciao /tʃaʊ/ *int. colloq.* goodbye; hello. [It.]
cicada /sɪˈkɑːdə, -ˈkeɪdə/ *n.* long insect with transparent wings that makes rhythmic chirping sound. [L]
cicatrice /ˈsɪkətrɪs/ *n.* scar left by healed wound. [F or L]
cicely /ˈsɪsəlɪ/ *n.* flowering plant allied to parsley and chervil. [L f. Gk *seselis*]
cicerone /tʃɪtʃəˈrəʊnɪ, sɪs-/ *n.* (*pl.* **ciceroni** /-iː/) guide to visitors of antiquities etc. [It. f. L *Cicero*, Roman statesman]
CID *abbr.* Criminal Investigation Department.
-cide *suffix* person or substance that kills (*regicide*, *insecticide*); killing (*homicide*). [L *caedo* kill]
cider *n.* drink of fermented apple-juice. [F ult. f. Heb., = strong drink]
cigar /sɪˈgɑː/ *n.* long thin roll of tobacco leaves for smoking. [F or Sp.]
cigarette /sɪgəˈret/, *US* **cigaret** *n.* thin cylinder of finely-cut tobacco etc. rolled in paper for smoking. [F dimin.]
cilium /ˈsɪlɪəm/ *n.* (*pl.* **cilia**) eyelash; similar fringe on leaf, insect's wing, etc.; hairlike vibrating organ on animal or vegetable tissue; **ciliary** *a.*; **ciliate** *a.* [L]
cinch *n. sl.* sure thing, certainty; easy task. [Sp. *cincha* saddle-girth]
cinchona /sɪŋˈkəʊnə/ *n.* a S. American evergreen tree or shrub; its bark, containing quinine; drug made from this. [Countess of *Chinchón*]
cincture /ˈsɪŋktʃə, -tʃʊə/ *literary* **1** *n.* girdle, belt, or border. **2** *v.t.* surround with cincture. [L (*cingo* gird)]
cinder *n.* residue of coal or wood etc. after burning; (in *pl.*) ashes. [OE *sinder* = slag]
Cinderella /sɪndəˈrelə/ *n.* person or thing of unrecognized or disregarded merit or beauty. [character in fairy-tale]
cine- *in comb.* cinematographic (*cine-camera*, *-film*, *-projector*). [abbr.]
cinema /ˈsɪnəmɑː, -mə/ *n.* theatre where motion-picture films are shown; production of films as an art or industry; **cinematic** /sɪnɪˈmætɪk/ *a.* [F (foll.)]
cinematograph /sɪnəˈmætəgrɑːf/ *n.* device for showing motion-picture film. [F (KINEMATIC)]
cinematography /sɪnəmæˈtɒgrəfɪ/ *n.* art of making motion-picture films; **cinematographer** *n.*; **cinematographic** /-ˈgræfɪk/ *a.*
cineraria /sɪnəˈreərɪə/ *n.* plant with bright flowers and ash-coloured down on leaves. [L (*cinis -ner-* ashes)]
cinerary /ˈsɪnərərɪ/ *a.* of ashes, esp. of urn holding ashes of dead after cremation.
cinnabar /ˈsɪnəbɑː/ *n.* red mercuric sulphide; vermilion; moth with reddish-marked wings. [L f. Gk]
cinnamon /ˈsɪnəmən/ *n.* spice from aromatic inner bark of SE Asian tree; this tree; yellowish-brown. [F f. L f. Gk]
cinque /sɪŋk/ *n.* the five on dice. [F f. L *quinque* five]
cinquefoil /ˈsɪŋkfɔɪl/ *n.* plant with compound leaf of five leaflets; *Archit.* five-cusped ornament in circle or arch. [L (prec., *folium* leaf)]
Cinque Ports /sɪŋk/ group of (orig. five) ports in SE England with ancient privileges. [L *quinque portus* five ports]
cipher /ˈsaɪfə/ **1** *n.* secret or disguised writing, thing so written, key to it; arithmetical symbol (0) of no value in itself but used to occupy vacant place in decimal etc. numeration; person or thing of no importance. **2** *v.t.* write in cipher. [F f. med.L f. Arab.]
circa /ˈsɜːkə/ *prep.* about (a specified date or number). [L]
circadian /sɜːˈkeɪdɪən/ *a. Physiol.* occurring about once per day. [prec., L *dies* day]
circle /ˈsɜːk(ə)l/ **1** *n.* round plane figure with circumference equidistant from centre at all points; circular or roundish structure, enclosure, etc.; curved upper tier of seats at theatre etc.; circular route (*lit.* or *fig.*); persons grouped round centre of interest; set, restricted group, class (*literary circles*); (in full **vicious circle**) unbroken sequence of reciprocal cause and effect or action and reaction; fallacy of proving by assuming proposition dependent on what is to be proved. **2** *v.* move in a circle (*about*, *around*, *round*); revolve round; form circle round, enclose, surround. **3 come full circle** return to starting-point. [F f. L dimin. (CIRCUS)]
circlet /ˈsɜːklɪt/ *n.* small circle; circular band esp. as ornament.
circuit /ˈsɜːkɪt/ *n.* line or course or distance enclosing an area; path of electric current, apparatus through which current passes; judge's itinerary through district to hold courts, such a district, lawyers following a circuit; chain of theatres, cinemas, etc., under single management; motor-racing track; sequence of sporting events or athletic exercises; group of Methodist churches forming minor administrative unit; **circuit-breaker** automatic device for interrupting electric circuit. [F f. L (CIRCUM-, *eo it-* go)]

circuitous /sɜ:'kju:ɪtəs/ *a.* indirect, going a long way round.

circuitry /'sɜ:kɪtrɪ/ *n.* system of electric circuits; equipment forming this.

circular /'sɜ:kjʊlə/ **1** *a.* having form of circle; moving or taking place along circle (*circular tour*); (of reasoning) depending on vicious circle; (of letter or notice) addressed to a number of people. **2** *n.* circular letter, leaflet, etc. **3 circular saw** rotating toothed disc for sawing wood etc. **4 circularity** /-'lærɪtɪ/ *n.* [F f. L (CIRCLE)]

circularize *v.t.* send circulars to.

circulate /'sɜ:kjʊleɪt/ *v.* be or put in circulation; send particulars to (several people); **circulator** *n.* [L (CIRCLE)]

circulation /sɜ:kjʊ'leɪʃ(ə)n/ *n.* movement to and fro, or from and back to starting-point, esp. that of blood in body from and to heart; transmission or distribution (of information, news, books, etc.); number of copies sold, esp. of newspapers; **in** (or **out of**) **circulation** participating (or not participating) in activities etc.

circulatory /sɜ:kjʊ'leɪtərɪ/ *a.* of circulation, esp. of the blood.

circum- *prefix* round, about. [L]

circumcise /'sɜ:kəmsaɪz/ *v.t.* cut off foreskin of (male person) as religious rite or surgical operation; **circumcision** /-'sɪʒ(ə)n/ *n.* [F f. L (*caedo* cut)]

circumference /sɜ:'kʌmfərəns/ *n.* line enclosing circle or circular object; distance round this; **circumferential** /-'renʃ(ə)l/ *a.* [F f. L (*fero* carry)]

circumflex /'sɜ:kəmfleks/ *n.* & *a.* (in full **circumflex accent**) mark (ˆ) over vowel to show contraction, length, or special quality. [L (FLEX)]

circumlocution /sɜ:kəmlə'kju:ʃ(ə)n/ *n.* roundabout expression, evasive talk; verbosity; **circumlocutory** /-'lɒkjʊtərɪ/ *a.* [F or L (LOCUTION)]

circumnavigate /sɜ:kəm'nævɪgeɪt/ *v.t.* sail round (esp. the world); **circumnavigation** /-'geɪʃ(ə)n/ *n.* [L (NAVIGATE)]

circumscribe /'sɜ:kəmskraɪb/ *v.t.* (of line etc.) enclose or outline; mark or lay down limits of, confine, restrict; draw (figure) round another so as to touch it at points without cutting it; **circumscription** /-'skrɪpʃ(ə)n/ *n.* [L (*scribo* write)]

circumspect /'sɜ:kəmspekt/ *a.* wary, cautious, taking everything into account; **circumspection** /-'spekʃ(ə)n/ *n.* [L (*specio spect-* look)]

circumstance /'sɜ:kəmstəns/ *n.* fact, occurrence, or condition, esp. (in *pl.*) connected with or affecting an event etc.; (in *pl.*) financial condition; ceremony, fuss; **in** (or **under**) **the circumstances** the state of affairs being what it is; **in** (or **under**) **no circumstances** not at all, never; **circumstanced** *a.* [F or L (*sto* stand)]

circumstantial /sɜ:kəm'stænʃ(ə)l/ *a.* (of account or story) giving full details; (of evidence) indicating a conclusion by inference from known facts hard to explain otherwise; **circumstantiality** /-ʃɪ'ælɪtɪ/ *n.*

circumvent /sɜ:kəm'vent/ *v.t.* evade, find way round; baffle, outwit; **circumvention** *n.* [L (*venio vent-* come)]

circus /'sɜ:kəs/ *n.* travelling show of performing animals, acrobats, clowns, etc.; *colloq.* scene of lively action; *colloq.* group of people in common activity, esp. sport; open space in town, on which streets converge; *hist.* arena for sports and games. [L, = ring]

cirque /sɜ:k/ *n.* deep bowl-shaped hollow at head of valley or on mountainside. [F (CIRCUS)]

cirrhosis /sɪ'rəʊsɪs/ *n.* chronic disease of liver, esp. suffered by alcoholics. [Gk *kirrhos* tawny]

cirriped /'sɪrɪped/ *n.* marine crustacean in valved shell, e.g. barnacle. [foll., L (*pes ped-* foot)]

cirrus /'sɪrəs/ *n.* (*pl.* **cirri** /-aɪ/) white wispy cloud, esp. at high altitude; tendril or appendage of plant or animal. [L, = curl]

cisalpine /sɪs'ælpaɪn/ *a.* on south (or Roman) side of Alps. [L (*cis-* on this side of)]

cissy var. of SISSY.

Cistercian /sɪ'stɜ:ʃ(ə)n/ **1** *n.* monk or nun of order founded as stricter branch of Benedictines. **2** *a.* of the Cistercians. [F (*Cîteaux* in France)]

cistern /'sɪstən/ *n.* tank for storing water, esp. in roof-space supplying taps or as part of flushing lavatory; underground reservoir. [F f. L (*cista* box f. Gk)]

cistus /'sɪstəs/ *n.* shrub with large white or red flowers. [L f. Gk]

citadel /'sɪtədel/ *n.* fortress, usu. on high ground protecting or dominating city; meeting-hall of Salvation Army. [F or It. dimin. (CITY)]

citation /saɪ'teɪʃ(ə)n/ *n.* citing or passage cited; mention in official dispatch; description of reasons for award. [foll.]

cite *v.t.* adduce as instance, quote (passage, book, or author) in support; mention in official dispatch; summon at law. [F f. L (*cieo* set in motion)]

citizen /'sɪtɪz(ə)n/ *n.* native or naturalized member *of* a State; inhabitant of a city; *US* civilian; **citizens' band** system of local intercommunication by individuals on special radio frequencies; **citizenry** *n.*; **citizenship** *n.* [AF (CITY)]

citrate /'sɪtreɪt/ *n.* salt of citric acid. [foll.]

citric /'sɪtrɪk/ *a.* derived from citrus fruit; **citric acid** sharp-tasting acid in lemon-juice etc. [F f. L (CITRUS)]

citron /'sɪtrən/ *n.* large yellow-skinned fruit like lemon; tree bearing it.

citronella /sɪtrə'nelə/ *n.* a fragrant oil; grass from S. Asia yielding it.

citrus /'sɪtrəs/ *n.* tree of group including citron, lemon, and orange; fruit of such tree. [L]

city /'sɪtɪ/ *n.* large town, esp. one created by royal charter and containing cathedral; **the City** part of London governed by Lord Mayor and Corporation, business quarter of this, commercial circles; **city fathers** officials administering city; **city-state** *hist.* city that is also an independent State. [F f. L *civitas* (CIVIC)]

civet /'sɪvɪt/ *n.* catlike animal of central Africa (in full **civet-cat**); strong musky perfume obtained from it. [F ult. f. Arab.]

civic /'sɪvɪk/ *a.* of a city; of citizens or citizenship; **civic centre** area where municipal offices etc. are situated; **civically** *adv.* [F or L (*civis* citizen)]

civics *n.pl.* study of rights and duties of citizenship.

civil /'sɪv(ə)l, -ɪl/ *a.* of or belonging to citizens; of ordinary citizens, non-military; polite, obliging, not rude; *Law* concerning private rights and not criminal offences; (of length of day, year, etc.) fixed by custom or law, not natural or astronomical; **civil defence** organization for protecting civilians in air raid or other enemy action; **civil disobedience** refusal to comply with certain law(s) as peaceful protest; **civil engineer** one who designs or maintains works of public utility, e.g. roads and bridges; **civil liberty** freedom of action subject to the law; **civil list** annual allowance by Parliament for sovereign's household expenses etc.; **civil marriage** one solemnized without religious ceremony; **civil rights** rights of citizens, esp. *US* of Blacks, to liberty, equality, etc.; **Civil Servant** member of Civil Service; **Civil Service** all non-military branches of State administration; **civil war** war between citizens of same country. [F f. L *civilis* (CIVIC)]

civilian /sɪ'vɪljən/ **1** *n.* person not in or of the armed services or police force. **2** *a.* of or for civilians.

civility /sɪ'vɪlɪtɪ/ *n.* politeness; act of politeness. [F f. L (CIVIL)]

civilization /sɪvɪlaɪ'zeɪʃ(ə)n/ *n.* advanced stage or system of social development; those peoples of the world regarded as having this; a people or nation (esp. of the past) regarded as element of social evolution (*ancient, Inca, civilization*). [foll.]

civilize /'sɪvɪlaɪz/ *v.t.* bring out of barbarous or primitive stage of society; enlighten, refine and educate. [F (CIVIL)]

civvies *n.pl. sl.* civilian clothes. [abbr.]

Civvy Street *n. sl.* civilian life. [abbr.]

cl. *abbr.* centilitre(s).

Cl *symb.* chlorine.

clack 1 *v.* make sharp sound as of boards struck together; chatter. **2** *n.* clacking noise or talk. [imit.]

clad *a.* clothed; provided with cladding. [*p.p.* of CLOTHE]

cladding *n.* protective coating or covering on structure, material, etc. [prec.]

cladistics /klæ'dɪstɪks/ *n.pl.* (usu. treated as *sing.*) study of connections between animal species by analysis of their common features. [Gk *klados* branch]

claim 1 *v.t.* demand as one's due or property; represent oneself as having, profess *to* (*claim knowledge, to be knowledgeable*); assert; have as achievement or consequence (*can claim two medals; the fire claimed many victims*); (of thing) deserve (attention etc.). **2** *n.* demand for thing considered one's due (*lay claim to; put in a claim*); right or title (*to* thing); assertion; thing (esp. land) claimed. **3 no claim(s) bonus** reduction of insurance premium after period without claim for payment. [F f. L *clamo* call out]

claimant *n.* person making claim, esp. in lawsuit.

clairvoyance /kleə'vɔɪəns/ *n.* supposed faculty of seeing mentally things or events in the future or out of sight; exceptional insight; **clairvoyant** *n.* & *a.* [F (CLEAR, *voir* see)]

clam 1 *n.* edible bivalve mollusc. **2** *v.i.* (**-mm-**) dig for clams. **3 clam up** *US* refuse to talk. [CLAMP¹]

clamber 1 *v.i.* climb laboriously with hands and feet. **2** *n.* difficult climb. [CLIMB]

clammy /'klæmɪ/ *a.* unpleasantly damp and sticky; **clammily** *adv.*; **clamminess** *n.* [*clam* to daub]

clamour /'klæmə/, *US* **clamor 1** *n.* loud or vehement shouting or noise; protest, demand. **2** *v.* make clamour; utter with clamour. **3 clamorous** *a.* [F f. L (CLAIM)]

clamp¹ 1 *n.* device, esp. brace or band of iron etc., for strengthening, pressing, or holding things together. **2** *v.t.* strengthen or fasten with clamp, fix firmly. **3 clamp down on** become stricter about, suppress; **clamp-down** *n.* act of doing this. [LG or Du.]

clamp[2] *n.* pile of bricks for burning; potatoes etc. stored under straw or earth. [Du., rel. to CLUMP]

clan *n.* group of families with common ancestor, esp. in Scotland; large family as social group; group with strong common interest; **clannish** *a.*; **clansman** *n.* [Gael.]

clandestine /klæn'destɪn/ *a.* surreptitious, secret. [F or L]

clang 1 *n.* loud resonant metallic sound as of bell, hammer, etc. **2** *v.i.* make clang. [imit.; cf. L *clango* resound]

clanger *n. sl.* mistake, blunder (*drop a clanger*).

clangour /'klæŋgə/ *US* **clangor** *n.* prolonged clanging; **clangorous** *a.*

clank 1 *n.* metallic sound as of metal striking metal. **2** *v.* (cause to) make clank. [imit.]

clap[1] **1** *v.* (**-pp-**) strike palms of one's hands, cause (hands) to clash, repeatedly as applause; applaud thus; put or place with vigour or determination (*clapped him in prison*; *clap a tax on whisky*). **2** *n.* act of clapping, esp. as applause; explosive sound, esp. of thunder; slap, pat. **3 clap eyes on** *colloq.* see; **clap on the back** strike (person) on back as encouragement or congratulation; **clapped out** *sl.* exhausted, worn out. [OE]

clap[2] *n. vulgar* venereal disease, esp. gonorrhoea. [F]

clapper *n.* tongue or striker of bell; **clapper-board** device in film-making that makes sharp clap for synchronizing picture and sound; **like the clappers** *sl.* very fast or hard. [CLAP[1]]

claptrap *n.* insincere or pretentious talk, nonsense.

claque /klæk/ *n.* hired group of applauders in theatre etc. [F]

claret /'klærət/ *n.* red wine esp. from Bordeaux; reddish-violet. [F (foll.)]

clarify /'klærɪfaɪ/ *v.* make or become clearer to see or easier to understand; free (liquid etc.) from impurity or opaqueness; **clarification** /-fɪ'keɪʃ(ə)n/ *n.* [F f. L (CLEAR)]

clarinet /klærɪ'net/ *n.* woodwind instrument with single reed; **clarinettist** (*US* **-etist**) *n.* [F dimin.]

clarion /'klærɪən/ *n.* clear rousing sound (often *attrib.*: *clarion call*); *hist.* shrill war-trumpet. [L (CLEAR)]

clarity /'klærɪtɪ/ *n.* clearness (esp. *fig.*).

clash 1 *n.* loud jarring sound as of weapons or metal objects being struck together; collision, conflict; discord of colours etc. **2** *v.* (cause to) make clashing sound; collide, coincide awkwardly; come into conflict or be at variance (*with*). [imit.]

clasp /klɑːsp/ **1** *n.* device with interlocking parts for fastening; grasp, handshake, embrace; bar on medal-ribbon. **2** *v.t.* fasten with clasp; grasp, hold closely, embrace. **3 clasp-knife** folding knife with catch to hold blade open. [OE]

class /klɑːs/ **1** *n.* any set of persons or things grouped together, or graded or differentiated (esp. by quality) from others (*first*, *second*, etc., *class*; *economy class*); division or order of society (*lower*, *middle*, *upper*, *working*, *professional*, etc., *class* or *classes*); distinction, high quality; set of students taught together, occasion when they meet, their course of instruction; division of candidates by merit in examination; grouping of animals or plants next below phylum. **2** *v.t.* place in a class. **3 class-conscious** aware of (one's place in) social class divisions; **in a class of its** (or **one's**) **own** unequalled, unique. [L *classis* assembly]

classic /'klæsɪk/ **1** *a.* of acknowledged excellence; outstandingly important, remarkably typical (*a classic example*); of ancient Greek and Roman art and society, resembling this, esp. in harmony and restraint; having historic associations. **2** *n.* classic work, example, writer, etc.; (in *pl.*) study of ancient Greek and Latin. **3 classically** *adv.* [F, or L *classicus* (prec.)]

classical *a.* of ancient Greek and Latin literature (cf. CLASSIC); (of language) having form used by ancient standard authors; (of music) serious or conventional (cf. *light*, *popular*), or of period from *c.* 1750–1800 (cf. *romantic*); simple and harmonious in style; **classicality** /-'kælɪtɪ/ *n.* [L (prec.)]

classicism /'klæsɪsɪz(ə)m/ *n.* following of classic style; classical scholarship, ancient Greek or Latin idiom; **classicist** *n.* [CLASSIC]

classify /'klæsɪfaɪ/ *v.t.* arrange in classes or categories; assign class to; designate as officially secret or not for general disclosure; **classification** /-fɪ'keɪʃ(ə)n/ *n.*; **classificatory** /-'keɪtərɪ/ *a.* [F (CLASS)]

classroom *n.* room where class of students is taught. [CLASS]

classy *a. colloq.* superior, stylish; **classily** *adv.*; **classiness** *n.*

clatter 1 *n.* sound as of hard objects struck together or falling; noisy talk. **2** *v.i.* make clatter; fall, move, etc., with clatter. [OE]

clause /klɔːz/ *n.* part of sentence, with subject and predicate; single statement in treaty, law, contract, etc.; **clausal** *a.* [F f. L *clausula* (CLOSE)]

claustrophobia /klɔːstrə'fəʊbɪə/ *n.*

morbid dread of confined places; **claustrophobic** *a.* [L (CLOISTER, -PHOBIA)]

clavichord /'klævɪkɔ:d/ *n.* early small keyboard instrument with very soft tone. [med.L (foll.)]

clavicle /'klævɪk(ə)l/ *n.* collar-bone. [L (*clavis* key)]

claw 1 *n.* pointed nail of animal's or bird's foot; foot armed with claws; pincers of shellfish; device for grappling, holding, etc. **2** *v.t.* scratch or maul or pull with claws; scratch with finger-nails. **3 claw back** regain laboriously or gradually; **claw-hammer** hammer with one side of head forked for extracting nails. [OE]

clay *n.* stiff sticky earth, esp. used for making bricks, pottery, etc.; substance of the human body; **clay pigeon** breakable disc thrown up from trap as target for shooting. [OE]

claymore *n. hist.* Scottish two-edged broadsword. [Gael., = great sword]

clean 1 *a.* free from dirt or contaminating matter, unsoiled; clear, not used, preserving what is regarded as original state (*clean air, page, clothes*); free from obscenity or indecency; attentive to personal hygiene and cleanness; complete, clear-cut; shapely or well-formed (*car has clean lines*); adroit, skilful; (of nuclear weapon) producing relatively little fall-out. **2** *adv.* completely, outright, simply; in a clean manner. **3** *v.* make or become clean. **4** *n.* process of cleaning. **5 clean-cut** sharply outlined; **clean out** clean thoroughly, *sl.* empty or deprive (esp. of money); **clean-shaven** without beard or moustache; **clean sheet** freedom from or removal from record of (past) commitments or imputations; **clean up** make clean or tidy, restore order or morality to, *sl.* acquire as or make profit; **clean-up** *n.* act of doing this; **come clean** *colloq.* confess; **make a clean breast of** see BREAST. [OE]

cleaner *n.* person employed to clean rooms; (usu. in *pl.*) establishment for cleaning clothes; device or substance for cleaning; **take to the cleaners** *sl.* defraud or rob of money, criticize ruthlessly.

cleanly[1] *adv.* in a clean manner.

cleanly[2] /'klenlɪ/ *a.* habitually clean, with clean habits; **cleanlily** *adv.*; **cleanliness** *n.*

cleanse /klenz/ *v.t.* make clean or pure.

clear 1 *a.* not clouded or murky or spotted; transparent; readily perceived by the senses or understood by the mind, unambiguous; able to discern readily and accurately (*a clear mind*); confident or convinced (*about, that*); (of conscience) free from guilt; (of road etc.) unobstructed, open; net, without deduction, complete (*a clear £1000; three clear days*); unhampered, free (*of* debt, commitments, etc.). **2** *adv.* clearly (*speak loud and clear*); completely (*he got clear away*); apart, out of contact (*stand clear*); *US* all the way *to*. **3** *v.* make or become clear; free from or *of* obstruction, suspicion, etc.; show or declare to be innocent (*of*); approve (person) for special duty, access to information, etc.; pass over or by safely or without touching; make (amount of money) as net gain or to balance expenses; pass (cheque) through clearing-house; pass through (customs office etc.). **4 clear the air** remove suspicion, tension, etc.; **clear away** remove completely, (of mist etc.) disappear; **clear-cut** sharply defined; **clear the decks** *fig.* prepare for action; **clearing bank** large bank belonging to clearing-house; **clearing-house** bankers' establishment where cheques etc. are exchanged, only balances being paid in cash, agency for collecting and distributing information etc.; **clear off** get rid of, complete payment of (debt etc.), *colloq.* go away; **clear out** empty, remove, *colloq.* go away; **clear-sighted** perceptive, sagacious; **clear up** tidy up, solve (mystery etc.), (of weather) become fine; **clear thing with** get approval or authorization of it with (person); **in the clear** free of suspicion or difficulty. [F f. L *clarus*]

clearance *n.* removal of obstructions etc.; space allowed for the passing of two objects or parts in machinery etc.; special authorization or permission (esp. for aircraft to take off or land, or for access to information etc.); clearing of person, ship, etc., by customs, certificate showing it; clearing of cheques.

clearing *n.* area in forest cleared for cultivation.

clearway *n.* main road other than motorway, on which vehicles may not ordinarily stop.

cleat *n.* projecting piece of metal, wood, etc., for fastening ropes or to secure woodwork; projecting piece on spar, gangway, etc., to prevent slipping. [OE]

cleavage /'kli:vɪdʒ/ *n.* hollow between woman's breasts; division, splitting; way in which thing tends to split. [foll.]

cleave[1] *v.* (*past* **clove** or **cleft** or **cleaved;** *p.p.* CLOVEN or CLEFT or **cleaved**) chop or break apart, split, come apart, esp. along grain or line of cleavage; make way through (water, air). [OE]

cleave[2] *v.i. archaic* stick fast or adhere *to*. [OE]

cleaver *n.* heavy chopping tool used by butchers. [CLEAVE[1]]
clef *n.* symbol showing pitch of music on staff; **alto** (or **C**) **clef** clef on third line (= middle C); **bass** (or **F**) **clef** clef on second line down (= bass F); **treble** (or **G**) **clef** clef on second line up (= treble G). [F f. L *clavis* key]
cleft[1] *a.* split, partly divided; **cleft palate** congenital split in roof of mouth; **in a cleft stick** in difficult position. [*p.p.* of CLEAVE[1]]
cleft[2] *n.* split, fissure. [CLEAVE[1]]
clematis /'klemətɪs/ *n.* cultivated climbing plant with white, pink, or purple flowers. [Gk]
clement /'klemənt/ *a.* mild (*clement weather*); merciful; **clemency** *n.* [L *clemens*]
clementine /'kleməntiːn/ *n.* a kind of small orange. [F]
clench **1** *v.t.* close (teeth, fingers) tightly; grasp firmly; clinch (nail, rivet). **2** *n.* clenching action; clenched state. [OE]
clerestory /'klɪəstərɪ/ *n.* upper row of windows in cathedral or large church, above level of aisle roofs. [*clear storey*]
clergy /'klɜːdʒɪ/ *n.* (usu. treated as *pl.*) men ordained as priests or ministers. [F (rel. to CLERIC) & eccl.L]
clergyman *n.* member of clergy, esp. of Church of England.
cleric /'klerɪk/ *n.* clergyman. [eccl.L f. Gk *klērikos*]
clerical *a.* of clergy or clergyman; of or done by clerks; **clerical collar** upright white collar fastening at back. [eccl. L (prec.)]
clerihew /'klerɪhjuː/ *n.* short comic verse usu. in two rhyming couplets. [E. *Clerihew* Bentley, its inventor]
clerk /klɑːk/ **1** *n.* person employed in office, bank, etc., to keep records, accounts, etc.; secretary, agent, of local council (*town clerk*), court, etc.; lay officer of church (*parish clerk*). **2** *v.i.* work as clerk. **3 clerk of (the) works** overseer of building works etc. **4 clerkly** *a.*; **clerkship** *n.* [OE & F (CLERIC)]
clever /'klevə/ *a.* skilful, talented, quick to understand and learn; adroit, dextrous; ingenious. [OE]
clew /kluː/ **1** *n. Naut.* lower or after corner of sail; small cords suspending hammock; *archaic* ball of thread or yarn. **2** *v.t. Naut.* haul *up* or let *down* (sail). [OE]
cliché /'kliːʃeɪ/ *n.* hackneyed phrase or opinion; metal casting of stereotype or electrotype. [F]
click **1** *n.* slight sharp sound as of switch being operated; catch in machinery. **2** *v.* make click; *sl.* become clear or understandable; be successful, become friendly *with* person, esp. of opposite sex. [imit.]
client /'klaɪənt/ *n.* person using services of lawyer, architect, or other professional person; customer. [L *cliens*]
clientele /kliːɒn'tel/ *n.* clients collectively; customers. [F & L (prec.)]
cliff *n.* steep rock-face, esp. on coast; **cliff-hanger** story etc. with strong element of suspense; **cliff-hanging** *a.* full of suspense. [OE]
climacteric /klaɪ'mæktərɪk/ *n.* period of life when physical powers begin to decline. [F or L f. Gk (CLIMAX)]
climate /'klaɪmɪt/ *n.* prevailing weather conditions of an area; region with certain weather conditions; prevailing trend of opinion or feeling; **climatic** /-'mætɪk/ *a.* **climatically** /-'mætɪkəlɪ/ *adv.* [F or L f. Gk *klima*]
climax /'klaɪmæks/ **1** *n.* event or point of greatest intensity or interest, culmination; sexual orgasm. **2** *v.* reach or bring to a climax. **3 climactic** /-'mæktɪk/ *a.* [L f. Gk, = ladder]
climb /klaɪm/ **1** *v.* ascend, mount, go or come *up*, esp. with use of one's hands; (of plant) grow up wall or other support by clinging or twining; rise in social rank etc. by one's own efforts. **2** *n.* action of climbing; hill etc. (to be) climbed. **3 climb down** descend with help of one's hands; retreat from position taken up in argument; **climb-down** *n.* such retreat; **climbing-frame** structure of joined bars etc. for children to climb on. [OE]
climber *n.* mountaineer; climbing plant; social aspirant.
clime /klaɪm/ *n. literary* region; climate. [L (CLIMATE)]
clinch **1** *v.* confirm or settle (argument or bargain) conclusively; (of boxers) come too close together for full-arm blow; *colloq.* embrace; secure (nail or rivet) by driving point sideways when through. **2** *n.* clinching; clinched state; *colloq.* embrace. [var. of CLENCH]
clincher *n.* decisive point that settles argument, proposition, etc.
cling *v.i.* (*past* and *p.p.* **clung**) maintain grasp, keep hold, resist separation; **cling to** adhere to, hold on to (support etc.), be reluctant to give up (friend, habit, belief). [OE]
clinic /'klɪnɪk/ *n.* private or specialized hospital; place or occasion for giving medical treatment or advice (*ante-natal clinic*); teaching of medicine or surgery at hospital bedside. [F f. Gk (*klinē* bed)]
clinical *a.* of or for the treatment of patients; dispassionate, coldly detached; **clinical death** death judged by observation of person's condition; **clinically** *adv.* [L f. Gk (prec.)]
clink[1] **1** *n.* sharp ringing sound, chink. **2** *v.* (cause to) make clink. [Du.; imit.]

clink[2] *n. sl.* prison, esp. in *in clink*. [orig. unkn.]
clinker *n.* mass of slag or lava; stony residue from burnt coal or coke. [Du. (CLINK[1])]
clinker-built (of boat) having external planks overlapping downwards and secured with clinched nails. [*clink*, dial. var. of CLINCH]
clip[1] **1** *n.* device for holding things together or for affixing something; piece of jewellery fastened by clip; set of attached cartridges for firearm. **2** *v.t.* (**-pp-**) fix with clip; grip tightly. **3 clip-on** attached by clip. [OE]
clip[2] **1** *v.t.* (**-pp-**) cut (hair, wool, etc.) short with shears or scissors; trim hair of; *colloq.* hit sharply; omit (letter etc.) from word; omit letters or syllables of (words pronounced); punch small piece from (ticket) to show that it has been used; cut from newspaper etc; *sl.* swindle, rob. **2** *n.* action of clipping; *colloq.* sharp blow; sequence from motion-picture film; yield of wool; *colloq.* speed, esp. rapid. **3 clip-joint** *sl.* club etc. charging exorbitant prices. [ON]
clipboard *n.* small portable board with spring clip for holding papers. [CLIP[1]]
clipper *n.* fast sailing-ship; (usu. in *pl.*) instrument for clipping hair. [CLIP[2]]
clipping *n.* piece clipped off; newspaper cutting.
clique /kli:k/ *n.* small exclusive group of people; **cliquish** *a.*; **cliquy** *a.* [F]
clitoris /ˈklɪtərɪs/ *n.* small erectile part of female genitals at upper end of vulva; **clitoral** *a.* [L f. Gk]
cloak **1** *n.* outdoor over-garment, usu. sleeveless, hanging loosely from shoulders; covering (*cloak of snow*). **2** *v.t.* cover with cloak; conceal, disguise. **3 cloak-and-dagger** involving intrigue and espionage; **under the cloak of** using as pretext. [F f. med.L (CLOCK)]
cloakroom *n.* room where outdoor clothes and luggage may be left by visitors; *euphem.* lavatory.
clobber[1] *n. sl.* clothing, personal belongings. [orig. unkn.]
clobber[2] *v.t. sl.* hit repeatedly, beat up; defeat; criticize severely. [orig. unkn.]
cloche /klɒʃ/ *n.* small translucent cover for protecting outdoor plants; woman's close-fitting bell-shaped hat. [F, = bell f. med.L (foll.)]
clock[1] **1** *n.* instrument for measuring time and indicating hours, minutes, etc., by hands on a dial or by displayed figures; clocklike measuring device, *colloq.* speedometer, taximeter, or stopwatch; *sl.* person's face; seed-head of dandelion. **2** *v.t.* time (race) with stopwatch; *sl.* hit. **3 clock golf** game in which golf ball is putted into hole from successive points round this; **clock in** (or **on**) register one's arrival at work, esp. by means of automatic clock; **clock off** (or **out**) register departure similarly; **clock (up)** *colloq.* attain or register (stated time, distance, or speed); **round the clock** all day, day and night. [LG or Du. f. med.L *clocca* bell]
clock[2] *n.* ornamental pattern on side of stocking or sock near ankle. [orig. unkn.]
clockwise *a.* & *adv.* moving in a curve corresponding in direction to the hands of a clock. [CLOCK[1]]
clockwork *n.* mechanism like that of clock, with spring and gears; *attrib.* driven by clockwork; **like clockwork** smoothly, with mechanical precision.
clod *n.* lump of earth, clay, etc. [var. of CLOT]
cloddish *a.* loutish, foolish, clumsy.
clodhoppers *n.pl. colloq.* large heavy shoes.
clog **1** *n.* shoe with thick wooden sole; *archaic* encumbrance. **2** *v.* (**-gg-**) impede; (cause to) become obstructed; choke *up*. [orig. unkn.]
cloister **1** *n.* covered walk, often with wall on one side and colonnade open to quadrangle on the other, esp. in convent, monastery, college, or cathedral; monastic life or seclusion. **2** *v.t.* seclude in convent etc. **3 cloistral** *a.* [F f. L *claustrum* (CLOSE[1])]
cloistered *a.* secluded, sheltered; monastic.
clone **1** *n.* group of plants or organisms produced asexually from one stock or ancestor; one such organism. **2** *v.t.* propagate as clone. **3 clonal** *a.* [Gk *klōn* twig]
clonk **1** *n.* abrupt heavy sound of impact. **2** *v.* make this sound; *colloq.* hit. [imit.]
close[1] /kləʊs/ **1** *a.* situated at short distance or interval; having strong or immediate relation or connection (*close friend*, *relative*, *resemblance*); in or almost in contact (*close combat*, *proximity*); dense, compact, with no or only slight intervals (*close formation*, *texture*, *writing*); in which competitors are almost equal (*close contest*, *election*); leaving no gaps or weaknesses, rigorous (*close confinement*, *reasoning*); concentrated, searching (*close attention*, *examination*); (of air etc.) oppressively warm or humid; closed, shut; limited to certain persons etc. (*close corporation*); hidden, secret, secretive; niggardly. **2** *adv.* closely, at short distance or interval (*they live close by*, *close to the church*). **3** *n.* enclosed space; street closed at one

end; precinct of cathedral; school playground. **4 at close quarters** very close together; **close call** = *close shave*; **close harmony** harmony in which notes of chord are close together; **close season** season when killing of game etc. is illegal; **close shave** (or **thing**) *fig.* narrow escape; **close-up** photograph etc. taken at close range. [F f. L *clausus* (*claudo* shut)]

close² /kləʊz/ **1** *v.* shut, block up; bring or come to an end; end day's business (at); bring or come closer or into contact (*close ranks*); make (electric circuit etc.) continuous. **2** *n.* conclusion, end. **3 closed book** subject one does not understand; **closed-circuit** (of television) transmitted by wires to restricted circuit of receivers; **close down** (of shop, factory, etc.) close, esp. permanently; **closed shop** business etc. where employees must belong to agreed trade union; **close in** enclose, approach, (of days) get successively shorter; **close up** move closer (*to*), shut, esp. temporarily, block up, (of aperture) grow smaller; **close with** make bargain with, join battle or start fighting with; **closing--time** time when public house etc. ends business. [F f. L (prec.)]

closet /ˈklɒzɪt/ **1** *n.* small cupboard or room; water-closet. **2** *v.t.* shut away, esp. in private conference or study. [F dimin. (prec.)]

closure /ˈkləʊʒə/ **1** *n.* closing, closed state; parliamentary procedure ending debate and taking vote. **2** *v.t.* apply closure to in debate. [F f. L (CLOSE²)]

clot 1 *n.* thick mass of coagulated liquid, esp. of blood exposed to air; *sl.* stupid person. **2** *v.* (**-tt-**) form into clots. **3 clotted cream** thick cream obtained by slow scalding. [OE]

cloth *n.* woven or felted material; piece of this for special purpose (*dishcloth, table-cloth*); fabric, esp. woollen, for clothes; status of clergy as shown by clothes; **the cloth** the clergy. [OE]

clothe /kləʊð/ *v.t.* (*past* and *p.p.* **clothed** or **clad**) put clothes on, provide with clothes; cover as with clothes. [OE]

clothes /kləʊðz, -əʊz/ *n.pl.* things worn to cover the body and limbs; bedclothes; **clothes-horse** frame for airing washed clothes; **clothes-line** rope or wire on which washed clothes are hung to dry; **clothes-peg** clip or forked device for securing clothes to a clothes-line. [OE]

clothier /ˈkləʊðɪə/ *n.* seller of men's clothes. [CLOTH]

clothing /ˈkləʊðɪŋ/ *n.* clothes collectively. [CLOTHE]

cloud 1 *n.* visible mass of condensed watery vapour floating high above ground; mass of smoke or dust; large moving mass of insects in sky; state of gloom, trouble, or suspicion. **2** *v.* cover or darken with clouds or gloom or trouble; become overcast or gloomy (*cloud over, up*). **3 cloud chamber** device containing vapour for tracking the paths of charged particles, X-rays, and gamma rays; **cloud-cuckoo-land** fanciful or ideal place; **cloud-hopping** movement of aircraft from cloud to cloud esp. for concealment; **under a cloud** under suspicion, out of favour; **with one's head in the clouds** day-dreaming. [OE]

cloudburst *n.* sudden violent rainstorm.

cloudy *a.* (of sky, weather) covered with clouds, overcast; not transparent, unclear; **cloudily** *adv.*; **cloudiness** *n.*

clout 1 *n.* heavy blow; *colloq.* power of effective action, influence; cloth, piece of clothing. **2** *v.t.* hit hard. [OE]

clove¹ *n.* dried bud of tropical myrtle, used as spice. [F f. L *clavus* nail (from shape)]

clove² *n.* small segment of compound bulb, esp. of garlic. [OE (CLEAVE¹)]

clove³ see CLEAVE¹.

clove hitch knot used for securing rope to spar or to another rope. [old *p.p.* of CLEAVE¹]

cloven /ˈkləʊv(ə)n/ *a.* split, partly divided; **cloven hoof** hoof that is divided, as of oxen or sheep or goats. [*p.p.* of CLEAVE¹]

clover *n.* trefoil plant used for fodder; **in clover** in ease and luxury. [OE]

clown 1 *n.* comic entertainer, esp. in pantomime or circus; person acting like clown. **2** *v.i.* behave like a clown. [orig. uncert.]

cloy *v.t.* satiate or sicken, esp. *with* richness, sweetness, or excess. [obs. *acloy* f. AF (ENCLAVE)]

club 1 *n.* heavy stick with one thick end, used as weapon etc.; stick with head used in golf; playing-card of suit (**clubs**) denoted by black trefoil; association of persons meeting periodically for shared activity (*tennis club*; *bridge club*); organization or premises offering members social amenities, meals and temporary residence, etc.; organization offering subscribers certain benefits (*book club*). **2** *v.* (**-bb-**) strike with club etc.; combine *together* or *with* esp. in making up sum of money for a purpose. **3 club-foot** congenitally deformed foot; **club-root** disease of cabbages etc. with swelling at base of stem. [ON]

clubbable *a.* sociable, fit for membership of a club.

clubhouse *n.* premises used by club.

cluck 1 *n.* guttural cry like that of hen. 2 *v.i.* emit cluck(s). [imit.]
clue /klu:/ 1 *n.* fact or idea that serves as guide, or suggests line of inquiry, in problem or investigation; piece of evidence etc. in detection of crime; word(s) indicating what is to be inserted in crossword. 2 *v.t.* provide clue to. 3 **clue in** (or **up**) *sl.* inform; **not have a clue** *colloq.* be ignorant or incompetent. [var. of CLEW]
clueless *a. colloq.* ignorant, stupid.
clump 1 *n.* cluster or mass (*clump of trees*). 2 *v.* form clump, arrange in clump; walk with heavy tread; *colloq.* hit. [LG or Du.]
clumsy /'klʌmzɪ/ *a.* awkward in movement or shape, ungainly; difficult to handle or use; tactless. [obs. *clumse* be numb with cold]
clung *past* and *p.p.* of CLING.
cluster 1 *n.* close group or bunch of similar people, animals, or things, brought or growing together. 2 *v.* bring or come into, be in, cluster(s); gather *round*. [OE]
clutch[1] 1 *v.* seize eagerly, grasp tightly; snatch *at*. 2 *n.* tight grasp; (in *pl.*) grasping hands, cruel or relentless grasp or control; (in motor vehicle) device for connecting engine to transmission, pedal operating this. [OE]
clutch[2] *n.* set of eggs for hatching; brood of chickens. [ON, = hatch]
clutter 1 *n.* crowded, untidy collection of things; untidy state. 2 *v.t.* (often with *up*) crowd untidily, fill with clutter. [rel. to CLOT]
cm. *abbr.* centimetre(s).
Cm *symb.* curium.
CMG *abbr.* Companion (of the Order) of St. Michael & St. George.
CND *abbr.* Campaign for Nuclear Disarmament.
co- *prefix* added to (1) nouns, with sense 'joint, mutual, common' (*co-author, coequality*), (2) adjectives and adverbs, with sense 'jointly, mutually' (*co-belligerent, coequal, coequally*), (3) verbs, with sense 'together with another or others' (*co-operate*). [COM-]
c/o *abbr.* care of.
CO *abbr.* Commanding Officer.
Co. *abbr.* company; county.
Co *symb.* cobalt.
coach 1 *n.* single-decker bus, usu. comfortably equipped for longer journeys; railway carriage; closed horse-drawn carriage; instructor or trainer in sport; private tutor. 2 *v.t.* train or teach as coach. [F f. Magyar]
coachwork *n.* bodywork of road or railway vehicle.
coagulate /kəʊ'ægjʊleɪt/ *v.* change from liquid to semisolid; clot, curdle; **coagulant** *n.*; **coagulation** /-'leɪʃ(ə)n/ *n.* [L (*coagulum* rennet)]
coal 1 *n.* hard black mineral, mainly carbonized plant matter, found below ground and used as fuel and in making gas, tar, etc.; piece of this, piece that is burning. 2 *v.* put coal into (ship etc.); take in supply of coal. 3 **coal-face** exposed surface of coal in mine; **coal gas** mixed gases extracted from coal and used for lighting and heating; **coal measures** seams of coal with intervening strata; **coal-mine** mine in which coal is dug; **coal-scuttle** container for coal to supply domestic fire; **coals to Newcastle** thing brought to place where already plentiful, unnecessary action; **coal tar** tar extracted from bituminous coal; **coal-tit** small greyish bird with dark head; **haul** (or **call**) **over the coals** reprimand; **heap coals of fire on person's head** cause him remorse by returning good for evil. [OE]
coalesce /kəʊə'les/ *v.i.* come together and form one whole; **coalescence** *n.*; **coalescent** *a.* [L (*alo* nourish)]
coalfield *n.* area yielding coal. [COAL]
coalition /kəʊə'lɪʃ(ə)n/ *n.* fusion into one whole; temporary alliance of political parties. [med.L (prec.)]
coaming /'kəʊmɪŋ/ *n.* raised border round ship's hatches etc. to keep out water. [orig. unkn.]
coarse *a.* rough or loose in texture, made of large particles; lacking refinement of manner or perception, crude, vulgar; inferior, common; (of language) obscene; **coarse fish** freshwater fish other than salmon and trout. [orig. unkn.]
coarsen *v.* make or become coarse.
coast 1 *n.* border of land near sea, seashore. 2 *v.i.* ride or move, usu. downhill, without use of power; *fig.* make progress without much effort; sail along coast. 3 **the coast is clear** there is no danger of being observed or caught. 4 **coastal** *a.* [F f. L *costa* side]
coaster *n.* ship that travels along coast; small tray or mat for bottle or glass.
coastguard *n.* body of men employed to keep watch on coasts, prevent smuggling, etc.; member of this.
coastline *n.* line of sea-shore, esp. with regard to its shape.
coat 1 *n.* outer garment with sleeves and often extending below hips, overcoat, jacket; natural covering, esp. animal's fur or hair; covering of paint etc. laid on a surface at one time. 2 *v.t.* cover *with* a coat or layer; (of paint etc.) form a covering to. 3 **coat of arms** heraldic bearings or shield of person or corporation; **coat**

of mail see MAIL²; **on person's coat-tails** undeservedly benefiting from success of another. [F f. Gmc]
coating *n.* layer of paint etc.; material for coats.
co-author /ˈkəʊɔːθə/ **1** *n.* joint author. **2** *v.t.* be joint author of. [co-]
coax *v.t.* persuade gradually or by flattery; get (thing) *out of* person thus; manipulate (thing) carefully or slowly. [obs. *cokes* a fool]
coaxial /kəʊˈæksɪəl/ *a.* having common axis; (of electric cable or line) transmitting by means of two concentric conductors separated by insulator. [co-]
cob *n.* roundish lump; = *corn-cob* (see CORN¹); sturdy riding-horse with short legs; male swan; large hazel-nut; loaf rounded on top. [orig. unkn.]
cobalt /ˈkəʊbɔːlt, -ɒlt/ *n.* a silvery-white metallic element; pigment made from this, its deep-blue colour. [G, prob. = *kobold* demon in mines]
cobber *n. Austral. & NZ colloq.* companion, friend. [orig. uncert.]
cobble¹ /ˈkɒb(ə)l/ **1** *n.* (in full **cobble-stone**) small rounded stone used for paving. **2** *v.t.* pave with cobbles. [f. COB]
cobble² /ˈkɒb(ə)l/ *v.t.* mend or patch up (esp. shoes); repair or put together roughly. [foll.]
cobbler *n.* one who mends shoes, esp. professionally; iced drink of wine, sugar, and lemon; fruit pie topped with scones. [orig. unkn.]
COBOL /ˈkəʊbɒl/ *n.* a computer language for use in commerce. [*Co*mmon *B*usiness *O*riented *L*anguage]
cobra /ˈkəʊbrə, ˈkɒ-/ *n.* a venomous hooded snake of India and Africa. [Port., f. L *colubra* snake]
cobweb *n.* fine network spun by spider; thread of this; **cobwebby** *a.* [obs. *coppe* spider]
coca /ˈkəʊkə/ *n.* a S. American shrub; its leaves chewed as stimulant. [Sp. f. Quechua]
cocaine /kɒˈkeɪn, kəʊ-/ *n.* drug from coca, used as local anaesthetic and as stimulant.
coccyx /ˈkɒksɪks/ *n.* (*pl.* **coccyges** /-dʒiːz/) small triangular bone at base of spinal column. [L f. Gk. = cuckoo (from shape of bill)]
cochineal /ˈkɒtʃɪniːl/ *n.* a scarlet dye; insects whose dried bodies yield this. [F or Sp. f. L *coccinus* scarlet f. Gk]
cock¹ **1** *n.* male bird, esp. of domestic fowl; *sl.* (as term of address) friend, fellow; *sl.* nonsense; *vulgar* penis; firing-lever in gun raised to be released by trigger, cocked position; tap, valve controlling flow. **2** *v.t.* raise or make upright or erect; turn or move (eye or ear) attentively or knowingly; set aslant, turn up brim of (hat); raise cock of (gun). **3 at half cock** only partly ready; **cocked hat** brimless triangular hat pointed at front, back, and top (**knock into a cocked hat** defeat utterly); **cock-a-doodle-doo** cock's crow; **cock-a-hoop** exultant; **cock-a-leekie** Scottish soup of cock boiled with leeks; **cock-and-bull story** one that is absurd or incredible; **cock a snook** see SNOOK; **cock-crow** dawn; **cock-eyed** *colloq.* crooked, askew, absurd, not practical; **cock-fight** fight between cocks as sport; **cock-shy** target for throwing at; a throw at this, *fig.* object of ridicule or criticism; **cock-up** *sl.* muddle, mistake. [OE & F]
cock² *n.* small conical pile of hay or straw. [perh. Scand.]
cockade /kɒˈkeɪd/ *n.* rosette etc. worn in hat as badge. [F (COCK¹)]
cockatoo /kɒkəˈtuː/ *n.* a crested parrot. [Du. f. Malay]
cockchafer /ˈkɒktʃeɪfə/ *n.* large pale-brown beetle. [COCK¹]
cocker *n.* (in full **cocker spaniel**) small spaniel with golden brown coat. [COCK¹]
cockerel /ˈkɒkər(ə)l/ *n.* a young cock. [dimin. of COCK¹]
cockle /ˈkɒk(ə)l/ **1** *n.* edible bivalve shellfish; its shell; pucker or wrinkle in paper, glass, etc.; (in full **cockle-shell**) small shallow boat. **2** *v.* make or become puckered. **3 warm the cockles of one's heart** make one rejoice. [F *coquille* f. med. L f. Gk (CONCH)]
cockney /ˈkɒknɪ/ **1** *n.* native of London, esp. of the East End; the dialect or accent used there. **2** *a.* of or characteristic of cockneys or their dialect. [*cokeney* 'cock's egg']
cockpit *n.* compartment for pilot (and crew) of aircraft or spacecraft; driver's seat in racing car; space for helmsman in some small yachts; arena of war or other conflict; place made for cock-fights. [COCK¹]
cockroach /ˈkɒkrəʊtʃ/ *n.* dark-brown beetle-like insect infesting esp. kitchens and bathrooms. [Sp. *cucaracha*]
cockscomb /ˈkɒkskəʊm/ *n.* crest of cock; see also COXCOMB. [COCK¹]
cocksure *a.* presumptuously or arrogantly confident; absolutely sure. [COCK¹]
cocktail /ˈkɒkteɪl/ *n.* mixed alcoholic drink, esp. of spirit with bitters etc.; appetizer containing shellfish or fruit. [orig. uncert.]
cocky *a.* conceited, arrogant; **cockily** *adv.*; **cockiness** *n.* [COCK¹]
coco /ˈkəʊkəʊ/ *n.* (*pl.* **cocos**) coconut palm. [Sp. & Port., = grimace]

cocoa /'kəʊkəʊ/ *n.* powder made from crushed cacao seeds, often with other ingredients; drink made from this; **cocoa bean** cacao seed; **cocoa butter** fatty substance got from this. [CACAO]

coconut /'kəʊkənʌt/ *n.* large brown seed of the coco, with hard shell and edible white lining enclosing milky juice; **coconut matting** matting made of fibre from coconut husks; **coconut shy** fairground side-show where balls are thrown to dislodge coconuts. [coco]

cocoon /kə'ku:n/ **1** *n.* silky case spun by insect larva to protect it as chrysalis, esp. that of silkworm; protective covering. **2** *v.t.* wrap or coat in cocoon. [F f. Prov. (*coca* shell)]

cocotte /kə'kɒt/ *n.* small fireproof dish for cooking and serving food. [F]

cod[1] *n.* (*pl.* same) large sea fish (also **codfish**); **cod-liver oil** oil from cod livers, rich in vitamins A and D. [orig. unkn.]

cod[2] *sl.* **1** *n.* parody; hoax. **2** *v.* (**-dd-**) perform hoax; parody. [orig. unkn.]

cod[3] *n. sl.* nonsense. [abbr. of CODSWALLOP]

COD *abbr.* cash (*US* collect) on delivery.

coda /'kəʊdə/ *n.* final passage of movement or piece of music, often elaborate and distinct; concluding section of ballet. [It. f. L *cauda* tail]

coddle /'kɒd(ə)l/ *v.t.* treat as an invalid; protect attentively, pamper; cook (egg) lightly. [*caudle* gruel f. F f. L *calidus* warm]

code 1 *n.* system of words, letters, or symbols used to represent others for secrecy or brevity; system of prearranged signals used to ensure secrecy in transmitting messages; set of instructions used in programming computer; systematic set of laws etc.; prevailing standard of moral behaviour. **2** *v.t.* put into code. [F f. L CODEX]

codeine /'kəʊdi:n/ *n.* alkaloid obtained from opium, used to relieve pain or induce sleep. [Gk *kōdeia* poppy-head]

codex /'kəʊdeks/ *n.* (*pl.* **codices** /-ɪsi:z/) ancient manuscript text in book form; collection of descriptions of medicinal drugs. [L, = tablet, book]

codger /'kɒdʒə/ *n. colloq.* person, esp. a strange one (*funny old codger*). [orig. uncert.]

codicil /'kəʊdɪsɪl/ *n.* addition to will explaining, modifying, or revoking (parts of) it. [L dimin. of CODEX]

codify /'kəʊdɪfaɪ/ *v.t.* arrange (laws etc.) systematically into a code; **codification** /-fɪ'keɪʃ(ə)n/ *n.*; **codifier** *n.* [CODE]

codling[1] /'kɒdlɪŋ/ *n.* (also **codlin**) a kind of cooking apple, usu. oblong and yellowish; moth whose larva feeds on apples. [AF *quer-de-lion* lion-heart]

codling[2] *n.* small codfish. [COD[1]]

codpiece *n. hist.* appendage like small bag or flap at front of man's breeches. [*cod* scrotum]

codswallop /'kɒdzwɒləp/ *n. sl.* nonsense. [orig. unkn.]

coeducation /kəʊedju:'keɪʃ(ə)n/ *n.* education of pupils of both sexes together; **coeducational** *a.* [co-]

coefficient /kəʊɪ'fɪʃənt/ *n. Math.* quantity placed before and multiplying another quantity; *Physics* multiplier or factor by which a property is measured (*coefficient of expansion, of friction*). [co-]

coelenterate /si:'lentəreɪt/ *n.* member of group of marine animals (including jellyfish and corals) with simple tube-shaped or cup-shaped body. [Gk *koilos* hollow, *enteron* intestine]

coenobite /'si:nəbaɪt/ *n.* member of a monastic community; **coenobitic** /-'bɪtɪk/ *a.*; **coenobitical** /-'bɪtɪk(ə)l/ *a.* [F or eccl.L f. Gk (*koinos bios* common life)]

coequal /kəʊ'i:kw(ə)l/ *a.* & *n. archaic* or *literary* equal. [L (co-)]

coerce /kəʊ'ɜ:s/ *v.t.* impel or force (*into* obedience etc.); **coercible** *a.*; **coercion** *n.* [L *coerceo* restrain]

coeval /kəʊ'i:v(ə)l/ **1** *a.* having same age, existing at same epoch. **2** *n.* coeval person, contemporary. **3 coevality** /-'vælɪtɪ/ *n.* [L (*aevum* age)]

coexist /kəʊɪg'zɪst/ *v.i.* exist together (*with*). [co-]

coexistence *n.* coexisting, esp. in **peaceful coexistence** mutual tolerance of nations professing different ideologies etc.; **coexistent** *a.*

coextensive /kəʊɪk'stensɪv/ *a.* extending over same space or time. [co-]

C. of E. *abbr.* Church of England.

coffee /'kɒfɪ/ *n.* drink made from the roasted and ground beanlike seeds of a tropical shrub; a cup of this; the seeds or the shrub; pale brown colour of coffee mixed with milk; **coffee bar** place serving coffee and light refreshments from counter; **coffee-break** interval from work for light refreshments; **coffee-mill** small machine for grinding roasted seeds; **coffee morning** morning gathering with drinking of coffee; **coffee-table** small low table; **coffee-table book** large expensive illustrated book. [Turk. f. Arab.]

coffer *n.* large strong box for valuables; (in *pl.*) treasury, funds; sunken panel in ceiling etc.; **coffer-dam** watertight enclosure pumped dry for work in building bridges etc., or for repairing ship. [F f. L *cophinus* basket f. Gk]

coffin /'kɒfɪn/ **1** *n.* box in which corpse is buried or cremated. **2** *v.t.* put in coffin. [F f. L (prec.)]

cog *n.* one of series of projections on edge of wheel or bar transferring motion by engaging with another series; unimportant member of organization etc.; **cog-wheel** wheel with cogs. [prob. Scand.]

cogent /ˈkəʊdʒənt/ *a.* convincing, compelling (*cogent argument, reason*); **cogency** *n.* [L *cogo* drive]

cogitate /ˈkɒdʒɪteɪt/ *v.* ponder, meditate; **cogitation** /-ˈteɪʃ(ə)n/ *n.*; **cogitative** *a.* [L *cogito*]

cognac /ˈkɒnjæk/ *n.* brandy, esp. that distilled in Cognac in W. France.

cognate /ˈkɒgneɪt/ **1** *a.* related to or descended from common ancestor; (of word) having same linguistic family or derivation. **2** *n.* relative; cognate word. **3** **cognate object** object whose meaning is not distinct from that of its verb (*live a good life*). [L *cognatus*]

cognition /kɒgˈnɪʃ(ə)n/ *n.* knowing, perceiving, or conceiving as an act or faculty distinct from emotion and volition; result of this; **cognitional** *a.*; **cognitive** /ˈkɒg-/ *a.* [L *cognitio* (foll.)]

cognizance /ˈkɒgnɪzəns/ *n.* knowledge or awareness, perception; sphere of observation or concern; distinctive device or mark. [F f. L *cognosco* get to know]

cognizant *a.* having knowledge or taking note of.

cognomen /kɒgˈnəʊmen/ *n.* nickname; ancient Roman's personal name or epithet (e.g. Marcus Tullius *Cicero*; P. Cornelius Scipio *Africanus*). [L]

cognoscente /kɒnjəˈʃentɪ/ *n.* (*pl.* ***cognoscenti***) connoisseur. [It.]

cohabit /kəʊˈhæbɪt/ *v.i.* live together as husband and wife (usu. of unmarried couple); **cohabitation** /-ˈteɪʃ(ə)n/ *n.* [L *habito* dwell]

cohere /kəʊˈhɪə/ *v.i.* (of parts or whole) stick together, remain united; (of reasoning etc.) be logical or consistent. [L (*haereo haes-* stick)]

coherent *a.* cohering; (of argument etc.) consistent, easily followed; (of radiation) having constant phase difference from other radiation, and so able to interfere with it; **coherence** *n.* [COHERE]

cohesion /kəʊˈhi:ʒ(ə)n/ *n.* sticking together; force with which parts cohere, tendency to cohere; **cohesive** *adj.*

cohort /ˈkəʊhɔ:t/ *n.* Roman military unit, one tenth of a legion; band of warriors; persons banded together. [F or L]

coif *n. hist.* close-fitting cap. [F f. L *cofia* helmet]

coiffeur /kwɑ:ˈfɜ:/ *n.* hairdresser; **coiffeuse** /-ˈfɜ:z/ *n. fem.* [F]

coiffure /kwɑ:ˈfjʊə/ *n.* hairstyle.

coign /kɔɪn/ *n.* projecting corner, chiefly in **coign of vantage** place affording good view. [old form of COIN]

coil **1** *v.* arrange or be arranged in spirals or concentric rings; move sinuously. **2** *n.* coiled length of rope etc.; coiled arrangement; single turn of coiled thing; flexible loop as contraceptive device in womb; coiled wire for passage of electric current. [F f. L (COLLECT[1])]

coin **1** *n.* small stamped disc of metal as official money; coins collectively. **2** *v.t.* make (money) by stamping metal; make (metal) into coins; invent (esp. new word). **3** **coin money** get money easily or quickly; **false coin** counterfeit money, anything spurious; **pay person in his own coin** reciprocate his behaviour. [F f. L *cuneus* wedge]

coinage *n.* coining; coins; system of coins in use; invention, coined word.

coincide /kəʊɪnˈsaɪd/ *v.i.* occur at same time; occupy same portion of space; agree or be identical (*with*). [L (INCIDENT)]

coincidence /kəʊˈɪnsɪdəns/ *n.* coinciding; remarkable concurrence of events or circumstances without apparent causal connection; **coincident** *a.*

coincidental /kəʊɪnsɪˈdent(ə)l/ *a.* occurring by, in the nature of, a coincidence; **coincidentally** *adv.*

coir /ˈkɔɪə/ *n.* coconut fibre used for ropes, matting, etc. [Malayalam *kāyar* cord]

coition /kəʊˈɪʃ(ə)n/ *n.* = COITUS. [L *coitio* (*eo* go)]

coitus /ˈkəʊɪtəs/ *n.* sexual intercourse; **coital** *a.* [L (prec.)]

coke[1] **1** *n.* solid substance left after gases have been extracted from coal. **2** *v.t.* convert (coal) into coke. [dial. *colk* core]

coke[2] *n. sl.* cocaine. [abbr.]

col *n.* depression in chain of mountains. [F f. L *collum* neck]

col- see COM-.

Col. *abbr.* Colonel.

col. *abbr.* column.

cola *n.* W. African tree with seed producing extract used as tonic etc.; carbonated drink flavoured with this. [W. Afr.]

colander /ˈkʌləndə/ *n.* perforated vessel used to strain off liquid in cooking. [L *colo* strain]

cold /kəʊld/ **1** *a.* of or at low temperature, esp. when compared with human body; not heated, cooled after heat; feeling cold; dead; *sl.* unconscious; lacking ardour, affection, or geniality; depressing, dispiriting, uninteresting; (of colour) suggestive of cold; remote from thing sought; (of scent in hunting) grown faint; unrehearsed. **2** *n.* prevalence of low temperature; cold condition; infectious illness of nose or throat or both, with catarrh and sneezing. **3** **cold-blooded** having body temperature varying as that of environment does, callous, cruel; **cold chisel** chisel for cutting cold metal; **cold comfort** poor consolation; **cold cream** ointment for cleansing and softening the skin; **cold frame** unheated frame for growing small plants; **cold shoulder** deliberate unfriendliness; **cold-shoulder** *v.t.* be unfriendly to; **cold storage** storage in refrigerator (**in cold storage** *fig.* put aside but still available); **cold sweat** state of sweating induced by fear or illness etc.; **cold war** hostility between nations without actual fighting; **get** (or **have**) **cold feet** become fearful or reluctant; **have person cold** *colloq.* have him at one's mercy; **in cold blood** see BLOOD; **leave one cold** fail to impress or excite one; **out in the cold** ignored, neglected; **throw** (or **pour**) **cold water on** be discouraging or depreciatory about. [OE]

cole *n.* cabbage. [ON f. L *caulis*]

coleopterous /kɒlɪ'ɒptərəs/ *a.* of the order of insects (comprising beetles and weevils) with front wings serving as sheaths. [L f. Gk (*koleon* sheath, *pteron* wing)]

coleslaw /'kəʊlslɔ:/ *n.* dressed salad of sliced raw cabbage. [COLE; Du. *sla* salad]

colic /'kɒlɪk/ *n.* severe spasmodic abdominal pain; **colicky** /'kɒlɪkɪ/ *a.* [F f. L (COLON[2])]

colitis /kɒ'laɪtɪs/ *n.* inflammation of lining of colon. [COLON[2]]

collaborate /kə'læbəreɪt/ *v.i.* work jointly (*with*), esp. at literary or artistic production; co-operate with enemy; **collaboration** /-'reɪʃ(ə)n/ *n.*; **collaborator** *n.* [L (LABOUR)]

collage /'kɒlɑ:ʒ/ *n.* form or work of art in which various materials are arranged and glued to a backing. [F, = gluing]

collagen /'kɒlədʒ(ə)n/ *n.* protein found in animal tissue and bone, yielding gelatin on boiling. [F f. Gk *kolla* glue]

collapse /kə'læps/ **1** *n.* tumbling down or falling in of structure, folding up, giving way; failure of plan etc.; physical or mental breakdown. **2** *v.* (cause to) undergo collapse; fold up. **3 collapsible** *a.* [L *labor laps-* slip]

collar /'kɒlə/ **1** *n.* neckband, upright or turned over, of coat or dress or shirt etc.; band of leather etc. round animal's (esp. dog's) neck; band or ring or pipe in machine etc. **2** *v.t.* seize (person) by collar, capture; *sl.* seize, appropriate. **3 collar-bone** bone joining breastbone and shoulder-blade. [AF f. L (*collum* neck)]

collate /kə'leɪt/ *v.t.* compare in detail (esp. texts, or one copy *with* another); collect and arrange systematically; **collator** *n.* [L (CONFER)]

collateral /kə'lætər(ə)l/ **1** *a.* side by side, parallel; additional but subordinate; contributory; connected but aside from main subject or course etc.; descended from same stock but by different line. **2** *n.* collateral person or security. **3 collateral security** additional security pledged as guarantee for repayment of money. [L (LATERAL)]

collation /kə'leɪʃ(ə)n/ *n.* collating; thing collated; light meal. [F f. L (CONFER)]

colleague /'kɒli:g/ *n.* fellow official or worker, esp. in a profession or business. [F f. L *collega*]

collect[1] /kə'lekt/ *v.* bring or come together, assemble, accumulate; systematically seek and obtain (books, stamps, etc.) for addition to others; get (contributions or tax etc.) from a number of people; call for, fetch; regain control of, concentrate, recover (*oneself*, one's thoughts, courage, etc.); (in *p.p.*) not perturbed or distracted. [F or L (*lego lect-* pick)]

collect[2] /'kɒlekt/ *n.* short prayer of Anglican or RC Church. [F f. L *collecta* (prec.)]

collection /kə'lekʃ(ə)n/ *n.* collecting; things collected, esp. systematically; money collected, esp. at meeting or church service. [COLLECT[1]]

collective /kə'lektɪv/ **1** *a.* formed by, constituting, or denoting a collection; taken as a whole, aggregate, common. **2** *n.* collective farm; collective noun. **3 collective bargaining** negotiation of wages etc. by organized body of employees; **collective farm** jointly operated amalgamation of several smallholdings; **collective noun** singular noun denoting collection or number of individuals (e.g. *cattle, flock, troop*); **collective ownership** ownership of land etc. by all for benefit of all. **4 collectivity** /-'tɪvɪtɪ/ *n.* [F or L (COLLECT[1])]

collectivism *n.* theory or practice of collective ownership of land and means of production; **collectivist** *n.*

collector /kə'lektə/ *n.* one who collects things of interest; one who collects money due (*rent-, tax-collector*); **collector's item** (or **piece**) thing of special interest to collectors. [AF f. med.L (COLLECT[1])]

colleen /kɒ'li:n/ *n. Ir.* girl. [Ir. *cailin*]

college /'kɒlɪdʒ/ *n.* establishment for higher or professional education; body of teachers and students within a university, their premises; small university; school; organized body of persons with shared functions and privileges. [F or L (COLLEAGUE)]

collegian /kə'li:dʒɪən/ *n.* member of college.

collegiate /kə'li:dʒɪət/ *a.* of or constituted as a college; **collegiate church** church endowed for chapter of canons but without bishop's see.

collide /kə'laɪd/ *v.i.* come into collision or conflict (*with*). [L *collido -lis-* clash]

collie /'kɒlɪ/ *n.* sheep-dog of orig. Scottish breed. [perh. f. *coll* COAL]

collier /'kɒlɪə/ *n.* coal-miner; coal ship, member of its crew. [COAL]

colliery *n.* coal-mine and its buildings.

collision /kə'lɪʒ(ə)n/ *n.* violent encounter of moving body, esp. ship or vehicle, with another or with fixed object; clashing of opposed interests etc.; **collision course** course or action bound to cause collision. [L (COLLIDE)]

collocate /'kɒləkeɪt/ *v.t.* place (esp. words) together or side by side; **collocation** /-'keɪʃ(ə)n/ *n.* [L (LOCUS)]

colloid /'kɒlɔɪd/ *n.* gluey substance; non-crystalline substance with very large molecules; finely divided substance dispersed in another; **colloidal** /kə'lɔɪd(ə)l/ *a.* [Gk *kolla* glue]

collop /'kɒləp/ *n.* slice of meat, escalope. [Scand.]

colloquial /kə'ləʊkwɪəl/ *a.* belonging or proper to ordinary or familiar conversation, not formal or literary; **colloquially** *adv.* [*L* (COLLOQUY)]

colloquialism *n.* colloquial word or phrase; use of these.

colloquium /kə'ləʊkwɪəm/ *n.* academic conference or seminar. [L (foll.)]

colloquy /'kɒləkwɪ/ *n.* talk, a conversation. [L (*loquor* speak)]

collusion /kə'lu:ʒ(ə)n/ *n.* secret agreement or co-operation, esp. for fraud or deceit; **collusive** *a.* [F or L (*ludo lus-* play)]

collywobbles /'kɒlɪwɒb(ə)lz/ *n.pl. colloq.* rumbling or pain in stomach; apprehensive feeling. [COLIC, WOBBLE]

cologne /kə'ləʊn/ *n.* eau-de-Cologne or other scented liquid. [abbr.]

colon[1] /'kəʊlən/ *n.* punctuation-mark (:), used esp. to mark illustration or antithesis. [L f. Gk, = clause]

colon[2] /'kəʊlən/ *n.* lower and greater part of large intestine; **colonic** /kə'lɒnɪk/ *a.* [F or L f. Gk]

colonel /'kɜ:n(ə)l/ *n.* officer commanding regiment, of rank next below brigadier; **colonelcy** *n.* [F f. It. *colonello* (COLUMN)]

colonial /kə'ləʊnɪəl/ **1** *a.* of a colony or colonies. **2** *n.* inhabitant of a colony. [COLONY]

colonialism *n.* policy of acquiring or maintaining colonies; *derog.* alleged policy of exploitation of colonies; **colonialist** *n.*

colonist /'kɒlənɪst/ *n.* settler in or inhabitant of a colony. [COLONY]

colonize /'kɒlənaɪz/ *v.* establish a colony (in); join a colony; **colonization** /-'zeɪʃ(ə)n/ *n.* [COLONY]

colonnade /kɒlə'neɪd/ *n.* row of columns, esp. supporting entablature or roof. [F (COLUMN)]

colony /'kɒlənɪ/ *n.* settlement or settlers in new country fully or partly subject to mother country; their territory; group of one nationality, occupation, etc., forming a community in a city; group of animals that live close together. [L *colonia* farm]

colophon /'kɒləfən/ *n.* tailpiece in manuscript or book, giving writer's or printer's name, date, etc.; publisher's imprint, esp. on title-page. [L f. Gk, = summit]

color *US* var. of COLOUR.

Colorado beetle /kɒlə'rɑ:dəʊ/ yellow and black beetle, larva of which is destructive to potato plant. [*Colorado* in U.S.A.]

coloration /kʌlə'reɪʃ(ə)n/ *n.* colouring; arrangement of colours. [F or L (COLOUR)]

coloratura /kɒlərə'tu:rə/ *n.* elaborate ornamentation of a vocal melody; soprano skilled in coloratura singing. [It. (COLOUR)]

colossal /kə'lɒs(ə)l/ *a.* gigantic, huge; *colloq.* remarkable, splendid; **colossally** *adv.* [foll.]

colossus /kə'lɒsəs/ *n.* (*pl.* **colossi** /-aɪ/, **-uses**) statue of much more than life size; gigantic person or personified empire. [L f. Gk]

colostomy /kə'lɒstəmɪ/ *n.* surgical operation on colon to construct artificial opening for evacuation of bowel. [COLON[2]]

colour /'kʌlə/ **1** *n.* sensation produced on eye by rays of light when resolved as by prism into different wavelengths; one, or any mixture, of the constituents into which light can be separated as in a spectrum or rainbow, sometimes including (loosely) black and white; use of all colours (not only black and white) as in photography; colouring substance, esp. paint; pigmentation of the skin, esp. when dark, this as ground of discrimination etc.; ruddiness of complexion; (in *pl.*) appearance or aspect (*see things in their true colours*); (in *pl.*) coloured ribbon, dress, etc., worn as symbol of school, club, team, etc., esp. by member of it; (in *pl.*) flag of regiment or ship; quality, mood, or variety in music, literature, etc.; show of reason, pretext (*lend colour to, under colour of*). **2** *v.* give colour to; paint, stain, dye; imbue with its own character (*an attitude coloured by experience*); misrepresent, exaggerate; take on colour, blush. **3 colour-bar** discrimination between white and non-white persons; **colour-blind** unable to distinguish certain colours; **colour-sergeant** senior sergeant of infantry company; **nail one's colours to the mast** persist, refuse to give in; **primary colours** red, green, violet, or for pigments red, blue, yellow; **secondary colours** mixtures of two primary colours; **show one's true colours** reveal true character or intentions; **under false colours** falsely, deceitfully; **with flying colours** very successfully. [F f. L *color*]

colourable *a.* plausible but false, specious, counterfeit.

colouration var. of COLORATION.

coloured 1 *a.* having colour; wholly or partly of non-white descent, (**Coloured**, in S. Africa) of mixed white and non-white descent. **2** *n.* coloured person, (**Coloured**, in S. Africa) person of mixed white and non-white descent.

colourful *a.* full of colour or interest, vivid.

colouring *n.* disposition of colours; substance giving colour; artist's use of colour; facial complexion.

colourless *a.* without colour; lacking character or vividness.

colt /kəʊlt/ *n.* young male horse; inexperienced player in team. [OE]

colter *US* var. of COULTER.

coltsfoot *n.* weed with large leaves and yellow flowers. [COLT]

columbine /ˈkɒləmbaɪn/ *n.* garden plant with flower like five clustered pigeons. [F f. L (*columba* pigeon)]

column /ˈkɒləm/ *n.* pillar, usu. of circular section and with base and capital; column-shaped object; vertical cylindrical mass of liquid or vapour; vertical division of page in printed matter; part of newspaper devoted to particular subject or by regular writer; vertical row of figures in accounts etc.; narrow-fronted deep arrangement of troops or armoured vehicles in successive lines; **columnar** /kəˈlʌmnə/ *a.* [F & L]

columnist /ˈkɒləmnɪst/ *n.* person regularly writing a newspaper column.

com- *prefix* (co- esp. before vowels; assimilated to **col-**, **con-**, or **cor-** before certain consonants) with, together, altogether. [L *com-*, *cum* with]

coma /ˈkəʊmə/ *n.* prolonged deep unconsciousness. [L f. Gk]

comatose /ˈkəʊmətəʊz/ *a.* in a coma; drowsy, sleepy.

comb /kəʊm/ **1** *n.* toothed strip of rigid material for tidying and arranging hair, or for keeping it in place; part of machine having similar design or purpose; red fleshy crest of fowl, esp. cock; honeycomb. **2** *v.t.* draw comb through (hair); dress (wool etc.) with comb; *colloq.* search (place) thoroughly; **comb out** remove with comb, *colloq.* search out and get rid of (anything unwanted). [OE]

combat /ˈkɒmbæt/ **1** *n.* fight, struggle, contest. **2** *v.* engage in contest (with); oppose, strive against. [F f. L (BATTLE)]

combatant /ˈkɒmbətənt/ **1** *a.* fighting, for fighting. **2** *n.* person engaged in fighting.

combative /ˈkɒmbətɪv/ *a.* pugnacious.

combe var. of COOMB.

combination /kɒmbɪˈneɪʃ(ə)n/ *n.* combining; combined state (*in combination with*); combined set of persons or things; sequence of numbers or letters used to open combination lock; motor cycle with side-car attached; (in *pl.*) single undergarment for body and legs; **combination lock** lock which can be opened only by specific sequence of movements. [F or L (*bini* pair)]

combine 1 /kəmˈbaɪn/ *v.* join together, unite for common purpose; possess (esp. qualities usu. distinct) together; form chemical compound; co-operate; **combining form** form of word used in combinations (e.g. *Anglo-* repr. *English*). **2** /ˈkɒmbaɪn/ *n.* combination of persons or firms acting together in business. **3 combine harvester** combined reaping and threshing machine.

combings /ˈkəʊmɪŋz/ *n.pl.* loose hair removed by brush or comb. [COMB]

combustible /kəmˈbʌstɪb(ə)l/ **1** *a.* capable of or used for burning. **2** *n.* combustible thing. **3 combustibility** /-ˈbɪlɪtɪ/ *n.* [F or med.L (foll.)]

combustion /kəmˈbʌstʃ(ə)n/ *n.* development of light and heat with chemical combination; burning, consumption by fire. [F or L *comburo -ust-* burn up]

come /kʌm/ *v.i.* (*past* **came**; *p.p.* **come**) move, be brought towards, or reach place thought of as near or familiar to speaker or hearer (*come and see me*; *shall we come to your house?*); reach specified situation or result (*you'll come to no harm*; *have come to believe it*; *total comes to £10*); reach or extend to specified point (*road comes within a mile of us*); traverse or accomplish (with cognate object: *have come a long way*); occur, happen, become present instead of future (*had it coming to him*; *how did you come to break your leg?*; *come to* *pass*); take or occupy specified position in space or time (*it comes on the third page*; *Nero came after Claudius*); become perceptible or known (*church came into sight*; *news comes as a surprise*; *it will come to me*); be available (*dress comes in three sizes*); become (*the handle came loose*); be descended, be result *of* (*comes from a rich family*; *that comes of complaining*); *colloq.* play the part of, behave like (with cognate object: *don't come the bully with me*); *sl.* have sexual orgasm; *colloq.* (in *subj.*) when specified time comes (*come Friday*, *tomorrow*); (in *imper.*) excl. of mild protest or encouragement; **come about** happen; **come across** meet or find by chance, *colloq.* be effective, *sl.* hand over money etc.; **come again** make second effort, *colloq.* (as *imper.*) what did you say?; **come along** make progress, (as *imper.*) hurry up; **come at** reach, get access to, attack; **come away** become detached, be left *with* (impression etc.); **come back** return, recur to memory; **come-back** *n.* return to previous (esp. successful) state, *colloq.* retort or retaliation; **come between** separate, interfere with relationship of; **come by** obtain, pay brief visit; **come clean** see CLEAN; **come down** lose position or wealth, be handed down by tradition, decide (*in favour of* etc.), amount basically *to*; **come-down** *n.* downfall, degradation; **come down on** criticize harshly, rebuke, punish; **come down with** begin to suffer from (disease); **come forward** advance, offer oneself for task, post, etc.; **come-hither** *a.* flirtatious, inviting; **come home to** see HOME; **come in** enter, take specified position in race etc. (*came in third*), become fashionable or seasonable, have a place or function, prove to be *handy* or *useful*, begin speaking esp. in radio transmission; **come in for** receive; **come into** enter, be brought into (collision, prominence, etc.), receive esp. as heir; **come of age** see AGE; **come off** be detached or detachable (from), fare (*badly*, *well*, etc.), succeed, occur; **come off it** *colloq.* stop talking or behaving like that; **come on** = *come upon*, advance, make progress, begin (*came on to rain*), appear on stage etc., (as *imper.*) hurry, follow me, please do what I ask, I defy you; **come-on** *n. sl.* enticement; **come out** emerge, become known, go on strike, be published, declare oneself (*for*, *against*, etc.), be satisfactorily visible in photograph etc., (of stain etc.) be removed, become covered *in* (rash etc.), attain specified result in examination etc., make début on stage or in society, be solved; **come out with** say, disclose; **come over** come from distance or across obstacle, change sides or opinion; (of feeling etc.) overtake or affect (person), *colloq.* feel suddenly (*come over faint*); **come round** pay informal visit, recover consciousness, be converted to other person's opinion, (of date) recur; **come to** amount to, be equivalent to, recover consciousness; **come to a head** see HEAD; **come to nothing** have no useful result in the end, fail; **come to one's senses** be sensible once more; **come true** see TRUE; **come up** arise, present itself, be mentioned or discussed; **come up against** be faced with or opposed by; **come upon** meet or find by chance, attack by surprise; **come-uppance** *colloq.* deserved punishment or retribution; **come up to** reach, be equal to (standard etc.); **come up with** present or produce (idea etc.), draw level with. [OE]

Comecon /ˈkɒmiːkɒn/ *n.* economic association of Communist countries. [abbr. of *Council for Mutual Economic Assistance*]

comedian /kəˈmiːdɪən/ *n.* humorous performer on stage, television, etc.; actor who plays comic parts; **comedienne** /-ɪˈen/ *n. fem.* [F]

comedy /ˈkɒmədɪ/ *n.* play or film of light amusing character, usu. representing everyday life, and with happy ending; humorous genre of drama; humour, amusing aspects of life. [F f. L f. Gk (COMIC)]

comely /ˈkʌmlɪ/ *a.* handsome, good-looking; **comeliness** *n.* [OE]

comer /ˈkʌmə/ *n.* one who comes (*first comers*); **all comers** anyone who applies, takes up challenge, etc. [COME]

comestibles /kəˈmestɪb(ə)lz/ *n.pl.* things to eat. [F f. L]

comet /ˈkɒmɪt/ *n.* hazy object usu. with starlike nucleus and with tail pointing away from sun, moving in path about sun. [F f. L f. Gk]

comfit /ˈkʌmfɪt/ *n. archaic* sweet consisting of nut etc. in sugar. [F f. L (CONFECTION)]

comfort /ˈkʌmfət/ **1** *n.* state of physical or mental well-being or contentment; relief of suffering or grief, consolation; person or thing that gives this; (in *pl.*) things that allow ease or well-being in life. **2** *v.t.* give comfort to, soothe in grief, console. [F f. L (*fortis* strong)]

comfortable *a.* giving ease and contentment; feeling at ease or free from pain, trouble, or hardship; sufficient, appreciable (*a comfortable income*; *won by a comfortable margin*); **comfortably** *adv.*

comforter *n.* one who comforts; baby's

dummy; *archaic* woollen scarf; **the Comforter** the Holy Spirit. [COMFORT]
comfrey /ˈkʌmfrɪ/ *n.* tall bell-flowered plant growing in damp, shady places. [F f. L]
comfy /ˈkʌmfɪ/ *a. colloq.* comfortable. [abbr.]
comic /ˈkɒmɪk/ **1** *a.* of or like comedy; designed to amuse, facetious, funny (*comic song*). **2** *n.* comedian; comic paper, esp. periodical with narrative mainly in pictures. **3 comic strip** sequence of drawings telling comic or adventure story in newspaper etc. **4 comical** *a.*; **comically** *adv.* [L f. Gk (*kōmos* revel)]
coming /ˈkʌmɪŋ/ **1** *a.* approaching, next (*in the coming week*; *this coming Sunday*); of potential importance (*coming man*). **2** *n.* arrival. [COME]
comity /ˈkɒmɪtɪ/ *n.* courtesy, friendship; association of nations etc.; **comity of nations** nations' friendly recognition of each other's laws and customs. [L (*comis* courteous)]
comma /ˈkɒmə/ *n.* punctuation-mark (,), indicating slight pause or break between parts of sentence. [L f. Gk, = clause]
command /kəˈmɑːnd/ **1** *v.* give formal order or instruction to, order (person *to do* thing, thing to *be done*, *that*); have authority over or control of; exercise command; have at one's disposal or within reach (skill, resources, etc.); deserve and get (respect, sympathy, etc.); dominate (strategic position) from superior height, look down over. **2** *n.* order given; exercise or tenure of authority, esp. naval or military; control, mastery, possession; forces or district under commander. **3 Command Paper** paper laid before parliament by royal command; **command performance** performance of film, show, etc., at royal request. [F f. L (MANDATE)]
commandant /kɒmənˈdænt, ˈkɒm-/ *n.* commanding officer, esp. of military academy or prisoner-of-war camp. [F or It. or Sp. (prec.)]
commandeer /kɒmənˈdɪə/ *v.t.* seize (esp. property) for military use; take arbitrary possession of. [S. Afr. Du. f. F (COMMAND)]
commander /kəˈmɑːndə/ *n.* one who commands, esp. naval officer next below captain; (in full **knight commander**) member of higher class in some orders of knighthood; **commander-in-chief** supreme commander, esp. of nation's forces. [F (COMMAND)]
commanding *a.* that commands; (of ability, appearance, etc.) exalted or impressive; (of position) giving wide view. [COMMAND]
commandment *n.* divine command, esp. (**Commandment**) one of the ten given to Moses (Exod. 20 : 1–17). [F (COMMAND)]
commando /kəˈmɑːndəʊ/ *n.* (*pl.* **commandos**) body of amphibious shock troops; member of this. [Port. (COMMAND)]
commemorate /kəˈmeməreɪt/ *v.t.* keep in memory by celebration or ceremony; be a memorial to; **commemoration** /-ˈreɪʃ(ə)n/ *n.* **commemorative** *a.* [L (MEMORY)]
commence /kəˈmens/ *v.* begin. [F f. Rmc f. L (COM-, INITIATE)]
commencement *n.* beginning; ceremony of degree conferment; *US* graduation ceremony.
commend /kəˈmend/ *v.t.* praise; recommend; entrust, commit; **commendation** /-ˈdeɪʃ(ə)n/ *n.*; **commendatory** *a.* [L (MANDATE)]
commendable *a.* praiseworthy; **commendably** *adv.*
commensurable /kəˈmenʃərəb(ə)l/ *a.* measurable by same standard (*with* or *to*); (of numbers) in ratio equal to ratio of integers; proportionate *to*. [L (MEASURE)]
commensurate /kəˈmenʃərət/ *a.* coextensive (*with*), proportionate (*to* or *with*). [L (MEASURE)]
comment /ˈkɒment/ **1** *n.* brief critical or explanatory remark or note, opinion. **2** *v.i.* write comments (*up*)*on*; utter (esp. critical) remarks (*on*, *that*); **3 no comment** *colloq.* I decline to say anything on the matter. [L]
commentary /ˈkɒməntərɪ/ *n.* series of descriptive comments on an event or performance, esp. for broadcasting while it is in progress (*running commentary*); set of explanatory notes on text etc. [L]
commentate /ˈkɒmənteɪt/ *v.i.* act as commentator. [foll.]
commentator *n.* speaker or writer of commentary; one who comments on current events. [L]
commerce /ˈkɒmɜːs/ *n.* buying and selling, all forms of trading, including banking, insurance, etc. [F or L (MERCER)]
commercial /kəˈmɜːʃ(ə)l/ **1** *a.* of, engaged in, commerce; concerned chiefly with financial profit; (of broadcasting) in which advertisements are included to provide finance; (of chemicals) unpurified. **2** *n.* broadcast advertisement. **3 commercial art** style of art used in advertising; **commercial traveller** firm's representative visiting shops etc. to obtain orders.
commercialism *n.* commercial practices and attitudes.

commercialize *v.t.* make commercial; seek to make profitable; **commercialization** /-'zeɪʃ(ə)n/ *n.*
Commie /'kɒmɪ/ *n. sl. derog.* Communist. [abbr.]
commination /kɒmɪ'neɪʃ(ə)n/ *n.* threatening of divine vengeance; **comminatory** /'kɒmɪnətərɪ/ *a.* [L (MENACE)]
commingle /kə'mɪŋg(ə)l/ *v. literary* mix together. [COM-]
comminute /'kɒmɪnju:t/ *v.t.* reduce to small fragments (*comminuted fracture*); divide (property) into small portions; **comminution** /-'nju:ʃ(ə)n/ *n.* [L (MINUTE²)]
commiserate /kə'mɪzəreɪt/ *v.i.* have or express sympathy *with* (person); **commiseration** /-'reɪʃ(ə)n/ *n.*; **commiserative** *a.* [L (MISER)]
commissar /'kɒmɪsɑ:/ *n. hist.* head of government department of USSR. [Russ. f. L (COMMIT)]
commissariat /kɒmɪ'seərɪət/ *n.* department responsible for supply of food etc. for army; food supplied; *hist.* government department of USSR. [foll.]
commissary /'kɒmɪsərɪ/ *n.* deputy, delegate; *US* store for supply of food etc. for army; *US* restaurant in film studio etc.; **commissarial** /-'seərɪəl/ *a.* [L (COMMIT)]
commission /kə'mɪʃ(ə)n/ **1** *n.* giving of authority to person to perform task; task so given, such person's authority or instructions; body or board of persons constituted to perform certain duties; warrant conferring authority, esp. that of officer in armed forces above a certain rank; pay or percentage received by agent; committing, performance (e.g. of crime). **2** *v.t.* empower by commission; employ (person *to do* piece of work); give (officer) command of ship; prepare (ship) for active service; bring (machine etc.) into operation. **3 commission-agent** bookmaker; **in** (or **out of**) **commission** (esp. of ship) ready (or not ready) for use. [F f. L (COMMIT)]
commissionaire /kəmɪʃə'neə/ *n.* uniformed attendant at door of theatre, office, etc. [F (foll.)]
commissioner *n.* member of a commission; official representing government in a district, department, etc.; one who has been commissioned; **Commissioner for Oaths** solicitor authorized to administer oaths in affidavits etc. [med.L (COMMISSION)]
commissure /'kɒmɪsjʊə/ *n.* joint between two bones; junction, seam. [L (foll.)]
commit /kə'mɪt/ *v.t.* (**-tt-**) be doer of (crime, blunder, etc.); entrust or consign for treatment or safe keeping; send (person) to prison; expose to risk, involve in course of action, pledge or dedicate *oneself* (*to* a course of action etc.); **commit to memory** learn by heart; **commit to paper** (or **writing**) write down. [L *committo -miss-*]
commitment *n.* act of committing or being committed; engagement or involvement that restricts freedom of action or choice; dedication or obligation to particular action, cause, etc.
committal *n.* action of committing, esp. to prison.
committed *a.* dedicated or pledged (*to* a particular action, cause, etc.).
committee /kə'mɪtɪ/ *n.* group of persons appointed by (and usu. out of) a larger body, to attend to special business or to manage business of club etc.; (**Committee**) House of Commons sitting as committee; **standing committee** one that is permanent during existence of appointing body. [COMMIT, -EE]
commode /kə'məʊd/ *n.* chamber-pot mounted in chair or with cover; chest of drawers. [F f. L (MODE)]
commodious /kə'məʊdɪəs/ *a.* roomy. [F or med.L (prec.)]
commodity /kə'mɒdɪtɪ/ *n.* article of trade, esp. product as opposed to service. [F or L (MODE)]
commodore /'kɒmədɔ:/ *n.* naval officer next below rear-admiral; commander of squadron or other division of fleet; president of yacht club. [Du. f. F (COMMANDER)]
common /'kɒmən/ **1** *a.* shared by, coming from, or affecting all concerned (*common cause, knowledge*; *by common consent*); of or belonging to the whole community, public (*common land*); occurring often (*a common experience*); ordinary, of the most familiar or numerous kind (*common cold, weed*); without special rank or position (*the common people*; *a common soldier*); of inferior quality, ill-bred, unrefined; *Gram.* (of noun) referring to any one of a class, (of gender) referring to individuals of either sex; *Math.* belonging to two or more quantities (*common denominator, factor*). **2** *n.* land belonging to a community; (piece of) unenclosed waste land; *sl.* common sense. **3 common ground** matters on which two or more (otherwise differing) parties agree, basis for argument; **common law** unwritten law based on custom and precedent; **common-law husband, wife** husband or wife recognized by common law without formal marriage; **Common Market** the European Economic Community; **common or garden** *colloq.* ordinary; **common-room** room for

social use of students or teachers at college etc.; **common sense** good practical sense esp. in everyday matters; **common time** *Mus.* four crotchets in a bar; **in common** shared by several (esp. as interest or characteristic), in joint use. [F f. L *communis*]

commonality /kɒmə'nælɪtɪ/ *n.* sharing of an attribute; common occurrence. [var. of foll.]

commonalty /'kɒmən(ə)ltɪ/ *n.* the common people; general body (of mankind etc.). [F f. med.L (COMMON)]

commoner *n.* one of the common people (below rank of peer); student without financial support from college. [med.L (COMMON)]

commonly *adv.* usually, frequently; ordinarily. [COMMON]

commonplace 1 *n.* event, topic, etc. that is ordinary or usual; trite remark. 2 *a.* ordinary; lacking originality or individuality; trite. [trans. L *locus communis*]

commons *n.pl.* the common people; **(Commons)** = *House of Commons*; provisions shared in common; **short commons** not enough food. [COMMON]

commonsensical /kɒmən'sensɪk(ə)l/ *a.* having or marked by common sense.

commonwealth *n.* independent State or community; republic or democratic State; federation of States; **the Commonwealth** republican government of Britain in 1649–60; **the (British) Commonwealth** association of UK with various independent States (previously subject to Britain) and dependencies; **Commonwealth Day** (formerly *Empire Day*) now celebrated on second Monday in March. [WEALTH]

commotion /kə'məʊʃ(ə)n/ *n.* noisy disturbance, confusion, uproar. [F or L (COM-)]

communal /'kɒmjʊn(ə)l/ *a.* shared between members of group or community; **communally** *adv.* [F f. L (foll.)]

commune[1] /'kɒmju:n/ *n.* group of people, not all of one family, sharing living arrangements and goods; small district of local government in France and certain other European countries. [F f. med.L (COMMON)]

commune[2] /kə'mju:n/ *v.i.* communicate mentally or spiritually, feel in close touch (*with*). [F (COMMON)]

communicable /kə'mju:nɪkəb(ə)l/ *a.* that can be communicated (*communicable disease*). [F or L (COMMUNICATE)]

communicant /kə'mju:nɪkənt/ *n.* one who receives Holy Communion (esp. regularly); one who imparts information. [foll.]

communicate /kə'mju:nɪkeɪt/ *v.* impart, transmit (news, heat, motion, feeling, disease, etc., *to*); have social dealings (*with*); succeed in conveying information; be connected (*rooms have a communicating door*); receive Holy Communion. [L (COMMON)]

communication /kəmju:nɪ'keɪʃ(ə)n/ *n.* communicating; information communicated; letter, message, etc.; social dealings; connection or means of access; (in *pl.*) science and practice of transmitting information; **communication cord** cord or chain for pulling by passenger to stop train in emergency.

communicative /kə'mju:nɪkətɪv/ *a.* ready and willing to talk and impart information.

communion /kə'mju:nɪən/ *n.* fellowship, having ideas and beliefs in common; mutual relation between members or parts of Church; body of Christians of same denomination (*Anglican communion*); **(Holy) Communion** Eucharist; **communion of saints** fellowship of Christians past and present. [F or L (COMMON)]

communiqué /kə'mju:nɪkeɪ/ *n.* official communication or report. [F, = communicated]

communism /'kɒmjʊnɪz(ə)m/ *n.* social system in which property is vested in the community and each member works for the common benefit; (usu. **Communism**) movement or political party advocating communism, communistic form of society established in USSR and elsewhere. [F (COMMON)]

communist /'kɒmjʊnɪst/ *n.* supporter of communism; (usu. **Communist**) member of Communist party; **communistic** /-'nɪstɪk/ *a.*

community /kə'mju:nɪtɪ/ *n.* body of people living in one place or district or country; group of people having religion, race, profession, etc., in common; commune; fellowship (*community of interest*); state of being shared or held in common; joint ownership or liability; **community centre** place providing social, recreational, and educational facilities for a neighbourhood; **community home** institution for housing young offenders; **community singing** organized singing in chorus by large gathering of people. [F f. L (COMMON)]

commute /kə'mju:t/ *v.* travel regularly by train or bus or car to and from one's daily work in city etc.; exchange (*for* something else); change (one form of payment or obligation) *for* or *into* another; change (punishment) *to* another less severe; **commutation** /kɒmjʊ'teɪʃ(ə)n/ *n.* [L (*muto* change)]

commuter *n.* one who commutes to and from work.

compact[1] **1** /kəm'pækt/ *a.* closely or neatly packed together; concise. **2** *v.t.* make compact. **3** /'kɒmpækt/ *n.* small flat case for face-powder. **4 compact disc** disc about 12 cm. in diameter from which sound can be reproduced by laser action. [L (*pango* fasten)]

compact[2] /'kɒmpækt/ *n.* agreement, contract. [L (PACT)]

companion /kəm'pænjən/ *n.* one who associates with or accompanies another; associate *in*, sharer *of*; member of some orders of distinction (*Companion of the Bath*); woman paid to live with and accompany another; handbook or reference book; thing that matches or accompanies another; **companion-way** staircase from ship's deck to saloon or cabins. [F f. Rmc (L *panis* bread)]

companionable *a.* sociable, friendly; **companionably** *adv.*

companionship *n.* state of being companions, friendly fellowship.

company /'kʌmpənɪ/ *n.* being with another or others; number of people assembled, guests; person's associate(s); body of persons combined for common (esp. commercial) object; group of actors etc.; subdivision of infantry battalion; **in company with** together with; **keep (person) company** remain with person to prevent his being alone; **part company** separate, cease dealing (*with*). [F (COMPANION)]

comparable /'kɒmpərəb(ə)l, (D) -'pær-/ *a.* that can be compared (*with* or *to*); **comparability** /-'bɪlɪtɪ/ *n.* [F f. L (COMPARE)]

comparative /kəm'pærətɪv/ **1** *a.* perceptible or estimated by comparison (*in comparative comfort*); of or involving comparison (*comparative philology*; *a comparative study*); considered in relation to each other (*their comparative merits*). **2** *n. Gram.* comparative degree or form. **3 comparative adjective** (or **adverb**) adjective (or adverb) in comparative degree; **comparative degree** form expressing higher degree of a quality (e.g. *braver*, *more quickly*). [L (foll.)]

compare /kəm'peə/ **1** *v.* estimate similarity of (one thing *with* or *to* another; two things); liken, regard as similar (*to*); bear comparison (*with*); *Gram.* form comparative and superlative degrees of (adjective, adverb). **2** *n. literary* comparison (*without compare*). **3 compare notes** exchange ideas or opinions. [F f. L (*compar* equal)]

comparison /kəm'pærɪs(ə)n/ *n.* comparing; **bear comparison** be able to be compared favourably *with*; **beyond comparison** impossible to compare because of superiority in quality; **degrees of comparison** *Gram.* positive, comparative, and superlative (of adjectives and adverbs).

compartment /kəm'pɑ:tmənt/ *n.* division separated by partitions, e.g. in railway carriage; watertight division of ship. [F f. It. f. L (PART)]

compartmental /kɒmpɑ:t'ment(ə)l/ *a.* of or divided into compartments or categories.

compartmentalize *v.t.* divide into compartments or categories.

compass /'kʌmpəs/ *n.* instrument showing direction of magnetic north and bearings from it; (often in *pl.*) instrument for taking measurements and describing circles, with two legs connected at one end by movable joint; circumference, boundary; area, extent, scope (*beyond my compass*); range of voice or musical instrument. [F f. L (*passus* pace)]

compassion /kəm'pæʃ(ə)n/ *n.* feeling of pity inclining one to be helpful or show mercy. [F f. eccl.L (PASSION)]

compassionate /kəm'pæʃənət/ *a.* sympathetic, showing compassion; **compassionate leave** leave granted on grounds of bereavement etc.

compatible /kəm'pætɪb(ə)l/ *a.* able to coexist (*with*); mutually tolerant; (of equipment etc.) able to be used in combination; **compatibility** /-'bɪlɪtɪ/ *n.* [F f. med.L, as COMPASSION]

compatriot /kəm'pætrɪət/ *n.* fellow-countryman. [F f. L *compatriota*]

compeer /kəm'pɪə/ *n.* person of equal standing; comrade. [F (PEER[2])]

compel /kəm'pel/ *v.t.* (-ll-) force or constrain; arouse irresistibly (*her courage compels admiration*). [L (*pello puls-* drive)]

compelling *a.* rousing strong interest or feeling of admiration.

compendious /kəm'pendɪəs/ *a.* comprehensive but brief. [F f. L (foll.)]

compendium /kəm'pendɪəm/ *n.* (*pl.* **compendia** or **-iums**) concise summary or abridgement; collection of table-games etc. [L]

compensate /'kɒmpənseɪt/ *v.* make suitable payment in return for (loss or damage etc.); recompense (person *for* thing); counterbalance; **compensatory** /kəm'pensətərɪ/ *a.* [L (*pendo pens-* weigh)]

compensation /kɒmpen'seɪʃ(ə)n/ *n.* compensating or being compensated; thing (esp. money) that compensates. [F f. L (prec.)]

compère /'kɒmpeə/ **1** *n.* person who

introduces artistes at variety show etc. **2** *v.t.* act as compère to. [F, = godfather]
compete /kəm'pi:t/ *v.i.* take part in contest, race, etc.; strive (*with* or *against* another or others). [L (*peto* seek)]
competence /'kɒmpətəns/ *n.* being competent, ability; sufficiency of means for living; legal capacity. [COMPETENT]
competency *n.* = COMPETENCE.
competent *a.* having the required ability, knowledge, or authority; effective, adequate. [F or L (COMPETE)]
competition /kɒmpə'tɪʃ(ə)n/ *n.* event in which persons compete; competing (*for*) by examination, in trade, etc.; those competing with one (*the competition is not very strong*). [L (COMPETE)]
competitive /kəm'petɪtɪv/ *a.* of or involving competition; (of prices etc.) comparable with those of rivals.
competitor /kəm'petɪtə/ *n.* one who competes; rival, esp. in trade. [F or L (COMPETE)]
compile /kəm'paɪl/ *v.t.* collect and arrange (information) into a list, volume, etc.; produce (book) thus; **compilation** /kɒmpɪ'leɪʃ(ə)n/ *n.* [F, or L *compilo* plunder]
complacent /kəm'pleɪsənt/ *a.* self-satisfied, calmly content; **complacence** *n.*; **complacency** *n.* [L (*placeo* please)]
complain /kəm'pleɪn/ *v.i.* express dissatisfaction (*about, at, that*); **complain of** say that one is suffering from (pain etc.), state grievance concerning. [F f. L (*plango* lament)]
complainant *n.* plaintiff in certain lawsuits.
complaint *n.* utterance of grievance; formal accusation; cause of dissatisfaction; illness. [F (COMPLAIN)]
complaisant /kəm'pleɪzənt/ *a.* inclined to please or defer to others; acquiescent; **complaisance** *n.* [F (COMPLACENT)]
complement **1** /'kɒmpləmənt/ *n.* that which makes a thing complete; full number required to man ship, fill conveyance, etc.; word(s) added to verb to complete predicate of sentence; deficiency of angle from 90°. **2** /'kɒmplɪment/ *v.t.* complete; form complement to. [L (*compleo* fill up)]
complementary /kɒmplə'mentərɪ/ *a.* completing, forming a complement; (of two or more things) complementing each other.
complete /kəm'pli:t/ **1** *a.* having all its parts, entire; finished; total, thorough, in every way (*a complete stranger, surprise*). **2** *v.t.* make complete; finish; fill in (form etc.). **3 complete with** having as noteworthy feature or addition (*diary complete with pencil*). **4 completion** *n.* [F or L (COMPLEMENT)]
complex /'kɒmpleks/ **1** *a.* consisting of several parts, composite; complicated. **2** *n.* a complex whole; group of usu. repressed ideas etc. causing abnormal behaviour or mental state. **3 complexity** /kəm'pleksɪtɪ/ *n.* [F, or L *complexus*]
complexion /kəm'plekʃ(ə)n/ *n.* natural colour, texture, and appearance of skin, esp. of face; character, aspect (*that puts a different complexion on the matter*). [F f. L (prec.)]
compliance /kəm'plaɪəns/ *n.* action in accordance with request, command, etc.; **in compliance with** according to. [COMPLY]
compliant *a.* complying, obedient. [COMPLY]
complicate /'kɒmplɪkeɪt/ *v.t.* make involved, intricate, or difficult. [L (*plico* to fold)]
complicated *a.* involved, intricate, difficult.
complication /kɒmplɪ'keɪʃ(ə)n/ *n.* involved condition; entangled state of affairs; complicating circumstance; secondary disease or condition aggravating an already existing one. [F or L (COMPLICATE)]
complicity /kəm'plɪsɪtɪ/ *n.* involvement in wrongdoing. [F (COMPLEX)]
compliment **1** /'kɒmplɪmənt/ *n.* polite expression of praise; act implying praise; (in *pl.*) formal greetings accompanying note, present, etc. **2** /'kɒmplɪment/ *v.t.* pay compliment to (person *on* achievement etc.), congratulate. [F, f. It. f. L (as COMPLEMENT)]
complimentary /kɒmplɪ'mentərɪ/ *a.* expressing compliment; given free of charge (*complimentary tickets*).
compline /'kɒmplɪn/ *n.* (office of) last of the canonical hours of prayer. [F f. L (COMPLY)]
comply /kəm'plaɪ/ *v.i.* act in accordance (*with* request or command). [It. f. Sp. f. L (*compleo* fill up)]
component /kəm'pəʊnənt/ **1** *a.* being one of the parts of a whole. **2** *n.* component part. [L (COMPOUND[1])]
comport /kəm'pɔ:t/ *v. literary* conduct or behave *oneself*; **comport with** suit, befit; **comportment** *n.* [L (*porto* carry)]
compose /kəm'pəʊz/ *v.* create in music or writing; make up, constitute; *Printing* set up (type), arrange (article etc.) in type; arrange artistically, neatly, or for specified purpose; make calm (*oneself*, feelings etc.); **composed of** made up of, consisting of. [F (POSE)]
composed *a.* calm, self-possessed; **composedly** /-ɪdlɪ/ *adv.*
composer *n.* one who composes (esp. music).
composite /'kɒmpəzɪt, -zaɪt/ **1** *a.* made

up of various parts; (of plant) having head of many flowers forming one bloom; *Archit.* of mixed Ionic and Corinthian style. **2** *n.* composite thing or plant. [F f. L (COMPOSE)]

composition /kɒmpə'zɪʃ(ə)n/ *n.* act or method of putting together into a whole, composing; thing composed, piece of writing or (esp.) music; constitution of a substance; arrangement of parts of picture etc.; compound artificial substance, esp. one serving purpose of natural one; financial compromise; **compositional** *a.*

compositor /kəm'pɒzɪtə/ *n.* one who sets up type for printing. [AF f. L (COMPOSE)]

compost /'kɒmpɒst/ **1** *n.* mixture of decayed organic matter used as fertilizer; mixture of soil and other ingredients for growing seedlings, cuttings, etc. **2** *v.t.* make into compost; treat with compost. [F f. L (COMPOSE)]

composure /kəm'pəʊʒə/ *n.* tranquil demeanour, calmness. [COMPOSE]

compote /'kɒmpəʊt, -pɒt/ *n.* fruit preserved or cooked in syrup. [F (COMPOSE)]

compound[1] **1** /'kɒmpaʊnd/ *n.* thing made up of two or more ingredients; substance consisting of two or more elements chemically united in fixed proportions; word formed by combination of words. **2** /kəm'paʊnd/ *v.* mix or combine (ingredients or elements); make up (a composite whole); increase or complicate (difficulty, offence, etc.); settle (matter) by mutual agreement; condone or conceal (offence, liability) for personal gain; come to terms (*with* person). **3** /'kɒmpaʊnd/ *a.* made up of two or more ingredients; combined, collective. **4 compound fracture** one complicated by wound; **compound interest** interest paid on principal and accumulated interest; **compound sentence** one with more than one subject or predicate. [F f. L *compono -pos-* put together]

compound[2] /'kɒmpaʊnd/ *n.* enclosure or fenced-in space; in India, China, etc., enclosure in which house or factory stands. [Port. or Du., f. Malay]

comprehend /kɒmprɪ'hend/ *v.t.* grasp mentally, understand; include. [F, or L *comprehendo* seize]

comprehensible *a.* that can be understood. [F or L (prec.)]

comprehension *n.* act or faculty of understanding; inclusion.

comprehensive 1 *a.* including much or all, inclusive. **2** *n.* comprehensive school. **3 comprehensive school** large secondary school providing courses for children of all abilities.

compress 1 /kəm'pres/ *v.t.* squeeze together; bring into smaller space. **2** /'kɒmpres/ *n.* pad of lint etc. pressed on to part of body to stop bleeding, relieve inflammation, etc. **3 compressible** /kəm'presɪb(ə)l/ *a.* [F or L (PRESS[1])]

compression /kəm'preʃ(ə)n/ *n.* compressing; reduction in volume of fuel mixture in internal-combustion engine before ignition.

compressor /kəm'presə/ *n.* machine for compressing air or other gases.

comprise /kəm'praɪz/ *v.t.* include, consist of; (**D**) compose, form parts of. [F (COMPREHEND)]

compromise /'kɒmprəmaɪz/ **1** *n.* settlement of dispute by mutual concession; intermediate way *between* conflicting courses, opinions, etc. **2** *v.* settle (dispute) or modify (principles) by compromise; bring (person or *oneself*) under suspicion or into danger by indiscreet action; make a compromise. [F f. L (PROMISE)]

comptroller /kən'trəʊlə/ *n.* (in titles of some financial officers) controller. [var. of CONTROLLER]

compulsion /kəm'pʌlʃ(ə)n/ *n.* compelling or being compelled; irresistible urge. [F f. L (COMPEL)]

compulsive /kəm'pʌlsɪv/ *a.* tending to compel; resulting or acting (as if) from compulsion, esp. contrary to one's conscious wishes; irresistible. [med.L (COMPEL)]

compulsory /kəm'pʌlsərɪ/ *a.* that must be done, required by the rules etc.; **compulsory purchase** obligatory purchase of land etc. by local authority; **compulsorily** *adv.*

compunction /kəm'pʌŋkʃ(ə)n/ *n.* pricking of conscience, slight regret or scruple. [F f. eccl.L (POINT)]

compute /kəm'pju:t/ *v.* reckon, calculate; use computer; **computation** /kɒmpju:'teɪʃ(ə)n/ *n.*

computer /kəm'pju:tə/ *n.* electronic apparatus for analysing or storing data, making calculations, or controlling machinery. [F or L *puto* reckon]

computerize *v.t.* equip with, perform or produce by, computer; **computerization** /-'zeɪʃ(ə)n/ *n.*

comrade /'kɒmreɪd, -rɪd/ *n.* associate or companion in some activity; fellow socialist or communist; **comradely** *a.*; **comradeship** *n.* [F f. Sp. (CHAMBER)]

con[1] *sl.* **1** *v.t.* (**-nn-**) persuade or swindle after winning person's confidence. **2** *n.* confidence trick. [abbr.]

con[2] *v.t.* (**-nn-**) peruse, study, learn by heart. [CAN[1]]

con[3] *v.t.*, (**-nn-**) direct steering of (ship). [orig. *cond* f. F (CONDUCT)]

con[4] 1 *adv.* & *prep.* (of argument or reason) against. **2** *n.* reason against (see PRO[2]). [L *contra* against]
con[5] *n. sl.* convict. [abbr.]
con- see COM-.
concatenate /kən'kætɪneɪt/ *v.t.* link together, form sequence of; **concatenation** /-'neɪʃ(ə)n/ *n.* [F or L (*catena* chain)]
concave /'kɒnkeɪv/ *a.* curved like interior of circle or sphere; **concavity** /-'kævɪtɪ/ *n.* [L (CAVE[1])]
conceal /kən'si:l/ *v.t.* keep secret or hidden; **concealment** *n.* [F f. L (*celo* hide)]
concede /kən'si:d/ *v.t.* admit to be true; grant (privilege, right, etc.); admit defeat in (contest, election, etc.). [F or L (CEDE)]
conceit /kən'si:t/ *n.* excessive pride in oneself; fanciful notion; far-fetched comparison. [CONCEIVE]
conceited *a.* having too high an opinion of one's qualities or attributes.
conceivable /kən'si:vəb(ə)l/ *a.* that can be (esp. mentally) conceived; **conceivably** *adv.* [foll.]
conceive /kən'si:v/ *v.* become pregnant; form (idea etc.) in the mind; (also with *of*) imagine, think of. [F f. L *concipio -cept-*]
concentrate /'kɒnsəntreɪt/ **1** *v.* employ all one's thought, attention, efforts (*on*); bring or come together to one place; increase strength of (liquid etc.) by removing water etc. **2** *n.* concentrated substance. [F f. L (CENTRE)]
concentrated *a.* (of liquid etc.) having more than natural or original strength, not diluted; intense.
concentration /kɒnsən'treɪʃ(ə)n/ *n.* concentrating or being concentrated; amount or strength of substance in mixture; mental state of exclusive attention; **concentration camp** place for detention of political prisoners etc.
concentric /kən'sentrɪk/ *a.* having the same centre; **concentrically** *adv.* [F or med.L (CENTRE)]
concept /'kɒnsept/ *n.* generalized idea or notion (*the concept of evolution*). [L (CONCEIVE)]
conception /kən'sepʃ(ə)n/ *n.* conceiving or being conceived; result of this, idea; **conceptional** *a.*; **conceptive** *a.* [F f. L (prec.)]
conceptual /kən'septjʊəl/ *a.* of mental conceptions or concepts; **conceptually** *adv.* [med.L (CONCEPT)]
conceptualize *v.t.* form a concept or idea of.
concern /kən'sɜ:n/ **1** *v.t.* be relevant or important to; affect, worry; relate to, be about. **2** *n.* thing of interest or importance to one (*it's no concern of mine*); related or interested condition or feeling, connection (*has a concern in politics*); (feeling of) anxiety or worry; (in *pl.*) one's affairs; business or firm; *colloq.* thing, contrivance. **3 be concerned in** take part in; **concern oneself** feel an interest or anxiety (*in*, *about*, etc.), have desire to deal *with*. **4 concernment** *n.* [F or L (*cerno* sift)]
concerned *a.* anxious or troubled (*am very concerned about her, to hear your story, that you are ill*); involved or interested; **concernedly** /-ɪdlɪ/ *adv.*; **concernedness** /-ɪdnɪs/ *n.*
concerning *prep.* about, regarding.
concert /'kɒnsət/ *n.* musical entertainment by usu. several performers; combination of voices or sounds; agreement, working together; **concert pitch** pitch internationally agreed for concert performance. [F f. It. (CONCERTO)]
concerted /kən'sɜ:tɪd/ *a.* effected by mutual agreement, done in co-operation; *Mus.* arranged in parts for voices or instruments.
concertina /kɒnsə'ti:nə/ **1** *n.* portable musical instrument resembling accordion but smaller. **2** *v.* compress or collapse in folds like those of concertina.
concerto /kən'tʃeətəʊ, -'tʃɜ:t-/ *n.* (*pl.* **concertos** or **-ti** /-ɪ/) musical composition for solo instrument(s) and orchestra. [It.]
concession /kən'seʃ(ə)n/ *n.* conceding; thing conceded, esp. grant of land for extraction of minerals, trading rights, etc.; reduction in price for certain category of person; **concessionary** *a.* [F or L (CONCEDE)]
concessionaire /kənseʃə'neə/ *n.* holder of concession. [F (prec.)]
concessive /kən'sesɪv/ *a. Gram.* expressing concession, of words such as *although* or *even if*. [L (CONCEDE)]
conch /kɒntʃ/ *n.* spiral shell of certain shellfish; such shellfish, esp. large gastropod. [L *concha* f. Gk *kogkhē*]
conchology /kɒŋ'kɒlədʒɪ/ *n.* study of shells and shellfish. [CONCH]
concierge /'kɒnsɪeəʒ/ *n.* door-keeper or porter (esp. of block of flats) in France etc. [F]
conciliate /kən'sɪlɪeɪt/ *v.t.* win over from anger or hostility, win goodwill of; reconcile (disagreeing parties); **conciliation** /-'eɪʃ(ə)n/ *n.*; **conciliator** *n.*; **conciliatory** *a.* [L (COUNCIL)]
concise /kən'saɪs/ *a.* (of speech, writing, style, etc.) brief but comprehensive in expression; **concision** /-'sɪʒ(ə)n/ *n.* [F or L (*caedo* cut)]
conclave /'kɒnkleɪv/ *n.* private meeting; meeting-place or assembly of cardinals for election of pope. [F f. L (*clavis* key)]

conclude /kən'klu:d/ *v.* bring or come to an end; arrange, settle finally (treaty etc.); draw conclusion (*that*). [L *concludo* (CLOSE[1])]

conclusion /kən'klu:ʒ(ə)n/ *n.* ending, end; judgement or opinion based on reasoning; settling or concluding (*of* peace etc.); proposition in logic reached from previous ones; **in conclusion** lastly, to conclude. [F or L (prec.)]

conclusive /kən'klu:sɪv/ *a.* decisive, completely convincing. [L (CONCLUDE)]

concoct /kən'kɒkt/ *v.t.* prepare, esp. by mixing variety of ingredients; invent (story or plot); **concoction** /-'kɒkʃ(ə)n/ *n.* [L (*coquo coct-* cook)]

concomitant /kən'kɒmɪtənt/ **1** *a.* accompanying. **2** *n.* accompanying thing. **3** **concomitance** *n.* [L (*comes comit-* companion)]

concord /'kɒŋkɔ:d/ *n.* agreement, harmony; *Mus.* chord or interval satisfactory in itself; *Gram.* agreement between words in gender, number, etc.; **concordant** /kən'kɔ:dənt/ *a.* [F f. L (*cor cord-* heart)]

concordance /kən'kɔ:dəns/ *n.* agreement; alphabetical index of words used by author or in book. [F f. med.L (prec.)]

concordat /kən'kɔ:dæt/ *n.* official agreement, esp. between Church and State. [F or L (CONCORD)]

concourse /'kɒŋkɔ:s/ *n.* crowd, gathering; large open area in railway station etc. [F f. L (CONCUR)]

concrete /'kɒŋkri:t/ **1** *n.* mixture of cement with sand and gravel, used in building. **2** *a.* existing in material form, real; definite, positive (*concrete evidence, proposals*); *Gram.* (of noun) denoting thing not quality or state etc. **3** *v.* cover with or embed in concrete; /kən'kri:t/ form into a mass, solidify. **4** **concrete music** music prepared from recorded (natural or man-made) sounds; **concrete poetry** poetry using typographical devices to enhance effect. [F or L (*cresco cret-* grow)]

concretion /kən'kri:ʃ(ə)n/ *n.* hard solid mass; forming of this by coalescence. [F f. L (prec.)]

concubine /'kɒŋkjʊbaɪn/ *n.* woman cohabiting with a man to whom she is not married; second wife in polygamous societies; **concubinage** /kən'kju:bɪnɪdʒ/ *n.* [F f. L (*cubo* lie)]

concupiscence /kən'kju:pɪsəns/ *n.* intense sexual desire; **concupiscent** *a.* [F f. L (*cupio* desire)]

concur /kən'kɜ:/ *v.i.* (-rr-) agree in opinion (*with*); happen together, coincide. [L (*curro* run)]

concurrence /kən'kʌrəns/ *n.* agreement; simultaneous occurrence of events.

concurrent *a.* existing or acting together or at the same time; running in same direction, (of three or more lines) meeting at or tending to one point.

concuss /kən'kʌs/ *v.t.* subject to concussion. [L (*quatio* shake)]

concussion /kən'kʌʃ(ə)n/ *n.* injury to brain caused by heavy blow, fall, etc.; violent shaking.

condemn /kən'dem/ *v.t.* express utter disapproval of; pronounce guilty, convict; sentence *to* punishment; pronounce unfit for use or habitation; assign unpleasant future or fate to; **condemnation** /kɒndem'neɪʃ(ə)n/ *n.*; **condemnatory** /kən'demnətərɪ/ *a.* [F f. L (DAMN)]

condensation /kɒnden'seɪʃ(ə)n/ *n.* condensing; condensed material (esp. water on cold windows etc.); abridgement. [L (foll.)]

condense /kən'dens/ *v.* make denser or more concentrated; change or be changed from gas or vapour into liquid; express in fewer words; **condensed milk** milk thickened by evaporation and sweetened. [F or L (DENSE)]

condenser *n.* apparatus or vessel for condensing vapour; *Electr.* = CAPACITOR; lens system for concentrating light.

condescend /kɒndɪ'send/ *v.i.* be gracious enough (*to do* thing) esp. while showing one's feeling of dignity or superiority; disregard one's superiority (*to* person). [F f. L (DESCEND)]

condescending *a.* patronizing, kind to inferiors.

condescension /kɒndɪ'senʃ(ə)n/ *n.* affability to inferiors; patronizing manner.

condign /kən'daɪn/ *a.* (of punishment etc.) severe and well-deserved. [F f. L (*dignus* worthy)]

condiment /'kɒndɪmənt/ *n.* seasoning or relish for food. [L *condio* pickle]

condition /kən'dɪʃ(ə)n/ **1** *n.* stipulation, thing upon the fulfilment of which something else depends; state of being of person or thing; state of physical fitness or (of things) fitness for use; ailment or abnormality (*heart condition*); (in *pl.*) circumstances, esp. those affecting the functioning or existence of something (*working conditions are good*). **2** *v.t.* bring into desired state or condition; make fit (esp. dogs or horses); train, accustom; impose condition on, be essential to. **3** **conditioned reflex** reflex response to non-natural stimulus, established by training; **in** (or **out of**) **condition** in good (or bad) condition;

on condition that with the condition that. [F f. L (*dico* say)]
conditional *a.* dependent (*on*); not absolute, containing a condition or stipulation; *Gram.* (of clause, mood, etc.) expressing a condition; **conditionally** *adv.* [F or L (prec.)]
condole /kən'dəʊl/ *v.i.* express sympathy (*with* person *on* loss etc.); **condolence** *n.* [L *condoleo* grieve with another]
condom /'kɒndəm/ *n.* contraceptive sheath. [orig. unkn.]
condominium /kɒndə'mɪnɪəm/ *n.* joint control of a State's affairs by other States; *US* building in which flats are individually owned. [L *dominium* lordship]
condone /kən'dəʊn/ *v.t.* forgive or overlook (offence or wrongdoing); **condonation** /kɒndə'neɪʃ(ə)n/ *n.* [L (*dono* give)]
condor /'kɒndɔ:/ *n.* large vulture of S. America. [Sp. f. Quechua]
conduce /kən'dju:s/ *v.i.* tend to lead or contribute *to* (result); **conducive** *a.* [L (foll.)]
conduct 1 /'kɒndʌkt/ *n.* behaviour (esp. in its moral aspect); manner of directing and managing (business, war). **2** /kən'dʌkt/ *v.* lead or guide; direct or manage (business etc.); be conductor of (orchestra etc.); transmit (heat, electricity, etc.) by conduction. **3 conduct oneself** act (*well*, *badly*, etc.). [L (*duco duct-* lead)]
conductance /kən'dʌktəns/ *n.* power of specified body to conduct electricity.
conduction /kən'dʌkʃ(ə)n/ *n.* transmission or conducting of heat, electricity, etc. [F or L (CONDUCT)]
conductive /kən'dʌktɪv/ *a.* having the property of conducting heat or electricity etc.; **conductivity** /kɒndʌk'tɪvɪtɪ/ *n.* [CONDUCT]
conductor *n.* person who directs performance of orchestra or choir etc.; person who collects fares in bus etc.; substance that conducts heat or electricity; **conductress** *n. fem.* (in 2nd sense). [F f. L (CONDUCT)]
conduit /'kɒndɪt, -djʊɪt/ *n.* channel or pipe for conveying liquids; tube or trough for protecting insulated electric wires. [F f. med.L (CONDUCT)]
cone *n.* solid figure with circular plane base, narrowing to a point; thing of similar shape, solid or hollow; dry fruit of pine or fir etc.; ice-cream cornet. [F f. L f. Gk]
coney var. of CONY.
confab /'kɒnfæb/ *colloq.* **1** *n.* confabulation. **2** *v.i.* (**-bb-**) confabulate. [abbr.]
confabulate /kən'fæbjʊleɪt/ *v.i.* converse, chat; **confabulation** /-'leɪʃ(ə)n/ *n.* [L (FABLE)]
confection /kən'fekʃ(ə)n/ *n.* dish or delicacy made with sweet ingredients; cake, sweet. [F f. L (*conficio* prepare)]
confectioner *n.* maker or retailer of confectionery.
confectionery *n.* confections, esp. sweets.
confederacy /kən'fedərəsɪ/ *n.* league or alliance, esp. of confederate States. [F (foll.)]
confederate /kən'fedərət/ **1** *a.* allied. **2** *n.* ally, esp. (in bad sense) accomplice; (**Confederate**) supporter of the Confederate States. **3** /-reɪt/ *v.* bring or come into alliance (*with*). **4 Confederate States** States which seceded from the US in 1860–1. [L (FEDERAL)]
confederation /kənfedə'reɪʃ(ə)n/ *n.* forming or being formed in alliance etc.; union or alliance of States.
confer /kən'fɜ:/ *v.* (**-rr-**) grant or bestow; hold a conference or discussion; **conferrable** *a.* [L *confero collat-* bring together]
conference /'kɒnfərəns/ *n.* consultation; meeting (esp. regular one) for discussion etc. [F or med.L (prec.)]
conferment /kən'fɜ:mənt/ *n.* conferring (of degree, honour, etc.). [CONFER]
confess /kən'fes/ *v.* acknowledge or own or admit (fault, wrongdoing, etc.); admit reluctantly (unwelcome fact etc.); declare one's sins formally, esp. to a priest; (of priest) hear confession of. [F f. L *confiteor -fess-*]
confessedly /kən'fesɪdlɪ/ *adv.* by personal or general admission.
confession /kən'feʃ(ə)n/ *n.* confessing (of offence, etc.; of sins to priest); thing confessed; declaration of one's religious beliefs, statement of one's principles (*confession of faith*).
confessional 1 *n.* enclosed stall in church in which priest sits to hear confession. **2** *a.* of confession.
confessor *n.* priest who hears confession and gives spiritual counsel; one who avows his religion.
confetti /kən'fetɪ/ *n.* small bits of coloured paper thrown by wedding guests at bride and bridegroom. [It.]
confidant /kɒnfɪ'dænt/ *n.* person trusted with knowledge of one's private affairs; **confidante** *n. fem.* [foll.]
confide /kən'faɪd/ *v.* tell (secret *to*); entrust (object of care, task, *to*); **confide in** talk confidentially to. [L *confido* trust]
confidence /'kɒnfɪdəns/ *n.* firm trust; feeling of reliance or certainty, sense of self-reliance, boldness; something told confidentially; **confidence man** one who robs by means of a confidence trick; **confidence trick** swindle in which victim is persuaded to trust swindler in some way; **in confidence** as a secret;

in person's confidence trusted with his secrets; **take into one's confidence** confide in. [L (prec.)]

confident *a.* feeling or showing confidence, bold. [F f. It. (CONFIDE)]

confidential /kɒnfɪ'denʃ(ə)l/ *a.* spoken or written in confidence; entrusted with secrets (*confidential secretary*); confiding; **confidentially** *adv.*; **confidentiality** /-ʃɪ'ælɪtɪ/ *n.*

configuration /kənfɪgjʊə'reɪʃ(ə)n/ *n.* manner of arrangement, shape, outline. [L (FIGURE)]

confine 1 /kən'faɪn/ *v.t.* keep or restrict within certain limits; imprison. 2 /'kɒnfaɪn/ *n.* (usu. in *pl.*) limit, boundary of area. 3 **be confined** be in childbirth. [F f. L (*finis* limit)]

confinement *n.* confining or being confined; childbirth.

confirm /kən'fɜ:m/ *v.t.* provide support for truth or correctness of; establish more firmly, encourage (person *in* opinion etc.); formally make definite or valid; administer rite of confirmation to; **confirmative** *a.*; **confirmatory** *a.* [F f. L (FIRM)]

confirmation /kɒnfə'meɪʃ(ə)n/ *n.* confirming; corroboration; religious rite confirming baptized person, esp. at age of discretion, as member of Christian Church.

confirmed *a.* firmly settled in some habit or condition (*confirmed bachelor, optimist*).

confiscate /'kɒnfɪskeɪt/ *v.t.* take or seize by authority; **confiscation** /-'keɪʃ(ə)n/ *n.* [L (FISCAL)]

conflagration /kɒnflə'greɪʃ(ə)n/ *n.* great and destructive fire. [L (FLAGRANT)]

conflate /kən'fleɪt/ *v.t.* blend or fuse together, esp. two variant texts into one. **conflation** /-'fleɪʃ(ə)n/ *n.* [L (*flo flat-* blow)]

conflict 1 /'kɒnflɪkt/ *n.* fight, struggle; clashing (*of* opposed principles etc.). 2 /kən'flɪkt/ *v.i.* struggle (*with*); clash, be incompatible. [L (*fligo flict-* strike)]

confluence /'kɒnfluəns/ *n.* place where two rivers meet; coming together, crowd of people. [L (*fluo* flow)]

confluent 1 *a.* flowing together, uniting. 2 *n.* stream joining another.

conform /kən'fɔ:m/ *v.* (cause to) fit or be suitable; comply with rules or general custom; **conform to** (or **with**) comply with, be in accordance with. [F f. L (FORM)]

conformable *a.* similar (*to*); consistent (*with*), adaptable (*to*).

conformation /kɒnfɔ:'meɪʃ(ə)n/ *n.* way in which thing is formed, structure.

conformist /kən'fɔ:mɪst/ *n.* one who conforms to an established practice; **conformism** *n.*

conformity *n.* conforming with established practice; agreement, suitability.

confound /kən'faʊnd/ 1 *v.t.* perplex, baffle; confuse; *archaic* defeat, overthrow. 2 *int.* of annoyance (*confound it!*). [F f. L *confundo -fus-* mix up]

confounded *a. colloq.* damned (*a confounded nuisance*).

confrère /'kɒnfreə/ *n.* fellow member of profession etc. [F f. med.L]

confront /kən'frʌnt/ *v.t.* meet or stand facing; face in hostility or defiance; (of difficulty etc.) present itself to; bring (person) face to face *with* (accusers etc.); **confrontation** /kɒnfrʌn'teɪʃ(ə)n/ *n.* [F f. med.L]

Confucian /kən'fju:ʃ(ə)n/ *a.* of Confucius or his philosophy; **Confucianism** *n.* [*Confucius*, Chin. philosopher]

confuse /kən'fju:z/ *v.t.* throw into disorder; disconcert, perplex, bewilder; mix up in the mind, fail to distinguish between; make indistinct (*confuse the issue*); **confusedly** /-ɪdlɪ/ *adv.* [CONFOUND]

confusion *n.* act or result of confusing.

confute /kən'fju:t/ *v.t.* prove (person or contention) to be in error; **confutation** /kɒnfjʊ'teɪʃ(ə)n/ *n.* [L]

congé /'kɔ:nʒeɪ/ *n.* unceremonious dismissal; leave-taking. [F f. L *commeatus* leave of absence]

congeal /kən'dʒi:l/ *v.* (cause to) become semi-solid by cooling; (of blood etc.) coagulate; **congelation** /kɒndʒɪ'leɪʃ(ə)n/ *n.* [F f. L (*gelo* freeze)]

congener /'kɒndʒɪnə/ *n.* thing or person of same kind or class. [L (GENUS)]

congenial /kən'dʒi:nɪəl/ *a.* pleasant because like oneself in temperament or interests; suited or agreeable (*to*); **congeniality** /-'ælɪtɪ/ *n.*; **congenially** *adv.* [COM-]

congenital /kən'dʒenɪt(ə)l/ *a.* existing or as such from birth (*congenital disease, idiot*); **congenitally** *adv.*

conger /'kɒŋgə/ *n.* large sea eel. [F f. L f. Gk *goggros*]

congeries /kən'dʒɪəri:z/ *n.* (*pl.* same) disorderly collection, mass, heap. [L (*congero* heap together)]

congest /kən'dʒest/ *v.t.* (usu. in *p.p.*) affect with congestion.

congestion /kən'dʒestʃ(ə)n/ *n.* abnormal accumulation or obstruction, esp. of traffic etc. or of blood in part of the body.

conglomerate /kən'glɒmərət/ 1 *a.* gathered into a rounded mass. 2 *n.* conglomerate mass; group or corporation formed by merging of separate firms.

3 /-'reɪt/ *v.* collect into a coherent mass. **4 conglomeration** /-'reɪʃ(ə)n/ *n.* [L (*glomus -eris* ball)]

congratulate /kən'grætjʊleɪt/ *v.t.* express pleasure at happiness or excellence or good fortune of (person *on* event etc.); **congratulate oneself** think oneself fortunate; **congratulatory** *a.* [L (*gratus* pleasing)]

congratulation /kəngrætjʊ'leɪʃ(ə)n/ *n.* congratulating; (usu. in *pl.*) expression of this.

congregate /'kɒŋgrɪgeɪt/ *v.* collect or gather into a crowd. [L (*grex greg-* flock)]

congregation /kɒngrɪ'geɪʃ(ə)n/ *n.* gathering of persons, esp. for religious worship; body of persons regularly attending a particular church etc. [F or L (prec.)]

congregational *a.* of a congregation; (**Congregational**) of or adhering to Congregationalism.

Congregationalism *n.* system of ecclesiastical organization whereby individual churches are largely self-governing; **Congregationalist** *n.* ¶ In England and Wales largely merged in United Reformed Church from 1972.

congress /'kɒŋgres/ *n.* formal meeting of delegates for discussion; (**Congress**) national legislative body, esp. of US; **congressional** /-'greʃən(ə)l/ *a.* [L (*gradior gress-* walk)]

congruent /'kɒŋgrʊənt/ *a.* suitable, agreeing (*with*); (of geometric figures) coinciding exactly when superimposed; **congruence** *n.*; **congruency** *n.* [F, or L (*congruo* agree)]

congruous /'kɒŋgrʊəs/ *a.* suitable, agreeing; fitting; **congruity** /-'gru:ɪtɪ/ *n.* [L (prec.)]

conic /'kɒnɪk/ *a.* of a cone; **conic section** figure formed by intersection of cone and plane. [L f. Gk (CONE)]

conical *a.* cone-shaped.

conifer /'kɒnɪfə, 'kəʊn-/ *n.* tree that bears cones; **coniferous** /kə'nɪfərəs/ *a.* [L (CONE)]

conjectural /kən'dʒektʃər(ə)l/ *a.* based on or involving conjecture. [foll.]

conjecture /kən'dʒektʃə/ **1** *n.* formation of opinion on incomplete grounds; guessing; guess. **2** *v.* guess. [F, or L *conjectura* (*jacio* throw)]

conjoin /kən'dʒɔɪn/ *v.* join, combine. [F f. L (JOIN)]

conjoint /'kɒndʒɔɪnt/ *a.* associated, conjoined.

conjugal /'kɒndʒʊg(ə)l/ *a.* of marriage or the relationship of husband and wife; **conjugally** *adv.* [L (*conjux* consort)]

conjugate /'kɒndʒʊgeɪt/ **1** *v.* give the different forms of verb; unite; become fused. **2** /-gət/ *a.* joined together, coupled, fused. **3** /-gət/ *n.* conjugate word or thing. [L (*jugum* yoke)]

conjugation /kɒndʒʊ'geɪʃ(ə)n/ *n.* *Gram.* system of verbal inflexion.

conjunct /kən'dʒʌŋkt/ *a.* joined together; combined; associated. [L (foll.)]

conjunction /kən'dʒʌŋkʃ(ə)n/ *n.* joining, connection; *Gram.* word used to connect clauses or sentences, or words in same clause (e.g. *and*, *but*, *if*); combination of events or circumstances; apparent proximity of two heavenly bodies to each other. [F f. L (CONJOIN)]

conjunctiva /kɒndʒʌŋk'taɪvə/ *n.* mucous membrane connecting eyeball and inner eyelids. [med.L (foll.)]

conjunctive /kən'dʒʌŋktɪv/ *a.* serving to join; *Gram.* of the nature of a conjunction. [L (CONJOIN)]

conjunctivitis /kəndʒʌŋktɪ'vaɪtɪs/ *n.* inflammation of the conjunctiva. [-ITIS]

conjuncture /kən'dʒʌŋktʃə/ *n.* combination of events; state of affairs. [F f. It. (CONJOIN)]

conjure /'kʌndʒə/ *v.* perform tricks which are deceptive or seemingly unnatural, esp. by movements of the hands; summon (a spirit) to appear; **conjure up** produce as if from nothing, evoke. [F f. L (*juro* swear)]

conjuror *n.* (also **conjurer**) skilled performer of conjuring tricks.

conk[1] *v.i.* *colloq.* in **conk out** (of machine etc.) break down; (of person) become exhausted and give up, faint, die. [orig. unkn.]

conk[2] *v.t.* *sl.* hit on the head. [perh. = CONCH]

conker *n.* horse-chestnut fruit; (in *pl.*) children's game played with these on strings. [dial. *conker* snail-shell]

conn *US* var. of CON[3].

connect /kə'nekt/ *v.* join (two things, or one *to* or *with* another); be joined (*with*); associate mentally or practically (*with*); (of train etc.) be synchronized at destination *with* another train etc. allowing passengers to transfer; put into communication by telephone; (usu. in *pass.*) unite or associate *with* others in relationships etc.; be meaningful or relevant; *colloq.* hit target with blow etc.; **connecting-rod** rod between piston and crankpin etc. in engine. [L (*necto nex-* bind)]

connected *a.* having specified relationships (*well connected*).

connection /kə'nekʃ(ə)n/ *n.* (also **connexion**) act of connecting; state of being connected or related; relation or association of ideas; connecting part; relative or close associate, group of associates or clients; connecting train etc.; *sl.* supplier of narcotics.

connective *a.* serving to connect, esp. of body tissue connecting and supporting organs etc.
connector *n.* thing that connects.
conning-tower *n.* raised structure of submarine containing periscope; armoured pilot-house on warship. [CON³]
connive /kə'naɪv/ *v.i.* (with *at*) disregard or tacitly consent to (wrongdoing); **connivance** *n.* [F, or L *conniveo* shut the eyes]
connoisseur /kɒnə'sɜː/ *n.* expert judge (*of* or *in* matters of taste, esp. in the fine arts). [F (*connaître* know)]
connote /kə'nəʊt/ *v.t.* (of word) imply in addition to the literal meaning; mean, signify; **connotation** /-'teɪʃ(ə)n/ *n.*; **connotative** /'kɒnəʊteɪtɪv/ *a.* [med.L (NOTE)]
connubial /kə'njuːbɪəl/ *a.* of marriage or the relationship of husband and wife. [L (*nubo* marry)]
conquer /'kɒŋkə/ *v.* overcome and control militarily; win, be victorious; overcome by effort; **conqueror** *n.* [F f. L *conquiro* win]
conquest /'kɒnkwest/ *n.* conquering; conquered territory; something won; person whose affections have been won; **the (Norman) Conquest** conquest of England by William of Normandy in 1066.
consanguineous /kɒnsæŋ'gwɪnɪəs/ *a.* descended from same ancestor, akin; **consanguinity** *n.* [L (*sanguis* blood)]
conscience /'kɒnʃəns/ *n.* moral sense of right and wrong, esp. as felt by person and affecting his behaviour; **conscience clause** clause in a law, ensuring respect for consciences of those affected; **conscience money** sum paid to relieve one's conscience, esp. about payment previously evaded; **conscience-stricken** (or **-struck**) made uneasy by bad conscience; **in all conscience** by any reasonable standard; **on one's conscience** causing one feelings of guilt. [F f. L (SCIENCE)]
conscientious /kɒnʃɪ'enʃəs/ *a.* (of person or conduct) obedient to conscience, scrupulous, assiduous; **conscientious objector** person who for reasons of conscience objects to military service etc. [F f. med.L (prec.)]
conscious /'kɒnʃəs/ **1** *a.* awake and aware of one's surroundings and identity; knowing, aware (*of* or *that*); (of actions, emotions, etc.) realized or recognized by the doer, intentional; (as *suffix*) aware of or concerned with (*class-conscious*). **2** *n. the* conscious mind. [L (*scio* know)]
consciousness *n.* awareness; person's conscious thoughts and feelings as a whole.
conscript **1** /kən'skrɪpt/ *v.t.* summon for compulsory State (esp. military) service. **2** /'kɒnskrɪpt/ *n.* conscripted person. **3** **conscription** /kən'skrɪpʃ(ə)n/ *n.* [F f. L (*scribo* write)]
consecrate /'kɒnsɪkreɪt/ *v.t.* make or declare sacred, dedicate formally to religious or divine purpose; devote *to* purpose; **consecration** /-'kreɪʃ(ə)n/ *n.* [L (SACRED)]
consecutive /kən'sekjʊtɪv/ *a.* following continuously; in unbroken or logical order; *Gram.* expressing consequence. [L (*sequor secut-* follow)]
consensus /kən'sensəs/ *n.* agreement in opinion; majority view (*consensus government*). [L (foll.)]
consent /kən'sent/ **1** *v.i.* express willingness, give permission, agree (*to*). **2** *n.* voluntary agreement, compliance, permission. **3** **age of consent** age at which consent to sexual intercourse is valid in law. [F f. L (*sentio* feel)]
consequence /'kɒnsɪkwəns/ *n.* what follows logically or effectively from some causal action or condition; importance; **in consequence** as a result (of); **take the consequences** accept whatever results from one's choice or action. [F f. L (CONSECUTIVE)]
consequent **1** *a.* following as a consequence (*on* or *upon*); logically consistent. **2** *n.* thing that follows another.
consequential /kɒnsɪ'kwenʃ(ə)l/ *a.* consequent; resulting indirectly; (of person, manner, etc.) self-important.
conservancy /kən'sɜːvənsɪ/ *n.* body controlling a port or river etc., or concerned with preservation of natural resources. [AF f. L (foll.)]
conservation /kɒnsə'veɪʃ(ə)n/ *n.* preservation, esp. of natural environment; **conservation of energy** principle that quantity of energy of any system of bodies not subject to external action remains constant. [F or L (CONSERVE)]
conservationist *n.* supporter or advocate of environmental conservation.
conservative /kən'sɜːvətɪv/ **1** *a.* tending to conserve; averse to rapid changes; (of views, taste, etc.) moderate, avoiding extremes; (of estimate etc.) purposely low. **2** *n.* conservative person; **(Conservative)** member or supporter of the Conservative Party. **3** **Conservative Party** political party disposed to maintain existing institutions and promote private enterprise; **conservatism** *n.* [L (CONSERVE)]
conservatoire /kən'sɜːvətwɑː/ *n.* (usu. European) school of music or other arts. [F f. It.]

conservatory /kən'sɜːvətərɪ/ *n.* greenhouse for tender plants, with communicating entrance from house; *US* = CONSERVATOIRE. [L & It. (foll.)]
conserve /kən'sɜːv/ **1** *v.t.* keep from harm, decay, or loss, esp. for future use. **2** *n.* jam, esp. made from fresh fruit. [F f. L (*servo* keep)]
consider /kən'sɪdə/ *v.t.* contemplate mentally, esp. in order to reach a conclusion; look attentively at; bring to or keep in mind; examine merits of (course of action, claim, candidate, etc.); make allowance or be thoughtful for (person, feelings, etc.); regard as; have the opinion *that*; (in *p.p.*, of opinion etc.) formed after careful thought; **all things considered** taking everything into account. [F f. L]
considerable *a.* not negligible, fairly great, in amount or extent etc.; of some importance; **considerably** *adv.*
considerate /kən'sɪdərət/ *a.* thoughtful for others, careful not to cause inconvenience or hurt. [L (CONSIDER)]
consideration /kənsɪdə'reɪʃ(ə)n/ *n.* careful thought; being considerate, kindness; fact or thing regarded as a reason; compensation, reward; **in consideration of** in return for, on account of; **take into consideration** make allowance for; **under consideration** being considered.
considering *prep.* in view of, taking into consideration; (*ellipt.*) *colloq.* in view of the circumstances (*that's good, considering*).
consign /kən'saɪn/ *v.t.* hand over or deliver; assign or commit *to* (misery, person's care, etc.); send (goods) *to*; **consignee** /-'niː/ *n.*; **consignor** *n.* [F f. L (SIGN)]
consignment *n.* consigning; goods consigned.
consist /kən'sɪst/ *v.i.* be composed *of*; have its essential features *in*; be consistent *with*. [L (*sisto* stand)]
consistency /kən'sɪstənsɪ/ *n.* degree of density, firmness, or solidity, esp. of thick liquids; being consistent. [F or L (prec.)]
consistent *a.* compatible or in harmony (*with*); (of person) constant to same principles of thought or action. [L (CONSIST)]
consistory /kən'sɪstərɪ/ *n.* council of cardinals, or of pope and cardinals. [AF f. L (CONSIST)]
consolation /kɒnsə'leɪʃ(ə)n/ *n.* act of consoling; consoling circumstance; **consolation prize** prize given to competitor who just fails to win a main prize; **consolatory** *a.* [F f. L (foll.)]
console[1] /kən'səʊl/ *v.t.* comfort, esp. in grief or disappointment. [F f. L (SOLACE)]
console[2] /'kɒnsəʊl/ *n.* bracket supporting a shelf etc.; cabinet with keys and stops of an organ; panel for switches, controls, etc.; cabinet for radio etc. equipment. [F]
consolidate /kən'sɒlɪdeɪt/ *v.* make or become strong or solid (*lit.* or *fig.*); combine (territories, companies, debts, etc.) into one whole; **consolidation** /-'deɪʃ(ə)n/ *n.*; **consolidator** *n.* [L (SOLID)]
consols /'kɒnsɒlz/ *n.pl.* British government securities. [abbr. of *consolidated annuities*]
consommé /kən'sɒmeɪ/ *n.* clear meat soup. [F]
consonance /'kɒnsənəns/ *n.* agreement or harmony. [F or L (*sono* SOUND[1])]
consonant 1 *n.* speech sound in which breath is at least partly obstructed, combining with vowel to form syllable; letter representing this. **2** *a.* in agreement or harmony *with*; agreeable *to*. **3 consonantal** /-'nænt(ə)l/ *a.*
consort[1] **1** /'kɒnsɔːt/ *n.* wife or husband, esp. of reigning monarch; ship sailing with another. **2** /kən'sɔːt/ *v.i.* associate or keep company (*with, together*); be in harmony (*with*). [F f. L (SORT)]
consort[2] /'kɒnsɔːt/ *n. Mus.* group of players or instruments. [var. of CONCERT]
consortium /kən'sɔːtɪəm/ *n.* (*pl.* **consortia**) association, esp. of several business companies. [L (CONSORT[1])]
conspectus /kən'spektəs/ *n.* general view or survey; synopsis. [L (*specio* look)]
conspicuous /kən'spɪkjʊəs/ *a.* clearly visible, attracting attention; noteworthy, striking. [as prec.]
conspiracy /kən'spɪrəsɪ/ *n.* act of conspiring; unlawful combination or plot; **conspiracy of silence** agreement to say nothing. [F f. L (CONSPIRE)]
conspirator /kən'spɪrətə/ *n.* one who takes part in a conspiracy; **conspiratorial** /-'tɔːrɪəl/ *a.*
conspire /kən'spaɪə/ *v.i.* combine secretly for unlawful or harmful purpose; (of events) seem to be working together. [F f. L (*spiro* breathe)]
constable /'kʌnstəb(ə)l/ *n.* policeman; policeman or policewoman of lowest rank; governor of royal castle; *hist.* principal officer of royal household; **Chief Constable** head of police force of county etc. [F f. L *comes stabuli* count of the stable]
constabulary /kən'stæbjʊlərɪ/ *n.* police force. [med.L (prec.)]
constancy /'kɒnstənsɪ/ *n.* quality of being unchanging and dependable; faithfulness. [L (foll.)]

constant 1 *a.* continuous (*needs constant attention*); frequently occurring (*receive constant complaints*); unchanging, faithful, dependable. **2** *n.* anything that does not vary; *Math.* & *Physics* quantity or number of constant value. **3 constantly** *adv.* [F f. L (*sto* stand)]

constellation /kɒnstə'leɪʃ(ə)n/ *n.* group of fixed stars; group of associated people etc. [F f. L (*stella* star)]

consternation /kɒnstə'neɪʃ(ə)n/ *n.* amazement or dismay causing mental confusion. [F or L (*sterno* throw down)]

constipate /'kɒnstɪpeɪt/ *v.t.* affect with constipation. [F or L (*stipo* cram)]

constipation /kɒnstɪ'peɪʃ(ə)n/ *n.* condition with hardened faeces and difficulty in emptying the bowels.

constituency /kən'stɪtjʊənsɪ/ *n.* body of voters who elect a representative; area so represented. [foll.]

constituent /kən'stɪtjʊənt/ **1** *a.* composing or helping to make a whole (*constituent part*); able to make or change a constitution (*constituent assembly, power*); electing a representative (*constituent body*). **2** *n.* constituent part; member of constituency. [L (foll.)]

constitute /'kɒnstɪtju:t/ *v.t.* compose, be the essence or components of; appoint, set up (assembly etc.) in legal form; form, establish (*does not constitute a precedent*). [L *constituo* establish]

constitution /kɒnstɪ'tju:ʃ(ə)n/ *n.* act or method of constituting, composition; form in which State is organized; body of fundamental principles by which a State or body is governed; condition of person's body as regards health, strength, etc. [F or L (prec.)]

constitutional **1** *a.* of or in harmony with or limited by the constitution. **2** *n.* walk taken regularly as healthy exercise. **3 constitutionality** /-'nælɪtɪ/ *n.*; **constitutionally** *adv.*

constitutive /'kɒnstɪtju:tɪv/ *a.* able to form or appoint, constituent; essential.

constrain /kən'streɪn/ *v.t.* urge irresistibly or by necessity; confine forcibly, imprison (*lit.* or *fig.*); (in *p.p.*, of voice, manner, etc.) forced, embarrassed. [F f. L (*stringo strict-* bind)]

constraint /kən'streɪnt/ *n.* act or result of constraining or being constrained; restriction; emotional etc. self-control.

constrict /kən'strɪkt/ *v.t.* compress, make narrow or tight; **constriction** *n.*; **constrictive** *a.* [L (CONSTRAIN)]

constrictor *n.* muscle that draws together or narrows a part; snake that kills by compressing.

construct **1** /kən'strʌkt/ *v.t.* make by fitting parts together, build, form (*lit.* or *fig.*); *Geom.* delineate (figure). **2** /'kɒnstrʌkt/ *n.* thing constructed, esp. by the mind. **3 constructor** /-'strʌktə/ *n.* [L (*struo struct-* build)]

construction /kən'strʌkʃ(ə)n/ *n.* constructing or thing constructed; syntactical connection of words in sentence; interpretation or explanation of statement or action; **constructional** *a.* [F f. L (prec.)]

constructive /kən'strʌktɪv/ *a.* tending to form basis for ideas, positive, helpful (*constructive arguments*); derived by inference. [L (CONSTRUCT)]

construe /kən'stru:/ *v.t.* interpret (words or actions); combine (words *with* others) grammatically; analyse syntax of (sentence); translate word for word. [L (CONSTRUCT)]

consubstantial /kɒnsəb'stænʃ(ə)l/ *a.* of one substance. [eccl.L (SUBSTANCE)]

consubstantiation /kɒnsəbstænʃɪeɪʃ(ə)n/ *n.* doctrine of presence of Christ's body and blood together with bread and wine in Eucharist.

consul /'kɒns(ə)l/ *n.* official appointed by State to live in foreign city and protect State's citizens and other interests there; *hist.* either of two annually-elected chief magistrates in ancient Rome; **consular** /-sjʊlə/ *a.*; **consulship** *n.* [L]

consulate /'kɒnsjʊlət/ *n.* position of consul; office or residence of consul.

consult /kən'sʌlt/ *v.* seek information or advice from (person, book, etc.); take counsel (*with*); take into consideration (feelings etc.). [F f. L *consulo consult-* take advice]

consultant *n.* person consulted for professional advice, esp. in branch of medicine; **consultancy** *n.*

consultation /kɒnsəl'teɪʃ(ə)n/ *n.* act or process of consulting; meeting for consulting.

consultative /kən'sʌltətɪv/ *a.* of or for consultation.

consume /kən'sju:m/ *v.t.* eat or drink; use up; destroy; (in *p.p.*) possessed by or entirely preoccupied *with* (envy etc.); **consumable** *a.* & *n.* [L (*consumo -sumpt-*)]

consumer *n.* one who consumes, esp. one who uses a product; person who buys or uses goods or services; **consumer research** investigation into needs and opinions of consumers.

consumerism *n.* protection or promotion of consumers' interests.

consummate **1** /kən'sʌmɪt/ *a.* complete; perfect; supremely skilled. **2** /'kɒnsəmeɪt/ *v.t.* make perfect or complete; complete (marriage) by sexual intercourse. **3 consummation** /-'meɪʃ(ə)n/ *n.* [L (*summus* utmost)]

consumption /kən'sʌmpʃ(ə)n/ *n.* consuming; purchase and use of goods etc.; amount consumed; wasting disease, esp. pulmonary tuberculosis. [F (CONSUME)]

consumptive /kən'sʌmptɪv/ **1** *a.* of or tending to consumption, affected with tuberculosis. **2** *n.* consumptive person. [med.L (as prec.)]

contact /'kɒntækt/ **1** *n.* condition or state of touching, meeting, or communicating; person who is, or may be, contacted for information, assistance, etc.; person likely to carry contagious disease through being near infected person; connection for passage of electric current. **2** /also kən'tækt/ *v.t.* get in touch with (person); begin communication or personal dealings with. **3 contact lens** small usu. plastic lens placed against eyeball to correct faulty vision. [L (*tango tact-* touch)]

contagion /kən'teɪdʒ(ə)n/ *n.* spreading of disease by bodily contact; disease so transmitted; corrupting moral influence. [as prec.]

contagious /kən'teɪdʒəs/ *a.* (of person) likely to transmit disease by bodily contact; (of disease) transmitted in this way.

contain /kən'teɪn/ *v.t.* have or hold, or have the capacity for holding, within itself; include, comprise; consist of or be equal to (*a pound contains 16 ounces*); enclose, prevent from moving or extending; control or restrain (feelings etc.); (of number) be divisible by (factor) without remainder. [F f. L (*teneo* hold)]

container *n.* box, jar, etc. for containing particular things; large boxlike receptacle of standard design for transport of goods.

containerize *v.t.* pack in or transport by container; **containerization** /-'zeɪʃ(ə)n/ *n.*

containment *n.* action or policy of preventing expansion of hostile country or influence.

contaminate /kən'tæmɪneɪt/ *v.t.* pollute, esp. with radioactivity; infect; **contaminant** *n.*; **contamination** /-'neɪʃ(ə)n/ *n.*; **contaminator** *n.* [L (*tamen-* rel. to *tango* touch)]

contemn /kən'tem/ *v.t. literary* despise; disregard. [F or L (*temno tempt-*)]

contemplate /'kɒntəmpleɪt/ *v.* survey with eyes or in mind; regard (event) as possible; intend; meditate; **contemplation** /-'pleɪʃ(ə)n/ *n.* [L]

contemplative /kən'templətɪv/ **1** *a.* of or given to (esp. religious) contemplation, meditative. **2** *n.* person devoted to religious contemplation. [F or L (prec.)]

contemporaneous /kəntempə'reɪnɪəs/ *a.* existing or occurring at the same time (*with*); **contemporaneity** /-'ni:ɪtɪ/ *n.* [L (COM-)]

contemporary /kən'tempərərɪ/ **1** *a.* belonging to same time or period; of same age; modern in style or design. **2** *n.* contemporary person or thing. [med.L (prec.)]

contempt /kən'tempt/ *n.* feeling that person or thing is worthless or beneath consideration, or deserving extreme reproach or scorn; condition of being held in contempt; (in full **contempt of court**) disrespect for or disobedience to court of law. [L (CONTEMN)]

contemptible *a.* deserving contempt; **contemptibly** *adv.* [F or L (prec.)]

contemptuous *a.* feeling or showing contempt. [med.L (CONTEMPT)]

contend /kən'tend/ *v.* struggle or compete; argue (*with*); assert or maintain (*that*). [F or L (TEND[1])]

content[1] /'kɒntent/ *n.* what is contained in thing, esp. in vessel, book, or house (usu. in *pl.*); capacity or volume; amount (of constituent) contained (*high fat content*); substance (of speech etc.) as distinct from form. [med.L (CONTAIN)]

content[2] /kən'tent/ **1** *predic. a.* satisfied, adequately happy; willing (*to do* thing). **2** *v.t.* make content, satisfy. **3** *n.* contented state, satisfaction. **4 to one's heart's content** to full extent of one's desires. [F f. L (CONTAIN)]

contented /kən'tentɪd/ *a.* satisfied; willing to be content *with*.

contention /kən'tenʃ(ə)n/ *n.* contending, argument or dispute; point contended for in argument. [F or L (CONTEND)]

contentious /kən'tenʃəs/ *a.* quarrelsome; likely to cause argument.

contentment *n.* satisfied state, tranquil happiness. [CONTENT[2]]

conterminous /kɒn'tɜ:mɪnəs/ *a.* having a common boundary (*with*). [L (TERMINUS)]

contest 1 /'kɒntest/ *n.* contending, strife; a competition. **2** /kən'test/ *v.* dispute (claim, statement); contend or compete for (prize, seat in parliament, etc.) or in (election). [L (*testis* witness)]

contestant /kən'testənt/ *n.* one who takes part in a contest.

context /'kɒntekst/ *n.* parts that precede and follow a word or passage and fix its precise meaning; circumstances; **out of context** without surrounding words and therefore misleading; **contextual** /-'tekstjʊəl/ *a.* [L (TEXT)]

contiguous /kən'tɪgjʊəs/ *a.* next (*to*); touching, in contact; **contiguity** /-'gju:ɪtɪ/ *n.* [L (CONTACT)]

continence /'kɒntɪnəns/ *n.* self-restraint, being continent. [foll.]

continent /'kɒntɪnənt/ **1** *n.* any of the

main continuous bodies of land (Europe, Asia, Africa, N. America, S. America, Australia, Antarctica). **2** *a.* exercising self-restraint, esp. sexually; able to control movements of the bowels and bladder. **3 the Continent** mainland of Europe as distinct from British Isles. [L (CONTAIN)]

continental /kɒntɪ'nent(ə)l/ *a.* of or characteristic of a continent; (**Continental**) characteristic of the Continent; **Continental breakfast** light breakfast of coffee and rolls etc.; **continental quilt** duvet; **continental shelf** shallow sea-bed bordering continent.

contingency /kən'tɪndʒənsɪ/ *n.* event that may or may not occur; unknown or unforeseen circumstance. [L (foll.)]

contingent 1 *a.* conditional or dependent (*on* or *upon* esp. an uncertain event or circumstance); that may or may not occur; fortuitous. **2** *n.* body of troops, ships, etc., forming part of larger group. [L (CONTACT)]

continual /kən'tɪnjʊəl/ *a.* constantly or frequently recurring; always happening; **continually** *adv.* [F (CONTINUE)]

continuance /kən'tɪnjʊəns/ *n.* continuing in existence or operation; duration.

continuation /kəntɪnjʊ'eɪʃ(ə)n/ *n.* act of continuing; thing that continues something else.

continue /kən'tɪnju:/ *v.* maintain, keep up, not stop (action etc.); resume, prolong (narrative, journey, etc., or abs.); prolong, be sequel to; remain, stay; not become other than (*weather continues fine*). [F f. L (CONTAIN)]

continuity /kɒntɪ'nju:ɪtɪ/ *n.* state of being continuous; logical sequence; detailed scenario of film; linkage between broadcast items. [F f. L (CONTINUOUS)]

continuo /kən'tɪnjʊəʊ/ *n.* (*pl.* **continuos**) *Mus.* continuous bass accompaniment played usu. on keyboard instrument. [It.]

continuous /kən'tɪnjʊəs/ *a.* without interval or break, uninterrupted; connected throughout in space or time. [L (CONTAIN)]

continuum /kən'tɪnjʊəm/ *n.* (*pl.* **continua**) thing of continuous structure. [L (as prec.)]

contort /kən'tɔ:t/ *v.t.* twist or force out of normal shape; **contortion** *n.* [L (*torqueo tort-* twist)]

contortionist /kən'tɔ:ʃənɪst/ *n.* performer who can twist his body into unusual positions.

contour /'kɒntʊə/ **1** *n.* outline; line on map joining points at same altitude; line separating differently-coloured parts of design. **2** *v.t.* mark with contour lines. [F f. It. *contornare* draw in outline]

contra- *prefix* against, opposed to. [L]

contraband /'kɒntrəbænd/ **1** *n.* smuggled goods, smuggling; prohibited trade. **2** *a.* forbidden to be imported or exported. [Sp. f. It.]

contraception /kɒntrə'sepʃ(ə)n/ *n.* prevention of pregnancy, use of contraceptives. [CONTRA-, CONCEPTION]

contraceptive /kɒntrə'septɪv/ **1** *a.* preventing pregnancy. **2** *n.* contraceptive device or drug.

contract 1 /'kɒntrækt/ *n.* written or spoken agreement, esp. one enforceable by law; document recording it. **2** /kən'trækt/ *v.* make or become smaller; make a contract (*with*); form or enter into (marriage, debt, etc.); catch or develop (illness); draw together (muscles, brow, etc.); shorten word by combination or elision (as *do not* to *don't*); arrange (work) to be done by contract. **3 contract bridge** form of bridge in which only tricks bid and won count towards game; **contract in** (or **out**) elect to enter (or not to enter) scheme or commitment. **4 contractable** *a.* (with ref. to disease); **contractible** *a.* (with ref. to making smaller or drawing together). [F f. L *contractus* (TRACT)]

contractile /kən'træktaɪl/ *a.* capable of or producing contraction; **contractility** /kɒntræk'tɪlɪtɪ/ *n.*

contraction /kən'trækʃ(ə)n/ *n.* act of contracting; shrinking, diminution; shortened word(s).

contractor /kən'træktə/ *n.* one who makes a contract, esp. to build houses etc. [L (CONTRACT)]

contractual /kən'træktjʊəl/ *a.* of or in the nature of a contract; **contractually** *adv.*

contradict /kɒntrə'dɪkt/ *v.* deny (statement), deny statement made by (person); (of facts, statements, etc.) be at variance or conflict with (others); **contradiction** *n.*; **contradictory** *n.* [L (*dico dict-* say)]

contradistinction /kɒntrədɪs'tɪŋkʃ(ə)n/ *n.* distinction by contrast; contrast. [CONTRA-]

contraflow /'kɒntrəfləʊ/ *n.* flow (esp. of road traffic) alongside, and in a direction opposite to, an established or usual flow.

contralto /kən'træltəʊ/ *n.* (*pl.* **contraltos**) female singer of lowest range; range sung by contralto. [It. (CONTRA-, ALTO)]

contraption /kən'træpʃ(ə)n/ *n.* machine or device, esp. a strange or cumbersome one. [orig. unkn.]

contrapuntal /kɒntrə'pʌnt(ə)l/ *a.* of or

in counterpoint; **contrapuntally** *adv.* [It.]

contrariwise /kən'treərɪwaɪz/ *adv.* on the other hand, in the opposite way; perversely. [foll.]

contrary /'kɒntrərɪ/ **1** *a.* opposed in nature, tendency, or direction; in opposition *to*; (of wind) impeding, unfavourable; /kən'treərɪ/ perverse, self-willed. **2** *n.* the opposite of a person or thing. **3** *adv.* in opposition or contrast *to* (*he acted contrary to my wishes*; *it happened contrary to expectation*). **4 on the contrary** in contrast to what has just been implied or stated; **to the contrary** to the opposite effect. [AF f. L (CONTRA-)]

contrast 1 /'kɒntrɑːst/ *n.* juxtaposition or comparison showing striking differences; difference so revealed; thing or person having noticeably different qualities (*to*); degree of difference between tones in photograph or television picture. **2** /kən'trɑːst/ *v.* set in opposition to reveal contrast; have or show contrast (*with*). [F f. It. f. L (*sto* stand)]

contravene /kɒntrə'viːn/ *v.t.* violate or infringe (law); contradict, conflict with; **contravention** /-'venʃ(ə)n/ *n.* [L (*venio* come)]

contretemps /kɔːntrətɑ̃/ *n.* unfortunate occurrence; unexpected mishap. [F]

contribute /kən'trɪbjuːt, (**D**) 'kɒn-/ *v.* give jointly with others (*to* common fund etc.); supply (article etc.) for publication with others; **contribute to** help to bring about; **contributor** *n.* [L (TRIBUTE)]

contribution /kɒntrɪ'bjuːʃ(ə)n/ *n.* act of contributing; thing contributed.

contributory /kən'trɪbjʊtərɪ/ *a.* that contributes; using contributions.

contrite /'kɒntraɪt/ *a.* penitent, feeling great guilt; **contrition** /kən'trɪʃ(ə)n/ *n.* [F f. L (TRITE)]

contrivance /kən'traɪvəns/ *n.* something contrived, esp. a device or plan; act of contriving. [foll.]

contrive /kən'traɪv/ *v.* devise, plan or make resourcefully or with skill; manage (*to do* thing). [F f. L]

control /kən'trəʊl/ **1** *n.* power of directing or restraining, self-restraint; means of restraining or regulating; (usu. in *pl.*) switches and other devices by which machine is controlled; place where something is controlled or verified; standard of comparison for checking results of experiment; personality said to direct actions and words of spiritualist medium. **2** *v.t.* have control of, regulate; serve as control to; check, verify. **3 control tower** tall building at airport from which air traffic is controlled; **in control** in charge (*of*); **out of control** unrestrained, without control; **under control** being controlled, in order. **4 controllable** *a.* [AF f. med.L, = keep copy of accounts (CONTRA-, ROLL)]

controller *n.* person or thing that controls; person in charge of expenditure.

controversial /kɒntrə'vɜːʃ(ə)l/ *a.* causing or subject to controversy. [L (CONTROVERT)]

controversy /'kɒntrəvɜːsɪ, (**D**) kən'trɒvəsɪ/ *n.* prolonged argument or dispute. [L (foll.)]

controvert /'kɒntrəvɜːt/ *v.t.* dispute, deny. [L (*verto vers-* turn)]

contumacy /'kɒntjʊməsɪ/ *n.* stubborn refusal to obey or comply; **contumacious** /kɒntjuː'meɪʃəs/ *a.* [L (*tumeo* swell)]

contumely /'kɒntjuːmlɪ/ *n.* insulting language or treatment; disgrace; **contumelious** /-'miːlɪəs/ *a.* [F f. L (prec.)]

contuse /kən'tjuːz/ *v.t.* bruise; **contusion** *n.* [L (*tundo tus-* thump)]

conundrum /kə'nʌndrəm/ *n.* riddle or hard question, esp. one with pun in its answer. [orig. unkn.]

conurbation /kɒnɜː'beɪʃ(ə)n/ *n.* extended urban area, esp. consisting of several towns and merging suburbs. [L *urbs* city]

convalesce /kɒnvə'les/ *v.i.* recover health after illness. [L (*valeo* be well)]

convalescent 1 *a.* recovering from illness. **2** *n.* convalescent person. **3 convalescence** *n.*

convection /kən'vekʃ(ə)n/ *n.* transmission of heat by movement of heated substance. [L (*veho vect-* carry)]

convector /kən'vektə/ *n.* heating appliance that circulates warm air by convection.

convene /kən'viːn/ *v.* summon or arrange (meeting etc.); assemble; **convener** *n.* [L (*venio vent-* come)]

convenience /kən'viːnɪəns/ *n.* quality of being convenient, suitability; freedom from difficulty or trouble; advantage; useful thing; lavatory, esp. a public one; **at one's convenience** at a time or place etc. that suits one; **convenience food** food requiring very little preparation. [L (as prec.)]

convenient *a.* serving one's comfort or interests, suitable, free of trouble or difficulty; available or occurring at a suitable time or place; *colloq.* well situated (*house is convenient for the shops*).

convent /'kɒnvənt/ *n.* religious community, esp. of nuns, under vows; building occupied by this. [F f. L (CONVENE)]

conventicle /kən'ventɪk(ə)l/ *n.* chiefly *hist.* secret meeting, esp. of religious dissenters. [L (as prec.)]

convention /kən'venʃ(ə)n/ *n.* formal assembly or conference; formal agreement or treaty; general agreement on social behaviour etc. by implicit consent of the majority; custom or customary practice. [F f. L (CONVENE)]

conventional *a.* depending on or according with convention; (of person) attentive to social conventions; usual, of agreed significance; not spontaneous or sincere or original; (of weapons or power) non-nuclear; **conventionalism** *n.*; **conventionality** /-'nælɪtɪ/ *n.*; **conventionalize** *v.t.*; **conventionally** *adv.*

converge /kən'vɜːdʒ/ *v.i.* come together or towards the same point; **converge on** (or **upon**) approach from different directions; **convergence** *n.*; **convergent** *a.* [L (*vergo* incline)]

conversant /kən'vɜːsənt/ *a.* well acquainted (*with* subject etc.). [F CONVERSE[1]]

conversation /kɒnvə'seɪʃ(ə)n/ *n.* informal exchange of ideas by spoken words; instance of this. [F f. L (CONVERSE[1])]

conversational *a.* of or in conversation; fond of conversation; colloquial; **conversationally** *adv.*

conversationalist *n.* person fond of or good in conversation.

converse[1] **1** /kən'vɜːs/ *v.i.* hold conversation, talk (*with* person). **2** /'kɒnvɜːs/ *n. archaic* conversation. [F f. L (CONVERT)]

converse[2] /'kɒnvɜːs/ **1** *a.* opposite, contrary, reversed. **2** *n.* converse statement, idea, or proposition. **3 conversely** *adv.* [L (CONVERT)]

conversion /kən'vɜːʃ(ə)n/ *n.* converting or being converted, esp. in belief or religion. [F f. L (foll.)]

convert 1 /kən'vɜːt/ *v.* change in form or function (*into*); cause (person) to change beliefs, opinion, party, etc.; change (money etc.) into different form or currency; make structural alterations in (building) for new purpose; complete (try in Rugby) by kicking a goal. **2** /'kɒnvɜːt/ *n.* person converted, esp. to new religion. [F f. L (*verto vers-* turn)]

convertible /kən'vɜːtɪb(ə)l/ **1** *a.* able to be converted. **2** *n.* motor car with folding or detachable roof. **3 convertibility** /-'bɪlɪtɪ/ *n.* [F f. L (prec.)]

convex /'kɒnveks/ *a.* with outline or surface curved like exterior of sphere or circle; **convexity** /-'veksɪtɪ/ *n.* [L]

convey /kən'veɪ/ *v.t.* transport or carry (goods, passengers, etc.); communicate (idea, meaning, etc.); transfer legal title to (property); transmit (sound etc.). [F f. L (*via* way)]

conveyance *n.* conveying; means of transport, vehicle; legal transfer of property, deed effecting this; (in legal sense) **conveyancer** *n.*, **conveyancing** *n.*

conveyor *n.* (also **conveyer**) person or thing that conveys; **conveyor belt** endless moving belt for conveying articles in factory etc.

convict 1 /kən'vɪkt/ *v.t.* prove or find guilty (*of* crime etc). **2** /'kɒnvɪkt/ *n.* convicted prisoner. [L (*vinco vict-* conquer)]

conviction /kən'vɪkʃ(ə)n/ *n.* convicting or being convicted; being convinced, convinced state; firm belief; **carry conviction** be persuasive. [L (prec.)]

convince /kən'vɪns/ *v.t.* firmly persuade (*of, that*); **convincible** *a.* [L (CONVICT)]

convivial /kən'vɪvɪəl/ *a.* fond of good company, sociable and lively; **conviviality** /-'ælɪtɪ/ *n.* [L (*vivo* live)]

convocation /kɒnvə'keɪʃ(ə)n/ *n.* convoking; assembly convoked, esp. provincial synod of Anglican clergy or legislative assembly of a university; **convocational** *a.* [L (foll.)]

convoke /kən'vəʊk/ *v.t.* call together; summon to assemble. [L (*voco* call)]

convoluted /'kɒnvəluːtɪd/ *a.* coiled, twisted; complex. [L (*volvo volut-* roll)]

convolution /kɒnvə'luːʃ(ə)n/ *n.* coiling; a coil or twist; complexity; sinuous fold in surface of the brain. [med.L (prec.)]

convolvulus /kən'vɒlvjʊləs/ *n.* twining plant, esp. bindweed. [L]

convoy /'kɒnvɔɪ/ **1** *v.t.* escort as protection. **2** *n.* convoying; group of ships, vehicles, etc., travelling together or escorted. [F (CONVEY)]

convulse /kən'vʌls/ *v.t.* (usu. in *pass.*) affect with convulsion; cause to laugh uncontrollably; **convulsive** *a.* [L (*vello vuls-* pull)]

convulsion /kən'vʌlʃ(ə)n/ *n.* violent irregular motion of limbs or body caused by involuntary contraction of muscles (often in *pl.*); violent disturbance; (in *pl.*) uncontrollable laughter. [F or L (prec.)]

cony /'kəʊnɪ/ *n.* rabbit; its fur. [F f. L *cuniculus*]

coo 1 *n.* soft murmuring sound like that of dove. **2** *v.* emit coo; talk or say in soft or amorous voice. **3** *int. sl.* expressing surprise or incredulity. [imit.]

cooee /'kuːɪ/ **1** *n.* sound used to attract attention. **2** *v.i.* emit cooee. **3** *int. colloq.* used to attract attention. [imit.]

cook /kʊk/ **1** *v.* prepare (food) by heating; undergo cooking; *colloq.* alter or falsify (accounts etc.). **2** *n.* one who cooks, esp. professionally or in specified way (*a good cook*). **3 cook (person's) goose** ruin his chances; **cook up** invent or concoct (story, excuse, etc.); **what's cook-**

ing? *colloq.* what is happening or planned? [OE f. L *coquus*]

cooker *n.* appliance or vessel for cooking food; fruit (esp. apple) suitable for cooking.

cookery *n.* art or practice of cooking; **cookery book** book with recipes and other cooking information.

cookie /'kʊkɪ/ *n.* *US* sweet biscuit. [Du. *koekje*]

cool 1 *a.* of or at fairly low temperature, fairly cold, not hot; suggesting or achieving coolness (*cool colours, clothes*); calm, unexcited; lacking enthusiasm, restrained, unfriendly (*got a cool reaction*); calmly audacious; *colloq.* at least *a* (*cost me a cool thousand*); *sl.* (esp. *US*) excellent. 2 *n.* coolness; cool air or place; *sl.* calmness, composure (*keep, lose, one's cool*). 3 *v.* (often with *down* or *off*) make or become cool. 4 **cooling tower** tall structure for cooling hot water before reuse, esp. in industry; **cool it** *sl.* relax, calm down; **cool off** calm down (**cooling-off period** interval to allow for change of mind before action). 5 **coolly** /'ku:llɪ/ *adv.* [OE]

coolant *n.* cooling agent, esp. fluid to remove heat from engine.

cooler *n.* vessel in which a thing is cooled; *US* refrigerator; *sl.* prison cell.

coolie /'ku:lɪ/ *n.* unskilled native labourer in Eastern countries. [perh. f. *kulī*, tribe in India]

coomb /ku:m/ *n.* valley on side of hill; short valley running up from coast. [OE]

coon *n.* racoon (*US*); *sl. derog.* (**R**) Black. [abbr.]

coop 1 *n.* cage for keeping poultry. 2 *v.t.* keep (fowl) in coop; (often with *in* or *up*) confine (person). [LG or Du., ult. f. L *cupa* basket]

co-op /'kəʊɒp/ *n.* *colloq.* co-operative society or shop. [abbr.]

cooper *n.* maker or repairer of casks and barrels. [LG or Du. (COOP)]

co-operate /kəʊ'ɒpəreɪt/ *v.i.* work or act together (*with* person); **co-operation** /-'reɪʃ(ə)n/ *n.*; **co-operator** *n.* [CO-]

co-operative /kəʊ'ɒpərətɪv/ 1 *a.* of or affording co-operation; willing to co-operate; (of business) owned and run jointly by its members with profits shared among them. 2 *n.* co-operative farm or society or business.

co-opt /kəʊ'ɒpt/ *v.t.* appoint to membership of body by invitation of existing members; **co-optation** /-'teɪʃ(ə)n/ *n.*; **co-option** *n.*; **co-optive** *a.* [L *co-opto* (*opto* choose)]

co-ordinate /kəʊ'ɔ:dɪnət/ 1 *a.* equal in rank or importance, esp. of parts of compound sentence; consisting of co-ordinate things. 2 *n.* co-ordinate thing; *Math.* (usu. **coordinate**) each of a system of magnitudes used to fix position of point, line, or plane; (in *pl.*) matching items of women's clothing. 3 /-neɪt/ *v.t.* make co-ordinate; bring (parts, movements, etc.) into proper relation; cause (limbs, parts, etc.) to function together or in proper order. 4 **co-ordination** /-'neɪʃ(ə)n/ *n.*; **co-ordinative** *a.*; **co-ordinator** *n.* [L *ordino* (ORDER)]

coot *n.* water-bird with horny white band on forehead; *colloq.* stupid person. [prob. LG]

cop *sl.* 1 *n.* policeman; capture or arrest (*it's a fair cop*). 2 *v.* (**-pp-**) catch or arrest (offender); receive, obtain, suffer; take, seize. 3 **cop it** get into trouble, be punished; **cop out** withdraw, give up, escape; **cop-out** *n.* cowardly evasion, escape; **not much cop** of little value or use. [F *caper* seize]

copal /'kəʊp(ə)l/ *n.* resin of tropical tree, used for varnish. [Sp. f. Aztec]

copartner /kəʊ'pɑ:tnə/ *n.* partner or associate; **copartnership** *n.* [CO-]

cope[1] *v.i.* deal effectively or contend *with*; *colloq.* manage successfully. [F (COUP)]

cope[2] 1 *n.* long cloaklike vestment worn by priest in ceremonies and processions. 2 *v.t.* cover with cope or coping. [OE f. L *cappa* CAP]

copeck /'kəʊpek/ *n.* Russian coin, one hundredth of a rouble. [Russ. *kopeika*]

Copernican /kə'pɜ:nɪkən/ *a.* of the system or theory that the planets (including the earth) move round the sun. [*Copernicus*, astronomer]

copier /'kɒpɪə/ *n.* person or machine that copies (esp. documents). [COPY]

co-pilot /'kəʊpaɪlət/ *n.* second pilot in aircraft. [CO-]

coping *n.* top (usu. sloping) row of masonry in wall; **coping-stone** stone used in coping. [COPE[2]]

coping saw D-shaped saw for cutting curves in wood. [COPE[1]]

copious /'kəʊpɪəs/ *a.* abundant, plentiful; producing much. [F or L (*copia* plenty)]

copper[1] 1 *n.* reddish-brown ductile metallic element; bronze coin; large metal vessel for boiling esp. laundry. 2 *a.* made of or coloured like copper. 3 *v.t.* cover with copper. 4 **copper beech** beech with copper-coloured leaves; **copper-bottomed** having bottom sheathed with copper (esp. of ship or pan), reliable or genuine. [OE f. L *cuprum*]

copper[2] *n.* *sl.* policeman. [COP]

copperhead *n.* venomous American or Australian snake with reddish-brown head. [COPPER[1]]

copperplate *n.* polished copper plate for engraving or etching; print made from this; fine style of handwriting.

coppice /ˈkɒpɪs/ *n.* area of small trees and undergrowth. [F f. med.L (COUP)]

copra /ˈkɒprə/ *n.* dried coconut-kernels. [Port. f. Malayalam]

copse *n.* = COPPICE. [shortened form]

Copt *n.* native Egyptian in and after Hellenistic period; native Christian of independent Egyptian Church. [(F f.) Arab.]

Coptic **1** *a.* of the Copts. **2** *n.* language of the Copts, now used only in Coptic Church.

copula /ˈkɒpjʊlə/ *n.* connecting word, esp. part of verb *be* connecting predicate with subject. [L]

copulate /ˈkɒpjʊleɪt/ *v.i.* have sexual intercourse (*with*); **copulation** /-ˈleɪʃ(ə)n/ *n.*

copy /ˈkɒpɪ/ **1** *n.* thing made to look like another, esp. piece of writing; specimen of book, magazine, etc.; matter to be printed; material for newspaper article; text of advertisement. **2** *v.* make copy (of); imitate, do same as. **3 copy-cat** *colloq.* slavish imitator; **copy-typist** typist working from copy; **copy-writer** writer of copy for publication, esp. publicity material. [F f. L *copia* transcript]

copy-book **1** *n.* book containing models of handwriting for learners to imitate. **2** *a.* tritely conventional; exemplary.

copyhold *n. hist.* tenure in accordance with transcript of manorial records; land so held.

copyist *n.* person who makes copies; imitator.

copyright **1** *n.* exclusive legal right to print, publish, perform, film, or record literary, artistic, or musical material. **2** *a.* protected by copyright. **3** *v.t.* secure copyright for (material).

coquette /kɒˈket/ **1** *n.* flirtatious woman or girl. **2** *v.i.* flirt. **3 coquetry** /ˈkɒkɪtrɪ/ *n.*; **coquettish** *a.* [F dimin. (COCK[1])]

cor *int. sl.* expressing astonishment, exasperation, etc. [corrupt. of GOD]

cor- see COM-.

coracle /ˈkɒrək(ə)l/ *n.* small boat of wickerwork covered with watertight material. [W]

coral /ˈkɒr(ə)l/ **1** *n.* hard red, pink, or white calcareous substance built up on sea-bed by marine polyps. **2** *a.* like coral in colour, red or pink. **3 coral island, reef** one formed by growth of coral. [F f. L f. Gk *korallion*]

coralline /ˈkɒrəlaɪn/ **1** *a.* of or like coral. **2** *n.* a seaweed with hard jointed stem. [F & It. (prec.)]

cor anglais /kɔː ˈɒŋgleɪ/ alto woodwind instrument of oboe family. [F]

corbel /ˈkɔːb(ə)l/ *n.* stone or timber projection from wall, acting as supporting bracket; **corbelled** *a.* [F dimin. (foll.)]

corbie /ˈkɔːbɪ/ *n. Sc.* raven, black crow. [F f. L *corvus* crow]

cord **1** *n.* thick string, piece of this; similar structure in body (*spinal cord*); ribbed fabric, esp. corduroy; (in *pl.*) corduroy trousers; electric flex; measure of cut wood (usu. 128 cu. ft., 3.6 cu. m.). **2** *v.t.* secure with cord; (in *p.p.*, of cloth) ribbed. [F f. L f. Gk *khordē* string]

cordial /ˈkɔːdɪəl/ **1** *a.* heartfelt, sincere; warm, friendly. **2** *n.* fruit-flavoured drink. **3 cordiality** /-ˈælɪtɪ/ *n.*; **cordially** *adv.* [L (*cor cord-* heart)]

cordite /ˈkɔːdaɪt/ *n.* cordlike smokeless explosive. [CORD]

cordon /ˈkɔːd(ə)n/ **1** *n.* line or circle of police, soldiers, guards, etc., esp. preventing access to or from area; ornamental cord or braid; fruit-tree trained to grow as single stem. **2** *v.t.* (often with *off*) enclose or separate with cordon of police etc. [It. & F (CORD)]

cordon bleu /kɔːdɒn ˈblɜː/ of highest class in cookery; cook of this class. [F]

corduroy /ˈkɔːdərɔɪ/ *n.* thick cotton fabric with velvety ribs; (in *pl.*) corduroy trousers. [*cord* = ribbed fabric]

core **1** *n.* horny central part of certain fruits, containing the seeds; central or most important part of anything; central region of the earth; region of fissile material in nuclear reactor; unit of structure in computer, storing one bit (see BIT[2]) of data; inner strand of electric cable; piece of soft iron forming centre of magnet or induction coil. **2** *v.t.* remove core from. [orig. unkn.]

coreopsis /kɒrɪˈɒpsɪs/ *n.* plant with daisy-like usu. yellow flowers. [Gk *koris* bug, *opsis* appearance (with ref. to seed)]

co-respondent /kəʊrɪˈspɒndənt/ *n.* person (esp. man) said to have committed adultery with respondent in divorce case. [co-]

corgi /ˈkɔːgɪ/ *n.* dog of short-legged Welsh breed with foxlike head. [W]

coriander /kɒrɪˈændə/ *n.* aromatic plant; its seeds used as flavouring. [F f. L f. Gk]

Corinthian /kəˈrɪnθɪən/ *a.* of ancient Corinth in southern Greece; *Archit.* of order characterized by acanthus-leaf capitals and ornate decoration, used esp. by the Romans. [L f. Gk]

cork **1** *n.* outer bark of a kind of S. European oak, a buoyant light-brown substance; bottle-stopper of cork or other material; float of cork. **2** *v.t.* (often with *up*) stop or confine; restrain (feelings etc.). [LG or Du. f. Sp. *alcorque*]

corkage *n.* charge made by restaurant etc. for serving wine (esp. when brought from elsewhere).

corked *a.* stopped with cork; (of wine) spoilt by decayed cork.

corker *n. sl.* splendidly fine person or thing.

corking *a. sl.* strikingly large or splendid.

corkscrew 1 *n.* spiral steel device for extracting corks from bottles; (often *attrib.*) thing with spiral shape. **2** *v.* move spirally, twist.

corm *n.* bulblike underground stem of certain plants. [L f. Gk *kormos* lopped tree-trunk]

cormorant /'kɔ:mərənt/ *n.* large black voracious sea-bird. [F f. L *corvus marinus* sea-raven]

corn[1] *n.* cereal before or after harvesting, esp. wheat, oats, or maize; grain or seed of cereal plant; *colloq.* something corny or trite; **corn-cob** cylindrical centre of ear of maize, to which grains are attached (**corn on the cob** maize cooked and eaten in this form); **corn dolly** symbolic or decorative figure made of plaited straw. [OE]

corn[2] *n.* small tender horny place on skin, esp. on toe. [AF f. L *cornu* horn]

corncrake *n.* bird with harsh grating cry. [CORN[1]]

cornea /'kɔ:nɪə/ *n.* transparent membrane covering iris and pupil of eyeball; **corneal** *a.* [med.L (CORN[2])]

corned *a.* preserved in salt or brine (*corned beef*). [CORN[1]]

cornel /'kɔ:n(ə)l/ *n.* hard-wooded tree. [G, ult. f. L *cornus*]

cornelian /kɔ:'ni:lɪən/ *n.* dull red variety of chalcedony. [F]

cornelian cherry /kɔ:'ni:lɪən/ a European berry-bearing tree. [CORNEL]

corner 1 *n.* place where converging sides or edges meet; projecting angle, esp. where two streets meet; internal space or recess formed by the meeting of two sides, esp. of a room; difficult position, esp. one with no escape; secluded or remote place; region or quarter, esp. a remote one; action or result of buying the whole available stock of a commodity; angle of ring in boxing etc., esp. one where contestant rests between rounds; free kick or hit from corner of field in football and hockey. **2** *v.* force (person) into difficult or inescapable position; establish corner in (commodity); (esp. of or in vehicle) go round corner. **3 corner-stone** stone in projecting angle of wall, foundation-stone, *fig.* indispensable part or basis. [AF f. L (CORN[2])]

cornet /'kɔ:nɪt/ *n.* brass instrument resembling trumpet but shorter and wider; conical wafer for holding ice-cream; **cornettist, cornetist** /-'netɪst/ *n.* [F dimin. f. L *cornu* (CORN[2])]

cornflakes *n.pl.* breakfast cereal of toasted flakes made from maize flour. [CORN[1]]

cornflour *n.* fine-ground flour made from maize, rice, etc.

cornflower *n.* plant (esp. blue-flowered kind) that grows wild in cornfields.

cornice /'kɔ:nɪs/ *n.* horizontal moulding in relief, esp. along top of internal wall or as topmost part of entablature. [F f. It.]

Cornish /'kɔ:nɪʃ/ **1** *a.* of Cornwall. **2** *n.* Celtic language of Cornwall. **3 Cornish pasty** seasoned meat and vegetables baked in pastry envelope. [*Cornwall* in S. England]

cornucopia /kɔ:njʊ'kəʊpɪə/ *n.* symbol of plenty consisting of horn overflowing with flowers, fruit, and corn; abundance. [L (CORN[2], COPIOUS)]

corny *a. colloq.* trite; feebly humorous; sentimental, old-fashioned; **cornily** *adv.*; **corniness** *n.* [CORN[1]]

corolla /kə'rɒlə/ *n.* whorl of petals forming inner envelope of flower. [L dimin. of *corona* crown]

corollary /kə'rɒlərɪ/ *n.* proposition that follows from one already proved; natural consequence (*of* something). [L, = gratuity (prec.)]

corona /kə'rəʊnə/ *n.* (*pl.* **coronae** /-i:/) small circle of light round sun or moon; gaseous envelope of sun, seen as ring of white light round moon in total eclipse of sun; any of various crownlike parts of the body; appendage in flower on top of seed or inner side of corolla; glow round electric conductor; **coronal** *a.* [L, = crown]

coronary /'kɒrənərɪ/ **1** *a.* of the arteries supplying blood to the heart. **2** *n.* coronary artery or thrombosis. **3 coronary thrombosis** blockage by blood-clot in coronary artery. [L (prec.)]

coronation /kɒrə'neɪʃ(ə)n/ *n.* ceremony of crowning sovereign or consort. [F f. med.L (CORONA)]

coroner /'kɒrənə/ *n.* officer holding inquest on deaths thought to be violent or accidental, and inquiries in cases of treasure trove. [AF (CROWN)]

coronet /'kɒrənɪt, -ət/ *n.* small crown; band of jewels worn as head-dress. [F dimin. (CROWN)]

corpora *pl.* of CORPUS.

corporal[1] /'kɔ:pər(ə)l/ *n.* non-commissioned army or RAF officer next below sergeant. [F f. It.]

corporal[2] /'kɔ:pər(ə)l/ *a.* of the human body; **corporal punishment** that in-

flicted on the body, esp. by beating; **corporality** /-'rælɪtɪ/ *n.* [F f. L (*corpus* body)]
corporate /'kɔ:pərət/ *a.* forming a corporation or group; of or belonging to a group. [L (prec.)]
corporation /kɔ:pə'reɪʃ(ə)n/ *n.* group of people authorized to act as an individual, esp. in business; civic authorities of borough, town, or city; *colloq.* protruding abdomen.
corporative /'kɔ:pərətɪv/ *a.* of a corporation; governed by or organized in corporations esp. of employers and employed.
corporeal /kɔ:'pɔ:rɪəl/ *a.* bodily, physical, material; **corporeality** /-'ælɪtɪ/ *n.*; **corporeally** *adv.*
corps /kɔ:/ *n.* (*pl.* same /kɔ:z/) a military force or division; group of persons engaged in special activity (*diplomatic corps*). [F (as CORPSE)]
corps de ballet /kɔ: də 'bæleɪ/ a company of ballet-dancers. [F]
corps diplomatique /kɔ: dɪpləmæ'ti:k/ diplomatic corps.
corpse *n.* dead (usu. human) body. [F f. L (CORPUS)]
corpulent /'kɔ:pjʊlənt/ *a.* bulky in body, fat; **corpulence** *n.* [L (foll.)]
corpus /'kɔ:pəs/ *n.* (*pl.* **corpora** /'kɔ:pərə/) body or collection of writings, texts, etc. [L, = body]
corpuscle /'kɔ:pʌs(ə)l/ *n.* minute body or cell in organism, esp. (in *pl.*) the red or white cells in the blood of vertebrates; **corpuscular** /-'pʌskjʊlə/ *a.* [L dimin. of prec.]
corral /kɒ'rɑ:l/ **1** *n.* enclosure for wild animals or (*US*) cattle or horses. **2** *v.t.* (**-ll-**) put or keep in corral. [Sp. & Port. (KRAAL)]
correct /kə'rekt/ **1** *a.* true, accurate; (of conduct) proper, in accordance with taste or standard. **2** *v.t.* set right (error, omission, etc.); mark errors in; substitute right thing for (wrong one); admonish (person); punish (person or fault); counteract (harmful or divergent tendency etc.); eliminate aberration from (lens etc.); bring into accordance with standard. **3 corrector** *n.* [F f. L (*rego rect-* guide)]
correction /kə'rekʃ(ə)n/ *n.* act or instance of correcting; thing substituted for what is wrong; *archaic* punishment. [F f. L (prec.)]
correctitude /kə'rektɪtju:d/ *n.* consciously correct behaviour. [CORRECT, RECTITUDE]
corrective **1** *a.* serving to correct or counteract something harmful. **2** *n.* corrective measure or thing. [F or L (CORRECT)]
correlate /'kɒrəleɪt/ **1** *v.* have or bring into a mutual relation or dependence (*with* or *to*). **2** *n.* each of two related or complementary things. **3 correlation** /-'leɪʃ(ə)n/ *n.* [med.L *correlatio*]
correlative /kɒ'relətɪv/ *a.* having a mutual relation; *Gram.* (of words) corresponding to each other and used regularly together (as *neither* and *nor*); **correlativity** /-'tɪvɪtɪ/ *n.*
correspond /kɒrɪ'spɒnd/ *v.i.* be analogous (*to*) or in agreement (*with*); communicate by interchange of letters (*with*). [F f. med.L]
correspondence *n.* agreement or similarity; communication by letters, letters sent or received; **correspondence course** course of study conducted by post.
correspondent *n.* person writing letters to another, esp. regularly; person employed by newspaper to write regularly on particular subject.
corridor /'kɒrɪdɔ:/ *n.* passage from which doors lead into rooms; passage in train giving access along its length; strip of territory of one State passing through that of another; route which aircraft must follow, esp. over foreign country; **corridors of power** places where covert influence is said to be exerted in government. [F f. It.]
corrie /'kɒrɪ/ *n.* *Sc.* round hollow on mountainside. [Gael.]
corrigendum /kɒrɪ'gendəm/ *n.* (*pl.* **corrigenda**) thing to be corrected, esp. error in book. [L *corrigo* (CORRECT)]
corrigible /'kɒrɪdʒɪb(ə)l/ *a.* able to be corrected; submissive; **corrigibly** *adv.* [F f. med.L (as prec.)]
corroborate /kə'rɒbəreɪt/ *v.t.* confirm or give support to (person, statement, belief); **corroboration** /-'reɪʃ(ə)n/ *n.*; **corroborative** *a.*; **corroborator** *n.*; **corroboratory** *a.* [L (*robur* strength)]
corroboree /kə'rɒbərɪ/ *n.* festive or warlike dance of Australian Aboriginals; noisy party. [Abor.]
corrode /kə'rəʊd/ *v.* wear away, esp. by chemical action; destroy gradually; decay. [F or L (*rodo ros-* gnaw)]
corrosion /kə'rəʊʒ(ə)n/ *n.* corroding, corroded part or substance; **corrosive** *a.* & *n.*
corrugate /'kɒrʊgeɪt/ *v.* (esp. in *p.p.*) form into alternate ridges and grooves, esp. to strengthen (*corrugated iron, paper*); **corrugation** /-'geɪʃ(ə)n/ *n.* [L (*ruga* wrinkle)]
corrupt /kə'rʌpt/ **1** *a.* morally depraved, wicked; influenced by or using bribery; (of text etc.) made suspect or unreliable by errors or alterations. **2** *v.* make or become corrupt. **3 corrup-**

tion *n.*; **corruptive** *a.* [F or L (*rumpo rupt-* break)]
corruptible *a.* able to be corrupted, esp. morally; **corruptibility** /-ˈbɪlɪtɪ/ *n.*
corsage /kɔ:ˈsɑ:ʒ/ *n. US* small bouquet worn by a woman. [F (CORPSE)]
corsair /ˈkɔ:seə/ *n.* pirate ship; pirate. [F (COURSE)]
corselette /ˈkɔ:slɪt/ *n.* woman's foundation garment combining corset and brassière. [f. CORSLET]
corset /ˈkɔ:sɪt/ *n.* close-fitting supporting undergarment worn esp. by woman; **corsetry** *n.* [F dimin. (CORPSE)]
corslet /ˈkɔ:slɪt/ *n.* garment (usu. tight-fitting) covering body; *hist.* armour covering body. [F dimin. (as prec.)]
cortège /kɔ:ˈteɪʒ/ *n.* procession, esp. for funeral. [F]
cortex /ˈkɔ:teks/ *n.* (*pl.* **cortices** /-ɪsi:z/) outer covering of kidney or other organ; outer grey matter of brain; **cortical** *a.*; **corticated** *a.* [L, = bark]
cortisone /ˈkɔ:tɪzəʊn/ *n.* hormone used medicinally against inflammation and allergy. [abbr. of chem. name]
corundum /kəˈrʌndəm/ *n.* extremely hard crystallized alumina, used esp. as abrasive. [Tamil f. Skr.]
coruscate /ˈkɒrəskeɪt/ *v.i.* sparkle, shine (*lit.* or *fig.*); **coruscation** /-ˈskeɪʃ(ə)n/ *n.* [L]
corvette /kɔ:ˈvet/ *n.* small naval escort-vessel; *hist.* flush-decked warship with one tier of guns. [F f. Du.]
corymb /ˈkɒrɪmb/ *n.* flat-topped cluster of flowers on long stem with stems lengthening away from centre. [F or L f. Gk]
cos[1] *n.* crisp lettuce with narrow leaves. [*Cos*, Greek island]
cos[2] *abbr.* cosine.
cos[3] *conj. colloq.* because. [abbr.]
cosh *colloq.* **1** *n.* heavy blunt weapon. **2** *v.t.* hit with a cosh. [orig. unkn.]
cosine /ˈkəʊsaɪn/ *n.* ratio of side adjacent to acute angle (in right-angled triangle) to hypotenuse. [co-]
cosmetic /kɒzˈmetɪk/ **1** *a.* designed to beautify skin, hair, etc.; *fig.* superficially improving or beneficial; (of body treatment or surgery) imitating or enhancing normal appearance. **2** *n.* cosmetic preparation, esp. for the face. **3 cosmetically** *adv.* [F f. Gk (COSMOS[2])]
cosmic /ˈkɒzmɪk/ *a.* of the cosmos, esp. as distinct from earth; of or for space travel; **cosmic rays** high-energy radiation from outer space. [COSMOS[1]]
cosmogony /kɒzˈmɒgənɪ/ *n.* origin of the universe; theory about this. [Gk (*-gonia* begetting)]
cosmology /kɒzˈmɒlədʒɪ/ *n.* science or theory of the universe; **cosmological** /-ˈlɒdʒɪk(ə)l/ *a.*; **cosmologist** *n.* [COSMOS[1], -LOGY]
cosmonaut /ˈkɒzmənɔ:t/ *n.* Russian astronaut. [prec., Gk *nautēs* sailor]
cosmopolitan /kɒzməˈpɒlɪt(ə)n/ **1** *a.* of or from many parts of the world; free from national limitations or prejudices. **2** *n.* cosmopolitan person. **3 cosmopolitanism** *n.* [Gk (*politēs* citizen)]
cosmos[1] /ˈkɒzmɒs/ *n.* the universe as a well-ordered whole. [Gk]
cosmos[2] /ˈkɒzmɒs/ *n.* garden plant with pink, white, or purple flowers. [Gk, = ornament]
Cossack /ˈkɒsæk/ *n.* member of a S. Russian people, famous as horsemen. [F f. Russ. f. Turk.]
cosset /ˈkɒsɪt/ *v.t.* pamper. [earlier = pet lamb, AF f. OE, = cottager]
cost 1 *v.t.* (*past* and *p.p.* **cost**) be obtainable for (certain sum), have as price (*what does it cost?*; *it cost her £5*); involve as loss or sacrifice (*it cost him his life, much effort*); (*past* and *p.p.* **costed**) fix or estimate cost of. **2** *n.* what thing costs, price; loss or sacrifice; (in *pl.*) legal expenses. **3 at all costs** no matter what the cost or risk may be; **cost-effective** effective in relation to its cost; **cost of living** level of prices esp. of basic necessities; **cost price** price paid for thing by one who later sells it. [F f. L *consto* stand at a price]
costal /ˈkɒst(ə)l/ *a.* of the ribs. [F f. L (*costa* rib)]
coster *n.* = COSTERMONGER. [as prec.]
costermonger /ˈkɒstəmʌŋgə/ *n.* person who sells fruit, vegetables, etc., from barrow in street. [*costard* large apple (as prec.)]
costive /ˈkɒstɪv/ *a.* constipated. [AF f. L (CONSTIPATE)]
costly *a.* costing much, expensive; **costliness** *n.* [COST]
costume /ˈkɒstju:m/ **1** *n.* style of dress, esp. as associated with particular place or time; set of clothes; clothes or garment for a particular activity (*swimming-costume*); actor's clothes for part. **2** *v.t.* provide with costume. **3 costume jewellery** jewellery made from artificial materials; **costume play** play in which actors wear historical costume. [F f. It. f. L (CUSTOM)]
costumier /kɒˈstju:mɪə/ *n.* one who makes or deals in costumes. [F (prec.)]
cosy /ˈkəʊzɪ/ **1** *a.* comfortable and warm, snug. **2** *n.* cover to keep a teapot or boiled egg hot. **3** (often with *along*) *colloq.* reassure, delude. **4 cosily** *adv.*; **cosiness** *n.* [orig. unkn.]
cot[1] *n.* bed with high sides for a baby or very young child; small light bed; **cot-death** unexplained death of sleeping baby. [Hindi]

cot² *n.* small shelter; cote; *poetic* cottage. [OE]
cote *n.* shelter for animals or birds. [OE]
coterie /'kəʊtərɪ/ *n.* exclusive group of people sharing interest. [F]
cotoneaster /kətəʊnɪ'æstə/ *n.* shrub or small tree bearing red or orange berries. [L *cotonium* quince]
cottage /'kɒtɪdʒ/ *n.* small simple house, esp. in the country; **cottage cheese** soft white cheese made from curds of skim milk without pressing; **cottage industry** one carried on at home; **cottage pie** dish of minced meat topped with mashed potato. [AF (COT²)]
cottager *n.* one who lives in a cottage.
cottar /'kɒtə/ *n.* (*also* **cotter**) *hist.* & *Sc.* farm-labourer having free use of cottage. [COT²]
cotter *n.* bolt or wedge for securing parts of machinery etc.; **cotter pin** cotter, split pin put through cotter to keep it in place. [orig. unkn.]
cotton /'kɒt(ə)n/ *n.* soft white fibrous substance covering seeds of certain plants; such a plant; thread or cloth made from this; **cotton on (to)** *sl.* understand; **cotton on to** *sl.* form liking or attachment for; **cotton wool** fluffy wadding of kind orig. made from raw cotton; **cottony** *a.* [F f. Arab.]
cotyledon /kɒtɪ'li:d(ə)n/ *n.* first leaf produced by plant embryo. [L f. Gk (*kotulē* cup)]
couch¹ 1 *n.* long bedlike seat with head-rest at one end, for reclining on; sofa; bed or resting-place. 2 *v.* express *in* words of a certain kind; lay as on couch; (of animal) lie, esp. in lair; lower (spear) to position for attack. [F f. L *colloco* lay in place]
couch² /ku:tʃ, kaʊtʃ/ *n.* (in full **couch-grass**) grassy weed with long creeping roots. [var. of QUITCH]
couchette /ku:'ʃet/ *n.* railway carriage with seats convertible into sleeping-berths; berth in this. [F, = little bed]
cougar /'ku:gə/ *n. US* puma. [F f. Guarani]
cough /kɒf/ 1 *v.* expel air or other matter from lungs with sudden sharp sound; (of engine etc.) make similar sound; *sl.* confess. 2 *n.* act or sound of coughing; condition of respiratory organs causing coughing. 3 **cough mixture** medicine to relieve cough; **cough up** eject or say with coughs, *sl.* bring out or give (money or information) reluctantly. [imit., rel. to Du. *kuchen*]
could /kʊd/ *v. aux.* 1 *past* of CAN. 2 feel inclined to (*I could throttle him*; *could not think of allowing it*). 3 **could be** *colloq.* that may be true. [CAN¹]
couldn't /'kʊd(ə)nt/ *colloq.* = *could not.*
coulomb /'ku:lɒm/ *n.* unit of electric charge. [*Coulomb*, physicist]
coulter /'kəʊltə/ *n.* vertical blade in front of ploughshare. [OE f. L *culter* knife]
council /'kaʊns(ə)l/ *n.* advisory, deliberative, or administrative body, a meeting of it; local administrative body of county, city, town, etc.; **council house** house owned and let by local council. [AF f. L *concilium*]
councillor /'kaʊnsələ/ *n.* member of (esp. local) council.
counsel /'kaʊns(ə)l/ 1 *n.* advice formally given; consultation esp. to seek or give advice; legal adviser, esp. barrister, a group of these. 2 *v.t.* (**-ll-**, *US* **-l-**) advise (person), recommend (course or action). 3 **counsel of despair** action to be taken when all else fails; **counsel of perfection** ideal but impracticable advice; **keep one's own counsel** not confide in others; **King's** (or **Queen's**) **Counsel** counsel to the Crown, taking precedence over other barristers; **take counsel** consult *with* person. [F f. L *consilium*]
counsellor /'kaʊnsələ/, *US* **counselor** *n.* adviser; *US* lawyer.
count¹ 1 *v.* find number of (things etc.), esp. by assigning successive numerals; repeat numerals in order (*count to ten*); include or be included in reckoning or consideration; have certain value or significance (*counts against you*; *counts for little*); regard or consider (*count it an honour*; *count ourselves lucky*). 2 *n.* counting, reckoning; total; each charge in a legal indictment. 3 **count on** rely on, expect; **count out** exclude, disregard, complete count of 10 seconds over (fallen boxer etc.), procure adjournment of (House of Commons) for lack of quorum; **count up** find total of; **keep** (or **lose**) **count** know (or not know) how many there have been; **out for the count** defeated, unconscious. [F f. L (COMPUTE)]
count² *n.* foreign nobleman equivalent in rank to earl. [F f. L *comes* companion]
countdown *n.* counting numerals backwards to zero, esp. before firing rocket etc. [COUNT¹]
countenance /'kaʊntɪnəns/ 1 *n.* facial expression, the face; composure of the face; moral support or approval. 2 *v.t.* give approval to (act); encourage or connive at (person or practice). 3 **keep one's countenance** maintain composure, esp. refrain from laughing. [F (CONTAIN)]
counter¹ *n.* long flat-topped fitment in shop etc. over which business is conducted with customers; small disc used in table-games for scoring etc.; token representing coin; device for counting; **under the counter** surreptitiously, esp. illegally. [COUNT¹]

counter[2] 1 *v.* oppose, contradict; baffle or frustrate (person or action) by an annoying move; give return blow in boxing. 2 *adv.* in the opposite direction or manner. 3 *a.* opposite. 4 *n.* return action or blow, countermove; stiff part of shoe or boot round heel; curved part of ship's stern. [foll.]

counter- *prefix* forming verbs, nouns, adjectives, and adverbs, implying retaliation or reversal (*counterstroke, counter-clockwise*), rivalry or opposition (*counter-attraction, counter-current*), reciprocity or correspondence (*countersign, counterpart*). [F f. L *contra* against]

counteract /kaʊntə'rækt/ *v.t.* neutralize or hinder by contrary action; **counteraction** *n.*; **counteractive** *a.* [COUNTER-]

counter-attack 1 *n.* attack made to meet another attack. 2 *v.* attack in reply.

counterbalance 1 *n.* weight or influence that balances another. 2 *v.t.* neutralize by contrary force or influence.

counter-clockwise *a.* & *adv.* = ANTI-CLOCKWISE.

counter-espionage /kaʊntə'respɪənɑːʒ/ *n.* action taken to frustrate enemy's spying.

counterfeit /'kaʊntəfɪt, -fiːt/ 1 *a.* made in imitation and of inferior material, usu. to defraud; not genuine, forged. 2 *n.* counterfeit thing. 3 *v.t.* make counterfeit of in order to defraud, forge. [F]

counterfoil /'kaʊntəfɔɪl/ *n.* part of cheque, receipt, etc., retained as record by person issuing it. [FOIL[2]]

counter-intelligence /'kaʊntərɪn'telɪdʒəns/ *n.* action taken to counter enemy's espionage or intelligence activity. [COUNTER-]

countermand /kaʊntə'mɑːnd/ 1 *v.t.* revoke or cancel (a command); summon back by contrary order. 2 *n.* command cancelling a previous one. [F f. L (MANDATE)]

countermarch 1 *n.* march in opposite direction. 2 *v.* (cause to) march back. (COUNTER-]

countermeasure *n.* action taken to counteract danger or threat.

counterpane /'kaʊntəpeɪn/ *n.* bedspread. [F f. med.L *culcita puncta* quilted mattress]

counterpart /'kaʊntəpɑːt/ *n.* person or thing like or naturally complementary to another; duplicate. [COUNTER-]

counterpoint /'kaʊntəpɔɪnt/ *n.* harmonious combination of simultaneous parts or voices in music; one part or voice added to another. [F f. med.L *contrapunctum* marked opposite]

counterpoise /'kaʊntəpɔɪz/ 1 *n.* balancing of each other by two weights or forces; counterbalancing weight or force. 2 *v.t.* counterbalance; compensate for. [F f. L *pensum* weight]

counter-productive /kaʊntəprə'dʌktɪv/ *a.* having the opposite of the desired effect. [COUNTER-]

counter-revolution *n.* revolution opposing a former one or reversing its results.

countersign 1 *v.t.* add confirming signature to (document already signed by another). 2 *n.* word required in answer to sentry's challenge; identifying mark. 3 **countersignature** /-'sɪg-/ *n.* [F f. It. (SIGN)]

countersink *v.t.* (*past* and *p.p.* **countersunk**) shape top of (screw-hole) with tapered enlargement so that screw-head lies level with or below surface; sink (screw etc.) in such a hole. [COUNTER-]

counter-tenor *n.* male singer of high voice with pure tone; range sung by him. [F f. It. (CONTRA-)]

countervail /'kaʊntəveɪl/ *v.t.* counterbalance; avail against. [AF f. L (*valeo* have worth)]

counterweight *n.* counterbalancing weight. [COUNTER-]

countess /'kaʊntɪs/ *n.* wife or widow of earl or count; woman holding rank of earl or count. [F f. L *comitissa* (COUNT[2])]

countless *a.* too many to be counted.

countrified /'kʌntrɪfaɪd/ *a.* rustic in appearance or manners. [foll.]

country /'kʌntrɪ/ *n.* territory of a nation, State of which one is a member, national population esp. as electors; land of a region with regard to its aspect or associations (*mountainous country*; *Hardy country*); open regions of fields and woods etc. as distinct from towns or the capital (often *attrib.*); = *country-and-western*; **country-and-western** rural or cowboy songs to guitar etc.; **country club** sporting and social club in rural area; **country dance** traditional English dance, often with couples face-to-face in lines; **go to the country** dissolve Parliament and hold general election. [F f. med.L *contrata* (*terra*) (land) lying opposite]

countryman *n.* person living in rural parts; fellow-member of State or district; **countrywoman** *n.*

countryside *n.* country districts.

country-wide *a.* extending throughout a nation.

county /'kaʊntɪ/ *n.* territorial division of country, forming chief unit of local administration and justice; *US* political and administrative division next below State; people of a county, esp. long-established families of high social level;

county council elected governing body of administrative county; **county court** local court for civil cases; **county town** town that is administrative centre of county. [F f. L *comitatus* (COUNT²)]

coup /ku:/ *n.* successful stroke or move, esp. = *coup d'état.* [F f. med.L *colpus* blow]

coup de grâce /ku: də 'grɑ:s/ finishing stroke. [F]

coup d'état /ku: deɪ'tɑ:/ sudden overthrowing of a government esp. by force.

coupé /'ku:peɪ/, *US* **coupe** /'ku:p/ *n.* closed two-door car with sloping back. [F (*couper* cut)]

couple /'kʌp(ə)l/ **1** *n.* man and woman who are engaged or married; pair of partners in dance etc.; two things, or *loosely* several things (*a couple of minutes; I'll take a couple*). **2** *v.t.* link or associate together; copulate. [F f. L COPULA]

couplet /'kʌplɪt/ *n.* two successive lines of verse, esp. when rhyming and of same length. [F dimin. (prec.)]

coupling /'kʌplɪŋ/ *n.* link connecting two railway vehicles or two parts of machinery; arrangement of items on gramophone record. [COUPLE]

coupon /'ku:pɒn/ *n.* small often detachable piece of printed paper entitling holder to specified goods or service or some concession; small printed form of application or entry for competition etc., usu. to be cut from advertisement etc. [F (*couper* cut)]

courage /'kʌrɪdʒ/ *n.* readiness to face and capacity to endure danger or difficulty, inherent ability to control or suppress fear or its disturbing effects; courageous mood or inclination; **have the courage of one's convictions** have courage to do what one believes to be right. [F f. L (*cor* heart)]

courageous /kə'reɪdʒəs/ *a.* having or showing courage.

courgette /kʊə'ʒet/ *n.* small green vegetable marrow. [F]

courier /'kʊrɪə/ *n.* special messenger; person employed to guide and assist group of tourists. [F f. It. f. L *curro curs-* run]

course /kɔ:s/ **1** *n.* onward movement in space or time; direction taken or intended (*ship's course; change course; on, off, course*); direction or channel followed by river etc.; successive development *of* events, ordinary sequence or order (*things must take their course*); line of conduct or action; series *of* lectures, lessons, etc., in a particular subject; each successive part of a meal; sequence of medical treatment (*course of injections*); = *golf-course,* RACECOURSE; continuous row of masonry at one level in a building. **2** *v.* use hounds to hunt (esp. hares); move or flow freely. **3 in course of** in the process of; **in due course** at about the expected time; **of course** as is or was to be expected, without doubt, admittedly. [F f. L *cursus* (prec.)]

courser *n.* fast-running African or Asian bird; *poetic* swift horse.

court /kɔ:t/ **1** *n.* courtyard; yard surrounded by houses, with entry from street; enclosed or marked area for some games, e.g. squash and tennis; (also **Court**) sovereign's establishment with courtiers and attendants, this as representing a country; reception at court; (in full **court of law**) judicial body hearing legal cases, place where this meets, *the* judges of a court. **2** *v.t.* treat flatteringly or with special attention; seek the favour or love of; seek to win, make oneself vulnerable to (*court popularity, disaster*). **3 court-card** playing-card that is king, queen, or jack; **court-house** building in which court of law is held, *US* building containing administrative offices of county; **court martial** (*pl.* **courts martial**) judicial court for trying offenders against military law; **court-martial** *v.t.* try by this; **Court of St James's** court of British sovereign; **court shoe** woman's light shoe with low-cut upper; **go to court** take legal action; **hold court** preside over one's admirers; **out of court** (of settlement) without reaching trial, *fig.* not worth discussing; **pay court to** court (person) to win favour; **put out of court** refuse to consider. [F f. L (COHORT)]

courteous /'kɜ:tɪəs/ *a.* polite, considerate. [F (prec.)]

courtesan /kɔ:tɪ'zæn/ *n.* prostitute with clients among wealthy or nobility. [F f. It. (COURT)]

courtesy /'kɜ:təsɪ/ *n.* courteous behaviour or act; **by courtesy of** by permission of (person); **courtesy light** light in car switched on when door is opened. [F (COURTEOUS)]

courtier /'kɔ:tɪə/ *n.* companion of sovereign at court. [AF (COURT)]

courtly *a.* polished or refined in manners; **courtliness** *n.* [COURT]

courtship *n.* courting, esp. of intended spouse or mate; period of courting.

courtyard *n.* space enclosed by walls or buildings.

couscous /'ku:sku:s/ *n.* N. African dish of crushed wheat or coarse flour steamed over broth, often with meat or fruit added. [F f. Arab.]

cousin /'kʌz(ə)n/ *n.* son or daughter of one's uncle or aunt (also **first cousin** or

cousin-german); *hist.* title used by one sovereign addressing another; **cousin once removed** son or daughter of one's cousin; **second cousin** son or daughter of one's parent's first cousin; **cousinly** *a.* [F f. L *consobrinus*]

couture /ku:'tjʊə/ *n.* design and making of high-quality fashionable clothes. [F]

couturier /ku:'tjʊərɪeɪ/ *n.* fashion designer; **couturière** /-ɪeə/ *n. fem.*

cove[1] **1** *n.* small bay or inlet of coast; sheltered recess; curved moulding at junction of ceiling and wall. **2** *v.t.* provide (room etc.) with cove; slope (sides of fireplace) inwards. [OE]

cove[2] *n. sl.* fellow, man. [cant]

coven /'kʌv(ə)n/ *n.* assembly of witches. [CONVENT]

covenant /'kʌvənənt/ **1** *n.* formal agreement, *Law* sealed contract; biblical compact between God and the Israelites. **2** *v.* agree, esp. by legal covenant (*with* person). [F, rel. to CONVENE]

covenanter *n.* one who covenants, esp. (**Covenanter**) adherent of the Scottish Presbyterian National Covenants of 1638 and 1643.

Coventry /'kɒvəntrɪ/ *n.* in **send person to Coventry** refuse to speak to or associate with him. [*Coventry* in England]

cover /'kʌvə/ **1** *v.t.* lie or extend over, form or occupy whole surface of; conceal or protect (a thing) by placing something on or in front of it; provide (person) with something that covers; protect, clothe; strew thoroughly *with*; enclose or include, deal with (subject); travel (specified distance etc.); be enough money to pay for (*£5 will cover your expenses*); investigate or describe as reporter; (of fortification or gun) protect from commanding position; keep gun aimed at, have within range of fire, protect by firing against enemy; protect or oppose (another player) in field-games; (of stallion etc.) mate with; deputize temporarily *for*; (in *p.p.*) wearing hat, having roof. **2** *n.* thing that covers, lid, top; binding of book, one board of this; envelope or other postal wrapping (*under separate cover*); shelter, protection; screen, pretence; pretended identity; funds from insurance to meet liability or contingent loss, protection by insurance; supporting force protecting another from attack; individual place-setting at meal; = *cover-point*. **3 cover charge** service charge per person in restaurant or club; **cover girl** girl whose picture appears on magazine covers; **covering letter** (or **note**) one sent with and explaining goods or documents; **cover note** temporary certificate of current insurance; **cover-point** fieldsman covering point; **cover up** conceal (thing or fact); **cover-up** *n.* concealment esp. of facts; **take cover** seek shelter; **under cover** in secret, sheltered from weather; **under cover of** hidden or protected by (e.g. darkness), with outward show of (e.g. friendship). [F f. L *cooperio*]

coverage *n.* area or amount covered or reached; reporting of events in newspaper etc.

coverall /'kʌvərɔ:l/ *n.* thing that covers entirely; (usu. in *pl.*) full-length protective garment.

coverlet /'kʌvəlɪt/ *n.* covering, esp. a bedspread. [AF (COVER, *lit* bed)]

covert /'kʌvət/ **1** *a.* disguised, not open or explicit (*covert glance*). **2** *n.* wood or thicket affording cover for game; feather covering base of bird's wing feather or tail feather. [F (COVER)]

covet /'kʌvɪt/ *v.t.* envy another the possession of, long to possess. [F, rel. to CUPID]

covetous /'kʌvɪtəs/ *a.* coveting, avaricious, grasping.

covey /'kʌvɪ/ *n.* brood of partridge, esp. flying together; small group *of* people. [F f. L (*cubo* lie)]

cow[1] *n.* (*pl.* **cows,** *archaic* **kine**) fully-grown female of any bovine animal, esp. of the domestic species used as source of milk and beef; female of other large animals, esp. elephant, whale, or seal; *vulgar derog.* woman; **cow-lick** projecting lock of hair; **cow-pat** flat round piece of cow-dung. [OE]

cow[2] *v.t.* intimidate, dispirit. [ON]

coward /'kaʊəd/ *n.* person easily giving way to fear and lacking courage. [F f. L *cauda* tail]

cowardice /'kaʊədɪs/ *n.* cowardly feelings or conduct.

cowardly *a.* of or like a coward, lacking courage; (of action) done against one who cannot retaliate.

cowbell *n.* bell hung round cow's neck. [COW[1]]

cowboy *n.* in western US, a man in charge of cattle; *colloq.* unscrupulous or reckless business man.

cowcatcher *n.* fender in front of locomotive for pushing aside obstacles on the line.

cower *v.i.* crouch or shrink back, esp. in fear; huddle up. [LG]

cowherd *n.* person who looks after cows at pasture. [COW[1]]

cowhide *n.* cow's hide; leather or whip made from this.

cowl *n.* monk's hood or hooded garment;

hood-shaped covering, esp. of chimney or shaft. [OE f. L *cucullus*]

cowling *n.* removable cover of engine in vehicle or aircraft.

co-worker *n.* one who works in collaboration with another. [co-]

cowpox *n.* disease of cows, whose virus is used in smallpox vaccination. [cow[1]]

cowrie /'kaʊrɪ/ *n.* tropical mollusc with bright shell; the shell used as money in Africa and S. Asia. [Urdu & Hindi]

cowslip *n.* wild plant with small yellow flowers. [obs. *slyppe* dung]

cox 1 *n.* coxswain, esp. of racing boat. **2** *v.* act as cox (of). [abbr.]

coxcomb /'kɒkskəʊm/ *n.* conceited showy person; *hist.* medieval jester's cap; **coxcombry** *n.* [= *cock's comb*]

coxswain /'kɒksweɪn, 'kɒks(ə)n/ **1** *n.* steersman of rowing-boat or other small boat; senior petty officer in small ship. **2** *v.* act as coxswain (of). [*cock* ship's boat, SWAIN]

coy *a.* affectedly modest or bashful; archly reticent. [F, rel. to QUIET]

coyote /kɔɪ'əʊtɪ, 'kɔɪəʊt/ *n.* N. American prairie-wolf. [Mex. Sp.]

coypu /'kɔɪpu:/ *n.* beaver-like water-rodent, orig. from S. America. [Araucan]

cozen /'kʌz(ə)n/ *v. literary* cheat, defraud; act deceitfully; **cozenage** *n.* [cant]

cozy *US* var. of COSY.

c.p. *abbr.* candle-power.

Cpl. *abbr.* Corporal.

c.p.s. *abbr.* cycles per second.

Cr *symb.* chromium.

crab 1 *n.* shellfish with ten legs, of which front pair are modified into pincers; flesh of this as food; (**Crab**) sign or constellation Cancer. **2** *v. colloq.* (**-bb-**) criticize adversely or captiously; act so as to spoil. **3 catch a crab** get oar jammed under water by faulty stroke in rowing; **crab-apple** fruit of crab-tree; **crab-louse** parasite infecting hairy parts of body; **crab-tree** apple tree with small fruit of harsh sour flavour. [OE]

crabbed /'kræbɪd/ *a.* bad-tempered, crabby; (of writing) difficult to read or decipher.

crabby *a.* irritable, morose; **crabbily** *adv.*; **crabbiness** *n.*

crabwise *adv.* sideways or backwards like a crab.

crack 1 *n.* sudden sharp explosive noise; sharp blow (*a crack on the head*); narrow opening; split or rift, partial break without parts separating entirely; *colloq.* joke. **2** *v.* (cause to) break partially, producing crack; (of surface) gape with cracks; hit sharply; (cause to) make sound of crack; break case of (nut); find solution to (code or problem); break into (safe etc.); tell (joke); (of voice) become harsh or change pitch through emotion or old age or at manhood; (of person) suddenly yield or cease to resist (esp. under torture etc.); (in *p.p.*) *colloq.* crazy, infatuated. **3 crack a bottle** open it and drink contents; **crack-brained** crazy; **crack down on** *colloq.* take severe measures against; **crack of dawn** daybreak; **crack up** *colloq.* have physical or mental breakdown, praise highly (usu. in *pass.* esp. in **not all it** etc. **is** etc. **cracked up to be**); **get cracking** *colloq.* make a start; **have a crack at** *colloq.* attempt. [OE]

cracker *n.* explosive firework; small paper toy in form of roll that makes cracking sound when the ends are pulled; thin crisp savoury biscuit, *US* biscuit.

crackers *predic. a. sl.* crazy.

crackle /'kræk(ə)l/ **1** *n.* sound of repeated slight cracks as of burning wood. **2** *v.i.* emit crackle.

crackling /'kræklɪŋ/ *n.* crisp skin of roast pork.

cracknel /'krækn(ə)l/ *n.* light crisp kind of biscuit. [F f. Du. (CRACK)]

crackpot *colloq.* **1** *a.* eccentric or unpractical. **2** *n.* crackpot person. [CRACK]

-cracy *suffix* in sense 'rule, ruling body, of'. [F f. L *-cratia* f. Gk (*kratos* power)]

cradle /'kreɪd(ə)l/ **1** *n.* small bed or cot for a baby, usu. on rockers; place regarded as origin of something (*cradle of art, of civilization*); supporting framework or structure. **2** *v.t.* place in cradle; contain or shelter as in cradle. [OE]

craft /krɑ:ft/ **1** *n.* special skill or technique; an occupation needing this; cunning, guile; (*pl.* same) ship or boat, aircraft or spacecraft. **2** *v.t.* make in skilful manner. [OE]

craftsman *n.* one who practises a craft; skilled person; **craftsmanship** *n.*

crafty *a.* guileful, ingenious; **craftily** *adv.*; **craftiness** *n.*

crag *n.* steep rugged rock; **craggy** *a.* [Celt.]

crake *n.* bird of the rail family, esp. corncrake. [ON, imit. of cry]

cram *v.* (**-mm-**) fill to excess; force (thing *in* or *into*); feed to excess; study intensively for examination. [OE]

cramp 1 *n.* sudden painful involuntary contraction of muscle(s); (in full **cramp-iron**) kind of clamp, esp. for holding masonry or timbers. **2** *v.t.* affect with cramp; restrict or confine narrowly; fasten with cramp. **3 cramp person's style** prevent him from acting freely or to his best ability. [F, f. LG or Du.]

cramped *a.* (of space) too narrow; (of

handwriting) small and with letters close together.
crampon /'kræmpən/ *US* **crampoon** *n.* iron plate with spikes, fixed to boot for climbing on ice. [F (CRAMP)]
cranberry /'krænbərɪ/ *n.* small acid red berry; shrub bearing it. [G *kranbeere* crane-berry]
crane 1 *n.* machine for moving heavy objects, usu. by suspending them from projecting arm or beam; large wading bird with long legs, neck, and bill. **2** *v.* stretch (one's neck) in order to see something. **3 crane-fly** two-winged insect with very long legs; **crane's-bill** wild geranium. [OE]
cranium /'kreɪnɪəm/ *n.* (*pl.* **crania**) bones enclosing the brain; skull; **cranial** *a.*; **craniology** /-'ɒlədʒɪ/ *n.* [med.L f. Gk]
crank 1 *n.* part of axle or shaft bent at right angles for converting reciprocal into circular motion, or vice versa; eccentric person. **2** *v.* cause to move by means of crank. **3 crank up** start (car engine) by turning a crank. [OE]
crankcase *n.* case enclosing crankshaft.
crankpin *n.* pin by which connecting-rod is attached to crank.
crankshaft *n.* shaft driven by crank.
cranky *a.* shaky; crotchety, eccentric; ill-tempered; **crankily** *adv.*; **crankiness** *n.*
cranny /'krænɪ/ *n.* chink, crevice; **crannied** *a.* [F]
crap *vulgar* **1** *n.* faeces; nonsense, rubbish. **2** *v.* (**-pp-**) defecate. **3 crappy** *a.* [Du.]
crape *n.* crêpe, usu. of black silk etc., esp. for mourning dress. [CRÊPE]
craps *n.pl.* US game of chance played with dice. [orig. uncert.]
crapulent /'kræpjʊlənt/ *a.* suffering or resulting from intemperance; **crapulence** *n.*; **crapulous** *a.* [L *crapula* inebriation]
crash[1] **1** *n.* sudden violent percussive noise; fall or impact accompanied by this; burst of loud sound; sudden downfall or collapse (esp. of government or a business); *attrib.* done rapidly or urgently (*crash course, programme*). **2** *v.* (cause to) fall or collide with a crash; (cause to) proceed with a crash (*he crashed into the room, crashed the trolley through the doors*); make noise of crash; (of aircraft or pilot) fall violently to land or sea; collapse financially; pass (instruction to stop, esp. red light); *colloq.* enter or take part in (party etc.) uninvited. **3** *adv.* with a crash. **4 crash-dive** *v.i.* (of submarine) submerge hurriedly in emergency, (of aircraft) dive and crash; **crash-dive** *n.* action of this; **crash-helmet** helmet worn to protect head in case of crash; **crash-land** (of aircraft or pilot) make emergency landing. [imit.]
crash[2] *n.* coarse plain linen or cotton fabric. [Russ.]
crashing *a. colloq.* overwhelming (*a crashing bore*). [CRASH[1]]
crass *a.* gross (*crass stupidity*); grossly stupid. [L *crassus* thick]
-crat *suffix* forming nouns meaning 'supporter or member of a -CRACY'. [F (-CRACY)]
crate 1 *n.* packing-case made of wooden slats, for conveying fragile goods; *sl.* old aircraft or car. **2** *v.t.* pack in crate. [perh. Du.]
crater *n.* mouth of volcano; bowl-shaped cavity, esp. that made by explosion of shell or bomb. [L f. Gk, = mixing-bowl]
-cratic *suffix* (also **-cratical**) forming adjectives from nouns in *-crat*. [-CRAT]
cravat /krə'væt/ *n.* short scarf or necktie. [F f. Serbo-Croatian, = Croat]
crave *v.* greatly desire, long *for*; ask earnestly for. [OE]
craven /'kreɪv(ə)n/ **1** *a.* cowardly, abject. **2** *n.* craven person. [perh. F f. L (*crepo* burst)]
craving *n.* strong desire, intense longing. [CRAVE]
craw *n.* crop of bird or insect; **stick in one's craw** be unacceptable. [LG or Du.]
crawfish /'krɔːfɪʃ/ *n.* large spiny sea-lobster. [var. of CRAYFISH]
crawl 1 *v.* progress with body on or close to ground, or on hands and knees; walk or move or (of time) pass slowly; *colloq.* seek favour by behaving in a servile way; be covered or filled *with*; (of skin etc.) creep. **2** *n.* crawling; slow rate of motion; high-speed swimming stroke. [orig. unkn.]
crayfish /'kreɪfɪʃ/ *n.* small lobster-like freshwater crustacean; crawfish. [F *crevice*]
crayon /'kreɪən/ **1** *n.* stick or pencil of coloured wax etc. for drawing. **2** *v.t.* draw or colour with crayons. [F (*craie* chalk)]
craze 1 *n.* great but usu. temporary enthusiasm; object of this. **2** *v.t.* make crazy. [perh. f. ON]
crazy *a.* insane; foolish, lacking sense (*a crazy idea*); *colloq.* extremely enthusiastic (*about*); (of building etc.) unsound; **crazy paving** paving made up of irregular pieces; **like crazy** *colloq.* like mad, very much; **crazily** *adv.*; **craziness** *n.*
creak 1 *n.* harsh strident noise, as of

unoiled hinge. **2** *v.i.* make or move with creak; be in poor condition. **3 creaky** *a.* [imit.]

cream 1 *n.* part of milk with high fat content; its yellowish-white colour; creamlike preparation or ointment; food or drink with consistency of or compared to cream; the best part *of*. **2** *v.* remove cream from (milk); make creamy; apply cosmetic cream to (skin); form cream or scum. **3 cream cheese** soft rich cheese made of cream and unskimmed milk; **cream off** remove best or required part of; **cream of tartar** purified tartar used in medicine and cooking. [F, f. L *cramum* & eccl. L *chrisma* CHRISM]

creamery /'kri:mərɪ/ *n.* place where dairy products are processed or sold.

creamy *a.* like cream; rich in cream; **creamily** *adv.*; **creaminess** *n.*

crease 1 *n.* line caused by folding or crushing; line defining position of bowler or batsman in cricket. **2** *v.* make creases in (dress etc.); develop creases; *sl.* stun, tire out. [CREST]

create /kri:'eɪt/ *v.* bring into existence; give rise to; originate (*actor creates a part*); invest (person) with rank (*was created a peer*); *sl.* make a fuss. [L *creo*]

creation /kri:'eɪʃ(ə)n/ *n.* creating; all created things; thing created, esp. by human intelligence; **the Creation** the creation of the world. [F f. L (prec.)]

creative *a.* able to create; inventive, imaginative; **creativity** /-'tɪvɪtɪ/ *n.* [CREATE]

creator *n.* one who creates; **the Creator** God. [F f. L (CREATE)]

creature /'kri:tʃə/ *n.* created being, esp. animal; person (*she's a lovely creature*); one in subservient position; **creature comforts** good food, clothes, surroundings, etc.

crèche /kreʃ/ *n.* day nursery for babies. [F]

credence /'kri:dəns/ *n.* belief; small table etc. for Eucharistic elements before consecration. [med.L (CREDO)]

credentials /krɪ'denʃ(ə)lz/ *n.pl.* letter(s) of introduction; evidence of achievement or trustworthiness. [med.L (prec.)]

credibility /kredɪ'bɪlɪtɪ/ *n.* being credible; **credibility gap** seeming difference between what is said and what is true. [foll.]

credible /'kredɪb(ə)l/ *a.* believable, worthy of belief. [L (CREDO)]

credit /'kredɪt/ **1** *n.* belief or confidence in person, words, or actions (*he, his story, deserves little credit*); source of approval or good reputation, the power or influence it gives (*she is a credit to the school*; *your offer does you credit*); acknowledgement of merit or achievement (*got little credit for his idea*); (usu. in *pl.*) acknowledgement of contributor's services to book, film, etc.; trust that person will pay later for goods supplied, power to buy in this way; person's financial standing, sum at person's disposal in bank; entry in account of sum paid into it, this sum, side of account recording such entries; *US* certificate of completion of course by student. **2** *v.t.* believe, take to be true or reliable; enter on credit side of account (amount *to* person, person *with* amount); attribute (thing *to* person). **3 credit card** card authorizing purchase of goods on credit; **credit person with** ascribe (quality or feeling) to him; **give person credit for** recognize that he may have; **on credit** by arrangement to pay later; **to one's credit** in one's favour. [F f. It. or L (CREDO)]

creditable *a.* praiseworthy; bringing honour or respect; **creditably** *a.*

creditor *n.* person to whom money is owed. [AF f. L (CREDIT)]

credo /'kri:dəʊ, 'kreɪ-/ *n.* (*pl.* **credos**) creed. [L, = I believe]

credulity /krɪ'dju:lɪtɪ/ *n.* inclination to believe too readily. [foll.]

credulous /'kredjʊləs/ *a.* too ready to believe; (of behaviour) showing credulity. [L (CREDO)]

creed *n.* system of religious belief; formal summary of Christian doctrine; set of beliefs or principles; **creedal** *a.* [OE f. L (CREDO)]

creek *n.* inlet on sea-coast; short arm of river; *Austral.* & *NZ* stream, brook; *US* tributary of river; **up the creek** *sl.* in difficulties, crazy. [ON & Du.]

creel *n.* fisherman's large wicker basket. [orig. unkn.]

creep 1 *v.i.* (*past* and *p.p.* **crept**) move slowly with body prone and close to ground; move stealthily or cautiously, advance very gradually; (of plant) grow along ground or up vertical surface; experience shivering sensation due to repugnance or fear (*makes my flesh creep, me creep all over*); develop gradually (*creeping inflation*). **2** *n.* act or spell of creeping; *sl.* unpleasant person; gradual change in shape of metal under stress. **3 the creeps** *colloq.* nervous feeling of revulsion or fear. [OE]

creeper *n.* person or thing that creeps; creeping or climbing plant; *sl.* soft-soled shoe.

creepy *a.* causing nervous revulsion or fear; having this feeling; **creepily** *adv.*; **creepiness** *n.*

creepy-crawly *n. colloq.* small creeping insect.
creese var. of KRIS.
cremate /krɪ'meɪt/ *v.t.* burn (corpse) to ashes; **cremation** *n.* [L *cremo* burn]
crematorium /kremə'tɔ:rɪəm/ *n.* (*pl.* **crematoria** or **-iums**) place where corpses are cremated.
crematory /'kremətərɪ/ **1** *a.* of or pertaining to cremation. **2** *n. US* crematorium.
crème de menthe /krem də 'mɑ̃t/ green peppermint liqueur. [F]
crenellated /'krenəleɪtɪd/ *a.* having battlements; **crenellation** /-'leɪʃ(ə)n/ *n.* [F *crenel* embrasure]
Creole /'kri:əʊl/ **1** *n.* descendant of European settlers in W. Indies or Central or S. America; white descendant of French settlers in southern US; person of mixed European and Negro descent; language spoken by Creoles. **2** *a.* that is a Creole; of Creoles; (**creole**) of local origin or production. [F f. Sp.]
creosote /'kri:əsəʊt/ **1** *n.* dark-brown oil distilled from coal tar, used as wood-preservative; colourless oily fluid distilled from wood tar, used as antiseptic. **2** *v.t.* treat with creosote. [G f. Gk words, = flesh-preserver]
crêpe /kreɪp/ *n.* gauzelike fabric with wrinkled surface; durable wrinkled sheet rubber used for shoe-soles etc.; **crêpe paper** thin crinkled paper; **crêpe Suzette** small sweet pancake served *flambé*. [F f. L (CRISP)]
crepitate /'krepɪteɪt/ *v.i.* make crackling sound; **crepitation** /-'teɪʃ(ə)n/ *n.* [L (*crepo* creak)]
crept *past* and *p.p.* of CREEP.
crepuscular /krɪ'pʌskjʊlə/ *a.* of twilight; (of animals) appearing or active in twilight; dim, not yet fully enlightened. [L *crepusculum* twilight]
crescendo /krɪ'ʃendəʊ/ *Mus.* **1** *adv.* with gradual increase of loudness. **2** *n.* (*pl.* **crescendos**) passage to be played this way; *fig.* progress towards a climax. [It. (foll.)]
crescent /'kresənt/ **1** *n.* waxing moon; moon as seen in first or last quarter; this as emblem of Turkey or Islam; anything of crescent shape, esp. street of houses. **2** *a.* increasing; crescent-shaped. [F f. L *cresco* grow]
cress *n.* any of various plants with pungent edible leaves. [OE]
crest **1** *n.* comb or tuft on bird's or animal's head; plume, esp. on helmet etc.; top of mountain, roof, or ridge; curl of foam on wave; device above shield and helmet on coat of arms, or on notepaper etc. **2** *v.* reach crest of; (of wave) form crest; serve as crest to, crown. [F f. L *crista*]
crestfallen *a.* dejected, abashed.
cretaceous /krɪ'teɪʃ(ə)s/ **1** *a.* of the nature of chalk; (**Cretaceous**) of the latest period of the Mesozoic era, with formation of chalk. **2** *n.* (**Cretaceous**) this period. [L (*creta* chalk)]
cretin /'kretɪn/ *n.* person with deformity and mental retardation caused by thyroid deficiency; *colloq.* stupid person; **cretinism** *n.*; **cretinous** *a.* [F *crétin* (CHRISTIAN)]
cretonne /'kretɒn/ *n.* printed cotton cloth used for chair-covers etc. [F (*Creton* in Normandy)]
crevasse /krɪ'væs/ *n.* deep open crack, esp. in ice of glacier. [F f. L *crepo* crack]
crevice /'krevɪs/ *n.* narrow opening or fissure, esp. in rock or building etc. [F (as prec.)]
crew[1] /kru:/ **1** *n.* body of persons manning ship, aircraft, etc.; these other than officers; group of people, esp. working together (*camera crew*). **2** *v.* act as crew (for); supply crew for. **3** **crew cut** closely cropped man's haircut; **crew neck** close-fitting round neckline, esp. of pullover. [F (L *cresco* increase)]
crew[2] see CROW.
crewel /'kru:əl/ *n.* thin worsted yarn for tapestry and embroidery; **crewel-work** design in this on linen. [orig. unkn.]
crib **1** *n.* wooden framework for animals' fodder; child's bed or cot; model of manger scene at Bethlehem; cards given by other players to dealer in cribbage; *colloq.* cribbage; *colloq.* plagiarism; literal translation for use of students. **2** *v.* (**-bb-**) confine in small space; pilfer; copy unfairly or without acknowledgement. [OE]
cribbage /'krɪbɪdʒ/ *n.* card-game for two or more persons, with 'crib'. [orig. unkn.]
crick **1** *n.* sudden painful stiffness in the neck or back. **2** *v.t.* cause crick in. [orig. unkn.]
cricket[1] /'krɪkɪt/ *n.* outdoor summer game played with ball, bats, and wickets between two sides of eleven players; **not cricket** *colloq.* not fair play. [orig. unkn.]
cricket[2] /'krɪkɪt/ *n.* jumping chirping insect. [F, imit.]
cricketer *n.* player of cricket. [CRICKET [1]]
crier /'kraɪə/ *n.* one who cries, esp. official making public announcements in lawcourts or street. [CRY]
crikey /'kraɪkɪ/ *int. sl.* expressing astonishment. [CHRIST]
crime *n.* act (usu. serious offence) punishable by law; evil act; such acts

collectively; *colloq.* a shame, senseless act. [F f. L *crimen*]
criminal /'krɪmɪn(ə)l/ **1** *n.* person guilty of crime. **2** *a.* of or involving or concerning crime; guilty of crime. **3 criminality** /-'nælɪtɪ/ *n.*; **criminally** *adv.*
criminology /krɪmɪ'nɒlədʒɪ/ *n.* scientific study of crime; **criminologist** *n.* [-LOGY]
crimp 1 *v.t.* press into small folds or ridges; corrugate; make waves in (hair). **2** *n.* crimped thing or form. [LG or Du.]
crimson /'krɪmz(ə)n/ **1** *a.* of rich deep red inclining to purple. **2** *n.* crimson colour. [ult. f. Arab. (KERMES)]
cringe /krɪndʒ/ *v.i.* shrink back in fear, cower; behave obsequiously (*to*). [rel. to CRANK]
crinkle /'krɪŋk(ə)l/ **1** *n.* wrinkle, crease. **2** *v.* form crinkles (in). **3 crinkly** *a.* [as prec.]
crinoline /'krɪnəlɪn, -li:n/ *n.* stiffened or hooped petticoat formerly worn to make long skirt stand out; stiff fabric of horsehair etc. used for linings, hats, etc. [F f. L *crinis* hair, *linum* thread]
cripple /'krɪp(ə)l/ **1** *n.* person who is permanently lame. **2** *v.t.* make a cripple of, lame; disable, weaken or damage seriously (*output crippled by strikes*). [OE]
crisis /'kraɪsɪs/ *n.* (*pl.* **crises** /-i:z/) decisive moment; time of danger or great difficulty. [L f. Gk, = decision]
crisp 1 *a.* hard but brittle; (of air) bracing; (of style or manner) lively, brisk and decisive; (of features etc.) neat, clear-cut; (of paper etc.) stiff and crackling; (of hair) closely curling. **2** *n.* thin fried slice of potato (sold in packets etc.). **3** *v.* make or become crisp. **4 crispy** *a.* [OE f. L *crispus* curled]
crispbread *n.* thin crisp biscuit of crushed rye etc.
criss-cross 1 *n.* pattern of crossing lines. **2** *a.* crossing, in cross lines (*criss-cross traffic*). **3** *adv.* crosswise, at cross purposes. **4** *v.* mark or form or move in criss-cross pattern. [*Christ's Cross*]
criterion /kraɪ'tɪərɪən/ *n.* (*pl.* **criteria**) principle or standard that thing is judged by. [Gk, = means of judging]
critic /'krɪtɪk/ *n.* one who censures; one who reviews or judges merit of literary, artistic, etc., works. [L *criticus* f. Gk *kritēs* judge]
critical *a.* fault-finding, censorious; expressing criticism; of or at a crisis, decisive, crucial; marking transition from one state etc. to another (*critical angle*); (of nuclear reactor) maintaining a self-sustaining chain reaction; **critical path** sequence of stages determining minimum time needed for complex operation; **critically** *adv.* [L (prec.)]
criticism /'krɪtɪsɪz(ə)m/ *n.* finding fault, censure; work of a critic; critical article, essay, or remark. [CRITIC]
criticize /'krɪtɪsaɪz/ *v.* find fault (with), censure; discuss critically.
critique /krɪ'ti:k/ *n.* critical essay or analysis; criticism. [F (CRITIC)]
croak 1 *n.* deep hoarse sound as of raven or frog. **2** *v.* utter or speak with croak; *sl.* die, kill. [imit.]
Croat /'krəʊæt/ *n.* native or inhabitant of Croatia in Yugoslavia; language of Croats; **Croatian** /-'eɪʃ(ə)n/ *a.* & *n.* [L f. Serbo-Croatian *Hrvat*]
crochet /'krəʊʃeɪ/ **1** *n.* needlework in which yarn is looped into pattern of stitches by means of hooked needle. **2** *v.* make in or do crochet. [F (CROTCHET)]
crock[1] *n.* *colloq.* inefficient or broken-down or worn-out person; worn-out vehicle, ship, etc. [orig. Sc.]
crock[2] *n.* earthenware pot or jar; broken piece of this. [OE]
crockery *n.* earthenware vessels, plates, etc. [CROCK[1]]
crocodile /'krɒkədaɪl/ *n.* large tropical amphibious reptile with thick skin, long tail, and very long jaws; its skin, used to make bags, shoes, etc.; *colloq.* line of schoolchildren etc. walking in pairs; **crocodile tears** insincere grief. [F f. L f. Gk *krokodilos*]
crocus /'krəʊkəs/ *n.* dwarf spring-flowering plant growing from corm, with yellow or purple or white flowers. [L f. Gk]
Croesus /'kri:səs/ *n.* person of great wealth. [king of anc. Lydia]
croft 1 *n.* enclosed piece of (usu. arable) land; small rented farm in Scotland or N. England. **2** *v.i.* farm croft; live as crofter. [OE]
crofter *n.* one who rents a croft.
croissant /'krwʌsɔ̃/ *n.* rich crescent-shaped bread roll. [F (CRESCENT)]
cromlech /'krɒmlek/ *n.* dolmen; circle of upright prehistoric stones. [W]
crone *n.* withered old woman. [Du. *croonje* carcass]
crony /'krəʊnɪ/ *n.* close friend. [Gk *khronios* long-lasting]
crook /krʊk/ **1** *n.* hooked staff of shepherd or bishop; bent or curved thing; hook; bend, curve; *colloq.* rogue, swindler; professional criminal. **2** *v.* bend, curve. [ON]
crooked /'krʊkɪd/ *a.* not straight or level; bent, curved, twisted; *colloq.* not straightforward, dishonest.
croon 1 *v.* hum or sing in low subdued voice and sentimental manner. **2** *n.* such singing. [LG or Du.]

crop 1 *n.* produce of cultivated plants, esp. cereals; season's total yield; group or amount produced at one time; handle of looped whip; hair cut very short; pouch in bird's gullet where food is prepared for digestion. **2** *v.* (**-pp-**) cut or bite off; cut (hair) very short; sow (land) *with* crop; (of land) bear crops (in specified way). **3 crop-eared** with ears or hair cut short; **crop up** occur unexpectedly or by chance. [OE]

cropper *n.* crop-producing plant of specified quality (*good, light, cropper*); **come a cropper** *sl.* fall heavily, fail badly.

croquet /'krəʊkeɪ/ **1** *n.* game played on lawn, with wooden balls that are driven through hoops with mallets; act of croqueting. **2** *v.* drive away (opponent's ball) by placing one's own against it and striking one's own. [as CROCKET]

croquette /krəʊ'ket/ *n.* fried breaded roll of potato, meat, etc. [F (*croquer* crunch)]

crore *n.* (in India) 10 million, one hundred lakhs.

crosier /'krəʊzɪə, -ʒə/ *n.* hooked staff carried by bishop as symbol of office. [F *croisier* cross-bearer & *crossier* crook-bearer]

cross 1 *n.* upright post with transverse bar, as used in antiquity for crucifixion; representation of this as emblem of Christianity, staff surmounted by cross; monument in form of cross; thing or mark of similar shape, esp. figure made by two short intersecting lines (+ or ×); = *sign of the cross* (see SIGN); decoration indicating rank in some orders of knighthood or awarded for personal valour (*Victoria, George, Cross*); intermixture of breeds, a hybrid; mixture or compromise *between* two or more things; crosswise movement of actor, football, boxer's fist, etc.; a trouble or annoyance. **2** *v.* go across (road, river, sea, any area), cross road etc.; (cause to) intersect or be across one another (*cross one's legs*); draw line(s) across; make sign of cross on or over (esp. *oneself*); pass in opposite or different directions; thwart, frustrate; anger by refusing to acquiesce; (cause to) interbreed; cross-fertilize (plants). **3** *a.* transverse, reaching from side to side; intersecting; contrary, opposed, reciprocal; annoyed or angry (*with*). **4 the Cross** that on which Christ was crucified, Christianity; **be at cross purposes** misunderstand or conflict with one another; **cross-bench** bench in Parliament for members not belonging to Government or main opposition party; **cross-bred** hybrid; **cross-breed** *v.* & *n.* produce hybrid of, hybrid animal or plant; **cross-check** *n.* & *v.* check by alternative method of verification; **cross-country** across fields, not keeping to main or direct roads; **cross-cut** diagonal cut, path, etc.; **cross-cut saw** saw for cutting across grain of wood; **cross-examination** process of cross-examining; **cross-examine** examine (esp. opposing witness in lawcourt) to check or extend previous testimony; **cross-eyed** having one or both eyes turned inwards; **cross-fertilize** fertilize (animal or plant) from one of a different species; **cross-grained** (of wood) with grain in crossing directions; (of person) perverse, intractable; **cross one's heart** make sign of cross over it as sign of sincerity; **cross-legged** with legs crossed, or with ankles crossed and knees apart; **cross one's mind** (of idea etc.) occur to one; **cross off** remove from list etc.; **cross out** cancel, obliterate; **cross-patch** *n.* bad-tempered person; **cross-ply** (of tyre) having fabric layers with cords lying crosswise; **cross-question** = *cross-examine*; **cross-reference** reference from one part of book etc. to another; **cross-section** transverse section, representation or diagram of thing as if cut through, *fig.* representative sample; **cross-stitch** stitch formed from two crossing stitches; **cross-talk** unwanted transfer of signals between communication channels, repartee; **cross-wind** wind blowing across direction of travel; **on the cross** diagonally. [OE f. ON, ult. f. L *crux*]

crossbar *n.* horizontal bar, esp. between uprights.

crossbill *n.* bird with bill whose jaws cross when closed.

crossbow *n.* bow fixed across wooden stock, with groove for arrow and mechanism for drawing and releasing string.

crosse *n.* netted crook used in lacrosse. [F]

crossfire *n.* firing of guns in two crossing directions; opposition, interrogation, etc., from several sides at once. [CROSS]

crossing *n.* place where things (esp. roads) cross; place at which one may cross (*pedestrian crossing*); travel across water (*we had a smooth crossing*).

crossroad *n.* (often in *pl.*) intersection of two roads; **at the crossroads** at point where decision must be made or course of action chosen.

crosswise *adv.* (also **crossways**) in the manner of a cross, across, with one crossing the other.

crossword *n.* puzzle in which vertically and horizontally crossing words indicated by clues have to be fitted into grid of squares.
crotch *n.* place where things (esp. legs of body or garment) fork. [CROOK]
crotchet /'krɒtʃɪt/ *n. Mus.* note equal to two quavers or half a minim. [F dimin. of *croc* (CROOK)]
crotchety *a.* peevish.
crouch 1 *v.* lower the body with knees bent close against chest; be in this position. **2** *n.* crouching. [F f. N (CROOK)]
croup[1] /kru:p/ *n.* inflammation of larynx and trachea of children, with hard cough and difficult breathing. [imit.]
croup[2] /kru:p/ *n.* rump (esp. of horse). [F (CROP)]
croupier /'kru:pɪə/ *n.* person in charge of gambling-table, raking in and paying out money. [F (prec.)]
croûton /'kru:tɒn/ *n.* small piece of fried or toasted bread served with soup etc. [F (CRUST)]
crow /krəʊ/ **1** *n.* large black bird of family including jackdaw, raven, and rook; cry of crow, crowing of cock. **2** *v.i.* (*past* in 1st sense also **crew** /kru:/) (of cock) utter loud shrill cry; (of baby) utter happy sounds; express gleeful satisfaction (*over*). **3 as the crow flies** in straight line; **crow's foot** wrinkle at outer corner of eye; **crow's-nest** barrel fixed at mast-head of sailing ship as shelter for look-out. [OE]
crowbar *n.* iron bar with flattened end, used as lever.
crowd 1 *n.* large number of people gathered together without orderly arrangement; mass of spectators, audience; *colloq.* company, set, lot. **2** *v.* (cause to) come together in a crowd; fill, occupy, cram (things *into* space, space etc. *with*); inconvenience by crowding or coming aggressively close to. **3 crowd out** keep out by crowding. **4 crowded** *a.* [OE]
crown 1 *n.* monarch's ornamental and usu. jewelled headdress; (often **Crown**) *the* monarch (esp. as head of State), *the* power or authority of the monarch; wreath for the head, as emblem of victory, reward for or consummation of effort; top part of thing, esp. of head or hat; highest or central point of arched or curved thing (*crown of the road*); part of tooth projecting from gum, artificial replacement for (part of) this; figure of crown as mark or emblem; British coin worth 25p (formerly 5 shillings); former size of paper, 504 × 384 mm. **2** *v.t.* put crown on (person or person's head), invest with regal crown or office; be a crown to, encircle or rest on the top of; be the consummation or reward or finishing touch to; *sl.* hit on the head; promote (piece in draughts) to king. **3 Crown Colony** colony subject to direct control by British government; **Crown Court** court of criminal jurisdiction in England and Wales; **Crown Derby** kind of china made at Derby and often marked with crown; **crown glass** optical glass of low refractive index (formerly also used in windows); **crown jewels** sovereign's regalia including crown, sceptre, and orb, used on ceremonial occasions; **Crown Prince** male heir to throne; **Crown Princess** wife of Crown Prince, female heir to throne; **crown wheel** wheel with teeth or cogs at right angles to its plane. [F f. L *corona*]
crozier var. of CROSIER.
CRT *abbr.* cathode-ray tube.
cruces *pl.* of CRUX.
crucial /'kru:ʃ(ə)l/ *a.* decisive, critical; *colloq.* (**D**) very important. [F f. L *crux crucis* cross]
crucible /'kru:sɪb(ə)l/ *n.* melting-pot for metals etc.; *fig.* severe test. [med.L (prec.)]
cruciferous /kru:'sɪfərəs/ *a.* (of plant) with four equal petals arranged crosswise. [L (CRUCIAL)]
crucifix /'kru:sɪfɪks/ *n.* model of the cross, esp. with figure of Christ on it. [F f. L (*cruci fixus* fixed to cross)]
crucifixion /kru:sɪ'fɪkʃ(ə)n/ *n.* crucifying or being crucified; **the Crucifixion** that of Christ. [eccl.L (prec.)]
cruciform /'kru:sɪfɔ:m/ *a.* cross-shaped. [L *crux crucis* cross]
crucify /'kru:sɪfaɪ/ *v.t.* put to death by fastening to a cross; persecute, torment; destroy in argument etc. [F (CRUCIFIX)]
crude /kru:d/ *a.* in the natural state, not refined; lacking finish, unpolished; rude, blunt; **crudity** *n.* [L *crudus* raw]
cruel /'kru:əl/ *a.* indifferent to or gratified by another's suffering; causing pain or suffering; **cruelly** *adv.*; **cruelty** *n.* [F f. L (prec.)]
cruet /'kru:ɪt/ *n.* small glass bottle for holding oil or vinegar for use at table; stand holding this and salt, pepper, and mustard pots. [AF dimin. (CROCK[2])]
cruise /kru:z/ **1** *v.i.* sail about without precise destination, or calling at series of places; (of motor vehicle or aircraft) travel at moderate economical speed; (of vehicle or driver) travel at random, esp. slowly. **2** *n.* cruising voyage. **3 cruise missile** one able to fly at low altitude and guide itself by reference to features of region traversed. [Du. (CROSS)]
cruiser *n.* warship of high speed and

medium armament; = *cabin cruiser* (see CABIN).
cruiserweight *n.* = *light heavyweight* (see HEAVYWEIGHT).
crumb /krʌm/ **1** *n.* small fragment, esp. of bread; small particle (*crumb of comfort*); soft inner part of bread; *sl.* objectionable person. **2** *v.* cover with breadcrumbs; crumble (bread). **3 crumby** *a.* [OE]
crumble /ˈkrʌmb(ə)l/ **1** *v.* break or fall into small fragments; (of power, reputation, etc.) gradually collapse. **2** *n.* dish of cooked fruit with crumbly topping. **3 crumbly** *a.*
crumbs /krʌmz/ *int.* expressing dismay or surprise. [CHRIST]
crummy *a. sl.* dirty, squalid; inferior, worthless; **crumminess** *n.* [var. of CRUMBY]
crumpet /ˈkrʌmpɪt/ *n.* flat soft cake of yeast mixture, toasted and eaten with butter; *sl.* head; *sl.* sexually attractive woman or women. [orig. uncert.]
crumple /ˈkrʌmp(ə)l/ *v.* crush or become crushed into creases; collapse, give way. [obs. *crump* curl up]
crunch **1** *v.* crush noisily with teeth; grind under foot (gravel, dry snow, etc.); make crunching sound. **2** *n.* crunching; a crunching sound; *colloq.* decisive event. **3 when it comes to the crunch** when there is a show-down. [imit.]
crupper *n.* strap holding harness back by passing under horse's tail. [F (CROUP[2])]
crusade /kru:ˈseɪd/ **1** *n.* any of several medieval military expeditions made by Europeans to recover the Holy Land from the Muslims; vigorous campaign in favour of a cause. **2** *v.* engage in crusade. [F (CROSS)]
cruse /kru:z/ *n. archaic* earthenware pot or jar. [OE]
crush **1** *v.* compress with violence, so as to break, bruise, etc.; reduce to powder by pressure; crumple, crease; defeat or subdue completely. **2** *n.* act of crushing; crowded mass of people; drink made from juice of crushed fruit; *sl.* infatuation. [F]
crust **1** *n.* hard outer part of bread, similar casing of anything; rocky outer skin of the earth; deposit, esp. from wine on bottle; *sl.* impudence. **2** *v.* cover with or form into crust; become covered with crust. [F f. L *crusta* rind, shell]
crustacean /krʌˈsteɪʃ(ə)n/ **1** *n.* member of group of hard-shelled mainly aquatic animals including crabs, lobsters, shrimps, etc. **2** *a.* of crustaceans.
crusty *a.* having a crisp crust; irritable, curt; **crustily** *adv.*; **crustiness** *n.*
crutch *n.* support for lame person, usually with cross-piece fitting under armpit; any support; crotch. [OE]
crux /krʌks/ *n.* (*pl.* **cruces** /ˈkru:si:z/) decisive point, crucial element of problem. [L, = cross]
cry /kraɪ/ **1** *v.* make loud or shrill sound, esp. to express pain, grief, etc., or to appeal for help; shed tears, weep; say or exclaim loudly or excitedly; (often with *out*) appeal, demand, show need, *for*; (of hawker etc.) proclaim (wares etc.) in street. **2** *n.* loud inarticulate utterance of grief, pain, fear, joy, etc.; loud excited utterance of words; urgent appeal or entreaty; spell of weeping; public demand or strong movement of opinion; watchword, rallying call; natural utterance of animal, esp. of hounds on scent; street-call of hawker etc. **3 cry-baby** person who weeps easily or without good reason; **cry down** disparage; **cry off** withdraw from promise or undertaking; **cry up** praise, extol; **cry wolf** see WOLF; **in full cry** in close pursuit. [F f. L *quirito*]
crying *a.* (esp. of injustice) flagrant, demanding redress.
cryogenics /kraɪəʊˈdʒenɪks/ *n.* branch of physics dealing with very low temperatures and their effects. [Gk *kruos* frost, *-genēs* born]
crypt /krɪpt/ *n.* vault, esp. one beneath church, used as burial-place. [L *crypta* f. Gk (*kruptos* hidden)]
cryptic *a.* secret, mysterious; obscure in meaning; **cryptically** *adv.*
cryptogam /ˈkrɪptəgæm/ *n.* plant with no true flowers or seeds, e.g. fern, moss, fungus; **cryptogamous** /-ˈtɒgəməs/ *a.* [F (CRYPT, Gk *gamos* marriage)]
cryptogram /ˈkrɪptəgræm/ *n.* thing written in cipher. [CRYPT, -GRAM]
cryptography /krɪpˈtɒgrəfɪ/ *n.* art of writing in or deciphering codes; **cryptographer** *n.*; **cryptographic** /-təˈgræfɪk/ *a.* [prec., -GRAPHY]
crystal /ˈkrɪst(ə)l/ **1** *n.* clear transparent colourless mineral; piece of this; highly transparent glass, flint glass, articles made of this; aggregation of molecules with definite internal structure and external form of solid enclosed by symmetrically arranged plane faces. **2** *a.* made of, like, clear as, crystal. **3 crystal ball** glass globe used in crystal-gazing; **crystal-gazing** concentrating one's gaze on a crystal to obtain picture by hallucination etc. [OE f. F f. L f. Gk]
crystalline /ˈkrɪstəlaɪn/ *a.* of or like or clear as crystal; having structure and form of a crystal; **crystallinity** /-ˈlɪnɪtɪ/ *n.* [F (prec.)]
crystallize /ˈkrɪstəlaɪz/ *v.* form into crystals; (of ideas or plans) become

definite; **crystallized fruit** fruit preserved in sugar; **crystallization** /-ˈzeɪʃ(ə)n/ *n.* [CRYSTAL]

crystallography /krɪstəˈlɒgrəfɪ/ *n.* science of crystal structure; **crystallographer** *n.*

crystalloid /ˈkrɪstəlɔɪd/ *n.* substance having crystalline structure.

c/s *abbr.* cycles per second.

Cs *symb.* caesium.

CSE *abbr.* Certificate of Secondary Education.

cu. *abbr.* cubic.

Cu *symb.* copper. [L *cuprum*]

cub 1 *n.* young of fox, bear, lion, etc.; ill-mannered young man; *colloq.* inexperienced newspaper reporter. **2** *v.* (**-bb-**) bring forth (cubs); hunt fox-cubs. **3 Cub (Scout)** member of junior branch of Scout Association. [orig. unkn.]

cubby-hole /ˈkʌbɪhəʊl/ *n.* very small room; small snug place. [LG]

cube 1 *n.* solid contained by six equal squares; cube-shaped block; product of a number multiplied by its square. **2** *v.t.* find cube of (number); cut (food) into small cubes. **3 cube root** number which produces a given number when cubed. [F or L f. Gk]

cubic *a.* of three dimensions; involving cube (and no higher power) of number; **cubic metre** etc. volume of a cube whose edge is one metre etc. [F or L (prec.)]

cubical /ˈkju:bɪk(ə)l/ *a.* cube-shaped.

cubicle /ˈkju:bɪk(ə)l/ *n.* small separate sleeping-compartment; enclosed space screened for privacy. [L (*cubo* lie)]

cubism /ˈkju:bɪz(ə)m/ *n.* style of art (esp. painting) in which objects are represented by juxtaposed geometrical figures; **cubist** *n.* [F (CUBE)]

cubit /ˈkju:bɪt/ *n.* ancient measure of length, approximately equal to length of forearm. [L *cubitum* elbow]

cuboid /ˈkju:bɔɪd/ **1** *a.* cube-shaped, like a cube. **2** *n.* rectangular parallelepiped. [Gk (CUBE)]

cuckold /ˈkʌkəʊld/ **1** *n.* husband of adulteress. **2** *v.t.* make cuckold of. **3 cuckoldry** *n.* [F]

cuckoo /ˈkʊku:/ **1** *n.* migratory bird with characteristic cry, depositing its eggs in nests of small birds. **2** *a. sl.* crazy, foolish. **3 cuckoo-pint** wild arum; **cuckoo-spit** froth exuded by larvae of certain insects on leaves, stems, etc. [F, imit.]

cucumber /ˈkju:kʌmbə/ *n.* long green fleshy fruit, used in salads; plant producing this. [F f. L]

cud *n.* half-digested food that ruminant chews at leisure; **chew the cud** reflect, ponder. [OE]

cuddle /ˈkʌd(ə)l/ **1** *v.* hug, embrace fondly; lie close and snug; nestle together. **2** *n.* prolonged and fond hug. **3 cuddlesome** *a.*; **cuddly** *a.* [orig. uncert.]

cudgel /ˈkʌdʒ(ə)l/ **1** *n.* short thick stick used as weapon. **2** *v.t.* (**-ll-**, *US* **-l-**) beat with cudgel. **3 cudgel one's brains** think hard about a problem; **take up the cudgels for** defend vigorously. [OE]

cue[1] **1** *n.* last words of actor's speech etc. as signal to another actor to begin; stimulus to perception etc.; signal, hint. **2** *v.t.* give cue to. **3 cue in** insert cue for, give information to. [orig. unkn.]

cue[2] **1** *n.* billiard-player's rod for striking the ball. **2** *v.* use cue (on). [var. of QUEUE]

cuff[1] *n.* thicker end part of sleeve; separate band worn round wrist; (in *pl.*) *colloq.* handcuffs; **cuff-link** one of pair of fasteners for shirt cuffs; **off the cuff** extempore, without preparation. [orig. unkn.]

cuff[2] **1** *v.t.* strike with open hand. **2** *n.* a cuffing blow. [perh. imit.]

Cufic var. of KUFIC.

cuirass /kwɪˈræs/ *n.* armour breastplate and back-plate fastened together. [F f. L (*corium* leather)]

cuisine /kwɪˈzi:n/ *n.* style or method of cooking. [F]

cul-de-sac /ˈkʌldəsæk, ˈkʊl-/ *n.* (*pl.* **culs-de-sac** *pr.* same) street or passage closed at one end. [F, = sack-bottom]

-cule *suffix* forming (orig. dimin.) nouns (*molecule*). [F or L]

culinary /ˈkʌlɪnərɪ/ *a.* of or for cooking. [L (*culina* kitchen)]

cull 1 *v.t.* pick (flower etc.), select; select from herd etc. and kill (surplus animals). **2** *n.* culling; animal(s) culled. [F (COLLECT[1])]

culminate /ˈkʌlmɪneɪt/ *v.i.* reach its highest point (*in*); **culmination** /-ˈneɪʃ(ə)n/ *n.* [L (*culmen* top)]

culottes /kju:ˈlɒts/ *n.pl.* woman's divided skirt. [F, = knee-breeches]

culpable /ˈkʌlpəb(ə)l/ *a.* deserving blame; **culpability** /-ˈbɪlɪtɪ/ *n.* **culpably** *adv.* [F f. L (*culpo* blame)]

culprit /ˈkʌlprɪt/ *n.* person accused of or guilty of offence. [perh. AF *culpable* (prec.)]

cult *n.* system of religious worship esp. as expressed in ritual; devotion or homage to person or thing. [F or L (foll.)]

cultivate /ˈkʌltɪveɪt/ *v.t.* prepare and use (soil) for crops; raise, produce (crops); apply oneself to improving or developing (the mind, an acquaintance, etc.), pay attention to, develop friendship of (person); **cultivation** /-ˈveɪʃ(ə)n/ *n.* [L (*colo cult-* till, worship)]

cultivator /ˈkʌltɪveɪtə/ *n.* device for breaking up ground; one who cultivates.

culture /ˈkʌltʃə/ **1** *n.* refined understanding of the arts and other human intellectual achievement; customs and civilization of a particular time or people; improvement by care and training; cultivation of plants, rearing of bees, silkworms, etc.; quantity of bacteria grown for study. **2** *v.t.* grow (bacteria) for study. **3 cultural** *a.* [F or L (CULTIVATE)]

cultured *a.* having or showing culture; **cultured pearl** pearl formed by oyster after insertion of foreign body into its shell.

culvert /ˈkʌlvət/ *n.* underground channel carrying water across road etc. [orig. unkn.]

cum /kʊm/ *prep.* with, together with, also used as (*bedroom-cum-study*). [L]

cumber *v.t. literary* hamper, hinder, inconvenience. [ENCUMBER]

cumbersome /ˈkʌmbəsəm/ *a.* hampering, awkward in size or weight or shape.

cumin /ˈkʌmɪn/ *n.* herb with aromatic seeds. [F f. L f. Gk]

cummerbund /ˈkʌməbʌnd/ *n.* sash worn round the waist. [Hindi & Pers.]

cumquat var. of KUMQUAT.

cumulate /ˈkju:mjʊleɪt/ *v.* accumulate; combine (catalogue entries etc). [L (CUMULUS)]

cumulative /ˈkju:mjʊlətɪv/ *a.* increasing or increased in amount, force, etc., by successive additions. [L (foll.)]

cumulus /ˈkju:mjʊləs/ *n.* (*pl.* **cumuli** /-aɪ/) form of cloud consisting of rounded masses heaped on horizontal base. [L, = heap]

cuneiform /ˈkju:nɪfɔ:m/ **1** *a.* (in ancient Babylonia etc.) of or using writing with impressed wedge-shaped strokes. **2** *n.* cuneiform writing. [F, or L (*cuneus* wedge)]

cunning **1** *a.* skilled in ingenuity or deceit, selfishly clever or crafty; ingenious (*a cunning device*); *US* attractive, quaint. **2** *n.* craftiness, skill in deceit. [CAN[1]]

cunt *n. vulgar* female genitals; unpleasant or stupid person. [orig. uncert.]

cup **1** *n.* small bowl-shaped container with handle, used for drinking from; its contents, amount that it holds; cup-shaped thing; flavoured wine, cider, etc.; ornamental vessel as prize for race etc.; one's fate or fortune. **2** *v.t.* (**-pp-**) form (esp. one's hands) into shape of cup; take or hold as in a cup. **3 Cup Final** final football etc. match in competition for cup. [OE f. med.L *cuppa*]

cupboard /ˈkʌbəd/ *n.* recess or piece of furniture with door and (usu.) shelves, in which things may be stored; **cupboard love** display of affection meant to secure some gain.

Cupid /ˈkju:pɪd/ *n.* Roman god of love represented as naked winged boy with bow and arrows. [L (*cupio* desire)]

cupidity /kjʊˈpɪdɪtɪ/ *n.* greed for gain. [F or L (prec.)]

cupola /ˈkju:pələ/ *n.* small dome on roof; furnace for melting metals; ship's or fort's revolving gun-turret. [It. f. L *cupa* cask]

cuppa /ˈkʌpə/ *n. colloq.* cup of (tea). [corrupt.]

cupreous /ˈkju:prɪəs/ *a.* of or like copper. [L (COPPER[1])]

cupric /ˈkju:prɪk/ *a.* of copper.

cupro-nickel /ˈkju:prəʊˈnɪk(ə)l/ *n.* alloy of copper and nickel.

cur *n.* worthless or snappish dog; contemptible person. [perh. ON *kurr* grumbling]

curable /ˈkjʊərəb(ə)l/ *a.* that can be cured. [CURE]

curaçao /ˈkjʊərəsəʊ/ *n.* liqueur flavoured with peel of bitter oranges. [*Curaçao*, Carib. island]

curacy /ˈkjʊərəsɪ/ *n.* curate's office or tenure of it. [CURATE]

curare /kjʊəˈrɑ:rɪ/ *n.* bitter extract of various plants, used by S. American Indians as poison on arrows. [Carib]

curate /ˈkjʊərət/ *n.* assistant to parish priest. [med.L *curatus* (CURE)]

curative /ˈkjʊərətɪv/ **1** *a.* tending or able to cure. **2** *n.* curative thing. [F f. med.L (prec.)]

curator /kjʊəˈreɪtə/ *n.* person in charge of museum or other collection. [AF or L (CURE)]

curb **1** *n.* check, restraint; strap etc. fastened to bit and passing under horse's lower jaw, used as check; border or edging, frame round top of well; kerb. **2** *v.t.* restrain; put curb on (horse). [F (CURVE)]

curd *n.* (often in *pl.*) coagulated substance formed by action of acids on milk, made into cheese or eaten as food. [orig. unkn.]

curdle /ˈkɜ:d(ə)l/ *v.* congeal, form into curds; **make one's blood curdle** fill one with horror. [orig. unkn.]

cure **1** *v.t.* restore to health; relieve (person) *of* disease; eliminate (disease, evil, etc.); preserve (meat, fruit, tobacco, or skins) by salting or drying etc.; vulcanize (rubber). **2** *n.* thing that cures; restoration to health; course of medicinal or healing treatment. [F f. L *cura* care]

curé /ˈkjʊəreɪ/ *n.* parish priest in France etc. [F]

curette /kjʊəˈret/ **1** *n.* surgeon's small scraping-instrument. **2** *v.t.* scrape with this. **3 curettage** *n.* [F (CURE)]

curfew /'kɜːfjuː/ *n.* signal or time after which people must remain indoors; *hist.* signal for extinction of fires at fixed evening hour. [F (COVER, L FOCUS)]

Curia /'kjʊərɪə/ *n.* papal court, government departments of Vatican. [L]

curie /'kjʊərɪ/ *n.* unit of radioactivity. [*Curie*, scientist]

curio /'kjʊərɪəʊ/ *n.* (*pl.* **curios**) rare or unusual object. [abbr. of foll.]

curiosity /kjʊərɪ'ɒsɪtɪ/ *n.* eager desire to know; inquisitiveness; strange or rare thing. [F f. L (foll.)]

curious /'kjʊərɪəs/ *a.* eager to know or learn; inquisitive; strange, surprising, odd. [F f. L (CURE)]

curium /'kjʊərɪəm/ *n.* artificial radioactive metallic element. [*Curie*, name of scientists]

curl 1 *v.* bend or coil into spiral; move in spiral form (*smoke curling upwards*); play curling. **2** *n.* coiled lock of hair; anything spiral or curved inwards; curling movement. **3 curl up** lie or sit with knees drawn up, *fig.* writhe with horror, shame, etc. [Du.]

curler *n.* device for curling the hair.

curlew /'kɜːljʊ/ *n.* wading bird with long slender bill. [F]

curlicue /'kɜːlɪkjuː/ *n.* decorative curl or twist. [CURLY, CUE² or Q]

curling *n.* game played on ice with large flat stones that are slid towards a mark. [CURL]

curly *a.* having or arranged in curls; moving in curves.

curmudgeon /kə'mʌdʒ(ə)n/ *n.* bad-tempered person [orig. unkn.]

currant /'kʌrənt/ *n.* dried fruit of small seedless grape, used in cookery; any of various shrubs producing black, red, or white berries, such a berry. [AF (*Corinth* in Greece)]

currency /'kʌrənsɪ/ *n.* money in use in a country; being current, prevalence. [foll.]

current 1 *a.* belonging to the present time, happening now (*current events*); (of money, opinion, rumour, word) in general circulation or use. **2** *n.* body of water, air, etc., moving in definite direction, esp. through stiller surrounding body; general tendency or course *of* events or opinions; movement of electrically charged particles. **3 current account** bank account from which money may be drawn without notice. [F f. L *curro curs-* run]

currently *adv.* at the present time.

curriculum /kə'rɪkjʊləm/ *n.* (*pl.* **curricula**) course (of study); **curriculum vitae** brief account of one's previous career. [L, = course]

curry¹ /'kʌrɪ/ **1** *n.* dish of meat, fish, eggs, etc., cooked with hot-tasting spices, usu. served with rice. **2** *v.t.* make (meat etc.) into a curry. **3 curry powder** preparation of turmeric and other spices for making curry. [Tamil]

curry² /'kʌrɪ/ *v.t.* groom (horse) with curry-comb; treat (tanned leather) to improve its properties; **curry-comb** metal brush for currying horse; **curry favour** ingratiate oneself. [F f. Gmc, rel. to READY]

curse 1 *n.* solemn utterance wishing person to suffer destruction or punishment; evil resulting from curse; violent exclamation of anger, profane oath; thing that causes evil or harm. **2** *v.* utter curse against; utter expletive curses. **3 the curse** *colloq.* menstruation; **be cursed with** have as a burden or source of harm. [OE]

cursed /'kɜːsɪd/ *a.* damnable, abominable.

cursive /'kɜːsɪv/ **1** *a.* (of writing) done with joined characters. **2** *n.* cursive writing. [med.L, = running (CURRENT)]

cursor /'kɜːsə/ *n.* transparent slide with hair-line, forming part of slide-rule; indicator on VDU screen, showing particular position in displayed matter. [L, = runner (as prec.)]

cursory /'kɜːsərɪ/ *a.* hasty, hurried; **cursorily** *adv.* [L (prec.)]

curt *a.* noticeably or rudely brief. [L *curtus* short]

curtail /kɜː'teɪl/ *v.t.* cut short, reduce; **curtailment** *n.* [corrupt. of obs. adj. *curtal* (as prec.)]

curtain /'kɜːt(ə)n/ **1** *n.* piece of cloth etc. hung up as screen, usu. movable sideways or upwards, esp. at window or between stage and auditorium of theatre; rise or fall of stage curtain at beginning or end of act or scene; (in *pl.*) *sl.* the end. **2** *v.t.* furnish or cover with curtains; shut *off* with curtain(s). **3 curtain-call** audience's summons to actor(s) to take bow after fall of curtain; **curtain-raiser** short opening theatre-piece, *fig.* preliminary event; **curtain-wall** plain wall of fortified place, connecting two towers etc. [F f. L *cortina*]

curtilage /'kɜːtɪlɪdʒ/ *n.* area attached to dwelling-house as part of its enclosure. [F (COURT)]

curtsy /'kɜːtsɪ/ **1** *n.* woman's or girl's salutation made by bending the knees and lowering the body. **2** *v.i.* make curtsy. [var. of COURTESY]

curvaceous /kɜː'veɪʃəs/ *a. colloq.* (of woman) having shapely curved figure. [CURVE]

curvature /'kɜːvətʃə/ *n.* curving; curved form. [F f. L (foll.)]

curve 1 *n.* line of which no part is

straight; surface of which no part is flat; curved form or thing; curved line on graph. **2** *v.* bend or shape so as to form a curve. [L *curvus* curved]

curvet /kɜːˈvet/ **1** *n.* horse's frisky leap. **2** *v.i.* (of horse) perform curvet. [It. dimin. (prec.)]

curvilinear /kɜːvɪˈlɪnɪə/ *a.* contained by or consisting of curved lines. [CURVE after *rectilinear*]

cushion /ˈkʊʃ(ə)n/ **1** *n.* mass of soft material stuffed into bag of cloth etc., used to make seat etc. more comfortable; means of protection against shock; lining of billiard-table rim; body of air supporting hovercraft etc. **2** *v.t.* provide or protect with cushion(s); mitigate adverse effects of. [F f. L *culcita* mattress]

cushy /ˈkʊʃɪ/ *a. colloq.* (of job etc.) pleasant and easy. [Hindi *ḳhūsh* pleasant]

cusp *n.* point at which two curves meet (e.g. horn of crescent moon). [L *cuspis -id-* point, apex]

cuss *colloq.* **1** *n.* curse; awkward or difficult person. **2** *v.* curse. [CURSE]

cussed /ˈkʌsɪd/ *a. colloq.* awkward and stubborn.

custard /ˈkʌstəd/ *n.* dish or sauce made with milk and beaten eggs, usu. sweetened; sweet sauce made with milk and flavoured cornflour. [obs. *crustade* (CRUST)]

custodian /kʌˈstəʊdɪən/ *n.* guardian or keeper, esp. of public building. [foll.]

custody /ˈkʌstədɪ/ *n.* guardianship, protective care; imprisonment; **take into custody** arrest; **custodial** /-ˈstəʊdɪəl/ *a.* [L (*custos -od-* guard)]

custom /ˈkʌstəm/ *n.* usual way of behaving or acting; established usage as a power or as having force of law; business patronage, regular dealings or customers; (in *pl.*) duty levied on imports, (often treated as *sing.*) government department or officials administering this; **custom-built** built to customer's order; **custom-house** office at port or frontier etc. at which customs duties are levied. [F f. L *consuetudo*]

customary *a.* in accordance with custom, usual; **customarily** *adv.* [med.L (prec.)]

customer *n.* person who buys goods or services from a shop or business; *colloq.* person one has to deal with (*awkward, ugly, customer*). [AF (CUSTOM)]

cut 1 *v.* (-**tt**-; *past* and *p.p.* **cut**) penetrate or wound with sharp-edged instrument; divide (*into* parts) with knife etc.; trim, detach part of, by cutting (corn, flowers, hair, etc.); cause physical or mental pain to (*cut him to the heart; cutting wind, irony*); make *loose, open*, etc. by cutting, execute or make (*cut a caper, dash, sorry figure*); reduce (prices, rates, time, etc.), reduce or cease (services etc.); shape or form (garment, gem, record) by cutting; cross, intersect (*two lines cut; line cuts circle at two points*); divide (pack of cards) into two; edit (film), stop the cameras in filming, go quickly *to* another shot; renounce (connection), ignore or refuse to recognize (person); absent oneself from (meeting etc.); hit (ball) with chopping motion; switch off (engine etc.); pass *through, across, round*, etc., esp. in hurry or as shorter way; *US* dilute, adulterate. **2** *n.* act of cutting, division or wound made by cutting, cutting remark; stroke with knife, sword, whip, etc.; reduction (in prices, wages, service, etc.), cessation (of power supply etc.); excision of part of play, film, book, etc.; *sl.* commission, share of profits etc.; way garment or hair is cut, style; piece of meat cut from carcass; stroke of ball in cricket etc. made by cutting; ignoring of or refusal to recognize person. **3 a cut above** noticeably superior to; **cut and dried** prepared in advance, ready, inflexible; **cut and run** *sl.* run away; **cut and thrust** lively interchange of argument; **cut back** reduce, prune; **cut-back** *n.* reduction; **cut both ways** serve both sides of argument etc.; **cut corners** do task etc. perfunctorily or incompletely; **cut down** reduce (expenses etc.); **cut in** interrupt, move in front of another vehicle (esp. in overtaking) leaving too little space; **cut it fine** see FINE[1]; **cut it out** *sl.* (in *imper.*) stop doing that; **cut one's losses** abandon unprofitable scheme before losses become too great; **cut no ice** *sl.* be of no importance or effect; **cut off** end abruptly, intercept, interrupt, prevent from continuing, disinherit; **cut-off** *n.* point at which thing is cut off, device for stopping flow; **cut out** remove, omit, cut and remove parts from larger whole, outdo or supplant, (cause to) cease functioning, (in *pass.*) be suited (*for* or *to*); **cut-out** *n.* thing cut out, device for automatic disconnection, release of exhaust gases, etc.; **cut-price** for sale at reduced price; **cut-rate** available at reduced rate; **cut a tooth** have tooth beginning to emerge from gum (**cut one's teeth on** acquire experience from); **cut up** cut into small pieces, (in *pass.*) be greatly distressed; **cut up rough** show anger or resentment. [OE]

cutaneous /kjuːˈteɪnɪəs/ *a.* of the skin. [L (CUTICLE)]

cutaway *a.* (of diagram etc.) having some parts absent to reveal interior; (of coat) with front below waist cut away.

cute *a. colloq.* clever, ingenious; *US* attractive, quaint. [ACUTE]
cuticle /'kju:tɪk(ə)l/ *n.* skin at base of finger-nail or toe-nail. [L dimin. (*cutis* skin)]
cutis /'kju:tɪs/ *n.* true skin beneath epidermis. [L]
cutlass /'kʌtləs/ *n. hist.* short sword with slightly curved blade. [F f. L *cultellus* dimin. (COULTER)]
cutlery /'kʌtlərɪ/ *n.* knives, forks, and spoons for use at table. [AF (as prec.)]
cutlet /'kʌtlɪt/ *n.* neck-chop of mutton or lamb; small piece of veal etc. for frying; flat cake of minced meat etc. [F dimin. f. L *costa* rib]
cutter *n.* tailor etc. who takes measurements and cuts cloth; small fast sailing-ship; small boat carried by large ship. [CUT]
cutthroat **1** *n.* murderer; razor with long blade set in handle. **2** *a.* intense and ruthless (*cutthroat competition*); (of card-game) three-handed.
cutting *n.* piece cut from newspaper etc.; piece cut from plant for propagation; excavated channel through high ground, for railway or road.
cuttlefish /'kʌt(ə)lfɪʃ/ *n.* ten-armed mollusc that ejects black fluid when threatened. [OE]
cutwater *n.* forward edge of ship's prow; wedge-shaped projection from pier or bridge. [CUT]
c.v. *abbr.* curriculum vitae.
cwm /ku:m/ *n.* (in Wales) = COOMB; cirque. [W]
cwt. *abbr.* hundredweight.
-cy *suffix* denoting status or condition (*bankruptcy, baronetcy*). [L *-cia*, Gk *-kia*]
cyanic /saɪ'ænɪk/ *a.* of or containing cyanogen. [CYANOGEN]
cyanide /'saɪənaɪd/ *n.* highly poisonous substance used in extraction of gold and silver. [foll.]
cyanogen /saɪ'ænədʒɪn/ *n.* inflammable poisonous gas. [F f. Gk *kuanos* blue mineral]
cyanosis /saɪə'nəʊsɪs/ *n.* blue discoloration of skin due to lack of oxygen in the blood. [-OSIS]
cybernetics /saɪbə'netɪks/ *n.* science of systems of control and communications in animals and machines. [Gk *kubernētēs* steersman]
cyclamate /'saɪkləmeɪt, 'sɪk-/ *n.* artificial sweetening agent. [chem. name]
cyclamen /'sɪkləmən/ *n.* plant with pink, red, or white flowers with reflexed petals. [L f. Gk]
cycle /'saɪk(ə)l/ **1** *n.* recurrent round or period (of events, phenomena, etc.); time needed for one such round or period; recurrent series of operations or states; series of songs, poems, etc., usu. on single theme; bicycle, tricycle, etc.; *Electr.* = HERTZ. **2** *v.i.* ride bicycle etc.; move in cycles. [F or L f. Gk *kuklos* circle]
cyclic /'saɪklɪk/ *a.* recurring in cycles; belonging to a chronological cycle; *Chem.* with constituent atoms forming ring. [F or L (prec.)]
cyclist /'saɪklɪst/ *n.* rider of bicycle. [CYCLE]
cyclo- *comb. form* of CYCLE.
cyclone /'saɪkləʊn/ *n.* system of winds rotating inwards to area of low barometric pressure; violent hurricane of limited diameter; **cyclonic** /-'klɒnɪk/ *a.* [Gk *kuklōma* wheel]
Cyclopean /saɪklə'pi:ən/ *a.* (of ancient masonry) made of massive irregular blocks. [L f. Gk (*Kuklōps* anc. one-eyed giant)]
cyclostyle /'saɪkləstaɪl/ **1** *n.* apparatus printing copies of writing from stencil. **2** *v.t.* print or reproduce with this. [CYCLO-]
cyclotron /'saɪklətrɒn/ *n.* apparatus for acceleration of charged atomic particles revolving in magnetic field. [CYCLO-, -TRON]
cygnet /'sɪgnɪt/ *n.* young swan. [AF dimin. f. F f. L *cygnus* swan f. Gk]
cylinder /'sɪlɪndə/ *n.* uniform solid or hollow body with straight sides and circular section; thing of this shape, e.g. container for liquefied gas etc., or part of machine, esp. piston-chamber in engine; **cylindrical** /-'lɪndrɪk(ə)l/ *a.* [L *cylindrus* f. Gk]
cymbal /'sɪmb(ə)l/ *n.* each of pair of concave brass plates forming musical instrument, clashed together or struck to make ringing sound; **cymbalist** /-bəlɪst/ *n.* [L f. Gk]
cyme /saɪm/ *n.* flower group with single terminal flower on each stem. [F f. L f. Gk *kuma* wave]
Cymric /'kɪmrɪk/ *a.* Welsh. [W *Cymru* Wales]
cynic /'sɪnɪk/ *n.* one who has little faith in human sincerity or goodness; (**Cynic**) ancient-Greek philosopher showing contempt for ease and pleasure; **cynical** *a.*; **cynically** *adv.*; **cynicism** /-sɪz(ə)m/ *n.* [L f. Gk (*kuōn* dog)]
cynosure /'saɪnəzjʊə,'sɪn-/ *n.* centre of attraction or admiration. [F, or L f. Gk, = dog's tail (name for Ursa Minor)]
cypher var. of CIPHER.
cypress /'saɪprəs/ *n.* coniferous tree with dark foliage, taken as symbol of mourning. [F f. L f. Gk]
Cypriot /'sɪprɪət/ **1** *n.* native or inhabitant of Cyprus; dialect of Greek used there. **2** *a.* of Cyprus. [*Cyprus* in E. Mediterranean]

Cyrillic /sɪ'rɪlɪk/ *a.* of alphabet used by Slavonic peoples of the Orthodox Church. [St *Cyril* d. 869]
cyst /sɪst/ *n.* sac formed in the body, containing morbid matter. [Gk *kustis* bladder]
cystic *a.* of the bladder; like a cyst.
cystitis /sɪs'taɪtɪs/ *n.* inflammation of the bladder. [-ITIS]
-cyte *suffix* denoting mature biological cell (*leucocyte*). [foll.]
cytology /saɪ'tɒlədʒɪ/ *n.* study of biological cells. [Gk *kutos* vessel]
cytoplasm /'saɪtəplæz(ə)m/ *n.* protoplasmic content of cell other than the nucleus.
czar var. of TSAR.
Czech /tʃek/ **1** *n.* native or language of Bohemia; = CZECHOSLOVAK. **2** *a.* of Bohemia; of Czechoslovakia. [Bohemian *Čech*]
Czechoslovak /tʃekə'sləʊvæk/ (also **Czechoslovakian** /-'vækɪən/) **1** *n.* native of Czechoslovakia. **2** *a.* of Czechoslovakia. [prec., SLOVAK]

D

D, d /di:/ *n.* (*pl.* **Ds, D's**) fourth letter; *Mus.* second note in diatonic scale of C major; *Rom. num.* 500; = DEE.
d. *abbr.* daughter; died; (former) penny [L DENARIUS].
'd *v. colloq.* (usu. after pronouns) had, would (*I'd, he'd*). [abbr.]
dab[1] **1** *v.* (**-bb-**) press (surface) briefly with sponge etc. without rubbing; press (sponge, brush; colour etc.) on surface thus, aim feeble blow (*at*), strike lightly. **2** *n.* dabbing; light blow; smear of paint etc.; (in *pl.*) *sl.* fingerprints. [imit.]
dab[2] *n.* & *a. colloq.* adept (*at*); **dab hand** expert. [orig. unkn.]
dab[3] *n.* a kind of flat-fish. [orig. unkn.]
dabble /'dæb(ə)l/ *v.* take casual interest or part (*in* subject or activity); wet partly or intermittently; moisten, stain; move feet or hands about in shallow water. [DAB[1]]
dabchick /'dæbtʃɪk/ *n.* small water-bird of grebe family. [OE]
dace *n.* (*pl.* same) small freshwater fish. [F *dars* (DART)]
dacha /'dætʃə/ *n.* country villa in Russia. [Russ.]
dachshund /'dækshʊnd/ *n.* dog of short-legged long-bodied breed. [G, = badger-dog]
dactyl /'dæktɪl/ *n.* a metrical foot (‑ˇˇ); **dactylic** /-'tɪlɪk/ *a.* [L f. Gk, = finger]
dad *n. colloq.* father. [imit. of child's *da da*]
Dada /'dɑ:dɑ:/ *n.* 20th-c. international movement in art and literature repudiating conventions; **Dadaism** *n.* [F (*dada* hobby-horse)]
daddy /'dædɪ/ *n. colloq.* father; oldest or most important person or thing; **daddy-long-legs** /-'lɒŋ-/ crane-fly. [DAD]
dado /'deɪdəʊ/ *n.* (*pl.* **dados**) lower part of room-wall when visibly distinct from upper part; plinth of column; cube of pedestal. [It. (DIE[1])]
daemon see DEMON.
daffodil /'dæfədɪl/ *n.* yellow narcissus with trumpet-shaped crown. [ASPHODEL]
daft /dɑ:ft/ *a. colloq.* silly, foolish, crazy. [OE, = meek]
dagger *n.* short pointed stabbing-weapon; *Printing* = OBELUS; **at daggers drawn** in bitter enmity; **look daggers at** glare angrily at. [orig. uncert.]
dago /'deɪgəʊ/ *n.* (*pl.* **dagos**) *sl. derog.* **(R)** foreigner, esp. Spaniard, Portuguese, or Italian. [Sp. *Diego* = James]
daguerreotype /də'gerəʊtaɪp/ *n.* early kind of photograph using chemically treated plate. [*Daguerre*, inventor]
dahlia /'deɪlɪə/ *n.* garden plant with bright flowers. [*Dahl*, botanist]
Dáil (Eireann) /dɔɪl ('eɪrən)/ *n.* lower house of parliament in Republic of Ireland. [Ir., = assembly (of Ireland)]
daily /'deɪlɪ/ **1** *a.* done or produced or occurring every day. **2** *adv.* every day, constantly. **3** *n.* daily newspaper; *colloq.* charwoman working daily. **4 daily bread** one's necessary food or livelihood. [DAY]
dainty /'deɪntɪ/ **1** *a.* delicately pretty; delicate of build or in movement; (of food) choice, tasty; (of person) fastidious, having delicate taste and sensibility. **2** *n.* choice morsel, delicacy. **3 daintily** *adv.* [F f. L (DIGNITY)]
daiquiri /'dækərɪ, 'daɪ-/ *n.* cocktail of rum, lime-juice, etc. [*Daiquiri* in Cuba]
dairy /'deərɪ/ *n.* place for processing and distribution of milk and its products; **dairy farm** one producing esp. dairy products; **dairy products** milk, cream, butter, cheese, etc. [OE]

dairymaid *n.* woman employed in dairy.
dairyman *n.* dealer in milk etc.
dais /'deɪɪs/ *n.* low platform usu. at upper end of room or hall. [F f. L DISCUS table]
daisy /'deɪzɪ/ *n.* small flower having yellow disc and white petals; **daisy wheel** disc with characters on circumference used as printer in word processors and typewriters. [OE, = *day's eye*]
Dalai lama see LAMA.
dale *n.* valley, esp. in N. England. [OE]
dally /'dælɪ/ *v.i.* delay, waste time; amuse oneself, play about or flirt (*with*); **dalliance** *n.* [F]
Dalmatian /dæl'meɪʃ(ə)n/ *n.* dog of large white breed with dark spots. [*Dalmatia* in Yugoslavia]
dam[1] **1** *n.* barrier checking flow of water to form reservoir, to prevent flooding, etc. **2** *v.t.* (**-mm-**) furnish or confine with dam; obstruct, block (*up*). [LG or Du.]
dam[2] *n.* mother, esp. of four-footed animal. [var. of DAME]
damage /'dæmɪdʒ/ **1** *n.* injury impairing value or usefulness of something, loss of what is desirable; *sl.* cost; (in *pl.*) sum claimed or awarded as compensation for loss or injury. **2** *v.t.* do harm to, injure. **3** **damageable** *a.* [F f. L *damnum*]
damascene /'dæməsi:n, -'si:n/ *v.t.* decorate (metal) esp. with inlaid gold or silver. [*Damascus* in Syria]
damask /'dæməsk/ **1** *n.* figured woven material, esp. white table-linen with designs shown by reflection of light. **2** *a.* made of damask; coloured like damask rose, velvety pink. **3** *v.t.* weave with figured designs. **4** **damask rose** a fragrant rose grown esp. to make attar. [AF f. L (as prec.)]
dame *n.* (title of) woman with rank of Knight Commander or holder of Grand Cross in Orders of chivalry (**Dame**); comic middle-aged woman in modern pantomime, usu. played by man; *archaic* or *US sl.* woman. [F f. L *domina* lady]
damn /dæm/ **1** *v.t.* curse (person or thing, or *absol.*; freq. = *may God damn*, or as *int.* of anger or annoyance); condemn, censure; doom to hell, cause damnation of; bring condemnation upon, be the ruin of, show to be guilty (*damning evidence*). **2** *n.* uttered curse; negligible amount (*don't give a damn*). **3** *a.* & *adv.* *colloq.* damned. **4** **damn all** *sl.* nothing at all; **damn(ed) well** as emphatic (*damn well do without*); **damn with faint praise** commend so feebly as to imply disapproval; **I'm damned if** *I do, will*, etc., *colloq.* I certainly do not, will not, etc.; **(well) I'm damned** *colloq.* I am astonished. [F f. L (*damnum* loss)]
damnable /'dæmnəb(ə)l/ *a.* hateful, annoying; **damnably** *adv.*
damnation /dæm'neɪʃ(ə)n/ **1** *n.* eternal punishment. **2** *int.* expressing anger or annoyance.
damned /dæmd/ **1** *a.* damnable. **2** *adv.* extremely (*damned hot*). **3** **do one's damnedest** do one's utmost.
damp **1** *n.* diffused moisture esp. as inconvenience or danger. **2** *a.* slightly or fairly wet. **3** *v.* make damp; take vigour or crispness out of, reduce vibration of, make flaccid or spiritless. **4** **damp course** layer of damp-proof material in wall near ground, preventing rise of damp. [LG]
damper *n.* device that reduces shock or noise; silencing-pad in piano mechanism, shock-absorber in vehicle, plate in flue controlling draught and combustion.
damsel /'dæmz(ə)l/ *n.* *archaic* young woman. [F dimin. (DAME)]
damson /'dæmz(ə)n/ *n.* small dark-purple plum; its colour; tree bearing it. [L (DAMASCENE)]
dan *n.* degree of proficiency in judo etc.; holder of this. [Jap.]
dance /dɑ:ns/ **1** *v.* move rhythmically, usu. to music, alone or with partner or set; move in lively way, skip; bob up and down; perform (specified dance); move up and down, dandle (child). **2** *n.* piece of dancing, special form of this, single round or turn of one; social gathering for dancing; tune for dancing to. **3** **dance attendance (on person)** follow or wait on obsequiously; **lead person a dance** cause him much trouble. **4** **dancer** *n.* [F]
d. and c. *abbr.* dilatation (of the cervix) and curettage (of the uterus).
dandelion /'dændɪlaɪən/ *n.* yellow-flowered wild plant with toothed leaves. [F f. L. = lion's tooth]
dander *n.* *colloq.* temper, indignation; **get one's dander up** be angry. [orig. uncert.]
dandle /'dænd(ə)l/ *v.t.* dance (child) on one's knees or in one's arms. [orig. unkn.]
dandruff /'dændrʌf/ *n.* dead skin in small scales among the hair; condition of having this. [orig. uncert.]
dandy /'dændɪ/ **1** *n.* man unduly devoted to smartness and fashion in dress etc.; *colloq.* excellent thing. **2** *a.* *colloq.* splendid, first-rate. [perh. name *Andrew*]
Dane *n.* native of Denmark; *hist.* invader of England in 9th–11th c.; **(Great) Dane** dog of large short-haired breed. [ON]
danger /'deɪndʒə/ *n.* liability or exposure to harm, thing that causes harm;

danger list list of those dangerously ill; **danger money** extra payment for dangerous work; **in danger of** likely to incur or suffer from. [F f. L *dominus* lord]

dangerous *a.* involving or causing danger.

dangle /'dæŋg(ə)l/ *v.* be loosely suspended, hold or carry suspending loosely; hold out enticingly (bait, temptation). [imit.]

Danish /'deɪnɪʃ/ **1** *a.* of Denmark, of the Danes or their language. **2** *n.* Danish language. **3 Danish blue** white cheese with blue veins; **Danish pastry** coiled yeast cake topped with icing, nuts, etc. [F f. L (DANE)]

dank *a.* disagreeably cold and damp. [prob. Scand.]

daphne /'dæfnɪ/ *n.* a kind of flowering shrub. [Gk]

dapper *a.* neat and precise, esp. in dress; sprightly. [LG or Du.]

dapple /'dæp(ə)l/ *v.t.* mark with rounded spots of colour or shade; **dapple-grey** *a.* & *n.* (horse) of grey with darker spots; **dappled** *a.* [orig. unkn.]

Darby and Joan /'dɑ:bɪ/ devoted old married couple; **Darby and Joan club** social club for elderly people. [people in 18th-c. poem]

dare 1 *v.t.* (3 *sing. pres.* usu. **dare** before expressed or implied infinitive without *to*) venture (*to*), have the courage or impudence (*to*) (*dare he do it?*; *if they dare to come*; *how dare you?*); defy, challenge (person) *to*. **2** *n.* act of daring, challenge. **3 I dare say** I think it probable (*that*). [OE]

daredevil 1 *n.* recklessly daring person. **2** *a.* recklessly daring.

daring 1 *n.* adventurous courage. **2** *a.* bold, adventurous, prepared to take risks.

dariole /'dærɪəʊl/ *n.* savoury or sweet dish cooked and served in small mould. [F]

dark 1 *a.* with little or no light; of deep or sombre colour; with brown or black skin, complexion, or hair; gloomy, dismal, remote or mysterious, secret; forbidding; *archaic* ignorant, unenlightened. **2** *n.* absence of light; lack of knowledge; dark place, e.g. in painting. **3 after dark** after nightfall; **Dark Ages** period preceding Middle Ages, esp. 5th–10th c., *fig.* period of unenlightenment; **dark horse** little-known person who is unexpectedly successful; **dark-room** room with light excluded, for photographic work; **in the dark** with no light, lacking information. [OE]

darken *v.* make or become dark; **never darken person's door** stay away from him.

darkness *n.* lack of light; wickedness (*powers of darkness*).

darling /'dɑ:lɪŋ/ **1** *n.* beloved or lovable person or thing, favourite. **2** *a.* beloved or prized, *colloq.* charming or pretty. [OE (DEAR)]

darn[1] **1** *v.t.* mend (cloth etc.) by stitching across hole. **2** *n.* place so mended. [orig. uncert.]

darn[2] *v.*, *n.*, *a.*, & *adv.*, **darned** *a.* & *adv.*, *sl.* mild forms of DAMN, DAMNED. [corrupt.]

darnel /'dɑ:n(ə)l/ *n.* a kind of weed growing in corn. [orig. unkn.]

darning *n.* things to be darned. [DARN[1]]

dart 1 *n.* small pointed missile used as weapon or in game; insect's sting; (in *pl.*) indoor game with feathered darts and target; darting motion; tapering stitched tuck in garment. **2** *v.* throw (missile); direct suddenly (glance etc.); go rapidly like missile (*out*, *in*, *past*, etc.). [F f. Gmc]

dartboard *n.* circular target in game of darts.

Darwinian /dɑ:'wɪnɪən/ *a.* of Darwin's doctrine of evolution of species; **Darwinism** /'dɑ:-/ *n.* [*Darwin*, naturalist]

dash 1 *v.* rush hastily or forcefully; strike with violence so as to shatter; fling (*against* etc.); knock, drive, throw, thrust (*away*, *off*, *out*, etc.); frustrate (hopes etc.), daunt, dispirit; *sl.* mild form of DAMN. **2** *n.* rush, onset, sudden advance (*made a dash for the door*); impetuous vigour; showy appearance or behaviour; *US* sprinting-race; horizontal stroke (—) in writing or printing to mark break in sense, omitted words, etc.; longer signal of two in Morse code; slight admixture (*dash of soda*); = DASHBOARD. **3 cut a dash** make brilliant show; **dash down** (or **off**) write down hurriedly. [imit.]

dashboard *n.* surface beneath windscreen of motor vehicle, containing instruments and controls.

dashing *a.* spirited, lively; showy.

dastardly /'dæstədlɪ/ *a.* cowardly, despicable. [orig. uncert.]

data /'deɪtə, 'dɑ:-/ *n.pl.* (also (**D**) treated as *sing.*, although *sing.* form is **datum**) known facts or things used as basis for inference or reckoning; quantities or characters operated on by computer etc.; **data bank** store or source of data; **data processing** automatic performance of operations on data; **data processor** machine that does this. [F f. L *data* (*do* give)]

database *n.* organized store of data for computer processing.

datable /'deɪtəb(ə)l/ *a.* capable of being dated (*to* a particular time). [foll.]

date[1] **1** *n.* day of the month; statement (usu. day, month, and year) in document etc. of time of composition or publication; period to which work of art etc. belongs; time at which thing happens or is to happen; *colloq.* engagement, appointment, *US* person with whom one has social engagement. **2** *v.* mark with date; refer (event, thing) *to* a time; have existed *from* a certain time; be recognizable as of a past or particular period, be or become or make or indicate to be out of date (*your clothes date you*); *colloq.* make a social engagement with. **3 date-line** north–south line partly along meridian 180° from Greenwich, east and west of which date differs, line in newspaper at head of dispatch or special article to show date and place of writing; **date-stamp** adjustable rubber stamp for recording date; **out of date** old-fashioned, obsolete; **to date** until now; **up to date** meeting or according to latest requirements or knowledge. [F (DATA)]

date[2] *n.* dark oblong single-stoned fruit of W. Asia and N. Africa; tree bearing it (also **date-palm**). [F f. L f. Gk (DACTYL; from shape of leaf)]

dative /'deɪtɪv/ *Gram.* **1** *n.* case expressing indirect object or recipient. **2** *a.* of or in the dative. [L (DATA)]

datum see DATA.

daub /dɔ:b/ **1** *v.t.* coat or smear (wall or other surface) with plaster or other sticky or greasy substance; paint crudely or unskilfully. **2** *n.* plaster or other substance daubed on surface, smear; crude painting. [F f. L (DE-, ALB)]

daughter /'dɔ:tə/ *n.* female child in relation to her parent(s); female descendant, female member *of* family etc.; woman who is regarded as the spiritual descendant of; **daughter-in-law** son's wife. [OE]

daunt /dɔ:nt/ *v.t.* discourage, intimidate. [F f. L *domito* (*domo* tame)]

dauntless *a.* not to be daunted, intrepid.

dauphin /'dɔ:fɪn/ *n. hist.* eldest son of King of France. [F f. L *delphinus* DOLPHIN, w. ref. to territorial name]

davenport /'dævənpɔ:t/ *n.* kind of writing-desk; *US* large sofa. [maker's name]

davit /'dævɪt/ *n.* crane on board ship, esp. one of pair used for suspending or lowering boat. [F (dimin. of *David*)]

Davy Jones's locker /'deɪvɪ 'dʒəʊnzɪz/ *sl.* bottom of the sea, esp. regarded as grave of drowned sailors. [orig. unkn.]

Davy lamp /'deɪvɪ/ miner's safety lamp with wire gauze enclosing flame. [inventor]

daw *n.* = JACKDAW. [OE]

dawdle /'dɔ:d(ə)l/ *v.i.* walk slowly and idly, delay, waste time. [orig. unkn.]

dawn 1 *n.* first light, daybreak, incipient gleam of something. **2** *v.i.* begin to be day, grow light; become evident, develop. **3 dawn chorus** early-morning bird-song; **dawn on** begin to be understood by. [OE]

day *n.* time between sunrise and sunset, daylight (*clear as day*); time during which work is normally done (*an 8-hour day*); period of 24 hours as unit of time; (in *sing.* or *pl.*) period (*to this day, the old days*), lifetime, period of prosperity etc. (*in my day, end one's days*); point of time in the future (*one day, some day*); date of specific festival, day associated with particular event or purpose (*Christmas day, pay-day*); day's endeavour, esp. as bringing success (*save the day*); **all in a day's work** part of normal routine; **at the end of the day** in the final reckoning; **call it a day** end a period of activity; **day-bed** (for daytime rest); **day-boy** (or **-girl**) school pupil living at home; **day-dream** *n.* & *v.i.* (indulge in) pleasant fantasy or reverie; **day in, day out** continuous(ly), routine(ly); **day nursery** one where children are looked after while mothers are at work; **day release** system of allowing employees days off work for education; **day-return** *a.* & *n.* (ticket) at reduced rate for journey both ways in one day; **day-room** one used during day only; **day-school** one for pupils living at home; **day-to-day** *attrib. a.* routine; **has had its day** is no longer useful; **late in the day** too late to be useful; **not one's day** day of successive misfortunes (for someone); **one day** see ONE; **one of these (fine) days** before long; **one of those days** day when things go badly; **on one's day** at one's peak of capability; **some day** in the future; **that will be the day** that will be worth waiting for, *iron.* that will never happen. [OE]

daybreak *n.* first light of day.

daylight *n.* light of day, dawn; open knowledge; visible interval e.g. between boats in a race; **daylight robbery** *colloq.* excessive charge or expense; **daylight saving** achieving of longer evening daylight esp. in summer by making clocks show later time; **scare** etc. **the (living) daylights out of** *sl.* terrify; **see daylight** begin to understand what was previously obscure.

daytime *n.* time of daylight.

daze 1 *v.t.* stupefy, bewilder. **2** *n.* state of being dazed. [ON]

dazzle /'dæz(ə)l/ **1** *v.t.* blind temporarily or confuse sight of by excess of light; impress or overpower (person) with knowledge, ability, etc. **2** *n.* bright blinding light. [f. prec.]

dB *abbr.* decibel(s).

DC *abbr.* direct current; District of Columbia.

D-Day /'di:deɪ/ *n.* day (6 June 1944) on which British and American forces invaded N. France; day on which an important operation is to begin. [*D* for *day*]

DDT /-'ti:/ *n.* white chlorinated hydrocarbon used as insecticide. [f. chem. name]

de- *prefix* in senses 'down', 'away' (*descend, deduct*), 'completely' (*denude*); added to verbs and derivs. to form verbs and nouns implying removal or reversal (*decentralize, de-ice, demoralization*). [L]

deacon /'di:kən/ *n.* (in Episcopal churches) minister of third order, below bishop and priest; (in Nonconformist churches) secular officer of congregation; (in early Church) minister of charity; **deaconess** /-'nes/ *n. fem.* [OE f. L f. Gk *diakonos* servant]

deactivate /di:'æktɪveɪt/ *v.t.* render inactive or less reactive. [DE-]

dead /ded/ **1** *a.* no longer alive, *colloq.* extremely tired or unwell; having lost sensation (*my fingers are dead*); (with *to*) unappreciative of, insensitive to; no longer effective or in use, extinct (*dead as the dodo*); extinguished or inactive (*dead match, volcano*); inanimate; lacking vigour, dull, lustreless, not resonant, no longer effervescent; quiet, lacking activity (*the dead season*); (of microphone or telephone etc.) not transmitting sounds; (of ball in games) out of play; abrupt, complete, exact, unqualified (*dead stop, calm, centre, certainty*). **2** *adv.* absolutely, extremely, completely, exactly (*dead right, tired, against, on target*). **3** *n.* time of silence or inactivity (*the dead of night*). **4 the dead** dead person(s), all who have died; **cut person dead** deliberately ignore his presence; **dead-and-alive** dull, spiritless; **dead beat** *colloq.* exhausted; **dead-beat** *n. colloq.* penniless person; **dead duck** *sl.* unsuccessful or useless person or thing; **dead end** closed end of passage etc., *fig.* course offering no prospects (often *attrib.* with hyphen); **dead hand** oppressive posthumous control; **dead head** faded flower-head, non-paying member of audience, useless person; **dead heat** (result of) race in which two or more competitors finish exactly level; **dead language** one no longer ordinarily spoken; **dead letter** law or practice no longer recognized; **dead loss** *colloq.* useless person or thing; **dead man's handle** controlling-handle on electric train, disconnecting power supply if released; **dead march** funeral march; **dead-pan** *a.* expressionless; **dead reckoning** (of ship's position by log or compass etc. when observations are impossible); **dead set** see SET[2]; **dead shot** one who never misses; **dead to the world** fast asleep, unconscious; **dead weight** inert mass, *fig.* debt not covered by assets; total weight carried on ship; **dead wood** *fig.* useless person(s) or thing(s). [OE]

deaden *v.* deprive of or lose vitality, force, brightness, feeling, etc., make insensitive *to*.

deadline *n.* time-limit.

deadlock **1** *n.* situation in which no progress can be made; type of lock requiring key to open or close it. **2** *v.* bring or come to standstill.

deadly **1** *a.* causing or able to cause fatal injury or serious damage; intense, extreme, as death; accurate (*deadly aim*). **2** *adv.* as if dead, extremely (*deadly pale, serious*).

deaf /def/ *a.* wholly or partly without hearing; declining to listen *to*; **the deaf** deaf people; **deaf-aid** hearing aid; **deaf-and-dumb alphabet** system of manual signs for communication with or among the deaf; **deaf mute** deaf and dumb person; **turn a deaf ear** be unresponsive. [OE]

deafen *v.t.* overpower with sound. make unable to hear, esp. temporarily.

deafening *a.* very loud.

deal[1] **1** *v.* (*past* and *p.p.* **dealt** /delt/) distribute or portion (*out, round*) to several people etc.; distribute (cards) to players; assign as share or deserts; administer, cause to be received (*deal a heavy blow* lit. or fig.); behave in specified way (*honourably, badly*, etc.) *with* or *by* person. **2** *n.* dealing or turn to deal at cards, round of play following this; *colloq.* business agreement, transaction (*do a deal with, it's a deal*); (*colloq.*) *a* large amount. **3 deal in** be a seller of; **deal with** do business with, take measures concerning (question, problem, person), treat (subject); **a good** (or **great**) **deal** a large amount (as *n.* or *adv.*: *a good deal of money, is a great deal better*); **raw** (or **rough**) **deal** harsh or unfair treatment. [OE]

deal[2] *n.* sawn fir or pine timber; deal board of standard size. [LG]

dealer *n.* person dealing at cards, trader (in *comb.* or with *in*: *cattle-dealer, dealer in tobacco*). [DEAL[1]]

dealings *n.pl.* (esp.) person's conduct or transactions.

dean[1] *n.* head of cathedral or collegiate-church chapter; fellow of college etc. with advisory and disciplinary functions; head of university faculty or department or of medical college; (**rural**) **dean** head of clergy in division of archdeaconry. [F f. L *decanus*]

dean[2] var. of DENE.

deanery *n.* dean's house or office; rural dean's group of parishes. [DEAN[1]]

dear **1** *a.* beloved or much esteemed (often *iron.*, or as polite form esp. at beginning of letters); precious *to*, cherished; earnest, deeply felt (in this sense usu. *superl.* or in *adv.*: *his dearest wish*; *would dearly like*); high in price, having high prices. **2** *n.* dear person (esp. as form of address). **3** *adv.* at high price or great cost (*cost him dear*; *will pay dear*). **4** *int.* expressing esp. surprise, distress, or pity (*dear me!*; *oh dear!*). [OE]

dearth /dɜːθ/ *n.* scarcity or lack, esp. of food.

death /deθ/ *n.* dying, final cessation of vital functions; being killed or killing, event which ends life; ceasing to be, annihilation (*death of one's hopes*); (also **Death**) personified power that annihilates; being dead, lack of spiritual life (*everlasting death*); **at death's door** close to death; **Black Death** 14th-c. plague epidemic in Europe; **catch one's death** *colloq.* catch serious chill etc.; **death-blow** lethal blow (*lit.* or *fig.*); **death certificate** official statement of cause and date and place of person's death; **death duty** tax levied on property after owner's death; **death-mask** cast taken of dead person's face; **death penalty** punishment by being put to death; **death rate** number of deaths per 1,000 of population per year; **death-trap** unsafe place, vehicle, etc.; **death-warrant** order for execution of condemned person, *fig.* anything that causes end of established practice etc.; **death-watch (beetle)** small beetle whose larva bores in wood with ticking sound, once supposed to portend death; **death-wish** desire (usu. unconscious) for death of oneself or another; **fate worse than death** subjection to rape; **put to death** kill or cause to be killed; **sure as death** quite certain; **to death** to the utmost, extremely (*bored to death*, *worked to death*). [OE]

deathbed *n.* bed on which one dies.

deathly **1** *a.* suggestive of death (*deathly silence*). **2** *adv.* in a deathly way (*deathly pale*).

deb *n. colloq.* débutante. [abbr.]

débâcle /deɪˈbɑːk(ə)l/ *n.* utter defeat or failure; sudden collapse; confused rout. [F]

debar /dɪˈbɑː/ *v.t.* (**-rr-**) exclude *from* admission or right. [F (BAR[1])]

debark /diːˈbɑːk/ *v.* land from a ship; **debarkation** /-ˈkeɪʃ(ə)n/ *n.* [F *débarquer*]

debase /dɪˈbeɪs/ *v.t.* lower in quality, value, or character; depreciate (coin) by alloying etc. [DE-, (A)BASE]

debatable /dɪˈbeɪtəb(ə)l/ *a.* open to discussion or dispute. [foll.]

debate /dɪˈbeɪt/ **1** *v.* discuss (question); hold formal argument, esp. in legislative or public meeting; consider different sides of question, ponder. **2** *n.* formal discussion on particular matter, open argument. [F (BATTLE)]

debauch /dɪˈbɔːtʃ/ **1** *v.t.* corrupt morally; make intemperate or sensually indulgent; deprave or debase (taste, judgement); (in *p.p.*) dissolute. **2** *n.* bout of sensual indulgence. [F]

debauchery *n.* excessive sensual indulgence.

debenture /dɪˈbentʃə/ *n.* acknowledgement of indebtedness, esp. bond of company acknowledging debt and providing for payment of interest at fixed intervals. [L *debentur* are owed]

debilitate /dɪˈbɪlɪteɪt/ *v.t.* enfeeble, enervate. [L (*debilis* weak)]

debility /dɪˈbɪlɪtɪ/ *n.* feebleness, esp. of health.

debit /ˈdebɪt/ **1** *n.* entry in account of sum owed; the sum itself or total of such sums. **2** *v.t.* enter on debit side of account (amount *against* or *to* person, person *with* amount). [F f. L *debitum* DEBT]

debonair /debəˈneə/ *a.* carefree, self-assured, cheerful in manner. [F]

debouch /dɪˈbaʊtʃ, -ˈbuːʃ/ *v.i.* (of troops, stream) issue from ravine, wood, etc., into open ground; (of river, road, etc.) merge into larger body or area (sea, square, etc.). [F (*bouche* mouth)]

debrief /diːˈbriːf/ *v.t.* interrogate (person, esp. pilot etc.) about completed undertaking. [BRIEF]

debris /ˈdebriː, ˈdeɪ-/ *n.* scattered fragments, rubbish, wreckage. [F (*briser* break)]

debt /det/ *n.* money etc. that is owed, obligation, state of owing (*in*, *out of*, *debt*); **debt of honour** one not legally recoverable, esp. sum lost in gambling; **in person's debt** under obligation to him. [F f. L (*debeo*, *debit-* owe)]

debtor /ˈdetə/ *n.* person owing money etc.

debug /diːˈbʌg/ *v.t.* (**-gg-**) remove bugs from; *sl.* remove concealed listening devices from (room etc.) or defects from (machine etc.). [DE-, BUG]

debunk /diːˈbʌŋk/ *v.t. colloq.* show good reputation of (person, institution, etc.) to be spurious; expose falseness of (claim etc.). [DE-, BUNK[3]]

début /'deɪbu:, -bju:/, *US* **debut** *n.* first appearance (as performer, in society, etc.). [F]
débutante /'debju:tɑ:nt/ *n.* young woman making social début.
Dec. *abbr.* December.
deca- *in comb.* tenfold. [Gk *deka* ten]
decade /'dekeɪd/ *n.* ten-year period; series or group of ten. [F f. L f. Gk (prec.)]
decadence /'dekədəns/ *n.* deterioration, decline (esp. of nation, art, or literature after reaching peak); decadent attitude or behaviour. [F f. L (DECAY)]
decadent *a.* declining, of a period of decadence; self-indulgent.
decaffeinated /di:'kæfɪneɪtɪd/ *a.* having had caffeine removed or reduced. [DE-]
decagon /'dekəgən/ *n.* plane figure with ten sides and angles; **decagonal** /-'kægən(ə)l/ *a.* [L f. Gk (DECA-, *-gōnos* -angled)]
decagram /'dekəgræm/ *n.* (also **decagramme**) metric unit of mass, equal to 10 grams. [DECA-]
decalitre /'dekəli:tə/ *n.* metric unit of capacity, equal to 10 litres.
Decalogue /'dekəlɒg/ *n.* the Ten Commandments. [F or L f. Gk (DECA-, LOGOS)]
decametre /'dekəmi:tə/ *n.* metric unit of length, equal to 10 metres. [DECA-]
decamp /dɪ'kæmp/ *v.i.* break up or leave camp; take oneself off, abscond. [F (CAMP¹)]
decanal /dɪ'keɪn(ə)l, 'dekə-/ *a.* of dean; of dean's or S. side of choir. [L (DEAN¹)]
decant /dɪ'kænt/ *v.* pour off (wine, liquid, solution) leaving sediment behind; *fig.* transfer as if by pouring. [L f. Gk (*kanthos* lip of jug)]
decanter *n.* stoppered glass flask into which wine or spirit is decanted.
decapitate /dɪ'kæpɪteɪt/ *v.t.* behead; **decapitation** /-'teɪʃ(ə)n/ *n.* [L (CAPITAL)]
decapod /'dekəpɒd/ *n.* ten-footed crustacean, e.g. crab. [F f. L f. Gk (DECA-, *pous pod-* foot)]
decarbonize /di:'kɑ:bənaɪz/ *v.t.* remove carbon from (internal-combustion engine etc.). [DE-]
decathlon /dɪ'kæθlɒn/ *n.* athletic contest in which each competitor takes part in all its 10 events. [DECA-, Gk *athlon* contest]
decay /dɪ'keɪ/ **1** *v.* (cause to) rot, decompose; (cause to) decline in quality, power, wealth, energy, beauty, etc.; (of substance) undergo change by radioactivity. **2** *n.* rotten or ruinous state; decline in health, loss of quality; radioactive change. [F (L *cado* fall)]
decease /dɪ'si:s/ chiefly *Law* **1** *n.* death. **2** *v.i.* die. [F f. L (*cedo* go)]
deceased **1** *a.* dead. **2** *n.* person who has died, esp. recently.
deceit /dɪ'si:t/ *n.* concealing of truth in order to mislead, dishonest trick; tendency to use deceit; **deceitful** *a.* [F f. L (*capio* take)]
deceive /dɪ'si:v/ *v.* make (person) believe what is false, mislead purposely; be unfaithful to, esp. sexually; use deceit; **deceive oneself** persist in mistaken belief.
decelerate /di:'seləreɪt/ *v.* reduce speed (of); **deceleration** /-'reɪʃ(ə)n/ *n.* [DE-, (AC)CELERATE]
December /dɪ'sembə/ *n.* twelfth month of year. [F f. L (*decem* ten, orig. 10th month of Roman year)]
decency /'di:sənsɪ/ *n.* correct and tasteful behaviour; compliance with recognized propriety; avoidance of obscenity; (in *pl.*) requirements of correct behaviour. [L (DECENT)]
decennial /dɪ'senj(ə)l/ *a.* lasting, recurring every, 10 years. [L (*decem* ten, *annus* year)]
decent /'di:sənt/ *a.* seemly, not immodest or obscene or indelicate; respectable; acceptable, good enough; *colloq.* kind, obliging. [F or L (*decet* is fitting)]
decentralize /di:'sentrəlaɪz/ *v.t.* transfer from central to local authority; distribute among local centres; **decentralization** /-'zeɪʃ(ə)n/ *n.* [DE-]
deception /dɪ'sepʃ(ə)n/ *n.* deceiving, being deceived; thing that deceives. [F or L (DECEIVE)]
deceptive /dɪ'septɪv/ *a.* apt to mislead, easily mistaken for something else.
deci- *in comb.* one-tenth. [L *decimus* tenth]
decibel /'desɪbel/ *n.* unit used in comparison of power levels in electrical communication or intensities of sound. [DECI-, BEL]
decide /dɪ'saɪd/ *v.* bring or come to a resolution (*to do* thing, *for* or *against*, *that*); settle (issue etc.) in favour of one side or another; give judgement (*between*, *for*, *in favour of*, *against*, *that*). [F or L (*caedo* cut)]
decided *a.* definite or unquestionable (usu. *attrib.*); (of person) having clear views, positive in judgement.
decidedly *adv.* undoubtedly, undeniably.
decider *n.* game, race, etc., to decide between competitors finishing equal in previous contest.
deciduous /dɪ'sɪdjʊəs/ *a.* (of tree) shedding its leaves annually; (of leaves, horns, teeth, etc.) shed periodically or normally. [L (*cado* fall)]
decigram /'desɪgræm/ *n.* (also

decigramme) metric unit of mass, equal to 0.1 gram. [DECI-]

decilitre /'desɪli:tə/ *n.* metric unit of capacity, equal to 0.1 litre.

decimal /'desɪm(ə)l/ **1** *a.* of tenths or ten, proceeding or reckoning by tens; of decimal coinage. **2** *n.* decimal fraction. **3** **decimal coinage** (or **currency**) one using decimal system; **decimal fraction** one with a power of 10 as denominator, esp. when written as figures after decimal point; **decimal point** dot placed after the unit figure in decimal notation; **decimal system** that in which each denomination or weight or measure is 10 times the value of the one immediately below it. [L (*decem* ten)]

decimalize *v.t.* express as decimal, convert to decimal system; **decimalization** /-'zeɪʃ(ə)n/ *n.*

decimate /'desɪmeɪt/ *v.t.* destroy one tenth of, (**D**) large proportion of; *hist.* kill one in ten of (mutinous or cowardly soldiers).

decimetre /'desɪmi:tə/ *n.* metric unit of length, equal to 0.1 metre. [DECI-]

decipher /dɪ'saɪfə/ *v.t.* convert (text written in cipher or unfamiliar script) into understandable script or language; establish meaning of (poor writing, anything puzzling). [DE-, CIPHER]

decision /dɪ'sɪʒ(ə)n/ *n.* act of deciding; settlement (of issue etc.); conclusion reached, resolve made; tendency to decide firmly. [F or L (DECIDE)]

decisive /dɪ'saɪsɪv/ *a.* that decides an issue or contributes to a decision (*decisive battle*); (of person, preference, etc.) decided, positive. [F f. med.L (DECIDE)]

deck **1** *n.* platform in ship covering (part of) hull's area at any level and serving as floor, ship's accommodation on particular deck; floor or compartment of bus etc.; component that carries magnetic tape, disc, etc., in sound-reproduction equipment or computer; *US* pack of cards; *sl.* ground. **2** *v.t.* furnish with, cover as, deck; (often with *out*) array, adorn. **3** **below deck(s)** in(to) space under main deck; **deck-chair** portable folding chair (orig. used on deck in passenger ships); **deck-hand** man employed on ship's deck in cleaning and odd jobs. **4** **-decker** *in comb.* having specified number of decks (*double-decker bus*). [Du., = cover]

declaim /dɪ'kleɪm/ *v.* speak or utter rhetorically or affectedly; practise oratory; inveigh *against*; **declamation** /deklə'meɪʃ(ə)n/ *n.*; **declamatory** /dɪ'klæmətərɪ/ *a.* [F or L (CLAIM)]

declaration /deklə'reɪʃ(ə)n/ *n.* declaring; emphatic or deliberate statement; formal announcement. [L (foll.)]

declare /dɪ'kleə/ *v.* announce openly or formally (*declare war, a dividend*); pronounce (*declared it invalid*); assert emphatically (*that*); acknowledge possession of (*dutiable goods, income*, etc.); (in *p.p.*) that is such by his own admission (*a declared atheist*); (in cricket) choose to close one's side's innings before all wickets have fallen; name trump suit in card-game; **declare oneself** reveal one's intentions or identity; **declarative** /-'klærətɪv/ *a.*; **declaratory** /-'klærətərɪ/ *a.* [L (*clarus* clear)]

declension /dɪ'klenʃ(ə)n/ *n.* variation of form of noun etc. to give its grammatical case; class by which noun etc. is declined; falling-off, deterioration. [F f. L (DECLINE)]

declination /deklɪ'neɪʃ(ə)n/ *n.* downward bend; angular distance of star etc. north or south of celestial equator; deviation of compass needle from true north; **declinational** *a.* [L (foll.)]

decline /dɪ'klaɪn/ **1** *v.* deteriorate, lose strength or vigour, decrease; refuse (invitation or challenge) formally and courteously, give or send refusal; slope downwards; bend down, droop; *Gram.* give forms of (noun or adjective) corresponding to cases. **2** *n.* declining, gradual loss of vigour etc., deterioration, decay. [F f. L (*clino* bend)]

declivity /dɪ'klɪvɪtɪ/ *n.* downward slope. [L (*clivus* slope)]

declutch /di:'klʌtʃ/ *v.i.* disengage clutch of motor vehicle. [DE-]

decoction /dɪ'kɒkʃ(ə)n/ *n.* boiling down to extract essence; the essence produced. [F or L (*coquo* boil)]

decode /di:'kəʊd/ *v.t.* convert (coded message) into understandable language. [DE-]

decoke /di:'kəʊk/ *colloq.* **1** *v.t.* decarbonize. **2** *n.* process of decarbonizing. [COKE[1]]

décolletage /deɪkɒl'tɑ:ʒ/ *n.* low neckline of woman's dress etc. [F (*collet* collar)]

décolleté /deɪ'kɒlteɪ/ *a.* having low neckline.

decompose /di:kəm'pəʊz/ *v.* decay, rot; separate (substance) into its elements; **decomposition** /-pə'zɪʃ(ə)n/ *n.* [F (DE-)]

decompress /di:kəm'pres/ *v.t.* subject to decompression. [DE-]

decompression /di:kəm'preʃ(ə)n/ *n.* release from compression; gradual reduction of air pressure on person who has been subjected to it (esp. underwater); **decompression chamber** enclosed space for this; **decompression**

sickness condition caused by sudden lowering of air pressure and formation of bubbles in the blood.

decongestant /di:kən'dʒestənt/ *n.* medicinal substance that relieves congestion.

decontaminate /di:kən'tæmɪneɪt/ *v.t.* remove (esp. radioactive) contamination from; **decontamination** /-'neɪʃ(ə)n/ *n.* [DE-]

décor /'deɪkɔ:, 'de-/ *n.* furnishing and decoration of room or stage. [F (foll.)]

decorate /'dekəreɪt/ *v.t.* furnish with adornments; paint, paper, etc., room or house; serve as adornment to; invest with order, medal, or other award; **Decorated style** ornate 14th-c. stage of English Gothic architecture; **decorative** *a.* [L (*decus -oris* beauty)]

decoration /dekə'reɪʃ(ə)n/ *n.* decorating, thing that decorates; medal etc. conferred and worn as honour; (in *pl.*) flags etc. put up on festive occasion. [F or L (prec.)]

decorator /'dekəreɪtə/ *n.* person who decorates, esp. one who paints or papers houses professionally. [DECORATE]

decorous /'dekərəs/ *a.* having or showing decorum. [L *decorus* seemly]

decorum /dɪ'kɔ:rəm/ *n.* behaviour or usage conforming with decency or politeness, seemliness. [as prec.]

decoy /'di:kɔɪ/ **1** *n.* thing or person used to lure an animal or other person into a trap or danger; bait, enticement. **2** /also dɪ'kɔɪ/ *v.t.* lure by means of a decoy. [Du.]

decrease 1 /dɪ'kri:s/ *v.* make or become smaller or fewer. **2** /'di:kri:s/ *n.* decreasing; amount by which thing decreases. [F f. L (DE-, *cresco* grow)]

decree /dɪ'kri:/ **1** *n.* official or authoritative order having legal force; judgement or decision of certain law-courts. **2** *v.t.* ordain by decree. **3 decree nisi** /'naɪsaɪ/ provisional order for divorce, made absolute unless cause to the contrary is shown within fixed period. [F f. L *decretum* (*cerno* sift); L *nisi* unless]

decrepit /dɪ'krepit/ *a.* weakened by age or hard use, dilapidated; **decrepitude** *n.* [L (*crepo* creak)]

decretal /dɪ'kri:t(ə)l/ *n.* papal decree. [L (DECREE)]

decry /dɪ'kraɪ/ *v.t.* disparage, depreciate. [CRY]

dedicate /'dedɪkeɪt/ *v.t.* devote to sacred person or purpose; devote (esp. *oneself*) to a special task or purpose; (of author or composer) address (book, piece of music, etc.) *to* person as honour or recognition; (in *p.p.*) devoted to vocation etc., having single-minded loyalty; **dedicatee** /-kə'ti:/ *n.*; **dedicator** *n.*; **dedicatory** *a.* [L (*dico* declare)]

dedication /dedɪ'keɪʃ(ə)n/ *n.* dedicating; words with which book etc. is dedicated. [F or L (prec.)]

deduce /dɪ'dju:s/ *v.t.* infer, draw as logical conclusion. [L (*duco duct-* lead)]

deduct /dɪ'dʌkt/ *v.t.* subtract, take away, withhold (portion or amount). [as prec.]

deductible *a.* that may be deducted, esp. from one's tax or taxable income.

deduction /dɪ'dʌkʃ(ə)n/ *n.* deducting, amount deducted; deducing, inferring of particular instances from general law; conclusion reached. [F or L (DEDUCE)]

deductive *a.* of or reasoning by deduction. [med.L (DEDUCE)]

dee *n.* letter D; thing shaped like this. [name of letter D]

deed *n.* thing consciously done; brave, skilful, or conspicuous act; actual fact, performance (*kind in word and deed*); document effecting legal transfer of ownership and bearing disposer's signature; **deed-box** strong box for keeping deeds and other documents; **deed of covenant** agreement to pay regular amount annually to charity etc., enabling charity to recover tax paid by donor on this amount of his income; **deed poll** deed made by one party only, esp. to change name. [OE, rel. to DO¹]

deem *v.t.* regard, consider, judge (*deem it my duty*; *deem it sufficient*). [OE]

deemster *n.* either of two judges in Isle of Man. [f. prec.]

deep 1 *a.* extending far down or in from top or surface or edge; extending to or lying at specified depth (*ankle-deep in mud*; *water 6ft. deep*; *soldiers drawn up six deep*); situated far down or back or in; coming or brought from far down or in (*deep breath, sigh*); low-pitched, full-toned, not shrill (*deep voice, note, bell*); intense, vivid, extreme (*deep disgrace, secret, sleep, colour*); heartfelt, absorbing (*deep feelings, interest*); fully absorbed or overwhelmed (*deep in thought, in debt*); profound, penetrating, difficult to understand (*deep thinker, thought, insight*). **2** *n.* deep place (esp. *the* sea) or state (*deep of the night*); position of fieldsman distant from batsman in cricket. **3** *adv.* deeply, far down or in (*dig deep*; *deep into the night*). **4 deep-fry** fry (food) in fat or oil that covers it; **deep-laid** (of scheme) secret and elaborate; **deep-rooted, -seated** (of feelings or convictions) firmly established, profound; **go off the deep end** give way to anger or emotion; **in deep water** in trouble or difficulty. [OE]

deepen *v.* make or become deep or deeper.
deep-freeze /di:p'fri:z/ **1** *n.* freezer; storage in freezer. **2** *v.t.* (*past* **deep-froze**; *p.p.* **deep-frozen**) store in deep-freeze.
deer *n.* (*pl.* same) four-footed ruminant animal of which the male usu. has antlers. [OE]
deerskin *n.* leather from deer's skin.
deerstalker /'dɪəstɔ:kə/ *n.* soft cloth cap with peaks in front and behind.
deface /dɪ'feɪs/ *v.t.* spoil appearance of; make illegible; **defacement** *n.* [F (FACE)]
de facto /di: 'fæktəʊ, deɪ/ in fact, existing in fact (whether by right or not). [L]
defalcate /'di:fælkeɪt/ *v.i.* misappropriate money; **defalcator** *n.* [med.L f. L *falx* sickle]
defalcation /di:fæl'keɪʃ(ə)n/ *n.* misappropriation of money; amount misappropriated; shortcoming.
defame /dɪ'feɪm/ *v.t.* attack good reputation of; speak ill of; **defamation** /defə'meɪʃ(ə)n/ *n*; **defamatory** /dɪ'fæmətərɪ/ *a.* [F f. L (*fama* report)]
default /dɪ'fɔ:lt, -'fɒlt/ **1** *n.* failure to fulfil an obligation, esp. to appear, pay, or act in some way. **2** *v.i.* fail to meet (esp. pecuniary) obligation. **3 go by default** be absent, be ignored because of absence; **in default of** because of or in case of lack or absence of. [F (FAIL)]
defaulter *n.* one who defaults, esp. soldier guilty of military offence.
defeat /dɪ'fi:t/ **1** *v.t.* overcome in battle or other contest; frustrate, baffle. **2** *n.* defeating or being defeated. [AF f. L (DIS-, FACT)]
defeatist *n.* one who expects or accepts defeat too readily; **defeatism** *n.*
defecate /'di:fɪkeɪt/ *v.* expel faeces from the bowels; **defecation** /-'keɪʃ(ə)n/ *n.* [L (*faex faecis* dregs)]
defect /dɪ'fekt/ **1** /also 'di:fekt/ *n.* lack of something essential, imperfection; shortcoming, failing. **2** *v.i.* abandon one's country or cause in favour of another. [L (*deficio -fect-* fail)]
defection /dɪ'fekʃ(ə)n/ *n.* abandonment of one's country or cause; **defector** *n.* [L (prec.)]
defective /dɪ'fektɪv/ *a.* having defects, imperfect, incomplete; mentally subnormal. [F or L (DEFECT)]
defence /dɪ'fens/, *US* **defense** *n.* defending, protection; means of resisting attack; justification, vindication; defendant's case in lawsuit, counsel for defendant; players in defending position in game; (in *pl.*) fortifications; **defence mechanism** body's reaction against disease organisms, mental process avoiding conscious conflict. [foll.]
defend /dɪ'fend/ *v.* resist attack made on, protect (person or thing, or *absol.*); uphold by argument, speak or write in favour of; conduct defence in lawsuit; **defender** *n.* [F f. L *defendo -fens-*]
defendant *n.* person accused or sued in a lawsuit. [F (prec.)]
defensible /dɪ'fensɪb(ə)l/ *a.* able to be defended or justified; **defensibility** /-'bɪlɪtɪ/ *n.*; **defensibly** *adv.* [L (DEFEND)]
defensive *a.* done or intended for defence, protective; **on the defensive** in attitude or position of defence, ready for criticism. [F f. med.L (DEFEND)]
defer[1] /dɪ'fɜ:/ *v.t.* (**-rr-**) put off to later time, postpone; **deferred payment** payment by instalments for goods supplied; **deferred shares** (or **stock**) shares or stock with least entitlement to dividend; **deferment** *n.*; **deferral** *n.* [orig. same as DIFFER]
defer[2] /dɪ'fɜ:/ *v.i.* (**-rr-**) yield or make concessions in opinion or action (*to* person). [F f. L *defero delat-* carry away]
deference /'defərəns/ *n.* courteous regard, compliance with another's wishes or advice; **in deference to** out of respect for.
deferential /defə'renʃ(ə)l/ *a.* showing deference; **deferentially** *adv.*
defiance /dɪ'faɪəns/ defying, open disobedience, bold resistance. [F (DEFY)]
defiant *a.* showing defiance.
deficiency /dɪ'fɪʃənsɪ/ *n.* being deficient; lack or shortage (*of*); thing lacking, deficit; **deficiency disease** disease caused by lack of some essential element in diet. [foll.]
deficient *a.* incomplete or insufficient in some essential respect (*deficient in vitamins*). [L (DEFECT)]
deficit /'defɪsɪt/ *n.* amount by which total falls short of what is required; excess of liabilities over assets. [F f. L (DEFECT)]
defile[1] /dɪ'faɪl/ *v.t.* make dirty, pollute; corrupt; **defilement** *n.* [earlier *defoul* f. F *defouler* trample down]
defile[2] /dɪ'faɪl/ **1** /also 'di:faɪl/ *n.* gorge or pass through which troops etc. can pass only in file. **2** *v.i.* march in file. [F (FILE[1])]
define /dɪ'faɪn/ *v.t.* give exact meaning of (word etc.); describe or explain scope of (*define one's position*); outline clearly, mark out the boundary of. [F f. L (*finis* end)]
definite /'defɪnɪt/ *a.* having exact and discernible limits; clear and distinct, not vague; **definite article** see ARTICLE. [L (prec.)]
definition /defɪ'nɪʃ(ə)n/ *n.* defining; statement of precise meaning of word etc.; degree of distinctness in outline of object or image. [F f. L (DEFINE)]

definitive /dɪ'fɪnɪtɪv/ *a.* (of answer, treaty, verdict, etc.) final, decisive, unconditional; (of edition of book etc.) most authoritative.
deflate /dɪ'fleɪt/ *v.* let out air or gas from (balloon, tyre, etc.); (cause to) lose confidence or conceit; apply deflation to (the economy), pursue policy of deflation. [DE-, INFLATE]
deflation /dɪ'fleɪʃ(ə)n/ *n.* deflating; reduction of amount of money in circulation to increase its value as measure against inflation; **deflationary** *a.*
deflect /dɪ'flekt/ *v.* turn aside from straight course or intended purpose; (cause to) deviate (*from*); **deflexion** *n.* (also **deflection**); **deflector** *n.* [L (*flecto* bend)]
deflower /di:'flaʊə/ *v.t.* deprive (woman) of virginity; ravage; remove flowers from (plant). [F f. L (FLOWER)]
defoliate /di:'fəʊlɪeɪt/ *v.t.* remove leaves from, esp. as military tactic; **defoliant** *n.*; **defoliation** /-'eɪʃ(ə)n/ *n.* [L (FOIL²)]
deform /dɪ'fɔ:m/ *v.t.* spoil appearance or form of, put out of shape; **deformation** /-'meɪʃ(ə)n/ *n.* [F f. L (FORM)]
deformed *a.* (of person or limb) misshapen.
deformity *n.* deformed state; malformation esp. of body or limb.
defraud /dɪ'frɔ:d/ *v.t.* cheat by fraud. [F or L (FRAUD)]
defray /dɪ'freɪ/ *v.t.* provide money to pay (cost or expense); **defrayal** *n.* [F f. med.L (*fredum* fine)]
defrost /di:'frɒst/ *v.t.* remove frost or ice from; unfreeze (frozen food). [DE-]
deft *a.* neatly skilful or dextrous, adroit. [var. of DAFT = 'meek']
defunct /dɪ'fʌŋkt/ *a.* no longer existing or in use; extinct, dead. [L (*fungor* perform)]
defuse /di:'fju:z/ *v.t.* remove fuse from (explosive, bomb); reduce tension or potential danger in (crisis, difficulty, etc.). [DE-]
defy /dɪ'faɪ/ *v.t.* resist openly, refuse to obey; (of thing) present insuperable obstacles to (*defy solution*, *definition*, *comparison*); challenge (person) to do or prove something. [F f. Rmc (L *fides* faith)]
degenerate /dɪ'dʒenərət/ **1** *a.* having lost the qualities that are normal and desirable or proper to its kind. **2** *n.* degenerate person or animal. **3** /-əreɪt/ *v.i.* become degenerate. **4 degeneracy** *n.* [L (*genus* race)]
degeneration /dɪdʒenə'reɪʃ(ə)n/ *n.* becoming degenerate; morbid deterioration of body tissue. [F f. L (prec.)]
degrade /dɪ'greɪd/ *v.* reduce to lower rank; bring into dishonour or contempt; reduce to lower organic type or simpler structure; **degradation** /degrə'deɪʃ(ə)n/ *n.* [F f. L (GRADE)]
degrading *a.* humiliating, lowering one's self-respect.
degree /dɪ'gri:/ *n.* stage in ascending or descending series; stage in intensity or amount (*to a high degree*); relative condition (*each good in its degree*); unit of measurement of angle or arc; unit in scale of temperature, hardness, etc.; academic diploma of proficiency in specified subject; *Law* grade of crime or criminality (*murder in the first degree*); step in direct genealogical descent; social or official rank; **by degrees** a little at a time, gradually; **comparative** and **superlative degree** see COMPARATIVE, SUPERLATIVE; **forbidden** (or **prohibited**) **degrees** number of degrees of descent too few to allow of marriage between two related persons. [F f. Rmc (L *gradus* step)]
dehumanize /di'hju:mənaɪz/ *v.t.* remove human characteristics from; make impersonal. [DE-]
dehydrate /di:'haɪdreɪt/ *v.* remove water or moisture from; make or become dry (*lit.* or *fig.*); **dehydration** /-'dreɪʃ(ə)n/ *n.* [Gk *hudōr* water]
de-ice /di:'aɪs/ *v.t.* remove ice from; prevent formation of ice on; **de-icer** *n.* [DE-]
deify /'di:ɪfaɪ/ *v.t.* make a god of; regard or worship as a god; **deification** /-fɪ'keɪʃ(ə)n/ *n.* [F f. L (*deus* god)]
deign /deɪn/ *v.i.* think fit, condescend, *to do* thing. [F f. L (*dignus* worthy)]
deism /'di:ɪz(ə)m/ *n.* belief in the existence of a god arising from conviction rather than revelation or dogma; **deist** *n.*; **deistic** /-'ɪstɪk/ *a.* [L *deus* god]
deity /'di:ɪtɪ, (D)'deɪ-/ *n.* divine status or nature; god; **the Deity** God. [F f. eccl.L]
déjà vu /'deɪʒɑ: 'vu:/ illusory feeling of having already experienced a present situation; something tediously familiar. [F, = already seen]
deject /dɪ'dʒekt/ *v.t.* (often in *p.p.*) put in low spirits, depress. [L (*jacio* throw)]
de jure /di: 'dʒʊərɪ, deɪ 'jʊəreɪ/ rightful; by right. [L]
dekko /'dekəʊ/ *n. sl.* a look (*let's have a dekko*). [Hindi]
delay /dɪ'leɪ/ **1** *v.* make or be late, hinder; postpone, defer; wait, loiter. **2** *n.* act or process of delaying; hindrance; time lost by inaction or inability to proceed. **3 delayed-action** *a.* operating after an interval of time. [F]
delectable /dɪ'lektəb(ə)l/ *a.* delightful, enjoyable; **delectably** *adv.* [F f. L (DELIGHT)]

delectation /di:lek'teɪʃ(ə)n/ *n.* enjoyment, delight (*for one's delectation*).

delegate 1 /'delɪgət/ *n.* person appointed as representative; member of deputation or committee. **2** /'delɪgeɪt/ *v.t.* appoint or send as representative; entrust (task) *to* representative. [L (LEGATE)]

delegation /delɪ'geɪʃ(ə)n/ *n.* delegating; body of delegates.

delete /dɪ'li:t/ *v.t.* cross out or remove (letter, word, etc.); **deletion** *n.* [L *deleo*]

deleterious /delɪ'tɪərɪəs/ *a.* harmful to body or mind. [L f. Gk]

delft *n.* a kind of glazed earthenware, usu. with blue decoration (also **delftware**). [*Delft* in Holland]

deliberate 1 /dɪ'lɪbərət/ *a.* intentional, fully considered; unhurried, slow and careful. **2** /dɪ'lɪbəreɪt/ *v.* think carefully (about); take counsel. [L (*libra* balance)]

deliberation /dɪlɪbə'reɪʃ(ə)n/ *n.* careful consideration; careful slowness. [F f. L (prec.)]

deliberative /dɪ'lɪbərətɪv/ *a.* of or for deliberation (*deliberative function, assembly*). [F or L (DELIBERATE)]

delicacy /'delɪkəsɪ/ *n.* delicateness; avoidance of immodesty or of giving offence; a choice food. [foll.]

delicate /'delɪkət/ *a.* fine or pleasing in texture or construction, exquisite; subtle, hard to discern (*delicate flavour, colour*); deft, sensitive (*delicate touch, instrument*); tender, easily harmed, liable to illness (*delicate skin, health, child*); requiring deftness or tact (*a delicate operation, subject, situation*); avoiding coarseness or impropriety; (esp. of actions) considerate. [F or L]

delicatessen /delɪkə'tes(ə)n/ *n.* shop selling prepared foods and delicacies; such food. [G f. F (prec.)]

delicious /dɪ'lɪʃəs/ *a.* highly pleasing, esp. to taste or smell. [F f. L (*deliciae* delight)]

delight /dɪ'laɪt/ **1** *v.* please greatly; take great pleasure *in*; be highly pleased *to do* thing. **2** *n.* great pleasure; thing that gives it. **3 delightful** *a.*; **delightfully** *adv.* [F f. L (*delecto*)]

delimit /dɪ'lɪmɪt/ *v.t.* fix limits or boundaries of; **delimitation** /-'teɪʃ(ə)n/ *n.* [F f. L (LIMIT)]

delineate /dɪ'lɪnɪeɪt/ *v.t.* show by drawing or description; **delineation** /-'eɪʃ(ə)n/ *n.*; **delineator** *n.* [L (LINE)]

delinquent /dɪ'lɪŋkwənt/ **1** *a.* committing an offence; failing in a duty. **2** *n.* offender (esp. *juvenile delinquent*). **3 delinquency** *n.* [L *delinquo* offend]

deliquesce /delɪ'kwes/ *v.i.* become liquid, melt; dissolve in moisture absorbed from the air; **deliquescence** *n.*; **deliquescent** *a.* [L (LIQUID)]

delirious /dɪ'lɪrɪəs/ *a.* affected with delirium; raving, wildly excited; ecstatic. [foll.]

delirium /dɪ'lɪrɪəm/ *n.* disordered state of mind with incoherent speech and hallucinations; mood of frenzied excitement; **delirium tremens** /'tri:menz/ form of delirium with tremors and terrifying delusions, caused by prolonged consumption of alcohol. [L (*lira* ridge between furrows)]

deliver /dɪ'lɪvə/ *v.t.* convey or distribute (letters or goods etc.) to destination(s); transfer possession of, give *up* or hand *over* to another; utter (speech or sermon); aim or launch (blow, attack, ball); set free, rescue (*from*); assist at birth of or in giving birth; **be delivered of** give birth to; **deliver the goods** *colloq.* carry out one's part of bargain. [F f. L (*liber* free)]

deliverance *n.* rescue, setting free.

delivery *n.* delivering, being delivered; periodical distribution of letters or goods etc.; manner of delivering ball, speech, etc. [AF (DELIVER)]

dell *n.* small wooded hollow. [OE]

delouse /di:'laʊs/ *v.t.* rid of lice. [DE-]

Delphic /'delfɪk/ *a.* of or like the ancient Greek oracle at Delphi; obscure, enigmatic. [*Delphi* in Greece]

delphinium /del'fɪnɪəm/ *n.* garden plant with tall spikes of usu. blue flowers. [Gk (DOLPHIN)]

delta /'deltə/ *n.* fourth letter of Greek alphabet (Δ,δ); triangular alluvial tract at river's mouth enclosed or watered by diverging outlets; **delta wing** triangular swept-back wing of aircraft. [Gk]

delude /dɪ'lu:d/ *v.t.* fool, deceive. [L (*ludo* mock)]

deluge /'delju:dʒ/ **1** *n.* great flood; heavy fall of rain; overwhelming rush (*a deluge of applications*). **2** *v.t.* flood; overwhelm. **3 the Deluge** Noah's flood. [F f. L *diluvium*]

delusion /dɪ'lu:ʒ(ə)n/ *n.* false belief or impression; vain hope; hallucination; **delusive** *a.* [DELUDE]

de luxe /də 'lʌks, 'lu:ks/ of superior kind or quality; sumptuous. [F, = of luxury]

delve *v.* search (*into* books etc.) for information; *archaic* dig. [OE]

demagnetize /di:'mægnɪtaɪz/ *v.t.* remove magnetization of; **demagnetization** /-'zeɪʃ(ə)n/ *n.* [DE-]

demagogue /'deməgɒg/, *US* **demagog** *n.* political agitator appealing to popular wishes or prejudices; **demagogic** /-'gɒgɪk/ *a.*; **demagogy** *n.* [Gk, = leader of people]

demand /dɪ'mɑ:nd/ **1** *n.* request made as of right or peremptorily; urgent claim (*many demands on my time*); popular desire for goods or services (*little demand for caviar in Bootle*). **2** *v.t.* make a demand for; insist on being told (*demanded her business*); require, call for (*job demands much patience*). **3 in demand** much sought after; **on demand** as soon as asked for. [F f. L (MANDATE)]

demanding *a.* requiring much skill or effort; making many demands.

demarcation /di:mɑ:'keɪʃ(ə)n/ *n.* marking of boundary or limits, esp. between work considered by trade unions to belong to different trades (*demarcation dispute*). [Sp. (*marcar* MARK[1])]

demean /dɪ'mi:n/ *v.t.* lower the dignity of (*would not demean myself*). [MEAN[2]]

demeanour /dɪ'mi:nə/, *US* **demeanor** *n.* bearing, outward behaviour. [F f. Rmc f. L *minor* threaten]

demented /dɪ'mentɪd/ *a.* driven mad, crazy. [F f. L (*mens* mind)]

dementia /dɪ'menʃə/ *n.* insanity with loss of intellectual power due to brain disease or injury; **dementia praecox** /'pri:kɒks/ schizophrenia. [L (prec.)]

demerara /demə'reərə/ *n.* a brown raw cane sugar. [*Demerara* in Guyana]

demerit /di:'merɪt/ *n.* fault, undesirable quality. [F or L (MERIT)]

demesne /dɪ'mi:n, -'meɪn/ *n.* land attached to mansion etc; region or domain; landed estate; possession (of land) as one's own. [F f. L *dominicus* (*dominus* lord)]

demi- /'demɪ/ *prefix* half-. [F f. L *dimidius* half]

demigod /'demɪgɒ:d/ *n.* partly divine being; offspring of mortal and god or goddess; godlike person. [GOD]

demijohn /'demɪdʒɒn/ *n.* large bottle in wicker case. [F]

demilitarize /di:'mɪlɪtəraɪz/ *v.t.* remove military organization or forces from (zone etc.); **demilitarization** /-'zeɪʃ(ə)n/ *n.* [DE-]

demi-monde /'demɪmɔ̃d/ *n.* women of doubtful repute in society; group behaving with doubtful legality etc. [F, = half-world]

demise /dɪ'maɪz/ **1** *n.* death (*lit.* or *fig.*); transfer of estate by lease or will. **2** *v.t.* transfer (estate or title) to another. [AF (DISMISS)]

demisemiquaver /demɪ'semɪkweɪvə/ *n.* note in music equal to half a semiquaver. [DEMI-]

demist /di:'mɪst/ *v.t.* clear mist from (windscreen etc.); **demister** *n.* [DE-]

demo /'deməʊ/ *n.* (*pl.* **demos**) *colloq.* (political etc.) demonstration. [abbr.]

demob /di:'mɒb/ *v.t.* (**-bb-**) *colloq.* demobilize. [abbr.]

demobilize /di:'məʊbɪlaɪz/ *v.t.* release from military service; **demobilization** /-'zeɪʃ(ə)n/ *n.* [F (DE-)]

democracy /dɪ'mɒkrəsɪ/ *n.* government by all the people, direct or representative; State having this; form of society ignoring hereditary class distinctions and tolerating minority views. [F f. L f. Gk (*dēmos* the people)]

democrat /'deməkræt/ *n.* advocate of democracy; (**Democrat**) *US* member of Democratic Party. [F (prec.)]

democratic /demə'krætɪk/ *a.* of or according to democracy; supporting or constituting democracy; **democratically** *adv.*; **democratize** /dɪ'mɒkrətaɪz/ *v.t.* [F f. med.L f. Gk (DEMOCRACY)]

demodulation /di:mɒdjʊ'leɪʃ(ə)n/ *n.* process of extracting modulating signal from modulated carrier wave. [DE-]

demography /dɪ'mɒgrəfɪ/ *n.* study of statistics of births, deaths, disease, etc., as illustrating conditions of life in communities; **demographic** /demə'græfɪk/ *a.*; **demographically** /demə'græfɪkəlɪ/ *adv.* [Gk *dēmos* the people, -GRAPHY]

demolish /dɪ'mɒlɪʃ/ *v.t.* pull or knock down (building); destroy; refute (theory); overthrow (institution); **demolition** /demə'lɪʃ(ə)n/ *n.* [F f. L (*moles* mass)]

demon /'di:mən/ *n.* devil, evil spirit; cruel or forceful person; personified evil passion; (also **daemon**) supernatural being in Greek mythology; **demonic** /dɪ'mɒnɪk/ *a.* [L f. Gk *daimōn* deity]

demonetize /di:'mʌnɪtaɪz/ *v.t.* withdraw (coin etc.) from use as money. [F (DE-, MONEY)]

demoniac /dɪ'məʊnɪæk/ **1** *a.* possessed by an evil spirit; of or like a demon; fiercely energetic, frenzied. **2** *n.* demoniac person. **3 demoniacal** /di:məʊ'naɪək(ə)l/ *a.* [F f. eccl.L (prec.)]

demonolatry /di:mə'nɒlətrɪ/ *n.* worship of demons. [DEMON, Gk *latreuō* worship]

demonology /di:mə'nɒlədʒɪ/ *n.* study of beliefs about demons. [-LOGY]

demonstrable /'demənstrəb(ə)l/ *a.* able to be shown or proved; **demonstrably** *adv.* [L (foll.)]

demonstrate /'demənstreɪt/ *v.* show evidence of; describe and explain by help of specimens or experiments; logically prove truth of; take part in public demonstration. [L (*monstro* show)]

demonstration /demən'streɪʃ(ə)n/ *n.* demonstrating; show of feeling; explanation of specimens and experiments as way of teaching; collective expression of opinion e.g. by public meeting; display of military force. [F or L (prec.)]

demonstrative /dɪ'mɒnstrətɪv/ *a.* showing or proving; given to or marked by open expression of feelings; *Gram.* (of adjective or pronoun) indicating person or thing referred to (e.g. *this, those*). [F f. L (DEMONSTRATE)]

demonstrator /'demənstreɪtə/ *n.* one who demonstrates; one who teaches by demonstration, esp. in laboratory. [L (DEMONSTRATE)]

demoralize /dɪ'mɒrəlaɪz/ *v.* weaken the morale of, dishearten; **demoralization** /-'zeɪʃ(ə)n/ *n.* [F]

demote /di:'məʊt/ *v.t.* reduce to lower rank or class; **demotion** *n.* [DE-, PROMOTE]

demotic /dɪ'mɒtɪk/ **1** *a.* popular, of the people; (of language) of popular simplified form. **2** *n.* form of modern Greek in everyday use; popular form of ancient Egyptian writing. [Gk (*dēmos* the people)]

demur /dɪ'mɜ:/ **1** *v.i.* (**-rr-**) raise objections, be unwilling. **2** *n.* objecting (usu. in **without demur**). [F f. L (*moror* delay)]

demure /dɪ'mjʊə/ *a.* quiet and serious or affectedly so. [F (prec.)]

demurrer /dɪ'mʌrə/ *n.* legal objection to relevance of opponent's point. [DEMUR]

den *n.* wild beast's lair; place of crime or vice; small private room for study etc. [OE]

denarius /dɪ'neərɪəs/ *n.* (*pl.* **denarii** /-rɪaɪ/) ancient Roman silver coin. [L (*deni* by tens)]

denary /'di:nərɪ/ *a.* of ten, decimal.

denationalize /di:'næʃənəlaɪz/ *v.t.* transfer (industry, institution, etc.) from national to private ownership; **denationalization** /-'zeɪʃ(ə)n/ *n.* [DE-]

denature /dɪ'neɪtʃə/ *v.t.* change properties of; make (alcohol) unfit for drinking. [F]

dendrochronology /dendrəʊkrə'nɒlədʒɪ/ *n.* chronology by study of annual growth-rings in timber. [Gk *dendron* tree]

dendrology /den'drɒlədʒɪ/ *n.* study of trees. [prec., -LOGY]

dene *n.* narrow wooded valley. [OE]

dengue /'deŋgɪ/ *n.* infectious tropical fever causing acute pain in joints. [W. Indian Sp. f. Swahili]

deniable /dɪ'naɪəb(ə)l/ *a.* that may be denied. [DENY]

denial /dɪ'naɪəl/ *n.* denying; refusal of request or wish; statement that thing is not true or existent; disavowal.

denier /'denjə/ *n.* unit for measuring fineness of silk, rayon, or nylon yarn. [orig. name of small coin; F f. L (DENARIUS)]

denigrate /'denɪgreɪt/ *v.t.* blacken the reputation of, defame; **denigration** /-'greɪʃ(ə)n/ *n.*; **denigrator** *n.* [L (*niger* black)]

denim /'denɪm/ *n.* twilled cotton fabric used for overalls, jeans, etc.; (in *pl.*) garment made of this. [F *de* of, *Nîmes* in France]

denizen /'denɪz(ə)n/ *n.* inhabitant or occupant (*of* place); foreigner admitted to residence and certain rights; naturalized foreign word, animal, or plant. [AF f. L *de intus* from within]

denominate /dɪ'nɒmɪneɪt/ *v.t.* give name to; call or describe (person or thing) as. [L (NOMINATE)]

denomination /dɪnɒmɪ'neɪʃ(ə)n/ *n.* name or designation, esp. characteristic or class name; Church or religious sect; class of units of measurement or money (*coins of small denominations*). [F or L (prec.)]

denominational *a.* of a particular religious denomination.

denominator /dɪ'nɒmɪneɪtə/ *n.* number below line in vulgar fraction, showing how many parts whole is divided into, divisor; **least** (or **lowest**) **common denominator** least common multiple of denominators of several fractions, *fig.* common feature of members of a group. [F or L (*nomen* name)]

denote /dɪ'nəʊt/ *v.t.* be the name for, be the sign or symbol of; indicate, give to understand; **denotation** /di:nə'teɪʃ(ə)n/ *n.* [F or L (NOTE)]

dénouement /deɪ'nu:mɔ̃/ *n.* unravelling of plot, esp. final resolution in play, novel, etc. [F (L *nodus* knot)]

denounce /dɪ'naʊns/ *v.t.* inform against, accuse publicly; announce withdrawal from (treaty etc.). [F f. L (*nuntius* messenger)]

de novo /dɪ 'nəʊvəʊ/ *adv.* afresh, starting again. [L]

dense *a.* closely compacted in substance; crowded together; crass, stupid. [F, or L *densus*]

density *n.* closeness of substance; degree of consistency measured by quantity of mass in unit volume; opacity of photographic image. [F or L (prec.)]

dent **1** *n.* depression in surface left by blow or pressure. **2** *v.t.* make dent in; become dented. [INDENT]

dental /'dent(ə)l/ *a.* of or for the teeth; of dentistry; (of consonant) pronounced with tongue-tip against upper front teeth or ridge of teeth; **dental floss** fine strong thread used to clean between teeth; **dental surgeon** dentist. [L (*dens dent-* tooth)]

dentate /'denteɪt/ *a.* toothed, having toothlike notches. [L (prec.)]

dentifrice /'dentɪfrɪs/ *n.* paste etc. for cleaning teeth. [F f. L (DENTAL)]

dentine /'denti:n/, *US* **dentin** /-tɪn/ *n.* hard dense tissue forming main part of teeth. [L (DENTAL)]
dentist /'dentɪst/ *n.* person who is qualified to treat the teeth, extract them and fit artificial ones, etc.; **dentistry** *n.* [F (DENTAL)]
dentition /den'tɪʃ(ə)n/ *n.* type and arrangement of teeth in a species etc.; teething. [L (DENTAL)]
denture /'dentʃə/ *n.* set of artificial teeth. [F (DENTAL)]
denude /dɪ'nju:d/ *v.t.* make naked or bare; strip *of* covering, property, etc.; **denudation** /di:nju:'deɪʃ(ə)n/ *n.* [L (*nudus* naked)]
denunciation /dɪnʌnsɪ'eɪʃ(ə)n/ *n.* denouncing; **denunciatory** /dɪ'nʌnsɪətərɪ/ *a.* [F or L (DENOUNCE)]
deny /dɪ'naɪ/ *v.t.* declare untrue or non-existent; disavow or repudiate; refuse (request, applicant, thing *to* person); **deny oneself** be abstinent. [F f. L (NEGATE)]
deodar /'di:ədɑ:/ *n.* Himalayan cedar. [Hindi f. Skr., = divine tree]
deodorant /dɪ'əʊdərənt/ **1** *a.* that removes or conceals unwanted odours. **2** *n.* deodorant substance. [ODOUR]
deodorize /dɪ'əʊdəraɪz/ *v.t.* destroy odour of; **deodorization** /-'zeɪʃ(ə)n/ *n.*
deoxyribonucleic acid /dɪɒksɪraɪbəʊnjʊ'kli:ɪk/ substance in chromosomes of most organisms, storing genetic information. [DE-, OXYGEN, RIBONUCLEIC]
dep. *abbr.* departs; deputy.
depart /dɪ'pɑ:t/ *v.* go away, leave; (of train or bus etc.) set out, leave; diverge or deviate (*depart from accepted view, custom*); **depart this life** die. [F f. L *dispertio* divide]
departed **1** *a.* bygone; deceased. **2** *n.* **the departed** the dead.
department *n.* separate part of complex whole, branch, esp. of municipal or State administration, university, or shop; administrative district in France etc.; area of activity; **department store** large shop supplying many kinds of goods from various departments; **departmental** /-'ment(ə)l/ *a.* [F (DEPART)]
departure /dɪ'pɑ:tʃə/ *n.* going away; deviation *from* (truth, standard); starting of train, aircraft, etc.; setting out on course of action or thought (*new departure*). [F (DEPART)]
depend /dɪ'pend/ *v.i.* (with *on* or *upon*, or *absol.*) be controlled or determined by (*success depends on hard work*); (with *on* or *upon*) be unable to do without, need for success etc. (*she depends on my help*), trust in. [F f. L (*pendeo* hang)]
dependable *a.* that may be depended on; **dependability** /-'bɪlɪtɪ/ *n.*
dependant *n.* one who depends on another for support. [F (DEPEND)]
dependence *n.* depending or being dependent; reliance.
dependency *n.* country or province controlled by another.
dependent **1** *a.* depending (*on*); unable to do without something (esp. a drug); maintained at another's cost; (of clause, phrase, or word) in subordinate relation to a sentence or word. **2** *n.* *US* = DEPENDANT. [DEPEND]
depict /dɪ'pɪkt/ *v.t.* represent in drawing or colours; portray in words, describe; **depiction** *n.* [L (PICTURE)]
depilate /'depɪleɪt/ *v.t.* remove hair from; **depilation** /-'leɪʃ(ə)n/ *n.* [L (*pilus* hair)]
depilatory /dɪ'pɪlətərɪ/ **1** *a.* that removes unwanted hair. **2** *n.* depilatory substance.
deplete /dɪ'pli:t/ *v.t.* empty, exhaust; reduce numbers or quantity of; **depletion** *n.* [L (*pleo* fill)]
deplorable /dɪ'plɔ:rəb(ə)l/ *a.* lamentable, regrettable; exceedingly bad, shocking; **deplorably** *adv.* [foll.]
deplore /dɪ'plɔ:/ *v.t.* regret deeply; find deplorable. [F or It. f. L (*ploro* wail)]
deploy /dɪ'plɔɪ/ *v.* spread (troops) out from column into line; bring (forces, arguments, etc.) into effective action; **deployment** *n.* [F f. L (*plico* fold)]
deponent /dɪ'pəʊnənt/ **1** *a.* (of verb, esp. in Greek and Latin) passive in form but active in meaning. **2** *n.* deponent verb; person making deposition under oath. [L *depono* put down, lay aside]
depopulate /di:'pɒpjʊleɪt/ *v.t.* reduce population of; **depopulation** /-'leɪʃ(ə)n/ *n.* [L (*populus* people)]
deport /dɪ'pɔ:t/ *v.t.* remove, esp. to another country, banish; behave or conduct *oneself* (in specified manner). [F f. L (*porto* carry)]
deportation /di:pɔ:'teɪʃ(ə)n/ *n.* removal (of unwanted person) to another country.
deportee /di:pɔ:'ti:/ *n.* person who has been or is to be deported. [-EE]
deportment /dɪ'pɔ:tmənt/ *n.* bearing, behaviour. [F (DEPORT)]
depose /dɪ'pəʊz/ *v.* remove from power, esp. dethrone; bear witness *that*, testify *to*, esp. on oath in court. [F f. L (foll.)]
deposit /dɪ'pɒzɪt/ **1** *n.* thing stored or entrusted for safe keeping; sum placed in bank; sum required and paid as pledge or first instalment; layer of precipitated matter, natural accumulation. **2** *v.t.* store or entrust for keeping (esp. sum in bank); pay as pledge; lay

down; (of water etc.) leave (matter) lying. **3 deposit account** savings account at bank requiring notice for withdrawal. [L (*pono posit-* put)]

depositary *n.* person to whom thing is entrusted. [L (prec.)]

deposition /depə'zɪʃ(ə)n, di:-/ *n.* deposing, esp. dethronement; sworn evidence, giving of this; taking down of Christ from the Cross. [F f. L (DEPOSIT)]

depositor /dɪ'pɒzɪtə/ *n.* person who deposits money or property. [DEPOSIT]

depository *n.* storehouse; = DEPOSITARY. [L (DEPOSIT)]

depot /'depəʊ/ *n.* storehouse, esp. for military supplies; headquarters of regiment; place where goods are deposited or from which goods, vehicles, etc., are dispatched; *US* railway or bus station. [F (DEPOSIT)]

deprave /dɪ'preɪv/ *v.t.* make morally bad, corrupt. [F or L (*pravus* crooked)]

depravity /dɪ'prævɪtɪ/ *n.* moral corruption, wickedness.

deprecate /'deprɪkeɪt/ *v.t.* express wish against or disapproval of; try to avert (person's anger etc.); **deprecation** /-'keɪʃ(ə)n/ *n.*; **deprecatory** *a.* [L (PRAY)]

depreciate /dɪ'pri:ʃɪeɪt/ *v.* diminish in value, price, or purchasing power; disparage, belittle. [L (PRICE)]

depreciation /dɪpri:sɪ'eɪʃ(ə)n/ *n.* decline in value, esp. due to wear and tear; allowance made for this.

depreciatory *a.* disparaging.

depredation /deprɪ'deɪʃ(ə)n/ *n.* (usu. in *pl.*) plundering, destruction. [F f. L (PREY)]

depress /dɪ'pres/ *v.t.* lower the spirits of, sadden; reduce activity of (esp. trade); press down (lever etc.); **depressed area** area of economic depression. [F f. L (PRESS[1])]

depressant 1 *a.* causing depression. 2 *n.* depressant agent or influence.

depression /dɪ'preʃ(ə)n/ *n.* state of extreme dejection, often with physical symptoms; long period of financial and industrial slump; lowering of atmospheric pressure, winds etc. caused by it; sunken place or hollow on a surface; pressing down.

depressive 1 *a.* tending to depress; involving mental depression. 2 *n.* person suffering from depression.

deprivation /deprɪ'veɪʃ(ə)n/ *n.* depriving; loss of desired thing. [foll.]

deprive /dɪ'praɪv/ *v.t.* prevent from use or enjoyment of; dispossess or strip of; **deprived child** child lacking normal home life; **deprival** *n.* [F f. L (PRIVATION)]

Dept. *abbr.* Department.

depth *n.* deepness; measurement from top down, from surface inwards, or from front to back; profundity, abstruseness, sagacity; intensity of colour, darkness, etc.; (often in *pl.*) deepest or most central part (*depths of the country*; *in the depth of winter*); **depth charge** bomb exploding under water, for dropping on submerged submarine etc.; **in depth** thoroughly; **in-depth** *a.* thorough; **out of one's depth** in water too deep to stand in; engaged on task beyond one's powers. [DEEP]

deputation /depjʊ'teɪʃ(ə)n/ *n.* body of persons appointed to represent others. [L (foll.)]

depute /dɪ'pju:t/ *v.t.* delegate (task) to person; appoint as one's deputy. [F f. L (*puto* consider)]

deputize /'depjʊtaɪz/ *v.i.* act as deputy (*for*). [foll.]

deputy /'depjʊtɪ/ *n.* person appointed to act for another; parliamentary representative in some countries. [var. of DEPUTE]

derail /dɪ'reɪl/ *v.t.* cause (train) to leave the rails; **derailment** *n.* [F (RAIL[1])]

derange /dɪ'reɪndʒ/ *v.t.* throw into confusion, disrupt; make insane; **derangement** *n.* [F (RANK[1])]

Derby /'dɑ:bɪ/ *n.* annual horse-race at Epsom; similar race elsewhere; important sporting contest. [Earl of *Derby*]

derelict /'derɪlɪkt/ 1 *a.* abandoned, left to fall into ruin (esp. of ship at sea or decrepit property). 2 *n.* abandoned property, esp. ship; person forsaken by society, social misfit. [L (RELINQUISH)]

dereliction /derɪ'lɪkʃ(ə)n/ *n.* abandoning or being abandoned; neglect *of duty*; shortcoming.

derestrict /di:rɪ'strɪkt/ *v.t.* remove restriction (esp. speed-limit) from. [DE-]

deride /dɪ'raɪd/ *v.t.* laugh scornfully at; treat with contempt; **derision** /-'rɪʒ(ə)n/ *n.* [L (*rideo* laugh)]

de rigueur /də 'ri:gɜ:/ required by custom or etiquette. [F]

derisive /dɪ'raɪsɪv/ *a.* scornful, scoffing (*derisive laughter*). [DERIDE]

derisory /dɪ'raɪsərɪ/ *a.* showing derision; deserving derision, too insignificant for serious consideration.

derivation /derɪ'veɪʃ(ə)n/ *n.* deriving; formation of word from word or root, tracing or statement of this. [F or L (DERIVE)]

derivative /dɪ'rɪvətɪv/ 1 *a.* derived from a source, not original. 2 *n.* derivative word or thing; *Math.* quantity measuring rate of change of another.

derive /dɪ'raɪv/ *v.* trace or obtain *from* a source; originate, be descended, *from*; show or assert descent or formation of (word etc.) *from*. [F or L (*rivus* stream)]

dermatitis /dɜ:mə'taɪtɪs/ *n.* inflammation of the skin. [Gk *derma* skin, -ITIS]

dermatology /dɜ:mə'tɒlədʒɪ/ *n.* study of the skin and its diseases; **dermatologist** *n.* [prec., -LOGY]

dermis /'dɜ:mɪs/ *n.* layer of skin below epidermis. [EPIDERMIS]

derogate /'derəgeɪt/ *v.i.* detract *from* (merit, right, etc.); **derogation** /-'geɪʃ(ə)n/ *n.* [L (*rogo* ask)]

derogatory /dɪ'rɒgətərɪ/ *a.* involving disparagement or discredit; depreciatory.

derrick /'derɪk/ *n.* kind of crane with arm pivoted at end to central post or floor; framework over oil-well etc., holding drilling machinery. [*Derrick*, hangman]

derring-do /derɪŋ'du:/ *n. literary* heroic courage or action. [*daring to do*]

derris /'derɪs/ *n.* tropical climbing plant; insecticide made from its powdered root. [L f. Gk]

derv *n.* fuel oil used in heavy road-vehicles. [*d*iesel-*e*ngined *r*oad *v*ehicle]

dervish /'dɜ:vɪʃ/ *n.* member of a Muslim religious order, vowed to poverty and chastity. [Turk. f. Pers., = poor]

desalinate /dɪ'sælɪneɪt/ *v.t.* remove salt from (esp. sea-water); **desalination** /-'neɪʃ(ə)n/ *n.* [SALINE]

descant 1 /'deskænt/ *n.* free treble part added to hymn tune; *poetic* song, melody. **2** /dɪs'kænt/ *v.i.* talk lengthily *upon.* [F f. L DIS-, *cantus* song (CHANT)]

descend /dɪ'send/ *v.* go or come down; slope downwards; make sudden attack or unexpected visit (*on*); sink or stoop *to* (unworthy act); pass by inheritance *to*; **be descended from** come by descent from (specified person etc.). [F f. L (*scando* climb)]

descendant *n.* person descended from another. [F (prec.)]

descent /dɪ'sent/ *n.* act or way of descending; downward slope; lineage, family origin; sudden attack; decline, fall.

describe /dɪ'skraɪb/ *v.t.* set forth in words, recite characteristics of; mark out, draw; move in (specified line or curve). [F f. L (*scribo* write)]

description /dɪ'skrɪpʃ(ə)n/ *n.* describing; account or verbal picture (*fits the description*); sort or class (*no food of any description*). [F f. L (prec.)]

descriptive /dɪ'skrɪptɪv/ *a.* serving or seeking to describe. [L (DESCRIBE)]

descry /dɪ'skraɪ/ *v.t.* catch sight of, succeed in discerning. [F (CRY)]

desecrate /'desɪkreɪt/ *v.t.* destroy or contemptuously disregard sacred character of; **desecration** /-'kreɪʃ(ə)n/ *n.*; **desecrator** *n.* [DE-, CONSECRATE]

desegregate /di:'segrɪgeɪt/ *v.t.* abolish racial segregation in; **desegregation** /-'geɪʃ(ə)n/ *n.* [DE-]

desert[1] /dɪ'zɜ:t/ *v.* abandon, leave without intention of returning; leave military service unlawfully; **desertion** *n.* [F f. L (*desero -sert-* leave)]

desert[2] /'dezət/ **1** *n.* dry barren often sand-covered area of land. **2** *a.* uninhabited, barren. [F f. L *desertus* (prec.)]

desert[3] /dɪ'zɜ:t/ *n.* deserving, being worthy of reward or punishment; (in *pl.*) deserved recompense. [F (DESERVE)]

deserve /dɪ'zɜ:v/ *v.* be entitled to, esp. by one's conduct or qualities (*deserves a present, a hiding*; *deserves better of them*). [F f. L (*servio* serve)]

deservedly /dɪ'zɜ:vɪdlɪ/ *adv.* as deserved, justly.

deserving *a.* worthy (*of*), worth rewarding or supporting.

déshabillé /deɪzæ'bi:eɪ/ *n.* state of being only partly dressed. [F, = undressed]

desiccate /'desɪkeɪt/ *v.t.* remove moisture from, dry (foodstuff) to preserve it; **desiccation** /-'keɪʃ(ə)n/ *n.* [L (*siccus* dry)]

desideratum /dɪsɪdə'reɪtəm/ *n.* (*pl.* **desiderata**) thing that is lacking but needed or desired. [L (DESIRE)]

design /dɪ'zaɪn/ **1** *n.* preliminary outline or drawing for something that is to be made; art of producing these; scheme of lines or shapes forming a decoration; general arrangement or layout; established form of a product; intention or purpose; mental plan, scheme of attack or approach. **2** *v.* prepare a design for; be a designer; intend or set aside for some purpose (*the remark was designed to offend*; *the course is designed for beginners*). **3 by design** on purpose; **have designs on** plan to harm or appropriate. [F f. L (*signum* mark)]

designate 1 /'dezɪgneɪt/ *v.t.* specify, indicate as having some function; describe as, give or serve as name or distinctive mark to; appoint to a position. **2** /'dezɪgnət/ *a.* appointed to but not yet installed in office (*bishop designate*). [L (prec.)]

designation /dezɪg'neɪʃ(ə)n/ *n.* designating; name or title. [F or L (prec.)]

designedly /dɪ'zaɪnɪdlɪ/ *adv.* intentionally. [DESIGN]

designer *n.* one who makes designs, esp. for clothes or manufactured products.

designing *a.* crafty, scheming.

desirable /dɪ'zaɪərəb(ə)l/ *a.* worth having or wishing for; causing desire; (of course of action) advisable. [foll.]

desire /dɪ'zaɪə/ **1** *n.* unsatisfied longing; feeling of potential pleasure or satisfaction in something; expression of this, request; object of desire; strong sexual urge. **2** *v.* have a desire for; ask for; *archaic* wish. **3 leaves much to be desired** is very imperfect. [F f. L *desidero* long for]

desirous *predic. a.* having a desire (*of*), wanting. [AF (prec.)]

desist /dɪ'zɪst, -'sɪst/ *v.i.* cease (*from* an action etc.). [F f. L *desisto*]

desk *n.* piece of furniture with flat or sloped surface serving as rest for writing or reading at; counter behind which receptionist or cashier sits; section of newspaper office dealing with specified topics; position of player in orchestra. [L (DISCUS) table]

desolate 1 /'desələt/ *a.* left alone, solitary; deserted, uninhabited, barren, dismal; forlorn and wretched. **2** /'desəleɪt/ *v.t.* depopulate, devastate; make (person) wretched. [L (*solus* alone)]

desolation /desə'leɪʃ(ə)n/ *n.* desolate or barren state; being forsaken, loneliness; grief, wretchedness. [L (prec.)]

despair /dɪs'peə/ **1** *n.* complete loss or absence of hope; thing that causes this. **2** *v.i.* lose all hope (*of*). [F f. L (*spero* hope)]

despatch var. of DISPATCH.

desperado /despə'rɑːdəʊ/ *n.* (*pl.* **desperadoes**, *US* **-os**) desperate or reckless person, esp. criminal. [foll.]

desperate /'despərət/ *a.* leaving no or little room for hope; extremely dangerous or serious (*desperate situation*); reckless from despair, violent, lawless; staking all on a small chance (*desperate remedy*). [L (DESPAIR)]

desperation /despə'reɪʃ(ə)n/ *n.* despair; reckless state of mind; readiness to take any action in desperate situation.

despicable /'despɪkəb(ə)l, dɪ'spɪk-/ *a.* deserving to be despised, contemptible. [L (*specio spect-* look at)]

despise /dɪ'spaɪz/ *v.t.* regard as inferior or worthless; feel contempt for. [F f. L (prec.)]

despite /dɪ'spaɪt/ **1** *prep.* in spite of. **2** *n. literary* disdain; malice or hatred. [F f. L (as prec.)]

despoil /dɪ'spɔɪl/ *v.t. literary* plunder, rob; **despoliation** /dɪspəʊlɪ'eɪʃ(ə)n/*n.* [F f. L (SPOIL)]

despondent /dɪ'spɒndənt/ *a.* in low spirits, dejected; **despondency** *n.* [L (SPONSOR)]

despot /'despɒt/ *n.* absolute ruler; tyrant. [F f. L f. Gk *despotēs* master]

despotic /de'spɒtɪk/ *a.* having unrestricted power, tyrannous; **despotically** *adv.*

despotism /'despətɪz(ə)m/ *n.* rule by a despot; country ruled by a despot.

dessert /dɪ'zɜːt/ *n.* sweet course of meal; course of fruit, nuts, etc., at end of dinner. [F (DIS-, SERVE)]

dessertspoon *n.* spoon between tablespoon and teaspoon in size; amount held by this; **dessertspoonful** *n.* (*pl.* **dessertspoonfuls**).

destination /destɪ'neɪʃ(ə)n/ *n.* place to which person or thing is going. [F or L (foll.)]

destine /'destɪn/ *v.t.* settle or determine the future of, appoint, set apart for a purpose (*was destined for high office, to be president*). [F f. L]

destiny /'destɪnɪ/ *n.* fate considered as a power; what is destined to happen to person etc.; predetermined course of events. [F f. L]

destitute /'destɪtjuːt/ *a.* without resources, in great need of food, shelter, etc.; devoid *of*; **destitution** /-'tjuːʃ(ə)n/ *n.* [L]

destroy /dɪ'strɔɪ/ *v.t.* pull or break down; make useless; kill (esp. sick etc. animal); nullify, neutralize effect of. [F f. L (*struo struct-* build)]

destroyer *n.* person or thing that destroys; fast heavily armed warship designed to escort other ships.

destruct /dɪ'strʌkt/ *US* **1** *v.* destroy (one's own equipment) deliberately; be destroyed thus. **2** *n.* action of destructing. **3 destructible** *a.* [L (DESTROY) or f. foll.]

destruction /dɪ'strʌkʃ(ə)n/ *n.* destroying or being destroyed; cause of this. [F f. L (DESTROY)]

destructive *a.* destroying, causing destruction; tending to destroy; merely negative, refuting etc. without amendment (*destructive criticism*).

desuetude /dɪ'sjuːɪtjuːd/ *n.* state of disuse. [F or L (*suesco* be accustomed)]

desultory /'desəltərɪ/ *a.* going constantly from one subject to another; disconnected, unmethodical; **desultorily** *adv.* [L *desultorius* superficial]

detach /dɪ'tætʃ/ *v.t.* unfasten or separate and remove (*from*); send (part of force) on separate mission. [F (as ATTACH)]

detached *a.* separate, standing apart; unemotional, impartial.

detachment *n.* detaching, being detached; lack of emotion or concern, impartiality; portion of army etc. separately employed. [F (DETACH)]

detail /'diːteɪl/ **1** *n.* item, small or subordinate particular; these collectively, treatment of them; minor decoration in building etc.; part of picture etc. shown alone; small military detachment. **2** *v.t.* give particulars of, relate circumstantially; assign for special duty. **3 in detail**

describing the individual parts or events fully. [F (TAIL²)]
detailed *a.* having or involving many details; thorough.
detain /dɪ'teɪn/ *v.t.* keep in confinement or under restraint; keep waiting, delay. [F f. L (*teneo* hold)]
detainee /dɪteɪ'ni:/ *n.* person detained in custody, usu. on political grounds.
detect /dɪ'tekt/ *v.i.* discover existence or presence of; discover (person) *in* performance of some wrong or secret act; **detector** *n.* [L (*tego tect-* cover)]
detection /dɪ'tekʃ(ə)n/ *n.* detecting or being detected; work of a detective.
detective /dɪ'tektɪv/ *n.* person, esp. member of police force, employed to investigate crimes. [DETECT]
détente /deɪ'tɑ̃t/ *n.* easing of strained relations, esp. between States. [F, = relaxation]
detention /dɪ'tenʃ(ə)n/ *n.* detaining or being detained; being kept in school after hours as punishment; **detention centre** institution for brief detention of young offenders. [F or L (DETAIN)]
deter /dɪ'tɜ:/ *v.t.* (**-rr-**) discourage or prevent (*from*) through fear or dislike of the consequences; **determent** *n.* [L (*terreo* frighten)]
detergent /dɪ'tɜ:dʒənt/ **1** *n.* cleansing agent, esp. synthetic substance used with water for removing dirt etc. **2** *a.* cleansing. [L (*tergeo* wipe)]
deteriorate /dɪ'tɪərɪəreɪt/ *v.* make or become worse; **deterioration** /-'reɪʃ(ə)n/ *n.* [L (*deterior* worse)]
determinant /dɪ'tɜ:mɪnənt/ **1** *a.* determining, decisive. **2** *n.* determining factor; quantity obtained by adding products of elements of a square matrix according to a certain rule. [L (DETERMINE)]
determinate /dɪ'tɜ:mɪnət/ *a.* limited, of definite scope or nature.
determination /dɪtɜ:mɪ'neɪʃ(ə)n/ *n.* firmness of purpose, resoluteness; process of deciding, determining, or calculating. [F f. L (DETERMINE)]
determine /dɪ'tɜ:mɪn/ *v.* find out or calculate precisely; settle, decide; be decisive factor in regard to (*demand determines supply*); decide firmly, resolve; **be determined** have resolved. [F f. L (*terminus* boundary)]
determined *a.* showing determination, resolute, unflinching.
determinism *n.* doctrine that human action is not free but determined by motives regarded as external forces acting on the will; **determinist** *n.*
deterrent /dɪ'terənt/ **1** *a.* deterring. **2** *n.* deterrent thing or factor. [DETER]
detest /dɪ'test/ *v.t.* hate, loathe; **detestation** /-'steɪʃ(ə)n/ *n.* [L *detestor* (*testis* witness)]
detestable *a.* intensely disliked, hateful.
dethrone /di:'θrəʊn/ *v.t.* remove from throne, depose; **dethronement** *n.* [DE-]
detonate /'detəneɪt/ *v.* (cause to) explode with loud report; **detonation** /-'neɪʃ(ə)n/ *n.* [L (*tono* thunder)]
detonator *n.* device for detonating explosive.
detour /'di:tʊə/ *n.* divergence from direct or intended route, roundabout course. [F (TURN)]
detract /dɪ'trækt/ *v.* take away (some amount) *from* a whole (*detracted a little from our enjoyment*); **detract from** reduce credit due to, depreciate; **detraction** *n.*; **detractor** *n.* [L (*traho tract-* draw)]
detriment /'detrɪmənt/ *n.* harm, damage; thing causing this; **detrimental** /-'ment(ə)l/ *a.* [F or L (TRITE)]
detritus /dɪ'traɪtəs/ *n.* matter produced by erosion, as gravel or rock-debris. [F f. L (prec.)]
de trop /də 'trəʊ/ not wanted, in the way. [F, = excessive]
deuce¹ /dju:s/ *n.* the two on dice or playing cards; in tennis, the score of 40 all, at which two consecutive points are needed to win. [F f. L *duo duos* two]
deuce² /dju:s/ *n.* misfortune, the Devil (*colloq.* used esp. as exclamation of surprise or annoyance: *who the deuce are you?*) [LG *duus* two (as worst throw at dice)]
deus ex machina /deɪʊs eks 'mækɪnə/ *n.* unexpected power or event saving seemingly impossible situation, esp. in play or novel. [L transl. Gk, = god from the machinery]
deuterium /djʊ'tɪərɪəm/ *n.* heavy isotope of hydrogen with mass about double that of ordinary hydrogen. [L f. Gk *deuteros* second]
Deutschmark /'dɔɪtʃmɑ:k/ *n.* currency unit in Federal Republic of Germany. [G (MARK²)]
devalue /di:'vælju:/ *v.t.* reduce value of, reduce value of (currency) in relation to other currencies or to gold; **devaluation** /-'eɪʃ(ə)n/ *n.* [DE-]
devastate /'devəsteɪt/ *v.t.* lay waste, cause great destruction to; **devastation** /-'steɪʃ(ə)n/ *n.* [L (*vasto* lay waste)]
devastating *a.* crushingly effective, overwhelming.
develop /dɪ'veləp/ *v.* make or become bigger or fuller or more elaborate or systematic; bring or come to active or visible state or to maturity, reveal or be revealed; begin to exhibit or suffer from (*develop a rattle, measles*); construct new

buildings on (land), convert (land) to new use so as to use its resources; treat (photographic film etc.) to make picture visible; **developing country** poor or primitive country that is developing better economic and social conditions. [F]

development *n*. developing or being developed; stage of growth or advancement; thing that has developed, esp. event or circumstance; full-grown state; developed land; *Mus*. part of movement in which themes are developed; **development area** one where new industries are encouraged in order to counteract unemployment there; **developmental** /-'ment(ə)l/ *a*.

deviant /'di:vɪənt/ **1** *a*. that deviates from the normal. **2** *n*. deviant person or thing. [foll.]

deviate /'di:vɪeɪt/ *v.i.* turn aside or diverge (*from* course of action, rule, etc.). [L (*via* way)]

deviation /di:vɪ'eɪʃ(ə)n/ *n*. deviating; departing from accepted political (esp. Communist) doctrine; **deviationist** *n*. [F f. med.L (prec.)]

device /dɪ'vaɪs/ *n*. thing made or adapted for a particular purpose; plan, scheme, trick; emblematic or heraldic design; **leave person to his own devices** leave him to do as he wishes. [F (DEVISE)]

devil /'dev(ə)l/ **1** *n*. supreme spirit of evil, Satan (usu. **the Devil**); evil spirit, demon, superhuman malignant being; personified evil spirit or force; wicked or cruel person, mischievously energetic, clever, or self-willed person; *colloq*. person, fellow (*lucky devil*; *poor devil*); personified evil quality; fighting spirit, mischievousness (*the devil is in him tonight*); *colloq*. something difficult or awkward; *colloq*. used as exclamation of surprise or annoyance (*who the devil are you?*); literary hack exploited by employer, junior legal counsel. **2** *v.t.* (**-ll-**, *US* **-l-**) cook (food) with hot seasoning; act as devil for (author or barrister); *US* harass, worry. **3 between the devil and the deep blue sea** in a dilemma; **devil-may-care** cheerful and reckless; **a devil of** *colloq*. a considerable or remarkable; **devil's advocate** one who tests proposition by arguing against it; **devil's own** very difficult or unusual (*devil's own job*); **the devil to pay** trouble to be expected; **give the Devil his due** acknowledge merits or achievement of person otherwise disfavoured; **play the devil with** cause severe damage to. [OE f. L f. Gk *diabolos* accuser, slanderer]

devilish **1** *a*. of or like a devil; mischievous. **2** *adv*. *colloq*. very, extremely.

devilment *n*. mischief, wild spirits.

devilry *n*. wickedness, reckless mischief; black magic.

devious /'di:vɪəs/ *a*. winding, circuitous; not straightforward, underhand. [L (*via* way)]

devise /dɪ'vaɪz/ *v.t.* plan or invent by careful thought; *Law* leave (real estate) by will. [F f. L (DIVIDE)]

devoid /dɪ'vɔɪd/ *predic. a*. (with *of*) quite lacking or free from. [F (VOID)]

devolution /di:və'lu:ʃ(ə)n/ *n*. delegation of power, esp. by central government to local or regional administration. [L (foll.)]

devolve /dɪ'vɒlv/ *v*. (of work or duties) pass or be passed on to another; (of property etc.) descend or pass (*to* or *upon*). [L (*volvo volut-* roll)]

Devonian /dɪ'vəʊnɪən/ **1** *a*. of the period in the Palaeozoic era after Silurian. **2** *n*. this period. [*Devon* in England]

devote /dɪ'vəʊt/ *v.t.* apply or give over *to* a particular activity or purpose. [L (*voveo vot-* vow)]

devoted *a*. showing devotion, very loyal or loving.

devotee /devə'ti:/ *n*. person who is devoted to something, enthusiast (*devotees of football*); very pious person.

devotion /dɪ'vəʊʃ(ə)n/ *n*. great love or loyalty, enthusiastic zeal; religious worship; (in *pl*.) prayers; **devotional** *a*. [F or L (DEVOTE)]

devour /dɪ'vaʊə/ *v.t.* eat hungrily or greedily; (of fire etc.) engulf, destroy; take in greedily with eyes or ears (*devour novel after novel*); absorb attention of (*am devoured by curiosity*). [F f. L (*voro* swallow)]

devout /dɪ'vaʊt/ *a*. earnestly religious; earnest, sincere. [F f. L (DEVOTE)]

dew *n*. atmospheric vapour condensing in small drops on cool surfaces between evening and morning; beaded or glistening moisture resembling this; **dew-claw** rudimentary inner toe of some dogs; **dew-point** temperature at which dew forms; **dew-pond** shallow, usu. artificial, pond once supposed to be fed by atmospheric condensation; **dewy** *a*. [OE]

dewberry *n*. bluish fruit like blackberry. [DEW]

dewdrop *n*. drop of dew.

dewlap *n*. fold of loose skin hanging from throat of cattle and other animals. [DEW, LAP¹]

dexter *a*. of or on right-hand side (observer's left) of shield etc. [L, = on the right]

dexterity /dek'sterɪtɪ/ *n.* skill in handling things; manual or mental adroitness. [F f. L (DEXTER)]

dextrous /'dekstrəs/ *a.* (also **dexterous**) having or showing dexterity. [L (as prec.)]

DFC *abbr.* Distinguished Flying Cross.

DFM *abbr.* Distinguished Flying Medal.

dg. *abbr.* decigram(s).

dharma /'dɑːmə/ *n.* (in India) social custom; right behaviour; Buddhist truth; Hindu moral law. [Skr., = decree, custom]

dhoti /'dəʊtɪ/ *n.* loincloth worn by male Hindus. [Hindi]

dhow /daʊ/ *n.* lateen-rigged ship of Arabian Sea. [orig. unkn.]

di-[1] *prefix* in sense 'two-', 'double-'. [Gk (*dis* twice)]

di-[2] *prefix* = DIS-.

dia- *prefix* (**di-** before vowel) in sense 'through' (*diaphanous*), 'apart' (*diacritical*); 'across' (*diameter*). [Gk (*dia* through)]

dia. *abbr.* diameter.

diabetes /daɪə'biːtiːz/ *n.* disease in which sugar and starch are not properly absorbed by the body. [L f. Gk]

diabetic /daɪə'betɪk/ **1** *a.* of or having diabetes, for diabetics. **2** *n.* person suffering from diabetes.

diabolic /daɪə'bɒlɪk/ *a.* (also **diabolical**) of the Devil; devilish, inhumanly cruel or wicked; fiendishly clever or cunning or annoying; **diabolically** *adv.* [F or L (DEVIL)]

diabolism /daɪ'æbəlɪz(ə)m/ *n.* worship of the Devil; sorcery. [Gk (DEVIL)]

diachronic /daɪə'krɒnɪk/ *a.* concerned with historical development of a subject; **diachronically** *adv.* [F f. Gk (*khronos* time)]

diaconal /daɪ'ækən(ə)l/ *a.* of a deacon. [eccl.L (DEACON)]

diaconate /daɪ'ækənət/ *n.* office of a deacon; body of deacons.

diacritical /daɪə'krɪtɪk(ə)l/ *a.* distinguishing, distinctive; **diacritical mark** (or **sign**) sign used to indicate different sounds or values of a letter (accent, diaeresis, cedilla, etc.). [Gk (CRITICISM)]

diadem /'daɪədem/ *n.* crown or headband worn as sign of sovereignty; sovereignty; crowning distinction or glory. [F f. L f. Gk (*deō* bind)]

diaeresis /daɪ'ɪərəsɪs/ *n.* (*pl.* **diaereses** /-iːz/) mark (as in *naïve*) over vowel indicating that it is sounded separately. [L f. Gk, = separation]

diagnose /'daɪəgnəʊz/ *v.t.* make diagnosis of (disease, mechanical fault, etc.); infer presence of (specified disease etc.) from symptoms. [foll.]

diagnosis /daɪəg'nəʊsɪs/ *n.* (*pl.* **diagnoses** /-iːz/) identification of disease by means of patient's symptoms, formal statement of this; ascertainment of cause of mechanical fault etc. [L f. Gk (*gignōskō* know)]

diagnostic /daɪəg'nɒstɪk/ **1** *a.* of or assisting diagnosis. **2** *n.* symptom. **3** **diagnostician** /-'stɪʃ(ə)n/ *n.* [Gk (prec.)]

diagonal /daɪ'ægən(ə)l/ **1** *a.* crossing a straight-sided figure from corner to corner, slanting, oblique. **2** *n.* straight line joining two opposite corners. **3** **diagonally** *adv.* [L f. Gk (*gōnia* angle)]

diagram /'daɪəgræm/ *n.* drawing showing general scheme or outline of an object and its parts; graphic representation of course or results of an action or process; **diagrammatic** /-grə'mætɪk/ *a.* [L f. Gk (-GRAM)]

dial /'daɪəl/ **1** *n.* plate on front of clock or watch, marking hours etc.; similar flat plate marked with a scale for measurement of something, and having a movable pointer indicating amount registered; movable disc on telephone, with numbers for making connection; plate or disc etc. on radio or television set for selecting wavelength or channel; *sl.* person's face. **2** *v.* (**-ll-**, *US* **-l-**) select or regulate by means of dial; make telephone connection by using dial; ring up (number etc.) thus. [L *diale* (*dies* day)]

dialect /'daɪəlekt/ *n.* form of speech peculiar to a particular region; subordinate variety of a language with non-standard vocabulary, pronunciation, or idioms; **dialectal** /-'lekt(ə)l/ *a.* [F or L f. Gk (*legō* speak)]

dialectic /daɪə'lektɪk/ *n.* logical discussion by question and answer as means of investigating truths in philosophy etc.; criticism dealing with metaphysical contradictions and their solutions; **dialectical** *a.* [F or L (prec.)]

dialogue /'daɪəlɒg/, *US* **dialog** *n.* conversation; written form of this; passage of conversation in novel etc.; discussion between representatives of two groups etc. [F or L f. Gk (*legō* speak)]

dialysis /daɪ'ælɪsɪs/ *n.* (*pl.* **dialyses** /-iːz/) separation of particles by differences in their ability to pass through suitable membrane; purification of blood by such means. [L f. Gk (*luō* set free)]

diamanté /dɪə'mɑ̃teɪ/ *a.* decorated with powdered crystal or other sparkling substance. [F (*diamant* diamond)]

diameter /daɪ'æmɪtə/ *n.* straight line passing from side to side through the centre of a circle or sphere; transverse measurement, width, thickness; unit of

linear magnifying power. [F f. L f. Gk (-METER)]
diametrical /daɪə'metrɪk(ə)l/ *a.* of or along a diameter; (of opposites etc.) complete, direct. [Gk (prec.)]
diamond /'daɪəmənd/ *n.* very hard transparent precious stone of pure crystallized carbon; rhombus; rhombus-shaped thing; playing-card of suit (**diamonds**) denoted by red rhombus; **diamond wedding** 60th (or 75th) anniversary of wedding. [F f. L f. Gk (ADAMANT)]
dianthus /daɪ'ænθəs/ *n.* flowering plant of kind including carnation. [Gk, = flower of Zeus]
diapason /daɪə'peɪs(ə)n, -z-/ *n.* entire compass of musical instrument or voice; fixed standard of musical pitch; either of two main organ-stops extending through whole compass. [L f. Gk, = through all (notes)]
diaper /'daɪəpə/ *n.* linen or cotton fabric with small diamond pattern; *US* baby's nappy. [F f. L f. Gk (*aspros* white)]
diaphanous /daɪ'æfənəs/ *a.* (of fabric etc.) light and delicate, and almost transparent. [L f. Gk (*phainō* show)]
diaphragm /'daɪəfræm/ *n.* muscular partition between thorax and abdomen in mammals; thin sheet used as partition etc.; vibrating disc in microphone or telephone or loudspeaker etc.; device for varying lens aperture in camera etc.; thin contraceptive cap fitting over cervix of uterus; **diaphragmatic** /-fræg'mætɪk/ *a.* [L f. Gk (*phragma* fence)]
diarist /'daɪərɪst/ *n.* one who keeps a diary. [DIARY]
diarrhoea /daɪə'ri:ə/, *US* **diarrhea** *n.* condition of excessively frequent and loose bowel movements. [L f. Gk (*rheō* flow)]
diary /'daɪərɪ/ *n.* daily record of events or thoughts; book for this or for noting future engagements. [L (*dies* day)]
Diaspora /daɪ'æspərə/ *n.* the Dispersion of the Jews; Jews thus dispersed. [Gk]
diastase /'daɪəsteɪs/ *n.* enzyme converting starch to sugar, important in digestion. [F f. Gk, = separation]
diastole /daɪ'æstəlɪ/ *n.* dilatation of the heart rhythmically alternating with systole to form pulse; **diastolic** /daɪə'stɒlɪk/ *a.* [L f. Gk (*stellō* place)]
diatom /daɪ'ætəm/ *n.* microscopic one-cell alga found as plankton and forming fossil deposits. [L f. Gk, = cut in half]
diatomic /daɪə'tɒmɪk/ *a.* consisting of two atoms; having two replaceable atoms or radicals. [DI-[1]]
diatonic /daɪə'tɒnɪk/ *a.* *Mus.* (of scale, interval, etc.) involving only notes proper to prevailing key without chromatic alteration. [F or L f. Gk (TONIC)]
diatribe /'daɪətraɪb/ *n.* forceful verbal attack, abusive criticism. [F f. L f. Gk (*tribō* rub)]
dibble /'dɪb(ə)l/ **1** *n.* (also **dibber**) hand-tool for making holes in ground for seeds or young plants. **2** *v.* prepare (soil), sow or plant, with dibble. [orig. uncert.]
dice 1 *n.* (properly *pl.* of DIE[2] but often as *sing.*) small cube with faces bearing usu. 1–6 spots used in games of chance; game played with one or more of these. **2** *v.* gamble with dice; take great risks (*dicing with death*); cut into small cubes. **3 no dice** *sl.* no success or prospect of it. [DIE[2]]
dicey *a. sl.* risky, unreliable.
dichotomy /daɪ'kɒtəmɪ/ *n.* division into two parts or kinds. [L f. Gk (*dikho-* apart, TOME)]
dichromatic /daɪkrə'mætɪk/ *a.* two-coloured; having vision sensitive to only two of three primary colours. [DI-[1]]
dick *n. sl.* detective. [abbr.]
dickens /'dɪkɪnz/ *n. colloq.* deuce, the Devil (esp. in exclamations). [prob. name *Dickens*]
Dickensian /dɪ'kenzɪən/ *a.* of Dickens or his works; resembling situations described in them. [novelist]
dicker *v.* bargain, haggle. [orig. uncert.]
dicky /'dɪkɪ/ **1** *a. sl.* unsound, likely to collapse or fail. **2** *n. colloq.* false shirt-front. [*Dicky* dimin. of *Richard*]
dicotyledon /daɪkɒtɪ'li:d(ə)n/ *n.* flowering plant having two cotyledons; **dicotyledonous** *a.* [DI-[1]]
dicta *pl.* of DICTUM.
Dictaphone /'dɪktəfəʊn/ *n.* (P) machine for recording and playing back dictated words. [DICTATE, PHONE]
dictate 1 /dɪk'teɪt/ *v.* say or read aloud (words to be written down or recorded); state or order with the force of authority; give peremptory orders. **2** /'dɪkteɪt/ *n.* (usu. in *pl.*) authoritative instruction (*dictates of conscience*). **3 dictation** /-'teɪʃ(ə)n/ *n.* [L *dicto* (*dico* say)]
dictator /dɪk'teɪtə/ *n.* ruler with (often usurped) unrestricted authority; person with supreme authority in any sphere; domineering person; **dictatorship** *n.* [L (prec.)]
dictatorial /dɪktə'tɔ:rɪəl/ *a.* of or like a dictator; imperious, overbearing. [L (as prec.)]
diction /'dɪkʃ(ə)n/ *n.* manner of enunciation in speaking or singing; choice of words and phrases in speech or writing. [F, or L *dictio* (*dico dict-* say)]
dictionary /'dɪkʃənərɪ/ *n.* book that

lists (usu. in alphabetical order) and explains the words of a language or gives equivalent words in another language; similar book explaining terms of a particular subject. [med.L (DICTION)]

dictum /ˈdɪktəm/ *n.* (*pl.* **dicta**) formal expression of opinion; saying. [L, neut. p.p. of *dico* say]

did *past* of DO[1].

didactic /dɪˈdæktɪk, daɪ-/ *a.* meant to instruct; (of person) tediously pedantic; **didacticism** /-tɪsɪz(ə)m/ *n.* [Gk (*didaskō* teach)]

diddle /ˈdɪd(ə)l/ *v.t. sl.* cheat, swindle. [prob. f. older *diddler* f. character in play]

didn't /ˈdɪd(ə)nt/ *colloq.* = *did not*.

die[1] /daɪ/ *v.i.* (*partic.* **dying** /ˈdaɪɪŋ/) cease to live, expire, lose vital force; cease to exist or function, disappear, fade away, (of flame) go out; wish longingly or intently (*I am dying for a drink, to see you*); be exhausted or tormented (*we were dying with laughter, of boredom*); **die away** become weaker or fainter to point of extinction; **die back** (of plant) decay from tip towards root; **die down** become less loud or strong; **die-hard** conservative or stubborn person; **die out** become extinct, cease to exist; **never say die** keep up courage, not give in. [ON]

die[2] *n.* **1** see DICE. **2** engraved device for stamping design on coins, medals, etc.; device for stamping, cutting, or moulding material into particular shape. **3 die-casting** process or product of casting from metal moulds; **the die is cast** irrevocable step is taken; **die-sinker** engraver of dies; **die-stamping** embossing paper etc. with die; **straight as a die** quite straight, very honest. [F f. L *datum* (*do* give)]

dielectric /daɪəˈlektrɪk/ **1** *a.* that does not conduct electricity. **2** *n.* dielectric substance usable for insulating. [DIA-]

dieresis *US* var. of DIAERESIS.

diesel /ˈdiːz(ə)l/ *n.* internal-combustion engine in which fuel is ignited by heat of air highly compressed (in full **diesel engine**); vehicle driven by, or fuel for, diesel engine; **diesel-electric** driven by electric current from generator driven by diesel engine; **diesel oil** heavy petroleum fraction used in diesel engines. [*Diesel*, engineer]

diet[1] /ˈdaɪət/ **1** *n.* the sort of foods one habitually eats; prescribed course of food to which person is restricted. **2** *v.* restrict oneself to a special diet, esp. in order to control one's weight; restrict (person) to a special diet. **3 dietary** *a.* [F f. L f. Gk *diaita* way of life]

diet[2] /ˈdaɪət/ *n.* congress; parliamentary assembly in certain countries. [L *dieta*]

dietetic /daɪəˈtetɪk/ *a.* of diet and nutrition. [L f. Gk (DIET[1])]

dietetics *n.pl.* scientific study of diet and nutrition.

dietitian /daɪəˈtɪʃ(ə)n/ *n.* (also **dietician**) expert in dietetics. [DIET[1]]

dif- *prefix* = DIS-.

differ *v.i.* be unlike; be distinguishable *from*; disagree in opinion (*from, with*). [F f. L *differo dilat-* bring apart]

difference /ˈdɪfrəns/ *n.* being different or unlike; point in which things differ, amount or degree of unlikeness; quantity by which amounts differ, the remainder left after subtraction; disagreement in opinion, dispute, quarrel; **make all the difference** be very important or significant; **split the difference** take average of two proposed amounts. [F f. L (prec.)]

different *a.* unlike, of other nature, form, or quality (*from* or (**D**) *to*); separate, distinct; unusual.

differential /dɪfəˈrenʃ(ə)l/ **1** *a.* of or showing or depending on a difference; constituting or relating to specific differences; *Math.* relating to infinitesimal differences. **2** *n.* agreed difference in wage between industries or between different classes of workers in same industry; difference between rates of interest etc. **3 differential calculus** method of calculating rates of change, maximum and minimum values, etc.; **differential (gear)** gear enabling motor vehicle's rear wheels to revolve at different speeds in rounding corners. [med.L (DIFFER)]

differentiate /dɪfəˈrenʃɪeɪt/ *v.* constitute difference between or in; recognize as different, distinguish, discriminate; develop differences, become different; *Math.* calculate derivative of; **differentiation** /-ˈeɪʃ(ə)n/ *n.*

difficult /ˈdɪfɪkəlt/ *a.* needing much effort or skill; troublesome, perplexing; not easy to please or satisfy. [foll.]

difficulty *n.* being difficult; difficult problem or thing, hindrance to progress; (often in *pl.*) trouble or distress, esp. shortage of money (*in difficulties*). [L *difficultas* (FACULTY)]

diffident /ˈdɪfɪdənt/ *a.* lacking self-confidence; excessively modest and reticent; **diffidence** *n.* [L *diffido* distrust]

diffract /dɪˈfrækt/ *v.t.* break up (beam of light) into series of dark and light bands or coloured spectra, or (beam of radiation or particles) into series of high and low intensities; **diffraction** *n.*; **diffractive** *a.* [L *diffringo* (FRACTION)]

diffuse 1 /dɪ'fju:s/ *a.* spread out, not concentrated; wordy, not concise. **2** /dɪ'fju:z/ *v.* spread widely or thinly; (esp. of fluids) intermingle by diffusion. **3 diffusible** /-z-/ *a.*; **diffusive** /-s-/ *a.* [F or L (FOUND[2])]

diffusion /dɪ'fju:ʒ(ə)n/ *n.* diffusing or being diffused; interpenetration of substances by natural movement of their particles. [L (prec.)]

dig 1 *v.* (**-gg-**; *past* and *p.p.* **dug**) break up and remove or turn over ground etc. with tool, hands, claws, etc.; break up (ground) thus; make (a way, hole, etc.) or obtain (things in the ground) by digging; excavate archaeologically; make way by digging *into*, *through*, *under*; thrust (sharp object) *into* something or *in*, prod or nudge (esp. *in the ribs*); make search (*for* information, *into* book etc.); *sl.* understand, experience, admire. **2** *n.* piece of digging; archaeological excavation; prod or nudge (esp. *in the ribs*); cutting or sarcastic remark; (in *pl.*) *colloq.* lodgings. **3 dig one's heels** (or **toes**) **in** be obstinate, refuse to give way; **dig in** mix into the soil by digging, *colloq.* begin eating or working energetically; **dig oneself in** dig defensive trench or pit, establish one's position; **dig out** (or **up**) get or find by digging (*lit.* or *fig.*); **dig up** break up soil of (fallow land). [OE]

digest 1 /dɪ'dʒest, daɪ-/ *v.* assimilate food in the stomach and bowels; understand and assimilate mentally; summarize. **2** /'daɪdʒest/ *n.* methodical summary, esp. of laws; periodical synopsis of current literature or news. **3 digestible** *a.* [L *digero -gest-*]

digestion /dɪ'dʒestʃ(ə)n/ *n.* process of digesting; power of digesting food. [L (prec.)]

digestive 1 *a.* of or aiding or having the function of digesting. **2** *n.* digestive substance. [F or L (DIGEST)]

digger *n.* one who digs; mechanical excavator; *colloq.* Australian or New Zealander.

digit /'dɪdʒɪt/ *n.* any numeral from 0 to 9; finger or toe. [L, = finger, toe]

digital *a.* of digits; **digital clock** (or **watch**) clock or watch that shows time by displayed digits; **digital computer** computer operating on data represented as series of digits; **digital recording** recording with sound-information represented in digits for more accurate transmission. [L (prec.)]

digitalis /dɪdʒɪ'teɪlɪs/ *n.* drug prepared from dried foxglove leaves, used as heart-stimulant. [as prec., from form of flowers]

dignified /'dɪgnɪfaɪd/ *a.* having or showing dignity. [foll.]

dignify /'dɪgnɪfaɪ/ *v.t.* confer dignity on, ennoble; give high-sounding name to (*school dignified with the name of college*). [F f. L (*dignus* worthy)]

dignitary /'dɪgnɪtərɪ/ *n.* person holding high rank or position, esp. ecclesiastical. [foll.]

dignity /'dɪgnɪtɪ/ *n.* composed and serious manner or style; being worthy of honour or respect; worthiness (*the dignity of labour*); high rank or position; **beneath one's dignity** not worthy enough for one to do; **stand on one's dignity** insist on being treated with respect. [F f. L (*dignus* worthy)]

digraph /'daɪgrɑ:f/ *n.* group of two letters representing one sound (e.g. *ph*, *ea*). [DI-[1], -GRAPH]

digress /daɪ'gres/ *v.i.* depart from the main subject temporarily in speech or writing; **digression** *n.* [L *digredior -gress-*]

dike 1 *n.* long wall or embankment against flooding; ditch; low wall of turf or stone. **2** *v.t.* provide or protect with dikes. [ON, = ditch]

diktat /'dɪktæt/ *n.* categorical statement or decree. [G, = DICTATE]

dilapidated /dɪ'læpɪdeɪtɪd/ *a.* in state of disrepair or ruin. [L (DI-[2], *lapis* stone)]

dilapidation /dɪlæpɪ'deɪʃ(ə)n/ *n.* state of disrepair, bringing or being brought into this state.

dilatation /daɪlə'teɪʃ(ə)n/ *n.* dilation; widening of cervix, e.g. for surgical curettage. [foll.]

dilate /daɪ'leɪt/ *v.* make or become wider or larger; speak or write at length; **dilation** *n.* [F f. L (*latus* wide)]

dilatory /'dɪlətərɪ/ *a.* given to or causing delay. [L *dilatorius* (DIFFER)]

dilemma /dɪ'lemə, daɪ-/ *n.* situation in which a choice has to be made between alternatives that are both undesirable; (D) difficult situation. [L f. Gk (*lemma* premiss)]

dilettante /dɪlɪ'tæntɪ/ *n.* (*pl.* **dilettanti** /-ɪ/ or **dilettantes**) one who dabbles in subject without serious study of it; **dilettantism** *n.* [It. (*dilettare* DELIGHT)]

diligence /'dɪlɪdʒəns/ *n.* careful and persevering effort or work; industrious character. [F f. L (foll.)]

diligent *a.* hard-working; showing care and effort. [F f. L (*diligo* love)]

dill *n.* yellow-flowered herb with scented leaves and seeds used for flavouring pickles. [OE]

dilly-dally /'dɪlɪdælɪ/ *v.i.* *colloq.* vacillate, dawdle. [redupl. of DALLY]

dilute /daɪ'lju:t/ **1** *v.t.* reduce strength of (fluid) by adding water or other solvent; weaken or reduce forcefulness of. **2** *a.* diluted. **3 dilution** *n.* [L *diluo -lut-* wash away]

diluvial /daɪˈluːvɪəl/ *a.* of a flood, esp. of the Flood in Genesis. [L (DELUGE)]

dim 1 *a.* faintly luminous or visible; indistinct, not clearly perceived or remembered; not seeing clearly (*eyes dim with tears*); *colloq.* stupid. **2** *v.* (**-mm-**) become or make dim. **3 dim-wit** *colloq.* stupid person; **dim-witted** stupid; **take a dim view of** *colloq.* disapprove of, feel gloomy about. [OE]

dime *n. US* ten-cent coin. [F f. L *decima* tenth (part)]

dimension /daɪˈmenʃ(ə)n/ *n.* measurable extent of any kind, as length, breadth, thickness, area or volume; (in *pl.*) size (*of great dimensions*); extent or scope in particular aspect (*gave the problem a new dimension*); **dimensional** *a.* [F f. L (*metior mens-* measure)]

diminish /dɪˈmɪnɪʃ/ *v.* make or become smaller or less (in fact or appearance); lessen the reputation of (person); **law of diminishing returns** fact that expenditure, taxation, etc., beyond a certain point does not produce proportionate yield. [F f. L (MINUTE[1])]

diminuendo /dɪmɪnjʊˈendəʊ/ *Mus.* **1** *adv.* with gradual decrease of loudness. **2** *n.* (*pl.* **diminuendos**) passage to be played this way. [It. (prec.)]

diminution /dɪmɪˈnjuːʃ(ə)n/ *n.* diminishing or being diminished; decrease. [F f. L (DIMINISH)]

diminutive /dɪˈmɪnjʊtɪv/ **1** *a.* remarkably small, tiny; (of word) implying smallness either actual or imputed in token of affection etc. **2** *n.* diminutive word.

dimple /ˈdɪmp(ə)l/ **1** *n.* small hollow or dent, esp. in cheek or chin. **2** *v.* produce dimples in; show dimples. [prob. OE]

din 1 *n.* prolonged loud and distracting noise. **2** *v.t.* (**-nn-**) force (information) *into* person by continually repeating it (*dinned it into him*); make din. [OE]

dinar /ˈdiːnɑː/ *n.* currency unit in Yugoslavia and in several countries of the Middle East and N. Africa. [Arab. & Pers. f. Gk f. L DENARIUS]

dine *v.* eat dinner; give dinner to, esp. socially; **dine out** dine away from home; **dining-car** railway coach in which meals are served; **dining-room** room in which meals are eaten. [F f. Rmc (DIS-, JEJUNE)]

diner *n.* person who dines; small dining-room; dining-car on train; *US* small restaurant.

ding-dong /ˈdɪŋdɒŋ/ **1** *n.* sound of alternating strokes as of two bells. **2** *a.* (of contest) in which each contestant alternately has the advantage. **3** *adv.* with vigour and energy. [imit.]

dinghy /ˈdɪŋɡɪ, -ŋɪ/ *n.* small boat carried by ship; small pleasure boat; small inflatable rubber boat. [Hindi]

dingle /ˈdɪŋɡ(ə)l/ *n.* deep wooded valley or dell. [orig. unkn.]

dingo /ˈdɪŋɡəʊ/ *n.* (*pl.* **dingoes**) wild or half-domesticated Australian dog. [Abor.]

dingy /ˈdɪndʒɪ/ *a.* dull-coloured, drab; dirty-looking; **dingily** *adv.*; **dinginess** *n.* [orig. uncert.]

dinkum /ˈdɪŋkəm/ *Austral. & NZ colloq.* **1** *a.* genuine, real. **2** *n.* work, toil. **3 dinkum oil** the honest truth. [orig. unkn.]

dinky /ˈdɪŋkɪ/ *a. colloq.* neat and attractive; small, dainty. [Sc. *dink*]

dinner *n.* chief meal of the day, whether at midday or evening; formal evening meal in honour of person or event; **dinner-jacket** man's short usu. black jacket for evening wear. [F (DINE)]

dinosaur /ˈdaɪnəsɔː/ *n.* extinct reptile of the Mesozoic era, often of enormous size. [L f. Gk *deinos* terrible, SAURIAN]

dint 1 *n.* dent. **2** *v.t.* mark with dints. **3 by dint of** by force or means of. [OE & ON]

diocese /ˈdaɪəsɪs/ *n.* district under pastoral care of bishop; **diocesan** /daɪˈɒsɪs(ə)n/ *a.* [F f. L f. Gk *dioikēsis* administration]

diode /ˈdaɪəʊd/ *n.* thermionic valve having two electrodes; semiconductor rectifier having two terminals. [DI-[1], ELECTRODE]

Dionysian /daɪəˈnɪzɪən/ *a.* sensual, wild, unrestrained. [L f. Gk (*Dionusos* god of wine)]

dioptre /daɪˈɒptə/ *n.* unit of refractive power of lens. [F f. L f. Gk (DIA-, *opsis* sight)]

diorama /daɪəˈrɑːmə/ *n.* scenic painting in which changes in colour and direction of illumination simulate sunrise etc.; small representation of scene with three-dimensional figures, viewed through window etc.; small-scale model or film-set. [DIA-, Gk *horaō* see]

dioxide /daɪˈɒksaɪd/ *n.* oxide containing two atoms of oxygen (*carbon dioxide*). [DI-[1]]

dip 1 *v.* (**-pp-**) put or let down into liquid, immerse; dye (fabric) thus, wash (sheep) in vermin-killing liquid; go under water and emerge quickly; go down, go below any surface or level; lower for a moment and then raise again; lower beam of (vehicle's headlights) to reduce dazzle; slope or extend downwards (*road dips after the bend*); put hand or ladle etc. *into* to take something out; look cursorily *into* (book etc.). **2** *n.* dipping or being dipped; liquid into which thing is dipped; *colloq.* bathe in sea etc.; downward slope of road etc.; depression in skyline etc.; sauce or dressing into which food is dipped before eating; candle made by dipping wick in tallow. **3 dip-stick** rod for measuring depth of liquid, esp. oil in vehicle's engine; **dip-switch** switch for dipping vehicle's headlights. [OE]

Dip. Ed. *abbr.* Diploma in Education.

diphtheria /dɪf'θɪərɪə/ *n.* acute infectious bacterial disease with inflammation of a mucous membrane esp. of throat. [L f. F f. Gk *diphthera* skin, hide]

diphthong /'dɪfθɒŋ/ *n.* union of two vowels (letters or sounds) pronounced in one syllable (as in *coin, loud, toy*); **diphthongal** /-'θɒŋg(ə)l/ *a.* [F f. L f. Gk (*phthoggos* voice)]

diploma /dɪ'pləʊmə/ *n.* certificate of qualification awarded by college etc.; document conferring honour or privilege. [L f. Gk, = folded paper (*diplous* double)]

diplomacy /dɪ'pləʊməsɪ/ *n.* management of international relations, skill in this; tact. [F (DIPLOMATIC)]

diplomat /'dɪpləmæt/ *n.* member of diplomatic service; tactful person. [F (foll.)]

diplomatic /dɪplə'mætɪk/ *a.* of or involved in diplomacy; tactful; **diplomatic immunity** exemption of diplomatic staff etc. abroad from arrest, taxation, etc.; **diplomatic service** branch of public service concerned with representation of country abroad; **diplomatically** *adv.* [F (DIPLOMA)]

diplomatist /dɪ'pləʊmətɪst/ *n.* diplomat. [DIPLOMAT]

dipper *n.* thing that dips; diving bird, esp. water ouzel. [DIP]

dipso /'dɪpsəʊ/ *n.* (*pl.* **dipsos**) *sl.* dipsomaniac. [abbr.]

dipsomania /dɪpsə'meɪnɪə/ *n.* abnormal craving for alcoholic liquor; **dipsomaniac** *n.* [Gk *dipsa* thirst]

dipterous /'dɪptərəs/ *a.* (of insect) having two wings. [L f. Gk (*pteron* wing)]

diptych /'dɪptɪk/ *n.* painting, esp. altarpiece, on two leaves closing like book. [L f. Gk, = pair of writing-tablets (*ptukhē* fold)]

dire *a.* dreadful, calamitous; ominous; urgent (*in dire need*). [L]

direct /dɪ'rekt, daɪ-/ **1** *a.* extending or moving in straight line or by shortest route, not crooked or oblique; straightforward, going straight to the point, frank, not ambiguous; without intermediaries, personal; (of descent) linear, not collateral; complete, greatest possible (*direct opposite, contrast*). **2** *adv.* in a direct way or manner (*deal with him direct*); by direct route (*train goes to London direct*). **3** *v.t.* control, govern movements of; order (person) *to do* thing, (thing) *to be done*; give orders (*that*); guide as adviser, principle, etc. (*duty directs my actions*); tell (person) the way (*to*); give indications for delivery of (letter etc. *to* person or place); point, aim, or turn (blow, attention, remark, effort, etc.) *to, at, towards* person or thing; supervise acting etc. of (play, film, etc.). **4 direct action** exertion of pressure on the community by action (e.g. strike or sabotage) seeking immediate effect, rather than by parliamentary means; **direct current** electric current flowing in one direction only; **direct debit** regular debiting of person's bank account at request of recipient; **direct-grant school** one receiving money from Government and not local authority; **direct object** primary object of action of transitive verb; **direct speech** words quoted as actually spoken, not as modified in reporting; **direct tax** tax levied on person bearing burden for it, esp. on income. [L *dirigo* (*rego rect-* guide)]

direction /dɪ'rekʃ(ə)n, daɪ-/ *n.* directing, supervision; (usu. in *pl.*) order or instruction; line along which, point to or from which, a person or thing moves or looks; tendency or scope of subject, aspect. [F or L (prec.)]

directional *a.* of or indicating direction; sending or receiving radio signals in one direction only.

directive /dɪ'rektɪv, daɪ-/ **1** *n.* general instruction for procedure or action. **2** *a.* serving to direct. [med.L (DIRECT)]

directly 1 *adv.* in a direct line or manner; at once, without delay. **2** *conj.* as soon as (*I came directly I heard*). [DIRECT]

director *n.* one who directs, esp. member of board managing affairs of company etc.; person who directs play, film, etc.; spiritual adviser; **directorial** /-'tɔ:rɪəl/ *a.*; **directorship** *n.*; **directress** *n. fem.* [AF f. L (DIRECT)]

directorate /dɪ'rektərət, daɪ-/ *n.* office of director; board of directors.

directory /dɪ'rektərɪ, daɪ-/ *n.* book with list of telephone subscribers, inhabitants of district, members of profession etc., with various details. [L (DIRECT)]

dirge *n.* slow mournful song; lament for the dead. [L *dirige* imper. (DIRECT), used in Office of the Dead]

dirigible /'dɪrɪdʒɪb(ə)l/ **1** *a.* capable of being guided. **2** *n.* dirigible balloon or airship. [DIRECT]

dirk *n.* a kind of dagger. [orig. unkn.]

dirndl /'dɜ:nd(ə)l/ *n.* woman's dress with tight waistband and full skirt; skirt of this. [G]

dirt *n.* unclean matter that soils; earth, soil; foul or malicious words or talk; excrement; **dirt cheap** *colloq.* very cheap; **dirt road** road without made surface; **dirt-track** racing track made of earth or rolled cinders etc.; **do person dirt** *sl.* harm or injure him maliciously; **treat person like dirt** treat him with contempt. [ON *drit* excrement]

dirty 1 *a.* soiled, unclean; sordid, lewd, obscene; despicable; dishonourable, unfair (*dirty trick*, *player*); (of weather) rough, squally; (of colour) not pure or clear. **2** *v.* make or become dirty. **3** *adv.* *sl.* very. **4 dirty look** *colloq.* look of disapproval or disgust; **dirty money** extra money paid to those who handle dirty materials; **dirty word** obscene word, word for something disapproved of (*charity is a dirty word*); **do the dirty on** play mean trick on. **5 dirtily** *adv.*; **dirtiness** *n.*

dis- *prefix* forming nouns, adjectives, and verbs, implying reversal of action or state (*disarrange*, *disorientate*), direct opposite of the simple word (*disadvantage*, *discourteous*), removal of thing or quality (*dismember*, *disable*), completeness or intensification of the action (*dispose*, *dissolve*). [F *des-* or L]

disability /dɪsə'bɪlɪtɪ/ *n.* thing or lack that prevents one's doing something; physical incapacity caused by injury or disease. [DIS-]

disable /dɪs'eɪb(ə)l/ *v.t.* deprive of an ability; (esp. in *p.p.*) cripple, deprive of or reduce power of acting, walking, etc.; **disablement** *n.*

disabuse /dɪsə'bju:z/ *v.t.* free *of* false idea etc., disillusion.

disadvantage /dɪsəd'vɑ:ntɪdʒ/ **1** *n.* unfavourable circumstance or condition; damage to one's interest or reputation. **2** *v.* put at a disadvantage. **3 disadvantageous** /-'teɪdʒəs/ *a.* [F (DIS-)]

disadvantaged *a.* in unfavourable conditions, esp. lacking normal social opportunities.

disaffected /dɪsə'fektɪd/ *a.* discontented; disloyal; **disaffection** *n.* [DIS-]

disagree /dɪsə'gri:/ *v.i.* hold different opinion; (of factors or circumstances) fail to correspond; **disagree with** differ in opinion from, have adverse effect on (*ice-cream disagrees with me*); **disagreement** *n.* [F (DIS-)]

disagreeable *a.* unpleasant, not to one's liking; bad-tempered. [F (prec.)]

disallow /dɪsə'laʊ/ *v.t.* refuse to allow or accept as valid, prohibit. [F (DIS-)]

disappear /dɪsə'pɪə/ *v.i.* cease to be visible, pass from sight or existence; **disappearance** *n.* [DIS-]

disappoint /dɪsə'pɔɪnt/ *v.t.* fail to fulfil desire or expectation of; frustrate (hope, purpose, etc.). [F (DIS-)]

disappointment *n.* person, thing, or event that disappoints; resulting distress.

disapprobation /dɪsæprə'beɪʃ(ə)n/ *n.* disapproval. [DIS-]

disapprove /dɪsə'pru:v/ *v.* have or express unfavourable opinion (*of*); **disapproval** *n.*

disarm /dɪs'ɑ:m/ *v.* deprive of weapons or the means of defence; reduce or give up one's own armaments; defuse (bomb); pacify hostility or suspicions of. [F (ARM²)]

disarmament /dɪs'ɑ:məmənt/ *n.* reduction of military forces and armaments.

disarrange /dɪsə'reɪndʒ/ *v.t.* bring into disorder; **disarrangement** *n.* [DIS-]

disarray /dɪsə'reɪ/ **1** *n.* disorder. **2** *v.t.* throw into disorder.

disassociate /dɪsə'səʊsɪeɪt/ *v.* = DISSOCIATE.

disaster /dɪ'zɑ:stə/ *n.* sudden or great misfortune; complete failure; **disastrous** *a.* [F f. It. f. L *astrum* star]

disavow /dɪsə'vaʊ/ *v.t.* disclaim knowledge of or responsibility for; **disavowal** *n.* [F (DIS-)]

disband /dɪs'bænd/ *v.* break up (group etc.); disperse; **disbandment** *n.* [obs. F (DIS-)]

disbar /dɪs'bɑ:/ *v.t.* (**-rr-**) deprive (barrister) of right to practise law; **disbarment** *n.* [DIS-]

disbelieve /dɪsbɪ'li:v/ *v.* refuse or be unable to believe; be sceptical.

disburden /dɪs'bɜ:d(ə)n/ *v.t.* relieve of burden; remove (load or anxiety) from.

disburse /dɪs'bɜ:s/ *v.t.* pay out (money); **disbursal** *n.*; **disbursement** *n.* [F (DIS-, BOURSE)]

disc *n.* thin flat circular object; round flat or apparently flat surface (*sun's disc*) or mark; layer of cartilage between vertebrae; gramophone record; **disc brake** brake consisting of disc operated by action of friction pads on it; **disc jockey** presenter of broadcast programme featuring gramophone records of popular music. [F, or L DISCUS]

discard 1 /dɪ'skɑ:d/ *v.t.* give up, put aside; reject as unwanted. **2** /'dɪskɑ:d/ *n.* discarded thing. [CARD¹]

discern /dɪ'sɜ:n/ *v.t.* perceive clearly with mind or senses; make out by thought or by gazing, listening, etc. [F f. L (*cerno cret-* separate)]

discerning *a.* having good judgement or insight.

discernment *n.* good judgement or insight.

discharge /dɪs'tʃɑ:dʒ/ **1** *v.* put forth,

send out, emit (missile, contents, etc.); release (prisoner), allow (patient, jury, etc.) to leave; dismiss from employment or office; acquit oneself of, pay, perform (duty or obligation); fire (gun); release electric charge of; relieve (bankrupt) of residual liability; *Law* cancel (order of court); remove cargo from (ship etc.), unload (cargo) from ship. **2** /also 'dɪs-/ *n.* discharging or being discharged; matter or thing discharged; release of electric charge, esp. with spark; written certificate of release, dismissal, etc. [F (DIS-)]

disciple /dɪ'saɪp(ə)l/ *n.* follower or adherent of a leader, teacher, etc.; one of Christ's followers. [OE f. L (*disco* learn)]

disciplinarian /dɪsɪplɪ'neərɪən/ *n.* one who enforces or believes in strict discipline. [foll.]

disciplinary /'dɪsɪplɪnərɪ, -'plɪn-/ *a.* of or enforcing discipline. [med.L (foll.)]

discipline /'dɪsɪplɪn/ **1** *n.* training or way of life aimed at self-control and conformity; maintaining of order among those in one's charge; control exercised over members of organization; punishment; branch of instruction or learning; system of rules for conduct. **2** *v.t.* train to obedience and order; punish. [F f. L *disciplina* (prec.)]

disclaim /dɪs'kleɪm/ *v.t.* renounce claim to, disown, deny (responsibility etc.). [AF (DIS-)]

disclaimer *n.* statement disclaiming something; renunciation.

disclose /dɪs'kləʊz/ *v.t.* make known; expose to view; **disclosure** *n.* [F (DIS-)]

disco /'dɪskəʊ/ *n.* (*pl.* **discos**) *colloq.* discothèque; dancing-party with records; equipment for this. [abbr.]

discolour /dɪs'kʌlə/, *US* **discolor** *v.* stain, tarnish, (cause to) change colour; **discoloration** /-'reɪʃ(ə)n/ *n.* [F or med.L (DIS-)]

discomfit /dɪs'kʌmfɪt/ *v.t.* disconcert, baffle, frustrate. [F (DIS-, CONFECTION)]

discomfort /dɪs'kʌmfət/ **1** *n.* lack of comfort; thing causing this. **2** *v.t.* make uncomfortable. [F (DIS-)]

discompose /dɪskəm'pəʊz/ *v.t.* disturb composure of; **discomposure** *n.* [DIS-]

disconcert /dɪskən'sɜ:t/ *v.t.* disturb self-possession of, fluster. [F (DIS-)]

disconnect /dɪskə'nekt/ *v.t.* break connection of; put out of action by disconnecting parts; **disconnection** *n.* [DIS-]

disconnected *a.* incoherent, having abrupt transitions (esp. of speech or writing).

disconsolate /dɪs'kɒnsələt/ *a.* forlorn, downcast, disappointed. [L (DIS-, SOLACE)]

discontent /dɪskən'tent/ **1** *n.* dissatisfaction; lack of contentment, grievance. **2** *v.t.* make dissatisfied. **3 discontentment** *n.* [DIS-, CONTENT[2]]

discontented *a.* dissatisfied, feeling discontent.

discontinue /dɪskən'tɪnju:/ *v.* (cause to) cease; cease from, give up; **discontinuance** *n.* [F f. med.L (DIS-)]

discontinuous *a.* lacking continuity in space or time, intermittent; **discontinuity** /-'nju:ɪtɪ/ *n.* [med.L (DIS-)]

discord /'dɪskɔ:d/ *n.* opposition of views, strife; harsh noise, clashing sounds; lack of harmony between notes sounded together. [F f. L (DIS-, *cor cord-* heart)]

discordant /dɪ'skɔ:dənt/ *a.* disagreeing; out of harmony, clashing; **discordance** *n.*

discothèque /'dɪskəʊtek/ *n.* nightclub etc. for dancing to recorded popular music. [F, = record-library]

discount 1 /'dɪskaʊnt/ *n.* amount deducted from full or normal price; amount deducted for immediate payment of sum not yet due (e.g. on bill of exchange). **2** /dɪ'skaʊnt/ *v.t.* disregard partly or wholly; give or receive sum with deduction of discount on (bill of exchange etc.); deduct amount from (price etc.). **3 at a discount** below full or normal price, *fig.* not at true value. [F or It. (DIS-, COUNT[1])]

discountenance /dɪ'skaʊntɪnəns/ *v.t.* refuse to approve of; disconcert (person). [DIS-]

discourage /dɪ'skʌrɪdʒ/ *v.t.* deprive of courage or confidence; dissuade, deter; show disapproval of; **discouragement** *n.* [F (DIS-)]

discourse 1 /'dɪskɔ:s/ *n.* conversation; speech or lecture; lengthy treatment of subject. **2** /dɪ'skɔ:s/ *v.i.* converse; speak or write at length on subject; utter a discourse. [L (*curro curs-* run)]

discourteous /dɪs'kɜ:tɪəs/ *a.* lacking courtesy; **discourtesy** *n.* [DIS-]

discover /dɪ'skʌvə/ *v.t.* acquire knowledge or sight of by effort or chance; be the first to do this in a particular case (*Cook discovered Australia*). [F f. L (DIS-)]

discovery *n.* discovering; thing discovered.

discredit /dɪs'kredɪt/ **1** *v.t.* harm good reputation of; refuse to believe; cause to be disbelieved. **2** *n.* harm to reputation, person or thing causing this; lack of credibility. [DIS-]

discreditable *a.* bringing discredit, shameful; **discreditably** *adv.*

discreet /dɪ'skri:t/ *a.* circumspect in speech or action; judicious, prudent; unobtrusive. [F f. L (DISCERN)]

discrepancy /dɪ'skrepənsɪ/ *n.* difference, failure to correspond, inconsistency; **discrepant** *a.* [L *discrepo* be discordant]

discrete /dɪ'skri:t/ *a.* separate, individually distinct, discontinuous. [L (DISCERN)]

discretion /dɪ'skreʃ(ə)n/ *n.* being discreet, good judgement, prudence; freedom or authority to act according to one's judgement; **discretionary** *a.* [F f. L (DISCERN)]

discriminate /dɪ'skrɪmɪneɪt/ *v.* make or see a distinction (*between*), esp. as basis for prejudice or unfair treatment (*discriminate against*); **discrimination** /-'neɪʃ(ə)n/ *n.*; **discriminatory** *a.* [L *discrimino* (DISCERN)]

discriminating *a.* showing good judgement, discerning.

discursive /dɪs'kɜ:sɪv/ *a.* wandering from topic to topic, digressive. [L (*curro curs-* run)]

discus /'dɪskəs/ *n.* heavy thick-centred disc thrown in athletic sports. [L f. Gk]

discuss /dɪs'kʌs/ *v.t.* consider (subject) by talking or writing about it; hold conversation about; **discussion** *n.* [L *discutio -cuss-* disperse]

disdain /dɪs'deɪn/ **1** *n.* scorn, contempt. **2** *v.t.* regard with disdain; refrain or refuse from disdain. **3 disdainful** *a.*; **disdainfully** *adv.* [F f. L (DE-, DEIGN)]

disease /dɪ'zi:z/ *n.* unhealthy condition of body or mind; illness, sickness; particular kind of this with special symptoms or location. [F (DIS-, EASE)]

diseased *a.* affected with disease; abnormal, disordered.

disembark /dɪsɪm'bɑ:k/ *v.* go or put ashore; **disembarkation** /-'keɪʃ(ə)n/ *n.* [F (DIS-)]

disembarrass /dɪsɪm'bærəs/ *v.t.* free from embarrassment; rid or relieve (*of*); **disembarrassment** *n.* [DIS-]

disembody /dɪsɪm'bɒdɪ/ *v.t.* free (soul, spirit, etc.) from body or concrete form; **disembodiment** *n.*

disembowel /dɪsɪm'baʊəl/ *v.t.* (-ll-, US -l-) remove bowels or entrails of; **disembowelment** *n.*

disenchant /dɪsɪn'tʃɑ:nt/ *v.t.* free from enchantment or illusion; **disenchantment** *n.* [F (DIS-)]

disencumber /dɪsɪn'kʌmbə/ *v.t.* free from encumbrance. [DIS-]

disengage /dɪsɪn'geɪdʒ/ *v.* detach, loosen, release from engagement; become detached; **disengagement** *n.*

disengaged *a.* at leisure, uncommitted; detached.

disentangle /dɪsɪn'tæŋg(ə)l/ *v.* free or become free of tangles or complications; **disentanglement** *n.*

disestablish /dɪsɪ'stæblɪʃ/ *v.t.* end established state of; deprive (Church) of State connection; **disestablishment** *n.*

disfavour /dɪs'feɪvə/, *US* **disfavor 1** *n.* dislike, disapproval; being disliked. **2** *v.t.* regard or treat with disfavour.

disfigure /dɪs'fɪgə/ *v.t.* spoil appearance of; **disfigurement** *n.* [F (DIS-)]

disfranchise /dɪs'fræntʃaɪz/ *v.t.* deprive of rights as citizen or of franchise held; **disfranchisement** *n.* [DIS-]

disgorge /dɪs'gɔ:dʒ/ *v.* eject from the throat; pour forth. [F (DIS-)]

disgrace /dɪs'greɪs/ **1** *n.* loss of favour or respect; downfall from position of honour, ignominy (*is in disgrace*); thing that causes this. **2** *v.t.* bring disgrace to, degrade; dismiss from favour or honour. [F f. It. (DIS-)]

disgraceful *a.* causing disgrace, shameful; **disgracefully** *adv.*

disgruntled /dɪs'grʌnt(ə)ld/ *a.* sulkily discontented. [DIS-, GRUNT]

disguise /dɪs'gaɪz/ **1** *v.t.* conceal identity of, make unrecognizable; conceal, obscure (*disguise one's intentions*). **2** *n.* practice of or material used in disguising; disguised state. [F (DIS-)]

disgust /dɪs'gʌst/ **1** *n.* strong aversion, repugnance. **2** *v.t.* cause disgust in. [F or It. (DIS-, GUSTO)]

dish 1 *n.* shallow flat-bottomed container for holding food; its contents; particular kind of food; (in *pl.*) all the utensils after use at a meal (*wash the dishes*); dish-shaped object or cavity; *colloq.* attractive girl or woman. **2** *v.t.* make dish-shaped; *colloq.* frustrate, outmanœuvre. **3 dish out** *sl.* distribute, esp. carelessly; **dish up** put (food) in dishes ready for serving, prepare to serve meal, *sl.* present as fact or argument; **dish-water** water in which dishes have been washed. [OE f. L DISCUS]

dishabille /dɪsə'bi:l/ var. of DÉSHABILLÉ.

disharmony /dɪs'hɑ:mənɪ/ *n.* lack of harmony, discord; **disharmonious** /-'məʊnɪəs/ *a.* [DIS-]

dishcloth *n.* cloth for washing dishes. [DISH]

dishearten /dɪs'hɑ:t(ə)n/ *v.t.* make despondent, cause to lose courage or confidence; **disheartenment** *n.* [DIS-]

dishevelled /dɪ'ʃev(ə)ld/, *US* **disheveled** *a.* ruffled and untidy; **dishevelment** *n.* [F (DIS-, *chevel* hair f. L *capillus*)]

dishonest /dɪs'ɒnɪst/ *a.* insincere, fraudulent; **dishonesty** *n.* [F (DIS-)]

dishonour /dɪs'ɒnə/ *US* **dishonor 1** *n.* loss of honour or respect, shame or disgrace; thing that causes this. **2** *v.t.* bring dishonour upon, disgrace; refuse to accept or pay (cheque etc.). [F f. Rmc or med.L (DIS-)]

dishonourable *a.* bringing dishonour, shameful, ignominious; **dishonourably** *adv.*
dishwasher *n.* machine for washing dishes; water wagtail. [DISH]
dishy *a. colloq.* very attractive.
disillusion /dɪsɪ'lu:ʒ(ə)n/ **1** *v.t.* free from illusion or mistaken belief. **2** *n.* being disillusioned. **3 disillusionment** *n.* [DIS-]
disincentive /dɪsɪn'sentɪv/ *n.* thing or factor discouraging contemplated action.
disincline /dɪsɪn'klaɪn/ *v.t.* make unwilling; **disinclination** /-klɪn'neɪʃ(ə)n/ *n.*
disinfect /dɪsɪn'fekt/ *v.t.* cleanse of infection, remove bacteria from; **disinfection** *n.* [F (DIS-)]
disinfectant **1** *a.* having disinfecting properties. **2** *n.* disinfecting substance.
disinflation /dɪsɪn'fleɪʃ(ə)n/ *n.* policy designed to counteract inflation without producing disadvantages of deflation; **disinflationary** *a.* [DIS-]
disingenuous /dɪsɪn'dʒenjʊəs/ *a.* insincere, not candid.
disinherit /dɪsɪn'herɪt/ *v.t.* reject as one's heir, deprive of right of inheritance (esp. by making new will); **disinheritance** *n.*
disintegrate /dɪ'sɪntɪgreɪt/ *v.* (cause to) separate into component parts, break up; deprive of or lose cohesion; (of nucleus) emit particle(s) or divide into smaller nuclei; **disintegration** /-'greɪʃ(ə)n/ *n.*; **disintegrator** *n.*
disinter /dɪsɪn'tɜ:/ *v.t.* (**-rr-**) dig up (esp. corpse) from the ground. [F (DIS-)]
disinterest /dɪs'ɪntərest/ *n.* impartiality; (**D**) lack of concern. [DIS-]
disinterested *a.* impartial, not in fluenced by involvement or advantage; (**D**) uninterested.
disjoin /dɪs'dʒɔɪn/ *v.t.* separate, disunite, part. [F (DIS-)]
disjoint /dɪs'dʒɔɪnt/ *v.t.* take to pieces at the joints; dislocate; disturb working or connection of.
disjointed *a.* (of talk) disconnected, incoherent.
disjunction /dɪs'dʒʌŋkʃ(ə)n/ *n.* disjoining, separation. [F or L (DIS-)]
disjunctive /dɪs'dʒʌŋktɪv/ *a.* involving separation; (of conjunction) indicating an alternative (e.g. *but*, *or*). [L (DIS-)]
disk var. of DISC.
dislike /dɪs'laɪk/ **1** *n.* feeling that person or thing is unpleasant, unattractive, etc.; object of this. **2** *v.t.* have dislike for, not like. [LIKE²]
dislocate /'dɪsləʊkeɪt/ *v.t.* disturb normal connection of (esp. joint in the body); disrupt, put out of order; **dislocation** /-'keɪʃ(ə)n/ *n.* [F or med.L (DIS-)]
dislodge /dɪs'lɒdʒ/ *v.t.* disturb or move from established position; **dislodgement** *n.* [F (DIS-)]
disloyal /dɪs'lɔɪəl/ *a.* unfaithful, lacking loyalty; **disloyally** *adv.*; **disloyalty** *n.*
dismal /'dɪzm(ə)l/ *a.* causing or showing gloom; miserable, dreary; *colloq.* feeble, inept. [AF f. L *dies mali* unlucky days]
dismantle /dɪs'mænt(ə)l/ *v.t.* pull down, take to pieces; deprive of defences, equipment, etc. [F (DIS-)]
dismay /dɪs'meɪ/ **1** *n.* feeling of intense disappointment and discouragement. **2** *v.t.* fill with dismay. [F f. Gmc (DIS-, MAY¹)]
dismember /dɪs'membə/ *v.t.* remove limbs from; partition (a country etc.), divide up; **dismemberment** *n.* [F (DIS-)]
dismiss /dɪs'mɪs/ *v.t.* send away, cause to leave one's presence, disperse; order to terminate employment or service, esp. with dishonour; put out of one's thoughts, cease to feel or discuss; treat (subject) summarily; reject (esp. lawsuit) without further hearing; put out (batsman or side) in cricket (usu. *for* stated score); **dismissal** *n.*; **dismissive** *a.* [F f. L (*mitto miss-* send)]
dismount /dɪs'maʊnt/ *v.* (cause to) get off or down from thing one is riding; unseat; remove (thing) from mounting. [DIS-]
disobedient /dɪsə'bi:dɪənt/ *a.* disobeying, rebellious; **disobedience** *n.* [F (DIS-)]
disobey /dɪsə'beɪ/ *v.* fail or refuse to obey; disregard (rule, order, etc.).
disoblige /dɪsə'blaɪdʒ/ *v.t.* refuse to consider convenience or wishes of. [F f. Rmc (DIS-)]
disorder /dɪs'ɔ:də/ **1** *n.* lack of order, confusion; commotion, riot; disturbance of normal state or function; ailment, disease. **2** *v.t.* put into disorder, upset. [F (DIS-, ORDAIN)]
disorderly *a.* untidy, eonfused; riotous, contrary to public order or morality.
disorganize /dɪs'ɔ:gənaɪz/ *v.t.* upset order or system of, throw into confusion; **disorganization** /-'zeɪʃ(ə)n/ *n.* [F (DIS-)]
disorient /dɪs'ɔ:rɪənt/ *v.* = DISORIENTATE.
disorientate /dɪs'ɔ:rɪenteɪt/ *v.t.* confuse (person) as to his bearings; **disorientation** /-'teɪʃ(ə)n/ *n.* [DIS-]
disown /dɪs'əʊn/ *v.t.* refuse to recognize or acknowledge, repudiate; reject connection with.
disparage /dɪ'spærɪdʒ/ *v.t.* speak slightingly of, belittle; bring discredit

on; **disparagement** *n.* [F (DIS-, *parage* rank)]

disparate /'dɪspərət/ *a.* essentially different, unrelated, not comparable. [L *disparo* separate]

disparity /dɪ'spærɪtɪ/ *n.* inequality, difference, incongruity. [F f. L (DIS-)]

dispassionate /dɪ'spæʃ(ə)nət/ *a.* free from emotion, impartial. [DIS-]

dispatch /dɪ'spætʃ/ **1** *v.t.* send off to a destination or for a purpose; give the death-blow to, kill; finish or dispose of promptly or quickly. **2** *n.* dispatching or being dispatched; promptness, efficiency; written (esp. official) message; news report sent to newspaper or news agency. **3 dispatch-box** case for carrying official documents; **dispatch-rider** official messenger on motor cycle. [It. *dispacciare* or Sp. *despachar*]

dispel /dɪ'spel/ *v.t.* (-ll-) drive away, scatter (esp. darkness, fog, fears). [L (*pello* drive)]

dispensable /dɪ'spensəb(ə)l/ *a.* that can be dispensed with. [med.L (DISPENSE)]

dispensary /dɪ'spensərɪ/ *n.* place (esp. room) where medicines are dispensed.

dispensation /dɪspen'seɪʃ(ə)n/ *n.* dispensing, distributing; ordering or management, esp. of the world by Providence; exemption from penalty, rule, or obligation. [F or L (foll.)]

dispense /dɪ'spens/ *v.* distribute, deal out, administer; make up and give out (medicine etc.); **dispense with** do without, make unnecessary. [F f. L (*pendo pens-* weigh)]

dispenser *n.* person who dispenses (esp. medicine); device for dispensing in fixed quantities.

disperse /dɪ'spɜ:s/ *v.* scatter; drive, go, or send in different directions; send to or station at different points; put in circulation, disseminate; separate (white light) into coloured constituents; **dispersal** *n.*; **dispersive** *a.* [L (DIS-, SPARSE)]

dispersion /dɪ'spɜ:ʃ(ə)n/ *n.* dispersing or being dispersed; **the Dispersion** the Jews dispersed among the Gentiles after Captivity in Babylon.

dispirit /dɪ'spɪrɪt/ *v.t.* (often in *p.p.*) make despondent. [DIS-]

displace /dɪs'pleɪs/ *v.t.* move from its place; oust, take the place of; remove from office; **displaced person** one who has had to leave his home country because of war, persecution, etc.

displacement *n.* displacing or being displaced; amount of fluid displaced by thing floating or immersed in it (*a ship with a displacement of 11,000 tons*); amount by which thing is shifted from its place.

display /dɪ'spleɪ/ **1** *v.t.* exhibit, show; reveal, betray, allow to appear. **2** *n.* displaying, thing(s) displayed, exhibition, show; ostentation; bird's special pattern of behaviour as means of visual communication. [F f. L (*plico* fold)]

displease /dɪs'pli:z/ *v.t.* arouse disapproval or indignation of, offend; be unpleasing to. [F (DIS-)]

displeasure /dɪs'pleʒə/ *n.* displeased feeling, indignation, dissatisfaction.

disport /dɪ'spɔ:t/ *v.* play, frolic, enjoy *oneself*. [AF (*porter* carry f. L)]

disposable /dɪ'spəʊzəb(ə)l/ **1** *a.* able to be disposed of; at one's disposal (*disposable income*); designed to be thrown away after use. **2** *n.* disposable article. [DISPOSE]

disposal /dɪ'spəʊz(ə)l/ *n.* disposing, disposing of; **at one's disposal** available. [foll.]

dispose /dɪ'spəʊz/ *v.* place suitably or in order, arrange; incline, make willing or desirous (*his candour disposed us to believe him*); bring (person, mind) into certain state (esp. in *pass.*, have a specified tendency of mind: *be well* or *ill disposed*; *not disposed to be lenient*); determine course of events (*man proposes, God disposes*); **dispose of** get rid of, deal with, finish, prove (argument etc.) incorrect. [F (POSE)]

disposition /dɪspə'zɪʃ(ə)n/ *n.* setting in order, arrangement; relative position of parts; temperament (*has a cheerful disposition*); natural tendency, inclination; (usu. in *pl.*) plan, preparations. [F f. L (DIS-)]

dispossess /dɪspə'zes/ *v.t.* deprive (person) of the possession *of*; oust, dislodge; **dispossession** *n.* [F (DIS-)]

disproof /dɪs'pru:f/ *n.* disproving, refutation. [DIS-]

disproportion /dɪsprə'pɔ:ʃ(ə)n/ *n.* lack of proportion; being out of proportion.

disproportionate /dɪsprə'pɔ:ʃənət/ *a.* out of proportion, relatively too large or small.

disprove /dɪs'pru:v/ *v.t.* prove to be false. [F (DIS-)]

disputable /dɪ'spju:təb(ə)l, 'dɪs-/*a.* open to question, uncertain. [F or L (DISPUTE)]

disputant /dɪ'spju:tənt/ *n.* person involved in dispute. [DISPUTE]

disputation /dɪspju:'teɪʃ(ə)n/ *n.* argument, debate; formal discussion of set question or thesis. [F or L (DISPUTE)]

disputatious *a.* fond of argument.

dispute /dɪ'spju:t/ **1** *v.* argue, debate; discuss, esp. heatedly, quarrel; question truth or validity of (claim etc.); contend for, strive to win (*disputed territory*); oppose, resist. **2** /also (D) 'dɪs-/ *n.*

controversy, debate; quarrel, difference of opinion. 3 **in dispute** being argued about. [F f. L (*puto* reckon)]
disqualify /dɪs'kwɒlɪfaɪ/ *v.t.* make or pronounce ineligible or unsuitable; debar from competition; **disqualification** /-fɪ'keɪʃ(ə)n/ *n.* [DIS-]
disquiet /dɪs'kwaɪət/ 1 *n.* uneasiness, anxiety. 2 *v.t.* cause disquiet to.
disquietude *n.* state of disquiet.
disquisition /dɪskwɪ'zɪʃ(ə)n/ *n.* long or elaborate treatise or discourse on subject. [F f. L (*quaero quisit-* seek)]
disregard /dɪsrɪ'gɑ:d/ 1 *v.t.* pay no attention to, treat as of no importance. 2 *n.* lack of attention, indifference, neglect. [DIS-]
disrepair /dɪsrɪ'peə/ *n.* bad condition due to lack of repairs (*is in disrepair, in a state of disrepair*).
disreputable /dɪs'repjʊtəb(ə)l/ *a.* of bad repute, not respectable in character or appearance; discreditable; **disreputably** *adv.*
disrepute /dɪsrɪ'pju:t/ *n.* lack of good repute, discredit.
disrespect /dɪsrɪ'spekt/ *n.* lack of respect, discourtesy; **disrespectful** *a.*; **disrespectfully** *adv.*
disrobe /dɪs'rəʊb/ *v.* remove clothes (from).
disrupt /dɪs'rʌpt/ *v.t.* interrupt flow or continuity of, bring disorder to; break apart; **disruption** *n.*; **disruptive** *a.* [L (RUPTURE)]
dissatisfaction /dɪsætɪs'fækʃ(ə)n/ *n.* lack of satisfaction or contentment; cause of this. [DIS-]
dissatisfy /dɪs'sætɪsfaɪ/ *v.t.* fail to satisfy, make discontented.
dissect /dɪ'sekt/ *v.t.* cut into pieces, esp. to examine parts or structure; analyse, examine or criticize in detail; **dissection** *n.*; **dissector** *n.* [L (SECTION)]
dissemble /dɪ'semb(ə)l/ *v.* conceal or disguise (intention, character, feeling, etc.), practise such concealment; talk or act hypocritically or insincerely. [F f. L (*simulo* SIMULATE)]
disseminate /dɪ'semɪneɪt/ *v.t.* scatter about, spread (esp. ideas) widely; **dissemination** /-'neɪʃ(ə)n/ *n.*; **disseminator** *n.* [L (DIS-, SEMEN)]
dissension /dɪ'senʃ(ə)n/ *n.* discord arising from difference of opinion. [F f. L (foll.)]
dissent /dɪ'sent/ 1 *v.i.* disagree openly, hold different view or belief (*from*), esp. in religion from established doctrine. 2 *n.* such difference of opinion; expression of this. [L (DIS-, *sentio* feel)]
dissenter *n.* one who dissents, esp. (**Dissenter**) protestant dissenting from Church of England.
dissentient /dɪ'senʃɪənt, -ʃənt/ 1 *a.* dissenting from established view. 2 *n.* dissentient person.
dissertation /dɪsə'teɪʃ(ə)n/ *n.* detailed discourse, esp. as submitted for higher degree in university. [L (*disserto* discuss)]
disservice /dɪs'sɜ:vɪs/ *n.* harmful action, esp. in misguided attempt to help. [DIS-]
dissident /'dɪsɪdənt/ 1 *a.* disagreeing, at variance. 2 *n.* person at variance esp. with established authority. 3 **dissidence** *n.* [F f. L (DIS-, *sedeo* sit)]
dissimilar /dɪ'sɪmɪlə/ *a.* unlike, not similar; **dissimilarity** /-'lærɪtɪ/ *n.* [DIS-]
dissimulate /dɪ'sɪmjʊleɪt/ *v.* dissemble; **dissimulation** /-'leɪʃ(ə)n/ *n.* [L (as DISSEMBLE)]
dissipate /'dɪsɪpeɪt/ *v.* dispel, disperse; squander, fritter away. [L]
dissipated *a.* given to dissipation, dissolute.
dissipation /dɪsɪ'peɪʃ(ə)n/ *n.* dissipating; frivolous or dissolute way of life. [F or L (DISSIPATE)]
dissociate /dɪ'səʊsɪeɪt, -ʃɪ-/ *v.* separate or disconnect in thought or fact; become dissociated; **dissociate oneself from** declare oneself unconnected with; **dissociation** /-'eɪʃ(ə)n/ *n.*; **dissociative** *a.* [L (DIS-, ASSOCIATE)]
dissoluble /dɪ'sɒljʊb(ə)l/ *a.* that can be disintegrated, loosened, or disconnected. [F or L (DIS-)]
dissolute /'dɪsəlu:t, -lju:t/ *a.* morally lax, licentious. [L (DISSOLVE)]
dissolution /dɪsə'lu:ʃ(ə)n, -'lju:-/ *n.* dissolving or being dissolved, esp. of partnership or of parliament for new election; breaking up, abolition (of institution); death. [F or L (foll.)]
dissolve /dɪ'zɒlv/ *v.* make or become liquid, esp. by immersion or dispersion in liquid; (cause to) disappear gradually; dismiss or disperse (assembly, esp. parliament); annul or put an end to (marriage, partnership); **dissolve into** give way to (tears or laughter). [L (DIS-, *solvo solut-* loosen)]
dissonant /'dɪsənənt/ *a.* not in harmony, harsh-toned; incongruous; **dissonance** *n.* [F or L (DIS-, *sono* SOUND[1])]
dissuade /dɪ'sweɪd/ *v.t.* give advice or exercise influence to discourage or divert (person *from*); **dissuasion** *n.*; **dissuasive** *a.* [L (DIS-, *suadeo* advise)]
dissyllable etc. var. of DISYLLABLE etc.
distaff /'dɪstɑ:f/ *n.* cleft stick holding wool or flax for spinning; **distaff side** female branch of family. [OE]
distance /'dɪstəns/ 1 *n.* extent of space between two points; being far off, remoteness; distant point (*to, from, a dis-*

tance); remoter field of vision (*in the distance*); space of time. **2** *v.t.* place or cause to seem far off; leave far behind in race etc. **3 at a distance** far off, not very near; **keep at a distance** remain aloof from; **keep one's distance** remain aloof. [F f. L (DIS-, *sto* stand)]

distant *a.* far away, at a specified distance (*10 miles distant*); remote in position, time, relationship, or concept (*distant prospect, past, cousin, hope*); avoiding familiarity, aloof. [F or L (prec.)]

distaste /dɪs'teɪst/ *n.* dislike, aversion (*for*). [DIS-]

distasteful *a.* causing distaste, disagreeable *to*; **distastefully** *adv.*

distemper[1] /dɪ'stempə/ **1** *n.* disease of dogs and some other animals, with catarrh and weakness. **2** *v.t. archaic* (usu. in *p.p.*) upset, derange. [L (DIS-, *tempero* mingle)]

distemper[2] /dɪ'stempə/ **1** *n.* a kind of paint using glue or size instead of oil-base, for use on walls. **2** *v.t.* paint with this. [F or L, = soak (see prec.)]

distend /dɪ'stend/ *v.* swell or stretch out by pressure from within; **distensible** *a.*; **distension** *n.* [L (TEND[1])]

distich /'dɪstɪk/ *n.* verse couplet. [L f. Gk (*stikhos* line)]

distil /dɪ'stɪl/, *US* **distill** *v.t.* (**-ll-**) purify or extract essence from (a substance) by vaporizing it with heat, then condensing it with cold and collecting the resulting liquid; make (whisky, essence, etc.) by distilling raw materials; (cause to) fall in drops; **distillation** /-'leɪʃ(ə)n/ *n.* [L (DE-, *stillo* drip)]

distiller *n.* one who distils, esp. maker of alcoholic liquor.

distillery *n.* place where alcoholic liquor is distilled.

distinct /dɪ'stɪŋkt/ *a.* not identical, separate, different in quality or kind; clearly perceptible, definite and unmistakable (*a distinct advantage*). [L (DISTINGUISH)]

distinction /dɪ'stɪŋkʃ(ə)n/ *n.* seeing or making a difference, discrimination; a difference seen or made; thing that differentiates; distinguished character, excellence (*a person of distinction*); showing of special consideration (*treat with distinction*); title or mark of honour. [F f. L (DISTINGUISH)]

distinctive *a.* distinguishing, characteristic.

distingué /dɪ'stæŋgeɪ/ *a.* having distinguished air or manners. [F (foll.)]

distinguish /dɪ'stɪŋgwɪʃ/ *v.* observe or identify a difference in (*distinguish fact from theory*); differentiate, draw distinctions (*between*); characterize, be a mark or property of; make out by listening, looking, etc.; make oneself prominent or noteworthy (*by* some achievement). [F or L (DIS-, *stinguo stinct-* extinguish)]

distinguished *a.* eminent, having distinction.

distort /dɪ'stɔ:t/ *v.t.* pull or twist out of shape; transmit (sound etc.) inaccurately; misrepresent (facts etc.); **distortion** *n.* [L (*torqueo tort-* twist)]

distract /dɪ'strækt/ *v.t.* draw away the attention of (person, mind, etc.); confuse, bewilder. [L (DIS-, *traho tract-* draw)]

distraction /dɪ'strækʃ(ə)n/ *n.* distracting or being distracted; thing that distracts the attention or impairs concentration; amusement, relaxation; mental confusion or distress. [F or L (prec.)]

distrain /dɪ'streɪn/ *v.i.* levy distraint (*upon* person or goods). [F f. L (DIS-, *stringo strict-* draw tight)]

distraint /dɪ'streɪnt/ *n.* seizure of goods as method of enforcing payment.

distrait /dɪ'streɪ/ *a.* (*fem.* ***distraite*** /-eɪt/) inattentive; distraught. [F (DISTRACT)]

distraught /dɪ'strɔ:t/ *a.* much troubled in mind; demented with worry etc. [as prec.]

distress /dɪ'stres/ **1** *n.* anguish or suffering caused by pain, sorrow, worry, or exhaustion; state of difficulty or helplessness; lack of money or necessaries; *Law* distraint. **2** *v.t.* cause distress to, make unhappy. **3 distressful** *a.* [F f. Rmc, rel. to DISTRAIN]

distressed *a.* affected by distress, impoverished; **distressed area** region of much poverty and unemployment.

distribute /dɪ'strɪbju:t, (D) 'dɪs-/ *v.t.* divide and give share of to each of a number; spread about, scatter, put at different points; arrange, classify; **distribution** /-'bju:ʃ(ə)n/ *n.* [L (*tribuo -but-* assign)]

distributive 1 *a.* of, concerned with, or produced by distribution; *Gram. & Logic* referring to each individual of a class, not to the class collectively. **2** *n.* distributive word (e.g. *each, neither, every*). [F or L (prec.)]

distributor *n.* one who distributes things, esp. agent who markets goods; device in internal-combustion engine for passing current to each sparking-plug in turn. [DISTRIBUTE]

district /'dɪstrɪkt/ *n.* region or territory regarded as a geographical or administrative unit (*the Peak District; postal district*); division of a county; **district attorney** *US* prosecuting officer of a district; **district nurse** local nurse visiting patients at home. [F f. L (DISTRAIN)]

distrust /dɪs'trʌst/ **1** *n.* lack of trust, suspicion. **2** *v.t.* feel distrust in. **3 distrustful** *a.* [DIS-]

disturb /dɪ'stɜ:b/ *v.t.* break the rest or quiet or calm of; agitate, worry; move from settled position; (in *p.p.*) emotionally or mentally unstable or abnormal. [F f. L (DIS-, *turba* tumult)]

disturbance *n.* interruption of tranquillity; agitation; tumult, uproar. [F (prec.)]

disunion /dɪs'ju:nɪən/ *n.* separation, lack of union; discord. [DIS-]

disunite /dɪsju:'naɪt/ *v.* remove unity from; (cause to) separate; **disunity** /-'ju:nɪtɪ/ *n.*

disuse **1** /dɪs'ju:z/ *v.t.* cease to use. **2** /dɪs'ju:s/ *n.* disused state. [F (DIS-)]

disyllable /dɪ'sɪləb(ə)l, daɪ-/ *n.* word or metrical foot of two syllables; **disyllabic** /-'læbɪk/ *a.* [F f. L f. Gk (DI-¹)]

ditch **1** *n.* long narrow excavated channel, esp. for drainage or to mark boundary. **2** *v.* make or repair ditches (*hedging and ditching*); drive (vehicle) into ditch; *sl.* make forced landing on sea, bring (aircraft) down thus; *sl.* abandon, discard, leave in the lurch; *sl.* defeat, frustrate. **3 dull as ditch-water** very dull. [OE]

dither /'dɪðə/ **1** *v.* be nervously hesitant or unsure; tremble, quiver. **2** *n.* state of dithering, nervous excitement or apprehension. [var. of *didder* DODDER¹]

dithyramb /'dɪθɪræm/ *n.* Greek choric hymn, wild in character; passionate or inflated poem, speech, or writing; **dithyrambic** /-'ræmbɪk/ *a.* [L f. Gk]

dittany /'dɪtənɪ/ *n.* herb formerly supposed to be of medicinal value. [F f. L f. Gk]

ditto *n.* (*pl.* **dittos**) the aforesaid, the same (in accounts, inventories, etc., or *colloq.*); **ditto marks** inverted commas etc. representing the word 'ditto'. [It. f. L (DICTUM)]

ditty /'dɪtɪ/ *n.* short simple song. [F f. L (DICTATE)]

diuretic /daɪjʊə'retɪk/ **1** *a.* causing increased secretion of urine. **2** *n.* diuretic drug. [F or L f. Gk (DIA, *oureō* urinate)]

diurnal /daɪ'ɜ:n(ə)l/ *a.* of the day, not nocturnal; daily; occupying one day. [L *diurnalis* (*dies* day)]

diva /'di:və/ *n.* great woman singer, prima donna. [It. f. L, = goddess]

divalent /daɪ'veɪlənt/ *a. Chem.* having a valence of two. [DI-¹, VALENCE]

divan /dɪ'væn/ *n.* low couch or bed without back or ends. [F or It. f. Turk. f. Arab. f. Pers.]

dive **1** *v.* plunge, esp. head first, into water; (of aircraft) plunge steeply downwards; (of submarine or diver) submerge; go down or out of sight suddenly; rush or move suddenly (*dived into a shop*); put one's hand *into* pocket, handbag, etc. **2** *n.* act of diving; sharp downward movement or fall; *colloq.* disreputable place, drinking-den. **3 dive-bomb** drop bombs from diving aircraft; **diving-bell** open-bottomed structure supplied with air, in which diver can be lowered into deep water; **diving-board** sprung board for diving from; **diving-suit** watertight suit, usu. with helmet and air-supply for work under water. [OE]

diver *n.* one who dives, esp. person who works under water in diving-suit; diving bird.

diverge /daɪ'vɜ:dʒ/ *v.i.* go in different directions from common point, become further apart; go aside *from* track or path; **divergence** *n.*; **divergent** *a.* [L (DI-², *vergo* incline)]

divers /'daɪvəz/ *a. archaic* various, several. [F f. L (foll.)]

diverse /daɪ'vɜ:s/ *a.* of different kinds, varied. [F f. L (DI-², *verto vers-* turn)]

diversify /daɪ'vɜ:sɪfaɪ/ *v.t.* make diverse, vary; spread (investment) over several enterprises or products; **diversification** /-fɪ'keɪʃ(ə)n/ *n.* [F f. med.L (prec.)]

diversion /daɪ'vɜ:ʃ(ə)n/ *n.* diverting something from its course; diverting of attention, manœuvre to achieve this; pastime, recreation; alternative route when road is temporarily closed to traffic; **diversionary** *a.* [L (DIVERSE)]

diversity /daɪ'vɜ:sɪtɪ/ *n.* being diverse; variety. [F f. L (DIVERSE)]

divert /daɪ'vɜ:t/ *v.t.* turn aside, deflect; distract (attention); entertain or amuse. [F f. L (DIVERSE)]

divest /daɪ'vest/ *v.t.* strip (person) *of* clothes; deprive or rid *of*. [F f. L (VEST)]

divide /dɪ'vaɪd/ **1** *v.* separate *into* parts, split or break up; separate (one thing) from another; become or be able to be divided; mark out into parts or groups, classify; cause to disagree, set at variance; distribute, share out, *with*, *among*, etc.; find how many times number contains another (*divide 20 by 5*); separate (assembly etc.) into two sets in voting, be thus separated. **2** *n.* watershed; *fig.* dividing line. [L *divido -vis-*]

dividend /'dɪvɪdend/ *n.* number to be divided; share of profits paid to shareholders or to winners in football pool; benefit from an action. [AF (prec.)]

divider *n.* screen etc. dividing room; (in *pl.*) measuring compasses. [DIVIDE]

divination /dɪvɪ'neɪʃ(ə)n/ *n.* insight into the unknown or future by allegedly supernatural means. [F or L (foll.)]

divine /dɪ'vaɪn/ **1** *a.* of, from, or like God or a god; sacred; *colloq.* excellent, delightful. **2** *n.* theologian or clergyman. **3** *v.* discover by intuition, inspiration, or guessing; foresee; practise divination. **4 divining-rod** = *dowsing-rod* (see DOWSE[1]). [F f. L *divinus*]

diviner *n.* one who practises divination.

divinity /dɪ'vɪnɪtɪ/ *n.* being divine; a god, godhead; theology. [F f. L (DIVINE)]

divisible /dɪ'vɪzɪb(ə)l/ *a.* able to be divided; **divisibility** /-'bɪlɪtɪ/ *n.* [F or L (DIVIDE)]

division /dɪ'vɪʒ(ə)n/ *n.* dividing or being divided; process of dividing number by another; disagreement or discord (*division of opinion*); (in parliament) separation of members into two sections for counting votes; one of parts into which thing is divided; major unit of administration or organization; **division sign** the sign ÷ indicating that one quantity is to be divided by another. [F f. L (DIVIDE)]

divisive /dɪ'vaɪsɪv/ *a.* tending to cause disagreement. [L (DIVIDE)]

divisor /dɪ'vaɪzə/ *n.* number by which another is to be divided. [F or L (DIVIDE)]

divorce /dɪ'vɔːs/ **1** *n.* legal dissolution of marriage; separation, severance of connected things. **2** *v.t.* legally dissolve marriage between; end marriage with (one's husband or wife) by divorce; detach, separate. [F f. L (DIVERSE)]

divorcee /dɪvɔː'siː/ *n.* divorced person. [-EE]

divot /'dɪvət/ *n.* piece of turf cut out by blow, esp. by head of golf-club. [orig. unkn.]

divulge /daɪ'vʌldʒ/ *v.t.* disclose or reveal (secret etc.); **divulgence** *n.* [L *divulgo* publish]

divvy /'dɪvɪ/ *colloq.* **1** *n.* dividend. **2** *v.* (with *up*) share out. [abbr.]

Dixie[1] /'dɪksɪ/ *n.* the southern States of the US. [orig. uncert.]

dixie[2] /'dɪksɪ/ *n.* large iron cooking-pot used by campers etc. [Hind. f. Pers.]

Dixieland *n.* Dixie; kind of jazz with strong two-beat rhythm. [DIXIE[1]]

DIY *abbr.* do-it-yourself.

dizzy /'dɪzɪ/ **1** *a.* giddy, feeling confused; making giddy (*dizzy heights, speed*). **2** *v.t.* make dizzy, bewilder. **3 dizzily** *adv.*; **dizziness** *n.* [OE]

DJ *abbr.* disc jockey; dinner-jacket.

dl. *abbr.* decilitre(s).

D-layer *n.* lowest stratum of ionosphere. [*D* arbitrary]

D. Litt. *abbr.* Doctor of Letters. [L *Doctor Litterarum*]

dm. *abbr.* decimetre(s).

D. Mus. *abbr.* Doctor of Music.

DNA *abbr.* deoxyribonucleic acid.

D-notice *n.* official request to news editors not to publish items on specified subjects, for reasons of security. [*de*fence, NOTICE]

do[1] /dʊ, *emphat.* duː/ *v.* (3 *sing. pres.* **does** /dʌz/; *past* **did**; *p.p.* **done** /dʌn/; *partic.* **doing**) **1** *v.t.* perform, carry out, achieve, complete (*do work, duty, a course*); produce, make, bring about, provide (*do copies, a painting; do lunches*); bestow, grant, impart (*do me a favour; does her credit; does no harm*); deal with, attend to, put in order (*do the dishes, one's hair*); work at, be occupied with (*do carpentry, chemistry*); work out, solve (*can you do this sum?*); traverse (*we did 50 miles today*); produce (play, opera, etc.: *the Company will do Fidelio*); play the part of, act like (*did Lear; do a Garbo*); satisfy, be suitable or convenient to (*that will do me nicely*); *colloq.* provide food etc. for (*they do one very well here*); cook, esp. to the right degree (*do it in the oven; did it to a turn*); translate or transform (*into* another language or medium); *colloq.* visit, see sights of (*do London, the night-clubs*); *sl.* cheat, swindle, rob (*did us out of £100; did the supermarket*); *sl.* prosecute, convict (*did him for shoplifting*); *sl.* undergo (term of imprisonment); exhaust, tire out, *sl.* defeat, ruin, kill. **2** *v.i.* act, proceed, perform deeds (*do as the Romans do; would do well to accept*); fare, get on (*mother and child doing well; they did badly out of it*); be suitable or acceptable, suffice, serve the purpose (*this money will do for the moment; it doesn't do to worry*); be in progress (*nothing doing*). **3** as auxiliary verb with infinitive or elliptically, (a) for emphasis (*I do want to; do tell me; I did go but she wasn't in*), (b) in inversion (*little does he know*), (c) in questions and negations (*do you understand?; he does not want to; don't be silly*), (d) elliptically or in place of verb (*you know her better than I do; I wanted to go and I did so; tell me, do*). **4 be done with** see DONE; **do away with** get rid of, abolish, kill; **do down** *colloq.* overcome, cheat, swindle; **do for** be satisfactory or sufficient for, *colloq.* destroy, ruin, kill, *colloq.* act as housekeeper for; **do-gooder** person meaning to do social good but unrealistic or intrusive in the process; **do in** *sl.* ruin, kill, *colloq.* exhaust, tire out; **do-it--yourself** *a.* & *n.* (work) done or to be done by amateur handyman at home; **do justice to** see JUSTICE; **do or die** persist regardless of danger; **do out** clean or redecorate (room); **do over** *sl.* attack, beat up; **do proud** see PROUD; **do something for** (or **to**) *colloq.* enhance appearance or quality of; **do up** fasten, wrap up, refurbish, renovate; **do with** use, treat (*what shall we do with this?*; *we could do with this*; *what did you do with it?*); **do without** forgo, manage without; **have done with** see DONE; **make do** see MAKE; **to do with** in connection with, related to (*what has that to do with it?*; *problem is to do with money*). [OE]

do[2] /du:/ *n.* (*pl.* **dos** or **do's**) elaborate event, party, or operation; *colloq.* swindle, hoax; **dos and don'ts** rules of behaviour; **fair dos** fair shares.

do[3] var. of DOH.

do.[4] *abbr.* ditto.

Dobermann pinscher /'dəʊbəmən 'pɪnʃə/ large dog of German breed with smooth coat and docked tail. [G]

doc *n. colloq.* doctor. [abbr.]

docile /'dəʊsaɪl/ *a.* submissive, easily managed; **docility** /də'sɪlɪtɪ/ *n.* [L (*doceo* teach)]

dock[1] **1** *n.* artificially enclosed body of water for loading, unloading, and repair of ships; (in *pl.*) range of docks with wharves and offices. **2** *v.* bring or come into dock; join (two or more spacecraft) together in space, become joined thus. **3** **in dock** *colloq.* in hospital or (of vehicle) laid up for repairs. [Du. *docke*]

dock[2] *n.* enclosure in criminal court for accused. [Flem. *dok* cage]

dock[3] *n.* a weed with broad leaves. [OE]

dock[4] *v.t.* cut short (animal's tail); reduce or take away part of (wages, supplies, etc.). [OE]

docker *n.* person employed to load and unload ships. [DOCK[1]]

docket /'dɒkɪt/ **1** *n.* document or label listing goods delivered or contents of package, or recording payment of customs dues etc. **2** *v.t.* enter on docket, label with docket. [orig. unkn.]

dockland *n.* district near docks. [DOCK[1]]

dockyard *n.* area with docks and equipment for building and repairing ships.

doctor /'dɒktə/ **1** *n.* qualified practitioner of medicine, physician; person who holds doctorate (*Doctor of Civil Law*). **2** *v.t.* treat medically; castrate or spay (animal); patch up (machinery etc.); tamper with or falsify. [F f. L (*doceo* teach)]

doctoral *a.* of or for degree of doctor.

doctorate /'dɒktərət/ *n.* higher university degree in any faculty, often honorary.

doctrinaire /dɒktrɪ'neə/ **1** *n.* person who applies principles pedantically without allowance for circumstances. **2** *a.* theoretical and unpractical. [F (foll.)]

doctrine /'dɒktrɪn/ *n.* what is taught, body of instruction; principle of religious or political etc. belief, set of such principles. [F f. L (DOCTOR)]

document **1** /'dɒkjʊmənt/ *n.* thing, esp. title-deed, writing, or inscription, that provides a record or evidence. **2** /'dɒkjʊment/ *v.t.* prove by or provide with documents. **3** **documentation** /-'teɪʃ(ə)n/ *n.* [F f. L (DOCTOR)]

documentary /dɒkjʊ'mentərɪ/ **1** *a.* consisting of documents (*documentary evidence*); providing a factual record or report. **2** *n.* documentary film.

dodder[1] *v.i.* tremble or totter, esp. from age; **dodderer** *n.*; **doddery** *a.* [obs. dial. *dadder*]

dodder[2] *n.* threadlike climbing parasitic plant. [orig. uncert.]

dodecagon /dəʊ'dekəgən/ *n.* plane figure with twelve sides and angles. [Gk *dōdeka* twelve, *-gōnos* angled)]

dodecahedron /dəʊdekə'hi:drən/ *n.* solid figure with twelve faces. [prec., Gk *hedra* base]

dodge **1** *v.* move quickly to one side, or *round*, *about*, or *behind* obstacle, to elude pursuer, blow, etc.; evade by cunning or trickery. **2** *n.* quick movement to avoid something; clever trick or expedient. [orig. unkn.]

dodgem /'dɒdʒəm/ *n.* small electrically-driven car in enclosure at fun-fair, in which driver tries to bump other cars and dodge those trying to bump his car. [prec., -EM]

dodgy *a. colloq.* awkward, unreliable, tricky. [DODGE]

dodo *n.* /'dəʊdəʊ/ (pl. **dodos**) large extinct bird of Mauritius etc.; **as dead as the** (or **a**) **dodo** entirely obsolete. [Port. *doudo* simpleton]

doe *n.* female of the fallow deer, reindeer, hare, or rabbit. [OE]

DOE *abbr.* Department of the Environment.

doer /'du:ə/ *n.* one who does something; one who acts rather than merely talking or thinking. [DO[1]]

does see DO[1]

doesn't /'dʌz(ə)nt/ *colloq.* = *does not.*

doff *v.t.* take off (hat or clothing). [*do off*]

dog **1** *n.* four-legged carnivorous animal of family akin to fox and wolf, and of many breeds wild and domesticated; male of this or of fox or wolf; person (*lucky dog*), despicable person (*dirty dog*); mechanical device for gripping. **2** *v.t.* (**-gg-**) follow closely and persistently, pursue, track. **3** **dog-collar** collar for dog, *colloq.* clerical collar; **dog days** hottest period of year; **dog-eared** (of book) with corners worn or battered with use; **dog-eat-dog** ruthless competition; **dog-end** *sl.* cigarette-end; **dog in the manger** one who clings to thing he cannot use, preventing others from enjoying it; **dog's breakfast** *colloq.* mess; **dog's**

life life of misery or harassment; **dog-star** chief star of constellation Canis Major or Minor, esp. Sirius; **dog-tired** tired out; **dog-watch** one of two-hour watches on ship (4–6 or 6–8 p.m.); **go to the dogs** *sl.* deteriorate, be ruined; **like a dog's dinner** *colloq.* smartly or flashily (dressed, arranged, etc.); **not a dog's chance** no chance at all. [OE]

dogcart *n.* two-wheeled driving-cart with cross seats back to back.

doge /dəʊdʒ/ *n. hist.* chief magistrate of Venice or Genoa. [F f. It. f. L *dux* leader]

dogfight *n.* close combat between fighter aircraft; uproar, fight like that between dogs. [DOG]

dogfish *n.* a kind of small shark.

dogged /'dɒgɪd/ *a.* tenacious, grimly persistent.

doggerel /'dɒgər(ə)l/ *n.* poor or trivial verse. [app. f. DOG]

doggie *n.* pet-name for dog. [DOG]

doggo *adv. sl.* in **lie doggo** lie motionless or hidden.

doggy 1 *a.* of or like a dog; devoted to dogs. **2** *n.* = DOGGIE.

doghouse *n.* dog's kennel (*US*); **in the doghouse** *sl.* in disgrace.

dogma /'dɒgmə/ *n.* principle or tenet or system of these, esp. as laid down by authority of a Church; arrogant declaration of opinion. [L f. Gk, = opinion]

dogmatic /dɒg'mætɪk/ *a.* of or in the nature of dogma; (given to) asserting dogmas or opinions; arrogant, intolerantly authoritative; **dogmatically** *adv.*

dogmatism /'dɒgmətɪz(ə)m/ *n.* tendency to be dogmatic; **dogmatist** *n.*

dogmatize /'dɒgmətaɪz/ *v.* speak dogmatically; express (principle etc.) as dogma. [F f. L f. Gk (DOGMA)]

dogrose *n.* a wild hedge-rose. [DOG]

dogsbody /'dɒgzbɒdɪ/ *n. colloq.* drudge.

dogwood *n.* shrub with dark red branches, greenish-white flowers, and purple berries, found in woods and hedgerows.

doh /dəʊ/ *n. Mus.* first note of diatonic scale. [It. *do*]

doily /'dɔɪlɪ/ *n.* small ornamental lace or paper mat used on plate for cakes etc. [*Doiley*, draper]

Dolby /'dɒlbɪ/ *n.* **(P)** system used in tape-recording to reduce unwanted sounds at high frequency. [inventor]

doldrums /'dɒldrəmz/ *n.pl.* low spirits; period of inactivity; equatorial ocean region often marked by calms. [perh. after *dull, tantrum*]

dole 1 *n.* charitable distribution, thing given sparingly or reluctantly; *colloq. the* benefit claimable by the unemployed from the State. **2** *v.t.* deal *out* sparingly. **3 on the dole** receiving State benefit for the unemployed. [OE]

doleful /'dəʊlfʊl/ *a.* mournful, sad; dreary, dismal; **dolefully** *adv.* [*dole* f. F f. L (*doleo* grieve)]

doll 1 *n.* small model of human figure, esp. baby or child, as child's toy; ventriloquist's dummy; *colloq.* pretty but silly young woman; *sl.* young woman. **2** *v. colloq.* dress *up* smartly. [pet form of *Dorothy*]

dollar /'dɒlə/ *n.* currency unit in the US and certain other countries. [LG *daler* f. G *taler*]

dollop /'dɒləp/ *n. colloq.* shapeless lump of food etc. [perh. Scand.]

dolly *n.* child's name for doll; movable platform for cine-camera; easy catch in cricket; **dolly-bird** *colloq.* attractive and stylish young woman. [DOLL]

dolman sleeve /'dɒlmən/ loose sleeve cut in one piece with body of garment. [Turk.]

dolmen /'dɒlmən/ *n.* megalithic tomb with large flat stone laid on upright ones. [F]

dolomite /'dɒləmaɪt/ *n.* mineral or rock of calcium magnesium carbonate. [F (de *Dolomieu*, geologist)]

dolour /'dɒlə/, *US* **dolor** *n. literary* sorrow, distress; **dolorous** *a.* [F f. L (*dolor* pain)]

dolphin /'dɒlfɪn/ *n.* sea mammal like porpoise but larger and with slender pointed snout. [L f. Gk *delphis -in-*]

dolt /dəʊlt/ *n.* stupid person. [prob. rel. to obs. *dol* = DULL]

Dom *n.* title prefixed to names of some RC dignitaries, and Benedictine and Carthusian monks. [L *dominus* master]

-dom *suffix* forming nouns, (1) from nouns or adjectives, denoting rank, condition, or domain (*earldom, freedom, kingdom*), (2) from nouns, denoting collective plural or in sense 'the ways of —s' (*officialdom*). [OE]

domain /də'meɪn/ *n.* area under one rule, realm; estate or lands under one control; sphere of control or influence. [F (DEMESNE)]

dome *n.* circular vault forming roof; dome-shaped thing. [F f. It. f. L *domus* house]

domed *a.* having dome(s), shaped like dome.

domestic /də'mestɪk/ **1** *a.* of the home or household or family affairs; of one's own country, not foreign or international; fond of home life; (of animal) kept by or living with man. **2** *n.* household servant. **3 domestic science** = *home economics.* **4 domestically** *adv.* [F f. L (*domus* home)]

domesticate /də'mestɪkeɪt/ *v.t.* tame

(animal) to live with humans; accustom to home life and management. [med.L (prec.)]

domesticity /dɒməs'tɪsɪtɪ/ *n.* being domestic; domestic or home life. [DOMESTIC]

domicile /'dɒmɪsaɪl/ *n.* dwelling-place; *Law* place of permanent residence, fact of residing. [F f. L (*domus* home)]

domiciled *a.* having domicile *at* or *in*.

domiciliary /dɒmɪ'sɪlɪərɪ/ *a.* of a dwelling-place (esp. of visit of doctor, officials, etc., to person's home). [F f. med.L (prec.)]

dominant /'dɒmɪnənt/ **1** *a.* dominating, prevailing; (of inherited characteristic) appearing in offspring even when a corresponding opposite characteristic is also inherited. **2** *n. Mus.* fifth note of diatonic scale of any key. **3 dominance** *n.* [F f. L (foll.)]

dominate /'dɒmɪneɪt/ *v.* have a commanding influence over; be the most influential or conspicuous; (of high place) have commanding position over; **domination** /-'neɪʃ(ə)n/ *n.* [L *dominor* (*dominus* lord)]

domineer /dɒmɪ'nɪə/ *v.i.* behave in arrogant and overbearing way. [Du. f. F (as prec.)]

Dominican /də'mɪnɪkən/ **1** *n.* friar or nun of order founded by St Dominic. **2** *a.* of St Dominic or his order. [L (*Dominic*)]

dominion /də'mɪnjən/ *n.* sovereignty, control; territory of sovereign or government, domain; *hist.* title of self-governing territories of British Commonwealth. [F f. med.L (*dominus* lord)]

domino /'dɒmɪnəʊ/ *n.* (*pl.* **dominoes**) any of 28 small oblong pieces marked with 0–6 pips in each half; (in *pl.*) game played with these; loose cloak with mask for upper part of face, worn at masquerades; **domino theory** theory that one (esp. political) event precipitates others in causal sequence, like row of dominoes falling over. [F, prob. as prec.]

don[1] *n.* university teacher, esp. senior member of college at Oxford or Cambridge; (**Don**) Spanish title prefixed to Christian name; **Don Juan** seducer of women, libertine. [Sp. f. L *dominus* lord]

don[2] *v.t.* (**-nn-**) put on (clothing). [*do on*]

donate /dəʊ'neɪt/ *v.t.* give or contribute (money etc.), esp. voluntarily to fund or institution. [foll.]

donation /dəʊ'neɪʃ(ə)n/ *n.* act of donating; amount donated. [F f. L (*donum* gift)]

done /dʌn/ *a.* completed; cooked; socially acceptable (*the done thing*); (as *int.* in reply to offer etc.) accepted; *colloq.* tired out (often with *in* or *up*); **be done with** have finished with, be finished with; **done for** in serious trouble; **have done with** finish dealing with, be rid of. [*p.p.* of DO[1]]

donjon /'dɒndʒ(ə)n/ *n.* great tower of castle. [*archaic* sp. of DUNGEON]

donkey /'dɒŋkɪ/ *n.* domestic ass; *colloq.* stupid person; **donkey engine** small auxiliary engine; **donkey jacket** workman's thick weatherproof jacket; **donkey's years** *colloq.* a very long time; **donkey-work** laborious part of a job. [perh. *Duncan* (cf. NEDDY)]

Donna /'dɒnə/ *n.* title of Italian or Spanish or Portuguese lady. [It. f. L *domina* mistress]

donnish *a.* like a college don; pedantic. [DON[1]]

donor /'dəʊnə/ *n.* one who gives or donates something; one who provides blood for transfusion, semen for insemination, or organ or tissue for transplantation. [AF f. L (DONATION)]

don't /dəʊnt/ *colloq.* = *do not*; (as *n.*) prohibition; see DO[2]. [DO[1]]

doodle /'du:d(ə)l/ **1** *v.i.* scribble or draw, esp. absent-mindedly. **2** *n.* scribble or drawing made by doodling. [orig. = foolish person]

doom **1** *n.* grim fate or destiny, death or ruin; condemnation. **2** *v.t.* condemn or destine *to*. [OE, = STATUTE]

doomsday /'du:mzdeɪ/ *n.* the day of the Last Judgement; **till doomsday** for ever.

door *n.* hinged, sliding, or revolving barrier for closing entrance to building or room or cupboard etc.; this as representing house etc. (*she lives two doors away*); doorway; entrance or exit, means of access or approach; **close** (or **open**) **the door to** create (or exclude) opportunity for; **door-keeper** = DOORMAN; **door-to-door** *a.* (of selling etc.) done at each house in turn. [OE]

doorbell *n.* bell in house rung at front door by visitors to signal arrival.

doorknob *n.* knob for turning to release latch of door.

doorman *n.* person on duty at door at entrance to large building.

doormat *n.* mat at entrance, for wiping shoes; feebly submissive person.

doorstep *n.* step leading to, point in front of, outer door of house etc.; **on one's doorstep** very close.

doorstop *n.* device for keeping door open or to prevent it from striking wall when opened.

doorway *n.* opening filled by door.

dope **1** *n.* thick liquid used as lubricant etc.; varnish; *sl.* drug, esp. narcotic; drug or stimulant given to athlete etc. to affect performance; *sl.* information; *sl.* stupid person. **2** *v.* treat with dope; give drug or stimulant to; take addictive drugs. [Du., = sauce]

dopey *a. colloq.* half asleep; stupefied (as) by a drug; stupid; **dopiness** *n.*

doppelgänger /ˈdɒp(ə)lgeŋə/ *n.* wraith of living person. [G, = double-goer]

Doppler effect apparent increase (or decrease) in frequency of sound, light, and other waves when source and observer become closer (or more distant). [*Doppler*, physicist]

dorado /dəˈrɑːdəʊ/ *n.* (*pl.* **dorados**) blue and silver sea-fish showing brilliant colours when it dies out of water. [Sp., = gilt]

Doric /ˈdɒrɪk/ **1** *a.* (of dialect) broad, rustic; *Archit.* of oldest and simplest of the Greek orders. **2** *n.* rustic English or esp. Scots. [L f. Gk (*Doris* in Greece)]

dormant /ˈdɔːmənt/ *a.* sleeping, lying inactive as in sleep; temporarily inactive; (of plants) alive but not actively growing; **dormancy** *n.* [F f. L *dormio* sleep]

dormer *n.* projecting upright window in sloping roof. [F (as prec.)]

dormitory /ˈdɔːmɪtərɪ/ *n.* sleeping-room with several beds, esp. in school or institution; (in full **dormitory town**) small town or suburb from which people travel to work in city etc. [L (as prec.)]

dormouse /ˈdɔːmaʊs/ *n.* (*pl.* **dormice**) small hibernating rodent resembling mouse and squirrel. [orig. unkn.]

dormy /ˈdɔːmɪ/ *a.* as many holes ahead in score in golf as there are holes left to play (*dormy two*). [orig. unkn.]

dorsal /ˈdɔːs(ə)l/ *a.* of or on the back (*dorsal fin*). [F or L (*dorsum* back)]

dory /ˈdɔːrɪ/ *n.* (also **John Dory**) an edible sea-fish. [F *dorée* = gilded]

dosage /ˈdəʊsɪdʒ/ *n.* giving of dose; size of dose. [foll.]

dose 1 *n.* amount of medicine to be taken at one time; amount of flattery, punishment, etc.; amount of radiation received by person or thing; *sl.* venereal infection. **2** *v.t.* give dose(s) of medicine to; treat (person or animal) *with*. [F f. L f. Gk *dosis* gift]

doss *v.i. sl.* sleep, esp. in doss-house; **doss down** *sl.* sleep on makeshift bed; **doss-house** *sl.* cheap lodging-house. [prob. orig. seat-back cover, F f. L *dorsum* back]

dossier /ˈdɒsɪə, -ɪeɪ/ *n.* set of documents containing information about person or event. [F]

dot 1 *n.* small round mark or spot; this as part of *i* or *j* or as decimal point; shorter signal of two in Morse code. **2** *v.t.* (**-tt-**) mark with dot(s), place dot over (letter); scatter like dots; partly cover as with dots (*sea dotted with ships*); *sl.* hit. **3 dotted line** line of dots on document to show place for signature; **dot the i's and cross the t's** be minutely accurate, emphasize details; **on the dot** exactly on time; **the year dot** *colloq.* far in the past. [OE]

dotage *n.* feeble-minded senility (*in his dotage*). [DOTE]

dotard /ˈdəʊtəd/*n.* person who is in his dotage. [foll.]

dote *v.i.* be silly or infatuated; **dote on** be excessively fond of. [orig. uncert.]

dotterel /ˈdɒtər(ə)l/ *n.* small migrant plover. [prec.]

dottle /ˈdɒt(ə)l/ *n.* remnant of unburnt tobacco in pipe. [DOT]

dotty *a. colloq.* feeble-minded, eccentric, silly; **dottiness** *n.*

double /ˈdʌb(ə)l/ **1** *a.* consisting of two parts or things, twofold, multiplied by two; twice as much or many (*double the amount, the number; double thickness*), having twice the usual quantity, size, strength, etc. (*double bed, whisky*); having some part double, (of flower) having more than one circle of petals; folded, stooping (*bent double*); ambiguous, deceitful, hypocritical (*double meaning; play a double game*); *Mus.* lower in pitch by an octave (*double bassoon*). **2** *adv.* at or to twice the amount etc. (*counts double*); two together (*sleep double*). **3** *n.* double quantity or thing, double measure of spirits etc., twice as much or many; counterpart of person or thing, person who looks exactly like another; (in *pl.*) game between two pairs of players; pair of victories over same team or of championships at same game etc.; system of betting in which winnings and stake from first bet are transferred to a second; doubling of opponent's bid in bridge; hit on narrow ring between the two outer circles in darts. **4** *v.* make or become double, increase twofold, multiply by two; amount to twice as much as; fold or bend over on itself, become folded; act (two parts) in the same play etc., be understudy etc. (*for*); play twofold role (*as*); turn sharply in flight or pursuit; (of ship) sail round (headland); make call in bridge increasing value of points to be won or lost on (opponent's bid). **5 at the double** running, hurrying; **double agent** one who spies simultaneously for two rival countries; **double back** take new direction opposite to previous one; **double-barrelled** (of gun) having two barrels, (of name) having two parts with hyphen; **double-bass** largest and lowest-pitched instrument of violin family; **double-breasted** (of coat etc.) having fronts that overlap to fasten across the breast; **double-check** verify twice or in two ways; **double chin** chin with a fold of loose flesh below it; **double cream** thick cream with high fat-content; **double-cross** *v.t.* & *n.* deceive or betray (person one is supposedly helping), act of doing this; **double-dealing** *n.* & *a.* deceit, esp. in business, practising deceit; **double-decker** see DECK; **double Dutch** gibberish; **double eagle** figure of two-headed eagle; **double-edged** having two cutting-edges, *fig.* damaging to user as well as his opponent; **double entry** system of book-keeping in which each transaction is entered as a debit in one account and a credit in another; **double figures** numbers from 10 to 99; **double glazing** two layers of glass in window to reduce heat loss and exclude noise; **double-jointed** having joints that allow unusual bending of fingers etc.; **double or quits** a gamble to decide whether player's loss or debt be doubled or cancelled; **double-park** park vehicle alongside one that is already parked at roadside; **double pneumonia** that affecting both lungs; **double-quick** *a.* & *adv.* very quick, very quickly; **double standard** rule or principle applied more strictly to some than to others (or to oneself); **double-stopping** sounding of two strings at once on violin etc.; **double take** delayed reaction to situation etc. immediately after one's first reaction; **double-talk** verbal expression that is (usu. deliberately) ambiguous or misleading; **double-think** mental capacity to accept contrary opinions at same time; **double time** payment of employee at twice normal rate; **double up** (cause to) bend or curl up with pain or (*lit.* or *fig.*) laughter, (cause to) share room, quarters, etc., with another or others. **6 doubly** *adv.* [F f. L *duplus*]

double entendre /du:bl ɑ:n'tɑ:ndrə/ phrase affording two meanings, one usu. indecent. [obs. F]

doublet /'dʌblɪt/ *n.* one of a pair of similar things; *hist.* man's short close-fitting jacket with or without sleeves. [F (prec.)]

doubloon /dʌb'lu:n/ *n. hist.* Spanish gold coin. [F or Sp. (DOUBLE)]

doubt /daʊt/ **1** *n.* feeling of uncertainty about something, undecided state of mind; inclination to disbelieve; uncertain state of things; lack of full proof or clear indication. **2** *v.* feel uncertain or undecided (about); hesitate to believe; call in question. **3 no doubt** certainly, probably, admittedly; **without (a) doubt** certainly. [F f. L *dubito* hesitate]

doubtful *a.* feeling doubt; causing doubt, unreliable, undecided.

doubtless *adv.* certainly, probably.

douche /du:ʃ/ **1** *n.* jet of liquid applied to part of the body for cleansing or for medicinal purpose; device for producing such jet. **2** *v.* treat with douche; use douche. [F f. It. f. L (DUCT)]

dough /dəʊ/ *n.* thick mixture of flour etc. and liquid, for baking; *sl.* money; **doughy** *a.* [OE]

doughnut *n.* small sweetened fried cake of dough.

doughty /'daʊtɪ/ *a. archaic* valiant, stout-hearted; **doughtily** *adv.*; **doughtiness** *n.* [OE]

dour /dʊə/ *a.* stern, severe, obstinate. [prob. Gael. *dúr* dull obstinate]

douse *v.t.* plunge into water, throw water over; extinguish (light). [orig. uncert.]

dove /dʌv/ *n.* bird with short legs, small head, and large breast; advocate of peace or peaceful policy; gentle or innocent person. [ON]

dovecote /'dʌvkɒt/ *n.* shelter with nesting-holes for domesticated pigeons.

dovetail *n.* joint formed by mortise with tenon shaped like dove's spread tail. **2** *v.* put together with dovetails; fit together or combine neatly.

dowager /'daʊədʒə/ *n.* woman with title or property derived from her late husband (*the dowager duchess*); *colloq.* dignified elderly lady. [F (DOWER)]

dowdy /'daʊdɪ/ *a.* (of clothes) unattractively dull; (of person) dressed in dowdy clothes; **dowdily** *adv.*; **dowdiness** *n.* [orig. unkn.]

dowel /'daʊəl/ **1** *n.* headless wooden or metal pin for holding two pieces of wood or stone together. **2** *v.t.* (**-ll-**, *US* **-l-**) fasten with dowel. [LG]

dowelling *n.* round rods for cutting into dowels.

dower 1 *n.* widow's share for life of husband's estate; *archaic* dowry. **2** *v.t. archaic* give dowry to; endow *with* talent etc. **3 dower house** smaller house near big one, forming part of widow's dower. [F f. L *dos* dowry]

down[1] **1** *adv.* at, in, or towards a lower place or a place regarded as lower, esp. the south or parts away from a capital or university (*fall down*; *down to the country*); in or into a low or weaker position or condition (*hit a man when he's down*; *team was three goals down*; *wife down with a cold*); from an earlier to a later time (*down to 1600*); to finer consistency or smaller amount or size (*boil, grind, wear, down*); cheaper, of lower value (*butter is down*; *shares are down*); into quiescence (*calm down*); in writing, in or into recorded form (*copy, put*, etc., *it down*; *I got it down on tape*; *you are* *down to speak next*); (of part of larger whole) paid, dealt with (*£5 down, £20 to pay*; *3 down, 6 to go*); with the current or wind. **2** *prep.* downwards along, through, or into; from top to bottom of; along (*walked down the road*); at or in a lower part of (*situated down the river, the street*). **3** *a.* directed downwards (*a down draught*); of travel away from a capital or centre (*the down train, platform*). **4** *v.t. colloq.* knock or bring down, swallow. **5** *n.* act of putting down; reverse of fortune (often in *ups and downs*). **6 down and out** penniless, destitute; **down-and-out** *n.* destitute person; **down-hearted** dejected; **down in the mouth** looking unhappy; **down on** holding in disfavour; **down payment** partial payment made at time of purchase; **down stage** at or to front of theatre stage; **down-to-earth** practical, realistic; **down tools** cease work, go on strike; **down to the ground** *colloq.* completely; **down under** in the antipodes, esp. Australia; **down with** *int.* of disgust with or rejection of stated person or thing; **have a down on** hold in disfavour. [earlier *adown* (DOWN³)]

down² *n.* first covering of young birds, bird's under-plumage; fine soft feathers or short hairs; fluffy substance. [ON]

down³ *n.* area of open rolling land (also **downland**); (in *pl.*) chalk uplands esp. of S. England. [OE]

downbeat **1** *n.* accented beat in music. **2** *a.* pessimistic, gloomy; relaxed. [DOWN¹]

downcast *a.* (of eyes) looking downwards; (of person) dejected.

downfall *n.* fall from prosperity or power; cause of this.

downgrade *v.t.* lower in rank.

downhill **1** *adv.* in descending direction. **2** *a.* sloping down, declining. **3 go downhill** deteriorate.

downpipe *n.* pipe for carrying rainwater from roof to drain.

downpour *n.* heavy fall of rain.

downright **1** *a.* plain, straightforward; utter, complete (*downright nonsense*). **2** *adv.* thoroughly, completely (*downright rude*).

Down's syndrome mongolism. [*Down*, physician]

downstairs **1** *adv.* down the stairs; to or on a lower floor. **2** *a.* situated downstairs. **3** *n.* downstairs floor. [DOWN¹]

downstream *a.* & *adv.* in direction in which stream flows.

downtown *US* **1** *a.* of lower or more central part of town or city. **2** *n.* downtown area.

downtrodden *a.* oppressed, badly treated.

downturn *n.* decline, esp. in economic or business activity.

downward /'daʊnwəd/ **1** *adv.* (also **downwards**) towards what is lower, inferior, less important, or later. **2** *a.* moving or extending downwards. [-WARD]

downwind *a.* & *adv.* in the direction in which the wind is blowing. [DOWN¹]

downy *a.* of or like down, soft and fluffy; *sl.* aware, knowing. [DOWN²]

dowry /'daʊərɪ/ *n.* property or money brought by a bride to her husband. [AF, = F *douaire* DOWER]

dowse¹ /daʊz/ *v.* search for underground water or minerals by holding a Y-shaped stick or rod (**dowsing-rod**) which dips abruptly when over right spot. [orig. unkn.]

dowse² var. of DOUSE.

doxology /dɒk'sɒlədʒɪ/ *n.* liturgical formula of praise to God. [L f. Gk (*doxa* glory)]

doyen /'dɔɪən/ *n.* senior member of a body of colleagues; **doyenne** /-'en/ *n. fem.* [F (DEAN¹)]

doz. *abbr.* dozen.

doze **1** *v.i.* be half asleep, sleep lightly. **2** *n.* short light sleep. **3 doze off** fall lightly asleep. [orig. unkn.]

dozen /'dʌz(ə)n/ *n.* (*pl.* after number **dozen**) twelve, set of twelve; **talk nineteen to the dozen** talk incessantly. [F f. L *duodecim* twelve]

dozy *a.* drowsy; *colloq.* stupid, lazy. [DOZE]

D. Phil. *abbr.* Doctor of Philosophy.

DPP *abbr.* Director of Public Prosecutions.

Dr *abbr.* Doctor.

drab **1** *a.* dull, uninteresting; of dull brownish colour. **2** *n.* drab colour. [obs. *drap* cloth f. F. f. L]

drachm /dræm/ *n.* weight formerly used by apothecaries, = ⅛ ounce. [F, or L f. Gk]

drachma /'drækmə/ *n.* (*pl.* **drachmas**) unit of currency of Greece; silver coin of ancient Greece. [L, f. Gk *drakhmē*]

Draconian /drə'kəʊnɪən/ *a.* (of laws) very harsh, cruel. [*Drakōn*, Athenian lawgiver]

draft /drɑ:ft/ **1** *n.* rough preliminary outline of scheme or written version of speech, document, etc.; written order for payment of money by bank, drawing of money by this; detachment from larger group for special duty or purpose, selection of this; *US* conscription. **2** *v.t.* prepare draft of (writing or scheme); select for special duty or purpose; *US* conscript. [phon. sp. of DRAUGHT]

draftsman *n.* one who drafts documents.

drag 1 *v.* (**-gg-**) pull along with effort or difficulty; (allow to) trail along the ground, proceed heavily or tediously; use grapnel, search (bottom of water) with grapnels, nets, etc.; *colloq.* take (person *to* place etc. esp. against his will); *colloq.* draw *on* or *at* (cigarette etc.). **2** *n.* obstruction to progress, retarding force, retarded motion; *colloq.* boring or tiresome person, duty, etc.; lure drawn before hounds as substitute for fox, hunt using this; apparatus for dredging etc.; = *drag-net*; *sl.* draw on cigarette etc.; *sl.* women's clothes worn by men. **3 drag one's feet** be deliberately slow or reluctant to act; **drag in** introduce (subject) irrelevantly; **drag-net** net drawn through river or across ground to trap fish or game, systematic hunt for criminals etc.; **drag on** continue tediously; **drag out** prolong at length; **drag race** acceleration race between cars over short distance; **drag up** *colloq.* introduce or revive (unwelcome subject). [OE or ON]

draggle /'dræg(ə)l/ *v.* make dirty or wet or limp by trailing; hang trailing. [prec.]

dragon /'drægən/ *n.* mythical monster like reptile, usu. with wings and able to breathe out fire; fierce person. [F f. L f. Gk, = serpent]

dragonfly *n.* large insect with long body and two pairs of transparent wings.

dragoon /drə'gu:n/ **1** *n.* cavalryman (orig. mounted infantryman); fierce fellow. **2** *v.t.* force *into* doing something. [F *dragon* (DRAGON)]

drain 1 *v.* draw off liquid from; draw off (liquid); flow or trickle away; dry or become dry as liquid flows away; exhaust of strength or resources; drink (liquid), empty (glass etc.) by drinking contents. **2** *n.* channel, conduit, or pipe carrying off liquid, sewage, etc.; constant outflow or expenditure (*a great drain on my income*). **3 down the drain** *colloq.* lost, wasted; **draining-board** sloping grooved surface beside sink on which washed dishes etc. are left to drain; **drain-pipe** pipe for carrying off surplus water or liquid sewage from a building. [OE (DRY)]

drainage *n.* draining; system of drains; what is drained off.

drake *n.* male duck. [orig. uncert.]

dram *n.* small drink of spirits; = DRACHM. [F, or L *drama* (DRACHM)]

drama /'drɑ:mə/ *n.* play for acting on stage or for broadcasting; art of writing and presenting plays; dramatic series of events; dramatic quality (*the drama of the situation*). [L f. Gk (*draō* do)]

dramatic /drə'mætɪk/ *a.* of drama; sudden and exciting or unexpected; vividly striking; (of gesture etc.) overdone or absurd. [L f. Gk (prec.)]

dramatics *n.pl.* (often treated as *sing.*) performance of plays; exaggerated behaviour.

dramatis personae /'dræmətɪs pɜ:'səʊnaɪ/ *n.pl.* characters in a play; list of these. [L, = persons of the drama]

dramatist /'dræmətɪst/ *n.* writer of dramas. [DRAMA]

dramatize /'dræmətaɪz/ *v.* make (novel etc.) into a play; make a dramatic scene of; behave dramatically; **dramatization** /-'zeɪʃ(ə)n/ *n.*

drank *past* of DRINK.

drape 1 *v.t.* cover loosely, hang, adorn, with cloth etc.; arrange (clothes, hangings) in graceful folds. **2** *n.* (in *pl.*) *US* curtains. [F f. L *drappus* cloth]

draper *n.* retailer of cloth, linen, etc.

drapery *n.* draper's trade or fabrics; clothing or hangings arranged in folds.

drastic /'dræstɪk, 'drɑ:-/ *a.* having a strong or far-reaching effect, severe. [Gk *drastikos* (DRAMA)]

drat *v.t. colloq.* (as *int.* of anger or annoyance) curse; **dratted** *a.* [(*Go*)*d rot*]

draught /drɑ:ft/ *n.* current of air in room etc., or in chimney; pulling, traction; depth of water needed to float ship; drawing of liquor from cask etc.; single act of drinking, amount so drunk; (in *pl.*) game for two played on chessboard with 24 pieces; drawing in of fishing-net, fish caught in this; **draught beer** beer drawn from cask, not bottled; **draught-horse** horse used for pulling heavy loads, cart, plough, etc.; **feel the draught** *sl.* feel the effect of financial or other difficulties. [DRAW]

draughtboard *n.* = CHESSBOARD.

draughtsman *n.* one who makes drawings, plans, or sketches; piece in game of draughts; **draughtsmanship** *n.*

draughty *a.* (of room etc.) letting in sharp currents of air.

draw 1 *v.* (*past* **drew** /dru:/; *p.p.* **drawn**) pull or cause to move towards or after one; pull (thing) up, over, or across; pull (curtains etc.) open or shut; attract, take in, bring to oneself or to something (*draw a deep breath*; *I felt drawn to her*; *drew my attention to the matter*; *the match drew large crowds*); suck *on* or *at* cigarette or pipe etc.; take out, remove (*draw a cork*, *pistol*, *sword*, *card*, or *absol.*); obtain or take from a source (*draw a salary*; *draw inspiration*; *drew £100 from my account*); trace (line or mark); produce (picture) by tracing lines and marks, represent (thing) thus, *absol.* make drawing(s); finish (contest or game) with neither side winning;

proceed or make one's way (*drew near the bridge*; *draw to a close*; *second horse drew ahead*, *drew level*); infer (conclusion); elicit, evoke, bring about (*draw criticism*; *draw ruin upon oneself*); induce (person) to reveal facts or feelings; haul up (water) from well; bring out (liquid from vessel, blood from body); extract liquid essence from; (of chimney etc.) promote or allow draught; (of tea) infuse; obtain by lot, *absol.* draw lots; make call *on* person or his skill etc.; compose or write out (document, cheque, etc.); formulate or perceive (comparison, distinctions); (of ship) require (specified depth of water) to float in; disembowel; search (cover) for game; drag (badger or fox) from hole. **2** *n.* act of drawing; person or thing that draws custom, attention, etc.; drawing of lots, raffle; drawn game; suck on cigarette etc. **3 draw a bead on** see BEAD; **draw back** withdraw from undertaking; **draw a blank** see BLANK; **draw in** (of days) become shorter, persuade to join; **draw in one's horns** become less assertive or ambitious; **draw the line at** set a limit (of tolerance etc.) at; **draw lots** see LOT; **draw on** approach, come near, lead to, allure; **draw out** prolong, elicit, induce to talk, (of days) become longer; **draw-string** one that can be pulled to tighten an opening; **draw up** compose or draft (document etc.), bring into order, come to a halt, make *oneself* stiffly erect; **quick on the draw** quick to react. [OE]

drawback *n.* thing that impairs satisfaction, disadvantage.

drawbridge *n.* bridge esp. over moat, hinged at one end for drawing up.

drawer /ˈdrɔːə/ *n.* one who or that which draws, esp. person who draws a cheque etc.; (also /drɔː/) boxlike storage compartment without lid, for sliding in and out of table etc. (*chest of drawers*); (in *pl.*) undergarment worn next to body below waist.

drawing *n.* art of representing by line with pencil etc.; picture etc. drawn thus; **drawing-board** board on which paper is stretched while drawing is made; **drawing-pin** flat-headed pin for fastening paper etc. to a surface.

drawing-room *n.* room for comfortable sitting or entertaining in a private house. [earlier *withdrawing-room*]

drawl 1 *v.* speak with drawn-out vowel-sounds. **2** *n.* drawling utterance or way of speaking. [LG or Du.]

drawn *a.* looking strained from fear or anxiety; (of butter) melted. [DRAW]

dray *n.* low cart without sides for heavy loads, esp. beer-barrels. [DRAW]

dread /dred/ **1** *v.t.* fear greatly; look forward to with great apprehension. **2** *n.* great fear or apprehension. **3** *a.* dreaded; *archaic* dreadful, awe-inspiring. [OE]

dreadful *a.* terrible; *colloq.* troublesome, very bad; **dreadfully** *adv.*

dream 1 *n.* series of pictures or events in mind of sleeping person; day-dream, fantasy; ideal or aspiration; beautiful or ideal person or thing. **2** *v.* (*past* and *p.p.* **dreamt** /dremt/ or **dreamed**) experience dream; imagine as in a dream; (with *neg.*) think of as a possibility (*would not dream of it*; *never dreamt he would come*); spend (time) *away* unpractically; be inactive or unpractical. **3 dream-land** ideal or imaginary land; **dream up** imagine, invent; **like a dream** *colloq.* easily, effortlessly. [OE]

dreamy *a.* dreamlike; given to dreaming or fantasy, vague; **dreamily** *adv.*; **dreaminess** *n.*

dreary *a.* dismal, dull, gloomy; **drearily** *adv.*; **dreariness** *n.* [OE]

dredge[1] 1 *n.* apparatus for bringing up oysters etc. or clearing out mud etc. from river or sea bottom. **2** *v.* bring *up* or clean out with dredge; use dredge. [orig. uncert.]

dredge[2] *v.t.* sprinkle with flour, sugar, etc. [earlier = sweetmeat, f. F]

dredger[1] *n.* dredge, boat with dredge. [DREDGE[1]]

dredger[2] *n.* container with perforated lid, used for sprinkling flour etc. [DREDGE[2]]

dregs *n. pl.* sediment, grounds, lees; worst or most useless part. [ON]

drench 1 *v.t.* make thoroughly wet; force (animal) to take dose of medicine. **2** *n.* dose of medicine for animal. [OE]

dress 1 *v.* put clothes upon; provide oneself with and wear clothes; put on one's clothes; put on evening dress; arrange or adorn (hair, shop window, etc.); clean or treat (wound etc.); prepare (bird or crab or salad) for cooking or eating; finish surface of (fabric, leather, stone); apply manure to; correct the alignment of (troops). **2** *n.* clothing, esp. the visible part of it; woman's or girl's garment of bodice and skirt; formal or ceremonial costume; external covering, outward form. **3 dress-circle** first gallery in theatre, where evening dress was formerly required; **dress down** scold, reprimand; **dress rehearsal** final rehearsal in full costume; **dress up** put on special clothes, make (thing) more attractive or interesting. [F f. L, rel. to DIRECT]

dressage /ˈdresɑːʒ/ *n.* training of horse in obedience and deportment; display of this. [F]

dresser[1] *n.* kitchen sideboard with shelves for dishes etc. [F (*dresser* prepare)]

dresser[2] *n.* one who helps to dress actors or actresses; surgeon's assistant in operations. [DRESS]

dressing *n.* putting one's clothes on; sauce or stuffing etc. for food; bandage, ointment, etc., for wound; manure etc. spread over land; substance used to stiffen textile fabrics during manufacture; **dressing down** scolding; **dressing-gown** loose gown worn when one is not fully dressed; **dressing-room** room for dressing or changing clothes, esp. in theatre etc., or attached to bedroom; **dressing-table** table with a mirror, for use while dressing or using make-up.

dressmaker *n.* person who makes women's clothes, esp. professionally; **dressmaking** *n.*

dressy *a.* smart, elegant, wearing stylish clothes; **dressily** *adv.*

drew *past* of DRAW.

drey /dreɪ/ *n.* squirrel's nest. [orig. unkn.]

dribble /'drɪb(ə)l/ **1** *v.* allow saliva to flow from the mouth; (cause to) flow in drops; move the ball forward in football or hockey with slight touches of the feet or stick. **2** *n.* act of dribbling; dribbling flow. [obs. *drib* = DRIP]

driblet /'drɪblɪt/ *n.* small amount.

dribs and drabs small scattered amounts.

drier /'draɪə/ *n.* device for drying hair, laundry, etc. [DRY]

drift 1 *n.* being driven along, esp. by current, slow movement or variation; mass of snow or sand driven along or heaped up by wind; general scope or tendency of person's words; merely waiting on events, inaction; slow deviation of vehicle or projectile etc. from course; fragments of rock heaped up by wind, water, etc. (*glacial drift*); *S. Afr.* ford. **2** *v.* be carried by or as if by current of air or water, (of current) cause to drift; heap or be heaped into drifts; move about casually or aimlessly. **3 drift-net** net used in sea-fishing and allowed to drift with tide. [ON & LG or Du.]

drifter *n.* aimless person; boat used for fishing with drift-net.

driftwood *n.* wood floating on moving water or washed ashore by it.

drill[1] **1** *n.* tool or machine for boring holes or sinking wells; instruction in military exercises; thorough training, esp. by repeated routine; *colloq.* recognized procedure (*what's the drill?*). **2** *v.* make (hole) with a drill; make hole in with drill; train or be trained by means of drill. [Du.]

drill[2] **1** *n.* small furrow; machine for making furrow, sowing, and covering seed; row of seeds so sown. **2** *v.t.* plant in drills. [orig. unkn.]

drill[3] *n.* strong twilled cotton or linen fabric. [G *drillich* f. L *trilix* having three threads]

drill[4] *n.* W. African baboon related to mandrill. [prob. native]

drily *a.* in a dry manner. [DRY]

drink 1 *v.* (*past* **drank;** *p.p.* **drunk**) swallow liquid, swallow (liquid); swallow contents of (vessel); take alcoholic liquor, esp. to excess; bring (*oneself*) to specified state by drinking; (of plant, sponge, etc.) absorb (moisture). **2** *n.* liquid for drinking; glass etc. or portion of this, esp. alcoholic; intoxicating liquor, excessive use of it (*has taken to drink*). **3 the drink** *sl.* the sea; **drink person's health** pledge good wishes to him by drinking; **drink in** listen to or understand eagerly; **drink to** drink toast to, wish success to; **drink up** drink all or remainder (of). **4 drinkable** *a.* [OE]

drip 1 *v.* (**-pp-**) fall or let fall in drops; be so wet (*with* liquid) as to shed drops. **2** *n.* small falling drop of liquid; liquid falling in drops, sound of this; = DRIP-FEED; *sl.* feeble or dull person. [Da. (cf. DROP)]

drip-dry 1 *v.* (leave to) dry easily when hung up. **2** *a.* made of fabric that will dry easily without creasing.

drip-feed 1 *n.* feeding by liquid a drop at a time, esp. intravenously. **2** *v.t.* apply drip-feed to.

dripping *n.* fat melted from roasting meat.

drive 1 *v.* (*past* **drove;** *p.p.* **driven** /'drɪv(ə)n/) urge in some direction by blows or threats or violence etc.; throw or cause to go in some direction; direct and control (vehicle or locomotive); convey in vehicle; operate motor vehicle, be competent to do so (*will you drive?*; *I don't drive*); travel in private vehicle; impel or carry along; hit (ball) forcibly; (of power-source) set or keep (machinery) going; force or hit (nail or stake) *into* ground, wood, etc.; bore (tunnel or horizontal cavity); urge (*oneself* or another) to overwork; force into a state of being (*mad* etc.); chase (wild beasts, enemy) from large area into small; be moved by wind, esp. rapidly (*driving rain*); carry on, conclude (*drove a roaring trade, a good bargain*); dash, rush, work hard *at*. **2** *n.* excursion or journey in vehicle; street or road, esp. scenic one; = DRIVEWAY; forcible stroke of ball; capacity or desire to achieve things, organized effort to some end; transmission of power to machinery, wheels of motor vehicle, etc.; position of steering-wheel of motor vehicle (*left-hand drive*); social event of numerous simultaneous card-games etc. **3 drive at** seek, intend, mean (*what is he driving at?*); **drive-in** *a.* & *n.* (cinema, bank, etc.) for use of customers seated in cars; **driving-licence** licence permitting one to drive motor vehicle; **driving-test** official test of competence to drive motor vehicle; **driving-wheel** wheel communicating motive power in machinery. [OE]

drivel /ˈdrɪv(ə)l/ **1** *n.* silly talk, nonsense. **2** *v.* (**-ll-**) talk drivel; run at nose or mouth. [OE]

driven *p.p.* of DRIVE.

driver *n.* person who drives (esp. motor vehicle); golf-club for driving from tee. [DRIVE]

driveway *n.* road serving as approach for vehicles, esp. private one to house etc.

drizzle /ˈdrɪz(ə)l/ **1** *n.* very fine rain. **2** *v.i.* (of rain) fall in very fine drops. **3 drizzly** *a.* [OE]

droll /drəʊl/ *a.* oddly or strangely amusing; **drolly** /ˈdrəʊl-lɪ/ *adv.* [F]

drollery *n.* quaint humour.

dromedary /ˈdrɒmɪdərɪ,ˈdrʌm-/ *n.* light one-humped (esp. Arabian) camel bred for riding. [F or L f. Gk *dromas -ados* runner]

drone 1 *n.* non-working male of honey-bee; idler; deep humming sound; bass-pipe of bagpipe or its continuous note. **2** *v.* make deep humming sound; speak or utter monotonously. [OE]

drool /dru:l/ *v.* dribble, slobber; show unrestrained admiration (*over*). [DRIVEL]

droop /dru:p/ **1** *v.* bend or hang downwards, esp. through tiredness or weakness; languish, flag; let (eyes or head) drop. **2** *n.* drooping attitude, loss of spirit. [ON (foll.)]

drop 1 *n.* small round portion of liquid such as hangs or falls separately or adheres to surface; thing in shape of drop, esp. sweet or pendant; (in *pl.*) liquid medicine to be measured by drops; minute quantity; glass etc. of intoxicating liquor; act of dropping, fall of prices, temperature, etc.; thing that drops or is dropped; distance dropped; *sl.* hiding-place for stolen or illicit goods etc.; *sl.* bribe. **2** *v.* (**-pp-**) fall by force of gravity from not being held; allow to fall, cease to hold; (cause to) fall in drops, shed (tears, blood); set down (passenger, parcel); sink to ground, esp. from exhaustion or injury; die; fall naturally *asleep*, (*back*) *into* habit, etc.; fall in direction, condition, amount, degree or pitch (*price, voice, wind, drops*); let (eyes) drop, lower (voice); fall or get left *back*, *behind*, etc., in race etc.; cease to associate with, abandon, no longer deal with or discuss; cease, lapse; utter or be uttered casually (*drop a hint*); send casually (*line, note*, etc.); come or go casually *by* or *in* as visitor, or *into* place; lose (money, esp. in gambling); omit in speech (*drop one's h's*); send (ball) or score (goal) in football by drop-kick; give birth to (esp. lamb); (chiefly in *p.p.*) place in lower position than usual (*dropped handlebars*); perform (curtsy). **3 at the drop of a hat** promptly, instantly; **drop a brick** see BRICK; **drop-curtain** painted curtain that can be lowered on to theatre stage; **drop-kick** kick at football made by dropping ball and kicking it as it touches ground; **drop off** fall asleep, drop (passenger); **drop on person** be severe with him; **drop out** cease to take active part; **drop-out** *n.* one who withdraws from conventional society; **drop scone** scone made by dropping spoonful of mixture on cooking surface. **4 droplet** *n.* [OE]

dropper *n.* device for releasing liquid in drops.

droppings *n.pl.* what falls or has fallen in drops, esp. dung of some animals and birds.

dropsy *n.* disease in which watery fluid collects in cavities or tissues of the body; **dropsical** *a.* [earlier *hydropsy* f. F f. L f. Gk (HYDRO-)]

dross *n.* scum separated from metals in melting; impurities, rubbish. [OE]

drought /draʊt/ *n.* abnormally prolonged spell without rain. [OE]

drove[1] *n.* herd or flock being driven or moving together; moving crowd. [OE (DRIVE)]

drove[2] *past* of DRIVE.

drover *n.* driver of cattle.

drown *v.* (cause to) suffocate by submersion in water or other liquid; flood, drench; alleviate (sorrow etc.) with drink; overpower (sound) with louder noise. [prob. OE]

drowse /draʊz/ *v.i.* be lightly asleep. [foll.]

drowsy /ˈdraʊzɪ/ *a.* very sleepy, almost asleep. [prob. OE]

drub *v.t.* (**-bb-**) beat, thrash; defeat thoroughly; **drubbing** *n.* [ult. f. Arab.]

drudge 1 *n.* one who does dull, laborious, or menial work. **2** *v.i.* work hard or laboriously, toil. **3 drudgery** *n.* [orig. uncert.]

drug 1 *n.* medicinal substance; narcotic, hallucinogen, or stimulant, esp. one causing addiction. **2** *v.* (**-gg-**) add drug to (food or drink); give drugs to, stupefy; take drugs as an addict. **3 drug on the**

market commodity that is plentiful but no longer in demand. [F]
drugget /ˈdrʌgɪt/ *n.* coarse woven fabric used for floor coverings etc. [F]
druggist *n.* pharmaceutical chemist. [DRUG]
drugstore *n. US* chemist's shop also selling light refreshments and other articles.
Druid /ˈdru:ɪd/ *n.* priest of an ancient Celtic religion; officer of a Gorsedd; **Druidical** /-ˈɪdɪk(ə)l/ *a.*; **Druidism** *n.* [F or L f. Celt.]
drum 1 *n.* percussion instrument consisting of skin stretched over ends of cylindrical frame or hollow hemisphere; sound produced by striking drum; (in *pl.*) percussion section of orchestra or band; cylindrical object or structure or container; ear-drum; segment of pillar. **2** *v.* (**-mm-**) play drum; make sound of drum, tap or beat continuously or rhythmically with fingers etc.; drive facts or lesson *into* person by persistence; (of bird or insect) make loud noise with wings. **3 drum brake** brake consisting of shoes acting on revolving drum; **drum major** leader of marching band; **drum majorette** female drum major; **drum out** dismiss with ignominy; **drum up** produce or obtain by vigorous effort. [LG]
drumhead *n.* skin of drum.
drummer *n.* player of drum.
drumstick *n.* stick for beating drum; lower joint of leg of cooked fowl.
drunk 1 *a.* lacking proper control of oneself from effects of alcoholic drink; overcome *with* joy, success, etc. **2** *n.* drunken person; *sl.* bout of drinking. [p.p. of DRINK]
drunkard /ˈdrʌŋkəd/ *n.* person who is habitually drunk.
drunken *a.* drunk, often drunk; involving or caused by excessive alcoholic drinking; **drunkenness** *n.*
drupe /dru:p/ *n.* fleshy or pulpy stone-fruit, e.g. plum or olive. [L f. Gk]
dry /draɪ/ **1** *a.* without moisture, not wet; not rainy, deficient in rainfall; not yielding liquid (*well, cow, is dry*); parched, dried up, *colloq.* thirsty; prohibiting or opposed to sale of alcoholic liquor at some or all times; unconnected with or not using liquid (*dry distillation, shampoo*); (of eyes) free from tears; solid, not liquid (*dry provisions*); without butter etc. (*dry bread*); (of liquid) having disappeared by evaporation, draining, wiping, etc.; (of wine) free from sweetness; plain, unelaborated, uninteresting (*dry facts; a dry book*); cold, impassive, (of wit) expressed with pretended seriousness. **2** *v.* make or become dry; preserve (food) by removal of moisture (*dried egg, fruit*). **3 dry battery** (or **cell**) battery or cell in which electrolyte is absorbed in a solid; **dry-clean** clean (clothes etc.) with organic solvents without using water; **dry dock** dry enclosure for building or repairing ships; **dry-fly** *a.* (of fishing) using artificial fly that floats; **dry ice** solid carbon dioxide used as refrigerant; **dry land** land as distinct from sea etc.; **dry measure** measure for dry goods; **dry out** make or become fully dry, (of drug addict etc.) undergo treatment to cure addiction; **dry rot** decayed state of wood when not well ventilated, fungi causing this, any moral or social decay; **dry run** *colloq.* rehearsal; **dry-shod** *a.* & *adv.* without wetting one's shoes; **dry up** dry washed dishes, make completely dry, cease to yield liquid, become unproductive, (of actor) forget lines, (in *imper.*) cease to talk. [OE]
dryad /ˈdraɪæd/ *n.* wood-nymph. [F f. L f. Gk (*drus* tree)]
dryer var. of DRIER.
dryly var. of DRILY.
drystone *a.* (of wall etc.) made without mortar. [DRY]
DSC *abbr.* Distinguished Service Cross.
D.Sc. *abbr.* Doctor of Science.
DSM *abbr.* Distinguished Service Medal.
DSO *abbr.* Distinguished Service Order.
d.t., d.t.'s *abbr.* delirium tremens.
dual /ˈdju:əl/ **1** *a.* composed of two parts, twofold, double. **2** *n. Gram.* dual number or form. **3 dual carriageway** road with dividing strip between traffic flowing in opposite directions; **dual-control** two linked sets of controls, enabling either of two persons to operate car or aircraft. **4 duality** /-ˈælɪtɪ/ *n.* [L (*duo* two)]
dub[1] *v.t.* (**-bb-**) make (person) a knight by touching his shoulders with a sword; give specified name to; smear (leather) with grease. [F]
dub[2] *v.t.* (**-bb-**) make alternative soundtrack of (film) esp. in a different language; add (sound effects, music) to film or broadcast. [abbr. of DOUBLE]
dubbin /ˈdʌbɪn/ *n.* (also **dubbing**) thick grease for softening and waterproofing leather. [DUB[1]]
dubiety /dju:ˈbaɪətɪ/ *n.* feeling of doubt. [L (foll.)]
dubious /ˈdju:bɪəs/ *a.* hesitating, doubtful; unreliable; of questionable or suspected character. [L (*dubium* doubt)]
ducal /ˈdju:k(ə)l/ *a.* of or like a duke. [F (DUKE)]
ducat /ˈdʌkət/ *n.* gold coin formerly current in most European countries. [It., or L *ducatus* DUCHY]

duchess /ˈdʌtʃɪs/ *n.* wife or widow of duke; woman holding rank of duke in her own right. [F f. med.L *ducissa* (DUKE)]

duchy /ˈdʌtʃɪ/ *n.* territory of duke or duchess; royal dukedom of Cornwall or Lancaster. [F f. med.L *ducatus* (DUKE)]

duck[1] **1** *n.* swimming-bird, esp. domesticated form of the mallard or wild duck, female of this; its flesh as food; score of 0 in cricket; *colloq.* (esp. as form of address) dear. **2** *v.* bob down, esp. to avoid being seen or hit; dip head under water and emerge; plunge (person) briefly in water; *colloq.* dodge or avoid (task etc.). **3 duck-boards** narrow path of wooden slats in trench or over mud; **ducks and drakes** game of making flat stone skim along surface of water (**play ducks and drakes with** squander); **like water off a duck's back** producing no effect. [OE]

duck[2] *n.* strong linen or cotton cloth; (in *pl.*) trousers made of this. [Du.]

duckbill *n.* platypus. [DUCK[1]]

duckling *n.* young duck.

duckweed *n.* plant that covers surface of still water.

ducky *n. colloq.* (esp. as form of address) dear.

duct 1 *n.* channel or tube for conveying fluid, cable, etc.; tube in the body conveying secretions etc. (*tear ducts*). **2** *v.t.* convey through duct. **3 ductless gland** gland secreting directly into the bloodstream. [L *ductus* (*duco duct-* lead)]

ductile /ˈdʌktaɪl/ *a.* (of metal) capable of being drawn into wire; pliable, docile; **ductility** /-ˈtɪlɪtɪ/ *n.* [F or L (prec.)]

dud *sl.* **1** *n.* thing that fails to work, useless thing; (in *pl.*) clothes, rags. **2** *a.* defective, useless. [orig. unkn.]

dude /dju:d/ *n. US* dandy; city man. [G dial. *dude* fool]

dudgeon /ˈdʌdʒ(ə)n/ *n.* resentment, indignation, usu. in **in high dudgeon** very angry. [orig. unkn.]

due 1 *a.* owing or payable as a debt or obligation; merited, appropriate; that ought to be given *to* person (*first place is due to Milton*); ascribable *to* cause, agent, etc. (*the difficulty is due to our ignorance*); under engagement *to do* something or arrive at certain time (*is due to speak tonight*; *train due at 7.30*); to be looked for or foreseen (*in due time*). **2** *adv.* (of point of compass) exactly, directly (*went due east*; *a due north wind*). **3** *n.* what one owes (*pay one's dues*); (usu. in *pl.*) fee or amount payable; person's right, what is owed him (*give him his due*). **4 become** (or **fall**) **due** become payable; **due to** (**D**) because of (*was late due to an accident*). [F f. L (*debeo* owe)]

duel /ˈdju:əl/ **1** *n.* formal fight with deadly weapons between two persons; two-sided contest. **2** *v.i.* (**-ll-**) fight duel. **3 duellist** *n.* [It. *duello* or L *duellum* war]

duenna /dju:ˈenə/ *n.* older woman acting as chaperon to girls, esp. in Spanish family. [Sp. f. L *domina* (DON[1])]

duet /dju:ˈet/ *n.* musical composition for two performers; the performers; **duettist** *n.* [G or It. f. L *duo* two]

duff[1] **1** *a. sl.* worthless, useless, counterfeit. **2** *n.* boiled pudding. [var. of DOUGH]

duff[2] *v.t. sl.* bungle. [perh. foll.]

duffer *n.* inefficient or stupid person. [orig. uncert.]

duffle /ˈdʌf(ə)l/ *n.* (also **duffel**) heavy woollen cloth; **duffle bag** cylindrical canvas bag closed by draw-string; **duffle coat** hooded overcoat of duffle, fastened with toggles. [*Duffel* in Belgium]

dug[1] *past* and *p.p.* of DIG.

dug[2] *n.* udder, teat. [orig. unkn.]

dugong /ˈdu:gɒŋ/ *n.* Asian sea-mammal. [Malay]

dug-out *n.* canoe made by hollowing tree-trunk; roofed shelter, esp. for troops in trenches. [DUG[1], OUT]

duke *n.* person holding highest hereditary title of nobility; sovereign prince ruling duchy or small State; **dukedom** *n.* [F f. L *dux* leader]

dulcet /ˈdʌlsɪt/ *a.* sweet-sounding. [F dimin. f. L *dulcis* sweet]

dulcimer /ˈdʌlsɪmə/ *n.* musical instrument with metal strings struck by two hand-held hammers. [F f. L (prec., *melos* song)]

dull 1 *a.* (of colour, light, sound, etc.) not bright or vivid or clear; (of weather) overcast; tedious, not interesting or exciting; (of pain) indistinctly felt; slow in understanding, stupid; listless, depressed; (of eyes, ears, etc.) lacking keen perception; (of edge) not sharp; (of trade etc.) slow, sluggish. **2** *v.* make or become dull. **3 dully** /ˈdʌl-lɪ/ *adv.* [LG or Du.]

dullard /ˈdʌləd/ *n.* mentally dull person.

duly /ˈdju:lɪ/ *adv.* in due time or manner; rightly, properly, sufficiently. [DUE]

dumb /dʌm/ *a.* unable to speak, either abnormally (of humans) or normally (of animals); temporarily silenced by surprise, shyness, etc.; stupid, ignorant; taciturn, reticent; not expressed in words (*dumb agony*); inarticulate, having no voice in government etc. (*the dumb millions*); giving no sound; **dumb show** gestures instead of speech; **dumb waiter** small movable set of shelves for serving food, lift for food etc. [OE]

dumb-bell *n.* short bar with weight at each end used in pairs for exercising muscles; *sl.* stupid person.

dumbfound /dʌm'faʊnd/ *v.t.* nonplus, make speechless with surprise. [DUMB, CONFOUND]

dumdum bullet /'dʌmdʌm/ soft-nosed bullet that expands on impact. [*Dum-Dum* in India]

dummy /'dʌmɪ/ **1** *n.* model of human form, esp. as used to display clothes or by ventriloquist; imitation object, object serving to replace real or normal one; baby's rubber teat; stupid person; person taking no real part, figure-head; player or imaginary player in some card-games, whose cards are exposed and played by partner. **2** *a.* sham, imitation. **3** *v.i.* use feigned pass or swerve in football etc. **4 dummy run** trial attempt, rehearsal. [DUMB]

dump 1 *v.t.* deposit as rubbish; put down firmly or clumsily; *colloq.* abandon or get rid of; sell (excess goods) in new market (esp. abroad) at lower price than in original market. **2** *n.* place or heap for depositing rubbish; accumulated pile of ore, earth, etc.; temporary store of ammunition etc.; *colloq.* unpleasant or dreary place. [orig. uncert.]

dumpling /'dʌmplɪŋ/ *n.* baked or boiled ball of dough, as part of stew or containing apple etc.; small fat person. [*dump* small round object]

dumps *n.pl. colloq.* low spirits, depression, usu. in **down in the dumps**. [LG or Du. (DAMP)]

dumpy /'dʌmpɪ/ *a.* short and stout; **dumpiness** *n.* [DUMPLING]

dun[1] **1** *a.* greyish-brown. **2** *n.* dun colour; dun horse. [OE]

dun[2] **1** *v.t.* (**-nn-**) ask persistently for payment of debt. **2** *n.* demand for payment. [obs. *dunkirk* privateer]

dunce *n.* one slow at learning, dullard. [*Duns* Scotus, schoolman]

dunderhead /'dʌndəhed/ *n.* stupid person. [orig. unkn.]

dune *n.* mound or ridge of sand etc. formed by wind. [F f. Du. (DOWN[3])]

dung 1 *n.* excrement of animals; manure. **2** *v.t.* apply dung to, manure, (land). **3 dung-beetle** beetle whose larvae develop in dung. [OE]

dungaree /dʌŋgə'ri:/ *n.* strong coarse cotton cloth; (in *pl.*) overalls or trousers made of this. [Hindi]

dungeon /'dʌndʒ(ə)n/ *n.* underground cell for prisoners. [orig. = *donjon*; F f. L (DON[1])]

dunghill *n.* heap of dung or refuse in farmyard. [DUNG]

dunk *v.t.* dip (bread etc.) into soup or beverage before eating it; immerse. [G *tunken* dip]

dunlin /'dʌnlɪn/ *n.* red-backed sandpiper. [DUN[1]]

dunnock /'dʌnək/ *n.* hedge-sparrow. [DUN[1]]

duo *n.* (*pl.* **duos**) pair of performers; = DUET. [It. f. L, = two]

duodecimal /dju:əʊ'desɪm(ə)l/ *a.* of twelfths or twelve; proceeding or reckoning by twelves. [L (*duodecim* twelve)]

duodenum /dju:əʊ'di:nəm/ *n.* first part of small intestine immediately below stomach; **duodenal** *a.* [med.L (prec.)]

duologue /'dju:əlɒg/ *n.* dialogue between two persons. [DUO, MONOLOGUE]

dupe 1 *n.* victim of deception. **2** *v.t.* deceive, trick. [F]

duple /'dju:p(ə)l/ *a.* of two parts; **duple time** *Mus.* that with two beats to the bar. [L *duplus*]

duplex /'dju:pleks/ *a.* having two parts; (of set of rooms) on two floors. [L, = double]

duplicate / 'dju:plɪkət/ **1** *a.* exactly like another example; existing in two examples, having two corresponding parts; doubled, twice as large or many; (of card-games) with same hands played by different players. **2** *n.* one of two things exactly alike, esp. that made after the other; second copy of letter or document. **3** /-keɪt/ *v.* make or be exact copy of; double, multiply by two; repeat (action etc.) esp. unnecessarily. **4 duplication** /-'keɪʃ(ə)n/ *n.* [L (DUPLEX)]

duplicator *n.* machine for producing documents in multiple copies.

duplicity /dju:'plɪsɪtɪ/ *n.* double-dealing, deceitfulness. [F or L (DUPLEX)]

durable /'djʊərəb(ə)l/ *a.* likely to last; (of goods) remaining useful for long period; resisting wear, decay, etc.; **durability** /-'bɪlɪtɪ/ *n.* [F f. L (*durus* hard)]

duration /djʊə'reɪʃ(ə)n/ *n.* time during which a thing continues. [F f. med.L (prec.)]

duress /djʊə'res/ *n.* use of force or threats, esp. illegally (*under duress*); imprisonment. [F f. L *durus* hard]

during /'djʊərɪŋ/ *prep.* throughout or at a point in the duration of. [F f. L (DURABLE)]

dusk *n.* darker stage of twilight. [OE]

dusky *a.* shadowy, dim; dark-coloured; **duskily** *adv.*; **duskiness** *n.*

dust 1 *n.* finely powdered earth or other matter; pollen, fine powder of any material; dead person's remains; confusion, turmoil. **2** *v.t.* clear of dust by wiping, clear furniture etc. of dust; sprinkle (powder or dust usu. over object, object *with* powder). **3 bite the dust** be killed; **dust bowl** area denuded of vegetation by drought and erosion and so reduced to desert; **dust-cart**

vehicle for collecting household refuse; **dust-cover** sheet or cloth to keep dust off furniture etc., = *dust-jacket*; **dust-jacket** paper wrapper on book; **dust-sheet** dust-cover for furniture; **dust-up** *colloq.* fight, disturbance; **shake the dust off one's feet** depart indignantly; **throw dust in person's eyes** mislead him. [OE]

dustbin *n.* container for household refuse.

duster *n.* cloth for dusting furniture etc.

dustman *n.* man employed by local authority or by contractor to empty dustbins.

dustpan *n.* pan into which dust is brushed from floor.

dusty *a.* covered with or full of dust; like dust; (of colour) dull or vague; **dusty answer** curt rejection of request; **not so dusty** *sl.* fairly good; **dustily** *adv.*; **dustiness** *n.*

Dutch[1] **1** *a.* of the Netherlands or its people or language; having Dutch characteristics. **2** *n.* the Dutch language. **3 the Dutch** *pl.* the people of the Netherlands; **Dutch auction** one in which price is reduced until buyer is found; **Dutch barn** farm shelter for hay etc., consisting of roof on poles; **Dutch cap** contraceptive diaphragm; **Dutch courage** courage induced by alcoholic drink; **Dutch elm disease** fungous disease of elms; **Dutch oven** metal box for cooking, of which open side is turned towards ordinary fire, covered cooking-pot; **Dutch treat** party, outing, etc., at which each participant pays for own share; **go Dutch** share expenses on outing etc.; **in Dutch** *sl.* in disgrace; **talk like a Dutch uncle** speak severely but kindly. [Du.]

dutch[2] *n. sl.* wife. [abbr. of DUCHESS]

Dutchman *n.* man of Dutch birth or nationality; **I'm a Dutchman** phrase implying refusal or disbelief. [DUTCH[1]]

duteous /ˈdju:tɪəs/ *a. literary* dutiful. [DUTY]

dutiable /ˈdju:tɪəb(ə)l/ *a.* requiring payment of duty.

dutiful /ˈdju:tɪf(ə)l/ *a.* doing or observant of one's duty, obedient; **dutifully** *adv.*

duty /ˈdju:tɪ/ *n.* moral or legal obligation, what one is bound or ought to do, binding force of what is right; business, office, function arising from these, engagement in these; deference, expression of respect to superior; tax levied on certain goods, imports, events, or services; **do duty for** serve as or pass for (something else); **duty-bound** obliged by duty; **duty-free shop** shop at airport etc. at which goods can be bought free of duty; **on** (or **off**) **duty** actually engaged (or not engaged) in one's regular work or some obligation. [AF (DUE)]

duvet /ˈdu:veɪ/ *n.* thick soft quilt used instead of bedclothes. [F]

dwarf /dwɔ:f/ **1** *n.* (*pl.* **dwarfs**) person, animal, or plant much below normal size; small mythological being with magical powers. **2** *a.* of a kind very small in size. **3** *v.t.* stunt in growth; make seem small by contrast or distance. [OE]

dwell *v.i.* (*past* and *p.p.* **dwelt**) live as occupant or inhabitant; **dwell on** (or **upon**) think or speak or write at length on. [OE, = lead astray]

dwelling *n.* house, residence.

dwindle /ˈdwɪnd(ə)l/ *v.i.* become gradually less or smaller; lose importance. [OE]

Dy *symb.* dysprosium.

dye /daɪ/ **1** *n.* substance used to change colour of hair, fabric, wood, etc.; colour produced by this. **2** *v.t.* (*partic.* **dyeing**) impregnate with dye; make (thing) specified colour thus (*dyed it yellow*). **3 dyed in the wool** out-and-out, unchangeable. [OE]

dying see DIE[1].

dyke var. of DIKE.

dynamic /daɪˈnæmɪk/ *a.* of motive force (opp. *static*); of force in actual operation (opp. *potential*); of dynamics; (of person) active, energetic; **dynamically** *adv.* [Gk (*dunamis* power)]

dynamics *n.pl.* (usu. treated as *sing.*) mathematical study of motion and the forces causing it; branch of any science in which forces or changes are considered; motive forces, physical or moral, in any sphere; *Mus.* gradations or amount of volume of sound.

dynamism /ˈdaɪnəmɪz(ə)m/ *n.* energizing or dynamic action or power.

dynamite /ˈdaɪnəmaɪt/ **1** *n.* high explosive of nitroglycerine mixed with inert absorbent; potentially dangerous person or thing. **2** *v.t.* charge or blow up with dynamite.

dynamo /ˈdaɪnəməʊ/ *n.* (*pl.* **dynamos**) machine converting mechanical into electrical energy, esp. by rotating coils of copper wire in magnetic field. [abbr. of *dynamo-electric machine*]

dynamometer /daɪnəˈmɒmɪtə/ *n.* instrument measuring energy expended. [F f. Gk (DYNAMIC)]

dynast /ˈdɪnəst/ *n.* ruler; member of dynasty. [L f. Gk]

dynasty /ˈdɪnəstɪ/ *n.* line of hereditary rulers; succession of leaders in any field; **dynastic** /-ˈnæstɪk/ *a.* [F or L f. Gk]

dyne /daɪn/ *n.* unit of force, the force that, acting for 1 second on mass of 1 g., gives it velocity of 1 cm. per sec. [F f. Gk *dunamis* force]

dys- *prefix* bad, difficult. [Gk]
dysentery /'dɪsəntrɪ/ *n.* disease with inflammation of the intestines, causing severe diarrhoea. [F or L f. Gk (*entera* bowels)]
dyslexia /dɪs'leksɪə/ *n.* abnormal difficulty in reading and spelling, caused by condition of the brain; **dyslexic** *a.* & *n.* [G (DYS-, *lexis* speech)]
dyspepsia /dɪs'pepsɪə/ *n.* indigestion; **dyspeptic** *a.* & *n.* [L f. Gk (DYS-, *pepto* digest)]
dysprosium /dɪs'prəʊzɪəm/ *n.* metallic element of lanthanide series. [Gk *dusprositos* hard to get at]
dystrophy /'dɪstrəfɪ/ *n.* defective nutrition; **muscular dystrophy** hereditary weakening and wasting of the muscles. [L f. Gk *-trophia* nourishment]

E

E, e /i:/ *n.* (*pl.* **Es, E's**) fifth letter; *Mus.* third note in diatonic scale of C major.
E. *abbr.* east, eastern.
e- *prefix* form of EX-[1] before consonants except *c, f, h, p, q, s.*
each 1 *a.* every one of two or more persons or things, regarded separately (*each man*; *on each occasion*; *five in each class*). **2** *pron.* each person or thing. **3 each other** one another; **each way** (of bet) backing horse etc. to win and to be placed. [OE]
eager /'i:gə/ *a.* full of keen desire, enthusiastic; **eager beaver** *colloq.* very or excessively diligent person. [F f. L *acer* keen]
eagle /'i:g(ə)l/ *n.* large bird of prey with keen vision and powerful flight; figure of eagle, esp. as symbol of US or *hist.* as Roman or French ensign; hole played in two under par or bogey in golf; **eagle-eye** keen sight or watchfulness. [F f. L *aquila*]
eaglet /'i:glɪt/ *n.* young eagle.
E. & O. E. *abbr.* errors and omissions excepted.
ear[1] *n.* organ of hearing in man and animals, esp. external part of this; faculty of discriminating sound (*an ear for music*); ear-shaped thing; **all ears** listening attentively; **ear-drum** internal membrane of ear; **ear-piercing** shrill; **ear-plug** piece of wax etc. placed in ear to protect against water, noise, etc.; **ear-ring** ornament worn on lobe of ear; **ear-splitting** extremely loud; **ear-trumpet** trumpet-shaped tube formerly used as aid to hearing by the partially deaf; **give one's ears** make any sacrifice; **have** (or **keep**) **an ear to the ground** be alert to rumours or trend of opinion; **have person's ear** have person's favourable attention; **up to the ears** *colloq.* deeply involved or occupied (*in*). [OE]
ear[2] *n.* seed-bearing head of a cereal plant. [OE]
earache *n.* pain in the inner ear. [EAR[1]]
earful *n. colloq.* copious talk; a reprimand.
earl /ɜ:l/ *n.* British nobleman ranking between marquis and viscount; **Earl Marshal** officer presiding over Heralds' college, with ceremonial duties; **earldom** *n.* [OE]
early /'ɜ:lɪ/ *a.* & *adv.* before the due, usual, or expected time (*was early for my appointment*; *train arrived early*); not far on in day or night or time (*early evening*; *seek an early opportunity for discussion*); not far on in a period, development, or process of evolution (*the early spring*; *the early part of the century*; *the early Christians*; *early man*); forward in flowering, ripening, etc. (*early peaches*); **early bird** *colloq.* one who arrives or gets up early; **early days** early in time for something (to happen etc.); **Early English (style)** first stage of English Gothic architecture (13th c.); **early on** at an early stage. [OE (ERE)]
earmark 1 *n.* identifying mark; owner's mark on ear of animal. **2** *v.t.* set aside for special purpose; mark (animal) with earmark. [EAR[1]]
earn /ɜ:n/ *v.t.* (of person, conduct, etc.) obtain or be entitled to as reward of work or merit; bring in as income or interest. [OE]
earnest[1] /'ɜ:nɪst/ *a.* ardently serious, showing intense feeling; **in earnest** serious, seriously, with determination. [OE]
earnest[2] /'ɜ:nɪst/ *n.* money paid as instalment, esp. to confirm contract; token, foretaste. [L *arrha* pledge]
earnings *n.pl.* money earned. [EARN]
earphone *n.* device put to or worn over ear to receive radio etc. communication. [EAR[1]]
earshot *n.* hearing-distance (*within earshot*).
earth /ɜ:θ/ **1** *n.* planet on which we live (also **Earth**); present abode of man, as

distinct from heaven and hell; land and sea, as distinct from sky; dry land, ground (*fell to earth*); soil, mould; connection to earth as completion of electrical circuit; hole of badger, fox, etc.; *colloq.* huge sum, vast amount (*costs the earth*). **2** *v.t.* connect (electrical circuit) to earth; cover (roots of plant) with earth. **3 come back to earth** return to realities; **earth-nut** any of various plants or their tubers, esp. peanut; **earth sciences** those concerned with the earth or part of it; **earth-shaking** having violent effect; **gone to earth** in hiding; **on earth** existing anywhere (*happiest man on earth*; *what on earth do you mean?*); **run to earth** find after long search. [OE]

earthbound *a.* attached (*lit.* or *fig.*) to the earth or earthly things; moving towards the earth.

earthen *a.* made of earth or baked clay.

earthenware *n.* pottery made of coarse baked clay.

earthly *a.* of the earth or man's life on it, terrestrial; **no earthly** *colloq.* absolutely no (*no earthly reason, use*); **not an earthly** *sl.* no chance whatever; **earthliness** *n.*

earthquake *n.* convulsion of earth's surface due to faults in strata or volcanic action.

earthwork *n.* artificial bank of earth in fortification or road-building.

earthworm *n.* common worm living in the ground.

earthy *a.* of or like earth or soil; gross, coarse (*earthy jokes*); worldly; **earthiness** *n.*

earwig *n.* small insect with pincers at tail end. [EAR[1]]

ease /i:z/ **1** *n.* freedom from pain or trouble; freedom from constraint; facility (*did it with ease*). **2** *v.* relieve from pain or anxiety; relax, slacken, make or become less burdensome; cause to move by gentle force (*ease into position*). **3 at ease** free from anxiety or constraint, (of soldiers etc.) in relaxed attitude, with feet apart; **ease off** (or **up**) become less burdensome or severe. [F f. L (ADJACENT)]

easel /'i:z(ə)l/ *n.* standing wooden support for artist's canvas, blackboard, etc. [Du. *ezel* ass]

easement *n.* legal right of way or similar right over another's ground or property. [F (EASE)]

easily /'i:zɪlɪ/ *adv.* without difficulty; by far (*easily the best*); very probably (*could easily snow*). [EASY]

east 1 *n.* point of horizon where sun rises at equinoxes, compass point corresponding to this, direction in which this lies; (usu. **East**) part of country or town lying to the east, regions or countries lying to the east of Europe, Communist States of eastern Europe. **2** *a.* towards, at, near, or facing east; coming from the east (*east wind*). **3** *adv.* towards, at, or near the east. **4 East End** eastern part of London; **east-north-east, east-south-east** (compass point) midway between east and north-east, or south-east; **east of** further east than; **to the east (of)** in an eastward direction (from). [OE]

Easter *n.* Christian festival (held on a variable Sunday in March or April) commemorating Christ's resurrection; **Easter egg** artificial usu. chocolate egg given as gift at Easter. [OE]

easterly /'i:stəlɪ/ *a.* & *adv.* in eastern position or direction; (of wind) blowing from the east. [EAST]

eastern /'i:st(ə)n/ *a.* of or in the east; **Eastern Church** Orthodox Church; **easternmost** *a.*

easterner *n.* native or inhabitant of the east.

eastward /'i:stwəd/ **1** *a.* & (also **eastwards**) *adv.* towards the east. **2** *n.* eastward direction or region. [-WARD]

easy /'i:zɪ/ **1** *a.* not difficult, achieved without great effort; free from pain, trouble, or anxiety; free from awkwardness, strictness, etc., relaxed and pleasant; compliant, obliging. **2** *adv.* with ease, in effortless or relaxed manner; (as *int.*) go carefully. **3 easy chair** large comfortable chair; **easy on the eye** pleasant to look at; **Easy Street** *colloq.* affluence; **go easy** be sparing or cautious (*with* or *on*); **I'm easy** *colloq.* I have no preference; **take it easy** proceed gently, relax. **4 easiness** *n.* [F (EASE)]

easygoing *a.* placid and tolerant, relaxed in manner.

eat 1 *v.* (*past* **ate** /et, eɪt/, *p.p.* **eaten**) take into the mouth, chew and swallow (food); consume food, take a meal; (often with *away*) destroy, consume; (also with *at*) trouble, vex (*what's eating her?*). **2** *n.* (in *pl.*) *colloq.* food, a meal. **3 eat one's heart out** suffer greatly from anxiety or longing; **eating apple** etc. one suitable for eating raw; **eat out** have meal away from home, esp. in restaurant; **eat up** eat or consume completely (*eat up your dinner*; *eaten up with jealousy*), traverse (distance) rapidly; **eat one's words** retract them abjectly. [OE]

eatable 1 *a.* that may be eaten. **2** *n.* (usu. in *pl.*) food.

eater *n.* one who eats (*a big eater*); eating apple etc.

eau-de-Cologne /əʊdəkə'ləʊn/ *n.*

perfume made orig. at Cologne. [F, = water of Cologne]

eaves /iːvz/ *n.pl.* projecting lower edge of roof. [OE]

eavesdrop *v.i.* listen secretly to private conversation; **eavesdropper** *n.*

ebb **1** *n.* outward movement of tide, away from land; decline, poor condition (*at a low ebb*). **2** *v.i.* flow back; recede, decline. [OE]

ebonite /ˈebənaɪt/ *n.* vulcanite. [foll.]

ebony /ˈebənɪ/ **1** *n.* hard heavy black wood of tropical tree. **2** *a.* made of ebony; black like ebony. [F f. L f. Gk]

ebullient /ɪˈbʌlɪənt/ *a.* exuberant, high-spirited; **ebullience** *n.*; **ebulliency** *n.* [L (BOIL[1])]

ebullition /ebəˈlɪʃ(ə)n/ *n.* boiling; sudden outburst of passion or emotion.

EC *abbr.* East Central.

eccentric /ɪkˈsentrɪk/ **1** *a.* odd or capricious in behaviour or appearance; not placed, not having its axis placed, centrally; (of circle) not concentric (*to* another circle); (of orbit) not circular. **2** *n.* eccentric person; disc fixed eccentrically on revolving shaft, for changing rotatory to to-and-fro motion. **3** **eccentrically** *adv.*; **eccentricity** /-ˈtrɪsɪtɪ/ *n.* [L f. Gk (CENTRE)]

Eccles cake /ˈek(ə)lz/ round cake of pastry filled with currants. [*Eccles* in N. England]

ecclesiastic /ɪkliːzɪˈæstɪk/ *n.* clergyman. [F or L f. Gk (*ekklēsia* church)]

ecclesiastical *a.* of the Church or clergy.

ECG *abbr.* electrocardiogram.

echelon /ˈeʃəlɒn/ *n.* formation of troops or ships, aircraft, etc., in parallel rows with end of each row projecting further than one in front; level or rank in an organization. [F, = ladder, f. L *scala*]

echidna /ɪˈkɪdnə/ *n.* Australian egg-laying animal like hedgehog. [Gk, = viper]

echinoderm /ɪˈkaɪnədɜːm/ *n.* sea animal of group including starfish and sea-urchin, some having spiny skins. [L f. Gk *ekhinos* sea-urchin, *derma* skin]

echo /ˈekəʊ/ **1** *n.* (*pl.* **echoes**) repetition of sound by reflection of sound-waves, secondary sound so produced; close imitation or imitator; reflected radio or radar beam. **2** *v.* (of place) resound with echo, repeat (sound) thus; (of sound) be repeated, resound; repeat (person's words), imitate opinions of. **3** **echo location** location of objects by reflected sound; **echo-sounder** sounding apparatus for determining depth of sea beneath ship by measuring time taken for echo to be received. [F or L f. Gk]

echoic /eˈkəʊɪk/ *a.* (of word) imitating sound it represents, onomatopoeic; **echoically** *adv.*

echt /ext/ *a.* genuine. [G]

éclair /eɪˈkleə, ɪ-/ *n.* finger-shaped cake of choux pastry filled with cream and iced. [F, = lightning]

éclat /ˈeɪklɑː/ *n.* brilliant success or display; renown, esteem. [F]

eclectic /ɪˈklektɪk/ **1** *a.* selecting ideas or beliefs from various sources. **2** *n.* eclectic person. **3** **eclectically** *adv.*; **eclecticism** /-sɪz(ə)m/ *n.* [Gk (*eklegō* pick out)]

eclipse /ɪˈklɪps/ **1** *n.* obscuring of light from one heavenly body by another; loss of light, brilliance, or importance. **2** *v.t.* (of heavenly body) cause eclipse of (another); intercept (light); *fig.* outshine, surpass. [F f. L f. Gk]

ecliptic /ɪˈklɪptɪk/ *n.* sun's apparent path among stars during year. [L f. Gk (prec.)]

eclogue /ˈeklɒg/ *n.* short pastoral poem. [L f. Gk (ECLECTIC)]

eco- *prefix* ecology, ecological (*ecoclimate*). [foll.]

ecology /iːˈkɒlədʒɪ/ *n.* study of organisms in relation to one another and to their surroundings; **ecological** /iːkəˈlɒdʒɪk(ə)l/ *a.*; **ecologist** *n.* [G f. Gk *oikos* house]

economic /iːkəˈnɒmɪk, ek-/ *a.* of economics; maintained for profit, on business lines; adequate to pay or recoup expenditure with some profit (*not economic to run buses on Sundays*; *an economic rent*); practical, considered with regard to human needs (*economic geography*); **economically** *adv.* [F or L f. Gk (ECONOMY)]

economical *a.* sparing in use of resources; avoiding waste; **economically** *adv.*

economics *n.pl.* (as *sing.*) science of production and distribution of wealth; application of this to particular subject (*the economics of publishing*).

economist /ɪˈkɒnəmɪst/ *n.* expert on or student of economics. [Gk (ECONOMY)]

economize /ɪˈkɒnəmaɪz/ *v.* be economical, make economies, reduce expenditure; (usu. with *on*) use sparingly.

economy /ɪˈkɒnəmɪ/ *n.* wealth and resources of a community, administration or condition of these; careful management of (esp. financial) resources, frugality, instance of this (*make little economies*). [F or L f. Gk *oikonomia* household management]

ecru /ˈeɪkruː/ *n.* light fawn colour. [F]

ecstasy /ˈekstəsɪ/ *n.* overwhelming feeling of joy, rapture; **ecstatic** /ekˈstætɪk/ *a.* [F f. L f. Gk *ekstasis* standing outside oneself]

ECT *abbr.* electroconvulsive therapy.

ecto- in *comb.* outside. [Gk *ektos*]
ectomorph /'ektəmɔ:f/ *n.* person with lean body. [Gk *morphē* form]
-ectomy *suffix* forming nouns, denoting surgical operation in which some part is removed (*hysterectomy*). [Gk *ektomē* (excision)]
ectoplasm /'ektəplæz(ə)m/ *n.* viscous substance supposed to emanate from body of spiritualistic medium during trance. [ECTO-, PLASMA]
ECU *abbr.* European Currency Unit.
ecumenical /i:kju:'menɪk(ə)l/ *a.* of or representing the whole Christian world; seeking world-wide Christian unity; **ecumenicalism** *n.*; **ecumenism** /i:'kju:mənɪz(ə)m/ *n.* [L f. Gk *oikoumenikos* of the inhabited earth]
eczema /'eksɪmə/ *n.* skin disorder with inflammation and itching. [L f. Gk]
-ed[1] *suffix* forming adjectives (1) from nouns, in sense 'having, wearing, etc.' (*diseased*, *talented*, *trousered*), (2) from phrases of adjective and noun (*good-humoured*, *three-cornered*). [OE]
-ed[2] *suffix* forming (1) past tense and past participle of weak verbs (*needed*), (2) participial adjectives (*escaped prisoner*, *pained look*. [OE]
ed. *abbr.* edited (by); edition; editor; educated.
Edam /'i:dæm/ *n.* round Dutch cheese, usu. pale yellow with red rind. [*Edam* in Holland]
eddy /'edɪ/ **1** *n.* area of water swirling in circular motion; smoke, fog, etc., moving like this. **2** *v.* move in eddies. [OE *ed-* again, back]
edelweiss /'eɪd(ə)lvaɪs/ *n.* Alpine plant with white flowers. [G, = noble-white]
Eden /'i:d(ə)n/ *n.* place of great delight or happiness, with reference to abode of Adam and Eve at Creation. [L f. Gk f. Heb. (orig. = delight)]
edentate /ɪ'denteɪt/ **1** *a.* having few or no teeth. **2** *n.* edentate animal, esp. mammal. [L (*dens dent-* tooth)]
edge /edʒ/ **1** *n.* cutting side of blade; sharpness, *fig.* effectiveness; edge-shaped thing, esp. crest of ridge; meeting-line of surfaces; boundary-line of region or surface, brink of precipice. **2** *v.* sharpen (tool etc.); give or form border to; insinuate (thing or *oneself*, *in* etc.); advance, esp. gradually and obliquely. **3 have the edge on** *colloq.* have an advantage over; **on edge** tense and irritable; **set one's teeth on edge** (of taste or sound) cause unpleasant nervous sensation; **take the edge off** dull, weaken, make less intense. [OE]
edgeways *adv.* (also **edgewise**) with edge foremost or uppermost; **get a word in edgeways** contribute to conversation dominated by another or others.
edging *n.* thing forming edge, border.
edgy *a.* irritable, anxious, on edge; **edgily** *adv.*; **edginess** *n.*
edible /'edɪb(ə)l/ **1** *a.* fit to be eaten. **2** *n.* edible thing. **3 edibility** /-'bɪlɪtɪ/ *n.* [L (*edo* eat)]
edict /'i:dɪkt/ *n.* order proclaimed by authority. [L (*edico* proclaim)]
edifice /'edɪfɪs/ *n.* building, esp. large imposing one. [F f. L (*aedis* dwelling)]
edify /'edɪfaɪ/ *v.t.* improve morally; benefit spiritually; **edification** /-fɪ'keɪʃ(ə)n/ *n.* [F f. L (*aedifico* build)]
edit /'edɪt/ *v.t.* assemble or prepare (written material), arrange or modify (another's work), for publication; act as editor of (newspaper etc.); prepare (data) for processing by computer; take extracts from and collate (film etc.) to form unified sequence; reword for a purpose. [F, ult. f. L *edo edit-* give out]
edition /ɪ'dɪʃ(ə)n/ *n.* edited or published form of a book etc.; the copies of a book, newspaper, etc., issued at one time; product of the same kind, person etc. resembling another (*a smaller edition of his brother*).
editor /'edɪtə/ *n.* one who edits; one who directs content and writing of newspaper or a particular section of one (*sports editor*); head of department of publishing house. [L (EDIT)]
editorial /edɪ'tɔ:rɪəl/ **1** *a.* of an editor or editing. **2** *n.* newspaper article commenting on current topic, written or sanctioned by editor. **3 editorially** *adv.*
EDP *abbr.* electronic data processing.
educate /'edju:keɪt/ *v.t.* train or instruct intellectually, morally, and socially; provide schooling for; **educated guess** one based on experience; **educable** *a.*; **educator** *n.*; **educative** *a.* [L *educo -are* rear]
education /edju:'keɪʃ(ə)n/ *n.* systematic instruction, course of this; development of character or mental powers; **educational** *a.* [F or L (prec.)]
educationist *n.* (also **educationalist**) expert in educational methods.
educe /ɪ'dju:s/ *v.t.* bring out, develop from latent or potential existence; **eduction** /ɪ'dʌkʃ(ə)n/ *n.* [L *educo -ere* draw out]
Edwardian /ed'wɔ:dɪən/ **1** *a.* of or characteristic of the reign of Edward VII (1901–10). **2** *n.* person of this period. [*Edward*]
-ee *suffix* forming nouns expressing (1) person affected by the verbal action (*addressee*, *employee*, *payee*), (2) person concerned with or described as (*absentee*, *bargee*, *refugee*), (3) object of smaller size (*bootee*). [F *-é* in p.p.]

EEC *abbr*. European Economic Community.
EEG *abbr*. electroencephalogram.
eel *n*. snakelike fish; evasive person. [OE]
-eer *suffix* forming (1) nouns in sense 'person concerned with' (*auctioneer*, *mountaineer*, *profiteer*), (2) verbs in sense 'be concerned with' (*electioneer*). [F *-ier* f. L *-arius*]
eerie /'ɪərɪ/ *a*. gloomy and strange, weird; **eerily** *adv*.; **eeriness** *n*. [OE]
ef- see EX-[1]
efface /ɪ'feɪs/ *v.t.* rub or wipe out (mark, recollection, impression); surpass, eclipse; **efface oneself** treat oneself as unimportant; **effacement** *n*. [F (FACE)]
effect /ɪ'fekt/ **1** *n*. result or consequence of action etc.; state of being operative; efficacy (*of no effect*); impression produced on spectator or hearer etc. (*lights gave a pretty effect*; *said it just for effect*); (in *pl*.) property; (in *pl*.) sounds and visual features giving realism to play, film, etc. **2** *v.t.* bring about, accomplish, cause to occur (*effect a change*, *cure*, *sale*). **3 bring** (or **carry**) **into effect** accomplish; **give effect to** make operative; **in effect** for practical purposes, in reality; **take effect** become operative; **to that effect** having that result or implication; **with effect from** coming into operation at (stated time). [F or L (FACT)]
effective *a*. having an effect, powerful in effect; striking, remarkable; actual, existing; operative. [L (prec.)]
effectual /ɪ'fektʃʊəl, -tjʊəl/ *a*. answering its purpose, sufficient to produce an effect; valid; **effectually** *adv*. [med.L (EFFECT)]
effeminate /ɪ'femɪnət/ *a*. (of a man) womanish in appearance or manner; **effeminacy** *n*. [L (*femina* woman)]
effervesce /efə'ves/ *v.i.* give off bubbles of gas; be energetic; **effervescence** *n*.; **effervescent** *a*. [L (FERVENT)]
effete /e'fi:t/ *a*. worn out, lacking vitality; feeble. [L]
efficacious /efɪ'keɪʃəs/ *a*. producing or able to produce the desired effect; **efficacy** /'efɪkəsɪ/ *n*. [L *efficax* (foll.)]
efficient /ɪ'fɪʃənt/ *a*. productive with minimum waste of effort; (of person) capable, acting effectively; producing effect (*efficient cause*); **efficiency** *n*. [L (*facio* make)]
effigy /'efɪdʒɪ/ *n*. sculpture or model of person; **burn person in effigy** burn figure representing him. [L *effigies* (*fingo* fashion)]
effloresce /eflɔ:'res/ *v.i.* burst into flower; (of substance) turn to fine powder on exposure to air; (of salts) come to the surface and crystallize; (of surface) become covered with salt particles; **efflorescence** *n*.; **efflorescent** *a*. [L (*flos flor-* FLOWER)]
effluence /'eflʊəns/ *n*. flowing out of light or electricity etc.; that which flows out. [F or med.L (foll.)]
effluent 1 *a*. flowing out. **2** *n*. thing that flows out, esp. stream from larger stream, or sewage. [L (*fluo flux-* flow)]
effluvium /e'flu:vɪəm/ *n*. (*pl*. **effluvia**) outflow of substance, esp. unpleasant or harmful one. [L (prec.)]
efflux /'eflʌks/ *n*. outflow. [med.L (EFFLUENT)]
effort /'efət/ *n*. strenuous physical or mental exertion; application of this, attempt; force exerted; *colloq*. something accomplished. [F f. Rmc (L *fortis* strong)]
effortless *a*. easily done, requiring no effort.
effrontery /ɪ'frʌntərɪ/ *n*. shameless insolence, impudence. [F f. L (*frons front-* forehead)]
effulgent /ɪ'fʌldʒənt/ *a*. radiant, bright; **effulgence** *n*. [L (*fulgeo* shine)]
effuse /ɪ'fju:z/ *v.t.* pour forth, send out (liquid, light, or *fig*.) [L (*fundo fus-* pour)]
effusion /ɪ'fju:ʒ(ə)n/ *n*. outpouring, esp. *derog*. of unrestrained literary work. [F or L (prec.)]
effusive /ɪ'fju:sɪv/ *a*. demonstrative, gushing. [EFFUSE]
eft *n*. newt. [OE]
EFTA /'eftə/ *abbr*. European Free Trade Association.
e.g. *abbr*. for example. [L *exempli gratia*]
egalitarian /ɪgælɪ'teərɪən/ **1** *a*. of or advocating equal rights for all. **2** *n*. egalitarian person. **3 egalitarianism** *n*. [F (*égal* equal)]
egg[1] *n*. oval body produced by female of birds etc. containing germ of new individual, esp. that of domestic fowl for eating; female ovum; *colloq*. person (qualified in some way: *good egg*; *tough egg*); **egg-cup** small cup for holding boiled egg; **egg-flip** (or **-nog**) drink of alcoholic spirit with beaten egg, milk, etc.; **egg-plant** plant with deep purple fruit used as vegetable, its fruit, aubergine; **with egg on one's face** *colloq*. made to look foolish; **eggy** *a*. [ON]
egg[2] *v.t.* urge (person) *on*. [ON (EDGE)]
egghead *n*. *colloq*. intellectual person. [EGG[1]]
eggshell 1 *n*. shell of an egg. **2** *a*. (of china) thin and fragile; (of paint) with slight gloss.
eglantine /'eglәntaɪn/ *n*. sweet-brier. [F, f. L *acus* needle]
ego /'i:gəʊ, 'e-/ *n*. (*pl*. **egos**) the self, the part of the mind that reacts to reality and has sense of individuality; self-

esteem; **ego-trip** *colloq*. activity undertaken to boost one's own self-esteem or feelings. [L, = I]

egocentric /egəʊ'sentrɪk/ *a*. self-centred. [CENTRE]

egoism /'egəʊɪz(ə)m/ *n*. self-interest as moral basis of behaviour; systematic selfishness; egotism; **egoist** *n*.; **egoistic** /-'ɪstɪk/ *a*.; **egoistically** /-'ɪstɪkəlɪ/ *adv*. [EGO]

egotism /'egətɪz(ə)m/ *n*. practice of talking too much about oneself; self-conceit; selfishness; **egotist** *n*.; **egotistic** /-'tɪstɪk/ *a*.; **egotistically** /-'tɪstɪkəlɪ/ *adv*. [EGO, -ISM, with intrusive *-t-*]

egregious /ɪ'gri:dʒəs/ *a*. outstandingly bad; *archaic* remarkable. [L (*grex greg-* flock)]

egress /'i:gres/ *n*. exit; right of going out. [L (*egredior -gress-* walk out)]

egret /'i:grɪt/ *n*. a kind of heron with long white feathers. [F *aigrette*]

Egyptian /ɪ'dʒɪpʃ(ə)n/ **1** *n*. native of Egypt; language of ancient Egyptians. **2** *a*. of Egypt. [*Egypt*]

Egyptology /i:dʒɪp'tɒlədʒɪ/ *n*. study of Egyptian antiquities; **Egyptologist** *n*. [-LOGY]

eh /eɪ/ *int*. *colloq*. expressing inquiry or surprise, or inviting assent, or asking for repetition or explanation. [instinctive excl.]

eider /'aɪdə/ *n*. large northern duck. [Icel.]

eiderdown *n*. quilt stuffed with down or other soft material.

eight /eɪt/ *a*. & *n*. one more than seven; symbol for this (8, viii, VIII); size etc. denoted by eight; eight-oared rowing-boat or its crew; **have one over the eight** *sl*. get slightly drunk. [OE]

eighteen /eɪ'ti:n/ *a*. & *n*. one more than seventeen; symbol for this (18, xviii, XVIII); size etc. denoted by eighteen; **eighteenth** *a*. & *n*. [OE]

eightfold *a*. & *adv*. eight times as much or as many; consisting of eight parts. [EIGHT]

eighth *a*. & *n*. next after seventh; one of eight equal parts of thing; **eighthly** *adv*.

eightsome *a*. for eight people; **eightsome reel** lively Scottish dance.

eighty /'eɪtɪ/ *a*. & *n*. eight times ten; symbol for this (80, lxxx, LXXX); (in *pl*.) numbers, years, degrees of temperature, from 80 to 89; **eightieth** *a*. & *n*. [OE]

einsteinium /aɪn'staɪnɪəm/ *n*. artificial radioactive metallic element. [*Einstein*, physicist]

eisteddfod /aɪs'teðvɒd/ *n*. annual congress of Welsh poets and musicians for competitions.

either /'aɪðə, 'i:ðə/ **1** *a*. & *pron*. one or the other of two (*either of you can go*; *you may have either book*); each of two (*houses on either side of the road*; *either will do*). **2** *adv*. or *conj*. as one possibility (*is either black or white*); as one choice or alternative, which way you will (*either come in or go out*); (with neg. or interrog.) any more than the other (*if you do not go, I shall not either*), moreover (*there is no time to lose, either*). [OE]

ejaculate /ɪ'dʒækjʊleɪt/ *v*. utter suddenly, exclaim; emit (esp. semen) from the body; **ejaculation** /-'leɪʃ(ə)n/ *n*.; **ejaculatory** *a*. [L *ejaculor* dart out]

eject /ɪ'dʒekt/ *v.t*. expel, compel to leave, dispossess (tenant); send out, emit; **ejection** *n*. [L *ejicio eject-* throw out]

ejector *n*. device for ejecting; **ejector seat** device for ejection of pilot of aircraft etc. in emergency.

eke *v.t*. (with *out*) make (living) or support (existence) with difficulty, supplement (income etc.). [OE]

elaborate **1** /ɪ'læbərət/ *a*. minutely worked out; highly developed or complicated. **2** /ɪ'læbəreɪt/ *v*. work out or explain in detail. **3** **elaboration** /-'reɪʃ(ə)n/ *n*. [L (LABOUR)]

élan /eɪ'lɑ̃/ *n*. vivacity, dash. [F]

eland /'i:lənd/ *n*. large African antelope. [Du.]

elapse /ɪ'læps/ *v.i*. (of time) pass by. [L *elabor elaps-* slip away]

elastic /ɪ'læstɪk/ **1** *a*. able to resume its normal bulk or shape after contraction, dilation, or distortion; springy; (of feelings or person) buoyant; flexible, adaptable. **2** *n*. elastic cord or fabric, usu. woven with strips of rubber. **3** **elastically** *adv*.; **elasticity** /-'stɪsɪtɪ/ *n*. [L f. Gk *elastikos* propulsive]

elasticated /ɪ'læstɪkeɪtɪd/ *a*. (of fabric) made elastic by weaving with rubber thread.

elastomer /ɪ'læstəmə/ *n*. natural or synthetic rubber or rubber-like plastic. [ELASTIC, after *isomer*]

elate /ɪ'leɪt/ *v.t*. inspirit, stimulate; (esp. in *p.p.*) make pleased or proud. [L *effero elat-* raise]

elbow /'elbəʊ/ **1** *n*. joint between forearm and upper arm; part of sleeve of garment covering elbow; elbow-shaped bend etc. **2** *v.t*. thrust or jostle (*oneself* or *one's way in*, *out*, etc.). **3** **elbow-grease** *colloq*. vigorous polishing, hard work; **elbow-room** plenty of room to move or work in; **out at (the) elbows** worn, ragged, poor. [OE (ELL, BOW[1])]

elder[1] **1** *a*. (of persons, esp. related ones) senior, of greater age. **2** *n*. (in *pl*.) persons of greater age or venerable because of age; official in early Christian Church and some modern Churches. **3** **elder**

statesman influential experienced person, esp. politician, of advanced age. [OE OLD)]
elder[2] *n.* tree with white flowers and dark berries. [OE]
elderberry *n.* berry of elder tree.
elderly *a.* somewhat old, past middle age. [ELDER[1]]
eldest *a.* first-born, oldest surviving.
eldorado /eldə'rɑ:dəʊ/ *n.* (*pl.* **eldorados**) imaginary land of great wealth, place of abundance or opportunity. [Sp. *el dorado* the gilded]
eldritch /'eldrɪtʃ/ *a. Sc.* weird, hideous. [orig. uncert.]
elecampane /elɪkæm'peɪn/ *n.* plant with bitter aromatic leaves and root. [L *enula* this plant, *campana* of the fields]
elect /ɪ'lekt/ **1** *v.t.* choose by voting; choose (thing, *to do* thing). **2** *a.* chosen; select, choice; (after noun) chosen but not yet in office (*president elect*). [L *eligo elect-* pick out]
election /ɪ'lekʃ(ə)n/ *n.* electing or being elected; process of electing, esp. Members of Parliament. [F f. L (prec.)]
electioneer /ɪlekʃə'nɪə/ *v.i.* take part in election campaign.
elective /ɪ'lektɪv/ *a.* chosen or appointed by election; (of body) having power to elect; optional, not urgently necessary.
elector /ɪ'lektə/ *n.* one who has right to elect or take part in election; (**Elector**) *hist.* any of German princes entitled to elect emperor; **electoral** *a.*
electorate /ɪ'lektərət/ *n.* body of electors; office or dominions of a German Elector.
electric /ɪ'lektrɪk/ **1** *a.* of, worked by, or charged with electricity; producing or capable of generating electricity; causing sudden and dramatic excitement (*news had an electric effect*). **2** *n.* electric light, vehicle, etc.; (in *pl.*) electrical equipment. **3 electric blanket** blanket heated by internal electric element; **electric chair** chair used to electrocute as form of execution; **electric eel** eel-like fish able to give electric shock; **electric eye** photoelectric cell operating relay when beam of light is broken; **electric fire** appliance giving heat from electrically charged wire coil or bar; **electric shock** effect of sudden discharge of electricity through body of person etc. [L f. Gk *ēlektron* amber]
electrical /ɪ'lektrɪk(ə)l/ *a.* of or concerned with electricity; suddenly exciting (*effect was electrical*); **electrically** *adv.*
electrician /ɪlek'trɪʃ(ə)n/ *n.* person whose profession is installing and maintaining electrical equipment.
electricity /ɪlek'trɪsɪtɪ/ *n.* form of energy occurring in elementary particles (electrons, protons) and hence in larger bodies containing them; supply of electricity; science of electricity.
electrify /ɪ'lektrɪfaɪ/ *v.t.* charge with electricity; convert (railway, factory, etc.) to use of electric power; suddenly excite or startle (*news was electrifying*); **electrification** /-fɪ'keɪʃ(ə)n/ *n.*
electro- in *comb.* of, by, or caused by electricity. [Gk ELECTRIC)]
electrocardiogram /ɪlektrəʊ'kɑ:dɪəʊgræm/ *n.* record of heartbeat traced by electrocardiograph. [G (ELECTRO-)]
electrocardiograph /ɪlektrəʊ'kɑ:dɪəʊgrɑ:f/ *n.* instrument recording electric currents generated by person's heartbeat.
electroconvulsive therapy /ɪlektrəʊkən'vʌlsɪv/ therapy using convulsive response to electric shocks. [ELECTRO-]
electrocute /ɪ'lektrəkju:t/ *v.t.* kill or execute by electric shock: **electrocution** /-'kju:ʃ(ə)n/ *n.* [ELECTRO-, after *execute*]
electrode /ɪ'lektrəʊd/ *n.* conductor through which electricity enters or leaves electrolyte, gas, vacuum, etc. [ELECTRIC, Gk *hodos* way]
electrodynamics /ɪlektrəʊdaɪ'næmɪks/ *n.pl.* (often as *sing.*) study of electricity in motion. [ELECTRO-]
electroencephalogram /ɪlektrəʊen'sefələʊgræm/ *n.* record traced by electroencephalograph. [G (ELECTRO-)]
electroencephalograph /ɪlektrəʊen'sefələʊgrɑ:f/ *n.* instrument recording electrical activity of the brain.
electrolyse /ɪ'lektrəʊlaɪz/, *US* **electrolyze** *v.t.* subject to or treat by electrolysis. [foll.]
electrolysis /ɪlek'trɒlɪsɪs/ *n.* chemical decomposition by electric action; breaking up of tumours, hair-roots, etc., by electric action; **electrolytic** /ɪlektrəʊ'lɪtɪk/ *a.* [ELECTRO-, -LYSIS]
electrolyte /ɪ'lektrəʊlaɪt/ *n.* solution able to conduct electric current, esp. in electric cell or battery; substance that can dissolve to produce this. [ELECTRO-, -LYTE]
electromagnet /ɪlektrəʊ'mægnɪt/ *n.* soft metal core made into magnet by electric current through coil surrounding it. [ELECTRO-]
electromagnetic /ɪlektrəʊmæg'netɪk/ *a.* having both electrical and magnetic properties; **electromagnetically** *adv.*
electromagnetism /ɪlektrəʊ'mægnətɪz(ə)m/ *n.* magnetic forces produced by electricity; study of these.
electromotive /ɪlektrəʊ'məʊtɪv/ *a.* producing or tending to produce electric current; **electromotive force** force set

up by difference of potential in electric circuit.

electron /ɪ'lektrɒn/ *n.* stable elementary particle with indivisible charge of negative electricity, found in all atoms and acting as carrier of electricity in solids; **electron lens** device for focusing stream of electrons by electric and magnetic fields; **electron microscope** microscope with high magnification and resolution using electron lenses; **electron-volt** unit of energy, amount gained by electron when accelerated through potential difference of one volt. [ELECTRIC, *-on*]

electronic /ɪlek'trɒnɪk/ *a.* produced by or involving flow of electrons; of electrons or electronics; **electronic music** music produced by electronic means and recorded on tape; **electronically** *adv.*

electronics *n.pl.* (as *sing.*) branch of physics and technology dealing with behaviour of electrons in vacuum, gas, semiconductor, etc.

electroplate /ɪ'lektrəʊpleɪt/ **1** *v.t.* coat with thin layer of silver, chromium, etc., by electrolysis. **2** *n.* objects so plated. [ELECTRO-]

electroscope /ɪ'lektrəskəʊp/ *n.* instrument for detecting and measuring electricity, esp. to indicate ionization of air by radioactivity.

electro-shock /ɪlektrəʊ'ʃɒk/ *n.* electric shock; **electro-shock therapy** medical treatment by means of electric shocks.

electrostatics /ɪlektrəʊ'stætɪks/ *n.pl.* (as *sing.*) study of electricity at rest.

electrotechnology /ɪlektrəʊtek'nɒlədʒɪ/ *n.* science of technological application of electricity.

electrotherapy /ɪlektrəʊ'θerəpɪ/ *n.* treatment of diseases by use of electricity.

elegant /'elɪgənt/ *a.* graceful in appearance or manner; tasteful, refined; **elegance** *n.* [F or L (ELECT)]

elegiac /elɪ'dʒaɪək/ **1** *a.* used for elegies; mournful. **2** *n.* (in *pl.*) elegiac verses. **3 elegiac couplet** dactylic hexameter and pentameter. [F or L (foll.)]

elegy /'elɪdʒɪ/ *n.* sorrowful poem or song; lament for the dead; poem in elegiac metre. [F, or L f. Gk]

element /'elɪmənt/ *n.* component part, contributing factor; any of about 100 substances that cannot be resolved by chemical means into simpler substances; any of the four substances (earth, water, air, and fire) in ancient and medieval philosophy, a being's natural abode or environment; wire that gives out heat in electric cooker, heater, etc.; (in *pl.*) atmospheric agencies, esp. wind and storm; (in *pl.*) rudiments of learning or of an art etc.; (in *pl.*) bread and wine of Eucharist; **in one's element** in one's accustomed or preferred surroundings, doing what one is skilled at and enjoys. [F f. L]

elemental /elɪ'ment(ə)l/ *a.* of or like the elements or the forces of nature, powerful, tremendous; basic, essential.

elementary /elɪ'mentərɪ/ *a.* dealing with simplest facts of subject, rudimentary; unanalysable; **elementary particle** any of several subatomic particles thought not to consist of simpler ones; **elementarily** *adv.*; **elementariness** *n.*

elephant /'elɪfənt/ *n.* largest living land animal, with trunk and ivory tusks. [F f. L f. Gk]

elephantiasis /elɪfən'taɪəsɪs/ *n.* skin disease causing gross enlargement of limb etc.

elephantine /elɪ'fæntaɪn/ *a.* of elephants; huge, clumsy, unwieldy. [L f. Gk (ELEPHANT)]

elevate /'elɪveɪt/ *v.t.* raise or lift up; enhance morally or intellectually; (in *p.p.*) exalted in rank or status. [L (*levo* lift)]

elevation /elɪ'veɪʃ(ə)n/ *n.* elevating or being elevated; height above given (esp. sea) level; high position; angle (esp. of gun or direction of heavenly body) with the horizontal; flat drawing showing one side of a building. [F or L (prec.)]

elevator *n.* hoisting-machine; movable part of tailplane for changing aircraft's altitude; *US* lift. [ELEVATE]

eleven /ɪ'lev(ə)n/ *a.* & *n.* one more than ten; symbol for this (11, xi, XI); size etc. denoted by eleven; team of eleven players at cricket, football, etc.; **eleven-plus** examination taken at age 11–12 before entering secondary school. [OE]

elevenfold *a.* & *adv.* eleven times as much or as many; consisting of eleven parts.

elevenses /ɪ'levənzɪz/ *n.* light refreshment about 11 a.m.

eleventh *a.* & *n.* next after tenth; one of eleven equal parts of thing; **eleventh hour** last possible moment.

elf *n.* (*pl.* **elves**) mythical dwarfish being; mischievous child; **elfish** *a.* [OE]

elfin *a.* of elves, elflike.

elicit /ɪ'lɪsɪt/ *v.t.* draw out (latent thing, esp. response etc.) [L *elicio*]

elide /ɪ'laɪd/ *v.t.* omit (vowel or syllable) in pronunciation. [L *elido elis-* crush out]

eligible /'elɪdʒɪb(ə)l/ *a.* fit or entitled to be chosen (*for* office, award, etc.); desirable or suitable, esp. for marriage; **eligibility** /-'bɪlɪtɪ/ *n.* [F f. L (ELECT)]

eliminate /ɪ'lɪmɪneɪt/ *v.t.* remove, get rid of; exclude from consideration; exclude from further stage of competition through defeat etc.; **elimination** /-'neɪʃ(ə)n/ *n.*; **eliminator** *n.* [L (*limen limin-* threshold)]

elision /ɪ'lɪʒ(ə)n/ *n.* omission of vowel or syllable in pronunciation (e.g. in *we'll*). [L (ELIDE)].

élite /eɪ'li:t/ *n.* select group or class; *the* best (of a group); size of letters in typewriting (12 per inch). [F (ELECT)]

élitism *n.* recourse to or advocacy of leadership or dominance by a select group.

elixir /ɪ'lɪksə/ *n.* alchemist's preparation designed to change metal into gold or (**elixir of life**) to prolong life indefinitely; remedy for all ills; aromatic medicinal drug. [L f. Arab.]

Elizabethan /ɪlɪzə'bi:θ(ə)n/ **1** *a.* of the time of Queen Elizabeth I or II. **2** *n.* person of this time. [*Elizabeth*]

elk *n.* large deer of N. Europe and Asia. [OE]

ell *n. hist.* measure = 45 in. [OE, = forearm]

ellipse /ɪ'lɪps/ *n.* regular oval, figure produced when cone is cut by plane making smaller angle with base than side of cone makes. [F f. L f. Gk *elleipsis* deficit]

ellipsis /ɪ'lɪpsɪs/ *n.* (*pl.* **ellipses** /-i:z/) omission of words needed to complete construction or sense; set of three dots etc. indicating such omission.

ellipsoid /ɪ'lɪpsɔɪd/ *n.* solid of which all plane sections through one axis are ellipses and all other plane sections are ellipses or circles.

elliptical /ɪ'lɪptɪk(ə)l/ *a.* of or in the form of an ellipse; of or containing an ellipsis; **elliptically** *adv.* [Gk (ELLIPSE)]

elm *n.* tree with rough serrated leaves; its wood. [OE]

elocution /elə'kju:ʃ(ə)n/ *n.* art or style of expressive speaking; **elocutionary** *a.*; **elocutionist** *n.* [L (*loquor* speak)]

elongate /'i:lɒŋgeɪt/ *v.t.* lengthen, extend, draw out; **elongation** /-'geɪʃ(ə)n/ *n.* [L (*longus* long)]

elope /ɪ'ləʊp/ *v.i.* run away to get secretly married; **elopement** *n.* [AF]

eloquence /'eləkwəns/ *n.* fluent and effective use of language. [F f. L (*loquor* speak)]

eloquent *a.* having eloquence; expressive (*of*).

else *adv.* (with indefinite or interrog. pronoun) besides (*nobody else knew*; *what else?*); instead (*what else could I say?*); otherwise, if not (*run, or else you will be late*); **or else** *colloq.* expressing threat or warning (*hand over the money or else*). [OE]

elsewhere *adv.* in or to some other place.

elucidate /ɪ'lu:sɪdeɪt/ *v.t.* throw light on, explain; **elucidation** /-'deɪʃ(ə)n/ *n.*; **elucidatory** *a.* [L (LUCID)]

elude /ɪ'lju:d/ *v.t.* escape adroitly from (danger etc.); avoid compliance with or fulfilment of (law, obligation, etc.); baffle (person or memory etc.); **elusion** *n.*; **elusive** *a.*; **elusory** *a.* [L (*ludo* play)]

elver *n.* young eel. [EEL, FARE]

elves *pl.* of ELF.

elvish *a.* = ELFISH.

Elysium /ɪ'lɪzɪəm/ *n.* (in Greek mythology) abode of the blessed after death; place of ideal happiness; **Elysian** *a.* [L f. Gk]

em *n. Printing* unit of measurement equal to space occupied by m. [name of letter *M*]

'em /əm/ *pron. colloq.* them.

em- see EN-.

emaciate /ɪ'meɪsɪeɪt, -ʃ-/ *v.t.* make thin or feeble; **emaciation** /-'eɪʃ(ə)n/ *n.* [L (*macies* leanness)]

emanate /'eməneɪt/ *v.* (cause to) originate or proceed (*from* source, person, etc.); **emanation** /-'neɪʃ(ə)n/ *n.* [L (*mano* flow)]

emancipate /ɪ'mænsɪpeɪt/ *v.t.* free from slavery or from (esp. political or social) restraint; **emancipation** /-'peɪʃ(ə)n/ *n.*; **emancipatory** /-'peɪtərɪ/ *a.* [L, = free from possession (*manus* hand, *capio* take)]

emasculate **1** /ɪ'mæskjʊleɪt/ *v.t.* castrate; deprive of strength or force. **2** /ɪ'mæskjʊlət/ *a.* castrated; effeminate; deprived of force. **3** **emasculation** /-'leɪʃ(ə)n/ *n.* [L (MALE)]

embalm /ɪm'bɑ:m/ *v.t.* preserve (corpse) from decay; preserve from oblivion; make fragrant; **embalmment** *n.* [F (BALM)]

embankment /ɪm'bæŋkmənt/ *n.* earth or stone bank keeping back water or carrying road, railway, etc. [EN-]

embargo /em'bɑ:gəʊ/ **1** *n.* (*pl.* **embargoes**) order forbidding foreign ships to enter, or any ships to leave, the country's ports; prohibition or restraint, esp. of commerce. **2** *v.t.* place under embargo. [Sp. (BAR¹)]

embark /ɪm'bɑ:k/ *v.* put or go on board ship (*for* destination); engage *in* or *on* enterprise. [F (BARQUE)]

embarkation /embɑ:'keɪʃ(ə)n/ *n.* embarking on ship.

embarrass /ɪm'bærəs/ *v.t.* make (person) feel awkward or ashamed; encumber; perplex; complicate (question etc.); **embarrassment** *n.* [F f. Sp. f. It. (BAR¹)]

embassy /'embəsɪ/ *n.* offices or residence of ambassador; ambassador and his staff; deputation to foreign government. [F (AMBASSADOR)]

embattled /ɪm'bæt(ə)ld/ *a.* prepared or arrayed for battle; fortified with battlements. [EN-]
embed /ɪm'bed/ *v.t.* (**-dd-**) fix firmly in surrounding mass. [EN-]
embellish /ɪm'belɪʃ/ *v.t.* beautify, adorn; enhance (narrative) with fictitious additions; **embellishment** *n.* [F (*bel*, BEAU)]
ember[1] *n.* (usu. in *pl.*) small piece of live coal etc. in dying fire. [OE]
ember[2] *a.* in **ember days** group of three days in each season, observed as days of fasting and prayer in some Churches. [OE]
embezzle /ɪm'bez(ə)l/ *v.t.* divert (money etc.) fraudulently to one's own use; **embezzlement** *n.* [AF]
embitter /ɪm'bɪtə/ *v.t.* arouse bitter feelings in; make bitter; **embitterment** *n.* [EN-]
emblazon /ɪm'bleɪz(ə)n/ *v.t.* = BLAZON; **emblazonment** *n.* [EN-]
emblem /'embləm/ *n.* symbol, heraldic or representative device; **emblematic** /-'mætɪk/ *a.* [L f. Gk, = insertion]
embody /ɪm'bɒdɪ/ *v.t.* make (idea etc.) actual or discernible; (of thing) be an expression of; include, comprise; **embodiment** *n.* [EN-]
embolden /ɪm'bəʊld(ə)n/ *v.t.* make bold, encourage. [EN-]
embolism /'embəlɪz(ə)m/ *n.* obstruction of artery etc. by clot of blood, air-bubble, etc. [L f. Gk]
embolus /'embələs/ *n.* (*pl.* **emboli** /-aɪ/) object causing embolism.
emboss /ɪm'bɒs/ *v.t.* carve or decorate with design in relief; **embossment** *n.* [BOSS[2]]
embrace /ɪm'breɪs/ **1** *v.t.* hold closely in the arms, esp. as sign of affection; (*absol.* of two people) embrace each other; clasp, enclose; accept, adopt (idea, belief, etc.); take in with the eye or mind. **2** *n.* holding in the arms, clasp. [F f. L (BRACE)]
embrasure /ɪm'breɪʒə/ *n.* bevelling of wall at sides of window etc.; opening in parapet for gun. [F (*embraser* splay)]
embrocation /embrə'keɪʃ(ə)n/ *n.* liquid for rubbing on the body to relieve muscular pain. [F or L f. Gk *embrokhē* lotion]
embroider /ɪm'brɔɪdə/ *v.t.* decorate (cloth etc.) with needlework; embellish (narrative). [AF f. Gmc]
embroidery *n.* embroidered work; inessential ornament.
embroil /ɪm'brɔɪl/ *v.t.* bring (affairs etc.) into confusion; involve (person) in hostility (*with* another); **embroilment** *n.* [F (*brouiller* mix)]
embryo /'embrɪəʊ/ **1** *n.* (*pl.* **embryos**) unborn or unhatched offspring; human offspring in first eight weeks from conception; rudimentary plant in a seed; thing in rudimentary stage. **2** *a.* undeveloped, immature. **3 in embryo** undeveloped. **4 embryonic** /-'ɒnɪk/ *a.* [L f. Gk (*bruō* grow)]
emend /ɪ'mend/ *v.t.* (seek to) correct or remove errors from (text etc.); **emendation** /-'deɪʃ(ə)n/ *n.* [L (*menda* fault)]
emerald /'emərəld/ *n.* bright-green precious stone; colour of this; **Emerald Isle** Ireland. [F f. L f. Gk *smaragdos*]
emerge /ɪ'mɜ:dʒ/ *v.i.* come up or out into view; become known or recognized, (of facts) be revealed; (of difficulty) occur; **emergence** *n.*; **emergent** *a.* [L (MERGE)]
emergency /ɪ'mɜ:dʒənsɪ/ **1** *n.* sudden state of danger, conflict, etc., requiring immediate action; condition needing immediate treatment, patient with this. **2** *a.* for use in emergency. [med.L (prec.)]
emeritus /ɪ'merɪtəs/ *a.* retired and retaining title as honour (*emeritus professor*). [L (*mereor* earn)]
emery /'emərɪ/ *n.* coarse corundum for polishing metal etc.; **emery-board** emery-coated nail-file. [F f. It. f. Gk]
emetic /ɪ'metɪk/ **1** *a.* that causes vomiting. **2** *n.* emetic medicine. [Gk (*emeō* vomit)]
EMF *abbr.* electromotive force.
emigrant /'emɪgrənt/ **1** *n.* one who emigrates. **2** *a.* emigrating. [foll.]
emigrate /'emɪgreɪt/ *v.i.* leave one's own country to settle in another; **emigration** /-'greɪʃ(ə)n/ *n.* [L (MIGRATE)]
émigré /'emɪgreɪ/ *n.* emigrant, esp. political exile. [F]
eminence /'emɪnəns/ *n.* distinction, recognized superiority; piece of rising ground; title used in addressing or referring to a cardinal (*His, Your, Eminence*). [L (EMINENT)]
éminence grise /eɪmɪnɑ̃s 'gri:z/ one who exercises power or influence without holding office. [F, = grey cardinal (orig. of Richelieu's secretary)]
eminent /'emɪnənt/ *a.* distinguished, notable, outstanding. [L *emineo* jut out]
emir /e'mɪə/ *n.* title of various Muslim rulers. [F (AMIR)]
emirate /'emɪərət/ *n.* rank, domain, or reign of an emir.
emissary /'emɪsərɪ/ *n.* person sent on special diplomatic mission. [L (foll.)]
emit /ɪ'mɪt/ *v.t.* (**-tt-**) send out (light, heat, etc.); utter (cry etc.); **emission** *n.*; **emissive** *a.* [L *emitto emiss-*]
emollient /ɪ'mɒlɪənt/ **1** *a.* softening or soothing the skin. **2** *n.* emollient substance. [L (*mollis* soft)]
emolument /ɪ'mɒljʊmənt/ *n.* fee from employment, salary. [F or L]

emote /ɪ'məʊt/ *v.i.* act with show of emotion. [foll.]
emotion /ɪ'məʊʃ(ə)n/ *n.* strong mental or instinctive feeling such as love or fear. [F (MOTION)]
emotional *a.* of or expressing emotion(s); liable to excessive emotion; **emotionalism** *n.*; **emotionally** *adv.*
emotive /ɪ'məʊtɪv/ *a.* of or tending to excite emotion; arousing feeling. [L (MOTION)]
empanel /ɪm'pæn(ə)l/ *v.t.* (-**ll**-) enter (jury) on panel. [EN-]
empathy /'empəθɪ/ *n.* power of identifying oneself mentally with (and so fully comprehending) person or object of contemplation; **empathetic** /-'θetɪk/ *a.*; **empathize** *v.* [PATHOS]
emperor /'empərə/ *n.* sovereign of an empire; **emperor penguin** largest known species of penguin. [F f. L (*impero* command)]
emphasis /'emfəsɪs/ *n.* (*pl.* **emphases** /-i:z/) special importance or prominence attached to thing (*emphasis on economy*); stress laid on word(s) to indicate special meaning or importance; vigour or intensity of expression, feeling, etc. [L f. Gk]
emphasize *v.t.* put emphasis on, stress.
emphatic /ɪm'fætɪk/ *a.* full of emphasis, forcibly expressive; (of words) bearing stress, used to give emphasis; **emphatically** *adv.*
emphysema /emfɪ'si:mə/ *n.* swelling due to air in body tissues. [L f. Gk (*emphusaō* puff up)]
empire /'empaɪə/ *n.* extensive group of States or countries under single supreme authority; supreme dominion; large commercial organization etc. owned or directed by one person; **the Empire** *hist.* the British Empire; **empire-building** deliberate accumulation of territory, authority, etc. [F f. L *imperium* dominion]
empirical /em'pɪrɪk(ə)l/ *a.* relying on observation and experiment, not on theory; **empirically** *adv.*; **empiricism** *n.*; **empiricist** *n.* [L f. Gk (*empeiria* experience)]
emplacement /ɪm'pleɪsmənt/ *n.* putting in position; platform for guns. [F (PLACE)]
employ /ɪm'plɔɪ/ **1** *v.t.* use services of (person) in return for payment; use (thing, time, energy, etc.) to good effect; keep occupied. **2** *n.* in **in the employ of** employed by. [F f. L *implicor* be involved]
employee /emplɔɪ'i:, -'plɔɪi/ *n.* person employed for wages. [-EE]
employment *n.* employing or being employed; one's regular trade or profession; **employment exchange** State office concerned with finding employment for those needing it. [EMPLOY]
emporium /em'pɔ:rɪəm/ *n.* (*pl.* **emporia, -ums**) centre of commerce, market; large shop, store. [L f. Gk (*emporos* merchant)]
empower /ɪm'paʊə/ *v.t.* give power or authority to. [EN-]
empress /'emprɪs/ *n.* wife or widow of emperor; woman emperor. [F (EMPEROR)]
empty /'emptɪ/ **1** *a.* containing nothing; (of house etc.) unoccupied or unfurnished; *colloq.* hungry; foolish, meaningless, vacuous. **2** *v.* remove contents of; transfer (contents of one thing *into* another); become empty; (of river) discharge itself. **3** *n.* empty bottle, box, etc. **4 empty-handed** having or bringing nothing; **empty-headed** foolish, lacking sense. **5 emptily** *adv.*; **emptiness** *n.* [OE]
empyrean /empaɪ'ri:ən/ **1** *n.* the highest heaven, as sphere of fire or abode of God. **2** *n.* of this. **3 empyreal** *a.* [L f. Gk (*pur* fire)]
EMS *abbr.* European Monetary System.
emu /'i:mju:/ *n.* large flightless Australian bird. [Port.]
emulate /'emjʊleɪt/ *v.t.* try to equal or excel; imitate; **emulation** /-'leɪʃ(ə)n/ *n.*; **emulative** *a.*; **emulator** *n.* [L (*aemulus* rival)]
emulous /'emjʊləs/ *a.* eagerly or jealously imitative (*of*); actuated by rivalry.
emulsify /ɪ'mʌlsɪfaɪ/ *v.t.* convert into an emulsion. [foll.]
emulsion /ɪ'mʌlʃ(ə)n/ *n.* fine dispersion of one liquid in another, esp. as paint, medicine, etc.; mixture of silver compound in gelatin etc. as coating for photographic plate or film; **emulsive** *a.* [F or L (*mulgeo* milk)]
en *n. Printing* unit of measurement equal to half an em. [name of letter *N*]
en- *prefix* (**em-** before *b, m, p*) **1** = IN-[1], forming verbs, (1) from nouns, in sense 'put into or on' (*engulf, entrust, embed*), (2) from nouns or adjectives, in sense 'bring into condition of' (*enslave*), often with suffix -EN (*enlighten*), (3) from verbs, in sense 'in, into, on' (*enfold*) or intensively (*entangle*). **2** in, inside (*energy, enthusiasm*). [F f. L *in-*; Gk]
-en *suffix* forming verbs, (1) from adjectives, usu. in sense 'make or become so or more so' (*deepen, moisten*), (2) from nouns (*happen, heighten*). [OE]
enable /ɪ'neɪb(ə)l/ *v.t.* give (person) means or authority (*to do* thing); make possible. [EN-]
enact /ɪ'nækt/ *v.t.* ordain, decree; play (part on stage or in life); **enactive** *a.* [EN-]

enactment *n.* law enacted.
enamel /ɪ'næm(ə)l/ **1** *n.* glasslike (usu. opaque) ornamental or preservative coating on metal; hard smooth coating, cosmetic simulating this; hard coating of teeth; painting done in enamel. **2** *v.t.* (**-ll-**, *US* **-l-**) coat, inlay, or portray with enamel. [AF f. Gmc]
enamour /ɪ'næmə/, *US* **enamor** *v.t.* (usu. in *p.p.*) inspire with love or liking (*of*). [F (*amour* love)]
en bloc /ɑ 'blɒk/ in a block, all at the same time. [F]
encamp /ɪn'kæmp/ *v.* settle in (esp. military) camp; **encampment** *n.* [EN-]
encapsulate /ɪn'kæpsjʊleɪt/ *v.t.* enclose (as) in a capsule; summarize, isolate; **encapsulation** /-'leɪʃ(ə)n/ *n.* [CAPSULE]
encase /ɪn'keɪs/ *v.t.* confine (as) in a case; **encasement** *n.* [EN-]
encash /ɪn'kæʃ/ *v.t.* convert into cash; **encashment** *n.*
encaustic /en'kɔːstɪk/ **1** *a.* (of painting) using pigments mixed with hot wax, which are burned in as inlay. **2** *n.* art or product of this. [L f. Gk (CAUSTIC)]
-ence *suffix* forming nouns denoting quality or state (*permanence*), an instance of this (*impertinence*), or action (*reference*). [F f. L]
enceinte /ɑ̃'sæ̃t/ *a.* pregnant. [F (CINCTURE)]
encephalitis /ensefə'laɪtɪs/ *n.* inflammation of the brain. [Gk *egkephalos* brain]
encephalogram /en'sefələʊgræm/ *n.* = ELECTROENCEPHALOGRAM.
encephalograph /en'sefələʊgrɑːf/ *n.* = ELECTROENCEPHALOGRAPH.
enchain /ɪn'tʃeɪn/ *v.t.* chain up; hold fast (attention, emotions). [F (EN-)]
enchant /ɪn'tʃɑːnt/ *v.t.* charm, delight; bewitch; **enchantment** *n.*; **enchantress** *n.fem.* [F [EN-)]
encircle /ɪn'sɜːk(ə)l/ *v.t.* surround; form a circle round; **encirclement** *n.* [EN-]
enclave /'enkleɪv/ *n.* territory of one State surrounded by that of another. [F f. L *clavis* key]
enclitic /en'klɪtɪk/ **1** *a.* (of word) pronounced with so little emphasis that it forms part of preceding word. **2** *n.* such a word (e.g. *not* in *cannot*). [L f. Gk (*klinō* lean)]
enclose /ɪn'kləʊz/ *v.t.* shut in on all sides, surround with wall or fence etc.; shut up in receptacle (esp. in envelope besides letter); (in *p.p.*, of religious community) secluded from the outside world. [F f. L (INCLUDE)]
enclosure /ɪn'kləʊʒə/ *n.* act of enclosing; enclosed space or area; thing enclosed with letter. [F (prec.)]
encode /ɪn'kəʊd/ *v.t.* put into code. [EN-]
encomium /en'kəʊmɪəm/ *n.* (*pl.* **encomiums**) formal or high-flown praise. [L f. Gk (*kōmos* revelry)]
encompass /ɪn'kʌmpəs/ *v.t.* surround; contain. [EN-]
encore /'ɒŋkɔː/ **1** *n.* audience's demand for further performance or repetition of item; such item. **2** *v.t.* call for encore of (item), call back (performer) for this. **3** /also -'kɔː/ *int.* again, once more. [F, = once again]
encounter /ɪn'kaʊntə/ **1** *v.t.* meet by chance or unexpectedly; meet as adversary. **2** *n.* meeting by chance or in conflict. [F f. L *contra* against]
encourage /ɪn'kʌrɪdʒ/ *v.t.* give courage or confidence to; urge; stimulate, promote; **encouragement** *n.* [F (EN-)]
encroach /ɪn'krəʊtʃ/ *v.i.* intrude (*on* or *upon*); advance gradually beyond due limits; **encroachment** *n.* [F (*croc* CROOK)]
encrust /ɪn'krʌst/ *v.* cover with or form a crust; overlay with crust of silver etc. [F (EN-)]
encumber /ɪn'kʌmbə/ *v.t.* be burden to; hamper, impede. [F f. Rmc]
encumbrance *n.* burden, impediment.
-ency *suffix* forming nouns denoting quality or state (*efficiency*, *presidency*). [L]
encyclical /ɪn'sɪklɪk(ə)l/ **1** *a.* for wide circulation. **2** *n.* papal encyclical letter. [L f. Gk (CYCLE)]
encyclopaedia /ensaɪkləʊ'piːdɪə/ *n.* (also **encyclopedia**) book or set of books giving information on many subjects, or on many aspects of one subject. [Gk *egkuklios* all-round, *paideia* education]
encyclopaedic *a.* (also **encyclopedic**) (of knowledge or information) comprehensive.
end **1** *n.* extreme limit, furthest point (*end of the line*); extreme part or surface of thing (*strip of wood with a nail in one end*); finish or conclusion, latter part (*end of the world*; *no end to his misery*); destruction, death (*met an untimely end*); purpose, object (*will do anything to achieve his ends*); result, outcome; remnant, piece left over (*cigarette-end*); half of sports pitch etc. occupied by one side; part or share with which person is concerned (*no problem at my end*). **2** *v.* bring or come to an end, finish; result *in*. **3 the end** *colloq.* limit of endurability; **end it all** *colloq.* commit suicide; **end on** with the end facing one or adjoining the end of next object; **end-product** final product of manufacture, transformation, etc.; **ends of the earth** remotest regions; **end to end** with end of one

adjoining end of next in series; **end up** reach certain state or action eventually (*ended up a drunkard*; *ended up making a fortune*); **in the end** finally; **keep one's end up** do one's part despite difficulties; **make ends meet** live within one's income; **no end** *colloq.* to a great extent; **no end of** *colloq.* much or many of; **on end** upright, continuously (*for three weeks on end*); **put an end to** stop, abolish, destroy. [OE]

endanger /ɪn'deɪndʒə/ *v.t.* bring into danger. [EN-]

endear /ɪn'dɪə/ *v.t.* make dear (*to*). [EN-]

endearment *n.* act or words expressing affection; liking, affection.

endeavour /ɪn'devə/, *US* **endeavor 1** *v.t.* try earnestly (*to do* thing). **2** *n.* earnest attempt. [EN-, F *devoir* owe]

endemic /en'demɪk/ **1** *a.* regularly or only found among (specified) people or in (specified) country. **2** *n.* endemic disease or plant. **3 endemically** *adv.* [F or L f. Gk (as DEMOTIC)]

ending *n.* end or final part, esp. of story; inflected final part of word. [END]

endive /'endɪv/ *n.* curly-leaved plant used in salads. [F f. L *endiva* f. Gk]

endless /'endlɪs/ *a.* without end, infinite; incessant; continual; *colloq.* innumerable; **endless belt** (or **chain**) etc. one with ends joined for continuous action over wheels etc. [OE (END)]

endmost *a.* nearest the end. [END]

endo- *in comb.* internal. [Gk *endon* within]

endocrine /'endəʊkraɪn, -ɪn/ *a.* (of gland) secreting directly into the blood. [Gk *krinō* sift]

endogenous /en'dɒdʒɪnəs/ *a.* growing or originating from within. [-GENOUS]

endomorph /'endəʊmɔ:f/ *n.* person with soft round build of body. [Gk *morphē* form]

endorse /ɪn'dɔ:s/ *v.t.* confirm, approve; write on back of (document etc.), esp. sign back of (cheque); enter details of conviction for offence on (licence); **endorsement** *n.* [L (*dorsum* back)]

endow /ɪn'daʊ/ *v.t.* bequeath or give permanent income to (person, institution, etc.); (esp. in *p.p.*) provide with talent or ability. [AF (DOWER)]

endowment *n.* endowing; endowed income; **endowment assurance** (or **insurance** or **policy** etc.) form of life insurance with payment of fixed sum to insured person on specified date, or to his estate if he dies earlier.

endpaper *n.* stout blank leaf of paper fixed across beginning or end of book and inside cover. [END]

endue /ɪn'dju:/ *v.t.* provide (person *with* qualities etc.). [F f. L (INDUCE)]

endurance /ɪn'djʊərəns/ *n.* power of enduring (*beyond endurance*); ability to withstand prolonged strain (*endurance test*). [F (foll.)]

endure /ɪn'djʊə/ *v.* undergo (pain etc.); tolerate, bear (*cannot endure him*); last. [F f. L (*durus* hard)]

endways *adv.* (also **endwise**) with end uppermost or foremost; end to end. [END]

enema /'enɪmə/ *n.* insertion of liquid through the anus into the rectum, esp. to expel its contents; liquid or syringe used for this. [L f. Gk (*hiēmi* send)]

enemy /'enəmɪ/ **1** *n.* person actively hostile to another; hostile nation or army, member of this; adversary, opponent. **2** *a.* of or belonging to an enemy. [F f. L (IN-[2], *amicus* friend)]

energetic /enə'dʒetɪk/ *a.* full of energy, powerfully active. [Gk (ENERGY)]

energize /'enədʒaɪz/ *v.t.* give energy to; provide (device) with energy for operation. [foll.]

energy /'enədʒɪ/ *n.* capacity for activity, force, vigour; ability of matter or radiation to do work. [F or L f. Gk (*ergon* work)]

enervate /'enəveɪt/ *v.t.* deprive of vigour or vitality; **enervation** /-'veɪʃ(ə)n/ *n.* [L (NERVE)]

enfant terrible /ɑ̃fɑ̃ tə'ri:bl/ person who causes embarrassment by indiscreet behaviour; unruly child. [F, = terrible child]

enfeeble /ɪn'fi:b(ə)l/ *v.t.* make feeble; **enfeeblement** *n.* [EN-]

enfilade /enfɪ'leɪd/ **1** *n.* gunfire directed along line from end to end. **2** *v.t.* direct enfilade at. [F (FILE[1])]

enfold /ɪn'fəʊld/ *v.t.* wrap (person *in* or *with*); clasp, embrace. [EN-]

enforce /ɪn'fɔ:s/ *v.t.* compel observance of (law etc.); impose (action or will etc. *on* person); persist in (demand etc.); **enforcement** *n.* [F f. L (FORCE[1])]

enfranchise /ɪn'fræntʃaɪz/ *v.t.* give (person) right to vote; give (town) municipal rights, esp. representation in parliament; free (slave etc.); **enfranchisement** /-ɪzmənt/ *n.* [F (FRANK[1])]

engage /ɪn'geɪdʒ/ *v.* employ or hire (person); employ busily, occupy (*engage one's attention*; *are you engaged tomorrow?*; *the bathroom*, *the line*, *is engaged*); bind by contract or by promise (esp. in *pass.* of marriage); arrange beforehand to occupy (room, seat, etc.); interlock (parts of gear etc.), (of gear etc.) become interlocked; come or bring (troops) into battle, come into battle with; take part (*engage in politics*); pledge oneself (*to do* thing, *that*). [F (GAGE[1])]

engagement *n.* engaging or being

engaged; appointment with another person; bethrothal; battle.

engaging *a.* attractive, charming.

engender /ɪn'dʒendə/ *v.t.* give rise to (feeling etc.). [GENUS]

engine /'endʒɪn/ *n.* mechanical contrivance of parts working together, esp. as source of power; railway locomotive (*is an engine-driver*); = *fire-engine*, *steam-engine*; *archaic* machine of war, instrument, means. [F f. L *ingenium* device]

engineer /endʒɪ'nɪə/ **1** *n.* person skilled in a branch of engineering; = *civil engineer*; person who makes or is in charge of engines or other equipment (*ship's engineer*); one who designs and constructs military works, esp. a soldier so trained. **2** *v.* act as engineer; construct, manage (bridge, work, etc.) as engineer; *colloq.* contrive, bring about. [F f. med.L (prec.)]

engineering *n.* application of science for control and use of power, esp. in roads and other works of public utility (*civil engineering*), machines (*mechanical engineering*), electrical apparatus (*electrical engineering*).

English /'ɪŋglɪʃ/ **1** *a.* of England or its people or language. **2** *n.* the language of England, now used in UK, US, and most Commonwealth countries. **3** *v.t.* (**english**) esp. *archaic* render into English. **4 the English** *pl.* the people of England; **the King's** (or **Queen's**) **English** English language correctly spoken or written; **Middle English** the language in use from *c.* 1150 to *c.* 1500; **Old English** that in use before *c.* 1150. [OE]

Englishman *n.* one who is English by birth, descent, or naturalization; **Englishwoman** *n. fem.*

engorged /ɪn'gɔ:dʒd/ *a.* crammed full; congested with blood. [F (EN-, GORGE)]

engraft /ɪn'grɑ:ft/ *v.t.* graft (shoot of one plant *on* or *into* another); implant; incorporate (thing *into* another). [EN-, IN-[1]]

engrave /ɪn'greɪv/ *v.t.* inscribe or cut (design) on hard surface; inscribe (surface) thus; impress deeply *on* memory. [GRAVE[2]]

engraving *n.* print made from engraved plate.

engross /ɪn'grəʊs/ *v.t.* absorb attention of, occupy fully; write out in large letters or in legal form; **engrossment** *n.* [AF (EN-)]

engulf /ɪn'gʌlf/ *v.t.* flow over and swamp, overwhelm. [EN-]

enhance /ɪn'hɑ:ns/ *v.t.* heighten or intensify (quality or power etc.); **enhancement** *n.* [AF f. Rmc f. L *altus* high]

enigma /ɪ'nɪgmə/ *n.* puzzling thing or person; riddle or paradox; **enigmatic** /-'mætɪk/ *a.* [L f. Gk]

enjoin /ɪn'dʒɔɪn/ *v.t.* command, order; impose (action *on* person); *Law* prohibit by injunction (*from doing* thing). [F f. L *injungo* attach]

enjoy /ɪn'dʒɔɪ/ *v.t.* take pleasure in; have use or benefit of; experience (*enjoy good health*); **enjoy oneself** experience pleasure; **enjoyment** *n.* [F]

enjoyable *a.* pleasant, giving enjoyment.

enkephalin /en'kefəlɪn/ *n.* either of two morphine-like peptides in the brain thought to be concerned with the perception of pain. [Gk *egkephalos* brain]

enkindle /ɪn'kɪnd(ə)l/ *v.t.* cause to blaze up, arouse. [EN-]

enlarge /ɪn'lɑ:dʒ/ make or become larger or wider; describe in greater detail; reproduce (photograph) on larger scale; **enlargement** *n.* [F (LARGE)]

enlighten /ɪn'laɪt(ə)n/ *v.t.* instruct or inform (person *on* subject); free from superstition etc. [EN-]

enlightenment *n.* enlightening; **the Enlightenment** 18th-c. philosophy of reason and individualism.

enlist /ɪn'lɪst/ *v.* enrol in armed services; secure as means of help or support; **enlistment** *n.* [EN-]

enliven /ɪn'laɪv(ə)n/ *v.t.* make lively or cheerful, inspirit; **enlivenment** *n.* [EN-]

en masse /ɑ̃ 'mæs/ all together. [F]

enmesh /ɪn'meʃ/ *v.t.* entangle (as) in net. [EN-]

enmity /'enmɪtɪ/ *n.* state or feeling of being an enemy, hostility. [F f. Rmc (ENEMY)]

ennoble /ɪ'nəʊb(ə)l/ *v.t.* make (person) a noble; make noble; **ennoblement** *n.* [F (EN-)]

ennui /ɒ'nwi:/ *n.* mental weariness caused by idleness or lack of interest, feeling of boredom. [F (ANNOY)]

enormity /ɪ'nɔ:mɪtɪ/ *n.* monstrous wickedness; dreadful crime; serious error; (**D**) great size. [F f. L (foll.)]

enormous /ɪ'nɔ:məs/ *a.* extraordinarily large, vast, huge. [L *enormis* (NORM)]

enough /ɪ'nʌf/ **1** *a.* as much or as many as required (*we have enough apples, sugar*; *we have apples, sugar, enough*). **2** *n.* amount or quantity that is enough (*we have enough of everything now*). **3** *adv.* to the required degree, adequately (*are you warm enough?*); fairly (*she sings well enough*); very, quite (*you know well enough what I mean*; *oddly enough*). **4 have had enough of** want no more of, be satiated with or tired of; **sure enough** undeniably, as expected. [OE]

en passant /ɑ̃ 'pæsɑ̃/ by the way. [F, = in passing]

enquire see INQUIRE; **enquiry** see INQUIRY.
enrage /ɪn'reɪdʒ/ *v.t.* make furious. [F (EN-)]
enrapture /ɪn'ræptʃə/ *v.t.* delight intensely. [EN-]
enrich /ɪn'rɪtʃ/ *v.t.* make rich or richer; increase strength or wealth or value of; **enrichment** *n.* [F (EN-)]
enrol /ɪn'rəʊl/, *US* **enroll** *v.* (-ll-) write name of (person) on list; enlist; incorporate as a member; enrol oneself; **enrolment** *n.* [F (EN-)]
en route /ɑ̃ 'ru:t/ on the way. [F]
ensconce /ɪn'skɒns/ *v.t.* settle (esp. *oneself*) comfortably. [SCONCE²]
ensemble /ɑ̃'sɑ̃b(ə)l/ *n.* thing viewed as sum of its parts; general effect of this; set of matching items of dress; group of actors, dancers, musicians, etc., performing together; *Mus.* concerted passage for ensemble. [F f. L (*simul* at same time)]
enshrine /ɪn'ʃraɪn/ *v.t.* enclose (as) in shrine; serve as shrine for. [EN-]
enshroud /ɪn'ʃraʊd/ *v.t.* cover completely (as) with shroud; hide from view. [EN-]
ensign /'ensaɪn, -s(ə)n/ *n.* banner or flag, esp. military or naval flag of nation; standard-bearer; *hist.* lowest commissioned infantry officer; *US* lowest commissioned officer in navy. [F (INSIGNIA)]
ensilage /'ensɪlɪdʒ/ *n.* = SILAGE. [F (SILO)]
enslave /ɪn'sleɪv/ *v.t.* make (person) a slave; **enslavement** *n.* [EN-]
ensnare /ɪn'sneə/ *v.t.* catch (as) in snare. [EN-]
ensue /ɪn'sju:/ *v.* happen later or as result. [F f. Rmc (L *sequor* follow)]
en suite /ɑ̃ 'swi:t/ forming single unit (*bedroom with bathroom en suite*). [F, = in sequence]
ensure /ɪn'ʃʊə/ *v.t.* make certain or secure; make safe (*against* risks). [AF (ASSURE)]
-ent *suffix* forming adjectives denoting attribution of action (*consequent*) or state (*existent*), and agent nouns (*president*). [F or L (*-ent-* partic. stem of vbs.)]
ENT *abbr.* ear, nose, and throat.
entablature /ɪn'tæblətʃə/ *n. Archit.* upper part supported by columns, including architrave, frieze, and cornice. [It. (TABLE)]
entail /ɪn'teɪl/ **1** *v.t.* necessitate or involve unavoidably (*the work entails much effort*); *Law* bequeath (estate) inalienably to named succession of beneficiaries. **2** *n.* entailed estate or succession. [TAIL²]
entangle /ɪn'tæŋg(ə)l/ *v.t.* cause to get caught in snare or tangle; involve in difficulties; complicate; **entanglement** *n.* [EN-]
entente /ɑ̃'tɑ̃t/ *n.* friendly understanding, esp. between States; **entente cordiale** entente esp. between Britain and France from 1904. [F]
enter *v.* go or come in or into; come on stage (esp. as direction: *enter Macbeth*); penetrate (*bullet entered his chest*); write (name, details, etc.) in list, book, etc.; become member of (society or profession); register, record name, as competitor (*entered for the long jump*; *entered the horse for the Derby*); admit, obtain admission for (child *at* school etc.); make known, present for consideration (*entered a protest*); record formally (before court of law etc.); **enter into** take part in (conversation etc.), subscribe to or become bound by (agreement, contract, etc.), form part of (calculation, plan, etc.), sympathize with (feelings); **enter on** (*or* **upon**) assume possession of (property) or functions of (office), begin, begin to deal with. [F f. L (*intra* within)]
enteric /en'terɪk/ *a.* of the intestines. [Gk (*enteron* intestine)]
enteritis /entə'raɪtɪs/ *n.* inflammation of the intestines. [-ITIS]
enterprise /'entəpraɪz/ *n.* undertaking, esp. bold or difficult one; readiness to be involved in such undertakings. [F f. L *prehendo* grasp]
enterprising *a.* showing enterprise; energetic and resourceful.
entertain /entə'teɪn/ *v.t.* amuse, occupy agreeably; receive as guest, receive guests; harbour, cherish, consider favourably (idea etc.). [F f. Rmc (*teneo* hold)]
entertainer *n.* one who provides entertainment, esp. professionally.
entertaining *a.* amusing, diverting.
entertainment *n.* entertaining; thing that entertains, esp. before public audience.
enthral /ɪn'θrɔ:l/, *US* **enthrall** *v.t.* (-ll-) captivate, please greatly; **enthralment** *n.* [EN-]
enthrone /ɪn'θrəʊn/ *v.t.* place on throne, esp. ceremonially; **enthronement** *n.* [EN-]
enthuse /ɪn'θju:z, -'θu:z/ *v. colloq.* be or make enthusiastic. [foll.]
enthusiasm /ɪn'θju:zɪæz(ə)m, -'θu:-/ *n.* intensity of feeling or interest, great eagerness. [F or L f. Gk (*entheos* inspired by god)]
enthusiast *n.* person full of enthusiasm for something. [F or eccl.L (prec.)]
enthusiastic /ɪnθju:zɪ'æstɪk, -θu:-/ *a.* having enthusiasm; **enthusiastically** *adv.*

entice /ɪn'taɪs/ *v.t.* persuade by offer of pleasure or reward; **enticement** *n.* [F f. L *titio* firebrand]
entire /ɪn'taɪə/ *a.* whole, complete; unbroken; unqualified, absolute; in one piece, continuous. [F f. L (INTEGER)]
entirely *adv.* wholly, solely.
entirety /ɪn'taɪərətɪ/ *n.* completeness; sum total (*of*); **in its entirety** in its complete form.
entitle /ɪn'taɪt(ə)l/ *v.t.* give (person) just claim (*to*); give title to; **entitlement** *n.* [AF f. L (TITLE)]
entity /'entɪtɪ/ *n.* thing with distinct existence; thing's existence in itself. [F or L (*ens ent-* being)]
entomb /ɪn'tu:m/ *v.t.* place in tomb; serve as tomb for; **entombment** *n.* [F (TOMB)]
entomology /entə'mɒlədʒɪ/ *n.* study of insects; **entomological** /-'lɒdʒɪk(ə)l/ *a.*; **entomologist** *n.* [Gk *entomon* insect]
entourage /ɒntʊə'rɑ:ʒ/ *n.* people attending important person. [F]
entr'acte /'ɒntrækt/ *n.* interval between acts of play; dance or music etc. performed then. [F]
entrails /'entreɪlz/ *n.pl.* bowels, intestines; inner parts of thing. [F f. L (*inter* among)]
entrance[1] /'entrəns/ *n.* going or coming in; place for entering; right of admission; coming of actor on stage. [F (ENTER)]
entrance[2] /ɪn'trɑ:ns/ *v.t.* enchant, delight; put into trance; **entrancement** *n.*; **entrancing** *a.* [EN-]
entrant /'entrənt/ *n.* one who enters examination, profession, etc. [F (ENTER)]
entrap /ɪn'træp/ *v.t.* (**-pp-**) catch (as) in trap; beguile. [EN-]
entreat /ɪn'tri:t/ *v.t.* ask earnestly, beg. [EN-]
entreaty *n.* earnest request.
entrecôte /'ɒntrəkəʊt/ *n.* boned steak cut off sirloin. [F, = between-rib]
entrée /'ɒntreɪ/ *n.* right of admission; dish served between fish and meat courses; *US* main dish of meal. [F]
entrench /ɪn'trentʃ/ *v.* establish firmly (in position, office, etc.); surround with trench as fortification; **entrenchment** *n.* [EN-]
entrepôt /'ɒntrəpəʊ/ *n.* warehouse for temporary storage of goods in transit. [F]
entrepreneur /ɒntrəprə'nɜ:/ *n.* one who undertakes a commercial enterprise with chance of profit or loss; contractor acting as intermediary; **entrepreneurial** *a.* [F (ENTERPRISE)]
entropy /'entrəpɪ/ *n.* measure of the unavailability of a system's thermal energy for conversion into mechanical work; measure of the degradation or disorganization of the universe. [G f. Gk (EN-, *tropē* transformation)]
entrust /ɪn'trʌst/ *v.t.* give (object of care) with trust; assign responsibility *to* (person). [EN-]
entry /'entrɪ/ *n.* going or coming in; liberty to do this; place of entrance, door, gate, etc.; passage between buildings; item entered in diary, list, etc., the recording of this; person or thing competing in race etc., list of such competitors. [F f. Rmc (ENTER)]
entwine /ɪn'twaɪn/ *v.t.* twine round, interweave. [EN-]
enumerate /ɪ'nju:məreɪt/ *v.t.* count; specify (items); **enumeration** /-'reɪʃ(ə)n/ *n.*; **enumerative** *a.* [L (NUMBER)]
enumerator *n.* person employed in census-taking.
enunciate /ɪ'nʌnsɪeɪt/ *v.t.* pronounce (words) clearly; state in definite terms; **enunciation** /-'eɪʃ(ə)n/ *n.* [L (*nuntio* announce)]
enuresis /enjʊə'ri:sɪs/ *n.* involuntary urination. [Gk *enoureō* urinate in]
envelop /ɪn'veləp/ *v.t.* wrap up; surround, cover on all sides; **envelopment** *n.* [F]
envelope /'envələʊp, 'ɒn-/ *n.* folded paper container for letter etc.; wrapper, covering; gas container of balloon or airship.
enviable /'envɪəb(ə)l/ *a.* such as to cause envy, desirable; **enviably** *adv.* [ENVY]
envious /'envɪəs/ *a.* feeling or showing envy. [AF (ENVY)]
environment /ɪn'vaɪərənmənt/ *n.* surroundings, esp. as affecting people's lives; conditions or circumstances of living; **environmental** /-'ment(ə)l/ *a.* [F *environ* surroundings]
environmentalist /ɪnvaɪərən'mentəlɪst/ *n.* one who is concerned with protection of the environment.
environs /ɪn'vaɪərənz/ *n.pl.* district round town etc.
envisage /ɪn'vɪzɪdʒ/ *v.t.* have mental picture of (thing not yet existent); conceive as possible or desirable. [F (VISAGE)]
envoy /'envɔɪ/ *n.* messenger or representative; (in full **envoy extraordinary**) diplomatic agent ranking below ambassador. [F (*envoyer* send f. L *via* way)]
envy /'envɪ/ **1** *n.* feeling of discontented longing aroused by another's better fortune etc.; object of this feeling. **2** *v.t.* feel envy of (person or his success etc.) [F f. L *invidia* (*video* see)]
enwrap /ɪn'ræp/ *v.t.* (**-pp-**) wrap or enfold (*in*). [EN-]
enzyme /'enzaɪm/ *n.* protein catalyst of

a specific biochemical reaction. [G f. Gk (ZYMOTIC)]

Eocene /'i:əʊsi:n/ **1** *a.* of the second geological epoch of the Tertiary period. **2** *n.* this epoch. [Gk *ēōs* dawn, *kainos* new]

eolian *US* var. of AEOLIAN.

eolithic /i:əʊ'lɪθɪk/ *a.* of the period preceding the palaeolithic age. [Gk *ēōs* dawn, *lithos* stone]

eon *US* var. of AEON.

EP *abbr.* extended-play (record).

epaulette /'epəlet/, *US* **epaulet** *n.* ornamental shoulder-piece worn on uniform. [F (*épaule* shoulder)]

épée /eɪ'peɪ/ *n.* sharp-pointed sword used (with end blunted) in fencing. [F (SPATHE)]

ephedrine /'efədrɪn/ *n.* alkaloid drug used to relieve asthma etc. [*Ephedra*, genus of plants yielding it]

ephemera /ɪ'femərə/ *n.pl.* things of only short-lived use. [L (foll.)]

ephemeral /ɪ'femər(ə)l/ *a.* lasting or living only a day or a few days; transitory. [Gk (EPI-, *hēmera* day)]

epi- *prefix* upon, above, in addition. [Gk]

epic /'epɪk/ **1** *n.* long poem narrating adventures or achievements of a heroic figure or a nation; book or film based on this. **2** *a.* of or like an epic; grand, heroic. [L f. Gk (*epos* song)]

epicene /'epɪsi:n/ **1** *a.* of, for, or denoting both sexes; having characteristics of both sexes or of neither sex. **2** *n.* epicene person. [L f. Gk (*koinos* common)]

epicentre /'epɪsentə/, *US* **epicenter** *n.* point at which earthquake reaches earth's surface; central point of difficulty. [Gk (CENTRE)]

epicure /'epɪkjʊə/ *n.* person of refined tastes in food and drink etc.; **epicurism** *n.* [med.L (foll.)]

Epicurean /epɪkjʊə'ri:ən/ **1** *a.* of Epicurus or his philosophy; (**epicurean**) fond of pleasure and luxury. **2** *n.* student or follower of Epicurus; (**epicurean**) person of epicurean tastes. **3** **Epicureanism** *n.* [*Epicurus* (3rd c. BC), Gk philosopher]

epidemic /epɪ'demɪk/ **1** *a.* (esp. of disease) prevalent among community at particular time. **2** *n.* epidemic disease. [F f. L f. Gk (*dēmos* the people)]

epidemiology /epɪdi:mɪ'ɒlədʒɪ/ *n.* branch of medicine concerned with control of epidemics. [-LOGY]

epidermis /epɪ'dɜ:mɪs/ *n.* outer layer of skin, cuticle; **epidermal** *a.* [L f. Gk (*derma* skin)]

epidiascope /epɪ'daɪəskəʊp/ *n.* optical projector giving images of both opaque and transparent objects. [EPI-, DIA-, -SCOPE]

epidural /epɪ'djʊər(ə)l/ **1** *a.* (of anaesthetic) injected in dura mater round spinal cord. **2** *n.* epidural injection. [EPI-, DURA (MATER)]

epiglottis /epɪ'glɒtɪs/ *n.* cartilage at root of tongue, depressed to cover windpipe in swallowing; **epiglottal** *a.* [Gk *glōtta* tongue]

epigram /'epɪgræm/ *n.* short poem with witty ending; pointed saying; **epigrammatic** /-grə'mætɪk/ *a.* [F or L f. Gk (-GRAM)]

epigraph /'epɪgrɑ:f/ *n.* inscription. [Gk (-GRAPH).

epigraphy /e'pɪgrəfɪ/ *n.* study of inscriptions.

epilepsy /'epɪlepsɪ/ *n.* nervous disorder with convulsions and often loss of consciousness; **epileptic** /epɪ'leptɪk/ *a.* & *n.* [F or L f. Gk (*lambanō* seize)]

epilogue /'epɪlɒg/ *n.* concluding part of book etc.; speech or short poem addressed to audience by actor at end of play. [F f. L f. Gk (*logos* speech)]

Epiphany /e'pɪfənɪ/ *n.* manifestation of Christ to the Magi, festival of this (6 Jan.); (**epiphany**) manifestation of a superhuman being. [F f. eccl.L f. Gk (*phainō* show)]

episcopacy /e'pɪskəpəsɪ/ *n.* government by bishops; **the episcopacy** the bishops. [EPISCOPATE]

episcopal /e'pɪskəp(ə)l/ *a.* of bishop(s); (of church) governed by bishops; **episcopally** *adv.* [F or eccl.L (BISHOP)]

episcopalian /epɪskə'peɪlɪən/ **1** *a.* of episcopacy. **2** *n.* adherent of episcopacy; member of episcopal church. **3** **episcopalianism** *n.*

episcopate /e'pɪskəpət/ *n.* office or tenure of bishop; **the episcopate** the bishops. [eccl.L (BISHOP)]

episiotomy /epɪsɪ'ɒtəmɪ/ *n.* surgical cut made at opening of vagina during childbirth, to aid delivery. [Gk *epision* pubic region]

episode /'epɪsəʊd/ *n.* incident in narrative, one part of several in serial story; incident or event as part of sequence; incidental narrative or series of events. [Gk (*eisodos* entrance)]

episodic /epɪ'sɒdɪk/ *a.* sporadic, occurring irregularly; incidental; **episodically** *adv.*

epistemology /epɪstɪ'mɒlədʒɪ/ *n.* theory of method or grounds of knowledge; **epistemological** /-'lɒdʒɪk(ə)l/ *a.* [Gk *epistēmē* knowledge]

epistle /ɪ'pɪs(ə)l/ *n.* any of letters in New Testament, written by apostles; (usu. *joc.*) any letter; poem etc. in form of letter. [F f. L f. Gk *epistolē* (*stellō* send)]

epistolary /ɪ'pɪstələrɪ/ *a.* of or suitable for letters. [F or L (prec.)]

epitaph /ˈepɪtɑ:f/ *n.* words inscribed on tomb or appropriate to dead person. [F f. L f. Gk (*taphos* tomb)]
epithelium /epɪˈθi:lɪəm/ *n.* (*pl.* **epithelia**) tissue forming outer layer of body or lining open cavity; epidermis of young cells; **epithelial** *a.* [Gk *thēlē* teat]
epithet /ˈepɪθet/ *n.* adjective expressing quality or attribute, descriptive word; **epithetic** /-ˈθetɪk/ *a.*; **epithetically** *adv.* [F or L f. Gk *tithēmi* put)]
epitome /eˈpɪtəmɪ/ *n.* person who embodies a quality etc., thing that represents another in miniature. [L f. Gk (*temno* cut)]
epitomize *v.t.* make or be an epitome of.
EPNS *abbr.* electroplated nickel silver.
epoch /ˈi:pɒk/ *n.* period of history etc. marked by notable events; beginning of era in history, life, etc.; division of geological period, corresponding to a series in rocks; **epoch-making** very important or remarkable; **epochal** *a.* [Gk, = pause]
eponym /ˈepəʊnɪm/ *n.* person after whom place etc. is named; **eponymous** /eˈpɒnɪməs/ *a.* [Gk (*onoma* name)]
epoxy /ɪˈpɒksɪ/ *a.* of or derived from a compound in which oxygen atom and two carbon atoms form ring; **epoxy resin** synthetic thermosetting resin. [EPI-, OXY-]
epsilon /ˈepsɪlən/ *n.* fifth letter of Greek alphabet (Ε, ε). [Gk]
Epsom salts /ˈepsəm/ magnesium sulphate used as purgative etc. [*Epsom* in S. England]
equable /ˈekwəb(ə)l/ *a.* even, not varying; (of climate) moderate; (of person) not easily disturbed; **equably** *adv.* [foll.]
equal /ˈi:kw(ə)l/ **1** *a.* the same in number, size, degree, merit, etc.; evenly balanced (*equal fight*); having same rights or status (*all men should be equal*); uniform in operation (*equal laws*). **2** *n.* person or thing equal to another, esp. person equal in rank or status. **3** *v.t.* (**-ll-**, *US* **-l-**) be equal to; achieve something that is equal to. **4 be equal to** have strength or capacity for. **5 equally** *adv.* [L *aequalis*]
equality /i:ˈkwɒlɪtɪ/ *n.* being equal. [F f. L (EQUAL)]
equalize /ˈi:kwəlaɪz/ *v.* make or become equal; (in games) reach opponent's score; **equalization** /-ˈzeɪʃ(ə)n/ *n.* [EQUAL]
equalizer *n.* goal etc. that equalizes.
equanimity /ekwəˈnɪmɪtɪ, i:k-/ *n.* mental composure; acceptance of fate. [L *aequus* even, *animus* mind]
equate /ɪˈkweɪt/ *v.t.* regard as equal or equivalent (*to* or *with*). [L *aequo aequat-* (EQUAL)]
equation /ɪˈkweɪʒ(ə)n/ *n.* equating, making equal, balancing; statement of equality between two mathematical expressions (conveyed by sign =); formula indicating chemical reaction by use of symbols. [F or L (prec.)]
equator /ɪˈkweɪtə/ *n.* imaginary line round the earth or other body, equidistant from poles; = *celestial equator* (see CELESTIAL). [F or med.L (EQUATE)]
equatorial /ekwəˈtɔ:rɪəl/ *a.* of or near the equator.
equerry /ˈekwərɪ/ *n.* officer of royal household attending members of royal family. [F *escurie* stable]
equestrian /ɪˈkwestrɪən/ **1** *a.* of horse-riding; on horseback. **2** *n.* rider or performer on horseback. [L *equestris* (*equus* horse)]
equi- *in comb.* equal. [L (EQUAL)]
equiangular /i:kwɪˈæŋgjʊlə/ *a.* having equal angles.
equidistant /i:kwɪˈdɪstənt/ *a.* at equal distances.
equilateral /i:kwɪˈlætər(ə)l/ *a.* having sides equal.
equilibrium /i:kwɪˈlɪbrɪəm/ *n.* (*pl.* **equilibria**) state of balance; composure. [LIBRA]
equine /ˈekwaɪn/ *a.* of or like a horse. [L (*equus* horse)]
equinoctial /i:kwɪˈnɒkʃ(ə)l, e-/ **1** *a.* of, happening at or near, an equinox. **2** *n.* = *celestial equator*. **3 equinoctial line** = *celestial equator*. [F or L (foll.)]
equinox /ˈi:kwɪnɒks, ˈe-/ *n.* time or date at which sun crosses equator and day and night are equal; **autumn equinox** that about 22 Sept.; **spring** (or **vernal**) **equinox** that about 20 Mar. [F f. L (*nox* night)]
equip /ɪˈkwɪp/ *v.t.* (**-pp-**) supply with what is needed. [F f. ON, rel. to SHIP]
equipage /ˈekwɪpɪdʒ/ *n.* requisites, outfit; carriage and horses with attendants. [F (prec.)]
equipment /ɪˈkwɪpmənt/ *n.* equipping; necessary outfit, tools, apparatus, etc. [F (EQUIP)]
equipoise /ˈekwɪpɔɪz, ˈi:k-/ *n.* equilibrium; counterbalancing thing. [EQUI-]
equitable /ˈekwɪtəb(ə)l/ *a.* fair, just; valid in equity rather than law; **equitably** *adv.* [F (EQUITY)]
equitation /ekwɪˈteɪʃ(ə)n/ *n.* riding on horse; horsemanship. [F or L (*equito* ride horse)]
equity /ˈekwɪtɪ/ *n.* fairness; principles of justice as supplementing law; value of shares issued by a company; (in *pl.*) stocks and shares not bearing fixed interest. [F f. L *aequitas* (EQUAL)]
equivalent /ɪˈkwɪvələnt/ **1** *a.* equal in

value, amount, importance, etc.; corresponding; meaning the same; having the same result. **2** *n.* equivalent thing, amount, etc. **3 equivalence** *n.* [F f. L (VALUE)]

equivocal /ɪ'kwɪvək(ə)l/ *a.* of double or doubtful meaning; of uncertain nature; questionable, dubious; **equivocally** *adv.* [L (*voco* call)]

equivocate /ɪ'kwɪvəkeɪt/ *v.i.* use equivocal terms to conceal truth; **equivocation** /-'keɪʃ(ə)n/ *n.*; **equivocator** *n.* [L (prec.)]

er /ɜ:, ə, etc./ *int.* expressing hesitation. [imit.]

-er[1] *suffix* forming nouns from nouns, adjectives, and verbs, in senses 'person, animal, or thing that does' (*maker*, *pointer*, *computer*), 'person or thing that has or is' (*three-decker*, *foreigner*), 'person concerned with' (*hatter*, *geographer*), 'person from' (*Londoner*, *villager*); also in slang distortion of word (*rugger*, *soccer*). [OE]

-er[2] *suffix* forming comparative of adjectives and adverbs (*wider*, *nicer*, *sooner*, *happier*). [OE]

ER *abbr.* Queen Elizabeth [L *Elizabetha Regina*]; King Edward [L *Edwardus Rex*].

Er *symb.* erbium.

era /'ɪərə/ *n.* system of chronology starting from noteworthy event (*Christian era*); historical or other period, date beginning this; major division of geological time. [L, = number (pl. of *aes* money)]

eradicate /ɪ'rædɪkeɪt/ *v.t.* root out, destroy completely; **eradicable** *a.*; **eradication** /-'keɪʃ(ə)n/ *n.*; **eradicator** *n.* [L (*radix -icis* root)]

erase /ɪ'reɪz/ *v.t.* rub out; obliterate, remove all traces of; remove recording from (magnetic tape). [L (*rado ras-* scrape)]

eraser *n.* thing that erases, esp. piece of rubber etc. for removing pencil marks.

erasure /ɪ'reɪʒə/ *n.* erasing; erased word etc.

erbium /'ɜ:bɪəm/ *n.* metallic element of lanthanide series. [*Ytterby* in Sweden]

ere /eə/ *prep.* & *conj.* (*archaic* or *poetic*) before (*ere noon*; *ere he went*). [OE]

erect /ɪ'rekt/ **1** *a.* upright, vertical; (of hair) bristling; (of penis etc.) enlarged and rigid from sexual excitement. **2** *v.t.* raise, set upright, build; establish (*erect a theory*). **3 erection** *n.* [L (*erigo erect-* set up)]

erectile *a.* that can become erect (esp. of body tissue by sexual excitement). [F (prec.)]

erg *n.* unit of work or energy. [Gk *ergon* work]

ergo /'ɜ:gəʊ/ *adv.* therefore. [L]

ergonomics /ɜ:gə'nɒmɪks/ *n.* study of efficiency of persons in their working environment. [Gk *ergon* work]

ergot /'ɜ:gət/ *n.* disease of rye etc. caused by fungus; drug prepared from the fungus. [F]

Erin /'ɪərɪn/ *n.* ancient or poetic name for Ireland. [Ir.]

ermine /'ɜ:mɪn/ *n.* animal of weasel family with brown fur turning white in winter; its white fur, used in robes of judges, peers, etc. [F]

erne /ɜ:n/, *US* **ern** *n.* sea eagle. [OE]

Ernie /'ɜ:nɪ/ *n.* device for drawing prize-winning numbers of Premium Bonds. [*e*lectronic *r*andom *n*umber *i*ndicator *e*quipment]

erode /ɪ'rəʊd/ *v.t.* wear away or destroy gradually; **erosion** *n.*; **erosive** *a.* [F or L (*rodo ros-* gnaw)]

erogenous /ɪ'rɒdʒɪnəs/ *a.* (esp. of areas of the body) causing sexual excitement. [Gk (foll.), -GENOUS]

erotic /ɪ'rɒtɪk/ *a.* of or causing sexual excitement or desire; **erotically** *adv.* [F f. Gk (*erōs* love)]

erotica /ɪ'rɒtɪkə/ *n.pl.* erotic literature or art.

eroticism /ɪ'rɒtɪsɪz(ə)m/ *n.* erotic character, sexual excitement.

err /ɜ:/ *v.i.* be mistaken or incorrect; do wrong, sin. [F f. L (*erro* stray, wander)]

errand /'erənd/ *n.* short journey for taking message, collecting goods, etc.; object of journey; **errand of mercy** journey to relieve distress etc. [OE]

errant /'erənt/ *a.* erring; travelling in search of adventure (*knight errant*); **errantry** *n.* (in 2nd sense). [ERR; in 2nd sense ult. f. L (*iter* journey)]

erratic /ɪ'rætɪk/ *a.* uncertain in movement; irregular in conduct or opinion etc.; **erratic block** large rock brought from a distance by glacier; **erratically** *adv.* [F f. L (ERR)]

erratum /e'rɑ:təm/ *n.* (*pl.* **errata**) error in printing or writing. [L (ERR)]

erroneous /ɪ'rəʊnɪəs/ *a.* incorrect. [F or L (ERR)]

error /'erə/ *n.* mistake; condition of being wrong in opinion or conduct (*led her into error*); wrong opinion; amount of inaccuracy in calculation or measurement. [F f. L (ERR)]

ersatz /'eəzæts/ *a.* & *n.* substitute; imitation. [G]

Erse /ɜ:s/ *a.* & *n.* Irish or Scottish Gaelic. [early Sc. form of *Irish*]

erstwhile /'ɜ:stwaɪl/ **1** *a.* former, previous. **2** *adv. archaic* formerly. [OE superl. (ERE), WHILE]

eructation /i:rʌk'teɪʃ(ə)n/ *n.* belching. [L (*ructo* belch)]

erudite /'eru:daɪt/ *a.* learned or showing great learning; **erudition** /-'dɪʃ(ə)n/ *n.* [L *eruditus* instructed (RUDE)]
erupt /ɪ'rʌpt/ *v.i.* break out suddenly or dramatically; (of volcano) shoot out lava etc.; (of rash) appear on skin; **eruption** *n.*; **eruptive** *a.* [L *erumpo erupt-* break out]
-ery, -ry *suffix* forming nouns denoting a class or kind (*greenery, machinery, citizenry*), employment, state or condition (*archery, dentistry, slavery, bravery*); place of work or cultivation or breeding (*brewery, orangery, rookery*), behaviour (*mimicry*), (often *derog.*) all that has to do with (*knavery, popery, tomfoolery*). [F f. L]
erysipelas /erɪ'sɪpɪləs/ *n.* acute inflammation of skin, with deep red coloration. [L f. Gk]
erythrocyte /ɪ'rɪθrəʊsaɪt/ *n.* red blood-corpuscle. [Gk *eruthros* red, -CYTE]
Es *symb.* einsteinium.
escalate /'eskəleɪt/ *v.* increase or develop (usu. rapidly) by stages; (cause to) become more intense; **escalation** /-'leɪʃ(ə)n/ *n.* [foll.]
escalator *n.* staircase with endless chain of steps moving up or down; **escalator clause** clause in contract providing for change in price etc. under certain conditions. [F f. Sp. (SCALE[1])]
escallop /ɪ'skæləp/ *n.* = SCALLOP. [foll.]
escalope /'eskəlɒp/ *n.* slice of boneless meat, esp. from leg of veal. [F, orig. = shell]
escapade /eskə'peɪd/ *n.* piece of daring or reckless adventure. [F f. Prov. or Sp. (foll.)]
escape /ɪ'skeɪp/ **1** *v.* get free of restriction or control, get free *from*; (of gas etc.) leak from container etc.; succeed in avoiding punishment etc.; elude, avoid (punishment, commitment, etc.); elude notice or memory of (*nothing escapes you; the name escapes me*); (of words etc.) issue unawares from (person, lips). **2** *n.* escaping; means or act or fact of escaping; leakage of gas etc.; temporary relief from reality or worry. **3 escape clause** one specifying conditions under which party to contract is free from obligations; **escape velocity** minimum velocity needed to escape from gravitational field of a body. [AF f. Rmc (L *cappa* CAPE[1])]
escapee /eskeɪ'pi:/ *n.* one who has escaped.
escapement *n.* part of watch or clock mechanism connecting and regulating motive power. [F (ESCAPE)]
escapism *n.* tendency to seek distraction or relief from reality; **escapist** *n.* [ESCAPE]
escapology /eskə'pɒlədʒɪ/ *n.* methods and technique of escaping from confinement; **escapologist** *n.*
escarpment /ɪ'skɑ:pmənt/ *n.* long steep slope at edge of plateau etc. [F f. It. (SCARP)]
eschatology /eskə'tɒlədʒɪ/ *n.* doctrine of death and afterlife; **eschatological** /-'lɒdʒɪk(ə)l/ *a.* [Gk *eskhatos* last]
escheat /ɪs'tʃi:t/ *hist.* **1** *n.* lapse of property to government etc. on owner's dying intestate without heirs; property so lapsing. **2** *v.* hand over or revert as an escheat; confiscate. [F f. L (*cado* fall)]
eschew /ɪs'tʃu:/ *v.t.* avoid, abstain from. [F f. Gmc, rel. to SHY[1]]
escort 1 /'eskɔ:t/ *n.* person or group of persons, vehicles, ships, etc., accompanying person or thing for protection or as courtesy; person accompanying another of opposite sex socially. **2** /ɪ'skɔ:t/ *v.t.* act as escort to. [F f. It.]
escritoire /eskrɪ'twɑ:/ *n.* writing-desk with drawers etc. [F f. L SCRIPTORIUM]
escudo /e'skju:dəʊ/ *n.* (*pl.* **escudos**) monetary unit of Portugal. [Sp. & Port., f. L *scutum* shield]
esculent /'eskjʊlənt/ **1** *a.* fit for food. **2** *n.* esculent substance. [L (*esca* food)]
escutcheon /ɪ'skʌtʃ(ə)n/ *n.* shield or emblem bearing coat of arms; **blot on one's escutcheon** stain on one's reputation. [AF f. L *scutum* shield]
Eskimo /'eskɪməʊ/ **1** *n.* (*pl.* **Eskimos** or same) member of people inhabiting Arctic coast of N. America and of E. Siberia; their language. **2** *a.* of the Eskimos or their language. **3 Eskimo dog** dog of powerful breed used by Eskimos to pull sledges etc. [Da. f. F f. Algonquian]
ESN *abbr.* educationally subnormal.
esophagus *US* var. of OESOPHAGUS.
esoteric /i:səʊ'terɪk/ *a.* intelligible only to those with special knowledge. [Gk (*esō* within)]
ESP *abbr.* extra-sensory perception.
espadrille /espə'drɪl/ *n.* light canvas shoe with plaited fibre sole. [F f. Prov. (ESPARTO)]
espalier /ɪ'spælɪə/ *n.* lattice-work along which branches of tree or shrub are trained; tree or shrub so trained. [F f. It.]
esparto /e'spɑ:təʊ/ *n.* coarse grass of Spain and N. Africa, used in paper-making. [Sp. f. L f. Gk *sparton* rope]
especial /ɪ'speʃ(ə)l/ *a.* special, exceptional. [F f. L (SPECIAL)]
especially *adv.* particularly, more than in other cases.
Esperanto /espə'ræntəʊ/ *n.* artificial universal language. [L *spero* hope]
espionage /'espɪənɑ:ʒ/ *n.* spying or use of spies. [F (SPY)]

esplanade /esplə'neɪd/ *n.* level open area, esp. as promenade or separating fortress from town. [F f. Sp. f. L (*planus* level)]

espousal /ɪ'spaʊz(ə)l/ *n.* espousing of cause; (often in *pl.*) betrothal, marriage. [F f. L (foll.)]

espouse /ɪ'spaʊz/ *v.t.* adopt or support (cause); marry, give (woman) in marriage. [F f. L (*spondeo* betroth)]

espresso /e'spresəʊ/ *n.* (*pl.* **espressos**) strong concentrated black coffee made under steam pressure; machine for making this. [It., = pressed out]

esprit /'espri:/ *n.* sprightliness; wit; ***esprit de corps*** /də 'kɔ:/ devotion and loyalty to body by its members. [F (SPIRIT)]

espy /ɪ'spaɪ/ *v.t.* catch sight of. [F (SPY)]

Esq. *abbr.* Esquire.

-esque *suffix* forming adjectives in sense 'after the style of' (*Schumannesque*). [F f. It. f. L *-iscus*]

esquire /ɪ'skwaɪə/ *n.* title added to man's surname when no other title is used, esp. as form of address in letters (usu. **Esquire**); *archaic* = SQUIRE. [F f. L (*scutum* shield)]

-ess *suffix* forming nouns denoting females (*actress, lioness*). [F f. L f. Gk *-issa*]

essay 1 /'eseɪ/ *n.* short prose composition on a subject; attempt. **2** /e'seɪ/ *v.t.* attempt. [F f. L *exigo* weigh; cf. ASSAY]

essayist /'eseɪɪst/ *n.* writer of essays.

essence /'esəns/ *n.* all that makes a thing what it is; indispensable quality or element; extract got by distillation etc.; perfume, scent; **in essence** fundamentally; **of the essence** indispensable. [F f. L (*esse* be)]

essential /ɪ'senʃ(ə)l/ **1** *a.* necessary, indispensable; of or constituting a thing's essence. **2** *n.* indispensable or fundamental element or thing. **3 essential oil** volatile oil with odour characteristic of plant from which it is extracted. **4 essentiality** /-ʃɪ'ælɪtɪ/ *n.*; **essentially** *adv.* [L (ESSENCE)]

-est *suffix* forming superlative of adjectives and adverbs (*widest, nicest, soonest, happiest*). [OE]

establish /ɪ'stæblɪʃ/ *v.t.* set up (system, business, etc.) on permanent basis; settle (person etc. *in* office etc.); cause to be generally accepted, place beyond dispute (custom, fact, etc.); **Established Church** Church recognized by State. [F f. L (STABLE)]

establishment *n.* establishing or being established; organized body permanently maintained (e.g. army, navy, civil service); business firm or public institution; household, staff of servants etc.; Church system established by law; **the Establishment** social group exercising authority or influence and resisting change.

estate /ɪ'steɪt/ *n.* landed property; residential or industrial area with integrated design or purpose; a person's assets and liabilities, esp. at death; property where rubber, tea, grapes, etc., are cultivated; class forming part of body politic and sharing in government; *archaic* state or condition (*holy estate of matrimony*); **estate agent** one whose business is sale or lease of houses and land, steward of estate; **estate car** motor car with interior extended at rear to accommodate passengers and goods; **estate duty** = *death duty*; **the Three Estates** Lords Spiritual, Lords Temporal, Commons. [F f. L (*sto stat-* stand)]

esteem /ɪ'sti:m/ **1** *v.t.* have high regard for, think favourably of; consider to be (*shall esteem it an honour*). **2** *n.* high regard or favour. [F f. L (ESTIMATE)]

ester *n.* chemical compound formed by interaction of an acid and an alcohol. [G]

estimable /'estɪməb(ə)l/ *a.* worthy of esteem. [F f. L (ESTEEM)]

estimate 1 /'estɪmət/ *n.* approximate judgement of number, amount, quality, character, etc.; price quoted for work etc. to be undertaken. **2** /'estɪmeɪt/ *v.t.* form an estimate or opinion of, form estimate *that*; fix by estimate (*at* so much). **3 estimator** *n.* [L *aestimo* fix price of]

estimation /estɪ'meɪʃ(ə)n/ *n.* estimating; judgement of worth. [F or L (prec.)]

estrange /ɪ'streɪndʒ/ *v.t.* cause (person) to turn away in feeling or affection (*from* another); **estrangement** *n.* [F f. L (STRANGE)]

estuary /'estjʊərɪ/ *n.* wide tidal mouth of river. [L (*aestus* tide)]

eta /'i:tə/ *n.* seventh letter of Greek alphabet (Η, η). [Gk]

ETA *abbr.* estimated time of arrival; /'eɪtə/ Basque separatist movement [Basque abbr.].

et al. *abbr.* and others. [L *et alii*]

etc. *abbr.* et cetera.

et cetera /et 'setərə/ and the rest, and so on. [L]

etceteras *n.pl.* extras, sundries.

etch *v.* reproduce (picture etc.) by engraving metal plate with acid, esp. to print copies; engrave (plate) with acid; practise this craft; *fig.* impress deeply (*on*). [Du. *etsen* f. G]

etching *n.* print made from etched plate; art of producing etched prints.

ETD *abbr.* estimated time of departure.

eternal /ɪ'tɜ:n(ə)l/ *a.* existing always, without end or (usu.) beginning; unchanging; constant, too frequent (*eternal arguments*); **the Eternal** God; **eternally** *adv.* [F f. L *aeternus*]

eternity /ɪ'tɜ:nɪtɪ/ *n.* infinite (esp. future) time; endless life after death; being eternal; *colloq.* very long time; **eternity ring** finger-ring with gems set all round it. [F f. L (prec.)]

-eth see -TH.

ethane /'eθeɪn, 'i:θ-/ *n.* a hydrocarbon gas of the paraffin series. [foll.]

ether /'i:θə/ *n.* volatile liquid produced by action of acids on alcohol, used as solvent or anaesthetic; clear sky, upper air; medium formerly assumed to permeate space and transmit electromagnetic radiation. [F or L f. Gk (*aithō* burn)]

ethereal /ɪ'θɪərɪəl/ *a.* light, airy; delicate, esp. in appearance; heavenly; **ethereally** *adv.* [L f. Gk (prec.)]

ethic /'eθɪk/ **1** *n.* set of moral principles (*the Quaker ethic*). **2** *a.* = ETHICAL. [F or L f. Gk (ETHOS)]

ethical *a.* relating to morals, esp. as concerning human conduct; morally correct; (of medicine or drug) not advertised to general public and usu. available only on doctor's prescription; **ethically** *adv.*

ethics *n.pl.* (also treated as *sing.*) science of morals in human conduct; moral principles or code.

ethnic /'eθnɪk/ *a.* of group of mankind having common national or cultural tradition; (of clothes etc.) resembling those of an ethnic group, primitive; **ethnical** *a.*; **ethnically** *adv.* [eccl.L f. Gk (*ethnos* nation)]

ethnology /eθ'nɒlədʒɪ/ *n.* comparative scientific study of human peoples; **ethnological** /-ə'lɒdʒik(ə)l/ *a.*; **ethnologist** *n.* [-LOGY]

ethos /'i:θɒs/ *n.* characteristic spirit or attitudes of a community etc. [Gk *ēthos* character]

ethyl /'eθɪl/ *n.* radical derived from ethane, present in alcohol and ether. [G (ETHER)]

ethylene /'eθɪli:n/ *n.* a hydrocarbon of the olefin series.

etiolate /'i:tɪəʊleɪt/ *v.t.* make (plant) pale by excluding light; give sickly hue to (person); **etiolation** /-'leɪʃ(ə)n/ *n.* [F f. L *stipula* straw]

etiology *US* var. of AETIOLOGY.

etiquette /'etɪket/ *n.* conventional rules of social behaviour or professional conduct. [F (TICKET)]

Etruscan /ɪ'trʌskən/ **1** *a.* of ancient Etruria in Italy. **2** *n.* native of Etruria; its language. [L *Etruscus*]

et seq. *abbr.* (also **et seqq.**) and the following (pages, matter, etc.). [L *et sequentia*]

-ette *suffix* forming nouns denoting smallness (*cigarette, kitchenette*), imitation or substitution (*flannelette, leatherette*), or female status (*suffragette, usherette*). [F]

étude /eɪ'tju:d/ *n.* short musical composition (usu. for one instrument). [F, = study]

etymology /etɪ'mɒlədʒɪ/ *n.* origin and development of a word in form and sense, account of this; study of origins of words; **etymological** /-'lɒdʒɪk(ə)l/ *a.*; **etymologist** *n.* [F f. L f. Gk (*etumos* true)]

eu- *prefix* well, easily. [Gk]

Eu *symb.* europium.

eucalyptus /ju:kə'lɪptəs/ *n.* (also **eucalypt**) tall evergreen tree; oil obtained from it, used as antiseptic etc. [EU-, Gk *kalyptos* covered]

Eucharist /'ju:kərɪst/ *n.* Christian sacrament in which bread and wine are consecrated and consumed; consecrated elements, esp. bread; **Eucharistic** /-'rɪstɪk/ *a.* [F f. eccl.L f. Gk, = thanksgiving]

euchre /'ju:kə/ *n.* American card-game. [orig. unkn.]

eugenic /ju:'dʒenɪk/ *a.* of or concerning eugenics; **eugenically** *adv.* [EU-, Gk *gen-* produce]

eugenics *n.pl.* science of improving the population by control of inherited qualities.

eulogize /'ju:lədʒaɪz/ *v.t.* extol, praise. [foll.]

eulogy /'ju:lədʒɪ/ *n.* speech or writing in praise of person; expression of praise; **eulogistic** /-'dʒɪstɪk/ *a.* [L f. Gk]

eunuch /'ju:nək/ *n.* castrated man, esp. at oriental harem or court. [L f. Gk, = bed-keeper]

euphemism /'ju:fɪmɪz(ə)m/ *n.* use of mild or indirect expression instead of direct or blunt one; such expression (e.g. *touched* for *mad*); **euphemistic** /-'mɪstɪk/ *a.*; **euphemistically** /-'mɪstɪkəlɪ/ *adv.* [Gk (*phēmē* speaking)]

euphonium /ju:'fəʊnɪəm/ *n.* tenor tuba. [foll.]

euphony /'ju:fənɪ/ *n.* pleasantness of sounds, esp. of words; pleasing sound; **euphonious** /-'fəʊnɪəs/ *a.* [F f. L f. Gk (*phōnē* sound)]

euphoria /ju:'fɒrɪə/ *n.* feeling of well-being, esp. one based on over-confidence; **euphoric** *a.* [Gk (*pherō* bear)]

euphuism /'ju:fju:ɪz(ə)m/ *n.* affected or high-flown style of writing; **euphuistic** /-'ɪstɪk/ *a.*; **euphuistically** /-'ɪstɪkəlɪ/ *adv.* [orig. of writing imitating Lyly's *Euphues*]

Eurasian /jʊə'reɪʒ(ə)n/ **1** *a.* of mixed

European and Asian parentage; of Europe and Asia. **2** *n.* Eurasian person. [*Europe, Asia*]

Euratom /jʊər'ætəm/ *n.* European Atomic Energy Community. [abbr.]

eureka /jʊə'ri:kə/ *int.* I have found (it) (announcing discovery etc.). [Gk *heurēka*]

Euro- /'jʊərəʊ/ *in comb.* Europe, European. [abbr.]

Eurocommunism *n.* Communism in countries of W. Europe, independent of Soviet influence.

Eurocrat /'jʊərəʊkræt/ *n.* bureaucrat of European Communities.

Eurodollar *n.* dollar held in bank in Europe etc.

European /jʊərə'pi:ən/ **1** *a.* of or in or extending over Europe. **2** *n.* native or inhabitant of Europe; descendant of such; person interested in Europe as a unity. [F f. L (*Europe*)]

europium /jʊə'rəʊpɪəm/ *n.* metallic element of lanthanide series. [*Europe*]

Eustachian tube /ju:'steɪʃjən/ narrow passage from pharynx to cavity of middle ear. [*Eustachi*, anatomist]

euthanasia /ju:θə'neɪzɪə/ *n.* bringing about of gentle and easy death in case of incurable and painful disease; such death. [Gk (*thanatos* death)]

eV *abbr.* electron-volt(s).

evacuate /ɪ'vækjʊeɪt/ *v.t.* send (people) away from place of danger; empty (place) thus; make empty; (of troops) withdraw from (place); empty (bowels); **evacuation** /-'eɪʃ(ə)n/ *n.* [L (VACUUM)]

evacuee /ɪvækju:'i:/ *n.* person sent away from place of danger. [-EE]

evade /ɪ'veɪd/ *v.t.* avoid or escape from, esp. by guile or trickery; avoid doing or answering directly. [F f. L *evado* escape]

evaluate /ɪ'væljʊeɪt/ *v.t.* find or state the number or amount of; appraise, assess; **evaluation** /-'eɪʃ(ə)n/ *n.* [F (VALUE)]

evanesce /i:və'nes, e-/ *v.i.* fade from sight, disappear. [L (*vanus* empty)]

evanescent *a.* (of impression etc.) quickly fading; **evanescence** *n.*

evangelical /i:væn'dʒelɪk(ə)l/ **1** *a.* of or according to the teaching of the gospel or the Christian religion; of the Protestant school maintaining that doctrine of salvation by faith is essence of gospel. **2** *n.* member of evangelical school. **3** **evangelicalism** *n.*; **evangelically** *adv.* [eccl. L f. Gk (EU-, ANGEL)]

evangelism /ɪ'vændʒəlɪz(ə)m/ *n.* preaching or promulgation of the gospel.

evangelist *a.* writer of one of the four gospels; preacher of the gospel; **evangelistic** /-'lɪstɪk/ *a.*

evangelize *v.t.* preach the gospel to; convert to Christianity; **evangelization** /-'zeɪʃ(ə)n/ *n.*

evaporate /ɪ'væpəreɪt/ *v.* turn into vapour; (cause to) lose moisture as vapour; *fig.* (cause to) be lost or disappear; **evaporated milk** unsweetened milk concentrated by partial evaporation and tinned; **evaporable** *a.*; **evaporation** /-'reɪʃ(ə)n/ *n.* [L (VAPOUR)]

evasion /ɪ'veɪʒ(ə)n/ *n.* evading; evasive answer etc. [F f. L (EVADE)]

evasive /ɪ'veɪsɪv/ *a.* seeking to evade; not direct in answer etc.

eve *n.* evening or day before festival etc. (*Christmas Eve*; *the eve of the funeral*); time just before an event (*on the eve of an election*); *archaic* evening. [= EVEN²]

even¹ /'i:v(ə)n/ **1** *a.* level, smooth; uniform in quality, constant; equal in amount, value, etc., equally balanced; in same plane or line (*with*); equable, calm (*even disposition, temper*); (of number such as 4, 6) integrally divisible by 2, bearing such number (*no parking on even dates*); not involving fractions (*in even dozens*). **2** *v.* (often with *up*) make or become even or equal. **3** *adv.* (*a*) inviting comparison of the negation, assertion, etc., with implied one that is less strong or remarkable: *never even opened* (let alone read) *the letter*; *does he even suspect* (not to say realize) *the danger?*; *ran even faster* (not just as fast as before); (*b*) introducing extreme case: *even you must realize it*; *might even cost £100.* **4** **be** (or **get**) **even with** have one's revenge on; **even chance** equal chance of success or failure; **even-handed** impartial, fair; **even money** (or **evens**) betting odds offering gambler chance of winning the amount he staked; **even now** now as well as previously, at this very moment; **even so** despite some other consideration. **5** **evenness** *n.* [OE]

even² /'i:v(ə)n/ *n. poetic* evening. [OE]

evening /'i:vnɪŋ/ *n.* end of day, esp. from sunset to bedtime (*this evening, tomorrow evening, during the evening*; *evening meal*); decline or last period (of life etc.); **evening dress** formal dress for evening wear; **evening primrose** plant with yellow flowers that open in evening; **evening star** planet, esp. Venus, conspicuous in West after sunset. [OE (prec.)]

evensong *n.* service of evening prayer in Church of England. [EVEN²]

event /ɪ'vent/ *n.* thing that happens or takes place, esp. one of importance; fact of thing occurring; item in (esp. sports) programme; **at all events, in any** (or **either**) **event** whatever happens; **in the event** as it turned out; **in the event**

of ... if ... happens or occurs; **in the event that** if. [L (*venio vent-* come)]
eventful *a.* marked by noteworthy events; **eventfully** *adv.*
eventide /ˈiːvəntaɪd/ *n. archaic* evening. [EVEN²]
eventual /ɪˈventʃʊəl/ *a.* occurring in due course or at last; **eventually** *adv.* [EVENT]
eventuality /ɪventʃʊˈælɪtɪ/ *n.* possible event or result.
eventuate /ɪˈventʃʊeɪt/ *v.i.* result, be the outcome.
ever /ˈevə/ *adv.* at all times, always (*ever hopeful*; *ever after*; *will last for ever*); at any time (*have you ever been to Paris?*; *nothing ever happens*; *as good as ever*); (as emphatic word) in any way, at all (*how ever did you do it?*); in comb. (*ever-present*, *ever-recurring*); **did you ever?** *colloq.* did you ever hear or see the like?; **ever since** throughout period since (then); **ever so** *colloq.* very (*ever so big*), very much (*thanks ever so*); **ever such a** *colloq.* a very (*ever such a nice man*). [OE]
evergreen 1 *a.* retaining green leaves throughout year. **2** *n.* evergreen tree or shrub.
everlasting /evəˈlɑːstɪŋ/ **1** *a.* lasting for ever; lasting a long time; (of flowers) keeping shape and colour when dried. **2** *n.* eternity; everlasting flower.
evermore *adv.* for ever, always.
every /ˈevrɪ/ *a.* each single (*heard every word*; *watched her every movement*); each at specified interval in series (*take every third one*; *comes every four days*); all possible, utmost degree of (*every prospect of success*); **every bit as** *colloq.* quite as; **every now and then** from time to time; **every one** each one; **every other** each second in series (*every other day*); **every so often** at intervals, occasionally. [OE (EVER, EACH)]
everybody *pron.* every person.
everyday *a.* occurring or used every day; ordinary, commonplace.
Everyman *n.* ordinary or typical person. [character in 15th-c. morality play]
everyone *pron.* everybody.
everything *pron.* all things (*everything depends on it*); thing of chief importance (*speed is everything*).
everywhere *adv.* in every place; *colloq.* in many places.
evict /ɪˈvɪkt/ *v.t.* expel (tenant) by legal process; **eviction** *n.* [L *evinco evict-* conquer]
evidence /ˈevɪdəns/ **1** *n.* indication, sign, facts available as proving or supporting notion etc.; *Law* information given personally or drawn from document etc. and tending to prove fact, testimony admissible in court. **2** *v.t.* indicate, be evidence of. **3 in evidence** conspicuous; **King's** (or **Queen's**) **evidence** evidence for the prosecution given by participant in a crime. [F f. L (*video* see)]
evident *a.* obvious, plain, manifest. [F or L (prec.)]
evidential /evɪˈdenʃ(ə)l/ *a.* of or providing evidence. [EVIDENCE]
evil /ˈiːv(ə)l, -ɪl/ **1** *a.* morally bad, wicked; harmful, tending to harm; disagreeable (*an evil temper*). **2** *n.* evil thing; wickedness. **3 evil eye** gaze or stare superstitiously believed to do material harm. **4 evilly** *adv.* [OE]
evildoer *n.* sinner; **evildoing** *n.*
evince /ɪˈvɪns/ *v.t.* indicate or exhibit (quality). [L (EVICT)]
eviscerate /ɪˈvɪsəreɪt/ *v.t.* disembowel; **evisceration** /-ˈreɪʃ(ə)n/ *n.* [L (VISCERA)]
evocative /ɪˈvɒkətɪv/ *a.* tending to evoke (esp. feelings or memories). [foll.]
evoke /ɪˈvəʊk/ *v.t.* inspire or draw forth (memories, response, etc.); **evocation** /evəˈkeɪʃ(ə)n/ *n.* [L (*voco* call)]
evolution /iːvəˈluːʃ(ə)n/ *n.* evolving; origination of species by development from earlier forms; gradual development of phenomenon, organism, etc.; change in disposition of troops or ships; **evolutionary** *a.* [L (*volvo volut-* roll)]
evolutionist *n.* advocate of evolution rather than creation of species.
evolve /ɪˈvɒlv/ *v.* develop gradually by natural process; work out or devise (theory, plan, etc.); unfold, open out; give off (gas, heat, etc.).
ewe /juː/ *n.* female sheep. [OE]
ewer /ˈjuːə/ *n.* water-jug with wide mouth. [AF f. Rmc (L *aqua* water)]
ex¹ *prep.* (of goods) sold from (*ex-works*); outside, without, exclusive of; **ex-directory** not listed in telephone directory at wish of subscriber; **ex dividend** (of stocks and shares) not including next dividend. [L, = out of]
ex² *n. colloq.* former husband or wife. [EX-¹]
ex-¹ *prefix* (**ef-** before *f*; E- before some consonants) forming (1) verbs in sense 'out', 'forth' (*exclude*, *exit*), 'upward' (*extol*), 'thoroughly' (*excruciate*), 'bring into a state' (*exasperate*), (2) nouns from titles of office, status, etc., in sense 'formerly' (*ex-convict*, *ex-president*, *ex-wife*). [L (prec.)]
ex-² *prefix* = 'out' (*exodus*). [Gk]
exacerbate /ekˈsæsəbeɪt/ *v.t.* make (pain, anger, etc.) worse; irritate (person); **exacerbation** /-ˈbeɪʃ(ə)n/ *n.* [L (*acerbus* sour)]
exact /ɪgˈzækt/ **1** *a.* accurate, correct in all details (*exact description*); precise, (of person) tending to precision. **2** *v.t.* demand and enforce payment etc. of;

demand, require urgently, insist on. **3 exact science** one in which absolute precision is possible. [L *exigo exact-* require]

exacting *a.* making great demands, calling for much effort.

exaction /ɪg'zækʃ(ə)n/ *n.* exacting (*of* money etc.), thing exacted; illegal or exorbitant demand, extortion.

exactitude *n.* exactness, precision.

exactly *adv.* accurately, precisely; (said in reply) I quite agree.

exaggerate /ɪg'zædʒəreɪt/ *v.t.* make (thing, or *absol.*) seem larger or greater than it really is, in speech or writing; enlarge or alter beyond normal or due proportions (*spoke with exaggerated politeness*); **exaggeration** /-'reɪʃ(ə)n/ *n.* [L (*agger* heap)]

exalt /ɪg'zɔ:lt/ *v.t.* raise in rank or power etc.; praise highly; make lofty or noble (*exalted aims, style*); **exaltation** /-'teɪʃ(ə)n/ *n.* [L (*altus* high)]

exam /ɪg'zæm/ *n. colloq.* examination (in 2nd sense). [abbr.]

examination /ɪgzæmɪ'neɪʃ(ə)n/ *n.* examining or being examined; testing of proficiency or knowledge by oral or written questions; formal questioning of witness etc. in lawcourt. [F f. L (foll.)]

examine /ɪg'zæmɪn/ *v.t.* inquire into nature or condition etc. of; look closely at; ask questions of, test proficiency of; **examinee** /-'ni:/ *n.* [F f. L (*examen* tongue of balance)]

example /ɪg'zɑ:mp(ə)l/ *n.* thing characteristic of its kind or illustrating general rule; person or thing or conduct worthy of imitation; fact or thing seen as warning to others; problem or exercise designed to illustrate rule; **for example** by way of illustration. [F f. L *exemplum* (EXEMPT)]

exasperate /ɪg'zæspəreɪt, -'zɑ:s-/ *v.t.* irritate intensely; **exasperation** /-'reɪʃ(ə)n/ *n.* [L (*asper* rough)]

ex cathedra /eks kə'θi:drə/ with full authority (esp. of papal pronouncement). [L, = from the chair]

excavate /'ekskəveɪt/ *v.t.* make (hole or channel) by digging, dig out (soil); reveal or extract by digging; **excavation** /-'veɪʃ(ə)n/ *n.*; **excavator** *n.* [L *excavo* (CAVE)]

exceed /ɪk'si:d/ *v.t.* be more or greater than, surpass; go beyond (limit etc.), do more than is warranted by (instructions etc.). [F f. L *excedo -cess-* go beyond]

exceedingly *adv.* very, extremely.

excel /ɪk'sel/ *v.* (-ll-) be superior to; be pre-eminent. [L *excello* be eminent]

excellence /'eksələns/ *n.* great worth or quality. [F or L (prec.)]

Excellency *n.* title used in addressing or referring to certain high officials (*Your, His, etc., Excellency*). [L (EXCEL)]

excellent *a.* extremely good. [F (EXCEL)]

excentric var. (in technical senses) of ECCENTRIC.

except /ɪk'sept/ **1** *v.t.* exclude from general statement or condition etc. **2** *prep.* not including, other than (*all failed except him; is all right except (that) it is too long*). **3** *conj. archaic* unless (*except he be born again*). [L *excipio -cept-* take out]

excepting *prep.* except.

exception /ɪk'sepʃ(ə)n/ *n.* excepting; thing or case excepted or apart, esp. thing not following general rule; **take exception** object (*to*); **with the exception of** except. [F f. L (EXCEPT)]

exceptionable *a.* open to objection.

exceptional *a.* forming an exception, unusual; outstanding; **exceptionally** *adv.*

excerpt 1 /'eksɜ:pt/ *n.* short extract from book, film, etc. **2** /ɪk'sɜ:pt/ *v.t.* take excerpts from. **3 excerption** /-'sɜ:pʃ(ə)n/ *n.* [L (*carpo* pluck)]

excess 1 /ɪk'ses/ *n.* fact of exceeding; amount by which one number or quantity exceeds another; overstepping of limits of moderation, esp. intemperance in eating or drinking; (usu. in *pl.*) outrageous or immoderate behaviour; extreme or improper degree (*in, to, excess*); agreed amount subtracted from any claim to be made under insurance. **2** /'ekses/ *a.* that exceeds a limit or given amount; required as an excess (*excess fare, postage*). **3 excess baggage** (or **luggage**) that exceeding weight-allowance and liable to extra charge; **in excess of** more than. [F f. L (EXCEED)]

excessive /ɪk'sesɪv/ *a.* too much, too great, more than what is normal or necessary.

exchange /ɪks'tʃeɪndʒ/ **1** *n.* act or process of giving one thing and receiving another in its place; giving of money for its equivalent in money of same or another country; central telephone office of district, where connections are effected; place where merchants, brokers, etc., gather to transact business; office where certain information is given, esp. = *employment exchange*; system of settling debts between persons (esp. in different countries) without use of money, by bills of exchange (see BILL[1]). **2** *v.* give or receive (thing) in place of (or *for*) another; give one and receive another of (things or persons; *exchange blows, glances, words*); make an exchange *with* someone else. **3 exchange rate** value of one currency in terms of another; **in exchange** as thing exchanged (*for*). **4 exchangeable** *a.* [F (CHANGE)]

exchequer /ɪks'tʃekə/ *n.* government department in charge of national revenue; royal or national treasury; one's private funds. [F f. med.L *scaccarium* chessboard]
excise[1] /'eksaɪz/ **1** *n.* duty or tax levied on goods produced or sold within the country, and on various licences etc. **2** *v.t.* charge excise on; make (person) pay excise. [Du. *excijs* f. Rmc (L CENSUS tax)]
excise[2] /ɪk'saɪz/ *v.t.* remove by cutting out or away (passage from book, tissue from the body, etc.); **excision** /-'sɪʒ(ə)n/ *n.* [L *excido* cut out]
excitable /ɪk'saɪtəb(ə)l/ *a.* (esp. of person) easily excited; **excitably** *adv.* [foll.]
excite /ɪk'saɪt/ *v.t.* rouse feelings or emotion of (person); bring into play, rouse up (feelings etc.); provoke or bring about (action etc.); stimulate (bodily organ etc.) to activity. [L (*cieo* stir up)]
excitement *n.* thing that excites; excited state of mind.
exciting *a.* arousing great interest or enthusiasm.
exclaim /ɪk'skleɪm/ *v.* cry out, esp. in anger, surprise, pain, etc.; utter or say in this manner. [F or L (CLAIM)]
exclamation /ekskləˈmeɪʃ(ə)n/ *n.* exclaiming; word(s) etc. exclaimed; **exclamation mark** punctuation mark (!) indicating exclamation. [F or L (prec.)]
exclamatory /ɪk'sklæmətərɪ/ *a.* of or serving as an exclamation.
exclude /ɪk'sklu:d/ *v.t.* shut or keep out from place or group or privilege etc.; remove from consideration (*no theory can be excluded*); make impossible, preclude; **exclusion** *n.* [L *excludo -clus-* shut out]
exclusive /ɪk'sklu:sɪv/ *a.* excluding, not inclusive; excluding all others (*exclusive right*); tending to exclude others, esp. socially; (of shops or goods) high-class, catering for the wealthy; (of goods for sale, newspaper article, etc.) not available or appearing elsewhere; **exclusive of** not counting; **exclusivity** /-'sɪvɪtɪ/ *n.* [med.L (prec.)]
excommunicate /ekskə'mju:nɪkeɪt/ **1** *v.t.* deprive (person) of membership and esp. sacraments of Church. **2** /-ət/ *a.* excommunicated. **3** /-ət/ *n.* excommunicated person. **4 excommunication** /-'keɪʃ(ə)n/ *n.* [L (COMMON)]
excoriate /eks'kɔ:rɪeɪt/ *v.t.* remove part of skin of (person) by abrasion etc.; strip off (skin); censure severely; **excoriation** /-'eɪʃ(ə)n/ *n.* [L (*corium* hide)]
excrement /'ekskrɪmənt/ *n.* faeces; **excremental** /-'ment(ə)l/ *a.* [F or L (EXCRETE)]
excrescence /ɪk'skresəns/ *n.* abnormal or morbid outgrowth on body or plant; ugly addition; **excrescent** *a.* [L (*cresco* grow)]
excreta /ek'skri:tə/ *n.pl.* faeces and urine. [L (foll.)]
excrete /ɪk'skri:t/ *v.t.* expel from the body as waste; **excretion** *n.*; **excretory** *a.* [L (*cerno cret-* sift)]
excruciating /ɪk'skru:ʃɪeɪtɪŋ/ *a.* acutely painful; *colloq.* (of humour etc.) shocking, poor. [L *crucio* torment]
exculpate /'ekskʌlpeɪt/ *v.t.* free from blame; clear (person *from* charge); **exculpation** /-'peɪʃ(ə)n/ *n.*; **exculpatory** /-'kʌlpətərɪ/ *a.* [med.L (L *culpa* blame)]
excursion /ɪk'skɜ:ʃ(ə)n/ *n.* short journey or ramble for pleasure and returning to starting-point. [L (*excurro* run out)]
excursive *a.* digressive.
excuse 1/ɪk'skju:z/ *v.t.* try to lessen blame attaching to (act or fault or person committing it), (of fact or circumstance) mitigate or justify thus; overlook or forgive (person or offence); release from an obligation or duty, gain exemption for; allow to leave (*will you excuse me?*). **2** /ɪk'skju:s/ *n.* reason put forward to mitigate or justify offence; apology (*make my excuses*). **3 be excused** be allowed to leave room etc., e.g. to go to the lavatory; **excuse me** polite apology for interrupting or disagreeing etc.; **excuse oneself** ask permission or apologize for leaving. [F f. L (*causa* accusation)]
ex-directory see EX[1].
ex dividend see EX[1].
execrable /'eksɪkrəb(ə)l/ *a.* abominable. [F f. L (foll.)]
execrate /'eksɪkreɪt/ *v.* express loathing for, detest; utter curses; **execration** /-'kreɪʃ(ə)n/ *n.* [L *ex(s)ecror* curse (SACRED)]
executant /ɪg'zekjʊtənt/ *n.* performer, esp. of music. [F (foll.)]
execute /'eksɪkju:t/ *v.t.* carry into effect, perform (plan, duty, etc.); produce (work of art); inflict capital punishment on; make (legal document) valid by signing, sealing, etc. [F f. L (*sequor* follow)]
execution /eksɪ'kju:ʃ(ə)n/ *n.* carrying out, performance; infliction of capital punishment; skill in or manner of performance. [F f. L (prec.)]
executioner *n.* one who carries out death sentence.
executive /ɪg'zekjʊtɪv/ **1** *a.* concerned with executing laws, agreements, etc., or with other administration or management. **2** *n.* person or body having executive authority or in executive position in business organization etc.; the executive branch of government etc. [med.L (EXECUTE)]

executor /ɪg'zekjʊtə/ *n.* person appointed by testator to carry out terms of will; **executorial** /-'tɔ:rɪəl/ *a.*; **executrix** *n. fem.*

exegesis /eksɪ'dʒi:sɪs/ *n.* (*pl.* **exegeses** /-i:z/) explanation, esp. of passage of Scripture; **exegetic** *a.* [Gk (*hēgeomai* lead)]

exemplar /ɪg'zemplə/ *n.* model, type; instance. [F f. L (EXAMPLE)]

exemplary *a.* fit to be imitated, very good; illustrative; serving as warning. [L (EXAMPLE)]

exemplify /ɪg'zemplɪfaɪ/ *v.t.* give or serve as an example of; **exemplification** /-fɪ'keɪʃ(ə)n/ *n.* [med.L (EXAMPLE)]

exempt /ɪg'zempt/ **1** *a.* free from an obligation or liability etc. imposed on others; (with *from*) not liable to. **2** *v.t.* make exempt (*from*). **3 exemption** *n.* [L (*eximo -empt-* take out)]

exequies /'eksɪkwɪz/ *n.pl.* funeral rites. [F f. L *exsequiae* (*exsequor* follow after)]

exercise /'eksəsaɪz/ **1** *n.* activity requiring physical effort, done to improve health, (often in *pl.*) particular bodily task devised for this; use or application (of mental faculty, right, etc.); practice (of virtue or function etc.); (often in *pl.*) military drill or manœvres. **2** *v.t.* use or apply (mental faculty, right, etc.); practise (virtue or function etc.); (cause to) take exercise, give exercise to; perplex, worry. [F f. L (*exerceo* keep busy)]

exert /ɪg'zɜ:t/ *v.t.* bring into use, bring to bear (influence, pressure, etc.); **exert oneself** use efforts or endeavours; **exertion** *n.* [L *exsero exsert-* put forth]

exeunt /'eksɪənt/ *v.i.* (as stage direction) they leave the stage; ***exeunt omnes*** /'ɒmni:z/ all go off. [L (EXIT)]

exfoliate /eks'fəʊlɪeɪt/ *v.i.* come off in scales or layers; (of tree) throw off bark thus; **exfoliation** /-'eɪʃ(ə)n/ *n.* [L (*folium* leaf)]

ex gratia /eks 'greɪʃə/ done or given as a concession, not from (esp. legal) obligation. [L, = from favour]

exhale /eks'heɪl/ *v.* breathe out; give off or be given off in vapour; **exhalation** /-hə'leɪʃ(ə)n/ *n.* [F f. L (*halo* breathe)]

exhaust /ɪg'zɔ:st/ **1** *v.t.* consume or use up the whole of; use up strength or resources of, tire out; empty (vessel etc. *of* contents); draw off (air); study or expound on (subject) completely. **2** *n.* expulsion or exit of steam or waste gases from engine etc.; such gases etc.; pipe or system through which they are expelled. **3 exhaustible** *a.* [L (*haurio haust-* drain)]

exhaustion /ɪg'zɔ:stʃ(ə)n/ *n.* exhausting or being exhausted; complete loss of strength. [L (prec.)]

exhaustive /ɪg'zɔ:stɪv/ *a.* that exhausts a subject; thorough, comprehensive. [EXHAUST]

exhibit /ɪg'zɪbɪt/ **1** *v.t.* show or display, esp. publicly; manifest (quality etc.). **2** *n.* thing exhibited, esp. in exhibition or as evidence in lawcourt. **3 exhibitor** *n.* [L *exhibeo -hibit-*]

exhibition /eksɪ'bɪʃ(ə)n/ *n.* exhibiting or being exhibited; public display of works of art etc.; scholarship, esp. from funds of school or college etc. [F f. L (prec.)]

exhibitioner *n.* student receiving exhibition.

exhibitionism *n.* tendency towards display or extravagant behaviour; perverted mental condition characterized by indecent exposure of genitals; **exhibitionist** *n.*

exhilarate /ɪg'zɪləreɪt/ *v.t.* enliven or gladden; **exhilaration** /-'reɪʃ(ə)n/ *n.* [L (*hilaris* cheerful)]

exhort /ɪg'zɔ:t/ *v.t.* urge or admonish earnestly; **exhortation** /egzɔ:'teɪʃ(ə)n/ *n.*; **exhortative** *a.*; **exhortatory** *a.* [F or L *exhortor* encourage]

exhume /eks'hju:m/ *v.t.* dig up or unearth (esp. buried corpse); **exhumation** /-'meɪʃ(ə)n/ *n.* [F f. L (*humus* ground)]

ex hypothesi /eks haɪ'pɒθəsɪ/ according to the hypothesis proposed. [L]

exigency /'eksɪdʒənsɪ/ *n.* (also **exigence**) urgent need or demand; emergency; **exigent** *a.* [F f. L (*exigo* EXACT)]

exiguous /eg'zɪgjʊəs/ *a.* scanty, small; **exiguity** /-'gju:ɪtɪ/ *n.* [L]

exile /'ekzaɪl, 'eg-/ **1** *n.* being expelled from one's native country; long absence abroad; person in exile. **2** *v.t.* send into exile. [F f. L]

exist /ɪg'zɪst/ *v.i.* have place in reality; (of circumstances etc.) occur, be found; live, sustain life; continue in being. [L *existo*]

existence *n.* fact or manner of existing or living; continuance in life or being; all that exists; **existent** *a.* [F or L (prec.)]

existential /egzɪ'stenʃ(ə)l/ *a.* of or relating to existence; concerned with human experience as viewed by existentialism; **existentially** *adv.* [L (prec.)]

existentialism *n.* philosophical theory emphasizing existence of the individual as free and responsible agent determining his own development; **existentialist** *n.* & *a.*

exit[1] /'eksɪt, 'egz-/ **1** *n.* act or right of going out; passage or door as way out; actor's departure from stage. **2** *v.i.* make one's exit. [L (*exeo exit-* go out)]

exit[2] /'eksɪt, 'egz-/ *v.i.* (as stage direction) he or she leaves the stage (*exit Macbeth*).

exo- *in comb.* external. [Gk *exō* outside]
exocrine /'eksəʊkraɪn, -ɪn/ *a.* (of gland) secreting through duct. [Gk *krinō* sift]
exodus /'eksədəs/ *n.* mass departure; (**Exodus**) that of Israelites from Egypt. [L f. Gk (*hodos* way)]
ex officio /eks ə'fɪʃɪəʊ/ by virtue of one's office; **ex-officio** of position held thus. [L]
exonerate /ɪg'zɒnəreɪt/ *v.t.* free or declare free from blame; **exoneration** /-'reɪʃ(ə)n/ *n.* [L (*onus, oner-* load)]
exorbitant /ɪg'zɔ:bɪtənt/ *a.* (of price or demand etc.) grossly excessive. [L (ORBIT)]
exorcize /'eksɔ:saɪz/ *v.t.* drive out (evil spirit) by invocation etc.; free (person or place) thus; **exorcism** *n.*; **exorcist** *n.* [F f. eccl.L f. Gk (*horkos* oath)]
exordium /ek'sɔ:dɪəm/ *n.* (*pl.* **exordiums**) introductory part of discourse or treatise. [L (*exordior* begin)]
exotic /ɪg'zɒtɪk/ **1** *a.* introduced from abroad, not native; remarkably strange or unusual. **2** *n.* exotic plant etc. **3 exotically** *adv.* [L f. Gk (*exō* outside)]
exotica /ɪg'zɒtɪkə/ *n.pl.* remarkably strange or rare objects.
expand /ɪk'spænd/ *v.* increase in size or bulk or importance; unfold or spread out; express at length (condensed notes, algebraic expression, etc.); be genial or effusive. [L (*pando pans-* spread)]
expanse /ɪk'spæns/ *n.* wide area or extent of land, space, etc.
expansible *a.* that can be expanded.
expansion /ɪk'spænʃ(ə)n/ *n.* expanding; enlargement, increase.
expansionism *n.* advocacy of expansion, esp. in territory; **expansionist** *n.*
expansive /ɪk'pænsɪv/ *a.* able or tending to expand; extensive; (of person etc.) effusive, genial.
expatiate /ɪk'speɪʃɪeɪt/ *v.i.* speak or write at length (*on*); **expatiation** /-'eɪʃ(ə)n/ *n.*; **expatiatory** *a.* [L (*spatium* SPACE)]
expatriate **1** /eks'pætrɪeɪt/ *v.t.* expel, remove *oneself*, from native country. **2** /-ət/ *a.* expatriated. **3** /eks'pætrɪət/ *n.* expatriated person. **4 expatriation** /-'eɪʃ(ə)n/ *n.* [L (*patria* native land)]
expect /ɪk'spekt/ *v.t.* regard as likely, assume as future event or occurrence; look for as due (*I expect co-operation*); *colloq.* think, suppose; **be expecting** *colloq.* be pregnant. [L (*specto* look)]
expectancy *n.* state of expectation; prospect or prospective chance.
expectant *a.* expecting, having expectation; pregnant.
expectation /ekspek'teɪʃ(ə)n/ *n.* looking forward, anticipation; what one expects; probability (*of* event); probable duration (*of* life); (in *pl.*) prospects of inheritance.
expectorant /ek'spektərənt/ **1** *a.* that causes one to expectorate. **2** *n.* expectorant medicine. [foll.]
expectorate /ek'spektəreɪt/ *v.* cough or spit out (phlegm etc.) from chest or lungs; spit; **expectoration** /-'reɪʃ(ə)n/ *n.* [L (*pectus pector-* breast)]
expedient /ɪk'spi:dɪənt/ **1** *a.* advantageous, advisable on practical rather than moral grounds; suitable, appropriate. **2** *n.* means of achieving an end, resource. **3 expedience** *n.*; **expediency** *n.* [foll.]
expedite /'ekspədaɪt/ *v.t.* assist progress of, hasten (action, measure, etc.); accomplish (business) quickly. [L *expedio* (*pes ped-* foot)]
expedition /ekspə'dɪʃ(ə)n/ *n.* journey or voyage for particular purpose, esp. exploration; people or ships etc. undertaking this; promptness, speed. [F f. L (prec.)]
expeditionary *a.* of or used in an expedition.
expeditious /ekspə'dɪʃəs/ *a.* acting or done with speed and efficiency.
expel /ɪk'spel/ *v.t.* (**-ll-**) send or drive out by force; lawfully compel (person) to leave school or country etc. [L (*pello puls-* drive)]
expend /ɪk'spend/ *v.t.* spend or use up (money, time, etc.) [L (*pendo pens-* weigh)]
expendable *a.* that may be sacrificed or dispensed with; not worth preserving.
expenditure /ek'spendɪtʃə/ *n.* expending (esp. of money); amount expended.
expense /ɪk'spens/ *n.* cost incurred; (in *pl.*) costs incurred in doing job etc., reimbursement for these; spending of money, thing on which money is spent; **at the expense of** so as to cause loss or damage or discredit to; **expense account** record of employee's expenses payable by employer. [F f. L *expensa* (EXPEND)]
expensive *a.* costing much, of high price.
experience /ɪk'spɪərɪəns/ **1** *n.* personal observation of or involvement with fact, event, etc.; knowledge or skill based on this; event that affects one (*a trying experience*). **2** *v.t.* have experience of, undergo; feel. [F f. L (*experior -pert-* try)]
experienced *a.* having had much experience; skilled from this (*an experienced driver*).
experiential /ɪkspɪərɪ'enʃ(ə)l/ *a.* involving or based on experience; **experientially** *adv.*
experiment /ɪk'sperɪmənt/ **1** *n.*

procedure tried on the chance of success, or to test hypothesis etc. or demonstrate known fact. **2** /also -ent/ *v.i.* make experiment (*on* or *with*). **3 experimentation** /-'teɪʃ(ə)n/ *n.* [F or L (EXPERIENCE)]

experimental /ɪksperɪ'ment(ə)l/ *a.* of, based on, or using experiment; in the nature of an experiment; **experimentalism** *n.*; **experimentally** *adv.*

expert /'ekspɜ:t/ **1** *a.* highly practised and skilful, or well-informed, in subject. **2** *n.* person expert in subject; *attrib.* of or being an expert (*expert evidence, witness*). [F f. L (EXPERIENCE)]

expertise /ekspɜ:'ti:z/ *n.* expert skill or knowledge or judgement. [F]

expiate /'ekspɪeɪt/ *v.t.* make amends for (wrong); pay the penalty of; **expiable** *a.*; **expiation** /-'eɪʃ(ə)n/ *n.*; **expiatory** *a.* [L *expio* (PIOUS)]

expiratory *a.* of breathing out. [foll.]

expire /ɪk'spaɪə/ *v.* (of period, validity of thing, etc.) come to an end; breathe out (air, or *absol.*); die; **expiration** /ekspɪ'reɪʃ(ə)n/ *n.* [F f. L (*spiro* breathe)]

expiry *n.* ceasing; end of validity of thing.

explain /ɪk'spleɪn/ *v.t.* make clear or intelligible, give meaning of; make known in detail; account for (conduct etc.); **explain away** minimize significance of; **explain oneself** justify one's conduct or attitude etc. [L *explano* (*planus* flat)]

explanation /eksplə'neɪʃ(ə)n/ *n.* explaining; statement or circumstance that explains.

explanatory /ɪk'splænətərɪ/ *a.* serving or intended to explain.

expletive /ɪk'spli:tɪv/ **1** *n.* oath or meaningless exclamation; word used to fill out sentence etc. **2** *a.* serving as expletive. [L (*expleo* fill out)]

explicable /'eksplɪkəb(ə)l, ɪk'splɪk-/ *a.* that can be explained. [foll.]

explicate /'eksplɪkeɪt/ *v.t.* explain or develop (idea etc.); **explication** /-'keɪʃ(ə)n/ *n.* [L *explico -plicit-* unfold]

explicit /ɪk'splɪsɪt/ *a.* expressly stated, not merely implied; stated in detail; definite; outspoken. [F or L (prec.)]

explode /ɪk'spləʊd/ *v.* expand suddenly with loud noise owing to release of internal energy, cause (gas or bomb etc.) to do this; give vent suddenly to emotion or violence; (of population etc.) increase suddenly or rapidly; expose or discredit (theory etc.); (usu. in *p.p.*) show parts of (diagram etc.) in relative positions but somewhat separated. [L *explodo -plos-* hiss off the stage]

exploit 1 /'eksplɔɪt/ *n.* bold or daring feat. **2** /ɪk'splɔɪt/ *v.t.* use or develop for one's own ends, take advantage of. **3 exploitation** /-'teɪʃ(ə)n/ *n.* [F f. L (EXPLICATE)]

explore /ɪk'splɔ:/ *v.t.* travel extensively through (country etc.) in order to learn or discover about it; inquire into; examine by touch; **exploration** /eksplə'reɪʃ(ə)n/ *n.*; **exploratory** /-'splɒr-/ *a.* [F f. L *exploro* search out]

explosion /ɪk'spləʊʒ(ə)n/ *n.* exploding; loud noise due to this; sudden outbreak of feeling etc.; rapid or sudden increase. [L (EXPLODE)]

explosive /ɪk'spləʊsɪv/ **1** *a.* able or tending or likely to explode; likely to cause violent outburst etc., dangerously tense. **2** *n.* explosive substance.

exponent /ɪk'spəʊnənt/ *n.* person who explains or interprets something; person who favours or promotes idea etc.; type or representative; raised symbol beside numeral indicating how many times it is to be multiplied by itself (e.g. $2^3 = 2 \times 2 \times 2$). [L *expono* EXPOUND]

exponential /ekspə'nenʃ(ə)l/ *a.* of or indicated by mathematical exponent; (of increase etc.) more and more rapid.

export /'ekspɔ:t/ **1** /also -'spɔ:t/ *v.t.* send out (goods) for sale in another country. **2** *n.* exporting; exported article; (usu. in *pl.*) amount exported. **3 exportation** /-'teɪʃ(ə)n/ *n.* [L (*porto* carry)]

expose /ɪk'spəʊz/ *v.t.* leave uncovered or unprotected, esp. from weather; reveal, make known or visible; show up (person or act etc.) in true (usu. unfavourable) light; subject *to* (criticism, danger, influence, etc.); allow light to reach (photographic film or plate); *hist.* leave (child) in the open to die; **expose oneself** expose one's body indecently. [F f. L (*pono* put)]

exposé /ek'spəʊzeɪ/ *n.* orderly statement of facts; revealing of discreditable thing. [F]

exposition /ekspə'zɪʃ(ə)n/ *n.* expounding, explanatory account; large public exhibition; *Mus.* part of movement in which themes are presented. [F or L (EXPOUND)]

ex post facto /eks pəʊst 'fæktəʊ/ retrospective(ly). [L, = from what is done afterwards]

expostulate /ɪk'spɒstjʊleɪt/ *v.i.* make reasoned protest, remonstrate; **expostulation** /-'leɪʃ(ə)n/ *n.*; **expostulatory** *a.* [L (POSTULATE)]

exposure /ɪk'spəʊʒə/ *n.* exposing or being exposed; exposing of photographic film or plate, duration of this, part of film exposed for one picture. [EXPOSE]

expound /ɪk'spaʊnd/ *v.t.* set forth in detail; explain, interpret. [F f. L (*pono posit-* place)]

express /ɪk'spres/ 1 *v.t.* represent or make known in words or by gestures, conduct, etc.; squeeze out (juice etc.); send by express service. **2** *a.* definitely stated, explicit; sent or delivered by specially fast service; (of train) travelling at high speed and with few stops. **3** *n.* express train etc.; *US* service for rapid transport of parcels etc. **4** *adv.* at high speed, by express. **5 express oneself** say what one means or thinks. **6 expressible** *a.* [F f. L *exprimo -press-* squeeze out]

expression /ɪk'spreʃ(ə)n/ *n.* expressing; word or phrase expressed; look or facial aspect; showing of feeling in manner of speaking or performing music; representation of feeling in art; symbols in mathematics expressing a quantity. [F (prec.)]

expressionism *n.* style of painting, music, etc., in which artist or writer seeks to express emotional experience rather than impressions of the physical world; **expressionist** *a.* & *n.*

expressive /ɪk'spresɪv/ *a.* serving to express (*words expressive of contempt*); full of expression (*an expressive look*). [F or med.L (EXPRESS)]

expressway *n.* *US* urban motorway. [EXPRESS]

expropriate /eks'prəʊprɪeɪt/ *v.t.* take away (property) from its owner; dispossess (person); **expropriation** /-'eɪʃ(ə)n/ *n.*; **expropriator** *n.* [L (*proprium* property)]

expulsion /ɪk'spʌlʃ(ə)n/ *n.* expelling or being expelled; **expulsive** *a.* [L (EXPEL)]

expunge /ɪk'spʌndʒ/ *v.t.* erase or remove (passage *from* book etc.). [L *expungo* prick out (for deletion)]

expurgate /'ekspɜːgeɪt/ *v.t.* remove (matter thought to be objectionable) from book etc.; remove (such matter); **expurgation** /-'geɪʃ(ə)n/ *n.*; **expurgator** *n.* [L (PURGE)]

exquisite /'ekskwɪzɪt, (D) ek'skwɪzɪt/ **1** *a.* extremely beautiful or delicate; highly sensitive (*exquisite taste*); acute, keen (*exquisite pleasure*). **2** *n.* person of refined (esp. affected) tastes. [L *exquiro -quisit-* seek out]

ex-serviceman /eks'sɜːvɪsmən/ *n.* former member of the armed services. [EX-[1]]

extant /ek'stænt, 'ek-/ *a.* still existing. [L *ex(s)to* exist]

extemporaneous /ekstempə'reɪnɪəs/ *a.* spoken or done without preparation. [EXTEMPORE]

extemporary /ɪk'stempərərɪ/ *a.* extemporaneous.

extempore /ek'stempərɪ/ *a.* & *adv.* without preparation, offhand. [L]

extemporize /ɪk'stempəraɪz/ *v.* speak or utter or perform extempore; **extemporization** /-'zeɪʃ(ə)n/ *n.*

extend /ɪk'stend/ *v.* lengthen in space or time, increase in scope; stretch or lay out at full length; reach or be continuous over certain area; have a certain scope (*permit does not extend to camping*); offer or accord feeling, invitation, etc., *to* person); **extended family** one including relatives living near; **extended-play** (of gramophone record) playing for longer than most singles; **extend oneself** (or **be extended**) be taxed to the utmost. [L *extendo -tens-* (TEND[1])]

extensible /ɪk'stensɪb(ə)l/ *a.* (also **extendible**) that can be extended.

extension /ɪk'stenʃ(ə)n/ *n.* extending or being extended; part enlarging or added on to main structure etc.; additional period of time; subsidiary telephone on same line as main one, its number; extramural instruction by university or college etc.

extensive /ɪk'stensɪv/ *a.* large; far-reaching. [F or L (EXTEND)]

extent /ɪk'stent/ *n.* space over which thing extends; large area; range, scope, or degree. [AF (EXTEND)]

extenuate /ɪk'stenjʊeɪt/ *v.t.* lessen seeming seriousness of (offence or guilt) by partial excuse; **extenuation** /-'eɪʃ(ə)n/ *n.* [L (*tenuis* thin)]

exterior /ɪk'stɪərɪə/ **1** *a.* outer, outward; coming from outside. **2** *n.* exterior part or aspect; outdoor scene in filming. [L]

exterminate /ɪk'stɜːmɪneɪt/ *v.t.* destroy utterly (disease, people, etc.); **extermination** /-'neɪʃ(ə)n/ *n.*; **exterminator** *n.* [L (TERMINAL)]

external /ek'stɜːn(ə)l/ **1** *a.* of or situated on the outside or visible part; coming from the outside or an outside source; of a country's foreign affairs; outside the conscious subject (*the external world*); (of medicine etc.) for use on outside of the body; of students taking examinations of, but not attending, a university. **2** *n.* (in *pl.*) external features or circumstances; non-essentials. **3 externality** /-'nælɪtɪ/ *n.*; **externally** *adv.* [L (*externus* outer)]

externalize *v.t.* give or attribute external existence to; **externalization** /-'zeɪʃ(ə)n/ *n.*

extinct /ɪk'stɪŋkt/ *a.* no longer existing, obsolete; no longer burning, (of volcano) no longer active. [L *ex(s)tinguo -stinct-* quench]

extinction /ɪk'stɪŋkʃ(ə)n/ *n.* making or becoming extinct, dying out.

extinguish /ɪk'stɪŋgwɪʃ/ *v.t.* cause (flame etc.) to die out; terminate, make extinct, destroy; wipe out (debt).

extinguisher *n.* = *fire extinguisher* (see FIRE).
extirpate /'ekstɜ:peɪt/ *v.t.* destroy, root out; **extirpation** /-'peɪʃ(ə)n/ *n.* [L *ex-(s)tirpo* (*stirps* stem of tree)]
extol /ɪk'stəʊl/ *v.t.* (-**ll**-) praise enthusiastically. [L (*tollo* raise)]
extort /ɪk'stɔ:t/ *v.t.* obtain (money, secret, etc.) by force or threats or intimidation etc. [L (*torqueo tort-* twist)]
extortion /ɪk'stɔ:ʃ(ə)n/ *n.* extorting, esp. of money; illegal exaction.
extortionate /ɪk'stɔ:ʃənət/ *a.* exorbitant; given to extortion.
extortioner *n.* one who practises extortion.
extra /'ekstrə/ **1** *a.* additional; more than is usual or necessary or expected. **2** *adv.* more than usually (*extra long*); additionally (*is charged extra*). **3** *n.* extra thing; thing charged extra (*drinks are an extra*); person engaged temporarily for minor part in film etc.; special issue of newspaper etc.; run in cricket not scored from hit with bat. **4 extra cover** fieldsman in cricket on line between cover-point and mid-off but beyond these. [prob. f. EXTRAORDINARY]
extra- *prefix* forming adjectives in sense 'outside', 'beyond the scope of'. [L *extra* outside]
extract 1 /ɪk'strækt/ *v.t.* take out by effort or force (anything firmly rooted); obtain (money, admission, etc.) against person's will; obtain (juice etc.) by pressure, distillation, etc.; derive (pleasure etc. *from*); quote or copy out (passage from book etc.); find (root of number). **2** /'ekstrækt/ *n.* short passage from book etc.; substance got by distillation etc.; concentrated preparation (*malt extract*). [L (*traho tract-* draw)]
extraction /ɪk'strækʃ(ə)n/ *n.* extracting, esp. of tooth; lineage (*of Indian extraction*). [F f. L (prec.)]
extractive /ɪk'stræktɪv/ *a.* of or involving extraction; **extractive industry** one obtaining minerals etc. from the ground. [EXTRACT]
extractor /ɪk'stræktə/ *n.* person or thing that extracts; **extractor fan** ventilating fan in window etc. to remove stale air.
extra-curricular /ekstrəkə'rɪkjʊlə/ *a.* not part of the normal curriculum. [EXTRA-]
extraditable /'ekstrədaɪtəb(ə)l/ *a.* liable to or (of crime) warranting extradition. [foll.]
extradite /'ekstrədaɪt/ *v.t.* hand over (person accused of crime) to State wishing to try him; **extradition** /-'dɪʃ(ə)n/ *n.* [F (TRADITION)]
extramarital /ekstrə'mærɪt(ə)l/ *a.* of sexual relationships outside marriage. [EXTRA-]
extramural /ekstrə'mjʊər(ə)l/ *a.* (of university teaching) additional to normal degree courses.
extraneous /ɪk'streɪnɪəs/ *a.* of external origin; not belonging (*to* matter in hand). [L *extraneus*]
extraordinary /ɪk'strɔ:dɪnərɪ, ekstrə-/ *a.* unusual or remarkable; out of usual course, additional; specially employed (*envoy extraordinary*); unusually great; **extraordinarily** *adv.* [L]
extrapolate /ek'stræpəleɪt/ *v.* estimate from known values, data, etc., (others which lie outside the range of those known); **extrapolation** /-'leɪʃ(ə)n/ *n.* [EXTRA-, INTERPOLATE]
extra-sensory /ekstrə'sensərɪ/ *a.* (of perception) derived by means other than known senses. [EXTRA-]
extra-terrestrial /ekstrətɪ'restrɪəl/ *a.* outside the earth or its atmosphere.
extravagant /ɪk'strævəgənt/ *a.* spending (esp. money) excessively; costing much; passing bounds of reason, absurd; **extravagance** *n.* [L *vagor* wander]
extravaganza /ekstrævə'gænzə/ *n.* fanciful literary, musical, or dramatic composition; spectacular theatrical production. [It.]
extravasate /ek'strævəseɪt/ *v.* force out (blood etc.) from its vessel; (of blood, lava, etc.) flow out; **extravasation** /-'seɪʃ(ə)n/ *n.* [L *vas* vessel]
extreme /ɪk'stri:m/ **1** *a.* reaching a high or the highest degree (*extreme age, danger*); severe, going to great lengths (*extreme measures*); politically far to the left or right; outermost, furthest from centre; utmost; last. **2** *n.* one or other of two things as remote or as different as possible, thing at either end; extreme degree; first or last of a series. **3 extreme unction** last rites in Roman Catholic and Orthodox Churches; **go to extremes** take extreme course of action; **in the extreme** to an extreme degree. [F f. L]
extremely *adv.* in an extreme degree, very.
extremist *n.* one who holds extreme (esp. political) views; **extremism** *n.*
extremity /ɪk'stremɪtɪ/ *n.* extreme point, end; extreme distress or difficulty; (in *pl.*) hands and feet. [F or L (EXTREME)]
extricate /'ekstrɪkeɪt/ *v.t.* free or disentangle (*from* difficulty etc.); **extricable** *a.*; **extrication** /-'keɪʃ(ə)n/ *n.* [L (*tricae* perplexities)]
extrinsic /ek'strɪnsɪk/ *a.* not inherent or intrinsic; extraneous, not belonging

(*to*); **extrinsically** *adv.* [L *extrinsecus* outwardly]

extrovert /'ekstrəvɜ:t/ **1** *a.* (also **extroverted**) directing thoughts and interests to things outside oneself; sociable, unreserved. **2** *n.* extrovert person. **3 extroversion** /-'vɜ:ʃ(ə)n/ *n.* [L *verto* turn]

extrude /ek'stru:d/ *v.t.* thrust or force out; shape (metal, plastics, etc.) by forcing through die; **extrusion** *n.*; **extrusive** *a.* [L *extrudo -trus-* thrust out]

exuberant /ɪg'zju:bərənt/ *a.* lively, effusive, high-spirited; (of plant etc.) prolific, luxuriant; (of health, emotion, etc.) overflowing, abundant; **exuberance** *n.* [F f. L (*uber* fertile)]

exude /ɪg'zju:d/ *v.* ooze out; give out (moisture); emit (smell); show (pleasure etc.) freely; **exudation** /-'deɪʃ(ə)n/ *n.* [L (*sudo* sweat)]

exult /ɪg'zʌlt/ *v.i.* rejoice greatly; **exultation** /-'teɪʃ(ə)n/ *n.* [L *ex(s)ulto* (*salio salt-* leap)]

exultant *a.* exulting, rejoicing.

-ey see -Y².

eye /aɪ/ **1** *n.* organ of sight in man and animals; iris of eye; region round eye (*black eye*); particular visual faculty (*have an eye for perspective*); thing like an eye, e.g. spot on peacock's tail or butterfly's wing, leaf-bud of potato; hole of needle; calm region in centre of hurricane etc. **2** *v.t.* (*partic.* **eyeing**) look at, observe (esp. with curiosity or suspicion). **3 all eyes** watching intently; **all my eye** *sl.* nonsense; **cast** (or **run**) **an eye over** examine quickly; **catch (person's) eye** succeed in attracting person's attention; **close** (or **shut**) **one's eyes to** ignore, disregard; **cry one's eyes out** weep bitterly; **do (person) in the eye** defraud or thwart; **eye for an eye** retaliation in kind; **eye-liner** cosmetic applied as line round eye; **eye-opener** surprising or revealing fact or circumstance; **eye-rhyme** correspondence of words in spelling but not in pronunciation (e.g. *dear* and *pear*); **eye-shade** device to protect eyes from strong light; **eye-shadow** cosmetic applied to skin round eyes; **eye-strain** weariness of eyes; **eye-tooth** canine tooth in upper jaw, below eye; **get one's eye in** become accustomed to prevailing conditions, esp. in sport; **half an eye** the slightest degree of perceptiveness; **have eyes for** be interested in, wish to acquire; **in** (or **through**) **the eyes of** from the point of view of, in the judgement of; **in the public eye** receiving much publicity; **keep an eye on** watch carefully, take care of; **keep an eye open** (or **out**) **for** watch for; **keep one's eyes open** (or *sl.* **peeled** or **skinned**) be watchful; **make eyes at** look at amorously or flirtatiously; **one in the eye** setback or discomfiture (*for* person); **see eye to eye** agree; **set eyes on** catch sight of; **turn a blind eye to** see BLIND; **up to the eyes** deeply engaged or involved *in*; **with an eye to** with a view to; **with one's eyes closed** (or **shut**) easily. [OE]

eyeball *n.* ball of the eye, within lids and socket; **eyeball to eyeball** *colloq.* confronting closely.

eyebath *n.* small cup shaped to fit round eye, for applying lotion to the eye.

eyebright *n.* plant formerly used as remedy for weak eyes.

eyebrow *n.* fringe of hair growing on ridge above eye-socket; **raise an eyebrow** (or **one's eyebrows**) show surprise or disbelief.

eyeful *n.* thing thrown or blown into eye (*eyeful of mud*); *colloq.* thorough look; *colloq.* visually striking person or thing.

eyeglass *n.* lens for defective eye.

eyehole *n.* socket containing eye; hole to look through.

eyelash *n.* any of hairs on edge of eyelid.

eyelet /'aɪlɪt/ *n.* small hole for passing cord or rope through; metal ring strengthening this. [F dimin. (*oil* eye f. L *oculus*)]

eyelid *n.* either of two folds of skin that can be moved together to cover the eye. [EYE]

eyepiece *n.* lens or lenses to which eye is applied at end of microscope, telescope, etc.

eyesight *n.* faculty or power of seeing.

eyesore *n.* thing that offends sight; ugly object etc.

eyewash *n.* lotion for the eye; *sl.* nonsense, insincere talk.

eyewitness *n.* person who can give evidence of incident from personal observation of it.

eyrie /'aɪərɪ, 'ɪərɪ/ *n.* nest of eagle or other bird of prey built high up; house etc. perched high up. [F *aire* lair f. L *agrum* piece of ground]

F

F, f /ef/ *n.* (*pl.* **Fs, F's**) sixth letter; *Mus.* fourth note in diatonic scale of C major.
F *abbr.* Fahrenheit; farad(s); Fellow of; fine (pencil-lead).
f. *abbr.* female; feminine; focal length; folio; following page etc.
f *abbr. Mus.* forte.
F *symb.* fluorine.
fa var. of FAH.
FA *abbr.* Football Association.
fab *a. colloq.* marvellous. [abbr. of FABULOUS]
Fabian /'feɪbɪən/ *a.* cautiously persistent (*Fabian policy*); of society of socialists (**Fabian Society**) aiming at gradual social change. [L (*Fabius*, Roman general)]
fable /'feɪb(ə)l/ *n.* story, esp. supernatural one, not based on fact; short moral tale esp. about animals; legendary tales (*in fable*; *fact and fable*); lie; thing only supposed to exist. [F f. L *fabula* discourse]
fabled *a.* celebrated in fable, legendary.
fabric /'fæbrɪk/ *n.* woven etc. material; walls, floor, and roof of building; structure (*lit.* or *fig.*); thing put together. [F f. L (*faber* metal-worker)]
fabricate /'fæbrɪkeɪt/ *v.t.* construct (esp. product in final shape); invent (story), forge (document); **fabrication** /-'keɪʃ(ə)n/ *n.*; **fabricator** *n.* [L (prec.)]
fabulous /'fæbjʊləs/ *a.* famed in fable, legendary; incredible, absurd; *colloq.* marvellous. [F or L (FABLE)]
façade /fə'sɑːd/ *n.* face or front of building; outward (esp. deceptive) appearance. [F (foll.)]
face **1** *n.* front of head from forehead to chin; expression of facial features; surface of thing, esp. functional surface of tool etc.; upper or forward-facing side, front; dial-plate of clock; composure, esteem (*we have very little face left*); effrontery, nerve; outward appearance, aspect; = TYPEFACE. **2** *v.* look or front towards, be opposite to; meet resolutely, not shrink from; present itself to (*the problem that faces us*); cover surface of (wall etc.) with facing, put facing on (garment etc.). **3 face card** = *court card*; **face-cloth** face-flannel, smooth-surfaced woollen cloth; **face-flannel** cloth for washing one's face; **face-lift** face-lifting, *fig.* procedure to improve appearance of thing; **face-lifting** operation for removing wrinkles by tightening skin of face; **face the music** see MUSIC; **face to face** facing, confronting each other; **face up to** accept (difficulty etc.) bravely; **face value** value printed or stamped on money, *fig.* what thing seems to mean or imply; **have the face** be shameless enough; **in (the) face of** despite; **lose face** be humiliated; **make** (or **pull**) **a face** grimace; **on the face of it** to outward appearances; **put a bold** (or **good**) **face on** accept (difficulty etc.) cheerfully; **save face** preserve esteem, avoid humiliation; **set one's face against** resist determinedly; **show one's face** let oneself be seen; **to person's face** openly in his presence. [F f. L *facies*]
faceless *a.* without identity, purposely not identifiable; lacking character.
facer *n.* sudden unexpected difficulty.
facet /'fæsɪt/ *n.* one aspect of problem etc.; one side of many-sided cut gem etc. [F (FACT)]
facetious /fə'siːʃəs/ *a.* intending or meant to be amusing, esp. inopportunely. [F f. L *facetia* jest]
facia /'feɪʃə/ *n.* instrument panel of motor vehicle; plate over shop-front with name etc. [FASCIA]
facial /'feɪʃ(ə)l/ **1** *a.* of or for the face. **2** *n.* beauty treatment for face. **3 facially** *adv.* [med.L (FACE)]
facile /'fæsaɪl/ *a.* easily achieved but of little value; easy, easily done; working easily, fluent. [F or L (*facio* do)]
facilitate /fə'sɪlɪteɪt/ *v.t.* make easy or less difficult; make (action or result) more easily achieved; **facilitation** /-'teɪʃ(ə)n/ *n.* [F f. It. (prec.)]
facility /fə'sɪlɪtɪ/ *n.* ease, absence of difficulty; fluency, dexterity; (esp. in *pl.*) opportunity or equipment for doing something. [F or L (FACILE)]
facing *n.* layer of material over part of garment etc., for contrast or strength; outer layer covering surface of wall etc. [FACE]
facsimile /fæk'sɪmɪlɪ/ *n.* exact copy of writing, picture, etc. [L, = make like]
fact *n.* thing that is known to be true or to exist; truth, reality; thing assumed as basis for argument (*his facts are disputable*); wrongful act (*before the fact*); **facts and figures** precise details; **facts of life** *colloq.* realities of a situation, knowledge of human sexual functions; **in fact** in reality, in short. [L *factum* (*facio* do)]
faction /'fækʃ(ə)n/ *n.* small group with special aims within larger one, esp. political; **factional** *a.* [F f. L (FACT)]

-faction *suffix* forming nouns of action from verbs in -FY (*petrifaction, satisfaction*). [L (FACT)]

factious /'fækʃəs/ *a.* of a faction, characterized by factions. [F or L (FACTION)]

factitious /fæk'tɪʃəs/ *a.* made for special purpose; artificial. [L (FACT)]

factor /'fæktə/ *n.* circumstance etc. contributing to a result; whole number etc. that when multiplied with another produces a given number; business agent; *Sc.* land-steward; agent, deputy. [F or L FACT)

factorial /fæk'tɔːrɪəl/ **1** *n.* product of a number and all whole numbers below it. **2** *a.* of a factor or factorial.

factorize *v.t.* resolve into factors; **factorization** /-'zeɪʃ(ə)n/ *n.*

factory /'fæktərɪ/ *n.* building(s) in which goods are manufactured; **factory farm** one employing industrial or intensive methods of rearing livestock. [Port. & L]

factotum /fæk'təʊtəm/ *n.* employee doing all kinds of work. [med.L (FACT, TOTAL)]

factual /'fæktjʊəl/ *a.* based on or concerning facts; **factually** *adv.* [FACT]

faculty /'fæk(ə)ltɪ/ *n.* aptitude or ability for particular activity; inherent mental or physical power; department of university teaching particular subject; *US* staff of university or college; authorization, esp. by Church authority. [F f. L (FACILE)]

fad *n.* craze; peculiar notion; **faddish** *a.* [prob. *fiddle-faddle*]

faddy *a.* having arbitrary likes and dislikes, esp. about food; **faddiness** *n.*

fade **1** *v.* (cause to) lose colour, freshness, or strength; disappear gradually; in films etc., bring (sound or picture) gradually *in* or *out* of perception. **2** *n.* action of fading. **3 fade away** (or **out**) become weaker or less distinct; die away; disappear. [F *fade* dull]

faeces /'fiːsiːz/ *n.pl.* waste matter discharged from bowels; **faecal** /'fiːk(ə)l/ *a.* [L]

faff *v.i. colloq.* fuss, dither. [imit.]

fag[1] **1** *v.* (**-gg-**) tire (*out*), exhaust; toil; as junior schoolboy, run errands for senior boy. **2** *n. colloq.* drudgery; *sl.* cigarette; schoolboy who fags. **3 fag-end** cigarette end. [orig. unkn.]

fag[2] *n. US sl.* homosexual. [abbr. of foll.]

faggot /'fægət/, *US* **fagot** *n.* ball or roll of seasoned chopped liver, etc., baked or fried; bundle of sticks, herbs, metal rods, etc.; *sl.* unpleasant woman; *US sl.* homosexual. [F f. It.]

fah /fɑː/ *n. Mus.* fourth note of major scale. [L *famuli*, word arbitrarily taken]

Fahrenheit /'færənhaɪt/ *a.* of scale of temperature on which water freezes at 32° and boils at 212°. [physicist]

faience /'faɪɑ̃s/ *n.* decorated and glazed earthenware and porcelain. [F f. It. (*Faenza* in Italy)]

fail **1** *v.* not succeed (*failed to persuade, in persuading*); be unsuccessful in (examination etc.); adjudge or be unsuccessful in examination etc.; disappoint, let down (*failed me in my need*); neglect, be unable (*failed to appear*); be absent or deficient (*supplies failed; words fail me*); cease functioning, break down (*engine failed*); become bankrupt. **2** *n.* failure in an examination. **3 fail-safe** reverting to safe condition in event of breakdown etc.; **without fail** for certain, whatever happens. [F f. L *fallo* deceive]

failed *a.* unsuccessful (*a failed actor*).

failing **1** *n.* fault, weakness. **2** *prep.* in default of, if not.

failure /'feɪljə/ *n.* failing, non-performance, lack of success; breaking down or ceasing to function (*engine, heart, failure*); running short of supply etc.; unsuccessful person or thing. [AF (FAIL)]

fain *archaic* **1** *predic. a.* willing or obliged (*to do* thing). **2** *adv.* gladly (*would fain*). [OE]

faint **1** *a.* indistinct, pale, dim; weak from hunger, etc.; timid; feeble. **2** *v.i.* lose consciousness, become faint. **3** *n.* act or state of fainting. **4 faint-hearted** cowardly, timid. [F (FEIGN)]

fair[1] **1** *a.* just, equitable, in accordance with rules; blond, light or pale in colour; of (only) moderate quality or amount; (of weather) fine and dry, (of wind) favourable; satisfactory, promising; clean, clear, unblemished (*write a fair copy*); beautiful. **2** *adv.* in a fair manner; exactly, completely. **3 fair and square** exactly, straightforwardly; **fair crack of the whip** fair chance to participate; **fair dos** see DO[2]; **fair game** thing one may reasonably or legitimately pursue etc.; **fair play** equitable conduct or conditions; **the fair sex** women; **fair-weather-friend** friend or ally who is unreliable in difficulties; **in a fair way to** likely to. [OE]

fair[2] *n.* periodical gathering for sale of goods, often with entertainments; = *fun-fair*; exhibition, esp. to promote particular products. [F f. L *feriae* holiday]

fairground *n.* outdoor area where fair is held.

fairing *n.* streamlining structure added to ship or aircraft. [FAIR[1]]

Fair Isle (of jersey etc.) knitted in a characteristic coloured design. [*Fair Isle* in Shetlands]

fairly *adv.* in a fair manner; moderately (*fairly good*); to a noticeable degree (*fairly narrow*). [FAIR[1]]

fairway *n.* navigable channel; part of golf-course between tee and green, kept free of rough grass.

fairy /'feərɪ/ *n.* small imaginary being with magical powers; *sl.* male homosexual; **fairy-cycle** small bicycle for children; **fairy godmother** benefactress; **fairy lights** small coloured lights esp. for outdoor decorations; **fairy ring** ring of darker grass caused by fungi; **fairy story** (or **-tale**) tale about fairies, incredible story, falsehood. [F (FAY, -ERY)]

fairyland /'feərɪlænd/ *n.* home of fairies; enchanted place.

fait accompli /feɪt ə'kɒmpli:/ *n.* thing that has been done and is past arguing against. [F]

faith *n.* complete trust, unquestioning confidence; strong belief, esp. in religious doctrine; religion (*the Christian faith*); things believed; loyalty, trustworthiness; **bad faith** dishonest intention; **faith-cure** (or **-healing** etc.) cure etc. depending on faith rather than treatment; **good faith** sincere intention. [F f. L *fides*]

faithful *a.* showing faith; loyal, trustworthy, constant; accurate (*a faithful account*); **the Faithful** believers in a religion, followers.

faithfully *adv.* in faithful manner; **yours faithfully** formula for ending business or formal letter.

faithless *a.* false, unreliable, disloyal; without religious faith.

fake 1 *n.* thing or person that is not genuine. 2 *a.* counterfeit, not genuine. 3 *v.t.* make (false thing) so that it appears genuine; feign. [G *fegen* sweep]

fakir /'feɪkɪə/ *n.* Muslim or Hindu religious mendicant or ascetic. [Arab., = poor man]

falchion /'fɔ:ltʃ(ə)n/ *n.* broad curved sword. [F f. L *falx* sickle]

falcon /'fɔ:lkən/ *n.* small hawk trained to hunt game-birds for sport. [F f. L *falco*]

falconry *n.* breeding and training of hawks.

fall /fɔ:l/ 1 *v.i.* (*past* **fell;** *p.p.* **fallen**) go or come down freely, descend; cease to stand, come suddenly to the ground from loss of balance etc.; become detached and descend, slope or hang down; become lower, subside (*the wind fell; prices will fall*); lose status or position (*fall from grace*); yield to temptation; succumb (*to*); be overthrown or vanquished, perish; (of face) show dismay or disappointment; take or have a particular direction or place (*accent falls on first syllable; friends fell behind*); occur (*Easter falls early this year*); come by chance or duty (*it falls to me to answer*); pass *in* or *into* a specified condition (*fall in love, into error, into a rage*); become (*fall a prey, victim, to; fall asleep, due, ill*); (of river) discharge *into*. 2 *n.* act or manner of falling; amount of fall, amount that falls; succumbing to temptation; overthrow (*the fall of Rome*); (esp. in *pl.*) waterfall; wrestling-bout, throw in this; *US* autumn. 3 **the Fall (of man)** Adam's sin and its results; **fall about** be helpless, esp. with laughter; **fall away** become few or thin, desert, vanish; **fall back** retreat; **fall back on** have recourse to in extremity; **fall down (on)** fail (in); **fall flat** be a failure, fail to win applause; **fall for** *colloq.* be captivated or deceived by; **fall foul of** collide or quarrel with; **fall guy** *sl.* easy victim, scapegoat; **fall in** (cause to) take one's place in military formation, (of building etc.) collapse; **fall into** take one's place in, begin (conversation *with*), be caught in (trap etc.); **fall in with** meet (by chance), agree or coincide with; **fall off** decrease, deteriorate; **fall on** (or **upon**) assault, meet; **fall on one's feet** get out of a difficulty successfully; **fall out** quarrel, result, occur, (cause) to leave one's place in military formation; **fall-out** *n.* radioactive debris in the air, from nuclear explosion; **fall over** stumble and come to the ground; **fall over backwards** see BACKWARDS; **fall over oneself** *colloq.* be eager or hasty, be very confused; **fall short** be deficient or inadequate; **fall short of** fail to reach or obtain; **fall through** fail, (of plan etc.) come to nothing; **fall to** begin (*they fell to work*); **fall to the ground** (of plan etc.) be abandoned, fail; **fall under** be classed among, be subjected to (scrutiny etc.). [OE]

fallacy /'fæləsɪ/ *n.* mistaken belief; faulty reasoning or misleading argument; tendency to mislead or delude; **fallacious** /fə'leɪʃəs/ *a.* [L (*fallo* deceive)]

fallible /'fælɪb(ə)l/ *a.* capable of making mistakes; **fallibility** /-'bɪlɪtɪ/ *n.*; **fallibly** *adv.* [med.L (prec.)]

Fallopian tube /fə'ləʊpɪən/ either of two tubes along which egg-cells travel from ovaries to womb. [*Fallopius*, anatomist]

fallow[1] /'fæləʊ/ 1 *a.* (of land) ploughed but left unsown; uncultivated. 2 *n.* fallow land. [OE]

fallow[2] /'fæləʊ/ *a.* of pale brownish or reddish yellow; **fallow deer** species smaller than red deer. [OE]

false /fɔ:ls, fɒls/ *a.* wrong, incorrect;

deceitful, treacherous, unfaithful *to*; deceptive; spurious, sham, artificial; improperly so called (*false acacia*); **false alarm** alarm needlessly given; **false pretences** misrepresentation(s) made with intent to deceive. [OE & F f. L *falsus* (FAIL)]

falsehood *n.* untrue thing; lie, lying.

falsetto /fɔːl'setəʊ, fɒl-/ *n.* (*pl.* **falsettos**) artificial voice above normal range, esp. by male tenor. [It. dimin. (FALSE)]

falsies /'fɔːlsɪz, 'fɒl-/ *n.pl. colloq.* pads etc. to make breasts seem larger. [FALSE]

falsify /'fɔːlsɪfaɪ, 'fɒl-/ *v.t.* fraudulently alter; misrepresent (facts etc.); **falsification** /-fɪ'keɪʃ(ə)n/ *n.* [F or med.L (FALSE)]

falsity *n.* being false. [FALSE]

falter /'fɔːltə/ *v.* stumble; move or function unsteadily; say or speak hesitatingly; lose strength. [orig. uncert.]

fame *n.* renown; state of being famous; *archaic* reputation. [F f. L *fama*]

famed *a.* famous, much spoken of (*for* good food etc.).

familial /fə'mɪlɪəl/ *a.* of or relating to a family or its members. [F f. L (FAMILY)]

familiar /fə'mɪlɪə/ **1** *a.* well acquainted *with*; well known (*to*); often encountered or experienced; informal, esp. excessively so. **2** *n.* intimate friend or spirit. **3** **familiar spirit** demon serving witch etc. **4** **familiarity** /-'ærɪtɪ/ *n.* [F f. L (FAMILY)]

familiarize *v.t.* make (person or oneself) familiar (*with* fact etc.); make well known; **familiarization** /-'zeɪʃ(ə)n/ *n.*

family /'fæmɪlɪ/ *n.* set of parents and children or of relatives; person's children; members of household; all descendants of one lineage; group of kindred peoples, related objects; group of allied genera of animals or plants; **family allowance** allowance paid by State etc. to parent of family, now replaced by *child benefit*; **family man** husband and father, domestic man; **family name** surname (esp. used as Christian name); **family planning** birth-control; **family tree** genealogical chart; **in the family way** *colloq.* pregnant. [L *familia*]

famine /'fæmɪn/ *n.* extreme scarcity, esp. of food. [F (*faim* f. L *fames* hunger)]

famish /'fæmɪʃ/ *v.* reduce or be reduced to extreme hunger; **be famished** (or **famishing**) *colloq.* be very hungry. [F f. Rmc (prec.)]

famous /'feɪməs/ *a.* well known, celebrated; *colloq.* excellent. [F f. L (FAME)]

fan[1] **1** *n.* mechanical apparatus with rotating blades for ventilation; device (usu. folding and sector-shaped when spread out) waved in hand to cool face etc.; anything spread out in this shape. **2** *v.* (**-nn-**) cool or kindle by agitating air around; blow gently upon; spread (*out*) in fan shape. **3** **fan belt** belt transmitting torque from motor-vehicle engine to fan which cools radiator; **fan-jet** = TURBOFAN; **fan tracery** (or **vaulting**) ornamental vaulting with fanlike ribs. [OE f. L *vannus* winnowing basket]

fan[2] *n.* devotee of specified amusement, performer, etc. (*football fan*); **fan club** one organized for a celebrity's admirers; **fan mail** letters to celebrity from fans. [abbr. of foll.]

fanatic /fə'nætɪk/ **1** *n.* person filled with excessive and often misguided enthusiasm for something. **2** *a.* excessively enthusiastic. **3** **fanatical** *a.*; **fanatically** *adv.*; **fanaticism** /-siz(ə)m/ *n.* [F or L (*fanum* temple)]

fancier /'fænsɪə/ *n.* connoisseur (*dog-fancier*). [FANCY]

fanciful /'fænsɪfʊl/ *a.* existing only in imagination or fancy; indulging in fancy; **fancifully** *adv.*

fancy /'fænsɪ/ **1** *n.* faculty of imagination; mental image; supposition; caprice; liking or whim (*passing fancy*). **2** *a.* elaborate, ornamental; unusual. **3** *v.t.* imagine; *colloq.* feel desire for (*fancy a doughnut*); *colloq.* find sexually attractive; *colloq.* have unduly high opinion of (*oneself*, one's ability, etc.); be inclined to think (*that*). **4** **fancy dress** costume for masquerading as different person etc. at party etc.; **fancy-free** not in love; **fancy man** *sl.* woman's lover, pimp; **fancy that!** (or **just fancy!**) how strange!; **fancy woman** *sl.* mistress. [contr. of FANTASY]

fandango /fæn'dæŋgəʊ/ *n.* (*pl.* **fandangoes**) lively Spanish dance, music for this. [Sp.]

fanfare /'fænfeə/ *n.* short showy or ceremonious sounding of trumpets etc. [F]

fang *n.* canine tooth, esp. of dog or wolf; serpent's venom-tooth; root of tooth or its prong. [OE]

fanlight *n.* small (orig. semi-circular) window over door or other window. [FAN[1]]

fanny /'fænɪ/ *n. sl.* female genitals; *US sl.* buttocks. [orig. unkn.]

fantail *n.* pigeon with fan-shaped tail. [FAN[1]]

fantasia /fæntə'zɪə, -'teɪzɪə/ *n.* musical or other composition in which form is subordinate to imagination, or which is based on familiar tunes. [It. (FANTASY)]

fantasize /'fæntəsaɪz/ *v.* imagine, create fantasy (about); day-dream. [FANTASY]

fantastic /fæn'tæstɪk/ extravagantly fanciful, fabulous; grotesque, quaint; *colloq*. excellent, extraordinary; **fantastically** *adv*. [F f. L f. Gk (foll.)]

fantasy /'fæntəsɪ/ *n*. imagination, esp. when extravagant; mental image, daydream; fanciful invention or composition, book or film etc. relating fanciful events. [F f. L f. Gk *phantasia* appearance]

far (*compar*. FURTHER, FARTHER; *superl*. FURTHEST, FARTHEST) **1** *adv*. at or to or by a great distance (*far away*, *off*, *out*); a long way (off) in space or time (*are you travelling far?*; *talked far into the night*); to a great extent or degree, by much (*far better*; *far too early*). **2** *a*. distant, remote (*a far country*); more distant (*the far end of the room*). **3 as far as** right to (a place), to the extent that; **by far** by a great amount; **far and away** by far; **far and wide** over a large area; **far-away** remote, (of look) dreamy, (of voice) sounding as if from distance; **a far cry** a long way; **Far East** China, Japan, and other countries of E. Asia; **far-fetched** (of explanation etc.) strained, unconvincing; **far-flung** extending far; **far from** very different from being, tending to the opposite of (*problem is far from easy*); **far gone** advanced in time, in advanced state of illness etc.; **far-off** remote; **far-out** distant, avant-garde, excellent; **far-reaching** of wide application or influence; **far-seeing** showing foresight, prudent; **far-sighted** far-seeing, seeing distant things most clearly; **go far** achieve much, be of great use, be successful in career etc.; **go too far** go beyond limits of reason, politeness, etc.; **in so far as** to the extent that; **so far** to such an extent, to this point, until now; **so far as** as far as, in so far as. [OE]

farad /'færəd/ *n*. fundamental unit of capacitance. [*Faraday*, physicist]

farce *n*. comedy based on ludicrously improbable events; this genre of theatre; absurdly futile proceedings or pretence; **farcical** *a*.; **farcically** *adv*. [F f. L *farcio* to stuff, used with ref. to interludes etc.]

fare 1 *n*. price charged to passenger on public transport; fare-paying passenger; food provided. **2** *v*. progress, get on (*how did he fare?*). **3 fare-stage** section of bus etc. route for which a fixed fare is charged, stop marking this. [OE]

farewell /feə'wel/ **1** *int*. goodbye! **2** *n*. leave-taking.

farina /fə'raɪnə, -'ri:nə/ *n*. flour or meal of corn, nuts, or starchy roots. [L]

farinaceous /færɪ'neɪʃəs/ *a*. of or like farina, starchy.

farm 1 *n*. area of land and its buildings used under one management for growing crops, rearing animals, etc.; any place for breeding animals (*trout-farm*, *mink-farm*); farmhouse. **2** *v*. use (land) for growing crops, rearing animals, etc.; breed (fish etc.) commercially; work as farmer; take proceeds of (tax) on payment of fixed sum. **3 farm-hand** worker on farm; **farm out** delegate (work) to others. [F *ferme* f. L *firma* fixed payment]

farmer *n*. owner or manager of farm.

farmhouse *n*. dwelling-place attached to farm.

farmost *a*. furthest. [FAR]

farmstead /'fɑ:msted/ *n*. farm and its buildings.

farmyard *n*. yard of farmhouse.

faro /'feərəʊ/ *n*. gambling card-game. [F *pharaon* PHARAOH]

farrago /fə'rɑ:gəʊ/ *n*. (*pl*. **farragos,** *US* **farragoes**) hotchpotch, medley. [L, = mixed fodder (*far* corn)]

farrier /'færɪə/ *n*. smith who shoes horses; **farriery** *n*. [F f. L (*ferrum* iron, horseshoe)]

farrow /'færəʊ/ **1** *v*. (of sow) give birth, give birth to (pigs). **2** *n*. farrowing; litter of pigs. [OE]

Farsi /'fɑ:sɪ/ *n*. the Persian language. [Pers.]

fart *vulgar* **1** *v*. emit wind from anus; *sl*. fool *about* or *around*. **2** *n*. emission of wind from anus; *sl*. contemptible person. [OE]

farther /'fɑ:ðə/ var. of FURTHER.

farthest /'fɑ:ðɪst/ var. of FURTHEST.

farthing /'fɑ:ðɪŋ/ *n*. *hist*. quarter of penny, coin of this value. [OE (FOURTH)]

farthingale /'fɑ:ðɪŋgeɪl/ *n*. *hist*. hooped petticoat. [F f. Sp. (*verdugo* rod)]

fasces /'fæsi:z/ *n*. bundle of rods with projecting axe-blade carried before Roman magistrate; symbol of authority. [L, pl. of *fascis* bundle]

fascia /'feɪʃə/ *n*. *Archit*. long flat surface of wood or stone; stripe, band; = FACIA. [L, = band, door-frame]

fascicle /'fæsɪk(ə)l/ *n*. instalment of book. [L dimin. (FASCES)]

fascinate /'fæsɪneɪt/ *v.t.* capture interest of; charm irresistibly; (of snake etc.) paralyse (victim) with fear; **fascination** /-'neɪʃ(ə)n/ *n*. [L (*fascinum* spell)]

Fascism /'fæʃɪz(ə)m/ *n*. extreme right-wing totalitarian political system or views, as orig. prevailing in Italy (1922–43); **Fascist** *n*. & *a*. [It. (*fascio* bundle, organized group)]

fashion /'fæʃ(ə)n/ **1** *n*. current popular custom or style, esp. in dress; manner of doing something. **2** *v.t.* form or make (*into*). **3 after a fashion** to some extent, barely adequately; **in fashion** fashionable at the present time; **out of fashion**

no longer fashionable. [F f. L *factio* (FACT)]

fashionable *a.* following or in keeping with current fashion; characteristic of or patronized by fashionable people; **fashionably** *adv.*

fast[1] /fɑ:st/ **1** *a.* rapid, quick-moving; capable of high speed (*a fast car*), enabling or causing quick motion (*a fast road*); (of clock etc.) showing time later than correct time; firm, fixed, firmly attached; (of colour) not fading when washed etc.; (of photographic film) needing only short exposure; (of person) immoral, dissipated; (of friend) close. **2** *adv.* quickly, in quick succession; firmly, tightly. **3 fast breeder (reactor)** reactor using mainly fast neutrons; **fast neutron** neutron with high kinetic energy; **fast one** *sl.* unfair or deceitful action. [OE]

fast[2] /fɑ:st/ **1** *v.i.* abstain from food or certain food, esp. as religious observance. **2** *n.* fasting; period of fasting. [OE]

fasten /'fɑ:s(ə)n/ *v.* secure or attach (one thing *to* another), fix *on*, join or close *up*; become tightly fixed; **fasten on** (or **upon**) seize on (pretext etc.). [OE (FAST[1])]

fastener /'fɑ:snə/ *n.* (also **fastening**) device that fastens something.

fastidious /fæ'stɪdɪəs/ *a.* very careful in matters of choice or taste; easily disgusted, squeamish. [L (*fastidium* loathing)]

fastness /'fɑ:stnɪs/ *n.* stronghold. [OE]

fat 1 *a.* very plump; well-fed; containing much fat; thick (*a fat book*); fertile. **2** *n.* oily or greasy substance found in animal bodies etc.; fat part of animal. **3** *v.t.* (**-tt-**) fatten. **4 a fat chance** *sl.* very little chance; **fat-head** *colloq.* stupid person; **the fat is in the fire** there will be trouble; **a fat lot** *sl.* very little; **kill the fatted calf** celebrate, esp. at prodigal's return; **live off the fat of the land** live luxuriously. [OE]

fatal /'feɪt(ə)l/ *a.* causing or ending in death (*fatal accident*); ruinous, disastrous, fateful; **fatally** *adv.* [F or L (FATE)]

fatalism *n.* belief that all that happens is predetermined and therefore inevitable; **fatalist** *n.*; **fatalistic** /-'lɪstɪk/ *a.*

fatality /fə'tælɪtɪ/ *n.* death by accident or in war etc.; fatal influence; predestined liability to disaster.

fate 1 *n.* irresistible power or force controlling all events; what is destined; person's destiny or fortune (*unhappy fate*); death, destruction. **2** *v.t.* (esp. in *pass.*) preordain (*was fated to win*). [It. & L *fatum*]

fateful *a.* controlled by fate; decisive, important; **fatefully** *adv.*

father /'fɑ:ðə/ **1** *n.* male parent; male guardian through adoption; (usu. in *pl.*) forefather; founder or originator, early leader; (in *pl.*) elders, leading members; (**Father**) God, esp. first person of Trinity; priest, esp. of religious order, or as title or form of address; venerable person, esp. as title in personifications (*Father Christmas, Thames, Time*). **2** *v.t.* beget; originate (scheme etc.); fix paternity of (child) or responsibility for (book, idea, etc.) *on* or *upon*. **3 father-figure** older man who is respected like a father, trusted leader; **father-in-law** (*pl.* **fathers-in-law**) one's wife's or husband's father; **Father of the House** member of House of Commons with longest continuous service; **Father's Day** day (usu. third Sunday in June) for special tribute to fathers; **Fathers (of the Church)** early and authoritative Christian writers; **Father Superior** see SUPERIOR. **4 fatherhood** *n.* [OE]

fatherland *n.* one's native country.

fatherly *a.* of or like a father.

fathom /'fæð(ə)m/ **1** *n.* measure of 6 feet, esp. in soundings. **2** *v.t.* comprehend; measure depth of (water). [OE]

fathomless *a.* too deep to fathom; incomprehensible.

fatigue /fə'ti:g/ **1** *n.* extreme tiredness; weakness in metals etc. from variations of stress; soldier's non-combatant duty, (in *pl.*) clothing worn for this. **2** *v.t.* cause fatigue in; tire. [F f. L *fatigo* exhaust]

fatstock *n.* livestock fattened for slaughter. [FAT]

fatten *v.* make or become fat.

fatty *a.* like or containing fat; **fatty acid** member of series of acids occurring in or derived from natural fats etc.

fatuous /'fætjʊəs/ *a.* silly, purposeless; **fatuity** /fə'tju:ɪtɪ/ *n.* [L *fatuus*]

faucet /'fɔ:sɪt/ *n.* tap for barrel etc.; *US* any tap. [F *fausset* vent-peg f. Prov. (*falsar* bore *v.*)]

fault /fɔ:lt, fɒlt/ **1** *n.* defect or blemish (in object, structure, person's character, etc.); offence or misdeed, responsibility or blame for this (*all my fault*); (in tennis etc.) incorrect serve; (in show-jumping) penalty for error; break in continuity of rock strata. **2** *v.* find fault with, blame; cause fault in (rock strata), (of rock) have fault. **3 at fault** blameworthy; **find fault with** criticize unfavourably; **to a fault** excessively (*generous to a fault*). [F f. L *fallo* deceive]

faultless *a.* without fault.

faulty *a.* having fault(s), imperfect; **faultily** *adv.*; **faultiness** *n.*

faun /fɔ:n/ *n.* Latin rural deity with goat's horns, legs, and tail. [F, or L *Faunus*]

fauna /ˈfɔːnə/ *n.* (*pl.* **faunas**) animals of a particular region or period. [L *Fauna*, fem. (prec.)]

faux pas /fəʊ ˈpɑː/ *n.* (*pl.* same /ˈpɑːz/) tactless mistake, blunder. [F = false step]

favour /ˈfeɪvə/, *US* **favor 1** *n.* liking, goodwill, approval; kind or helpful act (*do me a favour*); partiality; badge or ornament worn as mark of favour. **2** *v.t.* regard, treat, with favour or partiality; support, promote, prefer; oblige *with*; be to the advantage of, facilitate; (in *p.p.*) having unusual advantages, having specified attribute (*ill-favoured*). **3 in** (or **out of**) **favour** approved (or disapproved) of; **in favour of** in support of; to the advantage of. [F f. L (*faveo* be kind to)]

favourable /ˈfeɪvərəb(ə)l/, *US* **favorable** *a.* well disposed, approving; pleasing, satisfactory; helpful, suitable; **favourably** *adv.*

favourite /ˈfeɪvərɪt/, *US* **favorite 1** *a.* preferred to all others (*favourite book, colour*). **2** *n.* favourite person or thing, esp. person favoured by monarch or superior; (in sport) competitor thought most likely to win. [F f. It. (FAVOUR)]

favouritism *n.* unfair favouring of one person or group at expense of another.

fawn[1] **1** *n.* deer in its first year; light yellowish-brown colour. **2** *a.* fawn-coloured. **3** *v.* give birth to (fawn). [F f. L (FOETUS)]

fawn[2] *v.i.* (esp. of dog etc.) try to win affection by grovelling etc.; lavish caresses (*on* or *upon*); behave servilely. [OE]

fay *n. literary* fairy. [F f. L *fata pl.* Fates]

FBA *abbr.* Fellow of the British Academy.

FBI *abbr. US* Federal Bureau of Investigation.

Fe *symb.* iron. [L *ferrum*]

fealty /ˈfiːəltɪ/ *n.* duty of feudal tenant or vassal to his lord; allegiance. [F f. L (FIDELITY)]

fear 1 *n.* unpleasant emotion caused by exposure to danger, expectation of pain, etc.; alarm; dread, awe; danger, likelihood (*little fear of failure*). **2** *v.* have fear, expect with fear or anxiety (*they fear to go out; I fear we'll be late*); be afraid of; shrink from (*doing*); revere (God). **3 for fear of** because of the danger of; **no fear** *colloq.* certainly not; **without fear or favour** impartially. [OE]

fearful *a.* afraid, reluctant through fear; causing fear; *colloq.* extreme, annoying; **fearfully** *adv.*

fearless *a.* without fear, brave.

fearsome *a.* frightening, formidable.

feasible /ˈfiːzɪb(ə)l/ *a.* practicable, possible; **feasibility** /-ˈbɪlɪtɪ/ *n.*; **feasibly** *adv.* [F (L *facio* do)]

feast 1 *n.* large meal, banquet; joyful religious festival; something giving great pleasure. **2** *v.* partake of feast, eat and drink heartily (*on*); give feast to; give pleasure to, regale (*feast one's eyes on*). [F f. L (*festus* joy)]

feat *n.* remarkable act or achievement. [F f. L (FACT)]

feather /ˈfeðə/ **1** *n.* any of the appendages growing from bird's skin, with horny stem and fine strands on both sides, piece of this as decoration etc.; *collect.* plumage; game-birds. **2** *v.* cover or line with feathers; turn (oar) so that it passes through the air edgeways. **3 feather bed** mattress stuffed with feathers; **feather-bed** *v.t.* make things easy for, pamper; **feather-brained** (or **-headed**) stupid; **feather in one's cap** achievement to one's credit; **feather one's nest** enrich oneself; **in fine** (or **high**) **feather** in good spirits. **4 feathery** *a.* [OE]

feathering *n.* plumage; feathers of arrow; feather-like structure or marking.

featherweight *n.* boxing-weight with upper limit of 57 kg.; very light person or thing.

feature /ˈfiːtʃə/ **1** *n.* part of face, esp. with regard to appearance (usu. in *pl.*); characteristic or notable part of thing; prominent article in newspaper etc.; = *feature film*. **2** *v.* give prominence to; be feature of; be participant (*in*). **3 feature film** main film in cinema programme. [F, f. L *factura* formation (FACT)]

featureless *a.* lacking distinct features.

Feb. *abbr.* February.

febrile /ˈfiːbraɪl/ *a.* of fever. [F or L (*febris* fever)]

February /ˈfebrʊərɪ/ *n.* second month of year. [F f. L (*februa* purification feast)]

fecal, feces *US* var. of FAECAL, FAECES.

feckless /ˈfeklɪs/ *a.* feeble, incompetent, helpless. [Sc. feck (*effeck* var. of EFFECT)]

fecund /ˈfiːkənd/ *a.* prolific, fertile; fertilizing; **fecundity** /fɪˈkʌndɪtɪ/ *n.* [F or L]

fecundate /ˈfiːkəndeɪt/ *v.t.* make fecund, fertilize; **fecundation** /-ˈdeɪʃ(ə)n/ *n.*

fed *past* and *p.p.* of FEED.

federal /ˈfedər(ə)l/ *a.* of system of government in which several States unite but remain independent in internal affairs; of such States or their central government; relating to or favouring central as opposed to provincial government; (**Federal**) *US* of Northern States in Civil War; **federalism** *n.*; **federalist**

n.; **federalize** *v.t.*; **federally** *adv.* [L (*foedus* covenant)]

federate 1 /ˈfedəreɪt/ *v.* unite on federal basis or for common object. 2 /ˈfedərət/ *a.* so united.

federation /fedəˈreɪʃ(ə)n/ *n.* act of federating; federal group; **federative** /ˈfedərətɪv/ *a.* [F f. L (FEDERAL)]

fee *n.* sum payable to official or professional person for services; charge for joining society, taking examination, etc.; money paid for transfer to another employer of footballer etc.; (in *pl.*) regular payment for instruction at school etc.; *Law* inherited estate of land, unlimited (**fee simple**) or limited (**fee-tail**) as to class of heir. [AF, = F *feu* etc. f. L *feudum*, perh. f. Gmc]

feeble /ˈfi:b(ə)l/ *a.* weak; lacking strength, energy, or effectiveness; **feeble-minded** mentally deficient; **feebly** *adv.* [F f. L *flebilis* lamentable]

feed 1 *v.* (*past* and *p.p.* **fed**) supply with food, put food into mouth of; give as food to animals; take food, eat (esp. of animals, or *colloq.*); maintain supply of (material required *into* machine etc.), keep (machine, fire, etc.) supplied thus; comfort (person *with* hope etc.); send passes to (player) in football etc. 2 *n.* food for animals, measured allowance of this; feeding; meal (esp. for babies, or *colloq.*); material supplied to machines etc. 3 **fed up** *colloq.* discontented or bored (*with*); **feed on** consume, be nourished or strengthened by. [OE]

feedback *n.* return to input of part of output of system or process; signal so returned; information about result of experiment etc.; response.

feeder *n.* one (esp. animal) that feeds in specified way; feeding apparatus in machine; child's bib; tributary, branch road, railway line, etc., that links with main system.

feel 1 *v.* (*past* and *p.p.* **felt**) examine or search by touch; perceive by touch, have sensation of; be conscious of (emotion etc.); experience, be affected by (emotion or physical condition); seem, give impression of being (*water feels warm*); have vague or emotional impression (*I feel I am right*); consider, think (*I feel it useful*); be consciously, consider oneself (*I feel happy*); sympathize (*with*), have pity (*for*). 2 *n.* act of feeling; sense of touch; sensation characterizing a material, situation, etc. 3 **feel like** *colloq.* have wish for, be inclined towards; **feel up to** be ready for or capable of; **feel one's way** proceed cautiously (*lit.* or *fig.*). [OE]

feeler *n.* organ in certain animals for testing things by touch; tentative proposal or suggestion.

feeling 1 *n.* capacity to feel, sense of touch (*lost feeling in his arm*); emotion (*a feeling of anger*); (in *pl.*) emotional susceptibilities (*hurt my feelings*); opinion or notion (*my feelings on the subject*; *had a feeling she would be there*); sympathy with others; earnestness (*said with feeling*); common attitude (*the feeling of the meeting*). 2 *a.* sensitive, sympathetic; heartfelt. 3 **bad feeling** discontent, resentment.

feet *pl.* of FOOT.

feign /feɪn/ *v.t.* pretend; simulate. [F f. L *fingo fict-* mould, contrive]

feint /feɪnt/ 1 *n.* sham attack, blow, etc. to divert opponent's attention from main attack; pretence. 2 *v.i.* make a feint. 3 *a.* (of paper etc.) having faintly ruled lines. [F (prec.)]

feldspar /ˈfeldspɑ:/ *n.* common white or flesh-red mineral containing aluminium and other silicates; **feldspathic** /-ˈspæθɪk/ *a.* [G (*feld* field, *spat(h)* SPAR²)]

felicitate /fəˈlɪsɪteɪt/ *v.t.* congratulate. [L (*felix* happy)]

felicitation /fəlɪsɪˈteɪʃ(ə)n/ *n.* (usu. in *pl.*) congratulation.

felicitous /fəˈlɪsɪtəs/ *a.* well-chosen, apt. [foll.]

felicity /fəˈlɪsɪtɪ/ *n.* great happiness; pleasing manner or style. [F f. L (*felix* happy)]

feline /ˈfi:laɪn/ 1 *a.* of cats; catlike. 2 *n.* animal of cat family. 3 **felinity** /fɪˈlɪnɪtɪ/ *n.* [L (*feles* cat)]

fell¹ *v.t.* cut down (tree); strike down by blow or cut; stitch down (edge of seam). [OE]

fell² *n.* hill; stretch of hills or moorland, esp. in N. England. [ON]

fell³ *a.* ruthless, destructive; **at one fell swoop** in a single (deadly) action. [F (FELON)]

fell⁴ animal's skin or hide with hair. [OE]

fell⁵ *past* of FALL.

fellatio /feˈlɑ:tɪəʊ/ *n.* stimulation of penis by sucking. [L *fello* suck]

fellow /ˈfeləʊ/ 1 *n.* comrade or associate; counterpart, equal; *colloq.* man or boy; incorporated senior member of college, research student receiving fellowship; member of learned society. 2 *attrib.* or *a.* of same class, associated in joint action (*fellow-citizen*). 3 **fellow-feeling** sympathy with person whose experience etc. one shares; **fellow-traveller** sympathizer with but not member of political (esp. Communist) party. [OE f. ON]

fellowship *n.* friendly association with others, companionship; body of associates; position or income of fellow of college or learned society; stipend granted to graduate for period of research.

felon /'felən/ *n.* one who has committed a felony. [F f. med.L *fello*]

felony *n.* crime regarded by the law as grave; **felonious** /fə'ləʊnɪəs/ *a.*

felspar var. of FELDSPAR.

felt[1] **1** *n.* cloth of matted and pressed fibres of wool etc. **2** *v.* make into felt; cover with felt; become matted. **3 felt (-tip** or **-tipped) pen** pen with felt point. [OE]

felt[2] *past* and *p.p.* of FEEL.

felucca /fɪ'lʌkə/ *n.* small ship with lateen sails and/or oars, used on Mediterranean coasts. [It. f. Sp. f. Arab.]

female /'fi:meɪl/ **1** *a.* of the sex that can bear offspring or produce eggs; (of plants) fruit-bearing; of women or female animals or plants; (of screw, socket, etc.) made hollow to receive corresponding inserted part. **2** *n.* female person, animal, or plant. [F f. L dimin. of *femina* woman, assim. to *male*]

feminine /'femɪnɪn/ **1** *a.* of women; having qualities associated with women; *Gram.* of or denoting gender proper to women's names; (of rhyme or line-ending) having stressed syllable followed by unstressed one. **2** *n.* feminine gender or word. **3 femininity** /-'nɪnɪtɪ/ *n.* [F or L (prec.)]

feminism /'femɪnɪz(ə)m/ *n.* advocacy of women's rights on basis of equality of sexes; **feminist** *n.*

femme fatale /fæm fæ'tɑ:l/ *n.* dangerously attractive woman. [F]

femur /'fi:mə/ *n.* (*pl.* **femurs** or **femora** /'femərə/) thigh-bone; **femoral** /'femər(ə)l/ *a.* [L]

fen *n.* low marshy area of land; **the Fens** low-lying areas in Cambridgeshire etc. [OE]

fence 1 *n.* barrier or railing enclosing field, garden, etc.; structure for horse to jump over in competition etc.; guard or guide or gauge in machine; receiver of stolen goods. **2** *v.* surround (as) with fence; enclose or separate with fence (often with *in*, *off*, etc.); practise sport of fencing; be evasive. [DEFENCE]

fencing *n.* fences, material for fences; sword-fighting, esp. with foils as sport.

fend *v.* ward *off*, repel; provide *for* (esp. *oneself*). [DEFEND]

fender *n.* low frame bordering fireplace to keep in falling coals etc.; pad or bundle of rope etc. hung over vessel's side to protect it against impact; *US* bumper of motor vehicle.

fennel /'fen(ə)l/ *n.* yellow-flowered herb used for flavouring. [OE & F f. L (*fenum* hay)]

fenny *a.* characterized by fens. [FEN]

fenugreek /'fenju:gri:k/ *n.* leguminous plant with aromatic seeds. [F f. L, = Greek hay]

feoff /fef/ *n.* = FIEF. [F var. of FIEF]

feral /'fɪər(ə)l/ *a.* wild; uncultivated; in wild state after escape from captivity; brutal. [L *ferus* wild]

ferial /'fɪərɪəl/ *a.* (of day) not a festival or fast. [F, or L (*feria* FAIR[2])]

ferment 1 /'fɜ:ment/ *n.* fermentation; fermenting agent; excitement. **2** /fə'ment/ *v.* undergo or subject to fermentation; excite. [F, or L *fermentum* (FERVENT)]

fermentation /fɜ:men'teɪʃ(ə)n/ *n.* chemical change involving effervescence and production of heat, induced by organic substance such as yeast; excitement; **fermentative** /fə'mentətɪv/ *a.* [L (prec.)]

fermium /'fɜ:mɪəm/ *n.* artificial radioactive metallic element. [*Fermi*, physicist]

fern *n.* a kind of flowerless plant, usu. with feathery fronds; **ferny** *a.* [OE]

ferocious /fə'rəʊʃəs/ *a.* fierce, savage; **ferocity** /fə'rɒsɪtɪ/ *n.* [L *ferox*]

-ferous *suffix* forming adjectives (usu. as **-iferous**) in sense 'bearing, having' (*vociferous*). [L *fero* bear]

ferret /'ferɪt/ **1** *n.* small animal like weasel used in catching rabbits, rats, etc. **2** *v.* hunt with ferrets; rummage, search (*about* or *around*); search *out* (secret, criminal). [F f. L (*fur* thief)]

ferric /'ferɪk/ *a.* of iron; containing iron in trivalent form. [L *ferrum* iron]

Ferris wheel /'ferɪs/ giant revolving vertical wheel with passenger cars in amusement parks etc. [*Ferris*, inventor]

ferro- *in comb.* containing iron; of iron. [FERRIC]

ferroconcrete /ferəʊ'kɒŋkri:t/ *n.* reinforced concrete.

ferrous /'ferəs/ *a.* containing iron (*ferrous and non-ferrous metals*); containing iron in divalent form.

ferrule /'ferəl, -u:l/ *n.* metal ring or cap strengthening end of stick etc. [F f. L (*viriae* bracelet)]

ferry /'ferɪ/ **1** *v.* go or convey in boat across water; (of boat) pass to and fro across water; transport from one place to another, esp. as regular service. **2** *n.* boat etc. used for ferrying; place or service of ferrying. **3 ferryman** *n.* [ON]

fertile /'fɜ:taɪl/ *a.* (of soil) producing abundant vegetation or crops; fruitful; (of seed, egg, etc.) capable of becoming new individual; (of animals and plants) able to conceive young or produce fruit; (of mind) inventive; (of nuclear material) able to become fissile by capture of neutrons; **fertility** /fə'tɪlɪtɪ/ *n.* [F f. L]

fertilize /'fɜ:tɪlaɪz/ *v.t.* make (soil etc.) fertile; cause (plant or egg or female animal) to develop new individual by introducing pollen or sperm into; **fertilization** /-'zeɪʃ(ə)n/ *n.*

fertilizer *n.* chemical or natural substance added to soil to make it more fertile.

fervent /'fɜ:vənt/ *a.* ardent, impassioned; **fervency** *n.* [F f. L *ferveo* boil]

fervid /'fɜ:vɪd/ *a.* fervent. [L (prec.)]

fervour /'fɜ:və/, *US* **fervor** *n.* passion, zeal. [F f. L (FERVENT)]

festal /'fest(ə)l/ *a.* of a feast or festival; gay, joyous; **festally** *adv.* [F f. L (FEAST)]

fester *v.* make or become septic; cause continuing annoyance; rot, stagnate. [F f. L FISTULA]

festival /'festɪv(ə)l/ *n.* day or time of celebration; series of concerts, plays, etc. held regularly in a town etc. (*Bath Festival*). [F (foll.)]

festive /'festɪv/ *a.* of or characteristic of a festival; joyous. [L (FEAST)]

festivity /fe'stɪvɪtɪ/ *n.* gaiety, festive celebration; (in *pl.*) festive proceedings. [F or f. L (prec.)]

festoon /fe'stu:n/ **1** *n.* chain of flowers, ribbons, etc., hung in curve as decoration. **2** *v.t.* adorn with or form into festoons. [F f. It. (FESTIVE)]

Festschrift /'festʃrɪft/ *n.* (*pl.* **Festschriften, -schrifts**) published collection of writings in honour of a scholar. [G, = festival-writing]

fetal *US* var. of FOETAL.

fetch /fetʃ/ **1** *v.* go for and bring back (person or thing); be sold for (*fetched £10*); cause (blood, tears, etc.) to flow; draw (breath), heave (sigh); *colloq.* give (blow, slap, etc.). **2** *n.* act of fetching; dodge, trick. **3 fetch and carry** act as menial; **fetch up** *colloq.* arrive, stop, vomit. [OE]

fetching *a.* attractive.

fête /feɪt/ **1** *n.* outdoor function with sale of goods, amusements, etc., esp. to raise funds for some purpose. **2** *v.t.* honour or entertain lavishly. [F (FEAST)]

fetid /'fetɪd, 'fi:t-/ *a.* stinking. [L (*feteo* stink)]

fetish /'fetɪʃ/ *n.* object worshipped as magical by primitive peoples; thing evoking irrational devotion or respect; thing abnormally stimulating or attracting sexual desire; **fetishism** *n.*; **fetishist** *n.* [F f. Port. *feitiço* charm, f. L (FACTITIOUS)]

fetlock /'fetlɒk/ *n.* part of back of horse's leg above hoof where tuft of hair grows. [FOOT]

fetter 1 *n.* shackle for holding prisoner by the ankles; (in *pl.*) captivity; restraint. **2** *v.t.* put into fetters; restrict. [OE]

fettle /'fet(ə)l/ *n.* condition or trim (*in fine fettle*). [OE]

fetus *US* var. of FOETUS.

feu /fju:/ *Sc.* **1** *n.* perpetual lease at fixed rent; land so held. **2** *v.t.* grant (land) on feu. [F (FEE)]

feud[1] /fju:d/ **1** *n.* prolonged mutual hostility, esp. between families or groups. **2** *v.i.* conduct feud. [F f. Gmc (FOE)]

feud[2] /fju:d/ *n.* = FIEF. [L *feudum* FEE]

feudal /'fju:d(ə)l/ *a.* of social system in medieval Europe whereby vassal held land from superior in exchange for allegiance and service; **feudalism** *n.*; **feudalistic** /-'lɪstɪk/ *a.*

fever 1 *n.* abnormally high body temperature, often with delirium etc.; disease characterized by this; nervous agitation or excitement. **2** *v.t.* affect with fever or excitement. **3 fever pitch** state of extreme excitement. [OE & F f. L *febris*]

feverfew /'fi:vəfju:/ *n.* aromatic herb with feathery leaves, formerly used to reduce fever. [L *febrifuga* (prec., *fugo* drive away)]

feverish *a.* having symptoms of fever; excited, restless. [FEVER]

few 1 *a.* not many. **2** *n.* a small number. **3 a few** some, several; **few and far between** scarce; **a good** (or **quite a**) **few** a fair number (of); **no fewer than** as many as. [OE]

fey /feɪ/ *a.* strange, other-worldly; *Sc.* fated to die soon. [OE, = doomed to die]

fez *n.* (*pl.* **fezzes**) flat-topped conical red cap with tassel, worn by men in some Muslim countries. [Turk.]

ff. *abbr.* following pages etc.

ff *abbr. Mus.* fortissimo.

fiancé /fɪ'ɒnseɪ/ *n.* man or (**fiancée**) woman to whom a person is engaged to be married. [F]

fiasco /fɪ'æskəʊ/ *n.* (*pl.* **fiascos**) ludicrous or humiliating failure. [It., = bottle]

fiat /'faɪæt/ *n.* authorization; decree. [L, = let it be done]

fib 1 *n.* trivial lie. **2** *v.i.* (**-bb-**) tell fib. **3 fibber** *n.* [perh. f. redupl. of FABLE]

fibre /'faɪbə/, *US* **fiber** *n.* one of the threads or filaments forming animal and vegetable tissue and textile substance; piece of glass in form of thread; substance formed of fibres; character (*moral fibre*); **fibre optics** transmission of information by means of infra-red light signals along thin glass fibre. [F f. L *fibra*]

fibreboard *n.* flexible board made of compressed fibres of wood etc.

fibreglass *n.* textile fabric made from woven glass fibres; plastic containing glass fibres.
fibril /'faɪbrɪl/ *n.* small fibre. [dimin. of FIBRE]
fibroid /'faɪbrɔɪd/ **1** *a.* of or like fibrous tissue. **2** *n.* fibroid tumour in uterus. [FIBRE]
fibrosis /faɪ'brəʊsɪs/ *n.* development of excessive fibrous tissue. [FIBRE, -OSIS]
fibrositis /faɪbrə'saɪtɪs/ *n.* rheumatic inflammation of fibrous tissue. [FIBRE, -ITIS]
fibrous /'faɪbrəs/ *a.* of or like fibre. [FIBRE]
fibula /'fɪbjʊlə/ *n.* (*pl.* **fibulae** /-iː/) bone on outer side of lower leg; **fibular** *a.* [L, = brooch]
-fic *suffix* forming adjectives (usu. as **-ific**) in sense 'producing, making' (*prolific, pacific*). [F or L (*facio* make)]
-fication *suffix* forming nouns of action (usu. as **-ification**) from verbs in -FY (*purification, simplification*).
fiche /fiːʃ/ *n.* (*pl.* same) = MICROFICHE. [abbr.]
fickle /'fɪk(ə)l/ *a.* inconstant, changeable, esp. in loyalty; **fickly** *adv.* [OE]
fiction /'fɪkʃ(ə)n/ *n.* invented idea or statement or narrative; literature describing imaginary events and people; conventionally accepted falsehood; **fictional** *a.*; **fictionalize** *v.t.* [F f. L (FEIGN)]
fictitious /fɪk'tɪʃəs/ *a.* imagined or made up, not real or genuine.
fiddle /'fɪd(ə)l/ **1** *n. colloq.* stringed instrument played with bow, esp. violin; *sl.* instance of cheating or fraud. **2** *v.* play restlessly (*with*), move aimlessly (*about*); *sl.* cheat, swindle, falsify, get by cheating; play fiddle, play (tune) on fiddle. **3 as fit as a fiddle** in very good health; **play second fiddle** take subordinate role. [OE]
fiddle-faddle **1** *n.* trivial matters. **2** *v.i.* fuss, trifle. **3** *int.* nonsense. [redupl. of prec.]
fiddler *n.* player on fiddle; *sl.* swindler; small crab.
fiddlesticks *int.* nonsense.
fiddling *a.* petty, trivial.
fiddly *a. colloq.* awkward to do or use.
fidelity /fɪ'delɪtɪ/ *n.* faithfulness, loyalty; accuracy; precision in reproduction of sound. [F or L (*fides* faith)]
fidget /'fɪdʒɪt/ **1** *v.* move or act restlessly or nervously; be or make uneasy. **2** *n.* one who fidgets; (in *pl.*) fidgeting movements. **3** **fidgety** *a.* [obs. or dial. *fidge* twitch]
fiduciary /fɪ'djuːʃɪərɪ/ **1** *a.* of, or held or given in, trust; (of paper currency) depending for its value on public confidence or securities. **2** *n.* trustee. [L (*fiducia* trust)]
fie /faɪ/ *int.* expressing disgust or shame. [F f. L]
fief /fiːf/ *n.* land held under feudal system or in fee; one's sphere of operation or control. [F (FEE)]
field **1** *n.* area of open land, esp. for pasture or crops; area rich in some natural product, e.g. coalfield, oilfield; piece of land for specified purpose, esp. area marked out for games; participants in contest or sport; all competitors or all but specified one(s), fielding side in cricket; expanse of ice, sea, snow, etc.; place of battle or campaign; area of operation or activity, subject of study; area in which a force is effective (*gravitational, magnetic, field*), force exerted by such field; range of perception (*field of view*); background of picture, coin, flag, etc.; (in computers) part of a record, representing a unit of information; surface of escutcheon. **2** *attrib.* (of animal or plant) found in open country, wild; (of artillery etc.) light and mobile for use on campaign; carried out or working in the natural environment, not in laboratory etc. **3** *v.* act as fieldsman in cricket etc., stop and return (ball); select (team or individual) to play in a game; deal with (succession of questions etc.). **4** **field-day** military exercise or review, important or successful occasion; **field-events** athletic sports other than races; **field-glasses** binoculars for outdoor use; **Field Marshal** army officer of highest rank; **field officer** army officer of rank above captain and below general; **field sports** outdoor sports, esp. hunting, shooting, and fishing; **hold the field** not be superseded; **take the field** begin campaign. [OE]
fielder *n.* = FIELDSMAN.
fieldfare *n.* a kind of thrush.
fieldsman *n.* player (other than bowler) opposed to batsman in cricket etc.
fieldwork *n.* practical (as distinct from theoretical) work; temporary fortification.
fiend /fiːnd/ *n.* evil spirit, devil; very wicked or cruel person; *sl.* devotee or addict (*fresh-air fiend*); **fiendish** *a.* [OE]
fierce *a.* vehemently aggressive or frightening in temper or action, violent; eager, intense; strong or uncontrolled (*fierce heat*). [F f. L *ferus* savage]
fiery /'faɪərɪ/ *a.* consisting of fire, flaming; like fire in appearance, bright red; intensely hot; spirited, passionate, intense (*a fiery look, temper*); **fierily** *adv.*; **fieriness** *n.* [FIRE]

fiesta /fɪ'estə/ *n.* festival, holiday. [Sp.]
fife *n.* small shrill flute used in military music. [G *pfeife* PIPE or F *fifre*]
fifteen /fɪf'ti:n/ *a.* & *n.* one more than fourteen; symbol for this (15, xv, XV); size etc. denoted by fifteen; team of fifteen players, esp. in Rugby football; **fifteenth** *a.* & *n.* [OE (FIVE, -TEEN)]
fifth *a.* & *n.* next after fourth; one of five equal parts of thing; *Mus.* interval or chord spanning five consecutive diatonic notes (e.g. C to G); **fifth column** group working for an enemy within a country at war; **fifth columnist** member of this, traitor; **fifthly** *adv.* [OE (FIVE)]
fifty /'fɪftɪ/ *a.* & *n.* five times ten; symbol for this (50, l, L); (in *pl.*) numbers, years, degrees of temperature, from 50 to 59; **fifty-fifty** *a.* & *adv.* equal(ly); **fiftieth** *a.* & *n.* [OE]
fig[1] *n.* soft pear-shaped fruit; tree bearing it; thing of little value (*not worth a fig*); **fig-leaf** device for concealing something, esp. genitals. [F f. L *ficus*]
fig[2] *n.* dress or equipment (*in full fig*); condition (*in good fig*). [obs. *feague* (FAKE)]
fig. *abbr.* figure.
fight /faɪt/ **1** *v.* (*past* and *p.p.* **fought** /fɔ:t/) contend or struggle physically in war, battle, single combat, etc.; contend thus with (opponent); contend about (issue); campaign or strive determinedly to achieve (or *for*) something; strive to overcome (disease, fire, etc.); make (one's way) by fighting. **2** *n.* fighting, battle, combat; conflict, struggle, vigorous effort in face of difficulty; power or inclination to fight (*has no fight left*); boxing-match. **3 fight back** show resistance; **fighting chance** opportunity of succeeding by great effort; **fighting fit** fit and ready; **fight it out** settle issue by fighting over it until one side wins; **fight shy of** avoid. [OE]
fighter *n.* one who fights; fast military aircraft designed for attacking other aircraft.
figment /'fɪgmənt/ *n.* thing invented or existing only in the imagination. [L (FEIGN)]
figuration /fɪgjʊ'reɪʃ(ə)n/ *n.* act or mode of formation; ornamentation. [F or L (FIGURE)]
figurative /'fɪgjʊrətɪv, -gə-/ *a.* metaphorical, not literal; characterized by figures of speech; of pictorial or sculptural representation. [L (foll.)]
figure /'fɪgə/ **1** *n.* external form or bodily shape; person as seen but not identified, or as contemplated mentally (*figure of fun*; *public figure*); appearance as giving a certain impression (*cut a poor figure*); representation of human form in drawing, sculpture, etc., image; geometrical space enclosed by lines or surfaces; symbol of number, numeral, esp. 0–9; value, amount of money (*cannot put a figure on it*); (in *pl.*) arithmetical calculations; diagram, illustration; decorative pattern; series of movements forming a single unit in dancing etc.; succession of notes forming single idea in music. **2** *v.* appear or be mentioned, esp. prominently; represent in diagram or picture; imagine, picture mentally; embellish with pattern; mark with numbers or prices; calculate, do arithmetic; be symbol of; *US* understand, consider, *colloq.* be likely or understandable. **3 figure-head** carved image at ship's prow, person nominally at head but with no real power; **figure (of speech)** expression using words differently from literal meaning, esp. metaphor; **figure out** work out by arithmetic or logic. [F f. L *figura* (FEIGN)]
figurine /fɪgjʊ'ri:n/ *n.* statuette. [F f. It. (prec.)]
filament /'fɪləmənt/ *n.* threadlike strand or fibre; conducting wire or thread in electric bulb; **filamentary** /-'mentərɪ/ *a.* [F or L (*filum* thread)]
filbert /'fɪlbət/ *n.* nut of cultivated hazel; tree bearing it. [AF (because ripe about St *Philibert*'s day)]
filch *v.t.* pilfer, steal. [orig. unkn.]
file[1] **1** *n.* folder or box etc. for holding loose papers; its contents; collection of (usu. related) data stored under one reference in computer; line of people or things one behind the other. **2** *v.* place in file or among records; submit (application for divorce, petition, etc.); (of reporter) send (story etc.) to newspaper; walk in a line. [F f. L *filum* thread]
file[2] **1** *n.* tool with roughened steel surface for smoothing or shaping wood etc. **2** *v.t.* smooth or shape with file. [OE]
filial /'fɪlɪəl/ *a.* of or due from a son or daughter; **filially** *adv.* [F or L (*filius*, *-a* son, daughter)]
filibuster /'fɪlɪbʌstə/ **1** *n.* person engaging in unauthorized warfare against foreign State; one who obstructs progress in legislative assembly, such obstruction. **2** *v.i.* act as filibuster. [Du. (FREEBOOTER)]
filigree /'fɪlɪgri:/ *n.* fine ornamental work in gold etc. wire; similar delicate work. [F *filigrane* ult. f. L *filum* thread, *granum* seed]
filing *n.* (usu. in *pl.*) particle rubbed off by file. [FILE[2]]
Filipino /fɪlɪ'pi:nəʊ/ **1** *n.* (*pl.* **Filipinos**) native of the Philippine Islands. **2** *a.* of the Filipinos. [Sp., = Philippine]
fill 1 *v.* make or become full (*with*);

occupy completely, spread over or through; block up (cavity or hole), drill and put filling into (decayed tooth); appoint person to hold (vacant post); hold or discharge duties of (office etc.); carry out or supply (order, commission, etc.); occupy (vacant time); (of sail) be distended by wind. **2** *n.* as much as one wants or can bear of food etc. (*eat your fill*; *wept her fill*); enough to fill thing. **3 fill the bill** be suitable or adequate; **fill in** add information to complete (form or document etc.), complete (drawing etc.) within outline, fill (hole etc.) completely, act as substitute (*for*), spend (time) in temporary activity; **fill person in** *colloq.* give him required information; **fill out** enlarge to required size, become enlarged or plump; **fill up** make or become completely full, fill in (document), fill petrol tank of (car etc.). [OE]

filler *n.* material used to fill cavity or increase bulk; item filling space in newspaper etc.

fillet /'fɪlɪt/ **1** *n.* boneless piece of meat or fish; headband, hair ribbon; narrow strip or ridge; *Archit.* narrow flat band between mouldings. **2** *v.t.* remove bones from; divide (fish etc.) into fillets; bind or provide with fillet(s). [F f. L (*filum* thread)]

filling *n.* material used to fill cavity in tooth; material between bread in sandwich; **filling-station** establishment selling petrol etc. to motorists. [FILL]

fillip /'fɪlɪp/ **1** *n.* stimulus, incentive; flick with finger or thumb. **2** *v.* stimulate; flick. [imit.]

filly /'fɪlɪ/ *n.* young female horse; *sl.* lively young woman. [ON]

film 1 *n.* thin coating or covering layer; strip or sheet of plastic or other flexible base coated with light-sensitive emulsion for exposure in a camera; motion picture, story represented by this; (in *pl.*) the cinema industry; slight veil of haze etc.; dimness or morbid growth affecting eyes. **2** *v.* make film or motion picture of (scene, story, etc.); cover or become covered with a film. **3 film star** celebrated actor or actress in films; **film-strip** series of transparencies in a strip for projection. [OE]

filmy *a.* thin and translucent; **filmily** *adv.*; **filminess** *n.*

filter 1 *n.* device for removing impurities from a liquid or gas passed through it; = *filter tip*; screen for absorbing or modifying light, X-rays, etc.; device for suppressing electrical or sound waves of frequencies not required; arrangement for filtering traffic. **2** *v.* (cause to) pass through a filter; make way gradually (*through*, *into*, etc.), leak *out*; (of traffic) be allowed to pass in certain direction while other traffic is held up (esp. at traffic lights). **3 filter-paper** porous paper for filtering; **filter-tip** (cigarette with) filter for purifying smoke. [F f. L f. Gmc (FELT[1])]

filth *n.* repugnant or extreme dirt; obscenity. [OE (FOUL)]

filthy 1 *a.* extremely or disgustingly dirty; obscene; *colloq.* (of weather) very unpleasant. **2** *adv.* in filthy way (*filthy dirty*); *colloq.* extremely (*filthy rich*). **3 filthily** *adv.*; **filthiness** *n.*

filtrate /'fɪltreɪt/ **1** *v.t.* filter. **2** *n.* filtered liquid. **3 filtration** /-'treɪʃ(ə)n/ *n.* [FILTER]

fin *n.* thin flat organ on body of fish etc. for propelling and steering; similar projection on aircraft etc. for stability, or on motor car; underwater swimmer's flipper. [OE]

finagle /fɪ'neɪg(ə)l/ *v. colloq.* act or obtain dishonestly. [dial. *fainaigue* cheat]

final /'faɪn(ə)l/ **1** *a.* situated at the end, coming last; conclusive, decisive. **2** *n.* last or deciding heat or game in sports etc.; last edition of day's newspaper; (usu. in *pl.*) final examination. **3 final cause** ultimate purpose; **final clause** *Gram.* clause expressing purpose. **4 finally** *adv.* [F or L (*finis* end)]

finale /fɪ'nɑːlɪ/ *n.* last movement or section of piece of music or drama etc. [It. (prec.)]

finalist /'faɪnəlɪst/ *n.* competitor in final of competition etc. [FINAL]

finality /faɪ'nælɪtɪ/ *n.* quality or fact of being final. [F f. L (FINAL)]

finalize /'faɪnəlaɪz/ *v.t.* put into final form, complete; **finalization** /-'zeɪʃ(ə)n/ *n.* [FINAL]

finance /faɪ'næns, fɪ-, 'faɪ-/ **1** *n.* management of money; support in money for an enterprise; (in *pl.*) money resources. **2** *v.t.* provide capital for (person or enterprise). **3 finance company** (or **house**) company concerned mainly with providing money for hire-purchase transactions. [F (FINE[2])]

financial /faɪ'nænʃ(ə)l, fɪ-/ *a.* of finance; **financial year** year reckoned from 1 or 6 April for taxing and accounting; **financially** *adv.*

financier /faɪ'nænsɪə, fɪ-/ *n.* person engaged in large-scale finance. [F (FINANCE)]

finch *n.* any of several small songbirds. [OE]

find /faɪnd/ **1** *v.t.* (*past* and *p.p.* **found**) discover or get possession of by chance or effort; become aware of; obtain, succeed in obtaining (*cannot find the money, the time*); seek out and provide (*will find you a book*); ascertain by inquiry, calculation, etc.; perceive or experience (*find no sense in it*; *find difficulty in breathing*); regard or discover from experience (*finds England too cold*; *we find it pays*); (of jury, judge, etc.) decide and declare (*found him guilty*; *found for the plaintiff*); reach by natural process (*water finds its level*). **2** *n.* discovery; thing or person discovered, esp. when of value. **3 find oneself** discover that one is, discover one's vocation; **find fault with** see FAULT; **find one's feet** be able to walk, develop one's independent ability; **find out** discover or detect (wrongdoer etc.), get information (about). [OE]

finder *n.* one who finds; small telescope attached to large one to locate object; viewfinder.

finding *n.* (often in *pl.*) conclusion reached by inquiry etc.

fine[1] **1** *a.* of high quality; excellent, of notable merit (*a fine performance*; also *iron.*: *a fine friend you are!*); pure, refined; (of gold or silver) containing specified proportion of pure metal; of handsome appearance or size, beautiful, imposing; in good health (*I'm fine, thank you*); (of weather) bright, free from rain, fog, etc.; small, thin, or sharp of its kind, in small particles; (of speech) tritely complimentary, euphemistic; smart, showy, ornate; fastidious, affectedly refined. **2** *n.* fine weather; (in *pl.*) small particles in mining, milling, etc. **3** *adv.* finely; *colloq.* very well (*suits me fine*). **4** *v.* (often with *away*, *down*, *off*) make or become pure, clear, thinner, etc. **5 cut** (or **run**) **it fine** allow very little margin of time etc.; **fine arts** those appealing to the mind or sense of beauty, esp. painting, sculpture, and architecture; **fine-spun** delicate, (of theory) too subtle, unpractical; **fine-tooth comb** comb with narrow close-set teeth; **go over with a fine-tooth comb** search thoroughly; **not to put too fine a point on it** to speak bluntly. [F *fin* f. L *finio* FINISH]

fine[2] **1** *n.* sum of money (to be) paid as penalty. **2** *v.t.* punish by fine. **3 in fine** in sum. [F *fin* settlement of dispute (L *finis* end)]

finery /ˈfaɪnərɪ/ *n.* showy dress or decoration. [FINE[1]]

fines herbes /fiːnz ˈeəb/ mixed herbs used in cooking. [F, = fine herbs]

finesse /fɪˈnes/ **1** *n.* refinement; subtle or delicate manipulation; artful tact in handling difficulty; (in card-games) attempt to win trick by playing card that is not the highest held. **2** *v.* use or achieve by finesse; (in card-games) make a finesse (with). [F (FINE)]

finger /ˈfɪŋgə/ **1** *n.* any of the five terminal members of the hand, any of these excluding the thumb; part of glove for finger; finger-like object or structure; measure of liquor in glass, based on breadth of finger. **2** *v.t.* feel or turn about with the fingers; play (music or instrument) with the fingers. **3 finger-board** flat strip at top end of stringed instrument, against which strings are pressed to determine tones; **finger-bowl** small bowl for rinsing fingers during meal; **finger-mark** mark left on surface by finger; **finger-nail** nail at tip of finger; **finger-plate** plate fixed to door above handle to prevent finger-marks; **finger-stall** sheath to cover injured finger; **get** (or **pull** etc.) **one's finger out** *sl.* cease prevaricating and start to act; **put one's finger on** locate or identify exactly. [OE]

fingering *n.* manner or technique of using the fingers, esp. to play instrument; indication of this in musical score.

fingerprint **1** *n.* impression made on surface by fingertip, esp. as a means of identification. **2** *v.t.* record fingerprints of (person).

fingertip *n.* tip of finger; **have at one's fingertips** be thoroughly familiar with (subject etc.).

finial /ˈfɪnɪəl/ *n.* ornamental top to gable, canopy, etc. [AF (FINE[1])]

finicky /ˈfɪnɪkɪ/ *a.* (also **finical, finicking**) excessively detailed, fiddly; over-particular, fastidious. [perh. FINE[1]]

finis /ˈfɪnɪs, ˈfiːn-/ *n.* end, esp. of book. [L]

finish /ˈfɪnɪʃ/ **1** *v.* (often with *off* or *up*) bring or come to an end, come to the end of; complete manufacture of (cloth etc.) by surface treatment. **2** *n.* end, last stage; point at which race etc. ends; method, material, or texture used for surface treatment of wood, cloth, etc. **3 finishing-school** private school where girls are prepared for entry into fashionable society; **finish off** end, *colloq.* kill; **finish with** have no more to do with. [F f. L (*finis* end)]

finite /ˈfaɪnaɪt/ *a.* limited, not infinite; (of part of verb) having specific number and person. [L (prec.)]

Finn *n.* native of Finland. [OE]

finnan /ˈfɪnən/ *n.* haddock cured with smoke of green wood, turf, or peat. [*Findhorn*, *Findon*, in Scotland]

Finnic *a.* of the group of peoples or languages allied to the Finns or Finnish.

Finnish **1** *a.* of the Finns or their language. **2** *n.* language of the Finns. [FINN]

fiord /fjɔːd/ *n.* narrow inlet of sea between high cliffs. [Norw.]

fipple /ˈfɪp(ə)l/ *n.* plug at mouth-end of wind instrument; **fipple flute** flute played by blowing endwise, e.g. recorder. [orig. unkn.]

fir *n.* evergreen coniferous tree with needles placed singly on its shoots; its wood; **fir-cone** its fruit; **firry** *a.* [ON]

fire 1 *n.* state or process of combustion causing heat and light, active principle operative in this, flame or incandescence; destructive burning (*forest fire*); burning fuel in grate or furnace, electric or gas fire (see ELECTRIC, GAS); firing of guns; fervour, spirit, vivacity, poetic inspiration; burning heat, fever. **2** *v.* shoot (gun etc. or missile from it), shoot gun or missile (*at*), detonate (explosive); deliver or utter in rapid succession (*fired insults at her*); dismiss (employee) from job; set fire to with intention of destroying; catch fire; (of internal-combustion engine) undergo ignition; supply (furnace etc.) with fuel; stimulate (imagination); fill (person) with enthusiasm; bake or dry (pottery, bricks, etc.); become heated or excited; redden. **3 catch fire** ignite, start to burn; **fire-alarm** device giving warning of fire; **fire-ball** large meteor, ball of flame from nuclear explosion, energetic person; **fire-bomb** incendiary bomb; **fire-break** obstacle to spread of fire in forest etc.; **fire-brick** fireproof brick used in grate; **fire brigade** organized body of men trained and employed to extinguish fires; **fire-bug** *colloq.* pyromaniac; **fire-clay** clay used to make fire-bricks; **fire-drill** rehearsal of procedure to be used in case of fire; **fire-eater** conjuror who appears to swallow fire, quarrelsome person; **fire-engine** vehicle carrying equipment for fighting large fires; **fire-escape** emergency staircase or apparatus for escape from building on fire; **fire extinguisher** apparatus with jet for discharging liquid chemicals or foam to extinguish fire; **fire-guard** protective screen or grid placed in front of fire; **fire in one's belly** enthusiasm, ambition; **fire-irons** tongs, poker, and shovel, for tending domestic fire; **fire-lighter** piece of inflammable material used to help start fire in grate; **fire-power** destructive capacity of guns etc.; **fire-practice** fire-drill; **fire-raising** arson; **fire station** headquarters of fire brigade; **fire-storm** high wind or storm following fire caused by bombs; **fire-trap** building without proper provision for escape in case of fire; **fire-watcher** person keeping watch for fires, esp. those caused by bombs; **fire-water** *colloq.* strong alcoholic liquor; **on fire** burning, *fig.* excited; **open fire** start firing guns etc.; **set fire to** (or **on fire**) cause to burn or ignite; **set the world on fire** do something remarkable or sensational; **under fire** being fired on (by enemy etc.), being rigorously criticized or questioned. [OE]

firearm *n.* (usu. in *pl.*) gun, pistol, or rifle.

firebox *n.* fuel-chamber of steam-engine or boiler.

firebrand *n.* piece of burning wood; person who causes trouble.

firecracker *n. US* explosive firework.

firedamp *n.* miners' name for methane, which is explosive when mixed in certain proportion with air.

firedog *n.* andiron.

firefly *n.* a kind of beetle emitting phosphorescent light.

firelight *n.* light from fire in fireplace.

fireman *n.* member of fire brigade; one who tends furnace of steam-engine.

fireplace *n.* grate or hearth for domestic fire; its surrounding structure.

fireproof 1 *a.* able to resist fire or great heat. **2** *v.t.* make fireproof.

fireside *n.* area round fireplace; one's home or home-life.

firewood *n.* wood for use as fuel.

firework *n.* device containing combustible chemicals that cause explosions or spectacular effects; (in *pl.*) outburst of passion, esp. anger.

firing *n.* discharge of guns; fuel; **firing-line** front line in battle, leading part in activity etc.; **firing-squad** group that fires salute at military funeral or shoots condemned person.

firm¹ 1 *a.* solid, stable, steady, not fluctuating; resolute, determined; not easily shaken (*firm belief*); (of offer etc.) not liable to cancellation after acceptance. **2** *adv.* firmly (*stand firm*). **3** *v.* (cause to) become firm or secure. [F f. L *firmus*]

firm² *n.* business concern or its members. [Sp. and It. f. L *firma*; cf. prec.]

firmament /ˈfɜːməmənt/ *n.* sky regarded as a vault or arch. [F f. L (FIRM¹)]

first 1 *a.* foremost in time or order or importance (*first turning on the left*; *first cuckoo*; *first violins*); most willing or likely (*be the first to admit it*); basic, evident (*first principles*). **2** *n.* first person or thing; first occurrence of something notable; first-class honours in university degree. **3** *adv.* before anyone or anything else; before someone or something else (*must get this done first*); for the first time (*when did you first see her?*); in preference (*I'll see you damned first*). **4 at first** at the beginning; **at first hand** directly from original source; **first aid** help given to injured until medical treatment is available; **first blood** first success in contest; **first-born** *a.* & *n.* eldest, eldest child; **first class** best group or category, best accommodation in train, ship, etc., class of mail most quickly delivered, highest category of achievement in examination; **first-class** *a.* & *adv.* of or by the first class, excellent; **first-day cover** envelope with stamps postmarked on first day of issue; **first finger** that next to thumb; **first floor** see FLOOR; **first-foot** *n.* & *v.i. Sc.* (be) first person to cross threshold in New Year; **first-fruit** (usu. in *pl.*) first agricultural produce of season, first results of work etc.; **First Lady** *US* wife of President; **first light** dawn; **first night** first public performance of play etc.; **first offender** one against whom no previous conviction is recorded; **first officer** mate on merchant ship; **first past the post** winning election by having most votes though not necessarily absolute majority; **first person** see PERSON; **first-rate** excellent, *colloq.* very well (*feeling first-rate*); **in the first place** as the first consideration. [OE]

firsthand *a.* & *adv.* from original source, direct.

firstly *adv.* first, to begin with.

firth *n.* narrow inlet of sea; estuary. [ON (FIORD)]

fiscal /'fɪsk(ə)l/ **1** *a.* of public revenue. **2** *n.* legal official in some countries; *Sc.* = procurator fiscal. [F or L (*fiscus* treasury)]

fish[1] **1** *n.* (*pl.* usu. same) vertebrate cold-blooded animal with gills and fins living wholly in water; any animal living in water, e.g. cuttlefish, jellyfish; flesh of fish as food; *colloq.* person (*cold, queer, fish*); (**Fish** or **Fishes**) sign or constellation Pisces. **2** *v.* try to catch fish; do this in (river etc.); search (*for* thing) in water or concealed place; seek by indirect means *for* (compliments, secrets, etc.). **3 drink like a fish** drink esp. alcoholic liquor excessively; **fish cake** small fried cake of shredded fish and mashed potato; **fish-eye lens** wide-angled lens with distorting effect; **fish finger** small oblong piece of fish in batter or breadcrumbs; **fish-hook** barbed hook for catching fish; **fish-kettle** oval pan for boiling fish; **fish-meal** ground dried fish as fertilizer etc.; **fish-net** (of fabric) made with open mesh; **fish out** *colloq.* pull out from pocket etc.; **fish out of water** person not in his element; **fish-tail** thing shaped like fish's tail; **other fish to fry** more important things to do. [OE]

fish[2] *n.* piece of wood or iron etc. to strengthen mast, beam, etc.; **fish-plate** flat plate of iron etc. connecting railway rails. [F *ficher* f. L *figere* FIX]

fisher *n.* fishing animal; *archaic* fisherman. [OE]

fisherman *n.* man who earns living by fishing or who goes fishing for sport.

fishery *n.* place where fish are caught; business of fishing. [FISH[1]]

fishing *n.* sport of trying to catch fish; **fishing-line, -rod** line and rod with fish-hook, used in this.

fishmonger *n.* dealer in fish.

fishwife *n.* woman who sells fish.

fishy *a.* of or like fish; *sl.* dubious, suspect; **fishily** *adv.*; **fishiness** *n.*

fissile /'fɪsaɪl/ *a.* capable of undergoing nuclear fission; tending to split. [L (FISSURE)]

fission /'fɪʃ(ə)n/ **1** *n.* method of biological reproduction by division of cell etc.; = *nuclear fission*. **2** *v.* (cause to) undergo fission. **3 fission bomb** atomic bomb. [L (foll.)]

fissure /'fɪʃə/ **1** *n.* opening, esp. long and narrow one made by cracking or splitting; split, cleavage. **2** *v.* split, crack. [F, or L (*findo fiss-* cleave)]

fist *n.* tightly closed hand. [OE]

fisticuffs /'fɪstɪkʌfs/ *n.pl.* fighting with fists. [prob. f. obs. *fisty* (prec.), CUFF]

fistula /'fɪstjʊlə/ *n.* long pipelike ulcer; abnormal or surgically made passage in the body; **fistular** *a.*; **fistulous** *a.* [L, = pipe]

fit[1] **1** *a.* well suited or qualified, competent, worthy; in suitable condition, ready; in good health or condition; proper, befitting. **2** *v.* (**-tt-**) be in harmony with, befit; be or make of right size and shape (for), (of component) be correctly positioned (*that bit fits here*); adapt, make suitable or competent; supply (ship etc.) *with*. **3** *n.* way in which garment, component, etc., fits (*a bad, good, tight, fit*). **4 fit in** (cause to) be in suitable or harmonious place or relation (*with* other things, *to* space); find space or time for (object, engagement, etc.); **fit out** (or **up**) equip (*with*); **see** (or **think**) **fit** decide or choose (*to do* esp. arbitrary or foolish thing). [orig. unkn.]

fit[2] *n.* sudden seizure of epilepsy, hysteria, etc., usu. with unconsciousness; brief attack of illness or symptoms (*fit of coughing*); sudden short bout or burst (*fit of giggles, energy*); **by** (or **in**) **fits and starts** spasmodically; **have a fit** *colloq.* be greatly surprised or outraged; **in fits** laughing uncontrollably. [OE]

fitful *a.* active or occurring spasmodically or intermittently; **fitfully** *adv.*

fitment *n.* piece of fixed furniture.

fitter *n.* person concerned with fitting of clothes etc.; mechanic who fits together and adjusts machinery. [FIT[1]]

fitting **1** *n.* process of having garment etc. fitted; (in *pl.*) fixtures and fitments of a building. **2** *a.* proper, befitting.

five *a.* & *n.* one more than four; symbol for this (5, v, V); size etc. denoted by five; (in *pl.*) game in which ball is hit with gloved hand or bat against walls of court. [OE]

fivefold *a.* & *adv.* five times as much or as many; consisting of five parts.

fiver *n. colloq.* £5 note.

fix 1 *v.* make firm or stable, fasten, secure; implant (idea, memory) in the mind; place definitely or permanently; decide, settle, specify (price, date, etc.); direct steadily (eyes, attention, *on*); attract and hold (attention, person); single out (person *with one's eyes*); determine exact nature, position, etc., of; identify, locate; make (eyes or features) rigid, (of these) become rigid; congeal, stiffen; mend, repair; *colloq.* punish or kill; *colloq.* secure support of (person) or result of (race etc.) fraudulently; *sl.* inject (*oneself*) with narcotic; make (colour, photographic image, etc.) fast or permanent; (of plant) assimilate (nitrogen, carbon dioxide) by forming non-gaseous compound. **2** *n.* dilemma, difficult position; act of finding position, position found, by bearings etc.; *sl.* dose of narcotic drug. **3 be fixed (for)** *colloq.* be situated (as regards: *how are you fixed for money?*); **fixed star** star that appears to have fixed position; **fix on** (or **upon**) choose, decide on; **fix up** arrange, organize, accommodate. [L *figo fix-*]

fixate /fɪk'seɪt/ *v.t.* direct one's gaze on; (chiefly in *pass.*) cause to acquire abnormal attachment to persons or things. [L (FIX)]

fixation /fɪk'seɪʃ(ə)n/ *n.* act or process of being fixated; obsession, concentration on one idea; fixing, coagulation, process of combining gas to form solid. [med.L (FIX)]

fixative /'fɪksətɪv/ **1** *a.* tending to fix or secure. **2** *n.* fixative substance. [FIX]

fixedly /'fɪksɪdlɪ/ *adv.* in a fixed way, intently.

fixer *n.* person or thing that fixes; *colloq.* one who makes (esp. illicit) arrangements; substance for fixing photographic image etc.

fixings *n.pl. US* apparatus, equipment; trimmings of dress or dish.

fixity *n.* fixed state, stability, permanence.

fixture /'fɪkstʃə/ *n.* thing fixed in position; (in *pl.*) articles belonging to house etc.; sporting event or date fixed for it.

fizz 1 *v.i.* effervesce; hiss, splutter. **2** *n.* hissing sound; effervescence; *colloq.* effervescent drink. [imit.]

fizzle /'fɪz(ə)l/ **1** *v.i.* make feeble hiss. **2** *n.* fizzling sound. **3 fizzle out** end feebly. [imit.]

fizzy *a.* effervescent; **fizziness** *n.* [FIZZ]

fjord var. of FIORD.

fl. *abbr.* floruit; fluid.

flab *n. colloq.* fat, flabbiness. [imit. or f. FLABBY]

flabbergast /'flæbəgɑ:st/ *v.t. colloq.* astound, astonish. [orig. uncert.]

flabby /'flæbɪ/ *a.* limp and hanging loose; feeble; **flabbily** *adv.*; **flabbiness** *n.* [alt. of *flappy* (FLAP)]

flaccid /'flæksɪd/ *a.* flabby; drooping; **flaccidity** /-'sɪdɪtɪ/ *n.* [F or L (*flaccus* limp)]

flag[1] **1** *n.* piece of material, usu. oblong or square and attached by one edge to pole, rope, etc., used as country's emblem or as standard, signal, etc.; small metal plate showing that taxi is for hire. **2** *v.t.* (**-gg-**) inform or signal (as) with flag, esp. (often with *down*) signal (vehicle or driver) to stop; mark with flag or tag. **3 flag-day** day on which money is raised from passers-by etc. for a cause and small paper flags are given as tokens; **flag of convenience** foreign flag under which a ship is registered to avoid taxes etc.; **flag-officer** admiral, vice-admiral, or rear-admiral, or commodore of yacht-club; **flag of truce** white flag, indicating desire to parley; **flag-pole** flagstaff. [orig. unkn.]

flag[2] *v.i.* (**-gg-**) lose momentum or vigour; become limp or feeble. [orig. unkn.]

flag[3] **1** *n.* flagstone; (in *pl.*) pavement of these. **2** *v.t.* (**-gg-**) pave with flags. [prob. Scand.]

flag[4] *n.* plant with bladed leaf (e.g. iris), usu. growing on moist ground. [orig. unkn.]

flagellant /'flædʒələnt/ **1** *n.* one who flagellates himself or others. **2** *a.* of flagellation. [L *flagellum* whip]

flagellate /'flædʒəleɪt/ *v.t.* whip, flog, esp. as religious discipline or sexual stimulus; **flagellation** /-'leɪʃ(ə)n/ *n.*

flagellum /flə'dʒeləm/ *n. Bot.* runner, creeping shoot; *Biol.* lashlike appendage. [L, = whip]

flageolet /flædʒə'let/ *n.* fipple flute with two thumb-holes. [F f. Prov.]

flagon /'flægən/ *n.* large rounded vessel for holding liquids, usu. with handle and lid. [F f. L *flasco* FLASK]

flagrant /'fleɪgrənt/ *a.* glaringly bad; notorious or scandalous; **flagrancy** *n.* [F or L (*flagro* blaze)]

flagship *n.* ship that carries admiral and flies his flag; principal vessel of shipping-line. [FLAG[1]]

flagstaff *n.* pole on which flag is hoisted.

flagstone *n.* flat slab of stone for paving. [FLAG[3]]

flail 1 *n.* short heavy stick swinging at end of wooden staff, as implement for threshing. 2 *v.* wave or swing wildly; beat (as) with flail. [OE f. L *flagellum* whip]

flair *n.* natural ability or talent for selecting or doing what is best, useful, etc.; style, finesse. [F, = scent, f. L (FRAGRANT)]

flak *n.* anti-aircraft fire; barrage of criticism; **flak jacket** heavy protective jacket reinforced with metal. [G, *Fl*ieger *a*bwehr*k*anone 'aviator-defence-gun']

flake 1 *n.* small light piece, e.g. of snow; thin broad piece shaved or split off; dogfish as food. 2 *v.* take or come *away* or *off* in flakes; fall in or sprinkle with flakes. 3 **flake out** *colloq.* fall asleep or faint (as) with exhaustion. 4 **flaky** *a.* [orig. unkn.]

flambé /'flɒmbeɪ/ *a.* (of food) covered with spirit and served alight. [F (FLAME)]

flamboyant /flæm'bɔɪənt/ *a.* showy or florid in appearance or manner; **flamboyance** *n.* [F (as prec.)]

flame 1 *n.* ignited gas, tongue-shaped portion of this; visible combustion (*burst into flames*); bright light or (esp. red) colour; passion, esp. love; *colloq.* sweetheart. 2 *v.i.* burn with flames, blaze; (of person) explode in anger (*flame out*, *up*); shine or glow like flame. 3 **flame-thrower** weapon throwing spray of flame. [F f. L *flamma*]

flamenco /flə'meŋkəʊ/ *n.* (*pl.* **flamencos**) Spanish gypsy style of song or dance. [Sp., = Flemish]

flaming *a.* burning with flames; very hot or bright; *colloq.* passionate (*flaming row*); *colloq.* = DAMNED.

flamingo /flə'mɪŋgəʊ/ *n.* (*pl.* **flamingos**) tall long-necked wading-bird with pink, scarlet, and black plumage. [Port. f. Prov. (FLAME)]

flammable /'flæməb(ə)l/ *a.* inflammable; **flammability** /-'bɪlɪtɪ/ *n.* [L (FLAME)]

flan *n.* open sponge or pastry case filled or spread with fruit or savoury filling. [F f. L f. Gmc]

flange /flændʒ/ *n.* rim or projection, esp. for strengthening or attachment to other object. [orig. uncert.]

flank 1 *n.* fleshy part of side of body between ribs and hip; side of mountain etc.; left or right side of body of troops. 2 *v.t.* be or be posted at or move along flank or side of. [F f. Gmc]

flannel /'flæn(ə)l/ 1 *n.* a kind of woven woollen usu. napless cloth; (in *pl.*) flannel garments, esp. trousers; cloth used for washing oneself; *sl.* nonsense, flattery. 2 *v.* (**-ll-**, *US* **-l-**) wash with flannel; *sl.* flatter. [W *gwlanen* (*gwlān* wool)]

flannelette /flæn(ə)l'et/ *n.* napped cotton fabric resembling flannel.

flap 1 *v.* (**-pp-**) (cause to) swing or sway about, or move up and down; hit at (fly etc.) with flat object; *colloq.* (of ears) listen intently; *colloq.* be agitated or panicky. 2 *n.* flat broad piece attached at one edge, acting as cover, extension, etc.; aileron on aircraft; action or sound of flapping; light blow, usu. with something flat; *colloq.* state of agitation or fuss. 3 **flappy** *a.* [prob. imit.]

flapdoodle /'flæpdu:d(ə)l/ *n.* nonsense.

flapjack *n.* sweet oatcake; small pancake.

flapper *n.* broad flat device for killing flies, etc., flap; *colloq.* young esp. unconventional woman in 1920s.

flare 1 *v.* blaze with bright unsteady flame; burst into anger (*tempers flared*); (cause to) widen gradually. 2 *n.* flame or bright light used as signal or to illuminate target etc.; outburst of flame; dazzlingly unsteady light; gradual widening (e.g. in trousers or skirt). 3 **flare path** line of lights to guide aircraft landing or taking off; **flare up** burst into flame, become suddenly angry. [orig. unkn.]

flash 1 *n.* sudden short blaze of flame or light; brief outburst of feeling, transient display of wit etc.; an instant (*in a flash*); unscheduled news item on radio etc.; photographic flashlight; coloured cloth patch as emblem on military uniform. 2 *v.* give out a flash, gleam; burst suddenly into view or perception; send or reflect like a flash or in flashes (*her eyes flashed passion*); cause to shine briefly (*flash headlights*, *torch*); rush past suddenly; send (news etc.) by radio or telegraph; *colloq.* show suddenly or ostentatiously; *sl.* briefly display oneself indecently. 3 *a.* *colloq.* gaudy, showy, smart; *colloq.* connected with thieves etc. 4 **flash cube** set of four flashbulbs arranged as cube and operated in turn; **flash in the pan** seemingly brilliant but fleeting success, failure after promising start. [imit.]

flashback *n.* return to past event, esp. as scene in film.

flashbulb *n.* bulb giving bright light for flashlight photography.

flasher *n.* automatic device for flashing lights intermittently; *sl.* person who 'flashes' indecently.

flashing *n.* strip of metal acting as waterproofing at joint of roofing etc. [dial.]

flashlight *n.* device producing brief bright light for indoor etc. photography; electric torch. [FLASH]

flashpoint *n.* temperature at which vapour from oil etc. will ignite; point at which anger breaks out.

flashy *a.* gaudy, showy, cheaply attractive; **flashily** *adv.*; **flashiness** *n.*

flask /flɑ:sk/ *n.* = *vacuum-flask*; narrow-necked bulbous bottle as used in chemistry; small flat bottle for spirits, carried in pocket etc. [F & It. f. L *flasca, flasco*; cf. FLAGON]

flat 1 *a.* (-tt-) horizontal, level; spread out, lying at full length (*lying flat against the wall*; *flat on the floor*); smooth, without bumps or indentations; absolute, downright (*flat refusal*); dull, uninteresting, monotonous; (of drink) that has lost its effervescence; (of battery etc.) no longer able to generate electric current; (of tyre) deflated, esp. from puncture; *Mus.* below normal or correct pitch, (after note, indicating semitone lower, as *B flat*). 2 *adv.* in a flat manner (*lies flat*; *sings flat*); *colloq.* absolutely, completely, exactly (*turned it down flat*; *ten seconds flat*). 3 *n.* group of rooms, usu. on one floor, forming residence; flat thing or part, level ground; low land; *Mus.* note lowered by semitone, sign (♭) indicating this; *colloq.* flat tyre; section of stage scenery mounted on frame. 4 **the flat** season of flat races for horses; **flat feet** feet with less than normal arch beneath; **flat-fish** type of fish with flattened body, e.g. sole and plaice; **flat-footed** having flat feet, *colloq.* resolute, uninspired, unprepared; **flat-iron** heavy iron for pressing linen etc., heated by external means; **flat out** at top speed, using all one's strength or resources; **flat race** race over level ground, without jumps; **flat rate** unvarying rate or charge; **flat spin** nearly horizontal spin in aircraft, *colloq.* agitation or panic; **that's flat** *colloq.* that is definite. [ON]

flatlet *n.* small flat, usu. of one or two rooms.

flatten *v.* make or become flat; defeat or refute decisively, humiliate.

flatter *v.t.* pay exaggerated or insincere compliments to, esp. to win favour; cause to feel honoured; (of portrait etc.) represent (person) too favourably; **flatter oneself** smugly delude oneself (*that*). [F]

flattery *n.* exaggerated or insincere praise.

flatulent /ˈflætjʊlənt/ *a.* causing, caused by, or troubled with, formation of gas in alimentary canal; inflated, pretentious; **flatulence** *n.*; **flatulency** *n.* [F, or L (*flatus* blowing)]

flatworm *n.* type of worm with flattened body, e.g. tapeworm. [FLAT]

flaunt *v.* display proudly; show off, parade. [orig. unkn.]

flautist /ˈflɔ:tɪst/ *n.* flute-player. [It. (FLUTE)]

flavour /ˈfleɪvə/, *US* **flavor** 1 *n.* mingled sensation of smell and taste; distinctive taste; indefinable characteristic quality; slight admixture *of* a quality. 2 *v.t.* give flavour to, season. 3 **flavoursome** *a.* [F]

flavouring *n.* thing used to flavour food or drink.

flaw[1] 1 *n.* imperfection, blemish; crack, breach; invalidating defect in document etc. 2 *v.* make flaw in, spoil. [ON]

flaw[2] *n.* squall of wind. [LG or Du.]

flax *n.* blue-flowered plant cultivated for its seed and for textile fibre obtained from its stem; its fibre; **flax-seed** linseed. [OE]

flaxen *a.* of flax; pale yellow.

flay *v.t.* strip off skin or hide of; peel off; criticize severely. [OE]

flea *n.* small wingless jumping insect feeding on human and other blood; **flea-bite** slight injury or inconvenience; **flea-bitten** bitten by or infested with fleas, shabby; **a flea in one's ear** sharp reproof; **flea market** *colloq.* street market selling second-hand goods etc.; **flea-pit** *sl.* dingy dirty cinema etc. [OE]

fleck 1 *n.* small spot of colour; small particle, speck. 2 *v.t.* mark with flecks. [ON, or LG or Du.]

flection *US* var. of FLEXION.

fled *past* and *p.p.* of FLEE.

fledge *v.t.* provide (bird, arrow, etc.) with feathers or down; rear (young bird) until it can fly; (in *p.p.*) able to fly, *fig.* mature, independent, trained (*a fully-fledged pilot*). [obs. adj. *fledge* fit to fly]

fledgeling /ˈfledʒlɪŋ/ *n.* (also **fledgling**) young bird; inexperienced person.

flee *v.* (*past* and *p.p.* **fled**) run away (from), leave hurriedly; seek safety in flight; vanish. [OE]

fleece 1 *n.* woolly coat of sheep etc.; wool shorn from sheep in one shearing; soft fabric for lining etc. 2 *v.t.* strip or rob of money, property, etc.; remove fleece from (sheep). 3 **fleecy** *a.* [OE]

fleet 1 *n.* naval force, navy; group of ships under one commander; number of vehicles under one proprietor. 2 *a.* swift, nimble. [OE]

fleeting *a.* brief, passing rapidly (*fleeting glimpse, moment*).

Fleming /ˈflemɪŋ/ *n.* native of Flanders. [OE]

Flemish /ˈflemɪʃ/ 1 *a.* of Flanders or its people or language. 2 *n.* language of Flanders. [Du.]

flesh *n.* soft substance between skin and bones; tissue of animal bodies (excluding fish and sometimes fowl) as food; body as opposed to mind or soul; visible surface of human body; pulpy part of

fruit or plant; plumpness, fat; **the flesh** physical or sensual appetites; **flesh and blood** the human body, human nature, mankind (**one's flesh and blood** near relations); **flesh-coloured** yellowish pink; **flesh-wound** wound not reaching bone or vital organ; **in the flesh** in bodily form, in person. [OE]
fleshly *a.* mortal, worldly; sensual.
fleshpots *n.pl.* luxurious living.
fleshy *a.* of or like flesh, plump, pulpy; **fleshiness** *n.*
fleur-de-lis /flɜ:də'li:/ *n.* (also **-lys;** *pl.* **fleurs-** *pr.* same) heraldic lily of three petals; former royal arms of France. [F, = flower of lily]
flew *past* of FLY[1].
flex[1] *v.t.* bend (joint or limb); move (muscle) to bend joint. [L (*flecto flex-* bend)]
flex[2] *n.* flexible insulated wire. [abbr. of foll.]
flexible /'fleksɪb(ə)l/ *a.* that bends easily without breaking, pliable; adaptable to circumstances; manageable; **flexibility** /-'bɪlɪtɪ/ *n.*; **flexibly** *adv.* [F, or L *flexibilis* (FLEX[1])]
flexion /'flekʃ(ə)n/ *n.* bending; bent state or part. [f. L *flexio* (FLEX)]
flexitime /'fleksɪtaɪm/ *n.* system of flexible working hours. [FLEXIBLE]
flibbertigibbet /flɪbətɪ'dʒɪbɪt/ *n.* gossiping or frivolous person. [imit.]
flick 1 *n.* sudden release of bent finger or thumb; quick light blow or stroke; (in *pl.*) *colloq.* cinema performance. **2** *v.t.* strike or knock or move with a flick. **3 flick-knife** knife with blade that springs out when button etc. is pressed; **flick through** look cursorily through (book etc.). [imit.]
flicker 1 *v.i.* burn or shine unsteadily or fitfully; flutter, wave about; (of hope etc.) occur briefly. **2** *n.* flickering light or movement; brief spell (of hope, recognition, etc.). [OE]
flier var. of FLYER.
flight[1] /flaɪt/ *n.* act or manner of flying, movement or path of thing through the air, distance flown; journey made by aircraft or airline, esp. regularly; group of birds etc. flying together; volley (*of* arrows etc.); series (*of* stairs in straight line, *of* hurdles etc. for racing); act that is exceptional in effort or result (*flight of fancy*); tail of dart; **flight-deck** cockpit of large aircraft, deck of aircraft-carrier; **flight lieutenant** RAF officer next below squadron leader; **flight-recorder** electronic device in aircraft, recording information about its flight; **flight sergeant** RAF rank next above sergeant; **in the first** (or **top**) **flight** taking a leading place, excellent of its kind. [OE (FLY[1])]
flight[2] /flaɪt/ *n.* fleeing, escape from danger etc.; **put to flight** cause to flee; **take (to) flight** flee. [OE]
flightless *a.* (of bird) lacking power of flight. [FLIGHT[1]]
flighty *a.* (usu. of girl) frivolous, changeable; **flightily** *adv.*; **flightiness** *n.*
flimsy /'flɪmzɪ/ *a.* lightly or carelessly assembled; easily damaged or knocked apart; (of excuse etc.) unconvincing; **flimsily** *adv.*; **flimsiness** *n.* [orig. uncert.]
flinch *v.i.* draw back, shrink (*from* action); wince. [F f. Gmc]
fling 1 *v.* (*past* and *p.p.* **flung**) throw, esp. forcefully or hurriedly, hurl; put or send hurriedly or summarily (*flung them in prison*); put *on* or take *off* (clothes) hurriedly or casually; rush, go angrily or violently (*he flung out of the house*). **2** *n.* action of flinging; vigorous dance (*Highland fling*); short bout of self-indulgence. [ON]
flint *n.* a hard stone containing silica; piece of this, esp. as prehistoric tool or weapon; piece of hard alloy used to produce spark; anything hard and unyielding; **flinty** *a.* [OE]
flintlock *n.* old type of gun fired by spark from flint.
flip[1] **1** *v.* (**-pp-**) turn over quickly, flick; toss (thing) with jerk so that it turns over in the air. **2** *n.* action of flipping; *colloq.* short trip. **3 flip one's lid** lose self-control, go mad; **flip side** reverse side of gramophone record; **flip through** look cursorily through (book etc.). [prob. FILLIP]
flip[2] *n.* drink of heated beer and spirit. [perh. f. prec.]
flip[3] *a. colloq.* glib, flippant. [FLIP[1]]
flippant /'flɪpənt/ *a.* treating serious matter lightly, disrespectful; **flippancy** *n.* [FLIP[1]]
flipper *n.* limb used by turtle, seal, etc., in swimming; flat rubber etc. attachment worn on foot in underwater swimming; *sl.* hand. [FLIP[1]]
flipping *a.* & *adv. sl.* expressing mild annoyance.
flirt 1 *v.i.* behave (*with* person) in amorous or enticing manner without serious intentions; superficially interest oneself (*with* idea etc.); trifle *with* danger etc. **2** *n.* one who flirts amorously. **3 flirtation** /-'teɪʃ(ə)n/ *n.*; **flirtatious** /-'teɪʃəs/ *a.* [imit.]
flit 1 *v.i.* (**-tt-**) move lightly and rapidly (*about* etc.); make short flights; abscond, disappear secretly (esp. from abode to escape creditor). **2** *n.* act of flitting. [ON (FLEET)]
flitch *n.* side of bacon. [OE]

flitter *v.i.* flit about; **flitter-mouse** = BAT². [FLIT]

float 1 *v.* (cause to) rest or move on surface of liquid; move or be suspended *in* liquid or gas; *sl.* move about in leisurely way; hover *before* eye or mind; (of currency) (cause or allow to) have fluctuating exchange rate; start (company, scheme, etc.). **2** *n.* raft; floating device to control flow of water, petrol, etc.; structure enabling aircraft to float on water; cork or quill used on fishing-line as indicator; cork supporting edge of fishing-net; low-bodied lorry or cart, esp. used for display in procession; sum of money retained for minor expenditure or change-giving; tool for smoothing plaster; (in *sing.* or *pl.*) footlights in theatre. **3 floating dock** floating structure usable as dry dock; **floating kidney** one unusually movable; **floating population** population not settled in definite place; **floating rib** any of ribs not joined to breastbone; **floating voter** voter not supporting any political party. [OE]

floatation var. of FLOTATION.

flocculent /'flɒkjʊlənt/ *a.* like tufts of wool; in or showing tufts; **flocculence** *n.* [FLOCK²]

flock¹ **1** *n.* number of sheep, goats, or birds regarded as a group or unit; large crowd of people; number of people in care of priest or teacher etc. **2** *v.i.* move, assemble *together*, in large numbers. [OE]

flock² *n.* lock or tuft of wool etc.; wool or cotton waste used as stuffing. [F f. L *floccus*]

floe /fləʊ/ *n.* sheet of floating ice. [Norw.]

flog *v.t.* (**-gg-**) beat with whip, stick, etc.; *sl.* sell; **flog a dead horse** waste one's efforts; **flog to death** *colloq.* talk about or promote at tedious length. [orig. unkn.]

flood /flʌd/ **1** *n.* influx or overflowing of water beyond its normal confines, esp. over land; the water that overflows; outpouring, outburst of great quantity (*floods of abuse, tears, visitors*); inflow of tide; *colloq.* = FLOODLIGHT. **2** *v.* overflow, cover, or be covered, with flood; come (*in*) in great quantities; drive *out* (of home etc.) by flood; have uterine hæmorrhage. **3 the Flood** that described in Genesis; **flood-tide** rising tide. [OE]

floodgate *n.* gate for admitting or excluding water; restraint against tears etc.

floodlight **1** *n.* large powerful light (usu. one of several) to illuminate building, sportsground, etc. **2** *v.t.* illuminate with this. **3 floodlit** *a.*

floor /flɔ:/ **1** *n.* lower surface of room, on which one stands; bottom of sea, cave, etc.; rooms etc. on same level in building; part of legislative assembly etc. where members sit and speak; right to speak next in debate etc. (*have, be given, the floor*); level area; minimum of prices, wages, etc. **2** *v.t.* provide with floor; knock (person) down; baffle or nonplus; overcome. **3 first** (*US* **second**) **floor** floor above ground floor; **floor show** entertainment presented on floor of night-club etc.; **ground** (*US* **first**) **floor** floor on ground level. [OE]

floorboard *n.* long wooden board used for flooring.

floorcloth *n.* cloth for washing floors.

flooring *n.* boards etc. used as floor.

floozie *n.* (also **floosie**) *colloq.* girl or woman, esp. disreputable one. [orig. unkn.]

flop **1** *v.i.* (**-pp-**) fall or sit etc. (*down*) suddenly, awkwardly, or with slight thud; hang or sway limply or heavily; make dull flapping sound; *sl.* fail. **2** *n.* flopping motion or sound; *sl.* failure. **3** *adv.* with a flop. [var. of FLAP]

floppy *a.* tending to flop, not firm or rigid; **floppy disc** flexible disc for storage of machine-readable data; **floppiness** *n.*

flora /'flɔ:rə/ *n.* (*pl.* **floras**) plants of a particular region or period. [L, name of goddess of flowers]

floral /'flɔ:r(ə)l, 'flɒ-/ *a.* of or decorated with flowers; **florally** *adv.* [L]

Florentine /'flɒrəntaɪn/ **1** *a.* of Florence in Italy. **2** *n.* native of Florence. [F or L]

floret /'flɔ:rɪt/ *n.* small flower; one of the small flowers of a composite flower. [L *flos* FLOWER]

floribunda /flɒrɪ'bʌndə/ *n.* rose or other plant bearing dense clusters of flowers. [as prec.; cf. MORIBUND]

florid /'flɒrɪd/ *a.* ornate, elaborate, showy; ruddy, flushed. [F or L (FLOWER)]

florin /'flɒrɪn/ *n.* gold or silver coin, esp. former English two-shilling coin. [F f. It. *fiorino* (foll.)]

florist /'flɒrɪst/ *n.* one who deals in or grows flowers. [L *flos* FLOWER]

floruit /'flɒrʊɪt/ *n.* period or date at which person lived or worked. [L, = he or she flourished]

floss *n.* rough silk enveloping silkworm's cocoon; untwisted silk thread for embroidery; = *dental floss*; **floss silk** rough silk used in cheap goods; **flossy** *a.* [F *floche*]

flotation /fləʊ'teɪʃ(ə)n/ *n.* launching of a commercial enterprise etc. [FLOAT]

flotilla /flɒ'tɪlə/ *n.* small fleet; fleet of small ships. [Sp.]

flotsam /'flɒtsəm/ *n.* wreckage found

floating; **flotsam and jetsam** odds and ends, vagrants, etc. [AF (FLOAT)]

flounce[1] **1** *v.i.* go or move abruptly or angrily, with jerking movements (*flounced out of the room*). **2** *n.* flouncing movement. [orig. unkn.]

flounce[2] **1** *n.* ornamental frill round woman's skirt etc. **2** *v.t.* trim with flounces. [alt. of *frounce* pleat f. F]

flounder[1] **1** *v.i.* move or struggle helplessly or clumsily; progress with great difficulty, struggle. **2** *n.* act of floundering. [imit.]

flounder[2] *n.* flat-fish, esp. of small edible species. [AF, prob. Scand.]

flour 1 *n.* fine meal or powder made by milling and usu. sifting cereals, esp. wheat; fine soft powder. **2** *v.t.* sprinkle with flour. **3 floury** *a.* [diff. sp. of FLOWER 'best part']

flourish /'flʌrɪʃ/ **1** *v.* grow vigorously and healthily; prosper, thrive, be in prime; wave, brandish. **2** *n.* ornamental curve in writing; dramatic gesture with hand etc.; *Mus.* florid passage, fanfare. [F f. L *floreo* (*flos* FLOWER)]

flout 1 *v.* disobey scornfully (convention etc.); express contempt (for). **2** *n.* flouting speech or act. [Du. *fluiten* whistle (FLUTE)]

flow /fləʊ/ **1** *v.i.* glide along as a stream, move like liquid; gush out (*from* source); (of blood, money, electric current, etc.) circulate; move smoothly and steadily (*flowing traffic, music*); hang easily, undulate (*flowing hair, robe*); be plentiful (*the wine flowed*); be plentifully supplied *with* (*land flowing with milk and honey*); result (*from*); (of tide) rise. **2** *n.* flowing movement or mass; flowing liquid, amount of this; outpouring (*flow of words*); rise of tide (*ebb and flow*). **3 flow chart** (or **diagram** or **sheet**) diagram showing movement or development of things through a series of processes. [OE]

flower /'flaʊə/ **1** *n.* part of plant from which fruit or seed is developed; blossom (and stem) used esp. in groups for decoration; plant cultivated or noted for its flowers. **2** *v.* (cause to) bloom or blossom; reach peak. **3 the flower of** the best part of; **flowers of sulphur** fine powder produced when sulphur evaporates and condenses; **in flower** with the flowers out. [F f. L *flos flor-*]

flowerpot *n.* pot in which plant may be grown.

flowery *a.* abounding in flowers; (of language) ornate, elaborate; **floweriness** *n.*

flown *p.p.* of FLY[1].

flu /flu:/ *n. colloq.* influenza. [abbr.]

fluctuate /'flʌktjʊeɪt/ *v.i.* vary erratically, rise and fall; **fluctuation** /-'eɪʃ(ə)n/ *n.* [L (*fluctus* wave)]

flue /flu:/ *n.* smoke-duct in chimney; channel for conveying heat. [orig. unkn.]

fluent /'flu:ənt/ *a.* (of person) able to speak quickly and easily; (of speech) flowing easily, coming readily; **fluency** *n.* [L (*fluo* flow)]

fluff 1 *n.* light downy substance, e.g. that shed from fabric; *sl.* bungle or mistake (in performance etc.). **2** *v.* shake or puff into soft mass; *sl.* make mistake in, bungle. **3 fluffy** *a.* [prob. dial. alt. of *flue* fluff]

fluid /'flu:ɪd/ **1** *n.* substance, as gas or liquid, that is capable of flowing freely; fluid part or secretion. **2** *a.* able to flow freely; not solid or rigid, fluctuating (*situation is fluid*). **3 fluid ounce** one twentieth of a pint, *US* one sixteenth of a pint. **4 fluidity** /-'ɪdɪtɪ/ *n.* [F or L (FLUENT)]

fluke[1] /flu:k/ **1** *n.* thing that happens or succeeds by chance, piece of luck. **2** *v.t.* achieve, hit, etc., by fluke. **3 fluky** *a.* [orig. uncert.]

fluke[2] /flu:k/ *n.* flat-fish, flounder; parasitic worm found in sheep's liver. [OE]

fluke[3] /flu:k/ *n.* triangular flat end of anchor arm; lobe of whale's tail. [perh. f. prec.]

flummery /'flʌmərɪ/ *n.* sweet milk dish; nonsense, empty talk. [W *llymru*]

flummox /'flʌməks/ *v.t. colloq.* bewilder, disconcert. [orig. unkn.]

flung *past* and *p.p.* of FLING.

flunk *v. US colloq.* fail, esp. in examination. [orig. unkn.]

flunkey /'flʌŋkɪ/ *n.* (usu. *derog.*) footman; toady, snob; *US* cook, waiter, etc. [orig. uncert.]

fluoresce /flʊə'res/ *v.i.* be or become fluorescent. [foll.]

fluorescent *a.* (of substance) absorbing radiation and emitting it in the form of light; **fluorescent lamp** one with such substance; **fluorescence** *n.* [FLUORSPAR]

fluoridate /'flʊərɪdeɪt/ *v.t.* add traces of fluoride to (drinking-water etc.), esp. to prevent tooth-decay; **fluoridation** /-'deɪʃ(ə)n/ *n.* [foll.]

fluoride /'flʊəraɪd/ *n.* binary compound of fluorine. [FLUORINE]

fluorinate /'flʊərɪneɪt/ *v.t.* = FLUORIDATE; introduce fluorine into. [foll.]

fluorine /'flʊəri:n/ *n.* pale yellow corrosive gaseous element. [F (foll.)]

fluorspar /'flʊəspɑ:/ *n.* calcium fluoride as mineral. [*fluor* mineral used as flux (L, f. *fluo* flow)]

flurry /'flʌrɪ/ **1** *n.* gust, squall; sudden

burst of activity; nervous hurry, agitation. **2** *v.t.* confuse or agitate. [imit.]

flush[1] **1** *v.* (cause to) become red in the face, blush; cleanse (drain, lavatory, etc.) by flow of water; dispose of (thing) thus; (of water) rush or spurt out; inflame with pride or passion (*flushed with success*); make level. **2** *n.* reddening of the face, blush; feeling of feverish heat; rush of excitement or elation (*the first flush of victory*); rush of water; cleansing by flushing; freshness, vigour. **3** *a.* level, in same plane; *colloq.* having plenty of money etc. [perh. = foll.]

flush[2] *v.* (cause to) take wing and fly up or away; reveal, drive *out*. [imit.]

flush[3] *n.* hand of cards all of one suit; **straight flush** flush that is also a sequence; **royal flush** straight flush headed by ace. [F f. L (FLUX)]

fluster 1 *v.* confuse or agitate; make nervous; bustle. **2** *n.* confused or agitated state. [orig. unkn.]

flute /flu:t/ **1** *n.* woodwind instrument consisting of pipe with holes along it stopped by fingers or keys and mouth-hole in side; ornamental groove in pillar etc. **2** *v.* make grooves in; sing or speak etc. in flutelike tones; play (on) flute. **3** **fluty** *a.* [F]

fluting *n.* series of ornamental grooves.

flutter 1 *v.* flap (wings) in flying or trying to fly; wave or flap quickly and irregularly; move about restlessly; (of pulse) beat feebly and irregularly. **2** *n.* fluttering; state of nervous excitement; rapid fluctuation in pitch or loudness; *colloq.* small bet or speculation. [OE]

fluvial /'flu:vɪəl/ *a.* of or found in rivers. [L (*fluvius* river)]

flux *n.* continuous succession of changes (*state of flux*); flowing; inflow of tide; substance mixed with metal etc. to aid fusion. [F, or L *fluxus* (*fluo flux-* flow)]

fly[1] /flaɪ/ **1** *v.* (*past* **flew** /flu:/; *p.p.* **flown** /fləʊn/) move through the air by means of wings; (of aircraft etc. or occupants) travel through the air or space; transport in aircraft; (of cloud etc.) pass quickly through the air; go or move quickly, pass swiftly (*time flies*); *colloq.* depart hastily; (of flag, hair, etc.) wave; raise (flag) so that it waves; make (kite) rise and stay aloft; be driven or scattered, come or be forced suddenly *off*, *open*, etc. (*sent me flying*; *feathers flew*; *door flew open*); pass suddenly *into* (a rage etc.); hasten or spring violently (*at*, *on*, *to*, *upon*); flee (from). **2** *n.* flying; flap on garment, esp. trousers, to contain or cover fastening, (usu. in *pl.*) this fastening; flap at entrance of tent; (in *pl.*) space over proscenium in theatre; part of flag furthest from staff. **3** **fly-away** (of hair etc.) streaming, waving; **fly-by-night** *n.* & *a.* unreliable (person); **fly-half** stand-off half in Rugby football; **fly high** have high ambition; **fly in the face of** disregard or disobey openly; **fly a kite** see KITE; **fly off the handle** *colloq.* become uncontrollably angry; **fly-past** ceremonial flight of aircraft past person or place. [OE]

fly[2] /flaɪ/ *n.* two-winged insect; other winged insect, e.g. firefly, mayfly; disease of plants or animals caused by flies; natural or artificial fly as bait in fishing; **fly-blown** *a.* (of meat etc.) tainted by flies' eggs; **fly-fish** *v.i.* fish with fly; **fly in the ointment** minor irritation that spoils enjoyment; **fly on the wall** unnoticed observer; **fly-paper** sticky treated paper for catching flies; **fly-spray** liquid sprayed from canister to kill flies; **fly-trap** plant able to catch flies; **there are no flies on him** *sl.* he is very astute. [OE]

fly[3] *a. sl.* knowing, clever. [orig. unkn.]

flycatcher *n.* bird that catches insects in the air. [FLY[2]]

flyer *n.* airman; fast-moving animal or vehicle; ambitious or outstanding person. [FLY[1]]

flying 1 *n.* flight. **2** *a.* that flies; (of flag etc.) fluttering, waving; hasty (*flying visit*); (of animal) able to make long leaps by use of membranes etc.; (of vehicle etc.) designed for rapid movement. **3** **flying boat** seaplane with boat-like fuselage; **flying buttress** buttress slanting from separate column, usu. forming arch with wall it supports; **flying colours** see COLOUR; **flying fish** tropical fish with winglike fins, able to rise into the air; **flying fox** fruit-eating bat; **flying officer** RAF officer next below flight lieutenant; **flying picket** picket organized for moving from place to place; **flying saucer** unidentified saucer-shaped object reported as seen in the sky; **flying squad** police detachment or other body organized for rapid movement; **flying start** start in which starting-point is passed at full speed, *fig.* vigorous start giving initial advantage. [FLY[1]]

flyleaf *n.* blank leaf at beginning or end of book.

flyover *n.* bridge that carries one road or railway over another.

flysheet *n.* tract or circular of 2 or 4 pages.

flyweight *n.* boxing-weight with upper limit of 51 kg.; **light flyweight** this with upper limit of 48 kg. [FLY[2]]

flywheel *n.* heavy wheel on revolving shaft to regulate machinery or accumulate power. [FLY[1]]

FM *abbr.* Field Marshal; frequency modulation.

Fm *symb.* fermium.

f-number /ef/ *n.* ratio of focal length and effective diameter of lens, used in photography to calculate amount of light passing through lens. [*focal*]

FO *abbr.* Flying Officer; *hist.* Foreign Office.

foal 1 *n.* young of horse or related animal. **2** *v.* (of mare etc.) give birth to (foal). **3 in** (or **with**) **foal** (of mare etc.) pregnant. [OE]

foam 1 *n.* collection of small bubbles formed on or in liquid by agitation, fermentation, etc.; froth of saliva or perspiration; substance resembling foam, e.g. rubber or plastic in cellular mass. **2** *v.i.* emit foam, froth; run in a foam. **3 foam at the mouth** be very angry. **4 foamy** *a.* [OE]

fob[1] *n.* ornamental attachment to watch-chain, key-ring, etc.; small pocket for watch etc. in waistband of trousers. [G]

fob[2] *v.t.* (**-bb-**) now only in **fob off** deceive (person) into accepting or being satisfied (*with* inferior thing, excuse, etc.); palm or pass off (thing) *on* or *on to* person. [cf. obs. *fop* dupe]

f.o.b. *abbr.* free on board.

focal /'fəʊk(ə)l/ *a.* of or at a focus; **focal distance** (or **length**) distance between centre of mirror or lens and its focus; **focally** *adv.* [L (FOCUS)]

fo'c's(')le var. of FORECASTLE.

focus /'fəʊkəs/ **1** *n.* (*pl.* **focuses** or **foci** /'fəʊsaɪ/) point at which rays or waves meet after reflection or refraction; point from which rays etc. appear to proceed; point at which object must be situated for lens or mirror to give well-defined image; adjustment of eye or lens to give clear image; state of clear definition (*in, out of, focus*); centre of interest or activity etc. **2** *v.* (**-s-** or **-ss-**) bring into focus; adjust focus of (lens or eye); (cause to) converge to a focus; concentrate or be concentrated *on*. [L, = hearth]

fodder 1 *n.* dried hay or straw etc. for horses, cattle, etc. **2** *v.t.* give fodder to. [OE]

foe *n.* (chiefly *poetic*) enemy. [OE]

foetid /'fi:tɪd/ var. of FETID.

foetus /'fi:təs/ *n.* unborn or unhatched offspring, esp. human embryo more than eight weeks after conception; **foetal** *a.* [L *fetus* offspring]

fog 1 *n.* thick cloud of water droplets or smoke suspended at or near earth's surface; cloudiness obscuring image on photographic negative etc. **2** *v.* (**-gg-**) cover or become covered (as) with fog; perplex. **3 fog-bank** mass of fog at sea; **fog-bound** unable to leave because of fog; **fog-horn** horn sounding warning to ships in fog, *fig.* loud penetrating voice; **fog-lamp** powerful lamp for use in fog. [perh. ult. Scand.]

foggy *a.* full of fog; of or like fog, indistinct; **not have the foggiest** *colloq.* have no idea at all; **fogginess** *n.*

fogy /'fəʊgɪ/ *n.* (also **fogey**) old-fashioned person (usu. **old fogy**). [orig. unkn.]

foible /'fɔɪb(ə)l/ *n.* small weakness in person's character. [F (FEEBLE)]

foil[1] *v.t.* baffle, frustrate, defeat. [perh. f. F *fouler* trample]

foil[2] *n.* metal hammered or rolled into thin sheet; person or thing that enhances the qualities of another by contrast. [F f. L *folium* leaf]

foil[3] *n.* light blunt-edged sword used in fencing. [orig. unkn.]

foist *v.* fob (thing) (*off*) *on* person. [Du. *vuisten* take in the hand]

fold[1] /fəʊld/ **1** *v.* bend or close (flexible thing) over upon itself; bend part of (thing) *back* or *down*; become or be able to be folded; embrace (*in* arms or *to* breast); clasp (arms etc.) *about* or *round*; wrap, envelop; (in cookery) mix (ingredient) *in* without stirring or beating. **2** *n.* folding; folded part; line made by folding; hollow among hills; curvature of geological strata. **3 fold one's arms** place them across chest, together or entwined; **fold away** (or **up**) make compact by folding; **fold one's hands** clasp them; **fold up** collapse (*lit.* or *fig.*), cease to function. [OE]

fold[2] **1** *n.* = *sheep-fold*; body of believers, members of Church. **2** *v.t.* enclose (sheep) in fold. [OE]

-fold *suffix* forming adjectives and adverbs from cardinal numbers, in sense 'in amount multiplied by' (*repaid tenfold*), 'with so many parts' (*threefold blessing*). [orig. = folded in so many layers etc.]

folder *n.* folding cover or holder for loose papers; folded leaflet. [FOLD[1]]

foliaceous /fəʊlɪ'eɪʃəs/ *a.* of or like leaves; laminated. [L (FOIL[2])]

foliage /'fəʊlɪɪdʒ/ *n.* leaves, leafage. [F *feuillage* (*feuille* leaf)]

foliar /'fəʊlɪə/ *a.* of leaves; **foliar feed** feed supplied to leaves of plants. [as foll.]

foliate 1 /'fəʊlɪət/ *a.* leaflike, having leaves. **2** /'fəʊlɪeɪt/ *v.* split or beat into thin layers. **3 foliation** /-'eɪʃ(ə)n/ *n.* [L *folium* leaf]

folio /'fəʊlɪəʊ/ **1** *n.* (*pl.* **folios**) leaf of paper etc., esp. one numbered only on front; sheet of paper folded once making two leaves of book; book made of such sheets. **2** *a.* (of book etc.) made of folios, of largest size. **3 in folio** made of folios. [L, abl. of *folium* leaf]

folk /fəʊk/ **1** *n.* nation or people; people of specified class (*townsfolk*); (often in *pl.*) people in general; one's parents or relatives; = *folk-music*. **2** *attrib.* of popular origin (*folk-art*). **3 folk-music, -song** music or song traditional in a country, or in style of this. [OE]

folklore *n.* traditional beliefs etc. of a community; study of these.

folksy /'fəʊksɪ/ *a.* having characteristics of ordinary people or of folk-art; simple, unpretentious, friendly.

folkweave *n.* rough loosely woven fabric.

follicle /'fɒlɪk(ə)l/ *n.* small sac or vesicle in the body, esp. one containing hair-root; **follicular** /fɒ'lɪkjʊlə/ *a.* [L dimin. of *follis* bellows]

follow /'fɒləʊ/ *v.* go or come after (person or thing proceeding ahead); go or come *after*; go along (road etc.); come next in order or time (*my reasons follow, are as follows*); take as guide or leader, conform to; practise (trade or profession), undertake (course of study etc.); understand meaning or tendency of (argument, speaker); be aware of present state or progress of (events etc.); provide *with* sequel or successor; result *from*; be necessarily true as result of something else; **follow on** continue, (of cricket team) have to bat again immediately after first innings; **follow-on** *n.* instance of this; **follow out** carry out, adhere strictly to (instructions etc.); **follow suit** play card of suit led, conform to another's actions; **follow through** continue (action etc.) to its conclusion; **follow up** pursue, develop, supplement (one thing *with* another); **follow-up** *n.* further or continued action, measure, etc. [OE]

follower *n.* one who follows; supporter or devotee.

following **1** *n.* body of supporters or devotees. **2** *a.* that follows or comes after. **3** *prep.* after in time, as sequel to. **4 the following** what follows; now to be given or named (*answer the following questions*).

folly /'fɒlɪ/ *n.* foolishness; foolish act, behaviour, idea, etc.; costly ornamental building. [F *folie* (*fol* mad, FOOL)]

foment /fə'ment/ *v.t.* instigate or stir up (trouble, discontent, etc.); **fomentation** /-'teɪʃ(ə)n/ *n.* [F f. L (*foveo* heat, cherish)]

fond *a.* affectionate, loving; doting; (of hopes, beliefs, etc.) foolishly credulous or optimistic; **fond of** having a liking for. [obs. *fon* fool, be foolish]

fondant /'fɒndənt/ *n.* soft sweet of flavoured sugar. [F, = melting (FUSE[1])]

fondle /'fɒnd(ə)l/ *v.t.* caress. [FOND]

fondue /'fɒndju:, -du:/ *n.* dish of flavoured melted cheese. [F, = melted (FUSE[1])]

font[1] *n.* receptacle in church for baptismal water; **fontal** *a.* [OE f. Ir. f. L *fons font-* fountain]

font[2] *US* var. of FOUNT[1].

fontanelle /fɒntə'nel/, *US* **fontanel** *n.* membranous space in infant's skull at angles of parietal bones. [F f. L *fontanella* little FOUNTAIN]

food *n.* substance taken into animal or plant to maintain life and growth; solid food (*food and drink*); material for mental work (*food for thought*); **food poisoning** illness due to bacteria etc. in food eaten; **food processor** electric device for chopping and mixing food; **food value** nourishing power of a food. [OE]

foodstuff *n.* substance used as food.

fool[1] **1** *n.* person who acts or thinks unwisely or imprudently, stupid person; *hist.* jester, clown; dupe. **2** *v.* act in joking or teasing way; play or trifle (*about, around*); cheat or deceive (person) *out of* something or *into doing* thing. **3 act** (or **play**) **the fool** behave in silly way; **be no** (or **nobody's**) **fool** be shrewd or prudent; **fool's errand** fruitless errand; **fool's paradise** illusory happiness; **make a fool of** make (person) look foolish, trick or deceive. [F f. L *follis* bellows.]

fool[2] *n.* dessert of fruit crushed and mixed with cream or custard. [perh. f. prec.]

foolery *n.* foolish acts or behaviour. [FOOL[1]]

foolhardy *a.* rashly or foolishly bold, reckless; **foolhardiness** *n.*

foolish *a.* (of person or action) lacking good sense or judgement, unwise.

foolproof *a.* (of procedure, machine, etc.) so straightforward or simple as to be incapable of misuse or mistake.

foolscap /'fu:lskæp, -lz-/ *n.* size of paper, about 330 × 200 (or 400) mm. [f. watermark of *fool's cap*]

foot /fʊt/ **1** *n.* (*pl.* **feet**) end part of leg beyond ankle; lowest part of page, table, hill, etc., end of bed where feet are normally put; part of sock etc. covering foot; (*pl.* also **foot**) linear measure of 12 inches, 30.48 cm.; division of verse including one stressed syllable; step, pace, tread (*fleet of foot*); *hist.* infantry. **2** *v.t.* pay (bill). **3 feet of clay** fundamental weakness in person otherwise revered; **foot-and-mouth** (**disease**) contagious virus disease of cattle etc.; **foot-brake** foot-operated brake on vehicle; **foot-bridge** bridge for pedestrians only;

have one's feet on the ground be practical; **have one foot in the grave** be near death or very old; **my foot!** *colloq.* exclamation of contemptuous contradiction; **on foot** walking not riding; **put one's feet up** have a rest; **put one's foot down** be firm or insistent, accelerate motor vehicle; **put one's foot in it** blunder; **under one's feet** in the way (*lit.* & *fig.*); **under foot** on the ground. [OE]

footage *n.* length in feet, esp. of exposed cinema film.

football *n.* large inflated ball, usu. of leather; outdoor game between two teams, played with this; **football pool** form of gambling on results of football matches, entry money being awarded in prizes; **footballer** *n.*

footfall *n.* sound of footstep.

foothill *n.* one of low hills near bottom of mountain or range.

foothold *n.* place where foot can be supported securely; *fig.* secure initial position.

footing *n.* foothold, secure position (*lost his footing*); position or status of person in relation to others (*be on an equal footing*).

footlights *n.pl.* row of lights at front of stage at level of actors' feet.

footling /'fu:tlɪŋ/ *a. sl.* trivial, silly. [*footle*, orig. uncert.]

footloose *a.* free to act as one pleases. [FOOT]

footman *n.* liveried servant for attending at door or at table.

footnote *n.* note printed at foot of page.

footpad *n. hist.* unmounted highwayman.

footpath *n.* path for pedestrians, pavement.

footplate *n.* platform for driver and fireman in locomotive.

footprint *n.* impression left by foot or shoe.

footsore *a.* with sore feet, esp. from walking.

footstep *n.* step taken in walking; sound of this; **follow in person's footsteps** do as he did.

footstool *n.* stool for resting feet on when sitting.

footway *n.* path for pedestrians only.

footwear *n.* shoes, socks, etc.

footwork *n.* use or agility of feet in sports, dancing, etc.

fop *n.* dandy; **foppery** *n.*; **foppish** *a.* [perh. obs. *fop* fool]

for /fə, *emphat.* fɔ:/ **1** *prep.* in defence, support, or favour of; in the interest or to the benefit of (*I did it all for you*; *won a name for herself*); suitable or appropriate to (*a book for children*; *it is for you to say*); in respect or reference to, regarding, so far as concerns (*ready for dinner*; *for all I know*; *MP for Lincoln*; *nothing for it but to confess*; *usual for a tie to be worn*); at price of, in exchange with, corresponding to (*bought it for £5*; *took it back for a larger one*; *word for word*); as penalty or reward resulting from (*fined for speeding*; *decorated for bravery*); with a view to, in hope or quest of, in order to get (*did it for the money*; *go for a walk*; *send for a doctor*); in direction of, towards, to reach (*left for the station*); so as to have begun by (*meeting is at 7 for 8*); through or over (distance or period), during (*walked for two hours, two miles*); in the character of, as being (*for the last time*; *for one thing*; *know for a fact*); because of, on account of (*could not speak for laughing*); in spite of, notwithstanding (*for all his boasting*; *for all you know*); considering or making due allowance in respect of (*well done for a beginner*). **2** *conj.* seeing that, since, because. **3 be for it** *colloq.* be about to get punishment or other trouble; **for ever** for all time (see also FOREVER); **O** (or **oh**) **for** I wish I had. [OE, reduced form of FORE]

for- *prefix* forming verbs etc. meaning (1) away or off (*forget*, *forgive*); (2) prohibition (*forbid*); (3) abstention or neglect (*forgo*, *forsake*). [OE]

f.o.r. *abbr.* free on rail.

forage /'fɒrɪdʒ/ **1** *n.* food for horses and cattle; foraging. **2** *v.* go searching, rummage; collect forage (from). [F f. Gmc (FODDER)]

forasmuch /fɒrəz'mʌtʃ/ *adv.* in **forasmuch as** *archaic* since, because. [*for as much*]

foray /'fɒreɪ/ **1** *n.* sudden attack, raid. **2** *v.i.* make foray. [F (FODDER)]

forbade, forbad *past* of FORBID.

forbear[1] /fɔ:'beə/ *v.* (*past* **forbore;** *p.p.* **forborne**) abstain (from) or refrain (*could not forbear speaking out* or *from speaking out*; *forbore to mention it*). [OE (BEAR[1])]

forbear[2] var. of FOREBEAR.

forbearance *n.* patient self-control, tolerance. [FORBEAR[1]]

forbid /fə'bɪd/ *v.t.* (**-dd-;** past **forbade** /-'bæd/, **forbad;** *p.p.* **forbidden**) order not *to do* thing (*forbade him to leave*); refuse to allow (thing, or person to have thing); refuse person entry to. [OE (BID)]

forbidding *a.* uninviting, repellent, stern.

forbore *past* of FORBEAR[1].

forborne *p.p.* of FORBEAR[1].

force[1] **1** *n.* strength, power, impetus, intense effort; coercion, compulsion; military strength; organized body of soldiers, police, workers, etc.; binding power, validity, effect, precise significance; influence, efficacy (*force of habit*); measurable influence tending to cause motion of a body, intensity of this, *fig.* person or thing likened to this (*a force for good*). **2** *v.* constrain (person) by force or against his will; make way into or through by force, break open by force; drive or propel violently or against resistance; impose or press (thing) *on* or *upon* person; cause or produce by effort (*force a smile*); strain or increase to the utmost, overstrain; artificially hasten growth or maturity of (plant, pupil, etc.). **3 forced labour** compulsory labour usu. under harsh conditions; **forced landing** unavoidable landing of aircraft in emergency; **forced march** lengthy and vigorous march esp. by troops; **force-feed** feed (esp. prisoner) against his will; **force person's hand** make him act prematurely or unwillingly; **force the issue** make an immediate decision necessary; **in force** valid (*the laws now in force*), in great strength or numbers (*attacked in force*). [F f. L *fortis* strong]

force[2] *n. N. Engl.* waterfall. [ON]

forceful *a.* powerful and vigorous; (of speech) impressive, compelling; **forcefully** *adv.* [FORCE[1]]

force majeure /fɔ:s mæ'ʒɜ:/ irresistible force; unforeseen circumstances excusing from fulfilment of contract. [F]

forcemeat /'fɔ:smi:t/ *n.* meat etc. chopped and seasoned for stuffing or garnish. [FARCE]

forceps /'fɔ:seps/ *n.* (*pl.* same) surgical pincers. [L]

forcible *a.* done by or involving force; forceful; **forcibly** *adv.* [F (FORCE[1])]

ford 1 *n.* shallow place where river or stream may be crossed by wading, in motor vehicle, etc. **2** *v.t.* cross (water) thus. [OE]

fore 1 *a.* situated in front. **2** *n.* front part, bow of ship. **3** *int.* (in golf) as warning to person likely to be hit by ball. **4 fore and aft** at bow and stern, all over ship; **fore-and-aft** *a.* (of sail or rigging) lengthwise, not on yards; **to the fore** in front, conspicuous. [OE]

fore- *prefix* forming (1) verbs in senses 'in front' (*foreshorten*), 'beforehand' (*forewarn*), (2) nouns in senses 'situated in front' (*forecourt*), 'front part of' (*forehead*), 'of or near bow of ship' (*forecastle*), 'preceding' (*forerunner*).

forearm[1] /'fɔ:rɑ:m/ *n.* arm between elbow and wrist or fingertips. [ARM[1]]

forearm[2] /fɔ:r'ɑ:m/ *v.t.* arm beforehand, prepare. [ARM[2]]

forebear /'fɔ:beə/ *n.* (usu. in *pl.*) ancestor. [FORE-, obs. *beer* (BE)]

forebode /fɔ:'bəʊd/ *v.t.* be an advance sign of, portend; have presentiment of (usu. evil) or *that*. [FORE-]

foreboding *n.* expectation of trouble.

forecast /'fɔ:kɑ:st/ **1** *v.t.* (*past* and *p.p.* **forecast** or **-casted**) predict or estimate beforehand. **2** *n.* forecasting, prediction.

forecastle /'fəʊks(ə)l/ *n.* forward part of ship where formerly crew was accommodated.

foreclose /fɔ:'kləʊz/ *v.t.* take possession of mortgaged property of (person) when loan is not duly repaid; stop (mortgage) from being redeemable; exclude, prevent; **foreclosure** *n.* [F (L *foris* out, CLOSE[1])]

forecourt *n.* enclosed space in front of building; part of filling-station where petrol is dispensed. [FORE-]

foredoom /fɔ:'du:m/ *v.t.* doom or condemn beforehand.

forefather *n.* (usu. in *pl.*) ancestor, member of past generation of a family or people.

forefinger *n.* finger next to thumb.

forefoot *n.* front foot of animal.

forefront *n.* foremost part; leading position.

foregoing /fɔ:'gəʊɪŋ/ *a.* preceding, previously mentioned.

foregone /'fɔ:gɒn/ *a.* previous, preceding; **foregone conclusion** easily foreseen or predictable result.

foreground *n.* part of view or picture nearest observer; *fig.* most conspicuous position. [Du. (FORE-, GROUND[1])]

forehand 1 *n.* (in tennis etc.) stroke made with palm of hand facing opponent. **2** *a.* (also **forehanded**) of or made with this stroke. [FORE-]

forehead /'fɒrɪd, 'fɔ:hed/ *n.* part of face above eyebrows.

foreign /'fɒrən/ *a.* of or from or situated in or characteristic of a country or language other than one's own; dealing with other countries (*foreign affairs*); of another district, society, etc.; unfamiliar, strange, uncharacteristic; coming from outside (*foreign body*, *substance*); **foreign aid** money etc. given or lent by one country to another; **foreign legion** body of foreign volunteers in (esp. French) army; **Foreign and Commonwealth Office** UK government department dealing with foreign affairs; **Foreign Secretary** head of this. [F f. L (*foris* outside)]

foreigner *n.* person born in or coming from another country.

foreknow /fɔ:'nəʊ/ *v.t.* know beforehand; **foreknowledge** /fɔ:'nɒlɪdʒ/ *n.* [FORE-]

foreland *n.* promontory, cape.
foreleg *n.* front leg of animal.
forelimb *n.* front limb of animal.
forelock *n.* lock of hair just above forehead; **take time by the forelock** seize opportunity.
foreman *n.* workman supervising others; president and spokesman of jury.
foremast *n.* mast nearest bow of ship.
foremost 1 *a.* most advanced in position; most notable, best. 2 *adv.* in the first place, most importantly. [OE]
forename *n.* first or Christian name. [FORE-]
forenoon *n.* day till noon, morning.
forensic /fə'renzɪk/ *a.* of or used in courts of law; **forensic medicine** application of medical knowledge to legal problems; **forensically** *adv.* [L *forensis* (FORUM)]
foreordain /fɔ:rɔ:'deɪn/ *v.t.* destine beforehand; **foreordination** /-dɪ'neɪʃ(ə)n/ *n.* [FORE-]
forepaw *n.* front paw of animal.
foreplay *n.* stimulation preceding sexual intercourse.
forerunner *n.* predecessor; advance messenger.
foresail /'fɔ:seɪl, -s(ə)l/ *n.* principal sail on foremast.
foresee /fɔ:'si:/ *v.t.* (*past* **foresaw,** *p.p.* **foreseen**) see or be aware of beforehand; **in the foreseeable future** period ahead when circumstances are known.
foreshadow /fɔ:'ʃædəʊ/ *v.t.* be warning or indication of (future event).
foreshore *n.* shore between high- and low-water marks.
foreshorten /fɔ:'ʃɔ:t(ə)n/ *v.t.* show or portray (object) with the apparent shortening due to visual perspective.
foresight *n.* regard or provision for the future; foreseeing; front sight of gun.
foreskin *n.* loose skin covering end of penis.
forest /'fɒrɪst/ 1 *n.* large area of land covered chiefly with trees and undergrowth; trees in this; *fig.* dense concentration (of things). 2 *v.t.* plant with trees, make into forest. [F f. L *forestis* (FOREIGN)]
forestall /fɔ:'stɔ:l/ *v.t.* act in advance of in order to prevent; deal with beforehand. [FORE-, STALL]
forester *n.* officer in charge of forest; dweller in forest. [FOREST]
forestry *n.* science or management of forests.
foretaste *n.* taste or experience of something in advance. [FORE-]
foretell /fɔ:'tel/ *v.t.* (*past* and *p.p.* **foretold** /fɔ:'təʊld/) predict, prophesy; be precursor of.
forethought *n.* care or provision for the future; deliberate intention.
forever /fə'revə/ *adv.* continually, persistently (*is forever complaining*). [FOR]
forewarn /fɔ:'wɔ:n/ *v.t.* warn beforehand. [FORE-]
forewoman *n.* woman worker supervising others; woman foreman of jury.
foreword *n.* introductory remarks at beginning of book, often by person other than the author.
forfeit /'fɔ:fɪt/ 1 *n.* penalty, thing surrendered as penalty. 2 *v.t.* lose or surrender as penalty. 3 *a.* lost or surrendered as a forfeit. 4 **forfeiture** *n.* [F *forfaire* transgress f. L *foris* outside, *facio* do]
forgather /fɔ:'gæðə/ *v.i.* assemble, associate. [Du.]
forgave *past* of FORGIVE.
forge[1] 1 *v.t.* make or write in fraudulent imitation; shape (metal) by heating and hammering. 2 *n.* furnace etc. for melting and refining metal; workshop with this; blacksmith's workshop. [F f. L *fabrica* (FABRIC)]
forge[2] *v.i.* move forward gradually or steadily; **forge ahead** progress rapidly, take lead. [perh. alt. of FORCE[1]]
forgery /'fɔ:dʒərɪ/ *n.* act of forging; forged document etc. [FORGE[1]]
forget /fə'get/ *v.* (-**tt**-; *past* **forgot;** *p.p.* **forgotten,** *US* **forgot**) lose remembrance of or *about*, not remember; neglect or overlook; cease to think of; **forget oneself** put others' interests first, behave without due dignity. [OE]
forgetful *a.* apt to forget, neglectful; **forgetfully** *adv.*
forget-me-not *n.* plant with small blue flowers.
forgive /fə'gɪv/ *v.t.* (*past* **forgave;** *p.p.* **forgiven**) cease to feel angry or resentful towards (person) or about (offence); pardon; remit (debt). [OE]
forgiveness *n.* act of forgiving; state of being forgiven.
forgiving *a.* inclined readily to forgive.
forgo /fɔ:'gəʊ/ *v.t.* (*past* **forwent**; *p.p.* **forgone** /fɔ:'gɒn/ go without, relinquish; omit or decline to take or use (pleasure, advantage, etc.). [OE]
forgot *past* (and *US p.p.*) of FORGET.
forgotten *p.p.* of FORGET.
fork 1 *n.* pronged implement used in eating and cooking; similar much larger implement used for digging, lifting, etc.; divergence of stick, road, etc., into two parts, place of this, one of the two parts; forked support for bicycle wheel; pronged device pushed under load to be lifted. 2 *v.* form fork or branch by separating into two parts; take one road at fork; dig, lift, or throw with fork. 3 **fork-lift truck** vehicle with fork for

lifting and carrying loads; **fork out** *sl.* pay, usu. reluctantly. [OE f. L *furca* pitchfork]

forlorn /fɔ:'lɔ:n/ *a.* sad and abandoned; in pitiful state; **forlorn hope** faint remaining hope or chance. [*lorn* = p.p. of obs. *leese* LOSE; *forlorn hope* f. Du. *verloren hoop* lost troop]

form 1 *n.* shape, arrangement of parts, visible aspect; person or animal as visible or tangible; mode in which thing exists or manifests itself; printed document with blank spaces for information to be inserted; class in school; customary method; set order of words; species, kind; behaviour according to rule or custom (*good or bad form*); correct procedure (*he knows the form*); (of athlete, horse, etc.) condition of health and training; (in racing etc.) details of previous performances; *sl.* criminal record; one of the ways in which a word may be spelt, pronounced, or inflected; arrangement and style in literary or musical composition; bench; hare's lair. **2** *v.* fashion or shape; train or instruct; develop or establish as a concept, institution, or practice (*form an idea, an alliance, a habit*); organize (*into* a company etc.); be material of, make up, be *one of* or *part of*; take shape, come into existence; construct (word) by inflexion etc.; (of troops etc.; often with *up*) bring or move into formation. **3 on** (or **off**) **form** performing or playing well (or badly). [F f. L *forma*]

-form *suffix* forming adjectives (usu. as **-iform**) in senses 'having the form of' (*cuneiform*), 'having such a number of forms' (*uniform*).

formal /'fɔ:m(ə)l/ *a.* used or done or held in accordance with rules, convention, or ceremony (*formal dress, language, occasion*); excessively stiff or methodical; valid or correctly so called because of its form, explicit (*formal agreement, denial*); of or concerned with (outward) form, esp. as distinct from content or matter; perfunctory, following form only; precise, symmetrical (*formal garden*); **formally** *adv.* [L (FORM)]

formaldehyde /fɔ:'mældɪhaɪd/ *n.* aldehyde of formic acid, used as disinfectant and preservative. [FORMIC, ALDEHYDE]

formalin /'fɔ:məlɪn/ *n.* aqueous solution of formaldehyde.

formalism /'fɔ:məlɪz(ə)m/ *n.* strict or excessive adherence to or concern with form or forms; **formalist** *n.* [FORMAL]

formality /fɔ:'mælɪtɪ/ *n.* formal act, regulation, or custom (often lacking real significance); thing done simply to comply with rule; rigid observance of rules or convention.

formalize /'fɔ:məlaɪz/ *v.t.* make formal; give definite (esp. legal) form to; **formalization** /-'zeɪʃ(ə)n/ *n.*

format /'fɔ:mæt/ **1** *n.* shape and size (of book etc.); style or manner of arrangement or procedure; arrangement of data etc. for computer. **2** *v.t.* (**-tt-**) arrange in format, esp. for computer. [F f. G f. L *formatus* shaped (FORM)]

formation /fɔ:'meɪʃ(ə)n/ *n.* forming; thing formed; particular arrangement (e.g. of troops); set of rocks or strata with common characteristic. [F or L (FORM)]

formative /'fɔ:mətɪv/ *a.* serving to form or fashion; of formation.

forme *n.* body of type secured in chase for printing at one impression. [var. of FORM]

former *a.* of the past, earlier; **the former** (often *absol.*) the first or first-mentioned of two. [FOREMOST]

formerly *adv.* in former times.

Formica /fɔ:'maɪkə/ *n.* (**P**) hard durable plastic laminate used on surfaces. [orig. uncert.]

formic acid /'fɔ:mɪk/ colourless irritant volatile acid contained in fluid emitted by ants. [L *formica* ant]

formidable /'fɔ:mɪdəb(ə)l, (**D**) -'mɪd-/ *a.* inspiring fear or dread; likely to be difficult to overcome or deal with; **formidably** *adv.* [F or L (*formido* fear)]

formless *a.* without definite or regular form. [FORM]

formula /'fɔ:mjʊlə/ *n.* (*pl.* **formulas, -ae** /-i:/) set of chemical symbols showing constituents of substance; mathematical rule expressed in figures; fixed form of words, esp. one used on social or ceremonious occasions; form of words embodying or enabling agreement; list of ingredients; classification of racing car, esp. by engine capacity; *US* infant's food; **formulaic** /-'leɪɪk/ *a.* [L dimin. of *forma* FORM]

formulary /'fɔ:mjʊlərɪ/ *n.* collection of formulas or set forms. [F or med.L (prec.)]

formulate /'fɔ:mjʊleɪt/ *v.t.* express in a formula; express clearly and precisely; **formulation** /-'leɪʃ(ə)n/ *n.* [FORMULA]

fornicate /'fɔ:nɪkeɪt/ *v.i.* (of people not married to each other) have sexual intercourse voluntarily; **fornication** / -'keɪʃ(ə)n/ *n.*; **fornicator** *n.* [L (*fornix* brothel)]

forsake /fɔ:'seɪk/ *v.t.* (*past* **forsook** /-'sʊk/; *p.p.* **forsaken**) give up, renounce; withdraw help or companionship from. [OE]

forsooth /fɔ:'su:θ/ *adv. archaic* indeed, truly, no doubt. [OE (FOR, SOOTH)]

forswear /fɔːˈsweə/ *v.t.* (*past* **forswore;** *p.p.* **forsworn**) abjure, renounce; (in *p.p.*) perjured; **forswear oneself** perjure oneself. [OE]

forsythia /fɔːˈsaɪθɪə/ *n.* ornamental shrub with bright yellow flowers. [*Forsyth*, botanist]

fort *n.* fortified military building or position; **hold the fort** act as temporary substitute, cope with emergency. [F or It. (L *fortis* strong)]

forte[1] /ˈfɔːteɪ/ *n.* one's strong point, thing in which one excels. [fem. of F FORT]

forte[2] /ˈfɔːteɪ/ *Mus.* **1** *a.* & *adv.* loud, loudly. **2** *n.* loud playing or passage. [It. (FORT)]

fortepiano /ˈfɔːtɪpɪænəʊ/ *n.* = PIANOFORTE, esp. with ref. to instrument of 18th – early 19th c.

forth *adv.* (*archaic* exc. in set phrases) forward, into view (*bring, come, forth*); onwards in time (*henceforth*); forwards (*back and forth*); out from starting-point (*set forth*); **and so forth** see so[1]. [OE]

forthcoming *a.* approaching, coming or available soon; produced when wanted; (of person) informative or responsive.

forthright *a.* straightforward; outspoken; decisive. [OE]

forthwith /fɔːθˈwɪθ/ *adv.* at once, without delay. [FORTH]

fortification /fɔːtɪfɪˈkeɪʃ(ə)n/ *n.* act of fortifying; (usu. in *pl.*) defensive works, walls, etc. [F f. L (foll.)]

fortify /ˈfɔːtɪfaɪ/ *v.* strengthen physically, mentally, morally, etc.; erect or provide with fortifications; strengthen (wine) with alcohol; add extra nutrients, esp. vitamins, to (food). [F f. L (*fortis* strong)]

fortissimo /fɔːˈtɪsɪməʊ/ *Mus.* **1** *a.* & *adv.* very loud, very loudly. **2** *n.* very loud playing or passage. [It., superl. of FORTE[2]]

fortitude /ˈfɔːtɪtjuːd/ *n.* courage in pain or adversity. [F f. L (*fortis* strong)]

fortnight *n.* two weeks. [OE (*fourteen nights*)]

fortnightly **1** *a.* done, produced, or occurring once a fortnight. **2** *adv.* every fortnight. **3** *n.* fortnightly magazine etc.

FORTRAN *n.* a computer language used esp. for scientific calculations. [*For*mula *Tran*slation]

fortress /ˈfɔːtrɪs/ *n.* fortified building or town. [F f. L *fortis* strong]

fortuitous /fɔːˈtjuːɪtəs/ *a.* happening by chance, accidental; **fortuity** *n.* [L (*forte* by chance)]

fortunate /ˈfɔːtjʊnət, -tʃənət/ *a.* lucky, auspicious. [L *fortunatus* (foll.)]

fortune /ˈfɔːtjuːn, -tʃuːn/ *n.* chance or luck as force in human affairs; luck that befalls person or enterprise; good luck; person's destiny; prosperity, great wealth, huge sum of money; **fortune-teller** person who claims to foretell one's destiny; **make a fortune** become very rich. [F f. L *fortuna*]

forty /ˈfɔːtɪ/ *a.* & *n.* four times ten; symbol for this (40, xl, XL); (in *pl.*) numbers, years, degrees of temperature, from 40 to 49; **forty winks** short sleep; **fortieth** *a.* & *n.* [OE (FOUR)]

forum /ˈfɔːrəm/ *n.* public square or market-place in ancient Roman city used for judicial and other business; place of or meeting for public discussion; court, tribunal. [L]

forward /ˈfɔːwəd/ **1** *a.* lying in one's line of motion, onward or towards the front; relating to the future (*forward contract, delivery*); precocious, bold in manner, presumptuous; approaching maturity or completion; (of plant etc.) well advanced or early. **2** *n.* attacking player near the front in football, hockey, etc. **3** *adv.* (*a*) to the front, into prominence (*move, come, forward*); in advance, ahead (*send him forward*); onward so as to make progress (*not getting any further forward*); towards the future (*from this time forward*); (*b*) (also **forwards**) towards front in direction one is facing; in normal direction of motion or of traversal; with continuous forward motion (*backwards and forwards; rushing forward*). **4** *v.t.* send (letter etc.) on to further destination; dispatch (goods etc.); help to advance, promote. [OE (FORTH, -WARD)]

fosse *n.* long ditch or trench, esp. in fortification. [F f. L, = ditch]

fossil /ˈfɒs(ə)l/ **1** *n.* remains or impression of (usu. prehistoric) plant or animal hardened in rock; antiquated or unchanging person or thing. **2** *a.* of or like a fossil; dug from the ground (*fossil fuel*). [F f. L (*fodio foss-* dig)]

fossilize /ˈfɒsɪlaɪz/ *v.* (cause to) become fossil; **fossilization** /-ˈzeɪʃ(ə)n/ *n.*

foster **1** *v.t.* promote growth or development of; bring up (child that is not one's own); encourage or harbour (feeling); (of circumstances) be favourable to. **2** *a.* having family connection by fostering and not birth (*foster-brother, -child, -parent*). **3** **foster home** home in which foster-child is brought up. [OE (FOOD)]

fought *past* and *p.p.* of FIGHT.

foul **1** *a.* offensive, loathsome, stinking; filthy, soiled; *colloq.* disgusting, awful; (of language etc.) obscene, disgustingly abusive; (of weather) rough, stormy; containing noxious matter (*foul air, water*); clogged, choked; unfair, against rules (*by fair means or foul*); in collision;

(of rope etc.) entangled. **2** *n.* foul stroke or piece of play; collision, entanglement. **3** *adv.* unfairly, contrary to rules. **4** *v.* make or become foul; commit foul against (player); (cause to) become entangled; collide with. **5 foul-mouthed** using obscene or offensive language; **foul play** unfair play in sport, treacherous or violent act, esp. murder; **foul up** (cause to) become blocked or entangled, make a mess of (*lit.* or *fig.*). [OE]

foulard /fu:'lɑ:d/ *n.* thin soft material of silk etc.; handkerchief of this. [F]

found[1] *v.t.* establish, esp. with endowment, originate or initiate (institution etc.); be original builder of (town etc.); lay base of (building); construct or base (story, theory, rule, etc.) *on* or *upon*; **ill-founded** unjustified; **well-founded** justified, reasonable. [F f. L (*fundus* bottom)]

found[2] *v.t.* melt and mould (metal), fuse (materials for glass), make (thing) thus. [F f. L *fundo fus-* pour]

found[3] *past* and *p.p.* of FIND.

foundation /faʊn'deɪʃ(ə)n/ *n.* establishing, esp. of endowed institution; such institution (e.g. college, hospital, school) or its revenues; solid ground or base on which building rests; (in *sing.* or *pl.*) lowest part of building usu. below ground-level; basis, underlying principle; material or part on which other parts are overlaid; (in full **foundation garment**) woman's supporting undergarment, e.g. corset; **foundation-stone** stone laid ceremonially to celebrate founding of building, *fig.* basis. [F f. L (FOUND[1])]

founder *v.i.* (of horse or rider) fall to ground, fall from lameness, stick in mud etc.; (of plan etc.) fail; (of ship) fill with water and sink. [FOUND[1]]

foundling /'faʊndlɪŋ/ *n.* abandoned infant of unknown parents. [FIND]

foundry /'faʊndrɪ/ *n.* workshop for or business of casting metal. [FOUND[2]]

fount[1] /faʊnt, fɒnt/ *n.* set of printing-type of same face and size. [F (FOUND[2])]

fount[2] *n.* source; *poetic* spring, fountain. [back-form. f. foll.]

fountain /'faʊntɪn/ *n.* jet(s) of water made to spout for ornamental purposes or for drinking; structure provided for this; spring; source (*of* river, wisdom, etc.); **fountain-head** source; **fountain-pen** pen with reservoir holding ink. [F f. L *fontana* (*fons font-* spring)]

four /'fɔ:/ *a.* & *n.* one more than three; symbol for this (4, iv, IV); size etc. denoted by four; team of four, four-oared boat or its crew; **four-in-hand** vehicle with four horses driven by one person; **four-letter word** short word referring to sexual or excretory functions and regarded as vulgar or obscene; **four-poster** bed with four posts supporting canopy; **four-square** *a.* & *adv.* solidly based, steady, squarely, resolutely; **four-stroke** (of internal-combustion engine) having cycle of four strokes of piston, in which cylinder fires once; **on all fours** on hands and knees. [OE]

fourfold *a.* & *adv.* four times as much or as many; consisting of four parts.

foursome *n.* group of four persons; golf match between two pairs with partners playing same ball.

fourteen /fɔ:'ti:n/ *a.* & *n.* one more than thirteen; symbol for this (14, xiv, XIV); size etc. denoted by fourteen; **fourteenth** *a.* & *n.* [OE (FOUR, -TEEN)]

fourth *a.* & *n.* next after third; one of four equal parts of thing; **fourth estate** the press; **fourthly** *adv.* [OE (FOUR)]

fowl **1** *n.* (*pl.* **fowls** or *collect.* **fowl**) domestic cock or hen kept for eggs and flesh; flesh of birds as food; bird (*archaic* exc. in *comb.*, e.g. *guinea-fowl*). **2** *v.i.* hunt or shoot or snare wildfowl. [OE]

fox **1** *n.* wild four-legged animal of dog family with red fur and bushy tail; its fur; cunning person. **2** *v.t.* deceive, baffle; (esp. in *p.p.*) discolour (pages of book etc.) with brownish marks. **3 fox-terrier** a kind of short-haired terrier. [OE]

foxglove *n.* tall plant with purple or white flowers like glove-fingers.

foxhole *n.* hole in ground used as shelter against missiles or as firing-point.

foxhound *n.* a kind of hound bred and trained to hunt foxes.

foxtrot **1** *n.* ballroom dance with slow and quick steps, music for this. **2** *v.i.* (**-tt-**) dance foxtrot.

foxy *a.* foxlike; sly or cunning; reddish-brown; **foxily** *adv.*; **foxiness** *n.*

foyer /'fɔɪeɪ/ *n.* entrance hall or open space in theatre etc. [F, = hearth, home, f. L FOCUS]

Fr. *abbr.* Father; French.

fr. *abbr.* franc(s).

Fr *symb.* francium.

fracas /'frækɑ:/ *n.* (*pl.* same /-kɑ:z/, *US* **fracases**) noisy disturbance or quarrel. [F f. It.]

fraction /'frækʃ(ə)n/ *n.* numerical quantity that is not a whole number (e.g. $\frac{1}{2}$, 0.5); small part, piece, or amount; portion of mixture obtained by distillation etc.; **fractional** *a.*; **fractionally** *adv.* [F f. L (*frango fract-* break)]

fractious /'frækʃəs/ *a.* irritable, peevish. [prec. in obs. sense 'brawling']

fracture /'fræktʃə/ **1** *n.* breakage, esp.

of bone or cartilage. **2** *v*. cause fracture in, suffer fracture. [F or L (FRACTION)]

fragile /ˈfrædʒaɪl/ *a*. easily broken, weak; of delicate constitution, not strong; **fragility** /frəˈdʒɪlɪtɪ/ *n*. [F or L (prec.)]

fragment /ˈfrægmənt/ **1** *n*. part broken off; remains of otherwise lost or destroyed whole; extant remains or unfinished portion of book etc. **2** /also -ˈment/ *v*. break or separate into fragments. **3 fragmentary** *a*.; **fragmentation** /-ˈteɪʃ(ə)n/ *n*. [F or L (FRACTION)]

fragrance /ˈfreɪgrəns/ *n*. sweetness of smell; sweet scent. [F or L (*fragro* smell sweet)]

fragrant *a*. sweet-smelling.

frail *a*. fragile, delicate; transient; morally weak; **frailly** *adv*. [F f. L (FRAGILE)]

frailty *n*. frail quality; weakness, foible.

frame 1 *v.t.* construct, put together, or devise (complex thing, idea, theory, etc.); adapt or fit *to* or *into*; articulate (words); set in frame; serve as frame for; *sl*. concoct false charge or evidence against, devise plot against. **2** *n*. case or border enclosing picture, window, door, etc.; human or animal body, esp. with reference to size; basic rigid supporting structure of building, motor vehicle, aircraft, bicycle, etc.; (in *pl*.) structure of spectacles holding lenses; construction, build, structure; established order or system (*frame of society*); temporary condition (*frame of mind*); single complete image or picture on cinema film or transmitted in series of lines by television; boxlike structure of glass etc. for protecting plants; triangular structure for positioning balls in snooker etc., round of play in snooker etc.; *US sl*. = *frame-up*. **3 frame of reference** system of geometrical axes for defining position, set of standards or principles governing behaviour, thought, etc.; **frame-up** *colloq*. conspiracy to make innocent person appear guilty. [OE, = be helpful]

framework *n*. essential supporting structure; basic system.

franc *n*. unit of currency in France, Belgium, Switzerland, etc. [F (FRANK²)]

franchise /ˈfræntʃaɪz/ **1** *n*. right to vote in State election; full membership of corporation or State, citizenship; right or privilege granted to person or corporation; authorization to sell company's goods etc. in particular area. **2** *v.t.* grant franchise to. [F (*franc* FRANK¹)]

Franciscan /frænˈsɪskən/ **1** *a*. of order founded by St Francis of Assisi. **2** *n*. Franciscan friar or nun. [F f. L (*Franciscus* Francis)]

francium /ˈfræŋkɪəm/ *n*. radioactive metallic element. [*France*, discoverer's country]

Franco- *in comb*. French and (*Franco-German*). [L (FRANK²)]

franglais /ˈfrɒŋgleɪ/ *n*. corrupt version of French using many words and phrases borrowed from English. [F (*français* French, *anglais* English)]

frank¹ 1 *a*. candid, open, outspoken, undisguised, unmistakable. **2** *v.t.* mark (letter etc.) to record payment of postage. **3** *n*. franking signature or mark. [F f. L *francus* free (foll.)]

Frank² *n*. member of Germanic people that conquered Gaul in 6th c. [OE]

Frankenstein /ˈfræŋkənstaɪn/ *n*. (more correctly **Frankenstein's monster**) thing that becomes terrifying to its creator. [character in Mary Shelley's novel *Frankenstein*]

frankfurter /ˈfræŋkfɜːtə/ *n*. seasoned smoked sausage. [G (*Frankfurt* in Germany)]

frankincense /ˈfræŋkɪnsens/ *n*. aromatic gum resin burnt as incense. [F (FRANK¹ in obs. sense 'high quality', INCENSE²)]

frantic /ˈfræntɪk/*a*. wildly excited, frenzied; characterized by great hurry or anxiety, desperate, violent; *colloq*. extreme; **frantically** *adv*. [F f. L (FRENETIC)]

frappé /ˈfræpeɪ/ *a*. (esp. of wine) iced, chilled. [F]

fraternal /frəˈtɜːn(ə)l/ *a*. of brothers, brotherly; (of twins) developed from separate ova and not necessarily similar; **fraternally** *adv*. [L (*frater* brother)]

fraternity /frəˈtɜːnɪtɪ/ *n*. religious brotherhood; guild or group of people sharing interests or beliefs etc.; brotherliness; *US* students' society in college or university. [F or L (prec.)]

fraternize /ˈfrætənaɪz/ *v.i.* associate or make friends (*with*); (of troops) enter into friendly relations *with* enemy troops or inhabitants of occupied country; **fraternization** /-ˈzeɪʃ(ə)n/ *n*. [F & L (FRATERNAL)]

fratricide /ˈfrætrɪsaɪd/ *n*. killing of one's sister or brother; one who does this; **fratricidal** /-ˈsaɪd(ə)l/ *a*. [F or L (*frater* brother, -CIDE)]

Frau /fraʊ/ *n*. (*pl*. **Frauen**) German woman; title of German wife or widow, = Mrs. [G]

fraud /frɔːd/ *n*. criminal deception; dishonest artifice or trick; impostor; person or thing not fulfilling claim or expectation. [F f. L *fraus fraud*-]

fraudulent /ˈfrɔːdjʊlənt/ *a*. of, involving, or guilty of fraud; **fraudulence** *n*. [F or L (prec.)]

fraught /frɔ:t/ *a.* filled or attended *with* (danger etc.); *colloq.* causing or suffering anxiety or distress. [Du. *vracht* FREIGHT]

Fräulein /ˈfrɔɪlaɪn/ *n.* unmarried German woman; title of German spinster, = Miss. [G]

fray[1] *v.* (cause to) become worn through by rubbing; become ragged at edge (*lit.*, or *fig.* of nerves, temper, etc.). [F f. L *frico* rub]

fray[2] *n.* fight, conflict; brawl. [AFFRAY]

frazzle /ˈfræz(ə)l/ *n.* worn or exhausted state (*beaten to a frazzle*). [orig. uncert.]

freak 1 *n.* capricious or unusual idea, act, etc.; monstrosity, abnormal person or thing; unconventional person; one who freaks out; drug addict. **2** *v.* (with *out*) *sl.* (cause to) undergo hallucinations or strong emotional experience through drug-taking etc.; adopt unconventional life-style. **3 freakish** *a.* [prob. f. dial.]

freckle /ˈfrek(ə)l/ **1** *n.* light brown spot on skin. **2** *v.* spot or be spotted with freckles. [ON]

free 1 *a.* (*compar.* **freer** /ˈfri:ə/; *superl.* **freest** /ˈfri:ɪst/) not a slave or under the control of another, having personal rights and social and political liberty; (of State, citizens, or institutions) subject neither to foreign domination nor to despotic government; unrestricted, unimpeded, not confined or fixed; released or exempt *from*; spontaneous, unforced (*free offer, compliment*); not subject to tax etc.; costing nothing; not occupied or in use (*the bathroom is free now*); lavish, unstinted; permitted, at liberty, *to*; frank, unreserved; (of talk, stories, etc.) slightly indecent; familiar, impudent; (of literary style) not observing strict laws of form; (of translation) not literal; available to all; independent (*a free agent*); *Chem.* not combined (*free radical*); (of power or energy) disengaged, available. **2** *adv.* freely; without cost or payment. **3** *v.t.* make free, set at liberty; relieve *from*; rid or ease *of*; clear, disentangle. **4 free and easy** informal; **free-born** born as a free citizen; **Free Church** a nonconformist Church; **free enterprise** freedom of private business from State control; **free fall** movement under force of gravity only; **free fight** general fight in which all present may join, without rules; **free-for-all** free fight, unrestricted discussion etc.; **free hand** freedom to act at one's own discretion; **free-hand** *a.* (of drawing) done without instruments such as ruler or compasses; **free-handed** generous; **free house** inn or public house not controlled by a brewery and therefore able to sell any brand of beer etc.; **free kick** kick in football taken without interference from opponents, as minor penalty; **free lance** person whose services are available to any would-be employer, not one only; **free-lance** *a.* & *v.i.* of a free lance, act as a free lance; **free-loader** *sl.* sponger; **free love** sexual relations irrespective of marriage; **free market** market in which prices are determined by unrestricted competition; **free on board** (or **rail**) without charge for delivery to ship, railway wagon, etc.; **free port** one open to all traders, or free from duty on goods in transit; **free-range** (of hens etc.) given freedom of movement in seeking food etc.; **free speech** freedom to express opinions of any kind; **free-spoken** not concealing one's opinions; **free-standing** not supported by another structure; **free-style** (of swimming-race) in which any stroke may be used, (of wrestling) with few restrictions on the holds permitted; **free-thinker** one who rejects dogma or authority in religious belief; **free trade** trade left to its natural course without import restrictions etc.; **free vote** parliamentary vote in which members are not bound by party policy; **free wheel** driving-wheel of bicycle able to revolve with pedals at rest; **free-wheel** *v.i.* ride bicycle with pedals at rest, *fig.* move or act without constraint; **free will** power of acting without constraint of necessity or fate, ability to act at one's own discretion (*I did it of my own free will*); **free world** non-Communist countries' collective name for themselves. [OE]

-free *in comb.* free of or from (*duty-free*; *fancy-free*).

freeboard *n.* part of ship's side between water-line and deck. [FREE]

freebooter *n.* pirate. [Du. *vrijbuiter* (FREE, BOOTY)]

freedman *n.* emancipated slave. [FREE]

freedom /ˈfri:dəm/ *n.* condition of being free or unrestricted; personal or civic liberty; liberty of action (*to do* thing); frankness, undue familiarity; exemption (*from*); unrestricted use (*of* house etc.); honorary membership or citizenship (*freedom of the city*); **freedom of speech** right to express one's views freely. [OE]

freehold 1 *n.* holding of land or property in absolute possession. **2** *a.* owned thus. **3 freeholder** *n.* [FREE]

freeman *n.* one who is not slave or serf; one who has freedom of city etc.

Freemason /ˈfri:meɪs(ə)n/ *n.* member of international fraternity for mutual help and fellowship, with elaborate secret rituals; **Freemasonry** *n.*

freesia /'fri:zjə, -ʒə/ *n.* bulbous African plant with fragrant flowers. [*Freese*, physician]

freeway *n.* express highway, esp. with limited access. [FREE]

freeze 1 *v.* (*past* **froze**; *p.p.* **frozen**) turn into ice or other solid by cold; cover or become covered with ice; be or feel very cold; make or become rigid from cold; preserve (food) by refrigeration below freezing-point; adhere *to* or *together* by frost; (cause to) become motionless through fear, surprise, etc.; fix (prices, wages, etc.) at a certain level; make (assets) unavailable. **2** *n.* state of frost; coming or period of frost; fixing or stabilization of prices, wages, etc. **3 freeze-dry** freeze and dry by evaporation of ice in high vacuum; **freeze on to** *sl.* take or keep tight hold of; **freeze up** freeze completely, obstruct by formation of ice etc.; **freeze-up** *n.* period or conditions of extreme cold; **freezing-point** temperature at which liquid, esp. water, freezes. [OE]

freezer *n.* refrigerated container or compartment in which food is preserved at very low temperature.

freight /freɪt/ **1** *n.* transport of goods in containers or by water or air (or *US* by land); goods transported, cargo, load; charge for transport of goods. **2** *v.t.* transport (goods) by freight; load with freight. [LG or Du. *vrecht* var. of *vracht* FRAUGHT]

freighter *n.* ship or aircraft designed to carry freight; *US* freight-wagon.

freightliner *n.* train carrying goods in containers.

French 1 *a.* of France or its people or language; having French characteristics. **2** *n.* the French language; *euphem.* bad language (*excuse my French*); dry vermouth. **3 the French** *pl.* the people of France; **French bean** kidney or haricot bean used as unripe sliced pods or as ripe seeds; **French bread** bread in long crisp loaf; **French Canadian** native of French-speaking area of Canada; **French chalk** finely powdered talc used as marker, dry lubricant, etc.; **French dressing** salad dressing of seasoned oil and vinegar; **French fried potatoes** *US* potato chips (also **French fries**); **French horn** coiled brass wind instrument with wide bell; **French leave** absence without permission; **French letter** *colloq.* condom; **French polish** shellac polish for wood; **French window** glazed door in outside wall. [OE (FRANK²)]

Frenchify /'frentʃɪfaɪ/ *v.t.* (usu. in *p.p.*) make French in form, manners, etc.

Frenchman *n.* man of French birth or nationality; **Frenchwoman** *n. fem.*

frenetic /frə'netɪk/ *a.* frantic, frenzied; fanatic; **frenetically** *adv.* [F f. L f. Gk (*phrēn* mind)]

frenzy /'frenzɪ/ **1** *n.* wild excitement or agitation; delirious fury. **2** *v.t.* (usu. in *p.p.*) drive to frenzy. [F f. med.L (as prec.)]

frequency /'fri:kwənsɪ/ *n.* commonness of occurrence; frequent occurrence; rate of recurrence (of vibration etc.); number of cycles of carrier wave per second, band or group of such values; **frequency modulation** varying carrier-wave frequency. [foll.]

frequent 1 /'fri:kwənt/ *a.* occurring often or in close succession; habitual, constant. **2** /frɪ'kwent/ *v.t.* attend or go to habitually. [F, or L *frequens -ent-* crowded]

frequentative /frɪ'kwentətɪv/ *Gram.* **1** *a.* (of verb etc.) expressing frequent repetition or intensity of action. **2** *n.* frequentative verb etc.

fresco /'freskəʊ/ *n.* (*pl.* **frescos**) painting done in water-colour on wall or ceiling before plaster is dry. [It., = fresh]

fresh 1 *a.* newly made or obtained; other, different, not previously known or used (*start a fresh page*; *we need fresh ideas*); lately arrived *from*; not stale or musty or faded; (of food) not preserved by salting, tinning, freezing, etc.; not salty (*fresh water*); pure, untainted, refreshing (*fresh air*, *complexion*); (of wind) brisk; cheeky, amorously impudent; inexperienced. **2** *adv.* newly, recently (esp. in comb.: *fresh-baked*, *-caught*, *-cut*, etc.). [F f. Rmc f. Gmc]

freshen *v.* make or become fresh.

fresher *n.* freshman.

freshet /'freʃɪt/ *n.* stream of fresh water flowing into sea; flood of river.

freshman *n.* first-year student at university or (*US*) high school.

freshwater *a.* (of fish etc.) not of the sea.

fret¹ 1 *v.* (**-tt-**) worry, vex; be worried or distressed; wear or consume by gnawing or rubbing. **2** *n.* worry, vexation. [OE (FOR, EAT)]

fret² 1 *n.* ornamental pattern of continuous combinations of straight lines joined usu. at right angles. **2** *v.t.* (**-tt-**) adorn with fret or with carved or embossed work. [F *freter*]

fret³ *n.* bar or ridge on finger-board of guitar etc. to guide fingering. [orig. unkn.]

fretful *a.* constantly fretting, querulous; **fretfully** *adv.*

fretsaw *n.* narrow saw stretched on frame for cutting thin wood in patterns. [FRET²]

fretwork *n.* ornamental work in wood with fretsaw.

Freudian /'frɔɪdɪən/ **1** *a.* of Freud or his theory or method of psychoanalysis. **2** *n.* adherent of Freud. **3 Freudian slip** unintentional error that seems to reveal subconscious feelings. [*Freud*, psychologist]

Fri. *abbr.* Friday.

friable /'fraɪəb(ə)l/ *a.* easily crumbled; **friability** /-'bɪlɪtɪ/ *n.*

friar /'fraɪə/ *n.* member of certain non-enclosed RC orders of men (esp. Augustinians, Carmelites, Dominicans, and Franciscans); **friar's balsam** tincture of benzoin etc. used esp. for inhaling. [F f. L *frater* brother]

friary *n.* monastery of friars.

fricassee /'frɪkəsi:, -'si:/ **1** *n.* dish of stewed or fried pieces of meat served in thick sauce. **2** *v.t.* make fricassee of. [F]

fricative /'frɪkətɪv/ **1** *a.* (of consonant, e.g. *f, th*) sounded by friction of breath in narrow opening. **2** *n.* fricative consonant. [L (*frico* rub)]

friction /'frɪkʃ(ə)n/ *n.* rubbing of one object against another; resistance object encounters in moving over another; clash of wills, temperaments, opinions, etc.; **frictional** *a.* [F f. L (prec.)]

Friday /'fraɪdeɪ, -dɪ/ **1** *n.* day of week following Thursday. **2** *adv. colloq.* on Friday. **3 Fridays** on Friday, each Friday; **girl** (or **man**) **Friday** helper or follower. [OE]

fridge *n. colloq.* refrigerator. [abbr.]

friend /frend/ *n.* person with whom one enjoys mutual affection and regard (usu. exclusive of sexual or family bonds); sympathizer, helper; helpful thing or quality; one who is not an enemy (*friend or foe?*); some person already mentioned or under discussion (*my friend at the next table now left the room*); (usu. in *pl.*) regular contributor of money or other assistance to an institution; (**Friend**) member of the Society of Friends, Quaker. [OE]

friendly **1** *a.* acting as or like a friend, well-disposed, kindly; on amicable terms (*with*); characteristic of friends, showing or prompted by kindness. **2** *n.* = *friendly match.* **3** *adv.* in friendly manner. **4 friendly match** match played for enjoyment and not in competition; **Friendly Society** society for insurance against sickness etc. **5 friendliness** *n.*

friendship *n.* friendly relationship or feeling.

frier var. of FRYER.

Friesian /'fri:ʒjən/ *n.* one of a breed of large black-and-white dairy cattle orig. from Friesland. [var. of FRISIAN]

frieze /fri:z/ *n.* part of entablature between architrave and cornice; horizontal band of sculpture filling this; band of decoration, esp. along wall near ceiling. [F f. L *Phrygium* (*opus*) Phrygian (work)]

frigate /'frɪgɪt/ *n.* naval escort-vessel like large corvette; *hist.* warship next in size to ships of the line. [F f. It.]

fright /fraɪt/ *n.* sudden or extreme fear; instance of this (*you gave me a fright*); person or thing looking grotesque or ridiculous. [OE]

frighten *v.t.* fill with fright; force or drive (*away* or *off*) by fright.

frightful *a.* dreadful, shocking, ugly; *colloq.* extreme, extremely bad (*a frightful idea, rush*); **frightfully** *adv.*

frigid /'frɪdʒɪd/ *a.* lacking friendliness or enthusiasm, dull; (of woman) sexually unresponsive; (esp. of climate or air) cold; **frigidity** /-'dʒɪdɪtɪ/ *n.* [L (*frigus* n. cold)]

frill **1** *n.* strip of material gathered or pleated and fixed along one edge as trimming; (in *pl.*) unnecessary embellishments or accomplishments. **2** *v.t.* decorate with frill. **3 frilly** *a.* [orig. unkn.]

fringe **1** *n.* border or edging of tassels or loose threads; front hair hanging over forehead; margin or outer limit of area, population, etc.; area or part of minor importance. **2** *v.t.* adorn with fringe; serve as fringe to. **3 fringe benefit** employee's benefit additional to normal wage or salary. [F f. L *fimbria*]

frippery /'frɪpərɪ/ *n.* showy finery or ornament, esp. in dress; empty display in speech, literary style, etc. [F *friperie*]

Frisbee /'frɪzbɪ/ *n.* (**P**) concave plastic disc for skimming through air as outdoor game. [perh. f. name *Frisbie*]

Frisian /'frɪzɪən/ **1** *a.* of Friesland. **2** *n.* native or language of Friesland. [L *Frisii* n.pl. f. OFris. *Frīsa*]

frisk **1** *v.* leap or skip playfully; *sl.* feel over and search (person) for weapon etc. **2** *n.* playful leap or skip; *sl.* search of person. [F *frisque* lively]

frisky *a.* lively, playful; **friskily** *adv.*

frisson /'fri:sɒn/ *n.* emotional thrill. [F]

frith var. of FIRTH.

fritter[1] *v.t.* (usu. with *away*) waste (money, time, energy, etc.) triflingly or indiscriminately. [obs. *fritters* fragments]

fritter[2] *n.* small flat piece of fried batter containing meat or fruit etc. [F *friture* f. L (*frigo* FRY[1])]

frivolous /'frɪvələs/ *a.* paltry, trifling; lacking seriousness, silly; **frivolity** /-'vɒlɪtɪ/ *n.* [L]

frizz **1** *v.t.* form (hair) into mass of small curls. **2** *n.* frizzed hair or state. [F *friser*]

frizzle[1] /ˈfrɪz(ə)l/ *v.* fry or cook with sizzling noise; burn or shrivel (*up*). [obs. *frizz* (FRY[1], with imit. ending)]
frizzle[2] /ˈfrɪz(ə)l/ **1** *v.* form into tight curls. **2** *n.* frizzled hair. [FRIZZ]
frizzly *a.* (also **frizzy**) in tight curls.
fro *adv.* back, now only in **to and fro** (see TO[2]). [ON (FROM)]
frock **1** *n.* woman's or girl's dress; monk's or priest's gown; smock. **2** *v.t.* invest with priestly office. **3 frock-coat** man's long-skirted coat not cut away in front, military coat of this shape. [F f. Gmc]
frog[1] *n.* small smooth-skinned leaping amphibian without tail; (**Frog**) *derog.* Frenchman; horny substance in sole of horse's foot; **frog in one's throat** *colloq.* hoarseness. [OE]
frog[2] *n.* ornamental coat-fastening of spindle-shaped button and loop. [orig. unkn.]
frogman *n.* person equipped with rubber suit and flippers etc. for underwater swimming. [FROG[1]]
frogmarch **1** *v.t.* hustle forward holding and pinning arms from behind; carry in frogmarch. **2** *n.* carrying of person face downwards by four others each holding a limb.
frolic /ˈfrɒlɪk/ **1** *v.i.* (**-ck-**) play about cheerfully. **2** *n.* cheerful play; prank; merry party. [Du. *vrolijk* a. (*vro* glad)]
frolicsome *a.* merry, playful.
from /frəm, *emphat.* frɒm/ *prep.* expressing separation or origin, followed by: person, place, time, etc., that is starting-point of motion or action (*comes from Paris*; *dinner is served from 8*); place, object, etc., whose distance or remoteness is stated (*a long way from home*; *I am far from admitting it*); source, giver, sender (*draw water from the tap*; *quoted from Shaw*; *have not heard from her*); thing or person avoided, deprived, etc. (*took his gun from him*; *released him from prison*; *prevented from coming*); reason, cause, motive (*died from fatigue*; *did it from jealousy*); thing distinguished or unlike (*know black from white*); lower limit (*saw from 10 to 20 boats*); state changed for another (*from being the victim he became the attacker*); adverbs or prepositions of time or place (*from long ago*; *from abroad*; *from under the bed*); **from time to time** see TIME. [OE]
frond *n.* leaflike part of fern or palm. [L *frons frond-* leaf]
front /frʌnt/ **1** *n.* side or part normally nearer or towards spectator or direction of motion; any face of building, esp. that of main entrance; foremost part of army, line of battle, ground towards enemy, scene of actual fighting; sector of activity compared to military front, organized political group; appearance, face, demeanour; forward or conspicuous position; bluff, pretext; person etc. serving to cover subversive or illegal activities; promenade of seaside resort; forward edge of advancing mass of cold or warm air; auditorium of theatre. **2** *a.* of the front; situated in front. **3** *v.* have the front facing or directed (*on, to, towards, upon*); *sl.* act as front or cover *for*; furnish with front (*fronted with stone*). **4 front-bencher** a leading member of government or opposition in parliament; **front runner** contestant most likely to succeed; **in front** in an advanced or facing position; **in front of** before, in advance of, in presence of, confronting. [F f. L *frons front-* face]
frontage *n.* front of building; land abutting on street or water, or between front of building and road; extent of front; way a thing faces; outlook.
frontal *a.* of or on front (*frontal attack*); of front as seen by onlooker (*frontal view*); of forehead (*frontal bone*).
frontier /ˈfrʌntɪə/ *n.* border between two countries, district on each side of it; limits of attainment or knowledge in subject.
frontispiece /ˈfrʌntɪspi:s/ *n.* illustration facing title-page of book. [F or L (FRONT, *specio* look)]
frost **1** *n.* freezing, prevalence of temperature below freezing-point of water; frozen dew or vapour. **2** *v.* cover (as) with frost; injure (plant etc.) with frost; make (glass) non-transparent by giving it a rough frostlike surface. **3 frost-bite** injury to tissue of the body due to freezing; **frost-bitten** affected with this; **frost over** become covered with frost. [OE (FREEZE)]
frosting *n.* sugar icing for cakes.
frosty *a.* cold with frost; covered (as) with frost; unfriendly in manner; **frostily** *adv.*; **frostiness** *n.*
froth **1** *n.* foam; idle talk or idea. **2** *v.* emit or gather froth; make (beer etc.) froth. **3 frothy** *a.* [ON]
froward /ˈfrəʊəd/ *a. archaic* perverse, difficult to deal with. [FRO-, WARD]
frown **1** *v.* wrinkle brows, esp. in displeasure or deep thought. **2** *n.* action of frowning; look of displeasure or deep thought. **3 frown at** (or **on**) disapprove of. [F]
frowsty /ˈfraʊstɪ/ *a.* stuffy, fusty. [var. of foll.]
frowzy /ˈfraʊzɪ/ *a.* fusty; slatternly, dingy. [orig. unkn.]
froze, frozen *past* and *p.p.* of FREEZE.
FRS *abbr.* Fellow of the Royal Society.

fructify /ˈfrʌktɪfaɪ/ *v.* (cause to) bear fruit. [F f. L (FRUIT)]
fructose /ˈfrʌktəʊz/ *n.* sugar found in fruit juice, honey, etc. [L (FRUIT)]
frugal /ˈfruːg(ə)l/ *a.* sparing or economical, esp. as regards food; meagre, costing little; **frugality** /-ˈgælɪtɪ/ *n.*; **frugally** *adv.* [L]
fruit /fruːt/ **1** *n.* product of plant or tree that contains seed, this used as food; these products collectively; (usu. in *pl.*) vegetable products fit for food (*fruits of the earth*); produce of action, result; (in *pl.*) profits. **2** *v.* (cause to) bear fruit. **3 fruit-cake** one containing dried fruit; **fruit machine** coin-operated gambling machine, often using symbols representing fruit; **fruit sugar** fructose. [F f. L *fructus* (*fruor* enjoy)]
fruiterer *n.* dealer in fruit.
fruitful *a.* producing much fruit; producing good results, successful; **fruitfully** *adv.*
fruition /fruːˈɪʃ(ə)n/ *n.* bearing of fruit (*lit.* or *fig.*); realization of aims or hopes. [F f. L (FRUIT)]
fruitless /ˈfruːtlɪs/ *a.* not bearing fruit; useless, unsuccessful. [FRUIT]
fruity *a.* of fruit, tasting or smelling like fruit; (of voice etc.) of full rich quality; *colloq.* full of rough humour or (usu. scandalous) interest; **fruitily** *adv.*; **fruitiness** *n.*
frump *n.* unattractive dowdy woman; **frumpish** *a.* [perh. dial. *frumple* wrinkle]
frustrate /frʌˈstreɪt/ *v.t.* make (efforts) ineffective; prevent (person) from achieving purpose; (in *p.p.*) discontented because unable to achieve desires; **frustration** *n.* [L (*frustra* in vain)]
frustum /ˈfrʌstəm/ *n.* (*pl.* **frusta**) lower part of cone or pyramid whose top is cut off by plane parallel to base. [L, = piece cut off]
fry[1] **1** *v.* cook or be cooked in hot fat. **2** *n.* internal parts of animals usu. eaten fried (*lamb's fry*); fried food. **3 frying-pan** shallow pan used in frying (**out of the frying-pan into the fire** from bad situation to worse); **fry-up** miscellaneous fried food. [F f. L *frigo*]
fry[2] *n.* young or newly hatched fishes; **small fry** people of little importance, children. [ON, = seed]
fryer *n.* one who fries; vessel for frying esp. fish. [FRY[1]]
ft. *abbr.* foot, feet.
fuchsia /ˈfjuːʃə/ *n.* shrub with drooping red or purple or white flowers. [*Fuchs*, botanist]
fuck *vulgar* **1** *v.* have sexual intercourse (with); idle *about* or *around*. **2** *int.* expressing anger or annoyance. **3** *n.* act of or partner in sexual intercourse; slightest amount (*don't give a fuck*). **4 fuck off** go away; **fuck up** make a mess of. **5 fucking** *a.* & *adv.* (often as mere intensive). [orig. unkn.]
fuddle /ˈfʌd(ə)l/ **1** *v.t.* confuse or stupefy, esp. with alcoholic liquor. **2** *n.* confusion; intoxication. [orig. unkn.]
fuddy-duddy /ˈfʌdɪdʌdɪ/ *sl.* **1** *a.* old-fashioned or quaintly fussy. **2** *n.* such person. [orig. unkn.]
fudge **1** *n.* soft toffee-like sweet made of milk, sugar, and butter; nonsense. **2** *v.t.* put together in makeshift or dishonest way, fake. [orig. uncert.]
fuel /ˈfjuːəl/ **1** *n.* material for burning as fire or source of heat or power; material used as source of nuclear energy; food as source of energy; thing that sustains or inflames passion etc. **2** *v.* (**-ll-**, *US* **-l-**) supply with fuel; inflame (feeling etc.); take in or get fuel. **3 fuel cell** cell producing electricity direct from chemical reaction. [F f. L *focus* hearth]
fug *n. colloq.* stuffiness of air in room; **fuggy** *a.* [orig. unkn.]
fugitive /ˈfjuːdʒɪtɪv/ **1** *a.* fleeing, that runs or has run away; fleeting, transient; (of literature) of passing interest, ephemeral. **2** *n.* one who flees, e.g. from justice or enemy. [F f. L (*fugio* flee)]
fugue /fjuːg/ *n.* piece of music in which short melody or phrase is introduced by one part and successively taken up or developed by others; **fugal** *a.* [F, or It. (L *fuga* flight)]
führer /ˈfjʊərə/ *n.* tyrannical leader. [G]
-ful *suffix* forming (1) adjectives from nouns, in sense 'full of' (*beautiful*), 'having qualities of' (*masterful*), or from adjectives (*direful*); or from verbs in sense 'apt to' (*forgetful*); (2) nouns (*pl.* **-fuls**) in sense 'amount that fills' (*glassful, handful, spoonful*). [FULL[1]]
fulcrum /ˈfʊlkrəm/ *n.* (*pl.* **fulcra**) point on which lever is supported. [L (*fulcio* prop)]
fulfil /fʊlˈfɪl/, *US* **fulfill**, *v.t.* (**-ll-**) carry out (task, prophecy, promise, command, law); satisfy (conditions, desire, prayer); answer (purpose); **fulfil oneself** develop fully one's gifts and character; **fulfilment** *n.* [OE (FULL[1], FILL)]
full[1] /fʊl/ **1** *a.* holding all its limits will allow (*bucket is full, full of water*); having eaten to one's limit or satisfaction; abundant, copious, satisfying (*a full meal; full details*); having abundance *of* (*full of interest, mistakes, vitality*); engrossed in thinking *of* (*full of himself, of his subject*); complete, perfect, reaching specified or usual or utmost limit (*a full hour; full marks; full*

membership); (of tone) clear and deep; plump, rounded (*a full figure*); (of clothes) made of much material hanging in folds. **2** *adv.* very (*you know full well*); quite, fully (*full six miles*); exactly (*hit him full on the nose*). **3 full back** defensive player near goal in football, hockey, etc.; **full-blooded** vigorous, sensual, not hybrid; **full-blown** fully developed; **full board** provision of bed and all meals at hotel etc.; **full-bodied** rich in quality, tone, etc.; **full brother** (or **sister**) brother (or sister) with both parents the same; **full face** with all the face visible to spectator; **full house** large or full attendance at theatre etc., hand in poker with three of a kind and a pair; **full-length** not shortened or abbreviated, (of mirror or portrait) showing whole of human figure; **full moon** moon with whole disc illuminated, time when this occurs; **full pitch** = *full toss*; **full-scale** not reduced in size, complete; **full stop** punctuation mark (.) used at end of sentence or abbreviation, complete cessation; **full time** total normal duration of work etc.; **full-time** *a.* occupying or using whole of available working time; **full toss** ball pitched right up to batsman in cricket; **in full** without abridgement, to or for the full amount; **in full view** entirely visible; **to the full** to the utmost extent. [OE]

full² /fʊl/ *v.t.* clean and thicken (cloth). [foll.]

fuller *n.* one who fulls cloth; **fuller's earth** type of clay used in fulling. [OE f. L *fullo*]

fullness *n.* being full; **the fullness of time** the appropriate or destined time. [FULL¹]

fully *adv.* completely, entirely (*am fully aware*); no less than (*fully 60*); **fully-fashioned** (of women's clothing) shaped to fit the body.

fulmar /'fʊlmə/ *n.* Arctic sea-bird related to petrel. [ON (FOUL, *mar* gull)]

fulminant /'fʊlmɪnənt/ *a.* fulminating; (of disease) developing suddenly. [F or L (foll.)]

fulminate /'fʊlmɪneɪt/ *v.* express censure loudly and forcefully; explode violently, flash like lightning; **fulmination** /-'neɪʃ(ə)n/ *n.*; **fulminator** *n.* [L (*fulmen -min-* lightning)]

fulsome /'fʊlsəm/ *a.* (of flattery etc.) cloying, disgustingly excessive. [FULL¹]

fumble /'fʌmb(ə)l/ **1** *v.* use the hands awkwardly, grope about; handle clumsily or nervously. **2** *n.* act of fumbling. [LG *fummeln*]

fume 1 *n.* (usu. in *pl.*) exuded gas or smoke or vapour, esp. when harmful or unpleasant. **2** *v.* emit fumes; issue in fumes; be very angry; subject to fumes, esp. of ammonia to darken oak etc. [F f. L (*fumus* smoke)]

fumigate /'fju:mɪgeɪt/ *v.t.* disinfect or purify with action of fumes; **fumigation** /-'geɪʃ(ə)n/ *n.*; **fumigator** *n.* [L (prec.)]

fun *n.* lively or playful amusement; source of this; **for** (or **in**) **fun** not seriously; **make fun of** (or **poke fun at**) tease, ridicule. [obs. *fun, fon* (FOND)]

function /'fʌŋkʃ(ə)n/ **1** *n.* activity proper to person or institution or by which thing fulfils its purpose; official or professional duty; public ceremony or occasion; social gathering, esp. large one; *Math.* quantity whose value depends on varying values (of others). **2** *v.i.* fulfil function, operate. [F f. L (*fungor funct-* perform)]

functional *a.* of or serving a function; designed or intended to be practical rather than necessarily attractive or pleasing; affecting function of a bodily organ but not its structure; **functionally** *adv.*

functionalism *n.* belief in or stress on practical application of thing; **functionalist** *n.*

functionary *n.* person or official performing certain duties.

fund 1 *n.* permanently available stock (*fund of knowledge*); stock of money, esp. one set apart for a purpose; (in *pl.*) money resources. **2** *v.t.* provide with money; make (debt) permanent at fixed interest. **3 in funds** having money to spend. [L *fundus* bottom]

fundamental /fʌndə'ment(ə)l/ **1** *a.* of, affecting, or serving as base or foundation, essential, primary. **2** *n.* fundamental rule or principle (usu. in *pl.*); fundamental note. **3 fundamental note** lowest note of chord; **fundamental particle** elementary particle. **4 fundamentally** *adv.* [F or L (FOUND¹)]

fundamentalism *n.* strict maintenance of traditional Protestant beliefs; **fundamentalist** *n.*

funeral /'fju:nər(ə)l/ **1** *n.* burial or cremation of the dead with ceremonies; *sl.* one's (usu. unpleasant) concern (*that's your funeral*). **2** *attrib. a.* of or used at funerals. [F f. L (*funus funer-*)]

funerary /'fju:nərərɪ/ *a.* of or used at funeral(s). [L (prec.)]

funereal /fju:'nɪərɪəl/ *a.* of or appropriate to a funeral, dismal, dark; **funereally** *adv.*

fun-fair *n.* fair consisting of amusements and side-shows. [FUN]

fungicide /'fʌndʒɪsaɪd/ *n.* substance that kills fungus; **fungicidal** /-'saɪd(ə)l/ *a.* [FUNGUS]

fungoid /'fʌŋgɔɪd/ **1** *a.* fungus-like. **2** *n.* fungoid plant.
fungus /'fʌŋgəs/ *n.* (*pl.* **fungi** /-gaɪ/) mushroom, toadstool, or allied plant including moulds, feeding on organic matter; spongy morbid growth; **fungous** *a.* [L]
funicular /fju:'nɪkjʊlə/ **1** *a.* (of railway, esp. on mountain) operating by cable with ascending and descending cars counterbalanced. **2** *n.* such railway. [L *funiculus* dimin. of *funis* rope]
funk *sl.* **1** *n.* fear, panic; coward. **2** *v.* be afraid (of); try to evade. **3 blue funk** extreme panic. [orig. uncert.]
funky /'fʌŋkɪ/ *a. sl.* (esp. of music) down-to-earth, emotional; fashionable; having strong smell. [orig. uncert.]
funnel /'fʌn(ə)l/ **1** *n.* narrow tube or pipe widening at the top, for pouring liquid etc. into small opening; metal chimney on steam-engine or ship. **2** *v.* (**-ll-**, *US* **-l-**) (cause to) move (as) through funnel. [Prov. *fonilh* f. L (*in*)*fundibulum*]
funny /'fʌnɪ/ *a.* amusing, comical; strange, hard to account for; *colloq.* slightly unwell, eccentric, etc.; **funny-bone** part of elbow over which very sensitive nerve passes; **funnily** *adv.*; **funniness** *n.* [FUN]
fur **1** *n.* short fine soft hair of certain animals; animal skin with fur on it, used esp. for making or trimming clothes etc.; garment made or lined with this; *collect.* furred animals; crust or coating formed on tongue in sickness, in kettle by hard water, etc. **2** *v.* (**-rr-**) line or trim with fur (esp. in *p.p.*); (often with *up*: of kettle etc.) become coated with fur deposit. **3 make the fur fly** cause disturbance or dissension. [F f. Gmc]
furbelow /'fɜ:bɪləʊ/ *n.* gathered strip or pleated border of skirt or petticoat; (in *pl.*) showy ornaments. [F *falbala*]
furbish /'fɜ:bɪʃ/ *v.t.* (often with *up*) polish, clean up or renovate. [F f. Gmc]
furcate /'fɜ:keɪt/ **1** *a.* forked, branched. **2** *v.i.* fork, divide. **3 furcation** /-'keɪʃ(ə)n/ *n.* [L (FORK)]
furious /'fjʊərɪəs/ *a.* very angry, full of fury, raging, frantic. [F f. L (FURY)]
furl *v.* roll up and bind (sail etc.); become furled. [F *ferler*]
furlong /'fɜ:lɒŋ/ *n.* eighth of mile. [OE (FURROW, LONG)]
furlough /'fɜ:ləʊ/ **1** *n.* leave of absence, esp. granted to serviceman. **2** *v. US* grant furlough to; spend furlough. [Du. (FOR, LEAVE)]
furnace /'fɜ:nɪs/ *n.* enclosed structure for intense heating by fire, esp. of metals or water; very hot place. [F f. L *fornax* (*fornus* oven)]
furnish /'fɜ:nɪʃ/ *v.t.* provide (house or room etc.) with furniture; supply *with* thing. [F f. Gmc]
furnishings *n.* furniture and fitments in house or room etc.
furniture /'fɜ:nɪtʃə/ *n.* movable equipment of house or room etc., e.g. tables, chairs, and beds; ship's equipment; accessories, e.g. handles and lock on door. [F (FURNISH)]
furore /fjʊə'rɔ:rɪ/, *US* **furor** /-rɔ:/ *n.* uproar; enthusiastic admiration; fury. [It. f. L (FURY)]
furrier /'fʌrɪə/ *n.* dealer in or dresser of furs. [F]
furrow /'fʌrəʊ/ **1** *n.* narrow cut in ground made by plough; rut, groove, wrinkle; ship's track. **2** *v.t.* plough; make furrows in. [OE]
furry /'fɜ:rɪ/ *a.* like or covered with fur. [FUR]
further /'fɜ:ðə/ **1** *adv.* more far in space or time; more, to greater extent (*will enquire further*); in addition (*I may add further*). **2** *a.* more distant or advanced; more, additional (*send further details*). **3** *v.t.* promote or favour (scheme etc.). **4 further education** that for persons above school age. [OE (FORTH)]
furtherance *n.* furthering of scheme etc.
furthermore *adv.* in addition, besides.
furthermost *a.* most distant.
furthest /'fɜ:ðɪst/ **1** *a.* most distant. **2** *adv.* to or at the greatest distance.
furtive /'fɜ:tɪv/ *a.* done by stealth; sly, stealthy. [F or L (*fur* thief)]
fury /'fjʊərɪ/ *n.* wild and passionate anger, rage; violence of storm, disease, etc.; (in *pl.*, **Furies**) avenging goddesses of Greek mythology; avenging spirit; angry or malignant woman; **like fury** *colloq.* with great force or effort. [F f. L *furia*]
furze *n.* spiny evergreen shrub with yellow flowers, gorse; **furzy** *a.* [OE]
fuse[1] /fju:z/ **1** *v.* melt with intense heat; blend into whole by melting; mix or blend together; provide (electric circuit) with fuse(s), (of appliance) fail owing to melting of fuse, cause (appliance) to do this. **2** *n.* device with strip or wire of easily melted metal placed in electric circuit so as to interrupt excessive current by melting. [L (FOUND[2])]
fuse[2] /fju:z/ **1** *n.* device or component of combustible matter for detonating bomb etc. or explosive charge. **2** *v.t.* fit fuse to. [It. f. L *fusus* spindle]
fuselage /'fju:zəlɑ:ʒ/ *n.* body of aeroplane. [F (FUSE[2])]
fusible /'fju:zɪb(ə)l/ *a.* that can be melted; **fusibility** /-'bɪlɪtɪ/ *n.* [L (FUSE[1])]
fusil /'fju:zɪl/ *n. hist.* light musket. [F (L *focus* fire)]

fusilier /fju:zɪ'lɪə/ *n.* member of any of several British regiments formerly armed with fusils. [F (prec.)]
fusillade /fju:zɪ'leɪd/ *n.* continuous discharge of firearms; sustained outburst of criticism etc.
fusion /'fju:ʒ(ə)n/ *n.* fusing or melting together; blending, coalition; = *nuclear fusion*. [F or L (FUSE[1])]
fuss 1 *n.* excited commotion, bustle; excessive concern about trivial thing; sustained protest or dispute. **2** *v.* behave with nervous concern; agitate, worry. **3 make a fuss** complain vigorously; **make a fuss of** treat (person) with excessive attention etc. [orig. unkn.]
fusspot *n. colloq.* person given to fussing.
fussy *a.* inclined to fuss; over-elaborate, fastidious; **fussily** *adv.*; **fussiness** *n.*
fustian /'fʌstɪən/ **1** *n.* thick twilled cotton cloth usu. dyed dark; bombast. **2** *a.* made of fustian; bombastic, worthless. [F]
fusty /'fʌstɪ/ *a.* musty, stuffy, stale-smelling; antiquated; **fustiness** *a.* [F (*fust* barrel f. L *fustis* cudgel)]
futile /'fju:taɪl/ *a.* useless, ineffectual, frivolous; **futility** /-'tɪlɪtɪ/ *n.* [L *futilis* leaky, futile]
future /'fju:tʃə/ **1** *a.* about to happen or be or become; of time to come; *Gram.* (of tense) describing event yet to happen. **2** *n.* time to come; what will happen in the future; person's, country's, etc., future condition; prospect of success etc. (*there's no future in it*); *Gram.* future tense; (in *pl.*) goods etc. sold for future delivery. **3 in future** from this time onwards. [F f. L *futurus* fut. partic. of *sum* be]
futurism *n.* movement in art, literature, music, etc., departing from traditional forms so as to express movement and growth; **futurist** *n.*
futuristic /fju:tʃə'rɪstɪk/ *a.* suitable for the future, ultra-modern; of futurism.
futurity /fju:'tjʊərɪtɪ/ *n.* future time; (in *sing.* or *pl.*) future events.
futurology /fju:tʃə'rɒlədʒɪ/ *n.* forecasting of future, esp. from present trends in society. [-LOGY]
fuze *US* var. of FUSE[2].
fuzz *n.* fluff; fluffy or frizzed hair; *sl.* police, policeman. [prob. LG or Du.]
fuzzy *a.* like fuzz; blurred, indistinct; **fuzzily** *adv.*; **fuzziness** *n.*
-fy *suffix* forming (1) verbs from nouns, in senses 'make, produce' (*pacify*, *satisfy*), 'make into' (*deify*, *petrify*), (2) verbs from adjectives in sense 'bring or come into state' (*Frenchify*, *solidify*), (3) verbs in causative sense (*horrify*, *stupefy*). [L *facio* make]

G

G, g /dʒi:/ *n.* (*pl.* **Gs, G's**) seventh letter; *Mus.* fifth note in diatonic scale of C major.
g. *abbr.* gram(s); gravity, acceleration due to gravity.
Ga *symb.* gallium.
gab *n. colloq.* talk, chatter; **gift of the gab** eloquence, loquacity. [var. of GOB[2]]
gabardine /'gæbədi:n/ *n.* twill-woven cloth, esp. of worsted. [var. of GABERDINE]
gabble /'gæb(ə)l/ **1** *v.* talk or utter inarticulately or too fast. **2** *n.* fast unintelligible talk. [Du., imit.]
gabby *a. colloq.* talkative. [GAB]
gaberdine /'gæbədi:n/ *n. hist.* loose long upper garment worn esp. by Jews; = GABARDINE. [F]
gable /'geɪb(ə)l/ *n.* triangular upper part of wall at end of ridged roof; end wall with gable; gable-shaped canopy. [ON & F]
gad[1] *v.i.* (**-dd-**) go *about* idly or in search of pleasure. [obs. *gadling* companion]
gad[2] *int.* (also **by gad**) expressing surprise or emphatic assertion. [*God*]
gadabout /'gædəbaʊt/ *n.* one who gads about. [GAD[1]]
gadfly /'gædflaɪ/ *n.* fly that bites cattle; irritating person. [obs. *gad* spike]
gadget /'gædʒɪt/ *n.* small mechanical device or tool; **gadgetry** *n.* [orig. unkn.]
gadoid /'geɪdɔɪd/ **1** *a.* of the cod family. **2** *n.* gadoid fish. [Gk *gados* cod]
gadolinium /gædə'lɪnɪəm/ *n.* metallic element of lanthanide series. [*Gadolin*, mineralogist]
gadwall /'gædwɔ:l/ *n.* brownish-grey freshwater duck. [orig. unkn.]
Gael /geɪl/ *n.* Scottish Celt; Gaelic-speaking Celt. [Sc. Gael. *Gaidheal*]
Gaelic /'geɪlɪk, 'gæl-/ **1** *n.* Celtic language of Scotland and Ireland. **2** *a.* of Gaelic; of Gaels.
gaff[1] **1** *n.* stick with iron hook for landing large fish; barbed fishing-spear; spar to which head of fore-and-aft sail is bent. **2** *v.t.* seize (fish) with gaff. [Prov. *gaf* hook]
gaff[2] *n. sl.* now chiefly in **blow the gaff** divulge plot or secret. [orig. unkn.]

gaffe /gæf/ *n.* blunder, *faux pas.* [F]
gaffer *n.* old fellow (also as title or form of address); foreman, boss. [prob. GODFATHER]
gag 1 *n.* thing thrust into or tied across mouth to prevent speech or hold mouth open for operation; joke or comic scene in play, film, etc.; thing restricting free speech; parliamentary closure. **2** *v.* (**-gg-**) apply gag to; silence, deprive of free speech; make gags in play, film, etc.; choke, retch. [orig. uncert.]
gaga /'gɑːgɑː/ *a. sl.* senile; fatuous, slightly crazy. [F]
gage[1] *n.* pledge, thing deposited as security; symbol of challenge to fight, esp. glove thrown down. [F f. Gmc (WAGE, WED)]
gage[2] *n.* greengage. [abbr.]
gage[3] *US* & *Naut.* var. of GAUGE.
gaggle /'gæg(ə)l/ *n.* flock of geese; disorderly group. [imit.]
gaiety /'geɪətɪ/ *n.* being gay, mirth; merry-making, amusement; bright appearance. [F (GAY)]
gaily *adv.* in a gay manner. [GAY]
gain 1 *v.* obtain or secure (*gain advantage, one's object*); acquire (sum) as profits etc., earn; make a profit, be benefited, improve or advance *in* some respect; obtain as increment or addition (*gain momentum, weight*); (of clock etc.) become fast, or be fast by (specified time); come closer to something pursued, catch up *on* or *upon*; reach (desired place); win (land from sea, battle); persuade. **2** *n.* increase of wealth etc., profit, improvement; increase in amount; acquisition of wealth; (in *pl.*) sums of money got by trade etc. **3 gain ground** advance, catch up *on* (person pursued); **gain time** improve one's chances by causing or accepting a delay. [F f. Gmc]
gainful *a.* (of employment) paid; lucrative; **gainfully** *adv.*
gainsay /geɪn'seɪ/ *v.t.* deny, contradict. [ON (AGAINST, SAY)]
gait *n.* manner of walking; manner of forward motion of horse etc. [ON]
gaiter *n.* covering of cloth, leather, etc., for leg below knee, for ankle, or for part of machine etc. [F *guêtre*]
gal *n. colloq.* girl. [repr. var. pr.]
gal. *abbr.* gallon(s).
gala /'gɑːlə, 'geɪlə/ *n.* festive occasion; festive gathering for sports. [F, or It. f. Sp., f. Arab.]
galactic /gə'læktɪk/ *a.* of a galaxy or galaxies. [Gk (GALAXY)]
galantine /'gæləntiːn/ *n.* white meat boned, spiced, etc., and served cold. [F f. L]
galaxy /'gæləksɪ/ *n.* independent system of stars, gas, dust, etc., existing in space; (**Galaxy**) Milky Way; brilliant company (*of* beauties etc.). [F f. L f. Gk (*gala* milk)]
gale[1] *n.* very strong wind or storm; outburst esp. of laughter; *poetic* breeze. [orig. unkn.]
gale[2] *n.* usu. in **sweet-gale** bog myrtle. [OE]
gall[1] /gɔːl/ *n.* bile of animals; bitterness (*gall and wormwood*); *sl.* impudence; asperity, rancour; **gall-bladder** vessel containing bile. [ON]
gall[2] /gɔːl/ **1** *n.* sore made by chafing; mental soreness or its cause; place rubbed bare. **2** *v.t.* rub sore; vex, humiliate. [LG or Du. *galle*]
gall[3] /gɔːl/ *n.* growth produced by insects etc. on plants and trees, esp. on oak. [F f. L *galla*]
gallant /'gælənt/ **1** *a.* brave; fine, stately; /also gə'lænt/ very attentive to women. **2** /also gə'lænt/ *n.* ladies' man. [F (*galer* make merry)]
gallantry *n.* bravery; devotion to women; polite act or speech; sexual intrigue.
galleon /'gælɪən/ *n. hist.* ship of war (usu. Spanish). [Du. f. F or Sp. (GALLEY)]
gallery /'gælərɪ/ *n.* room or building for showing works of art; balcony, esp. in hall or church (*minstrels' gallery*); highest balcony in theatre, its occupants; covered walk partly open at side, colonnade; narrow passage in thickness of wall or on corbels, open towards interior of building; long narrow room or passage (*shooting-gallery*); group of spectators at golf match etc.; horizontal underground passage in mine etc.; **play to the gallery** seek to win approval by appealing to unrefined taste. [F f. It. f. L]
galley /'gælɪ/ *n.* long flat one-decked vessel usu. rowed by slaves or criminals (*hist.*); ancient Greek or Roman warship; kitchen in ship or aircraft; long tray for set-up type in printing; **galley (proof)** proof in long narrow form; **galley-slave** *fig.* drudge. [F f. L *galea*]
Gallic /'gælɪk/ *a.* of Gaul or the Gauls; French. [L *Gallicus*]
Gallicism /'gælɪsɪz(ə)m/ *n.* French idiom. [GALLIC]
gallinaceous /gælɪ'neɪʃəs/ *a.* of the order including domestic poultry, pheasants, etc. [L (*gallina* hen)]
gallium /'gælɪəm/ *n.* soft bluish-white metallic element. [perh. L *gallium* cock, tr. *Lecoq*, discoverer]
gallivant /gælɪ'vænt/ *v.i. colloq.* gad about. [perh. corrupt. of GALLANT 'to flirt']
Gallo- *in comb.* French. [L]
gallon /'gælən/ *n.* measure of capacity

(4546 cc; for wine, or US, 3785 cc); (usu. in *pl.*) *colloq.* large amount. [F]

gallop /'gæləp/ **1** *n.* fastest pace of horse etc., with all feet off ground together in each stride; ride at this pace. **2** *v.* (of horse etc. or its rider) go at a gallop; make (horse) gallop; read, talk, etc., fast; progress rapidly (*galloping consumption, inflation*). [F (WALLOP)]

gallows /'gæləʊz/ *n.pl.* (usu. treated as *sing.*) structure, usu. of two uprights and cross-piece, for the hanging of criminals. [ON]

gallstone /'gɔ:lstəʊn/ *n.* small hard mass forming in gall-bladder. [GALL¹, STONE]

Gallup poll /'gæləp/ assessment of public opinion by questioning representative sample, esp. as basis of forecasts of voting etc. [*Gallup*, statistician]

galop /'gæləp/ *n.* lively dance in duple time; music for this. [F (GALLOP)]

galore /gə'lɔ:/ *adv.* in plenty (*whisky galore*). [Ir.]

galosh /gə'lɒʃ/ *n.* overshoe usu. of rubber. [F]

galumph /gə'lʌmf/ *v.i. colloq.* go prancing in triumph; move noisily or clumsily. [coined by Lewis Carroll, perh. f. GALLOP, TRIUMPH]

galvanic /gæl'vænɪk/ *a.* producing an electric current by chemical action; (of electricity) produced by chemical action; *fig.* stimulating, full of energy, sudden and remarkable; **galvanically** *adv.* [foll.]

galvanize /'gælvənaɪz/ *v.t.* stimulate by or as by electricity; rouse forcefully (*into* action etc.); coat (iron) with zinc to protect from rust; **galvanization** /-'zeɪʃ(ə)n/ *n.* [*Galvani*, physiologist]

galvanometer /gælvə'nɒmɪtə/ *n.* instrument for measuring small electric currents.

gambit /'gæmbɪt/ *n.* chess opening in which player sacrifices pawn or piece; opening move in discussion etc.; trick, device. [It. *gambetto* tripping up]

gamble /'gæmb(ə)l/ **1** *v.* play games of chance for money; risk much in hope of great gain. **2** *n.* gambling; risky undertaking. **3 gamble away** lose by gambling; **gamble on** act in hope of (event). [GAME¹]

gambler *n.* one who gambles, esp. habitually.

gamboge /gæm'bu:ʒ, -'bəʊʒ/ *n.* gum resin used as yellow pigment and as purgative. [*Cambodia* in SE Asia]

gambol /'gæmb(ə)l/ **1** *v.i.* (-ll-, *US* -l-) jump about playfully. **2** *n.* caper. [*gambade* leap f. It. (*gamba* leg)]

game¹ **1** *n.* form of play or sport, esp. competitive one organized with rules, penalties, etc.; portion of play forming scoring unit e.g. in bridge or tennis; winning score in game, state of score (*game is two all*); (in *pl.*) series of athletic etc. contests (*Olympic Games*); scheme, undertaking, etc. (*so that's your game*); wild animals or birds hunted for sport or food, their flesh as food. **2** *a.* spirited, eager and willing; having the spirit or energy (*are you game for a walk?*). **3** *v.i.* gamble for money stakes. **4 the game is up** scheme is revealed or foiled; **give the game away** reveal intentions or secret; **make game of** ridicule; **on the game** *sl.* involved in prostitution or thieving. [OE]

game² *a.* (of leg, arm, etc.) crippled. [orig. unkn.]

gamecock *n.* cock bred and trained for cock-fighting. [GAME¹]

gamekeeper *n.* person employed to breed and protect game.

gamelan /'gæmələn/ *n.* SE Asian orchestra, mainly of percussion instruments; type of xylophone used in this. [Jav.]

gamesmanship *n.* art of winning games by gaining psychological advantage over opponent.

gamesome *a.* playful, sportive.

gamester /'geɪmstə/ *n.* gambler.

gamete /'gæmi:t/ *n.* mature germ-cell able to unite with another in sexual reproduction; **gametic** /gə'metɪk/ *a.* [Gk, = wife]

gamin /'gæmɪn/ *n.* street urchin; impudent child. [F]

gamine /gə'mi:n/ *n.* girl with mischievous charm. [F]

gamma /'gæmə/ *n.* third letter of Greek alphabet (Γ, γ); **gamma radiation** (or **rays**) X-rays of very short wavelength. [Gk]

gammon /'gæmən/ *n.* bottom piece of flitch of bacon including hind leg; pig's ham cured like bacon. [F (JAMB)]

gammy /'gæmɪ/ *a. sl.* = GAME² [dial. form of GAME²]

gamut /'gæmət/ *n.* whole series of recognized musical notes; compass of voice etc.; *fig.* entire range. [L *gamma ut*, words arbitrarily taken as names of notes]

gamy *a.* smelling or tasting like high game. [GAME¹]

gander *n.* male goose; *sl.* look, glance (*take a gander*). [OE]

gang¹ **1** *n.* band of persons associating for some (usu. criminal) purpose; set of workers, slaves, or prisoners; set *of* tools working in co-ordination. **2** *v.t.* arrange (tools etc.) to work in co-ordination. **3 gang up** act in concert (*with*); **gang up on** *colloq.* combine against. [ON]

gang[2] *v.i. Sc.* go; **gang agley** (of plan etc.) go wrong. [OE]
ganger *n.* foreman of gang of workers. [GANG[1]]
gangling /'gæŋglɪŋ/ *a.* (of person) loosely built, lanky. [frequent. of GANG[2]]
ganglion /'gæŋglɪən/ *n.* (*pl.* **ganglia**) enlargement or knot on nerve forming centre for reception and transmission of impulses; centre of activity etc.; **ganglionic** /-'ɒnɪk/ *a.* [Gk]
gangplank *n.* movable plank for walking into or out of boat etc. [GANG[1]]
gangrene /'gæŋgri:n/ **1** *n.* death of body tissue, usu. caused by obstructed blood-circulation; moral corruption. **2** *v.* affect or become affected with gangrene. **3 gangrenous** *a.* [F. f. L f. Gk]
gangster *n.* member of gang of violent criminals. [GANG[1]]
gangue /gæŋ/ *n.* valueless earth etc. in which ore is found. [F f. G (GANG[1])]
gangway *n.* passage esp. between rows of seats; opening in ship's bulwarks, bridge from this to shore. [GANG[1]]
gannet /'gænɪt/ *n.* large sea-bird. [OE]
gantlet /'gæntlɪt/ *n. US* var. of GAUNTLET[2].
gantry /'gæntrɪ/ *n.* structure supporting travelling crane, railway signals, equipment for rocket-launch, etc. [prob. *gawn* GALLON, TREE]
gaol /dʒeɪl/ **1** *n.* public prison; confinement in this. **2** *v.t.* put in gaol. [F f. Rmc (CAGE)]
gaolbird *n.* habitual criminal; prisoner.
gaolbreak *n.* escape from gaol.
gaoler *n.* person in charge of gaol or prisoners in it.
gap *n.* breach in hedge or fence or wall; empty space, interval; deficiency; wide divergence in views etc.; gorge or pass; **gappy** *a.* [ON]
gape 1 *v.i.* open mouth wide; (of mouth etc.) open or be open wide; stare *at*; yawn. **2** *n.* open-mouthed stare; yawn; open mouth. [ON]
garage /'gærɑ:dʒ, -ɑ:ʒ, -ɪdʒ/ **1** *n.* building for housing motor vehicle(s); establishment selling petrol etc., or repairing and selling motor vehicles. **2** *v.t.* put or keep (vehicle) in garage. [F]
garb 1 *n.* clothing, esp. of distinctive kind. **2** *v.t.* (usu. in *pass.* or *refl.*) dress, esp. in distinctive clothes. [F f. It. f. Gmc (GEAR)]
garbage /'gɑ:bɪdʒ/ *n.* refuse; domestic waste; foul or rubbishy literature etc. [AF]
garble /'gɑ:b(ə)l/ *v.t.* unintentionally distort or confuse (facts, messages, etc.); make (usu. unfair) selection from (facts or statements). [It. f. Arab.]
garden /'gɑ:d(ə)n/ **1** *n.* piece of ground for growing flowers, fruit, or vegetables; *attrib.* cultivated (*garden plants*); (esp. in *pl.*) grounds laid out for public enjoyment. **2** *v.i.* cultivate garden. **3 garden centre** establishment selling garden plants and equipment; **garden city** town laid out with many open spaces and trees; **garden party** party held on lawn or in garden. [F f. Rmc f. Gmc (YARD[2])]
gardener /'gɑ:dnə/ *n.* person who gardens; person employed to tend garden.
gardenia /gɑ:'di:nɪə/ *n.* tree or shrub with large fragrant white or yellow flowers; its flower. [*Garden*, naturalist]
garfish /'gɑ:fɪʃ/ *n.* (*pl.* same) fish with long spearlike snout. [OE, = spear-fish]
gargantuan /gɑ:'gæntjʊən/ *a.* gigantic. [*Gargantua*, giant in Rabelais]
gargle /'gɑ:g(ə)l/ **1** *v.* wash (throat) with liquid held there and kept in motion by breath. **2** *n.* liquid so used. [F (foll.)]
gargoyle /'gɑ:gɔɪl/ *n.* grotesque carved face or figure as spout from gutter of building. [F, = throat]
garibaldi /gærɪ'bɔ:ldɪ/ *n.* biscuit containing layer of currants. [*Garibaldi*, Italian nationalist]
garish /'geərɪʃ/ *a.* obtrusively bright, showy, gaudy. [obs. *gaure* stare]
garland /'gɑ:lənd/ **1** *n.* wreath, usu. of flowers, worn on head or hung on thing as decoration. **2** *v.t.* deck with garlands; crown with garland. [F]
garlic /'gɑ:lɪk/ *n.* plant with pungent bulb used in cookery; **garlicky** *a.* [OE, = spear-leek]
garment /'gɑ:mənt/ *n.* article of dress; outward covering. [F (GARNISH)]
garner 1 *v.t.* store; collect. **2** *n. literary* storehouse, granary (*lit.* or *fig.*). [F f. L (GRANARY)]
garnet /'gɑ:nɪt/ *n.* vitreous silicate mineral, esp. red kind used as gem. [F f. med. L *granatum* POMEGRANATE]
garnish /'gɑ:nɪʃ/ **1** *v.t.* decorate (esp. dish for table). **2** *n.* decorative addition. [F *garnir* f. Gmc]
garotte var. of GARROTTE.
garret /'gærɪt/ *n.* attic or room in roof, esp. dismal one. [F, = watch-tower (foll.)]
garrison /'gærɪs(ə)n/ **1** *n.* troops stationed in town etc. to defend it. **2** *v.t.* provide with or occupy as garrison. [F (*garir* defend, f. Gmc)]
garrotte /gə'rɒt/, *US* **garrote 1** *n.* Spanish capital punishment by strangulation; apparatus for this. **2** *v.t.* execute by garrotte. [Sp.]
garrulous /'gærʊləs/ *a.* talkative; **garrulity** /gə'ru:lɪtɪ/ *n.* [L]
garter *n.* band worn near knee to keep up sock etc.; **the Garter** highest order of

1 MILE = 1·609 K.METRES
1 YARD = 0.9144 METRE
1 FOOT = 0.3048 "
1 INCH 25·4 MILLIMETRES

---

1. METRE = 1·094 YARDS

...ir predecessors achieved and w

bought toothbrushes by mistake. While the

blocks and the estate deteriorate more th

on one block. Do you not think this is gr

who have been waiting years for signs of

the time and money it will be 20 years be

personally feel is unaceptable besides by

lucky one now will be in the same boat as

Before this propsal goes ahead don't you

given some sort of priority.

Leaseholders and Tenants should contact

persons," and get them to arrange a Gene

estate to discuss all aspects of <u>our est</u>

The following 2 items I believe should b

fairness to the greater majority.

1. The subsidence in the roadway and gr

229-244 Empire Court resulting in the

now, this should be rectified immediat

as to who is responsible to pay becaus

going to cost apart from the continue

tradesmen who have to visit the estate

English knighthood, badge or membership of this; **garter stitch** plain knitting stitch. [F]

gas 1 *n.* (*pl.* **gases** /'gæsɪz/) any airlike or completely elastic fluid, esp. (as distinct from 'vapours') one not liquid or solid at ordinary temperatures; such fluid (esp. *coal gas* or *natural gas*) used for lighting, heating, or cooking; nitrous oxide or other gas used as anaesthetic; poisonous gas used to disable enemy in war; *US colloq.* petrol, gasoline; *colloq.* idle talk, boasting. **2** *v.* (**-ss-**) expose to gas; poison or injure by gas; *colloq.* talk idly or boastfully. **3 gas chamber** room that can be filled with poisonous gas to kill animals or people; **gas fire** domestic heater burning gas; **gas-fired** using gas as fuel; **gas mask** device worn over head as protection against poison gas; **gas ring** hollow perforated ring fed with gas for cooking etc.; **step on the gas** *colloq.* accelerate motor vehicle. [Du. after Gk (CHAOS)]

gasbag *n.* container of gas; *sl.* idle talker.

gaseous /'gæsɪəs/ *a.* of or like gas.

gash 1 *n.* long deep cut, wound, or cleft. **2** *v.t.* make gash in, cut. [F]

gasholder /'gæshəʊldə/ *n.* large receptacle for storing gas, gasometer. [GAS]

gasify /'gæsɪfaɪ/ *v.t.* convert into gas; **gasification** /-fɪ'keɪʃ(ə)n/ *n.*

gasket /'gæskɪt/ *n.* sheet or ring of rubber etc. to seal junction of metal surfaces; small cord securing furled sail to yard. [F *garcette*]

gaslight *n.* light given by burning gas. [GAS]

gasoline /'gæsəli:n/ *n.* *US* petrol.

gasometer /gæ'sɒmɪtə/ *n.* large tank from which gas is distributed by pipes. [F *gazomètre* (GAS, -METER)]

gasp /gɑ:sp/ **1** *v.* catch breath with open mouth as in exhaustion or surprise; utter with gasps. **2** *n.* convulsive catching of breath. **3 at one's last gasp** at point of death, exhausted. [ON]

gassy *a.* of or like or full of gas; verbose. [GAS]

gastric /'gæstrɪk/ *a.* of the stomach; **gastric flu** *colloq.* intestinal disorder of unknown cause; **gastric juice** digestive fluid secreted by stomach glands. [F (foll.)]

gastro- *in comb.* stomach. [Gk *gastēr* stomach]

gastro-enteritis /gæstrəʊentə'raɪtɪs/ *n.* inflammation of stomach and intestine.

gastronome /'gæstrənəʊm/ *n.* connoisseur of eating and drinking. [F (as foll.)]

gastronomy /gæ'strɒnəmɪ/ *n.* science of good eating and drinking; **gastronomic** /-'nɒmɪk/ *a.* [F f. Gk (GASTRO-)]

gastropod /'gæstrəpɒd/ *n.* mollusc that moves by means of ventral organ, e.g. snail. [F (GASTRO-, Gk *pous pod-* foot)]

gasworks *n.pl.* place where gas for lighting and heating is manufactured. [GAS]

gate 1 *n.* barrier, usu. hinged, used to close opening made for entrance and exit through wall, fence, etc.; such opening; means of entrance or exit; numbered place of access to aircraft at airport; device regulating passage of water in lock etc.; number entering by payment at gates to see football match etc.; amount of money thus taken. **2** *v.t.* confine to college or school, esp. after fixed hour. **3 gate-leg(ged)** (of table) with legs in gatelike frame which swings back to allow top to fold down. [OE]

gateau /'gætəʊ/ *n.* (*pl.* **gateaus**) large rich cream-cake. [F]

gatecrasher *n.* uninvited intruder at party etc.; **gatecrash** *v.* [GATE]

gateway *n.* opening which can be closed with gate; means of access (*lit.* or *fig.*).

gather /'gæðə/ **1** *v.* bring or come together, assemble, accumulate; infer or deduce; summon up (energy etc.); pick, or collect as harvest; increase (speed); draw together in folds or wrinkles; develop purulent swelling. **2** *n.* (usu. in *pl.*) fold or pleat. **3 gather up** bring together, pick up from ground, draw into small compass. [OE]

gathering *n.* assembly; purulent swelling; group of leaves taken together in bookbinding.

GATT /gæt/ *abbr.* General Agreement on Tariffs and Trade.

gauche /gəʊʃ/ *a.* tactless, socially awkward. [F]

gaucherie /'gəʊʃəri:/ *n.* gauche manners or act. [F (prec.)]

gaucho /'gaʊtʃəʊ/ *n.* (*pl.* **gauchos**) mounted herdsman in S. American pampas. [Sp. f. Quechua]

gaud /gɔ:d/ *n.* showy ornament. [prob. F f. L *gaudeo* rejoice]

gaudy[1] /'gɔ:dɪ/ *a.* tastelessly showy; **gaudily** *adv.*; **gaudiness** *n.* [prob. GAUD]

gaudy[2] /'gɔ:dɪ/ *n.* annual entertainment, esp. college dinner for old members etc. [L *gaudium* joy]

gauge /geɪdʒ/ **1** *n.* standard measure esp. of capacity or contents of barrel, fineness of textile, diameter of bullet, or thickness of sheet metal; distance between rails or opposite wheels; instrument for measuring or marking parallel lines; capacity, extent; criterion, test;

Naut. position relative to wind. **2** *v.t.* measure exactly; measure content or capacity of (cask etc.); estimate (person or character). [F]

Gaul /gɔ:l/ *n.* inhabitant of ancient Gaul. [F f. Gmc]

Gaulish 1 *a.* of the Gauls. **2** *n.* their language.

gaunt /gɔ:nt/ *a.* lean, haggard; grim, desolate. [orig. unkn.]

gauntlet[1] /'gɔ:ntlɪt/ *n.* stout glove with long loose wrist; *hist.* armoured glove; **pick up the gauntlet** *fig.* accept challenge; **throw down the gauntlet** *fig.* issue challenge. [F dimin. of *gant* glove]

gauntlet[2] /'gɔ:ntlɪt/ *n.* only in **run the gauntlet** pass between rows of men who strike one with sticks etc. as punishment; undergo criticism etc. [Sw. *gatlopp* (*gata* lane, *lopp* course)]

gauss /gaʊs/ *n.* (*pl.* **gauss**) electromagnetic unit of magnetic induction. [*Gauss*, mathematician]

gauze /gɔ:z/ *n.* thin transparent fabric of silk, cotton, wire, etc.; **gauzy** *a.* [F (*Gaza* in Palestine)]

gave *past* of GIVE.

gavel /'gæv(ə)l/ *n.* hammer used for calling attention by auctioneer or chairman or judge. [orig. unkn.]

gavotte /gə'vɒt/ *n.* medium-paced dance in common time; music for this. [F f. Prov.]

gawk 1 *v.i. colloq.* stare stupidly. **2** *n.* awkward or bashful person. [obs. *gaw* GAZE]

gawky *a.* awkward or ungainly; **gawkily** *adv.*; **gawkiness** *n.*

gawp *v.i. colloq.* gawk. [YELP]

gay 1 *a.* light-hearted, sportive, mirthful; *colloq.* homosexual; showy, brilliant; dissolute. **2** *n. colloq.* homosexual person. [F]

gayety *US* var. of GAIETY.

gaze 1 *v.i.* look fixedly (*at* or *on*). **2** *n.* intent look. [orig. unkn.]

gazebo /gə'zi:bəʊ/ *n.* (*pl.* **gazebos**) summer-house, turret, etc., with wide view. [perh. joc. f. prec.]

gazelle /gə'zel/ *n.* small graceful antelope. [F f. Sp. f. Arab.]

gazette /gə'zet/ **1** *n.* newspaper (used in title); official publication with announcements etc. **2** *v.t.* announce appointment of (person) in official gazette; publish in official gazette. [F f. It.]

gazetteer /gæzɪ'tɪə/ *n.* geographical index. [F f. It. (prec.)]

gazump /gə'zʌmp/ *v.t. sl.* raise price after accepting offer from (buyer); *sl.* swindle. [orig. unkn.]

GB *abbr.* Great Britain.

GC *abbr.* George Cross.

GCE *abbr.* General Certificate of Education.

Gd *symb.* gadolinium.

GDP *abbr.* gross domestic product.

GDR *abbr.* German Democratic Republic.

Ge *symb.* germanium.

gear 1 *n.* set of toothed wheels that work together, esp. those connecting engine of vehicle to road wheels (often in *pl.*); particular setting of these; equipment, apparatus, tackle, etc.; *colloq.* clothing; rigging. **2** *v.t.* put in gear; provide with gear; adjust or adapt *to*; harness (often with *up*). **3 gear-lever** (or *US* **-shift**) lever used to engage or change gear; **high** (or **low**) **gear** setting of gears with faster (or slower) revolutions of driven part of vehicle relative to driving part; **in gear** with gears engaged; **out of gear** with gears disengaged, *fig.* out of order. [ON]

gearbox *n.* case enclosing gears of vehicle or other machine.

gearing *n.* set or arrangement of gears.

gearwheel *n.* toothed wheel in set of gears.

gecko /'gekəʊ/ *n.* (*pl.* **geckos**) tropical house-lizard. [Malay]

gee[1] *int.* (also **gee whiz**) expressing surprise etc. [perh. abbr. of *Jesus*]

gee[2] *int.* (usu. with *up*) command to horse etc. to start or go faster. [orig. unkn.]

gee-gee *n. colloq.* horse.

geese *pl.* of GOOSE.

geezer /'gi:zə/ *n. sl.* person, esp. old man. [dial. *guiser* mummer]

Geiger counter /'gaɪgə/ device for detecting and measuring radioactivity etc. [*Geiger*, physicist]

geisha /'geɪʃə/ *n.* Japanese girl trained to entertain men. [Jap.]

gel *n.* semi-solid colloidal solution or jelly. [foll.]

gelatine /'dʒeləti:n/ *n.* (also **gelatin** /-tɪn/) transparent tasteless substance got from skin, tendons, etc., and used in cookery, photography, etc. [F f. It. (JELLY)]

gelatinize /dʒɪ'lætɪnaɪz/ *v.* make or become gelatinous; coat or treat with gelatine.

gelatinous /dʒɪ'lætɪnəs/ *a.* like jelly, esp. in consistency.

geld /geld/ *v.t.* deprive (usu. male animal) of reproductive ability, castrate. [ON]

gelding *n.* gelded animal, esp. male horse.

gelignite /'dʒelɪgnaɪt/ *n.* nitro-glycerine explosive. [GELATINE, IGNEOUS]

gem 1 *n.* precious stone, esp. cut and polished or engraved; thing of great beauty or worth. **2** *v.t.* (**-mm-**) adorn with or as with gems. [F f. L *gemma* bud, jewel]

geminate /'dʒemɪneɪt/ **1** *v.t.* double, repeat; arrange in pairs. **2** /also -ət/ *a.* combined in pairs. **3 gemination** /-'neɪʃ(ə)n/ *n.* [L (foll.)]

Gemini /'dʒemɪnaɪ, -nɪ/ *n.* constellation and third sign of zodiac. [L, = twins]

gemma /'dʒemə/*n.* (*pl.* **gemmae** /-i:/) (in cryptogams) small cellular body that separates from mother-plant and starts a new one. [L, see GEM]

gemmation /dʒe'meɪʃ(ə)n/ *n.* reproduction by gemmae. [F (GEM)]

gen *sl.* **1** *n.* information. **2** *v.* (**-nn-**) (with *up*) gain or give information. [prob. *general* information]

-gen *suffix* forming nouns in sense 'that which produces' (*hydrogen*). [F f. Gk (*gignomai* become)]

Gen. *abbr.* General.

gendarme /'ʒɒndɑ:m/ *n.* soldier employed in police duties, esp. in France. [F (*gens d'armes* men of arms)]

gender *n. Gram.* classification (or one of the classes) corresponding roughly to the two sexes and sexlessness (see MASCULINE, FEMININE, NEUTER); *colloq.* sex. [F f. L GENUS]

gene *n.* unit of heredity in chromosome, controlling a particular inherited characteristic of an individual. [G]

genealogy /dʒi:nɪ'ælədʒɪ/ *n.* descent traced continuously from ancestor, pedigree; study of pedigrees; plant's or animal's line of development from earlier forms; **genealogical** /-'lɒdʒɪk(ə)l/ *a.*; **genealogist** *n.* [F f. L f. Gk (*genea* race)]

genera *pl.* of GENUS.

general /'dʒenər(ə)l/ **1** *a.* including or affecting all or most parts or cases or things; not partial or local or particular; not restricted or specialized (*general education, knowledge*); not limited in application, true of all or nearly all cases (*as a general rule*); involving only main features, not detailed (*general resemblance*); usual, prevalent (*the general feeling*); chief, head, with unrestricted authority (*general manager*; *Attorney General*). **2** *n.* army officer next below Field Marshal; = *lieutenant-general* or *major-general*; commander of army; strategist (*a good general*); chief of religious order, e.g. of Jesuits etc. **3 general election** election of representatives to parliament etc. from whole country; **general practitioner** doctor treating cases of all kinds in the first instance; **general staff** officers assisting a military commander at headquarters; **general strike** strike of workers in all or most trades; **in general** as a normal rule, usually, for the most part. [F f. L *generalis*]

generalissimo /dʒenərə'lɪsɪməʊ/ *n.* (*pl.* **generalissimos**) commander of combined military and naval and air force, or of several armies. [It. superl.]

generality /dʒenə'rælɪtɪ/ *n.* general statement or rule; general applicability, indefiniteness; majority or bulk *of.* [F f. L (GENERAL)]

generalize /'dʒenərəlaɪz/ *v.* speak in general or indefinite terms, form general notions; reduce to general statement; infer (rule etc.) from particular cases; bring into general use; **generalization** /-'zeɪʃ(ə)n/ *n.* [F (GENERAL)]

generally *adv.* in a general sense, without regard to particulars or exceptions (*generally speaking*); in most respects or cases (*made himself generally offensive*). [GENERAL]

generate /'dʒenəreɪt/ *v.t.* bring into existence, produce. [L (GENUS)]

generation /dʒenə'reɪʃ(ə)n/ *n.* procreation; production esp. of electricity; step in pedigree; all persons born about same time; average time in which children are ready to take place of parents (about 30 years); **generation gap** differences of opinion or attitude between different generations. [F f. L (prec.)]

generative /'dʒenərətɪv/ *a.* of procreation; productive. [F or L (prec.)]

generator /'dʒenəreɪtə/ *n.* machine for converting mechanical into electrical energy; apparatus for producing gas, steam, etc. [GENERATE]

generic /dʒɪ'nerɪk/ *a.* characteristic of or applied to a genus or class; not specific or special; **generically** *adv.* [F f. L (GENUS)]

generous /'dʒenərəs/ *a.* giving or given freely; magnanimous, unprejudiced; abundant, copious; **generosity** /-'rɒsɪtɪ/ *n.* [F f. L (GENUS)]

genesis /'dʒenɪsɪs/ *n.* origin, mode of formation or generation; (**Genesis**) first book of Old Testament, with account of Creation. [L f. Gk (*gen-* be produced)]

genetic /dʒɪ'netɪk/ *a.* of genetics or genes; of or in origin; **genetic code** system of storage of genetic information in chromosomes; **genetic engineering** manipulation of DNA to modify hereditary features; **genetically** *adv.* [GENESIS]

genetics *n.* study of heredity and variation in animals and plants; **geneticist** *n.*

genial /'dʒi:nɪəl/ *a.* jovial, kindly, sociable; (of climate etc.) mild, warm, conducive to growth; cheering; **geniality** /-'ælɪtɪ/ *n.*; **genially** *adv.* [L (GENIUS)]

genie /'dʒi:nɪ/ *n.* (*pl.* **genii** /-nɪaɪ/) jinnee,

sprite or goblin of Arabian tales. [F *génie* GENIUS; see JINNEE]

genital /ˈdʒenɪt(ə)l/ **1** *a.* of animal reproduction. **2** *n.* (in *pl.*; also **genitalia** /-ˈteɪlɪə/) external genital organs. [F or L (*gigno genit-* beget)]

genitive /ˈdʒenɪtɪv/ **1** *a. Gram.* (of case) corresponding to *of, from,* etc., with noun representing possessor, source, etc. **2** *n.* genitive case. [F or L (GENITAL)]

genius /ˈdʒi:nɪəs/ *n.* (*pl.* **geniuses**) exceptional intellectual or creative power or other natural ability or tendency; person having this; tutelary spirit of person, place, etc.; person or spirit influencing person powerfully for good or evil (*evil genius; good genius*); prevalent feeling or association etc. (*of* people or place). [L]

genocide /ˈdʒenəsaɪd/ *n.* deliberate extermination of a people or nation; **genocidal** *a.* [Gk *genos* race, -CIDE]

-genous *suffix* forming adjectives in sense 'produced' (*endogenous*). [-GEN]

genre /ˈʒɑ̃rə/ *n.* kind or style of art etc.; painting of scenes from ordinary life. [F (GENDER)]

gent *n. colloq.* gentleman; **gents** (in shops) men; **the Gents** *colloq.* men's public lavatory. [GENTLEMAN]

genteel /dʒenˈti:l/ *a.* affectedly stylish or refined; upper-class; **genteelly** *adv.* [F *gentil* (GENTLE)]

genteelism *n.* word used because thought to be less vulgar than usual word (e.g. *perspire* for *sweat*).

gentian /ˈdʒenʃ(ə)n/ *n.* mountain plant usu. with blue flowers. [OE f. L *gentiana* (*Gentius*, king of Illyria)]

gentile /ˈdʒentaɪl/ **1** *a.* not Jewish; heathen. **2** *n.* person not Jewish. [L *gentilis* (*gens* family)]

gentility /dʒenˈtɪlɪtɪ/ *n.* social superiority, good manners, upper-class habits. [F (foll.)]

gentle /ˈdʒent(ə)l/ *a.* not rough or severe, kind, mild (*a gentle nature*); moderate (*gentle breeze*); (of birth, pursuits, etc.) honourable, of or fit for gentlemen; quiet, requiring patience (*gentle art*); **gently** *adv.* [F *gentil* f. L (GENTILE)]

gentlefolk *n.pl.* people of good family.

gentleman *n.* man (in polite or formal use); chivalrous well-bred man; man of good social position or of wealth and leisure (*country gentleman*); man of gentle birth attached to royal household (*gentleman in waiting*); (in *pl.* as form of address), male audience or part of audience; **gentleman-at-arms** one of sovereign's bodyguard; **gentleman's** (or **-men's**) **agreement** agreement binding in honour but not enforceable.

gentlemanly *a.* behaving or looking like a gentleman, befitting a gentleman.

gentlewoman *archaic* woman of good birth or breeding.

gentry /ˈdʒentrɪ/ *n.* people next below nobility; *derog.* people (*these gentry*). [F (GENTLE)]

genuflect /ˈdʒenju:flekt/ *v.i.* bend the knee, esp. in worship; **genuflexion** /-ˈflekʃ(ə)n/ *n.* [L (*genu* knee, *flecto* bend)]

genuine /ˈdʒenju:ɪn/ *a.* really coming from its reputed source etc.; not sham; properly so called; pure-bred. [L]

genus /ˈdʒi:nəs/ *n.* (*pl.* **genera** /ˈdʒenərə/) group of animals or plants with common structural characteristics, usu. containing several species; (in logic) kind of things including subordinate kinds or species; *colloq.* kind, class. [L *genus -eris*]

geo- *in comb.* earth. [Gk *gē*]

geocentric /dʒi:əˈsentrɪk/ *a.* considered as viewed from the earth's centre; having the earth as centre; **geocentrically** *adv.* [GEO-]

geode /ˈdʒi:əʊd/ *n.* cavity lined with crystals; rock containing this. [L f. Gk *geōdēs* earthy]

geodesic /dʒi:əˈdesɪk/ *a.* (also **geodetic**) of geodesy; **geodesic line** shortest possible line on surface between two points. [foll.]

geodesy /dʒi:ˈɒdɪsɪ/ *n.* study of the shape and area of the earth. [L f. Gk *geōdaisia*]

geographical /dʒi:əˈgræfɪk(ə)l/ *a.* (also **geographic**) of geography; **geographical mile** 1′ of Latitude, about 1.85 km.; **geographically** *adv.* [foll.]

geography /dʒɪˈɒgrəfɪ/ *n.* science of earth's form, physical features, climate, population, etc.; features or arrangement of place; **geographer** *n.* [F or L f. Gk]

geology /dʒɪˈɒlədʒɪ/ *n.* science of earth's crust and strata and their relations; geological features of district; **geological** /-ˈlɒdʒɪk(ə)l/ *a.*; **geologist** *n.* [-LOGY]

geometric /dʒi:əˈmetrɪk/ *a.* (also **geometrical**) of geometry; **geometric progression** progression with constant ratio between successive quantities, e.g. 1, 3, 9, 27; **geometrically** *adv.* [F (foll.)]

geometry /dʒɪˈɒmɪtrɪ/ *n.* science of properties and relations of lines, surfaces, and solids; **geometer** *n.*; **geometrician** /-ˈtrɪʃ(ə)n/ *n.* [F f. L f. Gk (-METRY)]

geophysics /dʒi:əʊˈfɪzɪks/ *n.* physics of the earth. [GEO-]

Geordie /ˈdʒɔ:dɪ/ *n.* native of Tyneside. [name *George*]

George Cross /dʒɔ:dʒ/ decoration (esp. of civilians) for gallantry. [King *George* VI]

georgette /dʒɔ:'dʒet/ *n.* thin silky dress-material. [*Georgette* de la Plante, dress-maker]

Georgian[1] /'dʒɔ:dʒɪən/ *a.* of the time of Kings George I–IV or of George V and VI.

Georgian[2] /'dʒɔ:dʒɪən/ **1** *a.* of Georgia in USSR or US. **2** *n.* native or language of Georgia in USSR; native of Georgia in US.

geranium /dʒə'reɪnɪəm/ *n.* herb or shrub bearing fruit shaped like crane's bill; *pop.* cultivated pelargonium. [L f. Gk (*geranos* crane)]

gerbil /'dʒɜ:bɪl/ *n.* mouselike desert rodent with long hind legs. [F (JERBOA)]

geriatrics /dʒerɪ'ætrɪks/ *n.pl.* (usu. treated as *sing.*) branch of medical science dealing with old age and its diseases; **geriatric** *a.*; **geriatrician** /-'trɪʃ(ə)n/ *n.* [Gk *gēras* old age, *iatros* physician]

germ *n.* micro-organism or microbe, esp. one causing disease; portion of organism capable of becoming a new one, rudiment of animal or of plant in seed (*wheat germ*); *fig.* thing that may develop, elementary principle; **germ warfare** use of germs to spread disease in war. [F f. L *germen* sprout]

German[1] /'dʒɜ:mən/ **1** *a.* of Germany or its people or language. **2** *n.* native or language of Germany. **3 German measles** disease like mild measles; **German silver** white alloy of nickel, zinc, and copper; **High German** literary and cultured form of German; **Low German** dialects other than High German. [L *Germanus*]

german[2] /'dʒɜ:mən/ *a.* (placed after *brother*, *sister*, *cousin*) having full relationship, not half-brother etc. [F f. L *germanus*]

germander /dʒɜ:'mændə/ *n.* plant of mint family; **germander speedwell** speedwell with leaves like germander. [L f. Gk, = ground-oak]

germane /dʒɜ:'meɪn/ *a.* relevant *to* a subject. [var. of GERMAN[2]]

Germanic /dʒɜ:'mænɪk/ **1** *a.* having German characteristics; *hist.* of the Germans; of Scandinavians, Anglo-Saxons, or Germans. **2** *n.* primitive language of Germanic peoples. [GERMAN[1]]

germanium /dʒɜ:'meɪnɪəm/ *n.* brittle greyish-white semi-metallic element. [GERMAN[1]]

Germano- *in comb.* German.

germicide /'dʒɜ:mɪsaɪd/ *n.* substance that destroys germs; **germicidal** *a.* [-CIDE]

germinal /'dʒɜ:mɪn(ə)l/ *a.* of germs; in the earliest stage of development; productive of new ideas etc.; **germinally** *adv.* [GERM]

germinate /'dʒɜ:mɪneɪt/ *v.* (cause to) sprout or bud (*lit.* or *fig.*); **germination** /-'neɪʃ(ə)n/ *n.*; **germinative** *a.* [L (GERM)]

gerontology /dʒerɒn'tɒlədʒɪ/ *n.* scientific study of old age and process of ageing. [Gk *gerōn geront-* old man]

gerrymander /dʒerɪ'mændə/ **1** *v.t.* manipulate boundaries of (constituency etc.) so as to give undue influence to some party or class. **2** *n.* this practice. [*Gerry*, Governor of Massachusetts]

gerund /'dʒerənd/ *n.* verbal noun, in English ending in *-ing* (e.g. *smoking is bad for your health*). [L]

gerundive /dʒə'rʌndɪv/ *n.* form of Latin verb functioning as adjective with sense 'that should be done' etc.

gesso /'dʒesəʊ/ *n.* (*pl.* **gessoes**) gypsum as used in painting or sculpture. [It. (GYPSUM)]

Gestapo /ge'stɑ:pəʊ/ *n.* Nazi secret police; any comparable organization. [G *Ge*heime *Sta*ats*po*lizei]

gestation /dʒe'steɪʃ(ə)n/ *n.* carrying in womb; period of this, between conception and birth; development of idea etc. [L (*gesto* carry)]

gesticulate /dʒe'stɪkjʊleɪt/ *v.* use gestures instead of or to reinforce speech; express thus; **gesticulation** /-'leɪʃ(ə)n/ *n.* [L (foll.)]

gesture /'dʒestʃə/ **1** *n.* significant movement of limb or body; use of such movements esp. as rhetorical device; *fig.* action to evoke response or convey intention, usu. friendly. **2** *v.* gesticulate. [L *gestura* (*gero* wield)]

get /get/ *v.* (**-tt-**; past **got;** *p.p.* **got** or *archaic* & *US* **gotten**) come into possession of, receive or earn (*get a job*, *a living*, *£100 a week*, *first prize*); fetch or procure (*get my book for me*); go to reach or catch (train, bus, etc.); prepare (meal); receive (broadcast signal), establish communication by telephone etc. with; ascertain or calculate (*we get an average of 50*); experience or suffer, contract (illness), establish (idea etc.) in one's mind; (cause to) reach some state or become (*get wet*, *married*; *get her ready*); (cause to) come or go or arrive (*get back*, *down*, *up*, etc.; *got home*; *got them to Rome*; *got a message to her*); (in *perf.*) possess, have, be bound *to do* or *be* (*have not got a penny*; *has got nothing to say*; *you have got to say nothing*); induce *to do* thing (*get him to sign the form*); *colloq.* understand, perceive in argument (*did you get the joke?*, *I didn't get the last point*); *colloq.* attract or obsess or irritate; *colloq.* harm, injure, or kill, esp. in retaliation (*I'll get him for that*); develop inclination (with *infin.*: *one gets* *to like it*); (usu. of animals) beget; **get about** go from place to place, begin walking after illness etc., (of news) circulate; **get across** *colloq.* be or make effective or acceptable; **get across (person)** *sl.* annoy; **get along** live harmoniously (*together* or *with*); **get at** reach, get hold of, *colloq.* imply; **get away** escape, start; **get away with** escape blame or punishment for (thing one has done); **get back at** *colloq.* retaliate against; **get by** *colloq.* manage even if with difficulty, be acceptable; **get down** record in writing, swallow (thing); **get (person) down** depress, deject; **get down to** begin working on; **get going** *colloq.* begin moving or acting; **get his, hers,** etc. *sl.* be killed; **get hold of** grasp, secure, acquire or obtain, make contact with; **get in** arrive, win election, obtain place in college etc.; **get it** *sl.* be punished; **get off** (cause to) be acquitted, escape with little or no punishment, start, alight from (bus etc.); **get off with** *colloq.* achieve amorous or sexual relationship with, esp. abruptly or quickly; **get on** manage, make progress, live harmoniously, enter (bus etc.); **get on to** *colloq.* make contact with, understand or become aware of; **get out** transpire, become known, alight from vehicle; **get-out** *n.* means of avoiding something; **get out of** avoid or escape (duty etc.); **get over** = *get across*; **get over (thing)** recover from (illness or shock etc.), overcome (difficulty); **get (thing) over** (or **over with**) ensure prompt completion of (troublesome task etc.); **get one's own back** *colloq.* have one's revenge; **get rid of** see RID; **get round** evade (rule or law), coax or cajole (person), esp. to secure favour; **get round to** deal with (task etc.) in due course; **get somewhere** make progress, be initially successful; **get there** *sl.* succeed, understand what is meant; **get through** pass (examination etc.), finish or use up, make contact by telephone; **get through to** *colloq.* succeed in making (person) understand; **get-together** *colloq.* social gathering; **get up** rise from sitting etc., or from bed after sleeping, prepare or organize, work up (anger etc., subject for examination etc.), dress or arrange elaborately; **get-up** *n.* *colloq.* style or arrangement of dress etc. [ON]

get-at-able /get'ætəb(ə)l/ *a.* accessible.

getaway *n.* escape, esp. after a crime.

geum /'dʒi:əm/ *n.* kind of rosaceous plant. [L *gaeum*]

gewgaw /'gju:gɔ:/ *n.* gaudy plaything or ornament; showy trifle. [orig. unkn.]

geyser *n.* /'gaɪzə, 'geɪzə/ intermittent hot spring; /'gi:zə/ apparatus for heating water. [Icel. *Geysir* (*geysa* gush)]

ghastly /'gɑ:stlɪ/ **1** *a.* horrible, frightful; *colloq.* objectionable; deathlike, pallid; (of smile etc.) forced, grim. **2** *adv.* ghastlily (pale etc.). **3 ghastlily** *adv.*; **ghastliness** *n.* [obs. *gast* terrify]

ghat /gɔ:t/ *n.* (also **ghaut**) in India, steps leading to river, landing-place. [Hindi]

ghee /gi:/ *n.* Indian clarified butter made from milk of buffalo or cow. [Hindi f. Skr.]

gherkin /'gɜ:kɪn/ *n.* small cucumber for pickling. [Du.]

ghetto /'getəʊ/ *n.* (*pl.* **ghettos**) part of city occupied by minority group; *hist.* Jews' quarter in city; segregated group or area. [It.]

ghost /gəʊst/ **1** *n.* apparition of dead person or animal, disembodied spirit; emaciated or pale person; shadow or semblance (*not the ghost of a chance*); secondary or duplicated image in defective telescope or television-picture. **2** *v.* act as ghost writer (of, *for*). **3 ghost town** town with few or no remaining inhabitants; **ghost writer** writer doing work for which employer takes credit; **give up the ghost** die. **4 ghostliness** *n.*; **ghostly** *a.* [OE]

ghoul /gu:l/ *n.* person morbidly interested in death etc.; spirit in Muslim folklore preying on corpses. [Arab.]

GHQ *abbr.* General Headquarters.

ghyll var. of GILL[3].

GI /dʒi: 'aɪ/ **1** *n.* private soldier in US army. **2** *a.* of or for US servicemen. [*g*overnment (or *g*eneral) *i*ssue]

giant /'dʒaɪənt/ **1** *n.* an imaginary or mythical being of human form but superhuman size; person of great size, ability, strength, etc. **2** *a.* gigantic; (of animal, plant, etc.) of a very large kind. **3 giantess** *n.fem.* [F f. L f. Gk *gigas gigant-*]

gibber *v.i.* jabber inarticulately. [imit.]

gibberish *n.* unintelligible speech, meaningless sounds.

gibbet /'dʒɪbɪt/ **1** *n. hist.* gallows, post with arm on which executed criminal was hung. **2** *v.t.* put to death by hanging; expose or hang up on gibbet; hold up to contempt. [F *gibet*]

gibbon /'gɪbən/ *n.* long-armed SE Asian anthropoid ape. [F]

gibbous /'gɪbəs/ *a.* convex; (of moon or planet) having bright part greater than semicircle but less than circle; humpbacked. [L (*gibbus* hump)]

gibe 1 *v.* jeer or mock (at). **2** *n.* jeering remark, taunt. [perh. f. F *giber* handle roughly]

giblets /'dʒɪblɪts/ *n.pl.* edible organs etc. of bird, taken out and usu. cooked separately. [F *gibelet* game stew]

giddy /'gɪdɪ/ *a.* dizzy, tending to fall or

stagger; making dizzy (*giddy height, success*); mentally intoxicated, frivolous; flighty; **giddily** *adv.*; **giddiness** *n.* [OE]

gift /gɪft/ 1 *n.* thing given, present; natural ability or talent; giving; *colloq.* easy task. 2 *v.t.* endow with gifts; present *with* as gift; bestow as gift. 3 **gift token** (or **voucher**) voucher used as gift and exchangeable for goods; **gift-wrap** wrap attractively (as gift); **in person's gift** his to bestow. [ON (GIVE)]

gifted *a.* talented.

gig[1] /gɪg/ *n.* light two-wheeled one-horse carriage; light ship's-boat for rowing or sailing; rowing-boat esp. for racing. [prob. imit.]

gig[2] /gɪg/ *n. colloq.* engagement to play jazz etc., esp. for one night. [orig. unkn.]

giga- /ˈgɪgə, ˈgaɪgə/ *prefix* one thousand million. [Gk (GIANT)]

gigantic /dʒaɪˈgæntɪk/ *a.* giant-like, huge; **gigantically** *adv.* [L (GIANT)]

giggle /ˈgɪg(ə)l/ 1 *v.i.* laugh in small half-suppressed bursts. 2 *n.* such laugh; *colloq.* amusing person or thing, joke (*did it for a giggle*). 3 **giggly** *a.* [imit.]

gigolo /ˈʒɪgələʊ/ *n.* (*pl.* **gigolos**) young man paid by older woman to be escort or lover. [F]

gild[1] /gɪld/ *v.t.* (*p.p.* sometimes GILT[1] as adjective in lit. sense, otherwise **gilded**) cover thinly with gold; tinge with golden colour; **gild the lily** try to improve what is already satisfactory. [OE (GOLD)]

gild[2] var. of GUILD.

gill[1] /gɪl/ *n.* (usu. in *pl.*) respiratory organ in fish etc.; vertical radial plate on under-side of mushroom etc.; flesh below person's jaws and ears. [ON]

gill[2] /dʒɪl/ *n.* unit of liquid measure, equal to ¼ pint. [F]

gill[3] /gɪl/ *n.* deep ravine, usu. wooded; narrow mountain torrent. [ON]

gillie /ˈgɪlɪ/ *n.* man or boy attending sportsman in Scotland. [Gael.]

gillyflower /ˈdʒɪlɪflaʊə/ *n.* clove-scented flower, e.g. wallflower; clove-scented pink. [F *gilofre*]

gilt[1] /gɪlt/ 1 *a.* covered thinly with gold; gold-coloured. 2 *n.* gilding; gilt-edged security. 3 **gilt-edged** (of securities, stocks, etc.) having high degree of reliability. [GILD[1]]

gilt[2] /gɪlt/ *n.* young sow. [ON]

gimbals /ˈdʒɪmb(ə)lz/ *n.pl.* contrivance of rings and pivots for keeping instruments horizontal at sea. [var. of *gimmal* f. F *gemel* double finger-ring]

gimcrack /ˈdʒɪmkræk/ 1 *a.* showy but flimsy and worthless. 2 *n.* showy ornament etc., knick-knack. [orig. unkn.]

gimlet /ˈgɪmlɪt/ *n.* small tool with screw-tip for boring holes; **gimlet eye** eye with piercing glance. [F]

gimmick /ˈgɪmɪk/ *n.* trick or device, esp. to attract attention or publicity; **gimmickry** *n.*; **gimmicky** *a.* [orig. unkn.]

gimp /gɪmp/ *n.* twist of silk etc. with cord or wire running through it; fishing-line of silk etc. bound with wire. [Du.]

gin[1] *n.* spirit made from grain or malt and flavoured with juniper berries; **gin rummy** form of card-game rummy; **gin sling** *US* cold drink of gin flavoured and sweetened. [abbr. of *geneva* f. Du. f. F (JUNIPER)]

gin[2] 1 *n.* snare, trap; machine separating cotton from seeds; kind of crane and windlass. 2 *v.t.* (**-nn-**) treat (cotton) in gin; trap. [F (ENGINE)]

ginger /ˈdʒɪndʒə/ 1 *n.* hot spicy root used in cooking and medicine and preserved in syrup or candied; plant from which this comes; light reddish yellow; mettle, spirit; stimulation. 2 *v.t.* flavour with ginger; liven *up*. 3 **ginger-ale** (or **-beer** etc.) ginger-flavoured aerated drinks; **ginger group** group urging party or movement to more decided action; **ginger-nut** ginger-flavoured biscuit; **ginger-snap** thin brittle ginger-flavoured biscuit. 4 **gingery** *a.* [OE & F ult. f. Skr.]

gingerbread 1 *n.* ginger-flavoured treacle cake. 2 *a.* gaudy, tawdry.

gingerly 1 *a.* showing great care or caution. 2 *adv.* in gingerly manner. [perh. F *gensor* delicate]

gingham /ˈgɪŋəm/ *n.* plain-woven cotton cloth often striped or checked. [Du. f. Malay]

gingivitis /dʒɪndʒɪˈvaɪtɪs/ *n.* inflammation of the gums. [L *gingiva* GUM[1], -ITIS]

ginkgo /ˈgɪŋkəʊ/ *n.* (*pl.* **ginkgos**) tree with fan-shaped leaves and yellow flowers. [Jap. f. Chin., = silver apricot]

ginseng /ˈdʒɪnseŋ/ *n.* medicinal plant found in E. Asia and N. America; root of this. [Chin.]

gippy tummy /ˈdʒɪpɪ/ *colloq.* diarrhoea affecting visitors to hot countries. [EGYPTIAN]

gipsy var. of GYPSY.

giraffe /dʒɪˈrɑːf/ *n.* large four-legged African animal with long neck and forelegs. [F, ult. f. Arab.]

gird /gɜːd/ *v.t.* (*past* and *p.p.* **girded** or **girt**) encircle or attach or secure with belt or band; put (cord) *round*; enclose or encircle; **gird up one's loins** prepare for action. [OE]

girder *n.* iron or steel beam or compound structure for bridge-span etc.; beam supporting joists.

girdle[1] /ˈgɜːd(ə)l/ 1 *n.* belt or cord used to gird waist; corset; thing that surrounds; bony support for limbs (*pelvic girdle*). 2 *v.t.* surround with girdle. [OE]

girdle[2] /'gɜːd(ə)l/ *n.* (esp. *Sc.*) round iron plate set over fire or otherwise heated for baking etc. [var. of GRIDDLE]

girl /gɜːl/ *n.* female child; young woman; woman working in office, factory, etc.; female servant; man's girl-friend; **girl-friend** regular female companion; **girl guide** = GUIDE; **girlhood** *n.*; **girlish** *a.* [orig. uncert.]

girlie **1** *n.* little girl (as term of endearment). **2** *a.* (of publication etc.) depicting young women in erotic poses.

giro /'dʒaɪrəʊ/ *n.* (*pl.* **giros**) system of credit transfer between banks, post offices, etc. [G f. It.]

girt see GIRD.

girth /gɜːθ/ *n.* distance round thing; band round body of horse etc. securing saddle etc. [ON (GIRD)]

gist *n.* main substance or essence *of* a matter. [F f. L *jaceo* LIE[1]]

git /gɪt/ *n. sl.* silly or contemptible person. [*get* n., = fool]

give /gɪv/ **1** *v.* (*past* **gave;** *p.p.* **given** /'gɪv(ə)n/) transfer possession of gratuitously, confer ownership of; provide with or supply (without transferring ownership), administer (medicine), deliver (message), bestow (love); render or accord (benefit etc.); (in *imper.*) I prefer (*give me Wagner any time*); make over in exchange or payment; utter or perform (*gave a cry, a jump*); devote or addict (*gave her life, herself, to the poor*; *was given to drinking champagne*); pledge (one's word, honour); sanction marriage of (daughter etc.); consign, put (*give into custody*); present or offer or hold out (*gave him my hand*; *I'll give you an example*); provide (meal, party, etc.) as host; deliver (judgement etc.) authoritatively; impart, be source of (*give trouble*; *gave me his cold*); cause or allow to have (*gave me much pain*); yield as a result (*gives an average of 7*); (usu. in *p.p.*) assume or grant or specify (*he did well, given the circumstances*; *on a given straight line*); collapse or yield or shrink; (of window, road, etc.) look or lead (*on to, upon, into*). **2** *n.* elasticity, capacity for yielding. **3 give and take** exchange of talk or ideas, willingness to make concessions; **give away** transfer as gift, hand over (bride) to bridegroom at wedding, reveal (secret etc.) unintentionally; **give-away** *n. colloq.* thing given as gift or at low price, unintentional disclosure; **give in** yield, acknowledge defeat, hand in (document etc.) to proper official; **give it to (person)** *colloq.* scold or punish; **given name** *US* first or Christian name; **give off** emit (fumes etc.); **give or take** *colloq.* accept as margin of error in estimating; **give out** distribute, announce, emit, be exhausted, run short; **give over** devote, hand over, *colloq.* stop or desist; **give (person) to understand** inform or assure; **give tongue** speak one's thoughts, (of hounds) bark, esp. on tracing scent; **give up** cease from effort or activity, part with, resign or surrender, renounce hope (of), pronounce incurable or insoluble, deliver (fugitive etc.) to pursuers etc.; **give oneself up to** abandon oneself to (despair etc.), addict oneself to; **give way** yield under pressure, give precedence. **4 giveable** *a.* [OE]

gizzard /'gɪzəd/ *n.* bird's second stomach for grinding food; muscular stomach of some fish etc. [F]

glacé /'glæseɪ/ *a.* (of fruit) iced or sugared; (of cloth etc.) smooth, polished; **glacé icing** icing made from icing sugar and water. [F]

glacial /'gleɪʃ(ə)l/ *a.* of ice, characterized or produced by ice; *fig.* cold and forbidding; **glacial period** period when unusually large area was covered with ice-sheet; **glacially** *adv.* [F or L (*glacies* ice)]

glaciated /'gleɪsɪeɪtɪd/ *a.* covered with glaciers or ice-sheet; affected by friction of moving ice; **glaciation** /-'eɪʃ(ə)n/ *n.* [*glaciate* freeze f. L (prec.)]

glacier /'glæsɪə/ *n.* slowly moving river or mass of ice formed by accumulation of snow on higher ground. [F (GLACIAL)]

glad *a.* pleased (usu. *predic.*); expressing or causing pleasure (*glad cry, news*); ready and willing (*am glad to help*); **be glad of** find useful; **glad eye** *sl.* amorous glance; **glad hand** *colloq.* hearty welcome; **glad rags** *colloq.* best clothes. [OE]

gladden /'glæd(ə)n/ *v.t.* make glad.

glade *n.* clear open space in forest. [orig. unkn.]

gladiator /'glædɪeɪtə/ *n.* trained fighter in ancient Roman shows; **gladiatorial** /-ə'tɔːrɪəl/ *a.* [L (*gladius* sword)]

gladiolus /glædɪ'əʊləs/ *n.* (*pl.* **gladioli** /-aɪ/) plant with spikes of flowers and sword-shaped leaves. [L, dimin. of *gladius* (prec.)]

gladsome *a. poetic* cheerful, joyous. [GLAD]

Gladstone bag /'glædst(ə)n/ kind of light portmanteau. [*Gladstone*, statesman]

glair *n.* white of egg; viscous substance made from or resembling this. [F]

glamor *US* var. of GLAMOUR.

glamorize /'glæməraɪz/ *v.t.* make glamorous or attractive. [GLAMOUR]

glamour /'glæmə/ *n.* alluring or exciting beauty or charm; physical attractiveness, esp. feminine; **glamorous** *a.* [var. of GRAMMAR in obs. sense 'magic']

glance /glɑ:ns/ **1** *v.* look briefly (*at, down*, etc.); strike at an angle and glide off object (*glancing blow*; *ball glanced off his bat*); direct (one's eye *at, over*, etc.); refer briefly or indirectly to subject; (of light etc.) flash or dart. **2** *n.* brief look; flash or gleam; glancing stroke in cricket. [orig. uncert.]

gland *n.* organ secreting substances for use in body or for ejection; similar organ in plant. [F f. L *glandulae* pl.]

glanders /'glændəz/ *n.pl.* contagious disease of horses. [F *glandre* (prec.)]

glandular /'glændjʊlə/ *a.* of a gland or glands; **glandular fever** infectious disease with swelling of lymph-glands. [F (GLAND)]

glare 1 *v.i.* look fiercely or fixedly; shine oppressively. **2** *n.* fierce or fixed look; oppressive light; tawdry brilliance. [LG or Du.]

glaring *a.* shining oppressively; obvious or conspicuous (*glaring error*).

glass /glɑ:s/ **1** *n.* hard usu. brittle and transparent substance made by fusing sand with soda, potash, etc.; substance of similar properties, e.g. FIBREGLASS; glass objects collectively; glass drinking-vessel, its contents; object made of glass, esp. mirror, covering of watch-face, or lens; (in *pl.*) spectacles, binoculars; glazed frame for plants; barometer; microscope. **2** *v.t.* fit with glass. **3 glass-blowing** shaping semi-molten glass by blowing air into it through tube; **glass-cloth** cloth for drying glasses; **glass fibre** fabric made from or plastic reinforced by glass filaments; **glass-paper** paper coated with glass particles, for smoothing or polishing; **glass wool** mass of fine glass fibres for packing and insulation. [OE]

glasshouse *n.* greenhouse; *sl.* military prison.

glassware *n.* articles made of glass.

glassy *a.* like glass; (of eye or expression) dull and fixed.

Glaswegian /glæz'wi:dʒ(ə)n/ **1** *a.* of Glasgow. **2** *n.* native of Glasgow. [after *Norwegian*]

glaucoma /glɔ:'kəʊmə/ *n.* eye-condition with increased pressure in eyeball and gradual loss of sight; **glaucomatous** *a.* [L f. Gk (*glaukos* greyish blue)]

glaze 1 *v.* fit (window etc.) with glass or (building) with windows; cover (pottery etc.) with glaze; fix (colour *on* pottery) thus; put glaze on (cloth, pastry, etc.); cover (eye) with film; give glassy surface to; (of eye etc.) become glassy. **2** *n.* vitreous substance for glazing pottery; smooth shiny coating on materials or food; coat of transparent paint to modify underlying tone; surface formed by glazing. [GLASS]

glazier /'gleɪzɪə/ *n.* person who glazes windows etc. professionally.

GLC *abbr.* Greater London Council.

gleam 1 *n.* subdued or transient light; faint or momentary show (*of* humour, hope, etc.). **2** *v.i.* emit gleams. [OE]

glean *v.* acquire (facts etc.) in small amounts; gather (corn left by reapers). [F]

gleanings *n.pl.* things gleaned, esp. facts.

glebe *n.* portion of land going with clergyman's benefice and providing revenue. [L *gl(a)eba* clod, soil]

glee *n.* mirth, manifest joy; part-song for three or more (usu. male) voices; **glee club** society for singing part-songs. [OE]

gleeful *a.* joyful; **gleefully** *adv.*

glen *n.* narrow valley. [Gael.]

glengarry /glen'gærɪ/ *n.* kind of Highland cap with pointed front. [*Glengarry* in Highlands]

glib *a.* speaking or spoken quickly or fluently but without sincerity. [obs. *glibbery* slippery, perh. imit.]

glide 1 *v.* move smoothly and continuously; (of aircraft) fly without engine; go stealthily; pass gradually or imperceptibly; cause to glide. **2** *n.* gliding movement. **3 glide path** aircraft's line of descent to land. [OE]

glider *n.* light aircraft without engine.

glimmer 1 *n.* faint or intermittent light; (also **glimmering**) gleam (*of* hope etc.). **2** *v.i.* shine faintly or intermittently. [prob. Scand.]

glimpse 1 *n.* brief view (*of*); faint transient appearance. **2** *v.t.* have brief view of. [as prec.]

glint 1 *v.i.* flash, glitter. **2** *n.* brief flash of light. [prob. Scand.]

glissade /glɪ'sɑ:d, -'seɪd/ **1** *v.i.* make controlled slide down snow slope in mountaineering; make gliding step in dance. **2** *n.* glissading movement or step. [F]

glisten /'glɪs(ə)n/ **1** *v.i.* shine like wet or polished surface; glitter, sparkle. **2** *n.* glistening. [OE]

glitter 1 *v.i.* shine with bright tremulous light, sparkle; be showy or splendid (*with*). **2** *n.* glittering. [ON]

gloaming /'gləʊmɪŋ/ *n.* evening twilight. [OE]

gloat 1 *v.i.* look or ponder with greedy or malicious pleasure (*over* etc.). **2** *n.* act of gloating. [orig. unkn.]

global /'gləʊb(ə)l/ *a.* world-wide; all-embracing; **globally** *adv.* [F (foll.)]

globe *n.* spherical object, esp. *the* earth, or a representation of it with map on surface; thing shaped like this, e.g. lamp-shade or fish-bowl; **globe-fish** fish that inflates itself into globe form; **globe--flower** plant with spherical usu. yellow flowers; **globe-trotter** one who travels widely; **globe-trotting** such travel. [F, or L *globus*]

globular /'glɒbjʊlə/ *a.* globe-shaped; composed of globules. [foll.]

globule /'glɒbju:l/ *n.* small globe or round particle or drop. [F, or L *globulus*]

globulin /'glɒbju:lɪn/ *n.* protein found usu. associated with albumin in animal and plant tissues.

glockenspiel /'glɒkənspi:l/ *n.* set of bells or metal tubes or bars struck by hammers. [G, = bell-play]

gloom 1 *n.* partial or complete darkness; melancholy, depression. **2** *v.* look or be or make dark or dismal. [orig. unkn.]

gloomy *a.* dark or dim; depressed or depressing; **gloomily** *adv.*; **gloominess** *n.* [obs. *gloom* frown f. prec.]

glorify /glɔ:rɪfaɪ/ *v.t.* make glorious; extol; make (common or inferior thing) seem more splendid than it is; invest with radiance; **glorification** /-fɪ'keɪʃ(ə)n/ *n.* [F f. L (GLORY)]

glorious /glɔ:rɪəs/ *a.* possessing or conferring glory, splendid, illustrious; excellent (often *iron.*: *a glorious mess*).

glory /'glɔ:rɪ/ **1** *n.* renown, honourable fame; adoring praise; resplendent majesty, beauty, etc.; heavenly bliss and splendour; exalted or prosperous state; source of renown, special distinction; halo of saint etc. **2** *v.i.* take great pride (*in*). **3 glory-hole** *sl.* untidy room or cupboard etc.; **go to glory** *sl.* die, be destroyed. [AF *glorie* f. L *gloria*]

gloss[1] **1** *n.* lustre of surface; deceptively attractive appearance. **2** *v.t.* make glossy. **3 gloss over** seek to conceal; **gloss paint** paint giving glossy finish. [orig. unkn.]

gloss[2] **1** *n.* explanatory comment added to text, e.g. in margin; comment or paraphrase. **2** *v.* make such comment; add comment to (text or word etc.). [F (L *glossa* tongue)]

glossary /'glɒsərɪ/ *n.* dictionary or list of technical or special words; collection of glosses. [L (prec.)]

glossy *a.* having a gloss, shiny; **glossily** *adv.*; **glossiness** *n.* [GLOSS[1]]

glottal /'glɒt(ə)l/ *a.* of the glottis; **glottal stop** sound produced by sudden opening or shutting of glottis. [foll.]

glottis /'glɒtɪs/ *n.* opening at upper end of windpipe and between vocal cords. [Gk]

Gloucester /'glɒstə/ *n.* cheese made in Gloucestershire (now usu. **double Gloucester,** orig. richer kind). [*Gloucester* in England]

glove /glʌv/ **1** *n.* hand-covering, usu. with separated fingers, for protection, warmth, etc.; = *boxing-glove*. **2** *v.t.* cover or provide with glove(s). **3 with the gloves off** arguing or contending in earnest. [OE]

glover *n.* glove-maker.

glow /gləʊ/ **1** *v.i.* emit flameless light and heat; shine like thing intensely heated; show warm colour; burn *with* or indicate bodily heat or fervour. **2** *n.* glowing state; warmth of colour; ardour. **3 glow-worm** beetle whose wingless female emits light from end of abdomen. [OE]

glower /'glaʊə/ *v.i.* look angrily (*at*). [orig. uncert.]

gloxinia /glɒk'sɪnɪə/ *n.* American tropical plant with bell-shaped flowers. [*Gloxin*, botanist]

glucose /'glu:kəʊs, -əʊz/ *n.* sugar found in the blood or in fruit-juice etc. [F f. Gk *gleukos* sweet wine]

glue /glu:/ **1** *n.* sticky substance used as adhesive. **2** *v.t.* attach with glue; hold closely (*ear glued to the keyhole*). **3 gluey** *a.* [F f. L *glus* (GLUTEN)]

glum *a.* dejected, sullen. [var. of GLOOM]

glut 1 *v.t.* (**-tt-**) feed to the full, sate (person, stomach, desire); fill to excess; overstock (market). **2** *n.* excessive supply (*oil glut*); full indulgence, surfeit. [F *gloutir* swallow (GLUTTON)]

glutamate /'glu:təmeɪt/ *n.* salt or ester of glutamic acid, esp. sodium salt used to flavour food. [foll.]

glutamic acid /glu:'tæmɪk/ amino acid normally found in proteins. [foll.]

gluten /'glu:t(ə)n/ *n.* viscous part of flour left when starch is removed; viscous animal-secretion. [F, f. L *gluten -tin-* glue]

glutinous /'glu:tɪnəs/ *a.* sticky, gluelike, viscous. [F or L (prec.)]

glutton /'glʌt(ə)n/ excessive eater; person insatiably eager (*for* work etc.); voracious animal of weasel family; **gluttonous** *a.* [F f. L (*gluttio* SWALLOW[1])]

gluttony /'glʌtənɪ/ *n.* character or conduct of a glutton. [F (prec.)]

glyceride /'glɪsəraɪd/ *n.* compound ether of glycerine. [GLYCERINE]

glycerine /'glɪsəri:n/, *US* **glycerin** /-ɪn/ *n.* (also **glycerol**) colourless sweet viscous liquid obtained from fats, used as ointment etc. and in explosives. [F f. Gk *glukeros* sweet]

gm. *abbr.* gram(s).

G-man /'dʒi:mæn/ *n.* *US sl.* federal criminal-investigation officer. [*G*overnment]

GMT *abbr.* Greenwich Mean Time.

gnarled /nɑ:ld/ *a.* (of tree, hands, etc.) knobbly, rugged, twisted. [rel. to KNURL]
gnash /næʃ/ *v.* grind (one's teeth); (of teeth) strike together. [ON]
gnat /næt/ *n.* small two-winged biting fly. [OE]
gnaw /nɔ:/ *v.* (*p.p.* **gnawed** or **gnawn**) bite persistently (*at*, *into*, etc.); wear gradually *away* thus; corrode, wear away; (of pain etc.) torment. [OE]
gneiss /naɪs, gnaɪs/ *n.* coarse-grained metamorphic rock of quartz, feldspar, and mica. [G]
gnome /nəʊm/ *n.* subterranean spirit or goblin in folklore; figure of gnome; (esp. in *pl.*) *colloq.* person with sinister influence, esp. in finance. [F]
gnomic /'nəʊmɪk/ *a.* of maxims, sententious. [Gk (*gnōmē* opinion)]
gnomon /'nəʊmən/ *n.* rod or pin etc. of sundial, showing time by its shadow. [F or L f. Gk., = indicator]
gnostic /'nɒstɪk/ **1** *a.* of knowledge; having special mystical knowledge; (**Gnostic**) of Gnostics. **2** *n.* (**Gnostic**) early Christian heretic claiming mystical knowledge. **3 Gnosticism** /-tɪsɪz(ə)m/ *n.* [eccl.L f. Gk (*gnōsis* knowledge)]
GNP *abbr.* gross national product.
gnu /nu:/ *n.* oxlike antelope. [ult. Bantu *nqu*]
go[1] **1** /gəʊ/ *v.i.* (*past* **went;** *p.p.* **gone** /gɒn/; *partic.* GOING) start moving or be moving from one position or point in time to another, travel, proceed; (with *partic.*) make special trip for (*went fishing*); lie or extend in certain direction (*road goes to York*, *goes round a corner*); be functioning, moving, etc. (*clock will not go*); make specified motion or sound (*go like this with your leg*; *gun went bang*; *the bell will go*); be in specified state, habitually or for a time (*go armed*, *hungry*); pass into specified condition (*go bad*, *mad*, *sick*, *to sleep*), escape *free*, *unnoticed*, etc.; (of time or distance) pass, be traversed (*3 hours*, *3 miles*, *to go*); be regularly kept or put (*where do the forks go?*); fit, be able to be put (*the little one just goes in here*); (of number) be contained in another, esp. without remainder (*7 into 3 won't go*); be current (*the story goes*); be on the average (*good as these things go*); turn out, take a course or view (*things went well*; *vote went against her*); have specified form or wording (*forget how the next line goes*); be successful (*make the party go*); *colloq.* be acceptable or permitted, be accepted without question (*anything goes*; *what he says goes*); be sold (*they are going cheap*, *went for £5*); (of money or supplies etc.) be spent or used up; be relinquished or abolished; fail or decline, give way, collapse (*his hearing is going*; *the bulb has gone*; *the bridge has gone*); die; be allotted or awarded (*job went to his old rival*); contribute, tend, extend, reach (*it only goes to show*; *true as far as it goes*); carry action or commitment to certain point (*will go so far as to say*; *will go to £20*); (in *imper.*) *colloq.* or *US* proceed to (*go jump in the lake*). **2** *n.* animation, dash (*has plenty of go*); turn or try (*your go now*); success (*made a go of it*); *colloq.* vigorous activity (*it's all go*), state of affairs (*rum go*). **3** *a.* *colloq.* functioning properly. **4 go about** set to work at, be socially active, (with *partic.*) make a habit of; **go ahead** proceed immediately; **go-ahead** *n.* & *a.* permission to proceed, enterprising; **go along with** agree with; **go and** *colloq.* be so unwise etc. as to (*he went and sold it*); **go back on** fail to keep (promise etc.); **go begging** see BEG; **go-between** intermediary; **go by** be dependent on, be guided by; **go by default** see DEFAULT; **go down** descend or sink, be swallowed, be written down, leave university, find acceptance (*with*); **go down with** become ill with (disease); **go far** see FAR; **go for** like, prefer, choose, pass or be accounted as (*little* etc.), *sl.* attack; **go-getter** *colloq.* pushful enterprising person; **go-go** *colloq.* very active or energetic; **go-go dancer** performer of lively erotic dances at night-club etc.; **go halves** see HALF; **go in for** compete or engage in (competition, activity, etc.); **go into** become member of (profession etc.) or patient in (hospital etc.), investigate (matter); **go a long way** have much effect *towards*, (of supplies) last long, (of money) buy much; **go off** explode, deteriorate, fall asleep, (of event) succeed *well* etc., begin to dislike; **go on** continue (*doing* thing), persevere (*with*), talk at great length, proceed next *to do* thing; **go on at** *colloq.* nag; **go on** (or **upon**) judge by, base conclusions on; **go out** be extinguished, frequent society, be broadcast, cease to be fashionable, *US colloq.* lose consciousness, feel sympathy (*my heart went out to him*); **go over** examine or review, (of play etc.) be successful; **go round** pay informal visit *to*, be large enough or sufficient; **go slow** work at deliberately slow pace as industrial protest; **go-slow** *n.* such action; **go through** examine or revise, perform or undergo, spend or use up (money or supplies); **go through with** complete (undertaking); **go to** attend (school, church, etc.); **go too far** see FAR; **go under** succumb, fail; **go up** rise in price, explode, burn, enter university; **go with** match or suit, harmonize or

belong with; **go without** abstain from, tolerate lack (of); **on the go** *colloq.* in constant motion, active. [OE; *went* orig. past of WEND]

go² /gəʊ/ *n.* Japanese board-game. [Jap.]

goad 1 *n.* spiked stick for urging cattle; thing that torments or incites. **2** *v.t.* urge with goad; irritate; drive or stimulate (*into* action etc.). [OE]

goal *n.* structure into or through which ball is to be driven in certain games; point or points so won; object of effort; destination; point where race ends; **goal-line** line forming end-boundary of field of play. [orig. unkn.]

goalie *n. colloq.* goalkeeper. [foll.]

goalkeeper *n.* player defending goal. [GOAL]

goat *n.* small horned ruminant; (**Goat**) sign or constellation Capricorn; licentious man; *colloq.* foolish person; **get person's goat** *sl.* annoy him. [OE]

goatee /gəʊ'ti:/ *n.* beard like goat's.

goatherd *n.* one who tends goats.

goatsucker *n.* nightjar.

gob¹ *n. sl.* mouth; **gob-stopper** large hard sweet for sucking. [orig. uncert.]

gob² *n. vulgar* clot of slimy substance. [F *go(u)be* mouthful]

gobbet /'gɒbɪt/ *n.* extract from text, set for translation or comment. [F dimin. of *gobe* GOB²]

gobble¹ /'gɒb(ə)l/ *v.* eat hurriedly and noisily. [GOB²]

gobble² /'gɒb(ə)l/ *v.i.* (of turkey-cock) make gurgling sound in throat; speak thus. [imit.]

gobbledegook /'gɒbəldɪgu:k/ *n. sl.* pompous or unintelligible official or professional jargon. [imit. of turkey-cock]

goblet /'gɒblɪt/ *n.* drinking-vessel, esp. of glass, with foot and stem. [F dimin. of *gobel* cup]

goblin /'gɒblɪn/ *n.* mischievous ugly demon in folklore. [AF]

goby /'gəʊbɪ/ *n.* small fish with ventral fins joined to form disc or sucker. [L *gobius* f. Gk *kōbios* gudgeon]

god *n.* superhuman being worshipped as having power over nature and human affairs; (**God**) creator and ruler of universe in Christian and other monotheistic religions; image of a god, idol; person greatly admired or adored; **the gods** *colloq.* gallery of theatre; **God-fearing** earnestly religious; **God forbid** may it not be so; **God-forsaken** dismal, wretched; **God knows** we (or I) cannot know; **God willing** if circumstances allow. [OE]

godchild *n.* child or person in relation to godparent(s).

god-daughter *n.* female godchild.

goddess /'gɒdɪs/ *n.* female deity; adored woman.

godetia /gə'di:ʃə/ *n.* showy-flowered hardy annual. [*Godet*, botanist]

godfather *n.* male godparent. [GOD]

godhead *n.* divine nature, deity; **the Godhead** God.

godless *a.* not believing in a god or God; impious, wicked.

godlike *a.* like God or a god.

godly *a.* pious, devout; **godliness** *n.*

godmother *n.* female godparent.

godown /gə'daʊn/ *n.* warehouse in E. Asia, esp. in India. [Port. f. Malay]

godparent *n.* person who sponsors another (esp. a child) at baptism. [GOD]

godsend *n.* piece of unexpected good luck, useful or effective acquisition.

godson *n.* male godchild.

Godspeed *n.* expression of good wishes to person starting journey.

godwit /'gɒdwɪt/ *n.* wading bird like curlew but with straight or slightly up-curved bill. [orig. unkn.]

goer *n.* person or thing that goes (*slow goer*); lively or persevering person; regular attender of specified kind (*church-goer*). [GO]

goggle /'gɒg(ə)l/ **1** *v.* look with wide-open eyes; (of eyes) be rolled, project; roll (eyes). **2** *a.* (of eyes) protuberant, rolling. **3** *n.* (in *pl.*) spectacles for protecting eyes from glare, dust, etc. **4 goggle-box** *sl.* television set. [prob. imit.]

going /'gəʊɪŋ/ **1** *n.* state of ground for walking or riding on; rate of progress. **2** *a.* in action (*set the clock going*); existing, functioning, available (*going concern*; *the best brand going*); currently valid (*the going rate*). **3 get going** begin, start; **going on (for)** approaching (a time, age, etc.); **going-over** *colloq.* inspection or overhaul, *sl.* beating; **goings-on** strange behaviour or events; **going strong** continuing vigorously; **going to** about to, intending or likely to; **to be going on with** to start with, for present needs; **while the going is good** while circumstances are favourable. [partic. of GO¹]

goitre /'gɔɪtə/, *US* **goiter** *n.* morbid enlargement of thyroid gland. [F (L *guttur* throat)]

go-kart /'gəʊkɑ:t/ *n.* miniature racing car with skeleton body. [CART]

gold /gəʊld/ **1** *n.* a precious metallic element; its yellow colour; coins or articles made of gold, wealth; something precious or beautiful (*a heart of gold*); = *gold medal.* **2** *a.* of or coloured like gold. **3 gold-digger** *sl.* woman who wheedles money out of men; **gold-dust** gold in fine particles as often found naturally; **gold-field** area where gold is found;

gold foil gold beaten into thin sheet; **gold-leaf** gold beaten into very thin sheet; **gold medal** medal given usu. as first prize; **gold-mine** place where gold is mined, *fig*. source of wealth; **gold plate** vessels of gold, material plated with gold; **gold-plate** *v*. plate with gold; **gold-rush** rush to newly discovered gold-field; **gold standard** system by which value of money is based on that of gold. [OE]

goldcrest *n*. very small bird with golden crest.

golden *a*. of gold; yielding gold; coloured or shining like gold (*golden hair*); precious, excellent; **golden age** period of great cultural achievement; **golden eagle** large eagle with yellow-tipped head-feathers; **golden handshake** gratuity as compensation for dismissal or compulsory retirement; **golden jubilee** 50th anniversary; **golden mean** neither too much nor too little; **golden rod** plant with yellow flower-spikes; **golden rule** basic principle of action, esp. 'do as you would be done by'; **golden syrup** pale treacle; **golden wedding** 50th anniversary of wedding.

goldfinch *n*. songbird with yellow band across each wing.

goldfish *n*. small red Chinese carp.

goldsmith *n*. one who works in gold.

golf 1 *n*. game in which small hard ball is struck with clubs towards and into hole on each of successive smooth greens separated by fairways and rough ground. **2** *v.i.* play golf. **3 golf ball** ball used in golf, spherical unit carrying the type in some electric typewriters; **golf-course** (or **-links**) area of land on which golf is played. [orig. unkn.]

golliwog /'gɒlɪwɒg/ *n*. black-faced soft doll with bright clothes and fuzzy hair. [orig. uncert.]

golly[1] /'gɒlɪ/ *int*. expressing surprise. [GOD]

golly[2] /'gɒlɪ/ *n*. = GOLLIWOG. [abbr.]

golosh var. of GALOSH.

gonad /'gəʊnæd/ *n*. animal organ producing gametes, e.g. testis or ovary. [Gk (*gonē* seed)]

gondola /'gɒndələ/ *n*. light flat-bottomed Venetian canal-boat; car suspended from airship or balloon. [It.]

gondolier /gɒndə'lɪə/ *n*. rower of gondola. [F f. It. (prec.)]

gone *p.p.* of GO[1].

goner /'gɒnə/ *n. sl.* doomed or irrevocably lost person or thing. [prec.]

gonfalon /'gɒnfələn/ *n*. banner, often with streamers, hung from crossbar. [It.]

gong *n*. metal disc with turned rim giving resonant note when struck; saucer-shaped bell; *sl*. medal. [Malay]

gonorrhoea /gɒnə'ri:ə/, *US* **gonorrhea** *n*. venereal disease with inflammatory discharge from urethra or vagina. [L f. Gk, = semen-flux]

goo *n. sl.* viscous or sticky substance; *fig*. sickly sentiment. [orig. unkn.]

good /gʊd/ **1** *a*. having the right or required qualities, adequate; proper, expedient; commendable, worthy (esp. in *my good man* etc.); morally excellent, virtuous (*good works*); (of child) well-behaved; agreeable, enjoyable (*good news*; *have a good time*); suitable, efficient, competent (*a good driver*; *good at French*); thorough, considerable (*a good hiding*; *a good number*); valid, genuine, financially sound (*good money*; *his credit is good*); not less than (*waited a good hour*); used in exclamations (*good God!*, *gracious!*, etc.). **2** *adv. US colloq*. well (*doing pretty good*). **3** *n*. good quality or circumstance, esp. what is beneficial or morally right (*will do you good*; *up to no good*); (in *pl.*) movable property or merchandise, things to be transported. **4 the good** *pl*. good people; **the goods** things one has undertaken to supply (**have the goods on** have advantageous information about); **all in good time** in due course but without haste; **as good as** practically; **for good (and all)** finally, permanently; **good afternoon, day,** etc. forms used in greeting or parting; **good faith** honest or sincere intention; **good for** beneficial to, having good effect on, able to undertake or pay; **good-for-nothing** *a*. & *n*. worthless (person); **Good Friday** Friday before Easter Sunday, commemorating Crucifixion; **good-hearted** kindly, well-meaning; **good humour** genial mood; **good-humoured** genial; **good job** see JOB; **good-looking** handsome; **good nature** friendly disposition; **in good time** with no risk of being late; **good will** intention that good shall result (see also GOODWILL); **to the good** having as profit or benefit. [OE]

goodbye /gʊd'baɪ/, *US* **goodby 1** *int*. farewell (expressing good wishes on parting, ending telephone conversation, etc.). **2** *n*. (*pl*. **goodbyes,** *US* **goodbys**) parting, farewell. [*God be with you*]

goodly /'gʊdlɪ/ *a*. handsome; of imposing size etc.; **goodliness** *n*. [OE]

goodness *n*. virtue; excellence; kindness (*have the goodness to wait*); used instead of 'God' in exclamations (*goodness knows*). [OE]

goodwill *n*. kindly feeling; established reputation of business etc. as enhancing its value. [GOOD]

goody 1 *n.* (usu. in *pl.*) something good or attractive, esp. to eat; *colloq.* good or favoured person. 2 *int.* expressing childish delight.

goody-goody 1 *a.* obtrusively or smugly virtuous. 2 *n.* goody-goody person.

gooey *a. sl.* viscous or sticky; sentimental. [GOO]

goof *sl.* 1 *n.* foolish or stupid person; mistake. 2 *v.* blunder, bungle; idle. 3 **goofy** *a.* [ult. f. L *gufus* coarse]

googly /'gu:glɪ/ *n.* ball in cricket bowled so as to bounce in unexpected direction. [orig. unkn.]

goon *n. sl.* stupid person; hired ruffian. [orig. uncert.]

goosander /gu:'sændə/ *n.* duck with sharp serrated bill. [foll.]

goose *n.* (*pl.* **geese**) web-footed bird between duck and swan in size; female of this (cf. GANDER); flesh of goose as food; simpleton; (*pl.* **gooses**) tailor's smoothing iron (with handle like goose's neck); **goose-flesh** (or **-pimples**) bristling state of skin due to cold or fright; **goose-step** parading-step of marching soldiers with knees kept stiff. [OE]

gooseberry /'gʊzbərɪ/ *n.* small green sour berry; thorny shrub bearing it; **play gooseberry** be unwanted extra person. [orig. uncert.]

gopher /'gəʊfə/ *n.* American burrowing rodent, ground squirrel, or burrowing tortoise. [orig. uncert.]

Gordian /'gɔ:dɪən/ *a.* usu. in **cut the Gordian knot** solve problem by force or evasion. [*Gordius*, who tied a knot later cut by Alexander the Great]

gore[1] *n.* blood shed and clotted. [OE, = dirt]

gore[2] *v.t.* pierce with horn, tusk, etc. [orig. unkn.]

gore[3] 1 *n.* wedge-shaped piece in garment; triangular or tapering piece in umbrella etc. 2 *v.t.* shape with gore. [OE, = triangle of land]

gorge 1 *n.* narrow opening between hills; gorging, surfeit; contents of stomach. 2 *v.* feed greedily; satiate; choke up; devour greedily. 3 **one's gorge rises at** one is sickened by. [F, = throat]

gorgeous /'gɔ:dʒəs/ *a.* richly coloured, sumptuous; *colloq.* strikingly beautiful; *colloq.* very pleasant, splendid (*had a gorgeous time*). [F]

gorgon /'gɔ:gən/ *n.* frightening or repulsive woman; in Greek mythology, one of three snake-haired sisters whose look petrified beholder. [L f. Gk (*gorgos* terrible)]

Gorgonzola /gɔ:gən'zəʊlə/ *n.* a kind of rich blue-veined cheese. [*Gorgonzola* in Italy]

gorilla /gə'rɪlə/ *n.* large powerful anthropoid ape. [Gk, perh. f. Afr. = wild man]

gormandize /'gɔ:məndaɪz/ *v.* eat greedily. [GOURMAND]

gormless /'gɔ:mlɪs/ *a. colloq.* foolish, lacking sense. [obs. *gaumless* f. dial. *gaum* understanding]

gorse *n.* furze; **gorsy** *a.* [OE]

Gorsedd /'gɔ:seð/ *n.* meeting of Welsh etc. bards and druids (esp. as preliminary to eisteddfod). [W, lit. 'throne']

gory *a.* covered with blood; involving bloodshed; **gorily** *adv.*; **goriness** *n.* [GORE[1]]

gosh *int.* expressing surprise. [euphem. for GOD]

goshawk /'gɒshɔ:k/ *n.* large hawk with short wings. [OE (GOOSE, HAWK[1])]

gosling /'gɒzlɪŋ/ *n.* young goose. [ON (GOOSE)]

gospel /'gɒsp(ə)l/ *n.* teaching or revelation of Christ; (**Gospel**) each of four books of New Testament giving account of Christ's life, portion of this read at service; thing regarded as absolutely true (also **gospel truth**); principle one acts on or advocates. [OE (GOOD, SPELL[1] = news)]

gossamer /'gɒsəmə/ 1 *n.* filmy substance of small spiders' webs; delicate filmy material. 2 *a.* light and flimsy as gossamer. [orig. uncert.]

gossip /'gɒsɪp/ 1 *n.* idle talk; informal talk or writing esp. about persons or social incidents; person indulging in gossip. 2 *v.i.* talk or write gossip. 3 **gossip column** section of newspaper devoted to gossip about well-known people. 4 **gossipy** *a.* [OE, orig. 'godparent', hence 'familiar acquaintance']

got *past* and *p.p.* of GET.

Goth *n.* member of a Germanic tribe that invaded Roman Empire in 3rd–5th c.; uncivilized or ignorant person. [L f. Gk. f. Gothic]

Gothic 1 *a.* of the Goths; in the style of architecture prevalent in W. Europe in 12th–16th c., characterized by pointed arches; (of novel etc.) in a horrific style popular in 18th–19th c.; barbarous, uncouth. 2 *n.* Gothic language or architecture. [F or L (prec.)]

gotten see GET.

gouache /gu:'ɑ:ʃ/ *n.* painting with opaque pigments ground in water and thickened with gum and honey; these pigments. [F f. It.]

Gouda /'gaʊdə/ *n.* flat round cheese, usu. Dutch. [*Gouda* in Holland]

gouge /gaʊdʒ/ 1 *n.* chisel with concave blade. 2 *v.t.* cut with or as with gouge; force (*out*, esp. eye with thumb) with or as with gouge; force out eye of (person) thus. [F f. L *gubia*]

goulash /'gu:læʃ/ *n.* highly seasoned stew of meat and vegetables. [Magyar *gulyás-hús*, = herdsman's meat]

gourd /gʊəd/ *n.* fleshy usu. large fruit of a trailing or climbing plant; this plant; dried rind of this fruit used as bottle. [F, ult. f. L *cucurbita*]

gourmand /'gʊəmænd/ *n.* glutton; gourmet. [F]

gourmandise /'gʊəmɑ̃di:z/ *n.* gluttony.

gourmet /'gʊəmeɪ/ *n.* connoisseur of good or delicate food. [F]

gout *n.* disease with inflammation of joints, esp. of big toe; **gouty** *a.* [F f. L *gutta* drop]

govern /'gʌv(ə)n/ *v.* rule or control with authority, conduct policy and affairs of, be in charge or command of; influence or determine (person or course of action); be a standard or principle for; check or control; *Gram.* (esp. of verb or preposition) have (noun or its case) depending on it. [F f. L f. Gk *kubernaō* steer]

governance *n.* act or manner or function of governing. [F (prec.)]

governess /'gʌvənɪs/ *n.* woman employed to teach children in private household.

government *n.* act or manner or system of governing; form of organization of State; persons governing State; (usu. **Government**) particular ministry in office; **governmental** /-'ment(ə)l/ *a.*

governor *n.* ruler; official governing province, town, etc.; representative of Crown in colony; executive head of each State of US; officer commanding fortress etc.; head, or member of governing body, of institution; official in charge of prison; *sl.* one's employer or father; automatic regulator controlling speed of engine etc.; **Governor-General** representative of Crown in Commonwealth country that regards Queen as Head of State.

gown *n.* loose flowing garment, esp. long dress worn by woman; official robe of alderman, judge, clergyman, member of university, etc.; surgeon's overall. [F f. L *gunna* fur]

goy *n.* (*pl.* **goyim** or **goys**) Jewish name for non-Jew. [Heb., = people]

GP *abbr.* general practitioner.

GPO *abbr.* General Post Office.

gr. *abbr.* gram(s); grain(s); gross.

grab **1** *v.* (**-bb-**) seize suddenly; take greedily or unfairly; *sl.* attract attention of, impress; snatch (*at*); (of brakes) act harshly or jerkily. **2** *n.* sudden clutch or attempt to seize; mechanical device for clutching. [LG or Du.]

grace **1** *n.* attractiveness, esp. in elegance of proportion or manner or movement; courteous good will (*had the grace to apologize*); air or bearing; attractive feature, accomplishment (*social graces*); divine favour of inspiring influence, state of receiving this; goodwill, favour; delay granted as favour (*a year's grace*); thanksgiving before or after meal; (**Grace**) any of three sister goddesses in Greek myth, bestowers of beauty and charm. **2** *v.t.* add grace to; bestow honour on (*graced us with his presence*). **3 grace-and--favour house** etc. house etc. occupied by permission of sovereign; **grace-note** note embellishing melody; **His, Her, Your, Grace** titles used of or in addressing duke, duchess, or archbishop; **in person's good graces** in his favour; **with good** (or **bad**) **grace** as if willingly (or reluctantly). [F f. L *gratia*]

graceful *a.* having or showing grace or elegance; **gracefully** *adv.*

graceless *a.* lacking grace or elegance or charm.

gracious /'greɪʃəs/ **1** *a.* kind, indulgent and beneficent to inferiors; (of God) merciful, benign. **2** *int.* expressing surprise. **3 gracious living** elegant way of life. [F f. L (GRACE)]

gradate /grə'deɪt/ *v.* (cause to) pass by gradations from one shade to another; arrange in gradations. [foll.]

gradation /grə'deɪʃ(ə)n/ *n.* (usu. in *pl.*) stage of transition or advance; degree in rank, intensity, etc.; arrangement in gradations; **gradational** *a.* [L (foll.)]

grade **1** *n.* degree in rank, merit, proficiency, etc.; class of persons or things of same grade; mark indicating quality of student's work; slope; *US* class or form in school. **2** *v.* arrange in grades; give grade to (student); reduce (road etc.) to easy gradients; pass gradually (*up*, *down*, etc.) between grades or *into* a grade. **3 make the grade** succeed. [F, or L *gradus* step]

gradient /'greɪdɪənt/ *n.* amount of slope in road, railway, etc.; sloping road etc. [prob. prec.]

gradual /'grædjʊəl/ *a.* occurring by degrees, not rapid or steep or abrupt; **gradually** *adv.* [L (GRADE)]

gradualism *n.* policy of gradual change.

graduate **1** /'grædjʊət/ *n.* holder of academic degree. **2** /-eɪt/ *v.* take academic degree; move up *to* (higher grade of activity etc.); mark out in degrees or parts; arrange in gradations, apportion (tax) according to scale. **3 graduation** /-'eɪʃ(ə)n/ *n.* [med.L *graduor* take a degree (GRADE)]

Graeco-Roman /gri:kəʊ'rəʊmən/ *a.* of the Greeks and Romans.
graffito /grə'fi:təʊ/ *n.* (*pl.* **graffiti** /-ti:/) writing or drawing scribbled or scratched on wall etc. [It. (*graffio* scratching)]
graft[1] /grɑ:ft/ **1** *n.* shoot or scion from one plant or tree planted in slit made in another; piece of living tissue transplanted surgically; process of grafting; place where graft is inserted; *sl.* hard work. **2** *v.* insert (graft) *in* or *on*; transplant (living tissue); fix or join (thing) permanently to another; *sl.* work hard. [F f. L f. Gk *graphion* stylus]
graft[2] /grɑ:ft/ *colloq.* **1** *n.* practices, esp. bribery, used to secure illicit gains in politics or business; such gains. **2** *v.i.* seek or make such gains. [orig. unkn.]
Grail *n.* (usu. **Holy Grail**) in medieval legend, cup or platter used by Christ at Last Supper. [F f. L *gradalis* dish]
grain 1 *n.* fruit or seed of cereal; *collect.* wheat or allied food-grass, its fruit, corn; particle of salt, sand, etc.; unit of weight, 0.0648 gram; least possible amount (*not a grain of truth in it*); roughness of surface; texture in skin, wood, stone, etc.; pattern of lines of fibre in wood or paper, lamination in stone, etc. **2** *v.* paint in imitation of grain of wood etc.; give granular surface to; dye in grain; form into grains. **3 against the grain** contrary to one's natural inclination or feeling. **4 grainy** *a.* [F f. L *granum*]
grallatorial /grælə'tɔ:rɪəl/ *a.* of the long-legged wading birds. [L *grallator* walker on stilts (*grallae*)]
gram *n.* metric unit of mass, .001 of kilogram. [F *gramme* f. Gk *gramma* small weight]
-gram *suffix* forming nouns denoting thing (so) written or recorded (*diagram, monogram, telegram*); cf. -GRAPH. [Gk *gramma* thing written (*graphō* write)]
graminaceous /græmɪ'neɪʃəs/ *a.* of or like grass. [L (*gramen* grass)]
graminivorous /græmɪ'nɪvərəs/ *a.* feeding on grass, cereals, etc.
grammar /'græmə/ *n.* study or rules of a language's inflexions or other means of showing relation between words; book on grammar; observance or correct use of rules of grammar (*bad, good, grammar*); **grammar school** orig. a school founded for teaching Latin, now a secondary school with academic curriculum. [AF *gramere* f. L f. Gk (*gramma* letter)]
grammarian /grə'meərɪən/ *n.* expert in grammar or linguistics. [F (prec.)]
grammatical /grə'mætɪk(ə)l/ *a.* of or according to grammar; **grammatically** *adv.* [F or L f. Gk *grammatikos* (GRAMMAR)]
gramme var. of GRAM.
gramophone /'græməfəʊn/ *n.* instrument reproducing recorded sound by stylus resting on rotating grooved disc. [inversion of PHONOGRAM]
grampus /'græmpəs/ *n.* sea-animal resembling dolphin and famous for blowing. [F f. L (*crassus piscis* fat fish)]
gran *n. colloq.* grandmother. [abbr.]
granadilla /grænə'dɪlə/ *n.* passion-fruit. [Sp. dimin. of *granada* pomegranate]
granary /'grænərɪ/ *n.* storehouse for threshed grain; region producing, and esp. exporting, much corn. [L (GRAIN)]
grand 1 *a.* splendid, magnificent, imposing, dignified; main, of chief importance; of highest rank (*Grand Duke*); *colloq.* excellent, enjoyable; belonging to high society (*grand people*). **2** *n.* grand piano; *sl.* a thousand pounds, dollars, etc. **3 grand jury** *US* jury convened to decide whether evidence against accused justifies trial; **Grand National** annual steeplechase at Aintree, Liverpool; **grand opera** opera on serious theme, or in which entire libretto is sung; **grand piano** large full-toned piano with horizontal strings; **grand slam** see SLAM[2]; **grand total** sum of other totals; **grand tour** *hist.* tour of Europe. [AF f. L *grandis* full-grown]
grand- in *comb.* denoting second degree of ascent or descent in relationships.
grandad *n. colloq.* grandfather; elderly man.
grandam /'grændæm/ *n. archaic* grandmother, old woman. [AF (GRAND, DAME)]
grandchild *n.* one's child's child. [GRAND-]
grand-dad var. of GRANDAD.
granddaughter *n.* female grandchild.
grandee /græn'di:/ *n.* Spanish or Portuguese noble of high rank; great personage. [Sp., Port. *grande* (GRAND)]
grandeur /'grændjə, -ndʒə/ *n.* majesty, splendour, dignity, of appearance or bearing; high rank, eminence; nobility of character. [F (GRAND)]
grandfather *n.* male grandparent; **grandfather clock** clock in tall wooden case, worked by weights. [GRAND-]
grandiloquent /græn'dɪləkwənt/ *a.* pompous or inflated in language; **grandiloquence** *n.* [L (GRAND, *loquus* f. *loquor* speak)]
grandiose /'grændɪəʊs/ *a.* producing or meant to produce imposing effect; planned on large scale; **grandiosity** /-'ɒsɪtɪ/ *n.* [F f. It. (GRAND)]
grandma /'grændmɑ:/ *n. colloq.* grandmother. [GRAND-]

grand mal /grɑ̃ mɑ:l/ epilepsy with loss of consciousness. [F, = great sickness]
grandmaster *n.* chess-player of highest class. [GRAND]
grandmother *n.* female grandparent. [GRAND-]
grandpa /'grændpɑ:/ *n. colloq.* grandfather.
grandparent *n.* one's parent's parent.
Grand Prix /grɑ pri:/ any of several important international motor-racing events. [F, = great or chief prize]
grandsire *n. archaic* grandfather. [GRAND-]
grandson *n.* male grandchild.
grandstand *n.* main stand for spectators at racecourse etc.; **grandstand finish** close and exciting finish to race etc. [GRAND]
grange /greɪndʒ/ *n.* country house with farm-buildings. [F f. L *granica* (GRAIN)]
graniferous /grə'nɪfərəs/ *a.* producing grain or grainlike seed. [L (GRAIN)]
granite /'grænɪt/ *n.* granular crystalline rock of quartz, mica, etc., used for building; **granitic** /-'nɪtɪk/ *a.* [It. *granito* (GRAIN)]
granivorous /grə'nɪvərəs/ *a.* feeding on grain. [L (GRAIN)]
granny /'grænɪ/ *n. colloq.* (also **grannie**) grandmother; **granny flat** part of house, made into self-contained accommodation for a relative; **granny knot** reef-knot crossed the wrong way and therefore insecure. [dimin. *grannam* f. GRANDAM; -Y²]
grant /grɑ:nt/ **1** *v.t.* consent to fulfil (request etc.); give formally, transfer (property) legally; admit as true; concede, allow. **2** *n.* thing, esp. money, granted; granting; conveyance by written instrument. **3 take for granted** assume to be true or valid. [F *granter* var. of *creanter* f. L *credo* entrust]
grantor /grɑ:n'tɔ:/ *n.* person by whom property etc. is legally transferred.
granular /'grænjʊlə/ *a.* of or like grains or granules; **granularity** /-'lærɪtɪ/ *n.* [L (GRANULE)]
granulate /'grænjʊleɪt/ *v.* form into grains; roughen surface of; **granulation** /-'leɪʃ(ə)n/ *n.*
granule /'grænju:l/ *n.* small grain. [L dimin. of *granum* (GRAIN)]
grape *n.* berry (usu. green, purple, or black) growing in clusters on vine, used as fruit and in making wine; **grape hyacinth** small plant with cluster of flowers, usu. blue; **grape-shot** *hist.* small balls as scattering charge for cannon; **grape-vine** vine, *fig.* means of transmission of rumour. [F]
grapefruit *n.* (*pl.* same) large round yellow citrus fruit with acid juicy pulp.
graph /grɑ:f/ **1** *n.* diagram showing relation of two variable quantities each measured along one of a pair of axes. **2** *v.t.* plot or trace on graph. **3 graph paper** paper with network of lines as help in drawing graphs. [abbr. *graphic* formula]
-graph *suffix* forming nouns and verbs denoting thing written etc. in specified way (*holograph*), instrument that records (*telegraph*), write etc. in specified way (*photograph*). [F f. L f. Gk (*graphō* write)]
-grapher *suffix* forming nouns denoting person skilled in *-graphy* (*geographer*, *radiographer*). [Gk *-graphos* writer]
graphic /'græfɪk/ *a.* of writing, drawing, painting, etching, etc. (*graphic arts*); vividly descriptive; **graphically** *adv.* [L f. Gk (*graphē* writing)]
-graphic *suffix* (also **-graphical**) forming adjectives from nouns in *-graph* or *-graphy*. [Gk *-graphikos* (prec.)]
graphics *n.pl.* products of graphic arts; (usu. treated as *sing.*) use of diagrams in calculation and design. [GRAPHIC]
graphite /'græfaɪt/ *n.* crystalline allotropic form of carbon used in pencils, as lubricant, etc.; **graphitic** /-'ɪtɪk/ *a.* [G *graphit* f. Gk *graphō* write]
graphology /grə'fɒlədʒɪ/ *n.* study of handwriting esp. as guide to character; **graphologist** *n.* [Gk (GRAPHIC)]
-graphy *suffix* forming nouns denoting style or method of writing etc. (*stenography*), descriptive science (*geography*). [F or G f. L f. Gk *-graphia* writing]
grapnel /'græpn(ə)l/ *n.* instrument with iron claws for dragging or grasping; small anchor with several flukes. [AF f. F f. Gmc]
grapple /'græp(ə)l/ **1** *v.* grip with hands, come to close quarters with; contend *with* in close fight; try to deal *with* (problem); seize (as) with grapnel. **2** *n.* hold (as) in wrestling; close contest; clutching-instrument, grapnel. **3 grappling-iron** grapnel. [F *grapil* f. Prov. f. Gmc]
grasp /grɑ:sp/ **1** *v.* clutch, seize greedily; hold firmly; understand or realize (fact or meaning). **2** *n.* firm hold, grip; mastery (*of* subject); mental hold. **3 grasp at** try to seize, accept eagerly; **grasp the nettle** tackle difficulty boldly. [*grapse*, rel. to GROPE]
grasping *a.* avaricious.
grass /grɑ:s/ **1** *n.* any of a group of wild low-lying plants with green blades that are eaten by animals; any species of this (*Bot.* including cereals, reeds, and

bamboos); pasture land; grass-covered ground, lawn; grazing (*out to grass*); *sl.* marijuana; *sl.* person who 'grasses', informer. **2** *v.* cover with turf; *US* provide with pasture; *sl.* betray, inform police. **3 grass roots** fundamental level or source, ordinary people, rank and file of political party etc.; **grass snake** small non-poisonous snake; **grass widow** woman whose husband is away for prolonged period. **4 grassy** *a.* [OE]

grasshopper *n.* jumping insect with loud chirping sound.

grassland *n.* large open area covered with grass, esp. used for grazing.

grate[1] *v.* reduce to small particles by rubbing on rough surface; rub with harsh noise (*against* or *on*); grind (teeth); utter in harsh tone; sound harshly (*grating laugh*); have irritating effect (*on* person or nerves); creak. [F f. Gmc]

grate[2] *n.* fireplace or furnace; metal frame confining fuel in this. [F f. L *cratis* hurdle]

grateful /'greɪtfʊl/ *a.* thankful, feeling or showing gratitude; pleasant, acceptable; **gratefully** *adv.* [obs. *grate* f. L *gratus*]

gratify /'grætɪfaɪ/ *v.t.* please, delight; please by compliance; yield to (desire); **gratification** /-fɪ'keɪʃ(ə)n/ *n.* [F or L (GRATEFUL)]

grating *n.* framework of parallel or crossed bars, wires, lines ruled on glass, etc. [GRATE[2]]

gratis /'greɪtɪs, 'grɑ:-/ *a.* & *adv.* free, without charge. [L]

gratitude /'grætɪtju:d/ *n.* being thankful for and ready to return kindness. [F or L (GRATEFUL)]

gratuitous /grə'tju:ɪtəs/ *a.* given or done gratis; uncalled for, lacking good reason. [L, = spontaneous]

gratuity /grə'tju:ɪtɪ/ *n.* money given in recognition of services. [F or L (GRATEFUL)]

gravamen /grə'veɪmen/ *n.* (*pl.* **gravamens**) essence or worst part (*of* accusation); grievance. [L (*gravis* heavy)]

grave[1] *n.* hole dug for burial of corpse; mound or monument over this; death. [OE]

grave[2] *a.* serious, weighty, important; dignified, solemn; sombre; (of sound) low-pitched, not acute. [F, or L *gravis* heavy]

grave[3] *v.t.* (*p.p.* **graven** or **graved**) fix indelibly (*in* or *on* one's memory etc.); *archaic* engrave, carve; **graven image** idol. [OE]

grave[4] /grɑ:v, greɪv/ *n.* accent (`) over vowel to show quality or length. [GRAVE[2]]

grave[5] *v.t.* clean (ship's bottom) by burning and tarring; **graving dock** dry dock. [perh. F *grave, grève* shore]

gravel /'græv(ə)l/ **1** *n.* coarse sand and small stones, used for paths etc.; formation of crystals in bladder. **2** *v.t.* (**-ll-**, *US* **-l-**) lay with gravel; puzzle, nonplus. [F dimin. (GRAVE[5])]

gravelly *a.* like gravel; (of voice) deep and rough-sounding.

graven see GRAVE[3].

Graves /grɑ:v/ *n.* light wine from Graves in France.

gravestone *n.* stone (usu. inscribed) marking grave. [GRAVE[1]]

graveyard *n.* burial-ground.

gravid /'grævɪd/ *a.* pregnant. [L *gravidus* (GRAVE[2])]

gravimeter /grə'vɪmɪtə/ *n.* instrument measuring difference in force of gravity between two places. [F f. L (GRAVE[2])]

gravimetry /grə'vɪmɪtrɪ/ *n.* measurement of weight; **gravimetric** /grævɪ'metrɪk/ *a.*

gravitate /'grævɪteɪt/ *v.* move or be attracted (*to* or *towards*); move or tend by force of gravity (*towards*); sink by or as by gravity. [GRAVE[2]]

gravitation /grævɪ'teɪʃ(ə)n/ *n.* falling of bodies to earth; attraction of each particle of matter on every other; movement or tendency towards centre of this attraction; **gravitational** *a.*

gravity /'grævɪtɪ/ *n.* force that attracts body to centre of earth etc.; intensity of this; gravitational force; weight; importance, seriousness; solemnity; **gravity feed** supply of material by its fall under gravity. [F or L (GRAVE[2])]

gravy /'greɪvɪ/ *n.* juices exuding from meat in and after cooking; dressing for food, made of these; *sl.* unearned or unexpected money; **gravy-boat** boat-shaped vessel for gravy. [perh. erron. f. F *grané* (*grain* spice, GRAIN)]

gray *US* var. of GREY.

grayling *n.* silver-grey freshwater fish. [GREY, -LING]

graze[1] **1** *v.* suffer slight abrasion of (part of body); touch lightly in passing; move (*against*, *along*, etc.) with such contact. **2** *n.* abrasion. [perh. f. foll. 'take off grass close to ground']

graze[2] *v.* (of cattle etc.) eat growing grass; feed (cattle etc.) on growing grass; feed on (grass); pasture cattle. [OE (GRASS)]

grazier /'greɪzɪə/ *n.* one who feeds cattle for market; *Austral.* sheep-farmer. [GRASS]

grazing *n.* grassland suitable for pasturage. [GRAZE[2]]

grease /gri:s/ **1** *n.* oily or fatty matter esp. as lubricant; melted fat of dead animal. **2** /also gri:z/ *v.t.* smear or lubricate with grease. **3 grease-paint** make-up used by actors etc.; **grease person's palm** *colloq.* bribe him. [F f. L (*crassus* adj. fat)]

greasy *a.* of or like grease; smeared or covered with grease; having much or too much grease; slippery; (of person or manner) too unctuous; **greasily** *adv.*; **greasiness** *n.*

great /greɪt/ **1** *a.* of a size or amount or extent or intensity much above the normal or average (*made a great hole*; *take great care*; also contemptuously: *the great idiot*); important, pre-eminent (*the great advantage*; *Peter the Great*); remarkable in ability, character, etc. (*great man*; *great painter*); (also **greater**) larger of the name (*great auk*; *Great Malvern*; *greater celandine*); fully deserving the name of, doing a thing much or on a large scale (*great scoundrel*, *fiasco*; *great reader*, *traveller*); *colloq.* very enjoyable or satisfactory (*had a great time*); competent *at*, well-informed *on*. **2** *n.* great person or thing. **3 Great Bear** see BEAR[2]; **great circle** circle whose plane passes through centre of sphere on which circle lies; **Great Dane** see DANE; **a great deal** see DEAL[1]; **Great Russian** member or language or principal ethnic group in USSR; **Greats** Oxford BA course in classics and philosophy, final examination in this; **Great Seal** official seal used on important State papers; **Great War** war of 1914–18. [OE]

great- in *comb.* (of family relationships) one degree more remote (*great-aunt*; *great-grandfather*; *great-great-grandfather*).

greatcoat *n.* heavy overcoat.

greatly *adv.* by considerable amount, much (*greatly admired*; *greatly superior*).

greave *n.* (usu. in *pl.*) armour for shin. [F, = shin]

grebe *n.* a diving bird. [F]

Grecian /ˈgri:ʃ(ə)n/ *a.* (of architecture or facial outline) Greek; **Grecian nose** straight nose that continues line of forehead without dip. [F or L (*Graecia* Greece)]

greed *n.* excessive desire esp. for food or wealth. [foll.]

greedy *a.* showing greed, wanting or taking in excess; gluttonous; very eager (*to do* thing); **greedily** *adv.*; **greediness** *n.* [OE]

Greek 1 *a.* of Greece or its people or language, Hellenic. **2** *n.* native or language of Greece. **3 Greek cross** cross with four equal arms; **Greek god** paragon of male beauty; **Greek to me** incomprehensible to me. [OE f. Gmc f. L f. Gk *Graikos*]

green 1 *a.* of colour between blue and yellow, like that of grass; covered with leaves or grass; (of fruit etc. or wood) unripe or unseasoned; not dried, smoked, or tanned; inexperienced, gullible; pale, sickly-hued; jealous, envious; young, flourishing; not withered or worn out (*a green old age*). **2** *n.* green colour or pigment; green clothes or material (*dressed in green*); piece of grassy public land (*village green*); grassy area for special purpose (*putting-green*); (in *pl.*) green vegetables; vigour, youth (*in the green*). **3** *v.* make or become green. **4 green belt** area of open land for preservation round city; **green card** motorist's international insurance document; **green-eyed** jealous; **green fingers** skill in growing plants; **green light** signal to proceed on road etc., *colloq.* permission to go ahead with a project; **Green Paper** preliminary report of government proposals, for discussion; **green pound** value of the pound as currency exchange for agricultural produce in EEC; **green revolution** greatly increased crop production in developing countries; **green-room** room in theatre for actors off stage; **green-stick fracture** fracture, esp. in children, in which one side of bone is broken and one only bent; **green tea** tea made from steam-dried leaves. [OE]

greenery *n.* green foliage or growing plants.

greenfinch *n.* finch with green and yellow plumage.

greenfly *n.* green aphid; these collectively.

greengage *n.* round green plum. [Sir W. *Gage*]

greengrocer *n.* retailer of fruit and vegetables; **greengrocery** *n.*

greenhorn *n.* inexperienced person, new recruit.

greenhouse *n.* light structure with sides and roof mainly of glass, for rearing plants.

greenkeeper *n.* keeper of golf-course.

greensand *n.* green kind of sandstone.

greenstone *n.* green eruptive rock containing feldspar and hornblende; NZ kind of jade.

greenstuff *n.* vegetation, green vegetables.

greensward *n.* expanse of grassy turf.

Greenwich Mean Time /ˈgrenɪtʃ, ˈgrɪ-, -ɪdʒ/ mean time on the meridian of Greenwich in London, used as the international basis of time-reckoning.

greenwood *n.* woodlands in summer. [GREEN]
greet[1] *v.t.* address politely on meeting or arrival; salute, receive (person, news, etc., *with* reaction); (of a sight, sound, etc.) meet (eye, ear, etc.). [OE]
greet[2] *v.i. Sc.* weep. [OE]
greeting *n.* words, gestures, etc., used to greet a person; (often in *pl.*) expression of goodwill; **greetings card** decorative card sent to convey greetings. [GREET[1]]
gregarious /grɪ'geərɪəs/ *a.* fond of company; living in flocks or communities. [L (*grex gregis* flock)]
Gregorian /grɪ'gɔ:rɪən/ *a.* of the plainsong ritual music named after Pope Gregory I; **Gregorian calendar** calendar introduced in 1582 by Pope Gregory XIII.
gremlin /'gremlɪn/ *n. sl.* mischievous sprite said to interfere with machinery etc. [orig. unkn.]
grenade /grɪ'neɪd/ *n.* small bomb thrown by hand or shot from rifle. [F (POMEGRANATE)]
grenadier /grenə'dɪə/ *n. hist.* soldier armed with grenades; **Grenadiers** (or **Grenadier Guards**) first regiment of royal household infantry.
grew *past* of GROW.
grey /greɪ/ **1** *a.* of colour between black and white; dull, dismal; (of hair) turning white, (of person) with grey hair; aged, experienced, mature; ancient; anonymous, unidentifiable. **2** *n.* grey colour or pigment; grey clothes or material (*dressed in grey*); grey horse. **3** *v.* become or make grey. **4 Grey Friar** Franciscan; **grey matter** material of active part of brain, *colloq.* intelligence. [OE]
greyhound *n.* slender dog noted for swiftness and used in racing and coursing. [OE, = bitch-hound]
greylag *n.* European wild goose. [GREY]
grid *n.* grating; system of numbered squares printed on map and forming basis of map references; network of lines, electric-power connections, gas-supply lines, etc.; pattern of lines marking starting-places on car-racing track; wire network between filament and anode of thermionic valve; arrangement of town streets in rectangular pattern; gridiron. [GRIDIRON]
griddle /'grɪd(ə)l/ *n.* = GIRDLE[2]. [F f. L (*cratis* hurdle)]
gridiron /'grɪdaɪən/ *n.* cooking utensil of metal bars for broiling or grilling. [GRIDDLE]
grief *n.* deep or intense sorrow; cause of this; **come to grief** meet with disaster. [F (GRIEVE)]
grievance /'gri:vəns/ *n.* real or fancied ground of complaint. [F (prec.)]
grieve *v.* cause grief to; feel grief. [F f. L (GRAVE[2])]
grievous *a.* (of pain etc.) severe; causing grief; injurious; flagrant, heinous; **grievous bodily harm** *Law* serious injury. [F (prec.)]
griffin /'grɪfɪn/ *n.* fabulous creature with eagle's head and wings and lion's body. [F f. L f. Gk]
griffon /'grɪf(ə)n/ *n.* dog like terrier with coarse hair; large vulture; griffin. [F, = prec.]
grill 1 *n.* device on cooker for radiating heat downwards; gridiron; grilled food; grill-room; grille. **2** *v.* cook on gridiron or under grill; subject to or undergo torture or great heat; subject to severe questioning, esp. by police. **3 grill-room** small restaurant serving grills etc. [F (GRIDDLE)]
grille *n.* grating or latticed screen, esp. in door; metal grid protecting radiator of motor vehicle.
grilse *n.* young salmon that has been only once to the sea. [orig. unkn.]
grim *a.* of harsh or forbidding appearance; stern, merciless; ghastly, joyless (*grim smile*); unpleasant, unattractive. [OE]
grimace /grɪ'meɪs/ **1** *n.* distortion of face made in disgust etc. or to amuse. **2** *v.i.* make grimace. [F f. Sp.]
grime 1 *n.* soot or dirt ingrained in a surface, esp. skin. **2** *v.t.* blacken with grime, befoul. **3 grimy** *a.* [LG or Du.]
grin 1 *v.* (**-nn-**) smile broadly, showing teeth; make forced, unrestrained, or stupid smile; express by grinning. **2** *n.* act or action of grinning. **3 grin and bear it** take pain etc. stoically. [OE]
grind /graɪnd/ **1** *v.* (*past* and *p.p.* **ground**) crush to small particles; produce (flour) thus; oppress, harass with exactions; sharpen or smooth by friction; rub together gratingly; study hard, toil; produce or bring *out* with effort; turn handle of (barrel-organ). **2** *n.* grinding; hard dull work (*the daily grind*); size of ground particles. **3 grind to a halt** stop laboriously with sound of grating; **ground glass** glass made opaque by grinding. [OE]
grinder *n.* person or thing that grinds, esp. machine; molar tooth.
grindstone *n.* thick revolving disc used for grinding, sharpening, and polishing; kind of stone used for this; **keep one's nose to the grindstone** work hard and continuously.
grip 1 *v.* (**-pp-**) grasp tightly; take firm hold esp. by friction; compel attention of. **2** *n.* firm hold, grasp; grasping power;

way of clasping hands or of grasping or holding; mastery, intellectual hold (*get a grip on oneself, lose one's grip*); gripping part of machine etc.; part of weapon etc. that is held; hair-grip; *US* suitcase, travelling-bag. 3 **come** (or **get to) grips with** approach purposefully, begin to deal with. [OE (foll.)]

gripe 1 *v.* cause colic; affect with colic; *sl.* complain; clutch, grip; oppress. 2 *n.* colic (usu. *pl.*); *sl.* complaint; grip. 3 **gripe-water** medicine to cure colic in babies. [OE]

grisly /ˈgrɪzlɪ/ *a.* causing horror, disgust or fear; **grisliness** *n.* [OE]

grist *n.* corn to grind; **grist to the mill** source of profit or advantage. [OE (GRIND)]

gristle /ˈgrɪs(ə)l/ *n.* tough flexible tissue, cartilage; **gristly** *a.* [OE]

grit 1 *n.* particles of stone or sand, esp. as causing discomfort, clogging machinery, etc.; coarse sandstone; *colloq.* pluck, endurance. 2 *v.* (**-tt-**) spread grit on (icy roads etc.); clench (teeth); make grating sound. 3 **gritty** *a.* [OE]

grits *n.pl.* coarsely ground grain, esp. oatmeal; oats that have been husked but not ground. [OE]

grizzle /ˈgrɪz(ə)l/ *v.i. colloq.* (esp. of child) cry fretfully. [orig. unkn.]

grizzled /ˈgrɪz(ə)ld/ *a.* grey-haired or partly so. [*grizzle* grey f. F *grisel*]

grizzly /ˈgrɪzlɪ/ 1 *a.* grey, grey-haired. 2 *n.* grizzly bear. 3 **grizzly bear** large fierce bear of N. America.

groan 1 *v.* make deep sound expressing pain, grief, or disapproval; utter with groans; be loaded or oppressed (*groan under injustice*). 2 *n.* the sound made in groaning. [OE]

groat *n. hist.* silver coin worth four old pence. [LG or Du. (GREAT)]

groats *n.pl.* hulled or crushed grain, esp. oats. [OE]

grocer *n.* dealer in food and household provisions. [AF *grosser* f. L (*grossus* GROSS)]

grocery *n.* grocer's trade or shop; (in *pl.*) grocer's provisions.

grog *n.* drink of spirit (orig. rum) and water. [orig. uncert.]

groggy *a.* unsteady, tottering; **groggily** *adv.*; **grogginess** *n.*

grogram /ˈgrɒgrəm/ *n.* coarse fabric of silk, mohair, etc. [F *gros grain* coarse grain]

groin[1] 1 *n.* depression between belly and thigh; edge formed by vaults intersecting in roof; arch supporting vault. 2 *v.t.* build with groins. [orig. uncert.]

groin[2] *US* var. of GROYNE.

groom 1 *n.* person employed to take care of horses; bridegroom; one of certain officers of Royal Household. 2 *v.t.* curry or tend (horse); give neat appearance to (person etc.); prepare (person) *as* political candidate, *for* career, etc. [orig. unkn.]

groove 1 *n.* channel or hollow, esp. one made to guide motion or receive ridge; spiral cut in gramophone record for stylus; piece of routine, habit; *sl.* something excellent. 2 *v.* make groove or grooves in. [Du.]

groovy *a.* of or like a groove; *sl.* excellent.

grope *v.* feel about as in dark; search blindly (*lit.* or *fig.*); **grope one's way** proceed tentatively. [OE]

grosbeak /ˈgrəʊsbiːk/ *n.* hawfinch. [F *grosbec*, = large (GROSS) beak]

grosgrain /ˈgrəʊgreɪn/ *n.* corded fabric of silk etc. [F (GROGRAM)]

gros point /grəʊ ˈpwæ̃/ cross-stitch embroidery on canvas. [F (GROSS, POINT)]

gross /grəʊs/ 1 *a.* flagrant (*gross negligence*); total, not net (*gross tonnage*); (of manners, morals, person) coarse, unrefined, indecent; overfed, bloated; luxuriant, rank; thick, solid; (of senses etc.) dull. 2 *n.* (*pl.* same) twelve dozen. 3 *v.t.* produce as gross profit. 4 **gross domestic product** total value of goods produced and services provided in a country in one year; **gross national product** gross domestic product plus total of net income from abroad. [F f. L *grossus*]

grotesque /grəʊˈtesk/ 1 *a.* comically or repulsively distorted; incongruous, absurd. 2 *n.* decoration interweaving human and animal forms with foliage; comically distorted figure or design. [F f. It. (foll.)]

grotto /ˈgrɒtəʊ/ *n.* (*pl.* **grottoes**) picturesque cave; artificial or simulated cave. [It. *grotta* f. L (CRYPT)]

grotty /ˈgrɒtɪ/ *a. sl.* unpleasant, dirty, ugly, useless. [GROTESQUE]

grouch *colloq.* 1 *v.i.* grumble. 2 *n.* discontented person; fit of grumbling or the sulks. 3 **grouchy** *a.* [GRUDGE]

ground[1] 1 *n.* surface of the earth, esp. as contrasted with air around it; part of this specified in some way (*marshy, wet, ground*); position or area on earth's surface; foundation or motive; area of special kind or use (*camping-, cricket-ground*); surface worked upon in painting etc., predominant colour; (in *pl.*) enclosed land attached to house; (in *pl.*) dregs, esp. of coffee; electrical earth; bottom of sea; floor of room etc. 2 *attrib.* (in names of birds) terrestrial, (of animals) burrowing, lying on ground, (of plants) dwarfish, trailing. 3 *v.* run aground, strand; refuse authority for (airman or aircraft) to fly; instruct thoroughly (*in* subject); base (principle or conclusion *on* fact etc.); connect with earth as conductor; alight on ground; place, lay (esp. weapons) on ground. 4 **break new ground** treat subject previously not dealt with; **cover the ground** deal adequately with subject; **fall to the ground** (of plan etc.) fail; **get off the ground** make successful start; **give** (or **lose**) **ground** retreat, decline; **go to ground** (of fox etc.) enter burrow, (of person) withdraw from public notice; **ground bass** short theme in bass constantly repeated with upper parts of music varied; **ground floor** see FLOOR; **ground frost** frost on surface of ground or in top layer of soil; **ground-nut** N. American wild nut with edible tuber, peanut; **ground-plan** plan of building at ground level, general outline of scheme; **ground-rent** rent for land leased for building; **ground speed** aircraft speed relative to ground; **ground swell** heavy sea due to distant or past storm or earthquake; **ground water** water found in surface soil; **hold one's ground** not retreat. [OE]

ground[2] *past* and *p.p.* of GRIND.

grounding *n.* basic training or instruction in subject. [GROUND[1]]

groundless *a.* without motive or foundation.

groundsel /'graʊns(ə)l/ *n.* plant of which commonest species is used as food for cage-birds. [OE]

groundsheet *n.* waterproof sheet for spreading on ground. [GROUND[1]]

groundsman *n.* person who maintains sports ground.

groundwork *n.* preliminary or basic work.

group /gru:p/ 1 *n.* number of persons or things close together, or belonging or classed together; number of commercial companies under one owner; pop group; division of air force. 2 *v.t.* form into a group; place in a group or groups. 3 **group captain** RAF officer next below air commodore; **group therapy** therapy in which similarly affected patients are brought together to assist one another. [F f. It. *gruppo*]

grouse[1] *n.* (*pl.* same) game-bird with feathered feet; its flesh as food. [orig. uncert.]

grouse[2] *colloq.* 1 *v.i.* grumble, complain. 2 *n.* grumble. [orig. unkn.]

grout 1 *n.* thin fluid mortar. 2 *v.t.* apply grout to. [orig. uncert.]

grove *n.* small wood, group of trees. [OE]

grovel /'grɒv(ə)l/ *v.i.* (**-ll-**, *US* **-l-**) lie prone in abject humility; humble oneself. [foll.]

grovelling *a.* abject, base; prone. [ON *á grúfu* on one's face]

grow /grəʊ/ *v.* (*past* **grew;** *p.p.* **grown**) increase in size, height, amount, intensity, etc.; develop or exist as living plant or natural product; become gradually (*grow rich*); produce by cultivation; let (beard etc.) develop; (in *pass.*) be covered (*over* etc.) with growth; **growing pains** neuralgic pain in children's legs due to fatigue etc., *fig.* early difficulties in development of project etc.; **grown-up** *a.* & *n.* adult; **grow on** have increasing charm etc. for; **grow out of** become too large to wear (garment), become too mature to retain (habit etc.), develop from; **grow up** advance to maturity, (of custom) arise. [OE]

grower *n.* person growing produce, esp. fruit; plant that grows in specified way (*free grower*).

growl 1 *n.* guttural sound of anger; rumble; angry murmur, complaint. 2 *v.* make a growl. 3 **growl out** utter with growl. [prob. imit.]

grown *p.p.* of GROW.

growth /grəʊθ/ *n.* growing; increase in size or value; what has grown or is growing; tumour; **growth industry** industry developing faster than most others. [GROW]

groyne *n.* projecting structure of timber etc. to stop shifting of beach. [dial. *groin* snout f. F f. L]

grub 1 *n.* larva of insect, maggot; *sl.* food. 2 *v.* (**-bb-**) dig superficially; clear (ground) of roots etc., clear away (roots etc.); fetch *up* or *out* by digging (*lit.*, or *fig.* in books etc.); rummage. 3 **grub-screw** headless screw. [OE]

grubby *a.* dirty; full of grubs; **grubbily** *adv.*; **grubbiness** *n.*

grudge 1 *v.t.* be resentfully unwilling to give or allow. 2 *n.* feeling of resentment or ill will. [F]

gruel /'grʊəl/ *n.* liquid food of oatmeal etc. boiled in milk or water. [F f. Gmc]

gruelling *a.* exhausting.

gruesome /'gru:səm/ *a.* horrible, grisly, disgusting. [Scand.]

gruff *a.* (of voice) low and harsh; having a gruff voice; surly. [LG or Du. *grof* coarse]

grumble /'grʌmb(ə)l/ 1 *v.* complain peevishly; be discontented; make rumbling sound. 2 *n.* act or sound of grumbling. [obs. *grumme*]

grummet /'grʌmɪt/ *n.* insulating washer placed round electric conductor where it passes through hole in metal; *Naut.* ring usu. of twisted rope as fastening etc. [F]

grumpy /'grʌmpɪ/ *a.* morosely irritable; **grumpily** *adv.*; **grumpiness** *n.* [imit.]
grunt 1 *n.* low guttural sound characteristic of pig. **2** *v.* utter grunt; express discontent etc. thus; utter with grunt. [OE (imit.)]
Gruyère /'gru:jeə/ *n.* a kind of cheese, orig. Swiss, with many holes. [*Gruyère* in Switzerland]
gryphon var. of GRIFFIN.
G-string /'dʒi:strɪŋ/ *n.* narrow strip of cloth etc. covering genitals, attached to string round waist; string on violin etc. sounding note G. [G, STRING]
GT *n.* high-performance car. [It. *gran turismo* great touring]
guano /'gwɑ:nəʊ/ *n.* (*pl.* **guanos**) excrement of sea-fowl, used as manure; artificial manure, esp. that made from fish. [Sp. f. Quechua]
guarantee /gærən'ti:/ **1** *n.* formal promise or assurance, esp. that thing is of specified quality and durability; guarantor; guaranty; thing serving as security. **2** *v.t.* give or serve as guarantee for; provide with guarantee; give one's word; secure (thing *to* person). [WARRANT]
guarantor /'gærəntə, -'tɔ:/ *n.* giver of guaranty or security.
guaranty /'gærəntɪ/ *n.* undertaking, usu. written, to answer for payment of debt or performance of obligation by the person primarily liable; ground of security.
guard /gɑ:d/ **1** *v.* watch over and defend or protect; supervise (prisoners etc.) and prevent from escaping; keep (thoughts or speech) in check; take precautions (*against*). **2** *n.* state of vigilance or watchfulness; protector, sentry, *US* prison warder; railway official in charge of train; soldiers protecting place or person, escort, separate portion of army (*advance-guard*); device to prevent injury or accident (*fire-guard*); defensive posture or motion in boxing, fencing, etc.; (in *pl.*) household troops (*Foot, Horse*, etc., *Guards*). **3 on** (or **off**) **one's guard** ready (or not ready) against attack or challenge; **stand guard** act as sentry or guard (*over*). [F f. Gmc, rel. to WARD]
guarded *a.* (of remark etc.) cautious.
guardhouse *n.* building accommodating military guard or securing prisoners.
guardian /'gɑ:dɪən/ *n.* protector, keeper; person having legal custody of one incapable of managing his own affairs, or of his property; **guardianship** *n.* [F (GUARD, WARDEN)]
guardroom *n.* room with same purpose as guardhouse. [GUARD]
guardsman *n.* soldier belonging to guard or Guards.
guava /'gwɑ:və/ *n.* tropical American tree; its edible orange acid fruit. [Sp.]
gubbins /'gʌbɪnz/ *n.* gadget, equipment. [obs. *gobbons* fragments]
gubernatorial /gju:bənə'tɔ:rɪəl/ *a.* *US* of a governor. [L]
gudgeon[1] /'gʌdʒ(ə)n/ *n.* small freshwater fish used as bait; credulous person. [F f. L (*gobio* GOBY)
gudgeon[2] /'gʌdʒ(ə)n/ *n.* kind of pivot or metal pin; socket for rudder. [F dimin. (GOUGE)]
guelder rose /'geldə/ shrub with round bunches of white flowers. [Du. (*Gelderland* in Netherlands)]
Guernsey /'gɜ:nzɪ/ *n.* one of breed of cattle from Guernsey in Channel Islands; (**guernsey**) thick knitted woollen jersey; **Guernsey lily** kind of amaryllis.
guerrilla /gə'rɪlə/ *n.* person taking part in irregular fighting by small groups acting independently. [Sp. dimin. (WAR)]
guess /ges/ **1** *v.* estimate without calculation or measurement; form hypothesis about, conjecture, think likely; conjecture (answer to riddle etc.) rightly. **2** *n.* rough estimate, conjecture. **3 guess at** make guess concerning; **I guess** *US* I think it likely, I suppose. [orig. uncert.]
guesswork *n.* guessing, procedure based on this.
guest /gest/ *n.* person invited to visit one's house or have meal etc. at one's expense; person lodging at hotel etc.; performer not belonging to regular company; **guest-house** superior boarding-house. [ON]
guff *n. sl.* empty talk. [imit.]
guffaw /gʌ'fɔ:/ **1** *n.* boisterous laugh. **2** *v.i.* utter guffaw. [imit.]
guidance /'gaɪdəns/ *n.* guiding, being guided; advice on problems. [foll.]
guide /gaɪd/ **1** *n.* one who shows the way; hired conductor for tourists; person or thing by which others regulate movements; (**Guide**) member of girls' organization similar to Scouts; adviser; directing principle; book of rudiments; guidebook; rod etc. directing motion; thing marking position or guiding the eye. **2** *v.t.* act as guide to; be the principle or motive of; arrange course of (events). **3 guided missile** missile under remote control or directed by equipment within itself; **guide-dog** dog trained to guide blind person; **guided tour** tour accompanied by guide; **guide-line** directing principle. [F f. Gmc]
guidebook *n.* book of information for tourists.

Guider *n.* adult leader of Guides. [GUIDE]

guild /gɪld/ *n.* society for mutual aid or with common object; medieval association of craftsmen or merchants; **guild-hall** hall in which medieval guild met, town hall. [LG or Du. *gilde*]

guilder /'gɪldə/ *n.* currency unit of Netherlands; *hist.* gold coin of Netherlands and Germany. [alt. Du. *gulden* golden]

guile /gaɪl/ *n.* treachery, deceit; cunning, craftiness; **guileful** *a.*; **guileless** *a.* [F f. Scand.]

guillemot /'gɪlɪmɒt/ *n.* a kind of auk. [F]

guillotine /'gɪləti:n, -'ti:n/ **1** *n.* machine with blade sliding in grooves, used for beheading; machine for cutting paper, metal, etc.; method of preventing delay in Parliament by fixing times for voting on parts of Bill. **2** *v.t.* use guillotine on. [*Guillotin*, physician]

guilt /gɪlt/ *n.* fact of having committed specified or implied offence; culpability; feeling of culpability. [OE]

guiltless *a.* innocent; not having knowledge or possession *of*.

guilty *a.* having or showing or due to guilt; having committed offence (*of*); **guiltily** *adv.*; **guiltiness** *n.* [OE (prec.)]

guinea /'gɪnɪ/ *n.* sum of £1·05; *hist.* gold coin first coined for African trade; **guinea-fowl** domestic fowl with grey plumage spotted with white; **guinea-pig** S. American rodent kept as pet or for research in biology, person used as subject for experiment. [*Guinea* in W. Africa]

guipure /'gi:pʊə/ *n.* heavy lace of linen pieces joined by embroidery. [F]

guise /gaɪz/ *n.* assumed appearance, pretence; external appearance. [F f. Gmc (WISE²)]

guitar /gɪ'tɑ:/ *n.* musical instrument with six strings played with fingers or plectrum; **guitarist** *n.* [F or Sp. f. Gk *kithara* harp]

gulch *n.* *US* ravine, esp. with torrent. [orig. uncert.]

gulf *n.* large area of sea partly surrounded by land; deep hollow, chasm; wide difference of opinion etc.; **Gulf Stream** warm current from Gulf of Mexico to Europe. [F f. It. f. Gk *kolpos*]

gull¹ *n.* large sea-bird with webbed feet and long wings. [prob. W *gwylan*]

gull² *archaic* **1** *n.* fool, dupe. **2** *v.t.* cheat, fool. [perh. obs. *gull* yellow f. ON]

gullet /'gʌlɪt/ *n.* passage for food, extending from mouth to stomach. [F dimin. (L *gula* throat)]

gullible *a.* easily persuaded or deceived; **gullibility** /-'bɪlɪtɪ/ *n.* [GULL²]

gully /'gʌlɪ/ *n.* channel or ravine cut by water; gutter, drain; fielding-position in cricket between point and slips. [F *goulet* (GULLET)]

gulp **1** *v.* swallow (*down*) hastily, greedily, or with effort; keep *back* or *down* (tears etc.) with difficulty; make swallowing action with effort, choke. **2** *n.* act of gulping; large mouthful of liquid. [Du. *gulpen* (imit.)]

gum¹ **1** *n.* sticky substance secreted by some trees and shrubs, used esp. for sticking paper etc. together; chewing-gum; = *gum-drop*; = *gum arabic*; = *gum-tree*. **2** *v.t.* (**-mm-**) fasten with gum, apply gum to. **3 gum arabic** gum exuded by some kinds of acacia; **gum-drop** hard transparent sweet made of gelatine etc.; **gum-tree** tree that exudes gum, esp. eucalyptus (**up a gum-tree** in great difficulty); **gum up** *colloq.* interfere with, spoil (*gum up the works*). [F f. L f. Gk *kommi* f. Egypt. *kemai*]

gum² *n.* (often in *pl.*) firm flesh around roots of teeth. [OE]

gum³ *n.* chiefly in *sl.* oath **by gum!** [corrupt. of *God*]

gumboil *n.* small abscess on gum. [GUM²]

gumboot *n.* rubber boot. [GUM¹]

gummy¹ *a.* sticky, exuding gum.

gummy² *a.* toothless. [GUM²]

gumption /'gʌmpʃ(ə)n/ *n.* *colloq.* common sense; resource, initiative. [orig. unkn.]

gun **1** *n.* any kind of weapon consisting of metal tube for throwing missiles with explosive propellant; starting-pistol; device for discharging grease etc. on to desired point; member of shooting-party; *US* gunman. **2** *v.* (**-nn-**) shoot at or *down*; *colloq.* accelerate (engine etc.); go shooting. **3 at gunpoint** threatened by gun; **be gunning for** seek to attack or rebuke; **going great guns** acting vigorously and near success; **gun-carriage** wheeled support for gun; **gun cotton** explosive of cotton steeped in acids; **gun dog** dog trained to retrieve game in shoot; **gun-fight** *US* fight with firearms; **gun-metal** alloy formerly used for guns, bluish-grey colour of this; **stick to one's guns** maintain one's position. [perh. abbr. of Scand. *Gunnhildr* woman's name applied to cannon etc.]

gunboat *n.* small warship with heavy guns; **gunboat diplomacy** diplomacy backed by threat of force.

gunfire *n.* firing of guns.

gunman *n.* man armed with a gun, esp. in committing crime.

gunnel var. of GUNWALE.

gunner *n.* artillery soldier esp. as official term for private; naval warrant officer in charge of battery, magazine, etc.; airman who operates gun; game-shooter. [GUN]

gunnery *n.* construction and management of large guns; firing of guns.

gunny /'gʌnɪ/ *n.* coarse sacking usu. of jute fibre; sack made of this. [Hindi, Marathi]

gunpowder *n.* explosive powder of saltpetre, sulphur, and charcoal. [GUN]

gunroom *n.* room in warship for junior officers; room for sporting-guns etc. in house. [GUN]

gun-running *n.* systematic smuggling of guns and ammunition into a country; **gun-runner** *n.*

gunshot *n.* shot from gun; range of gun (*within gunshot*).

gunsmith *n.* maker and repairer of small firearms.

gunwale /'gʌn(ə)l/ *n.* upper edge of ship's or boat's side. [GUN, WALE (formerly used to support guns)]

guppy /'gʌpɪ/ *n.* small W. Indian fish. [*Guppy*, clergyman]

gurgle /'gɜ:g(ə)l/ **1** *n.* bubbling sound as of water from bottle. **2** *v.* make gurgles; utter with gurgles. [prob. imit.]

Gurkha /'gɜ:kə/ *n.* member of a Nepali people, forming regiments in British army. [Skr.]

gurnard /'gɜ:nəd/ *n.* sea-fish with large head, mailed cheeks, and finger-like pectoral rays. [F]

guru /'gʊru:/ *n.* Hindu spiritual teacher or head of religious sect; influential or revered teacher. [Hindi]

gush **1** *n.* sudden or copious stream; effusiveness. **2** *v.* flow (*out* etc.) with gush; emit gush of (water etc.); speak or behave effusively. [prob. imit.]

gusher *n.* oil-well emitting unpumped oil; effusive person.

gusset /'gʌsɪt/ *n.* piece let into garment etc. to strengthen or enlarge; strengthening iron bracket. [F]

gust **1** *n.* sudden violent rush of wind; burst of rain, smoke, anger, etc. **2** *v.i.* blow in gusts. **3 gusty** *a.* [ON]

gustatory /'gʌstətərɪ/ *a.* connected with sense of taste. [L (*gustus* taste)]

gusto /'gʌstəʊ/ *n.* zest, enjoyment in doing thing. [It. f. L (prec.)]

gut **1** *n.* intestine; (in *pl.*) bowels or entrails; (in *pl.*) *colloq.* pluck, force of character, staying power; material for violin etc. strings or surgical use made from intestines of animals; material for fishing-line made from intestines of silkworm; (in *pl.*) contents. **2** *a.* instinctive (*a gut reaction*); fundamental (*a gut issue*). **3** *v.t.* (**-tt-**) remove guts of (fish); remove or destroy internal fittings of (building); extract essence of (book etc.). **4 hate person's guts** dislike him intensely. [OE]

gutless *a. colloq.* lacking energy or courage.

gutsy *a. colloq.* courageous; *sl.* greedy.

gutta-percha /gʌtə'pɜ:tʃə/ *n.* tough plastic substance from latex of various Malayan trees. [Malay]

gutter **1** *n.* shallow trough below eaves, or channel at side of street, for carrying off rain-water; channel, groove. **2** *v.i.* (of candle) burn unsteadily and melt away rapidly. **3 the gutter** place of low breeding or vulgar behaviour; **gutter press** sensational journalism. [F f. L *gutta* drop]

guttering *n.* material for gutters.

guttersnipe *n.* street urchin.

guttural /'gʌtər(ə)l/ **1** *a.* throaty, harsh-sounding; (of consonants) produced in throat or by back of tongue and palate; of the throat. **2** *n.* guttural consonant (as *g*, *k*). **3 gutturally** *adv.* [F or med.L f. L *guttur* throat]

guv *n. sl.* governor. [abbr.]

guy[1] /gaɪ/ **1** *n.* effigy of Guy Fawkes burnt on 5 Nov.; *sl.* man; grotesquely-dressed person. **2** *v.t.* ridicule. [*Guy* Fawkes, conspirator]

guy[2] /gaɪ/ **1** *n.* rope or chain to secure tent or steady crane-load etc. **2** *v.t.* secure with guys. [prob. LG]

guzzle /'gʌz(ə)l/ *v.* eat or drink greedily. [prob. F *gosiller* (*gosier* throat)]

gybe /dʒaɪb/ *v.* (of fore-and-aft sail or boom) swing to other side; make (sail) gybe; (of boat etc.) change course thus. [Du.]

gym /dʒɪm/ *n. colloq.* gymnasium, gymnastics; **gym-slip** sleeveless tunic, usu. belted, worn by schoolgirls. [abbr.]

gymkhana /dʒɪm'kɑ:nə/ *n.* meeting for competition in sport, esp. horse-riding. [Hindi *gendkhāna* ball-house, assim. to foll.]

gymnasium /dʒɪm'neɪzɪəm/ *n.* (*pl.* **gymnasiums**) room etc. equipped for gymnastics. [L f. Gk (*gumnos* naked)]

gymnast /'dʒɪmnæst/ *n.* expert in gymnastics. [F or Gk (prec.)]

gymnastic /dʒɪm'næstɪk/ *a.* of gymnastics; **gymnastically** *adv.* [L f. Gk (GYMNASIUM)]

gymnastics *n.pl.* (occas. treated as *sing.*) exercises to develop muscles or demonstrate agility (also fig.: *mental gymnastics*).

gymp var. of GIMP.

gynaecology /gaɪnɪ'kɒlədʒɪ/ *n.* science of physiological functions and diseases of women; **gynaecological** /-kə'lɒdʒɪk(ə)l/ *a.*; **gynaecologist** *n.* [Gk *gunē gunaik-* woman, -LOGY]

gyp /dʒɪp/ *n.* only in **give person gyp**

colloq. severely punish or hurt him. [orig. uncert.]
gypsum /'dʒɪpsəm/ *n*. mineral used to make plaster of Paris or as fertilizer; **gypseous** *a*. [L f. Gk *gupsos*]
gypsy /'dʒɪpsɪ/ *n*. member of a wandering dark-skinned people in Europe; **gypsy's warning** cryptic or sinister warning. [EGYPTIAN]
gyrate /dʒaɪ'reɪt/ *v.i.* move in circle or spiral; **gyration** *n*.; **gyratory** /'dʒaɪrətərɪ/ *a*. [L f. Gk (GYRO-)]
gyrfalcon /'dʒɜ:fɔ:lkən/ *n*. large northern falcon. [F f. ON]
gyro /'dʒaɪrəʊ/ *n*. *colloq*. gyroscope. [abbr.]
gyro- *in comb*. rotation; gyroscopic. [Gk *guros* ring]
gyrocompass /'dʒaɪrəʊkʌmpəs/ *n*. compass giving true north and bearings from it by means of gyroscope.
gyroscope /'dʒaɪrəskəʊp/ *n*. rotating wheel whose axis is free to turn but maintains fixed direction unless perturbed, esp. for stabilization or to replace compass in ship etc.; **gyroscopic** /-'skɒpɪk/ *a*. [F (prec.)]

H

H, h /eɪtʃ/ *n*. (*pl*. **Hs, H's**) eighth letter.
H *abbr*. hard (pencil-lead).
h. *abbr*. hour(s); hecto-; hot.
H *symb*. hydrogen.
ha /hɑ:/ **1** *int*. expressing surprise, suspicion, triumph, etc. **2** *v.i.* see HUM. [imit.]
ha. *abbr*. hectare(s).
habeas corpus /heɪbɪəs 'kɔ:pəs/ *n*. writ requiring person to be brought before judge or into court, esp. to investigate lawfulness of his imprisonment. [L, = you must have the body]
haberdasher /'hæbədæʃə/ *n*. dealer in accessories of dress and in sewing-goods; **haberdashery** *n*. [prob. AF]
habiliments /hə'bɪlɪmənts/ *n.pl*. clothing, attire. [F f. *habiller* fit out (ABLE)]
habit /'hæbɪt/ *n*. settled or regular tendency or practice; practice that is hard to give up; mental constitution (*habit of mind*); dress, esp. of religious order; **habit-forming** causing addiction. [F f. L (*habeo habit-* have)]
habitable *a*. suitable for living in; **habitability** /-'bɪlɪtɪ/ *n*. [F f. L (*habito* INHABIT)]
habitat /'hæbɪtæt/ *n*. natural home of animal or plant. [L, = it inhabits]
habitation /hæbɪ'teɪʃ(ə)n/ *n*. house or home; inhabiting (*fit for human habitation*).
habitual /hə'bɪtjʊəl/ *a*. done constantly or as a habit; regular, usual; given to a habit (*habitual smoker*); **habitually** *adv*. [med.L (HABIT)]
habituate /hə'bɪtjʊeɪt/ *v.t.* accustom (to); **habituation** /-'eɪʃ(ə)n/ *n*. [L (HABIT)]
habitué /hə'bɪtjʊeɪ/ *n*. resident or frequent visitor (*of*). [F]
hachures /hæ'ʃjʊə/ *n.pl*. parallel lines used on maps to indicate degree of slope in hills. [F (HATCH[3])]
hacienda /hæsɪ'endə/ *n*. (in Spanish-speaking country) large estate etc. with dwelling-house. [Sp. f. L *facienda* things to be done]
hack[1] **1** *v*. cut or chop roughly; kick shin of (opponent at football); deal cutting blows (*at*). **2** *n*. kick with toe of boot, wound from this; mattock; miner's pick. **3 hacking cough** short dry frequent cough. [OE]
hack[2] **1** *n*. horse for ordinary riding; horse let out for hire; person hired to do dull routine work, esp. as writer. **2** *v*. ride on horseback at ordinary pace. **3** *a*. used as a hack; commonplace. [abbr. of HACKNEY]
hackle /'hæk(ə)l/ *n*. long feather(s) on neck of domestic cock etc.; steel comb for dressing flax etc.; **make person's hackles rise** make him very angry; **with his hackles up** angry, ready to fight. [OE]
hackney /'hæknɪ/ *n*. horse for ordinary riding; **hackney carriage** taxi. [perh. *Hackney* in London]
hackneyed /'hæknɪd/ *a*. (of phrase etc.) made commonplace or trite by long over-use.
hack-saw *n*. saw with narrow blade set in frame, for cutting metal. [HACK[1]]
had *past* and *p.p.* of HAVE.
haddock /'hædək/ *n*. (*pl*. same) sea-fish related to cod, used for food. [prob. F]
Hades /'heɪdi:z/ *n*. in Greek mythology, the underworld, abode of the spirits of the dead. [Gk (orig. a name of Pluto)]
hadji /'hædʒɪ/ *n*. (also **hajji**) Muslim who has been to Mecca as pilgrim. [Arab.]
hadn't /'hæd(ə)nt/ *colloq*. = *had not*.
haemal /'hi:m(ə)l/ *a*. of the blood. [Gk *haima* blood]

haematic /hiː'mætɪk/ *a.* of or containing blood.
haematite /'hiːmətaɪt/ *n.* ferric oxide as ore. [L (HAEMAL)]
haematology /hiːmə'tɒlədʒɪ/ *n.* study of the physiology of the blood. [-LOGY]
haemoglobin /hiːmə'gləʊbɪn/ *n.* oxygen-carrying substance in red blood-cells of vertebrates. [GLOBULIN]
haemophilia /hiːmə'fɪlɪə/ *n.* constitutional, usu. hereditary, tendency to bleed severely from even a slight injury, through failure of blood to clot normally; **haemophilic** *a.* [L f. Gk *haima* blood, *philia* loving]
haemophiliac *n.* person suffering from haemophilia.
haemorrhage /'hemərɪdʒ/ **1** *n.* escape of blood from blood-vessel, esp. when profuse. **2** *v.i.* undergo haemorrhage. [F f. L f. Gk (*haima* blood, *rhēgnumi* burst)]
haemorrhoid /'hemərɔɪd/ *n.* (usu. in *pl.*) swollen veins at or near the anus. [F f. L f. Gk (*haima* blood, *-rhoos* -flowing)]
hafnium /'hæfnɪəm/ *n.* metallic element resembling and usu. accompanying zirconium. [L *Hafnia* Copenhagen]
haft /hɑːft/ **1** *n.* handle (of dagger, knife, etc.). **2** *v.t.* furnish with haft. [OE]
hag *n.* ugly old woman; witch; **haggish** *a.* [OE]
haggard /'hægəd/ **1** *a.* looking exhausted and distraught from prolonged worry etc. **2** *n.* hawk caught when full-grown. [F *hagard*]
haggis /'hægɪs/ *n.* Scottish dish of offal boiled in bag with suet, oatmeal, etc. [orig. unkn.]
haggle /'hæg(ə)l/ **1** *v.* dispute or argue (esp. *about* or *over* price or terms). **2** *n.* haggling. [ON]
hagio- *in comb.* of saints. [Gk *hagios* holy]
hagiography /hægɪ'ɒgrəfɪ/ *n.* writing of saints' lives; **hagiographer** *n.* [-GRAPHY]
hagiology /hægɪ'ɒlədʒɪ/ *n.* literature of lives and legends of saints. [-LOGY]
hagridden *a.* afflicted by nightmares or fears. [HAG]
ha ha /hɑː 'hɑː/ repr. laughter. [OE]
ha-ha /'hɑːhɑː/ *n.* ditch with wall on inner side, forming boundary to park or garden without interrupting the view. [F]
haiku /'haɪkʊ/ *n.* (*pl.* same) Japanese three-part poem of usu. 17 syllables. [Jap.]
hail[1] **1** *n.* pellets of frozen rain falling in shower; shower *of* blows, missiles, questions, etc. **2** *v.* fall or send down as or like hail (*it is hailing*). [OE]
hail[2] **1** *int.* of greeting. **2** *v.* salute, greet *as* (*hail him king*); call to (person or ship) in order to attract attention; signal to (taxi etc.) to stop; originate, have come (*where does he hail from?*). **3** *n.* hailing. **4 be hail-fellow-well-met (with)** be very friendly or too friendly (with esp. strangers); **Hail Mary** = *Ave Maria* (see AVE); **within hail** close enough to be hailed. [ON *heill* (WASSAIL)]
hailstone *n.* pellet of hail. [HAIL[1]]
hailstorm *n.* prolonged period of heavy hail.
hair *n.* any of the fine threadlike strands growing from skin of animals, esp. from the human head; these collectively (*his hair is falling out*); elongated cell growing from surface of plant; thing resembling hair; very small quantity; **get in person's hair** encumber or annoy him; **hair-do** (*pl.* **-dos**) *colloq.* style or process of woman's hairdressing; **hair-grip** flat hairpin with ends close together; **hair-line** edge of person's hair on forehead etc., very narrow crack or line; **hair-piece** quantity of false hair augmenting person's natural hair; **hair-raising** terrifying; **hair's breadth** minute distance; **hair shirt** shirt of haircloth worn by penitents or ascetics; **hair-slide** clip for keeping hair in position; **hair-splitting** splitting hairs (see below); **hair-style** particular way of arranging hair; **hair-trigger** trigger set for release at slightest pressure; **keep one's hair on** *sl.* remain calm, not get angry; **let one's hair down** *colloq.* abandon restraint, behave wildly; **make one's hair stand on end** horrify one; **not turn a hair** remain unmoved or unaffected; **split hairs** make small and insignificant distinctions. [OE]
hairbrush *n.* brush for arranging the hair.
haircloth *n.* cloth woven from hair.
haircut *n.* cutting the hair; style of doing this.
hairdresser *n.* one whose business is to arrange and cut hair.
hairpin *n.* U-shaped pin for fastening the hair; **hairpin bend** sharp U-shaped bend in road.
hairspring *n.* fine spring regulating balance-wheel in watch.
hairy *a.* having much hair; made of hair; *sl.* unpleasant, difficult; **hairiness** *n.*
hajji var. of HADJI.
hake *n.* sea-fish like cod, used as food. [orig. uncert.]
halberd /'hælbəd/ *n. hist.* combined spear and battle-axe. [F f. G]
halcyon /'hælsɪən/ *a.* calm and peaceful (*halcyon days*); (of period) happy, prosperous. [L f. Gk, = kingfisher, reputed to calm the sea at midwinter]

hale[1] *a.* strong and healthy. [var. of WHOLE]

hale[2] *v.t. archaic* drag or draw forcibly. [F f. ON]

half /hɑːf/ **1** *n.* (*pl.* **halves** /hɑːvz/) either of two (esp. equal) parts into which a thing is divided; either of two equal periods of play in sports; half-price ticket, esp. for child; school term; *colloq.* = *half-back, half-pint*. **2** *a.* amounting to half (*half the men*; *half a pint* or *a half-pint*); forming a half (*a half share*). **3** *adv.* to the extent of half, *loosely* to some extent (*half dead with cold*; *I am half convinced*). **4 at half cock** when only half-ready; **by half** excessively (*too clever by half*); **by halves** without complete commitment (usu. after *neg.*: *they never do things by halves*); **go halves** share equally (*with*); **half-and-half** being half one thing and half another; **half-back** player between forwards and full back in football, hockey, etc.; **half-baked** not thoroughly thought out, foolish; **half-binding** binding of book with leather on spine and corners; **half-breed** (or **-caste**) person of mixed race; **half-brother** (or **-sister**) brother (or sister) with only one parent in common; **half-crown, half a crown** *hist.* coin or amount of 2s. 6d.; **half-hearted** lacking enthusiasm, feeble; **half hitch** knot formed by passing end of rope round its standing part and then through the bight; **half-life** time after which radioactivity etc. is half its original value; **half-mast** position of flag half-way up mast, as mark of respect for dead person; **half measures** measures lacking thoroughness; **half moon** moon when only half its disc is illuminated, time when this occurs, semicircular object; **half nelson** hold in wrestling with arm under opponent's arm and behind his back; **half-term** period about half-way through school term usu. with short holiday; **half-timbered** having walls with timber frame and brick or plaster filling; **half-time** time at which half of game or contest is completed, interval then occurring; **half-title** title or short title of a book, usu. printed on recto of leaf preceding title-leaf; **half-tone** black-and-white photographic illustration in which light and dark shades are reproduced by small and large dots; **half-track** propulsion system with wheels at front and endless driven belt at back, vehicle having this; **half-truth** statement conveying only part of the truth; **half-volley** return of ball in tennis as soon as it has touched the ground, ball in cricket so pitched that batsman may hit it as it bounces, hit so made; **half-way** *a.* & *adv.* at point equidistant between two others; **half-way house** compromise; **not half** by no means, *colloq.* not at all, *sl.* extremely, violently (*he didn't half swear*). [OE]

halfpenny /ˈheɪpnɪ/ *n.* (*pl.* as PENNY) coin worth half a penny; **halfpennyworth** *n.*

half-wit *n.* stupid or foolish person; **half-witted** *a.*

halibut /ˈhælɪbət/ *n.* large flat-fish used for food. [HOLY (perh. because eaten on holy days), *butt* flat-fish]

halitosis /hælɪˈtəʊsɪs/ *n.* unpleasant-smelling breath. [L (*halitus* breath)]

hall /hɔːl/ *n.* space or passage into which front entrance of house etc. opens; large room or building for meetings, meals, concerts, etc.; large country house, esp. with landed estate; university building used for residence or instruction of students, (in college etc.) common dining-room; large public room in palace etc.; building of guild. [OE]

hallelujah var. of ALLELUIA.

halliard var. of HALYARD.

hallmark **1** *n.* mark indicating standard of gold, silver, and platinum; distinctive feature, esp. of excellence. **2** *v.t.* stamp with hallmark. [HALL]

hallo /həˈləʊ/ **1** *int.* used in greeting, or to call attention or express surprise. **2** *n.* (*pl.* **hallos**) the cry 'hallo'. [var. of earlier *hollo*]

halloo /həˈluː/ **1** *int.* & *n.* cry used to urge on hounds, or to attract attention. **2** *v.* shout 'halloo'. [perh. *hallow* pursue with shouts]

hallow /ˈhæləʊ/ *v.* make or honour as holy. [OE (HOLY)]

Hallowe'en /hæləʊˈiːn/ *n.* 31 Oct., the eve of All Saints' Day.

hallucinate /həˈluːsɪneɪt/ *v.* (cause to) experience hallucinations; **hallucinant** *a.* & *n.*

hallucination /həluːsɪˈneɪʃ(ə)n/ *n.* illusion of seeing or hearing external object not actually present; **hallucinatory** /həˈluːsɪnətərɪ/ *a.* [L f. Gk]

hallucinogen /həˈluːsɪnədʒ(ə)n/ *n.* drug causing hallucinations; **hallucinogenic** /-ˈdʒenɪk/ *a.* [-GEN]

halm var. of HAULM.

halo /ˈheɪləʊ/ **1** *n.* (*pl.* **haloes**) disc or ring of light shown round head of sacred figure; glory round idealized person etc.; disc of diffused light round luminous body, esp. sun or moon. **2** *v.t.* surround with halo. [L f. Gk *halōs* threshing-floor, disc of sun or moon]

halogen /ˈhælədʒɪn/ *n.* any of the non-metallic elements fluorine, chlorine, bromine, iodine, and astatine which form a salt by simple union with a metal etc. [Gk *hals halos* salt, -GEN]

halt[1] /hɔːlt, hɒlt/ 1 *n.* stop (usu. temporary), interruption to progress; railway stopping-place for local services, without station buildings. 2 *v.* come or bring to a halt. 3 **call a halt** decide to stop. [G (HOLD)]

halt[2] /hɔːlt, hɒlt/ 1 *v.i.* walk hesitatingly; (of argument, verse, etc., esp. in *partic.*) be defective. 2 *a. archaic* lame. [OE]

halter /'hɔːltə/ 1 *n.* rope or strap with headstall, used for leading or tying up horse; woman's dress with top held up by strap passing round back of the neck. 2 *v.t.* put halter on (horse). [OE]

halve /hɑːv/ *v.t.* divide into two halves or parts; reduce by half; (in golf) draw (hole or match) with opponent. [HALF]

halves *pl.* of HALF.

halyard /'hæljəd/ *n.* rope for raising or lowering sail, yard, etc. [HALE[2]]

ham 1 *n.* upper part of pig's leg salted and dried or smoked for food; meat from this; back of thigh, thigh and buttock; *sl.* inexpert performer or actor; *colloq.* operator of amateur radio station (*radio ham*). 2 *v.* (**-mm-**) overact, exaggerate one's actions (*ham it up*). 3 **ham-fisted** (or **-handed**) *sl.* clumsy. [OE]

hamburger /'hæmbɜːgə/ *n.* flat round cake of minced beef served fried, often eaten in soft bread roll. [*Hamburg* in Germany]

Hamitic /hə'mɪtɪk/ *a.* of group of African languages including ancient Egyptian and Berber. [*Ham* (Gen. 10: 6 ff.)]

hamlet /'hæmlɪt/ *n.* small village, esp. one without church. [F *hamelet* dimin.]

hammer 1 *n.* tool with heavy metal head at right angles to handle, used for breaking, driving nails, etc.; similar contrivance, as for exploding charge in gun, striking strings of piano, etc.; auctioneer's mallet indicating by rap that article is sold; metal ball attached to a wire for throwing as athletic contest. 2 *v.* hit or beat (as) with hammer; strike loudly; utterly defeat. 3 **come under the hammer** be sold at auction; **hammer and sickle** symbols of industrial worker and peasant used as emblem of USSR; **hammer and tongs** with great vigour and commotion; **hammer-head** shark with lateral extensions of head bearing the eyes; **hammer out** devise (plan etc.) with great effort; **hammer-toe** toe bent permanently downwards. [OE]

hammock /'hæmək/ *n.* bed of canvas or rope network, suspended by cords at ends, used esp. on board ship. [Sp. f. Carib]

hammy *a. sl.* of or like ham actors. [HAM]

hamper[1] *n.* large basket usu. with hinged lid, esp. with contents of food. [F (*hanap* goblet f. Gmc)]

hamper[2] *v.t.* prevent free movement or activity of; impede, hinder. [orig. unkn.]

hamster *n.* small ratlike rodent with cheek-pouches for carrying grain. [G]

hamstring 1 *n.* any of five tendons at back of human knee; great tendon at back of quadruped's hock. 2 *v.t.* (*past* and *p.p.* **hamstringed** or **hamstrung**) cripple (person, animal) by cutting hamstring(s); impair activity or efficiency of. [HAM]

hand 1 *n.* end part of human arm beyond wrist, similar member of monkey; control, custody, disposal (*fell into my hands*; *is in good hands*); share in action, active support (*have a hand in*; *lend a hand*); agency (*the hand of God*); thing like hand, esp. pointer of clock or watch; right or left side or direction relative to person or thing; pledge of marriage; skill, person with reference to skill (*an old hand at debating*); style of writing, signature; person who does or makes something (*a picture by the same hand*); person etc. as source (*at first, second,* etc., *hand*); manual worker in factory, farm, etc.; playing-cards dealt to a player, such player, round of play; *colloq.* applause; forefoot of quadruped, forehock of pork; measure of horse's height, = 4 in. 2 *attrib.* operated by hand (*hand-drill*); held or carried by hand (*hand-mirror*); done by hand not by machine (*hand-knitted*). 3 *v.t.* deliver, transfer by hand or otherwise (*down, in, over,* etc.); serve or distribute *round.* 4 **all hands** entire crew of ship; **at hand** close by, about to happen; **by hand** by a person not a machine, delivered by messenger not by post; **change hands** see CHANGE; **from hand to mouth** satisfying only one's immediate needs; **get** (or **have** or **keep**) **one's hand in** become (or be or remain) in practice; **hand and** (or **in**) **glove** in collusion or association (*with*); **hand down** transmit (decision) from higher court etc.; **hand it to** *colloq.* award deserved praise to; **hand-me-down** clothing etc. passed on from someone else; **hand-out** *n.* something given free to needy person, statement given to press etc.; **hand-over-fist** *colloq.* with rapid progress; **hand-picked** carefully chosen; **hands down** with no difficulty; **hand to hand** (of fighting) at close quarters; **have one's hands full** be fully occupied; **in hand** at one's disposal, under one's control, receiving attention; **off one's hands** no longer one's responsibility; **on hand** available; **on one's hands** resting on one as a responsibility; **on the one** (or **the other**) **hand** as one (or another) point of view; **out of hand** out of control, peremptorily (*refused out of hand*); **put** (or **set** or **turn**) **one's hand to** start work on, engage in; **to hand** within reach. [OE]

handbag *n.* small bag for purse etc., carried esp. by women.

handball *n.* game with ball thrown by hand among players.

handbell *n.* small bell rung by hand.

handbill *n.* printed notice circulated by hand.

handbook *n.* short manual or guide-book.

handbrake *n.* brake operated by hand.

h. & c. *abbr.* hot and cold (water).

handcart *n.* small cart pushed or drawn by hand.

handclap *n.* clapping of the hands.

handcuff 1 *v.t.* put handcuffs on. **2** *n.* (in *pl.*) pair of lockable linked metal rings for securing prisoner's wrists.

handful *n.* quantity that fills the hand; small number (*of* people or things); *colloq.* troublesome person or task.

handicap /'hændɪkæp/ **1** *n.* disadvantage imposed on superior competitor(s) in order to make chances more equal; race or contest in which this is imposed; number of strokes by which golfer normally exceeds par for course; thing that makes progress or success difficult; a physical or mental disability. **2** *v.t.* (**-pp-**) impose handicap on; place (person) at disadvantage. [phr. *hand i'* (= in) *cap* describing a kind of sporting lottery]

handicapped *a.* suffering from a physical or mental disability.

handicraft /'hændɪkrɑ:ft/ *n.* work that requires both manual and artistic skill [earlier *handcraft*]

handiwork /'hændɪwɜ:k/ *n.* work done or thing made by the hands, or by a particular person. [OE]

handkerchief /'hæŋkətʃɪf, -tʃi:f/ *n.* (*pl.* **handkerchiefs, -chieves** /-tʃi:vs/) square of linen, cotton, etc., usu. carried in pocket for wiping nose etc. [HAND, KERCHIEF]

handle /'hænd(ə)l/ **1** *n.* part by which thing is held, carried, or controlled; fact that may be taken advantage of (*gave a handle to his critics*); *colloq.* personal title. **2** *v.* touch, feel, or move with the hands; manage or deal with (*knows how to handle people*); deal in (goods); discuss or write about (subject). **3 fly off the handle** *colloq.* lose one's self-control. [OE (HAND)]

handlebar *n.* (often in *pl.*) steering-bar of bicycle etc., with hand-grip at each end; **handlebar moustache** thick moustache with curved ends.

handler *n.* person who handles things; person who handles animals, esp. one in charge of trained police-dog etc.

handmade *a.* made by hand not machine. [hand]

handmaid *n.* (also **-maiden**) *archaic* female servant.

handrail *n.* narrow rail for holding as support on stairs etc.

handset *n.* telephone mouthpiece and ear-piece as one unit.

handshake *n.* shaking of person's hand with one's own as greeting etc.

handsome /'hænsəm/ *a.* good-looking; generous (*a handsome present*); (of price, fortune, etc.) considerable.

handspring *n.* somersault in which one lands first on hands and then on feet.

handstand *n.* balancing on one's hands with feet in the air or against wall.

handwriting *n.* writing with pen, pencil, etc.; person's particular style of this; **handwritten** *a.*

handy *a.* convenient to handle or use; ready to hand; clever with the hands; **handily** *adv.*; **handiness** *n.*

handyman *n.* person able to do odd jobs.

hang 1 *v.* (*past* and *p.p.* **hung** except as below) cause thing to be supported from above, esp. with lower part free; set up (door) on hinges; place (picture) on wall or in exhibition, attach (wallpaper) to wall; decorate (room etc.) *with* pictures, ornaments, etc.; (*past* and *p.p.* **hanged**) execute or kill (person or *oneself*) by suspending from rope round neck; *colloq.* (as imprecation) = DAMN, be damned (*I'll be hanged if*; *hang the expense*); let droop (*hang one's head*); be or remain hung (in various senses), be hanged. **2** *n.* way a thing hangs. **3 get the hang of** *colloq.* get the knack of, understand; **hang about** (or **around**) loiter, not move away; **hang back** show reluctance; **hang fire** be slow in taking action or in progressing; **hang heavily** (or **heavy**) (of time) pass slowly; **hang on** stick or hold closely (*to*), depend on (circumstance), remain in office or doing one's duty etc., attend closely to, *colloq.* not ring off in telephoning, *sl.* wait for a short time; **hang out** lean out (*of* window etc.), put on clothes-line etc.; **hang over** threaten (*danger hangs over us*); **hang together** be coherent, remain associated; **hang up** hang from hook etc., put aside, end telephone conversation, cause delay to; **hang-up** *n. sl.* emotional inhibition or problem; **hung parliament** one in which no party has clear majority; **not care** (or **give**) **a hang** *colloq.* not care at all. [OE]

hangar /'hæŋə, -ŋgə/ *n.* shed for housing aircraft etc. [F]

hangdog *a.* shamefaced. [HANG]

hanger *n.* person or thing that hangs; shaped piece of wood etc. from which clothes may be hung; **hanger-on** (*pl.* **hangers-on**) follower or dependant, esp. unwelcome one.

hang-glider *n.* frame used in hang-gliding.

hang-gliding *n.* sport of gliding while being suspended from airborne frame controlled by one's movements.

hanging *n.* execution by being hanged; (in *pl.*) draperies hung on wall etc.

hangman *n.* executioner who hangs condemned persons.

hangnail *n.* agnail.

hangover *n.* severe headache or other after-effects caused by excess of alcohol; amount left over.

hank *n.* coil or length of wool or thread etc. [ON]

hanker *v.i.* long *for*, crave *after*. [obs. *hank*]

hanky /'hæŋkɪ/ *n. colloq.* handkerchief. [abbr.]

hanky-panky /hæŋkɪ'pæŋkɪ/ *n. sl.* dishonest dealing, trickery; naughtiness. [orig. unkn.]

Hanoverian /hænəʊ'vɪərɪən/ *a.* of British sovereigns from George I to Victoria. [*Hanover* in Germany]

Hansard /'hænsɑ:d/ *n.* official report of proceedings in Parliament. [*Hansard*, its orig. printer]

Hansen's disease /'hænsənz/ leprosy. [*Hansen*, physician]

hansom /'hænsəm/ *n.* (in full **hansom cab**) *hist.* two-wheeled horse-drawn cab for two inside, with driver seated behind. [*Hansom*, architect]

hap *archaic* **1** *n.* chance, luck; chance occurrence. **2** *v.i.* (**-pp-**) come about by chance. [ON]

haphazard /hæp'hæzəd/ **1** *a.* done etc. by chance, random. **2** *adv.* at random. [prec.]

hapless *a.* unlucky.

happen /'hæpən/ *v.i.* occur (by chance or otherwise); have the (good or bad) fortune (*to do* thing); be the fate or experience of (*what happened to you?*); come by chance *on*.

happening *n.* event; improvised or spontaneous theatrical etc. performance.

happy /'hæpɪ/ *a.* feeling or showing pleasure or contentment; fortunate; (of words or behaviour) apt, pleasing; **happy event** birth of child; **happy-go-lucky** cheerfully casual; **happy medium** means of satisfactory avoidance of extremes; **happily** *adv.*; **happiness** *n.*

hara-kiri /hærə'kɪrɪ/ *n.* ritual suicide with disembowelment with sword, formerly practised by Samurai to avoid dishonour. [Jap. *hara* belly, *kiri* cutting]

harangue /hə'ræŋ/ **1** *n.* lengthy and earnest speech. **2** *v.* make a harangue (to). [F f. L, perh. f. Gmc]

harass /'hærəs/ *v.t.* trouble and annoy continually; make repeated attacks on (enemy); **harassment** *n.* [F]

harbinger /'hɑ:bɪndʒə/ *n.* person or thing that announces or signals the approach of another; forerunner. [F f. Gmc (foll.)]

harbour /'hɑ:bə/, *US* **harbor** **1** *n.* place of shelter for ships; shelter. **2** *v.t.* give shelter to (criminal etc.); keep in one's mind (unfriendly thought etc.). **3 harbour-master** officer in charge of harbour. [OE, = army shelter]

hard 1 *a.* firm, unyielding to pressure, solid, not easily cut; difficult to understand or *to do*; not easily allowing one *to* (*hard to please*); difficult to bear, (of season or weather) severe; strenuous, enthusiastic (*hard worker*); (of person) unfeeling, harsh; unpleasant to ear or eye (*hard voice, colours*); (of liquor) strongly alcoholic; (of drug) potent and addictive; (of water) containing mineral salts that make lathering difficult; established, not disputable (*hard facts*); (of currency, prices, etc.) high, not likely to fall in value; (of pornography) highly obscene; (of consonant) guttural (as *c* in *cat*, *g* in *go*). **2** *adv.* strenuously, intensively, copiously (*try, work, raining, hard*). **3 be hard on** be severe in treatment or criticism of; **hard and fast** (of rule or distinction) definite, unalterable; **hard-boiled** (of egg) boiled until white and yolk are solid; **hard by** close by; **hard case** intractable person, case of hardship; **hard cash** coins and banknotes not cheque etc.; **hard copy** printed material produced by computer, suitable for ordinary reading; **hard core** irreducible nucleus, heavy material as road-foundation; **hard-headed** practical, not sentimental; **hard-hearted** unfeeling; **hard labour** heavy manual work as punishment; **hard line** unyielding adherence to firm policy; **hard luck** see LUCK; **hard of hearing** somewhat deaf; **hard on** (or **upon**) close to in pursuit etc.; **hard pad** form of distemper in dogs etc.; **hard palate** front part of palate; **hard-pressed** closely pursued, burdened with urgent business; **hard put to it** in difficulty; **hard roe** see ROE[1]; **hard sell**

aggressive salesmanship; **hard shoulder** hardened strip alongside motorway for stopping on in emergency; **hard up** short of money, at a loss *for*; **hard-wearing** able to stand much wear. [OE]
hardback 1 *a.* bound in stiff covers. 2 *n.* hardback book.
hardbitten *a.* tough and tenacious.
hardboard *n.* stiff board made of compressed and treated wood-pulp.
harden *v.* make or become hard or harder, or (of attitude etc.) unyielding.
hardihood /'hɑ:dɪhʊd/ *n.* boldness, daring. [HARDY]
hardly *adv.* only with difficulty; scarcely, only just; harshly. [HARD]
hardship *n.* severe suffering or privation; circumstance causing this.
hardware *n.* tools and household articles of metal etc.; heavy machinery or weaponry; mechanical and electronic components of computer etc.
hardwood *n.* hard heavy wood from deciduous tree.
hardy /'hɑ:dɪ/ *a.* robust, capable of enduring difficult conditions; (of plant) able to grow in the open air all the year; **hardy annual** annual plant that may be sown in the open, a subject that comes up at regular intervals. [F *hardi* f. Gmc (HARD)]
hare 1 *n.* field mammal like rabbit, with long ears, short tail, hind legs longer than forelegs, and divided upper lip. 2 *v.i.* run rapidly. 3 **hare-brained** wild and foolish, rash. [OE]
harebell *n.* plant with pale-blue bell-shaped flowers.
harelip *n.* congenital fissure of the upper lip.
harem /'hɑ:ri:m/ *n.* women of a Muslim household, living in separate part of house; their quarters. [Arab., = sanctuary]
haricot /'hærɪkəʊ/ *n.* (in full **haricot bean**) white dried seed of variety of bean. [F]
hark *v.i.* listen attentively; **hark back** revert *to* subject. [prob. OE]
harlequin /'hɑ:lɪkwɪn/ 1 *a.* in varied colours. 2 *n.* (**Harlequin**) mute character in pantomime, usu. dressed in diamond-patterned costume. [F]
harlequinade /hɑ:lɪkwɪ'neɪd/ *n.* part of pantomime featuring Harlequin; piece of buffoonery.
harlot /'hɑ:lət/ *n. archaic* prostitute; **harlotry** *n.* [F, = knave]
harm 1 *n.* hurt, damage. 2 *v.t.* cause harm to. 3 **out of harm's way** in safety. [OE]
harmful *a.* causing harm.
harmless *a.* not able or likely to cause harm; inoffensive.
harmonic /hɑ:'mɒnɪk/ 1 *a.* of or relating to harmony; harmonious; produced by vibration of string etc. in aliquot part of its length (*harmonic tones, overtones*). 2 *n.* harmonic tone or overtone. 3 **harmonically** *adv.* [L f. Gk (HARMONY)]
harmonica *n.* mouth-organ. [L (as prec.)]
harmonious /hɑ:'məʊnɪəs/ *a.* sweet-sounding; forming a pleasing or consistent whole; free from disagreement or dissent. [HARMONY]
harmonium /hɑ:'məʊnɪəm/ *n.* keyboard musical instrument in which notes are produced by air driven through metal reeds by bellows operated by the feet. [F f. L (HARMONY)]
harmonize /'hɑ:mənaɪz/ *v.* add notes to melody to produce harmony; bring into or be in harmony (*with*); **harmonization** /-'zeɪʃ(ə)n/ *n.* [F (foll.)]
harmony /'hɑ:mənɪ/ *n.* combination of simultaneously sounded musical notes to produce chords and chord progressions, study of this; pleasing effect of apt arrangement of parts; agreement, concord; **in harmony (with)** in agreement (with). [F f. L f. Gk *harmonia* joining]
harness /'hɑ:nɪs/ 1 *n.* equipment of straps and fittings by which horse is fastened to cart etc. and controlled; similar arrangement for fastening thing to person. 2 *v.t.* put harness on (horse), attach by harness (*to*); utilize (river or other natural force) to produce electrical power etc. 3 **in harness** in the routine of daily work. [F f. ON, = army provisions]
harp 1 *n.* large upright stringed instrument played by plucking with the fingers. 2 *v.* talk repeatedly and tediously *on* (subject). 3 **harpist** *n.* [OE]
harpoon /hɑ:'pu:n/ 1 *n.* barbed spear-like missile with rope attached, for catching whales etc. 2 *v.* spear with harpoon. [F, f. L f. Gk *harpē* sickle]
harpsichord /'hɑ:psɪkɔ:d/ *n.* keyboard instrument in which strings are plucked mechanically. [F *harpechorde* f. L *harpa* harp, *chorda* string]
harpy /'hɑ:pɪ/ *n.* mythical monster with woman's head and body and bird's wings and claws; grasping unscrupulous person. [F or L f. Gk *harpuiai* snatchers]
harquebus /'hɑ:kwɪbəs/ *n. hist.* portable gun supported on tripod or forked rest. [F f. G, = hook-gun]
harridan /'hærɪd(ə)n/ *n.* bad-tempered old woman. [orig. uncert.]
harrier /'hærɪə/ *n.* hound used for hunt-

ing hares; (in *pl.*) cross-country runners; a kind of falcon. [HARE, HARRY]

harrow /'hærəʊ/ **1** *n.* heavy frame with iron teeth dragged over ploughed land to break up clods, cover seed, etc. **2** *v.t.* draw harrow over (land); distress greatly. [ON]

harry /'hærɪ/ *v.t.* ravage or despoil; harass. [OE]

harsh *a.* unpleasantly rough or sharp, esp. to the senses; severe, cruel. [LG]

hart *n.* male of (esp. red) deer, esp. after 5th year. [OE]

hartebeest /'hɑ:tɪbi:st/ *n.* large African antelope with curving horns. [Afrik.]

harum-scarum /heərəm 'skeərəm/ **1** *a.* wild and reckless. **2** *n.* such person. [rhyming form. on HARE, SCARE]

harvest /'hɑ:vɪst/ **1** *n.* gathering in of crops etc., season of this; season's yield; product of any action. **2** *v.* gather as harvest, reap. **3 harvest festival** thanksgiving festival in church for harvest; **harvest moon** full moon nearest to autumn equinox (22 or 23 Sept.); **harvest mouse** very small mouse nesting in stalks of standing corn. [OE]

harvester *n.* reaper; reaping-machine.

has see HAVE.

has-been *n. colloq.* person or thing of declined importance. [BEEN]

hash[1] **1** *n.* dish of cooked meat cut into small pieces and recooked; mixture, jumble; re-used material. **2** *v.t.* make (meat) into hash. **3 make a hash of** *colloq.* make a mess of, bungle; **settle person's hash** *colloq.* deal with and subdue him. [F *hacher* (*hache* HATCHET)]

hash[2] *n. colloq.* hashish. [abbr.]

hashish /'hæʃi:ʃ/ *n.* top leaves and tender parts of hemp, dried for smoking or chewing as narcotic. [Arab.]

hasn't /'hæz(ə)nt/ *colloq.* = *has not.*

hasp /hɑ:sp/ *n.* hinged metal clasp that fits over staple and is secured by padlock. [OE]

hassle /'hæs(ə)l/ *colloq.* **1** *n.* quarrel, struggle; difficulty. **2** *v.* quarrel; harass. [dial.]

hassock /'hæsək/ *n.* thick firm cushion for kneeling on; tuft of grass. [OE]

haste /heɪst/ **1** *n.* urgency of movement or action, hurry. **2** *v.i.* hasten. **3 in haste** quickly, hurriedly; **make haste** be quick. [F f. Gmc]

hasten /'heɪs(ə)n/ *v.* make haste, hurry; cause to occur or be ready or be done sooner.

hasty /'heɪstɪ/ *a.* hurried, acting too quickly; said, made, or done too quickly or too soon; **hastily** *adv.*; **hastiness** *n.*

hat *n.* covering for the head, esp. worn out of doors; **hat trick** taking of 3 wickets at cricket by same bowler with 3 successive balls,; scoring of 3 goals or winning of 3 victories by one person; **keep it under one's hat** keep it secret; **out of a hat** by random selection; **pass the hat round** collect contributions of money; **take off one's hat to** applaud; **talk through one's hat** *sl.* talk wildly or ignorantly. [OE]

hatband *n.* band of ribbon etc. round hat above brim.

hatch[1] *n.* opening in floor or wall etc.; opening or door in aircraft etc.; cover for hatchway. [OE]

hatch[2] **1** *v.* (of young bird or fish etc.) emerge from egg; (of egg) produce young animal; incubate (egg); devise (plot etc.). **2** *n.* hatching, a brood hatched. [perh. f. OE]

hatch[3] *v.t.* mark with close parallel lines; **hatching** *n.* [F *hacher* (HASH)]

hatchback *n.* car with sloping back hinged at top to form door. [HATCH[1]]

hatchet /'hætʃɪt/ *n.* light short-handled axe; **hatchet man** hired killer, person employed to make personal attacks. [F *hachette* dimin. of *hache* (HASH[1])]

hatchway *n.* opening in ship's deck for lowering cargo. [HATCH[1]]

hate **1** *n.* hatred; *colloq.* hated person or thing. **2** *v.t.* feel hatred towards; dislike greatly; *colloq.* be reluctant (*I hate to bother you*). [OE]

hateful *a.* arousing hatred.

hatred /'heɪtrɪd/ *n.* intense dislike or ill will.

hatter *n.* maker or seller of hats. [HAT]

haughty /'hɔ:tɪ/ *a.* arrogantly self-admiring and disdainful; **haughtily** *adv.*; **haughtiness** *n.* [*haught, haut* f. F, = high]

haul /hɔ:l/ **1** *v.* pull or drag forcibly; transport by lorry or cart etc.; turn ship's course; *colloq.* bring *up* for reprimand or trial. **2** *n.* hauling; amount gained or acquired; distance to be traversed (*a short haul*). [var. of HALE[2]]

haulage *n.* transport of goods; charge for this.

haulier /'hɔ:lɪə/ *n.* firm or person engaged in transport of goods by road.

haulm /hɔ:m/ *n. collect.* stems of potatoes, peas, beans, etc. [OE]

haunch /hɔ:ntʃ/ *n.* fleshy part of buttock and thigh; leg and loin of deer etc. as food. [F f. Gmc]

haunt /hɔ:nt/ **1** *v.t.* (of ghost) visit (place) regularly usu. reputedly leaving signs of presence; be persistently in (a place); (of memory etc.) linger in the mind of. **2** *n.* place frequented by person. [F f. Gmc]

hautboy /'əʊbɔɪ/ *n.* obs. name of OBOE. [F]

haute couture /əʊt ku:'tjʊə/ high

fashion; leading fashion houses collectively, or their products. [F]
haute cuisine /əʊt kwɪ'zi:n/ high-class cookery. [F]
hauteur /əʊ'tɜ:/ *n.* haughtiness of manner. [F (HAUGHTY)]
Havana /hə'vænə/ *n.* cigar made at Havana or elsewhere in Cuba.
have[1] /həv, *emphat.* hæv/ *v.* (3 *sing. pres.* **has** /həz, *emphat.* hæz/; *past* and *p.p.* **had** /həd, *emphat.* hæd/; *partic.* **having**) **1** *v.t.* hold in possession or at one's disposal; hold in a certain relationship (*have a sister, no equals*); contain as part or quality (*has blue eyes; house has three floors*); undergo, experience, enjoy, suffer (*had a good time, a shock, a headache*); engage in (activity: *have breakfast, an argument, sex, a try*); give birth to (baby); know (a language), conceive mentally (an idea etc.); receive (*had good news*), eat or drink (*have a cup of tea*); be burdened with or committed to (*have a job, my duty, to do*); be provided with (*have nothing to do, to wear*); cause (person or thing) to be, do, etc. (*had him dismissed; had us worried; had my hair cut; had a copy made*); accept or tolerate, permit to (usu. *neg.*: *I won't have it, will not have you say such things*); let (feeling etc.) be present (*have no doubt; have nothing against them*); be influenced by quality etc. (*have mercy on us*); *colloq.* have sexual intercourse with; *colloq.* deceive or get the better of. **2** as auxiliary verb with *p.p.* of verbs forming past tenses (*I have, had, shall have, seen; had I known I would have gone*). **3 had better** see BETTER; **have had it** *colloq.* have missed one's chance, have passed one's prime, have been killed; **have it** express view *that,* win decision, *colloq.* have found answer, possess advantage; **have it in for** *colloq.* be hostile or ill-disposed to; **have it off** *sl.* have sexual intercourse; **have it out** settle dispute by argument (*with*); **have on** wear (clothes), have (engagement), tease or hoax; **have to** (or *colloq.* **have got to**) be obliged to, must; **have up** bring (person) before court of justice or to be interviewed. [OE]
have[2] /hæv/ *n.* one who has (esp. wealth or resources); *sl.* swindle; **haves and have-nots** rich and poor.
haven /'heɪv(ə)n/ *n.* refuge; harbour, port. [OE]
haven't /'hæv(ə)nt/ *colloq.* = *have not.*
haver /'heɪvə/ *v.i.* hesitate, vacillate; talk foolishly. [orig. unkn.]
haversack /'hævəsæk/ *n.* strong canvas etc. bag carried on the back or over the shoulder. [F f. G, = oats-sack]
havoc /'hævək/ *n.* widespread destruction, great disorder. [AF f. F *havo(t)*]
haw[1] *n.* hawthorn berry. [OE]
haw[2] see HUM.
hawfinch *n.* large finch with powerful beak.
hawk[1] **1** *n.* bird of prey with rounded wings shorter than falcon's; person who advocates aggressive policy. **2** *v.* hunt with hawk. **3 hawk-eyed** keen-sighted. [OE]
hawk[2] *v.* clear the throat of phlegm noisily; bring up (phlegm) thus. [imit.]
hawk[3] *v.t.* carry (goods) about for sale. [foll.]
hawker *n.* one who hawks goods about. [LG or Du.]
hawser /'hɔ:zə/ *n.* thick rope or cable for mooring or towing a ship. [F, = hoist (L *altus* high)]
hawthorn *n.* thorny shrub with small dark red berries. [HAW[1]]
hay *n.* grass mown and dried for fodder; **hay fever** allergic disorder caused by pollen or dust; **hit the hay** *sl.* go to bed; **make hay of** throw into confusion; **make hay while the sun shines** seize opportunities for profit. [OE]
haymaking *n.* mowing grass and spreading it to dry; **haymaker** *n.*
haystack *n.* (also **hayrick**) packed pile of hay with pointed or ridged top.
haywire *a. colloq.* badly disorganized, out of control.
hazard /'hæzəd/ **1** *n.* danger or risk, source of this; obstacle on golf-course. **2** *v.t.* risk; venture (action or suggestion etc.). [F f. Sp. f. Arab.]
hazardous *a.* risky.
haze *n.* thin atmospheric vapour; mental confusion or obscurity. [HAZY]
hazel /'heɪz(ə)l/ *n.* bush or small tree bearing small edible nuts; light brown colour; **hazel-nut** *n.* [OE]
hazy *a.* misty; vague, indistinct; confused, uncertain; **hazily** *adv.*; **haziness** *n.* [orig. unkn.]
HB *abbr.* hard black (pencil-lead).
H-bomb /'eɪtʃbɒm/ *n.* hydrogen bomb. [*H* for hydrogen]
HCF *abbr.* highest common factor.
he /hi:/ **1** *pron.* (*obj.* HIM; *poss.* HIS; *pl.* THEY) the man or boy or male animal previously named or in question; person etc. of unspecified sex. **2** *n.* male, man. **3** *a.* (usu. with hyphen) male (*he-goat*). **4 he-man** masterful or virile man. [OE]
HE *abbr.* high explosive; His or Her Excellency; His Eminence.
He *symb.* helium.
head /hed/ **1** *n.* upper part of human body or foremost part of animal's body, containing mouth, sense-organs, and brain; seat of intellect, imagination;

mental aptitude (*good head for business*; *no head for heights*); *colloq.* headache; person, individual (*£5 a* or *per head*); individual animal, *collect.* animals (*20 head*); image of head on one side of coin, (usu. in *pl.*) this side turning up in toss of coin; height or length of head as measure; thing like head in form or position, e.g. striking part of tool, flattened top of nail, mass of leaves or flowers at top of stem, flat end of drum; foam on top of beer etc.; component on tape-recorder that touches moving tape in play and converts signals; upper end (of table, occupied by host; of lake, at which river enters; of bed etc., for one's head); front (of procession etc.); top or highest part (of stairs, list, page, etc.); chief person or ruler, master etc. of college, headmaster; position of command; confined body of water or steam, pressure exerted by this; bows of ship; promontory (esp. in place-names: *Beachy Head*); division in discourse, category; culmination, climax or crisis, fully developed top of boil etc. **2** *v.* be at head of or in charge of; strike (ball) with head in football; provide with head or heading; face or move (in specified direction); direct course (of). **3 come to a head** reach climax; **give person his head** let him move or act freely; **go to one's head** (of liquor) make one dizzy or slightly drunk, (of success) make one conceited; **head-dress** ornamental covering or band for the head; **head first** (of plunge etc.) with head foremost, *fig.* precipitately; **head for** be moving towards (place, or *fig.* trouble etc.); **head off** get ahead so as to intercept, forestall; **head-on** *a.* & *adv.* (of collision etc.) head to head or front to front; **head over heels** rolling body over in forward direction, topsy turvy, completely; **head-shrinker** *sl.* psychiatrist; **head start** advantage granted or gained at early stage; **head wind** wind blowing from directly in front; **in one's head** by thought, not in writing; **keep** (or **lose**) **one's head** keep (or lose) calm or self-control; **make head or tail of** (usu. *neg.*) understand; **off one's head** *colloq.* crazy; **off the top of one's head** *colloq.* impromptu, at random; **on one's (own) head** being one's responsibility; **over one's head** beyond one's understanding; **over person's head** to a position or authority higher than his; **put heads together** consult together; **turn person's head** make him conceited. [OE]

headache *n.* continuous pain in the head; *colloq.* worrying problem.

headboard *n.* upright panel along head of bed.

header *n.* heading of ball in football; *colloq.* dive or plunge with head first; brick etc. laid at right angles to face of wall.

headgear *n.* hat or head-dress.

heading *n.* title at head of page or section of book etc.; horizontal passage in mine.

headlamp *n.* = HEADLIGHT.

headland *n.* promontory.

headlight *n.* powerful light at front of motor vehicle or railway engine; beam from this.

headline *n.* heading at top of article or page, esp. in newspaper; (in *pl.*) most important items in broadcast news bulletin.

headlong *a.* & *adv.* with head foremost; in a rush.

headman *n.* chief man of tribe etc.

headmaster /hed'mɑ:stə/ *n.* principal master of school; **headmistress** *n. fem.*

headphone *n.* telephone or radio receiver held over ear(s) by band fitting over head.

headquarters *n.* (as *sing.* or *pl.*) place where military or other organization is centred.

headroom *n.* space or clearance above vehicle etc.

headship *n.* position of chief or leader, esp. of headmaster or headmistress.

headstall *n.* part of halter or bridle fitting round horse's head.

headstone *n.* stone set up at head of grave.

headstrong *a.* self-willed and obstinate.

headwaters *n.pl.* streams formed from sources of river.

headway *n.* progress; rate of progress of ship; headroom.

headword *n.* word forming heading.

heady *a.* (of liquor) potent; (of success etc.) likely to cause conceit; impetuous; **headily** *adv.*; **headiness** *n.*

heal *v.* (of wound or injury) become sound or healthy again, cause to do this; put right (differences etc.), alleviate (sorrow etc.); *archaic* cure. [OE (WHOLE)]

health /helθ/ *n.* state of being well in body or mind; person's mental or physical condition (*has poor health*); **health centre** headquarters of a group of local medical services; **health food** natural food thought to have health-giving qualities; **health service** public service providing medical care; **health visitor** trained person visiting babies or sick or elderly people at their homes. [OE (WHOLE)]

healthful *a.* conducive to good health, beneficial; **healthfully** *adv.*

healthy *a.* having or showing or

producing good health; beneficial; **healthily** *adv.*; **healthiness** *n.*

heap 1 *n.* number of things lying on one another; *colloq.* (esp. in *pl.*) large number or amount. **2** *v.* put (things *up* etc.) or become piled (*up*) in a heap; load with large quantities; give in large number (*heaped insults on him*). [OE]

hear *v.* (*past* and *p.p.* **heard** /hɜ:d/) perceive with the ear; listen to; listen judicially to (case, party); be informed (*that*); be told (*about*); grant (prayer), obey (order); **hear from** receive letter etc. from; **hear! hear!** expression of agreement or applause; **hear of** be told about, (with *neg.*) consider, allow (*will not hear of it, of your paying*). [OE]

hearer *n.* one who hears, esp. as member of audience.

hearing *n.* faculty of perceiving sounds; range within which sounds may be heard, presence (*within hearing*; *in my hearing*); opportunity to be heard, giving of case in lawcourt esp. before judge without jury; **hearing-aid** small sound-amplifier worn by deaf person.

hearken /'hɑ:kən/ *v.i. archaic* listen (*to*). [OE (HARK)]

hearsay *n.* rumour, gossip. [HEAR]

hearse /hɜ:s/ *n.* vehicle for conveying coffin at funeral. [F *herse* harrow f. L *hirpex* large rake]

heart /hɑ:t/ *n.* hollow muscular organ maintaining circulation of blood by rhythmic contraction and dilation; region of the heart, breast; centre of thought, feeling, and emotion (esp. love); capacity for feeling emotion (*has a tender heart*); courage, enthusiasm (*take, lose, heart*); central or innermost part, essence; compact head of cabbage etc.; heart-shaped thing, figure of heart, playing-card of suit (**hearts**) marked with red shape of heart; **at heart** in one's inmost feelings, basically; **break person's heart** distress him overwhelmingly; **by heart** in or from memory; **change of heart** change in one's feeling about something; **give** (or **lose**) **one's heart to** fall in love with; **have the heart to** (usu. with *neg.*) be insensitive or hard-hearted enough *to do* thing; **heart attack** sudden occurrence of heart failure; **heart-break** overwhelming distress; **heart-breaking**, **-broken** causing, affected by, this; **heart failure** failure of the heart to function properly; **heart-lung machine** machine which can temporarily take over functions of heart and lungs; **heart-rending** very distressing; **heart-searching** examination of one's own feelings and motives; **heart-strings** one's deepest feelings; **heart-throb** beating of heart, *colloq.* object of romantic affections; **heart-to-heart** candid; **heart-warming** emotionally rewarding or uplifting; **set one's heart on** want eagerly; **take to heart** be much affected by; **to one's heart's content** see CONTENT[2]; **with all one's heart** sincerely, with all goodwill. [OE]

heartache *n.* mental anguish.

heartbeat *n.* pulsation of heart.

heartburn *n.* burning sensation in chest, pyrosis.

hearten *v.* make or become more cheerful.

heartfelt *a.* sincere, deeply felt.

hearth /hɑ:θ/ *n.* floor of fireplace; area in front of this; the home. [OE]

heartily *adv.* in hearty manner; very (*heartily sick of it*). [HEARTY]

heartland *n.* central part of an area.

heartless *a.* unfeeling, pitiless.

heartsick *a.* despondent.

hearty *a.* strong, vigorous; (of meal or appetite) copious; warm, friendly; **heartiness** *n.* [HEART]

heat 1 *n.* being hot, form of energy arising from motion of bodies' molecules; hot weather; warmth of feeling, excitement, anger; preliminary or trial round in race or contest; receptive period of sexual cycle, esp. in female mammals; redness of skin with sensation of heat. **2** *v.* make or become hot, inflame. **3 heat shield** device to protect (esp. spacecraft) from excessive heat; **heat-stroke** illness caused by excessive heat; **heat wave** period of very hot weather. [OE]

heated *a.* (of person or discussion etc.) angry, inflamed with passion or excitement.

heater *n.* stove or other heating device.

heath *n.* area of flat uncultivated land with low shrubs; plant (e.g. heather) growing on heath. [OE]

heathen /'hi:ð(ə)n/ **1** *n.* one who is not member of a widely-held religion, esp. not Christian, Jew, or Muslim. **2** *a.* of heathens, having no religion. **3 the heathen** heathen people. [OE]

heather /'heðə/ *n.* low shrub with small usu. purple bell-shaped flowers. [orig. unkn.]

Heath Robinson /hi:θ 'rɒbɪns(ə)n/ absurdly ingenious and impracticable. [cartoonist]

heave 1 *v.* (*past* **heaved** or *Naut.* **hove**) lift or haul (heavy thing) with great effort; utter with effort (*heaved a sigh*); *colloq.* throw; *Naut.* haul by rope; rise and fall alternately like waves at sea; pant, retch. **2** *n.* heaving. **3 heave in sight** come into view; **heave to** bring (ship) or come to a standstill with ship's head to the wind. [OE]

heaven /'hev(ə)n/ *n.* place believed to be abode of God and of the righteous after death; (usu. **Heaven**) God, Providence; place or state of supreme bliss; something delightful; **the heavens** sky as seen from the earth, in which sun, moon, and stars appear; **heaven-sent** providential. [OE]

heavenly *a.* of heaven, divine; of the heavens or sky; *colloq.* very pleasing; **heavenly bodies** sun, stars, etc.

heavy /'hevɪ/ **1** *a.* of great or unusually high weight, difficult to lift; abundant, considerable (*a heavy crop*); severe, intense, extensive (*heavy fighting, frost, losses, sleep*); doing thing to excess (*heavy drinker*); striking, falling, with force (*heavy blows, sea, storm*); carrying heavy weapons (*the heavy brigade*); (of machinery, artillery, etc.) very large of its kind, large in calibre etc.; (of person, writing, music, etc.) serious or sombre in tone or attitude, dull, tedious; (of food or *fig.* of writings) hard to digest; dignified, stern (*heavy father*); of great density, esp. (of bread etc.) dense from not rising; (of ground) difficult to traverse; oppressive, hard to endure; ungraceful (*heavy features*), unwieldy. **2** *n.* villainous or tragic role or actor in play etc.; (usu. in *pl.*) serious newspaper, heavy vehicle. **3** *adv.* heavily (esp. in *comb.*: *heavy-laden*). **4 heavier-than-air** (of aircraft) weighing more than the air it displaces; **heavy-duty** *a.* intended to withstand hard use; **heavy going** slow or difficult progress; **heavy-handed** clumsy, oppressive; **heavy-hearted** sad, doleful; **heavy hydrogen** = DEUTERIUM; **heavy industry** that producing metal, machinery, etc.; **heavy metal** heavy guns, metal of high density; **heavy water** deuterium oxide; **make heavy weather of** exaggerate difficulty or burden presented by problem etc. **5 heavily** *adv.*; **heaviness** *n.* [OE]

heavyweight *n.* heaviest boxing-weight, with no upper limit; person of above average weight; person of influence or importance; **light heavyweight** boxing-weight with upper limit of 81 kg.

hebdomadal /heb'dɒməd(ə)l/ *a.* weekly. [L f. Gk (*hepta* seven)]

Hebraic /hi:'breɪɪk/ *a.* of Hebrew or the Hebrews. [L f. Gk (HEBREW)]

Hebraist /'hi:breɪɪst/ *n.* expert in Hebrew.

Hebrew /'hi:bru:/ **1** *n.* member of a Semitic people in ancient Palestine; their language; modern form of this used esp. in Israel. **2** *a.* of or in Hebrew; of the Jews. [F f. L f. Gk f. Heb.]

heck *n. colloq.* (in oaths) = HELL. [HELL]

heckle /'hek(ə)l/ *v.t.* interrupt and harass (public speaker). [var. of HACKLE]

hectare /'hektɑ:/ *n.* metric unit of square measure, 100 ares (2.471 acres). [F (HECTO-, ARE)]

hectic /'hektɪk/ *a.* busy and confused, excited; feverish; **hectically** *adv.* [F f. L f. Gk *hektikos* habitual]

hecto- *in comb.* hundred. [F f. Gk *hekaton*]

hectogram /'hektəgræm/ *n.* metric unit of mass, equal to 100 grams.

hector /'hektə/ **1** *v.t.* bully, intimidate. **2** *n.* bully. [*Hector* in *Iliad*]

hedge 1 *n.* fence or boundary formed by closely planted bushes or shrubs; protection against possible loss. **2** *v.* surround or bound with hedge; shut *in*; make or trim hedges; reduce one's risk of loss on bet etc. by compensating transactions on the other side; avoid committing oneself. **3 hedge-hop** fly at very low altitude; **hedge-sparrow** common brown-backed bird, dunnock. [OE]

hedgehog *n.* small insect-eating mammal with piglike snout and thick coat of spines, rolling itself up into a ball when attacked.

hedgerow *n.* row of bushes etc. forming hedge.

hedonic /hi:'dɒnɪk/ *a.* of pleasure. [Gk (foll.)]

hedonism /'hi:dənɪz(ə)m/ *n.* belief in pleasure as the proper aim; **hedonist** *n.*; **hedonistic** /-'nɪstɪk/ *a.* [Gk *hēdonē* pleasure]

heebie-jeebies /'hi:bɪdʒi:bɪz/ *n.pl. sl.* nervous depression or anxiety. [orig. unkn.]

heed 1 *v.* attend to, take notice of. **2** *n.* careful attention (*take heed*). [OE]

heedless *a.* not taking heed.

hee-haw /'hi:hɔ:/ **1** *n.* bray of donkey. **2** *v.i.* bray like donkey. [imit.]

heel[1] **1** *n.* back part of foot below ankle; part of sock covering heel, part of shoe etc. supporting heel; thing like heel in form or position, e.g. part of palm next to wrist, handle-end of violin bow; *sl.* rogue, villain. **2** *v.* Fit or renew heel on (shoe etc.); touch ground with heel, as in dancing; pass ball with heel in Rugby football. **3 at** (or **to**) **heel** (of dog or *fig.*) close behind, under control; **at** (or **on**) **the heels of** following closely after (person or event); **cool** (or **kick**) **one's heels** be kept waiting; **down at heel** (of shoe) with heel worn down, (of person) shabby; **take to one's heels** run away; **turn on one's heel** turn sharply round; **well-heeled** wealthy. [OE]

heel[2] **1** *v.* (of ship) tilt temporarily to one side; cause (ship) to do this. **2** *n.* act or amount of heeling. [prob. f. OE]

heel[3] var. of HELE.
heelball *n.* mixture of hard wax and lampblack used by shoemakers for polishing; this or similar mixture used in brass-rubbing. [HEEL[1]]
hefty /'heftɪ/ *a.* (of person) big and strong; (of thing) large, heavy, powerful; **heftily** *adv.*; **heftiness** *n.* [*heft* weight (HEAVE)]
hegemony /hɪ'gemənɪ/ *n.* leadership, esp. by one State of a confederacy. [Gk (*hēgemōn* leader)]
Hegira /'hedʒɪrə/ *n.* the flight of Muhammad from Mecca (AD 622), from which the Muslim era is reckoned. [L f. Arab.]
heifer /'hefə/ *n.* young cow, esp. one that has not had a calf. [OE]
heigh /heɪ/ *int.* expressing surprise or curiosity. [*heh*, imit.]
height /haɪt/ *n.* measurement from base to top or (of standing person) from head to foot; elevation (of object or position) above ground or sea level; high place or area; top; highest point, utmost degree. [OE (HIGH)]
heighten *v.* make or become higher or more intense.
heinous /'heɪnəs/ *a.* utterly odious or wicked. [F (*haïr* hate)]
heir /eə/ *n.* person entitled to property or rank as legal successor of its former owner; **heir apparent** heir whose claim cannot be set aside by the birth of another heir; **heir presumptive** one whose claim may be set aside thus; **heiress** *n. fem.* [F f. L (*heres hered-*)]
heirloom *n.* piece of personal property that has been in family for several generations; piece of property as part of inheritance.
Hejira var. of HEGIRA.
held *past* and *p.p.* of HOLD.
hele *v.t.* set (plant) in ground and cover its roots *in*. [OE]
helical /'helɪk(ə)l/ *a.* having form of helix. [HELIX]
helicopter /'helɪkɒptə/ *n.* aircraft lifted and propelled by engine-driven blades or rotors revolving horizontally. [F f. Gk (HELIX, *pteron* wing)]
helio- *in comb.* sun. [Gk *hēlios* sun]
heliocentric /hi:lɪəʊ'sentrɪk/ *a.* considered as viewed from sun's centre; regarding sun as centre.
heliograph /'hi:lɪəʊgrɑ:f/ **1** *n.* signalling device reflecting sun's rays in flashes; message sent by this. **2** *v.t.* send (message) thus. [-GRAPH]
heliotrope /'hi:lɪətrəʊp/ *n.* plant with small fragrant purple flowers; light purple colour. [L f. Gk (HELIO-, *trepō* turn)]
heliport /'helɪpɔ:t/ *n.* place where helicopters take off and land. [after *airport*]
helium /'hi:lɪəm/ *n.* light non-inflammable gas used in airships. [as HELIO-]
helix /'hi:lɪks/ *n.* (*pl.* **helices** /-lɪsi:z/) spiral (like corkscrew, or in one plane like watch-spring); **double helix** pair of parallel helices with common axis, esp. in structure of DNA molecule. [L f. Gk]
hell *n.* abode of the dead or of devils and condemned spirits in some beliefs; place or state of misery or wickedness; *colloq.* used as exclamation of surprise or annoyance (*who the hell are you?*; *a hell of a mess*); **beat** (or **knock**) **hell out of** pound heavily; **come hell or high water** no matter what the obstacles; **for the hell of it** just for fun; **get hell** *colloq.* be scolded or punished; **give person hell** scold or punish him; **hell-bent** recklessly determined (*on*); **hell-fire** fire(s) of hell; **hell for leather** at full speed (usu. of rider); **hell's angel** violent lawless youth, usu. one of gang on motor cycles. [OE]
hellebore /'helɪbɔ:/ *n.* plant with white or greenish flowers, of genus including Christmas rose. [F f. L f. Gk]
Hellene /'heli:n/ *n.* ancient Greek; native of modern Greece; **Hellenic** /-'li:nɪk/ *a.* [Gk]
Hellenism /'helɪnɪz(ə)m/ *n.* Greek character or culture (esp. of ancient Greece); **Hellenist** *n.*
Hellenistic /helɪ'nɪstɪk/ *a.* of the Greek language and culture of 4th–1st cc. BC.
hellish *a.* of or like hell; extremely unpleasant. [HELL]
hello var. of HALLO.
helm *n.* tiller or wheel by which ship's rudder is controlled; **at the helm** at the head of an organization etc., in control. [OE]
helmet /'helmɪt/ *n.* protective head-covering worn by policeman, fireman, diver, motor-cyclist, etc. [F f. Gmc]
helmsman /'helmzmən/ *n.* one who steers ship. [HELM]
helot /'helət/ *n.* serf, esp. in ancient Sparta. [L f. Gk]
help 1 *v.t.* provide (person etc.) with means towards what is needed or sought (*helped me with my work*; *helped me* (*to*) *pay my debts*); be of use or service to (person, or *absol.*); contribute to alleviating (pain or difficulty); prevent, remedy (*it can't be helped*); refrain from (*cannot help laughing*). **2** *n.* act of helping (*we need your help*; *come to our help*); person or thing that helps; domestic servant(s), employee(s); remedy etc. (*there is no help for it*). **3 cannot help oneself** cannot avoid undesired action; **help**

oneself (to) take without seeking help or permission; **help person out** give him help, esp. in difficulty; **help person to** serve him with (food at meal). [OE]
helpful *a.* giving help, useful; **helpfully** *adv.*
helping *n.* portion of food at meal.
helpless *a.* lacking help, defenceless; having or showing inability to act without help; unable to help oneself.
helpmate *n.* helpful companion or partner.
helter-skelter /heltə'skeltə/ 1 *adv.* in disorderly haste. 2 *n.* tall structure with external spiral track for sliding down. [imit.]
helve *n.* handle of weapon or tool. [OE]
hem[1] 1 *n.* border of cloth where edge is turned under and sewn down. 2 *v.t.* (**-mm-**) turn down and sew in edge of (cloth etc.). 3 **hem in** confine, restrict movement of; **hem-stitch** *n.* ornamental stitch, (*v.t.*) hem with this. [OE]
hem[2] 1 *int.* calling attention or expressing hesitation by slight cough. 2 *n.* utterance of this. 3 *v.i.* (**-mm-**) say *hem*, hesitate in speech. [imit.]
hemal etc. *US* var. of HAEMAL etc.
hemi- *prefix* half. [Gk, = L SEMI-]
hemipterous /he'mɪptərəs/ *a.* of insect order including aphids, bugs, and cicadas, with base of front wings thickened. [Gk *pteron* wing]
hemisphere /'hemɪsfɪə/ *n.* half a sphere; any half of the earth, esp. as divided by the equator (*Northern* or *Southern hemisphere*) or by line passing through poles (*Eastern* or *Western hemisphere*); **hemispherical** /-'sferɪk(ə)l/ *a.* [L f. Gk (HEMI-, SPHERE)]
hemline *n.* lower edge of skirt or dress. [HEM[1]]
hemlock /'hemlɒk/ *n.* poisonous plant with small white flowers; poison made from it. [OE]
hemp *n.* Asian herbaceous plant; its fibre used to make rope and stout fabrics; any of several narcotic drugs made from hemp plant. [OE]
hempen *a.* made of hemp.
hen *n.* female bird, esp. of the common domestic fowl; **hen-party** *colloq.* social gathering of women only. [OE]
henbane *n.* poisonous plant with unpleasant smell.
hence *adv.* from this time (*five years hence*); for this reason; *archaic* from here. [OE]
henceforth /hens'fɔ:θ/ *adv.* (also **henceforward**) from this time onwards.
henchman *n.* trusty supporter. [OE *hengest* horse, MAN)]
henge /hendʒ/ *n.* prehistoric monument of circle of massive stone or wood uprights. [*Stonehenge* in Wiltshire]
henna /'henə/ *n.* tropical shrub; reddish dye made from it and used esp. on the hair. [Arab.]
henpeck *v.t.* (of wife) domineer over (husband). [HEN]
henry /'henrɪ/ *n.* (*pl.* **henries**) unit of inductance. [*Henry*, physicist]
hep *a. sl.* aware of the latest trends and styles. [orig. unkn.]
hepatic /hɪ'pætɪk/ *a.* of the liver. [L f. Gk (*hēpar -atos* liver)]
hepatitis /hepə'taɪtɪs/ *n.* inflammation of the liver. [-ITIS]
hepta- *in comb.* seven. [Gk]
heptagon /'heptəgən/ *n.* plane figure with seven sides and angles; **heptagonal** /-'tægən(ə)l/ *a.* [Gk (HEPTA-, *-gōnos* -angled)]
her 1 *pron.* obj. case of SHE; *colloq.* = SHE (*it's her all right*). 2 *poss. a.* of or belonging to her; (in titles) that she is (*Her Majesty*). [OE dat. & gen. of SHE]
herald /'herəld/ 1 *n.* forerunner; messenger, bringer of news; official concerned with pedigrees and coats of arms; *hist.* official who made state proclamations, carried royal messages, etc. 2 *v.t.* proclaim approach of, usher in. 3 **heraldic** /he'rældɪk/ *a.* [F f. Gmc, = army-rule]
heraldry *n.* art or knowledge of a herald; armorial bearings.
herb *n.* plant whose stem is soft and dies down to the ground after flowering; plant whose leaves or seeds etc. are used for flavouring, food, medicine, scent, etc.; **herbiferous** /hɜ:'bɪfərəs/ *a.*; **herby** *a.* [F f. L *herba*]
herbaceous /hɜ:'beɪʃəs/ *a.* of or like herbs; **herbaceous border** garden border containing esp. perennial flowering plants. [L (prec.)]
herbage *n.* herbs collectively, esp. as pasture. [F f. med.L (HERB)]
herbal 1 *a.* of herbs in medicinal and culinary use. 2 *n.* manual describing these. [med.L (HERB)]
herbalist *n.* dealer in medicinal herbs; writer on herbs.
herbarium /hɜ:'beərɪəm/ *n.* systematic collection of dried plants; book, case, or room for these. [L (HERB)]
herbicide /'hɜ:bɪsaɪd/ *n.* toxic substance used to destroy unwanted vegetation. [-CIDE]
herbivore /'hɜ:bɪvɔ:/ *n.* herbivorous animal. [foll.]
herbivorous /hɜ:'bɪvərəs/ *a.* feeding on plants. [L *voro* devour]
herculean /hɜ:kjʊ'li:ən/ *a.* extremely strong; (of task) requiring great

strength. [*Hercules*, L alt. of Gk *Herakles*]

herd 1 *n*. a number of cattle or other animals feeding or staying together; large number of people, mob. **2** *v*. collect, go, or drive in a herd; tend (sheep or cattle). **3 herd instinct** tendency to remain or conform with the majority. [OE]

herdsman *n*. person who tends a herd of animals.

here 1 *adv*. in or at or to this place or position (*sit here*; *come here*); at this point (in speech, performance, writing, etc.). **2** *int*. calling attention or as command; as reply (= I am present) in roll-call. **3** *n*. this place (*lives near here*; *fill it up to here*). **4 here and there** in or to various places; **here goes** I am ready to begin; **here's to** I drink to the health of; **neither here nor there** of no importance. [OE]

hereabouts /ˈhɪərəbaʊts/ *adv*. (also **hereabout**) near this place.

hereafter /hɪərˈɑːftə/ **1** *adv*. in future, from now on. **2** *n*. the future; life after death.

hereby /hɪəˈbaɪ/ *adv*. by this means, as a result of this.

hereditable /hɪˈredɪtəb(ə)l/ *a*. that can be inherited. [F or L (HEIR)]

hereditary /hɪˈredɪtərɪ/ *a*. descending by inheritance; able to be transmitted from one generation to another; holding hereditary office. [L (HEIR)]

heredity *n*. biological transmission of physical or mental characteristics from parents to children; these characteristics; genetic constitution.

Hereford /ˈherɪfəd/ *n*. one of a breed of red and white beef cattle. [*Hereford* in England]

herein /hɪərˈɪn/ *adv*. *formal* in this place or document, etc.

hereinafter /hɪərɪnˈɑːftə/ *adv*. *formal* in later part of this document etc.

hereof /hɪərˈɒv/ *adv*. *archaic* of this.

heresy /ˈherɪsɪ/ *n*. opinion contrary to doctrine of Christian Church, or to accepted doctrine on any subject. [F f. L f. Gk (*hairesis* choice)]

heretic /ˈherɪtɪk/ *n*. one advocating a heresy (esp. in religion); **heretical** /hɪˈretɪk(ə)l/ *a*.

hereto /hɪəˈtuː/ *adv*. *archaic* to this.

heretofore /hɪətʊˈfɔː/ *adv*. *formal* formerly.

hereupon /hɪərəˈpɒn/ *adv*. after or in consequence of this.

herewith /hɪəˈwɪð/ *adv*. with this (esp. of enclosure in letter etc.).

heritable /ˈherɪtəb(ə)l/ *a*. that can be inherited or inherit; transmissible from parent to offspring. [F (HEIR)]

heritage /ˈherɪtɪdʒ/ *n*. what is or may be inherited; inherited circumstances or benefits; one's portion or lot.

hermaphrodite /hɜːˈmæfrədaɪt/ **1** *n*. person or animal having characteristics or organs of both sexes; plant in which same flower has stamens and pistils. **2** *a*. having such characteristics. **3 hermaphroditic** /-ˈdɪtɪk/ *a*. [L f. Gk, orig. the name of son of *Hermes* and *Aphrodite*]

hermetic /hɜːˈmetɪk/ *a*. with an airtight closure; **hermetically** *adv*. [L (*Hermes* Gk god regarded as founder of alchemy)]

hermit /ˈhɜːmɪt/ *n*. person (esp. early Christian) who lives in solitude; **hermit-crab** crab that lives in mollusc's cast-off shell; **hermitic** /-ˈmɪtɪk/ *a*. [F *ermite* or L f. Gk (*erēmos* solitary)]

hermitage *n*. place of hermit's retreat; secluded dwelling.

hernia /ˈhɜːnɪə/ *n*. protrusion of part of organ through aperture in enclosing membrane etc., esp. of abdomen. [L]

hero /ˈhɪərəʊ/ *n*. (*pl*. **heroes**) man admired for great deeds and noble qualities; chief male character in poem, play, or story; **hero-worship** excessive devotion to admired person. [L f. Gk *hērōs*]

heroic /hɪˈrəʊɪk/ **1** *a*. having characteristics of or suited to a hero, very brave. **2** *n*. (in *pl*.) over-dramatic talk or behaviour; (in *pl*.) heroic verse. **3 heroic verse** form used in epic poetry, e.g. iambic pentameter. **4 heroically** *adv*. [F or L f. Gk (prec.)]

heroin /ˈherəʊɪn/ *n*. sedative addictive drug prepared from morphine. [G]

heroine /ˈherəʊɪn/ *n*. female hero. [F or L f. Gk (HERO)]

heroism /ˈherəʊɪz(ə)m/ *n*. heroic conduct or qualities. [F *héroïsme* (HERO)]

heron /ˈherən/ *n*. wading bird with long neck and legs. [F f. Gmc]

heronry *n*. place where herons breed.

herpes /ˈhɜːpiːz/ *n*. virus disease causing blisters on the skin. [L f. Gk (*herpō* creep)]

Herr /heə/ *n*. (*pl*. **Herren**) German man; title of German man, = Mr. [G]

herring /ˈherɪŋ/ *n*. N. Atlantic fish used for food; **herring-bone** stitch or weave suggesting bones of herring, zigzag pattern; **herring gull** large gull with dark wing-tips. [OE]

hers /hɜːz/ *poss. pron*. of or belonging to her, the thing(s) belonging to her (*it is hers*; *hers are best*; *a friend of hers*). [HER]

herself /hɜːˈself/ *pron*. emphat. & refl. form of SHE and HER (*she went herself*; *she herself said it*; *she has hurt herself*; *ask the girl herself*); **be herself** behave in her normal manner, be in her normal health and spirits. [OE (HER, SELF)]

hertz *n.* (*pl.* same) unit of frequency, equal to one cycle per second. [*Hertz*, physicist]
hesitant /'hezɪtənt/ *a.* irresolute, hesitating; **hesitancy** *n.* [foll.]
hesitate /'hezɪteɪt/ *v.i.* feel or show uncertainty or reluctance, pause in doubt; be reluctant (*I hesitate to say so*); **hesitation** /-'teɪʃ(ə)n/ *n.* [L (*haero haes-* stick fast)]
hessian /'hesɪən/ *n.* strong coarse fabric of hemp or jute, sack-cloth. [*Hesse* in Germany]
het *a.* only in **het up** *sl.* excited, overwrought. [dial. = heated]
hetaera /hɪ'tɪərə/ *n.* (*pl.* **hetaerae** /-i:/) courtesan, esp. in ancient Greece. [Gk]
hetero- *in comb.* other, different. [Gk *heteros* other]
heterodox /'hetərəʊdɒks/ *a.* not orthodox; **heterodoxy** *n.* [L (HETERO-, Gk *doxa* opinion)]
heterodyne /'hetərəʊdaɪn/ *a.* relating to production of lower radio frequency from combination of two high frequencies. [HETERO-, Gk *dunamis* force]
heterogeneous /hetərəʊ'dʒi:nɪəs/ *a.* diverse in character; varied in content; **heterogeneity** /-dʒɪ'ni:ɪtɪ/ *n.* [L f. Gk (*genos* kind)]
heteromorphic /hetərəʊ'mɔ:fɪk/ *a.* of dissimilar forms; **heteromorphism** *n.* [HETERO-]
heterosexual /hetərəʊ'seksjʊəl/ **1** *a.* characterized by attraction to the opposite sex. **2** *n.* heterosexual person. **3** **heterosexuality** /-'ælɪtɪ/ *n.*
heuristic /hjʊə'rɪstɪk/ *a.* serving or helping to find out or discover; proceeding by trial and error. [Gk *heuriskō* find]
hew *v.* (*p.p.* **hewed** or **hewn**) chop or cut with axe, sword, etc.; cut into shape. [OE]
hexa- *in comb.* six. [Gk]
hexagon /'heksəgən/ *n.* plane figure with six sides and angles; **hexagonal** /-'ægən(ə)l/ *a.* [L f. Gk (HEXA-, *-gōnos* -angled)]
hexagram /'heksəgræm/ *n.* six-pointed star formed by two intersecting equilateral triangles. [HEXA-]
hexameter /hek'sæmɪtə/ *n.* line of six metrical feet.
hey /heɪ/ *int.* calling attention or expressing surprise or inquiry; **hey presto!** conjuror's formula in performing trick. [cf. HEIGH]
heyday /'heɪdeɪ/ *n.* time of greatest success or prosperity. [LG]
HF *abbr.* high frequency.
Hf *symb.* hafnium.
hg *abbr.* hectogram(s).
Hg *symb.* mercury. [L *hydrargyrum*]
HGV *abbr.* heavy goods vehicle.
HH *abbr.* double-hard (pencil-lead).
hi /haɪ/ *int.* calling attention or as greeting. [var. of HEY]
hiatus /haɪ'eɪtəs/ *n.* break or gap in sequence or series; break between two vowels coming together but not in same syllable. [L (*hio* gape)]
hibernate /'haɪbəneɪt/ *v.i.* (of animal) spend winter in dormant state; **hibernation** /-'neɪʃ(ə)n/ *n.* [L (*hibernus* of winter)]
Hibernian /haɪ'bɜ:nɪən/ **1** *a.* of Ireland. **2** *n.* native of Ireland. [L *Hibernia* f. Gk f. Celt.]
hibiscus /hɪ'bɪskəs/ *n.* cultivated shrub with large bright-coloured flowers. [Gk *hibiskos* marsh mallow]
hiccup /'hɪkʌp/ (also **hiccough**) **1** *n.* involuntary spasm of respiratory organs with abrupt cough-like sound. **2** *v.i.* make hiccup. [imit.]
hick *n.* *US colloq.* country bumpkin. [fam. form of *Richard*]
hickory /'hɪkərɪ/ *n.* N. American tree related to walnut; its hard wood. [Virginian *pohickery*]
hid *past* of HIDE[1].
hidalgo /hɪ'dælgəʊ/ *n.* (*pl.* **hidalgos**) member of lower nobility in Spain. [Sp. (*hijo dalgo* son of something)]
hidden *p.p.* of HIDE[1].
hide[1] **1** *v.* (*past* **hid**; *p.p.* **hidden**) put or keep out of sight, prevent from being seen; keep (fact etc.) secret (*from*); conceal oneself. **2** *n.* concealed place for observing wildlife. **3** **hide-and-seek** children's game in which player hides and is sought by others; **hide-out** *colloq.* hiding-place. [OE]
hide[2] *n.* animal's skin, raw or dressed; *colloq.* the human skin. [OE]
hidebound *a.* rigidly conventional, narrow-minded.
hideous /'hɪdɪəs/ *a.* very ugly, revolting. [AF *hidous*]
hiding[1] *n.* state of remaining hidden (*went into hiding*). [HIDE[1]]
hiding[2] *n.* *colloq.* a thrashing. [HIDE[2]]
hie /haɪ/ *v.i.* & *refl.* *archaic* or *poetic* go quickly. [OE]
hierarchy /'haɪərɑ:kɪ/ *n.* system in which grades of status or authority rank one above another; **hierarchical** /-'rɑ:kɪk(ə)l/ *a.* [L f. Gk (*hieros* sacred, *arkhō* rule)]
hieratic /haɪə'rætɪk/ *a.* of the priests (esp. of ancient Egyptian writing). [L f. Gk (*hiereus* priest)]
hieroglyph /'haɪərəglɪf/ *n.* picture or symbol representing word, syllable, or sound, used in ancient Egyptian and other writing. [foll.]
hieroglyphic /haɪərə'glɪfɪk/ **1** *a.* of or

written in hieroglyphs. **2** *n.* (in *pl.*) hieroglyphs, hieroglyphic writing. [F or L f. Gk (*hieros* sacred, *gluphō* carve)]

hi-fi /'haɪfaɪ/ *colloq.* **1** *a.* high fidelity. **2** *n.* high-fidelity equipment. [abbr.]

higgledy-piggledy /hɪg(ə)ldɪ'pɪg(ə)ldɪ/ *a.* & *adv.* disordered, in confusion. [orig. uncert.]

high /haɪ/ **1** *a.* of great upward extent (*a high building*); situated far above ground, sea level, etc. (*high altitude*); of specified upward extent (*one inch high*; *knee-high*); coming above normal level (*jersey with high neck*); (of physical action) done at or reaching a height (*high flight, kick*); of exalted rank or authority (*High Admiral*); extreme, intense, above the normal (*high fever, prices, temperature, wind*); extreme in opinion (*high Tory*); of superior quality (*high living, principles*); favourable (*high opinion*); (of time) far advanced, fully reached (*high summer*; *it is high time we left*); (of sound) shrill; (of meat etc.) beginning to go bad, (of game) hung until slightly decomposed and ready to cook; *colloq.* intoxicated by or *on* alcohol or drugs. **2** *n.* high or highest level or number; area of high pressure; *sl.* euphoric state caused by drug. **3** *adv.* far up, aloft; in or to high degree; at a high price; (of sound) at or to high pitch. **4 high and dry** aground, stranded; **high and low** everywhere (*searched high and low*); **high and mighty** *colloq.* pompous, arrogant; **high chair** young child's chair for meals, with long legs and usu. attached tray; **High Church** section of Church of England emphasizing ritual, priestly authority, and sacraments; **High Commission** embassy from one Commonwealth country to another; **High Commissioner** head of this; **High Court (of Justice)** supreme court for civil cases; **higher education** education at university etc.; **higher mammal, plant,** etc. those more highly developed; **high explosive** explosive with violent shattering effect; **high-falutin(g)** *colloq.* bombastic, pretentious; **high fidelity** reproduction of sound with quality close to the original; **high-flown** (of language etc.) extravagant, bombastic; **high-flyer, -flier** ambitious person, person or thing with potential for great achievements; **high-flying** ambitious; **high frequency** (in radio) 3–30 megahertz; **high-handed** overbearing; **high jump** athletic contest of jumping over high horizontal bar (**be for the high jump** be likely to receive severe punishment); **high-level** (of discussions etc.) conducted by persons of highest rank; **high-level language** computer language close to ordinary language and usu. not machine-readable; **high-minded** having high moral principles; **high-pitched** (of sound or voice) shrill, (of roof) steep; **high-powered** having or using great power, important or influential; **high pressure** high degree of activity or exertion, condition of atmosphere with pressure above average; **high priest** chief priest, head of cult; **high-rise** (of building) having many storeys; **high road** main road; **high school** secondary (esp. grammar) school; **high seas** open seas not under any country's jurisdiction; **high season** regular period of greatest number of visitors at resort etc.; **high-spirited** in high spirits, cheerful; **high spot** *colloq.* most important place or feature; **high street** principal street of town etc.; **high table** elevated table at public dinner or in college etc., for most important guests or members; **high tea** evening meal of tea and cooked food; **high-tech** *colloq.* characterized by high technology, (of interior design etc.) imitating styles more usual in industry etc.; **high technology** state of advanced technological development; **high tension** high voltage; **high tide** tide at highest level, time of this; **high treason** treason against one's ruler or country; **high-up** *colloq.* person of high rank; **high water** high tide; **high-water mark** level reached at high water, highest recorded point or value; **high wire** high tightrope; **on high** in or to high place or heaven. [OE]

highball *n.* *US* drink of spirits and soda etc. served with ice in tall glass.

highbrow *colloq.* **1** *a.* intellectual or highly cultural in interest or appeal. **2** *n.* highbrow person.

highland **1** *n.* (usu. in *pl.*) mountainous country, esp. (**Highlands**) of N. Scotland. **2** *a.* of highland or Scottish Highlands (*Highland dress*). **3 Highland cattle** breed with shaggy hair and long curved horns. [OE, = promontory (HIGH)]

highlander *n.* native or inhabitant of highlands or (**Highlander**) of Scottish Highlands.

highlight **1** *n.* moment or detail of vivid interest; outstanding feature; bright part of picture. **2** *v.t.* bring into prominence. [HIGH]

highly *adv.* in a high degree (*highly amusing, paid, probable*); favourably (*thinks highly of you*); **highly-strung** very sensitive and nervous.

highness *n.* title used in addressing or referring to a prince or princess (*Your,*

Her, etc., *Highness*); state of being high (esp. *fig*.).

highway *n*. public road; main route; conductor transmitting signals in computer; **Highway Code** set of rules issued officially for guidance of road-users; **King's** (or **Queen's**) **highway** public road regarded as protected by royal power.

highwayman *n*. *hist*. man, usu. mounted, who held up and robbed travellers on highway.

hijack /'haɪdʒæk/ **1** *v.t*. seize control of (vehicle or aircraft), esp. to force it to new destination; seize (goods in transit). **2** *n*. hijacking. [orig. unkn.]

hike 1 *n*. long walk, esp. across country. **2** *v.i*. go for a hike; walk laboriously. [orig. unkn.]

hilarious /hɪ'leərɪəs/ *a*. boisterously merry; extremely funny; **hilarity** /hɪ'lærɪtɪ/ *n*. [L f. Gk *hilaros*]

Hilary term /'hɪlərɪ/ university and law term beginning in January. [*Hilarius*, bishop (Anglican festival 13 Jan.)]

hill *n*. natural elevation of ground, not as high as mountain; sloping piece of road; heap or mound (*anthill*). [OE]

hill-billy *n*. folk music like that of southern US; *US colloq*. (often *derog*.) person from remote rural area in a southern State.

hillock /'hɪlək/ *n*. small hill, mound.

hillside *n*. sloping side of hill.

hilly *a*. having many hills; **hilliness** *n*.

hilt *n*. handle of sword, dagger, etc.; **up to the hilt** completely. [OE]

him *pron*. obj. case of HE[1]; *colloq*. = HE[1] (*it's him all right*). [OE, dat. of HE[1]]

himself /hɪm'self/ *pron*. emphat. & refl. form of HE[1] and HIM (for uses cf. HERSELF). [OE (HIM, SELF)]

hind[1] /haɪnd/ *a*. situated at the back (*hind legs*). [prob. f. OE]

hind[2] /haɪnd/ *n*. female of (esp. red) deer, esp. in and after third year. [OE]

hinder[1] /'hɪndə/ *v.t*. impede, prevent or retard progress of. [OE]

hinder[2] /'haɪndə/ *a*. rear, hind (*the hinder part*). [prob. f. OE]

Hindi /'hɪndɪ/ *n*. one of official languages of India, a literary form of Hindustani; group of spoken languages of northern India. [Urdu (*Hind* India)]

hindmost *a*. furthest behind. [HIND[1]]

hindquarters /haɪnd'kwɔ:təz/ *n.pl*. hind legs and adjoining parts of quadruped.

hindrance /'hɪndrəns/ *n*. thing that hinders; hindering, being hindered. [HINDER[1]]

hindsight *n*. wisdom after the event. [HIND[1]]

Hindu /hɪn'du:/ **1** *n*. adherent of Hinduism. **2** *a*. of the Hindus. [Urdu, f. Pers. (*Hind* India)]

Hinduism /'hɪndu:ɪz(ə)m/ *n*. religious and social system esp. in India, with worship of several gods and caste system.

Hindustani /hɪndʊ'stɑ:nɪ/ *n*. language based on Hindi, used in N. India and Pakistan. [HINDU, *-stān* country]

hinge /hɪndʒ/ **1** *n*. movable joint on which door, lid, etc. turns or swings; principle on which all depends. **2** *v*. attach or be attached by hinge; depend *on*. [HANG]

hinny /'hɪnɪ/ *n*. offspring of she-ass and stallion. [L *hinnus* f. Gk]

hint 1 *n*. slight or indirect indication or suggestion; small piece of practical information. **2** *v*. suggest slightly or indirectly. **3 broad hint** clear and unmistakable hint; **drop a hint** make hint; **hint at** refer indirectly to; **take a hint** understand hint. [obs. *hent* grasp]

hinterland /'hɪntəlænd/ *n*. district behind coast or river's banks; area served by port or other centre. [G]

hip[1] *n*. projection formed by pelvis and upper part of thigh-bone; **hip-bath** portable bath in which one sits immersed to the hips; **hip-bone** bone forming hip; **hip-flask** flattish flask for spirits, carried in hip-pocket; **hip-pocket** trouser-pocket just behind hip. [OE]

hip[2] *n*. fruit of (esp. wild) rose. [OE]

hip[3] *int*. used in cheering (*hip, hip, hurrah*). [orig. unkn.]

hip[4] *a*. *sl*. var. of HEP.

hippie /'hɪpɪ/ *n*. young person who rejects conventional ideas and society and adopts unusual style of dress, living habits, etc. [HIP[4]]

hippo /'hɪpəʊ/ *n*. (*pl*. **hippos**) *colloq*. hippopotamus. [abbr.]

Hippocratic oath /hɪpə'krætɪk/ oath of proper conduct taken by those beginning medical practice. [*Hippocrates*, Gk physician]

hippodrome /'hɪpədrəʊm/ *n*. music- or dance-hall; (in classical antiquity) course for chariot races, etc. [F or L f. Gk (*hippos* horse, *dromos* race)]

hippopotamus /hɪpə'pɒtəməs/ *n*. (*pl*. **hippopotamuses**) large African mammal with short legs and thick skin, inhabiting rivers etc. [L f. Gk (*hippos* horse, *potamos* river)]

hippy var. of HIPPIE.

hipster *a*. (of garment) hanging from the hips rather than the waist. [HIP[1]]

hire 1 *v.t*. obtain use of (thing) or services of (person) temporarily, for payment; (often with *out*) give use of thus. **2** *n*. hiring; payment for this. **3 for** (or **on**)

hire ready to be hired; **hire-purchase** system by which thing becomes hirer's after a number of payments. [OE]
hireling *n.* (usu. *derog.*) person who works for hire.
hirsute /'hɜ:sju:t/ *a.* hairy, shaggy. [L]
his /hɪz/ *poss. pron.* & *a.* of or belonging to him, the thing(s) belonging to him (*it is his*; *his are best*; *a friend of his*); (in titles) that he is (*His Majesty*). [OE, gen. of HE[1]]
Hispanic /hɪs'pænɪk/ *a.* of Spain (and Portugal); of Spain and other Spanish-speaking countries. [L (*Hispania* Spain)]
hiss 1 *n.* sharp sibilant sound, as of letter *s*. **2** *v.* make hiss; express disapproval (of) by hisses; utter with angry hiss. [imit.]
histamine /'hɪstəmɪn, -i:n/ *n.* chemical compound in body tissues, causing some allergic reactions. [HISTOLOGY, AMINE]
histogram /'hɪstəgræm/ *n.* statistical diagram in which frequency of values of a quantity is shown by columns. [Gk *histos* mast]
histology /hɪs'tɒlədʒɪ/ *n.* science of organic tissues. [Gk *histos* tissue]
historian /hɪ'stɔ:rɪən/ *n.* writer of history; person learned in history. [F (HISTORY)]
historic /hɪ'stɒrɪk/ *a.* famous or important in history or potentially so; *Gram.* (of tense) normally used of past events. [L f. Gk (HISTORY)]
historical *a.* of or concerning history or facts in history (*historical evidence*); having occurred in fact not legend or rumour; (of novel etc.) dealing with past period; (of study of subject) showing development over period of time; **historically** *adv.*
historicism /hɪ'stɒrɪsɪz(ə)m/ *n.* belief that historical events are governed by laws; tendency to stress historical development and influence of the past etc.
historicity /hɪstə'rɪsɪtɪ/ *n.* historical truth or authenticity.
historiography /hɪstɒrɪ'ɒgrəfɪ/ *n.* writing of history; study of this; **historiographer** *n.* [F or L f. Gk (foll., -GRAPH)]
history /'hɪstərɪ/ *n.* continuous record of (esp. public) events; study of the past involving human affairs or of any related thing, person, place, time, or activity; systematic or critical analysis of or research into past events etc.; similar record or account of natural phenomena; sequence of (esp. significant) past events in certain connection (*house has a history*); historical play etc.; **make history** do something memorable. [L f. Gk *historia* inquiry]
histrionic /hɪstrɪ'ɒnɪk/ **1** *a.* of acting; dramatic or theatrical in manner. **2** *n.* (in *pl.*) theatricals; dramatic behaviour intended to impress others. [L (*histrio* actor)]
hit 1 *v.* (-tt-; *past* and *p.p.* **hit**) strike with blow or missile; aim blow *at*; come against (thing) with force; have effect on (person), cause to suffer; propel (a ball etc.) with bat or club, to score runs or points; *colloq.* encounter (*hit a snag*), light upon, achieve, reach (*can't hit the high notes*); *sl.* attack, raid. **2** *n.* blow, stroke; shot that reaches its target; success, esp. in popularity. **3 hit-and-run** causing damage or injury and fleeing immediately; **hit back** retaliate; **hit below the belt** give unfair blow to, treat unfairly; **hit in the eye** be glaringly obvious to; **hit it off** get on well (*with* person); **hit list** *sl.* list of people to be killed or eliminated etc.; **hit man** *sl.* hired assassin; **hit the nail on the head** guess or explain precisely; **hit on** find (solution etc., esp. by chance); **hit-or-miss** aimed or done carelessly; **hit out** deal vigorous blows (*lit.* or *fig.*); **hit parade** list of best-selling records of popular music; **hit the right note** see NOTE; **hit the road** *sl.* depart; **make a hit** win popularity. [OE f. ON]
hitch 1 *v.* move (thing) with slight jerk; fasten or be fastened with loop or hook etc.; hitch-hike, obtain (a lift) in this way. **2** *n.* temporary difficulty, snag; slight jerk; any of various kinds of noose or knot. **3 get hitched** *sl.* get married. [orig. uncert.]
hitch-hike *v.* travel by seeking free rides in passing vehicles.
hither /'hɪðə/ **1** *adv.* to or towards this place. **2** *a.* situated on this side; the nearer (of two). **3 hither and thither** to and fro. [OE]
hitherto /hɪðə'tu:/ *adv.* until this time, up to now.
Hittite /'hɪtaɪt/ **1** *n.* member or language of an ancient people of Asia Minor and Syria. **2** *a.* of the Hittites. [Heb.]
hive 1 *n.* box etc. for housing bees; bees occupying hive; scene of busy activity. **2** *v.* place (bees) in hive; store (as) in hive. **3 hive off** separate from larger group. [OE]
hives *n.pl.* skin eruption, esp. nettle-rash. [orig. unkn.]
HM *abbr.* Her or His Majesty('s).
HMS *abbr.* Her or His Majesty's Ship.
HMSO *abbr.* Her or His Majesty's Stationery Office.
HNC *abbr.* Higher National Certificate.
HND *abbr.* Higher National Diploma.
ho /həʊ/ *int.* expressing triumph or scorn, or calling attention. [natural excl.]

Ho *symb.* holmium.
hoar *a.* grey with age; greyish-white; **hoar-frost** frozen water vapour on lawns etc. [OE]
hoard 1 *n.* carefully kept store of money etc. **2** *v.* amass and store in hoard. [OE]
hoarding *n.* temporary fence of light boards round building; structure erected to carry advertisements etc. [*hoard* f. F (HURDLE)]
hoarse *a.* (of voice) rough and deep-sounding, husky, croaking; having hoarse voice. [ON]
hoary *a.* (of hair) white or grey with age; having such hair, aged; (of joke etc.) old. [OE]
hoax 1 *v.* deceive, esp. by way of joke. **2** *n.* humorous or mischievous deception. [prob. contr. of HOCUS(-POCUS)]
hob *n.* flat metal shelf at side of fireplace, where kettle, pan, etc., can be heated; flat heating surface on cooker. [perh. var. of HUB]
hobbit /'hɒbɪt/ *n.* one of an imaginary race of half-sized persons in stories by J. R. R. Tolkien. [invented]
hobble /'hɒb(ə)l/ **1** *v.* (cause to) walk lamely; tie legs of (horse etc.) to limit its movement. **2** *n.* hobbling walk; rope etc. for hobbling a horse. [prob. LG]
hobby /'hɒbɪ/ *n.* occupation or activity pursued for pleasure, not as livelihood. [name *Robin*]
hobby-horse *n.* stick with horse's head, used as toy; figure of horse used in morris dance etc.; favourite subject or idea.
hobgoblin /'hɒbgɒblɪn/ *n.* mischievous or evil spirit; bugbear. [HOBBY, *goblin*]
hobnail *n.* heavy-headed nail for boot-soles. [HOB]
hob-nob *v.i.* (**-bb-**) associate or spend time (*with*). [*hab nab* have or not have]
hobo /'həʊbəʊ/ *n.* (*pl.* **hobos**) *US* wandering workman or tramp. [orig. unkn.]
Hobson's choice /'hɒbsənz/ option of taking what is offered or nothing. [*Hobson*, carrier who let out horses thus]
hock[1] *n.* joint of quadruped's hind leg between knee and fetlock. [OE]
hock[2] *n.* a German white wine. [*Hochheim* in Germany]
hock[3] *v.t. sl.* pawn; **in hock** in pawn, in prison, in debt. [Du.]
hockey /'hɒkɪ/ *n.* game played between two teams with hooked sticks and small hard ball. [orig. unkn.]
hocus-pocus /həʊkəs 'pəʊkəs/ *n.* trickery; typical formula used by conjurors. [sham L]
hod *n.* builder's light trough on pole for carrying bricks etc.; container for shovelling and holding coal. [F *hotte* pannier]
hodgepodge /'hɒdʒpɒdʒ/ var. of HOTCHPOTCH.
hoe 1 *n.* long-handled tool with blade, used for loosening soil or scraping up weeds etc. **2** *v.* (*partic.* **hoeing**) weed (crops), loosen (ground), dig up (weeds), with hoe. [F f. Gmc]
hog 1 *n.* castrated male pig; *colloq.* greedy person. **2** *v.* (**-gg-**) take greedily; hoard selfishly. **3 go the whole hog** *sl.* do thing thoroughly; **hog's back** steep-sided hill-ridge. **4 hoggish** *a.* [OE]
hogmanay /'hɒgmənеɪ/ *n. Sc.* New Year's Eve. [prob. F]
hogshead *n.* large cask; liquid or dry measure, usu. about 50 gallons. [HOG]
hogwash *n.* nonsense, rubbish.
ho-ho /həʊ'həʊ/ *int.* expressing surprise, triumph, or derision. [redupl. of HO]
hoick *v.t. sl.* lift or bring (*out*), esp. with jerk. [perh. var. of HIKE]
hoi polloi /hɔɪ pə'lɔɪ/ the masses, the common people. [Gk, = the many]
hoist 1 *v.t.* raise or haul up; lift with ropes and pulleys etc. **2** *n.* apparatus for hoisting things; hoisting. **3 hoist with one's own petard** caught by one's own trick etc. [*hoise* prob. f. LG]
hoity-toity /hɔɪtɪ'tɔɪtɪ/ *a.* haughty. [obs. *hoit* romp]
hokum /'həʊkəm/ *n. sl.* poor or crude theatrical plot or scenario; bunkum. [orig. unkn.]
hold[1] /həʊld/ **1** *v.* (*past* and *p.p.* **held**) keep fast in one's hands, arms, etc., grasp; keep or sustain (thing, *oneself*, one's head, etc.) in particular position or attitude; grasp so as to control (*hold the reins*); have capacity for, contain (*jug holds two pints*); have gained (qualification or achievement), have position of (job or office); possess or own (land, property, shares, etc.); occupy militarily, keep possession of against attack; conduct or celebrate (conversation, meeting, festival); keep (person) in place or condition (*hold him at bay, in suspense*); engross (person or attention); dominate (*holds the stage*); keep (person) *to* (promise etc.); detain in custody; remain unbroken (under pressure etc.), (of weather) continue fine, (of circumstance or condition) remain *good* or *true*; regard (*hold it cheap, dear*; *hold him in contempt, esteem*); think, believe, assert *that*, (of judge or court) decide (*that*); restrain (*hold your fire*); *colloq.* cease. **2** *n.* grasp (*lit.* or *fig.*: *catch, get, take*, etc., *hold of*); manner or means of holding, thing to hold by; means of influence (*on* or *over* person). **3 hold back** restrain, hesitate, refrain *from*; **hold down** repress, *colloq.* be competent enough to

keep (one's job); **hold forth** speak at length or tediously; **hold it!** cease action etc.; **hold it against person** regard it as to his discredit (*that*); **hold the line** not ring off (on telephone); **hold off** delay, keep one's distance, not begin; **hold on** maintain one's grasp, wait a moment, not ring off (on telephone); **hold out** offer (inducement etc.), (of supplies etc.) last, maintain resistance, continue to make demand *for*; **hold out on** *colloq.* refuse something to (person); **hold over** postpone; **hold one's own** maintain one's position, not be beaten; **hold up** hinder or obstruct, support or sustain, stop with force and rob; **hold-up** *n.* stoppage or delay, robbery by force; **hold water** (of reasoning) be sound, bear examination; **hold with** (usu. with *neg.*) approve of; **no holds barred** all methods permitted; **take hold** (of custom or habit) become established. [OE]

hold² /həʊld/ *n.* cavity below deck of ship for cargo. [OE (HOLLOW)]

holdall *n.* large soft travelling bag. [HOLD¹]

holdfast *n.* clamp securing object to wall etc.

holding *n.* tenure of land; land or stocks held; **holding company** one formed to hold shares of other companies, which it then controls.

hole 1 *n.* cavity in solid body; opening through or sunken place on surface; animal's burrow; small or gloomy place; *sl.* awkward situation; hollow or cavity into which ball etc. must be got in various games; (in golf) section of course between tee and hole. **2** *v.* make hole(s) in; pierce side of (ship); put into hole. **3 hole-and-corner** underhand; **hole in the heart** congenital defect in heart membrane; **hole up** *US sl.* hide oneself; **make a hole in** use large amount of (one's supply); **pick holes in** find fault with. **4 holey** *a.* [OE]

holiday /ˈhɒlɪdeɪ/ **1** *n.* day of break from one's normal work, esp. for recreation or festivity; (also in *pl.*) period of this, period of recreation away from home; religious festival. **2** *v.i.* spend a holiday. [OE (HOLY, DAY)]

holiness /ˈhəʊlmɪs/ *n.* being holy or sacred; **His Holiness** title of Pope. [HOLY]

holland /ˈhɒlənd/ *n.* smooth hard-wearing linen fabric; **brown holland** this fabric unbleached. [*Holland*, = Netherlands]

holler *v.* & *n.* *US colloq.* shout.

hollow /ˈhɒləʊ/ **1** *a.* having a cavity, not solid; sunken (*hollow cheeks*); empty, hungry; (of sound) echoing, as if made in or on hollow container; empty, worthless (*hollow victory*); insincere (*hollow laugh*). **2** *n.* hollow or sunken place, hole, valley. **3** *adv.* completely (*beat their opponents hollow*). **4** *v.* excavate (often with *out*); form into hollow shape. [OE]

holly /ˈhɒlɪ/ *n.* evergreen shrub with prickly leaves and red berries, used to decorate houses and churches at Christmas. [OE]

hollyhock /ˈhɒlɪhɒk/ *n.* tall plant with showy flowers. [HOLY, obs. *hock* mallow]

holmium /ˈhəʊlmɪəm/ *n.* metallic element of lanthanide series. [L *Holmia* Stockholm]

holm-oak /ˈhəʊməʊk/ *n.* evergreen oak with holly-like leaves, ilex. [dial. *holm* holly]

holocaust /ˈhɒləkɔːst/ *n.* large-scale destruction, esp. by fire. [F f. L f. Gk (*holos* whole, *kaustos* burnt)]

hologram /ˈhɒləgræm/ *n.* photographic pattern that gives a three-dimensional image when illuminated with coherent light. [Gk *holos* whole, -GRAM]

holograph¹ /ˈhɒləgrɑːf/ *v.t.* record as hologram; **holography** /-ˈlɒgrəfɪ/ *n.* [prec., after *telegraph*]

holograph² /ˈhɒləgrɑːf/ **1** *a.* wholly written by person named as author. **2** *n.* holograph document. [F or L f. Gk (*holos* whole, -GRAPH)]

hols /hɒlz/ *n. colloq.* holidays. [abbr.]

holster /ˈhəʊlstə/ *n.* leather case for pistol or revolver, usu. fixed to saddle or belt. [Du.]

holy /ˈhəʊlɪ/ *a.* morally and spiritually excellent and to be revered; belonging to or devoted to God; consecrated, sacred; **holier-than-thou** *colloq.* self-righteous; **Holy Communion** see COMMUNION; **Holy Ghost** = *Holy Spirit*; **Holy Grail** see GRAIL; **Holy Land** W. Palestine; **holy of holies** sacred inner chamber of Jewish temple, any place or retreat regarded as most sacred; **holy orders** see ORDER; **Holy See** papacy or papal court; **Holy Spirit** Third Person of the Trinity, God as spiritually acting; **Holy Week** week before Easter Sunday; **Holy Writ** holy writings esp. the Bible. [OE, rel. to WHOLE]

homage /ˈhɒmɪdʒ/ *n.* tribute, expression of reverence (*pay homage to*); (in feudal law) formal expression of allegiance. [F f. L (*homo* man)]

Homburg /ˈhɒmbɜːg/ *n.* man's hat with curled brim and lengthwise dent in crown. [*Homburg* in Germany]

home 1 *n.* place where one lives, fixed residence of family or household; native land; institution for persons needing care or rest etc. (*old people's home*); place where thing originates or is native or most common; finishing point in race; (in games) home match or win. **2** *a.* of or connected with one's home; carried on, done, or made, at home; in one's own country, not foreign; (of game) played on one's own ground etc. (*home match, win*). **3** *adv.* to or at one's home (*go home; is he home yet?*); to the point aimed at or as far as possible (*drove the nail home*). **4** *v.* (of pigeon etc.) make way home; (of vessel, missile, etc., often with *in*) be guided to destination or *on* target. **5 at home** in one's own house etc., at ease, familiar or well-informed (*in, on, with,* subject), available to callers; **at-home** *n.* reception of visitors within certain hours; **bring home to** cause to realize; **come home to** become realized by; **home and dry** having achieved one's aim; **Home Counties** counties closest to London; **home economics** study of household management; **home farm** farm worked by owner of estate containing other farms; **Home Guard** British volunteer army organized for defence in 1940; **home help** person who helps with housework etc.; **home-made** made at home; **Home Office** British government department dealing with law and order etc. in England and Wales; **Home Rule** government of a country or region by its own citizens; **Home Secretary** government minister in charge of Home Office; **home truth** (usu. unwelcome) truth about oneself heard from another. [OE]

homeland *n.* one's native land; area in South Africa reserved for Bantu.

homeless *a.* lacking a dwelling-place.

homely *a.* simple, plain, unpretentious; *US* (of facial appearance) unattractive; **homeliness** *n.*

homeopathy etc. *US* var. of HOMOEOPATHY etc.

homer *n.* homing pigeon.

Homeric /həʊˈmerɪk/ *a.* of the writings of Homer; of Bronze Age Greece as described in them. [L f. Gk]

homesick *a.* depressed by absence from home.

homespun 1 *a.* made of yarn spun at home; plain, simple. **2** *n.* homespun fabric.

homestead /ˈhəʊmsted/ *n.* house with outbuildings, farm.

homeward /ˈhəʊmwəd/ **1** *adv.* (also **homewards**) towards home. **2** *a.* going towards home. [-WARD]

homework *n.* work to be done at home by school pupil; preparatory work or study.

homicide /ˈhɒmɪsaɪd/ *n.* killing of one person by another; person who kills another; **homicidal** /-ˈsaɪd(ə)l/ *a.* [F f. L (*homo* man, -CIDE)]

homily /ˈhɒmɪlɪ/ *n.* sermon, moralizing lecture; **homiletic** /-ˈletɪk/ *a.* [F f. L f. Gk]

homing *a.* (of pigeon) trained to fly home from a distance; (of device) for guiding to target etc. [HOME]

hominid /ˈhɒmɪnɪd/ **1** *a.* of the mammal family of existing and fossil man. **2** *n.* member of this family. [L *homo homin-* man]

hominoid /ˈhɒmɪnɔɪd/ **1** *a.* manlike. **2** *n.* animal resembling man.

homo /ˈhəʊməʊ/ *n.* (*pl.* **homos**) *colloq.* homosexual. [abbr.]

homo- *in comb.* same. [Gk *homos* same]

homoeopathy /həʊmɪˈɒpəθɪ/ *n.* treatment of disease by minute doses of drugs that in a healthy person would produce its symptoms; **homoeopathic** /-ˈpæθɪk/ *a.* [Gk *homoios* like, PATHOS]

homogeneous /hɒməʊˈdʒiːnɪəs/ *a.* of the same kind; consisting of parts all of the same kind; **homogeneity** /-dʒɪˈniːɪtɪ/ *n.* [L (HOMO-, Gk *genos* kind)]

homogenize /həˈmɒdʒɪnaɪz/ *v.t.* make homogeneous; treat (milk) so that fat droplets are emulsified and cream does not separate.

homograph /ˈhɒməgrɑːf/ *n.* word spelt like another, but of different meaning or origin, e.g. BAT[1], BAT[2]. [HOMO-, -GRAPH]

homologous /hɒˈmɒləgəs/ *a.* having the same relation or relative position; corresponding; *Biol.* similar in position and structure but not necessarily in function. [L (HOMO-, Gk *logos* ratio)]

homology /hɒˈmɒlədʒɪ/ *n.* homologous state or relation.

homonym /ˈhɒmənɪm/ *n.* word of same spelling or sound as another but with different meaning, e.g. POLE[1], POLE[2]; THEIR, THERE; namesake. [L f. Gk (HOMO-, *onoma* name)]

homophone /ˈhɒməfəʊn/ *n.* word having same sound as another, but of different meaning or origin, e.g. SON, SUN. [HOMO-, Gk *phōnē* sound]

Homo sapiens /həʊməʊ ˈsæpɪenz/ modern man regarded as a species. [L, = wise man]

homosexual /həʊməʊˈseksjʊəl, hɒm-/ **1** *a.* feeling sexually attracted to people of same sex. **2** *n.* homosexual person. **3** **homosexuality** /-ˈælɪtɪ/ *n.* [HOMO-, SEXUAL]

Hon. *abbr.* Honorary; Honourable.

hone 1 *n.* whetstone for sharpening razors and tools. **2** *v.t.* sharpen on hone. [OE]

honest /ˈɒnɪst/ *a.* fair and sincere in character or behaviour, free of deceit or untruthfulness; fairly earned (*an honest living*); (of action etc.) sincere but undistinguished. [F f. L *honestus* (HONOUR)]

honestly *adv.* in honest way; really (*I don't honestly know*).

honesty *n.* being honest; truthfulness; plant with purple flowers and flat round semi-transparent seed-pods.

honey /'hʌnɪ/ *n.* sweet sticky fluid made by bees from nectar collected from flowers; its yellowish colour; sweetness, sweet thing, excellent person or thing; darling (esp. as form of address); **honey-bee** common hive-bee; **honeyed** *a.* [OE]

honeycomb 1 *n.* bees' wax structure of hexagonal cells for honey and eggs; pattern arranged hexagonally. **2** *v.t.* fill with cavities or tunnels; mark with honeycomb pattern. [OE]

honeydew *n.* sweet sticky substance found on leaves and stems, excreted by aphids; variety of melon with smooth pale skin and green flesh. [HONEY]

honeymoon 1 *n.* holiday of newly-married couple; initial period of enthusiasm or goodwill. **2** *v.i.* spend honeymoon.

honeysuckle *n.* climbing shrub with fragrant yellow and pink flowers.

honk 1 *n.* hooting cry of wild goose; sound of car horn. **2** *v.* (cause to) make honk. [imit.]

honky-tonk /'hɒŋkɪtɒŋk/ *n. colloq.* ragtime piano music; cheap or disreputable night-club. [perh. imit.]

honor etc. *US* var. of HONOUR etc.

honorarium /ɒnə'reərɪəm/ *n.* (*pl.* **honorariums**) voluntary payment for services without normal fee. [L (HONOUR)]

honorary /'ɒnərərɪ/ *a.* conferred as an honour (*honorary degree*); (of office or its holder) unpaid.

honorific /ɒnə'rɪfɪk/ *a.* conferring honour; implying respect.

honour /'ɒnə/ **1** *n.* high respect or public regard; adherence to what is right or an accepted standard of conduct (*code of honour*); nobleness of mind, magnanimity (*honour among thieves*); thing conferred as distinction, esp. official award for bravery or achievement; privilege (*have the honour to* or *of*); exalted position, esp. (**your, his, Honour**) of judge etc.; person or thing that brings honour (*an honour to her profession*); (of woman) chastity, reputation for this; (in *pl.*) mark of respect esp. at funeral; (in *pl.*) specialized degree-course or special distinction in examination; (in card-games) four or five highest-ranking cards; right of driving off first in golf. **2** *v.t.* respect highly; confer honour on; accept or pay (bill or cheque) when due. **3 do the honours** perform duties of host to guests etc.; **in honour of** as celebration for; **on one's honour** under moral obligation (*to do* thing). [F f. L *honor* repute]

honourable *a.* deserving, bringing, or showing honour; (**Honourable**) courtesy title of certain high officials, of the children of certain ranks of the nobility, and of MPs; **honourably** *adv.*

hooch *n. US colloq.* alcoholic liquor, esp. inferior or illicit whisky. [Alaskan]

hood[1] /hʊd/ **1** *n.* covering for head and neck, often forming part of garment; separate hoodlike garment worn as part of academic dress; thing resembling hood, e.g. folding soft roof over car; *US* bonnet of car. **2** *v.t.* cover with hood. [OE]

hood[2] /hʊd/ *n. US sl.* gangster, gunman. [abbr. of HOODLUM]

-hood *suffix* forming nouns of condition, quality, or grouping (*childhood, falsehood, sisterhood*). [OE]

hooded *a.* having a hood; (of animal) having a hoodlike part (*hooded crow*). [HOOD[1]]

hoodlum /'hu:dləm/ *n.* hooligan, young thug; gangster. [orig. unkn.]

hoodoo /'hu:du:/ *US* **1** *n.* bad luck; thing that brings or causes this; voodoo. **2** *v.t.* make unlucky, bewitch. [alt. of VOODOO]

hoodwink *v.t.* deceive, delude. [HOOD[1]]

hooey /'hu:ɪ/ *n.* & *int. sl.* nonsense. [orig. unkn.]

hoof /hu:f/ **1** *n.* (*pl.* **hoofs** or **hooves**) horny part of foot of horse etc. **2** *v.* (usu. as **hoof it**) *sl.* go on foot. [OE]

hoo-ha /'hu:hɑ:/ *n. sl.* commotion. [orig. unkn.]

hook /hʊk/ **1** *n.* bent or curved piece of wire or metal etc. for catching hold or for hanging things on; curved cutting instrument; hooklike thing, formation of land, bend in river, etc.; hooking stroke, short swinging blow in boxing. **2** *v.* grasp or secure with hook(s); catch with hook or *fig.* as if with hook; *sl.* steal; (in sports) send (ball) in curving or deviating path, (in Rugby football scrum) secure and pass (ball) backward with foot. **3 be hooked on** *sl.* be addicted to or captivated by; **by hook or by crook** by one means or another; **hook and eye** small metal hook and loop as dress-fastener; **hook it** *sl.* make off; **hook, line, and sinker** entirely; **hook-up** connection, esp. interconnection in broadcast transmission; **off the hook** *colloq.* out of difficulty or trouble. [OE]

hookah /'hʊkə/ *n.* oriental tobacco-pipe with long tube passing through water for cooling smoke as it is drawn through. [Urdu f. Arab., = casket]

hooked *a.* in shape of hook.

hooker[1] *n.* player in front row of scrum in Rugby football, who tries to hook ball; *US sl.* prostitute.

hooker[2] *n.* small Dutch or Irish fishing-vessel. [Du. *hoeker* (HOOK)]
hookey /ˈhʊkɪ/ *n.* in **play hookey** *US sl.* play truant. [orig. unkn.]
hookworm *n.* worm, male of which has hooklike spines, infesting humans and animals. [HOOK]
hooligan /ˈhu:lɪgən/ *n.* young ruffian. [orig. uncert.]
hoop 1 *n.* circular band of metal or wood etc. for binding cask etc., or forming part of a framework; large ring of wood etc., bowled along by child, or for circus performers to jump through; iron etc. arch used in croquet. **2** *v.t.* bind or encircle with hoop(s). **3 be put** (or **go**) **through the hoop** undergo ordeal. [OE]
hoop-la *n.* game in which rings are thrown in attempt to encircle prize.
hoopoe /ˈhu:pu:/ *n.* bird with fanlike crest and striped wings and tail. [F f. L *upupa* (imit. of its cry)]
hooray /hʊˈreɪ/ var. of HURRAH.
hoot 1 *n.* owl's cry; sound made by motor horn or steam whistle; shout expressing scorn or disapproval; *colloq.* laughter, cause of this. **2** *v.* utter hoot(s); greet or drive away with scornful hoots; sound (horn). **3 not care** (or **give** etc.) **a hoot** *sl.* not care at all. [imit.]
hooter *n.* siren, steam whistle, esp. as signal for work to begin or cease; car horn; *sl.* nose.
Hoover 1 *n.* **(P)** vacuum cleaner. **2** *v.t.* **(hoover)** clean (carpet etc.) with vacuum cleaner. [manufacturer]
hooves *pl.* of HOOF.
hop[1] **1** *v.* **(-pp-)** (of bird or animal) spring with two or all feet at once; (of person) jump on one foot; cross (ditch etc.) by hopping; *colloq.* make quick trip. **2** *n.* hopping movement; informal dance; short flight in aircraft. **3 hop in** (or **out**) *colloq.* get into (or out of) car; **hop it!** *sl.* go away!; **hopping mad** *colloq.* very angry; **on the hop** unprepared (*caught on the hop*). [OE]
hop[2] **1** *n.* climbing plant bearing cones; (in *pl.*) its ripe cones used to flavour beer. **2** *v.* **(-pp-)** flavour with hops. **3 hop-bind** (or **-bine**) climbing stem of hop. [LG or Du.]
hope 1 *n.* expectation and desire, e.g. for certain event(s) to occur; person, thing, or circumstance that encourages hope; what is hoped for. **2** *v.* feel hope; expect and desire; feel fairly confident. **3 hope against hope** cling to a mere possibility. [OE]
hopeful 1 *a.* feeling or causing hope; likely to succeed. **2** *n.* person who hopes or seems likely to succeed.
hopefully *adv.* in hopeful manner; **(D)** it is to be hoped.
hopeless *a.* feeling or admitting no hope; inadequate, incompetent.
hopper[1] *n.* one who hops; hopping insect; container tapering to base, with opening at base for discharging contents. [HOP[1]]
hopper[2] *n.* hop-picker. [HOP[2]]
hopscotch *n.* children's game of hopping over squares marked on ground to retrieve stone. [HOP[1], SCOTCH[2]]
horde *n.* large group, gang; troop of Tartar or other nomads. [Pol. f. Turk.]
horehound /ˈhɔ:haʊnd/ *n.* herb producing bitter juice used against coughs etc. [OE, = hoary herb]
horizon /həˈraɪz(ə)n/ *n.* line at which earth and sky appear to meet; limit of mental perception, experience, interest, etc.; **on the horizon** imminent, becoming apparent. [F f. L f. Gk (*horizō* bound)]
horizontal /hɒrɪˈzɒnt(ə)l/ **1** *a.* parallel to plane of horizon, at right angles to the vertical; at or concerned with same status, work, etc. **2** *n.* horizontal line etc. **3 horizontally** *adv.*
hormone /ˈhɔ:məʊn/ *n.* substance secreted internally and carried by blood or sap to an organ which it stimulates; similar synthetic substance; **hormonal** /-ˈməʊn(ə)l/ *a.* [Gk (*hormaō* impel)]
horn 1 *n.* hard outgrowth, often curved and pointed, from head of animal; each of two branched appendages on head of (esp. male) deer; hornlike projection on other animals, e.g. snail's tentacle; substance of which horns are made; wind instrument, orig. made of horn, now usu. brass; instrument sounding warning (*car horn*); receptacle or instrument made of horn; horn-shaped projection; extremity of moon or other crescent, arm of river etc.; either alternative of a dilemma. **2** *v.t.* furnish with horns; gore with horns. **3 horn in** *sl.* intrude, interfere; **horn of plenty** = CORNUCOPIA. [OE]
hornbeam *n.* tree with hard tough wood.
hornbill *n.* tropical bird with hornlike excrescence on bill.
hornblende /ˈhɔ:nblend/ *n.* black or green or dark brown mineral, constituent of granite etc.
hornet /ˈhɔ:nɪt/ *n.* large kind of wasp; **stir up a hornet's nest** cause angry outburst. [LG or Du.]
hornpipe *n.* lively dance, esp. associated with sailors; music for this. [HORN]
horny *a.* of or like horn; hard like horn, callous; *sl.* lecherous; **horniness** *n.*
horology /həˈrɒlədʒɪ/ *n.* art of measuring time or making clocks, watches, etc.;

horological /hɒrəˈlɒdʒɪk(ə)l/ *a.* [F f. L f. Gk (*hōra* time)]
horoscope /ˈhɒrəskəʊp/ *n.* forecast of person's future from diagram showing relative position of stars at birth; this diagram. [F f. L f. Gk (*hōra* time, *skopos* observer)]
horrendous /həˈrendəs/ *a.* horrifying. [L (HORRIBLE)]
horrible /ˈhɒrɪb(ə)l/ *a.* causing or exciting horror; *colloq.* unpleasant; **horribly** *adv.* [F f. L (*horreo* bristle, shudder at)]
horrid /ˈhɒrɪd/ *a.* horrible, revolting; *colloq.* unpleasant. [L (prec.)]
horrific /həˈrɪfɪk/ *a.* horrifying; **horrifically** *adv.* [F or L (HORRIBLE)]
horrify /ˈhɒrɪfaɪ/ *v.t.* arouse horror in, shock. [L (as prec.)]
horror /ˈhɒrə/ *n.* intense feeling of loathing and fear; intense dislike or dismay; person or thing causing horror; *colloq.* bad or mischievous person etc.; **the horrors** fit of depression or nervousness etc. [F f. L (HORRIBLE)]
hors-d'œuvre /ɔːˈdɜːvr/ *n.* appetizer served at beginning of meal. [F, = outside the work]
horse 1 *n.* large four-legged animal with long mane and tail, used for riding or to carry or pull loads; adult male horse, stallion; *collect.* (as *sing.*) cavalry; gymnastic vaulting-block; supporting frame (*clothes-horse*). 2 *v.i. colloq.* fool *around.* 3 **from the horse's mouth** (of information etc.) from original or authoritative source; **horse-box** closed vehicle for transporting horse(s); **horse-chestnut** tree with conical clusters of white or pink flowers, its dark brown fruit; **horse-fly** any of various insects troublesome to horses and cattle; **Horse Guards** cavalry brigade of household troops; **horse laugh** loud coarse laugh; **horse-radish** plant with pungent root used to make sauce; **horse sense** *colloq.* plain common sense; **horse-tail** tail of horse, plant resembling it; **horse-trading** *US* dealing in horses, shrewd bargaining; **on one's high horse** *colloq.* acting haughtily; **on horseback** mounted on a horse. [OE]
horseflesh *n.* flesh of horse as food; horses collectively.
horsehair *n.* hair from mane or tail of horse, used for padding etc.
horseman *n.* rider on horseback; skilled rider; **horsemanship** *n.*; **horsewoman** *n. fem.*
horseplay *n.* boisterous play.
horsepower *n.* (*pl.* same) unit for measuring power of engine, about 750 watts.
horseshoe *n.* U-shaped iron shoe for horse; thing of this shape.
horsewhip 1 *n.* whip for driving horses. 2 *v.t.* (**-pp-**) beat (person) with horsewhip.
horsy *a.* of or like a horse; concerned with or devoted to horses.
hortative /ˈhɔːtətɪv/ *a.* (also **hortatory**) tending or serving to exhort. [L (*hortor* exhort)]
horticulture /ˈhɔːtɪkʌltʃə/ *n.* art of garden cultivation; **horticultural** /-ˈkʌltʃər(ə)l/ *a.* [L *hortus* garden, CULTURE]
hosanna /həʊˈzænə/ *n.* shout of adoration. [L f. Gk f. Heb.]
hose /həʊz/ 1 *n.* flexible tube for conveying water (also **hose-pipe**); (*collect.* as *pl.*) stockings and socks (esp. in trade use); *hist.* breeches. 2 *v.t.* water or spray with hose. [OE]
hosier /ˈhəʊzɪə/ *n.* dealer in stockings and socks.
hosiery *n.* stockings and socks; knitted or woven underwear.
hospice /ˈhɒspɪs/ *n.* lodging for travellers, esp. one kept by a religious order; home for destitute or (esp. terminally) ill people. [F f. L (HOST²)]
hospitable /ˈhɒspɪtəb(ə)l/ *a.* giving or disposed to give hospitality; **hospitably** *adv.* [F, f. L *hospito* entertain (HOST²)]
hospital /ˈhɒspɪt(ə)l/ *n.* institution providing medical and surgical treatment and nursing care for ill or injured people; *hist.* charitable institution, hospice. [F f. L *hospitalis* (HOST²)]
hospitality /hɒspɪˈtælɪtɪ/ *n.* friendly and generous reception and entertainment of guests or strangers.
hospitalize /ˈhɒspɪtəlaɪz/ *v.t.* send or admit (patient) to hospital; **hospitalization** /-ˈzeɪʃ(ə)n/ *n.*
hospitaller /ˈhɒspɪtələ/ *n.* member of charitable religious order.
host¹ /həʊst/ *n.* large number of people or things; *archaic* army. [F f. L *hostis* enemy, army]
host² /həʊst/ 1 *n.* one who receives or entertains another as his guest; landlord of inn; animal or plant having parasite. 2 *v.t.* act as host to (person) or at (event). [F f. L *hospes -pitis* host, guest]
host³ /həʊst/ *n.* bread consecrated in the Eucharist. [F f. L *hostia* victim]
hostage /ˈhɒstɪdʒ/ *n.* person seized or held as security for fulfilment of condition(s). [F f. L *obses obsidis* hostage]
hostel /ˈhɒst(ə)l/ *n.* house of residence or lodging for students or other special groups (*youth hostel*). [F f. med.L (HOSPITAL)]
hostelry *n. archaic* inn.
hostess /ˈhəʊstɪs/ *n.* woman host; woman employed to entertain guests in

night-club etc.; stewardess in aircraft. [HOST²]

hostile /ˈhɒstaɪl/ *a.* of an enemy; unfriendly, opposed (*to*). [F or L (HOST¹)]

hostility /hɒˈstɪlɪtɪ/ *n.* being hostile, enmity; state of warfare; (in *pl.*) acts of warfare.

hot 1 *a.* having a relatively or noticeably high temperature; causing sensation of heat (*hot fever*); (of pepper, spices, etc.) pungent; (of person) feeling heat; ardent, eager, excited, passionate (*in hot pursuit*); having intense feeling, angry or upset; (of news etc.) fresh, recent; (of scent in hunting) strong; (of competitor, performer, feat) skilful, formidable; (of music) rhythmical and emotional; *sl.* (of goods) stolen, esp. if difficult to dispose of; *sl.* radioactive. **2** *v.* (**-tt-**) *colloq.* (often with *up*) make or become hot, become active or exciting. **3 hot air** *sl.* empty or boastful talk; **hot-blooded** ardent, passionate; **hot cross bun** bun marked with cross and eaten on Good Friday; **hot dog** *colloq.* hot sausage sandwiched in soft roll; **hot gospeller** *colloq.* eager preacher of gospel; **hot line** direct exclusive line of communication esp. for emergency; **hot money** capital frequently transferred; **hot potato** *colloq.* controversial or awkward matter or situation; **hot rod** motor vehicle modified to have extra power and speed; **hot seat** *sl.* position of difficult responsibility, electric chair; **hot stuff** *colloq.* formidably capable person, important person or thing, sexually attractive person; **hot-tempered** impulsively angry; **hot under the collar** angry, resentful, embarrassed; **hot water** *colloq.* difficulty or trouble; **hot-water bottle** rubber etc. container filled with hot water to warm bed etc.; **make it** (or **things** etc.) **hot for person** persecute him. [OE]

hotbed *n.* bed of earth heated by fermenting manure; place promoting growth of something (esp. unwelcome: *hotbed of vice*).

hotchpotch /ˈhɒtʃpɒtʃ/ *n.* confused mixture, jumble; mixed broth or stew. [F *hochepot* shake pot]

hotel /həʊˈtel/ *n.* establishment providing meals and accommodation for payment. [F (HOSTEL)]

hotelier /həʊˈtelɪə/ *n.* hotel-keeper.

hotfoot 1 *adv.* in eager haste. **2** *v.* (usu. with *it*) hurry eagerly. [HOT]

hothead *n.* impetuous person; **hotheaded** *a.*

hothouse *n.* heated building usu. largely of glass for rearing plants.

hotplate *n.* heated metal plate etc. (or set of these) for cooking food or keeping it hot.

hotpot *n.* meat and vegetables cooked in oven in closed pot.

Hottentot /ˈhɒt(ə)ntɒt/ *n.* member of a stocky Negroid people of SW Africa; their language. [Afrik.]

hound 1 *n.* dog used in hunting, foxhound; contemptible man. **2** *v.t.* harass or pursue; urge or incite. [OE]

hour /aʊə/ *n.* twenty-fourth part of day and night, 60 minutes; time of day, point in time (*came at the appointed hour*); (in *pl.* with preceding numerals in form *18.00, 20.30*, etc.) this number of hours and minutes past midnight on 24-hour clock; period set aside for some purpose (*lunch hour*; *keep regular hours*); (in *pl.*) fixed period of time for work, use of building, etc. (*office hours*; *opening hours*); short, indefinite period of time (*an idle hour*); *the* present time (*question of the hour*); time for action etc. (*the hour has come*); distance traversed in an hour (*two hours from London*); in RC Church, prayers said at one of seven fixed times of day; **the hour** the time o'clock, time of whole number of hours; **after hours** after normal business etc. hours. [F f. L f. Gk *hōra*].

hourglass *n.* reversible device with two glass bulbs containing sand that takes an hour to pass from upper to lower bulb.

houri /ˈhʊərɪ/ *n.* beautiful young woman of Muslim paradise. [F f. Pers. f. Arab.]

hourly 1 *a.* done or occurring every hour; frequent. **2** *adv.* every hour; frequently. [HOUR]

house 1 /haʊs/ *n.* (*pl.* /ˈhaʊzɪz/) building for human habitation; building for special purpose or for keeping animals or goods (*opera-house*; *summer-house*; *hen-house*); residential establishment, esp. religious order, university college, section of boarding-school etc.; division of day-school for games, competitions, etc.; royal family or dynasty (*House of York*); firm or institution, its place of business; legislative etc. assembly, building where it meets; audience or performance in theatre etc.; twelfth part of heavens in astrology. **2** /haʊz/ *v.t.* provide house or accommodation for; store (goods etc.); enclose or encase (part or fitting). **3 house-agent** agent for sale and letting of houses; **house arrest** detention in one's own house, not prison; **house-bound** unable to leave one's house; **house-dog** dog kept to guard house; **house-fly** common fly found in and around houses; **house martin** bird that builds mud nest on house walls; **house of cards** insecure scheme etc.; **House of Commons** elected assembly in parliament, building where it meets; **House of Keys** elected assembly in Isle of Man; **House of Lords** assembly of nobility and bishops in parliament, building where it meets; **house party** group of guests staying at country house etc.; **house-proud** attentive to care and appearance of the home; **house-room** space or provision in one's house (**would not give it house-room** would not have it in any circumstances); **house-trained** (of animals) trained to be clean in the house, *colloq.* well-mannered; **house-warming** party celebrating move to new home; **keep house** provide for a household; **like a house on fire** vigorously, successfully; **on the house** at the management's expense, free; **put** (or **set**) **one's house in order** make needed reforms; **shout** etc. **from the house-tops** announce publicly. [OE]

houseboat *n.* boat fitted up for living in.

housebreaking *n.* act of breaking into a building, esp. in daytime, to commit crime; **housebreaker** *n.* ¶ In 1968 statutorily replaced in UK (exc. Scotland) by BURGLARY.

housecoat *n.* woman's long dresslike garment for wear in the house.

household *n.* occupants of house regarded as unit; house and its affairs; **household troops** troops nominally employed to guard sovereign; **household word** familiar saying or name. [HOUSE, HOLD[1]]

householder *n.* person owning or renting a house; head of household.

housekeeper *n.* woman employed to manage household. [HOUSE]

housekeeping *n.* management of household affairs; money allowed for this.

housemaid *n.* woman servant in house; **housemaid's knee** inflammation of kneecap.

houseman *n.* resident doctor at hospital etc.

housemaster *n.* teacher in charge of house at boarding-school; **housemistress** *n. fem.*

housewife *n.* woman managing a household; /'hʌzɪf/ case for needles, thread, etc.; **housewifely** *a.* [HOUSE, WIFE = woman]

housework *n.* regular work done in housekeeping. [HOUSE]

housing /'haʊzɪŋ/ *n.* dwelling houses collectively, provision of these; shelter, lodging; casing for machinery etc.; **housing estate** residential area planned as a unit.

hove see HEAVE.

hovel /'hɒv(ə)l/ *n.* small miserable dwelling. [orig. unkn.]

hover /'hɒvə/ **1** *v.i.* (of bird etc.) remain in one place in the air; wait (*about, round*), wait close at hand. **2** *n.* hovering, state of suspense. [obs. *hove* hover]

hovercraft *n.* vehicle that travels over land or water on cushion of air provided by downward blast.

how *adv.* in what way, by what means (*how do you do it?*; *tell me how you do it*); in what condition, esp. of health (*how are you?*; *how do things stand?*); to what extent (*how far is it?*; *how we laughed!*); in whatever way, as (*do it how you can*); *colloq.* = that (*told us how he'd been in India*); **how about** what do you think of, would you like; **how do you do** a formal greeting; **how-do-you-do** *n. colloq.* awkward situation; **how many** what number; **how much** what amount, what price; **how's that?** how do you regard or explain that?, (said to umpire in cricket) is batsman out or not? [OE]

howbeit /haʊ'bi:ɪt/ *adv. archaic* nevertheless.

howdah /'haʊdə/ *n.* seat, usu. with canopy, for riding on back of elephant or camel. [Urdu f. Arab.]

however /haʊ'evə/ *adv.* in whatever way, to whatever extent; nevertheless. [HOW]

howitzer /'haʊɪtsə/ *n.* short gun for high-angle firing of shells. [Du. f. G f. Czech]

howl **1** *n.* long doleful cry of dog etc.; similar noise, e.g. made by strong wind; loud cry of pain, rage, derision, or laughter. **2** *v.* make howl; weep loudly; utter with howl. **3 howl down** prevent (speaker) from being heard by howling derision. [imit.]

howler *n. colloq.* glaring mistake.

howsoever /haʊsəʊ'evə/ *adv.* in whatsoever way, to whatsoever extent. [HOW]

hoy *int.* used to call attention. [natural cry]

hoyden /'hɔɪd(ə)n/ *n.* girl who behaves boisterously. [Du. *heiden* (HEATHEN)]

HP *abbr.* hire-purchase; (also **hp**) horsepower; (also **h.p.**) high pressure.

HQ *abbr.* headquarters.

HRH *abbr.* Her or His Royal Highness.

hr(s). *abbr.* hour(s).

HT *abbr.* high tension.

hub *n.* central part of wheel, from which spokes radiate; central point of interest, activity, etc. [orig. uncert.]

hubble-bubble /'hʌb(ə)lbʌb(ə)l/ *n.* simple form of hookah; bubbling sound; confused talk. [imit.]

hubbub /'hʌbʌb/ *n.* confused noise; disturbance. [perh. of Ir. orig.]

hubby /'hʌbɪ/ *n. colloq.* husband. [abbr.]
hubris /'hju:brɪs/ *n.* arrogant pride or presumption; **hubristic** /hju:'brɪstɪk/ *a.* [Gk]
huckaback /'hʌkəbæk/ *n.* strong linen or cotton fabric with rough surface, used for towels. [orig. unkn.]
huckleberry /'hʌk(ə)lbərɪ/ *n.* low shrub common in N. America; its blue or black fruit. [prob. alt. of *hurtleberry*, WHORTLEBERRY]
huckster 1 *n.* hawker; mercenary person. **2** *v.* haggle; be hawker. [prob. LG]
huddle /'hʌd(ə)l/ **1** *v.* heap or crowd together; nestle closely; curl one's body into small space. **2** *n.* confused mass. **3 go into a huddle** hold a close or secret conference. [perh. LG]
hue[1] *n.* colour, tint; variety or shade of colour. [OE]
hue[2] *n.* only in **hue and cry** loud outcry. [F (*huer* shout)]
huff 1 *n.* fit of petty annoyance. **2** *v.* blow; remove (opponent's piece) as forfeit in draughts. **3 in a huff** annoyed and offended. [imit. of blowing]
huffy *a.* apt to take offence; offended.
hug 1 *v.* (**-gg-**) hold closely in one's arms, usu. with affection; (of bear) squeeze between forelegs; keep close to (*ship hugged the shore*). **2** *n.* strong clasp with the arms; grip in wrestling. [prob. Scand.]
huge *a.* extremely large, enormous; (of abstract thing) very great. [F *ahuge*]
hugely *adv.* very much.
hugger-mugger /'hʌgəmʌgə/ **1** *a.* & *adv.* secret(ly); in confusion, confused. **2** *n.* confusion; secrecy. [orig. uncert.]
Huguenot /'hju:gənəʊ/ *n. hist.* French Protestant. [F]
huh /hʌ/ *int.* expressing disgust, surprise, etc. [imit.]
hula /'hu:lə/ *n.* Hawaiian woman's dance with flowing movements of the arms; **hula hoop** large hoop for spinning round the body. [Hawaiian]
hulk *n.* body of dismantled ship; *hist.* (in *pl.*) this used as prison; large clumsy-looking person or thing. [OE]
hulking *a. colloq.* bulky, clumsy.
hull[1] *n.* body of ship, airship, etc. [perh. rel. to HOLD[2]]
hull[2] **1** *n.* pod of peas or beans, husk of certain seeds or fruits, calyx of ripe strawberry, raspberry, etc. **2** *v.t.* remove hulls of (strawberries etc.). [OE]
hullabaloo /hʌləbə'lu:/ *n.* uproar. [redupl. of *hallo*, *hullo*, etc.]
hullo var. of HALLO.
hum 1 *v.* (**-mm-**) make low steady continuous sound like that of bee; sing wordless tune with closed lips; utter slight inarticulate sound, esp. of hesitation; *colloq.* be in active state (*things began to hum*); *sl.* smell unpleasantly. **2** *n.* humming sound; exclamation of hesitation; *sl.* bad smell. **3 hum and ha** (or **haw**) hesitate. [imit.]
human /'hju:mən/ **1** *a.* of or belonging to man; of or characteristic of man as opposed to God or animals or machines; showing better qualities of man. **2** *n.* human being. **3 human nature** general characteristics and feelings of mankind; **human rights** rights held to be claimable by any living person. [F f. L *humanus*]
humane /hjʊ'meɪn/ *a.* benevolent, compassionate, merciful; (of learning) tending to civilize; **humane killer** implement for painless slaughter of animals.
humanism *n.* belief or attitude emphasizing common human needs and seeking solely rational ways of solving human problems; system of thought concerned with human (not religious etc.) matters; literary culture, esp. in Renaissance; **humanist** *n.*; **humanistic** /-'nɪstɪk/ *a.*
humanitarian /hju:mænɪ'teərɪən/ **1** *a.* concerned with promoting human welfare. **2** *n.* humanitarian person. **3 humanitarianism** *n.*
humanity /hju:'mænɪtɪ/ *n.* human nature or (in *pl.*) qualities; the human race; humaneness; (in *pl.*) learning or literature concerned with human culture, formerly esp. Greek and Latin classics.
humanize *v.t.* make human or humane; **humanization** /-'zeɪʃ(ə)n/ *n.* [F (HUMAN)]
humanly *adv.* in a human manner; by human means, within human capabilities (*I will do it if it is humanly possible*). [HUMAN]
humble /'hʌmb(ə)l/ **1** *a.* having or showing a low estimate of one's own importance; of low social or political rank; (of thing) not large or elaborate. **2** *v.* make humble, lower rank or self-importance of. **3 eat humble pie** make a humble apology [*umbles* edible offal of deer]. **4 humbly** *adv.* [F f. L *humilis* (HUMUS)]
humbug /'hʌmbʌg/ **1** *n.* deceptive or false talk or behaviour; impostor; hard boiled sweet usu. flavoured with peppermint. **2** *v.* (**-gg-**) be or behave like an impostor. [orig. unkn.]
humdinger /'hʌmdɪŋə/ *n. sl.* remarkable person or thing. [orig. unkn.]
humdrum /'hʌmdrʌm/ *a.* dull, commonplace, monotonous. [HUM]
humerus /'hju:mərəs/ *n.* bone of upper arm; **humeral** *a.* [L, = shoulder]

humid /'hju:mɪd/ *a.* (of air or climate) damp; **humidify** /-'mɪdɪfaɪ/ *v.t.* [F, or L *humidus*]

humidifier /hju:'mɪdɪfaɪə/ *n.* device for keeping air moist in room etc.

humidity /hju:'mɪdɪtɪ/ *n.* dampness; degree of moisture, esp. in the atmosphere.

humiliate /hju:'mɪlɪeɪt/ *v.t.* harm the dignity or self-respect of; **humiliation** /-'eɪʃ(ə)n/ *n.* [L (HUMBLE)]

humility /hju:'mɪlɪtɪ/ *n.* humble attitude of mind; humbleness. [F (prec.)]

humming-bird *n.* small tropical bird, that makes humming sound with its wings. [HUM]

hummock /'hʌmək/ *n.* low hill or hump. [orig. unkn.]

hummus /'hʊməs/ *n.* hors d'œuvre made from ground chick-peas and sesame oil flavoured with lemon and garlic. [Turk.]

humor *US* var. of HUMOUR.

humoresque /hju:mə'resk/ *n.* light and lively musical composition. [G *humoreske*]

humorist *n.* writer or speaker noted for humour. [HUMOUR]

humorous /'hju:mərəs/ *a.* full of humour, amusing.

humour /'hju:mə/ **1** *n.* quality of being amusing; ability to appreciate the comic or amusing (*sense of humour*); state of mind (*is in a good humour*); each of four fluids (blood, phlegm, choler, melancholy) formerly held to determine person's physical and mental qualities. **2** *v.t.* keep (person) contented by indulging his wishes. **3 aqueous** (or **vitreous**) **humour** transparent substance before (or behind) lens of eye. [F f. L *humor* moisture]

hump **1** *n.* rounded protuberance on back of camel etc., or as abnormality on person's back; rounded raised mass of earth etc.; *sl.* fit of depression or annoyance (*it gives me the hump*). **2** *v.t.* form into hump; hoist or shoulder (one's pack etc.). [perh. LG or Du.]

humpback *n.* deformed back with hump; person with this; **humpback bridge** small bridge with steep ascent and descent; **humpbacked** *a.*

humph *int.* & *n.* inarticulate sound expressing doubt or dissatisfaction. [imit.]

humus /'hju:məs/ *n.* organic constituent of soil, formed by decomposition of dead leaves, plants, etc. [L, = ground]

Hun *n.* German (usu. *derog.*); vandal; one of Asiatic people who ravaged Europe in 4th–5th c.; **Hunnish** *a.* [OE]

hunch **1** *v.* bend or arch into a hump. **2** *n.* hump, hunk; intuitive feeling. [orig. unkn.]

hunchback *n.* humpback; **hunchbacked** *a.*

hundred /'hʌndrəd/ *a.* & *n.* ten times ten (*a*, *one*, *six*, etc., *hundred*); symbol for this (100, c, C); (in *pl.* **hundreds**) very many; *hist.* subdivision of county or shire with own court; **hundreds and thousands** tiny coloured sweets for decorating cake etc.; **hundredth** *a.* & *n.* [OE]

hundredfold *a.* & *adv.* a hundred times as much or as many; consisting of a hundred parts.

hundredweight *n.* (*pl.* same) measure of weight, 112 lb; **metric hundredweight** 50 kg; **short hundredweight** *US* 100 lb.

hung see HANG.

Hungarian /hʌŋ'geərɪən/ **1** *a.* of Hungary or its inhabitants. **2** *n.* native or inhabitant of Hungary; Magyar language. [med.L]

hunger /'hʌŋgə/ **1** *n.* discomfort or painful sensation caused by want of food; strong desire (*for*). **2** *v.i.* feel hunger; have craving (*for* or *after*). **3 hunger strike** refusal of food, esp. by prisoner(s), as form of protest. [OE]

hungry /'hʌŋgrɪ/ *a.* feeling or showing hunger; inducing hunger (*hungry work*); **hungrily** *adv.* [OE]

hunk *n.* large piece cut off (*a hunk of bread*). [prob. Du.]

hunkers /'hʌŋkəz/ *n.pl.* the haunches. [Sc.]

hunt **1** *v.* pursue (wild animals or game, or *absol.*) for sport or food; (of animal) pursue its prey; pursue with hostility; search for; make a search (*for*); search (district) for game; use (horse or hounds) for hunting; (of an engine) run alternately too fast and too slow. **2** *n.* hunting; association of people hunting, district where they hunt. [OE]

hunter *n.* one who hunts; horse ridden for hunting; watch with hinged metal cover protecting glass; **hunter's moon** first full moon after harvest moon.

huntsman *n.* hunter; person in charge of hounds.

hurdle /'hɜ:d(ə)l/ **1** *n.* portable rectangular frame with bars, for temporary fence etc.; each of series of upright frames to be jumped over in race; obstacle, difficulty; (in *pl.*) hurdle-race. **2** *v.* fence off with hurdles; run in hurdle-race. [OE]

hurdler /'hɜ:dlə/ *n.* one who runs in hurdle-races; one who makes hurdles.

hurdy-gurdy /'hɜ:dɪgɜ:dɪ/ *n.* portable musical instrument with droning sound, played by turning handle; *colloq.* barrel-organ. [imit.]

hurl 1 *v.t.* throw with great force; utter vehemently (*hurl insults*). 2 *n.* forceful throw. [imit.]

hurley *n.* (also **hurling**) Irish game somewhat resembling hockey; stick used in this. [prec.]

hurly-burly /'hɜ:lɪbɜ:lɪ/ *n.* boisterous activity, commotion. [HURL]

hurrah /hʊ'rɑ:/ *int.* & *n.* (also **hurray** /-'reɪ/) exclamation of joy or approval. [earlier *huzza*, orig. uncert.]

hurricane /'hʌrɪkən/ *n.* storm with violent wind, esp. W. Indian cyclone; wind of 73 m.p.h. or more; **hurricane lamp** lamp with flame protected from violent wind. [Sp. & Port. f. Carib.]

hurry /'hʌrɪ/ 1 *n.* great haste; eagerness, urgency; (with neg. or interrog.) need for haste (*what's the hurry?*). 2 *v.* move or act with eager or excessive haste; cause to move or proceed in this way (*away*, *along*, *into*, etc.); (in *p.p.*) hasty, done rapidly. 3 **hurry up** *colloq.* make haste; **in a hurry** hurrying, easily or readily (*you won't beat that in a hurry*). [imit.]

hurry-scurry /hʌrɪ'skʌrɪ/ 1 *n.* disorderly haste. 2 *a.* & *adv.* in confusion.

hurt 1 *v.* (*past* and *p.p.* **hurt**) cause pain or injury to; cause mental pain or distress to (person, feelings, etc.); suffer pain or harm (*my arm hurts*; *I hurt all over*). 2 *n.* injury, harm; offence to feelings. [F *hurter* knock]

hurtful *a.* causing (esp. mental) hurt; **hurtfully** *adv.*

hurtle /'hɜ:t(ə)l/ *v.* move or hurl rapidly or with clattering sound; come with a crash. [HURT]

husband /'hʌzbənd/ 1 *n.* married man in relation to his wife. 2 *v.t.* use economically. [OE, = house-dweller]

husbandry *n.* farming; management of resources.

hush 1 *v.* make or become silent or quiet. 2 *n.* silence. 3 **hush-hush** *colloq.* highly confidential, very secret; **hush-money** money paid to prevent disclosure of discreditable affair; **hush up** suppress public mention of (affair). [*husht* imit. int. taken as *p.p.*]

husk 1 *n.* dry outer covering of certain seeds and fruits; worthless outside part of anything. 2 *v.t.* remove husk(s) from. [prob. LG]

husky[1] /'hʌskɪ/ *a.* full of or dry as husks; (of person or voice) dry in the throat, hoarse; big and strong.

husky[2] /'hʌskɪ/ *n.* dog of powerful breed used in Arctic for pulling sledges. [perh. corrupt. of *Eskimo*]

hussar /hʊ'zɑ:/ *n.* soldier of a light cavalry regiment. [Magyar f. It. (CORSAIR)]

hussy /'hʌsɪ/ *n.* saucy girl; immoral woman. [contr. of HOUSEWIFE]

hustings /'hʌstɪŋz/ *n.* parliamentary election proceedings. [OE, = house of assembly, f. ON]

hustle /'hʌs(ə)l/ 1 *v.* push roughly, jostle; hurry (person *into* place, act, etc.); push one's way, bustle; *sl.* swindle, obtain by force. 2 *n.* hustling, bustle. [Du.]

hut 1 *n.* small simple or crude house or shelter; temporary housing for troops. 2 *v.t.* (**-tt-**) place (troops etc.) in huts; furnish with huts. [F *hutte* f. Gmc]

hutch *n.* boxlike pen for rabbits etc. [F *huche*]

hyacinth /'haɪəsɪnθ/ *n.* plant with fragrant bell-shaped (esp. purplish-blue) flowers; purplish-blue; **wild hyacinth** bluebell. [F f. L f. Gk]

hyaena var. of HYENA.

hybrid /'haɪbrɪd/ 1 *n.* offspring of two animals or plants of different species or varieties; thing composed of diverse elements, esp. word with parts from different languages. 2 *a.* bred as hybrid; cross-bred; heterogeneous. 3 **hybridism** *n.*; **hybridity** /-'brɪdɪtɪ/ *n.* [L]

hybridize *v.* subject (species etc.) to cross-breeding; produce hybrids; (of animal or plant) interbreed; **hybridization** /-'zeɪʃ(ə)n/ *n.*

hydra /'haɪdrə/ *n.* thing hard to get rid of; water-snake; freshwater polyp. [Gk, myth. snake whose many heads grew again when cut off]

hydrangea /haɪ'dreɪndʒə/ *n.* shrub with globular clusters of white, pink, or blue flowers. [L, f. Gk *hudōr* water, *aggos* vessel]

hydrant /'haɪdrənt/ *n.* pipe (esp. in street) with nozzle for hose, for drawing water from main. [HYDRO-]

hydrate /'haɪdreɪt/ 1 *n.* chemical compound of water with another compound or an element. 2 /also -'dreɪt/ *v.t.* combine chemically with water; cause to absorb water. 3 **hydration** /-'dreɪʃ(ə)n/ *n.* [F (HYDRO-)]

hydraulic /haɪ'drɔ:lɪk/ *a.* of water etc. conveyed through pipes or channels; operated by movement of liquid (*hydraulic brakes*, *lift*); **hydraulically** *adv.* [L f. Gk (*hudōr* water, *aulos* pipe)]

hydraulics *n.pl.* (usu. treated as *sing.*) science of conveyance of liquids through pipes etc., esp. as motive power.

hydride /'haɪdraɪd/ *n.* compound of hydrogen esp. with metal. [HYDRO-]

hydro /'haɪdrəʊ/ *n.* (*pl.* **hydros**) *colloq.* hotel etc. providing hydropathic treatment; hydroelectric power plant. [abbr.]

hydro- *in comb.* water, liquid; combined

with hydrogen. [Gk *hudro-* (*hudōr* water)]

hydrocarbon /haɪdrəʊ'kɑ:bən/ *n.* compound of hydrogen and carbon.

hydrocephalus /haɪdrə'sefələs/ *n.* condition (esp. in young children) with accumulation of fluid in cavity of cranium, which can impair mental faculties; **hydrocephalic** /-sɪ'fælɪk/ *a.* [Gk *kephalē* head]

hydrochloric /haɪdrəʊ'klɔ:rɪk/ *a.* containing hydrogen and chlorine (*hydrochloric acid*). [HYDRO-]

hydrochloride /haɪdrəʊ'klɔ:raɪd/ *n.* compound of organic base with hydrochloric acid.

hydrocyanic /haɪdrəʊsaɪ'ænɪk/ *a.* containing hydrogen and cyanogen; **hydrocyanic acid** prussic acid.

hydrodynamics /haɪdrəʊdaɪ'næmɪks/ *n.* science of forces acting on or exerted by liquids (esp. water); **hydrodynamic** *a.*

hydroelectric /haɪdrəʊɪ'lektrɪk/ *a.* developing electricity by utilization of water-power; (of electricity) produced thus; **hydroelectricity** /-'trɪsɪtɪ/ *n.*

hydrofoil /'haɪdrəfɔɪl/ *n.* boat equipped with device for raising hull out of water to enable rapid motion; this device.

hydrogen /'haɪdrədʒ(ə)n/ *n.* odourless tasteless gas, the lightest element, combining with oxygen to form water; **hydrogen bomb** immensely powerful bomb utilizing explosive fusion of hydrogen nuclei; **hydrogen peroxide** see PEROXIDE; **hydrogen sulphide** unpleasant-smelling poisonous gas formed by rotting animal matter; **hydrogenous** /-'drɒdʒɪnəs/ *a.* [F (HYDRO-, -GEN)]

hydrogenate /haɪ'drɒdʒɪneɪt/ *v.t.* charge with or cause to combine with hydrogen; **hydrogenation** /-'neɪʃ(ə)n/ *n.*

hydrography /haɪ'drɒgrəfɪ/ *n.* scientific study of seas, lakes, rivers, etc.; **hydrographer** *n.*; **hydrographic** /-'græfɪk/ *a.* [F (HYDRO-, -GRAPHY)]

hydrology /haɪ'drɒlədʒɪ/ *n.* science of the properties of water, esp. of its movement in relation to land. [HYDRO-, -LOGY]

hydrolyse /'haɪdrəlaɪz/, *US* **hydrolyze** *v.t.* decompose by hydrolysis. [foll.]

hydrolysis /haɪ'drɒlɪsɪs/ *n.* decomposition of a substance by chemical action of water. [Gk (*lusis* dissolving)]

hydrometer /haɪ'drɒmɪtə/ *n.* instrument for measuring density of liquids. [HYDRO-]

hydropathy /haɪ'drɒpəθɪ/ *n.* medical treatment by external and internal application of water; **hydropathic** /-'pæθɪk/ *a.* [PATHOS]

hydrophilic /haɪdrə'fɪlɪk/ *a.* having affinity for water; wettable by water. [Gk (*philos* loving)]

hydrophobia /haɪdrə'fəʊbɪə/ *n.* aversion to water, esp. as symptom of rabies in man; rabies, esp. in man; **hydrophobic** *a.* [-PHOBIA]

hydroplane /'haɪdrəpleɪn/ *n.* light fast motor boat designed to skim over surface of water; finlike device on submarine enabling it to rise or descend. [HYDRO-]

hydroponics /haɪdrə'pɒnɪks/ *n.* art of growing plants without soil, in sand etc. or liquid with added nutrients. [Gk *ponos* labour]

hydrosphere /'haɪdrəsfɪə/ *n.* waters of the earth's surface. [HYDRO-]

hydrostatic /haɪdrəʊ'stætɪk/ *a.* of the equilibrium of liquids and the pressure exerted by liquids at rest. [STATIC]

hydrostatics *n.pl.* branch of mechanics concerned with hydrostatic properties of liquids.

hydrous /'haɪdrəs/ *a.* (of substances) containing water. [HYDRO-]

hydroxide /haɪ'drɒksaɪd/ *n.* compound of element or radical with hydroxyl. [HYDRO-, OXIDE]

hydroxyl /haɪ'drɒksɪl/ *n.* radical containing hydrogen and oxygen.

hyena /haɪ'i:nə/ *n.* carnivorous mammal of Africa and Asia with shrill cry resembling laughter. [L f. Gk]

hygiene /'haɪdʒi:n/ *n.* principles of maintaining health, esp. by cleanliness; sanitary science; **hygienic** /-'dʒi:nɪk/ *a.*; **hygienist** *n.* [F f. Gk (*hugiēs* healthy)]

hygrometer /haɪ'grɒmɪtə/ *n.* instrument for measuring humidity of air or gas. [Gk *hugros* wet]

hygroscope /'haɪgrəskəʊp/ *n.* instrument indicating but not measuring humidity of air.

hygroscopic /haɪgrə'skɒpɪk/ *a.* of the hygroscope; (of substance) tending to absorb moisture from the air.

hymen /'haɪmen/ *n.* membrane partially closing external opening of vagina of virgin. [Gk *humēn* membrane]

hymenopterous /haɪmə'nɒptərəs/ *a.* of order of insects including ant, bee, wasp, etc., with four membranous wings. [Gk, = membrane-winged]

hymn /hɪm/ **1** *n.* song of praise, esp. to God. **2** *v.t.* praise or celebrate in hymns. [F f. L f. Gk]

hymnal /'hɪmn(ə)l/ *n.* book of hymns. [med.L (prec.)]

hymnology /hɪm'nɒlədʒɪ/ *n.* composition or study of hymns; **hymnologist** *n.* [HYMN, -LOGY]

hyoscine /'haɪəsi:n/ *n.* poisonous alkaloid from which a sedative is made, found in plants of nightshade family.

hyoscyamine /haɪəˈsaɪəmiːn/ *n.* poisonous alkaloid used as sedative, got from henbane. [Gk *huoskuamos* henbane (*hus huos* pig, *kuamos* bean)]

hyper- *prefix* in senses 'over', 'above', 'too'. [Gk *huper* over]

hyperactive /haɪpəˈræktɪv/ *a.* (of person) abnormally active.

hyperbola /haɪˈpɜːbələ/ *n.* plane curve produced when cone is cut by plane that makes larger angle with base than side of cone makes; **hyperbolic** /-ˈbɒlɪk/ *a.* [foll.]

hyperbole /haɪˈpɜːbəlɪ/ *n.* statement exaggerated for special effect; **hyperbolical** /-ˈbɒlɪk(ə)l/ *a.* [Gk (HYPER-, *ballō* throw)]

hypercritical /haɪpəˈkrɪtɪk(ə)l/ *a.* excessively critical; **hypercritically** *adv.* [HYPER-]

hypermarket /ˈhaɪpəmɑːkɪt/ *n.* very large self-service store usu. outside town. [F (HYPER-, MARKET)]

hypersensitive /haɪpəˈsensɪtɪv/ *a.* excessively sensitive; **hypersensitivity** /-ˈtɪvɪtɪ/ *n.* [HYPER-]

hypersonic /haɪpəˈsɒnɪk/ *a.* of speeds more than about five times that of sound; of sound frequencies above about 1,000 megahertz.

hypertension /haɪpəˈtenʃ(ə)n/ *n.* abnormally high blood pressure; great emotional tension.

hypertrophy /haɪˈpɜːtrəfɪ/ *n.* enlargement of organ etc. due to excessive nutrition; **hypertrophic** /-pəˈtrɒfɪk/ *a.* [HYPER-, Gk *trophē* food]

hyphen /ˈhaɪf(ə)n/ **1** *n.* sign (-) used to join words together (e.g. *fruit-tree, pick-me-up*), mark division of word at end of line, divide word into parts, etc. **2** *v.t.* join (words) with hyphen; write (word or words) with hyphen. [L f. Gk (HYPO-, *hen* one]

hyphenate /ˈhaɪfəneɪt/ *v.t.* hyphen; **hyphenation** /-ˈneɪʃ(ə)n/ *n.*

hypnosis /hɪpˈnəʊsɪs/ *n.* (*pl.* **hypnoses** /-iːz/) state like sleep in which the subject acts only on external suggestion; artificially produced sleep. [Gk *hupnos* sleep]

hypnotic /hɪpˈnɒtɪk/ **1** *a.* of or producing hypnosis; inducing sleep. **2** *n.* hypnotic drug or influence. **3 hypnotically** *adv.* [F f. L f. Gk (prec.)]

hypnotism /ˈhɪpnətɪz(ə)m/ *n.* production or process of hypnosis; **hypnotist** *n.*

hypnotize *v.t.* produce hypnosis in; fascinate, capture mind of (person).

hypo[1] /ˈhaɪpəʊ/ *n.* sodium thiosulphate (incorrectly called hyposulphite) used in photographic fixing. [abbr.]

hypo[2] /ˈhaɪpəʊ/ *n.* (*pl.* **hypos**) *sl.* = HYPODERMIC. [abbr.]

hypo- *prefix* in senses 'under', 'below', 'slightly'. [Gk *hupo* under]

hypocaust /ˈhaɪpəkɔːst/ *n.* space under floor in ancient-Roman houses, into which hot air was sent as form of heating. [L f. Gk (HYPO-, *kaustos* burnt)]

hypochondria /haɪpəˈkɒndrɪə/ *n.* abnormal anxiety about one's health. [L f. Gk, = soft parts of body below ribs (whence melancholy was thought to arise)]

hypochondriac **1** *n.* person suffering from hypochondria. **2** *a.* of hypochondria.

hypocrisy /hɪˈpɒkrɪsɪ/ *n.* simulation of virtue or goodness, insincerity. [F f. eccl. L f. Gk, = acting, feigning]

hypocrite /ˈhɪpəkrɪt/ *n.* person guilty of hypocrisy; **hypocritical** /-ˈkrɪtɪk(ə)l/ *a.*

hypodermic /haɪpəˈdɜːmɪk/ **1** *a.* of area beneath the skin; injected there, used for such injection. **2** *n.* hypodermic injection or syringe. **3 hypodermic syringe** syringe with hollow needle for injection beneath skin. [L f. Gk (HYPO-, *derma* skin)]

hypostasis /haɪˈpɒstəsɪs/ *n.* (*pl.* **hypostases** /-iːz/) underlying substance of thing as distinct from its attributes; any of the three persons of the Trinity. [eccl. L f. Gk (*stasis* standing)]

hypotension /haɪpəʊˈtenʃ(ə)n/ *n.* abnormally low blood pressure. [HYPO-]

hypotenuse /haɪˈpɒtənjuːz/ *n.* side opposite right angle of right-angled triangle. [L f. Gk, = subtending line]

hypothecate /haɪˈpɒθɪkeɪt/ *v.t.* pledge, mortgage; **hypothecation** /-ˈkeɪʃ(ə)n/ *n.* [L f. Gk (HYPO-, *tithēmi* place)]

hypothermia /haɪpəˈθɜːmɪə/ *n.* condition of having abnormally low body-temperature. [HYPO-, Gk *thermē* heat]

hypothesis /haɪˈpɒθɪsɪs/ *n.* (*pl.* **hypotheses** /-iːz/) proposition or supposition made from known facts as basis for reasoning or investigation. [L f. Gk, = foundation]

hypothesize *v.* form hypothesis; assume as hypothesis.

hypothetical /haɪpəˈθetɪk(ə)l/ *a.* of or based on hypothesis; supposed but not necessarily real or true; **hypothetically** *adv.*

hyssop /ˈhɪsəp/ *n.* small bushy aromatic herb formerly used medicinally; plant used for sprinkling in ancient-Jewish rites. [OE & F f. L f. Gk f. Semitic]

hysterectomy /hɪstəˈrektəmɪ/ *n.* surgical removal of the womb. [Gk *hustera* womb, -ECTOMY]

hysteria /hɪˈstɪərɪə/ *n.* wild uncontrollable emotion or excitement; functional disturbance of the nervous system, of psychoneurotic origin. [Gk *hustera* womb (since hysteria formerly associated with women)]

hysteric /hɪ'sterɪk/ *n.* hysterical person; (in *pl.*) fit of hysteria.

hysterical *a.* of or caused by hysteria; suffering from hysteria; **hysterically** *adv.*

Hz *abbr.* hertz.

I

I[1], **i** /aɪ/ *n.* (*pl.* **Is, I's**) ninth letter; *Rom. num.* 1.

I[2] /aɪ/ *pron.* of first person singular (*obj.* ME[1]; *poss.* MY, MINE[1]; *pl.* WE etc.). [OE]

I. *abbr.* Island(s); Isle(s).

I *symb.* iodine.

-ial *suffix* var. of -AL.

iambic /aɪ'æmbɪk/ **1** *a.* of or using iambuses. **2** *n.* (usu. in *pl.*) iambic verse. [F f. L f. Gk (foll.)]

iambus /aɪ'æmbəs/ *n.* (*pl.* **iambuses**) a metrical foot (⏑–). [L f. Gk, = lampoon]

-ian var. of -AN.

IBA *abbr.* Independent Broadcasting Authority.

Iberian /aɪ'bɪərɪən/ **1** *a.* of Iberia, the peninsula comprising Spain and Portugal. **2** *n.* native or language of ancient Iberia. [L *Iberia* f. Gk]

ibex /'aɪbeks/ *n.* wild goat of Alps etc. with large recurved horns. [L]

ibid. *abbr.* in the same book or passage etc. [L *ibidem* in the same place]

-ibility *suffix* forming nouns of quality corresponding to adjectives in *-ible*.

ibis /'aɪbɪs/ *n.* wading bird with curved bill. [L f. Gk]

-ible *suffix* forming adjectives in sense 'that may *or* may be' (*forcible, possible*). [F or L]

-ibly *suffix* forming adverbs corresponding to adjectives in *-ible*.

-ic *suffix* forming adjectives and nouns (*Arabic, classic, public; critic, mechanic, music*); *Chem.* combined in higher valence or degree of oxidation (*ferric, sulphuric*). [F or L or Gk]

-ical *suffix* forming adjectives esp. from nouns in *-ic* or *-y* (*comical, historical*). [-IC, -AL]

ice 1 *n.* frozen water; sheet of this on surface of water; portion of ice-cream or water-ice. **2** *v.* become covered (*over* or *up*) with ice; freeze; cover or mix with ice; cool in ice; cover (cake etc.) with icing. **3 break the ice** make a start, overcome formality; **ice age** glacial period; **ice-blue** very pale blue; **ice-breaker** ship designed to break through ice; **ice-cap** permanent covering of ice, e.g. in polar lands; **ice-cream** a sweet creamy frozen food; **ice-field** large expanse of floating ice; **ice hockey** form of hockey played on ice with puck instead of ball; **ice lolly** kind of water-ice on stick; **on ice** *colloq.* held in reserve, quite certain; **on thin ice** in risky situation. [OE]

iceberg /'aɪsbɜ:g/ *n.* huge floating mass of ice. [Du.]

icebox *n.* compartment in refrigerator for making or storing ice; *US* refrigerator. [ICE]

Icelander /'aɪsləndə/ *n.* native of Iceland in N. Atlantic.

Icelandic /aɪs'lændɪk/ **1** *a.* of Iceland. **2** *n.* language of Iceland.

ichneumon /ɪk'nju:mən/ *n.* mongoose of N. Africa etc., noted for destroying crocodiles' eggs; ichneumon-fly; **ichneumon-fly** insect that deposits its eggs in or on larva of another insect. [L f. Gk]

ichthyology /ɪkθɪ'ɒlədʒɪ/ *n.* study of fishes. [Gk *ikhthus* fish]

ICI *abbr.* Imperial Chemical Industries.

-ician *suffix* forming nouns chiefly in sense 'person skilled in', usu. corresponding to subject in *-ic(s)*. [F]

icicle /'aɪsɪk(ə)l/ *n.* tapering hanging spike of ice formed from dripping water. [ICE, obs. *ickle* icicle]

icing *n.* coating of sugar etc. on cake or biscuit; formation of ice on aircraft; **icing sugar** finely powdered sugar. [ICE]

icon /'aɪkɒn/ *n.* sacred painting, mosaic, etc., in the Orthodox Church. [L f. Gk]

iconoclast /aɪ'kɒnəklæst/ *n.* one who assails cherished beliefs; breaker of images; **iconoclasm** *n.*; **iconoclastic** /-'klæstɪk/ *a.* [L f. Gk (ICON, *klaō* break)]

iconography /aɪkə'nɒgrəfɪ/ *n.* illustration of subject by drawings etc.; study of portraits esp. of one person. [Gk (ICON)]

icosahedron /aɪkɒsə'hi:drən/ *n.* solid figure with 20 faces. [L f. Gk]

-ics *suffix* forming nouns denoting branches of study or action (*athletics, politics*). [F or L or Gk]

ictus /'ɪktəs/ *n.* rhythmical or metrical stress. [L, = stroke]

icy *a.* very cold; covered with or abounding in ice; (of tone or manner) unfriendly, hostile; **icily** *adv.*; **iciness** *n.* [ICE]

id *n.* a person's inherited psychological impulses. [L, = that]

-ide *suffix* forming names of binary chemical compounds of an element with another element or radical (*sodium chloride*; *calcium carbide*). [orig. in OXIDE]

idea /aɪ'dɪə/ *n.* plan or scheme formed by thinking; mental impression or conception; opinion or belief; vague notion, fancy (*I had no idea you were there*); ambition or aspiration (*have ideas*; *put ideas into a person's head*); archetype, pattern; **have no idea** *colloq.* be ignorant or incompetent. [L f. Gk, = form, kind]

ideal /aɪ'dɪəl/ **1** *a.* answering to one's highest conception; perfect; existing only in idea, visionary. **2** *n.* perfect type, conception of this; actual thing as standard for imitation. [F f. L (prec.)]

idealism *n.* forming or pursuing ideals, esp. unrealistically; representation of things in ideal form; imaginative treatment; philosophy in which object of external perception is held to consist of ideas; **idealist** *n.*; **idealistic** /-'lɪstɪk/ *a.* [F or G (prec.)]

idealize *v.t.* regard or represent as ideal or perfect; **idealization** /-'zeɪʃ(ə)n/ *n.* [IDEAL]

ideally *adv.* according to an ideal; in ideal circumstances.

idée fixe /i:deɪ 'fi:ks/ recurrent or dominating idea. [F, = fixed idea]

identical /aɪ'dentɪk(ə)l/ *a.* one and the same; agreeing in all details (*with* something else); (of twins) developed from a single fertilized ovum and thus of same sex and very similar in appearance; **identically** *adv.* [L *identicus* (IDENTITY)]

identification /aɪdentɪfɪ'keɪʃ(ə)n/ *n.* identifying; means of identifying; **identification parade** assembly of persons from whom suspect is to be identified. [foll.]

identify /aɪ'dentɪfaɪ/ *v.* establish identity of, recognize; treat (thing) as identical (*with*); associate (person, *oneself*) closely (*with* party, policy, etc.); associate oneself *with*; regard oneself as sharing characteristics *with* (another person); select; **identifiable** *a.* [med.L *identifico* (IDENTITY)]

Identikit /aɪ'dentɪkɪt/ *n.* (**P**) picture of person (esp. one wanted by police) assembled from descriptions. [foll., KIT[1]]

identity /aɪ'dentɪtɪ/ *n.* condition of being specified person or thing; absolute sameness; individuality, personality; equality of two algebraic expressions for all values of quantities, expression of this. [L *identitas* f. *idem* same]

ideogram /'ɪdɪəgræm/ *n.* character or symbol indicating the idea of a thing without expressing the sounds in its name. [IDEA, -GRAM]

ideograph /'ɪdɪəgrɑ:f/ *n.* ideogram; **ideographic** /-'græfɪk/ *a.*; **ideography** /-'ɒgrəfɪ/ *n.* [IDEA, -GRAPH]

ideologue /'aɪdɪəlɒg/ *n.* adherent of an ideology. [F (IDEA)]

ideology /aɪdɪ'ɒlədʒɪ/ *n.* ideas at basis of an economic or political theory or system, or characteristic of some class etc.; **ideological** /-'lɒdʒɪk(ə)l/ *a.*; **ideologist** *n.* [F (IDEA, -LOGY)]

ides /aɪdz/ *n. pl.* 15th day of March, May, July, Oct., 13th of other months, in ancient Roman calendar. [F f. L *Idus*]

idiocy /'ɪdɪəsɪ/ *n.* extreme mental imbecility; utter foolishness. [IDIOT]

idiom /'ɪdɪəm/ *n.* form of expression or usage peculiar to a language, esp. one whose meaning is not given by those of its separate words; language of a people; characteristic mode of expression in art etc. [F or L, f. Gk (*idios* own)]

idiomatic /ɪdɪə'mætɪk/ *a.* relating or conforming to idiom; characteristic of a language; **idiomatically** *adv.* [Gk (prec.)]

idiosyncrasy /ɪdɪə'sɪŋkrəsɪ/ *n.* attitude, form of behaviour, or mental or physical constitution, peculiar to a person; **idiosyncratic** /-'krætɪk/ *a.* [Gk (*idios* private, *sun* with, *krasis* mixture)]

idiot /'ɪdɪət/ *n.* person deficient in mind and incapable of rational conduct; *colloq.* stupid person; **idiotic** /-'ɒtɪk/ *a.*; **idiotically** /-'ɒtɪkəlɪ/ *adv.* [F f. L f. Gk, = private citizen, ignorant person]

idle /'aɪd(ə)l/ **1** *a.* not working; lazy, indolent; (of time etc.) unoccupied; useless, vain (*idle protest*); purposeless (*idle talk*); groundless (*idle rumour*). **2** *v.* be idle; move (*along*) idly; (of engine) run slowly without doing work; pass (time etc.) *away* in idleness. **3 idler** *n.*; **idly** *adv.* [OE]

idol /'aɪd(ə)l/ *n.* image of deity as object of worship; object of excessive or supreme devotion. [F f. L f. Gk]

idolater /aɪ'dɒlətə/ *n.* one who worships idols; devout admirer; **idolatrous** *a.*; **idolatry** *n.* [F f. L f. Gk (IDOL, *latreuō* worship]

idolize /'aɪdəlaɪz/ *v.t.* venerate or love excessively; treat as an idol; **idolization** /-'zeɪʃ(ə)n/ *n.* [IDOL]

idyll /'ɪdɪl/ *n.* short description usu. in verse of picturesque scene or incident esp. in rustic life; such scene or incident. [L f. Gk (*eidos* form)]

idyllic /ɪ'dɪlɪk/ *a.* of or like an idyll; peaceful and happy; **idyllically** *adv.*

i.e. *abbr.* that is to say. [L *id est*]

-ie see -Y[2].

if 1 *conj.* on the condition or supposition that, in the event that (*if he comes I will tell him*; *if you are tired we can rest*); with past tense, implying that condition is not fulfilled (*if I knew I would say*); even though (*I'll finish it, if it takes me all day*); whenever (*if I am not sure I ask*); whether (*see if you can find it*); expressing wish or surprise (*if you would close the door*; *if it isn't my old hat!*). 2 *n.* condition, supposition (*too many ifs about it*). [OE]

igloo /'ɪglu:/ *n.* Eskimo dome-shaped hut, esp. one built of snow. [Eskimo, = house]

igneous /'ɪgnɪəs/ *a.* produced by volcanic action; of fire. [L (*ignis* fire)]

ignite /ɪg'naɪt/ *v.* set fire to; catch fire; make intensely hot. [L *ignio ignit-* set on fire]

ignition /ɪg'nɪʃ(ə)n/ *n.* igniting; mechanism for or act of starting combustion in cylinder of internal-combustion engine. [F or L (prec.)]

ignoble /ɪg'nəʊb(ə)l/ *a.* dishonourable, base; of low birth or position; **ignobly** *adv.* [F or L (IN-², NOBLE)]

ignominious /ɪgnə'mɪnɪəs/ *a.* humiliating. [F or L (foll.)]

ignominy /'ɪgnəmɪnɪ/ *n.* dishonour, infamy. [F or L (IN-², L (*g*)*nomen* name)]

ignoramus /ɪgnə'reɪməs/ *n.* ignorant person. [L, = we do not know (IGNORE)]

ignorant /'ɪgnərənt/ *a.* lacking knowledge; uninformed; uncouth through lack of knowledge; **ignorance** *n.* [F f. L (foll.)]

ignore /ɪg'nɔ:/ *v.t.* refuse to take notice of; intentionally disregard. [F or L (*ignoro* not know)]

iguana /ɪg'wɑ:nə/ *n.* large tree lizard of W. Indies and S. America. [Sp. f. Carib]

iguanodon /ɪg'wɑ:nədɒn/ *n.* large herbivorous dinosaur.

ikon var. of ICON.

il-¹, ² see IN-¹, ².

ileum /'ɪlɪəm/ *n.* (*pl.* **ilea**) third and last portion of small intestine. [L *ilium*]

ilex /'aɪleks/ *n.* holm-oak; plant of genus including holly. [L]

iliac /'ɪlɪæk/ *a.* of the flank (*iliac artery*). [L (*ilia* flanks)]

ilk 1 *a. Sc.* same. 2 *n. colloq.* kind, sort. 3 **of that ilk** of ancestral estate with same name as family. [OE]

ill 1 *a.* out of health, sick; (of health) unsound; harmful (*ill effects*); hostile, unfavourable (*ill feeling*; *ill fortune*); irritable (*ill humour*, *temper*); improper, deficient (*with an ill grace*). 2 *adv.* badly, wrongly; unfavourably; scarcely (*can ill afford to do it*). 3 *n.* injury, harm, evil; (in *pl.*) misfortunes. 4 **ill-advised** (of action) unwise; **ill at ease** embarrassed, uncomfortable; **ill-bred** badly brought up, rude; **ill-disposed** unfavourably disposed (*towards*), disposed to evil; **ill-fated** destined to or bringing bad fortune; **ill-favoured** unattractive, objectionable; **ill-gotten** acquired by evil or unlawful means; **ill-mannered** having bad manners; **ill-natured** churlish, unkind; **ill-starred** unlucky; **ill-tempered** morose, irritable; **ill-timed** done or occurring at unsuitable time; **ill-treat** (or **-use**) treat badly or cruelly; **ill will** hostility, unkind feeling. [ON]

illegal /ɪ'li:g(ə)l/ *a.* not legal, contrary to law; **illegality** /ɪlɪ'gælɪtɪ/ *n.*; **illegally** *adv.* [IN-²]

illegible /ɪ'ledʒɪb(ə)l/ *a.* not legible; **illegibility** /-'bɪlɪtɪ/ *n.*; **illegibly** *adv.*

illegitimate /ɪlɪ'dʒɪtɪmət/ *a.* (of child) born of parents not married to each other; not authorized by law; improper; wrongly inferred; **illegitimacy** *n.*

illiberal /ɪ'lɪbər(ə)l/ *a.* intolerant, narrow-minded; without liberal culture, sordid; stingy; **illiberality** /-'rælɪtɪ/ *n.*; **illiberally** *adv.*

illicit /ɪ'lɪsɪt/ *a.* unlawful, forbidden.

illiterate /ɪ'lɪtərət/ 1 *a.* unable to read; uneducated. 2 *n.* illiterate person. 3 **illiteracy** *n.*

illness *n.* ill health, state of being ill; disease. [ILL]

illogical /ɪ'lɒdʒɪk(ə)l/ *a.* contrary to or devoid of logic; **illogicality** /-'kælɪtɪ/ *n.*; **illogically** *adv.* [IN-²]

illuminant /ɪ'lu:mɪnənt/ 1 *n.* means of illumination. 2 *a.* serving to illuminate. [L (*lumen* light)]

illuminate /ɪ'lu:mɪneɪt/ *v.t.* light up; enlighten spiritually or intellectually; help to explain (subject); shed lustre on; decorate with lights as sign of festivity; decorate (manuscript, initial letter, etc.) with gold or other bright colours; **illumination** /-'neɪʃ(ə)n/ *n.*; **illuminative** *a.*

illumine /ɪ'lju:mɪn/ *v.t. literary* light up; enlighten spiritually. [F f. L (ILLUMINANT)]

illusion /ɪ'lu:ʒ(ə)n, ɪ'lju:-/ *n.* false belief; something wrongly believed to exist; deceptive appearance; **illusive** *a.*; **illusory** *a.* [F f. L (*illudo* mock)]

illusionist *n.* producer of illusions, conjuror.

illustrate /'ɪləstreɪt/ *v.t.* provide (book, newspaper, etc.) with pictures; make clear esp. by examples or drawings; serve as example of; **illustrator** *n.* [L (*lustro* light up)]

illustration /ɪlə'streɪʃ(ə)n/ *n.* illustrating; picture or drawing in book etc.; explanatory example. [F f. L (prec.)]

illustrative /'ɪləstrətɪv/ *a.* explanatory (*of*). [ILLUSTRATE]

illustrious /ɪ'lʌstrɪəs/ *a.* distinguished, renowned. [L *illustris* (ILLUSTRATE)]

im-[1, 2] see IN-[1, 2].

image /'ɪmɪdʒ/ **1** *n.* imitation of object's external form, e.g. statue esp. as object of worship; reputation, general impression of person or thing; simile, metaphor; mental representation; optical counterpart produced by rays of light reflected from mirror etc.; counterpart in appearance (*he is the image of his father*); idea, conception. **2** *v.t.* describe or imagine vividly; make an image of, portray; reflect, mirror. [F f. L *imago imagin-*]

imagery *n.* figurative illustration; use of images in literature etc.; images, statuary, carving.

imaginary /ɪ'mædʒɪnərɪ/ *a.* existing only in imagination. [L (IMAGE)]

imagination /ɪmædʒɪ'neɪʃ(ə)n/ *n.* mental faculty forming images or concepts of objects not existent or present, creative faculty of the mind. [F f. L (IMAGINE)]

imaginative /ɪ'mædʒɪnətɪv/ *a.* having or showing a high degree of imagination.

imagine /ɪ'mædʒɪn/ *v.t.* form mental image of; picture to oneself (something non-existent or not present); conceive (*imagine him to be very cruel*); guess (*cannot imagine where he has gone*); *colloq.* suppose. [F f. L (IMAGE)]

imago /ɪ'meɪgəʊ/ *n.* (*pl.* **imagines** /-dʒɪni:z/) fully developed stage of insect, e.g. butterfly. [L (IMAGE)]

imam /ɪ'mɑ:m/ *n.* leader of prayers in mosque; title of some Muslim leaders. [Arab.]

imbalance /ɪm'bæləns/ *n.* lack of balance; disproportion. [IN-[2]]

imbecile /'ɪmbɪsi:l/ **1** *n.* person of abnormally weak intellect; stupid person. **2** *a.* mentally weak, idiotic; stupid. **3 imbecility** /-'sɪlɪtɪ/ *n.* [F f. L]

imbed var. of EMBED.

imbibe /ɪm'baɪb/ *v.t.* drink (esp. alcoholic liquor); absorb (ideas, moisture, etc.); inhale (air etc.). [L (*bibo* drink)]

imbroglio /ɪm'brəʊljəʊ/ *n.* (*pl.* **imbroglios**) complicated or confused situation; confused heap. [It. (IN-[1], BROIL[1])]

imbue /ɪm'bju:/ *v.t.* inspire or permeate (*with* feelings, opinions, or qualities); saturate or dye (*with*). [F, or L *imbuo*]

IMF *abbr.* International Monetary Fund.

imitate /'ɪmɪteɪt/ *v.t.* follow example of; mimic; make copy of; be like; **imitable** *a.*; **imitator** *n.* [L *imitor -tat-*]

imitation /ɪmɪ'teɪʃ(ə)n/ *n.* imitating; copy, counterfeit (often *attrib.*: *imitation leather*). [F or L (prec.)]

imitative /'ɪmɪtətɪv/ *a.* imitating; **imitative word** word whose sound reproduces a natural sound, e.g. *fizz*, or is otherwise suggestive, e.g. *blob*. [L (IMITATE)]

immaculate /ɪ'mækjʊlət/ *a.* pure, spotless; faultless, innocent; **immaculacy** *n.* [L (IN-[2], *macula* spot)]

immanent /'ɪmənənt/ *a.* inherent; (of God) permanently pervading the universe; **immanence** *n.* [L (IN-[1], *maneo* remain)]

immaterial /ɪmə'tɪərɪəl/ *a.* not material, not corporeal; unimportant, irrelevant; **immateriality** /-'ælɪtɪ/ *n.* [IN-[2]]

immature /ɪmə'tjʊə/ *a.* not mature; unripe; **immaturity** *n.*

immeasurable /ɪ'meʒərəb(ə)l/ *a.* not measurable; immense; **immeasurably** *adv.*

immediate /ɪ'mi:dɪət/ *a.* occurring at once (*immediate reply*); without intervening medium, direct, nearest, not separated by others (*the immediate future, my immediate neighbour*); **immediacy** *n.* [F or L (IN-[2])]

immediately 1 *adv.* without pause or delay; without intermediary. **2** *conj. colloq.* as soon as.

immemorial /ɪmɪ'mɔ:rɪəl/ *a.* ancient beyond memory or record (*from time immemorial*); very old. [IN-[2]]

immense /ɪ'mens/ *a.* vast, huge; immeasurably large; *colloq.* great (*an immense difference*); *sl.* very good; **immensity** *n.* [F f. L (*metior mens-* measure)]

immensely *adv.* in immense degree; *colloq.* very much.

immerse /ɪ'mɜ:s/ *v.t.* dip or plunge (*in* liquid); cause (person) to be completely under water, baptize thus; involve deeply (*in* thought, debt, etc.); embed. [L (*mergo mers-* dip)]

immersion /ɪ'mɜ:ʃ(ə)n/ *n.* immersing or being immersed; **immersion heater** electric heater designed to be immersed in liquid to be heated, esp. as fixture in hot-water tank.

immigrant /'ɪmɪgrənt/ **1** *n.* one who immigrates; descendant of recent (esp. coloured) immigrants. **2** *a.* immigrating; of immigrants. [foll.]

immigrate /'ɪmɪgreɪt/ *v.i.* come into a foreign country as settler; **immigration** /-'greɪʃ(ə)n/ *n.* [IN-[1]]

imminent /'ɪmɪnənt/ *a.* (of event, esp. danger) about to happen; **imminence** *n.* [L *immineo* be impending]

immiscible /ɪ'mɪsɪb(ə)l/ *a.* that cannot

be mixed (*with* another substance); **immiscibility** /-'bɪlɪtɪ/ *n.* [IN-²]

immobile /ɪ'məʊbaɪl/ *a.* immovable; motionless; **immobility** /ɪmə'bɪlɪtɪ/ *n.* [F f. L (IN-²)]

immobilize /ɪ'məʊbɪlaɪz/ *v.t.* make or keep immobile; keep (limb or patient) still for healing purposes; **immobilization** /-'zeɪʃ(ə)n/ *n.*

immoderate /ɪ'mɒdərət/ *a.* excessive, lacking moderation. [IN-²]

immodest /ɪ'mɒdɪst/ *a.* indecent; impudent; conceited; **immodesty** *n.*

immolate /'ɪməleɪt/ *v.t.* kill as sacrifice; **immolation** /-'leɪʃ(ə)n/ *n.* [L, = sprinkle with meal]

immoral /ɪ'mɒr(ə)l/ *a.* morally wrong, esp. in sexual matters; opposed to morality; depraved, dissolute; **immorality** /ɪmə'rælɪtɪ/ *n.*; **immorally** *adv.* [IN-²]

immortal /ɪ'mɔ:t(ə)l/ **1** *a.* not mortal, living for ever; divine; unfading; famous for all time. **2** *n.* immortal being, esp. (in *pl.*) gods of antiquity; person (esp. author) of enduring fame. **3 immortality** /-'tælɪtɪ/ *n.*; **immortalize** *v.t.*; **immortally** *adv.* [L (IN-²)]

immovable /ɪ'mu:vəb(ə)l/ *a.* that cannot be moved; unyielding; emotionless; motionless; (of property) consisting of land, houses, etc.; **immovability** /-'bɪlɪtɪ/ *n.*; **immovably** *adv.* [IN-²]

immune /ɪ'mju:n/ *a.* having immunity (*from* punishment or taxation; *against* infection or poison; *to* criticism). [L *immunis* exempt]

immunity *n.* ability of organism to resist and overcome infection; freedom or exemption (*from*).

immunize /'ɪmju:naɪz/ *v.t.* make immune, esp. against infection; **immunization** /-'zeɪʃ(ə)n/ *n.*

immunology /ɪmju:'nɒlədʒɪ/ *n.* study of resistance to infection.

immure /ɪ'mjʊə/ *v.t.* imprison; shut in. [F or L (*murus* wall)]

immutable /ɪ'mju:təb(ə)l/ *a.* unchangeable; **immutability** /-'bɪlɪtɪ/ *n.*; **immutably** *adv.* [L (IN-²)]

imp *n.* small devil; mischievous child. [OE, = young shoot]

impact 1 /'ɪmpækt/ *n.* collision, force of collision; strong effect or influence. **2** /ɪm'pækt/ *v.t.* press or fix firmly; (in *p.p.*, of tooth) wedged between another tooth and jaw. **3 impaction** /ɪm'pækʃ(ə)n/ *n.* [L (IMPINGE)]

impair /ɪm'peə/ *v.t.* damage, weaken; **impairment** *n.* [F f. L, = make worse (*pejor*)]

impala /ɪm'pɑ:lə/ *n.* (*pl.* same) small S. African antelope. [Zulu]

impale /ɪm'peɪl/ *v.t.* transfix (body) on or with pointed stake etc. esp. as capital punishment; **impalement** *n.* [F or L (*palus* PALE¹)]

impalpable /ɪm'pælpəb(ə)l/ *a.* not palpable; not easily grasped by the mind, intangible; (of powder) very fine; **impalpability** /-'bɪlɪtɪ/ *n.*; **impalpably** *adv.* [F or L (IN-²)]

impanel var. of EMPANEL.

impart /ɪm'pɑ:t/ *v.t.* give share of (thing *to*); communicate (news etc. *to*). [F f. L (PART)]

impartial /ɪm'pɑ:ʃ(ə)l/ *a.* fair, not partial; **impartiality** /-ʃɪ'ælɪtɪ/ *n.*; **impartially** *adv.* [IN-²]

impassable /ɪm'pɑ:səb(ə)l/ *a.* that cannot be traversed; **impassability** /-'bɪlɪtɪ/ *n.*; **impassably** *adv.*

impasse /'æmpɑ:s/ *n.* deadlock; position from which there is no escape. [F (PASS¹)]

impassible /ɪm'pæsɪb(ə)l/ *a.* not liable to pain or injury; impassive; **impassibility** /-'bɪlɪtɪ/ *n.*; **impassibly** *adv.* [F f. L (PASSION)]

impassioned /ɪm'pæʃ(ə)nd/ *a.* deeply moved, ardent. [It. *impassionato* (PASSION)]

impassive /ɪm'pæsɪv/ *a.* not feeling or showing emotion; serene; **impassivity** /-'sɪvɪtɪ/ *n.* [IN-²]

impasto /ɪm'pæstəʊ/ *n.* (*pl.* **impastos**) laying on of paint thickly. [It.]

impatient /ɪm'peɪʃənt/ *a.* not patient; showing lack of patience; intolerant (*of*); eager; **impatience** *n.* [F f. L (IN-²)]

impeach /ɪm'pi:tʃ/ *v.t.* accuse of treason or high crime before competent tribunal; call in question, disparage; **impeachment** *n.* [F *empecher* f. L (*pedica* fetter)]

impeccable /ɪm'pekəb(ə)l/ *a.* faultless; not liable to sin; **impeccability** /-'bɪlɪtɪ/ *n.*; **impeccably** *adv.* [IN-²]

impecunious /ɪmpɪ'kju:nɪəs/ *a.* having little or no money; **impecuniosity** /-'ɒsɪtɪ/ *n.* [PECUNIARY]

impedance /ɪm'pi:dəns/ *n.* total effective resistance of electric circuit etc. to alternating current. [foll.]

impede /ɪm'pi:d/ *v.t.* retard by obstructing, hinder. [L *impedio* (*pes ped-* foot)]

impediment /ɪm'pedɪmənt/ *n.* hindrance; defect in speech, esp. lisp or stammer. [L (prec.)]

impedimenta /ɪmpedɪ'mentə/ *n.pl.* encumbrances; baggage, esp. of army.

impel /ɪm'pel/ *v.t.* (**-ll-**) drive, force, urge; propel. [L (*pello* drive)]

impend /ɪm'pend/ *v.i.* (of event or danger) be imminent; hang (*over*). [L (*pendeo* hang)]

impenetrable /ɪm'penɪtrəb(ə)l/ *a.* not penetrable; inscrutable; impervious (*to* or *by* ideas etc.); **impenetrability** /-'bɪlɪtɪ/ *n.*; **impenetrably** *adv.* [IN-²]

impenitent /ɪm'penɪtənt/ *a.* not penitent; **impenitence** *n.*
imperative /ɪm'perətɪv/ **1** *a.* essential, urgently needed; *Gram.* of mood expressing command; peremptory. **2** *n.* imperative mood. [L (*impero* command)]
imperceptible /ɪmpə'septɪb(ə)l/ *a.* not perceptible, very slight or gradual; **imperceptibly** *adv.* [F or med.L (IN-[2])]
imperfect /ɪm'pɜ:fɪkt/ **1** *a.* not perfect, incomplete, faulty; *Gram.* of tense denoting action going on but not completed (esp. in past, e.g. *was doing*). **2** *n.* imperfect tense. [F f. L]
imperfection /ɪmpə'fekʃ(ə)n/ *n.* imperfectness; fault, blemish.
imperial /ɪm'pɪərɪəl/ *a.* of or characteristic of an empire or similar sovereign State; of an emperor; majestic; (of weights and measures) used (now or formerly) by statute in UK (*imperial gallon*); **imperially** *adv.* [F f. L (*imperium* dominion)]
imperialism *n.* imperial rule or system; (usu. *derog.*) policy of extending a country's influence by acquiring dependencies, or through trade, diplomacy, etc.; **imperialist** *n.*; **imperialistic** /-'lɪstɪk/ *a.*
imperil /ɪm'perɪl/ *v.t.* (-ll-, *US* -l-) endanger. [IN-[1]]
imperious /ɪm'pɪərɪəs/ *a.* domineering; urgent. [L (IMPERIAL)]
imperishable /ɪm'perɪʃəb(ə)l/ *a.* that cannot perish. [IN-[2]]
impermanent /ɪm'pɜ:mənənt/ *a.* not permanent; **impermanence** *n.*; **impermanency** *n.* [IN-[2]]
impermeable /ɪm'pɜ:mɪəb(ə)l/ *a.* not permeable; **impermeability** /-'bɪlɪtɪ/ *n.*
impersonal /ɪm'pɜ:sən(ə)l/ *a.* having no personality or personal feeling or reference; (of verb) used without definite subject (e.g. *it snows*); (of pronoun) = INDEFINITE; **impersonality** /-'nælɪtɪ/ *n.*; **impersonally** *adv.*
impersonate /ɪm'pɜ:səneɪt/ *v.t.* pretend to be (another person); play the part of; personify; **impersonation** /-'neɪʃ(ə)n/ *n.*; **impersonator** *n.* [IN-[1], L PERSONA]
impertinent /ɪm'pɜ:tɪnənt/ *a.* insolent, saucy; irrelevant; **impertinence** *n.* [IN-[2]]
imperturbable /ɪmpə'tɜ:bəb(ə)l/ *a.* not excitable, calm; **imperturbability** /-'bɪlɪtɪ/ *n.*; **imperturbably** *adv.*
impervious /ɪm'pɜ:vɪəs/ *a.* not affording passage (*to* water etc.); not responsive (*to* argument etc.).
impetigo /ɪmpɪ'taɪgəʊ/ *n.* contagious skin disease causing spots or pimples. [L (*impeto* assail)]
impetuous /ɪm'petjʊəs/ *a.* acting or done rashly or with sudden energy; moving violently or fast; **impetuosity** /-'ɒsɪtɪ/ *n.* [F f. L (foll.)]
impetus /'ɪmpɪtəs/ *n.* force with which body moves; impulse, driving force. [L (*impeto* assail)]
impiety /ɪm'paɪətɪ/ *n.* lack of piety or reverence. [F or L (IMPIOUS)]
impinge /ɪm'pɪndʒ/ *v.i.* make impact; encroach; **impingement** *n.* [L (*pango pact-* fix)]
impious /'ɪmpɪəs/ *a.* not pious; wicked. [L (PIOUS)]
impish *a.* of or like an imp; mischievous. [IMP]
implacable /ɪm'plækəb(ə)l/ *a.* not appeasable; **implacability** /-'bɪlɪtɪ/ *n.*; **implacably** *adv.* [F or L (IN-[2])]
implant 1 /ɪm'plɑ:nt/ *v.t.* plant, insert or fix (*in*); instil (idea etc.) *in* person's mind; insert (tissue etc.) in living body. **2** /'ɪmplɑ:nt/ *n.* thing implanted, esp. piece of tissue. **3 implantation** /-'teɪʃ(ə)n/ *n.* [F or L (PLANT)]
implausible /ɪm'plɔ:zɪb(ə)l/ *a.* not plausible; **implausibility** /-'bɪlɪtɪ/ *n.*; **implausibly** *adv.* [IN-[2]]
implement /'ɪmplɪmənt/ **1** *n.* tool, instrument, utensil. **2** /also -ment/ *v.t.* put (contract, decision, promise, etc.) into effect. **3 implementation** /-'teɪʃ(ə)n/ *n.* [L (*impleo* fulfil)]
implicate /'ɪmplɪkeɪt/ *v.t.* show (person) to be concerned (*in* charge, crime, etc.); involve; imply. [L (*plico* fold)]
implication /ɪmplɪ'keɪʃ(ə)n/ *n.* thing implied; implying; implicating.
implicit /ɪm'plɪsɪt/ *a.* implied though not expressed; absolute, unquestioning (*implicit obedience*). [F or L (IMPLICATE)]
implode /ɪm'pləʊd/ *v.* (cause to) burst inwards; **implosion** /-'pləʊʒ(ə)n/ *n.* [IN-[1]; cf. EXPLODE]
implore /ɪm'plɔ:/ *v.t.* entreat (person *to do* thing); beg earnestly for. [F or L (*ploro* weep)]
imply /ɪm'plaɪ/ *v.t.* indicate or suggest (*that* thing not stated is true); involve truth of (thing not stated); insinuate; mean. [F f. L (IMPLICATE)]
impolite /ɪmpə'laɪt/ *a.* uncivil, rude. [IN-[2]]
impolitic /ɪm'pɒlɪtɪk/ *a.* inexpedient, unwise.
imponderable /ɪm'pɒndərəb(ə)l/ **1** *a.* that cannot be estimated; weightless, very light. **2** *n.* imponderable thing. **3 imponderably** *adv.*
import 1 /ɪm'pɔ:t/ *v.t.* bring (esp. foreign goods) into a country; imply, mean. **2** /'ɪmpɔ:t/ *n.* article imported; (usu. in *pl.*) amount imported; importing; what is implied, meaning; importance. [L (*porto* carry)]
important /ɪm'pɔ:tənt/ *a.* of great effect

or consequence, momentous; (of person) having high rank or great authority; pompous; **importance** *n.* [F f. med.L (prec.)]

importation /ɪmpɔːˈteɪʃ(ə)n/ *n.* importing of goods, being imported. [IMPORT]

importunate /ɪmˈpɔːtjʊnət/ *a.* making persistent or pressing requests; **importunity** /ɪmpɔːˈtjuːnɪtɪ/ *n.* [L *importunus* inconvenient]

importune /ɪmˈpɔːtjuːn, -ˈtjuːn/ *v.t.* solicit (person) pressingly; solicit for immoral purpose. [F or med.L (prec.)]

impose /ɪmˈpəʊz/ *v.* lay (tax, duty, etc., *on* or *upon*); enforce compliance with; inflict; palm off (thing *upon* person); lay (pages of type) in proper order; **impose on** (or **upon**) take advantage of (person, his good nature, etc.), deceive, impress, overawe. [F f. L (*pono* put)]

imposing *a.* impressive, formidable, esp. in appearance.

imposition /ɪmpəˈzɪʃ(ə)n/ *n.* unfair demand or burden; tax, duty; work set as punishment at school; laying on of hands in blessing etc.; act of deception or taking advantage. [F or L (prec.)]

impossible /ɪmˈpɒsɪb(ə)l/ *a.* not possible; *loosely* not easy or convenient or credible; *colloq.* outrageous or intolerable (*impossible person*); **impossibility** /-ˈbɪlɪtɪ/ *n.*; **impossibly** *adv.* [F or L (IN-²)]

impost¹ /ˈɪmpəʊst/ *n.* tax or duty. [F f. med.L (IMPOSE)]

impost² /ˈɪmpəʊst/ *n.* upper course of pillar, carrying arch. [F or It. f. L (IMPOSE)]

impostor /ɪmˈpɒstə/ *n.* one who assumes a false character or personality; swindler. [F f. L (prec.)]

imposture /ɪmˈpɒstʃə/ *n.* deception, sham.

impotent /ˈɪmpətənt/ *a.* powerless; decrepit; (of male) without sexual power; **impotence** *n.* [F f. L (IN-²)]

impound /ɪmˈpaʊnd/ *v.t.* confiscate; take legal possession of; shut up (cattle etc.) in pound. [IN-¹]

impoverish /ɪmˈpɒvərɪʃ/ *v.t.* make poor; **impoverishment** *n.* [F (POVERTY)]

impracticable /ɪmˈpræktɪkəb(ə)l/ *a.* not practicable; **impracticability** /-ˈbɪlɪtɪ/ *n.*; **impracticably** *adv.* [IN-²]

impractical /ɪmˈpræktɪk(ə)l/ *a.* *US* not practical; not practicable; **impracticality** /-ˈkælɪtɪ/ *n.*

imprecate /ˈɪmprɪkeɪt/ *v.t.* invoke (evil *upon*); **imprecation** /-ˈkeɪʃ(ə)n/ *n.*; **imprecatory** *a.* [L (*precor* pray)]

imprecise /ɪmprɪˈsaɪs/ *a.* not precise; **imprecision** /-ˈsɪʒ(ə)n/ *n.* [IN-²]

impregnable /ɪmˈpregnəb(ə)l/ *a.* (of fortress etc., or *fig.*) safe against attack; **impregnability** /-ˈbɪlɪtɪ/ *n.*; **impregnably** *adv.* [F (IN-², L *prehendo* take)]

impregnate /ˈɪmpregneɪt/ *v.t.* fill or saturate (*with*); imbue (*with*); make (female) pregnant; fertilize (ovum); **impregnatable** *a.*; **impregnation** /-ˈneɪʃ(ə)n/ *n.* [L (PREGNANT)]

impresario /ɪmprɪˈsɑːrɪəʊ/ *n.* (*pl.* **impresarios**) organizer of public entertainment, esp. opera or concert. [It.]

impress¹ **1** /ɪmˈpres/ *v.t.* affect or influence deeply; affect (person) strongly (*with* idea etc.); fix, imprint (idea etc. *on* person); imprint or stamp (mark etc. *on* thing, thing *with* mark). **2** /ˈɪmpres/ *n.* mark impressed; characteristic quality. **3 impressible** *a.* [F (PRESS¹)]

impress² /ɪmˈpres/ *v.t.* *hist.* force to serve in army or navy; **impressment** *n.* [IN-¹, PRESS²]

impression /ɪmˈpreʃ(ə)n/ *n.* effect, esp. on mind or feelings; belief, esp. vague or mistaken; imitation of person or sound, done to entertain; impressing, mark impressed; unaltered reprint from standing type or plates; copies forming one issue of book, newspaper, etc.; print from type or engraving. [F f. L (IMPRESS¹)]

impressionable *a.* easily influenced; **impressionability** /-ˈbɪlɪtɪ/ *n.*; **impressionably** *adv.* [F (prec.)]

impressionism *n.* style of painting, music, or writing mainly concerned with mood or overall effect; **impressionist** *n.*; **impressionistic** /-ˈnɪstɪk/ *a.*

impressive /ɪmˈpresɪv/ *a.* able to excite deep feeling esp. of approval or admiration. [IMPRESS¹]

imprimatur /ɪmprɪˈmeɪtə/ *n.* licence to print, usu. from Roman Catholic Church; sanction. [L, = let it be printed]

imprint **1** /ɪmˈprɪnt/ *v.t.* set firmly (mark *on*, idea etc. *on* or *in* mind); stamp (thing *with* figure). **2** /ˈɪmprɪnt/ *n.* impression, stamp; publisher's name etc. on title-page of book. [F f. L (IMPRESSION)]

imprison /ɪmˈprɪz(ə)n/ *v.t.* put into prison; confine; **imprisonment** *n.* [F]

improbable /ɪmˈprɒbəb(ə)l/ *a.* not likely; **improbability** /-ˈbɪlɪtɪ/ *n.*; **improbably** *adv.* [IN-²]

improbity /ɪmˈprəʊbɪtɪ/ *n.* wickedness, dishonesty.

impromptu /ɪmˈprɒmptjuː/ **1** *a.* & *adv.* unrehearsed. **2** *n.* musical composition resembling improvisation; extempore performance. [F, f. L *in promptu* in readiness (PROMPT)]

improper /ɪmˈprɒpə/ *a.* unseemly, indecent; wrong, incorrect; **improper fraction** fraction with numerator greater than denominator. [F or L (IN-²)]

impropriety /ɪmprəˈpraɪətɪ/ *n.* incorrectness, unfitness, indecency; instance of this.

improve /ɪmˈpruːv/ *v.* make or become better; make good use of (occasion, opportunities); **improve on** (or **upon**) produce something better than; **improvable** *a.*; **improvement** *n.* [AF f. F *prou* profit]

improvident /ɪmˈprɒvɪdənt/ *a.* lacking foresight or care for the future; **improvidence** *n.* [F (IN-[2])]

improvise /ˈɪmprəvaɪz/ *v.t.* compose (verse, music, etc.) extempore; construct from materials not intended for the purpose; **improvisation** /-ˈzeɪʃ(ə)n/ *n.* [F or It. f. L (PROVIDE)]

imprudent /ɪmˈpruːdənt/ *a.* rash, indiscreet; **imprudence** *n.* [L (IN-[2])]

impudent /ˈɪmpjʊdənt/ *a.* impertinent, insolent; **impudence** *n.* [L (*pudeo* be ashamed)]

impugn /ɪmˈpjuːn/ *v.t.* challenge or call in question; **impugnment** *n.* [L (*pugno* fight)]

impulse /ˈɪmpʌls/ *n.* impelling, push; impetus; sharp force producing change of momentum (e.g. blow of hammer); wave of excitation in nerve; mental incitement; sudden tendency to act without reflection (*impulse buying*). [L (PULSE[1])]

impulsion /ɪmˈpʌlʃ(ə)n/ *n.* impelling, push; mental impulse; impetus. [F f. L (prec.)]

impulsive /ɪmˈpʌlsɪv/ *a.* tending to act on impulse; done on impulse; tending to impel. [F or L (prec.)]

impunity /ɪmˈpjuːnɪtɪ/ *n.* exemption from punishment or injurious consequences (*rob, drink, with impunity*). [L (*poena* penalty)]

impure /ɪmˈpjʊə/ *a.* mixed with foreign matter, adulterated; dirty; unchaste; **impurity** *n.* [L (IN-[2])]

impute /ɪmˈpjuːt/ *v.t.* attribute (fault etc.) *to*; **imputation** /-ˈteɪʃ(ə)n/ *n.* [F f. L (*puto* reckon)]

in 1 *prep.* expressing inclusion or position within limits of space, time, circumstance, etc. (*in England*; *in bed*; *in the rain*); during the time of (*in the night*; *in 1984*); within the time of (*will be back in two hours*); with respect to (*blind in one eye*; *good in parts*); as proportionate part of (*one in three failed*; *gradient of one in six*); with the form or arrangement of (*packed in tens*; *falling in folds*); as member of (*in the army*); concerned with (*in politics*); as content of (*there is something in what you say*); within the ability of (*does he have it in him?*); having condition of, affected by (*in bad health*; *in danger*); having as purpose (*in search of*; *in reply to*); by means of or using as material (*drawn in pencil*; *modelled in bronze*); having as language of expression or (of music) key (*written in French*; *symphony in C*); (of word) having as beginning or ending (*words in* un-); wearing as dress (*in blue*; *in a suit*); with the identity of (*found a friend in Mary*); (of animal) pregnant with (*in calf*); into (with verb of motion or change: *put it in the box*; *cut it in two*); introducing indirect object after verb (*believe in*, *engage in*, *share in*, etc.); forming adverbial phrases (*in any case*; *in reality*; *in short*). **2** *adv.* expressing position within limits or motion to such position: into room, house, etc. (*come in*); at home, in one's office, etc.; so as to be enclosed (*locked in*); in a publication (*is the advert in?*); on or to the inward side (*rub it in*); in fashion, season, or office, elected, exerting favourable action etc. (*long skirts are in*; *the SDP man got in*; *her luck was in*); (of man or side in cricket) having turn to bat; (of transport, season, harvest, order, etc.) having arrived or been received; (of fire) continuing to burn; designating effective action (*join in*; *tide is in*); as *suffix* denoting prolonged action esp. by large numbers (*sit-in*; *teach-in*). **3** *a.* internal, living in, inside; fashionable, esoteric (*the in thing to do*). **4 in all** see ALL; **in between** see BETWEEN; **in for** about to undergo, competing in or for; **in on** sharing in, privy to; **ins and outs** all the details (*of* procedure etc.); **in so far as** see FAR; **in that** because, in so far as; **in with** on good terms with; **nothing** (or **not much**) **in it** no (or little) advantage to be seen in one possibility over another. [OE]

in-[1] *prefix* (**il-** before *l*; **im-** before *b, m, p*; **ir-** before *r*) in, on, into, towards, within (*induce, influx, insight, intrude*). [prec. or L]

in-[2] *prefix* (**il-** etc. as prec.) added to adjectives in sense 'not', and to nouns in sense 'without', 'lacking'.

¶ The list at the foot of pp. 369–70 is of words that can be understood by reference to the simple word and the above; it does not include all derivatives of obvious formation (e.g. *inaccuracy* from *inaccurate*). Pronunciation and stress follow those of the main word.

inability
inaccurate
inaction
inactive
inadequate
inadmissible
inadvisable
inalienable
inapplicable

in. *abbr*. inch(es).
In *symb*. indium.
in absentia /ɪn æb'sentɪə/ in (his or her or their) absence. [L]
inaccessible /ɪnæk'sesɪb(ə)l/ *a*. not accessible; (of person) unapproachable; **inaccessibility** /-'bɪlɪtɪ/ *n*.; **inaccessibly** *adv*. [IN-²]
inadvertent /ɪnəd'vɜ:tənt/ *a*. unintentional; negligent, inattentive; **inadvertence** *n*.; **inadvertency** *n*. [IN-², ADVERT²]
inamorato /ɪnæmə'rɑ:təʊ/ *n*. (*fem*. **inamorata** /-tə/) lover. [It. *innamorato* (IN-¹, L *amor* love)]
inane /ɪ'neɪn/ *a*. silly, senseless; empty, void; **inanity** /ɪ'nænɪtɪ/ *n*. [L *inanis*]
inanimate /ɪn'ænɪmət/ *a*. not endowed with, or deprived of, animal life; spiritless, dull; **inanimation** /-'meɪʃ(ə)n/ *n*. [L (IN-²)]
inanition /ɪnə'nɪʃ(ə)n/ *n*. emptiness esp. from want of nourishment. [L (INANE)]
inapt /ɪn'æpt/ *a*. not suitable; unskilful; **inaptitude** *n*. [IN-²]
inarticulate /ɪnɑ:'tɪkjʊlət/ *a*. unable to express oneself clearly; (of speech) not articulate, indistinct; dumb; not jointed.
inasmuch /ɪnəz'mʌtʃ/ *adv*. in **inasmuch as** since, because. [*in as much*]
inattentive /ɪnə'tentɪv/ *a*. not paying attention; neglecting to show courtesy; **inattention** *n*. [IN-²]
inaugural /ɪ'nɔ:gjʊrəl/ **1** *a*. of inauguration. **2** *n*. inaugural speech or lecture. [F (foll.)]
inaugurate /ɪn'ɔ:gjʊreɪt/ *v.t.* admit formally to office, begin (undertaking), initiate public use of (building etc.), with ceremony; begin, introduce; **inauguration** /-'reɪʃ(ə)n/ *n*.; **inaugurator** *n*. [L (AUGUR)]
inboard /'ɪnbɔ:d/ **1** *adv*. within sides or towards centre of ship, aircraft, or vehicle. **2** *a*. situated inboard. [IN]
inborn *a*. naturally inherent, innate.
inbred *a*. inborn; produced by inbreeding.
inbreeding *n*. breeding from closely related animals or persons.
in-built *a*. built-in.
Inc. *abbr*. *US* Incorporated.
Inca /'ɪŋkə/ *n*. member of people of Peru before Spanish conquest. [Quechua, = lord]
incalculable /ɪn'kælkjʊləb(ə)l/ *a*. too great for calculation; not calculable beforehand, uncertain; **incalculability** /-'bɪlɪtɪ/ *n*.; **incalculably** *adv*. [IN-²]
incandesce /ɪnkæn'des/ *v*. (cause to) glow with heat. [foll.]
incandescent *a*. glowing with heat; shining; (of artificial light) produced by glowing filament etc.; **incandescence** *n*. [F f. L (*candeo* be white)]
incantation /ɪnkæn'teɪʃ(ə)n/ *n*. magical formula, spell, charm. [F f. L (*canto* sing)]
incapable /ɪn'keɪpəb(ə)l/ *a*. not capable; too honest etc. to do something; not capable of rational conduct (*drunk and incapable*); **incapability** /-'bɪlɪtɪ/ *n*.; **incapably** *adv*. [IN-²]
incapacitate /ɪnkə'pæsɪteɪt/ *v.t.* make incapable or unfit.
incapacity /ɪnkə'pæsɪtɪ/ *n*. inability, lack of power; legal disqualification.
incarcerate /ɪn'kɑ:səreɪt/ *v.t.* imprison; **incarceration** /-'reɪʃ(ə)n/ *n*. [med.L (*carcer* prison)]
incarnate /ɪn'kɑ:neɪt/ **1** /also -ət/ *a*. embodied in flesh, esp. in human form. **2** *v.t.* embody in flesh; put (idea etc.) into concrete form; be living embodiment of

inapposite
inappreciative
inapprehensible
inappropriate
inartistic
inaudible
inauspicious
incautious
incertitude
incoherent
incombustible
incommunicable
incommunicative
incomplete
incomprehensible
incomprehension
inconclusive
inconsonant
inconspicuous
incontrovertible
incorrect
incurious
indecipherable
indecorous
indefinable
indiscernible
indiscipline
indisputable
indistinguishable
indivisible
inedible
ineffaceable
ineffective
ineffectual
inefficacious
inelastic
inelegant
ineligible
inequitable
inequity
ineradicable
inessential
inexact
inexactitude
inexhaustible
inexpedient
inexpressive
inextinguishable
infertile
infrequent
inharmonious
inoperable
inoperative
inopportune
insanitary
insensitive
insentient
insufficient
insurmountable
insusceptible

(quality etc.). [L *incarnor* be made flesh (as CARNAGE)]
incarnation /ɪnkɑːˈneɪʃ(ə)n/ *n.* embodiment in flesh, esp. in human form; living type (*of* quality); **the Incarnation** incarnation of God in Christ.
incendiarism /ɪnˈsendɪərɪz(ə)m/ *n.* act(s) of arson. [foll.]
incendiary /ɪnˈsendɪərɪ/ **1** *a.* (of bomb) filled with material for causing fires; *fig.* inflammatory; of arson; guilty of arson. **2** *n.* incendiary bomb; incendiary person (*lit.* or *fig.*). [L (*incendo -cens-* kindle)]
incense[1] /ˈɪnsens/ **1** *n.* gum or spice giving sweet smell when burned; smoke of this esp. in religious ceremonial. **2** *v.t.* burn incense to; fumigate with incense; perfume as with incense. [F f. L *incensum* (prec.)]
incense[2] /ɪnˈsens/ *v.t.* make angry. [F f. L (INCENDIARY)]
incentive /ɪnˈsentɪv/ **1** *n.* motive or incitement; payment or concession encouraging effort in work. **2** *a.* inciting. [L, = setting the tune (*canto* sing)]
inception /ɪnˈsepʃ(ə)n/ *n.* beginning. [F or L (*incipio -cept-* begin)]
inceptive /ɪnˈseptɪv/ *a.* beginning; initial; (of verb) denoting beginning of action. [L (prec.)]
incessant /ɪnˈsesənt/ *a.* continual, repeated; unceasing. [F or L (*cesso* cease)]
incest /ˈɪnsest/ *n.* sexual intercourse of near relations. [L (*castus* chaste)]
incestuous /ɪnˈsestjʊəs/ *a.* of incest; guilty of incest.
inch **1** *n.* twelfth of (linear) foot, 2.54 cm.; used as unit of rainfall (= 1 inch depth of water) or as unit of map-scale (= 1 inch to 1 mile); small amount (*by inches*). **2** *v.* move gradually. **3 every inch** thoroughly (*is every inch a king*); **within an inch of his life** almost to death. [OE f. L *uncia* OUNCE[1]]
inchoate /ˈɪnkəʊət/ *a.* undeveloped; just begun; **inchoation** /-ˈeɪʃ(ə)n/ *n.* [L *inchoo, incoho* begin]
incidence /ˈɪnsɪdəns/ *n.* falling on or contact with a thing; range, scope, extent, or rate of occurrence or influence (*of* disease, tax, etc.); falling of line, ray, particles, etc., on surface. [F or med.L (foll.)]
incident **1** *n.* event or occurrence, esp. minor one; clash of armed forces (*frontier incident*); public event causing trouble; distinct piece of action in film, play, etc. **2** *a.* apt to occur, naturally attaching (*to*); (of rays etc.) falling (*on* or *upon*). [F or L (*cado* fall)]
incidental /ɪnsɪˈdent(ə)l/ *a.* having minor role in relation to more important thing or event etc., not essential; **incidental music** music played during or between the scenes of a play, film, etc.
incidentally *adv.* as an unconnected remark; in an incidental way.
incinerate /ɪnˈsɪnəreɪt/ *v.t.* consume by fire; **incineration** /-ˈreɪʃ(ə)n/ *n.* [med.L (*cinis ciner-* ashes)]
incinerator *n.* furnace or device for incineration.
incipient /ɪnˈsɪpɪənt/ *a.* beginning, in early stage. [L *incipio* begin]
incise /ɪnˈsaɪz/ *v.t.* make a cut in; engrave; **incision** /ɪnˈsɪʒ(ə)n/ *n.* [F f. L (*caedo* cut)]
incisive /ɪnˈsaɪsɪv/ *a.* sharp; clear and effective. [med.L (prec.)]
incisor /ɪnˈsaɪzə/ *n.* any of teeth between canine teeth.
incite /ɪnˈsaɪt/ *v.t.* urge or stir up (*to* action); **incitement** *n.* [F f. L (*cito* rouse)]
incivility /ɪnsɪˈvɪlɪtɪ/ *n.* rudeness; impolite act. [F or L (IN-[2])]
inclement /ɪnˈklemənt/ *a.* (of weather) severe or stormy; **inclemency** *n.*
inclination /ɪnklɪˈneɪʃ(ə)n/ *n.* tending or propensity; liking, affection; slope or slant (*of* line from the vertical, *to* another line); angle between lines; dip of magnetic needle. [F or L (foll.)]
incline **1** /ɪnˈklaɪn/ *v.* (cause to) lean, usu. from the vertical; bend forward or downward; dispose or influence (*his sincerity inclines me to trust him*; *am inclined to refuse*); have certain tendency. **2** /ˈɪnklaɪn/ *n.* slope; inclined plane. **3 inclined plane** sloping plane used e.g. to raise load with less force; **incline one's ear** listen favourably. [F f. L (*clino* bend)]
include /ɪnˈkluːd/ *v.t.* comprise or reckon in as part of a whole; put in certain category etc.; **inclusion** *n.* [L *includo -clus-* enclose (*claudo* shut)]
inclusive /ɪnˈkluːsɪv/ *a.* including (with *of*); including the limits stated (*pages 7 to 26 inclusive*); including all or much (*inclusive terms*). [med.L (prec.)]
incognito /ɪnkɒgˈniːtəʊ, ɪnˈkɒgnɪtəʊ/ **1** *adv.* under false name, with identity concealed. **2** *a.* acting incognito. **3** *n.* (*pl.* **incognitos**) pretended identity; person who is incognito. [It., = unknown (IN-[2], COGNITION)]
incognizant /ɪnˈkɒgnɪzənt/ *a.* unaware; **incognizance** *n.* [IN-[2]]
income /ˈɪnkʌm/ *n.* money received, esp. periodically or in year, from one's work, lands, investments, etc.;

income tax tax levied on income. [IN, COME]
incoming /'ɪnkʌmɪng/ *a.* coming in, esp. succeeding (*incoming tenant*).
incommensurable /ɪnkə'menʃ-ərəb(ə)l/ *a.* not commensurable; having no common measure integral or fractional (*with*); **incommensurability** /-'bɪlɪtɪ/ *n.* [L (IN-²)]
incommensurate /ɪnkə'menʃərət/ *a.* disproportionate, inadequate (*to*); incommensurable. [IN-²]
incommode /ɪnkə'məʊd/ *v.t.* inconvenience; annoy; impede. [F or L (IN-²)]
incommodious *a.* not affording comfort, inconvenient.
incommunicado /ɪnkəmju:nɪ'kɑ:dəʊ/ *a.* without means of communication; (of prisoner) in solitary confinement. [Sp. *incomunicado*]
incomparable /ɪn'kɒmpərəb(ə)l/ *a.* without an equal, matchless; **incomparably** *adv.* [IN-²]
incompatible /ɪnkəm'pætɪb(ə)l/ *a.* opposed, discordant, inconsistent (*with*); **incompatibility** /-'bɪlɪtɪ/ *n.*; **incompatibly** *adv.* [med.L (IN-²)]
incompetent /ɪn'kɒmpɪtənt/ **1** *a.* not qualified or able; not able to function; not legally qualified. **2** *n.* incompetent person. **3 incompetence** *n.* [F or L (IN-²)]
inconceivable /ɪnkən'si:vəb(ə)l/ *a.* that cannot be imagined; *colloq.* most unlikely; **inconceivably** *adv.* [IN-²]
incongruous /ɪn'kɒŋgrʊəs/ *a.* out of place, absurd; out of keeping (*with*); **incongruity** /-'u:ɪtɪ/ *n.* [L (IN-²)]
inconsequent /ɪn'kɒnsɪkwənt/ *a.* irrelevant; disconnected; not following logically; **inconsequence** *n.*
inconsequential /ɪnkɒnsɪ'kwenʃ(ə)l/ *a.* unimportant; inconsequent; **inconsequentially** *adv.* [IN-²]
inconsiderable /ɪnkən'sɪdərəb(ə)l/ *a.* not worth considering; of small size, amount, or value; **inconsiderably** *adv.* [F or L (IN-²)]
inconsiderate /ɪnkən'sɪdərət/ *a.* (of person or action) lacking in regard for others' feelings, thoughtless. [L (IN-²)]
inconsistent /ɪnkən'sɪstənt/ *a.* discordant or incompatible (*with*); acting at variance with one's own principles; **inconsistency** *n.* [IN-²]
inconsolable /ɪnkən'səʊləb(ə)l/ *a.* (of person, grief, etc.) that cannot be consoled; **inconsolably** *adv.* [F or L (IN-²)]
inconstant /ɪn'kɒnstənt/ *a.* fickle; variable; **inconstancy** *n.* [F f. L (IN-²)]
incontestable /ɪnkən'testəb(ə)l/ *a.* that cannot be disputed; **incontestably** *adv.* [F or med.L (IN-²)]
incontinent /ɪn'kɒntɪnənt/ *a.* unable to control excretions voluntarily; lacking self-restraint (esp. in sexual desire); **incontinence** *n.* [F or L (IN-²)]
inconvenience /ɪnkən'vi:nɪəns/ **1** *n.* lack of ease or comfort; cause or instance of this. **2** *v.t.* cause inconvenience to. [F f. L (IN-²)]
inconvenient *a.* unfavourable to ease or comfort; awkward, troublesome.
incorporate 1 /ɪn'kɔ:pəreɪt/ *v.* include as part or ingredient; unite (*in* one body, *with* others); form into a corporation; admit as member of company etc. **2** /ɪn'kɔ:pərət/ *a.* incorporated. **3 incorporation** /-'reɪʃ(ə)n/ *n.* [L (*corpus* body)]
incorporeal /ɪnkɔ:'pɔ:rɪəl/ *a.* without substance or material existence; **incorporeally** *adv.*; **incorporeity** /-'ri:ɪtɪ/ *n.*
incorrigible /ɪn'kɒrɪdʒɪb(ə)l/ *a.* (of person or habit) incurably bad; **incorrigibility** /-'bɪlɪtɪ/ *n.*; **incorrigibly** *adv.* [F or L (IN-²)]
incorruptible /ɪnkə'rʌptɪb(ə)l/ *a.* that cannot decay or be corrupted (esp. by bribery); **incorruptibility** /-'bɪlɪtɪ/ *n.*; **incorruptibly** *adv.*
increase 1 /ɪn'kri:s/ *v.* become or make greater or more numerous; advance (*in* power etc.). **2** /'ɪnkri:s/ *n.* growth, enlargement; (of people or animals or plants) multiplication. **3 on the increase** increasing. [F f. L (*cresco* grow)]
increasingly *adv.* more and more.
incredible /ɪn'kredɪb(ə)l/ *a.* that cannot be believed; *colloq.* surprising; **incredibility** /-'bɪlɪtɪ/ *n.*; **incredibly** *adv.* [L (IN-²)]
incredulous /ɪn'kredjʊləs/ *a.* unwilling to believe; **incredulity** /ɪnkrɪ-'dju:lɪtɪ/ *n.*
increment /'ɪnkrɪmənt/ *n.* amount of increase; profit; increase; **incremental** /-'ment(ə)l/ *a.* [L (*cresco* grow)]
incriminate /ɪn'krɪmɪneɪt/ *v.t.* indicate as guilty; charge with crime; **incrimination** /-'neɪʃ(ə)n/ *n*; **incriminatory** *a.* [L (CRIME)]
incrustation /ɪnkrʌs'teɪʃ(ə)n/ *n.* encrusting; crust, hard coating; deposit on a surface. [F or L (CRUST)]
incubate /'ɪnkjʊbeɪt/ *v.* hatch (eggs) by sitting on them or by artificial heat; sit on eggs; cause (bacteria etc.) to develop. [L (*cubo* lie)]
incubation /ɪnkjʊ'beɪʃ(ə)n/ *n.* incubating; development of disease germs before first symptoms appear.
incubator /'ɪnkjʊbeɪtə/ *n.* apparatus with artificial warmth for hatching eggs,

tending babies born prematurely, or developing bacteria.

incubus /ˈɪŋkjʊbəs/ *n.* (*pl.* **incubuses**) oppressive person or thing; evil spirit visiting sleeper; nightmare. [L (INCUBATE)]

inculcate /ˈɪnkʌlkeɪt/ *v.t.* implant (habit or idea *in* or *upon* person) by persistent urging; **inculcation** /-ˈkeɪʃ(ə)n/ *n.* [L (*calco* tread)]

inculpate /ˈɪnkʌlpeɪt/ *v.t.* incriminate; accuse, blame; **inculpation** /-ˈpeɪʃ(ə)n/ *n.*; **inculpatory** /ɪnˈkʌlpətərɪ/ *a.* [L (*culpa* fault)]

incumbency /ɪnˈkʌmbənsɪ/ *n.* office or tenure of incumbent. [foll.]

incumbent 1 *a.* resting as duty (*it is incumbent on you to do it*); lying or resting (*on*). 2 *n.* holder of office, esp. benefice. [L *incumbo* lie upon]

incunabulum /ɪnkjʊˈnæbjʊləm/ *n.* (*pl.* **incunabula**) early printed book, esp. from before 1501; (in *pl.*) early stages of thing. [L, (in *pl.*) = swaddling-clothes]

incur /ɪnˈkɜː/ *v.t.* (**-rr-**) bring on oneself (danger, blame, loss, etc.). [L (*curro* run)]

incurable /ɪnˈkjʊərəb(ə)l/ 1 *a.* that cannot be cured. 2 *n.* incurable person. 3 **incurability** /-ˈbɪlɪtɪ/ *n.*; **incurably** *adv.* [F or L (IN-²)]

incursion /ɪnˈkɜːʃ(ə)n/ *n.* invasion or attack, esp. sudden or brief; **incursive** *a.* [L (INCUR)]

incurve /ɪnˈkɜːv/ *v.t.* bend into curve; (esp. in *p.p.*) curve inwards; **incurvation** /-ˈveɪʃ(ə)n/ *n.* [IN-¹]

indebted /ɪnˈdetɪd/ *a.* owing debt or obligation (*to*). [F *endetté* (DEBT)]

indecent /ɪnˈdiːsənt/ *a.* offending against decency; unbecoming, unsuitable (*indecent haste*); **indecent assault** sexual attack not involving rape; **indecency** *n.* [F or L (IN-²)]

indecision /ɪndɪˈsɪʒ(ə)n/ *n.* lack of decision, hesitation; **indecisive** /-ˈsaɪsɪv/ *a.* [F (IN-²)]

indeclinable /ɪndɪˈklaɪnəb(ə)l/ *a.* (of words) having no inflexions. [F f. L (IN-²)]

indeed /ɪnˈdiːd/ 1 *adv.* in truth, really; admittedly. 2 *int.* expressing incredulity, surprise, etc. [IN, DEED]

indefatigable /ɪndɪˈfætɪgəb(ə)l/ *a.* unwearying, unremitting; **indefatigably** *adv.* [F or L (FATIGUE)]

indefeasible /ɪndɪˈfiːzɪb(ə)l/ *a.* (of right, possession, etc.) that cannot be forfeited or annulled; **indefeasibly** *adv.* [IN-²]

indefensible /ɪndɪˈfensɪb(ə)l/ *a.* that cannot be defended or justified; **indefensibly** *adv.*

indefinite /ɪnˈdefɪnɪt/ *a.* vague, undefined; unlimited; (of adjectives, adverbs, and pronouns) not determining the person etc. referred to (e.g. *some, someone, anyhow*); **indefinite article** see ARTICLE. [L (IN-²)]

indelible /ɪnˈdelɪb(ə)l/ *a.* that cannot be rubbed out; that makes indelible marks; **indelibly** *adv.* [F or L (*deleo* efface)]

indelicate /ɪnˈdelɪkət/ *a.* immodest, unrefined; tactless; **indelicacy** *n.* [IN-²]

indemnify /ɪnˈdemnɪfaɪ/ *v.t.* secure (person *from* or *against* loss); exempt from penalty (*for* actions); compensate; **indemnification** /-ˈkeɪʃ(ə)n/ *n.* [L *indemnis* free from loss]

indemnity /ɪnˈdemnɪtɪ/ *n.* security against damage or loss; exemption from penalty; compensation for damage. [F f. L (prec.)]

indent 1 /ɪnˈdent/ *v.* make notches, dents, or recesses in; start (line of print or writing) further from margin than others; make requisition (*on* person *for* thing), order goods by indent; write out (document) in duplicate. 2 /ˈɪndent/ *n.* official requisition for stores; order (esp. from abroad) for goods; indentation; indenture. [AF f. L (*dens dentis* tooth)]

indentation /ɪndenˈteɪʃ(ə)n/ *n.* indenting; notch; deep recess.

indention /ɪnˈdenʃ(ə)n/ *n.* indenting, esp. in printing; notch.

indenture /ɪnˈdentʃə/ 1 *n.* sealed agreement esp. (usu. in *pl.*) binding apprentice to master; formal list, certificate, etc. 2 *v.t.* bind by indentures. [AF (INDENT)]

independence /ɪndɪˈpendəns/ *n.* being independent. [foll.]

independent 1 *a.* not depending on authority or control (*of*); self-governing; not depending on another thing for validity etc., or on another person for one's opinion or livelihood; (of broadcasting, school, etc.) not supported from public funds; (of income or resources) making it unnecessary to earn one's living; unwilling to be under obligation to others; acting independently of any political party. 2 *n.* person who is politically independent. [IN-²]

indescribable /ɪndɪˈskraɪbəb(ə)l/ *a.* too unusual to be described; vague; **indescribably** *adv.*

indestructible /ɪndɪˈstrʌktɪb(ə)l/ *a.* that cannot be destroyed; **indestructibility** /-ˈbɪlɪtɪ/ *n.*; **indestructibly** *adv.*

indeterminable /ɪndɪˈtɜːmɪnəb(ə)l/ *a.* that cannot be ascertained or settled; **indeterminably** *adv.* [L (DETERMINE)]

indeterminate /ɪndɪˈtɜːmɪnət/ *a.* not

fixed in extent, character, etc.; left doubtful; **indeterminate vowel** vowel /ə/ heard in '*a* mom*e*nt *a*go'; **indeterminacy** *n.*

indetermination /ɪndɪtɜ:mɪ'neɪʃ(ə)n/ *n.* lack of determination.

index /'ɪndeks/ **1** *n.* (*pl.* **indexes** or **indices** /-ɪsi:z/) alphabetical list of subjects etc. with references, usu. at end of book; number indicating level of prices or wages as compared with some standard value; exponent of a number; pointer (*lit.* or *fig.*). **2** *v.t.* furnish (book) with index; enter in index; relate (wages etc.) to value of price index. **3 index finger** forefinger; **index-linked** related to value of price index. [L]

indexation /ɪndek'seɪʃ(ə)n/ *n.* making wages etc. index-linked.

India ink /'ɪndɪə/ *US* Indian ink; **India paper** thin tough opaque paper used for printing. [*India* in Asia]

Indiaman /'ɪndɪəmən/ *n. hist.* ship in trade with India or E. Indies.

Indian /'ɪndɪən/ **1** *a.* of India; of the subcontinent comprising India, Pakistan, and Bangladesh; of the original inhabitants of America and W. Indies. **2** *n.* native of India; original inhabitant of America or W. Indies, = *Red Indian.* **3 Indian clubs** pair of bottle-shaped clubs swung to exercise arms; **Indian corn** maize; **Indian file** single file; **Indian ink** a black pigment; **Indian summer** calm dry period in late autumn, *fig.* tranquil late period.

indiarubber /ɪndɪə'rʌbə/ *n.* rubber, esp. for rubbing out pencil marks etc.

indicate /'ɪndɪkeɪt/ *v.t.* point out, make known; be sign of, show presence of; require, call for (*stronger measures are indicated*); state briefly; **indication** /-'keɪʃ(ə)n/ *n.* [L (*dico* make known)]

indicative /ɪn'dɪkətɪv/ **1** *a.* suggestive *of*, giving an indication; *Gram.* (of mood) expressing statement, not command, wish, etc. **2** *n.* indicative mood or form. [F f. L (prec.)]

indicator /'ɪndɪkeɪtə/ *n.* person or thing that indicates; device indicating condition of machine etc.; board giving current information; device to show intended turn by vehicle. [INDICATE]

indicatory /ɪn'dɪkətərɪ/ *a.* indicative (*of*).

indices see INDEX.

indict /ɪn'daɪt/ *v.t.* accuse formally by legal process. [AF f. F f. Rmc (*dicto* DICTATE)]

indictable *a.* (of offence) making doer liable to be charged with crime; (of person) so liable.

indictment *n.* document stating alleged crimes; accusation. [AF (INDICT)]

indifference /ɪn'dɪfrəns/ *n.* lack of interest or attention; unimportance. [L (foll.)]

indifferent *a.* showing indifference or lack of interest; neither good nor bad; of poor quality or ability; unimportant. [F or L (IN-²)]

indigenous /ɪn'dɪdʒɪnəs/ *a.* native or belonging naturally (*to* place). [L]

indigent /'ɪndɪdʒənt/ *a.* needy, poor; **indigence** *n.* [F f. L (*egeo* need)]

indigestible /ɪndɪ'dʒestɪb(ə)l/ *a.* difficult or impossible to digest; **indigestibility** /-'bɪlɪtɪ/ *n.* [F or L (IN-²)]

indigestion /ɪndɪ'dʒestʃ(ə)n/ *n.* difficulty in digesting food; pain caused by this.

indignant /ɪn'dɪgnənt/ *a.* feeling or showing indignation. [L (*dignus* worthy)]

indignation /ɪndɪg'neɪʃ(ə)n/ *n.* scornful anger at supposed injustice, wickedness, etc. [F or L (prec.)]

indignity /ɪn'dɪgnɪtɪ/ *n.* humiliating treatment, insult; humiliating quality. [F or L]

indigo /'ɪndɪgəʊ/ *n.* (*pl.* **indigos**) deep violet-blue; dye of this colour. [Sp. & Port. f. L f. Gk *indikon* Indian (dye)]

indirect /ɪndɪ'rekt, -daɪ-/ *a.* not going straight to the point; (of road etc.) not straight; not directly aimed at (*indirect result*); **indirect object** person or thing affected by verbal action but not primarily acted on (e.g. *him* in *give him the book*); **indirect question** question in indirect speech; **indirect speech** reported speech; **indirect tax** tax paid in form of increased price for taxed goods. [F or med.L (IN-²)]

indiscreet /ɪndɪs'kri:t/ *a.* not discreet, revealing secrets; injudicious, unwary. [L (IN-²)]

indiscretion /ɪndɪs'kreʃ(ə)n/ *n.* indiscreet conduct or action. [F or L (IN-²)]

indiscriminate /ɪndɪs'krɪmɪnət/ *a.* done or acting without judgement or discrimination; **indiscrimination** /-'neɪʃ(ə)n/ *n.* [IN-²]

indispensable /ɪndɪ'spensəb(ə)l/ *a.* that cannot be dispensed with, necessary *to* or *for*; **indispensability** /-'bɪlɪtɪ/ *n.*; **indispensably** *adv.*

indisposed /ɪndɪ'spəʊzd/ *a.* slightly unwell; averse or unwilling; **indisposition** /-spə'zɪʃ(ə)n/ *n.*

indissoluble /ɪndɪ'sɒljʊb(ə)l/ *a.* that cannot be dissolved or destroyed, firm and lasting; **indissolubly** *adv.*

indistinct /ɪndɪ'stɪŋkt/ *a.* not distinct; confused, obscure.

indite /ɪn'daɪt/ *v.t.* put (speech etc.) into words; write (letter etc.). [F (INDICT)]

indium /'ɪndɪəm/ *n.* rare silver-white

soft metallic element occurring with zinc etc. [L *indicum* INDIGO]

individual /ɪndɪ'vɪdjʊəl/ **1** *a.* single; particular, not general; having distinct character; characteristic of particular person etc.; designed for use by one person. **2** *n.* single member of a class; single human being; *colloq.* person (*a tiresome individual*). [med.L (DIVIDE)]

individualism *n.* self-reliant action by individual; social theory favouring free action by individuals; egoism; **individualist** *n.*; **individualistic** /-'lɪstɪk/ *a.*

individuality /ɪndɪvɪdjʊ'ælɪtɪ/ *n.* separate existence; individual character, esp. when strongly marked.

individualize *v.t.* give individual character to.

individually *adv.* personally; distinctively; one by one.

Indo- *in comb.* Indian (and); **Indo-European** of the family of languages spoken over most of Europe and in N. India and Iran. [L f. Gk]

indoctrinate /ɪn'dɒktrɪneɪt/ *v.t.* imbue with a doctrine or opinion; teach, instruct; **indoctrination** /-'neɪʃ(ə)n/ *n.* [IN-[1]]

indolent /'ɪndələnt/ *a.* lazy, averse to exertion; **indolence** *n.* [L (*doleo* suffer pain)]

indomitable /ɪn'dɒmɪtəb(ə)l/ *a.* unyielding, stubbornly persistent; **indomitably** *adv.* [L (DAUNT)]

indoor *a.* of or done or for use in a building or under cover. [IN]

indoors *adv.* in(to) a building; under a roof.

indorse var. of ENDORSE.

indrawn /'ɪndrɔ:n/ *a.* drawn in; aloof. [IN]

indubitable /ɪn'dju:bɪtəb(ə)l/ *a.* that cannot be doubted; **indubitably** *adv.* [F or L (*dubito* doubt)]

induce /ɪn'dju:s/ *v.t.* prevail on, persuade; bring about; bring on (labour) artificially; produce by induction; infer as induction; **inducible** *a.* [L (*duco duct-* lead)]

inducement *n.* thing that induces; attraction, motive.

induct /ɪn'dʌkt/ *v.t.* install or initiate (*into* benefice or office etc.). [as INDUCE]

inductance /ɪn'dʌktəns/ *n.* amount of induction of electric current.

induction /ɪn'dʌkʃ(ə)n/ *n.* inducting or inducing; bringing on by artificial means; inferring of general law from particular instances; production of electric or magnetic state by proximity (without contact) of electrified or magnetized body, quantity giving measure of such influence; production of electric current by change of magnetic field; drawing of fuel mixture into cylinder(s) of internal-combustion engine. [F or L (INDUCE)]

inductive /ɪn'dʌktɪv/ *a.* (of reasoning etc.) based on or using induction; of electric or magnetic induction. [L (INDUCE)]

indue var. of ENDUE.

indulge /ɪn'dʌldʒ/ *v.* take pleasure freely (*in* activity etc.); yield freely to (desire etc.); gratify by compliance with wishes. [L *indulgeo* give free rein to]

indulgence *n.* indulging; privilege granted; (in RC Church) remission of punishment still due after sacramental absolution. [F f. L (prec.)]

indulgent *a.* indulging; lenient, willing to overlook faults etc.; too lenient. [F or L (INDULGE)]

indurate /'ɪndjʊəreɪt/ *v.* make or become hard; make callous; **induration** /-'reɪʃ(ə)n/ *n.*; **indurative** *a.* [L (*durus* hard)]

industrial /ɪn'dʌstrɪəl/ *a.* of or engaged in or for use in or serving the needs of industries; (of nation etc.) having highly developed industries; **industrial action** strike or other disruptive action used in industrial dispute; **industrial relations** relations between management and workers in industries; **industrially** *adv.* [INDUSTRY]

industrialism *n.* system involving prevalence of industries.

industrialist *n.* person engaged in management of industry.

industrialize *v.t.* make (nation etc.) industrial; **industrialization** /-'zeɪʃ(ə)n/*n.*

industrious /ɪn'dʌstrɪəs/ *a.* hard-working. [F or L (foll.)]

industry /'ɪndəstrɪ/ *n.* branch of trade or manufacture; trade or manufacture collectively; organized activity; diligence. [F or L]

indwelling *a.* permanently present in something. [IN-[1]]

-ine *suffix* forming adjectives in senses 'belonging to, of the nature of' (*Alpine*, *asinine*), and feminine nouns (*heroine*). [F, L & Gk]

inebriate /ɪ'ni:brɪət/ **1** *a.* drunken. **2** *n.* drunkard. **3** /-eɪt/ *v.t.* make drunk. **4** **inebriation** /-'eɪʃ(ə)n/ *n.*; **inebriety** /-'braɪətɪ/ *n.* [L (*ebrius* drunk)]

ineducable /ɪn'edjʊkəb(ə)l/ *a.* incapable of being educated, esp. through mental retardation. [IN-[2]]

ineffable /ɪn'efəb(ə)l/ *a.* too great for description in words; that must not be uttered; **ineffably** *adv.* [F or L (*effor* speak out)]

inefficient /ɪnɪ'fɪʃ(ə)nt/ *a.* not efficient or fully capable; **inefficiency** *n.* [IN-²]

ineluctable /ɪnɪ'lʌktəb(ə)l/ *a.* against which it is useless to struggle. [L (*luctor* strive)]

inept /ɪ'nept/ *a.* unskilful; absurd, silly; out of place; **ineptitude** *n.* [L (APT)]

inequable /ɪn'ekwəb(ə)l/ *a.* unfair; not uniform.

inequality /ɪnɪ'kwɒlɪtɪ/ *n.* lack of equality in any respect, variableness; unevenness of surface.

inert /ɪ'nɜ:t/ *a.* without inherent power of action, reaction, motion, or resistance; sluggish, slow. [L *iners -ert-* (ART)]

inertia /ɪ'nɜ:ʃə/ *n.* inertness; property by which matter continues in its existing state of rest or uniform motion in straight line unless that state is changed by external force; **inertia reel** reel allowing automatic adjustment of safety-belt rolled round it; **inertia selling** sending of goods not ordered in hope that they will not be refused; **inertial** *a.* [L (prec.)]

inescapable /ɪnɪ'skeɪpəb(ə)l/ *a.* that cannot be escaped or avoided; **inescapably** *adv.* [IN-²]

inestimable /ɪn'estɪməb(ə)l/ *a.* too good, great, etc., to be estimated; **inestimably** *adv.*

inevitable /ɪn'evɪtəb(ə)l/ *a.* unavoidable, bound to happen or appear; *colloq.* tiresomely familiar; **inevitability** /-'bɪlɪtɪ/ *n.*; **inevitably** *adv.* [L (*evito* avoid)]

inexcusable /ɪnɪk'skju:zəb(ə)l/ *a.* that cannot be excused or justified; **inexcusably** *adv.* [L (IN-²)]

inexorable /ɪn'eksərəb(ə)l/ *a.* relentless; that cannot be persuaded by entreaty; **inexorably** *adv.* [F or L (*exoro* entreat)]

inexpensive /ɪnɪk'spensɪv/ *a.* offering good value for the price. [IN-²]

inexperience /ɪnɪk'spɪərɪəns/ *n.* lack of experience or of knowledge or skill arising from experience; **inexperienced** *a.* [F f. L (IN-²)]

inexpert /ɪn'ekspɜ:t/ *a.* unskilful, lacking expertise.

inexpiable /ɪn'ekspɪəb(ə)l/ *a.* that cannot be expiated or appeased. [L (IN-²)]

inexplicable /ɪn'eksplɪkəb(ə)l, ɪnɪk'splɪk-/ *a.* that cannot be explained; **inexplicably** *adv.* [F or L (IN-²)]

inexpressible /ɪnɪk'spresɪb(ə)l/ *a.* that cannot be expressed in words; **inexpressibly** *adv.* [IN-²]

in extenso /ɪn eks'tensəʊ/ at full length. [L]

in extremis /ɪn eks'tri:mɪs/ at point of death; in great difficulties. [L]

inextricable /ɪn'ekstrɪkəb(ə)l/ *a.* that cannot be resolved or escaped from; that cannot be loosened; **inextricably** *adv.* [L (IN-²)]

infallible /ɪn'fælɪb(ə)l/ *a.* incapable of erring; (of Pope) incapable of erring in matters of doctrine expressed *ex cathedra*; **infallibility** /-'bɪlɪtɪ/ *n.*; **infallibly** *adv.* [L (IN-²)]

infamous /'ɪnfəməs/ *a.* notoriously vile or evil, abominable; **infamy** *n.* [L (IN-²)]

infant /'ɪnfənt/ *n.* child during earliest period of life; *Law* person under 18; thing in early stage of development; **infancy** *n.* [F f. L *infans* unable to speak]

infanta /ɪn'fæntə/ *n. hist.* daughter of Spanish or Portuguese king. [Sp. & Port. f. L (prec.)]

infanticide /ɪn'fæntɪsaɪd/ *n.* killing of infant soon after birth; one guilty of this. [F f. L (INFANT)]

infantile /'ɪnfəntaɪl/ *a.* of or like infants; **infantile paralysis** poliomyelitis. [F or L (INFANT)]

infantry /'ɪnfəntrɪ/ *n.* soldiers marching and fighting on foot. [F f. It. *infante* youth, foot-soldier (INFANT)]

infantryman *n.* soldier of infantry regiment.

infatuate /ɪn'fætjʊeɪt/ *v.t.* inspire with intense fondness and admiration; affect with extreme folly; **infatuation** /-'eɪʃ(ə)n/ *n.* [L (FATUOUS)]

infect /ɪn'fekt/ *v.t.* affect or contaminate with germ or virus or consequent disease; imbue with opinion or feeling etc. [L *inficio -fect-* taint]

infection /ɪn'fekʃ(ə)n/ *n.* infecting or being infected; instance of this, disease; communication of disease, esp. by agency of air, water, etc. [F or L (prec.)]

infectious *a.* infecting; able to be transmitted by infection.

infelicitous /ɪnfɪ'lɪsɪtəs/ *a.* not felicitous, unfortunate.

infelicity *n.* unhappiness; infelicitous expression or detail.

infer /ɪn'fɜ:/ *v.t.* (**-rr-**) deduce or conclude; **(D)** imply, suggest; **inferable** *a.* [L (*fero* bring)]

inference /'ɪnfərəns/ *n.* inferring; thing inferred; **inferential** /-'renʃ(ə)l/ *a.* [med.L (prec.)]

inferior /ɪn'fɪərɪə/ **1** *a.* lower in rank or quality etc. (*to*); of poor quality; situated below; written or printed below the line. **2** *n.* person inferior to another esp. in rank. [L compar. of *inferus* low]

inferiority /ɪnfɪərɪ'ɒrɪtɪ/ *n.* being inferior; **inferiority complex** unconscious feeling of inferiority to others, sometimes manifested in aggressive behaviour, *colloq.* sense of inferiority.

infernal /ɪn'fɜ:n(ə)l/ *a.* of hell; hellish;

colloq. detestable, annoying; **infernally** *adv.* [F f. L (*infernus* low)]
inferno /ɪn'fɜːnəʊ/ *n.* (*pl.* **infernos**) raging fire; scene of horror or distress; hell. [It., with reference to Dante's *Divine Comedy*, f. L (prec.)]
infest /ɪn'fest/ *v.t.* (of harmful persons or things, esp. vermin) overrun (place) in large numbers; **infestation** /-'teɪʃ(ə)n/ *n.* [F or L (*infestus* hostile)]
infidel /'ɪnfɪd(ə)l/ **1** *n.* disbeliever in religion or in a specified religion. **2** *a.* unbelieving; of infidels. [F or L (*fides* faith)]
infidelity /ɪnfɪ'delɪtɪ/ *n.* disloyalty esp. to one's husband or wife. [F or L (prec.)]
infield *n.* (in cricket) part of ground near wicket. [IN]
infighting *n.* hidden conflict in an organization; boxing within arms' length.
infilling *n.* placing of buildings in gaps between others.
infiltrate /'ɪnfɪltreɪt/ *v.* enter (territory, political party, etc.) gradually and imperceptibly; cause (troops etc.) to do this; pass (fluid) by filtration (*into*); permeate by filtration; **infiltration** /-'treɪʃ(ə)n/ *n.*; **infiltrator** *n.* [IN-¹]
infinite /'ɪnfɪnɪt/ *a.* boundless, endless; very great or many; **the Infinite** God; **the infinite** infinite space. [L (IN-²)]
infinitesimal /ɪnfɪnɪ'tesɪm(ə)l/ *a.* infinitely or very small; **infinitesimal calculus** that dealing with very small quantities; **infinitesimally** *adv.*
infinitive /ɪn'fɪnɪtɪv/ **1** *n.* verb form expressing verbal notion without particular subject, tense, etc. (often with *to*; e.g. *see* in *we came to see*, *let him see*). **2** *a.* having this form. **3** **infinitival** /-'taɪv(ə)l/ *a.* [L (IN-²)]
infinitude /ɪn'fɪnɪtjuːd/ *n.* infinity, being infinite. [L (INFINITE)]
infinity /ɪn'fɪnɪtɪ/ *n.* infinite number or extent; boundlessness. [F f. L (INFINITE)]
infirm /ɪn'fɜːm/ *a.* physically weak, esp. from age; weak, irresolute (*infirm of purpose*). [L (IN-²)]
infirmary *n.* hospital; sick-quarters in school etc.
infirmity *n.* being infirm; particular physical weakness.
infix /ɪn'fɪks/ *v.t.* fasten or fix in. [IN-¹]
in flagrante delicto /ɪn flægræntɪ de'lɪktəʊ/ in the very act of committing an offence. [L, = in blazing crime]
inflame /ɪn'fleɪm/ *v.* provoke to strong feeling (esp. anger); cause inflammation in; (cause to) catch fire; light up with or as with flame; make hot. [F f. L (IN-¹)]
inflammable /ɪn'flæməb(ə)l/ *a.* easily set on fire or excited; **inflammably** *adv.*
inflammation /ɪnflə'meɪʃ(ə)n/ *n.* inflaming, esp. condition of part of the body with heat, swelling, redness, and usu. pain. [L (INFLAME)]
inflammatory /ɪn'flæmətərɪ/ *a.* tending to cause anger etc.; of inflammation.
inflate /ɪn'fleɪt/ *v.t.* distend with air or gas; puff up (*with* pride etc.); raise (price) artificially; resort to inflation of (currency). [L *inflo -flat-*]
inflation /ɪn'fleɪʃ(ə)n/ *n.* inflating; general rise in prices; increase in supply of money regarded as cause of such a rise; **inflationary** *a.*
inflect /ɪn'flekt/ *v.t.* change pitch of (voice); modify (word) to express grammatical relation; bend, curve. [L (*flecto flex-* bend)]
inflection var. of INFLEXION.
inflective /ɪn'flektɪv/ *a.* of grammatical inflexion. [INFLECT]
inflexible /ɪn'fleksɪb(ə)l/ *a.* unbendable; unbending; **inflexibility** /-'bɪlɪtɪ/ *n.*; **inflexibly** *adv.* [L (IN-²)]
inflexion /ɪn'flekʃ(ə)n/ *n.* modulation of voice; inflected word; suffix etc. used to inflect; inflecting; **inflexional** *a.* [F or L (INFLECT)]
inflict /ɪn'flɪkt/ *v.t.* deal (blow etc.) *on*; impose or deliver forcibly *on* or *upon*; **infliction** *n.*; **inflictor** *n.* [L (*fligo flict-* strike)]
inflorescence /ɪnflə'resəns/ *n.* arrangement of flowers in relation to axis and to each other; collective flower of plant; flowering (*lit.* or *fig.*). [L (IN-¹, FLOURISH)]
inflow *n.* flowing in; that which flows in. [IN]
influence /'ɪnflʊəns/ **1** *n.* action invisibly exercised (*on*); ascendancy or moral power (*over* or *with*); thing or person exercising this. **2** *v.t.* exert influence on, affect. **3** **under the influence** *colloq.* drunk. [F or med.L (*influo* flow in)]
influential /ɪnflʊ'enʃ(ə)l/ *a.* having great influence; **influentially** *adv.* [med.L (prec.)]
influenza /ɪnflʊ'enzə/ *n.* acute virus disease usu. with fever and severe aching and catarrh, occurring in epidemics. [It. (prec.)]
influx /'ɪnflʌks/ *n.* flowing in, esp. of persons or things into a place. [F or L (FLUX)]
info /'ɪnfəʊ/ *n.* *colloq.* information. [abbr.]
inform /ɪn'fɔːm/ *v.* give information to; bring charge or complaint (*against*); (in *p.p.*) knowing the facts, enlightened. [F f. L (FORM)]
informal /ɪn'fɔːm(ə)l/ *a.* not formal; without formality; **informality** /-'mælɪtɪ/ *n.*; **informally** *adv.* [IN-²]
informant /ɪn'fɔːmənt/ *n.* giver of information. [L (INFORM)]

information /ɪnfə'meɪʃ(ə)n/ *n.* what is told, knowledge, items of knowledge, news; charge or complaint lodged with court etc.; telling; **information science** study of processes for storing and retrieving information; **information theory** study of transmission of information by signals. [F f. L (INFORM)]

informative /ɪn'fɔ:mətɪv/ *a.* giving information, instructive. [med.L (INFORM)]

informer *n.* one who informs against others.

infra /'ɪnfrə/ *adv.* below or further on in book etc. [L]

infra- /'ɪnfrə/ *prefix* below.

infraction /ɪn'frækʃ(ə)n/ *n.* infringement. [L (INFRINGE)]

infra dig. *colloq.* beneath one's dignity. [L *infra dignitatem*]

infra-red /ɪnfrə'red/ *a.* of or using rays with wavelength just below red end of visible spectrum. [INFRA-]

infrastructure *n.* subordinate parts of an undertaking, esp. permanent installations forming a basis of defence. [F (INFRA-, STRUCTURE)]

infringe /ɪn'frɪndʒ/ *v.* act contrary to (law, another's rights, etc.); encroach or trespass (*on*); **infringement** *n.* [L (*frango fract-* break)]

infuriate /ɪn'fjʊərɪeɪt/ *v.t.* make furious. [med.L (FURY)]

infuse /ɪn'fju:z/ *v.* cause to be saturated or filled *with* quality; instil (life, quality, etc., *into*); steep (tea etc.) in liquid to extract constituents, (of tea etc.) be steeped thus. [L *infundo -fus-* (FOUND²)]

infusible /ɪn'fju:zɪb(ə)l/ *a.* that cannot be melted; **infusibility** /-'bɪlɪtɪ/ *n.* [IN-²]

infusion /ɪn'fju:ʒ(ə)n/ *n.* infusing; liquid extract so obtained; infused element. [F or L (INFUSE)]

-ing¹ *suffix* forming nouns from verbs, usu. with sense of verbal action or its result (*asking, fighting, learning*). [OE]

-ing² *suffix* forming present participle of verbs (*asking, fighting*), often as adjective (*charming, strapping*). [OE]

ingenious /ɪn'dʒi:nɪəs/ *a.* clever at inventing, organizing, etc.; cleverly contrived. [F or L (*ingenium* cleverness)]

ingénue /'æ̃ʒeɪnju:/ *n.* artless young woman, esp. as stage role. [F (INGENUOUS)]

ingenuity /ɪndʒɪ'nju:ɪtɪ/ *n.* ingeniousness. [L (foll.); assoc. in Eng. with INGENIOUS]

ingenuous /ɪn'dʒenjʊəs/ *a.* artless; frank. [L *ingenuus* free-born, frank]

ingest /ɪn'dʒest/ *v.t.* take in by swallowing or absorbing; **ingestion** *n.* [L (*gero* carry)]

ingle-nook /'ɪŋg(ə)lnʊk/ nook providing seat beside recessed fireplace. [perh. Gael. *aingeal* fire, light]

inglorious /ɪn'glɔ:rɪəs/ *a.* shameful; not famous. [L (IN-²)]

ingoing *a.* going in. [IN]

ingot /'ɪŋgɒt/ *n.* mass, usu. oblong, of cast metal, esp. gold, silver, or steel. [orig. uncert.]

ingraft var. of ENGRAFT.

ingrained /ɪn'greɪnd, *attrib.* 'ɪn-/ *a.* (of habits, feelings, or tendencies) deeply rooted, inveterate; (of dirt etc.) deeply embedded. [GRAIN]

ingratiate /ɪn'greɪʃɪeɪt/ *v.t.* bring *oneself* into favour (*with*). [L *in gratiam* into favour]

ingratitude /ɪn'grætɪtju:d/ *n.* lack of due gratitude.

ingredient /ɪn'gri:dɪənt/ *n.* component part in mixture. [L *ingredior* enter into]

ingress /'ɪngres/ *n.* going in; right to go in. [L *ingressus* (prec.)]

ingrowing *a.* (of nail) growing into the flesh. [IN]

inguinal /'ɪŋgwɪn(ə)l/ *a.* of the groin. [L (*inguen* groin)]

inhabit /ɪn'hæbɪt/ *v.t.* dwell in, occupy. [F or L (HABIT)]

inhabitant *n.* person etc. who inhabits place. [F f. L (prec.)]

inhalant /ɪn'heɪlənt/ *n.* medicinal substance for inhaling. [L (foll.)]

inhale /ɪn'heɪl/ *v.* breathe in (air, gas, etc.); take (tobacco-smoke etc.) into lungs; **inhalation** /ɪnhə'leɪʃ(ə)n/ *n.* [L (*halo* breathe)]

inhaler *n.* inhaling-apparatus, esp. device for sending out vapour for inhaling.

inhere /ɪn'hɪə/ *v.i.* be inherent. [L (*haereo haes-* stick)]

inherent /ɪn'hɪərənt/ *a.* existing or abiding in something as essential quality or characteristic; **inherence** *n.*

inherit /ɪn'herɪt/ *v.t.* receive (property or rank) as heir; derive (qualities, problems, etc.) from parent, predecessor, etc.; **inheritor** *n.* [F f. L (*heres* heir)]

inheritance *n.* what is inherited; inheriting. [F (prec.)]

inhibit /ɪn'hɪbɪt/ *v.t.* hinder or restrain or prevent (action, process, or person); prohibit (*from doing*); **inhibitory** *a.* [L *inhibeo -hibit-* hinder]

inhibited *a.* subject to inhibition.

inhibition /ɪnhɪ'bɪʃ(ə)n/ *n.* inhibiting or being inhibited; restraint of direct expression of instinct; *colloq.* emotional resistance to thought or action. [F or L (INHIBIT)]

inhospitable /ɪn'hɒspɪtəb(ə)l, -'pɪt-/ *a.* not hospitable; (of place or climate) not affording shelter or favourable conditions; **inhospitably** *adv.* [F (IN-²)]

in-house 1 *adv.* within an institution. 2 *a.* done or existing in-house. [IN]
inhuman /ɪn'hju:mən/ *a.* brutal, unfeeling, barbarous; **inhumanity** /-'mænɪtɪ/ *n.* [L (IN-²)]
inimical /ɪ'nɪmɪk(ə)l/ *a.* hostile, harmful; **inimically** *adv.* [L (*inimicus* enemy)]
inimitable /ɪ'nɪmɪtəb(ə)l/ *a.* that cannot be imitated; **inimitably** *adv.* [F or L (IN-²)]
iniquity /ɪ'nɪkwɪtɪ/ *n.* wickedness; gross injustice; **iniquitous** *a.* [F f. L (*aequus* just)]
initial /ɪ'nɪʃ(ə)l/ 1 *a.* of or at the beginning; (of letter) at the beginning of a word. 2 *n.* initial letter, esp. (in *pl.*) those of a person's names. 3 *v.t.* (-ll-, -l-) mark or sign with initials. 4 **initially** *adv.* [L (*initium* beginning)]
initialism *n.* acronym.
initiate 1 /ɪ'nɪʃɪeɪt/ *v.t.* originate, begin, set going; admit (person) into society, office, etc.; instruct, esp. in rites or forms. 2 /ɪ'nɪʃɪət/ *n.* initiated person. 3 **initiation** /-'eɪʃ(ə)n/ *n.*; **initiator** *n.*; **initiatory** *a.* [L (*initium* beginning)]
initiative /ɪ'nɪʃɪətɪv/ *n.* ability to initiate things, enterprise (*has no initiative*); first step; power or right to begin (*have the initiative*). [F (prec.)]
inject /ɪn'dʒekt/ *v.t.* force (fluid, medicine, etc., *into* cavity etc.) by or as by syringe; fill (*with* fluid etc.) thus; administer medicine etc. to (person) thus; place (quality etc.) where needed in something; **injection** *n.*; **injector** *n.* [L *injicio -ject-* (*jacio* throw)]
injudicious /ɪndʒu:'dɪʃəs/ *a.* unwise, ill-judged. [IN-²]
injunction /ɪn'dʒʌŋkʃ(ə)n/ *n.* authoritative order; judicial process restraining person from specified act, compelling restitution, etc. [L (ENJOIN)]
injure /'ɪndʒə/ *v.t.* harm, damage; do wrong to. [INJURY]
injured *a.* harmed, damaged; (of voice) showing one is offended; wronged.
injurious /ɪn'dʒʊərɪəs/ *a.* wrongful; harmful; calumnious. [F or L (foll.)]
injury /'ɪndʒərɪ/ *n.* harm, damage; wrongful action or treatment; **injury time** extra playing-time added to football match etc. because of that lost in dealing with injuries. [AF f. L (IN-², *jus jur-* right)]
injustice /ɪn'dʒʌstɪs/ *n.* unfairness; unjust act; **do person an injustice** judge him unfairly. [F f. L (IN-²)]
ink 1 *n.* black or coloured fluid used for writing, printing, etc.; black liquid ejected by cuttlefish etc. 2 *v.t.* mark (*in, over*, etc.) with ink; cover with ink. 3 **ink out** obliterate with ink; **ink-well** pot for holding ink, fitted into hole in desk. [F f. L f. Gk *egkauston* Roman emperors' purple ink (EN-, CAUSTIC)]
inkling /'ɪŋklɪŋ/ *n.* hint, slight knowledge or suspicion (*of*). [orig. unkn.]
inkstand *n.* stand for one or more ink-bottles. [INK]
inky *a.* of ink; stained with ink; very black; **inkiness** *n.*
inland /'ɪnlənd, -lænd/ 1 *a.* in interior of country, remote from sea or border; within a country (*inland trade*). 2 /also -'lænd/ *adv.* in or towards interior of country. 3 *n.* interior of country. 4 **inland revenue** revenue from taxes and inland duties. [IN]
in-laws *n.pl. colloq.* relatives by marriage.
inlay 1 /ɪn'leɪ/ *v.t.* (*past* and *p.p.* **inlaid**) set or embed (pieces of wood or metal etc.) in another material so that the surfaces are level, forming a design; decorate (thing) thus. 2 /'ɪnleɪ/ *n.* inlaid material or work; filling shaped to fit tooth-cavity. [IN, LAY¹]
inlet /'ɪnlet/ *n.* small arm of sea, lake, or river; piece inserted; way in. [IN, LET¹]
in loco parentis /ɪn ləʊkəʊ pə'rentɪs/ in place of a parent. [L]
inmate *n.* any of occupants of house, hospital, prison, etc. [prob. INN, MATE¹]
in memoriam /ɪn mɪ'mɔ:rɪæm/ in memory of. [L]
inmost *a.* most inward. [OE (IN)]
inn *n.* house providing lodging etc. for payment, esp. for travellers; house providing alcoholic liquor; **Inn of Court** any of four legal societies admitting persons to practise at bar. [OE (IN)]
innards /'ɪnədz/ *n.pl. colloq.* inner parts, esp. entrails. [INWARD]
innate /ɪ'neɪt, 'ɪn-/ *a.* inborn, natural. [L (*natus* born)]
inner 1 *a.* interior, internal. 2 *n.* division of target next outside bull's-eye; shot striking this. 3 **inner city** central area of city, usu. with overcrowding and poverty; **inner man** (or **woman**) soul, mind, stomach; **inner tube** separate inflatable tube in pneumatic tyre. 4 **innermost** *a.* [OE, comparative of IN]
innings *n.* (*pl.* same) part of game of cricket etc. in which one side or player is batting; time of power etc. of political party etc.; period of person's chance to achieve something. [*in* v. = go in]
innkeeper *n.* keeper of inn. [INN]
innocent /'ɪnəsənt/ 1 *a.* without guilt, not guilty *of* a crime; sinless; without guile, harmless, affectedly so. 2 *n.* innocent person, esp. child. 3 **innocence** *n.* [F or L (*noceo* hurt)]
innocuous /ɪ'nɒkjʊəs/ *a.* harmless. [L *innocuus* (prec.)]

innovate /ˈɪnəveɪt/ *v.i.* bring in new methods, ideas, etc.; make changes *in*; **innovation** /-ˈveɪʃ(ə)n/ *n.*; **innovative** *a.*; **innovator** *n.*; **innovatory** *a.* [L (*novus* new)]

innuendo /ɪnjuːˈendəʊ/ *n.* (*pl.* **innuendoes**) allusive remark or hint, usu. disparaging. [L, = by nodding at (IN-[1], *nuo* nod)]

innumerable /ɪˈnjuːmərəb(ə)l/ *a.* too many to be counted; **innumerably** *adv.* [L (*numerus* number)]

innumerate *a.* not knowing basic mathematics and science; **innumeracy** *n.* [IN-[2]]

inoculate /ɪˈnɒkjʊleɪt/ *v.t.* treat (person or animal) with vaccine or serum, esp. as protection against disease; **inoculation** /-ˈleɪʃ(ə)n/ *n.* [L (*oculus* eye, bud)]

inoffensive /ɪnəˈfensɪv/ *a.* unoffending, not objectionable. [IN-[2]]

inoperable /ɪnˈɒpərəb(ə)l/ *a.* that cannot be cured by surgical operation. [F (IN-[2])]

inoperative /ɪnˈɒpərətɪv/ *a.* not working or taking effect. [IN-[2]]

inordinate /ɪˈnɔːdɪnət/ *a.* excessive. [L (ORDAIN)]

inorganic /ɪnɔːˈgænɪk/ *a.* (of chemical compound etc.) mineral not organic; without organized physical structure; extraneous; **inorganic chemistry** chemistry of inorganic substances. [IN-[2]]

in-patient *n.* patient residing in hospital during treatment. [IN]

input /ˈɪnpʊt/ **1** *n.* what is put in; place of entry of energy, information, etc. **2** *v.t.* (**-tt-**; *past* and *p.p.* **input** or **inputted**) put in or *into*; supply (data, programs, etc., *to* computer). [IN]

inquest /ˈɪnkwest/ *n.* inquiry held by coroner into cause of death; prolonged discussion after misfortune, failure, etc. [F f. Rmc (INQUIRE)]

inquietude /ɪnˈkwaɪɪtjuːd/ *n.* uneasiness. [F or L (QUIET)]

inquire /ɪnˈkwaɪə/ *v.* (also, esp. of informal question, **enquire**) ask question; seek information formally or searchingly; make inquiry *into*; **inquire after** ask about the health of. [F f. L (*quaero quisit-* seek)]

inquiry *n.* (also **enquiry** as prec.) investigation, esp. official (*hold an inquiry into*).

inquisition /ɪnkwɪˈzɪʃ(ə)n/ *n.* intensive investigation or inquiry; (**Inquisition**) *hist.* Roman Catholic tribunal for suppression of heresy, esp. that in Spain; **inquisitional** *a.* [F f. L (INQUIRE)]

inquisitive /ɪnˈkwɪzɪtɪv/ *a.* seeking knowledge; unduly curious, prying.

inquisitor /ɪnˈkwɪzɪtə/ *n.* one who questions searchingly; official investigator; officer of the Inquisition.

inquisitorial /ɪnkwɪzɪˈtɔːrɪəl/ *a.* of or like an inquisitor; prying; **inquisitorially** *adv.* [med.L (prec.)]

in re /ɪn ˈriː/ = RE[1]. [L]

INRI *abbr.* Jesus of Nazareth, King of the Jews. [L *Iesus Nazarenus Rex Iudaeorum*]

inroad *n.* hostile incursion; (often in *pl.*) encroachment, using up of resources etc. [IN]

inrush *n.* violent influx.

insalubrious /ɪnsəˈluːbrɪəs/ *a.* (of place or climate etc.) unhealthy. [L (IN-[2])]

insane /ɪnˈseɪn/ *a.* not sane, mad; very foolish; **insanity** /-ˈsænɪtɪ/ *n.*

insatiable /ɪnˈseɪʃəb(ə)l/ *a.* that cannot be satisfied, very greedy; **insatiably** *adv.* [F or L (IN-[2])]

insatiate /ɪnˈseɪʃɪət/ *a.* never satisfied. [L (IN-[2])]

inscribe /ɪnˈskraɪb/ *v.t.* write (words etc. *in* or *on* surface); mark (surface *with* characters); draw (geometrical figure) within another so that points of it lie on the other's boundary; enter name of (person) on list or in book; place informal dedication in or on (book etc.). [L (*scribo* write)]

inscription /ɪnˈskrɪpʃ(ə)n/ *n.* words inscribed; inscribing; **inscriptional** *a.* [L (prec.)]

inscrutable /ɪnˈskruːtəb(ə)l/ *a.* mysterious, impenetrable; **inscrutability** /-ˈbɪlɪtɪ/ *n.*; **inscrutably** *adv.* [L (*scrutor* search)]

insect /ˈɪnsekt/ *n.* any of many small invertebrate animals with six legs, two or four wings, and usu. body in three segments. [L (SECTION)]

insecticide /ɪnˈsektɪsaɪd/ *n.* substance for killing insects. [INSECT, -CIDE]

insectivore /ɪnˈsektɪvɔː/ *n.* animal that eats insects; plant that traps and absorbs insects; **insectivorous** /-ˈtɪvərəs/ *a.* [INSECT; L *voro* devour]

insecure /ɪnsɪˈkjʊə/ *a.* not secure or safe or dependable; given to constant anxiety; **insecurity** *n.* [L (IN-[2])]

inseminate /ɪnˈsemɪneɪt/ *v.t.* impregnate with semen; sow (seed etc., *lit.* or *fig.*, *in*); **insemination** /-ˈneɪʃ(ə)n/ *n.* [L (SEMEN)]

insensate /ɪnˈsenseɪt/ *a.* without sensibility; stupid; without physical sensation. [L (SENSE)]

insensible /ɪnˈsensɪb(ə)l/ *a.* unconscious; unaware (*of* or *to*); callous; too small or gradual to be perceived; **insensibility** /-ˈbɪlɪtɪ/ *n.*; **insensibly** *adv.* [F or L (IN-[2])]

inseparable /ɪnˈsepərəb(ə)l/ **1** *a.* that

cannot be separated; liking to be constantly together. **2** *n.* (usu. in *pl.*) inseparable person or thing, esp. friend. **3 inseparability** /-'bɪlɪtɪ/ *n.*; **inseparably** *adv.* [L (IN-²)]

insert 1 /ɪn'sɜ:t/ *v.t.* place or put (thing into another). **2** /'ɪnsɜ:t/ *n.* thing inserted. [L (*sero sert-* join)]

insertion /ɪn'sɜ:ʃ(ə)n/ *n.* inserting; thing inserted. [L (prec.)]

inset 1 /'ɪnset/ *n.* extra piece inserted in book, garment, etc.; small map etc. within border of larger one. **2** /ɪn'set/ *v.t.* (**-tt-**; *past* and *p.p.* **inset** or **insetted**) put in as inset; decorate with inset. [IN]

inshore *a.* & *adv.* near shore. [IN]

inside 1 *n.* inner side or part; position on inner side (*open the door from the inside*); (in *sing.* or *pl.*) *colloq.* stomach and bowels; (of path) side away from road. **2** *a.* of or on or in the inside; nearer to centre of games field. **3** *adv.* on or to or in the inside; *sl.* in prison. **4** *prep.* within, on the inside of; in less than (*inside an hour*). **5 inside information** information not accessible to outsiders; **inside job** *colloq.* burglary etc. by one living or working on the premises; **inside out** turned so that inner side becomes outer. [IN]

insider *n.* person within a group or society etc.; one who is in the secret.

insidious /ɪn'sɪdɪəs/ *a.* proceeding inconspicuously but harmfully; crafty. [L (*insidiae* ambush)]

insight *n.* mental penetration (*into* character etc.); piece of knowledge obtained by this. [IN-¹]

insignia /ɪn'sɪgnɪə/ *n.pl.* badges or emblems of rank, office, etc. [L (*signum* sign)]

insignificant /ɪnsɪg'nɪfɪkənt/ *a.* of no importance or meaning; worthless, trivial; **insignificance** *n.* [IN-²]

insincere /ɪnsɪn'sɪə/ *a.* not sincere or candid; **insincerity** /-'serɪtɪ/ *n.* [L (IN-²)]

insinuate /ɪn'sɪnjʊeɪt/ *v.t.* hint obliquely or unpleasantly; insert gradually or stealthily (*insinuate oneself into favour*); **insinuation** /-'eɪʃ(ə)n/ *n.* [L (*sinuo* curve)]

insipid /ɪn'sɪpɪd/ *a.* flavourless; dull, lifeless; **insipidity** /-'pɪdɪtɪ/ *n.* [F or L (SAPID)]

insist /ɪn'sɪst/ *v.* demand or maintain emphatically (*insist on going*, *on his innocence*; *insist that we go*, *that he is innocent*). [L (*sisto* stand)]

insistent *a.* insisting; forcing itself upon the attention; **insistence** *n.*

in situ /ɪn 'sɪtju:/ in its original place. [L]

insobriety /ɪnsə'braɪətɪ/ *n.* intemperance, esp. in drinking. [IN-²]

insofar /ɪnsəʊ'fa:/ *adv.* = *in so far* (see FAR).

insole *n.* inner sole of boot or shoe; removable inner sole for use in shoe. [IN]

insolent /'ɪnsələnt/ *a.* impertinently insulting; **insolence** *n.* [L (*soleo* be accustomed)]

insoluble /ɪn'sɒljʊb(ə)l/ *a.* that cannot be dissolved or solved; **insolubly** *adv.* [F or L (IN-²)]

insolvent /ɪn'sɒlvənt/ **1** *a.* unable to pay debts. **2** *n.* insolvent debtor. **3 insolvency** *n.* [IN-²]

insomnia /ɪn'sɒmnɪə/ *n.* habitual sleeplessness. [L (*somnus* sleep)]

insomniac *n.* person suffering from insomnia.

insomuch /ɪnsəʊ'mʌtʃ/ *adv.* to such an extent *that*; inasmuch *as*. [orig. *in so much*]

insouciant /ɪn'su:sɪənt/ *a.* carefree, unconcerned; **insouciance** *n.* [F (*souci* care)]

inspan /ɪn'spæn/ *v.t.* (**-nn-**) *S. Afr.* yoke (oxen etc.) in team to vehicle; harness animals to (wagon). [Du. (SPAN¹)]

inspect /ɪn'spekt/ *v.t.* examine, esp. closely or officially; **inspection** *n.* [L (*spicio spect-* look)]

inspector *n.* person employed to inspect or supervise; police officer next above sergeant; **inspector of taxes** official assessing income tax payable. [L (prec.)]

inspiration /ɪnspɪ'reɪʃ(ə)n/ *n.* inspiring; sudden brilliant idea; source of inspiring influence; divine influence, esp. in Scripture and poetry. [F f. L (INSPIRE)]

inspire /ɪn'spaɪə/ *v.t.* stimulate (person) to creative activity; animate (person etc. *with* feeling); instil thought or feeling into (person); breathe (air etc.) in. [F f. L (*spiro* breathe)]

inspirit /ɪn'spɪrɪt/ *v.t.* put life into, animate; encourage. [IN-¹]

inst. *abbr.* instant (*the 6th inst.*).

instability /ɪnstə'bɪlɪtɪ/ *n.* lack of stability or firmness. [F f. L (IN-²)]

install /ɪn'stɔ:l/ *v.t.* place (person) formally or ceremonially in office; fix or establish (person, equipment, etc.); **installation** /ɪnstə'leɪʃ(ə)n/ *n.* [L (STALL)]

instalment /ɪn'stɔ:lmənt/, *US* **installment** *n.* any of successive parts in which a sum is (to be) paid; any of the parts of a whole successively delivered, published, etc. [AF (*estaler* fix)]

instance /'ɪnstəns/ **1** *n.* example, illustration of general truth; particular case (*in this instance*). **2** *v.t.* cite as instance. **3 in the first instance** as the first stage (in a process). [F f. L *instantia* contrary example]

instant 1 *a.* immediate; (of food) that can be prepared easily for immediate use; urgent, pressing; of the current month (*the 6th instant*). **2** *n.* precise moment (*went that instant*); short time, moment (*in an instant*). [F f. L (*insto* be urgent)]

instantaneous /ɪnstən'teɪnɪəs/ *a.* occurring or done in an instant. [med.L (prec.)]

instantly *adv.* immediately, at once. [INSTANT]

instead /ɪn'sted/ *adv.* in place *of*; as a substitute. [IN]

instep *n.* top of foot between toes and ankle; part of shoe etc. over or under this. [ult. f. IN, STEP]

instigate /'ɪnstɪgeɪt/ *v.t.* incite or persuade; bring about (revolt, murder, etc.) thus; **instigation** /-'geɪʃ(ə)n/ *n.*; **instigator** *n.* [L (*stigo* prick)]

instil /ɪn'stɪl/, *US* **instill** *v.t.* (-ll-) put (ideas etc. *into* mind etc.) gradually; put in (liquid *into* thing) by drops; **instillation** /-'leɪʃ(ə)n/ *n.*; **instilment** *n.* [L (*stillo* drop)]

instinct 1 /'ɪnstɪŋkt/ *n.* innate propensity, esp. in lower animals, to seemingly rational acts; innate impulse or behaviour; intuition. **2** /ɪn'stɪŋkt/ *a.* filled or charged (*with* life, energy, etc.). **3 instinctive** /ɪn'stɪŋktɪv/ *a.*; **instinctual** /ɪn'stɪŋktjʊəl/ *a.* [L (*stinguo* prick)]

institute /'ɪnstɪtju:t/ **1** *n.* organized body for promotion of educational, scientific, or similar object; its building. **2** *v.t.* establish, found; initiate (inquiry etc.); appoint (person *to* or *into* benefice). [L (*statuo* set up)]

institution /ɪnstɪ'tju:ʃ(ə)n/ *n.* instituting or being instituted; organized body, esp. with charitable purpose; established law, custom, or practice; *colloq.* well-known person. [F f. L (prec.)]

institutional *a.* of or like an institution; typical of charitable institutions; **institutionally** *adv.*

institutionalize *v.t.* make institutional; place or keep (person needing care) in an institution.

instruct /ɪn'strʌkt/ *v.t.* teach or give information to (person *in* subject); direct, authorize; **instructor** *n.* [L *instruo -struct-* teach, furnish]

instruction /ɪn'strʌkʃ(ə)n/ *n.* instructing; (usu. in *pl.*) orders, authority; **instructional** *a.* [F f. L (prec.)]

instructive /ɪn'strʌktɪv/ *a.* tending to instruct, enlightening. [INSTRUCT]

instrument /'ɪnstrʊmənt/ *n.* tool or implement, esp. for delicate or scientific work; device for measuring or controlling function of machine or aircraft etc.; device for giving controlled musical sounds; thing used to perform a particular action; person so made use of; formal (esp. legal) document. [F or L (prec.)]

instrumental /ɪnstrʊ'ment(ə)l/ *a.* serving as instrument or means; (of music) performed on instruments; of or due to instrument (*instrumental error*); *Gram.* (of case) denoting means. [F f. med.L (prec.)]

instrumentalist *n.* performer on musical instrument.

instrumentality /ɪnstrʊmen'tælɪtɪ/ *n.* agency or means.

instrumentation /ɪnstrʊmen'teɪʃ(ə)n/ *n.* arrangement of music for instruments; provision of or operation with instruments. [F (INSTRUMENT)]

insubordinate /ɪnsə'bɔ:dɪnət/ *a.* disobedient, unruly; **insubordination** /-'neɪʃ(ə)n/ *n.* [IN-²]

insubstantial /ɪnsəb'stænʃ(ə)l/ *a.* lacking reality or solidity. [L (IN-²)]

insufferable /ɪn'sʌfərəb(ə)l/ *a.* intolerable; unbearably conceited; **insufferably** *adv.* [IN-²]

insular /'ɪnsjʊlə/ *a.* unable or unwilling to take a broad mental view; of or like islanders; of or forming an island; **insularity** /-'lærɪtɪ/ *n.* [L (foll.)]

insulate /'ɪnsjʊleɪt/ *v.t.* isolate, esp. with substance or device preventing passage of electricity, heat, or sound; **insulation** /-'leɪʃ(ə)n/ *n.*; **insulator** *n.* [L *insula* island]

insulin /'ɪnsjʊlɪn/ *n.* hormone produced in the pancreas, controlling sugar in body and used against diabetes.

insult 1 /ɪn'sʌlt/ *v.t.* abuse scornfully; offend self-respect or modesty of. **2** /'ɪnsʌlt/ *n.* insulting remark or action. [F or L (*insulto* leap on, assail)]

insuperable /ɪn'su:pərəb(ə)l/ *a.* (of barrier, difficulty, etc.) that cannot be surmounted or overcome; **insuperability** /-'bɪlɪtɪ/ *n.*; **insuperably** *adv.* [F or L (*supero* overcome)]

insupportable /ɪnsə'pɔ:təb(ə)l/ *a.* unbearable; unjustifiable; **insupportably** *adv.* [F (IN-²)]

insurance /ɪn'ʃʊərəns/ *n.* procedure or contract securing compensation for loss or damage or injury on payment of premium; business of this; sum paid to effect insurance. [F (ENSURE)]

insure /ɪn'ʃʊə/ *v.t.* effect insurance *against* or with respect to. [var. of ENSURE]

insured *n.* person protected by insurance.

insurer *n.* one who undertakes to pay insurance in consideration of premium.

insurgent /ɪn'sɜ:dʒənt/ **1** *n.* rebel. **2** *a.* in revolt, rebellious. **3 insurgence** *n.* [F f. L (*surgo surrect-* rise)]

insurrection /ɪnsə'rekʃ(ə)n/ *n.* rising

in open resistance to authority, incipient rebellion; **insurrectionist** *n.* [F f. L (prec.)]

intact /ɪn'tækt/ *a.* undamaged, unimpaired; entire; untouched. [L (*tango tact-* touch)]

intaglio /ɪn'tɑ:lɪəʊ/ *n.* (*pl.* **intaglios**) engraved design; gem with incised design. [It. (IN-[1], TAIL[2])]

intake *n.* action of taking in; place where water is taken into pipe, fuel or air into engine, etc.; persons or things or quantity taken in or received. [IN]

intangible /ɪn'tændʒɪb(ə)l/ *a.* that cannot be touched or mentally grasped; **intangibly** *adv.* [F or L (INTACT)]

integer /'ɪntɪdʒə/ *n.* whole number. [L, = untouched, whole]

integral /'ɪntɪgr(ə)l/ **1** *a.* of or necessary to a whole; complete, forming a whole; of or denoted by an integer. **2** *n.* quantity of which a given function is a derivative. **3** **integral calculus** branch of calculus concerned with finding integrals, their properties, etc. **4** **integrally** *adv.* [L (prec.)]

integrate /'ɪntɪgreɪt/ *v.* combine (parts) into a whole; bring or come into equal membership of society esp. disregarding race or religion; end segregation (of or at); complete by addition of parts; **integrated circuit** small piece of material replacing electric circuit of many components; **integration** /-'reɪʃ(ə)n/ *n.*

integrity /ɪn'tegrɪtɪ/ *n.* honesty; wholeness; soundness. [F or L (INTEGER)]

integument /ɪn'tegjʊmənt/ *n.* skin, husk, rind, or other covering. [L (*tego* cover)]

intellect /'ɪntɪlekt/ *n.* faculty of knowing and reasoning; understanding; person with good understanding. [F or L (INTELLIGENT)]

intellectual /ɪntɪ'lektjʊəl/ **1** *a.* of or requiring or using intellect; having highly-developed intellect. **2** *n.* intellectual person. **3** **intellectuality** /-'ælɪtɪ/ *n.*; **intellectualize** *v.t.*; **intellectually** *adv.* [L (prec.)]

intelligence /ɪn'telɪdʒəns/ *n.* intellect, understanding; quickness of understanding; information, news; collection of this, esp. for military purposes; persons engaged in such collection; **intelligence quotient** ratio of given person's intelligence to the normal or average. [F f. L (foll.)]

intelligent *a.* having or showing great intelligence, clever. [L (*intelligo -lect-* understand)]

intelligentsia /ɪntelɪ'dʒensɪə/ *n.* intellectuals as a class, esp. regarded as cultured and politically enterprising. [Russ. f. Pol. f. L (INTELLIGENCE)]

intelligible /ɪn'telɪdʒɪb(ə)l/ *a.* that can be understood; **intelligibility** /-'bɪlɪtɪ/ *n.*; **intelligibly** *adv.* [L (INTELLIGENT)]

intemperate /ɪn'tempərət/ *a.* lacking moderation; excessive in indulgence of appetite; addicted to drinking; **intemperance** *n.* [L (IN-[2])]

intend /ɪn'tend/ *v.t.* have as one's purpose or wish (*intend no harm*; *intend to stay*); plan or destine (person or thing *for* purpose, *as* something, *to do* thing). [F f. L (*tendo tens-*, *tent-* stretch)]

intended **1** *a.* done on purpose. **2** *n.* *colloq.* fiancé(e).

intense /ɪn'tens/ *a.* existing in high degree, violent, vehement (*intense desire, disgust, heat*); emotional; eager, ardent, strenuous; having a quality in high degree. [F or L (INTEND)]

intensify *v.* make or become (more) intense; **intensification** /-fɪ'keɪʃ(ə)n/ *n.*

intensity *n.* intenseness; amount of force, brightness, etc.

intensive *a.* thorough, vigorous; concentrated on one point or area (*intensive bombardment, study*); serving to increase production from given area (*intensive agriculture*); (of words) giving emphasis; of or in intensity; (as *suffix*) making much use of (*labour-intensive*); **intensive care** medical treatment with constant supervision of patient. [F or med.L (INTEND)]

intent /ɪn'tent/ **1** *n.* intention, purpose (*with intent to defraud*). **2** *a.* resolved or bent (*on*); attentively occupied (*on*); earnest, eager (*intent gaze*). **3** **to all intents and purposes** virtually, practically. [F or L (INTEND)]

intention /ɪn'tenʃ(ə)n/ *n.* thing intended; ultimate aim or purpose; intending (*done without intention*). [F f. L (INTEND)]

intentional *a.* done on purpose; **intentionally** *adv.* [F or med.L (prec.)]

inter /ɪn'tɜ:/ *v.t.* (**-rr-**) place (corpse etc.) in earth or tomb, bury. [F f. Rmc (L *terra* earth)]

inter- *prefix* between, among, mutually, reciprocally. [F or L (*inter* between, among)]

interact /ɪntər'ækt/ *v.i.* act on each other; **interaction** *n.*; **interactive** *a.*

inter alia /ɪntər 'eɪlɪə/ among other things. [L]

interbreed /ɪntə'bri:d/ *v.* breed with each other; cause animals to do this; produce (hybrid individual). [INTER-]

intercalary /ɪntə'kælərɪ/ *a.* (of day(s) or month) inserted to harmonize calendar with solar year; (of year) having such additions; interpolated. [L (foll.)]

intercalate /ɪn'tɜ:kəleɪt/ *v.t.* interpose;

insert (intercalary day etc.); **intercalation** /-'leɪʃ(ə)n/ *n.* [L (*calo* proclaim)]
intercede /ɪntə'si:d/ *v.i.* interpose on another's behalf, mediate; plead (*with* person *for* another). [F or L (CEDE)]
intercept /ɪntə'sept/ *v.t.* seize, catch, stop, in transit or progress; cut off (light etc. *from*); **interception** *n.*; **interceptive** *a.*; **interceptor** *n.* [L *intercipio -cept-* (*capio* take)]
intercession /ɪntə'seʃ(ə)n/ *n.* interceding; **intercessor** *n.* [F or L (INTERCEDE)]
interchange 1 /ɪntə'tʃeɪndʒ/ *v.t.* put (things) in each other's place; (of two persons) exchange (things) with each other; alternate. **2** /'ɪntətʃeɪndʒ/ *n.* exchange (*of* things) between persons etc.; alternation; junction of roads on different levels. **3** **interchangeable** *a.* [F (CHANGE)]
inter-city /ɪntə'sɪtɪ/ *a.* existing or travelling between cities. [INTER-]
intercom /'ɪntəkɒm/ *n. colloq.* system of intercommunication operating like telephone. [abbr.]
intercommunicate /ɪntəkə'mju:nɪkeɪt/ *v.i.* communicate mutually; have free passage into each other; **intercommunication** /-'keɪʃ(ə)n/ *n.* [AL (COMMUNICATE)]
intercommunion /ɪntəkə'mju:nɪən/ *n.* mutual communion, esp. between Christian denominations. [INTER-]
interconnect /ɪntəkə'nekt/ *v.* connect with each other; **interconnection** *n.*
intercontinental /ɪntəkɒntɪ'nent(ə)l/ *a.* connecting or travelling between continents.
intercourse /'ɪntəkɔ:s/ *n.* social communication between individuals; communication between countries etc., esp. in trade; = *sexual intercourse*. [F f. L (COURSE)]
interdenominational /ɪntədɪnɒmɪ'neɪʃən(ə)l/ *a.* of or involving more than one Christian denomination. [INTER-]
interdepartmental /ɪntədi:pɑ:t'ment(ə)l/ *a.* of more than one department.
interdependent /ɪntədɪ'pendənt/ *a.* dependent on each other; **interdependence** *n.*
interdict 1 /ɪntə'dɪkt/ *v.t.* forbid (action, thing *to* person); forbid use of; restrain (person *from doing* thing). **2** /'ɪntədɪkt/ *n.* authoritative prohibition; (in RC Church) sentence debarring person or place from ecclesiastical functions etc. **3** **interdiction** /-'dɪkʃ(ə)n/ *n.*; **interdictory** /-'dɪktərɪ/ *a.* [F f. L (*dico* say)]
interdisciplinary /ɪntədɪsɪ'plɪnərɪ/ *a.* of or involving different branches of learning. [INTER-]
interest /'ɪntrəst/ **1** *n.* concern or curiosity (*take an interest in*); quality causing this (*is of no interest to me*); thing towards which one feels it; advantage (*it is in your interest to go*); money paid for use of loan of money; legal concern, title, or right (*in* property); money stake (*in* a business); thing in which one has a stake or concern; principle which a party has in common, such party (*the brewing interest*); selfish pursuit of one's own welfare, self-interest. **2** *v.t.* arouse interest of; cause (person, esp. *oneself*) to be interested or involved (*in* thing). [F f. L, = it matters]
interested *a.* feeling interest or curiosity; having private interest, not impartial.
interesting *a.* causing curiosity, holding the attention.
interface *n.* surface forming common boundary of two regions; place or piece of equipment where interaction occurs between two systems etc. [INTER-]
interfere /ɪntə'fɪə/ *v.i.* meddle or intervene; obstruct, be an obstacle, clash (*with*); (of light-waves etc.) combine in different phases with partial or complete neutralization; **interfere with** molest or assault sexually. [F f. L *ferio* strike]
interference *n.* interfering; fading of received radio signals.
interferon /ɪntə'fɪərɒn/ *n.* protein inhibiting development of virus in cell.
interfuse /ɪntə'fju:z/ *v.* blend (things); (of two things) blend with each other; intersperse (thing *with* another); **interfusible** *a.*; **interfusion** *n.* [L (FUSE[1])]
interglacial /ɪntə'gleɪʃ(ə)l/ *n.* period between glacial periods. [INTER-]
interim /'ɪntərɪm/ **1** *n.* intervening time. **2** *a.* temporary, provisional. [L, = in the interim]
interior /ɪn'tɪərɪə/ **1** *n.* inner part, inside; inland region; inside of room etc. (*interior decoration*); picture of this; home affairs of a country (*Minister of the Interior*). **2** *a.* situated or coming from within; further in; inland; internal, domestic; existing in the mind. [L]
interject /ɪntə'dʒekt/ *v.t.* utter (words) abruptly or parenthetically. [L (*jacio ject-* throw)]
interjection /ɪntə'dʒekʃ(ə)n/ *n.* exclamation, esp. as part of speech (e.g. *ah, whew*). [F f. L (prec.)]
interlace /ɪntə'leɪs/ *v.* bind intricately together, interweave; cross each other intricately; **interlacement** *n.* [F (LACE)]
interlard /ɪntə'lɑ:d/ *v.t.* mix (writing or speech *with* unusual words or phrases). [F]
interleave /ɪntə'li:v/ *v.t.* insert leaves,

usu. blank, between leaves of (book). [LEAF]

interlinear /ɪntəˈlɪnɪə/ *a.* written or printed between lines of text. [med.L (LINEAR)]

interlink /ɪntəˈlɪŋk/ *v.* link together. [INTER-]

interlock /ɪntəˈlɒk/ **1** *v.* engage with each other by overlapping; lock or clasp in each other. **2** *a.* (of fabric) knitted with closely interlocking stitches. **3** *n.* such fabric. [LOCK[1]]

interlocutor /ɪntəˈlɒkjʊtə/ *n.* one who takes part in conversation. [L (*loquor* speak)]

interlocutory *a.* of dialogue; (of decree etc.) given in course of a legal action. [med.L (prec.)]

interloper /ˈɪntələʊpə/ *n.* intruder, one who thrusts himself into others' affairs, esp. for profit. [after *landloper* vagabond (Du. *loopen* run)]

interlude /ˈɪntəluːd/ *n.* pause between acts of play; something performed during this; intervening time or event of different character; piece of music played between verses of hymn etc. [med.L (*ludus* play)]

intermarry /ɪntəˈmærɪ/ *v.i.* (of tribes etc.) become connected by marriage; **intermarriage** *n.* [INTER-]

intermediary /ɪntəˈmiːdɪərɪ/ **1** *n.* mediator; intermediate thing. **2** *a.* acting as mediator; intermediate. [F f. It. f. L (foll.)]

intermediate /ɪntəˈmiːdɪət/ **1** *a.* coming between two things in time, place, character, etc. **2** *n.* intermediate thing; chemical compound formed by one reaction and then taking part in another. [med.L (MEDIUM)]

interment /ɪnˈtɜːmənt/ *n.* burial. [INTER]

intermezzo /ɪntəˈmetsəʊ/ *n.* (*pl.* **intermezzi** /-tsiː/) short connecting movement in musical work, or similar but independent piece; short light dramatic or other performance between acts of play etc. [It. (INTERMEDIATE)]

interminable /ɪnˈtɜːmɪnəb(ə)l/ *a.* tediously long; endless; **interminably** *adv.* [F or L (IN-[2])]

intermingle /ɪntəˈmɪŋg(ə)l/ *v.* mix together, mingle. [INTER-]

intermission /ɪntəˈmɪʃ(ə)n/ *n.* pause, cessation; interval in cinema etc. [F or L (foll.)]

intermittent /ɪntəˈmɪtənt/ *a.* occurring at intervals, not continuous. [L (*mitto miss-* let go)]

intermix /ɪntəˈmɪks/ *v.* mix together. [L (MIX)]

intern **1** /ɪnˈtɜːn/ *v.t.* oblige (prisoner, alien, etc.) to live within prescribed limits. **2** /ˈɪntɜːn/ *n.* *US* recent graduate or advanced student living in hospital and acting as assistant physician or surgeon. **3** **internment** *n.* [F (foll.)]

internal /ɪnˈtɜːn(ə)l/ *a.* of or in the inside or invisible part; relating or applied to interior of the body (*internal injury*); of a country's domestic affairs; of students attending a university as well as taking its examinations; used or applying within an organization; intrinsic; of mind or soul; **internal-combustion engine** engine in which motive power comes from explosion of gas or vapour with air in cylinder; **internal evidence** evidence derived from contents of the thing discussed; **internality** /-ˈnælɪtɪ/ *n.*; **internally** *adv.* [med.L (*internus* internal)]

international /ɪntəˈnæʃən(ə)l/ **1** *a.* existing or carried on between nations; agreed on or used by all or many nations. **2** *n.* contest, usu. in sport, between representatives of different nations; such representative; (**International**) any of four associations for socialist or communist action. **3** **internationality** /-ˈnælɪtɪ/ *n.*; **internationally** *adv.* [NATION]

internationalism *n.* advocacy of community of interests among nations; support of International; **internationalist** *n.*

internationalize *v.t.* make international; bring under protection or control of two or more nations.

internecine /ɪntəˈniːsaɪn/ *a.* mutually destructive. [L *internecinus* deadly (*neco* kill)]

internee /ɪntɜːˈniː/ *n.* person interned. [INTERN]

internist /ɪnˈtɜːnɪst/ *n.* specialist in internal diseases; *US* general practitioner. [INTERNAL]

interpenetrate /ɪntəˈpenɪtreɪt/ *v.* penetrate each other; pervade; **interpenetration** /-ˈtreɪʃ(ə)n/ *n.* [INTER-]

interpersonal /ɪntəˈpɜːsən(ə)l/ *a.* between persons.

interplanetary /ɪntəˈplænɪtərɪ/ *a.* between planets; of travel between planets.

interplay /ˈɪntəpleɪ/ *n.* reciprocal action.

Interpol /ˈɪntəpɒl/ *n.* International Criminal Police Commission. [abbr.]

interpolate /ɪnˈtɜːpəleɪt/ *v.t.* interject (remark) in talk; insert (words) in book etc., esp. misleadingly; make such insertions in (book etc.); insert (terms) in mathematical series, estimate (values) from known ones in same range; **interpolation** /-ˈleɪʃ(ə)n/ *n.*; **interpolator** *n.* [L *interpolo* furbish]

interpose /ɪntəˈpəʊz/ *v.* insert (thing

between others); say (words) as interruption, speak thus; exercise or advance (veto or objection) so as to interfere; intervene (*between* parties); **interposition** /-pəˈzɪʃ(ə)n/ *n.* [F f. L (*pono* put)]

interpret /ɪnˈtɜːprɪt/ *v.* explain (foreign or abstruse words, dream, etc.); make out or bring out meaning of; explain or understand in specified way; act as interpreter; **interpretation** /-ˈteɪʃ(ə)n/ *n.*; **interpretative** *a.*; **interpretive** *a.* [F or L (*interpres -pretis* explainer)]

interpreter *n.* one who interprets, esp. one who orally translates words of persons speaking different languages. [AF (prec.)]

interregnum /ɪntəˈregnəm/ *n.* (*pl.* **interregnums**) interval when usual government is suspended, esp. between successive reigns; interval, pause. [L (*regnum* reign)]

interrelated /ɪntərɪˈleɪtɪd/ *a.* related to each other; **interrelation** *n.* [INTER-]

interrogate /ɪnˈterəgeɪt/ *v.t.* question (person) esp. closely or formally; **interrogation** /-ˈgeɪʃ(ə)n/ *n.*; **interrogator** *n.* [L (*rogo* ask)]

interrogative /ɪntəˈrɒgətɪv/ **1** *a.* of or like or used in questions. **2** *n.* interrogative word (e.g. *who?*).

interrogatory /ɪntəˈrɒgətərɪ/ **1** *a.* questioning (*interrogatory tone*). **2** *n.* formal set of questions.

interrupt /ɪntəˈrʌpt/ *v.t.* act so as to break the continuous progress of (action, speech, person speaking, etc.); obstruct (view etc.); **interruption** *n.* [L (RUPTURE)]

intersect /ɪntəˈsekt/ *v.* divide (thing) by crossing it; (of lines, roads, etc.) cross each other. [L (SECTION)]

intersection /ɪntəˈsekʃ(ə)n/ *n.* place where two roads intersect; point or line common to lines or planes that intersect; intersecting.

interspace 1 /ˈɪntəspeɪs/ *n.* intervening space. **2** /ɪntəˈspeɪs/ *v.t.* put space or spaces between. [INTER-]

intersperse /ɪntəˈspɜːs/ *v.t.* diversify (thing or things *with* others scattered about); scatter (things *between* or *among*); **interspersion** *n.* [L (SPARSE)]

interstate /ˈɪntəsteɪt/ *a.* existing or carried on between States esp. of US. [INTER-]

interstellar /ɪntəˈstelə/ *a.* between stars.

interstice /ɪnˈtɜːstɪs/ *n.* intervening space; chink, crevice. [L *interstitium* (*sisto* stand)]

interstitial /ɪntəˈstɪʃ(ə)l/ *a.* of or in or forming interstices; **interstitially** *adv.*

intertwine /ɪntəˈtwaɪn/ *v.* twine closely together. [INTER-]

interval /ˈɪntəv(ə)l/ *n.* intervening time or space; pause, break, esp. between parts of performance; difference of pitch between two sounds; **at intervals** here and there, now and then. [L, = space between ramparts (*vallum*)]

intervene /ɪntəˈviːn/ *v.i.* occur in time between events; interfere, modify course or result of events; come in as extraneous thing; be situated *between* others. [L (*venio vent-* come)]

intervention /ɪntəˈvenʃ(ə)n/ *n.* intervening, interference, esp. by State; mediation.

interventionist *n.* one who favours intervention.

interview /ˈɪntəvjuː/ **1** *n.* conversation between reporter and person whose views he wishes to publish or broadcast; oral examination of applicant; meeting of persons face to face, esp. for consultation. **2** *v.t.* have interview with. **3 interviewee** /-vjuːˈiː/ *n.* [F *entrevue* (INTER-, *vue* sight)]

inter-war /ɪntəˈwɔː/ *a.* existing in period between two wars. [INTER-]

interweave /ɪntəˈwiːv/ *v.t.* weave together; blend intimately.

intestate /ɪnˈtesteɪt/ **1** *a.* not having made a will before death. **2** *n.* person who has died intestate. **3 intestacy** *n.* [L (TESTAMENT)]

intestine /ɪnˈtestɪn/ *n.* (in *sing.* or *pl.*) lower part of alimentary canal; **intestinal** *a.* [L (*intus* within)]

intimacy /ˈɪntɪməsɪ/ *n.* being intimate; intimate act, e.g. sexual intercourse. [foll.]

intimate /ˈɪntɪmət/ **1** *a.* closely acquainted, familiar (*intimate friend, friendship*); private and personal; having sexual relations *with*; (of knowledge) detailed, thorough; (of relations between things) close. **2** *n.* intimate friend. **3** /-eɪt/ *v.t.* state or make known; imply, hint. **4 intimation** /-ˈmeɪʃ(ə)n/ *n.* [L (*intimus* inmost)]

intimidate /ɪnˈtɪmɪdeɪt/ *v.t.* frighten, esp. in order to subdue or influence; **intimidation** /-ˈdeɪʃ(ə)n/ *n.*; **intimidator** *n.* [med.L (TIMID)]

into /ˈɪntʊ, -tə/ *prep.* expressing motion or direction to a point on or within (*crashed into the wall; went into the room*), or *fig.* (*will inquire into it*); expressing change of state (*turned into a dragon; divided into classes; pressed into agreement*); *colloq.* interested in. [OE (IN, TO)]

intolerable /ɪnˈtɒlərəb(ə)l/ *a.* that cannot be endured; **intolerably** *adv.* [F or L (IN-²)]

intolerant /ɪn'tɒlərənt/ *a.* not tolerant, esp. of views or beliefs differing from one's own; **intolerance** *n.* [L (IN-²)]

intonation /ɪntə'neɪʃ(ə)n/ *n.* intoning; modulation of voice, accent. [med.L (foll.)]

intone /ɪn'təʊn/ *v.t.* recite (prayers etc.) with prolonged sounds, esp. in monotone; utter with particular tone. [med.L (IN-¹)]

in toto /ɪn 'təʊtəʊ/ completely. [L]

intoxicant /ɪn'tɒksɪkənt/ **1** *n.* intoxicating substance. **2** *a.* intoxicating. [foll.]

intoxicate /ɪn'tɒksɪkeɪt/ *v.t.* make drunk; excite or elate beyond self-control; **intoxication** /-'keɪʃ(ə)n/ *n.* [med.L (TOXIC)]

intra- *prefix* within, on the inside. [L *intra* inside]

intractable /ɪn'træktəb(ə)l/ *a.* hard to control or deal with; difficult, stubborn; **intractability** /-'bɪlɪtɪ/ *n.*; **intractably** *adv.* [L (IN-²)]

intramural /ɪntrə'mjʊər(ə)l/ *a.* situated or done within walls; forming part of ordinary university work; **intramurally** *adv.* [L *murus* wall]

intransigent /ɪn'trænsɪdʒənt/ **1** *a.* uncompromising, stubborn. **2** *n.* intransigent person. **3** **intransigence** *n.* [F, f. Sp. *los intransigentes* extremists (IN-², TRANSACT)]

intransitive /ɪn'trænsɪtɪv/ *a.* (of verb) not taking direct object. [L (IN-²)]

intra-uterine /ɪntrə'ju:təraɪn, -rɪn/ *a.* within the womb. [INTRA-]

intravenous /ɪntrə'vi:nəs/ *a.* in or into vein(s).

in-tray *n.* tray for incoming documents. [IN]

intrepid /ɪn'trepɪd/ *a.* fearless, brave; **intrepidity** /ɪntrɪ'pɪdɪtɪ/ *n.* [F or L (*trepidus* alarmed)]

intricate /'ɪntrɪkət/ *a.* perplexingly entangled or complicated; **intricacy** *n.* [L (IN-¹, *tricae* tricks)]

intrigue /ɪn'tri:g/ **1** *v.* carry on underhand plot (*with*); use secret influence (*with*); rouse interest or curiosity of. **2** /also 'ɪn-/ *n.* underhand plotting or plot; *archaic* secret love affair. [F f. It. (prec.)]

intrinsic /ɪn'trɪnsɪk/ *a.* inherent, essential (*intrinsic value*); **intrinsically** *adv.* [F f. L *intrinsecus* inwardly]

intro- *prefix* into, inwards. [L]

introduce /ɪntrə'dju:s/ *v.t.* make (person, *oneself*) known by name *to* another, esp. formally; announce or present to audience; bring (custom etc.) into use; bring (bill) before Parliament etc.; extend understanding of (person *to* subject etc.) for first time; insert; bring in; usher in, bring forward; come just before start of; **introducible** *a.* [L (*duco* lead)]

introduction /ɪntrə'dʌkʃ(ə)n/ *n.* introducing; formal presentation of person to another; explanatory section at beginning of book etc.; introductory treatise; thing introduced. [F or L (prec.)]

introductory /ɪntrə'dʌktərɪ/ *a.* that introduces; preliminary. [L (INTRODUCE)]

introit /'ɪntrɔɪt/ *n.* psalm or antiphon sung or said while priest approaches altar for Eucharist. [F f. L *introitus* entrance]

introspection /ɪntrə'spekʃ(ə)n/ *n.* examining one's own thoughts; **introspective** *a.* [L (*specio spect-* look)]

introvert /'ɪntrəvɜ:t/ *n.* introverted person. [INTRO-]

introverted /'ɪntrəvɜ:tɪd/ *a.* principally interested in one's own thoughts; reserved, shy; **introversion** /-'vɜ:ʃ(ə)n/ *n.*

intrude /ɪn'tru:d/ *v.* force or come uninvited or unwanted (*into* or *on, upon*). [L (*trudo trus-* thrust)]

intruder *n.* one who intrudes; burglar; raiding aircraft.

intrusion /ɪn'tru:ʒ(ə)n/ *n.* intruding; influx of molten rock between strata etc.; **intrusive** *a.* [F or med.L (INTRUDE)]

intrust var. of ENTRUST.

intuition /ɪntju:'ɪʃ(ə)n/ *n.* immediate apprehension by the mind without reasoning; immediate apprehension by a sense; immediate insight; **intuitional** *a.* [L (*tueor tuit-* look)]

intuitive /ɪn'tju:ɪtɪv/ *a.* of, having, or perceived by, intuition. [med.L (prec.)]

inundate /'ɪnʌndeɪt/ *v.t.* flood or overwhelm (*with*); **inundation** /-'deɪʃ(ə)n/ *n.* [L (*unda* wave)]

inure /ɪ'njʊə/ *v.* accustom (*to* difficulty etc.); *Law* take effect; **inurement** *n.* [AF (IN, *eure* work f. L *opera*)]

in vacuo /ɪn 'vækjʊəʊ/ in a vacuum. [L]

invade /ɪn'veɪd/ *v.t.* enter (country) under arms to control or subdue it; swarm into; (of disease etc.) attack; encroach on (rights, esp. privacy). [L (*vado vas-* go)]

invalid¹ /'ɪnvəli:d/ **1** /also -ɪd/ *n.* person enfeebled or disabled by illness or injury. **2** /also -ɪd/ *a.* of or for invalids; being an invalid. **3** *v.t.* remove from active service, send away (*home* etc.), as an invalid; disable by illness. **4** **invalidism** *n.* [L (IN-²)]

invalid² /ɪn'vælɪd/ *a.* not valid; **invalidity** /-'lɪdɪtɪ/ *n.*

invalidate /ɪn'vælɪdeɪt/ *v.t.* make (argument, contract, etc.) invalid; **invalidation** /-'deɪʃ(ə)n/ *n.* [med.L (prec.)]

invaluable /ɪn'væljʊəb(ə)l/ *a.* beyond price, inestimable; **invaluably** *adv.* [IN-²]

invariable /ɪn'veərɪəb(ə)l/ *a.* unchangeable; always the same; constant; **invariably** *adv.* [F or L (IN-²)]

invasion /ɪn'veɪʒ(ə)n/ *n.* invading or being invaded; **invasive** *a.* [F or L (INVADE)]

invective /ɪn'vektɪv/ *n.* strong verbal attack. [F f. L (foll.)]

inveigh /ɪn'veɪ/ *v.i.* speak or write with strong hostility (*against*). [L *invehor -vect-* assail]

inveigle /ɪn'veɪg(ə)l/ *v.t.* entice, persuade by guile (*into*); **inveiglement** *n.* [AF f. F *aveugler* blind]

invent /ɪn'vent/ *v.t.* create by thought, originate (method or instrument); concoct (false story); **inventor** *n.* [L *invenio -vent-* come upon, find]

invention /ɪn'venʃ(ə)n/ *n.* inventing; thing invented; fictitious story; inventiveness. [L (prec.)]

inventive *a.* able to invent. [F or med.L (INVENT)]

inventory /'ɪnvəntərɪ/ **1** *n.* detailed list (of goods etc.); goods in this. **2** *v.t.* make inventory of; enter (goods) in inventory. [med.L (INVENT)]

inverse /ɪn'vɜːs, 'ɪn-/ **1** *a.* inverted in position or order or relation; (of proportion or ratio) between two quantities one of which increases in proportion as the other decreases. **2** *n.* inverted state; thing that is direct opposite (*of* another). [L (INVERT)]

inversion /ɪn'vɜːʃ(ə)n/ *n.* turning upside down; reversal of normal order, position, or relation; **inversive** *a.*

invert **1** /ɪn'vɜːt/ *v.t.* turn upside down; reverse position, order, or relation, of. **2** /'ɪnvɜːt/ *n.* homosexual. **3 inverted commas** quotation-marks. [L (*verto vers-* turn)]

invertebrate /ɪn'vɜːtɪbrət/ **1** *a.* without backbone or spinal column. **2** *n.* invertebrate animal. [IN-²]

invest /ɪn'vest/ *v.* apply or use (money) esp. for profit; provide or endue (person *with* qualities, insignia, or rank); clothe (person etc. *in* or *with*); cover as garment; lay siege to; **invest in** put money into (stocks etc.), *colloq.* buy. [F or L (*vestis* clothing)]

investigate /ɪn'vestɪgeɪt/ *v.* inquire into, examine; make systematic inquiry; **investigation** /-'geɪʃ(ə)n/ *n.*; **investigative** *a.*; **investigator** *n.*; **investigatory** *a.* [L (*vestigo* track)]

investiture /ɪn'vestɪtʃə/ *n.* formal investing of person(s) with honours or rank. [med.L (INVEST)]

investment *n.* investing; money invested; property etc. in which money is invested. [INVEST]

investor *n.* one who invests money.

inveterate /ɪn'vetərət/ *a.* (of habit etc.) deep-rooted; (of person) confirmed in habit etc.; **inveteracy** *n.* [L (*vetus* old)]

invidious /ɪn'vɪdɪəs/ *a.* likely to excite ill-will or indignation against the performer, possessor, etc. (*invidious task, position, honour*). [L *invidiosus* (ENVY)]

invigilate /ɪn'vɪdʒɪleɪt/ *v.i.* supervise examinees; **invigilation** /-'leɪʃ(ə)n/ *n.*; **invigilator** *n.* [L (VIGIL)]

invigorate /ɪn'vɪgəreɪt/ *v.t.* give vigour or strength to. [med.L (VIGOUR)]

invincible /ɪn'vɪnsɪb(ə)l/ *a.* unconquerable; **invincibility** /-'bɪlɪtɪ/ *n.*; **invincibly** *adv.* [F f. L (*vinco* conquer)]

inviolable /ɪn'vaɪələb(ə)l/ *a.* not to be violated or profaned; **inviolability** /-'bɪlɪtɪ/ *n.*; **inviolably** *adv.* [F or L (VIOLATE)]

inviolate /ɪn'vaɪələt/ *a.* not violated; **inviolacy** *n.* [L (VIOLATE)]

invisible /ɪn'vɪzɪb(ə)l/ *a.* that cannot be seen; **invisible exports** (or **imports**) items for which payment is made by or to another country but which are not goods; **invisibility** /-'bɪlɪtɪ/ *n.*; **invisibly** *adv.* [F or L]

invitation /ɪnvɪ'teɪʃ(ə)n/ *n.* inviting or being invited; letter or card etc. used to invite. [foll.]

invite **1** /ɪn'vaɪt/ *v.* ask (person) courteously to come (*to* a place or function, *in*, etc.) or to do something; solicit (suggestions etc.) courteously; tend to call forth (criticism etc.); attract, be attractive. **2** /'ɪnvaɪt/ *n. colloq.* invitation. [F or L]

inviting *a.* attractive, tempting.

invocation /ɪnvə'keɪʃ(ə)n/ *n.* invoking; appeal to Muse for inspiration; preacher's prefatory words 'In the name of the Father' etc.; **invocatory** /ɪn'vɒkətərɪ/ *a.* [F f. L (INVOKE)]

invoice /'ɪnvɔɪs/ **1** *n.* list of goods shipped or sent, or services rendered, with prices. **2** *v.t.* make invoice of (goods); send invoice to (person). [orig. pl. of obs. *invoy* (ENVOY)]

invoke /ɪn'vəʊk/ *v.t.* call on (deity etc.) in prayer or as witness; appeal to (law, person's authority, etc.); summon (spirit) by charms; ask earnestly for (vengeance etc.). [F f. L (*voco* call)]

involuntary /ɪn'vɒləntərɪ/ *a.* done without exercise of will; not controlled by will; **involuntarily** *adv.*; **involuntariness** *n.* [L (IN-²)]

involute /'ɪnvəluːt/ *a.* involved, intricate; spirally curled. [L (INVOLVE)]

involuted *a.* complicated, abstruse.

involution /ɪnvə'luːʃ(ə)n/ *n.* involving; intricacy; curling inwards; part so curled.

involve /ɪn'vɒlv/ *v.t.* cause (person or

thing) to share experience or effect (*in* situation, circumstances, etc.); imply, entail, make necessary; implicate (person *in* charge, crime, etc.); include or affect in its operation; (in *p.p.*) concerned (*in*); complicated in thought or form (*involved argument*, *sentence*); **involvement** *n.* [L (*volvo* roll)]

invulnerable /ɪn'vʌlnərəb(ə)l/ *a.* that cannot be wounded or hurt (esp. *fig.*); **invulnerability** /-'bɪlɪtɪ/ *n.*; **invulnerably** *adv.* [L (IN-²)]

inward /'ɪnwəd/ **1** *a.* directed towards the inside, going in; situated within; mental, spiritual. **2** *adv.* (also **inwards**) towards the inside; within mind or soul. [OE (IN-, -WARD)]

inwardly *adv.* on the inside; not aloud; in mind or soul. [OE (prec.)]

inwardness *n.* inner nature; spirituality. [INWARD]

inwrought /ɪn'rɔ:t, *attrib.* 'ɪn-/ *a.* (of fabric) decorated (*with* pattern); (of pattern) wrought (*in* or *on* fabric). [IN, WORK]

iodide /'aɪədaɪd/ *n.* binary compound of iodine. [IODINE]

iodine /'aɪədi:n, -ɪn/ *n.* halogen element forming black crystals and violet vapour; solution of this used as antiseptic. [F *iode* f. Gk *iōdēs* violet-like]

iodize /'aɪədaɪz/ *v.t.* impregnate with iodine.

IOM *abbr.* Isle of Man.

ion /'aɪən/ *n.* one of the electrically charged particles into which the atoms or molecules of certain substances are dissociated by solution in water, making the solution a conductor of electricity; similarly charged molecule of gas e.g. in air exposed to X-rays. [Gk, = going]

-ion *suffix* (appearing as **-sion, -tion, -xion,** and esp. -ATION) in nouns denoting verbal action (*excision*), an instance of this (*a suggestion*), or the resulting state (*vexation*) or product (*concoction*). [F or L]

Ionic[1] /aɪ'ɒnɪk/ *a.* of the order of Greek architecture characterized by column with scroll-shapes on either side of capital. [L f. Gk]

ionic[2] /aɪ'ɒnɪk/ *a.* of or using ions; **ionically** *adv.* [ION]

ionize /'aɪənaɪz/ *v.t.* convert or be converted into ion(s); **ionization** /-'zeɪʃ(ə)n/ *n.*

ionosphere /aɪ'ɒnəsfɪə/ *n.* ionized region of upper atmosphere reflecting radio waves; **ionospheric** /-'ferɪk/ *a.*

iota /aɪ'əʊtə/ *n.* ninth letter of Greek alphabet (Ι, ι); smallest possible amount. [Gk *iōta*]

IOU /aɪəʊ'ju:/ *n.* signed document acknowledging debt. [*I owe you*]

IOW *abbr.* Isle of Wight.

IPA *abbr.* International Phonetic Alphabet.

ipecacuanha /ɪpɪkækjʊ'ɑ:nə/ *n.* root of S. American plant, used as emetic or purgative. [Port., f. Tupi-Guarani, = emetic creeper]

ipso facto /ɪpsəʊ 'fæktəʊ/ by that very fact. [L]

IQ *abbr.* intelligence quotient.

ir-[1,2] see IN-[1,2].

Ir *symb.* iridium.

IRA *abbr.* Irish Republican Army.

Iranian /ɪ'reɪnɪən/ **1** *a.* of Iran (Persia); (of language) of family including Persian. **2** *n.* native of Iran. [Pers. *Īrān* Persia]

Iraqi /ɪ'rɑ:kɪ/ **1** *a.* of Iraq. **2** *n.* native or Arabic dialect of Iraq. [Arab.]

irascible /ɪ'ræsɪb(ə)l/ *a.* irritable, hot-tempered; **irascibility** /-'bɪlɪtɪ/ *n.*; **irascibly** *adv.* [F f. L *irascor* grow angry (*ira* anger)]

irate /aɪ'reɪt/ *a.* angry, enraged. [L *iratus* (as prec.)]

ire /'aɪə/ *n. literary* anger. [F f. L *ira*]

iridaceous /ɪrɪ'deɪʃəs/ *a.* of iris family. [IRIS]

iridescent /ɪrɪ'desənt/ *a.* showing rainbow-like colours; changing colour with position; **iridescence** *n.*

iridium /ɪ'rɪdɪəm/ *n.* hard white metallic element of platinum group.

iris /'aɪərɪs/ *n.* circular coloured membrane behind cornea of eye, with circular opening (pupil) in centre; perennial herbaceous plant usu. with tuberous roots, sword-shaped leaves, and showy flowers; diaphragm with hole of variable size. [L f. Gk *iris iridos* rainbow]

Irish /'aɪərɪʃ/ **1** *a.* of Ireland, of or like its people. **2** *n.* Celtic language of Ireland. **3 the Irish** *pl.* the people of Ireland; **Irish bull** = BULL³; **Irish stew** stew of mutton, potato, and onion. [OE]

Irishman *n.* man of Irish birth or descent; **Irishwoman** *n. fem.*

irk *v.t.* irritate or annoy or disgust (*it irks me that* ...). [orig. unkn.]

irksome *a.* tiresome, annoying.

iron /'aɪən/ **1** *n.* common strong grey metallic element; this as symbol of strength or firmness (*man of iron*; *will of iron*); tool of iron; implement with smooth flat base heated to smooth clothes etc.; golf-club with iron or steel head and sloping face; (in *pl.*) fetters, stirrups; (often in *pl.*) leg-support to rectify malformation etc. **2** *a.* of iron; very robust; unyielding, merciless. **3** *v.t.* smooth (clothes etc.) with iron. **4 Iron Age** period when weapons and tools were made of iron; **Iron Cross** German military decoration; **Iron Curtain** barrier to free passage of people and information between Soviet bloc and the West; **ironing-board** narrow folding table or stand for ironing clothes on; **iron lung** rigid case over patient's body for prolonged artificial respiration; **iron out** remove (difficulties etc.); **iron ration** small supply of tinned food etc. for use in emergency; **many irons in the fire** many undertakings or resources; **strike while the iron is hot** act promptly at good opportunity. [OE]

ironclad 1 *a.* covered in or protected with iron. 2 *n. hist.* ship cased with plates of iron.

ironic /aɪˈrɒnɪk/ *a.* (also **ironical**) using or displaying irony; **ironically** *adv.* [F or L f. Gk (IRONY)]

ironmaster *n.* manufacturer of iron. [IRON]

ironmonger *n.* dealer in hardware etc.; **ironmongery** *n.*

ironstone *n.* hard iron-ore; a kind of hard white pottery.

ironware *n.* things made of iron.

ironwork *n.* work in iron; things made of iron.

ironworks *n. pl.* (often treated as *sing.*) place where iron is smelted or iron goods are made.

irony /ˈaɪərənɪ/ *n.* expression of meaning by language of opposite or different tendency; ill-timed or perverse arrival of event or circumstance that would in itself be desirable; use of language with one meaning for privileged few and another for those addressed or concerned. [L, f. Gk *eirōneia* pretended ignorance]

irradiate /ɪˈreɪdɪeɪt/ *v.t.* subject to radiation; shine upon, light up; throw light on (subject); **irradiation** /-ˈeɪʃ(ə)n/ *n.* [L *irradio* shine on (*radius* ray)]

irrational /ɪˈræʃən(ə)l/ *a.* unreasonable, illogical; not endowed with reason; not commensurable with the natural numbers; **irrationality** /-ˈnælɪtɪ/ *n.*; **irrationally** *adv.* [L (IN-²)]

irreconcilable /ɪˈrekənsaɪləb(ə)l/ *a.* implacably hostile; incompatible; **irreconcilability** /-ˈbɪlɪtɪ/ *n.*; **irreconcilably** *adv.* [IN-²]

irrecoverable /ɪrɪˈkʌvərəb(ə)l/ *a.* that cannot be recovered or remedied; **irrecoverably** *adv.*

irredeemable /ɪrɪˈdiːməb(ə)l/ *a.* that cannot be redeemed; hopeless; **irredeemably** *adv.*

irredentist /ɪrɪˈdentɪst/ *n.* one who advocates restoration to his country of all territory formerly belonging to it. [It. (*irredenta* unredeemed)]

irreducible /ɪrɪˈdjuːsɪb(ə)l/ *a.* that cannot be reduced or simplified; **irreducibly** *adv.* [IN-²]

irrefutable /ɪˈrefjʊtəb(ə)l, ɪrɪˈfjuː-/ *a.* that cannot be refuted; **irrefutably** *adv.* [L (IN-²)]

irregular /ɪˈregjʊlə/ 1 *a.* unsymmetrical, uneven, varying (*irregular shape, surface, intervals*); contrary to rule, principle, or custom; (of troops) not in regular army; abnormal; (of verb, noun, etc.) not inflected normally; disorderly. 2 *n.* (in *pl.*) irregular troops. 3 **irregularity** /-ˈlærɪtɪ/ *n.* [F f. L (IN-²)]

irrelevant /ɪˈrelɪvənt/ *a.* not relevant (*to*); **irrelevance** *n.*; **irrelevancy** *n.* [IN-²]

irreligious /ɪrɪˈlɪdʒəs/ *a.* lacking or hostile to religion. [F or L (IN-²)]

irremediable /ɪrɪˈmiːdɪəb(ə)l/ *a.* that cannot be remedied; **irremediably** *adv.* [L (IN-²)]

irremovable /ɪrɪˈmuːvəb(ə)l/ *a.* that cannot be removed, esp. from office; **irremovably** *adv.* [IN-²]

irreparable /ɪˈrepərəb(ə)l/ *a.* that cannot be rectified or made good (*irreparable loss*); **irreparably** *adv.* [F f. L (IN-²)]

irreplaceable /ɪrɪˈpleɪsəb(ə)l/ *a.* that cannot be replaced. [IN-²]

irrepressible /ɪrɪˈpresɪb(ə)l/ *a.* that cannot be repressed or restrained; **irrepressibly** *adv.*

irreproachable /ɪrɪˈprəʊtʃəb(ə)l/ *a.* faultless, blameless; **irreproachably** *adv.* [F (IN-²)]

irresistible /ɪrɪˈzɪstɪb(ə)l/ *a.* too strong or delightful or convincing to be resisted; **irresistibly** *adv.* [med.L (IN-²)]

irresolute /ɪˈrezəluːt, -ljuːt/ *a.* hesitating; lacking in resoluteness; **irresolution** /-ˈluːʃ(ə)n/ *n.* [IN-²]

irrespective /ɪrɪˈspektɪv/ *a.* not taking account, regardless, *of*.

irresponsible /ɪrɪˈspɒnsɪb(ə)l/ *a.* acting or done without due sense of responsibility; not responsible for one's conduct; **irresponsibility** /-ˈbɪlɪtɪ/ *n.*; **irresponsibly** *adv.*

irretrievable /ɪrɪˈtriːvəb(ə)l/ *a.* that cannot be retrieved or recovered; **irretrievably** *adv.*

irreverent /ɪˈrevərənt/ *a.* lacking reverence; **irreverence** *n.* [L (IN-²)]

irreversible /ɪrɪˈvɜːsɪb(ə)l/ *a.* not reversible or alterable; **irreversibly** *adv.* [IN-²]

irrevocable /ɪˈrevəkəb(ə)l/ *a.* unalterable; gone beyond recall; **irrevocably** *adv.* [L (IN-²)]

irrigate /ˈɪrɪgeɪt/ *v.t.* water (land) with channels; (of stream etc.) supply (land) with water; supply (wound etc.) with constant flow of liquid; **irrigable** *a.*; **irrigation** /-ˈgeɪʃ(ə)n/ *n.*; **irrigator** *n.* [L (*rigo* moisten)]

irritable /ˈɪrɪtəb(ə)l/ *a.* easily annoyed;

(of organ etc.) sensitive; **irritability** /-ˈbɪlɪtɪ/ *n.*; **irritably** *adv.* [L (IRRITATE)]

irritant /ˈɪrɪtənt/ **1** *a.* causing irritation. **2** *n.* irritant substance. [foll.]

irritate /ˈɪrɪteɪt/ *v.t.* excite to anger, annoy; cause discomfort in (part of the body); *Biol.* stimulate (organ) to action; **irritation** /-ˈteɪʃ(ə)n/ *n.*; **irritative** *a.* [L *irrito*

irruption /ɪˈrʌpʃ(ə)n/ *n.* invasion, violent entry. [L (RUPTURE)]

is see BE.

-isation, -ise var. of -IZATION, -IZE.

ISBN *abbr.* international standard book number.

-ish *suffix* forming adjectives (1) from nouns, in senses 'having the qualities of' (*knavish*), 'of the nationality of' (*Danish*), (2) from adjectives, in sense 'somewhat' (*thickish*), (3) *colloq.* of approximate age or time (*fortyish*). [OE]

isinglass /ˈaɪzɪŋglɑːs/ *n.* kind of gelatin obtained from fish, esp. sturgeon, and used for jellies, glue, etc.; mica. [Du. *huisenblas* sturgeon's bladder]

Islam /ˈɪzlɑːm/ *n.* religion of Muslims, proclaimed by Muhammad; the Muslim world; **Islamic** /ɪzˈlæmɪk/ *a.* [Arab, = submission (to God)]

island /ˈaɪlənd/ *n.* piece of land surrounded by water; = *traffic island*; detached or isolated thing. [OE, orig. *iland*; *-s-* f. ISLE]

islander *n.* inhabitant of island.

isle /aɪl/ *n.* island, esp. small one (chiefly *poetic* and in names). [F *ile* f. L *insula*]

islet /ˈaɪlɪt/ *n.* small island; detached portion of tissue. [F (dimin.; prec.)]

ism /ˈɪz(ə)m/ *n.* (usu. *derog.*) any distinctive doctrine or practice. [foll.]

-ism *suffix* forming nouns, esp. expressing a system or principle (*Conservatism*, *jingoism*), a state or quality (*barbarism*, *heroism*), or a peculiarity in language (*Americanism*). [F f. L f. Gk (-IZE)]

isn't /ˈɪz(ə)nt/ *colloq.* = *is not*.

iso- *in comb.* equal. [Gk *isos* equal]

isobar /ˈaɪsəbɑː/ *n.* line on map connecting places with same atmospheric pressure; **isobaric** /-ˈbærɪk/ *a.* [Gk *baros* weight]

isochronous /aɪˈsɒkrənəs/ *a.* occupying equal time; occurring at same time. [ISO-]

isolate /ˈaɪsəleɪt/ *v.t.* place apart or alone; subject (patient with contagious or infectious disease) to quarantine; separate (substance) from compound; insulate (electrical apparatus); **isolation** /-ˈleɪʃ(ə)n/ *n.* [orig. in p.p., F f. It. f. L (INSULATE)]

isolationism *n.* policy of holding aloof from affairs of other countries or groups; **isolationist** *n.*

isomer /ˈaɪsəmɜː/ *n.* any of two or more substances whose molecules have same atoms in different arrangement; **isomeric** /-ˈmerɪk/ *a.*; **isomerism** /aɪˈsɒmərɪz(ə)m/ *n.* [G, f. Gk (*meros* share)]

isometric /aɪsəˈmetrɪk/ *a.* (of muscle action) developing tension while muscle is prevented from contracting; (of drawing etc.) with plane of projection at equal angles to three principal axes of object shown; of equal measure. [Gk *isometria* equality of measure]

isomorph /ˈaɪsəmɔːf/ *n.* substance having same form as another; **isomorphic** *a.*; **isomorphous** *a.* [ISO-, Gk *morphē* form]

isosceles /aɪˈsɒsɪliːz/ *a.* (of triangle) having two sides equal. [L (ISO-, Gk *skelos* leg)]

isotherm /ˈaɪsəθɜːm/ *n.* line on map connecting places with same temperature; **isothermal** /-ˈθɜːm(ə)l/ *a.* [F (ISO-, Gk *thermē* heat)]

isotope /ˈaɪsətəʊp/ *n.* any of two or more forms of an element differing from each other in atomic weight, and in nuclear but not chemical properties; **isotopic** /-ˈtɒpɪk/ *a.* [ISO-, Gk *topos* place]

isotropic /aɪsəˈtrɒpɪk/ *a.* having same physical properties in all directions; **isotropy** /aɪˈsɒtrəpɪ/ *n.* [ISO-, Gk *tropos* turn]

Israeli /ɪzˈreɪlɪ/ **1** *a.* of modern State of Israel in SW Asia. **2** *n.* Israeli person. [Heb.]

Israelite /ˈɪzrɪəlaɪt/ *n.* native of ancient Israel; Jew. [L f. Gk f. Heb.]

issue /ˈɪʃuː, ˈɪsjuː/ **1** *n.* outgoing, outflow; giving out or circulation (*of* shares, notes, stamps, etc.); quantity of coins, copies of newspaper, etc., circulated at one time; one of regular series of magazine etc. (*the May issue*); result, outcome; point in question, important topic of discussion or litigation; way out; place of emergence of stream etc.; *Law* progeny, children (*without male issue*). **2** *v.* go or come out; send forth, publish, put into circulation; give out (book, orders *to* subordinate); supply (thing *to* person, person *with* thing) esp. for official use; emerge from a condition; be derived or result (*from*); end or result (*in*). **3 at issue** in dispute, under discussion; **join** (or **take**) **issue** proceed to argue *with* person *on* point. [F f. L *exitus* (EXIT)]

-ist *suffix* forming personal nouns expressing adherent of creed etc. in *-ism* (*Marxist*, *fatalist*), person concerned with something (*pathologist*, *tobacconist*), person who uses a thing (*violinist*, *balloonist*, *motorist*), or person who does thing expressed by verb in *-ize* (*plagiarist*). [F & L f. Gk *istēs* (-IZE)]

isthmus /'ɪsməs/ *n.* narrow piece of land connecting two larger bodies of land; narrow connecting part; **isthmian** *a.* [L f. Gk]

it[1] *pron.* (*pl.* THEY) the thing (or occas. animal or child) previously named or in question (*took a stone and threw it*); the person in question (*who is it?*; *it is I*); as subject of impersonal verb (*it is raining*; *it is winter*; *it is two miles to Bath*); as substitute for deferred subject or object (*it is silly to think that*; *I take it that you agree*); as substitute for vague object (*brazen it out*); as antecedent to relative (*it was a fox that he saw*); exactly what is needed; extreme limit of achievement etc.; *colloq.* sexual intercourse, sex appeal; (in children's games) player who has to perform required feat; **that's it** *colloq.* that is what is required, the difficulty, the end. [OE]

it[2] *n. colloq.* Italian vermouth (*gin and it*). [abbr.]

Italian /ɪ'tæljən/ **1** *a.* of Italy. **2** *n.* native or language of Italy. **3 Italian vermouth** sweet vermouth. [It. *Italiano* (*Italia* Italy)]

Italianate /ɪ'tæljəneɪt/ *a.* of Italian style or appearance. [It. *Italianato*]

italic /ɪ'tælɪk/ **1** *a.* (of printed letters) of sloping kind now used esp. for emphasis and in foreign words; (of handwriting) compact and pointed like early Italian handwriting; (**Italic**) of ancient Italy. **2** *n.* letter in italic type; such type. [L *italicus* f. Gk (ITALIAN)]

italicize /ɪ'tælɪsaɪz/ *v.t.* print in italics.

itch **1** *n.* irritation in skin; contagious disease accompanied by this; impatient desire. **2** *v.i.* feel itch (*itching to tell you the news*). **3 itching palm** avarice. [OE]

itchy *a.* having or causing itch; **itchiness** *n.*

-ite *suffix* forming nouns in sense 'person or thing belonging to or connected with' (*Israelite*, *graphite*, *dynamite*). [F f. L f. Gk *-itēs*]

item /'aɪtəm/ *n.* any one of enumerated things; detached piece of news etc. [L, = likewise]

itemize *v.t.* state by items; **itemization** /-'zeɪʃ(ə)n/ *n.*

iterate /'ɪtəreɪt/ *v.t.* repeat, state repeatedly; **iteration** /-'reɪʃ(ə)n/ *n.*; **iterative** /-rətɪv/ *a.* [L (*iterum* again)]

-itic *suffix* forming adjectives corresponding to nouns in -ITE or -ITIS (*Semitic*, *arthritic*). [F f. L f. Gk *-itikos*]

itinerant /aɪ'tɪnərənt, ɪ-/ **1** *a.* travelling from place to place. **2** *n.* itinerant person. [L (*iter itiner-* journey)]

itinerary /aɪ'tɪnərərɪ, ɪ-/ *n.* route; record of travel; guidebook. [L (prec.)]

-itis *suffix* forming nouns, esp. names of inflammatory diseases (*appendicitis*) or *colloq.* of mental states fancifully regarded as diseases (*electionitis*). [Gk]

its *poss. pron.* & *a.* of it, of itself. [IT[1]]

it's *colloq.* = *it has, it is.*

itself /ɪt'self/ *pron.* emphat. and refl. form of IT[1]; **by itself** apart from its surroundings, automatically; **in itself** viewed in its essential qualities (*not in itself a bad thing*). [OE (IT[1], SELF)]

ITV *abbr.* independent television.

-ity *suffix* forming nouns of quality or condition (*humility*, *purity*) or instance of this (*a monstrosity*). [F f. L *-itas*]

IUD *abbr.* intra-uterine (contraceptive) device.

-ive *suffix* forming adjectives, esp. in sense 'tending to', and corresponding nouns (*suggestive*, *corrosive*, *palliative*, *coercive*, *talkative*). [F f. L *-ivus*]

ivory /'aɪvərɪ/ *n.* hard substance of tusks of elephant etc.; creamy-white colour of this; (usu. in *pl.*) article made of ivory; (usu. in *pl.*) *sl.* dice, billiard-ball, piano-key, tooth; **ivory tower** seclusion or withdrawal from harsh realities. [F f. L *ebur*]

ivy /'aɪvɪ/ *n.* climbing evergreen with shining usu. five-pointed leaves. [OE]

ixia /'ɪksɪə/ *n.* S. African iridaceous plant with large showy flowers. [L f. Gk]

-ization *suffix* forming nouns from verbs in *-ize*. [foll.]

-ize *suffix* forming verbs esp. in senses 'make or become such' (*Americanize*, *volatilize*), 'treat in such way' (*monopolize*, *pasteurize*). [F f. L f. Gk *-izō*]

J

J, j /dʒeɪ/ *n.* (*pl.* **Js, J's**) tenth letter.

J *abbr.* joule(s).

jab **1** *v.t.* (**-bb-**) poke roughly; thrust abruptly (thing *into*). **2** *n.* abrupt blow with pointed thing or fist; *colloq.* hypodermic injection. [var. of *job* = prod]

jabber **1** *v.* chatter volubly; utter

(words) fast and indistinctly. **2** *n.* chatter, gabble. [imit.]

jabot /'ʒæbəʊ/ *n.* ornamental frill or ruffle of lace etc. worn on front of shirt or blouse. [F]

jacaranda /dʒækə'rændə/ *n.* tropical American tree with hard scented wood, or one with blue flowers. [Tupi]

jacinth /'dʒæsɪnθ/ *n.* reddish-orange gem, variety of zircon. [F or L (HYACINTH)]

jack 1 *n.* device for lifting heavy objects, esp. wheel of vehicle off ground while changing it; court-card with picture of soldier or page; ship's flag, esp. one flown from bow and showing nationality; device using single plug to connect electrical circuit; device for turning spit; type of common man (*every man jack*); *sl.* policeman, detective; small white ball in bowls for players to aim at; = JACKSTONE, (in *pl.*) game of jackstones; pike, esp. young one; male of various animals. **2** *v.t.* (often with *up*) raise with or as with jack. **3 Jack Frost** frost personified; **jack in** (or **up**) *sl.* abandon (attempt etc.); **jack-in-the-box** toy figure that springs out of box when lid is lifted; **jack-in-office** self-important official; **jack of all trades** person who can do many different kinds of work; **jack-rabbit** *US* large prairie hare with very long ears; **Jack tar** sailor. [fam. form of JOHN]

jackal /'dʒækɔ:l, -(ə)l/ *n.* wild animal related to dog, formerly supposed to find prey for lion; one who does preliminary drudgery etc. for another. [Pers.]

jackanapes /'dʒækəneɪps/ *n.* pert or insolent fellow. [earlier *Jack Napes* for Duke of Suffolk]

jackass /'dʒækæs/ *n.* male ass; stupid person; **laughing jackass** kookaburra. [JACK]

jackboot *n.* large boot reaching above knee; military oppression, bullying behaviour.

jackdaw *n.* small bird of crow family.

jacket /'dʒækɪt/ *n.* sleeved short outer garment; thing similarly worn (*life-jacket*); outer covering round boiler etc. to prevent heat-loss etc.; = *dust-jacket*; skin of potato; animal's coat. [F]

jackknife 1 *n.* large clasp-knife; dive in which body is first bent at the waist and then straightened. **2** *v.i.* (of articulated vehicle) fold against itself in accidental skidding movement. [JACK]

jackpot *n.* accumulated prize or stakes in lottery, poker, etc.; **hit the jackpot** win remarkable luck or success.

jackstone *n.* small piece of metal etc. used with others in tossing-games; (in *pl.*) game with ball and jackstones.

Jacobean /dʒækə'bi:ən/ *a.* of James I's reign. [L (*Jacobus* James)]

Jacobite /'dʒækəbaɪt/ *n.* supporter of James II after his abdication, or of the Stuarts.

Jacquard /'dʒækɑ:d/ *n.* apparatus with perforated cards, fitted to loom to facilitate weaving of figured fabrics; fabric thus made. [inventor]

Jacuzzi /dʒə'ku:zɪ/ *n.* (**P**) large bath with underwater jets of water to massage the body. [name of inventor and manufacturers]

jade[1] *n.* a hard green, blue, or white stone, silicate of calcium and magnesium; green colour of jade. [F f. Sp. *ijada* f. L *ilia* flanks (named as cure for colic)]

jade[2] *n.* poor worn-out horse; hussy. [orig. unkn.]

jaded *a.* tired out, surfeited.

jadeite /'dʒeɪdaɪt/ *n.* jadelike silicate of sodium and aluminium. [JADE[1]]

jag[1] **1** *n.* sharp projection of rock etc. **2** *v.t.* (**-gg-**) cut or tear unevenly; make indentations in. [imit.]

jag[2] *n. sl.* drinking bout; period of indulgence in activity, emotion, etc. [orig. dial. = load]

jagged /'dʒægɪd/ *a.* with unevenly cut or torn edge. [JAG[1]]

jaguar /'dʒægjʊə/ *n.* large American carnivorous spotted animal of cat family. [Tupi]

jail etc. var. of GAOL etc.

Jain /dʒaɪn/ **1** *a.* of Indian religion having doctrines like those of Buddhism. **2** *n.* adherent of this religion. **3 Jainism** *n.*; **Jainist** *n.* [Hindi]

jalap /'dʒæləp/ *n.* purgative drug from tubers of a Mexican plant. [F f. Sp. (*Xalapa*, Mexican city, f. Aztec)]

jalopy /dʒə'lɒpɪ/ *n. colloq.* dilapidated old motor vehicle. [orig. unkn.]

jalousie /'ʒælu:zi:/ *n.* slatted blind or shutter to admit air and light but not rain etc. [F (JEALOUSY)]

jam[1] **1** *v.* (**-mm-**) squeeze or wedge (*into* a space); become wedged; cause (machinery) to become wedged etc. so that it cannot work, become thus wedged; force or thrust violently (*jam on the brakes*); push or cram together in compact mass; block (passage, road, etc.) by crowding; make (radio transmission) unintelligible by causing interference; *colloq.* (in jazz etc.) extemporize with other musicians. **2** *n.* squeeze, crush; stoppage (of machine etc.) due to jamming; crowded mass (*traffic jam*); *colloq.* awkward position, fix; *colloq.* improvised playing by group of musicians. **3 jam-packed** *colloq.* very full. [imit.]

jam[2] *n.* conserve of fruit and sugar

boiled until thick; *colloq.* something easy or pleasant (*money for jam*); **jam tomorrow** pleasant thing continually promised but usu. never produced. [perh. f. prec.]

jamb /dʒæm/ *n.* side post or side of doorway, window, or fireplace. [F *jambe* leg f. L]

jamboree /dʒæmbə'ri:/ *n.* celebration, merry-making; large rally of Scouts. [orig. unkn.]

jammy *a.* covered with jam; *colloq.* lucky; profitable. [JAM²]

Jan. *abbr.* January.

jangle /'dʒæŋg(ə)l/ **1** *v.* make, cause (bell etc.) to make, harsh metallic sound; irritate (nerves etc.) by discord etc. **2** *n.* harsh metallic sound. [F]

janitor /'dʒænɪtə/ *n.* doorkeeper, caretaker of building. [L (*janua* door)]

janizary /'dʒænɪzərɪ/ *n. hist.* member of Turkish infantry forming Sultan's guard etc. [Turk., = new troops]

January /'dʒænjʊərɪ/ *n.* first month of year. [AF f. L (*Janus*, guardian god of doors)]

Jap *a.* & *n. colloq.* (**R**) Japanese. [abbr.]

japan /dʒə'pæn/ **1** *n.* hard usu. black varnish, esp. of kind brought orig. from Japan. **2** *v.t.* (-**nn**-) varnish with japan; make black and glossy. [*Japan* in Asia]

Japanese /dʒæpə'ni:z/ **1** *n.* (*pl.* same) native or language of Japan. **2** *a.* of Japan. [prec.]

jape **1** *n.* practical joke. **2** *v.i.* play joke. [orig. unkn.]

japonica /dʒə'pɒnɪkə/ *n.* ornamental usu. red-flowered variety of quince. [JAPAN]

jar¹ **1** *v.* (-**rr**-) (of sound, words, manner, person, etc.) strike discordantly, grate (*on* or *upon* person, nerves, etc.); strike or make (thing) strike vibratingly (*against* etc.); (of body affected) vibrate gratingly; (of fact etc.) be at variance (*with*); quarrel. **2** *n.* jarring sound, shock, or thrill. [imit.]

jar² *n.* vessel of glass, earthenware, etc., usu. cylindrical; contents of this; *colloq.* glass (of beer etc.). [F f. Arab.]

jar³ *n.* only in **on the jar** ajar. [obs. CHAR¹ turn]

jardinière /ʒɑ:dɪ'njeə/ *n.* ornamental pot or stand for display of growing flowers; dish of mixed vegetables. [F]

jargon /'dʒɑ:gən/ *n.* words or expressions used by particular group or profession (*medical jargon*); barbarous or debased language; gibberish. [F]

jasmine /'dʒæsmɪn, 'dʒæz-/ *n.* shrub with white or yellow flowers. [F f. Arab. f. Pers.]

jasper *n.* red, yellow, or brown opaque quartz. [F f. L f. Gk *iaspis*]

jaundice /'dʒɔ:ndɪs/ **1** *n.* condition due to obstruction of bile and marked by yellowness of skin etc.; disordered (esp. mental) vision; envy. **2** *v.t.* affect with jaundice; *fig.* affect (person etc.) with envy, resentment, etc. [F (*jaune* yellow)]

jaunt /dʒɔ:nt/ **1** *n.* pleasure excursion. **2** *v.i.* take a jaunt. **3 jaunting car** two-wheeled horse-drawn vehicle used in Ireland. [orig. unkn.]

jaunty /'dʒɔ:ntɪ/ *a.* cheerful and self-confident; sprightly; **jauntily** *adv.*; **jauntiness** *n.* [F (GENTLE)]

Javanese /dʒɑ:və'ni:z/ **1** *n.* (*pl.* same) native or language of Java. **2** *a.* of Java. [*Java* in Indonesia]

javelin /'dʒævəlɪn, -vlɪn/ *n.* light spear thrown as weapon or in sports. [F]

jaw **1** *n.* bone or bones containing the teeth (*upper, lower, jaw*); (in *pl.*) mouth, its bones and teeth, mouth of valley etc., gripping parts of machine etc.; (in *pl.*) *fig.* grip (*jaws of death*); *colloq.* loquacity, long or sermonizing talk. **2** *v. sl.* speak esp. at length; admonish, lecture. **3 jaw-bone** lower jaw of mammals. [F]

jay *n.* noisy European bird with vivid plumage; silly chatterer; **jay-walk** walk in or across road without regard for traffic. [F f. L]

jazz **1** *n.* music of US Negro origin characterized by improvisation, syncopation, and regular or forceful rhythm; *sl.* pretentious talk or behaviour (*all that jazz*). **2** *v.* brighten or liven *up*; play or dance to jazz. [orig. uncert.]

jazzy *a.* of or like jazz; vivid, unrestrained.

jealous /'dʒeləs/ *a.* watchfully tenacious (*of* rights etc.); afraid, suspicious, resentful, of rivalry in love or affection; envious (*of* person or his advantages); (of God) intolerant of disloyalty; (of inquiry etc.) vigilant. [F f. med.L (ZEALOUS)]

jealousy *n.* jealous state or feeling; instance of this. [F (prec.)]

jean /dʒi:n, dʒeɪn/ *n.* twilled cotton cloth; (in *pl.* /dʒi:nz/) trousers of jean or denim. [F (L *Janua* Genoa)]

Jeep *n.* (**P**) small sturdy motor vehicle with four-wheel drive. [orig. US, f. initials of *general purposes*]

jeer **1** *v.* scoff (*at*); deride. **2** *n.* scoff, taunt. [orig. unkn.]

Jehovah /dʒə'həʊvə/ *n.* name of God in Old Testament; **Jehovah's Witness** member of a fundamentalist Christian sect. [Heb. *yahveh*]

jejune /dʒɪ'dʒu:n/ *a.* meagre, poor, barren; unsatisfying to the mind. [orig. = fasting (L *jejunus*)]

jejunum /dʒɪ'dʒu:nəm/ *n.* part of small

intestine between duodenum and ileum. [L (prec.)]

Jekyll and Hyde /ˈdʒekɪl/ person in whom two (opposing) personalities alternate. [character in story by R. L. Stevenson]

jell *v.i. colloq.* set as jelly; *fig.* take definite form. [back-form. f. JELLY]

jellaba /ˈdʒeləbə/ *n.* loose hooded woollen cloak (as) worn by Arab men. [Arab.]

jelly /ˈdʒelɪ/ **1** *n.* soft stiffish semitransparent food made of or with gelatin; similar preparation of fruit-juice, sugar, etc.; substance of similar consistency; *sl.* gelignite. **2** *v.* (cause to) set as jelly, congeal; set (food) in jelly (*jellied eels*). **3** **jelly baby** gelatinous sweet in shape of baby. [F *gelée* f. L (*gelo* freeze)]

jellyfish *n.* sea animal with stinging tentacles and gelatinous body.

jemmy /ˈdʒemɪ/ *n.* burglar's short crowbar. [name *James*]

jenny /ˈdʒenɪ/ *n.* = *spinning-jenny* (see SPIN); she-ass; **jenny wren** female wren. [name *Janet*]

jeopardize /ˈdʒepədaɪz/ *v.t.* endanger. [foll.]

jeopardy /ˈdʒepədɪ/ *n.* danger, esp. of severe harm. [obs. F *iu parti* divided play (JOKE, PART)]

jerbil var. of GERBIL.

jerboa /dʒɜːˈbəʊə/ *n.* small African jumping rodent with long hind legs. [L f. Arab.]

jeremiad /dʒerɪˈmaɪəd/ *n.* doleful complaint. [F f. eccl.L (foll.)]

Jeremiah /dʒerɪˈmaɪə/ *n.* dismal prophet, denouncer of the times. [Lamentations of *Jeremiah*, in OT]

jerk[1] **1** *n.* sharp sudden pull, twist, twitch, start, etc.; spasmodic twitch of muscle; *sl.* fool, stupid person. **2** *v.* move with a jerk; throw with suddenly arrested motion. [imit.]

jerk[2] *v.t.* cure (beef) by cutting in long slices and drying in the sun. [Sp. f. Quechua]

jerkin /ˈdʒɜːkɪn/ *n.* sleeveless jacket; *hist.* man's close-fitting jacket, often of leather. [orig. unkn.]

jerky *a.* having sudden abrupt movements; spasmodic; **jerkily** *adv.*; **jerkiness** *n.* [JERK[1]]

jeroboam /dʒerəˈbəʊəm/ *n.* wine-bottle of 6–12 times ordinary size. [*Jeroboam* in OT]

Jerry[1] /ˈdʒerɪ/ *n. sl.* German, German soldier, the Germans. [prob. alt. of *German*]

jerry[2] /ˈdʒerɪ/ *n. sl.* chamber-pot. [orig. unkn.]

jerry-builder *n.* builder of unsubstantial houses with bad materials; **jerry-building** *n.*; **jerry-built** *a.* [orig. uncert.]

jerrycan *n.* (also **jerrican**) a kind of (orig. German) petrol- or water-can. [JERRY[1]]

jersey /ˈdʒɜːzɪ/ *n.* knitted usu. woollen pullover or similar garment; plain-knitted (orig. woollen) fabric; (**Jersey**) animal of breed of dairy cattle from Jersey. [*Jersey* in Channel Islands]

Jerusalem artichoke /dʒəˈruːsələm/ kind of sunflower with edible root. [corrupt. of It. *girasole* sunflower]

jest **1** *n.* joke; fun; raillery, banter; object of derision. **2** *v.i.* joke, make jests. **3** **spoken in jest** not meant seriously. [F f. L *gesta* exploits]

jester *n.* (esp. *hist.*) professional joker of a court etc.

Jesuit /ˈdʒezjʊɪt/ *n.* member of Society of Jesus, a Roman Catholic order; **Jesuitical** /-ˈɪtɪk(ə)l/ *a.* [F or L (*Jesus*, founder of Christian religion)]

jet[1] **1** *n.* stream of water, steam, gas, flame, etc., shot esp. from small opening; spout or nozzle for emitting water etc. thus; jet engine or plane. **2** *v.* (**-tt-**) spurt out in jets; *colloq.* send or travel by jet plane. **3** **jet engine** engine using jet propulsion for forward thrust, esp. of aircraft; **jet lag** delayed bodily effects felt after long flight, esp. owing to difference of local time; **jet plane** plane with jet engine; **jet-propelled** having jet propulsion, *fig.* very fast; **jet propulsion** propulsion by backward ejection of high-speed jet of gas etc.; **jet set** wealthy élite frequently travelling by air. [F *jet(er)* f. L *jacto* throw]

jet[2] *n.* hard black lignite taking brilliant polish; **jet-black** deep glossy black. [F f. L f. Gk (*Gagai* in Asia Minor)]

jetsam /ˈdʒetsəm/ *n.* goods thrown out of ship to lighten it and washed ashore. [contr. of foll.]

jettison /ˈdʒetɪs(ə)n/ **1** *v.t.* throw (goods) overboard; drop (goods) from aircraft; *fig.* abandon. **2** *n.* jettisoning. [AF *getteson* (JET[1])]

jetty /ˈdʒetɪ/ *n.* pier or breakwater constructed to defend harbour etc.; landing-pier. [F *jetee* (JET[1])]

Jew /dʒuː/ **1** *n.* person of Hebrew descent or whose religion is Judaism; *colloq. derog.* (**R**) person who drives a hard bargain in trading, usurer. **2** *v.* (**jew**) *colloq. derog.* (**R**) drive a hard bargain, haggle, cheat. **3** **Jew's harp** small musical instrument held between the teeth. **4** **Jewess** *n. fem.* [F f. L *judaeus* f. Gk *ioudaios* f. Aram.]

jewel /ˈdʒuːəl/ **1** *n.* precious stone; personal ornament containing jewel(s); precious person or thing. **2** *v.t.* (**-ll-** exc.

US) adorn with jewels, fit (watch) with jewels for the pivot-holes. [F]

jeweller, *US* **jeweler** *n*. dealer in jewels or jewellery. [F (prec.)]

jewellery /ˈdʒuːəlrɪ/ *n*. (also **jewelry**) jewels collectively or as adornment. [F (JEWEL)]

Jewish *a*. of or like Jews; of Judaism. [JEW]

Jewry /ˈdʒʊərɪ/ *n*. Jews collectively. [AF *juerie*, F *juierie* (JEW)]

Jezebel /ˈdʒezəbel/ *n*. shameless woman. [*Jezebel* in OT]

jib 1 *n*. triangular staysail from outer end of jib-boom to top of foremast or from bowsprit to mast-head; projecting arm of crane. **2** *v*. (**-bb-**) pull (sail) round to other side of ship; (of sail) gybe; (of horse, *fig*. of person) stop and refuse to go on, move backwards or sideways instead of going on. **3 jib at** object strongly to; **jib-boom** spar run out from end of bowsprit. [orig. unkn.]

jibe var. of GIBE, GYBE.

jiff *n*. (also **jiffy**) *colloq*. short time, moment (*in a jiffy*). [orig. unkn.]

jig 1 *n*. lively jumping dance, music for this; appliance that holds a piece of work and guides the tools operating on it. **2** *v*. (**-gg-**) dance jig; move quickly up and down; work on or equip with jig. [orig. unkn.]

jigger[1] /ˈdʒɪgə/ *n*. measure of spirits etc.; small glass holding this; *sl*. (in billiards) cue-rest. [partly f. JIG]

jigger[2] /ˈdʒɪgə/ *n*. = CHIGOE. [corrupt.]

jiggered /ˈdʒɪgəd/ *a*. *colloq*. (as mild oath) confounded (*I'll be jiggered*). [euphem.]

jiggery-pokery /ˈdʒɪgərɪ ˈpəʊkərɪ/ *n*. *colloq*. deceitful or dishonest dealing, trickery. [orig. uncert.]

jiggle /ˈdʒɪg(ə)l/ *v*. rock or jerk lightly. [JIG]

jigsaw *n*. machine fretsaw; (also **jigsaw puzzle**) puzzle of picture pasted on board etc. and cut into irregular pieces to be reassembled. [JIG]

jilt *v.t.* abruptly reject or abandon (person formerly courted or proposed to). [orig. unkn.]

Jim Crow /krəʊ/ *derog*. (**R**) a Black; racial segregation esp. of Blacks. [nickname]

jim-jams /ˈdʒɪmdʒæmz/ *n.pl.* *sl.* delirium tremens; fit of depression or nervousness. [fanciful redupl.]

jingle /ˈdʒɪŋg(ə)l/ **1** *n*. mixed noise as of shaken keys or links; repetition of same sounds in words, short verse of this kind used in advertising etc. **2** *v*. make or cause (keys etc.) to make a jingle; (of writing) be full of alliterations, rhymes, etc. [imit.]

jingo /ˈdʒɪŋgəʊ/ *n*. (*pl*. **jingoes**) blustering patriot, supporter of bellicose policy; **jingoism** *n*.; **jingoist** *n*.; **jingoistic** /-ˈɪstɪk/ *a*. [conjuror's word]

jink 1 *v*. move elusively, dodge, elude by dodging. **2** *n*. act of jinking. **3 high jinks** boisterous fun. [orig. Sc.; imit.]

jinnee /dʒɪˈniː/ *n*. (*pl*. **jinn,** also used as *sing*.) (in Muslim mythology) spirit of supernatural power able to appear in human and animal forms. [Arab.]

jinx *n*. *colloq*. person or thing that seems to cause bad luck. [perh. var. of *jynx* wryneck, charm]

jitter *colloq*. **1** *v.i.* be nervous, act nervously. **2** *n*. (in *pl*.) extreme nervousness. **3 jittery** *a*. [orig. unkn.]

jitterbug 1 *n*. nervous person; popular dance like jive. **2** *v.t.* dance jitterbug.

jive *sl*. **1** *n*. fast lively jazz music, dance done to this. **2** *v.i.* dance to or play jive. [orig. uncert.]

Jnr. *abbr*. Junior.

job 1 *n*. piece of work (to be) done; position in paid employment; *sl*. a crime, esp. a robbery; *colloq*. difficult task; unscrupulous transaction. **2** *v*. (**-bb-**) do jobs, do piece-work; hire, let out for time or job; buy and sell (stock or goods) as middleman; deal corruptly with (matter). **3 bad** (or **good**) **job** unsatisfactory (or satisfactory) state of affairs; **job lot** miscellaneous group of articles, esp. bought together as speculation; **just the job** *sl*. precisely what is wanted; **make a (good) job of** do thoroughly or successfully. [orig. unkn.]

jobber *n*. = STOCKJOBBER; one who jobs.

jobbery *n*. corrupt dealing.

jobcentre *n*. government office displaying information about available jobs.

jobless *a*. unemployed.

Job's comforter /dʒəʊbz/ one who tries or purports to comfort but increases distress. [*Job* in OT]

Jock *n*. *sl*. Scotsman, esp. soldier. [Sc. form of JACK]

jockey /ˈdʒɒkɪ/ **1** *n*. rider, esp. professional, in horse-races. **2** *v*. cheat or manœuvre (person *into* or *out of*). **3 jockey for position** try to gain advantage esp. by skilful manœuvring or unfair action. [dimin. of prec.]

jock-strap *n*. support or protection for male genitals, worn esp. by sportsmen. [vulgar *jock* genitals]

jocose /dʒəˈkəʊs/ *a*. jocular; **jocosity** /-ˈkɒsɪtɪ/ *n*. [L (*jocus* jest)]

jocular /ˈdʒɒkjʊlə/ *a*. given to joking, humorous; **jocularity** /-ˈlærɪtɪ/ *n*.

jocund /ˈdʒɒkənd/ *a*. *literary* merry, cheerful; **jocundity** /dʒəˈkʌndɪtɪ/ *n*. [F f. L *jucundus* pleasant]

jodhpurs /ˈdʒɒdpəz/ *n.pl.* long riding-breeches, tight from knee to ankle. [*Jodhpur* in India]

jog 1 *v.* (**-gg-**) stimulate (person's memory); nudge (person); push or jerk; run slowly for exercise; walk, run, or ride with jolting gait; proceed laboriously (*on* or *along*). **2** *n.* spell of jogging; slow walk or trot; push or jerk or nudge. [prob. imit.]

joggle /'dʒɒg(ə)l/ **1** *v.* move to and fro in jerks. **2** *n.* slight shake.

jogtrot *n.* slow regular trot.

John Bull /dʒɒn/ English nation; typical Englishman. [character in satire]

johnny /'dʒɒnɪ/ *n. colloq.* fellow, man; **johnny-come-lately** newcomer, upstart. [dimin. of *John*]

joie de vivre /ʒwɑː də 'viːvrə/ feeling of exuberant enjoyment of life; high spirits. [F, = joy of living]

join 1 *v.* put together, fasten, unite (things, one *to* another, *together*); connect (points) by line etc.; become member of (club, army, etc.); take one's place with or in (company, procession, etc.); take part with others (*in* activity etc.); unite (persons, or one *with* or *to* another), be united in marriage, alliance, etc.; (of river, road, etc.) become continuous or connected with (another). **2** *n.* point, line, or surface of junction. **3 join battle** begin fighting; **join forces** combine efforts; **join up** enlist in army etc. [F f. L *jungo junct-*]

joiner *n.* maker of furniture and light woodwork; **joinery** *n.*

joint 1 *n.* place at which, means or device by which, two things join or are joined; structure by which two bones fit together; section of animal's carcass used for food; fissure in mass of rock; *sl.* place of meeting for drinking etc.; *sl.* marijuana cigarette. **2** *a.* belonging to or done by two or more persons etc. in common (*joint account, action*); sharing in possession etc. (*joint author, owner*). **3** *v.t.* connect by joint(s); divide (carcass) into joints or at a joint. **4 joint-stock company** company with capital held jointly by shareholders; **out of joint** dislocated, *fig.* out of order. [F (JOIN)]

jointure /'dʒɔɪntʃə/ **1** *n.* estate settled on wife for period during which she survives husband. **2** *v.t.* provide with jointure. [F f. L (JOIN)]

joist *n.* one of parallel timbers stretched from wall to wall to carry floor boards or ceiling. [F *giste* f. L (*jaceo* lie)]

jojoba /həʊ'həʊbə/ *n.* desert shrub with bean yielding oil similar to that of sperm whale. [Mex. Sp.]

joke 1 *n.* thing said or done to excite laughter, jest; ridiculous circumstance, person, etc. **2** *v.i.* make jokes. **3 no joke** a serious matter. [prob. L *jocus* jest]

joker *n.* one who jokes; extra playing-card used in some games; *sl.* person.

jokey *a.* inclined to joke; joking; ridiculous; **jokiness** *n.*

jollify /'dʒɒlɪfaɪ/ *v.* make or be merry; **jollification** /-fɪ'keɪʃ(ə)n/ *n.* [JOLLY]

jollity /'dʒɒlɪtɪ/ *n.* being jolly; merry-making. [F *joliveté* (foll.)]

jolly /'dʒɒlɪ/ **1** *a.* joyful, merry; festive, jovial; slightly drunk; *colloq.* (of person or thing) pleasant, delightful (also *iron.*: *a jolly shame*). **2** *adv. colloq.* very. **3** *v.t.* coax or humour (person) in friendly way (usu. with *along*). **4 Jolly Roger** pirates' black flag, usu. with skull and cross-bones. [F *jolif* gay, pretty]

jolly-boat /'dʒɒlɪbəʊt/ *n.* clinker-built ship's boat, smaller than cutter. [orig. unkn.]

jolt /dʒəʊlt/ **1** *v.* shake or dislodge with jerk (esp. person in moving vehicle); (of vehicle) move along with jerks; give mental shock to. **2** *n.* such jerk or shock. **3 jolty** *a.* [orig. unkn.]

Jonah /'dʒəʊnə/ *n.* person who brings, or is believed to bring, bad luck. [*Jonah* in OT]

jonquil /'dʒɒŋkwɪl/ *n.* species of narcissus with white or yellow fragrant flowers. [F or L (*juncus* rush plant)]

josh *US sl.* **1** *v.* make fun of; hoax; indulge in ridicule. **2** *n.* good-natured joke. [orig. unkn.]

joss *n.* Chinese idol; **joss-house** temple; **joss-stick** stick of fragrant tinder and clay for incense. [perh. ult. Port. *deos* f. L *deus* god]

jostle /'dʒɒs(ə)l/ **1** *v.* push or shove or knock (*against*), esp. in crowd; struggle (*with* person *for* thing). **2** *n.* jostling. [JOUST]

jot 1 *n.* small amount, whit (*not a jot*). **2** *v.t.* (**-tt-**) write (usu. *down*) briefly. [L f. Gk IOTA]

jotter *n.* small notebook or note-pad.

jottings *n.pl.* jotted notes.

joule /dʒuːl/ *n.* unit of work or energy. [*Joule*, physicist]

jounce *v.* bump, bounce, jolt. [orig. unkn.]

journal /'dʒɜːn(ə)l/ *n.* daily record of events or of business transactions and accounts; periodical (orig. daily newspaper); part of shaft or axle that rests on bearings. [F f. L (DIURNAL)]

journalese /dʒɜːnə'liːz/ *n.* hackneyed style of language characteristic of some newspaper writing.

journalist /'dʒɜːnəlɪst/ *n.* person employed to write for journal or newspaper; **journalism** *n.*; **journalistic** /-'lɪstɪk/ *a.*

journey /'dʒɜːnɪ/ **1** *n.* act of going from one place to another, esp. at long distance; distance travelled in specified time (*a day's journey*). **2** *v.i.* make a journey. [F *jornee* day, day's work or travel f. L (*diurnus* daily f. *dies* day)]

journeyman *n.* qualified mechanic or artisan working for another; sound but undistinguished workman.

joust /dʒaʊst/ **1** *n.* combat with lances between two mounted knights or men-at-arms. **2** *v.i.* engage in joust. [F f. L (*juxta* near)]

Jove *n.* Jupiter; **by Jove** exclamation of surprise. [L *Jupiter Jov-*]

jovial /'dʒəʊvɪəl/ *a.* merry, convivial, hearty; **joviality** /-'ælɪtɪ/ *n.*; **jovially** *adv.* [L *jovialis* (prec.)]

jowl *n.* jaw or jawbone; cheek (*cheek by jowl*); loose skin on throat, dewlap. [OE]

joy *n.* gladness, deep pleasure; cause of this; **joy-ride** *colloq.* pleasure-ride, usu. unauthorized, in car etc.; **no joy** *colloq.* no satisfaction or success; **joyful** *a.*; **joyfully** *adv.*; **joyous** *a.* [F f. L *gaudia* (*gaudeo* rejoice)]

joystick *n.* control-lever of aeroplane.

JP *abbr.* Justice of the Peace.

Jr. *abbr.* Junior.

jubilant /'dʒu:bɪlənt/ *a.* exultant, rejoicing; **jubilance** *n.* [L (*jubilo* shout)]

jubilation /dʒu:bɪ'leɪʃ(ə)n/ *n.* exultation, rejoicing.

jubilee /'dʒu:bɪli:/ *n.* anniversary (esp. 50th, *golden jubilee*); time of rejoicing. [F f. L f. Gk f. Heb.]

Judaic /dʒu:'deɪɪk/ *a.* of or characteristic of Jews. [L f. Gk (JEW)]

Judaism /'dʒu:deɪɪz(ə)m/ *n.* religion of the Jews.

Judaize /'dʒu:deɪaɪz/ *v.* make Jewish; follow Jewish customs.

Judas /'dʒu:dəs/ *n.* infamous traitor. [*Judas* Iscariot who betrayed Christ]

judder **1** *v.i.* shake noisily or violently. **2** *n.* instance of juddering. [imit.: cf. *shudder*]

judge /dʒʌdʒ/ **1** *n.* officer appointed to try causes in court of justice; person appointed to decide dispute or contest; person who decides a question; person fit to decide on merits of thing or question (*good judge of art*). **2** *v.* try (cause) in court of justice; pronounce sentence on (person); decide (contest, question); form opinion about, estimate; conclude or consider; act as judge. [F f. L *judex judic-*]

judgement *n.* (in law also **judgment**) critical faculty, discernment; good sense; opinion; decision of court of justice; judging of mankind by God; misfortune as sign of divine displeasure (*a judgement on you*). [F (prec.)]

judicature /'dʒu:dɪkətʃə/ *n.* administration of justice; judge's office; body of judges. [med.L (*judico* judge)]

judicial /dʒu:'dɪʃ(ə)l/ *a.* of or by a court of law; having the function of judgement (*judicial assembly*); of or proper to a judge; impartial; **judicially** *adv.* [L (*judicium* judgement)]

judiciary /dʒu:'dɪʃɪərɪ/ *n.* the judges of a State collectively.

judicious /dʒu:'dɪʃəs/ *a.* sensible, prudent. [F f. L (JUDICIAL)]

judo /'dʒu:dəʊ/ *n.* refined form of ju-jitsu. [Jap., = gentle way]

judoist *n.* student of or expert in judo.

jug **1** *n.* deep vessel for liquids with handle and often with shaped lip; *sl.* prison. **2** *v.t.* (**-gg-**) stew (hare) in covered vessel. [orig. uncert.]

juggernaut /'dʒʌgənɔ:t/ *n.* large heavy vehicle; overpowering force or object. [Hindi *Jagannath*, = lord of the world]

juggins /'dʒʌgɪnz/ *n.* *sl.* simpleton. [perh. f. surname]

juggle /'dʒʌg(ə)l/ **1** *v.* perform feats of dexterity (*with* objects), esp. by tossing and catching them keeping several in the air at once; manipulate or arrange (facts, figures, etc.) to suit purpose (also with *with*). **2** *n.* trick, deception. [F f. L (*jocus* jest)]

juggler /'dʒʌglə/ *n.* one who juggles, esp. to entertain. [F f. L *joculator* (prec.)]

Jugoslav var. of YUGOSLAV.

jugular /'dʒʌgjʊlə/ **1** *a.* of neck or throat. **2** *n.* jugular vein. **3** **jugular vein** either of two large veins in the neck, conveying blood from head. [L (*jugulum* collar-bone)]

juice /dʒu:s/ *n.* liquid content of fruit, vegetable, or meat; bodily secretion; *sl.* electricity, petrol. [F f. L]

juicy *a.* full of juice; *colloq.* interesting, esp. because scandalous; **juicily** *adv.*; **juiciness** *n.*

ju-jitsu /dʒu:'dʒɪtsu:/ *n.* Japanese system of unarmed combat using opponent's strength and weight to his disadvantage. [Jap. *jūjutsu* gentle skill]

ju-ju /'dʒu:dʒu:/ *n.* object venerated in W. Africa as charm or fetish; magic attributed to this. [perh. F *joujou* toy]

jujube /'dʒu:dʒu:b/ *n.* sweet fruit-flavoured lozenge of gelatin etc. [F, or med.L ult. f. Gk *zizuphon*]

juke-box /'dʒu:kbɒks/ *n.* machine that automatically plays selected gramophone record when coin is inserted. [Negro *juke* disorderly]

Jul. *abbr.* July.

julep /'dʒu:lep/ *n.* sweet drink esp. as vehicle for medicine; medicated drink; *US* iced and flavoured spirit and water, esp. *mint julep*. [F f. Pers. *gulāb* rose-water]

Julian /'dʒu:lɪən/ *a.* of Julius Caesar; **Julian calendar** calendar introduced by him, with year of 365 days and 366 every fourth year. [L (*Julius*)]

julienne /dʒu:lɪ'en/ **1** *n.* clear meat soup containing vegetables cut into thin strips; such vegetables. **2** *a.* cut into thin strips. [F (name *Jules* or *Julien*)]

Juliet cap /'dʒu:lɪət/ small network ornamental cap worn by brides etc. [*Juliet* in Shakespeare's *Romeo & Juliet*]

July /dʒu:'laɪ/ *n.* seventh month of year. [AF f. L (*Julius* Caesar)]

jumble /'dʒʌmb(ə)l/ **1** *v.t.* mix *up*, confuse. **2** *n.* confused heap etc., muddle; articles for jumble sale. **3 jumble sale** sale of miscellaneous articles, usu. second-hand, to raise funds for charity etc. [prob. imit.]

jumbo /'dʒʌmbəʊ/ **1** *n.* (*pl.* **jumbos**) big person, animal (esp. elephant), or thing (esp. = *jumbo jet*). **2** *a.* very large of its kind. **3 jumbo jet** large jet plane able to carry several hundred passengers. [prob. MUMBO-JUMBO]

jump 1 *v.* move up off ground etc. by sudden muscular effort; move suddenly with bound (*up*, *from*, *in*, *out*, etc.); give sudden movement from shock or excitement etc.; (of prices etc.) rise suddenly, cause to do this; pass over (obstacle etc.) by jumping; pass over (passage in book etc.); cause (thing, animal esp. horse) to jump; come *to* or arrive *at* (conclusion) hastily; (of train etc.) leave (rails); ignore and pass (red traffic-light etc.); abscond from (*jump bail*, *ship*); pounce upon or attack (person etc.); take summary possession of (claim allegedly forfeit etc.). **2** *n.* act of jumping; abrupt rise in price etc.; obstacle to be jumped esp. by horse; sudden transition; sudden movement caused by shock, excitement, etc. **3 have the jump on** *sl.* have an advantage over; **jump at** accept eagerly; **jump down person's throat** reprimand or contradict him severely; **jumped-up** *a.* upstart; **jump the gun** *colloq.* begin before signal is given, or prematurely; **jump-jet** jet aircraft that can take off and land vertically; **jump-lead** cable for conveying current from one battery to recharge or boost another; **jump-off** deciding round in show-jumping; **jump on** attack or criticize crushingly; **jump the queue** take unfair precedence; **jump suit** one-piece garment for whole body; **jump to it** act promptly and energetically; **one jump ahead** one stage ahead of rival etc. [imit.]

jumper[1] *n.* person or animal that jumps; short wire used to make or break electrical circuit.

jumper[2] *n.* knitted pullover; loose outer jacket worn by sailors. [prob. dial. *jump* short coat]

jumpy *a.* nervous, easily startled; making sudden movements; **jumpily** *adv.*; **jumpiness** *n.*

Jun. *abbr.* Junior; June.

junction /'dʒʌŋkʃ(ə)n/ *n.* joining; joint, joining-point; place where railway lines or roads meet; **junction box** box containing junction of electric cables etc. [L (JOIN)]

juncture /'dʒʌŋktʃə/ *n.* critical convergence of events or point of time; joining; joining-point.

June *n.* sixth month of year. [F, & L *Junius* (goddess *Juno*)]

jungle /'dʒʌŋg(ə)l/ *n.* land overgrown with tangled vegetation, esp. in tropics; area of such land; tangled mass; place of bewildering complexity or confusion or ruthless struggle; **jungly** *a.* [Hindi f. Skr.]

junior /'dʒu:nɪə/ **1** *a.* the younger (esp. appended to name for distinction between two persons of same name); inferior in age, standing, or position (*to*), of low or lowest position (*junior partner*); for younger children (*junior school*). **2** *n.* junior person; person acting or working in junior capacity (*the office junior*). [L, compar. of *juvenis* young]

juniper /'dʒu:nɪpə/ *n.* an evergreen shrub or tree, esp. with purple berry-like cones yielding an oil used for gin and medicine. [L *juniperus*]

junk[1] *n.* discarded articles, rubbish; anything regarded as of little value; *sl.* narcotic drug, esp. heroin; **junk food** food which is not nutritious. [orig. unkn.]

junk[2] *n.* flat-bottomed sailing vessel in China seas. [F f. Jav.]

junket /'dʒʌŋkɪt/ **1** *n.* dish of milk curdled by rennet and sweetened and flavoured; feast; *US* pleasure outing; *US* official's tour at public expense. **2** *v.i.* feast, make merry; *US* hold picnic or outing. [F *jonquette* rush-basket (used for junket) f. L *juncus* rush]

junkie *n. sl.* drug addict. [JUNK[1]]

junta /'dʒʌntə/ *n.* political clique or faction, esp. one holding power after revolution. [Sp. (JOIN)]

jural /'dʒʊər(ə)l/ *a.* of law; of (moral) rights and obligations. [L *jus jur-* law, right]

Jurassic /dʒʊə'ræsɪk/ **1** *a.* of the period in the Mesozoic era after Triassic, with prevalence of oolitic limestone. **2** *n.* this period. [F (*Jura* mountains)]

juridical /dʒʊə'rɪdɪk(ə)l/ *a.* of judicial proceedings; relating to law; **juridically** *adv.* [L (*jus jur-* law, *dico* say)]

jurisdiction /dʒʊərɪs'dɪkʃ(ə)n/ *n.* administration of justice (*over*); authority; extent of authority; territory over which it extends; **jurisdictional** *a.* [F & L (prec., DICTION)]

jurisprudence /dʒʊərɪs'pru:dəns/ *n.* science or philosophy of law; **jurisprudential** /-'denʃ(ə)l/ *a.* [L (prec., PRUDENT)]

jurist /'dʒʊərɪst/ *n.* one versed in law; **juristic** /-'rɪstɪk/ *a.* [F or med.L (*jus jur-* law)]

juror /'dʒʊərə/ *n.* member of jury; person taking oath. [F f. L (*juro* swear)]

jury /'dʒʊərɪ/ *n.* body of persons sworn to render verdict in court of justice or coroner's court; body of persons selected to award prizes in competition; **jury-box** enclosure for jury in court; **petty** (or **trial**) **jury** jury of twelve persons who try final issue of fact in civil or criminal cases and pronounce verdict.

jury-mast /'dʒʊərɪmɑ:st/ *n.* temporary mast replacing one broken or lost. [orig. unkn.]

jury-rigged /'dʒʊərɪrɪgd/ *a.* makeshift.

just **1** *a.* acting or done in accordance with what is morally right or proper; deserved, due (*a just reward*); well-grounded (*a just fear*); right in amount etc., proper (*just proportions*). **2** *adv.* exactly (*just what I need*); exactly or nearly at this or that moment, a little time ago (*he has just left*); barely, no more than (*I just caught the bus*); *colloq.* simply, merely (*we are just good friends*); positively, quite (*just splendid*); *sl.* really, indeed (*won't I just tell him*). **3** **just about** *colloq.* almost exactly, almost completely; **just in case** as a precaution; **just now** at this moment, a little time ago; **just so** exactly arranged, exactly as you say. [F f. L *justus* (*jus* right)]

justice /'dʒʌstɪs/ *n.* justness, fairness; exercise of authority in maintenance of right; judicial proceedings (*Court of Justice*; *was brought to justice*); judge or magistrate; **do justice to** treat fairly, appreciate duly; **do oneself justice** perform in manner worthy of one's abilities; **Justice of the Peace** unpaid lay magistrate appointed to hear minor cases; **Mr** (or **Mrs**) **Justice** —— title of High Court Judge. [F f. L *justitia* (prec.)]

justiciary /dʒʌ'stɪʃjərɪ/ *n.* administrator of justice; **Court of Justiciary** supreme criminal court in Scotland. [med.L (prec.)]

justifiable /'dʒʌstɪfaɪəb(ə)l/ *a.* that can be justified or defended. [F (foll)]

justify /'dʒʌstɪfaɪ/ *v.t.* show justice or truth of (person, act, statement, or claim); (of circumstances) be adequate ground for, warrant; adjust (line of type) to fill a space evenly; **justification** /-fɪ'keɪʃ(ə)n/ *n.*; **justificatory** /-fɪ'keɪtərɪ/ *a.* [F f. L (JUST, -FY)]

jut **1** *v.i.* (-**tt**-) project (*jut out*). **2** *n.* projection. [var. of JET[1]]

jute[1] *n.* fibre from bark of tropical plants, used for sacking, mats, etc. [Bengali]

Jute[2] *n.* member of Low German tribe that settled in Britain in 5th–6th c. [OE]

juvenile /'dʒu:vənaɪl/ **1** *a.* youthful; of or for young persons. **2** *n.* young person; actor playing such part. **3** **juvenile delinquency** violation of law by persons below age of legal responsibility; **juvenile delinquent** such offender. [L (*juvenis* young)]

juvenilia /dʒu:və'nɪlɪə/ *n.pl.* works produced by author or artist in youth.

juvenility /dʒu:və'nɪlɪtɪ/ *n.* youthfulness; youthful manner etc.

juxtapose /dʒʌkstə'pəʊz/ *v.t.* put side by side; **juxtaposition** /-pə'zɪʃ(ə)n/ *n.* [F f. L (*juxta* next, *pono* put)]

K

K, k /keɪ/ *n.* (*pl.* **Ks, K's**) eleventh letter.

K *abbr.* kelvin; king (in chess); unit of core-memory size in computers, = 1,024 (often taken as 1,000) words.

K. *abbr.* carat; King('s); Köchel (catalogue of Mozart's works).

K *symb.* potassium. [L *kalium*]

k *abbr.* kilo-.

Kaffir /'kæfə/ *n.* member or language of South African people of Bantu family; *derog.* Bantu inhabitant of South Africa. [Arab., = infidel]

kaftan var. of CAFTAN.

kaiser /'kaɪzə/ *n. hist.* emperor, esp. of Germany, Austria, or Holy Roman Empire. [L CAESAR]

kale *n.* hardy variety of cabbage with wrinkled leaves. [north. var. of COLE]

kaleidoscope /kə'laɪdəskəʊp/ *n.* tube containing mirrors and pieces of coloured glass etc. whose reflections produce patterns when the tube is rotated; **kaleidoscopic** /-'skɒpɪk/ *a.*;

kaleidoscopically /-'skɒpɪkəlɪ/ *adv.* [Gk *kalos* beautiful, *eidos* form; -SCOPE]
kaleyard /'keɪljɑ:d/ *n. Sc.* kitchen garden. [KALE]
kamikaze /kæmɪ'kɑ:zɪ/ *n.* in war of 1939–45, Japanese aircraft laden with explosives and suicidally crashed on target by pilot; pilot of this. [Jap., = divine wind]
kangaroo /kæŋgə'ru:/ *n.* Australian marsupial with hind quarters strongly developed for jumping; **kangaroo court** illegal court held by strikers, prisoners, etc. [Abor.]
kaolin /'keɪəlɪn/ *n.* fine white clay used for porcelain and in medicine. [F f. Chin. *kao-ling* high hill]
kapok /'keɪpɒk/ *n.* fine cotton-like material from tropical tree used as padding. [Malay]
kappa /'kæpə/ *n.* tenth letter of Greek alphabet (Κ,κ). [Gk]
kaput /kæ'pʊt/ *a. sl.* broken, ruined, done for. [G]
karakul /'kærəkʊl/ *n.* Asian sheep whose lambs have dark curled fleece; fur made from or resembling this. [Russ.]
karate /kə'rɑ:tɪ/ *n.* Japanese system of unarmed combat using hands and feet as weapons. [Jap., = empty hand]
karma /'kɑ:mə/ *n.* in Buddhism and Hinduism, sum of person's actions in one life, seen as determining fate in next. [Skr., = action, fate]
karoo /kə'ru:/ *n.* (also **karroo**) high plateau in S. Africa, waterless in dry season. [Hottentot]
kart *n.* = GO-KART.
katydid /'keɪtɪdɪd/ *n.* large green grasshopper common in US. [imit.]
kauri /'kaʊrɪ/ *n.* coniferous New Zealand timber-tree yielding gum.
kayak /'kaɪæk/ *n.* Eskimo one-man canoe of light wooden framework covered with sealskins; canoe developed from this. [Eskimo]
KBE *abbr.* Knight Commander of the Order of the British Empire.
KC *abbr.* King's Counsel.
kc/s *abbr.* kilocycles per second.
kea /'keɪə/ *n.* green New Zealand parrot said to attack sheep. [Maori, imit.]
kebab /kɪ'bæb/ *n.* (usu. in *pl.*) dish of small pieces of meat, vegetables, etc., cooked on skewer. [Urdu f. Arab.]
kedge 1 *v.* move (ship) by hawser attached to small anchor. **2** *n.* small anchor for this purpose. [orig. uncert.]
kedgeree /'kedʒərɪ, -'ri:/ *n.* European dish of fish, rice, hard-boiled eggs, etc.; Indian dish of rice, pulse, onions, eggs, etc. [Hindi]
keel 1 *n.* lengthwise timber or steel structure along base of ship, from which framework is built up. **2** *v.* turn (ship) keel upwards, (of ship) turn thus. **3 keel over** turn over, fall or collapse; **on an even keel** level, steady. [ON]
keelhaul *v.t.* haul (person) under keel as punishment; rebuke severely.
keelson var. of KELSON.
keen[1] *a.* (of person, desire, or interest) eager, ardent; (of the senses) acute, highly perceptive; (of knife or edge) sharp; (of wind etc.) piercingly cold; (of pain etc.) acute; (of sound, light, etc.) penetrating, vivid; (of price) competitively low; intellectually acute; **keen on** *colloq.* much attracted by; **keenness** *n.* [OE]
keen[2] 1 *n.* Irish funeral song accompanied with wailing. **2** *v.* utter the keen; bewail (person) thus. [Ir. *caoinim* wail]
keep 1 *v.* (*past* and *p.p.* **kept**) have continuous charge of, retain possession of, reserve (thing *for* future time etc.); (cause to) remain in specified condition, position, course, etc. (*keep cool*; *keep off the grass*; *keep them happy*); restrain, hold back *from*, detain; observe, pay due regard to (law, promise, appointment, etc.); conceal (secret etc.); own and manage (cows, bees, etc.); guard or protect (person, place, goal at football, etc.); provide for sustenance of (family, *oneself*, etc.); carry on, manage (shop etc.); maintain (house etc.) in proper order; preserve in being (*keep order*); continue to have or do (*keep company, guard*); continue to follow (way or course); (of food etc., also *fig.* of news etc.) remain in good condition; have (commodity) regularly on sale; maintain in return for sexual favours (*kept man, woman*); maintain (diary, accounts, etc.) by making requisite entries; remain in (*bed, room, house*, etc.); retain one's place in (saddle, one's seat, one's ground, etc.) against opposition. **2** *n.* maintenance, food; *hist.* tower, stronghold. **3 for keeps** *colloq.* permanently; **keep at** (cause to) work persistently at; **keep down** hold in subjection, keep low in amount; **keep in with** remain on good terms with; **keep on** continue (*doing*), nag *at*; **keep to** adhere to (course or promise), confine oneself to; **keep to oneself** avoid contact with others, keep (thing) secret; **keep under** repress; **keep up** maintain, prevent from sinking (esp. one's spirits etc.); **keep up with** achieve same pace as; **keep up with the Joneses** strive to remain on terms of obvious social equality with one's neighbours. [OE]
keeper *n.* person who keeps or looks

after something; custodian of museum or art gallery or forest; wicket-keeper.
keeping *n.* custody, charge (*in safe keeping*); agreement, harmony (*in, out of, keeping*).
keepsake *n.* thing kept in memory of its giver.
keg *n.* small cask or barrel; **keg beer** beer supplied from sealed metal container. [ON]
kelp *n.* large brown seaweed; calcined ashes of this yielding iodine etc. [orig. unkn.]
kelpie /'kelpɪ/ *n. Sc.* malevolent water-spirit usu. in form of horse; Australian sheepdog of Scottish origin. [orig. unkn.]
kelson /'kels(ə)n/ *n.* line of timber fixing ship's floor-timbers to keel. [LG (KEEL, SWINE as name of timber)]
Kelt[1] etc. var. of CELT etc.
kelt[2] *n.* salmon or sea trout after spawning. [orig. unkn.]
kelvin /'kelvɪn/ *n.* degree (equal to Celsius degree) of Kelvin scale; **Kelvin scale** scale of temperature with zero at absolute zero. [physicist]
ken 1 *v.t.* (**-nn-**) *Sc.* know. **2** *n.* range of knowledge or sight. [OE, = make known (CAN[1])]
kendo /'kendəʊ/ *n.* Japanese art of fencing with two-handed bamboo swords. [Jap., = sword-way]
kennel /'ken(ə)l/ **1** *n.* small shelter for dog; (in *pl.*) place where dogs are bred or boarded; pack of dogs. **2** *v.* (**-ll-**, *US* **-l-**) put or keep in a kennel. [AF f. L (*canis* dog)]
kepi /'kepɪ/ *n.* French military cap with horizontal peak.
kept *past* and *p.p.* of KEEP.
kerb *n.* stone edging to pavement or raised path. [var. of CURB]
kerbstone *n.* one of stones forming kerb.
kerchief /'kɜːtʃɪf/ *n.* square cloth used to cover head; handkerchief. [AF *courchef* (COVER, CHIEF)]
kerfuffle /kə'fʌf(ə)l/ *n. colloq.* fuss, commotion. [orig. Sc.]
kermes /'kɜːmɪz/ *n.* female of an insect, formerly taken to be a berry, that feeds on an evergreen oak; red dye made from dried bodies of these. [F f. Arab.]
kernel /'kɜːn(ə)l/ *n.* softer part within hard shell of nut or stone-fruit; seed within husk etc., e.g. grain of wheat; central or essential part of thing. [OE (CORN[1])]
kerosene /'kerəsiːn/ *n.* fuel-oil distilled from petroleum or from coal or bituminous shale, paraffin oil. [Gk *kēros* wax]
kestrel /'kestr(ə)l/ *n.* a kind of small falcon. [orig. uncert.]
ketch *n.* small sailing vessel with two masts. [CATCH]
ketchup /'ketʃəp/ *n.* thick spicy sauce made from tomatoes, mushrooms, etc. [Chin.]
ketone /'kiːtəʊn/ *n.* one of a class of organic compounds including acetone. [G *keton* alt. of *aketon* ACETONE]
kettle /'ket(ə)l/ *n.* vessel, usu. of metal with spout and handle, for boiling water; **a fine** (or **pretty** etc.) **kettle of fish** awkward state of affairs. [ON]
kettledrum *n.* drum consisting of inverted metal bowl with adjustable membrane stretched across.
key[1] /kiː/ **1** *n.* instrument, usu. of metal, for moving bolt of lock so that it locks or unlocks; similar implement for operating switch in form of lock, for winding clock etc., or for grasping screw, nut, etc.; one of set of levers or buttons pressed by finger in musical instrument, typewriter, etc.; *Mus.* system of notes based on material in a particular scale (*key of F major*), *fig.* general tone or style of thought or expression; solution to problem, explanation, word or system for solving cipher or code; thing or factor governing opportunity for or access to something, *attrib.* essential, of vital importance (*a key issue*); place that by its position gives control of sea, territory, etc.; piece of wood or metal inserted between others to secure them; mechanical device for making or breaking electric circuit; winged fruit of sycamore, ash, etc.; roughness of surface to help adhesion of plaster etc. **2** *v.* fasten (*in, on,* etc.) with pin, wedge, bolt, etc.; roughen (surface) to help adhesion of plaster etc.; align or link (thing *to* another). **3 key in** enter (data) by means of keyboard; **key money** payment required from incoming tenant nominally for provision of key to premises; **key-pad** miniature keyboard for holding in the hand; **key-ring** ring for keeping keys on; **key up** stimulate or excite (person). [OE]
key[2] /kiː/ *n.* reef, low island. [Sp. *cayo*]
keyboard *n.* set of keys on typewriter, piano, etc. [KEY[1]]
keyhole *n.* hole by which key is put into lock.
Keynesian /'keɪnzɪən/ *a.* of economic theories of J. M. Keynes, esp. regarding State control of the economy through taxes and the money supply.
keynote *n.* prevailing idea or tone in a speech etc.; lowest note in scale on which musical key is based. [KEY[1]]
keystone *n.* central locking stone in arch; central principle.
keyword *n.* key to cipher etc.

KG *abbr*. Knight of the Order of the Garter.
kg. *abbr*. kilogram(s).
KGB *n*. secret police of the USSR since 1953. [Russ. abbr., = committee of State security]
khaki /'kɑ:kɪ/ **1** *a*. dull brownish-yellow. **2** *n*. khaki cloth or uniform. [Urdu, = dusty]
khan /kɑ:n/ *n*. title of rulers and officials in Central Asia; **khanate** *n*. [Turki, = lord]
kHz *abbr*. kilohertz.
kibbutz /kɪ'bu:ts/ *n*. (*pl*. **kibbutzim** /-'tsi:m/) communal esp. farming settlement in Israel. [Heb., = gathering]
kibosh /'kaɪbɒʃ/ *n*. *sl*. nonsense; **put the kibosh on** put an end to. [orig. unkn.]
kick 1 *v*. thrust out, strike or propel forcibly, with foot or hoof; score (goal) by a kick; protest, show dislike (*against* or *at* treatment etc.); *sl*. abandon (habit). **2** *n*. kicking action or blow; recoil of gun when fired; *colloq*. resilience (*has no kick left*); *colloq*. temporary interest or enthusiasm (*on a health-food kick*), *colloq*. sharp stimulant effect, (usu. in *pl*.) thrill (*does it for kicks*). **3 kick about** (or **around**) treat (person) roughly, move idly from place to place, be unused or unwanted; **kick off** begin football match, *colloq*. make start; **kick-off** *n*. start esp. of football match; **kick out** *colloq*. expel forcibly, dismiss; **kick up** *colloq*. create or cause (fuss, trouble, etc.); **kick upstairs** promote (person) to ostensibly higher position to remove him from scene of real influence.
kickback *n*. recoil; *colloq*. payment for help in making profit or for showing favour etc.
kick-start 1 *n*. (also **-starter**) device to start engine of motor cycle etc. by downward thrust of pedal. **2** *v.t.* start (motor cycle etc.) thus.
kid 1 *n*. young goat; leather made from its skin; *colloq*. child. **2** *v*. (**-dd-**) give birth to young goat; *sl*. deceive or hoax. **3 handle** (or **treat** etc.) **with kid gloves** treat tactfully. [ON]
kidnap /'kɪdnæp/ *v.t.* (**-pp-**, *US* **-p-**) carry off (person) illegally esp. to obtain ransom; steal (child). [KID, *nap* = NAB]
kidney /'kɪdnɪ/ *n*. either of pair of glandular organs in abdominal cavity of mammals, birds, and reptiles, serving to remove waste products from the blood and excrete urine; animal's kidney as food; nature, kind, temperament; **kidney bean** kidney-shaped dwarf French bean, scarlet runner bean; **kidney machine** machine able to take over function of damaged kidney. [orig. unkn.]
kill 1 *v.t.* deprive of life or vitality, cause death of; put an end to (feelings etc.); switch off (light, engine, etc.); *colloq*. cause severe pain to (*my feet are killing me*); overwhelm with amusement; pass (time) unprofitably while waiting for future event; render ineffective; defeat totally (parliamentary bill). **2** *n*. act of killing; animal(s) killed, esp. in sport; destruction or disablement of submarine, aircraft, etc. **3 dressed to kill** dressed showily or alluringly. **4 killer** *n*. [perh. rel. to QUELL]
killing 1 *n*. causing death; rapid financial success. **2** *a*. *colloq*. highly amusing, exhausting.
killjoy *n*. person who spoils or questions others' enjoyment.
kiln *n*. furnace or oven for burning, baking, or drying, esp. for calcining lime, or firing pottery etc. [OE f. L *culina* kitchen]
kilo /'ki:ləʊ/ *n*. (*pl*. **kilos**) kilogram; kilometre. [F, abbr.]
kilo- *in comb*. thousand. [F f. Gk *khilioi*]
kilocycle /'kɪləsaɪk(ə)l/ *n*. = KILOHERTZ.
kilogram /'kɪləgræm/ *n*. metric unit of mass, approx. 2.205 lb.
kilohertz /'kɪləhɜ:ts/ *n*. unit of frequency, = 1,000 cycles per second.
kilolitre /'kɪləli:tə/ *n*. metric unit of capacity, 1,000 litres or approx. 35.31 cu.ft.
kilometre /'kɪləmi:tə, (D) kɪ'lɒmɪtə/ *n*. metric unit of length, 1,000 metres or approx. 0.62 mile.
kiloton /'kɪlətʌn/ *n*. unit of explosive force equal to 1,000 tons of TNT.
kilotonne /'kɪlətʌn/ *n*. metric unit equivalent to kiloton.
kilowatt /'kɪləwɒt/ *n*. unit of electrical power, equal to 1,000 watts; **kilowatt-hour** energy equal to one kilowatt working for one hour.
kilt 1 *n*. pleated usu. tartan skirt reaching from waist to knee, esp. worn by Highland man. **2** *v.t.* tuck up (skirts) round body; gather in vertical pleats. [Scand.]
kimono /kɪ'məʊnəʊ/ *n*. (*pl*. **kimonos**) long loose Japanese robe worn with sash; European dressing-gown modelled on this. [Jap.]
kin 1 *a*. one's relatives or family. **2** *predic. a*. related. **3 kinship** *n*. [OE]
-kin *suffix* forming diminutive nouns (*catkin, lambkin*). [Du.]
kind /kaɪnd/ **1** *n*. class of similar or related things, animals, etc.; natural way, fashion (*act after their kind*); character (*differ in degree but not in kind*). **2** *a*. of gentle or benevolent nature, friendly in one's conduct *to* (person etc.), considerate. **3 in kind** (of pay-

ment) in goods or produce, not money, (of repayment, esp. *fig.*) in same form as that received; **a kind of** something resembling (*a kind of musician*); **kind of** *colloq.* somewhat (*I'm kind of glad*). [OE]

kindergarten /ˈkɪndəgɑ:t(ə)n/ *n.* school for very young children. [G, = children's garden]

kindle /ˈkɪnd(ə)l/ *v.* light or set on fire; inspire or animate, arouse (feeling etc.); become kindled, flame, glow. [ON]

kindling *n.* small sticks etc. for lighting fire.

kindly[1] /ˈkaɪndlɪ/ *a.* kind, kind-hearted; (of climate) pleasant, genial; **kindliness** *n.* [KIND, -LY[1]]

kindly[2] /ˈkaɪndlɪ/ *adv.* in a kind way; **take kindly to** (usu. with *neg.*) be pleased by. [KIND, -LY[2]]

kindred /ˈkɪndrɪd/ **1** *n.* blood relationship; one's relations; resemblance in character. **2** *a.* related, allied, similar. **3 kindred spirit** person with feelings etc. like one's own. [OE, = kinship]

kine *archaic pl.* of cow[1].

kinematic /kɪnɪˈmætɪk/ *a.* of motion considered abstractly without reference to force or mass. [Gk *kinēma -matos* motion]

kinematics *n.pl.* science of pure motion.

kinetic /kɪˈnetɪk, kaɪ-/ *a.* of or due to motion; **kinetic art** form of visual art depending on moving components for effect; **kinetic energy** body's ability to do work by virtue of its motion. [Gk *kinetikos* (*kineo* move)]

kinetics *n.pl.* science of relations between motions of bodies and forces acting upon them.

king *n.* male sovereign (esp. hereditary) ruler of independent State; person or thing pre-eminent in specified field or class (*oil king*); *attrib.* large or largest kind of (*king penguin*); piece in chess that has to be protected from checkmate; crowned piece in draughts; court-card with picture of king; **King Charles spaniel** small black-and-tan spaniel; **King of Arms** chief herald at College of Arms and in Scotland; **king of beasts** lion; **king of birds** eagle; **king-post** upright post from tie-beam to top of rafter; **king-size(d)** larger than normal, very large; **kingly** *a.*; **kingship** *n.* [OE]

kingcup *n.* marsh marigold; buttercup.

kingdom *n.* territory or State ruled by king or queen; domain; division of natural world (*animal, vegetable, mineral, kingdom*); **kingdom-come** *sl.* the next world. [OE]

kingfisher *n.* small bird with brilliant plumage, which dives for fish. [KING]

kingpin *n.* vertical bolt used as pivot; essential person or thing.

kink 1 *n.* sudden bend or twist in something straight or smoothly curved; mental peculiarity or twist. **2** *v.* (cause to) form a kink. [LG or Du.]

kinky *a.* having kinks, *colloq.* bizarre, perverted (esp. sexually); **kinkily** *adv.*; **kinkiness** *n.*

kinsfolk /ˈkɪnzfəʊk/ *n.* one's blood relations. [KIN]

kinsman /ˈkɪnzmən/ *n.* (esp. male) blood relation; **kinswoman** *n. fem.* [KIN]

kiosk /ˈki:ɒsk/ *n.* light usu. outdoor structure for sale of newspapers, food, etc.; = *telephone kiosk*. [F f. Turk. f. Pers.]

kip *sl.* **1** *n.* a sleep; bed; common lodging-house. **2** *v.i.* (**-pp-**) sleep. [cf. Da. *kippe* mean hut]

kipper 1 *n.* kippered fish esp. herring; male salmon in spawning season. **2** *v.t.* cure (herring etc.) by splitting open, salting, drying and smoking. [orig. uncert.]

kirk *n. Sc. & N. Engl.* church; **kirk-session** lowest court in Church of Scotland and (*hist.*) other Presbyterian Churches, composed of ministers and elders; **The Kirk (of Scotland)** Church of Scotland as opposed to Church of England or to Episcopal Church in Scotland. [ON *kirkja* = E CHURCH]

kirsch(wasser) /ˈkɪəʃvʌsə/ *n.* brandy distilled from fermented juice of wild cherries. [G, = cherry (water)]

kismet /ˈkɪsmet, ˈkɪz-/ *n.* destiny, fate. [Turk. f. Arab.]

kiss 1 *n.* touch given with lips. **2** *v.t.* touch with the lips, esp. as sign of love, affection, greeting, or reverence; (absol., of two persons) touch each other's lips thus; touch gently. **3 kiss-curl** small curl of hair arranged on face or at nape; **kiss hands** greet sovereign thus; **kiss of death** apparently friendly act causing ruin; **kiss of life** mouth-to-mouth method of artificial respiration. [OE]

kisser *n. sl.* mouth or face.

kit 1 *n.* equipment or clothing required for particular activity or need (*football kit, first-aid kit*); soldier's or traveller's pack or equipment; set of parts sold together from which whole thing can be made (*model aeroplane kit*); *US* wooden tub. **2** *v.* (**-tt-**) equip or be equipped with kit (often with *out* or *up*). [Du.]

kitbag *n.* large, usu. cylindrical, bag for soldier's or traveller's kit.

kitchen /ˈkɪtʃɪn/ *n.* place where food is prepared and cooked; **kitchen garden** garden for growing fruit and vegetables. [OE f. L *coquina*]

kitchenette /kɪtʃɪ'net/ *n.* small room or alcove used as kitchen.
kite *n.* toy consisting of light framework with paper etc. stretched over it and flown in wind at end of long string; bird of prey of hawk family; **fly a kite** *colloq.* sound out public opinion. [OE]
Kitemark *n.* official kite-shaped mark on goods approved by British Standards Institution.
kith *n.* in **kith and kin** friends and relations. [OE, orig. 'knowledge' (CAN[1])]
kitsch /kɪtʃ/ *n.* worthless pretentiousness or bad taste in art; art of this type; **kitschy** *a.* [G]
kitten /'kɪt(ə)n/ **1** *n.* young of cat, of ferret, etc. **2** *v.* give birth to (kittens). **3** **have kittens** *colloq.* be very upset or nervous. [AF dimin. of *chat* CAT]
kittiwake /'kɪtɪweɪk/ *n.* a kind of small seagull. [imit. of its cry]
kitty /'kɪtɪ/ *n.* fund of money for communal use; pool in some card-games. [orig. unkn.]
kiwi /'ki:wi:/ *n.* flightless New Zealand bird with rudimentary wings and no tail; **(Kiwi)** *colloq.* New Zealander. [Maori]
kl. *abbr.* kilolitre(s).
Klaxon /'klæks(ə)n/ *n.* **(P)** powerful electric horn. [name of manufacturer]
kleptomania /kleptəʊ'meɪnɪə/ *n.* abnormal urge to steal, usu. without regard for need or profit; **kleptomaniac** *n.* & *a.* [Gk *kleptēs* thief]
kloof *n.* (in S. Africa) ravine or valley. [Du.]
km. *abbr.* kilometre(s).
knack *n.* acquired or intuitive faculty of doing a thing adroitly; trick; habit (*has a knack of offending people*). [orig. unkn.]
knacker **1** *n.* buyer of useless horses for slaughter, or of old houses etc. for materials. **2** *v.t.* (esp. in *p.p.*) *sl.* exhaust, wear out. [orig. unkn.]
knapsack /'næpsæk/ *n.* soldier's or traveller's bag, usu. of canvas, strapped to back. [G (*knappen* bite, SACK[1])]
knapweed /'næpwi:d/ *n.* weed with purple flowers on globular head. [KNOP]
knave *n.* unprincipled or dishonest person, rogue; jack in playing-cards; **knavish** *a.* [OE, orig. = boy, servant]
knavery *n.* conduct of knave.
knead *v.t.* work (moist flour, clay, etc.) into dough by pressing with hands; make (bread, pottery) thus; operate on using such motions (in massaging etc.). [OE]
knee **1** *n.* joint between thigh and lower leg in man; corresponding joint in animal; upper surface of thigh of sitting person (*sat on her knee*); part of garment covering knee. **2** *v.t.* touch or strike with the knee. **3** **bring person to his knees** reduce him to submission; **knee-breeches** breeches reaching to or just below knee; **knee-deep** immersed up to knees, *fig.* deeply involved *in*, so deep as to reach knees; **knee-high** so high as to reach knees; **knee-jerk** sudden involuntary kick caused by blow on tendon below knee; **knees-up** *colloq.* lively party with dancing. [OE]
kneecap *n.* convex bone in front of knee; protective covering for knee; **kneecapping** *n.* shooting in the legs as punishment.
kneel *v.i.* (*past* and *p.p.* **knelt** or *US* **kneeled**) rest or lower oneself on the knee(s). [OE (KNEE)]
kneeler *n.* hassock etc. for kneeling on.
knell *n.* sound of bell, esp. after death or at funeral; *fig.* omen of death or extinction. [OE]
knelt *past* & *p.p.* of KNEEL.
knew *past* of KNOW.
knickerbockers /'nɪkəbɒkəz/ *n.pl.* loose-fitting breeches gathered in at knee. [*Knickerbocker* pseud. of W. Irving, author of *History of New York*]
knickers *n.pl.* woman's or girl's undergarment covering body below waist and having separate legs or leg-holes. [abbr. of prec.]
knick-knack /'nɪknæk/ *n.* trinket or small ornament. [KNACK in obs. sense 'trinket']
knife **1** *n.* (*pl.* **knives**) cutting instrument or weapon consisting of metal blade with long sharpened edge fixed in handle; cutting-blade in machine. **2** *v.t.* cut or stab with knife. **3** **at knife-point** threatened by knife; **the knife** *colloq.* surgery; **have got one's knife into** be persistently malicious or vindictive towards; **knife-edge** sharp edge of knife, position of tense uncertainty about outcome; **knife-pleat** narrow flat pleat in overlapping series. [OE]
knight /naɪt/ **1** *n.* man raised to rank below baronetcy as reward for personal merit or services to Crown or country; *hist.* man raised to honourable military rank by king etc.; *hist.* military follower, esp. devoted to service of lady as her attendant or champion in war or tournament; chess piece usu. with shape of horse's head. **2** *v.t.* confer knighthood on. **3** **knight errant** medieval knight wandering in search of chivalrous adventures, *fig.* man of such spirit; **knight-errantry** practice or conduct of knight errant. [OE, orig. = boy]
knighthood *n.* rank or dignity of knight.
knightly *a.* of or like a knight; chivalrous.

knit *v.* (**-tt-**; *past* and *p.p.* **knitted** or (esp. *fig.*) **knit**) make (garment etc., or *absol.*) by interlocking loops of yarn or thread; form (yarn) into fabric etc. in this way; make (plain stitch) in knitting; wrinkle (brow); make or become close or compact, grow together. [OE]

knitting *n.* work being knitted; **knitting-needle** one of pair of slender pointed rods used in knitting by hand.

knitwear *n.* knitted garments.

knob *n.* rounded protuberance, esp. at end or on surface of thing, e.g. handle of door, drawer, etc., or for adjusting radio etc.; small lump (of butter etc.); **with knobs on** *sl.* that and more (often as emphatic or iron. agreement); **knobby** *a.* [MLG *knobbe* knot, knob]

knobbly /ˈnɒblɪ/ *a.* hard and lumpy. [*knobble*, dimin. of KNOB]

knobkerrie /ˈnɒbkerɪ/ *n.* short stick with knob at end as weapon of South African tribes. [Afrik. *knopkierie*]

knock 1 *v.* strike with audible sharp blow; make noise by striking door etc., to gain admittance; drive or send *in, out, off, on, over*, etc. by striking; make by knocking (*knock a hole in*); (of engine) make thumping or rattling noise, pink; *sl.* criticize or insult. **2** *n.* act or sound of knocking; sharp blow; sound of knocking in engine. **3 knock about** (or **around**) treat roughly, strike repeatedly, wander about aimlessly; **knock back** *sl.* eat or drink esp. hastily, disconcert; **knock down** strike (person) to ground, demolish, dispose of (article *to* bidder) by knock of hammer at auction; **knock-down** *a.* (of price) very low, (of furniture etc.) easily dismantled and reassembled, overwhelming; **knock-for-knock** (of insurance terms) each company paying its policy-holder in claim, regardless of liability; **knocking-shop** *sl.* brothel; **knock knees** abnormal inward curving of the legs at the knees; **knock-kneed** *a.* having this; **knock off** *colloq.* cease work, complete (piece of work etc.) quickly, deduct (sum from total), *sl.* steal or kill; **knock-on effect** decision about one instance as affecting other instances; **knock out** render unconscious by blow to head, disable (boxer) so that he is unable to recover in required time, defeat in knock-out competition, exhaust or disable, *sl.* astonish; **knock sideways** *colloq.* shock, astound; **knock spots off** *colloq.* easily surpass; **knock together** construct hurriedly; **knock up** make or arrange hastily, arouse (person) by knocking at door, score (runs) at cricket, *US sl.* make pregnant; **knock-up** *n.* practice game etc. [OE]

knockabout *a.* rough, boisterous.

knocker *n.* hinged metal device on door for knocking to call attention; (in *pl.*) *vulgar* woman's breasts.

knock-out 1 *a.* that knocks boxer etc. out, (of competition) in which loser of each round is eliminated. **2** *n.* blow that knocks boxer etc. out; *sl.* outstanding person or thing.

knoll /nəʊl/ *n.* hillock, mound. [OE]

knop *n.* ornamental knob; ornamental loop or tuft in yarn. [LG or Du.]

knot[1] **1** *n.* intertwining of parts of one or more ropes, strings, etc., to fasten them together; tangle (of hair, yarn, etc.); ribbon etc. tied with knot for ornament etc.; group or cluster (*of* persons or things); hard mass formed in tree-trunk where branch once grew out, corresponding cross-grained piece in board; difficulty or problem; that which forms or maintains a union, esp. marriage; unit of ship's or aircraft's speed equal to one nautical mile per hour. **2** *v.* (**-tt-**) tie in or with knot(s); make knots (esp. for fringe); make (fringe) thus; entangle; unite closely or intricately. **3 at a rate of knots** *colloq.* very fast; **knot-grass** weed with intricate creeping stems and pink flowers; **knot-hole** hole in wooden board, where knot has fallen out; **tie in knots** make (person) confused or baffled. [OE]

knot[2] *n.* small wading bird of sandpiper family. [orig. unkn.]

knotty *a.* full of knots; puzzling, difficult. [KNOT[1]]

know /nəʊ/ *v.* (*past* **knew**, *p.p.* **known** /nəʊn/) have in the mind, have learnt, be aware (of); have information (*about*); be acquainted with, have regular social contact with; have understanding of (language or subject); recognize or identify, be able to distinguish (one *from* another); have personal experience of (fear etc.); be subject to (*her joy knew no bounds*); **in the know** *colloq.* knowing secret or inside information; **know-all** *derog.* person who claims to know much; **know-how** practical knowledge or skill; **know of** be aware of, have heard of; **know one's own mind** know one's intentions firmly; **know what's what** have wide knowledge of the world; **you never know** it is always possible. [OE]

knowing *a.* having or showing knowledge or awareness; shrewd, clever.

knowingly *adv.* in knowing manner, intentionally, deliberately.

knowledge /ˈnɒlɪdʒ/ *n.* knowing; what is known (*of* person, thing, fact, or subject); sum of what is known to mankind (*every branch of knowledge*); person's

range of information; **to my knowledge** as far as I know.
knowledgeable *a.* having much knowledge, well-informed.
known *p.p.* of KNOW.
knuckle /'nʌk(ə)l/ **1** *n.* bone at finger-joint, esp. at root of finger; knee- or ankle-joint of animal, esp. with adjacent parts as joint of meat. **2** *v.* strike or press or rub with knuckles. **3 knuckle down** apply oneself earnestly (*to* work etc.); **knuckle-duster** metal guard worn over knuckles in fist-fighting esp. to increase violence of blow; **knuckle under** give in, submit; **near the knuckle** *colloq.* verging on indecency. [LG or Du. dimin. (*knoke* bone)]
knurl *n.* small projecting ridge etc. [LG or Du.]
KO *abbr.* knock-out.
koala /kəʊ'ɑ:lə/ *n.* Australian arboreal marsupial with thick grey fur and large ears. [Abor.]
kohl /kəʊl/ *n.* powder used in eastern countries to darken eyelids etc. [Arab.]
kohlrabi /kəʊl'rɑ:bɪ/ *n.* cabbage with turnip-like edible stem. [G f. It. f. L (COLE, RAPE²)]
kola var. of COLA.
kolkhoz /'kɒlkɒz/ *n.* collective farm in USSR. [Russ.]
koodoo var. of KUDU.
kook *n. US sl.* crazy or eccentric person; **kooky** *a.* [prob. CUCKOO]
kookaburra /'kʊkəbʌrə/ *n.* large Australian kingfisher with loud discordant cry. [Abor.]
kopje /'kɒpɪ/ *n.* (also **koppie**) (in S. Africa) small hill. [Afrik. *koppie*, Du. *kopje*, dimin. of *kop* head]
Koran /kɔ:'rɑ:n/ *n.* sacred book of Muslims. [Arab., = recitation]
kosher /'kəʊʃə/ **1** *a.* (of food or food-shop) fulfilling requirements of Jewish law; *colloq.* correct, genuine, legitimate. **2** *n.* kosher food or shop. [Heb., = proper]
kowtow /kaʊ'taʊ/ **1** *v.i.* act obsequiously (*to* person etc.); perform the kowtow. **2** *n.* Chinese custom of touching ground with head as sign of worship or submission. [Chin., = knock the head]
k.p.h. *abbr.* kilometres per hour.
Kr *symb.* krypton.
kraal /krɑ:l/ *n.* (in S. Africa) village of huts enclosed by fence; enclosure for sheep or cattle. [Afrik. f. Port. *curral*, of Hottentot orig.]
Kraut /kraʊt/ *n. sl. derog.* German. [SAUERKRAUT]
kremlin /'kremlɪn/ *n.* citadel within Russian town, esp. that of Moscow; **the Kremlin** the USSR Government. [F f. Russ.]
krill *n.* tiny planktonic crustaceans eaten by whales etc. [Norw. *kril* tiny fish]
kris /kri:s, krɪs/ *n.* Malay dagger with wavy blade. [Malay]
kromesky /krə'meskɪ/ *n.* minced meat or fish rolled in bacon and fried. [Pol. *kromeczka* small slice]
krona /'krəʊnə/ *n.* currency unit of Sweden (*pl.* **kronor**) and of Iceland (*pl.* **kronur**). [Sw. & Icel., = CROWN]
krone /'krəʊnə/ *n.* (*pl.* **kroner**) currency unit of Denmark and of Norway. [Da. & Norw., = CROWN]
krugerrand /'kru:gərɑ:nt/ *n.* S. African gold coin bearing portrait of Kruger. [*Kruger*, S. Afr. statesman]
krypton /'krɪptɒn/ *n.* rare inert gaseous element. [Gk (*kruptō* hide)]
Kt. *abbr.* Knight.
kudos /'kju:dɒs/ *n. colloq.* renown, glory. [Gk]
kudu /'ku:du:/ *n.* large white-striped spiral-horned African antelope. [Xhosa]
Kufic /'kju:fɪk/ **1** *n.* early form of Arabic alphabet, found esp. in inscriptions. **2** *a.* of or in this script. [*Cufa* in Iraq]
Ku-Klux-Klan /kju:klʌks'klæn/ *n.* US secret society hostile to Blacks. [orig. uncert.]
kukri /'kʊkrɪ/ *n.* heavy curved knife used by Gurkhas as weapon. [Hindi]
kümmel /'kʊm(ə)l/ *n.* liqueur flavoured with caraway and cumin seeds. [G (CUMIN)]
kumquat /'kʌmkwɒt/ *n.* plum-size orange-like fruit used in preserves. [Chin. *kin kü* gold orange]
kung fu /kʌŋ 'fu:/ Chinese form of karate. [Chin.]
kV *abbr.* kilovolt(s).
kW *abbr.* kilowatt(s).
kWh *abbr.* kilowatt-hour(s).
kyle /kaɪl/ *n.* narrow channel between island and mainland (or another island) in W. Scotland. [Gael. *caol* strait]

L

L, l /el/ *n.* (*pl.* **Ls, L's**) twelfth letter; L-shaped thing; *Rom. num.* 50.
L *abbr.* learner (driver).
L. *abbr.* Lake; Liberal; Licenciate of.

£ *abbr.* POUND[1] (money). [L *libra*]
l. *abbr.* left; line; litre(s).
la var. of LAH.
La *symb.* lanthanum.
lab. *n. colloq.* laboratory. [abbr.]
Lab. *abbr.* Labour.
label /'leɪb(ə)l/ **1** *n.* slip of paper etc. attached to object to give some information about it; general classifying phrase applied to persons etc. **2** *v.t.* (**-ll-**, *US* **-l-**) attach label to; assign to category; replace (atom) by usu. radioactive isotope for identification. [F]
labial /'leɪbɪəl/ **1** *a.* of the lips; of the nature of a lip; pronounced with partially or completely closed lips. **2** *n.* labial sound (e.g. *p, m, v*). [L (*labia* lips)]
labor etc. *US* var. of LABOUR etc.
laboratory /lə'bɒrətərɪ/ *n.* room or building used for scientific experiments and research. [L (foll.)]
laborious /lə'bɔːrɪəs/ *a.* needing much work or perseverance; showing signs of effort; hard-working. [F f. L (foll.)]
labour /'leɪbə/ **1** *n.* bodily or mental work, exertion; task; body of those doing (esp. manual or non-managerial) work, such body as a political force; (**Labour**) the Labour Party; pains of childbirth, process of giving birth. **2** *v.* exert oneself, work hard; have difficulty in maintaining normal motion or function; elaborate or work out (a point etc.) in excessive detail; suffer *under* (delusion etc.). **3 labour camp** place where prisoners must work as labourers; **Labour Day** day in honour of workers, often 1 May; **Labour Exchange** *colloq.* or *hist.* employment exchange; **Labour Party** political party representing esp. workers' interests; **labour-saving** designed to reduce or eliminate work. [F f. L *labor -oris*]
laboured *a.* showing signs of effort, not spontaneous.
labourer *n.* person who labours, esp. one employed to do unskilled manual work.
Labrador /'læbrədɔː/ *n.* retriever dog of breed with black or golden coat. [*Labrador* in Canada]
laburnum /lə'bɜːnəm/ *n.* ornamental tree with drooping yellow flowers. [L]
labyrinth /'læbərɪnθ/ *n.* complicated or confusing network of passages; tangled or intricate arrangement; complex cavity of inner ear; **labyrinthine** /læbə'rɪnθaɪn/ *a.* [F or L f. Gk]
lac *n.* resinous substance secreted by SE Asian insect as protective covering. [Hind.]
lace 1 *n.* cord or narrow strip threaded through holes or hooks for fastening or tightening shoes etc.; fabric or trimming in ornamental openwork design. **2** *v.t.* fasten or tighten with lace or laces; pass (cord etc.) *through*; trim with lace; add dash of spirits etc. to (drink); beat, lash. [F f. L *laqueus* noose]
lacerate /'læsəreɪt/ *v.t.* tear roughly (flesh etc.); wound (feelings); **laceration** /-'reɪʃ(ə)n/ *n.* [L (*lacer* torn)]
lachrymal /'lækrɪm(ə)l/ *a.* of tears (*lachrymal duct*). [L *lacrima* tear]
lachrymose /'lækrɪməʊs/ *a.* tearful, given to weeping.
lack 1 *n.* deficiency or want. **2** *v.t.* not have when needed, be without. **3 be lacking** be undesirably absent or deficient (*money is lacking, he is not lacking in courage*). [LG or Du.]
lackadaisical /lækə'deɪzɪk(ə)l/ *a.* languid, unenthusiastic; **lackadaisically** *adv.* [ALACK]
lackey /'lækɪ/ **1** *n.* obsequious follower; humble servant. **2** *v.t.* play lackey to. [F f. Catalan f. Sp.]
lacklustre /'læklʌstə/ *a.* lustreless, dull.
laconic /lə'kɒnɪk/ *a.* terse, using few words; **laconically** *adv.* [L f. Gk (*Lakōn* Spartan)]
lacquer /'lækə/ **1** *n.* hard shiny shellac or synthetic varnish; substance sprayed on hair to keep it in place. **2** *v.t.* coat with lacquer. [F *lacre* = LAC[1]]
lacrosse /lə'krɒs/ *n.* game like hockey with ball carried in crosse. [F (*la* the)]
lactate 1 /læk'teɪt/ *v.i.* secrete milk. **2** /'lækteɪt/ *n.* salt or ester of lactic acid.
lactation /læk'teɪʃ(ə)n/ *n.* suckling, secretion of milk. [L (LACTIC)]
lacteal /'læktɪəl/ **1** *a.* of milk; conveying chyle. **2** *n.* (in *pl.*) chyle-conveying vessels. [f. L *lacteus* (foll.)]
lactic /'læktɪk/ *a.* of milk; **lactic acid** acid found in sour milk. [L *lac lactis* milk]
lactose /'læktəʊs/ *n.* a sugar present in milk.
lacuna /lə'kjuːnə/ *n.* (*pl.* **lacunas, -æ**) gap or missing part, esp. in manuscript. [L (LAKE[1])]
lacy /'leɪsɪ/ *a.* like lace fabric, esp. in fineness. [LACE]
lad *n.* boy, young fellow; *colloq.* man. [orig. unkn.]
ladder 1 *n.* series of horizontal bars fixed between pair of long uprights, used for climbing up or down thing it rests against; vertical ladder-like flaw in stockings etc.; means of progress in career etc. **2** *v.* cause ladder in (stocking etc.), develop ladder. **3 ladder-back** chair with back made of horizontal bars between uprights. [OE]
lade *v.t.* (*p.p.* **laden**) load (ship), ship

(goods); (in *p.p.*) loaded or burdened (*with*); **bill of lading** detailed list of ship's cargo. [OE]

la-di-da /lɑːdɪˈdɑː/ *a. colloq.* pretentious or affected in manner or speech. [imit.]

ladle /ˈleɪd(ə)l/ **1** *n.* deep long-handled spoon for transferring liquids. **2** *v.t.* transfer with ladle. [OE]

lady /ˈleɪdɪ/ *n.* woman of good social standing, (as polite form) any woman; woman of polite or refined disposition; **(Lady)** title used as less formal prefix to name of peeress below duchess, or to Christian name of daughter of duke or marquis or earl, or to surname of wife or widow of baronet or knight; woman with authority in household (*lady of the house*); *archaic* wife; *attrib.* female (*lady doctor*); **the Ladies** (as *sing.*) women's public lavatory; **ladies' man** man fond of women's company; **Lady Chapel** Chapel dedicated to Our Lady; **Lady Day** 25 March; **lady-in-waiting** lady attending royal lady; **lady-killer** man given to making conquests of women; **lady's-maid** personal maidservant of lady; **lady's slipper** flower of orchid family, with flowers shaped like slipper or pouch; **Our Lady** the Virgin Mary. [OE, = loaf-kneader]

ladybird *n.* small round beetle, usu. reddish-brown with black spots.

ladylike *a.* like or appropriate to a lady.

ladyship *n.* title used in addressing or referring to woman with rank of Lady (*Your, Her, Ladyship*).

lag[1] **1** *v.i.* **(-gg-)** go too slow, not keep pace, fall behind others. **2** *n.* lagging, delay; *sl.* convict. [orig. uncert.]

lag[2] **1** *v.t.* **(-gg-)** enclose (boiler etc.) with heat-insulating material. **2** *n.* such material, insulating cover. [ON]

lager /ˈlɑːgə/ *n.* a kind of light beer. [G, = store]

laggard /ˈlægəd/ *n.* person who lags behind, procrastinator.

lagging *n.* material used to lag boiler etc.

lagoon /ləˈguːn/ *n.* salt-water lake separated from sea by sandbank or coral reef etc. [F, It., Sp., f. L LACUNA pool]

lah /lɑː/ *n. Mus.* sixth note of major scale. [L *labii*, word arbitrarily taken]

laicize /ˈleɪɪsaɪz/ *v.t.* make secular. [L f. Gk (LAY[2])]

laid *past* and *p.p.* of LAY[1].

lain *p.p.* of LIE[1].

lair *n.* sheltered place where wild animal habitually rests or eats; *fig.* hiding-place. [OE]

laird *n.* landowner in Scotland. [LORD]

laisser-faire /leɪseɪˈfeə/ *n.* policy of non-interference. [F, = let act]

laity /ˈleɪɪtɪ/ *n.* body of laymen, esp. in Church. [LAY[3]]

lake[1] *n.* large expanse of water surrounded by land; **Lake District** (or **the Lakes**) region round lakes in NW England. [F *lac* f. L *lacus*]

lake[2] *n.* pigment made from dye and mordant. [var. of LAC[1]]

lakh /læk/ *n.* (in India) 100,000 (esp. in *a lakh of rupees*). [Hind. *lākh* f. Skr.]

lam *v.* **(-mm-)** *sl.* hit hard, thrash. [perh. Scand.]

lama /ˈlɑːmə/ *n.* Tibetan or Mongolian Buddhist priest; **Dalai Lama** /ˈdælaɪ/ head lama of Tibet. [Tibetan]

lamasery /ləˈmɑːsərɪ/ *n.* lama monastery. [F]

lamb /læm/ **1** *n.* young sheep; its flesh as food; endearing, innocent, or vulnerable person. **2** *v.* give birth to lamb; (in *pass.*, of lamb) be born; tend (lambing ewes). **3** **The Lamb (of God)** Christ; **lamb's-wool** soft fine wool. [OE]

lambaste /læmˈbeɪst/ *v.t. colloq.* thrash, beat. [LAM, BASTE[1]]

lambda /ˈlæmdə/ *n.* eleventh letter of Greek alphabet (Λ, λ). [Gk]

lambent /ˈlæmbənt/ *a.* (of flame or light) playing about a surface; (of eyes, wit, etc.) gently brilliant; **lambency** *n.* [L *lambo* lick]

lame **1** *a.* (of person or limb) disabled or unable to walk normally, esp. by injury or defect in foot or leg; (of excuse etc.) unconvincing; (of metre) halting. **2** *v.t.* make lame, disable. **3** **lame duck** person or firm unable to cope without help. [OE]

lamé /ˈlɑːmeɪ/ *n.* fabric with gold or silver thread interwoven. [F]

lament /ləˈment/ **1** *n.* passionate expression of grief; elegy. **2** *v.* feel or express grief for or about; utter lament (*over, for*); (in *p.p.*) mourned for. [F or L (*lamentor*)]

lamentable /ˈlæməntəb(ə)l/ *a.* deplorable, regrettable; **lamentably** *adv.*

lamentation /læmenˈteɪʃ(ə)n/ *n.* lament, lamenting.

lamina /ˈlæmɪnə/ *n.* (*pl.* **laminae** /-iː/) thin plate or scale or layer; **laminar** *a.* [L]

laminate **1** /ˈlæmɪneɪt/ *v.* beat or roll into laminae, split into layers, overlay with metal plates, plastic layer, etc. **2** /ˈlæmɪnət/ *n.* laminated structure, esp. of layers fixed together. **3** /-ət/ *a.* in form of lamina or laminae. **4** **lamination** /-ˈneɪʃ(ə)n/ *n.*

Lammas /ˈlæməs/ *n.* first day of August, formerly kept as harvest festival. [OE (LOAF[1], MASS[2])]

lamp *n.* device or vessel for giving light or rays by use of electricity or gas or by

burning oil or spirit. [F f. L f. Gk *lampas* torch]
lampblack *n.* pigment made from soot.
lamplight *n.* light given by lamp.
lamplighter *n.* (usu. *hist.*) man who lights street lamps.
lampoon /læm'pu:n/ **1** *n.* piece of virulent or scurrilous satire on person. **2** *v.t.* write lampoon against. **3 lampoonist** *n.* [F *lampon*]
lamppost *n.* tall post supporting street lamp. [LAMP]
lamprey /'læmprɪ/ *n.* eel-like aquatic animal with sucker mouth. [F *lampreie* f. L *lampreda*]
lampshade *n.* shade placed over lamp.
Lancastrian /læŋ'kæstrɪən/ **1** *a.* of Lancashire or Lancaster; of family descended from John of Gaunt or of its supporters in the Wars of the Roses. **2** *n.* Lancastrian person. [*Lancaster* in Lancashire]
lance /lɑ:ns/ **1** *n.* long spear, esp. one used by horseman. **2** *v.t.* pierce with lance; apply surgical lancet to. **3 lance-corporal** NCO below corporal. [F f. L]
lanceolate /'lænsɪələt/ *a.* shaped like spearhead, tapering to each end.
lancer *n.* soldier of cavalry regiment orig. armed with lances; (in *pl.*) a kind of quadrille, music for this.
lancet /'lɑ:nsɪt/ *n.* surgical instrument with point and two edges for small incisions; narrow pointed arch or window.
land 1 *n.* solid part of earth's surface, not covered by water; ground, soil, expanse of country; this as basis for agriculture, building, etc.; landed property, (in *pl.*) estates; country, nation, State. **2** *v.* set or go ashore from ship etc.; bring (aircraft) to ground or other surface, come down thus; alight after jump etc.; (cause to) reach or find oneself in a certain place or situation (also with *up*); deliver (person blow etc.); present (person *with* problem etc.); bring (fish) to land, *fig.* win (prize), secure (appointment etc.). **3 how the land lies** what is the state of affairs; **land-agent** steward of estate, dealer in estates; **land-girl** woman doing farm-work, esp. in wartime; **land-line** means of telegraphic communication over land; **land-locked** almost or entirely enclosed by land; **land mass** large area of land; **land-mine** explosive mine laid in or on ground; **land on one's feet** overcome difficulty esp. by luck. [OE]
landau /'lændɔ:/ *n.* four-wheeled horse-drawn carriage with divided top. [*Landau* in Germany]
landed *a.* owning much land; consisting of land. [LAND]
landfall *n.* approach to land after sea or air journey.
landing *n.* process of coming or bringing to land; place for disembarking; area at top of flight of stairs or between flights; **landing-craft** naval craft for putting ashore troops and equipment; **landing-gear** undercarriage of aircraft; **landing-stage** platform for disembarking passengers and goods.
landlady *n.* woman landlord.
landless *a.* holding no land.
landlord *n.* person who lets rooms or keeps boarding-house, public house, etc.
landlubber *n.* person with little or no experience of ships and the sea.
landmark *n.* conspicuous and easily recognized feature of landscape; event marking important stage in process or history.
landowner *n.* owner of (esp. much) land.
landscape /'lændskeɪp, -nsk-/ **1** *n.* features of land-area as seen in broad view; picture of this, art of painting such pictures. **2** *v.* lay out or enhance (area of land) with natural features. **3 landscape gardening** laying-out of grounds to imitate natural scenery. [Du. (LAND, -SHIP)]
landslide *n.* landslip; overwhelming majority for one side in election. [LAND]
landslip *n.* sliding down of mass of land on slope or mountain.
landward /'lændwəd/ **1** *adv.* (also **landwards**) towards land. **2** *a.* going or facing towards land. [-WARD]
lane *n.* narrow road or street; passage between rows of people; strip of road for one line of traffic; strip of track or water for competitor in race; regular course followed by ship or aircraft. [OE]
language /'læŋgwɪdʒ/ *n.* words and their use, faculty of speech; system of words prevalent in one or more countries or in a profession etc.; method or style of expression; system of symbols and rules for computer programs; **language laboratory** room with tape-recorders etc. for learning foreign languages. [F f. L *lingua* tongue]
languid /'læŋgwɪd/ *a.* lacking vigour, uninclined to exert oneself; (of stream etc., or *fig.*) slow-moving, slack. [foll.]
languish /'læŋgwɪʃ/ *v.i.* lose or lack vitality; live *under* depressing conditions; pine (*for*). [F or L (*langeo* languish)]
languor /'læŋgə/ *n.* languid state, listlessness; soft or tender mood or effect; oppressive stillness of air; **languorous** *a.*
lank *a.* tall and lean; (of grass, hair, etc.) long and limp. [OE]
lanky *a.* ungracefully lean and tall or long; **lankiness** *n.*
lanolin /'lænəlɪn/ *n.* fat from sheep-

wool used in ointments. [G, f. L *lana* wool, OIL]

lantern /'lænt(ə)n/ *n.* transparent case holding a light and shielding it from wind etc.; light-chamber of lighthouse; erection on top of dome or room, with glazed sides; **lantern jaws** long thin jaws giving face hollow look. [F f. L f. Gk *lamptēr* torch]

lanthanide /'lænθənaɪd/ *n.* element of series from lanthanum or cerium to lutetium, with similar properties. [G (foll.)]

lanthanum /'lænθənəm/ *n.* metallic element, first of lanthanide series. [Gk *lanthanō* escape notice]

lanyard /'lænjəd/ *n.* short rope used on ship for securing or fastening; cord worn round neck or on shoulder to which knife etc. may be attached. [F *laniere*, assim. to YARD[1]]

Laodicean /leɪəʊdɪ'sɪən/ *a.* lacking zeal, esp. in religion or politics. [*Laodicea* in Asia Minor (Rev. 3:16)]

lap[1] **1** *n.* front of sitting person from waist to knees, part of dress covering this; one circuit of race-track etc.; *fig.* section of journey etc.; amount of overlap, overlapping part; single turn of thread etc. round reel etc. **2** *v.* (**-pp-**) be ahead of (competitor in race) by one or more laps; fold or wrap (garment *about* or *round*); enfold (*in* wraps); (esp. in *pass.*) enfold caressingly; cause to overlap. **3 in the lap of the gods** beyond human control; **in the lap of luxury** in great luxury; **in** (or **on**) **person's lap** as his responsibility; **lap-dog** small pet dog; **lap of honour** ceremonial circuit of race-track etc. by winner(s); **lap over** extend beyond (limit). [OE]

lap[2] **1** *v.* (**-pp-**) drink by scooping with the tongue (esp. of dogs and cats); drink (liquid, or *fig.*) greedily (usu. with *up*); (of waves etc.) flow in ripples, make lapping sound. **2** *n.* single act or amount of lapping; sound of wavelets. [OE]

lapel /lə'pel/ *n.* part of either side of coat-front etc. folded back against outer surface. [LAP[1]]

lapidary /'læpɪdərɪ/ **1** *a.* concerned with stones; engraved on stone. **2** *n.* cutter, polisher, or engraver, of gems. [L (*lapis lapid-* stone)]

lapis lazuli /'læpɪs 'læzju:lɪ/ *n.* bright blue gem, mineral, colour, and pigment. [prec. + *lazuli* as AZURE]

Laplander /'læplændə/ *n.* inhabitant of Lapland. [foll.]

Lapp *n.* member of a N. Scandinavian Mongol people; their language. [Sw.]

lappet /'læpɪt/ *n.* flap or fold of garment etc. or flesh; kind of large moth with side-lobed caterpillars. [LAP[1]]

lapse 1 *n.* slight mistake, slip of memory etc.; weak or careless decline to inferior state; passage *of* time. **2** *v.i.* fail to maintain position or standard; fall *back* (*into* inferior or previous state); (of right etc.) become no longer valid because not used or claimed or renewed; (in *p.p.*) that has lapsed. [L *lapsus* (*labor laps-* slip)]

lapwing /'læpwɪŋ/ *n.* peewit. [OE (LEAP, WINK; f. mode of flight)]

larboard /'lɑ:bəd/ *n.* & *a.* = PORT[4]. [orig. *ladboard*, perh. 'side on which cargo was taken in' (LADE)]

larceny /'lɑ:sənɪ/ *n.* theft of personal property; **larcenous** *a.* [AF f. L *latrocinium* (*latro* robber f. Gk)]

larch *n.* deciduous coniferous tree with bright foliage; its wood. [G *larche* f. L *larix*]

lard 1 *n.* pig fat prepared for use in cooking etc. **2** *v.t.* insert strips of bacon in (meat etc.) before cooking; garnish (talk etc.) *with* strange terms etc. [F = bacon, f. L *lardum*]

larder *n.* room or cupboard for storing food.

lardy *a.* like lard; **lardy-cake** cake made with lard, currants, etc.

large *a.* of considerable or relatively great size or extent; of the larger kind (*large intestine*); of wide range, comprehensive; doing thing on large scale (*large farmers*); **at large** at liberty, as a body or whole; with all details, without specific aim; **large-scale** made or occurring on large scale or in large amounts. [F f. L *largus* copious]

largely *adv.* to a great or preponderating extent (*is largely due to*).

largess /lɑ:'dʒes/ *n.* (also **largesse**) money or gifts freely given, esp. on occasion of rejoicing. [F f. Rmc f. L (LARGE)]

largo /'lɑ:gəʊ/ *Mus.* **1** *adv.* in slow tempo with broad dignified treatment. **2** *n.* (*pl.* **largos**) movement to be played this way. [It., = broad]

lariat /'lærɪət/ *n.* tethering rope; lasso. [Sp. *la reata*]

lark[1] *n.* kind of small songbird, esp. the skylark; **get up with the lark** get up early. [OE]

lark[2] *colloq.* **1** *n.* frolic or spree, amusing incident; affair, type of activity, etc. (*dislike this waiting lark*). **2** *v.i.* play (*about*). [orig. uncert.]

larkspur *n.* plant with spur-shaped calyx. [LARK[1]]

larn *v. joc.* var. of LEARN; *colloq.* teach. [dial.]

larrikin /'lærɪkɪn/ *n. Austral.* hooligan. [perh. *Larry* = *Lawrence*]

larva /'lɑ:və/ *n.* (*pl.* **larvae** /-i:/) insect in the stage between egg and pupa (e.g. caterpillar); **larval** *a.* [L, = ghost]

laryngeal /lə'rɪndʒɪəl/ *a.* of the larynx. [LARYNX]

laryngitis /lærɪn'dʒaɪtɪs/ *n.* inflammation of larynx. [foll., -ITIS]

larynx /'lærɪŋks/ *n.* cavity in throat holding vocal cords. [L f. Gk]

lasagne /lə'sænjə/ *n.* pasta in wide ribbon form. [It. pl., f. L *lasanum* cooking-pot]

Lascar /'læskə/ *n.* E. Indian seaman. [ult. Urdu *laškar* army, camp]

lascivious /lə'sɪvɪəs/ *a.* lustful; inciting to lust. [L]

laser /'leɪzə/ *n.* device giving strong beam of radiation in one direction. [*l*ight *a*mplification by *s*timulated *e*mission of *r*adiation]

lash 1 *v.* make sudden violent whiplike movement; pour or rush with great force; strike violently *at* or *against*; beat (with whip etc.); castigate in words; urge as with lash; fasten (*down*, *together*, etc.) with cord etc.; (of rain etc.) beat upon. **2** *n.* stroke with whip etc. (*lit.* or *fig.*); flexible part of whip; eyelash. **3 lash out** hit or speak out angrily, spend extravagantly. [imit.]

lashings *n.pl.sl.* a lot (*of*).

lass *n.* (also dimin. **lassie**) girl (esp. *Sc.*, *N. Engl.*, or *poetic*). [ON]

Lassa fever /'læsə/ acute virus disease, with fever, of tropical Africa. [*Lassa* in Nigeria]

lassitude /'læsɪtju:d/ *n.* languor, disinclination to exert or interest oneself. [F or L (*lassus* weary)]

lasso /læ'su:/ **1** *n.* (*pl.* **lassos**) noosed rope esp. for catching cattle. **2** *v.t.* catch with lasso. [Sp. *lazo* (LACE)]

last[1] /lɑ:st/ **1** *a.* after all others, coming at or belonging to the end; most recent, next before specified time (*last Christmas, Tuesday*; *last week*); only remaining (*our last chance*); least likely or suitable (*the last person I'd ask*); lowest in rank (*the last place*). **2** *adv.* after all others (esp in *comb.*: *last-mentioned*); on the last occasion before the present (*when did you last see him?*); lastly. **3** *n.* person or thing that is last, last-mentioned, most recent, etc.; last mention or sight (*shall never hear the last of it*); *the* end or last moment (*fighting to the last*), death; last performance of certain acts (*breathed his last*). **4 at (long) last** in the end, after much delay; **last ditch** place of final desperate defence; **last minute** (or **moment**) time just before decisive event; **last name** surname; **last rites** rites for dying person; **last straw** addition to burden or difficulty that makes it finally unbearable; **last word** final or definitive statement, latest fashion. [OE, = *latest*]

last[2] /lɑ:st/ *v.* remain unexhausted or adequate or alive for specified or long time (*food to last a week*); continue for specified time (*journey lasts an hour*); **last out** be strong enough or sufficient to last. [OE]

last[3] /lɑ:st/ *n.* shoemaker's model for shaping shoe etc. on; **stick to one's last** not meddle with what one does not understand. [OE]

lasting *a.* permanent, durable. [LAST[2]]

lastly *adv.* finally, in the last place. [LAST[1]]

lat. *abbr.* latitude.

latch 1 *n.* bar with catch and lever as fastening of gate etc.; spring-lock preventing door from being opened from outside without key after being shut. **2** *v.* fasten with latch. **3 latch on to** *colloq.* attach oneself to, understand; **on the latch** fastened by latch only. [OE]

latchkey *n.* key of outer door.

late 1 *a.* (*compar.* **later**, LATTER; *superl.* **latest**, LAST) after the due or usual time, occurring or done etc. thus; far on in day or night or time or period or development; flowering or ripening towards end of season; no longer alive or having specified status (*my late husband*); of recent date. **2** *adv.* after the due or usual time; far on in time, at or till late hour; at late stage of development; formerly but not now (*late of Durham*). **3 late in the day** *colloq.* at late stage in proceedings; **of late** recently. [OE]

lateen /lə'ti:n/ *a.* (of sail) triangular and on long yard at angle of 45° to mast; (of ship) rigged with such a sail. [F (*voile*) *latine* = Latin (sail)]

lately *adv.* in recent times, not long ago. [OE (LATE)]

latent /'leɪtənt/ *a.* concealed, dormant, existing but not developed or manifest; **latent heat** amount of heat lost or gained by substance changing from solid to liquid or from liquid to vapour, without change of temperature; **latency** *n.* [L (*lateo* be hidden)]

lateral /'lætər(ə)l/ **1** *a.* of or at or towards or from the side(s); descended from brother or sister of person in direct line. **2** *n.* lateral shoot or branch. **3 lateral thinking** seeking to solve problems by indirect or illogical methods. **4 laterally** *adv.* [L (*latus later-* side)]

latex /'leɪteks/ *n.* (*pl.* **latexes**) milky fluid of (esp. rubber) plant; synthetic substance like this. [L, = liquid]

lath /lɑ:θ/ *n.* (*pl.* /lɑ:ðz/) thin narrow strip of wood. [OE]

lathe /leɪð/ *n.* machine for shaping wood, metal, etc. by rotating article against cutting tools. [orig. uncert.]

lather /'lɑ:ðə/ **1** *n.* froth of soap etc. and

water; frothy sweat esp. of horse; state of agitation. **2** *v.* (of soap) form lather; cover with lather; thrash. [OE]

Latin /ˈlætɪn/ **1** *n.* language of ancient Rome and its empire. **2** *a.* of or in Latin; of the countries or peoples (e.g. France, Spain) using languages developed from Latin; of the Roman Catholic Church. **3 Latin America** parts of Central & S. America where Spanish or Portuguese is the main language; **Latin Church** Western Church. [F or L (*Latium* district about Rome)]

Latinate /ˈlætɪneɪt/ *a.* like or having character of Latin.

latish *a.* fairly late. [LATE].

latitude /ˈlætɪtjuːd/ *n.* angular distance on meridian, place's angular distance N. or S. of equator, (usu. in *pl.*) regions with reference to distance from equator; freedom from restriction in action or opinion. [L (*latus* broad)]

latitudinarian /lætɪtjuːdɪˈneərɪən/ **1** *a.* liberal, esp. in religion. **2** *n.* latitudinarian person.

latrine /ləˈtriːn/ *n.* communal lavatory, esp. in camp etc. [F f. L *latrina* (*lavo* wash)]

latter *a.* second-mentioned of two, last-mentioned of three or more; nearer to the end (*the latter part of the year*); recent; belonging to end of period, world, etc.; **the latter** (often *absol.*) the latter person or thing; **latter-day** modern, newfangled; **Latter-day Saints** Mormons' name for themselves. [OE, = later]

latterly *adv.* in the later part of life or a period; of late.

lattice /ˈlætɪs/ *n.* structure of crossed laths or bars with spaces between, used as screen, fence, etc.; regular arrangement of atoms or molecules; **lattice window** window with small panes set in diagonally crossing strips of lead. [F *lattis* (*latte* LATH)]

laud /lɔːd/ **1** *v.t.* praise, extol. **2** *n.* praise, hymn of praise; (in *pl.*) first religious service of day. [F f. L (*laus laud-*)]

laudable *a.* commendable; **laudability** /-ˈbɪlɪtɪ/ *n.*; **laudably** *adv.*

laudanum /ˈlɔːdnəm, ˈlɒd-/ *n.* tincture of opium. [L]

laudatory /ˈlɔːdətərɪ/ *a.* praising.

laugh /lɑːf/ **1** *v.* make sounds and movements usual in expressing lively amusement, scorn, etc.; utter with a laugh. **2** *n.* sound or act or manner of laughing; *colloq.* comical thing. **3 laugh at** ridicule; **laugh in** (or **up**) **one's sleeve** laugh secretly; **laugh off** get rid of (embarrassment or humiliation) with a jest. [OE]

laughable *a.* ludicrous, amusing; **laughably** *adv.*

laughing *n.* laughter; **laughing-gas** nitrous oxide as anaesthetic, with exhilarating effect when inhaled; **laughing-stock** person or thing generally ridiculed; **no laughing matter** serious thing.

laughter /ˈlɑːftə/ *n.* act or sound of laughing. [OE]

launch[1] /lɔːntʃ/ **1** *v.* set (vessel) afloat; hurl, send forth (weapon, rocket, etc.); start or set in motion (enterprise, person, etc.); go *forth* or *out* on an enterprise; burst (usu. *out*) *into* strong language etc. **2** *n.* launching of ship, rocket, etc. [AN *launcher* (LANCE)]

launch[2] /lɔːntʃ/ *n.* large motor-boat; man-of-war's largest boat. [Sp. *lancha*]

launcher *n.* structure to hold rocket etc. during launching. [LAUNCH[1]]

launder /ˈlɔːndə/ *v.* wash and iron (clothes etc.); transfer (funds) so as to conceal their illegal origin. [F (LAVE)]

launderette /lɔːnˈdret/ *n.* establishment with coin-operated automatic washing-machines for public use.

laundress /ˈlɔːndrɪs/ *n.* woman who launders, esp. professionally.

laundry /ˈlɔːndrɪ/ *n.* place for washing clothes; batch of clothes to be laundered. [F (LAUNDER)]

laureate /ˈlɒrɪət, ˈlɔː-/ **1** *a.* wreathed with laurel as honour. **2** *n.* = *Poet Laureate*. **3 laureateship** *n.* [foll.]

laurel /ˈlɒr(ə)l/ *n.* an evergreen shrub with dark glossy leaves; (in *sing.* or *pl.*) wreath of bay-leaves as emblem of victory or poetic merit (*win laurels* or *the laurel*); **look to one's laurels** take care not to lose pre-eminence; **rest on one's laurels** not seek further success. [F f. Prov. f. L *laurus* bay]

laurelled *a.* wreathed with laurel.

lav *n. colloq.* lavatory. [abbr.]

lava /ˈlɑːvə/ *n.* matter flowing from volcano and solidifying as it cools. [It. f. L *lavo* wash]

lavatory /ˈlævətərɪ, -trɪ/ *n.* receptacle for urine and faeces, usu. with means of disposal; room, building, or compartment with this; **lavatory paper** = *toilet paper*. [L (prec.)]

lave *v.t. literary* wash or bathe; (of water) wash against, flow along. [F f. L *lavo* wash]

lavender /ˈlævɪndə/ *n.* shrub with fragrant light purple flowers, these dried and used to scent linen etc.; light purple; **lavender-water** a light perfume. [AF f. L *lavandula*]

laver /ˈleɪvə, ˈlɑː-/ *n.* edible seaweed. [L]

lavish /ˈlævɪʃ/ **1** *v.t.* bestow or spend (money, effort, praise, etc.) abundantly. **2** *a.* giving or producing in large quantities, profuse (*of* praise etc., *in* giving etc.). [F *lavasse* deluge (LAVE)]

law *n.* rule enacted or customary in a community and recognized as enjoining or prohibiting certain actions; body of such rules; controlling influence of or obedience to this; such rules as a social system or subject of study, branch of this subject; *the* legal profession, *colloq. the* police; (in *pl.*) jurisprudence; judicial remedy, lawcourts providing it (*go to law*); divine commandment; rule of action or procedure; regularity in natural occurrences or phenomena, statement of perceived instance of this (*laws of nature*; *law of gravity*); binding injunction (*his word is law*); **be a law unto oneself** do what one feels is right, disregard custom; **law-abiding** obedient to the laws; **Law Lord** member of House of Lords qualified to perform its legal work; **lay down the law** be dogmatic or authoritarian; **take the law into one's own hands** redress grievance by one's own means, esp. by force. [OE f. N, = thing laid down]

lawcourt *n.* court of law (see COURT).

lawful *a.* conforming with or recognized by law; not illegal or (of child) illegitimate; **lawfully** *adv.*

lawgiver *n.* one who codifies body of laws.

lawless *a.* having no laws or no enforcement of them; disregarding laws, unbridled.

lawmaker *n.* legislator.

lawn[1] *n.* piece of grass kept mown and smooth in garden etc.; **lawn-mower** *n.* machine for cutting the grass of lawns; **lawn tennis** tennis played with soft ball on outdoor grass or hard court. [*laund* glade f. F f. Celt.]

lawn[2] *n.* fine linen or cotton. [*Laon* in France]

lawrencium /ləˈrensɪəm/ *n.* artificially produced transuranic metallic element. [*Lawrence*, physicist]

lawsuit *n.* prosecution of claim in lawcourt. [LAW]

lawyer /ˈlɔːjə, ˈlɔɪə/ *n.* person pursuing law as a profession; solicitor; expert at law. [LAW]

lax *a.* not strict, careless, slack; **laxity** *n.* [L *laxus* loose]

laxative /ˈlæksətɪv/ **1** *a.* tending to cause or facilitate evacuation of the bowels. **2** *n.* medicine for this. [F or L (prec.)]

lay[1] **1** *v.* (past and p.p. **laid**) place on a surface esp. horizontally or in proper or specified place; put or bring into required position or state (*lay carpet*); make by laying (*lay foundations*); locate (scene); (of hen bird) produce (egg, or *absol.*); cause to subside or lie flat; put down as wager, stake; impose (penalty or obligation or blame) *on*; apply (stress or emphasis) *on*; prepare or make ready (plan or trap); prepare (table) for meal; place or arrange fuel for (fire); cause to subside or lie flat (*storm has laid the corn*); coat or strew (surface) *with* material; *sl.* have sexual intercourse with (woman). **2** *n.* way or position or direction in which something lies; *sl.* woman partner in sexual intercourse. **3 in lay** (of hen) laying eggs regularly; **laid paper** paper with surface marked in fine ribs; **laid up** confined to bed or house; **lay about one** hit out on all sides; **lay a charge** make accusation; **lay aside** put to one side, cease to think of; **lay at the door of** impute to; **lay bare** expose, reveal; **lay claim to** claim as one's own; **lay down** put on ground, give up (office), formulate (rule), store (wine) in cellar, sacrifice (one's life); **lay one's hands on** obtain, acquire, be able to find; **lay hands on** seize or attack; **lay hold of** seize or grasp; **lay in** provide oneself with stock of; **lay into** *sl.* punish or scold harshly; **lay it on thick** (or **with a trowel**) *sl.* exaggerate greatly; **lay low** overthrow or humble; **lay off** discharge (workers) temporarily from shortage of work, *colloq.* desist; **lay-off** *n.* temporary discharge of workers; **lay on** provide or impose, inflict (blows), spread on (paint etc.); **lay open** break skin of, expose (*to* criticism etc.); **lay out** spread, expose to view, prepare (body) for burial, *colloq.* knock (person) unconscious, dispose (grounds etc.) according to a plan; **lay oneself out to** take pains to; **lay to rest** bury in grave; **lay up** store or save; **lay waste** ravage, destroy. [OE]

lay[2] *a.* non-clerical; not ordained into the clergy; not professionally qualified, esp. in law or medicine, of or done by such persons; **lay reader** layman licensed to conduct some religious services. [F f. L f. Gk (*laos* people)]

lay[3] *n.* minstrel's song, ballad. [F]

lay[4] *past* of LIE[1].

layabout *n.* habitual loafer or idler. [LAY[1]]

lay-by *n.* (*pl.* **lay-bys**) extra strip at side of open road for vehicles to park on.

layer 1 *n.* a thickness of matter, esp. one of several, spread over a surface; person etc. that lays; a shoot fastened down to take root while attached to the parent plant. **2** *v.t.* arrange, cut (hair), in layers; propagate (plant) as layer. [LAY[1]]

layette /leɪˈet/ *n.* clothes etc. prepared for new-born child. [F f. Du.]

lay figure jointed figure of human body used by artists for arranging drapery on etc.; unreal character in novel etc.; person lacking in individuality. [Du. (*led* joint)]

layman *n.* person not in holy orders; person without professional or special knowledge. [LAY²]

layout *n.* disposing or arrangement of ground, printed matter, etc.; thing arranged thus. [LAY¹]

layshaft *n.* second or intermediate transmission-shaft in machine.

laze 1 *v.i. colloq.* spend time doing nothing or relaxing. 2 *n.* spell of lazing. [back-form. f. LAZY]

lazy *a.* disinclined to work, doing little work; of or inducing idleness; **lazy-bones** lazy person; **lazily** *adv.*; **laziness** *n.* [perh. f. LG]

lb. *abbr.* pound(s) weight. [L *libra*]

l.b.w. *abbr.* leg before wicket.

l.c. *abbr.* in the passage etc. cited [L *loco citato*]; lower case.

LCM *abbr.* lowest common multiple.

L/Cpl. *abbr.* Lance-Corporal.

Ld. *abbr.* Lord.

lea *n. poetic* piece of meadow or pasture or arable land. [OE]

LEA *abbr.* Local Education Authority.

leach *v.t.* make (liquid) percolate through some material; subject (bark, ore, ash, soil) to action of percolating fluid; purge *away* or *out* thus. [OE]

lead¹ /li:d/ 1 *v.* (*past* and *p.p.* **led**) cause to go with one, guide or help to go, esp. by going in front or by taking person's hand or animal's halter etc.; direct the actions or opinions of, guide by persuasion or example or argument (*what led you to think that?*); provide access, bring (person, or *absol.*), *to* or *into* (*door leads into a small room*; *road leads to Lincoln*); pass or go through (life etc. of specified kind); have first place in, go first, be first in race or game; be in charge of (*leads a team of researchers*), be pre-eminent in some field; play (card, or *absol.*) as first player in trick, play one of (suit) thus; make (water etc.) go along certain course. 2 *n.* guidance given by going in front, example; leader's place (*has taken the lead*); amount by which competitor is ahead of others; clue (*first real lead in the case*); strap or cord for leading dog etc.; conductor (usu. a wire) conveying electric current to place of use; chief part in play etc., player of this; (in cards) act or right of playing first, card so played. 3 **lead by the nose** cajole (person) into compliance; **lead off** begin; **lead on** entice; **lead to** result in; **lead up the garden path** mislead; **lead up to** form preparation for or introduction to, direct conversation towards. [OE]

lead² /led/ 1 *n.* a heavy soft grey metallic element; graphite used in pencils, stick of this; lump of lead used for taking soundings in water; (in *pl.*) strips of lead covering roof, piece of lead-covered roof, lead frames holding glass of lattice etc.; metal strip in printing to give space between lines; *attrib.* made of lead. 2 *v.t.* cover or weight or frame or space with lead(s). 3 **lead pencil** pencil of graphite enclosed in wood; **lead-poisoning** acute or chronic poisoning by taking of lead into the body. [OE]

leaden /'led(ə)n/ *a.* of or like lead; heavy or slow; lead-coloured.

leader *n.* person or thing that leads, person followed by others; principal player in music group or of first violins in orchestra; leading article; shoot of plant at apex of stem or main branch; **leadership** *n.* [LEAD¹]

leading¹ *a.* chief, most important; **leading aircraftman** one ranking just below NCO; **leading article** newspaper-article giving editorial opinion; **leading light** prominent and influential person; **leading note** seventh note of diatonic scale; **leading question** one prompting desired answer.

leading² /'ledɪŋ/ *n.* covering or framework of lead. [LEAD²]

leaf 1 *n.* (*pl.* **leaves**) broad flat usu. green part of plant often on a stem; *collect.* leaves; state of having leaves out (*tree in leaf*); single thickness of paper, esp. in book with each side forming a page; very thin sheet of metal etc.; hinged flap of table etc.; extra section inserted to extend table. 2 *v.* put forth leaves. 3 **leaf-insect** insect with wings like plant-leaf; **leaf-mould** soil chiefly of decaying leaves; **leaf through** turn over pages of (book etc.). 4 **leafy** *a.* [OE]

leafage *n.* leaves of plants.

leaflet /'li:flɪt/ *n.* division of compound leaf, young leaf; sheet of paper (sometimes folded but not stitched) giving information, esp. for free distribution.

league¹ /li:g/ 1 *n.* people, countries, etc., combining for particular purpose; agreement to combine in this way; group of sports clubs which contend for championship; class of contestants. 2 *v.* join in league. 3 **in league** allied, conspiring. [F or It. f. L *ligo* bind]

league² /li:g/ *n. archaic* varying measure of travelling-distance, usu. about 3 miles. [L f. Celt.]

leak 1 *n.* hole through which liquid etc. passes wrongly in or out; liquid etc. passing through thus; similar escape of electric charge; the charge that escapes; disclosure of secret information. 2 *v.*

escape, let liquid etc. escape, out or in through opening; disclose (secret); **leak out** become known; **leaky** *a.* [LG or Du.]

leakage *n.* action or result of leaking.

lean[1] **1** *v.t.* (*past* and *p.p.* **leaned** or **leant** /lent/) be in or put in sloping position, incline from the perpendicular (*lean back, forward, out, over*, etc.); rest *against, on, upon*, for support; rely *on* or *upon*; be inclined or partial, have tendency, *to* or *towards*. **2** *n.* deviation from perpendicular, inclination. **3 lean on** *sl.* put pressure on (person) to make him co-operate; **lean over backwards** see BACKWARDS; **lean-to** building with roof resting against larger building or wall. [OE]

lean[2] **1** *a.* (of person or animal) thin, having no superfluous fat; (of meat) containing little fat; meagre. **2** *n.* lean part of meat. **3 lean years** period of scarcity. [OE]

leaning *n.* tendency or partiality. [LEAN[1]]

leap 1 *v.* (*past* and *p.p.* **leaped** /li:pt, lept/ or **leapt** /lept/) jump or spring forcefully. **2** *n.* forceful jump. **3 by leaps and bounds** with startlingly rapid progress; **leap in the dark** rash step or enterprise; **leap year** year with 366 days (including 29 Feb. as intercalary day). [OE]

leap-frog 1 *n.* game in which players in turn vault with parted legs over another who is bending down. **2** *v.* (**-gg-**) perform such a vault (over); *fig.* overtake alternately.

learn /lɜ:n/ *v.* (*past* and *p.p.* **learned** /lɜ:nd, lɜ:nt/, **learnt**) gain knowledge of, or skill in, by study, experience, or being taught; commit to memory; receive instruction, be informed (*of*), find out (*that, how*, etc.); *archaic* or *vulgar* teach. [OE]

learned /ˈlɜ:nɪd/ *a.* having much knowledge acquired by study; showing or requiring learning (*learned book*); concerned with interests of learned persons (*a learned society*).

learner *n.* one who is learning a subject or skill; **learner driver** one who is learning to drive a motor vehicle but has not yet passed driving test.

learning *n.* knowledge acquired by study.

lease 1 *n.* contract by which the owner of a building or land allows another to use it for a specified time, usu. in return for payment. **2** *v.t.* grant or take on lease. **3 a new lease of** (or *US* **on**) **life** improved prospect of living or of use after repair. [AF *les* (*lesser* let f. L *laxo* loosen)]

leasehold *n.* holding of property, or property held, by lease; **leaseholder** *n.*

leash 1 *n.* thong for holding dog; dog's lead. **2** *v.t.* put leash on; restrain. **3 straining at the leash** eager to begin. [F *lesse* (LEASE)]

least 1 *a.* smallest, slightest; very small (species or variety). **2** *n.* least amount. **3** *adv.* in the least degree. **4 at least** at all events, anyway, not less than; (**in**) **the least** at all (*not* (*in*) *the least offended*); **least common denominator, multiple** see DENOMINATOR, MULTIPLE; **to say the least** (**of it**) putting the case moderately. [OE, superl. of LESS]

leather /ˈleðə/ **1** *n.* material made from skin of animal by tanning etc.; leather cloth for polishing with; leather part(s) of something; *sl.* cricket-ball or football; *pl.* leggings, breeches. **2** *v.t.* cover with leather; polish or wipe with leather; beat, thrash. **3 leather-back** largest existing turtle with flexible shell; **leather-jacket** crane-fly grub with tough skin. [OE]

leathercloth *n.* strong fabric coated to resemble leather.

leatherette /leðəˈret/ *n.* imitation leather.

leathery *a.* like leather; tough.

leave[1] *v.* (*past* and *p.p.* **left**) go away (from), depart; cause to or let remain, depart without taking; cease to reside at or belong to or work for; abandon, forsake, desert; have remaining after one's death (*leaves a wife and two children*); bequeath; allow (person or thing) *to do* something without interference or assistance; commit or refer *to* someone else (*leave that to me*); abstain from consuming or dealing with, (in *pass.*) remain (*over*); deposit or entrust for attention, collection, etc., depute (person) to perform function in one's absence; cause to be or let remain in specified state (*left the door open*; *performance left her unmoved*); **leave alone** refrain from disturbing, not interfere with; **leave off** discontinue, come to or make an end; **leave out** omit; **left luggage** luggage deposited for later retrieval; **left-overs** *pl.* items (esp. food) remaining after rest has been used. [OE]

leave[2] *n.* permission; permission to be absent from duty, period for which this lasts; **on leave** legitimately absent from duty; **take (one's) leave (of)** bid farewell (to); **take leave of one's senses** go mad. [OE]

leaved *a.* having (esp. specified number of) leaves (*four-leaved clover*). [LEAF]

leaven /ˈlev(ə)n/ **1** *n.* substance (esp. yeast) used to make dough ferment and rise; *fig.* pervasive transforming influence, admixture *of* some quality. **2** *v.t.* ferment (dough) with leaven; permeate

and transform, modify *with* tempering element. [F f. L (*levo* raise)]
leaves *pl.* of LEAF.
leavings *n.pl.* things left over, esp. as worthless. [LEAVE[1]]
Lebanese /lebə'ni:z/ **1** *a.* of Lebanon. **2** *n.* (*pl.* same) native of Lebanon. [*Lebanon* in SW Asia]
lecher /'letʃə/ *n.* lecherous man, debauchee. [F *lecheor* f. Gmc (LICK)]
lecherous *a.* lustful, having strong or excessive sexual desire.
lechery *n.* unrestrained indulgence of sexual desire.
lectern /'lektз:n/ *n.* desk for holding bible or hymn-book in church; similar desk for lecturer etc. [F f. L (*lectrum* f. *lego* read)]
lectionary /'lekʃənərɪ/ *n.* list of portions of Scripture appointed to be read in churches. [med.L (prec.)]
lecture /'lektʃə/ **1** *n.* discourse giving information about subject to class or other audience; long serious speech esp. as scolding or reprimand. **2** *v.* deliver lecture(s); talk seriously or reprovingly to (a person). **3 lectureship** *n.* [F or L (prec.)]
lecturer *n.* one who lectures, esp. as university teacher.
led *past* & *p.p.* of LEAD[1].
ledge *n.* narrow horizontal projection or shelf. [orig. uncert.]
ledger *n.* tall narrow book in which a firm's accounts are kept. [Du.]
lee *n.* shelter given by neighbouring object (*under the lee of*); (in full **lee side**) sheltered side, side away from wind; **lee shore** shore to leeward of ship. [OE]
leech *n.* blood-sucking worm formerly used medicinally for bleeding; *fig.* person who sponges on another. [OE]
leek *n.* vegetable of onion family with cylindrical white bulb; this as Welsh national emblem. [OE]
leer 1 *v.i.* look slyly or lasciviously or maliciously. **2** *n.* leering look. [perh. obs. *leer* cheek]
leery *a.* knowing, sly, wary *of*.
lees /li:z/ *n.pl.* sediment of wine etc.; dregs. [F]
leeward /'li:wəd, *Naut.* 'lu:əd/ **1** *a.* & *adv.* on or towards the sheltered side. **2** *n.* leeward side or region. [LEE]
leeway *n.* ship's sideways drift leeward of desired course; allowable deviation or freedom of action.
left[1] **1** *a.* on or towards side of human body which corresponds to the position of west if one regards oneself as facing north; on or towards part of thing analogous to person's left side; politically of the left. **2** *adv.* on or to the left side. **3** *n.* left-hand part, region, or direction; left hand, blow with this; (often **Left**) political group or section favouring radical socialism, such radicals collectively. **4 have two left feet** be clumsy; **left bank** bank of river on left facing downstream; **left-hand** on or towards left side of person or thing; **left-handed** using left hand by preference as more serviceable, made by or for the left hand, turning to the left, awkward or clumsy, (of compliment) ambiguous, of doubtful sincerity; **left-hander** left-handed person or blow; **left wing** left side of football etc. team on field, left section of political party; **left-winger** person on left wing. [OE, orig. = weak, worthless]
left[2] *past* and *p.p.* of LEAVE[1].
leftism *n.* radical socialism; **leftist** *n.* [LEFT[1]]
leftmost *a.* furthest to the left.
leftward /'leftwəd/ **1** *adv.* (also **leftwards**) towards the left. **2** *a.* going towards or facing the left. [-WARD]
lefty *a. colloq.* left-winger in politics; left-handed person. [LEFT[1]]
leg *n.* each of the limbs on which a person or animal walks and stands; leg of animal as food; artificial leg; part of garment covering leg; support of chair, table, etc.; part of cricket field on side where striker places his feet; one section of a journey; each of several stages in competition etc.; one branch of forked object; *Naut.* run made on single tack; **give person a leg up** help him to mount horse etc. or get over obstacle or difficulty; **leg before wicket** (of batsman) out because of illegal obstruction of ball with part of body other than hand; **leg it** walk or run hard; **leg-pull** hoax; **not have a leg to stand on** be unable to support argument by facts or sound reasons; **on one's last legs** near death or end of usefulness etc.; **-legged** /legd, 'legɪd/ *a.* [ON]
legacy /'legəsɪ/ *n.* gift left in a will; something handed down by predecessor (*legacy of corruption*). [F f. L (*lego* bequeath, commit)]
legal /'li:g(ə)l/ *a.* of or based on law, concerned with, appointed or required or permitted, by law; **legal aid** payment from public funds for legal advice or proceedings; **legal separation** see SEPARATION; **legal tender** currency that cannot legally be refused in payment of debt; **legality** /lɪ'gælɪtɪ/ *n.*; **legally** /'li:gəlɪ/ *adv.* [F or L (*lex leg-* law)]
legalism *n.* excessive adherence to law or formula; **legalist** *n.*; **legalistic** /-'lɪstɪk/ *a.*
legalize /'li:gəlaɪz/ *v.t.* make lawful,

bring into harmony with law; **legalization** /-ˈzeɪʃ(ə)n/ *n.*

legate /ˈlegət/ *n.* ambassador (now only of Pope). [F f. L (*lego* depute)]

legatee /legəˈtiː/ *n.* recipient of legacy. [L *lego* bequeath]

legation /lɪˈgeɪʃ(ə)n/ *n.* body of deputies; diplomatic minister (esp. below ambassadorial rank) and his staff; diplomatic minister's residence; legateship. [L (LEGATE)]

legato /lɪˈgɑːtəʊ/ *Mus.* **1** *adv.* & *a.* in smooth manner. **2** *n.* (*pl.* **legatos**) smooth playing or passage. [It. = bound (L *ligo* bind)]

legend /ˈledʒənd/ *n.* story (true or invented) handed down from the past, myth; such stories collectively; inscription on coin or medal; caption; explanation on map etc. of symbols used. [F f. L *legenda* things to be read]

legendary *a.* of, based on, described in, a legend; *colloq.* remarkable, famous. [med.L (prec.)]

legerdemain /ledʒədəˈmeɪn/ *n.* sleight of hand, juggling; trickery, sophistry. [F, = light of hand]

leger line /ˈledʒə/ *Mus.* short line added for notes above or below range of staff. [var. of LEDGER]

legging *n.* (usu. in *pl.*) protective outer covering of leather etc. for leg from knee to ankle. [LEG]

leggy *a.* long-legged; **legginess** *n.*

leghorn /ˈleghɔːn, lɪˈgɔːn/ *n.* fine plaited straw; hat of this; (**Leghorn**) breed of domestic fowl. [*Leghorn* (*Livorno*) in Italy]

legible /ˈledʒɪb(ə)l/ *a.* clear enough to read, readable; **legibility** /-ˈbɪlɪtɪ/ *n.*; **legibly** *adv.* [L (*lego* read)]

legion /ˈliːdʒ(ə)n/ *n.* division of 3,000–6,000 men in ancient Roman army; other large organized body. [F f. L *legio -onis*]

legionary **1** *a.* of legion(s). **2** *n.* legionnaire.

legionnaire /liːdʒəˈneə/ *n.* member of legion; **legionnaires' disease** form of bacterial pneumonia first identified after outbreak at American Legion meeting in 1976. [F (LEGION)]

legislate /ˈledʒɪsleɪt/ *v.i.* make laws; **legislator** *n.* [foll.]

legislation /ledʒɪsˈleɪʃ(ə)n/ *n.* law-making; laws made. [L *lex legis* law, *latus* p.p. of *fero* carry]

legislative /ˈledʒɪslətɪv/ *a.* of or empowered to make legislation.

legislature /ˈledʒɪsleɪtʃə/ *n.* legislative body of a State.

legitimate /lɪˈdʒɪtɪmət/ *a.* (of child) born of parents married to each other; lawful, proper, regular, conforming to standard type; logically acceptable (*legitimate excuse*); **legitimate theatre** plays of established merit, plays containing spoken lines only as opposed to musical comedy etc.; **legitimacy** *n.* [L *legitimo* legitimize (*lex legis* law)]

legitimatize /lɪˈdʒɪtɪmətaɪz/ *v.t.* legitimize.

legitimize /lɪˈdʒɪtɪmaɪz/ *v.t.* make legitimate; serve as justification for; **legitimization** /-ˈzeɪʃ(ə)n/ *n.*

legume /ˈlegjuːm/ *n.* leguminous plant, fruit or edible part or pod of this. [F f. L *legumen -minis* pulse, bean (*lego* pick, gather, as being picked by hand)]

leguminous /lɪˈgjuːmɪnəs/ *a.* of family of plants with seeds in pods (e.g. peas, beans).

lei /ˈleɪiː/ *n.* Polynesian garland of flowers. [Hawaiian]

leisure /ˈleʒə/ *n.* free time, time at one's disposal, enjoyment of this; **at leisure** not occupied, in unhurried manner; **at one's leisure** when one has time. [AF *leisour* f. L *licet* it is allowed]

leisured *a.* having ample leisure.

leisurely **1** *a.* unhurried, relaxed. **2** *adv.* without hurry. **3 leisureliness** *n.*

leitmotiv /ˈlaɪtməʊtiːf/ *n.* (also **leitmotif**) theme associated throughout musical etc. composition with particular person or idea. [G (LEAD[1], MOTIVE)]

lemming /ˈlemɪŋ/ *n.* small arctic rodent renowned for rushing into sea and drowning during migration. [Norw.]

lemon[1] /ˈlemən/ *n.* pale-yellow oval fruit with acid juice; tree bearing it; lemon colour; *sl.* simpleton, something disappointing or unsuccessful; **lemon cheese** (or **curd**) thick creamy spread made from lemons; **lemony** *a.* [F *limon* f. Arab. (as LIME[2])]

lemon[2] /ˈlemən/ *n.* (in full **lemon sole**) a kind of plaice. [F *limande*]

lemonade /leməˈneɪd/ *n.* drink made from lemon-juice or synthetic substitute. [LEMON[1]]

lemur /ˈliːmə/ *n.* nocturnal mammal of Madagascar allied to monkeys. [L *lemures* ghosts]

lend *v.t.* (*past* and *p.p.* **lent**) grant (*to* person) use of (thing) on understanding that it or its equivalent shall be returned; allow use of (money) at interest; bestow or contribute (*lends a certain charm*); **lend an ear** listen; **lend a hand** help; **lend itself to** (of thing) be suitable for; **lend oneself to** accommodate oneself to. [OE (LOAN[1])]

length *n.* measurement or extent from end to end in space or time; distance thing extends; length of horse, boat, etc., as measure of lead in race; long stretch or extent; degree of thoroughness in action (*went to great lengths*); piece of certain length (*length of cloth*); quantity of vowel or syllable; (in cricket) distance from batsman at which ball pitches, proper amount of this; **at length** in detail, after a long time. [OE (LONG)]

lengthen *v.* make or become longer.

lengthways *adv.* (also **lengthwise**) in a direction parallel with a thing's length.

lengthy *a.* of unusual length; long and tedious; **lengthily** *adv.*; **lengthiness** *n.*

lenient /'li:nɪənt/ *a.* merciful, not severe, mild; **lenience** *n.*; **leniency** *n.* [L (*lenis* mild)]

lenity /'lenɪtɪ/ *n.* gentleness, mercifulness. [F or L (prec.)]

lens /lenz/ *n.* piece of transparent substance with one or both sides curved for concentrating or dispersing light-rays in optical instruments; combination of lenses in photography; transparent substance behind iris of eye. [L *lens lent-* lentil (from similarity of shape)]

Lent[1] *n.* period of fasting and penitence from Ash Wednesday to Easter Eve; **Lenten** *a.* [OE, = spring]

lent[2] *past* and *p.p.* of LEND.

lentil /'lentɪl/ *n.* a kind of leguminous plant; its edible seed. [F *lentille* f. L (LENS)]

lento /'lentəʊ/ *a.* & *adv. Mus.* slow, slowly. [It.]

Leo /'li:əʊ/ *n.* constellation and fifth sign of Zodiac. [OE f. L (LION)]

leonine /'li:ənaɪn/ *a.* of or like a lion. [F or L (prec.)]

leopard /'lepəd/ *n.* large African and S. Asian carnivorous animal of cat family with dark-spotted yellowish-fawn or black coat, panther. [F f. L f. Gk (*leōn* lion, *pardos* panther)]

leotard /'li:ətɑ:d/ *n.* close-fitting one-piece garment worn by dancers etc. [*Léotard*, trapeze artist]

leper /'lepə/ *n.* person with leprosy; *fig.* person shunned on moral grounds. [F *lepre* leprosy f. L f. Gk (*lepros* scaly)]

lepidopterous /lepɪ'dɒptərəs/ *a.* of the Lepidoptera or insects with four scale-covered wings including moths and butterflies; **lepidopterist** *n.* [Gk *lepis -idos* scale, *pteron* wing]

leprechaun /'leprəkɔ:n/ *n.* small mischievous sprite in Irish folklore. [Ir. (*lu* small, *corp* body)]

leprosy /'leprəsɪ/ *n.* chronic infectious disease of skin and nerves causing mutilations and deformities; **leprous** *a.* [LEPER]

lesbian /'lezbɪən/ **1** *n.* homosexual woman. **2** *a.* of homosexuality in women. **3 lesbianism** *n.* [*Lesbos*, island in Aegean]

lese-majesty /li:z'mædʒɪstɪ/ *n.* treason; insult to sovereign or ruler; presumptuous conduct. [F *lèse-majesté* f. L, = injured sovereignty]

lesion /'li:ʒ(ə)n/ *n.* damage; injury; morbid change in action or texture of an organ. [F f. L (*laedo laes-* injure)]

less 1 *a.* smaller in size, degree, duration, number, etc.; of smaller quantity, not so much (*less sugar*); (D) fewer (*less biscuits*). **2** *adv.* to smaller extent, in lower degree. **3** *n.* smaller amount or quantity or number (*cannot take less*; *for less than £10*). **4** *prep.* minus, deducting (*made £1,000 less tax*). [OE]

-less *suffix* forming adjectives and adverbs from nouns, in sense 'not having, without, free from' (*doubtless, powerless*) and from verbs, in sense 'unable to be —ed', 'not —ing' (*fathomless, tireless*). [OE]

lessee /le'si:/ *n.* person holding property by lease, tenant. [F (LEASE)]

lessen *v.* make or become less, diminish. [LESS]

lesser *a.* (usu. *attrib.*) not so great as the other or the rest (*the lesser evil*; *the lesser celandine*).

lesson /'les(ə)n/ *n.* spell of teaching; (in *pl.*) systematic instruction *in* subject; thing learnt by pupil; experience that serves to warn or encourage (*let that be a lesson to you*); passage from Bible read aloud during church service. [F *leçon* f. L (*lego lect-*)]

lessor /le'sɔ:/ *n.* person who lets a property by lease. [AF (LEASE)]

lest *conj.* in order that not, for fear that (*lest we forget*); that (*afraid lest we should be late*). [OE (LESS)]

let[1] **1** *v.* (-tt-; *past* and *p.p.* **let**) allow or enable or cause to, not prevent or forbid; allow or cause to pass *in* or *out* (*let the dog in*); grant use of (rooms, land, etc.) for rent or hire; allow or cause (liquid or air) to escape (*let blood*); award (contract for work); as auxiliary verb (with 1st and 3rd persons) expressing commands, appeals, etc. (*let us*, colloq. *let's, go*; *let it be done*; *let AB be equal to CD*; *just let him try*). **2** *n.* act of letting house, room, etc. (*a long let*). **3 let alone** apart from, far less or more (*difficult in French, let alone German*); **let alone** (or **be**) not interfere with, attend to, or do; **let down** lower, fail to support or satisfy, disappoint, lengthen (garment); **let-down** *n.* disappointment; **let down gently** not treat too severely; **let drop** (or **fall**) drop (esp. word or hint) intentionally or by accident; **let go** release, loose one's hold *of*, lose hold of; **let oneself go** abandon self-restraint; **let person in for** involve him in (loss or difficulty); **let loose** release, unchain; **let off** fire (gun) or explode (bomb), allow or cause (steam etc.) to escape, not punish or compel, punish *with* light penalty, excuse (person penalty or obligation); **let off steam** release pent-up energy or feeling; **let on** *colloq.* reveal secret, pretend; **let out** release from restraint, reveal (secret etc.), make (garment) looser, put out to rent or to contract; **let-out** *n.* opportunity to escape; **let up** *colloq.* become less intense or severe, relax one's efforts; **let-up** *n.* reduction in intensity, relaxation of effort; **to let** available for rent. [OE]

let[2] **1** *n.* obstruction of ball or player in tennis etc., requiring ball to be served again. **2** *v.t.* (-tt-; *past* and *p.p.* **letted** or **let**) *archaic* hinder, obstruct. **3 without let or hindrance** unimpeded. [OE]

-let *suffix* forming nouns usu. diminutive (*flatlet*) or denoting articles of ornament or dress (*anklet*). [F]

lethal /'li:θ(ə)l/ *a.* causing or sufficient to cause death; **lethally** *adv.* [L (*lethum* death)]

lethargy /'leθədʒɪ/ *n.* lack of energy or vitality; morbid drowsiness; **lethargic** /lɪ'θɑ:dʒɪk/ *a.*; **lethargically** /lɪ'θɑ:dʒɪkəlɪ/ *adv.* [F f. L f. Gk (*lēthargos* forgetful)]

letter 1 *n.* any of the symbols, representing sounds, of which written words are composed; written or printed communication usu. sent by post or messenger, (in *pl.*) addressed legal or formal document; precise terms of statement, strict verbal interpretation (*letter of the law*); (in *pl.*) literature, acquaintance with books, erudition. **2** *v.t.* inscribe letters on; classify with letters. **3 letter-bomb** terrorist explosive device in form of letter sent through post; **letter-box** box or slot into which letters are posted or delivered; **letter of credit** letter from bank authorizing bearer to draw money from another bank; **man of letters** scholar or author; **to the letter** with adherence to every detail. [F f. L *littera*]

lettered *a.* well read or educated.

letterhead *n.* printed heading on stationery, stationery with this.

letterpress *n.* printed words in illustrated book; printing from raised type.

lettuce /'letɪs/ *n.* garden plant with crisp leaves used as salad. [F f. L *lactuca* (*lac lact-* milk)]

leuco- *in comb.* white. [Gk *leukos* white]

leucocyte /'lju:kəʊsaɪt/ *n.* white or colourless corpuscle in blood.

leukaemia /lu:'ki:mɪə/, *US* **leukemia** *n.* progressive disease with abnormal accumulation of white corpuscles in tissues and usu. in blood. [G (Gk *leukos* white, *haima* blood)]

Levant /lɪ'vænt/ *n.* *the* East-Mediterranean region. [F, = point of sunrise, east (*lever* rise f. L *levo* lift)]

Levantine /lɪ'væntaɪn, 'levən-/ **1** *a.* of or trading to the Levant. **2** *n.* inhabitant of the Levant.

levee[1] /'levɪ/ *n.* *archaic* assembly of visitors or guests, esp. at formal reception; *hist.* sovereign's assembly for men only. [F *levé* var. of *lever* rising (LEVY)]

levee[2] /'levɪ/ *n.* embankment against river floods; river's natural embankment; landing-place. [F *levée* p.p. of *lever* raise (LEVY)]

level /'lev(ə)l/ **1** *n.* horizontal line or plane; height etc. reached, position on real or imaginary scale (*eye level*; *danger, noise, level*); social, moral, or intellectual standard; plane or rank of authority (*discussions at Cabinet level*); instrument for giving or testing a horizontal line or plane; level surface, flat country. **2** *a.* horizontal; on a level or equality (*with*); (of ground) flat and even, not bumpy; even, uniform; equable or well-balanced in quality, style, temper, judgement, etc. **3** *v.* (-ll-) make or become level, even, or uniform; place on same level, bring *up* or *down* to a standard; raze or demolish; aim (missile or gun); direct (accusation etc., or *absol.*, *at* or *against*). **4 do one's level best** *colloq.* do one's utmost; **find one's level** reach a position socially, intellectually, etc., suitable for one; **level-crossing** crossing of railway and road, or two railways, at same level; **level-headed** mentally well-balanced, sensible; **level off** (or **out**) make or become level; **level pegging** equality of scores or achievements; **on the level** *colloq.* honest(ly), without deception; **on a level with** in same horizontal plane as, equal with. [F f. L dimin. (*libra* balance)]

leveller *n.* one who advocates abolition of social distinctions.

lever 1 *n.* bar or other tool used for prizing; bar or other rigid structure used as lifting device of which one point (*fulcrum*) is fixed, another is connected with the force (*weight*) to be resisted or acted upon, and a third is connected with the force (*power*) applied; *fig.* means of moral pressure. **2** *v.* use lever; lift, move, etc., with lever (*along, out, up*, etc.). [AF f. L *levo* raise]

leverage *n.* action or power of lever; *fig.* means of accomplishing purpose.

leveret /'levərɪt/ *n.* young hare, esp. in first year. [AF dimin. of *levre* f. L *lepus lepor-* hare]

leviathan /lɪ'vaɪəθ(ə)n/ *n.* sea monster

(*Bibl.*); anything very large or powerful. [L f. Heb.]

Levis /'li:vaɪz/ *n.pl.* (**P**) type of (orig. blue) denim jeans or overalls reinforced with rivets. [*Levi* Strauss, manufacturer]

levitate /'levɪteɪt/ *v.* (cause to) rise and float in the air (esp. with reference to spiritualism); **levitation** /-'teɪʃ(ə)n/ *n.* [L *levis* light, after *gravitate*]

levity /'levɪtɪ/ *n.* disposition to make light of weighty matters, frivolity, lack of serious thought. [L (*levis* light)]

levy /'levɪ/ **1** *v.t.* impose or collect compulsorily (payment etc.); enrol (troops etc.); wage (war). **2** *n.* levying; payment etc. levied; (in *pl.*) troops levied. [F *levée*, p.p. of *lever* raise f. L *levo*]

lewd /lju:d/ *a.* lascivious; indecent, obscene. [OE, orig. = lay, vulgar, ill-mannered, base]

lexical /'leksɪk(ə)l/ *a.* of the words of a language; (as) of a lexicon. [LEXICON]

lexicography /leksɪ'kɒgrəfɪ/ *n.* compiling of dictionaries; **lexicographer** *n.* [foll., -GRAPHY]

lexicon /'leksɪkən/ *n.* dictionary, esp. of Greek, Hebrew, Syriac, or Arabic; individual's or author's vocabulary. [Gk (foll.)]

lexis /'leksɪs/ *n.* words, vocabulary; total stock of words in a language. [Gk, = word]

ley /leɪ/ *n.* land temporarily under grass. [LEA]

Leyden jar /'leɪd(ə)n/ a kind of electrical condenser with glass jar as dielectric between sheets of tin foil. [*Leiden* in Netherlands]

LF *abbr.* low frequency.

l.h. *abbr.* left hand.

Li *symb.* lithium.

liability /laɪə'bɪlɪtɪ/ *n.* being liable; troublesome person, handicap; (in *pl.*) debts etc. for which one is liable. [foll.]

liable /'laɪəb(ə)l/ *predic. a.* legally bound; subject or under obligation *to*; exposed or open *to* (something undesirable); apt or likely *to*; answerable *for*. [AF f. F f. L (*ligo* bind)]

liaise /lɪ'eɪz/ *v.i. colloq.* establish co-operation, act as link, *with* or *between*. [foll.]

liaison /lɪ'eɪzɒn/ *n.* communication or co-operation, esp. between military forces or units; illicit sexual relationship; egg-yolk thickening for sauces. [F (*lier* bind f. L as LIABLE)]

liana /lɪ'ɑ:nə/ *n.* climbing and twining plant in tropical forests. [F]

liar /'laɪə/ *n.* person who tells lies. [LIE[2]]

lias /'laɪəs/ *n.* a blue limestone rich in fossils; **liassic** /lɪ'æsɪk/ *a.* [F *liois*]

Lib. *abbr.* Liberal; *colloq.* liberation.

libation /laɪ'beɪʃ(ə)n/ *n.* pouring of drink-offering to god; such drink-offering. [L]

libel /'laɪb(ə)l/ **1** *n.* published false statement damaging to person's reputation, act of publishing it; false defamatory statement or representation. **2** *v.t.* (**-ll-**, *US* **-l-**) utter or publish libel against. **3 is a libel on** does injustice to. **4 libellous** *a.* [F f. L *libellus* dimin. of *liber* book]

liberal /'lɪbər(ə)l/ **1** *a.* given or giving freely, generous, not sparing *of*, abundant; open-minded, not prejudiced; not strict or rigorous; (of studies etc.) for general broadening of mind; favouring moderate political and social reform (*the Liberal Party*). **2** *n.* person of liberal views; (**Liberal**) member or supporter of the Liberal Party. **3 liberalism** *n.*; **liberality** /-'rælɪtɪ/ *n.*; **liberally** *adv.* [F f. L (*liber* free)]

liberalize /'lɪbərəlaɪz/ *v.t.* make more liberal or less strict; **liberalization** /-'zeɪʃ(ə)n/ *n.*

liberate /'lɪbəreɪt/ *v.t.* set at liberty, release (*from*); free (country) from oppressor or enemy occupation; free (person) from rigid social conventions; **liberation** /-'reɪʃ(ə)n/ *n.*; **liberator** *n.*

libertine /'lɪbəti:n/ **1** *n.* dissolute or licentious man. **2** *a.* licentious. [L, = freedman (*liber* free)]

liberty /'lɪbətɪ/ *n.* freedom from captivity, slavery, etc.; right or power to do as one pleases; right or privilege granted by authority; setting aside of rules or convention; **at liberty** free, not imprisoned, allowed *to do* thing; **take liberties** behave in unduly familiar manner (*with* person), deal *with* superficially. [F f. L (LIBERAL)]

libidinous /lɪ'bɪdɪnəs/ *a.* lustful. [L (foll.)]

libido /lɪ'bi:dəʊ/ *n.* (*pl.* **libidos**) psychic impulse or drive, esp. that associated with sexual desire; **libidinal** /lɪ'bɪdɪn(ə)l/ *a.* [L, = lust]

Libra /'li:brə/ *n.* constellation and seventh sign of zodiac. [L, = pound weight, balance]

librarian /laɪ'breərɪən/ *n.* person in charge of or assistant in library; **librarianship** *n.* [L (foll.)]

library /'laɪbrərɪ/ *n.* collection of books, public or private; room or building where these are kept; similar collection of films, records, computer routines, etc., or place where they are kept; series of books issued in similar bindings as set. [F f. L (*liber* book)]

libretto /lɪ'bretəʊ/ *n.* (*pl.* **libretti** /-ɪ/ or **librettos**) text of opera or other long musical vocal work; **librettist** *n.* [It., dimin. of *libro* book f. L *liber*]

lice *pl.* of LOUSE.

licence /ˈlaɪsəns/, *US* **license** *n.* permit from government etc. to own or do something or carry on some trade; leave or permission; excessive liberty of action; disregard of law or customs; writer's or artist's transgression of established rules for effect (*poetic licence*). [F f. L (*licet* it is allowed)]

license /ˈlaɪsəns/ *v.t.* grant licence to (person); authorize use of (premises) for certain purpose, esp. sale of alcoholic liquor; authorize publication of (book etc.) or performance of (play).

licensee /laɪsənˈsiː/ *n.* holder of licence, esp. to sell alcoholic liquor. [-EE]

licentiate /laɪˈsenʃɪət/ *n.* holder of certificate of competence to practise certain profession. [med.L (LICENCE)]

licentious /laɪˈsenʃəs/ *a.* immoral in sexual relations. [L (LICENCE)]

lichee var. of LITCHI.

lichen /ˈlaɪkən/ *n.* plant organism composed of fungus and alga in association, forming crust on rocks, tree-trunks, etc. [L f. Gk]

lich-gate /ˈlɪtʃgeɪt/ *n.* roofed gateway of churchyard where coffin awaits clergyman's arrival. [*lich* = corpse, GATE]

licit /ˈlɪsɪt/ *a.* not forbidden. [L (LICENCE)]

lick 1 *v.* pass tongue over; take *up* or *off*, make *clean*, by licking; (of flame etc.) play lightly over; *sl.* thrash, defeat, excel. **2** *n.* act of licking with tongue, blow with stick etc.; *sl.* (fast) pace (*at a lick*). **3 a lick and a promise** *colloq.* hasty performance of a task; **lick into shape** make presentable or efficient; **lick one's chops** (or **lips**) look forward with relish; **lick one's wounds** be in retirement after defeat; **lick person's boots** be servile to him. [OE]

licorice var. of LIQUORICE.

lid *n.* hinged or removable cover, esp. at top of container; = EYELID; *sl.* hat; **put the lid on** *sl.* be the culmination of, put a stop to; **-lidded** *a.* [OE]

lido /ˈliːdəʊ/ *n.* (*pl.* **lidos**) public open-air swimming-pool or bathing-beach. [*Lido*, near Venice]

lie[1] /laɪ/ **1** *v.i.* (*past* **lay;** *p.p.* **lain;** *partic.* **lying**) be in or assume horizontal position on supporting surface, be at rest on something; (of thing) be resting (flat) on surface; be kept or remain or be in specified state or place (*lie in ambush, in wait; books lay unread*); be situated (*village lies a mile to the south*); (of abstract thing) exist, be in certain position or manner (*answer lies in hard work*); be spread out to view; (of troops) be encamped *at, in*, or *near* etc. place; *Law* be admissible or sustainable. **2** *n.* way or direction or position in which thing lies. **3 lie down** assume lying position, have short rest; **lie-down** *n.* short rest; **lie down under** accept (insult etc.) without protest; **lie in** remain in bed in the morning, be brought to bed in childbirth; **lie-in** *n.* remaining in bed in the morning; **lie low** keep quiet or unseen, be discreet about one's intentions; **lie of the land** state of affairs; **lie with** be responsibility of; **take lying down** accept (insult etc.) without protest. [OE]

lie[2] /laɪ/ **1** *n.* intentional false statement (*tell a lie*); imposture, false belief. **2** *v.* (*partic.* **lying**) tell lies; (of thing) be deceptive. **3 give the lie to** serve to show falsity of (supposition etc); **lie-detector** instrument for determining whether person is telling the truth by measuring physiological changes. [OE]

lied /liːd/ *n.* (*pl.* ***lieder***) German song, esp. of Romantic period. [G]

lief *adv. archaic* gladly, willingly (usu. *had* or *would lief*). [OE, = dear]

liege (usu. *hist.*) **1** *a.* entitled to receive or bound to give feudal service or allegiance. **2** *n.* liege lord; (usu. in *pl.*) vassal, subject. **3 liege lord** feudal superior, sovereign. [F f. L prob. f. Gmc]

liegeman *n.* sworn vassal.

lien /ˈliːən/ *n.* right to hold another's property till debt on it is paid. [F f. L (*ligo* bind)]

lieu /ljuː/ *n.* only in **in lieu** instead or in the place (*of*). [F f. L *locus* place]

Lieut. *abbr.* lieutenant.

lieutenant /lefˈtenənt/ *n.* deputy or substitute acting for superior; army officer of rank next below captain, naval officer of rank next below lieutenant-commander; **lieutenant-colonel, -commander, -general** officers ranking next below colonel etc.; **lieutenancy** *n.* [F (LIEU place, TENANT holder)]

life *n.* (*pl.* **lives**) capacity for growth, functional activity, and continual change peculiar to animals and plants before death; state of existence as a living individual, living person (*sacrificed his life; lost three lives*); living things and their activity (*animal life; drawn from life; is there life on Mars?*); period during which life lasts, period from birth to present time or from present time to death (*have done so all my life; will remember you all my life*); individual's actions and fortunes, manner of existence or particular aspect etc. of this (*one's private life; village life*); energy, liveliness, animation (*full of life*); active part of existence, business and pleasures of the world (*we do see life*); written account of person's life, biography; time for which thing exists or continues to function; spiritual salvation, regenerate condition; *colloq.* sentence of imprisonment for life; **as large as life** life-size, *joc.* in person; **for dear life** to escape death or as if to do this; **for life** for the rest of one's life; **life-blood** blood necessary to life, vital factor or influence; **life cycle** cyclic series of changes undergone by an organism; **life-guard** expert swimmer employed to rescue bathers from drowning, bodyguard of soldiers; **Life Guards** regiment of household cavalry; **life insurance** insurance for sum paid on death of insured person; **life-jacket** jacket of buoyant material for supporting person in water; **life peer** peer whose title lapses on death; **life-preserver** short stick with heavily loaded end, life-jacket etc.; **life sciences** biology and related subjects; **life-size(d)** of same size as person or thing represented; **life-style** individual's way of life; **matter of life and death** issue on which person's living or dying depends, matter of great importance; **this life** earthly life. [OE]

lifebelt *n.* belt of buoyant or inflatable material for supporting person in water.

lifeboat *n.* specially constructed boat for rescuing those in distress at sea, launched from land; ship's small boat for use in emergency.

lifebuoy *n.* buoyant support for person in water.

lifeless *a.* lacking life, dead; lacking movement or vitality. [OE]

lifelike *a.* closely resembling person or thing represented. [LIFE]

lifeline *n.* rope used for life-saving, e.g. that attached to lifebuoy; sole means of communication or transport.

lifelong *a.* lasting a lifetime.

lifer *n. sl.* person sentenced to imprisonment for life; such sentence.

lifetime *n.* duration of person's life.

lift 1 *v.* raise or remove (*up, off, out*) to higher position; give upward direction to (eyes or face); elevate to higher plane of thought or feeling; (of fog etc.) rise, disperse; go up, be raised, yield to upward force; remove (barrier or restriction); steal; plagiarize (passage); dig up (potatoes etc.); (of floor) swell upwards, bulge; hold or have on high (*church lifts its spire*). **2** *n.* lifting; carrying of person without charge as passenger in vehicle; apparatus for raising and lowering persons or things from one floor to another in building; apparatus for carrying persons up or down mountain etc.; supporting or elevating influence, feeling of elation; upward force which air exerts on aircraft; transport by air, quantity thus transported. **3 lift down** pick up and bring to lower position; **lift-off** vertical take-off of spacecraft or rocket. [ON, rel. to LOFT]

ligament /ˈlɪgəmənt/*n.* band of tough fibrous tissue binding bones together. [L (*ligo* bind)]

ligature /ˈlɪgətʃə/ **1** *n.* tie or bandage (esp. in surgery); *Mus.* slur, tie; two or more letters joined, e.g. æ; bond, thing that unites. **2** *v.t.* bind or connect with ligature.

light[1] /laɪt/ **1** *n.* the natural agent (electromagnetic radiation) that stimulates sight and makes things visible; medium or condition of space in which this is present; appearance of brightness; source of light, e.g. sun, lamp, lighthouse; flame or spark serving to ignite, device producing this; traffic-light; aspect in which thing is viewed (*regarded it in a new light*); mental illumination, elucidation; spiritual illumination by divine truth; vivacity, enthusiasm, or inspiration in person's face, esp. in eyes; (in *pl.*) one's mental powers (*according to one's lights*); eminent person (*leading light*); bright parts of picture etc.; window or opening in wall to let light in; (in crossword etc.) word to be deduced from clues. **2** *a.* well provided with light, not dark; pale (*light blue*; *light-blue ribbon*). **3** *v.* (*past* **lit**; *p.p.* **lit** or (esp. as *attrib. a.*) **lighted**) set burning, begin to burn; (often with *up*) provide (room etc.) with light; show (person his) way or surroundings with a light; (cause eyes to) brighten with animation (usu. with *up*). **4 bring** (or **come**) **to light** reveal (or be revealed); **in a good** (or **bad**) **light** easily (or barely) visible, giving favourable, unfavourable, impression; **in the light of** drawing information from, with the help given by; **lighting-up time** time after which vehicles on road must show prescribed lights; **light meter** instrument for measuring intensity of light, esp. to show correct photographic exposure; **light pen** penlike photosensitive device held to screen of computer terminal for passing information on to it; **light up** begin to smoke cigarette etc., switch on lights; **light-year** distance light travels in one year (about 6 million million miles); **lit up** *sl.* drunk; **strike a light** produce spark or flame with match etc., also as *sl. int.* [OE]

light[2] /laɪt/ **1** *a.* of little weight, not heavy, easy to lift; relatively low in weight, amount, density, strength, etc. (*light arms, traffic, metal, blow, rain*); deficient in weight (*light coin*); carrying or suitable for small loads (*light rail-*

way); (of ship) unladen; carrying only light arms, armaments, etc.; (of food) easy to digest; easily borne or done (*light punishment, taxation, work*); intended only as entertainment, not profound (*light comedy, music*); (of sleep) easily disturbed; free from sorrow, cheerful (*light heart*); giddy (*light in the head*); nimble, quick-moving (*light of foot; light rhythm*); unchaste or wanton; (of building) elegant, graceful. **2** *adv.* in light manner (*tread light; sleep light*); with minimum load (*travel light*). **3** *v.i.* (*past* and *p.p.* **lit** or **lighted**) come by chance *on* or *upon*. **4 lighter-than-air** (of aircraft) weighing less than the air it displaces; **light-fingered** given to stealing; **light-footed** nimble; **light-headed** giddy, frivolous, delirious; **light-hearted** cheerful, (unduly) casual; **light industry** that producing small or light articles; **light into** attack; **light out** depart; **make light of** treat as unimportant. [OE]

lighten[1] *v.* make or become lighter; reduce weight or load of; bring relief to (heart, mind, etc.); mitigate (penalty).

lighten[2] *v.* shed light on; make or grow bright; shine brightly; emit lightning. [LIGHT[1]]

lighter[1] *n.* device for lighting cigarettes etc.

lighter[2] *n.* boat, usu. flat-bottomed, for transporting goods between ship and wharf etc. [Du. (LIGHT[2] 'unload')]

lighthouse *n.* tower or other structure containing beacon light to warn or guide ships at sea. [LIGHT[1]]

lighting *n.* equipment in room or street etc. for producing light; arrangement or effect of lights.

lightning 1 *n.* flash of bright light produced by electric discharge between clouds or cloud and ground. **2** *a.* very quick. **3 lightning conductor** (or *US* **rod**) metal rod or wire fixed to exposed part of building or to mast to divert lightning into earth or sea; **like (greased) lightning** *colloq.* with great speed. [LIGHTEN[2]]

lights /laɪts/ *n.pl.* lungs of sheep, pigs, etc., used as food esp. for pets. [LIGHT[2]; cf. LUNG]

lightship *n.* moored or anchored ship with beacon light. [LIGHT[1]]

lightsome *a.* gracefully light, agile, merry. [LIGHT[2]]

lightweight 1 *a.* below average weight; of little importance or influence. **2** *n.* lightweight person or thing; boxing-weight with upper limit of 60 kg.

ligneous /ˈlɪgnɪəs/ *a.* of the nature of wood; (of plants) woody. [L *lignum* wood]

lignite /ˈlɪgnaɪt/ *n.* brown coal of woody texture.

lignum vitae /lɪgnəm ˈvaɪtiː/ a hard-wooded tree. [L, = wood of life]

like[1] **1** *a.* having the qualities (or some of them) of another or each other or an original; resembling in some way, such as (*good books like David Copperfield*); characteristic of (*it was like her to do that*); in suitable state or mood for (*feel like working, a cup of tea*); *archaic* or *colloq.* likely (*as like as not*). **2** *prep.* in the manner of, to the same degree as (often in set phrases: *drink like a fish; swear like a trooper*). **3** *adv.* in the same manner *as* (*archaic*); *vulgar* so to speak (*by way of argument, like*). **4** *conj. colloq.* (**D**) as (*do it like I do*); *US* as if. **5** *n.* counterpart, equal, like person or thing; thing or things of same kind. **6 and the like** and similar things; **like anything** (or **blazes** etc.) *colloq.* very much, vigorously; **like hell** recklessly, *iron.* not at all; **like-minded** having same tastes, opinions, etc.; **the likes of** person such (esp. so humble) as; **more like it** nearer what is needed; **nothing like** in no way like; **something like** in some way like; **what is he** (or **it** etc.) **like?** what sort of person is he (or thing is it etc.)? [OE]

like[2] **1** *v.t.* find agreeable or pleasant (*like books, swimming; like to dance*; also *iron. I like his cheek!*); choose to have, prefer (*likes her coffee black*); wish or be inclined *to* (*should like to come*). **2** *n.* (usu. in *pl.*) thing(s) one likes or prefers. [OE]

-like *suffix* forming adjectives from nouns in sense 'similar to', 'characteristic of'.

¶ A hyphen is normally used when the first element is of more than one syllable or ends in *-l* (*eel-like, mouselike, tablelike*); but note *ladylike*.

likeable *a.* pleasant, easy to like; **likeably** *adv.* [LIKE[2]]

likelihood /ˈlaɪklɪhʊd/ *n.* probability; **in all likelihood** very probably. [foll.]

likely /ˈlaɪklɪ/ **1** *a.* probable, such as well might happen or be true; to be reasonably expected (*he is not likely to come*); promising, apparently suitable (*this is a likely spot*). **2** *adv.* probably. **3 not likely** *colloq.* certainly not, I refuse. [ON (LIKE[1])]

liken *v.t.* indicate or find resemblance of (one person or thing) *to* another. [LIKE[1]]

likeness *n.* resemblance; semblance or guise (*in the likeness of*); portrait, representation.

likewise *adv.* also, moreover; similarly (*do likewise*).

liking *n.* what one likes, one's taste (*is it*

to your liking?); regard, fondness, taste or fancy, *for*. [LIKE[2]]

lilac /'laɪlək/ 1 *n.* shrub with fragrant pale pinkish-violet or white blossoms; pale pinkish-violet colour. 2 *a.* of lilac colour. [F f. Sp. f. Arab. f. Pers.]

liliaceous /lɪlɪ'eɪʃəs/ *a.* of lily family. [LILY]

lilliputian /lɪlɪ'pju:ʃ(ə)n/ 1 *n.* diminutive person or thing. 2 *a.* diminutive. [*Lilliput*, place in Swift's 'Gulliver's Travels']

lilt 1 *n.* light pleasant rhythm, song or tune with this. 2 *v.* move or utter with lilt. [orig. unkn.]

lily /'lɪlɪ/ 1 *n.* bulbous plant with white or reddish or purplish often spotted flowers on tall slender stem; its flower; heraldic figure of lily. 2 *attrib.* delicately white. 3 **lily-livered** cowardly; **lily of the valley** spring plant with fragrant white bell-shaped flowers. [F f. L *lilium*]

limb[1] /lɪm/ *n.* arm, leg, or wing; large branch of tree; arm of cross; **out on a limb** isolated, stranded, at a disadvantage. [OE]

limb[2] /lɪm/ *n. Astron.* specified edge of sun etc. (*eastern, lower, limb*). [F, or L *limbus* hem, border]

limber[1] 1 *a.* flexible; lithe, agile. 2 *v.* make (oneself, part of body, etc.) supple; warm *up* in preparation for athletic etc. activity. [perh. foll.]

limber[2] 1 *n.* detachable front part of gun-carriage. 2 *v.t.* attach limber to (gun). [perh. L *limo -onis* shaft]

limbo[1] /'lɪmbəʊ/ *n.* (*pl.* **limbos**) in some Christian beliefs, a supposed abode of souls not condemned to hell but not admitted to heaven (e.g. because not baptized); intermediate state or condition of awaiting decision etc.; prison; state of neglect or oblivion. [L (*in*) *limbo* (LIMB[2])]

limbo[2] /'lɪmbəʊ/ *n.* (*pl.* **limbos**) W. Indian dance in which dancer bends backwards to pass under horizontal bar which is progressively lowered. [W. Indian word, perh. = LIMBER[1]]

lime[1] 1 *n.* white substance (calcium oxide) obtained by heating limestone and used for making mortar, as fertilizer, etc. 2 *v.t.* treat with lime. 3 **lime-kiln** kiln for heating limestone. [OE]

lime[2] *n.* round fruit like lemon but smaller and more acid; **lime green** pale green colour of lime. [F f. Arab.]

lime[3] *n.* ornamental tree with heart-shaped leaves and fragrant yellow blossom. [alt. of *line* = *lind* = LINDEN]

limelight *n.* intense white light obtained by heating cylinder of lime in oxyhydrogen flame, used formerly in theatres; **the limelight** *fig.* full glare of publicity. [LIME[1]]

limerick /'lɪmərɪk/ *n.* humorous five-line stanza. [orig. uncert.]

limestone *n.* rock composed mainly of calcium carbonate. [LIME[1]]

Limey /'laɪmɪ/ *n. US sl.* British person (orig. sailor) or ship. [LIME[2], because of enforced consumption of lime-juice in British Navy]

limit /'lɪmɪt/ 1 *n.* point, line, or level, beyond which something does not or may not extend or pass; greatest or smallest amount permitted. 2 *v.t.* set or serve as limit to, restrict *to*. 3 **be the limit** *sl.* be intolerable; **within limits** with some degree of freedom. [L *limes limit-* boundary, frontier]

limitation /lɪmɪ'teɪʃ(ə)n/ *n.* limiting or being limited; lack of ability (*know my limitations*); limiting rule or circumstance.

limited *a.* confined within limits; not great in scope or talents; (of monarchy etc.) subject to constitutional restrictions; **limited edition** production of limited number of copies; **limited (liability) company** company whose members are legally responsible only to limited degree for debts of company.

limn /lɪm/ *v.t.* paint (picture), portray. [*lumine* f. F f. L *lumino* ILLUMINATE]

limnology /lɪm'nɒlədʒɪ/ *n.* study of fresh waters and their organic life; **limnological** /-'lɒdʒɪk(ə)l/ *a.*; **limnologist** *n.* [Gk *limnē* lake]

limousine /lɪmʊ'zi:n/ *n.* motor car with closed body and partition behind driver; luxurious motor car. [F]

limp[1] 1 *v.i.* walk lamely; (of damaged ship etc.) proceed with difficulty; (of verse) be defective. 2 *n.* lame walk. [perh. obs. *limp-halt* (HALT[2])]

limp[2] *a.* not stiff or firm, easily bent; without will or energy. [perh. prec.]

limpet /'lɪmpɪt/ *n.* marine shellfish that sticks tightly to rocks; **limpet mine** mine attached to ship's hull and exploding after set time. [OE]

limpid /'lɪmpɪd/ *a.* clear, transparent; **limpidity** /-'pɪdɪtɪ/ *n.* [F or L]

linage /'laɪnɪdʒ/ *n.* number of lines in page etc.; payment by the line. [LINE[1]]

linchpin /'lɪntʃpɪn/ *n.* pin passed through axle-end to keep wheel in position; person or thing vital to an organization etc. [OE *lynis* = axle-tree]

linctus /'lɪŋktəs/ *n.* medicine, esp. soothing syrupy cough-mixture. [L (*lingo* lick)]

linden /'lɪnd(ə)n/ *n.* = LIME[3]. [OE *lind*(*e*)]

line[1] 1 *n.* long narrow mark traced on surface, its use in art; thing resembling such traced mark, band of colour, furrow, or wrinkle; straight or curved continuous extent of length without breadth, track of moving point; curve connecting all points having specified common property; straight line; limit, boundary (*dividing line*); mark limiting area of play in sports, starting-point in race; row of persons or things, direction as indicated by them, trend; *US* queue; piece of cord, rope, etc., serving usu. specified purpose (*fishing-line*); wire or cable for telephone or telegraph, connection by this; contour, outline, or lineament, shape to which garment is designed; course of procedure, conduct, thought, etc. (*don't take that line with me*); (in *pl.*) plan, draft, manner of procedure (*along these lines*); row of printed or written words, a verse; (in *pl.*) piece of poetry, words of actor's part, specified amount of text etc. to be written out as school punishment; single track of railway, one branch of railway system, whole system under one management; regular succession of buses, ships, aircraft, etc., plying between certain places, company conducting this; connected series of persons following one another in time (esp. several generations of family), lineage, stock; direction, course, track (*line of communication*); department of activity, province, branch of business; class of commercial goods (*a new line in hats*); connected series of military fieldworks, arrangement of soldiers side by side, ships etc. drawn up in battle array; one of the very narrow horizontal sections forming a television picture; level of base of most letters in printing; (as measure) $\frac{1}{12}$ inch. **2** *v.* mark with lines; position or stand at intervals along. **3 the Line** the equator; **all along the line** at every point; **bring, come, into line** make conform, conform; **drop person a line** send him short letter etc.; **get a line on** *colloq.* learn something about; **in line for** likely to receive; **in line with** in accordance with; **lay** (or **put**) **it on the line** speak frankly; **line-drawing** one done with pen or pencil; **line of fire** path of bullet etc. about to be shot; **line of vision** straight line along which observer looks; **line-out** in Rugby football, parallel lines of opposing forwards at right angles to touch-line for throwing in of ball; **line printer** machine that prints output from computer a line at a time; **line up** arrange or be arranged in line(s); **line-up** *n.* line of people for inspection, arrangement of persons in team etc.; **out of line** not in alignment, discordant. [OE & F f. L *linea* (*linum* flax)]

line² *v.t.* cover inside surface of (garment, box, etc.) with layer of usu. different material; serve as lining for; fill (purse, stomach, etc.). [obs. *line* linen, used for linings]

lineage /ˈlɪnɪɪdʒ/ *n.* lineal descent, ancestry. [F f. L (LINE¹)]

lineal /ˈlɪnɪəl/ *a.* in the direct line of descent or ancestry; linear; **lineally** *adv.*

lineament /ˈlɪnɪəmənt/ *n.* (usu. in *pl.*) distinctive feature or characteristic, esp. of face. [L (LINE¹)]

linear /ˈlɪnɪə/ *a.* of or in lines; long and narrow and of uniform breadth; **Linear A, B** forms of ancient writing in Crete and Greece; **linearity** /-ˈærɪtɪ/ *n.*

lineation /lɪnɪˈeɪʃ(ə)n/ *n.* marking with or arrangement of lines.

linen /ˈlɪnɪn/ **1** *n.* cloth woven from flax; *collect.* articles made (or orig. made) of linen, as sheets, shirts, undergarments, etc. **2** *a.* made of linen. [OE, rel. to L *linum* flax]

liner¹ *n.* ship or aircraft etc. carrying passengers on regular line; **liner train** fast freight train with detachable containers on permanently coupled wagons. [LINE¹]

liner² *n.* removable lining. [LINE²]

linesman *n.* umpire's or referee's assistant who decides whether ball falls within playing area or not. [LINE¹]

ling¹ *n.* a long slender sea-fish. [prob. Du.]

ling² *n.* a kind of heather. [ON]

-ling *suffix* forming nouns denoting person or thing connected with (*hireling*) or having the property of being (*weakling*) or undergoing (*starveling*), or denoting diminutive (*duckling*), often derog. (*lordling*). [OE, dimin. f. ON]

linger /ˈlɪŋgə/ *v.i.* be slow to depart, stay about, dally (*round* place or person; *over*, *on*, *upon*, subject etc.); (of ailment) be protracted; (of dying person or custom) be slow in dying. [ON (LONG)]

lingerie /ˈlæ̃ʒərɪ/ *n.* women's underwear and night-clothes. [F (*linge* linen)]

lingo /ˈlɪŋgəʊ/ *n.* (*pl.* **lingos**) *colloq.* foreign language; vocabulary of special subject or class of people. [prob. Port. *lingoa* f. L *lingua* tongue]

lingua franca /lɪŋgwə ˈfræŋkə/ language used by speakers whose native languages are different; system for mutual understanding. [It., = Frankish tongue]

lingual /ˈlɪŋgw(ə)l/ *a.* of or formed by the tongue; of speech or languages; **lingually** *adv.* [L *lingua* tongue, language]

linguist /ˈlɪŋgwɪst/ *n.* person skilled in languages or linguistics.

linguistic /lɪŋˈgwɪstɪk/ *a.* of the study of languages, of language; **linguistically** *adv.*

linguistics *n.* study of languages and their structure. [F or G (LINGUIST)]
liniment /ˈlɪnɪmənt/ *n.* embrocation, usu. made with oil. [L (*linio* smear)]
lining *n.* layer of material used to line surface. [LINE²]
link 1 *n.* one loop or ring of chain etc.; connecting part, thing or person that unites or provides continuity, one in series; state or means of connection; cuff-link. **2** *v.* connect or join (*together, to, with*); clasp or intertwine (hands or arms); be joined *on* or *in to* system, company, etc. **3 link up** connect or combine (*with*). [ON]
linkage *n.* system of links, linking, a link.
linkman *n.* person providing continuity in broadcast programme.
links *n.* (treated as *sing.* or *pl.*) golf-course. [OE, = rising ground]
Linnaean /lɪˈni:ən/ *a.* of Linnaeus or his system of classifying plants. [*Linnaeus*, naturalist]
linnet /ˈlɪnɪt/ *n.* a songbird, a common brown or grey finch. [F f. *lin* flax (flax-seeds being its food)]
lino /ˈlaɪnəʊ/ *n.* (*pl.* **linos**) linoleum. [abbr.]
linocut *n.* design cut in relief on block of linoleum; print made from this.
linoleum /lɪˈnəʊlɪəm/ *n.* floor-covering of canvas backing thickly coated with a preparation of linseed oil and powdered cork etc. [L *linum* flax, *oleum* oil]
Linotype /ˈlaɪnəʊtaɪp/ *n.* **(P)** composing-machine producing lines of words as single strips of metal, used esp. for newspapers. [= *line of type*]
linseed /ˈlɪnsi:d/ *n.* seed of flax; oil extracted from it and used in paint and varnish. [OE (LINE¹)]
linsey-woolsey /lɪnzɪˈwʊlzɪ/ *n.* fabric of coarse wool woven on cotton warp. [prob. *Lindsey* in Suffolk + WOOL]
lint *n.* linen with one side made fluffy by scraping, used for dressing wounds; fluff. [perh. f. F *linette* (*lin* flax)]
lintel /ˈlɪnt(ə)l/ *n.* horizontal timber or stone across top of door or window. [F (LIMIT)]
lion /ˈlaɪən/ *n.* large powerful tawny African and S. Asian carnivorous animal of cat family; brave or celebrated person; (**Lion**) sign or constellation Leo; **lion-heart** courageous person; **lion-hearted** brave; **lion's share** largest or best portion; **lioness** *n.fem.* [AF f. L *leo leon-* f. Gk]
lionize *v.t.* treat as celebrity.
lip 1 *n.* either of the fleshy parts forming edges of mouth-opening; edge of cup etc., edge of vessel shaped for pouring from; *sl.* impudence. **2** *v.t.* **(-pp-)** touch with lips, apply lips to; touch lightly. **3 bite one's lip** repress emotion, laughter, etc.; **curl one's lip** express scorn; **lip-read** (esp. of deaf person) understand speech entirely from observing speaker's lip-movements; **lip-service** insincere expression of support; **smack one's lips** part lips noisily in relish or anticipation, esp. of food. **4 lipped, -lipped** *a.* [OE]
lipstick *n.* small stick of cosmetic for colouring lips.
liquefy /ˈlɪkwɪfaɪ/ *v.* make or become liquid; **liquefaction** /-ˈfækʃ(ə)n/ *n.* [F f. L (LIQUID)]
liqueur /lɪˈkjʊə/ *n.* any of several strong sweet alcoholic spirits, variously flavoured. [F]
liquid /ˈlɪkwɪd/ **1** *a.* having a consistency like that of water or oil, flowing freely but not gaseous; having qualities of water in appearance (*liquid blue*); (of sounds) clear and pure; (of assets) easily converted into cash. **2** *n.* liquid substance; sound of *l* or *r*. **3 liquid crystal** liquid in state approaching that of crystalline solid. [L (*liqueo* be liquid)]
liquidate /ˈlɪkwɪdeɪt/ *v.t.* wind up affairs of (company or firm) by ascertaining liabilities and apportioning assets; pay off (debt); put an end to or get rid of (esp. by violent means); **liquidator** *n.* [med.L (prec.)]
liquidation /lɪkwɪˈdeɪʃ(ə)n/ *n.* liquidating of company etc.; **go into liquidation** (of company etc.) be wound up and have assets apportioned.
liquidity /lɪˈkwɪdɪtɪ/ *n.* state of being liquid or having liquid assets. [F or med.L (LIQUID)]
liquidize /ˈlɪkwɪdaɪz/ *v.t.* reduce to liquid state. [LIQUID]
liquidizer *n.* machine for making purées etc.
liquor /ˈlɪkə/ *n.* alcoholic (esp. distilled) drink; other liquid, esp. produced in cooking. [F f. L (LIQUID)]
liquorice /ˈlɪkərɪs, -ɪʃ/ *n.* black substance used as a sweet and in medicine; plant from whose root it is obtained. [AF *lycorys* f. L f. Gk *glukus* sweet, *rhiza* root]
lira /ˈlɪərə/ *n.* (*pl.* **lire** /-reɪ/ or **liras**) currency unit in Italy and in Turkey. [It. f. Prov. f. L *libra* pound]
lisle /laɪl/ *n.* fine smooth cotton thread for stockings etc. [*Lille* in France]
lisp 1 *n.* speech defect in which /s/ is pronounced /θ/ and /z/ is pronounced /ð/. **2** *v.* speak or say with a lisp. [OE]
lissom /ˈlɪsəm/ *a.* lithe, agile. [LITHE]
list¹ *n.* number of connected items, names, etc., written or printed together as record or to aid memory (*shopping*

list); selvage, this torn off and used; (in *pl.*) palisades enclosing area for tournament, *fig*. scene of contest. **2** *v.t.* make list of, enter in list. **3 enter the lists** issue or accept challenge; **listed building** one of historical etc. importance having official protection from demolition etc. [OE]

list² **1** *v.i.* (of ship etc.) lean over to one side. **2** *n.* listing position, tilt. [orig. unkn.]

listen /'lɪs(ə)n/ *v.i.* make effort to hear something, (often with *out*) wait alertly to hear something; hear with attention person speaking; give attention with ear *to* (person, sound, story); yield *to* request or advice or its author, take notice; **listen in** tap communication made by telephone, listen to radio broadcast. [OE]

listener /'lɪsnə/ *n.* one who listens; person listening to radio broadcast.

listless *a.* without energy or enthusiasm. [OE (obs. *list* inclination)]

lit *past & p.p.* of LIGHT¹ and LIGHT².

litany /'lɪtənɪ/ *n.* series of supplications to God recited by priest etc. with set responses by congregation; **the Litany** that in Book of Common Prayer. [F f. L *litania* f. Gk = prayer]

litchi /'li:tʃi:/ *n.* sweetish pulpy fruit in thin brown shell; tree (orig. Chinese) bearing this. [Chin.]

liter *US* var. of LITRE.

literacy /'lɪtərəsɪ/ *n.* ability to read and write. [LITERATE]

literal /'lɪtər(ə)l/ **1** *a.* taking words in their usual sense without metaphor or allegory; exactly corresponding to the original words (*literal translation*); (of person) prosaic, matter-of-fact; so called without exaggeration (*literal disaster*); *colloq*. (**D**) so called with some exaggeration or using metaphor (*a literal avalanche of mail*); of letter(s) of the alphabet. **2** *n.* = *literal error*. **3 literal error** misprint of a letter. **4 literally** *adv.* [F or L (*littera* letter)]

literalism *n.* insistence on literal interpretation, adherence to the letter; **literalist** *n.*

literary /'lɪtərərɪ/ *a.* of, concerned with, or interested in, literature or books or written composition; (of word or idiom) not colloquial, used chiefly by writers; **literariness** *n.* [L (LETTER)]

literate /'lɪtərət/ **1** *a.* able to read and write. **2** *n.* literate person.

literati /lɪtə'rɑ:ti:/ *n.pl.* men of letters, the learned class.

literature /'lɪtərətʃə/ *n.* written works, esp. of kind valued for form and style; the writings of a country or period or particular subject; literary production; *colloq*. printed matter, leaflets, etc.

lithe /laɪð/ *a.* flexible, supple. [OE]

lithium /'lɪθɪəm/ *n.* soft silver-white metallic element. [Gk *lithion* (*lithos* stone)]

litho /'laɪθəʊ/ *colloq*. **1** *n.* (*pl.* **lithos**) lithographic process. **2** *a.* lithographic. **3** *v.t.* lithograph. [abbr.]

lithograph /'lɪθəgrɑ:f/ **1** *n.* print produced by lithography. **2** *v.t.* produce lithographic print of. [foll.]

lithography /lɪ'θɒgrəfɪ/ *n.* process of printing from stone or metal surface so treated that ink adheres only to the design to be printed; **lithographer** *n.*; **lithographic** /-'græfɪk/ *a.*; **lithographically** /-'græfɪkəlɪ/ *adv.* [Gk *lithos* stone]

litigant /'lɪtɪgənt/ **1** *n.* party to lawsuit. **2** *a.* engaged in lawsuit. [foll.]

litigate /'lɪtɪgeɪt/ *v.* go to law, contest (point) at law; **litigation** /-'geɪʃ(ə)n/ *n.* [L (*lis lit-* lawsuit)]

litigious /lɪ'tɪdʒəs/ *a.* fond of litigation, contentious. [F or L (prec.)]

litmus /'lɪtməs/ *n.* blue colouring matter extracted from lichens that is turned red by acid and restored to blue by alkali; **litmus paper** paper stained with litmus and used as test for acids or alkalis. [ON, = dye-moss]

litotes /laɪ'təʊti:z/ *n.* ironic understatement, esp. using negative of its contrary (*I shan't be sorry* = *I shall be very glad*). [L f. Gk (*litos* plain, meagre)]

litre /'li:tə/ *n.* metric unit of capacity, equal to 1 cubic decimetre or about 1.75 pints. [F f. L f. Gk *litra*]

Litt.D. *abbr*. Doctor of Letters. [L *Litterarum Doctor*]

litter **1** *n.* refuse, esp. paper, discarded on streets etc.; odds and ends lying about; vehicle containing couch and carried on men's shoulders or by beasts of burden; kind of stretcher for sick and wounded; young animals brought forth at a birth; straw etc. as bedding for animals; straw and dung of farmyard. **2** *v.t.* make (place) untidy by discarding rubbish; give birth to (whelps etc. or *absol.*); provide (horse etc.) with litter as bedding; spread straw etc. on (stable-floor etc.). [AF f. L (*lectus* bed)]

litterbug *n.* (also **litter-lout**) person who carelessly leaves litter in street etc.

little /'lɪt(ə)l/ **1** *a.* (*compar*. LESS, LESSER, **littler**; *superl*. LEAST, **littlest**) small in size, amount, degree, etc., not great or big; often used to suggest fondness, condescension, etc. (*friendly little chap*; *silly little fool*); short in stature; of short distance or duration; relatively unimportant, operating on small scale (*the little man, shopkeeper*); young or younger (*little boy*; *my little brother*); smaller or smallest of the name (*little auk*; *little finger*); trivial, paltry, mean (*questions every little thing*); *a* certain though small amount of (*give me a little butter*). **2** *n.* not much, only a small amount (*got little out of it*); *a* certain but no great amount (*knows a little of everything*); short time or distance. **3** *adv.* (*compar.* LESS; *superl.* LEAST) to a small extent only (*little-known author*; *is little more than speculation*); not at all (*little does he know*). **4 Little Bear** see BEAR[2]; **little by little** by degrees; **little end** smaller end of connecting-rod, attached to piston; **the little people** fairies; **Little Russian** Ukrainian; **the little woman** *colloq.* one's wife. [OE]

littoral /ˈlɪtər(ə)l/ **1** *a.* of or on the shore. **2** *n.* region lying along the shore. [L (*litus litor-* shore)]

liturgy /ˈlɪtədʒɪ/ *n.* fixed form of public worship used in churches; *the* Book of Common Prayer; **liturgical** /-ˈtɜːdʒɪk(ə)l/ *a.*; **liturgically** /-ˈtɜːdʒɪkəlɪ/ *adv.* [F or L f. Gk = public worship]

live[1] /lɪv/ *v.* have life, be or remain alive; subsist or feed *on* (*lives on fruit*); depend for livelihood or subsistence or position *on* (*lives on his wife's earnings, on his reputation*); have one's home (*lives up the road, in a bungalow*); lead one's life or arrange one's habits in specified way (*live modestly, honestly, like a pauper*); (with cognate object) spend or pass (*live a virtuous life*); express in one's life (*live a lie*); enjoy life to the full (*this is really living*); (of thing) survive or endure; **live and let live** condone other's failings so as to secure same treatment for oneself; **live down** cause (past guilt or scandal etc.) to be forgotten by blameless conduct thereafter; **live it up** *colloq.* live gaily and extravagantly; **live off** derive support or sustenance from (*live off the land, off one's pension*); **live together** (esp. of unmarried man and woman) share home and have sexual relationship; **live up to** live or behave in accordance with (principles etc.). [OE]

live[2] /laɪv/ *attrib. a.* that is alive, living; actual, not pretended or toy (*a real live burglar*); burning or glowing (*live coals*); (of match, bomb, etc.) ready for use, not yet exploded or kindled; (of wire etc.) charged with or carrying electricity; (of performance, broadcast, etc.) transmitted during occurrence or undertaken with audience present (also *predic.*); of current or intense interest or importance (*a live issue*); (of component in machinery) moving or imparting motion; **live wire** highly energetic and forceful person. [ALIVE]

liveable /ˈlɪvəb(ə)l/ *a.* (of life) worth living; (of house, person, etc.) fit to live in or *with*. [LIVE[1]]

livelihood /ˈlaɪvlɪhʊd/ *n.* means of living, sustenance. [OE (LIFE)]

livelong /ˈlɪvlɒŋ/ *a.* in its entire length (*the livelong day*). [LIEF, LONG, assim. to LIVE[1]]

lively /ˈlaɪvlɪ/ *a.* full of life, vigorous, energetic; cheerful; keen (*a lively interest*); **liveliness** *n.* [OE]

liven /ˈlaɪv(ə)n/ *v.* make or become lively, cheer *up*. [LIFE]

liver[1] /ˈlɪvə/ *n.* large glandular organ in abdomen of vertebrates, secreting bile; flesh of some animals' liver as food; dark reddish-brown; **liver salts** salts for curing dyspepsia or biliousness; **liver sausage** sausage of cooked liver etc. [OE]

liver[2] /ˈlɪvə/ *n.* person who lives in specified way (*loose liver*). [LIVE[1]]

liveried /ˈlɪvərɪd/ *a.* wearing livery. [LIVERY]

liverish /ˈlɪvərɪʃ/ *a.* suffering from disorder of the liver; peevish, glum. [LIVER[1]]

Liverpudlian /lɪvəˈpʌdlɪən/ **1** *n.* native of Liverpool. **2** *a.* of Liverpool. [*Liverpool* in NW England]

liverwort /ˈlɪvəwɜːt/ *n.* round flat plant without stems or leaves and sometimes lobed like a liver; mosslike plant of same group. [LIVER[1]]

livery /ˈlɪvərɪ/ *n.* distinctive uniform worn by male servant or by member of City Company; distinctive guise or marking (*livery of grief*); allowance of fodder for horses; **at livery** (of horse) kept for owner for fixed charge; **livery stable** stable where horses are kept at livery or let out for hire. [AF *liveré*, p.p. of *livrer* DELIVER]

lives *pl.* of LIFE.

livestock /ˈlaɪvstɒk/ *n.* animals kept or dealt in for use or profit. [LIVE[1]]

livid /ˈlɪvɪd/ *a.* of bluish leaden colour; *colloq.* very angry. [F or L]

living /ˈlɪvɪŋ/ **1** *n.* being alive; livelihood; position held by clergyman, providing income. **2** *a.* having life; now alive, contemporary; (of likeness) lifelike, exact; (of language) still in vernacular use. **3 living-room** room for general day use; **living wage** wage on which one can live without privation; **within living memory** within memory of people still alive. [LIVE[1] (OE as *a.*)]

lizard /ˈlɪzəd/ *n.* reptile having usu. long body and tail, four legs and rough or scaly hide. [F *lesard* f. L *lacertus*]

LJ *abbr.* (*pl.* **L JJ**) Lord Justice.

'll *v. colloq.* (usu. after pronouns) shall, will (*I'll, he'll, that'll*). [abbr.]

llama /ˈlɑːmə/ *n.* S. American ruminant

kept as beast of burden and for its soft woolly hair. [Sp. f. Quechua]

LL B *abbr*. Bachelor of Laws. [L *legum baccalaureus*]

LL D *abbr*. Doctor of Laws. [L *legum doctor*]

LL M *abbr*. Master of Laws. [L *legum magister*]

Lloyd's /lɔɪdz/ *n*. incorporated society of underwriters in London; **Lloyd's Register** annual classified list of all ships. [*Lloyd*, proprietor of coffee-house where society orig. met]

ln *abbr*. natural logarithm.

lo /ləʊ/ *int. archaic* look; **lo and behold** introduction to mentioning surprising fact. [OE]

loach *n*. small freshwater fish. [F]

load 1 *n*. what is carried or to be carried; amount usu. or actually carried, this as weight or measure of some substances (*lorry-load of bricks*); weight of care, responsibility, etc.; amount of power carried by an electric circuit or supplied by a generating station; material object or force acting as a weight etc.; (in *pl.*) *colloq*. plenty (*of*). **2** *v*. put load on or aboard (vehicle, ship, person, animal, etc.); place (load) aboard ship, on vehicle, etc.; (of ship, vehicle, or person) take load aboard or *up*; burden, strain; supply or assail overwhelmingly *with* (*loaded her with gifts, praise, work*, etc.); put ammunition in (gun), film in (camera), cassette in (tape-recorder), etc., put (film etc.) *into* camera etc.; put (program or data etc.) in computer. **3 get a load of** *sl*. take note of; **loaded question** one put in such a way as to evoke required answer; **load line** = *Plimsoll line*. **4 -loader** *n*., **-loading** *a*. (of gun or machine: *breech-loader*; *front-loading*). [OE, = way]

loaded *a*. *sl*. rich; drunk; *US* drugged.

loadstone *n*. magnetic oxide of iron; piece of it used as magnet; thing that attracts.

loaf[1] *n*. (*pl*. **loaves**) quantity of bread baked alone or as separate or separable part of batch, usu. of standard weight; minced or chopped meat made in shape of loaf and cooked; *sl*. head. [OE]

loaf[2] *v.i*. spend time idly, hang about. [orig. uncert.]

loam *n*. rich soil of clay, sand, and decayed vegetable matter; **loamy** *a*. [OE]

loan 1 *n*. thing lent, esp. sum of money to be returned with or without interest; lending or being lent. **2** *v.t*. (**D**) lend. **3 loan-word** word adopted by one language from another in more or less modified form (e.g. *morale, naïve*); **on loan** being lent. [OE]

loath *predic. a*. averse, disinclined (*was loath to admit it*). [OE]

loathe /ləʊð/ *v.t*. regard with hatred and disgust; **loathing** *n*. [OE]

loathsome /ˈləʊðsəm/ *a*. arousing hatred and disgust; repulsive.

loaves *pl*. of LOAF[1].

lob 1 *v*. (**-bb-**) hit or throw (ball), hit or throw ball, slowly or in high arc. **2** *n*. such ball. [prob. LG or Du.]

lobar /ˈləʊbə/ *a*. of a lobe, esp. of the lung (*lobar pneumonia*). [LOBE]

lobate /ˈləʊbeɪt/ *a*. having lobe(s).

lobby /ˈlɒbɪ/ **1** *n*. entrance-hall, porch; ante-room, corridor; (in House of Commons) large hall open to public used esp. for interviews between MPs and others, (in full **division lobby**) each of two corridors to which members retire to vote; body of lobbyists. **2** *v*. seek to influence (MP etc.) to support one's cause, get (bill etc.) through, by interviews etc. in lobby; solicit members' votes or influence of (person); frequent parliamentary lobby for this purpose. [L *lobia* lodge]

lobbyist *n*. person who lobbies MP etc.

lobe *n*. the lower soft pendulous part of the outer ear; similar part of other organs, esp. brain, liver, and lung. [L f. Gk *lobos* lobe, pod]

lobelia /ləˈbiːlɪə/ *n*. herbaceous plant with brightly coloured flowers. [*Lobel*, botanist]

lobotomy /ləˈbɒtəmɪ/ *n*. incision into white tissue of frontal lobe of brain to relieve some cases of mental disorder. [LOBE]

lobscouse /ˈlɒbskaʊs/ *n*. sailor's dish of meat stewed with vegetables and ship's biscuit. [orig. unkn.]

lobster *n*. large edible sea crustacean with stalked eyes and heavy pincer-like claws, that turns from bluish-black to scarlet when boiled; its flesh as food; **lobster-pot** basket for trapping lobsters. [OE f. L *locusta* lobster, LOCUST]

lobworm /ˈlɒbwɜːm/ *n*. large earthworm used as fishing-bait. [LOB in obs. sense 'pendulous object']

local /ˈləʊk(ə)l/ **1** *a*. in regard to place; belonging to or existing in or peculiar to a particular place (*local history*); of one's own neighbourhood (*the local doctor*); of or affecting a part and not the whole (*local anaesthetic*); (of train, bus, etc.) stopping at all points on route. **2** *n*. inhabitant of particular district; local train, bus, etc.; (*colloq*.) *the* local public house. **3 local authority** body charged with administration of local government; **local colour** touches of detail in story etc. designed to provide convincing background; **local government**

system of administration of county or district etc. by elected representatives of those living there. **4 locally** *adv.* [F f. L (*locus* place)]

locale /ləʊ'kɑ:l/ *n.* scene or locality of operations or events. [F *local*]

locality /ləʊ'kælɪtɪ/ *n.* thing's position; site or scene of something, esp. in relation to surroundings; district. [F or L (LOCAL)]

localize /'ləʊkəlaɪz/ *v.t.* assign or confine to particular place; invest with characteristics of particular place; decentralize. [LOCAL]

locate /ləʊ'keɪt/ *v.t.* discover exact place of; establish in a place; state locality of. [L (LOCAL)]

location /ləʊ'keɪʃ(ə)n/ *n.* particular place; locating; **on location** (of filming) in natural setting rather than in studio.

locative /'lɒkətɪv/ *Gram.* **1** *n.* case expressing location. **2** *a.* of or in the locative. [LOCATE]

loc. cit. *abbr.* in the place cited. [L *loco citato*]

loch /lɒx, lɒk/ *n.* Scottish lake or landlocked arm of sea. [Gael.]

loci *pl.* of LOCUS.

lock[1] **1** *n.* mechanism for fastening door, lid, etc., with bolt that requires key of particular shape to work it; section of canal or river confined within sluiced gates for moving boats from one level to another; mechanism for exploding charge of gun; turning of front wheels of vehicle, maximum extent of this; interlocked or jammed state; wrestling-hold that keeps opponent's arm etc. fixed; (in full **lock forward**) player in second row of Rugby scrum. **2** *v.* fasten (door, box, etc.) with lock, shut *up* (house etc.) thus; shut (person or thing) *up*, *in*, *into*, or *out*, by locking; enclose or hold fast *in*; (of door etc.) be lockable; bring or come into rigidly fixed position, (cause to) jam or catch; store inaccessibly (*up* or *away*). **3 lock-keeper** person in charge of canal lock; **lock-knit** knitted with interlocking stitch; **lock-out** employer's procedure of refusing entry of workers to their place of work until certain terms are agreed to; **lock-stitch** secure sewing-machine stitch; **lock, stock, and barrel** whole of thing, completely; **under lock and key** locked up. [OE]

lock[2] *n.* portion of hair that hangs together; (in *pl.*) the hair of the head (*her golden locks*). [OE]

locker *n.* small lockable cupboard or compartment. [LOCK[1]]

locket /'lɒkɪt/ *n.* small ornamental case containing portrait or lock of hair and usu. hung from neck. [F dimin. of *loc* latch, LOCK[1]]

lockjaw *n.* form of tetanus in which jaws become rigidly closed. [LOCK[1]]

locksmith *n.* maker and mender of locks.

lock-up 1 *n.* premises that can be locked up; time or process of locking up; house or room for temporary detention of prisoners. **2** *a.* able to be locked up.

loco[1] /'ləʊkəʊ/ *n.* (*pl.* **locos**) *colloq.* locomotive engine. [abbr.]

loco[2] /'ləʊkəʊ/ *a. US sl.* crazy. [Sp.]

locomotion /ləʊkə'məʊʃ(ə)n/ *n.* motion or power of motion from place to place; travel, way (esp. artificial) of travelling. [L LOCUS, MOTION]

locomotive /'ləʊkəməʊtɪv/ **1** *n.* (in full **locomotive engine**) engine for drawing trains. **2** *a.* of or having or effecting locomotion, not stationary.

locum tenens /ləʊkəm 'ti:nenz/ (also *colloq.* **locum**) deputy acting esp. for doctor or clergyman. [L, = (one) holding place]

locus /'ləʊkəs/ *n.* (*pl.* **loci** /'ləʊsaɪ/) line or curve etc. made by all points satisfying certain conditions, or by defined motion of point or line or surface. [L, = place]

locus classicus /ləʊkəs 'klæsɪkəs/ best known or most authoritative passage on a subject. [L (prec.)]

locust /'ləʊkəst/ *n.* African or Asian grasshopper migrating in swarms and consuming all vegetation; person of devouring or destructive propensities; any of various kinds of tree and their fruit. [F f. L (*locusta* locust, LOBSTER)]

locution /lə'kju:ʃ(ə)n/ *n.* word or phrase or idiom; style of speech. [F or L (*loquor locut-* speak)]

lode *n.* vein of metal ore. [var. LOAD]

lodestar *n.* star used as guide in navigation, esp. pole-star; guiding principle, object of pursuit.

lodestone var. of LOADSTONE.

lodge 1 *n.* small house at entrance to park or grounds of large house, occupied by gate-keeper etc.; small house used in sporting seasons (*hunting lodge*); porter's room at entrance or gateway of factory, college, etc.; members or meeting-place of branch of society such as Freemasons; beaver's or otter's lair. **2** *v.* provide with temporary accommodation, reside or have one's quarters esp. as lodger; deposit (money etc.) for security; submit (complaint etc.) for attention; place (power etc.) in or *with* person; (cause to) stick or become embedded *in*. [F *loge*, rel. to LEAF]

lodger *n.* person receiving accommodation in another's house for payment.

lodging *n.* accommodation in hired

rooms, dwelling-place; (in *pl.*) room or rooms rented for lodging in.

loess /'ləʊɪs/ *n.* deposit of fine wind-blown soil esp. in basins of large rivers. [Swiss G, = loose]

loft 1 *n.* attic, room over stable esp. for hay and straw; gallery in church or hall (*organ-loft*); pigeon-house; backward slope on face of golf-club, a lofting stroke. **2** *v.t.* send (ball) in high arc. [ON, = air, upper room]

lofty *a.* (of things) towering, of imposing height; haughty or keeping aloof; exalted or noble (*lofty ideals*); **loftily** *adv.*; **loftiness** *n.*

log¹ 1 *n.* unhewn piece of felled tree, any large rough piece of wood esp. cut for firewood; floating device used to ascertain ship's speed; = *log-book*. **2** *v.t.* (**-gg-**) enter in ship's log-book; enter (data etc.) in regular record; attain (cumulative total thus recorded); cut into logs. **3 log-book** book in which details of voyage or journey or registration of vehicle are recorded; **log cabin** hut built of logs; **log in** (or **out**) begin (or finish) operations at terminal of multi-access computer; **sleep like a log** sleep soundly. [orig. unkn.]

log² *n.* logarithm. [abbr.]

logan /'ləʊgən/ *n.* (in full **logan-stone**) poised heavy stone rocking at a touch. [*logan* = (dial.) *logging*, = rocking]

loganberry /'ləʊgənberɪ/ *n.* dark-red fruit, hybrid of raspberry and American blackberry. [*Logan*, horticulturist]

logarithm /'lɒgərɪð(ə)m/ *n.* one of a series of arithmetic exponents tabulated to simplify computation by making it possible to use addition and subtraction instead of multiplication and division; **logarithmic** /-'rɪðmɪk/ *a.*; **logarithmically** /-'rɪðmɪkəlɪ/ *adv.* [L f. Gk *logos* reckoning, *arithmos* number]

loggerhead /'lɒgəhed/ *n.* usu. in **at loggerheads** disagreeing or disputing (*with*). [prob. dial. (*logger* wooden block)]

loggia /'ləʊdʒə/ *n.* open-sided gallery or arcade; open-sided extension to house. [It., = LODGE]

logic /'lɒdʒɪk/ *n.* science of reasoning; particular system or method of reasoning; chain of reasoning (regarded as sound or unsound), use of or ability in argument; inexorable force, compulsion (*the logic of facts*). [foll.]

-logic *suffix* (also **-logical**) forming adjectives corresponding esp. to nouns in -LOGY (*pathological*, *zoological*). [Gk *-logikos* (-LOGY)]

logical *a.* of or according to logic; correctly reasoned; defensible or explicable on ground of consistency; capable of correct reasoning; **logical positivism** see POSITIVISM; **logicality** /-'kælɪtɪ/ *n.*; **logically** *adv.* [F f. L f. Gk, = pertaining to reason (LOGOS)]

logician /lɒ'dʒɪʃ(ə)n/ *n.* user of or expert in logic.

-logist *suffix* forming nouns in sense 'person skilled in -logy' (*geologist*). [-LOGY, -IST]

logistics /lə'dʒɪstɪks/ *n. pl.* art of supplying and organizing (orig. military) services and equipment etc.; **logistic** *a.*; **logistically** *adv.* [F (*loger* lodge)]

logo /'ləʊgəʊ, 'lɒ-/ *n.* (*pl.* **logos**) *colloq.* logotype. [abbr.]

Logos /'lɒgɒs/ *n.* the Word of God, or Second Person of the Trinity. [Gk, = reason, discourse, utterance]

logotype /'lɒgəʊtaɪp/ *n.* non-heraldic design or symbol as badge of an organization; piece of type with this. [Gk *logos* word, TYPE]

logwood *n.* W. Indian tree; wood of this used in dyeing. [LOG¹]

-logy *suffix* forming nouns denoting subject of study (*biology*), or discourse (*trilogy*), or character of speech or language (*tautology*). [F or L or Gk *-logia* (LOGOS)]

loin *n.* (in *pl.*) side and back of body between ribs and hip-bones; (in *sing.*) joint of meat that includes the loin vertebrae. [F f. L *lumbus*]

loincloth *n.* cloth worn around hips, esp. as sole garment.

loiter *v.i.* stand about idly, linger; move or proceed indolently with frequent pauses. [Du.]

loll *v.* recline or sit or stand in lazy attitude; rest (one's head or limbs) lazily on something; hang (one's tongue) *out*, (of tongue) hang *out*. [imit.]

lollipop /'lɒlɪpɒp/ *n.* large round usu. flat boiled sweet on small stick; **lollipop lady** (or **man**) *colloq.* official using circular sign on stick to stop traffic for children to cross road. [orig. uncert.]

lollop /'lɒləp/ *v.i. colloq.* move in ungainly bounds; flop about. [prob. LOLL, TROLLOP]

lolly /'lɒlɪ/ *n. colloq.* lollipop; = *ice lolly*; *sl.* money. [abbr. of LOLLIPOP]

London clay /'lʌnd(ə)n/ geological formation in lower division of Eocene in SE England. [*London*, capital of UK]

Londoner /'lʌndənə/ *n.* native or inhabitant of London.

London pride a pink-flowered saxifrage.

lone *attrib. a.* solitary, without companions; uninhabited, lonely; **lone hand** hand played or player playing against the rest at cards, *fig.* person or action without allies; **lone wolf** loner. [ALONE]

lonely *a.* lacking friends or companions, despondent because of this; isolated, unfrequented, uninhabited; **loneliness** *n.*

loner *n.* person or animal preferring to act alone or not to associate with others.

lonesome *a.* lonely, causing loneliness.

long[1] **1** *a.* (*compar.* and *superl.* /-ŋg-/) measuring much from end to end in space or time; having specified length or duration (*2m. long*; *two weeks long*); seemingly more than the stated amount, lengthy, tedious (*ten long years*); lasting or reaching far back or forward in time (*long memory*); far-reaching, acting at a distance, involving great interval or difference; of elongated shape, remarkable for or distinguished by or concerned with length or duration; (of vowel or syllable) having the greater of two recognized durations; (of stocks etc.) bought in large quantities in advance, with expectation of rise in price. **2** *n.* a long interval or period (*will not take long*; *shall see you before long*); long syllable or vowel. **3** *adv.* for a long time (*have long thought so*); by a long time (*long ago*); throughout specified duration (*all day long*); (in *compar.*) after implied point of time (*shall not wait any longer*). **4 as** (or **so**) **long as** provided that; **in the long run** over long period, eventually; **the long and the short of it** all that need be said, the eventual outcome; **long-distance** travelling or operating between distant places; **long division** division of numbers with details of calculation written down; **long-drawn(-out)** prolonged; **long face** dismal expression; **long-haired** intellectual or hippie; **long-headed** shrewd, far-seeing; **long in the tooth** rather old; **long johns** *colloq.* long underpants; **long jump** athletic contest of jumping as far as possible along the ground in one leap; **long-life** (of milk etc.) treated to prolong period of usability; **long-lived** having a long life, durable; **long odds** very uneven odds; **long on** *colloq.* well supplied with; **long-playing** (of gramophone record) playing for about 15–30 minutes on each side; **long-range** having long range, relating to long period of future time; **long shot** wild guess or venture, bet at long odds (**not by a long shot** by no means); **long-sighted** able to see clearly only what is at a distance, having imagination or foresight; **long-standing** that has long existed; **long-suffering** bearing provocation patiently; **long suit** many cards of one suit in a hand, *fig.* one's strong point; **long-term** occurring in or relating to a long period of time; **long ton** see TON; **long wave** radio wave with length over 1,000 m.; **long-winded** (of speech or writing) tediously lengthy. [OE]

long[2] *v.i.* feel strong desire *for*; ardently wish *to*. [OE, = seem LONG[1] to]

long. *abbr.* longitude.

longboat *n.* largest boat carried by sailing ship. [LONG[1]]

longbow *n.* large bow drawn by hand and shooting long feathered arrow.

longeron /ˈlɒndʒərən/ *n.* (usu. in *pl.*) longitudinal member of aeroplane's fuselage. [F]

longevity /lɒnˈdʒevɪtɪ/ *n.* long life. [L (*longus* long, *aevum* age)]

longhand *n.* ordinary writing as distinct from typing, shorthand, etc. [LONG[1]]

longing /ˈlɒŋɪŋ/ *n.* intense desire. [LONG[2]]

longitude /ˈlɒŋgɪtju:d, ˈlɒndʒ-/ *n.* angular distance east or west from the meridian of Greenwich or other standard meridian to that of any place; *Astron.* body's or point's angular distance esp. along ecliptic. [L *longitudo* length (*longus* long)]

longitudinal /lɒŋgɪˈtju:dɪn(ə)l, lɒndʒ-/ *a.* of longitude; of or in length; lying longways; **longitudinally** *adv.*

long-shore *a.* found on the shore; employed along the shore, esp. near a port. [*along shore*]

longshoreman *n.* person employed in loading and unloading ships from shore.

longways *adv.* (also **longwise**) = LENGTHWAYS.

loo *n. colloq.* lavatory. [orig. uncert.]

loofah /ˈlu:fə/ *n.* dried pod of a kind of gourd used as rough sponge while bathing. [Arab.]

look /lʊk/ **1** *v.* use one's sight, turn one's eyes in some direction; make visual or mental search; have specified appearance, seem (*look a fool, foolish*); turn one's eyes on, contemplate or examine (*looked her in the eyes*); ascertain or observe by sight *what, how, whether*, etc.; (of thing) face or be turned in some direction; indicate (emotion etc.) by one's looks; take care or make sure *that*, expect *to do* thing. **2** *n.* act of looking, gaze or glance; (in *sing.* or *pl.*) appearance of face, expression, personal aspect; (of thing) appearance. **3** *int.* (also **look here!**) of protest or demanding attention. **4 look after** attend to, take charge of; **look one's age** seem as old as one really is; **look-alike** person or thing closely resembling another; **look down on** (or **down one's nose at**) regard with contempt or feeling of superiority; **look for** expect, try to find (*look for trouble*);

look forward to await (expected event) eagerly or with specified feelings; **look in** make short visit or call; **look-in** *n.* brief visit, chance of participation or success; **look into** investigate; **look on** regard (*as*), be spectator; **look oneself** seem to be in good health or spirits; **look out** be vigilant or prepared (*for*), search for and produce, have or afford outlook *on*, *over*, etc.; **look over** inspect; **look-see** *sl.* inspection; **look sharp** make haste; **look to** consider, be careful about, rely on; **look up** seek information about in reference book etc., improve in prospect, *colloq.* go to visit; **look up to** respect or admire (senior or superior person); **not like the look of** find alarming or suspicious. [OE]

looker *n.* person of specified appearance (*good-looker*); *colloq.* attractive woman; **looker-on** spectator.

looking-glass *n.* glass mirror.

look-out *n.* careful watch (*on the look-out for*); observation-post; person etc. stationed to keep watch; prospect (*it's a poor look-out*); person's own concern (*that's your look-out*).

loom[1] *n.* apparatus for weaving. [OE]

loom[2] *v.i.* appear dimly, be seen in vague and often magnified or threatening form (*lit.* or *fig.*). [prob. LG or Du.]

loon *n.* kind of diving bird; *sl.* crazy person (cf. foll.). [ON]

loony *n.* & *a.* *sl.* lunatic; **loony-bin** mental home or hospital. [abbr.]

loop 1 *n.* figure produced by curve, or doubled thread etc., that crosses itself; thing, path, etc., forming this figure; similarly shaped attachment or ornament used as fastening; metal ring etc. as handle etc.; contraceptive coil; skating figure or vertical aerobatic manœuvre describing shape of loop; complete circuit for electric current; endless strip of tape or film allowing continuous repetition; sequence of computer operations repeated until some condition is satisfied. **2** *v.* form (thread etc.) into loop; enclose (as) with loop, fasten with loops; form loop. **3 loop-line** railway or telegraph line that diverges from main line and joins it again; **loop the loop** perform aerobatic loop. [orig. unkn.]

loophole *n.* means of evading rule etc. without infringing letter of it; narrow vertical slit in wall of fort etc.

loopy *a.* *sl.* crazy, daft.

loose 1 *a.* not or no longer held by bonds or restraint; detached or detachable from its place, not held together or contained or fixed; slack, relaxed; inexact or indefinite, vague or incorrect (*loose grammar, style, translation*); not compact or dense (*loose scrum, soil*); morally lax. **2** *v.t.* free, untie, or detach; release; discharge (missile); relax (*loose hold*). **3 at a loose end** unoccupied; **loose cover** removable cover for armchair etc.; **loose-leaf** (of notebook etc.) with each leaf separately removable; **on the loose** enjoying oneself freely. [ON]

loosen *v.* make or become loose or looser; **loosen person's tongue** make him talk freely.

loot 1 *n.* booty, spoil; *sl.* money. **2** *v.* take loot (from), carry off (as) loot. [Hindi]

lop[1] *v.t.* (**-pp-**) cut away branches or twigs of; cut or strip *off* or *away*. [OE]

lop[2] *v.i.* (**-pp-**) hang limply; **lop-eared** having drooping ears. [rel. to LOB]

lope 1 *v.i.* run with long bounding stride. **2** *n.* long bounding stride. [ON, rel. to LEAP]

lopsided /lɒp'saɪdɪd/ *a.* with one side lower etc., unbalanced. [LOP[2]]

loquacious /lɒ'kweɪʃəs/ *a.* talkative; **loquacity** /-'kwæsɪtɪ/ *n.* [L (*loquor* speak)]

lord 1 *n.* master or ruler; *hist.* feudal superior, esp. of manor; peer of the realm or person entitled to title *Lord*; (**Lord**) prefixed as designation of marquis, earl, viscount, or baron, or (to Christian name) of younger son of duke or marquis. **2** *int.* (**Lord, good Lord,** etc.) expressing surprise, dismay, etc. **3 the Lord** God or Christ; **the Lords** = *House of Lords*; **live like a lord** live sumptuously; **Lord Bishop** ceremonious title of any bishop; **Lord Chamberlain** head of management in Royal Household; **Lord Chief Justice** president of Queen's Bench Division; **Lord (High) Chancellor** highest officer of the Crown, presiding in House of Lords etc.; **lord it over** domineer; **Lord Lieutenant** chief executive authority and head of magistrates in each county, *hist.* viceroy of Ireland; **Lord Mayor** title of mayor in some large cities; **Lord President of the Council** cabinet minister presiding at Privy Council; **Lord Privy Seal** senior cabinet minister without official duties; **Lord's day** Sunday; **Lord's Prayer** the Our Father; **Lords spiritual** bishops in House of Lords; **Lord's Supper** Eucharist; **Lords temporal** members of House of Lords not bishops; **Our Lord** Christ. [OE, = loaf-keeper (LOAF[1], WARD)]

lordly *a.* haughty, imperious; suitable for a lord; **lordliness** *n.*

lordship *n.* title used in addressing or referring to man with rank of Lord (*Your, His, Lordship*).

lore *n.* body of traditions and facts on a subject (*ghost lore*); *archaic* erudition. [OE (LEARN)]

lorgnette /lɔ:'njet/ *n.* pair of eyeglasses or opera-glasses held to eyes on long handle. [F (*lorgner* squint)]

lorn *a. archaic* desolate, forlorn. [OE, p.p. of LOSE]

lorry /'lɒrɪ/ *n.* large strong motor vehicle for transporting goods etc. [orig. uncert.]

lose /lu:z/ *v.* (*past* and *p.p.* **lost**) be deprived of, cease to have, esp. by negligence or misadventure; be deprived of (person) by death; become unable to find, fail to keep in sight or follow or mentally grasp; let or have pass from one's control or reach (*lose one's chance, composure, way*); get rid of (*have lost our pursuers*); fail to obtain or catch or perceive (*lose a train, a word*); be defeated in (game, race, lawsuit, battle); forfeit (stake, right to thing); spend (time, efforts, etc.) to no purpose; suffer loss or detriment, be the worse off; cause person the loss of (*will lose you your place*); (of clock etc.) become slow, become slow by (specified time); (in *pass.*) disappear, perish, die or be dead (*was lost at sea*; *is a lost art*); **be lost** (or **lose oneself**) **in** be engrossed in; **be lost on** be wasted on, not be noticed or appreciated by; **be lost to** be no longer affected by or accessible to (*lost to pity*; *lost to the world*); **get lost** *sl.* (usu. in *imper.*) go away; **lose out** *colloq.* be unsuccessful, not get full chance or advantage; **losing battle** (esp. *fig.*) battle in which defeat seems certain. [OE]

loser *n.* person who loses, esp. contest or game (*is a poor loser*); *colloq.* one who regularly fails.

loss *n.* losing or being lost; thing or amount lost; detriment resulting from losing; **at a loss** (*sold* etc.) for less than was paid for it; **be at a loss** be puzzled or uncertain; **loss-leader** article sold at a loss so as to attract customers.

lost *past* and *p.p.* of LOSE.

lot *n.* (1) *colloq.* (often in *pl.*) a large number or amount (*a lot of friends*; *lots of butter*; *works a lot*); much (*a lot better*); (2) each of a set of objects used in making chance selection; this method of deciding (*chosen by lot*); share or responsibility resulting from it; person's destiny, fortune, or condition; plot, allotment of land (*parking lot*); article or set of articles for sale at auction etc.; number or quantity of associated persons or things; **bad lot** person of bad character; **cast** (or **draw**) **lots** decide with lots; **throw in one's lot with** decide to share fortunes of; **the (whole) lot** the total number or quantity. [OE]

loth var. of LOATH.

Lothario /ləʊ'θeərɪəʊ/ *n.* (*pl.* **Lotharios**) libertine. [character in play]

lotion /'ləʊʃ(ə)n/ *n.* medicinal or cosmetic liquid preparation applied to skin. [F or L (*lavo lot-* wash)]

lottery /'lɒtərɪ/ *n.* means of raising money by selling numbered tickets and giving prizes to holders of numbers drawn at random; thing whose success is governed by chance. [Du. (LOT)]

lotto /'lɒtəʊ/ *n.* game of chance similar to bingo but with numbers drawn instead of called. [It.]

lotus /'ləʊtəs/ *n.* legendary plant inducing luxurious languor when eaten; kind of water-lily etc., esp. used symbolically in Hinduism and Buddhism; **lotus-eater** person given to indolent enjoyment; **lotus position** cross-legged position of meditation with feet resting on thighs. [L f. Gk]

loud **1** *a.* strongly audible, noisy; (of colours etc.) gaudy, obtrusive. **2** *adv.* loudly. **3** **loud hailer** electronic device for amplifying sound of voice so that it can be heard at a distance; **out loud** aloud (*laughed out loud*). [OE]

loudspeaker /laʊd'spi:kə/ *n.* apparatus that converts electrical impulses into sound.

lough /lɒk, lɒx/ *n. Ir.* lake, arm of sea. [Ir. (LOCH)]

lounge **1** *v.i.* recline comfortably; loll, stand or move about idly. **2** *n.* spell of or place for lounging; public room (e.g. in hotel) for lounging; place in airport etc. with seats for waiting passengers; sitting-room in house. **3** **lounge-suit** man's suit for ordinary day wear. [orig. uncert.]

lour *v.i.* frown, look sullen or (of sky etc.) dark and threatening. [orig. unkn.]

louse **1** *n.* (*pl.* **lice**) a kind of parasitic insect; *sl.* (*pl.* **louses**) contemptible person. **2** *v.t.* remove lice from. **3** **louse up** *sl.* spoil, mess up. [OE]

lousy /'laʊzɪ/ *a.* infested with lice; *sl.* disgusting, very bad; *sl.* swarming or well supplied *with*; **lousily** *adv.*; **lousiness** *n.*

lout *n.* hulking or rough-mannered fellow; **loutish** *a.* [orig. uncert.]

louvre /'lu:və/ *n.* (also **louver**) one of a set of overlapping slats arranged to admit air and exclude light or rain; domed erection on roof with side openings for ventilation etc. [F *lover* skylight]

lovable /'lʌvəb(ə)l/ *a.* inspiring love or affection. [LOVE]

lovage /'lʌvɪdʒ/ *n.* herb used for flavouring etc. [F *levesche* f. L *ligusticum* Ligurian]

love /lʌv/ **1** *n.* deep affection or fondness for person or thing; sexual passion, sexual relations; beloved one, sweetheart (often as form of address), *colloq*. person of whom one is fond; affectionate greetings (*give her my love*); (often **Love**) representation of Cupid; (in games) no score, nil. **2** *v*. feel love or deep fondness (for); delight in, admire, greatly cherish; be inclined, esp. as habit (*children love to dress up*), greatly like *to do* thing, find pleasure *doing* thing. **3 fall in love (with)** begin to feel great love (for); **for love** for pleasure not profit; **in love (with)** enamoured (of); **love-affair** romantic or sexual relationship between two people in love; **love-bird** parakeet esp. of kind seeming to show great affection for its mate; **love-child** illegitimate child; **love game** game in which loser makes no score; **love-hate relationship** intense emotional response involving ambivalent feelings of love and hate towards same object; **love-in-a-mist** blue-flowered garden plant; **love-lies-bleeding** garden plant with drooping spikes of purple-red bloom; **make love** have sexual intercourse, pay amorous attentions *to*; **not for love or money** not in any circumstances. [OE]

loveless *a*. unloving or unloved or both.

lovelorn *a*. pining from unrequited love.

lovely 1 *a*. exquisitely beautiful; *colloq*. pleasing, delightful. **2** *n*. *colloq*. pretty woman. **3 loveliness** *n*. [OE]

lover *n*. person (esp. man) in love with another; man with whom woman is having sexual relations; (in *pl*.) pair in love; one who likes or enjoys something (*lover of music; dog-lover*). [LOVE]

lovesick *a*. languishing with love.

lovey-dovey /lʌvɪˈdʌvɪ/ *a*. *colloq*. fondly affectionate and sentimental.

loving 1 *a*. feeling or showing love, affectionate. **2** *n*. affection, love. **3 loving-cup** two-handled drinking-cup passed round at banquets.

low¹ /ləʊ/ **1** *a*. not high or tall or reaching far up (*a low house*); not elevated in position (*low altitude; sun is low*); of or in humble rank or position (*of low birth*); of small or less than normal amount or extent or intensity (*low price, temperature, fever*); small or reduced in quantity (*stocks are low*); coming below normal level (*dress with low neck*); dejected, lacking vigour (*low spirits*); (of sound) not shrill or loud; not exalted or sublime, commonplace; unfavourable (*low opinion*); abject, mean, vulgar (*low cunning; low slang*); (in *compar*.) situated on less high land or to the south, (of geological period) earlier. **2** *n*. low or lowest level or number (*pound reached a new low*); area of low pressure. **3** *adv*. in or to low position (*lit*. or *fig*.); in low tone (*talk low*); (of sound) at or to low pitch. **4 low-born** of humble birth; **Low Church** section of Church of England giving low place to ritual, priestly authority, and sacraments; **low-class** of low quality or social class; **low comedy** that in which subject and treatment border on farce; **Low Countries** the Netherlands, Belgium, and Luxembourg; **low-down** *a*. abject, mean, dishonourable; **low-down** *n*. *sl*. relevant information (*on*); **lower case** see CASE²; **lower class** working class; **Lower House** larger and usu. elected body in legislature, esp. House of Commons; **lower mammal, plant** those less highly developed; **low frequency** (in radio) 30–300 kilohertz; **low-grade** of low quality; **low-key** restrained, lacking intensity; **low-level language** computer language close in form to machine-readable code; **low-pitched** (of sound) low, (of roof) having only slight slope; **low pressure** low degree of activity or exertion, condition of atmosphere with pressure below average; **low season** period of fewest visitors at resort etc.; **Low Sunday** Sunday after Easter; **low tide** tide of lowest level, time of this; **low water** low tide. [ON]

low² /ləʊ/ **1** *n*. sound made by cows, moo. **2** *v.i*. make this sound. [OE]

lowbrow *colloq*. **1** *a*. not intellectual or cultured. **2** *n*. lowbrow person. [LOW¹]

lower¹ *v*. let or haul down; make or become lower, reduce height or elevation of (*lower one's eyes*); degrade.

lower² var. of LOUR.

lowermost *a*. lowest. [LOW¹]

lowland 1 *n*. low-lying country. **2** *a*. of or in lowland. **3 lowlander** *n*.

lowly *a*. humble, unpretending; **lowliness** *n*.

loyal /ˈlɔɪəl/ *a*. faithful (*to*), steadfast in allegiance, devoted to legitimate sovereign etc.; **loyal toast** toast to sovereign; **loyally** *adv*.; **loyalty** *n*. [F f. L (LEGAL)]

loyalist *n*. one who remains loyal to legitimate sovereign etc., esp. in face of rebellion or usurpation; **loyalism** *n*.

lozenge /ˈlɒzɪndʒ/ *n*. small sweet or medicinal etc. tablet to be dissolved in the mouth; rhombus, diamond figure; lozenge-shaped object. [F]

LP *abbr*. long-playing (record).

L-plate /ˈelpleɪt/ *n*. sign bearing letter L, attached to front and rear of motor vehicle to indicate that it is being driven by a learner. [PLATE]

Lr *symb*. lawrencium.

LSD *abbr*. lysergic acid diethylamide, a powerful hallucinogenic drug.

£.s.d. /elesˈdiː/ *n*. pounds, shillings, and

pence (in former British currency); money, riches. [L *librae, solidi, denarii*]
LSE *abbr*. London School of Economics.
LT *abbr*. low tension.
Lt. *abbr*. Lieutenant; light.
Ltd. *abbr*. Limited.
Lu *symb*. lutetium.
lubber *n*. clumsy fellow, lout. [orig. uncert.]
lubberly *a*. awkward, unskilful; **lubberliness** *n*.
lubricant /'lu:brɪkənt/ *n*. oil or grease etc. used to reduce friction in machinery etc. [foll.]
lubricate /'lu:brɪkeɪt/ *v.t.* apply lubricant to; make slippery; **lubrication** /-'keɪʃ(ə)n/ *n*.; **lubricator** *n*. [L (*lubricus* slippery)]
lubricity /lu:'brɪsɪtɪ/ *n*. slipperiness; skill in evasion; lewdness. [F or L (prec.)]
lucerne /lu:'sɜ:n/ *n*. alfalfa. [F f. Prov., = glow-worm, with ref. to shiny seeds]
lucid /'lu:sɪd/ *a*. expressing or expressed clearly; sane; **lucidity** /-'sɪdɪtɪ/ *n*. [F or It. f. L (*lux luc-* light)]
Lucifer /'lu:sɪfə/ *n*. Satan. [prec., L *fero* bring]
luck *n*. chance regarded as bringer of good or bad fortune; circumstances of life (beneficial or not) brought by this; good fortune, success due to chance (*in, out of, luck*); **down on one's luck** in a period of bad fortune; **hard luck** worse fortune than one deserves; **push one's luck** take undue risks; **try one's luck** make a venture; **worse luck** unfortunately. [LG or Du.]
luckless *a*. invariably having bad luck; ending in failure.
lucky *a*. having or resulting from good luck, esp. as distinct from skill or design or merit; bringing good luck (*lucky charm*); **lucky dip** tub etc. containing articles of different value from which one chooses at random; **luckily** *adv*.
lucrative /'lu:krətɪv/ *a*. yielding considerable profits. [L (foll.)]
lucre /'lu:kə/ *n*. *derog*. pecuniary gain as motive. [F or L (*lucrum* gain)]
Luddite /'lʌdaɪt/ **1** *n*. member of bands of English artisans (1811–16) who raised riots for destruction of newly introduced machinery; person similarly engaged in seeking to obstruct progress. **2** *a*. of Luddites. [Ned *Lud*, destroyer of machinery]
ludicrous /'lu:dɪkrəs/ *a*. absurd, ridiculous, laughable. [L (*ludicrum* stage play)]
ludo /'lu:dəʊ/ *n*. simple game played with dice and counters on a special board. [L, = I play]
luff *v*. bring ship's head, bring head of (ship), nearer the wind; raise or lower (crane's jib). [F, prob. f. LG]
lug 1 *v*. (**-gg-**) drag or carry with effort or violence (*along* etc.); pull hard *at*. **2** *n*. hard or rough pull; projection on object by which it may be carried, fixed in place, etc.; *colloq*. ear. [prob. Scand.]
luggage /'lʌgɪdʒ/ *n*. suitcases, bags, etc., for containing traveller's belongings. [prec.]
lugger *n*. small ship with four-cornered sails. [LUG]
lugsail *n*. four-cornered sail on yard.
lugubrious /lu:'gu:brɪəs/ *a*. doleful. [L (*lugeo* mourn)]
lugworm *n*. large marine worm used as bait. [orig. unkn.]
lukewarm /'lu:kwɔ:m/ *a*. moderately warm, tepid; not enthusiastic, indifferent. [OE (now dial. *luke* warm), WARM]
lull 1 *v*. send to sleep, soothe; quiet (suspicion etc.) usu. by deception; (in *pass.*) be deluded *into* (undue confidence); (of storm or noise) lessen, fall quiet. **2** *n*. intermission in storm etc., temporary period of inactivity or quiet. [imit.]
lullaby /'lʌləbaɪ/ *n*. soothing song to send child to sleep. [prec.]
lumbago /lʌm'beɪgəʊ/ *n*. rheumatic pain in muscles of loins. [L (*lumbus* loin)]
lumbar /'lʌmbə/ *a*. of the loins. [med.L (prec.)]
lumber 1 *n*. disused and cumbersome articles; useless stuff; partly prepared timber. **2** *v*. encumber *with* (esp. of person *with* unwanted task or situation); fill *up* inconveniently, obstruct (place); move in blundering noisy way; cut and prepare forest timber. **3 lumber-jacket** jacket of kind worn by lumberjacks; **lumber-room** room in which disused articles are kept. [orig. uncert.]
lumberjack *n*. one who fells and removes lumber.
luminary /'lu:mɪnərɪ/ *n*. natural light-giving body, esp. sun or moon; person as source of intellectual or spiritual light. [F or L (*lumen lumin-* light)]
luminescent /lu:mɪ'nesənt/ *a*. emitting light without heat; **luminescence** *n*. [L (prec.)]
luminous /'lu:mɪnəs/ *a*. shedding light; phosphorescent and so visible in darkness; **luminosity** /-'nɒsɪtɪ/ *n*. [F or L (LUMINARY)]
lump[1] **1** *n*. compact mass of no particular or regular shape; protuberance or swelling on a surface; *sl*. great quantity, lot; heavy, dull, or ungainly person. **2** *v*. put together in a lump, collect in a lump; treat as all alike (often with *together*). **3 the lump** casual workers esp. in building trade who are paid

in lump sums; **in the lump** generally, taking things as a whole; **lump in one's throat** feeling of discomfort there due to anxiety or emotion; **lump sugar** sugar in small lumps or cubes; **lump sum** sum covering number of items, money paid down at once. [Scand.]

lump² *v.t. colloq.* put up with ungraciously (*you can like it or lump it*). [imit.]

lumpish *a.* heavy and clumsy; stupid, lethargic. [LUMP¹]

lumpy *a.* full of or covered with lumps; (of water) choppy; **lumpily** *adv.*; **lumpiness** *n.*

lunacy /'lu:nəsɪ/ *n.* insanity, mental unsoundness; great folly. [F f. L (foll.)]

lunar /'lu:nə/ *a.* of or like or concerned with the moon; **lunar (excursion) module** module for making journey from orbiting spacecraft to moon's surface and back; **lunar month** period of moon's revolution, esp. = LUNATION, *pop.* period of four weeks. [L (*luna* moon)]

lunate /'lu:neɪt/ *a.* cresent-shaped.

lunatic /'lu:nətɪk/ **1** *a.* insane; extremely reckless or foolish. **2** *n.* lunatic person. **3 lunatic asylum** *hist.* mental home or hospital; **lunatic fringe** fanatical or eccentric or visionary minority of party etc. [LUNACY]

lunation /lu:'neɪʃ(ə)n/ *n.* interval between new moons, about 29½ days. [med.L (LUNAR)]

lunch 1 *n.* midday meal; light refreshment at mid-morning. **2** *v.* take lunch, provide lunch for. [foll.]

luncheon /'lʌntʃ(ə)n/ *n. formal* midday meal; **luncheon meat** tinned meat loaf of pork etc.; **luncheon voucher** voucher given to employee as part of pay and exchangeable for food at certain restaurants and shops. [orig. uncert.]

lung *n.* either of the pair of air-breathing organs in man and most vertebrates. [OE, rel. to LIGHT²]

lunge 1 *n.* sudden forward movement of body in thrusting, hitting, or kicking; thrust; long rope on which horse is held and made to move in circle around its trainer. **2** *v.* deliver or make a lunge (*out*, *at*, etc.); drive (weapon etc.) violently in some direction; exercise (horse) on a lunge. [F *allonger* (*long* LONG)]

lupin /'lu:pɪn/ *n.* garden or fodder plant with long tapering spikes of flowers. [foll.]

lupine /'lu:paɪn/ *a.* of or like wolves. [L *lupinus* (*lupus* wolf)]

lupus /'lu:pəs/ *n.* ulcerous skin disease, esp. tuberculosis of skin. [L, = wolf]

lurch¹ 1 *n.* sudden lean or deviation to one side, stagger. **2** *v.i.* make lurch, stagger. [orig. Naut., of uncert. orig.]

lurch² *n.* only in **leave in the lurch** abandon (friend or ally) to an awkward situation, desert in difficulties. [obs. F *lourche* a kind of backgammon]

lurcher *n.* dog cross-bred between collie or sheep-dog and greyhound and used esp. by poachers. [LURK]

lure 1 *v.t.* entice (*away*, *into*); recall with lure. **2** *n.* thing used to entice; enticing quality *of* a pursuit etc.; falconer's apparatus for recalling hawk. [F f. Gmc]

lurid /'ljʊərɪd/ *a.* strong and glaring in colour; sensational, showy; horrifying (*lurid details*); ghastly, wan. [L]

lurk *v.i.* linger furtively or unobtrusively; lie in ambush, be hidden *in*, *under*, *about*, etc.; be latent (*lurking sympathy for*). [perh. f. LOUR]

luscious /'lʌʃəs/ *a.* richly sweet in taste or smell; (of style) over-rich; voluptuously attractive. [perh. rel. to DELICIOUS]

lush *a.* (of grass etc.) luxuriant and succulent; *fig.* luxurious. [orig. uncert.]

lust 1 *n.* strong sexual desire; passionate desire *for* or enjoyment *of* (*lust for power*, *of battle*); sensuous appetite regarded as sinful (*lusts of the flesh*). **2** *v.i.* have strong or excessive (esp. sexual) desire (with *after* or *for*). **3 lustful** *a.*; **lustfully** *adv.* [OE]

lustre /'lʌstə/, *US* **luster** *n.* gloss, shining surface; brilliance, splendour; iridescent glaze on pottery and porcelain; such pottery and porcelain; **lustrous** *a.* [F f. It. (L *lustro* illumine)]

lusty *a.* healthy and strong; vigorous, lively; **lustily** *adv.*; **lustiness** *n.* [LUST]

lutanist var. of LUTENIST.

lute¹ /lu:t/ *n.* guitar-like instrument with long neck and pear-shaped body, much used in 14th–17th c. [F f. Arab.]

lute² /lu:t/ **1** *n.* clay or cement for making joints airtight etc. **2** *v.t.* treat with lute. [F, or L *lutum* mud]

lutenist /'lu:tənɪst/ *n.* lute-player. [LUTE¹]

lutetium /lu:'ti:ʃəm/ *n.* heaviest element of lanthanide series. [*Lutetia*, anc. name of Paris]

Lutheran /'lu:θərən/ **1** *a.* of Luther, or the Protestant Reformation and doctrines associated with him. **2** *n.* follower or adherent of Luther, member of Lutheran Church. **3 Lutheranism** *n.* [Martin *Luther*, religious leader]

luxe /lʌks, lʊks/ *n.* luxury; cf. DE LUXE. [F, f. L *luxus*]

luxuriant /lʌg'zjʊərɪənt/ *a.* growing profusely; exuberant, florid; **luxuriance** *n.* [L (LUXURY)]

luxuriate /lʌg'zjʊərɪeɪt/ *v.i.* revel or feel keen delight *in*, abandon oneself to enjoyment or ease.

luxurious /lʌg'zjʊərɪəs/ *a.* supplied with luxuries, extremely comfortable; fond of luxury. [F f. L (foll.)]

luxury /'lʌkʃərɪ/ *n.* choice or costly surroundings, possessions, food, etc.; habitual use or enjoyment of these; thing desirable for comfort or enjoyment but not essential; *attrib.* comfortable and expensive (*luxury flat*). [F f. L (LUXE)]

LV *abbr.* luncheon voucher.

LXX *abbr.* Septuagint.

-ly[1] *suffix* forming adjectives esp. from nouns, in sense 'having qualities of' (*princely*, *manly*) or 'recurring at intervals of' (*daily*, *hourly*). [OE (LIKE[1])]

-ly[2] *suffix* forming adverbs from adjectives (*boldly*, *happily*, *miserably*). [OE (as prec.)]

Lyceum /laɪ'si:əm/ *n.* garden at Athens where Aristotle taught; his followers; his philosophy. [L f. Gk]

lychee /'laɪtʃi:/ var. of LITCHI.

lychgate var. of LICHGATE.

lye /laɪ/ *n.* water made alkaline with wood ashes; any alkaline solution for washing. [OE]

lying *partic.* of LIE[1] and LIE[2].

lymph /lɪmf/ *n.* colourless fluid from tissues or organs of body, containing white blood-cells; this fluid used as vaccine. [F, or L *lympha*]

lymphatic /lɪm'fætɪk/ *a.* of or secreting or conveying lymph; (of person) flabby, pale, sluggish.

lynch /lɪntʃ/ *v.t.* (of mob) execute or punish violently without lawful trial; **lynch law** such procedure by self-constituted illegal court. [orig. *US*, after *Lynch*, JP]

lynx /lɪŋks/ *n.* wild animal of cat family with short tail, spotted fur, and proverbially keen sight; **lynx-eyed** keen-sighted. [L f. Gk]

lyre /'laɪə/ *n.* ancient U-shaped stringed instrument used esp. for accompanying song; **lyre-bird** Australian bird, the male of which can spread its tail into lyre shape. [F f. L *lyra* f. Gk]

lyric /'lɪrɪk/ **1** *a.* (of poetry) expressing writer's emotions usu. briefly and in stanzas or groups of lines; (of poet) writing in this manner; or of for the lyre; meant to be sung, fit to be expressed in song, of the nature of song. **2** *n.* lyric poem; (esp. in *pl.*) words of song; (in *pl.*) lyric verses. [F or L (prec.)]

lyrical *a.* resembling, using language appropriate to, lyric poetry; songlike; *colloq.* highly enthusiastic; **lyrically** *adv.*

lyricist *n.* writer of (esp. popular) lyrics.

-lysis *suffix* forming nouns denoting disintegration or decomposition (*electrolysis*). [L f. Gk *lusis* loosening (*luō* loosen)]

-lyte *suffix* forming nouns denoting substances that can be decomposed (*electrolyte*). [L, f. Gk *lutos* loosed (*luō* loosen)]

M

M, m /em/ *n.* (*pl.* **Ms, M's**) thirteenth letter; *Rom. num.* 1,000.

M *abbr.* mega-; motorway.

M. *abbr.* Master; *Monsieur*.

m. *abbr.* metre(s); mile(s); million(s); milli-; minute(s); masculine; married; male.

'm *v. colloq.* = *am* in *I'm*. [abbr.]

ma /mɑ:/ *n. colloq.* mother. [abbr. of MAMMA]

MA *abbr.* Master of Arts.

ma'am /mæm, mɑ:m, məm/ *n.* madam (used esp. in addressing royal lady or officer in WRAC etc.). [abbr.]

mac *n. colloq.* mackintosh. [abbr.]

macabre /mə'kɑ:br/ *a.* grim, gruesome. [F]

macadam /mə'kædəm/ *n.* material for road-making with successive layers of compacted broken stone ; = *tar macadam* (see TAR[1]); **macadamize** *v.t.* [*McAdam*, surveyor]

macaroni /mækə'rəʊnɪ/ *n.* pasta formed into tubes; (*pl.* **macaronies**) 18th-c. dandy. [It. f. Gk]

macaroon /mækə'ru:n/ *n.* small cake or biscuit made with ground almonds or coconut. [F f. It. (MACARONI)]

macaw /mə'kɔ:/ *n.* American parrot with bright colours and long tail. [Port. *macao*]

McCoy /mə'kɔɪ/ *n. colloq.* only in **the real McCoy** the real thing, the genuine article. [orig. uncert.]

mace[1] *n.* staff of office, esp. symbol of Speaker's authority in House of Commons; *hist.* heavy club usu. having metal head and spikes. [F f. Rmc]

mace[2] *n.* dried outer covering of nutmeg as spice. [F f. L *macir*]

macédoine /'mæsɪdwɑ:n/ *n.* mixed fruit or vegetables, esp. cut up small or in jelly. [F]

macerate /'mæsəreɪt/ *v.* make or

become soft by soaking; waste away by fasting; **maceration** /-'reɪʃ(ə)n/ *n.* [L]
machete /mə'tʃetɪ, -'tʃeɪtɪ/ *n.* broad heavy knife used in Central America and W. Indies. [Sp. f. L]
machiavellian /mækɪə'velɪən/ *a.* elaborately cunning; deceitful, perfidious. [*Machiavelli*, political thinker]
machinate /'mækɪneɪt, 'mæʃ-/ *v.i.* lay plots, make intrigue; **machination** /-'neɪʃ(ə)n/ *n.*; **machinator** *n.* [L (foll.)]
machine /mə'ʃi:n/ **1** *n.* apparatus for applying mechanical power, having several parts each with definite function; bicycle, motor cycle, etc.; aircraft; computer; controlling system of an organization (*party machine*); person who acts mechanically. **2** *v.t.* make or operate on with machine (esp. of sewing or printing). **3 machine-readable** in form that computer can process; **machine tool** mechanically operated tool for working on metal, wood, or plastics. [F f. L f. Gk *mēkhanē*]
machine-gun 1 *n.* mounted automatic gun giving continuous fire. **2** *v.t.* (**-nn-**) shoot at with machine-gun.
machinery *n.* machines; mechanism; organized system (*of*), means arranged (*for*).
machinist *n.* one who operates a machine, esp. a sewing-machine or a machine tool; one who makes machinery. [F & MACHINE]
machismo /mə'tʃɪzməʊ/ *n.* assertive manliness, masculine pride. [Sp.]
Mach number /mɑ:k, mæk/ ratio of speed of body to speed of sound in surrounding medium. [*Mach*, physicist]
macho /'mætʃəʊ/ **1** *a.* manly, virile. **2** *n.* macho man; machismo. [MACHISMO]
mack var. of MAC.
mackerel /'mækər(ə)l/ *n.* (*pl.* same) sea-fish used as food; **mackerel sky** sky dappled with rows of small white fleecy clouds. [AF]
mackintosh /'mækɪntɒʃ/ *n.* waterproof coat or cloak; cloth waterproofed with rubber. [*Macintosh*, inventor]
macramé /mə'krɑ:mɪ/ *n.* art of knotting cord or string in patterns to make decorative articles; work so made. [Turk. f. Arab., = bedspread]
macro- *in comb.* long, large, large-scale. [Gk (*makros* long)]
macrobiotic /mækrəʊbaɪ'ɒtɪk/ *a.* relating to or following diet intended to prolong life. [Gk *bios* life]
macrocosm /'mækrəʊkɒz(ə)m/ *n.* universe; any great whole. [COSMOS]
macroeconomics /mækrəʊi:kə'nɒmɪks/ *n.* study of the economy as a whole. [MACRO-]
macron /'mækrɒn/ *n.* written or printed mark (¯) of long or stressed vowel. [Gk, neut. of *makros* long]
macroscopic /mækrəʊ'skɒpɪk/ *a.* visible to the naked eye; regarded in terms of large units. [MACRO-]
macula /'mækjʊlə/ *n.* (*pl.* **maculae** /-i:/) dark spot; spot, esp. permanent one, in skin; **maculation** /-'leɪʃ(ə)n/ *n.* [L, = spot, mesh]
mad *a.* with disordered mind, insane; (of person, conduct, idea) wildly foolish; wildly excited or infatuated (*about* or *on*); frenzied; *colloq.* angry; (of animal) rabid; wildly light-hearted; **like mad** *colloq.* with great energy or enthusiasm. [OE]
madam /'mædəm/ *n.* polite or respectful formal address or mode of reference to woman; *colloq.* conceited or precocious girl or young woman; woman brothel-keeper. [foll.]
Madame /'mædəm, mə'dɑ:m/ *n.* (*pl.* ***Mesdames*** /meɪ'dɑ:m, -'dæm/) title used of or to French-speaking woman, corresponding to Mrs or madam; (***madame***) madam. [F *ma dame* my lady]
madcap 1 *n.* wildly impulsive person. **2** *a.* wildly impulsive. [MAD]
madden *v.* make or become mad; irritate.
madder *n.* herbaceous plant with yellowish flowers; red dye obtained from its root; synthetic substitute for this dye. [OE]
made 1 *past* and *p.p.* of MAKE. **2** *a.* (of person) built or formed (*well-made*; *loosely-made*); successful (*made man*). **3 have it made** *sl.* be sure of success; **made for** ideally suited to; **made of** consisting of; **made of money** *colloq.* very rich. [MAKE]
Madeira /mə'dɪərə/ *n.* fortified white wine from island of Madeira.
Mademoiselle /mædəmwə'zel/ *n.* (*pl.* ***Mesdemoiselles*** /meɪdm-/) title used of or to unmarried French-speaking woman, corresponding to Miss or madam; (***mademoiselle***) young Frenchwoman, French governess. [F (*ma* my, *demoiselle* DAMSEL)]
madhouse *n.* mental home or hospital; scene of confused uproar. [MAD]
madly *adv.* in a mad manner; *colloq.* passionately, extremely.
madman *n.* man who is mad.
madonna /mə'dɒnə/ *n.* picture or statue of Virgin Mary. [It., = my lady]
madrigal /'mædrɪg(ə)l/ *n.* part-song for several voices, usu. without instrumental accompaniment. [It.]
madwoman *n.* woman who is mad. [MAD]
maelstrom /'meɪlstrɒm/ *n.* great whirlpool; confused state. [Du.]
maenad /'mi:næd/ *n.* bacchante; frenzied woman. [L f. Gk (*mainomai* rave)]
maestro /'maɪstrəʊ/ *n.* (*pl.* **maestri** /-i:/)

great composer, conductor, or teacher of music; masterly performer in any sphere. [It.]

Mae West /meɪ 'west/ *sl.* inflatable life-jacket. [film actress]

Mafia /'mæfiə, 'mɑ:-/ *n.* organized body of criminals, orig. in Sicily, now esp. in US; (**mafia**) group regarded as exerting hidden influence. [It. dial., = bragging]

Mafioso /mæfɪ'əʊsəʊ, mɑ:-/ *n.* (*pl.* **Mafiosi** /-si:/) member of Mafia. [It. (prec.)]

magazine /mægə'zi:n/ *n.* periodical publication (now usu. illustrated) containing contributions by various writers; store for arms, ammunition, and provisions, for use in war; store for explosives; chamber for holding supply of cartridges to be fed automatically to breech of gun, similar device in camera, slide-projector, etc. [F f. It. f. Arab.]

magenta /mə'dʒentə/ **1** *n.* shade of crimson; aniline dye of this colour. **2** *a.* of or coloured with magenta. [*Magenta* in Italy]

maggot /'mægət/ *n.* larva esp. of blue-bottle or cheese-fly; **maggoty** *a.* [perh. alt. of *maddock* f. ON]

Magi *pl.* of MAGUS.

magic /'mædʒɪk/ **1** *n.* supposed art of influencing course of events by occult control of nature or of spirits, witchcraft; conjuring tricks; inexplicable or remarkable influence; enchanting quality or phenomenon. **2** *a.* of magic; producing surprising results. **3** *v.t.* (**-ck-**) change or make (as if) by magic. **4 like magic** very rapidly; **magic away** cause to disappear (as if) by magic; **magic carpet** mythical carpet able to transport person on it to any place; **magic eye** photoelectric device used for automatic control; **magic lantern** simple form of image-projector using slides. [F f. L f. Gk *magikos* (MAGUS)

magical *a.* of magic; resembling, or produced as if by, magic; **magically** *adv.*

magician /mə'dʒɪʃ(ə)n/ *n.* one skilled in magic; conjuror. [F f. L (MAGIC)]

magisterial /mædʒɪ'stɪərɪəl/ *a.* imperious; having authority; of a magistrate; **magisterially** *adv.* [med.L (MASTER)]

magistracy /'mædʒɪstrəsɪ/ *n.* magisterial office; magistrates collectively. [foll.]

magistrate /'mædʒɪstreɪt/ *n.* civil officer administering law; person conducting court for minor cases and preliminary hearings (*magistrates' court*). [L (MASTER)]

magma /'mægmə/ *n.* (*pl.* **magmas** or **magmata**) fluid or semi-fluid material under earth's crust, from which igneous rock is formed by cooling. [L f. Gk (*massō* knead)]

Magna Charta /mægnə 'kɑ:tə/ (also **Magna Carta**) charter of liberty obtained from King John in 1215; any similar document of rights. [med.L, = great charter]

magnanimous /mæg'nænɪməs/ *a.* noble, generous, not petty, in feelings or conduct; **magnanimity** /-nə'nɪmɪtɪ/ *n.* [L (*magnus* great, *animus* mind)]

magnate /mægneɪt/ *n.* wealthy and influential person, esp. in business. [L (*magnus* great)]

magnesia /mæg'ni:ʃə/ *n.* magnesium oxide; hydrated magnesium carbonate, used as antacid and laxative. [*Magnesia* in Asia Minor]

magnesium /mæg'ni:zɪəm/ *n.* silver-white metallic element.

magnet /'mægnɪt/ *n.* piece of iron, steel, alloy, ore, etc., having properties of attracting iron and of pointing approximately north and south when suspended; loadstone; person or thing that attracts. [L f. Gk *magnēs -ētos* of Magnesia (MAGNESIA)]

magnetic /mæg'netɪk/ *a.* having properties of magnet; produced or acting by magnetism; capable of acquiring properties of or of being attracted by magnet; strongly attractive (*magnetic personality*); **magnetic field** area of influence of magnet; **magnetic mine** underwater mine detonated by approach of large mass of metal, e.g. ship; **magnetic needle** indicator made of magnetized steel on dial of compass; **magnetic north** point indicated by north end of magnetic needle; **magnetic pole** point near north or south pole where magnetic needle dips vertically; **magnetic storm** disturbance of earth's magnetic field by charged particles from sun etc.; **magnetic tape** plastic strip coated or impregnated with magnetic particles for recording and reproduction of signals; **magnetically** *adv.* [L (prec.)]

magnetism /'mægnɪtɪz(ə)m/ *n.* magnetic phenomena; science of these; natural agency producing them; great charm and attraction. [MAGNET]

magnetize *v.t.* give magnetic properties to; make into magnet; attract (*lit.* or *fig.*) as magnet does; **magnetization** /-'zeɪʃ(ə)n/ *n.*

magneto /mæg'ni:təʊ/ *n.* (*pl.* **magnetos**) electric generator using permanent magnets (esp. for ignition in internal-combustion engine). [abbr. of *magneto-electric*]

magnification /mægnɪfɪ'keɪʃ(ə)n/ *n.* magnifying; amount of this. [MAGNIFY]

magnificent /mæg'nɪfɪsənt/ *a.* splendid, stately; sumptuously constructed or adorned; splendidly lavish; *colloq.* fine, excellent; **magnificence** *n.* [F f. L *magnificus* (*magnus* great)]

magnify /'mægnɪfaɪ/ *v.t.* make (thing) appear larger than it is, as with lens; exaggerate; intensify; *archaic* extol; **magnifying glass** lens used to magnify; **magnifier** *n.* [F or L (prec.)]

magnitude /'mægnɪtju:d/ *n.* largeness; size; importance; degree of brightness of a star; class of stars arranged according to this (*first, seventh,* etc., *magnitude*); **of the first magnitude** very important. [L (*magnus* great)]

magnolia /mæg'nəʊlɪə/ *n.* tree with dark-green foliage and waxlike flowers. [*Magnol*, botanist]

magnum /'mægnəm/ *n.* bottle containing two reputed quarts of wine or spirits. [L, neut. of *magnus* great]

magnum opus /mægnəm 'əʊpəs/ great work of literature etc.; author's greatest work. [L]

magpie /'mægpaɪ/ *n.* a kind of crow with black-and-white plumage and long tail; random collector; chatterer. [*Mag* abbr. of woman's Christian name *Margaret*, PIE²]

Magus /'meɪgəs/ *n.* (*pl.* **Magi** /'meɪdʒaɪ/) priest of ancient Persia; sorcerer; (in *pl.*) the 'wise men' from the East (Matt. 2:1). [L f. Gk f. Pers.]

Magyar /'mægjɑ:/ **1** *n.* member of the people now predominant in Hungary; their language. **2** *a.* of this people. [native name]

maharaja /mɑ:hə'rɑ:dʒə/ *n.* (also **maharajah**) *hist.* title of some Indian princes. [Hindi, = great rajah]

maharanee /mɑ:hə'rɑ:nɪ/ *n.* (also **maharani**) *hist.* maharaja's wife or widow. [Hindi, = great ranee]

maharishi /mɑ:hə'rɪʃɪ/ *n.* great Hindu sage. [Hindi]

mahatma /mə'hætmə/ *n.* (in India etc.) person regarded with reverence; one of class of persons supposed by some Buddhists to have preternatural powers. [Skr., = great soul]

mah-jong /mɑ:'dʒɒŋ/ (also **-jongg**) *n.* game played with 136 or 144 pieces called tiles. [Chin. dial. *ma-tsiang* sparrows]

mahlstick /'mɑ:lstɪk/ var. of MAULSTICK.

mahogany /mə'hɒgənɪ/ *n.* reddish-brown wood used for furniture; its colour. [orig. unkn.]

Mahometan /mə'hɒmɪtən/ var. of MUHAMMADAN.

mahout /mə'haʊt/ *n.* (in India etc.) elephant-driver. [Hindi f. Skr.]

maid *n.* female servant; girl, young woman; **maid of all work** female servant doing general housework, person doing many jobs; **maid of honour** unmarried lady attending queen or princess, kind of small custard tart, *US* principal bridesmaid. [abbr. of foll.]

maiden /'meɪd(ə)n/ **1** *n.* girl, young unmarried woman; = *maiden over*; = *maiden horse*. **2** *a.* unmarried (*maiden aunt*); (of female animal) unmated; (of horse) that has never won race; (of race) open only to such horses; first (*maiden speech*). **3 maiden name** woman's surname before marriage; **maiden over** over in cricket in which no runs are scored. **4 maidenhood** *n.* [OE]

maidenhair *n.* fern with fine hairlike stalks and delicate fronds.

maidenhead *n.* virginity; hymen.

maidservant *n.* female servant. [MAID]

mail¹ **1** *n.* matter conveyed by post; this system of conveyance; letters, parcels, etc., sent, collected, or delivered at one place on one occasion; vehicle carrying post. **2** *v.t.* send by post. **3 mail-bag** large bag for carrying mail; **mailing list** list of persons to whom mail, esp. advertising matter, is to be posted; **mail order** purchase of goods by post. [F *male* wallet]

mail² *n.* armour composed of metal rings or plates; **coat of mail** jacket or tunic covered with mail. [F *maille* f. L *macula*]

maim *v.t.* cripple, disable, mutilate. [F *mahaignier*]

main **1** *a.* principal, most important; greatest in size or extent (*the main body of an army*); exerted to the full (*by main force*). **2** *n.* principal channel, duct, etc., for water, sewage, etc.; (usu. in *pl.*) principal cable for supply of electricity; *archaic* mainland, high seas (*Spanish main*). **3 have an eye to the main chance** consider one's own interests; **in the main** for the most part; **main brace** brace attached to main yard; **main line** important railway line linking large cities etc.; **main-topmast** mast above maintop; **main yard** yard on which mainsail is extended. [OE]

mainframe *n.* central processing unit of computer; (often *attrib.*) large computer as distinct from microcomputer etc.

mainland *n.* large continuous extent of land, excluding neighbouring islands etc.

mainly *adv.* for the most part, chiefly.

mainmast *n.* principal mast of ship.

mainsail /'meɪseɪl, -s(ə)l/ *n.* (in square-rigged vessel) lowest sail on mainmast; (in fore-and-aft rigged vessel) sail set on after part of mainmast.

mainspring *n.* principal spring of watch, clock, etc.; chief motivating force or incentive.
mainstay *n.* chief support; stay from maintop to foot of foremast.
mainstream *n.* principal current of river etc.; prevailing trend of opinion, fashion, etc.
maintain /meɪn'teɪn/ *v.t.* cause to continue, continue one's action in, retain in being; take action to preserve (machine, house, etc.) in good order; support, provide sustenance for; provide means for; assert as true; **maintained school** school supported from public funds. [F f. L *manus* hand, *teneo* hold]
maintenance /'meɪntɪnəns/ *n.* maintaining or being maintained; keeping equipment etc. in repair; provision of means to support life; alimony. [F (prec.)]
maintop *n.* platform above head of lower mainmast. [MAIN]
maisonette /meɪzə'net/ *n.* part of a house let or used separately (usu. not all on one floor); small house. [F *maisonnette*, dimin. of *maison* house]
maize *n.* a cereal plant of N. American origin; grain of this; yellow colour of its cobs. [F or Sp.]
Maj. *abbr.* Major.
majestic /mə'dʒestɪk/ *a.* stately and dignified, imposing; **majestically** *adv.* [foll.]
majesty /'mædʒɪstɪ/ *n.* stateliness of aspect, bearing, language, etc.; sovereign power; title used in addressing or referring to a king or queen or a sovereign's wife or widow (*Your*, *Her*, etc., *Majesty*; *Her Majesty the Queen Mother*). [F f. L *majestas* (MAJOR)]
majolica /mə'jɒlɪkə, -'dʒɒl-/ *n.* Italian earthenware of Renaissance period with coloured ornamentation on white enamel; modern imitation of this. [It., former name of Majorca]
major /'meɪdʒə/ **1** *a.* greater or relatively great in size or importance; of full legal age; *Mus.* (of scale) having intervals of a semitone above its third and seventh notes, (of interval) normal or perfect (cf. MINOR), (of key) based on major scale. **2** *n.* army officer next below lieutenant-colonel; officer in charge of section of band instruments (*trumpet major*); person of full legal age; *US* student's special course or subject. **3** *v.i. US* (of student) undertake study or qualify *in* as special subject. **4 major-general** army officer next below lieutenant-general. [L, compar. of *magnus* great]
major-domo /meɪdʒə'dəʊməʊ/ *n.* (*pl.* **major-domos**) chief steward of great household. [Sp. & It. f. med.L *major domus* highest official of household]
majority /mə'dʒɒrɪtɪ/ *n.* greater number or part (*of*); number by which votes for winning candidate etc. exceed those for next; number by which votes on one side exceed those on the other or on others combined; party etc. receiving greater or greatest number of votes; full legal age (*attained his majority*); rank of major; **majority rule** principle that greater number should exercise greater power. [F f. med.L (MAJOR)]
make 1 *v.* (*past* and *p.p.* MADE) construct, frame, create, from parts or other substance; bring about, cause to exist, give rise to (*make difficulties*, *a noise*); frame in the mind, feel (*make a judgement*); prepare (tea, coffee, etc.), arrange (bed) ready for use; arrange and light materials for (a fire); compose, write, or prepare (will, book, film, etc.); establish or enact (distinctions, rules, laws); gain, acquire, procure, obtain as result (*make money*, *a living*, *a profit*); secure advancement or success of (*his second novel made him*; *that made my day*); cause to be or become or seem (*made him a duke*; *made her happy*; *made it known*; *made fools of ourselves*); cause or compel (to); proceed (*towards* etc.), act as if with intention *to* (*he made to leave*); perform (an action etc.: *make an effort*, *a journey*, *a promise*, *a start*; *make war*); execute (bodily movement, e.g. a bow); consider to be, estimate as (*I make it an hour*); constitute, amount to (*2 and 2 make 4*); serve for, be adequate as (*makes a good teacher*); form or be reckoned as (*this makes the third time*); bring to (chosen value etc.); accomplish or achieve (distance, speed, score, etc.); achieve place in (team, prize-list, etc.); arrive at, come in sight of; *sl.* catch (train etc.). **2** *n.* way thing is made; origin of manufacture, brand. **3 make away with** get rid of, kill, squander; **make believe** pretend; **make-believe** *a.* & *n.* pretended, pretence; **make a day** (or **night** etc.) **of it** devote whole day etc. to an activity; **make do** manage with limited or inadequate means available; **make for** conduce to, proceed towards (place), attack; **make good** repay, repair, or compensate for, achieve (purpose), be successful; **make the grade** succeed; **make it** achieve one's purpose, be successful; **make much** (or **little**) **of** treat as important (or unimportant); **make nothing of** treat as trifling, be unable to understand or use or deal with; **make of** construct from, conclude to be the meaning or character of (*what do you make of this?*); **make off** depart

hastily; **make off with** carry away, steal; **make or break** cause success or ruin of; **make out** discern or understand, fare or progress, write out (document etc.) or fill in (form), prove or try to prove to be, pretend or claim; **make over** transfer possession of, refashion or convert to new purpose; **make time** contrive to find time to do something; **make up** put or get together, prepare, invent (story etc.), compensate (*for*), complete (amount originally deficient), form or constitute, apply cosmetics (to); **make (it) up** be reconciled; **make-up** *n.* cosmetics esp. as used by actors etc., way thing is made or composed, character or temperament; **make up to** court, curry favour with; **on the make** *sl.* intent on gain. [OE]

maker *n.* one who makes; (**Maker**) God.

makeshift 1 *n.* temporary substitute or device. 2 *a.* serving as this.

makeweight *n.* small quantity added to make up weight; person or thing supplying deficiency.

making *n.* (in *pl.*) earnings, profits; (in *pl.*) essential qualities for becoming (*he has the makings of a General*); **be the making of** ensure success or favourable development of; **in the making** in course of being made or formed. [OE (MAKE)]

mal- *prefix* bad (*malpractice*); badly (*maltreat*); faulty (*malfunction*); not (*maladroit*). [F *mal* badly f. L *male*]

malachite /'mæləkaɪt/ *n.* green mineral used for ornament. [F f. L f. Gk]

maladjusted /mælə'dʒʌstɪd/ *a.* (of person) not satisfactorily adjusted to environment and conditions of life; **maladjustment** *n.* [MAL-]

maladminister /mæləd'mɪnɪstə/ *v.t.* manage badly or improperly; **maladministration** /-'streɪʃ(ə)n/ *n.*

maladroit /mælə'drɔɪt, 'mæ-/ *a.* clumsy, bungling. [F (MAL-)]

malady /'mælədɪ/ *n.* disease or ailment (*lit.* or *fig.*). [F (*malade* sick)]

malaise /mæ'leɪz/ *n.* bodily discomfort, esp. without development of specific disease; uneasy feeling. [F (EASE)]

malapropism /'mæləprɒpɪz(ə)m/ *n.* ludicrous misuse of word esp. in mistake for one resembling it (e.g. *derangement of epitaphs* for *arrangement of epithets*). [f. Mrs *Malaprop* in Sheridan's *Rivals*]

malaria /mə'leərɪə/ *n.* recurrent fever transmitted by mosquito bite; **malarial** *a.* [It., = bad air]

malarkey /mə'lɑːkɪ/ *n.* *sl.* humbug, nonsense. [orig. unkn.]

Malay /mə'leɪ/ 1 *a.* of a people predominating in Malaysia and Indonesia. 2 *n.* member of this people; their language. [Malay *malāyu*]

malcontent /'mælkəntent/ 1 *n.* discontented person. 2 *a.* discontented. [F (MAL-)]

male 1 *a.* of the sex that can beget offspring by performing the fertilizing function; (of plants or flowers) containing stamens but no pistil; of men or male animals or plants; (of parts of machinery etc.) designed to enter or fill a corresponding hollow part (*male screw*). 2 *n.* male person or animal. [F f. L *masculus* (*mas* male)]

malediction /mælɪ'dɪkʃ(ə)n/ *n.* curse, uttering of curse; **maledictory** *a.* [L *maledictio* (MAL-)]

malefactor /'mælɪfæktə/ *n.* criminal; evil-doer; **malefaction** /-'fækʃ(ə)n/ *n.* [L (*male* badly, *facio fact-* do)]

malevolent /mə'levələnt/ *a.* wishing ill to others; **malevolence** *a.* [F or L (*volo* wish)]

malfeasance /mæl'fiːzəns/ *n.* misconduct, esp. in official capacity. [F (MAL-)]

malformation /mælfɔː'meɪʃ(ə)n/ *n.* faulty formation; **malformed** /-'fɔːmd/ *a.* [MAL-]

malfunction /mæl'fʌŋkʃ(ə)n/ 1 *n.* failure to function in normal manner. 2 *v.i.* function faultily.

malice /'mælɪs/ *n.* desire to harm or cause difficulty to others, ill-will; *Law* harmful intent (*malice aforethought*). [F f. L (*malus* bad)]

malicious /mə'lɪʃəs/ *a.* given to or arising from malice.

malign /mə'laɪn/ 1 *a.* (of thing) injurious; (of disease) malignant; malevolent. 2 *v.t.* slander, speak ill of. 3 **malignity** /-'lɪgnɪtɪ/ *n.* [F or L (*malus bad*)]

malignant /mə'lɪgnənt/ *a.* (of tumour) tending to spread and to recur after removal, cancerous; (of disease) very virulent (*malignant cholera*); feeling or showing intense ill-will; harmful; **malignancy** *n.* [L (prec.)]

malinger /mə'lɪŋgə/ *v.i.* pretend to be ill to escape duty. [F *malingre* sickly]

mall /mæl, mɔːl/ *n.* sheltered walk or promenade. [*The Mall*, street in London]

mallard /'mælɑːd/ *n.* (*pl.* same) kind of wild duck of which male has green head. [F]

malleable /'mælɪəb(ə)l/ *a.* (of metal etc.) that can be shaped by hammering; adaptable, pliable; **malleability** /-'bɪlɪtɪ/ *n.* [F f. med.L (foll.)]

mallet /'mælɪt/ *n.* hammer, usu. of wood; implement for striking croquet or polo ball. [F *mail* f. L *malleus* hammer]

mallow /'mæləʊ/ *n.* kind of flowering

plant with hairy stems and leaves. [OE f. L *malva*]

malmsey /'mɑ:mzɪ/ *n.* a strong sweet wine. [LG or Du. f. Gk (*Monemvasia* in Greece)]

malnutrition /mælnju:'trɪʃ(ə)n/ *n.* insufficient nutrition; condition where diet omits some foods necessary for health. [MAL-]

malodorous /mæl'əʊdərəs/ *a.* evil-smelling.

malpractice /mæl'præktɪs/ *n.* wrongdoing; illegal action for one's own benefit while in position of trust; improper or negligent treatment of patient by physician.

malt/mɔ:lt, mɒlt/ **1** *n.* grain, usu. barley, prepared by steeping, germination, and drying, for brewing etc.; *colloq.* malt liquor; malt whisky. **2** *v.t.* convert (grain) into malt. **3 malted milk** drink made from dried milk and extract of malt; **malt whisky** whisky made entirely from malted barley. [OE]

Maltese /mɔ:l'ti:z, mɒl-/ **1** *a.* of Malta. **2** *n.* (*pl.* same) native or language of Malta. **3 Maltese cross** cross with arms broadening outwards, often indented at ends.

Malthusian /mæl'θju:zɪən/ *a.* of Malthus's doctrine that population should be restricted to prevent increase beyond means of subsistence; **Malthusianism** *n.* [Malthus, clergyman]

maltreat /mæl'tri:t/ *v.t.* ill-treat; **maltreatment** *n.* [F (MAL-)]

malversation /mælvə'seɪʃ(ə)n/ *n.* corrupt behaviour in position of trust; corrupt administration (*of* public money etc.). [F f. L (*male* badly, *versor* behave)]

mama var. of MAMMA.

mamba /'mæmbə/ *n.* a kind of venomous African snake. [Zulu *imamba*]

mamma /mə'mɑ:/ *n. archaic* mother. [imit. of child's *ma, ma*]

mammal /'mæm(ə)l/ *n.* animal of class of warm-blooded vertebrates characterized by secretion of milk to feed young; **mammalian** /mə'meɪlɪən/ *a.* [L (*mamma* breast)]

mammary /'mæmərɪ/ *a.* of the breasts.

Mammon /'mæmən/ *n.* wealth regarded as idol or evil influence. [L f. Gk f. Aram.]

mammoth /'mæməθ/ **1** *n.* large extinct elephant, with hairy coat and curved tusks. **2** *a.* huge. [Russ.]

man 1 *n.* (*pl.* **men**) adult human male; human being, *collect.* the human race; human being of particular type or historical period (*Renaissance man*; *Java man*); (in indefinite or general application) person; individual person, esp. in role of assistant, opponent, or expert, or considered in terms of suitability (*he is your man*); husband (*man and wife*); (usu. in *pl.*) employee, workman; (usu. in *pl.*) members of armed forces, esp. those not officers; *colloq.* as form of address; one of set of objects used in playing chess, draughts, etc. **2** /usu. -mən/ *suffix* denoting man concerned or skilful with (*clergyman, oarsman*). **3** *v.t.* (**-nn-**) furnish with man or manpower for work or defence; act thus in respect of (*man the pumps*); fill (post). **4 as one man** in unison; **be one's own man** be independent; **man about town** fashionable socializer; **man-at-arms** *archaic* soldier; **man-hour** work done by one person in one hour; **man-hunt** organized search for person (esp. criminal); **man in the street** ordinary average man; **man-made** artificially made; **man-of-war** (*pl.* **men-of-war**) armed ship of country's navy; **man of the world** see WORLD; **man to man** candidly; **to a man** without exception. **5 mannish** *a.* [OE]

manacle /'mænək(ə)l/ **1** *n.* (usu. in *pl.*) fetter for the hand, handcuff; restraint. **2** *v.t.* fetter with manacles. [F f. L (*manus* hand)]

manage /'mænɪdʒ/ *v.* organize or regulate or be in charge of; succeed in achieving, contrive (*managed to come*; *managed a smile*); succeed with limited resources or means, be able to cope; (with *can* or *be able to*) cope with, do what is required regarding (*can you manage this matter, lunch on Friday?*); secure co-operation of (person) by tact, flattery, etc.; take control or charge of (person, animal, etc.); use or wield (tool etc.).; **manageable** *a.* [It. *maneggiare* f. L *manus* hand]

management *n.* managing or being managed; administration of business concerns or public undertakings; persons engaged in this.

manager *n.* person conducting a business, institution, etc.; person controlling activities of person or team in sport, entertainment, etc.; person who manages money, household affairs, etc., in specified way (*good manager*); **manageress** /-'res/ *n. fem.*; **managerial** /mænə'dʒɪərɪəl/ *a.*

mañana /mən'jɑ:nə/ *n.* & *adv.* tomorrow (as symbol of easy-going procrastination); indefinite future. [Sp.]

manatee /mænə'ti:/ *n.* large tropical aquatic mammal feeding on plants. [Sp. f. Carib]

Mancunian /mæŋ'kju:nɪən/ **1** *n.* native of Manchester. **2** *a.* of Manchester. [L *Mancunium*]

mandala /'mændələ/ *n.* circular figure as religious symbol of universe. [Skr.]
mandamus /mæn'deɪməs/ *n.* judicial writ issued as command to inferior court, or ordering person to perform public or statutory duty. [L, = we command]
mandarin /'mændərɪn/ *n.* influential person, esp. reactionary or secretive bureaucrat; *hist.* Chinese official; (**Mandarin**) former standard language of China; small flat orange with loose skin. [Port. f. Malay f. Hindi *mantrī*]
mandatary /'mændətərɪ/ *n.* holder or receiver of mandate. [L (foll.)]
mandate 1 /'mændeɪt/ *n.* authority to act for another; political authority supposed to be given by electors to government; judicial or legal command from superior. **2** /mæn'deɪt/ *v.t.* give authority to (delegate); commit (territory) *to* mandatary. [L *mandatum*, p.p. of *mando* command]
mandatory /'mændətərɪ/ *a.* compulsory; of or conveying a command; **mandatorily** *adv.* [L (prec.)]
mandible /'mændɪb(ə)l/ *n.* jaw, esp. lower jaw in mammals and fishes; upper or lower part of bird's beak; either half of crushing organ in mouth-parts of insect etc. [F or L (*mando* chew)]
mandolin /'mændəlɪn/ *n.* a kind of lute with paired metal strings, played with plectrum. [F f. It.]
mandrake /'mændreɪk/ *n.* narcotic plant with large yellow fruit. [prob. Du., ult. f. Gk *mandragoras*]
mandrel /'mændr(ə)l/ *n.* lathe-shaft to which work is fixed while being turned; cylindrical rod round which metal or other material is forged or shaped. [orig. unkn.]
mandrill /'mændrɪl/ *n.* a kind of large baboon. [prob. MAN, DRILL[4]]
mane *n.* long hair on neck of animal, esp. horse or lion; long hair of person. [OE]
manège /mə'neɪʒ/ *n.* riding-school; horsemanship; movements of trained horse. [F f. It. (MANAGE)]
maneuver *US* var. of MANŒUVRE.
manful *a.* brave, resolute; **manfully** *adv.* [MAN]
manganese /'mæŋgəni:z/ *n.* hard grey metallic element; oxide of this, a black mineral used in glass-making etc. [F f. It. (MAGNESIA)]
mange /meɪndʒ/ *n.* skin disease in hairy and woolly animals. [F (*mangier* eat f. L *manduco* chew)]
mangel-wurzel /'mæŋg(ə)l wɜ:z(ə)l/ *n.* a large beet used as cattle food. [G (*mangold* beet, *wurzel* root)]
manger /'meɪndʒə/ *n.* long open box or trough for horses or cattle to eat from. [F f. Rmc f. L (MANGE)]
mangle[1] /'mæŋg(ə)l/ *v.t.* hack or mutilate by blows; cut roughly so as to disfigure; spoil (text etc.) by gross blunders. [AF *ma(ha)ngler* prob. rel. to MAIM]
mangle[2] /'mæŋg(ə)l/ **1** *n.* machine of two or more cylinders for squeezing water from and pressing washed clothes etc. **2** *v.t.* press (clothes) in mangle. [Du. *mangel*]
mango /'mæŋgəʊ/ *n.* (*pl.* **mangoes**) tropical fruit with yellowish flesh; tree bearing this. [Port. f. Malay f. Tamil *mānkāy*]
mangrove /'mæŋgrəʊv/ *n.* tropical tree or shrub growing in shore-mud with many tangled roots above ground. [orig. unkn.]
mangy /'meɪndʒɪ/ *a.* having mange; squalid, shabby. [MANGE]
manhandle *v.t.* move by human effort alone; treat roughly. [MAN]
manhole *n.* opening (usu. with lid) giving man access to sewer, conduit, etc.
manhood *n.* state of being a man; manliness, courage; the men of a country.
mania /'meɪnɪə/ *n.* mental derangement marked by excitement and violence; great or excessive enthusiasm (*for*). [L f. Gk (*mainomai* be mad)]
-mania *suffix* forming nouns denoting (1) special type of mental disorder (*megalomania*); (2) enthusiasm or admiration.
maniac /'meɪnɪæk/ **1** *n.* person affected with mania. **2** *a.* of or affected with mania.
-maniac *suffix* forming nouns with sense 'person affected with -mania' and adjectives with sense 'affected with -mania'.
maniacal /mə'naɪək(ə)l/ *a.* of or like a mania or a maniac; **maniacally** *adv.*
manic /'mænɪk/ *a.* of or affected with mania; **manic-depressive** *a.* relating to mental disorder with alternating periods of elation and depression, (*n.*) person having such disorder.
manicure /'mænɪkjʊə/ **1** *n.* cosmetic treatment of the hands and finger-nails. **2** *v.t.* apply such treatment to (hands or person). **3 manicurist** *n.* [F f. L *manus* hand, *cura* care]
manifest /'mænɪfest/ **1** *a.* clear or obvious to eye or mind. **2** *v.* display or evince (quality or feeling) by one's acts etc.; (of thing) reveal *itself*; show plainly to eye or mind; be evidence of, prove; record in a manifest; (of ghost) appear. **3** *n.* cargo or passenger list. **4 manifestation** /-'steɪʃ(ə)n/ *n.* [F, or L *manifestus*]
manifesto /mænɪ'festəʊ/ *n.* (*pl.*

manifestos) public declaration of policy, esp. by political party. [It. (prec.)]
manifold /'mænɪfəʊld/ **1** *a.* many and various; having various forms, applications, component parts, etc. **2** *n.* pipe or chamber, in piece of mechanism, with several openings; manifold thing. [OE (MANY, FOLD)]
manikin /'mænɪkɪn/ *n.* little man, dwarf. [Du.]
manila /mə'nɪlə/ *n.* strong fibre of a Philippine tree; brown wrapping-paper made from this. [*Manila* in Philippines]
manipulate /mə'nɪpjʊleɪt/ *v.t.* handle, esp. with skill; arrange cleverly; manage (person, property, etc.) by dextrous (esp. unfair) use of influence etc.; **manipulable** *a.*; **manipulation** /-'leɪʃ(ə)n/ *n.*; **manipulator** *n.* [F (prec.)]
mankind /mæn'kaɪnd/ *n.* human species; /'mæn-/ men in general. [MAN]
manly *a.* having the qualities associated with a man (e.g. strength and courage); befitting a man; **manliness** *n.*
manna /'mænə/ *n.* substance miraculously supplied as food to Israelites in the wilderness (Exod. 16); unexpected benefit. [OE ult. f. Heb.]
manned *a.* (of spacecraft etc.) having human crew. [MAN]
mannequin /'mænɪkɪn/ *n.* person, usu. woman, employed by dressmaker etc. to model clothes; dummy for display of clothes in shop. [F, = MANIKIN]
manner *n.* way thing is done or happens; (in *pl.*) modes of life, conditions of society, behaviour in social intercourse, polite social behaviour (*good*, *bad*, etc., *manners*); outward bearing, style of utterance etc.; style in literature or art (*sketch in the manner of Rembrandt*); kind, sort (*not by any manner of means*); **all manner of** every kind of; **comedy of manners** comedy with satirical portrayal of manners of society; **in a manner of speaking** in some sense, to some extent, so to speak. [F f. L (*manus* hand)]
mannered *a.* behaving in specified way (*ill-*, *well-mannered*); full of mannerisms.
mannerism *n.* distinctive gesture or feature of style; excessive use of these in art etc.; **mannerist** *n.*
mannerly *a.* well-behaved, polite.
manœuvre /mə'nu:və/ **1** *n.* planned and controlled movement of vehicle or body of troops etc.; (in *pl.*) large-scale exercises of troops or ships; deceptive or elusive movement; skilful plan. **2** *v.* move (thing, esp. vehicle) carefully; perform manœuvres; cause (troops or ships) to do this; direct or force or manipulate (person or thing *into*, *out*, *away*, etc.) by scheming or adroitness; employ artifice. **3** **manœuvrability** /-vrə'bɪlɪtɪ/ *n.*; **manœuvrable** /-vrəb(ə)l/ *a.* [F f. med.L *manu operor* work with the hand]
manor /'mænə/ *n.* large landed estate or its house (also **manor-house**); *hist.* territorial unit under feudal control of a lord; *sl.* area for which a police unit is responsible; **manorial** /mə'nɔ:rɪəl/ *a.* [AF *maner* f. L *maneo* remain]
manpower *n.* number of persons available for work or military service. [MAN]
manqué /'mɑ̃keɪ/ *a.* (placed after noun) that might have been but is not (*an actor manqué*). [F]
mansard /'mænsɑ:d/ *n.* roof with each face having two slopes, the steeper below. [*Mansard*, architect]
manse *n.* ecclesiastical residence, esp. Scottish Presbyterian minister's house. [med.L (MANOR)]
manservant *n.* (*pl.* **menservants**) male servant. [MAN]
mansion /'mænʃ(ə)n/ *n.* large grand house; **the Mansion House** official residence of Lord Mayor of London. [F f. L (MANOR)]
manslaughter *n.* unlawful killing of human being without malice aforethought. [MAN]
mantel /'mænt(ə)l/ *n.* structure of wood or marble etc. above and around fireplace; = MANTELPIECE. [var. of MANTLE]
mantelpiece *n.* shelf over fireplace.
mantilla /mæn'tɪlə/ *n.* lace scarf worn by Spanish woman over hair and shoulders. [Sp. (MANTLE)]
mantis /'mæntɪs/ *n.* (in full **praying mantis**) predatory insect of species that holds forelegs in position suggesting hands folded in prayer. [Gk, = prophet]
mantle /'mænt(ə)l/ **1** *n.* loose sleeveless cloak; covering; fragile tube fixed round gas-jet to give incandescent light. **2** *v.t.* clothe in or as in mantle; conceal, envelop. [F, f. L *mantellum* cloak]
mantra /'mæntrə/ *n.* Hindu or Buddhist devotional incantation; Vedic hymn. [Skr., = instrument of thought]
mantrap *n.* trap for catching trespassers etc. [MAN]
manual /'mænjʊəl/ **1** *a.* of or done with the hands (*manual labour*); worked by hand, not by automatic equipment (*manual gear-change*). **2** *n.* handbook; reference book; organ keyboard played with hands not feet. **3** **manually** *adv.* [F f. L (*manus* hand)]
manufacture /mænjʊ'fæktʃə/ **1** *v.t.* produce (articles) by labour, esp. by machinery on large scale; invent or

fabricate (evidence or story etc.). **2** *n.* manufacturing of articles; branch of such industry (*woollen manufacture*). [F f. It., & L *manufactum* made by hand]
manure /mə'njʊə/ **1** *n.* fertilizer, esp. dung. **2** *v.t.* apply manure to (land). [AF *mainoverer* = MANŒUVRE]
manuscript /'mænjʊskrɪpt/ **1** *n.* book or document written by hand; author's copy, written by hand or typed, not printed; manuscript state (*is in manuscript*). **2** *a.* written by hand. [med.L *manuscriptus* written by hand]
Manx /mæŋks/ **1** *a.* of the Isle of Man. **2** *n.* Celtic language of Isle of Man. **3 the Manx** Manx people; **Manx cat** cat of tailless variety. [ON]
many /'menɪ/ **1** *a.* (*compar.* MORE, superl. MOST) great in number, numerous (*many people*; *many a time*; *there were many*). **2** *n.pl.* many people or things. **3 the many** the multitude of people; **a good many** a fair number; **a great many** a large number; **many's the** there are many —s that (*many's the tale he has told us*). [OE]
Maoism /'maʊɪz(ə)m/ *n.* Communist doctrines of Mao Zedong; **Maoist** *n.* [*Mao* Zedong, Chinese statesman]
Maori /'maʊrɪ/ **1** *n.* member of aboriginal people of New Zealand; their language. **2** *a.* of this people. [native name]
map **1** *n.* representation (usu. on flat surface) of earth's surface (or part of it); similar representation of the sky (showing positions of stars etc.) or of the moon etc.; diagram showing arrangement or components of thing. **2** *v.t.* (**-pp-**) represent on map. **3 map out** plan in detail. [L *mappa* napkin]
maple /'meɪp(ə)l/ *n.* a kind of tree or shrub grown for wood, ornament, shade, or sugar; its wood; **maple-leaf** emblem of Canada; **maple sugar** sugar obtained by evaporating sap of some kinds of maple; **maple syrup** syrup made by evaporating maple sap or dissolving maple sugar. [OE]
maquette /mə'ket/ *n.* preliminary model or sketch. [F f. It. (*macchia* spot)]
Maquis /'mɑ:ki:/ *n.* secret army of patriots in France during German occupation (1940–5); member of this. [F, = brushwood]
mar *v.t.* (-rr-) spoil, disfigure, impair perfection of. [OE]
Mar. *abbr.* March.
marabou /'mærəbu:/ *n.* kind of stork; its down as trimming etc. [foll.]
maraca /mə'rækə/ *n.* clublike gourd containing beans, beads, etc., held in the hand and shaken (usu. in pairs) as musical instrument. [Port.]
maraschino /mærə'ski:nəʊ/ *n.* (*pl.* **maraschinos**) a sweet liqueur made from cherries; **maraschino cherry** cherry preserved in this. [It.]
marathon /'mærəθ(ə)n/ *n.* long-distance foot-race, esp. of 26 miles 385 yards (42.195 km.); feat of endurance; undertaking of long duration. [*Marathon* in Greece, scene of decisive battle in 490 BC, whence messenger supposedly ran with news to Athens]
maraud /mə'rɔ:d/ *v.* make plundering raid (on); go about pilfering. [F (*maraud* rogue)]
marble /'mɑ:b(ə)l/ **1** *n.* a kind of limestone able to take high polish, used in sculpture and architecture; this as type of hardness or durability or smoothness (often *attrib.*); (in *pl.*) collection of sculptures (*Elgin Marbles*); small ball of glass etc. as toy; (in *pl.*) game using these. **2** *v.t.* stain or colour to look like variegated marble. [F f. L *marmor* f. Gk]
marbled *a.* looking like variegated marble; (of meat) streaked with fat.
marcasite /'mɑ:kəsaɪt/ *n.* crystalline iron sulphide; piece of this as ornament. [med.L f. Arab. f. Pers.]
March[1] third month of year; **March hare** hare in breeding season (*mad as a March hare*). [F f. L *Martius* of Mars]
march[2] **1** *v.* walk in military manner with regular and measured tread; advance thus *on* (place to be attacked); walk purposefully; (of events) proceed steadily; cause to march or walk. **2** *n.* marching of troops; uniform step of troops etc. (*quick march*); procession as protest or demonstration; long toilsome walk; progress (*of* events, time, mind); piece of music meant to accompany march; distance covered by troops, esp. in a day. **3 marching orders** command to troops to depart for war etc., dismissal; **march past** marching of troops in line past saluting-point at review. [F *marcher*]
march[3] **1** *n. hist.* boundary or frontier (often *pl.*); tract of land, often disputed, between two countries. **2** *v.i.* (of countries, estates, etc.) have common frontier *with*, border *upon*. [F f. Rmc f. Gmc]
marchioness /'mɑ:ʃənɪs/ *n.* marquis's wife or widow; woman holding rank of marquis in her own right. [med.L (prec.)]
Mardi Gras /mɑ:dɪ 'grɑ:/ Shrove Tuesday; merry-making then, at end of carnival. [F, = fat Tuesday]
mare[1] *n.* female of equine animal, esp. horse; **mare's nest** illusory discovery; **mare's tail** tall slender marsh plant, (in *pl.*) long straight streaks of cirrus cloud. [OE]

mare² /'mɑːrɪ/ *n.* (*pl.* **maria** /'mɑːrɪə/) large flat area on moon, once thought to be sea. [L, = sea]

margarine /mɑːdʒə'riːn, mɑːg-/ *n.* butter-substitute made from edible oils and animal fats. [F f. Gk *margaron* pearl]

marge *n. colloq.* margarine. [abbr.]

margin /'mɑːdʒɪn/ **1** *n.* edge or border of surface; plain space beside main body of print etc. on page; extra amount (of time, money, etc.) over and above the necessary or minimum (*by a narrow margin*; *margin of safety*; *profit margin*); condition near the limit below or beyond which a thing ceases to be possible (*on the margin of subsistence*). **2** *v.t.* furnish with margin or marginal notes. **3 margin of error** difference allowed for miscalculation or mischance. [L *margo -ginis*]

marginal *a.* written in margin; of or at edge; (of constituency) having elected MP with small majority; (of land) difficult to cultivate and yielding little profit; close to limit, esp. of profitability; barely adequate or provided for; **marginal cost** cost of producing one extra item of output. [med.L (prec.)]

marginalia /mɑːdʒɪ'neɪlɪə/ *n.pl.* marginal notes.

marginally *adv.* in or near margin; by a small margin. [MARGINAL]

marguerite /mɑːgə'riːt/ *n.* ox-eye daisy or similar flower. [F f. L *margarita* pearl (f. Gk)]

maria *pl.* of MARE².

marigold /'mærɪgəʊld/ *n.* any of various plants with golden or bright yellow flowers. [*Mary* (prob. the Virgin), *gold* (dial.) marigold]

marijuana /mærɪ'hwɑːnə/ *n.* (also **marihuana**) dried leaves and flowers and stems of common hemp, smoked as intoxicant. [Amer. Sp.]

marimba /mə'rɪmbə/ *n.* xylophone of peoples of Africa and Central America; modern orchestral instrument evolved from this. [Congo]

marina /mə'riːnə/ *n.* place with moorings for pleasure-yachts etc. [It. & Sp. f. L (MARINE)]

marinade /mærɪ'neɪd/ **1** *n.* mixture of wine, vinegar, oil, herbs, etc., for steeping meat or fish; meat or fish so steeped. **2** *v.t.* steep in marinade. [F f. Sp. (*marinar* pickle in brine; MARINE)]

marinate /'mærɪneɪt/ *v.t.* marinade. [It. or F (foll.)]

marine /mə'riːn/ **1** *a.* of, found in, or produced by the sea; of shipping or naval matters (*marine insurance*); for use at sea. **2** *n.* member of corps trained to serve on land or sea (*Royal Marines*); country's shipping, fleet, or navy (*mercantile marine*). [F f. L (MARE²)]

mariner /'mærɪnə/ *n.* seaman. [AF f. F f. med.L (prec.)]

marionette /mærɪə'net/ *n.* puppet worked by strings. [F (*Mary*)]

marital /'mærɪt(ə)l/ *a.* of marriage; of or between husband and wife; **maritally** *adv.* [L (*maritus* husband)]

maritime /'mærɪtaɪm/ *a.* situated or living or found near the sea; connected with the sea or seafaring. [L (MARE²)]

marjoram /'mɑːdʒərəm/ *n.* aromatic herb used in cookery. [F f. med.L]

mark¹ **1** *n.* stain, scar, spot, or other visible sign esp. as spoiling surface etc.; written or printed symbol, this as assessment of conduct or proficiency; feature indicating or distinguishing a feeling or quality (*mark of respect*); sign or symbol on thing to identify it or indicate its origin; cross etc. made in place of signature by illiterate person; lasting effect or influence (*war left its mark on the town*); unit of numerical award of merit in examination; target or other object to be aimed at, desired object; line etc. serving to indicate position; standard (*up to*, *below*, *the mark*); runner's starting-point in race; (followed by numeral) particular type or design of equipment etc. **2** *v.* make mark on; attach identifying mark or name to; give distinctive character to, be a feature of; allot marks to (student's work etc.); name or indicate (place on map, length of syllable, etc.) by sign or mark; attach figures indicating prices to (goods); (in *pass.*) have natural marks (*marked with dark spots*); see, notice, observe mentally (*mark my words*); (in sports) keep close to (opponent) to hinder him in play. **3 make one's mark** attain distinction; **mark down** make written note of, mark at lower price; **mark-down** *n.* reduction in price; **mark off** separate, mark limits of; **mark out** mark boundaries of, trace (course), destine, single out; **mark time** move feet as in marching but without advancing, occupy time routinely while awaiting events or opportunity; **mark up** mark at higher price; **mark-up** *n.* amount seller adds to cost-price of article to cover profit margin etc.; **off the mark** having made a start, irrelevant; **on the mark** ready to start. [OE]

mark² *n.* currency unit of Germany and of Finland. [G]

marked *a.* clearly noticeable or evident; **marked man** one singled out, esp. as object of attack etc.; **markedly** /-ɪdlɪ/ *adv.* [MARK¹]

marker *n.* thing marking position; person or thing that marks; scorer in game etc.

market /'mɑ:kɪt/ **1** *n.* gathering of people for purchase and sale of provisions, livestock, etc.; space or building used for this; demand (*for* commodity or service); place or group providing such demand; conditions as regards, or opportunity for, buying or selling; rate of purchase and sale. **2** *v.* sell; offer for sale; buy or sell goods in market. **3 in the market for** wishing to buy; **market-day** day on which market is regularly held; **market garden** place where vegetables are grown for market; **market-place** open space where market is held in town, *fig.* scene of actual dealings; **market price** price in current dealings; **market research** study of consumers' needs and preferences; **market town** town where market is held; **market value** value as saleable thing; **on the market** offered for sale. [Gmc f. L (*mercor* buy)]

marketable *a.* able or fit to be sold.

marking *n.* identification mark; colouring of animal's fur or feathers etc. [MARK[1]]

marksman *n.* skilled shot, esp. with rifle; **marksmanship** *n.*

marl 1 *n.* soil consisting of clay and lime, used as fertilizer. **2** *v.t.* apply marl to (ground). **3 marly** *a.* [F f. med.L *margila*]

marlinspike /'mɑ:lɪnspaɪk/ *n.* pointed tool used to separate strands of rope or wire. [*marling* f. Du. *marlen* f. *marren* bind]

marmalade /'mɑ:məleɪd/ *n.* preserve of citrus fruit, usu. oranges, made like jam. [F f. Port. (*marmelo* quince)]

marmoreal /mɑ:'mɔ:rɪəl/ *a.* of or like marble. [L (MARBLE)]

marmoset /'mɑ:məzet/ *n.* small monkey with bushy tail. [F]

marmot /'mɑ:mət/ *n.* burrowing rodent of squirrel family. [F f. L *mus* mouse, *mons* mountain]

marocain /'mærəkeɪn/ *n.* dress-fabric of crêpe type. [F, = Moroccan]

maroon[1] /mə'ru:n/ *a.* & *n.* brownish-crimson. [F *marron* chestnut, f. It. f. Gk]

maroon[2] /mə'ru:n/ *v.t.* put (person) ashore in desolate place and leave him there; (of person or natural phenomenon) cause (person) to be unable to leave place. [F *marron* wild person f. Sp. *cimarrón*]

marque /mɑ:k/ *n.* make of motor car, as opp. to specific type. [F, = MARK[1]]

marquee /mɑ:'ki:/ *n.* large tent used for party or exhibition etc. [F *marquise*]

marquess var. of MARQUIS.

marquetry /'mɑ:kɪtrɪ/ *n.* inlaid work in wood, ivory, etc. [F (MARQUE)]

marquis /'mɑ:kwɪs/ *n.* nobleman ranking between duke and (in UK) earl or (elsewhere) count. [F (MARCH[3])]

marquise /mɑ:'ki:z/ *n.* (in foreign nobility) marchioness.

marram /'mærəm/ *n.* a shore grass that binds sand. [ON, = sea-haulm]

marriage /'mærɪdʒ/ *n.* condition of man and woman legally united for purpose of living together and usu. procreating lawful offspring; act or ceremony etc. establishing this condition; particular matrimonial union (*by a previous marriage*); **marriage bureau** establishment arranging introductions between persons wishing to marry; **marriage certificate** certificate stating that marriage ceremony has taken place; **marriage guidance** counselling of married couples who have problems in living together harmoniously; **marriage lines** marriage certificate; **marriage of convenience** marriage not made primarily for love; **marriage settlement** arrangement securing property to wife. [F (*marier* MARRY)]

marriageable *a.* old enough to marry; (of age) fit for marriage.

marron glacé /mærɒn 'glɑ:seɪ/ *n.* chestnut preserved in sugar as a sweet. [F]

marrow /'mærəʊ/ *n.* gourd with whitish flesh, cooked as vegetable; fatty substance in cavities of bones; **to the marrow** right through. [OE]

marrowbone *n.* bone containing edible marrow.

marrowfat *n.* kind of large pea.

marry /'mærɪ/ *v.* take or join or give in marriage; enter into marriage; unite intimately, correlate as pair. [F f. L (*maritus* husband)]

Marsala /mɑ:'sɑ:lə/ *n.* dark sweet fortified wine. [*Marsala* in Sicily]

Marseillaise /mɑ:seɪ'jeɪz, -sə'leɪz/ *n.* national anthem of France. [F (*Marseille* in France)]

marsh *n.* low-lying watery land; **marsh gas** methane; **marsh mallow** shrubby herb, confection made from root of this; **marsh marigold** plant with golden flowers, growing in moist meadows; **marshy** *a.* [OE]

marshal /'mɑ:ʃ(ə)l/ **1** *n.* high-ranking officer of state or in armed forces (*Air Marshal, Earl Marshal, Field Marshal*); officer arranging ceremonies, controlling procedure at races, etc. **2** *v.t.* (**-ll-**, *US* **-l-**) arrange in due order (soldiers, facts, one's thoughts, etc.); conduct (person) ceremoniously. **3 marshalling yard** railway yard in which goods trains etc. are assembled; **Marshal of the RAF** highest rank in RAF. [F f. L f. Gmc]

marshmallow *n.* soft sweet made from sugar, albumen, gelatine, etc. [*marsh mallow*]

marsupial /mɑːˈsuːpɪəl/ **1** *n.* mammal of class in which females have a pouch in which to carry their young. **2** *a.* of this class. [L f. Gk *marsupion* pouch]

mart *n.* trade centre; auction-room; market. [Du. (MARKET)]

Martello tower /mɑːˈteləʊ/ circular fort usu. for coast-defence. [Cape *Mortella* in Corsica]

marten /ˈmɑːtɪn/ *n.* animal like weasel, with valuable fur. [Du. f. F]

martial /ˈmɑːʃ(ə)l/ *a.* of or appropriate to warfare; warlike, brave, fond of fighting; **martial arts** fighting sports such as judo and karate; **martial law** military government, by which ordinary law is suspended. [F, or L *martialis* of Mars]

Martian /ˈmɑːʃ(ə)n/ **1** *a.* of the planet Mars. **2** *n.* hypothetical inhabitant of Mars. [F or L]

martin /ˈmɑːtɪn/ *n.* bird of swallow family. [prob. St Martin, bishop]

martinet /mɑːtɪˈnet/ *n.* strict disciplinarian. [*Martinet*, drill-master]

Martini /mɑːˈtiːniː/ *n.* (**P**) vermouth; cocktail made of gin and vermouth. [*Martini* & Rossi, firm selling vermouth]

Martinmas /ˈmɑːtɪnməs/ *n.* St Martin's day, 11 Nov. [MASS²]

martyr /ˈmɑːtə/ **1** *n.* one who undergoes death penalty for persistence in Christian faith or obedience to law of Church, or undergoes death or suffering for any great cause. **2** *v.t.* put to death as martyr; torment. **3 martyr to** constant sufferer from (ailment). [OE f. L f. Gk *martur* witness]

martyrdom *n.* sufferings and death of martyr; torment. [OE (prec.)]

marvel /ˈmɑːv(ə)l/ **1** *n.* wonderful thing; wonderful example *of* (quality). **2** *v.i.* (**-ll-**, *US* **-l-**) feel surprise or wonder (*at* or *that*). [F f. L (*miror* wonder at)]

marvellous /ˈmɑːvələs/, *US* **marvelous** *a.* astonishing; excellent. [F (prec.)]

Marxism /ˈmɑːksɪz(ə)m/ *n.* doctrines of Marx, predicting abolition of private ownership of means of production, with provision of work and subsistence for all; **Marxian** *a.*; **Marxist** *n.* & *a.* [*Marx*, socialist]

marzipan /ˈmɑːzɪpæn/ *n.* paste of ground almonds, sugar, etc. [G f. It.]

mascara /mæˈskɑːrə/ *n.* cosmetic for darkening eyelashes etc. [It., = mask]

mascot /ˈmæskɒt/ *n.* person or animal or thing supposed to bring luck. [F f. Prov. (*masco* witch)]

masculine /ˈmæskjʊlɪn/ **1** *a.* of men; having qualities appropriate to a man; *Gram.* of gender proper to men's names; (of rhyme or line-ending) having final stressed syllable. **2** *n.* masculine gender or word. **3 masculinity** /-ˈlɪnɪtɪ/ *n.* [F f. L (MALE)]

maser /ˈmeɪzə/ *n.* device for amplifying microwaves. [*m*icrowave *a*mplification by *s*timulated *e*mission of *r*adiation]

mash 1 *n.* soft or confused mixture; mixture of boiled grain, bran, etc., given warm to horses etc.; *colloq.* mashed potatoes (*sausage and mash*); mixture of malt and hot water used in brewing; soft pulp made by crushing, mixing with water, etc. **2** *v.t.* reduce (potatoes etc.) to uniform mass by crushing; crush to a pulp; mix (malt) with hot water. [OE]

mask /mɑːsk/ **1** *n.* covering for all or part of face, worn as disguise, for protection, or (by surgeon etc.) to prevent infection of patient; respirator used to filter inhaled air or to supply gas for inhalation; likeness of person's face, esp. one made by taking mould from face (*death-mask*); *fig.* disguise or pretence (*throw off the mask*). **2** *v.t.* cover or disguise with mask; conceal or protect. **3 masking tape** adhesive tape used in painting to cover areas on which paint is not wanted. [F f. It. f. Arab.]

masochism /ˈmæsəkɪz(ə)m/ *n.* form of (esp. sexual) perversion in which sufferer derives pleasure from his own pain or humiliation; *colloq.* enjoyment of what appears to be painful or tiresome; **masochist** *n.*; **masochistic** /-ˈkɪstɪk/ *a.* [von Sacher-*Masoch*, novelist]

mason /ˈmeɪs(ə)n/ *n.* one who builds with stone; (**Mason**) Freemason. [F]

Masonic /məˈsɒnɪk/ *a.* of Freemasons.

masonry *n.* mason's work; stonework; (**Masonry**) Freemasonry.

masque /mɑːsk/ *n.* amateur dramatic and musical entertainment esp. in 16th–17th c. [var. of MASK]

masquer *n.* one who takes part in masquerade or masque.

masquerade /mɑːskəˈreɪd, mæs-/ **1** *n.* false show, pretence; masked ball. **2** *v.i.* appear in disguise, assume false appearance (*as*). [F f. Sp. (*máscara* mask)]

mass¹ 1 *n.* coherent body of matter of indefinite shape; dense aggregation of objects (*a mass of fibres*); (in *sing.* or *pl.*) large number or amount (*of*); unbroken expanse (*of* colour etc.); quantity of matter a body contains. **2** *v.* gather into mass; assemble into one body (*massed bands*). **3** *a.* of or relating to large numbers of persons or things, large-scale (*mass grave, hysteria*). **4 the mass** the majority (*of*); **the masses** the ordinary people; **in the mass** in the aggregate; **mass media** means of communication (e.g. newspapers or broadcasting) to large numbers of people; **mass production** production of large quantities of a standardized article by mechanical processes. [F f. L *massa* f. Gk]

mass² /mæs, mɑːs/ *n.* celebration of the Eucharist, esp. in RC Church; liturgy used in this; musical setting for parts of it. [OE f. L *missa* dismissal]

massacre /ˈmæsəkə/ **1** *n.* general slaughter (of persons, occas. of animals); utter defeat or destruction. **2** *v.t.* make a massacre of; murder (large number of people) cruelly or violently. [F]

massage /ˈmæsɑːʒ/ **1** *n.* rubbing, kneading, etc., of muscles and joints of body with the hands, to stimulate their action, cure strains, etc. **2** *v.t.* treat (part or person) thus. [F]

masseur /mæˈsɜː/ *n.* one who provides massage professionally; **masseuse** /-ˈsɜːz/ *n. fem.* [F (prec.)]

massif /ˈmæsiːf, -ˈsiːf/ *n.* mountain heights forming a compact group. [F (foll.)]

massive /ˈmæsɪv/ *a.* large and heavy or solid; substantial, imposing, unusually large; (of features, head, etc.) relatively large, of solid build. [F f. L (MASS¹)]

mast¹ /mɑːst/ *n.* long upright post set up on ship's keel to support sails; post or upright to support radio or television aerial; flag-pole (*half-mast*); **before the mast** as ordinary sailor. [OE]

mast² /mɑːst/ *n.* fruit of beech, oak, etc., esp. as food for pigs. [OE]

mastectomy /mæˈstektəmɪ/ *n.* surgical removal of a breast. [Gk *mastos* breast]

master /ˈmɑːstə/ **1** *n.* person having control of persons or things, esp. an employer, male head of household, head of college etc., owner of animal or slave, (in full **master mariner**) captain of merchant ship; male teacher or tutor, = SCHOOLMASTER; one who has or gets the upper hand (*we shall see which of us is master*); skilled workman, or one in business on his own account (*master carpenter, mason*); holder of university degree (*Master of Arts, Science,* etc.); revered teacher in philosophy etc.; great artist, picture by one; chess player of proved ability at international level; thing from which series of copies (e.g. of film or gramophone record) is made; (**Master**) title prefixed to name of boy not old enough to be called *Mr.* **2** *a.* commanding, superior (*a master spirit*); main, principal (*master bedroom*); controlling others (*master plan*). **3** *v.* overcome, conquer; gain knowledge of or skill in. **4 the Master** Christ; **master-key** key that opens several locks, each also having its own key; **Master of Ceremonies** person in charge of ceremonial or social occasion, person introducing speakers at banquet or performers at variety show; **Master of the Rolls** Court of Appeal judge in charge of Public Record Office; **master-stroke** outstandingly skilful act of policy etc.; **master-switch** switch controlling electricity etc. supply to entire system. [OE & F f. L *magister*]

masterful *a.* imperious, domineering; masterly; **masterfully** *adv.*

masterly *a.* worthy of a master, very skilful.

mastermind **1** *n.* person with outstanding intellect; person directing intricate operation. **2** *v.t.* plan and direct (scheme).

masterpiece *n.* outstanding piece of artistry; one's best work.

mastery *n.* dominion, sway; masterly skill or knowledge.

masthead *n.* highest part of ship's mast; title details of newspaper at head of front or editorial page. [MAST¹]

mastic /ˈmæstɪk/ *n.* gum or resin exuded from certain trees; type of cement. [F f. L f. Gk]

masticate /ˈmæstɪkeɪt/ *v.t.* grind (food) with teeth, chew; **mastication** /-ˈkeɪʃ(ə)n/ *n.*; **masticatory** *a.* [L f. Gk]

mastiff /ˈmæstɪf/ *n.* large strong kind of dog. [F f. L (*mansuetus* tame)]

mastodon /ˈmæstədɒn/ *n.* large extinct animal resembling elephant. [Gk *mastos* breast, *odous* tooth]

mastoid /ˈmæstɔɪd/ **1** *a.* shaped like woman's breast. **2** *n.* conical prominence on temporal bone behind ear (also **mastoid process**); *colloq.* inflammation of this. [Gk (*mastos* breast)]

masturbate /ˈmæstəbeɪt/ *v.* produce sexual orgasm or arousal (of) by stimulation of genitals other than by sexual intercourse; **masturbation** /-ˈbeɪʃ(ə)n/ *n.*; **masturbatory** *a.* [L]

mat¹ **1** *n.* piece of coarse material as floor-covering or for wiping shoes on, esp. doormat; piece of cork, rubber, plastic, etc., to protect surface from heat or moisture of object placed on it; piece of resilient material for landing on in gymnastics or wrestling. **2** *v.* (**-tt-**) make or become entangled in thick mass; cover or furnish with mats. **3 on the mat** *sl.* being reprimanded. [OE]

mat² var. of MATT.

matador /ˈmætədɔː/ *n.* bullfighter whose task is to kill bull. [Sp. f. *matar* kill (CHECKMATE)]

match¹ **1** *n.* contest or game of skill etc. in which persons or teams compete against each other; competitor able to contend with another as an equal; person equal to another in some quality; person or thing exactly like or corresponding to another; marriage; person viewed in regard to eligibility for marriage. **2** *v.* be equal, correspond in some essential respect (to); place (person etc.) in conflict or competition *against* or *with*; find material etc. that matches (another); find person or thing suitable for another. **3 match point** state of a game when one side needs only one more point to win the match, this point. [OE]

match[2] *n.* short thin piece of wood etc. tipped with composition that bursts into flame when rubbed on rough or specially prepared surface; fuse for firing cannon etc. [F *mesche*]

matchboard *n.* board with tongue cut along one edge and groove along the other, so as to fit with similar boards. [MATCH[1]]

matchbox *n.* box for holding matches. [MATCH[2]]

matchless *a.* incomparable. [MATCH[1]]

matchmaker *n.* person fond of scheming to bring about marriages.

matchstick *n.* stem of a match. [MATCH[2]]

matchwood *n.* wood suitable for matches; minute splinters.

mate[1] **1** *n.* companion, fellow worker; *colloq.* general form of address to an equal; one of a pair, esp. of birds; *colloq.* partner in marriage; subordinate officer on merchant ship; assistant to a worker (*plumber's mate*). **2** *in comb.* fellow member or joint occupant of (*team-mate*; *room-mate*). **3** *v.* come or bring together in marriage or for breeding; fit well (*with*). [LG]

mate[2] *n.* & *v.t.* = CHECKMATE. [F *mat* in *eschec mat* CHECKMATE]

mater *n. sl.* mother. [L]

material /mə'tɪərɪəl/ **1** *n.* matter from which thing is made; cloth, fabric; (in *pl.*) things needed for an activity (*building materials*); person or thing of specified kind or suitable for a purpose (*officer material*); (in *sing.* or *pl.*) information etc. to be used in writing book etc.; (in *sing.* or *pl.*) elements, constituent parts (*of* substance). **2** *a.* of matter, corporeal; concerned with bodily comfort etc. (*material well-being*); of conduct, point of view, etc.) not spiritual; important, essential, relevant. [F f. L (*materia* MATTER)]

materialism *n.* tendency to prefer material possessions and physical comfort to spiritual values; opinion that nothing exists but matter and its movements and modifications; **materialist** *n.*; **materialistic** /-'lɪstɪk/ *a.*

materialize *v.* become actual fact; appear, become visible; represent in or assume bodily form; **materialization** /-'zeɪʃ(ə)n/ *n.*

materially *adv.* substantially, considerably.

matériel /mətɪərɪ'el/ *n.* available means, esp. materials and equipment in warfare. [F]

maternal /mə'tɜ:n(ə)l/ *a.* of or like a mother, motherly; related through mother; of the mother in pregnancy and childbirth; **maternally** *adv.* [F or L (MATER)]

maternity /mə'tɜ:nɪtɪ/ *n.* motherhood; motherliness; *attrib.* for women in pregnancy or childbirth. [F f. med.L (prec.)]

matey **1** *a.* sociable, familiar and friendly (*with*). **2** *n. colloq.* (as form of address) mate. **3 matily** *adv.* [MATE[1]]

mathematics /mæθə'mætɪks/ *n.pl.* (also treated as *sing.*) abstract science of number, quantity, and space; (as *pl.*) use of this in calculation etc.; **mathematical** *a.*; **mathematically** *adv.*; **mathematician** /-mə'tɪʃ(ə)n/ *n.* [F or L f. Gk (*manthanō* learn)]

maths *n. colloq.* mathematics. [abbr.]

matinée /'mætɪneɪ/, *US* **matinee** *n.* afternoon performance at theatre or cinema; **matinée coat** baby's short coat. [F f. *matin* morning (foll.)]

matins /'mætɪnz/ *n.pl.* morning prayer, esp. in Church of England. [F f. L (*matutinus* of the morning)]

matriarch /'meɪtrɪɑ:k/ *n.* woman who is head of family or tribe; **matriarchal** /-'ɑ:k(ə)l/ *a.* [L *mater* mother]

matriarchy *n.* social organization in which mother is head of family and descent is reckoned through female line.

matricide /'meɪtrɪsaɪd/ *n.* killing of one's mother; one who kills his mother; **matricidal** /-'saɪd(ə)l/ *a.* [L (MATER, -CIDE)]

matriculate /mə'trɪkjʊleɪt/ *v.* admit (student) to membership of university; be thus admitted. [med.L (MATRIX)]

matriculation /mətrɪkjʊ'leɪʃ(ə)n/ *n.* matriculating; examination to qualify for this.

matrimony /'mætrɪmənɪ/ *n.* rite of marriage; state of being married; **matrimonial** /-'məʊnɪəl/ *a.*; **matrimonially** *adv.* [AF f. L *matrimonium* (MATER)]

matrix /'meɪtrɪks/ *n.* (*pl.* **matrices** /-ɪsi:z/) mould in which thing is cast or shaped; place in which thing is developed; mass of rock enclosing gems etc.; rectangular array of mathematical quantities treated as single quantity. [L, = womb]

matron /ˈmeɪtrən/ *n.* married woman, esp. one of dignity and sobriety; woman managing domestic arrangements of school etc.; woman in charge of nurses in hospital (¶ now usu. called *senior nursing officer*); **matron of honour** married woman attending bride at wedding; **matronly** *a.* [F f. L *matrona* (MATER)]

matt *a.* (of colour etc.) dull, not lustrous. [F (MATE²)]

matter 1 *n.* physical substance in general, as distinct from mind and spirit; particular substance (*colouring matter*); material for thought or expression; substance of book, speech, etc., as distinct from its manner or form; thing of specified kind (*reading matter*); affair or situation being considered, or considered in particular way (*a serious matter*; *a matter for concern*; *the matter of your overdraft*); quantity or extent *of* (*a matter of £50*); thing depending on conditions *of* (*a matter of time*); substance in or discharged from the body. **2** *v.i.* be of importance, have significance. **3 the matter** thing that is amiss (*what is the matter with him?*); **as a matter of fact** in reality (esp. to correct falsehood or misunderstanding); **for that matter** as far as that is concerned, and indeed also; **a matter of course** a thing to be expected; **matter-of-fact** unimaginative, prosaic; **no matter** it is of no importance. [AF f. L *materia* timber, substance]

matting *n.* fabric for mats. [MAT¹]

mattins *var. of* MATINS.

mattock /ˈmætək/ *n.* agricultural tool like pickaxe with an adze and a chisel edge as ends of head. [OE]

mattress /ˈmætrɪs/ *n.* fabric case filled with soft or firm or springy material, used on or as bed. [F f. It. f. Arab.]

maturate /ˈmætjʊreɪt/ *v.i.* (of boil etc.) come to maturation. [L (MATURE)]

maturation /mætjʊˈreɪʃ(ə)n/ *n.* maturing, development; formation of purulent matter. [F or med.L (foll.)]

mature /məˈtjʊə/ **1** *a.* with fully developed powers of body and mind, adult; complete in natural development, ripe; (of thought, intentions, etc.) duly careful and adequate; (of bill etc.) due for payment. **2** *v.* develop fully; ripen; perfect (plan etc.); (of bill etc.) become due for payment. **3 maturity** *n.* [L *maturus* timely]

matutinal /mætju:ˈtaɪn(ə)l/ *a.* of or occurring in the morning; early. [L (MATINS)]

maty var. of MATEY.

maudlin /ˈmɔ:dlɪn/ *a.* weakly or tearfully sentimental, esp. from drunkenness. [F *Madeleine* f. L (St Mary *Magdalen*)]

maul /mɔ:l/ **1** *v.t.* beat and bruise; handle roughly or carelessly; damage by criticism. **2** *n.* loose scrum in Rugby football; brawl; heavy hammer. [F f. L *malleus* hammer]

maulstick /ˈmɔ:lstɪk/ *n.* stick used to support the hand in painting. [Du. (*malen* paint)]

maunder /ˈmɔ:ndə/ *v.i.* talk in dreamy or rambling manner; move or act listlessly or idly. [orig. unkn.]

Maundy /ˈmɔ:ndɪ/ *n.* distribution of Maundy money; **Maundy money** specially minted silver coins distributed by the sovereign to the poor on Maundy Thursday; **Maundy Thursday** Thursday before Easter. [F *mandé* f. L (MANDATE)]

mausoleum /mɔ:səˈli:əm/ *n.* magnificent tomb. [*Mausolos*, King of Caria]

mauve /məʊv/ **1** *a.* pale purple. **2** *n.* mauve colour or dye. [F f. L (MALLOW)]

maverick /ˈmævərɪk/ *n.* unorthodox or independent person; unbranded calf or yearling. [*Maverick*, owner of unbranded cattle]

maw *n.* stomach, esp. of animal; jaws or throat of voracious animal. [OE]

mawkish /ˈmɔ:kɪʃ/ *a.* sentimental in feeble or sickly way. [obs. *mawk* MAGGOT]

max. *abbr.* maximum.

maxi- *in comb.* very large or long (*maxi-coat*). [abbr. MAXIMUM; cf. MINI-]

maxilla /mækˈsɪlə/ *n.* (*pl.* **maxillae** /-i:/) the jaw, esp. (in vertebrates) the upper one; **maxillary** *a.* [L]

maxim /ˈmæksɪm/ *n.* general truth or rule of conduct expressed in a sentence. [F or med.L (MAXIMUM)]

maximal /ˈmæksɪm(ə)l/ *a.* being or related to a maximum. [MAXIMUM]

maximize /ˈmæksɪmaɪz/ *v.t.* increase or enhance to the utmost; **maximization** /-ˈzeɪʃ(ə)n/ *n.* [L (foll.)]

maximum /ˈmæksɪməm/ **1** *n.* (*pl.* **maxima**) highest amount possible, attained, usual, etc. **2** *a.* that is a maximum. [L (*maximus* greatest)]

may¹ *v. aux.* (3 *sing. pres.* **may**; past MIGHT¹) expressing possibility (*it may be true*), permission (*you may not go*), wish (*may the best man win*), uncertainty (*who may you be?*). [OE]

May² *n.* fifth month of year; (**may**) hawthorn or its blossom; **May Day** 1 May esp. as festival with dancing, or as international holiday in honour of workers; **May queen** (or **Queen of the May**) girl chosen to be queen of games on May Day. [F f. L *Maius* of the goddess Maia]

Maya /'mɑ:jə/ *n.* member or language of ancient Central American Indian people; **Mayan** *a.* [native name]
maybe /'meɪbi:/ *adv.* perhaps, possibly. [*it may be*]
mayday /'meɪdeɪ/ *n.* international radio distress-signal used by ships and aircraft. [repr. pr. of F *m'aider* help me]
mayflower *n.* any of various flowers that bloom in May. [MAY²]
mayfly *n.* insect which lives briefly in spring.
mayhem /'meɪhem/ *n.* violent or damaging action; *hist.* crime of maiming a person. [AF *mahem* (MAIM)]
mayn't /'meɪənt/ *colloq.* = *may not.*
mayonnaise /meɪə'neɪz/ *n.* dressing made of egg-yolks, oil, vinegar, etc.; dish dressed with this. [F]
mayor /meə/ *n.* head of municipal corporation of city or borough; head of district council with status of borough; **mayoral** *a.* [F *maire* f. L (MAJOR)]
mayoralty /'meərəltɪ/ *n.* office of mayor; period of this. [F (prec.)]
mayoress /'meərɪs/ *n.* mayor's wife; lady fulfilling ceremonial duties of mayor's wife; woman mayor. [MAYOR]
maypole *n.* pole decked with ribbons, for dancing round on May Day. [MAY²]
mazarine /mæzə'ri:n/ *n.* & *a.* rich deep blue. [perh. Cardinal *Mazarin*, statesman]
maze *n.* labyrinth, network of paths and hedges designed as puzzle for those who try to penetrate it; confusion, confused mass, etc. [AMAZE]
mazurka /mə'zɜ:kə/ *n.* lively Polish dance in triple time; music for this. [F or G f. Pol.]
MB *abbr.* Bachelor of Medicine. [L *Medicinae Baccalaureus*]
MBE *abbr.* Member of the Order of the British Empire.
MC *abbr.* Master of Ceremonies; Military Cross.
MCC *abbr.* Marylebone Cricket Club.
MD *abbr.* Doctor of Medicine. [L *Medicinae Doctor*]
Md *symb.* mendelevium.
me¹ /mi:, mɪ/ *pron.* obj. case of I²; *colloq.* = I² (*it's me all right*). [OE, acc. & dat. of I²]
me² /mi:/ *n. Mus.* third note of major scale. [L *mira*, word arbitrarily taken]
mead *n.* alcoholic drink of fermented honey and water. [OE]
meadow /'medəʊ/ *n.* piece of grassland, esp. one used for hay; low well-watered ground, esp. near river; **meadowy** *a.* [OE]
meadowsweet *n.* fragrant flowering meadow plant.
meagre /'mi:gə/, *US* **meager** *a.* of poor quality and scanty in amount; (of person) lean. [AF *megre* f. L *macer*]
meal¹ *n.* occasion when food is eaten; food eaten on one occasion; **make a meal of** treat (task etc.) too laboriously or fussily; **meal-ticket** source of food or income. [OE]
meal² *n.* grain or pulse ground to powder; *Sc.* oatmeal; *US* maize flour. [OE]
mealie /'mi:lɪ/ *n.* (in S. Africa) maize. [Afrik. *milie*]
mealtime *n.* usual time of eating. [MEAL¹]
mealy *a.* of or like or containing meal; dry and powdery; **mealy-mouthed** not outspoken, afraid to use plain expressions. [MEAL²]
mean¹ *v.t.* (*past* and *p.p.* **meant** /ment/) have as one's purpose or intention; design or destine for a purpose (*is meant to be used, meant for you*); intend to convey or indicate or refer to; involve or portend (*it means we must wait; this means war*); signify or import, (of words) have as equivalent in same or another language; be of a specified importance to, esp. as source of benefit or object of affection etc.; **mean it** not be joking or exaggerating; **mean well** have good intentions. [OE]
mean² *a.* niggardly, not generous; ignoble, small-minded (*a mean trick*); (of capacity, understanding, etc.) inferior, poor; not imposing in appearance; malicious, ill-tempered; *US* vicious, nastily behaved; *US sl.* skilful; **no mean** a very good (*he is no mean scholar*). [OE]
mean³ **1** *n.* condition or quality or course of action equally removed from two opposite extremes; quotient of the sum of several quantities and their number; term between first and last of arithmetical etc. progression esp. of three terms. **2** *a.* (of quantity) equally far from two extremes. **3** **in the mean time** meanwhile; **mean sea level** level halfway between those of high and low water. [AF f. L *medianus* MEDIAN]
meander /mɪ'ændə/ **1** *v.i.* (of stream) wind about; wander at random. **2** *n.* (in *pl.*) sinuous windings of river; circuitous journey. [L f. Gk *Maiandros*, winding river in Phrygia]
meanie var. of MEANY.
meaning **1** *n.* what is meant, significance. **2** *a.* expressive, significant. **3** **meaningful** *a.*; **meaningless** *a.* [MEAN¹]
means *n.pl.* (usu. treated as *sing.*) that by which a result is brought about; money resources, wealth (*a man of means*); **by all means** certainly; **by means of** by the agency or instrumentality of; **by no means** not at all, certain-

ly not; **means test** official inquiry to establish need before financial assistance is given. [MEAN³]

meant *past* and *p.p.* of MEAN¹.

meantime *adv.* meanwhile. [MEAN³]

meanwhile *adv.* in the intervening period of time; at the same time.

meany *n. colloq.* niggardly or small-minded person. [MEAN²]

measles /ˈmi:z(ə)lz/ *n.* (as *pl.* or *sing.*) infectious virus disease marked by red rash. [LG *masele* or Du. *masel*]

measly /ˈmi:zlɪ/ *a.* of or affected with measles; *sl.* inferior or contemptible or worthless.

measure /ˈmeʒə/ **1** *n.* size or quantity found by measuring; system or unit of measuring; device for measuring, esp. rod, tape, or vessel marked with standard units; degree or extent; (often in *pl.*) suitable action to achieve some end; legislative enactment; that by which thing is computed; prescribed quantity or extent; poetical rhythm, metre; metrical group of dactyl or two disyllabic feet; *Mus.* bar or time-content of bar; *archaic* dance; mineral stratum (*coal measures*). **2** *v.* find extent or quantity of (thing) by comparison with fixed unit or with object of known size; be of specified size; ascertain size and proportions of (person) for clothes etc.; (often with *off* or *out*) determine or mark out (line of given length); estimate (quality, character, etc.) by some standard; deal *out* (thing *to* person); bring (*oneself*, one's strength, etc.) into competition *with*. **3 beyond measure** very much or great, exceedingly; **for good measure** in addition to what is necessary; **in some measure** partly, to some extent; **made to measure** made from measurements specially taken; **measure up (to)** reach necessary standard (for); **take person's measure** estimate his character, ability, etc. [F f. L *mensura* (*metior* measure)]

measured *a.* rhythmical, regular in movement (*measured tread*); (of language) carefully considered.

measurement *n.* act or result of measuring; (in *pl.*) detailed dimensions.

meat *n.* animal flesh as food; essence or chief part; **meat and drink** source of great pleasure *to*; **meat-safe** ventilated cupboard for storing meat. [OE]

meatball *n.* small ball of minced meat.

meaty *a.* like meat; full of substance; full of meat, fleshy; **meatiness** *n.*

Mecca /ˈmekə/ *n.* place one aspires to visit. [*Mecca*, holy city in Arabia]

mechanic /mɪˈkænɪk/ *n.* skilled worker, esp. one who makes or uses or repairs machinery. [F or L (MACHINE)]

mechanical *a.* of machines or mechanism; working or produced by machinery; (of person or action) like a machine, automatic, lacking originality; (of agency, principle, etc.) belonging to mechanics; of mechanics as a science; **mechanically** *adv.* [L (prec.)]

mechanics *n.pl.* (usu. treated as *sing.*) branch of applied mathematics dealing with motion and tendencies to motion; science of machinery; (as *pl.*) method of construction or operation. [MECHANIC]

mechanism /ˈmekənɪz(ə)m/ *n.* structure or parts of machine or other set of mutually adapted parts; mode of operation of process or machine. [Gk (MACHINE)]

mechanize /ˈmekənaɪz/ *v.t.* introduce or use machines in; equip with machines; give mechanical character to; **mechanization** /-ˈzeɪʃ(ə)n/ *n.* [MECHANIC]

Med *n. colloq.* Mediterranean Sea. [abbr.]

medal /ˈmed(ə)l/ *n.* piece of metal, usu. in form of coin, struck or cast with inscription and device to commemorate event etc., or awarded as distinction to soldier, athlete, etc. [F f. It. f. L (METAL)]

medalist *US* var. of MEDALLIST.

medallion /mɪˈdæljən/ *n.* large medal; thing so shaped, e.g. decorative panel, portrait. [F f. It. (MEDAL)]

medallist /ˈmedəlɪst/ *n.* winner of medal, usu. specified (*gold medallist*). [MEDAL]

meddle /ˈmed(ə)l/ *v.i.* busy oneself unduly (*with*), interfere (*in*). [F f. L (MIX)]

meddlesome *a.* fond of meddling.

media *pl.* of MEDIUM.

mediaeval var. of MEDIEVAL.

medial /ˈmi:dɪəl/ *a.* situated in the middle; **medially** *adv.* [L (*medius* middle)]

median /ˈmi:dɪən/ **1** *a.* medial. **2** *n.* straight line drawn from any vertex of triangle to middle of opposite side; medial number or point in series. [F or L (prec.)]

mediate 1 /ˈmi:dɪeɪt/ *v.* intervene (*between* two persons or groups) for purpose of reconciling them; bring about (result) thus. **2** /ˈmi:dɪət/ *a.* connected not directly but through some other person or thing. **3 mediation** /-ˈeɪʃ(ə)n/ *n.*; **mediator** *n.* [L (*medius* middle)]

medic /ˈmedɪk/ *n. colloq.* medical practitioner or student. [L *medicus* physician]

medical /ˈmedɪk(ə)l/ **1** *a.* of the science of medicine in general or as distinct from surgery. **2** *n. colloq.* medical examination. **3 medical certificate** certificate of fitness or unfitness to work etc.; **medical examination** examination to determine person's physical fitness; **medical officer** person in charge of health services of local authority or other organization. **4 medically** *adv*. [F or med.L (prec.)]

medicament /mɪ'dɪkəmənt/ *n*. substance used in curative treatment. [F or L (foll.)]

medicate /'medɪkeɪt/ *v.t.* treat medically; impregnate with medicinal substance; **medication** /-'keɪʃ(ə)n/ *n*.; **medicative** *a*. [L (MEDIC)]

medicinal /mɪ'dɪsɪn(ə)l/ *a*. of medicine; having healing properties; **medicinally** *adv*. [F f. L (foll.)]

medicine /'medsɪn, -ɪsɪn/ *n*. art of restoring and preserving health, esp. by means of remedial substances etc. as distinct from surgery; substance used in this, esp. one taken internally; **medicine-man** witch-doctor; **take one's medicine** submit to rebuke or punishment etc. [F f. L *medicina*]

medico /'medɪkəʊ/ *n*. (*pl*. **medicos**) *colloq*. medical practitioner or student. [It. f. L (MEDIC)]

medieval /medɪ'i:v(ə)l/ *a*. of or imitating the Middle Ages. [L *medium aevum* middle age]

mediocre /mi:dɪ'əʊkə/ *a*. of middling quality; second-rate. [F, or L *mediocris*]

mediocrity /mi:dɪ'ɒkrɪtɪ/ *n*. mediocre quality or person. [F f. L (prec.)]

meditate /'medɪteɪt/ *v*. exercise the mind in contemplation (*on* or *upon* subject), esp. with religious aim; plan mentally, design; **meditation** /-'teɪʃ(ə)n/ *n*.; **meditator** *n*. [L *meditor*]

meditative /'medɪtətɪv/ *a*. inclined to meditate; indicative of meditation.

Mediterranean /medɪtə'reɪnɪən/ *a*. of or characteristic of the sea between Europe and N. Africa, or of the countries in and round it. [L *mediterraneus* inland]

medium /'mi:dɪəm/ **1** *n*. (*pl*. **media** or **mediums**) middle quality or degree; intervening substance through which impressions are conveyed to senses, e.g. air; agency or means (in *pl*., or erron. as *sing*.) = *mass media*; material or form used by artist, composer, etc.; (*pl*. **mediums**) person claiming to have communication with spirits of the dead etc.; environment. **2** *a*. intermediate between two degrees or amounts; average, moderate. **3 medium wave** radio wave with length between 100 and 1,000 metres. [L (*medius* middle)]

mediumistic /mi:dɪə'mɪstɪk/ *a*. of a spiritualist medium.

medlar /'medlə/ *n*. fruit like small apple, eaten when decayed; tree bearing this. [F *medler* f. L f. Gk *mespilē*]

medley /'medlɪ/ *n*. varied mixture, miscellany; collection of musical items from various sources. [F *medlee* f. L (MEDDLE)]

medulla /mɪ'dʌlə/ *n*. bone or spinal marrow; hindmost section of brain; **medullary** *a*. [L]

medusa /mɪ'dju:zə/ *n*. (*pl*. **medusae** or **-as**) jellyfish. [L f. Gk *Medousa*, name of Gorgon]

meek *a*. humbly submissive. [ON]

meerschaum /'mɪəʃəm/ *n*. white substance resembling clay; tobacco-pipe with bowl made of this. [G, = sea-foam]

meet[1] **1** *v*. (*past* and *p.p.* **met**) come by accident or design into the company of, come face to face (with); go to place to be present at arrival of (person, train, etc.); come together or into contact (with); make the acquaintance of, be introduced (to); (of people or group) assemble; deal with or answer effectively (demand, objection, etc.), satisfy or conform with (person's wishes); pay (cost, bill at maturity); experience or receive (one's death, fate, etc.); oppose or be in opposition in contest etc. **2** *n*. meeting of persons and hounds for hunt. **3 meet the case** be adequate; **meet the eye** (or **ear**) be visible, (or audible) (**more in it than meets the eye** hidden qualities or complications); **meet person's eye** look into eyes of person looking at one; **meet person half-way** respond to his advances, make compromise with him; **meet up with** *colloq*. happen to meet (person); **meet with** experience, encounter, happen to meet. [OE]

meet[2] *a*. *archaic* fitting, proper. [METE]

meeting *n*. coming together; assembly of people, e.g. for discussion or (esp. of Quakers) worship; = *race-meeting*. [MEET[1]]

mega- *in comb*. large; one million. [Gk *megas* great]

megadeath /'megədeθ/ *n*. death of one million people (esp. as unit in estimating casualties of war).

megahertz /'megəhɜ:ts/ *n*. unit of frequency, equal to one million cycles per second.

megalith /'megəlɪθ/ *n*. large stone, esp. as monument or part of one; **megalithic** /-'lɪθɪk/ *a*. [Gk *lithos* stone]

megalomania /megələ'meɪnɪə/ *n*. mental disorder, involving exaggerated idea of one's own importance; passion for grandiose things; **megalomaniac** *n*. [Gk *megas* great, MANIA]

megaphone /'megəfəʊn/ *n*. large funnel-shaped device for sending sound of voice to a distance. [Gk *megas* great, *phōnē* sound]

megaton /'megətʌn/ *n*. unit of explosive

force equal to one million tons of TNT. [MEGA-]

megavolt /'megəvəʊlt/ *n.* unit of electromotive force equal to one million volts.

megawatt /'megəwɒt/ *n.* unit of electrical power equal to one million watts.

megohm /'megəʊm/ *n.* unit of electrical resistance equal to one million ohms.

meiosis /maɪ'əʊsɪs/ *n.* (*pl.* **meioses** /-i:z/) litotes; a process of division of cell nuclei forming gametes each containing half the normal number of chromosomes. [Gk (*meiōn* less)]

melamine /'meləmi:n/ *n.* resilient kind of plastic. [*melam* (arbitrary), AMINE]

melancholia /melən'kəʊlɪə/ *n.* mental disorder marked by depression and ill-founded fears. [L (MELANCHOLY)]

melancholic /melən'kɒlɪk/ *a.* melancholy; liable to melancholy. [F f. L f. Gk (foll.)]

melancholy /'melənkəlɪ/ **1** *n.* pensive sadness; mental depression; habitual or constitutional tendency to this. **2** *a.* sad, gloomy; saddening, depressing; (of words etc.) expressing sadness. [F f. L f. Gk (*melas* black, *kholē* bile)]

mélange /meɪ'lɑ̃ʒ/ *n.* medley. [F (*mêler* mix)]

melanin /'melənɪn/ *n.* dark pigment in hair, skin, etc. [Gk *melas* black]

Melba toast /'melbə/ thin crisp toast. [*Melba*, soprano]

mêlée /'meleɪ/ *n.* confused fight or struggle; muddle. [F (MEDLEY)]

mellifluous /me'lɪflʊəs/ *a.* sweet-sounding. [F or L (*mel* honey, *fluo* flow)]

mellow /'meləʊ/ **1** *a.* (of fruit) soft, sweet, and juicy; (of character) softened by age or experience; genial, jovial; (of sound or colour or light) free from harshness, soft and rich; (of wine) well-matured; (of earth) rich, loamy; partly intoxicated. **2** *v.* make or become mellow. [orig. unkn.]

melodic /mɪ'lɒdɪk/ *a.* of melody. [F f. L f. Gk (MELODY)]

melodious /mɪ'ləʊdɪəs/ *a.* of or producing melody; sweet-sounding. [F (MELODY)]

melodrama /'melədrɑ:mə/ *n.* play with sensational plot and crude appeals to emotions; such plays as genre; behaviour or occurrence suggestive of this; **melodramatic** /-drə'mætɪk/ *a.*; **melodramatically** /-drə'mætɪkəlɪ/ *adv.* [F f. Gk *melos* music, F *drame* DRAMA]

melody /'melədɪ/ *n.* sweet music; musical arrangement of words; arrangement of single notes in musically expressive succession; principal part in harmonized music. [F f. L f. Gk (*melos* song; ODE)]

melon /'melən/ *n.* sweet fruit of various gourds; gourd producing this. [F f. L f. Gk *mēlon* apple]

melt *v.* (*p.p.* **melted** or MOLTEN) change from solid to liquid by heat; dissolve; (of person, feelings, etc.) be affected by pity or love; soften (person, feelings, etc.); change imperceptibly *into* (another form); *colloq.* depart unobtrusively; **melt away** dwindle away, disappear by liquefaction; **melt down** melt (metal articles) to use metal as raw material, become liquid and lose structure; **melting-point** temperature at which solid melts; **melting-pot** *fig.* place of reconstruction or vigorous mixing. [OE]

meltdown *n.* melting of (and consequent damage to) structure, e.g. overheated core of nuclear reactor.

member *n.* person or thing belonging to a society or group; (**Member**) person formally elected to take part in proceedings of a parliament; part of complex structure; part or organ of the body. [F f. L *membrum* limb]

membership *n.* being a member; number of members; body of members.

membrane /'membreɪn/ *n.* pliable sheetlike tissue connecting or lining structures in animal or vegetable body; **membranous** *a.* [L *membrana* skin, parchment (MEMBER)]

memento /mɪ'mentəʊ/ *n.* (*pl.* **mementoes**) object serving as reminder or souvenir. [L, imper. of *memini* remember]

memo /'meməʊ/ *n.* (*pl.* **memos**) *colloq.* memorandum. [abbr.]

memoir /'memwɑ:/ *n.* record of events, written from personal knowledge or special sources of information; (usu. in *pl.*) autobiography; biography; essay on learned subject specially studied by the writer. [F *mémoire* (MEMORY)]

memorabilia /memərə'bɪlɪə/ *n.pl.* memorable or noteworthy things. [L (foll.)]

memorable /'memərəb(ə)l/ *a.* worth remembering; easily remembered; **memorably** *adv.* [F or L (*memor* mindful)]

memorandum /memə'rændəm/ *n.* (*pl.* **memoranda** or **-ums**) note or record made for future use; informal written message, esp. in business etc. [L, = to be remembered (prec.)]

memorial /mɪ'mɔ:rɪəl/ **1** *n.* object or institution or custom established in memory of person or event. **2** *a.* serving to commemorate. [F or L (MEMORY)]

memorize /'meməraɪz/ *v.t.* learn by heart. [foll.]

memory /'memərɪ/ *n.* faculty by which

things are recalled to or kept in the mind; this in an individual (*a good memory*); recovery of one's knowledge by mental effort; act of remembering; person or thing remembered; posthumous repute (*of happy memory*); length of time over which memory extends (*within living memory*); store for data in computer; **from memory** without verification; **in memory of** to keep alive the remembrance of. [F f. L *memoria* (*memor* mindful)]

memsahib /'memsɑːɪb, -ɑːb/ *n. hist.* European married lady as spoken of or to by Indians. [MA'AM, SAHIB]

men *pl.* of MAN.

menace /'menɪs/ **1** *n.* threat; dangerous or obnoxious person or thing. **2** *v.t.* threaten. [L *minax* (*minor* threaten)]

ménage /meɪ'nɑːʒ/ *n.* domestic establishment; ***ménage à trois*** /ɑː trwɑː/ household consisting of husband, wife, and lover of one of these. [F f. L (MANSION)]

menagerie /mɪ'nædʒərɪ/ *n.* collection of wild animals in captivity for exhibition etc. [F (prec.)]

mend 1 *v.* restore to sound condition, repair; regain health; improve (*mend matters*). **2** *n.* place where material etc. has been repaired. **3 mend one's fences** make peace with person; **on the mend** improving in health or condition. [AF (AMEND)]

mendacious /men'deɪʃəs/ *a.* untruthful, lying; **mendacity** /-'dæsɪtɪ/ *n.* [L *mendax*]

mendelevium /mendə'liːvɪəm/ *n.* artificially produced transuranic element. [*Mendeleev*, chemist]

Mendelian /men'diːlɪən/ *a.* of Mendel's theory of heredity by genes. [*Mendel*, botanist]

mendicant /'mendɪkənt/ **1** *a.* begging; (of friar) living solely on alms. **2** *n.* beggar; mendicant friar. [L (*mendicus* beggar)]

menfolk *n.* men in general; men in family. [MAN]

menhir /'menhɪə/ *n.* tall upright stone, usu. forming prehistoric monument. [Breton *men* stone, *hir* long]

menial /'miːnɪəl/ **1** *a.* (of work) degrading, servile. **2** *n.* lowly domestic servant. **3 menially** *adv.* [AF *meinie* retinue f. L (MANSION)]

meninges /mɪ'nɪndʒiːz/ *n.pl.* membranes enclosing brain and spinal cord. [Gk *mēnigx* membrane]

meningitis /menɪn'dʒaɪtɪs/ *n.* inflammation of meninges. [-ITIS]

meniscus /mɪ'nɪskəs/ *n.* (*pl.* **menisci** /-saɪ/) curved upper surface of liquid in tube; lens convex on one side, concave on the other. [Gk *mēniskos* crescent f. *mēnē* moon]

menopause /'menəpɔːz/ *n.* final cessation of menses; period of woman's life (usu. 40–50) when this occurs; **menopausal** *a.* [Gk *mēn* month, PAUSE]

menorah /mɪ'nɔːrə/ *n.* seven-branched candelabrum used in Jewish worship. [Heb., = candlestick]

menses /'mensiːz/ *n.pl.* monthly flow of blood etc. from lining of womb. [L, pl. of *mensis* month]

menstrual /'menstrʊəl/ *a.* of menstruation. [L (*menstruus* monthly)]

menstruate /'menstrʊeɪt/ *v.i.* discharge menses; **menstruation** /-'eɪʃ(ə)n/ *n.*

mensurable /'mensjʊrəb(ə)l/ *a.* measurable; having fixed limits. [F or L (MEASURE)]

mensuration /mensjʊə'reɪʃ(ə)n/ *n.* measuring; mathematical rules for finding lengths, areas, and volumes. [L (prec.)]

menswear *n.* clothes for men. [MAN]

-ment *suffix* forming nouns expressing result or means of verbal action (*fragment, ornament, treatment*); also forming nouns from adjectives (*merriment, oddment*). [F f. L *-mentum*]

mental /'ment(ə)l/ *a.* of the mind; done by the mind; caring for mental patients (*mental nurse*); *colloq.* affected with mental disorder; **mental age** degree of person's mental development expressed as age at which same degree is attained by average child; **mental deficiency** imperfect mental development leading to abnormally low intelligence; **mental patient** sufferer from mental illness; **mentally** *adv.* [F or L (*mens ment-* mind)]

mentality /men'tælɪtɪ/ *n.* mental character or outlook; mental ability.

menthol /'menθɒl/ *n.* camphor-like substance obtained from oil of peppermint etc., used as flavouring or to relieve local pain etc. [G f. L (MINT[1])]

mentholated /'menθəleɪtɪd/ *a.* treated with or containing menthol.

mention /'menʃ(ə)n/ **1** *v.t.* refer to briefly or by name. **2** *n.* mentioning (*make mention of*); formal acknowledgement of merit (*honourable mention*). **3 not to mention** and also. [F f. L *mentio*]

mentor /'mentɔː/ *n.* experienced and trusted adviser. [*Mentor* in *Odyssey*]

menu /'menjuː/ *n.* list of dishes available in restaurant etc. or to be served at meal; list of computer options displayed on screen. [F f. L (MINUTE[2])]

MEP *abbr.* Member of the European Parliament.

mephistophelean /mefɪstə'fiːlɪən/ *a.*

of or like Mephistopheles, fiendish. [*Mephistopheles*, evil spirit to whom in German legend Faust sold his soul]

mercantile /'mɜːkəntaɪl/ *a.* of trade, commercial; trading; **mercantile marine** merchant navy. [F f. It. f. L (MERCHANT)]

mercenary /'mɜːsɪnərɪ/ **1** *a.* working merely for money or other reward; hired. **2** *n.* hired soldier in foreign service. **3 mercenarily** *adv.* [L (MERCY)]

mercer *n.* dealer in textile fabrics. [AF f. L (*merx merc-* goods)]

mercerize /'mɜːsəraɪz/ *v.t.* treat (cotton fabric or thread) with caustic alkali to give greater strength and lustre. [*Mercer*, alleged inventor]

merchandise /'mɜːtʃəndaɪz/ **1** *n.* commodities of commerce; goods for sale. **2** *v.* promote sales of (goods etc.); trade. [F (foll.)]

merchant /'mɜːtʃənt/ *n.* wholesale trader, esp. with foreign countries; *US* & *Sc.* retail trader; *sl.* person fond of an activity etc. (*speed-merchant*); **merchant bank** bank dealing in commercial loans and financing; **merchant navy** shipping engaged in commerce; **merchant prince** wealthy merchant; **merchant ship** ship carrying merchandise. [F f. L (*mercor* trade *v.*)]

merchantable *a.* saleable.

merchantman *n.* merchant ship.

merciful /'mɜːsɪfʊl/ *a.* having or showing or feeling mercy; giving relief; **mercifully** *adv.* [MERCY]

merciless /'mɜːsɪlɪs/ *a.* pitiless, showing no mercy.

mercurial /mɜː'kjʊərɪəl/ *a.* (of person) volatile, ready-witted; of or containing mercury. [F or L (MERCURY)]

mercury /'mɜːkjʊrɪ/ *n.* silvery-white heavy normally liquid metallic element, used in thermometers, barometers, etc.; **mercuric** /-'kjʊərɪk/ *a.*; **mercurous** *a.* [L *Mercurius*, Roman messenger-god]

mercy /'mɜːsɪ/ *n.* forbearance or compassion shown to enemies or offenders in one's power; tendency to show mercy; act of mercy; thing to be thankful for; **at the mercy of** wholly in the power of, liable to danger or harm from; **mercy killing** killing out of mercy or pity for suffering person. [F f. L *merces* reward, pity]

mere[1] *attrib. a.* that is solely or no more or better than what is specified (*a mere boy*; *no mere theory*). [AF f. L *merus* unmixed]

mere[2] *n. poetic* lake. [OE]

merely *adv.* only, just. [MERE[1]]

meretricious /merɪ'trɪʃəs/ *a.* showily but falsely attractive. [L (*meretrix* prostitute)]

merganser /mɜː'gænsə/ *n.* a diving duck. [L *mergus* diver, *anser* goose]

merge *v.* combine *with*; join or blend gradually; (cause to) lose character or identity *in* something else. [L *mergo* dip]

merger *n.* combining, esp. of two commercial companies etc. into one. [AF (prec.)]

meridian /mə'rɪdɪən/ *n.* circle of constant longitude, passing through given place and the terrestrial poles; corresponding line on map or sky; *fig.* prime, full splendour. [F or L (*meridies* midday)]

meridional *a.* of the south, esp. of Europe, or its inhabitants; of a meridian. [F f. L (prec.)]

meringue /mə'ræŋ/ *n.* mixture of white of egg, sugar, etc., baked crisp. [F]

merino /mə'riːnəʊ/ *n.* (*pl.* **merinos**) variety of sheep with fine wool; soft woollen yarn or fabric orig. of merino wool. [Sp.]

merit /'merɪt/ **1** *n.* quality of deserving well; excellence, worth; (usu. in *pl.*) thing that entitles to reward or gratitude. **2** *v.t.* deserve (reward, punishment, consideration, etc.). [F f. L *meritum* value (*mereor* deserve)]

meritocracy /merɪ'tɒkrəsɪ/ *n.* government by persons selected for merit.

meritorious /merɪ'tɔːrɪəs/ *a.* praiseworthy. [L (MERIT)]

merlin /'mɜːlɪn/ *n.* a kind of small falcon. [AF]

mermaid *n.* legendary sea-creature with woman's head and trunk and fish's tail. [MERE[2] 'sea', MAID]

merry /'merɪ/ *a.* joyous, full of laughter or gaiety; *colloq.* slightly tipsy; **make merry** be festive; **merry-go-round** revolving machine with horses, cars, etc., for riding on at fair etc., revolving device in playground, cycle of bustling activities; **merry-making** festivity; **merrily** *adv.*; **merriment** *n.* [OE]

mesa /'meɪsə/ *n.* *US* high tableland with steep sides. [Sp., = table]

mésalliance /meɪ'zælɪɑ̃s/ *n.* marriage with social inferior. [F]

mescal /'meskæl/ *n.* peyote cactus; **mescal buttons** its disc-shaped dried tops. [Sp. f. Nahuatl]

mescaline /'meskəliːn/ *n.* hallucinogenic alkaloid present in mescal buttons.

Mesdames *pl.* of MADAME; also used as *pl.* of MRS.

Mesdemoiselles *pl.* of MADEMOISELLE.

mesembryanthemum /mɪzembrɪ'ænθɪməm/ *n.* a kind of plant with flowers opening at about noon. [Gk *mesēmbria* noon, *anthemon* flower]

mesh **1** *n.* open space in net, sieve, etc.;

network fabric; (in *pl.*) network, *fig.* trap or snare. **2** *v.* (of teeth of wheel) be engaged (*with* others); be harmonious; catch in net (*lit.* or *fig.*). **3 in mesh** (of teeth of wheels) engaged. [Du.]

mesmerize /'mezməraɪz/ *v.t.* hypnotize; fascinate, spellbind; **mesmerism** *n.* [*Mesmer*, physician]

meso- *in comb.* middle, intermediate. [Gk *mesos* middle]

mesolithic /mesə'lɪθɪk/ *a.* of Stone Age between palaeolithic and neolithic. [Gk *lithos* stone]

mesomorph /'mesəmɔ:f/ *n.* person with compact muscular body-build. [Gk *morphē* form]

meson /'mi:zɒn/ *n.* unstable elementary particle intermediate in mass between proton and electron. [MESO-]

Mesozoic /mesə'zəʊɪk/ **1** *a.* of the second geological era. **2** *n.* this era. [Gk *zōion* animal]

mess 1 *n.* dirty or untidy state of things; state of confusion, embarrassment, or trouble; something spilt; domestic animal's excreta; disagreeable concoction; group of people who take meals together, esp. in armed services; room where such meals are taken, meal so taken; portion of liquid or pulpy food. **2** *v.* make untidy or dirty, make a mess of (often with *up*); potter or fool *about* or *around*; interfere *with*; take one's meals (*with*). **3 make a mess of** bungle; **mess-jacket** short close-fitting coat worn at mess; **mess-kit** soldier's cooking and eating utensils. [F f. L *missus* course of meal (foll.)]

message /'mesɪdʒ/ *n.* communication sent or transmitted by one person to another; inspired or significant communication from prophet, writer, preacher, etc.; **get the message** *colloq.* understand what is meant. [F f. L *mitto miss-* send]

messenger /'mesɪndʒə/ *n.* one who carries a message.

Messiah /mɪ'saɪə/ *n.* promised deliverer of Jews; Christ regarded as this; liberator of oppressed people. [Heb., = anointed]

Messianic /mesɪ'ænɪk/ *a.* of the Messiah; inspired by hope or belief in a Messiah. [F (prec.)]

Messieurs *pl.* of MONSIEUR.

Messrs /'mesəz/ *n.* used as *pl.* of MR, esp. as prefix to name of firm or to list of men's names. [abbr. MESSIEURS]

messuage /'meswɪdʒ/ *n. Law* dwelling-house with outbuildings and land. [AF, = dwelling]

messy *a.* untidy or dirty; causing or accompanied by a mess; difficult to deal with; **messily** *adv.*; **messiness** *n.* [MESS]

met[1] *a. colloq.* meteorological; metropolitan; **the Met** the Meteorological Office, the Metropolitan Opera House (New York). [abbr.]

met[2] *past* and *p.p.* of MEET[1].

meta- *prefix* denoting position or condition behind, after, beyond, or transcending (*metacarpus*) or change of position or condition (*metabolism*). [Gk (*meta* with, after)]

metabolism /mɪ'tæbəlɪz(ə)m/ *n.* process by which food is built up into living material or used to supply energy in a living organism; **metabolic** /metə'bɒlɪk/ *a.* [META-, Gk *ballō* throw]

metabolize /mɪ'tæbəlaɪz/ *v.t.* process (food) in metabolism.

metacarpus /metə'kɑ:pəs/ *n.* (*pl.* **metacarpi** /-aɪ/) part of hand between wrist and fingers; set of bones in this; **metacarpal** *a.* [META-, CARPUS]

metal /'met(ə)l/ **1** *n.* any of a class of elements such as gold, iron, and tin, all crystalline when solid and usu. good conductors of heat and electricity; alloy of these; (in *pl.*) rails of railway-line; road-metal. **2** *a.* made of metal. **3** *v.t.* (**-ll-**, *US* **-l-**) furnish or fit with metal; make or mend (road) with road-metal. [F or L f. Gk *metallon* mine]

metalize *US* var. of METALLIZE.

metallic /mɪ'tælɪk/ *a.* of metal; characteristic of metals; sounding like struck metal; **metallically** *adv.* [F f. L f. Gk (METAL)]

metalliferous /metə'lɪfərəs/ *a.* (of rocks etc.) containing metal. [L (METAL)]

metallize /'metəlaɪz/ *v.t.* render metallic; coat with thin layer of metal. [METAL]

metallography /metə'lɒgrəfɪ/ *n.* descriptive science of metals.

metallurgy /mɪ'tælədʒɪ, 'metəlɜ:dʒɪ/ *n.* science of the properties of metals; art of working metals, esp. of extracting metals from ores; **metallurgical** /metə'lɜ:dʒɪk(ə)l/ *a.*; **metallurgist** *n.* [Gk *metallon* (METAL), *-ourgia* working]

metamorphic /metə'mɔ:fɪk/ *a.* of metamorphosis; (of rock) that has undergone transformation by natural agencies; **metamorphism** *n.* [META-, Gk *morphē* form]

metamorphose /metə'mɔ:fəʊz/ *v.t.* change in form, turn (*to* or *into* new form); change nature of. [F (foll.)]

metamorphosis /metə'mɔ:fəsɪs, -'fəʊsɪs/ *n.* (*pl.* **metamorphoses** /-i:z/) change of form, esp. by magic or natural development; change of character, conditions, etc. [L f. Gk (*morphē* form)]

metaphor /'metəfə/ *n.* application of name or descriptive term or phrase to object or action where it is not literally applicable (e.g. *a glaring error*);

metaphorical /-'fɒrɪk(ə)l/ *a.*; **metaphorically** /-'fɒrɪkəlɪ/ *adv.* [F or L f. Gk]
metaphysics /metə'fɪzɪks/ *n.pl.* (often treated as *sing.*) theoretical philosophy of existence and knowledge; **metaphysical** *a.* [F f. med.L f. Gk, as having followed physics in Aristotle's works]
metastasis /me'tæstəsɪs/ *n.* (*pl.* **metastases** /-i:z/) transfer of disease etc. from one part of the body to another. [L f. Gk, = removal]
metatarsus /metə'tɑ:səs/ *n.* (*pl.* **metatarsi** /-aɪ/) part of foot between ankle and toes; set of bones in this; **metatarsal** *a.* [META-, TARSUS]
mete *v.t.* allot or deal *out* (punishment, reward, etc.). [OE]
meteor /'mi:tɪə/ *n.* small mass of matter from outer space rendered luminous by compression of air on entering earth's atmosphere. [Gk *meteōros* lofty]
meteoric /mi:tɪ'ɒrɪk/ *a.* of meteors; like a meteor, dazzling, rapid, transient; **meteorically** *adv.*
meteorite /'mi:tɪəraɪt/ *n.* fallen meteor, fragment of rock or metal reaching earth's surface from outer space.
meteoroid /'mi:tɪərɔɪd/ *n.* body moving through space, of same nature as those which become visible as meteors.
meteorological /mi:tɪərə'lɒdʒɪk(ə)l/ *a.* of meteorology; **Meteorological Office** government department providing weather forecasts etc. [foll.]
meteorology /mi:tɪə'rɒlədʒɪ/ *n.* study of phenomena of atmosphere, esp. for weather forecasting; **meteorologist** *n.* [Gk *meteōrologia* (METEOR)]
meter[1] **1** *n.* instrument for recording amount of substance supplied or used, time spent, distance travelled, etc. **2** *v.t.* measure by meter. [METE]
meter[2] *US* var. of METRE.
-meter *suffix* forming names of automatic measuring instruments (*thermometer*, *voltmeter*) or of lines of verse with specified number of measures (*pentameter*). [Gk *metron* measure]
methane /'mi:θeɪn/ *n.* inflammable hydrocarbon gas of the paraffin series. [METHYL]
methinks /mɪ'θɪŋks/ *v.i. impers.* (*past* **methought** /mɪ'θɔ:t/) *archaic* it seems to me. [OE (ME[1], THINK)]
method /'meθəd/ *n.* special form of procedure esp. in mental activity; orderliness, regular habits; orderly arrangement of ideas. [F or L f. Gk (META-, *hodos* way)]
methodical /mɪ'θɒdɪk(ə)l/ *a.* characterized by method or order; **methodically** *adv.* [L f. Gk (prec.)]
Methodist /'meθədɪst/ *n.* member of a Protestant denomination originating in an 18th-c. evangelistic movement; **Methodism** *n.* [METHOD]
methodology /meθə'dɒlədʒɪ/ *n.* science of method; body of methods used in an activity.
methought *past* of METHINKS.
meths *n. colloq.* methylated spirit. [abbr.]
methyl /'meθɪl, 'mi:θaɪl/ *n.* chemical radical present in methane etc.; **methyl alcohol** a colourless volatile inflammable liquid. [G or F (Gk *methū* wine, *hulē* wood)]
methylated /'meθɪleɪtɪd/ *a.* mixed or impregnated with methyl alcohol; **methylated spirit** alcohol so treated to make it unfit for drinking.
meticulous /mɪ'tɪkjʊləs/ *a.* giving great or excessive attention to details, very careful and precise. [L (*metus* fear)]
métier /'meɪtjeɪ/ *n.* one's trade, profession, or field of activity; one's forte. [F f. L (MINISTER)]
metonymy /mɪ'tɒnɪmɪ/ *n.* substitution of name of attribute or adjunct for that of thing meant (e.g. *crown* for *king*). [L f. Gk (META-, *onuma* name)]
metre /'mi:tə/ *n.* metric unit of length, equal to about 39·4 in.; rhythm in poetry, any particular form of this; metrical group or measure. [F f. L f. Gk *metron* measure]
metric /'metrɪk/ *a.* of or based on the metre; = METRICAL; **metric hundredweight** see HUNDREDWEIGHT; **metric system** decimal measuring-system with metre, litre, and gram as units of length, capacity, and weight or mass; **metric ton** see TON; **metrically** *adv.* [F (prec.)]
-metric *suffix* (also **-metrical**) forming adjectives from nouns in *-meter* or *-metry*.
metrical *a.* of or composed in metre; of or involving measurement; **metrically** *adv.* [L f. Gk (METRE)]
metrication /metrɪ'keɪʃ(ə)n/ *n.* conversion to metric system. [METRIC]
metronome /'metrənəʊm/ *n.* instrument marking musical time at selected rate. [Gk *metron* measure, *nomos* law]
metropolis /mɪ'trɒpəlɪs/ *n.* chief city of a country or region, capital. [L f. Gk (*mētēr* mother, *polis* city)]
metropolitan /metrə'pɒlɪt(ə)n/ **1** *a.* of a metropolis; of or forming mother country as distinct from colonies etc. **2** *n.* bishop with authority over the bishops of a province; inhabitant of a metropolis.
-metry *suffix* forming names of procedures and systems involving measurement (*geometry*). [Gk (METRE)]
mettle /'met(ə)l/ *n.* quality or strength of

character, courage; **on one's mettle** incited to do one's best. [var. of METAL]
mettlesome *a.* spirited.
mew[1] **1** *n.* characteristic cry of cat. **2** *v.i.* utter mew. [imit.]
mew[2] *n.* a gull. [OE]
mews /mju:z/ *n.pl.* (treated as *sing.*) set of stabling round open yard or lane, now often converted into dwellings. [orig. sing. *mew* 'cage for hawks', F f. L *muto* change]
Mexican /'meksɪkən/ **1** *a.* of Mexico. **2** *n.* native of Mexico; language of Mexico, esp. Nahuatl. [Sp.]
mezzanine /'metsəni:n/ *n.* extra storey between two others, usu. between ground and first floors. [F f. It. f. L (MEDIAN)]
mezzo /'metsəʊ/ *adv.* (esp. *Mus.*) half, moderately; ***mezzo forte*** fairly loud; ***mezzo piano*** fairly soft; **mezzo-soprano** voice between soprano and contralto, singer with this voice. [It. f. L *medius* middle]
mezzotint /'metsəʊtɪnt/ *n.* method of engraving using a uniformly roughened plate, on which rough areas give shade and areas scraped smooth give light; print produced by this. [It. (prec., TINT)]
mf abbr. *mezzo forte.*
mg. *abbr.* milligram(s).
Mg *symb.* magnesium.
Mgr. abbr. *Monsignor*; *Monseigneur*.
MHz *abbr.* megahertz.
mi var. of ME[2].
miaow /mɪ'aʊ/ **1** *n.* cry of cat, mew. **2** *v.i.* make this cry. [imit.]
miasma /mɪ'æzmə, maɪ-/ *n.* (*pl.* **miasmata**) infectious or noxious escape of air etc. [Gk, = defilement]
mica /'maɪkə/ *n.* kind of mineral found as small glittering scales in granite etc. or in crystals separable into thin transparent plates. [L, = crumb]
mice *pl.* of MOUSE.
Michaelmas /'mɪkəlməs/ *n.* feast of St Michael, 29 Sept.; **Michaelmas daisy** aster flowering in autumn; **Michaelmas term** university and law term beginning near Michaelmas. [MASS[2]]
mickey /'mɪkɪ/ *n. sl.* in **take the mickey (out of)** tease or mock. [orig. uncert.]
Mickey Finn /mɪkɪ 'fɪn/ *sl.* strong alcoholic drink, esp. with added narcotic. [orig. uncert.]
mickle /'mɪk(ə)l/ *n.* (*archaic* or *Sc.*) large amount. [ON]
micky var. of MICKEY.
micro- *in comb.* small; one millionth of (*microgram*, *microsecond*). [Gk (*mikros* small)]
microbe /'maɪkrəʊb/ *n.* micro-organism, esp. bacterium causing disease or fermentation; **microbial** /-'rəʊbɪ(ə)l/ *a.*; **microbially** *adv.* [F f. Gk *mikros* small, *bios* life]
microbiology /maɪkrəʊbaɪ'ɒlədʒɪ/ *n.* study of micro-organisms. [MICRO-]
microchip /'maɪkrəʊtʃɪp/ *n.* tiny piece of semiconductor carrying many electrical circuits.
microcircuit /'maɪkrəʊsɜ:kɪt/ *n.* integrated circuit or other very small circuit.
microcomputer /maɪkrəʊkəm'pju:tə/ *n.* computer in which the central processor is a microprocessor.
microcosm /'maɪkrəkɒz(ə)m/ *n.* complex thing, esp. man, viewed as epitome of universe; miniature representation (*of*); **microcosmic** /-'kɒsmɪk/ *a.* [F or med.L f. Gk (COSMOS)]
microdot /'maɪkrəʊdɒt/ *n.* photograph of document etc. reduced to size of dot. [MICRO-]
microelectronics /maɪkrəʊi:lek'trɒnɪks/ *n.* design, manufacture, and use of microcircuits.
microfiche /'maɪkrəʊfi:ʃ/ *n.* (*pl.* same) small sheet of film bearing microphotograph of document etc. [MICRO-, F *fiche* slip of paper]
microfilm /'maɪkrəʊfɪlm/ **1** *n.* length of film bearing microphotograph of document etc. **2** *v.t.* record on this. [MICRO-]
microlight /'maɪkrəʊlaɪt/ *n.* a kind of motorized hang-glider.
micrometer /maɪ'krɒmɪtə/ *n.* instrument for measuring small lengths or angles. [F (MICRO-)]
micron /'maɪkrɒn/ *n.* one millionth of a metre. [Gk *mikros* small]
micro-organism /maɪkrəʊ'ɔ:gənɪz(ə)m/ *n.* organism not visible to naked eye, e.g. bacterium or virus. [MICRO-]
microphone /'maɪkrəfəʊn/ *n.* instrument for converting sound-waves into electrical energy which may be reconverted into sound elsewhere. [MICRO-, Gk *phōnē* sound]
microphotograph /maɪkrəʊ'fəʊtəgrɑ:f/ *n.* photograph reduced to very small size. [MICRO-]
microprocessor /maɪkrəʊ'prəʊsesə/ *n.* data processor contained on one or more microchips. [MICRO-]
microscope /'maɪkrəskəʊp/ *n.* instrument magnifying small objects by means of lens or lenses so as to reveal details invisible to the naked eye. [MICRO-, -SCOPE]
microscopic /maɪkrə'skɒpɪk/ *a.* too small to be visible without microscope; extremely small; of or by means of a microscope; **microscopically** *adv.*
microscopy /maɪ'krɒskəpɪ/ *n.* use of the microscope.

microsurgery /'maɪkrəʊsɜ:dʒərɪ/ *n.* intricate surgery using microscope to see tissue and instruments involved. [MICRO-]
microwave /'maɪkrəʊweɪv/ *n.* electromagnetic wave of length between about 30 cm. and 1 mm.; **microwave oven** oven using such waves to heat food quickly.
micturition /mɪktjʊə'rɪʃ(ə)n/ *n.* urination. [L]
mid *a.* in the middle of (usu. as comb.: *mid-air*; *mid-week*); that is in the middle, medium, half; **mid-off** (or **on**) position of fieldsman in cricket near bowler on off (or on) side. [OE]
midday /'mɪddeɪ/ *n.* noon; time near noon. [OE (MID, DAY)]
midden /'mɪd(ə)n/ *n.* dunghill, refuse-heap. [Scand. (MUCK)]
middle /'mɪd(ə)l/ **1** *attrib. a.* at equal distance from extremities; (of member of group) so placed as to have same number of members on each side; intermediate in rank, quality, etc.; average (*man of middle height*). **2** *n.* middle point or position or part; waist. **3 in the middle of** during or half-way through (activity or process); **middle age** middle part of normal life; **middle-aged** of middle age; **Middle Ages** period in Europe after Dark Ages, *c.*1000–1400; **middle C** C near middle of piano keyboard, note between treble and bass staves; **middle class** social class between upper and lower, including professional and business people; **middle ear** cavity behind ear-drum; **Middle East** area covered by countries from Egypt to Iran inclusive; **middle name** name between first name and surname, *fig.* person's most characteristic quality (*cunning is his middle name*); **middle-of-the-road** (of person or action) moderate, avoiding extremes; **middle school** school for children from about 9 to 13; **middle-sized** of medium size; **Middle West** region of US near northern Mississippi. [OE]
middleman *n.* any of traders who handle commodity between its producer and its customer; intermediary.
middleweight *n.* boxing-weight with upper limit of 75 kg; **light middleweight** this with upper limit of 71 kg.
middling **1** *a.* moderately good, fairly well in health. **2** *adv.* fairly, moderately.
midfield *n.* part of football pitch away from goals. [MID]
midge *n.* gnatlike insect. [OE]
midget /'mɪdʒɪt/ **1** *n.* extremely small person or thing. **2** *a.* extremely small.
midland /'mɪdlənd/ *a.* of the middle part of a country; **the Midlands** the inland counties of central England. [MID]
midnight /'mɪdnaɪt/ *n.* 12 o'clock at night; time near this; middle of the night; **midnight blue** very dark blue; **midnight sun** sun visible at midnight during summer in polar regions. [OE (MID, NIGHT)]
midriff /'mɪdrɪf/ *n.* region of front of the body just above waist. [OE, = mid-belly]
midshipman /'mɪdʃɪpmən/ *n.* naval officer ranking next above cadet. [MID]
midst *n.* middle part; **in the midst of** among, in the middle of. [MID]
midsummer /mɪd'sʌmə, 'mɪ-/ *n.* period of or near summer solstice, about 21 June; **Midsummer's Day** 24 June. [OE (MID, SUMMER)]
midway *adv.* in middle of distance between places. [MID]
midwicket /mɪd'wɪkɪt/ *n.* position in cricket on leg side opposite middle of pitch.
midwife *n.* (*pl.* **midwives**) person trained to assist women in childbirth; **midwifery** /-wɪfrɪ/ *n.* [orig. = with-woman]
midwinter /mɪd'wɪntə/ *n.* period of or near winter solstice, about 22 Dec. [OE (MID, WINTER)]
mien *n.* person's bearing or look. [prob. obs. *demean*]
might[1] /maɪt/ *v. aux.* used as *past tense* of MAY especially (1) in reported speech (*he said he might come*), (2) with perfect infinitive expressing possibility based on a condition not fulfilled (*if you had come I might have seen you*; *but for the radio we might not have known about it*), or based on an obligation not fulfilled (*you might have asked me*); also used *loosely* as = MAY (*you might like to see this* = *you may like* etc.); **might-have-been** event that might have happened but did not. [MAY[1]]
might[2] /maɪt/ *n.* great strength or power; **with might and main** with all one's power. [OE (MAY[1])]
mightn't /'maɪt(ə)nt/ *colloq.* = *might not.*
mighty **1** *a.* powerful, strong; massive, bulky; *colloq.* great, considerable. **2** *adv. colloq.* very. **3 mightily** *adv.*; **mightiness** *n.* [OE (MIGHT[2])]
mignonette /mɪnjə'net/ *n.* plant with small fragrant flowers. [F, dimin. of *mignon* small]
migraine /'mi:greɪn/ *n.* severe recurring form of headache, often with nausea and disturbance of vision. [F f. L f. Gk *hēmicrania* (HEMI-, CRANIUM)]
migrant /'maɪgrənt/ **1** *a.* that migrates. **2** *n.* migrant person or animal, esp. bird. [L *migro*]
migrate /maɪ'greɪt/ *v.i.* leave one place

and settle in another; (of bird or fish) come and go with the seasons; **migration** *n.*; **migratory** /'maɪgrətərɪ/ *a.*

mikado /mɪ'kɑ:dəʊ/ *n.* (*pl.* **mikados**) emperor of Japan. [Jap., = august door]

mike *n. colloq.* microphone. [abbr.]

milady /mɪ'leɪdɪ/ *n.* English noblewoman. [F f. *my Lady*]

milch *a.* giving milk; **milch cow** cow kept for milk, *fig.* source of regular or easy profit. [OE, rel. to MILK]

mild /maɪld/ **1** *a.* (of person) gentle in manner; not severe or harsh in action or effect; (of climate etc.) moderately warm; (of flavour etc.) not strong or bitter. **2** *n.* mild ale. **3 mild steel** steel that is tough but not easily tempered. [OE]

mildew /'mɪldju:/ **1** *n.* growth of minute fungi forming on surfaces exposed to damp. **2** *v.* taint or be tainted with mildew. **3 mildewy** *a.* [OE]

mile *n.* unit of linear measure, equal to 1,760 yds. or about 1.6 km.; *colloq.* great distance or amount (*miles better*); race extending over a mile. [OE, ult. f. L *mille* thousand]

mileage *n.* number of miles travelled; advantage to be derived from something.

miler *n.* person or horse specializing in races of one mile.

milestone *n.* stone set up beside road to mark distance in miles; significant event or stage in life or history.

milfoil /'mɪlfɔɪl/ *n.* plant with small white flowers and finely divided leaves, yarrow. [F f. L (MILE, FOIL²)]

milieu /'mi:ljɜ:/ *n.* (*pl.* **milieux** /-jɜ:z/) environment, state of life, social surroundings. [F]

militant /'mɪlɪtənt/ **1** *a.* aggressively active, combative; engaged in warfare. **2** *n.* militant person. **3 militancy** *n.* [F f. L (MILITATE)]

militarism /'mɪlɪtərɪz(ə)m/ *n.* military spirit; aggressive policy of reliance on military strength and means; **militarist** *n.*; **militaristic** /-'rɪstɪk/ *a.* [F (MILITARY)]

militarize /'mɪlɪtəraɪz/ *v.t.* make military or warlike; equip with military resources; imbue with militarism; **militarization** /-'zeɪʃ(ə)n/ *n.* [foll.]

military /mɪlɪtərɪ/ *a.* of or for or done by soldiers or the armed forces; **the military** (as *sing.* or *pl.*) the army (as distinct from police or civilians); **militarily** *adv.* [F f. L (*miles milit-* soldier)]

militate /'mɪlɪteɪt/ *v.i.* (of facts or evidence) tell or have force (*against*, rarely *in favour of*, conclusion etc.). [L (prec.)]

militia /mɪ'lɪʃə/ *n.* military force, esp. one raised from civil population and supplementing regular army in emergency. [L, = military service (MILITARY)]

milk 1 *n.* opaque white fluid secreted by female mammals for nourishment of their young; milk, esp. of cow, as food; milklike liquid, e.g. in coconut. **2** *v.t.* draw milk from (animal); exploit or extract money etc. from (person). **3 milk and honey** abundant means of prosperity; **milk and water** feeble or insipid or mawkish discourse or sentiment; **milk float** light low vehicle used in delivering milk; **milk run** routine expedition or mission; **milk shake** drink of milk and flavouring mixed or shaken until frothy; **milk-tooth** any of first temporary teeth in young mammals. [OE]

milkmaid *n.* woman who milks or works in dairy.

milkman *n.* man who sells or delivers milk.

milksop *n.* weak or timid man or youth.

milkweed *n.* any of various wild plants with milky juice.

milky *a.* of, like, or containing milk; (of liquid) cloudy, unclear; **Milky Way** luminous band of stars indistinguishable to naked eye; **milkiness** *n.*

mill 1 *n.* building fitted with mechanical apparatus for grinding corn; such apparatus; apparatus for grinding any solid substance to powder or pulp (*pepper-mill*); building fitted with machinery for manufacturing-processes etc. (*cotton mill*); such machinery. **2** *v.* grind (corn) in mill; produce (flour) in mill; produce regular markings on edge of (coin); cut or shape (metal) with rotating tool; (of people or animals) move (*about* or *around*) in aimless manner. **3 go** (or **put**) **through the mill** undergo (or cause to undergo) training or experience or suffering; **mill-pond** pond formed by damming stream to use water in mill; **mill-race** current of water that works mill-wheel; **mill-wheel** wheel used to drive water-mill. [OE f. Gmc f. L (*molo* grind)]

millennium /mɪ'lenɪəm/ *n.* (*pl.* **millenniums** or **-ia**) period of 1,000 years; Christ's prophesied reign of 1,000 years on earth (Rev. 20); coming time of justice and happiness; **millennial** *a.* [L *mille* thousand]

millepede /'mɪlɪpi:d/ *n.* small crawling animal with many legs; wood-louse. [L (*mille* thousand, *pes ped-* foot)]

miller *n.* one who works or owns a mill, usu. a corn-mill; **miller's thumb** a kind of small fish. [MILL]

millesimal /mɪ'lesɪm(ə)l/ **1** *a.* thousandth; consisting of thousandths.

2 *n.* thousandth part. [L (*mille* thousand)]
millet /'mɪlɪt/ *n.* cereal plant with small nutritious seeds; these seeds. [F dimin. f. L *milium*]
milli- *in comb.* thousand; one-thousandth. [L *mille* thousand]
milliard /'mɪljəd/ *n.* one thousand millions. [F (*mille* thousand)]
millibar /'mɪlɪbɑ:/ *n.* unit of pressure equal to one thousandth of a bar. [MILLI-, BAR²]
milligram /'mɪlɪgræm/ *n.* metric unit of mass, equal to 0.001 gram. [MILLI-]
millilitre /'mɪlɪli:tə/ *n.* metric unit of capacity, equal to 0.001 litre.
millimetre /'mɪlɪmi:tə/, *US* **millimeter** *n.* metric unit of length, equal to 0.001 metre or about 0.04 in.
milliner /'mɪlɪnə/ *n.* person who makes or sells women's hats; **millinery** *n.* [*Milan* in Italy]
million /'mɪljən/ *a.* & *n.* one thousand thousand (*a*, *one*, *six*, etc., *million*); a million pounds or dollars; (in *pl.* **millions**) very many; **millionth** *a.* & *n.* [F, prob. f. It. (*mille* thousand)]
millionaire /mɪljə'neə/ *n.* person possessing a million pounds, dollars, etc.; very rich person. [F *millionnaire* (prec.)]
millipede var. of MILLEPEDE.
millstone *n.* either of two circular stones for grinding corn; heavy burden or responsibility. [MILL]
milometer /maɪ'lɒmɪtə/ *n.* instrument for measuring number of miles travelled by a vehicle. [MILE, -METER]
milt *n.* reproductive gland or sperm of male fish; spleen of mammals. [OE]
mime 1 *n.* acting with gestures and without words; performance involving this. **2** *v.* perform in form of mime. [L f. Gk *mimos*]
mimeograph /'mɪmɪəgrɑ:f/ **1** *n.* apparatus for making copies from stencils. **2** *v.t.* reproduce by means of this. [Gk *mimeomai* imitate]
mimetic /mɪ'metɪk/ *a.* of or given to imitation or mimicry. [Gk *mimētikos* (prec.)]
mimic /'mɪmɪk/ **1** *v.t.* (**-ck-**) imitate (person, manner, etc.), esp. to entertain or ridicule; copy minutely or servilely; (of thing) resemble closely. **2** *n.* person skilled in imitation, esp. as entertainment. **3 mimicry** *n.* [L f. Gk *mimikos* (MIME)]
mimosa /mɪ'məʊzə/ *n.* any of several usu. tropical shrubs, esp. with small fragrant globular flower-heads. [L (MIME)]
min. *abbr.* minute(s); minimum; minim.
Min. *abbr.* Minister; Ministry.
mina /'maɪnə/ *n.* talking bird of starling family. [Hindi]
minaret /mɪnə'ret, 'mɪ-/ *n.* slender turret connected with mosque, from which muezzin calls at hours of prayer. [F or Sp. f. Turk. f. Arab.]
minatory /'mɪnətərɪ/ *a.* threatening, menacing. [L (*minor* threaten)]
mince 1 *v.* cut into very small pieces, esp. in machine; walk or speak in affected way. **2** *n.* minced meat. **3 mince pie** pie containing mincemeat; **not to mince matters** (or **one's words**) speak plainly. [F *mincier* f. L (MINUTE²)]
mincemeat *n.* mixture of currants, sugar, spices, suet, etc.; **make mincemeat of** defeat or refute utterly.
mind /maɪnd/ **1** *n.* seat of consciousness, thought, volition, and feeling; intellectual powers as distinct from will and emotions; remembrance (*bear*, *have*, *keep*, *in mind*); opinion, this as expressed (*speak one's mind*); way of thinking or feeling (*state of mind*; *the Victorian mind*); direction of thought or desires (*turn* etc. *one's mind to*); normal condition of mental faculties (*in one's right mind*; *lose one's mind*; *out of one's mind*); person as embodying mental faculties. **2** *v.* object to (usu. with neg. or interrog.: *do you mind if I smoke?*; *she said she did not mind my coming*; *I wouldn't mind a drink*); remember and take care (*mind you finish in time*); have charge of for a while; apply oneself to; concern oneself about (*mind my words*). **3 be in two minds** be undecided; **change one's mind** discard one's opinion etc. in favour of another; **do you mind?** *iron.* please stop that; **have a mind of one's own** be capable of independent opinion; **have a (good) mind to** feel (much) inclined or tempted to; **have in mind** think of, intend *to do* thing; **in one's mind's eye** in one's imagination; **make up one's mind** decide, resolve (*to*); **mind one's P's and Q's** be careful in speech or conduct; **mind out** be careful, (in *imper.*) let me pass; **mind-reader** one who claims to know another's thoughts; **mind (you)** please take note; **never mind** do not be troubled (about), I would rather not answer, you may ignore; **on one's mind** in one's thoughts, worrying one. [OE]
minded *a.* inclined to think in specified way or concern oneself with specified thing (*mechanically minded*; *car-minded*); having mind of specified kind (*high-minded*); disposed *to do* thing.
minder *n.* one whose business it is to attend to something, esp. a child or machinery.

mindful *a.* taking thought or care (*of* something); **mindfully** *adv.*
mindless *a.* lacking intelligence, stupid; heedless (*of*).
mine[1] *poss. pron.* of or belonging to me, the thing(s) belonging to me (*it is mine*; *mine are best*; *a friend of mine*). [OE]
mine[2] **1** *n.* excavation in earth for extracting metal, coal, salt, etc.; abundant source (*of* information etc.); receptacle filled with explosive placed in or on ground or in water for destroying enemy personnel, material, or ships. **2** *v.* obtain (metal, coal, etc.) from mine; dig in (earth etc.) for ore etc.; lay explosive mines under or in. [F]
minefield *n.* area where mines have been laid; *fig.* area presenting many unseen hazards.
minelayer *n.* ship or aircraft for laying mines.
miner *n.* one who works in a mine. [F (MINE[2])]
mineral /'mɪnər(ə)l/ **1** *n.* substance obtained by mining; natural inorganic substance in the earth; artificial mineral water or similar drink. **2** *a.* obtained by mining; not animal or vegetable. **3** **mineral water** water found in nature impregnated with mineral substance, artificial imitation of this, other non-alcoholic effervescent drink. [F or med.L (MINE[2])]
mineralogy /mɪnə'rælədʒɪ/ *n.* science of minerals; **mineralogical** /-rə'lɒdʒɪk(ə)l/ *a.*; **mineralogist** *n.*
minestrone /mɪnɪ'strəʊnɪ/ *n.* thick soup containing vegetables and pasta or rice. [It.]
minesweeper *n.* ship for clearing explosive mines from the sea. [MINE[2]]
mineworker *n.* miner.
Ming *n.* Chinese porcelain of time of Ming dynasty (1368–1644).
mingle /'mɪŋg(ə)l/ *v.* mix, blend; **mingle with** go about among. [OE]
mingy /'mɪndʒɪ/ *a. colloq.* mean, stingy; **mingily** *adv.* [prob. MEAN[2], STINGY]
mini /'mɪnɪ/ *n. colloq.* miniskirt; (**Mini;** **P**) type of small car. [abbr.]
mini- *in comb.* miniature, small of its kind (*minicar*; *mini-budget*).
miniature /'mɪnɪtʃə/ **1** *a.* much smaller than normal; represented on small scale. **2** *n.* small minutely finished portrait; miniature thing. **3** **in miniature** on a small scale. [It. f. L (*minium* red lead)]
miniaturist *n.* painter of miniatures.
miniaturize *v.t.* make miniature; produce in smaller version.
minibus /'mɪnɪbʌs/ *n.* small bus for about twelve passengers. [MINI-]
minicab /'mɪnɪkæb/ *n.* car like taxi but available only if ordered in advance.
minicomputer /mɪnɪkəm'pju:tə/ *n.* computer that is small in size and storage capacity.
minim /'mɪnɪm/ *n. Mus.* note half as long as semibreve; 1/60 of fluid drachm, about 1 drop. [L *minimus* least]
minimal /'mɪnɪm(ə)l/ *a.* being or related to a minimum; very small or slight; **minimally** *adv.*
minimize /'mɪnɪmaɪz/ *v.t.* reduce to minimum; estimate at smallest possible amount or degree; estimate or represent at less than true value or importance.
minimum /'mɪnɪməm/ **1** *n.* (*pl.* **minima**) least amount possible, attained, usual, etc. **2** *a.* that is a minimum. **3** **minimum lending rate** announced minimum rate of interest at which Bank of England lends money; **minimum wage** lowest wage allowed by law or agreement. [L (MINIM)]
minion /'mɪnjən/ *n. derog.* subordinate, assistant. [F *mignon*]
miniskirt /'mɪnɪskɜ:t/ *n.* skirt ending well above knees. [MINI-]
minister /'mɪnɪstə/ **1** *n.* person at head of a government department; clergyman, esp. in Presbyterian and Nonconformist churches; diplomatic agent usu. ranking below ambassador; person employed in execution *of* (purpose, will, etc.). **2** *v.* render aid or service (*to* person, cause, etc.). **3** **Minister of State** departmental senior minister between departmental head and junior minister. **4** **ministerial** /-'stɪərɪ(ə)l/ *a.* [F f. L, = servant]
ministration /mɪnɪ'streɪʃ(ə)n/ *n.* giving aid or service; ministering, esp. in religious matters; **ministrant** /'mɪnɪstrənt/ *a.* & *n.* [F or L (prec.)]
ministry /'mɪnɪstrɪ/ *n.* government department; building occupied by it; body of ministers of the government; period of government under one Prime Minister; office as religious minister, priest, etc.; period of tenure of this; ministering, ministration; **the ministry** the clerical profession. [L (MINISTER)]
mink *n.* small stoatlike animal; its fur; coat made from this. [Sw.]
minnesinger /'mɪnɪsɪŋə/ *n.* German lyric poet in 12th–14th cc. [G, = love-singer]
minnow /'mɪnəʊ/ *n.* small freshwater fish. [OE]
Minoan /mɪ'nəʊən/ **1** *a.* of Bronze-Age civilization in Crete and the Aegean (*c.* 3000–1100 BC). **2** *n.* person of this civilization. [*Minos*, legendary king of Crete]
minor /'maɪnə/ **1** *a.* lesser or relatively

less in size or importance; under full legal age; *Mus.* (of scale) having intervals of a semitone above its second and seventh notes, (of interval) less by a semitone than a major interval, (of key) based on minor scale. **2** *n.* person under full age; *US* student's subsidiary subject or course. **3** *v.i. US* (of student) undertake study *in* as subsidiary subject. [L, = less]

minority /maɪ'nɒrɪtɪ, mɪ-/ *n.* smaller number or part (*of*), esp. smaller party voting together against majority; state of having fewer than half the votes; small group of persons differing from others in race, religion, language, opinion on a topic, etc.; state of being under full legal age; period of this. [F or med.L (prec.)]

minster *n.* large or important church (*York Minster*); church of monastery. [OE (MONASTERY)]

minstrel /'mɪnstr(ə)l/ *n.* medieval singer or musician; (usu. in *pl.*) one of a band of public entertainers with blackened faces etc., performing songs and music ostensibly of Negro origin. [F f. Prov. f. L (MINISTER)]

minstrelsy /'mɪnstr(ə)lsɪ/ *n.* minstrel's art or poetry.

mint[1] *n.* aromatic herb used in cooking; peppermint; small sweet flavoured with this. [OE f. L *menta* f. Gk]

mint[2] **1** *n.* place where money is coined, usu. under State authority; vast sum or amount. **2** *v.t.* make (coin) by stamping metal; invent or coin (word or phrase). **3 in mint condition** as new, unsoiled. [OE f. L *moneta*]

minuet /mɪnjʊ'et/ *n.* slow stately dance in triple measure; music for this, or in same rhythm or style. [F dimin. (MENU)]

minus /'maɪnəs/ **1** *prep.* with subtraction of (symbol −); below zero (*temperature of minus 10°*); *colloq.* deprived of (*came back minus shoes and socks*). **2** *a.* (of number) less than zero, negative; having negative electrical charge; (in evaluating) rather worse than (*beta minus*). **3** *n.* minus sign; disadvantage; negative quantity. **4 minus sign** the symbol (−). [L, neuter of MINOR]

minuscule /'mɪnəskju:l/ **1** *a.* extremely small; lower-case. **2** *n.* lower-case letter. [F f. L dimin. (prec.)]

minute[1] /'mɪnɪt/ **1** *n.* period of 60 seconds, sixtieth part of hour; distance traversed in a minute (*10 minutes from the shops*); very brief portion of time; particular point of time (*came the minute you called*); sixtieth part of degree of measurement of angles; (in *pl.*) brief summary of proceedings of assembly, committee, etc.; official memorandum authorizing or recommending a course of action; rough draft, memorandum. **2** *v.t.* record in minutes; send minute to (person); make a note of. **3 the minute** *colloq.* the present time; **in a minute** very soon; **minute steak** thin slice of steak that can be cooked quickly; **up to the minute** having latest information, in the latest fashion. [F f. L (*minuo* lessen)]

minute[2] /maɪ'nju:t/ *a.* very small; precise, detailed. [L *minutus* (prec.)]

minutiae /maɪ'nju:ʃɪi:, mɪ-/ *n.pl.* very small or unimportant details. [L (MINUTE[1])]

minx /mɪŋks/ *n.* pert or mischievous or sly girl. [orig. unkn.]

Miocene /'mɪəsi:n/ **1** *a.* of the fourth geological epoch of the Tertiary period. **2** *n.* this epoch. [Gk *meiōn* less, *kainos* new]

miracle /'mɪrək(ə)l/ *n.* marvellous event ascribed to supernatural agency; remarkable occurrence; remarkable specimen (*of* some quality); **miracle play** dramatic representation in Middle Ages, based on Bible or lives of saints. [F f. L (*mirus* wonderful)]

miraculous /mɪ'rækjʊləs/ *a.* that is a miracle, supernatural; remarkable. [F or med.L (prec.)]

mirage /'mɪrɑ:ʒ/ *n.* optical illusion caused by atmospheric conditions, esp. appearance of sheet of water in desert or on hot road; illusory thing. [F f. L *miro* look at]

mire 1 *n.* swampy ground, bog; mud. **2** *v.t.* plunge in mire; involve in difficulties; defile, bespatter (*lit.* or *fig.*). **3 in the mire** in difficulties. [ON]

mirror /'mɪrə/ **1** *n.* polished surface (usu. of amalgam-coated glass) reflecting image; what gives faithful reflection or true description of thing (*hold the mirror up to*). **2** *v.t.* reflect as in mirror (*lit.* or *fig.*). **3 mirror image** reflection or copy in which left and right sides are reversed. [F f. L *miro* look at]

mirth *n.* merriment; laughter; **mirthful** *a.* [OE (MERRY)]

miry *a.* muddy; vile. [MIRE]

mis-[1] *prefix* to verbs and verbal derivatives, in sense 'amiss', 'badly', 'wrongly', 'unfavourably' (*mislead, misshapen, mistrust*). [OE]

mis-[2] *prefix* to verbs, adjectives, and nouns, in sense 'amiss', 'badly', 'wrongly', or negative (*misadventure, mischief*). [F f. L MINUS]

misadventure /mɪsəd'ventʃə/ *n.* piece of bad luck; death due to accident without crime or negligence. [F (MIS-[2])]

misalliance /mɪsə'laɪəns/ *n.* unsuitable alliance, esp. marriage with social inferior. [MIS-[1]]

misanthrope /'mɪsənθrəʊp, 'mɪz-/ *n.* hater of mankind; one who avoids human society; **misanthropic** /-'θrɒpɪk/ *a.*; **misanthropically** /-'θrɒpɪkəlɪ/ *adv.* [F f. Gk (*misos* hatred, *anthrōpos* man)]
misanthropy /mɪ'sænθrəpɪ, mɪ'z-/ *n.* condition or habits of misanthrope.
misapply /mɪsə'plaɪ/ *v.t.* apply (esp. funds) wrongly; **misapplication** /-æplɪ'keɪʃ(ə)n/ *n.* [MIS-[1]]
misapprehend /mɪsæprɪ'hend/ *v.t.* misunderstand (words or person); **misapprehension** /-ʃ(ə)n/ *n.*
misappropriate /mɪsə'prəʊprɪeɪt/ *v.t.* take wrongly, esp. apply (another's money) wrongly to one's own use; **misappropriation** /-'eɪʃ(ə)n/ *n.*
misbegotten /mɪsbɪ'gɒt(ə)n/ *a.* contemptible, disreputable; bastard.
misbehave /mɪsbɪ'heɪv/ *v.i.* behave improperly; **misbehaviour** *n.*
miscalculate /mɪs'kælkjʊleɪt/ *v.* calculate wrongly; **miscalculation** /-'leɪʃ(ə)n/ *n.* [MIS-[1]]
miscall /mɪs'kɔ:l/ *v.t.* call by wrong name.
miscarriage /mɪs'kærɪdʒ, 'mɪs-/ *n.* spontaneous abortion; delivery of foetus in 12th–28th week of pregnancy; miscarrying of plan etc.; **miscarriage of justice** failure of court to achieve justice. [foll.]
miscarry /mɪs'kærɪ/ *v.i.* (of person or scheme etc.) be unsuccessful; (of woman) have miscarriage; (of letter) fail to reach destination. [MIS-[1]]
miscast /mɪs'kɑ:st/ *v.t.* (*past* and *p.p.* **miscast**) allot unsuitable part to (actor).
miscegenation /mɪsɪdʒɪ'neɪʃ(ə)n/ *n.* interbreeding of races, esp. of Whites with non-Whites. [MIX, GENUS]
miscellaneous /mɪsə'leɪnɪəs/ *a.* of various kinds; of mixed composition or character. [L (*misceo* MIX)]
miscellany /mɪ'selənɪ/ *n.* mixture, medley; book containing various literary compositions etc. [F or L (prec.)]
mischance /mɪs'tʃɑ:ns/ *n.* bad luck, misfortune. [F (MIS-[2])]
mischief /'mɪstʃɪf/ *n.* troublesome but not malicious conduct, esp. of children (*get into mischief*); playful malice or archness (*eyes full of mischief*); harm or injury, esp. caused by person (*do someone a mischief*); **make mischief** create discord. [F (MIS-[2], *chever* happen)]
mischievous /'mɪstʃɪvəs/ *a.* (of person) disposed to mischief; (of conduct) playfully malicious, mildly troublesome; (of thing) having harmful effects.
miscible /'mɪsɪb(ə)l/ *a.* that can be mixed (*with*); **miscibility** /-'bɪlɪtɪ/ *n.* [med.L (MIX)]
misconceive /mɪskən'si:v/ *v.* have wrong idea or conception (of); **misconception** /-'sepʃ(ə)n/ *n.* [MIS-[1]]
misconduct /mɪs'kɒndʌkt/ *n.* improper conduct, esp. adultery.
misconstrue /mɪskən'stru:/ *v.t.* misinterpret; **misconstruction** *n.*
miscopy /mɪs'kɒpɪ/ *v.t.* copy wrongly.
miscount /mɪs'kaʊnt/ **1** *v.* make wrong count; count (things) wrongly. **2** *n.* wrong count, esp. of votes.
miscreant /'mɪskrɪənt/ *n.* vile wretch, villain. [F (MIS-[2], *creant* believer)]
misdeal /mɪs'di:l/ **1** *v.* (*past* and *p.p.* **misdealt** /-'delt/) make mistake in dealing (cards). **2** *n.* such mistake; misdealt hand.
misdeed /mɪs'di:d/ *n.* wrong or improper action. [OE (MIS-[1])]
misdemeanour /mɪsdɪ'mi:nə/, *US* **misdemeanor** *n.* misdeed; *Law* indictable offence, formerly (in UK) one less heinous than felony. [MIS-[1]]
misdirect /mɪsdɪ'rekt, -daɪ-/ *v.t.* direct wrongly; **misdirection** *n.*
misdoing /mɪs'du:ɪŋ/ *n.* misdeed.
mise en scène /mi:zɑ̃'seɪn/ *n.* scenery and properties of acted play; surroundings of an event. [F]
miser /'maɪzə/ *n.* person who hoards wealth, esp. one who lives miserably; **miserly** *a.* [L, = wretched]
miserable /'mɪzərəb(ə)l/ *a.* wretchedly unhappy or uncomfortable; contemptible or mean (*a miserable hovel*); causing wretchedness; **miserably** *adv.* [F f. L (prec.)]
misericord /mɪ'zerɪkɔ:d/ *n.* projection under seat in choir stall serving (when seat was turned up) to support person standing. [F f. L *misericordia* pity]
misery /'mɪzərɪ/ *n.* condition or feeling of extreme unhappiness or discomfort; cause of this; *colloq.* constantly grumbling or doleful person. [F or L (MISER)]
misfire /mɪs'faɪə/ **1** *v.i.* (of gun, motor engine, etc.) fail to go off or start action or function regularly; (of plan etc.) fail to have intended effect. **2** *n.* such failure. [MIS-[1]]
misfit *n.* person unsuited to his environment or work; garment etc. that does not fit properly.
misfortune /mɪs'fɔ:tʃu:n/ *n.* bad luck; instance of this.
misgive /mɪs'gɪv/ *v.t.* (*past* **misgave**; *p.p.* **misgiven**) (of person's mind, heart, etc.) fill (him) with suspicion or foreboding.
misgiving *n.* feeling of mistrust or apprehension.
misgovern /mɪs'gʌvən/ *v.t.* govern badly; **misgovernment** *n.*
misguided /mɪs'gaɪdɪd/ *a.* mistaken in thought or action.

mishandle /mɪs'hænd(ə)l/ *v.t.* deal with incorrectly or ineffectively; handle (person or thing) roughly or rudely.
mishap /'mɪshæp/ *n.* unlucky accident.
mishear /mɪs'hɪə/ *v.t.* (*past* and *p.p.* **misheard** /-hɜ:d/) hear incorrectly or imperfectly.
mishit 1 /mɪs'hɪt/ *v.t.* (**-tt-**; *past* and *p.p.* **mishit**) hit (ball) faultily or badly. **2** /'mɪshɪt/ *n.* faulty or bad hit.
mishmash /'mɪʃmæʃ/ *n.* confused mixture. [redupl. of MASH]
misinform /mɪsɪn'fɔ:m/ *v.t.* give wrong information to; **misinformation** /-fə'meɪʃ(ə)n/ *n.* [MIS-[1]]
misinterpret /mɪsɪn'tɜ:prɪt/ *v.t.* give wrong interpretation to; make wrong inference from; **misinterpretation** /-'teɪʃ(ə)n/ *n.*
misjudge /mɪs'dʒʌdʒ/ *v.* have wrong opinion of; judge wrongly; **misjudgement** *n.*.
mislay /mɪs'leɪ/ *v.t.* (*past* and *p.p.* **mislaid**) put (thing) by accident where it cannot readily be found.
mislead /mɪs'li:d/ *v.t.* (*past* and *p.p.* **misled**) lead astray, cause to go wrong in conduct or belief. [OE (MIS-[1])]
mismanage /mɪs'mænɪdʒ/ *v.t.* manage badly or wrongly; **mismanagement** *n.* [MIS-[1]]
mismatch 1 /mɪs'mætʃ/ *v.t.* match unsuitably or incorrectly. **2** /'mɪsmætʃ/ *n.* bad match.
misnomer /mɪs'nəʊmə/ *n.* name or term used wrongly; use of wrong name. [AF (MIS-[2], *nommer* to name)]
misogynist /mɪ'sɒdʒɪnɪst/ *n.* one who hates all women; **misogyny** *n.* [Gk *misos* hatred, *gunē* woman]
misplace /mɪs'pleɪs/ *v.t.* put in wrong place; bestow (affections or confidence) on wrong object; time (words or action) badly; **misplacement** *n.* [MIS-[1]]
misprint 1 /'mɪsprɪnt/ *n.* mistake in printing. **2** /mɪs'prɪnt/ *v.t.* print wrongly.
misprision /mɪs'prɪʒ(ə)n/ *n.* *Law* wrong act or omission; **misprision of treason** (or **of felony**) concealment of one's knowledge of treasonable (or felonious) intent. [AF (MIS-[2], *prendre* take)]
mispronounce /mɪsprə'naʊns/ *v.t.* pronounce (word etc.) wrongly; **mispronunciation** /-nʌnsɪ'eɪʃ(ə)n/ *n.* [MIS-[1]]
misquote /mɪs'kwəʊt/ *v.t.* quote inaccurately; **misquotation** /-'teɪʃ(ə)n/ *n.*
misread /mɪs'ri:d/ *v.t.* (*past* and *p.p.* **misread** /-'red/) read or interpret wrongly.
misrepresent /mɪsreprɪ'zent/ *v.t.* give false account of, represent wrongly; **misrepresentation** /-'teɪʃ(ə)n/ *n.*
misrule /mɪs'ru:l/ **1** *n.* bad government; disorder. **2** *v.t.* govern badly.
miss[1] **1** *v.* fail to hit or reach or catch (object); fail to catch (train etc.) or see (event) or meet (person); fail to keep (appointment) or seize (opportunity); fail to see or hear or understand; notice or regret loss or absence of; avoid (*missed being chosen*; *tried to miss the traffic*); (of engine) misfire; fail. **2** *n.* failure to hit or attain. **3 miss out** omit, leave out; **miss out (on)** *colloq.* fail to get benefit or enjoyment (from). [OE]
miss[2] *n.* girl or unmarried woman; (**Miss**) title of unmarried woman or girl; title of beauty queen from specified region (*Miss France*, *Miss World*). [MISTRESS]
missal /'mɪs(ə)l/ *n.* (in RC Church) book containing service for Mass for whole year; book of prayers. [L (*missa* MASS[2])]
missel-thrush /'mɪsəlθrʌʃ/ *n.* large thrush that feeds on mistletoe etc. berries. [OE *mistel* = mistletoe]
misshapen /mɪs'ʃeɪpən/ *a.* ill-shaped, deformed; distorted. [MIS-[1], *shapen* archaic = *shaped*]
missile /'mɪsaɪl/ *n.* object or weapon suitable for throwing at target or for discharge from machine; weapon directed by remote control or automatically. [L (*mitto miss-* send)]
missing *a.* not in its place, lost; (of person) not yet traced or confirmed as alive but not known to be dead; not present; **missing link** thing lacking to complete series; hypothetical intermediate type, esp. between man and apes. [MISS[1]]
mission /'mɪʃ(ə)n/ *n.* body of persons sent to conduct negotiations or propagate a religious faith; missionary post; task to be performed; journey for such purpose; operational sortie; dispatch of aircraft or spacecraft; a person's vocation. [F or L (as MISSILE)]
missionary 1 *a.* of religious etc. missions. **2** *n.* person doing missionary work. [L (prec.)]
missis /'mɪsɪz/ *n.* *vulgar*, as form of address to woman; **the missis** my or your wife. [MISTRESS]
missive /'mɪsɪv/ *n.* official or long and serious letter. [L (as MISSILE)]
misspell /mɪs'spel/ *v.t.* (*past* and *p.p.* **misspelt** or **misspelled**) spell wrongly. [MIS-[1]]
misspend /mɪs'spend/ *v.t.* (*past* and *p.p.* **misspent**) spend amiss or wastefully.
misstate /mɪs'steɪt/ *v.t.* state wrongly; **misstatement** *n.*
mist 1 *n.* water vapour near ground in droplets smaller than raindrops and causing obscuration of the atmosphere; condensed vapour obscuring wind-

screens etc.; dimness or blurring of sight caused by tears etc. **2** *v.* cover or become covered (as) with mist. [OE]

mistake /mɪ'steɪk/ **1** *n.* incorrect idea or opinion, thing incorrectly done or thought. **2** *v.* (*past* **mistook** /-'stʊk/; *p.p.* **mistaken**) misunderstand meaning or intention of; wrongly take (one *for* another); choose wrongly (*mistake one's vocation*). [ON (MIS-¹, TAKE)]

mistaken /mɪ'steɪken/ *a.* wrong in opinion (*you are mistaken*); ill-judged (*mistaken kindness*).

mister *n.* person without title of nobility etc. (*a mere mister*); *vulgar* as form of address to man. [MASTER; cf. MR]

mistime /mɪs'taɪm/ *v.t.* say or do (thing) at wrong time. [MIS-¹]

mistletoe /'mɪs(ə)ltəʊ/ *n.* parasitic plant growing on apple and other trees and bearing white berries. [OE, = mistletoe-twig (see MISSEL-THRUSH)]

mistook *past* of MISTAKE.

mistral /'mɪstr(ə)l, -'trɑ:l/ *n.* cold N. or NW wind in S. France. [F & Prov. f. L (MASTER)]

mistreat /mɪs'tri:t/ *v.t.* treat badly; **mistreatment** *n.*

mistress /'mɪstrɪs/ *n.* woman in authority or with power; female head of household; female teacher; woman having illicit sexual relationship with (usu. married) man. [F (*maistre* MASTER, -ESS)]

mistrial /mɪs'traɪəl/ *n.* trial vitiated by error. [MIS-¹]

mistrust /mɪs'trʌst/ **1** *v.t.* feel no confidence in, be suspicious of. **2** *n.* lack of confidence, suspicion. **3 mistrustful** *a.*; **mistrustfully** *adv.*

misty *a.* of or covered with mist; of dim outline; *fig.* obscure, vague; **mistily** *adv.*; **mistiness** *n.* [OE (MIST)]

misunderstand /mɪsʌndə'stænd/ *v.t.* (*past* and *p.p.* **misunderstood** /-'stʊd/) understand in wrong sense; (esp. in *p.p.*) misinterpret words or action of (person). [MIS-¹]

misunderstanding *n.* failure to understand correctly; slight disagreement or quarrel.

misusage /mɪs'ju:sɪdʒ/ *n.* wrong or improper usage, ill-treatment.

misuse 1 /mɪs'ju:z/ *v.t.* use wrongly, apply to wrong purpose, ill-treat. **2** /mɪs'ju:s/ *n.* wrong or improper use or application.

mite *n.* small arachnid, esp. of kind found in cheese etc.; modest contribution; small object or child. [OE]

miter *n. US* var. of MITRE.

mitigate /'mɪtɪgeɪt/ *v.t.* make milder or less intense or severe; **mitigation** /-'geɪʃ(ə)n/ *n.* [L (*mitis* mild)]

mitosis /maɪ'təʊsɪs, mɪt-/ *n.* (*pl.* **mitoses** /-i:z/ a process of division of cell nuclei in which two new nuclei each with the full number of chromosomes are formed; **mitotic** /-'tɒtɪk/ *a.* [L (Gk *mitos* thread)]

mitre /'maɪtə/ **1** *n.* tall deeply-cleft headdress worn by bishops and abbots, esp. as symbol of episcopal office; joint of two pieces of wood etc. at angle of 90°, such that line of junction bisects this angle. **2** *v.t.* bestow mitre on; join with mitre. [F f. L f. Gk *mitra* turban]

mitt *n.* glove with only one compartment for four fingers (also **mitten**); knitted or lace glove leaving fingers and thumb-tip bare; *sl.* hand; baseball-player's glove. [F f. L (MOIETY)]

mix 1 *v.* combine or put together (two or more substances or things) so that constituents of each are diffused among those of the other(s); prepare (compound, cocktail, etc.) by mixing ingredients; (of person) be harmonious or sociable (*with*), have dealings *with*, participate *in*; join, be mixed (*oil will not mix with water*); (of things) be compatible. **2** *n.* mixing, mixture; proportion of materials in a mixture; ingredients prepared commercially for making cake etc. or for process such as concrete-making. **3 be mixed up in** (or **with**) be involved in or with; **mix it** *colloq.* start fighting; **mix up** mix thoroughly, confuse; **mix-up** *n.* confusion, misunderstanding. [back-form. f. foll.]

mixed /mɪkst/ *a.* of diverse qualities or elements; (of group of persons) containing persons from various classes; for persons of both sexes (*mixed school, bathing*); **mixed bag** diverse assortment; **mixed blessing** thing having advantages but also disadvantages; **mixed doubles** (in tennis) doubles game with man and woman as partners on each side; **mixed farming** farming of both crops and livestock; **mixed feelings** mixture of pleasure and dismay at some event; **mixed grill** dish of various grilled meats and vegetables; **mixed marriage** marriage between persons of different race or religion; **mixed metaphor** combination of inconsistent metaphors; **mixed-up** *colloq.* mentally or emotionally confused, socially ill-adjusted. [F f. L (*misceo* mix)]

mixer *n.* device for mixing foods etc.; person who manages socially in specified way (*a good mixer*); drink to be mixed with another. [MIX]

mixture /'mɪkstʃə/ *n.* process or result of mixing; thing made by mixing; combination of ingredients, qualities, characteristics, etc.; **the mixture as**

before *fig.* the same treatment repeated. [F or L (MIXED)]
mizen /'mɪz(ə)n/ *n.* (also **mizen-sail**) lowest fore-and-aft sail of full-rigged ship's mizen-mast; **mizen-mast** mast next aft of mainmast. [F *misaine* f. It. (MEZZANINE)]
ml. *abbr.* millilitre(s); mile(s).
Mlle(s) abbr. *Mademoiselle, Mesdemoiselles.*
MLR *abbr.* minimum lending rate.
MM *abbr. Messieurs,* Military Medal.
mm. *abbr.* millimetre(s).
Mme(s) *abbr. Madame, Mesdames.*
Mn *symb.* manganese.
mnemonic /nɪ'mɒnɪk/ **1** *a.* of or designed to aid the memory. **2** *n.* mnemonic device; (in *pl.*) art of or system for improving memory. **3 mnemonically** *adv.* [L f. Gk (*mnēmōn* mindful)]
mo /məʊ/ *n. sl.* (*pl.* **mos**) moment. [abbr.]
MO *abbr.* Medical Officer; money order.
Mo *symb.* molybdenum.
moa /'məʊə/ *n.* extinct flightless New Zealand bird resembling ostrich. [Maori]
moan **1** *n.* long murmur expressing physical or mental suffering; low plaintive sound of wind etc.; complaint, grievance. **2** *v.* make moan(s); utter with moans. [OE]
moat *n.* defensive ditch round castle, town, etc., usu. filled with water. [F *mote* mound]
mob **1** *n.* disorderly crowd, rabble; *the* populace; *sl.* gang, associated group of persons. **2** *v.t.* (**-bb-**) (of mob) attack; crowd round in order to attack or admire. [L *mobile vulgus* excitable crowd]
mob-cap *n. hist.* woman's large indoor cap covering all the hair. [obs. *mob*, orig. = slut]
mobile /'məʊbaɪl/ **1** *a.* movable, not fixed, able to move (easily); (of face etc.) readily changing its expression; (of shop etc.) accommodated in a vehicle so as to serve various places; (of person) able to change one's social status. **2** *n.* decorative structure that may be hung so as to turn freely. **3 mobility** /mə'bɪlɪtɪ/ *n.* [F f. L (*moveo* move)]
mobilize /'məʊbɪlaɪz/ *v.* make (troops etc.) or become ready for active service; **mobilization** /-'zeɪʃ(ə)n/ *n.*
mobster *n. sl.* gangster. [MOB]
moccasin /'mɒkəsɪn/ *n.* soft heelless shoe as orig. worn by N. American Indians. [Amer. Ind.]
mocha /'mɒkə, 'məʊ-/ *n.* fine quality of coffee; flavouring made with this. [*Mocha*, port on Red Sea]
mock **1** *v.* ridicule, scoff (*at*), mimic contemptuously; jeer, defy or delude contemptuously. **2** *attrib. a.* sham, imitation (esp. without intent to deceive). **3 mocking-bird** bird that mimics notes of other birds; **mock orange** shrub with fragrant white flowers; **mock turtle soup** soup made from calf's head etc., to resemble turtle soup; **mock-up** experimental model or replica of proposed structure etc. [F *moquer*]
mockery *n.* derision; subject or occasion of this; counterfeit or absurdly inadequate representation (*of*); ludicrously or insultingly futile action etc.
mod *colloq.* **1** *n.* modification. **2** *a.* modern. **3 mod cons** modern conveniences. [abbr.]
modal /'məʊd(ə)l/ *a.* of mode or form, not of substance; *Gram.* of mood of verb, (of verb, e.g. *would*) used to express mood of another verb. [L (MODE)]
mode *n.* way or manner in which thing is done; method of procedure; prevailing fashion or custom; *Mus.* scale system. [F, & L *modus* measure]
model /'mɒd(ə)l/ **1** *n.* representation in three dimensions of existing person or thing or of proposed structure, esp. on smaller scale; simplified description of system for calculations etc.; figure in clay, wax, etc., to be reproduced in another material; particular design or style of structure, esp. of motor vehicle; person or thing proposed for imitation; person employed to pose for artist, or to display clothes etc. by wearing them; garment etc. by well-known designer, copy of this. **2** *a.* exemplary, ideally perfect. **3** *v.* (**-ll-**, *US* **-l-**) fashion or shape (figure) in clay, wax, etc.; form (thing) *after* or (*up*)*on* model; act or pose as model; (of person acting as model) display (garment). [F f. It. *modello* f. L (prec.)]
modem /'məʊdem/ *n.* combined device for modulation and demodulation, e.g. between computer and telephone line. [portmanteau word]
moderate /'mɒdərət/ **1** *a.* avoiding extremes, temperate in conduct or expression; fairly or tolerably large or good; (of wind) of medium strength; (of prices) fairly low. **2** *n.* one who holds moderate views in politics etc. **3** /-eɪt/ *v.* make less violent, intense, rigorous, etc.; become less vehement; act as moderator (of or to). [L]
moderation /mɒdə'reɪʃ(ə)n/ *n.* moderating; moderateness; **in moderation** in moderate manner or degree. [F f. L (prec.)]
moderator *n.* arbitrator, mediator, presiding officer; Presbyterian minister presiding over any ecclesiastical body. [L (MODERATE)]
modern /'mɒd(ə)n/ **1** *a.* of present and

recent times; in current fashion, not antiquated. **2** *n.* person living in modern times. **3 modern English** English from 1500 onwards. **4 modernity** /-'dɜ:nɪtɪ/ *n.* [F f. L (*modo* just now)]
modernism *n.* modern ideas or methods; **modernist** *n.*
modernize *v.* make modern, adapt to modern needs or habits; adopt modern ways or views; **modernization** /-'zeɪʃ(ə)n/ *n.*
modest /'mɒdɪst/ *a.* having humble or moderate estimate of one's own merits; diffident, bashful; decorous in manner and conduct; (of demand, statement, etc.) not excessive or exaggerated; unpretentious in appearance, amount, etc.; **modesty** *n.* [F f. L]
modicum /'mɒdɪkəm/ *n.* small quantity. [L (MODE)]
modification /mɒdɪfɪ'keɪʃ(ə)n/ *n.* modifying or being modified; change made; **modificatory** /'mɒd-/ *a.* [F or L (foll.)]
modify /'mɒdɪfaɪ/ *v.t.* make less severe or decided, tone down; make partial changes in; *Gram.* qualify sense of (word etc.). [F f. L (MODE)]
modish /'məʊdɪʃ/ *a.* fashionable. [MODE]
modiste /mɒ'di:st/ *n.* milliner, dressmaker. [F (MODE)]
modulate /'mɒdjʊleɪt/ *v.* regulate or adjust; moderate; adjust or vary tone or pitch of (speaking voice); alter amplitude or frequency of (wave) by wave of lower frequency to convey signal; *Mus.* pass from one key to another; **modulation** /-'leɪʃ(ə)n/ *n.* [L (foll.)]
module /'mɒdju:l/ *n.* standardized part or independent unit in construction esp. of furniture, building, spacecraft, or electronic system; **modular** *a.* [F, or L (as foll.)]
modulus /'mɒdjʊləs/ *n.* (*pl.* **moduli** /-aɪ/) constant factor or ratio. [L, = measure (MODE)]
modus operandi /'məʊdəs opə'rændɪ/ way person goes about task, way a thing operates. [L, = mode of working]
modus vivendi /'məʊdəs vɪ'vendɪ/ way of living or coping; arrangement whereby those in dispute can carry on pending settlement. [L, = mode of living]
mog *n.* (also **moggie**) *sl.* cat. [dial.]
mogul /'məʊg(ə)l/ *n. colloq.* important or influential person; (**Mogul**) Mongolian; **the (Great** or **Grand) Mogul** emperor of Delhi in 16th–19th cc. [Pers. & Arab. (MONGOL)]
mohair /'məʊheə/ *n.* hair of Angora goat; yarn or fabric from this. [ult. f. Arab., = choice]
Mohammedan var. of MUHAMMADAN.
moiety /'mɔɪɪtɪ/ *n.* (*Law* or *literary*) half; one of the two parts of a thing. [F f. L *medietas* (*medius* middle)]
moil *v.i.* drudge. [F f. L (*mollis* soft)]
moire /mwɑ:/ *n.* (also **moire antique**) watered fabric, usu. silk. [F (MOHAIR)]
moiré /'mwɑ:reɪ/ *a.* (of silk) watered; (of metal) having clouded appearance like watered silk. [F (prec.)]
moist *a.* slightly wet, damp; (of season) rainy. [F]
moisten /'mɔɪs(ə)n/ *v.* make or become moist.
moisture /'mɔɪstʃə/ *n.* liquid diffused in small quantity as vapour, within solid, or condensed on a surface. [F (MOIST)]
moisturize *v.t.* make less dry (esp. the skin by use of cosmetic).
moke *n. sl.* donkey. [orig. unkn.]
molar /'məʊlə/ **1** *a.* (usu. of mammal's back teeth) serving to grind. **2** *n.* molar tooth. [L (*mola* millstone)]
molasses /mə'læsɪz/ *n.* uncrystallized syrup drained from raw sugar; *US* treacle. [Port. f. L (*mel* honey)]
mold etc. *US* var. of MOULD[1–3] etc.
molder *US* var. of MOULDER.
mole[1] *n.* small burrowing mammal with usu. blackish velvety fur and very small eyes; *colloq.* spy established deep within an organization and usu. dormant for long period while attaining position of trust. [LG or Du.]
mole[2] *n.* small permanent dark spot on human skin. [OE]
mole[3] *n.* massive structure usu. of stone, as pier, breakwater, or causeway; artificial harbour. [F f. L *moles* mass]
mole[4] *n.* quantity of a substance containing as many molecules as there are atoms in 0.012 kg. of the isotope carbon-12 [G *mol* (*molekül* MOLECULE)]
molecular /mə'lekjʊlə/ *a.* of or relating to or consisting of molecules. **molecular weight** ratio between mass of one molecule of a substance and one-twelfth of mass of an atom of the isotope carbon-12; **molecularity** /-'lærɪtɪ/ *n.* [foll.]
molecule /'mɒlɪkju:l/ *n.* smallest particle (usu. a group of atoms) to which a substance can be reduced by subdivision without losing its chemical identity. [F f. L dimin. (MOLE[3])]
molehill *n.* small mound thrown up by mole in burrowing; **make a mountain out of a molehill** over-react to small difficulty. [MOLE[1]]
molest /mə'lest/ *v.t.* annoy or pester (person) in hostile or injurious way; **molestation** /-'steɪʃ(ə)n/ *n.* [F or L *molestus* troublesome]
moll *n. colloq.* prostitute; gangster's female companion. [pet-form of *Mary*]
mollify /'mɒlɪfaɪ/ *v.t.* appease, soften;

mollification /-fɪ'keɪʃ(ə)n/ *n.* [F or L (*mollis* soft)]

mollusc /'mɒləsk/, *US* **mollusk** *n.* one of the group of soft-bodied usu. hard-shelled animals including snails, oysters, etc. [F f. L *molluscus* soft]

mollycoddle /'mɒlɪkɒd(ə)l/ **1** *v.* coddle, pamper. **2** *n.* effeminate man or boy, milksop. [as MOLL; CODDLE]

molt *US* var. of MOULT.

molten /'məʊlt(ə)n/ *a.* melted, esp. made liquid by heat. [MELT]

molto /'mɒltəʊ/ *adv. Mus.* very. [It. f. L *multus* much]

molybdenum /mə'lɪbdɪnəm/ *n.* silver-white metallic element used in steel for making high-speed tools etc. [L f. Gk (*molubdos* lead)]

moment /'məʊmənt/ *n.* very brief portion of time; particular point of time (*I came the moment you called*); importance (*of great, little, moment*); product of force and distance of its line of action from centre of rotation; **at the moment** at this time, now; **in a moment** very soon; **man** etc. **of the moment** the one of importance at the time in question; **moment of truth** time of crisis or test. [F, f. L MOMENTUM]

momentary *a.* lasting only a moment; **momentarily** *adv.* [L (as prec.)]

momentous /mə'mentəs/ *a.* having great importance.

momentum /mə'mentəm/ *n.* (*pl.* **momenta**) quantity of motion of a moving body, product of its mass and its velocity; impetus gained by movement (*lit.* or *fig.*). [L (*moveo* move)]

Mon. *abbr.* Monday.

monad /'mɒnæd, 'məʊ-/ *n.* the number one, unit; ultimate unit of being (e.g. a soul, an atom, a person, God); **monadic** /mə'nædɪk/ *a.* [F or L f. Gk *monas -ados* unit]

monarch /'mɒnək/ *n.* sovereign with title of king, queen, emperor, empress, or equivalent; supreme ruler (*lit.* or *fig.*); **monarchic** /mə'nɑ:kɪk/ *a.*; **monarchical** /mə'nɑ:kɪk(ə)l/ *a.* [F or L f. Gk (MONO-, *arkhō* rule)]

monarchism *n.* advocacy of or principles of monarchy; **monarchist** *n.* [F (foll.)]

monarchy *n.* form of government with monarch at head; State with this. [L f. Gk (MONARCH)]

monastery /'mɒnəstərɪ/ *n.* residence of community of monks. [L *monasterium* f. Gk (*monos* alone)]

monastic /mə'næstɪk/ *a.* of or like monks, nuns, friars, etc.; of monasteries; **monastically** *adv.*; **monasticism** /mə'næstɪsɪz(ə)m/ *n.* [F or L f. Gk (prec.)]

Monday /'mʌndeɪ, -dɪ/ **1** *n.* day of week following Sunday. **2** *adv. colloq.* on Monday. **3 Mondays** on Mondays, each Monday. [OE]

monetarism /'mʌnɪtərɪz(ə)m/ *n.* control of money as chief method of stabilizing the economy; **monetarist** *n.* [foll.]

monetary /'mʌnɪtərɪ/ *a.* of the currency in use; (consisting) of money; **monetarily** *adv.* [F or L (foll.)]

money /'mʌnɪ/ *n.* current medium of exchange in form of coins and banknotes; (in *pl.* **moneys** or **monies**) sums of money; wealth, property viewed as convertible into money; rich person or people; **in the money** having or winning plenty of money; **make money** acquire wealth; **money-bag** bag for money (in *pl.* treated as *sing.*) *colloq.* wealthy person; **money-box** closed box for holding money dropped in through slit; **money-changer** one whose business it is to change money, esp. at official rate; **money for jam** *sl.* profit for little or no trouble; **money-grubber** person greedily intent on amassing money; **money-grubbing** *a.* & *n.* (given to) this practice; **money-lender** one whose business it is to lend money at interest; **money-making** *a.* & *n.* producing wealth, acquisition of wealth; **money-market** sphere of operation of dealers in short-dated loans, stocks, etc.; **money of account** unit of money used in accounting but not current as coin or note; **money order** order for payment of specified sum, issued by bank or Post Office; **money-spinner** thing that brings in much profit, a kind of small spider; **money's-worth** good value for one's money; **the one for one's money** the one that one prefers; **put money into** make investment in. [F f. L *moneta*]

moneyed *a.* wealthy; consisting of money.

monger /'mʌŋgə/ *n.* (chiefly *in comb.*) dealer or trader (*fishmonger*); *fig.* (usu. *derog.*) spreader (*scandalmonger, scaremonger*). [OE f. L *mango* dealer.]

Mongol /'mɒŋg(ə)l/ **1** *a.* of Asian people now inhabiting Mongolia; having Mongoloid characteristics; (**mongol**) suffering from mongolism. **2** *n.* Mongol person; (**mongol**) person suffering from mongolism. [native name]

Mongolian /mɒŋ'gəʊlɪən/ **1** *a.* of Mongolia, Mongol, Mongoloid. **2** *n.* native or language of Mongolia.

mongolism /'mɒŋgəlɪz(ə)m/ *n.* congenital mental deficiency with Mongoloid appearance. [MONGOL]

Mongoloid /'mɒŋgəlɔɪd/ **1** *a.* resembling Mongolians in racial origin or in having broad flat (yellowish) face; mongol. **2** *n.* Mongoloid person.

mongoose /'mɒŋgu:s/ *n.* (*pl.* **mongooses**) small carnivorous tropical mammal, esp. a species common in India, able to kill venomous snakes unharmed. [Marathi]

mongrel /'mʌŋgr(ə)l/ **1** *n.* dog of no definable type or breed; other animal or plant resulting from crossing of different breeds or types. **2** *a.* of mixed origin, nature, or character. [rel. to MINGLE]

monism /'mɒnɪz(ə)m/ *n.* any theory denying duality of matter and mind; **monist** *n.*; **monistic** /-'nɪstɪk/ *a.* [L f. Gk *monos* single]

monitor /'mɒnɪtə/ **1** *n.* pupil in school with disciplinary or other duties; television receiver used in selecting or verifying the broadcast picture; one who listens to and reports on foreign broadcasts etc.; detector of radioactive contamination. **2** *v.* act as monitor (of); maintain regular surveillance (over); regulate strength of (recorded or transmitted signal). **3 monitorial** /-'tɔ:rɪəl/ *a.* [L (*moneo* warn)]

monitory /'mɒnɪtərɪ/ *a.* giving or serving as a warning. [L *monitorius* (prec.)]

monk /mʌŋk/ *n.* member of community of men living apart under religious vows; **monkish** *a.* [OE f. L f. Gk *monakhos* (*monos* alone)]

monkey /'mʌŋkɪ/ **1** *n.* mammal of group closely allied to and resembling man, esp. small long-tailed member of order Primates; mischievous person, esp. child; *sl.* £500, *US* $500. **2** *v.* mimic or mock; fool *about* or *around*; tamper or play mischievous tricks (*with*). **3 monkey business** *sl.* mischief; **monkey-nut** peanut; **monkey-puzzle** prickly tree with interlaced branches; **monkey-tricks** *sl.* mischief; **monkey-wrench** wrench with adjustable jaw. [orig. unkn.]

monkshood /'mʌŋkshʊd/ *n.* poisonous plant with hood-shaped flowers. [MONK]

mono /'mɒnəʊ/ **1** *a.* monophonic. **2** *n.* (*pl.* **monos**) monophonic record, reproduction, etc. [abbr.]

mono- *in comb.* (before vowel usu. **mon-**) one, alone, single. [Gk (*monos* alone)]

monochromatic /mɒnəkrə'mætɪk/ *a.* (of light or other radiation) containing only one colour or wavelength; executed in monochrome; **monochromatically** *adv.*

monochrome /'mɒnəkrəʊm/ **1** *n.* picture done in one colour or different tints of this, or in black and white only. **2** *a.* having or using only one colour. [MONO-, Gk *khrōma* colour]

monocle /'mɒnək(ə)l/ *n.* single eyeglass. [F f. L (MONO-, *oculus* eye)]

monocotyledon /mɒnəkɒtɪ'li:d(ə)n/ *n.* flowering plant with single cotyledon; **monocotyledonous** *a.* [MONO-]

monocular /mə'nɒkjʊlə/ *a.* with or for one eye. [MONOCLE]

monody /'mɒnədɪ/ *n.* ode sung by single actor in Greek play; poem in which mourner bewails someone's death; **monodist** *n.* [L f. Gk (MONO-, ODE)]

monogamy /mə'nɒgəmɪ/ *n.* practice or state of being married to one person at a time; **monogamist** *n.*; **monogamous** *a.* [F f. L f. Gk (*gamos* marriage)]

monogram /'mɒnəgræm/ *n.* two or more letters, esp. person's initials, interwoven as device. [MONO-]

monograph /'mɒnəgrɑ:f/ *n.* separate treatise on single subject or aspect of it.

monolith /'mɒnəlɪθ/ *n.* single block of stone, esp. shaped into pillar etc.; person or thing like monolith in being massive, immovable, or solidly uniform; **monolithic** /-'lɪθɪk/ *a.* [F f. Gk (*lithos* stone)]

monologue /'mɒnəlɒg/ *n.* scene in drama where person speaks alone; dramatic composition for one performer; long speech by one person in a company. [F f. Gk *monologos* speaking alone]

monomania /mɒnə'meɪnɪə/ *n.* obsession of mind by one idea or interest; **monomaniac** *a.* [F (MONO-)]

monophonic /mɒnə'fɒnɪk/ *a.* (of reproduction of sound) using only one channel of transmission. [Gk *phōnē* sound]

monoplane /'mɒnəpleɪn/ *n.* aeroplane with one set of wings. [MONO-]

monopolist /mə'nɒpəlɪst/ *n.* one who has or advocates monopoly; **monopolistic** /-'lɪstɪk/ *a.* [MONOPOLY]

monopolize /mə'nɒpəlaɪz/ *v.t.* obtain exclusive possession or control of (trade or commodity); dominate or prevent others from sharing in (conversation etc.); **monopolization** /-'zeɪʃ(ə)n/ *n.* [foll.]

monopoly /mə'nɒpəlɪ/ *n.* exclusive possession of the trade in some commodity; this conferred as a privilege by State; exclusive possession, control, or exercise (*of*, US *on*); thing that is monopolized. [L f. Gk (*pōleō* sell)]

monorail /'mɒnəʊreɪl/ *n.* railway in which track consists of single rail. [MONO-]

monosyllable /'mɒnəsɪləb(ə)l/ *n.* word of one syllable; **monosyllabic** /-'læbɪk/ *a.*

monotheism /'mɒnəθi:ɪz(ə)m/ *n.* doctrine that there is only one god; **monotheist** *n.*; **monotheistic** /-'ɪstɪk/ *a.*

monotone /'mɒnətəʊn/ **1** *n.* sound or utterance continuing or repeated on one note without change of pitch; sameness in style of writing. **2** *a.* without change of pitch.

monotonous /mə'nɒtənəs/ *a.* lacking in variety, wearisome through sameness; **monotony** *n.*

monovalent /'mɒnəveɪlənt/ *a.* univalent.

monoxide /mə'nɒksaɪd/ *n.* oxide containing one oxygen atom.

Monseigneur /mɒnsen'jɜ:/ *n.* title given to eminent French person, esp. prince, cardinal, archbishop, or bishop. [F (*mon* my, SEIGNEUR)]

Monsieur /mə'sjɜ:/ *n.* (*pl.* ***Messieurs*** /me'sjɜ:/) title used of or to French-speaking man, corresponding to Mr or sir; Frenchman. [F (*mon* my, *sieur* lord)]

Monsignor /mɒn'si:njə/ *n.* title of various Roman Catholic prelates. [It. (MONSEIGNEUR)]

monsoon /mɒn'su:n/ *n.* wind in S. Asia, esp. in Indian Ocean, blowing from SW in summer and from NE in winter; rainy season accompanying SW monsoon. [Du. f. Port. f. Arab.]

monster **1** *n.* imaginary creature, usu. large and frightening, compounded of incongruous elements; misshapen animal or plant; inhumanly cruel or wicked person; animal or thing of huge size. **2** *a.* huge. [F f. L *monstrum* (*moneō* warn)]

monstrance /'mɒnstrəns/ *n.* (in RC Church) vessel in which Host is exposed for veneration. [L *monstro* show]

monstrosity /mɒn'strɒsɪtɪ/ *n.* misshapen animal or plant; outrageous thing; monstrousness. [L (foll.)]

monstrous /'mɒnstrəs/ *a.* like a monster, abnormally formed; huge; outrageously wrong or absurd, atrocious. [F or L (MONSTER)]

montage /mɒn'tɑ:ʒ/ *n.* selection, cutting, and piecing together as consecutive whole, of separate sections of cinema or television film; composite whole from juxtaposed pieces of music, photographs, etc.; production of this. [F (MOUNT)]

month /mʌnθ/ *n.* any of usu. 12 periods of time into which year is divided or any period between same dates in successive such portions; period of 28 days; **month of Sundays** very long period. [OE]

monthly **1** *a.* produced or occurring once every month. **2** *adv.* every month. **3** *n.* monthly periodical.

monument /'mɒnjʊmənt/ *n.* anything enduring that serves to commemorate or make celebrated, esp. structure or building; stone or other structure placed over grave or in church etc. in memory of the dead; written record. [F f. L (*moneo* remind)]

monumental /mɒnjʊ'ment(ə)l/ *a.* of or serving as monument; massive and permanent, extremely great, stupendous; **monumental mason** maker of tombstones etc.; **monumentally** *adv.*

moo **1** *n.* characteristic vocal sound of cow, low. **2** *v.i.* make this sound. [imit.]

mooch *v. sl.* loiter *about*, walk slowly *along*; steal. [prob. F *muchier* skulk]

mood[1] *n.* state of mind or feeling; (in *pl.*) fits of melancholy or bad temper; **in the mood** disposed or inclined. [OE]

mood[2] *n. Gram.* form(s) of verb serving to indicate whether it is to express fact, command, wish, etc. (*indicative, imperative, subjunctive, mood*); group of such forms, distinction of meaning expressed by this. [alt. of MODE]

moody *a.* gloomy, sullen, subject to moods; **moodily** *adv.*; **moodiness** *n.* [MOOD[1]]

moon **1** *n.* natural satellite of the earth, revolving round it monthly, illuminated by sun and reflecting some light to earth; this as visible in sky (*no moon tonight*), or as appearing in particular month or at particular time; *poetic* month; natural satellite of any planet. **2** *v.i.* move or look listlessly (*about, around*, etc.). **3 moon-face** round face like full moon; **moon over** act dreamily or absently because infatuated by; **moon-shot** launching of spacecraft travelling to the moon; **over the moon** in raptures, highly excited. [OE]

moonbeam *n.* ray of moonlight.

moonlight **1** *n.* light of moon. **2** *a.* lighted by the moon. **3** *v.i. colloq.* have two paid occupations, esp. one by day and one by night. **4 moonlight flit** hurried escape by night to avoid paying rent.

moonlit *a.* lighted by the moon.

moonshine *n.* visionary talk or ideas; illicitly distilled or smuggled alcoholic liquor.

moonstone *n.* feldspar with pearly appearance.

moonstruck *a.* deranged in mind.

moony *a.* of or like the moon; foolishly dreamy; **moonily** *adv.*

moor[1] /'mʊə, mɔ:/ *n.* tract of open waste ground esp. if covered with heather; tract of ground preserved for shooting. [OE]

moor[2] /'mʊə, mɔ:/ *v.t.* attach (boat etc.) to fixed object. [prob. LG]

Moor[3] /ˈmʊə, mɔː/ *n.* one of a Muslim people of NW Africa; **Moorish** *a.* [F f. L f. Gk *Mauros*]

moorage *n.* place or charge made for mooring. [MOOR[2]]

moorhen *n.* small water-hen. [MOOR[1]]

mooring *n.* (usu. in *pl.*) permanent anchors and chains laid down for ships to be moored to; place where vessel is moored. [MOOR[2]]

moorland *n.* country abounding in heather. [MOOR[1]]

moose /muːs/ *n.* (*pl.* same) N. American animal closely allied to or same as European elk. [Narragansett]

moot /muːt/ **1** *a.* debatable. **2** *v.t.* raise (question) for discussion. **3** *n. hist.* assembly. [OE]

mop 1 *n.* bundle of coarse yarn or cloth fastened at end of stick, for cleaning floors etc.; similarly shaped instrument for various purposes; thick head of hair like mop. **2** *v.t.* (**-pp-**) wipe or clean (as) with mop; wipe tears, sweat, etc., from (face etc.); wipe (tears etc.) thus. **3 mop up** wipe up (as) with mop, *sl.* absorb, *sl.* dispatch or make an end of, complete military occupation of (district etc.) by capturing or killing troops left there, capture or kill (stragglers). [orig. uncert.]

mope 1 *v.i.* be depressed and listless. **2** *n.* one who mopes; (in *pl.*) low spirits. **3 mopy** *a.* [orig. unkn.]

moped /ˈməʊped/ *n.* motorized bicycle. [Sw. *mo*tor, *ped*aler pedals]

moppet /ˈmɒpɪt/ *n.* (as term of endearment) baby or small child. [obs. *moppe* baby, doll]

moquette /mɒˈket/ *n.* upholstery fabric with raised loops or cut pile.

moraine /mɒˈreɪn/ *n.* area of debris carried down and deposited by glacier. [F]

moral /ˈmɒr(ə)l/ **1** *a.* concerned with goodness or badness of character or disposition or with the distinction between right and wrong; virtuous in general conduct; (of rights or duties etc.) founded on moral law; capable of moral action. **2** *n.* moral lesson of fable, story, event, etc.; (in *pl.*) moral habits, e.g. sexual conduct. **3 moral certainty** probability so great as to leave no reasonable doubt; **moral courage** courage to face disapproval rather than abandon right course of action; **moral law** conditions to be fulfilled by any right course of action; **moral philosophy** that concerned with ethics; **moral support** that giving psychological rather than physical help; **moral victory** defeat that has some of the satisfactory elements of victory. **4 morally** *adv.* [L (*mos mor-* custom)]

morale /mɒˈrɑːl/ *n.* mental attitude or bearing of person or group, esp. as regards confidence, discipline, etc. [F *moral* (prec.)]

moralist /ˈmɒrəlɪst/ *n.* one who practises or teaches morality; one who follows a natural system of ethics; **moralistic** /-ˈlɪstɪk/ *a.*

morality /mɒˈrælɪtɪ/ *n.* degree of conformity to moral principles; (esp. good) moral conduct; moralizing; science of morals, particular system of morals; **morality play** *hist.* drama teaching a moral lesson, with abstract qualities as main characters. [F or L (MORAL)]

moralize /ˈmɒrəlaɪz/ *v.* indulge in moral reflection or talk (*on* subject); interpret morally; make (more) moral; **moralization** /-ˈzeɪʃ(ə)n/ *n.* [F or med.L (MORAL)]

morass /məˈræs/ *n.* marsh or bog; *fig.* entanglement or confusion. [Du. *moeras* f. F (MARSH)]

moratorium /mɒrəˈtɔːrɪəm/ *n.* (*pl.* **moratoriums**) legal authorization to debtors to postpone payment; period of this; temporary prohibition or suspension (*on* activity). [L (*moror* delay)]

morbid /ˈmɔːbɪd/ *a.* (of mind, ideas, etc.) unwholesome, sickly; given to morbid feelings; *colloq.* melancholy; of the nature of or indicative of disease; **morbidity** /-ˈbɪdɪtɪ/ *n.* [L (*morbus* disease)]

mordant /ˈmɔːdənt/ **1** *a.* (of sarcasm etc.) caustic, biting, pungent; corrosive or cleansing; serving to fix colouring matter. **2** *n.* mordant acid or substance. [F f. L (*mordeo* bite)]

more /mɔː/ **1** *a.* greater in quantity or degree; additional or further (*bring some more water*). **2** *n.* greater quantity or number. **3** *adv.* in greater degree; again (*did it once more*); moreover; forming comparative of adjectives and adverbs, esp. those of more than one syllable (*more absurd*; *more easily*). **4 more and more** increasingly, increasingly great amount; **more of** to a greater extent (*more of a poet than a musician*); **more or less** in greater or less degree, approximately; **what is more** as an additional point, moreover. [OE]

moreish /ˈmɔːrɪʃ/ *a. colloq.* pleasant to eat, causing desire for more. [MORE]

morello /məˈreləʊ/ *n.* (*pl.* **morellos**) bitter kind of dark cherry. [It., = blackish]

moreover /mɔːˈrəʊvə/ *adv.* besides, in addition to that already said. [MORE]

mores /ˈmɔːriːz/ *n.pl.* customs or conventions regarded as characteristic of or essential to a community. [L pl. of *mos* custom]

morganatic /mɔːgəˈnætɪk/ *a.* (of marriage) between man of high rank and woman of lower rank, the wife and children having no claim to possessions or title of father; (of wife) so married; **morganatically** *adv.* [F, or G f. L *morganaticus* f. Gmc, = morning gift (from husband to wife on morning after consummation of marriage)]

morgue /mɔːg/ *n.* mortuary; (in journalism) repository where miscellaneous material for reference is kept. [F, orig. name of Paris mortuary]

moribund /'mɒrɪbʌnd/ *a.* at point of death (*lit.* or *fig.*). [L (*morior* die)]

Mormon /'mɔːmən/ *n.* member of religious body (Church of Jesus Christ of Latter-day Saints) based on revelation; **Mormonism** *n.* [*Mormon*, name of supposed author of book on which Mormonism is founded]

morn *n. poetic* morning. [OE]

mornay /'mɔːneɪ/ *n.* cheese-flavoured white sauce. [orig. uncert.]

morning /'mɔːnɪŋ/ *n.* early part of day, ending at noon or at hour of midday meal (*this morning*; *tomorrow morning*; *during the morning*; *morning coffee*); **morning after** *colloq.* time of hangover; **morning-after pill** contraceptive pill effective when taken some hours after intercourse; **morning coat** coat with front cut away to form tails; **morning dress** formal dress for man of morning coat and striped trousers; **morning glory** twining plant with trumpet-shaped flowers; **morning sickness** nausea in morning in early pregnancy; **morning star** planet esp. Venus, seen in east before sunrise. [MORN]

morocco /mə'rɒkəʊ/ *n.* (*pl.* **moroccos**) fine flexible leather of goatskin tanned with sumac. [*Morocco* in NW Africa]

moron /'mɔːrɒn/ *n.* adult with intelligence equal to that of average child of 8–12; *colloq.* very stupid person; **moronic** /mə'rɒnɪk/ *a.* [Gk *mōros* foolish]

morose /mə'rəʊs/ *a.* sullen, gloomy, and unsociable. [L (*mos mor-* manner)]

morpheme /'mɔːfiːm/ *n.* any of the smallest meaningful units of language (e.g. *in*, *come*, *-ing*, as distinct from *income*, *incoming*). [F f. Gk *morphē* form]

morphia /'mɔːfɪə/ *n.* morphine. [foll.]

morphine /'mɔːfiːn/ *n.* narcotic constituent of opium, used to alleviate pain. [G f. L *Morpheus* god of sleep]

morphology /mɔː'fɒlədʒɪ/ *n.* study of the forms of things, esp. of animals and plants and of words and their structure; **morphological** /-'lɒdʒɪk(ə)l/ *a.* [Gk *morphē* form]

morris dance /'mɒrɪs/ traditional dance in fancy costume with ribbons, bells, sticks, etc. [*morys* var. of *Moorish* (MOOR[3])]

morrow /'mɒrəʊ/ *n.* (*poetic*) *the* following day; **on the morrow of** in the time just following. [MORN]

Morse 1 *n.* the alphabet or code in which letters are represented by various combinations of two signs, e.g. dot and dash, long and short flash, etc. **2** *a.* of this alphabet or code. **3** *v.* signal by Morse code. [*Morse*, electrician]

morsel /'mɔːs(ə)l/ *n.* small piece or quantity; mouthful; fragment. [F f. L *morsus* bite]

mortal /'mɔːt(ə)l/ **1** *a.* subject to death; causing death, fatal; (of combat) fought to the death; accompanying death (*mortal agony*); (of enemy) implacable; (of pain, fear, affront, etc.) intense, very serious; *colloq.* whatsoever (*every mortal thing*); *colloq.* long and tedious (*two mortal hours*). **2** *n.* mortal being; human being. **3 mortal sin** sin that causes death of the soul or is fatal to salvation. [F or L (*mors mort-* death)]

mortality /mɔː'tælɪtɪ/ *n.* being subject to death; loss of life on large scale; number of deaths in given period etc.; **mortality rate** death rate. [F f. L (prec.)]

mortally *adv.* fatally, intensely. [MORTAL]

mortar /'mɔːtə/ **1** *n.* mixture of lime or cement, sand, and water, for joining stones or bricks; short large-bore cannon for throwing shells at high angles; vessel in which ingredients are pounded with pestle. **2** *v.t.* plaster or join with mortar; attack or bombard with mortars. **3 mortar-board** board for holding mortar, academic cap with stiff square top. [AF *morter* f. L *mortarium*]

mortgage /'mɔːgɪdʒ/ **1** *n.* conveyance of property by debtor to creditor as security for debt (esp. incurred by purchase of the property), with proviso that it shall be returned on payment of debt within certain period; deed effecting this; sum of money lent by this. **2** *v.t.* convey (property) by mortgage. **3 mortgageable** *a.* [F, = dead pledge (GAGE[1])]

mortgagee /mɔːgɪ'dʒiː/ *n.* creditor in mortgage.

mortgager /'mɔːgɪdʒə/ *n.* (*Law* **mortgagor**) debtor in mortgage.

mortice var. of MORTISE.

mortician /mɔː'tɪʃ(ə)n/ *n. US* undertaker. [L *mors mort-* death]

mortify /'mɔːtɪfaɪ/ *v.* cause (person) to feel humiliated, wound (feelings); bring (body, the flesh, passions, etc.) into subjection by self-denial or discipline; (of flesh) be affected by gangrene or necrosis; **mortification** /-fɪ'keɪʃ(ə)n/ *n.* [F f. L (prec.)]

mortise /ˈmɔːtɪs/ **1** *n.* hole in framework to receive end of another part, esp. tenon. **2** *v.t.* join securely, esp. by mortise and tenon; cut mortise in. **3 mortise lock** lock recessed in edge of door etc. [F f. Arab.]

mortuary /ˈmɔːtjʊərɪ/ **1** *n.* building in which dead bodies may be kept for a time. **2** *a.* of death or burial. [AF f. med.L (*mortuus* dead)]

mosaic[1] /məʊˈzeɪɪk/ **1** *n.* picture or pattern produced by juxtaposing small pieces of glass, stone, etc., of different colours; this form of art; diversified thing. **2** *a.* of or like mosaic. [F f. It. f. med.L f. Gk (MUSE[2])]

Mosaic[2] /məʊˈzeɪɪk/ *a.* of Moses. [F or L (*Moses* in OT)]

moselle /məʊˈzel/ *n.* a dry white wine produced in valley of Moselle in Germany.

Moslem /ˈmɒzləm/ var. of MUSLIM.

mosque /mɒsk/ *n.* Muslim place of worship. [F *mosquée* f. It. f. Arab.]

mosquito /mɒsˈkiːtəʊ/ *n.* (*pl.* **mosquitoes**) gnat, esp. one of which the female punctures skin of man and animals to suck their blood; **mosquito-net** net to keep off mosquitoes. [Sp. & Port. dimin. of *mosca* fly]

moss *n.* small flowerless plant growing in dense clusters in bogs or on surface of ground, trees, stones, etc.; *Sc. & N. Engl.* bog, esp. peat-bog; **moss-rose** variety of rose with mosslike growth on calyx and stalk; **mossy** *a.* [OE]

most /məʊst/ **1** *a.* greatest in quantity or degree; the majority of (*most people think so*). **2** *n.* the greatest quantity or degree; the majority. **3** *adv.* in the highest degree; forming superlative of adjectives and adverbs, esp. those of more than one syllable (*most absurd; most easily*). **4 at (the) most** as the greatest amount; **for the most part** in the main, usually; **make the most of** use or enjoy to the best advantage; **Most Reverend** title of archbishop or Irish RC bishop. [OE]

-most *suffix* forming adjectives with superlative sense from prepositions and other words indicating relative position (*foremost, inmost, topmost, uttermost*). [OE]

mostly *adv.* for the most part. [MOST]

mot /məʊ/ *n.* witty saying; ***mot juste*** /ʒuːst/ exactly appropriate expression. [F, = word]

MOT *abbr.* Ministry of Transport; (in full **MOT test**) *colloq.* compulsory annual test of motor vehicles of more than a specified age.

mote *n.* particle of dust. [OE]

motel /məʊˈtel/ *n.* roadside hotel or group of furnished cabins accommodating motorists and their vehicles. [*mo*tor ho*tel*]

motet /məʊˈtet/ *n.* short usu. unaccompanied Church anthem. [F (MOT)]

moth *n.* lepidopterous insect like butterfly but without knobbed antennae and mainly nocturnal; insect of this kind breeding in cloth etc., on which its larvae feed; **moth-eaten** damaged or destroyed by moths, antiquated, time-worn. [OE]

mothball *n.* small ball of naphthalene etc. placed in stored clothes to keep away moths; **in mothballs** stored out of use for considerable time.

mother /ˈmʌðə/ **1** *n.* female parent; quality or condition etc. that gives rise to something else (*necessity is the mother of invention*); head of female religious community; title used to or of an elderly woman. **2** *v.t.* give birth to, be the origin of; protect as a mother does. **3 Mother Carey's chicken** stormy petrel; **mother country** country in relation to its colonies; **mother earth** earth as mother of its inhabitants; **Mothering Sunday** fourth Sunday in Lent, with old custom of giving one's mother a gift; **mother-in-law** (*pl.* **mothers-in-law**) wife's or husband's mother; **mother-of-pearl** smooth shining iridescent substance forming inner layer of oyster etc. shell; **Mother's Day** = *Mothering Sunday*; **mother tongue** one's native language. **4 motherhood** *n.* [OE]

mothercraft *n.* skill in looking after one's children as a mother.

motherland *n.* one's native land.

motherly *a.* having or showing the good qualities of a mother; **motherliness** *n.*

mothproof **1** *a.* (of clothes) treated so as to repel moths. **2** *v.t.* treat (clothes) thus. [MOTH]

mothy *a.* infested with moths.

motif /məʊˈtiːf/ *n.* distinctive feature or dominant idea in artistic or literary or musical composition; ornament sewn separately on to garment; ornament on vehicle identifying maker etc. [F (MOTIVE)]

motion /ˈməʊʃ(ə)n/ **1** *n.* moving; manner of moving the body in walking etc.; change of posture, gesture; formal proposal in deliberative assembly; application, usu. interlocutory, for order from judge; evacuation of bowels; (in *sing.* or *pl.*) faeces. **2** *v.* direct (person) by gesture etc.; make such gesture (*to* person). **3 go through the motions** do thing perfunctorily or superficially; **in motion** not at rest, moving; **motion picture** film recording story or events with movement as in real life. [F f. L (MOVE)]

motionless *a.* not moving.

motivate /ˈməʊtɪveɪt/ *v.t.* supply motive to, be motive of; cause (person) to act in a particular way; stimulate interest of (person in activity); **motivation** /-ˈveɪʃ(ə)n/ *n.* [foll.]

motive /ˈməʊtɪv/ **1** *n.* what induces a person to act in a particular way; motif. **2** *a.* tending to initiate movement; concerned with movement. **3 motive power** moving or impelling power, esp. source of energy used to drive machinery. [F f. L *motivus* (MOVE)]

motley /ˈmɒtlɪ/ **1** *a.* diversified in colour; of varied character (*a motley crew*). **2** *n. hist.* jester's particoloured dress. [orig. unkn.]

moto-cross /ˈməʊtəʊkrɒs/ *n.* cross-country racing on motor cycles. [foll., CROSS]

motor /ˈməʊtə/ **1** *n.* thing that imparts motion; machine (esp. internal-combustion engine) supplying motive power for vehicle etc. or for other device with moving parts; = *motor car*. **2** *a.* giving or imparting or producing motion; driven by motor (*motor boat*); of or for motor vehicles. **3** *v.* go or convey in motor car. **4 motor bicycle** motor cycle, moped; **motor bike** *colloq.* = *motor cycle*; **motor car** small motor vehicle for carrying passengers; **motor cycle** two-wheeled motor-driven road vehicle without pedal propulsion; **motor-cyclist** rider of motor cycle; **motor nerve** nerve carrying impulses from brain or spinal cord to muscle; **motor vehicle** vehicle driven by a motor (esp. an internal-combustion engine). [L (MOVE)]

motorcade /ˈməʊtəkeɪd/ *n.* procession or parade of motor cars. [prec., after *cavalcade*]

motorist *n.* driver of motor car. [MOTOR]

motorize *v.* equip with motor transport; equip (device etc.) with motor.

motorman *n.* driver of (esp. underground) train.

motorway *n.* road designed for fast motor traffic.

mottle /ˈmɒt(ə)l/ *v.t.* (esp. in *p.p.*) mark with spots or smears of colour. [back-form. f. MOTLEY]

motto /ˈmɒtəʊ/ *n.* (*pl.* **mottoes**) maxim adopted as rule of conduct; phrase or sentence accompanying coat of arms; sentence inscribed on object; verses etc. in paper cracker. [It., as MOT]

mould[1] /məʊld/ **1** *n.* hollow container into which molten metal etc. is poured or soft material is pressed to harden in required shape; vessel used to give shape to puddings etc.; pudding etc. so shaped; form or shape, esp. of animal body; pattern or template used in making mouldings. **2** *v.t.* bring into particular shape or form; influence at early stage of development. [F *modle* f. L MODULUS]

mould[2] /məʊld/ *n.* furry growth of fungi on things of animal or vegetable origin that lie for some time in moist warm air. [ON]

mould[3] /məʊld/ *n.* loose earth, upper soil of cultivated land, esp. when rich in organic matter. [OE]

moulder *v.i.* decay to dust, rot or decline (*away*). [prec. or Scand.]

moulding *n.* moulded object, esp. ornamental strip of wood; ornamental variety of outline in cornices etc. of building; similar shape in woodwork etc. [MOULD[1]]

mouldy *a.* covered with mould; out-of-date, stale; *sl.* dull, miserable; **mouldiness** *n.* [MOULD[2]]

moult /məʊlt/ **1** *v.* (of bird) shed feathers, shed (feathers), in changing plumage; (of animal) shed hair, shell, etc. **2** *n.* moulting. [OE f. L *muto* change]

mound *n.* elevation of earth or stones, esp. of earth heaped over grave; hillock; heap or pile. [orig. unkn.]

mount[1] **1** *v.* get on (horse etc.) in order to ride; set on horseback; climb on to; ascend (hill, stairs, etc.); move upwards; rise to higher rank or power; increase in amount or intensity; put or fix in position for use or exhibition; put (picture) in mount or (gem etc.) in gold etc.; fix (object) on microscope slide; prepare (specimens etc.) for display or preservation; take action to effect (programme etc., esp. military offensive); place on guard (*mount guard over it*); put (play) on stage. **2** *n.* horse for person to ride; margin surrounding picture etc.; card on which drawing etc. is mounted; setting for gem etc. [F f. Rmc f. L (foll.)]

mount[2] *n.* mountain or hill (*archaic* exc. before name: *Mount Everest*). [OE & F f. L *mons mont-*]

mountain /ˈmaʊntɪn/ *n.* large high natural elevation of ground; large heap or pile, huge quantity *of*; large surplus stock (*butter mountain*); **mountain ash** tree bearing scarlet berries, rowan; **mountain dew** *colloq.* whisky esp. illicitly distilled; **mountain goat** white goatlike animal of Rocky Mountains etc.; **mountain lion** puma; **mountain sickness** malady caused by rarefied air at great heights. [F f. L (prec.)]

mountaineer /maʊntɪˈnɪə/ **1** *n.* one skilled in mountain-climbing. **2** *v.* climb mountains as recreation.

mountainous *a.* having many mountains; huge.
mountainside *n.* sloping side of mountain.
mountebank /'maʊntɪbæŋk/ *n.* swindler, charlatan; *hist.* itinerant quack. [It., = mount on bench]
mounted *a.* serving on horseback etc. (*mounted police*). [MOUNT[1]]
Mountie *n. colloq.* member of Royal Canadian Mounted Police. [abbr.]
mourn /mɔ:n/ *v.* feel or show deep sorrow or regret for (dead person, lost or regretted thing); grieve *for* or *over*. [OE]
mourner *n.* one who mourns; one who attends funeral.
mournful *a.* doleful, sad, expressing mourning; **mournfully** *adv.*
mourning *n.* expressing sorrow, esp. by wearing black clothes; such clothes.
mouse 1 *n.* (*pl.* **mice**) small rodent, esp. species infesting houses etc.; shy or timid person. **2** /also maʊz/ *v.i.* (of cat, owl, etc.) hunt mice. [OE]
mousetrap *n.* trap for catching mice; *colloq.* cheese of poor quality.
moussaka /mʊ'sɑ:kə, -sɑ:'kɑ:/ *n.* Greek dish of minced meat, aubergines, etc. [Gk or Turk.]
mousse /mu:s/ *n.* dish of cold whipped cream or similar substance flavoured with fruit, chocolate, or meat or fish purée. [F, = froth]
moustache /mə'stɑ:ʃ/ *n.* hair left to grow on man's upper lip. [F f. It f. Gk *mustax*]
mousy /'maʊsɪ/ *a.* greyish-brown; shy, timid; quiet. [MOUSE]
mouth 1 /maʊθ/ *n.* (*pl.* /maʊðz/) external orifice in head, with cavity behind it containing apparatus for biting and chewing and vocal organs; this cavity; similar opening, e.g. of cave, trumpet, volcano, etc.; place where river enters sea; individual as needing sustenance (*an extra mouth to feed*). **2** /maʊð/ *v.* utter or speak with affectation, declaim; grimace, move lips silently. **3 mouth-organ** thin rectangular musical instrument played by blowing and sucking air through it; **put words into person's mouth** tell him what to say, represent him as having said them; **take words out of person's mouth** say what he was about to say. [OE]
mouthful *n.* quantity of food that fills the mouth; small quantity (*of* food etc.); something difficult to say.
mouthpiece *n.* part of pipe, musical instrument, telephone, etc., placed between or near lips; person who speaks for another or others.
mouthwash *n.* liquid for rinsing mouth or gargling.
movable /'mu:vəb(ə)l/ *a.* that can be moved; varying in date from year to year (*movable feast*). [foll.]
move /mu:v/ **1** *v.* (cause to) change position or posture; put or keep in motion, rouse, stir; make a move in board-game, change position of (man or piece); go or pass (*about*, *away*, etc.) from place to place; move house; be socially active *in* specified group etc.; affect (person) *with* (emotion); prompt or incline (person *to* action, *to do*); stimulate (person *to* laughter, anger, etc.); cause (bowels) to be evacuated, (of bowels) be moved; propose (resolution, *that* thing be done) in deliberative assembly; initiate action; make request or application *for*; (of merchandise) be sold. **2** *n.* act or process of moving; change of residence, business premises, etc.; step taken to secure object; changing position of man or piece in board-game, player's turn to do this. **3 get a move on** *colloq.* hurry; **make a move** initiate action; **move house** change one's place of residence; **move in** take possession of new residence etc.; **move over** (or **up**) adjust one's position to make room for another; **on the move** progressing, moving about. [AF f. L *moveo*]
movement *n.* moving or being moved; moving part of mechanism; principal division of a musical work; body of persons with common object, campaign undertaken by these (*the peace movement*); motion of bowels.
movie *n. US sl.* motion picture.
moving *a.* emotionally affecting.
mow /məʊ/ *v.t.* (*p.p.* **mowed** or **mown**) cut (grass etc.) with scythe or machine; cut down grass of (lawn) or produce of (field) thus; **mow down** kill or destroy randomly or in great numbers. [OE]
mower *n.* mowing machine, esp. lawnmower; person who mows.
MP *abbr.* Member of Parliament.
mp *abbr. mezzo piano.*
m.p.g. *abbr.* miles per gallon.
m.p.h. *abbr.* miles per hour.
Mr /'mɪstə/ *n.* (*pl.* MESSRS) title of man without higher title, or prefixed to designation of office etc. (*Mr Jones*; *Mr Speaker*). [abbr. of MISTER]
Mrs /'mɪsɪz/ *n.* (*pl.* same or **Mesdames**) title of married woman without higher title. [abbr. of MISTRESS]
Ms /mɪz/ *n.* title of woman without higher title, whether or not married. [comb. of MRS, MISS[2]]
MS *abbr.* manuscript; multiple sclerosis.
M.Sc. *abbr.* Master of Science.
MSS /em'esɪz/ *abbr.* manuscripts.
Mt. *abbr.* Mount.

mu /mju:/ *n.* twelfth letter of Greek alphabet (M, μ). [Gk]

much 1 *a.* existing in great quantity (*much trouble*; *too much noise*). **2** *n.* great quantity (*much of that is true*); noteworthy or outstanding thing (*not much to look at*). **3** *adv.* in great degree (*much to my surprise*; *much better*; *much the best*; *I much regret it*); often, for a large part of one's time (*do you play much?*); approximately (*is much the same*). **4 as much** that amount (*as much again*; *I thought as much*); **a bit much** *colloq.* rather extreme or excessive; **much as** though ... much (*cannot come, much as I want to*); **much of a muchness** very nearly the same or alike; **not much of a** *colloq.* not a great, a somewhat poor. [MICKLE]

mucilage /ˈmju:sɪlɪdʒ/ *n.* viscous substance extracted from plants; adhesive gum. [F f. L (MUCUS)]

muck 1 *n.* farmyard manure; *colloq.* dirt, filth; *colloq.* mess. **2** *v.* manure; make dirty. **3 make a muck of** *sl.* bungle; **muck about** (or **around**) *sl.* potter or fool about, interfere *with*; **muck in** *colloq.* share tasks etc. equally (*with* another); **muck out** remove manure from; **muck-raking** searching out and revealing scandal; **muck sweat** *colloq.* profuse sweat; **muck up** *sl.* bungle, spoil. [Scand.]

muckle /ˈmʌk(ə)l/ var. of MICKLE.

mucky *a.* covered with muck, dirty. [MUCK]

mucous /ˈmju:kəs/ *a.* of or covered with mucus; **mucous membrane** skin lining nose and other cavities of the body; **mucosity** /-ˈkɒsɪtɪ/ *n.* [L *mucosus* (foll.)]

mucus /ˈmju:kəs/ *n.* slimy substance secreted by mucous membrane. [L]

mud *n.* wet soft earth; hard ground from drying of area of this; **fling** (or **throw** etc.) **mud** speak slanderously; **mud-flat** stretch of muddy land uncovered at low tide; **mud pack** cosmetic paste applied thickly to face; **one's name is mud** one is in disgrace. [G]

muddle /ˈmʌd(ə)l/ **1** *v.* bring into disorder, jumble (*up*); bewilder, confuse; act in confused and ineffective way; mismanage (matter). **2** *n.* disorder, muddled condition. **3 muddle along** (or **on**) progress in haphazard way; **muddle-headed** confused, stupid; **muddle through** succeed despite one's inefficiency etc. [perh. Du., rel. to prec.]

muddy 1 *a.* like mud; covered in or full of mud; confused, obscure. **2** *v.* make muddy. **3 muddily** *adv.*; **muddiness** *n.* [MUD]

mudguard *n.* curved strip or cover over wheel to protect rider etc. from being splashed by mud etc.

muesli /ˈmu:zlɪ/ *n.* food of crushed cereals, dried fruit, nuts, etc. [Swiss G]

muezzin /mu:ˈezɪn/ *n.* Muslim crier who proclaims hours of prayer usu. from minaret. [Arab.]

muff[1] *n.* tubular covering esp. of fur in which hands are put to keep them warm. [Du. *mof* f. med.L]

muff[2] *v.t.* bungle; miss (catch, ball, etc.); blunder in (theatrical part etc.).

muffin /ˈmʌfɪn/ *n.* light flat round yeast cake eaten toasted and buttered. [orig. unkn.]

muffle /ˈmʌf(ə)l/ *v.t.* wrap or cover for warmth or protection, or to deaden sound; (usu. in *p.p.*) repress, deaden sound of. [perh. F (*moufle* thick glove, MUFF[1])]

muffler *n.* scarf or wrap worn for warmth; thing used to deaden sound.

mufti /ˈmʌftɪ/ *n.* plain clothes worn by one who normally wears uniform (esp. *in mufti*). [Arab.]

mug[1] **1** *n.* drinking-vessel, usu. cylindrical and with handle and used without saucer; its contents; *sl.* face or mouth; *sl.* gullible person, simpleton. **2** *v.* (**-gg-**) attack and rob, esp. in public place. **3 a mug's game** unprofitable or senseless occupation. [Scand.]

mug[2] *v.* (**-gg-**) learn (subject) by concentrated study (with *up*). [orig. unkn.]

muggins /ˈmʌgɪnz/ *n.* (*pl.* **mugginses** or same) *colloq.* person who allows himself to be outwitted. [perh. surname]

muggy /ˈmʌgɪ/ *a.* (of weather etc.) oppressively humid and warm; **mugginess** *n.* [ON]

Muhammadan /məˈhæməd(ə)n/ **1** *a.* of Muhammad; Muslim. **2** *n.* a Muslim. [*Muhammad*, prophet]

mulatto /mju:ˈlætəʊ/ *n.* (*pl.* **mulattos**) person of mixed White and Black parentage. [Sp. *mulato* young mule]

mulberry /ˈmʌlbərɪ/ *n.* tree bearing purple or white edible berries, and leaves which are used to feed silkworms; fruit of this; dull purplish-red. [OE f. L *morum* mulberry, BERRY]

mulch 1 *n.* mixture of wet organic material spread to protect roots of newly planted trees etc. **2** *v.t.* treat with mulch. [OE, = soft]

mulct *v.t.* extract money from by fine or taxation or by fraudulent means. [F f. L *mulcta* fine]

mule[1] *n.* animal that is offspring of mare and male ass, or *loosely* of she-ass and stallion (*properly* HINNY); a kind of spinning-machine. [F f. L *mulus*]

mule[2] *n.* backless slipper. [F]

muleteer /mju:lɪ'tɪə/ *n.* mule-driver. [F *muletier* (MULE[1])]
mulish *a.* obstinate. [MULE[1]]
mull[1] *v.* ponder (*over*). [prob. Du.]
mull[2] *v.t.* make (wine or beer) into hot drink with sugar, spices, etc. [orig. unkn.]
mull[3] *n. Sc.* promontory (*Mull of Kintyre*). [orig. uncert.]
mullah /'mʊlə/ *n.* Muslim learned in Islamic theology and sacred law. [ult. Arab. *mawlā*]
mullet /'mʌlɪt/ *n.* sea-fish of various kinds valued for food (*red mullet*; *grey mullet*). [F *mulet* f. L *mullus* f. Gk]
mulligatawny /mʌlɪgə'tɔ:nɪ/ *n.* highly seasoned soup orig. from India. [Tamil, = pepper-water]
mullion /'mʌljən/ *n.* vertical bar dividing lights in window. [prob. F *moinel* middle (MEAN[3])]
multi- *prefix* many. [L (*multus* much, many)]
multi-access /mʌltɪ'ækses/ *a.* (of computer system) allowing access to central processor from several terminals at the same time.
multicoloured /mʌltɪ'kʌləd/ *a.* of many colours.
multifarious /mʌltɪ'feərɪəs/ *a.* many and various; having great variety. [L *multifarius*]
multiform /'mʌltɪfɔ:m/ *a.* having many forms, of many kinds. [MULTI-]
multilateral /mʌltɪ'lætər(ə)l/ *a.* (of agreement, treaty, etc.) in which three or more parties participate; having many sides.
multilingual /mʌltɪ'lɪŋgw(ə)l/ *a.* in or using or speaking many languages.
multimillionaire /mʌltɪmɪljə'neə/ *n.* person with fortune of several millions.
multinational /mʌltɪ'næʃən(ə)l/ **1** *a.* operating in several countries. **2** *n.* multinational company.
multiple /'mʌltɪp(ə)l/ **1** *a.* having several parts, elements, or components; many and various. **2** *n.* quantity that contains another some number of times without remainder (*56 is a multiple of 7*). **3 least** (or **lowest**) **common multiple** least quantity that is a multiple of two or more given quantities; **multiple-choice** (of question in examination) accompanied by several possible answers from which correct one is to be selected; **multiple sclerosis** see SCLEROSIS. [F f. L *multiplus* (foll.)]
multiplex /'mʌltɪpleks/ *a.* of many elements, manifold. [L (MULTI-, *-plex, -plicis* -fold)]
multiplicand /mʌltɪplɪ'kænd/ *n.* quantity to be multiplied by another. [med.L (MULTIPLY)]
multiplication /mʌltɪplɪ'keɪʃ(ə)n/ *n.* multiplying, esp. the arithmetical process; **multiplication sign** ×, as 2 × 3; **multiplication table** table of products of pairs of factors, esp. from 1 to 12. [F or L (MULTIPLY)]
multiplicity /mʌltɪ'plɪsɪtɪ/ *n.* manifold variety; great number *of*. [L (MULTIPLEX)]
multiplier /'mʌltɪplaɪə/ *n.* quantity by which multiplicand is multiplied. [foll.]
multiply /'mʌltɪplaɪ/ *v.* obtain from (number) another that is a specified number of times its value (*multiply 6 by 4 and get 24*); increase in number, esp. by procreation; produce large number of (instances); breed (animals); propagate (plants). [F f. L *multiplico* (MULTIPLEX)]
multi-purpose /mʌltɪ'pɜ:pəs/ *a.* serving many purposes. [MULTI-]
multiracial /mʌltɪ'reɪʃ(ə)l/ *a.* composed of or concerning people of several races.
multi-storey /mʌltɪ'stɔ:rɪ/ *a.* having several storeys.
multitude /'mʌltɪtju:d/ *n.* crowd of people; great number (*of*); **the multitude** the common people. [F f. L]
multitudinous /mʌltɪ'tju:dɪnəs/ *a.* very numerous; consisting of many individuals. [L (prec.)]
mum[1] *a. colloq.* silent (*keep mum*); **mum's the word** say nothing. [imit.]
mum[2] *v.i.* (**-mm-**) act in dumb show. [MLG *mummen*; cf. prec.]
mum[3] *n. colloq.* = MUMMY[2].
mumble /'mʌmb(ə)l/ **1** *v.* speak or utter indistinctly. **2** *n.* indistinct utterance. [MUM[1]]
mumbo-jumbo /mʌmbəʊ'dʒʌmbəʊ/ *n.* (*pl.* **mumbo-jumbos**) meaningless ritual; language or action intended to mystify or confuse; object of senseless veneration. [*Mumbo Jumbo*, supposed African idol]
mummer *n.* actor in traditional mime. [F *momeur* (MUM[1])]
mummery *n.* performance by mummers; ridiculous (esp. religious) ceremonial. [F *momerie* (prec.)]
mummify /'mʌmɪfaɪ/ *v.t.* preserve (body) as mummy; **mummification** /-fɪ'keɪʃ(ə)n/ *n.* [foll.]
mummy[1] /'mʌmɪ/ *n.* body of human being or animal embalmed for burial, esp. in ancient Egypt. [ult. f. Pers. *mūm* wax]
mummy[2] /'mʌmɪ/ *n. colloq.* mother. [imit. of child's pronunc.]
mumps *n.* infectious disease with swelling of neck and face. [imit. of mouth-shape]
munch *v.* eat steadily with marked action of jaws. [imit.]

mundane /mʌn'deɪn/ *a.* dull or routine; of this world, worldly. [F f. L (*mundus* world)]

municipal /mju:'nɪsɪp(ə)l *a.* of or concerning a municipality or its self-government; **municipally** *adv.* [L (*municipium* Roman city)]

municipality /mju:nɪsɪ'pælɪtɪ/ *n.* town or district having local self-government; governing body of this. [F (prec.)]

munificent /mju:'nɪfɪsənt/ *a.* (of giver or gift) splendidly generous; **munificence** *n.* (L (*munus* gift, -FIC)]

muniment /'mju:nɪmənt/ *n.* (usu. in *pl.*) document kept as evidence of rights or privileges. [F f. L (*munio* fortify)]

munition /mju:'nɪʃ(ə)n/ *n. pl.* military weapons, ammunition, equipment, and stores. [F f. L, = fortification (prec.)]

mural /'mjʊər(ə)l/ **1** *a.* of or like a wall; on a wall (*mural paintings*). **2** *n.* mural painting etc. [F f. L (*murus* wall)]

murder 1 *n.* intentional and unlawful killing of human being by another; *colloq.* highly troublesome or dangerous state of affairs. **2** *v.t.* kill (human being) unlawfully with malice aforethought; kill wickedly or inhumanly; *colloq.* spoil by bad performance, mispronunciation, etc.; *colloq.* utterly defeat. **3 cry blue murder** *sl.* make extravagant outcry; **get away with murder** *colloq.* do whatever one wishes. **4 murderer** *n.*; **murderess** *n. fem.* [OE]

murderous *a.* (of person, weapon, action, etc.) capable of or intent on or involving murder or great harm.

murk *n.* darkness, poor visibility. [prob. Scand.]

murky *a.* dark, gloomy; (of liquid etc.) thick and dirty; suspiciously obscure (*murky past*); **murkily** *adv.*; **murkiness** *n.*

murmur /'mɜ:mə/ **1** *n.* subdued continuous sound as of waves, brook, etc.; softly spoken or nearly inarticulate speech; subdued expression of discontent. **2** *v.* make murmur; utter (words) softly; complain in low tones. [F or L]

murmurous *a.* with murmuring sound.

murphy *n. sl.* potato. [Ir. surname]

murrain /'mʌrɪn/ *n.* infectious disease in cattle. [AF *moryn*]

muscadine /'mʌskədi:n, -daɪn/ *n.* musk-flavoured kind of grape. [prob. foll.]

muscat /'mʌskət/ *n.* muscadine; wine made from this. [F f. Prov. (MUSK)]

muscatel /mʌskə'tel/ *n.* muscadine; wine or raisin made from this.

muscle /'mʌs(ə)l/ **1** *n.* any of the contractile fibrous bands or bundles that produce movement in animal body; that part of the animal body which is composed of muscles, chief constituent of flesh; power, strength. **2** *v.i. sl.* force one's way *in*. **3 muscle-bound** with muscles stiff and inelastic through excessive exercise or training; **muscleman** man with highly-developed muscles, esp. as intimidator; **not move a muscle** be perfectly motionless. [F f. L dimin. of *mus* mouse]

Muscovite /'mʌskəvaɪt/ **1** *a.* of Moscow. **2** *n.* citizen of Moscow. [foll.]

Muscovy duck /'mʌskəvɪ/ crested duck with red markings on head. [*Muscovy*, principality of Moscow]

muscular /'mʌskjʊlə/ *a.* of or affecting muscles; having well-developed muscles; **muscularity** /-'lærɪtɪ/ *n.* [MUSCLE]

muse[1] /mju:z/ *v.* ponder, meditate; say meditatively. [F]

Muse[2] /mju:z/ *n.* any of nine sister goddesses in Greek and Roman mythology, presiding over branches of learning and the arts; (**muse**) poet's inspiring genius. [F or L f. Gk *mousa*]

museum /mju:'zi:əm/ *n.* building used for exhibition and storage of objects illustrating antiquities, natural history, arts, etc.; **museum piece** specimen of art, manufacture, etc. fit for a museum, old-fashioned person or machine, etc. [L f. Gk (prec.)]

mush[1] *n.* soft pulp; feeble sentimentality; *US* maize porridge. [app. var. of MASH]

mush[2] *v.i. N. Amer.* travel across snow with dog-sledge; (as command to sledge-dogs) get moving. [prob. corrupt. F *marchons* (MARCH[2])]

mushroom /'mʌʃrʊm/ **1** *n.* edible fungus with stem and domed cap. **2** *v.i.* spring up rapidly; expand and flatten like a mushroom cap; gather mushrooms. **3 mushroom cloud** cloud of mushroom shape, esp. from nuclear explosion. [F *mousseron* f. L]

mushy *a.* like mush, soft; feebly sentimental; **mushily** *adv.*; **mushiness** *n.* [MUSH[1]]

music /'mju:zɪk/ *n.* art of combining vocal and/or instrumental sounds in harmonious and expressive ways; sounds so produced; musical composition, printed or written score of this; pleasant natural sound; **face the music** face one's critics etc., not shirk consequences; **music centre** equipment combining radio, record-player, and tape-recorder; **music-hall** variety entertainment with singing, dancing, etc., hall or theatre for this; **music-stool** stool with adjustable height of seat, for pianist; **music to one's ears** what one is pleased to hear. [F f. L f. Gk (MUSE[1])]

musical **1** *a.* of music; (of sound etc.) melodious or harmonious; fond of or skilled in music; set to or accompanied by music. **2** *n.* film or play etc. with music and song as principal feature. **3** **musical box** box containing mechanism (usu. revolving toothed cylinder striking comblike metal plate) for playing certain tune when opened; **musical chairs** musical party game in which players are eliminated one by one. **4** **musicality** /-'kælɪtɪ/ *n.*; **musically** *adv.*

musician /mju:'zɪʃ(ə)n/ *n.* person skilled in music, esp. one practising it professionally; **musicianship** *n.* [F (MUSIC)]

musicology /mju:zɪ'kɒlədʒɪ/ *n.* study of history and forms of music as distinct from study to perform or compose it; **musicologist** *n.* [-LOGY]

musk *n.* substance secreted by male musk-deer used as basis of perfumes; plant which has or used to have musky smell; **musk-deer** small hornless ruminant of Central Asia; **musk-duck** duck with musky smell; **musk-melon** common yellow melon; **musk-ox** shaggy ruminant with curved horns; **musk-rat** large N. American aquatic rodent with musky smell, its fur; **musk-rose** rambling rose with musky fragrance. [L *muscus* f. Pers.]

musket /'mʌskɪt/ *n. hist.* infantryman's (esp. smooth-bored) light gun. [F f. It. *moschetto* crossbow bolt]

musketeer /mʌskɪ'tɪə/ *n.* soldier armed with musket.

musketry /'mʌskɪtrɪ/ *n.* muskets; art of using muskets or rifles; troops armed with muskets. [F (MUSKET)]

musky *a.* smelling like musk; **muskiness** *n.* [MUSK]

Muslim /'mʊzlɪm/ **1** *n.* follower of religion revealed by Muhammad, with Allah as God. **2** *a.* of Muslims or their religion. [Arab. (ISLAM)]

muslin /'mʌzlɪn/ *n.* fine delicately woven cotton fabric. [F f. It. (*Mussolo* Mosul in Iraq)]

musquash /'mʌskwɒʃ/ *n.* musk-rat; its fur. [Algonquian]

mussel /'mʌs(ə)l/ *n.* bivalve mollusc, esp. edible kind. [OE (MUSCLE)]

must[1] **1** *v. aux.* (*pres.* and *past* **must**; no other parts used) expressing obligation (*we must find it*), insistence (*I must ask you to leave*), rightness or advisability (*we must see what can be done*), certainty or likelihood (*we must win in the end; you must be her sister*). **2** *n. colloq.* thing that must be done, seen, etc. [OE]

must[2] *n.* grape-juice before end of fermentation; new wine. [OE f. L]

mustache *US* var. of MOUSTACHE.

mustang /'mʌstæŋ/ *n.* wild horse of Mexico and California. [Sp.]

mustard /'mʌstəd/ *n.* plant with yellow flowers; condiment made by grinding seeds of this and making them into paste with water or vinegar; brownish-yellow colour; **mustard gas** colourless oily liquid or its vapour, a powerful irritant; **mustard plaster** plaster containing mustard, applied to the skin as poultice. [F f. Rmc (MUST[2])]

muster **1** *v.* collect (orig. soldiers) for inspection, to check numbers, etc.; bring or come together; summon (courage, strength, etc.). **2** *n.* assembling of persons for inspection etc. **3** **pass muster** be accepted as adequate. [F f. L (*monstro* show)]

mustn't /'mʌs(ə)nt/ *colloq.* = *must not.*

musty *a.* mouldy, stale; antiquated; **mustily** *adv.*; **mustiness** *n.* [perh. alt. of *moisty* (MOIST)]

mutable /'mju:təb(ə)l/ *a.* liable to change; fickle; **mutability** /-'bɪlɪtɪ/ *n.* [L (*muto* change)]

mutant /'mju:tənt/ **1** *a.* resulting from mutation. **2** *n.* mutant form.

mutate /mju:'teɪt/ *v.* undergo mutation; cause to do this. [foll.]

mutation /mju:'teɪʃ(ə)n/ *n.* change, alteration; genetic change which when transmitted to offspring gives rise to heritable variation; mutant; umlaut. [L (*muto* change)]

mutatis mutandis /mu:'tɑ:tɪs mu:'tændɪs/ with due alteration of details (in comparing cases). [L]

mute /mju:t/ **1** *a.* silent, refraining from speech; not emitting articulate sound; (of person or animal) dumb; (of letter) not pronounced; not expressed in speech (*mute adoration*). **2** *n.* dumb person; actor whose part is in dumb show; device to deaden sound of musical instrument; mute consonant. **3** *v.t.* deaden or soften sound of (esp. musical instrument); tone down, make less intense. **4** **mute swan** common white swan. [F f. L *mutus*]

mutilate /'mju:tɪleɪt/ *v.t.* deprive (person or animal) of limb or organ; destroy use of (limb or organ); render (book etc.) imperfect by excision etc.; **mutilation** /-'leɪʃ(ə)n/ *n.*; **mutilator** *n.* [L (*mutilus* maimed)]

mutineer /mju:tɪ'nɪə/ *n.* one who mutinies. [F f. Rmc (MOVE)]

mutinous /'mju:tɪnəs/ *a.* rebellious, ready to mutiny.

mutiny /'mju:tɪnɪ/ **1** *n.* open revolt against authority, esp. by servicemen against officers. **2** *v.i.* engage in mutiny, revolt (*against*).

mutt *n. sl.* ignorant or stupid person; *derog.* dog. [abbr. of *mutton-head*]

mutter 1 *v.* speak low in barely audible manner; utter (words etc.) thus; murmur, grumble (*against* or *at*); say in secret. **2** *n.* muttering; muttered words. [rel. to MUTE]

mutton /'mʌt(ə)n/ *n.* flesh of sheep as food; **mutton dressed as lamb** middle-aged or elderly woman dressed to look young; **mutton-head** *colloq.* dull, stupid person; **muttony** *a.* [F f. med.L *multo* sheep]

mutual /'mju:tjʊəl/ *a.* (of feeling, action, etc.) felt or done by each to or towards the other (*mutual affection*); standing in (specified) relation to each other (*mutual well-wishers*); *colloq.* (**D**) common to two or more persons (*mutual friend*); **mutuality** /-'ælɪtɪ/ *n.*; **mutually** *adv.* [F f. L *mutuus* borrowed]

Muzak /'mju:zæk/ *n.* (**P**) system of music transmission for playing in public place; recorded light music as background. [MUSIC]

muzzle /'mʌz(ə)l/ **1** *n.* projecting part of animal's head including nose and mouth; open end of firearm; contrivance of strap or wire etc. put over animal's head to prevent its biting, eating, etc. **2** *v.t.* put muzzle on; impose silence on. [F *musel* f. med.L *musum*]

muzzy /'mʌzɪ/ *a.* confused, dazed; (of sound etc.) indistinct; **muzzily** *adv.*; **muzziness** *n.* [orig. unkn.]

MW *abbr.* megawatt(s).

my /maɪ/ *poss. a.* of or belonging to me; also in affectionate collocations (*my boy*; *my dear fellow*) and as exclamation of surprise. [MINE[1]]

Mycenaean /maɪsə'ni:ən/ **1** *a.* of late Bronze-Age civilization in Greece (*c.* 1500–1100 BC) depicted in Homeric poems and represented by finds at Mycenae. **2** *n.* person of this civilization. [L *Mycenaeus*]

mycology /maɪ'kɒlədʒɪ/ *n.* study of fungi; **mycologist** *n.* [Gk *mukēs* mushroom]

myna, mynah var. of MINA.

myopia /maɪ'əʊpɪə/ *n.* short-sightedness; **myopic** /-'ɒpɪk/ *a.* [Gk (*muō* shut, *ōps* eye)]

myriad /'mɪrɪəd/ *literary* **1** *n.* indefinitely great number; ten thousand. **2** *a.* innumerable. [L f. Gk (*murioi* 10,000)]

myrmidon /'mɜ:mɪd(ə)n/ *n.* hired ruffian, base servant. [*Myrmidons*, followers of Achilles]

myrrh /mɜ:/ *n.* gum resin used in perfumes, medicine, and incense. [OE f. L *myrrha* f. Gk]

myrtle /'mɜ:t(ə)l/ *n.* evergreen shrub with shiny leaves and white scented flowers. [L f. Gk *murtos*]

myself /maɪ'self/ *pron.* emphat. & refl. form of I[2], ME[1] (for uses cf. HERSELF). [OE (ME[1], SELF)]

mysterious /mɪ'stɪərɪəs/ *a.* full of or wrapped in mystery; (of person) enjoying mystery. [F (foll)]

mystery /'mɪstərɪ/ *n.* inexplicable or secret matter; secrecy or obscurity; practice of making a secret of things; fictional work dealing with puzzling event, esp. crime; religious truth divinely revealed, esp. one beyond human reason; religious rite, esp. (in *pl.*) Eucharist; (in *pl.*) secret religious rites of Greeks, Romans, etc.; miracle play; **make a mystery of** treat as impressive secret; **mystery tour** or **trip** pleasure excursion to unspecified destination. [F or L f. Gk *mustērion* (foll.)]

mystic /'mɪstɪk/ **1** *n.* one who seeks by contemplation and self-surrender to obtain union with or absorption into the Deity, or who believes in spiritual apprehension of truths beyond the understanding. **2** *a.* mysterious and awe-inspiring; spiritually allegorical or symbolic; occult, esoteric; of hidden meaning. [F or L f. Gk (*mustēs* initiated person)]

mystical *a.* of mystics or mysticism; having direct spiritual significance; **mystically** *adv.*

mysticism /'mɪstɪsɪz(ə)m/ *n.* beliefs of mystics.

mystify /'mɪstɪfaɪ/ *v.t.* bewilder, confuse utterly; **mystification** /-fɪ'keɪʃ(ə)n/ *n.* [F (MYSTIC or MYSTERY)]

mystique /mɪ'sti:k/ *n.* atmosphere of mystery and veneration attending some activity or person; a skill or technique impressive to the layman. [F (MYSTIC)]

myth /mɪθ/ *n.* traditional narrative usu. involving supernatural or fancied persons etc. and embodying popular ideas on natural or social phenomena etc.; such narratives collectively; imaginary person or thing; widely held but false notion; allegory (*Platonic myth*). [L f. Gk *muthos*]

mythical *a.* of or existing in myth; imaginary; **mythically** *adv.*

mythology /mɪ'θɒlədʒɪ/ *n.* body of myths; study of myths; **mythological** /mɪθə'lɒdʒɪk(ə)l/ *a.*; **mythologically** /mɪθə'lɒdʒɪkəlɪ/ *adv.*; **mythologist** *n.* [F or L f. Gk (MYTH)]

myxomatosis /mɪksəmə'təʊsɪs/ *n.* virus disease in rabbits. [Gk *muxa* mucus]

N

N, n /en/ *n.* (*pl.* **Ns, N's**) fourteenth letter; indefinite number; **to the nth degree** to the utmost.
N. *abbr.* New; North(ern).
N *abbr.* knight (in chess); newton(s).
n. *abbr.* name; neuter; note.
N *symb.* nitrogen.
Na *symb.* sodium. [L *natrium*]
NAAFI /'næfı/ *abbr.* Navy, Army, and Air Force Institutes (canteen for servicemen).
nab *v.t.* (**-bb-**) *sl.* catch (wrongdoer) in the act, arrest; seize, grab. [orig. unkn.]
nabob /'neıbɒb/ *n. hist.* Muslim official or governor under Mogul empire; *archaic* wealthy luxury-loving person, esp. one who has returned from India with fortune. [Port. or Sp. f. Urdu (NAWAB)]
nacre /'neıkə/ *n.* mother-of-pearl, shell-fish yielding this; **nacreous** *a.* [F]
nadir /'neıdıə/ *n.* point of heavens directly under observer, opposite to zenith; *fig.* lowest point, state or time of deepest depression etc. [F f. Arab., = opposite]
naevus /'ni:vəs/ *n.* (*pl.* **naevi** /-aı/) birth-mark in form of sharply-defined red mark in skin; = MOLE². [L]
nag¹ *v.* (**-gg-**) find fault or scold persistently (with *at*); worry (person) by nagging; (of pain etc.) be persistent. [dial.]
nag² *n. colloq.* horse (esp. for riding). [orig. unkn.]
naiad /'naıæd/ *n.* water-nymph. [L f. Gk]
naïf /nɑ:'i:f/ *a.* = NAÏVE. [F]
nail 1 *n.* horny covering of upper surface of tip of finger or toe; small metal spike hammered in to hold things together or serve as a peg or ornament. **2** *v.t.* fasten with nail(s); secure or catch or arrest (person, thing, attention, etc.); identify, esp. as being spurious; fix (eyes, attention, etc.) *to* or *on*. **3 nail down** bind (person *to* promise etc.), define precisely; **nail in person's coffin** thing hastening person's death; **on the nail** without delay (esp. of payment). [OE]
nainsook /'neınsʊk/ *n.* fine cotton fabric, orig. Indian. [Hindi]
naïve /nɑ:'i:v/ *a.* simple, unaffected, unconsciously artless; (of art etc.) straightforward in style, eschewing subtlety or conventional technique; ***naïveté*** /-'i:vteı/ *n.*; **naïvety** /-'i:vtı/ *n.* [F f. L *nativus* NATIVE]
naked /'neıkıd/ *a.* unclothed, nude; without usual covering or furnishings; unsheathed or unprotected (*naked flame*); undisguised (*naked truth*); (of eye) unassisted by telescope etc. [OE]
namby-pamby /næmbı'pæmbı/ **1** *a.* insipid, sentimental, weak, unmanly. **2** *n.* person of this kind. [derog. form. on name of *Ambrose* Philips, writer]
name 1 *n.* word by which individual person, animal, place, or thing is spoken of or to (*what is your name?*); word denoting object of thought, esp. one applicable to many individuals (*what is the name of those flowers?*); reputation (*a good name*); person as known, famed, etc. (*many great names in the cast*); family, clan. **2** *v.t.* give name to; state name of; mention, specify, cite; nominate or appoint. **3 call person names** address him abusively; **have to one's name** possess; **in the name of** invoking, as representing (*in God's name, in the name of the law*); **in name only** not in reality; **make a name for oneself** become famous; **name-day** day of saint after whom person is named; **name-dropping** familiar mention of famous names as form of boasting; **name-plate** plate with name inscribed on it, identifying occupant etc. **4 nameable** *a.* [OE]
nameless *a.* having no name or no known name; left unnamed (*persons who shall be nameless*); unmentionable, loathsome (*nameless horrors*).
namely *adv.* that is to say, in other words.
namesake *n.* person or thing with same name as another. [prob. orig. *for the name's sake*]
nancy /'nænsı/ *n. sl.* effeminate or homosexual man or boy. [*Nancy*, pet form of *Ann*]
nankeen /næŋ'ki:n/ *n.* yellow cotton cloth; colour of this. [*Nanking* in China]
nanny /'nænı/ *n.* child's nurse or minder; *colloq.* grandma; **nanny-goat** female goat. [as NANCY]
nano- /'nænəʊ, 'neınəʊ/ *in comb.* one thousand millionth. [L f. Gk *nanos* dwarf]
nap¹ 1 *n.* short period of light sleep, esp. during day. **2** *v.i.* (**-pp-**) have nap. **3 catch person napping** take him unawares, find him remiss. [OE]
nap² *n.* surface of cloth consisting of fibre-ends raised, cut even, and smoothed. [LG or Du.]
nap³ 1 *n.* a card-game like whist, with bidding; racing tip claimed to be almost a certainty. **2** *v.t.* (**-pp-**) name (horse) as almost certain winner. **3 go nap** make

the highest bid in nap, *fig.* risk everything. [*Napoleon*]

napalm /ˈneɪpɑːm/ **1** *n.* thickening agent made from naphthalene and coconut oil; jellied petrol made from this, used in bombs. **2** *v.t.* attack with napalm bombs. [NA(PHTHALENE), PALM]

nape *n.* back of the neck. [orig. unkn.]

naphtha /ˈnæfθə/ *n.* inflammable oil distilled from coal etc. [L f. Gk]

naphthalene /ˈnæfθəliːn/ *n.* white crystalline substance obtained in distilling coal-tar.

napkin /ˈnæpkɪn/ *n.* piece of linen etc. used at meals for wiping lips and fingers or protecting clothes; nappy. [F *nappe* f. L *mappa* (MAP) + -KIN]

nappy /ˈnæpɪ/ *n.* piece of material wrapped round waist and between legs of baby to hold or absorb its excreta. [NAPKIN]

narcissism /nɑːˈsɪsɪz(ə)m/ *n.* abnormal self-love or self-admiration; **narcissistic** /-ˈsɪstɪk/ *a.* [*Narkissos*, Gk youth who fell in love with his reflection]

narcissus /nɑːˈsɪsəs/ *n.* (*pl.* **narcissi** /-aɪ/) kind of flowering bulb including daffodil. [L f. Gk]

narcosis /nɑːˈkəʊsɪs/ *n.* insensible state, induction of this. [Gk (*narkē* numbness)]

narcotic /nɑːˈkɒtɪk/ **1** *a.* (of substance) inducing sleep or drowsiness or stupor, etc.; (of drug) affecting the mind. **2** *n.* narcotic substance, drug, or influence. [F or med.L f. Gk]

nard *n.* spikenard; plant yielding this. [L f. Gk]

nark *sl.* **1** *v.t.* annoy, infuriate. **2** *n.* police informer or spy. [Romany *nāk* nose]

narrate /nəˈreɪt/ *v.* recount, tell facts of, relate as story; write or speak narrative; **narration** *n.*; **narrator** *n.* [L *narro*]

narrative /ˈnærətɪv/ **1** *n.* spoken or written account of connected events in order of happening. **2** *a.* of or by narration. [F f. L (prec.)]

narrow /ˈnærəʊ/ **1** *a.* of small width in proportion to length; not broad; confined or confining (esp. *fig.*: *within narrow bounds*); careful, exact; with little margin (*narrow escape*); narrow-minded. **2** *n.* (usu. in *pl.*) narrow part of a sound, strait, river, pass, or street. **3** *v.* make or become narrower, lessen, contract. **4 narrow boat** canal boat; **narrow-minded** intolerant, prejudiced, rigid or restricted in one's views; **narrow seas** English Channel and Irish Sea. [OE]

narwhal /ˈnɑːw(ə)l/ *n.* Arctic mammal the male of which has a long tusk. [Du. f. Da.]

nasal /ˈneɪz(ə)l/ **1** *a.* of the nose; (of letter or sound) pronounced with nose passage open (e.g. *m*, *n*, *ng*); (of voice or speech) having many nasal sounds. **2** *n.* nasal letter or sound. **3 nasally** *adv.* [F or L (*nasus* nose)]

nasalize /ˈneɪzəlaɪz/ *v.* speak nasally; give nasal sound to.

nascent /ˈnæsənt/ *a.* in process of birth, incipient, not mature; **nascence** *n.*; **nascency** *n.* [L (NATAL)]

nasturtium /nəˈstɜːʃəm/ *n.* trailing garden plant with bright orange or yellow or red flowers. [L]

nasty /ˈnɑːstɪ/ *a.* highly unpleasant or disagreeable; (of person) unkind or malicious; difficult to deal with; **nasty piece of work** *colloq.* unpleasant or undesirable person; **nastily** *adv.*; **nastiness** *n.* [orig. unkn.]

Nat. *abbr.* National; Nationalist; Natural.

natal /ˈneɪt(ə)l/ *a.* of or concerning birth. [L *natalis* (*nascor nat-* be born)]

nation /ˈneɪʃ(ə)n/ *n.* community of people of mainly common descent, language, history, or political institutions and usu. sharing one territory and government; **nation-wide** extending over whole nation. [F f. L (NATAL)]

national /ˈnæʃən(ə)l/ **1** *a.* of a or the nation, affecting or concerning a whole nation. **2** *n.* citizen or subject of specified country; one's fellow countryman. **3 the National** the Grand National; **national anthem** song of patriotism or loyalty adopted by nation; **national debt** money owed by State, esp. to its citizens; **National Front** UK political organization with extreme reactionary views on immigration etc.; **national grid** network of high-voltage electric power-lines between major power-stations, metric system of geographical coordinates used in maps of British Isles; **National Guard** *US* State reserve force available for federal use; **National Health Service** system of national medical service financed by taxation; **National Insurance** system of compulsory contribution from employee and employer to provide State assistance in sickness, unemployment, retirement, etc.; **national park** area of countryside under State supervision to preserve its natural state for public enjoyment; **national service** service by conscription in armed forces; **nationally** *adv.* [F (prec.)]

nationalism *n.* patriotic feeling or principles or efforts; policy of national independence; **nationalist** *n.*

nationality /næʃəˈnælɪtɪ/ *n.* status of belonging to a particular nation (*has*

British nationality); distinctive national qualities; being national; ethnic group forming part of one or more political nations.

nationalize /ˈnæʃənəlaɪz/ *v.t.* make national, convert (industry, institution, etc.) to public ownership; **nationalization** /-ˈzeɪʃ(ə)n/ *n.*

native /ˈneɪtɪv/ **1** *a.* inborn or innate, natural *to*; of one's birth, belonging to one by right of birth (*native land*); born in a particular place, indigenous; of the natives of a place; (of metal etc.) found in pure or uncombined state. **2** *n.* one born in a particular place; a local inhabitant; member of non-European or less civilized native people; (in S. Africa) a Black; indigenous animal or plant. [L (NATAL)]

nativity /nəˈtɪvɪtɪ/ *n.* birth, esp. (**the Nativity**) that of Christ; festival celebrating birth of Christ. [F f. L (prec.)]

NATO /ˈneɪtəʊ/ *abbr.* (also **Nato**) North Atlantic Treaty Organization.

natter *colloq.* **1** *v.i.* chat, chatter idly. **2** *n.* chat, idle chatter. [imit., orig. dial.]

natterjack /ˈnætədʒæk/ *n.* a kind of small toad. [perh. f. prec.]

natty /ˈnætɪ/ *a.* neat and trim, dapper; **nattily** *adv.* [cf. NEAT[1]]

natural /ˈnætʃər(ə)l/ **1** *a.* of or concerned with or according to nature; provided or produced by nature (*natural resources*); conforming to ordinary course of nature, normal (*natural death*); physically existing (*the natural world*); innate, inherent, uncultivated (*natural state*); unaffected, easy-mannered; not surprising, to be expected (*natural consequence*); suited to be such by nature (*natural leader*); spontaneous or easy *to* (*comes natural to him*); related by nature only, illegitimate; *Mus.* (of note) not sharp or flat (*B natural*). **2** *n.* person or thing that seems naturally suited (*for* role, purpose, etc.); *Mus.* natural note, sign denoting this; pale fawn colour. **3** **natural gas** gas found in earth's crust, not manufactured; **natural history** study of animal and vegetable life; **natural law** correct statement of invariable sequence between specified conditions and specified phenomenon; **natural number** any whole number greater than 0; **natural science** science dealing with natural or material phenomena; **natural selection** process favouring survival of organisms best adapted to their environment; **natural year** see YEAR. [F f. L (NATURE)]

naturalism *n.* adherence to nature in art and literature; realism; action, morality, religion or philosophy based on nature alone; **naturalistic** /-ˈlɪstɪk/ *a.*

naturalist *n.* expert in natural history; adherent of naturalism.

naturalize *v.t.* admit (alien) to citizenship; adopt or introduce (foreign word, custom, plant, animal); free from conventions; **naturalization** /-ˈzeɪʃ(ə)n/ *n.* [F (NATURAL)]

naturally *adv.* in natural manner; of course, as might be expected. [NATURAL]

nature /ˈneɪtʃə/ *n.* phenomena of physical world as a whole, physical power causing these; (**Nature**) these personified; thing's essential qualities; person's or animal's innate character; kind or class (*things of this nature*); vital force, functions, or needs; **by nature** innately; **by** (or **in**) **the nature of things** inevitable, inevitably; **call of nature** need to urinate or defecate; **in a state of nature** in uncivilized or uncultivated state, totally naked; **nature trail** path through countryside planned to show interesting natural objects; **-natured** *a.* (*good-natured*). [F f. L *natura* (as NATAL)]

naturist *n.* nudist; **naturism** *n.*

naught /nɔːt/ **1** *n. archaic* nothing, nought. **2** *predic. a. archaic* worthless, useless. **3** **come to naught** not succeed, come to nothing; **set at naught** despise. [OE (NO[1], WIGHT)]

naughty /ˈnɔːtɪ/ *a.* badly behaved, disobedient, wicked; mildly indecent; **naughtily** *adv.*; **naughtiness** *n.* [prec.]

nausea /ˈnɔːzɪə/ *n.* inclination to vomit; loathing; **nauseous** *a.* [L f. Gk (*naus* ship)]

nauseate /ˈnɔːzɪeɪt/ *v.* affect with nausea, disgust; loathe, feel nausea (*at*).

nautch /nɔːtʃ/ *n.* performance of Indian dancing girls. [Hindi]

nautical /ˈnɔːtɪk(ə)l/ *a.* of sailors or navigation; **nautical mile** about 1.85 km.; **nautically** *adv.* [F *nautique* f. L f. Gk (*nautēs* sailor)]

nautilus /ˈnɔːtɪləs/ *n.* (*pl.* **nautiluses**, **-li** /-aɪ/) mollusc with spiral shell divided into compartments. [L f. Gk (prec.)]

naval /ˈneɪv(ə)l/ *a.* of the or a navy; of ships. [L (*navis* ship)]

nave[1] *n.* body of church (apart from choir or chancel, aisles, and transepts). [L (*navis* ship)]

nave[2] *n.* hub of wheel. [OE]

navel /ˈneɪv(ə)l/ *n.* hollow in belly left by detachment of umbilical cord; central point of anything; **navel orange** orange with navel-like formation on top. [OE]

navigable /ˈnævɪgəb(ə)l/ *a.* (of river etc.) affording passage for ships; (of ship etc.) seaworthy; (of balloon) steerable;

navigability /-'bɪlɪtɪ/ *n.*; **navigably** *adv.* [F or L (foll.)]
navigate /'nævɪgeɪt/ *v.* sail (in) ship; sail or steam in or through (sea or river); manage, direct course of (ship or aircraft); (in car etc.) assist driver by indicating correct route; **navigator** *n.* [L *navigo* (as NAVAL)]
navigation /nævɪ'geɪʃ(ə)n/ *n.* methods of determining ship's or aircraft's position and course by geometry and astronomy; **navigational** *a.* [F or L (prec.)]
navvy /'nævɪ/ **1** *n.* labourer employed in excavating for roads, railways, canals, etc. **2** *v.i.* work as navvy. [abbr. of *navigator*]
navy /'neɪvɪ/ *n.* a State's warships with their crews and organization; officers and men of the navy; *poetic* a fleet; **navy (blue)** dark blue as of naval uniforms. [F f. L *navia* ship (as NAVAL)]
nawab /nə'wɑ:b/ *n.* title of distinguished Muslim in Pakistan; *hist.* title of nobleman in India. [Urdu f. Arab. = deputies]
nay 1 *adv.* no (*archaic*); or rather, and even, and more than that. **2** *n.* the word 'nay'. **3 say nay** refuse, contradict. [ON, = not ever]
Nazarene /næzə'ri:n/ **1** *a.* of Nazareth. **2** *n.* person of Nazareth, esp. Christ; (in Jewish or Muslim use) Christian. [L f. Gk]
Nazi /'nɑ:tsɪ/ **1** *n.* member of German National Socialist Party led orig. by Hitler. **2** *a.* of this party. **3 Nazism** *n.* [repr. pronunc. of *Nati-* in G *Nationalsozialist*]
NB *abbr.* note well. [L *nota bene*]
Nb *symb.* niobium.
NCB *abbr.* National Coal Board.
NCO *abbr.* non-commissioned officer.
n.d. *abbr.* no date.
Nd *symb.* neodymium.
NE *abbr.* North-East(ern).
Ne *symb.* neon.
Neanderthal /nɪ'ændətɑ:l/ *a.* of a type of man found in palaeolithic Europe, with retreating forehead and massive brow-ridges. [valley in Germany]
neap *n.* (in full **neap tide**) tide at times of month when there is least difference between high and low water. [OE]
Neapolitan /nɪə'pɒlɪt(ə)n/ **1** *a.* of Naples. **2** *n.* native of Naples. [L f. Gk *Neapolis* Naples]
near 1 *adv.* to or at or within a short distance in space or time; closely (*as near as one can guess*). **2** *prep.* near to in space, time, condition, or semblance; (*in comb.*) resembling, intended as substitute for (*near-silk*), that is almost (*near-hysterical*). **3** *a.* close (*to*) in place or time (*the man near you, in the near future*); intimate, closely related; with little margin (*near escape*); (of way) direct; (of part of vehicle or horse or road) nearer to side of road when facing forward, usu. left; niggardly. **4** *v.* draw near (to), approach. **5 go near to do, come** or **go near (to) doing** nearly do; **near at hand** (or **near by**) not far off; **Near East** region comprising countries of eastern Mediterranean; **near miss** attempt or shot etc. just failing to be successful, narrowly avoided collision, bomb etc. only just missing target and having some effect; **near-sighted** short-sighted; **near thing** narrow escape. [ON, orig. = *nigher* (NIGH)]
nearby *a.* close in position.
nearly *adv.* almost; closely; **not nearly** nothing like.
neat *a.* tidy, clean, orderly, elegantly simple; (of alcoholic drink) undiluted; cleverly phrased, epigrammatic; cleverly done, dextrous. [F NET[2] f. L *nitidus* clean]
neaten *v.t.* make neat.
neath *prep. poetic* beneath. [abbr.]
nebula /'nebjʊlə/ *n.* (*pl.* **nebulae** /-i:/) luminous or dark patch in sky made by distant star-cluster or gas or dust; **nebular** *a.* [L, = mist]
nebulous *a.* cloudlike, vague, indistinct. [F or L (prec.)]
necessary /'nesəsərɪ/ **1** *a.* indispensable, required, that must be done; inevitable, determined by natural laws or predestination and not by free will. **2** *n.* (usu. *pl.*) thing without which life cannot be maintained or is unduly harsh. **3 the necessary** *sl.* money or action needed for a purpose. **4 necessarily** *adv.* [AF or L (*necesse* needful)]
necessitarianism /nɪsesɪ'teərɪənɪz(ə)m/ *n.* denial of free will and belief that all action is determined by causes; **necessitarian** *a.* & *n.* [NECESSITY]
necessitate /nɪ'sesɪteɪt/ *v.t.* make necessary, involve as condition or accompaniment or result. [med.L (NECESSITY)]
necessitous /nɪ'sesɪtəs/ *a.* poor, needy. [F or foll.]
necessity /nɪ'sesɪtɪ/ *n.* constraint or compulsion regarded as a law governing all human action; imperative need; constraining power of circumstances; indispensable thing; poverty, want, hardship; **of necessity** unavoidably. [F f. L (NECESSARY)]
neck 1 *n.* part of body connecting head with shoulders; narrow part or piece of anything (e.g. of bottle, violin, or land); part of garment around neck; length of horse's head and neck as measure of its lead in race; flesh of animal's neck as food; life (*save one's neck*); *sl.* impudence.

2 *v. sl.* kiss and caress amorously. **3 get it in the neck** *colloq.* suffer heavy blow, be severely reprimanded or punished; **neck and neck** running level in race; **up to one's neck** *colloq.* very deeply involved (*in*), very busy. [OE]

neckband *n.* strip of material round neck of garment.

neckerchief *n.* square of cloth worn round neck. [KERCHIEF]

necklace /'neklɪs/ *n.* ornament of beads, precious stones, etc., worn round neck.

necklet /'neklɪt/ *n.* ornament or fur garment for neck.

neckline *n.* outline of garment-opening at neck.

necktie *n.* band of material tied round shirt-collar.

necro- *in comb.* corpse. [Gk (*nekros* corpse)]

necromancy /'nekrəʊmænsɪ/ *n.* dealings with the dead as means of divination; magic; **necromancer** *n.* [F f. L f. Gk (NECRO-, *mantis* seer)]

necrophilia /nekrəʊ'fɪlɪə/ *n.* abnormal (esp. erotic) attraction to corpses. [NECRO-]

necropolis /ne'krɒpəlɪs/ *n.* cemetery, esp. an ancient one. [Gk (NECRO-, *polis* city)]

necrosis /ne'krəʊsɪs/ *n.* (*pl.* **necroses** /-i:z/) death of piece of bone or tissue; **necrotic** /-'krɒtɪk/ *a.* [Gk (*nekroō* kill)]

nectar /'nektə/ *n.* sweet fluid produced by plants and made into honey by bees; (in Greek and Roman mythology) drink of the gods; any delicious drink; **nectarous** *a.* [L f. Gk]

nectarine /'nektərɪn, -i:n/ *n.* a kind of peach with smooth downless skin. [prec.]

nectary /'nektərɪ/ *n.* plant's nectar-secreting organ. [NECTAR]

NEDC *abbr.* National Economic Development Council.

neddy /'nedɪ/ *n. colloq.* donkey; (**Neddy**) NEDC. [pet-form of name *Edward*]

née /neɪ/ *a.* born (used in adding married woman's maiden name after her surname: *Anne Hall, née Browne*). [F, fem. p.p. of *naître* be born]

need 1 *n.* circumstances requiring some course of action (*if need be*; *there is no need to worry*); requirement or want (*my needs are few*); time of difficulty or crisis (*friend in need*); destitution or poverty. **2** *v.* (in neg. and interrog. *to* can be omitted and 3 *sing. pres.* is **need**) be in need of, require; be under necessity or obligation (*need to sleep*, *need you ask?*; *he need not come*; *need she have spoken?*). **3 have need of** require; **need not have done** did not need to do (but did). [OE]

needful *a.* requisite; **the needful** *sl.* money, action required; **needfully** *adv.*

needle /'ni:d(ə)l/ **1** *n.* long slender piece of polished steel pointed at one end and with eye for thread, used in sewing; similar larger instrument of bone or plastic etc. without eye, used in knitting or crocheting etc.; piece of metal etc. transmitting vibrations from revolving gramophone record, = STYLUS; pointer of compass or other instrument; pointed end of hypodermic syringe; slender pointed leaf of fir or pine; sharp rock or peak; obelisk (*Cleopatra's Needle*); *sl.* fit of nervousness or irritation. **2** *v.t. colloq.* annoy or provoke. **3 needle game** (or **match**) game or match closely contested or arousing exceptional personal feeling; **needle-point** embroidery on canvas, lace made with needles, not bobbins. [OE]

needlecord *n.* finely ribbed corduroy fabric.

needless *a.* unnecessary, uncalled for. [NEED]

needlewoman *n.* seamstress; woman or girl who sews.

needlework *n.* sewing or embroidery.

needs *adv. archaic* of necessity (esp. in **must needs**). [NEED]

needy *a.* poor, destitute; **neediness** *n.*

ne'er /neə/ *adv. poetic* never. [contr.]

ne'er-do-well 1 *n.* good-for-nothing person. **2** *a.* good-for-nothing.

nefarious /nɪ'feərɪəs/ *a.* wicked. [L (*nefas* wrong)]

neg. *abbr.* negative.

negate /nɪ'geɪt/ *v.t.* nullify, deny the existence of. [L *nego* deny]

negation /nɪ'geɪʃ(ə)n/ *n.* denying; negative statement; absence or opposite of something actual or positive; negative or unreal thing. [F or L (prec.)]

negative /'negətɪv/ **1** *a.* expressing or implying denial, prohibition, or refusal (*negative answer*); lacking or consisting in lack of positive attributes; marked by absence of qualities (*negative reaction*); (of quantity in algebra) less than zero, to be subtracted from others or from zero; in direction opposite that regarded as positive; of or containing or producing the kind of electrical charge carried by electrons; of opposite nature to thing regarded as positive; (of photograph) having lights and shades of actual objects or scene reversed, or colours replaced by complementary ones. **2** *n.* negative statement or word; developed photographic film etc. bearing negative image from which positive pictures are obtained. **3** *v.t.* veto, refuse consent to; serve to disprove; contradict (statement); neutralize (effect). **4 in the**

negative with refusal, or negative statement or reply.

neglect /nɪ'glekt/ **1** *v.t.* pay too little or no attention to; leave uncared for; omit or leave undone, be remiss about. **2** *n.* neglecting or being neglected; disregard *of*; negligence. **3 neglectful** *a.*; **neglectfully** *adv.* [L *neglego -ect-*]

négligé /'neglɪʒeɪ/ *n.* woman's light flimsy dressing-gown. [F, p.p. of *négliger* = prec.]

negligence /'neglɪdʒəns/ *n.* lack of proper care, culpable carelessness; **negligent** *a.* [F or L (NEGLECT)]

negligible /'neglɪdʒɪb(ə)l/ *a.* too small or unimportant to be considered; **negligibly** *adv.* [F (NEGLECT)]

negotiable /nɪ'gəʊʃəb(ə)l/ *a.* that can be negotiated; open to discussion. [foll.]

negotiate /nɪ'gəʊʃɪeɪt/ *v.* confer with view to reaching agreement; arrange (affair), bring about (result) by conferring thus; get or give money value for (bill or cheque); get over or through (obstacle or difficulty); **negotiation** /-'eɪʃ(ə)n/ *n.*; **negotiator** *n.* [L (*negotium* business)]

Negrillo /ne'grɪləʊ/ *n.* (*pl.* **Negrillos**) one of dwarf Negro people in Central and S. Africa. [Sp. dimin. (NEGRO)]

Negrito /ne'gri:təʊ/ *n.* (*pl.* **Negritos**) one of small Negroid people in Malayo-Polynesian region. [Sp. (as prec.)]

Negritude /'ni:grɪtju:d/ *n.* quality of being a Negro; affirmation of the value of Negro culture. [F]

Negro /'ni:grəʊ/ **1** *n.* (*pl.* **Negroes**) member of black-skinned (orig.) African race of mankind. **2** *a.* of this race, black-skinned; occupied by or connected with Negroes. **3 Negress** *n.fem.* [Sp. & Port., f. L *niger nigri* black]

Negroid /'ni:grɔɪd/ **1** *a.* of group having characteristics typical of Negroes. **2** *n.* Negroid person.

negus /'ni:gəs/ *n.* hot sweetened wine with water. [*Negus*, its inventor]

neigh /neɪ/ **1** *n.* cry of horse. **2** *v.i.* utter neigh. [OE]

neighbour /'neɪbə/, *US* **neighbor 1** *n.* person who lives next door or near by; person or thing near or next to another; fellow human being; *attrib.* neighbouring. **2** *v.* adjoin, border (on). [OE (NIGH, rel. to BOOR)]

neighbourhood *n.* district, people of a district; vicinity; **in the neighbourhood of** approximately.

neighbourly *a.* like a good neighbour, friendly, helpful; **neighbourliness** *n.*

neither /'naɪðə, 'ni:ðə/ **1** *adv.* not either, not on the one hand (introducing one of two negative statements, the other often introduced by *nor*: *neither knowing nor caring*; *he did not go and neither did I*). **2** *a.* & *pron.* not either, not the one nor the other (*neither statement is true*; *neither of them heard*). **3** *conj. archaic* nor, not yet (*I do not know, neither can I guess*). [OE (NO, WHETHER)]

nelly /'nelɪ/ *n.* in **not on your nelly** *sl.* certainly not. [perh. woman's name]

nelson /'nels(ə)n/ *n.* wrestling hold in which arm is passed under opponent's arm from behind and the hand applied to his neck. [app. f. name *Nelson*]

nematode /'nemətəʊd/ *n.* slender unsegmented worm. [Gk *nēma* thread]

nem. con. *abbr.* with no one dissenting. [L *nemine contradicente*]

nemesis /'neməsɪs/ *n.* justice bringing deserved punishment. [Gk (*Nemesis* goddess of this)]

neo- *in comb.* new, modern, a new form of. [Gk (*neos* new)]

neoclassical /ni:əʊ'klæsɪk(ə)l/ *a.* of a revival of classical style or treatment in the arts.

neodymium /ni:ə'dɪmɪəm/ *n.* metallic element of lanthanide series. [NEO-, Gk *didumos* twin]

neolithic /ni:əʊ'lɪθɪk/ *a.* of later Stone Age. [Gk *lithos* stone]

neologism /ni:'ɒlədʒɪz(ə)m/ *n.* newly-coined word; word-coining. [Gk *logos* word]

neon /'ni:ɒn/ *n.* inert gaseous element giving orange-red glow when electricity is passed through it; **neon lamp** (or **light**) neon-filled tube used for bright lighting. [Gk, = new]

neophyte /'ni:əʊfaɪt/ *n.* new convert; religious novice; beginner. [L f. Gk (*phuton* plant)]

Neoplatonism /ni:əʊ'pleɪtənɪz(ə)m/ *n.* 3rd-c. mixture of Platonic ideas with oriental mysticism. [NEO-]

Neozoic /ni:əʊ'zəʊɪk/ *a.* of later period of geological history. [Gk *zōion* animal]

nephew /'nefju:, -v-/ *n.* one's brother's or sister's son. [F *neveu* f. L *nepos*]

nephritic /ne'frɪtɪk/ *a.* of or in the kidneys. [Gk *nephros* kidney]

nephritis /ne'fraɪtɪs/ *n.* inflammation of the kidneys. [-ITIS]

ne plus ultra /neɪ plʊs 'ʊltrɑ:/ furthest attainable point; acme, perfection. [L, = not further beyond]

nepotism /'nepətɪz(ə)m/ *n.* favouritism shown to relatives in conferring offices. [F f. It. (*nepote* NEPHEW)]

neptunium /nep'tju:nɪəm/ *n.* trans-uranic element produced when uranium atoms absorb bombarding neutrons. [*Neptune*, planet]

nereid /'nɪərɪɪd/ *n.* sea-nymph; long sea-worm or centipede. [L f. Gk]

nerve 1 *n.* fibrous connection conveying

impulses of sensation or of movement between brain or spinal cord and other parts of the body; material constituting these; courage, coolness in danger; *colloq.* impudent boldness; *pl.* nervousness; condition of mental and physical stress; *Bot.* rib of leaf. **2** *v.t.* give strength or courage or vigour to; brace (oneself) to face danger etc. **3 bundle of nerves** very nervous person; **get on person's nerves** irritate him; **lose one's nerve** become timid or irresolute; **nerve-cell** cell transmitting impulses in nerve tissue; **nerve-centre** group of closely connected ganglion-cells, *fig.* centre of control; **nerve gas** poison gas that affects nervous system; **nerve-racking** greatly straining the nerves; **strain every nerve** do one's utmost. [L *nervus* sinew, tendon, bowstring]

nerveless *a.* lacking vigour; (of style) diffuse.

nervous *a.* having delicate or disordered nerves, timid or anxious, highly strung; fearful (*of*); of the nerves, full of nerves; affecting or acting on the nerves; (of style) terse; **nervous breakdown** severe disorder of nerves, causing loss of emotional and mental stability; **nervous system** nerves and nerve-centres as a whole. [L (NERVE)]

nervy *a.* nervous, easily excited. [NERVE]

nescient /ˈnesɪənt/ *a.* not having knowledge (*of*); **nescience** *n.* [L (*ne-* not, *scio* know)]

ness *n.* headland. [OE]

-ness *suffix* forming nouns from adjectives, expressing state or condition (*happiness*) or an instance of this (*a kindness*), or material in a state (*foulness*). [OE]

nest 1 *n.* structure or place where bird lays eggs and shelters young; animal's or insect's building-place or lair; snug retreat or shelter; brood or swarm; group or set of similar objects, often of different sizes (*nest of tables*). **2** *v.* have or build nest; take wild birds' nests or eggs; (of objects) fit together or one inside another. **3 nest-egg** sum of money saved for the future. [OE]

nestle /ˈnes(ə)l/ *v.* settle oneself comfortably; press oneself against another in affection etc.; push (head or shoulder etc.) affectionately or snugly *in* or *into*; lie half hidden or embedded. [OE]

nestling /ˈnestlɪŋ/ *n.* bird too young to leave nest. [NEST]

net[1] **1** *n.* meshed fabric of twine or cord etc.; piece of this for catching fish, or keeping hair in place, or enclosing areas of ground, e.g. in sport. **2** *v.* (**-tt-**) catch or procure (as) with net; cover or confine with nets; put (ball) in net, esp. of goal; make cord etc. into net. [OE]

net[2] **1** *a.* remaining after necessary deductions; (of price) off which discount is not allowed; (of effect, result, etc.) ultimate, effective. **2** *v.t.* (**-tt-**) gain or yield (sum) as net profit. **3 net profit** actual profit after working expenses have been paid; **net weight** that excluding weight of wrappings etc. [F (NEAT[1])]

netball *n.* team game in which ball is to be thrown to fall through high horizontal ring from which net hangs. [NET[1]]

nether /ˈneðə/ *a.* lower, esp. in **nether regions** (or **world**) hell, the underworld. [OE]

nett var. of NET[2].

netting *n.* netted fabric; piece of this. [NET[1]]

nettle /ˈnet(ə)l/ **1** *n.* plant covered with stinging hairs; plant resembling this. **2** *v.t.* irritate or provoke. **3 nettle-rash** skin eruption like nettle-stings. [OE]

network 1 *n.* arrangement with intersecting lines and interstices, complex system of railways etc.; chain of interconnected persons or operations or electrical conductors; group of broadcasting stations connected for simultaneous broadcast of same programme. **2** *v.t.* broadcast thus. [NET[1]]

neural /ˈnjʊər(ə)l/ *a.* of the nerves; **neurally** *adv.* [Gk *neuron* nerve]

neuralgia /njʊəˈrældʒə/ *n.* intense intermittent pain in nerves esp. of face and head; **neuralgic** *a.*

neurasthenia /njʊərəsˈθiːnɪə/ *n.* debility of nerves causing fatigue etc.; **neurasthenic** *a.*

neuritis /njʊəˈraɪtɪs/ *n.* inflammation of nerve or nerves. [-ITIS]

neuro- *in comb.* nerve, nerves. [Gk *neuron* nerve]

neurology /njʊəˈrɒlədʒɪ/ *n.* scientific study of nerve systems; **neurological** /-ˈlɒdʒɪk(ə)l/ *a.*; **neurologist** *n.*

neurone /ˈnjʊərəʊn/ *n.* (also **neuron** /-rɒn/) a nerve-cell and its appendages.

neurosis /njʊəˈrəʊsɪs/ *n.* (*pl.* **neuroses** /-iːz/) disorder of nervous system producing depression or irrational behaviour. [-OSIS]

neurotic /njʊəˈrɒtɪk/ **1** *a.* caused by or suffering from neurosis; *colloq.* abnormally anxious or obsessive. **2** *n.* neurotic person. **3 neurotically** *adv.*

neuter /ˈnjuːtə/ **1** *a.* (of noun etc.) neither masculine nor feminine; (of plants) having neither pistils nor stamens; (of insects) sexually undeveloped. **2** *n.* a neuter word; the neuter gender; sexually undeveloped female insect, esp. bee or ant; castrated animal. **3** *v.t.* castrate. [F or L]

neutral /ˈnju:tr(ə)l/ **1** *a.* not helping or supporting either of two opposing sides, impartial; belonging to neutral State etc. (*neutral ships*); indistinct, vague, indeterminate; (of gear) in which engine is disconnected from driven parts; (of colours) not strong or positive, grey or fawn; *Chem.* neither acid nor alkaline; *Electr.* neither positive nor negative; *Biol.* sexually undeveloped, asexual. **2** *n.* neutral State or person; subject of neutral State; neutral gear. **3 neutrality** /-ˈtrælɪtɪ/ *n.* [F, or L *neutralis* of neuter gender]

neutralize *v.t.* make neutral, make ineffective by opposite force or effect, exempt or exclude (place) from sphere of hostilities; **neutralization** /-ˈzeɪʃ(ə)n/ *n.* [F (prec.)]

neutrino /nju:ˈtri:nəʊ/ *n.* (*pl.* **neutrinos**) elementary particle with zero electric charge and probably zero mass. [It., dimin. of *neutro* neutral (NEUTER)]

neutron /ˈnju:trɒn/ *n.* elementary particle of about same mass as proton but without electric charge. [NEUTRAL]

never /ˈnevə/ *adv.* at no time, on no occasion, not ever; not at all (*never fear*); *colloq.* surely not (*you never left the key in the lock!*); **never-never** *colloq.* hire-purchase; **well I never** exclamation of surprise. [OE, = not ever]

nevermore *adv.* at no future time.

nevertheless /nevəðəˈles/ *adv.* for all that, notwithstanding.

nevus *US* var. of NAEVUS.

new 1 *a.* of recent origin or arrival, made, invented, discovered, acquired, or experienced recently or now for the first time; in original condition, not worn or used; renewed or reformed (*new hope, life*), reinvigorated (*I feel a new man*); changed or different from previous one (*has a new job*), additional to other(s) already existing (*have you been to the new hotel?*); unfamiliar or strange (*was all new to me*); later, modern, *derog.* newfangled, advanced in method or doctrine (often preceded by *the*: *the new rich*); (in place-names) discovered or founded later than and named after (*New England*; *New Zealand*). **2** *adv.* (usu. as **new-**) newly, recently (*new-born*; *new-found*; *new-laid*). **3 the new mathematics** system using set theory (see SET²) in elementary teaching; **new moon** moon when first seen as crescent after conjunction with sun, time of such appearance; **new potatoes** earliest potatoes of new crop; **new star** nova; **new style** of date reckoned by Gregorian Calendar; **New Testament** part of Bible concerned with teachings of Christ and his earliest followers; **new town** town established as completely new settlement with government sponsorship; **New World** North and South America; **new year** year about to begin or just begun; first few days of year; **New Year's Day, Eve** 1 Jan., 31 Dec. [OE]

newcomer *n.* person recently arrived.

newel /ˈnju:əl/ *n.* supporting central post of winding stairs; top or bottom post of stair-rail. [F f. L (*nodus* knot)]

newfangled /nju:ˈfæŋg(ə)ld/ *a. derog.* different from what one is used to, objectionably new. [= new taken]

newly *adv.* recently, afresh, new-; **newly-weds** recently married couple(s). [NEW]

news /nju:z/ *n.pl.* (usu. treated as *sing.*) information about recent events, esp. when published or broadcast; broadcast report of news; new or interesting information; **news-stand** stall for sale of newspapers; **news-vendor** newspaper-seller. [NEW]

newsagent *n.* dealer in newspapers.

newscast *n.* radio or television broadcast of news reports.

newscaster *n.* person who reads newscast.

newsletter *n.* informal printed report issued to members of club or other group.

newspaper *n.* printed publication (usu. daily or weekly) containing news, advertisements, correspondence, etc.; the sheets of paper forming this (*wrapped in newspaper*).

Newspeak /ˈnju:spi:k/ *n.* ambiguous euphemistic language used esp. in political propaganda. [artificial official language in Orwell's *Nineteen Eighty-Four*]

newsprint *n.* type of paper on which newspapers are printed. [NEWS]

newsreel *n.* short film account of recent news.

newsworthy *a.* topical, noteworthy as news.

newsy *a. colloq.* full of news.

newt *n.* small tailed amphibian allied to salamander. [*a newt* f. *an ewt* (var. of *ewet* EFT)]

newton /ˈnju:t(ə)n/ *n.* unit of force, the force that acting for 1 second on mass of 1 kg. gives it a velocity of 1 metre per second. [*Newton*, scientist]

next 1 *a.* being or lying or living nearest (*to*); nearest in order or time, soonest come to (*next Friday*; *ask the next person you see*). **2** *adv.* in next place or degree (*put it next to mine*); on next occasion (*when I see you next*). **3** *n.* next person or thing. **4** *prep.* next to. **5 next-best** second-best; **next door** in the next room or house; **next of kin** closest living relative(s); **next to** almost (*next to nothing*); **the next world** life after death. [OE, superl. of NIGH]

nexus /'neksəs/ *n.* connected group or series. [L *necto nex-* bind]

NHS *abbr.* National Health Service.

NI *abbr.* National Insurance; Northern Ireland.

Ni *symb.* nickel.

niacin /'naɪəsɪn/ *n.* nicotinic acid. [contr.]

nib *n.* pen-point; (in *pl.*) crushed coffee- or cocoa-beans. [LG or Du.]

nibble /'nɪb(ə)l/ **1** *v.* take small bites at; eat in small amounts; bite gently or cautiously or playfully. **2** *n.* act of nibbling; very small amount of food. **3 nibble at** show cautious interest in. [LG or Du.]

nibs /nɪbz/ *n. sl.* in **his** etc. **nibs** with reference to important or self-important person. [orig. cant]

nice *a.* pleasant, agreeable, satisfactory, (of person) kind, good-natured; *iron.* bad or awkward (*a nice mess*); fine or subtle (*a nice distinction*); fastidious, delicately sensitive; **nice and** satisfactorily (*nice and warm*). [orig. = foolish, f. F f. L *nescius* ignorant]

nicety /'naɪsɪtɪ/ *n.* precision; subtle distinction or detail; **to a nicety** exactly. [F (NICE)]

niche /nɪtʃ, ni:ʃ/ *n.* shallow recess, esp. in wall; *fig.* comfortable or suitable position in life or employment. [F f. L *nidus* nest]

nick 1 *n.* small cut or notch; *sl.* prison, police station; *sl.* condition (*in good nick*). **2** *v.t.* make nick(s) in; *sl.* steal; *sl.* catch, arrest. **3 in the nick of time** only just in time. [orig. unkn.]

nickel /'nɪk(ə)l/ *n.* silver-white metallic element much used esp. in alloys; *US* five-cent piece; **nickel silver** alloy of nickel, zinc, and copper; **nickel steel** alloy of nickel with steel. [G]

nicker *n.* (*pl.* same) *sl.* £1 sterling. [orig. unkn.]

nick-nack var. of KNICK-KNACK.

nickname /'nɪkneɪm/ **1** *n.* familiar or humorous name given to person or thing instead of or as well as real name. **2** *v.t.* call (person or thing) by nickname; give nickname to. [EKE + NAME (*an eke = a nick-*)]

nicotine /'nɪkəti:n/ *n.* poisonous substance found in tobacco. [F (*Nicot*, introducer of tobacco into France)]

nicotinic acid /nɪkə'tɪnɪk/ vitamin of B group.

nictitate /'nɪktɪteɪt/ *v.i.* blink, wink; **nictitating membrane** third or inner eyelid of many animals; **nictitation** /-'teɪʃ(ə)n/ *n.* [L]

niece *n.* one's brother's or sister's daughter. [F f. L *neptis* granddaughter]

niff *n.* & *v.i. sl.* smell, stink; **niffy** *a.* [orig. dial.]

nifty /'nɪftɪ/ *a. sl.* smart, stylish; clever, adroit. [orig. unkn.]

niggard /'nɪgəd/ *n.* stingy person. [prob. of Scand. orig.]

niggardly *a.* stingy; **niggardliness** *n.*

nigger *n. derog.* (**R**) Negro, dark-skinned person; **nigger in the woodpile** hidden cause of trouble or inconvenience. [F *nègre* f. Sp. NEGRO]

niggle /'nɪg(ə)l/ *v.* fuss over details, find fault in petty way; irritate, nag. [orig. unkn.]

niggling *a.* petty, troublesome, nagging.

nigh /naɪ/ *adv., prep.,* & *a.* (*archaic* and *dial.*) = NEAR. [OE]

night /naɪt/ *n.* period of darkness between one day and the next, time from sunset to sunrise; nightfall; darkness of night; night or evening appointed for some activity (*first night of the Proms*); **make a night of it** spend most or all of night enjoying oneself; **night-club** club that is open at night and provides refreshment and entertainment; **night-dress** (or **-gown**) woman's or girl's loose garment worn in bed; **night-life** entertainment available at night in a town; **night-light** short thick candle or dim bulb kept burning in bedroom at night; **night-long** *a.* & *adv.* throughout the night; **night safe** safe with opening in outer wall of bank for deposit of money etc. when bank is closed; **night school** school providing evening classes for those working by day; **night-shirt** man's or boy's long shirt for sleeping in; **night-time** time of darkness; **night-watchman** person keeping watch by night, (in cricket) inferior batsman sent in near close of play to avoid dismissal of better one in adverse conditions. [OE]

nightcap *n.* cap worn in bed; hot or alcoholic drink taken at bedtime.

nightfall *n.* end of daylight.

nightie *n. colloq.* night-dress.

nightingale /'naɪtɪŋgeɪl/ *n.* small bird of thrush family, of which the male sings much at night. [OE, = night-singer]

nightjar *n.* nocturnal bird with harsh cry. [NIGHT]

nightly 1 *a.* happening or done or existing in the night; recurring every night. **2** *adv.* every night.

nightmare *n.* terrifying dream; *colloq.* terrifying or very unpleasant experience or situation; haunting fear; **nightmarish** *a*. [orig. female monster supposedly suffocating sleeper, incubus (*mare* goblin)]

nightshade *n*. any of several wild plants, some with poisonous berries. [OE]

nihilism /ˈnaɪlɪz(ə)m/ *n*. rejection of all religious and moral principles; doctrine that nothing has real existence; **nihilist** *n*.; **nihilistic** /-ˈlɪstɪk/ *a*. [L *nihil* nothing]

-nik *suffix* forming nouns denoting person associated with specified thing or quality (*beatnik*). [Russ. (as SPUTNIK) & Yiddish]

nil *n*. nothing, no number or amount, esp. as score in games. [L]

nimble /ˈnɪmb(ə)l/ *a*. quick and light in movement or action, agile; (of the mind) quick, clever; **nimbly** *adv*. [OE, = quick to take]

nimbus /ˈnɪmbəs/ *n*. (*pl*. **nimbi** /-aɪ/ or **nimbuses**) halo, aureole; storm-cloud. [L, = cloud]

nincompoop /ˈnɪnkəmpu:p/ *n*. foolish person. [orig. unkn.]

nine *a*. & *n*. one more than eight; symbol for this (9, ix, IX); size etc. denoted by nine; **the Nine** the Muses; **nine days' wonder** thing attracting interest for short time. [OE]

ninefold *a*. & *adv*. nine times as much or as many; consisting of nine parts.

ninepins *n.pl*. a kind of skittles.

nineteen /naɪnˈti:n/ *a*. & *n*. one more than eighteen; symbol for this (19, xix, XIX); size etc. denoted by nineteen; **nineteenth** *a*. & *n*. [OE (NINE, -TEEN)]

ninety /ˈnaɪntɪ/ *a*. & *n*. nine times ten; symbol for this (90, xc, XC); (in *pl*.) numbers, years, degrees of temperature, from 90 to 99; **ninetieth** *a*. & *n*. [OE]

ninny /ˈnɪnɪ/ *n*. foolish person. [orig. uncert.]

ninth /naɪnθ/ **1** *a*. next after eighth. **2** *n*. each of nine equal parts into which thing may be divided. **3 ninthly** *adv*. [NINE]

niobium /naɪˈəʊbɪəm/ *n*. rare metallic element usu. found associated with tantalum. [*Niobe* in Gk legend]

nip[1] **1** *v*. (**-pp-**) pinch or squeeze sharply, bite; pinch *off* (bud etc.); check growth of; (of the cold) pain or harm; *colloq*. go nimbly or quickly (*in*, *out*, *past*, etc.). **2** *n*. pinch, sharp squeeze, bite; biting coldness. [LG or Du.]

nip[2] *n*. small quantity of spirits. [*nipperkin* small measure]

Nip[3] *n*. & *a*. *sl*. *derog*. (**R**) Japanese. [NIPPONESE]

nipper *n*. claw of crab etc.; (in *pl*.) forceps, pincers, or other gripping or cutting tool; *colloq*. young child. [NIP[1]]

nipple /ˈnɪp(ə)l/ *n*. small projection in which mammary ducts of either sex of mammals terminate and from which in females milk is secreted for young; teat of feeding-bottle; nipple-like protuberance. [perh. f. *neb* tip]

Nipponese /nɪpɒˈni:z/ *n*. (*pl*. same) & *a*. Japanese. [Jap. *Nippon* Japan]

nippy *a*. *colloq*. nimble, quick; chilly, cold. [NIP[1]]

nirvana /nɜ:ˈvɑ:nə, nɪə-/ *n*. (in Buddhism & Hinduism) perfect bliss attained by extinction of individuality. [Skr., = extinction]

Nissen hut /ˈnɪs(ə)n/ *n*. tunnel-shaped hut of corrugated iron with cement floor. [*Nissen*, engineer]

nit *n*. louse or other parasite, its egg; *sl*. stupid person; **nit-picking** *n*. & *a*. *colloq*. petty fault-finding. [OE]

nitrate[1] /ˈnaɪtreɪt/ *n*. salt or ester of nitric acid; potassium or sodium nitrate as fertilizer. [F (NITRE)]

nitrate[2] /naɪˈtreɪt/ *v.t*. treat or combine or impregnate with nitric acid. [foll.]

nitre /ˈnaɪtə/ *n*. saltpetre. [F f. L f. Gk]

nitric /ˈnaɪtrɪk/ *a*. of or containing nitrogen; **nitric acid** pungent corrosive caustic liquid.

nitride /ˈnaɪtraɪd/ *n*. binary compound of nitrogen. [NITRE]

nitrify /ˈnaɪtrɪfaɪ/ *v.t*. turn into nitrite or nitrate; **nitrification** /-fɪˈkeɪʃ(ə)n/ *n*. [F (NITRE)]

nitrite /ˈnaɪtraɪt/ *n*. salt or ester of nitrous acid. [NITRE]

nitro- *in comb*. of or made with nitric acid or nitre or nitrogen; **nitro-glycerine** yellowish oily highly explosive liquid made by adding glycerine to nitric and sulphuric acids. [Gk (NITRE)]

nitrogen /ˈnaɪtrədʒ(ə)n/ *n*. gaseous element forming four-fifths of the atmosphere; **nitrogenous** /-ˈtrɒdʒɪnəs/ *a*. [F]

nitrous /ˈnaɪtrəs/ *a*. of or like or impregnated with nitre; **nitrous acid** liquid like nitric acid but containing less oxygen; **nitrous oxide** colourless gas used as anaesthetic, laughing-gas. [L (NITRE)]

nitty-gritty /nɪtɪˈgrɪtɪ/ *n*. *sl*. realities or basic facts of a matter. [orig. uncert.]

nitwit *n*. stupid person. [perh. NIT, WIT]

nix *n*. *sl*. nothing. [G colloq. *nix* = *nichts* nothing]

NNE *abbr*. north-north-east.

NNW *abbr*. north-north-west.

no[1] /nəʊ/ **1** *a*. not any (*there is no excuse*); not a, quite other than (*is no fool*); hardly any (*took no time*). **2** *adv*. as negative answer to question etc.: it is not so, I do not agree, I shall not, etc.; (with *compar*.)

by no amount, not at all (*no better*; *no more*); (after *or*) not (*pleasant or no, it is true*). **3** *n.* (*pl.* **noes**) the word *no*; a denial or refusal; negative vote. **4 no-ball** unlawfully delivered ball in cricket; **no go** it is hopeless or impossible; **no-go area** one to which entry is forbidden or restricted; **no man's land** space between two opposing armies, area not assigned to any owner; **no one** no person, nobody; **no way** *colloq.* it is impossible. [OE]

No² var. of NOH.

No. *abbr.* number. [L *numero*, abl. of *numerus* number]

No *symb.* nobelium.

nob¹ *n. sl.* person of wealth or high social standing; **nobby** *a.* [orig. unkn.]

nob² *n. sl.* head. [KNOB]

nobble /'nɒb(ə)l/ *v.t. sl.* tamper with (racehorse) to prevent its winning; dishonestly get possession of; catch (criminal). [dial. *knobble* beat]

nobelium /nəʊ'bi:lɪəm/ *n.* artificially produced transuranic element. [*Nobel*, as foll.]

Nobel prize /'nəʊbel/ each of six annual prizes (for physics, chemistry, medicine, literature, economics, and the promotion of peace). [*Nobel*, orig. donor]

nobility /nəʊ'bɪlɪtɪ/ *n.* nobleness of character, mind, birth, or rank; class of nobles; **the nobility** the aristocracy. [foll.]

noble /'nəʊb(ə)l/ **1** *a.* belonging to the aristocracy by birth or rank; of excellent character, free from pettiness or meanness, magnanimous; of imposing appearance. **2** *n.* nobleman, noblewoman. **3 noble metal** metal (e.g. gold) that resists chemical attack. [F f. L *nobilis*]

nobleman *n.* peer.

noblesse oblige /nəʊ'bles ɒ'bli:ʒ/ privilege entails responsibility. [F]

noblewoman *n.* peeress. [NOBLE]

nobody /'nəʊbədɪ/ *pron.* no person; person of no importance. [NO¹]

nock *n.* notch on bow or arrow for bowstring. [Du.]

nocturnal /nɒk'tɜ:n(ə)l/ *a.* of or in the night; done or active by night; **nocturnally** *adv.* [L (*nox noct-* night)]

nocturne /'nɒktɜ:n/ *n.* dreamy musical piece; picture of night scene. [F]

nod 1 *v.* (**-dd-**) incline head slightly and briefly in greeting, assent, or command; let head droop in drowsiness, be drowsy; incline (head); signify (assent etc.) by nod; (of flowers etc.) bend downwards and sway; make mistake due to momentary lack of alertness or attention. **2** *n.* nodding of the head. **3 nod off** fall asleep. [orig. unkn.]

noddle /'nɒd(ə)l/ *n. colloq.* head. [orig. unkn.]

noddy /'nɒdɪ/ *n.* simpleton; tropical seabird. [prob. obs. *noddy* foolish]

node *n.* knob on root or branch; point at which leaves spring; hard swelling; point or line of rest in vibrating body; point at which curve crosses itself; intersecting point of planet's orbit and ecliptic or of two great circles of celestial sphere; **nodal** *a.* [L *nodus* knot]

nodule /'nɒdju:l/ *n.* small rounded lump of anything; small node in plant; small knotty tumour, ganglion; **nodular** *a.* [L dimin. (prec.)]

Noel /nəʊ'el/ *n.* Christmas. [F, f. L (NATAL)]

nog¹ *n.* small block or peg of wood. [orig. unkn.]

nog² *n.* strong beer; = *egg-nog*. [orig. unkn.]

noggin /'nɒgɪn/ *n.* small mug; small (usu. ¼-pint) measure; *sl.* head. [orig. unkn.]

nogging *n.* brickwork in wooden frame. [NOG¹]

Noh /nəʊ/ *n.* traditional Japanese drama. [Jap.]

noise /nɔɪz/ **1** *n.* sound, esp. loud or unpleasant one; series of loud sounds; irregular fluctuations with transmitted signal; (in *pl.*) utterances, esp. conventional remarks (*polite noises*). **2** *v.t.* make public, spread (person's name, fact) *abroad*. [F f. L NAUSEA]

noiseless *a.* without a sound.

noisome /'nɔɪsəm/ *a. literary* noxious, disgusting esp. to smell. [ANNOY]

noisy *a.* full of or making or attended with noise; given to making noise; **noisily** *adv.*; **noisiness** *n.* [NOISE]

nomad /'nəʊmæd/ *n.* member of tribe roaming from place to place for pasture; wanderer; **nomadic** /-'mædɪk/ *a.* [F f. L f. Gk *nomas -ad-* (*nemō* pasture *v.*)]

nom de plume /nɒm də 'plu:m/ *n.* (*pl.* ***noms pr.*** same) writer's assumed name. [sham F, = pen-name]

nomen /'nəʊmen/ *n.* (in ancient Rome) second or family name, e.g. Marcus *Tullius* Cicero. [L, = name]

nomenclature /nəʊ'menklətʃə/ *n.* system of names or naming, terminology. [L (prec., *calo* call)]

nominal /'nɒmɪn(ə)l/ *a.* of or as or like a noun; of or in names; existing in name only, not real or actual; (of sum of money etc.) virtually nothing, much below actual value; **nominal value** face value; **nominally** *adv.* [F or L (NOMEN)]

nominalism *n.* philosophical doctrine that abstract concepts are mere names; **nominalist** *n.*; **nominalistic** /-'lɪstɪk/ *a.* [F (prec.)]

nominate /'nɒmɪneɪt/ *v.t.* appoint to or propose for election to office; name or appoint (date etc.); **nominator** *n.* [L (NOMEN)]
nomination /nɒmɪ'neɪʃ(ə)n/ *n.* nominating or being nominated; right of nominating. [F or L (prec.)]
nominative /'nɒmɪnətɪv/ *Gram.* **1** *n.* case expressing subject of verb. **2** *a.* of or in the nominative.
nominee /nɒmɪ'ni:/ *n.* person who is nominated. [NOMINATE]
non- *prefix* giving negative sense of words with which it is combined. [F f. L *non* not]
nonage /'nəʊnɪdʒ, 'nɒn-/ *n.* being under full legal age, minority; immaturity. [AF (NON-, AGE)]
nonagenarian /nəʊnədʒɪ'neərɪən, 'nɒn-/ *n.* person from 90 to 99 years old. [L (*nonageni* 90 each)]
nonagon /'nɒnəgɒn/ *n.* plane figure with nine sides and angles. [L *nonus* ninth, -GON]
non-aligned /nɒnə'laɪnd/ *a.* (of State) not in alliance with any major bloc. [NON-]
non-belligerent /nɒnbə'lɪdʒərənt/ **1** *a.* taking no active or open part in a war. **2** *n.* non-belligerent State.
nonce *n.* the time being, present, esp. in **for the nonce** for the occasion only; **nonce-word** word coined for one occasion. [*for then anes* for the one]
nonchalant /'nɒnʃələnt/ *a.* unmoved, calm and casual; **nonchalance** *n.* [F (*chaloir* be concerned)]
non-com. *abbr.* non-commissioned (officer).
non-combatant /nɒn'kɒmbətənt/ **1** *a.* not fighting, esp. in war as being civilian, army chaplain, etc. **2** *n.* such person. [NON-]
non-commissioned /nɒnkə'mɪʃ(ə)nd/ *a.* (esp. of officer) of grade below those with commissions.
non-committal /nɒnkə'mɪt(ə)l/ *a.* not committing oneself to definite opinion, course of action, etc.
non compos mentis /nɒn 'kɒmpɒs 'mentɪs/ *a.* not in one's right mind. [L, not having control of one's mind]
non-conductor /nɒnkən'dʌktə/ *n.* substance that does not conduct heat or electricity. [NON-]
nonconformist /nɒnkən'fɔ:mɪst/ *n.* one who does not conform to doctrine or discipline of an established Church, esp. (**Nonconformist**) member of (usu. Protestant) sect dissenting from Anglican Church; one who does not conform to a prevailing principle. [CONFORM]
nonconformity *n.* nonconformists or their principles etc.; failure to conform; lack of correspondence between things.
non-contributory /nɒnkən'trɪbjʊtərɪ/ *a.* not involving contributions. [NON-]
non-co-operation /nɒnkəʊɒpə'reɪʃ(ə)n/ *n.* failure or refusal to co-operate, esp. as political protest.
nondescript /'nɒndɪskrɪpt/ **1** *a.* indeterminate, lacking distinctive characteristics. **2** *n.* nondescript person or thing. [DESCRIBE]
none /nʌn/ **1** *pron.* not any (*none of this concerns me*), no one (*none of them has*, or *have, come*); no person(s) (*none can say*). **2** *a.* not any (usu. with reference supplied by earlier or later noun: *you have money, I have none*). **3** *adv.* by no amount (*none the wiser*). **4 none the less** nevertheless. [OE, = not one]
nonentity /nɒ'nentɪtɪ/ *n.* person or thing of no importance; non-existence, non-existent thing. [NON-]
nones /nəʊnz/ *n.pl.* 7th day of March, May, July, Oct., 5th of other months, in ancient Roman calendar. [L *nonus* ninth]
non-essential /nɒnɪ'senʃ(ə)l/ **1** *a.* not essential. **2** *n.* non-essential thing. [NON-]
nonesuch var. of NONSUCH.
non-event /nɒnɪ'vent/ *n.* event that turns out to be insignificant (usu. contrary to hopes or expectations). [NON-]
non-existent /nɒnɪg'zɪstənt/ *a.* not existing.
non-ferrous /nɒn'ferəs/ *a.* (of metal) not iron or steel.
non-fiction /nɒn'fɪkʃ(ə)n/ *n.* literary works dealing with fact.
non-interference /nɒnɪntə'fɪərəns/ *n.* = NON-INTERVENTION.
non-intervention /nɒnɪntə'venʃ(ə)n/ *n.* (esp. political) principle or practice of not interfering in others' disputes.
non-member *n.* one who is not a member.
non-moral /nɒn'mɒr(ə)l/ *a.* unconcerned with morality.
non-nuclear /nɒn'nju:klɪə/ *a.* not involving nuclei or nuclear energy.
nonpareil /'nɒnpər(ə)l/ **1** *a.* unrivalled or unique. **2** *n.* such person or thing. [F (*pareil* equal)]
non-party /nɒn'pɑ:tɪ/ *a.* independent of political parties. [NON-]
nonplus /nɒn'plʌs/ *v.t.* (-ss-) completely perplex. [L *non plus* not more]
non-profit-making /nɒn'prɒfɪt-/ *a.* (of enterprise) conducted with no view to gain. [NON-]
non-proliferation /nɒnprəlɪfə'reɪʃ(ə)n/ *n.* limitation of number esp. of nuclear weapons.
non-resistance /nɒnrɪ'zɪstəns/ *n.*

policy of not resisting even wrongly exercised authority.

nonsense /'nɒnsəns/ **1** *n.* absurd or meaningless words or ideas; foolish or extravagant scheme or behaviour. **2** *int.* you are talking nonsense. **3 nonsensical** /-'sensɪk(ə)l/ *a.*; **nonsensically** *adv.* [NON-]

non sequitur /nɒn 'sekwɪtə/ *n.* conclusion that does not logically follow from the premisses. [L, = it does not follow]

non-skid /nɒn'skɪd/ *a.* that does not, or is designed not to, skid. [NON-]

non-smoker /nɒn'sməʊkə/ *n.* person who does not smoke; compartment in train etc. where smoking is forbidden.

non-starter /nɒn'stɑ:tə/ *n. colloq.* idea or person not worth consideration.

non-stick /nɒn'stɪk/ *a.* (of saucepan etc.) to which food will not stick during cooking.

non-stop /nɒn'stɒp/ **1** *a.* (of train etc.) not stopping at intermediate stations; not ceasing, done without pausing. **2** *adv.* without stopping.

nonsuch /'nʌnsʌtʃ/ *n.* unrivalled person or thing, paragon; plant like lucerne. [*none such*]

nonsuit /nɒn'sju:t/ *Law* **1** *n.* stoppage of suit by judge as unsustainable. **2** *v.t.* subject (plaintiff) to nonsuit. [AF *no(un)suit* (NON-)]

non-U *a. colloq.* not characteristic of the upper class. [U²]

non-union /nɒn'ju:nɪən/ *a.* not belonging to, not made by members of, trade union. [NON-]

non-violent /nɒn'vaɪələnt/ *a.* abstaining from the use of violence to gain one's ends; **non-violence** *n.*

non-voting /nɒn'vəʊtɪŋ/ *a.* (of shares) not entitling holder to vote.

non-White /nɒn'waɪt/ **1** *a.* belonging to race other than White race. **2** *n.* non-White person.

noodle¹ /'nu:d(ə)l/ *n.* strip of pasta used in soups etc. [G]

noodle² /'nu:d(ə)l/ *n.* simpleton; *sl.* head. [orig. unkn.]

nook /nʊk/ *n.* secluded corner or recess. [orig. unkn.]

noon *n.* twelve o'clock in the day, midday. [OE f. L *nona* (*hora*) ninth (hour); orig. 3 p.m. (cf. NONES)]

noonday *n.* midday.

noose **1** *n.* loop in rope etc. with running knot; snare, bond. **2** *v.t.* catch with or enclose in noose. [F *no(u)s* f. L (NODE)]

nor *conj.* and not (*neither one thing nor the other*); and not either (*can neither read nor write*). [contr. of obs. *nother* (NO¹, WHETHER)]

nor' = NORTH, esp. in compounds (*nor'ward, nor'wester*). [abbr.]

Nordic /'nɔ:dɪk/ **1** *a.* of the tall blond long-headed Germanic people of Scandinavia. **2** *n.* Nordic person. [F (*nord* north)]

Norfolk jacket /'nɔ:fək/ man's loose single-breasted belted jacket. [*Norfolk* in England]

norm *n.* standard or pattern or type; standard amount (of work etc.); customary behaviour. [L *norma* carpenter's square]

normal /'nɔ:m(ə)l/ **1** *a.* conforming to a standard, regular, usual, typical; free from mental or emotional disorder; (of line) at right angles, perpendicular. **2** *n.* normal value of temperature etc. usual state, level, etc.; line at right angles. **3 normalcy** *n.*; **normality** /-'mælɪtɪ/ *n.* [F, or L *normalis* (prec.)]

normalize *v.* make or become normal; cause to conform; **normalization** /-'zeɪʃ(ə)n/ *n.*

normally *adv.* in normal manner; usually.

Norman /'nɔ:mən/ **1** *n.* native of Normandy; descendant of mixed Scandinavian and Frankish people established there in 10th c.; Norman French or style. **2** *a.* of the Normans; of their style of architecture, with rounded arches and heavy pillars. **3 Norman French** French as spoken by Normans or (after 1066) in English lawcourts. [F f. ON, = *Northman*]

normative /'nɔ:mətɪv/ *a.* of or establishing a norm. [F f. L (NORM)]

Norn *n.* each of three goddesses of destiny in Scandinavian mythology. [ON]

Norse **1** *n.* the Norwegian language; the Scandinavian language-group. **2** *a.* of ancient Scandinavia, esp. Norway. **3 Old Norse** Germanic language of Norway and its colonies, or of Scandinavia, until 14th c. **4 Norseman** *n.* [Du. *noor(d)sch* northern]

north **1** *n.* compass point 90 anticlockwise from east; direction in which this lies; (usu. **North**) part of country or town lying to the north. **2** *a.* towards, at, near, or facing north; coming from the north (*north wind*). **3** *adv.* towards, at, or near the north. **4 north country** northern part of England; **north of** further north than; **North Pole** northern end of earth's axis of rotation; **North Star** the pole-star (see POLE²); **to the north (of)** in a northward direction (from). [OE]

north-east **1** *n.* point midway between north and east; direction in which this lies; (**North-East**) part of country or town lying to the north-east. **2** *a.* of, towards, or coming from the north-east. 3 *adv.* towards, at, or near the north-east. 4 **north-north-east** direction midway between north and north-east. 5 **north-easterly** *a.* & *adv.*; **north--eastern** *a.*

northeaster /nɔ:θ'i:stə/ *n.* north-east wind.

northerly /'nɔ:ðəlɪ/ *a.* & *adv.* in northern position or direction; (of wind) blowing from the north.

northern /'nɔ:ð(ə)n/ *a.* of or in the north; **northern lights** = AURORA BOREALIS. [OE]

northerner *n.* inhabitant of the north.

Northman *n.* native of Scandinavia, esp. of Norway. [NORTH]

northward /'nɔ:θwəd/ 1 *a.* & (also **northwards**) *adv.* towards the north. 2 *n.* northward direction or region. [-WARD]

north-west 1 *n.* point midway between north and west; direction in which this lies; (**North-West**) part of country or town lying to the north-west. 2 *a.* of, towards, or coming from the north-west. 3 *adv.* towards, at, or near the north-west. 4 **north-north-west** direction midway between north and north-west. 5 **north-westerly** *a.* & *adv.*; **north--western** *a.*

northwester /nɔ:θ'westə/ *n.* north-west wind.

Norwegian /nɔ:'wi:dʒ(ə)n/ 1 *a.* of Norway. 2 *n.* native or language of Norway. [med.L *Norvegia* f. ON, = north way]

nor'-wester *n.* = NORTHWESTER. [NOR']

Nos. *abbr.* numbers. [cf. No.]

nose /nəʊz/ 1 *n.* organ above mouth on face or head of man or animal, used for smelling and breathing; sense of smell; ability to detect particular thing (*a nose for scandal*); odour or perfume, e.g. of wine; open end of tube, pipe, etc.; front end or projecting part of thing, e.g. of car or aircraft; *sl.* police informer. 2 *v.* perceive smell of, discover by smell, detect; thrust one's nose against or into; pry or search (*after*, *around*, etc.); make one's way cautiously forward. 3 **by a nose** by a very narrow margin; **keep one's nose clean** stay out of trouble; **pay through the nose** have to pay exorbitant price; **put person's nose out of joint** embarrass or disconcert him; **rub person's nose in it** remind him humiliatingly of error etc.; **turn up one's nose** show disdain; **under one's nose** right before one; **with one's nose in the air** haughtily. [OE]

nosebag *n.* bag containing fodder, hung on horse's head.

noseband *n.* lower band of bridle passing over horse's nose and attached to cheek-straps.

nosebleed *n.* a bleeding from the nose.

nose-cone *n.* cone-shaped nose of rocket etc.

nosedive 1 *n.* steep downward plunge by aeroplane; sudden plunge or drop. 2 *v.i.* make nosedive.

nosegay /'nəʊzgeɪ/ *n.* small bunch of flowers.

nosh *sl.* 1 *v.* eat. 2 *n.* food, esp. snack. 3 **nosh-up** large meal. [Yiddish]

nostalgia /nɒ'stældʒɪə/ *n.* homesickness; sentimental yearning for the past; **nostalgic** *a.*; **nostalgically** *adv.* [L f. Gk (*nostos* return home, *algos* pain)]

nostril /'nɒstrɪl/ *n.* either opening in nose. [OE, = nose-hole]

nostrum /'nɒstrəm/ *n.* quack remedy, patent medicine; pet scheme, esp. for political or social reform. [L, = of our own make]

nosy *a.* inquisitive, prying; **Nosy Parker** busybody; **nosily** *adv.*; **nosiness** *n.* [NOSE]

not *adv.* expressing negation (*I am not*, *do not know*; also *colloq.* —**n't** as in *don't*, *haven't*); expressing denial or refusal, or *ellipt.* for negative phrase etc. (*Are you mad? Not at all*; *Is she coming? I hope not*; *Is he upset? Not he*); **not at all** in polite reply to thanks, there is no need to thank me; **not half** see HALF; **not quite** almost, noticeably not (*not quite proper*). [contr. of NOUGHT]

notable /'nəʊtəb(ə)l/ 1 *a.* worthy of note, striking, remarkable, eminent. 2 *n.* eminent person. 3 **notability** /-'bɪlɪtɪ/ *n.*; **notably** *adv.* [F f. L (*noto* NOTE)]

notary /'nəʊtərɪ/ *n.* (in full **notary public**) person with authority to draw up deeds and perform other legal formalities; **notarial** /-'teərɪəl/ *a.* [L *notarius* secretary]

notation /nəʊ'teɪʃ(ə)n/ *n.* representing of numbers, quantities, sounds, etc., by symbols; any set of such symbols. [F or L (NOTE)]

notch 1 *n.* V-shaped indentation on edge or surface. 2 *v.t.* make notches in; record or score (as) with notches (often with *up*). [AF]

note 1 *n.* brief record of facts, topics, etc., as aid to memory, for use in writing, etc. (often in *pl.*); short or informal letter; short annotation or additional explanation in book etc.; = BANKNOTE, written promise of payment of various kinds; formal diplomatic communication; notice, attention (*worthy of note*); eminence (*person of note*); written sign representing pitch and duration of musical sound; single tone of definite pitch made by musical instrument, voice, etc.;

key of piano etc.; significant sound or feature of expression (*note of assurance, of optimism*); characteristic, distinguishing feature. **2** *v.t.* observe, notice, give attention to; (often with *down*) record as thing to be remembered or observed; (in *p.p.*) celebrated, well known *for*. **3 hit** (or **strike**) **the right note** speak or act in exactly the right manner. [F f. L *nota* mark *n.*, *noto* mark *v.*]

notebook *n.* small book for memoranda.

notecase *n.* wallet for holding banknotes.

notelet /'nəʊtlɪt/ *n.* small folded card or sheet for informal letter.

notepaper *n.* paper for writing letters.

noteworthy *a.* worthy of attention, remarkable.

nothing /'nʌθɪŋ/ **1** *n.* no thing (*I see nothing that I want*); not anything (*nothing has been done*); person or thing of no importance; non-existence, what does not exist; no amount, nought. **2** *adv.* not at all, in no way (*is nothing like as good*). **3 for nothing** at no cost, without payment, to no purpose; **have nothing on** be naked; **have nothing on (person)** possess no advantage over, be much inferior to; **nothing doing** *colloq.* no prospect of success or agreement. [OE (NO[1], THING)]

nothingness *n.* non-existence; worthlessness, triviality.

notice /'nəʊtɪs/ **1** *n.* heed or attention (*it escaped my notice*); intimation or warning, (esp. formal) announcement; displayed sheet etc. bearing announcement; formal declaration of intention to end agreement or leave employment at specified time; newspaper or magazine review, comment, or article. **2** *v.t.* perceive, observe; remark upon. **3 at short notice** with little warning; **notice-board** board for displaying notices; **take (no) notice** show (no) signs of interest; **take notice of** observe, act upon. [F f. L (*notus* known)]

noticeable *a.* noteworthy, perceptible; **noticeably** *adv.*

notifiable /'nəʊtɪfaɪəb(ə)l/ *a.* (of disease) that must be notified to health authorities. [foll.]

notify /'nəʊtɪfaɪ/ *v.t.* inform or give notice to (person *of* or *that*); make (thing) known; **notification** /-fɪ'keɪʃ(ə)n/ *n.* [F f. L (*notus* known)]

notion /'nəʊʃ(ə)n/ *n.* concept or idea, conception; vague view or opinion; understanding or inclination, intention. [L *notio* (as prec.)]

notional *a.* hypothetical, imaginary; **notionally** *adv.*

notorious /nəʊ'tɔ:rɪəs/ *a.* well known, esp. for unfavourable reason; **notoriety** /-tə'raɪɪtɪ/ *n.* [L (*notus* known)]

notwithstanding /nɒtwɪθ'stændɪŋ, -wɪð-/ **1** *prep.* in spite of, without prevention by. **2** *adv.* nevertheless. [NOT, WITHSTAND]

nougat /'nu:gɑ:/ *n.* sweet made from sugar or honey, nuts, and egg-white. [F f. Prov.]

nought /nɔ:t/ *n.* figure 0, cipher; (*poetic* or *archaic*) nothing; **noughts and crosses** a paper-and-pencil game. [OE (NOT, AUGHT)]

noun *n.* word used as name of person, place, or thing. [AF f. L NOMEN]

nourish /'nʌrɪʃ/ *v.t.* sustain with food (*lit.* or *fig.*); foster or cherish (feeling etc.). [F f. L *nutrio* feed]

nourishing *a.* containing much nourishment.

nourishment *n.* sustenance, food.

nous /naʊs/ *n. Philos.* mind or intellect; *colloq.* common sense, gumption. [Gk]

nouveau riche /nu:vəʊ 'ri:ʃ/ *n.* (*pl.* ***nouveaux riches*** *pr.* same) one who has recently acquired (usu. ostentatious) wealth. [F, = new rich]

Nov. *abbr.* November.

nova /'nəʊvə/ *n.* (*pl.* **novae** or **novas**) star showing sudden large increase of brightness and then subsiding. [L, = new]

novel /'nɒv(ə)l/ **1** *a.* of new kind, strange, hitherto unknown. **2** *n.* fictitious prose story published as complete book. [F f. L (*novus* new)]

novelette /nɒvə'let/ *n.* short novel.

novelist /'nɒvəlɪst/ *n.* writer of novels.

novella /nə'velə/ *n.* short novel or narrative story. [It. (NOVEL)]

novelty /'nɒvəltɪ/ *n.* newness; new thing or occurrence; small toy etc. of novel design. [NOVEL]

November /nəʊ'vembə/ *n.* eleventh month of year. [F f. L (*novem* nine)]

novena /nə'vi:na/ *n.* Roman Catholic devotion consisting of special prayers or services on nine successive days. [L (*novem* nine)]

novice /'nɒvɪs/ *n.* probationary member of religious order; new convert; beginner. [F f. L *novicius* (NOVEL)]

noviciate /nə'vɪʃɪət/ *n.* (also **novitiate**) period of being a novice; religious novice; novices' quarters. [F or L (prec.)]

now 1 *adv.* at the present or mentioned time; by this time; immediately (*I must go now*); on this further occasion (*what do you want now?*); under the present circumstances (*I cannot now agree*); in the immediate past (*just now*); (in narrative) then, next (*Caesar now marched south*); (without reference to time, giving various tones to sentence) surely,

I insist, I wonder, etc. (*now what do you mean by that?*; *oh, come now!*). **2** *conj.* (also with *that*) as a consequence of the fact (*now that I am grown up*; *now you mention it*). **3** *n.* this time, the present. **4 for now** until a later time; **now and again** (or **then**) from time to time, intermittently. [OE]

nowadays /ˈnaʊədeɪz/ **1** *adv.* at the present time or age, in these times. **2** *n.* the present time. [A[3]]

nowhere /ˈnəʊweə/ **1** *adv.* in or to no place. **2** *pron.* no place. **3 get nowhere** make no progress; **nowhere near** not nearly. [OE]

nowt *n.* (*colloq.* or *dial.*) nothing. [NOUGHT]

noxious /ˈnɒkʃəs/ *a.* harmful, unwholesome. [L (*noxa* harm)]

nozzle /ˈnɒz(ə)l/ *n.* spout of hose etc. for jet to issue from. [dimin. of NOSE]

Np *symb.* neptunium.

nr. *abbr.* near.

NS *abbr.* new style.

NSPCC *abbr.* National Society for the Prevention of Cruelty to Children.

NSW *abbr.* New South Wales.

n't see NOT.

NT *abbr.* New Testament; *Austral.* Northern Territory.

nth see N.

nu /nju:/ *n.* thirteenth letter of Greek alphabet (Ν, ν). [Gk]

nuance /ˈnju:ɑ̃s/ *n.* subtle difference in or shade of meaning, feeling, colour, etc. [F, ult. f. L *nubes* cloud]

nub *n.* small lump, esp. of coal (also **nubble**); point or gist (*of* matter or story); **nubbly** *a.* [KNOB]

nubile /ˈnju:baɪl/ *a.* (of woman) marriageable or sexually attractive; **nubility** /-ˈbɪlɪtɪ/ *n.* [L (*nubo* become wife)]

nuclear /ˈnju:klɪə/ *a.* of or relating to or constituting a nucleus; using nuclear energy; **nuclear bomb** = *atomic bomb*; **nuclear energy** energy released or absorbed during reactions in atomic nuclei; **nuclear family** father, mother, and child(ren); **nuclear fission** splitting of heavy atomic nucleus spontaneously or on impact of another particle, with release of energy; **nuclear fuel** source of nuclear energy; **nuclear fusion** union of atomic nuclei to form heavier nuclei, with release of energy, this process as source of energy; **nuclear physics** physics dealing with atomic nuclei; **nuclear power** power derived from nuclear energy, country possessing nuclear weapons; **nuclear reactor** see REACTOR. [NUCLEUS]

nucleate /ˈnju:klɪeɪt/ *v.* form into nucleus; form nucleus. [L (NUCLEUS)]

nucleic acid /nju:ˈkli:ɪk/ either of two acids (DNA and RNA) present in all living cells. [foll.]

nucleus /ˈnju:klɪəs/ *n.* (*pl.* **nuclei** /-aɪ/) central part or thing around which others collect, central part of atom, of seed, or of plant or animal cell; kernel, initial part meant to receive additions. [L, = kernel, dimin. of *nux nuc-* nut]

nude 1 *a.* naked, bare, unclothed. **2** *n.* picture or sculpture etc. of nude human figure; nude person; (**the nude**) unclothed state, representation of undraped human figure. **3 nudity** *n.* [L *nudus*]

nudge 1 *v.* prod gently with elbow to attract attention; push in gradual manner. **2** *n.* such prod or push. [orig. unkn.]

nudist *n.* person who advocates or practises going unclothed; **nudism** *n.* [NUDE]

nugatory /ˈnju:gətərɪ/ *a.* futile, trifling; inoperative, not valid. [L (*nugae* trifles)]

nugget /ˈnʌgɪt/ *n.* lump of gold etc. as found in the earth; something valuable. [app. dial. *nug* lump]

nuisance /ˈnju:səns/ *n.* source of trouble or annoyance; obnoxious act, circumstances, thing, or person. [F, = hurt (*nuire nuis-* f. L *noceo* hurt)]

null *a.* void, not valid; characterless, expressionless; non-existent; **nullity** *n.* [F, or L *nullus* none]

nullify /ˈnʌlɪfaɪ/ *v.t.* neutralize, invalidate; **nullification** /-fɪˈkeɪʃ(ə)n/ *n.*

numb /nʌm/ **1** *a.* deprived of feeling or power of motion. **2** *v.t.* make numb; stupefy, paralyse. [obs. *nome* p.p. of *nim* take (NIMBLE)]

number 1 *n.* count, sum, or aggregate of persons or things or abstract units (*a large number of people* etc.); arithmetical value showing position in series, symbol or figure representing this (*house, telephone*, etc., *number*); person or thing having place in series, esp. single issue of magazine, item in programme, etc.; numerical reckoning (*laws of number*); company, collection, group (*among our number*); (in *pl.*) numerical preponderance (*force of numbers*); *Gram.* classification of words by their singular or plural forms, particular such form. **2** *v.t.* count; assign number(s) to; have or amount to specified number; include *among*, *in*, or *with* some class; (in *pass.*) be restricted in number. **3 one's days are numbered** one does not have long to live; **have person's number** *sl.* understand him or his motives etc.; **one's number is up** *colloq.* one is doomed (to die); **number one** *colloq.* oneself, the most important (*the number one priority*); **number-plate** plate on vehicle giving registration number;

without number innumerable. [AF f. L *numerus*]
numberless *a.* innumerable.
numerable /ˈnju:mərəb(ə)l/ *a.* countable. [L (NUMBER)]
numeral /ˈnju:mər(ə)l/ **1** *n.* symbol denoting a number. **2** *a.* of or denoting a number. [L (NUMBER)]
numerate /ˈnju:mərət/ *a.* acquainted with basic principles of mathematics and science; **numeracy** *n.* [L *numerus* number, after *literate*]
numeration /nju:məˈreɪʃ(ə)n/ *n.* method or process of numbering; calculation. [L (NUMBER)]
numerator /ˈnju:məreɪtə/ *n.* number above line in vulgar fraction showing how many of the parts indicated by the denominator are taken. [F or L (NUMBER)]
numerical /nju:ˈmerɪk(ə)l/ *a.* of, in, or denoting number(s); **numerically** *adv.* [med.L (NUMBER)]
numerology /nju:məˈrɒlədʒɪ/ *n.* study of occult significance of numbers. [-LOGY]
numerous /ˈnju:mərəs/ *a.* many; consisting of many. [L (NUMBER)]
numinous /ˈnju:mɪnəs/ *a.* indicating presence of divinity; spiritual, awe-inspiring. [L (*numen* deity)]
numismatic /nju:mɪzˈmætɪk/ *a.* of coins or coinage or medals; **numismatist** /-ˈmɪz-/ *n.* [F f. L f. Gk *nomisma* coin]
numismatics *n.pl.* (usu. treated as *sing.*) study of coins or medals.
numskull *n.* stupid person. [NUMB]
nun *n.* member of community of women living apart under religious vows. [OE & F f. L *nonna*]
nuncio /ˈnʌnʃɪəʊ/ *n.* (*pl.* **nuncios**) papal ambassador. [It. f. L *nuntius* envoy]
nunnery *n.* convent of nuns. [AF (NUN)]
nuptial /ˈnʌpʃ(ə)l/ **1** *a.* of marriage or wedding. **2** *n.* (usu. in *pl.*) wedding. [F or L (*nubo nupt-* wed)]
nurse 1 *n.* person trained to assist doctors in caring for the sick or infirm; woman employed to take charge of young children. **2** *v.* work as a nurse; attend to (sick person); feed or be fed at the breast; hold or treat carefully; foster, promote development of; pay special attention to; (in *pass.*) be brought up (*in* some condition). **3 nursing home** privately run hospital or home for invalids, old people, etc. [F *nurice* f. L (NOURISH)]
nurseling *n.* (also **nursling**) infant that is being suckled.
nursemaid *n.* young woman in charge of a child or children.
nursery /ˈnɜ:sərɪ/ *n.* room or place equipped for young children; = *day nursery*; place where plants are reared for sale; **nursery rhyme** simple traditional song or story in rhyme for children; **nursery school** school for children, esp. those under five; **nursery slopes** slopes suitable for beginners at skiing. [prob. AF (NURSE)]
nurseryman *n.* owner of or worker in plant nursery.
nurture /ˈnɜ:tʃə/ **1** *n.* bringing up, fostering care; nourishment. **2** *v.t.* bring up, rear. [F f. *nourrir* (NOURISH)]
nut 1 *n.* fruit consisting of hard or tough shell around edible kernel, this kernel; pod containing hard seeds; small usu. hexagonal piece of metal with hole through it screwed on end of bolt to secure it; *sl.* head; *sl.* crazy person; small lump (of coal etc.). **2** *v.i.* (-tt-) seek or gather nuts. **3 do one's nut** *sl.* be very angry; **nut-case** *sl.* crazy person; **nuts and bolts** practical details. [OE]
nutation /nju:ˈteɪʃ(ə)n/ *n.* nodding; oscillation of earth's axis. [L *nuto* nod]
nutcracker *n.* (usu. in *pl.*) instrument for cracking nuts. [NUT]
nuthatch /ˈnʌthætʃ/ *n.* small climbing bird feeding on nuts, insects, etc.
nutmeg /ˈnʌtmeg/ *n.* hard aromatic seed of E. Indian tree, ground or grated as spice. [F (*nois* nut, *mugue* MUSK)]
nutria /ˈnju:trɪə/ *n.* skin or fur of coypu. [Sp., = otter]
nutrient /ˈnju:trɪənt/ **1** *a.* serving as or providing nourishment. **2** *n.* nutrient substance. [L *nutrio* nourish]
nutriment /ˈnju:trɪmənt/ *n.* nourishing food (*lit.* or *fig.*).
nutrition /nju:ˈtrɪʃ(ə)n/ *n.* food, nourishment; **nutritional** *a.* [F or L (NUTRIENT)]
nutritious /nju:ˈtrɪʃəs/ *a.* efficient as food. [L]
nutritive /ˈnju:trɪtɪv/ *a.* of nutrition; nutritious. [F f. med.L (NUTRIENT)]
nuts *a. sl.* crazy, mad; **nuts about** (or **on**) very fond of. [pl. of NUT]
nutshell *n.* hard exterior covering of nut; **in a nutshell** in a few words. [NUT]
nutter *n. sl.* crazy person.
nutty *a.* full of nuts; tasting like nuts; *sl.* crazy; **nuttily** *adv.*; **nuttiness** *n.*
nux vomica /nʌks ˈvɒmɪkə/ *n.* seed of E. Indian tree, yielding strychnine. [L (*nux* nut, VOMIT)]
nuzzle /ˈnʌz(ə)l/ *v.* prod or rub gently with the nose; press nose *into* or *against*; nestle, lie snug. [NOSE]
NW *abbr.* North-West(ern).
NY *abbr.* New York.
nylon /ˈnaɪlɒn/ *n.* strong light synthetic polymer; fabric of this; (in *pl.*) stockings of nylon. [invented word]

nymph /nɪmf/ *n.* mythological semi-divine maiden of sea, woods, etc.; *poetic* maiden; immature form of some insects. [F f. L f. Gk *nymphē* nymph, bride]

nympho /ˈnɪmfəʊ/ *n.* (*pl.* **nymphos**) *colloq.* nymphomaniac.

nymphomania /nɪmfəʊˈmeɪnɪə/ *n.* excessive sexual desire in women. [NYMPH, -MANIA]

nymphomaniac *n.* woman suffering from nymphomania.

NZ *abbr.* New Zealand.

O

O[1], **o** /əʊ/ *n.* (*pl.* **Os, O's**) fifteenth letter; (0) nought, zero.

O[2] /əʊ/ *int.* prefixed to name in vocative (*O God*) or expressing wish, entreaty, etc. (*O for a holiday*). [natural excl.]

o' /ə/ *prep.* of, on (esp. in phrases: *o'clock, will-o'-the-wisp*). [abbr.]

-o *suffix* forming usu. *sl.* or *colloq.* variants or derivatives (*beano*). [perh. OH as joc. suffix]

-o- terminal vowel of comb. forms (*Franco-Prussian, oscilloscope*). [orig. Gk]

O *abbr.* Old.

O *symb.* oxygen.

oaf *n.* (*pl.* **oafs**) awkward lout; **oafish** *a.* [ON (ELF)]

oak *n.* forest tree with hard wood, acorns, and lobed leaves; its wood; allied or similar tree (*holm-oak*); *attrib.* of oak; **oak-apple** (or **-gall**) kinds of excrescence produced on oak by gall-flies; **the Oaks** annual race at Epsom for fillies. [OE]

oakum /ˈəʊkəm/ *n.* loose fibre obtained by picking old rope to pieces and used esp. in caulking. [OE, = off-comb]

OAP *abbr.* old-age pension(er).

oar /ɔː/ *n.* pole with blade used to propel boat by leverage against water; rower; **put one's oar in** interfere. [OE]

oarsman *n.* rower; **oarsmanship** *n.*; **oarswoman** *n. fem.*

oasis /əʊˈeɪsɪs/ *n.* (*pl.* **oases** /-iːz/) fertile spot in desert; thing or circumstance offering relief in difficulty. [L f. Gk]

oast *n.* kiln for drying hops; **oast-house** building containing this. [OE]

oat *n.* (in *pl.*) hardy cereal grown as food; grain yielded by this; oat-plant or variety of it; **oat-grass** wild oat; **off one's oats** *colloq.* lacking appetite for food. [OE]

oatcake *n.* thin unleavened cake made of oatmeal.

oaten /ˈəʊt(ə)n/ *a.* made of oats or oat-stem.

oath *n.* (*pl.* /əʊðz/) solemn declaration or undertaking naming God etc. as witness; profanity, obscenity; **on** (or **under**) **oath** having made a solemn oath. [OE]

oatmeal *n.* meal made from oats. [OAT]

OAU *abbr.* Organization of African Unity.

ob- *prefix* (usu. **oc-** before *c*, **of-** before *f*, **op-** before *p*) esp. in words from Latin, expressing exposure, meeting, facing, direction, compliance, opposition, resistance, hindrance, concealment, finality, completeness. [L (*ob* towards, against, in the way of)]

ob. *abbr.* he or she died. [L *obiit*]

obbligato /ɒblɪˈɡɑːtəʊ/ *n.* (*pl.* **obbligatos**) *Mus.* part or accompaniment forming integral part of a composition. [It., = obligatory]

obdurate /ˈɒbdjʊrət/ *a.* hardened, stubborn; **obduracy** *n.* [L (*duro* harden)]

OBE *abbr.* Officer of the Order of the British Empire.

obedient /əʊˈbiːdɪənt/ *a.* obeying or ready to obey; submissive to another's will; **obedience** *n.* [F f. L (OBEY)]

obeisance /əʊˈbeɪsəns/ *n.* bow, curtsy, or other respectful gesture; homage; **obeisant** *a.* [F (OBEY)]

obelisk /ˈɒbəlɪsk/ *n.* tapering usu. four-sided stone pillar as monument. [L f. Gk (dimin. of foll.)]

obelus /ˈɒbələs/ *n.* (*pl.* **obeli** /-aɪ/) dagger-shaped mark of reference (†). [L f. Gk, = pointed pillar, spit]

obese /əʊˈbiːs/ *a.* very fat; **obesity** *n.* [L (*edo* eat)]

obey /əʊˈbeɪ/ *v.* carry out command of; do what one is told to do; carry out (command); be actuated by (force or impulse). [F *obéir* f. L *obedio* (*audio* hear)]

obfuscate /ˈɒbfʌskeɪt/ *v.t.* obscure or confuse (mind, topic, etc.); stupefy, bewilder; **obfuscation** /-ˈkeɪʃ(ə)n/ *n.* [L (*fuscus* dark)]

obituary /əˈbɪtjʊərɪ/ **1** *n.* notice of death(s); account of life of deceased person. **2** *a.* of or serving as obituary. [L *obitus* death]

object 1 /ˈɒbdʒɪkt/ *n.* material thing that can be seen or touched; person or thing to which action or feeling is directed (*object of attention*); thing sought or aimed at; *Gram.* noun or its equivalent governed by active transitive verb or by preposition; *Philos.* thing external to the thinking mind or subject. **2** /əb'dʒekt/ *v.* express opposition (*to*), feel or express dislike or reluctance (*to*); adduce as contrary or damaging (*to* or *against*). **3 no object** not forming an important or restricting factor (*time is no object*); **object-glass** lens in telescope etc. nearest to object observed; **object-lesson** striking practical example of some principle. **4 objector** /əb'dʒektə/ *n.* [L (*jacio -ject-* throw)]

objectify /ɒb'dʒektɪfaɪ/ *v.t.* make objective, embody.

objection /əb'dʒekʃ(ə)n/ *n.* expression or feeling of opposition or disapproval; objecting, adverse reason or statement. [F or L (OBJECT)]

objectionable *a.* open to objection; unpleasant, offensive; **objectionably** *adv.*

objective /əb'dʒektɪv/ **1** *a.* external to the mind, actually existing; dealing with outward things or exhibiting facts uncoloured by feelings or opinions; *Gram.* (of case or word) constructed as or appropriate to the object; aimed at. **2** *n.* something sought or aimed at; *Gram.* objective case. **3 objectivity** /ɒbdʒek'tɪvɪtɪ/ *n.* [med.L (OBJECT)]

objet d'art /ɒbʒeɪ 'dɑː/ *n.* (*pl.* ***objets d'art*** *pr.* same) small decorative object. [F, = object of art]

objurgate /'ɒbdʒɜːgeɪt/ *v.t. literary* chide or scold; **objurgation** /-'geɪʃ(ə)n/ *n.* [L (*jurgo* quarrel)]

oblate /'ɒbleɪt, ə'bleɪt/ *a. Geom.* (of spheroid) flattened at poles. [L (OB-, cf. PROLATE)]

oblation /əʊ'bleɪʃ(ə)n/ *n.* thing offered to divine being. [F or L (OFFER)]

obligate /'ɒblɪgeɪt/ *v.t.* (usu. in *p.p.*) bind (person) *to do* thing. [L (OBLIGE)]

obligation /ɒblɪ'geɪʃ(ə)n/ *n.* constraining power of law, duty, responsibility, etc.; duty or task; binding agreement; indebtedness for service or benefit; **under (an) obligation** owing gratitude. [F f. L (OBLIGE)]

obligatory /ə'blɪgətərɪ/ *a.* binding, compulsory; **obligatorily** *adv.* [L (foll.)]

oblige /ə'blaɪdʒ/ *v.* constrain or compel *to do* thing; be binding on; help or gratify with a small service; **be obliged to person** be indebted or grateful to him; **much obliged** thank you. [F f. L *obligo* bind]

obliging *a.* helpful, accommodating.

oblique /ə'bliːk/ **1** *a.* declining from the vertical or horizontal, diverging from straight line or course; not going straight to the point, roundabout, indirect; *Gram.* (of case) other than nominative or vocative. **2** *n.* oblique stroke (/). **3 obliquity** /ə'blɪkwɪtɪ/ *n.* [F f. L]

obliterate /ə'blɪtəreɪt/ *v.t.* blot out, destroy, leave no clear traces of; **obliteration** /-'reɪʃ(ə)n/ *n.*; **obliterator** *n.* [L *oblitero* erase (*litera* letter)]

oblivion /ə'blɪvɪən/ *n.* state of being forgotten or being oblivious. [F f. L (*obliviscor* forget)]

oblivious /ə'blɪvɪəs/ *a.* unaware or unconscious (with *of* or *to*). [L (prec.)]

oblong /'ɒblɒŋ/ **1** *a.* of rectangular shape with adjacent sides unequal. **2** *n.* oblong figure or object. [L *oblongus* somewhat long]

obloquy /'ɒbləkwɪ/ *n.* abuse; being generally ill spoken of. [L *obloquium* contradiction (*loquor* speak)]

obnoxious /əb'nɒkʃəs/ *a.* offensive, objectionable, disliked. [L (*noxa* injury)]

oboe /'əʊbəʊ/ *n.* woodwind double-reed instrument with piercing plaintive tone; **oboist** /-bəʊɪst/ *n.* [It. f. F *hautbois* (*haut* high, *bois* wood)]

obscene /əb'siːn/ *a.* offensively indecent; *Law* (of publication) tending to deprave or corrupt; *colloq.* highly offensive; **obscenity** /-'senɪtɪ/ *n.* [F, or L *obsc(a)enus* abominable]

obscure /əb'skjʊə/ **1** *a.* not clearly expressed or easily understood; dark, indistinct; hidden or unnoticed; (of person) undistinguished, hardly known. **2** *v.t.* make obscure or unintelligible; conceal. **3 obscurity** *n.* [F f. L]

obsequies /'ɒbsɪkwɪz/ *n. pl.* funeral rites. [AF f. L *obsequiae*]

obsequious /əb'siːkwɪəs/ *a.* servile, fawning. [L (*obsequor* comply with)]

observance /əb'zɜːvəns/ *n.* keeping or performance of law, duty, etc.; rite, ceremonial act. [F f. L (OBSERVE)]

observant *a.* acute in taking notice; attentive in observance.

observation /ɒbzə'veɪʃ(ə)n/ *n.* observing or being observed; comment or remark; facts or data, the recording of these; **observational** *a.* [L (OBSERVE)]

observatory /əb'zɜːvətərɪ/ *n.* building for astronomical or other observation.

observe /əb'zɜːv/ *v.* perceive, become aware of; watch carefully; follow or keep (rules etc.); celebrate or perform (occasion, rite, etc.); note and record (facts or data); remark. [F f. L (*servo* watch, keep)]

observer *n.* one who observes; interested spectator.

obsess /əb'ses/ *v.t.* preoccupy, haunt, fill mind of (person) continually; **obsessive** *a.* [L (*obsideo -sess-* besiege)]

obsession /əb'seʃ(ə)n/ *n.* obsessing or being obsessed; persistent idea or thought dominating person's mind; **obsessional** *a.*

obsidian /ɒb'sɪdɪən/ *n.* dark vitreous

lava. [L (*Obsius*, discoverer of similar stone)]

obsolescent /ɒbsə'lesənt/ *a.* becoming obsolete; **obsolescence** *n.* [L (*soleo* be accustomed)]

obsolete /'ɒbsəli:t/ *a.* no longer used, antiquated.

obstacle /'ɒbstək(ə)l/ *n.* thing obstructing progress. [F f. L (*obsto* stand in the way)]

obstetrician /ɒbste'trɪʃ(ə)n/ *n.* specialist in obstetrics. [foll.]

obstetrics /ɒb'stetrɪks/ *n.pl.* (usu. treated as *sing.*) branch of medicine and surgery dealing with childbirth; **obstetric** *a.* [L (*obstetrix* midwife f. *obsto* be present)]

obstinate /'ɒbstɪnət/ *a.* stubborn, intractable; firmly continuing in one's action or opinion despite persuasion; **obstinacy** *n.* [L (*obstino* persist)]

obstreperous /əb'strepərəs/ *a.* noisy, turbulent, unruly. [L (*obstrepo* shout at)]

obstruct /əb'strʌkt/ *v.* block up, make hard or impossible to pass; prevent or retard progress of, impede; **obstructor** *n.* [L *obstruo -struct-* block up]

obstruction /əb'strʌkʃ(ə)n/ *n.* obstructing, being obstructive; thing that obstructs, blockage; hindering or hindrance.

obstructive *a.* causing or intended to cause obstruction. [OBSTRUCT]

obtain /əb'teɪn/ *v.* acquire, secure, have granted to one, get; (of practice etc.) be in vogue, prevail. [F f. L (*teneo* hold)]

obtrude /əb'tru:d/ *v.* thrust (a matter or oneself) importunately forward (*on* or *upon* person or his notice); be or become obtrusive; **obtrusion** *n.* [L *obtrudo* thrust against]

obtrusive /əb'tru:sɪv/ *a.* obtruding oneself; unpleasantly noticeable.

obtuse /əb'tju:s/ *a.* dull-witted, slow to understand; of blunt shape, not sharp-pointed or sharp-edged; (of angle) more than 90° but less than 180°. [L (*obtundo -tus-* beat against, blunt)]

obverse /'ɒbvɜ:s/ *n.* side of coin or medal etc. that bears the head or principal design; front or proper or top side of a thing; counterpart. [L (*obverto -vers-* turn towards)]

obviate /'ɒbvɪeɪt/ *v.t.* clear away, make unnecessary, get round (danger or hindrance etc.). [L *obvio* prevent (*via* way)]

obvious /'ɒbvɪəs/ *a.* easily seen or recognized or understood. [L (*ob viam* in the way)]

oc- see OB-.

OC *abbr.* Officer Commanding.

ocarina /ɒkə'ri:nə/ *n.* small egg-shaped musical wind-instrument. [It. (*oca* goose)]

occasion /ə'keɪʒ(ə)n/ **1** *n.* special event or happening, particular time marked by this; reason, need; suitable juncture, opportunity; immediate but subordinate cause. **2** *v.t.* cause, esp. incidentally. **3 on occasion** now and then, when need arises. [F or L (*occido -cas-* go down)]

occasional *a.* happening irregularly and infrequently; made or intended for, or acting on, a special occasion; **occasionally** *adv.*

Occident /'ɒksɪdənt/ *n.* (*poetic* or *rhet.*) *the* West (esp. Europe and America) as opposed to the Orient. [F f. L *occidens -entis* setting, sunset, west]

occidental /ɒksɪ'dent(ə)l/ **1** *a.* of the Occident, western. **2** *n.* native or inhabitant of the Occident.

occiput /'ɒksɪpʌt/ *n.* back of the head; **occipital** /ɒk'sɪpɪt(ə)l/ *a.* [L (*caput* head)]

occlude /ɒ'klu:d/ *v.t.* obstruct, stop up; *Chem.* absorb (gases); **occlusion** *n.* [L *occludo -clus-* close up]

occult /ɒ'kʌlt/ *a.* involving the supernatural, mystical, magical; esoteric, recondite; **the occult** occult phenomena generally. [L *occulo -cult-* hide]

occupant /'ɒkjʊpənt/ *n.* person occupying a dwelling or office or position; **occupancy** *n.* [F or L (OCCUPY)]

occupation /ɒkjʊ'peɪʃ(ə)n/ *n.* profession or employment; occupying or being occupied, esp. by armed forces of another country. [AF f. L (OCCUPY)]

occupational *a.* of or connected with one's occupation; **occupational disease** (or **hazard**) disease or hazard to which a particular occupation renders one especially liable; **occupational therapy** mental or physical activity to assist recovery from disease or injury.

occupier /'ɒkjʊpaɪə/ *n.* person residing in house etc. as its owner or tenant. [AF or foll.]

occupy /'ɒkjʊpaɪ/ *v.t.* reside in, be tenant of; take up or fill (space or time or place); hold (position or office); take military possession of; place oneself in (building etc.) forcibly or without authority; keep (person or his time) filled with an activity. [F f. L *occupo* seize]

occur /ə'kɜ:/ *v.i.* (**-rr-**) come into being as event or process; be met with or found in some place or conditions; **occur to** come into the mind of. [L *occurro* befall]

occurrence /ə'kʌrəns/ *n.* occurring; thing that occurs, event. [F f. L (prec.)]

ocean /'əʊʃ(ə)n/ *n.* sea surrounding continents of the earth, esp. one of five named divisions of this (*Atlantic, Pacif*, *ic, Indian, Arctic*, and *Antarctic Oceans*); immense expanse or quantity; **ocean-going** (of ship) able to cross the ocean; **oceanic** /əʊʃɪ'ænɪk/ *a*. [F f. L f. Gk]

oceanography /əʊʃjə'nɒgrəfɪ/ *n*. study of oceans; **oceanographer** *n*.

ocelot /'əʊsɪlɒt/ *n*. leopard-like feline of S. & Central America. [F f. Nahuatl]

och /ɒx/ *int*. (*Sc. & Ir.*) = *oh, ah*. [Gael. & Ir.]

ochre /'əʊkə/, *US* **ocher** *n*. earth used as yellow or brown or red pigment; pale brownish-yellow colour; **ochreous** *a*. [F f. L f. Gk]

o'clock /ə'klɒk/ *adv*. = *of the clock*, used to specify hour (*six o'clock*). [o', CLOCK[1]]

Oct. *abbr*. October.

oct-, octa- *in comb*. eight. [L *octo*, Gk *oktō*]

octagon /'ɒktəgən/ *n*. plane figure with eight sides and angles; **octagonal** /-'tægən(ə)l/ *a*. [L f. Gk (OCTA-, *-gōnos* -angled)]

octahedron /ɒktə'hi:drən/ *n*. (*pl*. **octahedrons**) solid figure contained by eight plane faces and usu. by eight triangles; **octahedral** *a*. [Gk]

octane /'ɒkteɪn/ *n*. hydrocarbon compound of paraffin series occurring in petrol; **high-octane** (of fuel used in internal-combustion engines) not detonating rapidly during power stroke; **octane number** number indicating antiknock properties of fuel. [OCT-]

octave /'ɒktɪv/ *n*. *Mus*. note seven diatonic degrees from given note, interval between given note and its octave, series of notes filling this; eight-line stanza. [F f. L (*octavus* eighth)]

octavo /ɒk'teɪvəʊ/ *n*. (*pl*. **octavos**) size of book or page given by folding sheet of standard size three times to form eight leaves; book or sheet of this size. [L (prec.)]

octet /ɒk'tet/ *n*. (also **octette**) musical composition for eight performers; the performers; any group of eight. [It. or G (OCT-)]

octo- *in comb*. eight. [as OCTA-]

October /ɒk'təʊbə/ *n*. tenth month of year. [OE f. L (*octo* eight, orig. 8th month of Roman year)]

octogenarian /ɒktəʊdʒɪ'neərɪən/ *n*. person from 80 to 89 years old. [L (*octogeni* 80 each)]

octopus /'ɒktəpəs/ *n*. (*pl*. **octopuses**) sea mollusc with eight suckered tentacles. [Gk (OCTO-, *pous* foot)]

ocular /'ɒkjʊlə/ *a*. of or connected with the eyes or sight, visual. [F f. L (*oculus* eye)]

oculist /'ɒkjʊlɪst/ *n*. specialist in treatment of eye diseases and defects.

o.d. *abbr*. outer diameter.

odd *a*. extraordinary, strange, remarkable, eccentric; casual, occasional (*odd jobs; odd moments*); not normally noticed or considered, unconnected (*in some odd corner*); (of numbers such as 3 and 5) not integrally divisible by two, bearing such number (*no parking on odd dates*); left over when rest have been distributed or divided into pairs (*have got an odd sock*); detached from set or series (*a few odd volumes*); (appended to number, sum, weight, etc.) somewhat more than (*forty odd; forty-odd people*); by which round number, given sum, etc., is exceeded (*we have 102; what shall we do with the odd two?*); **odd man out** person or thing differing from all others of group in some respect. [ON *oddi* point, angle, third or odd number]

oddball *n*. *colloq*. eccentric person.

oddity /'ɒdɪtɪ/ *n*. strangeness, peculiar trait; strange person, thing, or event.

oddment *n*. odd article, something left over; (in *pl*.) odds and ends.

odds *n.pl*. (sometimes treated as *sing*.) ratio between amounts staked by parties to bet, based on expected probability either way; balance of advantage or probability (*the odds are against it*); advantageous difference (*it makes no odds*); **at odds** in conflict or at variance (*with*); **odds and ends** remnants, stray articles; **odds-on** state when success is expected to be more likely than failure; **over the odds** above generally agreed price etc. [ODD]

ode *n*. lyric poem of exalted style and tone. [F f. L f. Gk *ōidē* song]

odious /'əʊdɪəs/ *a*. hateful, repulsive. [foll.]

odium /'əʊdɪəm/ *n*. widespread dislike or disapproval felt towards person or action. [L, = hatred]

odometer /əʊ'dɒmɪtə/ *n*. instrument for measuring distance travelled by wheeled vehicle. [F f. Gk *hodos* way]

odoriferous /əʊdə'rɪfərəs/ *a*. diffusing a (usu. agreeable) odour. [L (foll.)]

odour /'əʊdə/, *US* **odor** *n*. smell or fragrance; favour or repute (*in bad odour*); **odorous** *a*. [F f. L *odor*]

odyssey /'ɒdɪsi:/ *n*. long adventurous journey. [title of Homeric epic on adventures of *Odysseus*]

OECD *abbr*. Organization for Economic Co-operation and Development.

OED *abbr*. Oxford English Dictionary.

oedema /i:'di:mə, ɪ'd-/ *n*. swollen state of tissue in the body; **oedematous** *a*. [L f. Gk (*oideō* swell)]

Oedipus complex /'i:dɪpəs/ subconscious sexual desire of child for parent of the opposite sex (esp. mother); **Oedipal**

a. [Gk *Oidipous*, who in ignorance married his mother]

o'er /ˈəʊə/ *prep.* & *adv.* (chiefly *poetic*) = OVER. [contr.]

oesophagus /iːˈsɒfəgəs/ *n.* (*pl.* **oesophagi** /-dʒaɪ/) canal from mouth to stomach, gullet. [Gk]

oestrogen /ˈiːstrədʒ(ə)n/ *n.* sex hormone maintaining or developing female bodily characteristics. [Gk *oistros* frenzy, -GEN]

of /əv, *emphat.* ɒv/ *prep.* expressing origin or cause (*paintings of Turner*; *people of Rome*; *died of cancer*); material or substance (*house of cards*; *built of bricks*); belonging, connection, or possession (*thing of the past*; *articles of clothing*; *master of the house*); identity or closer definition (*city of Rome*; *a pound of apples*; *a fool of a man*); removal or separation (*north of the city*; *got rid of them*; *robbed him of £10*); reference, direction, or respect (*beware of the dog*; *suspected of fraud*; *very good of you*; *short of money*); objective relation (*love of music*; *in search of peace*); partition, classification, or inclusion (*no more of that*; *part of the story*; *this sort of book*); description, quality, or condition (*the hour of prayer*; *man of tact*; *girl of ten*; *on the point of leaving*); **be of** possess, give rise to (*is of great interest*); **of all the nerve** (or **cheek** etc.) exclamation of indignation at person's impudence etc.; **of an evening** *colloq.* most evenings, at some time in the evenings; **of late** recently; **of old** formerly. [OE]

of- see OB-.

off 1 *adv.* away, at or to a distance (*drove off*; *3 miles off*); out of position, not on or touching or attached, loose, separate, gone (*has come off*; *take your coat off*); so as to be rid of (*sleep it off*); so as to break continuity or continuance, discontinued, stopped (*turn off the radio*; *take a day off*; *the meeting is off*); not available on menu etc. (*chips are off*); to the end, entirely, so as to be clear (*clear off*; *finish off*; *pay off*); situated as regards money, supplies, etc. (*not very well off*); off-stage (*noises off*); (of food etc.) beginning to decay. **2** *prep.* from, away or down or up from, not on (*fell off his chair*; *took something off the price*); temporarily relieved of or abstaining from (*off duty*; *off his food*) or not achieving (*off form*); using as source or means of support (*live off the land*); leading from, not far from (*a street off the Strand*); at a short distance to sea from (*sank off Cape Horn*). **3** *a.* far, further (*off side of the wall*); (of part of vehicle, animal, or road) further from side of road when facing forward, usu. right; (in cricket) designating half of field (as divided lengthways through pitch) to which striker's feet are pointed. **4** *n.* the off side in cricket; start of race. **5 a bit off** *sl.* rather annoying or unfair or unwell; **off and on** intermittently, now and then; **off-beat** eccentric, unconventional; **off chance** remote possibility; **off colour** not in good health, *US* somewhat indecent; **off-day** day when one is not at one's best; **off-key** out of tune, not quite suitable or fitting; **off-licence** shop selling alcoholic drink for consumption elsewhere, licence for this; **off-line** (of computer equipment or process) not directly controlled by or connected to central processor; **off-load** unload; **off-peak** used or for use at times other than those of greatest demand; **off-putting** *colloq.* disconcerting, repellent; **off-season** time when business etc. is slack; **off-stage** *a.* & *adv.* not on the stage and so not visible or audible to audience; **off-white** white with grey or yellowish tinge. [var. of OF]

Off. *abbr.* Office; Officer.

offal /ˈɒf(ə)l/ *n.* edible parts of carcass (esp. heart, liver, etc.) cut off as less valuable; refuse, scraps. [Du. *afval* (OFF, FALL)]

offcut *n.* remnant of timber etc. after cutting. [OFF]

offence /əˈfens/ *n.* illegal act, transgression; wounding of the feelings, umbrage (*give*, *take*, *offence*); aggressive action. [foll.]

offend /əˈfend/ *v.* cause offence to, upset; displease or anger; do wrong. [F f. L *offendo -fens-* strike against, displease]

offense *US* var. of OFFENCE.

offensive /əˈfensɪv/ **1** *a.* causing offence, insulting; disgusting; aggressive, attacking, (of weapon) meant for attacking. **2** *n.* aggressive attitude or action or campaign. [F or med.L (prec.)]

offer 1 *v.* present for acceptance or refusal or consideration; express readiness or show intention *to do* thing; provide, give opportunity for; attempt (violence, resistance, etc.); make available for sale; present to sight or notice; present by way of sacrifice; present itself, occur (*as opportunity offers*). **2** *n.* expression of readiness to do or give if desired, or to buy or sell (for certain amount); amount offered; proposal (esp. of marriage); bid. **3 on offer** for sale at certain (esp. reduced) price. [OE & F f. L *offero oblat-*]

offering *n.* thing offered as sacrifice or as token of devotion.

offertory /ˈɒfətərɪ/ *n.* offering of bread and wine at Eucharist; collection of money at religious service. [eccl.L (OFFER)]

offhand 1 *a.* curt or casual in manner; without preparation etc. 2 *adv.* in offhand way. 3 **offhanded** /-'hændɪd/ *a.* [OFF]

office /'ɒfɪs/ *n.* room or building used as place of business, esp. for clerical or administrative work; room or department for particular business (*ticket-office*); local centre of large business (*our London office*); position with duties attached to it, tenure of official position (*seek office*); quarters or staff or collective authority of a government department (*Foreign Office*); duty, task, function; piece of kindness, service (*through the good offices of*); authorized form of religious worship; (in *pl.*) parts of house devoted to household work, storage, etc. [F f. L *officium* (*opus* work, *facio -fic-* do)]

officer /'ɒfɪsə/ *n.* person holding position of authority or trust, esp. one with commission in armed services, in mercantile marine, or on passenger ship; policeman; holder of post in a society (e.g. president or secretary). [F f. L (prec.)]

official /ə'fɪʃ(ə)l/ 1 *a.* of an office or its tenure; characteristic of officials and bureaucracy; properly authorized. 2 *n.* person holding office or engaged in official duties. 3 **officialdom** *n.*; **officially** *adv.*[L (OFFICE)]

officialese /əfɪʃə'li:z/ *n.* jargon associated with officials.

officiate /ə'fɪʃɪeɪt/ *v.i.* act in an official capacity; perform divine service. [L (OFFICE)]

officious /ə'fɪʃəs/ *a.* asserting one's authority, domineering; intrusively kind.

offing *n.* more distant part of sea in view; **in the offing** not far away, likely to appear or happen. [OFF]

offish *a. colloq.* inclined to be aloof.

offprint *n.* printed copy of article etc. orig. forming part of larger publication.

offset 1 *n.* side-shoot from plant serving for propagation; compensation, consideration or amount diminishing or neutralizing effect of contrary one; sloping ledge in wall etc.; bend in pipe etc. to carry it past obstacle; (in full **offset process**) method of printing with transfer of ink from plate or stone to rubber surface and thence to paper. 2 /also -'set/ *v.t.* (**-tt-** *p.p.* **offset**) counterbalance, compensate; print by offset process. [OFF, SET[1]]

offshoot *n.* side-shoot or branch; derivative. [OFF]

offshore *a.* at sea some distance from shore; (of wind) blowing from land towards sea.

offside /ɒf'saɪd/ *a.* (of player in field game) in position where he may not play the ball.

offspring *n.* (*pl.* same) person's child or children or descendants; animal's young or descendants; *fig.* result. [OE (SPRING)]

oft /ɒft/ *adv. archaic* often. [OE]

often /'ɒf(ə)n/ *adv.* frequently, many times; at short intervals; in many instances; **every so often** from time to time.

ogee /'əʊdʒi:, -'dʒi:/ *n.* sinuous line of double continuous curve as in S; moulding with such section. [OGIVE]

ogive /'əʊdʒaɪv, -'dʒaɪv/ *n.* diagonal rib of vault; pointed arch. [F]

ogle /'əʊg(ə)l/ 1 *v.* look amorously (at). 2 *n.* amorous glance. [prob. LG or Du.]

ogre /'əʊgə/ *n.* man-eating giant in folklore; terrifying person; **ogress** *n. fem.*; **ogrish** /'əʊgərɪʃ/ *a.* [F]

oh /əʊ/ *int.* expressing surprise, pain, entreaty, etc. [var. of O[2]]

ohm /əʊm/ *n.* unit of electrical resistance. [*Ohm*, physicist]

OHMS *abbr.* On Her (or His) Majesty's Service.

oho /əʊ'həʊ/ *int.* expressing surprise or exultation. [O[2], HO]

-oid *suffix* forming adjectives and nouns in sense '(something) having the form of or resembling' (*Negroid, rhomboid, thyroid*). [Gk *eidos* form]

oil 1 *n.* any of various thick, viscous, usu. inflammable liquids insoluble in water; *US* petroleum; (often in *pl.*) = *oil colour*, *colloq.* picture painted in oil-colours. 2 *v.* apply oil to, lubricate, impregnate or treat with oil; supply oil to. 3 **oil-colour** (usu. in *pl.*) paint made by mixing powdered pigment in oil; **oil-fired** using oil as fuel; **oil-paint** = *oil-colour*; **oil-painting** art of painting, or picture painted, in oil-colours; **oil rig** equipment for drilling an oil well; **oil-slick** smooth patch of oil esp. on sea; **oil well** well from which mineral oil is drawn. [AF f. L *oleum* olive oil]

oilcake *n.* compressed linseed from which oil has been expressed, used as cattle food or manure.

oilcloth *n.* fabric, esp. canvas, waterproofed with oil.

oiled *a. sl.* drunk.

oilfield *n.* district yielding mineral oil.

oilskin *n.* cloth waterproofed with oil; garment of this, (in *pl.*) suit of this.

oily *a.* of or like oil, covered or soaked with oil; (of manner) fawning, subserviently ingratiating; **oiliness** *n.*

ointment /'ɔɪntmənt/ *n.* smooth greasy

healing or beautifying preparation for the skin. [F f. L (*unguo* annoint)]

OK /əʊˈkeɪ/ (also **okay**) *colloq.* **1** *a.* & *adv.* all right, satisfactory; (as *int.*) I agree. **2** *n.* approval, sanction. **3** *v.t.* approve, sanction, mark 'OK'. [orig. US, app. initials of *oll* (or *orl*) *korrect* joc. form of 'all correct']

okra /ˈəʊkrə, ˈɒk-/ *n.* tall orig. African plant with seed-pods used for food. [W. Afr. native name]

-ol *suffix* in names of alcohols and other chemical compounds. [(ALCOH)OL & L *oleum* oil]

old /əʊld/ *a.* advanced in age, far on in natural period of existence, not young or near its beginning; made long ago, long in use, worn or dilapidated or shabby from passage of time; having characteristics, experience, feebleness, etc., of age (*child has an old face*); practised, inveterate (*an old offender*; *old in crime*); belonging only or chiefly to the past, lingering on, former (*old times*; *old memories*); dating from far back, long established or known, ancient, primeval (*old as the hills*; *old friends*; *an old family*); (appended to period of time) of age (*is ten years old*; *ten-year-old girl*; *a ten-year-old*); (of language) as used in former or earliest times; *colloq.* as term of fondness or casual reference (*good old Jack*; *old chap, fellow*, etc.; *old bean, fruit, thing*, etc.); **the old** *pl.* old people; **of old** of or in past times; **old age** later part of normal life; **old-age pension** = *retirement pension*; **old-age pensioner** person receiving this; **old boy** former member of school, *colloq.* elderly man, (as form of address) = *old man*; **the old country** one's mother country; **old-fashioned** in or according to fashion or tastes no longer current, antiquated; **old girl** former member of school, *colloq.* elderly woman, *colloq.* as fond form of address; **Old Glory** *US* the Stars and Stripes; **old gold** dull brownish-gold colour; **old guard** original or past or conservative members of a group; **old hand** person with much experience; **old hat** *colloq.* thing tediously familiar; **old lady** *colloq.* one's mother or wife; **old maid** elderly spinster, prim and fussy person; **old man** *colloq.* one's father or husband or employer etc., *colloq.* as fond form of address; **old man's beard** a kind of clematis with grey fluffy hairs round seeds; **old master** great painter of former times, esp. of 13th–17th c. in Europe, painting by such a painter; **Old Nick** the Devil; **Old Pals Act** doctrine that friends should always help one another; **old school** older attitudes or people having them; **old school tie** necktie with characteristic pattern worn by members of a particular (usu. public) school, *fig.* sign of excessive loyalty to traditional values; **old style** of date reckoned by Julian calendar; **Old Testament** part of Bible concerned with Mosaic dispensation; **old-time** belonging to former times; **old-timer** person with long experience or standing; **old wives' tale** old but foolish belief; **old woman** *colloq.* wife or mother, *fig.* fussy or timid man; **Old World** Europe, Asia, and Africa; **old year** year just ended or about to end. [OE]

olden *a. archaic* old, of old.

oldie *n. colloq.* old person or thing.

oleaginous /əʊlɪˈædʒɪnəs/ *a.* having properties of or producing oil; oily (*lit.* or *fig.*). [F f. L (OIL)]

oleander /əʊlɪˈændə/ *n.* evergreen flowering Mediterranean shrub. [L]

oleaster /əʊlɪˈæstə/ *n.* wild olive. [L (OIL)]

olefin /ˈəʊləfɪn/ *n.* hydrocarbon of type containing less than maximum amount of hydrogen. [F *oléfiant* oil-forming]

O level ordinary level in GCE examination. [abbr.]

olfactory /ɒlˈfæktərɪ/ *a.* concerned with smelling (*olfactory nerves*). [L (*oleo* smell, *facio* make)]

oligarch /ˈɒlɪgɑːk/ *n.* member of oligarchy. [Gk (*oligoi* few)]

oligarchy *n.* government, or State governed, by small group of people; members of such government; **oligarchic(al)** *a.*; **oligarchically** *adv.* [F or L (prec.)]

Oligocene /ˈɒlɪgəsiːn/ **1** *a.* of the third geological epoch of the Tertiary period. **2** *n.* this epoch. [Gk *oligos* little, *kainos* new]

olio /ˈəʊlɪəʊ/ *n.* (*pl.* **olios**) mixed dish, hotchpotch, stew; medley. [Sp.]

olive /ˈɒlɪv/ **1** *n.* small oval hard-stoned fruit, green when unripe, and bluish-black when ripe; tree bearing it; its wood; leaves or branch or wreath of olive as emblem of peace; colour of unripe olive. **2** *a.* coloured like unripe olive (*olive green*); (of complexion) yellowish-brown. **3 olive-branch** *fig.* something done or offered as sign of wish to make peace; **olive oil** oil extracted from olives. [F f. L *oliva* f. Gk]

olivine /ˈɒlɪviːn/ *n.* a mineral, usu. olive-green, composed of magnesium iron silicate.

Olympiad /əˈlɪmpɪæd/ *n.* period of four years between Olympic games, used by ancient Greeks in dating events; celebration of modern Olympic games; regular international contest in chess etc. [F or L f. Gk *Olumpias -ad-* (OLYMPIC)]

Olympian /ə'lɪmpɪən/ **1** *a.* of Olympus, celestial; (of manners etc.) magnificent, condescending, superior; = OLYMPIC. **2** *n.* dweller in Olympus, Greek god; person of great attainments or superhuman calm. [Mt. *Olympus* in Greece, or foll.]

Olympic /ə'lɪmpɪk/ **1** *a.* of the Olympic Games. **2** *n.* (in *pl.*) Olympic Games. **3 Olympic Games** ancient-Greek athletic festival held at Olympia every four years; modern international revival of this. [L f. Gk (*Olympia* in S. Greece)]

OM *abbr.* (member of the) Order of Merit.

ombudsman /'ɒmbʊdzmən/ *n.* (*pl.* **ombudsmen**) official appointed to investigate individual's complaints against public authorities. [Sw., = legal representative]

omega /'əʊmɪgə/ *n.* last letter of Greek alphabet (Ω, ω); last of series, final development. [Gk (*ō mega* = great O)]

omelette /'ɒmlɪt/ *n.* beaten eggs cooked in frying pan and often served folded around savoury or sweet filling. [F]

omen /'əʊmən/ *n.* occurrence or object portending good or evil; prophetic significance (*is of good* etc. *omen*). [L]

omicron /ə'maɪkrən/ *n.* fifteenth letter of Greek alphabet (O, o). [Gk (*o micron* = small O)]

ominous /'ɒmɪnəs/ *a.* of evil omen, inauspicious. [L (OMEN)]

omission /ə'mɪʃ(ə)n/ *n.* omitting or being omitted; thing omitted. [F or L (foll.)]

omit /ə'mɪt/ *v.t.* (**-tt-**) leave out, not insert or include; leave undone, neglect *doing* or fail *to do* thing. [L *omitto omiss-*]

omni- *in comb.* all. [L (*omnis* all)]

omnibus /'ɒmnɪbəs/ **1** *n.* bus; volume containing several novels etc. previously published separately. **2** *a.* serving several objects at once, comprising several items. [F f. L, = for all]

omnifarious /ɒmnɪ'feərɪəs/ *a.* of all sorts. [OMNI-, MULTIFARIOUS]

omnipotent /ɒm'nɪpətənt/ *a.* all-powerful; **omnipotence** *n.* [F f. L (POTENT)]

omnipresent /ɒmnɪ'prezənt/ *a.* ubiquitous; **omnipresence** *n.* [L (PRESENT[1])]

omniscient /ɒm'nɪsɪənt/ *a.* knowing everything or much; **omniscience** *n.* [L (*scio* know)]

omnivorous /ɒm'nɪvərəs/ *a.* feeding on many kinds of food, esp. on both plants and flesh; *fig.* reading, observing, etc., whatever comes one's way. [L (*voro* devour)]

on 1 *prep.* (so as to be) supported by or attached to or covering or enclosing (*sat on the chair*; *hangs on the wall*; *put the cloth on the table*; *fell on his knees*); carried with, about the person of (*have you a pen on you?*); (of time) during, exactly at, contemporaneously with (*on 29 May*; *on the hour*; *on schedule*; *closed on Sundays*); immediately after or before, as a result of (*on arriving I saw you*; *on examination I found this*); (so as to be) having membership etc. of or residence at or in (*put her on the committee*; *lives on the continent*); supported financially by (*lives on a grant*); close to, just by (*house is on the shore*); in the direction of, against, so as to threaten, touching or striking (*marched on Rome*; *a punch on the nose*; *drew a knife on me*); having as axis or pivot (*turned on his heels*); having as basis or motive (*works on a ratchet*; *arrested on suspicion*); having as standard, confirmation, or guarantee (*is on my conscience*; *had it on good authority*; *did it on purpose*); concerning or about (*writes on history*); using or engaged with (*is on the pill*; *here on business*); so as to affect (*walked out on her*); at the expense of (*the drinks are on me*); added to (*ruin on ruin*; *five pence on a pint of beer*); in specified manner or style (*on the cheap*; *on fire*; *on the run*). **2** *adv.* on something (*put his hat on*); in appropriate direction, towards something (*look on*); further toward, in advanced position or state (*time is getting on*; *happened later on*); with continued movement or action (*we played on*); in operation or activity (*light, gas, is on*); being shown or performed (*good film on tonight*); forward (*end on*). **3** *a.* (in cricket) designating part of field on striker's side and in front of his wicket. **4** *n.* the on side in cricket. **5 be on** (of event) be due to take place, *colloq.* be willing to participate or approve, make bet, be practicable or acceptable; **be on at** *colloq.* nag or grumble at; **be on to** realize significance or intentions of; **on and off** intermittently, now and then; **on and on** continually, at tedious length; **on-line** (of computer equipment or process) directly controlled by or connected to central processor; **on time** punctual(ly); **on to** to a position on. [OE]

onager /'ɒnəgə/ *n.* wild ass. [L f. Gk (*onos* ass, *agrios* wild)]

onanism /'əʊnənɪz(ə)m/ *n.* masturbation. [F or L (*Onan*, Bibl. person)]

ONC *abbr.* Ordinary National Certificate.

once /wʌns/ **1** *adv.* on one occasion only;

at some point or period in the past; ever or at all (*if we once lose sight of him*); multiplied by one, by one degree. **2** *conj.* as soon as. **3** *n.* one time or occasion (*just the once*). **4 all at once** without warning, suddenly, all together; **at once** immediately, simultaneously; **(every) once in a while** from time to time; **for once** on this (or that) occasion, even if at no other; **once again** (or **more**) another time; **once and for all** in a final manner, esp. after much hesitation or uncertainty; **once or twice** a few times; **once-over** *colloq.* rapid preliminary inspection; **once upon a time** at some vague time in the past. [orig. gen. of ONE]

oncoming *a.* approaching from the front. [ON]

OND *abbr.* Ordinary National Diploma.

one /wʌn/ **1** *a.* single and integral in number; (with noun implied) single person or thing of kind expressed or implied (*one of the best*; *a nasty one*); particular but undefined, esp. as contrasted with another (*that is one view*; *from one moment to the next*); only such (*the one man who can do it*); forming a unity (*one and undivided*); identical, the same (*of one opinion*). **2** *n.* the lowest cardinal numeral, thing numbered with it; unity, a unit (*one is half of two*; *came in ones and twos*); single thing or person or example (often referring to noun previously expressed or implied: *the big dog and the small one*); drink (*have a quick one*); story or joke (*the one about the parrot with a wooden leg*). **3** *pron.* a person of specified kind (*loved ones*; *like one possessed*); any person, as representing people in general (*one is bound to lose in the end*); *colloq.* I. **4 all one** a matter of indifference (*to*); **at one** in agreement; **one another** each the other (as formula of reciprocity: *they hate one another*); **one-armed bandit** *sl.* fruit-machine with long handle; **one day** on unspecified day, at some unspecified future date; **one-horse** using a single horse, *sl.* small, poorly equipped; **one-man** involving or operated by only one man; **one-night stand** single performance of play etc. in a place; **one-off** *colloq.* made as the only one, not repeated; **one or two** *colloq.* a few; **one-sided** unfair, partial; **one-time** former; **one-to-one** with one member of one group corresponding to one of another; **one-track mind** mind preoccupied with one subject; **one-up** *colloq.* having a particular advantage; **one-upmanship** *colloq.* art of maintaining psychological advantage; **one-way** allowing movement, travel, etc., in one direction only. [OE]

oneness *n.* singleness, uniqueness; agreement; sameness, changelessness.

onerous /'ɒnərəs, 'əʊn-/ *a.* burdensome. [F f. L (ONUS)]

oneself /wʌn'self/ *pron.* reflexive and emphatic form of *one* (*kill oneself*; *do thing oneself*). [ONE]

ongoing *a.* continuing, in progress. [ON]

onion /'ʌnjən/ *n.* vegetable with edible bulb of pungent smell and flavour; **oniony** *a.* [AF f. L *unio -onis*]

onlooker *n.* spectator. [ON]

only /'əʊnlɪ/ **1** *attrib. a.* existing alone of its or their kind; best or alone worth knowing. **2** *adv.* solely, merely, exclusively, and no one or nothing more besides; no longer ago than (*saw her only yesterday*); not until (*arrives only on Tuesday*); with no better result than (*hurried home only to find her gone*). **3** *conj.* except that, but then (*I'll come, only I may be late*). **4 if only** I wish that; **only too** extremely. [OE (ONE)]

o.n.o. *abbr.* or near offer.

onomatopoeia /ɒnəmætə'pi:ə/ *n.* formation of word from sound that resembles that associated with the thing named (e.g. *cuckoo*, *sizzle*); **onomatopoeic** *a.* [L f. Gk (*onoma* name, *poieō* make)]

onrush *n.* onward rush. [ON]

onset *n.* attack; impetuous beginning.

onshore *a.* on the shore; (of wind) blowing from sea towards land.

onside *a.* (of player in field game) not offside.

onslaught /'ɒnslɔ:t/ *n.* fierce attack. [Du. (ON, *slag* blow)]

onto /'ɒntʊ/ *prep.* (**D**) = *on to.* [ON]

ontology /ɒn'tɒlədʒɪ/ *n.* branch of metaphysics dealing with the nature of being; **ontological** /-'lɒdʒɪk(ə)l/ *a.* [Gk *ont-* being]

onus /'əʊnəs/ *n.* burden, duty, responsibility. [L *onus oner-* load]

onward /'ɒnwəd/ **1** *adv.* (also **onwards**) further on; towards the front; with advancing motion. **2** *a.* directed onwards. [-WARD]

onyx /'ɒnɪks/ *n.* a kind of chalcedony with coloured layers. [F f. L f. Gk]

oodles /'u:d(ə)lz/ *n.pl. colloq.* very great amount. [orig. unkn.]

ooh /u:/ *int.* expressing surprise, delight, pain, etc. [natural excl.]

oolite /'əʊəlaɪt/ *n.* granular limestone; **oolitic** /-'lɪtɪk/ *a.* [F (Gk *ōion* egg)]

oomph /ʊmf/ *n. sl.* energy, enthusiasm; attractiveness, esp. sexual appeal. [orig. uncert.]

oops /ʊps, u:ps/ *int.* on making obvious mistake. [natural excl.]

ooze 1 *v.* (of fluid) trickle or leak slowly out, pass slowly through pores of a body; (of substance) exude moisture; exude or exhibit (a feeling) freely. **2** *n.* wet mud; sluggish flow. **3 oozy** *a.* [OE]

op *n. colloq.* operation. [abbr.]

op- see OB-.

OP *abbr.* Order of Preachers (Dominican).

op. *abbr.* opus.

opacity /əʊ'pæsɪtɪ/ *n.* opaqueness. [F f. L (OPAQUE)]

opal /'əʊp(ə)l/ *n.* precious stone usu. of milky or bluish colour with iridescent reflections. [F or L]

opalescent /əʊpə'lesənt/ *a.* iridescent; **opalescence** *n.*

opaline /'əʊpəlaɪn/ *a.* opal-like, opalescent.

opaque /əʊ'peɪk/ *a.* not transmitting light, impenetrable to sight; obscure. [L *opacus* shaded]

op art *colloq.* = *optical art.* [abbr.]

op. cit. *abbr.* in the work already quoted. [L *opere citato*]

OPEC *abbr.* Organization of Petroleum Exporting Countries.

open /'əʊpən/ **1** *a.* not closed or locked or blocked up, giving access; not covered or confined, exposed; expanded, unfolded, or spread out; (of fabric etc.) not close, with intervals; undisguised, manifest (*open scandal*); (of exhibition, shop, etc.) accessible to visitors or customers, ready for business; (of race, competition, scholarship, etc.) unrestricted as to who may compete; (of offer or vacancy) still available; communicative, frank; (of bowels) not constipated; (of return ticket) not restricted as to date of travel. **2** *n. the* open air, *the* country; open competition or championship. **3** *v.* make or become open or more open; start or establish or set going (business, account, bidding, campaign, etc.); make a start (*story opens with a murder*); begin speaking, writing, etc.; ceremonially declare (building etc.) open. **4 open air** outdoors; **open-and-shut** *colloq.* straightforward; **open book** person who is easily understood; **open day** day when public may visit place normally closed to them; **open-ended** without limit or restriction; **open person's eyes** make him realize something unexpected; **open-handed** generous; **open-hearted** frank and kindly; **open-heart surgery** surgery with heart exposed and blood made to bypass it; **open into** (of door etc.) give or have communication with (room etc.); **open letter** letter of protest etc. addressed to individual and printed in newspaper etc.; **open-minded** accessible to new ideas, unprejudiced; **open-mouthed** aghast with surprise etc.; **open on** (of door, window, etc.) give or get view of; **open out** unfold, develop, expand, accelerate, become communicative; **open-plan** (of house, office, etc.) with few interior walls; **open prison** prison with few physical restraints on prisoners; **open question** matter on which different views are legitimate; **open sandwich** one without top slice of bread; **open sea** expanse of sea away from land; **open secret** supposed secret known to many; **open society** one with freedom of belief; **open to** willing or liable to receive, available to; **Open University** one teaching mainly by broadcasting and correspondence, and open to those without scholastic qualifications; **open up** make accessible, bring to notice, reveal, accelerate, begin shooting or sounding; **open verdict** one affirming commission of crime but not specifying criminal or (in case of violent death) cause. [OE]

opencast *a.* (of mine or mining) with removal of surface layers and working from above, not from shafts.

opener *n.* device for opening tins, bottles, etc.

opening 1 *n.* aperture or gap; opportunity; beginning, initial part. **2** *a.* initial, first (*opening remarks*). **3 opening-time** time at which public houses may legally open for custom.

openly *adv.* publicly; frankly.

opera[1] /'ɒpərə/ *n.* drama set to music for singers and instrumentalists; this as a genre; place where it is performed; **opera-glasses** small binoculars for use at opera or theatre; **opera-hat** man's collapsible hat; **opera-house** theatre for operas. [It. f. L, = labour, work]

opera[2] *pl.* of OPUS.

operable /'ɒpərəb(ə)l/ *a.* that can be operated; suitable for treatment by surgical operation. [L (foll.)]

operate /'ɒpəreɪt/ *v.* function, be in action; perform surgical or military or financial operation; control, work; bring about; **operating-theatre** room for surgical operations. [L *operor* work (OPUS)]

operatic /ɒpə'rætɪk/ *a.* of or like an opera; **operatically** *adv.* [OPERA[1]]

operation /ɒpə'reɪʃ(ə)n/ *n.* action or method or scope of working or operating; active process, discharge of function; piece of work, esp. one in series (*begin operations*); a performance of surgery on patient; military manœuvre; financial transaction; validity (*in operation*). [F f. L (OPERATE)]

operational *a.* of or engaged in or used for operations; able or ready to function; **operational research** application of scientific principles to business etc. management; **operationally** *adv.*

operative /'ɒpərətɪv/ **1** *a.* in operation, having effect; practical; having principal relevance (*'may' is the operative word*); of or by surgery. **2** *n.* worker, artisan. [L (OPERATE)]

operator /'ɒpəreɪtə/ *n.* one who operates machine etc., esp. person making connections of lines in telephone exchange; person operating or engaging in business, *colloq.* person acting in some way (*shrewd operator*).

operculum /ə'pɜ:kjʊləm/ *n.* (*pl.* **opercula**) fish's gill-cover; lidlike structure in plant; valve closing mouth of shell. [L (*operio* cover *v.*)]

operetta /ɒpə'retə/ *n.* one-act or short opera; light opera. [It. dimin. of OPERA[1]]

ophidian /ə'fɪdɪən/ **1** *n.* member of suborder of reptiles including snakes; snake. **2** *a.* of this order; snakelike. [Gk *ophis* snake]

ophthalmia /ɒf'θælmɪə/ *n.* inflammation of the eye, esp. conjunctivitis. [L f. Gk (*ophthalmos* eye)]

ophthalmic /ɒf'θælmɪk/ *a.* of or for the eye; of or for or affected with ophthalmia; **ophthalmic optician** optician qualified to prescribe as well as dispense spectacles etc.

ophthalmology /ɒfθæl'mɒlədʒɪ/ *n.* scientific study of the eye and its diseases.

ophthalmoscope /ɒf'θælməskəʊp/ *n.* instrument for examining the eye.

opiate /'əʊpɪət/ **1** *a.* containing opium; narcotic, soporific. **2** *n.* drug containing opium and easing pain or inducing sleep; soothing influence. [L (OPIUM)]

opine /əʊ'paɪn/ *v.t.* express or hold opinion (*that*). [L *opinor* believe]

opinion /ə'pɪnjən/ *n.* belief based on grounds short of proof, view held as probable, what one thinks about something; piece of professional advice (*a second opinion*); estimate (*low opinion of*); **opinion poll** = GALLUP POLL. [F f. L (prec.)]

opinionated *a.* assertive or dogmatic in one's opinions.

opium /'əʊpɪəm/ *n.* drug made from juice of certain poppies, used esp. as narcotic or sedative. [L f. Gk *opion*]

opossum /ə'pɒsəm/ *n.* American marsupial; similar Australian marsupial living in trees. [Virginian Ind.]

opp. *abbr.* opposite.

opponent /ə'pəʊnənt/ *n.* one who opposes or belongs to opposing side. [L *oppono -posit-* set against]

opportune /'ɒpətju:n/ *a.* (of time) well-chosen or especially favourable; (of action or event) well-timed. [F f. L *opportunus* (of wind) driving towards PORT[1]]

opportunism *n.* adaptation of policy or judgement to circumstances or opportunity, esp. regardless of principle; **opportunist** *n.*

opportunity /ɒpə'tju:nɪtɪ/ *n.* good chance, favourable occasion; chance or opening offered by circumstances. [F f. L (OPPORTUNE)]

oppose /ə'pəʊz/ *v.t.* place in opposition or contrast *to*; set oneself against, resist, argue against; **as opposed to** in contrast with. [F f. L (OPPONENT)]

opposite /'ɒpəzɪt/ **1** *a.* (often with *to*) having position on the other or further side, facing or back to back; of contrary kind, diametrically different *to* or *from*. **2** *n.* opposite thing or person or term. **3** *adv.* in opposite position. **4** *prep.* opposite to. **5 opposite number** person holding equivalent position in another group or organization.

opposition /ɒpə'zɪʃ(ə)n/ *n.* resistance, antagonism, being hostile or in conflict or disagreement; contrast, antithesis; group or party of opponents or competitors; placing opposite; diametrically opposite position of two heavenly bodies; **the Opposition** chief parliamentary party opposed to that in office. [F f. L (POSITION)]

oppress /ə'pres/ *v.t.* govern or treat harshly or with cruel injustice, keep in subservience; weigh down with cares or unhappiness; **oppression** *n.*; **oppressor** *n.* [F f. L (PRESS)]

oppressive *a.* oppressing, harsh or cruel; (of weather) close and sultry. [F f. med.L (prec.)]

opprobrious /ə'prəʊbrɪəs/ *a.* (of language) severely scornful, abusive. [L (foll.)]

opprobrium /ə'prəʊbrɪəm/ *n.* disgrace, bad reputation; cause of this. [L, = infamy, reproach]

oppugn /ə'pju:n/ *v.t.* controvert, call in question. [L *oppugno* fight against]

opt *v.i.* make choice, decide (*for* alternative); **opt out (of)** choose not to participate (in). [F f. L *opto* choose, wish]

optative /ˈɒptətɪv/ *Gram.* **1** *a.* expressing wish (esp. of mood in Greek). **2** *n.* optative mood or form. [F f. L (prec.)]

optic /ˈɒptɪk/ *a.* of the eye or sight. [F or L f. Gk (*optos* seen)]

optical *a.* of sight, visual; aiding sight; of or according to optics; **optical art** art using contrasting colours to create illusion of movement; **optical fibre** thin glass fibre used in fibre optics; **optical illusion** involuntary mental misinterpretation of thing seen, due to its deceptive appearance (e.g. mirage); **optically** *adv.*

optician /ɒpˈtɪʃ(ə)n/ *n.* maker or prescriber of optical instruments, esp. spectacles. [F f. med.L (OPTIC)]

optics *n.pl.* (usu. treated as *sing.*) science of light and vision. [OPTIC]

optimal /ˈɒptɪm(ə)l/ *a.* best or most favourable. [L *optimus* best]

optimism /ˈɒptɪmɪz(ə)m/ *n.* hopeful view or disposition, tendency or inclination to expect favourable outcome; belief that the actual world is the best possible; belief that good must ultimately prevail over evil; **optimist** *n.* [F f. L *optimus* best]

optimistic /ɒptɪˈmɪstɪk/ *a.* showing optimism; hopeful; **optimistically** *adv.*

optimize /ˈɒptɪmaɪz/ *v.t.* make optimal; make the most of.

optimum /ˈɒptɪməm/ **1** *n.* (*pl.* **optima**) most favourable conditions (for growth etc.), best compromise. **2** *a.* = OPTIMAL. [L, neut. of *optimus* best]

option /ˈɒpʃ(ə)n/ *n.* choice, choosing; thing that is or may be chosen; liberty of choosing; right to buy or sell something at certain price within limited time; **keep** (or **leave**) **one's options open** remain uncommitted. [F or L (OPT)]

optional *a.* open to choice, not obligatory; **optionally** *adv.*

opulent /ˈɒpjʊlənt/ *a.* wealthy; abundant; luxurious; **opulence** *n.* [L (*opes* wealth)]

opus /ˈəʊpəs, ˈɒp-/ *n.* (*pl.* **opera** /ˈɒpərə/) musical composition numbered as one of composer's works (*Beethoven opus 15*). [L, = work]

or[1] *conj.* introducing alternative (*black or white*) or other name for same thing (*the lapwing or peewit*) or afterthought (*came in laughing — or was it crying?*). [OE]

or[2] *n.* gold (esp. in heraldry). [F f. L *aurum* gold]

-or *suffix* forming nouns denoting esp. agent (*actor, escalator*) or condition (*error, horror*). [F or L]

oracle /ˈɒrək(ə)l/ *n.* (in classical antiquity) place where deities were consulted through medium of priest etc. for advice or prophecy; the reply given; person or thing regarded as source of wisdom etc.; (**Oracle; P**) teletext service provided by IBA; **oracular** /ɒˈrækjʊlə/ *a.* [F f. L *oraculum* (*oro* speak)]

oral /ˈɔːr(ə)l/ **1** *a.* spoken, verbal, by word of mouth; done or taken by the mouth (*oral sex, contraceptive*). **2** *n.* *colloq.* spoken examination. **3** **orally** *adv.* [L (*os oris* mouth)]

orange /ˈɒrɪndʒ/ **1** *n.* roundish reddish-yellow juicy citrus fruit; its colour; tree bearing it; orange pigment. **2** *a.* orange-coloured. **3** **orange-blossom** fragrant white flowers of orange, traditionally worn by brides. [F f. Arab. *nāranj* f. Pers.]

orangeade /ɒrɪndʒˈeɪd/ *n.* drink made from orange-juice or synthetic substitute.

Orangeman /ˈɒrɪndʒmən/ *n.* member of political society formed in 1795 to support Protestantism in Ireland. [William of *Orange*]

orangery /ˈɒrɪndʒərɪ/ *n.* building or hothouse for orange-trees. [ORANGE]

orang-utan /ɔːræŋuːˈtæn/ *n.* large long-armed anthropoid ape of E. Indies. [Malay, = wild man]

oration /ɔːˈreɪʃ(ə)n/ *n.* a formal or ceremonial speech. [L *oratio* discourse, prayer (*oro* speak, pray)]

orator /ˈɒrətə/ *n.* maker of formal speech; skilful speaker. [F f. L (prec.)]

oratorical /ɒrəˈtɒrɪk(ə)l/ *a.* of or like oratory. [ORATORY]

oratorio /ɒrəˈtɔːrɪəʊ/ *n.* (*pl.* **oratorios**) musical composition usu. on sacred theme for solo voices, chorus, and orchestra. [It. f. eccl.L]

oratory /ˈɒrətərɪ/ *n.* art of or skill in public speaking; small private chapel. [F & L (*oro* speak, pray)]

orb *n.* sphere, globe; globe surmounted by cross as part of regalia; heavenly body; *poetic* eyeball. [L *orbis* ring]

orbicular /ɔːˈbɪkjʊlə/ *a.* spherical or circular. [L *orbiculus* dimin. of *orbis* (ORB)]

orbit /ˈɔːbɪt/ **1** *n.* curved course of planet, comet, satellite, etc., round another body; range or sphere of action. **2** *v.* go round in orbit; put into orbit. **3** **in orbit** moving in an orbit. [L (*orbitus* circular)]

orbital *a.* of orbit(s); (of road) passing round outside of city.

Orcadian /ɔːˈkeɪdɪən/ **1** *n.* native or inhabitant of Orkney. **2** *a.* of Orkney. [L *Orcades* Orkney Islands]

orch. *abbr.* orchestra, orchestrated by.
orchard /'ɔ:tʃəd/ *n.* enclosed piece of land planted with fruit-trees. [OE f. L *hortus* garden]
orchestra /'ɔ:kɪstrə/ *n.* body of musicians playing together on stringed, wind, and percussion instruments according to an established scheme; area in theatre etc. assigned to them; **orchestra-pit** such area in front of stage and on lower level. [L f. Gk, = area for chorus in drama]
orchestral /ɔ:'kestr(ə)l/ *a.* of or for or performed by an orchestra.
orchestrate /'ɔ:kɪstreɪt/ *v.t.* compose or arrange or score for orchestral performance; *fig.* arrange or combine (various elements) harmoniously; **orchestration** /-'streɪʃ(ə)n/ *n.*
orchid /'ɔ:kɪd/ *n.* any of various plants with brilliant flowers. [L f. Gk *orkhis*, orig. = testicle]
ordain /ɔ:'deɪn/ *v.t.* confer holy orders on; order or enact. [AF f. L *ordino* (ORDER)]
ordeal /ɔ:'di:l/ *n.* severe or testing trial or experience; *hist.* method of determining guilt by making suspect undergo physical harm, safe endurance of which betokened innocence. [OE]
order 1 *n.* state of regular arrangement and normal functioning; natural or moral or spiritual system with definite tendencies; arrangement of things relative to one another, sequence; prevalence of constitutional authority and obedience to law; system of rules or procedure; command, authoritative direction or instruction; direction to supply something, thing (to be) supplied; instruction to pay money or deliver property, signed by owner or responsible agent; social class or rank, its members; kind or sort (*skills of a high order*); religious fraternity with common rule of life; grade of Christian ministry; company of persons distinguished by particular honour or reward (*Order of the Bath*), insignia worn by members of this; stated form of divine service (*order of baptism*); mode of treatment in architecture, with decorations and established proportions between parts; grouping of animals or plants below class and above family. **2** *v.t.* put in order, regulate, arrange systematically; command, bid, prescribe; command or direct (person) to go *to, away, home*, etc.; direct manufacturer, tradesman, etc., to supply, or waiter etc. to serve; (of God, fate, etc.) ordain. **3 call to order** request to be orderly, declare (meeting) open; **holy orders** status of bishop, priest, or deacon; **in** (or **out of**) **order** in correct (or incorrect) sequence or position, according or not according to rules etc., in or not in good condition; **in order that** with the intention or to the end that; **in order to** with a view to, for the purpose of; **on order** ordered but not yet received; **Order in Council** sovereign's order on administrative matter given by advice of Privy Council; **order-paper** written or printed order of day's proceedings, esp. in parliament; **to order** as specified by customer. [F f. L *ordo ordin-* row, command, etc.]
orderly 1 *a.* methodically arranged or inclined, tidy; well-behaved. **2** *n.* soldier in attendance on officer; attendant in (esp. military) hospital. **3 orderly room** room in barracks, for company's business. **4 orderliness** *n.*
ordinal /'ɔ:dɪn(ə)l/ **1** *a.* (of a number) defining a thing's position in a series (e.g. *first, tenth, hundredth*). **2** *n.* ordinal number. [L (ORDER)]
ordinance /'ɔ:dɪnəns/ *n.* decree; religious rite. [F f. L (ORDAIN)]
ordinand /'ɔ:dɪnænd/ *n.* candidate for ordination. [L (ORDAIN)]
ordinary /'ɔ:dɪnərɪ/ **1** *a.* normal, customary, unexceptional, usual. **2** *n.* rule or book laying down order of divine service. **3 in the ordinary way** in normal circumstances, usually; **ordinary level** lowest level in GCE examination; **ordinary seaman** seaman of lower rating than able seaman; **out of the ordinary** unusual. [F & L (ORDER)]
ordinate /'ɔ:dɪnət/ *n. Math.* coordinate measured usu. vertically. [L (ORDAIN)]
ordination /ɔ:dɪ'neɪʃ(ə)n/ *n.* ordaining, conferring of holy orders. [F or L (ORDAIN)]
ordnance /'ɔ:dnəns/ *n.* artillery and military supplies; government department for military stores; **Ordnance Survey** government survey of UK producing accurate maps. [contr. of *ordinance*]
Ordovician /ɔ:də'vɪsɪən/ **1** *a.* of the period in the Palaeozoic era after Cambrian. **2** *n.* this period. [L *Ordovices* anc. British tribe in N. Wales]
ordure /'ɔ:djʊə/ *n.* dung. [F f. L *horridus* HORRID]
ore /ɔ:/ *n.* solid rock or mineral from which metal or other valuable substances may be extracted. [OE]
oregano /ɒrɪ'gɑ:nəʊ/ *n.* dried wild marjoram as seasoning. [Sp., = ORIGAN]
organ /'ɔ:gən/ *n.* musical instrument

consisting of pipes that sound when air is forced through them, operated by keyboards and pedals; similar electronic instrument without pipes; harmonium; part of animal or plant body serving particular function (*organs of speech*; *reproductive organs*); medium of communication (e.g. newspaper) representing a party or interest; **organ-grinder** player of barrel-organ; **organ-loft** gallery for organ. [F f. L f. Gk *organon* tool]

organdie /'ɔ:gəndɪ, -'gændɪ/ *n.* fine translucent muslin, usu. stiffened. [F]

organic /ɔ:'gænɪk/ *a.* of or affecting a bodily organ or organs; (of plants or animals) having organs or organized physical structure; (of food etc.) produced without use of artificial fertilizers or pesticides; systematic or organized (*an organic whole*); *Chem.* (of compound etc.) containing carbon in its molecules; constitutional, inherent, structural; **organic chemistry** chemistry of carbon compounds; **organically** *adv.* [F f. L f. Gk (ORGAN)]

organism /'ɔ:gənɪz(ə)m/ *n.* individual animal or plant; organized body. [F (as ORGANIZE)]

organist /'ɔ:gənɪst/ *n.* player of organ. [ORGAN]

organization /ɔ:gənaɪ'zeɪʃ(ə)n/ *n.* organized body or system or society; fact or manner of organizing or being organized. [med.L or foll.]

organize /'ɔ:gənaɪz/ *v.t.* give orderly structure to, systematize; initiate or make arrangements for, enlist (person or group) in this; make organic or make into living tissue. [F f. L (ORGAN)]

organza /ɔ:'gænzə/ *n.* thin stiff transparent dress-fabric of silk or synthetic fibre. [orig. uncert.]

orgasm /'ɔ:gæz(ə)m/ *n.* climax of sexual excitement; **orgasmic** /-'gæzmɪk/ *a.* [F or L f. Gk, = excitement]

orgy /'ɔ:dʒɪ/ *n.* drunken or licentious party or revelry; excessive indulgence in an activity; (in *pl.*) revelry or debauchery, (in ancient Greece and Rome) secret rites in worship of various gods, esp. Bacchus, with wild drinking etc.; **orgiastic** /-'æstɪk/ *a.* [F f. L f. Gk *orgia* pl.]

oriel /'ɔ:rɪəl/ *n.* windows projecting from wall of house at upper level. [F]

orient 1 /'ɔ:rɪənt/ *n.* **(Orient)** *the* East, the countries east of the Mediterranean, esp. E. Asia. **2** /'ɔ:rɪent/ *v.* adjust or establish *oneself* in relation to surroundings; place (building etc.) to face east; turn eastward or in specified direction; place or determine position of with regard to compass; bring into clearly understood relations, direct *towards*. [F f. L *oriens -entis* rising, sunrise, east]

oriental /ɔ:rɪ'ent(ə)l, ɒr-/ **1** *a.* of the Orient, of the eastern or E. Asian world or its civilization. **2** *n.* native or inhabitant of the Orient.

orientate /'ɔ:rɪenteɪt/ *v.* = ORIENT. [foll.]

orientation /ɔ:rɪen'teɪʃ(ə)n/ *n.* orienting or being oriented; position relative to surroundings. [ORIENT]

orienteering /ɔ:rɪən'tɪərɪŋ/ *n.* competitive sport of traversing rough country on foot with map and compass. [Sw.]

orifice /'ɒrɪfɪs/ *n.* aperture, mouth of cavity, vent. [F f. L (*os or-* mouth, *facio* make)]

origami /ɒrɪ'gɑ:mɪ/ *n.* art of folding paper intricately into decorative shapes. [Jap.]

origan /'ɒrɪgən/ *n.* (also **origanum** /-'gɑ:nəm/) wild marjoram. [L f. Gk]

origin /'ɒrɪdʒɪn/ *n.* source, starting-point, parentage; *Math.* point from which coordinates are measured. [F, or L *origo origin-* (*orior* rise)]

original /ə'rɪdʒɪn(ə)l/ **1** *a.* existing from the first, earliest, primitive, innate; that has served as a pattern, of which a copy or translation has been made; new in concept, not derived or imitative; inventive, creative. **2** *n.* pattern, original model, thing from which another is copied or translated. **3 original sin** innate sinfulness held to be common to all human beings in consequence of the Fall. **4 originality** /-'nælɪtɪ/ *n.*; **originally** *adv.* [F or L (prec.)]

originate /ə'rɪdʒɪneɪt/ *v.* have origin, begin; initiate or give origin to or be origin of; **origination** /-'neɪʃ(ə)n/ *n.*; **originator** *n.* [med.L (ORIGIN)]

oriole /'ɔ:rɪəʊl/ *n.* a kind of bird, esp. **(golden oriole)** with black and yellow plumage in the male. [F f. L (*aurum* gold)]

ormolu /'ɔ:məlu:/ *n.* gilded bronze; a gold-coloured alloy; articles made of or decorated with ormolu. [F *or moulu* powdered gold]

ornament 1 /'ɔ:nəmənt/ *n.* thing used to adorn or decorate; decoration, embellishment, mere display; quality or person bringing honour or distinction. **2** /'ɔ:nəment/ *v.* adorn, beautify. **3 ornamental** /-'ment(ə)l/ *a.*; **ornamentation** /-'teɪʃ(ə)n/ *n.* [F f. L (*orno* adorn)]

ornate /ɔ:'neɪt/ *a.* elaborately adorned; (of literary style) embellished with flowery language. [L (prec.)]

ornithology /ɔ:nɪ'θɒlədʒɪ/ *n.* scientific

study of birds; **ornithological** /-ˈlɒdʒɪk(ə)l/ *a.*; **ornithologist** *n.* [Gk *ornis ornith-* bird]

orotund /ˈɒrətʌnd/ *a.* (of utterance) dignified, imposing; pompous, boastful. [L *ore rotundo* with round mouth]

orphan /ˈɔːfən/ **1** *n.* child whose parents are dead. **2** *a.* being an orphan; of or for orphans. **3** *v.t.* make (child) an orphan. [L f. Gk, = bereaved]

orphanage *n.* institution for orphans.

Orphic /ˈɔːfɪk/ *a.* of Orpheus or the mystic religion associated with him; **Orphism** *n.* [*Orpheus*, legendary Gk poet and musician]

orrery /ˈɒrərɪ/ *n.* clockwork model of planetary system. [Earl of *Orrery*]

orris /ˈɒrɪs/ *n.* a kind of iris; **orris-root** violet-scented iris root used in perfumery etc. [alt. of IRIS]

ortho- *in comb.* right, straight, correct. [Gk *orthos* straight]

orthodontics /ɔːθəʊˈdɒntɪks/ *n.* correction of irregularities in teeth and jaws; **orthodontic** *a.*; **orthodontist** *n.* [Gk *odous odont-* tooth]

orthodox /ˈɔːθədɒks/ *a.* holding usual or currently accepted views, esp. on religion; generally approved, conventional; **Orthodox Church** the Eastern or Greek Church with Patriarch of Constantinople as head, and the national Churches of Russia, Romania, etc., in communion with it; **orthodoxy** *n.* [L f. Gk (*doxa* opinion)]

orthography /ɔːˈθɒgrəfɪ/ *n.* spelling (esp. with reference to its correctness); **orthographic** /-ˈgræfɪk/ *a.* [F f. L f. Gk]

orthopaedics /ɔːθəˈpiːdɪks/, *US* **orthopedics** *n.* branch of surgery dealing with correction of deformities of bones or muscles, orig. in children; **orthopaedic** *a.*; **orthopaedist** *n.* [F (Gk *pais paid-* child)]

orthoptic /ɔːˈθɒptɪk/ *a.* relating to correct or normal use of the eyes. [ORTHO-]

ortolan /ˈɔːtələn/ *n.* European bunting, eaten as delicacy. [F f. Prov. f. L (*hortus* garden)]

-ory *suffix* forming nouns denoting place (*dormitory*, *laboratory*), and adjectives and nouns in sense of (person or thing) relating to or involving verbal action (*accessory*, *compulsory*). [AF f. L]

OS *abbr.* old style; ordinary seaman; Ordnance Survey; outsize.

Os *symb.* osmium.

Oscar /ˈɒskə/ *n.* each of several statuettes awarded annually by Academy of Motion Picture Arts and Sciences for excellence in film acting, directing, etc. [man's name]

oscillate /ˈɒsɪleɪt/ *v.* (cause to) swing to and fro; vacillate, vary between extremes; (of electric current) undergo high-frequency alternations; **oscillation** /-ˈleɪʃ(ə)n/ *n.* [L (*oscillo* swing)]

oscillator *n.* instrument for producing oscillations.

oscillo- *in comb.* oscillation, esp. of electric current.

oscillograph /əˈsɪləgrɑːf/ *n.* device for recording oscillations.

oscilloscope /əˈsɪləskəʊp/ *n.* device for displaying oscillations, esp. on screen of cathode-ray tube.

-ose *suffix* forming adjectives denoting possession of a quality (*bellicose*, *morose*). [L]

osier /ˈəʊzɪə, ˈəʊʒə/ *n.* willow used in basketwork; shoot of this. [F]

-osis *suffix* forming nouns denoting process or condition (*metamorphosis*), esp. pathological state (*neurosis*, *thrombosis*). [L or Gk]

-osity *suffix* forming nouns from adjectives in -OSE or -OUS (*verbosity*, *curiosity*). [F or L]

Osmanli /ɒzˈmænlɪ, ɒs-/ *a.* & *n.* = OTTOMAN. [Turk.]

osmium /ˈɒzmɪəm/ *n.* heavy hard bluish-white metallic element. [Gk *osmē* smell]

osmosis /ɒzˈməʊsɪs/ *n.* (*pl.* **osmoses** /-iːz/) diffusion of fluid through semi-permeable partition into another fluid; **osmotic** /-ˈmɒtɪk/ *a.* [Gk *ōsmos* thrust, push]

osprey /ˈɒspreɪ/ *n.* large bird preying on fish in inland waters. [F, ult. f. L *ossifraga* (*os* bone, *frango* break)]

osseous /ˈɒsɪəs/ *a.* of bone, having bones, bony. [L (*os oss-* bone)]

ossicle /ˈɒsɪk(ə)l/ *n.* small bone or piece of hard substance in animal structure. [L dimin. (prec.)]

ossify /ˈɒsɪfaɪ/ *v.* turn into bone, harden; make or become rigid or callous or unprogressive; **ossification** /-fɪˈkeɪʃ(ə)n/ *n.* [F f. L (OSSEOUS)]

ostensible /ɒˈstensɪb(ə)l/ *a.* pretended, professed, put forward to conceal what is real; **ostensibly** *adv.* [F f. L (*ostendo -tens-* show)]

ostensive /ɒˈstensɪv/ *a.* directly showing. [L (prec.)]

ostentation /ɒstenˈteɪʃ(ə)n/ *n.* pretentious display of wealth etc., showing off; **ostentatious** *a.* [F f. L (OSTENSIBLE)]

osteo- *in comb.* bone. [Gk *osteon* bone]

osteopath /ˈɒstɪəpæθ/ *n.* practitioner of osteopathy. [foll.]

osteopathy /ɒstɪˈɒpəθɪ/ *n.* treatment of disease by manipulation of bones (esp.

spine) and muscle, their deformity being supposed cause. [OSTEO-, PATHOS]

ostler /'ɒslə/ *n.* person in charge of stabling horses at inn. [HOSTEL]

Ostpolitik /'ɒstpɒlɪti:k/ *n.* policy of a W. European country with regard to Communist countries of E. Europe. [G]

ostracize /'ɒstrəsaɪz/ *v.t.* exclude from society, refuse to associate with; **ostracism** *n.* [Gk (*ostrakon* potsherd, on which vote was recorded in anc. Athens etc. to expel dangerously powerful citizen)]

ostrich /'ɒstrɪtʃ/ *n.* large swift-running flightless African bird; person who refuses to acknowledge an awkward truth. [F (L *avis* bird, *struthio* (f. Gk) ostrich)]

OT *abbr.* Old Testament.

other /'ʌðə/ **1** *a.* not the same as one or some already mentioned or implied, separate in identity or distinct in kind (*other people*; *use other means*); alternative or further or additional (*has no other friends*); *the* only remaining (*open the other eye*; *where are the other two?*). **2** *n.* or *pron.* other person or thing (*give me one other*; *do good to others*). **3** *adv.* otherwise (*cannot do other than laugh*). **4 the other day** (or **night** etc.) a few days (or nights etc.) ago; **other than** different from; **other-worldly** concerned or preoccupied with life in another world. [OE]

otherwise **1** *adv.* in a different way (*could not have acted otherwise*); in other respects (*is otherwise quite healthy*); in different circumstances, or else (*hurry otherwise we'll be late*). **2** *a.* in a different state (*the truth is quite otherwise*). [OE (WISE²)]

otic /'əʊtɪk/ *a.* of or relating to the ear. [Gk (*ous ōt-* ear)]

otiose /'əʊʃɪəʊs, 'əʊt-/ *a.* not required, serving no practical purpose, functionless. [L (*otium* leisure)]

otter *n.* aquatic fish-eating mammal with webbed feet and thick brown fur; its fur. [OE]

Ottoman /'ɒtəmən/ **1** *a.* of dynasty of Osman (or Othman) I or his descendants or their empire; Turkish. **2** *n.* (*pl.* **Ottomans**) Turk of Ottoman period; (**ottoman**) cushioned seat without back or arms, often box with cushioned top. [F f. Arab.]

OU *abbr.* Open University; Oxford University.

oubliette /u:blɪ'et/ *n.* secret dungeon with trapdoor entrance. [F (*oublier* forget)]

ouch *int.* expressing sharp or sudden pain. [natural excl.]

ought¹ /ɔ:t/ *v. aux.* (as present and past, the only form now in use; *neg.* **ought not,** *colloq.* **oughtn't** /'ɔ:t(ə)nt/) expressing rightness or duty (*we ought to be thankful*; *we ought to have told him*), advisability (*you ought to see a dentist*), probability (*it ought to rain soon*). [OE, past tense of OWE]

ought² /ɔ:t/ *n. colloq.* figure 0, nought. [NOUGHT]

Ouija /'wi:dʒə/ *n.* (also **Ouija-board**) (**P**) board marked with alphabet and other signs used with movable pointer to obtain messages in spiritualistic seances. [F *oui*, G *ja*, yes]

ounce *n.* unit of weight, $\frac{1}{16}$ lb. or 28 g.; a very small quantity. [F f. L *uncia* twelfth part of pound or foot]

our *poss. a.* of or belonging to us; that we are concerned with or thinking of (*our friend here*); **Our Father** prayer beginning with these words (Matt. 6: 9–13); **Our Lady** Virgin Mary. [OE]

ours *poss. pron.* of or belonging to us, the thing(s) belonging to us (*it is ours*; *ours are best*; *a friend of ours*).

ourself /aʊə'self/ *pron.* corresponding to MYSELF when used by sovereign etc. (*we ourself*). [SELF]

ourselves /aʊə'selvz/ *pron.* emphat. and refl. form of WE, US (for uses cf. HERSELF).

-ous *suffix* forming adjectives in sense 'abounding in, characterized by, of the nature of' (*envious*, *glorious*, *mountainous*, *poisonous*); *Chem.* combined in lower valence etc. (*ferrous*, *sulphurous*). [F f. L (-OSE)]

ousel var. of OUZEL.

oust *v.t.* eject, drive out of office or power, seize the place of. [AF f. L *obsto* oppose]

out **1** *adv.* expressing movement or position beyond or regardless of stated or implied limits, or state other than the right or usual one: away from or not in a place, not at home, in one's office, etc.; so as to be excluded (*kept, locked, out*); in(to) the open, so as to be clear or perceptible (*someone came out*; *who called out?*; *epidemic has broken out*); to or at an end, completely (*sold out*; *tired out*; *hear me out*; *before the day is out*; *have not typed it out yet*); with distribution from centre (*give these out*); not in fashion, season, or office, not or no longer exerting favourable action etc. (*short skirts are out*; *Labour are out*; *her luck was out*); (of fire, light, etc.) not burning or functioning; (of idea etc.) excluded from consideration; in error (*total is £50 out*);

(of limb etc.) dislocated (*put her arm out*); (so as to be) unconscious (*knocked him out; is out cold*); (of jury) considering verdict in private; (of man or side in cricket) dismissed from batting; (of book etc.) published, available for purchase; (of flower) open; (of secret) revealed; (with superl.) among known examples (*the best game out*). **2** *prep.* out of (*look out the window*). **3** *n.* way of escape. **4** *a.* (of match) played away; (of island) away from mainland. **5** *int.* get out! **6** *v.t.* put out; *colloq.* eject forcibly; (in boxing) knock out. **7 out and about** active outdoors; **out and away** by far; **out and out** thoroughly; **out-and-out** *a.* complete, thorough; **out for** intent on, determined to get; **out of** from within, not within, from among, away from (*out of town*); beyond range of (*out of sight*), because of (*did it out of malice*), by use of (*made out of wood*), lacking (*out of breath, sugar*), so as to be deprived of (*swindled him out of £20*); **out of date** see DATE[1]; **out of doors** in(to) the open air; **out to** determined to. [OE]

out- *prefix* in senses 'out of, away from, outward'; 'external, separate'; 'so as to surpass or exceed'.

outage *n.* period of non-operation of power supply etc.

outback *n.* remote inland districts of Australia.

outbid /aʊt'bɪd/ *v.* (**-dd-**) bid higher than.

outboard *a.* towards outside of ship, aircraft, or vehicle; (of motor) attached externally to stern of boat, (of boat) using such motor.

outbreak *n.* breaking out of anger, war, disease, fire, etc.

outbuilding *n.* outhouse.

outburst *n.* bursting out, esp. of emotion in vehement words.

outcast 1 *n.* person cast out of home or rejected by society. **2** *a.* homeless, rejected.

outclass /aʊt'klɑ:s/ *v.t.* surpass in quality.

outcome *n.* result, issue.

outcrop *n.* emergence of stratum etc. at surface, stratum thus emerging; *fig.* noticeable manifestation.

outcry *n.* loud protest, clamour.

outdated /aʊt'deɪtɪd/ *a.* out of date, obsolete.

outdistance /aʊt'dɪstəns/ *v.t.* get far ahead of.

outdo /aʊt'du:/ *v.t.* (3 *sing. pres.* **outdoes** /-'dʌz/; *past* **outdid;** *p.p.* **outdone** /-'dʌn/) exceed, excel, surpass.

outdoor *a.* of or done or for use out of doors; fond of the open air.

outdoors 1 *n.* the open air. **2** *adv.* in(to) the open air.

outer *a.* further from the centre or the inside; external, exterior; **outer space** universe beyond earth's atmosphere; **outermost** *a.* [OUT]

outface /aʊt'feɪs/ *v.t.* disconcert by staring or by display of confidence. [OUT-]

outfall *n.* outlet of river, drain, etc.

outfield *n.* outer part of cricket or baseball pitch.

outfit *n.* set of equipment or clothes; *colloq.* group of persons, organization.

outfitter *n.* supplier of equipment, esp. men's clothes.

outflank /aʊt'flæŋk/ *v.t.* extend beyond flank of (enemy); outmanœuvre, outwit.

outflow *n.* outward flow; what flows out.

outfox /aʊt'fɒks/ *v.t.* outwit.

outgoing 1 *a.* going out; retiring from office; friendly. **2** *n.* (in *pl.*) expenditure.

outgrow /aʊt'grəʊ/ *v.t.* (*past* **outgrew;** *p.p.* **outgrown**) grow faster or taller than; grow too big for; be too old or developed for.

outgrowth /'aʊtgrəʊθ/ *n.* offshoot; natural product.

outhouse *n.* small building apart from main house.

outing *n.* pleasure-trip or excursion. [OUT]

outlandish /aʊt'lændɪʃ/ *a.* looking or sounding very strange or foreign, bizarre. [OE (*outland* foreign country)]

outlast /aʊt'lɑ:st/ *v.t.* last longer than. [OUT-]

outlaw 1 *n.* fugitive from law (orig. one placed beyond protection of law). **2** *v.t.* declare (person) outlaw; make illegal, proscribe.

outlay *n.* expenditure.

outlet *n.* means of exit or escape; means of expressing feelings; market for goods.

outline 1 *n.* rough draft, summary, sketch consisting of only contour lines; (in *sing.* or *pl.*) line(s) enclosing visible object, contour, external boundary; (in *pl.*) main features or principles. **2** *v.t.* draw or describe in outline; mark outline of.

outlive /aʊt'lɪv/ *v.t.* live longer than or beyond (period, date); live through (experience).

outlook *n.* view or prospect (esp. *fig.*); mental attitude.

outlying *a.* far from a centre, remote.

outmanœuvre /aʊtmə'nu:və/ *v.t.* outdo in manœuvring.

outmatch /aʊt'mætʃ/ *v.t.* be more than a match for.
outmoded /aʊt'məʊdɪd/ *a.* out of fashion; obsolete.
outnumber /aʊt'nʌmbə/ *v.t.* exceed in number.
outpace /aʊt'peɪs/ *v.t.* go faster than, outdo in contest.
out-patient *n.* patient not residing in hospital during treatment. [OUT]
outpost *n.* detachment stationed at some distance from army; distant branch or settlement. [OUT-]
output 1 *n.* amount produced; electrical power etc. delivered by apparatus; place where energy, information, etc., leaves a system; results etc. supplied by computer. **2** *v.* (*past* and *p.p.* **output** or **outputted**) (of computer) supply (results etc.).
outrage /'aʊtreɪdʒ/ **1** *n.* extreme or shocking violation of others' rights, sentiments, etc.; gross offence or indignity; fierce resentment (*at*). **2** *v.t.* subject to outrage, commit outrage against, shock and anger. [F (*outrer* exceed f. L *ultra* beyond)]
outrageous /aʊt'reɪdʒəs/ *a.* immoderate, shocking, grossly cruel or immoral or offensive. [F (prec.)]
outrank /aʊt'ræŋk/ *v.t.* be superior in rank to. [OUT-]
outré /'u:treɪ/ *a.* eccentric, violating decorum. [F, p.p. of *outrer* (OUTRAGE)]
outrider *n.* mounted attendant or motor-cyclist riding ahead of procession etc. [OUT-]
outrigger *n.* spar or framework projecting from or over ship's side; strip of wood fixed parallel to canoe to stabilize it, canoe with this.
outright 1 /aʊt'raɪt/ *adv.* altogether, entirely, not gradually; without reservation, openly. **2** /'aʊtraɪt/ *a.* complete, thorough. [OUT, RIGHT]
outrun /aʊt'rʌn/ *v.t.* (**-nn-**; *past* **outran**; *p.p.* **outrun**) run faster or further than; go beyond (point or limit). [OUT-]
outsell /aʊt'sel/ *v.t.* (*past* and *p.p.* **outsold** /-'səʊld/) sell more than; be sold in greater quantities than.
outset *n.* start, beginning; usu. in **at** (or **from**) **the outset.**
outshine /aʊt'ʃaɪn/ *v.t.* (*past* and *p.p.* **outshone** /-'ʃɒn/) shine brighter than; surpass in excellence etc.
outside 1 *n.* external side or surface, outer part(s); external appearance, outward aspect; all that is without (*impressions from the outside*); position on outer side (*open the gate from the outside*). **2** *a.* of or on or nearer the outside, outer; not belonging to some circle or institution (*outside help*); nearer to outside of games field (*outside left*); greatest existent or possible (*outside price*). **3** *adv.* on or to the outside; in or to the open air; not within or enclosed or included; not in prison. **4** *prep.* not in, to or at the outside or exterior of; external to, not included in, beyond the limits of. **5 at the outside** (of amounts) at the most; **outside broadcast** one not made from a studio.
outsider *n.* non-member of some circle, party, profession, etc.; competitor thought to have little chance.
outsize 1 *a.* unusually large. **2** *n.* outsize garment etc. or person.
outskirts *n.pl.* outer area of town etc.
outsmart /aʊt'smɑ:t/ *v.t.* outwit, be cleverer than.
outspan /aʊt'spæn/ *v.t.* (**-nn-**) *S. Afr.* unyoke, unharness.
outspoken /aʊt'spəʊkən/ *a.* given to or involving plain speaking, frank.
outspread /aʊt'spred/ **1** *a.* spread out, expanded. **2** *v.t.* spread out, expand.
outstanding /aʊt'stændɪŋ/ *a.* conspicuous, esp. from excellence; still to be dealt with.
outstay /aʊt'steɪ/ *v.t.* stay longer than.
outstretched /aʊt'stretʃt/ *a.* stretched out.
outstrip /aʊt'strɪp/ *v.t.* (**-pp-**) go faster than; surpass esp. competitively.
out-tray *n.* tray for outgoing documents. [OUT]
outvote /aʊt'vəʊt/ *v.t.* defeat by majority of votes.
outward /'aʊtwəd/ **1** *a.* situated on or directed towards the outside; going out; bodily, external, apparent. **2** *adv.* (also **outwards**) in an outward direction, towards the outside. **3 outward bound** going away from home. [OE (OUT-, -WARD)]
outwardly *adv.* on the outside; in appearance.
outwardness *n.* external existence, objectivity.
outweigh /aʊt'weɪ/ *v.t.* exceed in weight, value, importance, or influence. [OUT-]
outwit /aʊt'wɪt/ *v.t.* (**-tt-**) be too clever for, overcome by greater ingenuity.
outwork *n.* advanced or detached part of fortification.
outworn /aʊt'wɔ:n/ *a.* worn out, obsolete, exhausted.
ouzel /'u:z(ə)l/ *n.* small bird of thrush family (**ring ouzel**); a kind of diving bird (**water ouzel**). [OE, = blackbird]
ouzo /'u:zəʊ/ *n.* Greek drink of aniseed-flavoured spirits. [Gk]
ova *pl.* of OVUM.
oval /'əʊv(ə)l/ **1** *a.* egg-shaped, ellip-

soidal; having outline of egg, elliptical. **2** *n.* egg-shaped or elliptical closed curve; thing with oval outline. [L (OVUM)]

ovary /ˈəʊvərɪ/ *n.* either of two reproductive organs in which ova are produced in female animals; lower part of pistil in plant, from which fruit is formed; **ovarian** /-ˈveərɪən/ *a.*

ovation /əˈveɪʃ(ə)n/ *n.* enthusiastic applause or reception. [L (*ovo* exult)]

oven/ˈʌv(ə)n/ *n.* enclosed compartment for heating or cooking food etc. [OE]

ovenware *n.* dishes in which food can be cooked in oven.

over 1 *adv.* expressing movement or position or state above or beyond something stated or implied: outward and downward from brink or from erect position (*lean, fall, jump, knock, over*); so as to cover or touch whole surface (*paint it over*); so as to produce fold or reverse position, upside down (*bend, turn, it over*); across a street or other space (*is over in America*; *came, asked her, over for drinks*); with transference or change from one hand, part, etc., to another (*hand it over*; *went over to the enemy*); with motion above something, so as to pass across something (*climb, look, boil, over*); from beginning to end, with repetition, with detailed consideration (*read, think, it over*; *did it six times over*); too, in excess, in addition, besides (*shall have a little over*); apart, till later time (*hold over*); at an end, settled (*the battle is over*; *get it over with*); (in radio conversation etc.) it is your turn to transmit; (as umpire's call in cricket) change ends for bowling etc. **2** *prep.* above, in or to position higher than; out and down from, down from edge of (*fell over the cliff*); so as to clear, on or to the other side of (*look over the hedge*; *jump over the stream*); so as to cover (*hat over her eyes*); above and across (*flew over the Atlantic*; *bridge over the river*); across (*rode over the moor*); concerning (*argued over money*); while occupied with (*discuss it over dinner*); with or achieving superiority or preference to (*won a victory over the enemy*; *has no control over them*); throughout, so as to do completely (*looked over the house*; *went over the plans*); through duration of (*lost weight over the years*); beyond, more than (*cost over £10*); transmitted by (*heard it over the radio*); in comparison with (*gain of 20 over last year*). **3** *n.* sequence of six (or eight) balls in cricket, bowled between two calls of 'over', play resulting from this. **4** *a.* upper, outer, superior, extra (usu. as *prefix*: see OVER-). **5 all over** completely finished, over one's entire body, *fig.* typically (*that is Sykes all over*); **all over (person)** *colloq.* effusively attentive to; **over again** once again, again from the beginning; **over against** in opposite situation to, adjacent to, in contrast with; **over all** from end to end (see also OVERALL); **over and above** besides, not to mention; **over and over** repeatedly; **over to you** it is your turn to act. [OE]

over- *prefix* in senses (1) OVER; (2) upper, outer; (3) superior; (4) excessively.

¶ The list at the foot of the page is of words in sense (4) that can be understood readily from the sense of the main word. Pronunciation and stress (when not given) follow those of the main word.

overact /əʊvərˈækt/ *v.* act with exaggeration.

overall 1 *a.* from end to end (*overall length*); total, inclusive of all. **2** /also -ˈɔːl/ *adv.* in all parts, taken as a whole. **3** *n.* protective outer garment; (in *pl.*) protective outer trousers or suit.

overarm *a.* & *adv.* with arm raised above shoulder.

overawe /əʊvərˈɔː/ *v.t.* overcome with awe.

overbalance /əʊvəˈbæləns/ *v.* (cause to) lose balance and fall.

overbear /əʊvəˈbeə/ *v.t.* (*past* **overbore**; *p.p.* **overborne**) bear down by

over-active
overbid /-ˈbɪd/ *v.t.* & /ˈəʊvə-/ *n.*
overbold
over-careful
over-compensate
over-confident
overcook
overcrowd
overdevelop
over-eager
overeat
over-emphasize
over-enthusiastic
over-excite
over-exertion
over-expose
overfeed
overfond
overfull
overheat
over-indulgent
over-large
overload /-ˈləʊd/ *v.t.* & /ˈəʊvə-/ *n.*
over-long
overmuch *a.*, *adv.*, & *n.*
overnice
overpay
overpraise
over-produce
overripe
over-sensitive
overstock
overstrain
overstretch
overstuff
over-use *v.t.* & *n.*
over-value
overwind

weight or force; repress by power or authority.

overbearing *a.* domineering, bullying.

overblown /əʊvəˈbləʊn/ *a.* inflated or pretentious; (of flower) past its prime.

overboard *adv.* from within ship into water; **go overboard** *colloq.* show extreme enthusiasm.

overbook *v.t.* make too many bookings for (aircraft flight, hotel, etc., or *absol.*).

overcast /ˈəʊvəkɑːst/ *a.* (of sky) covered with cloud; (in sewing) edged with stitching to prevent fraying.

overcharge /əʊvəˈtʃɑːdʒ/ *v.t.* charge too high a price to (person) or for (thing); put excessive charge into.

overcoat *n.* warm outdoor coat.

overcome /əʊvəˈkʌm/ *v.* (*past* **overcame**; *p.p.* **overcome**) prevail over, master, be victorious; (in *p.p.*) greatly affected or made helpless (*by* or *with*).

overdo /əʊvəˈduː/ *v.t.* (3 *sing. pres.* **overdoes** /-ˈdʌz/; *past* **overdid**; *p.p.* **overdone** /-ˈdʌn/) carry to excess, go too far in; cook too much; exhaust; **overdo it** work too hard, exaggerate, carry action too far.

overdose *n.* excessive dose, esp. of drug.

overdraft *n.* overdrawing of bank account; amount by which account is overdrawn.

overdraw /əʊvəˈdrɔː/ (*past* **overdrew** /-ˈdruː/; *p.p.* **overdrawn**) *v.t.* draw more from (bank account) than amount in credit; (in *p.p.*) having overdrawn one's account.

overdress /əʊvəˈdres/ *v.* dress ostentatiously or with too much formality.

overdrive *n.* mechanism in vehicle providing gear ratio higher than that of usual gears.

overdue /əʊvəˈdjuː/ *a.* past due time for payment, arrival, etc.

overestimate 1 /əʊvəˈestɪmeɪt/ *v.t.* form too high an estimate of. 2 /-ət/ *n.* too high an estimate.

overfish /əʊvəˈfɪʃ/ *v.t.* fish (river etc.) to depletion.

overflow 1 /əʊvəˈfləʊ/ *v.* flow over (brim etc.); flood (surface or area); (of crowd etc.) extend beyond limits of (room etc.); (of receptacle etc.) be so full that contents overflow; (of kindness, harvest, etc.) be very abundant. 2 /ˈəʊvə-/ *n.* what overflows or is superfluous; outlet for excess liquid.

overfly /əʊvəˈflaɪ/ *v.t.* (*past* **overflew** /-ˈfluː/; *p.p.* **overflown** /-ˈfləʊn/) fly over or beyond (place or territory).

overgrown /əʊvəˈgrəʊn/ *a.* covered with plants, weeds, etc.; grown too big; **overgrowth** *n.*

overhang 1 /-ˈhæŋ/ *v.* (*past* and *p.p.* **overhung**) project or hang (over). 2 /ˈəʊvə-/ *n.* fact or amount of overhanging; overhanging part.

overhaul 1 /-ˈhɔːl/ *v.t.* check over thoroughly and make necessary repairs to; overtake. 2 /ˈəʊvə-/ *n.* thorough check with repairs if necessary.

overhead 1 /-ˈhed/ *adv.* above one's head, in the sky. 2 /ˈəʊvə-/ *a.* placed overhead. 3 /ˈəʊvə-/ *n.* (in *pl.*) routine administrative and maintenance expenses of a business.

overhear /əʊvəˈhɪə/ *v.t.* (*past* and *p.p.* **overheard**) hear unintentionally or without speaker's knowledge.

overjoyed /əʊvəˈdʒɔɪd/ *a.* filled with extreme joy.

overkill *n.* excess of capacity to kill or destroy.

overland 1 /-ˈlænd/ *adv.* by land. 2 /ˈəʊvə-/ *a.* entirely or mainly by land.

overlap 1 /-ˈlæp/ *v.* (**-pp-**) partly cover, cover and extend beyond; partly coincide. 2 /ˈəʊvə-/ *n.* overlapping; overlapping part or amount.

overlay 1 /-ˈleɪ/ *v.t.* (*past* and *p.p.* **overlaid**) lay over; cover surface of *with* coating etc. 2 /ˈəʊvə-/ *n.* thing laid over another.

overleaf /əʊvəˈliːf/ *adv.* on other side of leaf of book.

overlie /əʊvəˈlaɪ/ *v.t.* (*past* **overlay**; *p.p.* **overlain**; *partic.* **overlying**) lie on top of; smother (child) thus.

overlook /əʊvəˈlʊk/ *v.t.* fail to notice, ignore, condone; have view of from above; supervise.

overlord *n.* supreme lord.

overly *adv.* (chiefly *Sc.* & *US*) excessively, too.

overman /əʊvəˈmæn/ *v.t.* (**-nn-**) provide with too many people as staff or crew etc.

overnight 1 /-ˈnaɪt/ *adv.* during the course of a night; on preceding evening regarded from next day; *colloq.* instantly. 2 /ˈəʊvə-/ *a.* done or for use etc. overnight.

overpass *n.* road that passes over another by means of bridge.

overplay /əʊvəˈpleɪ/ *v.t.* give too much importance to; **overplay one's hand** act with overestimation of one's strength.

overpower /əʊvəˈpaʊə/ *v.t.* subdue, reduce to submission; **overpowering** *a.* extreme, too intense.

overprint 1 /-ˈprɪnt/ *v.t.* print over (something already printed). 2 /ˈəʊvə-/ *n.* thing overprinted.

overrate /əʊvəˈreɪt/ *v.t.* have too high an opinion of.

overreach /əʊvəˈri:tʃ/ *v.t.* outwit, circumvent; **overreach oneself** fail through excessive endeavour.

over-react /əʊvərɪˈækt/ *v.i.* respond more strongly than is justified.

override /əʊvəˈraɪd/ *v.t.* (*past* **overrode;** *p.p.* **overridden** /-ˈrɪd(ə)n/) have precedence or superiority over; intervene and make ineffective.

overrider *n.* either of pair of vertical attachments to bumper of car.

overrule /əʊvəˈru:l/ *v.t.* set aside (decision etc.) by superior authority; set aside decision of (person) thus.

overrun /əʊvəˈrʌn/ *v.t.* (**-nn-**; *past* **overran;** *p.p.* **overrun**) swarm or spread over; conquer (territory) by force of numbers; exceed (limit).

overseas *a.* & *adv.* across or beyond sea.

oversee /əʊvəˈsi:/ *v.t.* (*past* **oversaw;** *p.p.* **overseen**) superintend.

overseer /ˈəʊvəsɪə/ *n.* superintendent.

overset /əʊvəˈset/ *v.t.* (**-tt-**; *past* and *p.p.* **overset**) overturn, upset.

oversew /əʊvəˈsəʊ/ *v.t.* (*p.p.* **oversewn** or **oversewed**) sew (two edges) with stitches lying over them.

overshadow /əʊvəˈʃædəʊ/ *v.t.* appear much more prominent or important than; cast into shade.

overshoe *n.* outer protective shoe worn over ordinary shoe.

overshoot /əʊvəˈʃu:t/ *v.t.* (*past* and *p.p.* **overshot**) pass or send beyond (target or limit).

overshot *a.* (of wheel) turned by water flowing above it.

oversight *n.* failure to do or note something, inadvertent mistake; supervision.

over-simplify /əʊvəˈsɪmplɪfaɪ/ *v.t.* distort or misrepresent by putting in too simple terms.

oversleep /əʊvəˈsli:p/ *v.i.* (*past* and *p.p.* **overslept**) sleep beyond intended time of waking.

overspend /əʊvəˈspend/ *v.i.* (*past* and *p.p.* **overspent**) spend beyond one's means.

overspill *n.* what spills over or overflows; surplus population moving to new area.

overspread /əʊvəˈspred/ *v.t.* cover surface of; (in *pass.*) be covered *with.*

overstate /əʊvəˈsteɪt/ *v.t.* state too strongly, exaggerate; **overstatement** *n.*

overstay /əʊvəˈsteɪ/ *v.t.* stay longer than.

oversteer *n.* tendency of vehicle to turn more sharply than was intended.

overstep /əʊvəˈstep/ *v.t.* (**-pp-**) pass beyond (limit).

overstrung /əʊvəˈstrʌŋ/ *a.* (of person or nerves) too highly strung.

over-subscribed /əʊvəsəbˈskraɪbd/ *a.* (esp. of shares for sale) not enough to meet amount subscribed.

overt /əʊˈvɜ:t, ˈəʊ-/ *a.* done openly, unconcealed. [F, p.p. of *ovrir* open]

overtake /əʊvəˈteɪk/ *v.t.* (*past* **overtook** /-ˈtʊk/; *p.p.* **overtaken**) catch up and pass in same direction; (esp. of misfortune) come suddenly upon. [OVER-]

overtax /əʊvəˈtæks/ *v.t.* make excessive demands on; tax too highly.

overthrow **1** /-ˈθrəʊ/ *v.t.* (*past* **overthrew** /-ˈθru:/; *p.p.* **overthrown**) remove forcibly from power; put an end to (institution etc.); conquer, overcome; knock down, upset. **2** /ˈəʊvə-/ *n.* defeat, downfall.

overtime **1** *n.* time worked in addition to regular hours; payment for this. **2** *adv.* as or during overtime.

overtone *n.* subtle extra quality or implication; *Mus.* any of tones above lowest in harmonic series.

overture /ˈəʊvətjʊə/ *n.* orchestral piece opening opera etc., composition in this style; (often in *pl.*) opening of negotiations, formal proposal or offer. [F (OVERT)]

overturn /əʊvəˈtɜ:n/ *v.* (cause to) turn over or fall down, upset; overthrow, subvert. [OVER-]

overview *n.* general survey.

overweening /əʊvəˈwi:nɪŋ/ *a.* arrogant, presumptuous.

overweight **1** /-ˈweɪt/ *a.* more than allowed or normal or desired weight. **2** /ˈəʊvə-/ *n.* excess weight.

overwhelm /əʊvəˈwelm/ *v.t.* overpower, esp. with emotion or burden; overcome by force of numbers; bury or drown beneath huge mass.

overwork /əʊvəˈwɜ:k/ **1** *v.* (cause to) work too hard; weary or exhaust with too much work. **2** *n.* excessive work.

overwrought /əʊvəˈrɔ:t/ *a.* suffering nervous reaction from over-excitement.

ovi- *in comb.* egg, ovum. [OVUM]

oviduct /ˈəʊvɪdʌkt/ *n.* canal through which ova pass from ovary, esp. in oviparous animals.

oviform /ˈəʊvɪfɔ:m/ *a.* egg-shaped.

ovine /ˈəʊvaɪn/ *a.* of or like sheep. [L (*ovis* sheep)]

oviparous /əʊˈvɪpərəs/ *a.* producing young from eggs expelled from body before being hatched. [OVUM, L *-parus* bearing]

ovoid /ˈəʊvɔɪd/ *a.* (of solid) egg-shaped. [OVUM]

ovulate /ˈɒvjʊleɪt/ *v.i.* discharge ovum or ova from ovary; produce ova; **ovulation** /-ˈleɪʃ(ə)n/ *n.* [OVUM]

ovule /ˈəʊvju:l/ *n.* structure containing germ-cell in female plant. [OVUM]

ovum /ˈəʊvəm/ (*pl.* **ova**) female germ-cell in animals, from which by fertilization with male sperm the young is developed; egg, esp. of mammal or fish or insect. [L, = egg]

ow *int.* expressing sudden pain. [natural excl.]

owe /əʊ/ *v.t.* be under obligation to pay or repay (money, person money, gratitude, etc.; money etc. *to* person); be in debt (*for* thing); have duty to render (*owe allegiance*); be indebted for *to* person or thing (*owe success to good teachers, to luck*). [OE]

owing *predic. a.* owed, yet to be paid; **owing to** caused by, because of.

owl *n.* nocturnal bird of prey with large head and eyes and hooked beak; solemn wise-looking person. [OE]

owlet /ˈaʊlɪt/ *n.* small or young owl.

owlish *a.* like an owl; solemn and dull.

own /əʊn/ **1** *a.* (after possessive) in full ownership, not another's (*saw it with my own eyes*; *use your own pen*); also used to emphasize identity rather than possession (*cooks his own meals*); *absol.* private property etc. (*is that your own?*). **2** *v.* have as property, possess; acknowledge paternity, authorship, or possession of; admit as existent, valid, true, etc. **3 come into one's own** receive one's due, achieve recognition; **of one's own** belonging to one; **on one's own** alone, independent(ly), without help; **own to** confess to; **own up (to)** confess frankly (to). **4 -owned** *a.* (*State-owned*). [OE]

owner *n.* possessor; **owner-occupier** one who owns and occupies house; **ownership** *n.*

ox *n.* (*pl.* **oxen**) animal of kinds of large usu. horned cloven-footed ruminant kept for draught, milk, and meat; castrated male of domesticated species of ox; **ox-eye** any of several plants with flowers like eye of ox. [OE]

oxalic acid /ɒkˈsælɪk/ highly poisonous and sour acid orig. found in wood sorrel and other plants. [F f. L f. Gk *oxalis* wood sorrel]

Oxbridge 1 *n.* universities of Oxford and Cambridge, esp. in contrast to newer universities. **2** *a.* characteristic of these. [portmanteau word]

oxen *pl.* of ox.

Oxf. *abbr.* Oxford.

Oxfam *abbr.* Oxford Committee for Famine Relief.

Oxford blue /ˈɒksfəd/ dark blue, sometimes with purple tinge.

oxherd *n.* cowherd. [ox]

oxhide *n.* hide of ox, leather from this.

oxidation /ɒksɪˈdeɪʃ(ə)n/ n. oxidizing or being oxidized. [F (foll.)]

oxide /ˈɒksaɪd/ *n.* binary compound of oxygen. [F (OXYGEN)]

oxidize /ˈɒksɪdaɪz/ *v.* (cause to) combine with oxygen; make or become rusty; coat (metal) with oxide; **oxidization** /-ˈzeɪʃ(ə)n/ *n.* (= OXIDATION).

Oxon. *abbr.* of Oxford University. [L *Oxoniensis* (foll.)]

Oxonian /ɒkˈsəʊnɪən/ **1** *a.* of Oxford or Oxford University. **2** *n.* member of Oxford University; citizen of Oxford. [*Oxonia* Latinized name of *Ox(en)ford*]

oxtail *n.* tail of ox, much used for soup-making. [ox]

oxy-acetylene /ɒksɪəˈsetɪli:n/ *a.* of or using a mixture of oxygen and acetylene, esp. in cutting or welding of metals. [OXY(GEN)]

oxygen /ˈɒksɪdʒ(ə)n/ *n.* an odourless tasteless gaseous element essential to animal and vegetable life; **oxygen tent** tentlike enclosure supplying patient with air having increased oxygen content. [F *oxygène* f. Gk *oxus* sharp, -GEN (because thought to be present in all acids)]

oxygenate /ɒkˈsɪdʒəneɪt/ *v.t.* supply or treat or mix with oxygen, oxidize.

oxymoron /ɒksɪˈmɔ:rɒn/ *n.* figure of speech with pointed conjunction of apparent contradictions (e.g. *cheerful pessimist*). [Gk, = pointedly foolish (*oxus* sharp, *mōros* dull)]

oyez /əʊˈjes/ *int.* (also **oyes**) cry uttered usu. three times by public crier or court officer to call for attention. [AF imper. pl. of *oïr* hear f. L *audio*]

oyster *n.* bivalve mollusc used as food and in some types producing pearl; symbol of all one desires (*the world is her oyster*); white colour with grey tinge; **oyster-catcher** wading sea-bird. [F *oistre* f. L *ostrea* f. Gk]

oz. *abbr.* ounce(s). [It. (*onza* ounce)]

ozone /ˈəʊzəʊn/ *n.* form of oxygen with three atoms in molecule, having pungent smell; *pop.* invigorating air at seaside etc.; *fig.* exhilarating influence. [G f. Gk *ozō* smell *v.*]

P

P, p /piː/ *n.* (*pl.* **Ps, P's**) sixteenth letter.
P *abbr.* pawn (in chess).
p *abbr.* penny, pence.
p. *abbr.* page.
p *abbr. Mus.* PIANO².
P *symb.* phosphorus.
pa /pɑː/ *n. colloq.* father. [abbr. of PAPA]
PA *abbr.* personal assistant; public address.
p.a. *abbr.* per annum.
Pa *symb.* protactinium.
pabulum /'pæbjʊləm/ *n.* food, esp. for the mind. [L]
pace¹ 1 *n.* single step in walking or running; space traversed in this; speed in walking or running; rate of progression; manner of walking or running; any of various gaits of (esp. trained) horse etc. **2** *v.* walk with slow or regular pace; traverse by pacing; set pace for (rider, runner, etc.); measure (distance *out*) by pacing; (of horse) amble. **3 keep pace** advance at equal rate (*with*); **put person through his paces** test his qualities in action etc.; **set the pace** determine the speed, esp. by leading. [F *pas* f. L *passus*]
pace² /'peɪsɪ, 'pɑːtʃeɪ/ *prep.* (in announcing contrary opinion) with all due deference to (person named). [L, abl. of *pax* peace]
pacemaker *n.* runner etc. who sets pace in race; natural or electrical device for stimulating heart muscle. [PACE¹]
pacha var. of PASHA.
pachyderm /'pækɪdɜːm/ *n.* thick-skinned mammal, esp. elephant or rhinoceros; **pachydermatous** /-'dɜːmətəs/ *a.* [F f. Gk (*pakhus* thick, *derma* skin)]
pacific /pə'sɪfɪk/ *a.* characterized by or tending to peace, tranquil; (**Pacific**) of or adjoining the ocean between America to the east and Asia and Australia to the west. [F or L (*pax pacis* peace)]
pacifist /'pæsɪfɪst/ *n.* one who rejects war and violence and believes in resort to peaceful alternatives as means of settling disputes; **pacifism** *n.* [F (prec.)]
pacify /'pæsɪfaɪ/ *v.t.* appease (person, anger, etc.); bring (country etc.) to state of peace; **pacification** /-fɪ'keɪʃ(ə)n/ *n.*; **pacificatory** /pə'sɪfɪkətərɪ/ *a.* [F or L (PACIFIC)]
pack¹ 1 *n.* collection of things wrapped up or tied together for carrying; (usu. *derog.*) lot or set (*pack of idiots*); set of playing-cards; group of wild animals, hounds, etc.; organized group of Cub Scouts or Brownies; team's forwards in Rugby football; medicinal or cosmetic substance applied to the skin; area of large crowded pieces of floating ice in sea; method of packing. **2** *v.* put (things) together in bundle, bag, etc., for transport or storing; fill (bag or suitcase etc.) with clothes etc.; put closely together, crowd; cover (thing) with thing pressed tightly round; cram (space etc. *with*); fill (theatre etc.) with spectators; *sl.* carry (gun etc.), be capable of delivering (a punch) with skill or force; depart with one's belongings; (of animals) form pack. **3 pack-horse** horse for carrying packs; **pack it in** *sl.* end it, finish; **pack it up** *sl.* desist; **pack off** send or drive (person) away, esp. summarily; **pack-saddle** saddle adapted for supporting packs; **pack up** *sl.* stop working, break down, retire from contest, activity, etc.; **send packing** *colloq.* dismiss summarily. [LG or Du.]
pack² *v.t.* select (jury etc.) so as to secure biased decision in one's favour. [PACT]
package 1 *n.* bundle of things packed; parcel, box, etc., in which things are packed; = *package deal.* **2** *v.t.* make up into or enclose in a package. **3 package deal** transaction or proposals offered or agreed to as a whole; **package holiday** (or **tour** etc.) one with all arrangements made at inclusive price. [PACK¹]
packaging *n.* wrapping or container(s) for goods.
packet /'pækɪt/ *n.* small package; *colloq.* large sum of money won or lost; **packet-boat** mail-boat.
packing *n.* material used to pack esp. fragile articles.
packthread *n.* stout thread for sewing or tying up packs.
pact *n.* agreement, treaty. [F f. L *pactum*]
pad¹ 1 *n.* piece of soft stuff used to reduce friction or jarring, fill out hollows, hold or absorb liquid, etc.; number of sheets of blank paper fastened together at one edge; fleshy underpart of animal's foot; guard for leg and ankle in cricket etc.; flat surface for helicopter take-off or rocket launching; *sl.* lodging. **2** *v.t.* (**-dd-**) provide with pad or padding, stuff; lengthen or fill *out* (book etc.) with unnecessary material. **3 padded cell** room with padded walls in mental hospital. [prob. LG or Du.]
pad² *v.* (**-dd-**) walk with soft dull steady sound of steps; tramp along (road etc.) on foot; travel on foot. [LG *pad* PATH]

padding *n.* material used to pad. [PAD[1]]

paddle[1] /'pæd(ə)l/ **1** *n.* short broad-bladed oar used without rowlock; paddle-shaped instrument; fin, flipper; one of the boards fitted round circumference of paddle-wheel or mill-wheel; action or spell of paddling. **2** *v.* move on water, propel canoe, by means of paddles; row gently. **3 paddle-boat** boat propelled by paddle-wheel; **paddle-wheel** wheel for propelling ship, with boards round circumference so as to press backward against water. [orig. unkn.]

paddle[2] /'pæd(ə)l/ **1** *v.* walk barefoot in shallow water; dabble (feet or hands) in shallow water. **2** *n.* action or spell of paddling. [prob. LG or Du.]

paddock /'pædək/ *n.* small field, esp. for keeping horses in; turf enclosure adjoining racecourse where horses or cars are assembled before race. [*parrock*, var. of PARK]

paddy[1] /'pædɪ/ *n.* field where rice is grown (in full **paddy-field**); rice before threshing or in the husk. [Malay]

paddy[2] /'pædɪ/ *n. colloq.* rage, fit of temper; (**Paddy**) nickname for Irishman. [Ir. *Padraig* Patrick]

padlock /'pædlɒk/ **1** *n.* detachable lock hanging by pivoted hook on object fastened. **2** *v.t.* secure with padlock. [orig. unkn.]

padre /'pɑːdrɪ/ *n. colloq.* chaplain in army etc. [It., Sp., Port., = father, priest]

paean /'piːən/ *n.* song of praise or triumph. [L f. Gk]

paederast etc. var of PEDERAST etc.

paediatrics /piːdɪ'ætrɪks/ *n.pl.* branch of medicine dealing with children and their diseases; **paediatric** *a.*; **paediatrician** /piːdɪə'trɪʃ(ə)n/ *n.* [PAEDO-, Gk *iatros* physician]

paedo- *in comb.* child. [Gk *pais paid-* child]

paedophilia /piːdə'fɪlɪə/ *n.* sexual love directed towards children.

paella /pɑː'elə/ *n.* Spanish dish of rice, saffron, chicken, seafood, etc., cooked and served in large shallow pan. [Catalan, f. F f. L PATELLA]

pagan /'peɪgən/ **1** *a.* heathen; unenlightened, irreligious. **2** *n.* pagan person. **3 paganism** *n.* [L *paganus* (*pagus* country district)]

page[1] **1** *n.* leaf of book etc., one side of this; what is written or printed on this; episode that might fill page in written history etc. **2** *v.t.* paginate. [F, f. L *pagina*]

page[2] **1** *n.* boy or man, usu. in livery, employed to run errands, attend to door, etc.; boy employed as personal attendant of person of rank, bride, etc. **2** *v.t.* summon (as) by page. [F]

pageant /'pædʒənt/ *n.* brilliant spectacle, esp. elaborate parade; spectacular procession, or play performed in the open, illustrating historical events; tableau etc. on fixed stage or moving vehicle. [orig. unkn.]

pageantry *n.* spectacular show or display, what serves to make a pageant.

paginate /'pædʒɪneɪt/ *v.t.* assign numbers to pages of (book etc.); **pagination** /-'neɪʃ(ə)n/ *n.* [L (PAGE[1])]

pagoda /pə'gəʊdə/ *n.* Hindu or Buddhist temple or sacred building, esp. tower, in India and Far East; ornamental imitation of this. [Port.]

pah /pɑː/ *int.* expressing disgust or contempt. [natural utterance]

paid *past* and *p.p.* of PAY.

pail *n.* bucket; **pailful** *n.* [OE]

pain **1** *n.* suffering or distress of body or mind; (in *pl.*) careful effort (*take pains*); (in *pl.*) throes of childbirth; punishment. **2** *v.t.* inflict pain on; (in *p.p.*) expressing pain (*pained look*). **3 on pain of death** etc. with death etc. as penalty; **pain in the neck** (or **arse**) *colloq.* annoying or tiresome person or thing; **pain-killer** medicine for alleviating pain. [F *peine* f. L *poena* penalty]

painful *a.* causing or (esp. of part of body) suffering pain; causing trouble or difficulty, laborious; **painfully** *adv.*

painless *a.* not causing pain.

painstaking /'peɪnzteɪkɪŋ/ *a.* careful, industrious.

paint **1** *n.* colouring matter, esp. in liquid form for imparting colour to a surface. **2** *v.t.* cover surface of (wall, object, etc.) with paint; depict (object, scene, etc., or *absol.*) with paints; make (picture) thus; apply paint of specified colour to (*paint the door blue*); describe vividly, as if by painting; apply liquid or cosmetic to (face etc.); apply (liquid to skin etc.). **3 painted lady** orange-red butterfly with black and white spots; **paint out** efface with paint; **paint the town red** *sl.* enjoy oneself flamboyantly. [F f. L *pingo pict-*]

paintbox *n.* box holding dry paints for use by artist.

paintbrush *n.* brush for applying paint.

painter[1] *n.* one who paints, esp. as artist or decorator.

painter[2] *n.* rope attached to bow of boat for tying it to quay etc. [orig. unkn.]

painting *n.* art of using paint; painted picture. [PAINT]

pair **1** *n.* set of two persons or things used together or regarded as a unit; article consisting of two joined or corresponding parts (*pair of trousers*); engaged or married couple; mated couple of animals; other member of a pair; two playing-cards of same denomination; either or both of two MPs etc. on opposite sides absenting themselves from voting by mutual arrangement. **2** *v.* arrange or be arranged in couples; unite in love or marriage; (of animals) mate. **3 pair off** arrange or go off in pairs, form pair in voting. [F f. L *paria* (PAR)]

Paisley /'peɪzlɪ/ *a.* (of garment) having distinctive pattern of curved abstract figures. [*Paisley* in Scotland]

pajamas /pə'dʒɑːməz/ *US* var. of PYJAMAS.

Pak *n.* (also **Paki**) *sl. derog.* **(R)** Pakistani. [abbr.]

Pakistani /pɑːkɪ'stɑːnɪ, pæk-/ **1** *n.* native of Pakistan. **2** *a.* of Pakistan. [Hind.]

pal *colloq.* **1** *n.* friend, mate. **2** *v.i.* **(-ll-)** (with *up*) become friends, associate (*with*). [Romany]

palace /'pælɪs/ *n.* official residence of sovereign, president, archbishop, or bishop; splendid mansion, spacious building; **palace revolution** overthrow of sovereign etc. without civil war. [F f. L *palatium*]

paladin /'pælədɪn/ *n.* any of the Twelve Peers of Charlemagne's court; knight errant, champion. [F f. It. (PALATINE[1])]

palaeo- *in comb.* ancient, of ancient times. [Gk *palaios*]

Palaeocene /'pælɪəsiːn/ **1** *a.* of the first epoch of the Tertiary period. **2** *n.* this epoch. [prec., Gk *kainos* new]

palaeography /pælɪ'ɒgrəfɪ/ *n.* study of ancient writing and documents; **palaeographic** /-'græfɪk/ *a.* [F (prec.)]

palaeolithic /pælɪəʊ'lɪθɪk/ *a.* of the early part of the Stone Age. [Gk *lithos* stone]

palaeontology /pælɪɒn'tɒlədʒɪ/ *n.* study of life in geological past; **palaeontologist** *n.* [Gk *ōn, ont-* being]

Palaeozoic /pælɪəʊ'zəʊɪk/ **1** *a.* of the geological era containing the oldest forms of highly organized life. **2** *n.* this era. [Gk *zōion* animal]

palais /'pæleɪ/ *n.* public hall for dancing. [F, = hall]

palanquin /pælən'kiːn/ *n.* (also **palankeen**) *n.* eastern covered litter for one. [Port.]

palatable /'pælətəb(ə)l/ *a.* pleasant to taste; agreeable to the mind. [PALATE]

palatal /'pælət(ə)l/ **1** *a.* of the palate; (of a sound) made by placing tongue against palate. **2** *n.* palatal sound. **3 palatally** *adv.*

palate /'pælət/ *n.* structure closing upper part of mouth cavity in vertebrates; sense of taste; mental taste, liking. [L *palatum*]

palatial /pə'leɪʃ(ə)l/ *a.* like a palace, spacious, splendid; **palatially** *adv.* [L (as PALACE)]

palatinate /pə'lætɪneɪt/ *n.* territory under Count Palatine. [foll.]

Palatine /'pælətaɪn/ *a.* having local authority that elsewhere belongs only to sovereign (*Count Palatine*); **County palatine** territory subject to this (in England still of Lancashire and Cheshire). [F f. L (PALACE)]

palaver /pə'lɑːvə/ **1** *n.* fuss and bother, profuse or idle talk, cajolery; *sl.* affair, business; (esp. *hist.*) parley between African or other natives and traders etc. **2** *v.* talk profusely, flatter, wheedle. [Port. *palavra* f. L (PARABLE)]

pale[1] **1** *a.* (of person or complexion) of whitish or ashen appearance; (of colour) faint, light; faintly coloured; of faint lustre, dim. **2** *v.* grow or make pale; become feeble in comparison (*before* or *beside*). **3 pale-face** supposed N. American Indian name for white man. [F f. L *pallidus*]

pale[2] *n.* pointed piece of wood for fence etc., stake; boundary; **beyond the pale** outside bounds of acceptable behaviour. [F *pal* f. L *palus*]

paleo- *US* var. of PALAEO-.

palette /'pælət/ *n.* artist's thin wooden slab etc. used for laying and mixing colours on; **palette-knife** thin steel blade with handle for mixing colours or applying paint; kitchen knife with long blunt round-ended flexible blade. [F dimin. f. L *pala* spade]

palfrey /'pɔːlfrɪ/ *n. archaic* horse for ordinary riding, esp. for ladies. [F f. L (Gk *para* beside, L *veredus* horse)]

palimpsest /'pælɪmpsest/ *n.* writing-material or manuscript on which original writing has been effaced to make room for other writing; monumental brass turned and re-engraved on reverse side. [Gk (*palin* again, *psēstos* rubbed)]

palindrome /'pælɪndrəʊm/ *n.* word or verse etc. that reads the same backwards as forwards (e.g. *nurses run*); **palindromic** /-'drɒmɪk/ *a.* [Gk *palindromos* running back again (prec., *drom-* run)]

paling *n.* fence of pales; pale. [PALE[2]]

palisade /pælɪ'seɪd/ **1** *n.* fence of pales or of iron railings; strong pointed wooden stake. **2** *v.t.* enclose or furnish with palisade. [F (PALE[2])]

pall[1] /pɔːl/ *n.* cloth spread over coffin, hearse, or tomb; a kind of ecclesiastical vestment; *fig.* dark covering (*pall of smoke*). [OE f. L *pallium* cloak]

pall[2] /pɔːl/ *v.* become uninteresting; satiate, cloy; **pall on** cease to interest or attract. [APPAL]

palladium /pə'leɪdɪəm/ *n.* rare hard white metallic element of platinum group. [*Pallas*, name of asteroid]

pallbearer *n.* person helping to carry coffin at funeral. [PALL[1]]
pallet[1] /ˈpælɪt/ *n.* straw mattress; mean or makeshift bed. [AF f. L *palea* straw]
pallet[2] /ˈpælɪt/ *n.* portable platform for transporting and storing loads. [F (PALETTE)]
palliasse /ˈpælɪæs/ *n.* straw mattress. [F f. It. f. Rmc f. L (PALLET[1])]
palliate /ˈpælɪeɪt/ *v.t.* alleviate (disease) without curing; excuse, extenuate; **palliative** *a.* & *n.* [L *pallio* cloak *v.* (PALL[1])]
pallid /ˈpælɪd/ *a.* pale, esp. from illness. [L (PALE[1])]
pallor /ˈpælə/ *n.* pallidness, paleness. [L (*palleo* be pale)]
pally *a. colloq.* friendly; **palliness** *n.* [PAL]
palm[1] /pɑːm/ *n.* a kind of chiefly tropical tree with no branches and a mass of large leaves at the top; leaf of this as symbol of victory; supreme excellence, prize for this; **palm-oil** oil from various palms; **Palm Sunday** Sunday before Easter, celebrating Christ's entry into Jerusalem. [OE f. L *palma* PALM[2]]
palm[2] /pɑːm/ **1** *n.* inner surface of hand between wrist and fingers; part of glove that covers this. **2** *v.t.* conceal in the hand. **3 palm off** impose or thrust fraudulently *on* person, put (person) off *with*. **4 palmar** /ˈpælmə/ *a.* [F f. L *palma*]
palmate /ˈpælmeɪt/ *a.* shaped like palm of hand, having lobes etc. like spread fingers. [L *palmatus* (PALM[2])]
palmetto /pælˈmetəʊ/ *n.* (*pl.* **palmettos**) palm-tree esp. of small size. [Sp. *palmito* dimin. of *palma* PALM[1]]
palmistry /ˈpɑːmɪstrɪ/ *n.* divination from lines etc. in palm of hand; **palmist** *n.* [PALM[2]]
palmy *a.* of or like or abounding in palms; triumphant, flourishing. [PALM[1]]
palomino /pæləˈmiːnəʊ/ *n.* (*pl.* **palaminos**) golden or cream-coloured horse with light-coloured mane and tail. [Sp. (L *palumba* dove)]
palpable /ˈpælpəb(ə)l/ *a.* that can be touched or felt; readily perceived by senses or mind; **palpability** /-ˈbɪlɪtɪ/ *n.* **palpably** *adv.* [L *palpo* caress]
palpate /ˈpælpeɪt/ *v.t.* examine (esp. medically) by touch; **palpation** /-ˈpeɪʃ(ə)n/ *n.*
palpitate /ˈpælpɪteɪt/ *v.i.* pulsate, throb; tremble (*with* pleasure, fear, etc.). [L *palpito* frequent (PALPABLE)]
palpitation /pælpɪˈteɪʃ(ə)n/ *n.* throbbing, trembling; increased activity of heart due to exertion, agitation, or disease.
palsy /ˈpɔːlzɪ/ **1** *n.* paralysis, esp. with involuntary tremors; *fig.* cause or condition of utter helplessness. **2** *v.t.* affect with palsy. [F (PARALYSIS)]
paltry /ˈpɔːltrɪ/ *a.* worthless, contemptible, trifling; **paltriness** *n.* [*palt* rubbish]
pampas /ˈpæmpəs/ *n.pl.* large treeless plains in S. America; **pampas-grass** large ornamental grass orig. from S. America. [Sp. f. Quechua]
pamper *v.t.* over-indulge (person, taste, etc.); spoil (person) with luxury. [obs. *pamp* cram]
pamphlet /ˈpæmflɪt/ *n.* small usu. unbound booklet or leaflet containing information or treatise. [*Pamphilus*, name of medieval poem]
pamphleteer /pæmflɪˈtɪə/ *n.* writer of (esp. political) pamphlets.
pan[1] **1** *n.* metal or earthenware or plastic vessel used for cooking and other domestic purposes; panlike vessel in which substances are heated etc.; bowl of scales or of lavatory; part of lock that held priming in old guns; hollow in ground (*salt-pan*). **2** *v.t.* (**-nn-**) *colloq.* criticize severely. **3 pan out** (of gravel) yield gold; (of action etc.) turn out *well* etc., be successful. [OE]
pan[2] **1** *v.* (**-nn-**) swing (cine-camera) horizontally to give panoramic effect or follow moving object; (of cine-camera) be moved thus. **2** *n.* panning movement. [PANORAMA]
pan- *in comb.* all, relating to whole of continent, racial group, religion, etc. (*pan-American*). [Gk (*pan* neut. of *pas pantos* all)]
panacea /pænəˈsɪə/ *n.* universal remedy. [L f. Gk (PAN-, *-akēs* remedy]
panache /pəˈnæʃ/ *n.* assertively or flamboyantly confident style or manner. [F, = plume]
panama /ˈpænəmɑː/ *n.* hat of strawlike material made from leaves of a pine-tree. [*Panama* in Central America]
panatella /pænəˈtelə/ *n.* long thin cigar. [Amer. Sp., = long thin biscuit]
pancake *n.* thin flat batter-cake usu. fried in pan; flat cake (e.g. of make-up); **Pancake Day** Shrove Tuesday (on which pancakes are traditionally eaten); **pancake landing** landing of aircraft descending vertically in level horizontal position. [PAN[1], CAKE]
panchromatic /pænkrəˈmætɪk/ *a.* (of film etc.) sensitive to all visible colours of spectrum. [PAN-]
pancreas /ˈpænkrɪəs/ *n.* gland near stomach supplying digestive fluid and insulin; **pancreatic** /-ˈætɪk/ *a.* [L f. Gk (*kreas* flesh)]
panda /ˈpændə/ *n.* large rare bearlike black-and-white mammal of China (also **giant panda**); Indian racoon-like

animal; **panda car** police patrol car (orig. white with black stripes on doors). [Nepali]

pandemic /pæn'demɪk/ *a.* (of a disease) prevalent over whole country or world. [Gk (*dēmos* people)]

pandemonium /pændɪ'məʊnɪəm/ *n.* uproar, utter confusion; scene of this. [place in hell in Milton (PAN-, DEMON)]

pander 1 *v.i.* (with *to*) gratify or indulge person or weakness etc. **2** *n.* go-between in illicit love-affairs, procurer; one who panders. [*Pandare*, character in story of Troilus and Cressida]

Pandora's box /pæn'dɔːrəz/ thing that once activated will generate many unmanageable problems. [box in Gk myth. from which many ills were released on mankind]

p. & p. *abbr.* postage and packing.

pane *n.* single sheet of glass in window or door. [F *pan* f. L *pannus* a cloth]

panegyric /pænɪ'dʒɪrɪk/ *n.* laudatory discourse, eulogy; **panegyrical** *a.* [F f. L f. Gk (*agora* assembly)]

panel /'pæn(ə)l/ **1** *n.* distinct, usu. rectangular, section of surface (e.g. of wall, door, vehicle); strip of material as part of garment; team in broadcast or public quiz programme etc., body of experts assembled for discussion or consultation; list of jurors, jury. **2** *v.t.* (**-ll-**) cover or decorate with panels. **3 panel game** quiz etc. played by panel. [F f. L dimin. of *pannus* (PANE)]

panelling *n.* panelled work, wood for making panels.

panellist *n.* member of panel.

pang *n.* sudden sharp pain or painful emotion. [obs. *pronge*]

pangolin /pæŋ'gəʊlɪn/ *n.* scaly anteater. [Malay]

panic /'pænɪk/ **1** *n.* sudden uncontrollable fear or alarm; infectious fright. **2** *a.* of or connected with or resulting from panic. **3** *v.* (**-ck-**) affect or be affected with panic. **4 panic-stricken** (or **-struck**) affected with panic. **5 panicky** *a.* [F f. L f. Gk (*Pan*, rural god)]

panicle /'pænɪk(ə)l/ *n.* loose branching cluster of flowers. [L *paniculum* dimin. of *panus* thread]

panjandrum /pæn'dʒændrəm/ *n.* mock title of exalted personage. [invented wd.]

pannier /'pænɪə/ *n.* basket, esp. one of pair carried by beast of burden or on bicycle, motor cycle, etc. [F f. L (*panis* bread)]

panoply /'pænəplɪ/ *n.* complete suit of armour; *fig.* complete or splendid array. [F or L f. Gk (*hopla* arms)]

panorama /pænə'rɑːmə/ *n.* picture or photograph containing wide view; continuous passing scene; unbroken view of surrounding region (*lit.* or *fig.*); **panoramic** /-'ræmɪk/ *a.* [Gk *horama* view]

pan-pipe *n.* (in *sing.* or *pl.*) musical instrument made of series of reeds fixed together with mouthpieces in line. [*Pan*, Gk rural god]

pansy /'pænzɪ/ *n.* garden plant with flowers of various rich colours; *colloq.* effeminate man, male homosexual. [F *pensée* thought, pansy]

pant 1 *v.* breathe with short quick breaths; utter breathlessly; yearn; (of heart etc.) throb violently. **2** *n.* a panting breath; throb. [F, ult. f. Gk (FANTASY)]

pantaloons /pæntə'luːnz/ *n.pl.* (esp. *US*) trousers. [F f. It.]

pantechnicon /pæn'teknɪkən/ *n.* large van for transporting furniture. [TECHNIC; orig. as name of bazaar]

pantheism /'pænθiːɪz(ə)m/ *n.* belief that God is everything and everything God; **pantheist** *n.*; **pantheistic** /-'ɪstɪk/ *a.* [Gk *theos* god]

pantheon /'pænθɪən/ *n.* temple dedicated to all the gods; deities of a people collectively; building in which illustrious dead are buried or have memorials. [L f. Gk (*theion* divine)]

panther *n.* leopard. [F f. L f. Gk]

panties /'pæntɪz/ *n.pl. colloq.* short-legged or legless knickers worn by women and girls. [dimin. of PANTS]

pantihose /'pæntɪhəʊz/ *n.* women's tights.

pantile /'pæntaɪl/ *n.* curved roof-tile. [PAN[1]]

panto /'pæntəʊ/ *n. colloq.* pantomime. [abbr.]

pantograph /'pæntəgrɑːf/ *n.* instrument with jointed rods for copying plan etc. on any scale; jointed framework conveying current to electric vehicle from overhead wires. [PAN-, -GRAPH]

pantomime /'pæntəmaɪm/ *n.* dramatic entertainment usu. produced about Christmas and based on fairy-tale; gestures and facial expression used to convey meaning; **pantomimic** /-'mɪmɪk/ *a.* [F or L f. Gk (PAN-, MIME)]

pantry /'pæntrɪ/ *n.* room or cupboard in which crockery, cutlery, table-linen, etc., are kept; larder. [AF f. L (*panis* bread)]

pants *n.pl. colloq.* underpants, panties; trousers, slacks. [abbr. of *pantaloons*, F f. It. character in comedy]

pap[1] *n.* soft or semi-liquid food for infants or invalids; undemanding reading matter. [LG or Du.]

pap[2] *n.* (*archaic* or *dial.*) nipple of breast. [Scand.]

papa /pə'pɑː/ *n. archaic* father (esp. as child's word). [F f. L f. Gk]

papacy /ˈpeɪpəsɪ/ *n.* Pope's office or tenure; papal system. [med.L *papatia* (POPE)]

papal /ˈpeɪp(ə)l/ *a.* of the Pope or his office; **papally** *adv.* [F f. med.L (POPE)]

papaw /pəˈpɔː/ *n.* oblong orange edible fruit; palmlike tropical American tree bearing this. [Sp. & Port. *papaya*]

paper 1 *n.* substance in thin sheets made from pulp of wood or other fibrous material, used for writing or drawing or printing on, as wrapping material, etc.; document printed on paper; (in *pl.*) documents attesting identity or credentials; documents belonging to a person or relating to a matter; = NEWSPAPER; = WALLPAPER; piece of paper, esp. as wrapper etc.; set of questions to be answered at one session in examination, written answers to these; essay or dissertation, esp. one read to a learned society. **2** *a.* made of or flimsy like paper; existing only in theory (*paper profits*). **3** *v.t.* decorate (wall etc.) with paper. **4 on paper** in writing, in theory, to judge from written or printed evidence; **paper-boy** (or **-girl**) one who delivers or sells newspapers; **paper-chase** cross-country run in which runners follow trail of torn-up paper; **paper-clip** clip of bent wire or of plastic for holding a few sheets of paper together; **paper-hanger** one who decorates with wallpaper, esp. professionally; **paper-knife** blunt knife for opening letters etc.; **paper money** money in form of banknotes; **paper tiger** threatening but ineffectual person or thing. [AF f. L PAPYRUS]

paperback 1 *a.* bound in stiff paper, not boards. **2** *n.* paperback book.

paperweight *n.* small heavy object for keeping loose papers in place.

paperwork *n.* routine clerical or administrative work.

papery *a.* like paper in thinness or texture.

papier mâché /pæpjeɪ ˈmæʃeɪ/ moulded paper pulp used for boxes, trays, etc. [F, = chewed paper]

papilla /pəˈpɪlə/ *n.* (*pl.* **papillae** /-iː/) small nipple-like protuberance in or on the body. [L]

papillary /pəˈpɪlərɪ/ *a.* papilla-shaped.

papist /ˈpeɪpɪst/ *n.* advocate of papal supremacy; (usu. *derog.*) Roman Catholic. [F or L (POPE)]

papoose /pəˈpuːs/ *a.* N. American Indian young child. [Algonquin]

paprika /ˈpæprɪkə/ *n.* ripe red pepper; red condiment made from it. [Magyar]

papyrology /pæpɪˈrɒlədʒɪ/ *n.* study of ancient papyri; **papyrologist** *n.* [foll.]

papyrus /pəˈpaɪrəs/ *n.* (*pl.* **papyri** /-iː/) aquatic plant of sedge family; ancient writing material made from stem of this, manuscript written on it. [L f. Gk]

par *n.* average or normal amount, degree, condition, etc. (*feel below par*); equality, equal status or footing (*on a par with*); (in golf) number of strokes a first-class player should normally require for hole or course; face value of stocks and shares etc.; (in full **par of exchange**) recognized value of one country's currency in terms of another's. [L, = equal]

para /ˈpærə/ *n. colloq.* paratrooper. [abbr.]

para-[1] *prefix* beside (*parabola, paramilitary*); beyond (*paradox, paranormal*). [Gk]

para-[2] *in comb.* protect, ward off (*parachute, parasol*). [F f. It. f. L (*paro* defend)]

para. *abbr.* paragraph.

parable /ˈpærəb(ə)l/ *n.* narrative of imagined events used to illustrate moral or spiritual lesson; allegory. [F f. L *parabola* f. Gk, = comparison]

parabola /pəˈræbələ/ *n.* open plane curve formed by intersection of cone with plane parallel to its side. [Gk *parabolē* placing side by side (prec.)]

parabolic /pærəˈbɒlɪk/ *a.* of or expressed in parable; of or like parabola; **parabolically** *adv.* [L f. Gk (prec.)]

paracetamol /pærəˈsiːtəmɒl, -ˈset-/ *n.* compound forming white powder, used to reduce pain and relieve fever; tablet of this. [*para-acetylaminophenol*]

parachute /ˈpærəʃuːt/ **1** *n.* umbrella-shaped apparatus of silk etc. allowing person or heavy object to descend safely from a height, esp. from aircraft; *attrib.* (to be) dropped by parachute (*parachute troops*). **2** *v.* descend or convey by parachute. **3 parachutist** *n.* [F (PARA-[2], CHUTE)]

Paraclete /ˈpærəkliːt/ *n.* The Holy Spirit as advocate or counsellor. [F f. L f. Gk (PARA-[1], *kaleō* call)]

parade /pəˈreɪd/ **1** *n.* muster of troops for inspection; public procession; ostentatious display; public square or promenade; parade-ground. **2** *v.* assemble for parade; march through (streets etc.), march ceremonially, in procession; display ostentatiously. **3 parade-ground** place for muster of troops. [F f. It. & Sp. (L *paro* prepare)]

paradigm /ˈpærədaɪm/ *n.* example or pattern, esp. of inflexions of noun, verb, etc.; **paradigmatic** /-dɪgˈmætɪk/ *a.* [L f. Gk]

paradise /ˈpærədaɪs/ *n.* heaven; region or state of supreme bliss; garden of Eden; **paradisaical** /-dɪˈsaɪək(ə)l/ *a.* [F f. L f. Gk]

paradox /ˈpærədɒks/ *n.* seemingly absurd though perhaps actually well-founded statement; self-contradictory or essentially absurd statement; person or thing conflicting with preconceived notion of what is reasonable or possible; paradoxical nature; **paradoxical** /-ˈdɒksɪk(ə)l/ *a.* [L f. Gk (PARA-[1], *doxa* opinion)]

paraffin /ˈpærəfɪn/ *n.* inflammable waxy or oily substance obtained by distillation from petroleum and shale and used esp. as fuel; hydrocarbon of type containing maximum amount of hydrogen; **liquid paraffin** tasteless mild laxative; **paraffin wax** paraffin in solid form. [G f. L, = having little affinity]

paragon /ˈpærəgən/ *n.* model of excellence, supremely excellent person or thing; model (*of* virtue etc.). [F f. It. f. Gk]

paragraph /ˈpærəgrɑ:f/ **1** *n.* distinct section of piece of writing, beginning on new, usu. indented, line; symbol (usu. ¶) as reference mark; short separate item in newspaper. **2** *v.t.* arrange (piece of writing) in paragraphs. **3 paragraphic** /-ˈgræfɪk/ *a.* [F or L f. Gk (PARA-[1], -GRAPH)]

parakeet /ˈpærəki:t/ *n.* small usu. long-tailed parrot. [F (PARROT)]

parallax /ˈpærəlæks/ *n.* apparent difference in position or direction of object caused by change of point of observation; angular amount of this; **paralactic** /-ˈlæktɪk/ *a.* [F f. Gk, = change]

parallel /ˈpærəlel/ **1** *a.* (of lines or planes) continuously equidistant, (of line or plane) having this relation (*to* another); precisely similar, analogous, or corresponding. **2** *n.* person or thing precisely analogous to another; comparison (*drew a parallel between the two situations*); (in full **parallel of latitude**) each of the imaginary parallel circles of constant latitude on earth's surface, corresponding line on map; two parallel lines (‖) as reference mark. **3** *v.t.* (**-l-**) be parallel to, correspond to; represent as similar, compare; adduce parallel instance to. **4 in parallel** (of electric circuits) arranged so as to join at common points at each end; **parallel bars** pair of parallel rails on posts for gymnastics. [F f. L f. Gk, = alongside one another]

parallelepiped /pærəleˈlepɪped, -əˈpaɪped/ *n.* solid body of which each face is a parallelogram. [Gk (prec., *epipedon* plane surface)]

parallelism *n.* being parallel; correspondence. [PARALLEL]

parallelogram /pærəˈleləgræm/ *n.* four-sided plane rectilinear figure with opposite sides parallel. [F f. L f. Gk (PARALLEL)]

paralyse /ˈpærəlaɪz/, *US* **paralyze** *v.t.* affect with paralysis; *fig.* render powerless, cripple. [F f. Gk (PARA-[1], *luō* loosen)]

paralysis /pəˈrælɪsɪs/ *n.* nervous disease with impairment or loss of motor or sensory function of nerves; *fig.* state of utter powerlessness. [L f. Gk (PARA-[1], *luō* loosen)]

paralytic /pærəˈlɪtɪk/ **1** *a.* affected by paralysis; *sl.* very drunk. **2** *n.* person affected by paralysis. [F f. L f. Gk (prec.)]

paramedical /pærəˈmedɪk(ə)l/ *a.* (of services etc.) supplementing and supporting medical work. [PARA-[1]]

parameter /pəˈræmɪtə/ *n.* quantity constant in case considered, but varying in different cases; (esp. measurable or quantifiable) characteristic or feature. [L f. Gk PARA-[1], -METER]

paramilitary /pærəˈmɪlɪtərɪ/ *a.* of forces ancillary to and similarly organized to military forces. [PARA-[1]]

paramount /ˈpærəmaʊnt/ *a.* supreme; in supreme authority. [AF (*par* by, *amont* above; see AMOUNT)]

paramour /ˈpærəmʊə/ *n. archaic* illicit lover of married person. [F *par amour* by love]

paranoia /pærəˈnɔɪə/ *n.* mental disorder with delusions of grandeur, persecution, etc.; abnormal tendency to suspect and mistrust others. [Gk (NOUS)]

paranoiac /pærəˈnɔɪæk/ *a.* & *n.* (also **paranoic**) = PARANOID.

paranoid /ˈpærənɔɪd/ **1** *a.* affected by paranoia. **2** *n.* paranoid person.

paranormal /pærəˈnɔ:m(ə)l/ *a.* lying outside the range of normal scientific investigations etc. [PARA-[1]]

parapet /ˈpærəpɪt/ *n.* low wall at edge of roof, balcony, etc., or along sides of bridge etc.; defence of earth or stone to conceal and protect troops. [F or It. (PARA-[2], *petto* breast)]

paraphernalia /pærəfəˈneɪlɪə/ *n.pl.* miscellaneous belongings, accessories, etc. [L f. Gk (PARA-[1], *phernē* dower)]

paraphrase /ˈpærəfreɪz/ **1** *n.* free rendering or rewording of a passage. **2** *v.t.* express meaning of (passage) in other words. [F or L f. Gk (PARA-[1])]

paraplegia /pærəˈpli:dʒə/ *n.* paralysis of legs and part or whole of trunk. [Gk (PARA-[1], *plēssō* strike)]

paraplegic **1** *a.* of paraplegia. **2** *n.* one who suffers from paraplegia.

parapsychology /pærəsaɪˈkɒlədʒɪ/ *n.* study of mental phenomena outside sphere of ordinary psychology (hypnosis, telepathy, etc.). [PARA-[1]]

paraquat /ˈpærəkwɒt/ *n.* quick-acting herbicide, becoming inactive on contact with soil. [PARA-[1], QUATERNARY]

parasite /ˈpærəsaɪt/ *n.* animal or plant

living in or on another and drawing nutriment directly from it; person who lives off or exploits another or others; **parasitic** /-'sɪtɪk/ *a.*; **parasitically** /-'sɪtɪkəlɪ/ *adv.*; **parasitism** *n.* [L f. Gk (PARA-[1], *sitos* food)]

parasol /'pærəsɒl/ *n.* light umbrella used to give shade from sun. [F f. It. (PARA-[2], *sole* sun)]

paratrooper /'pærətru:pə/ *n.* member of paratroops. [foll.]

paratroops /'pærətru:ps/ *n.pl.* parachute troops. [contr.]

paratyphoid /pærə'taɪfɔɪd/ *n.* fever resembling typhoid but caused by different bacterium. [PARA-[1]]

parboil /'pɑ:bɔɪl/ *v.t.* partly cook by boiling; *fig.* overheat. [F f. L (*par-* = PER-, confused with PART)]

parcel /'pɑ:s(ə)l/ **1** *n.* goods etc. wrapped up in single package; bundle so wrapped; piece of land; quantity dealt with in one commercial transaction. **2** *v.t.* (**-ll-**, *US* **-l-**) wrap (*up*) as parcel; divide (*out*) into portions. [F f. L (PARTICLE)]

parch *v.* make or become hot and dry; roast (peas, corn, etc.) slightly. [orig. unkn.]

parchment /'pɑ:tʃmənt/ *n.* skin, esp. of sheep or goat, prepared for writing, painting, etc.; manuscript written on this; high-grade paper made to resemble parchment. [F f. L (*Pergamum*, now *Bergama*, in Turkey)]

pardon /'pɑ:d(ə)n/ **1** *n.* forgiveness; remission of legal consequences of crime or conviction; courteous forbearance. **2** *v.t.* forgive; make (esp. courteous) allowances for, excuse. **3 I beg your pardon,** *colloq.* **pardon (me)** formula of apology or disagreement, or request to repeat something said. [F f. L *perdono* (PER-, *dono* give)]

pardonable *a.* that may be pardoned, easily excused; **pardonably** *adv.*

pare /peə/ *v.t.* trim or shave by cutting away surface or edge; *fig.* diminish little by little (with *away* or *down*). [F f. L *paro* prepare]

paregoric /pærə'gɒrɪk/ *n.* camphorated tincture of opium. [L f. Gk, = soothing]

parent /'peərənt/ **1** *n.* one who has begotten or borne offspring, father or mother; person who has adopted a child; forefather; animal or plant from which others are derived; *fig.* source, origin. **2** *v.* be parent (of). **3 parent–teacher association** organization consisting of, and promoting good relations between, teachers and schoolchildren's parents. **4 parental** /pə'rent(ə)l/ *a.*; **parentally** /pə'rentəlɪ/ *adv.*; **parenthood** *n.* [F f. L (*pario* bring forth)]

parentage *n.* lineage, descent from parents.

parenthesis /pə'renθəsɪs/ *n.* (*pl.* **parentheses** /-i:z/) word or clause or sentence inserted as explanation or afterthought into a passage which is grammatically complete without it, and usu. marked off by brackets or dashes or commas; (in *pl.*) pair of round brackets ( ) used for this; *fig.* interlude, interval. [L f. Gk (PARA-[1], EN-, THESIS)]

parenthetic /pærən'θetɪk/ *a.* of or inserted as parenthesis; **parenthetically** *adv.*

par excellence /pɑ:r eksə'lɑ̃s/ *adv.* above all others that may be so called (*the fashionable quarter par excellence*). [F]

parfait /'pɑ:feɪ/ *n.* rich iced pudding of whipped cream, eggs, etc.; layers of ice-cream, fruit, etc., served in tall glass. [F (*parfait* PERFECT)]

parget /'pɑ:dʒɪt/ **1** *v.t.* plaster (wall etc.), esp. with ornamental pattern; roughcast. **2** *n.* plaster; roughcast. [F *pargeter* (*par* all over; *jeter* throw)]

pariah /'pærɪə, pə'raɪə/ *n.* member of low or no caste; *fig.* social outcast. [Tamil]

parietal /pə'raɪət(ə)l/ *a.* of the wall of the body or any of its cavities; **parietal bone** one of pair of bones forming part of skull. [F or L (*paries* wall)]

paring *n.* strip or piece cut off. [PARE]

parish /'pærɪʃ/ *n.* area having its own church and clergyman; district constituted for purposes of local government; inhabitants of parish; **parish clerk** official performing various duties concerned with church; **parish council** administrative body in civil parish; **parish register** book recording christenings, marriages, and burials, at parish church. [F f. L *parochia* f. Gk (*oikos* dwelling)]

parishioner /pə'rɪʃənə/ *n.* inhabitant of parish. [obs. *parishen* (prec.)]

parity /'pærɪtɪ/ *n.* equality, equal status or pay etc.; parallelism or analogy (*parity of reasoning*); equivalence of one currency in another, being at par. [F, or L *paritas* (PAR)]

park 1 *n.* large public garden in a town, for recreation; large enclosed piece of ground, usu. with woodland and pasture, attached to country house etc.; large tract of land kept in natural state for public benefit; area for motor cars etc. to be left in; *US* sports ground. **2** *v.t.* leave (vehicle, or *absol.*), usu. temporarily, in park or elsewhere; *colloq.* deposit and leave, usu. temporarily. **3 park oneself** *colloq.* sit down; **parking-lot** *US* outdoor area for parking vehicles; **parking-meter** coin-operated meter which receives fees for vehicle parked in street and indicates time available; **parking-ticket** notice of fine etc. imposed for parking vehicle illegally. [F f. Gmc]

parka /ˈpɑːkə/ *n.* skin jacket with hood, worn by Eskimos; similar windproof fabric garment worn by mountaineers etc. [Aleutian]

Parkinson's disease /ˈpɑːkɪns(ə)nz/ (also **Parkinsonism**) progressive disease of nervous system with tremor, muscular rigidity, and emaciation. [*Parkinson*, surgeon]

Parkinson's law /ˈpɑːkɪns(ə)nz/ notion that work will always take as long as the time available for it. [*Parkinson*, writer]

parkland *n.* open grassland with clumps of trees etc. [PARK]

parky /ˈpɑːkɪ/ *a. sl.* chilly. [orig. unkn.]

parlance /ˈpɑːləns/ *n.* way of speaking, phraseology. [F f. *parler* speak ult. f. L *parabola* (PARABLE)]

parley /ˈpɑːlɪ/ **1** *n.* conference for debating points in dispute, esp. discussion of terms for armistice etc. **2** *v.i.* hold parley (*with* enemy etc.). [F *parler* (prec.)]

parliament /ˈpɑːləmənt/ *n.* legislative assembly of a country; (**Parliament**) council forming with the Sovereign the supreme legislature of the UK, consisting of House of Commons and House of Lords. [F (prec.)]

parliamentarian /pɑːləmenˈteərɪən/ *n.* skilled debater in parliament.

parliamentary /pɑːləˈmentərɪ/ *a.* of, enacted or established by, parliament; (of language) admissible in parliament.

parlour /ˈpɑːlə/, *US* **parlor** *n.* sitting-room in private house; room in hotel, convent, etc., for private conversation; shop providing specified goods or services (*beauty parlour*); **parlour game** indoor game, esp. word-game. [AF (PARLEY)]

parlous /ˈpɑːləs/ *archaic* **1** *a.* perilous, hard to deal with. **2** *adv.* extremely. [PERILOUS]

Parmesan /pɑːmɪˈzæn, *attrib.* ˈpɑː-/ *n.* a kind of hard cheese made orig. at Parma and used esp. in grated form. [F f. It. (*parmegiano* of Parma)]

parochial /pəˈrəʊkɪəl/ *a.* of a parish; (of affairs, views, etc.) merely local, confined to a narrow area; **parochialism** *n.*; **parochially** *adv.* [F f. L (PARISH)]

parody /ˈpærədɪ/ **1** *n.* humorous exaggerated imitation of author, literary work, style, etc.; feeble imitation, travesty. **2** *v.t.* compose parody of, mimic humorously. **3 parodist** *n.* [L or Gk (PARA-¹, ODE)]

parole /pəˈrəʊl/ **1** *n.* release of prisoner temporarily for special purpose or completely before expiry of sentence, on promise of good behaviour; such promise; word of honour. **2** *v.t.* put (prisoner) on parole. [F, = word (PARLEY)]

parotid /pəˈrɒtɪd/ **1** *a.* situated near the ear. **2** *n.* parotid gland. **3 parotid gland** salivary gland in front of the ear. [F f. L f. Gk (PARA-¹, *ous ōt-* ear)]

paroxysm /ˈpærəksɪz(ə)m/ *n.* sudden attack or outburst (*of* rage, laughter, etc.); fit of disease; **paroxismal** /-ˈsɪzm(ə)l/ *a.* [F f. L f. Gk (*oxus* sharp)]

parquet /ˈpɑːkeɪ, -kɪ/ **1** *n.* flooring of wooden blocks arranged in pattern. **2** *v.t.* floor (room) thus. **3 parquetry** /-kɪtrɪ/ *n.* [F, dimin. of *parc* PARK]

parr /pɑː/ *n.* young salmon. [orig. unkn.]

parricide /ˈpærɪsaɪd/ *n.* one who kills a near relative, esp. a parent; act of this; **parricidal** /-ˈsaɪd(ə)l/ *a.* [F or L (cf. PARENT, PATER, -CIDE)]

parrot /ˈpærət/ **1** *n.* mainly tropical bird with short hooked bill, of which many species have vivid plumage and some can imitate words; person who mechanically repeats another's words or imitates his actions. **2** *v.t.* repeat mechanically. [F (dimin. of *Pierre* Peter)]

parry /ˈpærɪ/ **1** *v.t.* turn aside, ward off, avert (weapon, blow, awkward question), esp. with one's own weapon etc. **2** *n.* act of parrying. [prob. F f. It. *parare* ward off]

parse /pɑːz/ *v.t.* describe (word in context) grammatically, stating inflexion, relation to sentence, etc.; resolve (sentence) into its component parts and describe them grammatically. [perh. F *pars* parts (PART)]

parsec /ˈpɑːsek/ *n.* unit of stellar distance, equal to about 3.25 light-years. [PAR(ALLAX), SEC(OND)]

Parsee /pɑːˈsiː/ *n.* adherent of Zoroastrianism; descendant of Persians who fled to India in 7th–8th cc.; **Parseeism** *n.* [Pers., = Persian]

parsimony /ˈpɑːsɪmənɪ/ *n.* carefulness in use of money or resources; meanness, stinginess; **parsimonious** /-ˈməʊnɪəs/ *a.* [L (*parco pars-* spare)]

parsley /ˈpɑːslɪ/ *n.* herb used for seasoning and garnishing dishes. [F f. L f. Gk (*petra* rock, *selinon* parsley)]

parsnip /ˈpɑːsnɪp/ *n.* plant with pale yellow tapering root used as culinary vegetable; its root. [F f. L *pastinaca*]

parson /ˈpɑːs(ə)n/ *n.* rector; vicar or any beneficed clergyman; *colloq.* any (esp. Protestant) clergyman; **parson's nose** rump of (cooked) fowl. [F f. L (PERSON)]

parsonage *n.* parson's house.
part 1 *n.* some but not all of a thing or number of things; essential member or component (*part of the family*; *spare parts*); division of book, broadcast serial, etc., esp. as much as is issued etc. at one time; each of several equal portions of a whole (*recipe has 3 parts of sugar and 5 of flour*); portion allotted, share; person's share in action, his duty (*will have no part in it*); character assigned to actor on stage, words spoken by actor on stage, copy of these; *Mus.* melody or other constituent of harmony assigned to particular voice or instrument; side in agreement or dispute; portion of human or animal body; (in *pl.*) region, district (*am not from these parts*); (in *pl.*) abilities (*a man of parts*). **2** *v.* (cause to) divide or separate into parts; separate (hair of head on either side of parting) with comb; quit one another's company; *colloq.* part with one's money, pay. **3** *adv.* in part, partly. **4 for my part** so far as I am concerned; **in part** partly; **on the part of** proceeding from, done etc. by; **part and parcel** essential part *of*; **part-exchange** transaction in which article is given as part of payment for more expensive one; **part of speech** each of grammatical classes of words; **part-song** song for several voice-parts, often unaccompanied; **part time** less than full time; **part-time** *a.* occupying or using only part of available working time; **part-timer** *n.* one employed in part-time work; **part with** give up possession of, hand over; **play a part** be significant or contributory; **take in good part** not be offended by; **take part** assist or have share (*in*); **take the part of** support, back up. [F f. L *pars part-*]
partake /pɑːˈteɪk/ *v.i.* (*past* **partook** /-ˈtʊk/; *p.p.* **partaken**) take a share (*of* or *in* thing, *with* person); eat or drink some or *colloq.* all *of*; have some (*of* quality etc.: *his manner partakes of insolence*). [back-form. f. *partaker* = *part-taker*]
parterre /pɑːˈteə/ *n.* level space in garden occupied by flower-beds; pit of theatre. [F, = on the ground]
parthenogenesis /pɑːθməʊˈdʒenəsɪs/ *n.* reproduction from gametes without fertilization. [L f. Gk *parthenos* virgin]
Parthian shot /ˈpɑːθɪən/ remark or glance etc. reserved for moment of departure, like missile shot at enemy by retreating Parthian horseman. [*Parthia*, anc. Asian kingdom]
partial /ˈpɑːʃ(ə)l/ *a.* not complete, forming only part (*partial success*); biased, unfair; **partial eclipse** eclipse in which only part of the luminary is covered or darkened; **partial to** having a liking for; **partially** *adv.* [F f. L (PART)]
partiality /pɑːʃɪˈælɪtɪ/ *n.* bias, favouritism; fondness (*for*). [F f. med.L (prec.)]
participant /pɑːˈtɪsɪpənt/ *n.* participator. [foll.]
participate /pɑːˈtɪsɪpeɪt/ *v.i.* have share or take part (*in* thing); **participation** /-ˈpeɪʃ(ə)n/ *n.*; **participator** *n.* [L (*particips -cip-* taking PART)]
participle /ˈpɑːtɪsɪp(ə)l/ *n.* word formed from verb (e.g. *going*, *gone*, *being*, *been*) and used in compound verb-forms (e.g. *is being*, *has been*) or as an adjective (*going concern*, *painted wall*); **participial** /-ˈsɪpɪəl/ *a.* [F f. L (prec.)]
particle /ˈpɑːtɪk(ə)l/ *n.* minute portion of matter; least possible amount (*not a particle of sense*); minor part of speech, esp. short undeclinable one; common prefix or suffix such as *un-*, *-ship*. [L *particula* dimin. of *pars* PART]
particoloured /ˈpɑːtɪkʌləd/ *a.* partly of one colour, partly of another. [PART, COLOUR]
particular /pəˈtɪkjʊlə/ **1** *a.* relating to one person or thing as distinct from others, individual (*in this particular instance*); more than usual, special (*took particular trouble*); scrupulously exact, fastidious; detailed (*full and particular account*). **2** *n.* detail, item; (in *pl.*) information, detailed account. **3 in particular** especially, specifically. [F f. L (PARTICLE)]
particularity /pətɪkjʊˈlærɪtɪ/ *n.* quality of being individual or particular; fullness or minuteness of detail in description.
particularize *v.t.* name specially or one by one; specify (items); **particularization** /-ˈzeɪʃ(ə)n/ *n.* [F (PARTICULAR)]
particularly *adv.* especially, very. [PARTICULAR]
parting *n.* leave-taking, departure (often *attrib.*: *parting words*); dividing line of combed hair; division or separating. [PART]
partisan /pɑːtɪˈzæn, ˈpɑː-/ *n.* strong, esp. unreasoning, supporter of party, cause, etc.; guerrilla; **partisanship** *n.* [F f. It. (PART)]
partition /pɑːˈtɪʃ(ə)n/ **1** *n.* division into parts; such part; structure separating two such parts, thin wall. **2** *v.t.* divide into parts. **3 partition off** separate (part of room etc.) with partition. [F f. L (*partior* divide)]
partitive /ˈpɑːtɪtɪv/ *Gram.* **1** *a.* (of a word, form, etc.) denoting part of a group or quantity. **2** *n.* partitive word (e.g. *some, any*) or form. [F or med.L (as prec.)]

partly *adv.* with respect to a part, in some degree. [PART]

partner **1** *n.* one who shares or takes part with another or others, esp. in business firm with shared risks and profits; companion in dancing; player on same side in game; husband or wife. **2** *v.t.* be partner of, associate as partners. [alt. of *parcener* joint heir]

partnership *n.* state of being partners, joint business, pair of partners.

partook *past* of PARTAKE.

partridge /'pɑ:trɪdʒ/ *n.* game-bird, esp. the brown and grey varieties. [F *perdriz* f. L f. Gk *perdix*]

parturient /pɑ:'tjʊərɪənt/ *a.* about to give birth. [L (*pario part-* bring forth)]

parturition /pɑ:tjʊə'rɪʃ(ə)n/ *n.* act of bringing forth young, childbirth.

party /'pɑ:tɪ/ *n.* social gathering, usu. of invited guests; body of persons working or travelling together (*search-party*); group of people united in a cause, opinion, etc., esp. political group organized on national basis; person(s) forming one side in agreement or dispute; accessory (*to* action); *colloq.* person; **party line** policy adopted by a political party, telephone line shared by two or more subscribers; **party-wall** wall common to two buildings or rooms that it divides. [F f. Rmc (PART)]

pas /pɑ:/ *n.* (*pl.* same) step in dancing; ***pas de deux*** /də 'dɜ:/ dance for two persons. [F, = step]

PASCAL /pæ'skɑ:l/ *n.* computer language used in training. [*Pascal*, scientist]

paschal /'pæsk(ə)l, 'pɑ:-/ *a.* of the Jewish Passover; of Easter; **paschal lamb** lamb sacrificed at Passover, *fig.* Christ. [F f. L f. Heb.]

pasha /'pɑ:ʃə/ *n. hist.* title (placed after name) of Turkish officer of high rank. [Turk.]

Pashto /'pʌʃtəʊ/ **1** *n.* Iranian language of Pathans. **2** *a.* of or in this language. [Pashto]

pasque-flower /'pæsk/ *n.* a kind of anemone. [F *passe-fleur*]

pass[1] /pɑ:s/ **1** *v.* (*p.p.* **passed** or as *a.* PAST) move onward or past something, proceed; (cause to) be transferred from one person or place to another (*pass the butter*; *title passed to his son*); go past, leave (thing etc.) on one side or behind; overtake; surpass, be too great for (*it passes my comprehension*); get through, effect a passage; move, (cause to) go (*passed his hand over his face*; *passed a rope round it*); (cause to) go by; occur, elapse (*remark passed unnoticed*; *time passes slowly*); spend (time or period); (in football etc.) send (ball, or *absol.*) to player of one's own side; discharge from the body as or with excreta; be successful in (examination), satisfy examiner; change (*into* something, *from* one state *to* another); come to an end; die (usu. with *away*, *on*, *hence*, etc.); happen, be done or said (*heard what passed between them*); forgo one's turn or chance in game etc.; go uncensured, be accepted as adequate (*let the matter pass*); be accepted or currently known *as*; utter (criticism, judicial sentence, *upon*); adjudicate (*upon*); (of bill in parliament, proposal, etc.) be sanctioned, (of bill) be examined and approved by (House of Commons etc.), cause or allow (bill, candidate, etc.) to proceed after scrutiny; (cause to) circulate, be current. **2** *n.* act of passing; success in examination; status of degree without honours; written permission to pass into or out of a place, or to be absent from quarters; ticket etc. giving free entry or access etc.; (in football etc.) transference of ball to player of one's own side; thrust in fencing, juggling trick, passing of hands over anything, as in conjuring or hypnotism; critical position (*come to a fine pass*). **3 bring to pass** cause to happen; **come to pass** happen, occur; **in passing** by the way, in course of speech; **make a pass at** *colloq.* make amorous advances to; **pass by** go past, disregard, omit; **pass for** be accepted as; **pass off** (of feelings etc.) disappear gradually, (of proceedings) be carried through (in specified way), misrepresent (person or thing) *as* something false, evade or lightly dismiss (awkward remark etc.); **pass out** become unconscious, complete military training; **pass over** omit, ignore, or disregard, ignore claims of (person) to promotion etc.; **pass up** *colloq.* refuse or neglect (opportunity etc.). [F f. Rmc (L *passus* PACE[1])]

pass[2] /pɑ:s/ *n.* narrow passage through mountains. [var. of PACE[1]]

passable *a.* (barely) satisfactory, adequate; that can be passed. [PASS[1]]

passage /'pæsɪdʒ/ *n.* process or means of passing, transit; = PASSAGEWAY; liberty or right to pass through; right of conveyance as passenger by sea or air; journey by sea or air; transition from one state to another; short extract from book etc. or section of music; passing of bill etc. into law; (in *pl.*) interchange of words etc.; **passage of arms** fight, dispute. [F (PASS[1])]

passageway *n.* narrow way for passing along, esp. with walls on either side, corridor.

passbook *n.* book issued by bank or building society to account-holder recording sums deposited and withdrawn. [PASS¹]

passé /'pæseɪ/ *a.* behind the times; past the prime. [F]

passenger /'pæsɪndʒə/ *n.* traveller in or on public or private conveyance (other than driver, pilot, crew, etc.); *colloq.* member of team, crew, etc. who does no effective work. [F *passager* (PASSAGE)]

passer-by *n.* one who goes past, esp. by chance. [PASS¹]

passerine /'pæsəraɪn/ **1** *a.* of the sparrow order. **2** *n.* passerine bird. [L (*passer* sparrow)]

passim /'pæsɪm/ *adv.* throughout, at several points in, book or article etc. [L]

passion /'pæʃ(ə)n/ *n.* strong emotion; outburst of anger; sexual love; strong enthusiasm (*for*); (**Passion**) the sufferings of Christ on the Cross, narrative of this from Gospels, musical setting of this narrative; **passion-flower** plant with flower which was supposed to suggest instruments of Crucifixion; **passion-fruit** edible fruit of some species of passion-flower; **passion-play** miracle play representing Christ's Passion; **Passion Sunday** fifth Sunday in Lent. [F f. L (*patior pass-* suffer)]

passionate /'pæʃənət/ *a.* dominated by or easily moved to strong feeling; showing or caused by passion. [med.L (PASSION)]

passionless *a.* cold, lacking in passion. [PASSION]

passive /'pæsɪv/ *a.* suffering action, acted upon; offering no opposition, submissive; not active, inert; *Gram.* indicating that subject undergoes action of verb (e.g. in *he was seen*); **passive resistance** non-violent refusal to cooperate; **passive voice** *Gram.* that comprising passive forms of verbs; **passivity** /-'sɪvɪtɪ/ *n.* [F or L (PASSION)]

passkey *n.* private key to door or gate etc.; master-key. [PASS¹]

Passover /'pɑːsəʊvə/ *n.* Jewish spring festival commemorating liberation of Israelites from Egyptian bondage. [PASS¹, OVER]

passport /'pɑːspɔːt/ *n.* official document issued by government certifying holder's identity and citizenship, and entitling him to travel under its protection to and from foreign country; *fig.* thing that ensures admission (*passport to success*). [F *passeport* (PASS¹, PORT¹)]

password *n.* agreed secret word uttered to sentry etc. to allow one to proceed. [PASS¹]

past /pɑːst/ **1** *a.* gone by in time (*past years; the time is past*); recently gone by (*the past week*); relating to a former time (*past president*); *Gram.* expressing past action or state. **2** *n.* past time (esp. **the past**); what has happened in past times; person's past life or career, esp. if discreditable (*man with a past*); past tense. **3** *prep.* beyond in time or place; beyond range, duration, or compass of (*past belief, endurance*). **4** *adv.* so as to pass by (*hurried past*). **5 not put it past** *colloq.* believe it possible of (person); **past it** *sl.* incompetent or unusable through age; **past master** expert, former master of Freemasons' lodge etc. [PASS¹]

pasta /'pæstə/ *n.* dried flour paste produced in various shapes (e.g. lasagne, macaroni); cooked dish made from this. [It. (foll.)]

paste /peɪst/ **1** *n.* any moist fairly stiff mixture, esp. of powder and liquid; dough of flour with fat, water, etc.; adhesive of flour and water etc.; easily spread preparation of ground meat, fish, etc. (*anchovy paste*); hard vitreous composition used in making imitation gems. **2** *v.t.* fasten or coat with paste; *sl.* beat, thrash, bomb etc. heavily. **3 paste-up** document prepared for copying etc. by pasting various materials on a backing. [F f. L *pasta* lozenge f. Gk]

pasteboard *n.* stiff substance made by pasting together sheets of paper; *attrib.* unsubstantial, flimsy.

pastel /'pæst(ə)l/ *n.* crayon made of dried paste compounded of pigments with gum solution; drawing in pastel; light and subdued shade of colour. [F, or It. *pastello* dimin. of PASTA]

pastern /'pæstɜːn/ *n.* part of horse's foot between fetlock and hoof. [F f. L]

pasteurize /'pɑːstʃəraɪz/ *v.t.* subject (milk etc.) to process of partial sterilization by heating; **pasteurization** /-'zeɪʃ(ə)n/ *n.* [*Pasteur*, chemist]

pastiche /pæ'stiːʃ/ *n.* medley, esp. picture or musical composition, made up from various sources; literary or other work of art composed in style of well-known author. [F f. It. *pasticcio* f. L *pasta* PASTE]

pastille /'pæstɪl, -iːl/ *n.* small sweet or lozenge; small roll of aromatic paste burnt as fumigator etc. [F f. L]

pastime /'pɑːstaɪm/ *n.* recreation, hobby; sport, game. [PASS¹, TIME]

pastor /'pɑːstə/ *n.* minister in charge of church or congregation; person exercising spiritual guidance. [F f. L (*pasco past-* feed)]

pastoral /'pɑːstər(ə)l/ **1** *a.* of shepherds; of flocks and herds; (of land) used for pasture; (of poem, picture, etc.) portraying country life; of a pastor. **2** *n.* pastoral poem, play, picture, etc.; letter from pastor (esp.

bishop) to clergy or people. **3 pastorally** *adv.* [L *pastoralis* (prec.)]

pastorate /'pɑːstərət/ *n.* pastor's office or tenure; body of pastors. [PASTOR]

pastrami /pæ'strɑːmɪ/ *n.* seasoned smoked beef. [Yiddish]

pastry /'peɪstrɪ/ *n.* dough of flour, fat, and water used as base or covering for pies etc.; food, esp. cake, made wholly or partly with this; **pastry-cook** cook who makes pastry, esp. for public sale. [PASTE]

pasturage /'pɑːstʃərɪdʒ/ *n.* pasture-land, pasturing. [foll.]

pasture /'pɑːstʃə/ **1** *n.* land covered with grass etc. suitable for grazing animals; herbage for animals. **2** *v.* put (animals) to graze in pasture; (of animals) graze. [F f. L (PASTOR)]

pasty[1] /'pæstɪ/ *n.* pastry case with sweet or savoury filling. [F f. L (PASTE)]

pasty[2] /'peɪstɪ/ *a.* of or like or covered in paste; unhealthily pale (*pasty-faced*); **pastily** *adv.*; **pastiness** *n.* [PASTE]

pat 1 *v.t.* (-tt-) strike gently with hand or flat surface; flatten or mould thus. **2** *n.* light stroke or tap; sound made by this; small mass (esp. of butter) formed by patting. **3** *a.* apposite, opportune; known thoroughly and ready for any occasion. **4** *adv.* in pat manner, appositely. **5 have off pat** know or have memorized perfectly; **pat on the back** congratulatory acknowledgement. [prob. imit.]

Pat. *abbr.* Patent.

patch 1 *n.* piece of material or metal etc. put on to mend hole or as reinforcement; piece of plaster etc. put over wound; pad worn to protect injured eye; large or irregular distinguishable area on surface; period of time in terms of its characteristic quality (*went through a bad patch*); piece of ground; *colloq.* area assigned to particular policeman etc.; number of plants growing in one place; scrap, remnant. **2** *v.t.* put patch(es) on; (of material) serve as patch to; piece (things) together (*lit.* or *fig.*). **3 not a patch on** *colloq.* greatly inferior to; **patch-pocket** one made of piece of cloth sewn on garment; **patch up** repair with patches, settle (quarrel etc.) esp. hastily or temporarily, put together hastily. [perh. F, var. of PIECE]

patchwork *n.* needlework using small pieces of cloth with different designs, forming pattern; thing made of various small parts. [PATCH]

patchy *a.* uneven in quality; having or existing in patches; **patchily** *adv.*; **patchiness** *n.*

pate *n.* (*archaic* or *colloq.*) head, often as seat of intellect. [orig. unkn.]

pâté /'pæteɪ/ *n.* paste of meat etc.; pie, patty; **pâté de foie gras** /də fwɑː grɑː/ paste or pie of fatted goose liver. [F, = PASTY[1]]

patella /pə'telə/ *n.* (*pl.* **patellae** /-iː/) kneecap; **patellar** *a.* [L, = pan, dimin. of *patina* (foll.)]

paten /'pæt(ə)n/ *n.* shallow dish used for bread at Eucharist. [F, or L *patina*]

patent /'peɪtənt, 'pæ-/ **1** *n.* official document conferring right or title etc., esp. sole right to make or use or sell some invention; right granted by this; invention or process so protected. **2** *a.* conferred or protected by patent; (of food, medicine, etc.) proprietary; obvious, plain (*patent disapproval*); *colloq.* ingenious, well-contrived. **3** *v.t.* obtain patent for (invention). **4 patent leather** leather with glossy varnished surface; **patent office** government office issuing patents. [F f. L (*pateo* lie open)]

patentee /peɪtən'tiː/ *n.* one who takes out or holds a patent; person for time being entitled to benefit of patent.

pater *n. sl.* father. [L]

paternal /pə'tɜːn(ə)l/ *a.* of or like a father, fatherly; related through father; (of government etc.) limiting freedom and responsibility by well-meant regulations; **paternally** *adv.* [L (PATER)]

paternalism *n.* policy of governing in paternal way; **paternalistic** /-'lɪstɪk/ *a.*

paternity /pə'tɜːnɪtɪ/ *n.* fatherhood; one's paternal origin; *fig.* authorship, source. [F or L (PATER)]

paternoster /pætə'nɒstə/ *n.* the Our Father, esp. in Latin. [OE, f. L *pater noster* our father]

path /pɑːθ; *pl.* pɑːðz/ *n.* way or track laid down for walking or made by walking; line along which person or thing moves; course of action. [OE]

Pathan /pə'tɑːn/ *n.* member of a people inhabiting NW Pakistan and SE Afghanistan. [Hindi]

pathetic /pə'θetɪk/ *a.* arousing pity or sadness or contempt; miserably inadequate; **pathetic fallacy** crediting inanimate things with human emotions; **pathetically** *adv.* [F f. L f. Gk (*pathos* f. *paskhō* suffer)]

pathfinder *n.* explorer. [PATH]

pathogen /'pæθədʒ(ə)n/ *n.* agent causing disease; **pathogenic** /-'dʒenɪk/ *a.* [Gk *pathos* suffering, -GEN]

pathological /pæθə'lɒdʒɪk(ə)l/ *a.* of pathology; of or caused by physical or mental disorder (*pathological fear of spiders*); **pathologically** *adv.* [foll.]

pathology /pə'θɒlədʒɪ/ *n.* science of bodily diseases; **pathologist** *n.* [Gk *pathos* (PATHETIC)]

pathos /'peɪθɒs/ *n.* quality in speech,

writing, etc. that arouses pity or sadness. [Gk (PATHETIC)]
pathway *n.* footway or track, esp. one made by walking. [PATH]
patience /'peɪʃəns/ *n.* calm endurance of hardship, provocation, pain, delay, etc.; perseverance; game (usu. for one player) in which cards are brought into specified arrangement. [F f. L (PASSION)]
patient **1** *a.* having or showing patience. **2** *n.* person receiving (or registered to receive) medical treatment.
patina /'pætɪnə/ *n.* incrustation, usu. green, on surface of old bronze; similar alteration on other surfaces; gloss produced by age on woodwork. [It. f. L (PATEN)]
patio /'pætɪəʊ/ *n.* (*pl.* **patios**) paved usu. roofless area adjoining house; inner court open to sky in Spanish or Spanish-American house. [Sp.]
patisserie /pə'ti:sərɪ/ *n.* pastry-cook's shop or wares. [F f. L (PASTE)]
patois /'pætwɑ:/ *n.* (*pl.* same /-ɑ:z/) dialect of common people of a region, differing fundamentally from the literary language; jargon. [F]
patriarch /'peɪtrɪɑ:k/ *n.* male head of family or tribe; (in Orthodox & RC Churches) bishop of high rank; venerable old man; **the Patriarchs** men named in Genesis as ancestors of mankind or of tribes of Israel; **patriarchal** /-'ɑ:k(ə)l/ *a.* [F f. L f. Gk (*patria* family, *arkhēs* ruler)]
patriarchate /'peɪtrɪɑ:kət/ *n.* office or see or residence of ecclesiastical patriarch. [med.L (prec.)]
patriarchy *n.* patriarchal system of society, government, etc. [med.L f. Gk (PATRIARCH)]
patrician /pə'trɪʃ(ə)n/ **1** *n.* ancient Roman noble. **2** *a.* noble, aristocratic; of the ancient Roman nobility. [F f. L *patricius* (PATER)]
patricide /'pætrɪsaɪd/ *n.* = PARRICIDE. [L, alt. of *parricida*]
patrimony /'pætrɪmənɪ/ *n.* property inherited from father or ancestors; heritage (*lit.* or *fig.*); **patrimonial** /-'məʊnɪəl/ *a.* [F f. L (PATER)]
patriot /'pætrɪət, 'peɪ-/ *n.* one who is devoted to and ready to defend his country; **patriotic** /-'ɒtɪk/ *a.*; **patriotically** /-'ɒtɪkəlɪ/ *adv.*; **patriotism** *n.* [F f. L f. Gk (*patris* fatherland)]
patristic /pə'trɪstɪk/ *a.* of the early Christian writers or their work. [G f. L (PATER)]
patrol /pə'trəʊl/ **1** *v.* (-ll-) walk or travel around (area, or *absol.*) in order to protect or supervise it; act as patrol. **2** *n.* patrolling; person(s) or vehicle(s) assigned or sent out to patrol; unit of usu. six in Scout troop or Guide company. [G *patrolle* f. F]
patrolman *n. US* policeman of lowest rank.
patron /'peɪtrən/ *n.* one who gives financial or other support to a person or activity or cause; customer of shop, restaurant, etc.; **patron saint** saint regarded as protecting person or place etc. [F f. L *patronus* (PATER)]
patronage /'pætrənɪdʒ/ *n.* patron's or customer's support; right of bestowing or recommending for appointment; patronizing airs. [F (prec.)]
patronize /'pætrənaɪz/ *v.t.* act as patron towards, support; treat condescendingly. [F or med.L (PATRON)]
patronymic /pætrə'nɪmɪk/ *n.* name derived from that of father or male ancestor. [L f. Gk (*patēr* father, *onoma* name)]
patten /'pæt(ə)n/ *n.* shoe with sole set on iron ring etc. to raise wearer's foot out of wet etc. [F *patin*]
patter[1] **1** *v.i.* make rapid succession of taps, as rain on window-pane; run with short quick steps. **2** *n.* series of taps or short light steps. [PAT[1]]
patter[2] **1** *n.* language of profession or class; glib or deceptive speech of salesman etc.; rapid speech used by comedian or introduced into song. **2** *v.* repeat (prayers etc.) in rapid mechanical way; talk glibly. [orig. *pater*, = PATERNOSTER]
pattern /'pæt(ə)n/ **1** *n.* decorative design as executed on carpet, wallpaper, cloth, etc.; model or design or instructions from which thing is to be made (*sewing pattern*); excellent example or model; regular form or order (*behaviour pattern*); sample of cloth etc. **2** *v.t.* model (thing *after* or *on* design etc.); decorate with pattern. [PATRON]
patty /'pætɪ/ *n.* small pie or pasty; *US* small flat cake of minced meat etc. [F PÂTÉ, after PASTY[1]]
paucity /'pɔ:sɪtɪ/ *n.* smallness of quantity or supply. [F or L (*paucus* few)]
paunch /pɔ:ntʃ/ *n.* stomach, belly, esp. protruding one; **paunchy** *a.* [AF *pa(u)nche* f. L *pantex -tic-* bowels]
pauper /'pɔ:pə/ *n.* very poor person; *hist.* recipient of poor-law relief; **pauperism** *n.* [L, = poor]
pause /pɔ:z/ **1** *n.* interval of inaction or silence; temporary stop; *Mus.* character placed over note or rest indicating that it is to be lengthened indefinitely. **2** *v.i.* make pause; linger *upon* (word etc.). **3** **give pause to** cause to hesitate. [F, or L *pausa* f. Gk (*pauō* stop)]
pavan /pə'væn/ *n.* (also **pavane**) stately dance in slow duple time; music for this. [F f. Sp.]

pave *v.t.* cover (street, floor, etc.) with durable surface; **pave the way** make preparations (*for*). [F *paver*, ult. f. L *pavio* ram *v.*]

pavement *n.* paved surface or path, esp. (for pedestrians) at side of road. [F f. L *pavimentum* (prec.)]

pavilion /pəˈvɪljən/ *n.* light building in park etc. used as shelter; building on sports ground for players and spectators; ornamental building for public entertainment; large tent. [F f. L *papilio* butterfly]

paving *n.* paved surface; material for this. [PAVE]

pavlova /pævˈləʊvə/ *n.* meringue cake with cream and fruit. [*Pavlova*, Russ. ballerina]

paw 1 *n.* foot of animal having claws or nails; *colloq.* person's hand. **2** *v.* strike with paw; scrape (ground), scrape ground with hoof; *colloq.* touch or pass hand over awkwardly or rudely or indecently. [F *poue* f. Gmc]

pawky /ˈpɔːkɪ/ *a.* (*Sc.* & *dial.*) drily humorous; shrewd. [orig. unkn.]

pawl *n.* lever with catch for teeth of wheel or bar; *Naut.* short bar to prevent capstan etc. from recoiling. [LG or Du. *pal*]

pawn[1] *n.* chess-man of smallest size and value; unimportant person subservient to others' plans. [AF *poun* f. L *pedo -onis* foot-soldier]

pawn[2] **1** *v.t.* deposit (thing) as security for money borrowed; *fig.* pledge or stake. **2** *n.* state of being pawned (*in pawn*). [F *pan* f. Gmc]

pawnbroker *n.* one who lends money at interest on security of personal property deposited.

pawnshop *n.* pawnbroker's place of business.

pawpaw var. of PAPAW.

pay 1 *v.* (*past* and *p.p.* **paid**) hand over money to discharge debt etc.; give (person) what is due in discharge of debt or in return for goods or services; hand over (money owed *to* person); hand over the amount of (debt, wages, ransom, etc.); (of business etc.) yield adequate return to (person), be profitable or advantageous; render, bestow, or express (attention, respect, compliment, etc.); suffer or undergo (penalty etc. or *absol.*); be beneficial to (*it will pay you to come*); (usu. in *p.p.*) recompense (work, time, etc.: *paid holiday*); (esp. *Naut.*) let rope *out* or *away* by slackening it. **2** *n.* payment, wages. **3 in the pay of** employed by; **pay-as-you-earn** method of collecting income tax by deducting it at source from wages etc.; **pay back** repay, punish or have revenge on; **pay-bed** hospital bed whose use is paid for by user; **pay a call** see CALL; **pay for** hand over price of, bear cost of, be punished for; **pay in** pay into a bank account etc.; **paying guest** lodger; **pay off** pay in full and discharge (debt etc.), pay in full and dismiss or be rid of (person, crew, etc.), *colloq.* yield good results, succeed; **pay-off** *n. sl.* act of payment, climax, final reckoning; **pay-packet** packet containing employee's wages; **pay phone** coin-box telephone; **pay up** pay in full, pay full amount of (**paid-up member** one who has made all necessary payments for membership); **pay one's way** meet one's debts etc. as they arise. [F f. L *paco* appease (PEACE)]

payable *a.* that must or may be paid.

PAYE *abbr.* pay-as-you-earn.

payee /peɪˈiː/ *n.* person to whom money is (to be) paid. [PAY]

payload *n.* that part of (esp. aircraft's) load from which revenue is derived; destructive capacity of explosive carried by rocket etc.

paymaster *n.* official who pays troops, workers, etc.; **Paymaster General** minister at head of department of Treasury through which payments are made.

payment *n.* paying; amount paid; reward, recompense.

payola /peɪˈəʊlə/ *n.* bribe or bribery offered in return for illicit or unfair help in promoting commercial product.

payroll *n.* list of employees receiving regular pay.

Pb *symb.* lead. [L *plumbum*]

PC *abbr.* police constable; Privy Counsellor.

p.c. *abbr.* per cent; postcard.

pd. *abbr.* paid.

Pd *symb.* palladium.

PE *abbr.* physical education.

pea *n.* hardy climbing plant whose seeds grow in pods and are used for food; its seed; similar plant (*sweet pea*); **pea-green** bright green; **pea-shooter** toy tube from which dried peas are shot by blowing; **pea-souper** *colloq.* thick yellow fog. [PEASE taken as *pl.*]

peace *n.* quiet, tranquillity; mental calm; freedom from or cessation of war; treaty of peace between powers at war; freedom from civil disorder (*breach of the peace*); **at peace** in a state of friendliness, not in strife (*with*); **hold one's peace** keep quiet; **keep the peace** prevent or refrain from strife; **make one's peace** bring oneself back into friendly relations (*with*); **peace offering** gift or gesture made in the interests of peace; **peace-pipe** tobacco-pipe as token of peace among N. American

Indians; **peace-time** period when country is not at war. [F f. L *pax pac-*]
peaceable *a.* disposed or tending to peace; peaceful; **peaceably** *adv.* [F f. L *placibilis* pleasing (PLEASE)]
peaceful *a.* characterized by or concerned with peace; not violating or infringing peace; **peacefully** *adv.* [PEACE]
peacemaker *n.* one who brings about peace.
peach[1] *n.* round juicy fruit with downy yellowish or reddish skin; tree bearing it; its yellowish-pink colour; *sl.* person or thing of superlative merit, attractive young woman; **peach Melba** dish of ice-cream and peaches with liqueur or sauce; **peachy** *a.* [F f. L *persica* Persian (apple)]
peach[2] *v.i. sl.* turn informer, inform (*against* or *on* accomplice). [obs. *appeach* (IMPEACH)]
peacock *n.* male peafowl, bird with brilliant plumage and tail that can be expanded erect like a fan; **peacock blue** lustrous blue of peacock's neck. [pea (OE f. L *pavo*), COCK[1]]
peafowl *n.* kind of pheasant; peacock or peahen. [prec., FOWL]
peahen *n.* female of peafowl. [as prec., HEN]
pea-jacket /'pi:dʒækɪt/ *n.* sailor's short double-breasted overcoat of coarse woollen cloth. [Du. *pijjakker*]
peak[1] **1** *n.* pointed top, esp. of mountain; any shape or edge or part that tapers to form a point; projecting part (usu. at front) of brim of cap; highest point of achievement, intensity, etc.; *attrib.* maximum, most busy or intense etc. (*peak hours*). **2** *v.i.* reach highest value, quality, etc. [rel. to PICK]
peak[2] *v.i.* waste away; (in *p.p.*) pinched, drawn. [orig. unkn.]
peaky *a.* sickly, peaked; **peakiness** *n.*
peal **1** *n.* loud ringing of bell(s), esp. series of changes on set of bells; set of bells with different notes; loud outburst of sound, esp. of thunder or laughter. **2** *v.* (cause to) sound in a peal; utter sonorously. [APPEAL]
peanut *n.* plant bearing pods that ripen underground, containing seeds used as food and yielding oil; its seed; (in *pl.*) *sl.* paltry or trivial thing or amount, esp. of money; **peanut butter** paste of ground roasted peanuts. [PEA]
pear /peə/ *n.* yellowish-green fleshy fruit tapering towards stalk; tree bearing it. [OE, ult. f. L *pirum*]
pearl /pɜ:l/ **1** *n.* smooth lustrous mass, usu. white or bluish-grey, formed within shell of certain oysters and used as a gem; an imitation of this; thing like pearl in form; precious thing, finest example. **2** *a.* like pearl in form or colour. **3** *v.* fish for pearls; reduce (barley etc.) to small rounded grains; form pearl-like drops; sprinkle with pearly drops. **4 pearl barley** barley rubbed into small rounded grains; **pearl button** button of real or imitation mother-of-pearl; **pearl-diver** one who dives for oysters containing pearls. [F f. Rmc, prob. f. L *perna* leg]
pearly **1** *a.* like or adorned with pearls. **2** *n.* (in *pl.*) costermongers' clothes decorated with pearl buttons. **3 Pearly Gates** the gates of heaven; **pearly king, queen** costermonger, his wife, wearing pearlies.
peasant /'pezənt/ *n.* (in some rural agricultural countries) worker on land, farm labourer, small farmer; **peasantry** *n.* [AF *paisant* (*pais* country)]
pease /pi:z/ *n. archaic* peas; **pease-pudding** pudding of boiled peas, eggs, etc. [OE *pise* f. L *pisa*]
peat *n.* vegetable matter decomposed in water and partly carbonized, used for fuel, in horticulture, etc.; cut piece of this; **peaty** *a.* [perh. Celt., rel. to PIECE]
peatbog *n.* bog composed of peat.
pebble /'peb(ə)l/ *n.* small stone worn and rounded by action of water; **pebble-dash** mortar with pebbles in it as a coating for wall; **pebbly** *a.* [OE]
pecan /'pi:kən/ *n.* pinkish-brown smooth nut; hickory producing it. [Algonquian]
peccadillo /pekə'dɪləʊ/ *n.* (*pl.* **peccadilloes**) trifling offence, venial sin. [Sp. *pecadillo* dimin., f. L *pecco* sin *v.*]
peccary /'pekərɪ/ *n.* wild pig of tropical America. [Carib]
peck[1] **1** *v.* strike (*at*) or nip or pick up with beak; make (hole) with beak; kiss hastily or perfunctorily; *colloq.* eat (food or *absol.*) esp. in nibbling or listless fashion; carp *at.* **2** *n.* stroke or nip or mark made by beak; hasty or perfunctory kiss. **3 pecking order** social hierarchy, orig. as observed among domestic fowls. [prob. LG]
peck[2] *n.* measure of capacity for dry goods, = 2 gallons or 8 quarts; a lot (*a peck of trouble*). [AF]
pecker *n.* esp. in **keep your pecker up** *sl.* stay cheerful. [PECK[1]]
peckish *a. colloq.* hungry.
pectin /'pektɪn/ *n.* soluble gelatinous carbohydrate found in ripe fruits etc. and used as setting agent in jams and jellies. [Gk (*pēgnumi* make solid)]
pectoral /'pektər(ə)l/ **1** *a.* of or for the breast or chest (*pectoral fin, muscle*); worn on the breast (*pectoral cross*). **2** *n.* pectoral fin or muscle. [F f. L (*pectus -tor-* chest)]
peculate /'pekjʊleɪt/ *v.* embezzle

(money); **peculation** /-ˈleɪʃ(ə)n/ *n.*; **peculator** *n.* [L (foll.)]

peculiar /pɪˈkju:lɪə/ *a.* odd or strange; belonging exclusively *to*; belonging to the individual (*own peculiar brand of humour*); particular, especial. [L (*peculium* private property f. *pecu* cattle)]

peculiarity /pɪkju:lɪˈærɪtɪ/ *n.* being peculiar; characteristic; oddity, eccentricity.

pecuniary /pɪˈkju:nɪərɪ/ *a.* of or consisting of money; (of offence) having money penalty. [L (*pecunia* money f. *pecu* cattle)]

pedagogue /ˈpedəgɒg/ *n.* (*archaic* or *derog.*) schoolmaster, teacher. [L f. Gk (*pais paid-* child, *agō* lead)]

pedagogy /ˈpedəgɒdʒɪ/ *n.* science of teaching; **pedagogic** /-ˈgɒdʒɪk/ *a.*; **pedagogical** /-ˈgɒdʒɪk(ə)l/ *a.* [L f. Gk (prec.)]

pedal /ˈped(ə)l/ **1** *n.* lever or key operated by foot, esp. in bicycle or motor vehicle or some musical instruments (e.g. organ or harp). **2** *v.* (**-ll-**, *US* **-l-**) move or operate by means of pedals; ride bicycle; work (bicycle) by pedals. **3** *a.* /also ˈpi:-/ of the foot or feet. [F f. L (*pes ped-* foot)]

pedalo /ˈpedələʊ/ *n.* (*pl.* **pedalos**) small pedal-operated pleasure-boat.

pedant /ˈpedənt/ *n.* one who lays excessive emphasis on detailed points of learning or procedure, narrow-minded observer of form; **pedantic** /pɪˈdæntɪk/ *a.*; **pedantically** /pɪˈdæntɪkəlɪ/ *adv.*; **pedantry** *n.* [F f. It.]

peddle /ˈped(ə)l/ *v.* follow occupation of pedlar; sell as pedlar; *fig.* deal out in small quantities, retail; busy oneself with trifles. [back-form. f. PEDLAR; in sense 'trifle' orig. var. of PIDDLE]

peddler *n. US* var. of PEDLAR.

pederast /ˈpedəræst/ *n.* one who commits pederasty. [foll.]

pederasty *n.* sodomy with a boy. [Gk (*pais paid-* boy, *erastēs* lover)]

pedestal /ˈpedɪst(ə)l/ *n.* base supporting column or pillar or statue etc.; foundation or basis (*lit.* or *fig.*); **put on a pedestal** admire greatly. [F *piédestal* f. It. = foot of stall]

pedestrian /pɪˈdestrɪən/ **1** *n.* person who is walking, esp. in a street. **2** *a.* prosaic, dull; of walking, going or performed on foot; for walkers. **3 pedestrian crossing** part of road where crossing pedestrians have priority over traffic. **4 pedestrianism** *n.* [F or L (PEDAL)]

pediatric etc. *US* var. of PAEDIATRIC etc.

pedicure /ˈpedɪkjʊə/ *n.* care or treatment of the feet and toe-nails; person who practises this professionally. [F f. L *pes ped-* foot, *cura* care]

pedigree /ˈpedɪgri:/ *n.* genealogical table; ancestral line (esp. distinguished one) of person or animal; derivation (of word); ancient descent; *attrib.* having a recorded line of descent (*pedigree cattle*). [*pedegru* f. F *pied de grue* crane's foot, mark denoting succession in pedigrees]

pediment /ˈpedɪmənt/ *n.* triangular part crowning front of buildings, esp. over portico. [*periment*, perh. corrupt. of PYRAMID]

pedlar /ˈpedlə/ *n.* travelling vendor of small wares; seller of illegal drugs; *fig.* retailer (*of* gossip etc.). [alt. of obs. *pedder* f. dial. *ped* pannier]

pedo- *US* var. of PAEDO-.

pedometer /pɪˈdɒmɪtə/ *n.* instrument for estimating the distance travelled on foot by recording number of steps taken. [F (L *pes ped-* foot; -METER)]

peduncle /pɪˈdʌnk(ə)l/ *n.* stalk of flower, fruit, or cluster, esp. main stalk bearing solitary flower or subordinate stalks; **peduncular** /pɪˈdʌnkjʊlə/ *a.* [L *pedunculus* (prec.)]

pee *colloq.* **1** *v.* urinate. **2** *n.* urination; urine. [PISS]

peek 1 *v.i.* peep slyly (*in*, *out*, etc.), glance. **2** *n.* sly peep or glance. [orig. unkn.]

peel 1 *n.* rind, outer coating of certain fruits and vegetables. **2** *v.* remove or strip peel etc. from; take *off* (peel etc.); become bare of skin, bark, etc.; (of skin, surface, etc.) be shed or come *off* like peel; be able to be peeled; *sl.* (of person) strip for exercise etc. [OE f. L *pilo* strip of hair]

peeling *n.* piece peeled off, esp. skin of fruit.

peep[1] **1** *v.i.* look furtively or quickly (*at*, *into*, etc.), esp. through narrow opening or from concealed place; (of distant object etc.) appear gradually or partially, emerge. **2** *n.* brief or furtive glance; first appearance (*peep of day*). **3 Peeping Tom** furtive voyeur; **peep-show** small exhibition of pictures etc. viewed through lens in small eyehole. [orig. unkn.]

peep[2] **1** *n.* brief shrill chirp or squeak as of young birds. **2** *v.i.* make this sound. [imit.]

peer[1] *v.i.* look searchingly or with difficulty (*at*, *into*, etc.); *archaic* appear, come into view. [orig. unkn.]

peer[2] *n.* one who is equal to another in rank, standing, merit, etc.; member of one of the degrees (duke, marquis, earl, viscount, baron) of nobility in United Kingdom; noble of any country; **peer**

group person's associates of same status as he; **peer of the realm** one of class of peers whose adult members may sit in House of Lords. [F f. L *par* equal]
peerage *n.* the peers, nobility, aristocracy; rank of peer or peeress.
peeress /'pɪərɪs/ *n.* female holder of peerage, peer's wife.
peerless *a.* unequalled, superb.
peeve *sl.* **1** *v.* irritate, annoy; grumble. **2** *n.* cause of annoyance, mood of vexation. [back-form. f. PEEVISH]
peeved *a. sl.* annoyed, vexed. [foll.]
peevish *a.* irritable, querulous. [orig. unkn.]
peewit /'pi:wɪt/ *n.* a kind of plover named from its cry. [imit.]
peg 1 *n.* pin or bolt of wood, metal, etc., for holding things together or hanging things on or as stopper; = *clothes-peg*; any of series of pins or screws for adjusting tension in string of violin etc.; occasion or opportunity, pretext (*peg to hang argument on*); pin for marking position, e.g. on cribbage-board; drink, esp. of spirits. **2** *v.* (**-gg-**) fix (thing *down*, *in*, *out*, etc.) with peg; maintain or stabilize (prices etc.) at certain level; mark (score) with pegs on cribbage-board; mark *out* boundaries of. **3 off the peg** (of clothes) ready-made; **peg away** work persistently (*at*); **peg-board** board with holes and pegs for displaying or hanging things on; **peg-leg** artificial leg, person with this; **peg out** mark out boundaries of, *sl.* die; **square peg in a round hole** person not suited to surroundings, position, etc.; **take person down a peg (or two)** humble or humiliate him. [prob. LG or Du.]
PEI *abbr.* Prince Edward Island.
pejorative /pɪ'dʒɒrətɪv, 'pi:dʒə-/ **1** *a.* derogatory, disparaging. **2** *n.* pejorative word. [F f. L (*pejor* worse)]
peke *n. colloq.* Pekinese [abbr.]
Pekinese /pi:kɪ'ni:z/ *n.* (also **Pekingese;** *pl.* same) dog of short-legged snub-nosed breed with long silky hair. [*Peking* in China]
pelargonium /pelɑ:'gəʊnɪəm/ *n.* plant with showy flowers and usu. fragrant leaves. [L f. Gk *pelargos* stork]
pelf *n.* (usu. *derog.* or *joc.*) money, wealth. [F, rel. to PILFER]
pelican /'pelɪkən/ *n.* large water-bird with pouch in bill for storing fish; **pelican crossing** pedestrian crossing with traffic lights operated by pedestrians. [OE & F f. L f. Gk]
pelisse /pe'li:s/ *n.* woman's mantle with armholes or sleeves, reaching to ankles; fur-lined mantle or cloak, esp. as part of hussar's uniform. [F f. L *pellicia* (cloak) of fur (*pellis* skin)]
pellagra /pɪ'lægrə, -'leɪgrə/ *n.* deficiency disease with cracking of skin, often ending in insanity. [It. *pelle* skin]
pellet /'pelɪt/ *n.* small closely-packed ball of paper, bread, etc.; pill; small shot. [F *pelote* f. Rmc (L *pila* ball)]
pellicle /'pelɪk(ə)l/ *n.* thin skin; membrane; film. [F f. L dimin. (*pellis* skin)]
pell-mell /pel'mel/ *adv.* in disorder, confusedly; headlong, recklessly. [F *pêle-mêle*]
pellucid /pɪ'lju:sɪd, -'lu:-/ *a.* transparent, not distorting image or diffusing light; clear in style or expression or thought. [L (PER-)]
pelmet /'pelmɪt/ *n.* valance or pendent border (esp. over window or door to conceal curtain rods). [prob. F]
pelota /pɪ'ləʊtə/ *n.* Basque game with ball and wicker baskets in walled court. [Sp., = ball]
pelt[1] **1** *v.* attack or strike repeatedly with missiles; (of rain etc.) beat down fast; run fast. **2** *n.* pelting. **3 at full pelt** as fast as possible. [orig. unkn.]
pelt[2] *n.* animal skin, esp. with hair or fur still on it. [F, ult. f. L *pellis* skin]
pelvis /'pelvɪs/ *n.* basin-shaped cavity formed by bones of haunch with sacrum and other vertebrae; **pelvic** *a.* [L, = basin]
pen[1] **1** *n.* instrument for writing in ink, (orig. sharpened quill, now usu. device with reservoir and metal nib); writing, esp. as profession. **2** *v.t.* (**-nn-**) write (letter etc.). **3 pen-friend** friend acquired and known mainly or only from correspondence; **pen-name** literary pseudonym; **pen-pusher** clerical worker; **pen-pushing** clerical work. [F f. L *penna* feather]
pen[2] **1** *n.* small enclosure for cows, sheep, poultry, etc. **2** *v.t.* (**-nn-**) enclose, shut *up* or *in*; shut up (cattle etc.) in pen. [OE]
pen[3] *n.* female swan. [orig. unkn.]
penal /'pi:n(ə)l/ *a.* of or concerned with or used for punishment, esp. by law; (of offence) punishable; **penally** *adv.* [F or L (*poena* penalty)]
penalize /'pi:nəlaɪz/ *v.t.* inflict penalty on; place at comparative disadvantage; make or declare (action) penal.
penalty /'penəltɪ/ *n.* punishment for breach of law; fine or loss etc. incurred by this; disadvantage imposed by action or circumstances; disadvantage to which player or team in sport must submit for breach of rule; **penalty area** area in front of goal in football field in which foul by defenders involves award of penalty kick. [F f. med.L (PENAL)]
penance /'penəns/ *n.* act of self-mortification as expression of repentance; (in RC Church) sacrament involving

confession, absolution, and act of repentance imposed by priest; **do penance** perform such act. [PENITENT]
pence *pl.* of PENNY.
penchant /ˈpɑ̃ʃɑ̃/ *n.* inclination or liking (*for*). [F]
pencil /ˈpens(ə)l/ **1** *n.* instrument for drawing or writing, esp. of graphite, chalk, etc., enclosed in cylinder of wood or metal etc. case with tapering end; something used or shaped like this. **2** *v.t.* (**-ll-**, *US* **-l-**) write or draw or mark with pencil. [F *pincel* f. L *penicillum* paint-brush]
pendant /ˈpendənt/ *n.* hanging ornament, esp. one attached to necklace, bracelet, etc. [F partic. of *pendre* hang]
pendent *a.* hanging, overhanging; undecided, pending; **pendency** *n.*
pending **1** *a.* undecided, awaiting decision or settlement; about to come into existence (*patent pending*). **2** *prep.* until; during. [after F (PENDANT)]
pendulous /ˈpendjʊləs/ *a.* suspended, drooping, hanging down; oscillating. [L *pendulus* (*pendeo* hang)]
pendulum /ˈpendjʊləm/ *n.* body suspended so as to be free to swing, esp. rod with weighted end regulating movement of clock's works. [L neut. adj. (prec.)]
penetrable /ˈpenɪtrəb(ə)l/ *a.* that can be penetrated; **penetrability** /-ˈbɪlɪtɪ/ *n.* [foll.]
penetrate /ˈpenɪtreɪt/ *v.* make way into or through, pierce; permeate; imbue (*with*); see into or through (darkness etc.); explore or comprehend mentally; make a way (*into*, *through*, *to*); be absorbed by the mind. [L]
penetrating *a.* having or showing great insight; (of voice or sound) easily heard through or above other sounds, carrying.
penetration /penɪˈtreɪʃ(ə)n/ *n.* act or extent of penetrating; acute insight.
penguin /ˈpeŋgwɪn/ *n.* flightless seabird of southern hemisphere with wings developed into flippers for swimming under water. [orig. unkn.]
penicillin /penɪˈsɪlɪn/ *n.* antibiotic of group produced naturally on moulds. [L (PENCIL)]
peninsula /pɪˈnɪnsjʊlə/ *n.* piece of land almost surrounded by water or projecting far into the sea; **peninsular** *a.* [L (*paene* almost, *insula* island)]
penis /ˈpiːnɪs/ *n.* sexual and (in mammals) urinatory organ of male animal. [L]
penitent /ˈpenɪtənt/ **1** *a.* repentant. **2** *n.* repentant sinner; person doing penance under direction of confessor. **3** **penitence** *n.* [F f. L (*paeniteo* repent)]
penitential /penɪˈtenʃ(ə)l/ *a.* of penitence or penance.
penitentiary /penɪˈtenʃərɪ/ **1** *n.* *US* reformatory prison. **2** *a.* of penance; of reformatory treatment. [L (PENITENT)]
penknife *n.* small folding knife, esp. for carrying in pocket. [PEN¹]
penmanship *n.* skill or style in writing or handwriting; process of literary composition.
pennant /ˈpenənt/ *n.* tapering flag, esp. that flown at mast-head of vessel in commission; = PENNON. [blend of PENDANT and PENNON]
penniless /ˈpenɪlɪs/ *a.* having no money; poor, destitute. [PENNY]
pennon /ˈpenən/ *n.* long narrow flag, triangular or swallow-tailed; long pointed streamer of ship. [F f. L *penna* feather]
penny /ˈpenɪ/ *n.* (*pl.* **pennies** for separate coins, **pence** for sum of money) British bronze coin worth $\frac{1}{100}$ of a pound, or formerly a coin worth $\frac{1}{12}$ of a shilling; monetary unit represented by this; **in for a penny, in for a pound** thing once begun should be concluded at all costs; **pennies from heaven** unexpected benefits; **penny black** first adhesive postage stamp (1840), printed in black; **the penny drops** understanding dawns; **penny farthing** early type of bicycle with large front wheel and small rear one; **penny-pinching** *a.* niggardly, (*n.*) niggardliness; **penny whistle** one with six holes for different notes; **penny wise (and pound foolish)** careful or thrifty in small matters (but wasteful in large ones); **a pretty penny** a large sum of money; **two a penny** commonly found and of little value. [OE]
pennyroyal /penɪˈrɔɪəl/ *n.* creeping species of mint. [AF *puliol real* royal thyme]
pennyweight *n.* unit of weight equal to 24 grains, $\frac{1}{20}$ ounce troy. [PENNY]
pennywort *n.* plant with rounded leaves.
pennyworth *n.* as much as can be bought for a penny.
penology /piːˈnɒlədʒɪ/ *n.* study of punishment and prison management; **penologist** *n.* [L *poena* penalty]
pension¹ /ˈpenʃ(ə)n/ **1** *n.* periodic payment made by State to person above specified age (*retirement pension*) or to widowed or disabled person, or by employer to retired employee. **2** *v.t.* grant pension to. **3** **pension off** dismiss with pension, cease to employ (person) or use (thing). [F f. L (*pendo pens-* weigh)]
pension² /ˈpɑsɪɔ̃ː/ *n.* continental boarding-house. [F (prec.)]
pensionable *a.* entitled or (of employ-

ment etc.) entitling to a pension. [PENSION¹]

pensionary 1 *a.* of pension. 2 *n.* recipient of pension. [med.L (PENSION¹)]

pensioner *n.* recipient of (esp. retirement) pension. [F (PENSION¹)]

pensive /'pensɪv/ *a.* deep in thought. [F (*penser* think)]

pent *a.* closely confined, shut *in* or *up* (*pent-up fury*). [PEN²]

penta- *in comb.* five. [Gk (*pente* five)]

pentacle /'pentək(ə)l/ *n.* figure used as symbol, esp. in magic, e.g. pentagram. [med.L *pentaculum* (PENTA-)]

pentagon /'pentəgən/ *n.* plane figure with five sides and angles; **the Pentagon** five-sided Washington headquarters of leaders of US defence forces; **pentagonal** /-'tægən(ə)l/ *a.* [F, or L f. Gk *pentagōnon* (PENTA-)]

pentagram /'pentəgræm/ *n.* five-pointed star. [Gk (PENTA-)]

pentameter /pen'tæmɪtə/ *n.* line of five metrical feet. [L f. Gk (PENTA-)]

Pentateuch /'pentətju:k/ *n.* first five books of Old Testament. [Gk *teukhos* book]

pentathlon /pen'tæθlɒn/ *n.* athletic contest in which each competitor takes part in all its five events. [Gk (PENTA-, *athlon* contest)]

pentatonic /pentə'tɒnɪk/ *a.* of five-note musical scale. [PENTA-]

Pentecost /'pentɪkɒst/ *n.* Jewish harvest festival on fiftieth day after second day of Passover; Whit Sunday; **pentecostal** /-'kɒst(ə)l/ *a.* [OE & F f. L f. Gk *pentēkostē* fiftieth (day)]

penthouse /'penthaʊs/ *n.* house or flat on roof of tall building; sloping roof, esp. as subsidiary structure attached to wall of main building. [F *apentis* f. L (APPEND)]

penult /pɪ'nʌlt, 'pi:-/ *a.* & *n.* last but one (esp. of syllable). [abbr. (foll.)]

penultimate /pɪ'nʌltɪmət/ *a.* & *n.* last but one. [L *paenultimus* (*paene* almost, *ultimus* last)]

penumbra /pɪ'nʌmbrə/ *n.* (*pl.* **penumbrae** /-i:/ or **penumbras**) partly shaded region round shadow of opaque body, esp. of moon or earth in eclipse; partial shadow; **penumbral** *a.* [L *paene* almost, UMBRA]

penurious /pɪ'njʊərɪəs/ *a.* poor; scanty; grudging, stingy. [med.L (foll.)]

penury /'penjʊrɪ/ *n.* destitution, poverty; lack or scarcity (*of*). [L]

peon /'pi:ən, pju:n/ *n.* (in India etc.) office-messenger, attendant; (in Spanish America) day-labourer. [Port. & Sp., rel. to PAWN¹]

peony /'pi:ənɪ/ *n.* garden plant with large round red or pink or white flowers. [OE f. L f. Gk]

people /'pi:p(ə)l/ 1 *n.* all persons belonging to nation, race, tribe, or community (*a warlike people*; *English-speaking peoples*); (as *pl.*) persons in general (*not many people here today*); (as *pl.*) persons belonging to a place or forming a company or class etc.; (as *pl.*) *the* persons not having special rank or position in a country etc.; (as *pl.*) subjects, followers, members of congregation etc.; (as *pl.*) parents or other relatives (*has not told her people yet*); (as *sing.* or *pl.*) *the* body of enfranchised or qualified citizens. 2 *v.t.* fill with people, populate; (esp. in *p.p.*) inhabit. [AF f. L *populus*]

pep *sl.* 1 *n.* vigour, spirit. 2 *v.t.* (**-pp-**) fill with vigour, liven *up*. 3 **pep pill** pill containing stimulant drug; **pep talk** talk urging listener to greater effort or courage. 4 **peppy** *a.* [abbr. of foll.]

pepper 1 *n.* pungent aromatic condiment obtained from dried berries of certain plants; capsicum plant grown as vegetable, its fruit; *fig.* anything pungent. 2 *v.t.* sprinkle with or as with pepper; pelt with missiles. 3 **pepper-and-salt** *a.* (of cloth) woven so as to show small dots of dark and light colour intermingled; **pepper-mill** mill for grinding peppercorns by hand; **pepper-pot** small container with perforated lid for sprinkling pepper. [OE f. L *piper* f. Gk f. Skr.]

peppercorn *n.* dried pepper-berry; nominal or very low rent.

peppermint *n.* species of mint grown for its strong fragrant oil; lozenge or sweet flavoured with this; the oil itself.

peppery *a.* of or like or abounding in pepper, hot and spicy; *fig.* pungent, hot-tempered.

pepsin /'pepsɪn/ *n.* enzyme contained in gastric juice. [G, f. Gk *pepsis* digestion]

peptic /'peptɪk/ *a.* digestive; **peptic ulcer** ulcer in stomach or duodenum; **peptically** *adv.* [Gk *peptikos* able to digest]

peptide /'peptaɪd/ *n.* compound with linked amino acids with elimination of water molecules. [G f. Gk *peptos* cooked]

per *prep.* for each (*£1 per person*; *five miles per hour*); through or by or by means of (*per post*); **as per** in accordance with (*as per instructions*); **as per usual** *colloq.* as usual. [L]

per- *prefix* through or all over (*pervade*); completely, very (*perturb*); to destruction (*perdition*), to the bad (*pervert*). [L (prec.)]

peradventure /pərəd'ventʃə/ (*archaic* or *joc.*) 1 *adv.* perhaps; by chance. 2 *n.* uncertainty, chance, conjecture; doubt. [F (PER, ADVENTURE)]

perambulate /pə'ræmbjʊleɪt/ *v.* walk

through or over or about (place); walk about, or from place to place; **perambulation** /-'leɪʃ(ə)n/ *n.* [L *perambulo* (AMBLE)]

perambulator *n.* = PRAM.

per annum /pɜ:r 'ænəm/ *adv.* for each year. [L]

percale /pə'keɪl/ *n.* closely woven cotton fabric. [F]

per caput /pɜ: 'kæpʊt/ *adv.* & *a.* (also **per capita** /'kæpɪtə/) for each person. [L, = by head(s)]

perceive /pə'si:v/ *v.t.* apprehend with the mind or through one of the senses, observe, notice, understand. [F f. L *percipio -cept-* seize, understand]

per cent /pə'sent/, *US* **percent 1** *adv.* in every hundred. **2** *n.* percentage; one part in every hundred (*half a per cent*). [PER, CENT]

percentage *n.* rate or proportion per cent; proportion (*small percentage of people*).

perceptible /pə'septɪb(ə)l/ *a.* that can be perceived by the senses or intellect; **perceptibility** /-'bɪlɪtɪ/; **perceptibly** *adv.* [F or L (PERCEIVE)]

perception /pə'sepʃ(ə)n/ *n.* act or faculty of perceiving, instinctive recognition (*of* truth, aesthetic quality, etc.); *Philos.* action by which the mind refers its sensations to external object as cause; **perceptual** /pə'septʃʊəl/ *a.* [L (PERCEIVE)]

perceptive /pə'septɪv/ *a.* of perception; quick to perceive and comprehend; **perceptivity** /-'tɪvɪtɪ/ *n.* [med.L (PERCEIVE)]

perch[1] **1** *n.* branch or bar etc. serving as bird's resting-place; elevated or secure position; measure of length esp. for land, equal to 5½ yards. **2** *v.* rest or place on or as if on perch. [F f. L *pertica* pole]

perch[2] *n.* (*pl.* same) spiny-finned freshwater food-fish. [F f. L *perca* f. Gk]

perchance /pə'tʃɑ:ns/ *adv. archaic* by chance; possibly, maybe. [AF (*par* by)]

percipient /pə'sɪpɪənt/ *a.* perceiving, conscious; **percipience** *n.* [L (PERCEIVE)]

percolate /'pɜ:kəleɪt/ *v.* (of liquid) filter or ooze *through*, permeate; (of person or strainer) cause to filter through pores etc.; prepare (coffee) in percolator; **percolation** /-'leɪʃ(ə)n/ *n.* [L (*colum* sieve)]

percolator *n.* pot for making and serving coffee, in which boiling water is made to rise up central tube and down through drum of ground coffee.

percussion /pə'kʌʃ(ə)n/ *n.* forcible striking of one (usu. solid) body against another; (of music or instrument etc.) involving the striking of a resonating surface; group of such instruments in orchestra; gentle tapping of body in medical diagnosis; **percussion cap** small metal or paper device containing explosive powder and exploded by fall of hammer; **percussive** *a.* [F or L (*percutio -cuss-* strike)]

perdition /pə'dɪʃ(ə)n/ *n.* damnation; eternal death. [F or L (*perdo -dit-* destroy)]

peregrine /'perɪgrɪn/ *n.* a kind of falcon used for hawking. [L *peregrinus* foreign]

peremptory /pə'remptərɪ, 'perɪm-/ *a.* (of statement or command) admitting no denial or refusal; (of person etc.) dogmatic, imperious, dictatorial; **peremptorily** *adv.*; **peremptoriness** *n.* [AF f. L *peremptorius* deadly, decisive]

perennial /pə'renɪəl/ **1** *a.* lasting through the year; lasting long or for ever; (of plant) living for several years. **2** *n.* perennial plant. **3 perennially** *adv.* [L *perennis* (*annus* year)]

perfect /'pɜ:fɪkt/ **1** *a.* complete and with all necessary qualities; faultless, not deficient; exact, precise (*a perfect square*); *colloq.* excellent, most satisfactory (*a perfect day*); entire or unqualified (*a perfect fool*; *perfect nonsense*); *Gram.* (of tense) denoting completed event or action viewed in relation to the present (e.g. *he has gone*). **2** *n.* perfect tense. **3** /pə'fekt/ *v.t.* make perfect or complete. **4 perfect interval** *Mus.* interval of a fourth or fifth or octave in major or minor scale; **perfect pitch** see PITCH[1]. [F f. L *perficio -fect-* complete *v.*]

perfectible /pə'fektɪb(ə)l/ *a.* that can be perfected; **perfectibility** *n.* /-'bɪlɪtɪ/ *n.*

perfection /pə'fekʃ(ə)n/ *n.* making or being perfect; faultlessness; perfect person or thing, or manifestation (*of* quality etc.); **to perfection** exactly, completely. [F f. L (PERFECT)]

perfectionist *n.* one who aspires constantly to perfection; **perfectionism.**

perfidy /'pɜ:fɪdɪ/ *n.* breach of faith, treachery; **perfidious** /pə'fɪdɪəs/ *a.* [L *perfidia* (*fides* faith)]

perforate /'pɜ:fəreɪt/ *v.* make hole(s) through, pierce; make row of small holes in (paper etc.) so that part may be torn off easily; **perforation** /-'reɪʃ(ə)n/ *n.* [L *perforo* pierce through]

perforce /pə'fɔ:s/ *adv.* unavoidably, necessarily. [F *par* (= by) *force*]

perform /pə'fɔ:m/ *v.* carry into effect, be agent of, do; go through (some process), execute (function, piece of music, etc.); act in play, sing, etc.; function; **performing arts** those such as drama that require public performance. [AF (PER-, FURNISH)]

performance /pə'fɔ:məns/ *n.* process or manner of performing or functioning; execution (*of* duty etc.); notable or *colloq.* ridiculous action; performing of or in play etc.

perfume /ˈpɜːfjuːm/ **1** *n.* sweet smell; fragrant liquid, esp. for application to the body, scent. **2** *v.t.* impart sweet smell to. [F f. It. *parfumare* smoke through]

perfumer /pəˈfjuːmə/ *n.* maker or seller of perfumes; **perfumery** *n.*

perfunctory /pəˈfʌŋktərɪ/ *a.* done superficially or without care, for the sake of duty; (of person) acting thus; **perfunctorily** *adv.* [L (FUNCTION)]

pergola /ˈpɜːgələ/ *n.* arbour or covered walk formed of growing plants trained over trellis-work. [It.]

perhaps /pəˈhæps, præps/ *adv.* it may be, possibly. [HAP]

peri- *prefix* round, about. [Gk]

perianth /ˈperɪænθ/ *n.* outer part of flower. [F (Gk *anthos* flower)]

pericardium /perɪˈkɑːdɪəm/ *n.* (*pl.* **pericardia**) membranous sac enclosing the heart. [Gk (*kardia* heart)]

perigee /ˈperɪdʒiː/ *n.* point nearest to earth in orbit of moon or satellite round it. [F f. Gk *perigeion*]

perihelion /perɪˈhiːlɪən/ *n.* (*pl.* **perihelia**) point nearest to sun in orbit of planet or comet round it. [Gk PERI-, *hēlios* sun)]

peril /ˈperɪl/ *n.* serious and immediate danger; **perilous** *a.* [F f. L *periculum*]

perimeter /pəˈrɪmɪtə/ *n.* circumference or outline of closed figure; length of this; outer boundary of enclosed area. [F or L f. Gk (-METER)]

perineum /perɪˈniːəm/ *n.* region of the body between anus and scrotum or vulva; **perineal** *a.* [L f. Gk]

period /ˈpɪərɪəd/ **1** *n.* length or portion of time; distinct portion of history, life, etc.; time forming part of geological era; interval between recurrences of a phenomenon; time allocated for lesson in school; occurrence of menstruation, time of this; complete sentence, esp. one consisting of several clauses; = *full stop*; appended to statement, stressing its completeness (*we want the best, period*). **2** *a.* belonging to or characteristic of some past period (*period furniture*). [F f. L f. Gk (*hodos* way)]

periodic /pɪərɪˈɒdɪk/ *a.* appearing or occurring at intervals; **periodic table** arrangement of chemical elements by atomic number, with regular recurrence of properties. [F or L f. Gk (prec.)]

periodical **1** *a.* = PERIODIC. **2** *n.* magazine etc. published at regular intervals. **3** **periodically** *adv.*

periodicity /pɪərɪəˈdɪsɪtɪ/ *n.* tendency to recur at intervals.

peripatetic /perɪpəˈtetɪk/ **1** *a.* going from place to place, itinerant; (**Peripatetic**) Aristotelian. **2** *n.* (**Peripatetic**) Aristotelian. [F or L f. Gk (*pateō* walk)]

peripheral /pəˈrɪfər(ə)l/ *a.* of marginal or lesser importance; of a periphery. [foll.]

periphery /pəˈrɪfərɪ/ *n.* boundary of surface or area or subject etc.; region just outside or inside this. [L f. Gk (*pherō* bear)]

periphrasis /pəˈrɪfrəsɪs/ *n.* (*pl.* **periphrases** /-iːz/) roundabout way of speaking or phrase, circumlocution; **periphrastic** /perɪˈfræstɪk/ *a.* [L f. Gk (PHRASE)]

periscope /ˈperɪskəʊp/ *n.* apparatus with tube and mirrors by which observer in trench, submerged submarine, rear of crowd, etc., can see things otherwise out of sight; **periscopic** /-ˈskɒpɪk/ *a.* [-SCOPE]

perish /ˈperɪʃ/ *v.* be destroyed, suffer death or ruin; lose or cause (fabric etc.) to lose normal qualities, rot; cause distress to or be distressed by cold or exposure. [F f. L *pereo*]

perishable **1** *a.* liable to perish, subject to speedy decay. **2** *n.* (esp. in *pl.*) perishable goods (esp. foods).

perisher *n.* *sl.* annoying person, esp. child.

perishing *a.* *colloq.* intensely cold; *colloq.* confounded.

peritoneum /perɪtəʊˈniːəm/ *n.* (*pl.* **peritoneums**) membrane lining cavity of abdomen; **peritoneal** *a.* [L f. Gk (*peritonos* stretched round)]

peritonitis /perɪtəˈnaɪtɪs/ *n.* inflammation of peritoneum. [-ITIS]

periwig /ˈperɪwɪg/ *n.* (esp. *hist.*) wig. [alt. of PERUKE]

periwinkle[1] /ˈperɪwɪŋk(ə)l/ *n.* evergreen trailing plant with blue or white flowers. [AF f. L *pervinca*]

periwinkle[2] /ˈperɪwɪŋk(ə)l/ *n.* winkle. [orig. unkn.]

perjure /ˈpɜːdʒə/ *v. refl.* cause *oneself* to be guilty of perjury; (in *p.p.*) guilty of or involving perjury. [F f. L (*juro* swear)]

perjury *n.* wilful utterance of false statement while on oath.

perk[1] *v.* *colloq.* (cause to) recover courage or confidence (usu. with *up*); smarten *up*; raise (head etc.) briskly. [orig. unkn.]

perk[2] *n.* *colloq.* (usu. in *pl.*) perquisite. [abbr.]

perky *a.* *colloq.* lively and cheerful; **perkily** *adv.*; **perkiness** *n.* [PERK[1]]

perm[1] *colloq.* **1** *n.* permanent wave. **2** *v.t.* give permanent wave to. [abbr.]

perm[2] *colloq.* **1** *n.* permutation. **2** *v.t.* make permutation of. [abbr.]

permafrost /ˈpɜːməfrɒst/ *n.* permanently frozen subsoil in polar regions. [foll.]

permanency /'pɜːmənənsɪ/ *n.* permanent thing or arrangement. [foll.]

permanent /'pɜːmənənt/ *a.* lasting, intended to last or function, indefinitely; **permanent wave** long-lasting artificial wave in hair; **permanent way** finished road-bed of railway; **permanence** *n.* [F, or L *permaneo* remain to the end]

permeable /'pɜːmɪəb(ə)l/ *a.* admitting passage of liquid etc.; **permeability** /-'bɪlɪtɪ/ *n.* [foll.]

permeate /'pɜːmɪeɪt/ *v.* penetrate throughout, pervade, saturate; diffuse itself *among*, *through*, etc.; **permeation** /-'eɪʃ(ə)n/ *n.* [L *permeo* pass through]

Permian /'pɜːmɪən/ **1** *a.* of the period in the Palaeozoic era after Carboniferous. **2** *n.* this period. [*Perm* in Russia]

permissible /pə'mɪsɪb(ə)l/ *a.* that can be permitted; **permissibility** /-'bɪlɪtɪ/ *n.* [F or med.L (PERMIT)]

permission /pə'mɪʃ(ə)n/ *n.* consent or liberty (*to do* thing). [F or f. L *permissio* (PERMIT)]

permissive /pə'mɪsɪv/ *a.* tolerant or liberal, esp. in sexual matters; giving permission. [F or med.L (foll.)]

permit 1 /pə'mɪt/ *v.* (**-tt-**) give permission or consent to; authorize, allow; give opportunity (*weather permitting*); admit *of* (alteration, delay, etc.). **2** /'pɜː-mɪt/ *n.* written order giving permission to act, esp. for entry into a place; permission. [L *permitto -miss-* allow]

permutation /pɜːmjuː'teɪʃ(ə)n/ *n.* variation of order of set of things; any one such arrangement; combination or selection of specified number of items from larger group (esp. of matches in football pool). [F or L *permuto* change thoroughly]

pernicious /pə'nɪʃəs/ *a.* destructive, ruinous, fatal; **pernicious anaemia** severe progressive form of anaemia. [L (*pernicies* ruin)]

pernickety /pə'nɪkɪtɪ/ *a. colloq.* fastidious; over-precise. [orig. unkn.]

peroration /perə'reɪʃ(ə)n/ *n.* lengthy (esp. concluding) part of speech. [L (*oro* speak)]

peroxide /pə'rɒksaɪd/ **1** *n.* compound of oxygen with another element containing maximum proportion of oxygen; (in full **hydrogen peroxide**) colourless liquid used in water solution, esp. to bleach hair. **2** *v.t.* bleach (hair) with peroxide. [PER-]

perpendicular /pɜːpən'dɪkjʊlə/ **1** *a.* at right angles (*to* given line, plane, or surface); upright, vertical, (of ascent, cliff, etc.) very steep; (**Perpendicular**) of style of English Gothic architecture (14th–15th cc.) with vertical tracery in large windows. **2** *n.* perpendicular line; perpendicular position or direction. **3** **perpendicularity** /-'lærɪtɪ/ *n.* [L *perpendiculum* plumb-line]

perpetrate /'pɜːpɪtreɪt/ *v.t.* commit or perform (blunder, crime, hoax, thing regarded as outrageous); **perpetration** /-'treɪʃ(ə)n/ *n.*; **perpetrator** *n.* [L *perpetro* perform]

perpetual /pə'petjʊəl/ *a.* lasting for ever or indefinitely; unceasing; continuous; *colloq.* frequent, much repeated (*perpetual interruptions*); **perpetual motion** motion of hypothetical machine running for ever unless subject to external forces or wear; **perpetually** *adv.* [F f. L *perpetuus* continuous]

perpetuate /pə'petjʊeɪt/ *v.t.* make perpetual, cause to be always remembered; **perpetuation** /-'eɪʃ(ə)n/ *n.*; **perpetuator** *n.* [L *perpetuo*]

perpetuity /pɜːpɪ'tjuːɪtɪ/ *n.* state or quality of being perpetual; perpetual possession or position or annuity; **in perpetuity** for ever. [F f. L (PERPETUAL)]

perplex /pə'pleks/ *v.t.* greatly puzzle or disconcert (person); complicate or confuse (matter). [F, or L *perplexus* involved]

perplexedly /pə'pleksɪdlɪ/ *adv.* in perplexed manner.

perplexity *n.* perplexing or being perplexed; thing that perplexes. [F f. L (PERPLEX)]

per pro. *abbr.* by proxy, through an agent. [L *per procurationem*]

perquisite /'pɜːkwɪzɪt/ *n.* extra profit or allowance additional to main income etc.; customary extra right or privilege. [L *perquiro -quisit-* search diligently for]

perry /'perɪ/ *n.* drink made from fermented pear-juice. [F *peré* (PEAR)]

per se /pɜː 'seɪ/ by or in itself, intrinsically. [L]

persecute /'pɜːsɪkjuːt/ *v.t.* subject to constant hostility and ill-treatment, esp. on grounds of religious or political beliefs; harass, worry; **persecution** /-'kjuːʃ(ə)n/ *n.*; **persecutor** *n.* [F f. L (*persequor -secut-* pursue)]

persevere /pɜːsɪ'vɪə/ *v.i.* continue steadfastly, persist (*in* or *with*); **perseverance** *n.* [F f. L (SEVERE)]

Persian /'pɜːʃ(ə)n/ **1** *n.* native or inhabitant of (esp. ancient) Persia, now Iran. **2** *a.* of Persia or its people or language. **3 Persian cat** cat of breed with long silky hair; **Persian lamb** silky curled fur of young karakul. [F f. L (*Persia*)]

persiflage /'pɜːsɪflɑːʒ/ *n.* banter, light raillery. [F]

persimmon /pɜː'sɪmən/ *n.* an American or E. Asian tree; its edible orange plumlike fruit. [Algonquian]

persist /pə'sɪst/ *v.i.* continue firmly or obstinately (*in* opinion, course of action, *doing* thing), esp. in face of difficulty or objection; (of phenomenon etc.) continue in existence, survive; **persistence** *n.*; **persistent** *a.* [L (*sisto* stand)]

person /'pɜ:s(ə)n/ *n.* individual human being; living body of human being; *Gram.* one of three classes of personal pronouns, verb-forms, etc., denoting respectively person etc. speaking (**first person**), spoken to (**second person**), or spoken of (**third person**); God as Father or Son or Holy Ghost; **in person** physically present. [F f. L (foll.)]

persona /pɜ:'səʊnə/ *n.* (*pl.* **personae** /-i:/) aspect of one's personality as shown to or perceived by others. [L, = actor's mask]

personable *a.* pleasing in appearance or behaviour. [PERSON]

personage *n.* person, esp. important one.

persona grata /pɜ:səʊnə 'grɑ:tə/ person acceptable to certain others. [L]

personal /'pɜ:sən(ə)l/ *a.* one's own, individual, private; done or made etc. in person (*will give it my personal attention*); directed to or concerning an individual (*personal letter*); referring (esp. in hostile way) to an individual's private life or concerns, tending to do this (*personal remarks*; *let us not be personal*); of the body (*personal hygiene*); of or existing as a person (*a personal God*); *Gram.* of or denoting one of the three persons (*personal pronoun*); **personal column** column of private advertisements or messages in newspaper; **personal property** all property except land and those interests in land that pass to one's heirs. [F f. L (PERSONA)]

personality /pɜ:sə'nælɪtɪ/ *n.* distinctive character or qualities of a person; personal existence or identity, being a person; famous person, celebrity; (in *pl.*) personal remarks. [F f. L (as prec.)]

personalize *v.t.* make personal, esp. by marking with owner's name etc.; personify. [PERSONAL]

personally *adv.* in person (*will see to it personally*); for one's own part (*personally I have no objection*).

persona non grata /pɜ:səʊnə nɒn 'grɑ:tə/ person unacceptable to certain others. [L]

personate /'pɜ:səneɪt/ *v.t.* play the part of or pretend to be (person); **personation** /-'neɪʃ(ə)n/ *n.*; **personator** *n.* [L (PERSONA)]

personify /pɜ:'sɒnɪfaɪ/ *v.t.* represent (thing or abstraction) as having personal nature; symbolize (quality) by figure in human form; (esp. in *p.p.*) embody in one's own person or typically exemplify (quality); **personification** /-fɪ'keɪʃ(ə)n/ *n.* [F (PERSON)]

personnel /pɜ:sə'nel/ *n.* body of employees, staff in public undertaking, armed forces, office, etc.; **personnel department** department of firm etc. dealing with appointment and welfare of employees. [F, = personal]

perspective /pə'spektɪv/ **1** *n.* art of drawing solid objects on plane surface so as to give right impression of relative positions, size, etc.; picture so drawn; apparent relation between visible objects as to position, distance, etc.; mental view of relative importance of things; view or prospect (*lit.* or *fig.*). **2** *a.* of or in perspective. **3 in perspective** drawn or viewed according to the rules of perspective; correctly regarded as to relative importance. [L (*perspicio -spect-* look at)]

Perspex /'pɜ:speks/ *n.* (**P**) a tough light transparent plastic. [prec.]

perspicacious /pɜ:spɪ'keɪʃəs/ *a.* having mental penetration or discernment; **perspicacity** /-'kæsɪtɪ/ *n.* [L *perspicax* (PERSPECTIVE)]

perspicuous /pə'spɪkjʊəs/ *a.* easily understood, clearly expressed; expressing things clearly; **perspicuity** /pɜ:spɪ'kju:ɪtɪ/ *n.* [L (as prec.)]

perspiration /pɜ:spɪ'reɪʃ(ə)n/ *n.* sweat, sweating. [F (foll.)]

perspire /pə'spaɪə/ *v.* sweat. [F f. L (*spiro* breathe)]

persuade /pə'sweɪd/ *v.t.* cause (person) to do or believe something, induce; (in *p.p.*) convinced (*of* or *that*); **persuadable** *a.*; **persuasible** *a.* [L *persuadeo -suas-* induce]

persuasion /pə'sweɪʒ(ə)n/ *n.* persuading; persuasiveness; belief or conviction, sect holding particular religious belief. [L (PERSUADE)]

persuasive /pə'sweɪsɪv/ *a.* able or tending to persuade. [F or med.L (PERSUADE)]

pert *a.* saucy, impudent; jaunty, lively. [F *apert* f. L *apertus* open]

pertain /pə'teɪn/ *v.i.* relate or have reference *to*; belong as part or appendage or accessory *to*; be appropriate *to*. [F f. L *pertineo* belong to]

pertinacious /pɜ:tɪ'neɪʃəs/ *a.* determined in some belief or course, persistent, obstinate; **pertinacity** /-'næsɪtɪ/ *n.* [L *pertinax* (prec.)]

pertinent /'pɜ:tɪnənt/ *a.* relevant to the matter in hand; to the point; **pertinence** *n.*; **pertinency** *n.* [F or L (PERTAIN)]

perturb /pə'tɜ:b/ *v.t.* throw into confusion or disorder; disturb mentally; agitate; **perturbation** /-'beɪʃ(ə)n/ *n.* [F f. L]

peruke /pə'ru:k/ *n.* (esp. *hist.*) wig. [F f. It.]
peruse /pə'ru:z/ *v.t.* read or study, esp. thoroughly or carefully; **perusal** *n.* [USE]
pervade /pə'veɪd/ *v.t.* spread through, permeate, saturate; be rife among or through; **pervasion** *n.*; **pervasive** *a.* [L *pervado* penetrate]
perverse /pə'vɜ:s/ *a.* (of person or action) deliberately or stubbornly departing from what is reasonable or required; having this tendency, intractable. [F f. L (PERVERT)]
perversion /pə'vɜ:ʃ(ə)n/ *n.* perverting or being perverted; preference for abnormal form of sexual activity. [L (foll.)]
pervert 1 /pə'vɜ:t/ *v.t.* turn (thing) aside from proper use or nature; misapply (words etc.); lead astray from right behaviour or beliefs; (in *p.p.*) showing perversion. **2** /'pɜ:vɜ:t/ *n.* person who is perverted, esp. sexually. [F or L (*verto vers-* turn)]
pervious /'pɜ:vɪəs/ *a.* permeable, affording passage (*to*); accessible (*to* reason etc.). [L (*via* road)]
peseta /pə'seɪtə/ *n.* Spanish coin and currency unit. [Sp.]
pesky /'peskɪ/ *a. US colloq.* troublesome, annoying. [orig. unkn.]
peso /'peɪsəʊ/ *n.* (*pl.* **pesos**) silver coin and currency unit in several Latin-American countries and in Philippines. [Sp.]
pessary /'pesərɪ/ *n.* device worn in vagina to prevent uterine displacement or as contraceptive; vaginal suppository. [L f. Gk]
pessimism /'pesɪmɪz(ə)m/ *n.* tendency to take worst view or expect worst outcome; belief that the actual world is the worst possible, or that all things tend to be evil; **pessimist** *n.* [L *pessimus* worst]
pessimistic /pesɪ'mɪstɪk/ *a.* having or showing pessimism; **pessimistically** *adv.*
pest *n.* troublesome or annoying person or thing; insect or animal that is destructive to plants, food, etc.; *archaic* pestilence, plague. [F, or L *pestis* plague]
pester *v.t.* trouble or annoy, esp. with frequent or persistent requests. [prob. F *empestrer* encumber; infl. by PEST]
pesticide /'pestɪsaɪd/ *n.* substance for destroying harmful insects etc. [PEST, -CIDE]
pestiferous /pe'stɪfərəs/ *a.* noxious, pestilent; harmful, pernicious. [L (PEST)]
pestilence /'pestɪləns/ *n.* fatal epidemic disease, esp. bubonic plague. [F f. L *pestilentia* (foll.)]
pestilent *a.* destructive to life, deadly; harmful, esp. morally; *colloq.* troublesome, annoying. [L (PEST)]
pestilential /pestɪ'lenʃ(ə)l/ *a.* of pestilence, pestilent. [med.L (prec.)]
pestle /'pes(ə)l/ *n.* club-shaped instrument for pounding substances in a mortar. [F f. L *pistillum* (*pinso* pound)]
pestology /pe'stɒlədʒɪ/ *n.* scientific study of harmful insects and of methods of dealing with them. [PEST]
pet[1] 1 *n.* domesticated animal kept for pleasure or companionship; darling, favourite. **2** *a.* of or for or in the nature of a pet (*pet dog, food*); favourite or particular (*pet hate*); expressing fondness or familiarity (*pet name*). **3** *v.t.* (**-tt-**) fondle, esp. erotically; treat as pet. [orig. unkn.]
pet[2] *n.* offence at being slighted, ill-humour. [orig. unkn.]
petal /'pet(ə)l/ *n.* each division of corolla of flower; **petalled** *a.* [L f. Gk *petalon* leaf]
petard /pɪ'tɑ:d/ *n. hist.* small bomb used to blast down door etc. [F]
peter *v.i.* in **peter out** diminish gradually and come to an end. [orig. unkn.]
Peter Pan person who retains youthful features and seems not to age. [character in J. M. Barrie]
petersham /'pi:təʃəm/ *n.* thick ribbed silk ribbon. [Lord *Petersham*]
petiole /'petɪəʊl/ *n.* slender stalk joining leaf to stem. [F f. L]
petit bourgeois /pəti: 'bʊəʒwɑ:/ member of lower middle classes. [F]
petite /pə'ti:t/ *a.* (of woman) small and dainty in build. [F, = little]
petit four /pəti: 'fʊə/ (*pl.* ***petits fours*** *pr.* same) very small fancy cake. [F, = small oven]
petition /pə'tɪʃ(ə)n/ **1** *n.* asking, supplication; formal written request, esp. one signed by many people, appealing to authority in some cause; application to court for writ, order, etc. **2** *v.* make or address petition to; ask earnestly or humbly. [F f. L (*peto petit-* ask)]
petit mal /pəti: 'mɑ:l/ mild form of epilepsy. [F, = small sickness]
petit point /pəti: 'pwæ̃/ embroidery on canvas using small stitches. [F]
petrel /'petr(ə)l/ *n.* a kind of sea-bird that flies far from land. [orig. unkn.]
petrify /'petrɪfaɪ/ *v.* paralyse with fear, astonishment, etc.; turn or be turned into stone. [F f. L (*petra* f. Gk, = rock)]
petrochemical /petrəʊ'kemɪk(ə)l/ *n.* substance industrially obtained from petroleum or natural gas. [PETROLEUM]
petrodollar /'petrəʊdɒlə/ *n.* dollar available in petroleum-exporting country.
petrol /'petr(ə)l/ *n.* refined petroleum

used as fuel in motor vehicles, aircraft, etc.; **petrol station** = *filling station*. [F *pétrole* f. L (foll.)]

petroleum /pɪ'trəʊlɪəm/ *n.* hydrocarbon oil found in upper strata of earth, refined for use as fuel etc.; **petroleum jelly** translucent solid mixture of hydrocarbons obtained from petroleum and used as lubricant etc. [L f. Gk *petra* rock + L *oleum* oil)]

petticoat /'petɪkəʊt/ *n.* woman's or girl's undergarment hanging from waist or shoulders; *attrib.* feminine. [*petty coat*]

pettifogging /'petɪfɒgɪŋ/ *a.* quibbling or wrangling about petty points; practising legal chicanery. [orig. uncert.]

pettish *a.* peevish, petulant, irritable. [PET²]

petty /'petɪ/ *a.* unimportant, trivial; small-minded; minor, inferior, on a small scale; **petty cash** money kept for small cash items of receipt or expenditure; **petty jury** see JURY; **petty officer** naval NCO; **petty sessions** meeting of two or more magistrates for summary trial of certain offences. [F *petit* small]

petulant /'petjʊlənt/ *a.* peevishly impatient or irritable; **petulance** *n.* [F f. L (*peto* seek)]

petunia /pɪ'tju:nɪə/ *n.* plant with funnel-shaped flowers of vivid purple, red, white, etc. [F *petun* tobacco]

pew *n.* long backed bench or enclosed compartment in church; *colloq.* seat (*take a pew*). [F f. L PODIUM]

pewit var. of PEEWIT.

pewter /'pju:tə/ *n.* grey alloy of tin with lead or other metal; articles made of this. [F *peutre*]

peyote /peɪ'əʊtɪ/ *n.* a Mexican cactus; the hallucinogenic drug prepared from it. [Amer. Sp., f. Nahuatl]

pfennig /'pfenɪg/ *n.* small German coin worth $\frac{1}{100}$ of a mark. [G]

PG *abbr.* paying guest.

pH /pi:'eɪtʃ/ *n.* measure of acidity or alkaline level of a solution. [G *potenz* power, H *symb.* hydrogen]

phagocyte /'fægəʊsaɪt/ *n.* leucocyte etc. capable of absorbing foreign matter (esp. bacteria) in the body. [Gk *phag-* eat, *kutos* cell]

phalanger /fə'lændʒə/ *n.* (in Australia and New Zealand) tree-dwelling marsupial with webbed hind feet. [F f. Gk *phalaggion* spider's web]

phalanx /'fælænks/ *n.* (*pl.* **phalanxes**) (in Greek antiquity) line of battle, esp. body of infantry drawn up in close order; set of persons etc. forming compact mass, or banded together for common purpose. [L f. Gk]

phallus /'fæləs/ *n.* (*pl.* **phalluses**) image of (usu. erect) penis as symbol of generative power; **phallic** *a.* [L f. Gk]

phantasm /'fæntæz(ə)m/ *n.* illusion, phantom; **phantasmal** /-'tæzm(ə)l/ *a.* [F f. L (PHANTOM)]

phantasmagoria /fæntæzmə'gɔ:rɪə/ *n.* shifting scene of real or imagined figures; **phantasmagoric** /-'gɒrɪk/ *a.* [prob. F *fantasmagorie* (prec.)]

phantasy var. of FANTASY.

phantom /'fæntəm/ **1** *n.* ghost, apparition, spectre; image (*of*); vain show, form without substance or reality, mental illusion. **2** *a.* merely apparent, illusory. [F f. L f. Gk *phantasma*]

Pharaoh /'feərəʊ/ *n.* title of ruler of ancient Egypt. [L f. Gk f. Heb. f. Egypt.]

Pharisee /'færɪsi:/ *n.* member of ancient-Jewish sect distinguished by strict observance of traditional and written law; self-righteous person, hypocrite; **Pharisaic** /-'seɪɪk/ *a.* [OE & F ult. f. Heb.]

pharmaceutical /fɑ:mə'sju:tɪk(ə)l/ *a.* of or engaged in pharmacy; of the use or sale of medicinal drugs. [L f. Gk (*pharmakon* drug)]

pharmaceutics *n.pl* (usu. treated as *sing.*) = PHARMACY (first sense).

pharmacist /'fɑ:məsɪst/ *n.* person engaged in pharmacy. [PHARMACY]

pharmacology /fɑ:mə'kɒlədʒɪ/ *n.* science of action of drugs on the body; **pharmacological** /-'lɒdʒɪk(ə)l/ *a.*; **pharmacologist** *n.* [Gk *pharmakon* drug]

pharmacopoeia /fɑ:məkə'pi:ə/ *n.* book (esp. one officially published) containing list of drugs with directions for use; stock of drugs. [Gk (*pharmakopoios* drug-maker)]

pharmacy /'fɑ:məsɪ/ *n.* preparation and (esp. medicinal) dispensing of drugs; pharmacist's shop, dispensary. [F f. med.L f. Gk (*pharmakon* drug)]

pharyngitis /færɪn'dʒaɪtɪs/ *n.* inflammation of the pharynx. [foll.]

pharynx /'færɪŋks/ *n.* cavity behind mouth and nose; **pharyngeal** /-ɪn'dʒi:əl/ *a.* [L f. Gk]

phase /feɪz/ **1** *n.* stage of change or development; aspect of moon or planet, according to amount of illumination; stage in periodically recurring sequence of changes, e.g. of alternating current or light-vibrations. **2** *v.t.* carry out (programme etc.) in phases or stages. **3** **phase in** (or **out**) bring gradually into (or out of) use. [F f. L f. Gk *phasis* appearance]

Ph.D. *abbr.* Doctor of Philosophy. [L *philosophiae doctor*]

pheasant /'fezənt/ *n.* long-tailed game-bird. [F *faisan* f. L f. Gk (*Phasis*, river)]
phenol /'fi:nɒl/ *n.* hydroxyl derivative of aromatic hydrocarbons. [F]
phenomenal /fɪ'nɒmɪnəl/ *a.* of the nature of a phenomenon; extraordinary, remarkable; **phenomenally** *adv.* [PHENOMENON]
phenomenon /fɪ'nɒmɪnən/ *n.* (*pl.* **phenomena**) fact or occurrence that appears or is perceived, esp. thing the cause of which is in question; remarkable person or thing. [L f. Gk (*phainō* show)]
phew /fju:/ *int.* expressing relief, weariness, surprise, etc. [imit.]
phi /faɪ/ *n.* twenty-first letter of Greek alphabet (Φ, φ). [Gk]
phial /'faɪəl/ *n.* small glass bottle, esp. for liquid medicine. [F *fiole* f. L f. Gk]
phil- see PHILO-.
philadelphus /fɪlə'delfəs/ *n.* a kind of shrub, esp. mock orange. [L f. Gk]
philander /fɪ'lændə/ *v.i.* (of a man) flirt (*with* woman). [Gk (*anēr andr-* man)]
philanthropy /fɪ'lænθrəpɪ/ *n.* concern for welfare of mankind, esp. as shown by acts of benevolence; **philanthropic** /-'θrɒpɪk/ *a.*; **philanthropist** *n.* [L f. Gk *anthrōpos* human being]
philately /fɪ'lætəlɪ/ *n.* collecting and study of postage-stamps; **philatelist** *n.* [F f. Gk *atelēs* tax-free]
-phile *suffix* (also **-phil**) forming nouns and adjectives in sense 'one who is fond of' (*bibliophile*). [Gk *philos* dear, loving]
philharmonic /fɪlɑ:'mɒnɪk/ *a.* (in names of orchestras and music societies) fond of music. [F f. It. (HARMONIC)]
philippic /fɪ'lɪpɪk/ *n.* bitter invective. [L f. Gk (*Philip* II of Macedon)]
Philistine /'fɪlɪstaɪn/ **1** *n.* member of ancient Palestinian people; (usu. **philistine**) one who is hostile or indifferent to culture, or whose interests are material or commonplace. **2** *a.* (usu. **philistine**) hostile or indifferent to culture, commonplace, prosaic. **3 philistinism** /-mɪz(ə)m/ *n.* [F or L f. Gk f. Heb.]
philo- *in comb.* (**phil-** before vowel or *h*) liking, fond of. [Gk (*philos* friend)]
philology /fɪ'lɒlədʒɪ/ *n.* science of language, esp. in historical and comparative aspects; **philological** /-'lɒdʒɪk(ə)l/ *a.*; **philologist** *n.* [F f. L f. Gk (LOGOS)]
philosopher /fɪ'lɒsəfə/ *n.* one engaged or learned in philosophy or a branch of it; one who lives by philosophy or acts philosophically; **philosophers' stone** object imagined by alchemists as means of turning other metals into gold or silver. [F f. L f. Gk (PHILOSOPHY)]
philosophical /fɪlə'sɒfɪk(ə)l/ *a.* (also **philosophic**) of or according to philosophy; skilled in or devoted to philosophy; wise, serene, calm in adverse circumstances; **philosophically** *adv.* [L (as prec.)]
philosophize /fɪ'lɒsəfaɪz/ *v.i.* reason like philosopher; speculate, theorize; moralize. [F (foll.)]
philosophy /fɪ'lɒsəfɪ/ *n.* use of reason and argument in search for truth and knowledge of reality, esp. of the causes and nature of things, and of the principles governing existence, perception, human behaviour, and the material universe; particular system or set of beliefs reached by this; system of conduct in life. [F f. L f. Gk (PHILO-, *sophia* wisdom)]
philtre /'fɪltə/, *US* **philter** *n.* drink supposed to be able to excite sexual love. [F f. L f. Gk (*phileō* love)]
phlebitis /flɪ'baɪtɪs/ *n.* inflammation of walls of vein; **phlebitic** /-'bɪtɪk/ *a.* [Gk *phleps phleb-* vein]
phlegm /flem/ *n.* thick viscous substance secreted by mucous membranes of respiratory passages, discharged by coughing; *archaic* this substance regarded as a humour; calmness, sluggishness. [F f. L f. Gk *phlegma*]
phlegmatic /fleg'mætɪk/ *a.* calm, not easily agitated; sluggish; **phlegmatically** *adv.*
phlogiston /flɒ'dʒɪst(ə)n/ *n.* substance formerly supposed to cause combustion. [L f. Gk (*phlox phlog-* flame)]
phlox /flɒks/ *n.* plant with clusters of reddish or purple or white flowers. [L f. Gk (prec.)]
-phobe *suffix* forming nouns and adjectives in sense '(person) disliking or fearing' (*Anglophobe*). [L f. Gk (*phobos* fear)]
phobia /'fəʊbɪə/ *n.* persistent abnormal fear or dislike of something. [foll.]
-phobia *suffix* forming abstract nouns corresponding to adjectives in *-phobe* (*xenophobia*); **-phobic** *a.* [L f. Gk]
phoenix /'fi:nɪks/ *n.* mythical bird, the only one of its kind, that burnt itself on pyre and rose from the ashes with renewed youth to live again; unique person or thing. [OE & F f. Gk]
phone *colloq.* **1** *n.* & *v.* telephone. **2 phone-in** broadcast programme in which listeners participate by telephoning the studio. [abbr.]
phoneme /'fəʊni:m/ *n.* unit of significant sound in a language; **phonemic** /-'ni:mɪk/ *a.* [F f. Gk (*phōneō* speak)]
phonetic /fə'netɪk/ *a.* of or representing vocal sounds; (of spelling) corresponding to pronunciation; **phonetically** *adv.* [Gk (as prec.)]

phonetician /fəʊnɪ'tɪʃ(ə)n/ *n.* expert in phonetics.
phonetics *n.pl.* (usu. treated as *sing.*) study or representation of vocal sounds.
phoney /'fəʊnɪ/ *sl.* **1** *a.* sham, counterfeit, fictitious. **2** *n.* phoney person or thing. [orig. unkn.]
phonic /'fəʊnɪk, 'fɒ-/ *a.* of sound; of vocal sound; **phonically** *adv.* [Gk *phōnē* voice]
phono- *in comb.* sound. [Gk *phōnē* voice, sound]
phonograph /'fəʊnəgrɑ:f/ *n.* early form of gramophone; *US* gramophone.
phonology /fə'nɒlədʒɪ/ *n.* study of sounds in a language; **phonological** /-'lɒdʒɪk(ə)l/ *a.*
phony var. of PHONEY.
phosphate /'fɒsfeɪt/ *n.* salt or ester of phosphoric acid, esp. used as fertilizer. [F (PHOSPHORUS)]
phosphor /'fɒsfə/ *n.* synthetic fluorescent or phosphorescent substance. [G, f. L PHOSPHORUS]
phosphoresce /fɒsfə'res/ *v.i.* show phosphorescence. [foll.]
phosphorescence *n.* radiation similar to fluorescence but detectable after excitation ceases; emission of light without combustion or perceptible heat; **phosphorescent** *a.* [PHOSPHORUS]
phosphoric /fɒs'fɒrɪk/ *a.* of or containing phosphorus. [PHOSPHORUS]
phosphorous /'fɒsfərəs/ *a.* = PHOSPHORIC.
phosphorus /'fɒsfərəs/ *n.* non-metallic element existing in allotropic forms, including a yellowish waxlike substance luminous in the dark. [L f. Gk (*phōs* light, *-phoros* bringing)]
photo /'fəʊtəʊ/ *n.* (*pl.* **photos**) photograph; **photo finish** close finish of race with winner determined by scrutiny of photograph; any close-run thing. [abbr.]
photo- *in comb.* light; photography. [Gk *phōs phōt-* light]
photocopier /'fəʊtəʊkɒpɪə/ *n.* machine for photocopying.
photocopy 1 *n.* photographic copy of document etc. **2** *v.t.* make photocopy of.
photoelectric /fəʊtəʊɪ'lektrɪk/ *a.* with or using emission of electrons from substances exposed to light; **photoelectric cell** device using this effect to generate current; **photoelectricity** /-'trisɪtɪ/ *n.*
photofit *n.* composite picture like Identikit but using photographs.
photogenic /fəʊtəʊ'dʒenɪk, -'dʒi:nɪk/ *a.* apt to be a good subject for photographs; producing or emitting light; **photogenically** *adv.*
photograph /'fəʊtəgrɑ:f/ **1** *n.* picture formed by chemical action of light or other radiation on sensitive film. **2** *v.t.* take photograph of (person etc., or *absol.*).
photographer /fə'tɒgrəfə/ *n.* one who takes photographs, esp. professionally.
photographic /fəʊtə'græfɪk/ *a.* of or produced by photography; (of memory) recalling in detail from single sight; **photographically** *adv.*
photography /fə'tɒgrəfɪ/ *n.* taking and processing of photographs.
photogravure /fəʊtəgrə'vjʊə/ *n.* picture produced from photographic negative transferred to metal plate and etched in. [F *gravure* engraving]
photolithography /fəʊtəʊlɪ'θɒgrəfɪ/ *n.* lithography with plates made by photography. [PHOTO-]
photometer /fəʊ'tɒmɪtə/ *n.* instrument for measuring light; **photometric** /fəʊtə'metrɪk/ *a.*; **photometry** *n.*
photon /'fəʊtɒn/ *n.* quantum of electromagnetic radiation energy, proportional to frequency. [after *electron*]
photosensitive /fəʊtəʊ'sensɪtɪv/ *a.* reacting chemically etc. to light.
Photostat /'fəʊtəʊstæt/ **1** *n.* **(P)** photocopy. **2** *v.t.* **(photostat)** **(-tt-)** make Photostat of.
photosynthesis /fəʊtəʊ'sɪnθəsɪs/ *n.* process in which energy of sunlight is used by green plants to form complex substances from carbon dioxide and water.
phrase /freɪz/ **1** *n.* group of words forming a conceptual unit but not a sentence, equivalent to a noun or adjective or adverb; an idiomatic or short pithy expression; mode of expression; *Mus.* group of notes forming distinct unit within longer melody. **2** *v.t.* express in words; divide (music) into phrases, esp. in performance. **3** **phrase-book** book for travellers, listing phrases and their foreign equivalents. **4** **phrasal** *a.* [L f. Gk *phrasis* (*phrazō* tell)]
phraseology /freɪzɪ'ɒlədʒɪ/ *n.* choice or arrangement of words, mode of expression; **phraseological** /-'lɒdʒɪk(ə)l/ *a.*
phrenetic var. of FRENETIC.
phrenology /frɪ'nɒlədʒɪ/ *n.* study of external form of cranium as supposed indication of person's character and mental faculties; **phrenological** /frenə'lɒdʒɪk(ə)l/ *a.*; **phrenologist** *n.* [F f. L f. Gk (*phrēn* mind)]
phthisis /'θaɪsɪs/ *n.* progressive wasting disease, now esp. pulmonary tuberculosis. [L f. Gk (*phthinō* decay *v.*)]
phut /fʌt/ *n.* dull sound of impact, collapse of inflated object, etc.; **go phut** *colloq.* collapse, break down. [Hindi *phaṭna* burst]

phylactery /fɪ'læktərɪ/ *n.* small leather box containing Hebrew texts, worn by Jews at prayer. [F f. L f. Gk (*phulassō* guard)]

phylum /'faɪləm/ *n.* (*pl.* **phyla**) major division of animal or plant kingdom. [L f. Gk *phulon* race]

physic /'fɪzɪk/ *n.* art of healing; medical profession; *archaic* medicine. [F f. L f. Gk (*phusis* nature)]

physical /'fɪzɪk(ə)l/ *a.* of matter, material; of the body (*physical fitness*); of, or according to the laws of, nature; of physics; **physical chemistry** application of physics to study of chemistry; **physical geography** that dealing with natural features; **physical jerks** *colloq.* physical exercises; **physical science** study of inanimate natural objects; **physically** *adv.* [L (prec.)]

physician /fɪ'zɪʃ(ə)n/ *n.* doctor, esp. specialist in medical diagnosis and treatment; *fig.* healer. [F (PHYSIC)]

physicist /'fɪzɪsɪst/ *n.* expert in physics. [foll.]

physics /'fɪzɪks/ *n.pl.* (usu. treated as *sing.*) science dealing with properties and interactions of matter and energy; (as *pl.*) these properties. [L *physica* (pl.) f. Gk (PHYSIC)]

physiognomy /fɪzɪ'ɒnəmɪ/ *n.* features or type of face; art of judging character from facial or bodily features; external features of country etc.; **physiognomist** *n.* [F f. L f. Gk (PHYSIC, GNOMON)]

physiography /fɪzɪ'ɒgrəfɪ/ *n.* description of nature or natural phenomena, or of a class of objects; physical geography; **physiographer** *n.* [F (PHYSIC, -GRAPHY)]

physiology /fɪzɪ'ɒlədʒɪ/ *n.* science of functions and phenomena of living organisms and their parts; these functions; **physiological** /-'lɒdʒɪk(ə)l/ *a.*; **physiologist** *n.* [F or L (PHYSIC, -LOGY)]

physiotherapy /fɪzɪəʊ'θerəpɪ/ *n.* treatment of disease or injury or deformity by massage, exercises, heat, etc., not by drugs; **physiotherapist** *n.* [PHYSIC, THERAPY]

physique /fɪ'zi:k/ *n.* bodily structure and development. [F (PHYSIC)]

pi /paɪ/ *n.* sixteenth letter of Greek alphabet (Π, π); (π) *Math.* symbol of ratio of circumference of circle to diameter (approx. 3.14). [Gk]

pia mater /paɪə 'meɪtə/ *n.* delicate inner membrane enveloping brain and spinal cord. [L, = tender mother]

pianissimo /pɪæ'nɪsɪməʊ/ *Mus.* **1** *adv.* very softly. **2** *n.* passage to be played very softly. [It., superl. of PIANO²]

pianist /'pɪənɪst/ *n.* player of piano. [foll.]

piano¹ /pɪ'ænəʊ/ *n.* (*pl.* **pianos**) musical instrument with metal strings struck by hammers worked by pressing keys of keyboard; **piano-accordion** accordion with melody played on small piano-like keyboard. [It., abbr. of PIANOFORTE]

piano² /pɪ'ɑ:nəʊ/ *Mus.* **1** *adv.* softly. **2** *n.* passage to be played softly. [It. f. L *planus* flat, (of sound) soft]

pianoforte /pɪænəʊ'fɔ:tɪ/ *n.* piano. [It., *piano e forte* soft and loud]

Pianola /pɪə'nəʊlə/ *n.* **(P)** a kind of automatic mechanical piano. [dimin.]

pibroch /'pi:brɒk/ *n.* martial or funerary bagpipe music. [Gael.]

pica /'paɪkə/ *n.* unit of type-size (⅙ inch); size of letters in typewriting (ten per inch). [L (PIE²)]

picador /'pɪkədɔ:/ *n.* mounted man with lance in bullfight. [Sp.]

picaresque /pɪkə'resk/ *a.* (of style of fiction) dealing with adventures of rogues. [F f. Sp. *pícaro* rogue]

picayune /pɪkə'ju:n/ *US* **1** *n.* small coin; *colloq.* insignificant person or thing. **2** *a.* *colloq.* mean, contemptible, petty. [F *picaillon*]

piccalilli /pɪkə'lɪlɪ/ *n.* pickle of chopped vegetables, mustard, and spices. [orig. unkn.]

piccaninny /pɪkə'nɪnɪ/ *n.* small Black or Australian Aboriginal child. [W. Ind. Negro f. Sp. *pequeño* little]

piccolo /'pɪkələʊ/ *n.* (*pl.* **piccolos**) small flute, sounding an octave higher than the ordinary. [It., = small]

pick **1** *v.* select, esp. carefully or thoughtfully; detach (flower, fruit, etc.) from place of growing; make hole in or break surface of with fingers or sharp instrument; make (hole) thus; open (lock) with pointed instrument, esp. to force entry; probe or dig at to remove unwanted matter; eat (food) desultorily or in small bits; clear (bone or carcass) of its flesh. **2** *n.* picking, selection; right to select (*you have first pick*); best or most wanted part; = PICKAXE; instrument for picking; plectrum. **3** **pick and choose** select fastidiously; **pick at** find fault with, eat desultorily; **pick person's brains** extract ideas or information from him for one's own use; **pick holes in** find fault with (idea); **pick-me-up** tonic (*lit.* or *fig.*) to restore health or revive spirits; **pick off** pluck off, select and shoot (target or succession of targets) with care; **pick on** find fault with, nag at, select; **pick out** take from large number, identify or recognize, distinguish from surrounding objects, play (tune) by ear on piano etc.; **pick over** look over item by item, choose best from; **pick person's pocket** steal its contents from him; **pick a quarrel**

provoke or seize opportunity for one; **pick to pieces** criticize harshly; **pick up** take hold of and lift, learn routinely, stop for and take with one, take (cargo etc.) on board, (of police) catch and take into custody, acquire by chance or casually, encounter and get to know (person), manage to receive (broadcast signal etc.), improve, recover health, (of engine) recover speed; **pick-up** *n.* picking up, person met casually, part of record-player carrying stylus, small open motor truck. [PIKE]

pick-a-back /ˈpɪkəbæk/ var. of PIGGY-BACK.

pickaninny *US* var. of PICCANINNY.

pickaxe /ˈpɪkæks/ *n.* heavy iron tool with point at end and wooden handle at right angles to it, for breaking up hard ground etc. [F, rel. to PIKE]

picket /ˈpɪkɪt/ **1** *n.* one or more persons stationed by strikers outside place of work to dissuade others from entering; small body of troops acting as patrol, party of sentries; pointed stake driven into ground. **2** *v.* place or act as picket outside (place of work); post as military picket; tether (animal); secure (place) with stakes. [F (*piquer* prick)]

pickings *n.pl.* casual profits or perquisites; gains from pilfering; remaining scraps, gleanings. [PICK]

pickle /ˈpɪk(ə)l/ **1** *n.* food (esp. vegetable) preserved in brine or vinegar or similar liquor; the liquor used; *colloq.* plight (*in a pickle*). **2** *v.t.* preserve in or treat with pickle; (in *p.p.*) *sl.* drunk. [LG or Du. *pekel*]

pickpocket *n.* one who steals from people's pockets. [PICK]

picky *a. colloq.* excessively fastidious.

picnic /ˈpɪknɪk/ **1** *n.* pleasure outing including informal outdoor meal; the meal itself; *colloq.* something readily or easily accomplished. **2** *v.i.* (**-ck-**) take part in picnic. [F *pique-nique*]

picot /ˈpiːkəʊ/ *n.* small loop of twisted thread in edging to lace etc. [F, dimin. of *pic* peak, point]

picric acid /ˈpɪkrɪk/ yellow bitter substance used in dyeing and in explosives. [Gk *pikros* bitter]

Pict *n.* one of an ancient people of northern Britain. [L]

pictograph /ˈpɪktəgrɑːf/ *n.* (also **pictogram**) pictorial symbol used as form of writing; pictorial representation of statistics; **pictographic** /-ˈgræfɪk/ *a.* [L *pingo pict-* paint *v.*]

pictorial /pɪkˈtɔːrɪəl/ **1** *a.* of or expressed in a picture or pictures; illustrated. **2** *n.* periodical with pictures as main feature. [L *pictor* painter (foll.)]

picture /ˈpɪktʃə/ **1** *n.* likeness or representation of subject produced by painting or drawing or photography; portrait; beautiful object or person; scene, total visual or mental impression produced; image on television screen; cinema film; (in *pl.*) cinema, performance at cinema. **2** *v.t.* imagine (*to oneself*); represent in picture; describe graphically. **3 in the picture** fully informed or noticed; **picture postcard** postcard with picture on one side; **picture window** large window facing attractive view. [L (*pingo pict-* paint)]

picturesque /pɪktʃəˈresk/ *a.* striking and pleasant to look at; (of language) graphic, expressive. [F f. It. *pittoresco*, assim. to prec.]

piddle /ˈpɪd(ə)l/ *v.i.* work or act in trifling way; *colloq.* urinate. [orig. uncert.]

piddling *a. colloq.* trifling, trivial.

pidgin /ˈpɪdʒɪn/ *n.* simplified language used between persons of different nationality etc.; **pidgin English** jargon chiefly of English words used orig. between Chinese and Europeans. [corrupt. of *business*]

pi-dog var. of PYE-DOG.

pie[1] /paɪ/ *n.* dish of meat or fish or fruit etc., enclosed in or covered with pastry and baked; similar object (*mud pie*); confused mass of printers' type; chaos; **easy as pie** very easy; **pie chart** diagram representing various quantities as sectors of a circle; **pie in the sky** delusive prospect of future happiness. [orig. uncert.]

pie[2] /paɪ/ *n.* magpie. [F f. L *pica*]

piebald /ˈpaɪbɔːld/ **1** *a.* (of horse etc.) of two colours, esp. black and white, irregularly arranged. **2** *n.* piebald animal. [PIE[2], BALD]

piece /piːs/ **1** *n.* one of the distinct portions of which thing is composed or into which it is divided or broken; detached portion (*of* something); single example or specimen, item (*piece of writing*; *piece of news*); distinct section or area *of* (land etc.); one of the things of which a set is composed (*three-piece suite*); definite quantity in which thing is made up for sale etc.; fixed unit of work; a (usu. short) literary or dramatic or musical composition; coin; man in board-games, esp. chess-man (esp. other than pawn); firearm, artillery weapon; *derog.* person, esp. woman. **2** *v.t.* form into a whole, join pieces of (*together*). **3 go to pieces** lose self-control, collapse; **in one piece** not broken, unharmed; **of a piece** uniform or consistent (*with*); **piece-goods** textile fabrics woven in standard lengths; **piece of eight** *hist.* Spanish dollar; **piece-work** work paid at rate per piece; **say one's piece** give one's opinion, make prepared statement; **take to pieces** separate parts of, be divisible thus. [AF, prob. f. Celt.]

pièce de résistance /pɪes də re'zɪstɑ̃s/ the most important or remarkable item; main dish at meal. [F]

piecemeal /'pi:smi:l/ **1** *adv.* piece by piece or part at a time. **2** *a.* done etc. piecemeal. [PIECE, MEAL²]

pied /paɪd/ *a.* particoloured; **Pied Piper** delusive enticer. [PIE²]

pied-à-terre /pjeɪdɑ:'teə/ *n.* (*pl.* ***pieds-à-terre*** *pr.* same) place kept available as temporary quarters when needed. [F, lit. 'foot to earth']

pie-dog var. of PYE-DOG.

pier *n.* structure running out into sea and serving as promenade or landing-stage or breakwater; support of arch or of span of bridge, pillar; solid masonry between windows etc.; **pier-glass** large mirror of kind orig. placed between windows. [L *pera*]

pierce /pɪəs/ *v.* (of sharp instrument) penetrate; prick with or like sharp instrument; make hole in; force one's way through or into; penetrate *through*, *into*, etc. [F *percer* f. L]

piercing *a.* (of pain or cold etc.) intense, penetrating sharply; (of look or sound) sharp or shrill, fierce.

pierrot /'pɪərəʊ/ *n.* French pantomime character; itinerant minstrel. [F]

pietà /pɪeɪ'tɑ:/ *n.* picture or sculpture of Virgin Mary holding dead body of Christ on her lap. [It., = PIETY]

pietism /'paɪətɪz(ə)m/ *n.* pious sentiment; exaggeration or affectation of this. [G (foll.)]

piety /'paɪətɪ/ *n.* quality of being pious; act etc. showing this. [F f. L (PIOUS)]

piffle /'pɪf(ə)l/ *sl.* **1** *n.* nonsense, empty talk. **2** *v.i.* talk or act feebly, trifle. [imit.]

piffling *a.* trivial, worthless.

pig **1** *n.* wild or domesticated animal with broad snout, stout bristly body, and short legs; pork; *colloq.* greedy, dirty, or unpleasant person; *sl. derog.* policeman; oblong mass of metal (esp. iron or lead) from smelting-furnace. **2** *v.* (**-gg-**) live or behave like a pig (esp. **pig it**). **3** **pig in a poke** thing acquired or offered without previous sight or knowledge of it; **pig-iron** crude iron from smelting-furnace; **pig-nut** = *earth-nut*. [OE]

pigeon /'pɪdʒ(ə)n/ *n.* bird of dove family; simpleton; **pigeon-toed** having toes turned inwards. [F f. L *pipio -on-*]

pigeon-hole **1** *n.* one of set of compartments in cabinet or on wall for papers, letters, etc. **2** *v.t.* put in pigeon-hole; put aside for future consideration; classify mentally.

piggery *n.* place where pigs are bred; pigsty. [PIG]

piggish *a.* like a pig, greedy or dirty.

piggy *n.* little pig; **piggy bank** money-box in form of hollow pig.

piggy-back **1** *n.* ride on shoulders and back of another. **2** *adv.* by means of piggy-back. [earlier *pick-a-back*: orig. unkn.]

pigheaded *a.* obstinate, stubborn. [PIG]

piglet /'pɪglɪt/ *n.* small young pig.

pigment /'pɪgmənt/ **1** *n.* colouring-matter used as paint or dye; natural colouring-matter of animal or plant tissue. **2** *v.t.* colour (as) with pigment. **3** **pigmentary** *a.* [L *pingo* paint]

pigmentation /pɪgmən'teɪʃ(ə)n/ *n.* colouring, esp. excessive, of tissue by deposition of pigment.

pigmy var. of PYGMY.

pigskin *n.* pig's skin; leather made from this. [PIG]

pigsty *n.* = STY¹.

pigswill *n.* (also **pigwash**) swill of kitchen or brewery fed to pigs.

pigtail *n.* plait of hair hanging from back of head.

pike *n.* large voracious freshwater fish with long narrow snout (*pl.* same); peaked top of hill; *hist.* long wooden shaft with pointed metal head. [OE]

pikestaff *n.* wooden shaft of pike; **plain as a pikestaff** quite plain or obvious.

pilaff /'pɪlæf/ *n.* oriental dish of rice or wheat with meat, spices, etc. [Turk.]

pilaster /pɪ'læstə/ *n.* rectangular column, esp. one fastened into wall. [F f. It. f. L (PILE¹)]

pilau /pɪ'laʊ/ *var. of* PILAFF.

pilchard /'pɪltʃəd/ *n.* small sea-fish related to herring. [orig. unkn.]

pile¹ **1** *n.* heap of things lying one upon another; *colloq.* large quantity, esp. of money; grand or lofty building; (in full **funeral pile**) heap of wood etc. on which corpse is burnt; series of plates of dissimilar metals laid alternately to produce electric current; (in full **atomic pile**) nuclear reactor. **2** *v.* heap (things *on*, *up*, etc.); load (surface *with* things); rush confusedly in crowd *in*, *into*, or *on* vehicle, *out of* place etc. **3** **pile it on** *colloq.* exaggerate; **pile up** accumulate, cause (vehicle or aircraft) to crash; **pile-up** *n.* collision of several motor vehicles. [F f. L *pila*]

pile² *n.* pointed stake or post; heavy beam driven vertically into ground as support for bridge etc.; **pile-driver** machine for driving piles. [OE f. L *pilum* javelin]

pile³ *n.* soft surface of fabric with tangible depth formed by cut or uncut loops. [AF f. L *pilus* hair]

pile[4] *n.* (usu. in *pl.*) haemorrhoid. [L *pila* ball]

pilfer *v.* steal, esp. in small quantities. [F *pelfre*, rel. to PELF]

pilgrim /ˈpɪlgrɪm/ *n.* one who journeys to sacred place as act of religious devotion; traveller; **Pilgrim Fathers** English Puritans who founded colony in Massachusetts in 1620. [Prov. f. L (PEREGRINE)]

pilgrimage *n.* pilgrim's journey.

pill *n.* small ball or flat piece of medicinal substance for swallowing whole; something unpleasant that has to be done or endured; **the pill** *colloq.* contraceptive pill. [LG or Du. f. L (PILULE)]

pillage /ˈpɪlɪdʒ/ **1** *n.* plundering, esp. in war. **2** *v.* sack, plunder. [F (*piller* plunder)]

pillar /ˈpɪlə/ *n.* slender vertical structure of stone etc. used as support or ornament; upright mass of air, water, rock, etc.; person who is a main supporter (*pillar of the faith*); **from pillar to post** rapidly from one place or situation to another; **pillar-box** hollow pillar in which letters may be posted; **pillar-box red** bright red. [AF *piler* f. Rmc (L *pila* PILE[1])]

pillbox *n.* shallow cylindrical box for holding pills; small concrete shelter, mainly underground. [PILL]

pillion /ˈpɪljən/ *n.* seat for passenger behind motor-cyclist etc.; **ride pillion** ride on this as passenger. [Gael. *pillean* small cushion f. L *pellis* skin]

pillory /ˈpɪlərɪ/ **1** *n. hist.* wooden framework with holes for head and hands of offender exposed to public ridicule etc. **2** *v.t.* put in pillory; *fig.* expose to ridicule. [F]

pillow /ˈpɪləʊ/ **1** *n.* cushion used as support for head, esp. in bed; pillow-shaped block or support. **2** *v.t.* rest, or prop up, on pillow. [OE f. L *pulvinus* cushion]

pillowcase *n.* (also **pillowslip**) washable cover of linen etc. for pillow.

pillule var. of PILULE.

pilot /ˈpaɪlət/ **1** *n.* person who operates controls of aircraft; person qualified to take charge of ships entering or leaving a harbour; guide. **2** *v.t.* act as pilot of, guide. **3** *a.* experimental, or small-scale (*pilot scheme*). **4 pilot-light** small gas-burner kept alight and lighting larger burner when this is turned on, electric indicator light or control light; **pilot officer** lowest commissioned rank in RAF. [F f. L f. Gk]

pilule /ˈpɪljuːl/ *n.* small pill. [F f. L (*pila* ball)]

pimento /pɪˈmentəʊ/ *n.* (*pl.* **pimentos**) W. Indian tree, ground berry of which produces allspice; this spice; sweet pepper. [Sp. f. L (PIGMENT)]

pimp 1 *n.* one who solicits clients for prostitute or brothel. **2** *v.i.* act as pimp. [orig. unkn.]

pimpernel /ˈpɪmpənel/ *n.* small, esp. scarlet, annual plant with flowers closing in cloudy or rainy weather. [F f. Rmc (L *piper* PEPPER)]

pimple /ˈpɪmp(ə)l/ *n.* small hard inflamed spot on skin; similar slight swelling on surface; **pimply** *a.* [OE]

pin 1 *n.* thin usu. cylindrical piece of metal with sharp point and round flattened head for fastening together papers, fabrics, etc.; larger similar object of wood or metal for various purposes; thing of small value; (in golf) stick with flag on it marking position of hole; (in *pl.*) *colloq.* legs. **2** *v.t.* (**-nn-**) fasten with pin(s); fix responsibility for (deed *on* person); seize and hold fast (*against* wall etc.); transfix with pin, lance, etc. **3 pin-ball** game in which small metal balls are shot across sloping board and strike against pins; **pin down** make (person) declare intentions etc. clearly, restrict actions of (enemy etc.), specify (thing) precisely; **pin one's faith** (or **hopes**) **on** rely absolutely on; **pin-head** small or trifling thing, *colloq.* stupid person; **pin-hole** hole made by pin or into which peg fits; **pin-money** small sum of money, orig. that allowed to or earned by woman; **pins and needles** tingling sensation in limb recovering from numbness; **pin-stripe** very narrow stripe in cloth; **pin-table** table used in pin-ball; **pin-tuck** very narrow ornamental tuck; **pin-up** picture of attractive or famous person, pinned up on wall etc., such person; **pin-wheel** small Catherine wheel. [OE f. L *pinna* wing, feather]

pinafore /ˈpɪnəfɔː/ *n.* full-length apron; **pinafore dress** dress without collar and sleeves, worn over blouse or jumper. [PIN, AFORE]

pince-nez /ˈpæsneɪ/ *n.* (*pl.* same) pair of eyeglasses with spring that clips on nose. [F, = pinch-nose]

pincers /ˈpɪnsəz/ *n.pl.* (also **pair of pincers**) gripping-tool of two pivoted limbs forming jaws; similar organ of crustaceans etc.; **pincer movement** converging movement against enemy position. [foll.]

pinch 1 *v.* squeeze tightly between two surfaces, esp. between finger and thumb; (of cold, hunger, etc.) affect painfully, cause to shrivel; stint, be niggardly; *sl.* steal (thing); *sl.* arrest. **2** *n.* pinching, squeezing; stress of circumstances (*feel the pinch*); as much as can be taken up with tips of finger and thumb (*pinch of salt*). **3 at a pinch** in an emergency, if necessary; **pinch off** (or **out** etc.) remove by pinching. [F *pincer*]

pinchbeck 1 *n.* goldlike alloy of copper and zinc used in cheap jewellery etc. **2** *a.* counterfeit, sham. [*Pinchbeck*, watchmaker]

pincushion *n.* small cushion or pad for sticking pins into ready for use. [PIN]

pine[1] *n.* evergreen coniferous tree with needle-shaped leaves growing in clusters; its wood; **pine-cone** fruit of pine. [OE f. L *pinus*]

pine[2] *v.i.* languish, waste *away* from grief, disease, etc.; long eagerly. [OE]

pineal /'pɪnɪəl/ *a.* shaped like pine-cone; **pineal body** (or **gland**) conical gland in brain, of unknown function. [F f. L (PINE[1])]

pineapple /'paɪnæp(ə)l/ *n.* large juicy tropical fruit with yellow flesh and tough segmented skin; plant bearing this. [PINE[1], APPLE]

ping 1 *n.* abrupt single ringing sound. **2** *v.* (cause to) make this sound. [imit.]

ping-pong *n.* table tennis. [imit.]

pinion[1] /'pɪnjən/ *n.* small cog-wheel engaging with larger one; cogged spindle engaging with wheel. [F f. L *pinea* pinecone (PINE[1])]

pinion[2] /'pɪnjən/ **1** *n.* outer segment of bird's wing; *poetic* wing; flight-feather. **2** *v.t.* cut off pinion of (bird or its wing) to prevent flight; bind arms of (person), bind (arms); bind (person etc.) fast *to* (thing). [F f. L *pinna* PIN]

pink[1] **1** *n.* pale red colour; pink clothes or material (*dressed in pink*); garden plant with fragrant flowers; *the* peak or perfect condition (*the pink of health*). **2** *a.* of pale red colour; *sl.* mildly communist. **3 in the pink** *sl.* in very good health; **pink gin** gin flavoured with angostura bitters. [orig. unkn.]

pink[2] *v.t.* pierce slightly; cut scalloped or zigzag edge on; **pinking shears** dressmaker's serrated scissors for cutting zigzag edge. [perh. LG or Du.]

pink[3] *v.i.* (of vehicle engine) emit high-pitched explosive sounds when running faultily. [imit.]

pinnace /'pɪnɪs/ *n.* warship's or other ship's small boat. [F]

pinnacle /'pɪnək(ə)l/ *n.* small ornamental turret crowning buttress, roof, etc.; natural peak; *fig.* culmination, climax. [F f. L (*pinna* PIN)]

pinnate /'pɪnɪt/ *a.* (of compound leaf) with leaflets on each side of leaf-stalk. [L *pinnatus* feathered (as prec.)]

pinny /'pɪnɪ/ *n. colloq.* pinafore. [abbr.]

pin-point 1 *n.* point of pin; *fig.* something very small or sharp. **2** *v.t.* locate or designate with high precision. **3** *a.* (of target) small and requiring very accurate aim. [PIN]

pinprick *n.* trifling irritation.

pint /paɪnt/ *n.* measure of capacity of liquids etc., $\frac{1}{8}$ gal.; this quantity of liquid, esp. milk or beer; **pint-sized** *colloq.* small. [F]

pinta /'paɪntə/ *n. colloq.* pint of milk etc. [corrupt. of *pint of*]

pintail *n.* duck or grouse with pointed tail. [PIN]

pintle /'pɪnt(ə)l/ *n.* bolt or pin, esp. one on which some other part turns. [OE]

pioneer /paɪə'nɪə/ **1** *n.* original explorer or settler or investigator of subject etc.; initiator of enterprise. **2** *v.* be a pioneer; originate (course of action etc. followed later by others). [F *pionnier* (PAWN[1])]

pious /'paɪəs/ *a.* devout, religious; hypocritically virtuous; dutiful. [L]

pip[1] *n.* seed of apple, orange, grape, etc. [abbr. of PIPPIN]

pip[2] *n.* each spot on playing-cards, dice, or dominoes; star (up to three according to rank) on shoulder of army officer's uniform. [orig. unkn.]

pip[3] *v.t.* (**-pp-**) *colloq.* hit with shot; forestall, defeat narrowly or at last moment (also **pip at the post**). [orig. unkn.]

pip[4] *n.* short high-pitched sound, esp. produced electronically e.g. as time-signal. [imit.]

pip[5] *n.* disease of poultry, hawks, etc.; *sl.* fit of disgust, depression, or bad temper (*he gives me the pip*). [LG or Du.]

pipe 1 *n.* tube of wood, metal, etc., esp. for conveying water, gas, etc.; narrow tube with bowl at one end containing tobacco for smoking, quantity of tobacco held by this; wind-instrument of single tube, each tube by which sound is produced in organ; (in *pl.*) = BAGPIPES; tubular organ, vessel, etc., in animal body; boatswain's whistle, sounding of this; cask for wine, esp. as measure (usu. = 105 gal.). **2** *v.* convey (oil, water, gas, etc.) by pipes; transmit (recorded music etc.) by wire or cable for hearing elsewhere; play (tune etc., or *absol.*) on pipe(s); utter in shrill voice; lead or bring (person etc.) by sound of pipe; summon by sounding whistle; decorate or trim with piping; furnish with pipes. **3 pipe-cleaner** piece of flexible tuft-covered wire to clean inside a tobacco-pipe; **pipe down** *colloq.* be quiet or less insistent; **pipe-dream** unattainable or fanciful hope or scheme, as indulged in when smoking (orig. opium) pipe; **pipe up** begin to sing, play tune, etc. [OE f. Rmc (L *pipo* chirp)]

pipeclay *n.* fine white clay for tobacco-pipes or for whitening leather etc.

pipeline *n.* series of pipes conveying oil etc. to a distance; channel of supply of goods, information, etc.; **in the pipeline** being considered, prepared, etc.

pip emma /pɪp 'emə/ *colloq.* = P.M. [formerly signallers' names for letters *P.M.*]

piper *n.* one who plays on pipe, esp. bagpipes. [PIPE]

pipette /pɪ'pet/ *n.* slender tube for transferring or measuring small quantities of liquids. [F dimin. (PIPE)]

piping **1** *n.* length of pipe, system of pipes; pipelike fold enclosing cord, as decoration for edges or seams of upholstery etc.; ornamental cordlike lines of icing on cake. **2** *a.* in **piping hot** (of food or water) very hot. [PIPE]

pipit /'pɪpɪt/ *n.* small bird resembling lark. [imit.]

pippin /'pɪpɪn/ *n.* apple grown from seed. [F]

pip-squeak *n. sl.* insignificant or contemptible person or thing. [imit.]

piquant /'pi:kənt/ *a.* agreeably pungent, sharp, appetizing; pleasantly exciting to the mind; **piquancy** *n.* [F (*piquer* prick)]

pique /pi:k/ **1** *v.t.* wound the pride of, irritate; arouse (curiosity or interest). **2** *n.* ill-feeling, resentment, hurt pride. [F (as prec.)]

piquet /pɪ'ket/ *n.* card-game for two players with pack of 32 cards. [F]

piracy /'paɪərəsɪ/ *n.* activity of a pirate; infringement of copyright etc. [PIRATE]

piranha /pɪ'rɑ:nə, -njə/ *n.* voracious S. American freshwater fish. [Port.]

pirate /'paɪərət/ **1** *n.* seafaring robber attacking other ships etc.; ship used by pirate; one who infringes another's copyright or business rights or who broadcasts without authorization (*pirate radio station*). **2** *v.t.* plunder; reproduce (book etc.) or trade (goods) without due authorization. **3 piratical** /paɪ'rætɪk(ə)l/ *a.* [L *pirata* f. Gk]

pirouette /pɪru:'et/ **1** *n.* ballet-dancer's spin on one foot or point of toe. **2** *v.i.* perform pirouette. [F, = spinning-top]

piscatorial /pɪskə'tɔ:rɪəl/ *a.* of fishermen or fishing. [L (*piscator* angler f. *piscis* fish)]

Pisces /'paɪsi:z/ *n.* constellation and twelfth sign of zodiac. [L, *pl.* of *piscis* fish]

pisciculture /'pɪsɪkʌltʃə/ *n.* artificial rearing of fish. [L *piscis* fish]

piscina /pɪ'si:nə/ *n.* perforated stone basin near altar in church for carrying away water used in rinsing chalice etc.; fish-pond. [L (prec.)]

piss *vulgar* **1** *v.* urinate; discharge with urine; (in *p.p.*) drunk. **2** *n.* urination; urine. **3 piss off** *sl.* go away; annoy, depress. [F, imit.]

pistachio /pɪ'stæʃɪəʊ/ *n.* (*pl.* **pistachios**) nut with greenish edible kernel; tree yielding this. [Sp. & It. ult. f. Pers.]

piste /pi:st/ *n.* ski-track of compacted snow. [F, = racetrack]

pistil /'pɪstɪl/ *n.* female organ of flower, comprising ovary, style, and stigma; **pistillate** *a.* [F or L (PESTLE)]

pistol /'pɪst(ə)l/ **1** *n.* small gun. **2** *v.t.* (**-ll-**, *US* **-l-**) shoot with pistol. **3 pistol-grip** handle shaped like butt of pistol; **pistol-whip** beat with pistol. [F f. G f. Czech]

piston /'pɪst(ə)n/ *n.* sliding cylinder fitting closely in tube and moving up and down in it, used in steam and internal-combustion engine to impart motion, or in pump to receive motion; sliding valve in trumpet etc.; **piston-rod** rod by which piston imparts motion. [F, f. It. (PESTLE)]

pit **1** *n.* large hole in ground, esp. one made in digging for mineral etc. or for industrial purposes; coal-mine; covered hole as trap for animals; hollow on a surface; part of auditorium of theatre on floor of house, sunken part before stage, accommodating orchestra; sunken area in workshop floor for access to underside of motor vehicles; area to side of track where racing cars are refuelled etc. during race. **2** *v.t.* (**-tt-**) match or set in competition *against*; (esp. in *p.p.*) make pits or scars in; put into pit. **3 pit-head** top of coal-mine shaft, area surrounding this; **pit of the stomach** depression below breastbone. [OE f. L *puteus* well]

pita /'pi:tə/ *n.* a flat bread eaten esp. in Greece and the Middle East. [mod. Gk]

pit-a-pat /'pɪtəpæt/ **1** *n.* sound as of quick light steps or quick tapping. **2** *adv.* with this sound. [imit.]

pitch[1] **1** *v.* erect and fix (tent or camp), fix in definite position; throw or fling; cause (bowled ball in cricket) to strike ground at particular point, (of ball) strike ground thus; express in particular style or at particular level; fall heavily; (of ship etc.) plunge alternately backwards and forwards in lengthwise direction; *Mus.* set at particular pitch; *sl.* tell (tale, yarn). **2** *n.* act or process of pitching; area marked out for play in outdoor games, (in cricket) area between or near wickets; *Mus.* quality of sound governed by rate of vibration of string etc., degree of highness or lowness of tone; place at which street vendor etc. is stationed; approach taken in advertising or sales-talk; degree or intensity (*of* quality etc.); distance between successive ridges of screw, teeth of cog, etc.; degree of slope. 3 **absolute pitch** ability to recognize or reproduce the pitch of a note (also **perfect pitch**), fixed standard of pitch; **pitched battle** battle fought between armies in prepared positions and formations, *fig.* fierce argument; **pitched roof** one that is not flat; **pitch in** *colloq.* set to work vigorously; **pitch into** *colloq.* attack forcefully. [orig. uncert.]

pitch[2] 1 *n.* dark resinous substance from distillation of tar or turpentine, used for caulking seams of ships etc. 2 *v.t.* coat with pitch. 3 **pitch-black** (or **-dark**) black with no light at all; **pitch-pine** pine-tree yielding much resin. 4 **pitchy** *a.* [OE f. L *pix pic-*]

pitchblende /'pɪtʃblend/ *n.* uranium oxide found in pitchlike masses and yielding radium. [G (prec.)]

pitcher[1] *n.* large jug with handle or two ears and usu. a lip, for holding liquids; **pitcher-plant** plant with pitcher-shaped leaves. [F, rel. to BEAKER]

pitcher[2] *n.* player who delivers ball in baseball. [PITCH[1]]

pitchfork 1 *n.* long-handled fork with two prongs, used for pitching hay. 2 *v.t.* throw (as) with pitchfork; thrust (person) forcibly (*into* position, office, etc.).

piteous /'pɪtɪəs/ *a.* deserving or arousing pity. [F f. Rmc (PITY)]

pitfall *n.* unsuspected danger or difficulty; covered hole as trap for animals. [PIT]

pith *n.* spongy tissue in plant stems and branches or lining rind of orange etc.; *fig.* essential part; physical strength, vigour; **pith helmet** helmet made from dried pith of sola etc. [OE]

pithy *a.* terse, condensed and forcible; of or like pith.

pitiable /'pɪtɪəb(ə)l/ *a.* deserving or arousing pity or contempt; **pitiably** *adv.* [F (PITY)]

pitiful /'pɪtɪfʊl/ *a.* (of thing) causing pity; contemptible; **pitifully** *adv.* [PITY]

pitiless /'pɪtɪlɪs/ *a.* showing no pity.

piton /'pi:tɒn/ *n.* peg driven in rock or crack to support climber or rope. [F]

pittance /'pɪtəns/ *n.* very small allowance or remuneration. [F f. Rmc (PITY)]

pitter-patter /'pɪtəpætə/ *n.* & *adv.* = PIT-A-PAT. [imit.]

pituitary /pɪ'tju:ɪtərɪ/ 1 *a.* in **pituitary gland** small ductless gland at base of brain. 2 *n.* pituitary gland. [L (*pituita* phlegm)]

pity /'pɪtɪ/ 1 *n.* feeling of sorrow for another's suffering; cause for regret (*what a pity!*). 2 *v.t.* feel pity (often with contempt) for. 3 **take pity on** feel or act compassionately towards. [F f. L (PIETY)]

pivot /'pɪvət/ 1 *n.* short pin or shaft on which something turns or oscillates; cardinal or crucial person or point. 2 *v.* turn (as) on pivot; provide with pivot; hinge *on.* 3 **pivotal** *a.* [F]

pixie /'pɪksɪ/ *n.* (*also* **pixy**) supernatural being akin to fairy; **pixie hood** hood with pointed crown. [orig. unkn.]

pizza /'pi:tsə/ *n.* Italian dish of layer of dough baked with savoury topping. [It., = pie]

pizzicato /pɪtsɪ'kɑ:təʊ/ *Mus.* 1 *adv.* with string of violin etc. plucked instead of played with bow. 2 *n.* (*pl.* **pizzicatos**) note or passage to be played in this way. [It.]

pl. *abbr.* place; plate; plural.

placable /'plækəb(ə)l/ *a.* easily appeased, mild, forgiving; **placability** /-'bɪlɪtɪ/ *n.* [F or L (*placo* appease)]

placard /'plækɑ:d/ 1 *n.* large notice for public display. 2 *v.t.* put placards on (wall etc.); advertise by placards; display as placard. [F f. Du. *placken* glue *v.*]

placate /plə'keɪt/ *v.t.* conciliate, pacify; **placatory** *a.* [L *placo* appease]

place 1 *n.* particular part of space, part of space occupied by person or thing; city, town, village, etc.; residence, dwelling; (esp. in names) small group of houses round square etc., country-house with surroundings; building or area devoted to specified purpose (*place of amusement*); particular spot on surface etc. (*a sore place on his arm*); particular passage in book etc., point reached in reading (*have lost my place*); rank or station; space or seat etc. reserved for or taken by person in vehicle, at table, etc.; office or employment, duties or entitlements proper to this (*not my place to inquire into that*); proper or natural or suitable position; step in progression of argument, statement, etc. (*in the first place*); position of figure in series as indicating its value esp. in decimal notation; (in racing) position among placed competitors, esp. other than winner. 2 *v.t.* put in particular or proper place or state or order; identify by association with circumstances etc., assign to a class; put or give (*place an order*; *place trust in*); find employment or living etc. for; state position of (usu. any of first three horses or runners) in race. 3 **be placed** be among first three in race; **give place to** make room for, yield precedence to, be succeeded by; **go places** *colloq.* be successful; **in place** in right place, suitable; **in place of** in exchange for, instead of; **in places** at some places but not others; **out of place** in wrong place, unsuitable; **place-kick** kick in football with ball placed on ground; **place-mat** table-mat for person's place at table; **place-setting** set of cutlery or dishes for one person at table; **put person in his place** expose his presumption; **take place** occur; **take the place of** be substituted for. **4 placement** *n.* [F f. L *platea* broad way f. Gk]

placebo /plə'si:bəʊ/ *n.* (*pl.* **placebos**) medicine intended to cure by reassuring patient rather than by physiological effect; dummy pill etc. used in controlled trial. [L, = I shall be acceptable]

placenta /plə'sentə/ *n.* (*pl.* **placentae** /-ɪ/ or **placentas**) organ that develops in uterus of pregnant mammal and serves to nourish foetus; **placental** *a.* [L f. Gk, = flat cake]

placer /'pleɪsə, 'plæ-/ *n.* deposit of sand or gravel etc. containing valuable minerals in particles. [Amer. Sp.]

placid /'plæsɪd/ *a.* calm, peaceful; not easily disturbed; **placidity** /plə'sɪdɪtɪ/ *n.* [F or L (*placeo* please)]

placket /'plækɪt/ *n.* opening or slit in woman's skirt, for fastenings or access to pocket. [var. of PLACARD]

plagiarize /'pleɪdʒəraɪz/ *v.t.* take and use (another's thoughts or writings etc., or *absol.*) as one's own; **plagiarism** *n.*; **plagiarist** *n.* [L *plagiarius* kidnapper]

plague /pleɪg/ **1** *n.* deadly contagious disease; infestation *of* a pest; great trouble or affliction; *colloq.* nuisance. **2** *v.t.* affect with plague; *colloq.* bother or annoy. [L *plaga* stroke, infection]

plaice *n.* (*pl.* same) a kind of edible flatfish. [F f. L *platessa*]

plaid /plæd/ **1** *n.* long piece of twilled woollen cloth, usu. with chequered or tartan pattern, outer article of Highland costume; cloth used for this. **2** *a.* made of plaid; having plaidlike pattern. [Gael.]

plain **1** *a.* clear and unmistakable, easily perceived or understood; outspoken, straightforward; not intricate or ornate or decorated; undistinguished in appearance, not beautiful or good-looking; (of food) not rich or highly seasoned; not luxurious (*plain living*); unsophisticated (*a plain man*). **2** *n.* level tract of country; ordinary stitch in knitting. **3** *adv.* clearly, simply. **4** **plain chocolate** chocolate made without milk; **plain clothes** civilian clothes as distinct from uniform or official dress; **plain dealing** candour, straightforwardness; **plain flour** flour that does not contain raising agent; **plain sailing** simple situation or course of action; **plain-spoken** frank. **5** **plainness** *n.* [F f. L *planus*]

plainchant *n.* = PLAINSONG.

plainsong *n.* traditional church music in free rhythm depending on accentuation of words, and sung in unison.

plaint *n. Law* accusation, charge; *poetic* lamentation, complaint. [F *plaint(e)* f. L *plango* lament]

plaintiff /'pleɪntɪf/ *n.* party who brings suit into lawcourt. [F *plaintif* (foll.)]

plaintive /'pleɪntɪv/ *a.* mournful-sounding. [F (PLAINT)]

plait /plæt/ **1** *n.* interlacing of three or more strands of hair or ribbon or straw etc.; material thus interlaced. **2** *v.t.* form into plait. [F *pleit* f. L *plico* fold]

plan **1** *n.* method or procedure, esp. conceived beforehand, by which thing is to be done; large-scale detailed map of town or district; drawing etc. made by projection on horizontal surface of parts of building or structure; scheme of arrangement. **2** *v.* (**-nn-**) arrange or work out details of (procedure, enterprise, etc.) beforehand; make plans; make plan of or design for; (in *p.p.*) done in accordance with plan. **3** **plan on** *colloq.* aim at or envisage *doing*. [F]

planchette /plæn'ʃet/ *n.* small board on two castors, with pencil, said to trace letters etc. without conscious direction when person's fingers rest lightly on board. [F dimin. (PLANK)]

plane¹ **1** *n.* surface such that a straight line joining any two points in it lies wholly in it; level surface; level of attainment or knowledge etc.; = AEROPLANE; main aerofoil. **2** *a.* level as, or lying in, a plane. [L *planus* PLAIN]

plane² **1** *n.* tool for smoothing surface of wood by paring shavings from it. **2** *v.t.* make smooth with plane; pare *away* or *down* with plane. [F f. L (as prec.)]

plane³ *n.* a tall spreading broad-leaved tree. [F f. L *platanus* f. Gk]

planet /'plænɪt/ *n.* any of heavenly bodies in orbit round sun; **planetary** *a.* [F f. L f. Gk, = wanderer]

planetarium /plænɪ'teərɪəm/ *n.* (*pl.* **planetariums**) device for projecting image of night sky as seen at various times and places; building containing this.

plangent /'plændʒənt/ *a.* loud and reverberating; plaintive. [L (PLAINT)]

plank **1** *n.* long flat piece of timber; item of political or other programme. **2** *v.t.* furnish or cover with planks; *colloq.* put *down* roughly or violently, esp. pay (money, or *absol.*) *down* on the spot. **3** **walk the plank** *hist.* be made to walk blindfold into sea along plank laid over side of ship. [F f. L *planca*]

planking *n.* planks collectively; structure or surface of planks.

plankton /'plæŋkt(ə)n/ *n.* forms of organic life (chiefly microscopic) that drift or float in sea or fresh water. [G f. Gk, = wandering]

planning *n.* making plans, esp. with reference to controlled design of buildings and development of land. [PLAN]

plant /plɑ:nt/ **1** *n.* organism generally containing chlorophyll enabling it to live wholly on inorganic substances, and lacking power of voluntary movement; small organism of this kind as distinguished from tree or shrub; machinery and implements etc. used in industrial processes; factory and its equipment; *sl.* thing deliberately placed for discovery by others, hoax or trap. **2** *v.t.* place in ground or soil for growing; put plants or seeds into (ground); put or fix firmly in position (*in* or *on* ground etc.); station (person), esp. as spy; cause (idea etc.) to be established *in* the mind; deliver (blow or thrust) with deliberate aim; *sl.* conceal, esp. with view to misleading a later discoverer; settle or establish (colony, community, etc.). **3 plant oneself** take up position. [F f. L *planta*]

plantain[1] /'plæntɪn/ *n.* herb with broad flat leaves spread close to ground and seeds used for food for cage-birds. [F f. L *plantago*]

plantain[2] /'plæntɪn/ *n.* tropical banana-like fruit; treelike plant bearing this. [Sp.]

plantation /plɑ:n'teɪʃ(ə)n, plæn-/ *n.* extensive collection or area of cultivated trees or plants; estate for cultivation of cotton, tobacco, etc.; *hist.* colony. [F or L (PLANT)]

planter *n.* owner or manager of plantation; container for house plants. [PLANT]

plaque /plɑ:k, plæk/ *n.* flat tablet or plate of metal or porcelain etc. fixed on wall as ornament or memorial; film on teeth where bacteria proliferate. [F f. Du. *plak* tablet (PLACARD)]

plasma /'plæzmə/ *n.* colourless coagulable part of blood, lymph, or milk, in which corpuscles or fat-globules float; protoplasm; gas of positive ions and free electrons in about equal numbers. [L f. Gk (*plassō* shape *v.*)]

plaster /'plɑ:stə/ **1** *n.* soft mixture of lime, sand, and water, for spreading on walls etc. to form smooth surface and harden by drying; medicinal or protective substance spread on fabric and applied to the body; = *sticking-plaster* (see STICK[2]); = *plaster of Paris*. **2** *v.t.* cover (wall etc.) with plaster or similar substance; coat or daub, cover thickly; stick or fix (thing) like plaster on surface; make smooth with fixative etc.; *sl.* bomb or shell heavily; (in *p.p.*) *sl.* drunk. **3 plaster of Paris** fine white plaster of gypsum for making moulds or casts. [OE & F f. L f. Gk *emplastron*]

plasterboard *n.* board with core of plaster used for partitions, walls, etc.

plastic /'plæstɪk/ **1** *n.* synthetic resinous substance that can be given any permanent shape. **2** *a.* made of plastic (*plastic bag*); capable of being moulded; pliant, supple; giving form to clay or wax etc. **3 plastic arts** arts concerned with modelling or with representation of solid objects; **plastic bomb** one containing putty-like explosive; **plastic surgeon** specialist in plastic surgery; **plastic surgery** repair or replacement of damaged skin, muscle, etc., esp. by transfer of tissue. **4 plasticity** /plæ'stɪsɪtɪ/ *n.* [F or L f. Gk (PLASMA)]

Plasticine /'plæstɪsi:n/ *n.* **(P)** plastic substance used for modelling.

plasticize /'plæstɪsaɪz/ *v.* make or become plastic.

plasticizer *n.* substance that produces or promotes plasticity.

plate 1 *n.* shallow usu. circular vessel from which food is eaten or served; contents of this; similar vessel used for collection in churches etc.; *collect.* utensils of silver, gold, or other metal, objects of plated metal; piece of metal with name or inscription for affixing to something; illustration on special paper in book; thin sheet of metal, glass, etc., coated with sensitive film for photography; flat thin usu. rigid sheet of metal etc.; smooth piece of metal etc. for engraving, impression from this; silver or gold cup as prize for horse-race etc., such race; thin piece of plastic material, moulded to shape of gums etc., to which artificial teeth are attached; *colloq.* denture. **2** *v.t.* cover (other metal) with thin coat esp. of silver, gold, or tin; cover (esp. ship) with plates of metal. **3 on a plate** *colloq.* available with little trouble to recipient; **on one's plate** for one to deal with or consider; **plate glass** thick fine-quality glass for shop windows etc.; **plate-rack** rack in which plates are held to drain. [F f. L *platta* (*plattus* flat)]

plateau /'plætəʊ/ *n.* (*pl.* **plateaux** /-əʊz/) *n.* area of fairly level high ground; state of little variation after an increase. [F (prec.)]

plateful *n.* as much as a plate will hold; *colloq.* a great deal (of work etc.). [PLATE]

platelayer *n.* person employed in fixing and repairing railway rails.

platelet *n.* small colourless disc found in blood and involved in clotting.

platen /'plæt(ə)n/ *n.* plate in printing-press by which paper is pressed against type; corresponding part in typewriter etc. [F *platine* (PLATE)]

platform /ˈplætfɔːm/ *n.* raised level surface, esp. one from which speaker addresses audience, or one along side of line at railway station; floor area at entrance to bus; thick sole of shoe; declared policy of political party. [F (PLATE, FORM)]

platinum /ˈplætɪnəm/ *n.* white heavy metallic element that does not tarnish; **platinum blonde** woman with silvery-blonde hair, this colour. [earlier *platina* f. Sp. dimin. (*plata* silver)]

platitude /ˈplætɪtjuːd/ *n.* commonplace remark, esp. one solemnly delivered; **platitudinous** /-ˈtjuːdɪnəs/ *a.* [F (PLATE)]

Platonic /pləˈtɒnɪk/ *a.* of Plato or his philosophy; (**platonic**) confined to words or theory, not leading to action, harmless; (of love or friendship) purely spiritual, not sexual. [L f. Gk *Platōn* (5th c. BC), Gk philosopher]

Platonism /ˈpleɪtənɪz(ə)m/ *n.* philosophy of Plato or his followers; **Platonist** *n.*

platoon /pləˈtuːn/ *n.* subdivision of military company; group of persons acting together. [F *peloton*, dimin. of *pelote* PELLET]

platter *n.* flat dish or plate, esp. for food. [AF *plater* (PLATE)]

platypus /ˈplætɪpəs/ *n.* Australian egg-laying aquatic and burrowing mammal with ducklike beak and flat tail. [Gk, = flat foot]

plaudit /ˈplɔːdɪt/ *n.* (usu. in *pl.*) round of applause; emphatic expression of approval. [L *plaudite*, imper. of *plaudo plaus-* clap]

plausible /ˈplɔːzɪb(ə)l/ *a.* (of statement etc.) seeming reasonable or probable; (of person) persuasive but deceptive; **plausibility** /-ˈbɪlɪtɪ/ *n.*; **plausibly** *adv.* [L (prec.)]

play **1** *v.* occupy or amuse oneself pleasantly with some recreation, game, exercise, etc.; do this *with* another; act lightheartedly or flippantly *with* (feelings etc.); perform on (musical instrument), perform (piece of music etc.); cause (record, record-player, etc.) to produce sounds; perform role on stage (*in* drama etc.), perform (drama or role etc.) on stage; act in real life the part of (*play truant*; *play the fool*); give dramatic performance at (particular theatre or place); perform (trick or joke etc. *on* person); *sl.* co-operate, do what is wanted (*they wouldn't play*); gamble (on); take part in (game or recreation); compete with (another player or team) in game; occupy (specified position) in team for game, assign (player) to a position; move (piece) or display (playing-card) in one's turn in game; strike (ball etc., or *absol.*), execute (stroke) in game; move about in lively or unrestrained manner, touch gently (*on*); emit light, water, etc., (*on*); allow (fish) to exhaust itself pulling against line. **2** *n.* recreation, amusement, esp. as spontaneous activity of children; playing of game, action or manner of this; dramatic piece for the stage etc.; activity or operation; freedom of movement, space or scope for this; brisk, light, or fitful movement; gambling. **3 in** (or **out of**) **play** (of ball etc. in game) in (or not in) position for continued play according to rules; **make a play for** *sl.* seek to acquire; **make play with** use effectively or ostentatiously; **play about** (or **around**) behave irresponsibly; **play along** pretend to co-operate; **play at** perform or engage in half-heartedly; **play back** play (sounds recently recorded); **play-back** *n.* playing back of sound; **play by ear** perform (music) without having seen score, perform step by step according to results; **play down** minimize importance of; **played out** exhausted of energy or usefulness; **play fast and loose** act unreliably; **play for time** seek to gain time by delaying; **play the game** observe rules, behave honourably; **play havoc** (or **hell**) **with** *colloq.* affect adversely; **play into person's hands** act so as unwittingly to give him an advantage; **play the market** speculate in stocks etc.; **play off** oppose (person *against* another) esp. for one's own advantage, play extra match to decide draw or tie; **play-off** *n.* match played to decide draw or tie; **play on** take advantage of (person's feelings etc.); **play on words** pun; **play-pen** portable enclosure for young child to play in; **play safe** (or **for safety**) avoid risks; **play up** behave mischievously, annoy thus, put all one's energy into game; **play up to** flatter to win favour etc.; **play with fire** take foolish risks. [OE]

playbill *n.* poster announcing theatre programme.

playboy *n.* pleasure-seeking usu. wealthy man.

player *n.* person taking part in game; performer on musical instrument; actor; = *record-player*.

playfellow *n.* playmate.

playful *a.* fond of or inclined to play; done in fun.

playgoer *n.* one who goes often to theatre.

playground *n.* outdoor area for children to play on.

playgroup *n.* group of pre-school children who play regularly together under supervision.
playhouse *n.* theatre.
playing-card *n.* small oblong card with rounded corners used in games, one of set of usu. 52 divided into four suits.
playing-field *n.* field used for outdoor games.
playmate *n.* child's companion in play.
plaything *n.* toy or other thing to play with.
playtime *n.* time for play or recreation.
playwright *n.* dramatist.
PLC *abbr.* Public Limited Company.
plea *n.* appeal, entreaty; *Law* formal statement by or on behalf of defendant; excuse. [AF f. L *placitum* decree (PLEASE)]
pleach *v.t.* entwine or interlace (esp. branches to form hedge). [F f. L (PLEXUS)]
plead *v.* address lawcourt as advocate; maintain (cause) in lawcourt; declare oneself to be *guilty* or *not guilty* to charge, allege formally as plea (*plead insanity*); offer as excuse; make appeal or entreaty; **plead with** earnestly entreat. [AF *pleder* (PLEA)]
pleading *n.* (usu. in *pl.*) formal statement of cause of action or defence.
pleasant /'plezənt/ *a.* pleasing to mind or feelings or senses. [F (PLEASE)]
pleasantry *n.* jocularity; humorous speech; joking or polite remark. [F (prec.)]
please /pli:z/ *v.* **1** be agreeable to, make glad; give pleasure (*anxious to please*); think fit (*take as many as you please*); (with *it* as subject) be the inclination or wish of (*it did not please him to attend*). **2** (short for *may it please you*) used in polite requests (*come in, please*). **3 be pleased** be glad or willing (*to*), be satisfied *with*; **if you please** if you are willing, esp. *iron.* to indicate unreasonableness (*then, if you please, we had to pay*); **please oneself** do as one likes. [F *plaisir* f. L *placeo*]
pleasurable /'pleʒərəb(ə)l/ *a.* causing pleasure; **pleasurably** *adv.* [foll.]
pleasure /'pleʒə/ *n.* feeling of satisfaction or joy, enjoyment; source of pleasure or gratification; one's will or desire; sensual gratification; *attrib.* done or used for pleasure. [F (PLEASE)]
pleat **1** *n.* fold or crease, esp. flattened fold in cloth doubled upon itself. **2** *v.t.* make pleat(s) in. [PLAIT]
pleb *n. sl.* person of lower classes. [abbr. of foll.]
plebeian /plɪ'bi:ən/ **1** *n.* commoner, esp. in ancient Rome. **2** *a.* of low birth, of the common people; uncultured; coarse, ignoble. [L (*plebs plebis* common people)]
plebiscite /'plebɪsɪt/ *n.* direct vote of all electors of State on important public question. [F f. L *plebiscitum* (prec.)]
plectrum /'plektrəm/ *n.* (*pl.* **plectra**) small thin piece of horn or metal etc. for plucking strings of guitar etc. [L f. Gk (*plēssō* strike)]
pledge **1** *n.* thing given as security for fulfilment of contract, payment of debt, etc., and liable to forfeiture in case of failure; thing put in pawn; thing given as token of favour etc. or of something to come; solemn promise; drinking of health, toast. **2** *v.t.* deposit as security, pawn; promise solemnly by pledge of (one's honour, word, etc.); bind by solemn promise; drink to health of. [F f. Gmc]
Pleiades /'plaɪədi:z/ *n.pl.* cluster of stars in constellation Taurus. [L f. Gk]
Pleistocene /'pleɪstəsi:n/ **1** *a.* of the earlier epoch of the Quaternary period. **2** *n.* this epoch. [Gk *pleistos* most, *kainos* new]
plenary /'pli:nərɪ/ *a.* entire or unqualified (*plenary indulgence*); (of assembly) to be attended by all members. [L (*plenus* full)]
plenipotentiary /plenɪpə'tenʃərɪ/ **1** *n.* person (esp. diplomat) invested with full power of independent action. **2** *a.* having this power. [L (prec., POTENT)]
plenitude /'plenɪtju:d/ *n.* fullness, completeness; abundance. [F f. L (PLENARY)]
plenteous /'plentɪəs/ *a. literary* = PLENTIFUL. [F *plentivous* (PLENTY)]
plentiful /'plentɪfʊl/ *a.* existing in ample quantity; **plentifully** *adv.* [foll.]
plenty /'plentɪ/ **1** *n.* abundance, quite enough (*of* thing, or *absol.*). **2** *a. colloq.* plentiful. **3** *adv. colloq.* quite, fully. [F f. L *plenitas* (PLENARY)]
pleonasm /'pli:ənæz(ə)m/ *n.* use of words not needed to give the sense (e.g. *hear with one's ears*); **pleonastic** /-'næstɪk/ *a.* [L f. Gk (*pleon* more)]
plethora /'pleθərə/ *n.* over-abundance. [L f. Gk, = fullness]
pleura /'plʊərə/ *n.* (*pl.* **pleurae** /-i:/) membrane enveloping the lungs. [med.L f. Gk (*pleura* rib)]
pleurisy /'plʊərɪsɪ/ *n.* inflammation of the pleura; **pleuritic** /-'rɪtɪk/ *a.* [F f. L f. Gk (PLEURA)]
plexus /'pleksəs/ *n.* network of nerves or vessels in animal body (*solar plexus*). [L *plecto plex-* plait]
pliable /'plaɪəb(ə)l/ *a.* bending easily, supple; *fig.* yielding, compliant; **pliability** /-'bɪlɪtɪ/ *n.* [F (PLY[1])]
pliant /'plaɪənt/ *a.* = PLIABLE; **pliancy** *n.*

pliers /ˈplaɪəz/ *n.pl.* pincers with parallel flat surfaces for holding small objects, bending wire, etc. [dial. *ply* bend (prec.)]

plight[1] /plaɪt/ *n.* condition or state, esp. unfortunate one. [AF *plit* PLAIT]

plight[2] /plaɪt/ *v.t. archaic* (esp. in *p.p.*) pledge, engage *oneself* (*to* person). [OE]

plimsoll /ˈplɪms(ə)l/ *n.* rubber-soled canvas sports shoe. [foll.]

Plimsoll line (or **mark**) /ˈplɪms(ə)l/ marking on ship's side showing limit of legal submersion under various conditions. [*Plimsoll*, politician]

plinth *n.* lower square member of base of column; base supporting vase or statue etc. [F or L f. Gk, = tile]

Pliocene /ˈplaɪəsi:n/ **1** *a.* of the latest epoch of the Tertiary period. **2** *n.* this epoch. [Gk *pleiōn* more, *kainos* new]

PLO *abbr.* Palestine Liberation Organization.

plod 1 *v.i.* (**-dd-**) walk doggedly or laboriously, trudge; work slowly and steadily. **2** *n.* spell of plodding. [prob. imit.]

plonk[1] **1** *n.* heavy thud. **2** *v.t.* set down hurriedly or clumsily, put *down* firmly. [imit.]

plonk[2] *n. sl.* cheap or inferior wine. [orig. unkn.]

plop 1 *n.* sound as of smooth object dropping into water without splash. **2** *v.* (**-pp-**) (cause to) fall with a plop. **3** *adv.* with a plop. [imit.]

plosive /ˈpləʊsɪv/ **1** *a.* pronounced with sudden release of breath. **2** *n.* plosive sound. [EXPLOSIVE]

plot 1 *n.* defined and usu. small piece of ground; interrelationship of main events in play or novel or film etc.; conspiracy, secret plan. **2** *v.t.* (**-tt-**) make plan or map of; mark on chart or diagram; make (curve etc.) by marking out a number of points; plan or contrive (crime etc., or *absol.*); plan secretly. [OE, & F *complot*]

plough /plaʊ/ **1** *n.* implement for cutting furrows in soil and turning it up; implement resembling this (*snow-plough*). **2** *v.t.* turn up (earth, or *absol.*), bring *out* or *up* with plough; furrow or scratch (surface) as with plough; produce (furrow or line) thus; advance laboriously (through snow, book, etc.); move like plough violently (*through* or *into* obstacles); fail in examination. **3 the Plough** the Great Bear (see BEAR[2]) or its seven bright stars; **plough back** plough (grass etc.) into soil to enrich it, reinvest (profits) in business producing them. [OE]

ploughman *n.* man who guides plough; **ploughman's lunch** meal of bread and cheese etc.

ploughshare *n.* cutting-blade of plough.

plover /ˈplʌvə/ *n.* medium-sized wading bird, e.g. peewit. [AF f. Rmc (L *pluvia* rain)]

plow *US* var. of PLOUGH.

ploy *n. colloq.* cunning manœuvre to gain advantage. [orig. unkn.]

PLR *abbr.* Public Lending Right.

pluck 1 *v.* pick or pull out or away; strip (bird) of feathers; pull at, twitch; tug or snatch *at*; sound (string of musical instrument) with finger or plectrum; plunder, swindle. **2** *n.* courage, spirit; plucking, twitch; animal's heart and liver and lungs as food. **3 pluck up courage** summon up one's courage. [OE]

plucky *a.* brave, spirited; **pluckily** *adv.*; **pluckiness** *n.*

plug 1 *n.* piece of solid material fitting tightly into hole, used to fill gap or cavity or act as wedge or stopper; device of metal pins in insulated casing fitting into holes in socket for making electrical connection, *colloq.* the socket; = *sparking-plug* (see SPARK); *colloq.* favourable publicity for commercial product etc.; *colloq.* release-mechanism of water-closet flushing-apparatus; cake or stick of tobacco, piece of this for chewing. **2** *v.* (**-gg-**) stop (hole etc. *up*) with plug; *sl.* shoot or hit (person etc.); *colloq.* seek to popularize (song, policy, etc.) by constant recommendation; *colloq.* work steadily *away* (*at*). **3 plug in** connect electrically by inserting plug into socket; **plug-in** *a.* able to be connected thus. [LG or Du.]

plum *n.* roundish fleshy fruit with sweet pulp and flattish pointed stone; tree bearing it; dried fruit used in cooking (*plum-cake*); thing that is highly prized or best of its kind; **plum pudding** = *Christmas pudding*. [OE, ult. f. L (PRUNE[2])]

plumage /ˈplu:mɪdʒ/ *n.* bird's feathers. [F (PLUME)]

plumb /plʌm/ **1** *n.* ball of lead, esp. attached to end of line for finding depth of water or testing whether wall etc. is vertical. **2** *a.* vertical. **3** *adv.* exactly (*plumb in the centre*); vertically; *US sl.* quite, utterly. **4** *v.* sound or test with plumb; *fig.* reach or experience (*depth of* feeling etc.), discover facts about (matter); make vertical; work as plumber. **5 out of plumb** not vertical; **plumb-line** line with plumb attached. [F f. Rmc (L *plumbum* lead)]

plumber *n.* person who fits and repairs domestic apparatus of water-supply.

plumbing *n.* system or apparatus of

water-supply; work of plumber; *colloq.* lavatory installations.

plume /plu:m/ **1** *n.* feather, esp. large one used for ornament; ornament of feathers etc. attached to helmet or hat or worn in hair; something resembling this (*plume of smoke*). **2** *v.t.* furnish with plume(s); pride *oneself*; (of bird) preen (*itself* or its feathers). [F f. L *pluma*]

plummet /ˈplʌmɪt/ **1** *n.* plumb, plumb-line; sounding-lead; weight attached to fishing-line to keep float upright. **2** *v.i.* fall or plunge rapidly. [F (PLUMB)]

plummy *a.* of or abounding in plums; *colloq.* good, desirable; (of voice) sounding affectedly rich in tone. [PLUM]

plump[1] **1** *a.* having full rounded shape, fleshy. **2** *v.* make or become plump; fatten *out* or *up*. [LG or Du. *plomp* blunt]

plump[2] **1** *v.* drop or plunge with abrupt descent. **2** *n.* abrupt or heavy fall. **3** *adv.* with a plump. **4 plump for** choose, decide on. [LG or Du. *plompen*, imit.]

plumy /ˈplu:mɪ/ *a.* plumelike, feathery; adorned with plumes. [PLUME]

plunder 1 *v.t.* rob (place or person) forcibly of goods, esp. as in war; rob systematically; steal or embezzle (goods, or *absol.*). **2** *n.* violent or dishonest acquisition of property; property so acquired; *sl.* profit, gain. [G *plündern*]

plunge 1 *v.* thrust suddenly or violently (*into*); dive (*into*); (cause to) enter condition or embark on course impetuously (*plunged in gloom*; *plunged the country into chaos*); move suddenly and dramatically downward; move with a rush (*into* room, *down* stairs, etc.); *sl.* run up gambling debts. **2** *n.* plunging action or movement, dive. **3 take the plunge** take decisive step. [F f. Rmc (PLUMB)]

plunger *n.* part of mechanism that works with plunging or thrusting movement; rubber cup on handle for removal of blockages by plunging action; *sl.* reckless gambler.

pluperfect /plu:ˈpɜ:fɪkt/ *Gram.* **1** *a.* (of tense) denoting action completed prior to some past point of time (e.g. *he had said*). **2** *n.* pluperfect tense. [L (*plus quam perfectum* more than perfect)]

plural /ˈplʊər(ə)l/ **1** *a.* more than one in number; *Gram.* (of word or form) denoting more than one. **2** *n. Gram.* plural word or form, plural number. [F f. L (PLUS)]

pluralism *n.* holding more than one office at a time; form of society in which members of minority groups maintain independent traditions; **pluralist** *n.*; **pluralistic** /-ˈlɪstɪk/ *a.*

plurality /plʊəˈrælɪtɪ/ *n.* state of being plural; pluralism, benefice or office held with another; *US* majority that is not absolute.

pluralize /ˈplʊərəlaɪz/ *v.t.* make plural, express in plural.

plus 1 *prep.* with addition of (symbol +); (of temperature) above zero (*plus 2°*); *colloq.* with, having gained, possessing. **2** *a.* additional, extra; (after number) at least (*fifteen plus*), rather better than (*beta plus*); *Math.* positive; having positive electrical charge. **3** *n.* the symbol (+); additional quantity, positive quantity; an advantage. [L *plus plur-* more]

plus-fours /plʌsˈfɔ:z/ *n.pl.* long wide knickerbockers. [length increased by 4 in. to create overhang]

plush 1 *n.* cloth of silk or cotton, etc., with long soft nap. **2** *a.* made of plush; plushy. [F f. L (PILE[3])]

plushy *a.* stylish, luxurious; **plushiness** *n.*

plutocracy /plu:ˈtɒkrəsɪ/ *n.* government by the wealthy, State so governed; wealthy élite. [Gk (*ploutos* wealth)]

plutocrat /ˈplu:təkræt/ *n.* member of plutocracy; wealthy man; **plutocratic** /-ˈkrætɪk/ *a.*

plutonic /plu:ˈtɒnɪk/ *a.* (of igneous rocks) formed by crystallization of molten material at a great depth underground; **plutonic theory** theory attributing most geological phenomena to action of internal heat. [L *Pluto* god of underworld, f. Gk]

plutonium /plu:ˈtəʊnɪəm/ *n.* radioactive metallic element. [*Pluto*, planet]

pluvial /ˈplu:vɪəl/ *a.* of rain, rainy; *Geol.* caused by rain. [L (*pluvia* rain)]

ply[1] /plaɪ/ *n.* thickness or layer of cloth or wood etc.; strand of rope or yarn etc. [F *pli* (PLAIT)]

ply[2] /plaɪ/ *v.* use or wield (tool or weapon); work steadily (at); supply continuously *with* food or drink etc., approach repeatedly *with* questions etc.; (of vehicle etc.) travel regularly to and fro *between*, work (*route*) thus; (of taxi-driver etc.) attend regularly for custom (*ply for hire*). [APPLY]

Plymouth Brethren /ˈplɪməθ/ Calvinistic religious body with no formal creed and no official order of ministers. [*Plymouth* in Devon]

plywood /ˈplaɪwʊd/ *n.* strong thin board made by gluing layers with the direction of the grain alternating. [PLY[1]]

PM *abbr.* Prime Minister; post-mortem.

p.m. *abbr.* after noon. [L *post meridiem*]

Pm *symb.* promethium.

pneumatic /nju:ˈmætɪk/ *a.* filled with wind or air (*pneumatic tyre*); working by means of compressed air (*pneumatic drill*). [F or L f. Gk (*pneuma* wind)]

pneumonia /njuːˈməʊnɪə/ *n.* inflammation of one or both lungs. [L f. Gk (*pneumōn* lung)]

po /pəʊ/ *n.* (*pl.* **pos**) *colloq.* chamber-pot; **po-faced** solemn-faced, humourless. [POT]

PO *abbr.* Post Office; postal order; Petty Officer; Pilot Officer.

Po *symb.* polonium.

poach[1] *v.* cook (egg) without shell in or over boiling water; cook (fish etc.) by simmering in small amount of liquid. [F *pochier* (POKE)]

poach[2] *v.* catch (game or fish, or *absol.*) illegally; trespass or encroach *on* (property or idea etc. of another). [earlier *poche* (as prec.)]

pock *n.* eruptive spot on skin, esp. in smallpox; **pock-marked** bearing scars left by such spots. [OE]

pocket /ˈpɒkɪt/ **1** *n.* small bag sewn into or on clothing, for carrying small articles; pouchlike compartment in suitcase, car door, etc.; pecuniary resources (*it is beyond my pocket*); isolated group or area (*pockets of opposition*); cavity in earth filled with gold or other ore; pouch at corner or on side of billiard-table into which balls are driven; = *air pocket.* **2** *a.* of suitable size or shape for carrying in pocket; smaller than usual size. **3** *v.t.* put into (one's) pocket; appropriate, usu. dishonestly; confine as in pocket; submit to (injury or affront); conceal or suppress (feelings). **4 in person's pocket** close to or intimate with him, under his control; **in** (or **out of**) **pocket** having gained (or lost) in a transaction; **pocket-book** notebook, booklike case for papers or money carried in pocket; **pocket borough** *hist.* borough with election controlled by one person or family; **pocket-knife** knife with folding blade(s), for carrying in pocket; **pocket-money** money for minor expenses, esp. that allowed to children. [AF dimin. (POKE[2])]

pocketful *n.* (*pl.* **-fuls**) as much as a pocket will hold.

pod 1 *n.* long seed-vessel, esp. of pea or bean. **2** *v.* (**-dd-**) bear or form pods.; remove (seeds etc.) from pods. [orig. unkn.]

podgy /ˈpɒdʒɪ/ *a.* short and fat; plump, fleshy; **podginess** *n.* [*podge* short fat person]

podium /ˈpəʊdɪəm/ *n.* (*pl.* **podia**) continuous projecting base or pedestal round room or house etc.; rostrum. [L, f. Gk *podion* dimin. of *pous pod-* foot]

poem /ˈpəʊɪm/ *n.* metrical composition, usu. concerned with feeling or imaginative description; elevated composition in verse or prose; something with poetic qualities. [F or L f. Gk (*poieō* make)]

poesy /ˈpəʊɪsɪ/ *n. archaic* = POETRY. [F, ult. as prec.]

poet /ˈpəʊɪt/ *n.* writer of poems; one possessing high powers of imagination or expression etc.; **Poet Laureate** poet appointed to write poems for State occasions; **poetess** *n. fem.* [F f. L f. Gk *poiētēs* (POEM)]

poetaster /pəʊɪˈtæstə/ *n.* paltry or inferior poet. [POET, L *-aster* derog. suffix]

poetic /pəʊˈetɪk/ *a.* of or like poetry or poets; **poetic justice** well-deserved punishment or reward; **poetic licence** writer's or artist's transgression of established rules for effect; **poetically** *adv.* [F f. L f. Gk (POET)]

poetical *a.* poetic; written in verse (*poetical works*); **poetically** *adv.*

poetry /ˈpəʊɪtrɪ/ *n.* art or work of poet; poems collectively; poetic or tenderly pleasing quality. [med.L (POET)]

pogo /ˈpəʊgəʊ/ *n.* (*pl.* **pogos;** also **pogo stick**) stiltlike toy with spring, used for jumping about on. [orig. uncert.]

pogrom /ˈpɒgrəm/ *n.* organized massacre (orig. of Jews in Russia). [Russ.]

poignant /ˈpɔɪnjənt/ *a.* painfully sharp to senses or feeling, deeply moving; sharp or pungent in taste or smell; pleasantly piquant; arousing sympathy; **poignancy** *n.* [F f. L (POINT)]

poinsettia /pɔɪnˈsetɪə/ *n.* plant with large usu. scarlet bracts surrounding small yellow flowers. [*Poinsett*, diplomat]

point 1 *n.* sharp or tapered end of tool, weapon, pin, etc., tip or extreme end; that which in geometry has position but no magnitude; dot or other punctuation-mark, = *decimal point* (*four point six*, = 4.6); very small mark on surface; particular place or moment; stage or degree of progress or increase; level of temperature at which change of state occurs (*freezing-point*); precise moment, esp. for action (*when it came to the point he refused*); single item or particular; unit of scoring in games or of measuring value etc.; significant or essential thing, thing actually intended or under discussion (*what was the point of your question?*); salient feature of story, joke, remark, etc.; effectiveness, purpose, or value (*saw no point in staying*); distinctive feature or characteristic (*tact is not his good point*); one of 32 directions marked at equal distances on compass, corresponding direction towards horizon; (usu. in *pl.*) tapering movable rail to allow train to pass from one line to another; = *power point*; (usu. in *pl.*)

electrical contact device in distributor of motor vehicle; (in cricket) fieldsman on the off side near batsman, his position; tip of toe in ballet; promontory; prong of deer's horn; (in *pl.*) extremities of horse, dog, etc. **2** *v.* direct or aim (finger, weapon, etc.); direct attention (*to* or *at*); aim or be directed (*at, to, towards*); provide with point(s); give force to (words or actions); fill joints of (brickwork etc.) with smoothed mortar or cement; (of dog) indicate presence of game by acting as pointer. **3 at** (or **on) the point of** on the verge of; **beside the point** irrelevant(ly); **in point of** as a matter of (*fact* etc.); **make a point of** indicate necessity of, call particular attention to (action); **point-duty** (of policeman etc.) position at particular point to control traffic; **point of no return** point in journey or enterprise at which it becomes essential or more practical to continue to the end; **point of view** position from which thing is viewed, way of considering a matter; **point out** indicate, draw attention to; **point-to-point** horse-race over course defined only by certain landmarks; **point up** emphasize; **to the point** relevant(ly); **up to a point** to some extent but not completely. [F f. L (*pungo punct-* prick)]

point-blank **1** *a.* (of shot) aimed or fired at range very close to target, (of range) very close; (of remark etc.) blunt, direct. **2** *adv.* at point-blank range; bluntly, directly.

pointed *a.* sharpened or tapering to a point; (of remark etc.) having point, cutting, emphasized.

pointer *n.* thing that points, e.g. index hand of gauge etc.; rod for pointing to features on chart etc.; *colloq.* hint; dog of breed that on scenting game stands rigid looking towards it; (in *pl.*) two stars in Great Bear in line with pole-star.

pointillism /'pwæntɪlɪz(ə)m/ *n.* technique of impressionist painting using tiny dots of colour blended in viewer's eye; **pointillist** *n.* [F (*pointiller* mark with dots)]

pointing *n.* cement filling joints of brickwork; facing produced by this. [POINT]

pointless *a.* without point or force; lacking purpose or meaning. [POINT]

poise /pɔɪz/ **1** *v.* balance or be balanced; hold suspended or supported; carry (one's head etc.). **2** *n.* equilibrium; composure, self-possession; carriage (*of* head etc.). [F f. L (*pendo pens-* weigh)]

poison /'pɔɪz(ə)n/ **1** *n.* substance that when introduced into or absorbed by living organism causes death or injury, esp. one that kills by rapid action even in small quantity; harmful influence. **2** *v.t.* administer poison to; kill or injure or infect with poison; (esp. in *p.p.*) smear (weapon) with poison; corrupt or pervert (person or mind); spoil or destroy (person's pleasure etc.). **3 poison ivy** N. American climbing plant secreting irritant oil from leaves; **poison pen** anonymous writer of libellous or scurrilous letters, practice of writing these. **4 poisonous** *a.* [F f. L (POTION)]

poke[1] **1** *v.* thrust or push with hand, stick, etc.; thrust end of finger etc. against; make thrusts (*at* etc.); stir (fire) with poker; produce (hole etc. *in* thing) by poking; thrust or be thrust forward, protrude (*out, up,* etc.); pry or search (*about* or *into*); potter *about* or *around*. **2** *n.* poking, thrust, nudge. **3 poke fun at** ridicule; **poke one's nose into** pry or intrude into [LG or Du.]

poke[2] *n. dial.* bag, sack. [F dial.]

poker[1] *n.* stiff metal rod with handle, for stirring fire. [POKE[1]]

poker[2] *n.* card-game in which players bet on value of their hands; **poker-face** impassive countenance appropriate to poker-player, person with this. [orig. unkn.]

poky *a.* (of room etc.) small and cramped; **pokiness** *n.* [POKE[1]]

polar /'pəʊlə/ *a.* of or near either pole of earth or celestial sphere; having electric or magnetic polarity; directly opposite in character; **polar bear** large white bear living in Arctic regions; **polar circles** parallels at 23° 27′ from poles. [F or L (POLE[2])]

polarity /pəʊ'lærɪtɪ/ *n.* tendency of magnet etc. to point with its extremities to earth's magnetic poles or of body to lie with axis in particular direction; possession of two poles having contrary qualities; electrical condition of body as positive or negative; *fig.* attraction towards an object.

polarize /'pəʊləraɪz/ *v.* restrict vibrations of (light-waves etc.) so that they have different amplitudes in different planes; give electric or magnetic polarity to; divide into two opposing groups; **polarization** /-'zeɪʃ(ə)n/ *n.*

Polaroid /'pəʊlərɔɪd/ *n.* (**P**) material in thin sheets polarizing light passing through it; camera able to develop negative and produce print within short time of exposure.

polder /'pəʊldə/ *n.* piece of low-lying land reclaimed from sea or river, esp. in Netherlands. [Du.]

pole[1] *n.* long slender rounded piece of wood or metal, esp. with end placed in ground as support etc.; (as measure) =

PERCH[1]; **pole-jump** (or **-vault**) vault over high bar with help of pole held in hands; **up the pole** *sl.* in a difficulty, crazy. [OE f. L *palus* stake]

pole[2] *n.* either of ends of earth's axis of rotation, either of two points in celestial sphere about which stars appear to revolve, North Pole or South Pole; each of two opposite points on surface of magnet at which magnetic forces are concentrated; each of two terminals (positive and negative) of electric cell or battery etc.; each of two opposed principles; **be poles apart** differ greatly; **pole-star** star in Little Bear, near the North Pole in the sky, *fig.* thing serving as guide. [L f. Gk, = axis]

Pole[3] *n.* native or inhabitant of Poland. [G f. Pol.]

pole-axe 1 *n.* battle-axe with long handle; butcher's axe with hammer at back. 2 *v.t.* slaughter or strike with pole-axe. [LG or Du. (POLL, AXE)]

polecat /'pəʊlkæt/ *n.* small dark-brown mammal of weasel family; *US* skunk. [orig. unkn.]

polemic /pə'lemɪk/ 1 *n.* verbal attack; controversial discussion. 2 *a.* (also **polemical**) controversial, involving dispute. 3 **polemically** *adv.* [L f. Gk (*polemos* war)]

polemics *n.pl.* art or practice of controversial discussion.

police /pə'li:s/ 1 *n.* civil force responsible for maintaining public order; (as *pl.*) its members; force with similar functions of enforcing regulations (*military police*). 2 *v.t.* control (country etc.) by means of police; provide with police; keep order in, control. 3 **police state** totalitarian State controlled by political police supervising citizens' activities; **police station** office of local police force. [F f. L (foll.)]

policeman *n.* member of police force; **policewoman** *n. fem.*

policy[1] /'pɒlɪsɪ/ *n.* course of action adopted by government or party or person; prudent conduct, sagacity. [F f. L *politia* POLITY]

policy[2] /'pɒlɪsɪ/ *n.* contract of insurance; document containing this. [F *police* ult. f. Gk *apodeixis* proof]

polio /'pəʊlɪəʊ/ *n. colloq.* poliomyelitis. [abbr.]

poliomyelitis /pəʊlɪəʊmaɪɪ'laɪtɪs/ *n.* infectious viral inflammation of nerve cells in grey matter of spinal cord, with temporary or permanent paralysis. [Gk *polios* grey, *muelos* marrow]

polish[1] /'pɒlɪʃ/ 1 *v.* make or become smooth and glossy by rubbing; (esp. in *p.p.*) refine or improve, add finishing touches to. 2 *n.* substance used for polishing; smoothness or glossiness produced by friction; refinement, elegance. 3 **polish off** finish off quickly. [F f. L *polio*]

Polish[2] /'pəʊlɪʃ/ 1 *a.* of Poland, of the Poles or their language. 2 *n.* language of Poland. [POLE[3]]

polite /pə'laɪt/ *a.* having good manners, courteous; cultivated, cultured; refined, elegant. [L *politus* (POLISH[1])]

politic /'pɒlɪtɪk/ 1 *a.* (of action) judicious, expedient; (of person) prudent, sagacious; political (now only in *body politic*). 2 *v.i.* (**-ck-**) engage in politics. [F f. L f. Gk (as POLITY)]

political /pə'lɪtɪk(ə)l/ *a.* of or engaged in politics; of or affecting the State or its government; of public affairs; relating to person's or organization's status or influence (*a political decision*); **political asylum** see ASYLUM; **political economy** study of economic problems of government; **political geography** that dealing with boundaries and possessions of States; **political prisoner** person imprisoned for alleged political offence; **politically** *adv.* [L (prec.)]

politician /pɒlɪ'tɪʃ(ə)n/ *n.* one skilled in or concerned with politics, esp. professionally. [POLITIC]

politicize /pə'lɪtɪsaɪz/ *v.* engage in or talk politics; give political character to; **politicization** /-'zeɪʃ(ə)n/ *n.*

politico /pə'lɪtɪkəʊ/ *n.* (*pl.* **politicos**) politician or political enthusiast. [Sp.]

politics /'pɒlɪtɪks/ *n.pl.* (also treated as *sing.*) science and art of government; political affairs or life; political principles or practice. [POLITIC]

polity /'pɒlɪtɪ/ *n.* form or process of civil government; organized society, State. [L *politia* f. Gk (*politēs* citizen f. *polis* city)]

polka /'pɒlkə/ 1 *n.* lively dance of Bohemian origin; music for this. 2 *v.i.* dance the polka. 3 **polka dot** round dot as one of many forming regular pattern on textile fabric etc. [F & G f. Czech]

poll /pəʊl/ 1 *n.* voting at election; counting of voters at election; result of voting; number of votes recorded; = GALLUP POLL; human head. 2 *v.* take vote(s) of; (of candidate) receive (so many votes); give (vote); give one's vote; cut off top of (tree or plant), esp. make pollard of; (esp. in *p.p.*) cut off horns of (cattle). 3 **poll-tax** tax levied on every person. [perh. LG or Du.]

pollack /'pɒlæk/ *n.* marine food-fish related to cod. [orig. unkn.]

pollard /'pɒləd/ 1 *n.* animal that has cast or lost its horns; ox or sheep or goat of hornless breed; tree polled so as to produce close rounded head of young branches. **2** *v.t.* make (tree) pollard. [POLL]

pollen /ˈpɒlən/ *n.* powdery substance discharged from flower's anther in fine grains, each containing fertilizing element; **pollen count** index of amount of pollen in air published as warning to those allergic to it. [L]

pollinate /ˈpɒlɪneɪt/ *v.t.* sprinkle (plant) with pollen; **pollination** /-ˈneɪʃ(ə)n/ *n.*; **pollinator** *n.*

pollock var. of POLLACK.

pollster *n.* person who organizes Gallup poll. [POLL]

pollute /pəˈluːt/ *v.t.* make foul or impure; corrupt; **pollutant** *a.* & *n.*; **pollution** *n.* [L *polluo -lut-*]

polo /ˈpəʊləʊ/ *n.* game like hockey played on horseback with long-handled mallet; **polo neck** high round turned-over collar. [Balti, = ball]

polonaise /pɒləˈneɪz/ *n.* slow processional dance of Polish origin; music for this. [F (POLE³)]

polonium /pəˈləʊnɪəm/ *n.* radioactive metallic element forming last stage before lead in decay of radium. [med.L *Polonia* Poland]

polony/pəˈləʊnɪ/ *n.* sausage of partly cooked pork etc. [prob. *Bologna* in Italy]

poltergeist /ˈpɒltəgaɪst/ *n.* mischievous ghost or spirit manifesting itself by making noisy disturbance. [G]

poltroon /pɒlˈtruːn/ *n.* spiritless coward; **poltroonery** *n.* [F f. It. (*poltro* sluggard)]

poly /ˈpɒlɪ/ *n.* (*pl.* **polys**) *colloq.* polytechnic. [abbr.]

poly- *prefix* many (*polygamy*); polymerized (*polyester*). [Gk (*polus* many)]

polyandry /ˈpɒlɪændrɪ/ *n.* polygamy in which one woman has more than one husband; **polyandrous** /-ˈændrəs/ *a.* [Gk *anēr andr-* man]

polyanthus /pɒlɪˈænθəs/ *n.* cultivated flower from hybridized primulas. [Gk *anthos* flower]

polychromatic /pɒlɪkrəˈmætɪk/ *a.* many-coloured; (of radiation) consisting of more than one wavelength. [POLY-]

polychrome /ˈpɒlɪkrəʊm/ **1** *a.* in many colours. **2** *n.* polychrome work of art. [F f. Gk (POLY-)]

polyester /pɒlɪˈestə/ *n.* synthetic resin or fibre. [POLY-]

polyethylene /pɒlɪˈeθɪliːn/ *n.* polythene. [ETHYLENE]

polygamy /pəˈlɪgəmɪ/ *n.* practice of having more than one wife or (less usu.) husband at once; **polygamist** *n.*; **polygamous** *a.* [Gk *gamos* marriage]

polyglot /ˈpɒlɪglɒt/ **1** *a.* knowing or using or written in several languages. **2** *n.* polyglot person. [Gk *glōtta* tongue]

polygon /ˈpɒlɪgɒn/ *n.* figure with many (usu. five or more) sides and angles; **polygonal** /pəˈlɪgən(ə)l/ *a.* [L f. Gk (*-gōnos* angled)]

polygraph /ˈpɒlɪgrɑːf/ *n.* machine for reading physiological characteristics (e.g. pulse-rate), lie-detector. [POLY-]

polygyny /pəˈlɪdʒɪnɪ/ *n.* polygamy in which one man has more than one wife; **polygynous** *a.* [Gk *gunē* wife]

polyhedron /pɒlɪˈhiːdrən/ *n.* (*pl.* **polyhedra**) solid figure with many (usu. seven or more) faces; **polyhedral** *a.* [Gk *hedra* base]

polymath /ˈpɒlɪmæθ/ *n.* person of varied learning, great scholar. [Gk (*manthanō math-* learn)]

polymer /ˈpɒlɪmə/ *n.* compound whose molecule is formed from many repeated units of one or more compounds; **polymeric** /pɒlɪˈmerɪk/ *a.* [G, f. Gk *polumeros* having many parts]

polymerize *v.* combine or become combined into a polymer; **polymerization** /-ˈzeɪʃ(ə)n/ *n.*

polymorphous /pɒlɪˈmɔːfəs/ *a.* varying in individuals, passing through successive variations. [Gk *morphē* form]

polynomial /pɒlɪˈnəʊmɪəl/ **1** *a.* (of algebraic expression) consisting of three or more terms. **2** *n.* polynomial expression. [POLY-, BINOMIAL]

polyp /ˈpɒlɪp/ *n.* simple organism with tube-shaped body; small growth of mucous membrane. [F f. L f. Gk (*pous* foot)]

polyphony /pəˈlɪfənɪ/ *n. Mus.* contrapuntal combination of several individual melodies; **polyphonic** /pɒlɪˈfɒnɪk/ *a.* [Gk (*phōnē* sound)]

polystyrene /pɒlɪˈstaɪriːn/ *n.* a kind of hard plastic, a polymer of styrene. [*styrene* f. Gk *sturax* a resin]

polysyllabic /pɒlɪsɪˈlæbɪk/ *a.* having many syllables; marked by polysyllables. [med.L f. Gk]

polysyllable /ˈpɒlɪsɪləb(ə)l/ *n.* polysyllabic word.

polytechnic /pɒlɪˈteknɪk/ **1** *a.* giving instruction in many (including vocational) subjects at an advanced level. **2** *n.* polytechnic institution, esp. college. [F f. Gk (*tekhnē* art)]

polytheism /ˈpɒlɪθiːɪz(ə)m/ *n.* belief in or worship of more than one god; **polytheist** *n.*; **polytheistic** /-ˈɪstɪk/ *a.* [F f. Gk (*theos* god)]

polythene /ˈpɒlɪθiːn/ *n.* tough light plastic. [POLYETHYLENE]

polyunsaturated/pɒlɪʌnˈsætʃəreɪtɪd/ *a.* of those kinds of fat or oil that are not associated with the formation of cholesterol in the blood. [POLY-]

polyurethane /pɒlɪˈjʊərɪθeɪn/ *n.* synthetic resin or plastic used esp. as foam. [UREA, ETHANE]

polyvinyl chloride /pɒlɪˈvaɪnɪl/ vinyl plastic used as insulation or as fabric. [POLY-]

pom *n.* Pomeranian; = POMMY. [abbr.]

pomace /ˈpʌmɪs/ *n.* mass of crushed apples in cider-making. [L (*pomum* apple)]

pomade /pəˈmɑːd/ *n.* scented ointment for hair and skin of head. [F f. It. (prec.)]

pomander /pəˈmændə/ *n.* ball of mixed aromatic substances; round container for this. [AF f. med.L]

pomegranate /ˈpɒmɪgrænɪt/ *n.* tropical fruit with tough rind and reddish pulp enclosing many seeds; tree bearing it. [F *pome grenate* f. Rmc = many-seeded apple]

pomelo /ˈpʌmɪləʊ/ *n.* (*pl.* **pomelos**) variety of large citrus fruit. [orig. unkn.]

Pomeranian /pɒməˈreɪnɪən/ *n.* small dog of breed with long silky hair. [*Pomerania* in Germany & Poland]

pomfret-cake /ˈpʌmfrɪt, ˈpɒ-/ *n.* small round flat liquorice sweet. [*Pontefract* in Yorkshire]

pommel /ˈpʌm(ə)l/ **1** *n.* knob, esp. at end of sword-hilt; upward projecting front of saddle. **2** *v.t.* (**-ll-**, *US* **-l-**) = PUMMEL. [F dimin. (L *pomum* apple)]

pommy /ˈpɒmɪ/ *n.* (also **pommie**) (*Austral.* & *NZ sl.*) British person, esp. recent immigrant. [orig. uncert.]

pomp *n.* splendour, splendid display; specious glory. [F f. L f. Gk]

pom-pom[1] /ˈpɒmpɒm/ *n.* automatic quick-firing gun. [imit.]

pom-pom[2] var. of POMPON.

pompon /ˈpɒmpɒn/ *n.* decorative tuft or ball on hat or shoes etc.; dahlia etc. with small tightly-clustered petals. [F]

pompous /ˈpɒmpəs/ *a.* ostentatiously or affectedly grand or solemn; (of language) pretentious, unduly grand; **pomposity** /-ˈpɒsɪtɪ/ *n.* [F f. L (POMP)]

ponce **1** *n.* man who lives off prostitute's earnings; *sl.* effeminate or homosexual man. **2** *v.i.* act as ponce; *sl.* move *about* effeminately, mess *about*. [orig. unkn.]

poncho /ˈpɒntʃəʊ/ *n.* (*pl.* **ponchos**) cloak of blanket-like piece of cloth with slit in middle for head; similar garment. [S. Amer. Sp.]

pond *n.* small area of still water. [var. of POUND[3]]

ponder *v.* think over, consider; muse, be deep in thought. [F f. L *pondero* weigh]

ponderable *a.* having appreciable weight or significance. [L (prec.)]

ponderous *a.* heavy, unwieldy; (of style) dull, tedious. [L (*pondus -er-* weight)]

pondweed *n.* aquatic herb growing in still water. [POND]

pong *n.* & *v.i. colloq.* stink. [orig. unkn.]

poniard /ˈpɒnjəd/ *n.* dagger. [F *poignard* f. L (*pugnus* fist)]

pontiff /ˈpɒntɪf/ *n.* bishop, chief priest; the Pope. [F f. L *pontifex -fic-* priest]

pontifical /pɒnˈtɪfɪk(ə)l/ *a.* of or befitting a pontiff; pompously dogmatic; **pontifically** *adv.* [F or L (prec.)]

pontificate **1** /pɒnˈtɪfɪkeɪt/ *v.i.* be pompously dogmatic; play the pontiff. **2** /pɒnˈtɪfɪkət/ *n.* office of bishop or Pope; period of this. [L (PONTIFF)]

pontoon[1] /pɒnˈtuːn/ *n.* card-game in which players try to acquire cards with face-value totalling 21 and no more. [prob. corrupt. of VINGT-ET-UN]

pontoon[2] /pɒnˈtuːn/ *n.* flat-bottomed boat; each of several boats etc. used to support temporary bridge. [F f. L *ponto -on-* punt]

pony /ˈpəʊnɪ/ *n.* horse of any small breed; **pony-tail** hair drawn back, tied, and hanging down behind head; **pony-trekking** travelling across country on ponies for pleasure. [perh. F *poulenet* foal]

poodle /ˈpuːd(ə)l/ *n.* dog of breed with thick curling hair often elaborately clipped and shaved. [G *pudel*]

poof /pʊf/ *n. colloq.* effeminate or homosexual man. [orig. unkn.]

pooh /puː/ *int.* expressing contempt or impatience. [imit.]

pooh-pooh /puːˈpuː/ *v.t.* express contempt for, ridicule. [redupl. of prec.]

pool[1] *n.* small body of still water, usu. of natural formation; small shallow body of any liquid; deep place in river; swimming-pool. [OE]

pool[2] **1** *n.* common fund, e.g. of profits of separate firms or of players' stakes in gambling; common supply of persons, vehicles, commodities, etc., for sharing by group of people; group of persons sharing duties etc.; arrangement between competing parties to fix prices and share business; *US* game on billiard-table with usu. 16 balls. **2** *v.t.* put into common fund, share in common. **3 the pools** = *football pool*, esp. as conducted on weekly basis. [F *poule*]

poop *n.* stern of ship; aftermost and highest deck. [F *pupe* f. L *puppis*]

poor /pʊə/ *a.* lacking adequate money or means to live comfortably; deficient (*in* a possession or quality); scanty, inadequate, less good than is usual or expected (*is a poor driver*; *had a poor day*); deserving pity or sympathy, unfortunate (*poor chap*; *you poor thing*); paltry, inferior (*poor consolation*; *came a poor third*); spiritless, despicable; humble, insignificant; **Poor Law** *hist.* law concerning support of the poor from public funds; **poor man's** inferior or cheaper substitute for; **poor white** *US derog.* member of socially inferior group of white people. [F *povre* f. L *pauper*)

poorhouse *n. hist.* workhouse.

poorly 1 *adv.* in poor manner, badly. 2 *predic. a.* unwell.

pop[1] 1 *n.* sudden sharp explosive sound, as of cork when drawn; effervescing drink. 2 *v.* (**-pp-**) (cause to) make pop; go, move, or put abruptly *in*, *out*, *up*, etc.; *sl.* pawn. 3 *adv.* with sound of pop (*went pop*). 4 **pop-eyed** with eyes bulging or wide open; **pop off** *sl.* die; **pop the question** *colloq.* propose marriage; **pop-shop** *sl.* pawnbroker's shop; **pop-up** involving parts that pop up automatically (*pop-up book*). [imit.]

pop[2] *colloq.* 1 *a.* in popular modern style (*pop music*); performing popular music (*pop group*). 2 *n.* pop music or record. 3 **pop art** art based on modern popular culture and mass media. [abbr.]

pop[3] *colloq.* father; any older man. [PAPA]

popcorn *n.* maize which when heated bursts open to form fluffy balls. [POP[1]]

pope *n.* head of Roman Catholic Church (*the Pope*; *we have a new pope*). [OE f. L *papa* f. Gk *papas*]

popery /'pəʊpərɪ/ *n. derog.* papal system, Roman Catholic religion.

popgun *n.* child's toy gun firing cork etc. by action of compressed air. [POP[1]]

popinjay /'pɒpɪndʒeɪ/ *n.* fop, conceited person. [F *papingay* f. Sp. f. Arab.]

popish /'pəʊpɪʃ/ *a. derog.* of popery. [POPE]

poplar /'pɒplə/ *n.* tall slender tree with straight trunk and often tremulous leaves. [AF f. L *populus*]

poplin /'pɒplɪn/ *n.* plain-woven fabric usu. of cotton, with corded surface. [F *papeline*]

popper *n. colloq.* press-stud. [POP[1]]

poppet /'pɒpɪt/ *n. colloq.* (esp. as term of endearment) small or dainty person. [ult. f. L *pu(p)pa* doll]

popping-crease *n.* (in cricket) line in front of and parallel to wicket within which batsman stands. [POP[1]]

poppy /'pɒpɪ/ *n.* plant with showy esp. scarlet flowers, milky juice, and narcotic properties; **Poppy Day** Remembrance Sunday, on which artificial poppies are worn. [OE f. L *papaver*]

poppycock *n. sl.* nonsense. [Du. *pappekak*]

populace /'pɒpjʊləs/ *n.* the common people. [F f. It. (foll.)]

popular /'pɒpjʊlə/ *a.* liked or admired by many people; of or for the general public; prevalent among the general public (*popular fallacies*); **popular music** music appealing to contemporary popular taste; **popularity** /-'lærɪtɪ/ *n.* [AF or L (*populus* PEOPLE)]

popularize *v.t.* make popular; present (a subject) in readily understandable form; **popularization** /-'zeɪʃ(ə)n/ *n.*

populate /'pɒpjʊleɪt/ *v.t.* inhabit, form population of; supply with inhabitants. [med.L (PEOPLE)]

population /pɒpjʊ'leɪʃ(ə)n/ *n.* the inhabitants of a place or country etc.; total number of these; extent to which place is populated; **population explosion** large sudden increase of population. [L (PEOPLE)]

populist /'pɒpjʊlɪst/ *n.* adherent of political party claiming to represent all the people. [L *populus* people]

populous /'pɒpjʊləs/ *a.* thickly inhabited. [L *populosus* (PEOPLE)]

porcelain /'pɔːslɪn/ *n.* fine earthenware with translucent body and transparent glaze; articles made of this. [F f. It. dimin. (*porca* sow)]

porch *n.* covered approach to entrance of building. [F f. L *porticus*]

porcine /'pɔːsaɪn/ *a.* of or like pig. [F or L (PORK)]

porcupine /'pɔːkjʊpaɪn/ *n.* rodent with body and tail covered with erectile spines. [F *porc espin* f. L (PORK, SPINE)]

pore[1] *n.* minute opening in surface of skin or leaf etc. through which fluids may pass. [F f. L f. Gk *poros*]

pore[2] *v.i.* (with *over*) be absorbed in studying (book etc.), meditate or think intently about. [orig. unkn.]

pork *n.* flesh (esp. unsalted) of pig used as food; **pork pie** pie of minced pork etc., eaten cold; **pork-pie hat** hat with flat rimmed crown and brim turned up all round. [F f. L *porcus* pig]

porker *n.* pig raised for pork.

porky *a.* of or like pork; *colloq.* fleshy; **porkiness** *n.*

porn *n. colloq.* pornography. [abbr.]

porno /'pɔːnəʊ/ *colloq.* 1 *n.* pornography. 2 *a.* pornographic. [abbr.]

pornography /pɔː'nɒgrəfɪ/ *n.* explicit representation of sexual activity visually or descriptively to stimulate erotic rather than aesthetic feelings; film, literature, etc. containing this; **pornographic** /pɔːnə'græfɪk/ *a.* [Gk (*pornē* prostitute)]

porous /'pɔːrəs/ *a.* containing pores; able to be permeated by fluid or air; **porosity** /-'rɒsɪtɪ/ *n.* [F f. L (PORE[1])]

porphyry /'pɔːfɪrɪ/ *n.* hard rock composed of crystals of red or white feldspar in red matrix; **porphyritic** /-'rɪtɪk/ *a.* [ult. f. Gk (PURPLE)]

porpoise /'pɔ:pəs/ *n.* sea mammal related to whale, with blunt rounded snout. [F f. Rmc (PORK, L *piscis* fish)]

porridge /'pɒrɪdʒ/ *n.* food made by boiling oatmeal or cereal in water or milk; *sl.* imprisonment. [alt. of POTTAGE]

porringer /'pɒrɪndʒə/ *n. archaic* small soup-basin, esp. for child. [F *potager* (POTTAGE)]

port[1] *n.* harbour; town or place possessing harbour; **port of call** place where ship or person stops during journey. [OE f. L *portus*]

port[2] *n.* strong sweet usu. dark-red fortified wine. [*Oporto* in Portugal]

port[3] **1** *n.* left-hand side of ship or aircraft looking forward. **2** *v.t.* turn (helm) to port. **3 port tack** tack with wind on port side. [prob. orig. side turned to PORT[1]]

port[4] *n.* opening in ship's side for entrance or loading etc.; porthole. [F f. L *porta* gate]

port[5] *v.t.* carry (rifle) diagonally across and close to body. [F f. L *porto* carry]

portable /'pɔ:təb(ə)l/ **1** *a.* easily movable, convenient for carrying. **2** *n.* portable form of an article, e.g. television or typewriter. **3 portability** /-'bɪlɪtɪ/ *n.* [F or L (PORT[5])]

portage /'pɔ:tɪdʒ/ **1** *n.* carrying of boats or goods between two navigable waters; place at which this is necessary. **2** *v.t.* convey (boat or goods) over portage. [F or L (PORT[5])]

portal /'pɔ:t(ə)l/ *n.* gate or doorway etc., esp. elaborate one; **portal vein** vein conveying blood to liver or other organ except heart. [F f. L (PORT[4])]

portcullis /pɔ:t'kʌlɪs/ *n.* strong heavy grating sliding up and down in vertical grooves, lowered to block gateway in fortress etc. [F, = sliding door]

portend /pɔ:'tend/ *v.t.* foreshadow, as an omen; give warning of. [L *portendo* (PRO-[1], TEND[1])]

portent /'pɔ:tent/ *n.* omen, significant sign of something to come; prodigy, marvellous thing. [L *portentum* (prec.)]

portentous /pɔ:'tentəs/ *a.* being or like a portent; pompously solemn.

porter[1] *n.* person employed to carry luggage etc.; dark beer brewed from charred or browned malt. [F f. L (PORT[5])]

porter[2] *n.* doorman or gate-keeper, esp. of large building. [AF f. L (PORT[4])]

porterage *n.* hire of porters. [PORTER[1]]

porterhouse steak choice cut of beef.

portfolio /pɔ:t'fəʊlɪəʊ/ *n.* (*pl.* **portfolios**) case for loose drawings, sheets of paper, etc.; list of investments held by person or company etc.; office of minister of State; **Minister without portfolio** minister not in charge of any department of State. [It. *portafogli* sheet-carrier]

porthole *n.* aperture, usu. glazed, in ship's side for admission of light and air. [PORT[4]]

portico /'pɔ:tɪkəʊ/ *n.* (*pl.* **porticoes**) colonnade, roof supported by columns at regular intervals, usu. attached as porch to a building. [It. f. L *porticus* porch]

portion /'pɔ:ʃ(ə)n/ **1** *n.* part or share; amount of food allotted to one person; dowry; one's destiny or lot. **2** *v.* divide (thing) into portions; distribute *out*; give dowry to. [F f. L *portio*]

Portland cement /'pɔ:tlənd/ cement manufactured from chalk and clay. [Isle of *Portland* in Dorset]

Portland stone valuable building limestone.

portly *a.* corpulent and dignified. [PORT[5]]

portmanteau /pɔ:t'mæntəʊ/ *n.* (*pl.* **portmanteaus**) trunk for clothes etc., opening into two equal parts; **portmanteau word** factitious word blending sounds and combining meanings of two others (e.g. CHORTLE). [F (PORT[5], MANTLE)]

portrait /'pɔ:trɪt/ *n.* likeness of person or animal made by drawing or painting or photography; description in words; **portraitist** *n.* [F (PORTRAY)]

portraiture /'pɔ:trɪtʃə/ *n.* portraying; portrait; description in words.

portray /pɔ:'treɪ/ *v.t.* make picture of; describe in words; **portrayal** *n.* [F *portraire -trait* depict]

Portuguese /pɔ:tjʊ'gi:z/ **1** *a.* of Portugal or its people or language. **2** *n.* (*pl.* same) native or language of Portugal. **3 Portuguese man-of-war** jellyfish with sail-shaped crest and poisonous sting. [Port. f. med.L]

pose /pəʊz/ **1** *v.* assume certain attitude for artistic purposes or to impress others; set up or give oneself out *as* (expert etc.); put forward or present (question or problem); place (artist's model etc.) in certain attitude; puzzle (person) with question or problem. **2** *n.* attitude of body or mind; affectation or pretence. [F f. L *pauso* PAUSE, confused with L *pono* place]

poser *n.* puzzling question or problem.

poseur /pəʊ'zɜ:/ *n.* person who poses for effect or behaves affectedly. [F (*poser* POSE)]

posh **1** *a.* high-class, smart. **2** *v.t.* smarten *up*. [perh. *sl. posh* money, a dandy]

posit /'pɒzɪt/ *v.t.* assume as fact, postulate. [L (foll.)]

position /pə'zɪʃ(ə)n/ **1** *n.* place occupied by person or thing; proper place (*in, out of, position*); being advantageously placed (*manœuvring for position*); way in which thing or its parts are placed or arranged; mental attitude, way of looking at question; situation in relation to others (*puts one in an awkward position*); rank or status, high social standing; paid (official or domestic) employment; place where troops are posted for strategical purposes; configuration of chess-men etc. during game. **2** *v.t.* place in position. **3 positional** *a.* [F or L (*pono posit-* place)]

positive /'pɒzɪtɪv/ **1** *a.* formally or explicitly stated (*positive assertion*); definite, unquestionable (*proof positive*); (of person) convinced, confident or over-confident in opinion; absolute, not relative; *colloq.* downright, out-and-out (*it would be a positive miracle*); constructive (*a positive suggestion*); marked by presence and not absence of qualities (*positive reaction*); dealing only with matters of fact, practical (*positive philosophy*); tending in direction naturally or arbitrarily taken as that of increase or progress; (of quantity in algebra) greater than zero; of or containing or producing the kind of electrical charge produced by rubbing glass with silk; (of photograph) showing lights and shades or colours as in original image cast on film etc.; *Gram.* (of adjective or adverb) in primary form expressing simple quality without comparison. **2** *n.* positive adjective, photograph, quantity, etc. **3 positive vetting** intensive inquiry into background and character of candidate for senior post in civil service etc. [F or L (prec.)]

positivism *n.* philosophical system recognizing only positive facts and observable phenomena; **logical positivism** form of this in which symbolic logic is used and linguistic problems emphasized; **positivist** *n.*

positron /'pɒzɪtrɒn/ *n.* elementary particle with mass of electron and charge same as electron's but positive. [*posi*tive elec*tron*]

posse /'pɒsɪ/ *n.* body (*of* constables); strong force or company. [L, = be able]

possess /pə'zes/ *v.t.* hold as property, own; have (faculty or quality etc.); occupy or dominate mind of; **like one possessed** with great energy; **possessor** *n.* [F f. L *possideo possess-*]

possession /pə'zeʃ(ə)n/ *n.* possessing or being possessed; thing possessed; occupancy; (in *pl.*) property, wealth; subject territory; **take possession of** become owner or possessor of. [F or L (prec.)]

possessive /pə'zesɪv/ **1** *a.* showing desire to possess or retain what one possesses; *Gram.* (of word or form) indicating possession (e.g. *Anne's, my, mine*). **2** *n. Gram.* possessive case or word. [L (POSSESS)]

possibility /pɒsɪ'bɪlɪtɪ/ *n.* state or fact of being possible; thing that may exist or happen; capability of being used or of producing good results (*the scheme has possibilities*). [foll.]

possible /'pɒsɪb(ə)l/ **1** *a.* capable of existing, happening, being done, etc. **2** *n.* possible candidate, member of team, etc.; highest possible score esp. in shooting. [F or L (POSSE)]

possibly *adv.* perhaps; in accordance with possibility (*cannot possibly agree*).

possum /'pɒsəm/ *n. colloq.* = OPOSSUM; **play possum** pretend to be unconscious, feign ignorance. [abbr.]

post[1] /pəʊst/ **1** *n.* long stout piece of timber or metal set upright in ground etc. to support something, mark position or boundary, etc.; pole marking start or finish of race. **2** *v.t.* (also with *up*) attach (paper etc.) in prominent place; announce or advertise by placard or in published list. [OE f. L *postis*]

post[2] /pəʊst/ **1** *n.* official conveying of parcels, letters, etc.; single collection or delivery of these (*will try to catch the post*); place where letters etc. are dealt with (*take it to the post*). **2** *v.* put (letter etc.) into post (esp. in *p.p.*) supply (person) with information (*keep me posted*); enter (item) in ledger, complete (ledger) thus. **3 post-bag** mail-bag; **post-box** box for posting letters; **post-code** group of letters and numerals in postal address to assist sorting; **post-free** sent by post without charge, with postage prepaid; **post-haste** with great speed; **post office** building or room where postal business is carried on; **Post Office** public department or corporation responsible for postal services; **post-paid** on which postage has been paid. [F f. It. f. L (POSITION)]

post[3] /pəʊst/ **1** *n.* situation of paid employment; appointed place of soldier etc. on duty; defensible position, fort, trading station, force of soldiers occupying fort etc. **2** *v.t.* place (soldier etc.) at his post; appoint to post or command. **3 last post** military bugle-call at bedtime or funeral. [F (as prec.)]

post- *prefix* after, behind. [L *post* adv. & prep.]

postage *n.* amount charged for sending letter etc. by post; **postage stamp** official stamp for sticking on letter etc indicating amount of postage paid. [POST²]

postal *a.* of or by post; **postal code** = *post-code*; **postal order** kind of money order issued by Post Office; **postally** *adv.* [F (POST²)]

postcard *n.* card for sending by post without envelope. [POST²]

postdate /pəʊst'deɪt/ *v.t.* follow in time; give later than true date to. [POST-]

poster *n.* placard in public place; large printed picture. [POST¹]

poste restante /pəʊst re'stɑ̃t/ department in post office where letters are kept till called for. [F]

posterior /pɒ'stɪərɪə/ **1** *a.* later, coming after in series or order or time; hinder. **2** *n.* buttocks. [L compar. of *posterus* (POST-)]

posterity /pɒ'sterɪtɪ/ *n.* succeeding generations; person's descendants. [F f. L (prec.)]

postern /'pɒstɜ:n/ *n. archaic* back or side entrance. [F f. L (as prec.)]

postgraduate /pəʊst'grædjʊət/ **1** *a.* (of course of study) carried on after taking first degree. **2** *n.* student taking such course. [POST-]

posthumous /'pɒstjʊməs/ *a.* occurring after death; published after author's death; born after father's death. [L *postumus* last]

postilion /pə'stɪljən/ *n.* rider on near horse drawing coach etc. without coachman. [F f. It. (POST²)]

Post-Impressionism /pəʊstɪm'preʃənɪz(ə)m/ *n.* artistic aims and methods directed to expressing individual artist's conception of objects represented; **Post-Impressionist** *n.* [POST-]

postman *n.* one who delivers or collects letters etc. [POST²]

postmark **1** *n.* official mark on letter etc. cancelling stamp and giving place and date. **2** *v.t.* stamp with postmark.

postmaster *n.* official in charge of a post office; **postmistress** *n. fem.*

post-mortem /pəʊst'mɔ:təm/ **1** *n.* examination made after death, esp. to determine its cause; *colloq.* discussion after conclusion (of game, election, etc.). **2.** *adv.* & *a.* after death. [L]

postnatal /pəʊst'neɪt(ə)l/ *a.* of or concerning period after childbirth. [POST-]

postpone /pəʊst'pəʊn/ *v.t.* cause or arrange to take place at later time; **postponement** *n.* [L (*pono* place)]

postprandial /pəʊst'prændɪəl/ *a.* after lunch or dinner. [L *prandium* a meal]

postscript /'pəʊstskrɪpt/ *n.* additional paragraph, esp. at end of letter after signature. [L (SCRIPT)]

postulant /'pɒstjʊlənt/ *n.* candidate, esp. for admission to religious order. [F or L (foll.)]

postulate **1** /'pɒstjʊleɪt/ *v.t.* assume or require to be true, esp. as basis for reasoning; claim; take for granted. **2** /'pɒstjʊlət/ *n.* thing postulated. **3 postulation** /-'leɪʃ(ə)n/ *n.* [L *postulo*]

posture /'pɒstʃə/ **1** *n.* attitude of body or mind, relative position of parts esp. of body; condition or state (*of* affairs etc.). **2** *v.* assume posture, esp. for effect; dispose limbs of (person) in particular way. **3 postural** *a.* [F f. It. f. L (POSIT)]

post-war /pəʊst'wɔ:, *attrib.* 'pəʊst-/ *a.* occurring or existing after a war. [POST-]

posy /'pəʊzɪ/ *n.* small bunch of flowers. [contr. of POESY]

pot¹ **1** *n.* rounded vessel of earthenware or metal or glass, for holding liquids or solids or for cooking in; = *chamber-pot*, TEAPOT, etc.; contents of pot; total amount bet in game etc., *colloq.* large sum; *sl.* prize in athletic contest, esp. silver cup; = *pot-belly*. **2** *v.* (-tt-) plant in pot; sit (child) on chamber-pot; pocket (ball) in billiards etc.; shoot (*at*); hit or kill (animal) by pot-shot; seize or secure; abridge or epitomize; (esp. in *p.p.*) preserve (food) in sealed pot etc. (*potted shrimps*). **3 go to pot** *colloq.* deteriorate, be ruined; **pot-belly** protruding belly, person with this; **pot-boiler** piece of art, writing, etc., done merely to earn money; **pot-herb** herb whose leaves etc. are used in cooking; **pot-hole** deep hole in rock, rough hole worn in road surface; **pot-holing** exploring pot-holes in rock; **pot-hook** hook over fireplace for hanging or lifting pot, curved stroke in handwriting; **pot-hunter** sportsman who shoots at random, person who takes part in contest merely for sake of prize; **pot luck** whatever is available; **pot plant** plant grown in flower-pot; **pot-roast** *n.* piece of meat cooked slowly in covered dish, (*v.t.*) cook thus; **pot-shot** random shot, casual attempt; **potting-shed** shed in which plants are grown in pots for planting out later. [OE f. L]

pot² *n. sl.* marijuana. [Mex. Sp. *potiguaya*]

potable /'pəʊtəb(ə)l/ *a.* drinkable. [F or L (*poto* drink)]

potage /pɒ'tɑ:ʒ/ *n.* thick soup. [F (POT¹)]

potash /'pɒtæʃ/ *n.* any of various salts of potassium, esp. potassium carbonate. [Du. (POT¹, ASH¹)]

potassium /pə'tæsɪəm/ *n.* soft silver-white metallic element. [prec.]

potation /pə'teɪʃ(ə)n/ *n.* drinking; a drink. [F f. L (POTION)]

potato /pə'teɪtəʊ/ *n.* (*pl.* **potatoes**) plant with starchy tubers used as food; its tuber. [Sp. *patata* f. Taino *batata*]

poteen /pɒ'ti:n/ *n.* (in Ireland) whisky from illicit still. [Ir *poitín* dimin. (POT[1])]

potent /'pəʊtənt/ *a.* powerful, strong; (of reason) forceful, cogent; (of man) not sexually impotent; **potency** *n.* [L *potens -ent-* (POSSE)]

potentate /'pəʊtənteɪt/ *n.* monarch, or ruler with great power. [F or L (prec.)]

potential /pə'tenʃ(ə)l/ **1** *a.* capable of coming into being or action. **2** *n.* capacity for use or development, usable resources; quantity determining energy of mass in gravitational field, of charge in electric field, etc. **3 potentiality** /-ʃɪ'ælɪtɪ/ *n.*; **potentially** *adv.* [F or L (POTENT)]

potheen var. of POTEEN.

pother /'pɒðə/ *n. literary* noise, commotion, fuss. [orig. unkn.]

potion /'pəʊʃ(ə)n/ *n.* dose or draught of liquid medicine or of drug or poison. [F f. L (*poto* drink)]

pot-pourri /pəʊ'pʊrɪ/ *n.* scented mixture of dried petals and spices; musical or literary medley. [F, = rotten pot]

potsherd *n.* broken piece of earthenware (esp. in archaeology). [POT[1]]

pottage /'pɒtɪdʒ/ *n. archaic* soup, stew. [F (POT[1])]

potter[1] *v.i.* work, move *about* or *around*, in desultory manner. [dial. *pote* push]

potter[2] *n.* maker of earthenware vessels; **potter's wheel** horizontal revolving disc to carry clay during moulding. [OE (POT[1])]

pottery *n.* vessels etc. made of baked clay; potter's work or workshop. [F (prec.)]

potty[1] /'pɒtɪ/ *a. sl.* crazy, foolish; insignificant, trivial. [orig. unkn.]

potty[2] *n. colloq.* chamber-pot, esp. for child. [POT[1]]

pouch 1 *n.* small bag or detachable outside pocket; baggy area of skin (under eyes etc.); pocket-like receptacle in which marsupials carry young during lactation. **2** *v.t.* put or make into pouch; take possession of, pocket. [F (POKE[2])]

pouffe /pu:f/ *n.* large cushion as low seat; soft stuffed couch. [F]

poult /pəʊlt/ *n.* young domestic fowl, turkey, or game-bird. [contr. of PULLET]

poulterer /'pəʊltərə/ *n.* dealer in poultry and usu. game. [*poulter* (POULT)]

poultice /'pəʊltɪs/ **1** *n.* soft heated mass of bread or kaolin etc. applied to sore part of the body. **2** *v.t.* apply poultice to. [L *pultes* pl. of *puls* pottage]

poultry /'pəʊltrɪ/ *n.* domestic fowls, ducks, geese, turkeys, etc., esp. as source of food. [F (POULT)]

pounce 1 *v.i.* make sudden attack (*on*); *fig.* seize eagerly *on* (opportunity etc.) **2** *n.* pouncing, sudden swoop. [orig. unkn.]

pound[1] *n.* unit of weight, equal to 16 oz. avoirdupois (454 g.), 12 oz. troy (373 g.); (in full **pound sterling;** *pl.* **pounds** or **pound**) currency unit of UK; currency unit of some other countries; **pound note** bank note for one pound; **pound of flesh** any legal but morally offensive demand. [OE f. L *pondo*]

pound[2] *v.* crush or beat with repeated strokes; deliver heavy blows or gunfire (*at* or *on*); make one's way heavily (*along* etc.); (of heart) beat heavily. [OE]

pound[3] *n.* enclosure where stray animals or officially removed vehicles are kept until claimed. [OE]

poundage *n.* commission or fee of so much per pound sterling or weight. [POUND[1]]

pounder *n.* thing that, or gun carrying shell that, weighs a pound or (**-pounder**) so many pounds (*three-pounder*).

pour /pɔ:/ *v.* (cause to) flow esp. downwards in stream or shower; rain heavily; come or go in profusion or rapid succession (*crowd poured out*; *letters poured in*); discharge or send freely; utter at length or in a rush (*poured out his story*). [orig. unkn.]

pourboire /pʊə'bwɑ:/ *n.* gratuity, tip. [F]

pout 1 *v.* push forward one's lips as sign of displeasure or sulking; protrude (lips), (of lips) be pushed forward thus. **2** *n.* pouting expression. [orig. unkn.]

pouter *n.* a kind of pigeon with great power of inflating its crop.

poverty /'pɒvətɪ/ *n.* being poor, want; scarcity or lack; inferiority, poorness; **poverty line** minimum income level needed to secure necessities of life; **poverty-stricken** very poor; **poverty trap** situation in which increase of income incurs loss of State benefits, making real improvement impossible. [F f. L (PAUPER)]

POW *abbr.* prisoner of war.

powder 1 *n.* mass of fine dry particles; medicine or cosmetic in this form; gunpowder. **2** *v.t.* apply powder to; reduce to fine powder (*powdered milk*). **3 powder blue** pale blue; **powder-puff** soft pad for applying powder to skin; **powder-room** ladies' lavatory in public building. **4 powdery** *a.* [F f. L *pulvis -ver-* dust]

power 1 *n.* ability to do or act; particular faculty of body or mind; vigour, energy; active property or function (*high heating power*); *colloq.* large number or amount (*did me a power of good*); government, influence, or authority; ascendancy or control (*the party in power*); authorization, delegated authority (*power of attorney*); influential person, body, or thing; State having international influence; deity; capacity for exerting mechanical force (*horsepower*); mechanical or electrical energy as opposed to hand labour, *attrib.* operated by this; electricity supply (*power-cut*); product obtained by multiplying number by given number of factors equal to it (*the third power of 2* = 2^3 = 8); magnifying capacity of lens. **2** *v.t.* supply with mechanical or electrical energy. **3** **power-point** socket in wall etc. for connecting electrical device to mains; **power-station** building where electrical power is generated for distribution; **the powers that be** those in authority. [AF f. Rmc (L *posse* be able)]

powerful *a.* having great power or influence; **powerfully** *adv.*

powerhouse *n.* power-station; person etc. of great energy.

powerless *a.* without power; wholly unable.

powwow /ˈpaʊwaʊ/ **1** *n.* conference or meeting for discussion (orig. among N. American Indians). **2** *v.i.* hold powwow. [Algonquian]

pox *n.* virus disease with pocks (*chickenpox*; *smallpox*); *colloq.* syphilis. [alt. of *pocks* pl. of POCK]

pp. *abbr.* pages.

p.p. abbr. *per pro.*

pp *abbr.* pianissimo.

p.p.m. *abbr.* parts per million.

PPS *abbr.* Parliamentary Private Secretary; additional postscript [*post-postscript*].

PR *abbr.* proportional representation; public relations.

pr. *abbr.* pair.

Pr *symb.* praseodymium.

practicable /ˈpræktɪkəb(ə)l/ *a.* that can be done or used; possible in practice; **practicability** /-ˈbɪlɪtɪ/ *n.* [F (foll.)]

practical /ˈpræktɪk(ə)l/ **1** *a.* of or concerned with practice rather than theory; suited to use or action; (of person) inclined to action, able to do or make functional things well; that is such in effect, virtual (*is in practical control*). **2** *n.* practical examination or lesson. **3** **practical joke** humorous trick played on person. **4** **practicality** /-ˈkælɪtɪ/ *n.* [F or L f. Gk *praktikos* (*prassō* do)]

practically *adv.* virtually, almost; in a practical way.

practice /ˈpræktɪs/ *n.* habitual action or carrying on; repeated exercise to improve a skill, spell of this; habit, custom; action as opposed to theory; professional work of doctor, lawyer, etc.; **out of practice** temporarily lacking former skill etc. [foll.]

practise /ˈpræktɪs/, *US* **practice** *v.* perform habitually, carry out in action; do repeatedly as exercise to improve skill, exercise oneself in or on (thing requiring skill); pursue (profession, religion, etc.; also *absol.*); (in *p.p.*) experienced, expert. [F or med.L (PRACTICAL)]

practitioner /prækˈtɪʃənə/ *n.* person practising a profession, esp. medicine.

praenomen /priːˈnəʊmen/ *n.* ancient Roman's first or personal name (e.g. *Marcus* Tullius Cicero). [L (PRE-, NOMEN)]

praetor /ˈpriːtə/ *n.* ancient-Roman magistrate below consul. [F *préteur* or L]

praetorian guard /priːˈtɔːrɪən/ bodyguard of ancient-Roman emperor.

pragmatic /prægˈmætɪk/ *a.* dealing with matters from a practical point of view; treating facts of history with reference to their practical lessons; **pragmatically** *adv.* [L f. Gk *pragma -mat-* deed]

pragmatism /ˈprægmətɪz(ə)m/ *n.* matter-of-fact treatment of things; philosophy that evaluates assertions solely by practical consequences and bearing on human interests; **pragmatist** *n.* [Gk *pragma* (prec.)]

prairie /ˈpreərɪ/ *n.* large treeless area of grassland, esp. in N. America; **prairie-dog** N. American rodent with bark like dog's; **prairie oyster** raw egg seasoned and swallowed whole. [F f. Rmc (L *pratum* meadow)]

praise /preɪz/ **1** *v.t.* express warm approval or admiration of; glorify (God) in words. **2** *n.* praising, commendation. [F *preisier* f. L (*pretium* price)]

praiseworthy *a.* worthy of praise.

praline /ˈprɑːliːn/ *n.* sweet made by browning nuts in boiling sugar. [F]

pram *n.* four-wheeled carriage for a baby, pushed by person on foot. [abbr. of PERAMBULATOR]

prance /prɑːns/ **1** *v.i.* walk or behave in elated or arrogant manner; (of horse) raise forelegs and spring from hind legs. **2** *n.* prancing, prancing movement. [orig. unkn.]

prang *sl.* **1** *v.t.* crash (aircraft or vehicle); damage by impact; bomb (target) successfully. **2** *n.* act or instance of pranging. [imit.]

prank *n.* practical joke, piece of mischief. [orig. unkn.]

prankster *n.* person fond of playing pranks.

praseodymium /preɪsɪəˈdɪmɪəm/ *n.* metallic element of lanthanide series. [G f. Gk *prasios* green]

prat *n. sl.* fool; buttocks. [orig. unkn.]

prate **1** *v.i.* chatter, talk too much; talk foolishly or irrelevantly. **2** *n.* prating, idle talk. [LG or Du.]

prattle /ˈpræt(ə)l/ **1** *v.* chatter or say in childish way. **2** *n.* childish chatter; inconsequential talk. [LG *pratelen* (PRATE)]

prawn *n.* edible shellfish like large shrimp. [orig. unkn.]

pray *v.* say prayers, make devout supplication; entreat; ask earnestly (for); please (*pray tell me*); **praying mantis** see MANTIS. [F f. L *precor*]

prayer[1] /ˈpreə/ *n.* solemn request or thanksgiving to God or object of worship; formula used in praying (*the Lord's prayer*); act of praying; religious service consisting largely of prayers (*morning prayer*); entreaty to person; **prayer-book** book of set prayers; **prayer-mat** small carpet on which Muslims kneel to pray; **prayer-wheel** revolving cylindrical box inscribed with or containing prayers, used esp. by Buddhists of Tibet. [F f. L (PRECARIOUS)]

prayer[2] /ˈpreɪə/ *n.* one who prays.

pre- *prefix* before (in time, place, order, degree, or importance). [L *prae* before]

preach *v.* deliver sermon or religious address, deliver (sermon); give moral advice in obtrusive way; proclaim (the Gospel etc.); advocate or inculcate (quality or practice etc.). [F f. L *praedico* declare]

preamble /priːˈæmb(ə)l/ *n.* preliminary statement; introductory part of statute or deed etc. [F f. L (AMBLE)]

pre-arrange /priːəˈreɪndʒ/ *v.t.* arrange beforehand; **pre-arrangement** *n.* [PRE-]

prebend /ˈprebənd/ *n.* stipend of canon or member of chapter; portion of land or tithe from which this is drawn; **prebendal** *a.* [F f. L (*praebeo* grant)]

prebendary /ˈprebəndərɪ/ *n.* holder of prebend; honorary canon. [med.L (prec.)]

Precambrian /priːˈkæmbrɪən/ **1** *a.* of the geological era preceding Palaeozoic. **2** *n.* this era. [PRE-]

precarious /prɪˈkeərɪəs/ *a.* uncertain, dependent on chance; insecure, perilous. [L *precarius* (PRAY)]

pre-cast /priːˈkɑːst/ *a.* (of concrete) cast in blocks before use. [PRE-]

precaution /prɪˈkɔːʃ(ə)n/ *n.* action taken beforehand to avoid risk or ensure good result; **precautionary** *a.* [F f. L (CAUTION)]

precede /prɪˈsiːd/ *v.t.* come or go before in time, order, importance, etc.; cause to be preceded *by*. [F f. L (CEDE)]

precedence /ˈpresɪdəns/ *n.* priority in time or order etc.; right of preceding others. [foll.]

precedent /ˈpresɪdənt/ **1** *n.* previous case taken as example for subsequent cases or as justification. **2** *a.* preceding in time or order etc. [F (PRECEDE)]

precentor /prɪˈsentə/ *n.* one who leads singing or (in synagogue) prayers of congregation. [F, or L *precentor* (*cano* sing)]

precept /ˈpriːsept/ *n.* command, rule of conduct; writ, warrant. [L *praeceptum* maxim, order]

preceptor /prɪˈseptə/ *n.* teacher, instructor; **preceptorial** /-ˈtɔːrɪ(ə)l/ *a.* [L (prec.)]

precession /prɪˈseʃ(ə)n/ *n.* slow movement of axis of spinning body around another axis; **precession of the equinoxes** slow retrograde motion of equinoctial points along ecliptic, resulting early occurrence of equinoxes in each successive sidereal year. [L (PRECEDE)]

pre-Christian /priːˈkrɪstjən/ *a.* before Christianity. [PRE-]

precinct /ˈpriːsɪŋkt/ *n.* enclosed area, esp. around place of worship; (in full **pedestrian precinct**) area in town where traffic is prohibited; (in *pl.*) environs. [L (*praecingo -cinct-* encircle)]

preciosity /preʃɪˈɒsɪtɪ/ *n.* over-refinement in art, esp. in choice of words. [foll.]

precious /ˈpreʃəs/ **1** *a.* of great value or worth; beloved, much prized; affectedly refined; *colloq.* (often *iron.*) considerable (*did him a precious lot of good*). **2** *adv. colloq.* extremely, very (*had precious little left*). **3 precious metals** gold, silver, and platinum; **precious stone** piece of mineral having great value esp. as used in jewellery. [F f. L *pretium* price]

precipice /ˈpresɪpɪs/ *n.* vertical or steep face of rock, cliff, mountain, etc. [F or L (PRECIPITATE)]

precipitance /prɪˈsɪpɪtəns/ *n.* (also **precipitancy**) rash haste. [F (foll.)]

precipitate 1 /prɪˈsɪpɪteɪt/ *v.t.* hasten occurrence of, make occur prematurely; send rapidly *into* certain state or condition (*were precipitated into war*); throw down headlong; cause (substance) to be deposited in solid form from solution; condense (vapour) into drops which fall as rain etc. **2** /prɪˈsɪpɪtət/ *a.* headlong, violently hurried; (of person or act) hasty, rash, inconsiderate. **3** /prɪˈsɪpɪtət/ *n.* substance precipitated from solution; moisture condensed from vapour and falling as rain etc. [L (*praeceps -cipit-* headlong)]

precipitation /prɪsɪpɪˈteɪʃ(ə)n/ *n.* precipitating or being precipitated; rash haste; rain or snow etc. falling to ground, quantity of this. [F or L (prec.)]

precipitous /prɪˈsɪpɪtəs/ *a.* of or like

precipice, dangerously steep; precipitate. [F f. L (PRECIPITATE)]

précis /'preɪsi:/ **1** *n.* (*pl.* same /-i:z/) summary, abstract. **2** *v.t.* make précis of. [F]

precise /prɪ'saɪs/ *a.* accurately expressed; definite, exact; punctilious, scrupulous in being exact. [F f. L (*praecido* cut short)]

precisely *adv.* in precise manner, exactly; in exact terms; (as reply) quite so, as you say.

precision /prɪ'sɪʒ(ə)n/ *n.* accuracy, degree of refinement in measurement etc.; *attrib.* marked by or adapted for precision (*precision instruments*). [F or L (PRECISE)]

preclude /prɪ'klu:d/ *v.t.* prevent (*from*), make impossible. [L *praecludo* (CLOSE[1])]

precocious /prɪ'kəʊʃəs/ *a.* (of person) prematurely developed in some faculty or characteristic; (of action etc.) indicating such development; **precocity** /prɪ'kɒsɪtɪ/ *n.* [L *praecox, -cocis* early ripe]

precognition /pri:kɒg'nɪʃ(ə)n/ *n.* (supposed) foreknowledge, esp. of supernatural kind. [PRE-]

preconceive /pri:kən'si:v/ *v.t.* form (idea or opinion etc.) beforehand.

preconception /pri:kən'sepʃ(ə)n/ *n.* preconceived idea, prejudice.

pre-condition /pri:kən'dɪʃ(ə)n/ *n.* condition that must be fulfilled in advance.

precursor /pri:'kɜ:sə/ *n.* forerunner, harbinger; one who precedes in office etc. [L (*praecurro -curs-* run before)]

predacious /prɪ'deɪʃəs/ *a.* (of animal) predatory. [L *praeda* booty]

pre-date /pri:'deɪt/ *v.t.* antedate. [PRE-]

predator /'predətə/ *n.* predatory animal. [L (PREDACIOUS)]

predatory *a.* (of animal) preying naturally upon others; plundering or exploiting others.

predecease /pri:dɪ'si:s/ *v.t.* die earlier than (another person). [PRE-]

predecessor /'pri:dɪsesə/ *n.* former holder of office or position with respect to later holder; ancestor; thing to which another has succeeded. [F f. L *decessor* (as DECEASE)]

predestine /pri:'destɪn/ *v.t.* determine beforehand, ordain by divine will or as if by fate; **predestination** /-'neɪʃ(ə)n/ *n.* [F or eccl.L (PRE-)]

predetermine /pri:dɪ'tɜ:mɪn/ *v.t.* decree beforehand, predestine. [PRE-]

predicable /'predɪkəb(ə)l/ *a.* that may be predicated or affirmed. [med.L (PREDICATE)]

predicament /prɪ'dɪkəmənt/ *n.* difficult or unpleasant situation. [L (PREDICATE)]

predicant /'predɪkənt/ *a.* (of religious order) engaged in preaching. [L (foll.)]

predicate 1 /'predɪkeɪt/ *v.t.* assert or affirm as true or existent. **2** /'predɪkət/ *n.* (in logic) what is predicated (e.g. *mortal* in *all men are mortal*); *Gram.* what is said about the subject of a sentence etc. (e.g. *went home* in *John went home*). **3 predication** /-'keɪʃ(ə)n/ *n.* [L *praedico -dicat-* declare]

predicative /prɪ'dɪkətɪv/ *a.* forming part or all of the predicate (e.g. *old* in *the dog is old* but not in *the old dog*). [L (prec.)]

predict /prɪ'dɪkt/ *v.t.* foretell, prophesy; **predictor** *n.* [L *praedico -dict-* foretell]

predictable *a.* that can be predicted or is to be expected; **predictably** *adv.*

prediction /prɪ'dɪkʃ(ə)n/ *n.* predicting or being predicted; thing predicted.

predilection /pri:dɪ'lekʃ(ə)n/ *n.* preference or special liking (*for*). [F f. L (*praediligo* prefer)]

predispose /pri:dɪ'spəʊz/ *v.t.* influence favourably in advance; render liable or inclined (*to*) beforehand; **predisposition** /-pə'zɪʃ(ə)n/ *n.* [PRE-]

predominant /prɪ'dɒmɪnənt/ *a.* predominating; being strongest or main element; **predominance** *n.*

predominate /prɪ'dɒmɪneɪt/ *v.i.* have control (*over*); be superior; be strongest or main element. [med.L (DOMINATE)]

pre-eminent /pri:'emɪnənt/ *a.* excelling others, outstanding; **pre-eminence** *n.* [PRE-]

pre-empt /pri:'empt/ *v.t.* obtain (thing) by pre-emption; appropriate beforehand, forestall. [back-form. f. foll.]

pre-emption /pri:'empʃ(ə)n/ *n.* purchase or taking by one person or party before opportunity is offered to others. [med.L (*emo empt-* buy)]

pre-emptive /pri:'emptɪv/ *a.* pre-empting; (of military action) intended to prevent attack by disabling enemy.

preen *v.t.* (of bird) tidy (feathers) with beak; (of person) smarten (*oneself* or one's clothes etc.); **preen oneself** congratulate oneself, show self-satisfaction. [F]

pre-exist /pri:ɪg'zɪst/ *v.* exist beforehand or prior to; **pre-existence** *n.* [PRE-]

prefab /'pri:fæb/ *n. colloq.* prefabricated building. [abbr.]

prefabricate /pri:'fæbrɪkeɪt/ *v.t.* manufacture sections of (building etc.) prior to their assembly on a site. [PRE-]

preface /'prefəs/ **1** *n.* introduction to book stating subject, scope, etc.; preliminary part of a speech. **2** *v.t.* provide with preface; introduce or begin (event or speech) *with*; (of event etc.) lead up to (another). [F f. L *praefatio*]

prefatory /'prefətərɪ/ *a.* of or serving as preface, introductory.

prefect /'pri:fekt/ *n.* chief administrative officer of certain departments in France, Japan, etc.; senior pupil in school etc. authorized to maintain discipline. [F f. L (*praeficio -fect-* set in authority over)]

prefecture /'pri:fektjʊə/ *n.* district under government of prefect; prefect's office or tenure. [F or L (prec.)]

prefer /prɪ'fɜ:/ *v.t.* (**-rr-**) choose rather, like better (*prefer coffee to tea*); submit (information, accusation, etc.) for consideration; promote (person *to* office). [F f. L *praefero -lat-*]

preferable /'prefərəb(ə)l/ *a.* to be preferred; more desirable; **preferably** *adv.*

preference /'prefərəns/ *n.* preferring or being preferred; thing preferred; favouring of one person etc. before others; prior right, esp. to payment of debts; **in preference to** as thing preferred over (another); **preference shares** (or **stock**) shares or stock with greatest entitlement to dividend. [F f. med.L (PREFER)]

preferential /prefə'renʃ(ə)l/ *a.* of or involving preference; giving or receiving favour; **preferentially** *adv.*

preferment /prɪ'fɜ:mənt/ *n.* promotion to office. [PREFER]

prefigure /pri:'fɪgə/ *v.t.* represent or imagine beforehand. [PRE-]

prefix /'pri:fɪks/ **1** *n.* verbal element placed at beginning of a word to qualify meaning (e.g. *ex-*, *non-*); title placed before name (e.g. *Mr*). **2** *v.t.* add as introduction; join as prefix (*to* word). [L (FIX)]

preform /pri:'fɔ:m/ *v.t.* form beforehand. [PRE-]

pregnant /'pregnənt/ *a.* (of woman or female animal) having a child or young developing in womb; full of meaning, significant or suggestive (*a pregnant silence*); plentifully furnished *with* (*pregnant with danger*); fruitful in results; **pregnancy** *n.* [F, or L *praegnans*]

prehensile /prɪ'hensaɪl/ *a.* (of tail or limb) capable of grasping. [F f. L *prehendo -hens-* seize]

prehistoric /pri:hɪ'stɒrɪk/ *a.* of the period before written records; **prehistory** /-'hɪstərɪ/ *n.* [PRE-]

pre-ignition /pri:ɪg'nɪʃ(ə)n/ *n.* premature firing of explosive mixture in internal-combustion engine.

prejudge /pri:'dʒʌdʒ/ *v.t.* pass judgement on (person) before trial or proper enquiry; form premature judgement on.

prejudice /'predʒʊdɪs/ **1** *n.* preconceived opinion, bias (*against*, *in favour of*); injury that results or may result from some action or judgement (*to the prejudice of*). **2** *v.t.* impair validity of (right, claim, statement, etc.); (esp. in *p.p.*) cause (person) to have prejudice. **3 without prejudice (to)** without detriment to any existing right or claim. [F f. L (JUDGE)]

prejudicial /predʒʊ'dɪʃ(ə)l/ *a.* causing prejudice; detrimental (*to* rights, interests, etc.); **prejudicially** *adv.*

prelacy /'preləsɪ/ *n.* church government by prelates; prelates collectively; office or rank of prelate. [AF f. med.L (foll.)]

prelate /'prelət/ *n.* high ecclesiastical dignitary, e.g. bishop; **prelatical** /prɪ'lætɪk(ə)l/ *a.* [F f. L (PREFER)]

prelim /'pri:lɪm/ *n. colloq.* preliminary examination. [abbr.]

preliminary /prɪ'lɪmɪnərɪ/ **1** *a.* introductory, preparatory. **2** *n.* (usu. in *pl.*) preliminary action or arrangement. **3** *adv.* preparatory. **4 preliminarily** *adv.* [F or L (*limen* threshold)]

prelude /'prelju:d/ **1** *n.* action or event or situation serving as introduction (*to* another); introductory part of poem etc.; *Mus.* introductory movement or first piece of suite, short piece of music of similar type. **2** *v.* serve as prelude to; introduce (with a prelude). [F or L (*ludo lus-* play)]

pre-marital /pri:'mærɪt(ə)l/ *a.* of the time before marriage. [PRE-]

premature /'premətjʊə/ *a.* occurring or done before usual or proper time; too hasty; (of baby) born 3–12 weeks before expected time; **prematurity** /-'tjʊərɪtɪ/ *n.* [L (MATURE)]

premedication /pri:medɪ'keɪʃ(ə)n/ *n.* (also *colloq.* **pre-med**) medication in preparation for operation etc. [PRE-]

premeditate /pri:'medɪteɪt/ *v.t.* (esp. in *p.p.*) think out or plan beforehand; **premeditation** /-'teɪʃ(ə)n/ *n.* [L (MEDITATE)]

pre-menstrual /pri:'menstrʊəl/ *a.* of the time immediately before menstruation. [PRE-]

premier /'premɪə/ **1** *a.* first in importance or order or time. **2** *n.* Prime Minister, esp. in Great Britain. [F, = first]

première /'premɪeə/ **1** *n.* first performance or showing of play or film. **2** *v.t.* give première of. [F fem. (as prec.)]

premise /'premɪs/ *n.* = PREMISS; (in *pl.*) house or building with grounds and appurtenances; *Law* houses, lands, or tenements previously specified in document etc.; **on the premises** in the house etc. concerned. [F or L *praemissa* set in front]

premiss /'premɪs/ *n.* previous statement from which another is inferred. [var. of prec.]

premium /'pri:mɪəm/ *n.* amount to be paid for contract of insurance; sum added to interest, wages, etc.; reward or prize; **at a premium** above usual or nominal price, highly valued; **Premium (Savings) Bond** government security without interest but with chances of cash prizes; **put a premium on** provide or act as incentive to, attach special value to. [L *praemium* reward]

premolar /pri:'məʊlə/ **1** *n.* tooth nearer front of mouth than molars. **2** *a.* of these teeth. [PRE-]

premonition /pri:mə'nɪʃ(ə)n, pre-/ *n.* forewarning, presentiment; **premonitory** /prɪ'mɒnɪtərɪ/ *a.* [F or L (*moneo* warn)]

pre-natal /pri:'neɪt(ə)l/ *a.* of or concerning period before childbirth. [PRE-]

preoccupation /pri:ɒkjʊ'peɪʃ(ə)n/ *n.* state of being preoccupied; thing that engrosses one's mind. [F or L (as foll.)]

preoccupy /pri:'ɒkjʊpaɪ/ *v.t.* (of thought etc.) dominate or engross mind of, to exclusion of other thoughts. [L *praeoccupo* seize beforehand]

pre-ordain /pri:ɔ:'deɪn/ *v.t.* ordain or determine beforehand. [PRE-]

prep *colloq. n.* preparation of school work, period when this is done; **prep school** preparatory school. [abbr.]

preparation /prepə'reɪʃ(ə)n/ *n.* preparing or being prepared; specially prepared substance; work done by school pupils to prepare for lesson; (usu. in *pl.*) thing done to make ready. [F f. L (PREPARE)]

preparatory /prɪ'pærətərɪ/ **1** *a.* serving to prepare, introductory. **2** *adv.* in preparatory manner (esp. with *to*). **3 preparatory school** school preparing pupils for higher school or (*US*) for college or university. [L (foll.)]

prepare /prɪ'peə/ *v.t.* make or get ready for use, consideration, etc.; assemble (meal etc.) for eating; make (person) ready or disposed in some way (*prepared her for a shock*); get oneself ready or disposed (*prepare to jump*); **be prepared to** be disposed or willing to. [F or L (*paro* make ready)]

prepay /pri:'peɪ/ *v.t.* pay (charge) beforehand; pay postage on (letter or parcel etc.) beforehand; **prepayment** *n.* [PRE-]

prepense /prɪ'pens/ *a.* (usu. after noun) deliberate, intentional (*malice prepense*). [F *purpensé* premeditated]

preponderate /prɪ'pɒndəreɪt/ *v.i.* be greater in influence, quantity, or number; weigh more; predominate; **preponderance** *n.*; **preponderant** *a.* [L (*pondus -der-* weight)]

preposition /prepə'zɪʃ(ə)n/ *n.* word governing (and usu. preceding) noun or pronoun and expressing relation to another word or element (e.g. the man *on* the platform, came *after* dinner, went *by* train); **prepositional** *a.* [L (*praepono -posit-* place before)]

prepossess /pri:pə'zes/ *v.t.* (usu. in *pass.*, of idea etc.) take possession of (person); prejudice (usu. favourably and at first sight); **prepossession** *n.* [PRE-]

prepossessing *a.* attractive, appealing.

preposterous /prɪ'pɒstərəs/ *a.* utterly absurd, outrageous; contrary to nature, reason, or common sense. [L (= before behind)]

prepuce /'pri:pju:s/ *n.* foreskin; similar structure at tip of clitoris. [L *praeputium*]

Pre-Raphaelite /pri:'ræfəlaɪt/ *n.* member of group of 19th-c. artists emulating work of Italian artists before time of Raphael. [PRE-]

prerequisite /pri:'rekwɪzɪt/ **1** *a.* required as pre-condition. **2** *n.* prerequisite thing.

prerogative /prɪ'rɒgətɪv/ *n.* right or privilege exclusive to an individual or class. [F or L (*praerogo* ask first)]

Pres. *abbr.* President.

presage /'presɪdʒ/ **1** *n.* omen, portent; presentiment, foreboding. **2** /also prɪ'seɪdʒ/ *v.t.* portend, foreshadow; give warning of (event etc.) by natural means; (of person) predict or have presentiment of. [F f. L *praesagium*]

presbyter /'prezbɪtə/ *n.* (in Episcopal Church) minister of second order, priest; (in Presbyterian Church) elder. [eccl.L f. Gk, = elder]

Presbyterian /prezbɪ'tɪərɪən/ **1** *a.* (of Church) governed by elders all of equal rank, esp. national Church of Scotland. **2** *n.* member of Presbyterian Church; adherent of Presbyterian system. **3 Presbyterianism** *n.* [eccl.L *presbyterium* (as foll.)]

presbytery /'prezbɪtərɪ/ *n.* body of presbyters, esp. court next above kirk-session; eastern part of chancel; house of Roman Catholic priest. [F f. eccl.L f. Gk (PRESBYTER)]

pre-school /'pri:sku:l/ *a.* of time before child is old enough to attend school. [PRE-]

prescient /'presɪənt/ *a.* having foreknowledge or foresight; **prescience** *n.* [L *praescio* know before]

prescribe /prɪ'skraɪb/ *v.t.* lay down or impose authoritatively; advise use of (medicine etc.). [L *praescribo*]

prescript /'pri:skrɪpt/ *n.* ordinance, law, command. [L (prec.)]
prescription /prɪ'skrɪpʃ(ə)n/ *n.* prescribing; doctor's (usu. written) instruction for composition and use of medicine; medicine thus prescribed. [F f. L (PRESCRIBE)]
prescriptive /prɪ'skrɪptɪv/ *a.* prescribing; laying down rules; based on prescription; prescribed by custom. [L (PRESCRIBE)]
presence /'prezəns/ *n.* being present; place where person is (*admitted to her presence*); person's appearance or bearing, esp. when imposing; person or thing that is present; **presence of mind** calmness and self-command in sudden difficulty etc. [F f. L (foll.)]
present[1] /'prezənt/ **1** *a.* being in the place in question; now existing, occurring, or being such; now being considered etc. (*in the present case*); *Gram.* expressing action etc. now going on or habitually performed. **2** *n. the* time now passing; *Gram.* present tense. **3 at present** now; **by these presents** *Law* by this document (*know all men by these presents*); **for the present** just now, as far as the present is concerned; **present-day** of this time, modern. [F f. L *praesens -ent-*]
present[2] /'prezənt/ *n.* thing given. [F (prec.)]
present[3] /prɪ'zent/ *v.t.* introduce (person *to* another); introduce or offer or exhibit for attention or consideration; offer or give (thing *to* person) as gift; offer (compliments etc. *to*); (of circumstance) reveal (some quality etc.: *this presents some difficulty*); (of idea etc.) offer or suggest itself; deliver (cheque, bill, etc.) for acceptance or payment; aim (weapon *at*), hold out (weapon) in position for aiming; **present arms** hold rifle etc. vertically in front as salute; **present person with** present to him, cause him to have (*presents me with a problem*). [F f. L *praesento* (PRESENT[1])]
presentable /prɪ'zentəb(ə)l/ *a.* of good appearance, fit to be presented; **presentability** /-'bɪlɪtɪ/ *n.*; **presentably** *adv.*
presentation /prezən'teɪʃ(ə)n/ *n.* presenting or being presented; thing presented. [F f. L (PRESENT[3])]
presentiment /prɪ'zentɪmənt/ *n.* vague expectation, foreboding (esp. of evil). [F (PRE-)]
presently *adv.* soon, after a short time; *US & Sc.* at the present time, now. [PRESENT[1]]
preservative /prɪ'zɜ:vətɪv/ **1** *n.* substance for preserving perishable foodstuffs etc. **2** *a.* tending to preserve. [F f. med.L (foll.)]
preserve /prɪ'zɜ:v/ **1** *v.t.* keep safe or free from decay etc.; maintain in present state; retain (quality or condition); treat (food) to prevent decomposition or fermentation; keep (game etc.) undisturbed for private use. **2** *n.* preserved fruit, jam; place where game etc. is preserved; sphere regarded by person as being for him alone. **3 preservation** /prezə'veɪʃ(ə)n/ *n.* [F f. L (*servo* keep)]
preside /prɪ'zaɪd/ *v.i.* be chairman or president (*at* or *over* meeting); exercise control or authority. [F f. L (*sedeo* sit)]
presidency /'prezɪdənsɪ/ *n.* office of president; period of this. [Sp. or It. (as prec.)]
president /'prezɪdənt/ *n.* elected head of a republican State; person who is head of a society or council etc.; head of some colleges; *US* head of a university or company etc.; person in charge of a meeting; **presidential** /-'denʃ(ə)l/ *a.* [F f. L (PRESIDE)]
presidium /prɪ'sɪdɪəm/ *n.* standing committee in Communist organization. [Russ. f. L (PRESIDE)]
press[1] **1** *v.* apply steady force to (thing in contact); compress or squeeze (thing) to flatten or shape or smooth it or to extract juice etc.; squeeze (juice etc. *out of*, *from*, etc.); embrace or caress (*he pressed her hand*); exert pressure (*on*, *against*, etc.); be urgent, demand immediate action; make insistent demand *for*; crowd (*up*, *round*, etc.); hasten *on*, *forward*, etc.; (of enemy etc.) bear heavily on (esp. in *p.p.*); urge or entreat (*pressed him to stay*, *for an answer*; *will not press you*); urge (opinion or course of action *upon* person); force (offer, gift, etc., *upon*); insist on (*did not press the point*). **2** *n.* pressing (*gave it a slight press*); device for compressing, flattening, shaping, extracting juice, etc.; = *printing-press*; *the* art or practice of printing; *the* newspapers etc. generally; notice or publicity in newspapers (*got a good press*); printing-house or establishment; publishing company; crowding, crowd (*of* people etc.); pressure of affairs; large usu. shelved cupboard for clothes, books, etc. **3 be pressed for** have barely enough (*time* etc.); **go** (or **send**) **to press** go or send to be printed; **press agent** person employed to attend to advertising and press publicity; **press conference** interview given to body of journalists; **press-gallery** gallery for reporters esp. in legislative assembly; **press-stud** small fastening device engaged by pressing two parts together; **press-up** (usu. in

pl.) exercise in which prone body is raised from trunk upwards by pressing down on hands to straighten arms. [F f. L *premo press-*]

press² *v.t. hist.* force (man, or *absol.*) to serve in army or navy; bring into use as makeshift (*was pressed into service*). [obs. *prest* f. F, = loan]

press-gang 1 *n.* body of men employed to press men into army or navy service; other group using coercive methods. 2 *v.t.* force into service. [PRESS²]

pressing 1 *a.* urgent; urging strongly (*pressing invitation*). 2 *n.* thing made by pressing, esp. gramophone record; series of such made at one time. [PRESS¹]

pressure /ˈpreʃə/ 1 *n.* exertion of continuous force on or against body by another in contact with it, force so exerted; amount of this (expressed by force on unit area), esp. that of atmosphere; urgency (*work under pressure*); affliction or difficulty (*under financial pressure*); constraining influence (*put pressure on him*). 2 *v.t.* apply pressure to; coerce, persuade. 3 **pressure-cooker** sealed pan for cooking in short time under steam pressure; **pressure group** group seeking to influence policy by concerted action and propaganda. [L (PRESS¹)]

pressurize *v.t.* raise to high pressure; (esp. in *p.p.*) maintain normal atmospheric pressure in (aircraft cabin etc.) at high altitude; pressure (person); **pressurization** /-ˈzeɪʃ(ə)n/ *n.*

Prestel /preˈstel/ *n.* (**P**) computerized visual information system operated by British Telecommunications.

prestidigitator /prestɪˈdɪdʒɪteɪtə/ *n.* conjuror; **prestidigitation** /-ˈteɪʃ(ə)n/ *n.* [F (PRESTO, DIGIT)]

prestige /preˈstiːʒ/ 1 *n.* influence or good reputation derived from past achievements, associations, etc. 2 *a.* having or conferring prestige. [F, = illusion (as foll.)]

prestigious /preˈstɪdʒəs/ *a.* having or showing prestige. [L (*praestigiae* juggler's tricks)]

presto /ˈprestəʊ/ *Mus.* 1 *adv.* in quick tempo. 2 *n.* (*pl.* **prestos**) movement to be played this way. [It. f. L *praestus* quick]

pre-stressed /priːˈstrest/ *a.* (of concrete) strengthened by means of stretched wires within it. [PRE-]

presumably /prɪˈzjuːməblɪ/ *adv.* it is or may be reasonably presumed. [foll.]

presume /prɪˈzjuːm/ *v.* suppose to be true, take for granted; take the liberty, be impudent enough, venture (*may I presume to ask?*); be presumptuous; **presume on** (or **upon**) take advantage of or make unscrupulous use of (person's good nature etc.). [F f. L *praesumo*]

presumption /prɪˈzʌmpʃ(ə)n/ *n.* arrogance, presumptuous behaviour; presuming thing to be true, thing that is, or may be, presumed to be true; ground for presuming. [F f. L (prec.)]

presumptive /prɪˈzʌmptɪv/ *a.* giving grounds for presumption (*presumptive evidence*). [F f. L (PRESUME)]

presumptuous /prɪˈzʌmptjʊəs/ *a.* unduly or overbearingly confident. [F f. L (PRESUME)]

presuppose /priːsəˈpəʊz/ *v.t.* assume beforehand; imply; **presupposition** /-pəˈzɪʃ(ə)n/ *n.* [F (PRE-)]

pre-tax /priːˈtæks/ *a.* (of income) before deduction of taxes. [PRE-]

pretence /prɪˈtens/ *n.* pretending, make-believe; claim (*to* merit etc.); false profession of purpose, pretext; ostentation, show. [AF f. AL (foll.)]

pretend /prɪˈtend/ *v.* claim or assert falsely so as to deceive (*pretend knowledge, illness; pretended to be rich, that he was rich*); imagine to oneself in play (*pretended to be a dog, that it was night*); (in *p.p.*) falsely claimed to be such (*a pretended friend*); **pretend to** lay claim to (right or title), profess to have. [F, or L *praetendo* (TEND¹)]

pretender *n.* one who claims throne or title etc.

pretense *US* var. of PRETENCE.

pretension /prɪˈtenʃ(ə)n/ *n.* assertion of claim; justifiable claim; pretentiousness. [med.L (PRETEND)]

pretentious /prɪˈtenʃəs/ *a.* making excessive claim to great merit or importance; ostentatious. [F (as prec.)]

preterite /ˈpretərɪt/, *US* **preterit** *Gram.* 1 *a.* expressing past action or state. 2 *n.* preterite tense of verb. [F or L *praeteritum* past]

preternatural /priːtəˈnætʃər(ə)l/ *a.* outside the ordinary course of nature, supernatural. [L *praeter* beyond]

pretext /ˈpriːtekst/ *n.* ostensible reason, excuse offered. [L *praetextus* (TEXT)]

pretty /ˈprɪtɪ/ 1 *a.* attractive in a delicate way (*pretty girl, dress, song*); fine or good of its kind; *iron.* considerable (*a pretty penny*). 2 *adv.* fairly, moderately. 3 **pretty much** (or **nearly** or **well**) almost, very nearly; **pretty-pretty** too pretty. 4 **prettify** *v.t.*; **prettily** *adv.*; **prettiness** *n.* [OE]

pretzel /ˈprets(ə)l/ *n.* crisp knot-shaped salted biscuit. [G]

prevail /prɪˈveɪl/ *v.i.* be victorious or gain mastery (*against* or *over*); be the more usual or prominent; exist or occur in general use or experience; **prevail**

on (or **upon**) persuade. [L *praevaleo* (AVAIL)]

prevalent /'prevələnt/ *a.* generally existing or occurring, predominant; **prevalence** *n.* [as prec.]

prevaricate /prɪ'værɪkeɪt/ *v.i.* speak or act evasively or misleadingly; quibble, equivocate; **prevarication** /-'keɪʃ(ə)n/ *n.*; **prevaricator** *n.* [L, = walk crookedly]

prevent /prɪ'vent/ *v.t.* stop from happening or doing something, hinder, make impossible; stop or hinder *from doing* thing; **prevention** *n.* [L *praevenio -vent-* hinder]

preventative /prɪ'ventətɪv/ *a.* = PREVENTIVE.

preventive /prɪ'ventɪv/ **1** *a.* serving to prevent, esp. preventing disease. **2** *n.* preventive agent, measure, drug, etc. **3 preventive detention** imprisonment of habitual criminal for corrective training etc.; **Preventive Service** department of Customs concerned with prevention of smuggling.

preview /'pri:vju:/ **1** *n.* showing of film or play etc. before it is seen by the general public. **2** *v.t.* view or show in advance of public presentation. [PRE-]

previous /'pri:vɪəs/ *a.* coming before in time or order; prior *to*; done or acting hastily; **previous to** before (*had called previous to writing*). [L *praevius* (*via* way)]

pre-war /pri:'wɔ:, *attrib.* 'pri:-/ *a.* occurring or existing before a war. [PRE-]

prey /preɪ/ **1** *n.* animal that is hunted or killed by another for food; person or thing that falls a victim (*to* enemy, disease, fear, etc.). **2** *v.i.* **prey on** (or **upon**) seek or take as prey, (of disease or emotion etc.) exert harmful influence on. **3 beast** (or **bird**) **of prey** one that kills and devours other animals. [F f. L *praeda*]

price **1** *n.* amount of money for which thing is bought or sold; what must be given or done etc. to obtain or achieve something (*peace at any price*); odds in betting. **2** *v.t.* fix or find price of (thing for sale); estimate value of. **3 at a price** at a high cost; **price-fixing** maintaining of prices at certain level by agreement between competing sellers; **price on person's head** reward for his capture or death; **price-tag** label on item showing its price, cost of undertaking etc.; **what price...?** *colloq.* what is the chance of...?, the vaunted... has failed. [F f. L *pretium*]

priceless *a.* invaluable; *colloq.* very amusing or absurd.

pricey *a.* (*compar.* **pricier**; *superl.* **priciest**) *colloq.* expensive.

prick **1** *v.* pierce slightly, make small hole in; mark with pricks or dots; trouble mentally (*conscience is pricking me*); feel pricking sensation. **2** *n.* small hole or mark made by pricking; pain caused as by pricking; *vulgar* penis; *vulgar derog.* man. **3 prick up one's ears** (of dog) make ears erect when on alert, (of person) become suddenly attentive. [OE]

prickle /'prɪk(ə)l/ **1** *n.* small thorn; hard-pointed spine of hedgehog etc.; prickling sensation. **2** *v.* affect or be affected with sensation as of pricking. [OE]

prickly *a.* having prickles; (of person) irritable; tingling; **prickly heat** inflammation of skin near sweat glands with eruption of vesicles and prickly sensation, common in hot countries; **prickly pear** cactus with pear-shaped edible fruit, this fruit.

pride **1** *n.* feeling of elation or satisfaction at one's achievements or qualities or possessions etc.; object of this feeling; high or overbearing opinion of one's worth or importance; proper sense of what befits one's position, self-respect; best condition, prime; group or company (of lions etc.). **2** *v. refl.* (with *on* or *upon*) be proud of. **3 pride of place** most important or prominent position; **take pride in** be proud of. [OE (PROUD)]

prie-dieu /pri:'djɜ:/ *n.* kneeling-desk for prayer. [F, = pray God]

priest *n.* ordained minister of Roman Catholic or Orthodox Church, or of Anglican Church (above deacon and below bishop); official minister of non-Christian religion. [OE f. L PRESBYTER]

priestess /'prɪstɪs/ *n.* female priest of non-Christian religion.

priesthood *n.* office or position of priest; **the priesthood** priests in general.

priestly *a.* of or like or befitting a priest; **priestliness** *n.* [OE]

prig *n.* self-righteously correct or moralistic person; **priggery** *n.*; **priggish** *a.* [orig. unkn.]

prim *a.* (of person or manner) stiffly formal and precise, demure; prudish. [ult. f. F (PRIME[1])]

prima ballerina /'pri:mə/ chief female performer in ballet. [It.]

primacy /'praɪməsɪ/ *n.* pre-eminence; office of a primate. [F f. L (PRIMATE)]

prima donna /pri:mə 'dɒnə/ chief female singer in opera; temperamentally self-important person; **prima donna-ish** *a.* [It.]

prima facie /praɪmə 'feɪʃi:/ at first sight; (of evidence) based on the first impression. [L]

primal /'praɪm(ə)l/ *a.* primitive,

primeval; chief, fundamental; **primally** *adv.* [L (PRIME[1])]

primary /'praɪmərɪ/ **1** *a.* earliest, original; of the first importance, chief; of first rank in series, not derived; (**Primary**) of lowest or earliest series of geological strata; of first stage of biological development. **2** *n.* thing that is primary; primary feather; *US* primary election. **3 primary battery** battery producing electricity by irreversible chemical action; **primary colours** see COLOUR; **primary education** first stage of education in which rudiments of knowledge are taught; **primary election** *US* election to appoint party conference delegates or to select candidates for principal election; **primary feather** large flight-feather of bird's wing; **primary school** school where primary education is given. **4 primarily** *adv.* [L (PRIME[1])]

primate /'praɪmət, -eɪt/ *n.* archbishop; member of highest order of mammals, including man, apes, and monkeys. [F f. L *primas -at-* chief]

prime[1] **1** *a.* chief, most important; first-rate, excellent (*prime beef*); primary, fundamental. **2** *n.* state of highest perfection (*prime of life*); the best part; beginning; second canonical hour of prayer; prime number. **3 Prime Minister** chief minister of government; **prime number** natural number other than 1 that can be divided exactly only by itself and unity; **prime time** time at which television etc. audience is expected to be largest. [F f. L *primus* first]

prime[2] *v.t.* prepare (thing) for use or action; prepare (gun) for firing or (explosive) for detonation; pour (liquid) into pump to make it start working; prepare (wood etc.) for painting by applying substance that prevents paint from being absorbed; equip (person) with information; ply (person) with food or drink in preparation for something. [orig. unkn.]

primer[1] *n.* substance used to prime wood etc.

primer[2] *n.* elementary school-book for teaching children to read; small book introducing subject. [AF f. L (PRIME[1])]

primeval /praɪ'mi:v(ə)l/ *a.* of the first age of the world; ancient, primitive; **primevally** *adv.* [L (PRIME[1], *aevum* age)]

primitive /'prɪmɪtɪv/ **1** *a.* ancient, at an early stage of civilization (*primitive man*); undeveloped, crude, simple (*primitive methods*). **2** *n.* untutored painter with direct naïve style; picture by such painter. [F or L (PRIME[1])]

primogeniture /praɪməʊ'dʒenɪtʃə/ *n.* fact of being first-born child; right of succession or inheritance belonging to eldest son. [med.L (PRIME[1], L *genitura* birth)]

primordial /praɪ'mɔ:dɪəl/ *a.* existing at or from the beginning, primeval; **primordially** *adv.* [L (PRIME[1], *ordior* begin)]

primp *v.t.* make (hair etc.) tidy; smarten. [var. of PRIM]

primrose /'prɪmrəʊz/ *n.* plant bearing pale yellow spring flower; its flower; colour of this flower; **the primrose path** unjustified pursuit of ease or pleasure. [F & L, = first rose]

primula /'prɪmjʊlə/ *n.* herbaceous perennial with flowers of various colours. [L dimin. (PRIME[1])]

Primus /'praɪməs/ *n.* (**P**) brand of portable stove burning vaporized oil for cooking etc. [L, = first]

prince *n.* male member of royal family who is not reigning king; ruler, esp. of small State; nobleman of some countries; person outstanding of his kind (*prince of novelists*); **prince consort** husband of reigning queen who is himself a prince; **Prince of Wales** title usu. conferred on heir apparent to British throne, such heir; **Prince Regent** prince acting as regent, esp. the future George IV. [F f. L *princeps -cip-*]

princeling /'prɪnslɪŋ/ *n.* young or petty prince.

princely *a.* of or worthy of a prince; sumptuous, splendid.

princess /prɪn'ses, *attrib.* 'prɪn-/ *n.* wife of prince; female member of royal family who is not reigning queen; **princess royal** title conferrable on sovereign's eldest daughter. [F (PRINCE)]

principal /'prɪnsɪp(ə)l/ **1** *a.* (usu. *attrib.*) first in rank or importance, chief; main, leading (*the principal reason*). **2** *n.* chief person; head of some schools, colleges, and universities; leading performer in concert, play, etc.; capital sum as distinct from interest or income; person for whom another is agent; person directly responsible for a crime; civil servant of grade below Secretaries. **3 principal boy** leading male part in pantomime, usu. played by a woman; **principal parts** parts of verb from which all other parts can be deduced. **4 principally** *adv.* [F f. L (PRINCE)]

principality /prɪnsɪ'pælɪtɪ/ *n.* government of or State ruled by a prince; **the Principality** Wales. [F f. L (prec.)]

principle /'prɪnsɪp(ə)l/ *n.* fundamental truth or law as basis of reasoning or action; personal code of conduct (*man of high principle*), (in *pl.*) such rules of conduct (*has no principles*); general law in physics; law of nature forming basis for construction or working of machine; *Chem.* constituent of a substance, esp. one giving rise to some quality etc.; fundamental source, primary element; **in principle** as regards fundamentals but not necessarily in detail; **on principle** from settled moral motive. [AF f. L *principium* source]

principled *a.* based on or having (esp. praiseworthy) principles of behaviour.

prink *v.t.* smarten, dress *up*; (of bird) preen. [orig. unkn.]

print 1 *n.* indentation or mark on surface left by pressure of thing in contact; printed lettering or writing; words in printed form; printed publication, esp. newspaper; picture or design printed from block or plate; photograph produced from negative; printed cotton fabric. **2** *v.t.* produce (book, picture, etc., or *absol.*) by applying inked types or blocks or plates to paper etc.; express or publish in print; impress or stamp (surface, or mark or design *in* or *on* surface); write (words, letters, or *absol.*) without joining, in imitation of typography; produce (photograph) from negative; mark (textile fabric) with coloured design; impress (idea or scene etc. *on* mind or memory). **3 in** (or **out of**) **print** (of book etc.) available (or no longer available) from publisher; **printed circuit** electric circuit with lines of conducting material printed on flat insulating sheet. [F f. L *premo* (PRESS[1])]

printer *n.* one who prints books etc.; owner of printing-press; device that prints; **printer's devil** errand boy in printer's office.

printing *n.* production of printed books etc., single impression of book; printed letters or writing imitating them; **printing-press** machine for printing from types or plates etc.

printout *n.* computer output in printed form.

prior /'praɪə/ **1** *a.* earlier; coming before in time or order or importance (*to*). **2** *n.* superior of religious house or order; (in abbey) deputy of abbot. **3 prior to** before (*left prior to his arrival*). **4 prioress** *n. fem.* [F f. L, = earlier]

priority /praɪ'ɒrɪtɪ/ *n.* being earlier or antecedent; precedence in rank etc.; an interest having prior claim to attention. [F f. med.L (prec.)]

priory /'praɪərɪ/ *n.* monastery governed by prior or nunnery governed by prioress. [AF & med.L (PRIOR)]

prise /praɪz/ *v.t.* force open or out by leverage. [F (PRIZE[2])]

prism /'prɪz(ə)m/ *n.* solid figure whose two ends are equal parallel rectilinear figures, and whose sides are parallelograms; transparent body of this form, usu. triangular, with refracting surfaces at acute angle with each other; **prism binoculars** binoculars in which triangular prisms are used to shorten the instrument. [L f. Gk *prisma -mat-* thing sawn]

prismatic /prɪz'mætɪk/ *a.* of or like a prism; (of colours) formed or distributed (as if) by transparent prism. [F f. Gk (prec.)]

prison /'prɪz(ə)n/ *n.* place where person is kept in captivity, esp. building to which persons are consigned while awaiting trial or for punishment; custody, confinement. [F f. L (*prehendo* seize)]

prisoner /'prɪznə/ *n.* person kept in prison; (also **prisoner at the bar**) person in custody on criminal charge and on trial; captive; person or thing held in confinement or in another's grasp etc.; **prisoner of conscience** person in prison for act of conscientious protest etc.; **prisoner of State** prisoner confined for political reasons; **prisoner of war** one who has been captured in war; **take prisoner** seize and hold as prisoner. [AF (prec.)]

prissy /'prɪsɪ/ *a.* prim, prudish; **prissily** *adv.* [perh. PRIM, SISSY]

pristine /'prɪsti:n, -aɪn/ *a.* in original condition, unspoilt; (**D**) spotless, fresh as if new; ancient, primitive. [L *pristinus* former]

privacy /'prɪvəsɪ, 'praɪ-/ *n.* being alone or undisturbed, right to this; freedom from intrusion or public attention. [foll.]

private /'praɪvɪt/ **1** *a.* belonging to an individual, one's own, personal (*private property*); confidential, not to be disclosed to others (*private talks*); kept or removed from public knowledge or observation; not open to the public; (of place) secluded; (of person) not holding public office or official position; (of medical treatment) conducted outside State system, at patient's expense. **2** *n.* private soldier; (in *pl.*) genitals. **3 in private** privately, not in public; **private bill** parliamentary bill affecting individual or corporation only; **private company** one with restricted membership and no issue of shares; **private detective** one engaged privately, outside official police force; **private enterprise** business(es) not under State control; **private eye** *colloq.* private detective; **private hotel** one not obliged to take all comers; **private means** income from investments etc., apart from earned income; **private member** MP not holding government appointment;

private parts genitals; **private school** school supported wholly by fees and endowments; **private sector** part of economy free of direct State control; **private soldier** ordinary soldier, not officer. [L (*privo* deprive)]

privateer /praɪvəˈtɪə/ *n.* privately owned and commissioned warship; its commander.

privation /praɪˈveɪʃ(ə)n/ *n.* lack of comforts or necessaries of life. [L (PRIVATE)]

privative /ˈprɪvətɪv/ *a.* consisting in or showing loss or absence; *Gram.* indicating lack or absence. [F or L (PRIVATE)]

privatize /ˈpraɪvətaɪz/ *v.t.* denationalize; **privatization** /-ˈzeɪʃ(ə)n/ *n.* [PRIVATE]

privet /ˈprɪvɪt/ *n.* bushy evergreen shrub with smooth dark-green leaves, used for hedges. [orig. unkn.]

privilege /ˈprɪvɪlɪdʒ/ **1** *n.* special right or advantage or immunity belonging or granted to person or class or office; special benefit or honour (*is a privilege to meet you*). **2** *v.t.* invest with privilege. [F f. L (PRIVY, *lex leg-* law)]

privileged *a.* enjoying privilege(s); allowed (*to do* thing) as privilege or benefit.

privy /ˈprɪvɪ/ **1** *a.* hidden, secluded, secret. **2** *n.* (*archaic* or *US*) lavatory. **3** **Privy Council** body of advisers chosen by sovereign (in UK now chiefly honorary); **Privy Counsellor** member of Privy Council; **privy purse** allowance from public revenue for monarch's private expenses; **privy seal** State seal formerly affixed to documents of minor importance; **privy to** sharing in the secret of (person's plans etc.). **4** **privily** *adv.* [F *privé* f. L (PRIVATE)]

prize[1] **1** *n.* something that can be won in a competition or lottery etc.; reward given as symbol of victory or superiority; something striven for or worth striving for. **2** *a.* to which prize is awarded; excellent of its kind. **3** *v.t.* value highly. **4** **prize-fighter** professional boxer. [F (PRAISE)]

prize[2] *n.* ship or property captured in naval warfare. [F *prise* f. L *prehendo* seize]

prize[3] var. of PRISE.

pro[1] /prəʊ/ *n.* (*pl.* **pros**) *colloq.* professional. [abbr.]

pro[2] /prəʊ/ **1** *a.* & *prep.* (of argument or reason) for, in favour (of). **2** *n.* (*pl.* **pros**) reason for or in favour (esp. in **pros and cons**). [L, = for, on behalf of]

pro-[1] *prefix* substitute or deputy for, substituted for; (person) favouring or siding with; forwards (*produce*); forwards and downwards (*prostrate*); onwards (*proceed*); in front of (*protect*). [L *pro* in front (of), for]

pro-[2] *prefix* before (in time or place or order). [Gk *pro* before]

PRO *abbr.* public relations officer.

probability /prɒbəˈbɪlɪtɪ/ *n.* being probable; likelihood; probable or most probable event; extent to which event is likely to occur, measured by ratio of favourable cases to all possible cases; **in all probability** most probably. [F or L (foll.)]

probable /ˈprɒbəb(ə)l/ **1** *a.* that may be expected to happen or prove true; likely. **2** *n.* a probable candidate, member of team, etc.; **probably** *adv.* [F or L (PROVE)]

probate /ˈprəʊbeɪt/ *n.* official proving of will; verified copy of will with certificate as handed to executors. [L (*probo* PROVE)]

probation /prəˈbeɪʃ(ə)n/ *n.* testing of character or abilities of person (esp. of candidate for employment or membership); *Law* system of suspending sentence on certain offenders subject to good behaviour under supervision; **on probation** undergoing probation before full admission to employment or membership, or as criminal offender; **probation officer** official supervising offenders on probation; **probationary** *a.* [F f. L (prec.)]

probationer *n.* person on probation.

probative /ˈprəʊbətɪv/ *a.* affording proof. [L (PROVE)]

probe **1** *n.* blunt-ended surgical instrument for exploring wound etc.; unmanned exploratory spacecraft transmitting information about its environment; penetrating investigation. **2** *v.t.* explore with probe; penetrate (thing) with sharp instrument; examine or enquire into closely. [L *proba* (PROVE)]

probity /ˈprəʊbɪtɪ/ *n.* uprightness, honesty. [F or L (*probus* good)]

problem /ˈprɒbləm/ *n.* doubtful or difficult matter requiring solution; something hard to understand or accomplish or deal with; exercise in mathematics or chess etc. [F or L f. Gk *problēma, -mat-*]

problematic /prɒbləˈmætɪk/ *a.* (also **problematical**) attended by difficulty; doubtful, questionable; **problematically** *adv.* [F or L f. Gk (prec.)]

proboscis /prəˈbɒsɪs/ *n.* elephant's trunk; long flexible snout of tapir etc.; elongated part of mouth of some insects. [L f. Gk (*boskō* feed)]

procedure /prəˈsiːdjə, -dʒə/ *n.* mode of conducting business or legal action; series of actions conducted in certain order or manner; **procedural** *a.* [F (foll.)]

proceed /prə'si:d/ *v.i.* go forward or on further, make one's way; continue in an activity (*proceed with the work, to another question*), (of action) be carried on or continued; adopt course of action (*how shall we proceed?*); go on to say; start lawsuit *against* person; come forth or originate (*from*). [F f. L (*cedo cess-* go)]

proceeding *n.* action, piece of conduct; (in *pl.*) legal action, published report of discussions or conference.

proceeds /'prəʊsi:dz/ *n.pl.* money produced by sale or performance etc. [pl. of obs. *proceed n.* f. PROCEED]

process[1] /'prəʊses/ **1** *n.* course of action or proceeding, esp. series of stages in manufacture or other operation; progress or course (*in process of construction*); natural or involuntary operation or series of changes (*process of growing old*); action at law, summons or writ; natural appendage or outgrowth on organism. **2** *v.t.* treat (esp. to prevent decay) by particular process (*processed cheese*). [F f. L (PROCEED)]

process[2] /prə'ses/ *v.i. colloq.* walk in procession. [back-form. f. foll.]

procession /prə'seʃ(ə)n/ *n.* number of persons or vehicles etc. going along in orderly succession, esp. as ceremony or demonstration or festivity; action of this. [F f. L (PROCEED)]

processional 1 *a.* of processions; used or carried or sung in processions. **2** *n.* processional hymn. [med.L (prec.)]

processor /'prəʊsesə/ *n.* machine that processes things; **central processor** part of computer that controls and co-ordinates activities of other units and performs actions specified in program. [PROCESS[1]]

proclaim /prə'kleɪm/ *v.t.* announce or declare publicly or officially; declare (person) to be (king, traitor, etc.); reveal as being (*his accent proclaimed him a Scot*). [L (CLAIM)]

proclamation /prɒklə'meɪʃ(ə)n/ *n.* proclaiming; thing proclaimed.

proclivity /prə'klɪvɪtɪ/ *n.* tendency or natural inclination. [L (*clivus* slope)]

procrastinate /prə'kræstɪneɪt/ *v.i.* defer action; be dilatory; **procrastination** /-'neɪʃ(ə)n/ *n.*; **procrastinator** *n.* [L (*cras* tomorrow)]

procreate /'prəʊkrɪeɪt/ *v.t.* bring (offspring) into existence by natural process of reproduction; **procreation** /-'eɪʃ(ə)n/ *n.*; **procreative** *a.* [L (CREATE)]

Procrustean /prəʊ'krʌstɪən/ *a.* seeking to enforce uniformity by violent methods. [Gk *Prokroustēs* robber who fitted victims to bed by stretching or lopping]

proctor /'prɒktə/ *n.* each of two university officers at Oxford and Cambridge, appointed annually and having mainly disciplinary functions; **Queen's** (or **King's**) **Proctor** official who has right to intervene in probate, divorce, and nullity cases when collusion or suppression of facts is alleged; **proctorial** /-'tɔ:rɪəl/ *a.*; **proctorship** *n.* [PROCURATOR]

procuration /prɒkjʊə'reɪʃ(ə)n/ *n.* procuring; function or authorized action of attorney. [F or L (PROCURE)]

procurator /'prɒkjʊəreɪtə/ *n.* agent or proxy, esp. with power of attorney; **procurator fiscal** coroner and public prosecutor of district in Scotland; **procurator general** head of Treasury law department. [F, or L *procurator* agent]

procure /prə'kjʊə/ *v.* obtain by care or effort, acquire; bring about; act as procurer or procuress (of); **procurement** *n.* [F f. L (*curo* look after)]

procurer *n.* one who obtains women for prostitution; **procuress** *n. fem.* [F f. L PROCURATOR]

prod 1 *v.* (**-dd-**) poke with finger or end of stick etc.; stimulate to action; make prodding motion *at*. **2** *n.* poke or thrust; stimulus to action. [orig. unkn.]

prodigal /'prɒdɪg(ə)l/ **1** *a.* recklessly wasteful; extravagant, lavish. **2** *n.* prodigal person. **3 prodigal son** repentant wastrel, returned wanderer. **4 prodigality** /-'gælɪtɪ/ *n.* [L (*prodigus* lavish)]

prodigious /prə'dɪdʒəs/ *a.* marvellous; enormous; abnormal. [L (foll.)]

prodigy /'prɒdɪdʒɪ/ *n.* person with exceptional qualities or abilities, esp. precocious child; marvellous thing; wonderful example *of* (some quality). [L *prodigium* portent]

produce 1 /prə'dju:s/ *v.t.* bring forward for consideration or inspection or use; manufacture (goods) from raw materials etc.; bear or yield (offspring, fruit, harvest, etc.); bring into existence; cause or bring about (a reaction etc.); extend or continue (a line *to* a point). **2** /'prɒdju:s/ *n.* what is produced, esp. agricultural and natural products generally, amount of this. **3 producible** /-'dju:s-/ *a.* [L (*duco duct-* lead)]

producer /prə'dju:sə/ *n.* one who produces articles or produce; person who directs performance of play or broadcast programme; person in charge of financing and scheduling of film production.

product /'prɒdʌkt/ *n.* thing or substance produced by natural process or manufacture; result (*the product of his* *labours*); quantity obtained by multiplying. [L (PRODUCE)]

production /prə'dʌkʃ(ə)n/ *n.* producing, being produced or manufactured esp. in large quantities (*go into production*); total yield; thing produced, esp. literary or artistic work, play or film etc. [F f. L (PRODUCE)]

productive /prə'dʌktɪv/ *a.* of or engaged in production of goods; producing much; producing commodities of exchangeable value (*productive labour*); (with *of*) producing or giving rise to. [F or L (PRODUCE)]

productivity /prɒdʌk'tɪvɪtɪ/ *n.* capacity to produce; effectiveness of productive effort, esp. in industry.

proem /'prəʊem/ *n.* introductory discourse. [F or L f. Gk]

Prof. *abbr.* Professor.

profane /prə'feɪn/ **1** *a.* not sacred, secular; irreverent, blasphemous. **2** *v.t.* treat (sacred thing) with irreverence or disregard; violate or pollute (what is entitled to respect). **3 profanation** /-'neɪʃ(ə)n/ *n.* [F or L (*fanum* temple)]

profanity /prə'fænɪtɪ/ *n.* profane act or language, blasphemy.

profess /prə'fes/ *v.t.* claim openly to have (a quality or feeling); pretend; declare (*profess ignorance*); affirm one's faith in or allegiance to. [F f. L *profiteor -fess-* declare]

professed *a.* self-acknowledged (*a professed Christian*); alleged, ostensible; **professedly** /-sɪdlɪ/ *adv.*

profession /prə'feʃ(ə)n/ *n.* occupation, esp. in some branch of advanced learning or science (*medical profession*); body of persons engaged in this; declaration, avowal. [F f. L (PROFESS)]

professional **1** *a.* of or belonging to or connected with a profession; having or showing the skill of a professional; engaged in specified activity as one's main paid occupation (often as distinct from *amateur*). **2** *n.* professional person. **3 professionally** *adv.*

professionalism *n.* qualities or typical features of a profession or professionals.

professor /prə'fesə/ *n.* holder of university chair; *US* university teacher of high rank; one who makes profession (of religion etc.); **professorial** /-'sɔ:rɪəl/ *a.*; **professorship** *n.* [F or L (PROFESS)]

professoriate /prəfe'sɔ:rɪət/ *n.* the professors of a university etc.

proffer *v.t.* offer. [F (PRO-[1], OFFER)]

proficient /prə'fɪʃənt/ *a.* skilled or expert (*in* or *at*); **proficiency** *n.* [L *proficio -fect-* advance]

profile /'prəʊfaɪl/ *n.* outline (esp. of human face) as seen from one side; representation of this; short biographical or character sketch; **keep a low profile** remain inconspicuous. [It. *profilare* draw in outline]

profit /'prɒfɪt/ **1** *n.* advantage or benefit; pecuniary gain, excess of returns over outlay. **2** *v.* be beneficial (to); obtain advantage or benefit. **3 profit-sharing** sharing of profits esp. between employer and employed. [F f. L *profectus* (PROFICIENT)]

profitable *a.* beneficial; yielding profit, lucrative; **profitability** /-'bɪlɪtɪ/ *n.*; **profitably** *adv.*

profiteer /prɒfɪ'tɪə/ **1** *v.* make or seek excessive profits out of others' needs esp. in times of scarcity. **2** *n.* person who profiteers. [PROFIT]

profiterole /prə'fɪtərəʊl/ *n.* small hollow cake of choux pastry with sweet or savoury filling. [F dimin. (PROFIT)]

profligate /'prɒflɪgət/ **1** *a.* licentious, dissolute; recklessly extravagant. **2** *n.* profligate person. **3 profligacy** *n.* [L *profligo* ruin)]

pro forma /prəʊ 'fɔ:mə/ for form's sake; (in full **pro forma invoice**) invoice sent to purchaser in advance of goods for completion of business formalities. [L]

profound /prə'faʊnd/ *a.* having or showing great knowledge or insight; requiring much study or thought; deep, intense, far-reaching; **profundity** /-'fʌndɪtɪ/ *n.* [F f. L *profundus*]

profuse /prə'fju:s/ *a.* lavish, extravagant (*profuse thanks*); plentiful, copious (*profuse bleeding*); **profusion** *n.* [L (*fundo fus-* pour)]

progenitor /prə'dʒenɪtə/ *n.* ancestor; predecessor, original. [F f. L (*progigno* beget)]

progeny /'prɒdʒənɪ/ *n.* offspring; outcome, issue. [F f. L (as prec.)]

progesterone /'prəʊ'dʒestərəʊn/ *n.* sex hormone causing uterine changes in latter part of menstrual cycle and maintaining pregnancy. [G (PRO-[2], GESTATION)]

prognosis /prɒg'nəʊsɪs/ *n.* (*pl.* **prognoses** /-i:z/) forecast or advance indication, esp. of course of disease. [L f. Gk (*gignōskō* know)]

prognostic /prɒg'nɒstɪk/ **1** *n.* advance indication or omen; prediction. **2** *a.* foretelling, predictive (*of*). [F f. L (as prec.)]

prognosticate /prɒg'nɒstɪkeɪt/ *v.t.* foretell or foresee; (of thing) betoken; **prognostication** /-'keɪʃ(ə)n/ *n.*; **prognosticator** *n.* [med.L (as prec.)]

programme /'prəʊgræm/, *US* & in computing **program** **1** *n.* plan of intended proceedings; descriptive list or notice of series of events (*concert programme*);

such series of events; broadcast performance or entertainment (*television programme*); series of instructions to control operation of computer. **2** *v.t.* (**-mm-**) make programme of; express (problem) or instruct (computer etc.) by means of program. **3 programmatic** /-'mætɪk/ *a.* [L f. Gk (*graphō* write)]

progress 1 /'prəʊgres/ *n.* forward or onward movement; advance or development, esp. to better state; *archaic* State journey, esp. by royal person. **2** /prəʊ'gres/ *v.i.* move forward or onward; advance or develop, esp. to better state. **3 in progress** taking place, in course of occurrence. [L (*progredior -gress-* go forward)]

progression /prə'greʃ(ə)n/ *n.* progressing; succession, series. [F or L (prec.)]

progressive /prə'gresɪv/ **1** *a.* moving forward; proceeding steadily or step by step; favouring rapid political or social reform; advancing in social conditions, efficiency, etc. (*a progressive nation*); (of disease etc.) continuously increasing in severity or extent; (of card-game, dance, etc.) with periodic change of partners; (of taxation) at rates increasing with the sum taxed; *Gram.* (of tense) expressing action in progress. **2** *n.* advocate of progressive policy. [F or med.L (PROGRESS)]

prohibit /prə'hɪbɪt/ *v.t.* forbid or prevent; **prohibited degrees** see DEGREE; **prohibitor** *n.*; **prohibitory** *a.* [L *prohibeo -hibit-*]

prohibition /prəʊɪ'bɪʃ(ə)n/ *n.* forbidding or being forbidden; edict or order that forbids; forbidding by law of the manufacture and sale of intoxicants. [F or L (prec.)]

prohibitionist *n.* advocate of legal prohibition.

prohibitive /prə'hɪbɪtɪv/ *a.* prohibiting; (of prices, costs, taxes, etc.) extremely high. [F or L (PROHIBIT)]

project 1 /'prɒdʒekt/ *n.* plan or scheme; planned undertaking, esp. piece of individual research by student(s). **2** /prə'dʒekt/ *v.* plan or contrive (scheme etc.); cause (light or shadow or image) to fall on surface; send or throw outward or forward; protrude or jut out; imagine (thing or person or *oneself*) as having another's feelings, being in another situation or in the future, etc.; attribute (one's own feelings) to another person or thing, esp. unconsciously; extrapolate (results *to* future time etc.); make projection of (earth or sky etc.). [L *projicio -ject-* throw forth]

projectile /prə'dʒektaɪl/ **1** *n.* object to be hurled or projected forcibly, esp. from gun. **2** *a.* of or serving as projectile.

projection /prə'dʒekʃ(ə)n/ *n.* projecting or being projected; thing that projects or protrudes; representation on plane surface of (any part of) surface of earth or of celestial sphere; mental image viewed as objective reality.

projectionist *n.* person who operates projector.

projector /prə'dʒektə/ *n.* apparatus for projecting image of film etc. on screen.

prolapse 1 /'prəʊlæps/ *n.* (also **prolapsus**) slipping forward or downward of part or organ, esp. of womb or rectum. **2** /prə'læps/ *v.i.* undergo prolapse. [L (LAPSE)]

prolate /'prəʊleɪt/ *a.* (of spheroid) lengthened along polar diameter. [L, = brought forward, prolonged]

prolegomena /prəʊlɪ'gɒmɪnə/ *n.pl.* preliminary discourse or matter prefixed to book etc. [L f. Gk (*legō* say)]

proletarian /prəʊlɪ'teərɪən/ **1** *a.* of proletariat. **2** *n.* member of proletariat. [L (*proles* offspring)]

proletariat /prəʊlɪ'teərɪət/ *n.* class of industrial workers. [F (prec.)]

proliferate /prə'lɪfəreɪt/ *v.* reproduce itself or grow by multiplication of elementary parts; produce (cells) thus; increase rapidly in numbers etc.; **proliferation** /-'reɪʃ(ə)n/ *n.* [*proliferation* f. F (L *proles* offspring)]

prolific /prə'lɪfɪk/ *a.* producing much offspring or output; abundantly productive (*of*), abounding (*in*); **prolifically** *adv.* [med.L (as prec.)]

prolix /'prəʊlɪks/ *a.* lengthy, tediously wordy; **prolixity** /prə'lɪksɪtɪ/ *n.* [F or L]

prologue /'prəʊlɒg/ *n.* introduction to poem or play etc.; act or event serving as introduction (*to*). [F f. L f. Gk (LOGOS)]

prolong /prə'lɒŋ/ *v.t.* extend in duration or spatial length; **prolongation** /prəʊlɒŋ'geɪʃ(ə)n/ *n.* [L (*longus* long)]

prom *n. colloq.* promenade, promenade concert. [abbr.]

promenade /prɒmə'nɑːd/ **1** *n.* public place for walking, esp. paved area at seaside; leisure walk, esp. for pleasure. **2** *v.* take leisurely walk (through); lead (person) about a place, esp. for display. **3 promenade concert** concert with area for part of audience to stand and move about; **promenade deck** upper deck on passenger ship. [F]

promethium /prə'miːθɪəm/ *n.* artificial radioactive metallic element of lanthanide series. [*Prometheus* in Gk myth.]

prominence /'prɒmɪnəns/ *n.* being prominent; prominent thing. [F f. L (foll.)]

prominent *a.* jutting out, projecting;

conspicuous; distinguished, well-known. [L *promineo* project]

promiscuous /prə'mɪskjʊəs/ *a.* having casual sexual relations with many people; casual, indiscriminate; of mixed and indiscriminate composition or kinds; **promiscuity** /prɒmɪ'skju:ɪtɪ/ *n.* [L (*misceo* mix)]

promise /'prɒmɪs/ **1** *n.* assurance as to what one will or will not do, or of help or giving something; indication of future achievement or good result (*pupil of great promise*). **2** *v.* make promise, give assurance; give (person) promise of (thing); *colloq.* assure (*I promise you it will not be easy*); seem likely (*to do* thing). **3 promised land** Canaan, any place of expected happiness. [L *promissum* (*mitto miss-* send)]

promising *a.* likely to turn out well, hopeful, full of promise.

promissory /'prɒmɪsərɪ/ *a.* conveying or implying a promise; **promissory note** signed document containing written promise to pay stated sum. [med.L (PROMISE)]

promontory /'prɒməntərɪ/ *n.* point of high land jutting out into sea etc., headland. [L]

promote /prə'məʊt/ *v.t.* advance (person) to higher position or office; help forward or encourage (enterprise or result); publicize and sell (product); initiate (project); take necessary steps for passing of (private bill in parliament); **promotion** *n.*; **promotional** *a.* [L *promoveo -mot-*]

promoter *n.* one who promotes an enterprise financially, esp. formation of joint-stock company or holding of sporting event etc. [AF f. med.L (prec.)]

prompt **1** *a.* acting or done without delay or at once; punctual. **2** *adv.* punctually (*at six o'clock prompt*). **3** *v.t.* incite or move (person) to action; inspire or give rise to (feeling or action); help (actor etc. or *absol.*) by supplying words that come next; assist (hesitant person) with suggestion etc. **4** *n.* thing said to help memory esp. of actor. **5 prompt side** side of stage usu. to actor's left. **6 promptitude** *n.* [F or L]

prompter *n.* person unseen by audience who prompts actors.

promulgate /'prɒməlgeɪt/ *v.t.* make known to public, disseminate; proclaim (decree or news); **promulgation** /-'geɪʃ(ə)n/ *n.*; **promulgator** *n.* [L]

prone *a.* lying face downwards; lying flat, prostrate; disposed (*to*), liable or likely (*to*) (*prone to illness, to fall asleep*; *accident-prone*). [L]

prong *n.* each of two or more projecting pointed parts at end of fork etc. [orig. unkn.]

pronominal /prə'nɒmɪn(ə)l/ *a.* of or of the nature of a pronoun. [L (foll.)]

pronoun /'prəʊnaʊn/ *n.* word used instead of noun to designate (without naming) person or thing; pronominal adjective. [PRO-[1]]

pronounce /prə'naʊns/ *v.* utter or speak (words, or *absol.*), esp. with reference to correct or required manner; utter or declare formally; declare as one's opinion (*the food was pronounced excellent*); pass judgement; **pronounceable** *a.* (esp. of word or language). [F f. L (*nuntio* announce)]

pronounced *a.* noticeable or strongly marked (*pronounced tendency, limp*).

pronouncement *n.* formal statement, declaration.

pronto /'prɒntəʊ/ *adv. sl.* promptly, quickly. [Sp. f. L (PROMPT)]

pronunciation /prənʌnsɪ'eɪʃ(ə)n/ *n.* way in which word is pronounced; person's way of pronouncing words. [F or L (PRONOUNCE)]

proof **1** *n.* fact or evidence or argument sufficing or helping to establish fact or truth of something; proving, demonstration; test, trial; standard of strength in distilled alcoholic liquors; trial impression of printed matter for correction; photographic print made for selection. **2** *a.* impervious to penetration or damage or undesired action. **3** *v.t.* make proof of (printed work); make (thing) proof, esp. (fabric etc.) waterproof. **4** **-proof** *in comb.* in sense 'impervious', 'resistant', forming adjectives (*bullet-proof*; *waterproof*) and verbs (*sound-proof*). **5 proof-read** read and correct (printed proofs); **proof-reader** person who does this; **proof spirit** mixture of alcohol and water having standard strength. [F f. L *proba* (PROVE)]

prop[1] **1** *n.* rigid support, esp. not structural part of thing supported; person etc. depended on for help or support. **2** *v.t.* (-pp-) support (as) with prop (often with *up*). [LG or Du.]

prop[2] *n. colloq.* aircraft propeller. [abbr.]

prop[3] *n. colloq.* stage property in theatre. [abbr.]

propaganda /prɒpə'gændə/ *n.* organized scheme etc. for (often tendentious) propagation of a doctrine or practice; (usu. *derog.*) ideas etc. thus propagated; *colloq.* biased information; **propagandist** *n.* [It. f. L (foll.)]

propagate /'prɒpəgeɪt/ *v.* breed or reproduce from parent stock; (of plant etc.) reproduce (*itself*); disseminate (news or ideas etc.); transmit (vibration, earthquake, etc.); be propagated; **propagation** /-ˈgeɪʃ(ə)n/ *n.*; **propagator** *n.* [L *propago*]

propane /ˈprəʊpeɪn/ *n.* a hydrocarbon of the paraffin series. [*propionic acid* (PRO-², Gk *piōn* fat)]

propel /prəˈpel/ *v.t.* (**-ll-**) drive or push forward, give onward motion to; **propellent** *a.* [L (*pello puls-* drive)]

propellant *n.* propelling agent.

propeller *n.* (in full **screw-propeller**) revolving shaft with blades for propelling ship or aircraft.

propensity /prəˈpensɪtɪ/ *n.* inclination or tendency. [L *propensus* inclined]

proper /ˈprɒpə/ *a.* suitable, appropriate, fitting; correct or accurate (*proper way to do it*); respectable, in conformity with social standards; real or genuine, rightly so called; (usu. placed after noun) strictly so called (*outside the city proper*); belonging or relating exclusively or distinctively (*to*); *colloq.* thorough, complete (*a proper mess*); **proper fraction** fraction less than unity, with numerator less than denominator; **proper name** (or **noun**) name of individual person or place or thing. [F f. L *proprius* one's own]

properly *adv.* in suitable or correct manner; rightly; with decency or good manners (*behave properly*); *colloq.* thoroughly (*puzzled him properly*).

propertied *a.* having property, esp. of real estate. [foll.]

property /ˈprɒpətɪ/ *n.* thing owned, possession(s), esp. real estate; owned or being owned; attribute or quality; movable object used on theatre stage or in film. [F f. L *proprietas* (prec.)]

prophecy /ˈprɒfɪsɪ/ *n.* faculty of a prophet; prophetic utterance; foretelling of future events. [F f. L f. Gk (PROPHET)]

prophesy /ˈprɒfɪsaɪ/ *v.* speak as prophet; foretell future events; foretell. [F *profecier* (as prec.)]

prophet /ˈprɒfɪt/ *n.* inspired teacher, person regarded as revealer or interpreter of divine will; any of writers of Old Testament prophecy; one who foretells events; spokesman or advocate (*of* principle etc.); **the Prophet** Muhammad; **prophetess** *n. fem.* [F f. L f. Gk *prophētēs* spokesman]

prophetic /prəˈfetɪk/ *a.* (also **prophetical**) of a prophet; predicting or containing a prediction *of* (event etc.); **prophetically** *adv.* [F, or L (as prec.)]

prophylactic /prɒfɪˈlæktɪk/ **1** *a.* tending to prevent disease or other misfortune. **2** *n.* prophylactic medicine or course of action. [F f. Gk, = keeping guard before]

prophylaxis /prɒfɪˈlæksɪs/ *n.* preventive treatment against disease etc. [PRO-², Gk *phulaxis* guarding]

propinquity /prəˈpɪŋkwɪtɪ/ *n.* nearness in place; close kinship. [F or L (*prope* near)]

propitiate /prəˈpɪʃɪeɪt/ *v.t.* appease (offended person etc.); **propitiable** *a.*; **propitiation** /-ˈeɪʃ(ə)n/ *n.*; **propitiator** *n.* [L (PROPITIOUS)]

propitiatory /prəˈpɪʃətərɪ/ *a.* serving or intended to propitiate. [eccl.L (prec.)]

propitious /prəˈpɪʃəs/ *a.* favourable; auspicious; suitable *for* or favourable *to* (purpose). [F, or L *propitius*]

proponent /prəˈpəʊnənt/ *n.* person who puts forward a proposal; person who supports cause etc. [L (PROPOSE)]

proportion /prəˈpɔːʃ(ə)n/ **1** *n.* comparative part or share (*a large proportion of the earth's surface*); comparative relation, ratio (*proportion of births to the population*); correct relation of one thing to another or between parts of a thing (*exaggerated out of all proportion*); (in *pl.*) dimensions, size; equality of ratios between two pairs of quantities (*3 and 5 are in proportion with 9 and 15*). **2** *v.t.* give correct proportions to; make (one thing) proportionate *to* another. **3 proportionment** *n.* [F or L (PORTION)]

proportional *a.* in correct proportion, corresponding in degree or amount; **proportional representation** electoral system by which each party is represented in proportion to the votes it receives; **proportionally** *adv.* [L (prec.)]

proportionate /prəˈpɔːʃənət/ *a.* in due proportion (*to*).

proposal /prəˈpəʊz(ə)l/ *n.* act of proposing something; course of action etc. proposed; offer of marriage. [foll.]

propose /prəˈpəʊz/ *v.* put forward for consideration; have as one's plan or intention (*we propose to leave now*); make proposal; make offer of marriage (*to*); offer (person or person's health) as subject for drinking of toast; nominate (person) as member of society etc. [F f. L (*pono posit-* place)]

proposition /prɒpəˈzɪʃ(ə)n/ **1** *n.* proposal, scheme proposed; statement, assertion; *colloq.* thing to be considered or dealt with or undertaken; formal statement of theorem or problem often including demonstration. **2** *v.t. colloq.* put (esp. indecent) proposition to. [F or L (prec.)]

propound /prəˈpaʊnd/ *v.t.* offer for consideration, propose. [*propo(u)ne* f. L (PROPOSE)]

proprietary /prəˈpraɪətərɪ/ *a.* of a proprietor; holding property; held in private ownership; manufactured and sold by one particular firm, usu. under patent (*proprietary medicines*). [L *proprietarius* (PROPERTY)]

proprietor /prəˈpraɪətə/ *n.* holder of property, owner esp. of business; **proprietorial** /-ˈtɔːrɪəl/ *a.*; **proprietress** *n. fem.* [as prec.]

propriety /prəˈpraɪɪtɪ/ *n.* fitness, rightness; correctness of behaviour or morals; (in *pl.*) details of correct conduct (*must observe the proprieties*). [F (PROPERTY)]

propulsion /prəˈpʌlʃ(ə)n/ *n.* driving or pushing forward; **propulsive** *a.* [PROPEL]

pro rata /prəʊ ˈrɑːtə/ proportional; in proportion. [L]

prorogue /prəˈrəʊg/ *v.* discontinue meetings of (parliament etc.) without dissolving it; (of parliament etc.) be prorogued; **prorogation** /prəʊrəˈgeɪʃ(ə)n/ *n.* [F f. L *prorogo* extend]

prosaic /prəˈzeɪɪk/ *a.* like prose, lacking in poetic beauty; unromantic, commonplace, dull; **prosaically** *adv.* [F or L (PROSE)]

proscenium /prəʊˈsiːnɪəm/ *n.* (*pl.* **prosceniums, -nia**) part of theatre stage in front of drop or curtain, esp. with the enclosing arch. [L f. Gk (SCENE)]

proscribe /prəˈskraɪb/ *v.t.* denounce or forbid (practice etc.); outlaw; banish or exile. [L, = publish in writing]

proscription /prəˈskrɪpʃ(ə)n/ *n.* proscribing or being proscribed; **proscriptive** *a.*

prose /prəʊz/ **1** *n.* ordinary non-metrical form of (esp. written) language; dull or matter-of-fact quality. **2** *v.i.* talk tediously. **3 prose poem** elevated composition in prose. [F f. L *prosa* (*oratio*) straightforward (discourse)]

prosecute /ˈprɒsɪkjuːt/ *v.t.* institute legal proceedings against (person, or *absol.*) or with reference to (crime or claim etc.); carry on or be occupied with. [L *prosequor -secut-* pursue]

prosecution /prɒsɪˈkjuːʃ(ə)n/ *n.* institution and carrying on of legal proceedings; prosecuting party; prosecuting or being prosecuted. [F or L (prec.)]

prosecutor /ˈprɒsɪkjuːtə/ *n.* one who prosecutes, esp. in criminal court. [PROSECUTE]

proselyte /ˈprɒsɪlaɪt/ *n.* person converted from one opinion or belief etc. to another; Gentile convert to Jewish faith. [L *proselytus* f. Gk]

proselytism /ˈprɒsɪlɪtɪz(ə)m/ *n.* being a proselyte, practice of proselytizing.

proselytize /ˈprɒsɪlɪtaɪz/ *v.t.* seek to make proselyte of (person, or *absol.*).

prosody /ˈprɒsədɪ/ *n.* science of versification; study of speech-rhythms; **prosodic** /prəˈsɒdɪk/ *a.*; **prosodically** /prəˈsɒdɪkəlɪ/ *adv.*; **prosodist** *n.* [L f. Gk (*pros* to, ODE)]

prospect 1 /ˈprɒspekt/ *n.* what one is to expect, chance (of success etc.); extensive view of landscape etc.; mental scene; *colloq.* possible or likely customer etc. **2** /prəˈspekt/ *v.* explore or search (*for* gold etc.); look out *for*. [L (PROSPECTUS)]

prospective /prəˈspektɪv/ *a.* expected to be or occur, future, possible (*prospective husband*). [F or L (as prec.)]

prospector /prəˈspektə/ *n.* one who prospects for gold etc. [PROSPECT]

prospectus /prəˈspektəs/ *n.* printed document describing chief features of school or business etc. [L, = prospect, f. *prospicio -spect-* look forward]

prosper *v.* be successful, thrive. [F or L *prospero*]

prosperity /prɒˈsperɪtɪ/ *n.* prosperous state or condition, wealth. [foll.]

prosperous /ˈprɒspərəs/ *a.* successful or thriving, esp. financially; auspicious. [F f. L]

prostate /ˈprɒsteɪt/ *n.* (in full **prostate gland**) large gland round neck of bladder, accessory to male genital organs; **prostatic** /-ˈtætɪk/ *a.* [F f. Gk *prostatēs* one who stands before]

prosthesis /ˈprɒsθɪsɪs/ *n.* (*pl.* **prostheses** /-iːz/) making up of bodily deficiencies, e.g. by artificial limb; part supplied for this; **prosthetic** /-ˈθetɪk/ *a.* [L f. Gk, = placing in addition]

prostitute /ˈprɒstɪtjuːt/ **1** *n.* woman who engages in promiscuous sexual intercourse for payment; man who undertakes homosexual acts for payment. **2** *v.t.* make prostitute of (esp. *oneself*); sell or make use of (one's honour or abilities etc.) unworthily. **3 prostitution** /-ˈtjuːʃ(ə)n/ *n.* [L (*prostituo -tut-* offer for sale)]

prostrate 1 /ˈprɒstreɪt/ *a.* lying with face to ground, esp. in submission or humility; lying in horizontal position; overcome, overthrown (*prostrate with grief*); physically exhausted. **2** /prɒˈstreɪt/ *v.t.* throw *oneself* down prostrate; overcome, make submissive; (of fatigue etc.) reduce to extreme physical weakness. **3 prostration** /prɒˈstreɪʃ(ə)n/ *n.* [L *prosterno -strat-* throw in front]

prosy /ˈprəʊzɪ/ *a.* commonplace, tedious, wearisomely dull; **prosily** *adv.*; **prosiness** *n.* [PROSE]

protactinium /prəʊtækˈtɪnɪəm/ *n.* radioactive metallic element. [G (ACTINIUM)]

protagonist /prəʊˈtægənɪst/ *n.* chief

person in drama or plot of story; principal performer; (**D**) champion or advocate *of* course or method etc. [Gk (PROTO-, *agonistēs* actor)]

protean /'prəʊtɪən, -'ti:ən/ *a.* variable, versatile; taking many forms. [*Proteus*, Gk sea-god who took various shapes]

protect /prə'tekt/ *v.t.* defend or keep safe (*from* or *against* danger or injury etc.); guard (home industry) against competition by import duties on foreign goods. [L (*tego tect-* cover)]

protection /prə'tekʃ(ə)n/ *n.* protecting or being protected; person or thing that protects; system of protecting home industries; immunity from molestation obtained by payment under threat of violence, money so paid. [F or L (prec.)]

protectionism *n.* principle or practice of economic protection; **protectionist** *n.*

protective *a.* protecting, giving or intended for protection; **protective custody** detention of person actually or allegedly for his own protection. [PROTECT]

protector *n.* person or thing that protects; regent in charge of kingdom during minority or absence of sovereign; **protectorship** *n.*; **protectress** *n. fem.* [F f. L (PROTECT)]

protectorate /prə'tektərət/ *n.* office of protector of kingdom or State, period of this; protectorship of weak or underdeveloped State by stronger one; State thus protected.

protégé /'prɒteʒeɪ/ *n.* person to whom another is protector or patron; **protégée** *n. fem.* [F (PROTECT)]

protein /'prəʊti:n/ *n.* any of a class of nitrogenous compounds essential in all living organisms. [F & G f. Gk (*prōtos* first)]

pro tem /prəʊ 'tem/ colloq. *pro tempore*. [abbr.]

pro tempore /prəʊ 'tempərɪ/ for the time being (esp. of appointment). [L]

protest 1 /prəʊ'test/ *v.* express disapproval or dissent; *US* object to (decision etc.); declare solemnly or firmly, esp. in reply to accusation etc.; write or obtain protest in regard to (bill). **2** /'prəʊtest/ *n.* formal statement or action of disapproval or dissent; written declaration that bill has been presented and payment or acceptance refused. **3** **under protest** unwillingly and after making protests. **4** **protestor** /prə'testə/ *n.* [F f. L *protestor* declare formally]

Protestant /'prɒtɪstənt/ **1** *n.* member or adherent of any of the Christian bodies that separated from the Roman communion in the Reformation (16th c.) or their offshoots. **2** *a.* of Protestants. **3** **Protestantism** *n.* [L (prec.)]

protestation /prɒte'steɪʃ(ə)n/ *n.* solemn affirmation; protest. [F or L (PROTEST)]

proto- *in comb.* first. [Gk *prōtos*]

protocol /'prəʊtəkɒl/ **1** *n.* official formality and etiquette, observance of this; original draft of diplomatic document, esp. of agreed terms of treaty. **2** *v.* (**-ll-**) draw up protocol(s); record in protocol. [F f. L f. Gk (*kolla* glue)]

proton /'prəʊtɒn/ *n.* elementary particle with unit positive electric charge, forming part or (in hydrogen) whole of atomic nucleus. [Gk (*prōtos* first)]

protoplasm /'prəʊtəʊplæz(ə)m/ *n.* viscous translucent colourless substance forming main constituent of cells in organisms; **protoplasmic** /-'plæzmɪk/ *a.* [Gk (PROTO-, PLASMA)]

prototype /'prəʊtəʊtaɪp/ *n.* an original thing or person in relation to a copy or imitation or developed form; trial model, preliminary version, esp. of aeroplane etc. [F or L f. Gk (PROTO-)]

protozoon /prəʊtə'zəʊən/ *n.* (*pl.* **protozoa**) one-celled microscopic animal; **protozoan** *a.* & *n.* [PROTO-, Gk *zōion* animal]

protract /prə'trækt/ *v.t.* prolong, lengthen, make last long or longer; **protraction** *n.* [L (*traho tract-* draw)]

protractor *n.* instrument for measuring angles, usu. in form of graduated semicircle.

protrude /prə'tru:d/ *v.* (cause to) project from a surface; thrust forward; **protrusion** *n.*; **protrusive** *a.* [L (*trudo -trus-* thrust)]

protuberant /prə'tju:bərənt/ *a.* bulging out, prominent; **protuberance** *n.* [L (TUBER)]

proud *a.* feeling or showing pride (*proud of his new car*) or proper pride (*too proud to complain*); haughty, arrogant; feeling oneself greatly honoured (*am proud to know her*); marked by or causing pride (*a proud moment for us*); (of thing) imposing, splendid; slightly projecting; (of flesh) overgrown round healing wound; **do person** (or **oneself**) **proud** treat him (or oneself) with great generosity or honour. [OE f. F *prud* valiant]

prove /pru:v/ *v.* (*p.p.* **proved** or esp. *US*, *Sc.*, & *literary* **proven**) demonstrate to be true or certain by evidence or argument; emerge as, be found *to* (*will prove the best, to be the best*); establish validity of (will); rise or cause (dough) to rise; *archaic* test qualities of; **not proven** *Sc. Law* evidence is insufficient to establish guilt or innocence; **prove oneself**

demonstrate one's abilities etc. [F f. L (*probo* test, approve)]

provenance /ˈprɒvənəns/ *n.* origin or place of origin. [F (*provenir* f. L)]

Provençal /prɒvɒnˈsɑːl/ **1** *a.* of Provence. **2** *n.* inhabitant or language of Provence. [F (PROVINCE)]

provender /ˈprɒvɪndə/ *n.* fodder; *colloq.* food for humans. [F f. L (PREBEND)]

proverb /ˈprɒvɜːb/ *n.* short pithy saying in general use, stating truth or giving advice; person or thing that is widely known as exemplifying something. [F, or L *proverbium* (*verbum* word)]

proverbial /prəˈvɜːbɪəl/ *a.* of or expressed in proverbs; well-known, notorious; **proverbially** *adv.* [L (prec.)]

provide /prəˈvaɪd/ *v.* cause (person) to have possession or use of (*provided me with a car*); supply, make available; supply necessities of life (*has to provide for a large family*); make due preparation (*for* or *against* contingency); stipulate, give as condition; **provided** (or **providing**) **(that)** on the condition or understanding that. [L *provideo -vis-* foresee]

providence /ˈprɒvɪdəns/ *n.* foresight, timely care; beneficent care of God or nature; (**Providence**) God in this aspect. [F or L (PROVIDE)]

provident *a.* having or showing foresight; thrifty; **Provident Society** = *Friendly Society*. [L (PROVIDE)]

providential /prɒvɪˈdenʃ(ə)l/ *a.* of or by divine foresight or intervention; opportune, lucky; **providentially** *adv.* [PROVIDENCE]

provider /prəˈvaɪdə/ *n.* breadwinner of family etc. [PROVIDE]

province /ˈprɒvɪns/ *n.* each of the principal administrative divisions of certain countries; sphere of action or business, branch of learning; *hist.* territory outside Italy under Roman rule; **the provinces** whole of a country outside its capital city. [F f. L *provincia*]

provincial /prəˈvɪnʃ(ə)l/ **1** *a.* of a province or provinces; having restricted views or the interests or manners etc. attributed to inhabitants of the provinces. **2** *n.* inhabitant of a province or the provinces. **3 provincialism** *n.* [F f. L (prec.)]

provision /prəˈvɪʒ(ə)n/ **1** *n.* providing; preparation for future contingency (*made provision for their old age*); provided amount *of* something; (in *pl.*) supply of food and drink; formally stated condition or stipulation. **2** *v.t.* supply with provisions. [F f. L (PROVIDE)]

provisional *a.* providing for immediate needs only, temporary; **provisionally** *adv.*

proviso /prəˈvaɪzəʊ/ *n.* (*pl.* **provisos**) stipulation, clause giving stipulation in document; **provisory** *a.* [L, = it being provided]

provocation /prɒvəˈkeɪʃ(ə)n/ *n.* incitement to anger etc., irritation; cause of annoyance. [F or L (PROVOKE)]

provocative /prəˈvɒkətɪv/ *a.* tending or intended to arouse anger etc.; deliberately annoying. [F f. L (foll.)]

provoke /prəˈvəʊk/ *v.t.* rouse or incite (person) *to* feeling or action; annoy or irritate (person *into doing* thing); cause or give rise to (feeling or reaction etc.); tempt, allure. [F, or L *provoco* call forth]

provost /ˈprɒvəst/ *n.* head of some colleges; *Sc.* head of municipal corporation or burgh; (in full **provost marshal** /prəˈvəʊ/) head of military police in camp or on active service. [OE & F f. L *propositus* (*pono* place)]

prow *n.* part adjoining stem of boat or ship; pointed projecting front part. [F *proue* f. L *prora* f. Gk]

prowess /ˈpraʊɪs/ *n.* skill, expertise; valour, gallantry. [F (PROUD)]

prowl 1 *v.* go about stealthily in search of prey or to catch others unawares; traverse (place) thus; pace or wander restlessly. **2** *n.* prowling (*on the prowl*). [orig. unkn.]

prox. *abbr.* proximo.

proximate /ˈprɒksɪmət/ *a.* nearest, next before or after (in time or order, in causation etc.); approximate. [L (*proximus* nearest)]

proximity /prɒkˈsɪmɪtɪ/ *n.* nearness in space or time (*to*); neighbourhood. [F or L (prec.)]

proximo /ˈprɒksɪməʊ/ *a.* (in commerce) of next month (*the 3rd proximo*). [L, = in the next (*mense* month)]

proxy /ˈprɒksɪ/ *n.* person authorized to act for another; agency of such a person (*voted by proxy*); document authorizing person to vote on behalf of another; vote so given. [obs. *procuracy* procuration]

prude /pruːd/ *n.* person of extreme (esp. affected) propriety in conduct or speech, esp. as regards sexual matters; **prudery** *n.*; **prudish** *a.* [F (PROUD)]

prudent /ˈpruːdənt/ *a.* (of person or conduct) showing care and foresight; circumspect, discreet; **prudence** *n.* [F or L *prudens -ent-* (PROVIDENT)]

prudential /pruːˈdenʃ(ə)l/ *a.* of or involving or marked by prudence; **prudentially** *adv.*

prune[1] *v.t.* trim (tree etc.) by cutting away dead or overgrown branches etc., esp. to promote growth; lop (branches etc.) *off* or *away*; remove or reduce (what is regarded as superfluous or excessive), remove items thus from. [F *prooignier* f. Rmc (ROUND)]

prune[2] *n.* dried plum. [F f. L *prunum* f. Gk]

prurient /'prʊərɪənt/ *a.* given to or arising from indulgence of lewd ideas; **prurience** *n.* [L *prurio* itch]

Prussian /'prʌʃ(ə)n/ **1** *a.* of Prussia. **2** *n.* native of Prussia. **3 Prussian blue** deep blue pigment. [*Prussia*, former German State]

prussic /'prʌsɪk/ *a.* of or obtained from Prussian blue; **prussic acid** a highly poisonous liquid. [F]

pry /praɪ/ *v.i.* inquire impertinently *into* (person's affairs etc.); look or peer inquisitively (*into*). [orig. unkn.]

PS *abbr.* postscript.

psalm /sɑ:m/ *n.* sacred song, hymn; **(Book of) Psalms** book of these in Old Testament. [OE & F f. L *psalmus* f. Gk]

psalmist *n.* author of psalms. [L (prec.)]

psalmody /'sɑ:mədɪ, 'sælmədɪ/ *n.* practice or art of singing psalms etc., esp. in public worship.[L f. Gk (PSALM)]

Psalter /'sɔ:ltə, 'sɒ-/ *n.* the Book of Psalms; **(psalter)** copy or version of this. [OE & F f. L f. Gk *psaltērion* stringed instrument]

psaltery /'sɔ:ltərɪ, 'sɒ-/ *n.* ancient and medieval instrument like dulcimer but played by plucking strings. [F f. L (prec.)]

psephology /pse'fɒlədʒɪ, se-/ *n.* study of trends in elections and voting; **psephologist** *n.* [Gk *psēphos* pebble, vote]

pseud /sju:d/ *colloq.* **1** *a.* sham, spurious; insincere; having aspirations beyond true worth. **2** *n.* pseud person. [PSEUDO-]

pseudo /'sju:dəʊ/ *a.* & *n.* (*pl.* **pseudos**) = PSEUD. [foll.]

pseudo- *in comb.* false, apparent, supposed but not real. [Gk (*pseudēs* false)]

pseudonym /'sju:dənɪm/ *n.* fictitious name, esp. one assumed by author; **pseudonymity** /-'nɪmɪtɪ/ *n.*; **pseudonymous** /-'dɒnɪməs/ *a.* [F f. Gk (prec., *onuma* name)]

psi /psaɪ/ *n.* twenty-third letter of Greek alphabet (Ψ, ψ). [Gk]

psoriasis /sɔ:'raɪəsɪs/ *n.* skin disease with red scaly patches. [Gk (*psōra* itch)]

psst *int.* to attract attention surreptitiously. [imit.]

PSV *abbr.* public service vehicle.

psyche /'saɪkɪ/ *n.* the human soul or spirit; the human mind. [L f. Gk]

psychedelic /saɪkɪ'delɪk/ *a.* hallucinatory, expanding the mind's awareness; having intensely vivid colours or sounds etc. [Gk *psukhē* mind, *dēlos* clear]

psychiatric /saɪkɪ'ætrɪk/ *a.* (also **psychiatrical**) of or concerning psychiatry; **psychiatrically** *adv.* [foll.]

psychiatry /saɪ'kaɪətrɪ/ *n.* study and treatment of mental disease; **psychiatrist** *n.* [PSYCHO-, Gk *iatros* physician]

psychic /'saɪkɪk/ **1** *a.* psychical, able to exercise psychical or occult powers. **2** *n.* person susceptible to psychical influence, medium; (in *pl.*) study of psychical phenomena; **psychically** *adv.* [Gk *psukhē* soul, mind]

psychical *a.* of the soul or mind, of phenomena and conditions apparently outside domain of physical law (*psychical research*); **psychically** *adv.*

psycho- *in comb.* mind, soul. [Gk (PSYCHIC)]

psycho-analyse /saɪkəʊ'ænəlaɪz/ *v.t.* treat by psycho-analysis; **psycho-analyst** *n.*

psycho-analysis /saɪkəʊə'nælɪsɪs/ *n.* therapeutic method of treating mental disorders by investigating interaction of conscious and unconscious elements in the mind; **psycho-analytic** /-ænə'lɪtɪk/ *a.*; **psycho-analytical** /-ænə'lɪtɪk(ə)l/ *a.*

psychological /saɪkə'lɒdʒɪk(ə)l/ *a.* of the mind, of psychology; **psychological moment** the psychologically appropriate moment, *colloq.* the most appropriate time; **psychological warfare** warfare achieving aims by weakening enemy's morale; **psychologically** *adv.*

psychology /saɪ'kɒlədʒɪ/ *n.* science of human mind; treatise on or system of this; *colloq.* mental characteristics; **psychologist** *n.*

psychoneurosis /saɪkəʊnjʊə'rəʊsɪs/ *n.* neurosis esp. with indirect expression of emotional feelings; **psychoneurotic** /-'rɒtɪk/ *a.*

psychopath /'saɪkəpæθ/ *n.* person suffering from chronic mental disorder esp. with abnormal social behaviour; mentally or emotionally unstable person; **psychopathic** /-'pæθɪk/ *a.*

psychopathology /saɪkəʊpə'θɒlədʒɪ/ *n.* science of mental disorders.

psychopathy /saɪ'kɒpəθɪ/ *n.* state or condition of psychopath.

psychosis /saɪ'kəʊsɪs/ *n.* (*pl.* **psychoses** /-i:z/) severe mental derangement involving the whole personality. [Gk (PSYCHE)]

psychosomatic /saɪkəʊsə'mætɪk/ *a.* of mind and body; (of disease etc.) caused or aggravated by mental stress; **psychosomatically** *adv.* [PSYCHO-]

psychosurgery /saɪkəʊ'sɜ:dʒərɪ/ *n.* brain surgery as a means of treating mental disorder.

psychotherapy /saɪkəʊ'θerəpɪ/ *n.* treatment of mental disorder by psychological means; **psychotherapeutic** /-'pju:tɪk/ *a.*; **psychotherapist** *n.*

psychotic /saɪ'kɒtɪk/ **1** *a.* of or suffering from psychosis. **2** *n.* psychotic person. [PSYCHOSIS]

PT *abbr.* physical training.

pt. *abbr.* part; pint; point; port.

Pt *symb.* platinum.

PTA *abbr.* parent–teacher association.

ptarmigan /'tɑ:mɪgən/ *n.* bird of grouse family. [Gael.]

Pte. *abbr.* Private (soldier).

pterodactyl /terə'dæktɪl/ *n.* extinct winged reptile. [Gk *pteron* wing, DACTYL]

PTO *abbr.* please turn over.

Ptolemaic /tɒlə'meɪɪk/ *a.* of or according to the theory of Ptolemy that the earth is the stationary centre round which sun and stars revolve. [L f. Gk *Ptolemaios*, 2nd-c. astronomer]

ptomaine /'təʊmeɪn/ *n.* any of various amines (some toxic) in putrefying animal and vegetable matter. [F f. It. f. Gk *ptōma* corpse]

Pu *symb.* plutonium.

pub *n. colloq.* public house; **pub crawl** journey to several pubs with drinking at each. [abbr.]

puberty /'pju:bətɪ/ *n.* stage at which person becomes capable of procreation through natural development of reproductive organs; **pubertal** *a.* [F or L (*puber* adult)]

pubes /'pju:bi:z/ *n.* lower part of abdomen. [L]

pubescence /pju:'besəns/ *n.* arrival at puberty; soft down on plant or animal; **pubescent** *a.* [F or L (PUBES)]

pubic /'pju:bɪk/ *a.* of the pubes or pubis. [PUBES]

pubis /'pju:bɪs/ *n.* (*pl.* **pubes** /-i:z/) bone forming front of each half of pelvis. [L *os pubis* bone of the PUBES]

public /'pʌblɪk/ **1** *a.* of or concerning or for the use of the people as a whole; representing, done by or for, the people (*public assembly*, *expenditure*); open to general observation or knowledge, openly done or existing (*made her views public*); of or engaged in the people's affairs or service (*public prosecutor*). **2** *n.* the (members of the) community in general; section of the community (*the reading public*). **3 in public** openly, for all to see or know; **public-address system** system of loudspeakers etc. for speaker at large gathering; **public company** one with shares available to all buyers; **public house** place licensed for and mainly concerned with selling alcoholic drink for consumption on the premises; **public lending right** right of authors to payment when their books are lent by public libraries; **public relations** promotion of good relations between business etc. and the public; **public school** endowed independent school for fee-paying pupils, *US & Sc.* school managed by public authorities; **public servant** State official; **public-spirited** ready to do things for the benefit of people in general; **public transport** buses, trains, etc., available to public and having fixed routes; **public utility** organization supplying gas or electricity or water, etc., and regarded as a public service; **public works** building operations undertaken by the State. [F or L]

publican /'pʌblɪkən/ *n.* keeper of public house. [F f. L (prec.)]

publication /pʌblɪ'keɪʃ(ə)n/ *n.* issuing of book or periodical etc. to public; book etc. so issued; making publicly known. [F f. L (PUBLIC)]

publicist /'pʌblɪsɪst/ *n.* writer on or person skilled in current public affairs; expert in publicity.

publicity /pʌb'lɪsɪtɪ/ *n.* public attention or the means of attracting it, the business of advertising; being open to general observation, notoriety. [F (PUBLIC)]

publicize /'pʌblɪsaɪz/ *v.t.* make publicly known, esp. by advertisement. [PUBLIC]

publish /'pʌblɪʃ/ *v.t.* issue copies of (book or periodical etc., or *absol.*) for sale to public; make generally known, announce formally. [F f. L (PUBLIC)]

publisher *n.* person or firm that issues and distributes copies of book or periodical etc.

puce *a.* & *n.* brownish-purple. [F f. L *pulex* flea]

puck[1] *n.* rubber disc used in ice hockey. [orig. unkn.]

puck[2] *n.* mischievous sprite; **puckish** *a.* [OE]

pucker **1** *v.* (cause to) gather into wrinkles or folds or bulges, intentionally or as fault e.g. in sewing (often with *up*). **2** *n.* such wrinkle or bulge. [orig. unkn.]

pud /pʊd/ *n. colloq.* = PUDDING. [abbr.]

pudding /'pʊdɪŋ/ *n.* any sweet food made with sugar, eggs, etc., dessert; food of various kinds containing or enclosed in mixture of flour (or similar substance) and other ingredients and cooked by baking or boiling or steaming; a kind of sausage (*black pudding*); dumpy slow-witted person; **puddingy** *a.* [F f. L *botellus* sausage]

puddle /'pʌd(ə)l/ **1** *n.* small pool esp. of rain on road etc.; clay made into watertight coating. **2** *v.* make muddy; knead (clay and sand) with water into muddy mixture; stir (molten iron) to produce wrought iron by expelling carbon. **3** **puddly** *a.* [OE]

pudenda /pju:'dendə/ *n.pl.* genitals, esp. of woman. [L (*pudeo* be ashamed)]

puerile /'pjʊəraɪl/ *a.* childish; silly or immature; **puerility** /-'rɪlɪtɪ/ *n.* [F or L (*puer* boy)]

puerperal /pju:'ɜ:pər(ə)l/ *a.* of or due to childbirth; **puerperal fever** fever following childbirth and caused by uterine infection. [L (*puer* boy, *pario* bear)]

puff 1 *n.* short quick blast of breath or wind; sound (as) of this; drawing in of smoke from pipe etc.; small quantity emitted at a puff; = *powder-puff*; cake of light pastry (*cream puff*); unduly laudatory review or advertisement etc. **2** *v.* emit puff of air or breath; (of air etc.) come *out* or *up* in puffs; blow (smoke etc.) in puffs, smoke (pipe etc.) in puffs; emit puffs of smoke, (of steam-engine) move with puffs; breathe hard, pant; put out of breath (*arrived looking puffed*); blow (dust etc. or light object) *away* or *off* etc. with puff; make or become inflated, (cause to) swell (*out* or *up*); advertise (goods) with false or exaggerated praise. **3 puff-adder** large venomous African viper inflating upper part of body when excited; **puff-ball** fungus with ball-shaped spore-case; **puff pastry** light flaky pastry; **puff** (or **puffed**) **sleeve** short sleeve that is very full at shoulder; **puff up** elate, make proud (esp. in *p.p.*: *puffed up with pride*). [imit.]

puffin /'pʌfɪn/ *n.* N. Atlantic auk with short striped bill. [orig. unkn.]

puffy *a.* puffed out, swollen; short-winded; **puffily** *adv.*; **puffiness** *n.* [PUFF]

pug *n.* dog of dwarf breed with broad flat nose and wrinkled face; **pug-nosed** having short flattish nose. [orig. unkn.]

pugilist /'pju:dʒɪlɪst/ *n.* professional boxer; **pugilism** *n.*; **pugilistic** /-'lɪstɪk/ *a.* [L *pugil* boxer]

pugnacious /pʌg'neɪʃəs/ *a.* disposed to fight, aggressive; **pugnacity** /-'næsɪtɪ/ *n.* [L *pugnax -acis* (*pugno* fight)]

puisne /'pju:nɪ/ *n.* judge of superior court who is inferior in rank to chief justice. [F (cf. PUNY)]

puissance /'pwi:sɑ:ns/ *n.* (in show-jumping) test of horse's ability to jump high obstacles. [F (foll.)]

puissant /'pju:ɪsənt/ *a. literary* having great power or influence, mighty. [F f. Rmc (POTENT)]

puke *v.* & *n.* vomit. [imit.]

pukka /'pʌkə/ *a. colloq.* genuine; of good quality. [Hindi]

pulchritude /'pʌlkrɪtju:d/ *n. literary* beauty; **pulchritudinous** /-'tju:dɪnəs/ *a.* [L (*pulcher* beautiful)]

pule *v.i.* whimper, cry querulously or weakly. [imit.]

pull /pʊl/ **1** *v.* exert force on (thing) to move it to oneself or to origin of force; cause to move thus; exert such force; remove (cork or tooth) by pulling; damage (muscle etc.) by abnormal strain; move (boat) by pulling on oars, (of boat etc.) be caused to move, esp. in specified direction; proceed with effort (*up* hill etc.); bring out (weapon) for use (*on* person); check speed of (horse); attract (customers); draw (liquor) from barrel etc.; (in cricket) strike (ball) to leg side; (in golf) strike (ball) widely to the left; print (proof etc.). **2** *n.* act of pulling, force thus exerted; means of exerting influence, advantage; deep draught of liquor; prolonged effort, e.g. in going up hill; handle etc. for applying pull; printer's rough proof; pulling stroke in cricket or golf. **3 pull apart** (or **to pieces**) forcibly separate parts of, criticize severely; **pull back** (cause to) retreat; **pull down** demolish, humiliate; **pull a fast one** *sl.* gain advantage by unfair means; **pull in** earn or acquire, (of train etc.) enter station, (of vehicle) move to side of or off road, *colloq.* arrest; **pull-in** *n.* place for vehicle to pull in off road; **pull person's leg** deceive him playfully; **pull off** remove by pulling, succeed in achieving or winning; **pull oneself together** recover control of oneself; **pull out** depart, withdraw from undertaking, (of train etc.) leave station, (of vehicle) move from side of road, or from normal position to overtake; **pull one's punches** avoid using one's full force; **pull rank** take unfair advantage of seniority; **pull round** (or **through**) recover from illness; **pull strings** exert (esp. clandestine) influence; **pull up** (cause to) stop moving, reprimand, pull out of ground, check oneself; **pull one's weight** do one's fair share of work. [OE]

pullet /'pʊlɪt/ *n.* young domestic fowl, esp. hen that has begun to lay but not yet moulted. [F dimin. of *poule* f. L *pullus*]

pulley /'pʊlɪ/ *n.* grooved wheel for cord etc. to pass over, set in block and used for changing direction of force; wheel or drum fixed on shaft and turned by belt, used esp. to increase speed or power. [F *polie*, rel. to POLE²]

Pullman /'pʊlmən/ *n.* railway carriage or motor coach affording special comfort; sleeping-car. [*Pullman*, designer]

pullover *n.* knitted garment put on over the head. [PULL]

pullulate /'pʌljʊleɪt/ *v.i.* grow or develop, abound *with*; **pullulation** /-'leɪʃ(ə)n/ *n.* [L *pullulo* sprout]

pulmonary /'pʌlmənərɪ/ *a.* of or in or connected with the lungs; affected with or subject to lung-disease. [L (*pulmo -onis* lung)]

pulp 1 *n.* fleshy part of fruit, animal body, etc.; soft shapeless mass, esp. that of rags or wood etc., from which paper is made; *attrib.* (of magazine etc.) printed orig. on rough paper, often with sensational or poor-quality writing. **2** *v.* reduce to or become pulp. **3 pulpiness** *n.*; **pulpy** *a.* [L]

pulpit /'pʊlpɪt/ *n.* raised enclosed platform in church etc. from which preacher delivers sermon; **the pulpit** preachers or preaching. [L *pulpitum* platform]

pulsar /'pʌlsə/ *n.* cosmic source of regularly and rapidly pulsating radio signals. [*pulsating star*, after *quasar*]

pulsate /pʌl'seɪt, 'pʌl-/ *v.i.* expand and contract rhythmically, throb; vibrate, quiver, thrill; **pulsation** /-'seɪʃ(ə)n/ *n.*; **pulsatory** /'pʌlsətərɪ/ *a.* [F f. L (as foll.)]

pulse¹ 1 *n.* rhythmical throbbing of arteries as blood is propelled along them; each successive beat of arteries or heart, rate of this beat; single vibration of sound or light or electric current etc., esp. as signal; throb or thrill of life or emotion, latent feeling. **2** *v.i.* pulsate. [F f. L (*pello puls-* drive, beat)]

pulse² *n.* (as *sing.* or *pl.*) edible seeds of leguminous plants, e.g. peas, beans, lentils; any kind of these. [F f. L *puls*]

pulverize /'pʌlvəraɪz/ *v.* reduce or crumble to powder or dust; demolish, defeat utterly; **pulverization** /-'zeɪʃ(ə)n/ *n.* [L (*pulvis -ver-* dust)]

puma /'pju:mə/ *n.* large tawny American feline. [Sp. f. Quechua]

pumice /'pʌmɪs/ *n.* (also **pumice-stone**) light porous lava for removing stains from skin etc. or as powder for polishing; piece of this. [F *pomis* f. L *pumex -ic-*]

pummel /'pʌm(ə)l/ *v.t.* (**-ll-**, *US* **-l-**) strike repeatedly esp. with fist. [POMMEL]

pump¹ 1 *n.* machine or device of various kinds for raising or moving liquids or gases. **2** *v.* raise or remove (liquid or gas) with a pump; fill (tyre etc.) with air (often with *up*); remove water etc. from with a pump; work a pump; (cause to) move or pour (*out*) as if by pumping; elicit information from (person) by persistent questioning; move vigorously up and down as if pumping. [orig. uncert.]

pump² *n.* plimsoll; light shoe for dancing etc.; *US* court shoe. [orig. unkn.]

pumpernickel /'pʌmpənɪk(ə)l, 'pʊ-/ *n.* German wholemeal rye bread. [G]

pumpkin /'pʌmpkɪn/ *n.* large orange-coloured fruit used as vegetable; plant bearing it. [F *pompon* f. L f. Gk *pepōn* melon]

pun 1 *n.* humorous use of word to suggest different meanings, or of words of same sound with different meaning. **2** *v.i.* (**-nn-**) make pun (*on* word or subject). [orig. unkn.]

punch¹ 1 *v.t.* strike with fist; pierce hole in (metal, paper, ticket, etc.) as or with punch; pierce (hole) thus. **2** *n.* blow with fist; ability to deliver this; *sl.* vigour, effective force; instrument or machine for cutting holes or impressing design in leather, metal, paper, etc. **3 punch-ball** inflated ball held on stand etc. and punched as form of exercise; **punch** (or **punched) card** card perforated according to a code, for conveying instructions to computer etc.; **punch-drunk** stupefied through having been severely punched (*lit.* or *fig.*); **punch-line** words giving point of joke or story; **punch-up** fist-fight, brawl. [var. of *pounce* emboss]

punch² *n.* drink usu. of wine or spirits mixed with hot or cold water, spice, etc.; **punch-bowl** bowl in which punch is mixed, round deep hollow in hill. [orig. unkn.]

punch³ *n.* (in full **Suffolk punch**) short-legged thickset draught horse; **(Punch)** grotesque humpbacked figure in puppet-show called *Punch and Judy*; **as pleased** (or **proud) as Punch** showing great pleasure (or pride). [abbr. of *Punchinello*, chief character in It. puppet-show]

punchy *a.* having vigour, forceful. [PUNCH¹]

punctilio /pʌŋk'tɪlɪəʊ/ *n.* (*pl.* **punctilios**) delicate point of ceremony or honour; etiquette of such points; petty formality. [It. & Sp. (POINT)]

punctilious /pʌŋk'tɪlɪəs/ *a.* attentive to formality or etiquette; precise in behaviour. [F f. It. (as prec.)]

punctual /'pʌŋktjʊəl/ *a.* observant of appointed time; neither early nor late; **punctuality** /-'ælɪtɪ/ *n.*; **punctually** *adv.* [med.L (POINT)]

punctuate /'pʌŋktjʊeɪt/ *v.t.* insert punctuation marks in; interrupt at intervals (*sermon was punctuated with loud coughing*); emphasize, accentuate. [med.L (as prec.)]

punctuation /pʌŋktjʊ'eɪʃ(ə)n/ *n.* punctuating; system used for this; **punctuation mark** any of the marks (e.g. full stop and comma) used in writing to separate sentences and phrases etc. and clarify meaning.

puncture /'pʌŋktʃə/ **1** *n.* prick or pricking, esp. accidental piercing of pneumatic tyre; hole thus made. **2** *v.* make

puncture in, undergo puncture; prick or pierce. [L *punctura* (POINT)]
pundit /ˈpʌndɪt/ *n.* learned Hindu; learned expert or teacher; **punditry** *n.* [Hind. f. Skr.]
pungent /ˈpʌndʒənt/ *a.* having sharp or strong taste or smell; (of remarks) penetrating, biting, caustic; mentally stimulating; **pungency** *n.* [L (POINT)]
punish /ˈpʌnɪʃ/ *v.t.* cause (offender) to suffer for offence; inflict penalty for (offence); *colloq.* inflict severe blows on (opponent); tax severely, subject to severe treatment. [F f. L *punio*]
punishment *n.* punishing or being punished; loss or suffering inflicted in this; severe treatment or suffering.
punitive /ˈpju:nɪtɪv/ *a.* inflicting or intended to inflict punishment. [F or med.L (PUNISH)]
punk *n. colloq.* worthless person or thing; *colloq.* = *punk rock*, devotee of this; **punk rock** type of pop music using aggressive and outrageous effects. [orig. unkn.]
punkah /ˈpʌŋkə/ *n.* large swinging fan worked by cord or electrically. [Hindi]
punnet /ˈpʌnɪt/ *n.* small basket or container for fruit etc. [orig. unkn.]
punster *n.* habitual maker of puns. [PUN]
punt[1] **1** *n.* flat-bottomed shallow boat propelled by long pole thrust against bottom of river etc. **2** *v.* propel (punt) with pole; travel or convey in punt. [LG or Du.]
punt[2] **1** *v.t.* kick (football) after it has dropped from the hands and before it reaches the ground. **2** *n.* such kick. [orig. unkn.]
punt[3] *v.i.* (in some card-games) lay stake against bank; *colloq.* bet on horse etc., speculate in shares etc. [F *ponter*]
puny /ˈpju:nɪ/ *a.* undersized, weak, feeble. [F *puisné* born afterwards]
pup 1 *n.* young dog; young wolf, rat, seal, etc. **2** *v.t.* (**-pp-**) (of bitch etc.) bring forth (young, or *absol.*). **3 in pup** (of bitch) pregnant; **sell person a pup** swindle him esp. by selling thing on prospective value. [PUPPY]
pupa /ˈpju:pə/ *n.* (*pl.* **pupae** /-i:/) insect in passive phase between larva and imago; **pupal** *a.* [L, = doll]
pupil /ˈpju:pɪl/ *n.* one who is taught by another, schoolchild, disciple; circular opening in centre of iris of eye. [F, or L *pupillus, -illa* dimins. of *pupus* boy, *pupa* girl]
puppet /ˈpʌpɪt/ *n.* kind of doll representing human being etc. and moved by various means as entertainment; person whose acts are controlled by another; **puppet state** country that is apparently independent but actually under the control of another power; **puppetry** *n.* [var. of POPPET]
puppy /ˈpʌpɪ/ *n.* young dog; vain empty-headed young man; **puppy-fat** temporary fatness of child or adolescent. [F (POPPET)]
purblind /ˈpɜ:blaɪnd/ *a.* partly blind, dim-sighted; obtuse, dim-witted. [*pur(e)* (= utterly) *blind*]
purchase /ˈpɜ:tʃəs/ **1** *v.t.* buy; obtain or achieve (*with* a cost or sacrifice). **2** *n.* buying; thing bought; annual rent or return from land; firm hold on thing to move it or prevent it slipping, leverage. [AF (PRO-[1], CHASE[1])]
purdah /ˈpɜ:də/ *n.* system of screening Muslim or Hindu women from strangers by means of veil or curtain. [Urdu]
pure *a.* unmixed, unadulterated; of unmixed origin; morally or sexually undefiled; guiltless, sincere; mere, simple, nothing but, sheer; (of sound) not discordant, perfectly in tune; (of mathematics or science) dealing with abstract concepts and not practical applications. [F f. L *purus*]
purée /ˈpjʊəreɪ/ *n.* pulp of vegetables or fruit etc. reduced to smooth cream. [F]
purely *adv.* in pure manner; merely; solely, exclusively; entirely. [PURE]
purgative /ˈpɜ:gətɪv/ **1** *a.* serving to purify; strongly laxative. **2** *n.* purgative thing; laxative. [F or L (PURGE)]
purgatory /ˈpɜ:gətərɪ/ *n.* condition or place of spiritual cleansing, esp. (in RC Church) of souls departing this life in grace of God but having to expiate venial sins etc.; place or state of temporary suffering or expiation; **purgatorial** /-ˈtɔ:rɪəl/ *a.* [F f. med.L (foll.)]
purge 1 *v.t.* make physically or spiritually clean; remove by cleansing process; rid of persons regarded as undesirable; empty (bowels) or bowels of (person); *Law* atone for or wipe out (offence, esp. contempt of court). **2** *n.* act or process of purging; purgative. [F f. L *purgo* purify]
purify /ˈpjʊərɪfaɪ/ *v.t.* cleanse or make pure; make ceremonially clean; clear of extraneous elements; **purification** /-fɪˈkeɪʃ(ə)n/ *n.*; **purificatory** *a.* [F or L (PURE)]
purist /ˈpjʊərɪst/ *n.* stickler for or affecter of scrupulous purity, esp. in language or art; **purism** *n.*; **puristic** /-ˈrɪstɪk/ *a.* [F (PURE)]
Puritan /ˈpjʊərɪt(ə)n/ **1** *n. hist.* member of group of English Protestants who regarded Reformation as incomplete and sought to simplify forms of worship; (**puritan**) purist member of any party; person practising or affecting extreme strictness in religion or

morals. **2** *a.* (**puritan**) of Puritans; scrupulous in religion or morals. **3** **puritanical** /-tænɪk(ə)l/ *a.*; **puritanism** *n.* [L (foll.)]

purity /ˈpjʊərɪtɪ/ *n.* pureness, cleanness, freedom from physical or moral pollution. [F f. L (PURE)]

purl[1] **1** *n.* knitting-stitch with needle put into stitch in opposite to normal direction; chain of minute loops, picot. **2** *v.t.* make (stitch, or *absol.*) purl. [orig. unkn.]

purl[2] *v.i.* (of brook etc.) flow with swirling motion and babbling sound. [imit.]

purler *n. colloq.* headlong fall. [*purl* overturn]

purlieu /ˈpɜːljuː/ *n.* one's bounds or limits or usual haunts; *hist.* tract on border of forest; (in *pl.*) outskirts, outlying region. [AF *puralé* (*aller* go)]

purlin /ˈpɜːlɪn/ *n.* horizontal beam along roof. [AL *perlio*]

purloin /pɜːˈlɔɪn/ *v.t.* steal, pilfer. [AF *purloigner* (*loign* far)]

purple /ˈpɜːp(ə)l/ **1** *n.* colour between red and blue; (in full **Tyrian purple**) crimson colour obtained from some molluscs; purple robe, esp. as dress of emperor etc.; scarlet official dress of cardinal. **2** *a.* of purple or Tyrian purple colour. **3** *v.* make or become purple. **4** **born in the purple** born in reigning family, belonging to most privileged class; **purple heart** heart-shaped stimulant tablet; **purple passage** (or **patch**) ornate passage in literary composition. [OE f. L *purpura* f. Gk *porphura* shellfish yielding dye]

purport 1 /pəˈpɔːt/ *v.t.* profess, be intended to seem (*a letter purporting to come from her*); (of document or speech) have as its meaning, state. **2** /ˈpɜːpət/ *n.* ostensible meaning; sense or tenor of document or statement. [AF f. L (PRO-[1], PORT[5])]

purpose /ˈpɜːpəs/ **1** *n.* object to be attained, thing intended; intention to act; resolution, determination. **2** *v.t.* have as one's purpose, design, intend. **3** **on purpose** intentionally; **purpose-built** (or **-made** etc.) built etc. for a specific purpose; **to little** (or **no**) **purpose** with little (or no) result or effect; **to the purpose** relevant, useful. [F f. L *propono* PROPOSE]

purposeful *a.* having or indicating (conscious) purpose; intentional; resolute; **purposefully** *adv.*

purposely *adv.* on purpose.

purposive /ˈpɜːpəsɪv/ *a.* having or serving or done with a purpose; purposeful.

purr /pɜː/ **1** *v.* make low vibratory sound as of cat expressing pleasure; (of machinery etc.) make similar sound. **2** *n.* such sound. [imit.]

purse 1 *n.* small pouch of leather etc. for carrying money on the person; *US* handbag; money, funds; sum given as present or prize for contest. **2** *v.* (also with *up*) pucker or contract (lips or brow) in wrinkles; become wrinkled. **3** **hold the purse-strings** have control of expenditure. [OE f. L *bursa* f. Gk, = leather bag]

purser *n.* officer on ship who keeps accounts, esp. head steward in passenger vessel. [prec.]

pursuance /pəˈsjuːəns/ *n.* carrying out or observance (*of* plan, rules, etc.). [foll.]

pursuant *adv.* conformably *to* (*the Act* etc.). [F (as foll.)]

pursue /pəˈsjuː/ *v.* follow with intent to overtake or capture or do harm to; continue or proceed along (route or course of action); follow or engage in (study or other activity); proceed in compliance with (plan etc.); seek after, aim at; continue to investigate or discuss (topic); (of misfortune etc.) persistently assail; go in pursuit. [F f. L (*sequor* follow)]

pursuit /pəˈsjuːt/ *n.* pursuing; occupation or activity pursued. [F (SUIT)]

pursuivant /ˈpɜːsɪvənt/ *n.* officer of College of Arms below herald. [F (PURSUE)]

pursy[1] /ˈpɜːsɪ/ *a.* short-winded, puffy; corpulent. [AF *porsif* f. F *polsif* (L *pulso* PULSATE)]

pursy[2] *a.* puckered. [PURSE]

purulent /ˈpjʊərʊlənt/ *a.* of or containing or discharging pus; **purulence** *n.* [L (PUS)]

purvey /pəˈveɪ/ *v.t.* provide or supply (articles of food) as one's business; **purveyor** *n.* [AF f. L (PROVIDE)]

purview /ˈpɜːvjuː/ *n.* scope or range of document or scheme etc.; range of physical or mental vision. [AF p.p. (PURVEY)]

pus *n.* yellowish viscous matter produced from inflamed or infected tissue. [L *pus puris*]

push /pʊʃ/ **1** *v.* exert force on (thing) to move it away from oneself or from origin of force; cause to move thus; exert such force; thrust forward or upward, (cause to) project; move forward by force or persistence, make (one's way) thus; exert oneself, esp. to surpass others; urge or impel; tax abilities or tolerance of; pursue (claim etc.); promote use or sale or adoption of, e.g. by advertising; sell (drug) illegally. **2** *n.* act of pushing, force thus exerted; vigorous effort, military attack in force; enterprise, determination to succeed; use of influence to advance a person; pressure of affairs, crisis. **3** **be pushed**

for *colloq.* have very little of (*time* etc.); **push around** bully; **push-bike** *colloq.* pedal cycle; **push-button** *n.* button to be pushed esp. to operate electrical device, (*a.*) operated thus; **push-chair** folding chair on wheels, for pushing child in; **push for** demand; **push one's luck** see LUCK; **push off** push with oar etc. to get boat out into river etc., *sl.* go away; **push-over** *colloq.* opponent or difficulty easily overcome; **push-start** *n.* starting of motor vehicle by pushing it to turn engine, (*v.t.*) start (vehicle) thus; **push through** get completed or accepted quickly. [F f. L (PULSATE)]

pusher *n.* illegal seller of drugs.

pushful *a.* self-assertive, determined to succeed; **pushfully** *adv.*

pushing *a.* pushful; *colloq.* having nearly reached (specified age).

Pushtu /'pʌʃtu:/ *n.* & *a.* = PASHTO. [Pers.]

pushy *a. colloq.* pushful. [PUSH]

pusillanimous /pju:sɪ'lænɪməs/ *a.* lacking courage, timid; **pusillanimity** /-'nɪmɪtɪ/ *n.* [L (*pusillus* petty, ANIMUS)]

puss /pʊs/ *n.* cat (esp. as form of address); *colloq.* playful or coquettish girl. [LG or Du.]

pussy /'pʊsɪ/ *n.* cat (also **pussy-cat**); *vulgar* vulva; **pussy willow** willow with furry catkins.

pussyfoot *v.i.* move stealthily; act cautiously or non-committally.

pustulate /'pʌstjʊleɪt/ *v.* form into pustules. [L (foll.)]

pustule /'pʌstju:l/ *n.* pimple; **pustular** *a.* [F, or L *pustula*]

put /pʊt/ **1** *v.* (**-tt-**; *past* and *p.p.* **put**) move to or cause to be in specified place or position (*put it in your pocket*; *put your signature here*); bring into specified condition or state (*puts me in difficulty*); impose, submit for consideration or attention (*put a tax on wine*; *put the blame on us*; *put a stop to it*); substitute (one thing *for* another); express in specified way (*to put it mildly*); estimate (amount etc.) *at* so much; invest (money) *in* or *into*; bet (money or amount) *on*; hurl (esp. shot) from hand as athletic exercise. **2** *n.* throw of shot. **3 put about** spread (rumour etc.), put (ship) on opposite tack; **put across** make acceptable or effective or understood; **put away** lay aside for future use, *colloq.* imprison, *colloq.* kill (old or sick animal), *colloq.* consume (food or drink); **put back** restore to former place, return to harbour or shore, move back hands of (clock or watch); **put by** lay aside for future use; **put down** suppress by force, snub or humiliate, record or enter in writing, attribute *to*, consider *as*, kill (old or sick animal), allow to alight; **put-down** *n.* a snub; **put forward** suggest or propose, advance hands of (clock or watch); **put in** enter (claim etc.), *colloq.* spend (time), enter harbour or come to shore; **put in for** apply or be candidate for; **put it across** *sl.* trick or get the better of (person); **put it to person** challenge him to deny *that*; **put off** postpone, postpone engagement with (person), dissuade, repel, evade (person *with* excuse etc.), start from shore or ship; **put on** clothe oneself with, stage (play etc.), cause (electrical device or light etc.) to function, advance hands of (clock or watch), feign (emotion), increase one's weight by (so much); **put oneself in person's place** imagine oneself in his situation etc.; **put out** disconcert or annoy, extinguish (fire or light), cause (batsman or side) to be out, dislocate; **put (out) to sea** leave harbour; **put over** = *put across*; **put through** carry out or complete, connect by telephone; **put under** make unconscious; **put up** build, erect, raise (price etc.), lodge or be lodged (*at*), engage in (fight, struggle, etc.) as form of resistance, present (proposal), present oneself as candidate, provide (money as backer), offer for sale or competition, concoct; **put-up** *a.* fraudulently concocted; **put upon** *colloq.* unfairly burdened or deceived; **put person up to** instigate him in; **put up with** tolerate, submit to. [OE]

putative /'pju:tətɪv/ *a.* reputed or supposed (*his putative father*). [F or L (*puto* think)]

putrefy /'pju:trɪfaɪ/ *v.i.* become putrid, go bad; fester, suppurate; become morally corrupt; **putrefaction** /-'fækʃ(ə)n/ *n.*; **putrefactive** /-'fæktɪv/ *a.* [L *putreo* rot]

putrescent /pju:'tresənt/ *a.* in process of rotting, of or accompanying this process; **putrescence** *n.* [L (as foll.)]

putrid /'pju:trɪd/ *a.* decomposed, rotten; foul, noxious; corrupt; *sl.* of poor quality, very unpleasant; **putridity** /-'trɪdɪtɪ/ *n.* [L (*putreō* rot *v.*)]

putsch /pʊtʃ/ *n.* attempt at political revolution. [Swiss G]

putt **1** *v.* strike (golf-ball) gently to get it into or nearer to hole on putting-green. **2** *n.* such stroke. **3 putting-green** (in golf) smooth area of grass round a hole. [PUT]

puttee /'pʌtɪ/ *n.* long strip of cloth wound spirally round leg from ankle to knee for protection and support. [Hindi]

putter *n.* golf-club used in putting. [PUTT]

putty /'pʌtɪ/ **1** *n.* soft hard-setting paste of chalk powder and linseed oil for fixing glass, filling up holes in woodwork, etc. **2** *v.t.* fix or fill with putty. [F *potée* (POT)]

puzzle /ˈpʌz(ə)l/ **1** *n.* difficult or confusing problem; problem or toy designed to test knowledge or ingenuity. **2** *v.* confound or disconcert mentally; require much thought to comprehend (*a puzzling situation*). **3 puzzle about** (or **over**) be confused about, ponder about; **puzzle out** solve or understand by hard thought. **4 puzzlement** *n.* [orig. unkn.]

puzzler *n.* difficult question or problem.

PVC *abbr.* polyvinyl chloride.

PW *abbr.* Policewoman.

pyaemia /paɪˈi:mɪə/, *US* **pyemia** *n.* blood-poisoning with formation of abscesses in viscera. [L f. Gk *puon* pus, *haima* blood]

pye-dog /ˈpaɪdɒg/ *n.* vagrant mongrel of the East. [Hindi]

pygmy /ˈpɪgmɪ/ **1** *n.* one of a group of very short people in equatorial Africa; very small person or thing; insignificant person. **2** *a.* of pygmies; (of person or animal) dwarf. [L f. Gk]

pyjamas /pɪˈdʒɑ:məz/ *n.pl.* suit of loose trousers and jacket for sleeping in; **pyjama jacket** (or **top**), **pyjama trousers** garments forming pyjamas. [Urdu, = leg-clothing]

pylon /ˈpaɪlən/ *n.* tall structure erected as support (esp. for electric-power cables) or boundary or decoration. [Gk (*pulē* gate)]

pyorrhoea /paɪəˈrɪə/, US **pyorrhea** *n.* discharge of pus, esp. in disease of tooth-sockets. [Gk *puon* pus, *rheō* flow]

pyracantha /paɪərəˈkænθə/ *n.* evergreen thorny shrub with white flowers and scarlet berries. [L f. Gk]

pyramid /ˈpɪrəmɪd/ *n.* monumental (esp. ancient Egyptian) structure of stone etc. with square base and sloping sides meeting at apex; solid of this shape with base of three or more sides; pyramid-shaped thing or pile of things; **pyramid selling** system of selling goods in which agency rights are sold to increasing number of distributors at successively lower levels; **pyramidal** /-ˈræmɪd(ə)l/ *a.* [L f. Gk *puramis -mid-*]

pyre /ˈpaɪə/ *n.* heap of combustible material, esp. funeral pile for burning a corpse. [L f. Gk (PYRO-)]

pyrethrum /paɪˈri:θrəm/ *n.* chrysanthemum with finely divided leaves; insecticide from its dried flowers. [L f. Gk]

pyretic /paɪˈretɪk, pɪ-/ *a.* of or producing fever. [Gk *puretos* fever]

Pyrex /ˈpaɪreks/ *n.* **(P)** a hard heat-resistant glass. [invented word]

pyrexia /paɪˈreksɪə/ *n.* fever. [Gk *purexis*]

pyrites /paɪˈraɪti:z/ *n.* a mineral that is a sulphide of iron (*iron pyrites*) or of copper and iron (*copper pyrites*). [L f. Gk (PYRE)]

pyro- *in comb.* fire. [Gk (*pur* fire)]

pyromania /paɪrəʊˈmeɪnɪə/ *n.* uncontrollable impulse to start fires; **pyromaniac** *n.* & *a.*

pyrotechnics /paɪrəʊˈteknɪks/ *n.pl.* art of making fireworks; display of fireworks; any loud or brilliant display; **pyrotechnic** *a.*

pyrrhic /ˈpɪrɪk/ *a.* (of victory) won at too great cost. [*Pyrrhus* of Epirus, who defeated Romans thus in 279 BC]

Pythagoras' theorem /paɪˈθægərəs/ theorem that square on hypotenuse of right-angled triangle is equal to sum of squares on other two sides. [*Pythagoras* (6th c. BC), Gk philosopher]

python /ˈpaɪθ(ə)n/ *n.* large snake that crushes its prey. [L f. Gk name of monster]

pyx /pɪks/ *n.* vessel in which consecrated bread for Eucharist is kept. [L *pyxis* f. Gk (BOX)]

Q

Q, q /kju:/ *n.* (*pl.* **Qs, Q's**) seventeenth letter.

Q. *abbr.* Queen('s); question.

QC *abbr.* Queen's Counsel.

QED *abbr.* which was to be proved. [L *quod erat demonstrandum*]

QM *abbr.* quartermaster.

qr. *abbr.* quarter(s).

qt. *abbr.* quart(s).

qua /kweɪ, kwɑ:/ *conj.* in the capacity of. [L, = (in the way) in which]

quack[1] **1** *n.* harsh sound made by ducks. **2** *v.i.* utter quack; talk loudly and foolishly. [imit.]

quack[2] *n.* unskilled practiser of medicine, charlatan. [abbr. *quacksalver* f. Du. (prob. QUACK[1], SALVE[1])]

quackery *n.* quack methods.

quad /kwɒd/ *colloq.* **1** *n.* quadruplet; quadrangle; quadraphony. **2** *a.* quadraphonic. [abbr.]

Quadragesima /kwɒdrəˈdʒesɪmə/ *n.* first Sunday in Lent. [L *quadragesimus* fortieth]

quadrangle /'kwɒdræŋg(ə)l/ *n.* four-sided figure, esp. square or rectangle; four-sided court esp. in colleges; **quadrangular** /-'ræŋgjʊlə/ *a.* [F f. L (QUADRI-, ANGLE¹)]

quadrant /'kwɒdrənt/ *n.* quarter of circle's circumference; quarter of circle as cut by two diameters at right angles; quarter of sphere as cut by two planes intersecting at right angles at centre; graduated quarter-circular strip of metal etc.; instrument including this for taking angular measurements. [L *quadrans -ant-*]

quadraphonic /kwɒdrə'fɒnɪk/ *a.* (of sound-reproduction) using four transmission channels; **quadraphonically** *adv.*; **quadraphony** /-'rɒfənɪ/ *n.* [QUADRI-, (STEREO)PHONIC]

quadrate /'kwɒdreɪt/ *a.* square or rectangular. [L (*quadro* make square)]

quadratic /kwɒd'rætɪk/ **1** *a.* involving the square and no higher power of unknown quantity or variable (esp. *quadratic equation*). **2** *n.* quadratic equation. [F or L (prec.)]

quadrennial /kwɒd'renɪəl/ *a.* lasting four years; recurring every four years; **quadrennially** *adv.* [foll.]

quadrennium /kwɒd'renɪəm/ *n.* (*pl.* **quadrenniums**) period of four years. [L *quadriennium* (foll., *annus* year)]

quadri- *in comb.* four. [L (*quattuor* four)]

quadrilateral /kwɒdrɪ'lætər(ə)l/ **1** *a.* having four sides. **2** *n.* quadrilateral figure. [L (QUADRI-)]

quadrille /kwə'drɪl/ *n.* a square dance; music for it. [F]

quadriplegia /kwɒdrɪ'pli:dʒɪə/ *n.* paralysis of all four limbs; **quadriplegic** *a.* & *n.* [QUADRI-, Gk *plēgē* a blow]

quadroon /kwə'dru:n/ *n.* offspring of White and mulatto, person of one-quarter Negro blood. [Sp. (*cuarto* fourth)]

quadruped /'kwɒdrʊped/ *n.* four-footed animal, esp. mammal. [F or L (QUADRI-, *pes ped-* foot)]

quadruple /'kwɒdrʊp(ə)l/ **1** *a.* fourfold, having four parts, being four times as many or as much; (of time in music) having four beats in bar. **2** *n.* fourfold number or amount. **3** *v.* multiply by four. [F f. L (QUADRI-)]

quadruplet /'kwɒdrʊplɪt, -'ru:p-/ *n.* each of four children born at one birth.

quadruplicate /kwɒ'dru:plɪkət/ **1** *a.* fourfold; of which four copies are made. **2** /-eɪt/ *v.t.* multiply by four; make 4 copies of. **3 in quadruplicate** in four copies. [L (QUADRI-)]

quaff /kwɒf, kwɑ:f/ *v. literary* drain (cup etc.) in copious draughts; drink deeply. [perh. imit.]

quagmire /'kwægmaɪə, 'kwɒg-/ *n.* quaking bog, marsh, slough. [*quag* bog, MIRE]

quail¹ *n.* bird related to partridge. [F *quaille* f. med.L, prob. imit.]

quail² *v.i.* flinch, show fear. [orig. unkn.]

quaint *a.* piquantly or attractively unfamiliar or old-fashioned, daintily odd. [F *cointe* f. L (*cognosco* ascertain)]

quake 1 *v.i.* tremble, rock to and fro; (of person) shake or shudder (*with* fear etc.). **2** *n. colloq.* earthquake. [OE]

Quaker *n.* member of Society of Friends; **Quakerism** *n.*

qualification /kwɒlɪfɪ'keɪʃ(ə)n/ *n.* qualifying; accomplishment fitting person for a position or purpose; thing that modifies or limits (*statement with many qualifications*); **qualificatory** /'kwɒ-/ *a.* [F or med.L (foll.)]

qualify /'kwɒlɪfaɪ/ *v.* make competent or fit for position or purpose; make legally entitled; (of person) satisfy conditions or requirements (*for*); modify or make less absolute (statement etc.); moderate, mitigate, make less extreme; attribute a quality to, describe *as*. [F f. med.L f. L *qualis* such as, of what kind]

qualitative /'kwɒlɪtətɪv/ *a.* concerned with or depending on quality. [L (foll.)]

quality /'kwɒlɪtɪ/ *n.* degree of excellence; general excellence (*has quality*); attribute or faculty (*has many good qualities*); relative nature or character; (of voice or sound) timbre; *archaic* high social standing (*people of quality*). [F f. L (*qualis* such as, of what kind)]

qualm /kwɑ:m/ *n.* misgiving, uneasy doubt, scruple of conscience; momentary faint or sick feeling. [orig. uncert.]

quandary /'kwɒndərɪ/ *n.* perplexed state, practical dilemma. [orig. uncert.]

quango /'kwæŋgəʊ/ *n.* (*pl.* **quangos**) semi-public body with financial support from and senior appointments made by government. [abbr. of *quasi* (*autonomous*) *non-governmental organization*]

quanta *pl.* of QUANTUM.

quantify /'kwɒntɪfaɪ/ *v.t.* express as quantity; determine quantity of; **quantification** /-fɪ'keɪʃ(ə)n/ *n.* [med.L (QUANTITY)]

quantitative /'kwɒntɪtətɪv/ *a.* concerned with, measured or measurable by, quantity.

quantity /'kwɒntɪtɪ/ *n.* property of things that is measurable; size or extent or weight or amount or number; specified or considerable portion or number or amount (*a small quantity of* *blood*; *buys in quantity*); (in *pl.*) large amounts or numbers; length or shortness of vowel sounds or syllables; thing having quantity; **quantity surveyor** person who measures and prices work of builders. [F f. L (*quantus* how much)]

quantum /'kwɒntəm/ *n.* (*pl.* **quanta**) discrete unit quantity of energy proportional to frequency of radiation; required or desired or allowed amount; **quantum theory** theory assuming that energy exists in such units. [L (*quantus* how much)]

quarantine /'kwɒrənti:n/ **1** *n.* isolation imposed on ship or persons or animals to prevent infection or contagion; period of this. **2** *v.t.* put in quarantine. [It. (*quaranta* forty)]

quark /kwɑ:k/ *n.* component of elementary particles. [word used by Joyce in *Finnegans Wake*]

quarrel /'kwɒr(ə)l/ **1** *n.* severe or angry dispute or contention; break in friendly relations; cause of complaint (*have no quarrel against* or *with*). **2** *v.i.* (**-ll-**, *US* **-l-**) have quarrel, dispute fiercely (*with*); find fault *with*. [F f. L *querela* (*queror* complain)]

quarrelsome *a.* given to quarrelling.

quarry[1] /'kwɒrɪ/ **1** *n.* place from which stone is extracted for building etc. **2** *v.t.* extract (stone) from quarry. **3 quarry tile** unglazed floor-tile. [med.L f. F f. L *quadrum* square]

quarry[2] /'kwɒrɪ/ *n.* intended prey or victim, object of pursuit. [F f. L *cor* heart]

quart /kwɔ:t/ *n.* liquid measure, equal to a quarter of a gallon. [F f. L (*quartus* fourth)]

quarter /'kwɔ:tə/ **1** *n.* one of four equal parts into which a thing is divided; period of three months, esp. one ending on quarter-day; point of time 15 minutes before or after any hour; 25 US or Canadian cents, coin for this; division of town, esp. as occupied by particular class (*residential quarter*); point of compass, region at this; direction, district, source of supply (*help came from many quarters*); (in *pl.*) lodgings, abode, station of troops; one fourth of lunar month, moon's position between first two (**first quarter**) and last two (**last quarter**) of these; one of four parts into which carcass is divided; (in *pl.*) hind legs and adjoining parts of quadruped, hindquarters; mercy towards enemy etc. on condition of surrender; grain-measure of 8 bushels. **2** *v.t.* divide into quarters; *hist.* divide (body of executed person) thus; put (troops etc.) into quarters; provide with lodgings; place (coats of arms) on four parts of shield's surface. **3 cry quarter** ask for mercy; **quarter-day** any of four days beginning official quarter of year for fiscal purposes (in England 25 March, 24 June, 29 Sept., 25 Dec.; in Scotland 2 Feb., 15 May, 1 August, 11 Nov.); **quarter-final** match or round preceding semi-final; **quarter-light** small vertically-opening window in motor vehicle; **quarter sessions** *hist.* court with limited criminal and civil jurisdiction, usu. held quarterly. [AF f. L *quartarius* (prec.)]

quarterdeck *n.* part of ship's upper deck near stern, usu. reserved for officers.

quartering *n.* (often in *pl.*) coats of arms arranged on one shield to denote alliances of families.

quarterly **1** *adv.* once in each quarter of the year. **2** *a.* done or published or due quarterly. **3** *n.* quarterly publication.

quartermaster *n.* regimental officer in charge of quartering, rations, etc.; naval petty officer in charge of steering, signals, etc.

quarterstaff *n.* stout pole, six to eight feet long, formerly used as weapon.

quartet /kwɔ:'tet/ *n.* (also **quartette**) musical composition for four performers; the performers; any group of four. [F f. It. (QUART)]

quarto /'kwɔ:təʊ/ *n.* (*pl.* **quartos**) size of book or page given by twice folding sheet of standard size to form four leaves; book or sheet of this size. [L (QUART)]

quartz /kwɔ:ts/ *n.* silica in various mineral forms; **quartz clock** clock operated by electric vibrations of quartz crystal; **quartz lamp** quartz tube with mercury vapour as light-source. [G f. Slav.]

quasar /'kweɪzɑ:/ *n.* starlike object with large red-shift. [contr. of *quasi-stellar*]

quash /kwɒʃ/ *v.t.* annul, reject as not valid, esp. by legal procedure; suppress, crush. [F *quasser* f. L]

quasi- /'kweɪzaɪ/ *prefix* seeming(ly), not real(ly), almost. [L *quasi* as if]

quassia /'kwɒʃə/ *n.* S. American tree; its wood or bark or root; bitter tonic made from these. [*Quassi*, discoverer of its medicinal properties]

quaternary /kwə'tɜ:nərɪ/ **1** *a.* having four parts; (**Quaternary**) of the period in the Cainozoic era after Tertiary. **2** *n.* (**Quaternary**) this period. [L (*quaterni* four each)]

quatrain /'kwɒtreɪn/ *n.* four-line stanza. [F (*quatre* four)]

quatrefoil /'kætrəfɔɪl/ *n.* four-cusped figure; four-lobed leaf or flower. [AF (*quatre* four, FOIL[1])]

quattrocento /kwɑ:trəʊ'tʃentəʊ/ *n.* Italian art of 15th c. [It. = 400 used for 14—]

quaver 1 *v.* (of voice or sound) vibrate, shake, tremble, trill; sing (note or song) with quavering; say (*out*) in trembling tones. 2 *n.* tremulousness in speech; trill; *Mus.* note half as long as crotchet. [prob. imit.]

quavery *a.* (of voice etc.) tremulous.

quay /kiː/ *n.* artificial landing-place for loading and unloading ships. [F]

queasy /ˈkwiːzɪ/ *a.* feeling slight nausea; having easily upset digestion; (of food) causing nausea; (of conscience or person) over-scrupulous; **queasily** *adv.*; **queasiness** *n.* [orig. uncert.]

queen 1 *n.* female sovereign of kingdom; king's wife; woman or country or thing regarded as supreme of its kind; perfect fertile female of bee, ant, etc.; most powerful piece in chess; court-card with picture of queen; *sl.* male homosexual. 2 *v.t.* convert (pawn in chess) to queen when it reaches opponent's end of board, (of pawn) be thus converted. 3 **Queen-Anne** style of English design in early 18th c.; **queen consort** king's wife; **queen it** act the queen; **queen mother** king's widow who is mother of sovereign; **queen-post** either of two upright posts between tie-beam and main rafters. [OE]

queenly *a.* like or appropriate to a queen; **queenliness** *n.*

queer 1 *a.* strange, odd, eccentric; suspect, of questionable character; slightly ill, faint; *sl.* (esp. of man) homosexual. 2 *n. sl.* (esp. male) homosexual. 3 *v.t. sl.* spoil, put out of order. 4 **in Queer Street** *sl.* in debt or trouble or disrepute; **queer the pitch for** *sl.* secretly spoil the chances of. [orig. uncert.]

quell *v.t.* crush or put down (rebellion etc.); suppress (fear etc.). [OE]

quench *v.t.* satisfy (thirst) by drinking; extinguish (fire or light); cool esp. with water, cool (hot substance) rapidly in cold water etc.; stifle or suppress (desire etc.). [OE]

quern *n.* hand-mill for grinding corn etc. [OE]

querulous /ˈkwerʊləs/ *a.* complaining, peevish. [L *queror* complain]

query /ˈkwɪərɪ/ 1 *n.* a question; question mark or the word *query* spoken or written as mark of interrogation. 2 *v.t.* ask or inquire; call in question, dispute accuracy of. [L *quaere* imper. of *quaero* inquire]

quest 1 *n.* search or seeking, thing sought. 2 *v.i.* search (*about*) for something (esp. of dogs seeking game). [F (L *quaero quaesit-* seek)]

question /ˈkwestʃ(ə)n/ 1 *n.* sentence so worded or expressed as to seek information; doubt or dispute about matter, raising of such doubt etc.; matter to be discussed or decided; problem for solution, thing depending on conditions *of* (*a question of money, of time*). 2 *v.t.* ask questions of, subject to examination; call in question, throw doubt on. 3 **beyond (all) question** certainly; **call in question** express doubts about, dispute; **in question** being mentioned or discussed; **out of the question** impracticable, not worth considering; **question mark** punctuation mark (?) indicating question; **question-master** chairman of broadcast quiz etc.; **question time** period in parliament when MPs may question ministers. [F f. L (prec.)]

questionable *a.* of doubtful truth or validity or advisability, suspect; **questionably** *adv.*

questionnaire /kwestʃəˈneə/ *n.* formulated series of questions put to a number of people, esp. as part of survey. [F (QUESTION)]

queue /kjuː/ 1 *n.* line or sequence of persons or vehicles etc. awaiting their turn; pigtail. 2 *v.i.* (often with *up*) stand in or join queue. [F f. L *cauda* tail]

quibble /ˈkwɪb(ə)l/ 1 *n.* petty objection, trivial point of criticism; play on words, pun; equivocation, evasion, argument depending on ambiguity of word or phrase. 2 *v.i.* use quibbles. [orig. uncert.]

quiche /kiːʃ/ *n.* open tart with savoury filling. [F]

quick 1 *a.* taking only a short time to do thing or things (*quick worker*; *be quick*); arriving after only short time, prompt; with little interval (*in quick succession*); lively, alert, intelligent; (of temper) easily roused. 2 *adv.* quickly, at rapid rate, in fairly short time (*come as quick as you can*; *quick-drying paint*). 3 *n.* sensitive flesh below nails or skin or sore; seat of feeling or emotion (*cut to the quick*). 4 **quick-change** (of actor etc.) quickly changing costume or appearance to play another part; **quick-freeze** freeze (food) rapidly to preserve natural qualities in storage; **quick one** *colloq.* quickly drunk (esp. alcoholic) drink; **quick time** marching at about 120 paces a minute; **quick-witted** alert, quick to understand. [OE]

quicken *v.* make or become quicker, accelerate; give life or vigour to, rouse; (of woman or foetus) reach stage of pregnancy when movements of child can be felt.

quickie *n. colloq.* thing made or done quickly.

quicklime *n.* unslaked lime.

quicksand *n.* area of loose wet sand readily swallowing up heavy objects.

quickset 1 *a.* formed of live plants set to grow in hedge. 2 *n.* hedge formed thus.

quicksilver *n.* mercury; mercurial temperament.

quickstep *n.* ballroom dance with quick steps, music for this.

quid[1] *n.* (*pl.* same) *sl.* one pound sterling; **quids in** able to profit. [prob. L *quid* what]

quid[2] *n.* lump of tobacco for chewing. [dial., = CUD]

quiddity /ˈkwɪdɪtɪ/ *n.* essence of a thing; quibble, captious subtlety. [L *quidditas* (*quid* what)]

quid pro quo /kwɪd prəʊ ˈkwəʊ/ *n.* thing given as compensation. [L, = something for something]

quiescent /kwɪˈesənt/ *a.* inert, dormant; **quiescence** *n.* [foll.]

quiet /ˈkwaɪət/ 1 *a.* with little or no sound or motion; of gentle or peaceful disposition; unobtrusive, not showy; not overt, disguised; undisturbed, uninterrupted, free or far from vigorous action; informal (*quiet wedding*); enjoyed in quiet (*a quiet pipe*); not anxious or remorseful. 2 *n.* undisturbed state, tranquillity; repose; stillness, silence. 3 *v.* make or become quiet or calm. 4 **be quiet** *colloq.* cease talk etc.; **keep quiet** say nothing (*about*); **on the quiet** secretly. [F f. L (*quiesco* become calm)]

quieten *v.* make or become quiet.

quietism *n.* passive contemplative attitude to life, as form of religious mysticism; **quietist** *n.* & *a.* [It. (QUIET)]

quietude /ˈkwaɪɪtju:d/ *n.* quietness. [QUIET]

quietus /kwaɪˈi:təs/ *n.* release from life, final riddance (*get his* or *its quietus*). [med.L (QUIET)]

quiff *n.* lock of hair plastered down or brushed up on forehead. [orig. unkn.]

quill *n.* large feather of wing or tail; hollow stem of this; pen etc. made of quill; (usu. in *pl.*) porcupine's spine(s). [prob. LG *quiele*]

quilt 1 *n.* coverlet esp. of quilted material. 2 *v.t.* line (coverlet or garment) with padding held between two layers of cloth etc. by lines of sewing. [F *cuilte* f. L *culcita* cushion]

quin *n. colloq.* quintuplet. [abbr.]

quince *n.* acid pear-shaped fruit used in jams etc.; tree bearing it. [pl. of obs. *quoyn*, F f. L *Cydonia* in Crete]

quincentenary /kwɪnsenˈti:nərɪ/ 1 *n.* 500th anniversary, celebration of this. 2 *a.* of a quincentenary. [L *quinque* five]

quincunx /ˈkwɪnkʌŋks/ *n.* centre and four corner points of square or rectangle; five trees etc. so placed. [L, = five-twelfths]

quinine /ˈkwɪni:n/ *n.* a bitter drug obtained from cinchona bark and used to reduce fever and as tonic. [*quina* cinchona bark, Sp. *kina* bark f. Quechua]

Quinquagesima /kwɪŋkwəˈdʒesɪmə/ *n.* Sunday before Lent. [med.L (L *quinquagesimus* fiftieth)]

quinquennial /kwɪŋˈkwenɪəl/ *a.* lasting or recurring every five years; **quinquennially** *adv.* [L *quinquennis* (foll.)]

quinquennium /kwɪŋˈkwenɪəm/ *n.* (*pl.* **quinquenniums**) period of five years. [L (*quinque* five, *annus* year)]

quinquereme /ˈkwɪŋkwɪri:m/ *n.* ancient galley, prob. with five men at each oar. [L (*quinque* five, *remus* oar)]

quinsy /ˈkwɪnzɪ/ *n.* inflammation of throat esp. with abscess on tonsil(s). [F f. L *quinancia* f. Gk]

quintessence /kwɪnˈtesəns/ *n.* purest and most perfect form or manifestation or embodiment *of* a quality etc.; highly refined extract; **quintessential** /-tɪˈsenʃ(ə)l/ *a.*; **quintessentially** /-tɪˈsenʃəlɪ/ *adv.* [F f. L *quinta essentia* fifth substance (underlying the four elements)]

quintet /kwɪnˈtet/ *n.* musical composition for five performers; the performers; any group of five. [F f. It. (*quinto* fifth f. L *quintus*)]

quintuple /ˈkwɪntjʊp(ə)l/ 1 *a.* fivefold, having five parts, being five times as many or as much. 2 *n.* fivefold number or amount. 3 *v.* multiply by five. [F f. L *quintus* fifth]

quintuplet /ˈkwɪntjʊplɪt/ *n.* each of five children born at one birth.

quintuplicate /kwɪnˈtju:plɪkət/ *a.* fivefold, of which five copies are made.

quip 1 *n.* clever saying, epigram. 2 *v.i.* (**-pp-**) make quips. [perh. L *quippe* forsooth]

quire *n.* 25 (formerly 24) sheets of paper; one of the folded sheets that are fixed together in book-binding; **in quires** unbound. [F (*qua(i)er* f. L (QUATERNARY)]

quirk *n.* peculiarity of behaviour; trick of fate; flourish in writing; **quirky** *a.* [orig. unkn.]

quisling /ˈkwɪzlɪŋ/ *n.* fifth-columnist, traitor. [*Quisling*, renegade Norwegian Army officer]

quit 1 *v.t.* (**-tt-**) give up, let go, abandon; cease, stop; leave or depart from. 2 *predic. a.* rid *of*. 3 **quit oneself** behave *well* etc. [F f. L (QUIET)]

quitch *n.* weed with long creeping roots, couch-grass. [OE]

quite *adv.* completely, entirely, wholly; really, actually (*was quite a shock*); rather, to some extent; **quite a few** a fair number; **quite (so)** I grant the truth of that; **quite something** remarkable. [var. of QUIT]

quits *predic. a.* on even terms by retaliation or repayment; **call it** (or **cry**) **quits** acknowledge that things are now even, agree to stop quarrelling etc. [QUIT]
quittance /'kwɪtəns/ *n. archaic* release *from* obligation; acknowledgement of payment. [F (QUIT)]
quitter *n.* deserter; shirker, one who gives up easily. [QUIT]
quiver[1] /'kwɪvə/ **1** *v.i.* tremble or vibrate with slight rapid motion. **2** *n.* quivering motion or sound. [obs. *quiver* nimble]
quiver[2] /'kwɪvə/ *n.* case for holding arrows. [AF f. Gmc]
qui vive /ki: 'vi:v/ in **on the qui vive** on the alert. [F, = (long) live who? (as sentry's challenge)]
quixotic /kwɪk'sɒtɪk/ *a.* extravagantly and romantically chivalrous; **quixotically** *adv.* [Don *Quixote* in Cervantes' romance]
quiz 1 *n.* (*pl.* **quizzes**) test of knowledge in radio or television or other entertainment programme; interrogation, examination. **2** *v.t.* (**-zz-**) examine by questioning; *archaic* make sport of, mock at, regard critically or curiously. [orig. unkn.]
quizzical /'kwɪzɪk(ə)l/ *a.* expressing or done with mild or amused perplexity; strange, comical; **quizzically** *adv.*
quod *n. sl.* prison (*in quod*). [orig. unkn.]
quoin /kɔɪn/ *n.* angle or corner of building; corner-stone; wedge used in printing and gunnery. [var. of COIN]
quoit /kɔɪt/ *n.* ring thrown at mark or to encircle peg; (in *pl.*) game using these. [orig. unkn.]
quondam /'kwɒndæm/ *a.* that once was, sometime, former. [L adv., = formerly]
quorum /'kwɔ:rəm/ *n.* number of members that must be present to constitute valid meeting; **quorate** *a.* [L, = of whom]
quota /'kwəʊtə/ *n.* share to be contributed to or received from a total by one of the parties concerned; total number or amount required or permitted. [L *quotus* (*quot* how many)]
quotable /'kwəʊtəb(ə)l/ *a.* worth quoting. [QUOTE]
quotation /kwəʊ'teɪʃ(ə)n/ *n.* quoting; passage or price quoted; **quotation-marks** inverted commas (' ' or " ") used at beginning and end of quoted passages or words. [med.L (foll.)]
quote 1 *v.* cite or appeal to (author or book) in confirmation of some view; repeat or copy out passage from; repeat or copy out (passage); make quotations (*from* author or book etc.); adduce or cite *as*; enclose (words) in quotation-marks; state price of (usu. *at* figure). **2** *n. colloq.* passage or price quoted; (usu. in *pl.*) quotation-mark. [L *quoto* mark with numbers]
quoth /kwəʊθ/ *v.t. archaic* (only with *I* or *he* or *she* placed after) said. [OE]
quotidian /kwɒ'tɪdɪən/ *a.* daily; everyday, commonplace; (of fever) recurring every day. [F f. L (*quotidie* daily)]
quotient /'kwəʊʃənt/ *n.* result of division sum. [L *quotiens -ent-* how many times]
q.v. *abbr.* which see (in references). [L *quod vide*]
qy. *abbr.* query.

R

R,r /ɑ:/ *n.* (*pl.* **Rs, R's**) eighteenth letter; **the three Rs** reading, (w)riting, (a)rithmetic.
R *abbr.* registered as trade mark (also ®); rook (in chess).
R. *abbr. Regina* (*Elizabeth R.*); *Rex* (*George R.*); River.
r. *abbr.* right.
RA *abbr.* Royal Academician; Royal Academy; Royal Artillery.
Ra *symb.* radium.
rabbet /'ræbɪt/ **1** *n.* step-shaped channel etc. cut along edge or face of wood etc. usu. to receive edge or tongue of another piece. **2** *v.t.* join or fix with rabbet; make rabbet in. [F *rab(b)at* (REBATE[1])]
rabbi /'ræbaɪ/ *n.* Jewish religious leader; Jewish scholar or teacher esp. of the law; **rabbinical** /-'bɪnɪk(ə)l/ *a.* [Heb., = my master]
rabbit /'ræbɪt/ **1** *n.* mammal of hare family but smaller than hare, usu. living in burrows; *US* hare; *colloq.* poor performer at a game. **2** *v.i.* hunt rabbits; *sl.* talk pointlessly, waffle. **3 rabbit punch** short chop with edge of hand to opponent's nape. **4 rabbity** *a.* [orig. uncert.]
rabble /'ræb(ə)l/ *n.* disorderly crowd, mob; contemptible or inferior set of people; **the rabble** the lower or disorderly classes of the populace; **rabble-rouser** one who stirs up rabble in agitation for social or political change. [orig. uncert.]
Rabelaisian /ræbə'leɪzɪən/ *a.* of or like the French satirist Rabelais or his

writings, exuberant in style with coarse humour.

rabid /ˈræbɪd/ *a.* furious, raging; fanatical; of or affected with rabies, mad; **rabidity** /rəˈbɪdɪtɪ/ *n.* [L (*rabio* rave)]

rabies /ˈreɪbɪz/ *n.* contagious virus disease of dogs and other warm-blooded animals, transmittable to man usu. by bite, hydrophobia. [L (as prec.)]

RAC *abbr.* Royal Automobile Club.

raccoon var. of RACOON.

race[1] **1** *n.* contest of speed between runners, horses, vehicles, ships, etc.; (in *pl.*) series of these for horses, dogs, etc., at fixed time on regular course; contest between persons to be first to achieve something; strong current in sea or river; channel (*mill-race*). **2** *v.* take part in race; have race with, try to surpass in speed; compete in speed *with*; cause to race; go, (cause to) move or work, at full or excessive speed; take part in horse-racing (*a racing man*). **3 race-meeting** series of horse-races at one venue at fixed times; **race-track** course for racing horses, vehicles, etc. [ON]

race[2] *n.* each of the major divisions of mankind with distinct physical characteristics; fact or concept of division into races; group of persons or animals or plants connected by common descent; genus or species or breed or variety of animals or plants; **the human race** mankind; **race relations** relations between members of different races in same country or community; **race riot** outbreak of violence due to racial antagonism. [F f. It. *razza*]

racecourse *n.* ground for horse-racing. [RACE[1]]

racegoer *n.* one who frequents horse-races.

racehorse *n.* horse bred or kept for racing.

raceme /rəˈsiːm/ *n.* flower-cluster with flowers attached by short stalks at intervals along stem. [L *racemus* grape-bunch]

racial /ˈreɪʃ(ə)l/ *a.* of or characteristic of race; concerning or caused by race. [RACE[2]]

racialism *n.* belief in superiority of a particular race; antagonism between different races; **racialist** *n.* & *a.*

racially *adv.* in respect of race.

racism *n.* racialism; theory that human abilities etc. are determined by race; **racist** *n.* & *a.*

rack[1] **1** *n.* framework, usu. with rails or bars etc., for holding things; cogged or toothed bar or rail engaging with wheel or pinion etc.; *hist.* instrument of torture stretching victim's joints. **2** *v.t.* (of disease or pain) inflict suffering on; *hist.* torture (person) on rack; place on or in rack; shake violently, injure by straining. **3 on the rack** in pain or distress; **rack one's brains** try hard to remember or think of something; **rack-railway** mountain railway with cogged rail in which pinion on locomotive engages; **rack-rent** exorbitant rent. [LG or Du.]

rack[2] *n.* destruction (*go to rack and ruin*). [WRACK]

racket[1] /ˈrækɪt/ *n.* bat having round or oval frame strung with catgut or nylon etc., used in tennis or rackets etc.; (in *pl.*) ball-game with rackets in a court of four plain walls. [F *raquette* f. It. f. Arab.]

racket[2] /ˈrækɪt/ **1** *n.* disturbance, uproar, din; scheme for obtaining money etc. by dishonest means; *sl.* dodge, game, line of business. **2** *v.i.* move (*about*) noisily. [perh. imit.]

racketeer /rækɪˈtɪə/ *n.* one who operates a dishonest scheme; **racketeering** *n.*

rackety *a.* noisy, rowdy.

raconteur /rækɒnˈtɜː/ *n.* teller of anecdotes. [F (RECOUNT)]

racoon /rəˈkuːn/ *n.* N. American mammal with bushy tail, sharp snout, and greyish-brown fur. [Algonquian]

racquet var. of RACKET[1].

racy *a.* lively and vigorous in style; *US risqué*; of distinctive quality, retaining traces of origin. [RACE[2]]

RADA /ˈrɑːdə/ *abbr.* Royal Academy of Dramatic Art.

radar /ˈreɪdɑː/ *n.* system for detecting presence and position or movement of objects by sending out short radio waves which they reflect; apparatus used for this; **radar trap** arrangement using radar to detect vehicles etc. travelling faster than speed limit. [*ra*dio *d*etection *a*nd *r*anging]

raddle /ˈræd(ə)l/ **1** *n.* red ochre. **2** *v.t.* colour with raddle, or with much rouge crudely used. [rel. to RUDDY]

raddled *a.* worn out.

radial /ˈreɪdɪəl/ **1** *a.* of or arranged like rays or radii; having spokes or lines radiating from a centre; acting or moving along lines that diverge from a centre; (of tyre: also **radial-ply**) having fabric layers parallel and tread strengthened. **2** *n.* radial-ply tyre. **3 radially** *adv.* [med.L (RADIUS)]

radian /ˈreɪdɪən/ *n.* angle at centre of circle formed by radii of arc with length equal to radius. [RADIUS]

radiant /ˈreɪdɪənt/ **1** *a.* emitting rays of light; (of eyes or looks) beaming with joy or hope or love; (of beauty) splendid or dazzling; (of light) issuing in rays. **2** *n.* point or object from which light or heat radiates. **3 radiant heat** heat transmitted by radiation. **4 radiance** *n.*; **radiancy** *n.* [L (RADIUS)]

radiate 1 /'reɪdɪeɪt/ *v.* emit rays of light, heat, etc., (of light or heat) issue in rays; diverge or spread from central point; emit (light or heat) from central point; disseminate as from centre; exude or show clearly (joy etc.). **2** /'reɪdɪət/ *a.* having parts radially arranged.

radiation /reɪdɪ'eɪʃ(ə)n/ *n.* radiating; emission of energy as electromagnetic waves or as moving particles; energy thus transmitted, esp. invisibly; **radiation sickness** sickness caused by exposure to excessive radiation.

radiator /'reɪdɪeɪtə/ *n.* apparatus for heating room etc. by radiation of heat; engine-cooling apparatus in motor vehicle or aeroplane.

radical /'rædɪk(ə)l/ **1** *a.* fundamental, far-reaching, thorough (*radical change*); advocating radical reforms, holding extreme views, revolutionary; forming the basis, primary; of the root of a number or quantity; of the roots of words. **2** *n.* person holding radical views or belonging to radical party; group of atoms forming part of compound and remaining unaltered during its ordinary chemical changes; root of word; mathematical quantity forming or expressed as root of another. **3 radicalism** *n.*; **radically** *adv.* [L (RADIX)]

radicle /'rædɪk(ə)l/ *n.* part of plant embryo that develops into primary root; rootlet. [L (as prec.)]

radii *pl.* of RADIUS.

radio /'reɪdɪəʊ/ **1** *n.* (*pl.* **radios**) transmission and reception of messages etc. by electromagnetic waves without connecting wire; apparatus for receiving signals by radio; sound broadcasting; station engaged in this (*Radio Leeds*). **2** *a.* of or using or equipped with or sent by radio; of or concerned with stars or other celestial bodies from which radio waves are received or reflected (*radio astronomy*). **3** *v.* send (message) by radio; send message to (person) by radio; communicate or broadcast by radio. **4 radio star** celestial object emitting strong radio waves. [abbr. of *radiotelegraphy* etc.]

radio- *in comb.* connected with rays, radiation, radioactivity, or radio. [RADIUS]

radioactive /reɪdɪəʊ'æktɪv/ *a.* of or exhibiting radioactivity.

radioactivity /reɪdɪəʊæk'tɪvɪtɪ/ *n.* property of spontaneous disintegration of atomic nuclei usu. with emission of penetrating radiation or particles.

radio-carbon /reɪdɪəʊ'kɑ:bən/ *n.* radio-isotope of carbon, esp. that of mass 14 used in dating ancient organic materials.

radio-controlled /reɪdɪəʊkən'trəʊld/ *a.* controlled from a distance by radio.

radio-frequency *n.* frequency of radio waves, between about 10 kilohertz and 0.1 terahertz.

radiogram /'reɪdɪəʊgræm/ *n.* combined radio and gramophone; telegram sent by radio; picture obtained by X-rays etc.

radiograph /'reɪdɪəgrɑ:f/ **1** *n.* picture obtained by X-rays etc.; instrument for recording intensity of radiation. **2** *v.t.* obtain picture of by X-rays etc. **3 radiographer** /-'ɒgrəfə/ *n.*; **radiography** /-'ɒgrəfɪ/ *n.* [RADIO-, -GRAPH]

radio-isotope /reɪdɪəʊ'aɪsətəʊp/ *n.* radioactive isotope.

radiology /reɪdɪ'ɒlədʒɪ/ *n.* scientific study of X-rays and other high-energy radiation esp. as used in medicine; **radiologist** *n.*

radioscopy /reɪdɪ'ɒskəpɪ/ *n.* examination by X-rays etc. of objects opaque to light.

radio-telegraphy /reɪdɪəʊtɪ'legrəfɪ/ *n.* telegraphy using radio.

radio-telephony /reɪdɪəʊtɪ'lefənɪ/ *n.* telephony using radio.

radio-therapy /reɪdɪəʊ'θerəpɪ/ *n.* treatment of disease by radiation, esp. X-rays.

radish /'rædɪʃ/ *n.* plant with crisp pungent root eaten raw; this root. [OE f. L RADIX]

radium /'reɪdɪəm/ *n.* radioactive metallic element obtained from pitchblende etc., used esp. in luminous materials and in radio-therapy. [foll.]

radius /'reɪdɪəs/ *n.* (*pl.* **radii** /-ɪaɪ/) straight line from centre to circumference of circle or sphere; length of this; distance from a centre (*within a radius of 20 miles*); any of set of lines diverging from point like radii of circle; thicker and shorter bone in forearm on same side as thumb, corresponding bone in animal's foreleg or bird's wing. [L]

radix /'reɪdɪks/ *n.* (*pl.* **radices** /-si:z/) number or symbol used as basis of numeration scale. [L *radix -icis* root]

radon /'reɪdɒn/ *n.* gaseous radioactive inert element arising from disintegration of radium. [RADIUM]

RAF *abbr.* Royal Air Force.

raffia /'ræfɪə/ *n.* fibre from leaves of a kind of palm-tree, used for tying up plants and making mats and baskets etc.; this tree. [Malagasy]

raffish /'ræfɪʃ/ *a.* disreputable, rakish; tawdry. [*raff* rubbish]

raffle /'ræf(ə)l/ **1** *n.* sale of articles by

lottery, esp. for charity. **2** *v.t.* sell by raffle. [F *rafle* a dice-game]

raft /'rɑːft/ *n.* flat floating structure of wood or fastened logs etc., used in water for transport or as emergency boat. [ON]

rafter /'rɑːftə/ *n.* any of the sloping beams forming the framework of a roof. [OE]

rag[1] *n.* torn or frayed or worn piece of woven material; (in *pl.*) old or torn or worn clothes; *collect.* rags used as material for paper, stuffing, etc.; *derog.* newspaper; **in rags** much torn; **rag-and-bone man** itinerant dealer in old clothes, furniture, etc.; **rag-bag** bag for old rags, *fig.* miscellaneous collection; **rags to riches** poverty to affluence; **rag trade** *colloq.* the clothing business. [prob. back-form. f. RAGGED]

rag[2] **1** *n.* programme of stunts, parades, and entertainment, staged by students to collect money for charity; *colloq.* prank; *sl.* rowdy celebration, noisy disorderly scene. **2** *v.* **(-gg-)** *sl.* tease, play rough jokes on; *sl.* engage in rough play, be noisy and riotous. [orig. unkn.]

rag[3] *n.* piece of ragtime. [abbr.]

ragamuffin /'rægəmʌfın/ *n.* person in ragged dirty clothes. [prob. RAG[1]]

rage 1 *n.* fierce or violent anger; a fit of this; violent operation of natural force. **2** *v.i.* be fiercely angry; speak furiously or madly (*at* or *against*); (of wind or battle etc.) be violent, be at its height. **3 be all the rage** be temporarily very popular or fashionable. [F f. L RABIES]

ragged /'rægıd/ *a.* torn or frayed; (of person) in ragged clothes; having broken jagged outline or surface; faulty, imperfect, lacking finish or smoothness or uniformity; **run person ragged** exhaust or debilitate him. [ON]

raglan /'ræglən/ *n.* garment, esp. overcoat, in which sleeve runs up to the neck; **raglan sleeve** sleeve of this kind. [Lord *Raglan*]

ragout /'rægu:/ *n.* stew of meat and vegetables. [F]

ragtag (and bobtail) riff-raff, disreputable people. [RAG[1]]

ragtime *n.* form of jazz music of US Black origin with much syncopation.

ragwort /'rægwɜːt/ *n.* wild plant with yellow flowers and ragged leaves.

raid 1 *n.* rapid surprise attack, in warfare or to steal or do harm; surprise visit by police etc. to arrest suspected person(s) or seize illicit goods. **2** *v.* make raid (on). [Sc. form of ROAD]

rail[1] **1** *n.* level or sloping bar or series of bars used to hang things on, as top of banisters, as part of fence, as protection against contact or falling over, etc.; steel bar or continuous line of bars laid on ground usu. as one of two forming railway track; railway (*send it by rail*; *rail unions*). **2** *v.t.* furnish with rail; enclose (*in* or *off*) with rails. **3 off the rails** disorganized, out of order or control, crazy. [F *reille* f. L *regula* rule]

rail[2] *v.i.* complain fiercely or abusively (*at* or *against*). [F *railler*]

rail[3] *n.* small wading bird of various kinds. [F]

railcar *n.* self-propelled railway coach. [RAIL[1]]

railhead *n.* furthest point reached by railway under construction; point on railway at which road transport of goods begins or ends.

railing *n.* fence or barrier made of rails.

raillery /'reılərı/ *n.* good-humoured ridicule. [F *raillerie* (RAIL[2])]

railman *n.* railwayman. [RAIL[1]]

railroad *n. US* railway.

railway *n.* track or set of tracks of steel rails for passage of trains conveying passengers and goods; such system worked by single company; organization and personnel required for its working. [RAIL[1], WAY]

railwayman *n.* railway employee.

raiment /'reımənt/ *n. archaic* clothing. [*arrayment* (ARRAY)]

rain 1 *n.* condensed moisture of atmosphere falling in drops, fall of these; (in *pl.*) falls of rain, season of these; falling liquid or solid particles or objects (*lit.* or *fig.*), rainlike descent of these. **2** *v.* fall or send down as or like rain; (of sky, clouds, etc.) send down rain; supply in large quantities, overwhelm with (*it rained invitations*). **3 it rains** (or **is raining**) rain is falling; **rain forest** luxuriant tropical forest with heavy rainfall; **rain off** (esp. in *pass.*) cause to be cancelled because of rain; **rain-water** water collected from fallen rain. [OE]

rainbow /'reınbəʊ/ **1** *n.* arch of colours formed in sky by refraction and dispersion of sun's rays in falling rain or in spray or mist. **2** *a.* many-coloured. **3 rainbow trout** large trout orig. of Pacific coast of N. America. [OE (RAIN, BOW[1])]

raincoat *n.* waterproof or water-resistant coat. [RAIN]

raindrop *n.* single drop of rain.

rainfall *n.* fall of rain; quantity of rain falling within given area in given time.

rainy *a.* (of weather, day, region, etc.) in or on which rain is falling or much rain usually falls; **rainy day** time of special need in the future. [OE (RAIN)]

raise /reız/ **1** *v.t.* put or take into higher position; cause to rise or stand up or be vertical; construct or build up; levy or collect or bring together (*raise tax*, *money, an army*); cause to be heard or considered (*raise a shout, an objection*); set going or bring into being (*raise a protest, hopes*); bring up, educate; breed or grow; increase amount or value or strength of (*raised his offer, his voice*); promote to higher rank; multiply (quantity) *to* a power; cause (bread) to rise; (in card-game) bet more than (another player); abandon or force enemy to abandon (siege etc.); remove (barrier); cause (ghost etc.) to appear; *colloq.* find (person etc. wanted). **2** *n.* increase in stake or bid; *US* increase in salary. **3 raise from the dead** restore to life; **raise a laugh** cause others to laugh; **raise one's eyebrows** look supercilious or shocked; **raise the wind** procure money for a purpose. [ON]

raisin /ˈreɪz(ə)n/ *n.* partially dried grape. [F f. L (RACEME)]

raison d'être /reɪzɔ̃ ˈdetr/ purpose or reason that accounts for or justifies or originally caused thing's existence. [F]

raj /rɑːdʒ/ *n.* British sovereignty in India. [Hindi]

raja /ˈrɑːdʒə/ *n.* (also **rajah**) *hist.* Indian king or prince, noble or petty dignitary. [Hindi f. Skr.]

rake[1] **1** *n.* implement of pole with toothed cross-bar at end for drawing together hay etc. or smoothing loose soil or gravel; implement like this, e.g. to draw in money at gaming-table. **2** *v.* collect or gather (as) with rake; make tidy or smooth with rake; use rake; search thoroughly, ransack; direct gun-fire along (line) from end to end; scratch or scrape. **3 rake in** *colloq.* amass (profits etc.); **rake-off** *colloq.* commission or share, esp. in disreputable deal; **rake up** revive (esp. unwelcome memories etc.). [OE]

rake[2] *n.* dissipated or immoral man of fashion. [*rakehell* (RAKE[1], HELL)]

rake[3] **1** *v.* set or be set at sloping angle; (of mast or funnel) incline from perpendicular towards stern. **2** *n.* raking position or build; amount by which thing rakes. [orig. unkn.]

rakish *a.* like a rake; dashing, jaunty. [RAKE[2]]

rallentando /rælənˈtændəʊ/ *Mus.* **1** *adv.* with gradual decrease of speed. **2** *n.* (*pl.* **rallentandos**) passage to be played this way. [It.]

rally[1] /ˈrælɪ/ **1** *v.* bring or come together as support or for action; bring or come together again after rout or dispersion, (cause to) renew conflict; rouse or revive (courage etc.); recover after illness; (of share-prices etc.) increase after fall. **2** *n.* rallying or being rallied, esp. mass meeting of supporters or persons having a common interest; competition for motor vehicles, usu. over public roads; series of strokes in tennis etc. before point is decided. [F *rallier* (RE-, ALLY)]

rally[2] /ˈrælɪ/ *v.t.* subject to good-humoured ridicule. [F *railler* (RAIL[2])]

ram 1 *n.* uncastrated male sheep; (**Ram**) sign or constellation Aries; = *battering-ram* (see BATTER[1]); falling weight of pile-driving machine; hydraulic water-raising or lifting machine. **2** *v.t.* (**-mm-**) force or squeeze into place by pressure; beat or drive (*down* or *in* etc.) by heavy blows; (of ship or vehicle etc.) strike violently, crash against; dash or violently impel (thing) *against* or *into* etc. [OE]

RAM *abbr.* Royal Academy of Music; random-access memory.

Ramadan /ræməˈdɑːn/ *n.* ninth month of Muslim year, with strict fasting in daylight hours. [Arab.]

ramble /ˈræmb(ə)l/ **1** *v.i.* walk for pleasure; talk or write disconnectedly. **2** *n.* walk taken for pleasure. [Du. *rammelen*]

rambler *n.* one who rambles; straggling or climbing rose.

rambling *a.* that rambles; (of house, street, etc.) irregularly arranged; (of plant) straggling, climbing.

RAMC *abbr.* Royal Army Medical Corps.

ramekin /ˈræmɪkɪn/ *n.* small dish for baking and serving individual portion of food; food served in this. [F *ramequin*]

ramify /ˈræmɪfaɪ/ *v.* form branches or subdivisions or offshoots, branch out; (usu. in *pass.*) cause to branch out, arrange in branching manner; **ramification** /-fɪˈkeɪʃ(ə)n/ *n.* [F f. L (*ramus* branch)]

ramp[1] **1** *n.* slope joining two levels of ground or floor etc.; movable stairs for entering or leaving aircraft. **2** *v.* furnish or build with ramp; take threatening posture; rampage. [F *ramper* crawl]

ramp[2] *sl.* **1** *n.* swindle, racket, esp. involving exorbitant prices. **2** *v.* engage in ramp; subject (person etc.) to ramp. [orig. unkn.]

rampage 1 /ræmˈpeɪdʒ/ *v.i.* rush wildly or violently about; rage, storm. **2** /ˈræmpeɪdʒ/ *n.* wild or violent behaviour. **3 on the rampage** rampaging. **4 rampageous** /ræmˈpeɪdʒəs/ *a.* [perh. RAMP[1]]

rampant /ˈræmpənt/ *a.* (of lion etc. as heraldic charge; after noun) standing on left hind foot with fore-paws in air; unchecked, flourishing excessively; violent or extravagant in action or opinion; rank, luxuriant; **rampancy** *n.* [F (RAMP[1])]

rampart /'ræmpɑ:t/ *n.* defensive wall with broad top and usu. stone parapet; walkway on this; defence, protection. [F (*remparer* fortify)]
ramrod /'ræmrɒd/ *n.* rod for ramming down charge of muzzle-loaded firearm; thing that is very straight or rigid. [RAM, ROD]
ramshackle /'ræmʃæk(ə)l/ *a.* (usu. of house or vehicle) tumbledown, rickety. [rel. to RANSACK]
ran *past* of RUN.
ranch /rɑ:ntʃ/ **1** *n.* cattle-breeding establishment esp. in US and Canada; farm where other animals are bred (*mink ranch*). **2** *v.i.* farm on ranch. [Sp. *rancho* persons eating together]
rancid /'rænsɪd/ *a.* smelling or tasting like rank stale fat; **rancidity** /-'sɪdɪtɪ/ *n.* [L *rancidus* stinking]
rancour /'ræŋkə/, *US* **rancor** *n.* inveterate bitterness, malignant hate; **rancorous** *a.* [F f. L *rancor* (prec.)]
rand /rænd, rɑ:nt/ *n.* currency unit of S. African countries. [*the Rand* near Johannesburg]
R & D *abbr.* research and development.
random /'rændəm/ *a.* made or done etc. without method or conscious choice; **at random** without aim or purpose or principle; **random-access** (of computer memory or file) having all parts directly accessible, so that it need not read sequentially. [F *randon* (*randir* gallop)]
randy /'rændɪ/ *a.* lustful, eager for sexual gratification; *Sc.* loud-tongued, boisterous; **randily** *adv.*; **randiness** *n.* [perh. rel. to RANT]
ranee /'rɑ:nɪ/ *n.* raja's wife or widow. [Hindi (RAJ)]
rang *past* of RING².
range /reɪndʒ/ **1** *n.* area over which thing is found or has effect or relevance, scope; region between limits of variation, such limits; distance attainable or to be covered by gun or missile etc.; distance that can be covered by vehicle or aircraft without refuelling; distance between camera and subject to be photographed; row or series, esp. of mountains; open or enclosed area with targets for shooting; fireplace with ovens and hotplates for cooking; large open area for grazing or hunting. **2** *v.* place in row(s) or in specified arrangement; rove or wander; reach, lie, spread out, be found over specified area, vary between limits; traverse in all directions. **3 range-finder** instrument to determine distance of object for shooting or photographing. [F (RANK¹)]
ranger *n.* keeper of royal or national park, or of forest; member of body of mounted troops; (**Ranger**) senior Guide.
rangy /'reɪndʒɪ/ *a.* tall and slim.
rani var. of RANEE.
rank¹ 1 *n.* position in hierarchy, grade of advancement; distinct social class, grade of dignity or achievement; high social position; place in a scale; row or line; soldiers in single line abreast; place where taxis await customers; order, array. **2** *v.* have rank or place; classify, give certain grade to; arrange (esp. soldiers) in rank. **3 close ranks** maintain solidarity; **rank and file** ordinary undistinguished people; **the ranks** common soldiers. [F *ranc* f. Gmc]
rank² *a.* too luxuriant, coarse, choked with or apt to produce weeds or excessive foliage; foul-smelling, loathsome, corrupt; flagrant, virulent, gross, complete (*rank outsider*). [OE]
rankle /'ræŋk(ə)l/ *v.i.* (of envy or disappointment etc. or their cause) cause persistent annoyance or resentment. [F (*d*)*rancler* fester f. med.L *dra*(*cu*)*nculus* little serpent]
ransack /'rænsæk/ *v.t.* pillage or plunder (house, country, etc.); search thoroughly. [ON *rannsaka* (*rann* house, *saka* seek)]
ransom /'rænsəm/ **1** *n.* sum of money or other payment demanded or paid for release of prisoner; liberation of prisoner in return for this. **2** *v.t.* buy freedom or restoration of, redeem; hold to ransom; release for a ransom. **3 hold to ransom** keep prisoner and demand ransom, threateningly demand concessions from. [F f. L (REDEMPTION)]
rant 1 *v.* use bombastic language; declaim, recite theatrically; preach noisily. **2** *n.* piece of ranting. [Du.]
ranunculus /rə'nʌŋkjʊləs/ *n.* (*pl.* **ranunculuses**) plant of genus including buttercup. [L dimin. of *rana* frog]
RAOC *abbr.* Royal Army Ordnance Corps.
rap¹ 1 *n.* smart slight blow; knock, sharp tapping sound; *sl.* blame, punishment. **2** *v.* (**-pp-**) strike smartly; knock, make sound of rap; criticize adversely. **3 rap out** utter abruptly, express by raps. [prob. imit.]
rap² *n.* a small amount, the least bit (*don't care a rap*). [abbr. of Ir. *ropaire* counterfeit coin]
rapacious /rə'peɪʃəs/ *a.* grasping, extortionate, predatory; **rapacity** /rə'pæsɪtɪ/ *n.* [L *rapax* (foll.)]
rape¹ 1 *n.* forcible sexual intercourse with woman without her freely given consent; violent assault or interference. **2** *v.t.* commit rape on (person, usu. woman). [AF *raper* f. L *rapio* seize]
rape² *n.* plant grown as fodder and for

its seed from which oil is made. [L *rapum, rapa* turnip]

rapid /'ræpɪd/ **1** *a.* quick, swift; acting or completed in short time; (of slope) descending steeply. **2** *n.* (usu. in *pl.*) steep descent in river-bed with swift current. **3 rapidity** /rə'pɪdɪtɪ/ *n.* [L (RAPE¹)]

rapier /'reɪpɪə/ *n.* light slender sword used for thrusting. [prob. LG or Du. f. F *rapière*

rapine /'ræpaɪn/ *n.* plundering. [F or L (RAPE¹)]

rapist *n.* one who commits rape. [RAPE¹]

rapport /ræ'pɔː/ *n.* relationship or communication, esp. when useful and harmonious. [F (L *porto* carry)]

rapprochement /ræ'prɒʃmɑ̃/ *n.* resumption of harmonious relations esp. between States. [F (APPROACH)]

rapscallion /ræp'skæljən/ *n.* rascal. [perh. f. RASCAL]

rapt *a.* fully absorbed or intent, enraptured; carried away with feeling or lofty thought. [L *raptus* (RAPE¹)]

raptorial /ræp'tɔːrɪəl/ **1** *a.* predatory. **2** *n.* predatory animal or bird. [L *raptor* robber (RAPE¹)]

rapture /'ræptʃə/ *n.* ecstatic delight; (in *pl.*) great pleasure or enthusiasm or the expression of it; **rapturous** *a.* [F or med.L (RAPE¹)]

rare¹ *a.* seldom done or found or occurring, uncommon, unusual; exceptionally good; of less than usual density (*rare atmosphere*); **rare earth** lanthanide element, oxide of this. [L *rarus*

rare² *a.* (of meat) underdone. [OE]

rarebit *n.* = *Welsh rarebit*. [RARE¹]

rarefy /'reərɪfaɪ/ *v.* make or become less solid or dense; refine; make (idea etc.) subtle; **rarefaction** /-'fækʃ(ə)n/ *n.* [F or med.L (RARE¹)]

rarely *adv.* seldom, not often; exceptionally. [RARE¹]

raring /'reərɪŋ/ *a. colloq.* enthusiastic, eager (*to go* etc.). [partic. of *rare*, dial. var. of ROAR or REAR²]

rarity /'reərɪtɪ/ *n.* rareness; uncommon thing. [F or L (RARE¹)]

rascal /'rɑːsk(ə)l/ *n.* dishonest or mischievous person; **rascally** *a.* [F *rascaille* rabble]

rase var. of RAZE.

rash¹ *a.* reckless, impetuous, hasty, acting or done without due consideration. [prob. OE]

rash² *n.* eruption of spots or patches on skin; sudden widespread onset (*a rash of strikes*). [orig. unkn.]

rasher *n.* thin slice of bacon or ham. [orig. unkn.]

rasp /rɑːsp/ **1** *n.* coarse kind of file having separate teeth. **2** *v.* scrape with rasp, scrape roughly, scrape *off* or *away*; make grating sound; say gratingly; grate upon (person or his feelings). [F *raspe(r)*

raspberry /'rɑːzbərɪ/ *n.* small usu. red fruit like blackberry, bramble bearing this; *sl.* sound expressing derision or dislike; **raspberry-cane** raspberry plant. [orig. unkn.]

Rastafarian /ræstə'feərɪən/ **1** *n.* member of sect of Jamaican origin regarding Blacks as chosen people. **2** *a.* of this sect. [*Ras Tafari*, title of Emperor Haile Selassie of Ethiopia]

rat 1 *n.* rodent like large mouse; similar rodent (*musk-rat, water-rat*); *colloq.* unpleasant or treacherous person. **2** *v.i.* (**-tt-**) hunt or kill rats; act as informer. **3 rat on** desert or betray (person); **rat race** fiercely competitive struggle, esp. to maintain one's position in work or life; **smell a rat** begin to suspect treachery etc. [OE & F f. Rmc]

ratafia /rætə'fiːə/ *n.* liqueur flavoured with almonds or fruit-kernels; a kind of biscuit similarly flavoured. [F]

ratatouille /rɑːtɑː'tuːɪ/ *n.* Provençal stew of vegetables. [F dial.]

ratchet /'rætʃɪt/ *n.* set of teeth on edge of bar or wheel with catch allowing motion in one direction only; (in full **ratchet-wheel**) wheel with rim so toothed. [F *rochet* lance-head]

rate¹ 1 *n.* stated numerical proportion between two sets of things (the second usu. expressed as unity), esp. as measure of amount or degree (*moving at a rate of 50 m.p.h.*) or as basis of calculating an amount or value (*rate of exchange, of interest, of taxation*); fixed or appropriate charge or cost or value, measure of this (*postal rates; the rate for the job*); rapidity of movement or change (*increasing at a great rate*); class or rank (*first-* etc. *rate*); assessment by local authority levied on value of buildings and land owned or leased, (in *pl.*) amount payable. **2** *v.* estimate or assign worth or value of; consider, regard as; rank or be rated *as*; subject to payment of local rate, value for assessment of rates; *US* be worthy of, deserve. **3 at any rate** in any case, whatever happens; **at this rate** if this example is typical. [F f. L *rata* (RATIO)]

rate² *v.* scold angrily. [orig. unkn.]

rateable *a.* liable to rates; **rateable value** value at which house etc. is assessed for rates. [RATE¹]

ratepayer *n.* person liable to pay rates.

rather /'rɑːðə/ *adv.* by preference (*would rather not go*); more truly, as more likely alternative *than* (*is stupid rather than honest*); more precisely (*tonight, or rather, this evening*); slightly, to some extent (*became rather drunk*); *colloq.* (in answer) most certainly; **had rather** would rather. [OE compar. (*rathe* early)]

ratify /'rætɪfaɪ/ *v.t.* confirm or accept (agreement made in one's name) by formal consent, signature, etc.; **ratification** /-fɪ'keɪʃ(ə)n/ *n.* [F f. med.L (RATE[1])]

rating[1] *n.* placing in rank or class; estimated standing of person as regards credit etc.; non-commissioned sailor; amount fixed as local rate; relative popularity of broadcast programme as determined by estimated size of audience. [RATE[1]]

rating[2] *n.* angry reprimand. [RATE[2]]

ratio /'reɪʃɪəʊ/ *n.* (*pl.* **ratios**) quantitative relation between two similar magnitudes determined by the number of times one contains the other (*are in the ratio of three to two*). [L (*reor rat-* reckon)]

ratiocinate /rætɪ'ɒsɪneɪt/ *v.i.* reason, esp. using syllogisms; **ratiocination** /-'neɪʃ(ə)n/ *n.* [L (as prec.)]

ration /'ræʃ(ə)n/ **1** *n.* allowance or portion of food or clothing etc., esp. official allowance in time of shortage; (usu. in *pl.*) fixed daily allowance of food in armed forces etc. **2** *v.t.* limit (persons or provisions) to fixed ration; share (*out*) food etc. in fixed quantities. [F f. It. or Sp. f. L (RATIO)]

rational /'ræʃən(ə)l/ *a.* of or based on reason; sensible; endowed with reason; rejecting what is unreasonable or cannot be tested by reason in religion or custom; (of quantity or ratio) expressible as ratio of integers; **rationality** /-'nælɪtɪ/ *n.*; **rationally** *adv.* [L (as prec.)]

rationale /ræʃə'nɑ:l/ *n.* fundamental reason, logical basis. [neut. of L *rationalis* (prec.)]

rationalism /'ræʃənəlɪz(ə)m/ *n.* practice of treating reason as basis of belief and knowledge; **rationalist** *n.* & *a.*; **rationalistic** /-'lɪstɪk/ *a.* [RATIONAL]

rationalize *v.t.* offer rational but specious explanation of (behaviour or attitude); make logical and consistent; make (an industry) more efficient by reorganizing it to reduce or eliminate waste; explain (*away*) by rationalism; **rationalization** /-'zeɪʃ(ə)n/ *n.*

ratline /'rætlɪn/ *n.* (also **ratlin**) any of the small lines fastened across a sailing-ship's shrouds like ladder-rungs. [orig. unkn.]

ratsbane *n.* plant etc. poisonous to rats. [RAT]

rattan /rə'tæn/ *n.* palm with long thin many-jointed pliable stems; piece of rattan stem used as cane etc. [Malay]

rat-tat /ræt'tæt/ *n.* rapping sound, esp. of knocker. [imit.]

rattle /'ræt(ə)l/ **1** *v.* (cause to) give out rapid succession of short sharp hard sounds; cause such sounds by shaking something; move or travel with rattling noise; (usu. with *off*) say or recite rapidly; (usu. with *on*) talk in lively thoughtless way; *sl.* disconcert, alarm. **2** *n.* rattling sound; device or toy etc. for making rattling sound. [prob. LG or Du.]

rattlesnake *n.* poisonous American snake with rattling structure of horny rings in tail.

rattletrap *n.* rickety old vehicle etc.

rattling **1** *a.* brisk, vigorous (*a rattling pace*). **2** *adv.* remarkably (*a rattling good story*).

ratty *a.* relating to or infested with rats; *sl.* irritable, angry. [RAT]

raucous /'rɔ:kəs/ *a.* harsh-sounding, loud and hoarse. [L]

raunchy /'rɔ:ntʃɪ/ *a.* coarse, earthy, boisterous. [orig. unkn.]

ravage /'rævɪdʒ/ **1** *v.* devastate, plunder, make havoc (in). **2** *n.* devastation; (usu. in *pl.*) destructive effect *of*. [F alt. of RAVINE rush of water]

rave **1** *v.i.* talk wildly or furiously (as) in delirium; speak with rapturous admiration *about* or *over*, go into raptures. **2** *n.* *colloq.* highly enthusiastic review (of film or play etc.); *sl.* infatuation. **3 rave-up** *sl.* lively party; **raving beauty** *colloq.* excitingly beautiful person; **raving mad** *colloq.* completely mad. [prob. F dial. *raver*]

ravel /'rævəl/ **1** *v.* (**-ll-**, *US* **-l-**) entangle or become entangled; confuse or complicate (question or problem); fray out; disentangle, unravel, distinguish separate threads or subdivisions of (often with *out*). **2** *n.* tangle, knot, complication. [perh. Du. *ravelen*]

raven[1] /'reɪv(ə)n/ **1** *n.* large crow with glossy blue-black feathers and hoarse cry. **2** *a.* (usu. of hair) glossy black. [OE]

raven[2] /'ræv(ə)n/ *v.* plunder, seek *after* prey or booty; devour voraciously. [F *raviner* f. L (RAPINE)]

ravenous /'rævənəs/ *a.* very hungry; voracious; rapacious. [F (prec.)]

ravine /rə'vi:n/ *n.* deep narrow gorge. [F f. L (RAPINE)]

ravioli /rævɪ'əʊlɪ/ *n.* small pasta envelopes containing meat etc. [It.]

ravish /'rævɪʃ/ *v.t.* commit rape on (woman); enrapture, fill with delight; **ravishment** *n.* [F f. L (RAPE[1])]

raw *a.* uncooked; in natural state, not processed or manufactured; inexperienced, untrained; stripped of skin, having flesh exposed, sensitive to touch from being so exposed; (of atmosphere or day etc.) damp and chilly; crude in artistic quality, lacking finish; (of edge of cloth) without hem or selvage; **in the raw** in its natural state without mitigation (*life in the raw*), naked; **raw-boned** gaunt; **raw deal** see DEAL¹; **raw material** that from which process of manufacture makes articles; **touch person on the raw** wound his feelings on point where he is sensitive. [OE]

rawhide *n.* untanned leather; rope or whip of this.

Rawlplug /'rɔ:lplʌg/ *n.* (**P**) thin cylindrical plug for holding screw or nail in masonry. [*Rawl*ings, name of engineers]

ray¹ *n.* single line or narrow beam of light from small or distant source; straight line in which radiation is propagated to given point; (in *pl.*) radiation of specified type (*X-rays*); remnant or beginning of enlightening or cheering influence (*a ray of hope*); any of set of radiating lines or parts or things; marginal part of composite flower, e.g. daisy. [F f. L RADIUS]

ray² *n.* large flat sea-fish related to shark and used as food. [F *raie* f. L *raia*]

ray³ *n. Mus.* second note of major scale. [L *resonare*, word arbitrarily taken]

rayon /'reɪɒn/ *n.* textile fibre or fabric made from cellulose. [RAY¹]

raze *v.t.* completely destroy, tear down (usu. *to the ground*). [F f. L *rado ras-* scrape]

razor /'reɪzə/ *n.* instrument with sharp blade used in cutting hair esp. from skin; **razor-bill** auk with sharp-edged bill; **razor-blade** blade used in razor, esp. flat piece of metal with sharp edge(s) used in safety razor; **razor-edge** keen edge, sharp mountain ridge, critical situation (*on a razor-edge*), sharp line of division. [F *rasor* (prec.)]

razzle /'ræz(ə)l/ *n. sl.* spree or lively outing (*on the razzle*). [foll.]

razzle-dazzle *n. sl.* excitement, bustle, spree; *sl.* extravagant publicity. [redupl. of DAZZLE]

razzmatazz /ræzmə'tæz/ *n.* excitement, bustle; extravagant publicity; insincere actions, humbug. [prob. alt. of prec.]

Rb *symb.* rubidium.

RC *abbr.* Roman Catholic.

RCA *abbr.* Royal College of Art.

RCM *abbr.* Royal College of Music.

RCP *abbr.* Royal College of Physicians.

RCS *abbr.* Royal College of Science; Royal College of Surgeons; Royal Corps of Signals.

Rd. *abbr.* road.

re¹ /ri:/ *prep.* in the matter of (as first word in heading, esp. of legal document); *colloq.* about, concerning. [L, abl. of *res* thing]

re² /reɪ/ var. of RAY³.

're *abbr.* are (*we're, they're*).

re-¹ *prefix* (sometimes **red-** before vowels: *redolent*) in verbs and verbal derivatives denoting: in return, mutually (*react, resemble*), opposition (*repel, resist*), behind or after (*relic, remain*), retirement or secrecy (*recluse, reticence*), off, away, down (*recede, relegate, repress*), frequentative or intensive force (*redouble, refine, resplendent*), negative force (*recant, reveal*). [L]

re-² *prefix* attachable to almost any verb or its derivative in senses (1) once more, afresh, anew; (2) back, with return to previous state. A hyphen is normally used when the word begins in *e-* (*re-enact*), or to distinguish the compound from a more familiar one-word form (*re-form* = form again).

¶ The list at the foot of the page is of words in sense (1) that can be understood readily from the sense of the main word; it does not include all derivatives of obvious formation (e.g. *readjustment* from *readjust*). Pronunciation and stress follow those of the main word.

reacquaint	**reassign**	**reconsecrate**
readdress	**reattack**	**reconvene**
readjust	**reattempt**	**reconvert**
readmit	**rebid**	**recopy**
readopt	**rebind**	**re-cover**
reaffirm	**reborn**	**re-create**
reafforest	**rebroadcast**	**recross**
reallocate	**rebuild**	**redecorate**
reanimate	**recharge**	**redesign**
reappear	**recheck**	**redevelop**
reapply	**reclassify**	**redirect**
reappoint	**reclothe**	**rediscover**
reapportion	**recolour**	**redistribute**
rearrest	**recombine**	**redivide**
reassemble	**recommence**	**re-elect**
reassert	**reconquer**	**re-embark**
reassess	**reconquest**	**re-emerge**

RE *abbr*. Royal Engineers.

Re *symb*. rhenium.

reach 1 *v*. stretch out or extend (*out*); stretch out the hand etc., make reaching motion or effort (*lit*. or *fig*.); get as far as, attain to, arrive at; make contact with with the hand etc. or by telephone etc. (*was out all day and could not be reached*); hand, pass or take with outstretched hand (*reach me the book*); *Naut*. sail with wind abeam or abaft the beam. **2** *n*. act of reaching out; extent to which hand etc. can be reached out, influence be exerted, motion carried out, or mental powers be used; continuous extent, esp. part of river that can be looked along at once between two bends, or part of canal between locks; *Naut*. distance traversed in reaching. **3 reach-me-down** *a*. *colloq*. ready-made. [OE]

react /ri:'ækt/ *v.i*. respond *to* stimulus, undergo change or show behaviour due to some influence; be actuated by repulsion *against*, tend in reverse or backward direction. [RE-[1]]

reaction /ri:'ækʃ(ə)n/ *n*. reacting, responsive feeling; occurrence of condition after its opposite; tendency to oppose change or to return to former system, esp. in politics; interaction of substances undergoing chemical change.

reactionary 1 *a*. showing reaction, esp. in politics. **2** *n*. reactionary person.

reactivate /ri:'æktɪveɪt/ *v.t*. restore to state of activity.

reactive /ri:'æktɪv/ *a*. showing reaction.

reactor *n*. (in full **nuclear reactor**) assembly of materials in which controlled nuclear chain reaction releases energy.

read 1 *v*. (*past* and *p.p*. **read** /red/) reproduce mentally or vocally the words of (book, author, etc.); (be able to) convert into intended words or meaning (written or other symbol or things so expressed, or *absol*.); interpret mentally, declare interpretation of (*can read her thoughts*); find thing stated in print etc.; interpret (statement or action) in certain sense; assume as intended or deducible from writer's words; bring into specified state by reading (*read myself to sleep*); (of recording instrument) show (figure etc.); convey meaning when read (*name reads from left to right*); sound or affect hearer or reader when read (*reads like a translation*); study by reading (esp. subject at university); (in *p.p*. with active sense) versed in subject or literature by reading (*is very well read*); (of computer) copy or transfer (data). **2** *n*. spell of reading. **3 read between the lines** look for and find hidden meaning; **read into** assume to be implicit in (words); **read up** make special study of (subject); **take as read** dispense with actual reading or discussion of. [OE]

readable *a*. able to be read; interesting to read; **readably** *adv*.

reader *n*. one who reads, esp. aloud in

re-emphasize
re-enact
re-engage
re-enlist
re-enter
re-equip
re-establish
re-examine
re-explain
reface
refashion
refloat
re-form
reformulate
refurnish
regroup
rehang
rehear
reheat
rehouse
reimpose
reincorporate
reinsert
reinspect
reinstruct
reinter
reinterpret
reintroduce
reinvest
reinvestigate
reissue
rekindle
relabel
re-lay
relet
reline
reload
remake
remarry
remodel
rename
renationalize
renegotiate
renumber
reoccupy
reoccur
reopen
reorient
reorientate
repack
repaint
repaper
rephrase
replant
repolish
repopulate
repot
republish
repurchase
reread
resell
reset
resettle
reshape
reshuffle
re-sign
re-sort
respell
restart
restate
restock
resurvey
retell
retie
retrain
retranslate
retype
reunify
reunite
reuse
revalue
revisit
revitalize
rework

church; book of extracts for learning a language; device to produce image that can be read from microfilm etc.; university lecturer of higher grade; publisher's employee who reports on submitted manuscripts; printer's proof-corrector.

readership *n.* readers of newspaper etc.

readily /'redılı/ *adv.* without showing reluctance, willingly; without difficulty. [READY]

readiness *n.* ready or prepared state (*all is in readiness*); willingness; facility, quickness in argument or action.

reading *n.* entertainment at which thing is read; matter to be read, its specified quality (*makes dull reading*); literary knowledge; figure etc. given by recording instrument; interpretation or view taken *of* facts etc., interpretation of drama, music, etc.; one of three occasions on which a Bill must be presented to legislature for acceptance; **reading-room** room in club, library, etc., for those wishing to read. [OE (READ)]

ready /'redı/ **1** *a.* with preparations complete (*dinner is ready*); in fit state; willing or inclined or resolved (*always ready to complain*); within reach, easily secured (*a ready source of revenue*); fit for immediate use; prompt, enthusiastic (*ready acceptance*; *ready with excuses*); about *to* (*a bud just ready to burst*); provided beforehand. **2** *adv.* beforehand, so as not to require doing when the time comes. **3** *n. sl.* ready money. **4** *v.t.* make ready, prepare. **5 at the ready** ready for action; **make ready** prepare; **ready-made** (esp. of clothes) made for immediate wear, not to measure; **ready money** actual coin or notes, payment on the spot; **ready reckoner** book or table of results of arithmetical computations of kind commonly wanted in business etc. [OE]

reagent /ri:'eıdʒənt/ *n.* substance used to cause chemical reaction, esp. to detect another substance. [RE-[1]]

real[1] **1** *a.* actually existing as thing or occurring in fact, genuine, rightly so called, not artificial; *Law* consisting of immovable property such as land or houses (*real estate*); appraised by purchasing power (*real wages*). **2** *adv. Sc.* & *US colloq.* really, very. **3 real money** coin, cash; **real tennis** original form of tennis played on indoor court; **real time** actual time in process analysed by computer. [AF, & L *realis* (*res* thing)]

real[2] /reı'ɑ:l/ *n. hist.* silver coin in Spanish-speaking countries. [Sp. (ROYAL)]

realign /ri:ə'laın/ *v.* align again; regroup in politics etc.; **realignment** *n.* [RE-[2]]

realism *n.* practice of regarding things in their true nature and dealing with them as they are; fidelity to nature in representation, showing of life etc. as it is in fact; philosophical doctrine that abstract concepts have objective existence; **realist** *n.* [REAL[1]]

realistic /rıə'lıstık/ *a.* regarding things as they are, following a policy of realism; based on facts rather than ideals; **realistically** *adv.*

reality /rı'ælıtı/ *n.* what is real or existent or underlies appearances; real existence, being real; resemblance to original. [med.L or F (REAL[1])]

realize *v.t.* be fully aware of, present or conceive as real, understand clearly; convert into fact (usu. in *pass.*); convert into money; acquire (profit), be sold for (specified price); **realization** /-'zeıʃ(ə)n/ *n.* [REAL[1]]

really *adv.* in reality; indeed, I assure you; as expression of mild protest or surprise.

realm /relm/ *n.* kingdom; sphere or domain (*the realm(s) of fancy, poetry*). [F f. L REGIMEN]

realty *n.* real estate. [REAL[1]]

ream *n.* twenty quires of paper; (usu. in *pl.*) large quantity of writing. [F ult. f. Arab., = bundle]

reap *v.t.* cut or gather (crop, esp. grain) as harvest; harvest crop of (field etc.); receive as consequence of one's own or others' actions. [OE]

reaper *n.* person who reaps; machine for reaping; death personified.

reappraise /ri:ə'preız/ *v.t.* appraise again, reconsider; **reappraisal** *n.* [RE-[2]]

rear[1] **1** *n.* back part of anything; space behind, or position at back of, anything; *colloq.* buttocks. **2** *a.* at the back, in the rear. **3 bring up the rear** come last; **Rear-Admiral** see ADMIRAL; **rear-lamp** (or **-light**) light, usu. red, on back of vehicle. [prob. abbr. of REARWARD or REARGUARD (cf. VAN[2])]

rear[2] *v.* bring up and educate (children); breed and care for (animals); cultivate (crops); (of horse etc.) raise itself on hind legs; set upright, build, hold upwards; extend to great height. [OE]

rearguard *n.* body of troops detached to protect rear esp. in retreats; **rearguard action** engagement between rearguard and enemy (*lit.* or *fig.*). [F *rereguarde*]

rearm /ri:'ɑ:m/ *v.* arm again, esp. with improved weapons; **rearmament** *n.* [RE-[2]]

rearmost *a.* furthest back. [REAR[1]]

rearrange /ri:ə'reındʒ/ *v.t.* arrange

again in different way; **rearrangement** *n.* [RE-²]

rearward /'rɪəwəd/ 1 *n.* rear, esp. in prepositional phrases: *to the rearward of*; *in the rearward.* **2** *a.* to the rear. **3** *adv.* (also **rearwards**) towards the rear. [AF *rerewarde* = REARGUARD]

reason /'ri:z(ə)n/ **1** *n.* motive or cause or justification; fact adduced or serving as this; intellectual faculty by which conclusions are drawn from premisses; sanity (*has lost his reason*); sense, sensible conduct, what is right or practical or practicable, moderation. **2** *v.* form or try to reach conclusions by connected thought; use argument *with* person by way of persuasion; conclude or assert in argument *that*; persuade or bring by argument *into* or *out of* (*reasoned him out of his prejudice*); think *out* (consequences etc.); express in logical or argumentative form (*reasoned exposition*); embody reason in (amendment etc.). **3 by reason of** owing to; **in** (or **within**) **reason** within the bounds of moderation; **with reason** not unjustifiably. [F f. L *ratio*]

reasonable *a.* having or based on sound judgement or moderation; sensible, not expecting too much; not excessive, inexpensive; tolerable, fair; ready to listen to reason; **reasonably** *adv.*

reassure /ri:ə'ʃʊə/ *v.t.* restore confidence to, dispel apprehensions of; confirm in opinion or impression; **reassurance** *n.* [RE-²]

reave *v.t.* (*past* and *p.p.* **reft**) *archaic* (esp. in *p.p.*) forcibly deprive *of*; take by force or carry off (*away* or *from*). [OE]

rebate¹ /'ri:beɪt/ *n.* deduction from sum to be paid, discount; partial refund. [F *rabattre* (RE-¹, ABATE)]

rebate² /'ræbɪt, rɪ'beɪt/ var. of RABBET.

rebel 1 /'reb(ə)l/ *n.* person who fights against, resists, or refuses allegiance to, the established government; person or thing that resists authority or control; *attrib.* rebellious, of rebels, in rebellion. **2** /rɪ'bel/ *v.i.* (**-ll-**) act as rebel (*against*); feel or display repugnance (*against* custom etc.). [F f. L (RE-¹, *bellum* war)]

rebellion /rɪ'beljən/ *n.* open resistance to authority, esp. organized armed resistance to established government. [F f. L (prec.)]

rebellious /rɪ'beljəs/ *a.* in rebellion; disposed to rebel, defying lawful authority; (of thing) unmanageable, refractory.

rebirth /ri:'bɜ:θ/ *n.* new incarnation; spiritual enlightenment; revival. [RE-²]

rebound 1 /rɪ'baʊnd/ *v.i.* spring back after impact; (of action) have adverse effect *upon* doer. **2** /'ri:baʊnd/ *n.* act of rebounding, recoil; reaction after emotion (*on the rebound*). [F *rebonder* (BOUND¹)]

rebuff /rɪ'bʌf/ **1** *n.* rejection of one who makes advances, proffers help or sympathy, shows interest or curiosity, makes request, etc.; repulse, snub. **2** *v.t.* give rebuff to. [F f. It.]

rebuke /rɪ'bju:k/ **1** *v.t.* reprove sharply, subject to protest or censure. **2** *n.* rebuking or being rebuked. [AF]

rebus /'ri:bəs/ *n.* representation of a word (esp. a name) by pictures etc. suggesting its parts. [F f. L *rebus*, abl. pl. of *res* thing]

rebut /rɪ'bʌt/ *v.t.* (**-tt-**) refute or disprove (evidence or charge); force or turn back, check; **rebuttal** *n.* [AF *rebuter* (BUTT¹)]

recalcitrant /rɪ'kælsɪtrənt/ *a.* obstinately disobedient, objecting to restraint; **recalcitrance** *n.* [L *recalcitro* kick out (*calx* heel)]

recall /rɪ'kɔ:l/ **1** *v.t.* summon to return; bring back to attention etc.; recollect, remember; bring back *to* memory, serve as reminder of; revive, resuscitate; revoke or annul (action or decision). **2** /also 'ri:kɔ:l/ *n.* summons to come back; act of remembering, ability to remember; possibility of recalling, esp. in sense of annulling (*beyond recall*). [RE-²]

recant /rɪ'kænt/ *v.* withdraw and renounce (former belief or statement etc.) as erroneous or heretical; disavow former opinion, esp. with public confession of error; **recantation** /ri:kæn'teɪʃ(ə)n/ *n.* [L (CHANT)]

recap /'ri:kæp/ *colloq.* **1** *v.t.* (**-pp-**) recapitulate. **2** *n.* recapitulation. [abbr.]

recapitulate /ri:kə'pɪtjʊleɪt/ *v.* go briefly through again, summarize, go over main points or headings of. [L (CAPITAL)]

recapitulation /ri:kəpɪtjʊ'leɪʃ(ə)n/ *n.* recapitulating; *Mus.* part of movement in which themes from the exposition are restated. [F or L (prec.)]

recapture /ri:'kæptʃə/ **1** *v.t.* capture again or in return; re-experience (past emotion etc.). **2** *n.* act of recapturing. [RE-²]

recast /ri:'kɑ:st/ **1** *v.t.* (*past* and *p.p.* **recast**) put into new form, improve arrangement of. **2** *n.* recasting; recast form.

recce /'rekɪ/ *sl.* **1** *n.* reconnaissance. **2** *v.* reconnoitre. [abbr.]

recede /rɪ'si:d/ *v.i.* go or shrink back or further off; be left at increasing distance by observer's motion; slope backwards; decline in force or value etc. [L *recedo -cess-* (CEDE)]

receipt /rɪ'si:t/ **1** *n.* fact or action of receiving or being received; written acknowledgement of this, esp. of payment of money; (usu. in *pl.*) amount of money etc. received; *archaic* recipe. **2** *v.t.* place written receipt on (bill). [AF *receite* (foll.)]

receive /rɪ'si:v/ *v.t.* take or accept (proffered thing) into one's hands or possession, have sent to one; acquire or be provided with; have conferred or inflicted on one; bear up against, stand force or weight of, encounter with opposition; consent to hear (confession or oath) or consider (petition); accept (stolen goods knowingly, or *absol.*); admit, consent or prove able to hold, provide accommodation for, submit to, serve as receptacle of; admit to membership; be marked (*lit.* or *fig.*) more or less permanently with (impression etc.); convert (broadcast signals) into sound or picture; entertain (person as guest, company at formal reception, or *absol.*); greet or welcome, esp. in specified manner; (esp. in *p.p.*) give credit to, accept as authoritative or true; **be at** (or **on) the receiving end** *colloq.* bear the brunt of something unpleasant; **received pronunciation** form of English speech used (with local variations) by majority of educated English-speaking people. [F f. L *recipio -cept-* get back again]

receiver *n.* person appointed by court to administer property of bankrupt or insane person or property under litigation; person who receives stolen goods; part of machine or instrument that receives something (esp. part of telephone that contains ear-piece); radio or television receiving apparatus.

recent /'ri:sənt/ **1** *a.* not long past, that happened or began to exist or existed lately; not long established, lately begun, modern; (**Recent**) of the later epoch of the Quaternary period, including the present. **2** *n.* (**Recent**) this epoch. [F or L *recens -ent-*]

receptacle /rɪ'septək(ə)l/ *n.* container, containing place or space; common base of organs of flower, axis of cluster. [F or L (RECEIVE)]

reception /rɪ'sepʃ(ə)n/ *n.* receiving or being received; way in which person or thing is received (*got a cool reception*); social occasion for receiving guests, esp. after wedding; place where guests or clients are registered or welcomed on arrival at hotel or office etc.; receiving of broadcast signals; quality of this; **reception room** room available or suitable for receiving company or visitors. [F or L (RECEIVE)]

receptionist *n.* person employed to receive guests, patients, clients, etc.

receptive /rɪ'septɪv/ *a.* able or quick to receive impressions or ideas; **receptivity** /ri:sep'tɪvɪtɪ/ *n.* [F or med.L (RECEIVE)]

recess /rɪ'ses/ **1** *n.* space set back from line of wall; remote or secret place; temporary cessation from work, esp. of Parliament. **2** *v.* make a recess in; place in a recess; *US* take recess, adjourn. [L *recessus* (RECEDE)]

recession /rɪ'seʃ(ə)n/ *n.* temporary decline in economic activity or prosperity; receding or withdrawal from place or point. [L (prec.)]

recessional **1** *a.* sung while clergy and choir withdraw after service. **2** *n.* recessional hymn.

recessive /rɪ'sesɪv/ *a.* tending to recede; (of inherited characteristic) remaining latent when a dominant characteristic is present. [RECESS]

recherché /rə'ʃeəʃeɪ/ *a.* devised or got with care or difficulty; far-fetched. [F]

rechristen /ri:'krɪs(ə)n/ *v.t.* christen again; give new name to. [RE-²]

recidivist /rɪ'sɪdɪvɪst/ *n.* one who relapses into crime; **recidivism** *n.* [F f. L *recidivus* falling back (RECEDE)]

recipe /'resɪpɪ/ *n.* statement of ingredients and procedure for preparing dish etc. in cookery; medical prescription; expedient. [L, 2nd sing. imper. of *recipio* RECEIVE]

recipient /rɪ'sɪpɪənt/ *n.* person who receives something. [F f. It. or L (as prec.)]

reciprocal /rɪ'sɪprək(ə)l/ **1** *a.* in return (*reciprocal help*); mutual (*reciprocal love*); *Gram.* (of pronoun) expressing mutual relation (e.g. *each other*). **2** *n.* mathematical expression or function so related to another that their product is unity (*$\frac{1}{5}$ is the reciprocal of 5*). **3 reciprocally** *adv.* [L *reciprocus* moving to and fro]

reciprocate /rɪ'sɪprəkeɪt/ *v.* give and receive mutually, interchange; requite (affection etc.), make a return (*with* thing so given); (of part of machine) go with alternate backward and forward motion; **reciprocation** /-'keɪʃ(ə)n/ *n.* [L (prec.)]

reciprocity /resɪ'prɒsɪtɪ/ *n.* condition of being reciprocal; mutual action; give-and-take, esp. interchange of privileges. [F (RECIPROCAL)]

recital /rɪ'saɪt(ə)l/ *n.* act of reciting; detailed account *of* connected things or facts, narrative; performance of programme by one musician with or without accompanist (*piano recital*). [RECITE]

recitation /resɪ'teɪʃ(ə)n/ *n.* reciting; thing recited. [F or L (RECITE)]

recitative /resɪtə'ti:v/ *n.* musical declamation of kind usual in narrative and dialogue parts of opera and oratorio. [It. *recitativo* (foll.)]

recite /rɪ'saɪt/ *v.* repeat aloud or declaim (poem or passage) from memory; give recitation; enumerate. [F, or L *recito* read out]

reckless /'reklɪs/ *a.* regardless of consequences or danger etc., rash. [OE (*reck* concern oneself)]

reckon /'rekən/ *v.* count or compute by calculation; include or count *in* in computation; consider or regard; conclude after calculation or be confidently of the opinion (*that*); make calculations, cast up account or sum; **reckon on** rely or count or base plans on; **reckon with** take into account, settle accounts with (person). [OE]

reckoning *n.* counting or calculating; consideration or opinion; settlement of account; **day of reckoning** time when something must be atoned for or avenged.

reclaim /rɪ'kleɪm/ *v.t.* seek return of (one's property); bring under cultivation esp. from state of being under water; win back or away from vice or error or waste condition; **reclamation** /reklə'meɪʃ(ə)n/ *n.* [F f. L *reclamo* cry out against]

recline /rɪ'klaɪn/ *v.* (cause to) assume or be in horizontal or leaning position. [F, or L *reclino*]

recluse /rɪ'klu:s/ *n.* person given to or living in seclusion or isolation, esp. as religious discipline. [F f. L *recludo -clus-* shut away]

recognition /rekəg'nɪʃ(ə)n/ *n.* recognizing or being recognized. [L (RECOGNIZE)]

recognizable /'rekəgnaɪzəb(ə)l/ *a.* that can be identified or detected; **recognizably** *adv.* [RECOGNIZE]

recognizance /rɪ'kɒgnɪzəns/ *n.* bond by which person undertakes before court or magistrate to observe some condition, e.g. to appear when summoned; sum pledged as surety for such observance. [F (RE-[1])]

recognize /'rekəgnaɪz/ *v.t.* identify as known before; realize or discover nature of; realize or admit *that*; acknowledge existence or validity or character or claims of; show appreciation of, reward; treat *as*. [F f. L *recognosco*]

recoil /rɪ'kɔɪl/ **1** *v.i.* suddenly move or spring back, or shrink mentally, in horror or disgust or fear; rebound after impact; have adverse reactive effect *on* or *upon* (originator); (of gun) be driven backwards by discharge. **2** /also 'ri:kɔɪl/ *n.* act or fact or sensation of recoiling. [F *reculer* f. L *culus* buttocks]

recollect /rekə'lekt/ *v.t.* remember; succeed in remembering, call to mind. [L *recolligo* (COLLECT[1])]

recollection /rekə'lekʃ(ə)n/ *n.* act or power of recollecting; thing recollected; person's memory, time over which it extends (*happened within my recollection*). [F or med.L (prec.)]

recommend /rekə'mend/ *v.t.* suggest as fit for employment or favour or trial; advise (course of action etc.); (of qualities or conduct etc.) make acceptable or desirable; commend or entrust *to* person or his care; **recommendation** /-'deɪʃ(ə)n/ *n.* [med.L (RE-[1])]

recompense /'rekəmpens/ **1** *v.t.* make amends to (person) or for (loss etc.); requite, reward or punish (person or action). **2** *n.* reward, requital; retribution. [F f. L (COMPENSATE)]

reconcile /'rekənsaɪl/ *v.t.* make friendly after estrangement; (usu. in *refl.* or *pass.*) make acquiescent or contentedly submissive (*to* what is disagreeable); settle (quarrel etc.); harmonize, make compatible, show compatibility of by argument or in practice; **reconciliation** /-sɪlɪ'eɪʃ(ə)n/ *n.* [F or L (CONCILIATE)]

recondite /'rekəndaɪt/ *a.* (of subject or knowledge) abstruse, out of the way, little known; (of author or style) dealing in recondite knowledge or allusion, obscure. [L (*recondo -dit-* put away)]

recondition /ri:kən'dɪʃ(ə)n/ *v.t.* overhaul, renovate, make usable again. [RE-[2]]

reconnaissance /rɪ'kɒnɪsəns/ *n.* survey of region, esp. military examination to locate enemy or ascertain strategic features; preliminary survey. [F (as foll.)]

reconnoitre /rekə'nɔɪtə/, *US* **reconnoiter** *v.* make reconnaissance (of). [F (RECOGNIZE)]

reconsider /ri:kən'sɪdə/ *v.t.* consider again, esp. for possible change of decision; **reconsideration** /-'reɪʃ(ə)n/ *n.* [RE-[2]]

reconstitute /ri:'kɒnstɪtju:t/ *v.t.* reconstruct or reorganize; restore previous constitution of (dried food etc.) by adding water; **reconstitution** /-'tju:ʃ(ə)n/ *n.*

reconstruct /ri:kən'strʌkt/ *v.t.* build again; piece together (past events) into intelligible whole, by imagination or by re-enacting them; reorganize; **reconstruction** *n.*

record **1** /rɪ'kɔ:d/ *v.t.* set down for remembrance or reference, put in writing or other permanent form; convert (sound, broadcast programme, etc.) to permanent form for later reproduction. **2** /'rekɔ:d/ *n.* state of being recorded or preserved in writing etc.; piece of recorded evidence or information, account of fact preserved in permanent form, document or monument preserving it; official report of public or legal proceedings; known facts about person's past, list and details of previous offences; disc from which recorded sound can be reproduced; object serving as memorial, portrait, etc.; (often *attrib.*) best performance or most remarkable event of its kind on record. **3 for the record** officially; **go on record** state opinion openly so that it is published; **have a record** have been convicted on previous occasion; **off the record** unofficially, confidentially; **on record** officially recorded, publicly known; **recorded delivery** Post Office service whereby safe delivery is recorded by signature of recipient: **record-player** gramophone. [F f. L (*cor cord-* heart)]

recorder /rɪ'kɔ:də/ *n.* keeper of records; judge in certain courts; apparatus for recording, esp. = *tape-recorder*; a kind of vertical flute.

recording *n.* process by which audio or video signals are recorded for later reproduction; material or programme thus recorded.

recount /rɪ'kaʊnt/ *v.t.* narrate, tell in detail. [AF *reconter* (RE-[2], COUNT[1])]

re-count 1 /ri:'kaʊnt/ *v.t.* count again. **2** /'ri:kaʊnt/ *n.* re-counting, esp. of election votes. [RE-[2]]

recoup /rɪ'ku:p/ *v.t.* recover or regain (loss); compensate or reimburse for loss; **recoup oneself** recover loss; **recoupment** *n.* [F *recouper* cut back]

recourse /rɪ'kɔ:s/ *n.* resorting to possible source of help; person or thing resorted to; **have recourse to** turn to (person or thing) for help. [F f. L (COURSE)]

recover /rɪ'kʌvə/ *v.* regain possession or use or control of; come back to health or consciousness or normal state or position; obtain or secure by legal process; retrieve or make up for (loss or setback etc.); **recover oneself** regain calmness or consciousness or control of limbs. [AF *recoverer* f. L (RECUPERATE)]

recovery *n.* act or process of recovering or being recovered. [AF *recoverie* (as prec.)]

recreant /'rekrɪənt/ *literary* **1** *a.* craven, cowardly. **2** *n.* coward. [F f. *recroire* surrender f. L (CREED)]

recreation /rekrɪ'eɪʃ(ə)n/ *n.* process or means of refreshing or entertaining oneself, pleasurable activity; **recreational** *a.* [F f. L (CREATE)]

recriminate /rɪ'krɪmɪneɪt/ *v.i.* make mutual or counter accusations; **recrimination** /-'neɪʃ(ə)n/ *n.*; **recriminatory** *a.* [med.L (CRIME)]

recrudesce /ri:kru:'des, rek-/ *v.i.* (of disease or sore or discontent etc.) break out again; **recrudescence** *n.*; **recrudescent** *a.* [L (CRUDE)]

recruit /rɪ'kru:t/ **1** *n.* serviceman or servicewoman newly enlisted and not yet fully trained; new member of society etc.; beginner. **2** *v.* enlist (person) as recruit; enlist recruits for (army etc.); get or seek recruits; replenish or reinvigorate (numbers or strength etc.). **3 recruitment** *n.* [F dial. *recrute* (CREW)]

rectal /'rekt(ə)l/ *a.* of or by means of rectum. [RECTUM]

rectangle /'rektæŋg(ə)l/ *n.* four-sided plane rectilinear figure with four right angles, esp. other than square; **rectangular** /-'tæŋgjʊlə/ *a.* [F or med.L]

rectify /'rektɪfaɪ/ *v.t.* adjust or make right; purify or refine, esp. by repeated distillation; convert (alternating current) to direct current; **rectification** /-fɪ'keɪʃ(ə)n/ *n.*; **rectifier** *n.* [F f. L *rectus* straight, right]

rectilinear /rektɪ'lɪnɪə/ *a.* bounded or characterized by straight lines; in or forming a straight line. [L (prec.)]

rectitude /'rektɪtju:d/ *n.* moral uprightness, righteousness, correctness. [F or L (*rectus* right)]

recto /'rektəʊ/ *n.* (*pl.* **rectos**) right-hand page of open book; front of leaf. [L, = on the right]

rector /'rektə/ *n.* incumbent of Church of England parish where all tithes formerly passed to incumbent; head priest of a Roman Catholic church; head of university or college or religious institution; **rectorship** *n.* [F or L (*rego rect-* rule)]

rectory *n.* rector's house. [F or med.L (prec.)]

rectum /'rektəm/ *n.* (*pl.* **rectums**) final section of large intestine, terminating at anus. [L, = straight]

recumbent /rɪ'kʌmbənt/ *a.* lying down, reclining. [L (*cumbo* lie)]

recuperate /rɪ'kju:pəreɪt, -'ku:-/ *v.* recover from illness or exhaustion or loss etc.; regain (health or losses etc.); **recuperation** /-'reɪʃ(ə)n/ *n.*; **recuperative** *a.* [L *recupero*]

recur /rɪ'kɜ:/ *v.i.* (**-rr-**) occur again, be repeated; go back in thought or speech *to*; **recurring decimal** decimal fraction in which same figures are repeated indefinitely. [L (*curro* run)]

recurrent /rɪ'kʌrənt/ *a.* recurring, happening repeatedly; **recurrence** *n.*

recusant /'rekjʊzənt/ *n.* one who

refuses submission to authority or compliance with regulation, esp. *hist.* one who refused to attend Anglican services; **recusancy** *n.* [L *recuso* refuse]

recycle /ri:ˈsaɪk(ə)l/ *v.t.* return (material) to previous stage of cyclic process, esp. convert (waste) to reusable material. [RE-²]

red 1 *a.* of colour ranging from that of blood to pink or orange; flushed in face with shame, anger, etc.; (of eyes) sore or bloodshot; (of hair) reddish-brown, tawny; having to do with bloodshed, burning, violence, or revolution; **(Red)** Russian, Soviet; socialist or communist. **2** *n.* red colour or pigment; red clothes or material (*dressed in red*); a socialist or communist. **3 in the red** in debt; **red admiral** species of butterfly; **red-blooded** virile, vigorous; **red carpet** privileged treatment of important visitor; **red cell** (or **corpuscle**) erythrocyte; **red cent** *US* smallest (orig. copper) coin; **Red Crescent** equivalent of Red Cross in Muslim countries; **Red Cross** international organization bringing relief to victims of war or natural disaster; **red flag** symbol of danger or of revolution; **red-handed** in the act of committing crime or doing wrong etc.; **red hat** cardinal's hat, symbol of his office; **red herring** irrelevant distraction; **red-hot** heated to redness, highly exciting or excited, angry, (of news) fresh, completely new; **red-hot poker** garden plant with spikes of usu. red or yellow flowers; **Red Indian** N. American Indian, with reddish skin; **red lead** pigment made from red oxide of lead; **red-letter day** one that is pleasantly noteworthy or memorable (orig. festival marked in red on calendar); **red light** signal to stop on road or railway, *fig.* warning; **red-light district** one containing many brothels; **red meat** meat that is red when raw (e.g. beef and lamb); **red pepper** cayenne pepper, ripe fruit of capsicum plant; **red rag** thing that excites person's rage; **red rose** emblem of Lancashire or Lancastrians; **red-shift** movement of spectrum to longer wavelengths in light from distant galaxies etc.; **red squirrel** native English species with reddish fur; **red tape** excessive bureaucracy or formalities esp. in public business. **4 reddish** *a.* [OE]

red- see RE-¹.

redbreast *n.* robin. [RED]

redbrick *a.* (of university) founded relatively recently.

redcap *n.* member of military police.

redcoat *n. hist.* British soldier.

redcurrant *n.* small round red edible berry; shrub bearing it.

redden *v.* make or become red.

redeem /rɪˈdi:m/ *v.t.* recover by expenditure of effort or by stipulated payment; make single payment to cancel (regular charge or obligation); convert (tokens or bonds) into goods or cash; deliver from sin and damnation; make amends for, serve as compensating factor (*has one redeeming feature*); save *from* a defect; save *oneself* from blame; purchase freedom of (person), save (person's life) by ransom; save or rescue or reclaim; fulfil (promise). [F *redimer* or L (*emo* buy)]

redeemer *n.* one who redeems; **the Redeemer** Christ.

redemption /rɪˈdempʃ(ə)n/ *n.* redeeming or being redeemed; thing that redeems. [F f. L (REDEEM)]

redeploy /ri:dɪˈplɔɪ/ *v.t.* send (troops or workers etc.) to new place or task; **redeployment** *n.* [RE-²]

redhead *n.* person with red hair.

rediffusion /ri:dɪˈfju:ʒ(ə)n/ *n.* relaying of broadcast programmes esp. by wire from central receiver.

redo /ri:ˈdu:/ *v.t.* (*past* **redid**; *p.p.* **redone** /-ˈdʌn/) do again; redecorate.

redolent /ˈredələnt/ *a.* strongly smelling or suggestive or reminiscent *of*; fragrant; **redolence** *n.* [F or L (*oleo* smell)]

redouble /ri:ˈdʌb(ə)l/ **1** *v.* make or grow greater or more intense or numerous; double again a bid in bridge already doubled by opponent. **2** *n.* redoubling of a bid in bridge. [F (RE-¹)]

redoubt /rɪˈdaʊt/ *n.* outwork or fieldwork without flanking defences. [F *redoute* (REDUCE)]

redoubtable /rɪˈdaʊtəb(ə)l/ *a.* formidable, esp. as opponent. [F (DOUBT)]

redound /rɪˈdaʊnd/ *v.i.* make great contribution *to* one's credit or advantage etc.; come back or recoil *on* or *upon*. [F f. L (*unda* wave)]

redpoll *n.* bird with red forehead, similar to linnet. [RED]

redress /rɪˈdres/ **1** *v.t.* remedy or rectify (wrong or grievance etc.); readjust, set straight again. **2** *n.* reparation for wrong; redressing *of* grievance etc. **3 redress the balance** restore equality. [F (DRESS)]

redshank *n.* a large kind of sandpiper. [RED]

redskin *n.* Red Indian.

redstart *n.* small songbird with red tail. [RED, obs. *steort* tail]

reduce /rɪˈdju:s/ *v.* make or become smaller or less; bring by force or necessity *to* some state or action (*reduced him to despair*; *was reduced to borrowing*); convert to another (esp. simpler) form (*reduce to dust, to writing*); convert (fraction) *to* form with lowest terms; bring or simplify or adapt by classification or analysis *to* components etc. (*the dispute may be reduced to three issues*); subdue, bring back to obedience; make lower in status or rank; lessen one's weight or size; weaken (*is in a very reduced state*); impoverish (*reduced circumstances*); convert (oxide etc.) to metal; (in surgery) restore (dislocated etc. part) to proper position, remedy (dislocation etc.) thus; **reducible** *adv.* [L (*duco duct-* lead)]

reductio ad absurdum /rɪdʌktɪəʊ æd əb'sɜ:dəm/ *n.* proof of falsity by showing absurd logical consequence; carrying of principle to unpractical lengths. [L, = reduction to the absurd]

reduction /rɪ'dʌkʃ(ə)n/ *n.* reducing or being reduced; amount by which prices etc. are reduced; reduced copy of picture or musical score etc.; **reductive** *a.* [F or L (REDUCE)]

redundant /rɪ'dʌndənt/ *a.* superfluous; that can be omitted without loss of significance; (of worker) no longer needed for any available job and therefore liable to dismissal; **redundancy** *n.* [L (REDOUND)]

reduplicate /rɪ'dju:plɪkeɪt/ *v.t.* make double, repeat; repeat (word or syllable) exactly or with slight change (e.g. *hurly-burly*, *see-saw*); **reduplication** /-'keɪʃ(ə)n/ *n.*; **reduplicative** /-kətɪv/ *a.* [L (RE-²)]

redwing *n.* thrush with red flanks. [RED]

redwood *n.* very large N. American tree yielding reddish wood.

re-echo /ri:'ekəʊ/ *v.* echo repeatedly, resound. [RE-¹]

reed *n.* water or marsh plant with firm stem; tall straight stalk of this; vibrating part of some wind instruments; (usu. in *pl.*) such instrument; **reed-stop** reeded organ-stop. [OE]

reeded *a.* with vibrating reed.

reedy *a.* full of reeds; like reed; like reed-instrument in tone; **reediness** *n.*

reef¹ *n.* ridge of rock or sand etc. at or near surface of water; lode of ore, bedrock surrounding this. [LG or Du. f. ON]

reef² 1 *n.* one of several strips along top or bottom of sail that can be taken in or rolled up to reduce sail's surface in high wind. 2 *v.t.* take in reef(s) of (sail). 3 **reef-knot** double knot made symmetrically. [Du. f. ON]

reefer *n.* marijuana cigarette; thick double-breasted jacket.

reek 1 *v.i.* smell strongly or unpleasantly (*of*); have unpleasant or suspicious associations (*reeks of corruption*). 2 *n.* foul or stale smell; (esp. *Sc.*) smoke, vapour, visible exhalation. [OE]

reel 1 *n.* cylindrical device on which thread, silk, yarn, paper, film, wire, etc., are wound; quantity of thread etc. wound on a reel; device for winding and unwinding line as required, esp. in fishing; revolving part in various machines; lively folk or Scottish dance, music for this. 2 *v.* wind (thread, fishing-line, etc.) on reel; draw (fish etc.) *in* or *up* by use of reel; stand or walk or run unsteadily, be shaken physically or mentally, rock from side to side, or swing violently; dance a reel. 3 **reel off** say or recite very rapidly and without apparent effort. [OE]

re-entrant /ri:'entrənt/ *a.* (of angle) pointing inwards, reflex. [RE-²]

reeve¹ *n. hist.* chief magistrate of town or district. [OE]

reeve² *v.t.* (*past* **rove**) *Naut.* thread (rope or rod etc.) *through* ring or other aperture; fasten (rope or block etc.) thus. [prob. Du. *reven*]

reeve³ *n.* female ruff. [orig. unkn.]

ref *n. colloq.* referee in sports. [abbr.]

refectory /rɪ'fektərɪ, 'refɪk-/ *n.* room for meals, esp. in monastery or college; **refectory table** long narrow table. [L (*reficio* renew)]

refer /rɪ'fɜ:/ *v.* (-rr-) trace or ascribe *to* person or thing as cause or source, consider as belonging *to* certain date or place or class; send on or direct (person, question for decision), make appeal or have recourse, *to* some authority or source of information (*referred him, the problem, to his MP*; *for support I refer to Plato*); send (person) to medical specialist etc.; send proposal etc. *back to* lower body, court, etc.; (of person speaking) make allusion or direct attention *to*; interpret (statement) as being directed *to*; (of statement etc.) have relation *to*, be directed *to*; fail (candidate); **referred pain** pain felt in part of the body other than its true source; **referable** /also 'refərəb(ə)l/ *a.* [F f. L *refero relat-* carry back]

referee /refə'ri:/ 1 *n.* person to whom dispute is or may be referred for decision; umpire esp. in football or boxing; person willing to testify to character of applicant for employment etc. 2 *v.* act as referee (for).

reference /'refərəns/ *n.* referring of matter for decision or settlement or consideration to some authority; scope given to such authority; relation or respect or correspondence *to*; allusion *to*; direction to book etc. (or passage in it) where information may be found, book or passage so cited; act of looking up passage etc., or of referring to person etc. for information; written testimonial supporting applicant for employment etc., person giving this; **in** (or **with**) **reference to** regarding, as regards, about; **reference book** book for occasional consultation at particular points for particular information; **referential** /-'renʃ(ə)l/ *a.*

referendum /refə'rendəm/ *n.* (*pl.* **referendums**) referring of political question to electorate for direct decision by general vote. [L (REFER)]

referral /rɪ'fɜ:r(ə)l/ *n.* referring of person to medical specialist etc. [REFER]

refill 1 /ri:'fɪl/ *v.t.* fill again. **2** /'ri:fɪl/ *n.* new filling; material for this. [RE-²]

refine /rɪ'faɪn/ *v.* free from impurities or defects; make or become more polished or elegant or cultured. [RE-¹]

refined *a.* characterized by polish or elegance or subtlety.

refinement *n.* refining or being refined; fineness of feeling or taste; polish or elegance in behaviour or manner; instance of added development or improvement (*new car has many refinements*); piece of subtle reasoning, fine distinction.

refiner *n.* one who refines, esp. one whose business is to refine crude oil or sugar or metal etc.

refinery *n.* place where oil etc. is refined.

refit 1 /ri:'fɪt/ *v.* (-**tt**-) make or become fit again (esp. of ship undergoing renewal and repairs). **2** /'ri:fɪt/ *n.* refitting. [RE-²]

reflate /ri:'fleɪt/ *v.t.* cause reflation of (currency or economy etc.). [RE-², after DEFLATE, INFLATE]

reflation /ri:'fleɪʃ(ə)n/ *n.* inflation of financial system to restore previous condition after deflation; **reflationary** *a.* [RE-², after DEFLATION, INFLATION]

reflect /rɪ'flekt/ *v.* (of surface or body) throw back (heat or light or sound); (of mirror etc.) show image of, reproduce to eye or mind, correspond in appearance or effect to; (of action, result, etc.) show or bring (credit etc.) *on* person or method responsible, *absol.* bring discredit *on* person etc. responsible; go back in thought, meditate, or consult with oneself (*on* or *upon*, or *absol.*), remind oneself or consider (*that, how*, etc.). [F or L (*flecto flex-* bend)]

reflection /rɪ'flekʃ(ə)n/ *n.* (also **reflexion**) reflecting or being reflected; reflected light or heat or colour or image; discredit or thing bringing discredit; reconsideration (*on reflection*); idea arising in the mind, comment (*on* or *upon*). [F or L (prec.)]

reflective *a.* (of surface etc.) giving back reflection or image; (of mental faculties) concerned in reflection or thought, (of person or mood etc.) thoughtful, given to meditation. [REFLECT]

reflector *n.* piece of glass or metal etc. for reflecting light in required direction, e.g. red one on back of motor vehicle; telescope etc. using mirror to produce images, the mirror itself.

reflex /'ri:fleks/ **1** *a.* (of action) independent of the will, as automatic response to nerve-stimulation (e.g. sneeze); (of angle) exceeding 180°. **2** *n.* reflex action; sign or secondary manifestation (*law is a reflex of public opinion*); reflected light or image. **3 reflex camera** camera in which image is reflected by mirror to allow focusing up to moment of exposure. [L (REFLECT)]

reflexive /rɪ'fleksɪv/ *Gram.* **1** *a.* (of word or form) implying subject's action on himself or itself. **2** *n.* reflexive word or form, esp. pronoun (e.g. *myself*).

reform /rɪ'fɔ:m/ **1** *v.* make or become better by removal of faults or errors; abolish or cure (abuse or malpractice). **2** *n.* removal of faults or abuses, esp. of moral or political or social kind; improvement made or suggested. **3 Reformed Church** Protestant (esp. Calvinist) Church. [F or L (RE-²)]

reformation /refə'meɪʃ(ə)n/ *n.* reforming or being reformed, esp. radical change for the better in political or religious or social affairs; **the Reformation** 16th-c. movement for reform of abuses in Roman Church ending in establishment of Reformed or Protestant Churches.

reformative /rɪ'fɔ:mətɪv/ *a.* tending or intended to produce reform. [F or med.L (REFORM)]

reformatory /rɪ'fɔ:mətərɪ/ **1** *a.* reformative. **2** *n. US & hist.* institution to which young offenders are sent to be reformed. [REFORMATION]

reformer *n.* one who advocates or brings about (esp. political or social) reform.

refract /rɪ'frækt/ *v.t.* (of water or air or glass etc.) deflect (ray of light etc.) at certain angle when it enters obliquely from another medium of different density; **refraction** *n.*; **refractive** *a.* [L *refringo -fract-* break open]

refractor *n.* refracting medium or lens; telescope using lens to produce image.

refractory /rɪ'fræktərɪ/ *a.* stubborn, unmanageable, rebellious; (of disease or wound etc.) not yielding to treatment; (of substance) hard to fuse or work. [L (REFRACT)]

refrain¹ /rɪ'freɪn/ *v.i.* abstain or keep

oneself (*from* thing or action). [F f. L (*frenum* bridle)]

refrain[2] /rɪ'freɪn/ *n*. recurring phrase or lines esp. at end of stanzas; music accompanying this. [F f. L (REFRACT)]

refrangible /rɪ'frændʒɪb(ə)l/ *a*. that can be refracted. [L (REFRACT)]

refresh /rɪ'freʃ/ *v.t.* give fresh spirit or vigour to; revive (memory, esp. by consulting source of information). [F (FRESH)]

refresher *n*. extra fee to counsel in prolonged lawsuit; *colloq*. a drink; **refresher course** course reviewing previous studies, or giving instruction in modern methods etc.

refreshment *n*. refreshing or being refreshed in mind or body; thing (esp., usu. in *pl*., food or drink) that refreshes.

refrigerant /rɪ'frɪdʒərənt/ **1** *n*. substance used for refrigeration. **2** *a*. refrigerating. [F or L (foll.)]

refrigerate /rɪ'frɪdʒəreɪt/ *v*. make or become cool or cold; subject (food etc.) to cold in order to freeze or preserve; **refrigeration** /-'reɪʃ(ə)n/ *n*. [L *refrigero* (*frigus* cold)]

refrigerator *n*. cabinet or room in which food etc. is refrigerated.

reft see REAVE.

refuel /ri:'fju:əl/ *v*. (**-ll-**, *US* **-l-**) replenish fuel supply (of). [RE-[2]]

refuge /'refju:dʒ/ *n*. shelter from pursuit or danger or trouble; person or place etc. offering this. [F f. L *refugium* (*fugio* flee)]

refugee /refjʊ'dʒi:/ *n*. person taking refuge, esp. in foreign country from war or persecution or natural disaster. [F *réfugié* (prec.)]

refulgent /rɪ'fʌldʒənt/ *a*. shining, gloriously bright; **refulgence** *n*. [L *refulgeo* shine brightly]

refund 1 /ri:'fʌnd/ *v*. pay back (money or expenses); reimburse (person); make repayment. **2** /'ri:fʌnd/ *n*. refunding, repayment. [F or L (*fundo* pour)]

refurbish /ri:'fɜ:bɪʃ/ *v.t.* brighten up, redecorate. [RE-[2]]

refusal /rɪ'fju:z(ə)l/ *n*. refusing or being refused; right or privilege of deciding to take or leave a thing before it is offered to others (*first refusal*). [foll.]

refuse[1] /rɪ'fju:z/ *v*. withhold acceptance of or consent to (*refuse offer*, *orders*); indicate unwillingness (*to do* thing or *absol*.: *I refuse to go*; *I refuse*; *car refuses to start*); not grant request made by (person); (of horse) be unwilling to jump (fence etc., or *absol*.). [F, prob. f. L (RECUSANT)]

refuse[2] /'refju:s/ *n*. what is rejected as worthless, waste. [F (as prec.)]

refute /rɪ'fju:t/ *v.t.* prove falsity or error of (statement etc. or person advancing it); rebut by argument; **refutation** /refju:'teɪʃ(ə)n/ *n*. [L *refuto*]

regain /rɪ'geɪn/ *v.t.* obtain possession or use of after loss (*regain consciousness*, *one's balance*, *one's feet*); reach (place) again. [F (RE-[2])]

regal /'ri:g(ə)l/ *a*. of or by a king or kings; fit for a king, magnificent; **regality** /rɪ'gælɪtɪ/ *n*.; **regally** *adv*. [F or L (*rex reg-* king)]

regale /rɪ'geɪl/ *v.t.* entertain lavishly with feasting; entertain *with* talk etc.; (of beauty, flowers, etc.) give delight to. [F *regaler* (GALLANT)]

regalia /rɪ'geɪljə/ *n.pl.* insignia of royalty used at coronations; insignia of an order or of civic dignity. [med.L (REGAL)]

regard /rɪ'gɑ:d/ **1** *v.t.* gaze on steadily (usu. in specified way: *regarded her intently*); give heed to, take into account; look upon or contemplate mentally in specified way (*I regard him kindly*, *regard it as an imposition*). **2** *n*. gaze, steady or significant look; attention or care (*to* or *for*); esteem or kindly feeling or respectful opinion (*for*); respect, point attended to; (in *pl*.) expression of friendliness in letter etc., compliments. **3 as regards** about, concerning, in respect of; **in** (or **with**) **regard to** regarding, in respect of. [F *regard*(*er*) (GUARD)]

regardful *a*. mindful *of*.

regarding *prep*. about, concerning, in respect of.

regardless 1 *a*. without regard or consideration (*of*). **2** *adv*. without paying attention.

regatta /rɪ'gætə/ *n*. meeting for boat or yacht races. [It.]

regency /'ri:dʒənsɪ/ *n*. office of regent; commission acting as regent; regent's or regency commission's period of office; **the Regency** (in Britain) 1810–20. [med.L *regentia* (REGENT)]

regenerate 1 /rɪ'dʒenəreɪt/ *v*. generate again, bring or come into renewed existence; improve moral condition of, breathe new and more vigorous and spiritually higher life into (person or institution etc.); invest with new and higher spiritual nature. **2** /rɪ'dʒenərət/ *a*. spiritually born again, reformed. **3 regeneration** /-'reɪʃ(ə)n/ *n*.; **regenerative** *a*. [L (RE-[2])]

regent /'ri:dʒənt/ **1** *n*. person appointed to administer State during minority or absence or incapacity of monarch. **2** *a*. (placed after noun) acting as regent (*Prince Regent*). [F or L (*rego* rule)]

reggae /'regeɪ/ *n*. W. Indian style of music with strongly accented subsidiary beat. [orig. unkn.]

regicide /'redʒɪsaɪd/ *n.* one who kills or takes part in killing a king; killing of a king; **regicidal** /-'saɪd(ə)l/ *a.* [L (*rex reg-* king, -CIDE)]

regime /reɪ'ʒi:m/ *n.* method or system of government; prevailing order or system of things. [F (foll.)]

regimen /'redʒɪmen/ *n.* prescribed course of exercise, way of life, and esp. diet. [L (*rego* rule)]

regiment /'redʒɪmənt/ **1** *n.* permanent unit of army usu. commanded by Colonel and divided into several companies or troops or batteries; operational unit of artillery etc.; large array or number (usu. *of*). **2** /also -ment/ *v.t.* organize (esp. oppressively) in groups or according to a system; form into a regiment or regiments. **3 regimentation** /-'teɪʃ(ə)n/ *n.* [F f. L (prec.)]

regimental /redʒɪ'ment(ə)l/ **1** *a.* of a regiment. **2** *n.* (in *pl.*) military uniform, esp. of a particular regiment. **3 regimentally** *adv.*

Regina /rɪ'dʒaɪnə/ *n.* reigning queen (in titles of lawsuits, e.g. ***Regina* v. Jones** the Crown versus Jones). [L, = queen (REX)]

region /'ri:dʒ(ə)n/ *n.* area of land, or division of the earth's surface, having definable boundaries or characteristics (*region between Elbe and Rhine*; *a fertile region*); administrative district esp. in Scotland; part of the body (*the lumbar region*); sphere or realm *of* (*you are getting into the region of metaphysics*); **in the region of** approximately; **regional** *a.*; **regionally** *adv.* [F f. L (*rego* rule)]

register /'redʒɪstə/ **1** *n.* official list e.g. of births, marriages, and deaths, of shipping, of professionally qualified persons, of qualified voters in constituency; book in which items are recorded for reference; device recording speed, force, etc.; adjustable plate for widening or narrowing an opening and regulating draught, esp. in fire-grate; compass of voice or instrument, part of voice-compass; set of organ-pipes, sliding device controlling this; = *cash register*. **2** *v.* set down (name, fact, etc.) formally, record in writing; enter or cause to be entered in particular register; entrust (letter etc.) to post office for transmission by registered post; put one's name on electoral etc. register, or as guest in register kept by hotel etc.; (of instrument) record automatically, indicate; make mental note of; express (emotion) facially or by gesture; make impression on person's mind (*name did not register with me*). **3 registered nurse** nurse with State certificate of competence; **registered post** procedure with special precautions for safety and for compensation in case of loss; **register office** place where civil marriages are conducted. [F or L (*regero -gest-* transcribe, record)]

registrar /redʒɪ'strɑ:/ *n.* person charged with keeping register (esp. in university); doctor undergoing hospital training as specialist. [med.L (prec.)]

registration /redʒɪ'streɪʃ(ə)n/ *n.* registering or being registered; **registration mark** (or **number**) combination of letters and figures identifying motor vehicle. [F or med.L (REGISTER)]

registry /'redʒɪstrɪ/ *n.* place or office where registers or records are kept; **registry office** = *register office*. [med.L (REGISTER)]

Regius professor /'ri:dʒɪəs/ holder of chair founded by sovereign (esp. one at Oxford or Cambridge instituted by Henry VIII) or filled by Crown appointment. [L *regius* royal (REX)]

regress 1 /rɪ'gres/ *v.i.* move backwards; go back to earlier state. **2** /'ri:gres/ *n.* going back; relapse, backward tendency. [L *regredior -gress-* go back]

regression /rɪ'greʃ(ə)n/ *n.* backward movement; relapse, reversion; return to earlier stage of development; **regressive** *a.*

regret /rɪ'gret/ **1** *v.t.* (**-tt-**) feel or express sorrow or repentance or distress over (action or loss etc.); say with sorrow or remorse (*I regret to say she is dead*; *I regret that I killed her*). **2** *n.* feeling of sorrow or repentance etc. over action or loss etc. **3 give** (or **send** etc.) **one's regrets** decline invitation. [F *regretter*]

regretful *a.* feeling or showing regret; **regretfully** *adv.*

regrettable *a.* (of events or conduct) undesirable, unwelcome, deserving censure; **regrettably** *adv.*

regular /'regjʊlə/ **1** *a.* conforming to a rule or principle, systematic, harmonious, symmetrical; acting or done or recurring uniformly or calculably in time or manner, habitual, constant, orderly; conforming to a standard of etiquette or procedure; properly constituted or qualified, devoted exclusively or primarily to its nominal function (*regular army, soldier*); *Gram.* (of noun, verb, etc.) following normal type of inflexion; *colloq.* thorough, indubitable (*a regular hero*); bound by religious rule, belonging to religious or monastic order. **2** *n.* regular soldier; *colloq.* regular customer, visitor, etc.; one of the regular clergy. **3 regularity** /-'lærɪtɪ/ *n.*; **regularize** *v.t.* [F f. L (*regula* rule)]

regulate /'regjʊleɪt/ *v.t.* control by rule; subject to restrictions; adapt to requirements; alter speed of (machine or clock) so that it may work accurately; **regulator** *n.* [L (prec.)]

regulation /regjʊ'leɪʃ(ə)n/ **1** *n.* regulating or being regulated; prescribed rule. **2** *a.* in accordance with regulations, of correct type etc.; usual.

regurgitate /ri:'gɜ:dʒɪteɪt/ *v.t.* bring (swallowed food) up again to the mouth; cast or pour out again; **regurgitation** /-'teɪʃ(ə)n/ *n.* [med.L (*gurges -git-* whirlpool)]

rehabilitate /ri:hə'bɪlɪteɪt/ *v.t.* restore to effectiveness or normal life by training, esp. after imprisonment or illness; restore to privileges or reputation or proper condition; **rehabilitation** /-'teɪʃ(ə)n/ *n.* [med.L (RE-², ABILITY)]

rehash 1 /ri:'hæʃ/ *v.t.* put (old material) into new form without significant change or improvement. **2** /'ri:hæʃ/ *n.* rehashing; material rehashed. [RE-²]

rehearsal /rɪ'hɜ:s(ə)l/ *n.* rehearsing; trial performance or practice. [foll.]

rehearse /rɪ'hɜ:s/ *v.* practise (play etc. or part in it) for later public performance; hold rehearsal; train (person) by rehearsal; recite or say over; give list of, enumerate. [AF (HEARSE)]

Reich /raɪk, raɪx/ *n.* the former German State, esp. (**Third Reich**) the Nazi regime of 1933–45. [G, = empire]

reign /reɪn/ **1** *n.* sovereignty, rule; period during which sovereign reigns. **2** *v.i.* be king or queen; prevail (*silence reigns*). [F f. L *regnum* (REX)]

reimburse /ri:ɪm'bɜ:s/ *v.t.* repay (person who has expended money, person's expenses); **reimbursement** *n.* [RE-², *imburse* (PURSE)]

rein /reɪn/ **1** *n.* (in *sing.* or *pl.*) long narrow strap with each end attached to bit used to guide or check horse etc. in riding or driving; similar device to restrain child etc.; means of control. **2** *v.t.* check or manage with reins; pull *up* or *back* with reins, hold *in* (as) with reins; govern, restrain, control. **3 give free rein to** let (one's imagination etc.) have free scope; **keep a tight rein on** allow little freedom to. [F *rene* f. L (RETAIN)]

reincarnation /ri:ɪnkɑ:'neɪʃ(ə)n/ *n.* rebirth of soul in new body; **reincarnate** /-ɪn'kɑ:nɪt/ *a.* [RE-²]

reindeer /'reɪndɪə/ *n.* (*pl.* usu. same) subarctic deer with large antlers. [ON]

reinforce /ri:ɪn'fɔ:s/ *v.t.* strengthen or support, esp. by additional men or material or by increase of numbers or quantity or size etc.; **reinforced concrete** concrete with metal bars or wire etc. embedded to increase its strength. [F *renforcer*]

reinforcement *n.* reinforcing or being reinforced; thing that reinforces, (in *pl.*) reinforcing personnel or equipment etc.

reinstate /ri:ɪn'steɪt/ *v.t.* restore to or replace in lost position or privileges etc.; **reinstatement** *n.* [RE-², IN-¹]

reinsure /ri:ɪn'ʃʊə/ *v.* insure again (esp. of insurer securing himself by transferring risk to another insurer); **reinsurance** *n.* [RE-²]

reiterate /ri:'ɪtəreɪt/ *v.t.* say or do again or repeatedly; **reiteration** /-'reɪʃ(ə)n/ *n.* [L (ITERATE)]

reject 1 /rɪ'dʒekt/ *v.t.* refuse to accept or believe in; put aside or send back as not to be used or done or complied with etc. **2** /'ri:dʒekt/ *n.* person or thing rejected. **3 rejection** /rɪ'dʒekʃ(ə)n/ *n.* [L *reicio -ject-* throw back]

rejig /ri:'dʒɪg/ *v.t.* (**-gg-**) re-equip (factory etc.) for new kind of work. [RE-²]

rejoice /rɪ'dʒɔɪs/ *v.* feel great joy; be glad; take delight *in* or *at*; cause joy to (*will rejoice your heart*). [F *rejoir* (JOY)]

rejoin¹ /ri:'dʒɔɪn/ *v.* join together again, reunite; join (companion etc.) again. [RE-²]

rejoin² /rɪ'dʒɔɪn/ *v.* say in answer, retort; reply to charge or pleading in lawsuit. [F *rejoindre* (JOIN)]

rejoinder /rɪ'dʒɔɪndə/ *n.* what is said in reply or rejoined, retort. [AF (prec.)]

rejuvenate /rɪ'dʒu:vəneɪt/ *v.t.* make (as if) young again; **rejuvenation** /-'neɪʃ(ə)n/ *n.*; **rejuvenator** *n.* [L *juvenis* young]

relapse /rɪ'læps/ **1** *v.i.* fall back or sink again (*into* worse state after improvement). **2** *n.* act or fact of relapsing, esp. deterioration in patient's condition after partial recovery. [L (*labor laps-* slip)]

relate /rɪ'leɪt/ *v.* narrate or recount; bring into relation (*to* or *with*, or *absol.*); have reference *to*; bring oneself into relation *to*. [L (REFER)]

related *a.* connected, esp. by blood or marriage.

relation /rɪ'leɪʃ(ə)n/ *n.* what one person or thing has to do with another, way in which one stands or is related to another, kind of connection or correspondence or contrast or feeling that prevails between persons or things; (in *pl.*) dealings *with* others, sexual intercourse; relative, kinsman or kinswoman; = RELATIONSHIP; narration, a narrative; **in relation to** as regards. [F or L (REFER)]

relationship *n.* state of being related; condition or character due to being related; kinship (*lit.* or *fig.*).

relative /'relətɪv/ **1** *a.* considered in relation to something else (*relative density*); proportioned *to* something else (*supply is relative to demand*); implying comparison ('*heat*' *is a relative word*); comparative (*their relative merits*); having mutual relations, corresponding in some way, related to each other; having reference or relating *to* (*the facts relative to the issue*); *Gram.* (of word) referring to expressed or implied antecedent and attaching a subordinate clause to it, (of clause) attached to antecedent by relative word. **2** *n.* person connected by blood or marriage; species related to another by common origin; *Gram.* relative word, esp. pronoun. [F f. L (REFER)]

relativity /relə'tɪvɪtɪ/ *n.* being relative; theory based on the principle that all motion is relative and that light has constant velocity (also **special relativity**), theory extending this to gravitation and accelerated motion (**general relativity**).

relax /rɪ'læks/ *v.* make or become less stiff or rigid or tense; make or become less formal or strict (*rules will be relaxed*); reduce or abate (one's attention or efforts etc.); cease work or effort. [L *relaxo* (LAX)]

relaxation /ri:læk'seɪʃ(ə)n/ *n.* relaxing or being relaxed; recreation, amusements. [L (prec.)]

relay /'ri:leɪ/ **1** *n.* fresh set of people or horses substituted for tired ones; supply of material similarly used; relay race; device activating electric circuit; relayed message or transmission. **2** *v.t.* /also ri:'leɪ/ receive (message, broadcast, etc.) and transmit to others. **3 relay race** race between teams of which each member in turn covers part of the distance. [F *relai* f. L (RELAX)]

release /rɪ'li:s/ **1** *v.t.* set free, liberate, unfasten; allow to move from fixed position; make (information or recording etc.) public; issue (film etc.) for general exhibition. **2** *n.* liberation from restriction or duty or difficulty etc.; handle or catch etc. that releases part of machine etc.; document etc. made available for publication (*press release*); film or record etc., that is released; releasing of document or film etc. thus. [F *relesser* f. L (RELAX)]

relegate /'relɪgeɪt/ *v.t.* consign or dismiss to inferior position; transfer (sports team) to lower division of league etc.; banish; **relegation** /-'geɪʃ(ə)n/ *n.* [L *relego* send away]

relent /rɪ'lent/ *v.i.* relax severity, abandon harsh intention, yield to compassion. [med.L (*lentus* flexible)]

relentless *a.* unrelenting.

relevant /'relɪvənt/ *a.* bearing on or having reference *to* the matter in hand; **relevance** *n.* [L *relevo* (RELIEVE)]

reliable /rɪ'laɪəb(ə)l/ *a.* that may be relied on; **reliability** /-'bɪlɪtɪ/ *n.*; **reliably** *adv.* [RELY]

reliance /rɪ'laɪəns/ *n.* trust, confidence (*have* or *place reliance on* or *in*); **reliant** *a.*

relic /'relɪk/ *n.* surviving custom or belief etc. from a past age; object interesting because of age or associations; part of holy person's body or belongings kept after his death as object of reverence; memento, souvenir; (in *pl.*) what has survived destruction or wasting or use; (in *pl.*) dead body or remains of person. [F *relique* f. L *reliquiae* remains (RELINQUISH)]

relict /'relɪkt/ *n.* object surviving in primitive form. [F *relicte* (prec.)]

relief /rɪ'li:f/ *n.* alleviation of or deliverance from pain, distress, anxiety, etc.; feature etc. that diversifies monotony or relaxes tension; assistance given to persons in special danger or need or difficulty; replacing of person(s) on duty by another or others, person(s) thus bringing relief; thing supplementing another in some service (*relief bus*); method of moulding or carving or stamping in which design stands out from surface; piece of sculpture etc. in relief; representation of relief given by arrangement of line or colour or shading; reinforcement (esp. raising of siege) *of* besieged place; (esp. *Law*) redress of hardship or grievance; **relief map** map showing hills and valleys by shading or colouring etc. rather than by contour lines alone; **relief road** road by which traffic can avoid congested area. [F & It. (as foll.)]

relieve /rɪ'li:v/ *v.t.* bring or give or be relief to; mitigate tedium or monotony of; release (person) from duty by taking his place or providing a substitute; **relieve one's feelings** use strong language or vigorous behaviour when annoyed; **relieve oneself** urinate or defecate; **relieve a person of** take (burden or responsibility etc.) from him. [F f. L *relevo* raise again, alleviate]

relievo /rɪ'li:vəʊ/ *n.* (*pl.* **relievos**) relief in sculpture etc. [It. *rilievo* (RELIEF)]

religion /rɪ'lɪdʒ(ə)n/ *n.* belief in superhuman controlling power, esp. in a personal God or gods entitled to obedience and worship; expression of this in worship; particular system of faith and worship; thing that one is devoted to; life under monastic vows (*her name in religion is Sister Mary*). [F f. L *religio* bond]

religious /rɪ'lɪdʒəs/ **1** *a.* imbued with religion, pious, devout; of or concerned with religion; of or belonging to a monastic order; scrupulous, conscientious. **2** *n.* (*pl.* same) person bound by monastic vows. [F f. L *religiosus* (prec.)]

relinquish /rɪ'lɪŋkwɪʃ/ *v.t.* give up or cease from (habit or plan or belief etc.); resign or surrender (right or possession); relax hold of; **relinquishment** *n.* [F f. L *relinquo -lict-* leave behind]

reliquary /'relɪkwərɪ/ *n.* receptacle for relics. [F *reliquaire* (RELIC)]

relish /'relɪʃ/ **1** *n.* great liking or enjoyment (*for*); appetizing flavour, attractive quality; thing eaten with plainer food to add flavour; distinctive taste or tinge *of*. **2** *v.* get pleasure out of, enjoy greatly. [F *reles* remainder (RELEASE)]

relive /ri:'lɪv/ *v.t.* live (experience etc.) over again, esp. in imagination. [RE-[2]]

relocate /ri:ləʊ'keɪt/ *v.* locate in or move to a new place; **relocation** /-'keɪʃ(ə)n/ *n.*

reluctant /rɪ'lʌktənt/ *a.* unwilling or disinclined (*to do* thing); **reluctance** *n.* [L (*luctor* struggle)]

rely /rɪ'laɪ/ *v.i.* depend with confidence or assurance *on* or *upon*. [F f. L *religo* bind closely]

remain /rɪ'meɪn/ *v.i.* be left over after other parts have been removed or used or dealt with; be in same place or condition during further time (*will remain at home until Friday*), continue to be (*remained loyal*). [F f. L *remaneo*]

remainder /rɪ'meɪndə/ **1** *n.* residue, remaining persons or things; number left after subtraction or division; copies of book left unsold when demand has almost ceased. **2** *v.t.* dispose of (remainder of books) at reduced price. [AF (prec.)]

remains *n.pl.* what remains after other parts have been removed or used etc.; relics of antiquity, esp. of buildings; dead body. [F, & REMAIN]

remand /rɪ'mɑ:nd/ **1** *v.t.* send back (prisoner) into custody to allow further inquiry. **2** *n.* recommittal to custody. **3 on remand** in state of being remanded; **remand centre** (or **home**) institution to which young people are remanded. [L *remando*]

remark /rɪ'mɑ:k/ **1** *v.* say by way of comment; make comment *on* or *upon*; take notice of, regard with attention. **2** *n.* written or spoken comment, anything said; noticing (*worthy of remark*). [F *remarquer* (MARK[1])]

remarkable *a.* worth notice, exceptional, striking; **remarkably** *adv.* [F *remarquable* (prec.)]

REME *abbr.* Royal Electrical and Mechanical Engineers.

remedial /rɪ'mi:dɪəl/ *a.* affording or intended as a remedy; (of teaching) for slow or backward children; **remedially** *adv.* [L (foll.)]

remedy /'remɪdɪ/ **1** *n.* medicine or treatment *for* or *against* disease; means of counteracting or removing anything undesirable; redress, legal or other reparation. **2** *v.t.* rectify, make good. **3 remediable** /rɪ'mi:dɪəb(ə)l/ *a.* [AF f. L *remedium* (*medeor* heal)]

remember /rɪ'membə/ *v.t.* keep in the memory, not forget; bring back into one's thoughts (knowledge or experience etc., or *absol.*); think of (person) in some connection, esp. in making gift etc.; convey greetings from (*remember me to your mother*). [F f. L (MEMORY)]

remembrance /rɪ'membrəns/ *n.* remembering or being remembered; keepsake, souvenir; (in *pl.*) greetings conveyed through third person; **Remembrance Sunday** Sunday nearest 11 Nov., when those who were killed in the wars of 1914–18 and 1939–45 are commemorated. [F (prec.)]

remind /rɪ'maɪnd/ *v.t.* cause (person) to remember or think *of*. [RE-[2]]

reminder *n.* thing that reminds or is memento (*of*).

reminisce /remɪ'nɪs/ *v.i.* indulge in reminiscence. [foll.]

reminiscence *n.* remembering of things past; (in *pl.*) account of facts and incidents remembered, esp. in literary form. [L (*reminiscor* remember)]

reminiscent *a.* reminding or suggestive *of*; concerned with reminiscence.

remiss /rɪ'mɪs/ *a.* careless of duty, lax, negligent. [L (REMIT)]

remission /rɪ'mɪʃ(ə)n/ *n.* shortening of prison sentence on account of good behaviour; remitting of debt or penalty etc.; diminution of force or effect or degree (esp. of disease or pain); forgiveness (*of* sins etc.). [F or L (foll.)]

remit /rɪ'mɪt/ **1** *v.* (**-tt-**) cancel or refrain from exacting or inflicting (debt or punishment etc.); abate or slacken, cease partly or entirely; send (money etc.) in payment; refer (matter for decision etc.) *to* some authority; send back (case) to lower court; postpone or defer; pardon (sins etc.). **2** /also 'ri:mɪt/ *n.* item remitted for consideration; terms of reference of committee etc. [L *remitto -miss-*]

remittance *n.* money sent to person; sending of money.

remittent *a.* that abates at intervals.

remnant /'remnənt/ *n.* small remaining quantity; piece of cloth etc. left when greater part has been used or sold. [F (REMAIN)]

remold *US* var. of REMOULD.

remonstrate /'remənstreɪt/ *v.* make

protest (*with* person); **remonstrance** /rɪ'mɒnstrəns/ *n.*; **remonstration** /'streɪʃ(ə)n/ *n.* [med.L (*monstro* show)]

remorse /rɪ'mɔ:s/ *n.* deep regret for wrong committed; compunction, compassionate reluctance to inflict pain (esp. *without remorse*). [F f. med.L (*mordeo mors-* bite)]

remorseful *a.* filled with repentance; **remorsefully** *adv.*

remorseless *a.* without compassion.

remote /rɪ'məʊt/ *a.* far apart, far away in place or time; out-of-the-way, secluded; not closely related (*a remote ancestor*); slight, faint (*haven't the remotest idea*); aloof, not friendly; **remote control** control of apparatus etc. from a distance by means of electrically operated device, radio, etc. [L *remotus* (REMOVE)]

remould 1 /ri:'məʊld/ *v.t.* mould again, refashion; reconstruct tread of (tyre). **2** /'ri:məʊld/ *n.* remoulded tyre. [RE-²]

removal /rɪ'mu:v(ə)l/ *n.* act of removing or being removed; transfer of furniture etc. to different house. [foll.]

remove /rɪ'mu:v/ **1** *v.* take off or away from place occupied, convey to another place, change situation of; get rid of, dismiss; (in *p.p.*) distant or remote *from* (*the country was not far removed from anarchy*). **2** *n.* distance, degree of remoteness; stage in gradation, degree; a form or division in some schools. **3** **cousin once, twice,** etc., **removed** a cousin's child or parent, grandchild or grandparent, etc. [F f. L *removeo -mot-*]

remunerate /rɪ'mju:nəreɪt/ *v.t.* reward, pay for service rendered; serve as or provide recompense for (toil etc.) or to (person); **remuneration** /-'reɪʃ(ə)n/ *n.*; **remunerative** *a.* [L (*munus -ner-* gift)]

Renaissance /rɪ'neɪsəns, -sɑ̃s/ *n.* revival of art and letters in 14th–16th cc.; period of this; style of art and architecture developed by it; (**renaissance**) any similar revival. [F (*naissance* birth)]

renal /'ri:n(ə)l/ *a.* of the kidneys. [F f. L (*renes* kidneys)]

renascent /rɪ'næsənt/ *a.* springing up anew, being reborn; **renascence** *n.* [L (*renascor* be born again)]

rend *v.* (*past* and *p.p.* **rent**) *archaic* tear or wrench forcibly. [OE]

render *v.t.* cause to be or become (*rendered us helpless*); give or pay (money, service, etc.) esp. in return or as thing due; give (assistance); submit or send in; represent or portray, act (role), perform (music); translate; melt down (fat); cover (stone or brick) with first coat of plaster. [F f. Rmc (L *reddo* give back)]

rendezvous /'rɒndeɪvu:/ **1** *n.* (*pl.* same /-u:z/) agreed or regular meeting-place; meeting by agreement. **2** *v.i.* (3 *sing. pres.* **rendezvouses**/-u:z/, *past* **rendezvoused** /-u:d/, *partic.* **rendezvousing** /-u:ɪŋ/) meet at rendezvous. [F, = present yourselves]

rendition /ren'dɪʃ(ə)n/ *n.* rendering or interpretation of dramatic role, musical piece, etc. [F (RENDER)]

renegade /'renɪgeɪd/ *n.* one who deserts party or principles. [Sp. f. med.L (foll.)]

renege /rɪ'ni:g/ *v.* deny or renounce; **renege on** fail to keep (promise etc.), disappoint (person). [med.L (*nego* deny)]

renew /rɪ'nju:/ *v.t.* revive, make new again, restore to original state; reinforce or resupply or replace; repeat or re-establish (*renewed our acquaintance*); continue or resume after interruption (*renewed his efforts*); grant or be granted continuation of (licence, subscription, lease, etc.); recover (strength etc.); **renewal** *n.* [RE-²]

rennet /'renɪt/ *n.* curdled milk found in stomach of unweaned calf, or preparation of stomach-membrane or of plant, used in curdling milk for cheese or junket. [prob. OE (RUN)]

renounce /rɪ'naʊns/ *v.* consent formally to abandon (claim or right etc.); repudiate, refuse to recognize any longer; decline further association or disclaim relationship with. [F f. L (*nuntio* announce)]

renovate /'renəveɪt/ *v.t.* restore to good condition, repair; **renovation** /-'veɪʃ(ə)n/ *n.*; **renovator** *n.* [L (*novus* new)]

renown /rɪ'naʊn/ *n.* fame, high distinction. [F f. *renomer* f. L (NOMINATE)]

renowned *a.* famous, celebrated.

rent¹ 1 *n.* tenant's periodical payment to owner or landlord for use of land or premises; payment for use of equipment etc. **2** *v.* take or occupy or use at a rent (*from*); let or hire (*out*) for rent (*to*); be let *at* specified rent. [F f. Rmc (RENDER)]

rent² *n.* large tear in garment etc.; opening in clouds etc. [REND]

rent³ *past* and *p.p.* of REND.

rental /'rent(ə)l/ *n.* amount paid or received as rent; act of renting; income from rents. [AF or AL (RENT¹)]

rentier /'rɑ̃tɪeɪ/ *n.* person living on income from property or investments. [F]

renunciation /rɪnʌnsɪ'eɪʃ(ə)n/ *n.* renouncing; self-denial, giving up of what is wanted. [F or L (RENOUNCE)]

reorder /ri:'ɔ:də/ *v.t.* order again; put into new order. [RE-²]

reorganize /ri:'ɔ:gənaɪz/ *v.t.* organize in new way; **reorganization** /-'zeɪʃ(ə)n/ *n.*

rep¹ *n.* textile fabric with corded surface used in curtains and upholstery. [F *reps*]

rep[2] *n. colloq.* representative, esp. commercial traveller. [abbr.]
rep[3] *n. colloq.* repertory theatre or company. [abbr.]
repair[1] /rɪ'peə/ **1** *v.t.* restore to good condition after damage or wear; set right or make amends for (loss or wrong etc.). **2** *n.* restoring to sound condition (*house needs repair*); act or result of doing this (*repairs done while you wait*; *the repair is visible*); good or relative condition for working or using (*in repair*; *in bad repair*). [F f. L (*paro* make ready)]
repair[2] /rɪ'peə/ *v.i.* go or resort or have recourse *to*. [F f. L (REPATRIATE)]
reparable /'repərəb(ə)l/ *a.* (of loss etc.) that can be made good. [F f. L (REPAIR[1])]
reparation /repə'reɪʃ(ə)n/ *n.* making of amends, compensation.
repartee /repɑ:'ti:/ *n.* witty retort; making of witty retorts. [F *repartie* f. *repartir* reply promptly (PART)]
repast /rɪ'pɑ:st/ *n.* meal; food and drink for meal. [F f. L *repasco -past-* feed]
repatriate 1 /ri:'pætrɪeɪt/ *v.*• return (person) or be returned to native land. **2** /ri:'pætrɪət/ *n.* repatriated person. **3** **repatriation** /-'eɪʃ(ə)n/ *n.* [L *repatrio* go back home (*patria* native land)]
repay /ri:'peɪ/ *v.* (*past* and *p.p.* **repaid**) pay back (money); pay back money to (person); give in return or recompense; make recompense for (service etc.); requite (action); **repayment** *n.* [F (RE-[2])]
repeal /rɪ'pi:l/ **1** *v.t.* annul or revoke (law etc.). **2** *n.* repealing. [F (APPEAL)]
repeat /rɪ'pi:t/ **1** *v.* say or do or provide over again; say or recite or report (something heard or learnt); recur, appear again or repeatedly; (of food) be tasted intermittently for some time after being swallowed. **2** *n.* repeating, thing repeated; repeated broadcast programme; *Mus.* passage intended to be repeated, mark indicating this; pattern repeated in wallpaper etc. **3 repeat itself** recur in same form; **repeat oneself** say or do same thing over again. [F f. L (*peto* seek)]
repeatedly *adv.* many times over.
repeater *n.* person or thing that repeats, esp. firearm that fires several shots without reloading, or watch etc. that strikes last quarter etc. again when required; device that repeats a signal.
repel /rɪ'pel/ *v.t.* (**-ll-**) drive back, ward off, refuse admission or approach or acceptance to; be repulsive or distasteful to. [L *repello -puls-*]
repellent 1 *a.* that repels. **2** *n.* substance that repels (esp. insects etc.).
repent /rɪ'pent/ *v.* feel deep sorrow or regret about (one's wrong or omission etc.; also with *of*); wish one had not done or resolve not to continue (wrongful action etc., or *absol.*); **repentance** *n.*; **repentant** *a.* [F f. L *paeniteo*]
repercussion /ri:pə'kʌʃ(ə)n/ *n.* indirect effect or reaction of event or act; recoil after impact; echo. [F or L (RE-[2])]
repertoire /'repətwɑ:/ *n.* stock of pieces etc. that performer or company knows or is prepared to give; stock of regularly performed pieces, regularly used techniques, etc. [F f. L (foll.)]
repertory /'repətərɪ/ *n.* repertoire; theatrical performance of various plays for short periods by one company; store or collection, esp. of information or instances etc. [L (*reperio* find)]
repetition /repɪ'tɪʃ(ə)n/ *n.* repeating or being repeated; thing repeated; copy; **repetitious** *a.*; **repetitive** /rɪ'petɪtɪv/ *a.* [F or L (REPEAT)]
repine /rɪ'paɪn/ *v.i.* fret or be discontented (*at* or *against*). [PINE[2], after *repent*]
replace /rɪ'pleɪs/ *v.t.* put back in place; take place of, succeed, be substituted for; fill up place of (*with* or *by*), find or provide substitute for. [RE-[2]]
replacement *n.* replacing or being replaced; person or thing that takes the place of another.
replay 1 /ri:'pleɪ/ *v.t.* play (match, recording, etc.) over again. **2** /'ri:pleɪ/ *n.* replaying (of match, recording of incident in game, etc.). [RE-[2]]
replenish /rɪ'plenɪʃ/ *v.t.* fill up again (*with*); renew (supply etc.); **replenishment** *n.* [F *replenir* (*plein* full)]
replete /rɪ'pli:t/ *a.* filled or well supplied *with*; gorged or sated (*with*); **repletion** *n.* [F or L (*pleo* fill)]
replica /'replɪkə/ *n.* exact copy, esp. duplicate made by original artist of his picture etc.; model, esp. on smaller scale. [It. (*replicare* REPLY)]
reply /rɪ'plaɪ/ **1** *v.* make answer, respond, in word or action (*to*); say in answer. **2** *n.* act of replying; what is replied, response. [F f. L *replico* fold back]
report /rɪ'pɔ:t/ **1** *v.* bring back or give account of; state as fact or news, narrate or describe or repeat esp. as eye-witness or hearer etc.; relate as spoken by another; make official or formal statement about; specify (offence or offender) *to* authorities or *absol.*; present oneself (*to* person) as having returned or arrived; take down word for word or epitomize or write description of for publication; make or draw up or send in report; be responsible *to* (superior, supervisor, etc.). **2** *n.* account given or opinion formally expressed after investigation or consideration, description or epitome or reproduction of scene or speech or law case esp. for newspaper

publication or broadcast; common talk, rumour; way person or thing is spoken of (*things of good report*); periodical statement on school pupil's work, conduct, etc.; sound of explosion. **3 reported speech** speaker's words as given in report of them, with person and tense etc. adapted; **report progress** state what has been done so far. [F f. L (PORT[3])]

reporter *n.* person employed to gather and report news for newspaper or broadcast.

repose[1] /rɪ'pəʊz/ **1** *n.* cessation of activity or excitement or toil; sleep; peaceful or quiescent state, tranquillity. **2** *v.* rest (*oneself*); lay (one's head etc.) to rest; lie, esp. in sleep or death; give rest to; be supported or based *on*. [F *reposer* f. L (PAUSE)]

repose[2] /rɪ'pəʊz/ *v.t.* place (trust etc.) *in*. [RE-[1], POSE]

reposeful *a.* inducing or exhibiting repose; **reposefully** *adv.* [REPOSE[1]]

repository /rɪ'pɒzɪtərɪ/ *n.* place where things are stored or may be found, esp. warehouse or museum; receptacle; recipient *of* secrets etc. [F or L (REPOSE[2])]

repossess /ri:pə'zes/ *v.t.* regain possession of (esp. hire-purchase goods with arrears in payment); **repossession** *n.* [RE-[2]]

repp var. of REP[1].

reprehend /reprɪ'hend/ *v.t.* rebuke, blame. [L (*prehendo* seize)]

reprehensible /reprɪ'hensɪb(ə)l/ *a.* blameworthy; **reprehensibly** *adv.*

represent /reprɪ'zent/ *v.t.* stand for or correspond to, be specimen of, act as embodiment of, symbolize; present likeness or description of to mind or senses; state by way of expostulation or incentive (*represented to him the folly of it*); describe or depict *as*, declare *to be*, allege *that*; show, or play part of, on stage; be substitute or deputy for, be entitled to act or speak for, be elected as member of legislature by. [F or L (PRESENT[3])]

representation /reprɪzen'teɪʃ(ə)n/ *n.* representing or being represented; thing that represents; (esp. in *pl.*) statement made by way of allegation or to convey opinion; **representational** *a.*

representative /reprɪ'zentətɪv/ **1** *a.* typical of a class; containing typical specimens of all or many classes (*a representative collection*); consisting of elected deputies or representatives; based on representation of nation etc. by such deputies (*representative government*); serving as portrayal or symbol *of* (*groups representative of the virtues*). **2** *n.* sample or specimen or typical embodiment *of*; agent of person or firm or society; delegate, substitute; deputy in representative assembly. [F or med.L (REPRESENT)]

repress /rɪ'pres/ *v.t.* keep under, quell; suppress, prevent from sounding or bursting out or rioting; actively exclude (unwelcome thought) from conscious awareness; (usu. in *pass.*) subject (person) to suppression of his thoughts; **repression** *n.*; **repressive** *a.* [L (PRESS[1])]

reprieve /rɪ'pri:v/ **1** *v.t.* postpone or remit execution of (condemned person); give respite to. **2** *n.* reprieving or being reprieved; remission or commutation of capital sentence; warrant for this; respite. [*repry* f. F *reprendre -pris* take back]

reprimand /'reprɪmɑ:nd/ **1** *n.* official rebuke (*for* fault). **2** *v.t.* administer reprimand to. [F f. Sp. f. L (REPRESS)]

reprint 1 /ri:'prɪnt/ *v.t.* print again. **2** /'ri:prɪnt/ *n.* reprinting of book etc., book etc. reprinted. [RE-[2]]

reprisal /rɪ'praɪz(ə)l/ *n.* act of retaliation. [AF *reprisaille* f. med.L (REPREHEND)]

reprise /rɪ'pri:z/ *n.* repeated passage in music; repeated song etc. in musical programme. [F (REPRIEVE)]

reproach /rɪ'prəʊtʃ/ **1** *v.t.* express disapproval to (person) for fault etc.; rebuke or censure. **2** *n.* rebuke or censure; thing that brings disgrace or discredit; disgraced or discredited state. **3 beyond reproach** perfect, deserving no blame. [F *reproche(r)* f. L *prope* near]

reproachful *a.* inclined to or expressing reproach; **reproachfully** *adv.*

reprobate /'reprəbeɪt/ *n.* unprincipled or immoral person. [L (PROVE)]

reprobation /reprə'beɪʃ(ə)n/ *n.* strong condemnation.

reproduce /ri:prə'dju:s/ *v.* produce copy or representation of; cause to be seen or heard etc. again; produce further members of same species by natural means; produce offspring of (*oneself* or *itself*); **reproducible** *a.* [RE-[2]]

reproduction /ri:prə'dʌkʃ(ə)n/ *n.* reproducing; copy of painting etc.; *attrib.* (of furniture etc.) made in imitation of earlier style; **reproductive** *a.*

reproof /rɪ'pru:f/ *n.* blame (*a word, glance, of reproof*); rebuke, words expressing blame. [F *reprove* (foll.)]

reprove /rɪ'pru:v/ *v.t.* rebuke or scold (person or conduct etc.). [F *reprover* f. L (REPROBATE)]

reptile /'reptaɪl/ *n.* member of the class of cold-blooded vertebrates including snakes, lizards, crocodiles, turtles, and tortoises; mean, grovelling, or repulsive person; **reptilian** /rep'tɪlɪən/ *a.* [F or L (*repo rept-* creep)]

republic /rɪ'pʌblɪk/ *n.* a State in which

supreme power is held by the people or its elected representatives or by elected or nominated president, not by monarch etc. [F f. L (*res* concern; PUBLIC)]

republican 1 *a.* of or constituted as a republic; characteristic of republics; advocating or supporting republican government. **2** *n.* person advocating or supporting republican government; (**Republican**) *US* member of Republican Party. **3 republicanism** *n.*

repudiate /rɪ'pju:dɪeɪt/ *v.t.* disown, disavow, reject; refuse dealings with; deny; refuse to recognize or obey (authority or treaty) or discharge (obligation or debt); **repudiation** /-'eɪʃ(ə)n/ *n.*; **repudiator** *n.* [L (*repudium* divorce)]

repugnance /rɪ'pʌgnəns/ *n.* strong aversion or antipathy; inconsistency or incompatibility of ideas etc. [F or L (*pugno* fight)]

repugnant *a.* extremely distasteful; contradictory.

repulse /rɪ'pʌls/ **1** *v.t.* drive back (attack or attacking enemy) by force of arms; rebuff (friendly advances or their maker), refuse (request or offer, or its maker). **2** *n.* repulsing or being repulsed, rebuff. [L (REPEL)]

repulsion /rɪ'pʌlʃ(ə)n/ *n.* aversion, disgust; tendency of bodies to repel each other.

repulsive /rɪ'pʌlsɪv/ *a.* causing aversion or loathing, loathsome, disgusting. [F *répulsif* or REPULSE]

reputable /'repjʊtəb(ə)l/ *a.* of good repute, respectable; **reputably** *adv.* [F or med.L (REPUTE)]

reputation /repjʊ'teɪʃ(ə)n/ *n.* what is generally said or believed about person's or thing's character (*a reputation for honesty*); state of being well thought of, respectability; credit or discredit (*has the reputation of being a swindler*). [L (foll.)]

repute /rɪ'pju:t/ **1** *n.* reputation. **2** *v.t.* (in *pass.*) be generally considered (*is reputed to be the best*). [F or L (*puto* think)]

reputed *a.* said to be but possibly not (*her reputed father*); **reputed pint** etc. bottle of wine or spirits etc. sold as pint etc. but not guaranteed as imperial pint etc.

request /rɪ'kwest/ **1** *n.* asking for something (*came at his request*); thing asked for; state of being sought after, demand (*in great request*). **2** *v.t.* make request for (thing) or of (person); seek permission *to do* thing. **3 by** (or **on**) **request** in response to expressed wish; **request stop** place where bus etc. stops only on passenger's request. [F f. L (REQUIRE)]

requiem /'rekwɪem/ *n.* form of Mass for repose of souls of the dead; music for this. [L, = rest]

require /rɪ'kwaɪə/ *v.t.* need; depend on for success or fulfilment (*the work requires much patience*); lay down as imperative (*is required by the rules*); demand or insist on (*I require an answer*); instruct or command (*we require you to attend*). [F f. L *requiro -quisit-* seek]

requirement *n.* thing required; need.

requisite /'rekwɪzɪt/ **1** *a.* required by circumstances, necessary to success. **2** *n.* thing needed (*for* some purpose). [L (REQUIRE)]

requisition /rekwɪ'zɪʃ(ə)n/ **1** *n.* official order laying claim to use of property or materials; formal written demand that some duty should be performed; being called or put into service. **2** *v.t.* demand use or supply of esp. by requisition order. [F or L (REQUIRE)]

requite /rɪ'kwaɪt/ *v.t.* make return for (service), reward or avenge (wrong or injury etc.); make return to (person), repay with good or evil; **requital** *n.* [RE-[1], *quite* = QUIT]

reredos /'rɪədɒs/ *n.* ornamental screen covering wall behind altar. [AF (AR-REAR, *dos* back)]

re-route /ri:'ru:t/ *v.t.* send or carry by different route. [RE-[2]]

rerun 1 /ri:'rʌn/ *v.t.* (**-nn-**; past **reran;** *p.p.* **rerun**) run again. **2** /'ri:rʌn/ *n.* act of rerunning; repeat of film etc.

resale /ri:'seɪl/ *n.* sale of thing bought.

rescind /rɪ'sɪnd/ *v.t.* abrogate, revoke, cancel; **rescission** /-ʒ(ə)n/ *n.* [L *rescindo -sciss-* cut off]

rescript /'ri:skrɪpt/ *n.* Roman emperor's or Pope's written reply to appeal for decision; official edict or announcement. [L *rescribo -script-* reply in writing]

rescue /'reskju:/ **1** *v.t.* save or set free from danger or harm. **2** *n.* rescuing or being rescued. [F f. Rmc (L as RE-[1], EX-[1], QUASH)]

research /rɪ'sɜ:tʃ, (D) 'ri:sɜ:tʃ/ **1** *n.* systematic investigation into and study of materials and sources etc. in order to establish facts and reach new conclusions. **2** *v.* do research (into or for). [F (SEARCH)]

resemblance /rɪ'zembləns/ *n.* likeness or similarity. [AF (foll.)]

resemble /rɪ'zemb(ə)l/ *v.t.* be like, have similarity to or same appearance as. [F (*sembler* seem)]

resent /rɪ'zent/ *v.t.* feel indignation at or retain bitter feelings about (action or injury etc.); feel offended by (person). [F f. L (*sentio* feel)]

resentful *a.* feeling resentment; **resentfully** *adv.*

resentment *n.* indignant or bitter feelings. [F or It. (RESENT)]

reservation /rezə'veɪʃ(ə)n/ *n.* reserving or being reserved; thing reserved (e.g. room in hotel); express or tacit limitation or exception to agreement or acceptance etc.; strip of land between carriageways of road; *US* area of land reserved for occupation by Indian tribe. [F or L (foll.)]

reserve /rɪ'zɜ:v/ **1** *v.t.* put aside or keep back for later occasion or special use; order to be specially retained or allocated for particular person at particular time; retain or secure (*reserve the right to*); postpone delivery of (judgement). **2** *n.* thing reserved for future use, extra amount; limitation or exception attached to something (*accepted without reserve*); self-restraint, reticence, coolness of manner; company's profit added to capital; (in *sing.* or *pl.*) assets kept readily available; (in *sing.* or *pl.*) troops withheld from action to reinforce or protect others, forces outside regular ones but available in emergency; member of military reserve; extra player chosen as possible substitute in team; place reserved for special use, esp. as habitat (*game reserve*; *nature reserve*). **3** **in reserve** unused and available if needed; **reserve price** lowest acceptable price stipulated for item sold at auction. [F f. L (*servo* keep)]

reserved *a.* reticent, slow to reveal emotions or opinions, uncommunicative.

reservist *n.* member of military reserve.

reservoir /'rezəvwɑ:/ *n.* large natural or artificial lake as source of area's water supply; receptacle for liquid; supply of information etc. [F (RESERVE)]

reshuffle /ri:'ʃʌf(ə)l/ **1** *v.t.* shuffle (cards) again; interchange posts or responsibilities of (group of people). **2** *n.* reshuffling. [RE-²]

reside /rɪ'zaɪd/ *v.i.* have one's home or dwell permanently (in specified place); (of power or right etc.) be vested *in*; (of quality) be present or inherent *in*. [F or L or back-form. f. RESIDENT]

residence /'rezɪdəns/ *n.* residing (*take up residence*); place where one resides, abode *of*; house esp. of considerable pretension; **in residence** dwelling at specified place esp. for performance of duties or work. [F or med.L (foll.)]

resident **1** *n.* permanent inhabitant (*of* place); guest of hotel staying overnight. **2** *a.* having quarters on the spot (*resident housekeeper*); residing; in residence; located *in* (*feeling resident in the nerves*). [F or L (*sedeo* sit)]

residential /rezɪ'denʃ(ə)l/ *a.* suitable for or occupied by private houses (*residential area*); used as residence; based on or connected with residence; **residentially** *adv.* [RESIDENCE]

residual /rɪ'zɪdjʊəl/ **1** *a.* left as residue or residuum. **2** *n.* residual quantity. **3** **residually** *adv.* [RESIDUE]

residuary /rɪ'zɪdjʊərɪ/ *a.* of the residue of an estate (*residuary legatee*); residual. [RESIDUUM]

residue /'rezɪdju:/ *n.* remainder, what is left or remains over; what remains of estate after payment of charges, debts, and bequests. [F f. L *residuum* (foll.)]

residuum /rɪ'zɪdjʊəm/ *n.* (*pl.* **residua**) what remains, esp. substance left after combustion or evaporation. [L (RESIDENT)]

resign /rɪ'zaɪn/ *v.* give up office (often with *from*); relinquish or surrender (office or claim etc.); **resign oneself to** come to accept or tolerate. [F f. L (*signo* sign)]

resignation /rezɪg'neɪʃ(ə)n/ *n.* resigning esp. of an office; letter etc. conveying this; uncomplaining endurance of difficulty. [F f. med.L (prec.)]

resigned *a.* having resigned oneself, content to endure, full or indicative of resignation; **resignedly** /-nɪdlɪ/ *adv.* [RESIGN]

resilient /rɪ'zɪlɪənt/ *a.* resuming original form after compression etc.; (of person) readily recovering from shock or depression etc.; **resilience** *n.* [L (SALIENT)]

resin /'rezɪn/ **1** *n.* sticky substance secreted by many plants and trees; similar synthetic substance, esp. organic compound made by polymerization and used as plastic or in plastics. **2** *v.t.* rub or treat with resin. **3** **resinous** *a.* [L]

resist /rɪ'zɪst/ **1** *v.* withstand action or effect of, prevent course or progress of; abstain from (pleasure etc.); strive against, try to impede; refuse to comply with (*resist arrest*); offer opposition, refuse to comply. **2** *n.* protective coating of resistant substance. **3** **resistible** *a.* [F or L (*sisto* stop)]

resistance *n.* act of resisting, refusal to comply; power to resist (*resistance to wear and tear*); impeding or stopping effect exerted by material thing on another (*overcame the resistance of the air*); property of failing to conduct electricity or heat etc.; resistor; secret organization resisting authority, esp. in conquered country; **line of least resistance** easiest method or course; **resistant** *a.* [F f. L (prec.)]

resistor *n.* device having resistance to passage of electric current. [RESIST]

resit /riːˈsɪt/ *v.t.* (**-tt-;** *past* and *p.p.* **resat**) take (examination) again, usu. after failing. [RE-[2]]

resoluble /rɪˈzɒljʊb(ə)l/ *a.* that can be resolved; analysable *into.* [F or L (RESOLVE)]

resolute /ˈrezəluːt, -ljuːt/ *a.* determined, bold, not vacillating or shrinking. [L (RESOLVE)]

resolution /rezəˈluːʃ(ə)n, -ˈljuː-/ *n.* resolute temper or character; thing resolved on, intention; formal expression of opinion by legislative body or public meeting; solving *of* doubt or problem or question; separation into components; conversion *into* other form; *Mus.* causing discord to pass into concord; smallest interval measurable by a scientific instrument.

resolve /rɪˈzɒlv/ **1** *v.* make up one's mind, decide firmly (*resolved to leave, on leaving*), cause to do this (*events resolved him to leave*); (of assembly or meeting) pass a resolution *that*; (cause to) separate into constituent parts, analyse mentally; solve or explain or settle (doubt, argument, etc.); *Mus.* convert (discord) or be converted into concord. **2** *n.* firm mental decision or intention; determination. [L (SOLVE)]

resolved *a.* resolute, determined.

resonant /ˈrezənənt/ *a.* (of sound) echoing, resounding, continuing to sound, reinforced or prolonged by vibration or reflection; (of body or room etc.) tending to reinforce or prolong sounds esp. by vibration; (of place) resounding *with*; **resonance** *n.* [F or L (RESOUND)]

resonate /ˈrezəneɪt/ *v.i.* produce or show resonance, resound; **resonator** *n.* [L (as prec.)]

resort /rɪˈzɔːt/ **1** *n.* place frequented esp. for holidays or for specified purpose or quality (*health, seaside, resort*); thing to which recourse is had, expedient, recourse; frequenting or being frequented. **2** *v.i.* turn for aid *to* (*resort to force*); go in large numbers or often *to.* **3 in the last resort** when all else has failed, as final attempt. [F (*sortir* go out)]

resound /rɪˈzaʊnd/ *v.* (of place) ring or echo (*with*); (of voice or instrument or sound etc.) produce echoes, go on sounding, fill place with sound; (of reputation etc.) be much talked of, produce sensation (*through* place); (of place) re-echo (sound). [F or L (SOUND[1])]

resounding *a.* that resounds; notable or decisive (*a resounding success*).

resource /rɪˈsɔːs, -ˈzɔːs/ *n.* expedient or device (*escape was his only resource*); (usu. in *pl.*) means of supplying what is needed, stock that can be drawn on; (in *pl.*) country's collective sources of wealth or means for defence; skill in devising expedients (*full of resource*). [F (SOURCE)]

resourceful *a.* good at devising expedients; **resourcefully** *adv.*

respect /rɪˈspekt/ **1** *n.* deferential esteem felt or shown towards person or quality; heed or regard *of* or *for*; attention *to*; aspect or detail (*correct in nearly all respects*); reference or relation (*with respect to*); (in *pl.*) polite greetings (*give her my respects*). **2** *v.t.* regard with deference or esteem; avoid interfering with or harming, treat with consideration; refrain from offending (person or feelings). **3 in respect of** as concerns, with reference to; **pay one's respects** make polite visit; **pay one's last respects** show respect for dead person, esp. by attending funeral. [F or L (*respicio -spect-* look back at)]

respectable *a.* deserving respect; of fair social standing, honest and decent; fairly good or competent; reasonably good in condition or appearance etc.; appreciable in number or size etc.; **respectability** /-ˈbɪlɪtɪ/ *n*; **respectably** *adv.*

respectful *a.* showing deference; **respectfully** *adv.*

respecting *prep.* in respect of, concerning.

respective *a.* concerning or appropriate to each of several individually (*go to your respective places*); comparative (*were dealt with according to their respective ranks*). [F or med.L (RESPECT)]

respectively *adv.* for each separately or in turn, and in the order mentioned (*he and I contributed £10 and £1 respectively*).

respiration /respəˈreɪʃ(ə)n/ *n.* breathing; plant's absorption of oxygen and emission of carbon dioxide; single inspiration and expiration, a breath. [F or L (RESPIRE)]

respirator /ˈrespəreɪtə/ *n.* apparatus worn over mouth and nose to warm or filter or purify inhaled air; apparatus for maintaining artificial respiration. [RESPIRE]

respiratory /ˈrespəreɪtərɪ, rɪˈspaɪərət-/ *a.* of respiration.

respire /rɪˈspaɪə/ *v.* breathe air, inhale and exhale air; (of plant) carry out respiration; breathe (air etc.). [F or L (*spiro* breathe)]

respite /ˈrespaɪt, -ɪt/ **1** *n.* interval of rest or relief; delay permitted before the discharge of an obligation or suffering of a penalty. **2** *v.t.* grant or bring respite to. [F f. L (RESPECT)]

resplendent /rɪ'splendənt/ *a.* brilliant, dazzlingly or gloriously bright; **resplendence** *n.* [L (*splendeo* shine)]

respond /rɪ'spɒnd/ *v.i.* make answer; act or behave in answering or corresponding manner (*responded with a kick*; *vehicle responds to controls*); show sensitiveness *to* by behaviour or change (*does not respond to kindness*; *nerve responds to stimulus*); (of congregation) make set answers to priest etc. [L *respondeo -spons-*]

respondent 1 *n.* defendant, esp. in appeal or divorce case. 2 *a.* in position of defendant.

response /rɪ'spɒns/ *n.* answer given in word or act, reply; feeling or movement or change etc. caused by stimulus or influence; any part of the liturgy said or sung in answer to priest etc. [F or L (RESPOND)]

responsibility /rɪspɒnsɪ'bɪlɪtɪ/ *n.* being responsible (with *for* or *of*); charge for which one is responsible; responsible quality. [foll.]

responsible /rɪ'spɒnsɪb(ə)l/ *a.* liable to be called to account (*to* person, *for* thing); morally accountable for actions, capable of rational conduct; of good credit or position or repute, respectable, evidently trustworthy; being the primary cause *for*; involving responsibility (*a responsible task*); **responsibly** *adv.* [F f. L (RESPOND)]

responsive /rɪ'spɒnsɪv/ *a.* responding readily (*to* some influence), sympathetic; answering; by way of answer. [F or L (RESPOND)]

respray 1 /ri:'spreɪ/ *v.t.* spray again (esp. to change colour of paint on vehicle). 2 /'ri:spreɪ/ *n.* act or process of respraying. [RE-[2]]

rest[1] 1 *v.* cease from exertion or action etc., be still or asleep, esp. to refresh oneself or recover strength; give relief or repose to, allow to rest; lie or be supported *on* (or *upon*) or *against*; depend or rely; (of look etc.) alight or be steadily directed *on* or *upon*; place for support or foundation *on* or *upon*; (of subject) be left without further discussion; lie buried (*in* churchyard etc.); (in *p.p.*) refreshed or reinvigorated by resting. 2 *n.* repose or sleep; ceasing of exertion or action etc., period of resting; support for holding or steadying something; *Mus.* interval of silence, sign denoting this. 3 **at rest** not moving, not agitated or troubled (esp. of the dead); **be resting** (of actor) be out of work; **put** (or **set**) **person's mind at rest** relieve or reassure him; **rest one's case** conclude presentation of it; **rest-cure** rest usu. of some weeks in bed as medical treatment; **rest on one's oars** relax one's efforts. [OE]

rest[2] 1 *n.* (**the rest**) the remaining part(s) or individuals *of*, the remainder of some quantity or number, the others. 2 *v.i.* remain in specified state (*rest assured*). 3 **for the rest** as regards anything else; **rest with** be left in the hands or charge of (*it rests with you to decide*). [F *reste(r)* f. L (*sto* stand)]

restaurant /'restərɒnt/ *n.* public premises where meals or refreshments may be had; **restaurant car** dining-car. [F (RESTORE)]

restaurateur /restərə'tɜ:/ *n.* restaurant-keeper.

restful *a.* inducing rest, quiet, soothing; **restfully** *adv.* [REST[1]]

restitution /restɪ'tju:ʃ(ə)n/ *n.* restoring of thing to proper owner; reparation for injury (*make restitution*). [F or L]

restive /'restɪv/ *a.* fidgety, restless; (of horse) jibbing, refractory; (of person) unmanageable, rejecting control. [F (REST[2])]

restless *a.* finding or affording no rest; constantly in motion or fidgeting; uneasy, agitated. [OE (REST[1])]

restoration /restə'reɪʃ(ə)n/ *n.* restoring or being restored; model or drawing representing supposed original form of extinct animal, ruined building, etc.; **the Restoration** return of Charles II in 1660. [F or L (RESTORE)]

restorative /rɪ'stɒrətɪv/ 1 *a.* that tends to restore health or strength. 2 *n.* restorative food or medicine etc. [F (foll.)]

restore /rɪ'stɔ:/ *v.t.* bring back to original state by rebuilding or repairing etc.; bring back to health etc.; give back to original owner etc.; reinstate; bring back to former place or condition or use; make representation of supposed original state of (extinct animal, ruin, etc.). [F f. L *restauro*]

restrain /rɪ'streɪn/ *v.t.* check or hold in *from*, keep in check or under control or within bounds, repress, keep down; confine, imprison. [F f. L *restringo -strict-*]

restraint *n.* restraining or being restrained; agency or influence that restrains; self-control, avoidance of excess or exaggeration; reserve of manner; confinement, esp. because of insanity.

restrict /rɪ'strɪkt/ *v.t.* confine or limit; **restriction** *n.* [L (RESTRAIN)]

restrictive /rɪ'strɪktɪv/ *a.* restricting; **restrictive practice** agreement or practice that limits efficiency or output in industry. [F or med.L (prec.)]

restructure /ri:'strʌktʃə/ *v.t.* give new structure to; rebuild, rearrange. [RE-[2]]

result /rɪ'zʌlt/ 1 *n.* consequence, issue or outcome of something; satisfactory outcome (*get results*); quantity or formula obtained by calculation; (in *pl.*) list of scores or winners etc. in sporting events or examinations. **2** *v.i.* arise as actual or follow as logical consequence (*from*); have outcome or end in specified manner (*resulted badly, in a large profit*). [L *resulto* spring back]

resultant 1 *a.* resulting, esp. as total outcome of more or less opposed forces. **2** *n.* force etc. equivalent to two or more acting in different directions at same point.

resume /rɪ'zju:m/ *v.* begin again or go on (with) after interruption, begin to speak or work or use again, recommence; get or take again or back (*resumed her seat*). [F or L (*sumo sumpt-* take)]

résumé /'rezju:meɪ/ *n.* summary. [F (prec.)]

resumption /rɪ'zʌmpʃ(ə)n/ *n.* resuming; **resumptive** *a.* [F or L (RESUME)]

resurface /ri:'sɜ:fɪs/ *v.* put new surface on; return to surface. [RE-[2]]

resurgent /rɪ'sɜ:dʒənt/ *a.* rising or arising again; **resurgence** *n.* [L *resurgo -surrect-* rise again]

resurrect /rezə'rekt/ *v.t.* revive practice or memory of; take from grave; dig up. [foll.]

resurrection /rezə'rekʃ(ə)n/ *n.* rising from the dead, esp. (**Resurrection**) that of Christ; revival after disuse or inactivity or decay. [F f. L (RESURGENT)]

resuscitate /rɪ'sʌsɪteɪt/ *v.* revive from unconsciousness or apparent death; revive (old practice etc.); **resuscitation** /-'teɪʃ(ə)n/ *n.* [L (*suscito* raise)]

retail /'ri:teɪl/ **1** *n.* selling of things in small quantities to the public and usu. not for resale. **2** *a.* of retail. **3** *adv.* by retail (*buys wholesale and sells retail*). **4** *v.* sell by retail; (of goods) be retailed (esp. *at* or *for* specified price); /also ri:'teɪl/ recount, relate details of. [F f. *taillier* cut (TALLY)]

retain /rɪ'teɪn/ *v.t.* keep possession of, not lose, continue to have or practise or recognize; not abolish or discard or alter; keep in one's memory; keep in place, hold fixed; secure services of (person, esp. barrister) with preliminary payment. [AF f. L *retineo -tent-*]

retainer *n.* person or thing that retains; fee for retaining barrister etc.; *hist.* dependant or follower of person of rank.

retake /ri:'teɪk/ *v.t.* (*past* **retook**; *p.p.* **retaken**) take again; recapture. [RE-[2]]

retaliate /rɪ'tælɪeɪt/ *v.* repay (injury or insult etc.) in kind; attack in return; **retaliation** /-'eɪʃ(ə)n/ *n.*; **retaliatory** /-ljətərɪ/ *a.* [L (*talis* such)]

retard /rɪ'tɑ:d/ *v.t.* make slow or late, delay progress or accomplishment of; **retardation** /ri:tɑ:'deɪʃ(ə)n/ *n.* [F f. L (*tardus* slow)]

retarded *a.* backward in mental or physical development.

retch *v.i.* make motion as in vomiting, esp. involuntarily and without effect.

retention /rɪ'tenʃ(ə)n/ *n.* retaining or being retained. [F or L (RETAIN)]

retentive /rɪ'tentɪv/ *a.* tending to retain; (of memory) not forgetful. [F or med.L (RETAIN)]

rethink 1 /ri:'θɪŋk/ *v.t.* (*past* and *p.p.* **rethought** /-'θɔ:t/) consider afresh, esp. with view to making changes. **2** /'ri:θɪŋk/ *n.* rethinking, reassessment. [RE-[2]]

reticence /'retɪsəns/ *n.* avoidance of expressing all one knows or feels or more than is necessary; disposition to silence, taciturnity; **reticent** *a.* [L (*reticeo* keep silent)]

reticulate 1 /rɪ'tɪkjʊleɪt/ *v.* divide or be divided in fact or appearance into a network. **2** /rɪ'tɪkjʊlət/ *a.* reticulated. [L (*reticulum* dimin. of *rete* net)]

reticulation /rɪtɪkjʊ'leɪʃ(ə)n/ *n.* (usu. in *pl.*) netlike marking or arrangement.

retina /'retɪnə/ *n.* (*pl.* **retinas**) layer at back of eyeball sensitive to light; **retinal** *a.* [med.L (*rete* net)]

retinue /'retɪnju:/ *n.* body of attendants accompanying important person. [F (RETAIN)]

retire /rɪ'taɪə/ *v.* leave office or employment, esp. because of age (*retire from the army, on a pension*); withdraw, go away, retreat; seek seclusion or shelter (*retire from the world*); go to bed; cause (employee) to retire; withdraw (troops); (of batsman at cricket) voluntarily terminate or be compelled to suspend one's innings (*retired hurt*); **retire into oneself** become uncommunicative or unsociable. [F (*tirer* draw)]

retired *a.* who has retired (*a retired grocer*); withdrawn from society or observation, secluded.

retirement *n.* retiring; condition of having retired; seclusion; **retirement pension** pension paid by State to retired people above certain age.

retiring *a.* shy, fond of seclusion.

retort[1] /rɪ'tɔ:t/ **1** *n.* incisive or witty or angry reply. **2** *v.* say by way of retort; make retort; repay (insult or attack) in kind. [L (*retorqueo -tort-* twist)]

retort[2] /rɪ'tɔ:t/ *n.* vessel with long downward-bent neck for distilling liquids; vessel for heating coal to generate gas. [F f. med.L (as prec.)]

retouch /ri:'tʌtʃ/ *v.t.* improve (picture or photograph etc.) by fresh touches or alterations. [F (RE-[2])]

retrace /rɪ'treɪs/ *v.t.* go back over (*retrace one's steps*); trace back to source or beginning; recall the course of in memory. [F (RE-²)]

retract /rɪ'trækt/ *v.* draw or be drawn back or in; withdraw (statement or opinion etc.); **retraction** *n.* [L *retraho -tract-* draw back]

retractile /rɪ'træktaɪl/ *a.* capable of being retracted.

retread 1 /ri:'tred/ *v.t.* put fresh tread on (tyre). **2** /'ri:tred/ *n.* retreaded tyre. [RE-²]

retreat /rɪ'tri:t/ **1** *v.i.* go back, retire, relinquish a position (esp. of army etc.); recede. **2** *n.* act of retreating; withdrawal into privacy or security; place of shelter or seclusion; period of seclusion for prayer and meditation; military signal for retreating; bugle-call at sunset. **3 beat a retreat** retreat, abandon undertaking. [F f. L (RETRACT)]

retrench /rɪ'trentʃ/ *v.* reduce amount of (expense or its cause); cut down expenses, introduce economies; **retrenchment** *n.* [F (TRENCH)]

retrial /ri:'traɪəl/ *n.* retrying of a case. [RE-²]

retribution /retrɪ'bju:ʃ(ə)n/ *n.* requital usu. for evil done; vengeance; **retributive** /rɪ'trɪbjʊtɪv/ *a.* [L (TRIBUTE)]

retrieve /rɪ'tri:v/ **1** *v.* regain possession of, recover by investigation or effort of memory; find again (stored information); (of dog) find and bring in (killed or wounded game etc.); rescue *from* bad state etc., restore to flourishing state; repair or set right (loss or error etc.). **2** *n.* possibility of recovery (*beyond retrieve*). **3 retrieval** *n.* [F (*trouver* find)]

retriever *n.* dog of breed used for retrieving game.

retro- *prefix* backwards, back again, in return, behind. [L]

retroactive /retrəʊ'æktɪv/ *a.* having retrospective effect.

retrograde /'retrəgreɪd/ **1** *a.* directed backwards (*retrograde motion*); reverting esp. to inferior state, declining; reversed (*retrograde order*). **2** *v.i.* move backwards, recede; decline, revert. [L (*retrogradior -gress-* move backwards)]

retrogress /retrə'gres/ *v.i.* move backwards, deteriorate; **retrogression** /-eʃ(ə)n/ *n.*; **retrogressive** *a.* [RETRO-]

retro-rocket /'retrəʊrɒkɪt/ *n.* auxiliary rocket for slowing down spacecraft etc.

retrospect /'retrəspekt/ *n.* survey of or reference to past time or conditions; **in retrospect** when looked back on. [RETRO-, PROSPECT]

retrospection /retrə'spekʃ(ə)n/ *n.* action of looking back, esp. into the past.

retrospective /retrə'spektɪv/ *a.* looking back on or dealing with the past (*retrospective exhibition*); (of statute etc.) applying to the past as well as the future.

retroussé /rə'tru:seɪ/ *a.* (of nose) turned up at tip. [F]

retroverted /'retrəvɜ:tɪd/ *a.* (esp. of womb) turned backwards. [RETRO-, L *verto* turn]

retry /ri:'traɪ/ *v.* try (defendant or law case) again. [RE-²]

retsina /ret'si:nə/ *n.* resin-flavoured Greek wine. [mod.Gk]

return /rɪ'tɜ:n/ **1** *v.* come or go back; bring or put or send back; pay back or reciprocate, give in response; yield (profit); say in reply, retort; send (ball) back in cricket or tennis etc.; state or mention or describe officially, esp. in answer to writ or formal demand; (of constituency) elect as MP etc. **2** *n.* coming or going back; giving or sending or putting or paying back; thing given etc. back; = *return ticket*; (in *sing.* or *pl.*) proceeds or profit of undertaking, coming in of these; formal report compiled or submitted by order (*income-tax return*). **3 by return (of post)** by next available post in return direction; **in return** as exchange or reciprocal action; **many happy returns (of the day)** birthday or festival greeting; **returning officer** official conducting election in constituency and announcing name of person elected; **return match** second match between same opponents; **return ticket** ticket for journey to place and back to starting-point. [F f. Rmc (TURN)]

reunion /ri:'ju:njən/ *n.* reuniting or being reunited; social gathering esp. of people formerly associated. [F (RE-²)]

rev *colloq.* **1** *n.* revolution (of engine). **2** *v.* (**-vv-**) (of engine) revolve; rev up. **3 rev up** cause (engine) to run quickly, increase speed of revolution. [abbr.]

Rev. *abbr.* Reverend.

revalue /ri:'vælju:/ *v.t.* give new (esp. higher) value to (currency etc.); **revaluation** /-'eɪʃ(ə)n/ *n.* [RE-²]

revamp /ri:'væmp/ *v.t.* renovate, revise, patch up.

Revd *abbr.* Reverend.

reveal /rɪ'vi:l/ *v.t.* display or show, allow to appear; disclose or divulge; **reveal itself** come to sight or knowledge. [F or L (*velum* veil)]

reveille /rɪ'vælɪ/ *n.* military waking-signal. [F *réveillez* wake up]

revel /'rev(ə)l/ **1** *v.i.* (**-ll-**, *US* **-l-**) make merry, be riotously festive; take keen delight *in*. **2** *n.* (in *sing.* or *pl.*) revelling, merry-making, or instance of this. [F f. L (REBEL)]

revelation /revə'leɪʃ(ə)n/ *n.* revealing, esp. disclosing of knowledge to man by divine or supernatural agency; knowledge so disclosed; striking disclosure;

(**Revelation**; in full **The Revelation of St John the Divine**) last book of New Testament. [F or L (REVEAL)]

revelry /ˈrevəlrɪ/ *n.* revelling. [REVEL]

revenge /rɪˈvendʒ/ **1** *n.* retaliation for offence or injury; act of retaliation; desire for this, vindictive feeling; chance to win after earlier defeat. **2** *v.t.* inflict retaliation for (offence); avenge (person or *oneself*). **3 be revenged** obtain revenge. [F f. L (VINDICATE)]

revengeful *a.* eager for revenge; **revengefully** *adv.*

revenue /ˈrevənju:, -vɪn-/ *n.* income, esp. of large amount, from any source; (in *pl.*) items constituting this; State's annual income from which public expenses are met; department of civil service collecting this. [F *revenu(e)* (*revenir* return)]

reverberate /rɪˈvɜ:bəreɪt/ *v.* (of sound or light or heat) be returned or reflected; return (sound etc.) thus; **reverberant** *a.*; **reverberation** /-ˈreɪʃ(ə)n/ *n.*; **reverberative** *a.* [L (*verbero* beat)]

revere /rɪˈvɪə/ *v.t.* hold in deep and usu. religious or affectionate respect. [F or L (*vereor* fear)]

reverence /ˈrevərəns/ **1** *n.* revering or being revered, capacity for revering. **2** *v.t.* regard or treat with reverence. [F f. L (prec.)]

reverend /ˈrevərənd/ *a.* deserving reverence; **the Reverend** title of clergyman; **Reverend Mother** Mother Superior of convent. [F, or L *reverendus* (REVERE)]

reverent /ˈrevərənt/ *a.* feeling or showing reverence. [L (REVERE)]

reverential /revəˈrenʃ(ə)l/ *a.* of the nature of, due to, or characterized by reverence; **reverentially** *adv.* [med.L (REVERENCE)]

reverie /ˈrevərɪ/ *n.* fit of abstracted musing; being engaged in this. [F]

revers /rɪˈvɪə/ *n.* (*pl.* same /-ɪəz/) turned-back edge of garment revealing under-surface; material on this surface. [F (REVERSE)]

reversal /rɪˈvɜ:s(ə)l/ *n.* reversing or being reversed. [foll.]

reverse /rɪˈvɜ:s/ **1** *v.* turn the other way round or up or inside out, change to opposite character or effect; (cause to) travel backwards; make (engine etc.) work in contrary direction; revoke or annul (decree, act, etc.). **2** *a.* opposite or contrary in character or order, inverted, turned backwards, upside down. **3** *n.* *the* opposite or contrary; contrary of usual manner (*printed in reverse*); piece of misfortune, disaster, esp. defeat in battle; reverse gear or motion; reverse side; side of coin etc. bearing secondary design; verso of leaf. **4 reverse arms** hold rifles butt upwards; **reverse the charges** make recipient of telephone call responsible for payment; **reverse gear** gear used to make vehicle etc. travel backwards; **the reverse of** far from, not at all; **reversing light** white light at rear of vehicle, operated when vehicle is in reverse gear. **5 reversible** *a.* [F f. L (*verto vers-* turn)]

reversion /rɪˈvɜ:ʃ(ə)n/ *n.* legal right (esp. of original owner or his heirs) to possess or succeed to property on death of present possessor; return to previous state, esp. *Biol.* to earlier type. [F or L (prec.)]

revert /rɪˈvɜ:t/ *v.* return *to* former state or practice or subject etc.; (of property, office, etc.) return by reversion; **revertible** *a.*

revetment /rɪˈvetmənt/ *n.* facing of masonry on rampart or wall. [F *revêtement* (VEST)]

review /rɪˈvju:/ **1** *n.* general survey or assessment of subject or thing; retrospect, survey of the past; revision or reconsideration (*is under review*); display and formal inspection of troops etc.; published account or criticism of book etc.; periodical publication with critical articles on current events, the arts, etc. **2** *v.t.* survey or look back on; reconsider or revise; hold review of (troops etc.); write review of (book etc.). [F f. *revoir* (VIEW)]

reviewer *n.* writer of critical reviews of books etc.

revile /rɪˈvaɪl/ *v.t.* criticize abusively. [F (VILE)]

revise /rɪˈvaɪz/ **1** *v.t.* examine or re-examine and improve or amend (esp. written or printed matter); read again (work learnt or done) to improve one's knowledge. **2** *n.* printer's proof-sheet embodying corrections made in earlier proof. **3 Revised Standard Version** revision of Bible made in 1946–57; **Revised Version** revision of Bible made in 1870–84. [F, or L *reviso* (*video vis-* see)]

revision /rɪˈvɪʒ(ə)n/ *n.* revising or being revised; revised edition or form. [L (prec.)]

revisory /rɪˈvaɪzərɪ/ *a.* of revision. [REVISE]

revival /rɪˈvaɪv(ə)l/ *n.* reviving or being revived; new production of old play etc.; reawakening of religious fervour, campaign to promote this. [REVIVE]

revivalist *n.* one who promotes religious revival; **revivalism** *n.*

revive /rɪˈvaɪv/ *v.* come or bring back to consciousness or life or strength; come or bring back to existence or use or notice etc. [F or L (*vivo* live)]

revivify /riːˈvɪvɪfaɪ/ *v.t.* restore to life or strength or activity; **revivification** /-fɪˈkeɪʃ(ə)n/ *n.* [F or L (VIVIFY)]

revocable /ˈrevəkəb(ə)l/ *a.* that can be revoked. [F or L (REVOKE)]

revoke /rɪˈvəʊk/ **1** *v.* rescind or withdraw or cancel (decree or promise etc.); fail to follow suit in card-game when able to do so. **2** *n.* revoking in card-game. [F or L (*voco* call)]

revolt /rɪˈvəʊlt/ **1** *v.* rise in rebellion against authority; affect with strong disgust; feel strong disgust (*at* or *against*), turn in disgust *from*. **2** *n.* act of rebelling; state of insurrection (*in revolt*); sense of loathing; mood of protest or defiance. [F f. It. (REVOLVE)]

revolting *a.* disgusting, horrible.

revolution /revəˈluːʃ(ə)n/ *n.* forcible overthrow of government or social order, in favour of new system; any fundamental change or reversal of conditions; revolving; single completion of orbit or rotation, time taken for this; cyclic recurrence. [F or L (REVOLVE)]

revolutionary **1** *a.* involving great and usu. violent change; of or causing political revolution. **2** *n.* instigator or supporter of political revolution.

revolutionize *v.t.* introduce fundamental change to.

revolve /rɪˈvɒlv/ *v.* (cause to) turn round, esp. on axis; move in orbit; ponder (problem etc.) in the mind; **revolving door** door with several partitions turning round central axis. [L *revolvo -volut-*]

revolver *n.* pistol with revolving chambers enabling several shots to be fired without reloading.

revue /rɪˈvjuː/ *n.* theatrical entertainment of short usu. satirical items. [F (REVIEW)]

revulsion /rɪˈvʌlʃ(ə)n/ *n.* abhorrence; sudden violent change of feeling. [F or L (*vello vuls-* pull)]

reward /rɪˈwɔːd/ **1** *n.* return or recompense for service or merit, requital for good or evil; sum offered for detection of criminal, recovery of lost property, etc. **2** *v.t.* give reward to (person) or for (service etc.). [AF *reward(er)* REGARD]

rewarding *a.* (of an activity etc.) well worth doing.

rewind /riːˈwaɪnd/ *v.t.* (*past* and *p.p.* **rewound**) wind (film or tape etc.) back to the beginning. [RE-[2]]

rewire /riːˈwaɪə/ *v.t.* renew electrical wiring of (house etc.).

reword /riːˈwɜːd/ *v.t.* express in different words.

rewrite **1** /riːˈraɪt/ *v.t.* (*past* **rewrote**; *p.p.* **rewritten**) write again or differently. **2** /ˈriːraɪt/ *n.* thing rewritten.

Rex *n.* reigning king (in use as REGINA). [L, = king]

r.h. *abbr.* right hand.

Rh *symb.* rhodium.

rhapsodize /ˈræpsədaɪz/ *v.i.* utter or write rhapsodies. [foll.]

rhapsody /ˈræpsədɪ/ *n.* enthusiastic or extravagant utterance or composition; emotional irregular piece of music; **rhapsodic** /-ˈsɒdɪk/ *a.* [L f. Gk (*rhaptō* stitch, ODE)]

rhenium /ˈriːnɪəm/ *n.* rare metallic element of manganese group. [L *Rhenus* Rhine]

rhesus /ˈriːsəs/ *n.* small Indian monkey; **rhesus factor** antigen occurring in red blood cells of most persons and some animals; **rhesus-negative** (or **-positive**) not having (or having) rhesus factor. [*Rhesus*, mythical king of Thrace]

rhetoric /ˈretərɪk/ *n.* art of persuasive or impressive speaking or writing; language designed to persuade or impress (often with implication of insincerity or exaggeration etc.). [F f. L f. Gk (*rhētōr* orator)]

rhetorical /rɪˈtɒrɪk(ə)l/ *a.* expressed with view to persuasive or impressive effect, of the nature of rhetoric; **rhetorical question** question asked not for information but to produce effect (e.g. *who cares?*); **rhetorically** *adv.* [L f. Gk (prec.)]

rheumatic /ruːˈmætɪk/ *a.* of or caused by or suffering from rheumatism; **rheumatic fever** fever with pain in joints; **rheumatically** *adv.* [F or L f. Gk (*rheuma* stream)]

rheumaticky *a. colloq.* like or having rheumatism.

rheumatics *n.pl. colloq.* rheumatism.

rheumatism /ˈruːmətɪz(ə)m/ *n.* disease marked by inflammation and pain in the joints, muscles, or fibrous tissue.

rheumatoid /ˈruːmətɔɪd/ *a.* having the character of rheumatism; **rheumatoid arthritis** chronic progressive disease causing inflammation and stiffening of joints.

rhinestone /ˈraɪnstəʊn/ *n.* imitation diamond. [river *Rhine* in Germany]

rhino /ˈraɪnəʊ/ *n.* (*pl.* same or **rhinos**) *colloq.* rhinoceros. [abbr.]

rhinoceros /raɪˈnɒsərəs/ *n.* large thick-skinned quadruped with horn or two horns on nose. [L f. Gk (*rhis*, *rhin-* nose, *keras* horn)]

rhizome /ˈraɪzəʊm/ *n.* rootlike stem growing along or under ground and producing both roots and shoots. [Gk *rhizoma*]

rho /rəʊ/ *n.* seventeenth letter of Greek alphabet (Ρ, ρ). [Gk]

rhodium /'rəʊdɪəm/ *n.* hard white metallic element of platinum group. [Gk *rhodon* rose]

rhododendron /rəʊdə'dendrən/ *n.* evergreen shrub with large clusters of trumpet-shaped flowers. [L f. Gk (*rhodon* rose, *dendron* tree)]

rhomboid /'rɒmbɔɪd/ **1** *a.* like a rhombus. **2** *n.* quadrilateral of which only opposite sides and angles are equal. **3** **rhomboidal** *a.* [F or L f. Gk (foll.)]

rhombus /'rɒmbəs/ *n.* (*pl.* **rhombuses**) oblique equilateral parallelogram, e.g. diamond on playing-cards. [L f. Gk *rhombos*]

rhubarb /'ru:bɑ:b/ *n.* garden plant with fleshy leaf-stalks used like fruit; these stalks; root of a Chinese plant; purgative made from this. [F f. L f. Gk *rha* rhubarb, *barbaros* foreign]

rhyme /raɪm/ **1** *n.* identity of sound between endings of words or of verse-lines; (in *sing.* or *pl.*) verse having rhymes, use of rhyme; word providing a rhyme. **2** *v.* (of words or lines) have rhyme; (of word) act as rhyme *with* another; write rhymes; put or make (story etc.) into rhyme; treat (word) as rhyming *with.* **3** **rhyme-scheme** arrangement of rhymes within a piece of verse; **rhyming slang** slang which replaces words by rhyming words or phrases (e.g. *stairs* by *apples and pears*); **without rhyme or reason** lacking discernible sense or logic. [F *rime* f. L (RHYTHM)]

rhymester *n.* writer of (esp. simple) rhymes.

rhythm /'rɪð(ə)m/ *n.* measured flow of words and phrases in verse or prose determined by various relations of long and short or accented and unaccented syllables; aspect of musical composition concerned with periodical accent and the duration of notes; movement with regular succession of strong and weak elements; regularly recurring sequence of events; **rhythm and blues** popular music with blues themes and strong rhythm; **rhythm method** contraception by avoiding sexual intercourse near times of ovulation; **rhythmic** *a.*; **rhythmical** *a.*; **rhythmically** *adv.* [F or L f. Gk *rhuthmos*]

rib **1** *n.* each of the curved bones articulated in pairs to spine and protecting thoracic cavity and its organs; joint of meat from this part of animal; ridge or long raised piece often of stronger or thicker material across surface or through structure serving to support or strengthen; combination of plain and purl stitches producing ribbed somewhat elastic fabric. **2** *v.t.* (**-bb-**) provide with ribs; *colloq.* make fun of, tease. **3** **rib-cage** bones of thorax. [OE]

ribald /'rɪbəld/ *a.* (of language or its user) coarsely or disrespectfully humorous, obscene. [F (*riber* be licentious)]

ribaldry *n.* ribald talk.

riband /'rɪbənd/ *n.* ribbon. [F *riban*, prob. f. Gmc]

ribbed *a.* having ribs or riblike markings. [RIB]

ribbing *n.* ribs or riblike structure; *colloq.* teasing.

ribbon /'rɪbən/ *n.* narrow strip or band of fabric, used esp. for decoration; material in this form; ribbon of special colour etc. worn to indicate some honour or membership of a sports team etc.; long narrow strip of anything, e.g. inked material used in typewriter; (in *pl.*) ragged strips (*torn to ribbons*); **ribbon development** building of houses along road outwards from town or village. [var. of RIBAND]

ribonucleic acid /raɪbənju:'kli:ɪk/ substance controlling protein synthesis in cells. [*ribose* sugar, NUCLEIC]

rice *n.* kind of grass grown in marshes, esp. in Asia; seeds of this, used as food; **rice-paper** paper made from pith of an oriental tree and used for painting and in cookery. [F *ris* f. It. f. L f. Gk *oruza*]

rich *a.* having much wealth; splendid, costly, elaborate; valuable or copious; abundant or ample (*a rich supply of ideas*); (of soil or region etc.) abounding (*in* or *with* natural resources etc.), fertile; (of food or diet) containing much fat or spice etc.; (of mixture in internal-combustion engine) containing high proportion of fuel; (of colour or sound or smell) mellow and deep, strong and full; (of incident or assertion etc.) highly amusing or ludicrous. [OE & F]

riches *n.pl.* abundant means, valuable possessions. [F *richeise* (prec.)]

richly *adv.* in a rich way; fully, thoroughly (*richly deserves success*). [RICH]

Richter scale /'rɪktə/ scale for stating strength of earthquake. [*Richter*, seismologist]

rick[1] *n.* stack of hay etc. [OE]

rick[2] **1** *v.t.* sprain or strain slightly. **2** *n.* slight sprain or strain. [LG *wricken*]

rickets /'rɪkɪts/ *n.* (as *sing.* or *pl.*) children's deficiency disease with softening of bones. [orig. uncert.]

rickety /'rɪkɪtɪ/ *a.* shaky, weak-jointed, insecure; suffering from rickets; **ricketiness** *n.*

rickrack var. of RICRAC.

rickshaw /'rɪkʃɔ:/ *n.* (also **ricksha**) light two-wheeled hooded vehicle drawn by one or more persons. [abbr. *jinricksha(w)* f. Jap.]

ricochet /ˈrɪkəʃeɪ, -ʃet/ **1** *n.* skipping or rebounding of projectile, esp. shell or bullet, on surface; hit made after this. **2** *v.i.* (*past* **ricocheted** /-eɪd/; *partic.* **ricocheting** /-eɪɪŋ/) (of projectile) skip or rebound once or more on surface. [F]

ricrac /ˈrɪkræk/ *n.* zigzag braided trimming for garments. [RACK¹]

rid *v.t.* (**-dd-**; past and *p.p.* **rid**) make (person or place) free *of* (esp. in **be** or **get rid of**). [ON]

riddance *n.* ridding; **good riddance** welcome deliverance from unwanted person or thing.

ridden *p.p.* of RIDE.

riddle¹ /ˈrɪd(ə)l/ **1** *n.* question or statement testing ingenuity in divining its answer or meaning; puzzling fact or thing or person. **2** *v.i.* speak in or propound riddles. [OE (READ)]

riddle² /ˈrɪd(ə)l/ **1** *v.t.* make many holes in, esp. with gunshot; (in *p.p.*) filled or permeated *with* (errors etc.); pass through riddle. **2** *n.* coarse sieve. [OE]

ride 1 *v.* (*past* **rode;** *p.p.* **ridden** /ˈrɪd(ə)n/) sit on and control or be carried by horse etc.; travel on bicycle or in (esp. public) vehicle; be carried *on* horse or bicycle etc. or *in* vehicle; sit and travel on; be carried or conveyed by (*ship rides the waves*); traverse on horseback etc., ride over or through; lie at anchor, float buoyantly; (of moon etc.) seem to float, rest *in* or *on* while moving; yield to (blow) so as to reduce its impact; give ride to, cause to ride; (of rider) cause (horse etc.) to move forward (*at* fence etc.); (in *p.p.*) dominated or infested (with) (*ridden by guilt*; *rat-ridden cellar*). **2** *n.* journey in (esp. public) vehicle; spell of riding on horse, bicycle, person's back, etc.; path (esp. through woods) for riding on; quality of sensations when riding (*gives a bumpy ride*). **3 let thing ride** leave it undisturbed; **ride down** overtake or trample on horseback; **ride out** come safely through (storm etc., or danger or difficulty); **ride up** (of garment) work upwards when worn; **riding-light** light shown by ship at anchor; **take for a ride** *sl.* hoax or deceive. [OE]

rider *n.* one who rides; additional clause amending or supplementing document, corollary, recommendation etc. added to verdict; *Math.* problem arising as corollary of theorem etc.

ridge /rɪdʒ/ *n.* line of junction of two surfaces sloping upwards towards each other; long narrow hill-top, mountain range, watershed; any narrow elevation across surface; elongated region of high barometric pressure; raised strip of arable land, usu. one of set separated by furrows; **ridge-pole** horizontal pole of long tent; **ridgy** *a.* [OE]

ridgeway *n.* road along ridge.

ridicule /ˈrɪdɪkjuːl/ **1** *n.* making or being made object of derision and mockery. **2** *v.t.* make fun of, subject to ridicule, laugh at. [F or L (*rideo* laugh)]

ridiculous /rɪˈdɪkjʊləs/ *a.* deserving to be laughed at, unreasonable. [prec. or L *ridiculosus*]

riding /ˈraɪdɪŋ/ *n.* former division of Yorkshire (*East*, *North*, and *West Riding*). [OE f. ON, = third part]

Riesling /ˈriːzlɪŋ/ *n.* a kind of dry white wine. [G]

rife *predic. a.* of common occurrence, widespread; well provided *with*. [OE, prob. f. ON]

riffle /ˈrɪf(ə)l/ *v.* turn (pages) in quick succession; leaf quickly *through* pages. [perh. var. of RUFFLE]

riff-raff /ˈrɪfræf/ *n.* rabble, disreputable or undesirable persons. [F *rif et raf*]

rifle /ˈraɪf(ə)l/ **1** *n.* gun with long rifled barrel, esp. one fired from shoulder-level; (in *pl.*) riflemen. **2** *v.t.* search and rob; make spiral grooves in (gun or its barrel or bore) to make bullet spin. [F]

rifleman *n.* soldier armed with rifle.

rifling *n.* arrangement of grooves in rifle.

rift *n.* crack or split in an object; cleft in earth or rock; disagreement, breach in friendly relations; **rift-valley** steep-sided valley formed by subsidence of earth's crust. [Scand., rel. to RIVEN]

rig¹ 1 *v.t.* (**-gg-**) provide (ship) with spars and ropes etc.; fit with clothes or other equipment (often with *out* or *up*); set *up* hastily or as makeshift; assemble and adjust parts of (aircraft). **2** *n.* arrangement of ship's masts and sails etc.; equipment for special purpose, e.g. radio transmitter; = *oil rig*. **3 rig-out** *colloq.* outfit of clothes. [perh. Scand.]

rig² *v.t.* (**-gg-**) manage or conduct fraudulently (*a rigged election*); **rig the market** cause artificial rise or fall in prices. [orig. unkn.]

rigging *n.* ship's spars and ropes etc. [RIG¹]

right /raɪt/ **1** *a.* (of conduct etc.) just, required by morality or equity or duty; correct, true; in good or normal condition, sound, sane, satisfactory; well-advised, not mistaken; the preferable or most suitable, the less wrong or not wrong (*which is the right way?*); on or towards side of human body which corresponds to the position of east if one regards oneself as facing north; on or towards part of thing analogous to person's right side; of the side of fabric meant for show or use; (*archaic* or *colloq.*) real, properly so called (*made a right mess of it*). **2** *n.* justification, fair claim, being entitled to privilege or immunity, thing one is entitled to (*belongs to them by right*; *has no right to do it*); what is just, fair treatment, the juster cause; (in *pl.*) right condition, true state; right-hand part, region, or direction; right hand, blow with this; (often **Right**) political group or section favouring conservatism, conservatives collectively. **3** *v.t.* restore to proper or straight or vertical position; make reparation for or to, avenge (wrong or wronged person); vindicate, justify, rehabilitate; correct (mistakes etc.), correct mistakes in; (usu. *refl.*) set in order (*a fault that will right itself*). **4** *adv.* straight (*go right on*); *colloq.* immediately (*I'll be right back*); all the way *to* or *round* or *through* etc., completely *off* or *out* etc.; exactly, quite (*right in the middle*); on or to the right side; justly, properly, correctly, truly, satisfactorily; *archaic* very, to the full. **5 by right** (or **rights**) if right were done; **in one's own right** through one's own position or effort etc.; **in the right** having justice or truth on one's side; **on the right side of** in the favour of (person), somewhat less than (stated age); **put** (or **set**) **to rights** arrange in proper order; **right and left** on all sides; **right angle** angle of 90°, made by lines meeting with equal angles on either side (**at right angles** placed to form right angle); **right arm** one's most reliable helper; **right bank** bank of river on right facing downstream; **right hand** = *right-hand man*; **right-hand** *a.* on or towards right side of person or thing; **right-handed** using right hand by preference as more serviceable, made by or for the right hand, turning to the right; **right-hander** right-handed person or blow; **right-hand man** indispensable or chief assistant; **right-minded** having sound views and principles; **right of way** right established by usage to pass over another's ground, path subject to such right, precedence in passing granted to one vehicle etc. over another; **Right Reverend** title of bishop; **right wing** right side of football etc. team on field, right section of political party; **right-winger** person on right wing. [OE]

righteous /'raɪtʃəs/ *a.* (of person or conduct) morally right, virtuous, law-abiding. [OE]

rightful *a.* (of action etc.) equitable, fair; (of person) legitimately entitled to; position etc.) (of property etc.) that one is entitled to; **rightfully** *adv.* [OE]

rightism *n.* political conservatism; **rightist** *n.* [RIGHT]

rightly *adv.* justly, properly, correctly, justifiably.

rightmost *a.* furthest to the right.

rightward /'raɪtwəd/ **1** *adv.* (also **rightwards**) towards the right. **2** *a.* going towards or facing the right. [-WARD]

rigid /'rɪdʒɪd/ *a.* not flexible, that cannot be bent; inflexible, strict, harsh; **rigidity** /-'dʒɪdɪtɪ/ *n.* [F or L]

rigmarole /'rɪgmərəʊl/ *n.* rambling or meaningless talk or tale; lengthy procedure. [orig. *ragman roll* catalogue]

rigor /'raɪgɔː, 'rɪgə/ *n.* sudden chill with shivering; **rigor mortis** stiffening of body after death. [L (*rigeo* be stiff)]

rigour /'rɪgə/, *US* **rigor** *n.* severity, strictness, harshness; (in *pl.*) harsh measures or conditions; logical exactitude; strict enforcement *of* rules etc.; austerity of life; **rigorous** *a.* [F f. L (prec.)]

rile *v.t. colloq.* anger, irritate. [F f. L]

rill *n.* small stream. [prob. LG or Du.]

rim *n.* raised edge or border, margin, verge; outer edge of wheel, on which tyre is fitted. [OE]

rime[1] **1** *n.* frost; *poetic* hoar-frost. **2** *v.t.* cover with rime. [OE]

rime[2] var. of RHYME.

rimmed *a.* edged or bordered (*red-rimmed eyes*). [RIM]

rind /raɪnd/ *n.* tough outer layer or covering of fruit and vegetables, cheese, bacon, etc. [OE]

rinderpest /'rɪndəpest/ *n.* disease of ruminants (esp. cattle). [G]

ring[1] **1** *n.* circlet usu. of precious metal worn on finger; circular band of any material; line or band round, or rim of, cylindrical or circular object; mark or part etc. having form of circular band; enclosure for circus performance, boxing, betting at races, showing of cattle, etc.; persons or things arranged in a circle, such arrangement; combination of traders, politicians, spies, etc., acting together for control of operations; circular or spiral course. **2** *v.t.* encompass, encircle; put ring on (bird etc.). **3 the ring** bookmakers; **make** (or **run**) **rings round** do things much better than (another person); **ring-dove** large species of pigeon; **ring-finger** third finger esp. of left hand, on which wedding ring is usu. worn; **ring main** (or **circuit**) electrical circuit serving many sockets in continuous ring; **ring road** bypass encircling town. [OE]

ring[2] **1** *v.* (*past* **rang**; *p.p.* **rung**) give clear resonant sound (as) of bell; make (bell) ring; make telephone call (to); sound in specified way (*ring true*); (of place) resound (*with* sound, fame, talk, etc.); (of ears) be filled with sensation of ringing; sound (peal etc.) on bells; usher *in* or *out* with bell-ringing. **2** *n.* ringing sound or tone; act of ringing bell, sound caused by this; specified feeling conveyed by utterance; *colloq.* telephone call; set of (church) bells. **3 ring a bell** *colloq.* begin to revive a memory; **ring down** (or **up**) **the curtain** cause it to be lowered (or raised); **ring off** end telephone call; **ring up** call by telephone, record (amount) on cash register. [OE]

ringleader *n.* leading instigator in crime, mischief, etc. [RING[1]]

ringlet /ˈrɪŋlɪt/ *n.* curly lock of hair; **ringleted** *a.*

ringmaster *n.* person directing circus performance.

ringside **1** *n.* area immediately beside boxing ring. **2** *a.* (of seat etc.) close to scene of action.

ringworm *n.* contagious fungous skin-disease forming circular patches esp. on child's scalp.

rink *n.* area of natural or artificial ice for skating or game of curling etc.; floor for roller-skating; building containing either of these; strip of bowling-green; team in bowls or curling. [app. F *renc* RANK[1]]

rinse **1** *v.t.* wash out with clean water; wash lightly; put (clothes etc.) through clean water to remove soap etc.; clear (impurities) *out* or *away* by rinsing. **2** *n.* rinsing; solution for temporary tinting of hair. [F *rincer*]

riot /ˈraɪət/ **1** *n.* tumult, disorder, disturbance of the peace by a crowd; loud revelry; lavish display or enjoyment *of* (*a riot of emotion, colour, sound*); *colloq.* very amusing thing or person. **2** *v.i.* make or engage in riot. **3 read the Riot Act** put firm stop to insubordination etc.; **run riot** throw off all restraint, (of plants) grow or spread uncontrolled. **4 riotous** *a.* [F]

rip[1] **1** *v.* (**-pp-**) tear or cut (thing) quickly or forcibly away or apart (*ripped out the lining*; *ripped the book up*); make (hole etc.) thus, make long tear or cut in; come violently apart, split; rush along. **2** *n.* long tear or cut; act of ripping; stretch of rough water. **3 let rip** *colloq.* not check speed of or interfere with (person or thing), speak violently; **rip-cord** cord for releasing parachute from its pack; **rip off** *sl.* defraud, steal; **rip-off** *sl.* fraud, theft; **rip-roaring** wildly noisy; **rip-saw** saw for sawing wood along the grain. [orig. unkn.]

rip[2] *n.* dissolute person; worthless horse. [orig. uncert.]

RIP *abbr.* may he or she or they rest in peace. [L *requiesca(n)t in pace*]

riparian /raɪˈpeərɪən/ *a.* of or on river-bank. [L (*ripa* bank)]

ripe *a.* (of grain or fruit or cheese etc.) ready to be reaped or picked or eaten; mature, fully developed; (of person's age) advanced; fit or ready (*time is ripe for action*). [OE]

ripen *v.* make or become ripe.

riposte /rɪˈpɒst/ **1** *n.* retort; quick return thrust in fencing. **2** *v.i.* deliver riposte. [F f. It. (RESPOND)]

ripple /ˈrɪp(ə)l/ **1** *n.* ruffling of water's surface, small wave or series of waves; gentle lively sound that rises and falls (*ripple of laughter*); wavy appearance in hair etc. **2** *v.* (cause to) form or flow in ripples; show or sound like ripples. **3 ripply** *a.* [orig. unkn.]

rise /raɪz/ **1** *v.i.* (*past* **rose** /rəʊz/; *p.p.* **risen** /ˈrɪz(ə)n/) come or go up, grow or project or swell or incline upwards, become higher; reach higher position or level or intensity or amount; come to surface, become or be visible above surroundings or horizon; get up from lying or sitting or kneeling or from bed; (of meeting etc.) cease to sit for business; recover standing or vertical position, become erect, leave ground; come to life again; (of bread or cake etc.) swell by action of yeast etc.; cease to be quiet or submissive, rebel; (of wind) begin to blow; (of river etc.) have origin, begin to flow *from* or *in* or *at*; (of person's spirits) become more cheerful; (of fish) come to surface to feed. **2** *n.* act or manner or amount of rising; upward slope, hill; social advancement, upward progress, increase in power, rank, price, amount, height, wages, etc.; movement of fish to surface; origin. **3 get a rise out of** cause to display temper or characteristic behaviour; **give rise to** cause or induce or suggest; **rise to** develop powers equal to (occasion). [OE]

riser *n.* vertical piece between treads of staircase.

risible /ˈrɪzɪb(ə)l/ *a.* laughable, ludicrous; inclined to laugh. [L (*rideo ris-* laugh)]

rising **1** *a.* advancing to maturity or high standing (*rising generation*; *rising young lawyer*); approaching (specified age); (of ground) sloping upwards. **2** *n.* revolt, insurrection. [RISE]

risk **1** *n.* chance or possibility of loss or bad consequence (*health risk*; *risk of fire*); person or thing causing risk or regarded in relation to risk (*is a poor risk*). **2** *v.t.* expose to risk; accept the chance of (*risk a sprained ankle*); venture on. **3 at risk** exposed to danger; **run a** (or **the**) **risk** expose oneself to danger or loss etc. [F *risque(r)* f. It.]

risky *a.* full of risk; *risqué*; **riskily** *adv.*; **riskiness** *n.*

risotto /rɪ'zɒtəʊ/ *n.* (*pl.* **risottos**) Italian dish of rice with meat, stock, onions, etc. [It.]

risqué /'rɪskeɪ/ *a.* (of story etc.) slightly indecent. [F (RISK)]

rissole /'rɪsəʊl/ *n.* fried ball or cake usu. of meat mixed with bread crumbs etc. [F]

ritardando /ri:tɑ:'dændəʊ/ *adv.* & *n.* (*pl.* **ritardandos**) = RALLENTANDO. [It.]

rite *n.* religious or solemn observance; action required or usual in this; body of usages characteristic of a Church. [F, or L *ritus*]

ritual /'rɪtjʊəl/ **1** *n.* prescribed order of performing rites; performance of actions in rite; procedure regularly followed. **2** *a.* of or done as ritual or rites. **3 ritually** *adv.* [L (prec.)]

ritualism *n.* regular or excessive practice of ritual; **ritualist** *n.*; **ritualistic** /-'lɪstɪk/ *a.*; **ritualistically** /-'lɪstɪkəlɪ/ *adv.*

ritzy /'rɪtsɪ/ *a. colloq.* high-class, luxurious, ostentatiously smart. [*Ritz*, name of expensive hotels]

rival /'raɪv(ə)l/ **1** *n.* person competing with another for same objective; person or thing that equals another in quality. **2** *attrib. a.* being rival(s). **3** *v.t.* (**-ll-**, *US* **-l-**) be rival of or comparable to; seem or claim to be as good as. [L (*rivus* stream)]

rivalry *n.* being rivals, emulation.

riven /'rɪv(ə)n/ *a.* split, torn violently. [*p.p.* of *rive* f. ON]

river /'rɪvə/ *n.* copious natural stream of water flowing in channel to sea etc.; copious flow (*a river of lava*); **sell down the river** *colloq.* defraud or betray. [AF *rivere* f. Rmc (L *ripa* bank)]

riverside *n.* ground along river-bank.

rivet /'rɪvɪt/ **1** *n.* nail or bolt for holding together metal plates etc., its headless end being beaten out or pressed down when in place. **2** *v.t.* join or fasten with rivets; beat out or press down end of (nail or bolt); fix, make immovable; direct intently (one's eyes or attention etc. *on* or *upon*); engross (person or attention). [F (*river* fasten)]

rivulet /'rɪvjʊlɪt/ *n.* small stream. [F, perh. f. It. (L *rivus* stream)]

RM *abbr.* Royal Marines.

RMA *abbr.* Royal Military Academy.

RN *abbr.* Royal Navy.

Rn *symb.* radon.

RNA *abbr.* ribonucleic acid.

roach *n.* small freshwater fish of carp family. [F]

road *n.* line of communication between places for vehicles and riders, esp. one with prepared surface; way of getting to or achieving (*the road to York*, *ruin*); one's way or route; (usu. in *pl.*) piece of water near shore in which ships can ride at anchor; **one for the road** *colloq.* final (esp. alcoholic) drink before departure; **on the road** travelling, esp. as commercial traveller, itinerant performer, or vagrant; **road-block** barricade set up by authorities on road to stop and search traffic; **road fund licence** disc attesting payment of vehicle excise tax; **road-hog** reckless or inçonsiderate motorist or cyclist; **road-holding** stability of moving vehicle; **road show** theatrical performance by company on tour; **road test** test of vehicle by use on road; **road-works** construction or repair of roads. [OE (RIDE)]

roadie *n. colloq.* assistant of touring musical band, responsible for equipment.

roadside *n.* border of road.

roadstead *n.* road for ships.

roadster *n.* open car without rear seats.

roadway *n.* road; part of road intended for vehicles.

roadworthy *a.* (of vehicle) fit for use on road.

roam **1** *v.* ramble, wander; walk or travel unsystematically over or through or about. **2** *n.* act of roaming, ramble. [orig. unkn.]

roan **1** *a.* (of animal) with coat of which prevailing colour is thickly interspersed with another, esp. bay or sorrel or chestnut mixed with white or grey (*red roan*). **2** *n.* roan animal, esp. horse. [F]

roar **1** *n.* loud deep hoarse sound as of lion. **2** *v.* utter roar; say or shout (*out*) in roar; function with sound of roar; travel in vehicle at high speed with engine roaring. [OE]

roaring **1** *a.* noisy, riotous; brisk (*a roaring trade*). **2** *adv.* very (*roaring drunk*).

roast **1** *v.* cook (food, esp. meat) by exposure to open fire or in oven; heat (coffee-beans) before grinding; expose to fire or great heat; *US* censure; undergo roasting. **2** *attrib. a.* (of meat, potato, chestnut, etc.) roasted. **3** *n.* dish of roast meat; meat for roasting; roast meat; operation of roasting. [F *rost(ir)* f. Gmc]

roaster *n.* fowl etc. suitable for roasting; apparatus for roasting.

roasting *a.* very hot.

rob *v.t.* (**-bb-**) take unlawfully from or deprive *of*, esp. by force or threat of force (*robbed the safe*; *robbed her of her jewels*); deprive *of* what is due or normal (*was robbed of my sleep*); **robber** *n*. [F *rob(b)er* f. Gmc]

robbery *n*. act of robbing, esp. with force or threat of force.

robe 1 *n*. long loose outer garment; (often in *pl*.) long outer garment worn as indication of wearer's rank or office etc.; dressing-gown. **2** *v*. put on robes; clothe (person) in robe; dress. [F]

robin /'rɒbɪn/ *n*. small brown bird with red breast. [F pet name f. *Robert*]

robot /'rəʊbɒt/ *n*. automaton with human appearance or functioning like human; automatic mechanical device; machine-like person. [Czech]

robust /rəʊ'bʌst/ *a*. strong and sturdy, esp. in physique or construction; (of exercise etc.) vigorous, requiring strength. [F or L (*robur* strength)]

roc *n*. gigantic bird of Eastern legend. [Sp. f. Arab.]

rochet /'rɒtʃɪt/ *n*. surplice-like vestment of bishop or abbot. [F f. Gmc]

rock¹ *n*. hard part of earth's crust underlying soil; hard compact material of which rock consists; large detached stone; mass of rock projecting and forming hill, cliff, etc., or standing up into or out of water from bottom; hard sweet in cylindrical stick, usu. flavoured with peppermint; **on the rocks** *colloq*. short of money, (of marriage etc.) broken down, (of drink) served neat with ice; **rock-bottom** *colloq*. (of prices etc.) very lowest (level); **rock-bound** (of coast) having many rocks; **rock-cake** small fruit-cake with rugged surface; **rock-crystal** transparent colourless quartz usu. in hexagonal prisms; **rock-garden** garden (or part of it) with large stones and rock-plants; **rock-plant** plant growing on or among rocks; **rock salmon** dogfish as sold for food; **rock-salt** common salt as solid mineral. [F *roque*, *roche*]

rock² 1 *v*. move gently to and fro, set or keep or be in such motion; sway or shake with force, oscillate, reel; greatly disturb. **2** *n*. rocking motion; modern popular music with strong beat, = *rock and roll*. **3 rock and roll** popular music with strong beat and element of blues; **rock the boat** *see* BOAT; **rocking-chair** chair mounted on rockers or springs for gently rocking in; **rocking-horse** wooden horse on rockers or springs for child to rock on. [OE]

rocker *n*. device for rocking or being rocked; each of curved bars on which rocking-chair etc. is mounted; **off one's rocker** *sl*. crazy.

rockery *n*. pile of rough stones with soil between them for growing rock-plants on. [ROCK¹]

rocket /'rɒkɪt/ **1** *n*. firework or signal in form of cylindrical case that can be projected to height or distance by ignition of contents; projectile operating by reaction of continuous jet of gases released in combustion of propellant within it; device propelled by rocket, esp. bomb or spacecraft; *sl*. reprimand. **2** *v*. move rapidly upwards or away; bombard with rockets. [F *roquette* f. It.]

rocketry *n*. science or practice of rocket propulsion.

rocky¹ *a*. of or like rock; abounding in rocks. [ROCK¹]

rocky² *a*. *colloq*. unsteady, tottering; **rockily** *adv*. [ROCK²]

rococo /rə'kəʊkəʊ/ **1** *a*. of ornate style of art, music, and literature in Europe in 18th c. **2** *n*. this style. [F]

rod *n*. slender straight round stick or metal bar; cane or birch for use in flogging; = *fishing-rod*; (as measure) = PERCH¹; **make a rod for one's own back** cause trouble for oneself. [OE]

rode *past* of RIDE.

rodent /'rəʊdənt/ *n*. animal with strong incisors and no canine teeth (e.g. rat, squirrel, beaver); **rodent officer** official rat-catcher. [L *rodo* gnaw]

rodeo /rəʊ'deɪəʊ/ *n*. (*pl*. **rodeos**) exhibition of cowboys' skill in handling animals; round-up of cattle on ranch for branding etc. [Sp.]

rodomontade /rɒdəmɒn'teɪd/ *n*. boastful talk. [F f. It.]

roe¹ /rəʊ/ *n*. mass of eggs in female fish's ovary (**hard roe**); male fish's milt (**soft roe**). [LG or Du.]

roe² /rəʊ/ *n*. (*pl*. **roes** or **roe**) a small kind of deer. [OE]

roebuck *n*. male roe-deer. [ROE², BUCK¹]

roentgen /'rʌntjən/ *n*. unit of ionizing radiation. [*Röntgen*, physicist]

rogation /rə'geɪʃ(ə)n/ *n*. (usu. in *pl*.) litany of the saints chanted on the three days (**Rogation Days**) before Ascension Day. [L (*rogo* ask)]

roger /'rɒdʒə/ *int*. your message has been received and understood (used in telegraphy etc.); *sl*. I agree. [man's Christian name, code for *R*]

rogue /rəʊg/ *n*. dishonest or unprincipled person; mischievous person, esp. child; wild animal driven away or living apart from herd and of savage temper (*rogue elephant*); inferior or defective specimen among many acceptable ones; **rogues' gallery** collection of photographs of known criminals etc.; **roguish** *a*. [orig. unkn.]

roguery /'rəʊgərɪ/ *n*. roguish behaviour; cheating; mischief.

roister *v.i.* revel noisily, be uproarious. [F *rustre* f. L (RUSTIC)]

role /rəʊl/ *n.* actor's part; person's or thing's function. [F (foll.)]

roll /rəʊl/ **1** *n.* cylinder formed by turning flexible material over and over on itself without folding; thing of similar form (*sausage roll*; *roll of butter*); small individual portion of bread separately baked; official list or register; rolling motion or gait; spell of rolling; continuous rhythmic sound of thunder or drum; complete revolution of aircraft about longitudinal axis. **2** *v.* move or send or go in some direction by turning on axis; (of vehicle) advance or convey on wheels; (of person) be so conveyed; turn over and over into cylindrical or spherical shape, make thus (*rolled a cigarette*); flatten by passing under or between rollers; walk with swaying gait, (of ship or vehicle) sway to and fro sideways; undulate, show undulating surface or motion (*rolling hills*), go or propel or carry with such motion; sound with vibration or trill (*roll one's rs*). **3 be rolling in** have large supply of; **roll by** (or **on**) (of time) pass steadily; **roll-call** calling of list of names to establish presence; **rolled gold** thin coating of gold applied to base metal; **rolled into one** combined in one person etc.; **roll one's eyes** show the whites in various directions; **roll in** arrive in great numbers; **rolling-mill** machine or factory for rolling metal into shape; **rolling-pin** roller for pastry; **rolling-stock** stock of railway (or *US* road) vehicles; **rolling stone** person unwilling to settle for long in one place; **roll of honour** list of those honoured, esp. dead in war; **roll-on** *n.* light elastic corset, (*a.*) (of ship) on to which motor vehicles can be driven, (of cosmetic) applied from container with rotating ball in neck; **roll-top desk** desk with flexible cover sliding in curved grooves; **roll up** make into or form roll, *colloq.* arrive in vehicle or on scene; **strike off the rolls** debar from practising as solicitor. [F f. L *rotulus* dimin. (ROTA)]

roller *n.* hard cylinder for smoothing, spreading, crushing, etc.; small cylinder on which hair is rolled for setting; long swelling wave; **roller-coaster** switchback at fair etc.; **roller-skate** see SKATE[1]; **roller towel** towel with ends joined, hung on roller.

rollicking /ˈrɒlɪkɪŋ/ *a.* jovial and boisterous. [orig. unkn.]

rollmop *n.* rolled pickled herring fillet. [ROLL]

roly-poly /rəʊlɪˈpəʊlɪ/ **1** *n.* pudding made of sheet of suet pastry covered with jam etc., formed into roll, and boiled or baked. **2** *a.* (usu. of child) podgy, plump. [prob. ROLL]

rom. *abbr.* roman (type).

Roman /ˈrəʊmən/ **1** *a.* of ancient Rome or its territory or people; of medieval or modern Rome; Roman Catholic; **(roman)** (of type) of plain upright kind used in ordinary print; (of alphabet etc.) based on ancient-Roman system with letters A–Z. **2** *n.* inhabitant of Rome; citizen of ancient-Roman republic or empire; Roman Catholic; **(roman)** roman type. **3 Roman candle** tubular firework discharging coloured balls; **Roman Catholic** *a.* of part of Christian Church acknowledging the Pope as its head, (*n.*) member of this Church; **Roman Catholicism** beliefs and practice of this Church; **Roman nose** one with high bridge; **Roman numerals** Roman letters representing numbers (I=1, V=5, X=10, L=50, C=100, D=500, M=1,000). [L]

romance /rəˈmæns/ **1** *n.* episode or story centred on highly imaginative and emotive scenes of love or heroism etc., orig. long verse narrative written in a Romance language; such stories as genre, atmosphere characterizing them; love affair regarded in these terms; tendency to be influenced by romances, sympathetic imaginativeness; exaggeration or picturesque falsehood, instance of this; **(Romance)** vernacular language of old France mainly developed from Latin, or corresponding language of Italy, Spain, Provence, etc. **2** *a.* **(Romance)** of any of the languages descended from Latin (French, Italian, Spanish, etc.). **3** *v.i.* exaggerate or distort the truth, esp. fantastically. [F *romanz* f. Rmc (ROMANIC)]

Romanesque /rəʊməˈnesk/ **1** *n.* style of art and architecture prevalent in Europe *c.* 1050–1200, with massive vaulting and round arches. **2** *a.* of this style. [F (-ESQUE)]

Romanian /rəʊˈmeɪnɪən/ **1** *a.* of Romania. **2** *n.* native or language of Romania. [*Romania* in E. Europe]

Romanic /rəˈmænɪk/ **1** *n.* Romance. **2** *a.* of Romance; Romance-speaking; descended from, or inheriting civilization etc. of, the ancient Romans. [L *Romanicus* (ROMAN)]

romanize /ˈrəʊmənaɪz/ *v.t.* make Roman or Roman Catholic in character; put into Roman alphabet or roman type; **romanization** /-ˈzeɪʃ(ə)n/ *n.* [-IZE]

Romano- *in comb.* Roman. [ROMAN]

romantic /rəˈmæntɪk/ **1** *a.* of or characterized by or suggestive of romance (*romantic evening, scene, story*); (of person) given to romance, imaginative or visionary; (of art or music etc.) concerned more with feeling and emotion than with form and aesthetic qualities; (of idea etc.) fantastic, unpractical. **2** *n.* romantic person; romanticist. **3 romantically** *adv.* [F (ROMANCE)]

romanticism *n.* adherence to romantic style in art etc.

romanticist *n.* writer or artist of the romantic school.

romanticize *v.* make romantic; indulge in romance.

Romany /'rɒmənɪ/ **1** *n.* gypsy; the gypsy language. **2** *a.* of gypsies or their language. [Romany (*Rom* gypsy)]

romp 1 *v.i.* play about roughly and energetically; succeed easily (*romped home*). **2** *n.* spell of romping. [perh. RAMP[1]]

rompers *n.pl.* young child's play-garment usu. covering trunk only.

rondeau /'rɒndəʊ/ *n.* short poem with only two rhymes throughout and opening words used twice as refrain. [F (as foll.)]

rondel /'rɒnd(ə)l/*n.* rondeau, esp. of special form. [F (ROUND); cf. ROUNDEL]

rondo /'rɒndəʊ/ *n.* (*pl.* **rondos**) piece of music with leading theme which recurs several times. [It., f. F RONDEAU]

Röntgen rays /'rʌntjən/ X-rays. [*Röntgen*, physicist]

rood *n.* crucifix, esp. one raised on middle of rood-screen; quarter-acre; **rood-screen** carved screen separating nave and chancel. [OE]

roof 1 *n.* upper covering of building; top of covered vehicle; overhead rock in cave or mine etc. **2** *v.t.* cover (*in* or *over*) with roof; be roof of. **3 hit** (or **raise**) **the roof** *colloq.* become very angry; **roof-garden** garden on flat roof of building; **roof of the mouth** palate; **roof-rack** framework to carry luggage etc. on roof of car; **roof-top** outer surface of roof; **roof-tree** ridge-piece of roof. [OE]

roofing *n.* material used for roof.

rook[1] /rʊk/ **1** *n.* black bird of crow family, nesting in colonies. **2** *v.t.* win money from at cards etc. esp. by swindling; charge (customer) extortionately. [OE]

rook[2] /rʊk/ *n.* chess piece with battlement-shaped top. [F f. Arab.]

rookery *n.* colony of rooks or penguins or seals. [ROOK[1]]

rookie /'rʊkɪ/ *n. sl.* recruit. [corrupt.]

room /ru:m, rʊm/ **1** *n.* space available for or occupied by something; part of house enclosed by walls or partitions, people in this; *pl.* apartments or lodgings. **2** *v.i. US* have room(s), lodge. **3 rooming-house** lodging-house; **room-mate** person sharing room; **room service** provision of food etc. in hotel bedroom. [OE]

roomy /'ru:mɪ/ *a.* having much room, spacious; **roominess** *n.*

roost 1 *n.* bird's perching or resting place, esp. place where fowls sleep. **2** *v.i.* (of bird or person) settle for sleep, be perched or lodged for the night. **3 come home to roost** recoil upon originator. [OE]

rooster *n.* domestic cock.

root[1] **1** *n.* part of plant that attaches it to earth and conveys nourishment from soil; (in *pl.*) fibres or branches of this; small plant with root for transplanting; plant with edible root, such root; embedded part of hair, tooth, etc.; (in *pl.*) what causes close emotional attachment to a place; source or origin *of*; basis, means of continuance; number that when multiplied by itself a given number of times yields a given number, esp. = *square root*; value of quantity such that given equation is satisfied; ultimate element of language from which words have been made by addition or modification. **2** *v.* (cause to) take root; (esp. in *p.p.*) fix or establish firmly (*rooted objection*); drag or dig up by the roots. **3 root and branch** thoroughly, radically; **root out** find and get rid of; **root-stock** rhizome, plant into which graft is inserted, source from which offshoots have arisen; **take root** begin to draw nourishment from soil, *fig.* become established. [OE]

root[2] *v.* dig or turn up (ground etc.) with snout or beak in search of food (also with *up*); rummage, find or extract by rummaging (with *out* or *up*); **root for** *US sl.* encourage by applause or support. [OE & ON]

rope 1 *n.* stout cord made by twisting together strands of hemp or wire etc.; piece of this; quantity of similar things strung together. **2** *v.t.* fasten or secure or catch with rope; enclose with rope (with *in* or *off*); connect with rope. **3 the rope** halter for hanging a person; **know** (or **learn**) **the ropes** know (or learn) procedure for doing something; **rope in** persuade to take part; **rope-ladder** ladder made of two long ropes connected by rungs; **rope-walk** long piece of ground where ropes are made; **rope-walker** performer on tightrope. [OE]

ropy *a. colloq.* poor in quality; **ropiness** *n.*

Roquefort /'rɒkfɔ:/ *n.* (**P**) blue cheese orig. made from ewes' milk. [*Roquefort* in France]

rorqual /'rɔ:kw(ə)l/ *n.* whale with dorsal fin. [F f. Norw.]

rosaceous /rəʊ'zeɪʃəs/ *a.* of the large

family of plants of which the rose is the type. [L (ROSE[1])]

rosary /'rəʊzərɪ/ *n.* (in RC Church) form of devotion made up of repeated prayers; string of beads for keeping count in this. [L *rosarium* rose-garden]

rose[1] /rəʊz/ **1** *n.* prickly bush or shrub bearing fragrant flower usu. of red or yellow or white colour; its flower; flowering plant resembling this (*Christmas rose*); light crimson colour, pink; representation of the flower, design based on it; sprinkling-nozzle of hose or watering-can. **2** *a.* coloured like a pale red rose, of warm pink. **3 rose-bay** willow-herb; **rose-bud** bud of rose, pretty girl; **rose-bush** rose plant; **rose-coloured** pinkish red, *fig.* (of attitude) optimistic, sanguine; **rose-water** perfume made from roses; **rose-window** circular window with roselike tracery. [OE & F f. L *rosa*]

rose[2] *p.p.* of RISE.

rosé /'rəʊzeɪ/ *n.* light pink wine. [F]

roseate /'rəʊzɪət/ *a.* rose-coloured (*lit.* or *fig.*). [L *roseus* (ROSE[1])]

rosemary /'rəʊzmərɪ/ *n.* evergreen fragrant shrub used as culinary herb. [*rosmarine* (L *ros* dew, MARINE)]

rosery *n.* rose-garden. [ROSE[1]]

rosette /rə'zet/ *n.* rose-shaped ornament of ribbons etc., esp. as supporter's badge, or as award or symbol of award in competition; rose-shaped carving. [F dimin. (ROSE[1])]

rosewood *n.* any of several fragrant close-grained woods used in making furniture. [ROSE[1]]

Rosicrucian /rəʊzɪ'kru:ʃ(ə)n/ **1** *n.* member of 17th–18th-c. society devoted to secret lore, or of similar later society. **2** *a.* of Rosicrucians. [*Rosenkreuz*, supposed founder]

rosin /'rɒzɪn/ **1** *n.* resin, esp. in solid form. **2** *v.t.* rub etc. (esp. bow of violin etc.) with rosin. [alt. of RESIN]

RoSPA /'rɒspə/ *abbr.* Royal Society for the Prevention of Accidents.

roster /'rɒstə/ **1** *n.* list or plan showing turns of duty etc. **2** *v.t.* put on roster. [Du. *rooster*, lit. gridiron]

rostrum /'rɒstrəm/ *n.* (*pl.* **rostra**) platform for public speaking or for orchestral conductor. [L]

rosy /'rəʊzɪ/ *a.* rose-coloured, deep pink; cheerful, hopeful (*a rosy future*); **rosily** *adv.*; **rosiness** *n.* [ROSE[1]]

rot **1** *v.* (-**tt**-) undergo natural decomposition, putrefy; gradually perish from want of vigour or use; cause to rot, make rotten. **2** *n.* decay or rottenness (*dry rot*); *sl.* nonsense, absurd statement or argument; series of failures, rapid decline. **3** *int.* expressing incredulity or ridicule. **4** **rot-gut** inferior or harmful liquor. [OE]

rota /'rəʊtə/ *n.* list of persons acting, or duties to be done, in rotation; roster. [L, = wheel]

Rotarian /rəʊ'teərɪən/ **1** *n.* member of Rotary. **2** *a.* of Rotary. [foll.]

rotary /'rəʊtərɪ/ **1** *a.* acting by rotation (*rotary drill*, *pump*). **2** *n.* (**Rotary**, in full **Rotary International**) world-wide society of business men with many branches for international service to humanity, orig. named from members entertaining in rotation. **3 Rotary Club** local branch of Rotary. [med.L (ROTA)]

rotate /rəʊ'teɪt/ *v.* move round axis or centre, revolve; arrange (esp. crops) or take in rotation. [L (ROTA)]

rotation /rəʊ'teɪʃ(ə)n/ *n.* rotating or being rotated; recurrence, recurrent series or period, regular succession of various members of a group; growing of different crops in regular order to avoid exhausting soil; **rotational** *a.*

rotatory /'rəʊtətərɪ/ *a.* rotating; of rotation.

rote *n.* in **by rote** from habit, by mechanical process of memory. [orig. unkn.]

rotisserie /rə'tɪsərɪ/ *n.* cooking-device for roasting food on revolving spit. [F (ROAST)]

rotor /'rəʊtə/ *n.* rotary part of machine; horizontally-rotating vane of helicopter. [ROTA]

rotten /'rɒt(ə)n/ *a.* perishing from decay, falling to pieces or liable to break or tear from age or use; morally or politically corrupt, effete; inefficient, worthless; *colloq.* disagreeable, unpleasant; **rotten borough** *hist.* borough able to elect MP though having very few voters. [ON (ROT)]

rotter *n.sl.* objectionable or contemptible person. [ROT]

rotund /rəʊ'tʌnd/ *a.* (of person) plump, podgy; (of speech or literary style etc.) sonorous, grandiloquent; **rotundity** *n.* [L *rotundus* (ROTA)]

rotunda /rəʊ'tʌndə/ *n.* circular building or hall, esp. one with dome. [It. *rotonda* (prec.)]

rouble /'ru:b(ə)l/ *n.* currency unit of USSR. [F f. Russ.]

roué /'ru:eɪ/ *n.* debauchee, rake, esp. elderly one. [F]

rouge /ru:ʒ/ **1** *n.* red cosmetic used to colour cheeks and lips. **2** *v.* colour with rouge; adorn oneself with rouge. [F f. L *rubeus* red]

rough /rʌf/ **1** *a.* having uneven surface, not smooth or level; not mild or quiet or gentle; violent, boisterous, harsh (*rough manners*, *sea*, *weather*); severe, unpleasant, demanding (*had a rough time*);

deficient in finish etc., approximate, preliminary (*rough sketch*, *estimate*). **2** *adv.* in rough manner. **3** *n.* hardship (*take the rough with the smooth*); hooligan; rough ground; *the* unfinished or natural state. **4** *v.i.* turn (feathers etc.) *up* by rubbing; sketch *in*, shape or plan *out*, roughly. **5** **rough-and-ready** rough or crude but effective, not elaborate or over-particular; **rough-and-tumble** *a.* disorderly, irregular, (*n.*) disorderly fight; **rough deal** see DEAL[1]; **rough diamond** uncut diamond, person of good nature but rough manners; **rough-dry** *v.t.* dry (clothes) without ironing; **rough house** *sl.* disturbance, violent behaviour; **rough it** do without basic comforts; **rough justice** treatment that is approximately fair; **rough-rider** one who rides unbroken horses; **rough up** *sl.* attack (person) violently. [OE]

roughage *n.* indigestible material eaten to stimulate intestinal action.

roughcast **1** *n.* plaster of lime and gravel, used on outside walls. **2** *v.t.* (*past* and *p.p.* **roughcast**) coat with this.

roughen *v.* make or become rough.

roughneck *n. colloq.* driller on oil rig; *US sl.* rough person.

roughshod *a.* (of horse) having shoes with nail-heads projecting to prevent slipping; **ride roughshod over** treat inconsiderately or arrogantly.

roulette /ru:'let/ *n.* gambling game on table with ball falling at random into any of the numbered compartments round edge of revolving wheel. [F dimin. f. L ROTA]

round **1** *a.* shaped like circle or sphere or cylinder; done with circular motion; entire, continuous, complete; candid. **2** *n.* round object; revolving motion, circular or recurring course, series; group of houses etc. to which goods are regularly delivered; single provision (*of* drinks etc.) to each member of a group; one spell of play in game etc., one stage in competition; playing of all holes in golf-course once; ammunition to fire one shot; slice across loaf, sandwich made from whole slices of bread; rung of ladder; solid form of sculpture etc.; circumference or extent *of*; *Mus.* canon for voices at same pitch or in octaves. **3** *adv.* with circular motion (*wheels go round*); with return to starting-point or earlier state (*summer comes round*); with change to opposite position (*lit.* or *fig.*: *he turned round to look*; *soon won her round*); to or at or affecting all or many points of circumference or area or members of a company etc. (*may I look round?*; *pass it round*); in every direction from a centre or within a radius; by circuitous way (*go a long way round*); to person's house etc. (*ask him round*; *will be round soon*); measuring (specified distance) in girth. **4** *prep.* so as to encircle or enclose; with successive visits to; at or to points on the circumference of (*sat round the table*); in various directions from (*towns round Birmingham*); having as axis or central point; so as to pass in curved course, having thus passed, in position thus reached (*go, be, find him, round the corner*). **5** *v.* give or take round shape; make (number etc.) round by omitting units etc. (often with *off*, *down*, *up*); pass round (cape, corner, etc.). **6** **go the rounds** be passed from person to person; **in the round** with all features shown or considered, (of sculpture) with all sides shown, not in relief, (of theatre) with audience all round stage; **round about** all round, on all sides (of), approximately; **round and round** several times round; **round dance** dance with circular movement or in which dancers form ring; **round figure** (or **number**) figure or number without odd units; **round off** bring to complete state; **round on** attack unexpectedly, esp. verbally; **round robin** petition with signatures in circle to conceal order of writing; **round shoulders** shoulders bent forward so that back is rounded; **round-table conference** one with discussion by members round table; **round trip** trip to one or more places and back again; **round up** gather or bring together; **round-up** *n.* rounding up, summary. [F f. L (ROTUND)]

roundabout **1** *n.* road junction with traffic passing in one direction round central island; merry-go-round or other revolving structure for children. **2** *a.* circuitous.

roundel /'raʊnd(ə)l/ *n.* small disc, medallion; circular identifying mark; = RONDEAU. [F *rondel*(*le*) (ROUND)]

roundelay /'raʊndɪleɪ/ *n.* short simple song with refrain. [alt. of F *rondelet* dimin. (prec.)]

rounders *n.* game with bat and ball in which players run through round of bases. [ROUND]

Roundhead *n.* member of Parliamentary party in English Civil War.

roundly *adv.* bluntly, severely.

roundsman *n.* tradesman's employee delivering goods on regular round.

roundworm *n.* worm with rounded body.

rouse /raʊz/ *v.* (cause to) wake; stir (*up*), make active or excited. [orig. unkn.]

rousing *a.* exciting, stirring.

roustabout /'raʊstəbaʊt/ *n.* labourer

on oil rig; unskilled or casual labourer. [*roust* root out, rouse]

rout[1] **1** *n.* disorderly retreat of defeated troops. **2** *v.t.* put to flight, defeat utterly. [F (ROUTE)]

rout[2] var. of ROOT[2].

route /ru:t/ **1** *n.* way taken in getting from starting-point to destination. **2** *v.t.* (*partic.* **routeing**) send by particular route. **3 route march** training-march for troops. [F *route* road f. L *rupta* (*via*)]

routine /ru:'ti:n/ **1** *n.* regular course of procedure, unvarying performance of certain acts; set sequence in theatrical performance, esp. dance; sequence of instructions to computer. **2** *a.* performed as routine (*routine duties*). [F (prec.)]

roux /ru:/ *n.* (*pl.* same) mixture of fat and flour for making sauce etc. [F]

rove[1] *v.i.* wander without settled destination; (of eyes) look in changing directions; **roving eye** tendency to ogle. [prob. Scand.]

rove[2] *past* of REEVE[2].

rover[1] *n.* roving person, wanderer. [ROVE[1]]

rover[2] *n.* pirate. [LG or Du.]

row[1] /rəʊ/ *n.* line of persons or things; line of seats in theatre etc.; street with houses along one or each side; **in a row** *colloq.* in succession. [OE]

row[2] /rəʊ/ **1** *v.* propel (boat) with oars; convey (passenger) in boat thus. **2** *n.* spell of rowing. **3 row-boat** (or **rowing-boat**) boat propelled by oars. [OE]

row[3] /raʊ/ *colloq.* **1** *n.* loud noise or commotion; fierce quarrel or dispute; severe reprimand. **2** *v.* make or engage in row; reprimand. [orig. unkn.]

rowan /'rəʊən, 'raʊ-/ *n.* mountain ash; its scarlet berry. [Scand.]

rowdy 1 *a.* noisy and disorderly. **2** *n.* rowdy person. **3 rowdily** *adv.*; **rowdiness** *n.*; **rowdyism** *n.* [orig. unkn.]

rowel /'raʊəl/ *n.* spiked revolving disc at end of spur. [F f. L *rotella* dimin. (ROTA)]

rowlock /'rɒlək/ *n.* device for holding oar in place and serving as fulcrum. [*oarlock* (OE; OAR, LOCK[1])]

royal /'rɔɪəl/ **1** *a.* of or suited to or worthy of a king or queen; in service or under patronage of a king or queen (*Royal Air Force, Marines, Navy*); belonging to a king or queen, of family of a king or queen; splendid, on great scale, of exceptional size etc. **2** *n. colloq.* member of royal family. **3 royal blue** deep vivid blue; **Royal British Legion** national association of ex-members of armed forces, founded in 1921; **Royal Commission** commission of inquiry appointed by Crown at request of Government; **Royal Family** family to which sovereign belongs; **royal jelly** substance secreted by worker-bees and fed by them to future queen bees; **royal warrant** warrant authorizing tradesman to supply goods to specified royal person. **4 royally** *adv.* [F f. L (REGAL)]

royalist *n.* supporter of monarchy, or of the royal side in English Civil War.

royalty *n.* being royal; royal persons; member of royal family; sum paid to patentee for use of patent or to author etc. for each copy of his book etc. sold or for each public performance of his work; royal right (now esp. over minerals) granted by sovereign to individual or corporation. [F (ROYAL)]

r.p.m. *abbr.* revolutions per minute.

RSM *abbr.* Regimental Sergeant-Major.

RSPCA *abbr.* Royal Society for the Prevention of Cruelty to Animals.

RSV *abbr.* Revised Standard Version (of Bible).

RSVP *abbr.* (in invitation etc.) please answer. [F *répondez s'il vous plaît*]

rt. *abbr.* right.

Rt. Hon. *abbr.* Right Honourable.

Rt. Revd *abbr.* Right Reverend.

Ru *symb.* ruthenium.

rub 1 *v.* (**-bb-**) move one's hand or other object with firm pressure over surface of; apply (one's hand etc.) thus; clean or polish or make dry or bare by rubbing; apply (polish etc.) by rubbing; remove by rubbing (with *off* or *out*); use rubbing to make (substance) go *in* or *into* or *through* something; move or slide (objects) against each other; move with contact or friction *against* or *on*; chafe or make sore by rubbing; (of cloth, skin, etc.) become frayed or worn or sore or bare with friction. **2** *n.* action or spell of rubbing; impediment or difficulty (*there's the rub*). **3 rub along** *colloq.* cope or manage without undue difficulty; **rub down** dry or smooth or clean by rubbing; **rub it in** emphasize or repeat embarrassing fact etc.; **rub off on** be transferred to by contact (*lit.* or *fig.*); **rub shoulders with** associate with; **rub up** polish, brush up (subject etc.); **rub up the wrong way** irritate. [LG]

rubato /ru:'bɑ:təʊ/ *n. Mus.* temporary disregarding of strict tempo. [It., = robbed]

rubber[1] *n.* tough elastic substance made from latex of tropical plants or synthetically; piece of this or other substance for erasing pencil or ink marks; *sl.* condom; (in *pl.*) *US* galoshes; **rubber band** loop of rubber to hold papers etc. together; **rubber plant** plant yielding rubber, esp. of kind grown as house plant; **rubber stamp** device for inking and imprinting on surface, one who mechanically agrees

to others' actions, indication of such agreement; **rubber-stamp** *v.t.* approve (action) automatically without proper consideration; **rubbery** *a.* [RUB]
rubber[2] *n.* match of usu. three successive games between same sides or persons at bridge etc. or cricket. [orig. unkn.]
rubberneck *US colloq.* **1** *n.* inquisitive person; gaping sightseer. **2** *v.i.* behave as rubberneck. [RUBBER[1]]
rubbing *n.* reproduction or impression made of (esp. brass) relief design by placing paper over it and rubbing with pigment. [RUB]
rubbish /ˈrʌbɪʃ/ *n.* waste or worthless matter; absurd ideas or suggestions, nonsense (often as exclamation of contempt); **rubbishy** *a.* [AF *rubbous*]
rubble /ˈrʌb(ə)l/ *n.* waste or rough fragments of stone or brick etc.; **rubbly** *a.* [prob. AF *robel* f. F *robe* spoils]
rubella /rʊˈbelə/ *n.* German measles. [L *rubellus* reddish]
Rubicon /ˈru:bɪkɒn/ *n.* boundary; **cross the Rubicon** take action by which one becomes committed to an enterprise. [*Rubicon*, river on anc. frontier of Italy]
rubicund /ˈru:bɪkʌnd/ *a.* (of person or complexion) ruddy, high-coloured. [F or L (*rubeo* be red)]
rubidium /ru:ˈbɪdɪəm/ *n.* soft silvery metallic element. [L *rubidus* red]
rubric /ˈru:brɪk/ *n.* direction for conduct of divine service inserted in liturgical book; explanatory words; heading or passage in red or special lettering. [F or L (*ruber* red)]
ruby /ˈru:bɪ/ **1** *n.* rare precious stone with colour varying from deep crimson to pale rose; deep red colour. **2** *a.* deep red. **3 ruby wedding** 40th anniversary of wedding. [F *rubi* f. med.L]
ruche /ru:ʃ/ *n.* frill or gathering of lace etc. [F f. med.L f. Celt.]
ruck[1] *n.* main body of competitors not likely to overtake leaders; undistinguished crowd of persons or things. [app. Scand.]
ruck[2] *v.* crease or wrinkle (*up*). [ON]
rucksack /ˈrʌksæk,ˈrʊk-/ *n.* bag slung by straps from both shoulders and resting on back. [G]
ruction /ˈrʌkʃ(ə)n/ *n. colloq.* disturbance, tumult, row. [orig. unkn.]
rudder *n.* flat piece hinged vertically to stern of vessel or rear of aeroplane for steering. [OE]
ruddy /ˈrʌdɪ/ *a.* (of person or complexion) freshly or healthily red; reddish; *sl.* bloody, damnable; **ruddily** *adv.*; **ruddiness** *n.* [OE]
rude *a.* impolite or offensive; roughly made or done; primitive or uneducated; abrupt or sudden (*rude awakening*, *reminder*); vigorous or hearty (*rude health*). [F f. L *rudis*]
rudiment /ˈru:dɪmənt/ *n.* (in *pl.*) elements or first principles of knowledge or some subject; (in *pl.*) imperfect beginning of something undeveloped; part or organ imperfectly developed because it is vestigial or has no function (e.g. the breast in males); **rudimentary** /-ˈmentərɪ/ *a.* [F or L (prec.)]
rue[1] *v.t.* (*partic.* **ruing**) repent of, wish undone or non-existent. [OE]
rue[2] *n.* an evergreen shrub with bitter leaves. [F f. L *ruta* f. Gk]
rueful *a.* expressing sorrow, genuine or humorously affected; **ruefully** *adv.* [RUE[1]]
ruff[1] *n.* projecting starched frill worn round neck esp. in 16th c.; projecting or conspicuously coloured ring of feathers or hair round bird's or animal's neck; bird of sandpiper family; kind of pigeon. [perh. = ROUGH]
ruff[2] **1** *v.* trump at cards. **2** *n.* trumping. [F *ro(u)ffle*]
ruffian /ˈrʌfɪən/ *n.* violent lawless person; **ruffianism** *n.*; **ruffianly** *a.* [F f. It. *ruffiano*]
ruffle /ˈrʌf(ə)l/ **1** *v.* disturb smoothness or tranquillity of; upset calmness of (person); undergo ruffling. **2** *n.* frill of lace etc. worn esp. round wrist or neck. [orig. unkn.]
rufous /ˈru:fəs/ *a.* (esp. of animals) reddish-brown. [L *rufus*]
rug *n.* floor-mat of shaggy material or thick pile; thick woollen coverlet or wrap; **pull the rug from under** deprive of support, weaken, unsettle. [prob. Scand.]
Rugby /ˈrʌgbɪ/ *n.* (in full **Rugby football**) game played with oval ball that may be kicked or carried; **Rugby League** partly professional form with teams of 13; **Rugby Union** amateur form with teams of 15. [school in Warwickshire]
rugged /ˈrʌgɪd/ *a.* (esp. of ground) having rough uneven surface; (of features) irregular and strongly marked; (of manners etc.) unpolished, rough but sincere; harsh-sounding; (esp. of machine) sturdy. [prob. Scand.]
rugger /ˈrʌgə/ *n. colloq.* Rugby football. [RUGBY]
ruin /ˈru:ɪn/ **1** *n.* destroyed or wrecked state; downfall or elimination (*the ruin of my hopes*); complete loss of property or position (*bring to ruin*); (in *sing.* or *pl.*) remains of building etc. that has suffered ruin (*an old ruin*; *ancient ruins*); cause of ruin (*will be the ruin of us*). **2** *v.t.* bring to ruin, utterly impair or wreck;

(esp. in *p.p.*) reduce (place) to ruins. [F f. L (*ruo* fall)]

ruination /ruːɪ'neɪʃ(ə)n/ *n.* bringing to ruin, ruining or being ruined.

ruinous *a.* bringing ruin, disastrous; in ruins, dilapidated. [L (RUIN)]

rule 1 *n.* principle to which action conforms or is required to conform; prevailing custom, standard, normal state of things; government, dominion; graduated straight measure; thin line or dash in printing; code of discipline of religious order; *Law* order made by judge or court with reference to particular case only. **2** *v.* exercise decisive influence over, keep under control; have sovereign control of or *over*; pronounce authoritatively *that*; make parallel lines across (paper), make (straight line), with ruler etc. **3 as a rule** usually; **rule of thumb** one based on experience or practice, not on theory; **rule out** exclude, pronounce irrelevant or ineligible; **rule the roost** be in control, dominate. [F f. L *regula*]

ruler *n.* person exercising government or dominion; straight strip of wood, plastic, etc., used in drawing or measuring lines.

ruling *n.* authoritative pronouncement.

rum¹ *n.* spirit distilled from sugar-cane or molasses. [orig. unkn.]

rum² *a. colloq.* strange, odd. [orig. unkn.]

Rumanian /ruː'meɪnɪən/ var. of ROMANIAN.

rumba /'rʌmbə/ *n.* ballroom dance of Cuban origin; music for this. [Amer. Sp.]

rumble¹ /'rʌmb(ə)l/ **1** *v.i.* make continuous deep sound as of distant thunder; (of person or vehicle) go *along* etc. making such sound. **2** *n.* rumbling sound. [prob. Du. *rommelen*]

rumble² /'rʌmb(ə)l/ *v.t. sl.* see through (deception), detect. [orig. unkn.]

rumbustious /rʌm'bʌstɪəs/ *a. colloq.* boisterous, uproarious. [prob. var. of *robustious* f. ROBUST]

ruminant /'ruːmɪnənt/ **1** *n.* animal that chews the cud. **2** *a.* belonging to the ruminants; meditative. [foll.]

ruminate /'ruːmɪneɪt/ *v.i.* chew the cud; ponder, meditate; **rumination** /-'neɪʃ(ə)n/ *n.*; **ruminative** *a.* [L (*rumen* throat)]

rummage /'rʌmɪdʒ/ **1** *v.* search thoroughly or untidily (in); find among other things (with *out* or *up*). **2** *n.* search of this kind. **3 rummage sale** jumble sale. [F *arrumage* (*arrumer* stow cargo)]

rummy /'rʌmɪ/ *n.* card-game played usu. with two packs. [orig. unkn.]

rumour /'ruːmə/, *US* **rumor 1** *n.* general talk or report or hearsay, of doubtful accuracy. **2** *v.t.* (usu. in *pass.*) report by way of rumour. [F f. L *rumor* noise]

rump *n.* tail-end or buttocks of animal or person or bird; unimportant remnant, esp. of a parliament; **rump steak** cut of beef from rump. [prob. Scand.]

rumple /'rʌmp(ə)l/ *v.t.* crease, crumple. [Du. *rompelen*]

rumpus /'rʌmpəs/ *n. colloq.* row, uproar, brawl. [orig. unkn.]

run 1 *v.* (**-nn-**; *past* **ran**; *p.p.* **run**) go at pace faster than walk, never having both of a pair of feet on ground at once; flee; go or travel hurriedly, briefly, etc.; advance (as) by rolling or on wheels or smoothly or easily, be in action or operation (*left the engine running*); be current or operative (*lease runs for 99 years*); (of bus, train, etc.) travel or be travelling on its route (*train is running late*); extend, have course or order or tendency (*road runs along the ridge*; *prices are running high*); compete in race, finish race in specified position; seek election; (of liquid etc. or its container) flow or be wet; cause (water etc.) to flow, fill (bath) thus; spread rapidly or beyond proper place (*ink ran over the table*; *shiver ran down my spine*); (in cricket) traverse pitch to score run; traverse or make one's way through or over (course, race, distance); perform (errand); cause (machine or vehicle etc.) to operate, cause (business etc.) to be conducted; take (person) for journey in vehicle; cause to run or go (*ran his car into a tree*); enter (competitor *for* contest); smuggle (guns etc.); chase or hunt; allow (account) to accumulate for a time before paying. **2** *n.* act or spell of running; short excursion; distance travelled; general tendency; regular route; continuous or long stretch or spell or course; high general demand; quantity produced at one time; general or average type or class; point scored in cricket or baseball; permission for free use *of* (*had the run of the house*); animal's regular track, enclosure for fowls, range of pasture; ladder in stocking etc. **3 on the run** fleeing; **run across** encounter; **run away** flee, escape in haste, leave one's family etc.; **run down** knock down or collide with, reduce numbers of (staff etc.), (of unwound clock etc.) stop, (of person or health) become feeble from overwork or underfeeding, discover after search, disparage; **run-down** *n.* reduction in numbers, detailed analysis, (*a.*) decayed from prosperity; **run dry** cease to flow; **run for it** seek safety by fleeing; **run for one's money** some return for outlay or effort; **run in** run (new engine or vehicle) carefully in early stages, *colloq.* arrest; **run in the family** (of trait) be found in all or many members of it; **run into** collide with, encounter, reach as many as (*runs into 6 volumes*); **run low** (or **short**) become depleted, have few left; **run off** flee, produce (copies etc.) on machine, decide (race) after tie or heats, (cause to) flow away, write or recite fluently; **run-of--the-mill** *a.* ordinary, undistinguished; **run out** come to an end, become used up, exhaust one's stock *of*, jut out, put down wicket of (batsman who is running); **run out on** *colloq.* desert (person); **run over** overflow, study or repeat quickly, (of vehicle or driver) pass over, knock down or crush; **run through** examine or rehearse briefly, peruse, deal successively with; **run to** have money or ability for, reach (amount or number), (of person) show tendency to (fat etc.); **run up** accumulate (debt etc.) quickly, build or make hurriedly, raise (flag); **run-up** *n.* period preceding important event; **run up against** meet with (difficulty). [OE]

runaway *n.* & *a.* fugitive.

rune *n.* any letter of earliest Germanic alphabet; similar mark of mysterious or magic significance; **runic** *a.* [ON]

rung[1] *n.* cross-piece of ladder (*lit.* or *fig.*); short stick fixed as crossbar in chair etc. [OE]

rung[2] *p.p.* of RING[2].

runnel /'rʌn(ə)l/ *n.* brook; gutter. [OE]

runner *n.* person or horse that runs, esp. in race; messenger; creeping plant-stem that can take root; rod or groove or blade on which thing slides; sliding ring on rod etc.; long narrow ornamental cloth or rug; **runner bean** a kind of climbing bean; **runner-up** person or team finishing second in competition. [RUN]

running 1 *n.* action of runners in race etc.; way race proceeds. 2 *a.* continuous (*running battle*); consecutive (*three days running*). 3 **in, out of, the running** with good, no, chance of succeeding; **make the running** set the pace (*lit.* or *fig.*); **running commentary** oral description of events as they occur; **running knot** knot that slips along rope etc. and changes size of loop; **running repairs** minor repairs and replacements.

runny *a.* tending to run or flow; excessively fluid.

runt *n.* undersized person or animal; smallest of litter. [orig. unkn.]

runway *n.* specially prepared surface for taking off and landing of aircraft. [RUN]

rupee /ru:'pi:/ *n.* currency unit of India, Pakistan, etc. [Hind.]

rupture /'rʌptʃə/ 1 *n.* breaking, breach; breach of harmonious relations, disagreement and parting; abdominal hernia. 2 *v.* burst (cell or membrane etc.); sever (connection); affect with or suffer hernia. [F or L (*rumpo rupt-* break)]

rural /'rʊər(ə)l/ *a.* in or of or suggesting the country; **rural dean** see DEAN[1]; **rural district** *hist.* group of country parishes governed by elected council. [F or L (*rus rur-* the country)]

ruse /ru:z/ *n.* stratagem, trick. [F]

rush[1] 1 *v.* go or move or pass precipitately or with great speed; impel or carry along rapidly (*was rushed to hospital*); force (person) to act hastily; attack or capture by sudden assault; *sl.* overcharge (customer). 2 *n.* act of rushing, violent advance or attack; period of great activity; sudden migration of large numbers; strong run *on* or *for* a commodity; (in *pl.*) *colloq.* first print or showing of film after shooting. 3 **rush at** attack impetuously; **rush one's fences** act with undue haste; **rush-hour** time each day when traffic is heaviest. [AF *russher*, F *ruser* (prec.)]

rush[2] *n.* marsh plant with slender pith-filled stems, used for making chair-seats or baskets etc.; a stem of this; **rush candle** candle made by dipping pith of a rush in tallow; **rushy** *a.* [OE]

rushlight *n.* rush candle; faint glimmer of intelligence or knowledge.

rusk *n.* slice of bread rebaked as light biscuit, esp. for feeding infants. [Sp. or Port. *rosca* twist]

russet /'rʌsɪt/ 1 *a.* reddish-brown. 2 *n.* russet colour; rough-skinned russet apple. [F f. L *russus*]

Russian /'rʌʃ(ə)n/ 1 *a.* of Russia or its people or language. 2 *n.* native or language of Russia. 3 **Russian roulette** firing of revolver held to one's head after spinning cylinder with one chamber loaded; **Russian salad** salad of mixed diced vegetables with mayonnaise. [med.L (*Russia* in E. Europe)]

Russo- *in comb.* Russian.

rust 1 *n.* reddish or yellowish-brown corrosive coating formed on iron or steel by oxidation; plant-disease with rust-coloured spots; impaired state due to disuse or inactivity. 2 *v.* become rusty; affect with rust; lose quality or efficiency by disuse or inactivity. [OE]

rustic /'rʌstɪk/ 1 *a.* having appearance or manners of country people or peasants; unsophisticated, uncouth; of simple workmanship; made of untrimmed branches or rough timber (*rustic seat, bridge*). **2** *n.* countryman, peasant. **3** **rusticity** /-'tɪsɪtɪ/ *n.* [L (*rus* the country)]

rusticate /'rʌstɪkeɪt/ *v.* send down temporarily from university as punishment; retire to or live in the country; **rustication** /-'keɪʃ(ə)n/ *n.*

rustle /'rʌs(ə)l/ **1** *v.* (cause to) make gentle sound as of dry leaves blown in breeze; go with such sound; steal (cattle or horses). **2** *n.* rustling sound. **3** **rustle up** *colloq.* produce when needed. **4** **rustler** /'rʌslə/ *n.* [imit.]

rusty *a.* rusted, affected by rust; stiff with age or disuse; (of knowledge etc.) faded or impaired by neglect; rust-coloured; (of black clothes) discoloured by age; **rustily** *adv.*; **rustiness** *n.* [OE (RUST)]

rut[1] *n.* deep track made by passage of wheels; fixed pattern of behaviour difficult to change (*in a rut*). [prob. F (ROUTE)]

rut[2] **1** *n.* periodic sexual excitement of male deer etc. **2** *v.i.* (**-tt-**) be affected with rut. [F f. L (*rugio* roar)]

ruthenium /ru:'θi:nɪəm/ *n.* rare hard white metallic element of platinum group. [med.L *Ruthenia* Russia]

ruthless /'ru:θlɪs/ *a.* having no pity or compassion. [*ruth* pity f. RUE[2]]

rutted /'rʌtɪd/ *a.* marked with ruts. [RUT[1]]

RV *abbr.* Revised Version (of Bible).

-ry see -ERY.

rye /raɪ/ *n.* a cereal plant; grain of this, used for bread and fodder; (in full **rye whisky**) whisky distilled from rye. [OE]

rye-grass /'raɪgrɑ:s/ *n.* any of various kinds of fodder-grass. [alt. of *ray-grass*]

S

S, s /es/ *n.* (*pl.* **Ss, S's**) nineteenth letter; S-shaped thing.

S. *abbr.* south, southern.

s. *abbr.* second(s), (former) shilling(s) [orig. f. L *solidus*]; singular; son.

's *abbr.* has, is, us (*he's done it*; *it's time*; *let's go*).

S *symb.* sulphur.

SA *abbr.* Salvation Army; sex appeal; South Africa; South Australia.

Sabbatarian /sæbə'teərɪən/ *n.* person who observes sabbath strictly; **Sabbatarianism** *n.* [L (foll.)]

sabbath /'sæbəθ/ *n.* religious rest-day appointed for Jews on last day (Saturday) and for Christians on first day (Sunday) of week. [OE, ult. f. Heb., = rest]

sabbatical /sə'bætɪk(ə)l/ **1** *a.* of the sabbath; (of leave) granted at intervals to university teacher for study or travel etc. **2** *n.* period of sabbatical leave. [L f. Gk (prec.)]

saber *US* var. of SABRE.

sable /'seɪb(ə)l/ **1** *n.* small dark-furred Arctic mammal; its fur or skin; (in heraldry) the colour black. **2** *a.* black, gloomy. [F f. L f. Slav.]

sabot /'sæbəʊ/ *n.* heavy wooden or wooden-soled shoe. [F]

sabotage /'sæbətɑ:ʒ/ **1** *n.* malicious or wanton damage or destruction, esp. for industrial or political purpose. **2** *v.t.* commit sabotage on; destroy, spoil. [F (prec.)]

saboteur /sæbə'tɜ:/ *n.* one who commits sabotage. [F]

sabre /'seɪbə/ *n.* cavalry sword with curved blade; light fencing-sword with tapering blade; **sabre-rattling** display or threats of military force. [F f. G *sabel*]

sac *n.* membranous bag in animal or vegetable organism. [F or L (SACK[1])]

SAC *abbr.* Senior Aircraftman.

saccharin /'sækərɪn/ *n.* very sweet substance used as substitute for sugar. [G f. med.L *saccharum* sugar]

saccharine /'sækəri:n/ *a.* intensely sweet, cloying.

sacerdotal /sækə'dəʊt(ə)l/ *a.* of priests or priestly office. [F or L (*sacerdos -dot-* priest)]

sachet /'sæʃeɪ/ *n.* small bag or packet containing small portion of a substance or filled with perfumed substance for laying among clothes etc. [F dimin. (SAC)]

sack[1] **1** *n.* large strong bag, for storing or conveying goods; quantity contained in sack; woman's loose-fitting dress; *sl.* bed. **2** *v.t.* put into sack(s); *colloq.* dismiss from job etc. **3** **the sack** *colloq.* dismissal from job etc.; **hit the sack** *sl.* go to bed. [OE f. L *saccus* f. Gk]

sack[2] **1** *v.t.* plunder and destroy (captured town etc.). **2** *n.* sacking of town etc. [F *sac* f. It. *sacco* SACK[1]]

sack[3] *n. hist.* white wine formerly imported from Spain and Canary Islands. [orig. (*wyne*) *seck* f. F *vin sec* dry wine]

sackbut /'sækbʌt/ *n.* early form of trombone. [F]

sackcloth *n.* coarse fabric of flax or hemp; *fig.* mourning or penitential garb (esp. in *sackcloth and ashes*). [SACK[1]]

sacking *n.* material for making sacks, sackcloth.

sacral /'seɪkr(ə)l/ *a.* of the sacrum; of or for sacred rites. [SACRUM]

sacrament /'sækrəmənt/ *n.* symbolic religious ceremony or act, esp. baptism and Eucharist; (in full **Blessed** or **Holy Sacrament**) the Eucharist; sacred thing, influence, etc.; **sacramental** /-'ment(ə)l/ *a.* [F f. L (foll.)]

sacred /'seɪkrɪd/ *a.* connected with religion (*sacred music*); dedicated or appropriated to a god; dedicated *to* some person or purpose; safeguarded or required by religion or tradition, inviolable; **sacred cow** idea or institution unreasonably held to be above criticism. [p.p. of obs. *sacre* consecrate f. F *sacrer* f. L (*sacer* holy)]

sacrifice /'sækrɪfaɪs/ **1** *n.* giving up of something valued for sake of something else, thing given up thus, loss entailed; slaughter of animal or person, surrender of a possession, as offering to a deity; what is thus slaughtered or surrendered. **2** *v.* give up (thing) for sake of something else; devote *to*; offer or kill as sacrifice. **3 sacrificial** /-'fɪʃ(ə)l/ *a.* [F f. L (prec.)]

sacrilege /'sækrɪlɪdʒ/ *n.* violation of what is sacred; **sacrilegious** /-'lɪdʒəs/ *a.* [F f. L (SACRED, *lego* take)]

sacristan /'sækrɪstən/ *n.* person in charge of sacristy and church contents. [med.L (SACRED)]

sacristy /'sækrɪstɪ/ *n.* repository for church's vestments, vessels, etc. [F or It. or med.L (SACRED)]

sacrosanct /'sækrəʊsæŋkt/ *a.* most sacred, inviolable; **sacrosanctity** /-'sæŋkt-/ *n.* [L (SACRED, SAINT)]

sacrum /'seɪkrəm/ *n.* composite triangular bone forming back of pelvis. [L *os sacrum* sacred bone]

sad *a.* unhappy, sorrowful; causing sorrow; regrettable; deplorably bad, incorrigible; **sadden** *v.* [OE]

saddle /'sæd(ə)l/ **1** *n.* seat of leather etc., usu. raised at front and rear, fastened on horse etc. for riding; seat for rider of bicycle etc.; joint of meat consisting of the two loins; ridge rising to a summit at each end. **2** *v.t.* put saddle on (horse etc.); burden (person) *with* task etc.; put (burden etc.) *on* person. **3 saddle-bag** one of pair of bags laid across back of horse etc., bag attached behind saddle of bicycle etc.; **in the saddle** on horseback, *fig.* in office or control. [OE]

saddleback *n.* saddlebacked hill or roof; black pig with white stripe across back.

saddlebacked *a.* with concave upper outline.

saddler *n.* maker of or dealer in saddles etc.

saddlery /'sædlərɪ/ *n.* saddler's trade or goods.

Sadducee /'sædjʊsi:/ *n.* member of Jewish sect at time of Christ emphasizing traditional law and denying resurrection of the dead. [OE f. L f. Gk f. Heb.]

sadhu /'sɑ:du:/ *n.* Indian holy man, sage, or ascetic. [Skr.]

sadism /'seɪdɪz(ə)m/ *n.* enjoyment of cruelty to others; sexual perversion characterized by this; **sadist** *n.*; **sadistic** /sə'dɪstɪk/ *a.* [de *Sade*, author]

s.a.e. *abbr.* stamped addressed envelope.

safari /sə'fɑ:rɪ/ *n.* hunting or scientific expedition, esp. in Africa (*go on safari*); **safari park** area where wild animals are kept in the open for viewing. [Swahili f. Arab.]

safe 1 *a.* free of danger or injury; affording security or not involving risks; reliable, certain; prevented from escaping or doing harm (*have got him safe*); cautious, unenterprising. **2** *n.* strong lockable cabinet etc. for valuables; = *meat-safe*. **3 on the safe side** having margin of error against risks; **safe conduct** immunity from arrest or harm, document granting this; **safe deposit** building containing safes and strongrooms let separately; **safe period** time during and near menstrual period when conception is unlikely. [F *sauf* f. L *salvus*]

safeguard 1 *n.* proviso, circumstance, etc., that tends to prevent something undesirable. **2** *v.t.* guard or protect (rights etc.).

safety *n.* being safe, freedom from danger; **safety-belt** strap securing person safely, esp. = *seat-belt*; **safety-catch** device for locking gun-trigger or preventing accidental operation of machinery; **safety curtain** fireproof curtain in theatre to divide auditorium from stage in case of fire etc.; **safety lamp** miner's lamp so protected as not to ignite firedamp; **safety match** match that ignites only on specially prepared surface; **safety net** net placed to catch acrobat etc. in case of fall; **safety-pin** pin with point bent back to head and held in guard when closed; **safety razor** one with guard to prevent blade cutting skin; **safety-valve** valve releasing excessive pressure in boiler etc., *fig.* means of harmlessly releasing excitement, anger, etc. [F f. L (prec.)]

saffron /'sæfrən/ **1** *n.* orange-coloured stigmas of crocus used for colouring and flavouring; colour of this. **2** *a.* saffron-coloured. [F f. Arab.]

sag 1 *v.i.* (**-gg-**) sink or subside, esp. unevenly; have downward bulge or curve in middle; fall in price. **2** *n.* state or amount of sagging. [LG or Du.]

saga /ˈsɑːgə/ *n.* long story of heroic achievement, esp. medieval tale of Scandinavian heroes; series of connected books telling story of a family etc. [ON (SAW²)]

sagacious /səˈgeɪʃəs/ *a.* having or showing insight or good judgement; **sagacity** /-ˈgæsɪtɪ/ *n.* [L *sagax -acis*]

sage¹ *n.* kitchen herb with dull greyish-green leaves; **sage-brush** growth of plants in some alkaline regions of US. [F f. L SALVIA]

sage² **1** *a.* wise, judicious, experienced. **2** *n.* very wise man. [F f. L *sapio* be wise]

Sagittarius /sædʒɪˈteərɪəs/ *n.* constellation and ninth sign of zodiac. [L, = archer]

sago /ˈseɪgəʊ/ *n.* (*pl.* **sagos**) starch used in puddings etc.; palm with pith yielding this. [Malay]

sahib /sɑːb, ˈsɑːɪb/ *n. hist.* form of address to European men in India. [Urdu f. Arab., = lord]

said *past* and *p.p.* of SAY.

sail **1** *n.* piece of canvas or other material extended on rigging to catch the wind and propel vessel; ship's sails collectively; voyage or excursion in sailing-vessel; ship, esp. as discerned from its sails; wind-catching apparatus on windmill. **2** *v.* travel on water by use of sails or engine-power; navigate (sea, ship, etc.); set (toy boat) afloat; start on voyage; glide or move smoothly or in stately manner. **3 sail close to the wind** sail as nearly against wind as possible, *fig.* come close to indecency or dishonesty; **sailing-boat** (or **-ship**) one driven by sails; **sail into** attack physically or verbally with force; **under sail** with sails set. [OE]

sailboard *n.* a kind of surf board with a sail; **sailboarder** *n.*

sailboarding *n.* sport of riding on sailboard, windsurfing.

sailcloth *n.* canvas for sails; canvas-like dress material.

sailor *n.* seaman or mariner, esp. one below rank of officer; person considered as liable or not liable to sea-sickness (*bad* or *good sailor*). [orig. *sailer* (-ER¹)]

sailplane *n.* glider designed for soaring.

sainfoin /ˈsænfɔɪn/ *n.* pink-flowered fodder plant. [F (L *sanctus* holy, *foenum* hay)]

saint /seɪnt or often before name sənt/ (abbr. **St** or **S.**, in *pl.* **Sts** or **SS**) **1** *n.* holy or (in some Christian churches) canonized person regarded as having place in heaven; very virtuous person. **2** *attrib.* (*Saint* or *St Joan, John*, etc.). **3** *v.t.* canonize; call or regard as saint; (in *p.p.*) sacred, worthy of sainthood. **4 All Saints' Day** 1 Nov.; **St Bernard** dog of very large breed kept orig. in Alps to rescue travellers; **St John's wort** plant with yellow flowers; **St Leger** horse-race at Doncaster for 3-year-olds; **St Swithun's Day** 15 July, on which rain or lack of it is said to presage same for forty days; **St Valentine's Day** see VALENTINE; **St Vitus's dance** disease producing involuntary convulsive movements of the body. **5 sainthood** *n.* [F f. L *sanctus*]

saintly *a.* very holy or virtuous; **saintliness** *n.*

sake¹ *n.* in **for the sake of, for (person's) sake** out of consideration for, in the interest of, in order to please, honour, get, or keep; **for heaven's** (or **God's** etc.) **sake** exclamation of dismay or annoyance or supplication. [OE]

sake² /ˈsɑːkɪ/ *n.* Japanese fermented liquor made from rice. [Jap.]

salaam /səˈlɑːm/ **1** *n.* oriental salutation, 'Peace'; Indian obeisance, a bow with right palm on forehead; (in *pl.*) respectful compliments. **2** *v.i.* make salaam. [Arab.]

salacious /səˈleɪʃəs/ *a.* indecently erotic; lecherous; **salacity** /-ˈlæsɪtɪ/ *n.* [L *salax -acis* (SALIENT)]

salad /ˈsæləd/ *n.* mixture of raw or cooked vegetables, herbs, etc., usu. seasoned with oil, vinegar, etc., and often eaten with or including cold meat, cheese, etc.; vegetable or herb suitable for eating raw; **salad days** one's period of youthful inexperience; **salad-dressing** mixture of oil, vinegar, etc., used with salad. [F f. Prov. (L *sal* salt)]

salamander /ˈsæləmændə/ *n.* lizard-like animal formerly supposed to be able to live in fire; kind of tailed amphibian. [F f. L f. Gk]

salami /səˈlɑːmɪ/ *n.* highly-seasoned sausage, orig. Italian. [It.]

sal ammoniac /əˈməʊnɪæk/ *n.* ammonium chloride, hard white crystalline salt. [L (*sal* salt, *ammoniacus* of Jupiter Ammon)]

salary /ˈsælərɪ/ **1** *n.* fixed regular payment, usu. monthly or quarterly, made by employer to employee. **2** *v.t.* (esp. in *p.p.*) pay salary to. [AF f. L (*sal* salt)]

sale *n.* exchange of commodity for money etc., act or instance of selling; amount sold (*the sales were enormous*); occasion when goods are sold; offering of goods at reduced prices for a period; **for** (or **on**) **sale** offered for purchase; **sale of work** sale for charity etc. of goods provided by participants; **sale or return** arrangement by which retailer can return to wholesaler without payment any goods unsold; **sale-room** room in which auctions are held; **sales talk** persuasive talk to promote sale of goods or acceptance of idea etc. [OE]

saleable *a.* fit to be sold, finding purchasers; **saleability** /-'bɪlɪtɪ/ *n.*

salesman *n.* man employed to sell goods in shop etc. or as middleman between producer and retailer.

salesmanship *n.* skill in selling.

salesperson *n.* salesman or saleswoman.

saleswoman *n.* woman employed to sell goods.

Salic law /'sælɪk/ law excluding females from dynastic succession. [F or L (*Salii* a Frankish tribe)]

salicylic acid /sælɪ'sɪlɪk/ antiseptic and pain-killing substance. [F (L *salix* willow)]

salient /'seɪlɪənt/ **1** *a.* prominent, conspicuous; standing or pointing outwards. **2** *n.* salient angle; bulge in line of military attack or defence. [L *salio* leap]

saline /'seɪlaɪn/ **1** *a.* of salt or salts; containing or tasting of salt or salts. **2** *n.* saline substance, esp. medicine; salt lake, spring, etc. **3 salinity** /sə'lɪnɪtɪ/ *n.* [L (*sal* salt)]

saliva /sə'laɪvə/ *n.* the colourless liquid produced by glands in the mouth; **salivary** *a.* [L]

salivate /'sælɪveɪt/ *v.i.* secrete or discharge saliva esp. in excess; **salivation** /-'veɪʃ(ə)n/ *n.* [L *salivare* (prec.)]

sallow[1] /'sæləʊ/ **1** *a.* (esp. of complexion) of sickly yellow or pale brown. **2** *v.* grow or make sallow. [OE]

sallow[2] /'sæləʊ/ *n.* low-growing willow; a shoot or the wood of this. [OE]

sally /'sælɪ/ **1** *n.* rush from besieged place upon besiegers, sortie; excursion; lively or witty remark. **2** *v.i.* make a sally; go *forth* or *out* on journey or walk etc. [F *saillie* f. L (SALIENT)]

Sally Lunn /sælɪ 'lʌn/ *n.* kind of teacake. [perh. name of girl hawking them]

salmon /'sæmən/ **1** *n.* (*pl.* usu. same) large fish with orange-pink flesh highly valued for food and sport; the colour of its flesh. **2** *a.* orange-pink. **3 salmon-trout** sea trout. [F f. L *salmo*]

salmonella /sælmə'nelə/ *n.* kind of bacterium causing food poisoning. [*Salmon*, veterinary surgeon]

salon /'sælɒn/ *n.* reception-room of large house; meeting here of eminent people; room or establishment where hairdresser or couturier etc. receives clients. [F (foll.)]

saloon /sə'lu:n/ *n.* large room or hall for assemblies etc., or for specified purpose (*billiard saloon*); public room on ship; *US* drinking-bar; **saloon-bar** first-class bar in public house; **saloon car** motor car with closed body for driver and passengers. [F f. It. (*sala* hall)]

salsify /'sælsɪfɪ/ *n.* plant with long fleshy root cooked as vegetable. [F f. It.]

salt /sɔ:lt, sɒlt/ **1** *n.* sodium chloride, substance found in sea-water and got in crystalline forms by mining or by evaporation of sea-water etc., and used esp. to season or preserve food (also **common salt**); chemical compound of basic and acid radicals, acid with whole or part of its hydrogen replaced by metal or metal-like radical; (often in *pl.*) substance resembling common salt in taste, form, etc., (in *pl.*) such substance used as laxative; piquancy, pungency, wit; = *salt-cellar*; (also **old salt**) experienced sailor. **2** *a.* containing, tasting of, cured or preserved or seasoned with, salt. **3** *v.t.* cure, preserve, or season with salt or brine; sprinkle (road etc.) with salt; *sl.* make fraudulent entries in (accounts etc.). **4 salt away** (or **down**) *colloq.* save or put aside for the future; **salt-cellar** container for salt at table; **salt-lick** place where animals lick earth impregnated with salt; **salt-mine** mine yielding rock-salt, *fig.* place of unremitting toil; **the salt of the earth** the finest people, those who keep society wholesome; **salt-pan** hollow near sea where salt is got by evaporation; **take with a grain** (or **pinch**) **of salt** regard sceptically; **worth one's salt** deserving one's position, competent. [OE]

SALT /sɒlt/ *abbr.* Strategic Arms Limitation Talks.

salting *n.* marsh overflowed by sea. [SALT]

saltire /'sæltaɪə/ *n.* X-shaped cross dividing shield etc. into four sections. [F *sautoir* stile f. L (SALIENT)]

saltpetre /sɒlt'pi:tə/, *US* **saltpeter** *n.* white crystalline salty substance used as constituent of gunpowder, in preserving meat, and medicinally. [F f. L, = salt of rock]

salty *a.* containing or tasting of salt; piquant, pungent; **saltiness** *n.* [SALT]

salubrious /sə'lu:brɪəs/ *a.* health-giving, healthy; **salubrity** *n.* [L (*salus* health)]

saluki /sə'lu:kɪ/ *n.* tall slender silky-coated dog. [Arab.]

salutary /'sæljʊtərɪ/ *a.* producing good effects; **salutarily** *adv.* [F or L (SALUTE)]

salutation /sælju:'teɪʃ(ə)n/ *n.* sign or expression of greeting or respect; use of these; **salutatory** /sə'lju:tətərɪ/ *a.* [F or L (foll.)]

salute /sə'lu:t, -'lju:t/ **1** *n.* gesture of respect or homage or courteous recognition; prescribed movement of hand or firing of gun(s) etc. as formal or ceremonial sign of respect. **2** *v.t.* make salute to (person etc.); greet with polite gesture; express respect for, commend. [L (*salus -ut-* health)]

salvage /'sælvɪdʒ/ **1** *n.* rescue of property from loss at sea or from fire etc.; payment made or due for this; property so saved; saving and utilization of waste materials; materials salvaged. **2** *v.t.* save from wreck etc.; make salvage of. **3 salvageable** *a.* [F or L (SAVE)]

salvation /sæl'veɪʃ(ə)n/ *n.* act of saving or being saved, esp. from sin and its consequences; religious conversion; person or thing that saves from loss or calamity etc.; **Salvation Army** religious and missionary organization on quasi-military lines for revival of religion and helping the poor; **Salvationist** *n.* [F f. L (SAVE)]

salve[1] **1** *n.* healing ointment; thing that soothes or consoles. **2** *v.t.* soothe. [OE]

salve[2] *v.t.* save from wreck or fire etc.; **salvor** *n.* [back-form. f. SALVAGE]

salver *n.* tray, usu. metal, on which letters or refreshments etc., are handed. [F *salve* or Sp. *salva* assaying of food (SAVE)]

salvia /'sælvɪə/ *n.* garden plant of sage family, esp. species with red flowers. [L, = SAGE[1]]

salvo /'sælvəʊ/ *n.* (*pl.* **salvoes**) simultaneous discharge of guns or bombs; round of applause. [F f. It. *salva*]

sal volatile /və'lætɪlɪ/ solution of ammonium carbonate, used as restorative in fainting etc. [L, = volatile salt]

Samaritan /sə'mærɪt(ə)n/ *n.* charitable or helpful person (also **good Samaritan**); member of an organization helping people in difficulties. [L f. Gk (*Samareia* Samaria)]

samarium /sə'meərɪəm/ *n.* metallic element of lanthanide series. [ult. f. *Samarski*, official]

samba /'sæmbə/ **1** *n.* a ballroom dance of Brazilian origin. **2** *v.i.* dance samba. [Port.]

same 1 *a.* the identical, not different (*read the same book again*); unchanged, unvarying (*gave the same answer as before*); just mentioned (*these same people came again*). **2** *pron.* (**the same**) the same person or thing; the person or thing just mentioned. **3** *adv.* (**the same**) in the same way, similarly (*we all feel the same about it*). **4 all** (or **just**) **the same** nevertheless; **be all** (or **just**) **the same** make no difference (*to* person); **same here** *colloq.* the same applies to me, I agree. [OE]

samizdat /'sæmɪzdæt/ *n.* system of clandestine publication of banned literature in USSR. [Russ.]

samovar /'sæməvɑ:/ *n.* Russian tea-urn. [Russ.]

Samoyed /'sæməjed/ *n.* member of people of northern Siberia; dog of white Arctic breed. [Russ.]

sampan /'sæmpæn/ *n.* small boat used in Far East. [Chin.]

samphire /'sæmfaɪə/ *n.* cliff plant used in pickles. [F, = herb of St. Peter]

sample /'sɑ:mp(ə)l/ **1** *n.* small part or quantity intended to show what whole is like; specimen; illustrative or typical example. **2** *v.t.* take or give sample of; try qualities of; get representative experience of. [AF (EXAMPLE)]

sampler *n.* piece of embroidery worked in various stitches as specimen of proficiency. [F (EXEMPLAR)]

Samson /'sæms(ə)n/ *n.* person of great strength. [*Samson* in OT]

samurai /'sæmʊraɪ/ *n.* (*pl.* same) Japanese army officer; *hist.* member of military caste in Japan. [Jap.]

sanatorium /sænə'tɔ:rɪəm/ *n.* (*pl.* **sanatoriums**) establishment for treatment of invalids, esp. of convalescents and the chronically sick; accommodation for sick persons in school etc. [L (*sano* heal)]

sanctify /'sæŋktɪfaɪ/ *v.t.* consecrate, make or observe as holy; free from sin; justify, sanction; **sanctification** /-fɪ'keɪʃ(ə)n/ *n.* [F f. L (SAINT)]

sanctimonious /sæŋktɪ'məʊnɪəs/ *a.* making a show of righteousness or piety. [L *sanctimonia* sanctity]

sanction /'sæŋkʃ(ə)n/ **1** *n.* approval or encouragement given to action etc. by custom or tradition, express permission; confirmation or ratification of law etc.; penalty for disobeying a law or reward for obeying it, consideration helping to enforce obedience to any rule of conduct, (esp. in *pl.*) economic or military action to coerce a State to conform with (esp. international) agreement etc. **2** *v.t.* authorize, countenance, or agree to (action etc.); ratify, attach penalty or reward to (law). [F f. L (*sancio sanct-* make sacred)]

sanctity /'sæŋktɪtɪ/ *n.* holiness, sacredness. [F or L (SAINT)]

sanctuary /'sæŋktjʊərɪ/ *n.* holy place; holiest part of temple, part of chancel containing altar; place where birds or wild animals etc. are bred and protected; (esp. *hist.*) place of refuge. [F f. L (SAINT)]

sanctum /'sæŋktəm/ *n.* holy place; private room or study. [L (SAINT)]

sand 1 *n.* loose granular substance resulting from wearing down of esp. siliceous rocks and found on sea-shore, river-beds, deserts, etc.; (in *pl.*) grains of sand, expanse of sand, sandbank. 2 *v.t.* smooth or polish with sandpaper; sprinkle, cover, or treat with sand. 3 **sand-blast** *n.* jet of sand driven by compressed air or steam for cleaning glass or stone etc. surface, (*v.t.*) treat with this; **sand-castle** structure of sand made by or for child on sea-shore; **sand-dune** (or **-hill**) = DUNE; **sand-martin** bird nesting in sandy banks; **sand-pit** pit etc. containing sand for children to play in; **sand-yacht** yachtlike vehicle on wheels for use on sand. [OE]

sandal[1] /'sænd(ə)l/ *n.* shoe with openwork upper or no upper, usu. fastened with straps. [L f. Gk]

sandal[2] /'sænd(ə)l/ *n.* (in full **sandalwood**) scented wood; tree with this. [L, ult. f. Skr.]

sandbag 1 *n.* bag filled with sand esp. for making temporary defences. 2 *v.t.* (**-gg-**) defend or hit with sandbag(s). [SAND]

sandbank *n.* deposit of sand forming shallow place in sea or river.

sandman *n.* imaginary person causing sleepiness in children.

sandpaper 1 *n.* paper with abrasive coating for smoothing or polishing. 2 *v.t.* treat with sandpaper.

sandpiper *n.* bird inhabiting wet sandy places.

sandstone *n.* sedimentary rock of compressed sand.

sandstorm *n.* storm with clouds of sand raised by wind.

sandwich /'sænwɪdʒ/ 1 *n.* two or more slices of bread with filling between; cake of two or more layers with jam or cream etc. between. 2 *v.t.* put (thing, statement, etc.) between two others of different kind. 3 **sandwich course** course of training with alternate periods of practical and theoretical work. [Earl of *Sandwich*]

sandy *a.* having much sand; sand-coloured; (of hair) yellowish-red; **sandiness** *n.* [OE (SAND)]

sane *a.* of sound mind, not mad; (of views) moderate, sensible. [L *sanus* healthy]

sang *past* of SING.

sang-froid /sɑ̃'frwɑ:/ *n.* calmness in danger or difficulty. [F, = cold blood]

sangría /sæŋ'gri:ə/ *n.* Spanish drink of red wine with lemonade etc. [Sp., = bleeding]

sanguinary /'sæŋgwɪnərɪ/ *a.* accompanied by or delighting in bloodshed; bloody, bloodthirsty. [L *sanguis -guin-* blood]

sanguine /'sæŋgwɪn/ *a.* optimistic; (of complexion) bright and florid. [F f. L (prec.)]

Sanhedrin /'sænɪdrɪn/ *n.* highest court of justice and supreme council in ancient Jerusalem. [Heb. f. Gk *sunedrion* council]

sanitarium /sænɪ'teərɪəm/ *n.* *US* sanatorium. [foll.]

sanitary /'sænɪtərɪ/ *a.* of or aimed at or assisting the protection of health; hygienic; **sanitary towel** absorbent pad used during menstruation. [F f. L *sanitas* (SANE)]

sanitation /sænɪ'teɪʃ(ə)n/ *n.* sanitary conditions, maintenance or improvement of these; disposal of sewage and refuse etc. [irreg. f. prec.]

sanitize /'sænɪtaɪz/ *v.t.* make sanitary. [SANITARY]

sanity /'sænɪtɪ/ *n.* being sane. [L *sanitas* (SANE)]

sank *past* of SINK.

Sanskrit /'sænskrɪt/ 1 *n.* the ancient and sacred language of Hindus in India. 2 *a.* of or in Sanskrit. 3 **Sanskritic** /-'krɪtɪk/ *a.* [Skr., = composed]

Santa Claus /sæntə 'klɔ:z/ person said to fill children's stockings with presents on night before Christmas. [Du., = St. Nicholas]

sap[1] 1 *n.* vital juice circulating in plants; vigour, vitality; *sl.* foolish person. 2 *v.t.* (**-pp-**) drain or dry (wood) of sap; exhaust vigour of, weaken. [OE]

sap[2] 1 *n.* tunnel or trench to conceal assailants' approach to fortified place; insidious undermining of belief etc. 2 *v.* (**-pp-**) dig saps; undermine (wall etc.); destroy insidiously, weaken. [F *sappe* or It. *zappa* spade]

sapid /'sæpɪd/ *a.* savoury, palatable; (of writings etc.) not insipid or vapid; **sapidity** /-'pɪdɪtɪ/ *n.* [L *sapio* have savour]

sapient /'seɪpɪənt/ *a.* *literary* wise, pretending to be wise; **sapience** *n.* [F or L (*sapio* be wise)]

sapling *n.* young tree. [SAP[1]]

sapper *n.* one who digs saps; soldier of Royal Engineers (esp. as official term for private). [SAP[2]]

Sapphic /'sæfɪk/ *a.* of Sappho or her poetry, esp. (of stanza or verse) in four-line form with short fourth line. [F f. L f. Gk (*Sappho*, poetess of Lesbos)]

sapphire /'sæfaɪə/ 1 *n.* transparent blue precious stone; its bright blue colour. 2 *a.* of sapphire blue. [F f. L f. Gk]

sappy *a.* full of sap; young and vigorous. [SAP[1]]

saprophyte /'sæprəʊfaɪt/ *n.* vegetable organism living on dead organic matter. [Gk *sapros* rotten, *phuō* grow]

saraband /'særəbænd/ *n.* slow Spanish dance; music for this. [F f. Sp.]
Saracen /'særəs(ə)n/ *n.* Arab or Muslim of time of Crusades. [F f. L f. Gk]
sarcasm /'sɑːkæz(ə)m/ *n.* bitter or wounding remark or comment, esp. ironically worded; use of such remarks. [F or L f. Gk (*sarkazō* speak bitterly)]
sarcastic /sɑː'kæstɪk/ *a.* using or showing sarcasm; given to sarcasm; **sarcastically** *adv.*
sarcoma /sɑː'kəʊmə/ *n.* (*pl.* **sarcomata**) malignant tumour on connective tissue. [Gk (*sarx sark-* flesh)]
sarcophagus /sɑː'kɒfəgəs/ *n.* (*pl.* **sarcophagi** /-aɪ/) stone coffin. [L f. Gk, = flesh-consumer]
sardine /sɑː'diːn/ *n.* young pilchard or similar small fish often tinned tightly packed in oil; **like sardines** crowded close together. [F f. L]
sardonic /sɑː'dɒnɪk/ *a.* grimly jocular, full of bitter mockery, cynical; **sardonically** *adv.* [F f. L f. Gk]
sardonyx /'sɑːdənɪks/ *n.* onyx in which white layers alternate with yellow or orange ones. [L f. Gk]
sargasso /sɑː'gæsəʊ/ *n.* (*pl.* **sargassos**) seaweed with berry-like air-vessels. [Port.]
sarge *n. sl.* sergeant. [abbr.]
sari /'sɑːrɪ/ *n.* length of material draped round body, worn as main garment by Hindu women. [Hindi]
sarong /sə'rɒŋ/ *n.* Malay or Javanese garment of long strip of cloth tucked round waist or under armpits. [Malay]
sarsaparilla /sɑːsəpə'rɪlə/ *n.* tropical American smilax; its dried roots; tonic made from these. [Sp.]
sarsen /'sɑːs(ə)n/ *n.* sandstone etc. boulder, relict carried by ice in glacial period. [SARACEN]
sarsenet /'sɑːsnɪt/ *n.* soft silk fabric used esp. as lining. [AF f. *sarzin* SARACEN]
sartorial /sɑː'tɔːrɪəl/ *a.* of clothes or tailoring. [L *sartor* tailor]
sash[1] *n.* long strip or loop of cloth etc. worn over one shoulder or round waist esp. as part of uniform or insignia. [Arab., = muslin]
sash[2] *n.* frame holding glass in sash-window; **sash cord** strong cord attaching sash-weights to sash; **sash-weight** weight attached to each end of sash to balance it at any height; **sash-window** window usu. made to slide up and down in grooves. [CHASSIS]
sassafras /'sæsəfræs/ *n.* a medicinal bark; N. American tree with this. [Sp. or Port.]
Sassenach /'sæsənæx, -æk/ *n.* (*Sc. & Ir.*, usu. *derog.*) Englishman. [Gael. f. L (SAXON)]
sat *past & p.p.* of SIT.
Sat. *abbr.* Saturday.
Satan /'seɪt(ə)n/ *n.* the Devil. [OE f. L f. Gk f. Heb., = enemy]
satanic /sə'tænɪk/ *a.* of or like Satan, devilish, evil; **satanically** *adv.*
Satanism /'seɪtənɪz(ə)m/ *n.* worship of Satan; pursuit of evil.
satchel /'sætʃ(ə)l/ *n.* small bag usu. with shoulder-strap, esp. for carrying school-books. [F f. L (SACK[1])]
sate /seɪt/ *v.t.* satiate. [prob. dial. *sade* satisfy]
sateen /sæ'tiːn/ *n.* glossy cotton fabric woven like satin. [alt. of SATIN]
satellite /'sætəlaɪt/ *n.* heavenly or artificial body revolving round earth or other planet; follower, hanger-on, underling; small country etc. controlled by or dependent on another. [F, or L *satelles -lit-* attendant]
satiate /'seɪʃɪeɪt/ *v.t.* gratify fully, surfeit; **satiable** *a.*; **satiation** /-'eɪʃ(ə)n/ *n.* [L (*satis* enough)]
satiety /sə'taɪətɪ/ *n.* glutted state; feeling of having had too much; **to satiety** in excessive measure. [F f. L (prec.)]
satin /'sætɪn/ **1** *n.* silk etc. fabric with glossy surface on one side. **2** *a.* smooth as satin. **3** *v.t.* give glossy surface to (paper). **4 satiny** *a.* [F f. Arab.]
satinwood *n.* a kind of choice glossy timber.
satire /'sætaɪə/ *n.* use of ridicule or irony etc. to expose folly or vice etc.; work or composition using satire; **satirical** /sə'tɪrɪk(ə)l/ *a.* [F, or L *satira* medley]
satirist /'sætɪrɪst/ *n.* writer or performer of satires.
satirize /'sætɪraɪz/ *v.t.* attack with satire; describe satirically. [F (SATIRE)]
satisfaction /sætɪs'fækʃ(ə)n/ *n.* satisfying or being satisfied; thing that satisfies desire or gratifies feeling; thing that settles obligation or debt, or compensates for injury or loss. [F f. L (SATISFY)]
satisfactory /sætɪs'fæktərɪ/ *a.* adequate, giving satisfaction; **satisfactorily** *adv.* [F or med.L (foll.)]
satisfy /'sætɪsfaɪ/ *v.* fulfil expectations or desires of, be adequate; content, please; adequately fulfil or deal with (obligation or debt, expectation, etc.); put an end to (an appetite or want) by giving what is required, rid (person) similarly of an appetite or want; provide with adequate information or proof, convince (*that*); **satisfy oneself** become certain (*that*). [F f. L *satisfacio*]
satrap /'sætræp/ *n.* provincial governor in ancient Persian empire. [F or L f. Gk f. Pers.]

satsuma /sæt'su:mə/ *n.* a kind of mandarin orange. [*Satsuma*, province in Japan]
saturate /'sætʃəreɪt, -tjʊr-/ *v.t.* fill with moisture, cause to absorb or accept as much as possible; cause (substance) to absorb or hold or combine with greatest possible amount of another substance. [L (*satur* full)]
saturation /sætʃə'reɪʃ(ə)n, -tjʊr-/ *n.* act or result of being saturated; **saturation point** stage beyond which no more can be absorbed or accepted.
Saturday /'sætədeɪ, -dɪ/ **1** *n.* day of week following Friday. **2** *adv. colloq.* on Saturday. **3 Saturdays** on Saturdays, each Saturday. [OE f. L (foll.)]
Saturnalia /sætə'neɪlɪə/ *n.* ancient-Roman festival of Saturn, observed as time of unrestrained merry-making; (**saturnalia**) scene or time of wild revelry or tumult. [L pl. (*Saturnus* Rom. god)]
saturnine /'sætənaɪn/ *a.* of gloomy temperament or appearance. [F f. med.L (as prec.)]
satyr /'sætə/ *n.* (in Greek and Roman mythology) half-human half-animal woodland deity noted for lechery; lustful or sensual man. [F or L f. Gk]
sauce /sɔ:s/ **1** *n.* liquid or soft preparation used as relish with food; thing that adds piquancy or interest; impudence, impertinent speech or action. **2** *v.t. colloq.* be impudent to (person). [F f. Rmc (L *salsus* salted)]
saucepan *n.* metal cooking-vessel, usu. round and with long handle at side, for use on top of cooker etc.
saucer *n.* small shallow dish esp. for standing cup on; thing of this shape. [F f. L (SAUCE)]
saucy *a.* impudent, cheeky; *colloq.* stylish, smart-looking; **saucily** *adv.* [SAUCE]
sauerkraut /'saʊəkraʊt/ *n.* German dish of chopped pickled cabbage. [G]
sauna /'sɔ:nə/ *n.* Finnish-style steam-bath; building or room for this. [Finn.]
saunter /'sɔ:ntə/ **1** *v.i.* walk in leisurely way. **2** *n.* leisurely ramble or gait. [orig. unkn.]
saurian /'sɔ:rɪən/ **1** *n.* animal of lizard family. **2** *a.* of or like a lizard. [Gk *saura* lizard]
sausage /'sɒsɪdʒ/ *n.* minced meat seasoned and enclosed in cylindrical case of thin membrane; a length of this; sausage-shaped object; **not a sausage** *sl.* nothing at all; **sausage meat** minced and seasoned meat used in sausages or as stuffing; **sausage roll** sausage meat baked in cylindrical pastry-case. [F *saussiche* f. L (SAUCE)]
sauté /'səʊteɪ/ **1** *a.* quickly and lightly fried in little fat. **2** *n.* food cooked thus. **3** *v.t.* (*past* and *p.p.* **sautéd**) cook thus. [F (*sauter* jump)]
Sauternes /səʊ'tɜ:n/ *n.* sweet white French wine. [*Sauternes* in France]
savage /'sævɪdʒ/ **1** *a.* uncivilized, primitive; fierce, cruel; *colloq.* very angry. **2** *n.* member of savage tribe; brutal or barbarous person. **3** *v.t.* (of animal) attack savagely, maul; (of critic etc.) attack fiercely. [F f. Rmc (L *silva* a wood)]
savagery *n.* savage behaviour or state.
savannah /sə'vænə/ *n.* grassy plain in tropical or subtropical region. [Sp.]
savant /'sævənt/ *n.* learned person. [F]
save 1 *v.* rescue or preserve from danger or harm etc.; keep for future use or enjoyment (also with *up*); reduce or obviate need for, avoid wasting (*save fuel, time, labour*); relieve (person) from some need or obligation or experience; effect spiritual salvation of, preserve from damnation; avoid losing (match or game etc.); (in football etc.) prevent opponent from scoring (goal etc., or *absol.*). **2** *n.* (in football etc.) act of preventing opponent from scoring. **3** *prep.* except, but. **4** *conj. archaic* unless, except. **5 save-as-you-earn** method of saving by regular deduction from earnings. [AF f. L *salvo* (*salvus* safe)]
saveloy /'sævəlɔɪ/ *n.* highly seasoned dried sausage. [alt. of F *cervelat* f. It.]
saving 1 *n.* act of rescuing or preserving; (usu. in *pl.*) money saved. **2** *a.* that saves or redeems; that makes economical use of (labour etc.); (of clause etc.) stipulating exception or reservation. **3** *prep.* except, with the exception of; without offence to. **4 savings bank** bank paying interest on small deposits; **savings certificate** interest-bearing document issued by Government to savers. [SAVE]
saviour /'seɪvjə/, *US* **savior** *n.* deliverer, redeemer; person who saves others from harm or danger; **our** (or **the**) **Saviour** Christ. [F f. L (SAVE)]
savoir faire /sævwɑ: 'feə/ *n.* quickness to know and do the right thing, tact. [F]
savor *US* var. of SAVOUR.
savory[1] /'seɪvərɪ/ *n.* aromatic herb used in cookery. [OE f. L *satureia*]
savory[2] *US* var. of SAVOURY.
savour /'seɪvə/ **1** *n.* characteristic taste or flavour; power to affect the taste (*lit.* or *fig.*); suggestion or suspicion *of* a quality. **2** *v.* appreciate or perceive taste of (*lit.* or *fig.*), esp. lingeringly or with deliberation; suggest the presence *of* (*the reply savours of impertinence*). [F f. L *sapor*]

savoury /ˈseɪvərɪ/ 1 *a.* having appetizing taste or smell; (of food) having salt or piquant and not sweet taste. 2 *n.* savoury dish, esp. at end of meal or as appetizer. 3 **savouriness** *n.*

savoy /səˈvɔɪ/ *n.* cabbage with wrinkled leaves. [*Savoy* in SE France]

savvy /ˈsævɪ/ *sl.* 1 *v.* know. 2 *n.* knowingness, understanding. 3 *a. US* knowing, wise. [Black & Pidgin E, f. Sp.]

saw[1] 1 *n.* tool with toothed metal blade or edge for cutting wood, metal, stone, etc., by to-and-fro or rotary motion. 2 *v.* (*p.p.* **sawn** or **sawed**) cut (wood etc.) with saw; make (boards etc.) with saw; move to and fro, divide (the air etc.) with motion as of saw or person sawing. 3 **saw off** remove or reduce by sawing; **saw-tooth** (or **-toothed**) shaped like teeth of saw, serrated. [OE]

saw[2] *n.* old saying, maxim. [OE (SAY)]

saw[3] *past* of SEE[1].

sawdust *n.* powdery fragments of wood produced in sawing. [SAW[1]]

sawfish *n.* large sea fish with toothed end of snout.

sawmill *n.* mill for mechanical sawing of wood.

sawn *p.p.* of SAW[1].

sawyer *n.* workman who saws timber. [SAW[1]]

sax *n. colloq.* saxophone. [abbr.]

saxe /sæks/ *n.* (also **saxe blue**) light blue with greyish tinge. [F, = Saxony]

saxifrage /ˈsæksɪfrɪdʒ/ *n.* rock plant with tufted foliage. [F or L (*saxum* rock, *frango* break)]

Saxon /ˈsæks(ə)n/ 1 *a.* of Germanic people that conquered parts of England in 5th–6th cc.; = ANGLO-SAXON. 2 *n.* member of Saxon people; Saxon language; = ANGLO-SAXON. [F f. L *Saxo -onis*]

saxophone /ˈsæksəfəʊn/ *n.* keyed brass wind instrument with reed; **saxophonist** /-ˈsɒfənɪst/ *n.* [*Sax*, maker]

say 1 *v.* (*past* and *p.p.* **said** /sed/; 3 *sing. pres.* **says** /sez/) utter (specified words); speak words of; state or promise or prophesy (*that*); put into words, express (*cannot say what I feel*); convey information (*spoke for an hour but didn't say much*); indicate or show (*clock said ten o'clock*); adduce or plead (*much to be said on both sides*); form or give opinion or decision, decide about (*hard to say who it was*); select as example etc., take (amount etc.) as near enough, assume as true (*it will take a long time, say a month*). 2 *n.* what one wishes to say, opportunity of saying this (*have* or *say one's say*); share in discussion or decision (*had no say in the matter*); power of final decision. 3 **go without saying** be obvious; **I'll say** *colloq.* yes indeed; **I say** exclamation drawing attention, opening conversation, or expressing surprise; **say-so** power of decision, mere assertion; **says you** *sl.* I disagree; **that is to say** in other words. [OE]

SAYE *abbr.* save-as-you-earn.

saying *n.* frequent or proverbial remark. [SAY]

Sb *symb.* antimony. [L *stibium*]

s.c. *abbr.* small capitals.

sc. *abbr.* scilicet.

Sc *symb.* scandium.

scab 1 *n.* crust formed over sore in healing; kind of skin-disease or plant-disease; blackleg in strike. 2 *v.i.* (**-bb-**) form scab, heal over; act as blackleg. 3 **scabby** *a.* [ON; cf. SHABBY]

scabbard /ˈskæbəd/ *n.* sheath of sword etc. [AF]

scabies /ˈskeɪbiːz/ *n.* contagious skin-disease causing itching. [L]

scabious /ˈskeɪbɪəs/ *n.* a wild or garden flower. [med.L *scabiosa* (*herba*) named as curing scabies]

scabrous /ˈskeɪbrəs/ *a.* (of skin etc.) rough and scaly; indecent. [F or L]

scaffold /ˈskæfəld/ *n.* platform on which criminals are executed; scaffolding. [F f. Rmc (EX-[1], CATAFALQUE)]

scaffolding *n.* temporary structure of poles or tubes and planks providing platforms for building work; materials for this; any temporary framework.

scalar /ˈskeɪlə/ *Math.* 1 *a.* having magnitude but not direction. 2 *n.* scalar quantity. [L (SCALE[1])]

scalawag var. of SCALLYWAG.

scald[1] /skɔːld/ 1 *v.t.* burn with hot liquid or vapour; heat (esp. milk) to near boiling-point; rinse (vessel *out*) with boiling water. 2 *n.* injury to skin by scalding. [AF f. L *excaldo* (*calidus* hot)]

scald[2] var. of SKALD.

scale[1] 1 *n.* set of marks at measured distances on line for use in measuring etc.; rule determining intervals between these; piece of metal etc. on which they are marked; relative dimensions; ratio of reduction or enlargement in map, drawing, etc.; series of degrees, ladder-like arrangement, graded system (*high on the social scale*); *Mus.* set of sounds belonging to a key, arranged in order of pitch. 2 *v.t.* climb (wall, precipice, etc.) with ladder or by clambering; represent in dimensions different from but proportional to the actual ones. 3 **in scale** in proportion (*with* surroundings etc.); **on a large** (or **small**) **scale** to large (or small) extent; **scale down** (or **up**) make smaller (or larger) in proportion, reduce or increase in size; **to scale** with uniform reduction or enlargement. [L *scala* ladder]

scale[2] **1** *n.* any of the small thin horny overlapping plates protecting the skin of many fishes and reptiles; thin plate or flake resembling this; incrustation inside boiler etc.; tartar on teeth. **2** *v.* remove scale(s) from; form or drop off in scales. **3 scaly** *a.* [F *escale* f. Gmc (foll.)]

scale[3] **1** *n.* pan of weighing-balance; (in *pl.*) weighing instrument; **(the Scales)** sign or constellation Libra. **2** *v.t.* be found to weigh (specified amount). **3 pair of scales** simple balance; **tip** (or **turn) the scale(s)** outweigh opposite scale, *fig.* be decisive factor.

scalene /ˈskeɪli:n/ *a.* (of triangle etc.) having unequal sides. [L f. Gk *skalēnos* unequal]

scallion /ˈskæljən/ *n.* shallot; long-necked bulbless onion. [AF f. L (*Ascalon* in Palestine)]

scallop /ˈskɒləp/ **1** *n.* shellfish with two fan-shaped ridged shells; one shell of this used as container in which food is cooked and served; each of series of ornamental semi-circular curves edging fabric etc. **2** *v.t.* cook in scallop; ornament (material etc.) with scallops. [F ESCALOPE]

scalloping *n.* scallop-edging.

scallywag /ˈskælɪwæg/ *n.* scamp, rascal. [orig. unkn.]

scalp **1** *n.* skin and hair of top of head; this cut off as trophy by American Indian. **2** *v.t.* remove scalp of; criticize savagely; *US colloq.* resell at high or quick profit. [prob. Scand.]

scalpel /ˈskælp(ə)l/ *n.* small surgical knife. [F or L (*scalpo* scratch)]

scamp **1** *n.* rascal, rogue. **2** *v.t.* do (work etc.) perfunctorily or inadequately. [prob. Du.]

scamper **1** *v.i.* move or run hastily or impulsively. **2** *n.* act of scampering. [perh. prec.]

scampi /ˈskæmpɪ/ *n.pl.* large prawns. [It.]

scan **1** *v.* (**-nn-**) look at all parts of (thing) successively; look over quickly or cursorily; traverse (region) with controlled electronic or radar beam; resolve (picture) into its elements of light and shade for television transmission; test metre of (line etc. of verse) by examining nature and number of feet and syllables; (of line etc.) be metrically correct. **2** *n.* act or process of scanning. [L *scando* climb, scan]

scandal /ˈskænd(ə)l/ *n.* general feeling of (esp. moral) outrage or indignation; thing causing this; malicious gossip. [F f. L f. Gk, = snare]

scandalize *v.t.* offend moral feelings or sense of propriety of. [F or L f. Gk (prec.)]

scandalmonger *n.* person who disseminates scandal. [SCANDAL]

scandalous /ˈskændələs/ *a.* containing or arousing scandal, outrageous, shocking.

Scandinavian /skændɪˈneɪvɪən/ **1** *a.* of Scandinavia (Denmark, Norway, Sweden, Iceland). **2** *n.* native or inhabitant, or family of languages, of Scandinavia. [L]

scandium /ˈskændɪəm/ *n.* metallic element resembling those of lanthanide series. [L *Scandia* Scandinavia]

scansion /ˈskænʃ(ə)n/ *n.* metrical scanning. [L (SCAN)]

scant **1** *a.* barely sufficient, deficient. **2** *v.t. archaic* skimp, stint. [ON]

scanty *a.* of small amount or extent; barely sufficient; **scantily** *adv.*; **scantiness** *n.*

scapegoat /ˈskeɪpgəʊt/ *n.* person bearing blame due to others (with ref. to Lev. 16). [obs. *scape* escape]

scapula /ˈskæpjʊlə/ *n.* (*pl.* **scapulae** /-i:/) shoulder-blade. [L]

scapular /ˈskæpjʊlə/ **1** *a.* of the scapula. **2** *n.* monastic short cloak.

scar[1] **1** *n.* mark left by damage, esp. on skin by healed wound or on plant by loss of leaf etc.; lasting effect of grief etc. **2** *v.* (**-rr-**) mark with or form scar. [F *escharre* f. L f. Gk]

scar[2] *n.* precipitous craggy part of mountain side or cliff. [ON, = reef]

scarab /ˈskærəb/ *n.* kind of beetle; sacred dung-beetle of ancient Egypt; gem cut in form of beetle. [L *scarabaeus* f. Gk]

scarce /skeəs/ **1** *a.* not plentiful, insufficient for demand or need (usu. *predic.*); seldom found, rare. **2** *adv. literary* scarcely. **3 make oneself scarce** go away, keep out of the way. [AF *scars* f. Rmc (L *excerpto* EXCERPT)]

scarcely *adv.* hardly, not quite, only just; surely not (*can scarcely have known*); probably not (*I scarcely think so*).

scarcity *n.* being scarce, insufficiency.

scare **1** *v.* strike or be struck with sudden fear, startle and frighten; drive *away*, *off*, etc., by fright; (in *p.p.*) frightened (*of* or *to do* thing). **2** *n.* sudden outbreak of fear, esp. baseless general apprehension of some harm or misfortune. [ON]

scarecrow *n.* figure of man dressed in old clothes and set up in field to keep birds away; badly-dressed or grotesque person.

scaremonger *n.* person who starts or spreads scare(s).

scarf[1] *n.* (*pl.* **scarves**) long narrow strip of material worn for warmth or ornament round neck; square piece of material worn round neck or over woman's hair. [F *escarpe*]

scarf[2] **1** *n.* joint made by thinning ends of two pieces of timber etc. so that they overlap without increase of thickness and fastening them with bolts etc. **2** *v.t.* join with scarf. [prob. F *escarf*]

scarify[1] /ˈskeərɪfaɪ, ˈskæ-/ *v.t.* loosen surface of (soil etc.); make slight incisions in (skin etc.), cut off skin from; criticize etc. mercilessly; **scarification** /-fɪˈkeɪʃ(ə)n/ *n.* [F f. L f. Gk (*skariphos* stylus)]

scarify[2] /ˈskeərɪfaɪ/ *v.t. colloq.* scare, terrify. [SCARE]

scarlatina /skɑːləˈtiːnə/ *n.* scarlet fever. [It. (foll.)]

scarlet /ˈskɑːlɪt/ **1** *a.* of brilliant red colour inclining to orange. **2** *n.* scarlet colour or pigment; scarlet clothes or material (*dressed in scarlet*). **3 scarlet fever** infectious fever with scarlet rash; **scarlet runner** a kind of bean, scarlet-flowered climbing plant bearing this. [F *escarlate*]

scarp 1 *n.* steep slope, esp. inner side of ditch in fortification. **2** *v.t.* make steep or perpendicular. [It. *scarpa*]

scarper *v.i. sl.* escape, run away. [prob. It. *scappare* escape]

scary *a. colloq.* frightening. [SCARE]

scat[1] *v.i.* (**-tt-**) & *int. colloq.* depart quickly. [perh. abbr. of SCATTER]

scat[2] **1** *n.* wordless jazz singing using voice as instrument. **2** *v.i.* (**-tt-**) sing in this style. [prob. imit.]

scathe /skeɪð/ *archaic* **1** *v.t.* harm or injure. **2** *n.* harm or injury. [ON]

scathing *a.* (of look, criticism, etc.) harsh, severe.

scatology /skæˈtɒlədʒɪ/ *n.* preoccupation with the obscene or with excrement; **scatological** /skætəˈlɒdʒɪk(ə)l/ *a.* [Gk *skōr skat-* dung]

scatter 1 *v.* throw or send or go in many different directions; cover by scattering; rout or be routed; dissipate; deflect or diffuse (light or particles etc.); (in *p.p.*) not situated together, wide apart. **2** *n.* act of scattering; small amount scattered; extent of distribution esp. of shot. **3 scatter-brain** scatter-brained person; **scatter-brained** *a.* lacking concentration, disorganized, flighty. [prob. var. of SHATTER]

scatty /ˈskætɪ/ *a. sl.* scatter-brained; **scattily** *adv.*; **scattiness** *n.* [*scatter-brained*]

scaur var. of SCAR[2].

scavenge /ˈskævɪndʒ/ *v.* be or act as scavenger (of); remove dirt or waste or impurities etc. from. [back-form. f. foll.]

scavenger *n.* person who searches among or collects things unwanted by others; animal or bird that feeds on carrion. [AF *scawager*, rel. to SHOW]

Sc.D. *abbr.* Doctor of Science. [L *Scientiae Doctor*]

scenario /sɪˈnɑːrɪəʊ/ *n.* (*pl.* **scenarios**) script or synopsis of film, play, etc.; imagined sequence of future events. [It. f. L (foll.)]

scene /siːn/ *n.* place in which event or series of events takes place; portion of play during which action is continuous, portion of an act; similar portion of film, book, etc.; incident or part of person's life etc., description of this; agitated or bad-tempered conversation or behaviour, emotional outburst (*don't make a scene*); landscape or view spread out before spectator; piece of painted canvas, woodwork, etc., used to represent scene of action on stage etc., whole of these together, or place represented by them; *sl.* area or subject of activity or interest, way of life (*not my scene*); **behind the scenes** behind the stage, out of sight of the audience, *fig.* not known to the public, working secretly; **come on the scene** appear, arrive; **set the scene** describe location of events etc.; **scene-shifter** person engaged in changing scenes in theatre. [L f. Gk *skēnē* tent, stage]

scenery *n.* furnishings used in theatre to represent supposed scene of action; features (esp. picturesque) of landscape. [SCENARIO]

scenic *a.* picturesque; of or on the stage, of scenery; **scenically** *adv.* [L f. Gk (SCENE)]

scent /sent/ **1** *n.* characteristic odour, esp. pleasant one; liquid perfume; smell or trail left by animal, *fig.* line of investigation or pursuit; power of detecting or distinguishing smells or discovering presence of something. **2** *v.t.* discern by smell; sniff out; begin to suspect presence or existence of (*I scent trouble*); make fragrant, apply perfume to. **3 off the scent** misled by false information etc.; **scent out** discover by smelling about or by search. [F *sentir* perceive f. L (SENSE)]

scepter *US* var. of SCEPTRE.

sceptic /ˈskeptɪk/ *n.* person who doubts truth of (esp. religious) doctrine or theory etc.; person inclined to question truth of facts or statements or claims; philosopher who questions the possibility of knowledge; **scepticism** *n.* [F f. L f. Gk (*skeptomai* observe)]

sceptical *a.* of scepticism; inclined to disbelieve, doubtful, incredulous; **sceptically** *adv.*

sceptre /'septə/ *n.* staff borne as symbol of sovereignty. [F f. L f. Gk]

schadenfreude /'ʃɑ:dənfrɔɪdə/ *n.* malicious enjoyment of others' misfortunes. [G, lit. damage-joy]

schedule /'ʃedju:l/ **1** *n.* timetable or programme of planned events etc.; table of details or items, esp. as appendix to document. **2** *v.t.* make schedule of; include in schedule; appoint time for; include (building) in list of those to be preserved. **3 on schedule** to time, not late; **scheduled flight** one operated on regular timetable. [F f. L dimin. (*scheda* leaf f. Gk)]

schematic /skɪ'mætɪk/ **1** *a.* of or in the form of a scheme; in form of diagram or chart. **2** *n.* schematic diagram. **3 schematically** *adv.* [SCHEME]

schematize /'ski:mətaɪz/ *v.t.* put in schematic form. [Gk (SCHEME)]

scheme /ski:m/ **1** *n.* systematic arrangement proposed or in operation; outline, syllabus; plan of action; artful or underhand plan. **2** *v.* make plan or plans esp. in secret or underhand way; plan to bring about. [L f. Gk *skhēma -mat-* shape]

scherzo /'skeətsəʊ/ *n.* (*pl.* **scherzos**) vigorous, often playful, movement in symphony or sonata etc.; lively musical composition. [It., = jest]

schism /'sɪz(ə)m, 'skɪ-/ *n.* division of (esp. religious) group into opposing parties on grounds of doctrinal disagreement; **schismatic** /sɪz'mætɪk, skɪ-/ *a.* [F f. L f. Gk *skhisma -mat-* cleft]

schist /ʃɪst/ *n.* layered crystalline rock. [F f. L f. Gk (prec.)]

schizo /'skɪtsəʊ/ *n. colloq.* (*pl.* **schizos**) schizophrenic. [abbr.]

schizoid /'skɪtsɔɪd/ **1** *a.* of or resembling schizophrenia or a schizophrenic. **2** *n.* schizoid person. [foll.]

schizophrenia /skɪtsə'fri:nɪə/ *n.* mental disease marked by disconnection between thought, feelings, and actions; **schizophrenic** /-'frenɪk/ *a.* & *n.* [Gk *skhizō* split, *phrēn* mind]

schmaltz /ʃmɔ:lts/ *n.* sugary sentimentality. [Yiddish]

schnapps /ʃnæps/ *n.* a kind of strong gin. [G]

schnitzel /'ʃnɪts(ə)l/ *n.* veal cutlet. [G]

schnorkel var. of SNORKEL.

scholar /'skɒlə/ *n.* learned person in particular subject; person who learns (*an apt scholar*); student awarded money for education at school, college, etc.; **scholarly** *a.* [F f. L (SCHOOL)]

scholarship *n.* award of money towards education; learning or knowledge in subject; methods or achievements of scholars.

scholastic /skɒ'læstɪk/ *a.* of schools or education, academic; **scholastically** *adv.* [L f. Gk (SCHOOL)]

scholasticism *n.* belief in or system of precise definition of and deduction from dogma.

school[1] /sku:l/ **1** *n.* institution for educating children or giving instruction; *US* university, department of this; buildings or pupils of such institution; time during which teaching is done; process of being educated in school; circumstances or occupation serving to educate or discipline (*in the school of adversity*); branch of study at university (*the music school*); group of thinkers, artists, etc., sharing same principles, methods, characteristics, or inspiration; group of card-players or gamblers; medieval lecture-room. **2** *v.t.* educate; send to school; discipline; deliberately train or accustom (*to* patience etc.). **3 at school** in course of education at a school; **go to school** attend school regularly; **school age** age-range in which children normally attend school; **school-leaver** pupil who has left school; **school year** period when schools are in session, reckoned from autumn term. [OE & F f. L *schola* f. Gk]

school[2] /sku:l/ *n.* shoal of fish, whales, etc. [LG or Du.]

schoolchild *n.* (also **schoolboy, schoolgirl**) child who attends school. [SCHOOL[1]]

schoolhouse *n.* building of (esp. village) school.

schoolmaster *n.* male teacher in a school; **schoolmistress** *n. fem.*

schoolroom *n.* room used for lessons in school or private house.

schoolteacher *n.* teacher in a school.

schooner /'sku:nə/ *n.* fore-and-aft-rigged ship with more than one mast; large glass of sherry etc. [orig. uncert.]

schottische /ʃɒ'ti:ʃ/ *n.* a kind of slow polka. [G, = Scottish]

schwa /ʃwɑ:, ʃvɑ:/ *n.* indeterminate vowel sound (as in *a*noth*er*); symbol (ə) representing this. [G f. Heb.]

sciatic /saɪ'ætɪk/ *a.* of the hip; affecting hip or sciatic nerve; suffering from or liable to sciatica; **sciatic nerve** large nerve from pelvis to thigh. [F f. L f. Gk (*iskhion* hip)]

sciatica /saɪ'ætɪkə/ *n.* neuralgia of hip and thigh. [L (prec.)]

science /'saɪəns/ *n.* branch of knowledge involving systematized observation of and experiment with phenomena; systematic and formulated knowledge, pursuit or principles of this; organized body of knowledge on a subject; skilful technique; **science fiction**

fanciful fiction based on postulated scientific discoveries, environmental changes, etc., and often dealing with space travel or life on other planets. [F f. L (*scio* know)]

scientific /saɪən'tɪfɪk/ *a.* of science; used or engaged in science; following the systematic methods of science; having, using, or requiring trained skill; **scientifically** *adv.* [F or L (prec.)]

scientist /'saɪəntɪst/ *n.* student or expert in science. [SCIENCE, prec.]

Scientology /saɪən'tɒlədʒɪ/ *n.* religious system based on study of knowledge and seeking to develop highest potentialities of its members. [L *scientia* knowledge]

sci-fi /'saɪfaɪ/ *n. colloq.* science fiction. [abbr.]

scilicet /'saɪlɪset/ *adv.* that is to say (introducing word to be supplied or explanation of ambiguous word). [L]

scimitar /'sɪmɪtə/ *n.* curved oriental sword. [F & It.]

scintilla /sɪn'tɪlə/ *n.* sign or trace. [L, = spark]

scintillate /'sɪntɪleɪt/ *v.i.* sparkle, twinkle; talk or act with brilliance; **scintillation** /-'leɪʃ(ə)n/ *n.* [L (prec.)]

sciolism /'saɪəlɪz(ə)m/ *n.* superficial knowledge, display of this; **sciolist** *n.*; **sciolistic** /-'lɪstɪk/ *a.* [L *sciolus* dimin. of *scius* knowing]

scion /'saɪən/ *n.* shoot or plant, esp. one for grafting; descendant, young member *of* family. [F]

scissors /'sɪzəz/ *n.pl.* (also **pair of scissors**) cutting-instrument made of two blades so pivoted that their cutting edges close on what is to be cut. [F f. L (*caedo* cut, as CHISEL)]

sclerosis /sklɪə'rəʊsɪs/ *n.* abnormal hardening of body tissue; **disseminated** (or **multiple**) **sclerosis** sclerosis spreading to all or many parts of body; **sclerotic** *a.* [Gk (*sklēros* hard)]

scoff[1] **1** *v.i.* speak derisively; jeer or mock *at*. **2** *n.* mocking words, taunt. **3 scoffer** *n.* [perh. Scand.]

scoff[2] *sl.* **1** *v.* eat greedily. **2** *n.* food, meal. [Afrik. *schoff*, f. Du.]

scold /skəʊld/ **1** *v.* rebuke (esp. child); find fault noisily. **2** *n.* nagging or complaining woman. [prob. ON (SKALD)]

scolding *n.* severe rebuke.

scollop var. of SCALLOP.

sconce[1] *n.* wall-bracket holding candlestick or light-fitting. [F f. L (*ab*)*sconsa* covered (light)]

sconce[2] *n.* small fort or earthwork. [Du. *schans* brushwood]

scone /skɒn, skəʊn/ *n.* small soft cake of flour etc. baked quickly. [orig. uncert.]

scoop 1 *n.* short-handled deep shovel; ladle-shaped dipping-vessel with long handle; excavating part of digging-machine etc.; device for serving portions of ice-cream etc.; quantity taken with scoop; act or motion of scooping; large profit made quickly or by anticipating one's competitors; exclusive item in newspaper etc. **2** *v.t.* lift (*up*) or hollow (*out*) with or as with scoop; secure (large profit etc.) by sudden action or stroke of luck; forestall (rival newspaper etc.) with news scoop. [LG or Du.]

scoot *v.i. colloq.* run, dart, make off esp. hastily. [orig. unkn.]

scooter *n.* child's toy vehicle propelled by foot, consisting of footboard with wheel at front and back, and long steering-handle; (also **motor scooter**) low-powered motor cycle resembling child's scooter, with seat.

scope *n.* reach or sphere of observation or action; extent to which it is possible or permissible to range or develop etc.; opportunity, outlet. [It. f. Gk, = mark for shooting]

-scope *suffix* forming nouns denoting thing looked at or through (*telescope*), or instrument for observing or showing (*oscilloscope*). [Gk *skopeō* look at]

-scopic *suffix* forming adjectives with sense 'looking at' (*macroscopic*) or 'pertaining to instrument with name in -SCOPE' (*gyroscopic*).

-scopy *suffix* forming nouns with sense 'looking at' or 'use of an instrument whose name ends in -SCOPE'.

scorbutic /skɔ:'bju:tɪk/ *a.* of or like or affected with scurvy. [L *scorbutus* scurvy]

scorch 1 *v.* burn or discolour surface of with dry heat, become so burnt or discoloured; *sl.* go at very high speed. **2** *n.* mark made by scorching. **3 scorched earth policy** policy of burning one's crops etc. and removing or destroying anything that might be useful to an occupying enemy. [orig. unkn.]

scorcher *n. colloq.* very hot day.

score 1 *n.* number of points, goals, etc., made by player or side in game etc., detailed table of these; twenty, set of twenty (*a score*; *three score*), (in *pl.* **scores**) very many; copy of musical composition with parts on series of staves; music for musical comedy, film, etc.; point or reason or motive; *colloq.* remark or act by which person scores off another; scratch, notch, or line made on surface; record of money owing. **2** *v.* make (points etc.) in game; win or gain (success, victory, etc.); keep the score; allot score to (competitor etc.); enter in score, record esp. mentally (often with *up*); secure an advantage, be successful, have good luck; mark with incisions or lines; make (line etc.) with something that marks; *Mus.* orchestrate or arrange (*for* instruments). **3 keep the score** register score as it is made; **know the score** be aware of essential facts; **on that score** so far as that matter is concerned; **pay off old scores** get revenge; **score-board** (or **-book, -card, -sheet**) board etc. on which score is entered or displayed; **score off** *colloq.* humiliate, defeat in argument or repartee; **score out** delete. [OE f. ON (SHEAR)]

scorer *n.* one who keeps score.

scoria /'skɔːrɪə/ *n.* (*pl.* **scoriae** /-iː/) slag, clinker-like mass of lava; **scoriaceous** /-'eɪʃəs/ *a.* [L f. Gk]

scorn 1 *n.* disdain, contempt, derision; object of contempt. **2** *v.t.* hold in contempt, consider beneath notice; refuse or abstain from as unworthy. [F *escarnir* f. Gmc]

scornful *a.* contemptuous (*of*); **scornfully** *adv.*

Scorpio /'skɔːpɪəʊ/ *n.* constellation and eighth sign of zodiac. [L f. Gk (*skorpios* scorpion)]

scorpion /'skɔːpɪən/ *n.* lobster-like arachnid with jointed stinging tail; (**Scorpion**) sign or constellation Scorpio.

Scot *n.* native of Scotland. [OE f. L *Scottus*]

Scotch[1] **1** *a.* of Scotland or its inhabitants or language. **2** *n.* form of English used in (esp. Lowlands of) Scotland; Scotch whisky. **3 Scotch broth** soup made from beef or mutton with vegetables, pearl barley, etc.; **Scotch egg** hard-boiled egg enclosed in sausage-meat; **Scotch fir** (or **pine**) type of pine-tree; **Scotch kale** kind of kale with purplish leaves; **Scotch mist** thick mist and drizzle; **Scotch terrier** small rough-haired short-legged kind of terrier; **Scotch whisky** whisky distilled in Scotland. ¶ *Scots* or *Scottish* is generally preferred in Scotland, except in the special compounds given above. [SCOTTISH]

scotch[2] **1** *v.t.* decisively put an end to; frustrate (plan etc.); *archaic* wound without killing. **2** *n.* line on ground for hopscotch. [orig. unkn.]

scot-free *a.* unharmed, unpunished. [obs. *scot* tax]

Scots *a.* & *n.* Scottish. ¶ See note at SCOTCH.[1] [var. of SCOTTISH]

Scotsman *n.* native of Scotland; **Scotswoman** *n. fem.*

Scottie *n. colloq.* Scotsman, Scotch terrier. [SCOT]

Scottish *a.* of Scotland or its inhabitants.

scoundrel /'skaʊndr(ə)l/ *n.* unscrupulous person, villain; **scoundrelly** *a.* [orig. unkn.]

scour[1] **1** *v.t.* clean (hard surface) by rubbing; rub (rust or stain etc.) *away* or *off*; clear out (channel or harbour etc.) by flow through or over. **2** *n.* act or process of scouring. [LG or Du. f. F f. L (EX-[1], CURE)]

scour[2] *v.* search rapidly or thoroughly; hasten (over or along), esp. in search or pursuit. [orig. unkn.]

scourer *n.* abrasive pad or powder for scouring. [SCOUR[1]]

scourge /skɜːdʒ/ **1** *n.* person or thing regarded as bringer of vengeance or punishment; whip. **2** *v.t.* chastise, afflict; whip. [F f. L (EX-[1], *corrigia* whip)]

scouse *sl.* **1** *a.* of Liverpool. **2** *n.* native of Liverpool; Liverpool dialect. [LOBSCOUSE]

scout[1] **1** *n.* person, esp. soldier, sent out to get information about enemy etc.; act of seeking information; = *talent-scout*; (**Scout**) member of Scout Association, boys' organization intended to develop character; college servant at Oxford; *colloq.* fellow, person. **2** *v.i.* act as scout. **3 scout about** (or **around**) search (*for*). [F *escoute(r)* f. L *ausculto* listen]

scout[2] *v.t.* reject (idea etc.) with scorn. [Scand.]

Scouter *n.* adult leader in Scout Association. [SCOUT[1]]

scow *n.* flat-bottomed boat. [Du.]

scowl 1 *n.* sullen or bad-tempered look on one's face. **2** *v.i.* make a scowl. [Scand.]

scrabble /'skræb(ə)l/ **1** *v.i.* scratch or grope (*about*) to find or collect something. **2** *n.* act of scrabbling; (**Scrabble**; **P**) game in which players build up words from letter-blocks on a board. [Du.]

scrag 1 *n.* inferior end of neck of mutton (also **scrag-end**); skinny person or animal. **2** *v.t.* (**-gg-**) *sl.* strangle, hang; seize roughly by the neck; handle roughly, beat up. [orig. uncert.]

scraggy *a.* thin and bony; **scraggily** *adv.*; **scragginess** *n.*

scram *v.i.* (**-mm-**) *sl.* (esp. in *imper.*) go away. [perh. foll.]

scramble /'skræmb(ə)l/ **1** *v.* make one's way by clambering, crawling, etc.; struggle with competitors (*for* thing or share of it); mix together indiscriminately; cook (eggs) by heating them when broken with butter, milk, etc., in pan; change speech frequency of (telephone conversation etc.) so as to make it unintelligible without special receiver; move hastily; (of aircraft or pilots) take off quickly in emergency. **2** *n.* climb, walk, or motor-cycle race over rough ground; eager struggle or competition (*for* something). **3 scrambled egg** *colloq.* gold braid on officer's cap. [imit.]

scrambler *n.* device for scrambling telephone conversations.

scrap[1] **1** *n.* small detached piece, fragment; rubbish or waste material, discarded metal for reprocessing; (with neg.) smallest piece or amount (*not a scrap of evidence*); (in *pl.*) odds and ends, bits of uneaten food. **2** *v.t.* (**-pp-**) discard as useless. **3 scrap-book** book in which newspaper cuttings etc. are mounted; **scrap-merchant** dealer in scrap; **scrap-yard** place where scrap is collected. [ON (SCRAPE)]

scrap[2] *colloq.* **1** *n.* fight or rough quarrel. **2** *v.i.* (**-pp-**) have scrap. [perh. foll.]

scrape 1 *v.* make (thing) level or clean or smooth by causing hard edge to move across surface, apply (hard edge) thus; remove by scraping (with *away*, *off*, etc.); scratch or damage by scraping; dig (hollow etc.) by scraping; draw or move with sound (as) of scraping, produce such sound (from); move while barely touching (*car scraped past*); gain with effort or by parsimony; contrive to bring (*together*, *up*); manage with difficulty (with *along*, *by*, *through*, etc.); be economical; draw back foot in making clumsy bow (*bow and scrape*). **2** *n.* act or sound of scraping; scraped place; awkward predicament, esp. resulting from escapade. **3 scrape the barrel** use one's last resources. [ON]

scraper *n.* device used for scraping.

scraping *n.* (esp. in *pl.*) fragment produced by scraping.

scrappy *a.* consisting of scraps; incomplete; carelessly arranged; **scrappily** *adv.*; **scrappiness** *n.* [SCRAP[1]]

scratch 1 *v.t.* score surface of, or wound superficially, with sharp or pointed thing; get (oneself or part of one's body) scratched; make or form by scratching; scrape without marking, esp. with finger-nail to relieve itching; get (thing) *together*, *up*, etc., by scratching or with difficulty; strike *off*, *out*, or *through* with pencil etc.; remove (horse's name from list of entries for race, competitor's or *US* election candidate's name); withdraw from competition. **2** *n.* mark or wound or sound made by scratching; spell of scratching oneself; *colloq.* trifling wound; line from which competitors, esp. those not receiving handicap, start. **3** *a.* collected by chance, collected or made from whatever is available, heterogeneous (*scratch crew*, *meal*, *team*); with no handicap given (*scratch player*, *race*). **4 from scratch** from the beginning, without help or advantage; **scratch one's head** be perplexed; **scratch the surface** deal with matter only superficially; **up to scratch** up to required standard. [orig. uncert.]

scratchy *a.* tending to make scratches or scratching noise; tending to cause itchiness; (of drawing etc.) done in scratches or carelessly; **scratchily** *adv.*; **scratchiness** *n.*

scrawl 1 *v.* write in hurried untidy way; cross *out* thus. **2** *n.* hurried writing; scrawled note. [orig. uncert.]

scrawny *a.* lean, scraggy. [dial.]

scream 1 *v.* emit piercing cry (as) of pain or terror; speak or sing (words etc.) in such tone; make or move with shrill sound like scream; laugh uncontrollably; be blatantly obvious. **2** *n.* act or sound of screaming; *colloq.* irresistibly funny occurrence or person. [OE]

scree *n.* (in *sing.* or *pl.*) small loose stones; mountain slope covered with these. [ON, = landslip]

screech 1 *n.* harsh high-pitched scream. **2** *v.* utter with or make screech. **3 screech-owl** owl that screeches instead of hooting, esp. barn-owl. [OE (imit.)]

screed *n.* long tiresome harangue (esp. list of grievances) or letter. [prob. SHRED]

screen 1 *n.* fixed or movable upright partition for separating, concealing, or sheltering from draughts or excessive heat or light; thing used as shelter, esp. from observation; measure adopted for concealment, protection afforded by this; blank surface on which film, televised picture, radar image, etc., is projected; *the* cinema industry; = *sight-screen*, WINDSCREEN; large sieve or riddle; frame with fine wire netting to keep out flies, mosquitoes, etc.; system for showing presence or absence of disease, quality, etc.; *Printing* transparent finely-ruled plate or film used in half-tone reproduction. **2** *v.t.* shelter, hide partly or completely; protect from detection, censure, etc.; show (film etc.) on screen; prevent from causing electrical interference; sieve; test (person) for presence or absence of disease, quality, etc., esp. for reliability or loyalty. **3 screen off** shut off or hide with screen; **screen-printing** process like stencilling with ink forced through prepared sheet of fine material. [F]

screenplay *n.* script, adaptation of novel etc., for film.

screw /skru:/ **1** *n.* thin cylinder or cone with spiral ridge round the outside (**male screw**) or the inside (**female screw**); metal male screw with slotted head and sharp point for fastening things (esp. of wood) together; wooden or metal screw used to exert pressure; (in *sing.* or *pl.*) instrument of torture operating thus; propeller acting like screw; one turn of a screw; small twisted-up paper *of* tobacco etc.; (in billiards etc.) oblique curling motion of ball; *sl.* prison warder; *sl.* amount of salary or wages; *vulgar* sexual intercourse, partner in this. **2** *v.* fasten or tighten with screw(s); turn (screw); twist or turn round like screw; (of ball etc.) swerve; put the screws on, oppress; extort (consent, money, etc.) *out of*; contort or contract (one's face etc.); *vulgar* have sexual intercourse (with). **3 have a screw loose** *colloq.* be slightly crazy; **put the screws on** exert pressure (on), esp. to extort or intimidate; **screw-cap** (or **-top**) cap or top that screws on to bottle etc.; **screw up** contort or contract (one's eyes, face, etc.), summon up (one's courage), *sl.* bungle or mismanage. [F *escroue*]

screwball *n. US sl.* crazy or eccentric person.

screwdriver *n.* tool with shaped tip fitting into head of screw to turn it.

screwed *a.* twisted; *sl.* drunk.

screwy *a. sl.* crazy or eccentric; absurd.

scribble /'skrɪb(ə)l/ **1** *v.* write carelessly or hurriedly; be author or writer. **2** *n.* scrawl, hasty note etc. [L *scribillo* dimin. (foll.)]

scribe 1 *n.* ancient or medieval copyist of manuscripts; ancient-Jewish record-keeper or professional theologian and jurist; pointed instrument for making marks on wood etc. **2** *v.t.* mark with scribe. **3 scribal** *a.* [L *scriba* (*scribo* write)]

scrim *n.* open-weave fabric for lining or upholstery etc. [orig. unkn.]

scrimmage /'skrɪmɪdʒ/ **1** *n.* tussle, confused struggle, brawl. **2** *v.i.* engage in scrimmage. [SKIRMISH]

scrimp *v.* skimp. [orig. unkn.]

scrip *n.* provisional certificate of money subscribed entitling holder to dividends; *collect.* such certificates; extra share or shares instead of dividend. [abbr. of *subscription receipt*]

script 1 *n.* handwriting, written characters; type imitating handwriting; alphabet or system of writing; text of play or film etc.; examinee's written answer. **2** *v.t.* write script for (film etc.). **3 script-writer** writer for broadcasting or films etc. [F f. L *scriptum* (*scribo* write)]

scripture /'skrɪptʃə/ *n.* sacred writings; (**Scripture** or **the Scriptures**) the Bible; **scriptural** *a.* [L (prec.)]

scrivener /'skrɪvənə/ *n. hist.* drafter of documents, copyist, notary. [F *escrivein* f. L (SCRIBE) + -ER[1]]

scrofula /'skrɒfjʊlə/ *n.* disease with glandular swellings, prob. a form of tuberculosis; **scrofulous** *a.* [L (*scrofa* sow)]

scroll /skrəʊl/ **1** *n.* roll of parchment or paper esp. with writing; book of the ancient roll form; ornamental design imitating roll of parchment. **2** *v.t.* move (display on VDU screen) up or down as new material appears. [orig. (*sc*)*rowle* ROLL]

scrolled *a.* having scroll ornament.

Scrooge /skru:dʒ/ *n.* miser. [character in Dickens]

scrotum /'skrəʊtəm/ *n.* (*pl.* **scrota**) pouch of skin containing the testicles; **scrotal** *a.* [L]

scrounge *v. sl.* obtain (things) illicitly or by cadging. [dial. *scrunge* steal]

scrub[1] **1** *v.* (**-bb-**) rub hard so as to clean, esp. with hard brush; use brush thus; use water to remove impurities from; *sl.* scrap or cancel (plan, order, etc.). **2** *n.* scrubbing or being scrubbed. **3 scrub up** (of surgeon etc.) clean hands and arms by scrubbing before operation. [LG or Du.]

scrub[2] *n.* brushwood or stunted forest growth, land covered with this; stunted or insignificant person etc.; **scrubby** *a.* [SHRUB]

scrubber[1] *n.* apparatus for cleaning gases; *sl.* immoral or sluttish woman. [SCRUB[1]]

scrubber[2] *n. Austral.* inferior animal, esp. bullock, living in scrub country. [SCRUB[2]]

scruff *n.* back of the neck.

scruffy /'skrʌfɪ/ *a. colloq.* shabby, slovenly, untidy; **scruffily** *adv.*; **scruffiness** *n.* [*scruff* = SCURF]

scrum *n.* scrummage; **scrum-half** half-back who puts ball into scrum. [abbr.]

scrummage *n.* (in Rugby football) grouping of all forwards on each side to push against those of the other and seek possession of ball thrown on ground between them. [SCRIMMAGE]

scrumptious /'skrʌmpʃəs/ *a. colloq.* delicious, delightful. [orig. unkn.]

scrumpy /'skrʌmpɪ/ *n. colloq.* (orig. *dial.*) rough cider. [dial. *scrump* small apple]

scrunch *n.* & *v.* crunch. [alt. of CRUNCH]

scruple /'skru:p(ə)l/ **1** *n.* regard to morality or propriety of an action etc.; doubt or hesitation caused by this; weight of 20 grains. **2** *v.i.* feel or be influenced by scruples; (esp. with neg.) be reluctant because of scruples. [F or L]

scrupulous /'skru:pjʊləs/ *a.* careful to avoid doing wrong; conscientious or thorough even in small matters; punctilious, over-attentive to details;

scrupulosity /-ˈlɒsɪtɪ/ *n.* [F or L (prec.)]
scrutineer /skru:tɪˈnɪə/ *n.* person who scrutinizes ballot-papers. [SCRUTINY]
scrutinize /ˈskru:tɪnaɪz/ *v.t.* subject to scrutiny. [foll.]
scrutiny /ˈskru:tɪnɪ/ *n.* critical gaze, close investigation, examination into details; official examination of ballot-papers to check their validity or accuracy of counting. [L *scrutinium* (*scrutor* examine)]
scuba /ˈsku:bə/ *n.* self-contained underwater breathing apparatus. [acronym]
scud 1 *v.i.* (**-dd-**) run or fly straight and fast, skim along; *Naut.* run before the wind. **2** *n.* spell of scudding, scudding motion; vapoury driving clouds or shower. [perh. alt. of SCUT]
scuff 1 *v.* walk with dragging feet, shuffle; graze or brush against; mark or wear out (shoes etc.) thus. **2** *n.* mark of scuffing. [imit.]
scuffle /ˈskʌf(ə)l/ **1** *n.* confused struggle or disorderly fight at close quarters. **2** *v.i.* engage in scuffle. [prob. Scand. (SHOVE)]
scull 1 *n.* each of pair of small oars; oar used to propel boat from stern, usu. by twisting motion; (in *pl.*) sculling race. **2** *v.t.* propel (boat, or *absol.*) with sculls. [orig. unkn.]
sculler *n.* user of scull(s); boat for sculling.
scullery /ˈskʌlərɪ/ *n.* back kitchen; room in which dishes are washed etc. [AF *squillerie* (*escuele* dish f. L *scutella* salver)]
scullion /ˈskʌljən/ *n. archaic* cook's boy, dish-washer. [orig. unkn.]
sculpt *v. colloq.* sculpture. [abbr.]
sculptor *n.* one who sculptures; **sculptress** *n. fem.* [L (foll.)]
sculpture /ˈskʌlptʃə/ **1** *n.* art of forming representations in the round or in relief by chiselling stone, carving wood, modelling clay, casting metal, etc.; a work of sculpture. **2** *v.* represent in or adorn with sculpture; practise sculpture. **3 sculptural** *a.*; **sculpturally** *adv.* [L (*sculpo sculpt-* carve)]
scum 1 *n.* layer of dirt or froth or impurities etc. at top of liquid; worthless part, worthless person(s). **2** *v.* (**-mm-**) remove scum from; form scum (on). **3 scummy** *a.* [LG or Du.]
scupper 1 *n.* hole in ship's side to carry off water from deck. **2** *v.t. sl.* sink (ship or crew); defeat or ruin (plan etc.); kill. [perh. AF deriv. of F *escopir* spit]
scurf *n.* flakes of dead skin, esp. on scalp; **scurfy** *a.* [OE]
scurrilous /ˈskʌrɪləs/ *a.* grossly or obscenely abusive; **scurrility** /-ˈrɪlɪtɪ/ *n.* [F or L (*scurra* buffoon)]
scurry /ˈskʌrɪ/ **1** *v.i.* run or move hurriedly esp. with short quick steps, scamper. **2** *n.* act or sound of scurrying; flurry of rain or snow. [abbr. of *hurry-scurry* redupl. of HURRY]
scurvy /ˈskɜ:vɪ/ **1** *n.* deficiency disease from lack of vitamin C. **2** *a.* paltry, dishonourable, contemptible. **3 scurvily** *adv.*; **scurviness** *n.* [SCURF]
scut *n.* short tail, esp. of rabbit or hare or deer. [orig. unkn.]
scutter *v.i.* & *n. colloq.* scurry. [perh. alt. of SCUTTLE³]
scuttle¹ /ˈskʌt(ə)l/ *n.* receptacle for carrying and holding small supply of coal; part of motor-car body between windscreen and bonnet. [ON, f. L *scutella* dish]
scuttle² /ˈskʌt(ə)l/ **1** *n.* hole with lid in ship's deck or side. **2** *v.* let water in (ship), esp. to sink it. [obs. F *escoutille* f. Sp. *escotilla* hatchway]
scuttle³ /ˈskʌt(ə)l/ **1** *v.i.* scurry, flee from danger or difficulty. **2** *n.* hurried gait; precipitate flight or departure. [cf. dial. *scuddle* frequent. of SCUD]
Scylla and Charybdis /ˈsɪlə, kəˈrɪbdɪs/ two dangers or extremes such that one can be avoided only by approaching the other. [monster and whirlpool in Gk mythology]
scythe /saɪð/ **1** *n.* mowing and reaping implement with long curved blade swung over ground. **2** *v.t.* cut with scythe. [OE]
SDP *abbr.* Social Democratic Party.
SE *abbr.* south-east, south-eastern.
Se *symb.* selenium.
sea 1 *n.* expanse of salt water that covers most of earth's surface, any part of this as opposed to land or fresh water; named tract of salt water partly or wholly enclosed by land (*Dead Sea*); large inland lake (*Sea of Galilee*); waves of the sea, their motion or state (*rough sea*); vast quantity or expanse *of*. **2** *attrib.* living or used in or on or near the sea (often prefixed to name of marine animal, plant, etc., having superficial resemblance to what it is named after). **3 at sea** in ship on the sea, *fig.* perplexed, confused; **by sea** in ship(s); **go to sea** become a sailor; **on the sea** in ship at sea, situated on coast; **sea anchor** bag to retard drifting of ship; **sea anemone** large polyp with petal-like tentacles; **sea-bird** bird frequenting sea or land near sea; **sea-borne** conveyed by sea; **sea change** notable or unexpected transformation; **sea-cow** sirenian, walrus, hippopotamus; **sea-dog** old sailor, esp. Elizabethan captain; **sea-girt** surrounded by sea; **sea-green** bluish green; **sea-horse** small fish with head

suggestive of horse's, mythical creature with horse's head and fish's tail; **sea-kale** herb with young shoots used as vegetable; **sea-legs** ability to walk on deck of rolling ship; **sea-level** mean level of sea's surface, used in reckoning height of hills etc. and as barometric standard; **sea-lion** large, eared seal; **Sea Lord** naval member of Admiralty Board; **sea mile** = *nautical mile*; **sea-room** space for ship to turn etc. at sea; **sea-salt** salt produced by evaporating sea-water; **Sea Scout** member of maritime branch of Scout Association; **sea shell** shell of salt-water mollusc; **sea-shore** land close to sea; **sea-urchin** small sea-animal with prickly shell; **sea-way** ship's progress, place where ship lies in open water, inland waterway open to seagoing ships. [OE]

seaboard *n.* seashore or line of coast; coastal region.

seafarer *n.* sailor, traveller by sea.

seafaring *a.* & *n.* travelling by sea, esp. regularly.

seafood *n.* edible marine fish or shellfish.

seagoing *a.* (of ships) fit for crossing the sea; (of person) seafaring.

seagull *n.* = GULL[1].

seal[1] **1** *n.* piece of wax, lead, paper, etc., with stamped design, attached to document as guarantee of authenticity or to receptacle, envelope, etc., to prevent its being opened without owner's knowledge; engraved piece of metal etc. for stamping design on this; substance or device to close aperture etc.; act or gesture or event regarded as confirmation or guarantee; decorative adhesive stamp. **2** *v.t.* stamp or fasten with seal, close securely or hermetically; fix seal to; certify as correct with seal or stamp; confine securely (often with *up*); settle or decide (*his fate is sealed*). **3 sealing-wax** mixture of shellac and rosin softened by heating and used for seals; **seal off** prevent entry to and exit from (area); **seals of office** those held during tenure esp. by Lord Chancellor or Secretary of State; **set one's seal to** authorize or confirm. [AF f. L *sigillum*]

seal[2] **1** *n.* fish-eating amphibious sea mammal with flippers; = SEALSKIN. **2** *v.i.* hunt seals. [OE]

sealant *n.* material for sealing, esp. to make airtight or watertight. [SEAL[1]]

sealer *n.* ship or man engaged in hunting seals. [SEAL[2]]

sealskin *n.* skin or prepared fur of seal; garment made from this.

Sealyham /'siːlɪəm/ *n.* wire-haired short-legged terrier. [*Sealyham* in Wales]

seam 1 *n.* line where two edges join, esp. of cloth or boards; fissure between parallel edges; wrinkle; stratum of coal etc. **2** *v.t.* join by seam; (esp. in *p.p.*) mark or score with seam, fissure, or scar. **3 seam bowler** bowler in cricket who makes ball deviate by bouncing it off its seam. [OE]

seaman *n.* one whose occupation is on the sea; sailor, esp. below the rank of officer. [SEA]

seamanship *n.* skill in managing ship or boat.

seamstress /'semstrɪs/ *n.* woman who sews, esp. professionally. [OE (SEAM)]

seamy *a.* marked with or showing seams; **seamy side** disreputable or unattractive side. [SEAM]

seance /'seɪɑ̃s/ *n.* meeting for exhibition or investigation of spiritualistic phenomena. [F]

seaplane *n.* aircraft designed to take off from and land on water. [SEA]

seaport *n.* town with harbour.

sear *v.t.* scorch, cauterize; make (conscience or feelings etc.) callous. [OE]

search /sɜːtʃ/ **1** *v.* look through or go over thoroughly to find something; examine or feel over (person) to find anything concealed; probe or penetrate into (*lit.* or *fig.*); make search or investigation (*for*); (in *partic.*, of examination) thorough, leaving no loopholes. **2** *n.* act of searching, investigation. **3 in search of** trying to find; **search me** *colloq.* I do not know; **search out** look for, seek out; **search-party** group of people organized to look for lost person or thing; **search-warrant** official authority to enter and search a building. [AF f. L *circo* (CIRCLE)]

searchlight *n.* powerful outdoor electric light with concentrated beam that can be turned in any direction; light or beam from this.

seascape *n.* picture or view of the sea. [SEA]

seasick *a.* suffering from sickness or nausea from motion of ship etc.; **seasickness** *n.*

seaside *n.* sea-coast, esp. as holiday resort.

season /'siːz(ə)n/ **1** *n.* each of the divisions of the year (spring, summer, autumn, winter) associated with a type of weather and a stage of vegetation; proper or suitable time, time when something is plentiful or active or in vogue, = *high season*; time of year regularly devoted to an activity, or to social life generally (*London in the season*); indefinite period; *colloq.* = *season-ticket*. **2** *v.* flavour or make palatable with salt, herbs, etc.; enhance with wit etc.; temper or moderate; make or become suitable or in desired condition, esp. by exposure to air or weather. **3 in season** (of food) available in good condition and plentifully, (of animal) on heat; **season-ticket** ticket entitling holder to any number of journeys, admittances, etc., in a given period. [F f. L *satio* sowing]

seasonable *a.* suitable or usual to the season; opportune; meeting the needs of the occasion; **seasonably** *adv.*

seasonal *a.* of, depending on, or varying with the season; **seasonally** *adv.*

seasoning *n.* flavouring added to food.

seat 1 *n.* thing made or used for sitting on; buttocks, part of trousers etc. covering them; part of chair etc. on which sitter's weight directly rests; place for one person in theatre etc.; occupation of seat or right to occupy it, esp. as Member of House of Commons; part of machine that supports or guides another part; site or location (*seat of learning*); country mansion, esp. with large grounds; manner of sitting on horse etc. **2** *v.t.* cause to sit; provide sitting accommodation for (*bus seats 100 passengers*); (in *p.p.*) sitting; put or fit in position. **3 be seated** sit down; **by the seat of one's pants** by instinct rather than knowledge or logic; **seat-belt** belt securing person in seat of car or aircraft; **take a seat** sit down. **4 -seater** *in comb.* having specified number of seats. [ON (SIT)]

seating *n.* seats collectively, sitting accommodation.

seaward /ˈsiːwəd/ **1** *adv.* (also **seawards**) towards sea. **2** *a.* going or facing towards sea. **3** *n.* such direction or position. [-WARD]

seaweed *n.* plant growing in sea or in rocks on shore. [SEA]

seaworthy *a.* fit to put to sea.

sebaceous /sɪˈbeɪʃəs/ *a.* fatty, secreting or conveying oily matter. [L (*sebum* tallow)]

sec *a.* (of wine) dry. [F]

Sec. *abbr.* Secretary.

sec. *abbr.* second(s).

secateurs /sekəˈtɜːz/ *n.* pruning-clippers used with one hand. [F]

secede /sɪˈsiːd/ *v.i.* withdraw formally from a political or religious body. [L *secedo -cess-*]

secession /sɪˈseʃ(ə)n/ *n.* act of seceding; **secessionist** *n.* [F f. L (prec.)]

seclude /sɪˈkluːd/ *v.t.* keep (person or place or *oneself*) retired or away from company; screen from view. [L *secludo -clus-*]

seclusion /sɪˈkluːʒ(ə)n/ *n.* secluded state or place. [med.L (prec.)]

second[1] /ˈsekənd/ **1** *a.* next after first; other besides one or the first, additional (*ate a second cake*); of subordinate importance or position etc., inferior; *Mus.* performing lower or subordinate part (*second violins*); metaphorical, such as to be comparable to (*a second Callas*). **2** *n.* second person etc. in race or competition; another person or thing besides the previously mentioned or principal one; assistant to combatant in duel, boxing-match, etc.; (in *pl.*) second helping of food or second course of meal. **3** *v.t.* support, back up; formally support (nomination or resolution etc., or its proposer); /sɪˈkɒnd/ transfer (person) temporarily to another department etc. **4 second-best** *a.* & *n.* next after best (**come off second-best** fail to win); **second chamber** upper house of parliament; **second class** second best group or category or accommodation; **second-class** *a.* & *adv.* of or by the second or inferior class, position, quality, etc.; **second cousin** see COUSIN; **second fiddle** subordinate position; **second-hand** *a.* having had previous owner, not new, (of shop etc.) supplying such goods, (*adv.*) from a secondary source (**at second hand** indirectly); **second lieutenant** army officer next below lieutenant; **second nature** acquired tendency that has become instinctive; **second officer** assistant mate on merchant ship; **second person** see PERSON; **second-rate** rated in second class, inferior; **second sight** supposed power of perceiving future events; **second thoughts** new opinion or resolution reached after further consideration; **second wind** recovery of regular breathing during continued exertion after breathlessness, renewed capacity for effort after tiredness. [F f. L *secundus* (*sequor* follow)]

second[2] /ˈsekənd/ *n.* sixtieth part of minute of time or angle; *colloq.* very short time (*wait a second*). [F f. med.L *secunda* (*minuta*) secondary (minute)]

secondary /ˈsekəndərɪ/ *a.* coming after or next below what is primary; derived from or depending on or supplementing what is primary; (of education, school, etc.) for those who have had primary education; **secondary colours** see COLOUR; **secondary picketing** picketing of premises of firm not otherwise involved in the industrial dispute; **secondarily** *adv.* [L (SECOND[1])]

secondly *adv.* in the second place, furthermore. [SECOND[1]]

secondment /sɪˈkɒndmənt/ *n.* temporary transfer of person to another department etc.

secrecy /ˈsiːkrəsɪ/ *n.* keeping of secrets

as a fact, habit, or faculty; **sworn to secrecy** having promised to keep a secret. [foll.]

secret /'si:krɪt/ **1** *a.* kept or meant to be kept private or unknown or hidden from all or all but a few; acting or operating secretly; fond of secrecy. **2** *n.* thing kept or meant to be kept secret; mystery, thing for which explanation is unknown or not widely known; valid but not generally understood method for achieving something (*what's her secret?; the secret of success*). **3 in secret** in secret manner; **secret agent** spy acting for a country; **secret ballot** one in which voting is not made public; **secret police** police force operating in secret for political ends; **secret service** government department concerned with espionage; **secret society** one whose members are sworn to secrecy about it. [F f. L (*secerno secret-* separate)]

secretaire /sekrɪ'teə/ *n.* escritoire. [F (SECRETARY)]

secretariat /sekrə'teərɪət/ *n.* administrative office or department; its members or premises. [F f. med.L (foll.)]

secretary /'sekrətərɪ/ *n.* person employed by an individual or in an office etc. to assist with correspondence, keep records, make appointments, etc.; official appointed by a society etc. to conduct its correspondence, keep its records, etc.; principal assistant of government minister, ambassador, etc.; **secretary-bird** long-legged crested African bird; **Secretary-General** principal administrator of an organization; **Secretary of State** head of a major government department, *US* = Foreign Secretary; **secretarial** /-'teərɪəl/ *a.*; **secretaryship** *n.* [L *secretarius* (SECRET)]

secrete /sɪ'kri:t/ *v.t.* conceal; separate (substance) in gland etc. from blood or sap for function in the organism or for excretion. [SECRET]

secretion /sɪ'kri:ʃ(ə)n/ *n.* act of secreting; secreted substance. [F or L (SECRET)]

secretive /'si:krətɪv/ *a.* inclined to make or keep secrets, uncommunicative. [SECRET]

secretory /sɪ'kri:tərɪ/ *a.* of physiological secretion. [SECRETE]

sect *n.* body of persons sharing (usu. unorthodox) religious doctrines; religious denomination; followers of a particular philosophy or school of thought. [F or L (*sequor* follow)]

sectarian /sek'teərɪən/ **1** *a.* of or concerning a sect; bigoted or narrow-minded in following one's sect. **2** *n.* member of a sect. **3 sectarianism** *n.* [med.L *sectarius* adherent]

section /'sekʃ(ə)n/ **1** *n.* part cut off; one of the parts into which thing is divided or divisible or out of which a structure can be fitted together; subdivision of book, statute, group of people, etc.; *US* area of land, district of town; subdivision of army platoon; separation by cutting; cutting of solid by plane, resulting figure or area of this. **2** *v.t.* arrange in or divide into sections. **3 section-mark** sign (§) used to indicate start of section of book etc. [F or L (*seco sect-* cut)]

sectional *a.* of a section; made in sections; local rather than general; partisan; **sectionally** *adv.*

sector /'sektə/ *n.* distinct part or branch of an enterprise, of society or the economy, etc.; plane figure enclosed between two radii of circle, ellipse, etc., and the arc cut off by them; portion of area for military activity. [L (SECTION)]

secular /'sekjʊlə/ *a.* concerned with the affairs of this world, not spiritual or sacred; not ecclesiastical or monastic; occurring once in an age or century; **secularity** /-'lærɪtɪ/ *n.* [L (*saeculum* an age)]

secularism *n.* belief that morality or education should not be based on religion; **secularist** *n.*

secure /sɪ'kjʊə/ **1** *a.* untroubled by danger or fear; impregnable; reliable, certain not to fail or give way or get loose or be lost. **2** *v.t.* make secure or safe; fasten or close securely; succeed in obtaining. [L (*se* without, *cura* care)]

security *n.* secure condition or feeling; thing that guards or guarantees; safety of State, company, etc., against espionage, theft, or other danger; organization for ensuring this; thing deposited or pledged as guarantee of fulfilment of undertaking or payment of loan, to be forfeited in case of failure; (often in *pl.*) document as evidence of loan, certificate of stock, bond, etc.; **security risk** person whose presence may threaten security. [F or L (prec.)]

sedan /sɪ'dæn/ *n.* former enclosed chair for one person, carried on poles by two men (also **sedan-chair**); *US* enclosed motor car for four or more persons. [orig. uncert.]

sedate /sɪ'deɪt/ **1** *a.* tranquil and dignified, equable, serious. **2** *v.t.* put under sedation. [L (*sedo* settle, calm)]

sedation /sɪ'deɪʃ(ə)n/ *n.* calming, esp. by sedatives. [F or L (SEDATE)]

sedative /'sedətɪv/ **1** *a.* tending to calm or soothe. **2** *n.* sedative medicine etc. [F or med.L (SEDATE)]

sedentary /'sedəntərɪ/ *a.* sitting; (of work etc.) characterized by much sitting and little physical exercise; (of person) spending much time seated. [F or L (*sedeo* sit)]

sedge *n.* waterside or marsh plant resembling coarse grass; **sedgy** *a.* [OE]

sediment /'sedɪmənt/ *n.* matter that settles to bottom of liquid, dregs; matter carried by water or wind and deposited on surface of land; **sedimentary** /-'mentərɪ/ *a.*; **sedimentation** /-'teɪʃ(ə)n/ *n.* [F or L (*sedeo* sit)]

sedition /sɪ'dɪʃ(ə)n/ *n.* conduct or speech inciting to rebellion; **seditious** *a.* [F, or L *seditio*]

seduce /sɪ'dju:s/ *v.t.* tempt or entice into sexual activity or into wrongdoing; coax or lead astray. [L (*se-* away, *duco duct-* lead)]

seduction /sɪ'dʌkʃ(ə)n/ *n.* seducing or being seduced; tempting or attractive thing or quality. [F or L (prec.)]

seductive /sɪ'dʌktɪv/ *a.* tending to seduce, alluring, enticing.

sedulous /'sedjʊləs/ *a.* persevering, unremitting, painstaking; **sedulity** /sɪ'dju:lɪtɪ/ *n.* [L *sedulus* zealous]

sedum /'si:dəm/ *n.* fleshy-leaved plant with pink or white or yellow flowers, e.g. stonecrop. [L, = houseleek]

see[1] *v.* (*past* **saw;** *p.p.* **seen**) discern by use of the eyes, have or use such power of discerning; discern mentally, understand; ascertain (*must see what can be done*); consider, foresee (*can just see the result*); watch, look at (*see a film*); look at for information (*see page 12*); meet and recognize (*saw your mother in town*); give interview to; visit to consult (*should see a doctor*); be visited by (*is too ill to see anyone*); learn esp. from visual source (*I see you have been promoted*); reflect, wait until one knows more (*we shall have to see*); interpret or have opinion of (*I see things differently now*); find attractive (*can't think what she sees in him*); supervise, ensure (*see that it is done*); experience, have presented to one's attention; imagine (*cannot see him agreeing to it*); escort or conduct (*may I see you home?*); (in gambling, esp. poker) equal (a bet), equal bet of (player); **see about** attend to; **see after** take care of; **see the back of** be rid of (unwanted person or thing); **see into** investigate; **see the light** realize one's mistakes etc., undergo religious conversion; **see off** accompany to place of departure, ensure departure of (person); **see out** accompany out of a building etc., finish (project etc.) completely, wait until end of (period); **see over** inspect, tour and examine; **see red** become suddenly enraged; **see stars** see lights before one's eyes as result of blow on head; **see things** have hallucinations; **see through** not be deceived by, detect nature of; **see person through** support him during difficult time; **see thing through** finish it completely; **see-through** *a.* (esp. of clothing) transparent; **see to** attend to, put right; **see to it** ensure (*that*). [OE]

see[2] *n.* area under authority of bishop or archbishop; his office or jurisdiction. [AF *se*(*d*) f. L *sedes* seat]

seed 1 *n.* unit of reproduction of plant, capable of developing into another such plant; *collect.* seeds in any quantity, esp. as collected for sowing; semen; prime cause, beginning; offspring, descendants; (in tennis etc.) seeded player. **2** *v.* place seeds in; sow seeds; sprinkle (as) with seed; produce or drop seed; remove seeds from (fruit etc.); place crystal etc. in (cloud) to produce rain; (in tennis etc.) designate (strong competitor in knock-out competition) so that strong competitors do not meet each other in early rounds, arrange (order of play) thus. **3 go** (or **run**) **to seed** cease flowering as seed develops, *fig.* become degenerate or unkempt etc.; **seed-bed** bed of fine soil in which to sow seeds, *fig.* place of development; **seed-pearl** very small pearl; **seed-potato** potato kept for seed. [OE]

seedling *n.* young plant, esp. one raised from seed and not from cutting etc.

seedsman *n.* dealer in seeds.

seedy *a.* full of seed; going to seed; shabby-looking; *colloq.* unwell; **seedily** *adv.*; **seediness** *n.*

seeing 1 *n.* use of the eyes. **2** *conj.* (also **seeing that**) considering that, inasmuch as, because. [SEE[1]]

seek *v.* (*past* and *p.p.* **sought** /sɔ:t/) make search or inquiry (*for*); try or want to find or get or reach; endeavour or try (*seek to please*); *archaic* aim at, attempt; **seek out** look for and find, single out for companionship etc. [OE]

seem *v.i.* have the air or appearance or feeling of being; give certain impression as to action or state (*seems to be breathing, to like you*); **it seems** it appears to be true or the fact (*that*). [ON]

seeming *a.* apparent but perhaps not real.

seemly *a.* conforming to good taste, decorous; **seemliness** *n.* [ON (SEEM)]

seen *p.p.* of SEE[1].

seep *v.i.* ooze out, percolate slowly. [OE]

seepage *n.* act of seeping, quantity that seeps out.

seer *n.* one who sees; person who sees visions, prophet. [SEE[1]]

seersucker /'sɪəsʌkə/ *n.* striped material of linen or cotton etc. with puckered surface. [Pers.]

see-saw /'si:sɔ:/ **1** *n.* device for children, with long plank balanced on central support and child sitting at each end moving up and down alternately; game played on this; up-and-down or to-and-fro motion; contest in which the advantage repeatedly changes from one side to the other. **2** *v.i.* play on see-saw; move up and down as on see-saw; vacillate in policy etc. **3** *a.* & *adv.* with up-and-down or backward-and-forward motion. [redupl. of SAW[1]]

seethe /si:ð/ *v.* boil, bubble over; be very agitated, esp. with anger. [OE]

segment /'segmənt/ **1** *n.* part cut off or separable or marked off as though separable from the other parts of something; part of circle or sphere etc. cut off by line or plane intersecting it. **2** /also -'ment/ *v.* divide into segments. **3 segmental** /-'ment(ə)l/ *a.*; **segmentation** /-'teɪʃ(ə)n/ *n.* [L (*seco* cut)]

segregate /'segrɪgeɪt/ *v.* put or come apart from the rest, isolate; separate (esp. racial group) from the rest of the community. [L (*grex greg-* flock)]

segregation /segrɪ'geɪʃ(ə)n/ *n.* enforced segregating of racial groups in community; **segregationist** *n.*

seigneur /seɪn'jɜ:/ *n.* feudal lord; **seigneurial** *a.* [F f. L SENIOR]

seine /seɪn/ **1** *n.* fishing-net for encircling fish, with floats at top and weights at bottom edge. **2** *v.* fish or catch with seine. [OE & F f. L *sagena* f. Gk]

seise see SEIZE.

seismic /'saɪzmɪk/ *a.* (also **seismical**) *a.* of earthquakes; **seismically** *adv.* [Gk *seismos* earthquake (*seiō* shake)]

seismogram /'saɪzməgræm/ *n.* record given by seismograph.

seismograph /'saɪzməgrɑ:f/ *n.* instrument for showing force and direction etc. of earthquake.

seismography /saɪz'mɒgrəfɪ/ *n.* study or recording of seismic phenomena; **seismographer** *n.*

seismology /saɪz'mɒlədʒɪ/ *n.* = SEISMOGRAPHY; **seismologist** *n.*

seize /si:z/ *v.* take hold or possession (of), esp. forcibly or suddenly or by legal power; affect suddenly (*panic seized us*); comprehend quickly or clearly ; *Law* (also **seise** /si:z/) put in possession of; *Naut.* fasten by binding with turns of yarn etc.; **seized** (or **seised**) **of** possessing legally, aware or informed of; **seize on** (or **upon**) seize eagerly; **seize up** (of mechanism) become stuck or jammed from undue heat or friction etc. [F *saisir* f. Gmc]

seizure /'si:ʒə/ *n.* seizing or being seized; sudden attack of apoplexy etc., stroke.

seldom /'seldəm/ *adv.* rarely, not often. [OE]

select /sɪ'lekt/ **1** *v.t.* choose, esp. as best or most suitable. **2** *a.* chosen for excellence or fitness; (of society etc.) exclusive, cautious in admitting members. **3 select committee** small parliamentary committee appointed to conduct special inquiry. [L *seligo -lect-*]

selection /sɪ'lekʃ(ə)n/ *n.* selecting or being selected; selected person or thing; things from which choice may be made; process by which some animals or plants thrive more than others, as factor in evolution. [L *selectio* (prec.)]

selective *a.* using or characterized by selection; able to select; **selectivity** /-'tɪvɪtɪ/ *n.* [SELECT]

selector *n.* person who selects, esp. representative team; device in machinery making required selection of gear etc.

selenium /sɪ'li:nɪəm/ *n.* non-metallic element of sulphur group. [Gk *selēnē* moon]

self **1** *n.* (*pl.* **selves**) person's or thing's own individuality or essence (*showed his true self*; *is her old self again*); person or thing as object of introspection or reflexive action; one's own interests or pleasure, concentration on these; (in commerce, or *colloq.*) myself, yourself, herself, etc. (*cheque drawn to self*). **2** *a.* of same colour as the rest or throughout. [OE]

self- *prefix* expressing reflexive action in senses 'of or by oneself or itself', 'on, in, for, or relating to oneself or itself'.

self-abuse /selfə'bju:s/ *n.* masturbation.

self-addressed /selfə'dresd/ *a.* addressed to oneself.

self-appointed /selfə'pɔɪntɪd/ *a.* appointed by oneself to some office or capacity, not necessarily recognized by others.

self-assertive /selfə'sɜ:tɪv/ *a.* determined to assert oneself, one's rights, etc.; **self-assertion** *n.*

self-assured /selfə'ʃʊəd/ *a.* self-confident; **self-assurance** *n.*

self-catering /self'keɪtərɪŋ/ *a.* catering for oneself, providing one's own meals.

self-centred /self'sentəd/ *a.* preoccupied with oneself or one's own affairs.

self-confessed /selfkən'fesd/ *a.* openly confessing oneself to be.

self-confident /self'kɒnfɪdənt/ *a.* having confidence in one's own abilities; **self-confidence** *n.*

self-conscious /self'kɒnʃəs/ *a.* ill at ease or embarrassed from awareness of oneself, one's actions, etc.

self-contained /selfkən'teɪnd/ *a.*

complete in itself, (of accommodation) having all facilities unshared; (of person) not dependent on others, uncommunicative.

self-control /selfkən'trəʊl/ *n.* ability to restrain oneself or one's behaviour etc.

self-deception /selfdɪ'sepʃ(ə)n/ *n.* deceiving oneself, esp. about one's feelings etc.

self-defeating /selfdɪ'fi:tɪŋ/ *a.* that defeats its own purpose.

self-defence /selfdɪ'fens/ *n.* defence of oneself or one's reputation etc.

self-denial /selfdɪ'naɪəl/ *n.* going without pleasures etc. one would like.

self-determination /selfdɪtɜ:mɪ'neɪʃ(ə)n/ *n.* making of one's own decisions, esp. nation's right to determine its own allegiance or form of government.

self-discipline /self'dɪsɪplɪn/ *n.* discipline and training of oneself.

self-drive /self'draɪv/ *a.* (of hired vehicle) driven by hirer.

self-educated /self'edjʊkeɪtɪd/ *a.* educated by oneself, with little or no help from schools etc.

self-effacing /selfɪ'feɪsɪŋ/ *a.* modest and withdrawn; **self-effacement** *n.*

self-employed /selfɪm'plɔɪd/ *a.* working as owner of business etc.

self-esteem /selfɪ'sti:m/ *n.* good opinion of oneself.

self-evident /self'evɪdənt/ *a.* evident without proof or further explanation.

self-examination /selfɪgzæmɪ'neɪʃ(ə)n/ *n.* examination of oneself, esp. as regards conduct or intentions etc.

self-explanatory /selfɪk'splænətərɪ/ *a.* that needs no (further) explanation.

self-fulfilment /self-fʊl'fɪlmənt/ *n.* fulfilment of one's own hopes and ambitions etc.

self-governing /self'gʌvənɪŋ/ *a.* governing itself or oneself; **self-government** *n.*

self-help /self'help/ *n.* use of one's own abilities or resources to achieve success.

self-important /selfɪm'pɔ:tənt/ *a.* having high opinion of oneself, pompous; **self-importance** *n.*

self-imposed /selfɪm'pəʊzd/ *a.* (of task etc.) imposed on and by oneself.

self-improvement /selfɪm'pru:vmənt/ *n.* improvement of one's own position or disposition by one's own efforts.

self-induced /selfɪn'dju:sd/ *a.* induced by oneself or itself.

self-indulgent /selfɪn'dʌldʒənt/ *a.* greatly indulging one's own pleasures or desires etc.; **self-indulgence** *n.*

self-inflicted /selfɪn'flɪktɪd/ *a.* inflicted by and on oneself.

self-interest /self'ɪntrəst/ *n.* one's personal interest or advantage; **self-interested** *a.*

selfish *a.* deficient in consideration for others, concerned chiefly with one's own personal profit or pleasure; (of motive etc.) actuated by or appealing to self-interest. [SELF]

selfless *a.* disregarding oneself or one's own interests, unselfish.

self-made *a.* having risen from poverty or obscurity by one's own efforts. [SELF-]

self-opinionated /selfə'pɪnjəneɪtɪd/ *a.* stubbornly adhering to one's own opinions.

self-pity /self'pɪtɪ/ *n.* pity for oneself.

self-portrait /self'pɔ:trɪt/ *n.* portrait (artistic or literary) of oneself by oneself.

self-possessed /selfpə'zesd/ *a.* feeling or remaining calm and composed, esp. in difficulty; **self-possession** *n.*

self-preservation /selfprezə'veɪʃ(ə)n/ *n.* keeping oneself from death or harm, instinct for this.

self-propelled /selfprə'peld/ *a.* propelled by its own power.

self-raising /self'reɪzɪŋ/ *a.* (of flour) containing its own raising agent.

self-regard /selfrɪ'gɑ:d/ *n.* regard for oneself.

self-reliant /selfrɪ'laɪənt/ *a.* reliant on or confident in one's own abilities; **self-reliance** *n.*

self-reproach /selfrɪ'prəʊtʃ/ *n.* reproach or blame directed at oneself.

self-respect /selfrɪ'spekt/ *n.* respect for oneself, feeling that one is behaving with honour, dignity, etc.; **self-respecting** *a.*

self-restrained /selfrɪ'streɪnd/ *a.* able to restrain one's own emotions; **self-restraint** *n.*

self-righteous /self'raɪtʃəs/ *a.* conceitedly aware of or asserting one's own rightness.

self-sacrifice /self'sækrɪfaɪs/ *n.* sacrifice of one's own interests and wishes in favour of others'; **self-sacrificing** *a.*

selfsame *a. the* very same, identical.

self-satisfied /self'sætɪsfaɪd/ *a.* showing undue satisfaction with oneself or one's achievements; **self-satisfaction** /-'fækʃ(ə)n/ *n.*

self-sealing /self'si:lɪŋ/ *a.* sealing automatically; (of tyre etc.) having means of automatically sealing small punctures.

self-seeking /self'si:kɪŋ/ *a.* & *n.* seeking one's own welfare before that of others.

self-service /self'sɜ:vɪs/ *n.* (often *attrib.*) system in shop or restaurant etc.

by which customers serve themselves and pay for what they have taken.

self-starter /self'stɑ:tə/ *n.* electric device for starting internal-combustion engine.

self-styled *a.* using a title or name etc. that one has given oneself, esp. without authorization or right.

self-sufficient /selfsə'fɪʃənt/ *a.* able to supply one's own needs without outside help; **self-sufficiency** *n.*

self-supporting /selfsə'pɔ:tɪŋ/ *a.* that supports oneself or itself; self-sufficient.

self-taught /self'tɔ:t/ *a.* having taught oneself without formal help from a teacher etc.

self-willed /self'wɪld/ *a.* obstinately determined to follow one's own wishes, intentions, etc.; **self-will** *n.*

sell 1 *v.* (*past* and *p.p.* **sold** /səʊld/) make over or dispose of in exchange for money; keep stock of for sale (*do you sell candles?*); (of goods) be purchased (*these are selling well*); have specified price (*sells at* or *for £5*); betray or offer dishonourably for money or other reward; advertise or disseminate merits of; cause to be sold (*the author's name will sell many copies*). **2** *n. colloq.* manner of selling; deception, disappointment. **3 be sold on** be enthusiastic about; **selling-point** an advantage recommending a thing; **sell off** sell remainder of (goods) at reduced prices; **sell out** sell (all one's stock, shares, etc., or *absol.*), betray, be treacherous or disloyal; **sell-out** *n.* selling of all tickets for a show etc., a commercial success, betrayal; **sell short** disparage, underestimate; **sell up** sell one's business, house, etc. [OE]

seller *n.* one who sells; commodity that sells well or badly; **seller's market** trading conditions favourable to seller.

Sellotape /'seləʊteɪp/ **1** *n.* **(P)** adhesive usu. transparent cellulose or plastic tape. **2** *v.t.* (**sellotape**) fix with Sellotape. [CELLULOSE]

selvage /'selvɪdʒ/ *n.* specially woven edging to prevent cloth from unravelling. [SELF, EDGE]

selves *pl.* of SELF.

semantic /sɪ'mæntɪk/ *a.* of meaning in language; **semantically** *adv.* [F f. Gk (*sēmainō* mean *v.*)]

semantics *n.pl.* (usu. treated as *sing.*) branch of linguistics concerned with meaning.

semaphore /'seməfɔ:/ **1** *n.* system of signalling by holding the arms or two flags in certain positions according to alphabetic code; signalling apparatus of post with movable arm(s) etc. used on railways etc. **2** *v.* signal or send by semaphore. [F f. Gk *sēma* sign, *pherō* bear]

semblance /'sembləns/ *n.* outward or superficial appearance *of* something. [F (L *simulo* SIMULATE)]

semen /'si:mən/ *n.* reproductive fluid of males, containing spermatozoa. [L *semen semin-* seed]

semester /sɪ'mestə/ *n.* half-year course or term in (esp. German and US) universities. [G f. L *semestris* (*sex* six, *mensis* month)]

semi /'semɪ/ *n. colloq.* semi-detached house. [abbr.]

semi- *prefix* half, partly; occurring or appearing twice in specified period (*semi-annual*). [F or L]

semibreve /'semɪbri:v/ *n. Mus.* longest note in common use.

semicircle /'semɪsɜ:k(ə)l/ *n.* half of circle or of its circumference; **semicircular** /-'sɜ:kjʊlə/ *a.*

semicolon /semɪ'kəʊlən/ *n.* punctuation mark (;) of intermediate value between comma and full stop.

semiconductor /semɪkən'dʌktə/ *n.* substance that in certain conditions has electrical conductivity intermediate between insulators and metals.

semi-detached /semɪdɪ'tætʃd/ *a.* (of house) joined to another on one side only.

semifinal /semɪ'faɪn(ə)l/ *n.* match or round preceding final; **semifinalist** *n.*

seminal /'semɪn(ə)l/ *a.* of seed or semen or reproduction, germinal; (of ideas etc.) providing basis for future development. [F or L (SEMEN)]

seminar /'semɪnɑ:/ *n.* small class at university etc. for discussion and research; short intensive course of study. [G (foll.)]

seminary /'semɪnərɪ/ *n.* training-college for priests or rabbis etc.; **seminarist** *n.* [L (SEMEN)]

semi-permeable /semɪ'pɜ:mɪəb(ə)l/ *a.* (of a membrane etc.) allowing small molecules to pass through but not large ones. [SEMI-]

semiprecious /semɪ'preʃəs/ *a.* (of gem) less valuable than a precious stone.

semiquaver /'semɪkweɪvə/ *n. Mus.* note equal to half a quaver.

semi-skilled *a.* (of work or worker) having or needing some training but less than for skilled worker.

Semite /'si:maɪt/ *n.* member of any of the peoples supposedly descended from Shem (Gen. 10), including esp. Jews and Arabs; **Semitism** *n.* [L f. Gk *Sēm* Shem]

Semitic /sɪ'mɪtɪk/ *a.* of languages of the family including Hebrew and Arabic; of Semites, esp. of Jews.

semitone /ˈsemɪtəʊn/ *n.* half a tone in musical scale. [SEMI-]
semi-trailer /semɪˈtreɪlə/ *n.* trailer having wheels at back and supported at front by towing vehicle.
semitropical /semɪˈtrɒpɪk(ə)l/ *a.* subtropical.
semivowel /ˈsemɪvaʊəl/ *n.* sound intermediate between vowel and consonant (e.g. *w*, *y*); letter representing this.
semolina /seməˈliːnə/ *n.* hard grains left after milling of flour, used in milk puddings etc.; pudding made of this. [It. *semolino*]
sempstress var. of SEAMSTRESS.
SEN *abbr.* State Enrolled Nurse.
Sen. *abbr.* Senator; Senior.
senate /ˈsenɪt/ *n.* legislative body, esp. upper and smaller assembly in US and France etc.; governing body of university or (*US*) college; ancient-Roman State council. [F f. L *senatus* (*senex* old man)]
senator /ˈsenətə/ *n.* member of senate; **senatorial** /-ˈtɔːrɪəl/ *a.* [F f. L (prec.)]
send *v.* (*past* and *p.p.* **sent**) order or cause to go or be conveyed; send message or letter (*he sent to warn me*); (of God, Providence, etc.) grant or bestow or inflict, bring about, cause to be; *sl.* affect emotionally, put into ecstasy; **send away** dispatch, cause to depart, send money etc. to dealer *for* thing; **send down** rusticate or expel from university, put in prison; **send for** summon, order by post; **send in** cause to go in, submit (entry etc.) for competition etc.; **send off** get (letter or parcel etc.) dispatched, send away (*for* thing), attend departure of (person) as sign of respect etc., (of referee) order (player) to leave field and take no further part in game; **send-off** *n.* demonstration of goodwill etc. at departure of person, start of project, etc.; **send on** transmit to further destination or in advance of one's own arrival; **send up** cause to go up, transmit to higher authority, *colloq.* satirize, or ridicule by mocking; **send-up** *n. colloq.* satire or parody; **send word** send information. [OE]
senescent /sɪˈnesənt/ *a.* growing old; **senescence** *n.* [L (*senex* old)]
seneschal /ˈsenɪʃ(ə)l/ *n.* steward of medieval great house. [F f. L f. Gmc, = old servant]
senile /ˈsiːnaɪl/ *a.* of or characteristic of old age; having symptoms and weaknesses of old age; **senility** /sɪˈnɪlɪtɪ/ *n.* [F or L (as prec.)]
senior /ˈsiːnɪə/ **1** *a.* more or most advanced in age or standing; of high or highest position; (placed after person's name) senior to another of same name. **2** *n.* senior person; one's elder or superior. **3** **senior citizen** elderly person, esp. old-age pensioner; **senior nursing officer** person in charge of nursing services in hospital; **senior school** school for older children (esp. over 11); **senior service** Royal Navy. [L compar. of *senex* old]
seniority /siːnɪˈɒrɪtɪ/ *n.* state of being senior.
senna /ˈsenə/ *n.* cassia; laxative prepared from this. [Arab.]
señor /senˈjɔː/ *n.* (*pl.* ***Señores*** /-rez/) title used of or to Spanish-speaking man. [Sp. f. L SENIOR]
señora /senˈjɔːrə/ *n.* title used of or to Spanish-speaking married woman.
señorita /senjəˈriːtə/ *n.* title used of or to Spanish-speaking unmarried woman.
sensation /senˈseɪʃ(ə)n/ *n.* consciousness of perceiving or seeming to perceive some condition of one's body, senses, mind, feelings, etc.; stirring of emotions or intense interest among a community or group, cause or manifestation of this. [med.L (SENSE)]
sensational *a.* causing or intended to cause great public excitement etc.; of or causing sensation; **sensationally** *adv.*
sensationalism *n.* use of or interest in the sensational; **sensationalist** *n.*
sense 1 *n.* any of the bodily faculties through which sensation is caused; sensitiveness of all or any of these; ability to perceive or feel; consciousness *of* (*sense of having done well*, *of one's importance*); quick or accurate appreciation, understanding, or instinct (*sense of humour*; *moral sense*); practical wisdom or judgement, conformity to this, = *common sense*; meaning of word etc., intelligibility or coherence; prevailing opinion (*the sense of the meeting*); (in *pl.*) person's sanity or normal state of mind. **2** *v.t.* perceive by sense(s); be vaguely aware of; realize; (of machine etc.) detect. **3 come to one's senses** regain consciousness, be sensible after acting foolishly; **in a** (or **one**) **sense** if the statement is understood in a particular way; **make sense** be intelligible or practicable; **make sense of** show or find meaning of; **sense-organ** bodily organ conveying external stimuli to the sensory system. [L *sensus* (*sentio sens-* feel)]
senseless *a.* unconscious; wildly foolish; without meaning or purpose.
sensibility /sensɪˈbɪlɪtɪ/ *n.* capacity to feel physically or emotionally; (exceptional or excessive) sensitiveness or susceptibility; (in *pl.*) tendency to feel offended etc. [L (foll.)]
sensible /ˈsensɪb(ə)l/ *a.* having or showing wisdom or common sense, reasonable, judicious; perceptible by the

senses, great enough to be perceived; practical and functional (e.g. of clothing); aware *of*; **sensibly** *adv.* [F or L (SENSE)]

sensitive /ˈsensɪtɪv/ *a.* acutely affected by external stimuli or mental impressions, having sensibility *to*; (of person) easily offended or emotionally hurt; (of instrument etc.) responsive *to* or recording slight changes; (of photographic paper etc.) prepared so as to respond to action of light; (of topic etc.) subject to restriction of discussion to prevent embarrassment, ensure security, etc.; **sensitive plant** mimosa or other plant that droops or closes when touched, sensitive person. [F or med.L (SENSE)]

sensitivity /sensɪˈtɪvɪtɪ/ *n.* quality or degree of being sensitive.

sensitize /ˈsensɪtaɪz/ *v.t.* make sensitive; **sensitization** /-ˈzeɪʃ(ə)n/ *n.*

sensor *n.* device to detect or record or measure a physical property. [foll.]

sensory *a.* of sensation or the senses. [L (*sentio sens-* feel)]

sensual /ˈsensjʊəl/ *a.* of or connected with the body and the senses; given to or depending on gratification of the senses, self-indulgent, esp. sexually; indicating sensuality (*sensual lips*); **sensualism** *n.*; **sensually** *adv.* [L (SENSE)]

sensuality /sensjʊˈælɪtɪ/ *n.* gratification of the senses, self-indulgence.

sensuous /ˈsensjʊəs/ *a.* of or derived from or affecting the senses, esp. aesthetically. [L (SENSE)]

sent *past* & *p.p.* of SEND.

sentence /ˈsentəns/ **1** *n.* set of words (or occas. one word) containing or implying a subject and a predicate and expressing a statement, question, exclamation, or command; decision of lawcourt, esp. punishment allotted to person convicted in criminal trial, declaration of this. **2** *v.t.* declare sentence of (convicted person); declare condemned *to* punishment. **3 sentential** /-ˈtenʃ(ə)l/ *a.* (in *Gram.* sense). [F f. L *sententia* (*sentio* consider)]

sententious /senˈtenʃəs/ *a.* affectedly or pompously formal or moralizing; aphoristic; moralistic. [L (prec.)]

sentient /ˈsenʃənt/ *a.* capable of perception and feeling; **sentience** *n.*; **sentiency** *n.* [L *sentio* feel]

sentiment /ˈsentɪmənt/ *n.* a mental feeling; the sum of what one feels on some subject, verbal expression of this; an opinion as distinguished from the words meant to convey it; a view based on or coloured with emotion, such views collectively, esp. as an influence; tendency to be swayed by feeling rather than by reason; mawkish tenderness, display of this. [F f. med.L (prec.)]

sentimental /sentɪˈment(ə)l/ *a.* of or characterized by sentiment; showing or affected by emotion rather than reason; **sentimental value** value of thing to particular person because of its associations; **sentimentalism** *n.*; **sentimentalist** *n.*; **sentimentality** /-ˈtælɪtɪ/ *n.*; **sentimentalize** *v.*; **sentimentally** *adv.*

sentinel /ˈsentɪn(ə)l/ *n.* look-out, sentry. [F f. It.]

sentry /ˈsentrɪ/ *n.* soldier etc. stationed to keep guard; **sentry-box** wooden cabin large enough to shelter standing sentry; **sentry-go** duty of pacing up and down as sentry. [perh. f. obs. *centrinel*, var. of prec.]

sepal /ˈsep(ə)l/ *n.* division or leaf of calyx. [F f. L (foll., PETAL)]

separable /ˈsepərəb(ə)l/ *a.* able to be separated; **separability** /-ˈbɪlɪtɪ/ *n.* [F or L (foll.)]

separate /ˈsepərət/ **1** *a.* physically disconnected, forming unit that is or may be regarded as apart or by itself, distinct, individual. **2** *n.* (in *pl.*) separate articles of clothing suitable for wearing together. **3** /-eɪt/ *v.* make separate, sever; prevent union or contact of; go different ways; cease to live together as married couple; secede *from*; divide or sort into parts or sizes; remove or take *out* (one ingredient etc.) thus. **4 separative** *a.* [L *separo* v.]

separation /sepəˈreɪʃ(ə)n/ *n.* separating or being separate; (in full **judicial** or **legal separation**) arrangement by which husband and wife remain married but live apart. [F f. L (prec.)]

separatism *n.* policy of separation, esp. for political or ecclesiastical independence; **separatist** *n.* [SEPARATE]

separator /ˈsepəreɪtə/ *n.* machine for separating, e.g. cream from milk.

Sephardi /seˈfɑːdɪ/ *n.* (*pl.* **Sephardim**) Jew of Spanish or Portuguese descent; **Sephardic** *a.* [Heb., = Spaniard]

sepia /ˈsiːpɪə/ *n.* dark reddish-brown colour or paint. [L f. Gk, = cuttlefish]

sepoy /ˈsiːpɔɪ/ *n. hist.* native Indian soldier under European, esp. British, discipline. [Pers. *sipāhī* soldier]

sepsis /ˈsepsɪs/ *n.* septic condition. [Gk (SEPTIC)]

sept *n.* clan, esp. in Ireland. [alt. of SECT]

Sept. *abbr.* September.

September /sepˈtembə/ *n.* ninth month of year. [L (*septem* seven)]

septennial /sepˈtenɪəl/ *a.* lasting or recurring every seven years; **septennially** *adv.*

septet /sepˈtet/ *n.* musical composition for seven performers; the performers;

any group of seven. [G f. L *septem* seven]

septic /'septɪk/ *a.* putrefying, contaminated by bacteria; **septic tank** tank in which sewage is disintegrated through bacterial activity; **septically** *adv.* [L f. Gk (*sēpō* rot)]

septicaemia /septɪ'si:mɪə/, *US* **septicemia** *n.* blood-poisoning; **septicaemic** *a.* [prec., Gk *haima* blood]

septuagenarian /septjʊədʒɪ'neərɪən/ **1** *a.* from 70 to 79 years old. **2** *n.* septuagenarian person. [L *-arius* (*septuaginta* 70)]

Septuagesima /septjʊə'dʒesɪmə/ *n.* Sunday before Sexagesima. [L, = seventieth]

Septuagint /'septjʊədʒɪnt/ *n.* ancient-Greek version of Old Testament including Apocrypha. [L *septuaginta* seventy]

septum /'septəm/ *n.* (*pl.* **septa**) partition such as that between nostrils or the chambers of a poppy-fruit or shell. [L *s(a)eptum* (*saepio* enclose)]

septuple /'septjʊp(ə)l/ **1** *a.* sevenfold, having seven parts; being seven times as many or as much. **2** *n.* sevenfold number or amount. [L (*septem* seven)]

sepulchral /sɪ'pʌlkr(ə)l/ *a.* of a tomb or interment; gloomy, funereal. [F or L (foll.)]

sepulchre /'sepəlkə/, *US* **sepulcher 1** *n.* tomb esp. cut in rock or built of stone or brick. **2** *v.t.* place in sepulchre; serve as sepulchre for. [F f. L (*sepelio* bury)]

sepulture /'sepəltʃə/ *n.* burying, placing in grave. [F f. L (as prec.)]

sequel /'si:kw(ə)l/ *n.* what follows esp. as result; novel or film etc. that continues story of an earlier one. [F or L (*sequor* follow)]

sequence /'si:kwəns/ *n.* succession, order of succession; set of things belonging next to one another, unbroken series; part of cinema film dealing with one scene or topic. [L (prec.)]

sequential /sɪ'kwenʃ(ə)l/ *a.* forming sequence or consequence; **sequentially** *adv.* [SEQUENCE]

sequester /sɪ'kwestə/ *v.t.* seclude, isolate; sequestrate. [F or L (*sequester* trustee)]

sequestrate /sɪ'kwestreɪt/ *v.t.* confiscate; take temporary possession of (debtor's estate etc.); **sequestration** /si:kwe'streɪʃ(ə)n/ *n.*; **sequestrator** *n.* [L (prec.)]

sequin /'si:kwɪn/ *n.* circular spangle for attaching to dress; **sequinned** *a.* [F f. It. *zecchino* a gold coin f. Arab.]

sequoia /sɪ'kwɔɪə/ *n.* Californian coniferous tree of great height. [L f. *Sequoiah*, name of a Cherokee]

seraglio /se'rɑ:lɪəʊ/ *n.* (*pl.* **seraglios**) harem; *hist.* Turkish palace. [It. f. Turk. f. Pers.]

seraph /'serəf/ *n.* (*pl.* **seraphim** or **seraphs**) angelic being of highest order of the celestial hierarchy; **seraphic** /sə'ræfɪk/ *a.* [L f. Gk f. Heb.]

Serb *n.* & *a.* = SERBIAN. [Serbo-Croatian *Srb*]

Serbian /'sɜ:bɪən/ **1** *n.* native or inhabitant of Serbia; language of Serbia. **2** *a.* of Serbia.

Serbo-Croat /sɜ:bəʊ'krəʊæt/ (also **Serbo-Croatian** /-krəʊ'eɪʃ(ə)n/) **1** *n.* Slavonic language of Serbs and Croats. **2** *a.* of this language. [SERB, CROAT]

serenade /serə'neɪd/ **1** *n.* piece of music (suitable to be) sung or played at night, esp. by lover under his lady's window; orchestral suite for small ensemble. **2** *v.t.* sing or play serenade to. [F f. It. (SERENE)]

serendipity /serən'dɪpɪtɪ/ *n.* faculty of making happy discoveries by accident. [coined by Horace Walpole]

serene /sɪ'ri:n/ *a.* clear and calm; tranquil, unperturbed; **serenity** /sɪ'renɪtɪ/ *n.* [L]

serf *n. hist.* labourer not allowed to leave the land on which he worked; oppressed person, drudge; **serfdom** *n.* [F f. L *servus* slave]

serge *n.* durable twilled worsted etc. fabric. [F f. L (SILK)]

sergeant /'sɑ:dʒənt/ *n.* non-commissioned Army or RAF officer next below warrant officer; police officer below inspector; **(regimental) sergeant-major** warrant officer assisting adjutant of regiment or battalion. [F f. L *serviens -ent-* servant (SERVE)]

serial /'sɪərɪəl/ **1** *n.* story published or broadcast etc. in regular instalments. **2** *a.* of or in or forming series; (of story etc.) in form of serial; (of music) using transformations of a series of notes (see SERIES). **3 serial number** number identifying item in series. **4 serially** *adv.* [SERIES]

serialize *v.t.* publish or produce in instalments.

series /'sɪəri:z, -ɪz/ *n.* (*pl.* same) number of similar or related things, events, etc.; set of geological strata with common characteristic; arrangement of the twelve notes of the chromatic scale as basis for serial music; **in series** in ordered succession, (of set of electrical circuits) arranged so that same current passes through each circuit. [L (*sero* join)]

serif /'serɪf/ *n.* slight projection finishing off stroke of printed letter (as in T contrasted with T). [orig. uncert.]

serio-comic /sɪərɪəʊ'kɒmɪk/ *a.* combining the serious and the comic. [foll.]

serious /'sɪərɪəs/ *a.* thoughtful, earnest; important, demanding thought; not slight or negligible (*a serious injury*); sincere, in earnest; not (merely) frivolous. [F, or L *seriosus*]

serjeant /'sɑːdʒənt/ *n.* (also **serjeant--at-law**) *hist.* barrister of highest rank; **serjeant-at-arms** official of court or city or parliament, with ceremonial duties. [SERGEANT]

sermon /'sɜːmən/ *n.* spoken or written discourse on religion or morals etc., esp. delivered from pulpit; admonition, reproof. [F f. L *sermo -mon-* speech]

sermonize *v.* deliver moral lecture (to).

serous /'sɪərəs/ *a.* of or like serum, watery; (of gland etc.) having serous secretion; **serosity** /-'rɒsɪtɪ/ *n.* [SERUM]

serpent /'sɜːpənt/ *n.* snake esp. of large kind; sly or treacherous person; old bass wind instrument roughly in form of S. [F f. L (*serpo* creep)]

serpentine /'sɜːpəntaɪn/ **1** *a.* of or like serpent, coiling, tortuous; cunning, treacherous. **2** *n.* soft usu. dark green rock, sometimes mottled.

serrated /sə'reɪtɪd/ *a.* with toothed edge like a saw; **serration** *n.* [L (*serra* saw)]

serried /'serɪd/ *a.* (of ranks of soldiers) close together. [*serry* press close f. F *serrer* to close]

serum /'sɪərəm/ *n.* (*pl.* **sera** or **serums**) amber-coloured liquid which separates from clot when blood coagulates, esp. used for inoculation; watery fluid in animal bodies. [L, = whey]

servant /'sɜːvənt/ *n.* person who carries out orders of employer, esp. person employed in house on domestic duties or as personal attendant; devoted follower, person willing to serve another. [F partic. of *servir* (foll.)]

serve 1 *v.* be servant to; do service for (person or community etc.); carry out duty (*served on six committees*); be employed (*in* organization), be member of armed forces (*served in the air force*); be useful to or serviceable for, meet requirements, perform function; go through due period of (office, apprenticeship, prison sentence, etc.); set out or present (food) for those about to eat it; act as waiter (*at* table); attend to (customer in shop); supply (person *with*); treat or act towards (person) in specified way; make legal delivery of (writ etc.); (in tennis etc.) deliver (ball) to begin or resume play; keep (gun etc.) firing; (of animal) copulate with (female). **2** *n.* act or manner of serving ball in tennis etc.; person's turn to serve. **3 serve person right** be his deserved punishment or misfortune; **serve up** offer for acceptance. [F *servir* f. L *servio*]

server *n.* one who serves; celebrant's assistant at religious service.

servery *n.* room from which meals etc. are served.

service /'sɜːvɪs/ **1** *n.* doing of work, or work done, for another or for a community etc., assistance or benefit given to someone, readiness to perform this; provision or system of supplying some public need, e.g. transport (*bus service*) or (in *pl.*) supply of water, gas, electricity, etc.; being a servant, employment or position as servant; employment in public organization or Crown department, such organization or department; (in *pl.*) the armed forces; *attrib.* of the kind issued to the armed forces (*service rifle*); ceremony of worship, form of liturgy for this; provision of what is necessary for due maintenance of machine etc. or process; assistance or advice given to customers after sale of goods; serving of food etc., extra charge nominally made for this; set of dishes, plates, etc., required for serving meal (*tea-service*); serve in tennis etc., game in which one serves. **2** *v.t.* provide service for, esp. maintain or repair (car or machine etc.). **3 at person's service** ready to serve him; **in service** employed as servant, in use; **of service** useful, helpful; **on active service** serving in armed forces in wartime; **see service** have experience of serving esp. in armed forces, (of thing) be much used; **service area** area beside major road for supply of petrol, refreshments, etc., area served by broadcasting station; **service charge** additional charge for service rendered; **service flat** flat in which domestic service and sometimes meals are provided by the management; **service industry** one providing services not goods; **service road** road serving houses lying back from main road; **service station** place beside road selling petrol and oil etc. to motorists. [F, or L *servitium* (*servus* slave)]

serviceable *a.* useful or usable, able to render service; durable, suited for use rather than ornament; **serviceability** /-'bɪlɪtɪ/ *n.*; **serviceably** *adv.*

serviceman *n.* man in armed forces; man providing service or maintenance.

servicewoman *n.* woman in armed services.

serviette /sɜːvɪ'et/ *n.* table-napkin. [F (SERVE)]

servile /'sɜːvaɪl/ *a.* of or like slaves; slavish, fawning, completely dependent; **servility** /-'vɪlɪtɪ/ *n.* [L (*servus* slave)]

serving *n.* quantity of food for one person. [SERVE]
servitor /'sɜːvɪtə/ *n. archaic* servant, attendant. [F f. L (SERVE)]
servitude /'sɜːvɪtjuːd/ *n.* slavery, subjection. [F f. L (*servus* slave)]
servo /'sɜːvəʊ/ *n.* (*pl.* **servos**) servo-motor or -mechanism. [foll.]
servo- *in comb.* means of powered automatic control of larger system (*servo-assisted, -mechanism, -motor*). [F f. L *servus* slave]
sesame /'sesəmɪ/ *n.* annual E. Indian plant with oil-yielding seeds; its seeds; (also **open sesame**) magic words used to cause door to open, magical or mysterious means of access to what is usu. inaccessible. [L f. Gk]
sesqui- /seskwɪ/ *prefix* denoting 1½ (*sesquicentenary*). [L]
sessile /'sesaɪl/ *a.* (of flower or leaf or eye etc.) attached directly by base without stalk or peduncle; fixed in one position, immobile. [L (foll.)]
session /'seʃ(ə)n/ *n.* assembly for deliberative or judicial business, single meeting for such purpose; period during which such meetings are regularly held; academic year, *US* university term; period devoted to an activity (*dance session*); **in session** assembled for business, not on vacation; **sessional** *a.* [F or L (*sedeo sess-* sit)]
sestet /ses'tet/ *n.* last six lines of sonnet; sextet. [It. (L *sextus* sixth)]
set[1] *v.* (**-tt-**; *past* and *p.p.* **set**) **1** *v.t.* put or lay or stand in certain position etc.; apply (one thing) to another (*set pen to paper*); fix ready or in position, dispose suitably for use or action or display; adjust hands of (clock or watch) to show right time; adjust (alarm-clock) to sound at required time; fix or arrange or mount, make (device) ready to act; lay (table) for meal; arrange (hair) while damp so that it dries in required style; insert (jewel) in ring, framework, etc.; ornament or provide (surface) *with*; bring by placing or arranging or other means into specified state, cause to be (*set things in motion*; *set it on fire*); represent (story etc.) as happening at certain time or place; cause (person or oneself) *to do* specified thing; start (person etc.) *doing* something; present or impose as work to be done or matter to be dealt with; exhibit as type or model (*set an example*); initiate (fashion etc.); establish (a record etc.); determine or decide; appoint or establish (*set him in authority*); join or attach or fasten; put parts of (broken or dislocated bone, limb, etc.) into correct position for healing, deal thus with (fracture or dislocation); (in full **set to music**) provide (words etc.) with music for singing; arrange (type), or type for (book); cause (hen) to sit on eggs, place (eggs) for hen to sit on. **2** *v.i.* (of cement, jelly, etc.) harden or solidify; (of sun, moon, etc.) move towards or below earth's horizon; (of tide, current, etc.) have certain motion or direction; (of face) assume hard expression; (of eyes etc.) become motionless; show or feel certain tendency (*opinion is setting against it*); (of blossom) form into fruit, (of fruit) develop from blossom, (of tree) develop fruit; (of dancer) take position facing partner; (of hunting dog) take rigid attitude indicating presence of game; (*vulgar* or *dial.*) sit. **3 set about** begin or take steps towards; **set against** consider or reckon (thing) as counterpoise or compensation for; **set apart** separate, differentiate, reserve; **set aside** put to one side, keep for future use, disregard or reject, annul; **set back** place further back in place or time, impede or reverse progress of, *sl.* cost (person) specified amount; **set-back** *n.* reversal or arrest of progress, relapse; **set down** record in writing, allow to alight, attribute *to*, explain or describe to oneself *as*; **set eyes on** see EYE; **set foot in** (or **on**) enter or go to (place etc.); **set forth** begin journey or expedition, make known, expound; **set in** begin (and seem likely to continue), become established, insert; **set off** begin journey, detonate (bomb etc.), initiate, stimulate, cause (person) to start laughing, talking, etc., serve as adornment or foil to, enhance, use as compensating item *against*; **set on** (or **upon**) attack violently, cause or urge to attack; **set out** begin journey, aim or intend *to do* something, demonstrate or arrange or exhibit, mark out, declare; **set sail** hoist sail, begin voyage; **set to** begin doing something vigorously, esp. fighting or arguing or eating; **set-to** *n.* (*pl.* **set-tos**) fight or argument; **set up** place in position or view, organize or start (business etc.), establish in some capacity, supply with needs, begin making (a loud sound), cause (condition or situation), prepare (task etc. for another), restore or enhance health of (person), establish (a record); **set-up** *n.* arrangement or organization, manner or structure or position of these. [OE]
set[2] *n.* **1** number of things or persons that belong together or resemble one another or are usually found together, collection or group; section of society consorting together or having similar interests etc.; collection of implements,

vessels, etc., needed for a specified purpose (*cricket set*; *tea-set*); radio or television receiver; (in tennis etc.) group of games counting as unit towards match for player or side that wins greater number of games; *Math.* collection of things sharing a property. **2** direction or position in which something sets or is set; setting, stage furniture, etc., for play or film etc.; setting of hair or *poetic* sun. **3** (also **sett**) badger's burrow; granite paving-block; young plant or bulb ready to be planted. **4 dead set** determined attack or initiative; **set theory** *Math.* study or use of sets. [sense 1 f. F *sette* f. L (SECT); senses 2–3 f. SET[1]]

set[3] *a.* prescribed or determined in advance, fixed, unchanging, unmoving; (of phrase or speech etc.) having invariable or predetermined wording, not extempore; prepared for action; **set on** (or **upon**) determined to get or achieve etc.; **set piece** formal or elaborate arrangement esp. in art or literature, fireworks arranged on scaffolding etc.; **set square** right-angled triangular plate for drawing lines esp. at 90°, 45°, or 30°. [p.p. of SET[1]]

sett see SET[2].

settee /se'ti:/ *n.* long seat, with back and usu. arms, for more than one person. [orig. uncert.]

setter *n.* dog of long-haired breed trained to stand rigid when it scents game. [SET[1]]

setting *n.* position or manner in which thing is set; immediate surroundings of house etc.; place and time, scenery, etc., of story, drama, etc.; frame etc. for jewel; music to which words are set; cutlery etc. for one person at table.

settle[1] /'set(ə)l/ *v.* establish or become established in abode or place or way of life; (cause to) sit or come down to stay for some time; bring to or attain fixity, certainty, composure, or quietness; determine or decide or agree upon; resolve (dispute etc.); deal effectively with, get rid of; terminate (lawsuit) by mutual agreement; pay (money owed, account, etc., or *absol.*); subside, come down esp. on surface, or to or towards bottom of a liquid; establish or become colonists or dwellers in (country etc., or *absol.*); (in *p.p.*) not soon changing (*settled weather*); **settle down** become settled after disturbance or movement etc., adopt regular or secure style of life, apply oneself *to* (work etc.); **settle for** accept or agree to (esp. a less desirable alternative); **settle up** pay (money, account, etc., or *absol.*); **settle with** pay all or part of amount due to (creditor), get revenge on. [OE (SIT)]

settle[2] /'set(ə)l/ *n.* bench with high back and often with box below seat. [OE]

settlement *n.* settling or being settled; place occupied by settlers; political or financial etc. agreement, arrangement ending dispute; terms on which property is given to person, deed stating these, amount or property given. [SETTLE[1]]

settler *n.* one who goes to live in a new country.

seven /'sev(ə)n/ *a.* & *n.* one more than six; symbol for this (7, vii, VII); size etc. denoted by seven; **the seven seas** all the seas of the world. [OE]

sevenfold *a.* & *adv.* seven times as much or as many; consisting of seven parts.

seventeen /sevən'ti:n/ *a.* & *n.* one more than sixteen; symbol for this (17, xvii, XVII); size etc. denoted by seventeen; **seventeenth** *a.* & *n.* [OE]

seventh *a.* & *n.* next after sixth; one of seven equal parts of thing; **seventh-day Adventist** member of sect of Adventists observing sabbath on Saturday; **seventh heaven** state of intense joy; **seventhly** *adv.* [SEVEN]

seventy /'sevəntɪ/ *a.* & *n.* seven times ten; symbol for this (70, lxx, LXX); (in *pl.*) numbers, years, degrees of temperature, from 70 to 79; **seventieth** *a.* & *n.* [OE]

sever /'sevə/ *v.* divide or break or make separate, esp. by cutting; end employment contract of (person). [AF f. L (SEPARATE)]

several /'sevr(ə)l/ *a.* & *pron.* a few, more than two but not many; separate or respective (*went our several ways*); **severally** *adv.* [AF f. L (*separ* distinct)]

severance *n.* severing, severed state; **severance pay** amount paid to employee on termination of contract [SEVER].

severe /sɪ'vɪə/ *a.* harsh and rigorous in attitude or treatment (*severe critic, discipline*); serious (*severe shortage*); vehement or extreme or forceful (*a severe winter, illness, storm*); arduous or exacting (*severe competition*); unadorned, plain in style; **severity** /sɪ'verɪtɪ/ *n.* [F, or L *severus*]

Seville orange /'sevɪl/ bitter orange used for marmalade. [*Seville* in Spain]

sew /səʊ/ *v.* (*p.p.* **sewn** or **sewed**) fasten, join, enclose, or make with stitches; use needle and thread or sewing-machine; **sew up** join or enclose by sewing, *colloq.* (esp. in *p.p.*) arrange or finish dealing with (a project etc.). [OE]

sewage /'sju:ɪdʒ, 'su:-/ *n.* waste matter conveyed in sewers; **sewage farm** (or

works) place where sewage is treated. [foll.]

sewer /'sju:ə, 'su:-/ *n.* conduit, usu. underground, for carrying off drainage water and waste matter. [AF *sever(e)* f. Rmc (EX-[1], *aqua* water)]

sewerage /'sju:ərɪdʒ, 'su:-/ *n.* system of or drainage by sewers.

sewing-machine *n.* machine for sewing or stitching. [SEW]

sewn *p.p.* of SEW.

sex 1 *n.* either of the main divisions (male and female) into which living things are placed on the basis of their reproductive functions; fact of belonging to one of these; males or females collectively; sexual instincts, desires, etc., or their manifestation; *colloq.* sexual intercourse. **2** *a.* of or pertaining to sex; arising from difference or consciousness of sex. **3** *v.t.* determine sex of; (in *p.p.*) having sexual appetite (*highly sexed*). **4 sex appeal** sexual attractiveness; **sex maniac** person needing excessive gratification of sexual desires; **sex-starved** lacking adequate sexual gratification. [F, or L *sexus*]

sexagenarian /seksədʒɪ'neərɪən/ **1** *a.* from 60 to 69 years old. **2** *n.* sexagenarian person. [L *-arius* (*sexaginta* 60)]

Sexagesima /seksə'dʒesɪmə/ *n.* Sunday before Quinquagesima. [L, = sixtieth]

sexism *n.* prejudice or discrimination against people (esp. women) because of their sex; **sexist** *a.* & *n.* [SEX]

sexless *a.* neither male nor female; lacking sexual desire or attractiveness.

sexology /sek'sɒlədʒɪ/ *n.* study of sexual life or relationships; **sexologist**.

sextant /'sekstənt/ *n.* instrument with graduated arc of 60 used in navigation and surveying for measuring angular distance of objects by means of mirrors. [L *sextans -ntis* sixth part]

sextet /sek'stet/ *n.* musical composition for six performers; the performers; any group of six. [alt. of SESTET after L *sex* six]

sexton /'sekst(ə)n/ *n.* person who looks after church and churchyard, often acting as bell-ringer and grave-digger. [F *segerstein* f. L *sacristanus*]

sextuple /'sekstjʊp(ə)l/ **1** *a.* sixfold, having six parts; being six times as many or as much. **2** *n.* sixfold number or amount. [med.L (*sex* six)]

sextuplet /'sekstjʊplɪt/ *n.* each of six children born at one birth.

sexual /'seksjʊəl, 'sekʃ-/ *a.* of sex or the sexes or the relations between them; **sexual intercourse** insertion of man's penis into woman's vagina, usu. followed by ejaculation of semen; **sexuality** /-'ælɪtɪ/ *n.*; **sexually** *adv.* [L (SEX)]

sexy *a.* sexually attractive or stimulating; **sexily** *adv.*; **sexiness** *n.*

sez *sl.* says (*sez you*).

SF *abbr.* science fiction.

sf *abbr.* sforzando.

sforzando /sfɔ:t'sændəʊ/ *a.* & *adv. Mus.* with sudden emphasis. [It.]

Sgt. *abbr.* Sergeant.

sh *int.* hush.

shabby /'ʃæbɪ/ *a.* faded and worn, dingy, dilapidated; contemptible, dishonourable (*a shabby trick*); **shabbily** *a.*; **shabbiness** *n.* [rel. to SCAB]

shack *n.* roughly built hut or cabin; **shack up** *sl.* cohabit *with* or *together*. [perh. Mex. *jacal* wooden hut]

shackle /'ʃæk(ə)l/ **1** *n.* metal loop or link, closed by bolt, to connect chains etc.; fetter enclosing ankle or wrist; restraint, impediment. **2** *v.t.* fetter; impede, restrain. [OE]

shad *n.* (*pl.* **shads** or **shad**) large edible fish. [OE]

shade 1 *n.* comparative darkness (and usu. coolness) caused by shelter from direct light and heat; place or area sheltered from sun; darker part of picture etc.; a colour, esp. with regard to its depth or as distinguished from one nearly like it; slight amount or difference (*am a shade better today*); translucent cover for lamp etc.; screen excluding or moderating light; ghost. **2** *v.* screen from light; cover or moderate or exclude light of; darken, esp. with parallel pencil lines to represent shadow etc.; change or pass by degrees (*away* or *off* or *into*). **3 in the shade** in comparative obscurity. [OE]

shadow /'ʃædəʊ/ **1** *n.* shade or patch of shade; dark figure projected by body intercepting rays of light; one's inseparable attendant or companion, person secretly following another; slightest trace (*not a shadow of a doubt*); weak or insubstantial remnant (*is a shadow of his former self*); shaded part of picture; gloom or sadness. **2** *v.t.* cast shadow over; secretly follow and watch all movements of. **3 shadow-boxing** boxing against imaginary opponent as form of training; **Shadow Cabinet, Chancellor,** etc. members of opposition party serving as spokesmen for affairs for which Cabinet ministers have responsibility. [OE (prec.)]

shadowy *a.* having or like shadow; vague, indistinct.

shady /'ʃeɪdɪ/ *a.* giving or situated in shade; disreputable, of doubtful honesty; **shadily** *adv.*; **shadiness** *n.* [SHADE]

shaft /ʃɑ:ft/ *n.* arrow or spear, its long slender stem; remark intended to hurt or stimulate (*shafts of wit*); ray (*of* light); bolt (*of* lightning); stem or handle of tool, implement, etc.; long narrow space, usu. vertical, for access to a mine, for a lift in a building, for ventilation, etc.; long and narrow part supporting or connecting or driving part(s) of greater thickness etc.; column, esp. between base and capital; one of pair of poles between which horse is harnessed to vehicle. [OE]

shag *n.* rough growth or mass of hair; coarse tobacco; (crested) cormorant. [OE]

shaggy *a.* hairy, rough-haired, unkempt; **shaggy-dog story** long inconsequential narrative or joke; **shaggily** *adv.*; **shagginess** *n.*

shagreen /ʃæ'gri:n/ *n.* a kind of untanned leather with granulated surface; shark-skin. [var. of CHAGRIN]

shah *n.* former ruler of Iran. [Pers.]

shake 1 *v.* (*past* **shook** /ʃʊk/; *p.p.* **shaken**) move violently or quickly up and down or to and fro; (cause to) tremble or vibrate; agitate or shock, *colloq.* upset composure of; weaken or impair, make less convincing or firm or courageous; (of voice etc.) make tremulous or rapidly alternating sounds, trill; make threatening gesture with (one's fist, stick, etc.); *colloq.* shake hands (*we shook on the bargain*). **2** *n.* shaking or being shaken; jerk or shock; = *milk shake*; *Mus.* trill; *colloq.* moment (*in two shakes*). **3 the shakes** fit of trembling; **no great shakes** *colloq.* not very good or significant; **shake down** settle or cause to fall by shaking, settle down, become established; **shake hands** clasp hands (*with* person), esp. when meeting or parting, in reconciliation or congratulation, or as sign of bargain; **shake one's head** move one's head from side to side in refusal, denial, disapproval, or concern; **shake off** get rid of (unwanted thing), evade (person); **shake out** empty by shaking, spread or open (sail, flag, etc.) by shaking; **shake up** mix (ingredients) by shaking, restore to shape by shaking, disturb or make uncomfortable, rouse from lethargy, apathy, conventionality, etc.; **shake-up** *n.* upheaval, reorganization. **4 shakeable** *a.* [OE]

shaker *n.* person or thing that shakes; container for shaking together ingredients of cocktails etc.

Shakespearian /ʃeɪk'spɪərɪən/ *a.* of Shakespeare. [*Shakespeare*, dramatist]

shako /'ʃækəʊ/ *n.* (*pl.* **shakos**) cylindrical peaked military hat with plume. [F f. Magyar]

shaky *a.* unsteady, apt to shake, trembling; unsound, infirm; unreliable, wavering; **shakily** *adv.*; **shakiness** *n.* [SHAKE]

shale *n.* soft rock that splits easily, resembling slate; **shaly** *a.* [G (SCALE³)]

shall /ʃ(ə)l, *emphat.* ʃæl/ *v. aux.* (3 *sing.* **shall**, *archaic* 2 *sing.* **shalt** as below; *past* SHOULD) expressing (1) future action or state etc., esp. in first person (*I shall return soon*) and also in other persons to imply strong assertion rather than wish (*they shall go*; *you shall regret this*), (2) command or duty (*thou shalt not steal*; *they shall obey*); **shall I?** do you want me to? [OE]

shallot /ʃə'lɒt/ *n.* onion-like plant with growing cluster of small bulbs. [F (SCALLION)]

shallow /'ʃæləʊ/ **1** *a.* of little depth; superficial, trivial. **2** *n.* (often in *pl.*) shallow place. **3** *v.* become or make shallow. [OE]

shalom /ʃə'ləʊm/ *n.* & *int.* Jewish salutation at meeting or parting. [Heb.]

shalt see SHALL.

sham **1** *v.* (**-mm-**) feign, pretend; pretend to be. **2** *n.* imposture, pretence; person or thing pretending or pretended to be that he or it is not. **3** *a.* pretended, counterfeit. [orig. unkn.]

shaman /'ʃæmən/ *n.* witch-doctor, priest claiming to communicate with gods etc.; **shamanism** *n.* [Russ.]

shamateur /'ʃæmətə/ *n.* sports player classed as amateur though often profiting like professional. [SHAM, AMATEUR]

shamble /'ʃæmb(ə)l/ **1** *v.i.* walk or run with shuffling or awkward gait. **2** *n.* shambling gait. [perh. rel. to foll.]

shambles *n.pl.* (usu. treated as *sing.*) *colloq.* mess, muddle; butcher's slaughter-house; scene of carnage. [pl. of *shamble* stall, OE f. L *scamellum* bench]

shambolic /ʃæm'bɒlɪk/ *a. colloq.* chaotic, disorganized. [prec. (after SYMBOLIC)]

shame **1** *n.* feeling of distress or humiliation caused by consciousness of one's guilt or folly etc.; capacity for experiencing this feeling; state of disgrace or discredit; person or thing that brings disgrace etc., thing that is wrong or regrettable. **2** *v.t.* bring shame on, make ashamed; put to shame; force by shame (*shamed him into admitting it*). **3 for shame!** reproof to person for not showing shame; **put to shame** disgrace or humiliate by revealing superior qualities etc. [OE]

shamefaced *a.* showing shame; bashful, shy.

shameful *a.* disgraceful, scandalous; **shamefully** *adv.*

shameless *a.* having or showing no shame; impudent.

shammy /ˈʃæmɪ/ *n.* chamois-leather. [CHAMOIS]
shampoo /ʃæmˈpuː/ **1** *n.* liquid or cream used to lather and wash hair; similar liquid or chemical for washing car or carpet etc. **2** *v.t.* wash with shampoo. [Hind.]
shamrock /ˈʃæmrɒk/ *n.* trefoil, used as national emblem of Ireland. [Ir.]
shandy /ˈʃændɪ/ *n.* mixture of beer and lemonade or ginger-beer. [orig. unkn.]
shanghai /ʃæŋˈhaɪ/ *v.t.* force (person) to be sailor on ship, usu. by trickery; put into detention or awkward situation by trickery. [*Shanghai* in China]
shank *n.* leg; lower part of leg; shin-bone; shaft or stem, long narrow part of implement etc.; **Shanks's mare** (or **pony**) one's own legs as means of conveyance. [OE]
shan't /ʃɑːnt/ *colloq.* = *shall not.*
shantung /ʃænˈtʌŋ/ *n.* soft undressed Chinese silk, usu. undyed. [*Shantung*, Chinese province]
shanty[1] /ˈʃæntɪ/ *n.* hut, cabin, shack; **shanty town** town consisting of shanties. [orig. unkn.]
shanty[2] /ˈʃæntɪ/ *n.* song sung by sailors while hauling ropes etc. [prob. F *chanter* (CHANT)]
shape 1 *n.* external form or appearance, total effect produced by thing's outlines; specific form or guise; description or sort or way (*not in any shape or form*); definite or proper arrangement; condition (*in bad or good shape*), good condition (*keep in shape*); person or thing as seen, esp. indistinctly seen or imagined; mould or pattern; jelly etc. shaped in mould; piece of material, paper, etc., made or cut in a particular form. **2** *v.* give a certain shape or form to, fashion, create; adapt or make conform *to*; give signs of future shape or development; frame mentally, imagine; assume or develop into shape; direct (one's life, course, etc.). **3 shape up** take (specified) form, show promise, make good progress. [OE]
shapeless *a.* lacking definite shape or shapeliness.
shapely *a.* well formed or proportioned; of elegant or pleasing shape or appearance; **shapeliness** *n.*
shard *n.* broken piece of pottery or glass etc. [OE]
share[1] **1** *n.* portion that person gives to or receives from common amount or commitment; each of the equal parts into which a company's capital is divided entitling owner to proportion of profits. **2** *v.* get or have or give share (of), participate *in*; divide and distribute (often with *out*); give away part of. **3** **share-out** division and distribution, esp. of profits or proceeds. [OE, rel. to SHEAR]
share[2] *n.* ploughshare. [OE (as prec.)]
shareholder *n.* owner of shares in a company. [SHARE[1]]
shark *n.* large voracious sea-fish; rapacious person, swindler. [orig. unkn.]
sharkskin *n.* skin of shark; smooth dull-surfaced fabric.
sharp 1 *a.* having edge or point able to cut or pierce; tapering to point or edge; abrupt or steep or angular; well-defined, clean-cut; severe or intense, (of voice etc.) shrill and piercing, (of words or temper etc.) harsh or acrimonious; acute, quick to perceive or comprehend; quick to take advantage, artful, unscrupulous or dishonest; (of food etc.) acid or pungent in taste; vigorous or brisk; *Mus.* (of note) above correct or normal pitch (*C sharp*). **2** *n. Mus.* sharp note, sign indicating this; *colloq.* swindler, cheat. **3** *adv.* punctually (*at six o' clock sharp*); suddenly (*pulled up sharp*); at a sharp angle (*turn sharp right*); *Mus.* above true pitch (*sings sharp*). **4 sharp practice** dishonest or barely honest dealings. [OE]
sharpen *v.* make or become sharp.
sharper *n.* swindler, esp. at cards.
sharpish *a.* & *adv. colloq.* fairly sharp(ly), quite quickly.
sharpshooter *n.* skilled marksman.
shatter *v.* break suddenly in pieces; severely damage or destroy (*has shattered my hopes*); greatly upset or discompose; **be shattered** *colloq.* (of person) be exhausted. [rel. to SCATTER]
shave 1 *v.* (*p.p.* **shaved** or, esp. as *a.*, **shaven** /ˈʃeɪv(ə)n/) cut (growing hair) from face etc. with razor, remove hair from face etc. (of); cut thin slices from surface of (wood etc.) to shape it; pass close to without touching, miss narrowly. **2** *n.* shaving or being shaved; narrow miss or escape (esp. **close shave**); tool for shaving wood etc. [OE]
shaver *n.* thing that shaves, esp. electric razor; *colloq.* young lad.
Shavian /ˈʃeɪvɪən/ **1** *a.* of or characteristic of the writer G. B. Shaw. **2** *n.* admirer of Shaw. [*Shavius*, L form of Shaw]
shaving *n.* (esp. in *pl.*) thin strip cut off surface of wood etc. [SHAVE]
shawl 1 *n.* piece of fabric, usu. rectangular and often folded into triangle, worn over shoulders etc. or wrapped round baby. **2** *v.t.* (esp. in *p.p.*) put shawl on (person). [Urdu f. Pers.]
she /ʃiː/ **1** *pron.* (*obj.* HER; *poss.* HER, HERS; *pl.* THEY) the woman or girl or female animal (or thing regarded as female, e.g.

ship) previously named or in question. **2** *n.* female, woman. **3** *a.* (usu. with hyphen) female (*she-ass*). [OE]

sheaf 1 *n.* (*pl.* **sheaves**) group of things laid lengthways together and usu. tied, esp. bundle of corn-stalks tied after reaping. **2** *v.t.* = SHEAVE. [OE]

shear 1 *v.* (*past* **sheared**; *p.p.* **shorn** or **sheared**) cut with scissors or shears etc.; remove or take off by cutting; clip wool off (sheep etc.); strip bare *of*, deprive *of*; distort, be distorted, or break (*off*). **2** *n.* strain produced by pressure in structure of substance; (in *pl.*; also **pair of shears**) clipping or cutting instrument shaped like scissors. [OE]

sheath *n.* (*pl.* /ʃi:ðz/) close-fitting cover, esp. for blade of knife; condom; woman's close-fitting dress; **sheath-knife** dagger-like knife carried in sheath. [OE]

sheathe /ʃi:ð/ *v.t.* put into sheath; encase or protect with sheath.

sheave *v.t.* make into sheaves. [SHEAF]

sheaves *pl.* of SHEAF.

shebeen /ʃɪ'bi:n/ *n. Ir.* unlicensed house selling alcoholic liquor. [Ir.]

shed[1] *n.* one-storied structure for storage or shelter or as workshop etc. [SHADE]

shed[2] *v.t.* (**-dd-**; past and *p.p.* **shed**) let or cause to fall off (*tree sheds leaves*); take off (clothes); reduce (electrical power load) by disconnection etc.; cause to fall or flow (*shed blood, tears*); disperse, diffuse, radiate; **shed light on** help to explain. [OE]

sheen *n.* gloss, lustre, brightness; **sheeny** *a.* [OE, = beautiful]

sheep *n.* (*pl.* **sheep**) animal with thick woolly coat, esp. kept in flocks for its wool or meat; bashful or timid or silly person; (usu. in *pl.*) member of minister's congregation; **sheep-dip** preparation for cleansing sheep of vermin etc., place where sheep are dipped in this; **sheep-dog** dog trained to guard and herd sheep, dog of breed suitable for this; **sheep-fold** enclosure for sheep. [OE]

sheepish *a.* bashful; embarrassed through shame.

sheepshank *n.* knot used to shorten rope temporarily.

sheepskin *n.* garment or rug of sheep's skin with wool on; leather of sheep's skin used in bookbinding etc.

sheer[1] **1** *a.* mere or unqualified (*sheer luck*); (of cliff or ascent etc.) perpendicular; (of textile) very thin, diaphanous. **2** *adv.* perpendicularly, directly (*rises sheer from the water*). [OE]

sheer[2] *v.i.* swerve or change course; **sheer off** go away, esp. from person etc. that one dislikes or fears. [orig. uncert.]

sheet[1] **1** *n.* large rectangular piece of cotton or other fabric, used esp. in pairs as inner bedclothes; broad usu. flat piece of material (e.g. paper or glass); wide expanse of water, ice, flame, falling rain, etc.; set of unseparated postage stamps; newspaper. **2** *v.* provide or cover with sheets; form into sheets; (of rain etc.) fall in sheets. **3 sheet metal** metal formed into thin sheets by rolling, hammering, etc.; **sheet music** music published in separate sheets. [OE]

sheet[2] *n.* rope or chain attached to lower corner of sail for securing or controlling it; **sheet anchor** second anchor for use in emergencies, person or thing depended on as last hope. [OE, rel. to prec.]

sheeting *n.* material for making sheets. [SHEET[1]]

sheikh /ʃeɪk, ʃi:k/ *n.* chief, head of Arab tribe or family or village; Muslim leader; **sheikhdom** *n.* [Arab.]

sheila /'ʃi:lə/ *n. Austral.* & *NZ sl.* young woman, girl. [orig. uncert.]

shekel /'ʃek(ə)l/ *n.* currency unit of Israel; ancient Jewish etc. weight and silver coin; (in *pl.*) *colloq.* money, riches. [Heb.]

sheldrake /'ʃeldreɪk/ *n.* (*pl.* **shelduck**) bright-plumaged wild duck. [prob. dial. *sheld* pied, DRAKE]

shelduck *n.* female sheldrake.

shelf *n.* (*pl.* **shelves**) horizontal board or slab etc. projecting from wall or forming one tier of bookcase or cupboard; ledge, horizontal steplike projection in cliff face etc.; reef or sandbank; **on the shelf** (esp. of person) no longer active or of use, (of woman) past age when she might be married; **shelf-life** time for which stored thing remains usable; **shelf-mark** mark on book to show its place in library. [LG]

shell 1 *n.* hard outer case of nut-kernel, egg, seed, fruit, or animal such as crab or snail or tortoise; framework or case for something; walls or framework of unfinished or gutted building, ship, etc.; explosive projectile for firing from large gun etc.; hollow case containing explosives for cartridge, firework, etc.; light rowing-boat for racing. **2** *v.t.* take out of shell, remove shell or pod from; fire shells at. **3 come out of one's shell** become more sociable and less shy; **shell out** *sl.* pay out (money); **shell-shock** nervous breakdown resulting from prolonged exposure to battle conditions. **4 shell-less** *a.*; **shelly** *a.* [OE]

shellac /ʃə'læk/ **1** *n.* resinous substance used for making varnish etc. **2** *v.t.* (**-ck-**) varnish with shellac. [SHELL, LAC]

shelled *a.* having a shell; deprived of its shell. [SHELL]

shellfish *n.* (*pl.* same) water animal with shell (mollusc or crustacean).
Shelta /ˈʃeltə/ *n.* ancient hybrid cant language of Irish gypsies and pipers, Irish and Welsh travelling tinkers, etc. [orig. unkn.]
shelter 1 *n.* protection from danger or the elements etc.; place providing this. **2** *v.* provide with shelter; take shelter *in* or *from* etc.; defend *from* blame or difficulty etc.; protect (industry etc.) from competition. [orig. unkn.]
shelve *v.* put (books etc.) on shelf; abandon or defer consideration of (plan etc.), remove (person) from active work etc.; fit (cupboard or library etc.) with shelves; (of ground etc.) slope gently. [SHELF]
shelves *pl.* of SHELF.
shelving *n.* shelves collectively; material for shelves.
shemozzle /ʃɪˈmɒz(ə)l/ *n. sl.* rumpus, brawl; muddle. [Yiddish]
shenanigan /ʃɪˈnænɪgən/ *n. colloq.* nonsense; trickery; high-spirited behaviour. [orig. unkn.]
shepherd /ˈʃepəd/ **1** *n.* man who tends sheep; spiritual leader, priest. **2** *v.t.* tend (sheep), lead spiritually; marshal or conduct or drive (crowd etc.) like sheep. **3 shepherd's pie** = *cottage pie.* **4 shepherdess** *n. fem.* [OE (SHEEP, HERD)]
Sheraton /ˈʃerət(ə)n/ *n.* style of furniture introduced in England *c.* 1790. [furniture-maker]
sherbet /ˈʃɜːbət/ *n.* oriental drink of sweetened diluted fruit-juices; fizzy flavoured drink, the powder for this. [Turk. & Pers. f. Arab.]
sherd *n.* = POTSHERD. [OE]
sheriff /ˈʃerɪf/ *n.* chief executive officer of Crown in county, with legal and ceremonial duties; honorary officer elected annually in some towns; *Sc.* (also **sheriff-depute**) chief judge of county or district; *US* chief law-enforcing officer of county. [OE (SHIRE, REEVE¹)]
Sherpa /ˈʃɜːpə/ *n.* member of a Himalayan people living on borders of Nepal and Tibet. [native name]
sherry /ˈʃerɪ/ *n.* white usu. fortified wine orig. from S. Spain, a glass of this. [*Xeres* in Spain]
Shetland pony /ˈʃetlənd/ small hardy rough-coated pony. [*Shetland Islands*, NNE of Scotland]
shew *archaic* var. of SHOW.
shibboleth /ˈʃɪbəleθ/ *n.* old-fashioned doctrine or formula of party or sect; catchword; word or custom or principle etc., regarded as revealing person's orthodoxy etc. [Heb. (Judg. 12:6)]
shield 1 *n.* piece of defensive armour carried in hand or on arm to protect the body when fighting; person or thing that gives protection; representation of shield as heraldic device displaying coat of arms; trophy in form of shield; protective plate or screen in machinery etc. **2** *v.t.* protect or defend. [OE]
shift 1 *v.* change or move from one position to another; change form or character; pass (responsibility etc.) on to someone else; *sl.* move quickly, consume (food or drink); *US* change gear in motor vehicle. **2** *n.* change of position or form or character; group of workers working at same time, period for which they work; expedient, stratagem, resource; trick or piece of evasion; woman's loose straight dress; change of position of typewriter type-bars to type capitals etc.; displacement of lines of spectrum; *US* gear-change in motor vehicle. **3 make shift** manage in less than ideal circumstances; **shift for oneself** depend on one's own efforts; **shift one's ground** take new position in argument etc. [OE]
shiftless *a.* lazy and inefficient; lacking resourcefulness.
shifty *a.* evasive, deceitful, untrustworthy; **shiftily** *adv.*; **shiftiness** *n.*
Shiite /ˈʃiːaɪt/ **1** *n.* member of Muslim branch esp. in Iran, rejecting first three Sunnite caliphs. **2** *a.* of this branch. [Arab. *Shiah* = party]
shillelagh /ʃɪˈleɪlə, -lɪ/ *n.* Irish cudgel. [*Shillelagh* in Ireland]
shilling /ˈʃɪlɪŋ/ *n.* former British currency unit and coin worth $\frac{1}{20}$ of a pound; monetary unit in E. African countries. [OE]
shilly-shally /ˈʃɪlɪʃælɪ/ *v.i.* vacillate, hesitate or be undecided. [*shall I?*]
shim 1 *n.* thin wedge used in machinery etc. to make parts fit. **2** *v.t.* (**-mm-**) fit or fill up thus. [orig. unkn.]
shimmer 1 *n.* tremulous or faint light. **2** *v.i.* shine with shimmer. [OE]
shin 1 *n.* front of leg below knee. **2** *v.* (**-nn-**) climb (*up* or *down* tree etc.) by clinging with arms and legs. **3 shin-bone** inner and usu. larger of two bones from knee to ankle. [OE]
shindig /ˈʃɪndɪg/ *n.* (also **shindy**) *colloq.* festive gathering, esp. boisterous one; brawl, disturbance, noise. [perh. alt. of SHINTY]
shine 1 *v.* (*past* and *p.p.* **shone** /ʃɒn/) emit or reflect light, be bright, glow; (of sun, star, etc.) be clearly visible; be brilliant, excel; cause to shine (in certain direction etc.); (*p.p.* **shined**) polish to produce shine. **2** *n.* brightness, lustre, polish; light, sunshine. **3 take a shine to** *colloq.* take a liking to. [OE]
shiner *n. colloq.* black eye.

shingle[1] /ˈʃɪŋg(ə)l/ *n.* pebbles in a mass, as on sea-shore; **shingly** *a.* [orig. uncert.]
shingle[2] /ˈʃɪŋg(ə)l/ **1** *n.* rectangular piece of wood used as roof-tile; shingled hair, shingling of hair. **2** *v.t.* roof with shingles; cut (woman's hair) short so that it tapers from back of head to nape of neck, cut hair of (person or head) thus. [L *scindula*]
shingles /ˈʃɪŋg(ə)lz/ *n.pl.* (usu. treated as *sing.*) acute painful viral inflammation of nerve ganglia, with skin eruption often forming girdle round middle of body. [L *cingulum* belt]
Shinto /ˈʃɪntəʊ/ *n.* Japanese religion revering ancestors and nature-spirits; **Shintoism** *n.*; **Shintoist** *n.* [Chin., = way of the Gods]
shinty /ˈʃɪntɪ/ *n.* game like hockey but with taller goals; stick or ball used in it. [orig. uncert.]
shiny *a.* having shine; (of clothes) with nap worn off; **shinily** *adv.*; **shininess** *n.* [SHINE]
ship 1 *n.* large seagoing vessel; *colloq.* spacecraft, *US* aircraft. **2** *v.* (**-pp-**) send or take or put in ship; transport (goods) by ship; deliver (goods) to agent for forwarding; fix (mast, rudder, etc.) in its place on ship; embark; (of sailor) engage for service on ship; take (oars) from row-locks and lay them inside boat. **3 ship-canal** canal constructed to admit large ships; **ship's boat** small boat carried on ship; **ship water** have water come into boat etc. over gunwale; **when one's ship comes home** (or **in**) when one's fortune is made. [OE]
-ship *suffix* forming nouns denoting quality or condition (*friendship, hardship*), status or office or honour (*authorship, lordship*), tenure of office (*chairmanship*), skill in certain capacity (*workmanship*), collective individuals of group (*membership*). [OE]
shipboard *n.* esp. in **on shipboard** on board ship. [SHIP]
shipbuilder *n.* person engaged in business of building ships; **shipbuilding** *n.*
shipload *n.* quantity of cargo or passengers that ship can carry.
shipmate *n.* person belonging to or sailing on same ship as another.
shipment *n.* placing of goods on ship; amount shipped.
shipowner *n.* person owning or having shares in ship(s).
shipper *n.* one who ships goods, esp. in import or export. [OE]
shipping *n.* ships collectively; transport of goods, esp. by ship. [SHIP]
shipshape *adv.* & *predic. a.* in good order, neat and tidy.
shipwreck 1 *n.* destruction of ship at sea by storm, striking rocks, etc.; remains of ship destroyed thus; ruin or ending *of* plans etc. **2** *v.* (cause to) suffer shipwreck.
shipwright *n.* shipbuilder; ship's carpenter.
shipyard *n.* place where ships are built.
shire *n.* county; **shire-horse** heavy powerful draught-horse. [OE]
shirk *v.t.* avoid or get out of (duty or work etc., or *absol.*) from laziness, cowardice, etc. [G *schurke* scoundrel]
shirt *n.* loose sleeved garment of cotton etc. for upper part of body; **keep one's shirt on** *sl.* keep one's temper; **put one's shirt on** *sl.* bet all one's money on (horse etc.); **shirt dress** woman's dress with bodice like shirt. [OE]
shirting *n.* material for shirts.
shirtwaister *n.* = *shirt dress.*
shirty *a. sl.* angry, bad-tempered; **shirtily** *adv.*; **shirtiness** *n.*
shish kebab /ʃɪʃ kɪˈbæb/ pieces of meat and vegetable grilled on skewers. [Turk. (KEBAB)]
shit *vulgar* **1** *v.* (**-tt-**; past and *p.p.* **shit**) defecate; get rid of as excrement. **2** *n.* faeces; act of defecating; nonsense; despicable person. **3** *int.* expressing anger or annoyance. [OE]
shiver[1] /ˈʃɪvə/ **1** *v.* tremble with cold or fear etc. **2** *n.* momentary shivering movement. **3 the shivers** attack of shivering, feeling of fear or horror. [orig. uncert.]
shiver[2] /ˈʃɪvə/ **1** *n.* (usu. in *pl.*) small fragment, splinter. **2** *v.* break into shivers. [rel. to dial. *shive* slice]
shivery *a.* characterized or affected by shivers; **shiveriness** *n.* [SHIVER[1]]
shoal[1] **1** *n.* multitude, great number, esp. of fish swimming together. **2** *v.i.* (of fish) form shoal or shoals. [Du.; cf. SCHOOL[2]]
shoal[2] **1** *n.* shallow place in sea; submerged sandbank esp. that shows at low water; (usu. in *pl.*) hidden danger. **2** *v.i.* become shallow. [OE]
shock[1] **1** *n.* violent collision or concussion or impact; sudden and disturbing physical or mental impression; acute state of prostration following sudden violent emotion, severe injury, etc., = *electric shock*; violent tremor of earth's surface in earthquake; great disturbance of or injury to organization, stability, etc. **2** *v.* affect (person) with electrical or mental shock; appear horrifying or outrageous to. **3 shock absorber** device on vehicle etc. for absorbing vibration and shock; **shock therapy** (or **treatment**) psychiatric treatment by means of shock induced artificially by

electricity or drugs; **shock wave** air-wave caused by explosion or by body moving faster than sound. [F *choc, choquer*]

shock[2] 1 *n.* group of corn-sheaves propped up together in field. 2 *v.t.* arrange (corn) in shocks. [LG or Du.]

shock[3] *n.* unkempt or shaggy mass of hair. [orig. unkn.]

shocker *n. colloq.* person or thing that shocks; very bad specimen of something; sordid or sensational novel, film, etc. [SHOCK[1]]

shocking *a.* causing shock; scandalous; *colloq.* very bad.

shod *past* and *p.p.* of SHOE.

shoddy /ˈʃɒdɪ/ *a.* of poor quality, counterfeit, shabby; **shoddily** *adv.*; **shoddiness** *n.* [orig. unkn.]

shoe /ʃuː/ 1 *n.* outer foot-covering of leather etc., esp. one not reaching above ankle; thing like shoe in shape or use; metal rim nailed to horse's hoof; = *brake-shoe* (see BRAKE[1]). 2 *v.t.* (*past* and *p.p.* **shod**; *partic.* **shoeing**) fit (horse etc.) with shoe(s); (in *p.p.*) having shoes etc. of a specified kind (*rough-shod*). 3 **in person's shoes** in his position or predicament; **shoe-lace** cord for lacing shoe; **shoe-string** shoe-lace, *colloq.* small or inadequate amount of money (esp. as capital); **shoe-tree** shaped block for keeping shoe in shape. [OE]

shoehorn *n.* curved piece of horn or metal etc. for easing heel into shoe.

shoemaker *n.* person whose business is making and repairing boots and shoes; **shoemaking** *n.*

shone *past* and *p.p.* of SHINE.

shoo 1 *int.* sound used to frighten animals away. 2 *v.* utter such sound; drive *away* thus. [imit.]

shook *past* of SHAKE.

shoot 1 *v.* (*past* and *p.p.* **shot**) cause (weapon, or *absol.*) to discharge missile; kill or wound (person or animal) with missile from weapon; discharge or send out rapidly; hunt game etc. with gun; come or go swiftly or suddenly or abruptly; (of pain) pass with stabbing sensation; pass swiftly down (rapids etc.) or under (bridge); (in football etc.) score (goal), take shot at goal; take film or photograph of; (of plant) put forth buds, (of bud) appear; (as *int.*) *US* say what you have to say. 2 *n.* young branch or sucker, new growth of plant; expedition or party for shooting game, land in which game is shot; chute. 3 **be** (or **get**) **shot of** be rid of; **shoot down** kill (person) cold-bloodedly by shooting, cause (aircraft or its pilot) to fall to ground by shooting, argue effectively against (proposal etc.); **shooting-brake** estate car; **shooting-gallery** place for shooting at targets with rifles etc.; **shooting star** small meteor moving rapidly; **shooting-stick** walking-stick with handle folding out to form small seat; **shoot one's mouth off** *sl.* talk freely or indiscreetly; **shoot up** rise or grow rapidly, destroy or terrorize by shooting; **the whole shoot** *sl.* everything. [OE]

shop 1 *n.* place for retail sale of goods or services etc.; place where manufacturing or repairing is done; one's work or profession as a subject of conversation (*talk shop*); *sl.* institution, establishment, place of business, etc. 2 *v.* (**-pp-**) go to shops to make purchases etc.; *sl.* inform against, esp. to police. 3 **all over the shop** *sl.* in great disorder, scattered everywhere; **shop around** look for best bargain; **shop-assistant** employee in retail shop; **shop-floor** production area in factory etc., workers as distinct from management; **shop-soiled** soiled or faded by display in shop; **shop-steward** official of trade union elected by fellow-workers as their spokesman. [F *eschoppe* f. LG]

shopkeeper *n.* owner or manager of shop.

shoplifter *n.* person who steals goods from shop in guise of customer; **shoplifting** *n.*

shopping *n.* going to shops; goods bought in shops; **shopping centre** area or complex with concentration of shops.

shopwalker *n.* supervisor in large shop.

shore[1] *n.* land that adjoins sea or large body of water; **on shore** ashore. [LG or Du.]

shore[2] 1 *n.* prop, beam set obliquely against wall or ship etc. as support. 2 *v.t.* support or hold *up* with shores. [LG or Du.]

shorn *p.p.* of SHEAR.

short 1 *a.* measuring little from end to end in space or time, or from head to foot; not far-reaching, acting near at hand; (of person's memory) retaining only things from the immediate past; (of temper) easily lost; concise, brief; curt or uncivil; deficient or insufficient (*we are one short*), scarce (*supplies are short*); (of alcoholic drink) small and concentrated, made with spirits; less than the stated or usual amount etc. (*short weight*; *short rations*); (of pastry etc.) easily crumbled; (of vowel or syllable) having the less of two recognized durations, having sound that is not long; (of odds in betting) nearly even; (of sale in stocks etc.) effected with borrowed stock in expectation of acquiring stock later at lower price. **2** *adv.* abruptly or suddenly, before the natural or expected time or place, in short manner. **3** *n.* short thing, esp. short syllable or vowel; short film; *colloq.* short circuit, short drink. **4** *v.* short-circuit. **5 be caught** (or **taken**) **short** be put at disadvantage, *colloq.* need suddenly to go to lavatory; **come** (or **fall**) **short of** fail to reach or amount to; **for short** as a short name; **in short** briefly; **short-change** *v.t.* rob or cheat esp. by giving insufficient change; **short circuit** electric circuit through small resistance, esp. instead of through normal circuit; **short-circuit** *v.* cause short circuit in, have short circuit, shorten or avoid by taking short cut; **short cut** shorter way or method than that usually followed; **short division** division without writing down details of calculation; **short for** serving as abbreviation of; **short-handed** undermanned, with insufficient help; **short list** list of selected candidates from which final choice will be made; **short-list** *v.t.* put on short list; **short-lived** having a short life, ephemeral; **short of** not having enough of (*short of money*), less than (*little short of a miracle*), distant from (*two miles short of home*), without going so far as (*did everything short of destroying it*); **short on** *colloq.* deficient in (*short on tact*); **short-range** having short range, relating to short period of future time; **short shrift** curt attention or treatment; **short sight** ability to see clearly only what is comparatively near; **short-sighted** having short sight, lacking imagination or foresight; **short-tempered** easily becoming angry; **short-term** occurring in or relating to a short period of time; **short wave** radio wave with length 100–10 m.; **short-winded** easily becoming breathless. [OE]

shortage *n.* deficiency; amount of this.

shortbread *n.* rich crumbly biscuit made with flour, butter, and sugar.

shortcake *n.* shortbread; cake of short pastry usu. served with fruit.

shortcoming *n.* failure to reach required standard, deficiency.

shorten *v.* make or become short or shorter.

shortening *n.* fat used for making short pastry.

shortfall *n.* deficit.

shorthand *n.* method of rapid writing used in dictation etc.; abbreviated or symbolic mode of expression.

shorthorn *n.* one of breed of cattle with short horns.

shortly *adv.* soon, in a short time; in a short manner. [OE]

shorts *n.pl.* trousers reaching only above knees; *US* underpants.

shorty *n.* (also **shortie**) *colloq.* person or garment shorter than average. [SHORT]

shot[1] *n.* discharge of gun etc., sound of this; attempt to hit something by shooting or throwing etc.; stroke or kick in ball-game; attempt to do something (*had a shot at canoeing*); possessor of specified skill in shooting (*a good shot*); single missile for gun etc., esp. non-explosive projectile; small lead pellet of which several are used for single charge, (as *pl.*) these collectively; heavy metal ball thrown in shot-put; photograph, film sequence taken by one camera; launch of space-rocket; injection of drug etc.; *colloq.* dram of spirits; **like a shot** very quickly, without hesitation, willingly; **shot in the arm** stimulus or encouragement; **shot in the dark** a mere guess; **shot-put** (or **putting the shot**) athletic contest of throwing heavy metal ball. [OE]

shot[2] **1** *past* & *p.p.* of SHOOT. **2** *a.* that has been shot; (of fabric) woven or dyed so as to show different colours at different angles. **3 shot through** permeated or suffused (*with*). [SHOOT]

shotgun *n.* gun for firing small shot at short range; **shotgun wedding** one that is enforced, esp. because of bride's pregnancy. [SHOT[1]]

should /ʃəd, *emphat.* ʃʊd/ *v. aux.* (3 *sing.* **should**) past tense of SHALL, used esp. in reported speech (*I said I should be home by evening*) or to express obligation (*I should tell you*; *you should have been more careful*), condition (*if it should happen*; *I should have been killed if I had gone*), likelihood (*they should be there by now*), or tentative suggestion (*I should like to disagree*). [SHALL]

shoulder /ˈʃəʊldə/ **1** *n.* part of body to which arm or wing or foreleg is attached, either lateral projection below or behind neck; part of garment covering shoulder; animal's upper foreleg as joint of meat; (in *pl.*) body regarded as bearing burden, blame, etc.; part or projection resembling human shoulder; strip of land adjoining metalled road-surface. **2** *v.* push with one's shoulder, make way thus; take burden on one's shoulders, assume responsibility or blame for. **3 put one's shoulder to the wheel** make strong effort; **shoulder arms** move rifle to position with barrel against shoulder and butt in hand; **shoulder-blade** either large flat bone of upper back; **shoulder-strap** strap passing over shoulder to support something, strap from shoulder to collar of garment, esp. with indication of military rank; **shoulder to shoulder** side by side, with united effort; **straight from the shoulder** (of blow) well delivered, (of criticism etc.) frank or direct. [OE]

shouldn't /'ʃʊd(ə)nt/ *colloq.* = *should not.*

shout 1 *n.* loud utterance or vocal sound calling attention or expressing joy or excitement etc.; (*Austral. & NZ colloq.*) one's turn to buy a round of drinks. **2** *v.* emit shout, speak or say or call loudly; (*Austral. & NZ colloq.*) buy drinks etc. for. **3 shout down** reduce to silence by shouting. [perh. rel. to SHOOT]

shove /ʃʌv/ 1 *v.* push vigorously; *colloq.* put casually (*shove it in a drawer*). **2** *n.* act of shoving. **3 shove-halfpenny** game in which coins etc. are pushed along marked board; **shove off** start from shore in boat, *colloq.* depart. [OE]

shovel /'ʃʌv(ə)l/ **1** *n.* implement like spade for scooping up coal etc.; machine or part of machine with similar function. **2** *v.t.* (**-ll-**, *US* **-l-**) move with or as with shovel; move vigorously in large quantities (*shovel food into mouth*). **3 shovelful** *a.* [OE]

shovelboard *n.* game played esp. on ship's deck by pushing discs over marked surface.

shoveller /'ʃʌvələ/ *n.* duck with shovel-like beak.

show /ʃəʊ/ 1 *v.* (*p.p.* **shown** or **showed**) allow or cause to be seen; disclose or manifest (*will show the dirt*; *showed great alarm*; *showed himself a rogue*); offer for inspection (*show me your ticket*); put on view, display; produce (*showed a large profit*); point out (*showed her the sights*); cause to understand (*show me how to do it*); demonstrate or prove (*shows that you are wrong*); afford (specified treatment: *showed me kindness*; *showed no mercy*); conduct (person *in* or *out*, *round*, etc.); be or become visible or noticeable (*stain will never show*); have specified appearance (*it shows white at a distance*). **2** *n.* showing; spectacle, exhibition, pageant, display; *colloq.* public entertainment or performance; *sl.* concern, undertaking, business (*a bad* or *good* or *poor show*); outward appearance, impression produced; ostentation, mere display; discharge of blood from vagina at start of menstruation or childbirth. **3 show business** the entertainment or theatrical profession; **show-case** glazed case for displaying exhibits; **show-down** final test or battle etc., disclosure of achievements or possibilities; **show one's hand** reveal one's intentions; **show house** one house in estate etc., furnished and prepared for inspection; **show-jumping** competitive jumping on horseback; **show off** display to advantage, act in flamboyant way in order to impress; **show-off** *n.* person who shows off; **show of hands** raising of hands to vote for or against proposal etc.; **show-piece** excellent specimen suitable for display; **show-place** attractive or much visited place; **show trial** judicial trial regarded as intended mainly to impress public opinion; **show up** make or be visible or conspicuous, expose or humiliate, *colloq.* appear or arrive. [OE]

shower 1 *n.* brief fall of rain or snow etc., or of bullets, stones, dust, etc.; sudden copious arrival of gifts or honours etc.; (in full **shower-bath**) bath in which water is sprayed from above, room or device for this; *sl.* contemptible or unpleasant person or group; *US* party for giving gifts, esp. to prospective bride. **2** *v.* descend in a shower; discharge (water or missiles etc.) in shower; lavishly bestow (gifts etc. *on* or *upon*); use shower-bath. [OE]

showery *a.* (of weather) with many showers.

showing *n.* display or performance; quality or appearance of performance or achievement etc.; evidence or putting of case. [SHOW]

showman *n.* proprietor or organizer of public entertainment; person skilled in showmanship.

showmanship *n.* capacity for exhibiting one's goods or capabilities to best advantage.

shown *p.p.* of SHOW.

showroom *n.* room where goods are displayed or kept for inspection. [SHOW]

showy *a.* making good or conspicuous display; gaudy; **showily** *adv.*; **showiness** *n.*

shrank *past* of SHRINK.

shrapnel /'ʃræpn(ə)l/ *n.* fragments of exploded bombs or shells; artillery shell containing metal pieces which it scatters on explosion. [*Shrapnel*, inventor]

shred 1 *n.* piece torn or scraped or broken off, scrap or fragment; least amount (*not a shred of evidence*). **2** *v.t.* (**-dd-**) tear or cut into shreds. [OE]

shrew /ʃru:/ *n.* small mouselike animal with long snout; bad-tempered or scolding woman. [OE]

shrewd /ʃru:d/ *a.* showing astute powers of judgement, clever and judicious. [perh. f. obs. *shrew* curse *v.*, f. prec.]

shrewish *a.* scolding, bad-tempered.

shriek 1 *n.* shrill scream or sound. **2** *v.* make a shriek, say in shrill tones. [ON]

shrift *n. archaic* confession and absolution; **short shrift** see SHORT. [OE (SHRIVE)]

shrike *n.* bird with strong hooked and toothed bill. [OE]

shrill 1 *a.* piercing and high-pitched in sound; *fig.* sharp, unrestrained. **2** *v.* utter with or make shrill sound. **3 shrilly** *adv.* [orig. uncert.]

shrimp 1 *n.* small edible crustacean, pink when boiled; *colloq.* very small person. **2** *v.i.* go in search of shrimps. [orig. uncert.]

shrine *n.* place for special worship or devotion; tomb or casket containing sacred relics; place hallowed by some memory or association etc. [OE f. L *scrinium* bookcase]

shrink 1 *v.* (*past* **shrank**; *p.p.* **shrunk** or, esp. as *a.*, **shrunken**) become or make smaller, esp. by action from moisture or heat or cold; flinch or draw back (*from*). **2** *n.* act of shrinking; *sl.* psychiatrist. **3 shrink-wrap** enclose (article) in material that shrinks tightly round it. [OE]

shrinkage *n.* process or degree of shrinking; (in commerce) allowance for loss by theft or wastage etc.

shrive *v.t.* (*past* **shrove**; *p.p.* **shriven** /ˈʃrɪv(ə)n/) *archaic* hear confession of and give absolution to; submit *oneself* for this. [OE f. L *scribo* write]

shrivel /ˈʃrɪv(ə)l/ *v.* (-**ll**-, *US* -**l**-) contract into wrinkled or curled-up state. [perh. ON]

shroud 1 *n.* wrapping for a corpse; something that conceals; (in *pl.*) ropes supporting ship's mast. **2** *v.t.* clothe (corpse) for burial; cover or conceal. [OE, = garment]

shrove *past* of SHRIVE.

Shrovetide *n.* Shrove Tuesday and the two preceding days. [foll.]

Shrove Tuesday day before Ash Wednesday, on which it was customary to be shriven. [SHRIVE]

shrub *n.* woody plant smaller than tree and usu. with separate stems from or near root; **shrubby** *a.* [OE]

shrubbery *n.* area planted with shrubs.

shrug 1 *v.* (-**gg**-) slightly and momentarily raise (one's shoulders) to express indifference or doubt etc. **2** *n.* shrugging movement. **3 shrug off** dismiss as unimportant. [orig. unkn.]

shrunk *p.p.* of SHRINK.

shrunken see SHRINK.

shudder 1 *n.* sudden or convulsive shivering or quivering; vibrating motion. **2** *v.i.* experience shudder; feel strong repugnance or fear etc. (*I shudder to think of it*); have vibrating motion. [LG or Du.]

shuffle /ˈʃʌf(ə)l/ **1** *v.* move (esp. one's feet) with dragging or sliding motion or with difficulty; intermingle or rearrange (esp. cards); keep shifting one's position; prevaricate, be evasive. **2** *n.* shuffling action or movement; general change of relative positions; shuffling dance. **3 shuffle off** remove or get rid of. [LG]

shun *v.t.* (-**nn**-) keep clear of, avoid, eschew. [OE]

shunt 1 *v.* move (train etc.) to another track, (of train) be shunted; move or put aside, redirect. **2** *n.* shunting or being shunted; conductor joining two points of electrical circuit for diversion of current; (in surgery) alternative path for circulation of blood; *sl.* collision of vehicles. [perh. SHUN]

shush 1 *int.* hush! **2** *v.* call for silence (from), be silent. [imit.]

shut *v.* (-**tt**-; *past* and *p.p.* **shut**) move (door, window, lid, etc.) into position to block opening; (of door etc.) move or admit of being moved thus; shut door or lid etc. of (room, box, eye, etc.); bring (book, telescope, etc.) into folded-up or contracted state; catch or pinch (finger, dress, etc.) by shutting something on it; bar access to (place); **be shut of** be rid of; **shut down** cease operation of (factory etc.), (of factory etc.) cease working; **shut-down** *n.* this process; **shut-eye** *n. sl.* sleep; **shut off** stop flow of (water, gas, etc.), separate *from* society etc.; **shut out** exclude, prevent, block; **shut up** close securely or permanently, imprison (person), put (thing) away in box etc., *colloq.* (esp. in *imper.*) stop talking; **shut up shop** cease business or work for the day or permanently. [OE]

shutter 1 *n.* movable hinged cover for window; device that opens and closes lens aperture of camera. **2** *v.t.* provide with shutters. **3 put up the shutters** cease business for the day or permanently.

shuttle /ˈʃʌt(ə)l/ **1** *n.* weaving-implement by which weft-thread is carried between threads of warp; thread-carrier in sewing-machine; train or bus or aircraft etc. used in shuttle service; = *space-shuttle*. **2** *v.* (cause to) move to and fro like shuttle. **3 shuttle service** transport system operating to and fro over relatively short distance. [OE (SHOOT)]

shuttlecock *n.* rounded piece of cork etc. with feathers attached, or similar device of plastic, struck to and fro in badminton.

shy[1] /ʃaɪ/ **1** *a.* self-conscious or uneasy in company, bashful; easily startled, wary; (as *suffix*) showing fear or distaste of (*work-shy*). **2** *v.* start aside in alarm (*at* or *away from*). **3** *n.* act of shying. [OE]

shy[2] *v.t.* & *n. colloq.* fling or throw. [orig. unkn.]

Shylock /'ʃaɪlɒk/ *n.* hard-hearted usurer. [character in Shakespeare]

shyster /'ʃaɪstə/ *n. colloq.* person who acts unscrupulously or unprofessionally. [orig. uncert.]

si = TE. [F f. It.]

SI *abbr.* international system of units of measurement. [F *Système International*]

Si *symb.* silicon.

Siamese /saɪə'mi:z/ **1** *a.* of Siam or its people or language. **2** *n.* native or language of Siam. **3 Siamese cat** cat of breed with short pale fur and dark markings; **Siamese twins** two persons joined together at birth, any very closely associated pair. [*Siam* (now Thailand) in Asia]

sib *n.* sibling. [OE, = akin]

sibilant /'sɪbɪlənt/ **1** *a.* sounded with a hiss; hissing. **2** *n.* sibilant letter or sound. **3 sibilance** *n.*; **sibilancy** *n.* [L]

sibling *n.* one of two or more children having one or both parents in common. [SIB]

sibyl /'sɪbɪl/ *n.* pagan prophetess. [F or med.L f. Gk]

sibylline /'sɪbɪlaɪn/ *a.* uttered by or characteristic of a sibyl; mysteriously prophetic. [L (prec.)]

sic /sɪk/ *adv.* thus used or spelt etc. (used in brackets to confirm or call attention to form of quoted words). [L, = so]

sick 1 *a.* ill, feeling effects of disease; vomiting or tending to vomit; of or for those who are sick (*sick-bed, -leave, -pay, -room,* etc.); greatly distressed or disgusted (*makes me sick*); surfeited or tired *of*; (of humour) finding amusement in, or making fun of, misfortune or macabre things. **2** *v.t. colloq.* vomit (esp. with *up*). **3** *n. colloq.* vomit. **4 fall** (or **take**) **sick** become ill; **sick and tired** fed up, utterly tired *of*; **sick-bay** place in institution or on ship etc. for those who are sick. [OE]

sicken *v.* make or become sick or disgusted etc.; **sicken for** be in first stages of (illness).

sickle /'sɪk(ə)l/ *n.* implement with curved blade and short handle used for reaping or lopping etc.; **sickle cell** sickle-shaped red blood-corpuscle, esp. as found in severe hereditary anaemia. [OE]

sickly *a.* liable to be ill, of weak health; unhealthy-looking, faint, pale; causing ill-health; inducing or connected with nausea; mawkish, weakly sentimental; **sickliness** *n.* [SICK]

sickness *n.* being ill; disease; vomiting.

side 1 *n.* any of the surfaces bounding an object, esp. vertical inner or outer surface or one of those distinguished from top and bottom or front and back or ends; one of the lines bounding a triangle, rectangle, etc.; either surface of thing regarded as having only two; amount of writing filling one side of sheet of paper; right or left part of person's or animal's body; direction (*from every side*; *on all sides*); part of object or place etc. that faces specified direction or is on observer's right or left; region to right or left of (or nearer or further than) a real or imaginary dividing line; marginal part or area of thing; partial aspect of thing, aspect differing from or opposed to other aspects (*all sides of the question*; *look on the bright side*); each of two sets of opponents at war or competing in some way, cause represented by this; line of descent through one parent (*cousin on my mother's side*); (in billiards etc.) spinning motion given to ball by striking it on one side; *sl.* assumption of superiority, swagger (*puts on side*). **2** *in comb.* situated at or directed to or from a side (*side-door, -table*; *side-glance*); secondary or minor or incidental (*side-effect, -issue, -road, -street*). **3** *v.i.* take part or be on same side *with*. **4 -sided** having specified number or type of sides. **5 by the side of** close to or compared with; **let the side down** act in way that frustrates colleagues' efforts or fails to support them; **on one side** not in the main or central position, aside; **on the side** as a sideline; **on the — side** somewhat (*on the large side*); **side by side** standing close together, esp. for mutual encouragement; **side-car** passenger car attachable to side of motor cycle; **side-drum** small double-headed drum; **side-saddle** *n.* saddle enabling rider to have both feet on same side of horse, (*adv.*) sitting thus on horse; **side-show** small show at a fair or exhibition, minor or subsidiary activity or affair; **side-slip** *n.* skid, movement sideways, (*v.i.*) move sideways, esp. of aircraft in downward manœuvre; **side-splitting** causing hearty laughter; **side-step** *n.* step sideways, (*v.t.*) avoid by stepping sideways, evade (issue etc.); **side-swipe** *n.* glancing blow along side, indirect or incidental criticism etc., (*v.t.*) hit with side-swipe; **side-track** *v.t.* divert (person) from main course or issue; **side-whiskers** those growing on cheek; **side wind** wind coming from one side. [OE]

sideboard *n.* table or flat-topped chest with drawers and cupboards for china etc.

sideburns *n.pl.* short side-whiskers.
sidekick *n. US colloq.* close friend or associate.
sidelight *n.* light from side; each of pair of small lights at front of vehicle; light at side of moving ship.
sideline *n.* work etc. carried on in addition to one's main activity; (in *pl.*) lines bounding sides of football pitch etc., space just outside these; place for spectators as opposed to participants.
sidelong **1** *a.* directed to the side, oblique. **2** *adv.* to the side.
sidereal /saɪ'dɪərɪəl/ *a.* of or determined by means of the stars; **sidereal day** time between successive passages of any given star over meridian. [L (*sidus sider-* star)]
sidesman *n.* assistant churchwarden who takes collection etc. [SIDE]
sidewalk *n. US* pavement at side of road.
sideways *a.* & *adv.* with side foremost; to or from a side.
siding *n.* short railway track to side of railway line, used for shunting.
sidle /'saɪd(ə)l/ *v.i.* walk obliquely, move timidly or furtively. [SIDELONG]
SIDS *abbr.* sudden infant death syndrome.
siege *n.* surrounding and blockading of fortified place; surrounding by police etc. of house occupied by gunman etc.; **lay siege to** conduct siege of; **raise siege** end it. [F *sege* seat]
sienna /sɪ'enə/ *n.* a kind of clay used as pigment; its colour of reddish-brown (**burnt sienna**) or yellowish-brown (**raw sienna**). [*Siena* in Italy]
sierra /sɪ'erə/ *n.* long jagged mountain-chain in Spain or Spanish America. [Sp. f. L *serra* saw]
siesta /sɪ'estə/ *n.* afternoon nap or rest, esp. in hot countries. [Sp. f. L *sexta* (*hora*) sixth (hour)]
sieve /sɪv/ **1** *n.* utensil with network or perforated bottom through which liquids or fine particles can pass while solid or coarser matter is retained. **2** *v.t.* sift. [OE]
sift *v.* separate with or cause to pass through sieve; sprinkle (flour etc.) from sieve etc.; subject (information etc.) to close scrutiny or analysis; (of snow etc.) fall as if from sieve. [OE]
sigh /saɪ/ **1** *n.* long deep audible breath expressing sadness, weariness, longing, relief, etc.; act of making this; sound resembling it. **2** *v.* make a sigh; express with sighs; yearn *for* (person or thing desired or lost). [OE]
sight /saɪt/ **1** *n.* faculty of seeing; act of seeing or being seen; range of vision, region open to vision; way of regarding, opinion (*found favour in her sight*); thing seen or visible or worth seeing; (**a sight**) unsightly or ridiculous-looking person or thing; (in *pl.*) noteworthy or attractive features of town etc.; precise aim with gun or observation with optical instrument, device for assisting this; *colloq. a* great quantity (*is a sight too clever*). **2** *v.t.* get sight of, observe presence of; aim (gun etc.) with sights. **3** **at first sight** on first glimpse or impression; **at** (or **on**) **sight** as soon as person or thing is seen; **catch sight of** begin to see or be aware of; **in sight** visible, imminent; **set one's sights on** be determined to acquire or achieve etc.; **a sight for sore eyes** person or thing one is delighted to see; **sight-read** read (music) at sight; **sight-screen** (in cricket) large white screen placed near boundary in line with wicket to help batsman see ball; **sight unseen** without previous inspection. [OE (SEE[1])]
sightless *a.* blind.
sightly *a.* attractive to look at; **sightliness** *n.*
sightseer *n.* person visiting sights of place; **sightseeing** *n.*
sigma /'sɪgmə/ *n.* eighteenth letter of Greek alphabet (Σ, σ or, when final, ς). [L f. Gk]
sign /saɪn/ **1** *n.* thing indicative or suggestive of a quality or state etc. (*a sign of weakness*), thing perceived as indicating future state or occurrence (*first signs of winter*); symbol or word etc. representing a phrase, idea, instruction, etc.; mark traced on surface etc.; motion or gesture used instead of words to convey information, demand, etc.; one of the twelve divisions of the zodiac; publicly displayed symbol or device giving information (*road-sign*), = SIGNBOARD. **2** *v.* write one's name on (document) to show its authenticity or one's agreement or acceptance; write (one's name) thus; engage or be engaged by signing contract (often with *on* or *up*); indicate or communicate by gesture (*signed to me to leave*). **3** **sign away** relinquish right to by signing; **sign-language** series of signs used by deaf or dumb people for communication; **sign of the Cross** movement of hand in representation of Cross; **sign off** end work or contract etc.; **sign on** register to obtain unemployment benefit. [F f. L *signum*]
signal /'sɪgn(ə)l/ **1** *n.* sign (esp. prearranged one) conveying information or giving instruction, message made up of such signs; device on railway giving instructions or warnings to train-drivers etc.; event which causes immediate activity (*her arrival was the signal for*

cheering); transmitted electrical impulses or radio waves, sequence of these. **2** *v.* (**-ll-**) make signal or signals (to); transmit or announce by signal; direct (person *to do* thing) by signal. **3** *a.* remarkably good or bad, noteworthy. **4** **signal-box** building from which railway signals are controlled. [F f. L (prec.)]

signalize *v.t.* make noteworthy or remarkable.

signaller *n.* signalman.

signally *adv.* remarkably, notably.

signalman *n.* person responsible for displaying or operating signals.

signatory /'sɪgnətərɪ/ **1** *a.* that has signed an agreement, esp. a treaty. **2** *n.* signatory party, esp. State. [L (SIGN)]

signature /'sɪgnətʃə/ *n.* person's name or initials used in signing; act of signing; *Mus.* sign put after clef to indicate key or time; section of a book made from one sheet folded and cut, letter or figure indicating sequence of these; **signature tune** tune used esp. in broadcasting to announce a particular programme or performer etc. [med.L (prec.)]

signboard *n.* board with name or symbol etc. displayed outside shop or hotel etc. [SIGN]

signet /'sɪgnɪt/ *n.* small seal; **signet ring** finger-ring with signet set in it. [F or med.L (SIGN)]

significance /sɪg'nɪfɪkəns/ *n.* being significant; meaning, import; importance. [F or L (SIGNIFY)]

significant *a.* having or conveying a meaning, esp. a suggestive or noteworthy one; important; **significant figure** *Math.* digit conveying information about a number containing it, and not a zero filling vacant place at beginning or end. [L (SIGNIFY)]

signify /'sɪgnɪfaɪ/ *v.* be sign or indication of; mean, have as meaning; communicate, make known; be of importance; **signification** /'fɪ'keɪʃ(ə)n/ *n.* [F f. L (SIGN)]

signor /'si:njɔ:/ *n.* (*pl.* **signori** /-ri:/) title used of or to Italian man. [It. f. L (SENIOR)]

signora /si:n'jɔ:rə/ *n.* title used of or to Italian married woman.

signorina /si:njə'ri:nə/ *n.* title used of or to Italian unmarried woman.

signpost **1** *n.* post bearing sign, esp. one indicating direction. **2** *v.t.* provide with signpost(s). [SIGN]

Sikh /si:k/ *n.* member of Indian monotheistic sect. [Hindi, = disciple]

silage /'saɪlɪdʒ/ *n.* storage in silo; green fodder so stored. [alt. of ENSILAGE after *silo*]

silence /'saɪləns/ **1** *n.* absence of sound; abstinence from speech or noise; avoidance of mentioning a thing, betraying a secret, etc. **2** *v.t.* make silent, esp. by coercion or superior argument. **3** **in silence** without speech or other sound. [F f. L (SILENT)]

silencer *n.* device for reducing noise made by gun or vehicle's exhaust etc.

silent *a.* making or accompanied by little or no sound or speech; **silent majority** those of moderate opinions who rarely make themselves heard. [L (*sileo* be silent)]

silhouette /sɪlu:'et/ **1** *n.* picture of person or thing showing outline only, usu. done in solid black on white or cut from paper; dark shadow or outline of person or thing against lighter background. **2** *v.t.* represent or (usu. in *pass.*) show in silhouette. [*Silhouette*, politician]

silica /'sɪlɪkə/ *n.* mineral occurring as quartz and as main constituent of sandstone and other rocks; **siliceous** /sɪ'lɪʃəs/ *a.* [L *silex -lic-* flint]

silicate /'sɪlɪkeɪt/ *n.* compound of metal(s), silicon, and oxygen.

silicon /'sɪlɪkən/ *n.* non-metallic element occurring in silica and silicates; **silicon chip** microchip made of silicon.

silicone /'sɪlɪkəʊn/ *n.* one of many organic compounds of silicon, used esp. in polishes, paints, lubricants, etc.

silicosis /sɪlɪ'kəʊsɪs/ *n.* lung disease caused by inhaling dust containing silica. [-OSIS]

silk *n.* fine soft lustrous fibre produced by silkworms; thread or cloth made from this; (in *pl.*) kinds or garments of such cloth, esp. as worn by jockey in horse-owner's colours; *colloq.* King's or Queen's Counsel, as having right to wear silk gown; *attrib.* made of silk; **silk hat** tall cylindrical hat covered with silk plush; **silk-screen printing** = *screen-printing*; **take silk** become King's or Queen's Counsel. [OE f. L *sericus* f. Gk *Seres* an oriental people]

silken *a.* of or resembling silk; soft or smooth or lustrous.

silkworm *n.* caterpillar that spins cocoon of silk.

silky *a.* soft and smooth like silk; suave; **silkily** *adv.*; **silkiness** *n.*

sill *n.* slab of wood or stone etc. at foot of window or doorway etc. [OE]

sillabub var. of SYLLABUB.

silly /'sɪlɪ/ **1** *a.* foolish, imprudent, unwise; weak-minded; (in cricket, of fielder or position) very close to batsman. **2** *n.* *colloq.* foolish person. **3** **sillily** *adv.*; **silliness** *n.* [OE, = happy]

silo /'saɪləʊ/ *n.* (*pl.* **silos**) pit or airtight structure in which green crops are stored for fodder; tower or pit for storage of cement or grain etc.; underground place where guided missile is kept ready for firing. [Sp. f. L]

silt 1 *n.* sediment deposited by water in a channel or harbour etc. 2 *v.* block or be blocked (*up*) with silt. [perh. Scand.]

Silurian /saɪ'ljʊərɪən/ 1 *a.* of the period in the Palaeozoic era after Ordovician. 2 *n.* this period. [*Silures*, British tribe]

silvan /'sɪlv(ə)n/ *a.* of the woods; having woods, rural. [F or L (*silva* a wood)]

silver 1 *n.* white lustrous precious metallic element; coins or articles made of or looking like silver; colour of silver; silver medal. 2 *a.* of or coloured like silver. 3 *v.* coat or plate with silver; give silvery appearance to; provide (mirror-glass) with backing of tin amalgam etc.; (of hair) turn grey or white. 4 **silver birch** common birch with silver-coloured bark; **silver-fish** silver-coloured fish, silvery wingless insect; **silver jubilee** 25th anniversary; **silver lining** consolation or hopeful feature in misfortune; **silver medal** medal of silver awarded as second prize; **silver paper** tin foil; **silver plate** articles plated with silver; **silver-plated** plated with silver; **silver sand** fine pure sand used in gardening; **silver wedding** 25th anniversary of wedding. [OE]

silverside *n.* upper (and usu. best) side of round of beef.

silversmith *n.* one who makes articles in silver.

silverware *n.* articles made of or plated with silver.

silvery *a.* like silver in colour or appearance; having clear gentle ringing sound.

silviculture /'sɪlvɪkʌltʃə/ *n.* cultivation of forest trees. [F f. L *silva* forest, CULTURE]

simian /'sɪmɪən/ 1 *a.* resembling ape or monkey. 2 *n.* ape or monkey. [L *simia* ape]

similar /'sɪmɪlə/ *a.* like, alike; having resemblance (*to*); of same kind, nature, shape, or amount; **similarity** /-'lærɪtɪ/ *n.* [F or L (*similis* like)]

simile /'sɪmɪlɪ/ *n.* comparison of one thing with another as illustration or ornament (e.g. *as brave as a lion*); use of such comparison. [L, neut. of *similis* like]

similitude /sɪ'mɪlɪtju:d/ *n.* guise, outward appearance; comparison, expression of comparison. [F or L (prec.)]

simmer 1 *v.* be or keep bubbling or boiling gently; be in state of suppressed anger or laughter. 2 *n.* simmering condition. 3 **simmer down** become less agitated. [perh. imit.]

simnel /'sɪmn(ə)l/ *n.* rich ornamental cake baked esp. at Easter, Christmas, and Mid-Lent, often with marzipan layer and decoration. [F f. L or Gk]

simony /'saɪmənɪ/ *n.* buying or selling of ecclesiastical offices. [F f. L (*Simon Magus*; Acts 8:18)]

simoom /sɪ'mu:m/ *n.* hot dry dust-laden desert wind. [Arab.]

simper 1 *v.* smile in silly or affected way; express by or with simpering. 2 *n.* such smile. [orig. unkn.]

simple /'sɪmp(ə)l/ *a.* easily understood or done, presenting no difficulty; not complicated or elaborate, without luxury or sophistication; not compound, consisting of or involving only one element or operation etc.; absolute, unqualified, straightforward (*the simple truth*); foolish or ignorant, gullible, feeble-minded; **simple fracture** fracture of bone only; **simple interest** interest paid on principal only; **simple-minded** ingenuous, feeble-minded, unsophisticated; **simple sentence** one with single subject and predicate. [F f. L *simplus*]

simpleton *n.* stupid or gullible person.

simplicity /sɪm'plɪsɪtɪ/ *n.* fact or quality of being simple.

simplify /'sɪmplɪfaɪ/ *v.t.* make simple or less difficult; **simplification** /-fɪ'keɪʃ(ə)n/ *n.* [F f. med.L (SIMPLE)]

simplistic /sɪm'plɪstɪk/ *a.* excessively or affectedly simple or simplified; **simplistically** *adv.* [SIMPLE]

simply *adv.* in simple manner; absolutely, without doubt (*simply astonishing*); merely (*was simply trying to please*).

simulate /'sɪmjʊleɪt/ *v.t.* pretend to be or have or feel; imitate or counterfeit; imitate conditions of (situation etc.) e.g. for training; **simulation** /-'leɪʃ(ə)n/ *n.*; **simulator** *n.* [L (SIMILAR)]

simultaneous /sɪməl'teɪnɪəs/ *a.* occurring or operating at the same time (*with*); **simultaneity** /-tə'ni:ɪtɪ/ *n.* [L (*simul* at the same time)]

sin[1] 1 *n.* breaking of divine or moral law, esp. by conscious act; such act; offence against good taste or propriety etc. 2 *v.i.* (-**nn**-) commit sin, offend *against*. [OE]

sin[2] /saɪn/ *abbr.* sine.

since 1 *prep.* throughout, or at point in, period between (specified time or event) and time present or being considered (*must have happened since yesterday*; *had been going on since June*). 2 *conj.* during or in the time after (*what have you been doing since we met?*); for the reason that, because. 3 *adv.* from that time or event until now (*have not seen her since*); ago (*happened many years since*). [OE, = after that]

sincere /sɪn'sɪə/ *a.* free from pretence or deceit; genuine, honest, frank; **sincerity** /sɪn'serɪtɪ/ *n.* [L]

sincerely *adv.* in sincere manner; **yours sincerely** formula for ending informal letter.

sine *n.* ratio of side opposite acute angle (in right-angled triangle) to hypotenuse. [L SINUS]

sinecure /'saɪnɪkjʊə/ *n.* position that requires little or no work but usu. yields profit or honour. [L *sine cura* without care]

sine die /saɪnɪ 'daɪi:, sɪneɪ 'di:eɪ/ *adv.* (of business adjourned indefinitely) with no appointed date. [L]

sine qua non /sɪneɪ kwɑ: 'nəʊn/ *n.* indispensable condition or qualification. [L, = without which not]

sinew /'sɪnju:/ *n.* tough fibrous tissue joining muscle to bone; piece of this; (in *pl.*) muscles, bodily strength; thing that strengthens or sustains. [OE]

sinewy *a.* having strong sinews.

sinful *a.* committing or involving sin; wicked; **sinfully** *adv.* [SIN]

sing *v.* (*past* **sang**; *p.p.* **sung**) utter musical sounds with the voice, esp. words with set tune; utter or produce by singing; (of wind, kettle, etc.) make humming or buzzing or ringing sound; (of ears) be affected with ringing or buzzing sound; *sl.* act as informer; **sing of** celebrate (hero or event etc.) in verse or song; **sing out** shout; **sing the praises of** praise enthusiastically or continually. [OE]

singe /sɪndʒ/ **1** *v.* (*partic.* **singeing**) burn superficially or lightly; burn off tips or ends of (hair etc.). **2** *n.* superficial burn; act of singeing. [OE]

Singhalese var. of SINHALESE.

single /'sɪŋg(ə)l/ **1** *a.* one only, not double or multiple; united, undivided; designed for or used or done by one person etc.; one by itself (*a single tree*); regarded separately (*every single thing*); not married; (of ticket) valid for outward journey only, not return; (with neg. or interrog.) even one (*did not see a single person*); (of flower) having only one circle of petals. **2** *n.* single thing, or item in series; single ticket; pop record with one piece of music on each side; hit for one run in cricket; (usu. in *pl.*) game with one player on each side. **3** *v.t.* choose *out* for special attention etc. **4 single-breasted** (of coat etc.) having only one set of buttons and overlapping little across breast; **single combat** duel; **single file** file of persons in one line; **single-handed** *adv.* without help from another, (*a.*) done single-handed; **single-minded** having or intent on only one purpose. **5 singly** *adv.* [F f. L *singulus*]

singlet /'sɪŋglɪt/ *n.* man's sleeveless garment worn under or instead of shirt. [after *doublet*]

singleton /'sɪŋg(ə)lt(ə)n/ *n.* single person or thing, esp. player's only card of a suit. [after *simpleton*]

singsong 1 *a.* uttered with monotonous rhythm or cadence. **2** *n.* singsong manner; informal gathering for singing. [SING, SONG]

singular /'sɪŋgjʊlə/ **1** *a.* unique, much beyond the average, extraordinary; eccentric, strange; *Gram.* (of word or form) denoting one person or thing. **2** *n.* *Gram.* singular word or form, singular number. **3 singularity** /-'lærɪtɪ/ *n.* [F f. L (prec.)]

Sinhalese /sɪŋhə'li:z/ **1** *a.* of an Aryan people from N. India now forming majority of population of Sri Lanka. **2** *n.* member or language of this people. [Skr.]

sinister /'sɪnɪstə/ *a.* suggestive of evil, looking malignant or villainous; wicked, criminal; of evil omen; of or on left-hand side (observer's right) of shield etc. [F or L, = left]

sink 1 *v.* (*past* **sank**; *p.p.* **sunk** or as *a.* SUNKEN) fall or come slowly downwards; disappear below horizon; go or penetrate below surface esp. of liquid, (of ship) go to bottom of sea etc.; settle down comfortably (*sank into a chair*); gradually lose strength or value or quality etc., decline, (of voice) descend in pitch; cause or allow to sink or penetrate; cause failure of (plan etc.) or discomfiture of (person); dig (well), bore (shaft); engrave (die); invest (money); cause (ball) to enter pocket in billiards, hole at golf, etc., achieve this by (stroke); overlook or forget (*sank their differences*). **2** *n.* fixed basin with water-supply and outflow pipe; place where foul liquid collects; place of rampant vice etc. **3 sink in** penetrate or make way in, become gradually comprehended; **sinking fund** money set aside for gradual repayment of debt; **sunk fence** fence formed by, or along bottom of, ditch. [OE]

sinker *n.* weight used to sink fishing-line or sounding-line.

sinner *n.* one who sins. [SIN]

Sinn Fein /ʃɪn 'feɪn/ *n.* political movement and party advocating independent republican government for whole of Ireland. [Ir., = we ourselves]

Sino- /saɪnəʊ/ *in comb.* Chinese (and) (*Sino-American*; *Sinophobia*). [Gk *Sinai* the Chinese]

sinologue /'sɪnəlɒg, 'saɪ-/ *n.* person skilled in sinology. [F (prec.)]

sinology /sɪ'nɒlədʒɪ, saɪ-/ *n.* study of Chinese language and history etc.; **sinologist** *n.* [SINO-]

sinter 1 *n.* solid coalesced by heating. **2** *v.* form into sinter. [G (CINDER)]

sinuous /'sɪnjʊəs/ *a.* with many curves, undulating, meandering; **sinuosity** /-'ɒsɪtɪ/ *n.* [F or L (foll.)]

sinus /'saɪnəs/ *n.* cavity of bone or tissue, esp. in skull communicating with nostrils. [L, = recess, curve]

sinusitis /saɪnə'saɪtɪs/ *n.* inflammation of sinus. [-ITIS]

-sion see -ION.

sip 1 *v.* (**-pp-**) drink in repeated small mouthfuls or spoonfuls. **2** *n.* small mouthful of liquid; act of taking this. [perh. var. of SUP]

siphon /'saɪf(ə)n/ **1** *n.* pipe or tube shaped like inverted V or U with unequal legs to convey liquid from container to lower level by atmospheric pressure; bottle from which aerated water is forced out by pressure of gas. **2** *v.* conduct or flow (as) through siphon. [F or L f. Gk]

sir *n.* polite or respectful form of address or reference to a man; (**Sir**) titular prefix to name of a knight or baronet. [foll.]

sire 1 *n.* male parent of animal, esp. stallion kept for breeding; *archaic* as form of address to a king; *archaic* father or male ancestor. **2** *v.t.* (esp. of stallion) beget. [F, f. L SENIOR]

siren /'saɪərən/ *n.* device for making loud prolonged signal or warning sound; the sound made; (in Greek mythology) any of several women or winged creatures whose singing lured unwary sailors on to rocks; dangerously fascinating woman, temptress; *attrib.* irresistibly tempting. [F f. L f. Gk]

sirenian /saɪ'ri:nɪən/ **1** *a.* of an order of large aquatic plant-eating mammals. **2** *n.* member of this order.

sirloin /'sɜ:lɔɪn/ *n.* upper and choicer part of loin of beef; *US* rump steak. [F (SUR-², LOIN)]

sirocco /sɪ'rɒkəʊ/ *n.* (*pl.* **siroccos**) hot moist wind in S. Europe. [F f. It. f. Arab.]

sirup *US* var. of SYRUP.

sis *n. colloq.* sister. [abbr.]

sisal /'saɪs(ə)l/ *n.* fibre from leaves of agave. [*Sisal*, port of Yucatán]

siskin /'sɪskɪn/ *n.* small songbird. [Du.]

sissy /'sɪsɪ/ **1** *n.* effeminate or cowardly person. **2** *a.* characteristic of sissy. [SIS]

sister *n.* woman or girl in relation to other sons and daughters of her parents; close woman friend or associate; female fellow member of class or sect or human race; member of sisterhood, esp. nun; female hospital nurse in authority over others, *colloq.* any female nurse; *attrib.* of same type or design or origin etc. (*sister nations, ship, university*); **sister-in-law** (*pl.* **sisters-in-law**) one's husband's or wife's sister, one's brother's wife; **sisterly** *a.* [OE]

sisterhood *n.* relationship (as) of sisters; society of women bound by monastic vows or devoting themselves to religious or charitable work.

Sisyphean /sɪsɪ'fi:ən/ *a.* (of toil) endless and fruitless like that of Sisyphus (whose task in Hades was to push uphill a stone that at once rolled down again). [L f. Gk]

sit *v.* (**-tt-**; *past* and *p.p.* **sat**) take or be in a position in which the body is supported more or less upright by buttocks resting on ground or raised seat etc.; cause to sit, place in sitting position; (of bird) perch, (of animal) rest with hind legs bent and body close to ground; (of bird) remain on nest to hatch eggs; be engaged in occupation in which sitting position is usual, pose *for* portrait, be Member of Parliament *for* constituency, be candidate *for* examination, etc.; undergo (examination); (of parliament or court etc.) be in session; be in more or less permanent position or condition; (of clothes etc.) fit or hang in certain way; keep or have one's seat on (horse etc.); **be sitting pretty** be comfortably or advantageously placed; **sit at person's feet** be his pupil; **sit back** relax one's efforts; **sit down** sit after standing, cause to sit, suffer tamely (*under* humiliation etc.); **sit-down** *a.* (of meal) eaten sitting; **sit-down strike** strike in which workers refuse to leave their place of work; **sit in** occupy place as protest; **sit-in** *n.* such protest; **sit in judgement** assume right of judging others, be censorious (*on* or *over* others); **sit in on** be present as guest or observer at (meeting); **sit on** be member of (committee etc.), hold session or inquiry concerning, *colloq.* delay action about, *sl.* repress or rebuke or snub; **sit on the fence** remain neutral or undecided; **sit out** take no part in (dance etc.), stay till the end of (esp. ordeal), sit outdoors; **sit tight** *colloq.* remain firmly in one's place, not yield; **sit up** rise from lying to sitting position, sit firmly upright, not go to bed (until later than usual time), *colloq.* become interested or aroused etc.; **sit-upon** *colloq.* buttocks; **sit well on** suit or fit. [OE]

sitar /'sɪtɑ:, sɪ'tɑ:/ *n.* Indian instrument like guitar, with long neck. [Hindi]

sitcom /'sɪtkɒm/ *n. colloq.* situation comedy. [abbr.]

site 1 *n.* ground on which town or building stood or stands or is to stand; place of

or for specified activity (*camping site*). **2** *v.t.* locate, place. [AF, or L *situs*]
sitter *n.* one who sits, esp. for a portrait; = *baby-sitter*; *sl.* easy catch or shot. [SIT]
sitting 1 *n.* time during which person or assembly etc. sits continuously; clutch of eggs. **2** *a.* having sat down; (of animal or bird) not running or flying. **3 sitting duck** (or **target**) person or thing easily attacked; **sitting-room** room for sitting in, space enough to accommodate seated persons; **sitting tenant** one already occupying house etc.
situate 1 /'sɪtjʊeɪt/ *v.t.* put in a certain position or circumstances (usu. in *p.p.*); establish or indicate place of, put in a context. **2** /'sɪtjʊət/ *a.* (*archaic* or *Law*) situated. [L *situo* (SITE)]
situation /sɪtjʊ'eɪʃ(ə)n/ *n.* place and its surroundings; set of circumstances, state of affairs, condition; employee's position or job; **situation comedy** broadcast comedy in which humour derives from characters' difficulties and misunderstandings; **situational** *a.* [F, or med.L (prec.)]
six *a.* & *n.* one more than five; symbol for this (6, vi, VI); size etc. denoted by six; (in cricket) hit scoring six runs; **at sixes and sevens** in confusion or disagreement; **hit** (or **knock**) **for six** *colloq.* utterly surprise or overwhelm; **six-gun** (or **-shooter**) *US* revolver with six chambers. [OE]
sixfold *a.* & *adv.* six times as much or as many; consisting of six parts. [SIX]
sixpence *n.* sum of 6p; *formerly* sum of 6d., silver coin worth this.
sixpenny *a.* costing or worth sixpence.
sixteen /sɪks'ti:n/ *a.* & *n.* one more than fifteen; symbol for this (16, xvi, XVI); size etc. denoted by sixteen; **sixteenth** *a.* & *n.* [OE]
sixth *a.* & *n.* next after fifth; one of six equal parts of thing; **sixth form** form in secondary school for pupils over 16; **sixth-form college** college with special courses for such pupils; **sixth sense** supposed faculty giving intuitive or extrasensory knowledge; **sixthly** *adv.* [SIX]
sixty /'sɪkstɪ/ *a.* & *n.* six times ten; symbol for this (60, lx, LX); (in *pl.*) numbers, years, degrees of temperature, from 60 to 69; **sixtieth** *a.* & *n.* [OE]
size[1] **1** *n.* relative bigness or extent of thing, dimensions or magnitude; each of the classes into which similar things are divided according to size (*takes size 8*). **2** *v.t.* sort in sizes or according to size. **3 size up** estimate size of, *colloq.* form judgement of; **that is the size of it** *colloq.* that is the truth of the matter. **4 -sized** of specific size (*large-sized*). [ASSIZE]
size[2] **1** *n.* gelatinous solution used in glazing paper, stiffening textiles, etc. **2** *v.t.* treat with size. [perh. = prec.]
sizeable *a.* fairly large. [SIZE[1]]
sizzle /'sɪz(ə)l/ **1** *v.i.* make spluttering or hissing noise as of frying; *colloq.* be in state of great heat or excitement etc. **2** *n.* sizzling sound. [imit.]
SJ *abbr.* Society of Jesus.
sjambok /'ʃæmbɒk/ *n.* (in S. Africa) rhinoceros-hide whip. [Afrik. f. Malay f. Urdu]
skald /skɔ:ld, skɒld/ *n.* ancient-Scandinavian poet. [ON]
skate[1] **1** *n.* each of pair of steel blades (or of boots with blades attached) for gliding on ice; (in full **roller-skate**) each of pair of metal frames with small wheels, fitted to shoes for riding on hard surface. **2** *v.* move on skates, perform (specified figure) on skates. **3 get one's skates on** *sl.* make haste; **skate on thin ice** behave rashly, risk danger etc.; **skate over** refer fleetingly to, disregard. [Du. *schaats* f. F]
skate[2] *n.* (*pl.* **skate**) kind of ray. [ON]
skate[3] *n. sl.* (also **cheap skate**) contemptible or dishonest person. [orig. uncert.]
skateboard *n.* short narrow board on roller-skate wheels for riding on while standing. [SKATE[1]]
skedaddle /skɪ'dæd(ə)l/ *colloq.* **1** *v.i.* depart quickly. **2** *n.* hurried departure. [orig. unkn.]
skein /skeɪn/ *n.* loosely coiled bundle of yarn or thread; flock of wild geese etc. in flight. [F *escaigne*]
skeleton /'skelɪt(ə)n/ *n.* hard framework of bones of animal or thing; supporting framework or structure of thing; very thin person or animal; remaining part of something after life or usefulness is gone; outline sketch, epitome; *attrib.* having only the essential or minimum number of persons or parts etc. (*skeleton crew, plan, staff*); **skeleton in the cupboard** discreditable or embarrassing fact kept secret; **skeleton key** key designed to fit many locks; **skeletal** *a.* [Gk (*skellō* dry up)]
skep *n.* wooden or wicker basket, quantity contained in this; straw or wicker beehive. [ON]
skeptic *US* var. of SCEPTIC.
skerry /'skerɪ/ *n.* reef, rocky island. [ON]
sketch 1 *n.* rough or unfinished drawing or painting; rough draft or general outline; short usu. humorous play; short descriptive piece of writing. **2** *v.* make or give sketch of; draw sketches. **3 sketch-book** pad of drawing-paper; **sketch in** indicate briefly or in outline; **sketch-**

-map roughly drawn map with few details. [Du. *schets* or G *skizze* ult. f. Gk *skhedios* extempore]

sketchy *a.* like a sketch; unsubstantial or imperfect esp. through haste; **sketchily** *adv.*; **sketchiness** *n.*

skew 1 *a.* set askew, oblique, distorted. **2** *n.* slant. **3** *v.* make skew; distort; move obliquely. **4 on the skew** askew. [F (ESCHEW)]

skewbald /'skju:bɔ:ld/ **1** *a.* (of animal) with irregular patches of white and another colour. **2** *n.* skewbald animal, esp. horse. [orig. uncert.]

skewer 1 *n.* long pin designed for holding meat compactly together while cooking. **2** *v.t.* fasten together or pierce (as) with skewer. [orig. uncert.]

skew-whiff /skju:'wɪf/ *a. colloq.* askew. [SKEW]

ski /ski:/ **1** *n.* (*pl.* **skis**) each of pair of long narrow pieces of wood etc. fastened under feet for travelling over snow; similar device under vehicle. **2** *v.i.* (*past* and *p.p.* **ski'd** or **skied** /ski:d/; *partic.* **skiing**) travel on skis. **3 ski-jump** steep slope levelling off before sharp drop to allow skier to leap through the air; **ski-lift** device for carrying skiers up slope, usu. on seats hung from overhead cable; **ski-run** slope prepared for skiing. **4 skier** *n.* [Norw. f. ON]

skid 1 *v.* (**-dd-**) (of vehicle etc.) slide esp. sideways or obliquely on slippery road etc.; cause (vehicle) to skid. **2** *n.* act of skidding; piece of wood etc. serving as support or fender etc.; braking device, esp. wooden or metal shoe on wheel; runner beneath aircraft for use when landing. **3 on the skids** *colloq.* about to be discarded or defeated; **put the skids under** hasten downfall or failure of; **skid-pan** slippery surface prepared for vehicle-drivers to practise control of skidding; **skid row** *US sl.* district frequented by vagrants. [orig. unkn.]

skiff *n.* light rowing or sculling boat. [F *esquif* (SHIP)]

skilful *a.* having or showing skill; **skilfully** *adv.* [foll.]

skill *n.* expertness, practised ability, facility in an action. [ON, = difference]

skilled *a.* skilful; (of worker) highly trained or experienced; (of work) requiring skill or special training.

skillet /'skɪlɪt/ *n.* small metal cooking-pot with long handle and usu. legs; *US* frying-pan. [F]

skillful *US* var. of SKILFUL.

skim *v.* (**-mm-**) take cream or scum from surface of (liquid); take (cream etc.) from surface of liquid; keep touching lightly or nearly touching (surface) in passing over; go thus *along* or *over* surface, glide along; read or look at cursorily; **skim milk** milk from which cream has been skimmed. [F (SCUM)]

skimp *v.* supply (person etc.) with or use meagre or insufficient amount (of); be parsimonious. [cf. SCRIMP]

skimpy *a.* meagre, insufficient; **skimpily** *adv.*; **skimpiness** *n.*

skin 1 *n.* flexible continuous covering of human or animal body; skin (with or without hair) removed from animal, material made from this; colour or complexion of skin; outer layer or covering; film like skin on surface of liquid; container for liquid, made of animal's skin; ship's planking or plating. **2** *v.* (**-nn-**) remove skin from; cover or become covered (as) with skin; *sl.* fleece or swindle. **3 be (all) skin and bone** be very thin; **by the skin of one's teeth** by a very narrow margin; **get under person's skin** *colloq.* interest or annoy him intensely; **have a thick** (or **thin**) **skin** be insensitive (or sensitive) to criticism etc.; **no skin off one's nose** *colloq.* of no consequence to one; **save one's skin** avoid death or harm etc.; **skin-deep** superficial, not deep or lasting; **skin-diver** one who swims underwater without diving-suit, usu. with aqualung and flippers; **skin-diving** such swimming; **skin-flick** *sl.* pornographic film; **skin-graft** surgical transplanting of skin, skin thus transferred; **skin-tight** very close-fitting. [ON]

skinflint *n.* miserly person.

skinful *n. colloq.* enough alcoholic liquor to make one drunk.

skinhead *n.* youth with close-cropped hair.

skinny *a.* thin or emaciated; **skinniness** *n.*

skint *a. sl.* having no money left. [= *skinned*]

skip[1] **1** *v.* (**-pp-**) move along lightly, esp. by taking two steps with each foot in turn; jump lightly from the ground e.g. so as to clear skipping-rope; move quickly from one subject or point to another; omit in reading or dealing with; *colloq.* not participate in; *colloq.* leave hurriedly. **2** *n.* skipping movement or action. **3 skip it!** *sl.* abandon topic etc.; **skipping-rope** length of rope (usu. with two handles) revolved over head and under feet while jumping as game or exercise. [prob. Scand.]

skip[2] *n.* large container for refuse etc.; cage or bucket etc. in which men or materials are raised or lowered in mines etc. [var. of SKEP]

skipper 1 *n.* captain of ship, esp. of small trading or fishing vessel; captain of aircraft; captain of side in games. **2** *v.t.*

act as captain of. [LG or Du. *schipper* (SHIP)]

skirl 1 *n.* shrill sound characteristic of bagpipes. 2 *v.i.* make skirl. [prob. Scand.]

skirmish /'skɜːmɪʃ/ 1 *n.* minor fight esp. between small or outlying parts of armies or fleets; short argument or contest of wit etc. 2 *v.i.* engage in skirmish. [F f. Gmc]

skirt 1 *n.* woman's outer garment hanging from the waist; part of coat etc. that hangs below waist; hanging part round base of hovercraft; edge, border, extreme part. 2 *v.* go or lie along or round the edge of; avoid dealing with (issue etc.). 3 **bit of skirt** *sl.* woman; **skirting-board** narrow board etc. along bottom of room-wall; **skirt of beef** diaphragm etc. as food, meat from lower flank. [ON (SHIRT)]

skit *n.* light, usu. short, piece of satire or burlesque. [perh. ON (SHOOT)]

skittish /'skɪtɪʃ/ *a.* lively, playful; (of horse etc.) nervous, inclined to shy. [perh. as prec.]

skittle /'skɪt(ə)l/ *n.* pin used in skittles; (in *pl.*) game played with usu. nine wooden pins set up to be bowled or knocked down. [orig. unkn.]

skive *v. sl.* evade (a duty); **skive off** depart evasively. [ON]

skivvy /'skɪvɪ/ *n. colloq. derog.* female domestic servant. [orig. unkn.]

skua /'skjuːə/ *n.* large predatory sea-bird. [ON]

skulduggery /skʌl'dʌgərɪ/ *n.* trickery; unscrupulous behaviour. [orig. unkn.]

skulk *v.i.* move stealthily, lurk, or hide, esp. in cowardly or sinister way, or to shirk duty. [Scand.]

skull *n.* bony case of brain of vertebrate; bony framework of head, representation of this; head as site of intelligence; **skull and cross-bones** representation of skull with two thigh-bones crossed below it as emblem of piracy or death; **skull-cap** small close-fitting peakless cap. [orig. unkn.]

skunk *n.* black American animal with white stripes and bushy tail, emitting powerful stench when attacked; contemptible person. [Amer. Ind.]

sky /skaɪ/ 1 *n.* (in *sing.* or *pl.*) region of the atmosphere and outer space seen from the earth (in *sing.* or *pl.*). 2 *v.t.* hit (cricket ball) high into air. 3 **sky-blue** *a.* & *n.* bright clear blue; **sky-diving** parachuting in which parachute is opened only at last safe moment; **sky-high** (as if) reaching the sky, very high; **sky-rocket** *n.* rocket exploding high in air, (*v.i.*) rise very steeply or rapidly; **sky-writing** legible smoke-trails from aeroplane; **to the skies** without reserve (*praise to the skies*). [ON, = cloud]

Skye /skaɪ/ *n.* short-legged long-haired Scotch terrier. [*Skye*, Scottish island]

skyjack *v.t. sl.* hijack (aircraft). [SKY]

skylark 1 *n.* lark that soars while singing. 2 *v.i.* play tricks and practical jokes.

skylight *n.* window in roof.

skyline *n.* outline of hills, buildings, etc., defined against sky.

skyscraper *n.* very tall building.

skyward /'skaɪwəd/ *adv.* (also **skywards**) & *a.* towards the sky. [-WARD]

slab *n.* flat thick usu. square or rectangular piece of solid matter. [orig. unkn.]

slack[1] 1 *a.* lacking firmness or tautness; lacking energy or activity; sluggish; negligent; (of tide etc.) neither ebbing nor flowing. 2 *n.* slack period, part of rope, etc.; *colloq.* spell of inactivity; (in *pl.*) informal trousers. 3 *v.* slacken; *colloq.* take a rest, be lazy. 4 **slack off** loosen, (cause to) lose vigour; **slack up** reduce speed. [OE]

slack[2] *n.* coal-dust. [prob. LG or Du.]

slacken *v.* make or become slack, slack *off*. [SLACK[1]]

slacker *n.* shirker, indolent person.

slag 1 *n.* refuse left after ore has been smelted etc. 2 *v.* (**-gg-**) form slag. 3 **slag-heap** hill of refuse from mine etc. 4 **slaggy** *a.* [LG]

slain *p.p.* of SLAY.

slake *v.t.* assuage or satisfy (thirst, revenge, etc.); disintegrate (lime) by combination with water. [OE (SLACK)]

slalom /'slɑːləm/ *n.* ski-race down zigzag course with artificial obstacles; obstacle race in canoes. [Norw.]

slam[1] 1 *v.* (**-mm-**) shut (esp. door) with loud bang; put or knock or move with similar sound or violently; *sl.* criticize severely, hit, beat, gain easy victory over. 2 *n.* sound or action of slamming. [prob. Scand.]

slam[2] *n.* gaining of every trick at cards; **grand slam** winning of 13 tricks in bridge, winning of all of group of championships in a sport. [orig. uncert.]

slander /'slɑːndə/ 1 *n.* malicious false and injurious utterance about person; uttering of this. 2 *v.t.* utter slander about. 3 **slanderous** *a.* [F *esclandre* (SCANDAL)]

slang 1 *n.* words and phrases, or particular meanings of these, in common informal use but generally not regarded as standard in a language; such expressions used by specified profession or class etc. 2 *v.* use abusive language (to). 3 **slangy** *a.* [orig. unkn.]

slant /slɑːnt/ 1 *v.* slope; lie or go

obliquely to vertical or horizontal, cause to do this; present (information) in biased or unfair way. **2** *n.* slope, oblique position; point of view, esp. biased one. **3** *a.* sloping, oblique. **4 on a** (or **the**) **slant** aslant. [Scand.]

slantwise *adv.* aslant.

slap 1 *v.* (**-pp-**) strike with palm of hand or flat object, or so as to make similar noise; lay forcefully (*slapped the money on the table*); put hastily or carelessly (*slap paint on the walls*). **2** *n.* blow with palm of hand or flat object; slapping sound. **3** *adv.* directly, suddenly, fully (*ran slap into her*; *hit me slap in the eye*). **4 slap and tickle** *colloq.* lively esp. amorous amusement; **slap-bang** violently, noisily, headlong; **slap person down** *colloq.* snub or reprimand him; **slap-happy** *colloq.* cheerfully casual or flippant; **slap in the face** a rebuff or insult; **slap on the back** congratulations; **slap-up** *a. colloq.* lavish, first-class. [LG, imit.]

slapdash 1 *a.* hasty and careless. **2** *adv.* in slapdash manner.

slapstick *n.* boisterous knockabout comedy.

slash 1 *v.* make sweeping cut(s) with knife etc.; make long gash(es) in or sweeping cut(s) at; reduce (prices etc.) drastically; (in *partic.*) vigorously incisive or effective; censure vigorously. **2** *n.* slashing cut or stroke. [orig. unkn.]

slat *n.* thin narrow piece of wood or plastic etc., esp. used in overlapping series as in a fence or Venetian blind. [F *esclat* splinter]

slate 1 *n.* a kind of metamorphic rock easily split into flat smooth plates; piece of such plate used as roofing-material or for writing on; colour of slate. **2** *v.t.* cover with slates; *colloq.* criticize severely; *US* make arrangements for (event etc.); *US* nominate for office etc. **3 clean slate** no discreditable history; **clean the slate** remove obligations, grievances, etc. **4 slaty** *a.* [F *esclate* fem. of *esclat* (SLAT)]

slattern /ˈslætɜːn/ *n.* slovenly woman; **slatternliness** *n.*; **slatternly** *a.* [orig. uncert.]

slaughter /ˈslɔːtə/ **1** *n.* killing of animals for food; killing of many persons or animals at once or continuously. **2** *v.t.* kill thus; *colloq.* defeat utterly. [ON (SLAY)]

slaughterhouse *n.* place for slaughter of animals as food.

Slav /slɑːv/ **1** *n.* member of group of peoples in Central and Eastern Europe speaking Slavonic languages. **2** *a.* of the Slavs. [L *Sclavus*, ethnic name]

slave 1 *n.* person who is owned by another and has to serve him; drudge, person working very hard; helpless victim *of* or *to* some dominating influence (*slave of fashion*; *slave to his passions*); part of machine directly controlled by another. **2** *v.i.* work very hard (*at* or *over*). **3 slave-driver** overseer of slaves at work, hard taskmaster; **slave labour** forced labour; **slave-trade** procuring, transporting, and selling slaves, esp. African Blacks. [F *esclave* f. L *Sclavus* SLAV (captive)]

slaver[1] *n.* ship or person engaged in slave-trade.

slaver[2] /ˈslævə/ **1** *n.* saliva running from mouth; flattery, drivel. **2** *v.i.* let saliva run from mouth, dribble; show excessive sentiment *over*. [LG or Du.]

slavery /ˈsleɪvərɪ/ *n.* condition or work of slave; drudgery; custom of having slaves. [SLAVE]

slavish *a.* of or like slaves; without originality. [SLAVE]

Slavonic /sləˈvɒnɪk/ **1** *a.* of the group of languages including Russian and Polish and Czech; of Slavs. **2** *n.* Slavonic group of languages. [SLAV]

slay *v.t.* (*past* **slew** /sluː/; *p.p.* **slain**) kill. [OE]

sleazy *a.* squalid, tawdry; slatternly; **sleazily** *adv.*; **sleaziness** *n.* [orig. unkn.]

sled *n.* & *v.* (**-dd-**) *US* sledge. [LG]

sledge 1 *n.* vehicle on runners instead of wheels for conveying loads or passengers esp. over snow. **2** *v.* travel or convey by sledge. [Du. *sleedse*]

sledge-hammer /ˈsledʒhæmə/ *n.* large heavy hammer; *attrib.* heavy or powerful (*sledge-hammer blow, argument*). [OE *sledge*, rel. to SLAY]

sleek 1 *a.* (of hair or skin etc.) smooth and glossy; looking well-fed and comfortable; ingratiating. **2** *v.t.* make sleek. [var. of SLICK]

sleep 1 *n.* natural recurring condition of mind and body in which eyes are closed, muscles and nerves relaxed, and consciousness suspended; a period of sleeping; state like sleep, rest or quiet, death. **2** *v.* (*past* and *p.p.* **slept**) be in state of sleep, fall asleep; spend the night *at* or *in* etc.; provide sleeping accommodation for (*house sleeps six*); have sexual intercourse in bed *together* or *with*; be inactive or dead. **3 go to sleep** enter state of sleep, (of limb) become numbed; **last sleep** death; **put to sleep** anaesthetize, kill (animal) painlessly; **sleep around** *colloq.* be sexually promiscuous; **sleep in** remain asleep later than usual in the morning; **sleeping-bag** lined or padded bag to sleep in esp. when camping etc.; **sleeping-car** (or **-carriage**) railway coach with beds or berths; **sleeping**

partner one not sharing in actual work of a firm; **sleeping-pill** pill to induce sleep; **sleeping sickness** tropical disease causing extreme lethargy; **sleep off** get rid of (headache etc.) by sleeping; **sleep on** not decide (question) until next day; **sleep-walker** person who walks about while asleep; **sleep-walking** this condition. [OE]

sleeper *n.* one who sleeps; each of the beams on which railway rails run; sleeping-car, berth in this; ring worn in pierced ear to keep hole from closing.

sleepless *a.* lacking sleep; unable to sleep; continually active.

sleepy *a.* ready for sleep, about to fall asleep; lacking activity or bustle (*a sleepy little town*); **sleepily** *adv.*; **sleepiness** *n.*

sleet 1 *n.* snow and rain together; hail or snow melting as it falls. **2** *v.i.* fall as sleet. **3 it sleets** (or **is sleeting**) sleet is falling. **4 sleety** *a.* [OE]

sleeve *n.* part of garment that encloses arm; cover of gramophone record; tube enclosing rod or smaller tube; wind-sock; **up one's sleeve** concealed but ready for use; **sleeved** *a.* [OE]

sleigh /sleɪ/ **1** *n.* sledge, esp. one for riding on. **2** *v.i.* travel on sleigh. [Du. *slee* (SLEDGE)]

sleight /slaɪt/ *n.* esp. in **sleight-of-hand** dexterity, conjuring. [ON (SLY)]

slender *a.* of small girth or breadth; gracefully thin; relatively small, scanty, meagre, inadequate. [orig. unkn.]

slept *past* and *p.p.* of SLEEP.

sleuth /slu:θ/ *n.* detective; **sleuth-hound** bloodhound. [ON]

slew[1] /slu:/ **1** *v.* turn or swing forcibly or with effort (*round*) to new position. **2** *n.* such turn. [orig. unkn.]

slew[2] *past* of SLAY.

slice 1 *n.* thin broad or wedge-shaped piece cut from something; share or part; implement with broad flat blade for serving fish etc. or for scraping or chipping; (in golf) slicing stroke. **2** *v.* cut into slices; cut (piece) *off*; cut (*into* or *through*) with or like a knife; (in golf) strike (ball) so that it deviates away from one. [F *esclice* f. Gmc]

slick 1 *a. colloq.* skilful or efficient, esp. superficially or pretentiously so; shrewd, wily; sleek, smooth. **2** *n.* smooth patch of oil esp. on sea. **3** *v.t. colloq.* make sleek or smart; flatten *down* (one's hair etc.). [OE]

slide 1 *v.* (*past* and *p.p.* **slid**) (cause to) move along smooth surface with constant friction on same part of thing moving; move or go smoothly or quietly (*down* or *in* or *out* etc.); pass gradually or imperceptibly (*to* or *into* a state or condition); glide over ice on feet without skates. **2** *n.* act of sliding; inclined plane down which goods etc., or children in play, slide; track for sliding esp. on ice; part of machine or instrument that slides; thing slid into place, esp. mounted transparency viewed by means of projector etc., or glass holding object for microscope; = *hair-slide*. **3 let things slide** be negligent, allow deterioration; **slide over** barely touch upon (delicate subject etc.); **slide-rule** ruler with sliding central strip, graduated logarithmically to make rapid calculations; **sliding scale** scale of fees or taxes or wages etc. that varies as a whole according to changes in some standard. [OE]

slight /slaɪt/ **1** *a.* small, inconsiderable, not serious or important, inadequate; slender, frail-looking. **2** *v.t.* treat (person etc.) with disrespect or as not worth attention; markedly ignore. **3** *n.* act of slighting. [ON]

slim 1 *a.* slender; not fat or overweight; clever, artful. **2** *v.i.* (**-mm-**) make oneself slimmer by dieting, exercise, etc. [LG or Du.]

slime *n.* thick slippery mud or similar substance. [OE]

slimline *a.* of slender design. [SLIM]

slimy /ˈslaɪmɪ/ *a.* like slime; covered with or full of slime; disgustingly obsequious; **slimily** *adv.*; **sliminess** *n.* [SLIME]

sling[1] **1** *n.* strap etc. used to support or raise thing; bandage supporting injured arm; strap or string used to throw small stone etc. **2** *v.t.* (*past* & *p.p.* **slung**) hurl, throw; suspend with sling, arrange so as to be held or moved from above. **3 sling-back** shoe held in place by strap above and behind heel; **sling one's hook** *sl.* make off. [ON, or LG or Du.]

sling[2] *n. US* sweetened drink of spirits (esp. gin) and water. [orig. unkn.]

slink *v.i.* (*past* & *p.p.* **slunk**) move in stealthy or guilty or sneaking manner. [OE]

slinky *a.* stealthy; (of garment) close-fitting and sinuous; **slinkily** *adv.*; **slinkiness** *n.*

slip 1 *v.* (**-pp-**) slide unintentionally or momentarily, lose footing or balance; go with sliding motion (*the catch slips into place*); get away by being slippery or hard to grasp or not grasped; make one's way quietly or unobserved (*in* or *out* or *away* etc.); make careless or casual mistake; fall below normal standard; place stealthily or casually or with sliding motion (*slipped a coin into his hand*); release from restraint or connection; move (stitch) to the other needle without knitting it; pull (garment etc.) hastily *on* or *off*, evade, escape from (*dog slips his collar*; *point slipped my mind*). **2** *n.* act of slipping; accidental or slight error; loose covering or garment, e.g. petticoat; reduction in movement or speed of pulley or propeller etc.; (in *sing*. or *pl.*) slope on which boats are landed or ships are repaired etc.; (in cricket) fieldsman close behind wicket, (in *sing*. or *pl.*) this part of ground. **3 give person the slip** escape from or evade him; **let slip** release accidentally or deliberately, miss (opportunity), utter inadvertently; **slip-case** (or **-cover**) fitted cover for book or furniture etc.; **slip-knot** knot that can be undone at a pull, running knot; **slip of the pen** (or **tongue**) small mistake in which something is written (or said) unintentionally; **slip-on** (of shoes or clothes) that can be easily slipped on or off; **slipped disc** disc between vertebrae that has become displaced and causes lumbar pain; **slip-road** road for entering or leaving motorway etc.; **slip-stream** current of air or water driven back by propeller or moving vehicle; **slip up** *colloq.* make mistake; **slip-up** *n. colloq.* mistake, blunder. [prob. f. LG *slippen*]

slip² *n.* small piece of paper, esp. for writing on; cutting taken from plant for grafting or planting; **slip of a girl** etc. small slim girl etc. [LG or Du.]

slip³ *n.* finely ground clay mixed with water for coating or decorating earthenware. [OE, = slime]

slipper *n.* light soft shoe for indoor wear. [SLIP¹]

slippery *a.* difficult to grasp because of smoothness or wetness etc.; (of surface) on which slipping is likely; (of person) unreliable, unscrupulous; **slipperiness** *n.* [OE & G]

slippy *a. colloq.* slippery; **look slippy** look sharp, make haste. [SLIP¹]

slipshod *a.* slovenly, careless; having shoes down at heel.

slipway *n.* slip used for building ships or as landing-stage.

slit 1 *n.* straight narrow incision or opening. **2** *v.t.* (**-tt-**; *past* & *p.p.* **slit**) make slit in; cut into strips. [OE]

slither /'slɪðə/ **1** *v.i.* slip or slide unsteadily. **2** *n.* act of slithering. **3 slithery** *a.* [alt. of *slidder* (SLIDE)]

sliver /'slɪvə/ **1** *n.* thin strip or piece of wood etc. **2** *v.* break off as sliver; break or form into slivers. [OE]

slob *n. colloq.* large and coarse or stupid person. [Ir. *slab* mud]

slobber 1 *v.* slaver; show excessive sentiment *over*. **2** *n.* slaver. **3 slobbery** *a.* [Du.]

sloe /sləʊ/ *n.* blackthorn; its small bluish-black fruit. [OE]

slog 1 *v.* (**-gg-**) hit hard and usu. wildly; work or walk doggedly (*away* etc.). **2** *n.* hard random hit; hard steady work, spell of this. [orig. unkn.]

slogan /'sləʊgən/ *n.* short catchy phrase used in advertising etc.; party cry, watchword. [Gael., = war-cry]

sloop *n.* small one-masted fore-and-aft-rigged vessel. [Du. *sloep*]

slop 1 *v.* (**-pp-**) spill or flow over edge of vessel, allow to do this; make (floor etc.) wet or messy by slopping; carry slops *out* (in prison etc.); gush, be effusive (*over* person); move *about* in slovenly manner. **2** *n.* liquid spilled or splashed; sentimental utterance; (in *pl.*) dirty water or liquid, waste contents of kitchen or bedroom vessels; (in *sing*. or *pl.*) unappetizing liquid food. **3 slop-basin** basin for dregs of cups at table; **slop-pail** pail for removing bedroom or kitchen slops. [OE]

slope 1 *n.* inclined position or direction or state; piece of rising or falling ground; difference in level between two ends or sides of thing; place for skiing on side of mountain etc. **2** *v.* have or take slope, slant; cause to slope. **3 slope arms** place rifle in sloping position against shoulder; **slope off** *sl.* go away, esp. to evade work etc. [*aslope* crosswise]

sloppy *a.* wet, watery, too liquid; unsystematic, careless; untidy, ill-fitting; weakly emotional; **sloppily** *adv.*; **sloppiness** *n.* [SLOP¹]

slosh 1 *v.* splash or flounder (*about*); *sl.* hit esp. heavily; *colloq.* pour (liquid) clumsily, pour liquid on. **2** *n.* slush; sound or act of splashing; *sl.* heavy blow. [var. of SLUSH]

sloshed *a. sl.* drunk.

slot 1 *n.* slit or other aperture in machine etc. for something (esp. coin) to be inserted; slit etc. into which something fits or in which something works; allotted place in an arrangement or scheme. **2** *v.* (**-tt-**) put or be placed (as if) into slot; provide with slot(s). **3 slot-machine** machine worked by insertion of coin, esp. delivering small purchased articles or providing amusement. [F *esclot* hollow of breast]

sloth /sləʊθ/ *n.* laziness, indolence; S. American slow-moving arboreal mammal. [SLOW]

slothful *a.* lazy; **slothfully** *adv.*

slouch 1 *v.* stand or move or sit in drooping ungainly fashion; bend one side of brim of (hat) downwards. **2** *n.* slouching posture or movement; downward bend of hat-brim; *sl.* incompetent or slovenly worker etc. **3 slouch hat**

hat with wide flexible brim. [orig. unkn.]

slough[1] /slaʊ/ *n.* swamp, miry place; **Slough of Despond** state of hopeless depression. [OE]

slough[2] /slʌf/ **1** *n.* dead skin or other part of animal (esp. snake) cast off. **2** *v.* cast or drop (*off*) as slough. [orig. unkn.]

Slovak /ˈsləʊvæk/ **1** *n.* native or language of Slovakia. **2** *a.* of the Slovaks. [native name]

sloven /ˈslʌv(ə)n/ *n.* untidy, lazy, or careless person. [orig. uncert.]

slovenly 1 *a.* careless and untidy, unmethodical. **2** *adv.* in slovenly manner. **3 slovenliness** *n.*

slow /sləʊ/ **1** *a.* taking a relatively long time to do thing or things, acting or moving or done without speed, not quick; not conducive to speed (*a slow road*); (of clock etc.) showing time earlier than correct time; dull-witted, not understanding readily; uninteresting, tedious; slack or sluggish (*business is slow*); (of fire or oven) giving little heat; (of photographic film) needing long exposure; lacking inclination (*slow to take offence*). **2** *adv.* slowly (used when *slow* gives the essential point, as in *go slow*). **3** *v.* (with *down* or *up*) move or act or work less quickly or energetically than before, cause to do this. **4 slow-down** action of slowing down; **slow motion** speed of film in which actions appear much slower than usual, simulation of this in real action. [OE]

slowcoach *n.* slow or indolent person.

slow-worm /ˈsləʊwɜːm/ *n.* small European legless lizard. [OE; not f. SLOW]

sludge *n.* thick greasy mud; muddy or slushy sediment; sewage; **sludgy** *a.* [cf. SLUSH]

slue var. of SLEW[1].

slug[1] *n.* small gastropod like snail but without shell; bullet of irregular shape; missile for airgun; (in printing) metal bar used in spacing, line of type in Linotype printing; *US* tot of liquor. [Scand.]

slug[2] *US* **1** *v.* (**-gg-**) hit hard. **2** *n.* hard hit. [cf. SLOG]

sluggard /ˈslʌgəd/ *n.* lazy person. [SLUG[1]]

sluggish *a.* inert, slow-moving.

sluice /sluːs/ **1** *n.* (also **sluice-gate**) sliding gate or other contrivance for regulating flow or level of water; water regulated by this; (also **sluice-way**) artificial water-channel; place for rinsing; rinsing. **2** *v.* provide or wash with sluice(s); rinse; pour water freely upon; (of water) rush out (as) from sluice. [F *escluse* f. L (EXCLUDE)]

slum 1 *n.* overcrowded, squalid, and poor district or house in city. **2** *v.i.* (**-mm-**) live in slumlike conditions; visit slum(s) esp. in search of amusement. **3 slummy** *a.* [orig. unkn.]

slumber *v.* & *n.* sleep (*lit.* or *fig.*); **slumberous** *a.*; **slumbrous** *a.* [OE]

slump 1 *n.* sudden severe or prolonged fall in prices and values and demand for goods etc. **2** *v.i.* undergo slump; sit or fall down limply. [imit.]

slung *past* & *p.p.* of SLING[1].

slunk *past* & *p.p.* of SLINK.

slur 1 *v.* (**-rr-**) sound or write (words, musical notes, etc.) so that they run into one another; put slur upon (person or character); pass lightly or deceptively *over*. **2** *n.* imputation of wrongdoing, reproach; act of slurring; *Mus.* curved line joining notes to be slurred. [orig. unkn.]

slurp *colloq.* **1** *v.t.* eat or drink noisily. **2** *n.* sound of slurping. [Du.]

slurry /ˈslʌrɪ/ *n.* thin semi-liquid mixture of cement, mud, etc. [rel. to dial. *slur* thin mud]

slush *n.* thawing snow; watery mud; silly sentiment; **slush fund** fund for illegal purposes, esp. bribery; **slushy** *a.* [orig. unkn.]

slut *n.* slovenly woman; **sluttish** *a.* [orig. unkn.]

sly /slaɪ/ *a.* crafty, wily, underhand, secretive; knowing, mischievous; **on the sly** secretly; **slyly** *adv.*; **slyness** *n.* [ON, rel. to SLAY]

Sm *symb.* samarium.

smack[1] **1** *n.* sharp slap or blow; hard hit; sharp sound as of surface struck by flat object; loud kiss. **2** *v.t.* slap; move with smack. **3** *adv. colloq.* with a smack; suddenly, directly, violently. **4 smack in the eye** rebuff. [imit.]

smack[2] **1** *v.i.* have flavour or suggestion (*of*). **2** *n.* flavour or suggestion (*of*). [OE]

smack[3] *n.* single-masted sailing-boat. [LG or Du.]

smacker *n. sl.* loud kiss; *sl.* £1, *US* $1. [SMACK[1]]

small /smɔːl/ **1** *a.* not large or big; not great in importance or amount or power etc.; not much, insignificant (*paid small attention to details*; *no small thing*); consisting of small particles (*small shot*); doing thing on small scale (*small farmer*); socially undistinguished, poor or humble; mean, ungenerous, paltry. **2** *n. the* slenderest part of something (esp. **small of the back**); (in *pl.*) *colloq.* small articles of laundry, esp. underwear. **3** *adv.* into small pieces (*chop it small*). **4 feel** (or **look**) **small** be humiliated or ashamed; **small arms** portable firearms; **small beer** insignificant thing; **small change** coins, esp. low denominations as opposed to notes; **small fry** see FRY[2]; **small hours** period soon after midnight; **small-minded** narrow or selfish in outlook; **small--scale** made or occurring on a small scale; **small talk** social conversation on unimportant matters; **small-time** unimportant, petty. [OE]

smallholder *n.* owner or user of smallholding.

smallholding *n.* piece of agricultural land smaller than farm.

smallpox *n.* acute contagious disease with fever and pustules usu. leaving permanent scars.

smarm *v.t. colloq.* smooth, plaster *down* (hair etc.); flatter fulsomely. [dial.]

smarmy *a. colloq.* ingratiating.

smart 1 *a.* clever, ingenious, quick-witted; bright and fresh in appearance, neat, fashionable; stylish, conspicuous in society; quick, brisk; painfully severe, sharp, vigorous. **2** *v.i.* feel or give acute pain or distress; rankle; suffer *for* (one's behaviour etc.). **3** *n.* bodily or mental sharp pain, stinging sensation. **4 look smart** make haste; **smart alec** conceited know-all. [OE]

smarten *v.* make or become smart (usu. with *up*).

smash 1 *v.* break (*up*) into pieces; bring or come to sudden or complete destruction or defeat or disaster; move with great force (*into* or *through* etc.); break *in* with crushing blow; hit (ball etc.) with great force, esp. downwards. **2** *n.* act or sound of smashing; very successful play or song etc. **3** *adv.* with a smash. **4 smash-and-grab** *colloq.* (of robbery) in which thief smashes window and seizes goods; **smash-up** complete smash, violent collision. [imit.]

smasher *n. colloq.* very pleasing or beautiful person or thing.

smashing *a. colloq.* excellent, wonderful, beautiful.

smattering /ˈsmætərɪŋ/ *n.* slight knowledge of something. [orig. unkn.]

smear 1 *v.t.* daub or stain with greasy or sticky substance; smudge; discredit or defame, seek to do this. **2** *n.* action or result of smearing; material smeared on microscope slide etc. for examination, specimen of this; discrediting or defaming, attempt at this. **3 smeary** *a.* [OE]

smell 1 *n.* faculty by which odours or scents are perceived; quality in substances that is perceived by this; unpleasant odour; act of inhaling to ascertain smell. **2** *v.* (*past & p.p.* **smelt** or **smelled**) perceive or detect or examine by smell; emit odour; seem by smell to be (*smells bad*); be redolent *of* (*smells of fish*); stink; have or use sense of smell. **3 smelling-salts** sharp-smelling substances sniffed to relieve faintness etc.; **smell out** seek or discover by smelling or investigation; **smell a rat** see RAT. [OE]

smelly *a.* evil-smelling, stinking; **smelliness** *n.*

smelt[1] *v.t.* extract metal from (ore) by melting; extract (metal) thus. [LG or Du. (MELT)]

smelt[2] *n.* small edible green and silver fish. [OE]

smelt[3] *past & p.p.* of SMELL.

smidgen /ˈsmɪdʒ(ə)n/ *n. colloq.* small bit or amount. [perh. f. synonym *smitch*]

smilax /ˈsmaɪlæks/ *n.* a climbing plant. [L f. Gk]

smile 1 *v.* make or have facial expression of amusement or pleasure or affection, usu. with parting of lips and upward turning of their ends; express by smiling (*smiled a welcome*); give (smile) of specified kind; be propitious, look favourably (*on*). **2** *n.* act of smiling; smiling expression or aspect. **3 smile on** (or **at**) look encouragingly on, (of circumstance etc.) favour. [perh. Scand.]

smirch 1 *v.t.* besmirch, bring discredit to. **2** *n.* blot, stain. [orig. unkn.]

smirk 1 *n.* silly or conceited smile. **2** *v.i.* give smirk. [OE]

smite *v.* (*past* **smote**; *p.p.* **smitten** /ˈsmɪt(ə)n/) *archaic* strike or hit; chastise, defeat; have sudden effect on; seize *with* disease or emotion etc. [OE]

smith *n.* worker in metal (*tinsmith*); blacksmith; one who creates something (*song-smith*). [OE]

smithereens /smɪðəˈriːnz/ *n.pl.* small fragments. [dial. *smithers*]

smithy /ˈsmɪðɪ/ *n.* blacksmith's workshop, forge. [SMITH]

smitten *p.p.* of SMITE.

smock 1 *n.* loose overall; (also **smock--frock**) loose shirtlike garment often ornamented with smocking. **2** *v.t.* decorate with smocking. [OE]

smocking *n.* ornamentation on cloth made by gathering it tightly with stitches.

smog *n.* fog intensified by smoke; **smoggy** *a.* [portmanteau word]

smoke 1 *n.* visible vapour from burning substance; act or period of smoking tobacco; *colloq.* cigarette or cigar. **2** *v.* emit smoke or visible vapour; inhale and exhale smoke of cigarette or cigar or pipe, do this habitually, use (cigarette etc.) thus; darken or preserve by action of smoke. **3 go up in smoke** come to nothing; **smoke-bomb** bomb that emits dense smoke on exploding; **smoke out** drive out by means of smoke, drive out of hiding or secrecy etc.; **smoke-stack** chimney or funnel for discharging smoke of locomotive or steamer. [OE]

smokeless *a.* having or producing no smoke.

smoker *n.* person who smokes tobacco habitually; part of railway coach in which smoking is allowed.

smokescreen *n.* cloud of smoke concealing (esp. military) operations; device or ruse for disguising activities.

smoky *a.* producing or emitting much smoke; covered or filled with smoke; obscured (as) with smoke; suggestive of or having the colour of smoke; **smokily** *adv.*; **smokiness** *n.*

smolder *US* var. of SMOULDER.

smooch /smu:tʃ/ *colloq.* 1 *n.* period of slow dancing close together or of kissing and caressing. 2 *v.i.* engage in smooch. [imit.]

smooth /smu:ð/ 1 *a.* having even surface, free from roughness or projections or lumps or indentations; that can be traversed without hindrance; (of water etc.) free from waves; not harsh or jerky (*smooth breathing, driving*); unaffected by difficulties or adverse conditions (*smooth journey*); (of person or behaviour etc.) equable, polite, conciliatory, flattering. 2 *v.* make or become smooth (often with *down* or *out*); get rid of (impediments etc.; often with *away* or *over*). 3 *adv.* smoothly. 4 *n.* smoothing touch or stroke (*gave her skirt a smooth*). 5 **smooth-tongued** insincerely flattering. [OE]

smorgasbord /'smɔ:gəsbɔ:d/ *n.* Swedish hors-d'œuvres; buffet meal with variety of dishes. [Sw.]

smote *past* of SMITE.

smother /'smʌðə/ 1 *v.* suffocate, stifle; overwhelm *with* gifts or kindness etc.; cover entirely *in* or *with*; extinguish (fire) by heaping with ashes etc.; have difficulty in breathing; (also with *up*) suppress or conceal. 2 *n.* cloud of smoke or dust etc.; obscurity caused by this. [OE]

smoulder /'sməʊldə/ 1 *v.i.* burn slowly without flame or in suppressed way (often *fig.* of discontent etc.). 2 *n.* such burning. [orig. unkn.]

smudge 1 *n.* blurred or smeared mark or blot etc. 2 *v.* make smudge on or of; become smeared or blurred. 3 **smudgy** *a.* [orig. unkn.]

smug *a.* self-satisfied, complacent, consciously respectable. [LG *smuk* pretty]

smuggle /'smʌg(ə)l/ *v.t.* import or export (goods) illegally, esp. without paying customs duties; convey secretly *in* or *out* etc. [LG]

smut 1 *n.* small flake of soot, spot or smudge made by this; obscene talk or pictures or stories; cereal-disease turning parts of plant to black powder. 2 *v.* (**-tt-**) mark or infect with smuts; contract smut disease. 3 **smutty** *a.* [orig. unkn.]

Sn *symb.* tin.

snack *n.* slight or casual or hurried meal; **snack-bar** place where snacks are sold. [Du.]

snaffle /'snæf(ə)l/ 1 *n.* simple bridle-bit without curb. 2 *v.t.* put snaffle on; *sl.* take, steal. [prob. LG or Du.]

snag 1 *n.* unexpected or hidden obstacle or drawback; jagged or projecting point or stump, esp. as possible danger; tear in material caused by snag. 2 *v.t.* (**-gg-**) catch or tear on snag. 3 **snagged** *a.*; **snaggy** *a.* [prob. Scand.]

snail *n.* slow-moving mollusc with spiral shell; **snail's pace** very slow movement. [OE]

snake 1 *n.* long limbless reptile; (also **snake in the grass**) treacherous person, secret enemy. 2 *v.i.* move or twist etc. like snake. 3 **snake-charmer** person appearing to make snakes move to music etc.; **snakes and ladders** game with counters moved along board with sudden advances up 'ladders' or returns down 'snakes' depicted on the board. [OE]

snaky *a.* of or like a snake; sinuous, winding; cunning, treacherous; **snakily** *adv.*

snap 1 *v.* (**-pp-**) break suddenly or with sharp crack; (cause to) emit sudden sharp sound; open or close with snapping sound; say something irritably or spitefully; make sudden audible bite; bite off; move quickly; take snapshot of. 2 *n.* act or sound of snapping; catch that fastens with a snap; crisp brittle cake or biscuit; = SNAPSHOT; (also **cold snap**) sudden brief spell of cold weather; card-game in which players call 'snap' when two similar cards are exposed (also as *int.* at unexpected similarity of two things); vigour, liveliness. 3 *adv.* with snapping sound. 4 *a.* done or taken quickly or unexpectedly (*snap decision*). 5 **snap fastener** = *press-stud* (see PRESS[1]); **snap one's fingers at** defy, regard with contempt; **snap out of** *sl.* throw off (mood etc.) by sudden effort; **snap up** pick up or buy hastily or eagerly. [prob. LG or Du.]

snapdragon *n.* plant with bag-shaped flower like dragon's mouth.

snapper *n.* any of several food-fish.

snappish *a.* inclined to snap; irritable, petulant.

snappy *a. colloq.* brisk, full of zest; neat and elegant; **make it snappy** be quick; **snappily** *adv.*

snapshot *n.* photograph taken informally or casually.

snare 1 *n.* trap, esp. with noose, for catching birds or animals; thing that tempts or exposes one to danger or failure etc.; (often in *pl.*) arrangement of twisted gut or wire etc. stretched across lower head of side-drum to produce rattling sound; (also **snare drum**) drum fitted with snares. **2** *v.t.* catch in snare; ensnare. [ON]

snarl[1] **1** *v.* make angry growl with bared teeth; speak irritably or cynically. **2** *n.* act or sound of snarling. [*snar* f. LG]

snarl[2] **1** *v.* (often with *up*) twist, tangle; confuse and hamper movement of (traffic etc.). **2** *n.* tangle. **3 snarl-up** confusion or jam of traffic etc. [SNARE]

snatch 1 *v.* seize quickly or eagerly or unexpectedly; obtain quickly or with difficulty; carry suddenly *away* or *from* etc. **2** *n.* act of snatching; fragment of song or talk etc.; short spell of activity etc. **3 snatch at** try to seize; take (offer etc.) eagerly. [rel. to SNACK]

snazzy /'snæzɪ/ *a. sl.* smart, stylish, excellent; **snazzily** *adv.*; **snazziness** *n.* [orig. unkn.]

sneak 1 *v.* go or convey furtively; *sl.* steal unobserved; *sl.* tell tales, esp. at school. **2** *n.* cowardly underhand person; *sl.* tell-tale, esp. at school. **3** *a.* acting or done without warning; secret. **4 sneak-thief** petty thief, person who steals from open windows etc. **5 sneaky** *a.* [orig. uncert.]

sneakers *n.pl.* soft-soled shoes.

sneaking *a.* (esp. of feeling or suspicion etc.) unavowed; persistent and puzzling.

sneer 1 *n.* derisive smile or remark. **2** *v.* make a sneer (*at*); utter sneeringly. [perh. LG or Du.]

sneeze 1 *n.* sudden involuntary expulsion of air from nose and mouth caused by irritated nostrils. **2** *v.i.* make sneeze. **3 not to be sneezed at** *colloq.* not contemptible, worth having. [OE]

snick 1 *v.t.* make small notch or incision in; (in cricket) deflect (ball) slightly with bat. **2** *n.* such notch or deflection. [*snickersnee* long knife ult. f. Du.]

snicker *v.i.* & *n.* snigger. [imit.]

snide *a. colloq.* sneering, slyly derogatory; counterfeit; *US* mean, underhand. [orig. unkn.]

sniff 1 *v.* draw up air audibly through nose; smell (scent etc.), smell scent of, by sniffing; take (*up*) into the nose by sniffing. **2** *n.* act or sound of sniffing. **3 sniff at** try the smell of; show contempt for or disapproval of. [imit.]

sniffle /'snɪf(ə)l/ **1** *v.i.* sniff repeatedly or slightly. **2** *n.* act of sniffling; (in *pl.*) cold in the head causing sniffling. [imit.; cf. SNIVEL]

sniffy *a. colloq.* disdainful; **sniffily** *adv.*; **sniffiness** *n.* [SNIFF]

snifter *n. sl.* small drink of alcoholic liquor. [dial. *snift* sniff]

snigger 1 *n.* half-suppressed laugh. **2** *v.i.* utter snigger. [SNICKER]

snip 1 *v.* (**-pp-**) cut with scissors or shears esp. in small quick strokes. **2** *n.* act of snipping; piece snipped off; *sl.* something cheaply acquired or easily done. [LG or Du. (imit.)]

snipe 1 *n.* (*pl.* **snipes** or *collect.* **snipe**) wading bird with long straight bill. **2** *v.i.* fire shots from hiding usu. at long range; make sly critical attack *at*. [prob. Scand.]

snippet /'snɪpɪt/ *n.* small piece cut off; (usu. in *pl.*) scrap or fragment of information or knowledge etc., short extract from book etc. [SNIP]

snitch *v.t. sl.* steal. [orig. unkn.]

snivel /'snɪv(ə)l/ **1** *v.i.* (**-ll-**, *US* **-l-**) weep with sniffling; show maudlin emotion; run at the nose. **2** *n.* act of snivelling; running mucus. [OE]

snob *n.* person who has exaggerated respect for social position or wealth or who despises those he considers to have inferior position or tastes etc.; **snobbery** *n.*; **snobbish** *a.* [orig. unkn.]

snog *sl.* **1** *n.* spell of kissing and caressing. **2** *v.i.* (**-gg-**) engage in this. [orig. unkn.]

snood *n.* loose net worn by woman to keep hair in place. [OE]

snook /snu:k/ *n. colloq.* contemptuous gesture with thumb to nose and fingers spread, esp. in **cock a snook at** make this gesture at, show contempt for. [orig. unkn.]

snooker 1 *n.* game played with 15 red and 6 other coloured balls on billiard-table; position in this game where direct shot would lose points. **2** *v.t.* subject (player) to snooker; *sl.* (esp. in *pass.*) thwart, defeat. [orig. unkn.]

snoop *colloq.* **1** *v.i.* pry into other's private affairs; sneak *about* or *around* looking for infractions of the law or rules. **2** *n.* act of snooping. **3 snoopy** *a.* [Du.]

snoot *n. sl.* nose. [SNOUT]

snooty /'snu:tɪ/ *a. colloq.* supercilious, haughty, snobbish. [orig. unkn.]

snooze 1 *n.* short sleep esp. in daytime. **2** *v.i.* take snooze. [orig. unkn.]

snore 1 *n.* snorting or grunting sound in breathing during sleep. **2** *v.i.* make such sounds. [imit.]

snorkel /'snɔ:k(ə)l/ **1** *n.* device for supplying air to underwater swimmer or submerged submarine. **2** *v.i.* (**-ll-**, *US* **-l-**) swim with snorkel. [G *schnorkel*]

snort 1 *n.* explosive sound made by sudden forcing of breath through nose, esp. expressing indignation or incredulity; similar sound made by engine etc.; *colloq.* small drink of liquor. 2 *v.* make a snort; express or utter with a snort. [imit.]

snorter *n. sl.* something notably vigorous or difficult etc.

snot *n. vulgar* nasal mucus; *sl.* contemptible person. [prob. LG or Du.]

snotty *a. sl.* running or foul with nasal mucus; *sl.* contemptible, bad-tempered, supercilious; **snottily** *adv.*; **snottiness** *n.*

snout *n.* projecting nose (and mouth) of animal; *derog.* human nose; pointed front of thing. [LG or Du.]

snow /snəʊ/ 1 *n.* frozen vapour falling to earth in light white flakes; fall of this, layer of it on ground; thing resembling snow in whiteness or texture etc.; *sl.* cocaine. 2 *v.* fall as or like snow; come in large numbers or quantities. 3 **it snows** (or **is snowing**) snow is falling; **snow-berry** garden shrub with white berries; **snow-blind** temporarily blinded by glare from snow; **snow-bound** prevented by snow from going out or travelling; **snow-capped** (of mountain) covered at top with snow; **snow-drift** bank of snow heaped by wind; **snowed in** (or **up**) snow-bound; **snowed under** covered (as) with snow, overwhelmed with quantity, work, etc.; **snow goose** arctic white goose; **snow-line** level above which snow never melts entirely; **snow-plough** device for clearing road or railway of snow; **snow-shoe** flat device like racket attached to boot for walking on snow without sinking in; **snow-white** pure white. [OE]

snowball 1 *n.* snow pressed together into a ball for throwing in play. 2 *v.* throw or pelt with snowballs; increase rapidly. 3 **snowball-tree** guelder rose.

snowdrop *n.* plant with white drooping flowers blooming in early spring.

snowfall *n.* amount of fallen snow.

snowflake *n.* each of the small collections of crystals in which snow falls.

snowman *n.* figure resembling man, made of compressed snow.

snowmobile /ˈsnəʊməbiːl/ *n.* motor vehicle, esp. with runners or Caterpillar tracks, for travel over snow.

snowstorm *n.* heavy fall of snow, esp. with high wind.

snowy *a.* of or like snow; (of weather etc.) with much snow; **snowy owl** large white owl.

SNP *abbr.* Scottish National Party.

Snr. *abbr.* Senior.

snub 1 *v.t.* (**-bb-**) rebuff or humiliate with sharp words or marked lack of cordiality. 2 *n.* act of snubbing. 3 *a.* (of nose) short and stumpy or turned up. [ON, = chide]

snuff[1] 1 *v.* remove snuff from (candle). 2 *n.* charred part of candle-wick. 3 **snuff it** *sl.* die; **snuff out** extinguish (candle) by covering or pinching flame, kill or put an end to (hopes etc.), *sl.* die. [orig. unkn.]

snuff[2] 1 *n.* powdered tobacco or medicine taken by sniffing it up nostrils; a sniff. 2 *v.* take snuff; sniff. 3 **snuff-box** small box for holding snuff; **snuff-coloured** of dark yellowish-brown. [Du.]

snuffer *n.* device for snuffing or extinguishing candle. [SNUFF[1]]

snuffle /ˈsnʌf(ə)l/ 1 *v.* make sniffing sounds; speak or say nasally or whiningly; breathe noisily (as) through partly blocked nose. 2 *n.* snuffling sound or tone. [prob. LG or Du. (as SNUFF[2])]

snug 1 *a.* cosy, comfortable, sheltered, well-enclosed or placed or arranged; close-fitting; (of income etc.) adequate for comfort. 2 *n.* bar-parlour of inn. [prob. LG or Du.]

snuggery *n.* snug place, esp. person's private room.

snuggle /ˈsnʌg(ə)l/ *v.* settle or draw into warm, comfortable position.

so[1] /səʊ/ *adv.* & *conj.* in this or that way, in the manner or position or state described or implied, to that or to such an extent (*why are you laughing so?*; *did not expect to arrive so soon*); to a great or notable degree (*I am so glad*); (with verbs of saying or thinking etc.) thus, this, that (*I think so*; *so he said*); consequently, therefore (*he'd gone so I couldn't ask him*); indeed, in actual fact (*you said it was good, and so it is*); also (*I was wrong, but so were you*); **and so on** (or **forth**) and others of the same kind, and in other similar ways; **or so** approximately (*50 or so*); **so as to** in order to, in such a way as to; **so be it** expression of acceptance of or resignation to event etc.; **so-called** called or named thus (but perhaps wrongly or inaccurately); **so long** *colloq.* goodbye; **so many** (or **much**) a definite number (or amount), nothing but; **so much for** that is all that need be said or done about; **so-so** *a.* & *adv.* only moderately good or well; **so that** in order that; **so to say** (or **speak**) expression of reserve or apology for exaggeration or neologism etc.; **so what?** that is irrelevant or of no importance. [OE]

so[2] var. of SOH.

-so *suffix* = -SOEVER.

soak 1 *v.* make or become thoroughly

wet through saturation with or in liquid; (of rain etc.) drench; take (liquid) *in* or *up*; absorb (knowledge etc.); drink heavily; *sl.* extort money from. **2** *n.* soaking; *colloq.* hard drinker. **3 soak-away** arrangement for disposal of water by percolation through soil; **soak oneself in** absorb (liquid or *fig.* knowledge etc.); **soak through** (of moisture) penetrate, make thoroughly wet. [OE]

so-and-so /'səʊənsəʊ/ *n.* (*pl.* **so-and-so's**) particular person or thing not needing to be specified; *colloq.* unpleasant or objectionable person. [so¹]

soap 1 *n.* cleansing substance yielding lather when rubbed in water. **2** *v.t.* apply soap to; rub with soap. **3 soap-box** makeshift stand for street orator; **soap-flakes** flakes of soap prepared for washing clothes etc.; **soap opera** sentimental domestic broadcast serial; **soap powder** powder, esp. with additives, for washing clothes etc. [OE]

soapstone *n.* steatite.

soapsuds = SUDS.

soapy *a.* of or like soap; containing or smeared with soap; unctuous, flattering; **soapily** *adv.*; **soapiness** *n.*

soar *v.i.* fly or rise high; reach high level or standard; fly without flapping wings or using engine. [F *essorer* f. L (EX-¹, AURA)]

sob 1 *v.* (**-bb-**) draw breath in convulsive gasps usu. with weeping; utter with sobs. **2** *n.* act or sound of sobbing. **3 sob-story** *colloq.* narrative meant to evoke sympathy; **sob-stuff** *colloq.* pathos, sentimental writing or behaviour. [imit.]

sober 1 *a.* not drunk; not given to drink; moderate, tranquil, serious, sedate; not exaggerated; (of colour etc.) quiet and inconspicuous. **2** *v.* make or become sober (often with *down* or *up*). [F f. L]

sobriety /sə'braɪətɪ/ *n.* being sober. [F or L (prec.)]

sobriquet /'səʊbrɪkeɪ/ *n.* nickname. [F]

Soc. *abbr.* Socialist; Society.

soccer /'sɒkə/ *n. colloq.* Association football. [Assoc.]

sociable /'səʊʃəb(ə)l/ *a.* fitted for or liking the society of other people; (of manner or behaviour etc.) friendly; **sociability** /-'bɪlɪtɪ/ *n.*; **sociably** *adv.* [F or L (*socius* comrade)]

social /'səʊʃ(ə)l/ **1** *a.* of society or its organization, concerned with mutual relations of (classes of) human beings; living in organized communities, unfitted for solitary life; needing companionship, gregarious, interdependent. **2** *n.* social gathering, esp. one organized by club etc. **3 social climber** person seeking to gain higher rank in society; **social contract** agreement to co-operate for social benefits, esp. involving submission to restrictions on individual liberty; **social democrat** advocate of gradual advance towards socialism; **social science** scientific study of human society and social relationships; **social security** State assistance to those lacking adequate means or welfare; **social services** welfare services provided by the State, including education, health, housing, pensions, etc.; **social work** organized work to alleviate social problems; **social worker** person engaged in this. **4 socially** *adv.* [F or L (prec.)]

socialism *n.* political and economic theory of social organization advocating State ownership and control of natural resources and commercial activities; policy or practice based on this theory; **socialist** *n.*; **socialistic** /-'lɪstɪk/ *a.* [F (as prec.)]

socialite /'səʊʃəlaɪt/ *n.* person prominent in fashionable society. [SOCIAL]

socialize /'səʊʃəlaɪz/ *v.* behave sociably; make social; organize in socialistic manner; **socialization** /-'zeɪʃ(ə)n/ *n.*

society /sə'saɪətɪ/ *n.* organized and interdependent community, the system and organization of living in this; the distinguished or fashionable members of a community, the upper classes; mixing with other people, companionship, company; association of persons sharing common aim or interest etc.; **Society of Friends** Christian sect with no written creed or ordained ministers, formerly noted for plain dress and simple living; **Society of Jesus** Jesuits. [F f. L (as prec.)]

socio- *in comb.* of society or sociology (and). [L (as prec.)]

sociology /səʊsɪ'ɒlədʒɪ/ *n.* study of society and social problems; **sociological** /-sɪə'lɒdʒɪk(ə)l/ *a.*; **sociologist** *n.* [F (as prec.)]

sock¹ *n.* short stocking, usu. not reaching the knee; insole; **pull one's socks up** *colloq.* make an effort to improve; **put a sock in it** *sl.* be quiet. [OE f. L *soccus* slipper f. Gk]

sock² *sl.* **1** *v.t.* hit (person) hard. **2** *n.* hard blow. **3 sock it to** attack or address (person) vigorously. [orig. unkn.]

socket /'sɒkɪt/ *n.* natural or artificial hollow for something to fit into or stand firm or revolve in, esp. device receiving plug or light-bulb etc. to make electrical connection. [AF]

Socratic /sə'krætɪk/ *a.* of Socrates or his philosophy; **Socratic irony** pose of ignorance assumed to entice others into refutable statements; **Socratic method** dialectic, procedure by question and answer. [L f. Gk *Sōkratēs* (5th-c. BC), Gk philosopher]

sod[1] *n.* turf, piece of turf; surface of ground; **under the sod** in the grave. [LG or Du.]

sod[2] *vulgar* **1** *n.* unpleasant or despicable person; fellow. **2** *v.* (**-dd-**) damn; (in *partic.*) damned. **3 sod off** go away. [abbr. of SODOMITE]

soda /ˈsəʊdə/ *n.* compound of sodium in common use; (also **soda-water**) water made effervescent with carbon dioxide and used as drink alone or with spirits etc.; **soda-bread** bread leavened with baking-soda; **soda-fountain** device supplying soda-water, shop equipped with this. [perh. L *sodanum* f. Arab.]

sodden /ˈsɒd(ə)n/ *a.* saturated with liquid, soaked through; rendered stupid or dull etc. with drunkenness. [obs. p.p. of SEETHE]

sodium /ˈsəʊdɪəm/ *n.* soft silver-white metallic element; **sodium bicarbonate** white crystalline compound used in baking-powder; **sodium hydroxide** compound of sodium with hydroxyl; **sodium lamp** lamp giving yellow light from electrical discharge in sodium vapour. [SODA]

sodomite /ˈsɒdəmaɪt/ *n.* person practising sodomy. [F f. L f. Gk (as foll.)]

sodomy /ˈsɒdəmɪ/ *n.* abnormal sexual act, esp. between males or between person and animal. [L (*Sodom*; Gen. 18, 19)]

soever /səʊˈevə/ *adv. literary* of any possible kind or extent (*how great soever it may be*). [SO[1], EVER]

-soever *suffix* in sense of SOEVER (*whosoever*, *howsoever*).

sofa /ˈsəʊfə/ *n.* couch with raised ends and back. [F, ult. f. Arab.]

soffit /ˈsɒfɪt/ *n.* under-surface of arch or lintel etc. [F or It. (SUFFIX)]

soft 1 *a.* not hard, yielding to pressure; malleable, plastic, easily cut; (of cloth etc.) smooth or fine in texture, not rough; (of air etc.) mild, balmy; (of water) free from mineral salts and hence good for washing etc.; (of light or colour etc.) not brilliant or glaring; (of sound) not loud or strident; (of consonant) sibilant (as *c* in *ice*, *g* in *age*); (of outline etc.) not sharply defined; (of action or manner etc.) gentle, conciliatory, complimentary, amorous; (of heart or feelings etc.) compassionate, sympathetic; (of character etc.) feeble, effeminate, silly, sentimental; *sl.* (of job etc.) easy; (of drug) not likely to cause addiction; (of currency, prices, etc.) likely to depreciate; (of pornography) not highly obscene. **2** *adv.* softly. **3 be soft on** *colloq.* be lenient towards, be infatuated with; **soft-boiled** (of egg) boiled with yolk still soft; **soft drink** non-alcoholic drink; **soft furnishings** curtains and rugs etc.; **soft-hearted** tender, compassionate; **soft option** the easier alternative; **soft palate** back part of palate; **soft pedal** pedal on piano, making tone softer; **soft-pedal** *v.* refrain from emphasizing; **soft roe** see ROE[1]; **soft sell** restrained salesmanship; **soft-soap** *v. colloq.* persuade (person) with flattery; **soft-spoken** speaking with soft voice; **soft spot** sentimental affection *for*; **soft touch** *sl.* person readily parting with money when asked. [OE]

soften /ˈsɒf(ə)n/ *v.* make or become soft or softer; **soften up** make weaker by preliminary attack, make more persuasible by preliminary approaches etc.

softie *n. colloq.* weak or silly person.

software *n.* programs etc. for computer.

softwood *n.* wood of coniferous tree.

softy var. of SOFTIE.

soggy /ˈsɒgɪ/ *a.* sodden, saturated; **soggily** *adv.*; **sogginess** *n.* [dial. *sog* marsh]

soh /səʊ/ *n. Mus.* fifth note of major scale. [L *solve*, word arbitrarily taken]

soigné /swɑːˈnjeɪ/ *a.* (*fem.* ***soignée***) carefully finished or arranged, well-groomed. [F]

soil[1] *n.* upper layer of earth in which plants grow; ground belonging to nation, territory (*on British soil*). [AF f. L *solium* seat, *solum* ground]

soil[2] **1** *v.* make or become dirty, smear or stain with dirt; defile, bring discredit to. **2** *n.* dirty mark; filth, refuse matter. **3 soil-pipe** discharge-pipe of water-closet. [F *soill(i)er* ult. f. L *sus* pig]

soirée /ˈswɑːreɪ/ *n.* evening party esp. for conversation or music. [F]

sojourn /ˈsɒdʒɜːn/ **1** *n.* temporary stay. **2** *v.i.* make sojourn. [F f. Rmc (L SUB-, *diurnum* day)]

sol *n.* liquid solution or suspension of colloid. [SOL(UTION)]

sola /ˈsəʊlə/ *n.* pithy-stemmed E. Indian swamp plant; **sola topi** sun-helmet made from its pith. [Urdu]

solace /ˈsɒləs/ **1** *n.* comfort in distress or disappointment or tedium. **2** *v.t.* give solace to. [F f. L *solatium* (*solor* console)]

solan /ˈsəʊlən/ *n.* large gooselike gannet. [ON]

solar /ˈsəʊlə/ *a.* of or reckoned by the sun; **solar battery** (or **cell**) device converting solar radiation into electricity; **solar day** interval between meridian transits of sun; **solar plexus** complex of radiating nerves at pit of stomach; **solar system** the sun and the heavenly bodies whose motion is governed by it; **solar year** see YEAR. [L (*sol* sun)]

solarium /sə'leərɪəm/ *n.* (*pl.* **solaria**) place for enjoyment or medical use of sunshine. [L (SOLAR)]

sold *past* & *p.p.* of SELL.

solder /'səʊldə, 'sɒ-/ **1** *n.* fusible alloy used to join less fusible metals or wires etc. **2** *v.t.* join with solder. **3 soldering-iron** tool to melt and apply solder. [F f. L (SOLID)]

soldier /'səʊldʒə/ **1** *n.* member of army; (also **common soldier**) private or NCO in army; military commander of specified ability (*a great soldier*). **2** *v.i.* serve as soldier. **3 soldier of fortune** adventurous person ready to serve any State or person, mercenary; **soldier on** *colloq.* persevere doggedly. **4 soldierly** *a.* [F f. *sou(l)de* (soldier's) pay f. L (SOLID)]

soldiery *n.* soldiers esp. of a specified character.

sole[1] **1** *n.* under-surface of foot; part of shoe or sock etc. below foot, esp. part other than heel; lower surface or base of plough, golf-club head, etc. **2** *v.t.* provide (shoe etc.) with sole. [OE f. L *solea* sandal]

sole[2] *n.* flat-fish used as food. [F f. Rmc f. L (as prec., from its shape)]

sole[3] *a.* one and only, single, exclusive. [F f. L *solus*]

solecism /'sɒlɪsɪz(ə)m/ *n.* offence against grammar or idiom or etiquette; **solecistic** /-'sɪstɪk/ *a.* [F or L f. Gk]

solemn /'sɒləm/ *a.* serious and dignified (*a solemn occasion*); formal, accompanied by ceremony; mysteriously impressive; (of person) serious or cheerless in manner; **solemnness** *n.* [F f. L *solemnis*]

solemnity /sə'lemnɪtɪ/ *n.* being solemn; solemn rite. [F f. L (prec.)]

solemnize /'sɒləmnaɪz/ *v.t.* duly perform (ceremony esp. of marriage); make solemn; **solemnization** /-'zeɪʃ(ə)n/ *n.* [F f. med.L (SOLEMN)]

solenoid /'səʊlənɔɪd/ *n.* cylindrical coil of wire acting as magnet when carrying electric current. [F f. Gk *sōlēn* tube]

sol-fa /sɒl'fɑ:/ *n.* system of syllables representing musical notes. [*sol* var. of SOH, FA]

soli see SOLO.

solicit /sə'lɪsɪt/ *v.* ask repeatedly or earnestly for or seek or invite (business etc.); accost (person) and offer one's services as prostitute; **solicitation** /-'teɪʃ(ə)n/ *n.* [F f. L (*sollicitus* anxious)]

solicitor *n.* member of legal profession competent to advise clients and instruct barristers but not appearing as advocate except in certain lower courts; **Solicitor-General** law officer below Attorney-General or Lord Advocate. [F (prec.)]

solicitous *a.* anxious or concerned; eager *to do* thing, desirous *of*. [L (SOLICIT)]

solicitude *n.* being solicitous. [F f. L (prec.)]

solid /'sɒlɪd/ **1** *a.* firm and stable in shape, not liquid or fluid; of such material throughout, not hollow; of the same substance throughout (*solid silver*); of strong material or construction or build, not flimsy or slender etc.; having three dimensions; concerned with solids (*solid geometry*); sound and reliable (*solid arguments*); sound but without special flair etc. (*solid piece of work*); financially sound; (of time) uninterrupted (*worked for six solid hours*); unanimous, undivided; (of printing) without spaces between lines etc.). **2** *n.* solid substance or body; (in *pl.*) solid food. **3 solid-state** *a.* using electronic properties of solids (e.g. semiconductor) to replace those of valves. [F, or L *solidus*]

solidarity /sɒlɪ'dærɪtɪ/ *n.* unity or agreement of feeling or action, esp. among individuals with a common interest; mutual dependence. [F (prec.)]

solidify /sə'lɪdɪfaɪ/ *v.* make or become solid; **solidification** /-fɪ'keɪʃ(ə)n/ *n.* [SOLID]

solidity /sə'lɪdɪtɪ/ *n.* state of being solid, firmness.

solidus /'sɒlɪdəs/ *n.* (*pl.* **solidi** /-aɪ/) oblique stroke (/). [L (SOLID)]

soliloquize *v.i.* utter a soliloquy. [foll.]

soliloquy /sə'lɪləkwɪ/ *n.* talking without or regardless of hearers, esp. in a play; period of this. [L (as SOLIPSISM, *loquor* speak)]

solipsism /'sɒlɪpsɪz(ə)m/ *n.* view that the self is all that exists or can be known; **solipsist** *n.* [L *solus* alone, *ipse* self]

solitaire /sɒlɪ'teə/ *n.* jewel set by itself, ear-ring etc. with this; game played on special board by one person who removes objects one at a time after jumping others over them; *US* card-game for one person. [F f. L (foll.)]

solitary /'sɒlɪtərɪ/ **1** *a.* living alone, not gregarious, without companions, lonely; secluded, unfrequented; single, sole. **2** *n.* recluse; *sl.* solitary confinement. **3 solitary confinement** isolation in separate cell. **4 solitarily** *adv.*; **solitariness** *n.* [L *solitarius* (*solus* alone)]

solitude /'sɒlɪtju:d/ *n.* being solitary; solitary place. [F, or L *solitudo* (as prec.)]

solo /'səʊləʊ/ **1** *n.* (*pl.* **solos**) piece or passage of music performed by one person with or without subordinate accompaniment (*pl.* also **soli** /-i:/); performance by one person, esp. unaccompanied flight by pilot in aircraft; (in full **solo whist**) card-game like whist in which one player may oppose the others. **2** *a.* & *adv.* performed as solo, unaccompanied, alone. [It. f. L (SOLE[3])]

soloist /'səʊləʊɪst/ *n.* performer of solo, esp. in music.

Solomon /'sɒləmən/ *n.* very wise person; **Solomon's seal** flowering plant esp. with drooping green and white flowers. [*Solomon*, king of Israel]

solstice /'sɒlstɪs/ *n.* either time when sun is furthest from equator; **summer solstice** about 21 June; **winter solstice** about 22 Dec. [F f. L (*sol* sun, *stit-* stand)]

soluble /'sɒljʊb(ə)l/ *a.* that can be dissolved (esp. in water) or solved; **solubility** /-'bɪlɪtɪ/ *n.*; **solubly** *adv.* [as foll.]

solute /'sɒlju:t/ *n.* dissolved substance. [L (SOLVE)]

solution /sə'lu:ʃ(ə)n, -'lju:-/ *n.* solving or means of solving a problem or difficulty; conversion of solid or gas into liquid by mixture with liquid; state resulting from this; dissolving or being dissolved. [F f. L (foll.)]

solve *v.t.* find action or course that removes or effectively deals with (problem or difficulty). [L *solvo solut-* release]

solvent 1 *a.* able to dissolve or form a solution with something; having enough money to meet one's liabilities. **2** *n.* solvent liquid etc. **3 solvency** *n.*

somatic /sə'mætɪk/ *a.* of the body, not of the mind; **somatically** *adv.* [Gk (*sōma -mat-* body)]

sombre /'sɒmbə/, *US* **somber** *a.* dark, gloomy, dismal. [F f. Rmc (SUB-, UMBRA)]

sombrero /sɒm'breərəʊ/ *n.* (*pl.* **sombreros**) broad-brimmed hat worn esp. in Latin American countries. [Sp. (prec.)]

some /səm, *emphat.* sʌm/ **1** *a.* an unspecified amount or number of (*some apples, bread; some of them*); that is unknown or unnamed (*some day; some fool has locked the door*); approximately (*waited some 20 minutes*); a considerable amount or number of (*went to some trouble; travelled some miles*); at least a small amount of (*do have some consideration*); such to a certain extent (*that is some help*); *sl.* notably such (*I call that some opera*). **2** *pron.* some people or things, some number or amount. **3** *adv. colloq.* to some extent (*do it some more*). [OE]

-some *suffix* forming (1) adjectives in senses 'adapted to, productive of' (*cuddlesome, fearsome*), 'characterized by being' (*fulsome*), 'apt to' (*tiresome, meddlesome*); (2) nouns from numerals in sense 'group of' (*foursome*). [OE]

somebody *n.* & *pron.* some person; person of importance. [SOME]

somehow *adv.* in some unspecified or unknown way; for some reason or other.

someone *n.* & *pron.* somebody.

someplace *adv. US* somewhere.

somersault /'sʌməsɒlt/ **1** *n.* leap or roll in which the head is turned over the heels. **2** *v.i.* perform somersault. [F (*sobre* above, *saut* jump)]

something *n.* & *pron.* some unspecified or unknown thing (*something has happened*); a known or understood but unexpressed quantity or quality or extent (*there is something about it I do not like; is something of a fool*); important or notable person or thing; **see something of** meet (person) occasionally or for short time. [OE (SOME, THING)]

sometime 1 *adv.* at some time; formerly. **2** *a.* former. [SOME]

sometimes *adv.* at some times.

somewhat *adv.* to some extent.

somewhere *adv.* in or to some place.

somnambulism /sɒm'næmbjʊlɪz(ə)m/ *n.* sleep-walking; **somnambulant** *a.*; **somnambulist** *n.* [L *somnus* sleep, *ambulo* walk]

somnolent /'sɒmnələnt/ *a.* sleepy, drowsy; inducing drowsiness; **somnolence** *n.* [F or L (prec.)]

son /sʌn/ *n.* male child in relation to his parent(s); male descendant, male member *of* family etc.; person who is regarded as inheriting an occupation or quality etc. (*sons of freedom*); form of address esp. to boy; **son-in-law** daughter's husband; **the Son of God** (or **of Man**) Christ. [OE]

sonar /'səʊnɑ:/ *n.* system of detecting objects under water by reflected or emitted sound; apparatus for this. [*so*und *na*vigation (and) *r*anging]

sonata /sə'nɑ:tə/ *n. Mus.* composition for one or two instruments, normally with three or four movements. [It., = sounded]

son et lumière /sɒn eɪ lu:'mjeə/ *n.* entertainment by night at historic building etc. with recorded sound and lighting effects to give dramatic narrative of its history. [F, = sound and light]

song *n.* singing, vocal music; piece of music for singing, short poem etc. set to music or meant to be sung; musical composition suggestive of a song; **for a song** very cheaply; **song and dance** rigmarole, commotion; **song thrush** common thrush noted for singing. [OE (SING)]

songbird *n.* bird with melodious cry.

songster *n.* singer; songbird; **songstress** *n.fem.*

sonic /'sɒnɪk/ *a.* of or involving sound or sound-waves; **sonic bang** (or **boom**) noise made when aircraft passes speed of sound; **sonic barrier** = *sound barrier* (see SOUND[1]). [L *sonus* sound]

sonnet /'sɒnɪt/ *n.* poem of 14 lines, in English usu. having 10 syllables per line. [F, or It. *sonetto* (SOUND[1])]

sonny /'sʌnɪ/ *n. colloq.* familiar form of address to young boy. [SON]

sonorous /'sɒnərəs, sə'nɔ:rəs/ *a.* having a loud or full or deep sound; (of speech etc.) imposing; **sonority** /sə'nɒrɪtɪ/ *n.* [L]

soon *adv.* after no long interval of time (*shall soon know the result*); relatively early (*must you go so soon?*); (after *as* or in compar.) readily or willingly (*I would just as soon, I would sooner, stay at home*); **as** (or **so**) **soon as** at the moment that, not later than, as early as (*I came as soon as I heard the news; did not arrive as* or *so soon as I expected*); **sooner or later** at some future time, eventually. [OE]

soot /sʊt/ **1** *n.* black powdery substance rising in smoke and deposited by it on surfaces. **2** *v.t.* cover with soot. [OE]

sooth *n. archaic* truth. [OE]

soothe /su:ð/ *v.t.* calm (person or feelings etc.); soften or mitigate (pain etc.). [OE]

soothsayer /'su:θseɪə/ *n.* one who foretells the future, diviner. [SOOTH]

sooty *a.* covered with soot; black or brownish-black. [SOOT]

sop **1** *n.* piece of bread etc. soaked in gravy etc.; thing given or done to pacify or bribe; milksop. **2** *v.* (-**pp**-) soak (*up*). [OE]

sophism /'sɒfɪz(ə)m/ *n.* false argument, esp. one intended to deceive. [F f. L f. Gk (*sophos* wise)]

sophist /'sɒfɪst/ *n.* captious or fallacious reasoner, quibbler; **sophistic** /-'fɪstɪk/ *a.* [L f. Gk (prec.)]

sophisticate **1** /sə'fɪstɪkeɪt/ *v.t.* (esp. in *p.p.*) make (person etc.) worldly-wise, cultured, or refined; make (equipment or techniques etc.) highly developed or complex. **2** /sə'fɪstɪkət/ *a.* sophisticated. **3** /sə'fɪstɪkət/ *n.* sophisticated person. **4** **sophistication** /səfɪstɪ'keɪʃ(ə)n/ *n.* [med.L (prec.)]

sophistry /'sɒfɪstrɪ/ *n.* use of sophisms, a sophism. [SOPHIST]

sophomore /'sɒfəmɔ:/ *n. US* second-year university or high-school student. [*sophom* obs. var. of SOPHISM]

soporific /sɒpə'rɪfɪk/ **1** *a.* tending to produce sleep. **2** *n.* soporific drug or influence. **3** **soporifically** *adv.* [L *sopor* sleep]

sopping *a.* drenched (*clothes are sopping, sopping wet*). [SOP]

soppy *a.* soaked with water; *colloq.* mawkishly sentimental, silly; **soppily** *adv.*; **soppiness** *n.*

soprano /sə'prɑ:nəʊ/ *n.* (*pl.* **sopranos**) female or boy singer of highest range; range sung by these; instrument of high or highest pitch in its family. [It. (*sopra* above)]

sorbet /'sɔ:bət/ *n.* water-ice; sherbet. [F f. It. f. Turk. f. Arab.]

sorcerer /'sɔ:sərə/ *n.* magician, wizard; **sorceress** *n. fem.*; **sorcery** *n.* [F *sourcier* (SORT)]

sordid /'sɔ:dɪd/ *a.* dirty, squalid; ignoble, mean, mercenary. [F, or L *sordidus*]

sore **1** *a.* (of part of the body) painful from injury or disease; (of person) suffering pain, aggrieved or vexed (*at*); (of subject etc.) causing distress or annoyance; *archaic* grievous or severe (*in sore need*). **2** *n.* sore place on the body; source of distress or annoyance. **3** *adv. archaic* grievously, severely. [OE]

sorely *adv.* very much (*sorely tempted*); severely (*sorely vexed*).

sorghum /'sɔ:gəm/ *n.* tropical cereal grass. [It. *sorgo*]

sorority /sə'rɒrɪtɪ/ *n.* devotional sisterhood; *US* women's society in university or college. [L (*soror* sister)]

sorrel[1] /'sɒr(ə)l/ *n.* sour-leaved herb. [F f. Gmc (SOUR)]

sorrel[2] /'sɒr(ə)l/ **1** *a.* of light reddish-brown colour. **2** *n.* this colour; sorrel animal, esp. horse. [F]

sorrow /'sɒrəʊ/ **1** *n.* mental distress caused by loss or disappointment etc.; thing causing sorrow. **2** *v.i.* feel sorrow, mourn. [OE]

sorrowful *a.* feeling or causing sorrow; **sorrowfully** *adv.*

sorry /'sɒrɪ/ *a.* **1** *predic.* pained or regretful or penitent (*about* or *for* or *that*); feeling pity or sympathy or mild contempt (*for* person); as expression of apology. **2** *attrib.* wretched, paltry. **3** **sorry for oneself** *colloq.* dejected. [OE (SORE)]

sort **1** *n.* group of things etc. with common attributes, kind, variety; *colloq.* person of specified sort (*a good sort*). **2** *v.t.* arrange according to sort. **3** **of a sort** (or **of sorts**) not fully deserving the name (*a holiday of sorts*); **out of sorts** slightly unwell, in low spirits; **sort of** *colloq.* as it were, to some extent; **sort out** separate into sorts, select (things of one or more sorts) from miscellaneous group, disentangle, put into order, solve, *sl.* deal with or punish. [F f. L *sors sort-* lot]

sortie /'sɔ:tɪ/ *n.* sally, esp. from besieged garrison; operational flight by military aircraft. [F]

SOS /esəʊ'es/ *n.* (*pl.* **SOSs**) international code-signal of extreme distress; urgent appeal for help etc. [letters easily recognized in Morse]

sostenuto /sɒstəˈnuːtəʊ/ *Mus.* **1** *adv.* in sustained or prolonged manner. **2** *n.* (*pl.* **sostenutos**) passage to be played in this way. [It.]

sot *n.* habitual drunkard; **sottish** *a.* [OE & F f. L]

sotto voce /ˈsɒtəʊ ˈvəʊtʃɪ/ in an undertone. [It.]

sou /suː/ *n.* former French coin of low value; *colloq.* very small amount of money; **not a sou** no money at all. [F f. L (SOLID)]

soubrette /suːˈbret/ *n.* pert maidservant etc. in comedy; actress taking this part. [F]

soubriquet var. of SOBRIQUET.

soufflé /ˈsuːfleɪ/ *n.* light spongy dish usu. made with stiffly beaten egg-whites. [F, = blown]

sough /sʌf, saʊ/ **1** *n.* moaning or whispering sound as of wind in trees. **2** *v.i.* make this sound. [OE]

sought *past* & *p.p.* of SEEK.

souk /suːk/ *n.* market-place in Muslim countries. [Arab.]

soul /səʊl/ *n.* spiritual or immaterial part of man, often regarded as immortal; moral or emotional or intellectual nature of person or animal; personification or pattern (*she is the soul of discretion*); an individual (*not a soul in sight*); person regarded with familiarity or pity etc. (*a good soul; poor soul*); person regarded as animating or essential part (*life and soul*); emotional or intellectual energy or intensity, esp. as revealed in work of art; Black American culture or music etc.; **All Souls' Day** 2 Nov.; **soul-destroying** deadeningly monotonous etc.; **soul food** traditional food of American Blacks; **soul mate** person ideally suited to another; **soul music** a kind of jazz played in strong emotional style; **soul-searching** examining one's own emotions or motives; **upon my soul** exclamation of surprise. [OE]

soulful *a.* having or expressing or evoking deep feeling; **soulfully** *adv.*

soulless *a.* lacking sensitivity or noble qualities; undistinguished, uninteresting.

sound[1] **1** *n.* sensation caused in the ear due to vibration of surrounding air or other medium; vibrations causing this sensation; what is or may be heard; idea or impression conveyed by words (*don't like the sound of it*); mere words. **2** *v.* (cause to) emit sound; utter, pronounce; convey an impression when heard (*you sound worried*); give audible signal for (alarm etc.); test (lungs etc.) by noting sound produced. **3** **sound barrier** high resistance of air to objects moving at speeds near that of sound; **sound effects** sounds other than speech or music produced artificially for film or broadcast etc.; **sounding-board** canopy projecting sound towards an audience, means of disseminating opinions etc.; **sound off** *colloq.* talk loudly, express one's opinions forcefully; **sound wave** wave of condensation and rarefaction, by which sound is transmitted in air etc. [F f. L *sonus*]

sound[2] **1** *a.* healthy, not diseased or injured or rotten; (of opinion or policy etc.) correct, orthodox, well-founded; financially secure; undisturbed (*sound sleep*); thorough (*sound thrashing*). **2** *adv.* soundly (*sound asleep*). [OE]

sound[3] *v.t.* test depth or quality of bottom of (sea or river etc.); (also with *out*) inquire (esp. cautiously or discreetly) into opinions or feelings of (person). [F f. L (SUB-, *unda* wave)]

sound[4] *n.* strait (of water). [OE, = swimming]

sounding *n.* measurement of depth of water; (in *pl.*) region near enough to shore to allow sounding. [SOUND[3]]

soundproof **1** *a.* impervious to sound. **2** *v.t.* make soundproof. [SOUND[1]]

soundtrack *n.* strip on cinema film or videotape for recording sound; the sound itself.

soup /suːp/ **1** *n.* liquid food made by stewing bones, vegetables, etc. **2** *v.t.* (usu. with *up*) *colloq.* increase power of (engine etc.), enliven. **3** **in the soup** *sl.* in difficulties or trouble; **soup-kitchen** establishment supplying free soup etc. to the poor or in times of distress; **soup-plate** large deep plate. **4** **soupy** *a.* [F]

soupçon /ˈsuːpsɔ̃/ *n.* very small quantity, trace or tinge. [F (SUSPICION)]

sour **1** *a.* having acid taste or smell (as from unripeness or fermentation; (of person or temper) peevish or morose; (of earth) dank; (of thing) unpleasant. **2** *v.* make or become sour. **3** **go** (or **turn**) **sour** turn out badly, lose one's keenness (*on*); **sour grapes** said when a person disparages what he desires but cannot attain. [OE]

source /sɔːs/ *n.* place from which thing comes or is got; person or book etc. providing information; place from which river or stream issues; **at source** at point of origin or issue. [F (SURGE)]

sourpuss *n. sl.* bad-tempered person. [SOUR]

souse /saʊs/ **1** *v.* immerse in pickle or other liquid; soak (thing *in* liquid); (in *p.p.*) *sl.* drunk. **2** *n.* pickle made with salt; *US* food in pickle; plunge or soaking in water. [F f. Gmc (SALT)]

soutane /su:'tɑ:n/ *n.* cassock of Roman Catholic priest. [F f. It. (*sotto* under)]
south 1 *n.* point of horizon at 90 clockwise from east; compass point corresponding to this; direction in which this lies; (usu. **South**) part of country or town lying to the south. **2** *a.* towards, at, near, or facing south; coming from the south (*south wind*). **3** *adv.* towards, at, or near the south. **4 South African** of Republic of South Africa, native or inhabitant of this; **south of** further south than; **South Pole** southern end of earth's axis of rotation; **South Sea** southern Pacific Ocean; **to the south (of)** in a southward direction (from). [OE]
south-east 1 *n.* point midway between south and east; direction in which this lies; (**South-East**) part of country or town lying to the south-east. **2** *a.* of, towards, or coming from the south-east. **3** *adv.* towards, at, or near the south-east. **4 south-south-east** direction midway between south and south-east. **5 south-easterly** *a.* & *adv.*; **south-eastern** *a.*
southeaster *n.* south-east wind.
southerly /'sʌðəlɪ/ *a.* & *adv.* in southern position or direction; (of wind) blowing from the south.
southern /'sʌð(ə)n/ *a.* of or in the south; **Southern Cross** constellation in S. hemisphere with stars forming cross; **southern lights** = AURORA AUSTRALIS.
southerner *n.* native or inhabitant of the south.
southpaw *colloq.* **1** *a.* left-handed. **2** *n.* left-handed person, esp. boxer.
southward /'saʊθwəd/ **1** *a.* & (also **southwards**) *adv.* towards the south. **2** *n.* southward direction or region. [-WARD]
south-west 1 *n.* point midway between south and west; direction in which this lies; (**South-West**) part of country or town lying to the south-west. **2** *a.* of, towards, or coming from the south-west. **3** *adv.* towards, at, or near the south-west. **4 south-south-west** direction midway between south and south-west. **5 south-westerly** *a.* & *adv.*; **south-western** *a.*
southwester *n.* south-west wind.
souvenir /su:və'nɪə/ *n.* thing kept as reminder of place or person or event. [F]
sou'wester /saʊ'westə/ *n.* waterproof hat with broad flap at back; south-west wind. [SOUTHWESTER]
sovereign /'sɒvrɪn/ **1** *n.* supreme ruler, esp. monarch; British gold coin (now rarely used) worth nominally £1. **2** *a.* supreme, possessing supreme power; independent (*sovereign States*); royal; very good or effective (*a sovereign remedy*); unmitigated (*sovereign contempt*). **3 sovereignty** *n.* [F *soverain* (SUPER-)]
soviet /'səʊvɪət, 'sɒv-/ **1** *n.* council elected in district of USSR. **2** *a.* (**Soviet**) of the Soviet Union. **3 Soviet Union** USSR. [Russ.]
sow[1] /səʊ/ *v.t.* (*past* **sowed**; *p.p.* **sown** or **sowed**) put (seed) on or in the earth for purpose of growth; plant (land *with* seed); initiate or arouse (*sow hatred*). [OE]
sow[2] /saʊ/ *n.* adult female pig. [OE]
soy *n.* sauce made from pickled soya beans; (also **soy bean**) soya bean. [Jap.]
soya /'sɔɪə/ *n.* leguminous plant yielding edible flour and oil; **soya bean** seed of this plant. [Du. f. Malay (as prec.)]
sozzled /'sɒz(ə)ld/ *a. sl.* very drunk. [dial. *sozzle* slop together, imit.]
spa /spɑ:/ *n.* curative mineral spring; place with this. [*Spa* in Belgium]
space 1 *n.* continuous expanse in which things exist and move; amount of this taken by a particular thing or available for particular purpose; interval between points or objects; interval of time (*within a space of 10 minutes*); expanse of paper used in writing or printing etc.; = *outer space*; large area (*open spaces*); blank between printed, typed, or written words etc.; (in printing) piece of metal separating words etc. **2** *attrib.* of or used for travel etc. in outer space (*space flight, rocket, travel*). **3** *v.t.* set or arrange at intervals; put spaces between; spread *out* with more or wider spaces between. **4 space age** era of space travel; **space shuttle** spacecraft for repeated use e.g. between earth and space station; **space station** artificial satellite as base for operations in outer space; **space-time** fusion of concepts of space and time as four-dimensional continuum. [F *espace* f. L *spatium*]
spacecraft *n.* vehicle for travelling in outer space.
spaceman *n.* space traveller.
spaceship *n.* spacecraft.
spacesuit *n.* sealed pressurized suit allowing wearer to survive in outer space.
spacious /'speɪʃəs/ *a.* having ample space, roomy. [F or L (SPACE)]
spade[1] *n.* digging-tool with sharp-edged broad usu. metal blade; similar tool for various purposes; **call a spade a spade** speak plainly or bluntly; **spadeful** *n.* [OE]
spade[2] *n.* playing-card of suit (**spades**) denoted by black figures shaped like inverted heart with short stem. [It. *spade* pl. f. L f. Gk, = sword]
spadework *n. fig.* hard preparatory work. [SPADE[1]]

spaghetti /spəˈgetɪ/ *n.* pasta in long thin sticks. [It.]
Spam *n.* (**P**) tinned meat made from ham. [*sp*iced h*am*]
span[1] **1** *n.* full extent from end to end; maximum lateral extent of aeroplane or its wing; each part of bridge between supports; maximum distance between tips of thumb and little finger, esp. as measure = 9 in. **2** *v.t.* (**-nn-**) extend from side to side or end to end of; bridge (river etc.). [OE]
span[2] see SPICK.
spandrel /ˈspændr(ə)l/ *n.* space between curve of arch and the surrounding rectangular moulding or framework, or between curves of adjoining arches and moulding above. [orig. uncert.]
spangle /ˈspæŋg(ə)l/ **1** *n.* small piece of glittering material, esp. one of many as ornament of dress etc. **2** *v.t.* cover (as) with spangles (esp. in *p.p.*). [obs. *spang* f. Du.]
Spaniard /ˈspænjəd/ *n.* native of Spain. [F (*Espaigne* Spain)]
spaniel /ˈspænj(ə)l/ *n.* dog of breed with long silky coat and drooping ears. [F f. Rmc (*Hispania* Spain)]
Spanish /ˈspænɪʃ/ **1** *a.* of Spain or its people or language. **2** *n.* the Spanish language. **3 the Spanish** *pl.* the people of Spain; **Spanish fly** dried insect used in medicine etc.; **Spanish Main** *hist.* NE coast of S. America and adjoining part of Caribbean Sea. [*Spain* in Europe]
spank 1 *v.* slap on buttocks; (of horse etc.) move briskly. **2** *n.* slap given in spanking. [imit.]
spanker *n. Naut.* fore-and-aft sail on after side of mizen-mast.
spanking 1 *n.* process of spanking or being spanked. **2** *a. colloq.* striking, excellent; brisk. **3** *adv. colloq.* strikingly, excellently.
spanner *n.* tool for turning nut on bolt etc.; **spanner in the works** upsetting element or influence. [G]
spar[1] *n.* stout pole as used for ship's mast etc.; main longitudinal beam of aeroplane wing. [ON *sperra* or F *esparre*]
spar[2] **1** *v.i.* (**-rr-**) make motions of attack and defence with closed fists, use the hands (as) in boxing; engage in argument etc. **2** *n.* sparring motion; boxing-match; **sparring-partner** boxer employed to practise with another in training, person with whom one enjoys arguing. [OE]
spar[3] *n.* easily split crystalline mineral. [LG]
spare 1 *v.* refrain from hurting or destroying or using or bringing into operation; dispense with, afford to give, do without; let (person) have (thing etc. esp. that one does not need); abstain from inflicting (*spare me this task*); be frugal or grudging (with). **2** *a.* superfluous, not required for normal or immediate use; reserved for emergency or occasional use; (of person etc.) lean, thin; frugal. **3** *n.* spare part. **4 go spare** *sl.* become very angry; **not spare oneself** exert one's utmost efforts; **spare part** duplicate to replace lost or damaged part; **spare-rib** closely-trimmed rib of meat, esp. pork; **spare time** leisure; **spare tyre** *colloq.* circle of fatness round or above waist. [OE]
sparing *a.* frugal; grudging; restrained.
spark 1 *n.* fiery particle thrown from burning substance, or still visibly alight in ashes, or struck by impact of flint etc.; flash of light between electric conductors etc.; such discharge serving to fire explosive mixture in internal-combustion engine; flash of wit etc.; minute amount *of* a quality etc. (*not a spark of life*); lively person. **2** *v.* emit spark(s); (also with *off*) stir into activity, initiate. **3 spark-** (or **sparking-)plug** device for making spark in internal-combustion engine. [OE]
sparkle /ˈspɑːk(ə)l/ **1** *v.i.* emit or seem to emit sparks; glitter, glisten; scintillate; (of wine) effervesce. **2** *n.* sparkling, glitter.
sparkler *n.* sparkling usu. hand-held firework; *sl.* diamond.
sparrow /ˈspærəʊ/ *n.* small brownish-grey bird; **sparrow-hawk** a small hawk. [OE]
sparse *a.* thinly scattered, infrequent; **sparsity** *n.* [L *spargo spars-* scatter]
Spartan /ˈspɑːt(ə)n/ **1** *a.* of Sparta in ancient Greece; austere, rigorous. **2** *n.* native of Sparta; austere or rigorous person. [L]
spasm /ˈspæz(ə)m/ *n.* sudden involuntary muscular contraction; sudden convulsive movement or emotion etc.; brief spell *of*. [F, or L f. Gk (*spaō* pull)]
spasmodic /spæzˈmɒdɪk/ *a.* of or occurring in spasms, intermittent; **spasmodically** *adv.* [Gk (prec.)]
spastic /ˈspæstɪk/ **1** *a.* suffering from cerebral palsy with spasm of muscles. **2** *n.* spastic person. **3 spastically** *adv.* [L f. Gk (SPASM)]
spat[1] *n.* (usu. in *pl.*) short gaiter covering the instep and reaching a little above the ankle. [abbr. of *spatterdash* (SPATTER)]
spat[2] *n.* spawn of shellfish, esp. of oyster. [AF]
spat[3] *n. US colloq.* petty or brief quarrel. [prob. imit.]
spat[4] *past* & *p.p.* of SPIT[1].

spate *n.* river-flood; large or excessive amount. [orig. unkn.]

spathe /speɪð/ *n.* large bract(s) enveloping flower-cluster. [L f. Gk]

spatial /'speɪʃ(ə)l/ *a.* of space; **spatially** *adv.* [L (SPACE)]

spatter 1 *v.* splash or scatter in drips. **2** *n.* spattering; pattering. [imit.]

spatula /'spætjʊlə/ *n.* implement with broad flexible blade used esp. by artists and in cookery. [L dimin. (SPATHE)]

spavin /'spævɪn/ *n.* disease of horse's hock with hard bony swelling; **spavined** *a.* [F]

spawn 1 *v.* (of fish or frog or mollusc etc.) produce (eggs), be produced as eggs or young; *derog.* produce (offspring); *fig.* produce or generate in large numbers. **2** *n.* eggs of fish, frogs, etc.; *derog.* human or other offspring; white fibrous matter from which fungi grow. [AF *espaundre* (EXPAND)]

spay *v.t.* sterilize (female animal) by removing ovaries. [AF (ÉPÉE)]

speak *v.* (*past* **spoke**; *p.p.* **spoken**) utter words in ordinary voice; hold conversation, make a speech; utter or pronounce (words); use (specified language) in speaking; make known in words; make mention *about* or *of*; convey idea (*actions speak louder than words*); **generally** (or **strictly** etc.) **speaking** in the general (or strict etc.) sense of the words; **not** (or **nothing**) **to speak of** not (or nothing) worth mentioning; **on speaking terms** sufficiently friendly or acquainted to hold conversation; **speak for** act as spokesman for, speak in defence of, bespeak; **speak for itself** be sufficient evidence; **speaking clock** telephone service giving exact time in words; **speak out** (or **up**) speak loudly or freely, give one's opinion etc. without hesitation or fear; **speak volumes (for)** be very significant (in terms of). [OE]

speakeasy *n. US sl.* place where alcoholic liquor is sold illicitly.

speaker *n.* one who speaks, esp. in public; person of specified skill in speech-making; one who speaks specified language; = LOUDSPEAKER; (**Speaker**) presiding officer of legislative assembly.

spear 1 *n.* thrusting or hurling weapon of stout staff with point usu. of steel. **2** *v.t.* pierce or strike (as) with spear. [OE]

spearhead /'spɪəhed/ **1** *n.* pointed tip of spear; person or group leading an attack or challenge etc. **2** *v.t.* act as spearhead of (attack etc.).

spearmint *n.* common garden mint used in cookery and to flavour chewing-gum.

spec *n. colloq.* speculation; **on spec** as a speculation. [abbr.]

special /'speʃ(ə)l/ **1** *a.* of particular or peculiar kind, not general; for particular purpose; exceptional in amount or degree etc. **2** *n.* special constable, edition of newspaper, dish on menu, etc. **3 Special Branch** police department dealing with political security; **special constable** person assisting police in routine duties or in emergencies; **special correspondent** one appointed by newspaper to report on special event or facts; **special delivery** delivery of mail in advance of regular delivery; **special edition** edition of newspaper, including later news than ordinary edition; **special licence** licence allowing marriage to take place within short time without banns; **special pleading** biased reasoning. **4 specially** *adv.* [F (ESPECIAL) or L (foll.)]

specialist *n.* one who specializes in particular branch of a profession, esp. medicine.

speciality /speʃɪ'ælɪtɪ/ *n.* special feature; special thing or activity; special product; subject in which one specializes.

specialize /'speʃəlaɪz/ *v.* devote oneself to a particular branch of a profession or discipline (with *in*); become or make special; **specialization** /-'zeɪʃ(ə)n/ *n.* [F (SPECIAL)]

specialty *n.* speciality.

specie /'spi:ʃi:, -ʃɪ/ *n.* coin as opposed to paper money. [foll.]

species /'spi:ʃi:z, -ʃɪz/ *n.* (*pl.* same) class of things having some common characteristics; group of animals or plants within genus, differing only in minor ways from others; a kind or sort. [L (*specio* look)]

specific /spɪ'sɪfɪk/ **1** *a.* particular or clearly defined (*a specific purpose*); exact, giving full details (*was specific about his wishes*); peculiar, relating to a particular thing; (of medicine etc.) having distinct effect in curing a certain disease. **2** *n.* specific detail or aspect; specific medicine. **3 specific gravity** ratio between the weight of a substance and that of the same volume of a substance used as a standard (usu. water or air). **4 specifically** *adv.*; **specificity** /-'fɪsɪtɪ/ *n.* [L (prec.)]

specification /spesɪfɪ'keɪʃ(ə)n/ *n.* (usu. in *pl.*) detail of design and materials etc. (to be) used in machine or project etc. [med.L (foll.)]

specify /'spesɪfaɪ/ *v.t.* name expressly, mention definitely; include in specifications. [F or L (SPECIFIC)]

specimen /'spesɪmɪn/ *n.* individual or

part taken as example of class or whole, esp. when used for investigation; sample of urine for testing; *colloq.* (usu. *derog.*) person of specified sort. [L (*specio* look)]

specious /'spi:ʃəs/ *a.* apparently good or sound but not really so; plausible. [L (as prec.)]

speck 1 *n.* small spot or stain; particle. **2** *v.t.* (esp. in *p.p.*) mark with specks. [OE]

speckle /'spek(ə)l/ **1** *n.* speck, esp. one of many markings on skin etc. **2** *v.t.* (esp. in *p.p.*) mark with speckles. [Du. *spekkel*]

specs *n.pl. colloq.* spectacles. [abbr.]

spectacle /'spektək(ə)l/ *n.* object of sight, esp. of public attention; striking or impressive or ridiculous sight; a public show; (in *pl.*) pair of lenses to correct or assist defective sight, set in frame to rest on nose and ears. [F f. L (*specio spect-* look)]

spectacled *a.* wearing spectacles.

spectacular /spek'tækjʊlə/ **1** *a.* of or like a public show, striking, lavish. **2** *n.* spectacular performance.

spectator /spek'teɪtə/ *n.* one who watches a show or game or incident etc.; **spectator sport** sport which attracts many spectators. [F or L (SPECTACLE)]

specter *US* var. of SPECTRE.

spectra *pl.* of SPECTRUM.

spectral /'spektr(ə)l/ *a.* of spectres or spectra; ghostlike; **spectrally** *adv.* [foll.]

spectre /'spektə/ *n.* ghost; haunting presentiment (*the spectre of ruin*). [F, or L *spectrum* (*specio* look)]

spectrometer /spek'trɒmɪtə/ *n.* spectroscope that can be used for measuring observed spectra. [G or F (prec., METER)]

spectroscope /'spektrəskəʊp/ *n.* instrument for producing and examining spectra; **spectroscopic** /-'skɒpɪk/ *a.*; **spectroscopically** /-'skɒpɪkəlɪ/ *adv.*; **spectroscopy** /-'trɒskəpɪ/ *n.* [G or F (SPECTRE, SCOPE)]

spectrum /'spektrəm/ *n.* (*pl.* **spectra**) band of colours as seen in rainbow etc.; image formed by rays of light etc. in which parts are arranged according to wavelength; entire or wide range of anything arranged by degree or quality etc. [L (*specio* look)]

speculate /'spekjʊleɪt/ *v.i.* indulge in conjectural thought or talk or writing (*on* or *upon* or *about*); engage in risky financial transactions; **speculation** /-'leɪʃ(ə)n/ *n.*; **speculative** *a.*; **speculator** *n.* [L *specula* watch-tower (SPECTRE)]

sped *past* & *p.p.* of SPEED.

speech *n.* act or faculty or manner of speaking; talk or address given in public; language of a nation or group etc.; **speech-day** annual celebration at school with speeches, distribution of prizes, etc.; **speech therapy** treatment to improve defective speech. [OE (SPEAK)]

speechify /'spi:tʃɪfaɪ/ *v.i. colloq.* make speech(es).

speechless *a.* silent, temporarily unable to speak through emotion or surprise etc.

speed 1 *n.* rapidity of movement, quick motion; rate of motion or action; gear appropriate to a range of speeds on bicycle etc.; relative sensitivity of photographic film to light, light-gathering power of lens; *sl.* stimulant drug; *archaic* success, prosperity. **2** *v.* (*past* & *p.p.* **sped**) go or send quickly; (of motorist etc.; *past* & *p.p.* **speeded**) travel at illegal or dangerous speed; *sl.* be under influence of stimulant drug; *archaic* be or make prosperous or successful. **3 at full speed** as fast as one can go or work; **at speed** moving quickly; **speed limit** maximum permitted speed of vehicle on road etc.; **speed merchant** *colloq.* motorist etc. who travels at high speed; **speed up** (cause to) move or work faster. [OE]

speedboat *n.* motor boat designed for high speed.

speedo /'spi:dəʊ/ *n.* (*pl.* **speedos**) *colloq.* = SPEEDOMETER. [abbr.]

speedometer /spi:'dɒmɪtə/ *n.* device indicating speed of vehicle. [SPEED, -O-, -METER]

speedster *n.* person who travels at high speed, esp. illegally. [SPEED, -STER]

speedway *n.* motor-cycle racing, arena for this; *US* road or track for fast traffic. [SPEED, WAY]

speedwell *n.* small plant with usu. bright-blue flowers. [SPEED, WELL[1]]

speedy *a.* rapid, prompt, not long delayed; **speedily** *adv.*; **speediness** *n.* [SPEED]

speleology /spelɪ'ɒlədʒɪ, spi:-/ *n.* scientific study of caves. [F f. L f. Gk *spēlaion* cave]

spell[1] *n.* words used as charm or incantation etc.; effect of these; fascination exercised by person or activity. [OE]

spell[2] *v.* (*past* & *p.p.* **spelt** or **spelled**) write or name correctly the letters of (word); (of letters) make up (word); (of circumstances etc.) have as consequence, involve (*floods spell ruin to the farmer*); **spell out** make out (words etc.) laboriously or slowly, spell aloud, explain in detail. [F f. Gmc, rel. to prec.]

spell[3] 1 *n.* period of time or work; period of some activity (*a spell of resting*); period of certain type of weather (*cold *spell*). **2** *v.t.* relieve or take turns with (person etc.). [OE, = substitute]

spellbound *a.* held as if by a spell, fascinated. [SPELL[1]]

spelling *n.* way word is spelt, esp. correctly; person's ability to spell correctly. [SPELL[2]]

spelt[1] *n.* a kind of wheat giving very fine flour. [OE]

spelt[2] see SPELL[2].

spend *v.* (*past* & *p.p.* **spent**) pay out (money); use up, consume (material or energy etc.); pass or occupy (time etc.); (in *p.p.*) having lost original force or strength; **spend a penny** *colloq.* urinate or defecate. [OE f. L (EXPEND)]

spendthrift *n.* extravagant person.

sperm *n.* (*pl.* **sperms** or **sperm**) semen; spermatozoon; **sperm whale** large whale yielding spermaceti. [L f. Gk *sperma -mat-*]

spermaceti /spɜ:mə'setɪ/ *n.* white waxy substance used for ointments etc. [med.L (L as prec., *ceti* of whale)]

spermatozoon /spɜ:mətə'zəʊən/ *n.* (*pl.* **spermatozoa**) fertilizing element in semen. [SPERM, Gk *zōion* animal]

spermicide /'spɜ:mɪsaɪd/ *n.* substance killing spermatozoa; **spermicidal** *a.* [SPERM, -CIDE]

spew *v.* vomit; (cause to) gush out. [OE]

sphagnum /'sfægnəm/ *n.* (*pl.* **sphagna**) moss growing in bogs and peat, used as packing etc. [L f. Gk *sphagnos*]

sphere *n.* solid figure with every point on its surface equidistant from centre, surface of this; globe, ball; field of action or influence or existence; one's place in society; each of the revolving shells in which heavenly bodies were formerly thought to be set. [F f. L f. Gk *sphaira* ball]

spherical /'sferɪk(ə)l/ *a.* shaped like sphere, of spheres; **spherically** *adv.* [L f. Gk (prec.)]

spheroid /'sfɪərɔɪd/ *n.* body like sphere but not perfectly spherical; **spheroidal** /-'rɔɪd(ə)l/ *a.* [L f. Gk (SPHERE)]

sphincter /'sfɪŋktə/ *n.* ring of muscle closing and opening orifice. [L f. Gk]

sphinx /sfɪŋks/ *n.* (in Egyptian antiquity) figure with lion's body and man's or animal's head; (**Sphinx**) winged monster in Greek mythology with woman's head and lion's body, who posed riddle solved by Oedipus; enigmatic or inscrutable person; **the Sphinx** colossal Egyptian sphinx near the Pyramids at Giza. [L f. Gk]

spice 1 *n.* aromatic or pungent vegetable substance used to flavour food; spices collectively; touch, flavour, piquant quality. **2** *v.t.* flavour with spice; enhance *with* wit etc. [F *espice* f. L SPECIES]

spick and span /spɪk ən 'spæn/ clean and tidy; smart and new. [emphat. extension of obs. *span new* (ON, = new as a chip)]

spicy *a.* of or flavoured with spice; piquant, improper; **spicily** *adv.*; **spiciness** *n.* [SPICE]

spider /'spaɪdə/ *n.* eight-legged arthropod, many species of which spin webs esp. to capture insects as food; thing resembling spider; **spider-crab** crab with long thin legs; **spider-man** man working at great height on building; **spider monkey** monkey with long limbs and long prehensile tail. [OE (SPIN)]

spidery *a.* of or like a spider; very thin or long.

spiel *sl.* **1** *n.* speech or story, esp. glib or long one. **2** *v.* speak lengthily or glibly. [G, = game]

spigot /'spɪgət/ *n.* small peg or plug; device for controlling flow of liquor from cask etc. [SPIKE[2]]

spike[1] **1** *n.* sharp point; pointed piece of metal, e.g. one of set forming top of iron fence or worn on bottom of running-shoe to prevent slipping; (in *pl.*) running-shoes fitted with spikes; large nail; pointed metal rod standing upright on base and used e.g. to hold unused matter in newspaper office. **2** *v.t.* put spikes on or into; fix on spike; *colloq.* add alcohol to (drink); *hist.* plug vent of (gun) with spike. **3 spike person's guns** spoil his plans. [LG or Du. (SPOKE[1])]

spike[2] *n.* ear of corn; long cluster of flowers with short stalks on central stem. [L *spica*]

spikenard /'spaɪknɑ:d/ *n.* tall sweet-smelling plant; aromatic ointment formerly made from this. [med.L (SPIKE[2], NARD]

spiky *a.* like a spike, having spike(s); *colloq.* rigid, dogmatic, touchy, bad-tempered; **spikily** *adv.*; **spikiness** *n.* [SPIKE[1]]

spill[1] **1** *v.* (*past* & *p.p.* **spilt** or **spilled**) allow (liquid or powder etc.) to fall or run out from container esp. accidentally or wastefully; (of liquid etc.) run out thus; shed (others' blood); throw from saddle or vehicle; *sl.* disclose (information etc.). **2** *n.* spilling or being spilt; being thrown from saddle etc.; tumble, fall. **3 spill the beans** see BEAN; **spill over** be surplus or excessive. [OE]

spill[2] *n.* thin strip of wood or paper etc. for lighting a fire or pipe. [LG or Du.]

spillage *n.* action of spilling; amount spilt. [SPILL[1]]

spillikin /'spɪlɪkɪn/ *n.* splinter of wood etc.; (in *pl.*) game in which heap of thin rods is removed by taking one at a time without disturbing the others. [SPILL²]

spillway *n.* passage for surplus water from dam. [SPILL¹]

spin 1 *v.* (**-nn-**; *past* and *p.p.* **spun**) turn rapidly on its own axis, cause to do this; draw out and twist (raw cotton or wool etc.) into threads, make (yarn) thus; (of spider or silkworm) make (web or cocoon) by emitting viscous thread; (of person's head etc.) be in a whirl through dizziness or astonishment; toss (coin); = *spin-dry*; tell or compose (story etc.). **2** *n.* revolving motion, whirl; secondary revolving or twisting motion e.g. of cricket or tennis ball; short or brisk excursion, esp. in motor vehicle; rotating dive of aircraft. **3 spin bowler** (in cricket) bowler who imparts spin to ball; **spin-drier** machine for drying clothes by spinning them in rotating drum; **spin-dry** dry (clothes) thus; **spinning-jenny** *hist.* machine for spinning fibres with more than one spindle at a time; **spinning-wheel** household device for spinning yarn or thread, with spindle driven by wheel with crank or treadle; **spin-off** *n.* incidental or secondary result or benefit, esp. in technology; **spin out** prolong (speech or discussion etc.); **spun silk** cheap material of short-fibred and waste silk, often mixed with cotton. [OE]

spina bifida /ˈspaɪnə ˈbɪfɪdə/ congenital defect of spine, with protruding membranes. [L, = cleft spine]

spinach /ˈspɪnɪdʒ/ *n.* vegetable with succulent leaves cooked as food. [prob. Du. f. F, ult. f. Pers.]

spinal /ˈspaɪn(ə)l/ *a.* of the spine; **spinal column** spine; **spinal cord** cylindrical nervous structure within spine. [L (SPINE)]

spindle /ˈspɪnd(ə)l/ *n.* slender rod or bar, often with tapered ends, to twist and wind thread; pin or axis that revolves or on which thing revolves; **spindle-shanks** person with long thin legs; **spindle-tree** tree with hard wood used for spindles. [OE (SPIN)]

spindly *a.* long or tall and thin.

spindrift /ˈspɪndrɪft/ *n.* spray blown along surface of sea. [Sc. var. of *spoondrift* f. obs. *spoon* scud]

spine *n.* series of vertebrae extending downwards from skull, backbone; sharp needle-like outgrowth of animal or plant; part of book's cover or jacket that encloses its page-fastening; sharp ridge or projection; **spine-chiller** spine-chilling book or film etc.; **spine-chilling** frighteningly thrilling or exciting. [F *espine* f. L *spina*]

spineless *a.* lacking backbone; lacking resoluteness or strength of character, feeble.

spinet /spɪˈnet/ *n. hist.* small harpsichord with one string to each note. [F f. It. *spinetta* dimin. (SPINE)]

spinnaker /ˈspɪnəkə/ *n.* large triangular sail carried opposite mainsail of racing-yacht running before wind. [*Sphinx*, yacht first using it]

spinner *n.* person or thing that spins, esp. manufacturer engaged in cotton-spinning; spin bowler; (in fishing) revolving bait as lure. [SPIN]

spinneret /ˈspɪnəret/ *n.* spinning-organ of spider etc.; device for forming synthetic fibre.

spinney /ˈspɪnɪ/ *n.* small wood, thicket. [F f. L *spinetum* (SPINE)]

spinster *n.* unmarried woman; (elderly) woman thought unlikely to marry. [orig. = woman who spins]

spiny *a.* having (many) spines; **spininess** *n.* [SPINE]

spiraea /spaɪˈrɪə/ *n.* garden plant related to meadowsweet. [L f. Gk (foll.)]

spiral /ˈspaɪər(ə)l/ **1** *a.* coiled in a plane or as round a cylinder or cone, having this shape. **2** *n.* spiral curve; a progressive rise or fall usu. resulting from interaction of factors. **3** *v.i.* (**-ll-**, *US* **-l-**) move in spiral course. **4 spiral staircase** staircase rising round central axis. **5 spirally** *adv.* [F or L (*spira* coil f. Gk)]

spirant /ˈspaɪərənt/ **1** *a.* uttered with continuous expulsion of breath. **2** *n.* spirant consonant. [L *spiro* breathe]

spire *n.* tapering structure like tall cone or pyramid rising above tower; any tapering body. [OE]

spirit /ˈspɪrɪt/ **1** *n.* person's animating principle or intelligence; person's soul; person from intellectual or moral viewpoint; disembodied person or incorporeal being; person's mental or moral nature; attitude or mood (*approached it in the wrong spirit*); courage, self-assertion, vivacity; (in *pl.*) state of mind (*in high spirits*); tendency prevailing at a particular time etc. (*spirit of the age*); principle or purpose underlying the form of a law etc.; volatile liquid got by distillation; purified alcohol; (usu. in *pl.*) strong distilled alcoholic liquor, e.g. whisky and gin. **2** *v.t.* convey *away* or *off* etc. rapidly or mysteriously. **3 in spirit** inwardly; **spirit gum** quick-drying gum for attaching false hair; **spirit-lamp** lamp burning methylated or other volatile spirit instead of oil; **spirit-level** device with glass tube nearly filled with liquid used to test levelness by position of air-bubble. [AF f. L *spiritus* (SPIRANT)]

spirited *a.* full of spirit, lively,

courageous; having specified spirits or disposition (*poor-spirited*).

spiritless *a.* lacking vigour or courage.

spiritual /'spɪrɪtjʊəl/ **1** *a.* of or concerned with the spirit; religious, divine, inspired. **2** *n.* religious song esp. of American Blacks. **3 spirituality** /-'ælɪtɪ/ *n.*; **spiritually** *adv.* [F f. L (SPIRIT)]

spiritualism *n.* belief that spirits of the dead communicate with the living, esp. through mediums; **spiritualist** *n.*; **spiritualistic** /-'lɪstɪk/ *a.*

spirituous /'spɪrɪtjʊəs/ *a.* alcoholic, distilled as well as fermented. [SPIRIT]

spirt var. of SPURT.

spit[1] **1** *v.* (**-tt-**; *past* & *p.p.* **spat** or **spit**) eject from the mouth; eject saliva from the mouth, do this as gesture of contempt; utter (oaths or threats etc.) vehemently; make noise as of spitting; (of fire or gun etc.) throw out with explosion; (of rain) fall lightly. **2** *n.* spittle; spitting. **3 the** (**dead** or **very**) **spit** spitting image *of*; **spit and polish** soldier's cleaning and polishing work; **spit it out** *colloq.* speak candidly or louder; **spitting image** exact counterpart or likeness (*of* person). [OE]

spit[2] **1** *n.* rod on which meat is fixed for roasting over fire etc.; long narrow strip of land projecting into sea. **2** *v.t.* (**-tt-**) pierce (as) with spit. [OE]

spite 1 *n.* ill will, malice. **2** *v.t.* hurt or harm or frustrate (person) through spite. **3 in spite of** notwithstanding, regardless of. [F (DESPITE)]

spiteful *a.* full of spite, malicious; **spitefully** *adv.*

spitfire *n.* person of fiery temper. [SPIT[1]]

spittle /'spɪt(ə)l/ *n.* saliva esp. as ejected from mouth. [SPIT[1]]

spittoon /spɪ'tu:n/ *n.* vessel to spit into.

spiv *n.* man, esp. flashily-dressed one, living from shady dealings rather than regular work; **spivish** *a.* [orig. unkn.]

splash 1 *v.* agitate (liquid) so that drops of it fly about; wet or stain by splashing; (of liquid) fly about in drops; move *about* or *along* etc. with splashing of liquid; jump or fall (*into* water etc.) with splashing; decorate with scattered colour; display (news) prominently; spend (money) recklessly or ostentatiously. **2** *n.* act or noise of splashing; quantity of liquid splashed; mark etc. made by splashing; patch of colour; prominent or ostentatious display; *colloq.* small quantity of soda-water etc. (in drink). **3 make a splash** attract much attention; **splash-down** alighting of spacecraft on sea; **splash out** *colloq.* spend money freely. **4 splashy** *a.* [imit.]

splatter *v.* & *n.* splash esp. with continuous or noisy action; spatter. [imit.]

splay 1 *v.* spread apart, (of opening) have sides diverging; make (opening) have divergent sides. **2** *n.* surface at oblique angle to another. **3** *a.* splayed. [DISPLAY]

spleen *n.* abdominal organ maintaining proper condition of blood; moroseness, irritability. [F *esplen* f. L f. Gk *splēn*]

spleenwort *n.* a kind of fern.

splendid /'splendɪd/ *a.* magnificent, gorgeous, sumptuous, glorious, brilliant; *colloq.* excellent, very fine; dignified, impressive. [F or L (SPLENDOUR)]

splendiferous /splen'dɪfərəs/ *a. colloq.* splendid. [foll.]

splendour /'splendə/, *US* **splendor** *n.* splendidness, great or dazzling brightness. [AF or L (*splendeo* shine)]

splenetic /splɪ'netɪk/ *a.* bad-tempered, peevish; **splenetically** *adv.* [L (SPLEEN)]

splenic /'spli:nɪk, 'sple-/ *a.* of or in the spleen. [F or L f. Gk (SPLEEN)]

splice 1 *v.t.* join pieces of (ropes) by interweaving strands; join (pieces of wood or tape etc.) in overlapping position; *colloq.* (esp. in *pass.*) join in marriage. **2** *n.* junction made by splicing. [prob. Du. *splissen*]

splint 1 *n.* strip of wood etc. bound to limb, esp. to keep broken bone in right position while it heals. **2** *v.t.* secure with splint. [LG or Du.]

splinter 1 *n.* small sharp piece broken off wood or glass etc. **2** *v.* break or become broken into splinters. **3 splinter group** small (esp. political) group that has broken away from a larger one. **4 splintery** *a.* [Du., rel. to prec.]

split 1 *v.* (**-tt-**; *past* and *p.p.* **split**) break, esp. lengthwise or with the grain or plane of cleavage; break forcibly; divide into parts or thicknesses etc.; remove or be removed by breaking or dividing (*off*); divide into disagreeing or hostile parties (*on* or *over* issue); cause fission of (atom); *sl.* betray secrets, inform (*on*). **2** *n.* act or result of splitting; disagreement or schism; dish made of bananas etc. split open, with ice-cream etc.; (in *pl.*) feat of sitting down or leaping with legs widely spread out at right angles to body; half bottle of mineral water; half glass of liquor. **3 be splitting** (of head) feel acute pain from headache; **split hairs** see HAIR; **split infinitive** one with adverb etc. inserted between *to* and verb; **split-level** built or having components at more than one level; **split pea** pea dried and split for cooking; **split personality** change of personality as in schizophrenia; **split pin** pin or bolt etc. held in place by splaying of its split end; **split second** very brief moment; **split one's sides** laugh heartily; **splitting**

headache very severe headache; **split up** separate, esp. (of married couple etc.) cease living together. [Du.]

splodge var. of SPLOTCH.

splosh *colloq.* 1 *v.* move with splashing. 2 *n.* act or noise of this; quantity of water suddenly dropped or thrown down. [imit.]

splotch *n.* & *v.t.* daub, blot, smear. [orig. uncert.]

splurge 1 *n.* noisy or ostentatious display or effort. 2 *v.i.* make splurge. [prob. imit.]

splutter 1 *v.* speak or emit with spitting sound; emit spitting sounds; speak rapidly or incoherently. 2 *n.* spluttering speech or sound. [SPUTTER]

spoil 1 *v.* (*past* and *p.p.* **spoilt** or **spoiled**) make or become useless or unsatisfactory; diminish person's enjoyment of (*the news spoilt his evening*); harm the character of (person) by indulgence; (of food etc.) go bad. 2 *n.* (in *sing.* or *pl.*) plunder, stolen goods; profits, advantages accruing from success or official position. 3 **be spoiling for** seek eagerly or aggressively (*is spoiling for a fight*); **spoil-sport** one who spoils others' enjoyment. [F *espoille* n., *-llier* v. f. L *spolio*]

spoiler *n.* device on aircraft to retard it by interrupting air flow; similar device on vehicle to increase contact with ground at speed.

spoke[1] 1 *n.* any of the bars or rods running from hub to rim of wheel; rung of ladder. 2 *v.t.* provide with spokes; obstruct (wheel etc.) by thrusting spoke in. 3 **put a spoke in person's wheel** hinder or thwart his purpose. [OE]

spoke[2] *past* of SPEAK.

spoken 1 *p.p.* of SPEAK. 2 *a.* speaking in specified way (*soft-*, *well-spoken*). [SPEAK]

spokeshave *n.* tool for planing curved surfaces. [SPOKE[1]]

spokesman /'spəʊksmən/ *n.* one who speaks for others, esp. to express a group's views. [SPOKE[2]]

spoliation /spəʊlɪ'eɪʃ(ə)n/ *n.* plundering, pillage. [L (SPOIL)]

spondee /'spɒndi:/ *n.* a metrical foot (– –); **spondaic** /-'deɪɪk/ *a.* [F, or L *spondeus* f. Gk]

sponge /spʌndʒ/ 1 *n.* sea animal with porous body-wall and tough elastic skeleton; this skeleton or piece of porous rubber etc. used as absorbent in bathing, cleansing surfaces, etc.; thing of spongelike absorbency or consistency; sponge-cake; act of sponging. 2 *v.* wipe or cleanse with sponge; wipe *out* or efface (as) with sponge; soak *up* (water etc.) with or like sponge; live parasitically off others (often with *off* or *on*). 3 **sponge-bag** waterproof bag for toilet articles; **sponge-cake** (or **-pudding**) light cake (or pudding) of spongelike consistency; **sponge rubber** rubber made porous like sponge; **throw in** (or **up**) **the sponge** abandon contest, admit defeat. 4 **spongeable** *a.* [OE & F f. L *spongia* f. Gk]

sponger *n.* person who habitually sponges on others.

spongy *a.* like sponge, porous, elastic, absorbent; **spongily** *adv.*; **sponginess** *n.*

sponsor /'spɒnsə/ 1 *n.* person who makes himself responsible for another, presents candidate for baptism, introduces legislation, or contributes to charity in return for specified activity by another; advertiser who pays for broadcast which includes advertisement of his goods. 2 *v.t.* be sponsor for. 3 **sponsorial** /spɒn'sɔ:rɪəl/ *a.*; **sponsorship** *n.* [L (*spondeo spons-* pledge)]

spontaneous /spɒn'teɪnɪəs/ *a.* acting or done or occurring without external cause or incitement; automatic, instinctive, natural; (of style or manner) gracefully natural and unconstrained; **spontaneous combustion** ignition of substance caused by chemical changes within it; **spontaneity** /spɒntə'ni:ɪtɪ/ *n.* [L (*sponte* of one's own accord)]

spoof *n.* & *v.t.* *colloq.* parody; hoax, swindle. [invented word]

spook *n. colloq.* ghost. [LG or Du.]

spooky *a. colloq.* ghostly, eerie; **spookiness** *n.*

spool 1 *n.* reel on which something is wound, e.g. yarn or magnetic tape; revolving cylinder of angler's reel. 2 *v.t.* wind on spool. [F *espole*, or LG or Du. *spole*]

spoon 1 *n.* utensil with oval or round bowl and handle for conveying food (esp. liquid) to mouth, for stirring, etc.; spoon-shaped thing; (in full **spoon-bait**) revolving spoon-shaped metal fish-lure. 2 *v.* take liquid (*up* or *out*) with spoon; hit (ball) feebly upwards; *colloq.* behave in amorous way, esp. foolishly. 3 **spoon-feed** feed (baby etc.) with spoon, give such extensive help etc. to (person) that he need make no effort for himself. 4 **spoonful** *n.* [OE]

spoonbill *n.* wading-bird with broad flat tip of bill.

spoonerism /'spu:nərɪz(ə)m/ *n.* transposition, usu. accidental, of initial letter etc. of two or more words. [*Spooner*, scholar]

spoor *n.* animal's track or scent. [Du.]

sporadic /spə'rædɪk/ *a.* occurring only here and there or occasionally; **sporadi-**

cally *adv.* [med.L f. Gk (*sporas -ad-* dispersed)]

spore *n.* minute reproductive cell of cryptogamous plants; resistant form of bacterium etc. [Gk *spora* seed]

sporran /'spɒrən/ *n.* pouch worn in front of kilt. [Gael. f. L (PURSE)]

sport 1 *n.* outdoor game or competitive activity, usu. involving physical exertion, e.g. cricket, racing, hunting; these collectively; (in *pl.*) meeting for competing in sports, esp. athletics; amusement, diversion, fun; *colloq.* good fellow, sporting person; animal or plant differing from normal type. **2** *v.* engage in sport; wear or exhibit, esp. ostentatiously. **3 in sport** jestingly; **make sport of** ridicule; **sports car** low-built fast car; **sports coat** (or **jacket**) man's jacket for informal wear. [DISPORT]

sporting *a.* interested or concerned in sport; sportsmanlike; **a sporting chance** some possibility of success.

sportive *a.* playful.

sportsman *n.* person fond of sport; person who behaves fairly and generously; **sportsmanlike** *a.*; **sportsmanship** *n.*

sporty *a. colloq.* fond of sport; *colloq.* rakish, showy; **sportily** *adv.*; **sportiness** *n.* [SPORT]

spot 1 *n.* small roundish area or mark differing in colour or texture etc. from the surface it is on; blemish or pimple; particular place, definite locality; particular part of one's body or aspect of one's character; *colloq.* one's (regular) position in an organization or programme etc.; flaw in one's character; *colloq.* small quantity of something (*a spot of lunch, of trouble*); drop (*of* rain etc.); = SPOTLIGHT. **2** *v.* (**-tt-**) mark or become marked with spots; make spots, rain slightly; *colloq.* pick out, recognize, catch sight of; watch for and take note of (trains, talent, etc.); (in *p.p.*) marked or decorated with spots. **3 in a** (**tight** etc.) **spot** *colloq.* in difficulty; **on the spot** at scene of action or event, *colloq.* in position such that response or action is required; **spot cash** money paid immediately on sale; **spot check** sudden or random check; **spot-on** *colloq.* precise, on target; **spotted dick** suet pudding containing currants; **spot welding** welding between points of metal surfaces in contact. [perh. LG or Du.]

spotless *a.* absolutely clean or pure.

spotlight 1 *n.* beam of light directed on small area; lamp projecting this; full attention or publicity. **2** *v.t.* (*past* and *p.p.* **spotlit**) direct spotlight on; make conspicuous, draw attention to.

spotty *a.* marked with spots; patchy, irregular; **spottily** *adv.*; **spottiness** *n.*

spouse /spaʊz/ *n.* husband or wife. [F f. L *sponsus -sa* (as SPONSOR)]

spout 1 *n.* projecting tube or lip through which liquid etc. is poured or issues from teapot, jug, roof-gutter, fountain, etc.; jet or column of liquid etc. **2** *v.* discharge or issue forcibly or in jet; utter in declamatory manner. **3 up the spout** *sl.* useless, ruined, in trouble, pawned. [Du.]

sprain 1 *v.t.* wrench (ankle or wrist etc.) and so cause pain or swelling. **2** *n.* such injury. [orig. unkn.]

sprang *past* of SPRING.

sprat *n.* small sea-fish. [OE]

sprawl 1 *v.* sit or lie or fall with limbs flung out or in ungainly way; spread (one's limbs) thus; (of plant or town or writing etc.) be of irregular or straggling form. **2** *n.* sprawling position or movement or mass. [OE]

spray[1] **1** *n.* water or other liquid flying in small drops; liquid preparation to be applied in this way with atomizer etc.; device for such application. **2** *v.t.* throw (liquid) in form of spray; sprinkle (object) thus, esp. (plants etc.) with insecticides. **3 spray-gun** gunlike device for spraying paint etc. [orig. uncert.]

spray[2] *n.* sprig of plant or small branch of tree, esp. graceful one with flowers and leaves used as ornament; artificial ornament in similar form. [OE]

spread /spred/ **1** *v.* (*past* and *p.p.* **spread**) open or extend surface of (often with *out*); cause to cover larger surface, display thus; have wide or specified or increasing extent; (cause to) become widely known or felt (*rumours are spreading*; *they are spreading rumours*); cover surface of (*bread spread with butter*); lay (table). **2** *n.* action or capability or extent of spreading; diffusion (*spread of learning*); breadth; increased bodily girth (*middle-aged spread*); range of prices or rates etc.; *colloq.* elaborate meal; paste for spreading on bread etc.; bedspread; printed matter spread across more than one column. **3 spread eagle** figure of eagle with legs and wings extended as emblem; **spread-eagle** *v.t.* place (person) in position with arms and legs spread out, defeat utterly; **spread oneself** be lavish or discursive. [OE]

spree *n.* lively outing, esp. with much spending of money (*shopping spree*); bout of fun or drinking etc. [orig. unkn.]

sprig 1 *n.* small branch, shoot; ornament resembling this, esp. on fabric; (usu. *derog.*) young man. **2** *v.t.* (**-gg-**) ornament with sprigs (*sprigged muslin*). [LG *sprick*]

sprightly /'spraɪtlɪ/ *a.* vivacious, lively, brisk; **sprightliness** *n.* [SPRITE]

spring 1 *v.* (*past* **sprang**; *p.p.* **sprung**) rise rapidly or suddenly, leap; move rapidly (as) by action of a spring; originate or arise (*from* ancestors or source etc.); (cause to) act or appear suddenly or unexpectedly; present (thing or circumstance etc.) suddenly or unexpectedly (with *on*); contrive escape of (person *from* prison etc.); rouse (game) from covert etc.; develop (leak); (of wood etc.) split; (usu. in *p.p.*) provide with springs. **2** *n.* jump, leap; recoil; elasticity; elastic device usu. of bent or coiled metal used esp. to drive clockwork or for cushioning furniture or in vehicles; first season of year, when vegetation begins to appear; early stage *of* life etc.; place where water or oil etc. wells up from the earth, basin or flow so formed; motive for or origin of action or custom etc. **3 spring balance** one that measures weight by tension of spring; **spring chicken** young fowl for eating, youthful person; **spring-clean** *n.* thorough cleaning of house esp. in spring, (*v.t.*) clean (house) thus; **spring onion** young onion eaten raw; **spring tide** tide at times of month when there is greatest difference between high and low water; **spring up** come into being, appear. [OE]

springboard *n.* springy board giving impetus in leaping or diving etc.; *fig.* source of impetus.

springbok /'sprɪŋbɒk/ *n.* S. African gazelle. [Afrik. f. Du.]

springer *n.* small spaniel of breed used to spring game. [SPRING]

springtime *n.* season of spring.

springy *a.* elastic, springing back quickly when squeezed or stretched; **springily** *adv.*; **springiness** *n.*

sprinkle /'sprɪŋk(ə)l/ **1** *v.t.* scatter in small drops or particles; subject (ground or object) to sprinkling (*with* liquid etc.); (of liquid etc.) fall thus on; distribute in small amounts. **2** *n.* light shower (*of* rain etc.). [orig. uncert.]

sprinkler *n.* device for sprinkling water on lawn or to extinguish fires.

sprinkling *n.* a small thinly distributed number or amount.

sprint 1 *v.* run short distance, run (specified distance), at full speed. **2** *n.* such run; similar short effort in cycling, swimming, etc. [ON]

sprit *n.* small diagonal spar from mast to upper outer corner of sail. [OE]

sprite *n.* elf, fairy. [*sprit*, contr. of SPIRIT]

spritsail /'sprɪts(ə)l/ *n.* sail extended by sprit. [SPRIT]

sprocket /'sprɒkɪt/ *n.* each of several teeth on wheel engaging with links of chain. [orig. unkn.]

sprout 1 *v.* put forth (shoots or hair etc.); begin to grow. **2** *n.* shoot of plant; (in *pl.*) *colloq.* = *Brussels sprouts*. [OE]

spruce[1] /spru:s/ **1** *a.* neat in dress and appearance, smart. **2** *v.* make or become smart (usu. with *up*). [perh. foll.]

spruce[2] /spru:s/ *n.* conifer with dense conical foliage; its wood. [obs. *Pruce* Prussia]

sprung *p.p.* of SPRING.

spry /spraɪ/ *a.* (*compar.* **spryer**; *superl.* **spryest**) lively, nimble; **spryly** *adv.* [orig. unkn.]

spud 1 *n.* small narrow spade for weeding; *sl.* potato. **2** *v.t.* (**-dd-**) remove (weeds *up* or *out*) with spud. [orig. unkn.]

spue var. of SPEW.

spume *n.* & *v.i.* froth, foam; **spumy** *a.* [F, or L *spuma*]

spun *p.p.* of SPIN.

spunk *n.* touchwood; *colloq.* mettle, spirit; *sl.* semen. [orig. unkn.]

spunky *a. colloq.* brave, spirited.

spur 1 *n.* device with small spike or spiked wheel attached to rider's heel for urging horse forward; stimulus, incentive; spur-shaped thing, esp. hard projection on cock's leg, projection from mountain or mountain range, branch road or railway. **2** *v.* (**-rr-**) prick (horse) with spur; incite or stimulate; ride hard (*on* or *forward* etc.); (esp. in *p.p.*) provide with spurs. **3 on the spur of the moment** on a momentary impulse. [OE]

spurge *n.* plant with acrid milky juice. [F *espurge* f. L (EXPURGATE)]

spurious /'spjʊərɪəs/ *a.* not genuine, not what it purports to be. [L]

spurn *v.t.* reject with disdain, treat with contempt; repel with one's foot. [OE]

spurt 1 *v.* (cause to) gush out in jet or stream; make a spurt. **2** *n.* sudden gushing out, jet; short sudden effort or increase of pace in racing etc. [orig. unkn.]

sputnik /'spʊtnɪk, 'spʌ-/ *n.* Russian artificial earth satellite. [Russ.]

sputter 1 *v.* splutter, make series of quick explosive sounds. **2** *n.* sputtering sound. [Du. (imit.)]

sputum /'spju:təm/ *n.* (*pl.* **sputa**) saliva; expectorated matter esp. used to diagnose disease. [L]

spy /spaɪ/ **1** *n.* person secretly collecting and reporting information on activities or movements of enemy or competitor etc.; person keeping secret watch on others. **2** *v.* discern, esp. by careful observation; act as spy (*on* person or proceedings); pry (*into* secret etc.). **3 spy out** explore or discover, esp. secretly. [F *espie(r)* f. Gmc]

spyglass *n.* small telescope.

spyhole *n.* peep-hole.

sq. *abbr.* square.

Sqn. Ldr. *abbr.* Squadron Leader.

squab /skwɒb/ **1** *n.* short fat person; young esp. unfledged pigeon or other bird; stuffed cushion, esp. as part of seat in motor car; sofa, ottoman. **2** *a.* short and fat, squat. [perh. Scand.]

squabble /'skwɒb(ə)l/ **1** *n.* petty or noisy quarrel. **2** *v.i.* engage in squabble. [prob. imit.]

squad /skwɒd/ *n.* small group of people sharing task etc., esp. small number of soldiers. [F *escouade* f. It. (SQUARE)]

squaddie *n.* (also **squaddy**) *sl.* recruit, private.

squadron /'skwɒdrən/ *n.* organized body of persons etc., esp. cavalry division of two troops; detachment of warships employed on particular service; unit of RAF with 10 to 18 aircraft; **squadron leader** officer commanding RAF squadron, next below wing commander. [It. *squadrone* (SQUAD)]

squalid /'skwɒlɪd/ *a.* dirty, filthy; mean or poor in appearance; wretched, sordid. [L]

squall /skwɔ:l/ **1** *n.* sudden or violent wind-storm, esp. with rain or snow or sleet; discordant cry, scream (esp. of baby). **2** *v.* utter (with) squall; scream. [prob. alt. of SQUEAL after BAWL]

squalor /'skwɒlə/ *n.* filthy or squalid state. [L]

squander /'skwɒndə/ *v.t.* spend wastefully. [orig. unkn.]

square 1 *n.* rectangle with four equal sides; object or arrangement of (approximately) this shape; open (usu. four-sided) area surrounded by buildings; product of number multiplied by itself (*16 is the square of 4*); L- or T-shaped instrument for obtaining or testing right angles; *sl.* conventional or old-fashioned person. **2** *a.* having shape of a square; having or in form of a right angle (*square corner*), angular and not round; designating unit of measure equal to area of square whose side is one of the unit specified (*square foot, metre*); level or parallel (*with*); at right angles (*to*); having breadth nearer length or height than is usual (*a man of square frame*); properly arranged, settled; (also **all square**) not in debt, with no money owed, (of scores etc.) balanced, equal; fair and honest; direct or uncompromising (*met with a square refusal*); *sl.* conventional or old-fashioned. **3** *adv.* squarely (*hit him square on the jaw*); fairly, honestly. **4** *v.* make square; multiply (number) by itself; adjust, make or be suitable *to* or consistent *with*, reconcile; mark out in squares; settle or pay (bill etc.); place (shoulders etc.) squarely facing forwards; *colloq.* pay or bribe (person); make scores of (match etc.) equal. **5 back to square one** *colloq.* back to starting-point with no progress made; **on the square** *colloq.* honest(ly), fair(ly); **out of square** not at right angles; **square-bashing** *sl.* military drill on barrack-square; **square the circle** construct square equal in area to given circle, *fig.* do what is impossible; **square dance** dance with usu. four couples facing inwards from four sides; **square deal** fair bargain or treatment; **square leg** (in cricket) position of fieldsman at some distance on batsman's legside and nearly opposite stumps; **square meal** substantial and satisfying meal; **square measure** measure expressed in square units; **square-rigged** with principal sails at right angles to length of ship; **square root** number that multiplied by itself gives a specified number; **square up** settle account etc.; **square up to** move towards (person) in fighting attitude, face and tackle (difficulty) resolutely. [F *esquare* (L EX[1], *quadra*)]

squash[1] /skwɒʃ/ **1** *v.* crush or squeeze flat or into pulp; force or make one's way (*into*) by squeezing; crowd; silence (person) with crushing retort etc. **2** *n.* crowd, crowded state; sound (as) of something being squashed; drink made of crushed fruit; (in full **squash rackets**) game played with rackets and small ball in closed court. **3 squashy** *a.* [F *esquasser* (EX-[1], QUASH)]

squash[2] /skwɒʃ/ *n.* trailing annual plant; gourd of this. [Narragansett]

squat /skwɒt/ **1** *v.* (**-tt-**) sit on one's heels, or on ground with knees drawn up, or in hunched posture; put into squatting position; *colloq.* sit down; act as squatter. **2** *a.* (of person etc.) short and thick, dumpy; squatting. **3** *n.* squatting posture; place occupied by squatters; being squatter. [F *esquatir* flatten]

squatter *n.* person who takes unauthorized possession of unoccupied premises etc.; Australian sheep-farmer.

squaw *n.* N. American Indian woman or wife. [Narragansett]

squawk 1 *n.* loud harsh cry esp. of bird; complaint. **2** *v.i.* utter squawk. [imit.]

squeak 1 *n.* short high-pitched cry or sound; (also **narrow squeak**) narrow escape, success barely attained. **2** *v.* make a squeak; utter (words) shrilly; *colloq.* pass narrowly *by* or *through* etc.; *sl.* turn informer. [imit. (SQUEAL, SHRIEK)]

squeaky *a.* making squeaking sound; **squeakily** *adv.*; **squeakiness** *n.*

squeal 1 *n.* prolonged shrill sound or cry. **2** *v.* make a squeal; utter (words) with squeal; *sl.* turn informer, protest vociferously. [imit.]

squeamish /'skwi:mɪʃ/ *a.* easily nauseated or disgusted or offended; fastidious, overscrupulous. [AF *escoymos*]
squeegee /skwi:'dʒi:/ **1** *n.* instrument with rubber edge or roller on a long handle, used to remove liquid from surfaces. **2** *v.t.* treat with squeegee. [*squeege*, alt. of foll.]
squeeze 1 *v.* exert pressure on from opposite or all sides; extract (moisture) out of by squeezing; reduce size of or alter shape of by squeezing; force, or make one's way, into or through small or narrow space; harass or put pressure on (person), obtain by entreaty or extort (money etc.) *out of.* **2** *n.* squeezing or being squeezed; close embrace; crowd, crowded state; small quantity produced by squeezing; extortion or exaction; restriction on borrowing and investment in financial crisis. [orig. unkn.]
squelch 1 *v.* make sucking sound as of treading in thick mud; move with squelching sound; disconcert, silence. **2** *n.* act or sound of squelching. [imit.]
squib *n.* small firework burning with hissing sound and usu. with final explosion; short satirical composition; **damp squib** unsuccessful attempt to impress etc. [perh. imit.]
squid *n.* ten-armed marine cephalopod. [orig. unkn.]
squiffy /'skwɪfɪ/ *a. sl.* slightly drunk. [orig. unkn.]
squiggle /'skwɪg(ə)l/ *n.* short curling line, esp. in handwriting; **squiggly** *a.* [imit.]
squill *n.* bulbous plant resembling lily. [L *squilla* f. Gk]
squint 1 *v.i.* have the eyes turned in different directions, have squint; look esp. obliquely or with half-shut eyes (*at* etc.). **2** *n.* abnormality of an eye which does not turn to match the other's direction; stealthy or sidelong glance; *colloq.* glance, look; oblique opening in church wall affording view of altar. [obs. *asquint*, perh. f. Du. *schuinte* slant]
squire 1 *n.* country gentleman, esp. the chief landowner in country district; woman's escort or gallant; *hist.* knight's attendant. **2** *v.t.* (of man) attend or escort (woman). [ESQUIRE]
squirearchy /'skwaɪərɑ:kɪ/ *n.* landowners collectively.
squirm 1 *v.i.* wriggle, writhe; show or feel embarrassment or discomfiture. **2** *n.* squirming movement. [imit.]
squirrel /'skwɪr(ə)l/ **1** *n.* bushy-tailed usu. arboreal rodent; its fur. **2** *v.t.* (**-ll-**, US **-l-**) hoard (*away*). [AF f. L (*sciurus* f. Gk)]
squirt 1 *v.* eject (liquid etc.) in a jet; be ejected thus. **2** *n.* jet of water etc.; device for ejecting this; *colloq.* insignificant self-assertive person. [imit.]
squish 1 *n.* slight squelching sound. **2** *v.i.* move with squish. **3 squishy** *a.* [imit.]
Sr. *abbr.* Senior; Señor.
Sr *symb.* strontium.
SRN *abbr.* State Registered Nurse.
SS *abbr.* Saints; steamship; *hist.* Nazi special police force [G *Schutz-Staffel*]
SSE *abbr.* south-south-east.
SSW *abbr.* south-south-west.
St *abbr.* Saint.
St. *abbr.* Street.
st. *abbr.* stone.
stab 1 *v.* (**-bb-**) pierce or wound with (usu. short) pointed tool or weapon; aim blow with such weapon (*at*); cause sensation like being stabbed (*stabbing pain*); hurt or distress (person or feelings etc.). **2** *n.* act or result of stabbing; wound or harm; *colloq.* attempt. **3 stab in the back** treacherous or slanderous attack. [orig. unkn.]
stability /stə'bɪlɪtɪ/ *n.* being stable. [F f. L (STABLE)]
stabilize /'steɪbɪlaɪz/ *v.* make or become stable; **stabilization** /-'zeɪʃ(ə)n/ *n.*
stabilizer *n.* device to keep ship or aircraft or child's bicycle steady.
stable /'steɪb(ə)l/ **1** *a.* firmly fixed or established, not easily moved or changed or destroyed; resolute, constant. **2** *n.* building in which horses are kept; place where racehorses are kept and trained; racehorses of particular stable; persons or products etc. having common origin or affiliation; such origin or affiliation. **3** *v.t.* put or keep (horse) in stable. **4 stable-companion** (or **-mate**) horse of same stable, member of same organization. **5 stably** *adv.* [F *estable* f. L (*sto* stand)]
stabling *n.* accommodation for horses.
staccato /stə'kɑ:təʊ/ *Mus.* **1** *adv.* & *a.* with each sound or spoken phrase sharply distinct from the others. **2** *n.* (*pl.* **staccatos**) staccato piece of music etc. [It.]
stack 1 *n.* pile or heap, esp. in orderly arrangement; = HAYSTACK; *colloq.* large quantity (*a stack of work*; *has stacks of money*); = *chimney-stack*; = *smoke-stack*; tall factory chimney; stacked group of aircraft; part of library where books are compactly stored; high detached rock esp. off coast of Scotland. **2** *v.t.* pile in stack or stacks; arrange (cards) secretly for cheating, manipulate (circumstances etc.) to one's advantage; cause (aircraft) to fly round same point at different levels while waiting to land. [ON]
stadium /'steɪdɪəm/ *n.* athletic or sports

ground with tiers of seats for spectators. [L f. Gk]

staff /stɑ:f/ **1** *n.* stick or pole esp. as weapon or support or as symbol of office; group of persons carrying on work under manager etc.; those in authority in a school etc.; body of officers in army etc. assisting officer in high command (*general staff*); (*pl.* also **staves**) *Mus.* set of usu. five parallel lines to indicate pitch of notes by position. **2** *v.t.* provide (institution etc.) with staff. **3 staff college** college where officers are trained for staff duties; **staff nurse** nurse ranking just below a sister; **staff sergeant** senior sergeant in cavalry or engineers. [OE]

stag *n.* male deer; person who seeks to buy new shares and sell at once for profit; **stag-beetle** beetle with branched mandibles like antlers; **stag-party** party for men only. [OE]

stage 1 *n.* point or period of development or process; platform, esp. raised one on which plays etc. are performed before audience; (**the stage**) the acting or theatrical profession, dramatic art or literature; scene of action; regular stopping-place on route, distance between two of these; section of space-rocket with separate means of propulsion. **2** *v.t.* present (play etc.) on stage; organize and carry out (*staged a demonstration*). **3 stage-coach** *hist.* large closed coach running regularly by stages between two places; **stage direction** instruction in a play about actor's movement, sounds heard, etc.; **stage fright** nervousness on facing audience esp. for first time; **stage-hand** person handling scenery etc. in theatre; **stage-manage** be stage-manager of, *fig.* arrange and control for effect; **stage-manager** person responsible for lighting and mechanical arrangements etc. on stage; **stage-struck** having obsessive wish to be actor or actress; **stage whisper** an aside, loud whisper meant to be heard by others than person addressed. [F *estage* f. Rmc (L *sto* stand)]

stagecraft *n.* skill or experience in writing or staging plays.

stager *n.* (esp. **old stager**) experienced person.

stagflation /stæg'fleɪʃ(ə)n/ *n.* state of inflation without corresponding increase of demand and employment. [STAGNATION, INFLATION]

stagger 1 *v.* (cause to) walk or move unsteadily; (of news etc.) shock or confuse (person); arrange (events or hours of work etc.) so that they do not coincide; arrange (objects) so that they are not in line. **2** *n.* staggering movement; (in *pl.*) disease, esp. of horses and cattle, causing staggering. [ON]

staggering *a.* astonishing, bewildering.

staghound *n.* large hound used in hunting deer. [STAG]

staging /'steɪdʒɪŋ/ *n.* presentation of play etc.; platform or support, esp. temporary one; shelves for plants in greenhouse; **staging post** regular stopping-place, esp. on air route. [STAGE]

stagnant /'stægnənt/ *a.* (of liquid) motionless, having no current; showing no activity, dull, sluggish; **stagnancy** *n.* [L (*stagnum* pool)]

stagnate /stæg'neɪt/ *v.i.* be or become stagnant; **stagnation** *n.*

stagy /'steɪdʒɪ/ *a.* theatrical, artificial, exaggerated. [STAGE]

staid *a.* quiet and sober in character or manner, sedate. [p.p. of STAY]

stain 1 *v.* discolour or be discoloured by action of liquid sinking in; spoil or damage (reputation or character etc.); colour (wood or glass etc.) with substance that penetrates the material; treat (microscopic specimen) with colouring agent. **2** *n.* act or result of staining; blot or blemish; damage to reputation etc.; substance used in staining. [*distain* f. F f. Rmc (DIS-, TINGE)]

stainless *a.* without stains; not liable to stain; **stainless steel** steel containing much chromium, resisting rust and corrosion.

stair *n.* each of a set of fixed indoor steps; (in *pl.*) set of these; **stair-rod** rod for securing carpet in angle between two steps. [OE]

staircase *n.* flight of stairs and supporting structure; part of building containing staircase.

stairway *n.* a flight of stairs; way up this.

stake 1 *n.* stout stick pointed for driving into ground as support or marker etc.; *hist.* post to which person was tied to be burnt alive, (**the stake**) this death as punishment; money etc. wagered on event; interest or concern, esp. financial; (in *pl.*) money offered as prize in horse-race, the race itself. **2** *v.t.* secure or support with stakes; mark (area) *off* or *out* with stakes; establish (claim); wager (money etc. *on* event); *US colloq.* give financial or other support to. **3 at stake** wagered, risked, to be won or lost; **stake out** place under surveillance. [OE]

stakeholder *n.* third party with whom money etc. wagered is deposited.

Stakhanovite /stə'kɑ:nəvaɪt/ *n.* worker (esp. in USSR) whose high output wins special awards; **Stakhanovism** *n.* [*Stakhanov*, coal-miner]

stalactite /'stæləktaɪt/ *n.* icicle-like deposit of calcium carbonate hanging from roof of cave etc. [Gk (*stalactos* dripping)]

stalagmite /'stæləgmaɪt/ *n.* deposit like stalactite rising like spike from floor of cave etc. [Gk (*stalagma* that which drops)]

stale 1 *a.* not fresh; musty, insipid, or otherwise the worse for age or use; trite or unoriginal (*stale joke, news*); (of athlete or musician etc.) having ability impaired by excessive exertion or practice. **2** *v.* become or make stale. [AF (*estaler* halt)]

stalemate 1 *n.* state of chess-game counting as draw, in which one player cannot move without going into check; deadlock in proceedings. **2** *v.t.* bring (player) to stalemate; bring to standstill. [obs. *stale* (prec.), MATE[2]]

stalk[1] /stɔ:k/ *n.* stem, esp. main stem of herbaceous plant or slender stem supporting leaf or flower or fruit etc.; similar support of organ etc. in animals. [dimin. of obs. *stale* rung]

stalk[2] /stɔ:k/ **1** *v.* pursue or approach (wild animal, or enemy) stealthily; stride, walk in stately or haughty manner. **2** *n.* stalking of game; imposing gait. **3 stalking-horse** horse behind which hunter hides, pretext concealing one's real intentions or actions. [OE, rel. to STEAL]

stall[1] /stɔ:l/ **1** *n.* stable or cowhouse, compartment for one animal in this; trader's booth in market etc.; fixed seat in choir or chancel, more or less enclosed at back and sides; (usu. in *pl.*) each of seats on ground floor of theatre; compartment for one person in shower-bath, one horse at start of race, etc.; stalling of engine or aircraft, condition resulting from this. **2** *v.* (of motor vehicle or its engine) stop because of inadequate fuel-supply or overloading of engine etc.; (of aircraft) get out of control because speed is insufficient; cause (engine etc.) to stall; put or keep (cattle etc.) in stall(s). [OE]

stall[2] /stɔ:l/ *v.* play for time when being questioned etc.; delay or obstruct (person). [*stall* decoy, perh. rel. to prec.]

stallion /'stæljən/ *n.* uncastrated male horse. [F f. Gmc (STALL[1])]

stalwart /'stɔ:lwət/ **1** *a.* strongly built, sturdy; courageous, resolute. **2** *n.* stalwart person, esp. loyal uncompromising partisan. [OE, = place-worthy]

stamen /'steɪmen, -mən/ *n.* male fertilizing organ of flowering plant. [L, = warp-thread]

stamina /'stæmɪnə/ *n.* ability to endure prolonged physical or mental strain. [L, pl. of prec.]

stammer 1 *v.* speak with halting articulation, esp. with pauses or rapid repetitions of same syllable; (often with *out*) utter (words) thus. **2** *n.* act or habit of stammering. [OE]

stamp 1 *v.* bring down (one's foot) heavily on ground etc., crush or flatten thus; walk *about* etc. with heavy steps; impress (pattern or mark etc.) on surface; impress (surface) with pattern or mark etc.; affix postage or other stamp to; assign specific character to, mark out. **2** *n.* instrument for stamping; mark or design made by this; (in full **postage stamp**) small adhesive piece of paper showing amount paid, affixed to letters etc. to be posted; mark impressed on or label etc. fixed to commodity as evidence of quality etc.; act or sound of stamping of foot; characteristic mark or quality. **3 stamp-collector** collector of postage stamps; **stamp-duty** duty imposed on certain kinds of legal document; **stamping-ground** favourite haunt or place of action; **stamp on** impress on (the memory etc.), suppress; **stamp out** produce by cutting out with die etc., put an end to, destroy. [OE]

stampede /stæm'pi:d/ **1** *n.* sudden hurried movement of (usu. frightened) cattle or people etc.; uncontrolled or unreasoning action by large number of people. **2** *v.* (cause to) take part in stampede. [Sp. f. Gmc, rel. to prec.]

stance /stɑ:ns, stæns/ *n.* attitude or position of body esp. when hitting a ball etc.; standpoint, attitude. [F f. It. STANZA]

stanch /stɑ:ntʃ/ *v.t.* stop flow of (blood etc.); stop flow from (wound). [F *estanchier* (STAUNCH)]

stanchion /'stɑ:nʃ(ə)n/ *n.* upright post or support; device for confining cattle in stall etc. [AF]

stand 1 *v.* (*past* and *p.p.* **stood** /stʊd/) have or take or maintain upright position, esp. on feet or base; be situated (*the house stands on a corner*); be of specified height; be in specified condition (*stands accused; stands in need of help*); set upright or in specified position (*stood it on the floor*); move to and remain in specified position, *fig.* take specified attitude (*stand aside, aloof*); maintain position, avoid falling or moving or being moved; assume stationary position, cease to move; remain valid or unaltered; *Naut.* hold specified course; endure or tolerate (*cannot stand noise, that fellow*); provide (person) with (thing, esp. drink) at one's own expense; act as (*stand proxy*). **2** *n.* act or condition of standing; resistance to attack or compulsion (*make a stand*); position or *fig.* attitude adopted; rack or pedestal etc. on or in which things may be placed; stall in market etc.; standing-place for vehicles; raised structure for persons to sit or stand on; *US* witness-box; halt made by touring-company etc. to give performance(s); (in cricket) prolonged stay at wicket by two batsmen; group *of* growing trees etc. **3 as it stands** in its present condition, in present circumstances; **stand by** stand ready for action, stand near, look on without interfering, uphold or support (person), adhere to (promise etc.); **stand-by** *n.* (*pl.* **stand-bys**) person or thing ready if needed in emergency etc.; **stand corrected** accept that one was wrong; **stand down** withdraw from position or candidacy; **stand for** represent or signify or imply, be candidate for (esp. public office), *colloq.* endure or tolerate; **stand one's ground** not yield; **stand in** deputize (*for*); **stand-in** *n.* deputy or substitute esp. for actor or actress; **stand off** move or keep away, temporarily dispense with services of (employee); **stand-off half** half-back in Rugby football who forms link between scrum-half and three-quarters; **stand-offish** cold or distant in manner; **stand on** insist on, observe scrupulously; **stand on one's own (two) feet** be self-reliant or independent; **stand out** be prominent or outstanding, persist in resistance (*against*) or support (*for*); **stand to** stand ready for action, abide by, be likely or certain to; **stand to reason** be obvious or logical; **stand up** come to or remain in or place in standing position, be valid, *colloq.* fail to keep appointment with; **stand-up** *a.* (of meal) eaten standing, (of fight) violent and thorough, (of collar) upright, not turned down; **stand up for** support, side with; **stand up to** face (opponent) courageously, be resistant to harmful effects of (use or wear etc.); **take one's stand** base argument or reliance *on*. [OE]

standard /'stændəd/ **1** *n.* object or quality or measure serving as basis or example or principle to which others should conform or by which others are judged; required or specified level of excellence etc. (*not up to standard*; *of a low standard*); ordinary procedure etc.; distinctive flag; upright support or pipe; treelike shrub with (or grafted on) upright stem. **2** *a.* serving or used as standard; having recognized and permanent value, authoritative; of normal or prescribed quality or size etc.; (of language) conforming to established educated usage. **3 standard-bearer** person who carries a distinctive flag, prominent leader in cause; **standard lamp** domestic lamp on tall upright with base; **standard of living** degree of material comfort enjoyed by person or group; **standard time** that established in a country or region by law or custom and based on longitude. [AF (EXTEND, with sense infl. by prec.)]

standardize *v.t.* cause to conform to a standard; **standardization** /-'zeɪʃ(ə)n/ *n.*

standing 1 *n.* status or esteem, high repute; duration (*of long standing*). **2** *a.* that stands, upright; established, permanent (*standing army*); (of jump or start) performed from rest without run-up; (of water) stagnant. **3 standing committee** see COMMITTEE; **standing joke** object of permanent ridicule; **standing order** instruction to banker to make regular payments, or to newsagent etc. for regular supply of a periodical etc.; **standing orders** rules governing procedure in Parliament or council etc.; **standing room** space to stand in.

standpipe *n.* vertical pipe for fluid to rise in.

standpoint *n.* point of view.

standstill *n.* stoppage, inability to proceed.

stank *past* of STINK.

stannary /'stænərɪ/ *n.* tin-mine. [L *stannum* tin]

stanza /'stænzə/ *n.* group of (usu. four or more rhymed) lines as repeated metrical unit. [It.]

staphylococcus /stæfɪlə'kɒkəs/ *n.* (*pl.* **staphylococci** /-aɪ/) form of pus-producing bacterium; **staphylococcal** *a.* [Gk (*staphulē* bunch of grapes, *kokkos* berry]

staple¹ /'steɪp(ə)l/ **1** *n.* U-shaped metal bar or piece of wire with pointed ends, driven into wood etc. to hold something or into sheets of paper to fasten them together. **2** *v.t.* fasten or furnish with staple. [OE]

staple² /'steɪp(ə)l/ **1** *a.* main or principal (*staple diet*); important as product or export. **2** *n.* important (usu. principal) article of commerce in a district or country; chief element or material; fibre of cotton or wool etc. as determining its quality (*of fine, long, staple*). [F *estaple* market f. LG or Du. (prec.)]

star 1 *n.* celestial body appearing as luminous point in night sky; large self-luminous gaseous ball such as the sun is; celestial body regarded as influencing person's fortunes etc.; thing resembling star in shape or appearance; figure or object with radiating points e.g. as decoration or mark of rank or showing category of excellence; famous or brilliant person, esp. actor or actress or other performer; principal performer in play or film etc. **2** *v.* (**-rr-**) mark or adorn (as) with star(s); present or perform as star actor etc. **3 star-dust** multitude of stars looking like dust; **star-gazer** *colloq.* astronomer or astrologer; **Star of David** figure of two interlaced equilateral triangles used as Jewish symbol; **Stars and Stripes** national flag of US; **star-studded** covered with stars, including many famous people; **star turn** main item in an entertainment etc. [OE]

starboard /ˈstɑːbəd/ **1** *n.* right-hand side of ship or aircraft looking forward. **2** *v.t.* turn (helm) to starboard. **3 starboard tack** tack with wind on starboard side. [OE, = *steer board*]

starch 1 *n.* white carbohydrate in cereals, potatoes, and all other plants except fungi; preparation of this for stiffening linen etc.; stiffness of manner, formality. **2** *v.t.* stiffen (as) with starch. [OE, rel. to STARK]

starchy *a.* of or like starch, containing much starch; stiff or formal in manner; **starchily** *adv.*; **starchiness** *n.*

stardom *n.* position or fame of star actor etc. [STAR]

stare 1 *v.* look fixedly with eyes wide open, esp. with curiosity or surprise or horror; reduce (person) to specified condition by staring (*stared him into silence*). **2** *n.* staring gaze. **3 stare person in the face** be clearly evident or imminent. [OE]

starfish *n.* star-shaped sea creature. [STAR]

stark 1 *a.* desolate, bare; sharply evident (*in stark contrast*); downright, sheer (*stark madness*); completely naked; *archaic* stiff, rigid. **2** *adv.* completely, wholly (*stark mad*). [OE]

starlet /ˈstɑːlɪt/ *n.* young film actress likely to become star. [STAR]

starlight *n.* light from stars.

starling /ˈstɑːlɪŋ/ *n.* small blackish-brown bird noted for its chatter and mimicry. [OE]

starlit *a.* lighted by stars; with stars visible. [STAR]

starry *a.* full of or bright with stars; **starry-eyed** *colloq.* bright eyed, romantic but unpractical.

start 1 *v.* set in motion or action, cause beginning of (*start work, a fire, crying, to cry*); set oneself in motion or action, begin journey etc.; cause (machine etc.) to begin operating; (of engine etc.) begin running; cause or enable (person) to commence business etc.; found or establish; give signal to (competitors) to start in race; conceive (baby); make sudden movement from surprise or pain etc.; spring *out* or *up* etc.; rouse (game etc.) from lair; (of timber etc.) be loose or displaced, cause (timber) to do this. **2** *n.* beginning; place where race is begun; advantage granted in beginning a race; advantageous initial position in life or business etc.; sudden movement of surprise or pain etc. **3 for a start** as a thing to start with; **starting-block** shaped block against which runner braces feet at start of race; **starting-price** final odds before start of horse-race etc.; **start off** begin, start to move; **start out** begin, begin journey; **start up** rise suddenly, come or bring into existence or action. [OE]

starter *n.* device for starting engine of motor vehicle etc.; person giving signal for start of race; horse or competitor starting in race; first course of meal.

startle /ˈstɑːt(ə)l/ *v.t.* give shock or surprise to. [OE]

starve *v.* (cause to) die of hunger or suffer from lack of food; *colloq.* feel very hungry (*I'm starving*); (cause to) be deprived or short *of* something needed or wanted; compel by starving (*into* surrender etc.); **starvation** /-ˈveɪʃ(ə)n/ *n.* [OE, = die]

starveling /ˈstɑːvlɪŋ/ *n.* starving person or animal.

stash *sl.* **1** *v.t.* conceal, put *away* in safe place. **2** *n.* hiding-place; thing hidden. [orig. unkn.]

stasis /ˈsteɪsɪs, ˈstæ-/ *n.* (*pl.* **stases** /-iːz/) stoppage of flow or circulation. [Gk]

state 1 *n.* existing condition or position of thing or person; *colloq.* excited or agitated mental condition (*was in a real state*); (often **State**) organized political community under one government, such community forming part of federal republic, civil government; pomp. **2** *a.* of or concerned with the State or its ceremonial occasions. **3** *v.t.* say or express, esp. fully or clearly, in speech or writing; fix or specify (date or time etc.); *Mus.* play (theme etc.) esp. for the first time. **4 in** (or **into**) **a state** in (or into) an excited or anxious or untidy condition; **lie in state** be laid in public place of honour before burial; **the States** the USA. [partly ESTATE, partly L *status*]

stateless *a.* having no nationality or citizenship.

stately *a.* dignified, imposing; **stately home** large grand house, esp. one open to public; **stateliness** *n.*

statement *n.* stated or being stated; expression in words, thing stated; formal account of facts, esp. of transactions in bank account or of amount due to tradesman.

stateroom *n.* state apartment; large private cabin in passenger ship.
statesman *n.* person skilled in affairs of State; sagacious far-sighted politician; **statesmanlike** *a.*; **statesmanship** *n.*
static /'stætɪk/ **1** *a.* stationary, not acting or changing; concerned with bodies at rest or forces in equilibrium. **2** *n.* static electricity; atmospherics. **3 static electricity** electricity not flowing as current. **4 statically** *adv.* [Gk *statikos* (*sta-* stand)]
statics *n.pl.* (usu. treated as *sing.*) science of static bodies or forces; static.
station /'steɪʃ(ə)n/ **1** *n.* place or building etc. where person or thing stands or is placed or where a particular activity, esp. a public service, is based or organized; regular stopping-place on railway line, the buildings of this; establishment engaged in broadcasting; military or naval base, inhabitants of this; position in life, rank or status; *Austral.* large sheep or cattle farm. **2** *v.t.* assign station to; put in position. **3 station-master** official in charge of railway station; **Stations of the Cross** series of scenes from the Passion as points of successive prayers in some churches; **station-wagon** *US* estate car. [F f. L (*sto stat-* stand)]
stationary *a.* not moving; not intended to be moved; not changing in amount or quantity. [L (prec.)]
stationer *n.* dealer in stationery.
stationery *n.* writing materials, office supplies, etc.; **Stationery Office** government publishing-house in UK.
statistic /stə'tɪstɪk/ *n.* statistical fact or item. [G (STATE)]
statistical *a.* of or concerned with statistics; **statistically** *adv.*
statistics *n.pl.* numerical facts systematically collected; (usu. treated as *sing.*) science of collecting or using statistics; **statistician** /stætɪ'stɪʃ(ə)n/ *n.*
statuary /'stætjʊərɪ/ **1** *a.* of or for statues. **2** *n.* statues; making or maker of statues. [L (foll.)]
statue /'stætju:, 'stætʃu:/ *n.* sculptured or moulded or cast figure of person or animal etc., usu. of or above life size. [F f. L (*sto* stand)]
statuesque /stætjʊ'esk, stætʃ-/ *a.* like, or having dignity or beauty of, a statue.
statuette /stætjʊ'et, stætʃ-/ *n.* small-scale statue.
stature /'stætjə, 'stætʃə/ *n.* height of (esp. human) body; eminence, mental or moral quality. [F f. L (*sto* stand)]
status /'steɪtəs/ *n.* rank or social position, relation to others, relative importance; superior social etc. position; **status quo** the existing or unchanged situation; **status symbol** possession etc. regarded as indicating person's high status. [L (as prec.)]
statute /'stætju:t/ *n.* law passed by legislative body; rule of corporation or founder intended as permanent; **statute-book** the statute law, book(s) containing this; **statute law** a statute, the statutes collectively; **statute mile** 1760 yds., about 1.6 km. [F f. L (*statuo* set up)]
statutory /'stætjʊtərɪ/ *a.* enacted or required by statute; **statutorily** *adv.*
staunch /stɔ:ntʃ/ *a.* trustworthy, loyal; (of ship or joint etc.) watertight, airtight. [F *estanche*]
stave 1 *n.* each of the curved pieces of wood forming sides of a cask or pail etc.; *Mus.* staff; stanza, verse. **2** *v.t.* (*past* & *p.p.* **stove** or **staved**) break a hole in, knock out of shape. **3 stave in** crush by forcing inwards; **stave off** avert or defer (danger or misfortune etc.). [STAFF]
staves see STAFF.
stay[1] **1** *v.* continue to be in same place or condition, not depart or change; dwell temporarily (*at* or *in* etc.); (cause to) stop or pause; postpone (judgement etc.); assuage (hunger etc.) esp. for short time; show endurance. **2** *n.* action or period of staying; suspension or postponement of execution of a sentence etc. **3 stay-at-home** *a.* remaining habitually at home, (*n.*) person who does this; **stay the course** endure struggle etc. to the end; **stay in** remain indoors; **staying-power** endurance; **stay the night** remain until next day; **stay put** *colloq.* remain where it is placed or where one is. [AF f. L *sto* stand]
stay[2] *n.* prop or support; rope etc. supporting mast or flagstaff etc.; tie-piece in aircraft; (in *pl.*) corset, esp. stiffened with whalebone etc. [F & OE f. Gmc]
stayer *n.* person or animal with great endurance. [STAY[1]]
staysail /'steɪseɪl, -s(ə)l/ *n.* sail extended on stay. [STAY[2]]
STD *abbr.* subscriber trunk dialling.
stead /sted/ *n.* only in **in person's** (or **thing's**) **stead** instead of him (or it), as a substitute; **stand in good stead** be advantageous or serviceable to (person). [OE, = place]
steadfast /'stedfɑ:st/ *a.* constant, firm, unwavering. [OE (prec.)]
steady /'stedɪ/ **1** *a.* firmly in position, not tottering or rocking or wavering; done or operating or happening in uniform and regular manner (*steady pace*; *steady increase*); constant, persistent; serious and dependable in behaviour. **2** *v.* make or become steady. **3** *adv.* steadily. **4** *n.* *colloq.* regular boy-friend or girl-friend. **5 go steady with** *colloq.* have as regular

boy-friend or girl-friend; **steady on!** be careful!; **steady state** unvarying condition, esp. in physical process. **6 steadily** *adv.*; **steadiness** *n.* [STEAD]

steak /steɪk/ *n.* thick slice of meat (esp. beef) or fish, usu. grilled or fried; beef from front of animal, cut for stewing or braising; **steak-house** restaurant specializing in meat steaks. [ON]

steal 1 *v.* (*past* **stole**; *p.p.* **stolen**) take (another's property) illegally or without permission, esp. secretly; obtain surreptitiously or by surprise (*stole a kiss*); gain insidiously or artfully etc.; move or come (*away* or *up* etc.) silently or gradually. **2** *n. US colloq.* stealing, theft; *colloq.* (unexpectedly) easy task or good bargain. **3 steal a march on** gain advantage over by acting surreptitiously or anticipating; **steal a person's thunder** forestall him; **steal the show** outshine other performers esp. unexpectedly. [OE]

stealth /stelθ/ *n.* secret or surreptitious behaviour. [OE (prec.)]

stealthy *a.* practising or done by stealth; **stealthily** *adv.*; **stealthiness** *n.*

steam 1 *n.* gas into which water is changed by boiling; condensed vapour formed from this; power obtained from steam; *colloq.* power or energy. **2** *v.* give out steam; cook or treat with steam; move by power of steam; *colloq.* work or move vigorously or rapidly. **3 steam-engine** engine or locomotive driven by steam; **steam-hammer** forging-hammer worked by steam; **steam iron** electric iron emitting steam from its flat surface; **steam radio** *colloq.* radio broadcasting regarded as antiquated by comparison with television; **steam train** train pulled by steam-engine; **steam up** cover or become covered with condensed steam (**be** or **get** etc. **steamed up** *sl.* be or get excited or agitated). [OE]

steamboat *n.* steam-driven boat.

steamer *n.* steamship; container for steaming food etc.

steamroller 1 *n.* heavy slow-moving locomotive with roller used in road-making; *fig.* crushing power or force. **2** *v.t.* crush or move along as with steam-roller.

steamship *n.* steam-driven ship.

steamy *a.* of or like or full of steam; *colloq.* erotic; **steamily** *adv.*; **steaminess** *n.*

steatite /ˈsti:ətaɪt/ *n.* a kind of usu. grey talc with greasy feel. [F f. Gk *stear steat-* tallow]

steed *n. literary* horse. [OE]

steel 1 *n.* malleable alloy of iron and carbon, used for tools, weapons, machines, etc.; steel rod for sharpening knives; *literary* (not in *pl.*) sword; great strength or firmness (*a grip like steel*; *nerves of steel*). **2** *a.* of or like steel. **3** *v.t.* harden or make resolute (*steel oneself* or *one's heart*). **4 steel band** band of musicians, orig. W. Indian, with instruments made from oil-drums; **steel wool** mass of steel shavings used as abrasive. [OE]

steely *a.* of or like steel; inflexibly severe; **steeliness** *n.*

steelyard *n.* weighing-apparatus with graduated arm along which a weight is moved. [STEEL, YARD[1]]

steep[1] 1 *a.* sloping sharply, hard to climb (*steep hill, stairs*); (of rise or fall) rapid; *colloq.* exorbitant, unreasonable, exaggerated, incredible. **2** *n.* steep slope, precipice. [OE]

steep[2] 1 *v.t.* soak or bathe in liquid. **2** *n.* action of, or liquid for, steeping. **3 steep in** pervade or imbue with, make deeply acquainted with (subject etc.). [OE]

steepen *v.* make or become steep. [STEEP[1]]

steeple /ˈsti:p(ə)l/ *n.* tall tower, esp. surmounted by spire, above roof of church. [OE (STEEP[1])]

steeplechase 1 *n.* horse-race with obstacles such as fences and ditches to jump; cross-country foot-race. **2** *v.i.* take part in steeplechase.

steeplejack *n.* person who repairs steeples, tall chimneys, etc.

steer[1] *v.* guide (vehicle or ship etc.) by means of wheel or rudder etc.; direct or guide (one's course, or other people) in specified direction; **steer clear of** take care to avoid; **steering-column** column on which steering-wheel is mounted; **steering committee** committee deciding order of business, general course of operations, etc.; **steering-wheel** wheel by which vehicle, vessel, etc., is steered. [OE]

steer[2] *n.* young male ox, esp. bullock. [OE]

steerage *n.* steering; part of ship formerly assigned to passengers travelling at cheapest rate. [STEER[1]]

steersman *n.* one who steers ship.

stein /staɪn/ *n.* large earthenware mug esp. for beer. [G]

stela /ˈsti:lə/ *n.* (also **stele** /-i:/; *pl.* **stelae** /-i:/) ancient upright slab or pillar, usu. inscribed and sculptured, esp. as gravestone. [L & Gk]

stellar /ˈstelə/ *a.* of a star or stars. [L (*stella* star)]

stem[1] 1 *n.* main body or stalk of plant; stalk supporting fruit or flower or leaf; stem-shaped part, e.g. slender part of wineglass between body and foot, tube of tobacco-pipe, vertical stroke in letter or musical note; root or main part of noun or verb etc., to which case-endings etc. are added; main upright timber at bow of ship (*from stem to stern*). **2** *v.i.* (**-mm-**) spring or originate *from*. [OE]

stem[2] *v.* (**-mm-**) check or stop, make headway against. [ON]

Sten *n.* (also **Sten gun**) lightweight machine-gun. [*S T* (inventors' initials) + *-en* as in BREN]

stench *n.* offensive or foul smell. [OE (STINK)]

stencil /'stens(ə)l/ **1** *n.* thin sheet in which pattern is cut, used to produce corresponding pattern on surface beneath it by applying ink or paint etc.; pattern so produced. **2** *v.t.* (**-ll-**, *US* **-l-**) produce (pattern) with stencil; mark (surface) thus. [F f. L *scintilla* spark]

stenography /ste'nɒgrəfɪ/ *n.* writing of shorthand; **stenographer** *n.* [Gk *stenos* narrow]

stentorian /sten'tɔ:rɪən/ *a.* (of voice etc.) loud and powerful. [*Stentor*, herald in Trojan War]

step 1 *n.* complete action of moving and placing one leg in walking or running; distance covered by this; unit of movement in dancing; measure taken, esp. one of several in course of action (*a wise step*; *took steps to prevent it*); surface on which foot is placed in ascending or descending, stair or tread; (in *pl.*) step-ladder; short distance (*only a step from my door*); mark or sound made by foot in walking etc.; manner of stepping; degree in scale of promotion or precedence etc. **2** *v.* (**-pp-**) lift and set down foot or alternate feet as in walking; go or come in specified direction by stepping; *fig.* make progress in specified way (*stepped into a new job*); measure (distance *off* or *out*) by stepping; perform (dance). **3 break step** get out of step; **in step** putting foot to ground at the same time as others, esp. in marching, *fig.* conforming to the actions etc. of others; **keep step** remain in step; **mind** (or **watch**) **one's step** take care; **out of step** not in step; **step by step** gradually, cautiously; **step down** resign; **step in** enter, intervene; **step-ladder** short self-supporting ladder with flat steps; **step on it** *sl.* go or act faster; **step out** take long brisk steps, go out to enjoy oneself socially; **stepping-stone** raised stone usu. as one of series as means of crossing stream etc., *fig.* means of progress; **step up** come up or forward, increase rate or volume etc. [OE]

step- *prefix* denoting relationship like the one specified but resulting from parent's remarriage. [OE, = orphaned]

stepbrother *n.* male child of one's step-parent's previous marriage.

stepchild *n.* spouse's child by previous marriage.

stepdaughter *n.* female stepchild.

stepfather *n.* male step-parent.

stephanotis /stefə'nəʊtɪs/ *n.* fragrant tropical climbing plant. [L f. Gk]

stepmother *n.* female step-parent. [STEP-]

step-parent *n.* mother's or father's later spouse.

steppe *n.* level treeless plain. [Russ.]

stepsister *n.* female child of one's step-parent's previous marriage. [STEP-]

stepson *n.* male stepchild.

-ster *suffix* denoting agent (*gangster*, *youngster*). [OE, orig. fem.]

stereo /'sterɪəʊ, 'stɪər-/ **1** *n.* (*pl.* **stereos**) stereophonic record-player etc.; stereophony; stereoscope; stereotype. **2** *a.* stereophonic; stereoscopic. [abbr.]

stereo- *in comb.* solid, having three dimensions. [Gk *stereos* solid]

stereophonic /sterɪəʊ'fɒnɪk, stɪər-/ *a.* using two or more channels so that sound has effect of being distributed; **stereophonically** *adv.*; **stereophony** /-'ɒfənɪ/ *n.*

stereoscope /'sterɪəskəʊp, 'stɪər-/ *n.* device by which two slightly different photographs etc. are viewed together, giving impression of depth and solidity; **stereoscopic** /-'skɒpɪk/ *a.*; **stereoscopically** /-'skɒpɪkəlɪ/ *adv.*

stereotype /'sterɪəʊtaɪp, 'stɪər-/ **1** *n.* unduly fixed mental impression; conventional idea or opinion or character etc.; printing-plate cast from mould of composed type. **2** *v.t.* formalize, make typical or conventional (usu. in *p.p.*); print from stereotype, make stereotype of. [F (STEREO-)]

sterile /'steraɪl/ *a.* not able to produce seed or offspring, barren; free from living micro-organisms; without result, unproductive (*a sterile discussion*); **sterility** /-'rɪlɪtɪ/ *n.* [F or L]

sterilize /'sterɪlaɪz/ *v.t.* make sterile; deprive of power of reproduction; **sterilization** /-'zeɪʃ(ə)n/ *n.*

sterling /'stɜ:lɪŋ/ **1** *a.* of or in British money (*pound sterling*); (of coin or precious metal) genuine, of standard value or purity; (of person or qualities etc.) of solid worth, genuine, reliable. **2** *n.* British money (*paid in sterling*). **3 sterling silver** silver of 92½% purity. [OE, = penny]

stern[1] *a.* severe, grim, enforcing discipline or submission. [OE]

stern[2] *n.* rear part of ship or boat; any rear part; **stern-post** central upright timber etc. of stern, usu. bearing rudder. [ON (STEER[1])]

sternum /'stɜ:nəm/ *n.* (*pl.* **sternums** or **sterna**) breastbone; **sternal** *a.* [Gk *sternon* chest]

steroid /'stɪərɔɪd, 'ste-/ *n.* any of various organic compounds including some hormones and vitamins. [foll.]

sterol /'stɪərɒl, 'ste-/ *n.* complex solid alcohol important in vitamin synthesis. [CHOLESTEROL etc. f. Gk *stereos* stiff]

stertorous /'stɜ:tərəs/ *a.* (of breathing etc.) laboured and noisy. [L *sterto* snore]

stet *v.* (**-tt-**) (usu. as instruction written on proof-sheet etc.) ignore or cancel correction or alteration, let original form stand. [L, = let it stand]

stethoscope /'steθəskəʊp/ *n.* instrument used in listening to heart, lungs, etc.; **stethoscopic** /-'skɒpɪk/ *a.* [F f. Gk *stēthos* breast]

stetson /'stets(ə)n/ *n.* slouch hat with very wide brim and high crown. [*Stetson*, hat-maker]

stevedore /'sti:vədɔ:/ *n.* man employed in loading and unloading ships. [Sp. *estivador*]

stew 1 *v.* cook by long simmering in closed vessel with liquid; *colloq.* swelter. 2 *n.* dish of stewed meat etc.; *colloq.* agitated or angry state. 3 **stew in one's own juice** suffer consequences of one's own actions. [F *estuver* f. Rmc]

steward /'stju:əd/ 1 *n.* person employed to manage another's property; person responsible for supplies of food etc. for college or club etc.; passengers' attendant on ship or aircraft or train; official in charge of race-meeting or show etc. 2 *v.* act as steward (of). 3 **stewardship** *n.* [OE, = house-warden]

stewardess *n.* female steward, esp. on ship or aircraft.

stewed *a.* cooked by stewing; (of tea) bitter or strong from infusing for too long; *sl.* drunk. [STEW]

stick[1] *n.* short slender branch or piece of wood, esp. trimmed for use as support or as weapon; thin rod of wood etc. for particular purpose (*drumstick*); *colloq.* piece of wood as part of house or furniture (*a few sticks of furniture*); implement used to propel ball in hockey or polo etc.; gear-lever; conductor's baton; more or less cylindrical piece of thing, e.g. celery or dynamite; punishment, esp. by beating; adverse criticism; *colloq.* person, esp. one who is dull or unsociable; **stick insect** insect with twiglike body. [OE]

stick[2] *v.* (*past* and *p.p.* **stuck**) insert or thrust (thing or its point) *in* or *into* etc., stab; fix *on* or *upon* pointed thing, be fixed (as) by pointed end *in* or *into* or *on* etc.; fix or become or remain fixed by adhesive etc.; lose or deprive of power of motion or action through friction or jamming or other impediment; *colloq.* put or remain in specified position or place; *colloq.* (of accusation etc.) be convincing or regarded as valid; *sl.* endure or tolerate; **be stuck for** be at a loss for or in need of; **be stuck on** *sl.* be captivated by; **be stuck with** *colloq.* be unable to get rid of; **get stuck in** (or **into**) *sl.* begin in earnest; **stick around** *sl.* linger, remain at same place; **stick at** *colloq.* persevere with; **stick at nothing** allow nothing, esp. no scruples, to deter one; **stick by** (or **with**) stay close or faithful to; **sticking-plaster** adhesive plaster for wounds etc.; **stick-in-the-mud** *colloq.* unprogressive or old-fashioned person; **stick in one's throat** be against one's principles; **stick it out** *colloq.* endure something unpleasant; **stick one's neck out** expose oneself to danger or censure etc. by acting boldly; **stick out** (cause to) protrude; **stick out for** persist in demanding; **stick to** remain fixed on or to, remain faithful to, keep to (subject etc.); **stick together** *colloq.* remain united or mutually loyal; **stick up** (cause to) protrude, be or make erect, fasten to upright surface, *sl.* rob or threaten with gun; **stick-up** *n. sl.* robbery with gun; **stick up for** support or defend (person or cause). [OE]

sticker *n.* adhesive label; persistent person.

stickleback /'stɪk(ə)lbæk/ *n.* small spiny-backed fish. [OE, = thorn-back]

stickler *n.* person who insists on something (*a stickler for punctuality*). [*obs. stickle* be umpire]

sticky *a.* tending or intended to stick or adhere; glutinous, viscous; (of weather) humid; *colloq.* making or likely to make objections; *sl.* very unpleasant or painful (*came to a sticky end*); **sticky wicket** difficult or awkward circumstances; **stickily** *adv.*; **stickiness** *n.* [STICK[2]]

stiff 1 *a.* rigid, not flexible, hard to bend or move etc.; hard to cope with, needing strength or effort (*stiff climb, test*); severe or strong (*stiff breeze, penalty*); (of person or manner) formal, constrained; (of muscle or limb etc., or person as regards these) aching when used, owing to previous exertion; (of an alcoholic or medicinal drink) strong; *colloq.* to an extreme degree (*bored stiff*). 2 *n. sl.* corpse; *sl.* foolish or useless person (*big stiff*). 3 **stiff-necked** obstinate or haughty; **stiff upper lip** firmness, fortitude; **stiff with** *sl.* abundantly provided with. [OE]

stiffen *v.* make or become stiff.

stifle /'staɪf(ə)l/ *v.* smother, cause or experience constraint of breathing or suppression of utterance etc. [orig. uncert.]

stigma /ˈstɪgmə/ *n.* (*pl.* **stigmas** except as below) mark or sign of disgrace or discredit; part of pistil that receives the pollen in pollination; (in *pl.* **stigmata** /ˈstɪgmətə/) marks corresponding to those left on Christ's body by the Crucifixion. [L f. Gk *stigma -mat-* brand, dot]

stigmatize /ˈstɪgmətaɪz/ *v.t.* describe as unworthy or disgraceful. [F or med.L f. Gk (prec.)]

stile *n.* arrangement of steps allowing people but not animals to climb over fence or wall. [OE]

stiletto /stɪˈletəʊ/ *n.* (*pl.* **stilettos**) short dagger; pointed instrument for making eyelets etc.; **stiletto heel** long tapering heel of shoe. [It. dimin. (STYLE)]

still[1] 1 *a.* without motion or sound, calm or tranquil; (of wine etc.) not effervescing. **2** *n.* silence (*in the still of the night*); ordinary static photograph (as opposed to motion picture), esp. single shot from cinema film. **3** *adv.* without moving (*sit still*); even till or at a particular time (*why are you still here?*); nevertheless, all the same; even, yet, increasingly (*urged to still greater efforts*). **4** *v.* make or become still, quieten. **5** **still birth** birth of dead child; **still life** (*pl.* **still lifes**) painting of inanimate objects, e.g. fruits. [OE]

still[2] *n.* apparatus for distilling spirituous liquors etc.; **still-room** room for distilling, housekeeper's store-room in large house. [obs. *still* v. = DISTIL]

stillborn *a.* born dead; abortive. [STILL[1]]

stilt *n.* each of a pair of poles with supports for feet enabling user to walk at a distance above the ground; each of a set of piles or posts supporting building etc. [LG or Du.]

stilted *a.* (of literary style etc.) stiff and unnatural, bombastic; standing on stilts.

Stilton /ˈstɪlt(ə)n/ *n.* rich blue-veined cheese. [*Stilton* in Cambridgeshire]

stimulant /ˈstɪmjʊlənt/ **1** *a.* that stimulates, esp. that increases bodily or mental activity. **2** *n.* stimulant substance or influence. [L (foll.)]

stimulate /ˈstɪmjʊleɪt/ *v.t.* animate, excite, arouse; **stimulation** /-ˈleɪʃ(ə)n/ *n.*; **stimulative** *a.*; **stimulator** *n.* [L (foll.)]

stimulus /ˈstɪmjʊləs/ *n.* (*pl.* **stimuli** /-aɪ/) stimulating thing or effect. [L, = goad]

sting **1** *n.* sharp wounding organ of insect or snake or nettle; inflicting of wound with this, the wound itself or the pain caused by it; wounding or painful quality or effect; pungency or vigour; *sl.* swindle, robbery. **2** *v.* (*past* and *p.p.* **stung**) wound or pierce with sting, be able to do this; give or feel tingling physical pain or sharp mental pain; incite by such mental effect (*was stung into replying*); *sl.* involve (person) in expense, swindle. **3** **stinging-nettle** nettle that stings; **sting in the tail** unexpected pain or difficulty at the end; **sting-ray** broad flat-fish with stinging tail. [OE]

stinger *n.* thing that stings, esp. sharp painful blow.

stingy /ˈstɪndʒɪ/ *a.* niggardly, mean; **stingily** *adv.*; **stinginess** *n.* [prob. f. STING]

stink **1** *v.i.* (*past* **stank** or **stunk**; *p.p.* **stunk**) have strong offensive smell; *colloq.* be or seem very unpleasant. **2** *n.* strong offensive smell; *colloq.* loud complaint or fuss (*kick up a stink about it*). **3** **stink-bomb** device emitting stink when exploded; **stink out** drive (person etc.) out by stink, fill (place) with stink. [OE]

stinker *n.* person or thing that stinks; *sl.* very objectionable person or thing, difficult task, letter etc. conveying strong disapproval.

stinking **1** *a.* that stinks; *sl.* very objectionable. **2** *adv. sl.* extremely and usu. objectionably (*stinking rich*).

stint **1** *v.t.* supply (food or aid etc.) in niggardly amount or grudgingly; keep (person etc.) thus supplied. **2** *n.* limitation of supply or effort (*without stint*); fixed or allotted amount of work (*daily stint*); small sandpiper. [OE]

stipend /ˈstaɪpend/ *n.* salary, esp. of clergyman. [F, or L *stipendium*]

stipendiary /staɪˈpendjərɪ, stɪ-/ **1** *a.* receiving stipend. **2** *n.* person receiving stipend. **3** **stipendiary magistrate** paid professional magistrate. [L (prec.)]

stipple /ˈstɪp(ə)l/ **1** *v.* draw or paint etc. with dots instead of lines; roughen surface of (paint or cement etc.). **2** *n.* stippling, effect of stippling. [Du.]

stipulate /ˈstɪpjʊleɪt/ *v.* demand or specify as part of bargain or agreement; **stipulate for** mention or insist upon as essential; **stipulation** /-ˈleɪʃ(ə)n/ *n.* [L *stipulor*]

stir[1] **1** *v.* (**-rr-**) move spoon etc. round and round in (liquid etc.) to mix ingredients; move esp. slightly, be or begin to be in motion; rise from sleep; arouse or inspire or excite (emotions etc., or person as regards these). **2** *n.* act of stirring; commotion, excitement, sensation. **3** **stir in** mix (ingredient) with substance by stirring; **stir one's stumps** *colloq.* begin to walk or to move faster; **stir up** mix thoroughly by stirring, stimulate. [OE]

stir[2] *n. sl.* prison. [orig. unkn.]

stirrup /'stɪrəp/ *n.* horse-rider's foot-rest; **stirrup-cup** drink offered to person about to depart, orig. on horseback; **stirrup-leather** (or **-strap**) strap attaching stirrup to saddle; **stirrup-pump** hand-operated water-pump with foot-rest, used to extinguish small fires. [OE, = climbing-rope]

stitch 1 *n.* single pass of needle, or result of this, in sewing or knitting or crocheting etc.; thread etc. between two needle-holes; particular method of sewing or knitting etc.; least bit of clothing (*hadn't a stitch on*); acute pain in side induced by running etc. **2** *v.* sew, make stitches (in). **3 in stitches** *colloq.* laughing uncontrollably; **stitch in time** timely remedy; **stitch up** join or mend by sewing. [OE (STICK¹)]

stoat *n.* ermine, esp. when fur is brown. [orig. unkn.]

stock 1 *n.* store of goods etc. ready for sale or distribution etc.; supply of things for use; equipment or raw material for trade etc. (*rolling-stock*); farm animals or equipment; capital of a business company, shares in this; money lent to government at fixed interest, right to receive such interest; one's reputation or popularity (*his stock is rising*); line of ancestry (*comes of Cornish stock*); liquid made by stewing bones, vegetables, etc., as basis for soup etc.; base or support or handle for implement or machine etc.; butt of rifle etc.; plant into which a graft is inserted; main trunk of tree etc.; fragrant-flowered cruciferous plant; (in *pl.*) supports for ship during building; (in *pl.*) *hist.* timber frame with holes for feet in which offenders were locked as public punishment; wide band of material worn round neck. **2** *a.* kept in stock and regularly available; perpetually repeated, hackneyed, conventional. **3** *v.* have (goods) in stock; provide (shop or farm etc.) with goods or equipment or livestock; fit (gun etc.) with stock. **4 in** (or **out of**) **stock** available (or not available) immediately for sale etc.; **on the stocks** in construction or preparation; **stock-car** specially strengthened car for use in racing in which deliberate bumping is allowed; **stock exchange** place where stocks and shares are publicly bought and sold, dealers working there; **stock-in-trade** all requisites of a trade or profession; **stock-market** stock exchange, transactions on this; **stock-pot** pot for making soup stock; **stock-room** room for storing goods; **stock-still** motionless; **stock-taking** making inventory of stock in shop etc., review of one's position and resources; **stock up** provide with or get stocks or supplies; **stock up with** gather stock of (food or fuel etc.); **take stock** make inventory of one's stock, make review or estimate (*of* situation etc.). [OE]

stockade /stɒ'keɪd/ **1** *n.* line or enclosure of upright stakes. **2** *v.t.* fortify with stockade. [F f. Sp. (STAKE)]

stockbreeder *n.* farmer who raises livestock. [STOCK]

stockbroker *n.* person who buys and sells stocks and shares for clients; **stockbroking** *n.*

stockholder *n.* owner of stocks or shares.

stockinet /stɒkɪ'net/ *n.* (also **stockinette**) elastic knitted material. [prob. *stocking-net*]

stocking *n.* covering for foot and all or part of leg, usu. woven or knitted of wool or nylon etc.; differently-coloured lower part of leg of horse etc.; **in one's stocking** (or **stockinged**) **feet** wearing stockings but no shoes; **stocking mask** nylon stocking worn over head as criminal's disguise; **stocking-stitch** alternate rows of plain and purl. [STOCK]

stockist *n.* one who stocks (certain) goods for sale.

stockjobber *n.* member of stock exchange buying and selling stocks to profit from price-fluctuations, and dealing only with stockbrokers.

stockpile 1 *n.* accumulated stock of goods etc. held in reserve. **2** *v.t.* accumulate stockpile of.

stocky *a.* short and strongly built; **stockily** *adv.*; **stockiness** *n.*

stockyard *n.* enclosure for sorting or temporary keeping of cattle.

stodge /stɒdʒ/ *colloq.* **1** *n.* food esp. of thick heavy kind; unimaginative person or work. **2** *v.* stuff (oneself) with food etc.; trudge through mud etc. [imit., after *stuff* and *podge*]

stodgy *a.* (of food) heavy and thick, indigestible; dull and uninteresting; **stodgily** *adv.*; **stodginess** *n.*

Stoic /'stəʊɪk/ **1** *n.* member of ancient Greek school of philosophy which sought virtue as greatest good and control of one's feelings and passions; (**stoic**) stoical person. **2** *a.* of the Stoics. [L f. Gk (*stoa* portico)]

stoical *a.* having or showing great self-control in adversity; **stoically** *adv.*

Stoicism /'stəʊɪsɪz(ə)m/ *n.* philosophy of the Stoics; (**stoicism**) stoical attitude.

stoke *v.* (often with *up*) feed and tend (fire or furnace etc.); *colloq.* consume food, esp. steadily and in large quantities. [back-form. f. STOKER]

stokehold *n.* compartment in which steamer's fires are tended.
stokehole *n.* space for stokers in front of furnace.
stoker *n.* one who stokes fires, esp. on steamer or steam-engine. [Du.]
STOL *abbr.* short take-off and landing.
stole[1] *n.* woman's long garment like scarf, worn over the shoulders; strip of silk etc. worn similarly as vestment by priest. [OE f. L *stola* f. Gk]
stole[2] *past* of STEAL.
stolen *p.p.* of STEAL.
stolid /'stɒlɪd/ *a.* lacking or concealing emotion or animation; not easily excited or moved; **stolidity** /-'lɪdɪtɪ/ *n.* [F or L]
stomach /'stʌmək/ **1** *n.* internal organ in which chief part of digestion occurs; one of several digestive organs of animal; lower front of body; appetite or inclination. **2** *v.t.* endure, put up with. **3 stomach-ache** pain in belly, esp. in bowels; **stomach-pump** syringe for emptying stomach or forcing liquid into it; **stomach upset** temporary slight digestive disorder. [F f. L f. Gk]
stomacher *n. hist.* pointed front-piece of woman's dress, often jewelled or embroidered. [prob. F (prec.)]
stomp 1 *n.* lively jazz dance with heavy stamping. **2** *v.* tread heavily (on); dance stomp. [STAMP]
stone 1 *n.* solid non-metallic mineral matter of which rock is made; small piece of this; piece of stone of definite shape or for particular purpose; thing resembling stone in hardness or form, e.g. hard morbid concretion in the body or hard case of kernel in some fruits; = *precious stone*; (*pl.* same) weight of 14lb. **2** *a.* made of stone. **3** *v.t.* pelt with stones; remove stones from (fruit). **4 cast** (or **throw**) **stones** make aspersions on character etc.; **leave no stone unturned** try every possible means; **Stone Age** period when weapons and tools were made of stone; **stone-cold** completely cold; **stone-dead** completely dead; **stone-deaf** completely deaf; **stone-fruit** fruit with flesh or pulp enclosing stone; **a stone's throw** a short distance. [OE]
stonechat *n.* small brown bird with black and white markings.
stonecrop *n.* creeping rock-plant.
stoned *a. sl.* very drunk.
stonemason *n.* dresser of or builder in stone.
stonewall *v.i.* obstruct discussion etc. with evasive answers; (in cricket) bat with excessive caution.
stoneware *n.* pottery made from very siliceous clay or from clay and flint.
stonework *n.* masonry.
stony *a.* full of stones; hard, rigid; unfeeling, uncompromising; **stony-broke** *sl.* entirely without money; **stonily** *adv.*; **stoniness** *n.*
stood *past* & *p.p.* of STAND.
stooge *colloq.* **1** *n.* butt, foil, esp. for comedian; assistant or subordinate, esp. for routine or unpleasant work. **2** *v.i.* move *about* or *around* etc., esp. aimlessly; act as stooge *for*. [orig. unkn.]
stool *n.* seat without back or arms, usu. for one person; = FOOTSTOOL; (usu. in *pl.*) faeces; root or stump of tree or plant from which shoots spring; **stool-ball** game resembling cricket; **stool-pigeon** pigeon as decoy, police informer. [OE]
stoop[1] *v.* bend (one's head or body) forwards and downwards; carry one's head and shoulders bowed forward; deign or condescend *to do* thing, descend or lower oneself *to* (some conduct). **2** *n.* stooping posture. [OE]
stoop[2] *n. US* porch or small veranda or steps in front of house. [Du. *stoep*]
stop 1 *v.* (**-pp-**) put an end to progress or motion or operation (of); effectively hinder or prevent (*from*); discontinue (*stop talking*), come to an end (*supplies suddenly stopped*); (cause to) cease action, defeat; *sl.* receive (blow etc.); remain, stay for short time; block or close up (hole or leak etc., often with *up*); not permit or supply as usual (wages or food etc.); (in full **stop payment of** or **on**) instruct bank to withhold payment on (cheque); put filling in (tooth); *Mus.* obtain desired pitch from (string of violin etc.) by pressing at appropriate point with finger. **2** *n.* stopping or being stopped; place where bus or train etc. regularly stops; sign to show pause in written matter, esp.= *full stop*; device for stopping motion at particular point; *Mus.* change of pitch effected by stopping string, (in organ) row of pipes of one character, knob etc. operating these; (in optics and photography) diaphragm, effective diameter of lens or device reducing this; (of sound) = PLOSIVE. **3 pull out all the stops** make extreme effort; **put a stop to** intervene to end (practice etc.); **stop at nothing** be ruthless or unscrupulous; **stop-go** alternate suppression and stimulation of progress; **stop off** (or **over**) break one's journey; **stopping train** train stopping at many intermediate stations; **stop-press** late news inserted in newspaper after printing has begun; **stop-watch** timer with mechanism for instantly starting and stopping it, used in timing races etc. [OE]
stopcock *n.* externally operated valve to regulate flow in pipe etc.

stopgap *n.* temporary substitute.
stopoff *n.* (also **stopover**) a break in one's journey.
stoppage *n.* condition of being blocked or stopped.
stopper *n.* plug for closing bottle etc.
stopping *n.* filling for a tooth.
storage /ˈstɔːrɪdʒ/ *n.* storing of goods etc., method of storing or the space available for it; cost of storing; storing of data; **storage battery** (or **cell**) battery (or cell) for storing electricity; **storage heater** electric heater accumulating heat outside peak hours for later release. [foll.]
store 1 *n.* quantity of something ready to be drawn on; (in *pl.*) articles for particular purpose accumulated for use, supply of them or place where they are kept; large shop selling many different kinds of goods; warehouse for temporary keeping of furniture etc.; device in computer for storing retrievable data. **2** *v.t.* put in store; accumulate for future use (often with *up* or *away*); stock or provide with something useful. **3 in store** kept in readiness, coming in the future, destined or intended *for*; **set store by** consider to be important; **store-room** room in which stores are kept, esp. for household. [F *estore(r)* f. L *instauro* renew]
storehouse *n.* place where things are stored.
storekeeper *n.* storeman; *US* shopkeeper.
storey /ˈstɔːrɪ/ *n.* any of the parts into which a building is divided horizontally, the whole of the rooms etc. having a continuous floor; thing forming horizontal division; **-storeyed** *a.* [AL (HISTORY, perh. with ref. to tier of painted windows)]
storied /ˈstɔːrɪd/ *a.* celebrated in or associated with stories or legends. [STORY]
stork *n.* tall usu. white wading bird, with long legs. [OE]
storm 1 *n.* violent disturbance of atmosphere with strong winds and usu. with thunder and rain or snow etc.; violent disturbance or commotion in human affairs etc.; violent shower of missiles or blows; outburst of feeling or applause etc.; direct assault on (and capture of) defended place by troops etc. **2** *v.* rage, be violent, bluster; move violently or angrily (*stormed out of the room*); attack or capture by storm. **3 storm-centre** centre of storm or cyclone, subject etc. upon which agitation is concentrated; **storm-cloud** heavy rain-cloud, something threatening; **storm-door** additional outer door; **storm in a teacup** great excitement over trivial matter; **storm petrel** small black and white petrel of N. Atlantic, person whose arrival foreshadows trouble; **storm-trooper** member of storm-troops; **storm-troops** shock-troops, Nazi political militia; **take by storm** capture by storm, quickly captivate. [OE]
stormy *a.* of or affected by storms; (of wind etc.) violent; full of feeling or outbursts (*a stormy meeting*); **stormily** *adv.*; **storminess** *n.*
story /ˈstɔːrɪ/ *n.* account of imaginary or past events, narrative, tale, anecdote; past course of life of person or institution etc.; (also **story-line**) narrative or plot of novel or play etc.; facts or experiences that deserve narration; *colloq.* fib. [AF *estorie* f. L (HISTORY)]
stoup /stuːp/ *n.* holy-water basin; *archaic* flagon, beaker. [ON]
stout 1 *a.* rather fat, corpulent, bulky; of considerable thickness or strength; brave, resolute, vigorous, staunch. **2** *n.* strong dark beer. [AF f. Gmc]
stove[1] *n.* closed apparatus burning fuel or electricity for heating or cooking; **stove-enamel** heat-proof enamel; **stove-pipe** pipe conducting smoke and gases from stove to chimney. [LG or Du.]
stove[2] see STAVE.
stow /stəʊ/ *v.t.* pack (goods etc.) tidily in right or convenient place(s); *sl.* (esp. as command) abstain or cease from; **stow away** place (thing) where it will not cause obstruction, be stowaway on ship etc. [BESTOW f. OE, = place]
stowage *n.* stowing, place for this.
stowaway *n.* person who hides on board ship or aircraft etc. to travel free or escape unseen.
strabismus /strəˈbɪzməs/ *n.* squinting, squint. [Gk (*strabos* squinting)]
straddle /ˈstræd(ə)l/ **1** *v.* sit or stand (across) with legs wide apart; part (one's legs) widely; drop shots or bombs short of and beyond (target etc.). **2** *n.* act of straddling. [STRIDE]
strafe /strɑːf/ **1** *v.t.* bombard, harass with gunfire. **2** *n.* act of strafing. [G, = punish]
straggle /ˈstræg(ə)l/ **1** *v.i.* lack or lose compactness or tidiness; be or become dispersed or sporadic; trail behind others in march or race etc. **2** *n.* straggling group. **3 straggly** *a.* [orig. uncert.]
straight /streɪt/ **1** *a.* extending uniformly in same direction, without curve or bend etc.; direct; successive (*three straight wins*); level, tidy, in proper order or place or condition (*put things straight*); honest, candid; (of thinking etc.) logical, unemotional; (of drama

etc.) ordinary, without music; unmodified, (of drink) undiluted; *colloq*. (of music) classical; *sl*. (of person etc.) conventional, respectable, heterosexual. **2** *n*. straight part of something, esp. concluding stretch of racecourse; straight condition; sequence of five cards in poker; *sl*. straight person. **3** *adv*. in a straight line, direct; in right direction, correctly. **4 go straight** live honest life after being criminal; **on the straight** direct, not on the bias; **straight away** immediately; **straight eye** ability to draw or cut etc. in straight line or detect deviation from the straight; **straight face** expression concealing or not showing feeling etc.; **straight fight** contest between two candidates only; **straight man** member of comic act who makes remarks for comedian to joke about; **straight off** *colloq*. immediately, without hesitation. [orig. p.p. of STRETCH]

straighten /'streɪt(ə)n/ *v*. make or become straight; **straighten up** stand erect after bending.

straightforward /streɪt'fɔːwəd/ *a*. honest, frank; (of task etc.) uncomplicated.

strain[1] **1** *v*. stretch tightly, make or become taut or tense; exercise (*oneself*, one's senses, thing, etc.) intensely or excessively, press to extremes, make intensive effort; distort from true intention or meaning; overtask or injure by over-use or excessive demands; clear (liquid) of solid matter by passing it through sieve etc., filter (solids) *out* from liquid. **2** *n*. act of straining, force exerted in straining; injury caused by straining muscle etc.; severe demand on mental or physical strength or resources, exertion needed to meet this; snatch or spell of music or poetry; tone or tendency in speech or writing. [F *estrei(g)n-* f. L *stringo*]

strain[2] *n*. breed or stock of animals, plants, etc.; moral tendency as part of character. [OE, = begetting]

strained *a*. constrained, forced, artificial; (of relationship) mutually distrustful or impatient. [STRAIN[1]]

strainer *n*. device for straining liquids.

strait **1** *n*. (in *sing*. or *pl*.) narrow passage of water connecting two large bodies of water; (usu. in *pl*.) difficulty, trouble, distress. **2** *a*. *archaic* narrow, limited, strict. **3 strait-laced** severely virtuous, puritanical. [F *estreit* f. L (STRICT)]

straiten /'streɪt(ə)n/ *v.t*. restrict; (in *p.p.*) of or marked by poverty.

strait-jacket **1** *n*. strong garment put on violent person to confine arms; restrictive measures. **2** *v.t*. restrain with strait-jacket; severely restrict.

stramonium /strə'məʊnɪəm/ *n*. drug used to treat asthma; plant yielding it. [orig. unkn.]

strand[1] **1** *v*. run aground; (in *p.p.*) in difficulties, esp. without money or means of transport. **2** *n*. margin of sea or lake or river, esp. foreshore. [OE]

strand[2] *n*. any of the threads or wires twisted round each other to make rope or cable etc.; single thread or strip of fibre; lock of hair; element or strain in any composite whole. [orig. unkn.]

strange /streɪndʒ/ *a*. unusual, peculiar, surprising, eccentric; unfamiliar, alien, foreign; unaccustomed *to*; not at ease. [F *estrange* f. L *extraneus*]

stranger /'streɪndʒə/ *n*. person in place or company that he does not know or belong to or where he is unknown; person one does not know; **a** (or **no**) **stranger to** unaccustomed (or accustomed) to. [F *estrangier* f. L (prec.)]

strangle /'stræŋg(ə)l/ *v.t*. squeeze windpipe or neck of, esp. so as to kill; hamper, suppress. [F *estrangler* f. L *strangulo* f. Gk]

stranglehold *n*. strangling or deadly grip; firm or exclusive control.

strangulate /'stræŋgjʊleɪt/ *v.t*. prevent circulation through (vein or intestine etc.) by compression. [L (STRANGLE)]

strangulation /stræŋgjʊ'leɪʃ(ə)n/ *n*. strangling; strangulating.

strap **1** *n*. strip of leather etc., often with buckle, for holding things in place etc.; thing like this for keeping garment in place; loop for grasping to steady oneself in moving vehicle. **2** *v.t*. (**-pp-**) secure or bind (*up* etc.) with strap; flog with strap. [dial., = STROP]

strapping *a*. big, tall, sturdy.

strata *pl*. of STRATUM.

stratagem /'strætədʒəm/ *n*. cunning plan or scheme; trickery. [F f. L f. Gk (*stratēgos* general)]

strategic /strə'tiːdʒɪk/ *a*. of or serving the ends of strategy; (of materials) essential in war; (of bombing) designed to disorganize or demoralize the enemy; **strategic weapons** missiles etc. that can reach the enemy's home territory rather than for use at close quarters or in battle; **strategically** *adv*. [as foll.]

strategy /'strætɪdʒɪ/ *n*. the art of war, esp. planning of movements of troops and ships etc. into favourable positions; plan of action or policy in business or politics etc. (*economic strategy*); **strategist** *n*. [F f. Gk (as STRATAGEM)]

strath *n*. *Sc*. broad valley. [Gael. *strath*]

strathspey /stræθ'speɪ/ *n*. a slow Scot-

tish dance; music for this. [prec., *Spey* river in Scotland]
stratify /'strætɪfaɪ/ *v.t.* (esp. in *p.p.*) arrange in strata or grades etc.; **stratification** /-fɪ'keɪʃ(ə)n/ *n.* [F (STRATUM)]
stratigraphy /strə'tɪgrəfɪ/ *n.* study of archaeological or geological strata; relative position of such strata; **stratigraphic** /-'græfɪk/ *a.* [STRATUM]
stratosphere /'strætəsfɪə/ *n.* layer of atmosphere above troposphere; **stratospheric** /-'sferɪk/ *a.* [foll.]
stratum /'strɑ:təm, 'streɪ-/ *n.* (*pl.* **strata**) layer of rock or atmosphere etc.; social grade or class. [L (*sterno* strew)]
straw *n.* dry cut stalks of grain as material for bedding, packing, fodder, etc.; single stalk or piece of straw; thin hollow tube for sucking drink through; insignificant thing; pale yellow colour of straw; **catch at a straw** try hopeless expedient in desperation; **straw in the wind** slight hint of future developments; **straw poll** (or **vote**) unofficial ballot as test of opinion. [OE]
strawberry /'strɔ:bərɪ/ *n.* pulpy red fruit having surface studded with yellow seeds; plant bearing this; **strawberry-mark** reddish birthmark. [OE (prec., for unkn. reason)]
stray 1 *v.i.* wander from the right place, become separated from one's companions etc., go astray; deviate morally (*from* correct course etc.). **2** *n.* strayed animal or person or thing. **3** *a.* strayed, lost; isolated, found or occurring occasionally; unwanted, unintentional. [AF *strey* (ASTRAY)]
streak 1 *n.* long thin usu. irregular line or band, esp. distinguished by colour; flash of lightning; strain or element in character; spell or series (*winning streak*). **2** *v.* mark with streaks; move very rapidly; *colloq.* run naked through public place. [OE, = pen-stroke]
streaky *a.* full of streaks; (of bacon) with alternate streaks of fat and lean; **streakily** *adv.*; **streakiness** *n.*
stream 1 *n.* flowing body of water, esp. a small river; flow of a fluid or of a mass of people; current or direction in which things are moving or tending (*against the stream*); group of schoolchildren having same level of ability. **2** *v.* move as stream; run with liquid; (of banner or hair etc.) float or wave in the wind; emit stream of (blood etc.); arrange (schoolchildren) in streams. **3 on stream** in active operation or production. [OE]
streamer *n.* long narrow flag; long narrow ribbon of paper; banner headline.
streamline *v.t.* give (vehicle etc.) form which presents least resistance to motion; make simple or more efficient or better organized.
street *n.* public road in a city or town or village, this with the houses or buildings on each side; persons who live or work in a particular street; **on the streets** working as prostitute; **streets ahead** (**of**) *colloq.* much superior (to); **street-walker** prostitute seeking customers in street; **up one's street** *colloq.* within one's range of interest or knowledge, to one's liking. [OE f. L *strata* (*via*)]
streetcar *n.* *US* tram.
strength *n.* quality or extent or manner of being strong; what makes one strong; number of persons present or available; full complement (*below strength*); **from strength to strength** with ever-increasing success; **in strength** in large numbers; **on the strength of** relying on, on the basis of. [OE (STRONG)]
strengthen /'streŋθ(ə)n/ *v.* make or become stronger.
strenuous /'strenjʊəs/ *a.* making or requiring great exertions, energetic. [L]
streptococcus /streptə'kɒkəs/ *n.* (*pl.* **streptococci** /-aɪ/) bacterium causing serious infections; **streptococcal** *a.* [Gk *streptos* twisted, *kokkos* berry]
streptomycin /streptə'maɪsɪn/ *n.* antibiotic effective against some disease-producing bacteria. [prec., Gk *mukēs* fungus]
stress 1 *n.* pressure or tension, quantity measuring this; demand on physical or mental energy, distress caused by this; emphasis, esp. on syllable or word. **2** *v.t.* lay stress on, emphasize; subject to stress. **3 lay stress on** indicate as important. [DISTRESS, or F *estresse* (STRICT)]
stressful *a.* causing stress; **stressfully** *adv.*
stretch 1 *v.* draw or be drawn or admit of being drawn out into greater length or size; make or become taut; place or lie at full length or spread out; extend (one's limbs, or *absol.*), thrust out limbs and tighten muscles after being relaxed; have specified length or extension, extend; strain or exert extremely or excessively, exaggerate (*stretch the truth*). **2** *n.* stretching or being stretched; continuous extent or expanse or period; *sl.* period of imprisonment; *US* straight part of race-track. **3** *a.* able to stretch, elastic (*stretch fabric*). **4 stretch one's legs** exercise oneself by walking; **stretch out** extend (hand or foot etc.), last for longer period, prolong; **stretch a point** agree to something not normally allowed. [OE]
stretcher *n.* framework of two poles with canvas between, for carrying person in lying position; any of various

devices for stretching; brick etc. laid along face of wall.

stretchy *a. colloq.* able or tending to stretch; **stretchiness** *n.*

strew /struː/ *v.t.* (*p.p.* **strewn** or **strewed**) scatter or spread about over a surface; spread (surface) with scattered things. [OE (STRAW)]

stria /ˈstraɪə/ *n.* (*pl.* **striae** /-iː/) slight furrow or ridge on surface. [L]

striated /straɪˈeɪtɪd/ *a.* marked with striae; **striation** *n.*

stricken /ˈstrɪkən/ *a.* affected or overcome with illness or misfortune etc. (*stricken with measles*; *grief-stricken*). [p.p. of STRIKE]

strict *a.* precisely limited or defined, without exception or deviation; requiring complete obedience or exact performance; **strictly speaking** if one uses words in their strict sense. [L *stringo strict-* draw tight]

stricture /ˈstrɪktʃə/ *n.* (usu. in *pl.*) critical or censorious remark (*on* or *upon*). [L (as prec.)]

stride 1 *v.* (*past* **strode**; *p.p.* **stridden** /ˈstrɪd(ə)n/) walk with long steps; cross with one step; bestride. 2 *n.* single long step, length of this; gait as determined by length of stride; (usu. in *pl.*) progress (*has made great strides*). 3 **get into one's stride** settle into efficient rate of work; **take in one's stride** manage without difficulty. [OE]

strident /ˈstraɪdənt/ *a.* loud and harsh; **stridency** *n.* [L *strido* creak]

strife *n.* conflict, struggle between opposed persons or things. [F *estrif* (STRIVE)]

strike 1 *v.* (*past* **struck**; *p.p.* **struck** or STRICKEN) subject to impact, deliver (blow) or inflict blow on, come or bring sharply into contact with, propel or divert with blow; (cause to) penetrate (*struck terror into him*); ignite (match) or produce (sparks etc.) by rubbing; make (coin) by stamping; produce (musical note) by striking; (of clock) indicate (time) by sounding of bell etc., (of time) be indicated thus; attack suddenly, (of disease) afflict; cause to become suddenly (*was struck dumb*); reach or achieve (*strike a balance*); agree on (bargain); put oneself theatrically into (attitude); discover or come across, find (oil etc.) by drilling; come to attention of or appear to (*it strikes me as silly*); (of employees) engage in strike, cease work as protest; lower or take down (flag or tent etc.); take specified direction; secure hook in mouth of (fish) by jerking tackle. 2 *n.* act of striking; employees' concerted refusal to work until some grievance is remedied, similar refusal to participate in some other expected activity; sudden find or success; attack, esp. from the air. 3 **be struck on** *sl.* be infatuated with; **on strike** taking part in industrial strike; **strike-breaker** person working or engaged in place of strikers; **strike home** deal effective blow, have intended effect; **strike off** remove with stroke, delete (name etc.) from list; **strike out** hit out, act vigorously, delete (item or name etc.); **strike pay** allowance paid to strikers by trade union; **strike up** start (an acquaintance, a conversation, etc.) esp. casually, begin playing (a tune etc.). [OE, = rub, go]

striker *n.* person or thing that strikes; employee on strike; (in football) player whose main function is to try to score goals.

striking *a.* impressive, attracting attention.

Strine *n.* comic transliteration of Australian speech; Australian English, esp. uneducated type. [= *Australian* in Strine]

string 1 *n.* twine or narrow cord; piece of this or similar material used for tying or holding together, pulling, etc.; piece of catgut or wire etc. on musical instrument, producing note by vibration; (in *pl.*) stringed instruments in orchestra etc.; *attrib.* relating to or consisting of stringed instruments (*string quartet*); (in *pl.*) awkward condition or complication (*the offer has no strings*); set of things strung together, series or line of persons or things; group of racehorses trained at one stable; tough piece connecting two halves of bean-pod etc. 2 *v.* (*past* and *p.p.* **strung**) supply with string(s); tie with string; thread (beads etc.) on string; arrange in or as string; remove strings from (bean); place string ready for use on (bow); *fig.* (esp. in *p.p.*) tighten *up* or make ready or excited (nerves, resolution, etc.). 3 **on a string** under one's control or influence; **string along** *colloq.* deceive; **string along with** *colloq.* keep company with; **string-course** raised horizontal band of bricks etc. on building; **string up** hang up on strings etc., kill by hanging; **string vest** vest of material with large meshes. [OE]

stringed *a.* (of musical instruments) having strings.

stringent /ˈstrɪndʒənt/ *a.* (of rules etc.) strict, severe, leaving no loophole for discretion; **stringency** *n.* [L (STRICT)]

stringer *n.* longitudinal structural member in framework esp. of ship or aircraft; newspaper correspondent not on regular staff. [STRING]

stringy *a.* like string, fibrous; **stringiness** *n.*

strip[1] **1** *v.* (**-pp-**) remove clothes or covering from; undress oneself; deprive (person) of property or titles; leave bare of accessories or fittings; remove old paint from; damage thread of (screw) or teeth of (gear). **2** *n.* act of stripping, esp. of undressing in strip-tease; *colloq.* clothes worn by members of sports team. **3 strip club** club where strip-tease is performed; **strip down** remove accessory fittings of or take apart (machine etc.); **strip-tease** entertainment in which performer gradually undresses before audience. [OE]

strip[2] *n.* long narrow piece; **strip cartoon** = *comic strip*; **strip light** tubular fluorescent lamp; **tear person off a strip** *sl.* rebuke him. [LG *strippe* strap]

stripe *n.* long narrow band or strip differing in colour or texture from the surface on either side of it; chevron etc. denoting military rank; *archaic* (usu. in *pl.*) blow with scourge or lash. [perh. LG or Du.]

striped *a.* marked with stripes.

stripling *n.* youth not fully grown. [STRIP[2]]

stripper *n.* person or thing that strips something; device or solvent for removing paint etc.; strip-tease performer. [STRIP[1]]

stripy *a.* striped. [STRIPE]

strive *v.i.* (*past* **strove**; *p.p.* **striven** /ˈstrɪv(ə)n/) try hard (*strive to succeed*); struggle or contend (*with* or *against*). [F *estriver*]

strobe *n. colloq.* stroboscope. [abbr.]

stroboscope /ˈstrəʊbəskəʊp/ *n.* lamp producing rapid series of flashes; device using this to determine speeds of rotation etc.; **stroboscopic** /-ˈskɒpɪk/ *a.* [Gk *strobos* whirling]

strode *past* of STRIDE.

stroke 1 *n.* act of striking; sudden disabling attack esp. of apoplexy; action or movement esp. as one of series or in game etc.; slightest such action (*has not done a stroke of work*); highly effective effort or action or occurrence *of* specified kind (*a stroke of diplomacy, genius, luck*); sound made by a striking clock; movement in one direction of pen or paintbrush etc.; detail contributing to general effect; mode or action of moving oar in rowing; mode of moving limbs in swimming; (in full **stroke oar**) oarsman nearest stern, who sets time of stroke; act or spell of stroking. **2** *v.t.* pass hand gently along surface of (hair or fur etc.); act as stroke of (boat or crew). **3 at a stroke** by a single action; **on the stroke (of)** punctually (at). [OE, rel. to STRIKE]

stroll /strəʊl/ **1** *v.i.* saunter, walk in leisurely way. **2** *n.* short leisurely walk. **3 strolling players** actors etc. going from place to place performing. [prob. G (*strolch* vagabond)]

strong 1 *a.* (*compar.* and *superl.* /-ŋg-/) having power of resistance, not easily damaged or overcome or disturbed, tough, firm, healthy; capable of exerting great force or of doing much, muscular, powerful; forceful or powerful in effect (*strong wind, protest*); decided, firmly held (*strong suspicion*); (of argument etc.) convincing, striking; powerfully affecting the senses or emotions (*strong light, acting*); (of solution or drink etc.) containing large proportion of the substance in water or other solvent; (of group) having specified number (*200 strong*). **2** *adv.* strongly, vigorously. **3 strong-arm** using force; **strong-box** strongly made small chest for valuables; **strong language** forceful language, swearing; **strong-minded** having a determined mind; **strong point** fortified position, thing at which one excels; **strong-room** strongly built room for storage and protection of valuables; **strong suit** suit at cards in which one can take tricks, *fig.* thing at which one excels; **strong verb** verb forming inflexions by vowel-change within stem. [OE]

stronghold *n.* fortified place; secure refuge; centre of support for a cause etc.

strontium /ˈstrɒntɪəm/ *n.* soft silver-white metallic element; **strontium 90** radioactive isotope of strontium concentrated selectively in bones when ingested. [*Strontian* in Scotland]

strop 1 *n.* device, esp. strip of leather, for sharpening razors. **2** *v.t.* (**-pp-**) sharpen on or with strop. [LG or Du.]

stroppy /ˈstrɒpɪ/ *a. sl.* bad-tempered, awkward to deal with. [orig. uncert.]

strove *past* of STRIVE.

struck *past* & *p.p.* of STRIKE.

structural /ˈstrʌktʃər(ə)l/ *a.* of a structure or framework; used in construction of buildings etc.; **structurally** *adv.* [STRUCTURE]

structuralism *n.* doctrine that structure rather than function is important.

structure /ˈstrʌktʃə/ **1** *n.* manner in which thing is constructed; supporting framework or essential parts; thing constructed, complex whole, a building. **2** *v.t.* give structure to, organize. [F or L (*struo struct-* build)]

strudel /ˈstru:d(ə)l/ *n.* confection of thin pastry filled esp. with apple. [G]

struggle /ˈstrʌg(ə)l/ **1** *v.i.* throw one's limbs or body about in violent effort to get free; make violent or determined efforts under difficulties; strive hard; contend *with* or *against*; make one's way with difficulty *along* or *up* etc.; (esp. in *partic.*) have difficulty in getting one's living or recognition. **2** *n.* act or period of struggling; hard or confused contest. [orig. uncert.]

strum 1 *v.* (**-mm-**) play on (stringed or keyboard instrument) esp. carelessly or unskilfully. **2** *n.* sound or spell of strumming. [imit.; cf. THRUM²]

strumpet /'strʌmpɪt/ *n. archaic* prostitute. [orig. unkn.]

strung *past* & *p.p.* of STRING.

strut 1 *n.* bar forming part of framework and designed to resist compression; strutting gait. **2** *v.* (**-tt-**) walk in stiff pompous way; brace with struts. [OE]

'struth /stru:θ/ *int. colloq.* exclamation of surprise. [*God's truth*]

strychnine /'strɪkni:n/ *n.* highly poisonous alkaloid used in small doses as stimulant. [F f. L f. Gk *struchnos* nightshade]

stub 1 *n.* remnant of pencil or cigarette etc. after use; counterfoil of cheque or receipt etc.; stump, stunted tail etc. **2** *v.t.* (**-bb-**) strike (one's toe) against something; (usu. with *out*) extinguish (cigarette etc.) by pressing lighted end against something. [OE]

stubble /'stʌb(ə)l/ *n.* lower part of cereal stalks left in the ground after harvest; short stiff hair esp. on unshaven face; **stubbly** *a.* [AF f. L *stupula*]

stubborn /'stʌbən/ *a.* obstinate, inflexible, intractable; **stubbornness** *n.* [orig. unkn.]

stubby *a.* short and thick; **stubbiness** *n.* [STUB]

stucco /'stʌkəʊ/ **1** *n.* (*pl.* **stuccoes**) plaster or cement for coating walls or moulding into architectural decorations. **2** *v.t.* coat with stucco. [It.]

stuck *past* & *p.p.* of STICK².

stuck-up *a.* conceited, snobbish. [STICK²]

stud¹ 1 *n.* large-headed nail, boss, or knob, projecting from a surface esp. for ornament; device for fixing separate collar to shirt. **2** *v.t.* (**-dd-**) set (as) with studs; **studded with** thickly set or strewn with (jewels etc.). [OE, = post]

stud² *n.* number of horses kept for breeding etc., place where these are kept; stallion; *sl.* young man (esp. one noted for sexual prowess); = *stud poker*; **at stud** (of stallion) available for breeding on payment of fee; **stud-book** book containing pedigrees of horses; **stud-farm** farm where horses are bred; **stud poker** poker with betting after dealing of successive cards face up. [OE]

studding-sail /'stʌns(ə)l/ *n.* extra sail set in light winds. [LG or Du.]

student /'stju:dənt/ *n.* person who is studying, esp. at university or other place of higher education; *attrib.* studying in order to become (*student nurse*). [L (STUDY)]

studio /'stju:dɪəʊ/ *n.* (*pl.* **studios**) workroom of painter or photographer etc.; place where cinema films or recordings are made or from where television or radio programmes are made or produced; **studio couch** divan-like couch that can be converted into a bed. [It. f. L (STUDY)]

studious /'stju:dɪəs/ *a.* assiduous in study or reading; painstaking; careful and deliberate. [L (foll.)]

study /'stʌdɪ/ **1** *n.* giving one's attention to acquiring information or knowledge, esp. from books, (in *pl.*) pursuit of academic knowledge; piece of work, esp. drawing, done as practice or experiment; portrayal in literature or other art-form of an aspect of behaviour or character etc.; *Mus.* composition designed to develop player's skill; room used for reading, writing, etc.; thing worth observing closely (*his face was a study*); thing that is or deserves to be investigated (*the proper study of mankind is man*). **2** *v.* make a study of, investigate or examine (subject); apply oneself to study (*for* examination etc.); scrutinize or earnestly contemplate (visible object); try to learn (words of one's role etc.); take pains to achieve (result) or pay regard to (subject or principle etc.); (in *p.p.*) deliberate, intentional, affected (*with studied politeness*). [F *estudie(r)* f. L *studium*]

stuff 1 *n.* material that thing is made of, substance or things or belongings of indeterminate kind or quality or not needing to be specified; particular knowledge or activity (*know* or *do one's stuff*); woollen fabric; *sl.* money. **2** *v.* pack (receptacle) tightly, force or cram (thing *in* or *into*); fill out skin of (animal or bird etc.) with material to restore original shape; fill (fowl or rolled meat etc.) with minced seasoning etc. before cooking; fill (person or *oneself*) with food, eat greedily; push, esp. hastily or clumsily; (usu. in *pass.*) block *up* (nose etc.); *sl.* dispose of as unwanted (*you can stuff the job*). **3 get stuffed** *sl.* go away, shut up; **stuff and nonsense** exclamation of incredulity or ridicule; **stuffed shirt** *colloq.* pompous person. [F *estoffe(r)* f. Gk *stuphō* pull together]

stuffing *n.* padding used to stuff cushions etc.; savoury mixture used to stuff fowl etc.

stuffy *a.* (of room etc.) lacking ventilation or fresh air; (of nose etc.) stuffed up;

colloq. prim and pompous, old-fashioned or narrow-minded; **stuffily** *adv.*; **stuffiness** *n.*

stultify /ˈstʌltɪfaɪ/ *v.t.* make ineffective or useless, impair; make foolish or absurd; negate, neutralize; **stultification** /-fɪˈkeɪʃ(ə)n/ *n.* [L (*stultus* foolish)]

stumble /ˈstʌmb(ə)l/ **1** *v.i.* lurch forward or have partial fall from catching or striking or misplacing foot, walk with repeated stumbling; make mistake or repeated mistakes in speaking etc.; come accidentally *on* or *upon* or *across*. **2** *n.* act of stumbling. **3 stumbling-block** obstacle or circumstance causing difficulty or hesitation. [cogn. with STAMMER]

stump 1 *n.* projecting remnant of cut or fallen tree; similar remnant of broken branch or amputated limb or worn-down pencil etc.; (in cricket) each of the three uprights of a wicket. **2** *v.* (of question etc.) be too hard for, puzzle (*colloq.*); (in *p.p.*) at a loss, baffled; (in cricket) put (batsman) out by touching stumps with ball while he is outside his crease; walk (as) on wooden leg; traverse (district) making political speeches. **3 stump up** *sl.* pay or produce (money required, or *absol.*). [LG or Du.]

stumpy *a.* short and thick; **stumpiness** *n.*

stun *v.t.* (**-nn-**) knock senseless, stupefy; bewilder, shock. [F (ASTONISH)]

stung *past* & *p.p.* of STING.

stunk see STINK.

stunner *n. colloq.* stunning person or thing. [STUN]

stunning *a. colloq.* extremely good or attractive.

stunt¹ *v.t.* retard growth or development of, dwarf. [obs. *stunt* foolish, short]

stunt² *colloq.* **1** *n.* something unusual done to attract attention; trick or daring manœuvre. **2** *v.i.* perform stunts. **3 stunt man** man employed to take actor's place in performing dangerous stunts. [orig. unkn.]

stupefy /ˈstjuːpɪfaɪ/ *v.t.* make stupid or insensible; stun with astonishment; **stupefaction** /-ˈfækʃ(ə)n/ *n.* [F f. L (*stupeo* be amazed)]

stupendous /stjuːˈpendəs/ *a.* amazing or prodigious, esp. by its size or degree. [L (prec.)]

stupid /ˈstjuːpɪd/ *a.* unintelligent, slow-witted, foolish; typical of stupid persons; uninteresting, boring; in a state of stupor; **stupidity** /-ˈpɪdɪtɪ/ *n.* [F or L (as prec.)]

stupor /ˈstjuːpə/ *n.* dazed or torpid or helplessly amazed state. [L (STUPEFY)]

sturdy /ˈstɜːdɪ/ *a.* robust, hardy, strongly built; **sturdily** *adv.*; **sturdiness** *n.* [F *esturdi*]

sturgeon /ˈstɜːdʒ(ə)n/ *n.* large edible fish yielding caviare. [AF f. Gmc]

stutter 1 *v.* stammer, esp. by involuntarily repeating first consonants of words; (often with *out*) utter (words) thus. **2** *n.* act or habit of stuttering. [dial. *stut*]

sty¹ /staɪ/ *n.* enclosure for pigs; filthy room or dwelling. [OE]

sty² /staɪ/ *n.* inflamed swelling on edge of eyelid. [OE]

Stygian /ˈstɪdʒɪən/ *a.* of or like the Styx or Hades; gloomy, murky. [L f. Gk (*Styx*, river encompassing Hades]

style /staɪl/ **1** *n.* kind or sort, esp. in regard to appearance and form (*an elegant style of house*); manner of writing or speaking or doing; distinctive manner of person or school or period; correct way of designating person or thing; superior quality or manner (*did it in style*); fashion in dress etc.; pointed implement for scratching or engraving; *Bot.* narrow extension of ovary supporting stigma. **2** *v.* design or make etc. in particular (esp. fashionable) style; designate in specified way. [F f. L *stilus*]

stylish *a.* fashionable; elegant; superior.

stylist *n.* person concerned with style, esp. writer having or aiming at good literary style, or designer of fashionable styles; hairdresser who styles hair.

stylistic /staɪˈlɪstɪk/ *a.* of literary or artistic style; **stylistically** *adv.*

stylized *a.* (of work of art etc.) made to conform to rules of a conventional style.

stylus *n.* (*pl.* **styluses**) needle-like point for producing or following groove in gramophone record; pointed writing-implement. [L (STYLE)]

stymie /ˈstaɪmɪ/ **1** *n.* situation in golf when opponent's ball is between one's own ball and the hole; difficult situation. **2** *v.t.* subject (person) to stymie; obstruct, thwart. [orig. unkn.]

styptic /ˈstɪptɪk/ **1** *a.* serving to check or reduce bleeding. **2** *n.* styptic substance. [L f. Gk (*stuphō* contract)]

styrene /ˈstaɪriːn/ *n.* liquid hydrocarbon easily polymerized and used in making plastics etc. [Gk *sturax* a resin]

suasion /ˈsweɪʒ(ə)n/ *n.* persuasion, esp. in **moral suasion** strong recommendation appealing to moral sense. [F or L (*suadeo suas-* urge)]

suave /swɑːv/ *a.* urbane, gracious, refined; **suavity** *n.* [F, or L *suavis*]

sub *colloq.* **1** *n.* submarine; subscription; substitute; sub-editor. **2** *v.* (**-bb-**) act as substitute (*for* someone); sub-edit. [abbr.]

sub- *prefix* at or to or from lower position (*subordinate, submerge, subtract*);

secondary or inferior position (*subclass, sub-lieutenant, subtotal*); nearly, more or less (*subarctic*). [L]

subaltern /'sʌb(ə)ltən/ *n.* officer of rank next below captain. [L (ALTERNATE)]

subaqua /sʌb'ækwə/ *a.* (of sport etc.) taking place under water. [SUB-]

subaquatic /sʌbə'kwætɪk/ *a.* underwater.

subaqueous /sʌb'eɪkwɪəs/ *a.* subaquatic.

subatomic /sʌbə'tɒmɪk/ *a.* occurring in an atom; smaller than an atom.

subconscious /sʌb'kɒnʃəs/ **1** *n.* part of the mind that is not fully conscious but is able to influence actions etc. **2** *a.* of the subconscious.

subcontinent /sʌb'kɒntɪnənt/ *n.* landmass of great extent not classed as continent.

subcontract 1 /sʌb'kɒntrækt/ *n.* arrangement by which one who has contracted to do work arranges for it to be done by others. **2** /sʌbkən'trækt/ *v.* make subcontract (for). **3 subcontractor** /'sʌbkəntræktə/ *n.*

subculture /'sʌbkʌltʃə/ *n.* social group or its culture within a larger culture.

subcutaneous /sʌbkju:'teɪnɪəs/ *a.* under the skin.

subdivide /sʌbdɪ'vaɪd/ *v.* divide again after first division. [L (SUB-)]

subdivision /'sʌbdɪvɪʒ(ə)n/ *n.* subdividing; subordinate division.

subdue /səb'dju:/ *v.t.* conquer, suppress, tame; (esp. in *p.p.*) make softer or gentler or less intense. [F f. L *subduco*]

sub-edit /sʌb'edɪt/ *v.t.* act as sub-editor of. [SUB-]

sub-editor /sʌb'edɪtə/ *n.* assistant editor; one who prepares material for printing in newspaper or book etc.; **subeditorial** /-'tɔ:rɪ(ə)l/ *a.*

subfusc /'sʌbfʌsk/ **1** *n.* dull-coloured formal clothing in some universities. **2** *a.* dull-coloured. [L (*fuscus* dark brown)]

subhuman /sʌb'hju:mən/ *a.* less than human; not fully human. [SUB-]

subject /'sʌbdʒekt/ **1** *n.* theme of discussion or description or representation, matter (to be) treated or dealt with, person (to be) studied or thought about; person under political rule, any member of a State except the sovereign; person owing obedience to another; circumstance or person or thing that gives occasion *for* specified feeling or action (*is a subject for ridicule*); branch of study (*her subject is history*); *Logic & Gram.* the term about which something is predicated in a proposition, noun or noun-equivalent with which verb of sentence is made to agree in number etc.; *Philos.* the conscious self as opposed to all that is external to the mind, the substance as opposed to the attributes of something; a principal theme in a piece of music; (esp. in medicine) person with specified usu. undesirable bodily or mental tendency (*a hysterical subject*). **2** *a.* under control or government, owing obedience *to*; liable or exposed *to*; (with *to*) conditional upon. **3** *adv.* (with *to*) conditionally upon (*subject to your approval I shall go tomorrow*). **4** /səb'dʒekt/ *v.t.* expose or make liable *to*; subdue, make one's political subject. **5 subjection** /səb'dʒekʃ(ə)n/ *n.* [F f. L *subicio -ject-* (*jacio* throw)]

subjective /səb'dʒektɪv/ *a.* of or due to the consciousness or thinking or percipient subject as opposed to real or external things, not objective, imaginary; giving prominence to or depending on personal opinions or idiosyncrasy; *Gram.* of the subject; **subjectivity** /-'tɪvɪtɪ/ *n.* [L (as prec.)]

subjoin /səb'dʒɔɪn/ *v.t.* add (anecdote or illustration etc.) at the end. [F f. L *subjungo -junct-*]

sub judice /sʌb 'dʒu:dɪsɪ/ under judicial consideration, not yet decided (and therefore not to be commented on). [L]

subjugate /'sʌbdʒʊgeɪt/ *v.t.* conquer, bring into subjection or bondage; **subjugation** /-'geɪʃ(ə)n/ *n.*; **subjugator** *n.* [L (*jugum* yoke)]

subjunctive /səb'dʒʌŋktɪv/ *Gram.* **1** *a.* (of mood) expressing wish or supposition or possibility (e.g. *if I were you*; *suffice it to say*). **2** *n.* subjunctive mood or form. [F or L (SUBJOIN)]

sublease 1 /'sʌbli:s/ *n.* lease granted to subtenant. **2** /sʌb'li:s/ *v.t.* lease by sublease. [SUB-]

sublet /sʌb'let/ *v.t.* (**-tt-**; *past* and *p.p.* **sublet**) let to subtenant.

sublimate 1 /'sʌblɪmeɪt/ *v.t.* divert energy of (primitive impulse etc.) into culturally higher activity; sublime (a substance); refine, purify. **2** /'sʌblɪmət/ *n.* sublimed substance. **3 sublimation** /-'meɪʃ(ə)n/ *n.* [L (foll.)]

sublime /sə'blaɪm/ **1** *a.* of the highest or most exalted sort, awe-inspiring; characteristic of one who has no fear of consequences (*sublime indifference*). **2** *v.* convert (substance) from solid into vapour by heat (and usu. allow to solidify again), (of substance) undergo this process; purify or make sublime. **3 sublimity** /-'blɪmɪtɪ/ *n.* [L *sublimis*]

subliminal /sʌb'lɪmɪn(ə)l/ *a.* below threshold of consciousness; too faint or rapid to be consciously perceived; **subliminally** *adv.* [L *limen -min-* threshold]

sub-machine-gun /sʌbmə'ʃi:ngʌn/ *n.* lightweight machine-gun held in the hand. [SUB-]

submarine /sʌbmə'ri:n, 'sʌb-/ **1** *n.* a ship, esp. an armed warship, equipped to operate below surface of the sea. **2** *a.* existing or occurring or done below surface of the sea. [SUB-, MARINE]

submerge /səb'mɜ:dʒ/ *v.* place or go beneath water; flood, inundate; **submergence** *n.*; **submersion** *n.* [L (*mergo mers-* dip)]

submersible /səb'mɜ:sɪb(ə)l/ **1** *a.* capable of submerging. **2** *n.* submersible vessel.

submicroscopic /sʌbmaɪkrə'skɒpɪk/ *a.* too small to be seen by microscope. [SUB-]

submission /səb'mɪʃ(ə)n/ *n.* submitting or being submitted; thing submitted; submissiveness. [F, or L *submissio* (SUBMIT)]

submissive /səb'mɪsɪv/ *a.* willing to submit, unresisting, meek.

submit /səb'mɪt/ *v.* (**-tt-**) surrender (oneself) to the control or authority of another; cease to resist or oppose; present for consideration or decision; subject (person or thing) *to* a process or treatment. [L (*mitto miss-* send)]

subnormal /'sʌbnɔ:m(ə)l/ *a.* below or less than normal, esp. in intelligence. [SUB-]

subordinate /sə'bɔ:dɪnət/ **1** *a.* of inferior importance or rank, secondary, subservient. **2** *n.* subordinate person. **3** /-eɪt/ *v.t.* make or treat as subordinate (usu. *to*). **4 subordinate clause** clause serving as noun or adjective or adverb within a sentence. **5 subordination** /-'neɪʃ(ə)n/ *n.* [L (ORDAIN)]

suborn /sə'bɔ:n/ *v.t.* induce esp. by bribery to commit perjury or other crime. [L (*orno* equip)]

subpoena /səb'pi:nə/ **1** *n.* writ commanding person's attendance in lawcourt. **2** *v.t.* (*past* & *p.p.* **subpoenaed** /-nəd/) serve subpoena on. [L, = under penalty]

sub rosa /sʌb 'rəʊzə/ in confidence or secretly. [L, = under the rose]

subscribe /səb'skraɪb/ *v.* pay (specified sum) esp. regularly for membership of an organization, receipt of a publication, etc.; agree to pay (such sum); contribute *to* a fund or *for* a purpose; write (esp. one's name) at foot of document etc.; sign (document) thus; **subscribe to** arrange to receive (periodical etc.) regularly, agree with (opinion or resolution). [L (*scribo script-* write)]

subscriber *n.* one who subscribes; person paying regular sum for hire of telephone; **subscriber trunk dialling** making of trunk-calls by subscriber without assistance of operator.

subscript /'sʌbskrɪpt/ **1** *a.* written or printed below. **2** *n.* subscript number or symbol.

subscription /səb'skrɪpʃ(ə)n/ *n.* amount subscribed; act of subscribing; **subscription concert** concert (usu. one of series) paid for mainly by those who subscribe in advance.

subsequent /'sʌbsɪkwənt/ *a.* following a specified or implied event; **subsequent to** later than, after. [F or L (*sequor* follow)]

subservient /səb'sɜ:vɪənt/ *a.* subordinate *to*, servile, obsequious; of use in minor role; **subservience** *n.* [L *subservio*]

subside /səb'saɪd/ *v.i.* sink or settle to a lower level, or to the bottom; (of ground) cave in, sink; become less active or intense or prominent; (of person) sink into chair etc.; **subsidence** /səb'saɪdəns, 'sʌbsɪdəns/ *n.* [L *subsido*]

subsidiary /səb'sɪdɪərɪ/ **1** *a.* serving to help or supplement, not of primary importance; (of company) controlled by another. **2** *n.* subsidiary company or thing or person. [L (SUBSIDY)]

subsidize /'sʌbsɪdaɪz/ *v.t.* provide with subsidy; reduce cost of with subsidy. [foll.]

subsidy /'sʌbsɪdɪ/ *n.* money contributed by State or public body etc. to keep prices at desired level or to assist in meeting expenses etc. [AF or F f. L (*subsidium* help)]

subsist /səb'sɪst/ *v.i.* exist, continue to exist, get sustenance or livelihood (*on* food etc., *by* occupation). [L *subsisto*]

subsistence /səb'sɪstəns/ *n.* subsisting, means of this; **subsistence farming** farming in which almost all crops are consumed by farmer's household; **subsistence level** (or **wage**) level (or wage) merely enough to provide bare necessities of life.

subsoil /'sʌbsɔɪl/ *n.* soil immediately below surface soil. [SUB-]

subsonic /sʌb'sɒnɪk/ *a.* relating to speeds less than that of sound; **subsonically** *adv.*

substance /'sʌbstəns/ *n.* particular kind of material having more or less uniform properties; essence of what is spoken or written (*the substance of his remarks*); reality, solidity; wealth and possessions (*person of substance*); content as distinct from form; **in substance** in the main points. [F f. L *substantia*]

substantial /səb'stænʃ(ə)l/ *a.* of real importance or value, of considerable amount; of solid structure; having substance, actually existing; well-to-do; es-

sential, virtual; **substantially** *adv.* [F or L (prec.)]
substantiate /səb'stænʃɪeɪt/ *v.t.* support or prove the truth of; **substantiation** /-'eɪʃ(ə)n/ *n.* [med.L (SUBSTANCE)]
substantive /'sʌbstəntɪv/ **1** *a.* having independent existence, not subordinate; actual, real, permanent. **2** *n.* noun. **3** **substantival** /-'taɪv(ə)l/ *a.* [F or L (SUBSTANCE)]
substitute /'sʌbstɪtju:t/ **1** *n.* person or thing acting or serving in place of another. **2** *v.t.* put or use or serve as a substitute (*for*). **3** *a.* acting as substitute. **4** **substitution** /-'tju:ʃ(ə)n/ *n.* [L *substituo -tut-*]
substratum /'sʌbstrɑ:təm, -streɪ-/ *n.* (*pl.* **substrata**) underlying layer or substance. [L (SUB-)]
subsume /səb'sju:m/ *v.t.* include (instance etc.) under a particular rule or class. [L (*sumo* take)]
subtenant /'sʌbtenənt/ *n.* person renting room or house etc. from one who is a tenant of it; **subtenancy** *n.* [SUB-]
subtend /səb'tend/ *v.t.* (of line) be opposite (angle or arc). [L (TEND[1])]
subterfuge /'sʌbtəfju:dʒ/ *n.* evasion or trickery to escape censure or defeat etc.; use or instance of this. [F or L]
subterranean /sʌbtə'reɪnɪən/ *a.* underground. [L (*terra* land)]
subtitle /'sʌbtaɪt(ə)l/ **1** *n.* subordinate or additional title of book etc.; caption of cinema film etc., esp. translating foreign dialogue. **2** *v.t.* provide with subtitle(s). [SUB-]
subtle /'sʌt(ə)l/ *a.* hard to detect or describe, fine or delicate (*a subtle distinction, flavour*); ingenious, clever; **subtlety** *n.* [F f. L *subtilis*]
subtopia /sʌb'təʊpɪə/ *n.* unsightly suburbs, esp. disfiguring a rural area. [SUB(URB), (U)TOPIA]
subtract /səb'trækt/ *v.t.* deduct (number etc. *from* greater number); **subtraction** *n.* [L (TRACT)]
subtropical /sʌb'trɒpɪk(ə)l/ *a.* bordering on the tropics; characteristic of subtropical regions. [SUB-]
suburb /'sʌbɜ:b/ *n.* outlying district of city. [F or L (*urbs* city)]
suburban /sə'bɜ:bən/ *a.* of or characteristic of suburbs; provincial in outlook; **suburbanite** *n.* [L (prec.)]
Suburbia /sə'bɜ:bɪə/ *n.* (usu. *derog.*) the suburbs and their inhabitants. [SUBURB]
subvention /səb'venʃ(ə)n/ *n.* subsidy. [F f. L (*subvenio* assist)]
subversive /səb'vɜ:sɪv/ **1** *a.* attempting subversion. **2** *n.* subversive person. [med.L (foll.)]
subvert /səb'vɜ:t/ *v.t.* weaken or overthrow authority of (government etc.), attempt to do this; **subversion** *n.* [F or L (*verto vers-* turn)]
subway /'sʌbweɪ/ *n.* underground passage, esp. for pedestrians; *US* underground railway. [SUB-]
suc- *prefix* assimilated form of SUB- before *c* in words from Latin (*succumb*).
succeed /sək'si:d/ *v.* have success (*in*); prosper or be successful; come next to in time or order, be subsequent (to); come by inheritance or in due order (*to* office or title). [F, or L *succedo -cess-* come after]
success /sək'ses/ *n.* favourable outcome, accomplishment of what was aimed at, attainment of wealth or fame or position; thing or person that turns out well; outcome (*ill success*). [L (prec.)]
successful *a.* having success, prosperous; **successfully** *adv.*
succession /sək'seʃ(ə)n/ *n.* a following in order; series of things one after another (*a succession of defeats*); succeeding to the throne or an office or inheritance, right of doing this, series of persons having such right; **in succession** one after another; **in succession to** as successor of. [F or L (SUCCEED)]
successive /sək'sesɪv/ *a.* following in succession, consecutive. [med.L (SUCCEED)]
successor /sək'sesə/ *n.* person or thing that succeeds (*to*) another. [F f. L (SUCCEED)]
succinct /sək'sɪŋkt/ *a.* concise, brief. [L (*cingo cinct-* gird)]
succour /'sʌkə/, *US* **succor** *literary* **1** *n.* help given in time of need. **2** *v.t.* give succour to. [F f. L (*curro* run)]
succulent /'sʌkjʊlənt/ **1** *a.* juicy; lively or interesting; (of plant) thick and fleshy. **2** *n.* succulent plant. **3** **succulence** *n.* [L (*succus* juice)]
succumb /sə'kʌm/ *v.i.* give way (*to*), be overcome; die (*succumbed to cancer*). [F or L (*cumbo* lie)]
such **1** *a.* of the kind or degree indicated or suggested (*there is no such thing; am not such a fool as to think so*); of the same kind (*books and papers and such things*); so great or extreme (*was in such a hurry*). **2** *pron.* such person(s) or thing(s). **3** **as such** as being what has been specified, in itself; **such-and-such** (person or thing) of particular kind but not needing to be specified; **such as** for example (*insects, such as bees*). [OE, = so like]
suchlike **1** *a.* of the same kind. **2** *pron.* (usu. *pl.*) things of this kind.
suck **1** *v.* draw (liquid) into the mouth by using lip muscles; draw liquid from (thing) thus; squeeze and extract flavour from (sweet etc.) in the mouth by using tongue; use sucking action or make

sucking sound (*sat sucking at his pipe*); draw sustenance from (*suck the breast*); derive advantage from; imbibe or gain (knowledge or advantage etc.). **2** *n.* act or period of sucking. **3 suck dry** exhaust of contents by sucking; **suck up** absorb; **suck up to** *sl.* seek favour of, flatter. [OE]

sucker *n.* side shoot springing from plant's root or stem below ground; organ in animals or part of apparatus for adhering by suction to surfaces; *sl.* gullible or easily deceived person.

suckle /'sʌk(ə)l/ *v.t.* feed (young) from breast or udder.

suckling *n.* unweaned child or animal.

sucrose /'sju:krəʊz, 'su:-/ *n.* sugar obtained from sugar-cane, sugar-beet, etc. [F *sucre* sugar]

suction /'sʌkʃ(ə)n/ *n.* sucking; production of partial vacuum causing adhesion of surfaces or enabling external atmospheric pressure to force liquid etc. in. [L (*sugo suct-* suck)]

Sudanese /su:də'ni:z/ **1** *a.* of Sudan. **2** *n.* (*pl.* same) native of Sudan. [*Sudan* in NE Africa]

sudden /'sʌd(ə)n/ *a.* done or occurring etc. abruptly or unexpectedly; **all of a sudden** suddenly; **sudden death** *colloq.* decision (esp. in drawn contest) by result of single event; **suddenness** *n.* [AF f. L *subitaneus*]

sudorific /sju:də'rɪfɪk, su:-/ **1** *a.* causing sweating. **2** *n.* sudorific drug. [L (*sudor* sweat)]

suds /sʌdz/ *n.pl.* froth of soap and water; **sudsy** *a.* [prob. LG *sudde* or Du. *sudse* marsh, bog]

sue /sju:, su:/ *v.* begin lawsuit against (person); make application (*to* person or court, *for* redress or favour). [AF *suer* f. Rmc (L *sequor* follow)]

suede /sweɪd/ *n.* kid or other skin with flesh side rubbed to a nap; cloth imitating it. [F, = Sweden]

suet /'sju:ɪt, 'su:-/ *n.* hard fat of kidneys and loins of oxen or sheep etc.; **suety** *a.* [AF f. L *sebum*]

suf- *prefix* assimilated form of SUB- before *f* in words from Latin (*suffice*).

suffer *v.* experience adverse effects of (something unpleasant); undergo (change etc.); experience pain or grief or discomfort etc.; tolerate; *archaic* permit, allow (*to* come etc.). [F f. Rmc (L *suffero*)]

sufferance *n.* tacit consent, abstention from objection; **on sufferance** tolerated but not supported. [AF or F f. L (prec.)]

suffice /sə'faɪs/ *v.* be enough or adequate; meet the needs of (person etc.); **suffice it to say** I will content myself with saying *that*. [F f. L *sufficio*]

sufficiency /sə'fɪʃənsɪ/ *n.* a sufficient amount. [L (foll.)]

sufficient *a.* sufficing, adequate. [F or L (SUFFICE)]

suffix /'sʌfɪks/ **1** *n.* letter(s) added at end of word to form derivative. **2** *v.t.* append, esp. as suffix. [L (*figo fix-* fasten)]

suffocate /'sʌfəkeɪt/ *v.* impede or stop breathing of (person etc.), choke or kill thus; be or feel suffocated; **suffocation** /-'keɪʃ(ə)n/ *n.* [L *suffoco* (*fauces* throat)]

suffragan /'sʌfrəgən/ *n.* bishop appointed to assist diocesan bishop; bishop in relation to his archbishop. [AF & F f. L (foll.)]

suffrage /'sʌfrɪdʒ/ *n.* right of voting in political elections; short prayer or petition. [F, or L *suffragium*]

suffragette /sʌfrə'dʒet/ *n. hist.* woman who agitated for women's suffrage.

suffuse /sə'fju:z/ *v.t.* (of colour or moisture etc.) spread throughout or over; **suffusion** *n.* [L (FOUND²)]

Sufi /'su:fɪ/ *n.* Muslim mystic; **Sufic** *a.*; **Sufism** *n.* [Arab.]

sug- *prefix* assimilated form of SUB- before *g* in words from Latin (*suggest*).

sugar /'ʃʊgə/ **1** *n.* sweet crystalline substance from sugar-cane, sugar-beet, and other plants, used in cookery, confectionery, etc.; soluble usu. sweet crystalline carbohydrate, e.g. glucose; something to reconcile person to what is unpalatable; *US colloq.* (as term of address) darling, sweetheart. **2** *v.t.* sweeten or coat with sugar. **3 sugar-beet** beet from whose roots sugar is made; **sugar-cane** perennial tropical grass with very tall stems from which sugar is made; **sugar-daddy** *sl.* elderly man who lavishes gifts on a young woman; **sugar-loaf** conical moulded mass of sugar; **sugar soap** alkaline compound for cleaning or removing paint. [F f. It. f. med.L f. Arab.]

sugary *n.* containing or resembling sugar; attractively or excessively sweet or pleasant; **sugariness** *n.*

suggest /sə'dʒest/ *v.t.* put forward for consideration or as a possibility, propose tentatively (*that*); cause (idea) to present itself, bring (idea) into the mind; **suggest itself** come into the mind. [L *suggero -gest-*]

suggestible *a.* open to (esp. hypnotic) suggestion; that may be suggested; **suggestibility** /-'bɪlɪtɪ/ *n.*

suggestion /sə'dʒestʃ(ə)n/ *n.* suggesting; thing suggested; insinuation of a belief or impulse into the mind; a hint or slight trace (*of*). [F f. L (SUGGEST)]

suggestive /sə'dʒestɪv/ *a.* conveying a suggestion (*of*); suggesting something indecent. [SUGGEST]

suicidal /su:ɪ'saɪd(ə)l, sju:-/ *a.* of or tending to suicide; (of person) liable to commit suicide; extremely foolhardy, destructive to one's own interests etc.; **suicidally** *adv.* [foll.]

suicide /'su:ɪsaɪd, 'sju:-/ *n.* intentional killing of oneself, an instance of this; person who does this; action destructive to one's own interests or reputation etc. [L *sui* of oneself, -CIDE]

sui generis /sjʊaɪ 'dʒenərɪs/ of its own kind, unique. [L]

suit /su:t, sju:t/ **1** *n.* set of clothes for wearing together, esp. of same cloth and consisting of jacket and trousers or skirt; clothing for particular purpose (*spacesuit*); set *of* pyjamas, armour, etc.; any of the four sets (spades, hearts, diamonds, clubs) into which pack of cards is divided; lawsuit; *archaic* suing, seeking of woman's hand in marriage. **2** *v.* satisfy, meet requirements or interest of, agree with; go well with, be in harmony with; be convenient or agreeable; adapt or make appropriate *to*; (in *p.p.*) appropriate *to*, well adapted or having the right qualities *for*. **3 suit oneself** do as one chooses, find something that satisfies one. [AF *suite* f. Rmc; see SUE]

suitable *a.* suited *for* or *to*; right or appropriate for the purpose or occasion etc.; **suitability** /-'bɪlɪtɪ/ *n.*; **suitably** *adv.*

suitcase *n.* case for carrying clothes etc., usu. with handle and flat hinged lid.

suite /swi:t/ *n.* set of rooms or furniture; group of attendants; *Mus.* set of instrumental pieces. [F (as SUIT)]

suitor /'su:tə, 'sju:-/ *n.* man wooing woman; plaintiff or petitioner. [AF f. L]

sulfa var. of SULPHA.

sulfur *US* var. of SULPHUR.

sulk 1 *v.i.* be sulky. **2** *n.* (usu. in *pl.*) sulky fit. [perh. back-form. f. foll.]

sulky *a.* sullen and unsociable from resentment or bad temper; **sulkily** *adv.*; **sulkiness** *n.* [perh. obs. *sulke* hard to dispose of]

sullen /'sʌlən/ *a.* passively resentful, stubbornly ill-humoured, unresponsive; **sullenness** *n.* [AF (*sol* SOLE²)]

sully /'sʌlɪ/ *v.t.* spoil purity or splendour of (reputation etc.). [F *souiller* (SOIL¹)]

sulpha /'sʌlfə/ *a.* sulphonamide (*sulpha drugs*). [abbr.]

sulphate /'sʌlfeɪt/ *n.* salt of sulphuric acid. [F f. L SULPHUR]

sulphide /'sʌlfaɪd/ *n.* binary compound of sulphur. [SULPHUR]

sulphite /'sʌlfaɪt/ *n.* salt of sulphurous acid. [F (SULPHATE)]

sulphonamide /sʌl'fɒnəmaɪd/ *n.* a type of antibiotic drug. [G *sulfon* (as SULPHUR), AMIDE]

sulphur /'sʌlfə/ *n.* pale-yellow non-metallic element burning with suffocating smell and blue flame; pale slightly greenish yellow colour; yellow butterfly. [AF f. L]

sulphureous /sʌl'fjʊərɪəs/ *a.* of or like sulphur. [L (SULPHUR)]

sulphuric /sʌl'fjʊərɪk/ *a.* containing sulphur in a higher valency; **sulphuric acid** dense oily highly acid and corrosive fluid. [F (SULPHUR)]

sulphurous /'sʌlfərəs/ *a.* of or like sulphur; containing sulphur in a lower valency; **sulphurous acid** unstable weak acid used as reducing and bleaching agent. [SULPHUR]

sultan /'sʌlt(ə)n/ *n.* Muslim sovereign; (also **sweet sultan**) a sweet-scented plant. [F or med.L f. Arab.]

sultana /sʌl'tɑ:nə/ *n.* a kind of seedless raisin; sultan's wife, mother, concubine, or daughter. [It.]

sultanate /'sʌltənət/ *n.* position of, or territory ruled by, sultan. [SULTAN]

sultry /'sʌltrɪ/ *a.* (of weather etc.) hot and close; (of person etc.) passionate, sensual; **sultrily** *adv.*; **sultriness** *n.* [obs. *sulter* v., rel. to SWELTER]

sum 1 *n.* total resulting from addition of items; a particular amount of money (*the sum of £5*); problem in arithmetic, working out of this; whole amount; substance, summary. **2** *v.t.* (**-mm-**) find sum of. **3 in sum** briefly, in summary; **sum up** find or give total of, express briefly or summarize, form or express judgement or opinion of (person or situation), (esp. of judge) recapitulate evidence or argument. [F f. L *summa*]

sumac /'ʃu:mæk/ *n.* shrub yielding leaves which are dried and ground for use in tanning and dyeing; these leaves. [F f. Arab.]

summarize /'sʌməraɪz/ *v.t.* make or be a summary of. [foll.]

summary /'sʌmərɪ/ **1** *n.* brief account giving chief points. **2** *a.* brief, without details or formalities. **3 summarily** *adv.* [L (SUM)]

summation /sʌ'meɪʃ(ə)n/ *n.* finding of total; summarizing. [SUM]

summer 1 *n.* warmest season of the year; mature stage of life etc. **2** *a.* characteristic of or suitable for summer. **3 summer-house** light building in garden etc. providing shade in summer; **summer school** series of lectures etc. in summer, esp. at university; **summer-time** season or weather of summer; **summer time** time shown by clocks advanced in summer for daylight saving. **4 summery** *a.* [OE]

summit /'sʌmɪt/ *n.* highest point, top; highest level of achievement or status; (in full **summit meeting**) conference of

heads of governments. [F f. L *summus* highest]
summon /'sʌmən/ *v.t.* demand presence of, call together; command (person) to appear in lawcourt; call upon *to do* thing (*summoned them to surrender*); **summon up** gather (one's strength or courage or energy etc., esp. *to do* thing). [F f. L *summoneo*]
summons 1 *n.* authoritative call to attend or do something, esp. to appear before judge or magistrate. **2** *v.t.* serve with summons.
sump *n.* casing holding oil in internal-combustion engine; pit or well for reception of (esp. superfluous) water or oil or other liquid in mines or machinery etc. [LG or Du.]
sumptuary /'sʌmptʊərɪ/ *a.* limiting (esp. private) expenditure. [L (*sumptus* cost)]
sumptuous /'sʌmptʊəs/ *a.* rich and costly; suggesting costliness. [F f. L (prec.)]
sun 1 *n.* the star round which the earth travels and from which the earth receives light and warmth; this light or warmth (*let in the sun*); any fixed star. **2** *v.* (**-nn-**) expose (oneself) to the sun. **3 place in the sun** favourable situation or condition; **sun-glasses** spectacles with tinted lenses to protect eyes from sunlight or glare; **sun-god** the sun worshipped as a deity; **sun-lamp** lamp giving ultra-violet rays for therapy or artificial sun-tan; **sun lounge** room designed to receive much sunlight; **sun-roof** roof with sliding section in saloon car; **sun-tan** tanning of skin by exposure to sun; **sun-tanned** tanned by sun; **sun-trap** sunny place, esp. sheltered from wind; **sun-up** *US* sunrise; **under the sun** anywhere in the world. [OE]
Sun. *abbr.* Sunday.
sunbathe *v.i.* expose one's body to the sun. [SUN]
sunbeam *n.* ray of the sun.
sunburn *n.* inflammation of skin from exposure to sun; **sunburnt** *a.*
sundae /'sʌndeɪ/ *n.* confection of ice-cream with fruit, syrup, etc. [perh. f. foll.]
Sunday /'sʌndeɪ/ **1** *n.* day of week following Saturday, Christian day of rest and worship; newspaper published on Sundays. **2** *adv. colloq.* on Sunday. **3 Sunday best** one's best clothes (kept for Sunday use); **Sunday school** school held on Sundays for religious instruction of children; **Sundays** on Sundays, each Sunday. [OE]
sunder *v.t.* sever. [OE (cf. ASUNDER)]
sundial *n.* instrument showing time by shadow of pointer in sunlight. [SUN]
sundown *n.* sunset.
sundry /'sʌndrɪ/ **1** *a.* various, several. **2** *n.* (in *pl.*) oddments, accessories, items not needed to be specified. **3 all and sundry** everyone. [OE, rel. to SUNDER]
sunfish *n.* large globular fish. [SUN]
sunflower *n.* tall garden-plant with large golden-rayed flowers.
sung *p.p.* of SING.
sunk *past* & *p.p.* of SINK.
sunken *a.* lying below level of surrounding area; (of cheeks etc.) shrunken, hollow. [p.p. of SINK]
sunless *a.* without sunshine. [SUN]
sunlight *n.* light from sun.
sunlit *a.* illuminated by sunlight.
Sunni /'sʌnɪ/ *n.* member of Muslim branch accepting law based on Muhammad's acts but not written by him; **Sunnite** *n.* & *a.* [Arab. *Sunna* = way, rule]
sunny *a.* bright with or as sunlight; exposed to or warm with the sun; happy, cheerful; **sunnily** *adv.*; **sunniness** *n.* [SUN]
sunrise *n.* sun's rising, moment of this.
sunset *n.* sun's setting, moment of this; western sky with colours of sunset.
sunshade *n.* parasol or awning.
sunshine *n.* direct light of sun, area illuminated by it; fair weather; cheerfulness or bright influence.
sunspot *n.* dark patch on sun's surface.
sunstroke *n.* acute prostration from excessive heat of sun.
sup 1 *v.* (**-pp-**) drink by sips or spoonfuls; take supper; *colloq.* drink (beer etc.). **2** *n.* mouthful of liquid; *colloq.* drink of beer etc. [OE]
sup- *prefix* assimilated form of SUB- before *p* in words from Latin (*support*).
super /'su:pə, 'sju:-/ **1** *a. sl.* excellent, splendid. **2** *n. colloq.* supernumerary; superintendent. [abbr.]
super- *prefix* above or beyond or over (*superstructure, supernormal*); to a great or extreme degree (*superabundant, supertanker*); higher in status (*superintendent*). [L]
superannuate /su:pə'rænjʊeɪt, sju:-/ *v.t.* dismiss or discard as too old; send into retirement with pension; (in *p.p.*) too old for work or use. [L (*annus* year)]
superannuation /su:pərænjʊ'eɪʃ(ə)n, sju:-/ *n.* pension, payment made to obtain this.
superb /su:'pɜ:b, sju:-/ *a.* magnificent, splendid; *colloq.* excellent. [F or L, = proud]
supercargo /'su:pəkɑ:gəʊ, 'sju:-/ *n.* (*pl.* **supercargoes**) person in merchant ship managing sales etc. of cargo. [Sp. *sobrecargo*]
supercharge /'su:pətʃɑ:dʒ, 'sju:-/ *v.t.* charge to extreme or excess (*with*

energy etc.); use supercharger on. [SUPER-]

supercharger *n.* device forcing extra air or fuel into internal-combustion engine.

supercilious /su:pəˈsɪlɪəs, sju:-/ *a.* contemptuous, haughty. [L *supercilium* eyebrow]

superconductivity /su:pəkɒndʌkˈtɪvɪtɪ, sju:-/ *n.* absence of electrical resistance in some substances at temperatures near absolute zero. [SUPER-]

supererogation /su:pərerəˈgeɪʃ(ə)n, sju:-/ *n.* doing of more than duty requires. [L *supererogo* pay in addition]

superficial /su:pəˈfɪʃ(ə)l, sju:-/ *a.* of or on the surface only; without depth of knowledge or feeling etc.; (of measure) square; **superficiality** /-ʃɪˈælɪtɪ/ *n.*; **superficially** *adv.* [L (FACE)]

superfine /ˈsu:pəfaɪn, ˈsju:-/ *a.* extremely fine or refined. [L (FINE¹)]

superfluity /su:pəˈflu:ɪtɪ, sju:-/ *n.* superfluous amount or thing; being superfluous. [F f. L (foll.)]

superfluous /su:ˈpɜ:flʊəs, sju:-/ *a.* more than is needed or wanted, useless. [L (*fluo* flow)]

supergrass /ˈsu:pəgrɑ:s, ˈsju:-/ *n. sl.* large-scale police informer. [SUPER-]

superhuman /su:pəˈhju:mən, sju:-/ *a.* exceeding (normal) human capacity or power. [L (SUPER-)]

superimpose /su:pərɪmˈpəʊz, sju:-/ *v.t.* lay or place (thing) on top of something else (often with *on*); **superimposition** /-pəˈzɪʃ(ə)n/ *n.* [SUPER-]

superintend /su:pərɪnˈtend, sju:-/ *v.* manage, watch and direct (work etc.); **superintendence** *n.* [L (SUPER-)]

superintendent *n.* one who superintends; director of institution etc.; police officer above rank of inspector. [L (prec.)]

superior /su:ˈpɪərɪə, sju:-/ **1** *a.* higher in rank or quality etc. (*to*); better or greater in some respect; high-quality (*made of superior leather*); priggish (*with a superior air*); unlikely to yield or not resorting *to* (bribery or temptation etc.); situated above; written or printed above the line. **2** *n.* person superior to another esp. in rank; head of monastery etc. (esp. *Father* or *Mother Superior*). **3 superiority** /-ˈɒrɪtɪ/ *n.* [F f. L compar. (SUPER-)]

superlative /su:ˈpɜ:lətɪv, sju:-/ **1** *a.* of the highest order or degree, excellent. **2** *n. Gram.* superlative degree or form. **3 superlative adjective** (or **adverb**) adjective (or adverb) in superlative degree; **superlative degree** form expressing the highest or a very high degree of a quality (e.g. *bravest, most quickly*). [F f. L]

superman /ˈsu:pəmæn, ˈsju:-/ *n.* man of superhuman powers or achievement. [SUPER-]

supermarket /ˈsu:pəmɑ:kɪt, ˈsju:-/ *n.* large self-service store usu. selling food and some household goods.

supernatural /su:pəˈnætʃər(ə)l, sju:-/ *a.* of or manifesting phenomena not explicable by natural or physical laws; **supernaturally** *adv.* [med.L (SUPER-)]

supernova /su:pəˈnəʊvə, sju:-/ *n.* (*pl.* **supernovae** /-i:/ or **-vas**) star that suddenly increases very greatly in brightness. [SUPER-]

supernumerary /su:pəˈnju:mərərɪ, sju:-/ **1** *a.* in excess of normal number; engaged for extra work; (of actor) appearing in unimportant part. **2** *n.* supernumerary person or thing. [L (NUMBER)]

superphosphate /su:pəˈfɒsfeɪt, sju:-/ *n.* fertilizer made from phosphate rock. [SUPER-]

superpower /ˈsu:pəpaʊə, ˈsju:-/ *n.* extremely powerful nation. [SUPER-]

superscribe /ˈsu:pəskraɪb, ˈsju:-/ *v.t.* write (inscription) at top of or outside document etc. [L (*scribo* write)]

superscript /ˈsu:pəskrɪpt, ˈsju:-/ **1** *a.* written or printed above. **2** *n.* superscript number or symbol.

superscription /su:pəˈskrɪpʃ(ə)n, sju:-/ *n.* superscribed words.

supersede /su:pəˈsi:d, sju:-/ *v.t.* take the place of; put or use another in place of; **supersession** /-ˈseʃ(ə)n/ *n.* [F f. L *supersedeo*]

supersonic /su:pəˈsɒnɪk, sju:-/ *a.* of or having a speed greater than that of sound; **supersonically** *adv.* [SUPER-]

superstition /su:pəˈstɪʃ(ə)n, sju:-/ *n.* belief in the existence or power of the supernatural; irrational fear of the unknown or mysterious; misdirected reverence; a religion or practice or opinion based on such tendencies; widely held but wrong idea; **superstitious** *a.* [F or L]

superstructure /ˈsu:pəstrʌktʃə, ˈsju:-/ *n.* structure built on top of something else. [SUPER-]

supertax /ˈsu:pətæks, ˈsju:-/ *n.* & *v.t.* surtax.

supervene /su:pəˈvi:n, sju:-/ *v.i.* occur as interruption in or change from some state; **supervention** *n.* [L *supervenio*]

supervise /ˈsu:pəvaɪz, ˈsju:-/ *v.t.* superintend, oversee; **supervision** /-ˈvɪʒ(ə)n/ *n.*; **supervisor** *n.*; **supervisory** *a.* [L *supervideo -vis-*]

supine /ˈsu:paɪn, ˈsju:-/ **1** *a.* lying face upwards; inactive, indolent. **2** *n.* Latin verbal noun used only in accusative and ablative cases. [L]

supper *n.* light evening meal. [F *souper*]

supplant /sə'plɑ:nt/ *v.t.* take the place of, esp. by underhand means. [F, or L *supplanto* trip up]

supple /'sʌp(ə)l/ *a.* flexible, pliant; **supplely** *adv.* [F f. L *supplex*]

supplement /'sʌplɪmənt/ **1** *n.* thing or part added to remedy deficiencies or amplify information; separate addition to newspaper etc. **2** /also -'ment/ *v.t.* provide supplement for. **3 supplemental** /-'ment(ə)l/ *a.*; **supplementary** /-'mentərɪ/ *a.*; **supplementation** /-'teɪʃ(ə)n/ *n.* [L (*suppleo* SUPPLY)]

suppliant /'sʌplɪənt/ **1** *n.* supplicating person. **2** *a.* supplicating. [F f. L (as foll.)]

supplicate /'sʌplɪkeɪt/ *v.* petition humbly to (person) or for (thing); make petition *to* or *for*; **supplication** /-'keɪʃ(ə)n/ *n.*; **supplicatory** *a.* [F f. L *supplico* (SUPPLE)]

supply /sə'plaɪ/ **1** *v.t.* furnish or provide (thing needed, person *with* thing, etc.); meet or make up for (deficiency or need etc.). **2** *n.* providing of what is needed; stock, store, amount of something provided or obtainable (*in short supply*); (in *pl.*) collected necessaries for army, expedition, etc.; person, esp. schoolteacher or clergyman, acting as temporary substitute for another. **3 on supply** (of schoolteacher etc.) acting as supply; **supply and demand** quantities available and required, as factors regulating price of commodities. [F f. L *suppleo* fill up]

support /sə'pɔ:t/ **1** *v.t.* carry all or part of weight of, keep from falling or sinking or failing; provide for (*support oneself, a family*); strengthen, encourage, give help or corroboration to; speak in favour of (a resolution etc.); be actively interested in (particular team or sport); take secondary part to (actor etc.); endure, tolerate. **2** *n.* supporting or being supported; person or thing that supports. **3 in support of** so as to support; **supporting film** less important film in cinema programme. [F f. L (*porto* carry)]

supporter *n.* person or thing that supports, esp. person supporting team or sport.

supportive *a.* providing support or encouragement.

suppose /sə'pəʊz/ *v.t.* assume, be inclined to think (*I suppose she'll be back*); take as a possibility or hypothesis (*let us suppose you are right*; *suppose* or *supposing you are right*); (in *imper.*) as formula of proposal (*suppose we try again*); (of theory or result etc.) require as condition; (in *p.p.*) generally accepted as being so (*their supposed incomes policy*); **be supposed to** be expected or required to, *colloq.* (with *neg.*) ought not to, not be allowed to. [F (POSE)]

supposedly /sə'pəʊzɪdlɪ/ *adv.* as is generally supposed.

supposition /sʌpə'zɪʃ(ə)n/ *n.* thing supposed; supposing.

suppositious /sʌpə'zɪʃəs/ *a.* hypothetical.

supposititious /səpɒzɪ'tɪʃəs/ *a.* spurious. [L (*pono posit-* place)]

suppository /sə'pɒzɪtərɪ/ *n.* medical preparation inserted into rectum or vagina to melt. [L *suppositorius* placed underneath]

suppress /sə'pres/ *v.t.* end the activity or existence of, esp. forcibly; prevent (information or feelings or reaction etc.) from being seen or heard or known; partly or wholly eliminate (electrical interference etc.), equip (device) to reduce such interference due to it; **suppressible** *a.*; **suppression** *n.*; **suppressor** *n.* [L (PRESS[1])]

suppurate/'sʌpjʊreɪt/ *v.i.* form pus, fester; **suppuration** /-'reɪʃ(ə)n/ *n.* [L (PUS)]

supra /'su:prə/ *adv.* above or further back in book etc. [L]

supra- *prefix* above.

supranational /su:prə'næʃən(ə)l/ *a.* transcending national limits.

supremacy /su:'preməsɪ, sju:-/ *n.* being supreme, highest authority. [foll.]

supreme /su:'pri:m, sju:-/ *a.* highest in authority or rank; greatest, most important; (of penalty or sacrifice etc.) involving death; **Supreme Court** highest judicial court in State etc. [L]

supremo /su:'pri:məʊ, sju:-/ *n.* (*pl.* **supremos**) supreme leader or ruler. [Sp., = SUPREME]

sur-[1] *prefix* assimilated form of SUB- before *r* in words from Latin (*surrogate*).

sur-[2] *prefix* = SUPER- (*surcharge, surface, surrealism*). [F]

surcease /sɜ:'si:s/ *archaic* **1** *n.* cessation. **2** *v.i.* cease. [F *sursis* p.p. f. L (SUPERSEDE)]

surcharge /'sɜ:tʃɑ:dʒ/ **1** *n.* additional charge or payment; mark printed on postage stamp changing its value; additional or excessive load. **2** /also -'tʃɑ:dʒ/ *v.t.* exact surcharge from; exact (sum) as surcharge; mark (postage stamp) with surcharge; overload. [F (SUR-[2])]

surd **1** *a.* (of number) irrational; (of sound) uttered with breath and not voice (e.g. *f, k, p, s, t*). **2** *n.* surd number, esp. root of integer; surd sound. [L, = deaf]

sure /ʃʊə, ʃɔ:/ **1** *a.* having or seeming to have adequate reason for belief; convinced (*of* or *that*); having certain prospect or confident anticipation or satisfactory knowledge *of*; reliable or unfailing; certain (*to do* thing); undoubtedly true or truthful. **2** *adv. colloq.* certainly. **3 be sure to** take care to, not fail to; **for sure** *colloq.* without doubt; **make sure** make or become certain, ensure; **sure enough** *colloq.* in fact, certainly; **sure-fire** *colloq.* certain to succeed; **sure-footed** never stumbling or making a mistake; **to be sure** it is undeniable or admitted. [F f. L *securus*]

surely *adv.* with certainty or safety; as appeal to likelihood or reason (*surely that can't be right*).

surety /'ʃʊərətɪ/ *n.* person who makes himself responsible for another's performance of an undertaking or payment of debt. [F f. L]

surf 1 *n.* foam of sea breaking on shore or reefs. **2** *v.i.* go surf-riding. **3 surf-riding** sport of being carried over surf to shore on board etc. [orig. unkn.]

surface /'sɜ:fɪs/ **1** *n.* the outside of a thing; any of the limits terminating a solid; the top of a liquid or of soil etc.; outward aspect, what is apprehended of something on casual view or consideration; *Geom.* that which has length and breadth but no thickness. **2** *attrib. a.* of the surface (*surface area*); superficial (*surface politeness*). **3** *v.* give (special) surface to (road, paper, etc.); rise to the surface; become visible or known; *colloq.* become conscious; bring (submarine) to the surface. **4 come to the surface** become perceptible after being hidden; **surface mail** mail carried overland and by sea; **surface tension** tension of surface of liquid, tending to minimize its surface area. [F (SUR-²)]

surfboard *n.* long narrow board used in surf-riding. [SURF]

surfeit /'sɜ:fɪt/ **1** *n.* excess esp. in eating or drinking, resulting satiety. **2** *v.* overfeed; (cause to) be wearied (*with*) through excess. [F (SUR-², FEAT)]

surge 1 *v.i.* move to and fro (as) in waves; move suddenly and powerfully (*forwards, upwards*, etc.). **2** *n.* powerful wave; surging motion; impetuous onset. [F f. L *surgo* rise]

surgeon /'sɜ:dʒ(ə)n/ *n.* person skilled in surgery; naval or military medical officer. [AF f. L *chirurgia* surgery f. Gk (*kheir* hand, *ergō* work)]

surgery /'sɜ:dʒərɪ/ *n.* manual or instrumental treatment of injuries or disorders of the body; place where or time when doctor or dentist etc. gives advice and treatment, or MP or lawyer etc. is available for consultation. [F (as prec.)]

surgical /'sɜ:dʒɪk(ə)l/ *a.* of or by surgeons or surgery; (of appliance) used for surgery or in conditions suitable for surgery; **surgical spirit** methylated spirits used for cleansing etc.; **surgically** *adv.* [F (SURGEON)]

surly /'sɜ:lɪ/ *a.* bad-tempered, unfriendly, churlish; **surlily** *adv.*; **surliness** *n.* [obs. *sirly* haughty (SIR)]

surmise /sə'maɪz/ **1** *n.* conjecture. **2** *v.* make conjecture (about), infer doubtfully. [AF f. L *supermitto -miss-* accuse]

surmount /sə'maʊnt/ *v.t.* overcome, get over (difficulty or obstacle); (in *p.p.*) capped or crowned (*by* or *with*). [F (SUR-²)]

surname /'sɜ:neɪm/ **1** *n.* name common to all members of a family, person's hereditary name. **2** *v.t.* give surname to. [obs. *surnoun* f. AF (SUR-²)]

surpass /sə'pɑ:s/ *v.t.* outdo, be greater or better than; (in *partic.*) pre-eminent, matchless. [F (SUR-²)]

surplice /'sɜ:plɪs/ *n.* loose white linen vestment worn by clergy and choristers. [AF f. L (SUPER-, PELISSE)]

surplus /'sɜ:pləs/ **1** *n.* amount left over when requirements have been met; excess of revenue over expenditure. **2** *a.* exceeding what is needed or used. [AF f. L (PLUS)]

surprise /sə'praɪz/ **1** *n.* unexpected or astonishing thing; emotion caused by this; catching of person etc. unprepared; (*attrib.*, of attack or visit etc.) unexpected, made or done etc. without warning. **2** *v.t.* affect with surprise, turn out contrary to expectations of; shock, scandalize; capture or attack by surprise; come upon (person) off his guard (*surprised him in the act*); startle (person) by surprise *into* conduct or act or *into doing* thing. **3 by surprise** unexpectedly. [F]

surrealism /sə'rɪəlɪz(ə)m/ *n.* 20th-c. movement in art and literature aiming at expressing the subconscious mind; **surrealist** *n.* & *a.*; **surrealistic** /-'lɪstɪk/ *a.*; **surrealistically** /-'lɪstɪkəlɪ/ *adv.* [SUR-², REAL¹]

surrender /sə'rendə/ **1** *v.* hand over, relinquish possession of; abandon (hope etc.); accept enemy's demand for submission; submit (*to*); give up rights under (insurance policy) in return for smaller sum received immediately. **2** *n.* surrendering. **3 surrender oneself to** give way to (an emotion); **surrender to one's bail** duly appear in lawcourt after release on bail. [AF (SUR-²)]

surreptitious /sʌrəp'tɪʃəs/ *a.* done by stealth, underhand. [L (*surripio* seize secretly)]

surrogate /'sʌrəgət/ *n.* deputy, esp. of bishop; substitute. [L (*rogo* ask)]

surround /sə'raʊnd/ **1** *v.t.* come or be all round. **2** *n.* border or edging, esp. area between walls and carpet; floor-covering for this. **3 surrounded by** (or **with**) having on all sides. [AF f. L (SUR-², *unda* wave)]

surroundings *n.pl.* things in neighbourhood of, or conditions affecting, a person or thing.

surtax /'sɜːtæks/ **1** *n.* additional tax, esp. on incomes above a certain amount. **2** *v.t.* impose surtax on. [F (SUR-²)]

surveillance /sɜː'veɪləns/ *n.* close observation, esp. of suspected person. [F (SUR-², *veiller* watch)]

survey 1 /sə'veɪ/ *v.t.* take or present a general view of; examine condition of (building etc.); determine boundaries, extent, ownership, etc., of (district etc.). **2** /'sɜːveɪ/ *n.* act or result of surveying; inspection or investigation; map or plan made by surveying. [AF f. L (SUPER-, *video* see)]

surveyor /sə'veɪə/ *n.* one who surveys land and buildings, esp. professionally.

survival /sə'vaɪv(ə)l/ *n.* surviving; relic. [foll.]

survive /sə'vaɪv/ *v.* continue to live or exist; live or exist longer than; come alive through or continue to exist in spite of (danger or accident etc.); **survivor** *n.* [AF *survivre* f. L (SUPER-, *vivo* live)]

sus *sl.* **1** *n.* suspicion; suspect. **2** *v.* (**-ss-**) investigate, inspect (often with *out*). [abbr.]

sus- *prefix* assimilated form of SUB- before *c*, *p*, or *t*, in words from Latin (*suspend*).

susceptibility /səseptɪ'bɪlɪtɪ/ *n.* being susceptible; (in *pl.*) person's sensitive feelings. [foll.]

susceptible /sə'septɪb(ə)l/ *a.* impressionable, sensitive, easily moved by emotion; *predic.* open or liable or sensitive *to*, admitting *of* (proof etc.); **susceptibly** *adv.* [L (*suscipio -cept-* take up)]

suspect 1 /sə'spekt/ *v.t.* have an impression of the existence or presence of, half believe *to be*, be inclined to think (*that*); mentally accuse *of*; doubt the innocence or genuineness or truth of. **2** /'sʌspekt/ *n.* suspected person. **3** /'sʌspekt/ *a.* subject to suspicion or distrust. [L *suspicio -spect-*]

suspend /sə'spend/ *v.t.* hang up; keep inoperative or undecided for a time; debar temporarily from function or office etc. [F, or L *suspendo -pens-*]

suspended *a.* (of judicial sentence) remaining unenforced on condition of good behaviour; (of solid in fluid) sustained or floating between top and bottom.

suspender *n.* attachment to hold up stocking or sock by its top; (in *pl.*) *US* pair of braces; **suspender belt** woman's undergarment with suspenders.

suspense /sə'spens/ *n.* state of anxious uncertainty or expectation. [F f. L (SUSPEND)]

suspension /sə'spenʃ(ə)n/ *n.* suspending or being suspended; means by which vehicle is supported on its axles; substance consisting of particles suspended in fluid; **suspension bridge** bridge with roadway suspended from cables supported by towers. [F or L (SUSPEND)]

suspicion /sə'spɪʃ(ə)n/ *n.* feeling of one who suspects; suspecting or being suspected; slight trace (*of*); **above suspicion** too obviously good etc. to be suspected; **under suspicion** suspected. [AF f. L (SUSPECT)]

suspicious /sə'spɪʃəs/ *a.* prone to or feeling suspicion; indicating or justifying suspicion. [AF & F f. L (prec.)]

sustain /sə'steɪn/ *v.t.* bear weight of, support, esp. for long period; endure, stand; undergo or suffer (defeat or injury etc.); (of court etc.) uphold or decide in favour of (objection etc.); substantiate or corroborate (statement or charge); keep up (effort etc.). [AF *sustenir* f. L]

sustenance /'sʌstɪnəns/ *n.* nourishment, food; means of support. [AF (prec.)]

sutler *n. hist.* camp-follower selling food etc. [Du. *soeteler*]

suttee /sʌ'tiː/ *n.* former act or custom of Hindu widow sacrificing herself on her husband's funeral pyre; Hindu widow doing this. [Hindi & Urdu f. Skr. *satī* faithful wife]

suture /'suːtʃə/ **1** *n.* joining of edges of wound by stitching; thread etc. used for this. **2** *v.t.* stitch (wound). [F, or L (*suo sut-* sew)]

suzerain /'suːzəreɪn/ *n.* feudal overlord; sovereign or State having some control over other State that is internally autonomous; **suzerainty** *n.* [F]

svelte /svelt/ *a.* slender, lissom, graceful. [F f. It.]

SW *abbr.* south-west, south-western.

swab /swɒb/ **1** *n.* mop or other absorbent device for cleaning or mopping up; absorbent pad used in surgery; specimen of morbid secretion taken for examination. **2** *v.t.* (**-bb-**) clean with swab; take *up* (moisture) with swab. [Du.]

swaddle /'swɒd(ə)l/ *v.t.* swathe (esp. infant) in garments or bandages etc.; **swaddling-clothes** narrow bandages formerly wrapped round new-born child to restrain its movements. [SWATHE]

swag *n.* ornamental festoon of flowers etc., representation of this; *sl.* booty of burglars etc.; *Austral.* traveller's bundle. [prob. Scand.]

swagger 1 *v.i.* walk or behave arrogantly or self-importantly. 2 *n.* swaggering gait or behaviour; smartness. 3 *a. colloq.* smart or fashionable; (of coat) cut with loose flare from shoulders. 4 **swagger-stick** short cane carried by military officer. [prec.]

Swahili /swɑːˈhiːlɪ/ *n.* a Bantu people of Zanzibar and adjacent coasts, a member of this people; language spoken by them, used widely in E. Africa. [Arab.]

swain *n. archaic* a country youth; *poetic* young lover or suitor. [ON, = lad]

swallow[1] /ˈswɒləʊ/ 1 *v.* cause or allow (food etc.) to pass down one's throat; perform muscular movement (as) of swallowing something; accept meekly or credulously (assertion or affront etc.); repress (one's pride etc.); pronounce (sounds) indistinctly; (often with *up*) engulf or absorb, exhaust, cause to disappear. 2 *n.* act of swallowing; amount swallowed. [OE]

swallow[2] /ˈswɒləʊ/ *n.* migratory swift-flying bird with forked tail; **swallow-dive** dive with arms outspread till close to water; **swallow-tail** deeply forked tail, butterfly etc. with this. [OE]

swam *past* of SWIM.

swami /ˈswɑːmɪ/ *n.* Hindu religious teacher. [Hindi f. Skr.]

swamp /swɒmp/ 1 *n.* piece of waterlogged ground. 2 *v.t.* overwhelm, flood, or soak with water; overwhelm or make invisible etc. with excess or large amount of something. 3 **swampy** *a.* [orig. uncert.]

swan /swɒn/ 1 *n.* large web-footed usu. white water-bird with long flexible neck; poet. 2 *v.i.* (**-nn-**) *sl.* go aimlessly or casually (*around* or *off* etc.). 3 **swan-song** person's final composition or performance etc.; **swan-upping** annual taking up and marking of Thames swans. [OE]

swank *colloq.* 1 *n.* ostentation, swagger. 2 *v.i.* behave with swank. 3 **swanky** *a.* [orig. unkn.]

swannery /ˈswɒnərɪ/ *n.* place where swans are kept. [SWAN]

swansdown /ˈswɒnzdaʊn/ *n.* down of swan used in trimmings etc.; thick cotton cloth with soft nap on one side.

swap /swɒp/ 1 *v.* (**-pp-**) exchange or barter. 2 *n.* act of swapping; thing suitable for swapping. [orig. = 'hit', imit.]

sward /swɔːd/ *n. literary* expanse of short grass. [OE, = skin]

swarm[1] /swɔːm/ 1 *n.* large number of insects or birds or persons moving in a cluster; (in *pl.*) great numbers *of*; cluster of bees leaving the hive with queen to form new home. 2 *v.i.* move in or form swarm; (of place) be crowded or infested *with*. [OE]

swarm[2] /swɔːm/ *v.i.* climb *up* (rope or tree etc.) by clasping or clinging with hands and knees etc. [orig. unkn.]

swarthy /ˈswɔːðɪ/ *a.* dark, dark-complexioned. [obs. *swarty* (*swart* black f. OE)]

swashbuckler /ˈswɒʃbʌklə/ *n.* swaggering bully or ruffian; **swashbuckling** *a.* & *n.* [*swash* strike noisily, BUCKLER]

swastika /ˈswɒstɪkə/ *n.* symbol formed by cross with equal arms each continued as far again at right angles and all in same direction, esp. as symbol of Nazis. [Skr.]

swat /swɒt/ 1 *v.t.* (**-tt-**) hit hard; crush (fly etc.) with blow. 2 *n.* act of swatting. [dial. var. of SQUAT]

swatch /swɒtʃ/ *n.* sample, esp. of cloth; collection of samples. [orig. unkn.]

swath /swɔːθ/ *n.* (*pl.* /swɔːθs, swɔːðz/) ridge of grass or corn etc. lying after being cut; space left clear after one passage of mower etc.; broad strip. [OE]

swathe[1] /sweɪð/ *v.t.* bind or enclose in bandages or garments etc. [OE]

swathe[2] /sweɪð/ *n.* = SWATH.

swatter *n.* implement for swatting flies. [SWAT]

sway 1 *v.* (cause to) move in different directions alternately, oscillate irregularly, waver; control motion or direction of, have influence or rule over. 2 *n.* swaying motion; rule or government. [orig. uncert.]

swear /sweə/ *v.* (*past* **swore;** *p.p.* **sworn**) state or promise solemnly or on oath; *colloq.* say emphatically (*swore he hadn't done it*); cause to take oath (*swore him to secrecy*); use profane or obscene language (*at* person); **swear by** appeal to as witness in taking oath, *colloq.* have great confidence in; **swear in** induct into office etc. by administering oath; **swear off** *colloq.* promise to abstain from (drink etc.); **swear to** *colloq.* say that one is certain of; **swear-word** profane or obscene word. [OE]

sweat /swet/ 1 *n.* moisture exuded through pores of the skin, esp. from heat or nervousness; state or period of sweating; *colloq.* state of anxiety (*in a sweat*); *colloq.* drudgery, effort, laborious task or undertaking; condensed moisture on a surface. 2 *v.* (*past* & *p.p.* **sweated,** *US* **sweat**) exude sweat; be terrified, suffering, etc.; (of wall etc.) exhibit surface moisture; emit like sweat; make (horse or athlete etc.) sweat by exercise; (cause to) drudge or toil. 3 **sweat-band** band of absorbent material inside hat or round wrist etc. to soak up sweat; **sweat blood** work strenuously, be extremely anxious; **sweated labour** labour employed for long hours at low wages; **sweat out** *colloq.* endure to the end; **sweat-shirt** sleeved cotton sweater; **sweat-shop** place in which sweated labour is used. **4 sweaty** *a.* [OE]

sweater *n.* jersey or pullover.

swede *n.* large yellow-fleshed turnip orig. from Sweden; (**Swede**) native of Sweden. [LG or Du.]

Swedish 1 *a.* of Sweden or its people or language. **2** *n.* the language of Sweden.

sweep 1 *v.* (*past* and *p.p.* **swept**) clean or clear (room or area etc.) with or as with a broom, clean room etc. thus; collect or remove (dirt or litter etc.) by sweeping; push *aside* or *away* etc. (as) with a broom; carry *along* or *down* etc. in impetuous course; clear *off* or *away* etc. forcefully; traverse swiftly or lightly, impart sweeping motion to; swiftly cover or affect; glide swiftly, speed along with unchecked motion, go majestically; have continuous extent (*coast sweeps northward*). **2** *n.* act or motion of sweeping; curve in road, sweeping line of hill, etc.; range or scope; = *chimney-sweep*; sortie by aircraft; *colloq.* sweepstake; long oar. **3 make a clean sweep of** completely abolish or expel, win all prizes etc. in; **sweep away** abolish swiftly; **sweep the board** win all the money in gambling-game, win all possible prizes etc.; **swept-wing** (of aircraft) having wings placed at acute angle to axis. [OE]

sweeper *n.* one who cleans by sweeping; device for sweeping carpet etc.; (in football) defensive player positioned close to goalkeeper.

sweeping 1 *a.* wide in range or effect (*sweeping changes*); taking no account of particular cases or exceptions (*sweeping statement*). **2** *n.* (in *pl.*) dirt etc. collected by sweeping.

sweepstake *n.* form of gambling on horse-races etc. in which all competitors' stakes are paid to winners; race with betting of this kind; prize(s) won in sweepstake.

sweet 1 *a.* tasting like sugar or honey; (of wine) having sweet or fruity taste; smelling pleasant like rose or perfume; (of sound etc.) melodious or harmonious; fresh, not salt or sour or bitter or stinking; highly gratifying or attractive, amiable, pleasant; *colloq.* pretty or charming. **2** *n.* small shaped piece of sweet food esp. made with sugar or chocolate; sweet dish forming course of meal; (in *pl.*) delights, gratifications; (esp. as form of address) darling, sweetheart. **3 be sweet on** *colloq.* be fond of or in love with; **sweet-and-sour** cooked in sauce with both sweet and sour ingredients; **sweet-brier** small wild rose; **sweet corn** sweet-flavoured maize; **sweet pea** climbing garden plant with fragrant flowers in many colours; **sweet potato** tropical climbing plant with sweet tuberous roots used for food, root of this; **sweet talk** *US* flattery; **sweet-talk** *v.t. US* persuade by flattery; **sweet tooth** liking for sweet-tasting things; **sweet-william** garden plant with clustered fragrant flowers. [OE]

sweetbread *n.* pancreas or thymus gland of animal, esp. as food.

sweeten *v.* make or become sweet or sweeter.

sweetener *n.* substance used to sweeten food or drink (also **sweetening**); *colloq.* bribe.

sweetheart *n.* one of a pair of lovers (also as term of endearment).

sweetie *n. colloq.* a sweet; sweetheart.

sweetmeat *n.* a sweet, a small fancy cake.

swell 1 *v.* (*p.p.* **swollen** /'swəʊlən/ or **swelled**) grow bigger or louder or more intense, cause to do this, rise or raise up from surrounding surface, bulge *out*; (of heart) feel like bursting with emotion. **2** *n.* act or state of swelling; heaving of sea with waves that do not break; crescendo, mechanism in organ etc. for obtaining crescendo or diminuendo; *colloq.* person of distinction or of dashing or fashionable appearance; protuberant part. **3** *a. colloq.* fine, splendid, excellent; *colloq.* smart, fashionable. **4 swelled** (or **swollen**) **head** *colloq.* conceit; **swell with** be hardly able to restrain (pride etc.). [OE]

swelling *n.* protuberance, esp. abnormal bulge on the body.

swelter 1 *v.i.* be uncomfortably hot. **2** *n.* sweltering condition. [OE]

swept *past* & *p.p.* of SWEEP.

swerve 1 *v.* (cause to) change direction, esp. suddenly. **2** *n.* swerving movement. [OE, = scour]

swift 1 *a.* quick, rapid; speedy or prompt (*was swift to act*). **2** *n.* swift-flying bird with long wings. [OE]

swig *colloq.* **1** *v.* (**-gg-**) drink in large draughts. **2** *n.* swallow of drink, esp. of large amount. [orig. unkn.]

swill 1 *v.* rinse or flush (*out*); drink greedily. **2** *n.* rinsing; mainly liquid refuse as pig-food; inferior liquor. [OE]

swim 1 *v.* (**-mm-**; *past* **swam**; *p.p.* **swum**) propel the body through water by working arms and legs, or fins etc.; traverse (stretch of water or its distance) thus; float on or at surface of liquid; appear to undulate or reel or whirl; have dizzy effect or sensation (*head was swimming*); be flooded (*in* or *with* liquid). **2** *n.* spell or act of swimming; main current of affairs.

3 in the swim engaged in or acquainted with what is going on; **swimming-bath** (or **-pool**) pool constructed for swimming; **swim-suit** bathing-suit. [OE]

swimmingly *adv.* with easy and unobstructed progress.

swindle /'swɪnd(ə)l/ **1** *v.* cheat (person, money *out of* person, person *out of* money). **2** *n.* act of swindling; person or thing represented as what it is not. **3 swindler** *n.* [back-form. f. *swindler* f. G]

swine *n.* (*pl.* same) pig; *colloq.* disgusting or contemptible person or thing. [OE]

swing 1 *v.* (*past* and *p.p.* **swung**) move with to-and-fro or curving motion, cause to do this, sway, hang so as to be free to sway; (cause to) oscillate or revolve; move by gripping something and leaping etc.; go with swinging gait; move *round* to opposite direction; change from one opinion or mood to another; attempt to hit or punch (*at* person etc.); play (music) with swing rhythm; *sl.* be lively or up to date or promiscuous, enjoy oneself; have decisive influence on (voting etc.); *sl.* (be competent to) deal with or achieve; *sl.* be executed by hanging. **2** *n.* act or motion or extent of swinging; swinging or smooth gait or rhythm or action; seat slung by ropes or chains etc. for swinging on or in, spell of swinging thus; smooth rhythmic jazz or jazzy dance-music, rhythmic feeling or drive of jazz; amount by which votes or points scored etc. change from one side to another. **3 in full swing** fully active; **swing-boat** boat-shaped swing at fairs; **swing bridge** bridge that can be swung aside to let ships pass; **swing-door** door able to open in either direction and close itself when released; **swing the lead** *sl.* malinger; **swing-wing** aircraft wing that can move from right-angled to rear-slanting position. [OE, = beat *v.*]

swingeing /'swɪndʒɪŋ/ *a.* (of a blow) forcible; huge or far-reaching (*swingeing economies*). [*swinge* strike f. OE]

swinish *a.* bestial; filthy. [SWINE]

swipe 1 *v. colloq.* hit hard and recklessly; *sl.* steal. **2** *n. colloq.* reckless hard hit or attempt to hit. [perh. var. of SWEEP]

swirl 1 *v.* move or flow or carry along with whirling motion. **2** *n.* swirling motion; twist, curl. [perh. LG or Du.]

swish 1 *v.* swing (scythe or stick etc.) audibly through the air or through grass etc.; cut (flower etc.) *off* thus; move with or make swishing sound. **2** *n.* swishing action or sound. **3** *a. colloq.* smart, fashionable. [imit.]

Swiss 1 *a.* of Switzerland or its people. **2** *n.* (*pl.* same) native of Switzerland. **3 Swiss roll** thin flat sponge-cake spread with jam etc. and rolled up. [F *Suisse*]

switch 1 *n.* device for making and breaking connection in electric circuit; transfer, change-over, deviation; flexible shoot cut from tree, light tapering rod; device at junction of railway tracks for transferring train from one track to another. **2** *v.* turn (electrical device) *on* or *off*; change or transfer (position or subject etc.); reverse positions of (*then switched glasses*); swing or snatch (thing) suddenly; whip or flick with switch. **3 switched-on** *sl.* up to date, aware of what is going on, excited, under the influence of drugs. [LG]

switchback *n.* railway at fair etc. in which train's ascents are effected by momentum of previous descents; railway or road with alternate sharp ascents and descents.

switchboard *n.* apparatus for varying connections between electric circuits, esp. in telephony.

swivel /'swɪv(ə)l/ **1** *n.* coupling between two parts enabling one to revolve without the other. **2** *v.* (**-ll-**, *US* **-l-**) turn (as) on swivel. **3 swivel chair** chair with seat turning horizontally. [OE]

swizz *n. sl.* swindle, disappointment. [orig. unkn.]

swizzle /'swɪz(ə)l/ *n. colloq.* compounded intoxicating drink esp. of rum or gin and bitters made frothy; *sl.* swizz; **swizzle-stick** stick used for frothing or flattening drinks. [orig. unkn.]

swollen see SWELL.

swoon *v.i.* & *n.* faint. [OE]

swoop 1 *v.i.* descend rapidly (*down*) like bird of prey; make sudden attack (*on*). **2** *n.* swooping or snatching movement or action. [OE]

swop var. of SWAP.

sword /sɔːd/ *n.* weapon with long blade and hilt with hand-guard; **the sword** war, military power; **cross swords** have fight or dispute (*with*); **put to the sword** kill, esp. in war; **sword-dance** dance in which performer brandishes swords or steps about swords laid on ground; **sword of Damocles** /'dæməkliːz/ imminent danger; **sword-play** fencing, repartee or lively arguing; **sword-stick** hollow walking-stick containing blade that can be used as sword. [OE]

swordfish *n.* large sea-fish with sword-like upper jaw.

swordsman *n.* person of (usu. specified) skill with a sword; **swordsmanship** *n.*

swore *past* of SWEAR.

sworn 1 *p.p.* of SWEAR. **2** *a.* bound (as) by oath (*sworn enemies*). [SWEAR]

swot *sl.* **1** *v.* (**-tt-**) study hard. **2** *n.* person who swots; hard study. **3 swot up** study (subject) hard or hurriedly. [dial. var. of SWEAT]
swum *p.p.* of SWIM.
swung *past* & *p.p.* of SWING.
sybarite /ˈsɪbəraɪt/ *n.* self-indulgent or luxury-loving person; **sybaritic** /-ˈrɪtɪk/ *a.* [*Sybaris*, anc. city in S. Italy]
sycamore /ˈsɪkəmɔː/ *n.* large maple; *US* plane-tree; wood of these. [F f. L f. Gk]
sycophant /ˈsɪkəfænt/ *n.* flatterer, toady; **sycophancy** *n.*; **sycophantic** /-ˈfæntɪk/ *a.* [F or L f. Gk]
syl- *prefix* assimilated form of SYN- before *l.*
syllabary /ˈsɪləbərɪ/ *n.* list of characters representing syllables. [SYLLABLE]
syllabic /sɪˈlæbɪk/ *a.* of or in syllables; **syllabically** *adv.* [F or L f. Gk (SYLLABLE)]
syllabification /sɪlæbɪfɪˈkeɪʃ(ə)n/ *n.* division into or utterance in syllables. [L (SYLLABLE)]
syllable /ˈsɪləb(ə)l/ *n.* unit of pronunciation forming whole or part of word and usu. having one vowel-sound often with consonant(s) before or after; character(s) representing syllable; least amount of speech or writing; **in words of one syllable** simply, plainly. [AF f. L f. Gk (*lambanō* take)]
syllabub /ˈsɪləbʌb/ *n.* dish of cream or milk curdled or whipped with wine etc. [orig. unkn.]
syllabus /ˈsɪləbəs/ *n.* (*pl.* **syllabuses**) programme or conspectus of a course of study, teaching, etc. [L, erron. f. Gk *sittuba* label]
syllepsis /sɪˈlepsɪs/ *n.* (*pl.* **syllepses** /-iːz/) figure of speech applying word to two others in different senses (e.g. *took the oath and his seat*), or to two others of which it grammatically suits one only (e.g. *neither you nor he knows*). [L f. Gk (as SYLLABLE)]
syllogism /ˈsɪlədʒɪz(ə)m/ *n.* form of reasoning in which from two propositions a third is deduced; **syllogistic** /-ˈdʒɪstɪk/ *a.* [F or L f. Gk (*logos* reason)]
sylph /sɪlf/ *n.* elemental spirit of the air; slender graceful woman or girl. [L]
sylvan var. of SILVAN.
sylviculture var. of SILVICULTURE.
sym- *prefix* assimilated form of SYN- before *b, m, p* (*sympathy*).
symbiosis /sɪmbɪˈəʊsɪs, -baɪ-/ *n.* (*pl.* **symbioses** /-iːz/) (usu. mutually advantageous) association of two different organisms living attached to each other or one within the other (also *fig.* of co-operating persons); **symbiotic** /-ˈɒtɪk/ *a.* [L f. Gk (SYM-, *bios* life)]
symbol /ˈsɪmb(ə)l/ *n.* thing generally regarded as typifying, representing, or recalling something (*white is a symbol of purity*); mark or character taken as conventional sign of some object or idea or process etc.; **symbolic** /-ˈbɒlɪk/ *a.*; **symbolically** /-ˈbɒlɪkəlɪ/ *adv.* [L f. Gk]
symbolism *n.* symbols, use of symbols; artistic movement or style using symbols to express ideas, emotions, etc.; **symbolist** *n.*
symbolize *v.t.* be symbol of; represent by means of symbols. [F (SYMBOL)]
symmetry /ˈsɪmɪtrɪ/ *n.* correct proportion of parts, beauty resulting from this; structure that allows object to be divided into parts of equal shape and size, possession of such structure; repetition of exactly similar parts facing each other or a centre; **symmetric** /-ˈmetrɪk/ *a.*; **symmetrical** /-ˈmetrɪk(ə)l/ *a.*; **symmetrically** /-ˈmetrɪkəlɪ/ *adv.* [F or L f. Gk]
sympathetic /sɪmpəˈθetɪk/ *a.* of or showing or expressing sympathy; due to sympathy; likeable; not antagonistic; **sympathetic magic** magic seeking to affect person through associated object; **sympathetically** *adv.* [SYMPATHY]
sympathize /ˈsɪmpəθaɪz/ *v.i.* feel or express sympathy (*with*). [F (foll.)]
sympathy /ˈsɪmpəθɪ/ *n.* being simultaneously affected with the same feeling as another; capacity for this; sharing (*with* person etc.) in emotion or sensation or condition; compassion or approval (*for*); (in *sing.* or *pl.*) agreement (*with* person etc.) in opinion or desire; **in sympathy** having or showing or resulting from sympathy (*with* another). [L f. Gk, = fellow-feeling]
symphony /ˈsɪmfənɪ/ *n.* elaborate composition for full orchestra, usu. with several movements; instrumental passage in oratorio etc.; *US* = *symphony orchestra*; **symphony orchestra** large orchestra playing symphonies etc.; **symphonic** /-ˈfɒnɪk/ *a.* [F f. L f. Gk]
symposium /sɪmˈpəʊzɪəm/ *n.* (*pl.* **symposia**) conference, or collection of essays etc., on a particular subject; philosophical or other friendly discussion. [L f. Gk (*sumpotēs* fellow-drinker)]
symptom /ˈsɪmptəm/ *n.* aspect of physical or mental condition as sign of disease or injury; sign of the existence of something. [L f. Gk (*piptō* fall)]
symptomatic /sɪmptəˈmætɪk/ *a.* serving as a symptom; **symptomatically** *adv.*
syn- *prefix* in senses 'together', 'at the same time', 'alike', etc. [Gk (*sun* with)]
synagogue /ˈsɪnəgɒg/ *n.* meeting-place

of Jewish assembly for religious observance and instruction, the assembly itself; **synagogal** *a.*; **synagogical** /-'gɒgɪk(ə)l, -'gɒdʒɪk(ə)l/ *a.* [F f. L f. Gk, = assembly]

sync /sɪŋk/ (also **synch**) *colloq.* **1** *n.* synchronization. **2** *v.t.* synchronize. [abbr.]

synchromesh /'sɪŋkrəʊmeʃ/ **1** *n.* system of gear-changing, esp. in motor vehicles, in which gear-wheels revolve at the same speed during engagement. **2** *a.* of this system. [abbr. of *synchronized mesh*]

synchronic /sɪŋ'krɒnɪk/ *a.* concerned with a subject as it exists at a particular time; **synchronically** *adv.* [L (SYNCHRONOUS)]

synchronism /'sɪŋkrənɪz(ə)m/ *n.* being or treating as synchronous or synchronic; synchronizing. [Gk (SYNCHRONOUS)]

synchronize /'sɪŋkrənaɪz/ *v.* make or be synchronous with; **synchronization** /-'zeɪʃ(ə)n/ *n.*

synchronous /'sɪŋkrənəs/ *a.* existing or occurring at same time (*with*); having same or proportional speed. [L f. Gk (*khronos* time)]

syncopate /'sɪŋkəpeɪt/ *v.t.* displace beats or accents in (music); shorten (word) by dropping interior letter(s); **syncopation** /-'peɪʃ(ə)n/ *n.* [L (foll.)]

syncope /'sɪŋkəpɪ/ *n.* syncopation; unconsciousness through fall of blood-pressure. [L f. Gk (SYN-, *koptō* strike, cut off)]

syncretic /sɪŋ'kretɪk/ *a.* attempting, esp. inconsistently, to unify or reconcile differing schools of thought; **syncretism** /'sɪŋkrɪtɪz(ə)m/ *n.*; **syncretize** /'sɪŋkrɪtaɪz/ *v.* [L f. Gk]

syndic /'sɪndɪk/ *n.* any of various university or government officials. [F f. L (*syndicus* f. Gk, = advocate)]

syndicalism /'sɪndɪkəlɪz(ə)m/ *n.* movement for transferring means of production and distribution to workers' unions; **syndicalist** *n.* [F (prec.)]

syndicate **1** /'sɪndɪkət/ *n.* combination of persons or commercial firms to promote some common interest; association supplying material simultaneously to a number of periodicals; committee of syndics. **2** /'sɪndɪkeɪt/ *v.t.* form into a syndicate; publish (material) through a syndicate. **3** **syndication** /-'keɪʃ(ə)n/ *n.* [F f. L (SYNDIC)]

syndrome /'sɪndrəʊm/ *n.* group of concurrent symptoms of disease; characteristic combination of opinions or emotions etc. [L f. Gk (SYN-, *dromos* course)]

synecdoche /sɪ'nekdəkɪ/ *n.* figure of speech in which part is named but the whole is understood, or conversely (*new faces in the team*; *England beat India at cricket*). [L f. Gk]

synod /'sɪnəd/ *n.* church council of senior clergy and officials. [L f. Gk, = meeting]

synonym /'sɪnənɪm/ *n.* word or phrase that means exactly or nearly the same as another in the same language. [L f. Gk (*onoma* name)]

synonymous /sɪ'nɒnɪməs/ *a.* having the same meaning (*with*).

synopsis /sɪ'nɒpsɪs/ *n.* (*pl.* **synopses** /-iːz/) summary, outline. [L f. Gk (*opsis* view)]

synoptic /sɪ'nɒptɪk/ *a.* of or giving synopsis; **Synoptic Gospels** those of Matthew, Mark, and Luke; **synoptically** *adv.* [Gk (prec.)]

synovia /saɪ'nəʊvɪə/ *n.* thick sticky fluid lubricating body joints etc.; **synovial** *a.* [L]

syntax /'sɪntæks/ *n.* grammatical arrangement of words, rules or analysis of this; **syntactic** /-'tæktɪk/ *a.*; **syntactically** /-'tæktɪkəlɪ/ *adv.* [F or L f. Gk, = arrangement]

synthesis /'sɪnθɪsɪs/ *n.* (*pl.* **syntheses** /-iːz/) combining of elements into a whole, result of this; artificial production of (esp. organic) substances from simpler ones. [L f. Gk (SYN-)]

synthesize /'sɪnθɪsaɪz/ *v.t.* make synthesis of.

synthesizer *n.* electronic musical instrument producing a great variety of sounds.

synthetic /sɪn'θetɪk/ **1** *a.* produced by synthesis, unnatural, artificial; *colloq.* affected or insincere. **2** *n.* synthetic substance. **3** **synthetically** *adv.*

syphilis /'sɪfɪlɪs/ *n.* a contagious venereal disease; **syphilitic** /-'lɪtɪk/ *a.* [*Siphylus*, character in poem 1530]

Syriac /'sɪrɪæk/ **1** *n.* language of ancient Syria. **2** *a.* of or in Syriac. [L f. Gk]

Syrian /'sɪrɪən/ **1** *a.* of Syria. **2** *n.* native of Syria. [F f. L f. Gk]

syringa /sɪ'rɪŋgə/ *n.* mock orange; *Bot.* lilac. [L (foll.)]

syringe /'sɪrɪndʒ, -'rɪndʒ/ **1** *n.* device for drawing in liquid by suction and then ejecting it in fine stream. **2** *v.t.* sluice or spray with syringe. [L *syringa* f. Gk *surigx -rigg-* pipe]

syrup /'sɪrəp/ *n.* thick liquid of water (nearly) saturated with sugar; this flavoured or medicated; condensed sugar-cane juice, molasses, treacle; excessive sweetness of manner; **syrupy** *a.* [F or L f. Arab. (SHERBET)]

system /'sɪstəm/ *n.* complex whole, set of connected things or parts, organized

body of things; set of organs in the body with common structure or function; the human or animal body as a whole; method, considered principles of procedure or classification; orderliness; major group of geological strata; **get thing out of one's system** be rid of its effects; **systems analysis** analysis of an operation in order to use computer to improve its efficiency. [F or L f. Gk *sustēma -mat-*]
systematic /sɪstəˈmætɪk/ *a.* methodical, according to a system, deliberate; **systematically** *adv.* [F f. L f. Gk (prec.)]
systematize /ˈsɪstəmətaɪz/ *v.t.* make systematic; **systematization** /-ˈzeɪʃ(ə)n/ *n.*
systemic /sɪsˈtemɪk/ *a.* of the bodily system as a whole; (of insecticide etc.) entering plant tissues via roots and shoots; **systemically** *adv.* [SYSTEM]
systole /ˈsɪstəlɪ/ *n.* contraction of heart rhythmically alternating with diastole to form pulse; **systolic** /sɪˈstɒlɪk/ *a.* [L f. Gk (*stellō* place)]

T

T, t /tiː/ *n.* (*pl.* **Ts, T's**) twentieth letter; T-shaped thing (*T-joint*); **cross the t's** be minutely accurate; **to a T** exactly, to a nicety.
t. *abbr.* ton(s); tonne(s).
T *symb.* tritium.
ta /tɑː/ *int. colloq.* thank you. [infantile form]
TA *abbr.* Territorial Army.
Ta *symb.* tantalum.
tab 1 *n.* small flap or strip attached for grasping or fastening or hanging up, or for identification; *colloq.* account, tally; *US colloq.* bill, price. **2** *v.t.* (**-bb-**) provide with tabs. **3 keep a tab** (or **tabs**) **on** keep account of, have under observation or in check. [prob. dial.; cf. TAG]
tabard /ˈtæbəd/ *n.* herald's short official coat emblazoned with arms of sovereign; woman's or girl's garment of similar shape; *hist.* knight's short emblazoned garment worn over armour. [F]
tabby /ˈtæbɪ/ *n.* grey or brownish cat with dark stripes; a kind of watered silk. [F f. Arab.]
tabernacle /ˈtæbənæk(ə)l/ *n.* tent used as sanctuary by Israelites in wilderness; canopied niche or receptacle esp. for Eucharistic elements; Nonconformist meeting-house. [F or L (TAVERN)]
tabla /ˈtæblə, ˈtɑːblə/ *n.* pair of small Indian drums played with hands. [Hind. f. Arab., = drum]
table /ˈteɪb(ə)l/ **1** *n.* piece of furniture with flat top and one or more legs, providing level surface for putting things on; food provided at table (*keeps a good table*); set of facts or figures systematically arranged esp. in columns, matter contained in such set; flat surface for working on or for machinery etc.; slab of wood or stone etc., matter inscribed on it. **2** *v.t.* bring forward for discussion or consideration; postpone consideration of (matter). **3 at table** taking a meal at a table; **on the table** submitted for discussion or consideration; **table-cloth** cloth spread on table, esp. for meals; **table licence** licence to serve alcoholic drinks with meals only; **table-linen** table-cloths, napkins, etc.; **table tennis** indoor game based on lawn tennis, played with small bats and ball bouncing on table divided by net; **turn the tables (on)** reverse relations (with), esp. pass from weaker to stronger position; **under the table** drunk. [F f. L *tabula* board]
tableau /ˈtæbləʊ/ *n.* (*pl.* **tableaux** /-əʊz/) picturesque presentation; group of silent motionless persons arranged to represent a scene; dramatic or effective situation suddenly brought about. [F, = picture, dimin. of prec.]
table d'hôte /tɑːbl ˈdəʊt/ meal at fixed time and price in hotel etc., with less choice of dishes than à la carte. [F, = host's table]
tableland *n.* plateau of land. [TABLE]
tablespoon *n.* large spoon for serving food; amount held by this; **tablespoonful** *n.* (*pl.* **tablespoonfuls**).
tablet /ˈtæblɪt/ *n.* small measured and compressed amount of substance, esp. of a medicine or drug; small flat piece of soap etc.; small slab, esp. for display of inscription. [F f. L dimin. (TABLE)]
tabloid /ˈtæblɔɪd/ *n.* newspaper, usu. popular in style, printed on sheets of half size. [prec.]
taboo /təˈbuː/ **1** *n.* system or act of setting person or thing apart as sacred or accursed; prohibition or restriction imposed by social custom. **2** *a.* avoided or prohibited, esp. by social custom (*taboo word*). **3** *v.t.* put under taboo; exclude or prohibit by authority or social influence (*the subject was tabooed*). [Tongan]

tabor /ˈteɪbə/ *n.* small drum, esp. used to accompany pipe. [F]
tabu var. of TABOO.
tabular /ˈtæbjʊlə/ *a.* of or arranged in tables or lists. [L (TABLE)]
tabulate /ˈtæbjʊleɪt/ *v.t.* arrange (figures or facts) in tabular form; **tabulation** /-ˈleɪʃ(ə)n/ *n.*
tabulator *n.* person or thing that tabulates; device on typewriter for advancing to sequence of set positions in tabular work.
tacho /ˈtækəʊ/ *n.* (*pl.* **tachos**) *colloq.* tachometer. [abbr.]
tachograph /ˈtækəgrɑːf/ *n.* device in motor vehicle for recording speed and travel-time. [Gk *takhos* speed]
tachometer /tæˈkɒmɪtə/ *n.* instrument for measuring velocity or speed of rotation (esp. of vehicle engine).
tacit /ˈtæsɪt/ *a.* understood or implied without being stated (*tacit agreement*). [L (*taceo* be silent)]
taciturn /ˈtæsɪtɜːn/ *a.* reserved in speech, saying little, uncommunicative; **taciturnity** /-ˈtɜːnɪtɪ/ *n.* [F or L (prec.)]
tack[1] **1** *n.* small sharp broad-headed nail; *US* drawing-pin; long stitch used in fastening cloths etc. lightly or temporarily together; direction in which ship moves as determined by position of its sails, temporary change of direction in sailing to take advantage of side wind etc.; course of action or policy (*try another tack*); sticky condition of varnish etc. **2** *v.* fasten (*down* etc.) with tacks; stitch (pieces of cloth etc.) lightly together; annex or append (thing *to* or *on to* another); change ship's course (*about*) by turning head to wind, make series of such tacks; change one's conduct or policy etc. [prob. rel. to F *tache* clasp, nail]
tack[2] *n.* riding-harness, saddles, etc. [TACKLE]
tackle /ˈtæk(ə)l/ **1** *n.* equipment for a task or sport (*fishing-tackle*); mechanism, esp. of ropes, pulley-blocks, hooks, etc., for lifting weights, managing sails, etc. (*block and tackle*); windlass with its ropes and hooks. **2** *v.t.* try to deal with (problem or difficulty); grapple with or try to overcome (opponent); enter into discussion with (person esp. *about* or *on* awkward matter); (in football etc.) intercept or stop (player running with ball). [LG]
tacky *a.* (of glue or varnish etc.) in the sticky stage before complete dryness; **tackiness** *n.* [TACK[1]]
tact *n.* adroitness in dealing with others or with difficulties due to personal feeling; intuitive perception of right thing to do or say. [F f. L (*tango tact-* touch)]
tactful *a.* having or showing tact; **tactfully** *adv.*
tactic /ˈtæktɪk/ *n.* piece of tactics. [Gk *taktikē* (TACTICS)]
tactical *a.* of tactics; (of bombing) done in immediate support of military or naval operations; adroitly planning or planned; **tactically** *adv.* [Gk *taktikos* (TACTICS)]
tactician /tækˈtɪʃ(ə)n/ *n.* expert in tactics. [foll.]
tactics *n.pl.* (also treated as *sing.*) art of disposing armed forces esp. in contact with enemy; procedure adopted in carrying out scheme or achieving some end. [Gk *taktika* (*tassō* arrange)]
tactile /ˈtæktaɪl/ *a.* of or connected with the sense of touch; perceived by touch; **tactility** /-ˈtɪlɪtɪ/ *n.* [L (TACT)]
tactless *a.* having or showing no tact. [TACT]
tadpole *n.* larva of frog or toad etc. at stage of living in water and having gills and tail. [TOAD, POLL]
taffeta /ˈtæfɪtə/ *n.* fine lustrous silk or silklike fabric. [F or med.L f. Pers.]
taffrail /ˈtæfreɪl/ *n.* rail round ship's stern. [Du. *taffereel* panel]
Taffy /ˈtæfɪ/ *n. colloq.* Welshman. [supposed W pronunc. of *Davy* = *David*]
tag[1] **1** *n.* loop or flap or label for handling or hanging or marking a thing; metal or plastic point of shoelace etc. used to assist insertion; loose or ragged end; trite quotation, stock phrase. **2** *v.* (**-gg-**) provide with tag; join or attach (*to* or *on to*); *colloq.* follow closely, trail behind. **3 tag along** *colloq.* go along (*with*). [orig. unkn.]
tag[2] **1** *n.* children's game of chasing and touching. **2** *v.t.* (**-gg-**) touch in game of tag. [orig. unkn.]
tagliatelle /tɑːljɑːˈtelɪ/ *n.* ribbon-shaped form of pasta. [It.]
tail[1] **1** *n.* hindmost part of animal, esp. when prolonged beyond the rest of the body; thing like tail in form or position, e.g. part of shirt below waist, hanging part of back of coat, end of procession, etc.; rear part of aeroplane or rocket; luminous train of comet; inferior or weaker part of anything; (in *pl.*) *colloq.* tailcoat, evening dress including this; (usu. in *pl.*) reverse of coin turning up in toss; *sl.* person following or shadowing another. **2** *v.t.* remove stalks of (fruit etc.); *sl.* shadow, follow closely. **3 on person's tail** closely following him; **tail away** (or **off**) become fewer or smaller or slighter, fall behind or away in scattered line, end inconclusively; **tail-back** long line of traffic extending back from an obstruction; **tail-board** hinged or removable back of lorry etc.;

tail-end hindmost or lowest or last part; **tail-gate** = *tail-board*, door at back of motor vehicle; **tail-light** (or **-lamp**) light at rear of motor vehicle or bicycle; **tail-spin** spin of aircraft, state of panic; **tail wind** wind blowing in the direction of travel of a vehicle or aircraft etc.; **turn tail** turn one's back, run away; **with one's tail between one's legs** humiliated or dejected by defeat etc. [OE]

tail[2] **1** *n.* limitation of ownership, esp. of estate limited to a person and his heirs. **2** *a.* so limited (*estate tail*; *fee-tail*). **3 in tail** under such limitation. [F f. *tailler* cut (TALLY)]

tailcoat *n.* man's coat with long skirt divided at back into tails and cut away in front, worn as part of formal dress. [TAIL[1]]

tailor /ˈteɪlə/ **1** *n.* maker of clothes, esp. one who makes men's outer garments to order. **2** *v.* make (clothes) as tailor; make or adapt for special purpose; work as or be tailor; (esp. in *p.p.*) make clothes for. **3 tailor-bird** small Asian bird sewing leaves together to form nest; **tailor-made** made specially by tailor, *fig.* entirely suited to purpose. [AF *taillour* (prec.)]

tailored *a.* (of woman's suit etc.) simple and well fitted.

tailpiece *n.* final part of thing; decoration in blank space at end of chapter etc. [TAIL[1]]

tailpipe *n.* rear section of exhaust pipe of motor vehicle.

tailplane *n.* horizontal aerofoil at tail of aircraft.

taint 1 *n.* spot or trace of decay or infection or some bad quality; corrupt condition, infection. **2** *v.* affect with taint; affect slightly *with*; become tainted. [F f. L (TINGE)]

take 1 *v.* (*past* **took** /tʊk/; *p.p.* **taken**) lay hold of, get into one's hands; acquire, get possession of, capture or win; get use of by purchase or formal agreement (*take lodgings*); use as means of transport (*took a taxi*); regularly buy (newspaper etc.); obtain after fulfilling conditions (*take a degree*); occupy (*take a chair*); consume as food or medicine (*took tea, the pills*); be successful or effective (*the inoculation did not take*); require or use up (*will only take a minute*; *these things take time*); cause to come or go with one, convey (*take the book home*; *the bus will take you all the way*); remove, dispossess person of; catch or be infected with (fire or fever etc.); experience or be affected by (*take fright, pleasure*); find out and note (name and address, temperature); grasp mentally, understand (*I take your point*; *I took him to mean yes*); treat or regard in specified way (*took the news calmly*; *took it badly*); accept or submit to (*take the offer, a joke, the risk*), choose or assume (*took a different view*; *took a job*; *took the initiative*); derive (*takes its name from the inventor*); subtract (*take 3 from 9*); perform or effect (*take notes*; *take an oath, a decision, a look*); occupy or engage oneself in (*took a rest*); conduct (*took morning prayers*); deal with in certain way (*took the corner too fast*); teach or be taught or examined in (subject); make by photography, photograph (person or thing); use as instance (*let us take Napoleon*); *Gram.* have or require as part of construction (*this verb takes an object*); copulate with (woman). **2** *n.* amount taken or caught; scene or sequence of film photographed at one time without stopping camera. **3 take after** resemble (parent etc.); **take against** begin to dislike; **take away** remove or carry elsewhere, subtract; **take-away** *a.* (of food) bought at a restaurant for eating elsewhere, (*n.*) restaurant selling this; **take back** retract (statement), convey to original position, carry (person) in thought to past time; **take down** write down (spoken words), remove (structure) by separating into pieces; **take for** regard as being (*do you take me for a fool?*); **take-home pay** that received by employee after deduction of tax etc.; **take in** receive as lodger etc.; undertake (work) at home, include, make (garment etc.) smaller, understand, cheat; **take in hand** undertake, start doing or dealing with, undertake control or reform of; **take in vain** use (person's name) lightly or profanely; **take it** assume *that*, *colloq.* endure punishment etc. bravely; **take it or leave it** accept it or not; **take it out of** exhaust strength of, have revenge on; **take it out on** relieve frustration by attacking or treating harshly; **take it on** (or **upon**) **oneself** venture or presume (*to do* thing); **taken by** (or **with**) attracted or charmed by; **taken ill** suddenly affected by illness; **take off** remove (clothing) from body, deduct, mimic humorously, jump from ground, become airborne, have (day) as holiday; **take-off** *n.* act of becoming airborne, act of mimicking, place from which one jumps; **take oneself off** depart; **take on** undertake (work), engage (employee), agree to oppose at game, acquire (new meaning etc.), *colloq.* show strong emotion; **take out** remove, escort on an outing, get (licence or summons etc.) issued; **take person out of himself** make him forget his worries etc.; **take**

over succeed to management or ownership of, assume control; **take-over** *n.* assumption of control (esp. of business); **take one's time** not hurry; **take to** begin or fall into habit of (*took to smoking*), have recourse to, adapt oneself to, form liking for; **take up** become interested or engaged in (pursuit), adopt as protégé, occupy (time or space), begin (residence etc.), resume after interruption, interrupt or question (speaker), accept (offer etc.); shorten (garment); **take person up on** accept (his offer etc.); **take up with** begin to associate with. [OE f. ON]

taker *n.* one who takes bet or accepts offer etc.

taking 1 *a.* attractive, captivating. **2** *n.* (in *pl.*) amount of money taken in business.

talc *n.* translucent mineral often found in thin glasslike plates; talcum powder. [F, or med.L *talcum*, f. Arab. f. Pers.]

talcum /'tælkəm/ *n.* talc; **talcum powder** powdered talc for toilet use, usu. perfumed. [med.L (prec.)]

tale *n.* narrative or story, esp. fictitious; report of alleged fact, often malicious or in breach of confidence. [OE]

talebearer *n.* person who maliciously gossips or reveals secrets.

talent /'tælənt/ *n.* special aptitude or faculty; high mental ability; persons of talent; ancient weight and unit of currency, esp. among Greeks; **talent-scout** seeker-out of talent esp. for entertainment industries. [OE & F f. L f. Gk]

talented *a.* having great ability.

talisman /'tælızmən/ *n.* object supposed to be endowed with magic powers esp. of averting evil from or bringing good luck to its holder; **talismanic** /-'mænık/ *a.* [F & Sp. f. Gk]

talk /tɔ:k/ **1** *v.* converse or communicate ideas by spoken words (*to* or *with* someone); have the power of speech; express or utter or discuss in words; use (a language) in speech; bring into specified condition etc. by talking (*talked him into it, out of the difficulty*); betray secrets; gossip (*people will talk*); have influence (*money talks*). **2** *n.* conversation, talking; particular mode of speech (*baby-talk*); informal address or lecture; rumour or gossip, its theme (*there is talk of a new baby*); (often in *pl.*) discussion. **3 now you're talking** *colloq.* your proposal etc. is acceptable; **talk back** reply defiantly; **talk down** silence (person) by greater loudness or persistence, speak patronizingly *to*, bring (pilot or aircraft) to landing by radio instructions from the ground; **talking book** recorded reading of book, esp. for the blind; **talk out** block course of (bill in parliament) by prolonging discussion to time of adjournment; **talk over** discuss at length; **talk person over** (or **round**) win him over by talking; **talk to** *colloq.* reprove; **you can** (or **can't**) **talk** *colloq.* you are just as bad yourself. [TALE or TELL]

talkative /'tɔ:kətıv/ *a.* fond of talking.

talking-to *n.* *colloq.* reproof, reprimand.

tall /tɔ:l/ *a.* of more than average height; of specified height (*he is six feet tall*); higher than surrounding objects; *colloq.* extravagant or excessive (*a tall story*); **talk tall** talk extravagantly or boastfully; **a tall order** an unreasonable demand, a difficult task; **walk tall** be proud. [OE, = swift]

tallboy *n.* tall chest of drawers.

tallow /'tæləʊ/ *n.* harder kinds of (esp. animal) fat melted down for use in making candles, soap, etc.; **tallowy** *a.* [LG]

tally /'tælı/ **1** *v.i.* agree or correspond (*with*). **2** *n.* reckoning of debt or score; mark registering fixed number of objects delivered or received; such number as unit; *hist.* piece of wood scored across with notches for items of an account; ticket or label for identification; corresponding thing, counterpart, duplicate (*of*). [AF *tallie* f. L *talea* rod]

tally-ho /tælı'həʊ/ **1** *int.* huntsman's cry to hounds on seeing fox. **2** *n.* (*pl.* **tally-hos**) utterance of this. **3** *v.* utter cry of 'tally-ho'; indicate (fox) or urge (hounds) with this. [cf. F *taïaut*]

Talmud /'tælmʊd/ *n.* body of Jewish civil and ceremonial law and tradition; **Talmudic** /-'mʊdık/ *a.*; **Talmudist** *n.* [Heb., = instruction]

talon /'tælən/ *n.* claw, esp. of bird of prey. [F, = heel f. L *talus* ankle]

TAM *abbr.* television audience measurement.

tamarind /'tæmərınd/ *n.* tropical tree with fruit whose acid pulp is used for cooling or medicinal drinks; this fruit. [med.L f. Arab., = Indian date]

tamarisk /'tæmərısk/ *n.* evergreen shrub with feathery branches. [L]

tambour /'tæmbʊə/ *n.* drum; circular frame for holding fabric taut while it is being embroidered. [F (TABOR)]

tambourine /tæmbə'ri:n/ *n.* percussion instrument of hoop with parchment stretched over one side and jingling discs in slots round the hoop. [F, dimin. of prec.]

tame 1 *a.* (of animal) domesticated, not wild or shy; insipid, lacking spirit or interest, dull; (of person) amenable and available. **2** *v.t.* make tame, domesticate, break in; subdue, humble. **3 tameable** *a.* [OE]

Tamil /'tæmɪl/ **1** *n.* member of a people inhabiting S. India and Sri Lanka; their language. **2** *a.* of this people or language. [native name]
tam-o'-shanter /tæmə'ʃæntə/ *n.* round Scottish cap, usu. woollen. [hero of poem by Burns]
tamp *v.t.* pack or ram down tightly. [*tampion* stopper for gun-muzzle f. F *tampon*]
tamper *v.i.* only in **tamper with** meddle with, make unauthorized changes in; exert secret or corrupt influence upon, bribe. [var. of TEMPER]
tampon /'tæmpən/ **1** *n.* plug of cotton-wool etc. used to absorb secretions or stop haemorrhage. **2** *v.t.* plug with tampon. [F (TAMP)]
tam-tam /'tæmtæm/ *n.* large metal gong. [Hindi]
tan[1] **1** *n.* brown colour in sunburnt skin; yellowish-brown colour; bark, esp. of oak, bruised and used to tan hides. **2** *a.* yellowish-brown. **3** *v.* (**-nn-**) make or become brown by exposure to sun; convert (raw hide) into leather by soaking in liquid containing tannic acid or by use of mineral salts etc.; *sl.* beat, thrash. [OE, prob. f. med.L *tanno*, perh. f. Celt.]
tan[2] *abbr.* tangent.
tandem /'tændəm/ **1** *n.* bicycle with two or more seats one behind another; group of two persons or machines etc. with one behind or following the other; carriage driven tandem. **2** *adv.* with two or more horses harnessed one behind another (*drive tandem*). **3 in tandem** one behind another. [L, = at length]
tandoor /'tændʊə/ *n.* clay oven. [Hind.]
tandoori /tæn'dʊərɪ/ *n.* food cooked over charcoal in tandoor.
tang *n.* strong taste or flavour or smell; characteristic quality; projection on blade of tool by which blade is held firm in handle. [ON *tange* point]
tangent /'tændʒənt/ *n.* straight line that meets a curve or curved surface at a point but if extended does not intersect it at that point; ratio of sides opposite and adjacent to angle in right-angled triangle; **at a tangent** diverging from previous course of action or thought etc. [L *tango tact-* touch]
tangential /tæn'dʒenʃ(ə)l/ *a.* of or along a tangent; divergent; peripheral; **tangentially** *adv.*
tangerine /tændʒə'ri:n/ *n.* kind of small flattened orange; its deep orange-yellow colour. [*Tangier* in Morocco]
tangible /'tændʒɪb(ə)l/ *a.* perceptible by touch; definite, clearly intelligible, not elusive or visionary; **tangibility** /-'bɪlɪtɪ/ *n.*; **tangibly** *adv.* [F or L (TANGENT)]
tangle /'tæŋg(ə)l/ **1** *v.* intertwine (threads or hairs etc.), or become involved, in confused mass; become involved (esp. in conflict) *with*; entangle; complicate (*a tangled affair*). **2** *n.* confused mass of intertwined threads etc.; confused state. [orig. uncert.]
tangly *a.* tangled.
tango /'tæŋgəʊ/ **1** *n.* (*pl.* **tangos**) slow S. American ballroom dance; music for this. **2** *v.i.* dance tango. [Amer. Sp.]
tangram /'tæŋgræm/ *n.* Chinese puzzle square cut into seven pieces to be combined into various figures. [orig. unkn.]
tangy *a.* having strong, usu. acid, taste or flavour or smell. [TANG]
tank *n.* large receptacle usu. for liquid or gas; armoured motor vehicle carrying guns and moving on Caterpillar tracks; **tank up** fill tank of vehicle etc., *sl.* drink heavily. [orig. Ind. = pond, f. Gujarati]
tankard /'tæŋkəd/ *n.* tall mug, esp. silver or pewter mug for beer. [prob. Du. *tankaert*]
tanker *n.* ship or aircraft or road vehicle for carrying liquids, esp. mineral oils, in bulk. [TANK]
tanner *n.* one who tans hides. [TAN]
tannery *n.* place where hides are tanned.
tannic /'tænɪk/ *a.* of tan; **tannic acid** tannin. [F *tannique* (foll.)]
tannin /'tænɪn/ *n.* any of several astringent substances obtained from oak-galls and various tree-barks, used in preparing leather and in making ink etc. [F *tanin* (TAN)]
Tannoy /'tænɔɪ/ *n.* (**P**) type of public-address system. [orig. uncert.]
tansy /'tænzɪ/ *n.* aromatic herb with yellow flowers. [F f. med.L f. Gk *athanasia* immortality]
tantalize /'tæntəlaɪz/ *v.t.* torment with disappointment, raise and then dash the hopes of; **tantalization** /-'zeɪʃ(ə)n/ *n.* [TANTALUS]
tantalum /'tæntələm/ *n.* rare hard white metallic element.
tantalus /'tæntələs/ *n.* stand in which spirit-decanters are locked up but visible. [*Tantalus*, mythical king punished in Hades with sight of inaccessible water and fruit]
tantamount /'tæntəmaʊnt/ *predic. a.* equivalent *to*. [It. *tanto montare* amount to so much]
tantra /'tæntrə/ *n.* any of a class of Hindu or Buddhist mystical and magical writings. [Skr., = doctrine]
tantrum /'tæntrəm/ *n.* outburst of bad temper or petulance. [orig. unkn.]
Taoism /'taʊɪz(ə)m, 'tɑ:əʊ-/ *n.* a Chinese philosophy advocating humility and religious piety; **Taoist** *n.* [Chin. *dao* right way]

tap[1] **1** *n.* device by which flow of liquid or gas from pipe or vessel can be controlled; act of tapping telephone etc. **2** *v.t.* (**-pp-**) provide (cask) with tap; let out (liquid) thus; draw sap from (tree) by cutting into it; obtain information or supplies from, establish communication or trade with; draw current from (telegraph or telephone wires etc.) to detect message; make screw-thread in. **3 on tap** ready to be drawn off by tap, *colloq.* ready for immediate use; **tap-root** tapering root growing vertically downwards. [OE]

tap[2] **1** *v.* (**-pp-**) strike gentle but audible blow (*at* or *on* door etc.); strike lightly (*tapped his teeth with a pencil*); cause (thing) to strike lightly *against* etc. (*tapped his stick against the window*). **2** *n.* light blow, rap; sound of this. **3 tap-dance** *n.* & *v.i.* dance with sharp rhythmical tapping of feet. [imit.]

tape 1 *n.* narrow strip of woven cotton etc. used as flat string; such strip stretched across racing-track at finishing-line; strip of paper or of transparent film etc. coated with adhesive for fastening packages etc.; = *magnetic tape*; tape-recording; long strip of paper printed or punched to convey messages; tape-measure. **2** *v.t.* tie up or join with tape; record on magnetic tape; measure with tape. **3 have person** (or **thing**) **taped** *sl.* understand him (or it) fully; **tape-machine** machine for receiving and recording telegraph messages; **tape-measure** strip of tape or thin flexible metal marked for measuring length; **tape-record** record (sounds) on magnetic tape; **tape-recorder** apparatus for recording sounds on magnetic tape and afterwards reproducing them; **tape-recording** such record or reproduction. [OE]

taper 1 *n.* wick coated with wax etc. for conveying flame. **2** *v.* diminish in thickness towards one end; cause to do this. **3 taper off** make or become gradually less. [OE]

tapestry /'tæpɪstrɪ/ *n.* thick textile fabric in which coloured weft threads are woven (orig. by hand) to form pictures or designs; embroidery imitating this, usu. in wools on canvas; piece of such embroidery; **tapestried** *a.* [*tapissery* f. F *tapis* carpet]

tapeworm *n.* tapelike worm living as parasite in intestines. [TAPE]

tapioca /tæpɪ'əʊkə/ *n.* starchy substance in hard white grains obtained from cassava and used for puddings etc. [Tupi-Guarani]

tapir /'teɪpə, -pɪə/ *n.* piglike mammal of tropical America and Malaya, with short flexible snout. [Tupi]

tappet /'tæpɪt/ *n.* cam or other projecting part used in machinery to give intermittent motion. [TAP[2]]

taproom *n.* room in which alcoholic drinks are available on tap. [TAP[1]]

tar[1] **1** *n.* dark thick inflammable liquid distilled from wood or coal etc. and used as preservative of wood and iron, antiseptic, etc.; similar substance formed in combustion of tobacco etc. **2** *v.t.* (**-rr-**) cover with tar. **3 tar and feather** smear with tar and then cover with feathers as punishment; **tar macadam** road-materials of stone or slag bound with tar; **tarred with the same brush** having same faults. [OE]

tar[2] *n. colloq.* sailor. [TARPAULIN]

taradiddle /'tærədɪd(ə)l/ *n. colloq.* petty lie; nonsense. [cf. DIDDLE]

tarantella /tærən'telə/ *n.* rapid whirling S.Italian dance; music for this. [It. (*Taranto* in Italy)]

tarantula /tə'ræntjʊlə/ *n.* large black spider of S. Europe; large hairy tropical spider. [med.L (as prec.)]

tarboosh /tɑː'buːʃ/ *n.* cap like fez. [Arab. f. Pers.]

tardy /'tɑːdɪ/ *a.* slow to act or come or happen, delaying or delayed beyond right or expected time; **tardily** *adv.*; **tardiness** *n.* [F f. L *tardus* slow]

tare[1] *n.* vetch, esp. as corn-weed or fodder; (in *pl.*) injurious corn-weed. [orig. unkn.]

tare[2] *n.* allowance made for weight of box etc. in which goods are packed; weight of motor vehicle without fuel or load. [F f. med.L f. Arab.]

target /'tɑːgɪt/ *n.* mark or person or object fired at, esp. round or rectangular object divided by concentric circles; objective or result aimed at (*export target*); butt for scorn etc. [dimin. of *targe* shield f. F f. Gmc]

tariff /'tærɪf/ *n.* table of fixed charges (*hotel tariff*); duty on particular class of imports or exports; list of duties or customs to be paid. [F ult. f. Arab., = notification]

tarlatan /'tɑːlət(ə)n/ *n.* thin stiff open muslin. [F; prob. orig. Ind.]

Tarmac /'tɑːmæk/ **1** *n.* (**P**) tar macadam; runway etc. made of this. **2** *v.t.* (**tarmac; -ck-**) apply Tarmac to. [abbr.]

tarn *n.* small mountain lake. [ON]

tarnish /'tɑːnɪʃ/ **1** *v.* lessen or destroy lustre of (metal etc.); impair (reputation etc.); (of metal etc.) lose lustre. **2** *n.* loss of lustre; blemish, stain. [F *ternir* (*terne* dark)]

taro /'tɑːrəʊ/ *n.* (*pl.* **taros**) tropical plant of arum family with tuberous root used as food esp. in Pacific islands. [Polynesian]

tarot /ˈtærəʊ/ *n.* (in *sing.* or *pl.*) game played with pack of 78 cards used also for fortune-telling; any card in this. [F]
tarpaulin /tɑːˈpɔːlɪn/ *n.* waterproof cloth esp. of tarred canvas; sheet or covering of this. [TAR[1], PALL[1]]
tarradiddle var. of TARADIDDLE.
tarragon /ˈtærəgən/ *n.* plant related to wormwood, used to flavour salads and vinegar. [med.L f. Gk]
tarry[1] /ˈtɑːrɪ/ *a.* of or smeared with tar; **tarriness** *n.* [TAR[1]]
tarry[2] /ˈtærɪ/ *v.i. archaic* defer coming or going, linger, be tardy, stay, wait. [orig. unkn.]
tarsal /ˈtɑːs(ə)l/ *a.* of the tarsus. [foll.]
tarsus /ˈtɑːsəs/ *n.* (*pl.* **tarsi** /-aɪ/) the ankle-bones; shank of bird's leg. [Gk]
tart[1] *n.* round of pastry with jam etc. on top; pie with fruit or sweet filling. [F *tarte*]
tart[2] **1** *n. sl.* prostitute, immoral woman. **2** *v. colloq.* dress *up* gaudily, smarten *up*. [prob. abbr. of SWEETHEART]
tart[3] *a.* of acid taste; cutting, bitter (*a tart reply*). [OE]
tartan /ˈtɑːt(ə)n/ *n.* pattern of coloured stripes crossing at right angles, esp. distinctive pattern worn by Scottish Highlanders to denote their clan; cloth woven in such pattern. [orig. uncert.]
tartar[1] /ˈtɑːtə/ *n.* hard deposit that forms on the teeth; substance deposited in cask by fermentation of wine. [med.L f. Gk]
Tartar[2] /ˈtɑːtə/ **1** *n.* member of a group of Central Asian peoples including Mongols and Turks; violent-tempered or savage person. **2** *a.* of Tartars; of Central Asia E. of Caspian Sea. **3 tartar sauce** sauce of mayonnaise and chopped gherkins etc. [F or med.L]
tartaric /tɑːˈtærɪk/ *a.* of tartar or tartaric acid; **tartaric acid** organic acid present in many plants, esp. unripe grapes. [F f. med.L (TARTAR[1])]
tartlet /ˈtɑːtlɪt/ *n.* small tart. [F (TART[1])]
Tarzan /ˈtɑːz(ə)n/ *n.* man of great agility and powerful physique. [character in stories by E. R. Burroughs]
task /tɑːsk/ **1** *n.* piece of work to be done. **2** *v.t.* make great demands on (person's powers etc.). **3 take to task** rebuke, scold; **task force** unit specially organized for task. [F *tasque* f. med.L *tasca*, prob. = *taxa* TAX]
taskmaster *n.* one who imposes task or burden.
tassel /ˈtæs(ə)l/ *n.* tuft of hanging threads or cords etc. attached as ornament to cushion or scarf etc.; tassel-like catkin etc. [F *tas(s)el* clasp]
taste /ˈteɪst/ **1** *n.* sensation caused in the tongue etc. by soluble substance placed on it; faculty of perceiving this sensation; small portion of food or drink taken as sample; slight experience (*taste of success*); liking or predilection; aesthetic discernment in art or literature or conduct, conformity to its dictates (*has taste*; *has good* or *bad taste*). **2** *v.* discern or test flavour of (food etc., or *absol.*) by taking it into the mouth; eat or drink a small portion of; perceive flavour of (*cannot taste with a cold*); have experience of; have specified flavour (*tastes bitter*, *of aniseed*). **3 taste-bud** any of the cells on the surface of the tongue by which things are tasted; **to one's taste** pleasing or suitable. [F f. Rmc]
tasteful *a.* having, or done in, good taste; **tastefully** *adv.*
tasteless *a.* lacking flavour; having, or done in, bad taste.
taster *n.* person employed to judge teas or wines etc. by tasting them.
tasty *a.* pleasing in flavour, appetizing; **tastily** *adv.*; **tastiness** *n.*
tat[1] *n.* tatty things; tatty person; tattiness. [back-form f. TATTY]
tat[2] *v.* (**-tt-**) do tatting; make by tatting. [orig. unkn.]
ta-ta /tæˈtɑː/ *int. colloq.* goodbye. [orig. unkn.]
tatter *n.* (usu. in *pl.*) rag, irregularly torn piece of cloth or paper etc.; **in tatters** (of argument etc.) ruined, demolished. [ON]
tattered *a.* in tatters.
tatting /ˈtætɪŋ/ *n.* a kind of knotted lace made by hand with small shuttle and used for trimming etc.; process of making this. [orig. unkn.]
tattle /ˈtæt(ə)l/ **1** *v.i.* prattle, chatter, gossip idly. **2** *n.* gossip, idle talk. [Flem. *tatelen*, imit.]
tattoo[1] /təˈtuː/ *n.* evening drum or bugle signal recalling soldiers to quarters; elaboration of this with music and marching as entertainment; rapping, drumming. [earlier *tap-too* f. Du. *taptoe*, lit. 'close the tap' (of cask)]
tattoo[2] /təˈtuː/ **1** *v.t.* mark (skin) with indelible design by puncturing and inserting pigment; make (design) thus. **2** *n.* such design. [Polynesian]
tatty /ˈtætɪ/ *a. colloq.* tattered, shabby, inferior; tawdry. [orig. Sc., = shaggy, app. rel. to TATTER]
tau /taʊ, tɔː/ *n.* nineteenth letter of Greek alphabet (Τ, τ). [Gk]
taught *past* and *p.p.* of TEACH.
taunt /tɔːnt/ **1** *n.* thing said to anger or wound a person. **2** *v.t.* assail with taunts, reproach (person with conduct etc.) contemptuously. [F *tant pour tant* tit for tat, smart rejoinder]
taupe /təʊp/ *n.* grey with tinge of another colour, usu. brown. [F, = MOLE]

Taurus /'tɔːrəs/ *n.* constellation and second sign of zodiac. [L, = bull]
taut /tɔːt/ *a.* (of rope etc.) tight, not slack; (of nerves) tense; (of ship etc.) in good condition; **tauten** *v.* [perh. = TOUGH]
tautology /tɔː'tɒlədʒɪ/ *n.* saying of same thing twice over in different words, esp. as fault of style (e.g. *arrived one after the other in succession*); **tautological** /tɔːtə'lɒdʒɪk(ə)l/ *a.*; **tautologous** /-ləgəs/ *a.* [L f. Gk (*tauto* the same)]
tavern /'tæv(ə)n/ *n. literary* inn, public house. [F f. L *taberna*]
tawdry /'tɔːdrɪ/ *a.* showy but worthless, gaudy; **tawdrily** *adv.*; **tawdriness** *n.* [*tawdry lace* f. *St Audrey's lace*]
tawny /'tɔːnɪ/ *a.* of orange-brown colour; **tawniness** *n.* [AF *tauné* (TAN)]
tax 1 *n.* contribution to State revenue legally levied on persons or property or business; strain or heavy demand *on* or *upon* (person, energies, etc.). **2** *v.t.* impose tax on (persons or goods etc.); pay tax on (*income taxed at source*); make heavy demands on (person's powers or resources etc.); charge (person *with* fault, *with doing* thing); call to account. **3 tax-deductible** (of expenses) that may be paid out of income before deduction of income tax; **tax-free** exempt from taxes; **tax haven** place where income tax is low; **tax return** declaration of income for taxation purposes. [F f. L *taxo* censure, compute]
taxation /tæk'seɪʃ(ə)n/ *n.* imposition or payment of tax. [F f. L (prec.)]
taxi /'tæksɪ/ **1** *n.* (in full **taxi-cab**) motor car plying for hire and usu. fitted with taximeter. **2** *v.* (*partic.* **taxiing**) (of aircraft or pilot) go along ground or surface of water under machine's own power before or after flying; go or convey in taxi. [abbr. of *taximeter cab*]
taxidermy /'tæksɪdɜːmɪ/ *n.* art of preparing, stuffing, and mounting skins of animals with lifelike effect; **taxidermist** *n.* [Gk *taxis* arrangement, *derma* skin]
taximeter /'tæksɪmiːtə/ *n.* automatic fare-indicator fitted to taxi. [F (TAX)]
taxman /'tæksmæn/ *n.* inspector or collector of taxes.
taxonomic /tæksə'nɒmɪk/ *a.* (also **taxonomical**) of or using taxonomy; **taxonomically** *adv.* [foll.]
taxonomy /tæk'sɒnəmɪ/ *n.* classification, esp. in biology; principles of this; **taxonomist** *n.* [F f. Gk *taxis* arrangement, *-nomia* distribution]
taxpayer *n.* one who pays taxes. [TAX]
TB *abbr.* tubercle bacillus, *colloq.* tuberculosis.
Tb *symb.* terbium.
T-bone /'tiːbəʊn/ *n.* T-shaped bone, esp. in steak from thin end of loin. [T, BONE]
Tc *symb.* technetium.
te /tiː/ *n. Mus.* seventh note of major scale. [*si*, F f. It.]
Te *symb.* tellurium.
tea *n.* evergreen shrub or small tree grown in India, China, etc.; its dried leaves; drink made by infusing tea-leaves in boiling water; similar drink made from leaves of other plants or from other substance; afternoon meal at which tea is the main feature; **tea-bag** small porous bag of tea for infusion; **tea-chest** light metal-lined wooden box in which tea is transported; **tea-cloth** cloth for tea-table, tea-towel; **tea-leaf** leaf of tea esp. (in *pl.*) after infusion or as dregs, (as *rhyming sl.*) thief; **tea-room** (or **-shop**) place where tea and light refreshments are served to the public; **tea-rose** rose with scent like tea; **tea-towel** towel for drying washed crockery etc. [prob. Du. *tee* f. Chin.]
teacake *n.* light usu. sweet bun eaten at tea, often toasted.
teach *v.* (*past* and *p.p.* **taught** /tɔːt/) give systematic information to (person) or about (subject or skill); practise this professionally; enable (person) to do something by instruction and training (*taught me to swim, how to dance*); advocate as moral etc. principle (*Christ taught forgiveness*); induce (person) by example or punishment (*not*) *to do* thing (*that will teach you not to lie*), *colloq.* make (person) disinclined *to do* thing (*that will teach you to lie*); **teach-in** lecture and discussion, or series of these, on subject of public interest. [OE]
teachable *a.* apt at learning; (of subject) that can be taught.
teacher *n.* one who teaches, esp. in a school.
teaching *n.* what is taught, doctrine; teachers' profession.
teacup *n.* cup from which tea is drunk. [TEA]
teak *n.* heavy durable timber; Asian tree yielding this. [Port. f. Malayalam]
teal *n.* (*pl.* same) small freshwater duck. [orig. unkn.]
team 1 *n.* set of players forming one side in game (*cricket team*); set of persons working together; set of draught animals. **2** *v.* join (*up*) as team or in common action (*with*). **3 team-mate** fellow member of team; **team spirit** willingness to act for group's rather than individual's benefit; **team-work** combined effort, co-operation. [OE]
teamster *n.* driver of team of animals; *US* lorry-driver.
teapot *n.* pot with handle and spout and

lid, in which tea is brewed and from which it is poured. [TEA]

tear[1] /teə/ **1** *v.* (*past* **tore;** *p.p.* **torn**) pull apart with some force (*tear it in half; tore up the letter*); make (hole or rent thus); pull violently or with some force (*away* or *off* etc.); violently disrupt (*country was torn by civil war*); go or travel hurriedly or impetuously (*tore across the road*); undergo tearing (*curtain tore down the middle*). **2** *n.* hole made by tearing, damage caused by tearing; torn part of cloth etc. **3 be torn between** have difficulty choosing between; **tear oneself away** leave in spite of strong desire to stay; **tear one's hair** pull it in anger or frustration or despair. [OE]

tear[2] /tɪə/ *n.* drop of clear salty liquid serving to moisten and wash the eye and falling from it in sorrow or distress etc.; **in tears** weeping; **tear-drop** single tear; **tear-gas** gas that disables by causing severe irritation to the eyes; **tear-jerker** *colloq.* story etc. calculated to evoke sadness or sympathy; **without tears** presented so as to be learned or done easily. [OE]

tearaway *n.* reckless hooligan. [TEAR[1]]

tearful *a.* in or given to or accompanied with tears; **tearfully** *adv.* [TEAR[2]]

tearing *a.* extreme or overwhelming (*in a tearing hurry*). [TEAR[1]]

tease /ti:z/ **1** *v.t.* irritate playfully or maliciously with trivial jests or deceptions; pick (wool etc.) into separate fibres; dress (cloth) esp. with teasels. **2** *n. colloq.* person fond of teasing others. **3 tease out** separate by disentangling. [OE]

teasel /ˈti:z(ə)l/ *n.* plant with prickly flower-heads; such head dried and used for raising nap on cloth; device used thus. [OE (prec.)]

teaser *n. colloq.* hard question or task. [TEASE]

teaspoon *n.* small spoon for stirring tea; amount held by this; **teaspoonful** *n.* (*pl.* **teaspoonfuls**). [TEA]

teat *n.* mammary nipple esp. of animal; device, esp. of rubber, for sucking milk from bottle. [F f. Gmc]

teazle var. of TEASEL.

tec *n. sl.* detective. [abbr.]

Tech /tek/ *n. colloq.* technical college or school. [abbr.]

technetium /tekˈni:ʃəm/ *n.* artificially produced radioactive metallic element. [Gk *tekhnētos* artificial]

technical /ˈteknɪk(ə)l/ *a.* of or involving the mechanical arts and applied sciences (*technical college, education*); of or relating to a particular subject or craft etc. or its techniques (*technical terms*); (of book or discourse etc.) using technical language, requiring special knowledge to be understood; such in strict interpretation (*technical assault*); **technically** *adv.* [L f. Gk (*tekhnē* art)]

technicality /teknɪˈkælɪtɪ/ *n.* being technical; technical expression; technical point or detail (*was acquitted on a technicality*).

technician /tekˈnɪʃ(ə)n/ *n.* expert in practical application of science; person skilled in technique of an art or craft; person employed to look after technical equipment in laboratory etc.

Technicolor /ˈteknɪkʌlə/ *n.* **(P)** a process of colour cinematography; vivid colour, artificial brilliance. [TECHNICAL, COLOR]

technique /tekˈni:k/ *n.* mechanical skill in art; means of achieving one's purpose (esp. skilfully); mode of artistic expression in music, painting, etc. [F (TECHNICAL)]

technocracy /tekˈnɒkrəsɪ/ *n.* government or control of society or industry by technical experts. [Gk *tekhnē* art]

technocrat /ˈteknəkræt/ *n.* exponent or advocate of technocracy.

technological /teknəˈlɒdʒɪk(ə)l/ *a.* of or using technology; **technologically** *adv.* [foll.]

technology /tekˈnɒlədʒɪ/ *n.* study or use of the mechanical arts and applied sciences; these subjects collectively; **technologist** *n.* [Gk *tekhnologia* systematic treatment (*tekhnē* art)]

tectonics /tekˈtɒnɪks/ *n.pl.* (usu. treated as *sing.*) study of the earth's structural features as a whole. [L f. Gk (*tektōn* craftsman)]

Ted *n. colloq.* Teddy boy. [abbr.]

teddy bear /ˈtedɪ/ soft toy bear. [*Teddy*, pet-name of *Theodore* Roosevelt]

Teddy boy /ˈtedɪ/ *colloq.* youth with supposedly Edwardian style of dress. [*Teddy*, pet-form of *Edward*]

tedious /ˈti:dɪəs/ *a.* tiresomely long, wearisome. [F or L (foll.)]

tedium /ˈti:dɪəm/ *n.* tediousness. [L *taedium* (*taedet* it bores)]

tee[1] *n.* letter T. [phon. sp.]

tee[2] **1** *n.* cleared space from which golf ball is struck at beginning of play for each hole; small support of wood or plastic from which ball is thus struck; mark aimed at in bowls, quoits, etc. **2** *v.t.* place (ball) on golf tee. **3 tee off** play ball from tee, start, begin. [orig. unkn.]

teem[1] *v.i.* be abundant; be full, swarm (*with*). [OE, = give birth to]

teem[2] *v.i.* (of water etc.) flow copiously, pour. [ON]

-teen *suffix* forming numerals 13–19. [OE (ten)]

teenage /'ti:neɪdʒ/ *a.* of or characteristic of teenagers. [TEENS, AGE]

teenager *n.* person in teens.

teens /ti:nz/ *n.pl.* years of one's age from 13 to 19. [-TEEN]

teeny /'ti:nɪ/ *a. colloq.* tiny. [var. of TINY]

teeny-bopper /'ti:nɪbɒpə/ *n. colloq.* teenager, usu. girl, following latest fashions. [TEENS, BOP]

teeter *v.i.* totter, move unsteadily. [dial. *titter*]

teeth *pl.* of TOOTH.

teethe /ti:ð/ *v.i.* grow or cut teeth, esp. milk-teeth; **teething-ring** small ring for infant to bite on while teething; **teething troubles** initial troubles in an enterprise etc. [TEETH]

teetotal /ti:'təʊt(ə)l/ *a.* of or advocating teetotalism. [redupl. of TOTAL]

teetotalism *n.* total abstinence from intoxicants.

teetotaller *n.* person advocating or practising teetotalism.

tele- *in comb.* far, at a distance; television. [Gk (*tēle* far off)]

telecommunication /telɪkəmju:nɪ'keɪʃ(ə)n/ *n.* communication over long distances by cable, telegraph, telephone, or broadcasting; (usu. in *pl.*) this branch of technology.

telegram /'telɪgræm/ *n.* message sent by telegraph and then usu. delivered in written form. [-GRAM]

telegraph /'telɪgrɑ:f/ **1** *n.* transmitting messages or signals to a distance esp. by making and breaking electrical connection; apparatus for this. **2** *v.* send message by telegraph (to); send (message) thus; send instruction to by telegraph (*telegraphed her to come*). [F (-GRAPH)]

telegraphic /telɪ'græfɪk/ *a.* of telegraphs or telegrams; economically worded; **telegraphically** *adv.*

telegraphist /tɪ'legrəfɪst/ *n.* person skilled or employed in telegraphy.

telegraphy /tɪ'legrəfɪ/ *n.* use or construction of telegraph.

telemeter /'telɪmi:tə/ *n.* apparatus for recording readings of an instrument and transmitting it by radio. [TELE-]

teleology /telɪ'ɒlədʒɪ/ *n.* view that developments are due to purpose or design that is served by them; study of final causes; **teleological** /-'lɒdʒɪk(ə)l/ *a.* [Gk *telos* end]

telepath /'telɪpæθ/ *n.* person able to communicate by telepathy. [foll.]

telepathy /tɪ'lepəθɪ/ *n.* communication between minds otherwise than by known senses; **telepathic** /telɪ'pæθɪk/ *a.* [PATHOS]

telephone /'telɪfəʊn/ **1** *n.* apparatus for transmitting sound (esp. speech) to a distance by wire or cord or radio, esp. by converting to electrical signals; transmitting and receiving instrument used in this; the system of communication by network of telephones. **2** *v.* speak to (person) by telephone; send (message) by telephone; make telephone call. **3 telephone-box** (or **booth** or **kiosk**) boxlike kiosk containing telephone for public use; **telephone directory** (or **book**) book listing names and numbers of people who have telephones; **telephone number** number assigned to particular telephone and used in making connections to it. **4 telephonic** /-'fɒnɪk/ *a.*; **telephonically** /-'fɒnɪkəlɪ/ *adv.* [PHONO-]

telephonist /tɪ'lefənɪst/ *n.* operator in telephone exchange or at switchboard.

telephony /tɪ'lefənɪ/ *n.* use or system of telephones.

telephoto /telɪ'fəʊtəʊ/ *a.* = TELEPHOTOGRAPHIC. [TELE-]

telephotographic /telɪfəʊtə'græfɪk/ *a.* of or for or using telephotography.

telephotography /telɪfə'tɒgrəfɪ/ *n.* photographing of distant objects with combined lenses giving large image.

teleprinter /'telɪprɪntə/ *n.* device for typing and transmitting telegraph messages, and for receiving and typing them.

telescope /'telɪskəʊp/ **1** *n.* optical instrument using lenses or mirrors or both to make distant objects appear nearer and larger; (in full **radio telescope**) directional aerial system for collecting radio waves from celestial objects. **2** *v.* press or drive (sections of tube, colliding vehicles, etc.) together so that one slides into another like sections of telescope; close or be driven or be capable of closing thus; compress so as to occupy less space or time. [It. (-SCOPE)]

telescopic /telɪ'skɒpɪk/ *a.* of or made with telescope (*telescopic observations*); consisting of sections which telescope (*telescopic umbrella*); **telescopic sight** telescope used for sighting on rifle etc.; **telescopically** *adv.*

teletext /'telɪtekst/ *n.* news and information service from computer source transmitted to television screens of subscribers. [TELE-]

Teletype /'telɪtaɪp/ *n.* (**P**) a kind of teleprinter.

televise /'telɪvaɪz/ *v.t.* transmit by television. [foll.]

television /'telɪvɪʒ(ə)n, -'vɪʒ(ə)n/ *n.* system for reproducing on a screen visual images transmitted (with sound) by radio signals; (in full **television set**) device for receiving these signals;

television broadcasting generally; **televisual** /-ˈvɪzjʊəl/ *a.* [VISION]

telex /ˈteleks/ **1** *n.* system of telegraphy using teleprinters and public telecommunication network. **2** *v.t.* send by telex; communicate with by telex. [TELE (PRINTER), EX(CHANGE)]

tell *v.* (*past* and *p.p.* **told** /təʊld/) relate or narrate in speech or writing (*tell me a story*); make known, express in words, divulge (*tell me your name*); utter (*tell lies*); give information or description (*of* or *about*); direct or order (person) *to do* thing; reveal secret; decide, determine, distinguish; assure (*it's not easy, I can tell you*); produce noticeable effect (*on*); **tell off** *colloq.* reprimand, scold; **tell on** *colloq.* inform against; **tell tales** report discreditable fact about another; **tell the time** read it from face of clock or watch; **you're telling me** *sl.* I am well aware of what you say. [OE (TALE)]

teller *n.* person employed to receive and pay out money in bank etc.; person appointed to count votes.

telling *a.* having marked effect, striking.

tell-tale 1 *n.* person who discloses another's private affairs or misdeeds; automatic registering device. **2** *a.* that reveals or betrays (*a tell-tale smile*).

tellurium /teˈljʊərɪəm/ *n.* rare silver-white element. [L *tellus -ur-* earth]

telly /ˈtelɪ/ *n.* *colloq.* television; television set. [abbr.]

temerity /tɪˈmerɪtɪ/ *a.* rashness. [L (*temere* rashly)]

temp *n. colloq.* temporary employee, esp. secretary. [abbr.]

temper 1 *n.* habitual or temporary disposition of mind esp. as regards composure; irritation or anger (*in a fit of temper*); tendency to have fits of anger (*have a temper*); composure or calmness (*keep, lose, one's temper*); condition of metal as regards hardness and elasticity. **2** *v.t.* bring (metal or clay) to proper hardness or consistency; moderate or mitigate (*temper justice with mercy*). **3 in a bad temper** angry, peevish; **in a good temper** in an amiable mood. [OE f. L *tempero* mingle]

tempera /ˈtempərə/ *n.* method of painting using emulsion e.g. of pigment with egg, esp. in fine art on canvas. [It.]

temperament /ˈtemprəmənt/ *n.* person's distinct nature and character, esp. as determined by physical constitution and permanently affecting behaviour. [L (TEMPER)]

temperamental /temprəˈment(ə)l/ *a.* of temperament; liable to erratic or moody behaviour; **temperamentally** *adv.*

temperance /ˈtempərəns/ *n.* moderation or self-restraint esp. in eating and drinking; abstinence or partial abstinence from alcoholic drink. [AF f. L (TEMPER)]

temperate /ˈtempərət/ *a.* avoiding excess; moderate; of mild temperature. [L (TEMPER)]

temperature /ˈtemprɪtʃə/ *n.* degree or intensity of heat of a body in relation to others esp. as shown by thermometer or perceived by touch; *colloq.* body temperature above normal (*have a temperature*); degree of excitement in discussion etc. [F or L (TEMPER)]

tempest /ˈtempɪst/ *n.* violent storm. [F f. L (*tempus* time)]

tempestuous /temˈpestjʊəs/ *a.* stormy, turbulent. [L (prec.)]

template /ˈtempleɪt/ *n.* thin board or metal plate used as guide in cutting or drilling. [orig. *templet*, dimin. of *temple* device in loom to keep cloth stretched]

temple[1] /ˈtemp(ə)l/ *n.* building devoted to worship, or treated as dwelling-place, of god or gods; **Inner** and **Middle Temple** two Inns of Court in London. [OE & F (L *templum*)]

temple[2] /ˈtemp(ə)l/ *n.* flat part of either side of head between forehead and ear. [F f. L]

tempo /ˈtempəʊ/ *n.* (*pl.* **tempos** or **tempi** /-iː/) speed at which music is or should be played, esp. as characteristic (*waltz tempo*); rate of motion or activity. [It., f. L *tempus -por-* time]

temporal /ˈtempər(ə)l/ *a.* of worldly as opposed to spiritual affairs, secular; of or denoting time; of temple(s) of the head (*temporal bone*). [F or L (foll.)]

temporary /ˈtempərərɪ/ **1** *a.* lasting or meant to last only for a limited time. **2** *n.* person employed temporarily. **3 temporarily** *adv.*; **temporariness** *n.* [L (*tempus -por-* time)]

temporize /ˈtempəraɪz/ *v.i.* avoid committing oneself, act so as to gain time; comply temporarily with requirements of occasion. [F f. med.L (prec.)]

tempt *v.t.* entice or incite (person) to do wrong or forbidden thing; allure, attract; risk provoking (fate or Providence); **be tempted to** be strongly disposed to; **tempter** *n.*; **temptress** *n. fem.* [F f. L *tempto*, *tento* try, test]

temptation /tempˈteɪʃ(ə)n/ *n.* tempting or being tempted, incitement esp. to wrongdoing; attractive thing or course of action; *archaic* putting to the test (*lead us not into temptation*).

tempting *a.* attractive, inviting.

ten *a.* & *n.* one more than nine; symbol for this (10, x, X); size etc. denoted by ten. [OE]

tenable /'tenəb(ə)l/ *a.* that can be maintained against attack or objection; (of office etc.) that can be held *for* period or *by* class of person; **tenability** /-'bılıtı/ *n.* [F (*tenir* hold)]

tenacious /tı'neıʃəs/ *a.* keeping firm hold (*of* property, principles, life, etc.); (of memory) retentive; holding tightly, not easily separable, tough; **tenacity** /tı'næsıtı/ *n.* [L *tenax -acis* (*teneo* hold)]

tenancy *n.* tenant's position. [foll.]

tenant /'tenənt/ *n.* person who rents land or property from landlord; occupant of place; **tenant farmer** one farming hired land. [F (as TENABLE)]

tenantry *n.* tenants of estate etc.

tench *n.* (*pl.* same) European freshwater fish of carp family. [F f. L *tinca*]

tend[1] *v.i.* be apt or inclined, serve, or conduce (*to* action or quality etc., *to do* thing); be moving, be directed, hold a course (*lit.* or *fig.*: *tends in our direction, to the same conclusion*). [F f. L *tendo tens-* or *tent-* stretch]

tend[2] *v.t.* take care of, look after (person esp. invalid, animals esp. sheep, machine). [ATTEND]

tendency /'tendənsı/ *n.* tending, leaning, inclination (*to* or *towards*). [med.L (TEND[1])]

tendentious /ten'denʃəs/ *a. derog.* (of writing etc.) designed to advance a cause.

tender[1] *a.* easily cut or chewed, not tough (*tender steak*); easily hurt or wounded, susceptible to pain or grief (*a tender heart*); delicate, fragile, sensitive; loving, affectionate (*wrote tender verses*); requiring tact (*a tender subject*); (of age) early, immature; **tender spot** subject on which one is touchy. [F f. L *tener*]

tender[2] **1** *v.* make offer of or present for acceptance (money in payment, one's services or resignation); send in a tender (*for* execution of work etc.). **2** *n.* offer, esp. in writing to execute work or supply goods at fixed price. **3 put out to tender** seek offers in respect of (work etc.). [F (TEND[1])]

tender[3] *n.* one who looks after people or things; vessel attending larger one and carrying stores etc.; truck attached to steam locomotive and carrying coal etc. [TEND[2]]

tenderfoot *n.* novice, newcomer. [TENDER[1]]

tenderize *v.t.* make tender, esp. make (meat) tender by beating etc. [TENDER[1]]

tenderloin *n.* middle part of pork loin; *US* undercut of sirloin. [TENDER[1]]

tendon /'tend(ə)n/ *n.* cord of strong tissue attaching muscle to bone etc. [F, or med.L *tendo* f. Gk]

tendril /'tendrıl/ *n.* one of the slender leafless shoots by which some climbing plants cling. [prob. F *tendrillon*, ult. rel. to L *tener* TENDER[1]]

tenement /'tenımənt/ *n.* dwelling-place, esp. set of rooms held separately from rest of house; house divided into and let in tenements. [F f. med.L (*teneo* hold)]

tenet /'tenıt/ *n.* doctrine held by group or person. [L, = he holds]

tenfold *a.* & *adv.* ten times as much or as many; consisting of ten parts. [TEN]

tenner *n. colloq.* £10 note.

tennis /'tenıs/ *n.* game played by two or four players with rackets and soft ball on open court divided by net. [prob. F *tenez* take! (as server's call)]

tenon /'tenən/ *n.* projection shaped to fit into mortise. [F (*tenir* hold f. L, as foll.)]

tenor /'tenə/ *n.* male singer of range between baritone and alto or countertenor; range sung by him; instrument with equivalent range; general purport *of* document or speech; prevailing course of one's life or habits. [F f. L (*teneo* hold)]

tenpin bowling form of skittles similar to ninepins.

tense[1] **1** *a.* stretched to tightness, strained or highly strung (*tense muscle, nerves, emotion*); causing tenseness (*a tense moment*). **2** *v.* make or become tense. [L *tensus* (TEND[1])]

tense[2] *n.* form taken by verb to indicate time (also continuance or completeness) of action etc.; set of such forms for various persons and numbers. [F f. L *tempus* time]

tensile /'tensaıl/ *a.* of tension; capable of being stretched; **tensile strength** resistance to breaking under tension; **tensility** /-'sılıtı/ *n.* [med.L (TENSE[1])]

tension /'tenʃ(ə)n/ *n.* stretching or being stretched; mental strain or excitement; strained (political or social etc.) state or relation; effect produced by forces pulling against each other (*surface tension*); electromotive force (*high, low, tension*). [F or L (TEND[1])]

tent *n.* portable shelter or dwelling of canvas or cloth etc. supported by poles and by ropes attached to pegs driven into ground; cover etc. resembling tent. [F *tente* f. L (TEND[1])]

tentacle /'tentək(ə)l/ *n.* long slender flexible appendage of animal, used for feeling, grasping, or moving; thing used like tentacle as feeler etc.; **tentacled** *a.* [L (TEMPT)]

tentative /'tentətıv/ *a.* done by way of trial, experimental, hesitant, not definite (*tentative suggestion*). [med.L (TEMPT)]

tenter *n.* cloth-stretching frame. [AF f. med.L *tentorium* (TEND[1])]

tenterhooks *n.pl.* hooks to which cloth is fastened on tenter; **on tenterhooks** in state of suspense, distracted by uncertainty.

tenth *a.* & *n.* next after ninth; one of ten equal parts of thing; **tenthly** *adv.* [TEN]

tenuous /ˈtenjʊəs/ *a.* slight, of little substance (*tenuous connection*); (of distinction etc.) over-subtle; thin, slender, small; rarefied; **tenuity** /-ˈjuːɪtɪ/ *n.* [L *tenuis*]

tenure /ˈtenjə/ *n.* condition, or form of right or title, under which (esp. real) property is held; holding (*of* office or property), period of this; permanent appointment of teacher etc. [F (*tenir* hold f. L *teneo*)]

tepee /ˈtiːpiː/ *n.* N. American Indian's conical tent. [Dakota]

tepid /ˈtepɪd/ *a.* slightly warm; unenthusiastic; **tepidity** /tɪˈpɪdɪtɪ/ *n.* [L]

tequila /teˈkiːlə/ *n.* Mexican liquor from agave. [*Tequila* in Mexico]

tera- /ˈterə/ *prefix* one million million. [Gk *teras* monster]

terbium /ˈtɜːbɪəm/ *n.* metallic element of lanthanide series. [*Ytterby* in Sweden]

tercel /ˈtɜːs(ə)l/ *n.* male hawk. [F f. Rmc dimin. of L *tertius* third]

tercentenary /tɜːsenˈtiːnərɪ/ *n.* three-hundredth anniversary; celebration of this. [L *ter* 3 times]

terebinth /ˈterɪbɪnθ/ *n.* S. European tree yielding turpentine. [F or L f. Gk]

teredo /təˈriːdəʊ/ *n.* (*pl.* **teredos**) mollusc that bores into submerged timber. [L f. Gk]

tergiversation /tɜːdʒɪvɜːˈseɪʃ(ə)n/ *n.* change of party or principles, apostasy; making of conflicting statements. [L (*tergum* back, *verto* turn)]

term 1 *n.* word used to express definite concept, esp. in branch of study etc.; (in *pl.*) language used, mode of expression (*answered in no uncertain terms*); (in *pl.*) relation or footing (*we are on good terms*); (in *pl.*) conditions or stipulations (*did it on my terms*); (in *pl.*) charge or price; limited period of some state or activity (*term of office*; *three-year term*); period of action or of contemplated results (*in the short term*); period during which instruction is given in school or university, or during which lawcourt holds sessions; word or words that may be subject or predicate of a logical proposition; *Math.* each quantity in ratio or series, item of compound algebraic expression; *archaic* appointed limit. **2** *v.t.* denominate, call. **3 bring to terms** cause to accept conditions; **come to terms** yield, give way; **come to terms with** reconcile oneself with (difficulty etc.); **in terms of** in the language peculiar to, using as basis of expression or thought; **terms of reference** points referred to an individual or body of persons for decision or report, scope of inquiry etc., definition of this. [F f. L TERMINUS]

termagant /ˈtɜːməgənt/ *n.* overbearing woman, virago. [F *Tervagan* f. It.]

terminable /ˈtɜːmɪnəb(ə)l/ *a.* that may be terminated. [TERMINATE]

terminal /ˈtɜːmɪn(ə)l/ **1** *a.* of or forming the last part or terminus (*terminal section, joint, station*); forming or undergoing last stage of fatal disease; of or done etc. each term (*terminal examinations*). **2** *n.* terminating thing, extremity; terminus for trains or long-distance buses; = *air terminal*; point of connection for closing electric circuit; apparatus for transmission of messages to and from computer or communications system etc. **3 terminally** *adv.* [L (TERMINUS)]

terminate /ˈtɜːmɪneɪt/ *v.* bring or come to an end; end *in*; **terminator** *n.*

termination /tɜːmɪˈneɪʃ(ə)n/ *n.* ending; way something ends; word's final letter(s). [F or L (prec.)]

terminology /tɜːmɪˈnɒlədʒɪ/ *n.* system of terms used in a particular subject; science of proper use of terms; **terminological** /-nəˈlɒdʒɪk(ə)l/ *a.* [G (foll.)]

terminus /ˈtɜːmɪnəs/ *n.* (*pl.* **termini** /-aɪ/) station at end of railway or bus route; point at end of pipeline etc. [L, = end, limit, boundary]

termite /ˈtɜːmaɪt/ *n.* small antlike insect destructive to timber. [L *termes -mitis*]

tern *n.* sea-bird like gull but usu. smaller and with forked tail. [Scand.]

ternary /ˈtɜːnərɪ/ *a.* composed of three parts. [L (*terni* 3 each)]

terrace /ˈterəs/ *n.* raised level space, natural or artificial, esp. for walking, standing, or cultivation; row of houses on raised level or built in one block of uniform style (*terrace house*); flight of wide shallow steps as for spectators at sports ground. [F f. L *terra* earth]

terraced *a.* formed into or having terrace(s); **terraced roof** flat roof esp. of Eastern house.

terracotta /terəˈkɒtə/ *n.* unglazed usu. brownish-red pottery used as ornamental building-material and in statuary; statuette of this; its colour. [It., = baked earth]

terra firma /terə ˈfɜːmə/ dry land, firm ground. [L]

terrain /teˈreɪn/ *n.* tract of land as regards its natural features. [F f. Rmc f. L (TERRENE)]

terrapin /'terəpɪn/ *n.* edible freshwater tortoise of N. America. [Algonquian]

terrarium /te'reərɪəm/ *n.* (*pl.* **terrariums**) place for keeping small land animals; sealed transparent globe etc. containing growing plants. [f. L *terra* earth, after *aquarium*]

terrazzo /tɪ'rætsəʊ/ *n.* (*pl.* **terrazzos**) flooring-material of stone chips set in concrete and given a smooth surface. [It., = terrace]

terrene /te'ri:n/ *a.* of earth, earthly; terrestrial. [AF f. L *terrenus* (*terra* earth)]

terrestrial /tə'restrɪəl/ *a.* of or on the earth (*terrestrial globe, life*); of or on dry land (*terrestrial birds*). [L *terrestris* (prec.)]

terrible /'terɪb(ə)l/ *a.* causing or fit to cause terror, dreadful; *colloq.* very great or bad (*a terrible bore*); *colloq.* very incompetent (*terrible at tennis*). [F f. L (*terreo* frighten)]

terribly *adv.* in a terrible manner; *colloq.* very, extremely (*he was terribly nice about it*).

terrier /'terɪə/ *n.* small active dog bred orig. for turning out foxes etc. from their earths. [F (*chien*) *terrier* f. med.L (L *terra* earth)]

terrific /tə'rɪfɪk/ *a.* causing terror; *colloq.* of great size or intensity; *colloq.* excellent (*did a terrific job*); **terrifically** *adv.* [L (TERRIBLE)]

terrify /'terɪfaɪ/ *v.t.* frighten severely.

terrine /tə'ri:n/ *n.* pâté or similar food; earthenware vessel holding this. [F f. Rmc f. L *terra* earth]

territorial /terɪ'tɔ:rɪəl/ **1** *a.* of territory or districts. **2** *n.* (**Territorial**) member of Territorial Army. **3 Territorial Army** volunteer reserve force organized by localities; **territorial waters** waters under a State's jurisdiction, esp. part of sea within stated distance of shore. **4 territorially** *adv.* [L (foll.)]

territory /'terɪtərɪ/ *n.* extent of land under jurisdiction of ruler or State; (**Territory**) organized division of a country esp. if not yet admitted to full rights of a State; sphere of action or thought, province; area over which commercial traveller etc. operates; area defended by animal against others of same species, or by team or player in game. [L (*terra* land)]

terror /'terə/ *n.* extreme fear; person or thing causing terror; *colloq.* formidable person, troublesome person or thing; **terror-stricken** (or **-struck**) affected with terror. [F f. L (*terreo* frighten)]

terrorism *n.* practice of using violent and intimidating methods, esp. to achieve political ends; **terrorist** *n.* [F (prec.)]

terrorize *v.t.* fill with terror; coerce by terrorism; **terrorization** /-'zeɪʃ(ə)n/ *n.* [TERROR]

terry /'terɪ/ *n.* pile fabric with loops uncut, used esp. for towels. [orig. unkn.]

terse *a.* concise, brief and forcible in style; curt. [L (*tergo ters-* wipe)]

tertiary /'tɜ:ʃərɪ/ **1** *a.* of third order or rank etc.; (**Tertiary**) of the earlier period in the Cainozoic era. **2** *n.* bird's flight-feather of third row; (**Tertiary**) the Tertiary period. [L (*tertius* third)]

Terylene /'terɪli:n/ *n.* (**P**) synthetic polyester used as textile fibre. [*terephthalic* acid + ETHYLENE]

tessellated /'tesəleɪtɪd/ *a.* of or resembling mosaic; having finely chequered surface. [L (*tessella* dimin. of TESSERA)]

tessellation /tesə'leɪʃ(ə)n/ *n.* arrangement of polygons without gaps or overlapping, esp. in repeating pattern.

tessera /'tesərə/ *n.* (*pl.* **tesserae** /-i:/) each of the small cubes or blocks of which mosaic consists. [L f. Gk]

test[1] **1** *n.* critical examination or trial of person's or thing's qualities; means or standard or circumstances suitable for or serving such examination; minor examination esp. in school; *colloq.* test match. **2** *v.t.* put to the test, make trial of; try severely, tax; *Chem.* examine by means of reagent. **3 put to the test** cause to undergo test; **stand the test** not fail or incur rejection; **test case** case whose decision is taken as settling other cases involving same question of law; **test match** cricket or Rugby match between teams of certain countries, usu. one of series in tour; **test out** put to practical test; **test paper** minor examination-paper, *Chem.* paper impregnated with substance changing colour under known conditions; **test pilot** pilot who tests performance of newly designed aircraft; **test-tube** thin glass tube closed at one end used for chemical tests etc.; **test-tube baby** *colloq.* baby conceived by artificial insemination, or developing elsewhere than in a mother's body. [F f. L *testu(m)* = *testa* (foll.)]

test[2] *n.* hard continuous shell of some invertebrates. [L *testa* pot, tile, shell]

testa /'testə/ *n.* (*pl.* **testae** /-i:/) seed-coat. [L (prec.)]

testaceous /te'steɪʃəs/ *a.* having hard continuous shell.

testacy /'testəsɪ/ *n.* being testate. [TESTATE]

testament /'testəmənt/ *n.* a will (usu. **last will and testament**); *colloq.* written statement of one's beliefs etc.; covenant, dispensation; (**Testament**) division of the Bible (see OLD, NEW). [L *testamentum* will (TESTATE)]

testamentary /testə'mentərɪ/ *a.* of or by or in a will. [L (prec.)]

testate /'testeɪt/ **1** *a.* having left a valid will at death. **2** *n.* testate person. [L (*testor* testify f. *testis* witness)]

testator /te'steɪtə/ *n.* person who has made a will, esp. one who dies testate. [AF f. L (prec.)]

testicle /'testɪk(ə)l/ *n.* male organ that secretes spermatozoa etc., esp. one of pair in scrotum behind penis of man and most mammals. [L, dimin. of *testis* witness (of virility)]

testify /'testɪfaɪ/ *v.* (of person or thing) bear witness (*to* fact or state or assertion, *against* person etc.); give evidence; affirm or declare; (of thing) be evidence of. [L *testificor* (*testis* witness)]

testimonial /testɪ'məʊnɪəl/ *n.* certificate of character or conduct or qualifications; gift presented to person (esp. in public) as mark of esteem. [F (foll.)]

testimony /'testɪmənɪ/ *n.* oral or written statement under oath or affirmation; declarations or statements (*the testimony of history*); evidence, demonstration. [L *testimonium* (*testis* witness)]

testis /'testɪs/ *n.* (*pl.* **testes** /-i:z/) testicle. [L, = witness (cf. TESTICLE)]

testosterone /te'stɒstərəʊn/ *n.* male sex hormone produced in the testicles. [TESTIS, STEROL]

testy *a.* irascible, short-tempered; **testily** *adv.*; **testiness** *n.* [AF f. F *teste* head (TEST²)]

tetanus /'tetənəs/ *n.* bacterial disease with continuous painful contraction of some or all voluntary muscles. [L f. Gk (*teinō* stretch)]

tetchy /'tetʃɪ/ *a.* peevish, irritable, touchy; **tetchily** *adv.*; **tetchiness** *n.* [*teche* blemish, fault]

tête-à-tête /teɪtɑ:'teɪt/ **1** *n.* private conversation or interview usu. between two persons. **2** *adv.* together in private. **3** *a.* private, confidential; concerning only two persons. [F, lit. head-to-head]

tether /'teðə/ **1** *n.* rope or chain by which animal is tied while grazing. **2** *v.t.* tie (animal) with tether. **3 at the end of one's tether** having reached the limit of one's patience or endurance etc. [ON]

tetra- *in comb.* four. [Gk (*tettares* 4)]

tetrad /'tetræd/ *n.* group of four. [Gk (TETRA-)]

tetragon /'tetrəgən/ *n.* plane figure with four sides and angles; **tetragonal** /-'rægən(ə)l/ *a.* [Gk (TETRA-, *-gōnos* -angled)]

tetrahedron /tetrə'hi:drən/ *n.* four-sided solid, triangular pyramid; **tetrahedral** *a.* [Gk (TETRA-, *hedra* base)]

tetralogy /te'trælədʒɪ/ *n.* group of four related literary or dramatic works. [Gk (TETRA-)]

tetrameter /te'træmɪtə/ *n.* line of verse of four measures. [L f. Gk (TETRA-)]

Teuton /'tju:t(ə)n/ *n.* member of a Teutonic nation, esp. a German. [L *Teutones*, anc. tribe of N. Europe]

Teutonic /tju:'tɒnɪk/ *a.* of Germanic peoples or languages; allegedly characteristic of these peoples; German. [F f. L (prec.)]

text *n.* main body of book as distinct from notes, appendices, etc.; original words of author or document, esp. as distinct from paraphrase or commentary; passage of Scripture quoted or used as subject of sermon etc.; subject, theme; (in *pl.*) books prescribed for study. [F f. L (*texo text-* weave)]

textbook **1** *n.* book for use in studying, esp. standard account of subject. **2** *a.* exemplary, accurate; instructively typical.

textile /'tekstaɪl/ **1** *n.* woven material. **2** *a.* of weaving (*textile industry*); woven (*textile fabrics*). [L (TEXT)]

textual /'tekstjʊəl/ *a.* of or in or concerning a text; **textually** *adv.* [med.L (TEXT)]

texture /'tekstʃə/ *n.* quality of a surface or substance when felt or looked at; arrangement of threads in textile fabric; **textural** *a.*; **texturally** *adv.* [L (TEXT)]

-th *suffix* (**-eth** after *-ty*) added to simple numbers from *four* onwards to form ordinal and fractional numbers. [OE]

Th *symb.* thorium.

Thai /taɪ/ **1** *n.* native or language of Thailand. **2** *a.* of Thailand. [Thai, = free]

thalidomide /θə'lɪdəmaɪd/ *n.* sedative drug found in 1961 to cause malformation of limbs of embryo when taken by mother early in pregnancy. [ph*thali*mi-do*glutarimide*]

thallium /'θælɪəm/ *n.* rare soft white metallic element. [Gk *thallos* green shoot]

than /ðən, *emphat.* ðæn/ *conj.* introducing second element in comparison (*you are taller than he, than he is*; *we like you better than her*), or statement of difference (*anyone other than me*). [OE, orig. = THEN]

thane *n. hist.* one who held land from English king or other superior by military service; *hist.* one who held land from Scottish king and ranked below earl, clan-chief. [OE]

thank **1** *v.t.* express gratitude to (person *for* thing); hold responsible (*you can thank yourself for that*). **2** *n.* (in *pl.*) gratitude, expression of gratitude, (as formula) thank you (*thanks very much*).

3 thank goodness (or **heavens** etc.) *colloq.* expressions of relief etc.; **thank you** polite formula acknowledging gift or service etc. [OE]

thankful *a.* grateful, pleased; expressive of thanks; **thankfully** *adv.*

thankless *a.* not expressing or deserving thanks; (of task etc.) giving no pleasure or profit.

thanksgiving *n.* expression of gratitude, esp. to God; **Thanksgiving (Day)** fourth Thursday in Nov. in US.

that /ðət, *emphat.* ðæt/ **1** *pron.* (*pl.* **those** /ðəʊz/) the person or thing indicated or named or understood (*who is that?*; *I heard that*); coupled or contrasted with *this* (*would you like this or that?*); the one, the person, etc. (*a doll like that in the window*); used to introduce defining clause instead of *which* or *whom* (*the book that I sent you*; *the man that I saw*). **2** *a.* (*pl.* **those**) designating the person or thing indicated etc. (in use as for the *pron.*). **3** *adv.* to such a degree, so (*have done that much*). **4** *conj.* introducing subordinate clause indicating esp. statement or hypothesis (*he said that I was crazy*), purpose (*he lives that he may eat*), or result (*am so sleepy that I cannot keep my eyes open*). **5 all that** very (*not all that good*); **that's that** that is settled or finished. [OE]

thatch 1 *n.* roofing of straw or reeds or similar material; *colloq.* hair of the head. **2** *v.t.* roof with thatch. [OE]

thaw 1 *v.* release or escape from frozen state, warm into liquid state or into life or animation or cordiality. **2** *n.* thawing; warmth of weather that thaws. [OE]

the /*before vowel* ðɪ; *before consonant* ðə; *emphat.* ðiː/ **1** *a.* serving to particularize as needing no further identification (*have you seen the newspaper?*), to describe as unique (*the Queen*; *the Thames*), to assist in defining with adjective (*Alfred the Great*) or (stressed) distinguish as the best-known (*do you mean the Kipling?*), to indicate following defining clause or phrase (*the horse you mention*); to confer generic or representative or distributive value on (*the cat loves comfort*; *the stage*; *5p in the pound*); or to precede adjective used *absol.* (*nothing but the best*). **2** *adv.* (preceding comparatives in expressions of proportional variation) in or by that (or such) degree, on that account (*the more the merrier*; *am not the more inclined to help him because he is poor*). [OE]

theatre /'θɪətə/, *US* **theater** *n.* building or outdoor area for dramatic performances; writing and production of plays; room or hall for lectures etc. with seats in tiers; operating-theatre; scene or field of action (*the theatre of war*); **theatre weapons** weapons intermediate between tactical and strategic. [F or L f. Gk *theatron*]

theatrical /θɪ'ætrɪk(ə)l/ **1** *a.* of or for theatre or acting; (of person or manner etc.) calculated for effect, showy. **2** *n.* (in *pl.*) dramatic performances (esp. *amateur theatricals*). **3 theatricality** /-'kælɪtɪ/ *n.*; **theatrically** *adv.* [L f. Gk (prec.)]

thee /ðiː/ *pron.* obj. case of THOU. [OE]

theft *n.* stealing; act or instance of this. [OE (THIEF)]

their /ðeə/ *poss. a.* of or belonging to them. [ON]

theirs *poss. pron.* of or belonging to them, the thing(s) belonging to them (*it is theirs*; *theirs are best*; *a friend of theirs*).

theism /'θiːɪz(ə)m/ *n.* belief in divine creation and conduct of the universe without denial of revelation as in deism; **theist** *n.*; **theistic** /-'ɪstɪk/ *a.*; **theistically** /-'ɪstɪkəlɪ/ *adv.* [Gk *theos* god]

them /ð(ə)m, *emphat.* ðem/ **1** *pron.* obj. case of THEY; *colloq.* = THEY (*it's them all right*). **2** *a. vulgar* those. [ON]

theme *n.* subject or topic (*of* talk etc.); *Mus.* dominating melody in a composition; *US* school exercise on given subject; **theme song** (or **tune**) recurrent melody in musical play or film, signature tune; **thematic** /θɪ'mætɪk/ *a.*; **thematically** /θɪ'mætɪkəlɪ/ *adv.* [L f. Gk *thema -mat-*]

themselves /ðəm'selvz/ *pron.* emphat. & refl. form of THEY and THEM (for uses cf. HERSELF, ITSELF). [THEM, SELF]

then /ðen/ **1** *adv.* at that time; next, after that, and also; in that case (*then you should have told me*); used to imply grudging or impatient concession (*all right then, have it your own way*), or to resume a narrative etc. (*the policeman, then, knocked on the door*). **2** *a.* existing at that time (*the then Duke*). **3** *n.* that time (*before*, *until*, etc., *then*). **4 then and there** immediately and on the spot. [OE]

thence /ðens/ *adv.* from that place; for that reason. [OE]

thenceforth /ðens'fɔːθ/ *adv.* (also **thenceforward**) from that time on.

theo- *in comb.* God or god. [Gk (*theos* god)]

theocracy /θɪ'ɒkrəsɪ/ *n.* form of government by God or god directly or through a priestly order etc.; **theocratic** /θɪə'krætɪk/ *a.*; **theocratically** /θɪə'krætɪkəlɪ/ *adv.*

theodolite /θɪ'ɒdəlaɪt/ *n.* surveying-instrument for measuring horizontal and vertical angles with rotating telescope. [orig. unkn.]

theologian /θi:ə'ləʊdʒɪən/ *n.* expert in theology. [F (foll.)]

theology /θɪ'ɒlədʒɪ/ *n.* study or system of (esp. Christian) religion; **theological** /θi:ə'lɒdʒɪk(ə)l/ *a.* [F f. L f. Gk (THEO-)]

theorem /'θɪərəm/ *n.* general proposition not self-evident but demonstrable by argument, esp. in mathematics; rule in algebra etc., esp. one expressed by symbols or formulae. [F or L f. Gk (*theōreō* look at)]

theoretical /θɪə'retɪk(ə)l/ *a.* concerned with knowledge but not with its practical application; based on theory rather than experience; **theoretically** *adv.* [L f. Gk (THEORY)]

theoretician /θɪərɪ'tɪʃ(ə)n/ *n.* person concerned with theoretical part of a subject.

theorist /'θɪərɪst/ *n.* holder or inventor of a theory. [THEORY]

theorize /'θɪəraɪz/ *v.i.* evolve or indulge in theories.

theory /'θɪərɪ/ *n.* supposition or system of ideas explaining something, esp. one based on general principles independent of particular things to be explained (*atomic theory*; *theory of evolution*); speculative (esp. fanciful) view (*one of my pet theories*); sphere of abstract knowledge or speculative thought (*this is all very well in theory*); exposition of principles of a science etc. (*the theory of music*); collection of propositions to illustrate principles of a branch of mathematics (*probability theory*). [L f. Gk (THEOREM)]

theosophy /θɪ'ɒsəfɪ/ *n.* any of various philosophies professing to achieve knowledge of God by spiritual ecstasy, direct intuition, or special individual relations, esp. one following Hindu and Buddhist teachings and seeking universal brotherhood; **theosophical** /θɪə'sɒfɪk(ə)l/ *a.*; **theosophist** *n.* [med.L f. Gk (*theosophos* wise concerning God)]

therapeutic /θerə'pju:tɪk/ *a.* of or for or contributing to the cure of disease; **therapeutically** *adv.* [F or L f. Gk (*therapeuō* wait on, cure)]

therapeutics *n.pl.* (usu. treated as *sing.*) branch of medicine concerned with treatment and remedying of ill health.

therapy /'θerəpɪ/ *n.* curative medical treatment; **therapist** *n.* [Gk *therapeia* healing]

there /ðeə/ **1** *adv.* in or at or to that place or position (*put it there*; *go over there*); at that point (in speech, performance, writing, etc.); in that respect (*I agree with you there*); used for emphasis in calling attention (*hello there!*); used as introductory word, usu. with *be*, indicating fact or existence of something (*there was much to see*). **2** *n.* that place (*lives near there*; *the tide comes up to there*). **3** *int.* expressing confirmation, satisfaction, reassurance, etc. [OE]

thereabouts /'ðeərəbaʊts/ *adv.* (also **thereabout**) near that place; near that number or quantity etc.

thereafter /ðeər'ɑ:ftə/ *adv. formal* after that.

thereby /ðeə'baɪ/ *adv.* by that means, as a result of that; **thereby hangs a tale** much could be said about that.

therefore /'ðeəfɔ:/ *adv.* for that reason, accordingly, consequently.

therein /ðeər'ɪn/ *adv. formal* in that place etc.; in that respect.

thereof /ðeər'ɒv/ *adv. formal* of that or it.

thereto /ðeə'tu:/ *adv. formal* to that or it; in addition.

thereupon /ðeərə'pɒn/ *adv.* in consequence of that; soon or immediately after that.

therm *n.* unit of heat, esp. statutory unit of calorific value in gas-supply (100,000 British thermal units). [Gk *thermē* heat]

thermal 1 *a.* of or for or producing heat. **2** *n.* rising current of heated air (used by gliders to gain height). **3 thermal unit** unit for measuring heat (**British thermal unit** amount of heat needed to raise 1 lb. of water 1°F). **4 thermally** *adv.* [F (prec.)]

thermionic valve /θɜ:mɪ'ɒnɪk/ device giving flow of electrons in one direction from heated substance, used esp. in rectification of current and in radio reception. [THERMO-, ION]

thermo- *in comb.* heat. [Gk]

thermocouple /'θɜ:məkʌp(ə)l/ *n.* device for measuring temperatures by means of the thermoelectric voltage developing between two pieces of wire of different metals joined to each other at each end.

thermodynamics /θɜ:mədaɪ'næmɪks/ *n.pl.* (usu. treated as *sing.*) science of relations between heat and other forms of energy.

thermoelectric /θɜ:məʊɪ'lektrɪk/ *a.* producing electricity by difference of temperatures.

thermometer /θə'mɒmɪtə/ *n.* instrument for measuring temperature, esp. graduated narrow glass tube containing mercury or alcohol. [F (THERMO-, -METER)]

thermonuclear /θɜ:məʊ'nju:klɪə/ *a.* relating to nuclear reactions that occur only at very high temperatures; (of bomb etc.) using such reactions. [THERMO-]

thermoplastic /θɜ:məʊ'plæstɪk/ **1** *a.*

becoming plastic on heating and hardening on cooling. **2** *n.* thermoplastic substance.

Thermos /ˈθɜːmɒs/ *n.* (**P**) vacuum flask (*Thermos flask*). [Gk *thermos* hot]

thermosetting /θɜːməʊˈsetɪŋ/ *a.* (of plastics) setting permanently when heated. [THERMO-]

thermostat /ˈθɜːməstæt/ *n.* device for automatic regulation of temperature; **thermostatic** /-ˈstætɪk/ *a.*; **thermostatically** /-ˈstætɪkəlɪ/ *adv.* [THERMO-, Gk *statos* standing]

thesaurus /θɪˈsɔːrəs/ *n.* (*pl.* **thesauri** /-aɪ/) dictionary or encyclopaedia; list of words or concepts arranged according to sense. [L f. Gk (TREASURE)]

these *pl.* of THIS.

thesis /ˈθiːsɪs/ *n.* (*pl.* **theses** /-iːz/) proposition to be maintained or proved; dissertation, esp. by candidate for degree. [L f. Gk, = putting]

Thespian /ˈθespɪən/ **1** *a.* of tragedy or drama. **2** *n.* actor or actress. [*Thespis*, Greek tragedian]

theta /ˈθiːtə/ *n.* eighth letter of Greek alphabet (Θ, θ). [Gk]

thews /θjuːz/ *n.pl. literary* person's muscular strength. [OE, = habit]

they /ðeɪ/ *pron.* (*obj.* THEM; *poss.* THEIR, THEIRS) *pl.* of HE, SHE, IT[1]; people in general (*they say*); those in authority (*they have raised the fees*). [ON]

thick 1 *a.* of great or specified depth between opposite surfaces; (of line etc.) broad, not fine; arranged closely, crowded together, dense; densely covered or filled (*air thick with snow*); firm in consistency, containing much solid matter, made of thick material (*a thick coat*); muddy, cloudy, impenetrable by sight; *colloq.* stupid, dull; (of voice) indistinct; *colloq.* intimate, very friendly. **2** *n.* thick part of anything. **3** *adv.* thickly (*snow was falling thick*). **4 a bit thick** *sl.* unreasonable, intolerable; **in the thick of it** in the busiest part of an activity or fight etc.; **thick-headed** stupid; **thick-skinned** not sensitive to reproach or criticism; **through thick and thin** under all conditions, in spite of all difficulties. [OE]

thicken *v.* make or become thick or thicker; become more complicated (*the plot thickens*).

thickening *n.* becoming thick or thicker; thickened part; substance used to thicken gravy.

thicket /ˈθɪkɪt/ *n.* tangle of shrubs or trees. [OE (THICK)]

thickness *n.* being thick; extent to which thing is thick; layer of material of known thickness (*three thicknesses of cardboard*).

thickset *a.* set or growing closely together; heavily or solidly built.

thief *n.* (*pl.* **thieves** /θiːvz/) one who steals esp. secretly and without violence. [OE]

thieve *v.* be a thief; steal (thing). [OE (prec.)]

thievery *n.* stealing. [THIEF]

thievish *a.* given to stealing.

thigh /θaɪ/ *n.* part of leg between hip and knee. [OE]

thimble *n.* metal or plastic cap, usu. with closed end, worn to protect finger and push needle in sewing. [OE (THUMB)]

thimbleful *n.* (*pl.* **thimblefuls**) small quantity, esp. of liquid to drink.

thin 1 *a.* having opposite surfaces close together, of small thickness or diameter; (of line) narrow, fine; made of thin material (*a thin dress*); lean, not plump; not dense or copious (*thin haze, hair*); of slight consistency; weak, lacking an important ingredient (*thin blood, voice*); (of excuse etc.) flimsy, transparent. **2** *adv.* thinly (*cut the bread very thin*). **3** *v.* (**-nn-**) make or become thin or thinner. **4 have a thin time** *sl.* have a wretched or uncomfortable time; **thin on the ground** few in number, rare; **thin on top** balding; **thin out** make or become fewer or less crowded; **thin-skinned** sensitive to reproach or criticism. **5 thinness** *n.* [OE]

thine /ðaɪn/ *archaic* **1** *poss. pron.* of or belonging to thee, the thing(s) belonging to thee. **2** *poss. a.* form of THY before vowel. [OE]

thing *n.* whatever is or may be thought about or perceived; an inanimate material object (*take that thing away*); unspecified object or item (*a few things to buy*); an act or idea or utterance (*a silly thing to do, think, say*); an event (*an unfortunate thing to happen*); a quality (*patience is a useful thing*); (with ref. to a person) expressing pity or contempt or affection (*poor thing!*; *a dear old thing*); specimen or type of something (*the latest thing in hats*); one's special interest or concern (*not my thing at all*); *colloq.* something remarkable (*now there's a thing!*); (in *pl.*) personal belongings or clothing (*where have I left my things?*), equipment (*painting things*); (in *pl.*) affairs in general (*not in the nature of things*), circumstances or conditions (*things look good*); (with following adjective) all that is so describable (*things Greek*); **the thing** what is conventionally proper or fashionable, what is needed or required or to be considered (*the thing is, shall we go or not?*); **do one's own thing** *colloq.* pursue one's own interests or inclinations; **have**

a thing about *colloq.* be obsessed or prejudiced about; **make a thing of** regard as essential, cause a fuss about. [OE]

thingummy /ˈθɪŋəmɪ/ *n.* (also **thingumajig** etc.) *colloq.* person or thing whose name one has forgotten or does not know.

think 1 *v.* (*past* and *p.p.* **thought** /θɔːt/) be of the opinion (*we think he will come*); judge or consider (*is thought to be a fraud*); exercise the mind (*let me think for a moment*); (with *of* or *about*) consider, be or become aware of, form or entertain the idea of, imagine to oneself; have half-formed intention (*I think I'll stay*); form conception of; reduce to specified condition by thinking (*cannot think away a toothache*); recognize presence or existence of (*child thought no harm*). **2** *n. colloq.* act of thinking (*let me have a think*). **3 think again** revise one's plans or opinions; **think aloud** utter one's thoughts as soon as they occur; **think better of** change one's mind about (intention) after reconsideration; **think little** (or **nothing**) **of** consider insignificant; **think much** (or **well** or **highly** etc.) **of** have a high opinion of; **think out** consider carefully, produce (idea etc.) by thinking; **think over** reflect upon in order to reach decision; **think through** reflect fully upon (problem etc.); **think twice** use careful consideration, avoid hasty action etc.; **think up** *colloq.* devise, produce by thought. [OE]

thinker *n.* one who thinks, esp. in specified way (*an original thinker*); person with skilled or powerful mind.

thinking 1 *a.* using thought or rational judgement. **2** *n.* opinion or judgement.

think-tank *n.* body of experts providing advice and ideas on national and commercial problems.

thinner *n.* volatile liquid used to make paint etc. thinner. [THIN]

thiosulphate /θaɪəˈsʌlfeɪt/ *n.* sulphate in which some oxygen is replaced by sulphur. [Gk *theion* sulphur]

third *a.* & *n.* next after second; one of three equal parts of thing; **third degree** long and severe questioning esp. by police to obtain information or a confession; **third man** fielder in cricket near boundary behind slips; **third party** another party besides the two principals, bystander etc.; **third-party** *a.* (of insurance) covering damage or injury suffered by person other than the insured; **third person** third party, *Gram.* see PERSON; **third-rate** inferior, very poor; **Third Reich** see REICH; **Third World** underdeveloped countries of Asia, Africa, and Latin America; **thirdly** *adv.* [OE (THREE)]

thirst 1 *n.* desire for a drink; suffering caused by lack of drink; strong desire or craving. **2** *v.i.* feel thirst, have strong desire (*for* or *after*). [OE]

thirsty *a.* feeling thirst; (of country or season) dry, parched; eager (*for* or *after*); *colloq.* causing thirst (*thirsty work*); **thirstily** *adv.*; **thirstiness** *n.* [OE (prec.)]

thirteen /θɜːˈtiːn/ *a.* & *n.* one more than twelve; symbol for this (13, xiii, XIII); size etc. denoted by thirteen; **thirteenth** *a.* & *n.* [OE (THREE)]

thirty /ˈθɜːtɪ/ *a.* & *n.* three times ten; symbol for this (30, xxx, XXX); (in *pl.*) numbers, years, degrees of temperature, from 30 to 39; **Thirty-nine Articles** statements assented to by those taking orders in Church of England; **thirtieth** *a.* & *n.* [OE (THREE)]

this /ðɪs/ **1** *pron.* (*pl.* **these** /ðiːz/) the person or thing close at hand or indicated or already named or understood (*can you see this?*; *this is Mr. Brown*); (contrasted with *that*) the person or thing nearer to hand or more immediately in mind. **2** *a.* (*pl.* **these**) designating the person or thing close at hand etc. (in use as for the *pron.*); (of time) the present or current (*I am busy all this week*); *colloq.* (in narrative) a previously unspecified (*then up comes this policeman*). **3** *adv.* to this degree or extent (*knew him when he was this high*; *did not reach this far*). **4 this and that** various ones, various things. [OE]

thistle /ˈθɪs(ə)l/ *n.* prickly herbaceous plant usu. with globular heads of purple flowers; this as Scottish national emblem. [OE]

thistledown *n.* light fluffy stuff containing thistle-seeds and blown about in the wind. [DOWN[2]]

thistly *a.* overgrown with thistles. [THISTLE]

thither /ˈðɪðə/ *adv. archaic* to or towards that place. [OE]

thole *n.* (in full **thole-pin**) pin in gunwale of boat as fulcrum for oar; each of two such pins forming rowlock. [OE]

thong *n.* narrow strip of hide or leather. [OE]

thorax /ˈθɔːræks/ *n.* (*pl.* **thoraces** /-rəsiːz/) part of the body between neck and abdomen; **thoracic** /-ˈræsɪk/ *a.* [L f. Gk]

thorium /ˈθɔːrɪəm/ *n.* radioactive metallic element. [*Thor*, Scand. god of thunder]

thorn *n.* stiff sharp-pointed projection on plant; thorn-bearing shrub or tree; **a thorn in one's flesh** (or **side**) a constant annoyance. [OE]

thorny *a.* abounding in thorns; (of subject) hard to handle without offence; **thornily** *adv.*; **thorniness** *n.* [OE (prec.)]

thorough /'θʌrə/ *a.* complete and unqualified, not merely superficial, acting or done with great care and completeness; absolute (*a thorough rogue*). [THROUGH]

thoroughbred 1 *a.* of pure breed; high-spirited. 2 *n.* thoroughbred animal, esp. horse.

thoroughfare *n.* road or path open at both ends esp. for traffic.

thoroughgoing *a.* uncompromising, extreme.

those *pl.* of THAT.

thou /ðaʊ/ *pron.* of second person singular: now replaced by YOU except in some formal, liturgical, and poetic uses. [OE]

though /ðəʊ/ 1 *conj.* despite the fact that (*though it was early we went to bed*; ellipt. *though annoyed, I agreed*); even supposing that (*ask him though he may refuse*); and yet, nevertheless. 2 *adv.* however, all the same. [ON]

thought¹ /θɔ:t/ *n.* process or power or manner of thinking, faculty of reason; way of thinking associated with a particular time or people etc.; sober reflection, consideration (*gave it much thought*); idea or reasoning produced by thinking; intention (*had no thought of resigning*); (usu. in *pl.*) what one is thinking, one's opinion; **a thought** somewhat (*a thought more careful*); **in thought** meditating; **thought-reader** person supposedly able to perceive another's thoughts. [OE (THINK)]

thought² *past* and *p.p.* of THINK.

thoughtful *a.* engaged in or given to meditation; (of book or writer etc.) giving signs of careful thought; (of person or conduct) considerate; **thoughtfully** *adv.* [THOUGHT¹]

thoughtless *a.* careless of consequences or of others' feelings; caused by lack of thought.

thousand /'θaʊzənd/ *a.* & *n.* ten hundred (*a*, *one*, *six*, etc., *thousand*); symbol for this (1,000, m, M); (in *pl.* **thousands**) very many; **thousandth** *a.* & *n.* [OE]

thousandfold *a.* & *adv.* a thousand times as much or as many; consisting of a thousand parts.

thraldom /'θrɔ:ldəm/ *n.* bondage. [foll.]

thrall /θrɔ:l/ *n.* slave (*of* or *to* a person or thing); slavery (*in thrall*). [OE f. ON]

thrash *v.* beat severely with stick or whip; defeat thoroughly in a contest; thresh (corn etc.); act like flail, deliver repeated blows; move violently *about* or *around*; **thrash out** discuss to conclusion. [OE]

thread /θred/ 1 *n.* spun-out cotton or silk or glass etc., yarn; length of this; thin cord of twisted yarns used esp. in sewing and weaving; anything regarded as threadlike with ref. to its continuity or connectedness (*the thread of life, of an argument*); spiral ridge of screw. 2 *v.t.* pass thread through eye of (needle); put (beads) on thread; arrange (material in strip form, e.g. film) in proper position on equipment; pick one's way through (maze, crowded place, etc.); make (one's way) thus. [OE (THROW)]

threadbare *a.* (of cloth) so worn that nap is lost and threads are visible; (of person) wearing such clothes; hackneyed.

threadworm *n.* small threadlike worm infesting intestines.

threat /θret/ *n.* declaration of intention to punish or hurt; indication of something undesirable coming (*there is a threat of rain*); person or thing as likely cause of harm etc. [OE]

threaten *v.t.* make threat(s) against; be sign or indication of (something undesirable); announce one's intention (*to do* undesirable or unexpected thing); give warning of infliction of (harm etc., or *absol.*). [OE]

three *a.* & *n.* one more than two; symbol for this (3, iii, III); size etc. denoted by three; **three-cornered** triangular, (of contest etc.) between three parties each for himself; **three-decker** warship with three gun-decks, sandwich with three slices of bread, three-volume novel; **three-dimensional** having or appearing to have length, breadth, and depth; **three-legged race** race between pairs with right leg of one tied to other's left leg; **three-ply** *n.* & *a.* (wool etc.) having three strands, (plywood) having three layers; **three-point turn** method of turning vehicle round in narrow space by moving forwards, backwards, and forwards; **three-quarter** any of three or four players just behind half-backs in Rugby football; **three-quarters** three parts out of four; **three Rs** see R; **three-way** involving three ways or participants. [OE]

threefold *a.* & *adv.* three times as much or as many; consisting of three parts.

threepence /'θrepəns/ *n.* sum of three pence.

threepenny /'θrepənɪ/ *a.* costing or worth three pence; **threepenny bit** former coin worth 3d.

threescore *n.* *archaic* sixty.

threesome *n.* group of three persons.

threnody /'θrenədɪ/ *n.* song of lamentation esp. on person's death. [Gk]
thresh *v.* beat out or separate grain from (corn etc.); move violently *about* or *around*; **threshing-floor** hard level floor for threshing esp. with flails. [OE]
threshold /'θreʃəʊld/ *n.* strip of wood or stone forming bottom of doorway and crossed in entering house etc.; point of entry or beginning; limit below which stimulus causes no reaction. [OE (THRASH in sense 'tread')]
threw *past* of THROW.
thrice *adv. archaic* three times; (esp. in *comb.*) highly (*thrice-blessed*). [THREE]
thrift *n.* frugality, economical management; the sea-pink. [ON (THRIVE)]
thriftless *a.* wasteful.
thrifty *a.* economical; **thriftily** *adv.*; **thriftiness** *n.*
thrill 1 *n.* wave or nervous tremor of emotion or sensation (*a thrill of joy, of recognition*); throb, pulsation. **2** *v.* (cause to) feel thrill; quiver or throb (as) with emotion. [OE, = pierce, rel. to THROUGH]
thriller *n.* exciting or sensational story or play etc., esp. one involving crime or espionage.
thrips *n.* a kind of small insect harmful to plants. [L f. Gk, = woodworm]
thrive *v.i.* (*past* **throve** or **thrived;** *p.p.* **thriven** /'θrɪv(ə)n/ or **thrived**) prosper, flourish; grow rich; (of animal or plant) grow vigorously. [ON]
throat *n.* windpipe, gullet; front part of neck containing this; narrow passage or entrance or exit; **cut one's own throat** bring about one's own downfall; **ram** (or **thrust**) **down a person's throat** force (thing) on his attention. [OE]
throaty *a.* (of voice) deficient in clarity, hoarsely resonant; **throatily** *adv.*; **throatiness** *n.*
throb 1 *v.i.* (**-bb-**) palpitate, pulsate esp. with more than usual force or rapidity; vibrate or quiver with persistent rhythm or with emotion. **2** *n.* throbbing; palpitation, (esp. violent) pulsation. [imit.]
throe *n.* (usu. in *pl.*) violent pang, esp. of childbirth or death; **in the throes of** *colloq.* struggling with the task of. [OE, alt. of orig. *throwe* perh. by assoc. w. *woe*]
thrombosis /θrɒm'bəʊsɪs/ *n.* (*pl.* **thromboses** /-i:z/) coagulation of blood in blood-vessel or organ during life; **thrombotic** /-'bɒtɪk/ *a.* [Gk, = curdling]
throne 1 *n.* chair of State for sovereign or bishop etc.; sovereign power (*came to the throne*). **2** *v.t.* enthrone. [F f. L f. Gk]
throng 1 *n.* crowd of people; multitude (*of* people or things) esp. in small space. **2** *v.* come in great numbers; flock into or crowd round or fill (as) with crowd. [OE]
throstle /'θrɒs(ə)l/ *n.* song-thrush. [OE]
throttle /'θrɒt(ə)l/ **1** *n.* valve controlling flow of fuel or steam etc. in engine; lever or pedal operating this valve; throat, gullet, windpipe. **2** *v.t.* choke, strangle; prevent utterance etc. of; control (engine or steam etc.) with throttle. **3 throttle back** (or **down**) reduce speed of (engine or vehicle) by throttling. [prob. THROAT]
through /θru:/ **1** *prep.* from end to end or side to side of, going in one side or end and out the other of; between or among (*swam through the waves*); from beginning to end of (*read through the letter*; *went through many difficulties*); by reason or agency or means or fault of (*lost it through carelessness*); *US* up to and including (*Monday through Friday*). **2** *adv.* through a thing, from side to side or end to end or beginning to end; so as to be connected by telephone (*will put you through*). **3** *a.* (concerned with) going through, esp. of travel where whole journey is made without change of line or vehicle etc. or with one ticket; (of traffic) going through a place to its destination. **4 be through** have finished (*with*), cease to have dealings (*with*), have no further prospects; **through and through** thoroughly, completely. [OE]
throughout /θru:'aʊt/ **1** *prep.* right through, from end to end of. **2** *adv.* in every part or respect.
throughput *n.* amount of material put through a process, esp. in manufacturing or computing.
throve see THRIVE.
throw /θrəʊ/ **1** *v.* (*past* **threw** /θru:/; *p.p.* **thrown**) propel with some force through the air or in a particular direction; force violently into specified position or state (*ship was thrown on the rocks*; *threw himself down*); compel to be in specified condition (*was thrown out of work*); turn or move (part of the body) quickly or suddenly (*threw her arm out*); project or cast (light, a shadow, a spell, etc.); bring to the ground in wrestling, (of horse) unseat (rider); *colloq.* disconcert (*the question threw me for a moment*); put (clothes etc.) carelessly or hastily *on* or *off* etc.; cause (dice) to fall on table, obtain (specified number) thus; cause to pass or extend suddenly to another state or position (*threw in the army*; *threw a bridge across the river*); move (switch or lever) so as to operate it; shape (round pottery) on wheel; have (fit or tantrum etc.); *sl.* give (a party); *US* lose (contest or race etc.) intentionally.

2 *n.* act of throwing; distance thing is or may be thrown; being thrown in wrestling. **3 throw away** part with as useless or unwanted, waste or fail to make use of (opportunity etc.); **throw-away** *a.* meant to be thrown away after use; **throw back** revert to ancestral character, (usu. in *pass.*) compel to rely *on*; **throw-back** *n.* reversion to ancestral character, instance of this; **throw in** interpose (word or remark), include at no extra cost, throw (football) from edge of pitch where it has gone out of play; **throw off** discard, contrive to get rid of, write or utter in offhand manner; **throw oneself at** energetically seek friendship or love of; **throw oneself into** engage vigorously in; **throw oneself on** (or **upon**) rely completely on; **throw open** cause to be suddenly or widely open, make accessible (*to*); **throw out** put out forcibly or suddenly, throw away, reject (proposal etc.), confuse or distract (person); **throw over** desert, abandon; **throw together** assemble hastily, bring into casual contact; **throw up** abandon, resign from, vomit, erect hastily, bring to notice. [OE, = twist]

thru *US* var. of THROUGH.

thrum[1] **1** *v.* (**-mm-**) play (stringed instrument) monotonously or unskilfully; drum or tap idly (on). **2** *n.* such playing; resulting sound. [imit.]

thrum[2] *n.* unwoven end of warp-thread, or the whole of such ends, left when finished web is cut away; any short loose thread. [OE]

thrush[1] *n.* kind of small bird, e.g. blackbird, nightingale, or esp. song-thrush or missel-thrush. [OE]

thrush[2] *n.* fungoid infection of throat esp. in children, or of vagina. [orig. unkn.]

thrust 1 *v.* (*past* and *p.p.* **thrust**) push with sudden impulse or with force; impose (thing) forcibly *on*, enforce acceptance of (thing) *on*; pierce or stab, make sudden lunge *at*; make (one's way) forcibly. **2** *n.* sudden or forcible push or lunge; forward force exerted by propeller or jet etc.; strong attempt to penetrate enemy's line or territory; remark aimed at a person; stress between parts of arch etc.; chief theme, gist (*of* remarks etc.). **3 thrust oneself** (or **one's nose**) **in** obtrude, interfere. [ON]

thud 1 *n.* low dull sound as of blow on non-resonant thing. **2** *v.i.* (**-dd-**) make thud; fall with thud. [prob. OE]

thug *n.* vicious or brutal ruffian; (**Thug**) *hist.* member of religious organization of robbers and assassins in India; **thuggery** *n.* [Hindi]

thulium /'θu:lɪəm/ *n.* metallic element of lanthanide series. [L *Thule* remote northern region]

thumb /θʌm/ **1** *n.* short thick finger set apart from the other four; part of glove for thumb. **2** *v.* wear or soil (pages etc.) with thumb (*a well-thumbed novel*); turn over pages with or as with thumb (*thumbed through the directory*); request or get (lift in passing vehicle) by indicating desired direction with thumb; use thumb in gesture. **3 thumb-index** set of lettered grooves cut down side of dictionary etc. to assist use; **thumb-nail sketch** brief verbal description; **thumb one's nose** cock a snook (*at*); **thumbs down** gesture of rejection; **thumbs up** gesture or exclamation of satisfaction; **under a person's thumb** completely dominated by him. [OE]

thumbscrew *n.* instrument of torture for squeezing thumbs.

thump 1 *v.* beat or strike heavily esp. with fist; deliver blows *at* or *on* etc. **2** *n.* heavy blow; sound of this. [imit.]

thumping *a. colloq.* big (*a thumping majority*, *lie*, etc.).

thunder 1 *n.* loud noise heard after lightning and due to disturbance of air by discharge of electricity; resounding loud deep noise (*thunders of applause*); (in *sing.* or *pl.*) authoritative censure or threats. **2** *v.* give forth thunder (esp. *it thunders*, *is thundering*); make noise like thunder; move with loud noise; make violent threats etc. *against* etc.; utter (threats etc.) loudly. **3 steal person's thunder** forestall him by using his own words before he can; **thunder-cloud** storm-cloud charged with electricity and producing thunder and lightning. [OE]

thunderbolt *n.* flash of lightning with crash of thunder; supposed bolt or shaft as destructive agent esp. as attribute of god. [BOLT[1]]

thunderclap *n.* crash of thunder; sudden terrible event or news. [CLAP[1]]

thundering *a. colloq.* very big or great. [THUNDER]

thunderous *a.* like thunder; very loud.

thunderstorm *n.* storm with thunder and lightning and usu. heavy rain or hail.

thunderstruck *a.* amazed.

thundery *a.* (of weather etc.) oppressive.

thurible /'θjʊərɪb(ə)l/ *n.* censer. [F or L (*thus thur-* incense)]

Thur(s). *abbr.* Thursday.

Thursday /'θɜ:zdeɪ/ **1** *n.* day of week following Wednesday. **2** *adv. colloq.* on Thursday. **3 Thursdays** on Thursdays, each Thursday. [OE]

thus /ðʌs/ *adv. formal* in this way;

accordingly, as a result or inference; to this extent, so (*thus far*; *thus much*). [OE]

thwack 1 *v.t.* hit with heavy blow. **2** *n.* heavy blow. [imit.]

thwart /θwɔːt/ **1** *v.t.* frustrate or foil (person or purpose etc.) **2** *n.* rower's seat. [ON, = across]

thy /ðaɪ/ *poss. a.* of or belonging to thee: now replaced by YOUR except in some formal, liturgical, and poetic uses. [THINE]

thyme /taɪm/ *n.* any of several herbs with fragrant aromatic leaves. [F f. L f. Gk]

thymol /'θaɪmɒl/ *n.* antiseptic made from oil of thyme.

thymus /'θaɪməs/ *n.* lymphoid organ near base of neck. [Gk]

thyroid /'θaɪrɔɪd/ *n.* thyroid gland; **thyroid cartilage** large cartilage of larynx, projection of which in man forms Adam's apple; **thyroid gland** large ductless gland near larynx secreting a hormone which regulates growth and development, extract from this gland of animals used in treating goitre etc. [F or Gk (*thureos* oblong shield)]

thyself *pron.* emphat. & refl. form of THOU and THEE: now replaced in general use by YOURSELF (cf. at THOU). [THY]

ti var. of TE.

Ti *symb.* titanium.

tiara /tɪ'ɑːrə/ *n.* jewelled ornamental band worn on front of woman's hair; Pope's three-crowned diadem; **tiaraed** *a.* [L f. Gk]

tibia /'tɪbɪə/ *n.* (*pl.* **tibiae** /-iː/) shinbone; **tibial** *a.* [L]

tic *n.* habitual spasmodic contraction of muscles esp. of face; kind of neuralgia. [F f. It.]

tick[1] **1** *n.* slight recurring click, esp. that of watch or clock; *colloq.* moment, instant; small mark set against items in list etc. in checking. **2** *v.* (of clock etc.) make ticks; mark (item, usu. *off*) with tick. **3 tick off** *sl.* reprimand; **tick over** (of engine or *fig.*) idle; **tick-tack** kind of manual semaphore signalling by racecourse bookmakers; **tick-tock** ticking of large clock etc.; **what makes a person tick** his motivation. [prob. imit.]

tick[2] *n.* parasitic arachnid or insect on animals. [OE]

tick[3] *n. colloq.* credit (*buy goods on tick*). [app. abbr. of TICKET in *on the ticket*]

tick[4] *n.* cover of mattress or pillow; ticking. [LG or Du., ult. f. Gk *thēkē* case]

ticker *n. colloq.* heart, watch, tape-machine; **ticker-tape** *US* paper strip from tape-machine; this or similar material thrown from windows to greet a celebrity. [TICK[1]]

ticket /'tɪkɪt/ **1** *n.* written or printed piece of paper or card entitling holder to enter place, participate in event, travel by public transport, etc. (*theatre, library, lottery, railway, cloakroom, -ticket*); certificate of discharge from army or of qualification as ship's master, pilot, etc.; label attached to thing and giving price etc.; official notification of traffic offence etc. (*parking ticket*); list of candidates put forward by one group, esp. political party; principles of a party. **2** *v.t.* attach ticket to. **3 the ticket** *sl.* the correct or desirable thing. [obs. F *étiquet*]

ticking *n.* stout usu. striped linen or cotton material to cover mattresses etc. [TICK[4]]

tickle /'tɪk(ə)l/ **1** *v.* apply light touches or stroking to (person or part of his body) so as to excite nerves and usu. produce laughter and spasmodic movement; feel this sensation; excite agreeably, amuse, divert. **2** *n.* act or sensation of tickling. **3 tickled pink** (or **to death**) *colloq.* extremely amused or pleased. [prob. dial. *tick* touch or tap lightly]

ticklish *a.* sensitive to tickling; (of matter or person to be dealt with) difficult, requiring careful handling.

tidal /'taɪd(ə)l/ *a.* of or due to or like or affected by the tide; **tidal wave** exceptionally large ocean wave (e.g. one caused by earthquake), widespread manifestation of feeling etc.; **tidally** *adv.* [TIDE]

tidbit *US* var. of TITBIT.

tiddler *n. colloq.* small fish, esp. stickleback or minnow; *colloq.* unusually small thing. [perh. rel. to *tiddly* 'little']

tiddly *a. sl.* slightly drunk. [orig. unkn.]

tiddly-wink /'tɪdlɪwɪŋk/ *n.* counter flicked by another into cup etc. on centre of table in game; **tiddly-winks** this game. [perh. rel. to prec.]

tide 1 *n.* regular rise and fall of sea due to attraction of moon and sun; water as moved by this; trend of opinion or fortune or events (*go with* or *against the tide*); time or season (*archaic* except in *noontide, Christmastide*, etc.). **2** *v.i.* be carried by the tide. **3 tide-mark** mark made by tide at high water, *colloq.* line of dirt round bath, or on body of person showing extent of washing; **tide person over** help him through temporary need or difficulty; **tide-table** list of times of high tide at a place; **turn the tide** reverse trend of events. [OE, = time]

tideway *n.* tidal part of river.

tidings /'taɪdɪŋz/ *n.* (as *sing.* or *pl.*) news. [OE, prob. f. ON]

tidy 1 *a.* neat, orderly, methodically arranged or inclined; *colloq.* considerable (*cost a tidy sum*). **2** *n.* receptacle for odds and ends; cover for chair-back etc. **3** *v.t.* put in good order, make (*oneself*, a room, etc.) tidy. **4 tidily** *adv.*; **tidiness** *n.* [TIDE; orig. = timely]

tie /taɪ/ **1** *v.* (*partic.* **tying**) attach or fasten with string or cord etc.; form (string, ribbon, shoe-lace, necktie, etc.) into knot or bow, form (knot or bow) thus; restrict or limit (person) in some way (*was tied to his work*); make same score as another competitor (*tied with her for second place*); bind (rafters etc.) by cross-piece etc.; *Mus.* unite notes by tie. **2** *n.* cord or chain etc. used for fastening; necktie; thing that unites or restricts persons (*family ties*; *ties of friendship*); equality of score or draw or dead heat among competitors; match between any pair of players or teams; rod or beam holding parts of structure together (also **tie-beam** etc.); *Mus.* curved line above or below two notes of same pitch that are to be joined as one. **3 tie-break** means of deciding winner when competitors have tied; **tied cottage** dwelling occupied subject to tenant's working for its owner; **tie-dye** method of producing dyed patterns by tying string etc. to protect parts of fabric from dye; **tie in** (or **up**) agree or be closely associated *with*, cause to do this; **tie-pin** ornamental pin holding tie in place; **tie up** bind or fasten with cord etc., invest or reserve (capital etc.) so that it is not immediately available for use, obstruct, (usu. in *pass.*) fully occupy (person). [OE]

tier *n.* row or rank or unit of structure, as one of several placed one above another (*tiers of seats*); **tiered** *a.* [F *tire* (*tirer* draw, elongate)]

tiercel var. of TERCEL.

tiff *n.* slight or petty quarrel. [orig. unkn.]

tiffin /'tɪfɪn/ *n.* (in India) lunch. [obs. *tiff* take small drink]

tiger /'taɪgə/ *n.* large Asian animal of cat family, with yellowish and black stripes; fierce or energetic or formidable person; **tiger-cat** any moderate-sized feline resembling tiger, e.g. ocelot; **tiger-lily** tall garden lily with dark-spotted orange flowers; **tiger-moth** moth with richly spotted and streaked wings. [F f. L f. Gk]

tight /taɪt/ **1** *a.* closely held or drawn or fastened or fitting or constructed (*tight knots*; *cork is too tight*; *tight joint, ship*); impermeable, impervious, esp. (in *comb.*) to specified thing (*airtight, watertight*); tense, stretched; *colloq.* drunk; (of money or materials) not easily obtainable; produced by or requiring great exertion or pressure (*a tight squeeze*); (of precautions, programme, etc.) stringent, demanding; *colloq.* presenting difficulties (*tight corner, place, spot*); *colloq.* stingy. **2** *adv.* tightly (*hold tight*; *tight fitting*). **3 tight-fisted** stingy; **tight-lipped** with lips compressed to restrain emotion or speech. [ON]

tighten *v.* make or become tighter.

tightrope *n.* rope stretched tightly high above ground, on which acrobats perform.

tights *n.pl.* thin close-fitting elastic garment covering legs and lower part of body, worn by women in place of stockings; similar garment worn by dancer, acrobat, etc. [TIGHT]

tigress /'taɪgrɪs/ *n.* female tiger. [TIGER]

tike var. of TYKE.

tilde /'tɪldə/ *n.* mark (~) put over letter, e.g. Spanish *n* when pronounced *ny* (as in *señor*). [Sp. f. L (TITLE)]

tile 1 *n.* thin slab of concrete or baked clay etc. used in series for covering roof or pavement etc.; similar slab of other material, e.g. cork, for covering floor etc.; thin flat piece used in game (esp. mah-jong). **2** *v.t.* cover with tiles. **3 on the tiles** *sl.* on a spree. [OE f. L *tegula*]

tiling *n.* process of fixing tiles; area of tiles.

till[1] **1** *prep.* up to or as late as (*wait till six o'clock*); up to the time of (*true till death*). **2** *conj.* up to the time when (*wait till I arrive*); so long that (*laughed till I cried*). [ON, rel. to TILL[3]]

till[2] *n.* drawer for money in shop or bank etc., esp. with device recording amount of each purchase. [orig. unkn.]

till[3] *v.t.* cultivate (land). [OE, = strive]

tillage *n.* preparation of land for crop-bearing; tilled land.

tiller *n.* bar by which rudder is turned. [AF *telier* weaver's beam]

tilt 1 *v.* (cause to) assume sloping position or heel over; strike or thrust or run *at* with weapon; engage in contest *with*. **2** *n.* tilting; sloping position; (of medieval knights etc.) charging with lance against opponent or at mark; attack esp. with argument or satire (*have a tilt at*). **3 (at) full tilt** at full speed, with full force. [OE, = unsteady]

tilth *n.* tillage, cultivation (*lit.* or *fig.*); tilled soil. [OE (TILL[3])]

timber *n.* wood prepared for building, carpentry, etc.; piece of wood, beam, esp. as rib of vessel; large standing trees; (esp. as *int.*) tree about to fall; **timber-line** line above which no trees grow. [OE, = building]

timbered *a.* made wholly or partly of timber; (of country) wooded.

timbre /tæ̃br,'tæmbə/ *n.* distinctive character of musical sound or voice apart from its pitch and intensity. [F f. Rmc f. Gk (TYMPANUM)]

timbrel /ˈtɪmbr(ə)l/ *n. archaic* tambourine.

time 1 *n.* indefinite continued existence of the universe in past, present, and future regarded as a whole; progress of this as affecting persons or things; portion of time belonging to particular events or circumstances (*in the time of Disraeli*; *in prehistoric times*); allotted or available portion of time (*had no time to discuss it*); point of time esp. in hours and minutes (*the time is 3.30*); time or amount of time as reckoned by conventional standards (*time allowed is one hour*; *7 a.m. local time*); occasion (*the only time I saw him*); expressing multiplication (*three times four is twelve*; *is three times as big as mine*); lifetime (*will last my time*); (in *sing.* or *pl.*) conditions of life or of a period (*hard times*; *went through a bad time*); prison sentence (*is doing time*); apprenticeship (*served his time*); period of gestation, date of childbirth or of death; measured time spent in work; *Mus.* duration of note, style of movement depending on beats in bar, rate of performance. **2** *v.t.* choose time for, do at chosen or correct time; arrange time of arrival of; ascertain time taken by. **3 against time** with utmost speed so as to finish by specified time; **ahead of time** earlier than expected; **all the time** during all the time. referred to (despite some contrary expectation etc.); **at one time** in a known but unspecified past period, simultaneously; **at the same time** simultaneously, nevertheless; **at times** intermittently; **behind the times** old-fashioned, antiquated; **for the time being** until some other arrangement is made; **from time to time** occasionally; **half the time** *colloq.* as often as not; **have a time of it** undergo trouble or difficulty; **have no time for** be unable or unwilling to spend time on, dislike; **in no time** very soon or quickly; **in time** not late, punctual, sooner or later, in accordance with time of music etc.; **keep time** move or sing etc. in time; **lose time** waste time; **on time** in accordance with timetable, punctual(ly); **pass the time of day** *colloq.* exchange greeting or casual remarks; **time after time** on many occasions, in many instances; **time and (time) again** on many occasions; **time and a half** rate of payment for work at 1½ times normal rate; **time-and-motion** concerned with measuring efficiency of industrial and other operations; **time bomb** bomb designed to explode at pre-set time; **time-clock** clock with device for recording workers' hours of work; **time exposure** exposure of photographic film for longer than an instant; **time-honoured** esteemed by tradition or custom; **time-lag** interval of time between cause and effect; **time-limit** limit of time within which thing must be done; **time of one's life** period of exceptional enjoyment; **time out of mind** from before anyone can remember; **time-server** one who, esp. for selfish ends, adapts himself to opinions of the time or of persons in power; **time-sharing** use of computer by several persons for different operations at one time, use of holiday home by several joint owners who contract to use it each at different time of year; **time-signal** audible indication of exact time of day; **time signature** *Mus.* indication of time following clef; **time-switch** switch acting automatically at pre-set time; **time was** there was a time; **time zone** range of longitudes where a common standard time is used. [OE]

timekeeper *n.* one who records time, esp. of workers or in game; watch or clock as regards its accuracy (*a poor timekeeper*).

timeless *a.* not affected by the passage of time.

timely *a.* opportune, coming at the right time; **timeliness** *n.*

timepiece *n.* clock or watch.

timer *n.* person or device that measures time taken.

timetable *n.* list of times at which events will take place, esp. arrival of buses or trains etc., or series of lessons in school etc.

timid /ˈtɪmɪd/ *a.* easily frightened, apprehensive; **timidity** /tɪˈmɪdɪtɪ/ *n.* [F or L (*timeo* fear)]

timing *n.* way thing is timed. [TIME]

timorous /ˈtɪmərəs/ *a.* timid; frightened. [F f. med.L (TIMID)]

timpani /ˈtɪmpəniː/ *n.pl.* kettledrums; **timpanist** *n.* [It., pl. of *timpano* = TYMPANUM]

tin 1 *n.* silvery-white metallic element used esp. in alloys and in making tin plate; container made of tin or tin plate esp. for preserving food; = *tin plate.* **2** *v.t.* (**-nn-**) pack (food) in tin for preservation; cover or coat with tin. **3 tin foil** foil made of tin, aluminium, or tin alloy, and used to wrap food for cooking, keeping fresh, etc.; **tin god** object of unjustified veneration; **tin hat** *sl.* modern soldier's steel helmet; **tin-opener** tool for opening tins; **tin-pan alley** world of composers and publishers of popular music; **tin plate** sheet iron or sheet steel coated with tin; **tin-tack** tinned iron tack; **tin whistle** = *penny whistle*. [OE]

tincture /ˈtɪŋktʃə/ **1** *n.* slight flavour or trace (*of* thing, *fig. of* moral quality etc.), tinge (*of* colour); medicinal solution *of* drug in alcohol (*tincture of quinine*). **2** *v.t.* colour slightly, tinge, flavour; affect slightly (*with* quality). [L (TINGE)]

tinder *n.* dry substance that readily catches fire from spark; **tinder-box** box containing tinder, flint, and steel, for kindling fires; **tindery** *a.* [OE]

tine *n.* prong or tooth or point of fork, comb, antler, etc. [OE]

tinge **1** *v.t.* colour or affect slightly (*with*). **2** *n.* tendency to or trace of some colour; slight admixture of a feeling or quality. [L *tingo tinct-* dye]

tingle /ˈtɪŋg(ə)l/ **1** *v.i.* feel slight pricking or stinging or throbbing sensation esp. in ears or hands; cause this (*the reply tingled in his ears*). **2** *n.* tingling sensation. [prob. TINKLE]

tinker **1** *n.* itinerant mender of kettles and pans etc.; *Sc. & Ir.* gypsy; *colloq.* mischievous person or animal; spell of tinkering. **2** *v.i.* work in amateurish or clumsy fashion *at* or *with* (thing) by way of repair or alteration; work as tinker. **3** **don't care a tinker's curse** (or **damn**) do not care at all. [orig. unkn.]

tinkle /ˈtɪŋk(ə)l/ **1** *n.* sound of or as of small bell; *colloq.* telephone call (*give him a tinkle*). **2** *v.* (cause to) make tinkle. [imit.]

tinny *a.* of or like tin; (of metal object) flimsy, insubstantial; sounding like struck tin; **tinnily** *adv.*; **tinniness** *n.* [TIN]

tinpot *a. colloq.* cheap, inferior.

tinsel /ˈtɪns(ə)l/ **1** *n.* glittering decorative metallic strips, threads, etc.; superficial brilliance or splendour. **2** *a.* showy, gaudy, flashy. **3** **tinselled** *a.* [F *estincelle* f. L SCINTILLA]

tinsmith *n.* worker in tin and tin plate. [TIN]

tint **1** *n.* a variety of a colour, esp. made by adding white; tendency towards or admixture of a different colour (*red with a blue tint*); faint colour spread over surface. **2** *v.t.* apply tint to, colour (*with*). [*tinct* (TINGE)]

tintinnabulation /tɪntɪnæbjʊˈleɪʃ(ə)n/ *n.* ringing or tinkling of bells. [L *tintinnabulum* bell]

tiny /ˈtaɪnɪ/ *a.* very small or slight; **tinily** *adv.*; **tininess** *n.* [orig. unkn.]

-tion see -ION.

tip[1] **1** *n.* extremity or end, esp. of small or tapering thing; small piece or part attached to end of thing; leaf-bud of tea. **2** *v.t.* (**-pp-**) provide with tip. **3** **on the tip of one's tongue** just about to be said, or remembered and spoken; **tip of the iceberg** small evident part of something much larger. [ON]

tip[2] **1** *v.* (**-pp-**) lean or slant (often *over* or *up*), cause to do this; overturn or cause to overbalance (*into* etc.); discharge (contents of truck or jug etc.) thus; make small present of money to, esp. for service given; name as likely winner of race or contest etc.; strike or touch lightly. **2** *n.* small money present, esp. for service given; private or special information (e.g. about horse-race or stock-market); small or casual piece of advice; slight push or tilt; place where material (esp. refuse) is tipped; light stroke. **3** **tip person off** give him a hint or special information or warning; **tip-off** *n.* such information etc.; **tip-up** able to be tipped, e.g. of seat in theatre to allow passage past; **tip person the wink** give him private information. [perh. Scand.; partly f. prec.]

tippet /ˈtɪpɪt/ *n.* covering of fur etc. for the shoulders worn by women and as part of some official costumes. [prob. TIP[1]]

tipple /ˈtɪp(ə)l/ **1** *v.* drink intoxicating liquor habitually; drink (liquor) repeatedly in small amounts. **2** *n. colloq.* drink, esp. strong. [orig. unkn.]

tipstaff *n.* sheriff's officer; metal-tipped staff carried by him. [TIP[1]]

tipster *n.* one who gives tips about horse-races etc. [TIP[2]]

tipsy /ˈtɪpsɪ/ *a.* slightly intoxicated; caused by or showing intoxication (*a tipsy lurch*); **tipsy-cake** sponge-cake soaked in wine or spirits and served with custard; **tipsily** *adv.*; **tipsiness** *n.* [TIP[2]]

tiptoe **1** *n.* the tips of the toes (*on tiptoe*). **2** *v.i.* walk on tiptoe or very stealthily. **3** *adv.* on tiptoe, with heels off the ground. [TIP[1]]

tiptop /ˈtɪptɒp, -ˈtɒp/ *colloq.* **1** *a.* excellent. **2** *n.* highest point of excellence. **3** *adv.* excellently. [TIP[1], TOP[1]]

TIR *abbr.* Transport International Routier. [F, = international road transport]

tirade /taɪˈreɪd, tɪ-/ *n.* long vehement denunciation or declamation. [F f. It.]

tire[1] *v.* make or grow weary; exhaust patience or interest of, bore. [OE]

tire[2] *n.* band of metal placed round rim of wheel to strengthen it; *US* = TYRE. [prob. ATTIRE]

tired *a.* weary, exhausted, ready for sleep; (of idea etc.) hackneyed; **tired of** bored or fed up with (thing or *doing* thing). [TIRE[1]]

tireless *a.* of inexhaustible energy.

tiresome *a.* wearisome, tedious; *colloq.* annoying.

tiro /'taɪərəʊ/ *n.* (*pl.* **tiros**) beginner, novice. [L, = recruit]

'tis /tɪz/ *archaic* it is. [contr.]

tissue /'tɪʃu:,'tɪsju:/ *n.* any of the coherent substances of which animal or plant bodies are made (*muscular tissue*); tissue-paper; disposable piece of thin soft absorbent paper for wiping, drying, etc.; fine woven esp. gauzy fabric; connected series (*of* lies etc.); **tissue-paper** thin soft unsized paper for wrapping etc. [F *tissu* p.p. of *tistre* weave f. L (TEXT)]

tit[1] *n.* any of various small birds (e.g. *blue tit, coal-tit*). [abbr. of TITMOUSE]

tit[2] *n.* usu. in **tit for tat** blow for blow, retaliation. [= TIP[2] *for tap*]

tit[3] *n. vulgar* nipple, (in *pl.*) woman's breasts. [OE]

Titan /'taɪt(ə)n/ *n.* person of very great strength or intelligence or importance. [L f. Gk, member of giant race]

titanic /taɪ'tænɪk/ *a.* gigantic, colossal; **titanically** *adv.* [Gk (prec.)]

titanium /taɪ'teɪnɪəm, tɪ-/ *n.* grey metallic element.

titbit *n.* dainty morsel; piquant item of news etc. [prob. dial. *tid* tender]

titfer *n. sl.* hat. [abbr. of *tit for tat* (see TIT[2]), rhyming sl.]

tithe /taɪð/ **1** *n.* one tenth of annual produce of land or labour formerly taken as tax for support of clergy and church; tenth part. **2** *v.* subject to tithes; pay tithes. **3 tithe barn** barn built to hold tithes paid in kind. [OE, = tenth]

Titian /'tɪʃ(ə)n/ *a.* (of hair) bright golden auburn. [*Titian*, painter]

titillate /'tɪtɪleɪt/ *v.t.* excite pleasantly; tickle; **titillation** /-'leɪʃ(ə)n/ *n.* [L]

titivate /'tɪtɪveɪt/ *v.t. colloq.* adorn, smarten, put finishing touches to (esp. *oneself*); **titivation** /-'veɪʃ(ə)n/ *n.* [earlier *tid-*, perh. f. TIDY after *cultivate*]

title /'taɪt(ə)l/ *n.* name of book or work of art, heading of chapter or poem or document etc.; contents of title-page of book; a book regarded in terms of its title; caption or credit title of film; form of nomenclature indicating person's status (e.g. *professor*, *queen*) or used as form of address or reference (e.g. *Lord*, *Mr*, *Your Grace*); a championship in sport; right to ownership of property with or without possession, facts constituting this, just or recognized claim (*to*); **title-deed** legal instrument as evidence of right; **title-page** page at beginning of book giving title and particulars of authorship etc.; **title-role** part in play etc. that gives it its name (e.g. *Othello*). [F f. L *titulus*]

titled *a.* having title of nobility or rank.

titmouse *n.* (*pl.* **titmice**) = TIT[1]. [OE *tit* little, *mose* titmouse, assim. to MOUSE]

titrate /taɪ'treɪt/ *v.t.* ascertain amount of constituent in (substance) by using standard reagent; **titration** /-'reɪʃ(ə)n/ *n.* [F (*titre* title)]

titter 1 *v.i.* laugh covertly, giggle. **2** *n.* such laugh. [imit.]

tittle /'tɪt(ə)l/ *n.* small written or printed stroke or dot; particle, whit (esp. *not one jot or tittle*). [L (TITLE)]

tittle-tattle /'tɪt(ə)ltæt(ə)l/ **1** *n.* petty gossip. **2** *v.i.* engage in this. [redupl. of TATTLE]

tittup /'tɪtəp/ **1** *v.i.* go friskily or jerkily, bob up and down, canter. **2** *n.* such gait or movement. [prob. imit.]

titular /'tɪtjʊlə/ *a.* of or related to a title; existing or being such in title only (*titular ruler, sovereignty*). [F (TITLE)]

tizzy /'tɪzɪ/ *n. sl.* state of nervous agitation (*in a tizzy*). [orig. unkn.]

Tl *symb.* thallium.

Tm *symb.* thulium.

TNT *abbr.* trinitrotoluene.

to[1] /tə, *before vowel* tʊ, *emphat.* tu:/ *prep.* **1** introducing noun, expressing what is reached or approached or touched (*went to Paris; fell to the ground; five minutes to six*); expressing what is aimed at (*throw it to me*); expressing what is followed (*made to order*); expressing what is considered or affected (*am used to that; is nothing to me*); expressing what is caused or produced (*tear to pieces*); expressing what is compared (*nothing to what it might be; equal to the occasion*); expressing what is increased (*add one to another*); expressing what is included or involved (*that is all there is to it*). **2** introducing infinitive (*to err is human; I like to think so; the first to arrive*), or infinitive expressing purpose or consequence or cause (*we eat to live; wise enough to know; am sorry to hear*); as substitute for *to* + infinitive (*meant to tell you but forgot to*). [OE]

to[2] /tu:/ *adv.* to or in normal or required position or condition (*come to; heave to*); (of door) in nearly closed position; **to and fro** backwards and forwards, repeatedly, between same places. [OE]

toad *n.* froglike amphibian breeding in water but living chiefly on land; repulsive person; **toad-in-the-hole** sausages or other meat baked in batter. [OE]

toadflax *n.* plant with yellow or purple flowers.

toadstool *n.* fungus, usu. poisonous, with round top and slender stalk.

toady 1 *n.* sycophant, obsequious hanger-on. **2** *v.* behave servilely (*to*); fawn upon. **3 toadyism** *n.* [contr. of *toad-eater*]

toast 1 *n.* bread in slices browned on both sides by heat; person or thing in whose honour company is requested to drink; call to drink or instance of drinking thus. **2** *v.t.* brown (bread, teacake, cheese, etc.) by heat; warm (one's feet, *oneself*) at fire etc.; drink to the health or in honour of. **3 have a person on toast** *sl.* have him at one's mercy; **toasting-fork** long-handled fork for making toast; **toast-master** person announcing toasts at public dinner; **toast-rack** rack for holding slices of toast at table. [F *toster* roast f. L (TORRID)]

toaster *n.* electrical device for making toast.

tobacco /tə'bækəʊ/ *n.* (*pl.* **tobaccos**) plant of American origin with narcotic leaves used for smoking, chewing, or snuff; its leaves esp. as prepared for smoking. [Sp. *tabaco*, of Amer. Ind. orig.]

tobacconist /tə'bækənɪst/ *n.* dealer in tobacco and cigarettes etc.

toboggan /tə'bɒgən/ **1** *n.* long light narrow sledge for going downhill esp. over snow. **2** *v.i.* ride on toboggan. [Can. F f. Algonquian]

toby jug /'təʊbɪ/ jug or mug in form of old man with three-cornered hat. [fam. form of name *Tobias*]

toccata /tə'kɑ:tə/ *n.* musical composition for keyboard instrument designed to exhibit performer's touch and technique. [It., = touched]

tocsin /'tɒksɪn/ *n.* alarm-signal; bell used to sound alarm. [F *touquesain*, *toquassen* f. Prov., ult. rel. to TOUCH, SIGN]

tod *n. sl.* usu. in **on one's tod** alone, on one's own. [*on one's Tod Sloan*, rhyming sl.]

today /tə'deɪ/ **1** *adv.* on this present day; nowadays, in modern times. **2** *n.* this present day; modern times. [OE]

toddle /'tɒd(ə)l/ **1** *v.i.* walk with small child's short unsteady steps; *colloq.* (usu. with *off*) depart. **2** *n.* toddling walk. [orig. unkn.]

toddler *n.* child who is just beginning to walk.

toddy /'tɒdɪ/ *n.* drink of spirits with hot water and sugar. [Hind. (*tār* palm)]

to-do /tə'du:/ *n.* commotion, fuss. [TO[1]]

toe 1 *n.* any of the five terminal members of the foot; corresponding part of animal or bird; part of footwear that covers toes; lower end or tip of implement etc. **2** *v.t.* touch with the toes. **3 on one's toes** alert, eager; **toe-cap** reinforced part of shoe covering toes; **toe-hold** slight foothold, small beginning or advantage; **toe the line** conform esp. under pressure. [OE]

toff *n. sl.* distinguished or well-dressed person. [perh. TUFT in archaic sl. sense 'titled undergraduate']

toffee /'tɒfɪ/ *n.* a kind of firm or hard sweet made by boiling sugar, butter, etc.; small piece of this; **can't do a thing for toffee** *sl.* is incompetent at it; **toffee-apple** toffee-coated apple on stick; **toffee-nosed** *sl.* snobbish, pretentious. [orig. unkn.]

tog *sl.* **1** *n.* (usu. in *pl.*) garment. **2** *v.t.* (**-gg-**) dress (*out* or *up*). [app. orig. cant & ult. rel. to L TOGA]

toga /'təʊgə/ *n.* ancient Roman citizen's loose flowing outer garment; **toga'd** *a.* [L]

together /tə'geðə/ *adv.* in company or conjunction (*walking together*; *were at school together*); simultaneously (*both exclaimed together*); one with another (*fighting together*); into conjunction, so as to unite (*sew them together*; *put two and two together*); into company or companionship; *colloq.* well organized or controlled; uninterruptedly (*he could talk for hours together*); **together with** as well as, and also. [OE (TO, GATHER)]

togetherness *n.* being together; feeling of belonging together.

toggle /'tɒg(ə)l/ *n.* device for fastening with cross-piece which can pass through hole or loop in one position but not in another; **toggle-switch** electric switch with projecting lever to be moved usu. up and down. [orig. unkn.]

toil 1 *v.i.* work laboriously or incessantly; make slow painful progress. **2** *n.* severe labour, drudgery. [AF *toil(er)* dispute]

toilet /'tɔɪlɪt/ *n.* lavatory; process of washing oneself, dressing, etc. (*make one's toilet*); **toilet-paper** paper for cleaning oneself after excreting; **toilet-roll** roll of toilet-paper; **toilet soap** soap for washing oneself; **toilet-training** training of young child to use lavatory; **toilet water** scented liquid used after washing. [F *toilette* dimin. of *toile* cloth]

toiletries /'tɔɪlɪtrɪz/ *n.pl.* articles used in making one's toilet.

toils /tɔɪlz/ *n.pl.* net or snare. [*toil* f. F (TOILET)]

toilsome /'tɔɪlsəm/ *a.* involving toil. [TOIL]

Tokay /tə'keɪ/ *n.* a sweet Hungarian wine. [*Tokaj* in Hungary]

token /'təʊkən/ **1** *n.* indication, thing serving as symbol or reminder or keepsake or distinctive mark or guarantee (*as a token of* or *in token of my affection or esteem*); voucher exchangeable for goods; anything used to represent something else, esp. money. **2** *a.* nominal or perfunctory (*token effort*); conducted briefly to demonstrate strength of feeling (*token resistance, strike*). **3 by this** (or **the same**) **token** similarly, moreover, in corroboration of what I say. [OE]

tokenism *n.* granting minimum concessions; making only a token effort.

told /təʊld/ *past* and *p.p.* of TELL.

tolerable /'tɒlərəb(ə)l/ *a.* not beyond endurance; fairly good; **tolerably** *adv.* [F f. L (TOLERATE)]

tolerance /'tɒlərəns/ *n.* willingness or ability to tolerate, forbearance; permissible variation in dimension or weight.

tolerant *a.* disposed or accustomed to tolerate others or their acts or opinions, enduring or patient *of*.

tolerate /'tɒləreɪt/ *v.t.* allow the existence or occurrence of without authoritative interference, leave unmolested; not be harmed by; find or treat as endurable. [L *tolero*]

toleration /tɒlə'reɪʃ(ə)n/ *n.* tolerating, esp. allowing of differences in religious opinion without discrimination. [F f. L (prec.)]

toll[1] /təʊl/ *n.* charge payable for permission to pass barrier or use bridge or road etc.; cost or damage caused by disaster or incurred in achievement; **take its toll** be accompanied by loss or injury etc.; **toll-bridge** bridge at which toll is charged; **toll-gate** gate preventing passage until toll is paid; **toll-road** road maintained by tolls collected on it. [OE f. med.L *toloneum* f. Gk (*telos* tax)]

toll[2] /təʊl/ **1** *v.* (of bell) sound with slow uniform succession of strokes (*for* death or dead person); ring (bell or knell) or strike (hour) or announce or mark (death etc.) thus. **2** *n.* tolling or stroke of bell. [prob. OE, orig. (now dial.) = entice, pull]

tolu /tə'lju:, 'təʊlju:/ *n.* fragrant brown balsam from S. American tree. [*Tolu* in Colombia]

toluene /'tɒljʊi:n/ *n.* colourless aromatic liquid hydrocarbon derivative of benzene, orig. obtained from tolu, used in manufacture of explosives etc.

toluol /'tɒljʊɒl/ *n.* commercial grade of toluene.

tom *n.* (in full **tom-cat**) male cat; **Tom, Dick, and Harry** (usu. *derog.*) persons taken at random, ordinary people (usu. preceded by *any* or *every*); **Tom Thumb** diminutive person. [abbr. of name *Thomas*]

tomahawk /'tɒməhɔ:k/ *n.* N. American Indian war-axe. [Renape]

tomato /tə'mɑ:təʊ/ *n.* (*pl.* **tomatoes**) glossy red or yellow pulpy edible fruit; plant bearing this. [ult. f. Mex. *tomatl*]

tomb /tu:m/ *n.* a grave; burial-vault; sepulchral monument; **the tomb** state of death. [AF *tumbe* f. L f. Gk]

tombola /tɒm'bəʊlə/ *n.* a kind of lottery with tickets and prizes. [F or It.]

tomboy *n.* rough boyish girl. [TOM]

tombstone *n.* stone standing or laid over grave, usu. with epitaph. [TOMB]

tome *n.* large book or volume. [F f. L f. Gk (*temnō* cut)]

tomfool /tɒm'fu:l/ **1** *a.* extremely foolish. **2** *n.* fool. [TOM]

tomfoolery *n.* foolish behaviour.

Tommy /'tɒmɪ/ *n.* British private soldier. [*Tommy Atkins*, name used in specimens of completed official forms]

tommy-gun /'tɒmɪgʌn/ *n.* a submachine-gun. [*Thompson*, manufacturer]

tommy-rot /'tɒmɪrɒt/ *n. sl.* nonsense. [TOM]

tomography /tə'mɒgrəfɪ/ *n.* method of radiography displaying details of a selected plane within the body. [Gk *tomē* a cutting]

tomorrow /tə'mɒrəʊ/ **1** *adv.* on the day after today; at some future time. **2** *n.* the day after today; the near future. [TO, MORROW]

tomtit *n.* tit, esp. blue tit. [TOM, TIT[1]]

tom-tom /'tɒmtɒm/ *n.* primitive drum beaten with the hands; tall drum used in jazz bands etc. [Hindi *tamtam*, imit.]

ton /tʌn/ *n.* measure of weight, 2240 lb. (**long ton**) or 2000 lb. (**short ton**) or 1000 kg. (**metric ton**); unit of measurement for ship's tonnage; (usu. in *pl.*) *colloq.* large number or amount (*tons of people, money*); *sl.* speed of 100 m.p.h.; *sl.* £100; **ton-up boys** motor-cyclists who travel at high speed; **weighs a ton** is very heavy. [diff. sp. of TUN]

tonal /'təʊn(ə)l/ *a.* of or relating to tone or tonality; **tonally** *adv.* [med.L (TONE)]

tonality /tə'nælɪtɪ/ *n.* relationship between notes of a musical scale, observance of single tonic key as basis of a composition; colour-scheme of picture.

tone **1** *n.* musical or vocal sound, esp. with reference to pitch, quality, and strength; modulation of the voice to express a particular feeling or mood (*impatient, suspicious, tone*); manner of expression in writing; *Mus.* musical sound, esp. of definite pitch and character, interval of major second, e.g. C–D; general effect of colour or of light and shade in picture, tint or shade of colour; prevailing character of morals and sentiments etc. in a group; proper firmness of bodily organs, state of good or specified health. **2** *v.* give desired tone to, modify tone of, attune (*to*); be in harmony (esp. of colour) *with*. **3** **tone-deaf** unable to perceive differences of musical pitch accurately; **tone down** make or become softer in tone of sound or colour, make (statement etc.) less harsh or emphatic; **tone poem** orchestral composition with descriptive subject; **tone up** make or become stronger in tone of sound or colour, make (statement etc.) more emphatic. [F f. L f. Gk *tonos* (*teino* stretch)]

tongs /tɒŋz/ *n.pl.* instrument with two arms for grasping and holding. [OE]

tongue /tʌŋ/ *n.* fleshy muscular organ in the mouth used in tasting, licking, swallowing, and (in man) speech; tongue of ox etc. as food; faculty of or tendency in speech (*a ready, a sharp, tongue*); language of nation etc. (*native tongue*); thing like tongue in shape, e.g. long low promontory, strip of leather under laces in shoe, clapper of bell, pin of buckle; projecting strip on wooden etc. board fitting into groove of another; **find** (or **lose**) **one's tongue** be able (or unable) to express oneself after shock etc.; **hold one's tongue** remain silent; **tongue-tie** speech impediment due to malformation of tongue; **tongue-tied** too shy or embarrassed to speak, having tongue-tie; **tongue-twister** sequence of words difficult to pronounce quickly and correctly; **with one's tongue in one's cheek** insincerely or ironically. [OE]

tonguing *n. Mus.* use of tongue to articulate certain notes in playing wind instrument.

tonic /ˈtɒnɪk/ **1** *n.* invigorating medicine; anything serving to invigorate; = *tonic water*; keynote in music. **2** *a.* serving as a tonic, invigorating; of or founded on the keynote in music. **3 tonic sol-fa** musical notation used esp. in teaching singing; **tonic water** carbonated drink with quinine. [F f. Gk (TONE)]

tonight /təˈnaɪt/ **1** *adv.* on the present or approaching evening or night. **2** *n.* the present evening or night, the evening or night of today. [OE]

tonnage /ˈtʌnɪdʒ/ *n.* ship's internal cubic capacity or freight-carrying capacity; charge per ton on cargo or freight. [TON]

tonne /tʌn, ˈtʌnɪ/ *n.* metric ton of 1000kg. [F (TON[1])]

tonsil /ˈtɒns(ə)l/ *n.* either of two small organs, one on each side of root of the tongue; **tonsillar** /ˈtɒnsɪlə/ *a.* [F or L]

tonsillectomy /tɒnsɪˈlektəmɪ/ *n.* surgical removal of the tonsils. [-ECTOMY]

tonsillitis /tɒnsɪˈlaɪtɪs/ *n.* inflammation of the tonsils. [-ITIS]

tonsorial /tɒnˈsɔːrɪəl/ *a.* of a barber or his work. [L (*tondeo tons-* shave)]

tonsure /ˈtɒnʃə/ **1** *n.* shaving of crown of head or entire head as clerical or monastic symbol; bare patch so made. **2** *v.t.* give tonsure to. [F or L (prec.)]

too *adv.* to a greater extent than is desirable or permissible (*shoes are too small; he is too late*); *colloq.* extremely (*you are too kind*); in addition, moreover (*may I come too?; I did it without help, too*); **none too** rather less than (*none too good*); **too bad** see BAD; **too much** intolerable; **too much for** more than a match for, more than can be endured by. [stressed form of TO]

took *past* of TAKE.

tool 1 *n.* mechanical implement, usu. held in the hand, for working on something; simple machine, e.g. lathe; thing used in occupation or pursuit (*the computer as a research tool*); person used as mere instrument by another; *sl.* penis. **2** *v.* dress (stone) with chisel; impress design on (leather book-cover); *sl.* drive or ride (*along* or *around* etc.) esp. in casual or leisurely manner. **3 tool-pusher** worker directing drilling on oil rig. [OE]

toot 1 *n.* short sharp sound as or like that of horn or trumpet. **2** *v.* sound (horn etc.) thus; give out such sound. [prob. imit.]

tooth *n.* (*pl.* **teeth**) each of a set of hard bony structures in jaws of most vertebrates, used for biting and chewing; toothlike part or projection, e.g. cog of gear-wheel, point of saw or comb etc.; sense of taste, appetite; (in *pl.*) force or effectiveness (*new law has been given teeth*); **armed to the teeth** completely and elaborately armed or equipped; **fight tooth and nail** fight very fiercely; **get one's teeth into** devote oneself seriously to; **in the teeth of** in spite of (opposition or difficulty etc.), in opposition to (instructions etc.), directly against (the wind etc.); **tooth-comb** = *fine-tooth comb* (see FINE[1]); **tooth-powder** powder for cleaning teeth. [OE]

toothache *n.* pain in a tooth or teeth.

toothbrush *n.* brush for cleaning teeth.

toothless *a.* having no teeth, esp. in old age.

toothpaste *n.* paste for cleaning teeth.

toothpick *n.* small sharp instrument for removing food etc. lodged between teeth.

toothsome *a.* (of food) delicious.

toothy *a.* having large or numerous or prominent teeth.

tootle /ˈtuːt(ə)l/ *v.i.* toot gently or repeatedly; *colloq.* move casually *along, around,* etc. [TOOT]

tootsy /ˈtʊtsɪ/ *n. joc.* or *childish* foot. [orig. uncert.]

top[1] **1** *n.* highest point or part; upper surface, thing forming upper part, cover or cap of container etc.; highest rank, foremost place or position; person holding such rank etc.; garment for upper part of body; (usu. in *pl.*) leaves etc. of plant grown chiefly for its root (*turnip tops*); utmost degree or intensity (*called out at the top of his voice*); = *top gear*; platform round head of lower mast of ship; *predic.* (in *pl.*) person or thing of very best quality. **2** *a.* highest in position or degree or importance. **3** *v.t.* (**-pp-**) furnish with top or cap; be higher than, be superior to, surpass; be at the top of (*top the list*); reach top of (hill etc.); hit (ball in golf) above centre. **4 at the top** in the highest rank of a profession etc.; **on top** above, in superior position; **on top of** fully in control of, in close proximity to, in addition to; **on top of the world** exuberant; **over the top** over parapet of trench, into final or decisive state or state of excess; **top brass** *colloq.* high-ranking officers; **top dog** *colloq.* victor, master; **top drawer** high social position or origin; **top-dress** apply manure or fertilizer on the top of (earth), not dig it in; **top-flight** in highest rank of achievement; **top gear** highest gear; **top hat** tall silk hat; **top-heavy** overweighted at top and so in danger of falling; **top-hole** *sl.* first-rate; **top-level** of or at highest rank or level; **top-notch** *colloq.* first-rate; **top off** put an end or finishing touch to; **top out** put highest stone on (building); **top secret** of the highest secrecy; **top up** fill up (partly empty container), add extra money or items etc. to. [OE]

top[2] *n.* toy, usu. conical or pear-shaped with sharp point at bottom on which it rotates when set in motion. [OE]

topaz /'təʊpæz/ *n.* a gem of various colours, esp. yellow. [F f. L f. Gk]

topcoat *n.* overcoat; outer coat of paint etc. [TOP[1]]

tope[1] *n.* a kind of small shark. [perh. Corn.]

tope[2] *v.i. archaic* drink intoxicating liquor to excess, esp. habitually; **toper** *n.* [orig. uncert.]

topgallant /tɒp'gælənt/ *n.* mast, sail, yard, or rigging, immediately above topmast and topsail. [TOP[1]]

topi /'təʊpɪ/ *n.* (also **topee**) sun-helmet, esp. sola topi. [Hindi, = hat]

topiary /'təʊpɪərɪ/ **1** *n.* art of clipping shrubs etc. into ornamental shapes. **2** *a.* of this art. [F f. L *topiarius* landscape-gardener f. Gk *topos* place]

topic /'tɒpɪk/ *n.* theme for discussion, subject of conversation or discourse. [L f. Gk (*topos* place, commonplace)]

topical *a.* dealing with current topics; **topicality** /-'kælɪtɪ/ *n.*; **topically** *adv.*

topknot *n.* tuft or crest or bow of ribbon etc. worn or growing on head. [TOP[1]]

topless *a.* without a top; (of woman's clothing) leaving the breasts bare, (of woman) so clothed.

topmast *n.* part of mast next above lower mast.

topmost *a.* uppermost, highest.

topography /tə'pɒgrəfɪ/ *n.* natural and artificial features of a district; knowledge or description of these; **topographer** *n.*; **topographical** /tɒpə'græfɪk(ə)l/ *a.* [L f. Gk (*topos* place)]

topology /tə'pɒlədʒɪ/ *n.* study of geometrical properties unaffected by changes of shape and size; **topological** /tɒpə'lɒdʒɪk(ə)l/ *a.* [G f. Gk *topos* place]

topper *n. colloq.* top hat. [TOP[1]]

topping 1 *n.* decorative cream etc. on top of cake etc. **2** *a. colloq.* excellent.

topple /'tɒp(ə)l/ *v.* fall (*over* or *down*) from vertical to horizontal position; cause to do this; overthrow. [TOP[1]]

topsail /'tɒps(ə)l/ *n.* square sail next above lowest; fore-and-aft sail on gaff. [TOP[1]]

topside *n.* outer side of round of beef; side of ship above water-line.

topsoil *n.* top layer of soil.

topsy-turvy /tɒpsɪ'tɜːvɪ/ *adv.* & *a.* upside-down; in utter confusion. [TOP[1], obs. *terve* topple]

toque /təʊk/ *n.* woman's brimless hat. [F]

tor *n.* rocky hill-top. [OE]

torch *n.* electric lamp with battery etc. in portable case; piece of resinous wood or twisted flax etc. soaked in tallow etc. for carrying lighted in hand; source of inspiration or edification; **carry a torch for** feel (esp. unreturned) love for. [F *torche* f. L (as TORT)]

tore *past* of TEAR[1].

toreador /'tɒrɪədɔː/ *n.* bullfighter, esp. on horseback. [Sp. (*toro* bull f. L *taurus*)]

torment 1 /'tɔːment/ *n.* severe bodily or mental suffering (*is in torment*; *suffer torments*); cause of this. **2** /tɔː'ment/ *v.t.* subject to torment; tease or worry excessively. **3 tormentor** *n.* [F f. L *tormentum* (as TORT)]

tormentil /'tɔːməntɪl/ *n.* trailing herb with yellow flowers. [F f. med.L]

torn *p.p.* of TEAR[1].

tornado /tɔː'neɪdəʊ/ *n.* (*pl.* **tornadoes**) violent storm over small area, esp. rotatory one travelling in narrow path; loud outburst. [Sp. *tronada* thunderstorm]

torpedo /tɔː'piːdəʊ/ **1** *n.* (*pl.* **torpedoes**) cigar-shaped self-propelled underwater missile fired at ship from the air or water and exploding on impact. **2** *v.t.* destroy or attack with torpedo; ruin (policy or institution etc.) with sudden effect. **3 torpedo-boat** small fast warship armed with torpedoes. [L, = electric ray (TORPOR)]

torpid /ˈtɔːpɪd/ *a.* sluggish, inactive, apathetic; (of hibernating animal) dormant; numb; **torpidity** /-ˈpɪdɪtɪ/ *n.* [L (foll.)]

torpor /ˈtɔːpə/ *n.* apathy; being dormant. [L (*torpeo* be numb)]

torque /tɔːk/ *n.* twisting or rotary force esp. in machine; twisted metal necklace worn by ancient Britons, Gauls, etc. [L (as TORT)]

torr *n.* (*pl.* same) unit of pressure, $\frac{1}{760}$ of atmosphere. [*Torricelli*, physicist]

torrent /ˈtɒrənt/ *n.* rushing stream of water or lava etc.; (usu. in *pl.*) great downpour of rain; violent flow (*of* abuse, questions, etc.); **torrential** /təˈrenʃ(ə)l/ *a.* [F f. It.]

torrid /ˈtɒrɪd/ *a.* (of land etc.) parched by sun, very hot; intense, passionate; **torrid zone** the tropics. [F or L (*torreo tost-* parch)]

torsion /ˈtɔːʃ(ə)n/ *n.* twisting, esp. of one end of thing while other is held; **torsional** *a.* [F f. L (as TORT)]

torso /ˈtɔːsəʊ/ *n.* (*pl.* **torsos**) trunk of human body or of statue; statue lacking head and limbs; unfinished or mutilated work. [It. f. L *thyrsus* rod]

tort *n.* breach of legal duty, other than under contract, with liability for damages; **tortious** /ˈtɔːʃəs/ *a.* [F f. med.L *tortum* wrong f. L *torqueo tort-* twist]

tortilla /tɔːˈtiːljə/ *n.* Latin American thin flat maize cake eaten hot. [Sp., = little cake]

tortoise /ˈtɔːtəs/ *n.* slow-moving reptile of land or fresh water, with body in horny shell. [F f. med.L *tortuca*]

tortoiseshell /ˈtɔːtəʃel/ **1** *n.* yellowish-brown mottled and clouded shell of certain turtles; cat or butterfly with markings suggesting tortoiseshell. **2** *a.* having such markings.

tortuous /ˈtɔːtjʊəs/ *a.* winding, indirect; involved, complicated; **tortuosity** /-ˈɒsɪtɪ/ *n.* [F f. L (as TORT)]

torture /ˈtɔːtʃə/ **1** *n.* infliction of severe bodily pain esp. as punishment or means of persuasion; severe physical or mental pain. **2** *v.t.* subject to torture; force out of natural shape or meaning, distort. [F f. L *tortura* twisting (as TORT)]

Tory /ˈtɔːrɪ/ **1** *n.* member of Conservative party; *hist.* member of political party in 17th–19th cc. opposed to Whigs and giving rise to Conservative party. **2** *a.* Conservative. **3 Toryism** *n.* [orig. = Irish outlaw]

tosh *n. sl.* nonsense, rubbish. [orig. unkn.]

toss 1 *v.* move with fitful to-and-fro motion, fling or roll or wave about; cast or throw lightly or carelessly (*to* person, *aside*, *away*, etc.); throw up (ball etc.) with the hand; (of bull etc.) throw (person) up with the horns; throw (head) back esp. in contempt or impatience; throw (coin) into the air to decide choice etc. by the way it falls, settle question or dispute with (person *for* thing) thus; coat (food) with dressing etc. by gentle shaking. **2** *n.* tossing of ball, coin, head, etc.; throw from horseback etc. **3 argue the toss** dispute a choice already made; **take a toss** be thrown by horse etc.; **toss off** compose or finish rapidly and effortlessly, drink (liquor) in one draught; **toss up** toss coin; **toss-up** *n.* tossing of coin, *colloq.* doubtful matter. [orig. unkn.]

tot[1] *n.* small child; dram of liquor. [orig. dial.]

tot[2] *v.* (**-tt-**) add (usu. *up*); (of items) mount up; **totting-up** adding of separate items, esp. of convictions towards disqualification from driving; **tot up to** amount to. [abbr. of TOTAL or L *totum* the whole]

total /ˈtəʊt(ə)l/ **1** *a.* complete, comprising the whole (*the total number of persons*); absolute, unqualified (*was in total ignorance*). **2** *n.* total number or quantity. **3** *v.* (**-ll-**, *US* **-l-**) find total of; amount in number to; amount *to*. [F f. med.L (*totus* entire)]

totalitarian /təʊtælɪˈteərɪən/ *a.* relating to form of government permitting no rival loyalties or parties; **totalitarianism** *n.* [foll.]

totality /təʊˈtælɪtɪ/ *n.* total; being total. [med.L (TOTAL)]

totalizator /ˈtəʊtəlaɪzeɪtə/ *n.* device showing number and amount of bets staked on race to enable total to be divided among those betting on winner; this betting system. [foll.]

totalize *v.t.* combine into a total. [TOTAL]

totally *adv.* completely.

tote[1] *n. sl.* totalizator. [abbr.]

tote[2] *v.t.* convey, or carry as load (gun or supplies etc.); **tote bag** large bag for parcels etc. [orig. US; prob. dial.]

totem /ˈtəʊtəm/ *n.* natural object, esp. animal, adopted as emblem of clan or individual, esp. among N. American Indians; image of this; **totem-pole** pole on which totems are carved or painted or hung; **totemic** /-ˈtemɪk/ *a.* [Algonquian]

totemism *n.* stage of development of which totems are characteristic; **totemistic** /-ˈmɪstɪk/ *a.*

t'other /ˈtʌðə/ *a.* & *pron. colloq.* the other. [(*tha*)*t other*]

totter 1 *v.i.* stand or walk unsteadily or feebly; (of tower etc., or *fig.* of State or system etc.) be shaken, be on the point of falling. **2** *n.* unsteady or shaky movement or gait. **3 tottery** *a.* [Du.]

toucan /'tu:kən/ *n.* tropical American bird with large bill. [Tupi]

touch /tʌtʃ/ **1** *v.* move or be placed so as to meet at one or more points; put one's hand etc. so as to meet thus, cause (two things) to meet thus, establish this relation towards (thing *with* one's hand etc.); strike lightly, affect with such stroke; reach as far as, esp. momentarily; approach in excellence (*nobody can touch him for speed*); (with neg.) move or harm or affect or attempt in any degree, have any dealings with; affect with tender or painful feelings; (in *p.p.*) slightly crazy; affect slightly, modify; strike (keys or strings of musical instrument). **2** *n.* act or fact of touching (*felt a touch on my arm*; *got a touch to the ball*); faculty of perception through response of the brain to contact esp. with fingers; light stroke of pencil etc. in drawing; small amount, tinge or trace; manner of touching keys or strings, response of keys etc. to this; distinctive manner of workmanship or procedure (*personal touch*); mental correspondence, communication (*in*, *out of*, *touch*); part of football field beyond side limits; *sl.* act of getting money from person, person from whom money may be got. **3 finishing touch** (or **touches**) final details completing and enhancing piece of work etc.; **touch-and-go** uncertain as regards result, risky; **touch at** (of ship) call at (port etc.); **touch bottom** reach bottom of water with feet, reach lowest or worst point; **touch down** (of aircraft) reach ground in landing; **touch person for** *sl.* get (money) from him; **touch-judge** linesman in Rugby football; **touch-line** side limit of football field; **touch off** explode by touching with match etc., initiate (process) suddenly; **touch on** (or **upon**) refer to or mention briefly or casually, verge on; **touch-paper** paper impregnated with nitre to burn slowly and ignite firework etc.; **touch-type** use typewriter without looking at keys; **touch up** correct or improve with minor additions; **touch wood** put hand on something wooden in superstitious belief of averting bad luck. [F *tochier*]

touchdown *n.* act of touching down by aircraft.

touché /'tu:ʃeɪ/ *int.* acknowledging hit by fencing-opponent or justified retort by another in discussion. [F, = *touched*]

touching **1** *a.* arousing sympathy or tender feelings. **2** *prep.* concerning.

touchstone *n.* dark schist or jasper for testing alloys by marks they make on it; criterion.

touchwood *n.* readily inflammable rotten wood or similar substance.

touchy *a.* apt to take offence, over-sensitive; **touchily** *adv.*; **touchiness** *n.*

tough /tʌf/ **1** *a.* hard to break or cut or tear or chew; able to endure hardship, hardy; stubborn, unyielding; difficult (*a tough job*); *colloq.* acting sternly or vigorously (*get tough with*); *colloq.* (of luck etc.) hard; *US sl.* vicious, ruffianly; (of clay etc.) stiff, tenacious. **2** *n.* tough person, esp. ruffian. [OE]

toughen *v.* make or become tough or tougher.

toupee /'tu:peɪ/ *n.* wig or artificial patch of hair worn to cover bald part of head. [F]

tour /tʊə/ **1** *n.* pleasure journey including stops at various places and ending where it began; journey or expedition with any of these characteristics (*go on a tour of inspection*); spell of military or diplomatic duty. **2** *v.* go on a tour; travel through (country etc.) so. **3 on tour** going from place to place to give performances etc. [F f. L (TURN)]

tour de force /tʊə də 'fɔ:s/ great feat of strength or skill. [F]

tourism *n.* visiting places as tourist; provision of tours or services for tourists, esp. commercially. [TOUR]

tourist *n.* holiday traveller; **tourist class** low class of passenger accommodation in ship or aircraft etc.

touristy *a.* *derog.* suitable for or frequented by tourists.

tourmaline /'tʊəməlɪn, -i:n/ *n.* mineral with unusual electric properties and used as gem. [F, f. Sinh.]

tournament /'tʊənəmənt/ *n.* contest of skill between a number of competitors (*chess tournament*); medieval spectacle in which two sides contended with usu. blunted weapons; modern display of military exercises, contests, etc. (*Royal Tournament*). [F (TOURNEY)]

tournedos /'tʊənədəʊ/ *n.* (*pl.* same) small fillet of beef in strip of suet. [F]

tourney /'tʊənɪ/ **1** *n.* tournament. **2** *v.i.* take part in tournament. [F (TURN)]

tourniquet /'tʊənɪkeɪ/ *n.* bandage etc. for stopping flow of blood through artery by compression. [F]

tousle /'taʊz(ə)l/ *v.t.* pull about roughly, make (hair or clothes) untidy. [dial. *touse*]

tout **1** *v.* pester possible customers with requests (*for* orders); solicit custom of (person) or for (thing); spy out movements and condition of racehorses in training. **2** *n.* person who touts. [OE, = peep]

tow[1] /təʊ/ **1** *v.t.* pull along behind, esp. with rope etc. **2** *n.* towing or being towed. **3 in tow** being towed, *colloq.* accompanying or under charge of a person; **on tow** being towed; **tow-bar** bar by which caravan etc. is attached to vehicle towing it; **tow-path** path beside river or canal, orig. for towing. [OE]

tow[2] /təʊ/ *n.* fibres of flax or hemp prepared for spinning; **tow-headed** having head of very light-coloured or tousled hair. [LG *touw*]

towards /tə'wɔ:dz/ *prep.* (also **toward**) in the direction of (*walked towards the house*); as regards, in relation to (*his attitude towards death*); for or for the purpose of (*offered something towards the expenses*); near (*towards noon; toward the end of our journey*). [OE, = future (TO, -WARD)]

towel /'taʊəl/ **1** *n.* absorbent cloth or paper etc. for drying with after washing. **2** *v.* (**-ll-**, *US* **-l-**) wipe or dry with towel. **3 throw in the towel** admit defeat. [F *toaille* f. Gmc]

towelling, *US* **toweling** *n.* material for towels.

tower 1 *n.* tall structure often forming part of castle, church, or other large building; similar structure housing machinery etc. (*control, cooling, tower*); tower block; fortress etc. having a tower. **2** *v.i.* extend high in the air, be of great height; be much more important or eminent (*towered over his contemporaries*). **3 tower block** tall building containing offices or dwelling-places; **tower of strength** person who gives strong and reliable support. [F f. L f. Gk *turris*]

towering *a.* high, lofty; (of rage etc.) violent.

town *n.* large concentrated collection of dwellings, densely populated settlement; this as distinct from the country or suburbs; London or the chief city or town of a neighbourhood (*went up to town*), central business area of a neighbourhood; **go to town** act or work with energy and enthusiasm; **on the town** *colloq.* on a spree in town; **town clerk** officer of town corporation, in charge of records etc.; **town crier** person making official announcements in public places; **town gas** manufactured inflammable gas for domestic use; **town hall** building for town's official business, often also used for public entertainment etc.; **town house** residence in town, esp. of person with a house in the country; house in (esp. terraced) group in town; **town planning** planning for regulated growth and improvement of towns. [OE]

townee /taʊ'ni:/ *n.* (also **townie** /'taʊnɪ/) *derog.* inhabitant of a town.

townscape *n.* picture of a town; visual appearance of town(s).

townsfolk *n.* inhabitants of town(s).

township *n.* formerly in UK, a small town or village that formed part of a large parish; *US & Canada* administrative division of county, or district six miles square; *Austral. & NZ* small town or settlement.

townsman *n.* inhabitant of a town; **townswoman** *n. fem.*

townspeople *n.pl.* inhabitants of a town.

toxaemia /tɒk'si:mɪə/, *US* **toxemia** *n.* blood-poisoning; condition of abnormally high blood-pressure in pregnancy. [as foll., Gk *haima* blood]

toxic /'tɒksɪk/ *a.* of or caused by or acting as poison; **toxicity** /tɒk'sɪsɪtɪ/ *n.* [L f. Gk *toxikon* poison for arrows]

toxicology /tɒksɪ'kɒlədʒɪ/ *n.* science of poisons; **toxicological** /-'lɒdʒɪk(ə)l/ *a.*; **toxicologist** *n.*

toxin /'tɒksɪn/ *n.* poison esp. of animal or vegetable origin; poison secreted by micro-organism and causing particular disease.

toy 1 *n.* thing to play with, esp. for children; trinket or curiosity, trifling thing or thing meant only for amusement. **2** *a.* that is a toy; (of dog) of diminutive breed; hardly deserving the name, not meant for serious use. **3** *v.i.* play or fiddle or dally *with* (thing, or idea etc.). [orig. unkn.]

trace[1] **1** *n.* mark left behind, as track of animal, footprint, or line made by moving pen; perceptible sign of what has existed or happened; small quantity (*contains traces of soda*). **2** *v.t.* follow path or establish position of; discover course or development or origin of from evidence etc.; discover from vestiges or signs (*cannot trace any such papers*); pursue one's way along (path etc.), (of pen etc.) mark (line etc.); copy (drawing etc.) by marking its lines on piece of transparent paper placed over it; sketch, mark out outline of, form (letters etc.) laboriously. **3 trace element** substance occurring or required, esp. in soil, only in minute amounts. **4 traceable** *a.* [F f. Rmc (L *traho* draw)]

trace[2] *n.* each of two side-straps or chains or ropes by which horse draws vehicle; **kick over the traces** become insubordinate or reckless. [F *trais*, pl. of TRAIT]

tracer *n.* bullet that leaves a trail of smoke etc. by which its course may be observed; artificial radioisotope whose course in human body etc. can be followed by radiation it produces. [TRACE[1]]

tracery *n.* stone ornamental open-work esp. in head of Gothic window; decorative lacelike pattern suggesting this.

trachea /trəˈkiːə, ˈtreɪkɪə/ *n.* the windpipe. [L f. Gk]

tracheotomy /treɪkɪˈɒtəmɪ, træk-/ *n.* surgical incision of trachea.

tracing *n.* traced copy of map or drawing etc.; process of making this. [TRACE[1]]

track 1 *n.* mark or series of marks left by person or animal or vehicle etc. in passing along, (in *pl.*) such marks, esp. footprints; path or rough road, esp. one established by use; course taken (*track of comet*; *followed in his track*); course of action or procedure; prepared racing-path; racecourse for horses etc.; continuous railway-line; band round wheels of tank or tractor etc.; = SOUNDTRACK; groove on gramophone record; particular recorded section of gramophone record or magnetic tape. **2** *v.* follow track or course of; trace (course or development etc.) from vestiges; (of cine-camera) move along set path while taking picture. **3 in one's tracks** *colloq.* where one stands, then and there; **keep** (or **lose**) **track** follow (or fail to follow) course or development (*of*); **make tracks** *sl.* go away; **make tracks for** *sl.* go in pursuit of or towards; **off the track** away from the subject in hand; **track down** reach or capture by tracking; **track event** (in athletics) event taking place on the track, e.g. running; **track record** person's past achievements; **track suit** suit worn by athletes etc. while training or before or after competing. [F *trac*]

tracklement /ˈtræk(ə)lmənt/ *n.* article of food, esp. jelly, for eating with meat. [orig. uncert.]

tract[1] *n.* region or area of indefinite (usu. large) extent; bodily organ or system (*digestive tract*). [L (*traho tract-* draw)]

tract[2] *n.* essay or pamphlet, esp. on religious subject. [app. L *tractatus* f. *tracto* handle]

tractable /ˈtræktəb(ə)l/ *a.* (of person or material etc.) easily handled, manageable; **tractability** /-ˈbɪlɪtɪ/ *n.* [L f. *tracto* handle]

traction /ˈtrækʃ(ə)n/ *n.* hauling; pulling force; therapeutic sustained pull on limb etc.; **traction-engine** steam or diesel engine for drawing heavy load on road or across fields etc. [F or med.L (TRACT[1])]

tractor /ˈtræktə/ *n.* powerful motor vehicle for pulling farm machinery or other heavy equipment; traction-engine. [as prec.]

trad *colloq.* **1** *a.* traditional. **2** *n.* traditional jazz. [abbr.]

trade 1 *n.* exchange of goods for money or other goods; business done with specified class or at specified time (*tourist, Christmas, trade*); business carried on for earnings or profit (esp. as distinct from a profession), skilled handicraft; the persons engaged in a particular trade (*the book trade*; *trade enquiries only*); (usu. in *pl.*) trade wind. **2** *v.* engage in trade (*in* commodity or *with* person etc.), buy and sell; exchange (goods) in commerce; have a transaction (*with* person). **3 trade in** give (used article) in part payment for another; **trade-in** *n.* article given in this way; **trade mark** device or word(s) legally registered or established by use to distinguish goods of a particular manufacturer etc.; **trade name** name by which a thing is known in the trade, or given by manufacturer to proprietary article, or under which business is carried on; **trade off** exchange as compromise; **trade on** (or **upon**) derive advantage from, esp. unfairly or unscrupulously; **trade price** that charged by manufacturer etc. to retailer; **trade secret** device or technique used in trade and giving advantage because not generally known; **Trades Union Congress** official representative body of British trade unions; **trade union** (*pl.* **trade unions**) organized association of work-people of a trade or group of allied trades formed to protect and promote their common interests; **trade-unionism** system of trade unions; **trade-unionist** member of trade union; **trade wind** constant wind blowing towards equator from north-east or south-east. [LG, = track (TREAD)]

trader *n.* person or ship engaged in trade.

tradescantia /trædɪsˈkæntɪə/ *n.* perennial plant with large blue, white, or pink flowers. [*Tradescant*, naturalist]

tradesman *n.* person engaged in trade, esp. shopkeeper. [TRADE]

trading *n.* engaging in trade, buying and selling; **trading estate** area designed to be occupied by industrial and commercial firms; **trading stamp** stamp given by tradesman to customer and exchangeable in quantity for various articles or for cash.

tradition /trəˈdɪʃ(ə)n/ *n.* opinion or belief or custom handed down from one generation to another esp. orally; this process of handing down; artistic or literary principle based on usage or experience. [F or L (*trado -dit-* hand on, betray)]

traditional *a.* of or based on or obtained by tradition; (of jazz) based on early style; **traditionally** *adv.*

traditionalism *n.* great or excessive respect for tradition; **traditionalist** *n.* [F or prec.]

traduce /trəˈdjuːs/ *v.t.* misrepresent, slander; **traducement** *n.* [L, = disgrace]

traffic /ˈtræfɪk/ **1** *n.* coming and going of persons and vehicles and goods by road, rail, air, sea, etc.; vehicles coming and going; trade, esp. in illicit goods (*the traffic in drugs*); number or amount of persons or goods conveyed; use of a service, amount of this (*telephone traffic*); dealings between persons etc. **2** *v.* (**-ck-**) trade, engage in traffic (*in* commodity); deal in, barter. **3 traffic island** paved etc. area in road to direct traffic and provide refuge for pedestrians; **traffic-light** signal controlling road traffic by coloured lights; **traffic warden** person employed to control movement and parking of road vehicles. [F f. It.]

tragacanth /ˈtrægəkænθ/ *n.* vegetable gum used in pharmacy etc. [F f. L f. Gk]

tragedian /trəˈdʒiːdɪən/ *n.* author of or actor in tragedy. [F (TRAGEDY)]

tragedienne /trədʒiːdɪˈen/ *n.* actress in tragedy.

tragedy /ˈtrædʒɪdɪ/ *n.* drama of elevated theme and diction and with unhappy ending; sad event, serious accident, calamity. [F f. L f. Gk]

tragic /ˈtrædʒɪk/ *a.* of tragedy; tragical.

tragical *a.* sad, calamitous, greatly distressing; **tragically** *adv.*

tragicomedy /trædʒɪˈkɒmɪdɪ/ *n.* drama of mixed tragic and comic events; **tragicomic** *a.*; **tragicomically** *adv.* [F or It. f. L (TRAGIC, COMEDY)]

trail 1 *v.* draw or be drawn along behind; drag (*oneself* or one's limbs) along wearily etc., walk wearily (*along* etc.); hang loosely, (of plant) hang or spread downwards; be losing in contest; follow the trail of, pursue, shadow. **2** *n.* track or scent or other sign of passage left behind; beaten path, esp. through wild region; thing that trails or is trailed behind; long line of people or things following behind something. **3 trail arms** let rifle etc. hang balanced in hand and parallel to ground; **trail away** (or **off**) diminish or become fainter; **trail-blazer** pioneer, one who blazes a trail (see BLAZE[2]); **trailing edge** rear edge of aircraft's wing. [F or LG]

trailer *n.* cart etc. drawn by vehicle and used to carry load; set of short extracts from film shown in advance to advertise it; person or thing that trails; *US* caravan.

train 1 *n.* series of railway carriages or trucks drawn by a locomotive; succession or series of persons or things (*wagon train*; *train of thought*); body of followers, retinue; thing drawn along behind or forming hinder part, esp. elongated part of woman's skirt or of official robe. **2** *v.* bring to desired standard of performance or behaviour by instruction and practice; undergo this process (*she trained as a nurse*); teach and accustom *to do* thing; bring or come to physical efficiency by exercise and diet; guide growth of (plant etc.) *along* or *up* etc.; point or aim (gun or camera *on* object etc.). **3 in train** arranged, in preparation; **train-bearer** person holding up train of another's robe; **train-spotter** collector of locomotive-numbers seen. [F f. Rmc (L *traho* draw)]

trainee /treɪˈniː/ *n.* person being trained, esp. for occupation.

trainer *n.* person who trains horses or athletes etc.; aircraft or device simulating it used to train pilots.

training *n.* process by which one is trained for sport or contest or occupation.

traipse *v.i. colloq.* tramp or trudge wearily; *colloq.* go *about* on errands. [orig. unkn.]

trait /treɪ/ *n.* distinguishing feature in character, appearance, habit, or portrayal. [F, f. L *tractus* (TRACT[1])]

traitor /ˈtreɪtə/ *n.* person guilty of betrayal, one who acts disloyally (*to* country or cause etc.); **traitorous** *a.*; **traitress** *n. fem.* [F f. L *traditor* (as TRADITION)]

trajectory /ˈtrædʒɪktərɪ, trəˈdʒek-/ *n.* path of body (e.g. comet or bullet) moving under given forces. [med.L f. L *traicio -ject-* throw across]

tram *n.* (also **tramcar**) passenger vehicle running on rails in public road; four-wheeled car used in coal-mines. [LG & Du. *trame* beam]

tramlines *n.pl.* rails for tram; *colloq.* pair of parallel lines at edge of tennis or badminton court.

trammel /ˈtræm(ə)l/ **1** *n.* a kind of fishing-net; (usu. in *pl.* and *fig.*) impediment to movement or action (*the trammels of routine*). **2** *v.t.* (**-ll-**, *US* **-l-**) hamper. [F *tremail* f. med.L *tremaculum*]

tramp 1 *v.* walk with firm heavy tread;

walk laboriously across or along (country or streets), cover (distance) thus; go on walking expedition; live as tramp. **2** *n.* person who tramps the roads as vagrant; sound (as) of person walking or marching; long walk; *sl.* dissolute woman; freight-vessel, esp. steamer, on no regular line. [Gmc]

trample /ˈtræmp(ə)l/ *v.* tread repeatedly with heavy or crushing steps (*on*); crush or harm thus. [prec.]

trampoline /ˈtræmpəliːn/ **1** *n.* stretched canvas sheet connected by springs to horizontal frame, used for jumping in acrobatics etc. **2** *v.i.* use trampoline. [It. *trampolino*]

tramway *n.* rails for tram. [TRAM]

trance /trɑːns/ *n.* sleeplike state without response to stimuli; hypnotic or cataleptic state; mental abstraction from external things, rapture, ecstasy. [F (*transir* f. L *transeo* pass over)]

tranny /ˈtrænɪ/ *n. sl.* transistor radio. [abbr.]

tranquil /ˈtræŋkwɪl/ *a.* serene, calm, undisturbed; **tranquillity** /-ˈkwɪlɪtɪ/ *n.*; **tranquilly** *adv.* [F or L]

tranquillize, *US* **tranquilize** *v.t.* make tranquil esp. by drug.

tranquillizer, *US* **tranquilizer** *n.* drug used to diminish anxiety and induce calmness.

trans- *prefix* across, through, beyond, to or on farther side of. [L]

transact /trænˈzækt, trɑː-/ *v.t.* perform or carry through (business). [L (ACT)]

transaction /trænˈzækʃ(ə)n, trɑː-/ *n.* transacting of business; piece of esp. commercial business done; (in *pl.*) reports of discussions and lectures at meetings of learned society.

transalpine /trænzˈælpaɪn, trɑː-/ *a.* on north side of the Alps. [L]

transatlantic /trænzətˈlæntɪk, trɑː-/ *a.* crossing or beyond the Atlantic; American; *US* European. [TRANS-]

transceiver /trænˈsiːvə, trɑː-/ *n.* combined radio transmitter and receiver. [TRANSMITTER, RECEIVER]

transcend /trænˈsend, trɑː-/ *v.t.* be beyond range or domain or grasp of (experience or belief or description etc.); excel, surpass. [F or L (*scando* climb)]

transcendent *a.* of supreme merit or quality; (of God) existing apart from, or not subject to limitations of, material universe; **transcendence** *n.*; **transcendency** *n.*

transcendental /trænsenˈdent(ə)l, trɑː-/ *a.* a priori, not based on experience, intuitively accepted, innate in the mind; consisting of or dealing in or inspired by abstraction; **Transcendental Meditation** technique of meditation and relaxation based on yoga; **transcendentally** *adv.* [med.L (prec.)]

transcendentalism *n.* philosophy or belief taking account of transcendental things; **transcendentalist** *n.*

transcontinental /trænzkɒntɪˈnent(ə)l, trɑː-/ *a.* extending across a continent. [TRANS-]

transcribe /trænˈskraɪb, trɑː-/ *v.t.* copy out; reproduce (shorthand etc.) in ordinary writing; *Mus.* adapt (composition) for voice or instrument other than that for which it was originally written. [L *transcribo -script-*]

transcript /ˈtrænskrɪpt, ˈtrɑː-/ *n.* written copy. [F f. L (prec.)]

transcription /trænˈskrɪpʃ(ə)n, trɑː-/ *n.* transcribing; transcript; something transcribed. [F or L (TRANSCRIBE)]

transducer /trænzˈdjuːsə, trɑː-/ *n.* any device which produces an output signal (e.g. a voltage) in response to a different sort of input signal (e.g. pressure). [L (as DUCT)]

transept /ˈtrænsept, ˈtrɑː-/ *n.* part of cruciform church at right angles to nave; either arm of this (*north, south, transept*). [L (SEPTUM)]

transfer 1 /trænsˈfɜː, trɑː-/ *v.* (-**rr**-) convey or remove or hand over from one person or place to another; make over possession of (property or rights etc.); convey (design etc.) from one surface to another; move (person) to, change or be moved to, another group; go from one station or route or conveyance to another in order to continue journey; change (meaning) by extension or metaphor. **2** /ˈtrænsfɜː, ˈtrɑː-/ *n.* transferring or being transferred; document effecting conveyance of property or right; design or picture that is or can be conveyed from one surface to another. **3 transferable** /-ˈfɜːrəb(ə)l/ *a.* [F or L (*fero lat-* carry)]

transference /ˈtrænsfərəns, ˈtrɑː-/ *n.* action of transferring.

transfiguration /trænsfɪgəˈreɪʃ(ə)n, trɑː-/ *n.* transfiguring or being transfigured; (**Transfiguration**) that of Christ (Matt. 17:2), celebrated on 6 Aug. [F or L (foll.)]

transfigure /trænsˈfɪgə, trɑː-/ *v.t.* change appearance of, esp. to something nobler or more beautiful; make more spiritual or elevated. [F or L]

transfix /trænsˈfɪks, trɑː-/ *v.t.* pierce with lance etc.; (of horror etc.) paralyse faculties of (person). [L (FIX)]

transform /trænsˈfɔːm, trɑː-/*v.t.* make considerable change in form or appearance or character of; change voltage of (electric current); **transformation** /-fə'meɪʃ(ə)n/ *n.* [F or L]

transformer *n.* apparatus for reducing or increasing voltage of alternating current.

transfuse /træns'fju:z, trɑ:-/ *v.t.* cause (fluid or colour or influence etc.) to permeate *into*; imbue by such permeation *with*; inject (blood or other liquid) into blood-vessel to replace that lost; **transfusion** /-'fju:ʒ(ə)n/ *n.* [L (FOUND²)]

transgress /træns'gres, trɑ:-/ *v.* violate, infringe, go beyond bounds set by (commandment, law, limitation, etc.); sin; **transgression** *n.*; **transgressor** *n.* [F, or L *transgredior -gress-*]

transient /'trænsɪənt, 'trɑ:-/ *a.* quickly passing away, fleeting; **transience** *n.* [L (TRANCE)]

transistor /træn'sɪstə, trɑ:-/ *n.* semiconductor device with three electrodes and same functions as thermionic valve but smaller and consuming less power; (in full **transistor radio**) portable radio set equipped with transistors. [TRANS(FER), (RES)ISTOR]

transistorize *v.t.* equip with transistors (rather than valves).

transit /'trænsɪt, 'trɑ:-/ *n.* going or conveying or being conveyed across or over or through (*goods damaged in transit*); passage or route (*the overland transit*); apparent passage of heavenly body across disc of another or meridian of place; **transit camp** camp for temporary accommodation of soldiers, refugees, etc. [L (TRANCE)]

transition /træn'sɪʃ(ə)n, trɑ:-/ *n.* passage or change from one state or action or subject or set of circumstances to another; period during which one style of art develops into another, esp. of architecture between Norman and Early English; **transitional** *a.*; **transitionally** *adv.* [F or L (prec.)]

transitive /'trænsɪtɪv, 'trɑ:-/ *a.* (of verb) taking direct object expressed or understood. [L (TRANSIT)]

transitory /'trænsɪtərɪ, 'trɑ:-/ *a.* passing, not long-lasting, merely temporary; **transitorily** *adv.*; **transitoriness** *n.* [AF *transitorie* f. L (TRANSIT)]

translate /træns'leɪt, trɑ:-/ *v.t.* express the sense of (word or text etc.) in another language, in plainer words, or in another form of representation (*translates emotion into music, speech into sign language*); infer or declare significance of, interpret; remove (bishop) to another see; move from one person or place or condition to another; **translation** *n.*; **translator** *n.* [L (TRANSFER)]

transliterate /træns'lɪtəreɪt, trɑ:-/ *v.t.* represent (word etc.) in corresponding characters of another alphabet or language; **transliteration** /-'reɪʃ(ə)n/ *n.*; **transliterator** *n.* [L *littera* letter]

translucent /træns'lu:sənt, trɑ:-/ *a.* allowing light to pass through, esp. without being transparent; **translucence** *n.*; **translucency** *n.* [L (*luceo* shine)]

transmigrate /trænsmaɪ'greɪt, trɑ:-/ *v.i.* (of soul) pass into different body; migrate; **transmigration** *n.* [L]

transmissible /træns'mɪsɪb(ə)l, trɑ:-/ *a.* transmittable. [L (TRANSMIT)]

transmission /træns'mɪʃ(ə)n, trɑ:-/ *n.* transmitting or being transmitted; broadcast programme; gear transmitting power from engine to axle in motor vehicle.

transmit /træns'mɪt, trɑ:-/ *v.t.* (**-tt-**) pass on, hand on, transfer, communicate (*transmit the message, the parcel, the title, the disease*); allow to pass through, be a medium for, serve to communicate (heat, light, sound, electricity, emotion, signal, news); **transmittable** *a.* [L (*mitto miss-* send)]

transmitter *n.* equipment used to transmit message, signal, etc.; person or thing that transmits.

transmogrify /træns'mɒgrɪfaɪ, trɑ:-/ *v.t.* transform esp. in magical or surprising manner; **transmogrification** /-fɪ'keɪʃ(ə)n/ *n.* [orig. unkn.]

transmutation /trænsmju:'teɪʃ(ə)n, trɑ:-/ *n.* transmuting or being transmuted; **transmutation of metals** turning of other metals into gold as alchemists' aim. [F or L (foll.)]

transmute /træns'mju:t, trɑ:-/ *v.t.* change form or nature or substance of, convert into different thing. [L (*muto* change)]

transoceanic /trænsəʊʃɪ'ænɪk, trɑ:-/ *a.* crossing or beyond the ocean. [TRANS-]

transom /'trænsəm/ *n.* cross-beam, esp. horizontal bar above door or above or in window; window above this. [F *traversin* (TRAVERSE)]

transparency /træns'pærənsɪ, trɑ:-/ *n.* being transparent; picture (esp. photograph) to be viewed by light passing through it. [med.L (foll.)]

transparent /træns'pærənt, trɑ:-/ *a.* that can be clearly seen through because allowing light to pass through without diffusion; (of disguise or pretext etc.) easily seen through; evident or obvious (*transparent sincerity*); easily understood; free from affectation or disguise. [F f. med.L f. L (*pareo* appear)]

transpire /træns'paɪə, trɑ:-/ *v.* (of secret or fact etc.) come to be known; (**D**) occur, happen; emit (vapour or moisture) through pores of skin etc.; be emitted thus; **transpiration** /-prɪ'reɪʃ(ə)n/ *n.* [F or med.L, f. L *spiro* breathe]

transplant 1 /træns'plɑ:nt, trɑ:-/ *v.t.* uproot and replant elsewhere (often *fig.*); transfer (living tissue or organ) and implant in another part of body or in another (human or animal) body. 2 /'trænsplɑ:nt, 'trɑ:-/ *n.* transplanting of tissue or organ; thing transplanted. 3 **transplantation** /-plɑ:n'teɪʃ(ə)n/ *n.* [L]

transport 1 /træns'pɔ:t, trɑ:-/ *v.t.* take (person or goods etc.) from one place to another; *hist.* deport (criminal) to penal colony; (esp. in *p.p.*) affect with strong emotion (*transported with joy*). 2 /'trænspɔ:t, 'trɑ:-/ *n.* transporting; means of conveyance (*the transport has arrived*); ship or aircraft employed to carry soldiers, stores, etc.; vehement emotion (*in transports of delight*). 3 **transport café** café providing meals for drivers of esp. commercial motor vehicles. 4 **transportable** *a.* [F or L (PORT[5])]

transportation /trænspɔ:'teɪʃ(ə)n, trɑ:-/ *n.* transporting; *hist.* deporting of convicts; *US* means of conveyance.

transporter *n.* vehicle used to transport other vehicles, heavy machinery, etc.; **transporter bridge** bridge carrying vehicles across water on suspended platform.

transpose /træns'pəʊz, trɑ:-/ *v.t.* cause (two or more things) to change places; change position of (thing) in series; change natural or existing order or position of (word or words) in sentence; put (music) into different key; **transposition** /-pə'zɪʃ(ə)n/ *n.* [F (POSE)]

transsexual /trænz'seksjʊəl, trɑ:-/ 1 *a.* having physical characteristics of one sex and psychological characteristics of the other. 2 *n.* transsexual person. 3 **transsexualism** *n.* [TRANS-]

trans-ship /træn'ʃɪp, trɑ:-/ *v.t.* (**-pp-**) transfer from one ship or conveyance to another; **trans-shipment** *n.*

transubstantiation /trænsəbstænʃɪ'eɪʃ(ə)n, trɑ:-/ *n.* conversion of Eucharistic elements wholly into body and blood of Christ. [med.L (TRANS-, SUBSTANCE)]

transuranic /trænsjʊə'rænɪk, trɑ:-/ *a.* (of element) having higher atomic number than uranium. [TRANS-]

transverse /'trænzvɜ:s, 'trɑ:-, -'vɜ:s/ *a.* situated or arranged or acting in crosswise direction. [L *transverto -vers-* turn across]

transvestism /trænz'vestɪz(ə)m, trɑ:-/ *n.* clothing oneself in garments of opposite sex. [L *vestio* clothe]

transvestite /trænz'vestaɪt, trɑ:-/ *n.* person given to transvestism.

trap[1] 1 *n.* device, often baited, for catching animals; trick betraying person into speech or act (*is this question a trap?*); arrangement to catch unsuspecting person, e.g. speeding motorist; device for effecting sudden release e.g. of greyhound in race, of ball to be struck at, of clay pigeon to be shot at; curve in drainpipe etc. serving when filled with liquid to seal it against return of gas; two-wheeled carriage (*pony and trap*); = *trapdoor*; *sl.* mouth (*shut your trap*). 2 *v.t.* (**-pp-**) catch in trap; stop and retain in or as in trap; furnish (place) with traps. [OE]

trap[2] *n.* kind of dark volcanic rock. [Sw.]

trapdoor *n.* door in floor or ceiling or roof. [TRAP[1]]

trapeze /trə'pi:z/ *n.* crossbar suspended by cords as swing for acrobatics etc. [F f. L (foll.)]

trapezium /trə'pi:zɪəm/ *n.* (*pl.* **trapezia** or **-iums**) quadrilateral with only one pair of sides parallel; *US* trapezoid. [L f. Gk *trapezion*]

trapezoid /'træpɪzɔ:ɪd/ *n.* quadrilateral with no sides parallel; *US* trapezium. [Gk (prec.)]

trapper *n.* person who traps wild animals esp. for furs. [TRAP[1]]

trappings /'træpɪŋz/ *n.pl.* ornamental accessories; harness of horse esp. when ornamental. [*trap* f. F *drap* cloth]

Trappist /'træpɪst/ *n.* monk of an order noted for silence. [La *Trappe* in Normandy]

traps *n.pl. colloq.* baggage, belongings (usu. *pack up one's traps*). [prob. TRAPPINGS]

trash *n.* worthless or waste stuff, rubbish; worthless person or people; **trash-can** *US* dustbin; **trashy** *a.* [orig. unkn.]

trattoria /trætə'ri:ə/ *n.* Italian eating-house. [It.]

trauma /'trɔ:mə/ *n.* (*pl.* **traumas**) emotional shock; morbid condition of body caused by wound or external violence. [Gk, = wound]

traumatic /trɔ:'mætɪk/ *a.* of or causing trauma; *colloq.* unpleasant (*a traumatic experience*); **traumatically** *adv.* [L f. Gk (prec.)]

travail /'træveɪl/ 1 *n. literary* painful or laborious effort; *archaic* pangs of childbirth. 2 *v.i. literary* make painful or laborious effort; *archaic* suffer pangs of childbirth. [F *travailler* f. med.L *trepalium*]

travel /'træv(ə)l/ 1 *v.* (**-ll-**, *US* **-l-**) go from one place to another, make journey esp. of some length or abroad; journey along or through (country), cover (distance) in travelling; *colloq.* withstand long journey (*wines that travel badly*); go from place to place as salesman (*for* firm or *in* commodity); move or proceed in specified manner or at specified rate; *colloq.* move quickly; pass esp. in deliberate or systematic manner from point to point (*his eye travelled over the scene*); (of machine or part) move or operate in specified way. **2** *n.* travelling, esp. in foreign countries, spell of this (often in *pl.*); range, rate, or mode of motion of part in machinery. **3 travel agency** (or **agent**) agency (or agent) making arrangements for travellers; **travelling crane** crane able to move along overhead support. [orig. = prec.]

travelled *a.* experienced in travelling.

traveller, *US* **traveler** *n.* person who travels or is travelling; commercial traveller; gypsy; **traveller's cheque,** *US* **traveler's check** cheque for fixed amount, encashable on signature usu. in many countries; **traveller's joy** wild clematis; **traveller's tale** incredible and probably untrue story.

travelogue /'trævəlɒg/ *n.* film or illustrated lecture with narrative of travel. [TRAVEL, after *monologue*]

traverse 1 /trə'vɜːs/ *v.* travel or lie across (*traversed the country*; *pit traversed by beam*); consider or discuss whole extent of (subject); turn (large gun) horizontally. **2** /'trævəs/ *n.* sideways movement, traversing; thing that crosses another. **3 traversal** /trə'vɜːs(ə)l/ *n.* [F (TRANSVERSE)]

travesty /'trævɪstɪ/ **1** *n.* grotesque misrepresentation or imitation. **2** *v.t.* make or be travesty of. [F (*travestir* disguise, f. It.)]

trawl 1 *n.* large wide-mouthed fishing-net dragged by boat along bottom. **2** *v.* fish with trawl or seine; catch by trawling. [prob. Du. *traghel* drag-net]

trawler *n.* boat for use with trawl.

tray *n.* flat shallow vessel usu. with raised rim for carrying dishes etc. or containing small articles, papers, etc.; shallow lidless box forming compartment of trunk. [OE]

treacherous /'tretʃərəs/ *a.* guilty of or involving treachery; (of weather, ice, memory, etc.) not to be relied on, likely to fail or give way. [F f. *trichier* cheat (TRICK)]

treachery /'tretʃərɪ/ *n.* violation of faith or trust esp. by secret desertion of the cause to which one professes allegiance.

treacle /'triːk(ə)l/ *n.* syrup produced in refining sugar; molasses; **treacly** *a.* [orig. = antidote for snake-bite (F f. L f. Gk)]

tread /tred/ **1** *v.* (*past* **trod**; *p.p.* **trodden** or **trod**) set down one's foot, walk or step, (of foot) be set down; walk on, press or crush with the feet; perform (steps etc.) by walking, make (hole etc.) by treading; (of male bird) copulate with (hen, or *absol.*). **2** *n.* manner or sound of walking; top surface of step or stair; part of wheel that touches ground or rails, part of rail that wheels touch, thick moulded part of vehicle tyre for gripping road, part of sole of boot etc. similarly moulded. **3 tread the boards** be an actor; **tread on air** feel elated; **tread on person's corns** (or **toes**) offend his feelings or privileges; **tread water** maintain upright position in water by moving feet and hands. [OE]

treadle /'tred(ə)l/ *n.* lever worked by foot and imparting motion to machine. [OE (prec.)]

treadmill *n.* device for producing motion by stepping on movable steps on revolving cylinder, formerly used as prison punishment; monotonous routine work. [TREAD]

treason /'triːz(ə)n/ *n.* violation by subject of allegiance to sovereign or State; breach of faith, disloyalty. [AF *treisoun* f. L (TRADITION)]

treasonable *a.* involving or guilty of treason; **treasonably** *adv.*

treasonous *a.* treasonable.

treasure /'treʒə/ **1** *n.* precious metals or gems, hoard of these, accumulated wealth; thing valued for rarity, workmanship, associations, etc. (*art treasures*); *colloq.* beloved or highly valued person. **2** *v.t.* store (*up*) as valuable (*lit.*, or *fig.* in memory); value highly. **3 treasure-hunt** search for treasure, game in which players seek hidden object; **treasure trove** treasure of unknown ownership found hidden. [F f. L f. Gk *thēsauros*]

treasurer *n.* person in charge of funds of society or municipality etc. [AF (prec.)]

treasury *n.* place where treasure is kept; funds or revenue of a State or institution or society; (**Treasury**) department managing public revenue of a country, offices and officers of this; **Treasury bench** front bench in Parliament occupied by Prime Minister, Chancellor of the Exchequer, etc.; **treasury bill** bill of exchange issued by government to raise money for temporary needs. [F *tresorie* (TREASURE)]

treat 1 *v.* act or behave towards or deal with (person or thing) in a certain way (*treated me kindly*; *treat it as a joke*); deal with or apply process to (*treat it with acid*); apply medical care or attention to; present or deal with (subject) in literature or art; provide with food or drink or entertainment at one's own expense (*treated us to dinner*); negotiate (*with* person); give spoken or written exposition *of*. **2** *n*. thing (esp. unexpected or unusual) that gives great pleasure; entertainment designed to do this; treating of others to food etc. (*it's my treat*). **3 stand treat** bear expense of entertainment etc. [F *traitier* f. L *tracto* handle]

treatise /'tri:tɪs, -ɪz/ *n*. written work dealing formally and systematically with a subject. [AF (as prec.)]

treatment *n*. process or manner of behaving towards or dealing with a person or thing; medical care or attention; manner of treating subject in literature or art.

treaty /'tri:tɪ/ *n*. formally concluded and ratified agreement between States; agreement between persons esp. for purchase of property. [AF f. L (as TREAT)]

treble /'treb(ə)l/ **1** *a*. threefold, triple, three times as much or many (*treble the amount*); (of voice) high-pitched; *Mus*. soprano (esp. of boy's voice or boy, or of instrument). **2** *n*. treble quantity or thing; hit at darts on narrow ring between the two middle circles on the board, scoring treble; soprano, esp. boy's voice or boy; high-pitched voice. **3** *v*. multiply or be multiplied by three. **4 trebly** *adv*. [F f. L (TRIPLE)]

tree 1 *n*. perennial plant with single woody self-supporting stem (*trunk*) usu. unbranched for some distance above ground; piece or frame of wood etc. for various purposes (*shoe-tree*); family tree. **2** *v.t.* force (animal, *fig*. person) to take refuge in tree. **3 grow on trees** be plentifully available without effort; **tree-creeper** small creeping bird feeding on insects in tree-bark; **tree-fern** large fern with upright woody stem; **tree-house** structure in tree for children to play in; **tree-ring** ring in cross-section of tree, from one year's growth; **tree surgeon** one who treats decayed trees in order to preserve them. [OE]

trefoil /'trefɔɪl, 'tri:-/ *n*. a kind of plant with leaves of three leaflets (clover, shamrock, etc.); three-lobed thing esp. ornamentation in tracery etc. [AF (TRI-, FOIL²)]

trek (orig. *S. Afr*.) **1** *v.i.* (**-kk-**) travel arduously; migrate or journey with one's belongings in ox-wagons. **2** *n*. such journey, each stage of it; organized migration of body of persons. [Du., = draw]

trellis /'trelɪs/ *n*. lattice or grating of light wooden or metal bars used esp. as support for fruit-trees or creepers and often fastened against wall. [F f. Rmc (TRI-, L *licium* warp-thread)]

trematode /'tremətəʊd/ *n*. kind of parasitic flatworm. [Gk (*trēma* hole)]

tremble /'tremb(ə)l/ **1** *v.i.* shake involuntarily with fear or excitement or weakness; be in state of apprehension; move in quivering manner (*leaves tremble in the breeze*). **2** *n*. trembling, quiver (*a tremble in her voice*). [F f. med.L (TREMULOUS)]

trembler *n*. automatic vibrator for making and breaking electric circuit.

trembly *a. colloq*. trembling.

tremendous /trɪ'mendəs/ *a*. awe-inspiring, overpowering; *colloq*. remarkable or considerable. [L *tremendus* to be trembled at (TREMOR)]

tremolo /'tremələʊ/ *n*. (*pl*. **tremolos**) tremulous effect in playing music or singing. [It. (TREMULOUS)]

tremor /'tremə/ *n*. shaking, quivering; thrill (of fear or exultation etc.); **earth tremor** slight earthquake. [F & L (*tremo* tremble)]

tremulous /'tremjʊləs/ *a*. trembling, quivering. [L *tremulus* (prec.)]

trench 1 *n*. long narrow usu. deep ditch, esp. one dug by troops to stand in and be sheltered from enemy's fire. **2** *v.t.* dig trench or trenches in (ground); dig (soil or garden) thus so as to bring subsoil to the top. **3 trench coat** soldier's lined or padded waterproof coat, *US* loose belted raincoat; **trench mortar** light simple mortar throwing bomb from one's own into enemy trenches. [F *trenche, -ier* cut]

trenchant /'trentʃənt/ *a*. (of style or language etc.) incisive, terse, vigorous; **trenchancy** *n*.

trencher *n. hist*. wooden platter for serving food.

trencherman *n*. feeder, eater (*good trencherman*).

trend 1 *n*. general direction and tendency (esp. of events or opinion etc.). **2** *v.i.* bend or turn away in specified direction; be chiefly directed, have general and continued tendency. **3 trend-setter** person who leads the way in fashion etc. [OE]

trendy *colloq*. **1** *a*. fashionable. **2** *n*. fashionable person. **3 trendily** *adv*.; **trendiness** *n*.

trepan /trɪ'pæn/ **1** *n*. surgeon's cylindrical saw for removing part of skull. **2** *v.t.* (**-nn-**) perforate (skull) with trepan. [med.L f. Gk *trupanon* auger]

trepidation /trepɪ'deɪʃ(ə)n/ *n*. fear; perturbation of mind; tremulous agitation, flurry. [L (*trepidus* flurried)]

trespass /'trespəs/ **1** *v.i.* make unlawful or unwarrantable intrusion (esp. *on* or *upon* land); make unwarrantable claims *on* (*shall trespass on your hospitality*). **2**

n. act of trespassing; *archaic* sin or offence. [F f. med.L (TRANS-, PASS)]

tress *n.* lock of human (esp. female) hair; (in *pl.*) head of such hair. [F]

trestle /'tres(ə)l/ *n.* supporting structure for table etc. consisting of two frames fixed at an angle or hinged or of bar supported by two divergent pairs of legs; trestle-work; **trestle-table** table of board or boards laid on trestles or other supports; **trestle-work** open braced framework to support bridge etc. [F f. Rmc (L *transtrum* cross-beam)]

trews /tru:z/ *n.pl.* close-fitting usu. tartan trousers. [Ir. & Gael. (TROUSERS)]

TRH *abbr.* Their Royal Highnesses.

tri- *in comb.* three, three times. [L & Gk]

triad /'traɪæd, -əd/ *n.* group of three (esp. notes in chord); the number three; Chinese secret society, usu. criminal; **triadic** /-'ædɪk/ *a.*; **triadically** /-'ædɪkəlɪ/ *adv.* [F or L f. Gk]

trial /'traɪəl/ *n.* judicial examination and determination of issues between parties by judge with or without jury; process or mode of testing qualities, experimental treatment, test (*will give you a trial*); sports match to test ability of players who may be selected for an important team; trying thing or experience or person; **on trial** to be chosen or retained only if suitable; **trial and error** repeated trials till one succeeds; **trial run** preliminary testing of vehicle or vessel etc. [AF (TRY)]

triangle /'traɪæŋg(ə)l/ *n.* plane figure with three sides and angles; any three things not in a straight line, with the imaginary lines joining them (*a triangle of beacons*); implement etc. of this shape; musical instrument of steel rod bent into triangle sounded by striking with small steel rod; situation etc. involving three persons. [F, or L (TRI-)]

triangular /traɪ'æŋgjʊlə/ *a.* triangle-shaped, three-cornered; (of contest or treaty etc.) between three persons or parties; (of pyramid) having three-sided base. [L (prec.)]

triangulate /traɪ'æŋgjʊleɪt/ *v.t.* divide (area) into triangles for surveying purposes; **triangulation** /-'leɪʃ(ə)n/ *n.*

Triassic /traɪ'æsɪk/ **1** *a.* of the earliest period of the Mesozoic era. **2** *n.* this period. [TRIAD]

tribe *n.* group of (esp. primitive) families under recognized chief and usu. claiming common ancestor; any similar natural or political division; (usu. *derog.*) set or number of persons esp. of one profession etc. or family (*the whole tribe of actors*); **tribal** *a.*; **tribalism** *n.*; **tribally** *adv.* [F or L *tribus*]

tribesman *n.* member of a tribe or of one's own tribe.

tribology /trɪ'bɒlədʒɪ, traɪ-/ *n.* study of friction, wear, lubrication, and design of bearings. [Gk (*tribō* rub)]

tribulation /trɪbjʊ'leɪʃ(ə)n/ *n.* great affliction. [F f. L (*tribulum* threshing-sledge)]

tribunal /traɪ'bju:n(ə)l, trɪ-/ *n.* board appointed to adjudicate in some matter; court of justice; seat or bench for judge or judges. [F or L (TRIBUNE[1])]

tribune[1] /'trɪbju:n/ *n.* popular leader or demagogue; official in ancient Rome chosen by the people to protect their liberties (*tribune of the people*); Roman legionary officer (*military tribune*); **tribunate** *n.* [L *tribunus* (TRIBE)]

tribune[2] /'trɪbju:n/ *n.* bishop's throne in basilica; apse containing this; dais, rostrum. [F f. It. f. med.L *tribuna* (TRIBUNAL)]

tributary /'trɪbjʊtərɪ/ **1** *n.* river or stream flowing into larger river or lake; person or State paying or subject to tribute. **2** *a.* that is a tributary; contributory. [L (foll.)]

tribute /'trɪbju:t/ *n.* thing said or done or given as mark of respect or affection etc.; payment made periodically by one State or ruler to another as sign of dependence; obligation to pay this. [L *tributum* (*tribuo -ut-* assign, orig. divide between TRIBES)]

trice *n.* only in **in a trice** in an instant. [*trice* haul up, f. LG & Du.]

triceps /'traɪseps/ *n.* muscle (esp. in upper arm) with three points of attachment. [L (*caput* head)]

trichinosis /trɪkɪ'nəʊsɪs/ *n.* disease caused by hairlike worms in muscles. [Gk *thrix trikh-* hair]

trichology /trɪ'kɒlədʒɪ/ *n.* study of hair; **trichologist** *n.*

trichromatic /traɪkrə'mætɪk/ *a.* three-coloured; (of vision) having normal three colour-sensations (red, green, purple). [TRI-]

trick **1** *n.* thing done to fool or outwit or deceive; optical or other illusion (*trick of the light*); special technique, knack or way of doing something; unusual action (e.g. begging) learned by animal; mischievous or foolish or discreditable act, practical joke (*a mean trick to play*); peculiar or characteristic habit (*has a trick of repeating himself*); cards played in one round of card-game, winning of round; *attrib.* done to deceive or mystify (*trick photography*). **2** *v.t.* deceive or mislead or outwit; (of thing) foil or baffle, take by surprise. **3 do the trick** *colloq.* achieve what is required; **how's tricks?** *sl.* how are you?, how are things?; **trick out** (or **up**) decorate, esp. showily. [F]

trickery *n.* deception, use of tricks.
trickle /'trɪk(ə)l/ **1** *v.* flow in drops or in small stream; cause to do this; come or go slowly or gradually (*information trickles out*). **2** *n.* trickling flow. **3 trickle charger** accumulator-charger that works at steady slow rate from mains. [prob. imit.]
trickster *n.* deceiver, rogue. [TRICK]
tricksy *a.* full of tricks, playful.
tricky *a.* requiring care and adroitness; crafty, deceitful; **trickily** *adv.*; **trickiness** *n.*
tricolour /'trɪkələ/, *US* **tricolor** *n.* flag of three colours, esp. French national flag of blue, white, and red. [F (TRI-)]
tricot /'trɪkəʊ, 'tri:-/ *n.* knitted fabric. [F]
tricycle /'traɪsɪk(ə)l/ **1** *n.* three-wheeled pedal-driven vehicle; three-wheeled motor vehicle for disabled driver. **2** *v.i.* ride on tricycle. **3 tricyclist** *n.* [CYCLE]
trident /'traɪdənt/ *n.* three-pronged spear. [L (*dens dent-* tooth)]
Tridentine /trɪ'dentaɪn/ *a.* of the Council of Trent, held at Trento in Italy 1545–63, esp. as basis of RC orthodoxy. [med.L (*Tridentum* Trento)]
triennial /traɪ'enɪəl/ *a.* lasting, or recurring every, three years; **triennially** *adv.* [L (*annus* year)]
trier /'traɪə/ *n.* one who perseveres in his attempts (*a real trier*); tester. [TRY]
trifle /'traɪf(ə)l/ **1** *n.* thing of slight value or importance; small amount esp. of money (*was sold for a trifle*); confection of sponge-cake with custard, jelly, fruit, cream, etc. **2** *v.i.* talk or act frivolously. **3 a trifle** somewhat (*seems a trifle annoyed*); **trifle with** treat with flippancy or derision, toy with. [orig. *trufle* f. F = *truf(f)e* deceit]
trifling *a.* unimportant, petty; frivolous.
triforium /traɪ'fɔ:rɪəm/ *n.* (*pl.* **triforia**) arcade or gallery above nave and choir arches. [AL]
trigger **1** *n.* movable device for releasing spring or catch and so setting mechanism (esp. that of gun) in motion; agent that sets off a chain reaction. **2** *v.t.* (often with *off*) set (action or process) in motion, initiate, precipitate. **3 quick on the trigger** quick to respond; **trigger-happy** apt to shoot on slight provocation. [*tricker* f. Du. *trekker* (*trekken* pull)]
trigonometry /trɪgə'nɒmɪtrɪ/ *n.* branch of mathematics dealing with relations of sides and angles of triangle, and with relevant functions of any angles; **trigonometric** /-nə'metrɪk/ *a.*; **trigonometrical** /-nə'metrɪk(ə)l/ *a.*; **trigonometrically** /-nə'metrɪkəlɪ/ *adv.* [Gk (*trigōnon* triangle)]

trike *n. colloq.* tricycle. [abbr.]
trilateral /traɪ'lætər(ə)l/ *a.* having three sides; affecting or between three parties. [L (TRI-)]
trilby /'trɪlbɪ/ *n.* soft felt hat with narrow brim and lengthwise dent in crown. [*Trilby*, character in novel by G. du Maurier]
trilingual /traɪ'lɪŋgw(ə)l/ *a.* speaking or able to speak three languages; written in three languages. [TRI-]
trill **1** *n.* quavering or vibratory sound (e.g. quick alternation of notes in singing, bird's warbling, pronunciation of *r* with vibration of tongue). **2** *v.* produce trill; warble (song) or pronounce (*r* etc.) with trill. [It.]
trillion /'trɪljən/ *n.* (*pl.* **trillion**) million million million; *US* (and increasingly *Brit.*) million million; **trillionth** *a.* & *n.* [F or It. (TRI-, MILLION, after *billion*)]
trilobite /'traɪləbaɪt/ *n.* a kind of fossil arthropod. [TRI-, Gk *lobos* lobe]
trilogy /'trɪlədʒɪ/ *n.* group of three related literary or operatic works. [Gk (TRI-)]
trim **1** *v.* (**-mm-**) set in good order, make neat or of required size and form, esp. by cutting away irregular or unwanted parts; (with *off* or *away*) remove (such parts); ornament, decorate; adjust balance of (ship or aircraft) by arrangement of its cargo etc.; arrange (sails) to suit wind; hold middle course in politics or opinion, associate oneself with currently prevailing views; *colloq.* rebuke sharply, thrash, get the better of in bargain etc. **2** *n.* state of readiness or fitness (*in perfect, fighting, trim*); ornament or decorative material; trimming of hair etc. **3** *a.* neat, spruce; in good order, well arranged or equipped. [OE, = make firm]
trimaran /'traɪməræn/ *n.* vessel like catamaran, with three hulls side by side. [CATAMARAN]
trimeter /'trɪmɪtə/ *n.* line of verse of three measures. [L f. Gk (TRI-)]
trimming *n.* ornamentation, decoration; (in *pl.*) *colloq.* usual accompaniments, esp. of main course of meal. [TRIM]
Trinitarian /trɪnɪ'teərɪən/ *n.* believer in the Trinity. [med.L (TRINITY)]
trinitrotoluene /traɪnaɪtrə'tɒljʊi:n/ *n.* (also **trinitrotoluol**) a high explosive. [NITRO-, TOLUENE]
trinity /'trɪnɪtɪ/ *n.* being three; group of three; **the Trinity** the three persons of the Godhead (Father, Son, Holy Spirit); **Trinity Sunday** Sunday next after Whit Sunday; **Trinity term** university and law term beginning after Easter. [F f. L *trinitas* (*trinus* threefold)]

trinket /'trɪŋkɪt/ *n.* trifling ornament, esp. one worn on the person. [orig. unkn.]

trio /'tri:əʊ/ *n.* (*pl.* **trios**) musical composition for three performers; the performers; any group of three. [F & It., f. L]

trip 1 *v.* (**-pp-**) walk or dance with quick light steps, (of rhythm) run lightly; (often with *up*) stumble or cause to stumble, make slip or blunder; (with *up*) detect (person) in blunder; take a trip to a place; *colloq.* have visionary experience caused by drug; release (part of machine) suddenly by knocking aside catch etc. **2** *n.* journey or excursion, esp. for pleasure; stumble or blunder, tripping or being tripped up; nimble step; *colloq.* visionary experience caused by drug; contrivance for tripping mechanism etc. **3 trip-wire** wire stretched close to ground, operating alarm etc. when disturbed. [F f. Du. *trippen* skip, hop]

tripartite /traɪ'pɑ:taɪt/ *a.* consisting of three parts; shared by or involving three parties. [L (*partior* divide)]

tripe *n.* first or second stomach of ruminant, esp. ox, as food; *sl.* worthless or trashy thing, rubbish. [F]

triple /'trɪp(ə)l/ **1** *a.* threefold, consisting of three parts or involving three parties; being three times as many or as much; (of time in music) having three beats in bar. **2** *n.* threefold number or amount; set of three. **3** *v.* multiply by three. **4 triple jump** athletic contest comprising hop, step, and jump. **5 triply** *adv.* [F or L *triplus* f. Gk]

triplet /'trɪplɪt/ *n.* one of three children or animals born at a birth; set of three things, esp. of equal notes played in time of two or verses rhyming together.

triplex *a.* triple, threefold. [L]

triplicate /'trɪplɪkət/ **1** *a.* existing in three examples; having three corresponding parts; tripled. **2** *n.* one of three things exactly alike. **3** /-keɪt/ *v.t.* make in three copies; multiply by three. **4 triplication** /-'keɪʃ(ə)n/ *n.* [L (prec.)]

tripod /'traɪpɒd/ *n.* three-legged stand for camera etc.; stool or table or utensil resting on three feet or legs. [L f. Gk, = three-footed]

tripos /'traɪpɒs/ *n.* honours examination for BA degree at Cambridge University.

tripper *n.* person who goes on a pleasure trip or excursion. [TRIP]

triptych /'trɪptɪk/ *n.* picture or carving on three panels, usu. hinged vertically together. [after DIPTYCH]

trireme /'traɪri:m/ *n.* ancient warship, prob. with three men at each oar. [F or L (*remus* oar)]

trisect /traɪ'sekt/ *v.t.* divide into three (usu. equal) parts; **trisection** *n.* [L *seco sect-* cut]

trite *a.* (of phrase, opinion, etc.) hackneyed, worn out by constant repetition. [L *tero trit-* rub]

tritium /'trɪtɪəm/ *n.* heavy radioactive isotope of hydrogen with mass about three times that of ordinary hydrogen. [Gk *tritos* third]

triumph /'traɪəmf/ **1** *n.* state of being victorious, great success or achievement; supreme example (*a triumph of engineering*); joy at success, exultation; processional entry of victorious general into ancient Rome. **2** *v.i.* gain victory, be successful, prevail; exult; (of Roman general) ride in triumph. [F f. L]

triumphal /traɪ'ʌmf(ə)l/ *a.* of or used in or celebrating a triumph. [F or L (prec.)]

triumphant /traɪ'ʌmfənt/ *a.* victorious, successful; exultant.

triumvir /'traɪəmvɪə, -'ʌmvə/ *n.* member of a triumvirate. [L (*tres* three, *vir* man)]

triumvirate /traɪ'ʌmvərət/ *n.* board or ruling group of three men, esp. in ancient Rome. [L (prec.)]

trivalent /traɪ'veɪlənt/ *a.* having a valence of three. [TRI-]

trivet /'trɪvɪt/ *n.* iron tripod or bracket for cooking-pot or kettle to stand on; **as right as a trivet** *colloq.* in perfectly good state. [app. L *tripes* three-footed]

trivia /'trɪvɪə/ *n.pl.* trifles, trivialities. [as foll.]

trivial /'trɪvɪəl/ *a.* of small value or importance, trifling; (of person) concerned only with trivial things; **triviality** /-'ælɪtɪ/ *n.*; **trivially** *adv.* [L *trivialis* commonplace (*trivium* three-way street-corner)]

trochee /'trəʊki:/ *n.* a metrical foot (– ˘); **trochaic** /trə'keɪɪk/ *a.* [L f. Gk, = running]

trod, trodden *past* and *p.p.* of TREAD.

troglodyte /'trɒglədaɪt/ *n.* cave-dweller. [L f. Gk (*trōglē* hole)]

troika /'trɔɪkə/ *n.* Russian vehicle with team of three horses abreast; such team; group of three persons esp. as administrative council. [Russ.]

Trojan /'trəʊdʒ(ə)n/ **1** *a.* of ancient Troy in Asia Minor. **2** *n.* inhabitant of Troy; person who works or fights or endures courageously (*like a Trojan*). **3 Trojan Horse** hollow wooden horse used by Greeks to enter Troy, person or device insinuated to bring about enemy's downfall. [L (*Troia* Troy)]

troll[1] /trəʊl/ *n.* supernatural being, giant or dwarf, in Scandinavian mythology. [ON]

troll[2] /trəʊl/ *v.* sing out in carefree jovial

manner; fish by drawing bait along in water. [cf. F *troller* to quest]

trolley /ˈtrɒlɪ/ *n.* small table or stand on wheels or castors for serving food, transporting luggage, etc.; low truck running on rails; trolley-wheel; **trolley-bus** electric bus using trolley-wheel; **trolley-wheel** wheel attached to pole etc. for collecting current from overhead electric wire to drive vehicle. [dial., perh. f. prec.]

trollop /ˈtrɒləp/ *n.* disreputable girl or woman. [cf. archaic *trull* prostitute]

trolly var. of TROLLEY.

trombone /trɒmˈbəʊn/ *n.* large brass wind instrument with sliding tube; **trombonist** *n.* [F or It. (*tromba* trumpet)]

trompe-l'œil /trɒmp ˈlʌi:/ **1** *a.* (of still-life painting etc.) designed to make spectator think objects represented are real. **2** *n.* such painting etc. [F, lit. 'deceives the eye']

-tron *suffix* forming nouns denoting elementary particles or particle accelerators. [ELECTRON]

troop 1 *n.* assembled company, assemblage of persons or animals; (in *pl.*) soldiers, armed forces; cavalry unit commanded by captain; unit of artillery and armoured formation; group of three or more Scout patrols. **2** *v.i.* come together or move in a troop (*in, out, off,* etc.). **3 troop the colour** transfer flag ceremonially at public mounting of garrison guards; **troop-ship** ship for transporting troops. [F *troupe*]

trooper *n.* private soldier in cavalry or armoured unit; *Austral. hist. & US* mounted or motor-borne policeman; cavalry horse; troop-ship; **swear like a trooper** swear extensively or forcefully.

trope *n.* figurative use of a word. [L f. Gk *tropos* (*trepō* turn)]

trophy /ˈtrəʊfɪ/ *n.* thing kept as prize or memento of contest or success; arms etc. of vanquished army set up as memorial of victory; group of things arranged for ornamental display. [F f. L f. Gk *tropaion*]

tropic /ˈtrɒpɪk/ **1** *n.* parallel of latitude 23° 27′ north (**tropic of Cancer**) or south (**tropic of Capricorn**) of the equator; corresponding circle on celestial sphere where sun appears to turn after reaching greatest declination. **2** *a.* tropical. **3 the tropics** region between tropics of Cancer and Capricorn. [L f. Gk *tropē* turn]

tropical *a.* of or peculiar to or suggestive of the tropics; **tropically** *adv.*

troposphere /ˈtrɒpəsfɪə/ *n.* layer of atmospheric air extending about seven miles upwards from earth's surface, in which temperature falls with increasing height. [Gk *tropos* turn]

trot 1 *v.* (**-tt-**) (of person) run at moderate pace esp. with short strides; (of horse) proceed at steady pace faster than walk lifting each diagonal pair of legs alternately; *colloq.* walk, go; cause (horse or person) to trot; traverse (distance) at trot. **2** *n.* action or exercise of trotting (*proceed at a trot; went for a trot*). **3 on the trot** *colloq.* continually busy (*kept him on the trot*), in succession (*five weeks on the trot*); **trot out** cause (horse) to trot to show his paces, produce or introduce (as if) for inspection and approval; **the trots** *sl.* diarrhoea. [F]

troth /trəʊθ/ *n. archaic* faith, loyalty; truth; **pledge** (or **plight**) **one's troth** pledge one's word esp. in marriage or betrothal. [OE (TRUTH)]

trotter *n.* horse bred or trained for trotting; (usu. in *pl.*) animal's foot as food. [TROT]

troubadour /ˈtru:bədɔ:/ *n.* French medieval lyric poet singing of chivalry and gallantry. [F f. Prov. (*trobar* find, compose)]

trouble /ˈtrʌb(ə)l/ **1** *n.* difficulty or distress, vexation, affliction (*have been through much trouble; am having trouble with my teeth*); inconvenience, unpleasant exertion, bother; cause of this (*his mother is a great trouble to him*); cause of annoyance or concern (*the trouble with you is you can't say no*); faulty condition or operation (*kidney, engine, trouble*); (in *pl.*) public disturbances. **2** *v.* cause distress to, agitate, disturb; be disturbed or worried (*don't trouble about it*); afflict, cause pain etc. to; subject or be subjected to inconvenience or unpleasant exertion (*sorry to trouble you*). **3 ask** (or **look**) **for trouble** *colloq.* behave rashly or incautiously or indiscreetly etc.; **in trouble** involved in matter likely to bring censure or punishment, *colloq.* pregnant while unmarried; **trouble-maker** person who habitually causes trouble; **trouble-shooter** person who traces and corrects faults in machinery etc., mediator in dispute. [F f. L (TURBID)]

troublesome *a.* causing trouble, annoying.

troublous /ˈtrʌbləs/ *a. literary* full of troubles, agitated, disturbed (*troublous times*). [L (TROUBLE)]

trough /trɒf/ *n.* long narrow open receptacle for water, animal feed, etc.; channel or hollow comparable to this; elongated region of low barometric pressure. [OE]

trounce *v.t.* defeat heavily; beat, thrash; punish severely. [orig. unkn.]

troupe /tru:p/ *n.* company of actors or acrobats etc. [F, = TROOP]
trouper *n.* member of theatrical troupe; staunch colleague.
trousers /'traʊzəz/ *n.pl.* two-legged outer garment reaching from waist usu. to ankles; **trouser-suit** woman's suit of trousers and jacket; **troused** *a.* [in *pl.* after *drawers*; Ir. & Gael. *triubhas* trews]
trousseau /'tru:səʊ/ *n.* (*pl.* **trousseaus**) bride's collection of clothes etc. [F (TRUSS)]
trout *n.* (*pl.* usu. same) fish related to salmon; **old trout** *sl. derog.* old woman. [OE f. L *tructa*]
trove *n.* = *treasure trove.* [AF *trové* f. *trover* find]
trow /traʊ, trəʊ/ *v.t. archaic* think, believe. [OE, rel. to TRUCE]
trowel /'traʊəl/ *n.* flat-bladed tool for spreading mortar or splitting bricks; scoop for lifting small plants or earth. [F f. med.L *truella* f. L *trulla*]
troy *n.* (in full **troy weight**) system of weights used for precious metals and gems, with pound of 12 ounces or 5760 grains. [prob. *Troyes* in France]
truant /'tru:ənt/ **1** *n.* child who absents himself from school; person missing from work etc. **2** *a.* (of person or conduct etc.) shirking, idle, wandering. **3 play truant** stay away as truant. **4 truancy** *n.* [F, prob. f. Celt.]
truce /'tru:s/ *n.* temporary cessation of hostilities; agreement for this. [orig. *trewes* pl.; OE, = covenant (TRUE)]
truck[1] *n.* strong vehicle for heavy goods; open railway wagon; hand-cart, porter's barrow. [perh. f. TRUCKLE]
truck[2] **1** *n.* dealings (*have no truck with*); barter, exchange. **2** *v. archaic* barter, exchange. [F *troquer*]
truckle /'trʌk(ə)l/ *v.i.* submit obsequiously (*to*); **truckle-bed** low bed on wheels, that may be pushed under another, esp. as formerly used by servants etc. [AF *trocle* f. L *trochlea* pulley f. Gk]
truculent /'trʌkjʊlənt/ *a.* pugnacious, defiant; aggressive, savage; fierce; **truculence** *n.*; **truculency** *n.* [L (*trux truc-* fierce)]
trudge /trʌdʒ/ **1** *v.* go on foot esp. laboriously; traverse (distance) thus. **2** *n.* trudging walk. [orig. unkn.]
true /tru:/ **1** *a.* in accordance with fact or reality (*a true story*); genuine, rightly or strictly so called, not spurious or counterfeit etc.; loyal or faithful (*to*); accurately conforming *to* (a type or standard); correctly positioned or balanced, upright, level. **2** *adv.* truly (*tell me true*); accurately (*aim true*); without variation (*breed true*). **3 come true** actually happen or be the case; **true-blue** *a.* extremely loyal or orthodox, (*n.*) such person; **true-love** sweetheart; **true north** north according to the earth's axis, not magnetic north; **true to life** accurately representing it. [OE]
truffle /'trʌf(ə)l/ *n.* edible subterranean fungus with rich flavour; round sweet made of chocolate mixture covered with cocoa etc. [prob. Du. f. F]
trug *n.* shallow oblong garden-basket usu. of wood strips. [perh. dial. var. of TROUGH]
truism /'tru:ɪz(ə)m/ *n.* statement too obviously true or too hackneyed to be worth making; statement that repeats idea already implied in one of its terms (e.g. *there's no need to be unnecessarily careful*). [TRUE]
truly *adv.* sincerely, genuinely (*am truly grateful*); really, indeed (*truly, I do not know*); faithfully, loyally (*served him truly*); accurately, truthfully (*is not truly depicted*); rightly, properly (*well and truly*). [OE (TRUE)]
trump[1] **1** *n.* playing-card of suit temporarily ranking above others; advantage esp. involving surprise; *colloq.* helpful or excellent person. **2** *v.t.* defeat (card or its player) with trump. **3 trump card** card belonging to, or turned up to determine, trump suit, *fig.* valuable resource; **trump up** fabricate or invent (accusation or excuse etc.); **turn up trumps** *colloq.* turn out better than expected, be greatly successful or helpful. [corrupt. of TRIUMPH in same (now obs.) sense]
trump[2] *n. archaic* trumpet-blast; **the last trump** trumpet-blast to wake the dead on Judgement Day. [F *trompe*]
trumpery /'trʌmpərɪ/ **1** *a.* showy but worthless, delusive, shallow. **2** *n.* worthless finery; rubbish. [F *tromperie* deceit]
trumpet /'trʌmpɪt/ **1** *n.* metal tubular or conical wind instrument with flared mouth and bright penetrating tone; trumpet-shaped thing (*ear-trumpet*); sound (as) of trumpet. **2** *v.* blow trumpet; (of enraged elephant etc.) make loud sound as of trumpet; proclaim loudly (person's or thing's merit). **3 trumpet-call** urgent summons to action; **trumpet-major** chief trumpeter of cavalry regiment. [F dimin. (TRUMP[2])]
trumpeter *n.* one who sounds a trumpet, esp. cavalry soldier giving signals. [prec. or F]
truncate /trʌŋ'keɪt/ *v.t.* cut top or end from; **truncation** /-'keɪʃ(ə)n/ *n.* [L (TRUNK)]
truncheon /'trʌntʃ(ə)n/ *n.* short club carried by policeman; staff or baton as symbol of authority. [F *tronchon* stump (TRUNK)]

trundle /'trʌnd(ə)l/ *v.* roll or move esp. heavily or noisily. [var. of obs. or dial. *trendle* (TREND)]

trunk *n.* main stem of tree as distinct from branches and roots; person's or animal's body apart from limbs and head; large luggage-box with hinged lid; *US* boot of motor car; elephant's elongated prehensile nose; (in *pl.*) men's close-fitting shorts worn for swimming, boxing, etc.; **trunk-call** telephone call on trunk-line with charges according to distance; **trunk-line** main line of railway, telephone system, etc.; **trunk-road** important main road. [F *tronc* f. L *truncus* cut short]

truss 1 *n.* supporting framework of roof or bridge etc.; surgical appliance worn to support hernia; bundle of hay or straw; compact cluster of flowers or fruit. **2** *v.t.* tie up (fowl) compactly for cooking; tie (person) up with arms to sides; support (roof or bridge etc.) with truss or trusses. [F]

trust 1 *n.* firm belief in reliability or truth or strength etc. of a person or thing, state of being relied on; confident expectation; thing or person committed to one's care, resulting obligation; *Law* trusteeship, board of trustees, property committed to trustee(s); association of several companies for purpose of united action to prevent competition. **2** *v.* have trust in, believe in, rely on character or behaviour of, place reliance *in*; consign (thing *to* person etc.) with trust; confidently leave (thing *with* person etc. for safe keeping or use); hope earnestly (*I trust you are well, to hear from you shortly*). **3 on trust** on credit; **take on trust** accept (assertion etc.) without evidence or investigation; **trust to** place (esp. undue) reliance on. [ON]

trustee /trʌs'ti:/ *n.* person or member of board given possession of property with legal obligation to administer it solely for purposes specified; State made responsible for government of an area; **trusteeship** *n.* [-EE]

trustful *a.* full of trust or confidence, not feeling or showing suspicion; **trustfully** *adv.* [TRUST]

trusting *a.* having trust, trustful.

trustworthy *a.* deserving of trust, reliable; **trustworthiness** *n.*

trusty 1 *a. archaic* trustworthy. **2** *n.* prisoner who is given special privileges for good behaviour. **3 trustily** *adv.*; **trustiness** *n.*

truth /tru:θ/ *n.* (*pl.* /-ðz, -θs/) quality or state of being true or truthful; what is true (*tell us the whole truth*; *the truth is that I forgot*); **in truth** *literary* truly, really. [OE (TRUE)]

truthful *a.* habitually speaking the truth; (of story etc.) true; **truthfully** *adv.*

try /traɪ/ **1** *v.* make effort with view to success (*try to be on time*; *I shall try*); make effort to achieve (*tried my best*); test (quality of thing) by use or experiment, test qualities of (person or thing); make severe demands on (person etc.); examine effectiveness or usefulness of for purpose (*try soap, kicking it, the off-licence*); investigate and decide (case or issue) judicially, subject (person) to trial (*for* murder etc.). **2** *n.* effort to accomplish something; (in Rugby football) touching-down of ball by player behind goal-line, scoring points and entitling his side to a kick at goal. **3 try and** *colloq.* try to; **try for** apply or compete for, seek to reach or attain; **try one's hand** see how skilful one is, esp. at first attempt; **try it on** *colloq.* test another's patience; **try on** put on (clothes etc.) to see if they fit; **try-on** *n. colloq.* act of 'trying it on', attempt to deceive; **try out** put to the test, test thoroughly; **try-out** *n.* experimental test. [orig. = separate, distinguish (F *trier* sift)]

trying *a.* endurable only with difficulty; exhausting; exasperating.

tryst /trɪst, traɪst/ *n. archaic* time and place for meeting, esp. of lovers. [F]

tsar /zɑ:/ *n.* title of former emperor of Russia. [Russ., ult. f. L *Caesar*]

tsetse /'tsetsɪ/ *n.* African fly carrying disease (esp. sleeping sickness) to man and animals by biting. [Tswana]

T-shirt /'ti:ʃɜ:t/ *n.* short-sleeved casual shirt having form of T when spread out. [T, SHIRT]

T-square /'ti:skweə/ *n.* T-shaped instrument for drawing or testing right angles. [T, SQUARE]

TT *abbr.* Tourist Trophy; tuberculin-tested; teetotal; teetotaller.

tub 1 *n.* open flat-bottomed usu. round vessel; *colloq.* bath; *colloq.* clumsy slow boat. **2** *v.* (**-bb-**) plant or bath or wash in tub. **3 tub-thumper** ranting preacher or orator. [prob. LG or Du.]

tuba /'tju:bə/ *n.* low-pitched brass wind instrument. [It. f. L, = trumpet]

tubby *a.* tub-shaped, (of person) short and fat; **tubbiness** *n.* [TUB]

tube 1 *n.* long hollow cylinder, natural or artificial structure having approximately this shape with open or closed ends and serving for passage of fluid etc. or as receptacle (*a tube of toothpaste*; *test-tube*); *colloq.* underground railway; inner tube (*tubeless tyre*); cathode-ray tube, e.g. in television set; *US* thermionic valve. **2** *v.t.* equip with tubes; enclose in tube. **3 the tube** *US* television. [F or L]

tuber *n.* thick round root (e.g. of dahlia) or underground stem (e.g. of potato), freq. bearing buds. [L, = hump, swelling]

tubercle /'tju:bək(ə)l/ *n.* small rounded swelling in plant or organ of body, esp. as characteristic of tuberculosis in lungs; **tubercle bacillus** bacillus causing tuberculosis. [L *tuberculum* dimin. of prec.]

tubercular /tju:'bɜ:kjʊlə/ *a.* of or affected with tuberculosis. [L (prec.)]

tuberculin /tju:'bɜ:kjʊlɪn/ *n.* preparation from cultures of tubercle bacillus used for treatment and diagnosis of tuberculosis; **tuberculin-tested** (of milk) from cows shown by tuberculin test to be free of tuberculosis.

tuberculosis /tju:bɜ:kjʊ'ləʊsɪs/ *n.* infectious bacterial disease marked by tubercles, esp. in lungs. [TUBERCLE]

tuberculous /tju:'bɜ:kjʊləs/ *a.* of or having or caused by tubercles or tuberculosis.

tuberose /'tju:bərəʊz/ *n.* plant with fragrant creamy-white flowers. [L (TUBER)]

tuberous *a.* having tubers; of or like a tuber. [F or L (as prec.)]

tubing *n.* length of tube or quantity of tubes. [TUBE]

tubular /'tju:bjʊlə/ *a.* tube-shaped; having or consisting of tubes; (of furniture etc.) made of tubular pieces. [foll.]

tubule /'tju:bju:l/ *n.* small tube in plant or animal body. [L *tubulus* dimin. as TUBE]

TUC *abbr.* Trades Union Congress.

tuck 1 *v.t.* draw or fold or turn outer or end parts of (cloth or clothes etc.) close together or so as to be held (often with *in* or *up*); draw together into small compass (*tucked her legs under her*); cover snugly and comfortably *in* or *up*; stow (thing) away in specified way (*tucked it in a corner*; *tucked it out of sight*); make stitched fold in (material or garment). **2** *n.* flattened usu. stitched fold in material or garment etc.; *sl.* eatables, esp. cakes and sweets. **3 tuck in** *sl.* eat food heartily; **tuck-in** *n. sl.* large meal; **tuck into** *sl.* eat (food) heartily; **tuck-shop** shop selling sweets etc. to schoolchildren. [LG or Du.]

tucker 1 *n.* piece of lace or linen etc. in or on woman's bodice (*hist.* except in **best bib and tucker** one's best clothes); *Austral. colloq.* food. **2** *v.t. US colloq.* tire (*out*).

-tude *suffix* forming abstract nouns (*altitude, attitude, solitude*). [F or L]

Tudor /'tju:də/ *a.* of the royal family of England ruling 1485–1603; of the architectural style of this period, esp. with half-timbering and elaborately decorated design of houses. [Owen *Tudor*]

Tue(s). *abbr.* Tuesday.

Tuesday /'tju:zdeɪ, -dɪ/ **1** *n.* day of week following Monday. **2** *adv. colloq.* on Tuesday. **3 Tuesdays** on Tuesdays, each Tuesday. [OE]

tufa /'tju:fə/ *n.* porous rock formed round springs of mineral water; tuff. [It. (foll.)]

tuff *n.* rock formed from volcanic ashes. [F f. It. f. L *tofus*]

tuffet /'tʌfɪt/ *n.* tuft. [var. of foll.]

tuft *n.* bunch or collection of threads or grass or feathers or hair etc. held or growing together at the base; **tufty** *a.* [prob. F *tofe*]

tug 1 *v.* (**-gg-**) pull hard, pull violently *at*; tow (vessel) by means of tugboat. **2** *n.* hard or violent or jerky pull (also *fig.*: *felt a great tug at parting*); tugboat. **3 tug of love** *colloq.* dispute over custody of child; **tug of war** trial of strength between two sides pulling opposite ways on a rope, *fig.* decisive or severe contest. [rel. to TOW[1]]

tugboat *n.* small powerful vessel for towing others.

tuition /tju:'ɪʃ(ə)n/ *n.* teaching or instruction, esp. as thing to be paid for; fee for this. [F f. L (*tueor tuit-* look after)]

tulip /'tju:lɪp/ *n.* bulbous spring-flowering plant with showy cup-shaped flowers; its flower; **tulip-tree** tree with tulip-like flowers. [Turk. *tul(i)band* TURBAN (f. its shape) f. Pers.]

tulle /tju:l/ *n.* soft fine silk net for veils and dresses. [*Tulle* in France]

tum *n. colloq.* stomach. [abbr. of TUMMY]

tumble /'tʌmb(ə)l/ **1** *v.* fall suddenly or headlong; fall rapidly in amount etc. (*prices tumbled*); roll or toss to and fro; move or rush in headlong or blundering fashion; overturn, fling or push roughly or carelessly; perform acrobatic feats, esp. somersaults; rumple or disarrange. **2** *n.* sudden or headlong fall; somersault or other acrobatic feat; untidy or confused state. **3 tumble-drier** machine for drying washing in heated rotating drum; **tumble to** *colloq.* grasp meaning of (idea etc.). [LG *tummeln*]

tumbledown *a.* falling or fallen into ruin, dilapidated.

tumbler *n.* drinking-glass with no handle or foot; acrobat; part of mechanism of lock; a kind of pigeon that turns over backwards in flight.

tumbrel /'tʌmbr(ə)l/ *n.* (also **tumbril**) open cart in which condemned persons were conveyed to guillotine during French Revolution. [F (*tomber* fall)]

tumescent /tjʊ'mesənt/ *a.* swelling; **tumescence** *n.* [L (as TUMOUR)]
tumid /'tju:mɪd/ *a.* swollen, inflated; (of style etc.) inflated, bombastic; **tumidity** /-'mɪdɪtɪ/ *n.*
tummy /'tʌmɪ/ *n. colloq.* stomach; **tummy-button** *colloq.* navel. [childish pr.]
tumour /'tju:mə/, *US* **tumor** *n.* abnormal or morbid swelling in the body; **tumorous** *a.* [L (*tumeo* swell)]
tumult /'tju:mʌlt/ *n.* riot, angry demonstration of a mob; uproar or din e.g. of waves or crowd; conflict of emotions in the mind. [F or L (prec.)]
tumultuous /tjʊ'mʌltjʊəs/ *a.* vehement, uproarious, making tumult.
tumulus /'tju:mjʊləs/ *n.* (*pl.* **tumuli** /-aɪ/) ancient sepulchral mound. [L (as TUMOUR)]
tun *n.* large cask for wine; brewer's fermenting-vat. [OE]
tuna /'tju:nə/ *n.* (*pl.* same) tunny; (also **tuna-fish**) flesh of tunny as food. [Amer. Sp.]
tundra /'tʌndrə/ *n.* vast level treeless Arctic region where subsoil is frozen. [Lappish]
tune 1 *n.* melody with or without harmony; correct pitch or intonation in singing or playing, adjustment of instrument to obtain this (*sings in tune*; *piano is out of tune*). **2** *v.t.* put (instrument) in tune; adjust (radio receiver etc.) to particular wavelength of signals; adjust (engine etc.) to run smoothly and efficiently; adjust or adapt (thing *to* purpose etc.). **3 call the tune** have control of events; **change one's tune** change one's style of language or manner esp. from insolent to respectful tone; **in** (or **out of**) **tune with** harmonizing (or clashing) with; **to the tune of** to the considerable sum or amount of; **tune in** set radio receiver to right wavelength to receive signal; **tune up** (of orchestra) bring instruments to proper or uniform pitch, bring to most efficient condition, begin to play or sing; **tuning-fork** two-pronged steel fork giving particular note when struck. [TONE]
tuneful *a.* melodious, musical; **tunefully** *adv.*
tuner *n.* person who tunes instruments, esp. pianos.
tungsten /'tʌŋst(ə)n/ *n.* heavy refractory metallic element. [Sw., = heavy stone]
tunic /'tju:nɪk/ *n.* close-fitting short coat of police or military uniform; loose garment, often sleeveless (*gym-tunic*). [F or L]
tunnel /'tʌn(ə)l/ **1** *n.* artificial underground passage through hill or under road etc., esp. for railway or road; underground passage dug by burrowing animal. **2** *v.* (**-ll-**, *US* **-l-**) make tunnel through (hill etc.), make one's way thus. [F dimin. of *tonne* TUN]
tunny /'tʌnɪ/ *n.* large edible sea-fish. [F *thon* f. Prov. f. L f. Gk *thunnos*]
tup 1 *n.* male sheep, ram. **2** *v.t.* (**-pp-**) (of ram) copulate with (ewe). [orig. unkn.]
Tupi /'tu:pɪ/ **1** *n.* member of American Indian people in Amazon valley; their language. **2** *a.* of this people. [Tupi]
tuppence /'tʌpəns/ *n.* = TWOPENCE. [phon. sp.]
tuppenny /'tʌpənɪ/ *a.* = TWOPENNY. [phon. sp.]
turban /'tɜ:bən/ *n.* man's head-dress of cotton or silk wound round cap, worn esp. by Muslims and Sikhs; woman's head-dress or hat resembling this. [ult. f. Turk. f. Pers.; cf. TULIP]
turbid /'tɜ:bɪd/ *a.* (of liquid or colour, *fig.* of style etc.) muddy, thick, not clear or limpid or lucid; **turbidity** /-'bɪdɪtɪ/ *n.* [L (*turba* crowd)]
turbine /'tɜ:baɪn/ *n.* rotary motor driven by flow of water or gas. [F f. L *turbo -in-* spinning-top, whirlwind]
turbo- /'tɜ:bəʊ/ *in comb.* turbine.
turbofan *n.* jet-engine with additional thrust from cold air drawn in by fan.
turbo-jet *n.* jet engine in which jet also operates turbine-driven air-compressor; aircraft with this.
turbo-prop *n.* jet engine in which turbine is used as in turbo-jet and also to drive propeller; aircraft with this. [PROP²]
turbot /'tɜ:bət/ *n.* large European flat-fish valued as food. [F f. Sw.]
turbulent /'tɜ:bjʊlənt/ *a.* disturbed, in commotion; (of flow of air etc.) varying irregularly; tumultuous; insubordinate, riotous; **turbulence** *n.* [L (*turba* crowd)]
Turco- *in comb.* Turkish. [med.L (TURK)]
turd *n. vulgar* ball or lump of excrement; contemptible person. [OE]
tureen /tjʊə'ri:n/ *n.* deep covered dish for soup. [TERRINE]
turf 1 *n.* (*pl.* **turfs** or **turves**) layer of grass etc. with earth and matted roots as surface of grassland; piece of this cut from ground; slab of peat for fuel. **2** *v.t.* plant (ground) with turf; *sl.* throw (person or thing) *out.* **3 the turf** the racecourse, horse-racing; **turf accountant** bookmaker. **4 turfy** *a.* [OE]
turgescent /tɜ:'dʒesənt/ *a.* becoming turgid; **turgescence** *n.* [L (foll.)]
turgid /'tɜ:dʒɪd/ *a.* swollen, inflated, enlarged; (of language) pompous, bombastic; **turgidity** /-'dʒɪdɪtɪ/ *n.* [L (*turgeo* swell)]

Turk *n.* native of Turkey; member of Central Asian people from whom Ottomans derived, speaking Turkic languages; (**R**) ferocious, wild, or unmanageable person; **Turk's head** turban-like ornamental knot. [orig. unkn.]

turkey /ˈtɜːkɪ/ *n.* large orig. American bird bred as food; its flesh; **turkey-cock** male turkey. [*Turkey*, whence orig. imported]

Turkey carpet woollen carpet with thick pile and bold design.

Turki /ˈtɜːkɪ/ **1** *a.* of a group of languages and peoples including Turkish. **2** *n.* this group. **3 Turkic** *a.* [Pers. (TURK)]

Turkish 1 *a.* of Turkey or the Turks or their language. **2** *n.* this language. **3 Turkish bath** hot-air or steam bath followed by washing, massage, etc., (in *sing.* or *pl.*) building for this; **Turkish carpet** Turkey carpet; **Turkish coffee** coffee made strong, black, and very sweet; **Turkish delight** sweet of lumps of flavoured gelatine coated in powdered sugar; **Turkish towel** towel made of cotton terry. [TURK]

Turko- var. of TURCO-.

turmeric /ˈtɜːmərɪk/ *n.* E. Indian plant of ginger family; its aromatic root powdered as flavouring or stimulant or dye. [perh. F *terre mérite*]

turmoil /ˈtɜːmɔɪl/ *n.* din and bustle and confusion. [orig. unkn.]

turn 1 *v.i.* move round a point or axis (*wheel turns*); be moved round thus (*key turns*); change in position so that a different side or end becomes outermost or uppermost etc., be inverted or reversed (*turned inside out, upside-down*); take new direction (*turn left here*); have recourse *to* (*turned to drink*); change in nature or form or condition (*turned into a dragon*); become (*turned hostile*); (of hair or leaves) change colour; (of milk) become sour; (of stomach) be nauseated; (of head) be giddy. **2** *v.t.* cause to move round a point or axis (*turn the wheel, key in lock*); cause to be inverted or reversed in position etc. (*turned the box upside-down*); give new direction to (*turn your face this way*); aim in certain way (*turned the hose on them*); move to other side of, go round (*turned the corner*); pass age or time of (*has turned 40, 4 o'clock*); send or put, cause to go (*was turned loose; turn it out into a basin*); cause to be changed in nature etc. (*turned him into a frog*); cause to become (*turned him angry*); perform (somersault); remake (garment) with former inner side out; make (profit); divert (bullet); blunt (edge of knife etc.); translate (*turn it into French*); make (milk) sour, (stomach) nauseated, (head) giddy; shape (object) on lathe; give (esp. elegant) form to (*turn a compliment*). **3** *n.* act or fact or process of turning; point of turning or change; change of tide from ebb to flow or flow to ebb; change in course of events; tendency, formation (*is of a mechanical turn of mind*); turning of road; opportunity or obligation etc. that comes successively to each of several persons etc. (*your turn will come; my turn to read*); short walk or ride (*take a turn in the garden*); short performance on stage or in circus etc.; service of specified kind (*did me a good turn*); purpose (*served my turn*); *colloq.* momentary nervous shock or ill feeling (*gave me quite a turn*); *Mus.* ornament of principal note with those above and below it; one round in coil of rope etc. **4 at every turn** continually; **by turns** in rotation, alternately; **in turn** in succession; **in one's turn** when one's turn comes; **out of turn** before or after one's turn, at inappropriate moment; **take turns** act etc. alternately; **to a turn** perfectly; **turn about** move so as to face in new direction; **turn-about** *n.* turning about, abrupt change of policy etc.; **turn against** make or become hostile to; **turn and turn about** alternately; **turn away** send away, reject; **turn back** begin or cause to retrace one's steps; **turn-buckle** device for tightly connecting parts of metal rod or wire; **turn down** reject, reduce volume or strength of (sound or heat etc.) by turning knob etc., fold down; **turn in** hand in or return, register (score etc.), *colloq.* go to bed, *colloq.* abandon (plan etc.); **turn off** stop flow or operation of by means of tap or switch etc., move (tap etc.) thus; enter side-road, *colloq.* cause to lose interest; **turn on** start flow or operation of by means of tap or switch etc., move (tap etc.) thus, be suddenly hostile to, *colloq.* arouse interest or emotion of, excite sexually, depend on; **turn out** expel, extinguish (electric light etc.), dress or equip (*well turned out*), produce (goods etc.), empty or clean out (room etc.), empty (pocket), *colloq.* get out of bed, *colloq.* go out of doors, prove to be the case, result (*turned out to be true*); **turn-out** *n.* number of people at meeting etc., set of clothes or equipment; **turn over** reverse position of, hand over, transfer, consider carefully, start running of (engine etc.); **turn over a new leaf** improve one's conduct; **turn round** move so as to face in new direction, unload and reload (ship etc.); **turn-round** *n.* process of loading and unloading; **turn to** set about one's work; **turn up** increase volume or strength of (sound or heat etc.) by turning knob etc., discover or reveal, be found, happen or present itself, fold over or upwards; **turn-up** *n.* lower turned up end of trouser leg, *colloq.* unexpected happening. [OE & F f. L *torno* (*tornus* lathe f. Gk)]

turncoat *n.* one who changes sides.

turner *n.* lathe-worker.

turnery *n.* objects made on lathe; work with lathe.

turning *n.* place where roads meet, road meeting another; use of lathe; (in *pl.*) chips or shavings from lathe; **turning-circle** smallest circle in which vehicle can turn; **turning-point** point at which decisive change occurs.

turnip /'tɜ:nɪp/ *n.* plant with globular root used as vegetable and fodder; its root; **turnip-tops** its leaves used as vegetable; **turnipy** *a.* [dial. *neep* (OE f. L *napus*)]

turnkey *n.* gaoler. [TURN]

turnover *n.* turning over; amount of money taken in business, amount of business done; pie or tart made by turning half of pastry over filling; number of persons entering or leaving employment etc.

turnpike *n US* road on which toll is collected at gates.

turnstile *n.* admission-gate with arms revolving on post.

turntable *n.* circular revolving platform for gramophone record being played or to reverse locomotive etc.

turpentine /'tɜ:pəntaɪn/ *n.* resin got from various trees (orig. terebinth); (in full **oil of turpentine**) volatile pungent oil distilled from this resin, used in mixing paints and varnishes and in medicine. [F f. L (TEREBINTH)]

turpitude /'tɜ:pɪtju:d/ *n.* baseness, depravity, wickedness. [F or L (*turpis* disgraceful)]

turps *n. colloq.* oil of turpentine. [abbr.]

turquoise /'tɜ:kwɔɪz, -kwɑ:z/ *n.* precious stone, usu. opaque and greenish-blue; greenish-blue colour. [F, = Turkish]

turret /'tʌrɪt/ *n.* small tower esp. as decorative addition to building; low flat usu. revolving armoured tower for gun and gunners in ship or aircraft or fort or tank; rotating holder for tools in lathe etc. [F dimin. (TOWER)]

turtle /'tɜ:t(ə)l/ *n.* sea reptile with flippers and horny shell; its flesh used for soup; **turn turtle** capsize; **turtle-neck** high close-fitting neck of knitted garment. [alt. of earlier *tortue* (TORTOISE)]

turtle-dove /'tɜ:t(ə)ldʌv/ *n.* wild dove noted for its soft cooing and affection for its mate. [OE f. L *turtur*]

Tuscan /'tʌskən/ **1** *a.* of Tuscany; *Archit.* of least ornamented order. **2** *n.* inhabitant or classical Italian language of Tuscany. [F f. L]

tusk *n.* long pointed tooth esp. projecting from mouth as in elephant, walrus, or boar. [OE]

tussle /'tʌs(ə)l/ **1** *n.* struggle, scuffle. **2** *v.i.* engage in tussle. [orig. Sc. & N. Engl., perh. dimin. of *touse* (TOUSLE)]

tussock /'tʌsək/ *n.* clump of grass etc.; **tussocky** *a.* [perh. dial. *tusk* tuft]

tut *int.*, *n.*, & *v.* = TUT-TUT. [imit. of click of tongue]

tutelage /'tju:tɪlɪdʒ/ *n.* guardianship; being under this; instruction, tuition. [L *tutela* (TUTOR)]

tutelary /'tju:tɪlərɪ/ *a.* serving as guardian, giving protection. [L (prec.)]

tutor /'tju:tə/ **1** *n.* private teacher, esp. in general charge of person's education; university teacher supervising studies or welfare of assigned undergraduates; book of instruction in a subject. **2** *v.* act as tutor to; work as tutor; restrain, discipline. **3 tutorship** *n.* [F or L (*tueor tut-* watch)]

tutorial /tju:'tɔ:rɪəl/ **1** *a.* of or as tutor. **2** *n.* period of individual tuition given by college tutor. **3 tutorially** *adv.* [L *tutorius* (prec.)]

tutti /'tʊti:/ *Mus.* **1** *adv.* with all voices or instruments together. **2** *n.* passage to be performed this way. [It., pl. of *tutto* all]

tut-tut **1** *int.* expressing rebuke, impatience, or contempt. **2** *n.* such exclamation. **3** *v.i.* (**-tt-**) exclaim thus. [TUT]

tutu /'tu:tu:/ *n.* ballet dancer's short skirt of stiffened frills. [F]

tu-whit, tu-whoo /tʊ'wɪt tʊ'wu:/ *n.* alleged cry of owl. [imit.]

tuxedo /tʌk'si:dəʊ/ *n.* (*pl.* **tuxedos**) *US* dinner-jacket. [*Tuxedo* Park in US]

TV *abbr.* television.

twaddle /'twɒd(ə)l/ **1** *n.* useless or dull writing or talk. **2** *v.i.* indulge in this. [earlier *twattle*, alt. of TATTLE]

twain *a.* & *n. archaic* = TWO. [OE, masc. of TWO]

twang **1** *n.* sound made by plucked string of musical instrument or bow; quality of voice compared to this (esp. *nasal twang*). **2** *v.* emit twang; cause to twang. [imit.]

'twas /twɒz, twəz/ *archaic* it was. [contr.]

twat /twæt, twɒt/ *n. vulgar* female genitals; unpleasant or stupid person. [orig. unkn.]

tweak **1** *v.t.* pinch and twist or jerk. **2** *n.* such action. [prob. dial. *twick*, TWITCH]

twee *a.* affectedly dainty or quaint. [childish pr. of SWEET]

tweed *n.* rough-surfaced woollen cloth

freq. of mixed colours; (in *pl.*) suit of tweed. [alt. of *tweel* (Sc. var. of TWILL)]

tweedy *a.* fond of wearing tweed; heartily informal.

'tween *prep.* between. [abbr.]

tweet 1 *n.* chirp of small bird. **2** *v.i.* make chirping noise. [imit.]

tweeter *n.* loudspeaker for high frequencies.

tweezers /'twi:zəz/ *n.pl.* small pair of pincers for taking up small objects, plucking out hairs, etc. [orig. *tweezes* pl. of obs. *tweeze* case for small instruments]

twelfth 1 *a.* next after eleventh. **2** *n.* one of twelve equal parts of thing. **3 Twelfth night** eve of Epiphany, formerly a time of festivities. [OE (foll.)]

twelve *a.* & *n.* one more than eleven; symbol for this (12, xii, XII); size etc. denoted by twelve; **the Twelve** the Apostles. [OE]

twelvefold *a.* & *adv.* twelve times as much or as many; consisting of twelve parts.

twelvemonth *n.* year.

twenty /'twentɪ/ *a.* & *n.* twice ten; symbol for this (20, xx, XX); (in *pl.*) numbers, years, degrees of temperature, from 20 to 29; **twentieth** *a.* & *n.* [OE]

'twere /twɜ:, twə/ *archaic* it were. [contr.]

twerp *n. sl.* stupid or objectionable person. [orig. unkn.]

twice *adv.* two times, on two occasions; in double degree or quantity (*twice as good*; *is twice the man he was*). [OE (TWO)]

twiddle /'twɪd(ə)l/ **1** *v.t.* twirl randomly or idly about. **2** *n.* act of twiddling. **3 twiddle one's thumbs** make them rotate round each other esp. for want of anything to do. **4 twiddly** *a.* [prob. imit.]

twig[1] *n.* small branch or shoot of tree or shrub; **twiggy** *a.* [OE]

twig[2] *v.t.* (**-gg-**) *colloq.* understand, catch meaning or nature (of); perceive, observe. [orig. unkn.]

twilight /'twaɪlaɪt/ *n.* light from sky when sun is below horizon, esp. in the evening; period of this; faint light; state of imperfect understanding; period of decline or destruction; **twilight zone** decrepit urban area, area between others in position and character. [TWO, LIGHT[1]]

twilit /'twaɪlɪt/ *a.* dimly illuminated by twilight.

twill *n.* fabric so woven as to have a surface of parallel ridges. [OE, = two-thread]

'twill *archaic* it will. [contr.]

twilled *a.* woven as twill. [TWILL]

twin 1 *n.* each of a closely related or associated pair esp. of children or animals born at a birth; exact counterpart of person or thing. **2** *a.* forming, or being one of, such a pair (*twin brothers*). **3** *v.* (**-nn-**) join intimately together, pair (with); bear twins. **4 twin bed** one of a pair of single beds; **twin-engined** having two engines; **the Twins** Gemini; **twin set** woman's matching cardigan and jumper; **twin towns** two towns, usu. in different countries, establishing special links. [OE (TWO)]

twine 1 *n.* strong thread of strands of hemp or cotton etc. twisted together; coil, twist. **2** *v.* make (string etc.) by twisting strands; weave (garland); garland (brow etc.) *with*; coil or wind *round* or *about* something; (of plant) grow thus. [OE]

twinge /twɪndʒ/ *n.* sharp momentary local pain or pang. [OE]

twinkle /'twɪŋk(ə)l/ **1** *v.* (of star or light etc.) shine with rapidly intermittent gleams; (of eyes) sparkle; (of feet in dancing) move rapidly; emit (light) in quick gleams. **2** *n.* sparkle or gleam of eyes; slight flash of light; short rapid movement. **3 in a twinkling** (or **in the twinkling of an eye**) in an instant. [OE]

twirl 1 *v.* spin or swing or twist quickly and lightly round. **2** *n.* twirling motion; flourish made with pen. [orig. uncert.]

twist 1 *v.* change the form of by rotating one end and not the other or the two ends opposite ways, undergo such change, make or become spiral, distort, warp, wrench; (with *off*) break off by twisting; wind (strands) about each other, make (rope etc.) thus; take curved course, make one's way in winding manner; distort or misrepresent meaning of (words); *colloq.* cheat. **2** *n.* twisting, twisted state; thing formed by twisting; point at which thing twists or bends; peculiar tendency of mind or character etc. **3 round the twist** *sl.* crazy; **twist person's arm** *colloq.* coerce him; **twist person round one's little finger** persuade or manage him very easily. [rel. to TWIN, TWINE]

twister *n. colloq.* swindler.

twisty *a.* full of twists; **twistily** *adv.*; **twistiness** *n.*

twit[1] *n. sl.* foolish person. [orig. dial., perh. f. foll.]

twit[2] *v.t.* (**-tt-**) reproach or taunt, usu. good-humouredly. [OE]

twitch 1 *v.* (of features or muscles etc.) move or contract spasmodically; give short sharp pull (at). **2** *n.* sudden involuntary contraction or movement; sudden pull or jerk; *colloq.* state of nervousness. [prob. OE]

twitter 1 *v.* (esp. of bird) utter succession of light tremulous sounds; utter or express thus. **2** *n.* twittering; *colloq.* tremulously excited state. [imit.]

'twixt *prep. archaic* = BETWIXT. [abbr.]

two /tu:/ *a.* & *n.* one more than one; symbol for this (2, ii, II); size etc. denoted by two; **in two** in or into two pieces; **put two and two together** make inference from known facts; **that makes two of us** *colloq.* that is true of me also; **two-dimensional** having or appearing to have length and breadth but no depth; **two-edged** double-edged; **two-faced** insincere; **two-handed** used with both hands or by two persons; **two-piece** suit of clothes or woman's bathing-suit comprising two separate parts; **two-ply** (of wool etc.) of two strands, layers, or thicknesses; **two-step** ballroom dance in march or polka time; **two-stroke** (of internal-combustion engine) having power cycle completed in one up-and-down movement of piston; **two-time** *sl.* swindle, deceive (esp. by infidelity). [OE]

twofold *a.* & *adv.* twice as much or as many; consisting of two parts.

twopence /'tʌpəns/ *n.* sum of two pence; thing of little value (*don't care twopence*).

twopenny /'tʌpənɪ/ *a.* costing two pence; cheap, worthless; **twopenny-halfpenny** /tʌpnɪ'heɪpnɪ/ contemptible, insignificant.

twosome *n.* pair or couple of persons.

'twould /twʊd/ *archaic* it would. [contr.]

-ty[1] *suffix* forming nouns denoting quality or condition (*cruelty, faculty, plenty, safety*); cf. -ITY. [F f. L *-tas -tatis*]

-ty[2] *suffix* = tens (*twenty, ninety*). [OE]

tycoon /taɪ'ku:n/ *n.* business magnate. [Jap., = great lord]

tying *partic.* of TIE.

tyke /taɪk/ *n.* low or objectionable fellow. [ON]

tympanum /'tɪmpənəm/ *n.* (*pl.* **tympana**) ear-drum; middle ear; space enclosed in pediment or between lintel and arch above. [L f. Gk *tumpanon* drum]

Tynwald /'tɪnwɒld/ *n.* Isle of Man annual assembly proclaiming newly enacted laws. [ON, = assembly-field]

type /taɪp/ **1** *n.* class of things having common characteristics; person or thing or event serving as illustration or symbol or characteristic specimen of another or of a class; object, conception, or work of art serving as model for subsequent artists; piece of metal etc. with raised letter or character on its upper surface for use in printing, a kind or size of such pieces, set or supply of these; *colloq.* person, esp. one of specified character (*a strange type*); (as *suffix*) resembling, functioning as (*ceramic-type material; Cheddar-type cheese*). **2** *v.* write with typewriter; assign to a type; be type or example of. **3** **type-cast** cast (actor) in role appropriate to his nature or previous theatrical successes. [F or L f. Gk *tupos* impression]

typeface *n.* set of types in one design; inked surface of types.

typescript *n.* typewritten text or document.

typesetter *n.* compositor; machine for setting type; **typesetting** *n.*

typewriter *n.* machine with keys for producing printlike characters one at a time on paper inserted round roller.

typewritten *a.* produced with a typewriter.

typhoid /'taɪfɔɪd/ *n.* (in full **typhoid fever**) infectious bacterial fever attacking intestines. [TYPHUS]

typhoon /taɪ'fu:n/ *n.* violent hurricane in E. Asian seas. [Chin., = great wind, & Arab.]

typhus /'taɪfəs/ *n.* an infectious fever. [Gk, = stupor]

typical /'tɪpɪk(ə)l/ *a.* serving as characteristic example, representative; characteristic, serving to distinguish a type; symbolical; **typically** *adv.* [med.L (TYPE)]

typify /'tɪpɪfaɪ/ *v.t.* be representative example of; represent by type; **typification** /-fɪ'keɪʃ(ə)n/ *n.* [L (TYPE)]

typist /'taɪpɪst/ *n.* (esp. professional) user of typewriter. [TYPE]

typography /taɪ'pɒgrəfɪ/ *n.* printing as an art; style and appearance of printed matter; **typographical** /-'græfɪk(ə)l/ *a.*; **typographically** /-'græfɪkəlɪ/ *adv.* [F (TYPE)]

tyrannical /tɪ'rænɪk(ə)l/ *a.* given to or characteristic of tyranny; **tyrannically** *adv.* [F f. L f. Gk (TYRANT)]

tyrannize /'tɪrənaɪz/ *v.* exercise tyranny (*over* person etc.); rule (person etc.) despotically. [F (TYRANT)]

tyrannosaur /tɪ'rænəsɔ:/ *n.* dinosaur with very short front legs and large head, that walked on hind legs. [TYRANT, after *dinosaur*]

tyrannous /'tɪrənəs/ *a.* tyrannical. [L (TYRANT)]

tyranny /'tɪrənɪ/ *n.* cruel and arbitrary use of authority; rule by tyrant; period of this; State thus ruled. [F f. med.L f. Gk (foll.)]

tyrant /'taɪrənt/ *n.* oppressive or cruel ruler; person exercising power arbitrarily or cruelly. [F f. L f. Gk *turannos*]

tyre /taɪə/ *n.* rubber covering, usu. inflated, placed round wheel to form soft contact with road. [TIRE²]

Tyrian /'tɪrɪən/ **1** *a.* of ancient Tyre in Phoenicia. **2** *n.* native of ancient Tyre. **3** **Tyrian purple** see PURPLE. [L (*Tyrus* Tyre)]

tyro var. of TIRO.

U

U¹, u /juː/ *n.* (*pl.* **Us, U's**) twenty-first letter; U-shaped object or curve.

U² /juː/ *a. colloq.* upper-class; supposedly characteristic of upper class. [abbr.]

U *symb.* uranium.

ubiquitous /juː'bɪkwɪtəs/ *a.* present everywhere or in several places simultaneously; often encountered; **ubiquity** *n.* [L (*ubique* everywhere)]

U-boat /'juːbəʊt/ *n. hist.* German submarine. [G *untersee* undersea]

UCCA *abbr.* Universities Central Council on Admissions.

udder *n.* baglike milk-secreting organ of cow etc., with several teats. [OE]

UDI *abbr.* unilateral declaration of independence.

UFO /'juːfəʊ/ *abbr.* unidentified flying object.

ugh /ʌh, ʊh/ *int.* expressing disgust or horror, or sound of cough or grunt. [imit.]

ugli /'ʌglɪ/ *n.* mottled green and yellow citrus fruit. [UGLY]

uglify /'ʌglɪfaɪ/ *v.t.* make ugly. [foll.]

ugly /'ʌglɪ/ *a.* unpleasing or repulsive to see or hear; unpleasantly suggestive, threatening, dangerous; morally repulsive, vile, discreditable; **ugly customer** unpleasantly formidable person; **ugly duckling** person who turns out to be more beautiful or talented etc. than was at first expected; **uglily** *adv.*; **ugliness** *n.* [ON]

UHF *abbr.* ultra-high frequency.

UHT *abbr.* ultra heat treated (of milk, for long keeping).

UK *abbr.* United Kingdom.

ukase /juː'keɪz/ *n.* arbitrary command; *hist.* edict of Russian government. [Russ.]

Ukrainian /juː'kreɪnɪən/ **1** *a.* of the Ukraine. **2** *n.* native or language of the Ukraine. [*Ukraine* in western USSR]

ukulele /juːkə'leɪlɪ/ *n.* small four-stringed guitar. [Hawaiian]

ulcer *n.* open sore on external or internal surface of body; corroding or corrupting influence; **ulcerous** *a.* [L *ulcus -cer-*]

ulcerate /'ʌlsəreɪt/ *v.* form ulcer (in or on); **ulceration** /-'reɪʃ(ə)n/ *n.* [L (prec.)]

-ule *suffix* of diminutives (*globule, granule*). [L]

ulna /'ʌlnə/ *n.* (*pl.* **ulnae** /-iː/) thinner and longer bone in forearm on side opposite to thumb; corresponding bone in animal's foreleg or bird's wing; **ulnar** *a.* [L]

ulster *n.* long loose overcoat of rough cloth. [*Ulster* in Ireland]

Ulsterman /'ʌlstəmən/ *n.* native of Ulster; **Ulsterwoman** *n. fem.*

ult. *abbr.* ultimo.

ulterior /ʌl'tɪərɪə/ *a.* (esp. of motive) beyond what is obvious or admitted. [L, = further]

ultimate /'ʌltɪmət/ *a.* last, final, beyond which no other exists or is possible; fundamental, primary, unanalysable. [L (*ultimus* last)]

ultimatum /ʌltɪ'meɪtəm/ *n.* (*pl.* **ultimatums**) final statement of terms, rejection of which may lead to war or end of co-operation etc. [L (ULTIMATE)]

ultimo /'ʌltɪməʊ/ *a.* (in commerce) of last month (*the 28th ultimo*). [L, = in the last (*mense* month)]

ultra- *prefix* extremely, excessively (*ultra-conservative, ultra-modern*); beyond. [L *ultra* beyond]

ultra-high /'ʌltrəhaɪ/ *a.* (of frequency) between 300 and 3000 megahertz.

ultramarine /ʌltrəmə'riːn/ **1** *n.* brilliant blue pigment orig. from lapis lazuli; colour of this. **2** *a.* of this colour. [It. & L, = beyond sea, whence lapis lazuli was brought]

ultramontane /ʌltrə'mɒnteɪn/ **1** *a.* situated south of the Alps; advocating supreme papal authority. **2** *n.* ultramontane person. [med.L (MOUNTAIN)]

ultrasonic /ʌltrə'sɒnɪk/ *a.* pitched above upper limit of human hearing; **ultrasonically** *adv.* [ULTRA-]

ultrasonics *n.* science of ultrasonic waves.

ultrasound /'ʌltrəsaʊnd/ *n.* ultrasonic waves.

ultraviolet /ʌltrə'vaɪələt/ *a.* (of radiation) just beyond violet end of visible spectrum; of or using such radiation.

ululate /'juːljʊleɪt/ *v.i.* howl, wail; **ululation** /-'leɪʃ(ə)n/ *n.* [L]

umbel /'ʌmb(ə)l/ *n.* flower-cluster in which stalks nearly equal in length spring from common centre and form flat or curved surface as in carrot; **umbellate** *a.* [F, or L *umbella* sunshade]

umbelliferous /ʌmbəˈlɪfərəs/ *a.* bearing umbels.

umber 1 *n.* pigment like ochre but darker and browner; colour of this. **2** *a.* of this colour. [F or It., f. L *umbra* shadow]

umbilical /ʌmˈbɪlɪk(ə)l/ *a.* of navel; **umbilical cord** flexible cordlike structure attaching foetus to placenta. [F or foll.]

umbilicus /ʌmˈbɪlɪkəs/ *n.* navel. [L]

umbra /ˈʌmbrə/ *n.* (*pl.* **umbrae** /-iː/ or **umbras**) total shadow cast by moon or earth in eclipse. [L, = shadow]

umbrage /ˈʌmbrɪdʒ/ *n.* offence, sense of slight or injury (*take umbrage at*). [F f. L (prec.)]

umbrella /ʌmˈbrelə/ *n.* light portable device for protection against weather, consisting of collapsible usu. circular canopy of cloth mounted on central stick; protection, means of this; coordinating agency. [It. dimin. (UMBRA)]

umlaut /ˈʊmlaʊt/ *n.* vowel-change (e.g. *mann* to *männer* in German); mark like diaeresis indicating this. [G]

umpire /ˈʌmpaɪə/ **1** *n.* person chosen to settle disputes and enforce rules, esp. in cricket and other games. **2** *v.* act as umpire (in). [F *nonper* not equal (PEER²)]

umpteen /ʌmpˈtiːn, ˈʌm-/ *a. sl.* many; an indefinite number of; **umpteenth** *a.* [-TEEN]

'un /ən/ *pron. colloq.* one (*that's a good 'un*). [ONE]

un- *prefix* added to (1) adjectives and their derivative nouns and adverbs, in sense 'not' (*unusable, uneducated, unyielding, unofficial*), or in sense 'the reverse of' with implication of praise or blame (*unsociable, unselfish*); (2) verbs, denoting action contrary to or annulling that of the simple verb (*unlock, untie*); (3) nouns, forming verbs in senses 'deprive of', 'divest (oneself) of', 'release from' (*unfrock, unleash*), or 'cause to be no longer' (*unman*); (4) nouns, in senses 'lack of' or 'the reverse of' (*unbelief, unemployment*).

¶ The number of words that can be formed with this prefix is unlimited and only a selection can be given here. The list at the foot of this and the following pages is of words in sense (1) that can be understood readily from the sense of the main word; it does not include all derivatives of obvious formation (e.g. *unapproachability* from *unapproachable*). Pronunciation and stress follow those of the main word.

unabashed
unabated
unabridged
unacceptable
unaccommodating
unacknowledged
unacquainted
unadorned
unadventurous
unaffiliated
unafraid
unaided
unalterable
unaltered
unambiguous
unambitious
unannounced
unanswered
unappetizing
unappreciative
unapproachable
unarguable
unattainable
unattractive
unauthorized
unavailable
unavoidable
unbeatable
unbelievable
unbiased
unbleached
unblemished
unblinking
unbound
unbreakable
unbusinesslike
unceasing
uncertified
unchallengeable
unchallenged
unchangeable
unchanged
unchanging
uncharacteristic
uncharted
unchecked
unchivalrous
uncircumcised
uncivilized
unclaimed
unclassified
unclouded
uncombed
uncomfortable
uncommitted
uncomplaining
uncomplimentary
unconcealed
unconfined
unconfirmed
uncongenial
unconnected
unconquerable
unconstrained
uncontaminated
uncontested
uncontrollable
uncontrolled
uncontroversial
unconverted
unconvinced
unconvincing
uncooked
uncooperative
uncoordinated
uncorroborated
uncorrupted
uncounted
undamaged
undated
undaunted
undefended
undefiled
undefined
undelivered
undemanding
undemocratic
undeserving
undesigned
undetectable
undetected
undeterred
undeveloped

UN *abbr*. United Nations.
unable /ʌn'eɪb(ə)l/ *a*. not able (*to do* thing). [UN-]
unaccompanied /ʌnə'kʌmpənɪd/ *a*. (of music) without accompaniment; alone, without escort.
unaccomplished /ʌnə'kʌmplɪʃt/ *a*. lacking accomplishments.
unaccountable /ʌnə'kaʊntəb(ə)l/ *a*. that cannot be explained, strange; (of person) not responsible; **unaccountably** *adv*.
unaccounted /ʌnə'kaʊntɪd/ *a*. (with *for*) unexplained.
unaccustomed /ʌnə'kʌstəmd/ *a*. not accustomed (*to*); not usual (*his unaccustomed silence*).
unadopted /ʌnə'dɒptɪd/ *a*. (of road) not taken over for maintenance by local authority.
unadulterated /ʌnə'dʌltəreɪtɪd/ *a*. pure.
unadvised /ʌnəd'vaɪzd/ *a*. indiscreet, rash; not advised; **unadvisedly** /-zɪdlɪ/ *adv*.
unaffected /ʌnə'fektɪd/ *a*. free from affectation, sincere; not affected (*by*).
unalloyed /ʌnə'lɔɪd/ *a*. (of pleasure etc.) pure, sheer.
unanimous /ju:'nænɪməs/ *a*. all of one mind, agreeing in opinion; (of opinion or vote etc.) formed or held etc. by all; **unanimity** /ju:nə'nɪmɪtɪ/ *n*. [L (*unus* one, *animus* mind)]
unanswerable /ʌn'ɑ:nsərəb(ə)l/ *a*. that cannot be refuted; **unanswerably** *adv*.
unarmed /ʌn'ɑ:md/ *a*. not armed, without weapons.
unashamed /ʌnə'ʃeɪmd/ *a*. feeling no guilt, shameless; **unashamedly** /-mɪdlɪ/ *adv*.
unasked /ʌn'ɑ:skt/ *a*. not asked (for), not requested or invited.
unassailable /ʌnə'seɪləb(ə)l/ *a*. that cannot be attacked or questioned; **unassailably** *adv*.
unassuming /ʌnə'sju:mɪŋ/ *a*. making little of one's own merits or status, modest.
unattached /ʌnə'tætʃt/ *a*. not engaged or married; not belonging to a particular regiment or church or club or college.
unattended /ʌnə'tendɪd/ *a*. not attended (*to*); not accompanied.
unavailing /ʌnə'veɪlɪŋ/ *a*. ineffectual.
unaware /ʌnə'weə/ *a*. not aware (*of* or *that*).
unawares *adv*. unexpectedly, without noticing.
unbacked /ʌn'bækt/ *a*. not supported, having no backers (esp. in betting); having no back or backing.
unbalanced /ʌn'bælənst/ *a*. (of the mind or person) unstable, deranged.

undignified
undiluted
undiminished
undiplomatic
undisciplined
undisclosed
undiscovered
undiscriminating
undisguised
undismayed
undisputed
undistinguished
undisturbed
undivided
undressed
undrinkable
uneaten
uneconomic
uneconomical
unedifying
unedited
uneducated
unembarrassed
unemotional
unemphatic
unenlightened
unenterprising
unenthusiastic
unenviable
unessential
uneventful
unexpected
unexpired
unexplained
unexplored
unexposed
unexpressed
unexpurgated
unfading
unfamiliar
unfashionable
unfathomable
unfavourable
unfed
unfeigned
unfeminine
unfenced
unfermented
unfinished
unfitting
unflattering
unflinching
unforeseen
unforgettable
unforgivable
unforgiving
unforthcoming
unfortified
unfrequented
unfriendly
unfruitful
unfulfilled
ungallant
ungenerous
ungentlemanly
ungrateful
ungrudging
unhampered
unharmed
unheeded
unhelpful
unhesitating
unhistorical
unhoped-for
unhurried
unhurt
unhygienic
unidentified
unilluminated
unillustrated
unimaginable
unimaginative
unimpaired
unimpeded
unimportant
unimpressive
uninflected
uninfluenced
uninhabitable
uninhabited
uninhibited
uninitiated
uninjured

unbar /ʌn'bɑː/ *v.t.* (**-rr-**) remove bar from (gate etc.); unlock or open.
unbearable /ʌn'beərəb(ə)l/ *a.* that cannot be endured; **unbearably** *adv.*
unbeaten /ʌn'biːt(ə)n/ *a.* not beaten; (of record etc.) not surpassed.
unbecoming /ʌnbɪ'kʌmɪŋ/ *a.* indecorous, not befitting (person, *to* or *for* person); not suited to the wearer (*an unbecoming hat*).
unbeknown /ʌnbɪ'nəʊn/ *a.* (also **unbeknownst**) *colloq.* not known; **unbeknown to** without the knowledge of.
unbelief /ʌnbɪ'liːf/ *n.* incredulity, disbelief esp. in divine revelation or in particular religion; **unbeliever** *n.*
unbelieving /ʌnbɪ'liːvɪŋ/ *a.* atheistic or agnostic; unduly incredulous.
unbend /ʌn'bend/ *v.* (*past* & *p.p.* **unbent**) change from bent position, straighten; relax (mind etc.) from strain or exertion or severity; become affable; *Naut.* unfasten (cable), untie (rope).
unbending *a.* inflexible, austere.
unbidden /ʌn'bɪd(ə)n/ *a.* not commanded or invited.
unbind /ʌn'baɪnd/ *v.t.* (*past* and *p.p.* **unbound**) release from bonds or binding; unfasten, untie.
unblock /ʌn'blɒk/ *v.t.* remove obstruction from.
unblushing /ʌn'blʌʃɪŋ/ *a.* shameless.
unbolt /ʌn'bəʊlt/ *v.t.* release (door etc.) by drawing back bolt(s).
unborn /ʌn'bɔːn/ *a.* not yet born; future.
unbosom /ʌn'bʊz(ə)m/ *v.t.* disclose (secrets etc.); **unbosom oneself** disclose one's thoughts, secrets, etc.
unbounded /ʌn'baʊndɪd/ *a.* infinite.
unbridle /ʌn'braɪd(ə)l/ *v.t.* remove bridle from (horse, or *fig.* tongue etc.).
unbridled *a.* (of insolence, tongue, etc.) unrestrained.
unbroken /ʌn'brəʊkən/ *a.* not broken; not tamed (*unbroken horse*); not interrupted (*unbroken silence*); not surpassed (*unbroken record*).
unbuckle /ʌn'bʌk(ə)l/ *v.t.* release the buckle(s) of (strap, shoe, etc.).
unburden /ʌn'bɜːd(ə)n/ *v.t.* relieve (*oneself* or one's conscience etc.) by confession etc. (*to* person).
unbutton /ʌn'bʌt(ə)n/ *v.t.* open (shirt etc.), open shirt etc. of (person), by taking buttons out of buttonholes.
uncalled-for /ʌn'kɔːldfɔː/ *a.* offered

unintelligent
unintelligible
unintentional
uninteresting
uninterrupted
uninvited
unjustifiable
unknowable
unlabelled
unladylike
unlawful
unlicensed
unlighted
unlovable
unlovely
unloving
unmarried
unmatched
unmeant
unmerciful
unmerited
unmethodical
unmindful
unmixed
unmodified
unmounted
unmourned
unnamed
unneighbourly
unnoticed
unobjectionable
unobservant
unobserved
unobtainable
unoccupied
unopened
unopposed
unorganized
unoriginal
unorthodox
unpalatable
unpardonable
unpatriotic
unperturbed
unplanned
unpleasing
unpolished
unpredictable
unprejudiced
unprepared
unprepossessing
unpresentable
unpriced
unprivileged
unproductive
unprofitable
unprogressive
unpromising
unpronounceable
unpropitious
unprotected
unproved
unprovided
unpublished
unpunctual
unpunished
unquenchable
unquestioned
unquiet
unquotable
unrealistic
unrealizable
unreasoned
unreasoning
unreciprocated
unrecognizable
unrecorded
unredeemed
unrefined
unreflecting
unreformed
unregenerate
unregistered
unregretted
unregulated
unrehearsed
unrelated
unreliable
unremarkable
unrepentant
unrepresentative
unrepresented
unresisting
unresolved
unresponsive
unrestrained
unrestricted
unrevised
unrewarded
unripe
unromantic
unruffled

impertinently or unnecessarily (*uncalled-for remark*).

uncanny /ʌn'kænɪ/ *a.* weird, mysterious; **uncannily** *adv.*; **uncanniness** *n.*

uncared-for /ʌn'keədfɔ:/ *a.* neglected.

unceremonious /ʌnserɪ'məʊnɪəs/ *a.* lacking ceremony or formality; abrupt in manner, discourteous.

uncertain /ʌn'sɜ:t(ə)n/ *a.* not certainly knowing or known; not to be depended on; changeable (*uncertain temper*); **uncertainty** *n.*

unchain /ʌn'tʃeɪn/ *v.t.* release from chains.

uncharitable /ʌn'tʃærɪtəb(ə)l/ *a.* censorious, severe in judgement; **uncharitably** *adv.*

unchristian /ʌn'krɪstjən/ *a.* contrary to Christian principles.

uncial /'ʌnsɪəl, 'ʌnʃ(ə)l/ **1** *a.* of or written in kind of writing with characters partly resembling modern capitals, found in manuscripts of 4th–8th cc. **2** *n.* uncial letter or manuscript. [L (*uncia* inch)]

uncivil /ʌn'sɪvɪl/ *a.* ill-mannered, rude; **uncivilly** *adv.* [UN-]

unclasp /ʌn'klɑ:sp/ *v.t.* loosen clasp(s) of; release grip of (hand etc.).

uncle /'ʌŋk(ə)l/ *n.* brother or brother-in-law of one's father or mother; *colloq.* unrelated friend of a parent; *sl.* pawnbroker; **Uncle Sam** *colloq.* US government. [AF f. L *avunculus*]

unclean /ʌn'kli:n/ *a.* not clean; foul; ceremonially impure; unchaste. [UN-]

unclose /ʌn'kləʊz/ *v.* open.

unclothe /ʌn'kləʊð/ *v.t.* remove clothes from, uncover.

uncoil /ʌn'kɔɪl/ *v.* draw out or become drawn out after having been coiled, unwind.

uncoloured /ʌn'kʌləd/ *a.* having no colour(s); not influenced *by*.

uncome-at-able /ʌnkʌ'mætəb(ə)l/ *a.* *colloq.* not accessible or attainable.

uncommon /ʌn'kɒmən/ *a.* unusual, remarkable.

uncommunicative /ʌnkə'mju:nɪkətɪv/ *a.* reserved, taciturn.

uncompromising /ʌn'kɒmprəmaɪzɪŋ/ *a.* refusing to compromise, unyielding, inflexible.

unconcern /ʌnkən'sɜ:n/ *n.* freedom from anxiety; indifference, apathy; **unconcerned** *a.*; **unconcernedly** /-nɪdlɪ/ *adv.*

unconditional /ʌnkən'dɪʃən(ə)l/ *a.* not subject to conditions, absolute

unsafe
unsaleable
unsalted
unsatisfactory
unsatisfied
unsatisfying
unscalable
unscarred
unscheduled
unscholarly
unsealed
unseeded
unselfconscious
unsentimental
unserviceable
unshakeable
unshaven
unshockable
unshorn
unsigned
unsized
unskilful
unsmiling
unsmoked
unsoiled
unsold
unsolved
unsorted
unsought
unspecified
unspoiled
unspoken
unsporting
unsportsmanlike
unstained
unstamped
unstarched
unstated
unsterilized
unstinted
unstoppable
unstrained
unsubstantiated
unsuccessful
unsuitable
unsullied
unsupported
unsure
unsurpassed
unsusceptible
unsuspecting
unsuspicious
unsweetened
unswept
unsymmetrical
unsympathetic
unsystematic
untainted
untalented
untameable
untamed
untarnished
untasted
unteachable
untenable
unthankful
untied
untilled
untiring
untouched
untraceable
untraced
untrained
untrammelled
untranslatable
untrodden
untrustworthy
untruthful
untuned
unturned
untutored
unvaccinated
unvaried
unvarying
unventilated
unverified
unwanted
unwashed
unwatered
unwavering
unweaned
unwedded
unwelcome
unwept
unwomanly
unworkable
unwound
unwrought
unwrung

(*unconditional surrender*); **unconditionally** *adv*.
unconditioned *a*. not subject to or determined by conditions; **unconditioned reflex** instinctive response to stimulus.
unconscionable /ʌnˈkɒnʃənəb(ə)l/ *a*. having no conscience; contrary to conscience; unreasonably excessive; **unconscionably** *adv*. [UN-, CONSCIENCE]
unconscious /ʌnˈkɒnʃəs/ **1** *a*. not conscious, not aware; done or spoken etc. without conscious intention (*unconscious humour*). **2** *n*. the part of the mind not normally accessible to consciousness. [UN-]
unconsidered /ʌnkənˈsɪdəd/ *a*. disregarded; not based on consideration.
unconstitutional /ʌnkɒnstɪˈtju:ʃən(ə)l/ *a*. (of measures or acts etc.) not in accordance with a country's constitution; **unconstitutionally** *adv*.
unconventional /ʌnkənˈvenʃən(ə)l/ *a*. not bound by convention or custom; unusual; **unconventionally** *adv*.
uncork /ʌnˈkɔ:k/ *v.t.* draw cork from (bottle); *colloq*. give vent to (feelings).
uncouple /ʌnˈkʌp(ə)l/ *v.t.* release from couples or couplings.
uncouth /ʌnˈku:θ/ *a*. (of person or appearance or manner) strikingly lacking in ease and polish. [OE, = unknown]
uncover /ʌnˈkʌvə/ *v*. remove cover or covering from; lay bare, disclose; take off one's cap or hat. [UN-]
uncritical /ʌnˈkrɪtɪk(ə)l/ *a*. disinclined or not competent to criticize; not according to principles of criticism; **uncritically** *adv*.
uncross /ʌnˈkrɒs/ *v.t.* remove from crossed position.
uncrossed /ʌnˈkrɒst/ *a*. not crossed; not thwarted.
uncrowned /ʌnˈkraʊnd/ *a*. not crowned; **uncrowned king** person having power but not title of king.
unction /ˈʌŋkʃ(ə)n/ *n*. anointing for medical or religious purposes (*extreme unction*); thing used in anointing; soothing words or thought; fervent or sympathetic quality in words or tone caused by or causing deep emotion; pretence of this. [L (*ungo unct-* anoint)]
unctuous /ˈʌŋktjʊəs/ *a*. full of (esp. simulated) unction; greasy, oily. [med.L (prec.)]
uncurl /ʌnˈkɜ:l/ *v*. straighten out from curled state or position. [UN-]
uncut /ʌnˈkʌt/ *a*. not cut; (of book) with leaves not cut open or with untrimmed margins; (of film) not censored; (of diamond) not shaped; (of fabric) with loops of pile not cut.
undeceive /ʌndɪˈsi:v/ *v.t.* free (person) from deception or *of* error.
undecided /ʌndɪˈsaɪdɪd/ *a*. not settled; irresolute.
undemonstrative /ʌndɪˈmɒnstrətɪv/ *a*. not given to showing strong feelings, reserved.
undeniable /ʌndɪˈnaɪəb(ə)l/ *a*. that cannot be denied or disputed; **undeniably** *adv*.
under 1 *prep*. in or to a position lower than (*lay under the table*; *drove under a bridge*); within or on the inside of (surface etc.); at the foot of (high wall); less than (*did it in under an hour*); inferior to, of lower rank than (*no one under a bishop*); in position or act of supporting or sustaining (*sank under the load*; *is now under repair*); governed or commanded by (*fought under Wellington*; *England under Henry VII*); on condition of (*under protest*); liable to, bound by (*under oath*; *under the impression that*); in accordance with (*under our agreement*); as determined by (*under the circumstances*); in the form of (*under an assumed name*); in the category of (*is classified under biology*); (of field etc.) planted with (crop); propelled by (*under sail*). **2** *adv*. in or into lower place or subordinate position; in or into unconsciousness. **3** *a*. lower (*under surface*). [OE]
under- *prefix* in senses (1) UNDER; (2) lower, inner; (3) inferior, subordinate; (4) insufficient(ly), incomplete(ly).
underachieve /ʌndərəˈtʃi:v/ *v.i.* do less than was expected (esp. scholastically).
underarm *a*. & *adv*. (in sport, esp. cricket) with arm below shoulder-level.
underbelly *n*. under-surface of animal etc. esp. as vulnerable to attack.
underbid 1 /ʌndəˈbɪd/ *v.t.* (**-dd-**; *past* and *p.p.* **underbid**) make lower bid than; (in bridge) bid less on (one's hand, or *absol.*) than its strength warrants. **2** /ˈʌndəbɪd/ *n*. such bid.
undercarriage *n*. structure under aircraft, usu. retractable, for support during and after landing; supporting frame of vehicle.
undercharge /ʌndəˈtʃɑ:dʒ/ *v.t.* charge too little for (thing) or to (person); put too little (explosive, electric, etc.) charge into.
undercliff *n*. terrace or lower cliff formed by landslip.
underclothes *n.pl.* clothes worn under others, esp. next to skin.
underclothing *n*. underclothes collectively.
undercoat *n*. layer of paint or (in animals) coat of hair under another.
undercover /ʌndəˈkʌvə/ *a*. surrep-

titious; spying esp. by working among those observed.

undercroft *n.* crypt. [obs. *croft* f. L]

undercurrent *n.* current below surface; underlying trend or influence or feeling, esp. one opposite to one perceived. [UNDER-]

undercut 1 /ʌndə'kʌt/ *v.t.* (-**tt**-; *past* and *p.p.* **undercut**) sell or work at lower price than; strike (ball) to make it rise high; cut away part below. 2 /'ʌndəkʌt/ *n.* under-side of sirloin.

underdeveloped /ʌndədɪ'veləpt/ *a.* not fully developed; (of country etc.) below its potential economic level.

underdog *n.* person etc. losing fight or in state of inferiority or subjection.

underdone /ʌndə'dʌn/ *a.* not thoroughly done, esp. lightly or insufficiently cooked.

underemployed /ʌndərɪm'plɔɪd/ *a.* not fully occupied.

underestimate 1 /ʌndə'restɪmeɪt/ *v.t.* form too low an estimate of. 2 /-mət/ *n.* estimate that is too low.

underexpose /ʌndərɪk'spəʊz/ *v.t.* (esp. in photography) expose for too short a time; **underexposure** *n.*

underfed /ʌndə'fed/ *a.* insufficiently fed.

underfelt *n.* felt for laying under carpet.

underfloor *a.* situated beneath the floor.

underfoot /ʌndə'fʊt/ *adv.* under one's feet, on the ground.

undergarment *n.* piece of underclothing.

undergo /ʌndə'gəʊ/ *v.t.* (*past* **underwent**; *p.p.* **undergone** /-'gɒn/) be subjected to, endure.

undergraduate /ʌndə'grædjʊət/ *n.* member of university who has not taken first degree.

underground 1 /ʌndə'graʊnd/ *adv.* beneath surface of ground; in or into secrecy or hiding. 2 /'ʌndəgraʊnd/ *a.* situated underground; secret, hidden. 3 /'ʌndəgraʊnd/ *n.* underground railway; secret group or activity, esp. aiming at subversion.

undergrowth *n.* dense growth of shrubs etc., esp. under large trees.

underhand *a.* secret; deceptive; = UNDERARM.

underlay 1 /ʌndə'leɪ/ *v.t.* (*past* and *p.p.* **underlaid**) lay thing under (another) to support or raise. 2 /'ʌndəleɪ/ *n.* thing laid under another (esp. under carpet).

underlie /ʌndə'laɪ/ *v.t.* (*past* **underlay**; *p.p.* **underlain**; *partic.* **underlying**) lie under (stratum etc.); be basis of (doctrine or conduct etc.); exist beneath superficial aspect of.

underline 1 /ʌndə'laɪn/ *v.t.* draw line under (word etc.); emphasize. 2 /'ʌndəlaɪn/ *n.* line placed under word or illustration.

underling /'ʌndəlɪŋ/ *n.* (usu. *derog.*) subordinate. [-LING]

undermanned /ʌndə'mænd/ *a.* having too few people as crew or staff. [UNDER-]

undermentioned /ʌndə'menʃ(ə)nd/ *a.* mentioned at later place in book etc.

undermine /ʌndə'maɪn/ *v.t.* make excavation under; wear away base of; weaken or wear out (health etc.) imperceptibly; injure (person etc.) by secret or insidious means.

undermost *a.* lowest, furthest underneath. [UNDER]

underneath /ʌndə'ni:θ/ 1 *prep.* at or to lower place than; on inside of. 2 *adv.* at or to lower place; inside. 3 *n.* lower surface or part. [OE (NETHER)]

undernourished /ʌndə'nʌrɪʃd/ *a.* insufficiently nourished; **undernourishment** *n.* [UNDER-]

underpants *n.pl.* undergarment for lower body and part of legs.

under-part *n.* lower or subordinate part.

underpass *n.* road etc. passing under another.

underpay /ʌndə'peɪ/ *v.t.* (*past* and *p.p.* **underpaid**) pay too little to (person) or for (thing).

underpin /ʌndə'pɪn/ *v.t.* (-**nn**-) support from below with masonry etc.; *fig.* support, strengthen.

underprivileged /ʌndə'prɪvɪlɪdʒd/ *a.* less privileged than others, not enjoying normal living standard or rights.

underproof *a.* containing less alcohol than proof spirit does.

underrate /ʌndə'reɪt/ *v.t.* have too low an opinion of.

underscore 1 /ʌndə'skɔ:/ *v.t.* = UNDERLINE *v.* 2 /'ʌndəskɔ:/ *n.* = UNDERLINE *n.*

undersea *a.* below (surface of) sea.

underseal 1 *v.t.* seal under-part of (esp. motor vehicle against rust etc.). 2 *n.* protective coating for this.

under-secretary /ʌndə'sekrətərɪ/ *n.* subordinate official, esp. junior minister or senior civil servant.

undersell /ʌndə'sel/ *v.t.* (*past* and *p.p.* **undersold**) sell at lower price than (another seller).

under-sexed /ʌndə'seksd/ *a.* having less than normal sexual desire.

undershirt *n.* undergarment worn under shirt, vest.

undershoot /ʌndə'ʃu:t/ *v.t.* (*past* and *p.p.* **undershot**) (of aircraft) land short of (runway etc.).

undershot *a.* (of wheel) turned by

water flowing under it; (of lower jaw) projecting beyond upper jaw.

under-side *n.* lower or under side or surface.

undersigned *a.* whose signature is appended.

undersized *a.* of less than usual size.

underskirt *n.* skirt worn under another, petticoat.

underslung *a.* supported from above.

underspend /ʌndə'spend/ *v.* (*past* and *p.p.* **underspent**) spend less than (amount); spend too little.

understaffed /ʌndə'stɑ:ft/ *a.* having too few staff.

understand /ʌndə'stænd/ *v.* (*past* and *p.p.* **understood**) perceive meaning of (words or language or person); perceive significance or explanation or cause of; be sympathetically aware of character or nature of, know how to deal with (*quite understand your difficulty*; *cannot understand him at all*); infer esp. from information received, take as implied or for granted (*but I understood that expenses were to be paid*; *am I to understand that you refuse?*); supply (word) mentally; have understanding in general or in particular. [OE (STAND)]

understanding 1 *n.* power of thought, intelligence; ability to understand; agreement, thing agreed upon; harmony in opinion or feeling; sympathetic awareness or tolerance. **2** *a.* having understanding or insight or good judgement; able to be sympathetic to others' feelings.

understate /ʌndə'steɪt/ *v.t.* express in greatly or unduly restrained terms, represent as being less than it really is; **understatement** *n.* [UNDER-]

understeer *n.* tendency of vehicle to turn less sharply than was intended.

understudy 1 *n.* one who studies another's role or duties so as to act in his absence. **2** *v.t.* study (role etc.) thus; act as understudy to (person).

undertake /ʌndə'teɪk/ *v.t.* (*past* **undertook** /ʌndə'tʊk/; *p.p.* **undertaken**) agree to perform, make oneself responsible for, engage in; accept obligation (*to do* thing); guarantee or affirm *that*. [TAKE]

undertaker /'ʌndəteɪkə/ *n.* one who professionally makes arrangements for funerals.

undertaking /ʌndə'teɪkɪŋ/ *n.* work etc. undertaken, enterprise; promise; /'ʌn-/ management of funerals.

undertone *n.* subdued tone; underlying quality or feeling. [UNDER-]

undertow *n.* current below sea-surface in opposite direction to surface current.

undervalue /ʌndə'vælju:/ *v.t.* value insufficiently.

undervest *n.* vest (undergarment).

underwater /ʌndə'wɔ:tə/ **1** *a.* situated or done under water. **2** *adv.* under water.

underwear *n.* underclothes.

underweight 1 /ʌndə'weɪt/ *a.* below normal or suitable weight. **2** /'ʌndəweɪt/ *n.* insufficient weight.

underwood *n.* undergrowth.

underworld *n.* those who live by organized crime and immorality; mythical abode of the dead under the earth.

underwrite *v.t.* (*past* **underwrote**; *p.p.* **underwritten**) sign and accept liability under (insurance policy esp. on shipping etc.); accept (liability) thus; undertake to finance or support.

underwriter *n.* insurer, esp. of shipping.

undeserved /ʌndɪ'zɜ:vd/ *a.* not deserved (as reward or punishment); **undeservedly** /-vɪdlɪ/ *adv.* [UN-]

undesirable /ʌndɪ'zaɪərəb(ə)l/ **1** *a.* unpleasant, objectionable. **2** *n.* undesirable person. **3 undesirably** *adv.*

undetermined /ʌndɪ'tɜ:mɪnd/ *a.* undecided.

undies /'ʌndɪz/ *n.pl.* *colloq.* (esp. woman's) underclothes. [abbr.]

undine /'ʌndi:n/ *n.* female water-spirit. [L *unda* wave]

undo /ʌn'du:/ *v.t.* (*past* **undid**; *p.p.* **undone** /-'dʌn/) unfasten (coat or parcel etc.); unfasten garment(s) of (person); annul (*cannot undo the past*); ruin prospects or reputation or morals of. [UN-]

undoing *n.* cause of ruin; ruin; reversal of what has been done.

undone /ʌn'dʌn/ *a.* not done; not fastened; *archaic* ruined.

undoubted /ʌn'daʊtɪd/ *a.* certain, not questioned.

undreamed /ʌn'dri:md/ *a.* (also **undreamt** /-'dremt/) not dreamed or thought (*of*).

undress /ʌn'dres/ **1** *v.* take off one's clothes; take off clothes of (person). **2** *n.* ordinary dress as opposed to full dress or uniform; casual or informal dress.

undue /ʌn'dju:/ *a.* excessive, disproportionate; **unduly** *adv.*

undulate /'ʌndjʊleɪt/ *v.i.* have wavy motion or look; **undulation** /-'leɪʃ(ə)n/; **undulatory** *a.* [L (*unda* wave)]

undying /ʌn'daɪɪŋ/ *a.* immortal; never-ending. [UN-]

unearned /ʌn'ɜ:nd/ *a.* not earned; **unearned income** income from interest payments etc. as opposed to salary or wages or fees.

unearth /ʌn'ɜ:θ/ *v.t.* discover by search or in course of digging or rummaging.

unearthly /ʌn'ɜ:θlɪ/ *a.* supernatural, mysterious; *colloq.* absurdly early or inconvenient (*at this unearthly hour*); **unearthliness** *n.*

uneasy /ʌn'i:zɪ/ *a.* disturbed or uncomfortable in mind or body; disturbing (*uneasy suspicion*); **uneasily** *adv.*; **uneasiness** *n.*

uneatable /ʌn'i:təb(ə)l/ *a.* not able to be eaten, esp. because of its condition.

unemployable /ʌnɪm'plɔɪəb(ə)l/ *a.* unfitted by character etc. for paid employment.

unemployed /ʌnɪm'plɔɪd/ *a.* temporarily out of work; lacking employment; not in use.

unemployment /ʌnɪm'plɔɪmənt/ *n.* lack of employment; **unemployment benefit** payment made by State to unemployed person.

unencumbered /ʌnɪn'kʌmbəd/ *a.* (of estate) having no liabilities on it.

unending /ʌn'endɪŋ/ *a.* having or apparently having no end.

unequal /ʌn'i:kw(ə)l/ *a.* not equal (*to*); of varying quality; not with equal advantage to both sides (*unequal contest*); **unequally** *adv.*

unequalled *a.* superior to all others.

unequivocal /ʌnɪ'kwɪvək(ə)l/ *a.* not ambiguous, plain, unmistakable; **unequivocally** *adv.*

unerring /ʌn'ɜ:rɪŋ/ *a.* not erring or failing or missing the mark.

UNESCO /ju:'neskəʊ/ *abbr.* (also **Unesco**) United Nations Educational, Scientific, and Cultural Organization.

unethical /ʌn'eθɪk(ə)l/ *a.* unscrupulous in professional conduct; **unethically** *adv.* [UN-]

uneven /ʌn'i:v(ə)n/ *a.* not level or smooth; not uniform or equable; (of contest) unequal.

unexampled /ʌnɪg'zɑ:mp(ə)ld/ *a.* without precedent.

unexceptionable /ʌnɪk'sepʃənəb(ə)l/ *a.* with which no fault can be found; **unexceptionably** *adv.*

unexceptional /ʌnɪk'sepʃən(ə)l/ *a.* not out of the ordinary; **unexceptionally** *adv.*

unfailing /ʌn'feɪlɪŋ/ *a.* not failing; not running short; constant; reliable.

unfair /ʌn'feə/ *a.* not equitable or honest or impartial.

unfaithful /ʌn'feɪθfʊl/ *a.* adulterous; not loyal, treacherous; **unfaithfully** *adv.*

unfasten /ʌn'fɑ:s(ə)n/ *v.* make or become loose; open fastening(s) of; detach.

unfeeling /ʌn'fi:lɪŋ/ *a.* lacking sensitivity, unsympathetic, cruel.

unfetter /ʌn'fetə/ *v.t.* release from fetters.

unfit /ʌn'fɪt/ **1** *a.* not fit (*to do* thing, *for* purpose). **2** *v.t.* (-**tt**-) make unsuitable (*for*).

unfitted *a.* not fit; not fitted; not furnished with fittings.

unfix /ʌn'fɪks/ *v.t.* release or loosen from fixed state; detach.

unflappable /ʌn'flæpəb(ə)l/ *a. colloq.* imperturbable; **unflappability** /-'bɪlɪtɪ/ *n.*

unfledged /ʌn'fledʒd/ *a.* (of person) inexperienced; (of bird) not fledged.

unfold /ʌn'fəʊld/ *v.* open fold(s) of, spread out; reveal (thoughts etc.); become opened out; develop.

unformed /ʌn'fɔ:md/ *a.* not formed; shapeless.

unfortunate /ʌn'fɔ:tjʊnət, -tʃənət/ **1** *a.* unlucky; unhappy; regrettable. **2** *n.* unfortunate person.

unfounded /ʌn'faʊndɪd/ *a.* without foundation (*unfounded hopes, rumour*).

unfreeze /ʌn'fri:z/ *v.* (*past* **unfroze**; *p.p.* **unfrozen**) (cause to) thaw.

unfrock /ʌn'frɒk/ *v.t.* deprive of ecclesiastical status.

unfurl /ʌn'fɜ:l/ *v.* spread out (sail etc.); become spread out.

unfurnished /ʌn'fɜ:nɪʃt/ *a.* not supplied (*with*); without furniture.

ungainly /ʌn'geɪnlɪ/ *a.* awkward-looking, clumsy; **ungainliness** *n.* [obs. *gain* straight (ON)]

unget-at-able /ʌnget'ætəb(ə)l/ *a. colloq.* inaccessible. [UN-]

ungird /ʌn'gɜ:d/ *v.t.* release girdle of.

ungodly /ʌn'gɒdlɪ/ *a.* impious, wicked; *colloq.* outrageous; **ungodliness** *n.*

ungovernable /ʌn'gʌvənəb(ə)l/ *a.* uncontrollable, violent.

ungracious /ʌn'greɪʃəs/ *a.* not kindly or courteous.

ungrammatical /ʌngrə'mætɪk(ə)l/ *a.* contrary to rules of grammar; **ungrammatically** *adv.*

unguarded /ʌn'gɑ:dɪd/ *a.* incautious, thoughtless; not guarded.

unguent /'ʌŋgwənt/ *n.* soft substance used as ointment or for lubrication. [L (*unguo* anoint)]

ungulate /'ʌŋgjʊlət/ **1** *a.* hoofed. **2** *n.* hoofed mammal. [L (*ungula* hoof, claw)]

unhallowed /ʌn'hæləʊd/ *a.* not consecrated; not sacred, wicked. [UN-]

unhand /ʌn'hænd/ *v.t.* take one's hands off (person), let go of.

unhappy /ʌn'hæpɪ/ *a.* not happy, miserable; unfortunate; unsuccessful; **unhappily** *adv.*; **unhappiness** *n.*

unharness /ʌn'hɑ:nɪs/ *v.t.* remove harness from.

unhealthy /ʌn'helθɪ/ *a.* not in good health; (of place etc.) harmful to health; unwholesome; *sl.* dangerous to life; **unhealthily** *adv.*; **unhealthiness** *n.*

unheard *a.* not heard; **unheard-of** unprecedented.
unhinge /ʌn'hɪndʒ/ *v.t.* take (door etc.) off its hinges; (esp. in *p.p.*) make (person or mind) crazy.
unhitch /ʌn'hɪtʃ/ *v.t.* release from hitched state; unhook, unfasten.
unholy /ʌn'həʊlɪ/ *a.* impious, wicked; *colloq.* frightful or outrageous; **unholiness** *n.*
unhook /ʌn'hʊk/ *v.t.* remove from hook(s); unfasten by releasing hook(s).
unhorse /ʌn'hɔːs/ *v.t.* throw (rider) from horse.
unhouse /ʌn'haʊz/ *v.t.* deprive of shelter, drive from house.
unhuman /ʌn'hjuːmən/ *a.* not human; superhuman; inhuman.
uni- *in comb.* one, having or consisting of one. [L (*unus* one)]
Uniat /'juːnɪæt/ **1** *a.* of Church in E. Europe and Near East acknowledging Pope's supremacy but following its own ritual. **2** *n.* member of such Church. [Russ. *uniyat* f. L *unio* UNION]
unicameral /juːnɪ'kæmər(ə)l/ *a.* with one legislative chamber. [CHAMBER]
UNICEF /'juːnɪsef/ *abbr.* United Nations Children's (orig. Emergency) Fund.
unicellular /juːnɪ'seljʊlə/ *a.* (of organism) consisting of one cell. [UNI-]
unicorn /'juːnɪkɔːn/ *n.* mythical animal resembling horse with single straight horn. [F f. L (*cornu* horn)]
unidea'd /ʌnaɪ'dɪəd/ *a.* having no ideas. [UN-]
unification /juːnɪfɪ'keɪʃ(ə)n/ *n.* unifying or being unified. [UNIFY or F or It.]
uniform /'juːnɪfɔːm/ **1** *a.* not changing in form or character, unvarying; conforming to same standard or rule. **2** *n.* distinctive clothing worn by members of same school or organization. **3 uniformity** /-'fɔːmɪtɪ/ *n.* [F or L (FORM)]
unify /'juːnɪfaɪ/ *v.t.* reduce to unity or uniformity. [F or L (UNI-)]
unilateral /juːnɪ'lætər(ə)l/ *a.* done by or affecting only one side or party; **unilaterally** *adv.* [UNI-]
unimpeachable /ʌnɪm'piːtʃəb(ə)l/ *a.* giving no opportunity for censure; **unimpeachably** *adv.* [UN-]
uninformed /ʌnɪn'fɔːmd/ *a.* not informed; ignorant.
uninspired /ʌnɪn'spaɪəd/ *a.* not inspired; (of oratory etc.) commonplace.
uninterested /ʌn'ɪntrəstɪd/ *a.* not interested; unconcerned, indifferent.
uninviting /ʌnɪn'vaɪtɪŋ/ *a.* unattractive, repellent.
union /'juːnjən/ *n.* uniting or being united; a whole resulting from combination of parts or members; such political combination (esp. US or UK or USSR); = *trade union*; marriage; concord, agreement; (**Union**) general social club and debating society at some universities and colleges; *Math.* totality of members of two or more sets; **Union Jack** national flag of UK with combined crosses of three patron saints. [F or L (*unus* one)]
unionist *n.* member of trade union; advocate of trade unions; advocate of union esp. between Britain and Northern Ireland (formerly between Britain and Ireland); **unionism** *n.*
unionize *v.t.* bring under trade-union organization or rules; **unionization** /-'zeɪʃ(ə)n/ *n.*
unique /jʊ'niːk/ *a.* being the only one of its kind, having no like or equal or parallel; (**D**) unusual. [F f. L *unicus* (*unus* one)]
unisex /'juːnɪseks/ **1** *n.* tendency of the human sexes to become indistinguishable in dress etc. **2** *a.* designed to be suitable for both sexes. [UNI-]
unison /'juːnɪs(ə)n/ *n.* coincidence in pitch; combination of voices or instruments at same pitch (esp. **in unison**); agreement (*acting in perfect unison*). [F or L (*sonus* SOUND[1])]
unit /'juːnɪt/ *n.* individual thing or person or group regarded as single and complete; quantity chosen as standard for expressing other quantities (*unit of heat*; *mass per unit volume*); smallest share in unit trust; device with specified function in complex mechanism; piece of furniture for fitting with others like it or made of complementary parts; group with special function in an organization; **unit price** price charged for each unit of goods supplied; **unit trust** company investing in varied stocks the combined contributions from many persons. [L *unus* one]
Unitarian /juːnɪ'teərɪən/ **1** *n.* one who believes that God is one person not a Trinity; member of religious body maintaining this. **2** *a.* of Unitarians. **3 Unitarianism** *n.* [L *unitas* unity]
unitary /'juːnɪtərɪ/ *a.* of a unit or units; marked by unity or uniformity. [UNIT or UNITY]
unite /jʊ'naɪt/ *v.* join together, make or become one, combine, consolidate, amalgamate; agree or combine or cooperate (*in*); **United Kingdom** Great Britain and Northern Ireland; **United Nations** international peace-seeking organization; **United States (of America)** republic in N. America. [L *unio -it-* (*unus* one)]
unity /'juːnɪtɪ/ *n.* oneness, being one or single or individual, due interconnection of parts; harmony between persons

etc.; thing forming a complex whole; the number 'one'. [F f. L (*unus* one)]

univalent /ju:nɪ'veɪlənt/ *a.* having chemical valence of one. [UNI-, VALENCE]

univalve /'ju:nɪvælv/ **1** *a.* having one valve. **2** *n.* univalve mollusc. [UNI-]

universal /ju:nɪ'vɜ:s(ə)l/ *a.* of or belonging to or done etc. by all persons or things in the world or in the class concerned, applicable to all cases; **universal coupling** (or **joint**) one which can transmit power by a shaft at any selected angle; **universality** /-'sælɪtɪ/ *n.*; **universally** *adv.* [F or L (UNIVERSE)]

universe /'ju:nɪvɜ:s/ *n.* all existing things; the whole creation; all mankind. [F f. L *universus* combined into one]

university /ju:nɪ'vɜ:sɪtɪ/ *n.* educational institution instructing or examining students in many branches of advanced learning, and conferring degrees; members of this collectively. [F f. L (prec.)]

unjust /ʌn'dʒʌst/ *a.* not just, not fair. [UN-]

unkempt /ʌn'kempt/ *a.* of untidy or uncared-for appearance. [= *uncombed*]

unkind /ʌn'kaɪnd/ *a.* not kind; harsh, cruel. [UN-]

unknot /ʌn'nɒt/ *v.t.* (**-tt-**) release knot(s) of, untie.

unknowing /ʌn'nəʊɪŋ/ *a.* not knowing, unconscious (*of*).

unknown /ʌn'nəʊn/ **1** *a.* not known, unfamiliar. **2** *n.* unknown thing or person; unknown quantity. **3 unknown quantity** person or thing whose nature or significance etc. cannot be determined; **unknown to** without the knowledge of (*did it unknown to me*).

unlace /ʌn'leɪs/ *v.t.* undo lace(s) of; unfasten or loosen thus.

unladen /ʌn'leɪd(ə)n/ *a.* not laden; **unladen weight** weight of vehicle etc. when not loaded with goods.

unlatch /ʌn'lætʃ/ *v.t.* release latch of; open thus.

unlearn /ʌn'lɜ:n/ *v.t.* discard from one's memory; rid oneself of (habit, false information, etc.).

unlearned[1] /ʌn'lɜ:nɪd/ *a.* not well educated.

unlearned[2] /ʌn'lɜ:nd/ *a.* (also **unlearnt**) (of lesson etc.) not learnt.

unleash /ʌn'li:ʃ/ *v.t.* release from leash or restraint; set free to engage in pursuit or attack (*lit.* or *fig.*).

unleavened /ʌn'lev(ə)nd/ *a.* not leavened; made without yeast or other raising agent.

unless /ʌn'les/ *conj.* if not, except when. [= *on less*]

unlettered /ʌn'letəd/ *a.* illiterate. [UN-]

unlike /ʌn'laɪk/ **1** *a.* not like, different from; uncharacteristic of (*such behaviour is unlike him*). **2** *prep.* differently from (*unlike his wife, he enjoys cooking*). **3 unlike signs** *Math.* plus and minus.

unlikely /ʌn'laɪklɪ/ *a.* improbable (*unlikely tale*); not to be expected *to do* thing; unpromising (*unlikely candidate*).

unlimited /ʌn'lɪmɪtɪd/ *a.* boundless, unrestricted; very great or numerous.

unlined /ʌn'laɪnd/ *a.* without lines; without lining.

unlisted /ʌn'lɪstɪd/ *a.* not in published list, esp. of telephone numbers or Stock Exchange prices.

unload /ʌn'ləʊd/ *v.t.* remove load from (ship etc., or *absol.*); remove (load) from ship etc.; remove charge from (firearm etc.); *colloq.* get rid of.

unlock /ʌn'lɒk/ *v.t.* release lock of (door etc., or *fig.* mind etc.); release or disclose by unlocking (*lit.* or *fig.*).

unlooked-for /ʌn'lʊktfɔ:/ *a.* not expected.

unloose /ʌn'lu:s/ *v.t.* (also **unloosen**) loose.

unlucky /ʌn'lʌkɪ/ *a.* not lucky or fortunate or successful; wretched; bringing bad luck; ill-judged; **unluckily** *adv.*

unmake /ʌn'meɪk/ *v.t.* (*past* and *p.p.* **unmade**) destroy, annul; (in *p.p.*) not made.

unman /ʌn'mæn/ *v.t.* (**-nn-**) deprive of manly qualities (e.g. self-control, courage), cause to weep etc.

unmanageable /ʌn'mænɪdʒəb(ə)l/ *a.* not (easily) managed or manipulated or controlled (*unmanageable child, material, situation*); **unmanageably** *adv.*

unmanned /ʌn'mænd/ *a.* not manned; overcome by emotion etc.

unmannerly /ʌn'mænəlɪ/ *a.* without good manners, showing lack of good manners; **unmannerliness** *n.*

unmarked /ʌn'mɑ:kt/ *a.* not marked; not noticed.

unmask /ʌn'mɑ:sk/ *v.* remove mask from; expose true character of; remove one's mask.

unmeaning /ʌn'mi:nɪŋ/ *a.* without meaning.

unmeant /ʌn'ment/ *a.* not intended.

unmentionable /ʌn'menʃənəb(ə)l/ *a.* that cannot (properly) be mentioned; **unmentionably** *adv.*

unmistakable /ʌnmɪ'steɪkəb(ə)l/ *a.* that cannot be mistaken or doubted, clear; **unmistakably** *adv.*

unmitigated /ʌn'mɪtɪgeɪtɪd/ *a.* not modified; absolute.

unmoral /ʌn'mɒr(ə)l/ *a.* not concerned with morality; **unmorally** *adv.*

unmoved /ʌn'mu:vd/ *a.* not moved; not

changed in purpose; not affected by emotion.
unmusical /ʌn'mju:zɪk(ə)l/ *a.* not pleasing to the ear; unskilled in or indifferent to music; **unmusically** *adv.*
unmuzzle /ʌn'mʌz(ə)l/ *v.t.* remove muzzle from.
unnameable /ʌn'neɪməb(ə)l/ *a.* too bad to be named.
unnatural /ʌn'nætʃər(ə)l/ *a.* contrary to (the usual course of) nature, not normal; lacking natural feelings; extremely cruel or wicked, monstrous; artificial; affected; **unnaturally** *adv.*
unnecessary /ʌn'nesəsərɪ/ *a.* not necessary; more than is necessary; **unnecessarily** *adv.*
unnerve /ʌn'nɜ:v/ *v.t.* deprive of strength or resolution.
unnumbered /ʌn'nʌmbəd/ *a.* not numbered or counted; countless.
UNO *abbr.* United Nations Organization.
unobtrusive /ʌnəb'tru:sɪv/ *a.* not making oneself or itself noticed. [UN-]
unoffending /ʌnə'fendɪŋ/ *a.* harmless, innocent.
unofficial /ʌnə'fɪʃ(ə)l/ *a.* not officially authorized or confirmed; **unofficial strike** strike not formally approved by strikers' trade union; **unofficially** *adv.*
unpack /ʌn'pæk/ *v.t.* open and remove contents of (luggage etc., or *absol.*); take (thing) out thus.
unpaged /ʌn'peɪdʒd/ *a.* with pages not numbered.
unpaid /ʌn'peɪd/ *a.* (of debt or person) not paid.
unparalleled /ʌn'pærəleld/ *a.* having no parallel or equal.
unparliamentary /ʌnpɑ:lə'mentərɪ/ *a.* contrary to parliamentary usage; **unparliamentary language** oaths, abuse.
unperson /'ʌnpɜ:s(ə)n/ *n.* one whose name or existence is denied or ignored.
unpick /ʌn'pɪk/ *v.t.* undo stitching of (garment etc.).
unpin /ʌn'pɪn/ *v.t.* (**-nn-**) unfasten or detach by removing pin(s).
unplaced /ʌn'pleɪst/ *a.* not placed as one of first three in race etc.
unplayable /ʌn'pleɪəb(ə)l/ *a.* (of ball in games) that cannot be played or returned etc.
unpleasant /ʌn'plezənt/ *a.* disagreeable.
unplug /ʌn'plʌg/ *v.t.* (**-gg-**) disconnect (electrical device) by removing its plug from socket; unstop.
unplumbed /ʌn'plʌmd/ *a.* not plumbed; not fully explored or understood.
unpointed /ʌn'pɔɪntɪd/ *a.* having no point(s); not punctuated; (of written Hebrew etc.) without vowel points; (of masonry) not pointed.
unpolitical /ʌnpə'lɪtɪk(ə)l/ *a.* not concerned with politics; **unpolitically** *adv.*
unpopular /ʌn'pɒpjʊlə/ *a.* not popular; disliked by the public or by people in general; **unpopularity** /'lærɪtɪ/ *n.*
unpractical /ʌn'præktɪk(ə)l/ *a.* not practical; (of person) without practical skill.
unpractised /ʌn'præktɪst/ *a.* not experienced or skilled; not put into practice.
unprecedented /ʌn'presɪdentɪd/ *a.* for which there is no precedent; unparalleled; novel.
unpremeditated /ʌnprɪ'medɪteɪtɪd/ *a.* not deliberately planned.
unpretending /ʌnprɪ'tendɪŋ/ *a.* = UNPRETENTIOUS.
unpretentious /ʌnprɪ'tenʃəs/ *a.* not given to display, making little show.
unprincipled /ʌn'prɪnsɪp(ə)ld/ *a.* lacking or not based on good moral principles.
unprintable /ʌn'prɪntəb(ə)l/ *a.* too indecent or libellous or blasphemous to be printed.
unprofessional /ʌnprə'feʃən(ə)l/ *a.* contrary to professional etiquette; not belonging to one's or a profession; **unprofessionally** *adv.*
unprompted /ʌn'prɒmptɪd/ *a.* spontaneous.
unprovoked /ʌnprə'vəʊkt/ *a.* without provocation.
unputdownable /ʌnpʊt'daʊnəb(ə)l/ *a.* *colloq.* (of book) so engrossing that reader cannot put it down.
unqualified /ʌn'kwɒlɪfaɪd/ *a.* not competent (*not qualified to give an answer*); not legally or officially qualified (*an unqualified practitioner*); not modified, complete (*an unqualified success*).
unquestionable /ʌn'kwestʃənəb(ə)l/ *a.* that cannot be questioned or doubted; **unquestionably** *adv.*
unquestioning /ʌn'kwestʃənɪŋ/ *a.* asking no questions; done etc. without asking questions.
unquote /ʌn'kwəʊt/ *v.i.* terminate passage that is within quotation-marks.
unravel /ʌn'ræv(ə)l/ *v.t.* (**-ll-**) cause to be no longer ravelled or tangled or intertwined; probe and solve (mystery etc.); undo (fabric, esp. knitted one); become disentangled or unknitted.
unread /ʌn'red/ *a.* (of book etc.) not read; (of person) not well-read.
unreadable /ʌn'ri:dəb(ə)l/ *a.* too dull or too difficult to be worth reading.
unready /ʌn'redɪ/ *a.* not ready; not prompt in action; **unreadily** *adv.*; **unreadiness** *n.*

unreal /ʌn'rɪəl/ *a.* not real; imaginary, illusory; **unreality** /-'ælɪtɪ/ *n.*
unreason /ʌn'ri:z(ə)n/ *n.* lack of reasonable thought or action.
unreasonable /ʌn'ri:zənəb(ə)l/ *a.* exceeding the bounds of reason (*unreasonable demands*); not guided by or listening to reason; **unreasonably** *adv.*
unreel /ʌn'ri:l/ *v.* unwind from reel.
unrelenting /ʌnrɪ'lentɪŋ/ *a.* not relenting or yielding; unmerciful; not abating or relaxing.
unrelieved /ʌnrɪ'li:vd/ *a.* lacking the relief given by contrast or variation.
unremitting /ʌnrɪ'mɪtɪŋ/ *a.* incessant, never slackening.
unremunerative /ʌnrɪ'mju:nərətɪv/ *a.* not (sufficiently) profitable.
unrepeatable /ʌnrɪ'pi:təb(ə)l/ *a.* that cannot be repeated or done etc. again; too indecent to be said again.
unrequited /ʌnrɪ'kwaɪtɪd/ *a.* (of love etc.) not returned.
unreserved /ʌnrɪ'zɜ:vd/ *a.* not reserved; without reserve or reservation; **unreservedly** /-vɪdlɪ/ *adv.*
unrest /ʌn'rest/ *n.* disturbed or agitated condition.
unrighteous /ʌn'raɪtʃəs/ *a.* not upright or honest or just; evil, wicked.
unrip /ʌn'rɪp/ *v.t.* (**-pp-**) open by ripping.
unrivalled /ʌn'raɪv(ə)ld/ *a.* having no equal, peerless.
unroll /ʌn'rəʊl/ *v.* open out from rolled-up state; display or be displayed thus.
unruly /ʌn'ru:lɪ/ *a.* not easily controlled or disciplined, refractory; **unruliness** *n.* [RULE]
unsaddle /ʌn'sæd(ə)l/ *v.t.* remove saddle from; throw from saddle.
unsaid /ʌn'sed/ *a.* not uttered.
unsaturated /ʌn'sætʃəreɪtɪd/ *a. Chem.* able to combine with hydrogen to form a third substance by joining of molecules.
unsavoury /ʌn'seɪvərɪ/ *a.* unpleasant, distasteful; morally offensive.
unsay /ʌn'seɪ/ *v.t.* (*past* and *p.p.* **unsaid** /ʌn'sed/) retract (statement).
unscathed /ʌn'skeɪðd/ *a.* without suffering injury.
unscientific /ʌnsaɪən'tɪfɪk/ *a.* not in accordance with scientific principles; **unscientifically** *adv.*
unscramble /ʌn'skræmb(ə)l/ *v.t.* restore from scrambled state, interpret (scrambled transmission etc.).
unscreened /ʌn'skri:nd/ *a.* (of coal) not passed through sieve.
unscrew /ʌn'skru:/ *v.t.* unfasten by removing screw(s); loosen (screw).
unscripted /ʌn'skrɪptɪd/ *a.* (of speech etc.) delivered without prepared script.
unscrupulous /ʌn'skru:pjʊləs/ *a.* having no scruples, unprincipled.
unseal /ʌn'si:l/ *v.t.* break seal of, open (letter, receptacle, etc.).
unseasonable /ʌn'si:zənəb(ə)l/ *a.* not seasonable; untimely, inopportune; **unseasonably** *adv.*
unseat /ʌn'si:t/ *v.t.* remove from (esp. parliamentary) seat; dislodge from seat, esp. on horseback.
unseeing /ʌn'si:ɪŋ/ *a.* unobservant; blind.
unseemly /ʌn'si:mlɪ/ *a.* indecent; unbecoming; **unseemliness** *n.*
unseen /ʌn'si:n/ **1** *a.* not seen, invisible; (of translation) to be done without preparation. **2** *n.* unseen translation.
unselfish /ʌn'selfɪʃ/ *a.* regardful of others' interests rather than one's own.
unsettle /ʌn'set(ə)l/ *v.t.* disturb settled state or arrangement of, discompose; derange.
unsettled *a.* not (yet) settled; liable or open to change or further discussion; (of bill etc.) unpaid.
unsex /ʌn'seks/ *v.t.* deprive (esp. woman) of qualities of her or his sex.
unshackle /ʌn'ʃæk(ə)l/ *v.t.* release from shackles; set free.
unsheathe /ʌn'ʃi:ð/ *v.t.* remove (knife etc.) from sheath.
unshrinkable /ʌn'ʃrɪŋkəb(ə)l/ *a.* (of fabric etc.) not liable to shrink.
unshrinking /ʌn'ʃrɪŋkɪŋ/ *a.* unhesitating, fearless.
unsighted /ʌn'saɪtɪd/ *a.* not sighted or seen; prevented from seeing.
unsightly /ʌn'saɪtlɪ/ *a.* unpleasant to look at, ugly; **unsightliness** *n.*
unskilled /ʌn'skɪld/ *a.* not having or needing special skill or training.
unsociable /ʌn'səʊʃəb(ə)l/ *a.* not sociable, disliking company of others; **unsociably** *adv.*
unsocial /ʌn'səʊʃ(ə)l/ *a.* not social; not suitable for or seeking society; outside normal working day (*unsocial hours*); **unsocially** *adv.*
unsolicited /ʌnsə'lɪsɪtɪd/ *a.* not asked for; given or done voluntarily.
unsophisticated /ʌnsə'fɪstɪkeɪtɪd/ *a.* artless, simple, natural.
unsound /ʌn'saʊnd/ *a.* not sound; unhealthy; rotten, weak; ill-founded, fallacious; **of unsound mind** insane.
unsparing /ʌn'speərɪŋ/ *a.* lavish; merciless.
unspeakable /ʌn'spi:kəb(ə)l/ *a.* that words cannot express; indescribably bad or good; **unspeakably** *adv.*
unstable /ʌn'steɪb(ə)l/ *a.* not stable, changeable; mentally or emotionally unbalanced; **unstably** *adv.*
unsteady /ʌn'stedɪ/ *a.* not steady or firm; changeable, fluctuating; not

uniform or regular; **unsteadily** *adv.*; **unsteadiness** *n.*

unstick /ʌn'stɪk/ *v.t.* (*past* and *p.p.* **unstuck**) separate (thing stuck to another); **come unstuck** *colloq.* fail, come to grief.

unstitch /ʌn'stɪtʃ/ *v.t.* undo stitches of.

unstop /ʌn'stɒp/ *v.t.* (**-pp-**) free from obstruction; remove stopper from.

unstoppable *a.* that cannot be stopped or prevented.

unstressed /ʌn'strest/ *a.* not pronounced with stress.

unstring /ʌn'strɪŋ/ *v.t.* (*past* and *p.p.* **unstrung**) remove or relax string(s) of (bow, harp, etc.); take (beads etc.) off string; (esp. in *p.p.*) unnerve.

unstructured /ʌn'strʌktʃəd/ *a.* not structured, informal.

unstudied /ʌn'stʌdɪd/ *a.* easy, natural, spontaneous.

unsubstantial /ʌnsəb'stænʃ(ə)l/ *a.* having little or no solidity or reality.

unsuited /ʌn'sju:tɪd/ *a.* not fit (*for* purpose); not adapted (*to*).

unsung /ʌn'sʌŋ/ *a.* not celebrated in song.

unswerving /ʌn'swɜ:vɪŋ/ *a.* steady, constant.

untangle /ʌn'tæŋg(ə)l/ *v.t.* free from tangle, disentangle.

untapped /ʌn'tæpt/ *a.* not (yet) tapped or used (*untapped resources*).

untaught /ʌn'tɔ:t/ *a.* not instructed by teaching; not acquired by teaching.

untether /ʌn'teðə/ *v.t.* release (animal) from tether.

unthink /ʌn'θɪŋk/ *v.t.* (*past* and *p.p.* **unthought** /ʌn'θɔ:t/) retract in thought.

unthinkable /ʌn'θɪŋkəb(ə)l/ *a.* that cannot be imagined or grasped by the mind; *colloq.* highly unlikely or undesirable; **unthinkably** *adv.*

unthinking /ʌn'θɪŋkɪŋ/ *a.* thoughtless; unintentional, inadvertent.

unthread /ʌn'θred/ *v.t.* take thread out of (needle).

unthrone /ʌn'θrəʊn/ *v.t.* dethrone.

untidy /ʌn'taɪdɪ/ *a.* not neat or orderly; **untidily** *adv.*; **untidiness** *n.*

untie /ʌn'taɪ/ *v.t.* (*partic.* **untying**) undo (knot etc.); undo cords of (parcel etc.); liberate from bonds or attachment.

until /ʌn'tɪl/ *prep.* & *conj.* = TILL[1] (used esp. when its clause or phrase stands first, *until you told me I had no idea of it*, and in formal style, *resided there until his decease*). [ON (TILL[1])]

untimely /ʌn'taɪmlɪ/ *a.* inopportune; (of death) premature; **untimeliness** *n.* [UN-]

unto /'ʌntʊ, 'ʌntə/ *prep. archaic* = TO (in all uses except as sign of infinitive). [UNTIL, with *to* replacing *til*]

untold /ʌn'təʊld/ *a.* not told; not (able to be) counted or measured (*untold misery*). [UN-]

untouchable /ʌn'tʌtʃəb(ə)l/ **1** *a.* that may not be touched. **2** *n.* member of hereditary Hindu group held to defile members of higher caste on contact.

untoward /ʌntə'wɔ:d/ *a.* inconvenient, awkward, unlucky; perverse, refractory.

untravelled /ʌn'træv(ə)ld/ *a.* that has not travelled; that has not been travelled over or through.

untried /ʌn'traɪd/ *a.* not tried or tested; inexperienced.

untroubled /ʌn'trʌb(ə)ld/ *a.* calm, tranquil.

untrue /ʌn'tru:/ *a.* not true; contrary to fact; not faithful or loyal (*to*); deviating from accepted standard; **untruly** *adv.*

untruth /ʌn'tru:θ/ *n.* being untrue; false statement, lie.

untuck /ʌn'tʌk/ *v.t.* free (bedclothes etc.) from being tucked in or up.

untwine /ʌn'twaɪn/ *v.* untwist, unwind.

untwist /ʌn'twɪst/ *v.* open from twisted or spiralled state.

unused /ʌn'ju:zd/ *a.* not in use, never having been used; /-'ju:st/ not accustomed *to*.

unusual /ʌn'ju:ʒʊəl/ *a.* not usual; remarkable; **unusually** *adv.*

unutterable /ʌn'ʌtərəb(ə)l/ *a.* inexpressible, beyond description; **unutterably** *adv.*

unvarnished /ʌn'vɑ:nɪʃt/ *a.* not varnished; plain and straightforward (*the unvarnished truth*).

unveil /ʌn'veɪl/ *v.* remove veil from; remove concealing drapery from (statue etc.) as part of ceremony; reveal; remove one's veil.

unversed /ʌn'vɜ:st/ *a.* not experienced or skilled *in*.

unvoiced /ʌn'vɔɪst/ *a.* not spoken; (of consonant etc.) not voiced.

unwarrantable /ʌn'wɒrəntəb(ə)l/ *a.* indefensible, unjustifiable; **unwarrantably** *adv.*

unwarranted /ʌn'wɒrəntɪd/ *a.* unauthorized; unjustified.

unwary /ʌn'weərɪ/ *a.* not cautious; not aware (*of* possible danger etc.); **unwarily** *adv.*; **unwariness** *n.*

unwearying /ʌn'wɪərɪɪŋ/ *a.* persistent.

unwell /ʌn'wel/ *a.* not in good health; indisposed.

unwholesome /ʌn'həʊlsəm/ *a.* not promoting, or detrimental to, physical or moral health; unhealthy, unsalubrious; unhealthy-looking.

unwieldy /ʌn'wi:ldɪ/ *a.* cumbersome or clumsy or hard to manage owing to size or shape or weight; **unwieldily** *adv.*; **unwieldiness** *n.* [*wieldy* active f. WIELD]

unwilling /ʌn'wɪlɪŋ/ *a.* not willing or inclined, reluctant.

unwind /ʌn'waɪnd/ *v.* (*past* and *p.p.* **unwound**) draw out or become drawn out after having been wound; *colloq.* relax.

unwinking /ʌn'wɪŋkɪŋ/ *a.* not winking; vigilant.

unwise /ʌn'waɪz/ *a.* foolish, imprudent.

unwished /ʌn'wɪʃt/ *a.* not wished (usu. *for*).

unwitting /ʌn'wɪtɪŋ/ *a.* unaware of the state of the case (*an unwitting offender*); unintentional. [OE (WIT)]

unwonted /ʌn'wəʊntɪd/ *a.* not customary or usual. [UN-]

unworkmanlike /ʌn'wɜ:kmənlaɪk/ *a.* amateurish.

unworldly /ʌn'wɜ:ldlɪ/ *a.* not worldly; spiritual; **unworldliness** *n.*

unworn /ʌn'wɔ:n/ *a.* that has not been worn or impaired by wear.

unworthy /ʌn'wɜ:ðɪ/ *a.* not worthy or befitting the character (*of*); discreditable, unseemly; **unworthily** *adv.*; **unworthiness** *n.*

unwrap /ʌn'ræp/ *v.* (**-pp-**) remove wrapping from; open; unfold; become unwrapped.

unwritten /ʌn'rɪt(ə)n/ *a.* not written; (of law etc.) resting on custom or judicial decision, not on statute.

unyielding /ʌn'ji:ldɪŋ/ *a.* not yielding; firm, obstinate.

unyoke /ʌn'jəʊk/ *v.* release (as) from yoke; cease work.

unzip /ʌn'zɪp/ *v.* (**-pp-**) open by undoing of zip-fastener.

up 1 *adv.* at, in, or towards a higher place or a place regarded as higher, esp. the north or a capital or university (*high up in the air*; *went up to Cambridge*); to or in erect position or condition (*stood it up*); to or in prepared or required position (*wound up his watch*); in a stronger or winning position or condition (*team was three goals up*; *am £5 up*); to place or time in question or where speaker etc. is (*child came up to her*; *has been fine up till now*); completely or effectually (*burn, eat, speak, tear, use, up*); in state of completion (*time is up*); into compact or accumulated or secure state (*pack, save, tie, up*); in or into condition of activity or progress (*stirred up trouble*; *the hunt is up*); out of bed (*are you up yet?*); happening, esp. unusually (*something is up*); before magistrate etc.; (of road etc.) being repaired; (of jockey) in saddle. **2** *prep.* upwards along, through, or into; from bottom to top of; along (*walked up the road*); at or in a higher part of (*situated up the river, the street*). **3** *a.* directed upwards (*up stroke*); of travel towards a capital or centre (*the up train, platform*). **4** *v.* (**-pp-**) *colloq.* start esp. abruptly or unexpectedly to say or do something (*he ups and says*); *colloq.* raise, esp. abruptly (*they upped their prices*). **5** *n.* spell of good fortune. **6 all up with** hopeless for (person); **on the up-and-up** *colloq.* steadily improving, honest(ly); **up against** close to, in or into contact with, *colloq.* confronted with (difficulty etc.); **up and about** (or **up and doing**) having risen from bed, active; **up-and-coming** *colloq.* (of person) making good progress and likely to succeed; **up and down** to and fro (along); **up-and-over** (of door) opened by being raised and pushed back into horizontal position; **up for** available for or being considered for (office etc.); **up in** *colloq.* knowledgeable about; **ups and downs** rises and falls, alternate good and bad fortune; **up stage** at or to back of theatre stage; **up to** until, not more than, equal to, incumbent on, capable of, occupied or busy with; **up to date** see DATE[1]; **up with** *int.* of support for stated person or thing. [OE]

up- *prefix* in senses of UP, added (1) as adverb to verbs and verbal derivatives, = 'upwards' (*upcurved*, *update*); (2) as preposition to nouns forming adverbs and adjectives (*up-country*, *uphill*); (3) as adjective to nouns (*upland*, *up-stroke*). [OE (prec.)]

upbeat 1 *n.* unaccented beat in music. **2** *a. colloq.* optimistic, cheerful.

upbraid /ʌp'breɪd/ *v.t.* chide or reproach (person *with* or *for* fault etc.). [OE (BRAID = brandish)]

upbringing *n.* bringing up (of child), education. [obs. *upbring* to rear]

up-country *adv.* & *a.* inland. [UP-]

upcurved *a.* curved upwards.

update /ʌp'deɪt/ *v.t.* bring up to date.

up-end /ʌp'end/ *v.* set or rise up on end.

upfield *adv.* in or to position farther along field.

upgrade /ʌp'greɪd/ *v.t.* raise in rank etc.

upheaval /ʌp'hi:v(ə)l/ *n.* violent change or disruption. [*upheave*]

uphill 1 /ʌp'hɪl/ *adv.* up a slope. **2** /'ʌphɪl/ *a.* sloping up, ascending; arduous. [UP-]

uphold /ʌp'həʊld/ *v.t.* (*past* and *p.p.* **upheld**) support, hold up; confirm (decision etc.).

upholster /ʌp'həʊlstə/ *v.t.* provide (chair etc.) with upholstery. [foll.]

upholsterer *n.* one whose trade it is to upholster. [obs. *upholster* (*uphold* keep in repair)]

upholstery *n.* textile covering, padding, springs, etc., for furniture. [UPHOLSTER]

upkeep *n.* maintenance in good condition; cost or means of this. [UP-]

upland /'ʌplənd/ **1** *n.* higher part of country. **2** *a.* of this part.

uplift **1** /ʌp'lɪft/ *v.t.* raise. **2** /'ʌplɪft/ *n. colloq.* elevating influence.

upon /ə'pɒn/ *prep.* = ON (*upon* is sometimes more formal, and is preferred in *once upon a time* and *upon my word*). [*up on*]

upper **1** *a.* higher in place, situated above another part; higher in rank or dignity etc. (*the upper class*). **2** *n.* upper part of boot or shoe. **3 on one's uppers** *colloq.* extremely short of money; **upper case** see CASE²; **the upper crust** *colloq.* the aristocracy; **upper-cut** *n.* & *v.t.* hit upwards with arm bent; **the upper hand** dominance, control; **Upper House** higher house in legislature, esp. House of Lords. [UP]

uppermost **1** *a.* highest; predominant. **2** *adv.* at or to the highest or most prominent position.

uppish *a.* self-assertive, arrogant. [UP]

uppity /'ʌpɪtɪ/ *a. colloq.* uppish.

upright **1** *a.* erect, vertical; (of piano) with vertical strings; strictly honourable or honest. **2** *n.* post or rod fixed upright esp. as support to some structure; upright piano. [OE]

uprising *n.* insurrection. [UP-]

uproar *n.* tumult, violent disturbance. [Du., = commotion]

uproarious /ʌp'rɔ:rɪəs/ *a.* very noisy; provoking loud laughter.

uproot /ʌp'ru:t/ *v.t.* pull (plant etc.) up from ground; displace (person) from accustomed location; eradicate. [UP-]

uprush *n.* upward rush.

upset **1** /ʌp'set/ *v.t.* (**-tt-**; *past* and *p.p.* **upset**) overturn; disturb composure or digestion of; disrupt. **2** /'ʌpset/ *n.* disturbance; surprising result.

upshot *n.* outcome, conclusion.

upside-down /ʌpsaɪd'daʊn/ *adv.* & *a.* with upper part where lower part should be, inverted; in or into total disorder. [*up so down*, prob. = 'up as if down']

upsilon /'ju:psɪlɒn, ʌp'saɪlən/ *n.* twentieth letter of Greek alphabet (Υ, υ). [Gk]

upstage /ʌp'steɪdʒ/ **1** *a.* & *adv.* nearer back of theatre stage; snobbish(ly). **2** *v.t.* move upstage from (actor) to make him face away from audience; divert attention from (person) to oneself. [UP-]

upstairs /ʌp'steəz/ **1** *adv.* to or on upper floor. **2** *a.* situated upstairs. **3** *n.* upper floor.

upstanding /ʌp'stændɪŋ/ *a.* standing up; strong and healthy; honest.

upstart **1** *n.* person who has risen suddenly to prominence, esp. one who behaves arrogantly. **2** *a.* that is an upstart; of upstarts.

upstate *US* **1** *a.* of part of state remote from large cities, esp. northern part. **2** *n.* this part.

upstream **1** *adv.* against flow of stream etc. **2** *a.* moving upstream.

up-stroke *n.* stroke made or written upwards.

upsurge *n.* upward surge.

upswept *a.* (of hair) combed to top of head.

upswing *n.* upward movement or trend.

upsy-daisy /'ʌpsɪdeɪzɪ/ *int.* of encouragement to child who is being lifted or has fallen. [earlier *up-a-daisy*]

uptake *n. colloq.* understanding (usu. in **quick** (or **slow**) **on the uptake**). [UP-]

upthrust *n.* upward thrust; upward displacement of part of the earth's crust.

uptight /'ʌptaɪt, ʌp'taɪt/ *a. colloq.* nervously tense, angry; *US colloq.* rigidly conventional.

uptown *US* **1** *a.* of residential part of town or city. **2** *adv.* in or into this part. **3** *n.* this part.

upturn **1** /'ʌptɜ:n/ *n.* upward trend, improvement. **2** /ʌp'tɜ:n/ *v.t.* turn up or upside-down.

upward /'ʌpwəd/ **1** *adv.* (also **upwards**) towards what is higher, superior, more important, or earlier. **2** *a.* moving or extending upwards. [OE (UP, -WARD)]

upwind *a.* & *adv.* against the wind. [UP-]

uranium /jʊə'reɪnɪəm/ *n.* heavy grey radioactive metallic element, capable of nuclear fission and used as source of nuclear energy. [*Uranus*, name of planet]

urban /'ɜ:bən/ *a.* of, or living or situated in, a town or city; **urban guerrilla** terrorist operating in urban area by kidnapping etc. [L (*urbs* city)]

urbane /ɜ:'beɪn/ *a.* courteous, elegant. [F or L (prec.)]

urbanity /ɜ:'bænɪtɪ/ *n.* urbane quality.

urbanize /'ɜ:bənaɪz/ *v.t.* render urban; remove rural quality of (district); **urbanization** /-'zeɪʃ(ə)n/ *n.* [F (URBAN)]

urchin /'ɜ:tʃɪn/ *n.* mischievous or needy boy; sea-urchin. [F f. L *ericius* hedgehog]

Urdu /'ʊədu:, 'ɜ:du:/ *n.* language related to Hindi but with many Persian words, used esp. in Pakistan. [Hind.]

-ure *suffix* forming nouns of action (*censure, seizure*) or result (*creature, scripture*), and collective nouns (*legislature, nature*). [F & L]

urea /'jʊərɪə, -'rɪə/ *n.* soluble colourless crystalline compound contained esp. in urine. [F *urée* f. Gk *ouron* urine]

ureter /jʊə'ri:tə/ *n.* duct by which urine passes from kidney to bladder. [F f. Gk (*oureō* urinate)]
urethra /jʊə'ri:θrə/ *n.* duct by which urine passes from bladder. [L f. Gk (prec.)]
urge 1 *v.t.* drive forcibly (*on*), hasten; encourage or entreat earnestly or persistently; advocate (action or argument etc.) emphatically (*on* or *upon* person), mention earnestly as reason or justification. **2** *n.* urging impulse or tendency; strong desire. [L *urgeo*]
urgent *a.* requiring immediate action or attention; importunate; **urgency** *n.* [F (prec.)]
uric /'jʊərɪk/ *a.* of urine; **uric acid** constituent of urine. [F *urique* (URINE)]
urinal /jʊə'raɪn(ə)l, 'jʊərɪn(ə)l/ *n.* place or receptacle for urination. [F f. L (URINE)]
urinary /'jʊərɪnərɪ/ *a.* of or relating to urine. [med.L (URINE)]
urinate /'jʊərɪneɪt/ *v.i.* discharge urine; **urination** /-'neɪʃ(ə)n/ *n.*
urine /'jʊərɪn/ *n.* fluid secreted by kidneys and discharged from bladder. [F f. L *urina*]
urn *n.* vase with foot and usu. rounded body, esp. for storing ashes of the dead or as vessel or measure; large vessel with tap, in which tea or coffee etc. is made or kept hot. [L *urna*]
urogenital /jʊərə'dʒenɪt(ə)l/ *a.* of urinary and reproductive systems. [Gk *ouron* urine]
urology /jʊə'rɒlədʒɪ/ *n.* study of urinary system.
Ursa Major /'3:sə/ = *Great Bear* (see BEAR²). [L]
Ursa Minor = *Little Bear* (see BEAR²).
ursine /'3:saɪn/ *a.* of or like a bear. [L (*ursus* bear)]
us /əs, *emphat.* ʌs/ *pron.* obj. case of WE; *colloq.* = WE (*it's us all right*); *colloq.* = ME¹ (*give us a kiss*). [OE]
US *abbr.* United States.
USA *abbr.* United States of America.
usable /'ju:zəb(ə)l/ *a.* that can be used. [F (USE¹)]
usage /'ju:sɪdʒ/ *n.* manner of using or treating (*damaged by rough usage*); customary practice esp. in use of a language. [F (USE²)]
use¹ /ju:z/ *v.* cause to act or serve for a purpose, bring into service; treat in specified manner (*they used her shamefully*); exploit selfishly; (in *past* /often ju:st/) had as one's or its constant or frequent practice or state (*I used to be an archaeologist*; *it used not* or *did not use to rain often*); (in *p.p.* /ju:st/) familiar by habit, accustomed *to* (*not used to hard work, to sharing*); **use up** consume completely, use the whole of, find use for (remainder). [F *user* f. frequent. of L *utor us-*]
use² /ju:s/ *n.* using or being used; right or power of using (*lost the use of his right arm*); ability to be used, purpose for which thing can be used; custom or usage (*long use has reconciled me to it*); **have no use for** be unable to find a use for, dislike, be contemptuous of; **in use** being used; **make use of** use, benefit from; **out of use** not being used. [F *us* f. L *usus* (as prec.)]
used *a.* second-hand. [USE¹]
useful *a.* of use, serviceable, producing or able to produce good results; *colloq.* creditable, efficient; **make oneself useful** perform useful services; **usefully** *adv.* [USE²]
useless *a.* serving no purpose, unavailing.
usher 1 *n.* person who shows people to their seats in hall or theatre etc.; doorkeeper of court etc.; officer walking before person of rank. **2** *v.t.* act as usher to; announce or show *in* etc. (*lit.* or *fig.*). [F f. L (*ostium* door)]
usherette /ʌʃə'ret/ *n.* female usher esp. in cinema.
USSR *abbr.* Union of Soviet Socialist Republics.
usual /'ju:ʒʊəl/ *a.* such as commonly occurs, customary, habitual; **as usual** as commonly occurs; **the** (or **my** etc.) **usual** *colloq.* a person's usual drink etc.; **usually** *adv.* [F or L (USE²)]
usurer /'ju:ʒərə/ *n.* one who practises usury. [F (USURY)]
usurious /jʊ'ʒʊərɪəs/ *a.* of or involving or practising usury. [USURY]
usurp /jʊ'z3:p/ *v.t.* seize or assume (throne or power etc.) wrongfully; **usurpation** /ju:zə'peɪʃ(ə)n/ *n.* [F f. L]
usury /'ju:ʒərɪ/ *n.* lending of money at interest, esp. at exorbitant or illegal rate; interest at this rate. [AF or med.L (USE²)]
utensil /ju:'tens(ə)l/ *n.* implement or vessel, esp. for domestic use. [F f. med.L (USE¹)]
uterine /'ju:təraɪn/ *a.* of the uterus. [L (foll.)]
uterus /'ju:tərəs/ *n.* (*pl.* **uteri** /-aɪ/) womb. [L]
utilitarian /jʊtɪlɪ'teərɪən/ **1** *a.* designed to be useful for a purpose rather than attractive, severely practical; of utilitarianism. **2** *n.* adherent of utilitarianism. [UTILITY]
utilitarianism *n.* doctrine that actions are right if they are useful or for benefit of majority.
utility /ju:'tɪlɪtɪ/ **1** *n.* usefulness, profitableness; useful thing; = *public utility*. **2** *a.* severely practical and standardized;

made or serving for utility. **3 utility room** room containing large fixed domestic appliances, e.g. washing-machine; **utility vehicle** vehicle serving various functions. [F f. L (*utilis* useful f. as USE[1])]

utilize /'ju:tɪlaɪz/ *v.t.* make use of, turn to account; **utilization** /-'zeɪʃ(ə)n/ *n.* [F f. It. (prec.)]

utmost /'ʌtməʊst/ **1** *a.* furthest, extreme, greatest. **2** *n.* the utmost point or degree etc. **3 do one's utmost** do all that one can. [OE, = *outmost*]

Utopia /ju:'təʊpɪə/ *n.* imagined perfect place or state of things; **Utopian** *a.* [title of book by Thomas More, f. Gk *ou* not, *topos* place]

utricle /'ju:trɪk(ə)l/ *n.* cell or small cavity in animal or plant. [F or L dimin. (*uter* bag)]

utter[1] *attrib. a.* complete, total, absolute. [OE, compar. adj. of OUT]

utter[2] *v.* express in words; emit audibly; put (esp. forged money) into circulation. [Du.]

utterance *n.* uttering; power or manner of speaking; thing spoken.

uttermost *a.* utmost. [UTTER[1]]

U-turn /'ju:tɜ:n/ *n.* turning a vehicle in U-shaped course so as to face opposite direction; reversal of policy. [U, TURN]

UV *abbr.* ultraviolet.

uvula /'ju:vjʊlə/ *n.* (*pl.* **uvulae** /-i:/) fleshy part of soft palate hanging above throat; **uvular** *a.* [L dimin. of *uva* grape]

uxorious /ʌk'sɔ:rɪəs/ *a.* greatly or excessively fond of one's wife. [L (*uxor* wife)]

V

V, v /vi:/ *n.* (**Vs, V's**) twenty-second letter; V-shaped thing; *Rom. num.* 5.

V *abbr.* volt(s).

v. *abbr.* verse; versus; very; *vide.*

V *symb.* vanadium.

vac *n. colloq.* vacation. [abbr.]

vacancy /'veɪkənsɪ/ *n.* being vacant; unoccupied post or place. [foll. or L *vacantia*]

vacant *a.* not filled or occupied; not mentally active, showing no interest; **vacant possession** possession of house etc. unoccupied. [F or L (foll.)]

vacate /və'keɪt/ *v.t.* leave vacant, cease to occupy (post, house, etc.). [L *vaco* be empty]

vacation /və'keɪʃ(ə)n/ **1** *n.* fixed period of cessation from work esp. in universities and lawcourts; *US* holiday; vacating. **2** *v.i. US* take holiday. [F or L (prec.)]

vaccinate /'væksɪneɪt/ *v.t.* inoculate with vaccine to procure immunity from disease, esp. smallpox; **vaccination** /-'neɪʃ(ə)n/ *n.*; **vaccinator** *n.* [foll.]

vaccine /'væksi:n, -sɪn/ *n.* virus of cowpox used in vaccination; any preparation similarly used. [L (*vacca* cow)]

vacillate /'væsɪleɪt/ *v.i.* fluctuate in opinion or resolution; **vacillation** /-'leɪʃ(ə)n/ *n.*; **vacillator** *n.* [L]

vacuole /'vækjʊəʊl/ *n.* tiny cavity in organ or cell, containing air or fluid etc. [F, dimin. of L *vacuus* empty]

vacuous /'vækjʊəs/ *a.* expressionless; unintelligent; empty; **vacuity** /və'kju:ɪtɪ/ *n.* [L *vacuus* empty]

vacuum /'vækjʊəm/ **1** *n.* (*pl.* **vacua** or **vacuums**) space entirely devoid of matter; space or vessel from which air has been completely or partly removed by pump etc.; absence of normal or previous content; (*pl.* **vacuums**) *colloq.* vacuum cleaner. **2** *v. colloq.* use vacuum cleaner (on). **3 vacuum brake** brake worked by exhaustion of air; **vacuum cleaner** apparatus for removing dust etc. by suction; **vacuum flask** vessel with double wall enclosing vacuum so that liquid in inner receptacle retains its temperature; **vacuum-packed** sealed after partial removal of air; **vacuum tube** tube with near-vacuum for free passage of electric current.

vade-mecum /vɑ:dɪ'meɪkəm, veɪdɪ'mi:kəm/ *n.* handbook etc. carried constantly for use. [F f. L, = go with me]

vagabond /'vægəbɒnd/ **1** *n.* wanderer, esp. idle one. **2** *a.* having no fixed habitation, wandering. [F or L (*vagor* wander)]

vagary /'veɪgərɪ/ *n.* caprice, eccentric act or idea. [L *vagor* wander]

vagina /və'dʒaɪnə/ *n.* (*pl.* **vaginae** /-i:/ or **vaginas**) canal between womb and vulva of female mammal; **vaginal** *a.* [L, = sheath]

vagrant /'veɪgrənt/ **1** *n.* person without settled home or regular work. **2** *a.* wandering, roving. **3 vagrancy** *n.* [AF]

vague /veɪg/ *a.* of uncertain or ill-defined meaning or character; (of person or mind) imprecise, inexact in thought or expression or understanding. [F, or L *vagus* wandering]

vain *a.* conceited (*of* one's beauty etc.);

empty, trivial (*vain boasts, triumphs*); useless, followed by no good result (*in the vain hope of dissuading him*); **in vain** without result or success. [F f. L *vanus*]
vainglory /veɪn'glɔ:rɪ/ *n.* extreme vanity, boastfulness; **vainglorious** *a.* [after F *vaine gloire*, L *vana gloria*]
valance /'væləns/ *n.* short curtain round frame or canopy of bedstead or above window. [prob. AF (*valer* descend)]
vale *n.* (*archaic* exc. in place-names) valley. [F *val* f. L *vallis*]
valediction /vælɪ'dɪkʃ(ə)n/ *n.* bidding farewell; words used in this; **valedictory** *a.* [L (*vale* farewell)]
valence[1] /'veɪləns/ *n.* combining- or replacing- power of an atom as compared with hydrogen atom. [L *valentia* power]
valence[2] var. of VALANCE.
valency /'veɪlənsɪ/ *n.* unit of combining power of an atom; this power. [L *valentia* power]
valentine /'væləntaɪn/ *n.* sentimental or comic missive sent, often anonymously, to person of opposite sex on St Valentine's day (14 Feb.); sweetheart chosen on this day. [*Valentine*, name of two saints]
valerian /və'lɪərɪən/ *n.* any of various kinds of flowering herb. [F f. med.L]
valet /'vælɪt, -leɪ/ **1** *n.* gentleman's personal attendant. **2** *v.* act as valet (to). [F *va(s)let*, rel. to VARLET, VASSAL]
valetudinarian /vælɪtju:dɪ'neərɪən/ **1** *n.* person of poor health or unduly anxious about his health. **2** *a.* that is a valetudinarian. **3 valetudinarianism** *n.* [L (*valetudo* health)]
valiant /'væljənt/ *a.* (of person or conduct) brave. [F f. L *valeo* be strong]
valid /'vælɪd/ *a.* (of reason, objection, etc.) sound, defensible; legally acceptable, executed with proper formalities (*valid contract, passport*); **validity** /və'lɪdɪtɪ/ *a.* [F or L (prec.)]
validate /'vælɪdeɪt/ *v.t.* make valid, ratify; **validation** /-'deɪʃ(ə)n/ *n.* [med.L (prec.)]
valise /və'li:z/ *n.* kitbag; *US* small portmanteau. [F f. It.]
valley /'vælɪ/ *n.* low area more or less enclosed by hills and usu. with stream. [F (VALE)]
valour /'vælə/, *US* **valor** *n.* courage esp. in battle; **valorous** *a.* [F f. L (*valeo* be strong)]
valuable /'væljʊəb(ə)l/ **1** *a.* of great value or price or worth (*valuable property, information, assistance*). **2** *n.* (usu. in *pl.*) valuable thing. **3 valuably** *adv.* [VALUE]
valuation /væljʊ'eɪʃ(ə)n/ *n.* estimation (esp. by professional valuer) of a thing's worth; worth so estimated. [foll.]
value /'vælju:/ **1** *n.* worth or desirability or utility, or qualities on which these depend; worth as estimated (*sets a high value on his time*); amount of money or goods for which thing can be exchanged in open market; equivalent of a thing, what represents or is represented by or may be substituted for a thing; (also **value for money**) something well worth the money spent; ability of a thing to serve a purpose or cause an effect (*news value*); (in *pl.*) one's principles or standards, one's judgement of what is valuable or important in life; *Mus.* duration of sound signified by note; *Math.* amount denoted by algebraic term or expression. **2** *v.t.* estimate value of, appraise (professionally); have high or specified opinion of, attach importance to. **3 value added tax** tax on amount by which value of an article has been increased at each stage of its production; **value judgement** subjective estimate of quality etc. [F p.p. of *valoir* be worth f. L *valeo* be well]
valueless *a.* having no value.
valuer *n.* one who estimates or assesses values, esp. professionally.
valve *n.* device for controlling passage of fluid through pipe etc., esp. automatic device allowing movement in one direction only; membranous part of organ etc. allowing flow of blood etc. in one direction only; = THERMIONIC VALVE; device to vary length of tube in trumpet etc.; each of two shells of oyster or mussel etc. [L *valva* leaf of folding door]
valvular /'vælvjʊlə/ *a.* of or like a valve; forming or having a valve or valves.
vamoose /və'mu:s/ *v.i. US sl.* depart hurriedly. [Sp. *vamos* let us go]
vamp[1] **1** *n.* upper front part of boot or shoe. **2** *v.* repair, furbish usu. *up*; make *up* by patching or from odds and ends; improvise musical accompaniment (to). [AF (F *avantpié* front of the foot)]
vamp[2] *colloq.* **1** *n.* unscrupulous flirt; woman who exploits men. **2** *v.* allure, exploit (man); act as vamp. [abbr. foll.]
vampire /'væmpaɪə/ *n.* ghost or reanimated corpse supposed to suck blood of sleeping persons; person who preys ruthlessly on others; **vampire bat** tropical (esp. S. American) bat actually or supposedly biting animals and persons and lapping their blood. [F or G f. Magyar]
van[1] *n.* covered vehicle for conveying goods etc.; railway carriage for luggage or for use of guard. [abbr. CARAVAN]
van[2] *n.* vanguard; forefront. [abbr.]

vanadium /və'neɪdɪəm/ *n.* hard grey metallic element used to strengthen steel. [ON *Vanadís*, name of the Scandinavian goddess Freyja]

Van Allen belt /væn 'ælən/ (also **Van Allen layer**) each of two regions of intense radiation partly surrounding earth at heights of several thousand kilometres. [*Van Allen*, physicist]

vandal /'vænd(ə)l/ *n.* one who wilfully or maliciously destroys or damages works of art or other property; **vandalism** *n.* [*Vandals*, Gmc tribe that sacked Rome in 5th c.; L f. Gmc]

vandalize /'vændəlaɪz/ *v.t.* destroy or damage (property etc.) as vandal.

Vandyke beard /væn'daɪk/ neat pointed beard. [*Van Dyck*, painter]

Vandyke brown /væn'daɪk/ deep rich brown.

vane *n.* weather-vane; blade of screw propeller or windmill etc. [dial. var. of obs. *fane* banner]

vanguard /'vængɑ:d/ *n.* foremost part of army or fleet advancing or ready to do so; leaders of movement, of opinion, etc. [F *avan(t) garde* (*avant* before, GUARD)]

vanilla /və'nɪlə/ *n.* substance obtained from vanilla-pod or synthetically and used to flavour ices, chocolate, etc.; tropical climbing orchid with fragrant flowers; fruit of this; **vanilla-pod** this fruit. [Sp. dimin. (*vaina* pod)]

vanish /'vænɪʃ/ *v.i.* disappear; cease to exist; **vanishing-cream** emollient that leaves no visible trace when rubbed into skin; **vanishing-point** point at which receding parallel lines viewed in perspective appear to meet, stage of complete disappearance. [F f. L (VAIN)]

vanity /'vænɪtɪ/ *n.* conceit and desire for admiration because of one's personal attainments or attractions; futility, unsubstantiality, unreal thing (*the vanity of human achievements*); ostentatious display; **vanity bag** (or **case**) bag or case carried by woman and containing small mirror, make-up, etc. [F f. L (VAIN)]

vanquish /'væŋkwɪʃ/ *v.t. literary* conquer, overcome. [F f. L *vinco*]

vantage /'vɑ:ntɪdʒ/ *n.* = ADVANTAGE (esp. in tennis); **vantage-point** place affording good view. [F (ADVANTAGE)]

vapid /'væpɪd/ *a.* insipid, lacking interest, flat; **vapidity** /və'pɪdɪtɪ/ *n.* [L *vapidus*]

vapor *US* var. of VAPOUR.

vaporize /'veɪpəraɪz/ *v.* convert or be converted into vapour; **vaporization** /-'zeɪʃ(ə)n/ *n.* [VAPOUR]

vaporous /'veɪpərəs/ *a.* in the form of or consisting of vapour. [L (foll.)]

vapour /'veɪpə/ *n.* moisture or other substance diffused or suspended in air, e.g. mist, smoke; gaseous form of a normally liquid or solid substance; **vapour trail** trail of condensed water from aircraft etc. [F, or L *vapor* steam]

vapoury *a.* resembling vapour.

variable /'veərɪəb(ə)l/ **1** *a.* that can be varied or adapted (*rod of variable length*; *the pressure is variable*); apt to vary, not constant, unsteady (*variable mood, temper, fortune*); (of mathematical quantity) indeterminate, able to assume different numerical values. **2** *n.* variable thing or quantity. **3 variability** /-'bɪlɪtɪ/ *n.*; **variably** *adv.* [F f. L (VARY)]

variance /'veərɪəns/ *n.* difference of opinion, dispute (*at variance among ourselves*); discrepancy.

variant 1 *a.* differing in form or details from that named or considered; differing thus among themselves (*forty variant types of pigeon*). **2** *n.* variant form, spelling, type, etc. [F (VARY)]

variation /veərɪ'eɪʃ(ə)n/ *n.* varying; departure from a former or normal condition or action or amount or from a standard or type (*prices are subject to variation*); extent of this; thing that varies from a type; music produced by repeating theme in changed or elaborated form. [F or L (VARY)]

varicoloured /'veərɪkʌləd/ *a.* variegated in colour; of various or different colours. [L *varius* VARIOUS]

varicose /'værɪkəʊs/ *a.* (of vein etc.) permanently and abnormally dilated. [L (*varix* varicose vein)]

varied /'veərɪd/ *a.* showing variety. [VARY]

variegated /'veərɪgeɪtɪd/ *a.* marked with irregular patches of different colours; **variegation** /-'geɪʃ(ə)n/ *n.* [L (VARIOUS)]

variety /və'raɪətɪ/ *n.* diversity, absence of uniformity, many-sidedness; quantity or collection of different things (*for a variety of reasons*); class of things differing in some common qualities from the rest of a larger class to which they belong; specimen or member of such class; different form *of* thing, quality, etc.; subspecies; mixed series of dances, songs, comedy acts, etc. (*variety show*). [F or L (foll.)]

various /'veərɪəs/ *a.* different, diverse (*too various to form a group*); more than one, several (*for various reasons*). [L *varius*]

varlet /'vɑ:lɪt/ *n. archaic* menial, rascal. [F var. of *vaslet* VALET]

varnish /'vɑ:nɪʃ/ **1** *n.* resinous solution used to give hard shiny transparent coating; other preparation for similar purpose; external appearance or display without underlying reality. **2** *v.t.* apply varnish to; gloss over (fact). [F *vernis* f. med.L or med.Gk]

varsity /'vɑːsɪtɪ/ *n.* (*colloq.*, esp. w. ref. to sports) university. [abbr.]

vary /'veərɪ/ *v.* make different, modify, diversify; undergo change, become or be different, be of different kinds. [F, or L *vario* (VARIOUS)]

vas *n.* (*pl.* **vasa** /'veɪsə/) duct, vessel; **vas deferens** /'defərenz/ (*pl.* **vasa deferentia** /defə'rentɪə/) sperm duct of testicle. [L, = vessel]

vascular /'væskjʊlə/ *a.* of or containing vessels for conveying blood, sap, etc. [L *vasculum* dimin. of VAS]

vase /vɑːz/ *n.* vessel, usu. tall and circular, used as ornament or container (*flower-vase*). [F f. L (VAS)]

vasectomy /və'sektəmɪ/ *n.* removal of part of each vas deferens esp. for sterilization of patient. [VAS]

Vaseline /'væsəliːn/ *n.* (**P**) type of petroleum jelly used as ointment etc. [G *wasser* water, Gk *elaion* oil]

vassal /'væs(ə)l/ *n.* humble dependant; *hist.* holder of land by feudal tenure. [F f. med.L f. Celt.]

vassalage *n.* vassal's condition. [F (prec.)]

vast /vɑːst/ *a.* immense, huge, very great. [L]

vat *n.* large tank or other vessel, esp. for holding liquids or something in liquid in process of brewing, tanning, dyeing, etc.; **vatful** *n.* [dial. var. of obs. *fat* f. OE]

VAT /viː eɪ tiː, væt/ *abbr.* value added tax.

vaudeville /'vɔːdəvɪl, 'vəʊd-/ *n.* variety entertainment; light stage-play with interspersed songs. [F]

vault /vɔːlt, vɒlt/ **1** *n.* arched roof; vault-like covering (*the vault of heaven*); underground chamber as place of storage, of interment beneath church or in cemetery, etc,; act of vaulting. **2** *v.* leap, spring, esp. while resting on the hand(s) or with help of pole; spring over (gate etc.) thus; (esp. in *p.p.*) make in form of vault, furnish with vault(s). [F f. Rmc (L *volvo* roll)]

vaulting *n.* arched work in vaulted roof or ceiling; **vaulting horse** wooden block to be vaulted over by gymnasts.

vaunt /vɔːnt/ *literary* **1** *v.* boast. **2** *n.* boast. [F f. L (VAIN)]

VC *abbr.* Victoria Cross.

VD *abbr.* venereal disease.

VDU *abbr.* visual display unit.

've *v. colloq.* (usu. after pronouns) have (*I've, they've*). [abbr.]

veal *n.* calf's flesh as food. [F f. L (*vitulus* calf)]

vector /'vektə/ *n.* quantity having direction as well as magnitude; carrier of disease; **vectorial** /-'tɔːrɪəl/ *a.* [L (*veho vect-* carry)]

Veda /'veɪdə, 'viːdə/ *n.* (in *sing.* or *pl.*) most ancient Hindu scriptures; **Vedic** *a.* [Skr., = knowledge]

veer **1** *v.i.* change direction esp. (of wind) clockwise; change in opinion or course. **2** *n.* change of direction. [F *virer*]

veg /vedʒ/ *n. colloq.* vegetable(s). [abbr.]

vegan /'viːgən/ **1** *a.* eating no animals or animal products. **2** *n.* vegan person. [VEGETARIAN]

vegetable /'vedʒɪtəb(ə)l/ **1** *n.* plant, esp. herbaceous plant or part of one used for food, e.g. cabbage, potato, turnip, bean; person living monotonous life, one who is incapable of normal intellectual activity through injury etc. **2** *a.* of or derived from or relating to plant life. [F or L (VEGETATE)]

vegetal /'vedʒɪt(ə)l/ *a.* of or of the nature of plants. [med.L (VEGETATE)]

vegetarian /vedʒɪ'teərɪən/ *n.* one who abstains from animal food, esp. that obtained by killing animals; **vegetarianism** *n.* [VEGETABLE]

vegetate /'vedʒɪteɪt/ *v.i.* live uneventful or monotonous life; grow as plants do. [L *vegeto* animate]

vegetation /vedʒɪ'teɪʃ(ə)n/ *n.* plants collectively, plant life. [med.L (prec.)]

vegetative /'vedʒɪtətɪv/ *a.* concerned with growth and development rather than sexual reproduction; of vegetation. [F or med.L (VEGETATE)]

vehement /'viːəmənt/ *a.* showing or caused by strong feeling, ardent (*a vehement protest, desire*); **vehemence** *n.* [F or L]

vehicle /'viːɪk(ə)l/ *n.* carriage or conveyance used on land or in space; thing or person used as medium for thought or feeling or action (*used the pulpit as a vehicle for his political opinions*); liquid etc. as medium for suspending pigments, drugs, etc.; **vehicular** /vɪ'hɪkjʊlə/ *a.* [F or L (*veho* carry)]

veil /veɪl/ **1** *n.* piece of usu. more or less transparent material attached to woman's hat or otherwise forming part of head-dress, esp. to conceal face or protect against sun, dust, etc.; piece of linen etc. as part of nun's head-dress; curtain, esp. that separating sanctuary in Jewish Temple; disguise, pretext. **2** *v.t.* cover with veil; partly conceal (*veiled threat, resentment*). **3 beyond the veil** in the unknown state of life after death; **draw a veil over** avoid discussing or calling attention to; **take the veil** become nun. [AF f. L *velum*]

vein /veɪn/ *n.* any of the tubes by which blood is conveyed to heart; *pop.* any blood-vessel (*has royal blood in his* *veins*); rib of leaf or insect's wing; streak or stripe of different colour in wood, marble, cheese, etc.; fissure in rock filled with ore; distinctive character or tendency, mood (*said this in a humorous vein*); **veined** *a.*; **veiny** *a.* [F f. L *vena*]

Velcro /'velkrəʊ/ *n.* (P) fastener for clothes etc. consisting of two strips of nylon fabric, one smooth and one burred, which adhere when pressed together. [F *velours croché* hooked velvet]

veld /velt/ *n.* (also **veldt**) open country. [Afrik. (FIELD)]

vellum /'veləm/ *n.* fine parchment orig. from skin of calf; manuscript on this; smooth writing-paper imitating vellum. [F *velin* (VEAL)]

velocity /vɪ'lɒsɪtɪ/ *n.* speed, esp. in a given direction (usu. of inanimate things). [F or L (*velox* swift)]

velour /və'lʊə/ *n.* (also **velours**) plush-like woven fabric or felt. [F]

velvet /'velvɪt/ **1** *n.* closely woven fabric with thick short pile on one side; furry skin on growing antler. **2** *a.* of, like, or soft as, velvet. **3 on velvet** in advantageous or prosperous position; **velvet glove** outward gentleness cloaking inflexibility. **4 velvety** *a.* [F f. med.L f. L *villus* shaggy hair]

velveteen /velvɪ'ti:n/ *n.* cotton fabric with pile like velvet.

Ven. *abbr.* Venerable (as title of archdeacon).

venal /'vi:n(ə)l/ *a.* (of person) that may be bribed; (of conduct etc.) characteristic of venal person; **venality** /vi:'nælɪtɪ/ *n.*; **venally** *adv.* [L (*venum* thing for sale)]

vend *v.t.* offer (small wares) for sale; **vending-machine** machine for automatic retail of small articles; **vendible** *a.* [F, or L *vendo* sell]

vendetta /ven'detə/ *n.* blood feud; prolonged bitter hostility. [It. f. L (VINDICTIVE)]

vendor *n.* (esp. in law) one who sells. [AF (VEND)]

veneer /vɪ'nɪə/ **1** *v.t.* cover (wood) with thin coating of finer wood. **2** *n.* thin coating; superficial disguise. [obs. *fineer* f. G f. F (FURNISH)]

venerable /'venərəb(ə)l/ *a.* entitled to veneration on account of character, age, associations, etc. (*venerable priest, relics, beard, ruins*); title of archdeacon in Church of England. [F or L (foll.)]

venerate /'venəreɪt/ *v.t.* regard with deep respect; **veneration** /-'reɪʃ(ə)n/ *n.*; **venerator** *n.* [L *veneror* revere]

venereal /vɪ'nɪərɪəl/ *a.* of sexual desire or intercourse; relating to venereal disease; **venereal disease** disease contracted chiefly by sexual intercourse with person already infected; **venereally** *adv.* [L (*Venus Vener-* goddess of love)]

Venetian /vɪ'ni:ʃ(ə)n/ **1** *a.* of Venice. **2** *n.* native or dialect of Venice. **3 venetian blind** window-blind of adjustable horizontal slats. [F or med.L (*Venetia* Venice)]

vengeance /'vendʒəns/ *n.* punishment inflicted or retribution exacted for wrong to oneself or to person etc. whose cause one supports; **with a vengeance** in a higher degree than was expected or desired (*punctuality with a vengeance*). [F f. *venger* f. L (VINDICATE)]

vengeful *a.* vindictive, seeking vengeance; **vengefully** *adv.* [obs. *venge* avenge (prec.)]

venial /'vi:nɪəl/ *a.* (of sin or fault) pardonable, excusable, not mortal; **veniality** /vi:nɪ'ælɪtɪ/ *n.*; **venially** *adv.* [F f. L (*venia* forgiveness)]

venison /'venɪs(ə)n/ *n.* deer's flesh as food. [F f. L *venatio* hunting]

Venn diagram diagram using overlapping and intersecting circles etc. to show relationships between mathematical sets. [*Venn*, logician]

venom /'venəm/ *n.* poisonous fluid of snakes, scorpions, etc.; malignity, virulence of feeling or language or conduct; **venomous** *a.* [F f. L *venenum*]

venous /'vi:nəs/ *a.* of, full of, or contained in, veins. [L (VEIN)]

vent¹ **1** *n.* hole or opening allowing motion of air etc. out of or into confined space; anus esp. of lower animal; outlet, free passage or play (*gave vent to his indignation*). **2** *v.t.* make vent in (cask etc.); give vent or free expression to. **3 vent one's spleen on** scold or ill-treat without cause. [F f. L *ventus* wind]

vent² *n.* slit in garment, esp. in lower edge of back of coat. [F *fente* f. L *findo* cleave]

ventilate /'ventɪleɪt/ *v.t.* cause air to circulate freely in (room etc.); submit (question, grievance, etc.) to public consideration and discussion; **ventilation** /-'leɪʃ(ə)n/ *n.* [L *ventilo* blow, winnow (VENT¹)]

ventilator *n.* appliance or aperture for ventilating room etc.

ventral /'ventr(ə)l/ *a.* of or on the abdomen; **ventrally** *adv.* [*venter* abdomen f. L]

ventricle /'ventrɪk(ə)l/ *n.* cavity in the body, hollow part of organ, esp. in brain or heart. [L *ventriculus* dimin. of *venter* belly]

ventricular /ven'trɪkjʊlə/ *a.* of or shaped like ventricle.

ventriloquism /ven'trɪləkwɪz(ə)m/ *n.*

act or art of speaking or uttering sounds in such a manner that they appear not to come from the speaker; **ventriloquist** *n*.; **ventriloquize** *v.i.* [L (*venter* belly, *loquor* speak)]

venture /'ventʃə/ **1** *n*. undertaking of risk; commercial speculation. **2** *v*. dare, not be afraid; dare to go etc. or to make or put forward (*shall not venture out, an opinion, a step*); expose to risk, stake; take risks. **3 at a venture** at random, without previous consideration; **venture on** dare to engage in, to make, etc.; **Venture Scout** senior Scout. [ADVENTURE]

venturesome *a*. disposed to take risks; risky.

venue /'venju:/ *n*. appointed meeting-place esp. for match; county etc. within which jury must be gathered and cause tried. [F f. *venir* (L *venio* come)]

veracious /və'reɪʃəs/ *a*. speaking, or disposed to speak, the truth; (of statement etc.) that is or is meant to be true; **veracity** /və'ræsɪtɪ/ *n*. [L *verax* (*verus* true)]

veranda /və'rændə/ *n*. open roofed platform along side of house. [Hindi f. Port. *varanda*]

verb *n*. word used to indicate action, state, or occurrence (e.g. *fly, become, happen*). [F, or L *verbum* word]

verbal *a*. of or concerned with words; oral, not written; of, or of the nature of, a verb; (of translation) literal; **verbal noun** noun derived from verb and partly sharing its constructions, e.g. nouns in -ING[1]; **verbally** *adv*. [F or L (prec.)]

verbalism *n*. minute attention to words.

verbalize *v*. express in words; be verbose. [F, or VERBAL]

verbatim /vɜ:'beɪtɪm/ *adv*. & *a*. in exactly the same words. [med.L (VERB)]

verbena /vɜ:'bi:nə/ *n*. plant of a genus of herbs and small shrubs. [L]

verbiage /'vɜ:bɪɪdʒ/ *n*. needless accumulation of words. [F (VERB)]

verbose /vɜ:'bəʊs/ *a*. using or expressed in more words than are needed; **verbosity** /vɜ:'bɒsɪtɪ/ *n*. [L (VERB)]

verdant /'vɜ:dənt/ *a*. (of grass etc.) green, fresh-coloured; (of field etc.) covered with green grass etc.; (of person) unsophisticated, raw, green; **verdancy** *n*. [perh. F *verdeant* f. L (*viridis* green)]

verdict /'vɜ:dɪkt/ *n*. decision of jury on issue of fact in civil or criminal cause; decision, judgement. [AF *verdit* (*ver* true, *dit* f. L DICTUM saying)]

verdigris /'vɜ:dɪgrɪs, -ri:s/ *n*. green deposit on copper or brass. [F, = green of Greece]

verdure /'vɜ:djə/ *n*. green vegetation; greenness of this; **verdurous** *a*. [F *verd* green]

verge[1] *n*. brink or border (usu. *fig*.; *on the verge of destruction*); grass edging of road, flower-bed, etc. [F, f. L *virga* rod]

verge[2] *v.i.* incline downwards or in specified direction; **verge on** border on, approach closely. [L *vergo* bend]

verger *n*. official in church who acts as caretaker and attendant; officer who bears staff before bishop etc. [AF (VERGE[1])]

verify /'verɪfaɪ/ *v.t.* establish truth or correctness of by examination or demonstration (*verify the statement, his figures*); (of event etc.) bear out, fulfil (prediction or promise); **verifiable** *a*.; **verification** /-fɪ'keɪʃ(ə)n/ *n*. [F f. med.L (VERY)]

verily /'verɪlɪ/ *adv*. *archaic* really, truly. [VERY]

verisimilitude /verɪsɪ'mɪlɪtju:d/ *n*. appearance of being true or real (*verisimilitude is not proof*). [L (*verus* true, *similis* like)]

veritable /'verɪtəb(ə)l/ *a*. real, rightly so called (*a veritable boon*); **veritably** *adv*. [F (foll.)]

verity /'verɪtɪ/ *n*. true statement, esp. one of fundamental import; *archaic* truth. [F, f. L *veritas* truth]

vermicelli /vɜ:mɪ'selɪ, -'tʃelɪ/ *n*. pasta made in long slender threads. [It. dimin. pl. f. L *vermis* worm]

vermicide /'vɜ:mɪsaɪd/ *n*. drug that kills worms. [L *vermis* worm]

vermiform /'vɜ:mɪfɔ:m/ *a*. worm-shaped; **vermiform appendix** small blind tube extending from caecum in man and some other mammals. [med.L (prec.)]

vermilion /və'mɪljən/ **1** *n*. cinnabar; brilliant red pigment made esp. from this; colour of this. **2** *a*. of this colour. [F f. L *vermiculus* dimin. of *vermis* worm]

vermin /'vɜ:mɪn/ *n*. (usu. treated as *pl*.) mammals and birds injurious to game, crops, etc., e.g. foxes, mice, owls; noxious or parasitic worms or insects; vile persons. [F f. L *vermis* worm]

verminous *a*. of the nature of or infested with vermin. [prec. or L *verminosus*]

vermouth /'vɜ:məθ/ *n*. wine flavoured with aromatic herbs. [F f. G (WORMWOOD)]

vernacular /və'nækjʊlə/ **1** *n*. language or dialect of the country; language of a particular class or group; homely speech. **2** *a*. (of language) of one's native country, not of foreign origin or of learned formation. [L *vernaculus* native]

vernal /'vɜ:n(ə)l/ *a*. of, in, or appropriate

to spring; **vernally** *adv*. [L (*ver* the spring)]
vernier /'vɜːnɪə/ *n*. small movable graduated scale for obtaining fractional parts of subdivisions on fixed scale of barometer etc. [*Vernier*, mathematician]
veronal /'verən(ə)l/ *n*. sedative drug. [G (*Verona* in Italy)]
veronica /və'rɒnɪkə/ *n*. speedwell. [med.L (prob. St. *Veronica*)]
verruca /və'ruːkə/ *n*. (*pl*. **verrucae** /-siː/ or **verrucas**) wart or similar protuberance. [L]
versatile /'vɜːsətaɪl/ *a*. turning easily or readily from one subject or occupation to another, capable of dealing with many subjects, having many uses; **versatility** /-'tɪlɪtɪ/ *n*. [F or L (*verto vers-* turn)]
verse *n*. metrical composition; stanza of metrical lines; metrical line; each of the short numbered divisions of the Bible. [OE & F f. L *versus* (prec.)]
versed /vɜːst/ *a*. experienced or skilled *in*. [F or L (*versor* be engaged in)]
versicle /'vɜːsɪk(ə)l/ *n*. each of short sentences in liturgy said or sung by priest etc. and alternating with responses. [F or L dimin. (VERSE)]
versify /'vɜːsɪfaɪ/ *v*. turn into or express in verse; compose verses; **versification** /-fɪ'keɪʃ(ə)n/ *n*. [F f. L (VERSE)]
version /'vɜːʃ(ə)n/ *n*. account of a matter from particular person's point of view; book or work etc. in particular edition or translation (*Authorized Version*); particular variant *of*. [F or med.L f. L *verto vers-* turn]
verso /'vɜːsəʊ/ *n*. (*pl*. **versos**) left-hand page of open book, back of leaf (cf. RECTO). [L, abl. p.p. of *verto* turn]
versus /'vɜːsəs/ *prep*. (esp. *Law* and in sport) against (*Rex versus Crippen*; *Surrey versus Kent*). [L (VERSE)]
vertebra /'vɜːtɪbrə/ *n*. (*pl*. **vertebrae** /-iː/) each segment of backbone; **vertebral** *a*. [L (*verto* turn)]
vertebrate /'vɜːtɪbrət, -reɪt/ **1** *a*. having spinal column. **2** *n*. vertebrate animal. [L *vertebratus* jointed (prec.)]
vertex /'vɜːteks/ *n*. (*pl*. **vertices** /-ɪsiːz/ or **vertexes**) highest point, top, apex; each angular point of triangle, polygon, etc.; meeting-point of lines that form an angle. [L, = whirlpool, crown of head (*verto* turn)]
vertical /'vɜːtɪk(ə)l/ **1** *a*. at right angles to plane of horizon; in direction from top to bottom of picture etc.; of or at the vertex. **2** *n*. vertical line or plane. **3 vertical take-off** take-off of aircraft directly upwards. **4 vertically** *adv*. [F or L (prec.)]
vertiginous /vɜː'tɪdʒɪnəs/ *a*. of or causing vertigo. [L (foll.)]
vertigo /'vɜːtɪgəʊ/ *n*. (*pl*. **vertigos**) dizziness. [L, = whirling (*verto* turn)]
vervain /'vɜːveɪn/ *n*. herbaceous plant of verbena genus esp. one with small blue, white, or purple flowers. [F f. L (VERBENA)]
verve *n*. enthusiasm, vigour, esp. in artistic or literary work. [F]
very /'verɪ/ **1** *adv*. in a high degree (*that is very good*; *did it very easily*); in the fullest sense (with superlative adjectives or *own*: *will do my very best*; *it is your very own book*). **2** *a*. real, true, actual, truly such (*the very thing we need*; *caught in the very act*; *those were his very words*; *have reached the very end*). **3 not very** in a low degree, far from being; **very good** (or **well**) formula of consent or approval; **very high frequency** (in radio) 30–300 megahertz; **Very Reverend** title of dean; **the very same** emphatically the same. [F *verai* f. L *verus* true]
Very light /'verɪ, 'vɪərɪ/ flare projected from pistol for signalling or temporarily illuminating part of battlefield etc. [*Very*, inventor]
vesicle /'vesɪk(ə)l/ *n*. small bladder or blister or bubble. [F or L]
vespers *n.pl*. evening service. [L *vesper* evening]
vessel /'ves(ə)l/ *n*. hollow receptacle esp. for liquid, e.g. cask, cup, pot, bottle, dish; ship or boat, esp. large one; duct or canal etc. holding or conveying blood or sap etc. [F f. L dimin. (VAS)]
vest 1 *n*. knitted or woven undergarment worn on upper part of body; (*US* and in commerce) waistcoat. **2** *v*. furnish (person *with* powers or property etc.); clothe (oneself), esp. in vestments. **3 vest in** (of property, rights, etc.) come into the possession of (person); **vest** (property or powers) **in a person** confer formally on him an immediate fixed right of present or future possession of; **vest-pocket** of size suitable for the (waistcoat-) pocket. [F f. It. f. L *vestis* garment]
vestal /'vest(ə)l/ **1** *a*. chaste, pure. **2** *n*. chaste woman; vestal virgin. **3 vestal virgin** virgin consecrated to Vesta and vowed to chastity. [L (*Vesta*, Roman goddess of hearth and home)]
vested *a*. (of interests or rights) securely held by right or by long association; **a vested interest in** an expectation of benefiting from. [VEST]
vestibule /'vestɪbjuːl/ *n*. antechamber, hall, lobby, next to outer door of building; *US* enclosed entrance to railway-carriage. [F or L]
vestige /'vestɪdʒ/ *n*. trace, evidence, sign; slight amount, particle; part or

organ of animal or plant, now degenerate but well developed in ancestors; **vestigial** /-ˈtɪdʒɪəl/ *a.* [F f. L *vestigium* footprint]

vestment /ˈvestmənt/ *n.* any of the official garments of clergy, choristers, etc., worn during divine service, esp. chasuble; garment, esp. official or state robe. [F f. L (VEST)]

vestry /ˈvestrɪ/ *n.* room or building attached to church for keeping vestments in; *hist.* meeting of parishioners usu. in vestry for parochial business, body of parishioners meeting thus.

vet *colloq.* **1** *n.* veterinary surgeon. **2** *v.t.* (**-tt-**) make careful and critical examination of (scheme, work, candidate, etc.); examine or treat (animal). [abbr.]

vetch *n.* plant of pea family largely used for fodder. [F f. L *vicia*]

vetchling *n.* plant related to vetch.

veteran /ˈvetərən/ *n.* person who has grown old in or had long experience of (esp. military) service or occupation (*a veteran of two world wars*; *a veteran golfer*); *US* ex-service man; **veteran car** car made before 1916, or before 1905. [F or L (*vetus -er-* old)]

veterinarian /vetərɪˈneərɪən/ *n.* veterinary surgeon. [L (foll.)]

veterinary /ˈvetərɪnərɪ/ **1** *a.* of or for diseases of farm and domestic animals, or their treatment. **2** *n.* veterinary surgeon. **3 veterinary surgeon** one skilled in such treatment. [L (*veterinae* cattle)]

veto /ˈvi:təʊ/ **1** *n.* (*pl.* **vetoes**) constitutional right to reject a legislative enactment, right of permanent member of UN Security Council to reject a resolution, such rejection, official message conveying this; prohibition (*put a* or *one's veto on*). **2** *v.t.* exercise veto against, forbid authoritatively. [L, = I forbid]

vex *v.t.* anger by slight or petty annoyance, irritate; *archaic* grieve, afflict. [F f. L *vexo* afflict]

vexation /vekˈseɪʃ(ə)n/ *n.* vexing or being vexed; annoying or distressing thing. [F or L (prec.)]

vexatious /vekˈseɪʃəs/ *a.* such as to cause vexation; *Law* not having sufficient grounds for action and seeking only to annoy defendant.

vexed *a.* (of question) much discussed. [VEX]

VHF *abbr.* very high frequency.

via /ˈvaɪə/ *prep.* by way of, through (*London to Rome via Paris*; *sent it via his secretary*). [L, abl. of *via* way]

viable /ˈvaɪəb(ə)l/ *a.* capable of living or existing or (of foetus etc.) maintaining life; (of plan etc.) feasible esp. from economic standpoint; **viability** /-ˈbɪlɪtɪ/ *n.* [F (*vie* life f. L *vita*)]

viaduct /ˈvaɪədʌkt/ *n.* bridgelike structure, esp. series of arches, carrying railway or road across valley or dip in ground. [L *via* way, after *aqueduct*]

vial /ˈvaɪəl/ *n.* small (usu. cylindrical glass) vessel esp. for holding liquid medicines. [PHIAL]

viand /ˈvaɪənd/ *n.* (usu. in *pl.*) article of food. [F f. L (*vivo* live)]

viaticum /vaɪˈætɪkəm/ *n.* Eucharist given to person dying or in danger of dying. [L (*via* way)]

vibes *n.pl. colloq.* vibraphone; *colloq.* vibrations. [abbr.]

vibrant /ˈvaɪbrənt/ *a.* vibrating; thrilling *with* (action etc.); resonant. [L (VIBRATE)]

vibraphone /ˈvaɪbrəfəʊn/ *n.* percussion instrument of metal bars with motor-driven resonators and metal tubes giving vibrato effect. [VIBRATO]

vibrate /vaɪˈbreɪt/ *v.* move unceasingly to and fro, esp. rapidly; (of sound) throb (*on* ear, *in* memory, etc.); quiver (*with* passion etc.); move to and fro like pendulum, oscillate; cause to do this. [L *vibro* shake]

vibration /vaɪˈbreɪʃ(ə)n/ *n.* vibrating; (in *pl.*) mental (esp. occult) influence. [L (prec.)]

vibrato /vɪˈbrɑ:təʊ/ *n.* (*pl.* **vibratos**) tremulous effect in pitch of singing or of playing stringed or wind instrument. [It. (VIBRATE)]

vibrator /vaɪˈbreɪtə/ *n.* thing that vibrates or causes vibration, esp. electric or other instrument used in massage. [VIBRATE]

vibratory *a.* causing vibration.

viburnum /vɪˈbɜ:nəm/ *n.* a kind of shrub, usu. with white flowers. [L, = wayfaring-tree]

vicar /ˈvɪkə/ *n.* incumbent of Church of England parish where tithes formerly belonged to chapter or religious house or layman; **vicar apostolic** Roman Catholic missionary or titular bishop; **vicar-general** official assisting or representing bishop esp. in administrative matters; **Vicar of Christ** the Pope. [AF f. L *vicarius* substitute (VICE[3])]

vicarage *n.* vicar's house.

vicarial /vɪˈkeərɪəl/ *a.* of or serving as vicar.

vicarious /vɪˈkeərɪəs/ *a.* experienced imaginatively through another person; acting or done for another; deputed, delegated. [L (VICAR)]

vice[1] *n.* evil (esp. grossly immoral) conduct, depravity; evil habit, particular form of depravity (*drunkenness is not* *among his vices*); defect or blemish; **vice squad** police department enforcing laws against prostitution etc. [F f. L *vitium*]

vice² *n.* instrument with two jaws between which thing may be gripped so as to leave hands free to work on it. [F *vis* innscrew f. L *vitis* vine]

vice³ /ˈvaɪsɪ/ *prep.* in the place of, in succession to. [L, abl. of (*vix*) *vicis* change]

vice- *prefix* forming nouns in senses 'acting as substitute or deputy for' (*vice-president*), 'next in rank to' (*vice-admiral*). [as prec.]

vice-chancellor /vaɪsˈtʃɑːnsələ/ *n.* deputy chancellor (esp. of university, discharging most administrative duties).

vicegerent /vaɪsˈdʒerənt/ **1** *a.* exercising delegated power. **2** *n.* vicegerent person, deputy. [med.L (L *gero* carry on)]

viceregal /vaɪsˈriːg(ə)l/ *a.* of viceroy; **viceregally** *adv.* [REGAL, after VICEROY]

vicereine /ˈvaɪsreɪn/ *n.* viceroy's wife; woman viceroy. [F (VICE-, *reine* queen)]

viceroy /ˈvaɪsrɔɪ/ *n.* ruler on behalf of sovereign in colony, province, etc. [F (VICE-, *roy* king)]

viceroyalty /vaɪsˈrɔɪəltɪ/ *n.* office of viceroy. [F (ROYALTY)]

vice versa /ˈvaɪsɪ ˈvɜːsə/ with order of terms changed, the other way round. [L, = the position being reversed]

Vichy water /ˈviːʃiː/ effervescent mineral water from Vichy in France.

vicinage /ˈvɪsɪnɪdʒ/ *n.* neighbourhood, surrounding district; relation of neighbours. [F f. L *vicinus* neighbour]

vicinity /vɪˈsɪnɪtɪ/ *n.* surrounding district; nearness (*to*); **in the vicinity (of)** near. [L (prec.)]

vicious /ˈvɪʃəs/ *a.* of the nature of or addicted to vice; bad-tempered, spiteful (*vicious dog, remark*); (of language or reasoning etc.) faulty or unsound; **vicious circle** see CIRCLE; **vicious spiral** see SPIRAL. [F f. L (VICE¹)]

vicissitude /vɪˈsɪsɪtjuːd/ *n.* change of circumstances, esp. of fortune. [F or L (VICE³)]

victim /ˈvɪktɪm/ *n.* person or thing injured or destroyed in pursuit of an object, in gratification of a passion etc., or as result of event or circumstance (*the victims of disease, of a road accident*); prey, dupe (*the numerous victims of the confidence trick*); living creature sacrificed to deity or in religious rite. [L]

victimize *v.t.* single out (person) for punishment or unfair treatment, esp. dismissal; make (person etc.) a victim; **victimization** /-ˈzeɪʃ(ə)n/ *n.*

victor /ˈvɪktə/ *n.* winner in battle or contest. [AF or L (*vinco vict-* conquer)]

victoria /vɪkˈtɔːrɪə/ *n.* low light four-wheeled carriage with collapsible top; **Victoria Cross** decoration awarded for conspicuous bravery in armed services. [Queen *Victoria*]

Victorian **1** *a.* of the time of Queen Victoria. **2** *n.* person, esp. writer, of this time. [*Victoria*]

victorious /vɪkˈtɔːrɪəs/ *a.* conquering, triumphant; marked by victory. [AF f. L (VICTOR)]

victory /ˈvɪktərɪ/ *n.* defeating one's enemy in battle or war or one's opponent in contest.

victual /ˈvɪt(ə)l/ **1** *n.* (usu. in *pl.*) food, provisions. **2** *v.* (**-ll-**, *US* **-l-**) supply with victuals; obtain stores; eat victuals. [F f. L (*victus* food)]

victualler /ˈvɪtlə/ *n.* one who furnishes victuals; **licensed victualler** innkeeper licensed to sell alcoholic liquor etc. [F (prec.)]

vicuña /vɪˈkjuːnə/ *n.* S. American mammal like llama, with fine silky wool; cloth made from its wool; imitation of this. [Sp. f. Quechua]

vide /ˈvɪdeɪ, ˈvaɪdɪ/ *v.t.* (as instruction in reference to passage in book etc.) see, consult. [L (*video* see)]

videlicet /vɪˈdelɪset/ *adv.* = VIZ. [L *video* see, *licet* it is allowed]

video /ˈvɪdɪəʊ/ **1** *a.* relating to recording or broadcasting of photographic images. **2** *n.* (*pl.* **videos**) such recording or broadcasting; apparatus for recording or playing videotapes; a videotape. [L, = I see]

videotape **1** *n.* magnetic tape suitable for records of television pictures and sound. **2** *v.t.* make recording of (broadcast material etc.) with this.

vie /vaɪ/ *v.i.* (*partic.* **vying** /ˈvaɪɪŋ/) carry on rivalry (*with* another). [prob. F (ENVY)]

Vietnamese /vɪetnəˈmiːz/ **1** *a.* of Vietnam. **2** *n.* (*pl.* same) native or language of Vietnam. [*Vietnam* in SE Asia]

view /vjuː/ **1** *n.* inspection by eye or mind, visual or mental survey; power of seeing, range of vision (*came into view*); what is seen, prospect, picture etc. representing this; manner of considering a subject, opinion, mental attitude. **2** *v.* survey with eyes or mentally, form mental impression or judgement of; watch television. **3 have in view** have as one's object, bear (circumstance) in mind in forming judgement etc.; **in view of** having regard to, considering; **on view** being shown (for observation or inspection); **with a view to** with the hope or intention of. [AF f. L (*video* see)]

viewdata *n.* news and information service from computer source to which

television screen is connected by telephone link.
viewer *n.* one who views; person watching television; device for looking at film transparencies etc.
viewfinder *n.* device on camera showing area covered by lens in taking photograph.
viewpoint *n.* point of view, standpoint.
vigil /ˈvɪdʒɪl/ *n.* keeping awake during time usually given to sleep, esp. to keep watch or pray (*keep vigil*); eve of a festival, esp. eve that is a fast. [F f. L *vigilia*]
vigilance *n.* watchfulness, caution; **vigilance committee** *US* self-appointed body for maintenance of order etc.; **vigilant** *a.* [F or L (prec.)]
vigilante /vɪdʒɪˈlæntɪ/ *n.* member of vigilance committee or similar body. [Sp., = vigilant]
vignette /viːnˈjet/ *n.* illustration not in definite border; photograph etc. with background gradually shaded off; short description, character-sketch. [F dimin. (VINE)]
vigour /ˈvɪgə/, *US* **vigor** *n.* active physical or mental strength or energy; healthy growth; trenchancy, animation; **vigorous** *a.* [F f. L (*vigeo* be lively)]
Viking /ˈvaɪkɪŋ/ *n.* Scandinavian trader and pirate of 8th–10th cc. [ON]
vile *a.* disgusting; morally base, depraved; *colloq.* abominably bad (*vile weather*). [F f. L *vilis* cheap, base]
vilify /ˈvɪlɪfaɪ/ *v.t.* defame, speak evil of; **vilification** /-fɪˈkeɪʃ(ə)n/ *n.* [L (prec.)]
villa /ˈvɪlə/ *n.* detached or semi-detached house in residential district; country residence; house for holiday-makers at seaside etc. [It. & L]
village /ˈvɪlɪdʒ/ *n.* group of houses etc. larger than hamlet and smaller than town. [F f. L (prec.)]
villager *n.* inhabitant of village.
villain /ˈvɪlən/ *n.* person guilty or capable of great wickedness; *colloq.* rascal. [F f. L (VILLA)]
villainous *a.* worthy of a villain; wicked; *colloq.* abominably bad.
villainy *n.* villainous behaviour. [F (VILLAIN)]
villein /ˈvɪlɪn/ *n. hist.* feudal tenant entirely subject to lord or attached to manor; **villeinage** *n.* [var. of VILLAIN]
vim *n. colloq.* vigour. [perh. L, acc. of *vis* energy]
vinaigrette /vɪnɪˈgret/ *n.* vinaigrette sauce; small bottle for smelling-salts; **vinaigrette sauce** salad dressing of oil and vinegar. [F dimin. (VINEGAR)]
vindicate /ˈvɪndɪkeɪt/ *v.t.* clear of blame or suspicion; establish existence or merits or justice of (one's courage, conduct, assertion, etc.); **vindication** /-ˈkeɪʃ(ə)n/ *n.*; **vindicator** *n.*; **vindicatory** *a.* [L *vindico* claim]
vindictive /vɪnˈdɪktɪv/ *a.* tending to seek revenge. [L *vindicta* vengeance (prec.)]
vine *n.* climbing or trailing plant with woody stem, bearing grapes; slender trailing or climbing stem. [F *vi(g)ne* f. L *vinea* vineyard]
vinegar /ˈvɪnɪgə/ *n.* sour liquid got from wine, cider, etc., by fermentation and used as condiment or for pickling; sour behaviour or character; **vinegary** *a.* [F, = sour wine (EAGER)]
vinery /ˈvaɪnərɪ/ *n.* greenhouse for grape-vines. [VINE]
vineyard /ˈvɪnjɑːd/ *n.* plantation of grape-vines, esp. for wine-making. [VINE, YARD²]
vingt-et-un /væ̃teɪˈɜː/ *n.* = PONTOON¹. [F, = twenty-one]
vinous /ˈvaɪnəs/ *a.* of or like or due to wine; addicted to wine. [L *vinum* wine]
vintage /ˈvɪntɪdʒ/ **1** *n.* gathering of grapes for wine-making; season of this; season's produce of grapes; wine made from this; wine of high quality kept separate from others; year etc. when thing was made etc.; thing made etc. in particular year etc. **2** *a.* of high quality; of a past season. **3 vintage car** car made 1917–30. [F *vendange* f. L (*vinum* wine)]
vintner *n.* wine-merchant. [AL f. F f. med.L f. L *vinetum* vineyard (*vinum* wine)]
vinyl /ˈvaɪnɪl/ *n.* one of a group of plastics, made by polymerization, esp. polyvinyl chloride. [L *vinum* wine]
viol /ˈvaɪəl/ *n.* early stringed musical instrument, like violin but held vertically. [F f. Prov.]
viola¹ /vɪˈəʊlə/ *n.* instrument of violin family, larger than violin and of lower pitch. [It. & Sp. (prec.)]
viola² /ˈvaɪələ/ *n.* any plant of group including violet and pansy, esp. cultivated hybrid. [L, = violet]
violate /ˈvaɪəleɪt/ *v.t.* disregard, fail to comply with, act against dictates or requirements of (oath, treaty, law, or conscience); treat (sanctuary etc.) profanely or with disrespect; break in upon, disturb (person's privacy etc.); rape; **violable** *a.*; **violation** /-ˈleɪʃ(ə)n/ *n.*; **violator** *n.* [L *violo*]
violence /ˈvaɪələns/ *n.* being violent; violent conduct or treatment; unlawful use of force; **do violence to** act contrary to, outrage. [F f. L (foll.)]
violent /ˈvaɪələnt/ *a.* involving great physical force (*a violent storm*; *came into violent collision*); intense, vehement (*violent pain, abuse, contrast, dislike*); (of

death) resulting from external force or from poison. [F f. L]

violet /'vaɪələt/ **1** *n.* plant with usu. purple, blue, or white flowers; colour seen at end of spectrum opposite red, blue with slight admixture of red; pigment or clothes or material of this colour. **2** *a.* of this colour. [F dimin. of *viole* VIOLA²]

violin /vaɪə'lɪn/ *n.* musical instrument with four strings of treble pitch played with bow; player of this; **violinist** *n.* [It. dimin. of VIOLA¹]

violist¹ /'vaɪəlɪst/ *n.* viol-player. [VIOL]

violist² /vɪ'əʊlɪst/ *n.* viola-player. [VIOLA¹]

violoncello /vaɪələn'tʃeləʊ, vi:ə-/ *n.* (*pl.* **violoncellos**) = CELLO. [It., dimin. of foll.]

violone /vɪə'ləʊnɪ/ *n.* double-bass viol. [It. (VIOLA¹)]

VIP *abbr.* very important person.

viper *n.* small venomous snake; malignant or treacherous person. [F or L]

virago /vɪ'rɑ:gəʊ/ *n.* (*pl.* **viragos**) fierce or abusive woman. [OE f. L, = female warrior]

viral /'vaɪər(ə)l/ *a.* of or caused by virus. [VIRUS]

virgin /'vɜ:dʒɪn/ **1** *n.* person (esp. woman) who has had no sexual intercourse; picture or statue of the Virgin Mary; (**Virgin**) sign or constellation Virgo. **2** *a.* of or befitting or being a virgin; not yet used etc. **3 the Virgin** Christ's mother the Blessed Virgin Mary. [F f. L *virgo -gin-*]

virginal **1** *a.* that is or befits a virgin. **2** *n.* (usu. in *pl.*) legless spinet in box. [F or L (prec.)]

Virginia creeper /və'dʒɪnɪə/ vine cultivated for ornament. [*Virginia* in US]

virginity /və'dʒɪnɪtɪ/ *n.* state of being a virgin. [F f. L (VIRGIN)]

Virgo /'vɜ:gəʊ/ *n.* constellation and sixth sign of zodiac. [OE f. L (VIRGIN)]

virile /'vɪraɪl/ *a.* having masculine vigour or strength; of or having procreative power; of man as distinct from woman or child; **virility** /vɪ'rɪlɪtɪ/ *n.* [F or L (*vir* man)]

virtual /'vɜ:tjʊəl/ *a.* that is such for practical purposes though not in name or according to strict definition (*is the virtual manager of the business*); **virtually** *adv.* [med.L (foll.)]

virtue /'vɜ:tju:/ *n.* goodness, uprightness, moral excellence; particular form of this; chastity esp. of woman; good quality (*has the virtue of being adjustable*); efficacy (*no virtue in such drugs*); **by** (or **in**) **virtue of** on the strength of, on the ground of. [F f. L (VIRILE)]

virtuoso /vɜ:tjʊ'əʊsəʊ/ *n.* (*pl.* **virtuosi** /-i:/) person skilled in technique of a fine art, esp. music; **virtuosity** /-'ɒsɪtɪ/ *n.* [It. (foll.)]

virtuous /'vɜ:tjʊəs/ *a.* possessing or showing moral rectitude; chaste. [F f. L (VIRTUE)]

virulent /'vɪrʊlənt/ *a.* strongly poisonous; (of disease) violent; bitterly hostile; **virulence** *n.* [L (foll.)]

virus /'vaɪərəs/ *n.* any of numerous kinds of very simple organisms smaller than bacteria, often able to cause diseases; *fig.* poison, source of disease. [L, = poison]

visa /'vi:zə/ *n.* endorsement on passport etc. esp. as permitting holder to enter or leave a country; **visaed** *a.* [F f. L, = seen]

visage /'vɪzɪdʒ/ *n. literary* face, countenance. [F f. L *visus* sight]

vis-à-vis /vi:zɑ:'vi:/ **1** *prep.* in relation to; opposite to. **2** *adv.* facing one another. **3** *n.* person or thing facing another. [F, = face to face (prec.)]

viscera /'vɪsərə/ *n.pl.* internal organs of the body; **visceral** *a.* [L]

viscid /'vɪsɪd/ *a.* glutinous, sticky. [L (as VISCOUS)]

viscose /'vɪskəʊz/ *n.* cellulose in highly viscous state (for making into rayon etc.). [L (VISCOUS)]

viscosity /vɪs'kɒsɪtɪ/ *n.* quality or degree of being viscous. [F or med.L (VISCOUS)]

viscount /'vaɪkaʊnt/ *n.* British nobleman ranking between earl and baron; **viscountcy** *n.* [AF (VICE-, COUNT²)]

viscountess *n.* viscount's wife or widow; woman with own rank of viscount.

viscous /'vɪskəs/ *a.* glutinous, sticky; semifluid; not flowing freely. [L (*viscum* birdlime)]

vise *US* var. of VICE².

visibility /vɪzɪ'bɪlɪtɪ/ *n.* being visible; range or possibility of vision as determined by conditions of light and atmosphere. [F or L (foll.)]

visible /'vɪzɪb(ə)l/ *a.* that can be seen by the eye or perceived or ascertained; (of exports etc.) consisting of actual goods; **visibly** *adv.* [F or L (as foll.)]

vision /'vɪʒ(ə)n/ *n.* act or faculty of seeing, sight; thing or person seen in dream or trance; thing seen vividly in the imagination (*the romantic visions of youth*); imaginative insight; statesmanlike foresight, sagacity in planning; person etc. of unusual beauty; what is seen on television screen. [F f. L (*video vis-* see)]

visionary **1** *a.* given to seeing visions or to indulging in fanciful theories; existing only in vision or in imagination; not practicable. **2** *n.* visionary person.

visit /'vɪzɪt/ **1** *v.* go or come to see (person or place etc., or *absol.*) socially or on business etc.; reside temporarily with (person) or at (place); be visitor; (of disease or calamity etc.) come upon, attack; punish (person or sin), inflict punishment for (sin) *upon* person. **2** *n.* act of visiting, temporary residence with person or at place; occasion of going *to* doctor etc.; formal or official call. [F f. L (VISION)]

visitant *n.* visitor, esp. supposedly supernatural one; migratory bird resting temporarily in an area.

visitation /vɪzɪ'teɪʃ(ə)n/ *n.* official visit of inspection; trouble or difficulty regarded as divine punishment; **(Visitation)** visit of Virgin Mary to Elizabeth, festival of Visitation.

visitor *n.* one who visits person or place; migratory bird; **visitors' book** book in which visitors to a hotel or church etc. write their names and addresses and sometimes remarks.

visor /'vaɪzə/ *n.* movable part of helmet covering face; shield at top of vehicle windscreen to protect eyes from bright sunshine; *hist.* mask. [AF *viser* (as VISAGE)]

vista /'vɪstə/ *n.* long narrow view as between rows of trees; mental view of long succession of events. [It.]

visual /'vɪzjʊəl, 'vɪʒj-/ *a.* of or concerned with or used in seeing; **visual aid** film etc. as aid to learning; **visual display unit** device displaying output or input of computer; **visually** *adv.* [L (*visus* sight)]

visualize *v.t.* make visible esp. to one's mind (thing not visible to the eye); **visualization** /-'zeɪʃ(ə)n/ *n.*

vital /'vaɪt(ə)l/ **1** *a.* of or concerned with or essential to organic life (*vital functions*); essential to existence of a thing or to the matter in hand (*question of vital importance*); full of life or activity; affecting life; fatal to life or to success etc. (*a vital error*); **(D)** important. **2** *n.* (in *pl.*) the body's vital organs, e.g. heart and brain. **3 vital statistics** number of births, marriages, deaths, etc., *colloq.* measurements of woman's bust, waist, and hips. [F f. L (*vita* life)]

vitalism *n.* doctrine that life originates in a vital principle distinct from physical forces; **vitalist** *n.*; **vitalistic** /-'lɪstɪk/ *a.* [F or prec.]

vitality /vaɪ'tælɪtɪ/ *n.* liveliness, animation; ability to sustain life. [L (VITAL)]

vitalize /'vaɪtəlaɪz/ *v.t.* endow with life; infuse with vigour; **vitalization** /-'zeɪʃ(ə)n/ *n.* [VITAL]

vitally *adv.* essentially, indispensably.

vitamin /'vɪtəmɪn, 'vaɪt-/ *n.* any of a number of substances present in many foodstuffs and essential to normal growth and nutrition (*vitamin A, B, C,* etc.). [G f. L (VITAL), AMINE]

vitaminize *v.t.* introduce vitamins into (food).

vitiate /'vɪʃɪeɪt/ *v.t.* impair quality or efficiency of, debase; make invalid or ineffectual (*a single word may vitiate a contract*); **vitiation** /-'eɪʃ(ə)n/ *n.* [L (VICE¹)]

viticulture /'vɪtɪkʌltʃə, 'vaɪt-/ *n.* grape-growing. [L *vitis* vine]

vitreous /'vɪtrɪəs/ *a.* of, or of nature of, glass; **vitreous humour** see HUMOUR. [L (*vitrum* glass)]

vitrify /'vɪtrɪfaɪ/ *v.* change into glass or glassy substance esp. by heat; **vitrifaction** /-'fækʃ(ə)n/ *n.*; **vitrification** /-fɪ'keɪʃ(ə)n/ *n.* [F or med.L (prec.)]

vitriol /'vɪtrɪəl/ *n.* sulphuric acid or a sulphate; caustic or hostile speech or criticism.

vitriolic /vɪtrɪ'ɒlɪk/ *a.* (of speech or criticism) caustic or hostile.

vituperate /vɪ'tju:pəreɪt, vaɪ-/ *v.* revile, abuse; **vituperation** /-'reɪʃ(ə)n/ *n.*; **vituperative** *a.*; **vituperator** *n.* [L]

viva¹ /'vaɪvə/ *n.* & *v.t.* (*past* and *p.p.* **vivaed**) *colloq.* = VIVA VOCE. [abbr.]

viva² /'vi:və/ **1** *int.* long live. **2** *n.* cry of this as salute etc. [It., = let live]

vivacious /vɪ'veɪʃəs/ *a.* sprightly, lively, animated; **vivacity** /vɪ'væsɪtɪ/ *n.* [L *vivax* (*vivo* live)]

vivarium /vaɪ'veərɪəm/ *n.* (*pl.* **vivaria**) place artificially prepared for keeping animals in (nearly) their natural state. [L]

viva voce /vaɪvə 'vəʊtʃɪ/ **1** *a.* oral. **2** *adv.* orally. **3** *n.* oral examination. **4** *v.t.* **(viva-voce)** examine orally. [med.L, = with the living voice]

vivid /'vɪvɪd/ *a.* (of light or colour) strong, intense; (of mental faculty, description, or impression) clear, lively, graphic. [L]

vivify /'vɪvɪfaɪ/ *v.t.* give life to (esp. *fig.*), enliven, animate. [F f. L]

viviparous /vɪ'vɪpərəs, vaɪ-/ *a.* bringing forth young alive. [L (*vivus* alive, *pario* produce)]

vivisect /'vɪvɪsekt/ *v.t.* perform vivisection on. [foll.]

vivisection /vɪvɪ'sekʃ(ə)n/ *n.* dissection or other painful treatment of living animals for scientific research; **vivisectionist** *n.*; **vivisector** /'vɪvɪsektə/ *n.* [L *vivus* living; DISSECTION]

vixen /'vɪks(ə)n/ *n.* female fox; spiteful woman. [OE (FOX)]

viz. /vɪz, or by substitution 'neɪmlɪ/ *adv.* namely, that is to say, in other words.

[abbr. of VIDELICET; *z* = med.L symb. for abbr. of *-et*]

vizier /vɪ'zɪə, 'vɪzɪə/ *n.* high official in some Muslim countries. [ult. f. Arab.]

vizor var. of VISOR.

V neck V-shaped neckline on garment, esp. pullover. [V]

vocable /'vəʊkəb(ə)l/ *n.* word, esp. w. ref. to form not meaning. [F or L (*voco* call)]

vocabulary /və'kæbjʊlərɪ/ *n.* words used by a language or book or branch of science or author; list of these, arranged alphabetically with definitions or translations; range of words known to an individual (*his vocabulary is limited*); set of artistic or stylistic forms or techniques. [med.L (prec.)]

vocal /'vəʊk(ə)l/ **1** *a.* of or concerned with or uttered by the voice (*vocal communication, music*); expressing one's feelings freely in speech (*was very vocal about her rights*). **2** *n.* (in *sing.* or *pl.*) sung part or piece of music. **3 vocal cords** voice-producing part of larynx. **4 vocally** *adv.* [L (VOICE)]

vocalic /və'kælɪk/ *a.* of or consisting of a vowel or vowels.

vocalist *n.* singer.

vocalize *v.t.* form (sound) or utter (word) with voice; **vocalization** /-'zeɪʃ(ə)n/ *n.*

vocation /və'keɪʃ(ə)n/ *n.* divine call to, or sense of fitness for, a career or occupation; employment, trade, profession; **vocational** *a.* [F or L (*voco* call)]

vocative /'vɒkətɪv/ **1** *n.* case of noun used in addressing or invoking person or thing. **2** *a.* of or in the vocative.

vociferate /və'sɪfəreɪt/ *v.* utter noisily; shout, bawl; **vociferation** /-'reɪʃ(ə)n/ *n.*; **vociferator** *n.* [L (VOICE, *fero* bear)]

vociferous /və'sɪfərəs/ *a.* noisy, clamorous; loud and insistent in speech.

vodka /'vɒdkə/ *n.* alcoholic spirit distilled esp. in Russia from rye etc. [Russ.]

vogue /vəʊg/ *n.* *the* prevailing fashion; popular use or reception (*has had a great vogue*); **in vogue** in fashion, generally current; **vogue-word** word currently fashionable. [F f. It.]

voice 1 *n.* sound formed in larynx and uttered by the mouth, esp. human utterance in speaking or singing etc.; ability to produce this (*has lost her voice*); use of voice, utterance in spoken or written form (*gave voice to his feelings*), opinion so expressed; right to express opinion, agency by which opinion is expressed; *Gram.* set of verbal forms showing whether verb is active or passive. **2** *v.t.* give utterance to, express; utter with vibration of vocal cords (e.g. *b, d*). **3 in good voice** in proper vocal condition for singing or speaking; **voice-over** narration in film etc. not accompanied by picture of speaker; **with one voice** unanimously. [F f. L *vox voc-*]

voiceless *a.* dumb, speechless; (of sound) uttered without vibration of vocal cords (e.g. *f, p*).

void 1 *a.* empty, vacant; (of contract etc.) invalid, not legally binding (*null and void*). **2** *n.* empty space, vacuum. **3** *v.t.* render void; excrete. **4 void of** lacking, free from. [F]

voile /vɔɪl, vwɑːl/ *n.* thin semi-transparent dress-material. [F, = VEIL]

vol. *abbr.* volume.

volatile /'vɒlətaɪl/ *a.* evaporating rapidly; changeable, fickle; lively, gay; apt to break out into violence; **volatility** /-'tɪlɪtɪ/ *n.* [F or L (*volo* fly)]

volatilize /və'lætɪlaɪz/ *v.* turn into vapour; **volatilization** /-'zeɪʃ(ə)n/ *n.*

vol-au-vent /'vɒləʊvɑ̃/ *n.* (usu. small) round case of puff pastry filled with savoury mixture. [F, lit. 'flight in the wind']

volcanic /vɒl'kænɪk/ *a.* of or like or produced by volcano; **volcanically** *adv.* [F (foll.)]

volcano /vɒl'keɪnəʊ/ *n.* (*pl.* **volcanoes**) mountain or hill having openings in earth's crust through which lava, steam, etc., are or have been expelled; state of things likely to cause violent outburst. [It. f. L *Volcanus* Vulcan, Roman god of fire]

vole *n.* small herbivorous rodent. [orig. *vole-mouse* f. Norw. *voll* field]

volition /və'lɪʃ(ə)n/ *n.* act or faculty of willing; **volitional** *a.*; **volitionally** *adv.* [F or med.L (*volo* wish)]

volley /'vɒlɪ/ **1** *n.* simultaneous discharge of a number of weapons; bullets etc. thus discharged at once; noisy emission (*of* oaths etc.) in quick succession; playing of ball in tennis, football, etc., before it touches ground; full toss. **2** *v.t.* return or send by volley. **3 volley-ball** game for two teams of six sending large ball by hand over net. [F *volée* f. L *volo* fly]

volt /vəʊlt/ *n.* unit of electromotive force, difference of potential that would carry one ampere of current against one ohm resistance. [*Volta*, physicist]

voltage *n.* electromotive force expressed in volts.

volte-face /vɒlt'fɑːs/ *n.* complete reversal of position in argument or opinion. [F f. It.]

voltmeter *n.* instrument measuring electric potential in volts. [VOLT]

voluble /'vɒljʊb(ə)l/ *a.* with vehement or incessant flow of words (*voluble ex-*

cuses, spokesman); **volubility** /-ˈbɪlɪtɪ/ *n.*; **volubly** *adv.* [F or L (*volvo* roll)]

volume /ˈvɒljuːm/ *n.* set of sheets of paper, usu. printed, bound together and containing part of a work or one or more works; solid content, bulk; space occupied by gas or liquid; amount or quantity *of*; quantity or power of sound; moving mass *of* water or smoke etc. [F f. L *volumen* (prec., ancient books being in roll form)]

volumetric /vɒljʊˈmetrɪk/ *a.* of measurement by volume; **volumetrically** *adv.* [VOLUME, METRIC]

voluminous /vəˈljuːmɪnəs, vəˈluː-/ *a.* (of book or writer) running to many volumes or great length; (of drapery etc.) loose and ample. [L (VOLUME)]

voluntary /ˈvɒləntərɪ/ **1** *a.* done or acting or able to act of one's own free will, not constrained or compulsory, intentional; unpaid (*voluntary work*); (of institution) supported by voluntary contributions; (of school) built by voluntary institution but maintained by LEA; brought about by voluntary action; (of movement, muscle, or limb) controlled by the will. **2** *n.* organ solo played before, during, or after church service. **3** **voluntarily** *adv.*; **voluntariness** *n.* [F or L (*voluntas* will)]

volunteer /vɒlənˈtɪə/ **1** *n.* person who voluntarily undertakes task or enters military etc. service. **2** *v.* undertake or offer (one's services, remark, etc.; *to do* thing) voluntarily; be volunteer. [F (prec.)]

voluptuary /vəˈlʌptʊərɪ/ *n.* person given up to luxury and sensual pleasure. [L (foll.)]

voluptuous /vəˈlʌptʊəs/ *a.* of, tending to, occupied with, or derived from, sensuous or sensual pleasure. [F or L (*voluptas* pleasure)]

volute /vəˈljuːt/ *n.* spiral scroll in stonework as ornament of esp. Ionic capital. [F or L (*volvo -ut-* roll)]

vomit /ˈvɒmɪt/ **1** *v.* eject (matter) from stomach through mouth; be sick; (of volcano, chimney, etc.) eject violently, belch forth. **2** *n.* matter vomited from stomach. [F or L]

voodoo /ˈvuːduː/ **1** *n.* use of or belief in religious witchcraft as practised among Blacks esp. in W. Indies. **2** *v.t.* affect by voodoo, bewitch. [Dahomey]

voracious /vəˈreɪʃəs/ *a.* greedy in eating, ravenous; very eager in some activity (*a voracious reader*); **voracity** /vəˈræsɪtɪ/ *n.* [L *vorax* (*voro* devour)]

vortex /ˈvɔːteks/ *n.* (*pl.* **vortexes** or **vortices** /-ɪsiːz/) whirlpool, whirlwind, whirling motion or mass; thing viewed as swallowing those who approach it (*the vortex of society*); **vortical** /-ɪk(ə)l/ *a.*; **vortically** /-ɪkəlɪ/ *adv.* [L (= VERTEX)]

votary /ˈvəʊtərɪ/ *n.* person vowed or devoted to the service *of* a god or cult or pursuit; **votaress** /-rɪs/ *n.* [L (foll.)]

vote **1** *n.* formal expression of choice or opinion in election of candidate, passing of law, etc., signified by ballot or show of hands etc.; (**the vote**) the right to vote, esp. in State election; opinion expressed by majority of votes (*a vote of confidence*); collective votes given by or for particular group (*the Welsh vote; the Labour vote*). **2** *v.* give one's vote (*for* or *against*); enact or resolve by majority of votes; grant (sum of money etc.) by vote; *colloq.* pronounce by general consent, announce one's proposal (*that*). **3** **vote down** defeat (proposal etc.) by votes; **vote in** elect by votes. [L *votum* (*voveo vot-* vow)]

voter *n.* person with right to vote at election; person voting.

votive /ˈvəʊtɪv/ *a.* given or consecrated in fulfilment of vow (*votive offering*). [L (VOTE)]

vouch *v.i.* answer *for*, be surety *for* (*will vouch for the truth of this, for him, for his honesty*). [F *vo(u)cher* (L *voco* call)]

voucher *n.* document exchangeable for goods or services as token of payment made or promised; document establishing payment of money or truth of accounts. [AF or prec.]

vouchsafe /vaʊtʃˈseɪf/ *v.t.* condescend to grant or *to do* thing. [VOUCH, SAFE]

vow **1** *n.* solemn promise esp. in form of oath to deity or saint (*under a vow; monastic vows*). **2** *v.t.* promise solemnly; *archaic* declare, esp. solemnly. [F *vou(er)* (VOTE)]

vowel /ˈvaʊəl/ *n.* speech-sound made with vibration of vocal cords but without audible friction (cf. CONSONANT); letter or letters representing this, as *a, e, i, o, u, aw, ah.* [F f. L (VOCAL)]

vox populi /vɒks ˈpɒpjʊliː, -laɪ/ public opinion, general verdict, popular belief. [L, = the people's voice]

voyage /ˈvɔɪɪdʒ/ **1** *n.* expedition to a distance, esp. by water or air or in space. **2** *v.i.* make voyage. [F f. L VIATICUM]

voyeur /vwɑːˈjɜː/ *n.* one who obtains sexual gratification from looking at others' sexual actions or organs; **voyeurism** *n.* [F (*voir* see)]

vs. *abbr.* versus.

V sign gesture made with the raised hand with first and second fingers forming a V, expressing victory or approval, or vulgar derision. [V]

VSO *abbr.* Voluntary Service Overseas.

VTO *abbr.* vertical take-off.
VTOL *abbr.* vertical take-off and landing.
vulcanite /ˈvʌlkənaɪt/ *n.* hard black vulcanized rubber. [foll.]
vulcanize /ˈvʌlkənaɪz/ *v.t.* make (rubber etc.) stronger and more elastic by treating with sulphur at high temperature; **vulcanization** /-ˈzeɪʃ(ə)n/ *n.* [*Vulcan* (VOLCANO)]
vulcanology /vʌlkəˈnɒlədʒɪ/ *n.* scientific study of volcanoes.
vulgar /ˈvʌlgə/ *a.* of or characteristic of the common people, coarse (*vulgar word, expression*); in common use, generally prevalent (*vulgar errors*); **vulgar fraction** fraction expressed by numerator and denominator, not decimally; **vulgar tongue** *the* national or vernacular language. [L (*vulgus* common people)]
vulgarian /vʌlˈgeərɪən/ *n.* vulgar (esp. rich) person.
vulgarism *n.* word or expression in coarse or uneducated use; instance of coarse or uneducated behaviour.
vulgarity /vʌlˈgærɪtɪ/ *n.* being vulgar. [L or VULGAR]
vulgarize /ˈvʌlgəraɪz/ *v.t.* make vulgar; spoil by making too common or frequented or well known; **vulgarization** /-ˈzeɪʃ(ə)n/ *n.* [VULGAR]
Vulgate /ˈvʌlgeɪt, -gət/ *n.* 4th-c. Latin version of Bible. [L (VULGAR)]
vulnerable /ˈvʌlnərəb(ə)l/ *a.* that may be wounded or harmed; exposed *to* damage by weapon or criticism etc.; having won a game towards rubber at contract bridge and therefore liable to higher penalties; **vulnerability** /-ˈbɪlɪtɪ/ *n.*; **vulnerably** *adv.* [L (*vulnus -er-* wound)]
vulpine /ˈvʌlpaɪn/ *a.* of or like a fox; crafty, cunning. [L (*vulpes* fox)]
vulture /ˈvʌltʃə/ *n.* large bird of prey feeding chiefly on carrion and reputed to gather with others in anticipation of a death; rapacious person. [AF f. L]
vulva /ˈvʌlvə/ *n.* external female genitals. [L]
vv. *abbr.* verses; volumes.
vying *partic.* of VIE.

W

W, w /ˈdʌb(ə)lju:/ *n.* (*pl.* **Ws, W's**) twenty-third letter.
W *abbr.* watt(s); west(ern).
w. *abbr.* wicket(s); wide(s); with.
W *symb.* tungsten. [*wolframium*, Latinized name]
WA *abbr.* Western Australia.
wacky *sl.* **1** *a.* crazy. **2** *n.* crazy person. [orig. dial., = left-handed]
wad /wɒd/ **1** *n.* lump of soft material to keep things apart or in place or to block hole; collection of banknotes or documents placed together; *sl.* bun, sandwich. **2** *v.t.* (**-dd-**) fix or stuff with wad; stuff or line or protect with wadding. [orig. uncert.]
wadding *n.* soft material usu. of cotton or wool for stuffing quilts, packing fragile articles in, etc.
waddle /ˈwɒd(ə)l/ **1** *v.i.* walk with short steps and swaying motion. **2** *n.* waddling walk. [foll.]
wade 1 *v.i.* walk through water or some impeding medium; *fig.* progress slowly or with difficulty. **2** *n.* spell of wading. **3 wade in** *colloq.* make vigorous intervention or attack; **wade through** read (book etc.) through in spite of dullness etc., ford on foot. [OE]
wader *n.* (esp.) long-legged water-bird; (in *pl.*) high waterproof fishing-boots.
wadi /ˈwɒdɪ/ *n.* rocky watercourse in N. Africa etc., dry except in rainy season. [Arab.]
wafer 1 *n.* very thin light crisp sweet biscuit; disc of unleavened bread used in Eucharist; disc of red paper stuck on law papers instead of seal. **2** *v.t.* fasten or seal with wafer. **3 wafer-thin** very thin. [AF *wafre* f. Gmc]
waffle[1] /ˈwɒf(ə)l/ **1** *n.* aimless verbose talk or writing. **2** *v.i.* indulge in waffle. [dial., = yelp]
waffle[2] /ˈwɒf(ə)l/ *n.* small crisp batter cake; **waffle-iron** utensil, usu. of two hinged shallow metal pans, for baking waffles. [Du.]
waft /wɒft/ **1** *v.t.* convey smoothly (as) through air or along water. **2** *n.* whiff *of* perfume etc. [obs. *wafter* convoy (ship) f. LG or Du. *wachter* (*wachten* to guard)]
wag 1 *v.* (**-gg-**) shake or wave to and fro. **2** *n.* single wagging motion (*with a wag of his tail*); facetious person. **3 tongues wag** there is talk. [OE]
wage 1 *n.* (in *sing.* or *pl.*) workman's periodical pay (*wages of £100 a week*). **2** *v.t.* carry on (war etc.). **3 wage-earner** one who works for a wage; **wage freeze** ban on wage-increases. [AF f. Gmc]
wager *n.* & *v.* bet. [AF (prec.)]
waggish *a.* playful, facetious. [WAG]

waggle /'wæg(ə)l/ *v. colloq.* wag.
waggly *a.* unsteady.
wagon /'wægən/ *n.* (also **waggon**) four-wheeled vehicle for heavy loads usu. drawn by horses; open railway truck; tea-trolley; **hitch one's wagon to a star** utilize powers higher than one's own; **on the (water-)wagon** *sl.* (temporarily) teetotal. [Du. (WAIN)]
wagoner *n.* (also **waggoner**) driver of wagon.
wagonette /wægə'net/ *n.* (also **waggonette**) four-wheeled open horse-drawn carriage with facing side-seats.
wagtail *n.* kind of small bird with long tail in frequent motion. [WAG]
waif *n.* homeless and helpless person, esp. abandoned child; ownerless object or animal; **waifs and strays** homeless or neglected children, odds and ends. [AF; prob. Scand.]
wail 1 *n.* prolonged plaintive inarticulate loud high-pitched cry of pain or grief etc.; sound resembling this. **2** *v.i.* utter or make wail or persistent or bitter lamentations or complaints. [ON]
wain *n. archaic* wagon. [OE]
wainscot /'weɪnskət/ *n.* boarding or wooden panelling on lower part of room-wall. [LG *wagenschot* (*wagen* wagon)]
wainscoting *n.* wainscot, material for it.
waist *n.* part of human body below ribs and above hips; narrowness marking this; circumference of waist; similar narrow part in middle of violin, wasp, etc.; part of garment corresponding to waist; part of garment between neck and waist; blouse, bodice; part of ship between forecastle and quarterdeck; **waist-deep** (or **-high**) up to waist (*in* water etc.). [OE (WAX²)]
waistband *n.* strip of cloth forming waist of garment.
waistcoat *n.* close-fitting waist-length garment without sleeves or collar, worn usu. by men over shirt and under jacket.
waistline *n.* outline or size of body at waist.
wait 1 *v.* defer action or departure in expectation of something happening or some person etc. (*wait until the door opens*; *wait for me*); do this for (specified time); await (opportunity, one's turn, etc.); defer (meal) until person's arrival; park vehicle for short time at side of road etc.; act as waiter or attendant. **2** *n.* act or time of waiting; watch for enemy; (in *pl.*) street singers of Christmas carols. **3 lie in wait** be hidden and ready (*for*); **wait and see** await progress of events; **waiting game** postponing action for greater effect; **waiting-list** list of applicants etc. for thing not immediately available; **waiting-room** room where people can wait, e.g. at railway station or surgery; **wait on** (or **upon**) await convenience of, be attendant or respectful visitor to; **wait up (for)** not go to bed (until arrival or happening of); **you wait!** expression of threat or warning. [F f. Gmc (WAKE¹)]
waiter *n.* man who takes orders and brings food etc. at hotel or restaurant tables.
waitress *n.* female waiter.
waive *v.t.* refrain from insisting on or using (right or claim etc.). [AF *weyver* (WAIF)]
waiver *n.* waiving.
wake¹ 1 *v.* (*past* **woke** or **waked**; *p.p.* **waked** or **woken**) cease or cause to cease to sleep (often with *up*); become or cause to become alert or attentive (often with *up*); be awake (*archaic* except as **waking**); disturb with noise; evoke (echo). **2** *n.* (in Ireland) watch by corpse before burial, attendant lamentations and merry-making; (usu. in *pl.*) annual holiday in (industrial) N. England. **3 wake-robin** wild arum. [OE]
wake² *n.* track left by moving ship on water; turbulent air left by moving aircraft; **in the wake of** following, as result or in imitation of. [LG f. ON]
wakeful /'weɪkfʊl/ *a.* unable to sleep, sleepless, vigilant; **wakefully** *adv.* [WAKE¹]
waken *v.* make or become awake. [ON]
wale *n.* = WEAL¹; ridge on corduroy etc.; *Naut.* broad thick timber along ship's side. [OE]
walk /wɔ:k/ **1** *v.* move by lifting and setting down each foot in turn with one foot always on ground at any time; travel or go on foot, take exercise thus; traverse (distance) in walking; tread floor or surface of; cause to walk with one. **2** *n.* act of walking, ordinary human gait; slowest gait of animal; person's action in walking; spell or distance of walking; excursion on foot; place or track meant or fit for walking. **3 walk (all) over** *colloq.* defeat easily, take advantage of; **walk away from** easily outdistance; **walk away** (or **off**) **with** *colloq.* steal, win easily; **walk into** *colloq.* encounter through unwariness; **walk of life** one's occupation; **walk on air** feel elated; **walk-on part** part involving appearance on stage but no speaking; **walk out** depart suddenly or angrily; **walk-out** *n.* sudden angry departure, esp. as protest or strike; **walk out on** desert, abandon; **walk-over** *n.* easy victory; **walk the streets** be prostitute. [OE]
walkabout *n.* informal stroll among

crowd by visiting member of royal family etc.; period of wandering by Australian Aboriginal.

walker *n.* one who walks; framework for person unable to walk unaided.

walkie-talkie /'wɔ:kɪtɔ:kɪ/ *n.* small portable radio transmitting and receiving set.

walking-stick *n.* stick held, or used as a support, when walking.

walkway *n.* passage or path for walking along.

wall /wɔ:l/ **1** *n.* continuous narrow upright structure of stone or brick etc. enclosing or protecting or separating a building or room or field or town etc.; thing like wall in appearance or effect; outermost layer of animal or plant organ or cell etc.; steep mountain-side. **2** *v.t.* block *up* (aperture etc.) with wall; (esp. in *p.p.*) provide or protect with wall, shut *in* or *off* thus. **3 go to the wall** fare badly in competition; **up the wall** *colloq.* crazy, furious; **wall-board** board made from wood-pulp etc. and used to cover walls; **wall game** Eton form of football played beside wall; **walls have ears** beware of eavesdroppers; **wall-to--wall** covering whole floor of room; **with one's back to the wall** at bay. **4 wall-less** *a.* [OE f. L *vallum* rampart]

wallaby /'wɒləbɪ/ *n.* small species of kangaroo. [Aboriginal]

wallah /'wɒlə/ *n. sl.* person connected with a specified occupation or task, (in *comb.*) -man. [Hindi]

wallet /'wɒlɪt/ *n.* flat case for holding banknotes etc. [AF]

wall-eye /'wɔ:laɪ/ *n.* eye with iris whitish or streaked, or with outward squint; **wall-eyed** *a.* [ON]

wallflower *n.* plant with fragrant flowers; *colloq.* partnerless woman at dance. [WALL]

Walloon /wɒ'lu:n/ **1** *n.* member or language of a people in Belgium and neighbouring part of France. **2** *a.* of the Walloons; in Walloon. [F f. L f. Gmc]

wallop /'wɒləp/ *sl.* **1** *v.t.* thrash, beat; (in *partic.*) big. **2** *n.* heavy blow; beer. [F *waloper* f. Gmc; earlier senses 'boil', GALLOP]

wallow /'wɒləʊ/ **1** *v.i.* roll about in mud, sand, water, etc.; take gross delight *in*. **2** *n.* act of wallowing; place where animals go to wallow. [OE]

wallpaper *n.* paper for pasting on room-walls, often decoratively printed. [WALL]

walnut /'wɔ:lnʌt/ *n.* nut with kernel in pair of boat-shaped shells; tree bearing this, its timber used in cabinet-making. [OE, = foreign nut]

walrus /'wɔ:lrəs/ *n.* long-tusked amphibious arctic mammal; **walrus moustache** long thick drooping moustache. [Du.]

waltz /wɔ:ls, wɒls/ **1** *n.* ballroom dance for couples, with graceful flowing melody in triple time; music for this. **2** *v.i.* dance waltz; dance *in* or *out* or *round* etc. in joy etc.; move easily or casually. [G *walzer*]

wampum /'wɒmpəm/ *n.* strings of shell-beads formerly used by N. American Indians for money or ornament. [Algonquian]

wan /wɒn/ *a.* pale, colourless, weary-looking; **wanness** *n.* [OE, = dark]

wand /wɒnd/ *n.* magician's or music-conductor's baton; slender rod or staff carried as sign of office etc. [ON]

wander /'wɒndə/ *v.i.* go from place to place without settled route or aim; go aimlessly *in*, *off*, etc.; diverge from right way (*lit.* or *fig.*); talk or think irrelevantly or incoherently, be inattentive or delirious; **wandering Jew** person always on the move. [OE (WEND)]

wanderlust *n.* eager desire or fondness for travelling or wandering. [G]

wane **1** *v.i.* (of moon) decrease in apparent size; decrease in size or splendour, lose power or importance. **2** *n.* process of waning. **3 on the wane** declining. [OE]

wangle /'wæŋg(ə)l/ *sl.* **1** *v.t.* secure (favour or desired result) by scheming or contrivance. **2** *n.* act of wangling. [orig. unkn.]

wank *vulgar* **1** *v.i.* masturbate. **2** *n.* act of masturbation. [orig. unkn.]

Wankel engine /'wæŋk(ə)l/ engine with continuously rotating eccentric shaft. [*Wankel*, engineer]

want /wɒnt/ **1** *v.* have desire for, wish for possession or presence of; require or need (*want a holiday*; *hair wants cutting*; *want to go by bus*); should or ought (*you want to be careful*); lack, be insufficiently supplied with; be in want (*for*). **2** *n.* desire for something, thing desired; lack or deficiency *of* (*for want of anything better*); poverty. **3 in want of** needing; **not want to** be unwilling (*does not want to come*), ought not to (*you don't want to overdo it*); **wanted (by the police)** sought by police as suspected criminal. [ON]

wanting *a.* lacking in quality or quantity, unequal to requirements; absent; deficient.

wanton /'wɒnt(ə)n/ **1** *a.* licentious, unchaste; (of cruelty, damage, etc.) purposeless, unprovoked; capricious, sportive (*wanton child*, *wind*, *mood*); luxuriant, wild (*wanton profusion*, *growth*). **2** *n.* licentious person. **3** *v.i.* be capricious or sportive. [earlier *wantowen*, = undisciplined]

wapiti /ˈwɒpɪtɪ/ *n.* large N. American deer. [Cree]

war /wɔː/ **1** *n.* strife usu. between nations conducted by force; military or naval or air attacks and suspension of ordinary relations involved in this, period of this; hostility between persons; efforts against crime, disease, etc. **2** *v.i.* (**-rr-**) *archaic* make war. **3 at war** engaged in war (*with* enemy); **go to war** begin hostile operations; **have been in the wars** *colloq.* show signs of injury; **war-cry** phrase or name shouted in battle, party catchword; **war-dance** dance performed by primitive peoples before war or after victory; **war-horse** trooper's horse, *fig.* veteran soldier; **war memorial** monument to those killed in a war; **war of nerves** attempt to wear down opponent by gradual destruction of morale; **war-paint** paint put on body esp. by N. American Indians before battle; **war-path** march of N. American Indians to make war (**on the war-path** engaged in conflict, taking hostile attitude). [AF f. Gmc]

warble /ˈwɔːb(ə)l/ **1** *v.* sing (esp. of bird) or speak in gentle continuous trilling manner. **2** *n.* warbling sound. [F *werble(r)* f. Gmc (WHIRL)]

warbler *n.* any of several small birds.

ward /wɔːd/ **1** *n.* separate room or division in hospital etc.; administrative division esp. for elections; minor etc. under care of guardian or court; (in *pl.*) notches and projections in key and lock to prevent opening by wrong key; *archaic* guarding, defending, guardianship. **2** *v.t.* (usu. **ward off**) parry (blow), avert (danger etc.); *archaic* guard, defend. [OE]

-ward *suffix* (also **-wards**) added to nouns of place or destination and to adverbs of direction and forming adverbs (usu. in *-wards*) meaning 'towards the place etc.' (*backwards*, *homewards*), adjectives (usu. in *-ward*) meaning 'turned or tending towards' (*downward*, *onward*), and less commonly nouns meaning 'the region towards or about' (*look to the eastward*). [OE]

warden /ˈwɔːd(ə)n/ *n.* president or governor of institution, e.g. hospital or college; official with supervisory duties. [AF & F (GUARDIAN)]

warder /ˈwɔːdə/ *n.* gaoler; **wardress** *n. fem.* [AF f. F (GUARD)]

wardrobe /ˈwɔːdrəʊb/ *n.* place, esp. large cupboard, where clothes are kept; person's stock of clothes; **wardrobe master** (or **mistress**) one who has charge of actor's or company's costumes. [F]

wardroom /ˈwɔːdruːm/ *n.* officers' quarters in warship. [WARD]

-wards see -WARD.

wardship *n.* tutelage. [WARD]

ware *n.* manufactured articles (esp. pottery) of kind specified (*Delft ware*, *kitchen ware*, *hardware*); (in *pl.*) what one has for sale. [OE]

warehouse /ˈweəhaʊs/ **1** *n.* building in which goods are stored or shown for sale. **2** /also -haʊz/ *v.t.* place or keep in warehouse.

warfare *n.* state of war, campaigning. [WAR]

warhead *n.* explosive head of missile.

warlike *a.* fond of or skilful in war; military.

warlock /ˈwɔːlɒk/ *n. archaic* sorcerer. [OE, = traitor]

warm /wɔːm/ **1** *a.* of or at a fairly high temperature; (of person) at natural temperature, or with skin temperature raised by exercise or excitement or external heat; (of clothes) serving to keep one warm; (of work or exercise etc.) serving to make one warm; (of feelings or behaviour etc.) excited or hearty etc.; (of reception or welcome etc.) vigorous and emphatic, by being either heartily friendly or strongly hostile; (of position etc.) difficult or dangerous; (of colour) suggesting warmth esp. by presence of red or yellow; (of scent in hunting) fresh and strong, (of seeker in children's game etc.) close to thing sought or guessed at. **2** *v.* make or become warm. **3** *n.* act of warming; warmth of atmosphere. **4 warm-blooded** (of animals) having blood temperature well above that of environment, *fig.* ardent; **warm-hearted** affectionate, sympathetic; **warming-pan** flat closed vessel holding live coals, formerly used for warming beds; **warm up** make or become warm, esp. (cause to) reach temperature of efficient working, prepare for performance by exercise or practice, reheat (food); **warm-up** *n.* process of warming up. [OE]

warmonger /ˈwɔːmʌŋgə/ *n.* one who seeks to cause war. [WAR]

warmth *n.* being warm; moderate heat; affection, friendly feeling; strength of feeling, either approving or disapproving. [WARM]

warn /wɔːn/ *v.t.* put (person) on guard (*against* person or thing or *doing*), give (person) timely notice (*of* danger or consequences, *that* thing may happen or is happening); **warn off** tell (person) to keep away (from). [OE]

warning *n.* what is said or done or occurs to warn person. [OE]

warp /wɔːp/ **1** *v.* make or become crooked or twisted esp. by uneven shrinkage or expansion; distort or pervert (person's mind), suffer such distortion (*warped sense of humour*); haul (ship) along by rope fixed to external point. **2** *n.* threads stretched in loom to be crossed by weft; contorted state of warped wood etc.; mental perversion or bias; rope used in warping a ship. [OE]

warrant /ˈwɒrənt/ **1** *n.* thing that authorizes an action; written authorization to receive or supply money or goods or services or to carry out arrest or search; certificate of service rank held by warrant-officer. **2** *v.t.* serve as warrant for, justify; guarantee, answer for genuineness etc. of. **3 I('ll) warrant (you)** I am certain, no doubt; **warrant-officer** officer between commissioned officers and NCOs. [F *warant* f. Gmc]

warranty *n.* authority or justification; seller's undertaking that thing sold is his and fit for use etc., often accepting responsibility for repairs needed over a period. [AF *warantie* (prec.)]

warren /ˈwɒrən/ *n.* piece of ground abounding in rabbit burrows; densely populated or labyrinthine building or district. [AF *warenne* f. Celt.]

warring /ˈwɔːrɪŋ/ *a.* rival, antagonistic. [WAR]

warrior /ˈwɒrɪə/ *n.* person famous or skilled in war; fighting man (esp. of primitive peoples); *attrib.* (of nation etc.) martial. [F dial. *werreior* (WAR)]

warship *n.* ship for use in war. [WAR]

wart /wɔːt/ *n.* small hardish roundish growth on skin; protuberance on skin of animal, surface of plant, etc.; **wart-hog** African wild pig; **warts and all** *colloq.* with no attempt to conceal blemishes or inadequacies; **warty** *a.* [OE]

wartime *n.* period when war is being waged. [WAR]

wary /ˈweərɪ/ *a.* on one's guard, circumspect; cautious (*of*), showing caution; **warily** *adv.*; **wariness** *n.*

was see BE.

wash /wɒʃ/ **1** *v.* cleanse with liquid, esp. water; take (stain etc.) *out* or *off* or *away* thus; wash clothes or oneself or one's face and/or hands; (of fabric or dye) bear washing without damage; (of argument etc.) stand scrutiny (*that doesn't* or *won't wash*); (of stain etc.) be taken *off* or *out* by washing; moisten, (of river etc.) touch with its waters; (of moving liquid) carry in specified direction, go sweeping or splashing *along* or *over* etc.; sift (ore) by action of water; brush thin coat of water-colour over. **2** *n.* washing or being washed; treatment at laundry (*send clothes to the wash*); quantity of clothes for washing; motion of agitated water or air, esp. due to passage of vessel or aircraft; kitchen slops given to pigs; thin or weak or inferior or animals' liquid food; liquid to spread over surface to cleanse or heal or colour; thin coat of water-colour. **3 come out in the wash** eventually become satisfactory; **wash one's dirty linen in public** let private quarrels or difficulties become generally known; **wash down** clean by washing, accompany or follow (food) *with* drink; **washed out** faded by washing, limp, enfeebled; **washed up** *sl.* defeated, having failed; **wash one's hands (of)** renounce responsibility (for); **wash-leather** chamois or similar leather for washing windows etc.; **wash out** clean inside of by washing, *colloq.* cancel; **wash-out** *n.* breach in railway or road caused by flood, *sl.* complete failure; **wash up** wash (dishes etc., or *absol.*) after use, (of sea) carry on to shore. [OE]

washable *a.* that can be washed without being damaged.

washer *n.* flat ring of leather or rubber or metal etc. to tighten joint and prevent leakage; washing-machine.

washerwoman *n.* woman whose occupation is washing clothes etc.

washing *n.* clothes to be washed; **washing-machine** machine for washing clothes; **washing-powder** powder of soap or detergent for washing clothes; **washing-soda** sodium carbonate, used (dissolved in water) for washing and cleaning; **washing-up** process of washing dishes etc. after use, dishes etc. for washing.

washy *a.* too watery or weak; lacking vigour; **washily** *adv.*; **washiness** *n.*

wasn't /ˈwɒz(ə)nt/ *colloq.* = *was not.*

wasp /wɒsp/ *n.* stinging insect with black and yellow stripes, slender waist and buzzing flight; **wasp-waist** very slender waist. [OE]

WASP /wɒsp/ *abbr. US* (usu. *derog.*) White Anglo-Saxon Protestant.

waspish /ˈwɒspɪʃ/ *a.* irritable, snappish. [WASP]

wassail /ˈwɒseɪl, -s(ə)l/ *archaic* **1** *n.* merry-making, festive drinking. **2** *v.i.* make merry. [ON *ves heill* be in good health (WHOLE)]

wastage /ˈweɪstɪdʒ/ *n.* amount wasted; loss by use or wear or leakage; loss of employees other than by redundancy. [foll.]

waste **1** *v.* use to no purpose or for inadequate result or extravagantly; fail to use (opportunity); give (advice etc.) without effect (*on* person); wear gradually away, make or become weak; lay waste; treat as waste. **2** *a.* superfluous, no longer serving a purpose; not inhabited or cultivated. **3** *n.* act of wasting;

waste material; waste region; diminution by use or wear; waste-pipe. **4** **go** (or **run**) **to waste** be wasted; **waste paper** spoiled or valueless paper; **waste-paper basket** receptacle for waste paper; **waste-pipe** pipe to carry off waste esp. from washing etc.; **waste product** useless by-product of organism or manufacture. [F f. L (VAST)]

wasteful *a.* extravagant, causing or showing waste; **wastefully** *adv.*

wasteland *n.* unproductive or useless area of land.

waster *n.* wasteful person; *sl.* wastrel.

wastrel /ˈweɪstr(ə)l/ *n.* good-for-nothing person.

watch /wɒtʃ/ **1** *n.* small portable timepiece for carrying on one's person; state of alert or constant observation or attention; *Naut.* four-hour spell of duty, part of crew taking it; *hist.* watchman or watchmen. **2** *v.* be on the watch, be vigilant, look or wait attentively *for*; keep eyes fixed on, keep under observation, follow observantly; look out for; await (opportunity). **3 on the watch** waiting for expected or feared occurrence; **watch-dog** dog kept to guard property etc., person etc. acting as guardian of others' rights etc.; **watches of the night** time when one lies awake; **watching brief** brief of barrister who follows case for client not directly concerned; **watch it** *colloq.* be careful; **watch-night service** religious service on last day of year; **watch out** be on one's guard; **watch over** look after, protect; **watch-tower** tower from which observation can be kept. [OE (WAKE[1])]

watchful *a.* accustomed to be watching, on the watch; **watchfully** *adv.*

watchmaker *n.* person who makes and repairs watches and clocks.

watchman *n.* man employed to look after empty building etc. at night.

watchword *n.* phrase summarizing some party principle.

water /ˈwɔːtə/ **1** *n.* colourless liquid compound of oxygen and hydrogen; liquid consisting chiefly of this and found in seas and rivers, in rain, and in human tears etc.; expanse of water, sea or lake or river; (in *pl.*) part of sea or river, mineral water at spa etc.; state of tide; solution of specified substance in water (*lavender water*); transparency and brilliance of diamond. **2** *attrib.* found in or near water; of or for or worked by water; involving or using or yielding water. **3** *v.* give water to (animal), supply (plant etc.) with water; take in supply of water; (of mouth or eyes) secrete water; (in *p.p.*, of silk etc.) having irregular wavy gloss. **4 by water** using ship etc. for travel or transport; **like water** lavishly, recklessly; **make one's mouth water** cause flow of saliva, create appetite or desire; **make** (or **pass**) **water** urinate; **mouth-watering** appetizing; **under water** in and covered by water; **water-bed** mattress of rubber or plastic etc. filled with water; **water-biscuit** thin crisp unsweetened biscuit made from flour and water; **water-buffalo** common domestic Indian buffalo; **water bus** river or lake boat carrying passengers on regular run; **water-cannon** device giving powerful water-jet to disperse crowd etc.; **water-clock** clock measuring time by flow of water; **water-closet** lavatory with means of flushing pan with water; **water-colour** pigment diluted with water and not oil, picture painted or art of painting with this; **water-cooled** cooled by circulation of water; **water-diviner** dowser; **water down** dilute, make less forceful or horrifying; **water-glass** solution of sodium or potassium silicate esp. for preserving eggs; **water-hammer** knocking noise in pipe when tap is turned off; **water-hole** shallow depression in which water collects; **water-ice** flavoured and frozen water and sugar etc.; **watering-can** portable container with long spout, for watering plants; **watering-place** pool where animals drink, spa or seaside resort; **water-jump** place where horse in steeplechase etc. must jump over water; **water-level** surface of water in reservoir etc., height of this, water-table, level using water to determine horizontal; **water-lily** aquatic plant with floating leaves and flowers; **water-line** line along which surface of water touches ship's side; **water-meadow** meadow periodically flooded by stream; **water-melon** large melon with smooth green skin, red pulp, and watery juice; **water-mill** mill worked by water-wheel; **water-pistol** toy pistol shooting jet of water; **water polo** game played by swimmers with ball like football; **water-power** mechanical force from weight or motion of water; **water-rat** water-vole; **water-rate** charge for use of public water-supply; **water-ski** ski on which person towed by motor boat can skim water-surface; **water-softener** apparatus for softening hard water; **water-table** plane below which ground is saturated with water; **water-tower** tower with elevated tank to give pressure for distributing water; **water under the bridge** irrevocable past; **water-vole** aquatic kind of vole like rat;

water-wheel wheel driven by water to work machinery, or used to raise water; **water-wings** inflated supports for beginners at swimming. [OE]

watercourse *n.* brook or stream; bed of this.

watercress *n.* cress growing in springs etc., with pungent leaves used in salads.

waterfall *n.* stream falling over precipice or down steep height.

waterfowl *n.* (usu. as *pl.*) water birds.

waterfront *n.* part of town adjoining river etc.

waterlogged *a.* saturated with water; (of boat etc.) barely able to float from being saturated or filled with water.

Waterloo /wɔːtəˈluː/ *n.* decisive defeat or contest. [*Waterloo* in Belgium, where Napoleon was defeated]

waterman *n.* boatman plying for hire; oarsman as regards skill in keeping boat balanced. [WATER]

watermark 1 *n.* faint design in paper to show maker etc. **2** *v.t.* mark with this.

waterproof 1 *a.* impervious to water. **2** *n.* such garment or material. **3** *v.t.* make waterproof.

watershed *n.* line between waters flowing to different river basins; turning-point in affairs. [*shed* ridge]

waterside *n.* margin of sea or lake or river. [WATER]

waterspout *n.* gyrating column of water and spray between sea and cloud.

watertight *a.* closely fastened or fitted so as to prevent passage of water; (of argument etc.) unassailable.

waterway *n.* navigable channel.

waterworks *n.* establishment for management of water-supply; *sl.* shedding of tears; *sl.* urinary system.

watery *a.* of or consisting of water; containing too much water; thin in consistency; vapid, uninteresting; (of colour) pale; (of sun or moon or sky) rainy-looking; **wateriness** *n.*

watt /wɒt/ *n.* unit of power, rate of working of one joule per second, corresponding to electric circuit where electromotive force is one volt and current one ampere; **watt-hour** energy of one watt applied for one hour. [*Watt*, engineer]

wattage *n.* amount of electrical power expressed in watts.

wattle[1] /ˈwɒt(ə)l/ *n.* Australian acacia with pliant boughs and golden flowers used as national emblem; interlaced rods and twigs for fences etc.; **wattle and daub** wickerwork plastered as building-material. [OE]

wattle[2] /ˈwɒt(ə)l/ *n.* fleshy appendage on head or throat of turkey etc. [orig. unkn.]

wave 1 *v.* move (hand etc.) to and fro in greeting or as signal; show sinuous or sweeping motion as of flag or tree or cornfield in wind; give such motion to; wave hand or held thing *to* person as signal or greeting; tell or direct (person) thus (*waved her away*; *waved her to come*), express thus; give undulating form to (hair etc.), have such form. **2** *n.* ridge of water between two depressions; long body of water curling into arched form and breaking on shore; thing compared to this, e.g. body of persons in one of successive advancing groups; gesture of waving; waving of hair; temporary increase of influence or condition (*heat wave*; *wave of enthusiasm*); disturbance of particles in fluid medium to form ridges and troughs for propagation of motion, heat, light, sound, etc., single curve in this; undulating line or outline. **3 wave aside** dismiss as intrusive or irrelevant; **wave down** wave to (vehicle or driver) as signal to stop. [OE]

waveband *n.* range of wavelengths between certain limits.

wavelength *n.* distance between crests of successive waves; this as distinctive feature of radio waves from a transmitter or *fig.* a person's way of thinking.

wavelet *n.* small wave.

waver *v.i.* be or become unsteady or irresolute, begin to give way; (of light) flicker. [ON (WAVE)]

wavy *a.* having waves or alternate contrary curves; **wavily** *adv.*; **waviness** *n.* [WAVE]

wax[1] **1** *n.* sticky plastic yellowish substance secreted by bees as material of honeycomb; this bleached and purified for candles, modelling, etc.; any similar substance. **2** *v.t.* cover or treat with wax. **3 be wax in person's hands** be entirely subservient to him. [OE]

wax[2] *v.i.* (of moon) increase in apparent size; become larger or stronger; pass into specified state or mood (*wax lyrical*); **wax and wane** undergo alternate increases and decreases. [OE]

wax[3] *n. sl.* fit of anger. [orig. uncert.]

waxen *a.* having smooth pale translucent surface as of wax; *archaic* made of wax. [WAX[1]]

waxwing *n.* any of several small birds with red tips like sealing-wax to some wing-feathers.

waxwork *n.* object, esp. lifelike dummy, modelled in wax; making of such objects; (in *pl.*) exhibition of wax dummies.

waxy *a.* resembling wax in consistency or surface; *sl.* in a rage, easily enraged; **waxily** *adv.*; **waxiness** *n.* [WAX[1, 3]]

way 1 *n.* road or track for passing along;

course or route for reaching a place, esp. best one (*asked the way to London*); method or plan for attaining object; person's desired or chosen course of action; travelling-distance, length (to be) traversed; unimpeded opportunity to advance, space free of obstacles, region over which advance is desired or natural; advance in some direction, impetus, progress; being engaged, or time spent, in movement from place to place; specified direction (usu. in adverbial phrase without preposition: *step this way*); chosen or desired or habitual behaviour; normal course of events (*that is always the way*); scope or range, line of occupation or business; specified condition or state (*things are in a bad way*); respect (*is useful in some ways*); (in *pl.*) structure of timber etc. down which new ship is launched. **2** *adv. colloq.* far (*way off the target*). **3 by the way** incidental(ly), irrelevant(ly); **by way of** by means of, as a form or method of, passing through; **come one's way** become available to one; **go out of one's way** make special effort, act without compulsion; **in a way** not altogether or completely; **in the way** obstructing, inconvenient; **lead** (or **show**) **the way** act as guide or leader; **look the other way** ignore what one should notice; **make one's way** go, prosper; **make way for** allow to pass, be superseded by; **on one's way** in the process of travelling or approaching; **on the way** travelling or approaching, having progressed, (of baby) conceived but not yet born; **on the way out** *colloq.* about to disappear or become unfashionable; **out of the way** unusual, not obstructing, remote, disposed of; **under way** in motion or progress; **way back** *colloq.* long ago; **way-bill** list of passengers or parcels conveyed; **way-leave** right of way rented to another; **way of life** principles or habits governing one's actions; **way-out** *colloq.* unusual, progressive, excellent; **ways and means** methods of achieving something, (in parliament) means of providing money. [OE]

wayfarer *n.* traveller, esp. on foot; **wayfaring** *n.*

waylay *v.t.* (*past* and *p.p.* **waylaid**) lie in wait for; stop to rob or talk to.

-ways *suffix* forming adjectives and adverbs of direction or manner (*sideways*).

wayside *n.* side of road; land at side of road.

wayward *a.* childishly self-willed, capricious. [AWAY, -WARD]

WC *abbr.* water-closet; West Central.

W/Cdr. *abbr.* Wing Commander.

we /wi:, wɪ/ *pron.* (*obj.* US; *poss.* OUR, OURS) *pl.* of I²; = I² in royal proclamations etc. and in newspaper editorials; I and you or others; **we and they** the groups including and opposed to us. [OE]

weak *a.* deficient in strength or power or number or cogency or resolution or vigour; **weak ending** unstressed syllable in normally stressed place at end of verse-line; **weak-kneed** lacking resolution; **weak-minded** mentally deficient, lacking resolution; **weak moment** time when one is unusually compliant or temptable; **weak point** (or **spot**) place where defences are assailable, flaw in argument or character or resistance to temptation; **weak verb** verb forming inflexions by suffix, not by vowel-change only. [ON]

weaken *v.* become or make weak or weaker.

weakling *n.* feeble person or animal.

weakly *a.* sickly, not robust; **weakliness** *n.*

weakness *n.* weak point; self-indulgent liking *for*.

weal¹ **1** *n.* ridge raised on flesh by whip etc. **2** *v.t.* mark with weal. [WALE]

weal² *n.* welfare (*for the public weal*). [OE]

wealth /welθ/ *n.* riches, being rich; abundance or profusion *of*. [OE]

wealthy *a.* having abundance esp. of money; **wealthily** *adv.*; **wealthiness** *n.*

wean *v.t.* accustom (infant or other young mammal) to food other than (mother's) milk; disengage *from* habit etc. by enforced discontinuance. [OE, = accustom]

weapon /ˈwepən/ *n.* thing designed or used or usable for inflicting bodily harm (e.g. gun or cosh); means employed for getting the better in a conflict; **weaponry** *n.* [OE]

wear /weə/ **1** *v.* (*past* **wore**; *p.p.* WORN) have on one's person as clothing or ornament etc. (*wears a hat, a watch, lipstick*); have as one's look or countenance (*wore a frown*); *colloq.* (usu. with neg.) tolerate; injure surface of, partly obliterate or alter, by rubbing or stress or use; suffer such injury or change; rub or be rubbed *off* or *away*; (of water etc.) make (hole etc.) by constant dripping or rubbing etc.; exhaust; (with *down*) overcome by persistence; endure continued use or life *well* etc.; (of time) pass, esp. tediously; (of ship) fly (flag). **2** *n.* wearing or being worn; things worn, fashionable or suitable apparel (*sportswear, footwear*); damage from continuous use (also **wear and tear**). **3 wear one's heart on one's sleeve** show one's feelings openly; **wear off** lose effectiveness or intensity; **wear out** use or be used until no longer usable, tire or be tired out; **wear thin** (of patience etc.) begin to fail. [OE]

wearisome /ˈwɪərɪsəm/ *a.* tedious, tiring by monotony or length. [foll.]

weary /ˈwɪərɪ/ **1** *a.* unequal to or disinclined for further exertion or endurance; disgusted at continuing *of*; tiring, tedious. **2** *v.* make or grow weary. **3 wearily** *adv.*; **weariness** *n.* [OE]

weasel /ˈwi:z(ə)l/ *n.* small ferocious carnivorous animal related to stoat and ferret. [OE]

weather /ˈweðə/ **1** *n.* state of atmosphere at a place and time (as regards heat, cloudiness, dryness, sunshine, wind, and rain etc.); *attrib.* windward. **2** *v.* expose to or affect by atmospheric changes; be discoloured or worn thus; come safely through (storm, *lit.* or *fig.*); get to windward of (cape etc.). **3 keep a weather eye open** be watchful; **make heavy weather of** find trying or needlessly difficult; **under the weather** *colloq.* indisposed; **weather-beaten** affected by exposure to weather; **weather-board** sloping board at bottom of door to keep out rain, horizontal board on wall, overlapping one next below it; **weather forecast** prediction of weather for next few hours or longer; **weather-vane** weathercock. [OE]

weathercock *n.* revolving pointer on church spire etc. to show direction of wind; inconstant person.

weatherman *n.* meteorologist, esp. one who broadcasts weather forecast.

weatherproof *a.* resistant to wind and rain.

weave[1] **1** *v.* (*past* **wove**; *p.p.* **woven**) form (fabric) by interlacing long threads in two directions, form (thread) into or make fabric thus; make (facts etc.) *into* story or connected whole, make (story etc.) thus. **2** *n.* style of weaving. [OE]

weave[2] *v.i.* move repeatedly from side to side, take intricate course to avoid obstructions; **get weaving** *sl.* begin action, hurry. [ON (WAVE)]

weaver *n.* one whose occupation is weaving; a kind of tropical bird building elaborately interwoven nests. [WEAVE[1]]

web *n.* woven fabric, amount woven in one piece; complex series (*a web of lies*); cobweb, gossamer, or similar product of spinning creature; membrane between toes of animal or swimming bird; large roll of paper for printing; thin flat connecting part in machinery; **web-footed** having toes connected by web; **webbed** *a.* [OE]

webbing *n.* strong narrow closely-woven fabric for belts etc.

wed *v.* (**-dd-**; *p.p.* occas. **wed**) marry; *fig.* unite; (in *p.p.*) of marriage (*wedded life*), obstinately attached or devoted *to* a pursuit etc. [OE, = pledge]

Wed. *abbr.* Wednesday.

wedding /ˈwedɪŋ/ *n.* marriage ceremony; **wedding breakfast** meal etc. between wedding and departure for honeymoon; **wedding-cake** rich iced cake distributed to wedding guests and absent friends; **wedding-ring** ring worn by married person from time of wedding ceremony. [OE (WED)]

wedge 1 *n.* piece of wood or metal with sharp edge at one end, used esp. to split wood or widen aperture or tighten loose parts or adjust level by having the thin edge inserted and the thicker part forced to follow; sector-shaped area or volume, persons or things or substance filling this; golf-club with wedge-shaped head. **2** *v.t.* force *open* or *apart* with wedge; fix firmly with wedge; pack or thrust (thing, or *oneself*) tightly *in* or *into* etc. **3 the thin end of the wedge** a change or procedure etc. that appears small or insignificant but will open the way to greater changes etc. [OE]

Wedgwood /ˈwedʒwʊd/ *n.* **(P)** a kind of fine pottery esp. with white cameo design; its characteristic blue colour. [*Wedgwood*, potter]

wedlock /ˈwedlɒk/ *n.* the married state; **born in** (or **out of**) **wedlock** born of married (or unmarried) parents. [OE, = marriage vow]

Wednesday /ˈwenzdeɪ, -dɪ/ **1** *n.* day of week following Tuesday. **2** *adv. colloq.* on Wednesday. **3 Wednesdays** on Wednesdays, each Wednesday. [OE]

wee *a.* little (esp. *Sc.*); *colloq.* tiny. [OE]

weed 1 *n.* wild herb growing where it is not wanted; thin weak-looking person or horse; *sl.* marijuana; *archaic* tobacco. **2** *v.* rid of weeds or inferior parts or members; cut off or uproot weeds; sort *out* (inferior parts etc.) for removal. **3 weed-killer** substance used to destroy weeds. [OE]

weeds /wi:dz/ *n.pl.* deep mourning worn by widow. [OE, = garment]

weedy *a.* full of weeds; growing freely like a weed; thin and weak. [WEED]

week *n.* seven-day period reckoned usu. from Saturday midnight; any seven-day period; the six days between Sundays; the five days Monday–Friday, period of work then done (*35-hour week*); **a week (from) today, Monday,** etc. (or **today, Monday,** etc., **week**) seven days after today, Monday, etc. [OE]

weekday *n.* day other than Sunday.

weekend /wi:kˈend, ˈwi:-/ *n.* Sunday and

(part of) Saturday (or slightly longer period) esp. for holiday or visit.

weekly 1 *a.* done, produced, or occurring every week. 2 *adv.* every week. 3 *n.* weekly newspaper or periodical.

weeny /'wi:nɪ/ *a. colloq.* tiny. [WEE]

weep 1 *v.* (*past* & *p.p.* **wept**) shed tears (*for* or *over*); weep for, bewail; be covered with or send forth drops, come or send forth in drops, exude; (of tree, usu. in *partic.*) having drooping branches. 2 *n.* fit or spell of weeping. [OE]

weepy *a. colloq.* inclined to weep, tearful.

weevil /'wi:vɪl/ *n.* destructive granary-beetle. [LG]

wee-wee /'wi:wi:/ *sl.* 1 *n.* urination; urine. 2 *v.i.* urinate. [orig. unkn.]

weft *n.* threads woven across warp to make fabric; yarn for these; thing woven. [OE (WEAVE[1])]

weigh /weɪ/ *v.* find weight of; balance in hands (as if) to guess weight of; estimate relative value or importance or desirability of, compare *with* or *against*; be equal to (specified weight), have (specified) importance, exert influence, be heavy or burdensome; **weigh anchor** see ANCHOR; **weigh down** bring down by weight (*lit.* or *fig.*); **weigh (heavy) on** be burdensome or depressing to; **weigh in** be weighed (of boxer before contest, or jockey after race); **weigh in with** *colloq.* advance (argument etc.) confidently; **weigh out** take definite weight of, (of jockey) be weighed before race; **weigh up** *colloq.* form estimate of; **weigh with** be regarded as important by; **weigh one's words** choose those which precisely express one's meaning. [OE, = carry]

weighbridge *n.* weighing-machine for vehicles on road.

weight /weɪt/ 1 *n.* tendency of bodies to fall to earth; quantitative expression of a body's weight, a scale of such weights (*troy weight*); body of known weight for use in weighing; heavy body esp. used in mechanism etc.; load or burden; influence, importance; (in athletics) = SHOT[1]. 2 *v.t.* attach a weight to, hold down with a weight; impede or burden *with*. 3 **throw one's weight about** (or **around**) *colloq.* be self-assertive; **weight-lifting** sport or exercise of lifting heavy objects; **worth one's weight in gold** exceedingly helpful. 4 **weightless** *a.* [OE]

weighting *n.* extra pay in special cases.

weighty *a.* heavy, momentous; (of utterances etc.) deserving consideration or carrying weight; influential, authoritative; **weightily** *adv.*; **weightiness** *n.*

weir /wɪə/ *n.* dam across river to retain water or regulate flow. [OE]

weird /wɪəd/ *a.* uncanny, supernatural; *colloq.* queer, incomprehensible; connected with fate; **the weird sisters** the Fates, witches. [OE, = destiny]

welch var. of WELSH[2].

welcome /'welkəm/ 1 *int.* of greeting (*welcome home, to England*, etc.). 2 *n.* saying 'welcome', kind or glad reception. 3 *v.t.* receive with signs of pleasure. 4 *a.* that one receives with pleasure (*welcome guest, news*); *predic.* ungrudgingly permitted *to do* thing or given right *to* thing, acquitted of obligation for favour etc. (*you're welcome to use my car* or *to the use of it*). 5 **make welcome** receive hospitably; **outstay one's welcome** stay too long as visitor etc.; **you are welcome** there is no need of thanks. [OE]

weld 1 *v.t.* hammer or press (pieces of iron etc. usu. heated but not melted) into one piece, join by fusion with electric arc etc., form by welding into some article, *fig.* fashion effectually *into* a whole. 2 *n.* welded joint. [alt. f. WELL[2] after p.p.]

welfare /'welfeə/ *n.* good fortune, happiness, health and prosperity (*of* person or community etc.); maintenance of persons in such condition, money given for this purpose; **Welfare State** country ensuring welfare of all citizens by social services operated by government; **welfare work** organized effort for welfare of class or group. [WELL[1], FARE]

welkin *n. poetic* sky. [OE, = clouds]

well[1] 1 *adv.* (*compar.* BETTER; *superl.* BEST) in right or satisfactory way (*have worked well*); in kind way (*treated me well*); thoroughly, carefully (*polish it well*); with heartiness or approval (*speak well of*); probably, reasonably (*you may well be right*); to a considerable extent (*is well over forty*). 2 *a.* in good health; *predic.* in satisfactory state or position; *predic.* advisable (*it would be well to inquire*). 3 *int.* expressing surprise or resignation etc., used esp. after pause in speaking. 4 **let well alone** avoid needless change or disturbance; **well-advised** prudent; **well and truly** decisively, completely; **well-appointed** having all necessary equipment; **well away** having made considerable progress; **well-behaved** having good manners; **well-being** welfare; **well--born** of noble family; **well-bred** having or showing good breeding or manners; **well-connected** related to good families; **well-disposed** having good disposition or friendly feeling (*towards*); **well done!** cry of commendation; **well-groomed** with carefully tended hair, clothes, etc.; **well-heeled** *colloq.* wealthy; **well-informed** having much knowledge or information about a subject; **well-intentioned** having or showing good intentions; **well-judged** opportunely or skilfully or discreetly done; **well-known** known to many; **well-made** strongly built, shapely; **well-mannered** having good manners; **well-meaning** (or **-meant**) well-intentioned (but ineffective); **well off** fortunately situated, fairly rich; **well-oiled** *sl.* drunk; **well-preserved** in good condition, (of old person) showing little sign of age; **well-read** having read (and learned) much; **well-rounded** complete and symmetrical; **well-spoken** ready or refined in speech; **well-to-do** prosperous; **well-tried** often tested with good results; **well-trodden** frequented; **well-wisher** person who wishes one well; **well-worn** much worn by use, (of phrase etc.) trite; **well worth** certainly worth *doing* thing. [OE]

well² 1 *n.* shaft sunk into ground to obtain water or oil; enclosed space like well-shaft, e.g. in middle of building for stairs or lift, or light and air; *fig.* source *of*; (in *pl.*) spa; ink-well; *archaic* water-spring; *US* railed space in law-court. 2 *v.i.* spring (*out* or *up*) as from fountain. 3 **well-head** (or **-spring**) source. [OE]

wellies /'welɪz/ *n.pl. colloq.* wellingtons. [abbr.]

wellington /'welɪŋt(ə)n/ *n.* waterproof rubber boot usu. reaching knee. [Duke of *Wellington*]

Welsh¹ 1 *a.* of Wales; in the Welsh language. 2 *n.* the Welsh language. 3 **the Welsh** Welsh people; **Welsh rabbit** (or by folk etym. **rarebit**) dish of melted cheese on toast. [OE, = foreign]

welsh² *v.i.* (of loser of bet, esp. bookmaker) decamp without paying; evade an obligation; **welsh on** fail to carry out promise to (person), fail to honour (obligation). [orig. unkn.]

Welshman *n.* one who is Welsh by birth or descent; **Welshwoman** *n. fem.* [WELSH¹]

welt 1 *n.* leather rim sewn to shoe-upper for sole to be attached to; = WEAL¹; heavy blow; ribbed or reinforced border of garment. 2 *v.t.* provide with welt; raise weals on, thrash. [orig. unkn.]

welter¹ 1 *v.i.* roll or lie prostrate or be soaked *in.* 2 *n.* general confusion; disorderly mixture or contrast. [LG or Du.]

welter² *n.* heavy rider or boxer. [orig. unkn.]

welterweight *n.* boxing-weight with upper limit of 67 kg.

wen *n.* benign tumour on skin esp. of scalp. [OE]

wench *n. archaic* girl or young woman. [abbr. *wenchel* (OE, = child)]

wend *v.* now only in **wend one's way** go (*to*). [OE, = turn]

Wendy house /'wendɪ/ children's small houselike tent or structure for playing in. [character in Barrie's *Peter Pan*]

went *past* of GO¹.

wept *past* & *p.p.* of WEEP.

were see BE.

weren't /wɜ:nt/ *colloq.* = *were not.*

werewolf /'wɪəwʊlf/ *n.* (also **werwolf**; *pl.* **-wolves**) mythical being who at times changes from person to wolf.

Wesleyan /'wezlɪən/ *hist.* 1 *a.* of Protestant denomination founded by John Wesley. 2 *n.* member of this denomination. [*Wesley*, evangelist]

west 1 *n.* point of horizon where sun sets at equinoxes, compass point corresponding to this, direction in which this lies; (usu. **West**) part of country or town lying to the west; European civilization, non-Communist States of Europe and N. America. 2 *a.* towards, at, near, or facing west; coming from the west (*west wind*). 3 *adv.* towards, at, or near the west. 4 **go west** *sl.* be killed or destroyed etc.; **to the west (of)** in a westward direction (from); **West Country** SW England; **West End** fashionable part of London; **West Indian** native or inhabitant of West Indies; **west-north-west** (compass point) midway between west and north-west; **west of** in a westward direction from; **West Side** *US* western part of Manhattan; **west-south-west** (compass point) midway between west and south-west. [OE]

westering *a.* (of sun) nearing the west.

westerly /'westəlɪ/ *a.* & *adv.* in western position or direction; (of wind) blowing from the west.

western /'west(ə)n/ 1 *a.* of or in the west. 2 *n.* film or novel about cowboys in western North America. 3 **westernize** *v.t.*; **westernmost** *a.*

westerner *n.* native or inhabitant of the west.

westward /'westwəd/ 1 *a.* & (also **westwards**) *adv.* towards the west. 2 *n.* westward direction or region. [-WARD]

wet 1 *a.* soaked or covered with water or other liquid; (of weather etc.) rainy; (of paint etc.) not yet dried; used with water (*wet shampoo*); *sl.* feeble, inept, mistaken. 2 *v.t.* (**-tt-**; *past* & *p.p.* **wet** or **wetted**) make wet. 3 *n.* liquid that wets something; rainy weather; *sl.* dull or feeble person; *sl.* a drink. 4 **wet behind the ears** immature, inexperienced; **wet**

blanket person or thing damping or discouraging enthusiasm, cheerfulness, etc.; **wet dream** erotic dream with involuntary emission of semen; **wet-nurse** *n.* woman employed to suckle another's child, (*v.t.*) suckle thus, *fig.* treat as if helpless; **wet suit** rubber garment worn by skin-divers etc. to keep warm; **wet through** (or **to the skin**) with clothes soaked. [OE]

wether /'weðə/ *n.* castrated ram. [OE]

Wg. Cdr. *abbr.* Wing Commander.

whack *colloq.* **1** *v.t.* strike or beat forcefully. **2** *n.* sharp or resounding blow; *sl.* share. **3 have a whack at** *sl.* attempt. [imit.]

whacked *a. colloq.* tired out.

whacking *sl.* **1** *a.* large. **2** *adv.* very (*great* etc.).

whale 1 *n.* fishlike marine mammal, esp. large one hunted for oil, whalebone, etc. **2** *v.i.* hunt whales. **3 a whale** *colloq.* very good *at* or keen *on*; **a whale of** *colloq.* an exceedingly good or fine etc.; **whale-oil** oil from blubber of whales. [OE]

whalebone *n.* elastic horny substance from upper jaw of some whales.

whaler *n.* whaling ship or seaman.

wham *int.* expressing forcible impact. [imit.]

wharf /wɔːf/ **1** *n.* (*pl.* **wharfs**) platform to which ship may be moored to load and unload. **2** *v.t.* moor (ship) at or store (goods) on wharf. [OE]

wharfage *n.* accommodation at wharf, fee for this.

wharfinger /'wɔːfɪndʒə/ *n.* owner or keeper of wharf.

what /wɒt/ **1** *a.* asking for choice from indefinite number or for statement of amount or number or kind (*what books have you read?*; *what news have you?*); *colloq.* = WHICH (*what book have you taken?*); how great or remarkable (*what a fool you are!*); the or any ... that (*lend me what money you can*). **2** *pron.* what thing or things? (*what is your name?*; *I don't know what you mean*); = *what did you say?* (asking for remark to be repeated); how much (*what he must have suffered!*); that or those which, a or the or any thing which (*what followed was worse*; *tell me what you think*). **3** *adv.* to what extent (*what does it matter?*). **4 what about** what is the news of or your opinion of; **what-d'you-call-it** substitute for name not recalled; **what ever** what at all or in any way (*what ever do you mean?*; see also WHATEVER); **what for?** for what reason? (**give person what for** severely scold him); **what have you** anything else similar; **what not** other similar things; **what's-his** (or **-its)-name** = *what-d'you-call-it*; **what's what** what is useful or important etc.; **what with** because of (usu. several things). [OE]

whatever /wɒt'evə/ *a.* & *pron.* = WHAT (in relative uses) with emphasis on indefiniteness (*lend me whatever you can, whatever money you can*); though anything (*we are safe whatever happens*); (with neg. or interrog.) at all, of any kind (*there is no doubt whatever*).

whatsoever /wɒtsəʊ'evə/ *a.* & *pron.* = WHATEVER.

wheat *n.* cereal bearing dense four-sided seed-spikes from which much bread is made; its grain. [OE]

wheatear *n.* a kind of small migratory bird. [WHITE, ARSE]

wheaten *a.* made of wheat. [OE]

wheatmeal *n.* wholemeal flour made from wheat.

wheedle /'wiːd(ə)l/ *v.t.* coax by flattery or endearments; get (thing) *out of* person or cheat (person) *out of* thing by wheedling. [orig. uncert.]

wheel 1 *n.* circular frame or disc arranged to revolve on axle and used to facilitate motion of vehicle or for various mechanical purposes; wheel-like thing; motion as of wheel, esp. movement of line of men with one end as pivot. **2** *v.* turn on axis or pivot, swing round in line with one end as pivot; (cause to) change direction or face another way (also with *round*); push or pull (wheeled thing esp. barrow or bicycle or pram, or its load or occupant); go in circles or curves. **3 at the wheel** driving a vehicle or directing a ship, in control of affairs; **on (oiled) wheels** smoothly; **wheel and deal** *US* engage in political or commercial scheming; **wheel-house** steersman's shelter; **wheel-spin** rotation of vehicle's wheels without traction; **wheels within wheels** intricate machinery, *fig.* indirect or secret agencies. [OE]

wheelbarrow *n.* shallow open box with shafts and one wheel for carrying loads etc.

wheelbase *n.* distance between axles of vehicle.

wheelchair *n.* invalid's chair on wheels.

wheelies *n.pl. colloq.* riding bicycle for short distance with front wheel off ground.

wheelwright *n.* maker of wheels.

wheeze 1 *v.i.* breathe with audible whistling sound. **2** *n.* sound of wheezing; *sl.* clever scheme, actor's interpolated joke etc. [ON, = hiss]

wheezy *a.* wheezing or sounding like a wheeze; **wheezily** *adv.*; **wheeziness** *n.*

whelk *n.* spiral-shelled marine mollusc. [OE]

whelm *v.t. poetic* engulf, crush with weight. [OE]

whelp 1 *n.* young dog, puppy; *archaic* cub; ill-mannered child or youth. **2** *v.i.* bring forth whelp(s) or (*derog.*) child. [OE]

when 1 *adv.* at what time?, on what occasion?, how soon?; (preceded by *time* etc.) at or on which (*there are times when I could laugh*). **2** *conj.* at the or any time that, as soon as (*come when you like*; *come when ready*); although (*walks when he could ride*); after which, and then, but just then (*I was about to leave when you called out*). **3** *pron.* what time? (*till when can you stay?*); which time (*since when it has been better*). **4** *n.* time, occasion (*fixed the where and when*). [OE]

whence 1 *adv.* from what place?; (preceded by *place* etc.) from which. **2** *conj.* to the place from which (*return whence you came*); and thence (*whence it follows that*). [OE (WHEN)]

whenever /wen'evə/ *conj.* & *adv.* at whatever time, on whatever occasion; every time that.

whensoever /wensəʊ'evə/ *conj.* & *adv.* = WHENEVER.

where /weə/ **1** *adv.* in or to what place or position?; in what direction or respect (*showed me where it concerns us*); (preceded by *place* etc.) in or to which (*places where they meet*). **2** *conj.* in or to the or any place or direction or respect in which (*go where you like*; *delete where applicable*); and there (*reached Crewe, where the car broke down*). **3** *pron.* what place? (*where do you come from?*). **4** *n.* place, scene of something (see WHEN **4**). [OE]

whereabouts 1 /weərə'baʊts/ *adv.* approximately where. **2** /'weərəbaʊts/ *n.* (as *sing.* or *pl.*) person's or thing's location roughly defined.

whereas /weər'æz/ *conj.* in contrast or comparison with the fact that; (esp. in legal preambles) taking into consideration the fact that.

whereby /weə'baɪ/ *conj.* by what or which means.

wherefore 1 *adv. archaic* for what reason?; for which reason. **2** *n.* reason (*the whys and wherefores*).

wherein /weər'ɪn/ *conj. formal* in what or which place or respect.

whereof /weər'ɒv/ *adv.* & *conj. formal* of what or which.

whereupon /weərə'pɒn/ *conj.* immediately after which.

wherever /weər'evə/ (also **wheresoever**) **1** *adv.* in or to whatever place. **2** *conj.* in every place that.

wherewithal /'weəwɪðɔ:l/ *n. colloq.* money etc. needed for a purpose.

wherry /'werɪ/ *n.* light rowing-boat usu. for carrying passengers; large light barge. [orig. unkn.]

whet *v.t.* (-tt-) sharpen (scythe etc., appetite or desire). [OE]

whether /'weðə/ *conj.* introducing the first or both of alternative possibilities (*I do not know whether he has come, whether he has come or not, whether he has come or whether he has stayed*; *I shall go whether or not you come with me*); **whether or no** whether it is so or not. [OE]

whetstone *n.* shaped stone for tool-sharpening. [WHET]

whew /hwju:/ *int.* expressing surprise, consternation, or relief. [imit.]

whey /weɪ/ *n.* watery liquid left when milk forms curds. [OE]

which 1 *a.* asking for choice from definite set of alternatives (*which Bob do you mean?*; *say which book you prefer*); being the one just referred to, and this or these (*ten years, during which time he spoke to nobody*). **2** *pron.* which person(s) or thing(s)? (*which of you is responsible?*; *say which you prefer*); which thing or things (*the house, which is empty, has been damaged*); used in relative sense in place of THAT after *in* or *that* (*there is the house in which I was born*; *that which you have just seen*). [OE]

whichever /wɪtʃ'evə/ *a.* & *pron.* any which (*take whichever* or *whichever one you like*).

whiff *n.* puff of air or smoke or odour; trace of scandal etc.; small cigar. [imit.]

Whig *n. hist.* member of the British reforming and constitutional party succeeded in mid-19th c. by Liberals; **Whiggery** *n.*; **Whiggish** *a.*; **Whiggism** *n.* [*whiggamores*, nickname of 17th-c. Sc. rebels]

while 1 *n.* space of time, time spent in some action (*a long while ago*; *waited a while*; *all this while*). **2** *conj.* during the time that, for as long as, at the same time as (*while I was in the bath burglars broke in*; *was drowned while bathing*); in spite of the fact that, at the same time (*while I want to believe it, I cannot*). **3** *v.t.* pass (time etc.) *away* in leisurely or interesting manner. **4** *adv.* (preceded by *time* etc.) during which (*the summer while I was abroad*). **5 between whiles** in the intervals; **for a while** for some time; **in a while** soon; **once in a while** occasionally; **the while** during some other action; **worth (one's) while** worth the time or effort spent. [OE]

whilom /'waɪləm/ *archaic* **1** *adv.* formerly. **2** *a.* former. [OE]

whilst /waɪlst/ *adv.* & *conj.* while. [WHILE]

whim *n.* sudden fancy, caprice. [orig. unkn.]

whimper 1 *v.i.* make feeble querulous or frightened sounds. 2 *n.* such sound. [imit.]

whimsical /ˈwɪmzɪk(ə)l/ *a.* capricious, fantastic; **whimsicality** /-ˈkælɪtɪ/ *n.*; **whimsically** *adv.* [foll.]

whimsy /ˈwɪmzɪ/ *n.* whim. [orig. uncert.]

whin *n.* (in *sing.* or *pl.*) furze. [Scand.]

whinchat *n.* a small songbird.

whine 1 *n.* dog's or child's long-drawn wail; similar shrill prolonged sound; querulous tone or talk. 2 *v.i.* emit or utter whine. [OE]

whinge /wɪndʒ/ *v.i.* whine, grumble peevishly. [OE]

whinny /ˈwɪnɪ/ 1 *n.* gentle or joyful neigh. 2 *v.i.* give whinny.

whip 1 *n.* lash attached to stick for urging on animals or punishing; person appointed to control discipline and tactics of MPs in his party, his written notice requesting attendance at division etc. (variously underlined according to degree of urgency: *three-line whip*), party discipline and instructions (*asked for the Labour whip*); food made with whipped cream etc.; = WHIPPER-IN. 2 *v.* (**-pp-**) strike or urge on with whip; beat (cream or eggs etc.) into froth; (with adverb or preposition) move suddenly or unexpectedly or rapidly (*whipped behind the door*; *whipped out a knife*); *sl.* excel, defeat; bind with spirally wound twine; sew with overcast stitches. 3 **have the whip hand** have advantage or control; **whip in** bring (hounds) together; **whip on** urge into action; **whip-round** *colloq.* appeal for contributions from a group of people; **whip up** incite, stir up. [LG or Du.]

whipcord *n.* tightly twisted cord.

whiplash *n.* lash of whip; **whiplash injury** injury to neck caused by jerk of head in collision.

whipper-in *n.* huntsman's assistant who manages hounds.

whipper-snapper /ˈwɪpəsnæpə/ *n.* small child; insignificant but presumptuous person.

whippet /ˈwɪpɪt/ *n.* cross-bred dog of greyhound type used for racing. [perh. *whippet* move briskly, f. *whip it*]

whipping-boy *n.* scapegoat; *hist.* boy educated with young prince and punished instead of him. [WHIP]

whipping-top *n.* top kept spinning by blows of lash.

whippoorwill /ˈwɪppʊəwɪl/ *n.* American nightjar. [imit.]

whippy *a.* flexible, springy; **whippiness** *n.* [WHIP]

whipstock *n.* handle of whip.

whirl 1 *v.* swing round and round, revolve rapidly; send or travel swiftly in orbit or curve; convey or go rapidly *away* etc. in car etc.; (of brain, senses, etc.) seem to spin round. 2 *n.* whirling movement; state of intense activity (*the social whirl*) or confusion (*my mind is in a whirl*). [ON & LG or Du.]

whirligig /ˈwɜːlɪgɪg/ *n.* spinning or whirling toy; merry-go-round; revolving motion.

whirlpool *n.* circular eddy of water.

whirlwind *n.* whirling mass or column of air; *attrib.* very rapid.

whirlybird /ˈwɜːlɪbɜːd/ *n. sl.* helicopter.

whirr 1 *n.* continuous rapid buzzing or softly clicking sound. 2 *v.i.* make this sound. [Scand.]

whisk 1 *v.* brush *away* or *off* with sweeping movement; whip (cream or eggs etc.); take *away* or *off* with sudden motion; convey or go (esp. out of sight) lightly or quickly; wave or lightly brandish. 2 *n.* utensil for whisking eggs or cream; bunch of grass, twigs, bristles, etc., to remove dust or flies; whisking motion. [Scand.]

whisker *n.* (usu. in *pl.*) hair of man's face, esp. on cheek; bristle(s) on face of cat etc.; *colloq.* small distance (*within a whisker of*). [f. prec.]

whiskey *Ir.* & *US* var. of WHISKY.

whisky /ˈwɪskɪ/ *n.* spirit distilled esp. from malted barley. [abbr. of *usquebaugh*, Gael. = water of life]

whisper 1 *v.* use breath instead of vocal cords, talk or say in barely audible tone or secret or confidential way; (of leaves or wind or water) rustle or murmur. 2 *n.* whispering speech or sound, thing whispered. 3 **it is whispered** there is a rumour. [OE]

whist *n.* a card-game usu. for four players; **whist drive** party for progressive whist. [alt. *whisk* with ref. to the silence (*whist!*) usual in the game]

whistle /ˈwɪs(ə)l/ 1 *n.* clear shrill sound made by forcing breath through small hole between nearly closed lips; similar sound made by bird or wind or missile or instrument; instrument used to produce it as signal etc. 2 *v.* emit whistle, give signal or express surprise or derision thus, summon or give signal to (dog etc.) thus, produce (tune) or produce tune thus. 3 **whistle for** *colloq.* seek or desire in vain; **whistle-stop** *US* small unimportant town on railway, politician's brief pause for electioneering speech on tour. [OE]

whit[1] *n.* particle, least possible amount (*not a whit better*). [app. = WIGHT]

Whit[2] *a.* connected with or belonging to or following Whit Sunday; **Whit Sunday** 7th Sunday after Easter, commemorating Pentecost. [OE, = white]

white 1 *a.* reflecting all light, of the colour of milk or fresh snow; approaching this condition, pale esp. in the face; (**White**) of the human group having light-coloured skin, of or reserved for such persons; albino (*white mouse*); (of hair) having lost its colour; *fig.* innocent, unstained. **2** *n.* white colour or pigment; white clothes or material (*dressed in white*); white ball or man in game, player of this; translucent or white part round yolk of egg; visible part of eyeball round iris; (**White**) White person. **3 bleed white** drain of wealth etc.; **white admiral** species of butterfly; **white ant** termite; **white cell** (or **corpuscle**) leucocyte; **white coffee** coffee with milk or cream; **white-collar** (of worker) not engaged in manual labour; **white elephant** useless possession; **white feather** symbol of cowardice; **white flag** symbol of surrender; **White Friar** Carmelite; **white-headed boy** highly favoured person; **white heat** temperature at which metal is white, state of intense passion or activity; **white hope** person expected to achieve much; **white horses** white-crested seawaves; **white-hot** at white heat; **white lead** mixture of lead carbonate and hydrated lead oxide used as pigment; **white lie** harmless or trivial untruth; **white light** colourless light, e.g. ordinary daylight; **white matter** fibrous part of brain and spinal cord; **white noise** noise containing many frequencies with about equal energies; **white-out** dense blizzard esp. in polar regions; **White Paper** Government report giving information; **white pepper** pepper made by grinding ripe or husked berry; **White Russian** native or inhabitant of Belorussia in western USSR; **white sale** sale of household linen; **white sauce** sauce of flour, melted butter, and milk or cream; **white slave** woman tricked or forced into prostitution; **white spirit** light petroleum as solvent; **white sugar** purified sugar; **white tie** man's white bow-tie in full evening dress; **white whale** northern whale, white when adult. [OE]

whitebait *n.* small silvery-white food-fish.

whiten *v.* make or become white.

whitewash 1 *n.* solution of lime or whiting for whitening walls etc.; concealing of mistakes or faults. **2** *v.t.* cover with whitewash; conceal mistakes or faults of or in.

whitewood *n.* light-coloured wood, esp. prepared for staining etc.

whither /ˈwɪðə/ *archaic* **1** *adv.* to what place or state?; (preceded by *place* etc.) to which. **2** *conj.* to the or any place to which (*go whither you will*); and thither.

whiting[1] *n.* small white-fleshed food-fish. [Du., rel. to WHITE]

whiting[2] *n.* (also **whitening**) ground chalk used in whitewashing, plate-cleaning, etc. [WHITE]

whitlow /ˈwɪtləʊ/ *n.* inflamed sore on finger. [orig. *white* FLAW[1]]

Whitsun /ˈwɪts(ə)n/ **1** *n.* = WHITSUNTIDE. **2** *a.* = WHIT[2]. [WHIT[2], SUN(DAY)]

Whitsuntide *n.* weekend or week including Whit Sunday.

whittle /ˈwɪt(ə)l/ *v.* pare (wood) with repeated slicings of knife, use knife thus (often *at* object); (often with *away* or *down*) reduce by repeated subtractions. [dial. *thwittle*]

whiz 1 *n.* sound made by body moving through air at great speed. **2** *v.i.* (**-zz-**) move with or make a whiz. **3 whiz-kid** *colloq.* brilliant or highly successful young person. [imit.]

who /hu:/ *pron.* (*obj.* **whom** /hu:m/, *colloq.* **who**; *poss.* **whose** /hu:z/) what or which person(s), what sort of person(s) (*who called?*; *you know who it was*; *who am I to object?*); (person) that (*anyone who wishes can come*; *the man whom*, colloq. *who, you saw*); and or but he, they, etc. (*gave it to Tom, who sold it to Jim*); **who's who** who or what each person is (*know who's who*), list with facts about notable persons. [OE]

WHO *abbr.* World Health Organization.

whoa /wəʊ/ *int.* used to stop horse etc. [HO]

whodunit /hu:ˈdʌnɪt/ *n. colloq.* detective or mystery story or play etc. [= *who done* (illiterate for *did*) *it?*]

whoever /hu:ˈevə/ *pron.* (*obj.* **whomever** /hu:mˈevə/, *colloq.* **whoever**; *poss.* **whosever** /hu:zˈevə/) the or any person(s) who (*whoever comes is welcome*); though anyone (*whoever else objects, I do not*). [WHO]

whole /həʊl/ **1** *a.* in uninjured or unbroken or intact or undiminished state; not less than, all there is of; (of blood or milk etc.) with no part removed. **2** *n.* thing complete in itself; all there is of thing; all members etc. *of.* **3 as a whole** as a unity, not as separate parts; **on the whole** taking everything relevant into account; **whole foods** foods not artificially processed or refined; **whole-hearted** completely devoted, done with all possible effort or sincerity; **a whole lot** *colloq.* a great amount; **whole number** number got by adding units, without fractions; **whole wheat** wheat not separated into parts by bolting. [OE]

wholemeal *n.* meal not deprived of constituents by bolting.

wholesale 1 *n.* selling of things in large quantities to be retailed by others. 2 *a.* & *adv.* by wholesale; on a large scale. 3 *v.t.* sell wholesale. [*by whole sale*]

wholesome /'həʊlsəm/ *a.* promoting physical or mental or moral health; prudent (*wholesome respect*). [OE (WHOLE)]

wholly /'həʊllɪ/ *adv.* entirely, without limitation, purely.

whom *pron.* obj. case of WHO.

whoop /hu:p, wu:p/ 1 *n.* loud cry (as) of excitement etc.; long rasping indrawn breath in whooping cough. 2 *v.i.* utter whoop. 3 **whooping cough** infectious bacterial disease, esp. of children, with short violent cough followed by whoop; **whoop it up** *colloq.* engage in revelry, *US* make a stir. [imit.]

whoopee /wʊ'pi:/ *int.* expressing exuberant joy; **make whoopee** /'wʊpɪ/ *colloq.* rejoice noisily or hilariously. [imit.]

whoops /wʊps/ *int.* on making obvious mistake or losing balance.

whop *v.t.* (**-pp-**) *sl.* thrash, defeat. [orig. unkn.]

whopper *n. sl.* big specimen, great lie.

whopping *a. sl.* very big.

whore /hɔ:/ *n.* prostitute; sexually immoral woman; **whore-house** brothel. [OE]

whorl /wɜ:l/ *n.* ring of leaves round stem; one turn of spiral. [app. var. of WHIRL]

whortleberry /'wɜ:t(ə)lberɪ/ *n.* bilberry. [orig. unkn.]

whose /hu:z/ 1 *pron.* of or belonging to which person (*whose is this book?*). 2 *a.* of whom (*whose book is this?*; *the man, whose name was Tim*).

whosoever /hu:səʊ'evə/ *pron.* (*obj.* **whomsoever** /hu:msəʊ'evə/; *poss.* **whosesoever** /hu:zsəʊ'evə/) = WHOEVER. [OE]

why /waɪ/ 1 *adv.* for what reason or purpose (*why are you tired?*; *don't know why he came*); (preceded by *reason* etc.) for which (*reasons why he did it*). 2 *int.* expressing surprised discovery or recognition (*why, it's you!*), impatience (*why, of course I do*), reflection (*why, yes, I think so*), objection (*why, what is wrong with it?*), etc. 3 *n.* reason. [OE]

WI *abbr.* West Indies; Women's Institute.

wick *n.* strip or thread feeding flame with fuel. [OE]

wicked /'wɪkɪd/ *a.* sinful, iniquitous, immoral; spiteful; playfully malicious; *colloq.* very bad. [orig. uncert.]

wicker *n.* plaited osiers etc. as material for baskets etc. [Scand.]

wickerwork *n.* wicker, things made of this.

wicket /'wɪkɪt/ *n.* small door or gate esp. beside or in larger one or closing lower part only of doorway; (in cricket) three stumps with bails in position defended by batsman, ground between two wickets, state of this, batsman's avoidance of being out; **wicket-keeper** fieldsman stationed close behind batsman's wicket. [AF *wiket* = F *guichet*]

wide 1 *a.* having sides far apart, broad, not narrow (*wide river, sleeve, angle*); extending far, not restricted (*wide experience, range*); open to full extent (*wide eyes*); far from target etc., not within reasonable distance *of* (*wide shot, wide of target*); (appended to measurement) in width (*3ft. wide*); (as *suffix*) extending to whole of (*world-wide*). 2 *adv.* widely, to full extent (*open your mouth wide, wide awake*); far from target etc. (*shot wide*). 3 *n.* wide ball. 4 **give a wide berth to** see BERTH; **to the wide** completely; **wide awake** *colloq.* wary, knowing; **wide ball** (in cricket) one judged by umpire to be beyond batsman's reach; **wide-eyed** surprised, naïve; **wide of the mark** incorrect, irrelevant; **wide open** exposed (*to* attack etc.); **the wide world** all the world as great as it is. [OE]

widen *v.* make or become wider.

widespread *a.* widely distributed.

widgeon /'wɪdʒ(ə)n/ *n.* a kind of wild duck. [orig. uncert.]

widow /'wɪdəʊ/ 1 *n.* woman who has lost her husband by death and not married again. 2 *v.t.* make into widow or widower; (in *p.p.*) bereft by death of husband or wife. 3 **widowhood** *n.* [OE]

widower *n.* man who has lost his wife by death and not married again.

width *n.* measurement from side to side; strip of material of full width; large extent; liberality of views etc.; **widthways** *adv.* [WIDE]

wield *v.t.* control, command, hold and use (*power, sceptre, a formidable pen,* etc.). [OE]

Wiener schnitzel /'vi:nə 'ʃnɪts(ə)l/ veal cutlet breaded, fried, and garnished. [G]

wife *n.* (*pl.* **wives**) married woman esp. in relation to her husband (*my wife, is a* *good wife*); *archaic* woman. [OE, = woman]

wifely *a.* befitting a wife.

wig[1] *n.* artificial head of hair. [abbr. of PERIWIG]

wig[2] *v.t.* (**-gg-**) *colloq.* rebuke sharply (esp. *a wigging*). [orig. uncert.]

wigeon var. of WIDGEON.

wiggle /ˈwɪg(ə)l/ *colloq.* **1** *v.* (cause to) move from side to side. **2** *n.* act of wiggling. **3 wiggly** *a.* [LG or Du. *wiggelen*]

wight /waɪt/ *n. archaic* a person. [OE, = creature, thing]

wigwam /ˈwɪgwæm/ *n.* N. American Indian's hut or tent. [Ojibwa]

wilco /ˈwɪlkəʊ/ *int.* expressing compliance or agreement. [abbr. *will comply*]

wild /waɪld/ **1** *a.* in original natural state, not civilized or domesticated or cultivated or populated (*wild cat, strawberry, landscape*); tempestuous, unrestrained, disorderly, uncontrolled (*wild night, hair, confusion*); intensely eager, frantic (*wild delight, enthusiasm*); *colloq.* infuriated; haphazard, ill-aimed, rash (*wild guess, shot, venture*). **2** *adv.* in wild manner. **3** *n.* wild tract, desert. **4 in the wilds** *colloq.* far from towns etc.; **run wild** grow or stray unchecked or undisciplined; **sow one's wild oats** indulge in youthful follies before maturity; **wild about** enthusiastically devoted to; **wild-goose chase** foolish or hopeless quest; **Wild West** western US in time of lawlessness. [OE]

wildcat **1** *n.* hot-tempered or violent person. **2** *a.* reckless, financially unsound; (of strike) sudden and unofficial.

wildebeest /ˈwɪldəbi:st/ *n.* gnu. [Afrik. (WILD, BEAST)]

wilderness /ˈwɪldənɪs/ *n.* desert, uncultivated region; confused assemblage *of*; **voice in the wilderness** unheeded advocate of reform. [OE (WILD, DEER)]

wildfire *n. hist.* combustible liquid used in war; **spread like wildfire** spread with extraordinary speed. [WILD]

wildfowl *n.* game-bird(s).

wildlife *n.* wild animals collectively.

wile **1** *n.* (usu. in *pl.*) stratagem, trick. **2** *v.t.* lure *away, into*, etc. [perh. Scand.]

wilful /ˈwɪlfʊl/ *a.* intentional, deliberate (*wilful murder, waste, disobedience*); obstinate, headstrong; **wilfully** *adv.* [WILL]

will **1** *v. aux.* (3 *sing. pres.* **will**; *past* WOULD) expressing future statement or order (strictly only in second and third persons: cf. SHALL; *you will regret this*; *you will leave at once*); expressing speaker's intention (*I will return soon*). **2** *v.t.* wish or desire (*come when you will*; *will you have a sweet*); choose or have tendency or custom (*will sit there for hours*; *boys will be boys*). **3** *v.t.* (with regular forms **wills, willed**, etc.) intend unconditionally, impel by will-power; bequeath by will. **4** *n.* faculty by which one decides what to do; fixed desire or intention (*will to live*); determination to implement one's wishes (*has a strong will*); arbitrary discretion; disposition towards others (*ill will*); written directions in legal form for disposition of one's property after death; *archaic* what is desired or ordained by person. **5 at will** whenever one wishes; **will-power** control by deliberate purpose over impulse; **with a will** vigorously. [OE]

willful *US* var. of WILFUL.

willies /ˈwɪlɪz/ *n.pl. sl.* nervous discomfort (*gives me the willies*). [orig. unkn.]

willing **1** *a.* ready to consent or undertake; given or done etc. by willing person. **2** *n.* cheerful intention (*show willing*). [WILL]

will-o'-the-wisp /wɪləðəˈwɪsp/ *n.* phosphorescent light seen on marshy ground; elusive person. [= *William of the torch*]

willow /ˈwɪləʊ/ *n.* waterside tree with pliant branches yielding osiers and timber for cricket-bats; **willow-herb** plant with leaves like willow; **willow-pattern** conventional Chinese design of blue on white china etc. [OE]

willowy *a.* having willows; lithe and slender.

willy-nilly /wɪlɪˈnɪlɪ/ *adv.* whether one likes it or not. [= *will I, nill* (obs. for *will not*) *I*]

wilt **1** *v.* (cause to) wither, droop. **2** *n.* plant-disease causing wilting. [orig. dial.]

wily /ˈwaɪlɪ/ *a.* crafty, cunning; **wilily** *adv.*; **wiliness** *n.* [WILE]

wimple /ˈwɪmp(ə)l/ *n.* linen or silk headdress covering neck and sides of face, worn now by nuns. [OE]

win **1** *v.* (**-nn-**; *past* & *p.p.* **won** /wʌn/) secure as result of fight or contest or bet or effort; be victorious in (fight etc.); be the victor, make one's way or become (*through, free*, etc.) by successful effort. **2** *n.* victory in game. **3 win over** persuade, gain support of; **win one's spurs** *hist.* gain knighthood, *fig.* gain distinction or fame; **win the day** be victorious in battle (*lit.* or *fig.*); **win through** (or **out**) overcome obstacles; **you can't win** *colloq.* there is no way to succeed. [OE, = toil]

wince **1** *n.* start or involuntary shrinking movement showing pain or distress. **2** *v.i.* give wince. [AF f. Gmc, rel. to WINK]

wincey /ˈwɪnsɪ/ *n.* lightweight fabric of

wool and cotton or linen. [app. alt. *woolsey* in LINSEY-WOOLSEY]

winceyette /wɪnsɪ'et/ *n.* lightweight napped flannelette.

winch 1 *n.* crank of wheel or axle; windlass. **2** *v.t.* lift with winch. [OE]

wind[1] **1** *n.* air in natural motion; scent carried by this and indicating presence; artificially produced air-current esp. for sounding a wind instrument, air (to be) so used, wind instruments in orchestra etc.; breath as needed in exertion or speech, power of breathing without difficulty; point below centre of chest where blow temporarily paralyses breathing; gas generated in bowels; empty talk. **2** *v.t.* exhaust wind of by exertion or blow, renew wind of by rest; make breathe quick and deep by exercise; detect presence of by scent. **3 get wind of** begin to suspect; **get** (or **have**) **the wind up** *sl.* become (or be) frightened; **in the wind** about to happen; **like the wind** swiftly; **put the wind up** *sl.* alarm, frighten; **take the wind out of person's sails** frustrate him by anticipating his action or remark; **wind-break** row of trees etc. to break force of wind; **wind-cheater** jacket designed to give protection against wind; **wind instrument** musical instrument sounded by blowing of air-current; **wind-jammer** merchant sailing-ship; **wind-sock** canvas cylinder or cone on mast to show direction of wind; **wind-swept** exposed to high winds; **wind-tunnel** tunnel-like device to produce air-stream past models of aircraft etc. for study of wind effects. [OE]

wind[2] /waɪnd/ **1** *v.* (*past* & *p.p.* **wound**) go in spiral or curved or crooked course; make (one's way) thus; coil, wrap closely, provide with coiled thread etc.; surround (as) with coil; wind up (clock etc.). **2** *n.* bend or turn in course; single turn when winding. **3 wind down** unwind (*lit.* or *fig.*), lower by winding; **winding-sheet** sheet in which corpse is wrapped for burial; **wind off** unwind; **wind up** coil whole of, tighten coiling or coiled spring of or *fig.* tension or intensity of, bring to a conclusion, end, arrange affairs of and dissolve (company), *colloq.* arrive finally. [OE]

windbag *n. colloq.* person who says much of little value. [WIND[1]]

windfall *n.* fruit blown to the ground by the wind; unexpected good fortune, esp. a legacy.

windlass /'wɪndləs/ *n.* machine with horizontal axle for hauling or hoisting. [AF f. ON, = winding-pole]

windmill *n.* mill worked by wind acting on its sails; **tilt at windmills** attack imaginary enemy. [WIND[1]]

window /'wɪndəʊ/ *n.* opening in wall etc. usu. with glass for admission of light etc.; the glass itself; space for display behind window of shop; window-like opening; **window-box** box placed outside window for cultivating ornamental plants; **window-dressing** art of arranging display in shop-window etc., *fig.* adroit presentation of facts etc. to give falsely favourable impression; **window envelope** envelope with opening or transparent part allowing address inside to show; **window-shopping** looking at goods displayed in shop-windows without buying anything. [ON, = wind-eye]

windpipe *n.* air-passage from throat to lungs. [WIND[1]]

windscreen *n.* screen of glass at front of motor vehicle.

Windsurfer *n.* **(P)** board like surfboard with sail; **(windsurfer)** one engaged in windsurfing.

windsurfing *n.* sport of riding on Windsurfer.

windward /'wɪndwəd/ **1** *a.* & *adv.* in the direction from which the wind is blowing. **2** *n.* windward direction. **3 get to windward of** place oneself there to avoid smell of or *fig.* gain advantage over. [WIND[1]]

windy *a.* exposed to or stormy with wind; generating or characterized by flatulence; wordy; *sl.* nervous, frightened; **windily** *adv.*; **windiness** *n.* [OE (WIND[1])]

wine 1 *n.* fermented grape-juice as alcoholic drink, fermented drink resembling it made from other fruits etc.; dark red colour of red wine. **2** *v.* drink wine; entertain to wine. **3 wine-bibber** tippler; **wine-cellar** cellar for storing wine, its contents. [OE]

wineglass *n.* glass for wine, usu. with stem and foot.

winepress *n.* press in which grapes are squeezed in making wine.

winesap *n.* large red American winter apple.

wineskin *n.* whole skin of goat etc. sewn up and used to hold wine.

wing 1 *n.* one of the limbs or organs by which flying is effected; winglike supporting part of aircraft; projecting part of building, battle array, etc.; (in *pl.*) sides of theatre stage; (in football etc.) player at either end of line, side part of playing area; extreme section of political party; mudguard of motor vehicle; air-force unit of several squadrons or groups. **2** *v.* travel or traverse on wings; equip with wings, enable to fly, send in flight; wound in wing or arm. **3 on the wing** flying; **spread one's wings** develop one's powers fully; **take wing** fly away; **take under one's wing** treat as protégé; **wing-case** horny cover of insect's wing; **wing-chair** one with side pieces at top of high back; **wing-collar** man's high stiff collar with turned-down corners; **wing commander** RAF officer next below group captain; **wing-nut** nut with projections for fingers to turn it on screw; **wing-span** (or **-spread**) measurement right across wings. [ON]

winger *n.* (in football etc.) wing player.

wink 1 *v.* close and open (eye or eyes), wink eye(s), wink one eye to convey message to or *at* person; (of light) twinkle. **2** *n.* act of winking; short sleep. **3 tip person the wink** give (person) information privately; **wink at** purposely avoid seeing, pretend not to notice. [OE]

winker *n.* flashing indicator on motor vehicle.

winkle /'wɪŋk(ə)l/ **1** *n.* small edible sea snail. **2** *v.t.* (with *out*) extract or eject. **3 winkle-picker** *sl.* long pointed shoe. [abbr. of PERIWINKLE²]

winner *n.* one who wins; successful thing. [WIN]

winning 1 *a.* having or bringing victory; attractive (*a winning smile*). **2** *n.* (in *pl.*) money won. **3 winning-post** post marking end of race.

winnow /'wɪnəʊ/ *v.t.* blow (grain) free of chaff etc. by air-current, blow (chaff etc.) *out* or *away* or *from* (often *fig.* of sifting evidence etc.). [OE (WIND¹)]

wino /'waɪnəʊ/ *n.* (*pl.* **winos**) *sl.* an alcoholic. [WINE]

winsome /'wɪnsəm/ *a.* (of person or looks or manner) winning, engaging. [OE, = joyous]

winter 1 *n.* coldest and last season of the year. **2** *a.* characteristic of or fit for winter. **3** *v.i.* pass winter (*at* or *in* place). **4 winter garden** garden or conservatory of plants flourishing in winter; **winter-green** a kind of plant remaining green all winter; **winter sports** sports performed on snow or ice, e.g. skiing. [OE]

wintry *a.* characteristic of winter, lacking warmth; **wintriness** *n.*

winy *a.* wine-flavoured. [WINE]

wipe 1 *v.* clean or dry surface of by rubbing; rub (cloth) over surface; put (liquid etc.) on to surface by rubbing; clear or remove by wiping (often with *away* or *off* etc.). **2** *n.* act of wiping. **3 wipe the floor with** *sl.* inflict humiliating defeat on; **wipe off** annul (debt); **wipe out** avenge (insult etc.), destroy, annihilate. [OE]

wiper *n.* device for keeping windscreen clear of rain etc.

wire 1 *n.* metal drawn out into slender flexible rod or thread, piece of this; length of wire used for fencing or to carry electric current, etc.; *colloq.* telegram. **2** *v.* provide, fasten, strengthen, with wire; *colloq.* telegraph. **3 get one's wires crossed** become confused and misunderstand; **wire-haired** (esp. of dog) with stiff or wiry hair; **wire netting** netting of wire twisted into meshes; **wire-tapping** tapping of telephone wires; **wire wool** mass of fine wire for cleaning; **wire-worm** destructive larva of a beetle. [OE]

wireless *n.* radio, radio receiving set.

wiring *n.* system of wires providing electrical circuits.

wiry *a.* tough and flexible as wire, sinewy, untiring; **wirily** *adv.*; **wiriness** *n.*

wisdom /'wɪzdəm/ *n.* experience and knowledge together with power of applying them; sagacity, prudence, common sense; wise sayings; **wisdom tooth** hindmost molar usu. cut at about 20 years of age. [OE (foll.)]

wise¹ /waɪz/ *a.* having or showing or dictated by wisdom, having knowledge, suggestive of wisdom; *US sl.* alert, crafty; **be** (or **get**) **wise to** *sl.* become aware of; **none the wiser** knowing no more than before; **put wise** (**to**) *sl.* inform (of); **wise after the event** (of person) who explains but has failed to foresee; **wise man** wizard, esp. one of the Magi. [OE]

wise² /waɪz/ *n. archaic* way or manner or degree; **in no wise** not at all. [OE]

-wise /waɪz/ *suffix* forming adjectives and adverbs of manner (*crosswise, clockwise, lengthwise*) or respect (*moneywise*).

wiseacre /'waɪzeɪkə/ *n.* one who affects to be wise. [Du. *wijsseggher* soothsayer]

wisecrack *colloq.* **1** *a.* smart pithy remark. **2** *v.i.* make wisecrack. [WISE¹]

wish 1 *v.* have or express desire or aspiration *for* (*wish for happiness*); have as desire or aspiration (*I wish* (*that*) *I could sing*); want or demand (*wish to see him, it done* or *to be done*); be inclined *well* or *ill* to person (*wish her well*); say one hopes for (specified fortune) to happen to someone (*wish you success, a pleasant journey*); *colloq.* foist (*up*)*on* person. **2** *n.* desire or request, expression of this; thing desired. **3 best** (or **good**) **wishes** hopes felt or expressed for another's happiness etc.; **wish-fulfilment** tendency for subconscious desire to be satisfied in fantasy. [OE]

wishbone *n.* forked bone between neck and breast of bird, object of similar shape.

wishful *a.* desiring (*to do* thing); **wish-**

ful thinking belief founded on wishes rather than facts; **wishfully** *adv.*

wishy-washy /ˈwɪʃɪwɒʃɪ/ *a.* feeble in quality or character. [WASH]

wisp *n.* small bundle or twist of straw etc.; small separate quantity of smoke or hair etc.; small thin person; **wispy** *a.* [orig. uncert.]

wistaria /wɪˈstɪərɪə/ *n.* (also **wisteria**) climbing shrub with blue, purple, or white hanging flowers. [*Wistar*, anatomist]

wistful *a.* yearningly or mournfully expectant or wishful; **wistfully** *adv.* [app. assim. of obs. *wistly* 'intently' to *wishful*]

wit 1 *n.* intelligence, quick understanding (in *sing.* or *pl.*); unexpected combining or contrasting of ideas or expressions, power of giving pleasure by this; person possessing such power. **2** *v.* (*sing. pres.* **wot**; *past* & *p.p.* **wist**; *partic.* **witting**) *archaic* know. **3 at one's wit's** (or **wits'**) **end** utterly at a loss or in despair; **have** (or **keep**) **one's wits about one** be alert; **live by one's wits** live by ingenious or crafty expedients, without settled occupation; **out of one's wits** mad; **to wit** that is to say, namely. [OE]

witch *n.* sorceress, woman supposed to have dealings with devil or evil spirits; old hag; fascinating girl or woman; **witch-doctor** tribal magician of primitive people; **witches' sabbath** supposed midnight orgy of the Devil and witches; **witch-hunt** search for and persecution of supposed witches or persons suspected of unpopular or unorthodox views. [OE]

witchcraft *n.* use of magic.

witchery *n.* witchcraft, power exercised by beauty or eloquence or the like.

with /wɪð/ *prep.* expressing instrumentality or means (*cut with a knife*), cause (*shiver with fear*), possession (*man with red hair*), circumstances (*sleep with the window open*), manner (*behave with courage*), material (*made with gold*), agreement and disagreement (*sympathize with*; *incompatible with*); company and parting of company (*mix with*; *dispense with*); antagonism (*quarrel with*); **in** (or **out** etc.) **with** take or send or put (person or thing) in (or out etc.); **with it** *colloq.* up to date, conversant with modern ideas etc.; **with that** thereupon. [OE]

withal /wɪˈðɔːl/ *archaic* **1** *adv.* moreover, as well. **2** *prep.* (placed later than its expressed or omitted object) with (*what shall he fill his belly withal?*). [WITH, ALL]

withdraw /wɪðˈdrɔː/ *v.* (*past* **withdrew** /wɪðˈdruː/; *p.p.* **withdrawn** /wɪðˈdrɔːn/) pull or take aside or back; discontinue, cancel, remove, take away; retract; retire or go apart; (in *p.p.*) unsociable; **withdrawal** *n.* [WITH = away]

withe /wɪθ, wɪð, waɪð/ *n.* tough flexible shoot used for tying bundle of wood etc. [OE]

wither /ˈwɪðə/ *v.* make or become dry and shrivelled; deprive of or lose vigour or freshness; blight with scorn etc. [app. var. of WEATHER]

withers /ˈwɪðəz/ *n.pl.* ridge between horse's shoulder-blades. [obs. *wither* against (the collar)]

withershins /ˈwɪðəʃɪnz/ *adv.* (esp. *Sc.*) contrary to the sun's course (and hence unlucky). [G, = contrary direction]

withhold /wɪðˈhəʊld/ *v.t.* (*past* & *p.p.* **withheld**) hold back, restrain; refuse to give or grant or allow. [WITH = away]

within /wɪˈðɪn/ **1** *adv.* inside, indoors. **2** *prep.* inside, not out of or beyond; not transgressing or exceeding; not further off than (*within two miles, ten days*). **3 within one's grasp** close enough to be grasped or obtained; **within reach** (or **sight**) **of** near enough to be reached (or seen). [OE (WITH, IN)]

without /wɪˈðaʊt/ **1** *prep.* not having or feeling or showing; with freedom from; in absence of; with neglect or avoidance of; *archaic* outside. **2** *adv. archaic* outside, out-of-doors. [OE (WITH, OUT)]

withstand /wɪðˈstænd/ *v.t.* (*past* & *p.p.* **withstood** /wɪðˈstʊd/) oppose, hold out against. [OE (WITH, STAND)]

withy /ˈwɪðɪ/ *n.* = WITHE.

witless *a.* foolish, crazy. [WIT]

witness /ˈwɪtnɪs/ **1** *n.* person giving sworn testimony; person attesting another's signature to a document; person present, spectator; testimony, evidence, confirmation; person or thing whose existence etc. serves as testimony *to* or proof *of*. **2** *v.* be witness to authenticity of (document or signature); be spectator of; serve as evidence or indication of; be witness *against* or *for* or *to*. **3 bear witness to** (or **of**) attest truth of; **call to witness** appeal to for confirmation etc.; **witness-box** (or *US* **-stand**) enclosure in lawcourt from which witness gives evidence. [OE (WIT)]

witter *v.i. colloq.* speak with annoying lengthiness on trivial matters. [orig. unkn.]

witticism /ˈwɪtɪsɪz(ə)m/ *n.* witty remark. [WITTY]

wittingly /ˈwɪtɪŋlɪ/ *adv.* with knowledge of what one is doing. [WIT]

witty /ˈwɪtɪ/ *a.* showing verbal wit; **wittily** *adv.*; **wittiness** *n.* [OE (WIT)]

wives *pl.* of WIFE.

wizard /ˈwɪzəd/ **1** *n.* person of extra-

ordinary powers, genius; magician, conjurer. **2** *a. sl.* wonderful. **3 wizardry** *n.* [WISE[1]]
wizened /'wɪz(ə)nd/ *a.* (of person or face etc.) shrivelled-looking. [OE]
WNW *abbr.* west-north-west.
WO *abbr.* Warrant Officer.
woad *n.* plant yielding a blue dye; the dye itself.
wobble /'wɒb(ə)l/ **1** *v.i.* sway from side to side, stand or go unsteadily, stagger; waver, vacillate. **2** *n.* wobbling motion; rocking movement. **3 wobbly** *a.* [cf. LG *wab(b)eln*]
wodge *n. colloq.* chunk, lump. [alt. f. WEDGE]
woe *n.* affliction, bitter grief, (in *pl.*) calamities; **woe betide** see BETIDE; **woe is me** alas. [OE]
woebegone /'wəʊbɪgɒn/ *a.* dismal-looking. [WOE, *begone* = surrounded]
woeful *a.* feeling affliction, afflicting; very bad; **woefully** *adv.* [WOE]
wog *n. sl.* (**R**) native of Middle East; foreigner. [orig. unkn.]
wok *n.* bowl-shaped frying-pan used esp. in Chinese cookery. [Chin.]
woke *past* of WAKE[1].
woken *p.p.* of WAKE[1].
wold /wəʊld/ *n.* high open uncultivated or moorland tract. [OE]
wolf /wʊlf/ **1** *n.* (*pl.* **wolves**) wild animal related to dog, preying on sheep etc. and hunting in packs. **2** *v.t.* devour greedily (*down*). **3 cry wolf** raise false alarm; **keep the wolf from the door** avert starvation; **wolf in sheep's clothing** hypocrite; **wolf-whistle** whistle by man sexually admiring woman. [OE]
wolfhound *n.* dog of kind used (orig.) to hunt wolves.
wolfram /'wʊlfrəm/ *n.* tungsten (ore). [G]
wolfsbane *n.* aconite. [WOLF]
wolverine /'wʊlvəri:n/ *n.* N. American animal of weasel family.
woman /'wʊmən/ *n.* (*pl.* **women** /'wɪmɪn/) adult human female; the female sex; feminine emotions; *attrib.* female (*woman doctor*); (as *suffix*) woman concerned or dealing or skilful with or describable as (*countrywoman, needlewoman, Welshwoman*); *colloq.* charwoman; **Women's Lib** movement urging liberation of women from domestic duties and subservient status; **women's rights** position of legal and social equality with men. [OE]
womanhood *n.* female maturity; womanly instinct; womankind.
womanish *a.* effeminate, unmanly.
womanize *v.i.* philander, consort illicitly with women.
womankind *n.* (also **womenkind**) women in general.
womanly *a.* having or showing qualities befitting a woman; **womanliness** *n.*
womb /wu:m/ *n.* organ of conception and gestation in woman and other female mammals. [OE]
wombat /'wɒmbæt/ *n.* burrowing herbivorous Australian marsupial. [Aboriginal]
women *pl.* of WOMAN.
womenfolk *n.* women in general; women in family. [WOMAN]
won *past* & *p.p.* of WIN.
wonder /'wʌndə/ **1** *n.* strange or remarkable thing or specimen or event etc.; emotion excited by what is unexpected or unfamiliar or inexplicable. **2** *v.* be filled with wonder or great surprise; be surprised to find (*that*); desire or be curious to know (*wonder who it was*). **3 I wonder** I very much doubt it; **no** (or **small**) **wonder** this event is quite natural; **work** (or **do**) **wonders** do miracles, succeed remarkably. [OE]
wonderful *a.* very remarkable or admirable; **wonderfully** *adv.* [OE]
wonderland *n.* fairyland; land of surprises or marvels.
wonderment *n.* surprise.
wondrous /'wʌndrəs/ *poetic* **1** *a.* wonderful. **2** *adv.* wonderfully.
wonky /'wɒŋkɪ/ *a. sl.* crooked; unsteady, loose; unreliable. [fanciful]
won't /wəʊnt/ *colloq.* = *will not.*
wont *archaic* **1** *predic. a.* accustomed (*to do* thing). **2** *n.* what is customary, one's habit. [OE]
wonted *attrib. a.* habitual, usual.
woo *v.t.* court, seek the hand or love of; try to win (fame, fortune, etc.); coax or importune *to*. [OE]
wood /wʊd/ *n.* hard fibrous substance in trunks and branches of tree or shrub, timber or fuel of this; (in *sing.* or *pl.*) growing trees densely occupying a tract of land; wooden cask for wine etc.; wooden-headed golf-club; = BOWL[2]; **cannot see the wood for the trees** fail to grasp main issue from over-attention to details; **out of the wood** out of danger or difficulty; **wood-louse** small land crustacean with many legs; **wood-pigeon** ring-dove; **wood-pulp** wood fibres prepared for paper-making; **wood-shed** shed where wood for fuel is stored. [OE]
woodbine *n.* honeysuckle.
woodchuck *n.* N. American marmot.
woodcock *n.* game-bird related to snipe.
woodcut *n.* relief cut on wood; print made from this.

wooded *a.* having woods or many trees.
wooden *a.* made of wood; like wood; stiff or clumsy, expressionless; **wooden-headed** stupid; **woodenness** *n.*
woodland *n.* wooded country, woods.
woodman *n.* forester.
woodpecker *n.* bird that taps tree-trunks in search of insects.
woodpile *n.* pile of wood, esp. for fuel.
woodruff *n.* a white-flowered plant with fragrant leaves.
woodwind *n.* orchestral wind instruments made (orig.) of wood.
woodwork *n.* making of things in wood; things made of wood.
woodworm *n.* beetle larva that bores in wood.
woody *a.* wooded; like or of wood; **woody nightshade** a kind of nightshade with poisonous red berries; **woodiness** *n.*
woof[1] /wʊf/ **1** *n.* gruff bark of dog. **2** *v.i.* give woof. [imit.]
woof[2] /wu:f/ *n.* = WEFT. [OE (WEB)]
woofer /ˈwʊfə/ *n.* loudspeaker for low frequencies. [WOOF[1]]
wool /wʊl/ *n.* fine soft wavy hair from fleece of sheep etc., woollen yarn or cloth or garments, wool-like substance; **pull the wool over person's eyes** deceive him; **wool-gathering** absent-mindedness. [OE]
woollen, *US* **woolen** **1** *a.* made wholly or partly of wool. **2** *n.* woollen fabric; (in *pl.*) woollen garments. [OE]
woolly **1** *a.* bearing wool, like wool; (of sound) indistinct; (of thought) vague or confused. **2** *n. colloq.* woollen (esp. knitted) garment. **3** **woolly-bear** large hairy caterpillar. **4** **woolliness** *n.* [WOOL]
Woolsack *n.* Lord Chancellor's wool-stuffed seat in House of Lords; his position.
wop *sl.* **(R)** South-European (esp. Italian) immigrant in US. [orig. unkn.]
Worcester sauce /ˈwʊstə/ a pungent sauce. [*Worcester* in England]
word /wɜ:d/ **1** *n.* meaningful element of speech usu. shown with space on either side of it when written or printed; speech, esp. as distinct from action; one's promise or assurance; (in *sing.* or *pl.*) thing said, remark, conversation; (in *pl.*) text of song or actor's part; (in *pl.*) angry talk; news, message; command, password, motto; unit of expression in computer. **2** *v.t.* put into words, select words to express. **3** **the Word (of God)** the Bible; **in a** (or **one**) **word** briefly; **in other words** expressing the same thing differently; **in so many words** explicitly, bluntly; **take person's word for it** believe his statement without investigation etc.; **take person at his word** act on assumption that he meant exactly what he said; **(upon) my word** exclamation of surprise or consternation; **word-blindness** = DYSLEXIA; **word for word** in exactly the same or (of translation) corresponding words; **word-game** game involving making or selection etc. of words; **word of honour** assurance given upon one's honour; **word of mouth** speech (only); **word-perfect** knowing one's part etc. by heart; **word processor** device for storing text entered from keyboard, incorporating corrections, and providing printout. [OE]
wording *n.* form of words used.
wordy *a.* using many or too many words; consisting of words; **wordily** *adv.*; **wordiness** *n.*
wore *past* of WEAR.
work /wɜ:k/ **1** *n.* application of mental or physical effort to a purpose, use of energy; task to be undertaken, the materials for this; thing done or made by work, result of action; employment or occupation etc., esp. as means of earning income; literary or musical composition, (in *pl.*) all such by an author or composer etc.; doings or experiences of specified kind (*good work!*); things made of specified material or with specified tools etc. (*ironwork*; *needlework*); (in *pl.*) operative part of clock or machine, *sl.* all that is available; (in *pl.*) operations of building or repair (*road works*); (in *pl.*, often treated as *sing.*) place of manufacture; *Theol.* (usu. in *pl.*) meritorious act; (usu. in *pl.* or in *comb.*) defensive structure (*earthwork*). **2** *v.* do work, be engaged in bodily or mental activity; be employed in certain work (*works in industry*; *works as a secretary*); make efforts (*works for peace*); be craftsman (*in material*); operate or function, esp. effectively (*how does this machine work?*; *cannot make it work*; *idea will not work*); carry on, manage, control (*work a mine*); put or keep in operation or at work, cause to toil (*works his staff hard*); bring about, produce as result (*worked miracles*); knead, hammer, bring to desired shape or consistency; do, or make by, needlework etc.; (cause to) progress or penetrate, or make (one's way), gradually or with difficulty in specified way (*worked his way through the crowd*; *work it into the mixture*); gradually become (*loose* etc.) by constant movement; artificially excite (*worked himself into a rage*); solve (sum) by mathematics; purchase with one's labour instead of money (*work one's passage*); be in

motion or agitated, ferment, have influence (*on* or *upon*). **3 at work** in action, engaged in work; **give person the works** give or tell him everything, treat him harshly; **have one's work cut out** be faced with hard task; **make short work of** quickly accomplish or dispose of; **work-basket** basket containing sewing materials; **work-force** workers engaged or available, number of these; **work in** find place for in composition or structure; **work-load** amount of work to be done; **work of art** fine picture or poem or building etc.; **work off** get rid of by work or activity; **work out** solve (sum) or find (amount) by calculation, be calculated *at*, have result (*plan worked out well*), provide for all details of (*has worked out a scheme*), attain with difficulty, exhaust with work; **work-out** *n.* practice or test, esp. in boxing; **work over** examine thoroughly, *colloq.* treat with violence; **work-room** room in which work is done; **work-shy** disinclined to work; **work study** system of assessing jobs so as to get best results for employees and employers; **work to rule** follow rules of one's occupation with pedantic precision to reduce efficiency, usu. as protest; **work-to-rule** *n.* process of this; **work up** bring gradually to efficient state, advance gradually *to* (climax), elaborate or excite by degrees, mingle (ingredients), learn (subject) by study; **work wonders** see WONDER. [OE]

workable *a.* that can be worked or will work or is worth working; **workably** *adv.*

workaday *a.* ordinary, everyday, practical.

workaholic /wɜːkəˈhɒlɪk/ *n. colloq.* person addicted to working.

workday *n.* day on which work is usu. done.

worker *n.* one who works, esp. manual or industrial employee; neuter bee or ant.

workhouse *n. hist.* public institution for poor in parish.

working 1 *a.* engaged in work, esp. in manual or industrial labour (*working man*); functioning or able to function (*working model*). **2** *n.* activity of work; functioning; mine or quarry. **3 working capital** that actually used in a business; **working class** class of people who are employed for wages, esp. in manual or industrial work; **working day** workday, part of the day devoted to work; **working knowledge** knowledge adequate to work with; **working order** condition in which machine works; **working party** group of people appointed to advise on some question.

workman *n.* man employed to do manual labour; person in respect of skill in job (*a good workman*).

workmanlike *a.* showing practised skill.

workmanship *n.* degree of skill in doing task or of finish in product made.

workmate *n.* one engaged in same work as another.

workpeople *n.pl.* people employed in labour for wages.

workpiece *n.* thing worked on with tool or machine.

worksheet *n.* paper for recording work done or in progress; paper listing questions or activities for students etc. to work through.

workshop *n.* room or building in which manufacture is done; place for concerted activity, such activity (*a dance workshop*).

world /wɜːld/ *n.* the earth, or a heavenly body like it; the universe, all that exists; time or state or scene of human existence; secular interests and affairs; human affairs, active life; average or respectable people or their customs or opinions; all that concerns or all who belong to specified class or sphere of activity (*the world of sport*); vast amount (*of*); *attrib.* affecting many nations, of all nations (*world politics*; *world champion*); **bring** (or **come**) **into the world** give birth to (or be born); **in the world** of all or at all (*what in the world is it?*); **man** (or **woman**) **of the world** person experienced and practical in human affairs; **out of this world** *colloq.* extremely good etc.; **think the world of** have very high regard for; **this world** mortal life; **world-beater** person or thing surpassing all others; **world-famous** known throughout the world; **world war** war involving many important nations; **world-wide** covering or known in all parts of the world. [OE]

worldly *a.* temporal, earthly (*worldly goods*); engrossed in temporal affairs, esp. pursuit of wealth and pleasure; **worldly-wise** prudent as regards one's own interests; **worldliness** *n.*

worm /wɜːm/ **1** *n.* any of several types of creeping invertebrate animal with long slender bodies and no limbs; larva of insect, esp. in fruit or wood; (in *pl.*) intestinal parasites; insignificant or contemptible person; spiral part of screw. **2** *v.* move with crawling motion; insinuate *oneself* into favour etc.; (with *out*) obtain (secret etc.) by cunning persistence. **3 worm-cast** convoluted mass of earth from earthworm; **worm-eaten** full of worm-holes; **worm-hole** hole left by passage of worm; **worm's-eye view** view from below or from humble position. [OE]

wormwood /'wɜ:mwʊd/ *n.* a woody herb with bitter aromatic taste; bitter mortification, source of this. [OE; cf. VERMOUTH]

wormy *a.* full of worms; worm-eaten; **worminess** *n.* [WORM]

worn 1 *p.p.* of WEAR. 2 *a.* damaged by use or wear; looking tired and exhausted. [WEAR]

worrisome /'wʌrɪsəm/ *a.* causing worry. [foll.]

worry /'wʌrɪ/ 1 *v.* give way to anxiety; harass, importune, be a trouble or anxiety to; (of dog etc.) shake or pull about with the teeth; (in *p.p.*) uneasy. 2 *n.* thing that causes anxiety or disturbs tranquillity; disturbed state of mind, anxiety. 3 **worry beads** string of beads manipulated with fingers to occupy or calm oneself. [OE, = strangle]

worse /wɜ:s/ 1 *a.* more bad; *predic.* in or into worse health, in worse condition (*is getting worse, is none the worse for it*). 2 *adv.* more badly or ill. 3 *n.* worse thing(s) (*you might do worse than accept*). 4 **from bad to worse** into even worse state; **worse luck** see LUCK; **the worse** worse condition (*a change for the worse*); **the worse for wear** damaged by use, injured. [OE]

worsen /'wɜ:s(ə)n/ *v.* make or become worse.

worship /'wɜ:ʃɪp/ 1 *n.* homage or service paid to a deity; acts, rites, or ceremonies of this; adoration or devotion. 2 *v.* (**-pp-**, *US* **-p-**) adore as divine, honour with religious rites; idolize or regard with adoration; attend public worship; be full of adoration. 3 **your** (or **his**) **Worship** title of respect used to (or of) certain magistrates etc. [OE (WORTH, -SHIP)]

worshipful *a. archaic* (esp. in old titles of companies or officers) honourable, distinguished; **worshipfully** *adv.*

worst /wɜ:st/ 1 *a.* most bad. 2 *adv.* most badly. 3 *n.* worst part or possibility (*prepare for the worst*). 4 *v.t.* get the better of, defeat. 5 **at its** etc. **worst** in the worst state; **at (the) worst** in the worst possible case; **do your worst** expression of defiance; **get the worst of it** be defeated; **if the worst comes to the worst** if the worst happens. [OE (WORSE)]

worsted /'wʊstɪd/ *n.* fine woollen yarn; fabric made from this. [*Worste(a)d* in Norfolk]

wort /wɜ:t/ *n. archaic* (except in names) plant (*liverwort*); infusion of malt before it is fermented into beer. [OE]

worth /wɜ:θ/ 1 *predic. a.* (governing noun like *prep.*) of value equivalent to (*worth £1, a lot of money*); such as to justify or repay (*worth doing, the trouble*); possessing, having property amounting to (*is worth a million pounds*). 2 *n.* what person or thing is worth, (high) merit (*of great worth*); equivalent of money in commodity (*ten pounds' worth of petrol*). 3 **for all one is worth** *colloq.* with utmost efforts; **for what it is worth** without guarantee of its truth or value; **worth it** worth while; **worth one's salt** having merit; **worth (one's) while** see WHILE. [OE]

worthless *a.* without value or merit.

worthwhile /wɜ:θ'waɪl/ *a.* that is worth the time or effort spent.

worthy /'wɜ:ðɪ/ 1 *a.* estimable or deserving respect (*lived a worthy life*); (of person) entitled to (condescending) recognition (*a worthy old couple*); deserving (*of* or *to be* or *to do* thing) adequate or suitable to the dignity etc. *of* (*in words worthy of the occasion*); (as *suffix* forming adjectives) deserving of, suitable for (*noteworthy, seaworthy*). 2 *n.* worthy person; person of some distinction in his country, time, etc. 3 **worthily** *adv.*; **worthiness** *n.*

wot see WIT.

would /wəd, *emphat.* wʊd/ *v. aux.* (3 *sing.* **would**) past tense of WILL, used esp. in reported speech (*he said he would be home by evening*) or to express habitual action (*he would wait for her every evening*), condition (*she would have been killed if she had gone*), question (*would they like it?*), polite request (*would you come in please?*), or probability (*she would be over fifty by now*); **would-be** desiring or aspiring to be. [WILL]

wouldn't /'wʊd(ə)nt/ *colloq.* = *would not.*

wound[1] /wu:nd/ 1 *n.* injury done to living tissue by cut or blow etc.; injury to reputation or pain inflicted on feelings. 2 *v.t.* inflict wound on. [OE]

wound[2] *past* and *p.p.* of WIND[2].

wove *past* of WEAVE[1].

woven *p.p.* of WEAVE[1].

wow[1] 1 *int.* expressing astonishment or admiration. 2 *n. sl.* sensational success. [imit.]

wow[2] *n.* slow pitch-fluctuation in sound-reproduction, perceptible in long notes. [imit.]

w.p.b. *abbr.* waste-paper basket.

WPC *abbr.* woman police constable.

w.p.m. *abbr.* words per minute.

WRAC *abbr.* Women's Royal Army Corps.

wrack *n.* seaweed cast up or growing on

shore; destruction. [LG or Du. *wrak*; cf. WRECK]

WRAF *abbr.* Women's Royal Air Force.

wraith *n.* ghost; spectral appearance of living person supposed to portend his death. [orig. unkn.]

wrangle /'ræŋg(ə)l/ **1** *n.* noisy argument or altercation or dispute. **2** *v.i.* engage in wrangle. [LG or Du.]

wrap 1 *v.* (**-pp-**) envelop in folded or soft encircling material (often with *up*), arrange or draw (pliant covering) *round* or *about* person etc. **2** *n.* shawl or scarf or other such addition to clothing. **3 under wraps** in secrecy; **wrap over** (of garment) overlap itself when worn; **wrapped up in** engrossed or absorbed in; **wrap up** finish off (matter), put on wraps (*mind you wrap up well*). [orig. unkn.]

wrapper *n.* paper cover for sweet or book or posted newspaper; loose enveloping robe or gown.

wrapping *n.* (esp. in *pl.*) wraps, wrappers, enveloping garments; **wrapping paper** strong or decorative paper for wrapping parcels.

wrasse /ræs/ *n.* a bright-coloured sea-fish. [Corn. *wrach*]

wrath /rɒθ, rɔːθ/ *n.* extreme anger. [OE (WROTH)]

wrathful *a.* extremely angry; **wrathfully** *adv.*

wreak *v.t.* give play to (*vengeance, one's anger* etc., usu. *upon* enemy); cause (damage etc.). [OE, = avenge]

wreath *n.* (*pl.* /riːθs, riːðz/) flowers or leaves fastened in a ring esp. as ornament for head or building or for laying on grave etc.; curl or ring of smoke or cloud or soft fabric. [OE (WRITHE)]

wreathe /riːð/ *v.* encircle as or with or like wreath; wind (one's arms etc.) *round* person etc.; (of smoke etc.) move in wreaths.

wreck 1 *n.* destruction or disablement esp. of ship; ship that has suffered wreck; greatly damaged or disabled building or thing or person; wretched remnant *of*. **2** *v.* cause wreck of (ship, hopes, etc.); suffer wreck; (in *p.p.*) involved in wreck. [AF *wrec* f. Gmc]

wreckage *n.* wrecked material; remnants of wreck.

wrecker *n.* one who tries from shore to bring about shipwreck in order to plunder or profit by wreckage.

wren[1] *n.* small short-winged usu. brown songbird. [OE]

Wren[2] *n.* member of Women's Royal Naval Service. [initials *WRNS*]

wrench 1 *n.* violent twist or oblique pull or tearing off; tool like spanner for gripping and turning nuts etc.; *fig.* painful uprooting or parting. **2** *v.t.* inflict wrench on, pull (*off* or *away* etc.) with wrench; distort (facts) to suit a theory etc. [OE]

wrest *v.t.* distort into accordance with one's interests or views; wrench away (weapon) or snatch (victory) or extract (consent) *from* opponent etc. [OE]

wrestle /'res(ə)l/ **1** *n.* contest in which two opponents grapple and try to throw each other to the ground esp. as athletic sport under code of rules; hard struggle. **2** *v.* take part in wrestle (with); struggle *with* or *against*, do one's utmost to deal *with* (temptation, task, etc.). **3 wrestler** *n.*; **wrestling** *n.* [OE]

wretch *n.* unfortunate or pitiable person; miscreant or conscienceless person (often as playful term of depreciation). [OE, = outcast]

wretched /'retʃɪd/ *a.* unhappy or miserable; of bad quality or no merit, contemptible; unsatisfactory or displeasing.

wrick var. of RICK[2].

wriggle /'rɪg(ə)l/ **1** *v.* (of worm etc.) twist or turn body with short writhing movements, go *along* etc. thus; (of person or animal) make wriggling motions, make way *through* etc. thus; *fig.* practise evasion; move (*oneself*, one's hand, etc.) with wriggling action. **2** *n.* act of wriggling. **3 wriggle out of** avoid on some pretext. **4 wriggly** *a.* [LG *wriggelen*]

wright /raɪt/ *n. archaic* (except in *comb.*) maker or builder (*playwright, wheelwright*). [OE (WORK)]

wring 1 *v.t.* (*past* & *p.p.* **wrung**) squeeze tightly, squeeze and twist esp. to remove liquid (*out*); break by twisting; distress, torture; extract by squeezing; (with *out* or *from*) obtain by pressure or importunity, extort. **2** *n.* act of wringing. **3 wring one's hands** clasp them as gesture of great distress; **wringing (wet)** so wet that water can be wrung out; **wring neck of** kill (chicken etc.) by twisting its head; **wring person's hand** clasp it forcibly or press it with emotion. [OE]

wringer *n.* device for wringing water from washed clothes etc.

wrinkle /'rɪŋk(ə)l/ **1** *n.* crease in skin such as is produced by age; similar mark in other flexible surface; *colloq.* useful tip, clever expedient. **2** *v.* make wrinkles in; form wrinkles. **3 wrinkly** *a.* [OE]

wrist *n.* joint connecting hand with arm; part of garment covering this; (also **wrist-work**) working of hand without moving arm; **wrist-watch** small watch worn on strap etc. round wrist. [OE]

wristlet *n.* band or ring to strengthen or guard or adorn wrist.

writ[1] *n.* form of written command to act or not act in some way. [OE, rel. to WRITE]

writ[2] *archaic p.p.* of WRITE, esp. in **writ large** in magnified or emphasized form. [foll.]

write *v.* (*past* **wrote**; *p.p.* **written**) mark paper or other surface with symbols, letters, or words; form or mark (such symbols etc.); form or mark symbols of (word or sentence, or document etc.); fill or complete (sheet or cheque etc.) with writing; put (data) into computer store; (esp. in *p.p.*) indicate (quality or condition) by appearance (*has guilt written all over him*); compose for written or printed reproduction or publication, be engaged in such literary composition; write and send letter (*to* person or *for* thing wanted); *US* or *colloq.* write and send letter to (person); convey (news etc.) by letter; state in book etc.; **write down** record in writing, write as if for inferiors, disparage in writing, reduce nominal value of; **write off** write and send letter, cancel record of (bad debt etc.), completely destroy (vehicle etc.); **write-off** *n.* thing written off, esp. vehicle too badly damaged to be repaired; **write out** write in full or in finished form; **write up** write full account of, praise in writing; **write-up** *n.* written or published account, review. [OE]

writer *n.* one who writes or has written something; one who writes books, author; **writer's cramp** muscular spasm caused by excessive writing.

writhe /raɪð/ *v.i.* twist or roll oneself about (as) in acute pain; suffer mental torture (*under* or *at* insult etc., *with* shame etc.). [OE]

writing *n.* written words etc., handwriting; written document; (in *pl.*) author's works; **in writing** in written form; **writing on the wall** ominous event or sign; **writing-paper** paper for writing (esp. letters) on. [WRITE]

written *p.p.* of WRITE.

WRNS *abbr.* Women's Royal Naval Service.

wrong 1 *a.* mistaken, not true, in error; unsuitable, less or least desirable (*wrong road, decision*); contrary to law or morality (*is wrong to steal*); amiss, out of order, in bad or abnormal condition (*something wrong with my heart, car, life*). **2** *adv.* (usu. placed last) in wrong manner or direction, with incorrect result (*played the piece all wrong*). **3** *n.* what is morally wrong; wrong or unjust action. **4** *v.t.* treat unjustly; mistakenly attribute bad motives to. **5 do wrong** sin; **do wrong to** misjudge (person); **get (hold of) the wrong end of the stick** misunderstand completely; **get person wrong** misunderstand him; **go wrong** take wrong path, stop functioning properly, cease virtuous behaviour; **in the wrong** responsible for quarrel, mistake, or offence; **on the wrong side of** out of favour with (person), somewhat more than (stated age); **wrong-headed** perverse and obstinate; **wrong side** worse or undesired or unusable side; **wrong side out** inside out; **wrong way round** in opposite or reverse of normal or desirable orientation, sequence, etc. [OE]

wrongdoer *n.* person guilty of breach of law or morality; **wrongdoing** *n.*

wrongful *a.* unwarranted, unjustified; **wrongfully** *adv.*

wrong'un /ˈrɒŋən/ *n. colloq.* person of bad character; googly.

wrote *past* of WRITE.

wroth /rəʊθ, rɒθ/ *predic. a. literary* angry. [OE]

wrought /rɔːt/ **1** *archaic past* and *p.p.* of WORK. **2** *a.* (of metals) beaten out or shaped by hammering. **3 wrought iron** tough malleable form of iron suitable for forging or rolling, not cast. [WORK]

wrung *past* and *p.p.* of WRING.

WRVS *abbr.* Women's Royal Voluntary Service.

wry /raɪ/ *a.* (*compar.* **wryer**; *superl.* **wryest**) distorted, turned to one side; (of face, smile, etc.) contorted in disgust, disappointment, or mockery; (of humour) dry and mocking; **wryly** *adv.*; **wryness** *n.* [OE]

wryneck *n.* small bird able to turn head over shoulder.

WSW *abbr.* west-south-west.

wt. *abbr.* weight.

wych- *prefix* in names of trees with pliant branches (**wych-alder, -elm, -hazel**). [OE, = bending]

Wykehamist /ˈwɪkəmɪst/ **1** *a.* of Winchester College. **2** *n.* member of Winchester College. [William of *Wykeham*, founder]

X

X, x /eks/ *n.* (*pl.* **Xs, X's**) twenty-fourth letter; *Rom. num.* ten; (as *x*) first unknown quantity in algebra; cross-shaped symbol esp. used to indicate position (*X marks the spot*) or incorrectness or to symbolize a kiss or vote, or as signature of person who cannot write.

Xe *symb.* xenon.

xenon /'zenɒn/ *n.* heavy inert gaseous element. [Gk, neut. of *xenos* strange, foreign]

xenophobia /zenə'fəʊbɪə/ *n.* morbid dislike of foreigners; **xenophobic** *a.* [Gk *xenos* strange(r)]

xerography /zɪə'rɒgrəfɪ, ze'r-/ *n.* dry copying process in which powder adheres to areas remaining electrically charged after exposure of surface to light from image of document to be copied. [Gk *xēros* dry]

Xerox /'zɪərɒks, 'zer-/ **(P) 1** *n.* a certain process of xerography; a copy made using this process. **2** *v.t.* **(xerox)** reproduce by this process.

xi /saɪ, gzaɪ, zaɪ/ *n.* fourteenth letter of Greek alphabet (Ξ, ξ). [Gk]

-xion see -ION.

Xmas /'krɪsməs, 'eksməs/ *n.* = CHRISTMAS. [abbr., with X for initial chi of Gk *Khristos* Christ]

X-ray /'eksreɪ/ **1** *n.* (in *pl.*) electromagnetic radiation of short wavelength, able to pass through opaque bodies; photograph made by X-rays, esp. showing position of bones etc. by their greater absorption of the rays. **2** *v.t.* photograph or examine or treat with X-rays. [X, orig. with ref. to unkn. nature]

xylophone /'zaɪləfəʊn/ *n.* musical instrument of graduated wooden or metal bars struck with small wooden hammer(s); **xylophonist** *n.* [Gk *xulon* wood]

Y

Y, y /waɪ/ *n.* (*pl.* **Ys, Y's**) twenty-fifth letter; (as *y*) second unknown quantity in algebra; Y-shaped thing.

-y[1] *suffix* forming adjectives from nouns and adjectives, in senses 'full of', 'having the quality of', 'addicted to' (*messy, icy, horsy, boozy*), and from verbs in senses 'inclined to', 'apt to' (*runny, sticky*). [OE]

-y[2] *suffix* (also **-ey, -ie**) forming dimin. nouns, pet names, etc. (*granny, Sally, nightie, Mickey*). [orig. Sc.]

-y[3] *suffix* forming nouns denoting state or quality (*orthodoxy, modesty*). [F f. L or Gk]

Y *symb.* yttrium.

yacht /jɒt/ **1** *n.* light sailing-vessel; larger usu. power-driven vessel used for private pleasure excursions, cruising, etc. **2** *v.i.* race or cruise in yacht. **3 yacht-club** club esp. for yacht-racing. [Du. (*jaghtschip*, lit. pursuit-ship)]

yachtsman *n.* person who yachts.

yah *int.* expressing derision or defiance. [imit.]

yahoo /jə'hu:/ *n.* bestial person. [race of brutes in *Gulliver's Travels*]

Yahveh /'jɑ:veɪ/ *n.* (also **Yahweh**) = JEHOVAH.

yak *n.* long-haired Tibetan ox. [Tibetan]

Yale *n.* **(P)** (in full **Yale lock**) type of lock for doors etc., with revolving barrel. [*Yale*, inventor]

yam *n.* tropical or subtropical climbing plant, edible starchy tuber of this; sweet potato. [Port. or Sp.]

yammer *colloq.* or *dial.* **1** *n.* lament, wail, grumble; voluble talk. **2** *v.i.* utter yammer. [OE]

yank[1] *v.t.* & *n.* pull with a jerk. [orig. unkn.]

Yank[2] *n. colloq.* = YANKEE. [abbr.]

Yankee /'jæŋkɪ/ *n. colloq.* inhabitant of US, American; *US* inhabitant of New England or of northern states. [perh. Du. *Janke* dimin. of *Jan* John, used derisively; or repr. Amer. Ind. pronunc. of *English*]

yap 1 *v.i.* **(-pp-)** bark shrilly or fussily; *colloq.* talk noisily or foolishly or complainingly. **2** *n.* sound of yapping. [imit.]

yapp *n.* bookbinding with projecting limp leather cover. [*Yapp*, bookseller]

yarborough /'jɑ:bərə/ *n.* whist or bridge hand with no card above a 9. [Earl of *Yarborough*]

yard[1] *n.* unit of linear measure (3 ft., 0.9144 metre), this length of material; square or cubic yard; spar slung across mast for sail to hang from; **yard-**

-arm either end of ship's yard. [OE, = stick]

yard[2] *n.* piece of enclosed ground esp. attached to building(s) or used for particular purpose; *US* garden of house. [OE, = enclosure]

yardage *n.* number of yards of material etc. [YARD[1]]

yardstick *n.* rod a yard long usu. divided into inches etc.; standard of comparison.

yarmulka /'jɑːmʌlkə/ *n.* skull-cap worn by Jewish men. [Yiddish]

yarn **1** *n.* spun thread, esp. for knitting or weaving etc.; *colloq.* story, traveller's tale, anecdote. **2** *v.i. colloq.* tell yarns. [OE]

yarrow /'jærəʊ/ *n.* a kind of perennial herb, esp. milfoil. [OE]

yashmak /'jæʃmæk/ *n.* veil concealing face except eyes, worn by some Muslim women. [Arab.]

yaw **1** *v.i.* (of ship or aircraft etc.) fail to hold straight course; go unsteadily. **2** *n.* yawing of ship etc. from course. [orig. unkn.]

yawl *n.* a kind of ship's boat or sailing- or fishing-boat. [LG or Du. *jol(le)*]

yawn **1** *v.i.* open the mouth wide and inhale esp. in sleepiness or boredom; (of chasm etc.) gape, be wide open. **2** *n.* act of yawning. [OE]

yaws /jɔːz/ *n.pl.* (usu. treated as *sing.*) contagious tropical skin-disease with raspberry-like swellings. [orig. unkn.]

Yb *symb.* ytterbium.

yd(s). *abbr.* yard(s).

ye[1] /jɪ, jiː/ *pron. archaic pl.* of THOU.

ye[2] /jiː, or as THE/ *a. pseudo-archaic* = THE (*ye olde tea-shoppe*). [f. old use of obs. *y*-shaped letter for *th*]

yea /jeɪ/ *archaic* **1** *adv.* yes. **2** *n.* the word 'yea'. **3 yea and nay** shilly-shally; **yeas and nays** affirmative and negative votes. [OE]

yeah /jeə/ *adv. colloq.* yes. [casual pronunc. of YES]

year /jɪə, jɜː/ *n.* time occupied by the earth in one revolution round the sun, approx. 365¼ days; period from 1 Jan. to 31 Dec. inclusive; period of same length as this starting at any point (*four years ago*; *school year*); (in *pl.*) age, time of life (*young for his years*); (usu. in *pl.*) very long time; group of students entering college etc. in same academic year; **year-book** annual publication having current information on a subject. [OE]

yearling *n.* animal between one and two years old.

yearly **1** *a.* done or produced or occurring every year; of or lasting a year. **2** *adv.* once every year.

yearn /jɜːn/ *v.i.* be filled with longing or compassion or tenderness. [OE]

yeast *n.* greyish-yellow fungous substance obtained esp. from fermenting malt liquors and used as fermenting agent, to raise bread, etc. [OE]

yeasty *a.* frothy; in a ferment; working like yeast; (of talk etc.) light and superficial; **yeastily** *adv.*; **yeastiness** *n.*

yell **1** *n.* loud sharp cry of pain, anger, fright, encouragement, delight, etc.; shout. **2** *v.* make or utter with yell. [OE]

yellow /'jeləʊ/ **1** *a.* of the colour of buttercups or lemons or yolks; having yellow skin or complexion; *colloq.* cowardly. **2** *n.* yellow colour or pigment; yellow clothes or material (*dressed in yellow*). **3** *v.* turn yellow. **4 yellow fever** tropical virus disease with fever and jaundice; **yellow flag** flag displayed by ship in quarantine; **yellow pages** section of telephone directory on yellow paper and listing business subscribers according to goods or services they offer; **yellow spot** point of acutest vision in retina; **yellow streak** trace of cowardice. [OE]

yellowhammer *n.* bunting of which male has yellow head, neck, and breast.

yelp **1** *n.* sharp shrill cry (as) of dog in pain or excitement. **2** *v.i.* utter yelp. [OE]

yen[1] *n.* (*pl.* same) Japanese monetary unit. [Jap. f. Chin.]

yen[2] **1** *n.* longing or yearning. **2** *v.i.* (**-nn-**) feel longing. [Chin.]

yeoman /'jəʊmən/ *n.* man holding and cultivating small landed estate; member of yeomanry force; **Yeoman of the Guard** member of sovereign's bodyguard; **yeoman('s) service** efficient or useful help in need; **yeomanly** *a.* [OE, prob. = young man]

yeomanry *n.* body of yeomen; *hist.* volunteer cavalry force raised from yeoman class.

yes **1** *adv.* serving to indicate that the answer to the question is affirmative, the statement etc. made is correct, the request or command will be complied with, or the person summoned or addressed is present; (**yes?**) indeed? is that so? what do you want? **2** *n.* the word *yes*. **3 say yes** grant request, confirm statement; **yes and** form for introducing stronger phrase (*he came home drunk, yes and was sick*); **yes-man** *colloq.* weakly acquiescent person. [OE, = *yea let it be*]

yester- *in comb.* of yesterday, that is last past (*yester-eve, yestermorn*); **yester-year** last year, the recent past. [OE]

yesterday /'jestədeɪ, -dɪ/ **1** *adv.* on the day before today, in the recent past. **2** *n.* the day before today, the recent past. [OE (prec., DAY)]

yet 1 *adv*. as late as, or until, now or then (*there is yet time*; *his best work yet*); (with neg. or interrog.) so soon as, or by, now or then (*it is not time yet*; *have you finished yet?*); again, in addition (*more and yet more*); in the remaining time available (*I will do it yet*); (with compar.) even (*a yet more difficult task*); nevertheless, and or but in spite of that. **2** *conj*. but at the same time, but nevertheless. [OE]

yeti /'jetɪ/ *n*. = *Abominable Snowman*.

yew *n*. dark-leaved evergreen coniferous tree; its wood. [OE]

Yid *n*. *sl. derog*. **(R)** Jew. [back-form. f. foll.]

Yiddish /'jɪdɪʃ/ **1** *n*. language used by Jews in or from Europe, orig. a German dialect with words from Hebrew etc. **2** *a*. of this language. [G *jüdisch* Jewish]

Yiddisher **1** *n*. person speaking Yiddish. **2** *a*. speaking Yiddish.

yield **1** *v*. produce or return as fruit or profit or result (*land yields crops*; *investment yields 15%*); give up, surrender, concede (*yield fortress*, *oneself prisoner*); make submission (*to*); be inferior or confess inferiority *to* (*yielded to persuasion*); give right of way (*to* other traffic). **2** *n*. amount yielded or produced. [OE, = pay]

yippee /'jɪpi:/ *int*. expressing delight or excitement. [natural excl.]

YMCA *abbr*. Young Men's Christian Association.

yob *n*. (also **yobbo** /'jɒbəʊ/ *pl*. **yobbos**) *sl*. lout, hooligan. [back sl. for BOY; cf. -O]

yodel /'jəʊd(ə)l/ **1** *v*. (**-ll-**, *US* **-l-**) sing with melodious inarticulate sounds and frequent changes between falsetto and normal voice in manner of Swiss mountain-dwellers. **2** *n*. yodelling cry. [G]

yoga /'jəʊgə/ *n*. Hindu system of philosophic meditation and asceticism designed to effect reunion with the universal spirit; system of physical exercises and breathing control used in yoga. [Hind. f. Skr., = union]

yoghurt /'jɒgət/ *n*. semi-solid sourish food prepared from milk fermented by added bacteria. [Turk.]

yogi /'jəʊgɪ/ *n*. devotee of yoga. [Hind. (YOGA)]

yoicks *int*. used by huntsman to urge on hounds. [orig. unkn.]

yoke **1** *n*. wooden cross-piece fastened over necks of two oxen etc. and attached to plough or wagon to be drawn; pair *of* oxen etc. (*pl*. often same after numeral); object like yoke in form or function, e.g. wooden shoulder-piece for carrying pair of pails, top section of dress or skirt etc. from which the rest hangs; sway, dominion, servitude; bond of union esp. of marriage. **2** *v*. put yoke on; couple or unite (pair); link (one *to* another); match or work together. [OE]

yokel /'jəʊk(ə)l/ *n*. rustic, country bumpkin. [perh. dial.]

yolk /jəʊk/ *n*. yellow internal part of egg. [OE (YELLOW)]

Yom Kippur /jɒm kɪ'pʊə/ most solemn religious fast day of Jewish year, Day of Atonement. [Heb.]

yomp *v.i. sl*. march with heavy equipment over difficult terrain. [orig. unkn.]

yon *archaic* **1** *a*. & *adv*. yonder. **2** *pron*. yonder person or thing. [OE]

yonder **1** *adv*. over there, at some distance in that direction, in the place indicated by pointing etc. **2** *a*. situated yonder.

yoo-hoo /'ju:hu:/ *int*. expressing desire to attract person's attention. [natural excl.]

yore *n*. now only in **of yore** formerly, in or of old days. [OE, = long ago]

york *v.t*. (in cricket) bowl out with yorker. [back-form. f. foll.]

yorker *n*. (in cricket) ball that pitches immediately under bat. [prob. with ref. to practice of Yorkshire cricketers]

Yorkist /'jɔ:kɪst/ **1** *a*. of family descended from 1st Duke of York or party supporting it in Wars of Roses. **2** *n*. adherent of Yorkist family esp. in Wars of Roses. [1st Duke of *York*]

Yorkshire pudding /'jɔ:kʃə/ baked batter eaten with roast beef.

Yorkshire terrier /'jɔ:kʃə/ small shaggy blue and tan toy kind of terrier.

you /ju:, jʊ/ *pron*. of second person singular and plural (*obj*. **you**; *poss*. YOUR, YOURS); the person(s) or thing(s) addressed; (as *voc*. with noun in excl. statement: *you fools!*); (in general statements) one, a person, anyone, everyone (*it's bad at first, but you get used to it*); **you and yours** you together with your family, property, etc. [OE, orig. obj. case of YE[1]]

young /jʌŋ/ **1** *a*. not far advanced in life or development or existence, not yet old; immature, inexperienced; representing young people (*Young Liberals* etc.); felt in or characteristic of youth (*young love*); distinguishing son from father (*young Jones*) or (in *compar*.) one person from another of the same name (*the younger Pitt*). **2** *n. collect*. offspring, esp. of animals before or soon after birth. **3** **the young** *pl*. young people. [OE]

youngster *n*. child, young person.

your /jɔ:, jʊə/ *poss. a*. of or belonging to you; *colloq*. (usu. *derog*.) much talked of, well known (*none so fallible as your self-styled expert*). [OE]

yours *poss. pron.* of or belonging to you, the thing(s) belonging to you (*it is yours*; *yours are best*; *a friend of yours*); **yours ever, faithfully, sincerely, truly,** etc. formulas preceding signature of letter.
yourself /jɔ:'self, jʊə'self/ *pron.* (*pl.* **yourselves**) emphat. and refl. form of YOU (for uses cf. HERSELF).
youth /ju:θ/ *n.* (*pl.* /ju:ðz/) being young, period between childhood and adult age, vigour or enthusiasm or inexperience or other characteristic of this period; young man; (as *pl.*) young people collectively (*the youth of the country*); **youth club** place for young people's leisure activities; **youth hostel** place where (esp. young) holiday-makers can put up cheaply for the night; **youth hosteller** user of youth hostel. [OE (YOUNG)]
youthful *a.* young or (still) having the characteristics of youth; **youthfully** *adv.*
yowl 1 *n.* loud wailing cry (as) of cat or dog in distress. **2** *v.i.* utter yowl. [imit.]
Yo-yo /'jəʊjəʊ/ *n.* (**P**; *pl.* **Yo-yos**) toy consisting of pair of discs with deep groove between them in which string is attached and wound, and which can be made to fall and rise. [orig. unkn.]
yr. *abbr.* year(s); younger; your.
yrs. *abbr.* years; yours.
ytterbium /ɪ'tɜ:bɪəm/ *n.* metallic element of lanthanide series. [*Ytterby* in Sweden]
yttrium /'ɪtrɪəm/ *n.* metallic element resembling those of lanthanide series.
yucca /'jʌkə/ *n.* white-flowered garden plant. [Carib.]
Yugoslav /'ju:gəslɑ:v/ **1** *a.* of Yugoslavia. **2** *n.* native or inhabitant of Yugoslavia. [G f. Serb. *jug* south; SLAV]
yule *n.* (in full **yule-tide**) *archaic* the Christmas festival; **yule-log** large log burnt in hearth on Christmas Eve. [OE]
yummy *a. colloq.* tasty, delicious. [foll.]
yum-yum /jʌm'jʌm/ *int.* expressing pleasure from eating or prospect of eating. [natural excl.]
YWCA *abbr.* Young Women's Christian Association.

Z

Z, z /zed/ *n.* (*pl.* **Zs, Z's**) twenty-sixth letter; (as *z*) third unknown quantity in algebra.
zabaglione /zɑ:bɑ:'ljəʊneɪ/ *n.* Italian sweet of whipped and heated egg yolks, sugar, and wine. [It.]
zany /'zeɪnɪ/ **1** *a.* comically idiotic, crazily ridiculous. **2** *n.* buffoon, jester; *hist.* clown's attendant. [F or It.]
zap *v.t. sl.* (**-pp-**) hit, attack, kill. [imit.]
Zarathustrian /zærə'θʊstrɪən/ *a.* & *n.* = ZOROASTRIAN. [*Zarathustra*, Persian founder of religion]
zeal *n.* earnestness or fervour in advancing cause or rendering service; hearty persistent endeavour; **zealous** /'zeləs/ *a.* [L f. Gk *zēlos*]
zealot /'zelət/ *n.* extreme partisan, fanatic; **zealotry** *n.*
zebra /'zebrə, 'zi:brə/ *n.* African quadruped related to ass and horse, with black and white stripes; *attrib.* with alternate dark and pale stripes; **zebra crossing** striped street-crossing where pedestrians have precedence over vehicles. [It. or Port., f. Congolese]
zebu /'zi:bu:/ *n.* humped ox of Asia and Africa. [F]
zed *n.* letter Z. [F f. L f. Gk ZETA]
zee *n. US* letter Z. [var. of ZED]
Zen *n.* form of Buddhism emphasizing value of meditation and intuition. [Jap., = meditation]
zenana /zɪ'nɑ:nə/ *n.* part of house for seclusion of women of high-caste families in India and Iran. [Hind. f. Pers.]
Zend *n.* interpretation of the Avesta; **Zend-Avesta** Zoroastrian sacred writings (**Avesta**) and interpretation (**Zend**). [Pers.]
zenith /'zenɪθ, 'zi:-/ *n.* point of heavens directly above observer; highest point (of power or prosperity etc.). [F or L f. Arab.]
zephyr /'zefə/ *n.* mild gentle breeze; fine cotton fabric; athlete's jersey. [F or L f. Gk, = west wind]
Zeppelin /'zepəlɪn/ *n.* German large dirigible airship of early 20th c. [Count F. von *Zeppelin*, airman]
zero /'zɪərəʊ/ *n.* (*pl.* **zeros**) figure 0, nought; point on scale of thermometer etc. from which positive or negative quantity is reckoned; (in full **zero-hour**) hour at which planned, esp. military, operation is timed to begin, crucial or decisive moment; **zero in on** take aim at, focus attention on; **zero-rated** on which no value added tax is charged. [F or It. f. Sp. f. Arab. (CIPHER)]
zest *n.* piquancy, stimulating flavour or quality; keen enjoyment or interest,

relish *for*, gusto; piece of orange or lemon peel as flavouring. [F]

zeta /'zi:tə/ *n.* sixth letter of Greek alphabet (Z, ζ). [Gk]

zeugma /'zju:gmə/ *n.* figure of speech using verb or adjective with two nouns, to one of which it is strictly applicable while the word appropriate to the other is not used (*with weeping eyes and* [sc. *grieving*] *hearts*; (loosely) = SYLLEPSIS. [L f. Gk, = a yoking (*zugon* yoke)]

ziggurat /'zɪgəræt/ *n.* pyramidal tower in ancient Mesopotamia, surmounted by temple. [Assyr.]

zigzag /'zɪgzæg/ **1** *a.* with abrupt alternate right and left turns (*zigzag line, road*). **2** *n.* zigzag line, thing forming zigzag line or having sharp turns. **3** *adv.* with zigzag course. **4** *v.i.* (**-gg-**) move in zigzag course. [F f. G]

zillion /'zɪljən/ *n. US* indefinite large number. [prob. after *million*]

zinc 1 *n.* white metallic element used as component of brass and as coating for sheet iron. **2** *v.t.* (**-c-** /-k-/ or **-k-** or **-ck-**) coat or treat with zinc. [G *zink*]

zing *colloq.* **1** *n.* vigour, energy. **2** *v.i.* move swiftly or shrilly. [imit.]

zinnia /'zɪnɪə/ *n.* garden plant with showy flowers. [*Zinn*, physician and botanist]

Zion /'zaɪən/ *n.* ancient Jerusalem, its holy hill; the Jewish religion; the Christian Church; the kingdom of Heaven. [OE f. L f. Heb.]

Zionism *n.* movement for the re-establishment and development of a Jewish nation in what is now Israel; **Zionist** *n.*

zip 1 *n.* light fast sound; energy, vigour; (in full **zip-fastener**) fastening device of two flexible strips with interlocking projections closed or opened by sliding clip pulled along them. **2** *v.* (**-pp-**) fasten (*up*) with zip-fastener; move with zip or at high speed. [imit.]

Zip code *US* system of postal codes. [*z*one *i*mprovement *p*lan]

zipper *n.* zip-fastener.

zircon /'zɜ:kən/ *n.* zirconium silicate of which some translucent varieties are used as gems. [G *zirkon*, prob. ult. f. Arab.]

zirconium /zɜ:'kəʊnɪəm/ *n.* a grey metallic element.

zither /'zɪðə/ *n.* stringed instrument with flat sound-box, placed horizontally and played with fingers and plectrum. [G f. L (as GUITAR)]

Zn *symb.* zinc.

zodiac /'zəʊdɪæk/ *n.* belt of the heavens including all apparent positions of sun, moon, and planets as known to ancient astronomers, and divided into 12 equal parts (called **signs of the zodiac**); diagram of these signs; **zodiacal** /zə'daɪək(ə)l/ *a.* [F f. L f. Gk (*zōion* animal)]

zombie /'zɒmbɪ/ *n.* corpse said to be revived by witchcraft; *colloq.* dull or apathetic person. [W. Afr.]

zone 1 *n.* area having particular features, properties, purpose, or use (*danger, erogenous, smokeless, zone*); any well-defined region of more or less beltlike form; area between two concentric circles; encircling band of colour etc.; *archaic* girdle or belt. **2** *v.t.* encircle as or with zone; arrange or distribute by zones; assign to particular area. **3 zonal** *a.* [F or L f. Gk *zōnē* girdle]

zoo *n.* zoological garden. [abbr.]

zoological /zəʊə'lɒdʒɪk(ə)l, zu:ə-/ *a.* of zoology; **zoological garden**(**s**) public garden or park with collection of animals for exhibition and study; **zoologically** *adv.* [foll.]

zoology /zəʊ'ɒlədʒɪ, zu:-/ *n.* scientific study of animals; **zoologist** *n.* [L f. Gk *zōion* animal]

zoom 1 *v.i.* move quickly, esp. with buzzing sound; cause aeroplane to mount at high speed and steep angle; (of camera) change (esp. quickly) from long shot to close-up. **2** *n.* aeroplane's steep climb. **3 zoom lens** lens allowing camera to zoom by varying focus. [imit.]

zoophyte /'zəʊəfaɪt/ *n.* plantlike animal, esp. coral, jellyfish, or sponge. [Gk (*zōion* animal, *phuton* plant)]

Zoroastrian /zɒrəʊ'æstrɪən/ **1** *a.* of Zoroaster or Zarathustra or the dualistic religious system taught by him. **2** *n.* follower of Zoroaster; adherent of Zoroaster's religious system. **3 Zoroastrianism** *n.* [*Zoroaster*, Persian founder of religion]

Zr *symb.* zirconium.

zucchini /zu:'ki:nɪ/ *n.* (*pl.* same or **zucchinis**) courgette. [It., pl. of *zucchino* dimin. of *zucca* gourd]

Zulu /'zu:lu:/ **1** *n.* member or language of a S. African Bantu people. **2** *a.* of this people. [native name]

zygote /'zaɪgəʊt/ *n.* cell formed by union of two gametes. [Gk *zugōtos* yoked (ZEUGMA)]

zymotic /zaɪ'mɒtɪk, zɪ-/ *a.* of fermentation. [Gk *zumē* leaven]

APPENDIX I

Weights and Measures

1. *British and American, with Approximate Metric Equivalents*

Linear Measure

1 inch	= 25.4 millimetres exactly
1 foot = 12 inches	= 0.3048 metre exactly
1 yard = 3 feet	= 0.9144 metre exactly
1 (statute) mile = 1,760 yards	= 1.609 kilometres

Square Measure

1 square inch	= 6.45 sq. centimetres
1 square foot = 144 sq. in.	= 9.29 sq. decimetres
1 square yard = 9 sq. ft.	= 0.836 sq. metre
1 acre = 4,840 sq. yd.	= 0.405 hectare
1 square mile = 640 acres	= 259 hectares

Cubic Measure

1 cubic inch	= 16.4 cu. centimetres
1 cubic foot = 1,728 cu. in.	= 0.0283 cu. metre
1 cubic yard = 27 cu. ft.	= 0.765 cu. metre

Capacity Measure

BRITISH	
1 pint = 20 fluid oz.	
= 34.68 cu. in.	= 0.568 litre
1 quart = 2 pints	= 1.136 litres
1 gallon = 4 quarts	= 4.546 litres
1 peck = 2 gallons	= 9.092 litres
1 bushel = 4 pecks	= 36.4 litres
1 quarter = 8 bushels	= 2.91 hectolitres
AMERICAN DRY	
1 pint = 33.60 cu. in.	= 0.550 litre
1 quart = 2 pints	= 1.101 litres
1 peck = 8 quarts	= 8.81 litres
1 bushel = 4 pecks	= 35.3 litres
AMERICAN LIQUID	
1 pint = 16 fluid oz.	
= 28.88 cu. in.	= 0.473 litre
1 quart = 2 pints	= 0.946 litre
1 gallon = 4 quarts	= 3.785 litres

Avoirdupois Weight

1 grain	= 0.065 gram
1 dram	= 1.772 grams
1 ounce = 16 drams	= 28.35 grams

1 pound = 16 ounces	
= 7,000 grains	= 0.4536 kilogram
1 stone = 14 pounds	= 6.35 kilograms
1 quarter = 2 stones	= 12.70 kilograms
1 hundredweight = 4 quarters	= 50.80 kilograms
1 short ton = 2,000 pounds	= 0.907 tonne
1 (long) ton = 20 hundredweight	= 1.016 tonnes

2. *Metric, with Approximate British Equivalents*

Linear Measure

1 millimetre	= 0.039 inch
1 centimetre = 10 mm.	= 0.394 inch
1 decimetre = 10 cm.	= 3.94 inches
1 metre = 10 dm.	= 1.094 yards
1 decametre = 10 m.	= 10.94 yards
1 hectometre = 100 m.	= 109.4 yards
1 kilometre = 1,000 m.	= 0.6214 mile

Square Measure

1 square centimetre	= 0.155 sq. inch
1 square metre	= 1.196 sq. yards
1 are = 100 square metres	= 119.6 sq. yards
1 hectare = 100 ares	= 2.471 acres
1 square kilometre	= 0.386 sq. mile

Cubic Measure

1 cubic centimetre	= 0.061 cu. inch
1 cubic metre	= 1.308 cu. yards

Capacity Measure

1 millilitre	= 0.002 pint (British)
1 centilitre = 10 ml.	= 0.018 pint
1 decilitre = 10 cl.	= 0.176 pint
1 litre = 10 dl.	= 1.76 pints
1 decalitre = 10 l.	= 2.20 gallons
1 hectolitre = 100 l.	= 2.75 bushels
1 kilolitre = 1,000 l.	= 3.44 quarters

Weight

1 milligram	= 0.015 grain
1 centigram = 10 mg.	= 0.154 grain
1 decigram = 10 cg.	= 1.543 grains
1 gram = 10 dg.	= 15.43 grains
1 decagram = 10 g.	= 5.64 drams
1 hectogram = 100 g.	= 3.527 ounces
1 kilogram = 1,000 g.	= 2.205 pounds
1 tonne (metric ton) = 1,000 kg.	= 0.984 (long) ton

3. *Temperature*

Fahrenheit: water boils (under standard conditions) at 212° and freezes at 32°.
Celsius or Centigrade: water boils at 100° and freezes at 0°.
Kelvin: water boils at 373.15 K and freezes at 273.15 K.
To convert Centigrade into Fahrenheit: multiply by 9, divide by 5, and add 32.
To convert Fahrenheit into Centigrade: subtract 32, multiply by 5, and divide by 9.
To convert Centigrade into Kelvin: add 273.15.

4. *The Power Notation*

10^2 or ten squared = $10 \times 10 = 100$
10^3 or ten cubed = $10 \times 10 \times 10 = 1{,}000$
$10^4 = 10 \times 10 \times 10 \times 10 = 10{,}000$
10^{10} = 1 followed by ten noughts = 10,000,000,000
$10^{-2} = 1/10^2 = 1/100$
$10^{-10} = 1/10^{10} = 1/10{,}000{,}000{,}000$

5. *Chemical Notation*

The symbol for a molecule shows the symbols for the elements contained in it (C = carbon, H = hydrogen, etc.), each followed by a subscript numeral denoting the number of atoms of the element in the molecule where this number is more than one. For example, the water molecule (H_2O) contains two atoms of hydrogen and one of oxygen.

APPENDIX II

The Greek Alphabet

Capital	*Lower-case*	*English transliteration*
Α	α	a
Β	β	b
Γ	γ	g
Δ	δ	d
Ε	ε	e
Ζ	ζ	z
Η	η	ē
Θ	θ	th
Ι	ι	i
Κ	κ	k
Λ	λ	l
Μ	μ	m
Ν	ν	n
Ξ	ξ	x
Ο	ο	o
Π	π	p
Ρ	ρ	r
Σ	σ, (at end of word) ς	s
Τ	τ	t
Υ	υ	u
Φ	φ	ph
Χ	χ	kh
Ψ	ψ	ps
Ω	ω	ō

ʽ (rough breathing) over vowel = prefixed h (ἁ = ha)
over rho = suffixed h (ῥ = rh)

ʼ (smooth breathing) over vowel or rho: not transliterated

ͅ (iota subscript) under vowel = suffixed i (ᾳ = ai)

The Russian Alphabet

Capital	*Lower-case*	*English transliteration*
А	а	a
Б	б	b
В	в	v
Г	г	g
Д	д	d
Е	е	e
Ё	ё	ë
Ж	ж	zh
З	з	z
И	и	i
Й	й	ĭ
К	к	k
Л	л	l
М	м	m
Н	н	n
О	о	o
П	п	p
Р	р	r
С	с	s
Т	т	t
У	у	u
Ф	ф	f
Х	х	kh
Ц	ц	ts
Ч	ч	ch
Ш	ш	sh
Щ	щ	shch
Ъ	ъ	″('hard sign')
Ы	ы	y
Ь	ь	′ ('soft sign')
Э	э	é
Ю	ю	yu
Я	я	ya

APPENDIX III

Principal Countries of the World

Country	*Inhabitant* (*name in general use*)	*Capital*	*Monetary unit*
Afghanistan	Afghan	Kabul	afghani
Albania	Albanian	Tirana	lek
Algeria	Algerian	Algiers	dinar
Angola	Angolan	Luanda	kwanza
Argentina	Argentinian or Argentine	Buenos Aires	peso
Australia	Australian	Canberra	dollar
Austria	Austrian	Vienna	schilling
Bangladesh	Bangladeshi	Dhaka (Dacca)	taka
Belgium	Belgian	Brussels	franc
Bolivia	Bolivian	La Paz	peso
Brazil	Brazilian	Brasilia	cruzeiro
Bulgaria	Bulgarian	Sofia	lev
Burma	Burmese	Rangoon	kyat
Cambodia	Cambodian	Phnom Penh	riel
Canada	Canadian	Ottawa	dollar
Chile	Chilean	Santiago	peso
China	Chinese	Beijing (Peking)	yuan
Colombia	Colombian	Bogotá	peso
Costa Rica	Costa Rican	San José	colón
Cuba	Cuban	Havana	peso
Cyprus	Cypriot	Nicosia	pound
Czechoslovakia	Czechoslovak	Prague	koruna
Denmark	Dane	Copenhagen	krone
Dominican Republic		Santo Domingo	peso
Ecuador	Ecuadorean	Quito	sucre
Egypt	Egyptian	Cairo	pound
El Salvador	Salvadorean	San Salvador	colón
Ethiopia	Ethiopian	Addis Ababa	dollar
Finland	Finn	Helsinki	markka
France	Frenchman, Frenchwoman	Paris	franc
Gambia, The	Gambian	Banjul	dalasi
German Democratic Republic (East Germany)	East German	East Berlin	mark
Germany, Federal Republic of (West Germany)	West German	Bonn	mark

Country	*Inhabitant* (*name in general use*)	*Capital*	*Monetary unit*
Ghana	Ghanaian	Accra	cedi
Greece	Greek	Athens	drachma
Guatemala	Guatemalan	Guatemala	quetzal
Guinea	Guinean	Conakry	sily
Haiti	Haitian	Port au Prince	gourde
Honduras	Honduran	Tegucigalpa	lempira
Hong Kong		Victoria	dollar
Hungary	Hungarian	Budapest	forint
Iceland	Icelander	Reykjavik	króna
India	Indian	Delhi	rupee
Indonesia	Indonesian	Jakarta	rupiah
Iran	Iranian	Tehran	toman (= 10 rials)
Iraq	Iraqi	Baghdad	dinar
Ireland, Republic of	Irishman[1], Irishwoman[1]	Dublin	pound (punt)
Israel	Israeli	Jerusalem	shekel
Italy	Italian	Rome	lira
Jamaica	Jamaican	Kingston	dollar
Japan	Japanese	Tokyo	yen
Jordan	Jordanian	Amman	dinar
Kenya	Kenyan	Nairobi	shilling
Korea, North	North Korean	Pyongyang	won
Korea, South	South Korean	Seoul	won
Kuwait	Kuwaiti	Kuwait	dinar
Laos	Laotian	Vientiane	kip
Lebanon	Lebanese	Beirut	pound
Liberia	Liberian	Monrovia	dollar
Libya	Libyan	Tripoli	dinar
Luxemburg	Luxemburger	Luxemburg	franc
Madagascar	Malagasy	Antananarivo	franc malgache
Malawi	Malawian	Lilongwe	kwacha
Malaysia	Malaysian	Kuala Lumpur	dollar
Malta	Maltese	Valletta	pound
Mauritius	Mauritian	Port Louis	rupee
Mexico	Mexican	Mexico City	peso
Mongolia	Mongolian	Ulan Bator	tugrik
Morocco	Moroccan	Rabat	dirham
Mozambique	Mozambican	Maputo	escudo
Nepal	Nepalese	Kathmandu	rupee
Netherlands	Dutchman, Dutchwoman	Amsterdam	gulden
New Zealand	New Zealander	Wellington	dollar

[1] May also denote an inhabitant of Northern Ireland.

Country	*Inhabitant (name in general use)*	*Capital*	*Monetary unit*
Nicaragua	Nicaraguan	Managua	córdoba
Nigeria	Nigerian	Lagos	naira
Norway	Norwegian	Oslo	krone
Pakistan	Pakistani	Islamabad	rupee
Panama	Panamanian	Panama City	balboa
Papua New Guinea	Papua New Guinean	Port Moresby	kina
Paraguay	Paraguayan	Asunción	guarani
Peru	Peruvian	Lima	sol
Philippines	Filipino, Filipina	Manila	peso
Poland	Pole	Warsaw	zloty
Portugal	Portuguese	Lisbon	escudo
Romania	Romanian	Bucharest	leu
Saudi Arabia	Saudi Arabian	Riyadh	riyal
Seychelles	Seychellois, Seychelloise	Victoria	rupee
Sierra Leone	Sierra Leonean	Freetown	leone
Singapore	Singaporean	Singapore	dollar
South Africa	South African	Pretoria; Cape Town	rand
Spain	Spaniard	Madrid	peseta
Sri Lanka	Sri Lankan	Colombo	rupee
Sudan	Sudanese	Khartoum	pound
Sweden	Swede	Stockholm	krona
Switzerland	Swiss	Berne	franc
Syria	Syrian	Damascus	pound
Taiwan	Taiwanese	Taipei	dollar
Tanzania	Tanzanian	Dar es Salaam	shilling
Thailand	Thai	Bangkok	baht
Tonga	Tongan	Nuku'alofa	pa'anga
Tunisia	Tunisian	Tunis	dinar
Turkey	Turk	Ankara	lira
Uganda	Ugandan	Kampala	shilling
Union of Soviet Socialist Republics	Russian, Soviet	Moscow	rouble
United Kingdom	Briton	London	pound
United States of America	American	Washington	dollar
Uruguay	Uruguayan	Montevideo	peso
Venezuela	Venezuelan	Caracas	bolívar
Vietnam	Vietnamese	Hanoi	dong
Yugoslavia	Yugoslav	Belgrade	dinar
Zaïre	Zaïrean	Kinshasa	zaïre
Zambia	Zambian	Lusaka	kwacha
Zimbabwe	Zimbabwean	Harare	dollar

APPENDIX IV

Counties of the United Kingdom

(with abbreviations in general use)

ENGLAND

Avon
Bedfordshire (Beds.)
Berkshire (Berks.)
Buckinghamshire (Bucks.)
Cambridgeshire (Cambs.)
Cheshire (Ches.)
Cleveland
Cornwall (Corn.)
Cumbria
Derbyshire (Derby.)
Devon
Dorset
Durham (Dur.)
East Sussex
Essex
Gloucestershire (Glos.)
Greater London
Greater Manchester
Hampshire (Hants)
Hereford & Worcester
Hertfordshire (Herts.)
Humberside
Isle of Wight (IOW)
Kent
Lancashire (Lancs.)
Leicestershire (Leics.)
Lincolnshire (Lincs.)
Merseyside
Norfolk
Northamptonshire (Northants)
Northumberland (Northumb.)
North Yorkshire
Nottinghamshire (Notts.)
Oxfordshire (Oxon.)
Shropshire
Somerset (Som.)
South Yorkshire
Staffordshire (Staffs.)
Suffolk
Surrey
Tyne and Wear
Warwickshire (War.)
West Midlands
West Sussex
West Yorkshire
Wiltshire (Wilts.)

NORTHERN IRELAND

Antrim
Armagh
Down
Fermanagh (Ferm.)
Londonderry
Tyrone

SCOTLAND

Regions

Borders
Central
Dumfries & Galloway
Fife
Grampian
Highland
Lothian
Strathclyde
Tayside

Islands Areas

Orkney
Shetland
Western Isles

WALES

Clwyd
Dyfed
Gwent
Gwynedd
Mid Glamorgan
Powys
South Glamorgan
West Glamorgan

APPENDIX V

States of the USA

(with official and official postal abbreviations)

Alabama (Ala., AL)
Alaska (Alas., AK)
Arizona (Ariz., AZ)
Arkansas (Ark., AR)
California (Calif., CA)
Colorado (Col., CO)
Connecticut (Conn., CT)
Delaware (Del., DE)
Florida (Fla., FL)
Georgia (Ga., GA)
Hawaii (HI)
Idaho (ID)
Illinois (Ill., IL)
Indiana (Ind., IN)
Iowa (Ia., IA)
Kansas (Kan., KS)
Kentucky (Ky., KY)
Louisiana (La., LA)
Maine (Me., ME)
Maryland (Md., MD)
Massachusetts (Mass., MA)
Michigan (Mich., MI)
Minnesota (Minn., MN)
Mississippi (Miss., MS)
Missouri (Mo., MO)
Montana (Mont., MT)
Nebraska (Nebr., NB)
Nevada (Nev., NV)
New Hampshire (NH)
New Jersey (NJ)
New Mexico (N. Mex., NM)
New York (NY)
North Carolina (NC)
North Dakota (N. Dak., ND)
Ohio (OH)
Oklahoma (Okla., OK)
Oregon (Oreg., OR)
Pennsylvania (Pa., PA)
Rhode Island (RI)
South Carolina (SC)
South Dakota (S. Dak., SD)
Tennessee (Tenn., TN)
Texas (Tex., TX)
Utah (UT)
Vermont (Vt., VT)
Virginia (Va., VA)
Washington (Wash., WA)
West Virginia (W. Va., WV)
Wisconsin (Wis., WI)
Wyoming (Wyo., WY)

APPENDIX VI

Books of the Bible

OLD TESTAMENT

Genesis (Gen.)
Exodus (Exod.)
Leviticus (Lev.)
Numbers (Num.)
Deuteronomy (Deut.)
Joshua (Josh.)
Judges (Judg.)
Ruth
First Book of Samuel (1 Sam.)
Second Book of Samuel (2 Sam.)
First Book of Kings (1 Kgs.)
Second Book of Kings (2 Kgs.)
First Book of Chronicles (1 Chr.)
Second Book of Chronicles (2 Chr.)
Ezra
Nehemiah (Neh.)
Esther
Job
Psalms (Ps.)
Proverbs (Prov.)
Ecclesiastes (Eccles.)
Song of Songs, Song of Solomon, Canticles (S. of S., Cant.)
Isaiah (Isa.)
Jeremiah (Jer.)
Lamentations (Lam.)
Ezekiel (Ezek.)
Daniel (Dan.)
Hosea (Hos.)
Joel
Amos
Obadiah (Obad.)
Jonah
Micah (Mic.)
Nahum (Nah.)
Habakkuk (Hab.)
Zephaniah (Zeph.)
Haggai (Hag.)
Zechariah (Zech.)
Malachi (Mal.)

APOCRYPHA

First Book of Esdras (1 Esd.)
Second Book of Esdras (2 Esd.)
Tobit
Judith
Rest of Esther (Rest of Esth.)
Wisdom of Solomon (Wisd.)
Ecclesiasticus, Wisdom of Jesus the Son of Sirach (Ecclus., Sir.)
Baruch
Song of the Three Children (S. of III Ch.)
Susanna (Sus.)
Bel and the Dragon (Bel & Dr.)
Prayer of Manasses (Pr. of Man.)
First Book of Maccabees (1 Macc.)
Second Book of Maccabees (2 Macc.)

NEW TESTAMENT

Gospel according to St Matthew (Matt.)
Gospel according to St Mark (Mark)
Gospel according to St Luke (Luke)
Gospel according to St John (John)
Acts of the Apostles (Acts)
Epistle to the Romans (Rom.)
First Epistle to the Corinthians (1 Cor.)
Second Epistle to the Corinthians (2 Cor.)
Epistle to the Galatians (Gal.)

Epistle to the Ephesians (Eph.)
Epistle to the Philippians (Phil.)
Epistle to the Colossians (Col.)
First Epistle to the Thessalonians (1 Thess.)
Second Epistle to the Thessalonians (2 Thess.)
First Epistle to Timothy (1 Tim.)
Second Epistle to Timothy (2 Tim.)
Epistle to Titus (Tit.)
Epistle to Philemon (Philem.)
Epistle to the Hebrews (Heb.)
Epistle of James (Jas.)
First Epistle of Peter (1 Pet.)
Second Epistle of Peter (2 Pet.)
First Epistle of John (1 John)
Second Epistle of John (2 John)
Third Epistle of John (3 John)
Epistle of Jude (Jude)
Revelation, Apocalypse (Rev., Apoc.)

APPENDIX VII

Punctuation Marks

1. Comma (,)

This is used:

1.1 To separate main clauses when the second is not closely identified with the first, e.g. *Cars will turn here, and coaches will go straight on.*

1.2 To avoid momentary misunderstanding, e.g. *In the valley below, the villages looked very small.*

1.3 In a sentence which would mean something different without the comma, e.g. *He did not go to church, because he was playing golf.*

1.4 Between adjectives qualifying a noun, except when the last adjective is more closely related to the noun, e.g. *a cautious, eloquent man* but *a distinguished foreign author.*

1.5 To separate items in a list of more than two items, e.g. *potatoes, peas, and carrots.*

1.6 Before or after a salutation or vocative, e.g. *Come here, boy*; *Dear Sir, Thank you for your letter.*

1.7 To mark the beginning and end of a parenthetical word or phrase, e.g. *It appears, however, that they were wrong.*

1.8 Before a quotation, e.g. *I boldly cried out, 'Woe to this city!'*

1.9 In numbers of four or more figures, to separate each group of three consecutive figures, starting from the right, e.g. 10,135,793.

2. Semicolon (;)

This separates two or more clauses which are of more or less equal importance and are linked as a pair or series, e.g. *To err is human; to forgive, divine.*

3. Colon (:)

This is used:

3.1 To separate main clauses when there is a step forward from the first to the second, as from introduction to main theme, from cause to effect, or from premiss to conclusion, e.g. *Country life is the natural life: it is there that you will find real friendship.*

3.2 To introduce a list of items (a dash should not be added), and after expressions such as *namely, for example, to resume, to sum up, the following.*

3.3 Before a quotation, e.g. *Then he wrote these words: 'I have named none to their disadvantage.'*

4. Period, Full Point, Full Stop (.)

This is used:

4.1 At the end of all sentences which are not questions or exclamations.

4.2 After many abbreviations and initials. If such a point closes a sentence, it also serves as the sentence's full point, e.g. . . . *cats etc.* but (. . . *cats etc.*).

5. Question Mark (?)

This is used:

5.1 After any sentence which asks a question, but not after an indirect question, e.g. *What is it?* but *I asked what it was.*

5.2 Before a word etc. whose accuracy is doubted, e.g. *Julius Caesar, born ?100* BC.

6. Exclamation Mark (!)

This is used after an exclamatory word, phrase, or sentence expressing absurdity, command, contempt, disgust, emotion, enthusiasm, pain, sorrow, a wish, or wonder.

7. Apostrophe (')

This is used:

7.1 To show the possessive case, e.g. *John's book.*

7.2 To show an omission, e.g. *John's angry.*

7.3 At the end of a quotation: see following section.

8. Quotation Marks

8.1 A quotation is normally preceded by a turned comma (') and followed by an apostrophe. Double marks are used for a quotation within a quotation. The apostrophe should come after any punctuation mark which is part of the quotation, but before any mark which is not, e.g. '*He asked "Where are we?"*' but '*Did he say "Here we are"?*' Quotation marks are only used when the exact words of the original are quoted.

8.2 Quotation marks are used when citing titles of articles, series, chapters, essays, poems, and songs, but not for titles of books of the Bible.

8.3 They may be used to enclose slang and technical terms.

9. Parentheses ( )

These enclose:

9.1 Interpolations and remarks made by the writer of the text himself, e.g. *He is (as he always was) a rebel.*

9.2 An authority, definition, explanation, reference, or translation.

9.3 In a report of a speech, interruptions by the audience.

9.4 Reference letters or figures, e.g. (1), (*a*).

10. Square Brackets [ ]

These enclose material added by someone other than the author, often by way of explanation, e.g. *He* [*Bloggs*] *fell down.*

11. Dash (—)

This is used:

11.1 Instead of the parentheses in 9.1 above.

11.2 Instead of the colon in 3.1 above.

11.3 To indicate pauses in hesitant speech, or the ending and resumption of a sentence interrupted by another speaker.

11.4 To replace an omitted word.

12. Hyphen (-)

This is used:

12.1 In compounds used attributively, e.g. *He is a well-known man* but *The man is well known.*

12.2 In compounds formed from words which have a syntactical relationship, e.g. *weight-carrying*, *punch-drunk*.

12.3 To join a prefix to a proper name, e.g. *anti-Darwinian.*

12.4 To prevent misconceptions by linking words, e.g. *twenty-odd people.*

12.5 To prevent misconceptions by separating a prefix from the main word, e.g. *One player resigned, but later he re-signed.*

12.6 To separate letters representing similar sounds, e.g. *sword-dance*, *radio-isotope.*

12.7 To represent a common second element in all but the last word of a list, e.g. *two-, three-, or fourfold.*

12.8 At the end of a line in printing, to indicate that the last word has been divided.

13. Ellipsis, Marks of Omission (. . .)

These are used to show an omission. If the omission follows a complete sentence, the three points are preceded by the full point of the sentence, but if it follows an incomplete sentence a fourth point should not be added.

OXFORD

OXFORD PAPERBACK REFERENCE

Details of other reference books available in Oxford Paperbacks are given on the following pages. A complete list of Oxford Paperbacks, including books in the World's Classics, Twentieth-Century Classics, Oxford Shakespeare, Oxford Authors, Past Masters, and OPUS series, as well as Oxford Paperback Reference, can be obtained from the General Publicity Department, Oxford University Press, Walton Street, Oxford OX2 6DP.

In the USA, complete lists are available from the Paperbacks Marketing Manager, Oxford University Press, 200 Madison Avenue, New York, NY 10016.

A Dictionary of Modern English Usage

H. W. Fowler

Second Edition
Revised by Sir Ernest Gowers

This is the first paperback edition of Fowler's *Modern English Usage*, which for over fifty years has been the standard work on the correct but easy and natural use of English in speech or writing. It deals with points of grammar, syntax, style, and the choice of words; with the formation of words and their spelling and inflexions; with pronunciation; and with punctuation and typography. But most of all Fowler is renowned for the iconoclasm and wit with which he writes.

'Let me beg readers as well as writers to keep the revised Fowler at their elbows. It brims with useful information.' Raymond Mortimer, *Sunday Times*

'Fowler is still the best available authority. For those who think that it matters to make their writing shipshape and water-tight, there is still no alternative. Apart from that, we read him because he was a funny, quirky, witty man, who used words to express complicated meanings with beautiful conciseness.' *Books and Bookmen*

The King's English

Third Edition

H. W. Fowler and F. G. Fowler

Generations of students, scholars, and professional writers have gone to *The King's English* for answers to problems of grammar or style. The Fowler brothers were particularly concerned to clarify the more problematic and obscure rules and principles inherent in English vocabulary and composition, and also to illustrate with examples the most common blunders and traps. They wrote with characteristic good sense and liveliness, and this book has become a classic reference work.

The Concise Oxford Dictionary of Quotations

Second Edition

This new edition of *The Concise Oxford Dictionary of Quotations* is drawn from the third edition of the best-selling *Oxford Dictionary of Quotations*, published in 1979. Collected here are 5800 well-known quotations by 1100 authors, ranging in time from the 8th century BC to the 1970s, and in space from Russia to South Africa and from China to Mexico. The reader can refer to a particular quotation, or a selection of quotations on a certain subject, guided by a useful index. The book provides 'excellent browsing' among a varied company where Chekhov rubs shoulders with Chesterton, Lord Palmerston with Dorothy Parker, and Wodehouse with Wittgenstein.

The Concise Oxford Dictionary of Proverbs

John Simpson

Many proverbs come to us with the wisdom of ages behind them, and new ones are continually being created. John Simpson's compilation embraces some 1000 English-language proverbs in use today. Those who love words will be fascinated to trace the origins – both old and new – of many familiar phrases.

'A work of scholarship and good humour, which deserves a place on the shelves of anyone interested in twentieth-century English usage.' *British Book News*

'Brilliantly arranged . . . I recommend it without hesitation to all students of the English language and lovers of literature, as well as to pedants, crossword fanatics and those who like to prove people wrong in argument.' Auberon Waugh, *Sunday Telegraph*

The Concise Oxford Dictionary of English Literature

Second Edition
Revised by Dorothy Eagle

This handy and authoritative reference book is essential for anyone who reads and enjoys English literature. It contains concise yet informative entries on English writers from the *Beowulf* poet to Samuel Beckett and W. H. Auden, defines literary movements and genres, and refers the reader to sources for more than a thousand characters from books and plays. It also includes a host of sources of influence on English literary achievement such as foreign books and writers, art, and major historical events.

The Concise Oxford Dictionary of English Literature is an abridgement of Paul Harvey's classic *Oxford Companion to English Literature*.

The Concise Oxford Dictionary of French Literature

Edited by Joyce M. H. Reid

This abridgement of the classic *Oxford Companion to French Literature* preserves the unique quality of the original work and at the same time extends its scope with the addition of some 150 new entries to bring it up to date. The *Dictionary* retains the distinctive features of the *Companion*, including its coverage of a great variety of major and minor writers, genres, and movements in French literature. Like its parent volume, the *Dictionary* contains entries on other relevant aspects of French history, philosophy, and culture.

The Concise Oxford Companion to the Theatre

Edited by Phyllis Hartnoll

The Concise Oxford Companion to the Theatre is an essential handbook for the theatre-goer or the drama student. It contains entries on actors and actresses from Sarah Bernhardt to Alec McCowen; on theatrical companies and theatre buildings from the Abbey Theatre in Dublin to the Yvonne Arnaud Theatre in Guildford; and on dramatists from Sophocles to Samuel Beckett. The range of the volume is international, and also includes explanations of technical terms, and notes on practical and historical aspects of stagecraft and design.

For this concise version, based on Phyllis Hartnoll's third edition of *The Oxford Companion to the Theatre*, all the articles have been considered afresh, and most have been recast and rewritten, often with the addition of new material.

The Concise Oxford Dictionary of Music

Third Edition

Michael Kennedy

The third edition of this famous music dictionary had been thoroughly updated and revised. Biographies and technical terms alike—nearly everything has been written afresh. There is a vastly increased coverage of early music, and of music and musicians of the twentieth century. The articles on major composers now include comprehensive lists of works. As a result, this will prove the indispensable compact music dictionary for the 1980s.

The Concise Oxford Dictionary of Opera

Second Edition

Harold Rosenthal and John Warrack

Since its first publication *The Concise Oxford Dictionary of Opera* has established itself as an invaluable source of information on all aspects of opera. It contains entries on individual operas, composers, librettists, singers, conductors, technical terms, and other general subjects connected with opera and its history. This enlarged second edition includes many new articles on composers and performers, details of casts at first performances, and much additional information on the development of opera in different countries. Many of the existing entries have been rewritten and updated.

'You will . . . discover here an enormous amount of information not available elsewhere.' *Daily Telegraph*

The Oxford Dictionary of Saints

David Hugh Farmer

This fascinating book provides concise accounts of the lives, cults, and artistic associations of about a thousand saintly figures either native to Great Britain and Ireland, or who lived or have been venerated there. It includes the great saints of early Christendom and the major figures of the medieval Church, as well as little-known local saints and those to whom a church is dedicated or who appear in the calendars of the Book of Common Prayer and other such missals.

'[David Hugh Farmer] breathes life into his scholarship and has produced a dictionary which makes compulsive reading.' *Tablet*

'Even those who do not believe in the saints . . . will be able to enjoy and to profit from this splendid book.' *The Economist*

The Concise Oxford Dictionary of the Christian Church

Edited by E. A. Livingstone

This is the abridged version of the second edition of *The Oxford Dictionary of the Christian Church*. It makes available for the general reader the vast majority of the entries in the parent volume. The range of the *Concise Dictionary* is considerable. It includes the major Christian feasts and denominations; historical accounts of the lives of the saints; résumés of Patristic writings; and histories of heretical sects. It also outlines the opinions of major theologians and moral philosophers, and explores many related subjects.

The Oxford Literary Guide to the British Isles

Dorothy Eagle and Hilary Carnell

This is the first paperback edition of the best-selling *Oxford Literary Guide to the British Isles*. It lists hundreds of places in Britain and Ireland and gives details of their connections with the lives and works of famous writers. It provides maps, precise directions, and opening times for the tourist. Not only is it an indispensable companion to every journey, but its endlessly fascinating facts and anecdotes are also a delight for the armchair traveller.

'Anyone who can read or write will find the *Guide* a sure way of wallowing unashamedly in a rich nostalgia for . . . our literary heritage.' *Times Literary Supplement*

The Oxford Dictionary of English Christian Names

Third Edition

E. G. Withycombe

What's in a name? This 'standard reference work for those approaching the font' (*Scotsman*) is equally at home on the family bookshelf and in the scholar's library. Personal names from Aaron to Zoë that have survived in use from the end of the fourteenth century are listed alphabetically. Each entry includes early forms of the name, its equivalents in other languages, pet forms, and etymology, together with an account of its introduction into England and subsequent history, frequency of occurrence, and fluctuations in fashion. Some of the commoner Irish, Gaelic, and Welsh names have also been included. The introduction discusses the general history of personal names, and an appendix lists common words derived from Christian names.